Auditing, Assurance and Ethics Handbook 2013

Chartered Accountants Program

Auditing, Assurance and Ethics Handbook 2013

Incorporating all the Standards
as at 1 December 2012

Technical Editor
Stephanie Kemp

GAA
Global Accounting Alliance

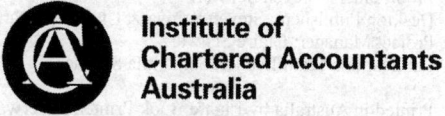

Institute of
Chartered Accountants
Australia

ISBN 1-11845-2380

Published in Australia by John Wiley & Sons Australia, Ltd, Milton, Queensland 4064

Typeset and edited by Institute of Chartered Accountants Australia, Sydney, New South Wales 2000
Proofreaders: Steven Schwarz
Desktop Publishers: Steven Schwarz, Claire Schwarz
Project Manager: Claire Schwarz
Publications Team Leader: Samantha Skinner

Printed in Australia by Ligare Book Printer, Riverwood, Sydney 2210

Foreword

The *Auditing Assurance and Ethics Handbook 2013* from the Institute of Chartered Accountants Australia (the Institute) is an essential reference tool designed to meet the demands of today's dynamic economic environment.

Developed for Chartered Accountants, accountancy students and other professionals working in Australian business, the handbook is a complete and comprehensive guide to both the ethical and audit and assurance requirements members must comply with.

The handbook includes the Australian Auditing and Assurance Standards and Guidance Statements and Professional and Ethical Standards issued up to 1 December 2012.

Significant new AUASB material in this year's edition includes the Standards on Assurance Engagements ASAE 3410 *Assurance Engagements on Greenhouse Gas Statements*, ASAE 3420 *Assurance Engagements to Report on the Compilation of Pro Forma Historical Financial Information included in a Prospectus or other Document* and ASAE 3450 *Assurance Engagements involving Corporate Fundraisings and/or Prospective Financial Information*, the Standard on Related Services ASRS 4450 *Comfort Letter Engagements* and Guidance Statement GS 020 *Special Considerations in Auditing Financial Instruments*.

The new ethical material includes APESB Guidance Note GN 40 *Ethical Conflicts in the Workplace — Considerations for Members in Business* but the APESB has also significantly revised a number of its existing pronouncements during 2012, updates for which are included in this book.

A companion to this handbook is the Institute's *Financial Reporting Handbook 2013*, containing the Australian Accounting Standards. Together, these handbooks are part of the suite of products and services available to Institute members and the student and business community.

I am confident you will find the *Auditing, Assurance and Ethics Handbook 2013* a valuable addition to your reference material.

Tim Gullifer FCA

President

Institute of Chartered Accountants Australia

1 January 2013

About the Technical Editor

Stephanie Kemp, MA (Dunelm), FCA is a consultant with Westworth Kemp Consultants specialising in financial reporting and auditing standards. For a number of years, she was part of the Leadership and Quality Team at the Institute of Chartered Accountants Australia. Stephanie is the author of numerous articles in the Institute's journal *Charter*, and has provided regular technical updates to accounting professionals via the Institute's electronic newsletter *Accounting and Audit News Today* (ANT). Before joining the team at the Institute, Stephanie worked as an auditor, and then in the internal quality control and technical sections of medium and large accounting firms in the United Kingdom and Australia.

Contents

AUSTRALIAN AUDITING STANDARDS (ASAs) *(cont.)*

Internal Control

GUIDANCE STATEMENTS (GSs) *(cont.)*

ACCOUNTING PROFESSIONAL AND ETHICAL STANDARDS BOARD STATEMENTS (APES)

MISCELLANEOUS PROFESSIONAL STATEMENTS

MATERIAL FOR MEMBERS OF THE INSTITUTE OF CHARTERED ACCOUNTANTS AUSTRALIA

Introduction

The selection and arrangement of the material contained in the Chartered Accountants *Auditing, Assurance and Ethics Handbook 2013* has been directed towards meeting the needs of students, academics and practitioners. The major features of this Handbook are listed below.

Overview

This section provides an overview of the major developments in Australian Auditing and Assurance Standards and Professional and Ethical Standards, that have occurred during 2012. The book's new title reflects the important role that the Professional and Ethical Standards have for members both in public practice and in business.

Introductory comments

Detailed introductory comments have been prepared outlining the history behind particular Auditing and Assurance Standards, Guidance Statements and APESB Standards. Cross-references to equivalent publications of the International Federation of Accountants (IFAC) and the IAASB have been included. Editorial notes have also been included indicating the major differences from the prior version.

Understanding Financial Statement Audits: A Guide for Financial Statement Users

This paper, originally published by the International Federation of Accountants (IFAC) in conjunction with the International Auditing Practices Committee provides an overview of the audit process and the relationship between preparers, users and auditors of financial statements. It was updated for the 2012 edition of this book by the Institute of Chartered Accountants Australia to reflect contemporary Australian auditing practices and is exclusive to the *Auditing Assurance and Ethics Handbook.*

Due process for the issue of auditing standards and other guidance

The due process for the development and issue of Australian Auditing and Assurance Standards and Guidance Statements is outlined in the information document, *AUASB Functions and Processes*, available on the AUASB website auasb.gov.au. AUASB pronouncements are generally based on equivalent pronouncements prepared by the IAASB, but some are developed solely for Australia by the AUASB in response to specific Australian issues. Both the IAASB and the AUASB employ an extensive due process involving discussion papers and exposure drafts. The AUASB also seeks comments on IAASB exposure drafts and considers them in preparing its own submission to the IAASB.

Authority of AUASB pronouncements

The AUASB is an independent statutory agency established under s. 277A of the *Australian Securities and Investments Commission Act 2001*, which has the power under s. 336 of the *Corporations Act 2001* to make auditing standards for the purposes of corporations legislation. The majority of the ASA auditing standards are legally enforceable by virtue of s. 307A of the *Corporations Act 2001* – 'the auditor ... must conduct the audit or review in accordance with the auditing standards'. For entities that do not come within the scope of the *Corporations Act 2001*, the applicability of auditing standards to members of the Institute of Chartered Accountants Australia (the Institute), CPA Australia and the Institute of Public Accountants (IPA) is set out in APES 210 *Conformity with Auditing and Assurance Standards*.

The AUASB issues a variety of pronouncements:

- Framework pronouncements, such as the *Foreword*, *Glossary* and *Framework for Assurance Engagements*;
- Standards;
- Guidance Statements; and
- Other publications.

The level of authority of the various auditing pronouncements issued by the AUASB and reproduced in this book is described in the *Foreword to AUASB Pronouncements*.

The current structure of AUASB standards is as follows:

- *Australian Auditing Standards* (ASAs);
- *Standards on Review Engagements* (ASREs);
- *Standards on Assurance Engagements* (ASAEs); and
- *Standards on Related Services* (ASRSs).

The Standards contain basic principles and essential procedures, together with related guidance. ASA 100 *Preamble to AUASB Standards*, supplemented by ASA 101 *Preamble to Australian Auditing Standards*, the interpretive preamble for the 'Clarity' Standards operative from 1 January 2010, sets out the AUASB's intentions as to how the AUASB Standards are to be understood, interpreted and applied. It also identifies those AUASB Standards that have the force of law for the purposes of the *Corporations Act 2001*, which are:

- those in the ASA series (apart from ASA 805 *Special Considerations – Audits of Single Financial Statements and Specific Elements, Accounts or Items of a Financial Statement* and ASA 810 *Engagements to Report on Summary Financial Statements*);
- ASQC 1 *Quality Control for Firms that Perform Audits and Reviews of Financial Reports and Other Financial Information, and Other Assurance Engagements*;
- ASRE 2410 *Review of a Financial Report Performed by the Independent Auditor of the Entity*; and
- ASRE 2415 *Review of a Financial Report – Company Limited by Guarantee*.

The AUASB also issues Guidance Statements, which, like the predecessor Board's Auditing Guidance Statements (AGSs), some of which are still in use, do not have the force of law and impose no further obligations, but provide guidance on procedural matters or industry or entity specific issues.

Other publications issued by the AUASB comprise:

- *AUASB Functions and Processes*, a description of how the AUASB works;
- *Principles of convergence with the IAASB and harmonisation with the NZAuASB*
- *Explanatory Guides*, which provide additional information about specific aspects of the standards;
- *AUASB Bulletins*, which are issued to raise a general awareness of matters that are of interest to auditors and assurance practitioners;
- *Bases of Conclusions*, which explain the rationale behind decisions taken during the development of the AUASB's standards; and
- Other publications on the audit and assurance implications of emerging issues.

As part of its due process, which is described in the *AUASB Functions and Processes*, the AUASB also produces *Exposure Drafts*, which are draft Standards made available to the public for comment, and other consultation documents.

For more information on the structure and authority of the AUASB and to see AUASB exposure drafts, visit the Board's website auasb.gov.au.

Authority of APESB pronouncements

The Accounting Professional and Ethical Standards Board (APESB) was established by the Institute and CPA Australia in February 2006 in order to create an independent and more transparent body with responsibility for setting professional and ethical standards applicable to the accounting profession. Its pronouncements are mandatory for members of those bodies and the IPA.

The APESB has assumed responsibility for the Miscellaneous Professional Statements (the APS series), which were originally issued by the Institute and CPA Australia and are now being phased out as they are replaced by APESB Standards.

It is also responsible for the profession's ethical rulings on matters such as independence, changes in professional appointment, fees, advertising, etc. which are contained in APES 110 *Code of Ethics for Professional Accountants*. APES 110 is mandatory for members of the Institute, CPA Australia and the IPA.

ASA 102 *Compliance with Ethical Requirements when Performing Audits, Reviews and Other Assurance Engagements* requires that auditors comply with 'relevant ethical requirements'. The definition of 'relevant ethical requirements' and guidance in ASA 102 makes it clear that for Corporations Act engagements auditors must be particularly mindful of APES 110 and ethical requirements in any other relevant legislation.

The APESB also issues Guidance Notes containing material to assist members in complying with relevant APESB standards. Guidance Notes may target the needs of a specific segment of the accounting profession.

For more information on the structure and authority of the APESB and to see APESB exposure drafts, visit their website apesb.org.au.

Availability of pronouncements

As the development and issue of Auditing Standards and Guidance Statements and ethical pronouncements is a year-round process, and the lead time required for typesetting, printing and distribution is lengthy, there is always the likelihood that the AUASB or APESB will finalise new or revised standards and statements between issues of this Handbook. The Boards also regularly issue exposure drafts for public comment. New publications can be obtained by download from the AUASB website at auasb.gov.au or the APESB website at apesb.org.au.

Further supporting materials for the Chartered Accountants *Auditing Assurance and Ethics Handbook 2013*, can be found on the Institute's website charteredaccountants.com.au. The website contains commentary and links to relevant material issued after 1 December 2012.

Stephanie Kemp, FCA

Technical Consultant

Sydney

December 2012

About the Institute of Chartered Accountants Australia

The Institute is the professional body for Chartered Accountants in Australia and members operating throughout the world.

Representing more than 70,000 current and future professionals and business leaders, the Institute has a pivotal role in upholding financial integrity in society. Members strive to uphold the profession's commitment to ethics and quality in everything they do, alongside an unwavering dedication to act in the public interest.

Chartered Accountants hold diverse positions across the business community, as well as in professional services, government, not-for-profit, education and academia. The leadership and business acumen of members underpin the Institute's deep knowledge base in a broad range of policy areas impacting the Australian economy and domestic and international capital markets.

The Institute of Chartered Accountants Australia was established by Royal Charter in 1928 and today has around 60,000 members and more than 12,000 talented graduates working and undertaking the Chartered Accountants Program.

The Institute is a founding member of the Global Accounting Alliance (GAA), which is an international coalition of accounting bodies and an 800,000-strong network of professionals and leaders worldwide.

charteredaccountants.com.au

For Institute enquiries

National Customer Service Centre

Ph: 1300 137 322 within Australia
+61 2 9290 5660 if overseas
Fax: +61 2 9262 4841
Email: service@charteredaccountants.com.au

Operating Hours

8:30am – 6.00pm AEST/AEDST
Monday to Friday (excluding national public holidays)

Overview

Influences on Auditing in 2012

In 2012, Audit Quality has been a recurring theme as regulators and standard setters have reflected on the aftermath of the 2008-9 financial crisis. The AUASB published Bulletins on *Auditing Considerations in a Prolonged Uncertain Economic Environment* and *Professional Scepticism in an Audit of a Financial Report*.

The focus on audit quality has been reflected in legislative changes, with the passing of the *Corporations Legislation Amendment (Audit Enhancement) Act 2012*, which has made structural changes to the audit environment and expanded the powers of the Australian Securities and Investments Commission (ASIC). The Act requires firms with more than ten significant audits to publish an annual transparency report, removes duplication of audit inspection responsibilities by the FRC and ASIC, allows ASIC to issue an audit deficiency report in respect of a firm that has been inspected and allows ASIC to communicate directly with audited bodies. It also permits an extension to the five-year rotation period, where independence and quality would not be impaired. Regulations accompanying the Act specify the form and content of the transparency reports.

Standards development has been in areas other than the traditional financial report audit, with new standards being issued for assurance engagements on statements of greenhouse gas emissions and in the context of fundraisings, particularly assurance on prospective and pro forma information. The Board is currently working on assurance for water accounting reports.

The Clarity Standards, based on the IAASB's Clarity Project that became operative on 1 January 2010 in Australia are now firmly embedded in Australian audit practice and the AUASB has almost completed reissuing Guidance Statements to support the standards. For further information about the Clarity Project and the 2010 reissue of the standards, refer to the Overview section of the *Auditing and Assurance Handbook 2010* and to the Institute's website, charteredaccountants.com.au. A table that cross-references the old and new standards and international standards is included at the end of this Overview.

Influences on Ethics in 2012

Work has been continuing on the professional and ethical standards affecting members of the accounting bodies with the Accounting Professional and Ethical Standards Board (APESB) having now almost completed its project to revise and reissue the various professional and ethical statements inherited from the profession as APES standards.

The APESB's table that cross-references its standards to the old APS statements can be found at the end of this Overview.

The APESB also issued its first Guidance Note during 2012 for members in business.

Snapshot of the Changes

New and Revised Material

Framework and policy documents – new

- *Principles of Convergence to International Standards of the International Auditing and Assurance Standards Board (IAASB) and Harmonisation with the Standards of the New Zealand Auditing and Assurance Standards Board (NZAuASB)*
- *AUASB Functions and Processes* (not included in this book, but available on the AUASB website)

Framework and policy documents – revised

- *Foreword to AUASB Pronouncements*

Assurance pronouncements, including auditing and assurance standards – new

- ASA 2012-1 *Amending Standard to ASA 570 Going Concern*
- ASAE 3410 *Assurance Engagements on Greenhouse Gas Statements*
- ASAE 3420 *Assurance Engagements to Report on the Compilation of Pro Forma Historical Financial Information included in a Prospectus or other Document*
- ASAE 3450 *Assurance Engagements involving Corporate Fundraisings and/or Prospective Financial Information*

Assurance pronouncements, including auditing and assurance standards – revised

- ASA 570 *Going Concern* (compiled)

Standards on related services – new

- ASRS 4450 *Comfort Letter Engagements*

Guidance Statements (GSs) – new

- GS 020 *Special Considerations in Auditing Financial Instrtuments*

Accounting Professional & Ethical Standards Board Standards (APESs) – revised

- APES 110 *Code of Ethics for Professional Accountants* (compiled)
- APES 225 *Valuation Services*

Accounting Professional & Ethical Standards Board Guidance Notes (GNs) – new

- GN 40 *Members in Business Guidance Note*

Material Withdrawn

The following pronouncements have been withdrawn or superseded:

Auditing Guidance Statements (AGSs) – withdrawn

- AGS 1030 *Auditing Derivative Financial Instruments*

Auditing Standards (AUS) – superseded

- AUS 804 *The Audit of Prospective Financial Information* (superseded from 1 July 2013 when ASAEs 3420 and 3450 become operative)

Auditing Guidance Statements (AGSs) – superseded

- AGS 1062 *Reporting in Connection with Proposed Fundraisings* (superseded from 1 July 2013 when ASAEs 3420 and 3450 become operative)

Forthcoming Publications

The AUASB at its 26 November 2012 meeting approved for issue Guidance Statement GS 021 *Engagements under the National Greenhouse and Energy Reporting, Clean Energy and Related Schemes*. The GS is expected to be issued in December, but was not available at the time of going to press. It will be available from auasb.gov.au.

Exposure Drafts

The AUASB and the APESB both regularly issue exposure drafts.

The AUASB issues international exposure drafts by the IAASB for local comment as the international standards form the basis of the AUASB's standards. The AUASB then feeds back comments to the IAASB in its own submission. It also requests comments on its own drafts dealing with local issues. Exposure drafts can be downloaded from the AUASB website at auasb.gov.au.

The APESB also regularly issues exposure drafts, which can be downloaded from apesb.org.au. Some are based on the work of the International Ethics Standards Board for Accountants (IESBA) and others are written by the APESB to address local issues.

The Changes in Detail

New and revised Framework Documents

Foreword to AUASB Pronouncements

The revised *Foreword* was issued in November 2012, and sets out an overview of the pronouncements and other publications issued by the AUASB. In this version, the processes and procedures followed by the AUASB have been moved to a separate document.

The description of the Board's due process that was included in the original *Foreword* has been expanded and moved to a new document, *AUASB Functions and Processes*, also issued in November and available on the AUASB website. It sets out the Board's functions and powers, its relationships with other bodies, such as the Government and the New Zealand Auditing and Assurance Standards Board (NZAuASB) and how it operates and develops standards.

Principles of Convergence and Harmonisation

Principles of Convergence to International Standards of the International Auditing and Assurance Standards Board (IAASB) and Harmonisation with the Standards of the New Zealand Auditing and Assurance Standards Board (NZAuASB) was issued in November 2012 and applies from July 2012. The document responds to the strategic objective set by the Financial Reporting Council for the AUASB to use ISAs in developing Australian standards, reflected in the AUASB's own twin objectives of adopting international standards unless there are strong reasons not to and working with the NZAuASB towards the establishment of harmonised standards across the two countries.

New and revised Auditing and Assurance Standards

ASA 2012-1 *Amending Standard to ASA 570 Going Concern* and ASA 570 *Going Concern (compiled)*

ASA 2012-1 was issued in July 2012 to make minor editorial improvements to the diagram in [Aus] Appendix 1 *Going Concern, Linking Going Concern Considerations and Types of Audit Opinions* of ASA 570.

ASAE 3410 *Assurance Engagements on Greenhouse Gas Statements*

ASAE 3410 was issued in June 2012 to assist auditors performing work on greenhouse gas emissions statements under the new carbon legislation effective from 1 July 2012. It provides detailed requirements and related guidance for assurance practitioners when identifying, assessing and responding to risks of material misstatement in these types of engagements and provides illustrative assurance reports on greenhouse gas statements. Because these engagements are likely to be undertaken by a multidisciplinary team, it also addresses the integration of other experts into the engagement. It is operative for periods ending on or after 1 July 2012 and is based on ISAE 3410 of the same name.

It is supplemented by GS 021 *Engagements under the National Greenhouse and Energy Reporting, Clean Energy and Related Schemes*, due to be released in December 2012. GS 021 relates the requirements of the assurance standard to the specific terms of the Australian legislation and regulations.

ASAE 3420 *Assurance Engagements to Report on the Compilation of Pro Forma Historical Financial Information included in a Prospectus or other Document*

ASAE 3420 was issued in November 2012. It provides detailed requirements and related guidance for auditors when determining whether to accept an engagement to report on the compilation of pro forma historical financial information, the appropriate level of assurance, how the engagement is to be performed and what to include in the assurance report and includes illustrative appendices. It is operative for engagements commencing on or after 1 July 2013 and conforms with the international standard ISAE 3420.

ASAE 3450 *Assurance Engagements involving Corporate Fundraisings and/or Prospective Financial Information*

ASAE 3450 was issued in November 2012. It applies where an assurance practitioner is asked to report on historical, prospective or pro forma financial information that has been prepared for inclusion in a document such as a prospectus and also to any assurance report on prospective financial information. It provides detailed requirements and related guidance for auditors when determining whether to accept such an engagement, the appropriate level of assurance, how the engagement is to be performed and what to include in the assurance report. It replaces AUS 804 *The Audit of Prospective Financial Information* and AGS 1062 *Reporting in Connection with Proposed Fundraisings* and is operative for engagements commencing on or after 1 July 2013 and has no international equivalent.

New Standard on Related Services

ASRS 4450 *Comfort Letter Engagements*

ASRS 4450 was issued in May 2012 for auditors to follow when providing a comfort letter to certain requesting parties in respect of financial information related to, and/or included in, an offering document. It provides detailed requirements and related guidance for auditors when determining whether to accept a comfort letter engagement, how it is to be performed and how and what to report. Illustrative appendices are provided to assist auditors with reporting. It is operative for engagements commencing on or after 1 July 2013 and there is no international equivalent, but it was based on the US standard SAS 72, *Letters for Underwriters and Certain Other Requesting Parties.*

ASRS 4450 is supported by the 'Explanatory Guide to applying ASRS 4450 Comfort Letter Engagements', which provides additional information on when to apply the standard and is available from the AUASB website

New Guidance Statements (GSs)

GS 020 *Special Considerations in Auditing Financial Instruments*

GS 020 was issued in May 2012. It provides extensive explanatory background on financial instruments and then goes on to give guidance to auditors on the special considerations relating to their audit, such as when financial instruments are held at valuation.

It is applicable from the date of issue and replaces AGS 1030 *Auditing Derivative Financial Instruments*. It conforms with International Auditing Practice Note (IAPN) 1000 *Special Considerations in Auditing Financial Instruments*.

Revised Accounting Professional & Ethical Standards Board Standards (APESs)

APES 110 *Code of Ethics for Professional Accountants (compiled)*

An amendment to APES 110 was issued in December 2011 and has now been incorporated into a compiled version of APES 110. The definition of Public Interest Entity (PIE) was amended and an Australian paragraph added to provide guidance on which entities in Australia are, or are likely to be, Public Interest Entities. The amended definition is effective from 1 January 2013.

APES 225 *Valuation Services*

The revised APES 225 *Valuation Services* was issued in May 2012. It provides additional guidance to practitioners in respect of the three types of valuation services engagements, particularly the difference between a full scope and a limited scope valuation engagement and new requirements relating to engagement letters. A diagram and new examples have been included as an Appendix to provide guidance on distinguishing between the different types of engagement. The new standard is effective for valuation engagements or assignments commencing on or after 1 September 2012 with earlier adoption permitted.

New Accounting Professional & Ethical Standards Board Guidance Note (GN)

APES GN 40 *Ethical Conflicts in the workplace – Considerations for Members in Business*

APES GN 40 was issued in March 2012. It provides assistance to members in business in addressing a range of ethical issues, including potential conflicts of interest arising from responsibilities to employers, their preparation and reporting of information, financial interests and whistle blowing. It provides guidance on the application of fundamental principles contained in APES 110: *Code of Ethics for Professional Accountants* (the Code), and includes 21 case studies providing examples of ethical issues experienced in the commercial, public and not-for-profit sectors. It includes a new section that provides guidance for members in business regarding their professional obligations in relation to whistle blowing. It supersedes GN 1 *Members in Business Guidance Statement*, which the APESB inherited from the accounting profession and has no international equivalent.

Historical Development of the Standards

Both the APESB and the AUASB are in the process of reissuing the standards and guidance that they have inherited from predecessor Standard setters. The following tables compare the old and new Standards for both Boards.

Comparison of APES Standards with their predecessor APS Standards and Guidance Notes (GNs)

New Accounting Professional and Ethical Standards (APESs)		Equivalent Professional Standards (APSs) and Joint Guidance Notes (GNs)	
APES Number	**APES Title**	**APS/GN Number**	**APS/GN Title**
All Members			
APES 110	Code of Ethics for Professional Accountants	–	Joint Code of Professional Conduct
APES 205	Conformity with Accounting Standards	APS 1	Conformity with Accounting Standards and UIG Consensus Views
APES 210	Conformity with Auditing and Assurance Standards	APS 1.1	Conformity with Auditing Standards
APES 215	Forensic Accounting Services	APS 11 GN2	Statement of Forensic Accounting Standards Forensic Accounting
APES 220	Taxation Services	APS 6	Statement of Taxation Standards
APES 225	Valuation Services	No equivalent APS	
No equivalent APES		APS 12	Statement of Financial Advisory Service Standards
Members in Public Practice			
APES 305	Terms of Engagement	APS 2	Terms of Engagement
APES 310	Dealing with Client Monies	APS 10 GN 3	Trust Accounts Operation of Trust Accounts
APES 315	Compilation of Financial Information	APS 9	Statement on Compilation of Financial Reports
APES 320	Quality Control for Firms	APS 5	Statement of Quality Control for Firms
APES 325	Risk Management for Firms	N3 (Institute document)	Risk Management Guidelines
APES 330	Insolvency Services	APS 7	Statement of Insolvency Standards
APES 345	Reporting on Prospective Financial Information Prepared in Connection with a Disclosure Document	F2	Prospectuses and Reports on Profit Forecasts

New Accounting Professional and Ethical Standards (APESs)		Equivalent Professional Standards (APSs) and Joint Guidance Notes (GNs)	
APES Number	**APES Title**	**APS/GN Number**	**APS/GN Title**
APES 350	Participation by Members in Public Practice in Due Diligence Committees in connection with a Public Document	No equivalent APS	
Members in Business			
GN 40	Ethical Conflicts in the Workplace – Considerations for Members in Business	GN 1	Members in Business Guidance Statement
Professional Standards withdrawn and not replaced			
No equivalent APES		APS 3	Compatibility of Australian Accounting Standards and International Accounting Standards (withdrawn Feb 2007)
No equivalent APES		APS 8	Statement of Management Consulting Services Standard (withdrawn June 2008)

Comparison of ASA Auditing Standards with their predecessor AUS Standards

A table cross-referencing the old, new and international Standards follows:

2009 ASA number (operative 1/1/10)	Title	Current equivalent International Standard	2006 ASA number	Title	Equivalent old AUS series Standard
	Foreword to AUASB Pronouncements			Foreword to AUASB Pronouncements	AUS 102
	AUASB Glossary			AUASB Glossary	AUS 104
	Framework for Assurance Engagements	International Framework for Assurance Engagements		Framework for Assurance Engagements	AUS 108
ASQC 1	Quality Control for Firms that Perform Audits and Reviews of Financial Reports and Other Financial Information, and Other Assurance Engagements.	ISQC 1			
ASA 100	Preamble to AUASB Standards		ASA 100	Preamble to AUASB Standards	
ASA 101	Preamble to Australian Auditing Standards				
ASA 102	Compliance with Ethical Requirements when Performing Audits, Reviews and Other Assurance Engagements				
ASA 200	Overall Objectives of the Independent Auditor and the Conduct of an Audit in Accordance with Australian Auditing Standards	ISA 200	ASA 200	Objective and General Principles Governing an Audit of a Financial Report	AUS 202
ASA 210	Agreeing the Terms of Audit Engagements	ISA 210	ASA 210	Terms of Audit Engagements	AUS 204
ASA 220	Quality Control for an Audit of a Financial Report and Other Historical Financial Information	ISA 220	ASA 220	Quality Control for Audits of Historical Financial Information	AUS 206
ASA 230	Audit Documentation	ISA 230	ASA 230	Audit Documentation	AUS 208

2009 ASA number (operative 1/1/10)	Title	Current equivalent International Standard	2006 ASA number	Title	Equivalent old AUS series Standard
ASA 240	The Auditor's Responsibilities relating to Fraud in an Audit of a Financial Report	ISA 240	ASA 240	The Auditor's Responsibility to Consider Fraud in an Audit of a Financial Report	AUS 210
ASA 250	Consideration of Laws and Regulations in an Audit of a Financial Report	ISA 250	ASA 250	Consideration of Laws and Regulations in an Audit of a Financial Report	AUS 218
ASA 260	Communication with Those Charged with Governance	ISA 260	ASA 260	Communication of Audit Matters with Those Charged with Governance	AUS 710
ASA 265	Communicating Deficiencies in Internal Control to Those Charged with Governance and Management	ISA 265			
ASA 300	Planning an Audit of a Financial Report	ISA 300	ASA 300	Planning an Audit of a Financial Report	AUS 302
ASA 315	Identifying and Assessing the Risks of Material Misstatement through Understanding the Entity and its Environment	ISA 315	ASA 315	Understanding the Entity and its Environment and Assessing the Risks of Material Misstatement	AUS 402
ASA 320	Materiality in Planning and Performing an Audit	ISA 320	ASA 320	Materiality and Audit Adjustments	AUS 306
ASA 330	The Auditor's Responses to Assessed Risks	ISA 330	ASA 330	The Auditor's Procedures in Response to Assessed Risks	AUS 406
ASA 402	Audit Considerations Relating to an Entity Using a Service Organisation	ISA 402	ASA 402	Audit Considerations Relating to Entities Using Service Organisations	AUS 404
ASA 450	Evaluation of Misstatements Identified during the Audit	ISA 450			
ASA 500	Audit Evidence	ISA 500	ASA 500	Audit Evidence	AUS 502

2009 ASA number (operative 1/1/10)	Title	Current equivalent International Standard	2006 ASA number	Title	Equivalent old AUS series Standard
ASA 501	Audit Evidence – Specific Considerations for Inventory and Segment Information	ISA 501	ASA 501	Existence and Valuation of Inventory	AUS 506
ASA 502	Audit Evidence – Specific Considerations for Litigation and Claims	ISA 501	ASA 508	Enquiry Regarding Litigation and Claims	AUS 508
ASA 505	External Confirmations	ISA 505	ASA 505	External Confirmations	AUS 504
ASA 510	Initial Audit Engagements – Opening Balances	ISA 510	ASA 510	Initial Engagements – Opening Balances	AUS 510
ASA 520	Analytical Procedures	ISA 520	ASA 520	Analytical Procedures	AUS 512
ASA 530	Audit Sampling	ISA 530	ASA 530	Audit Sampling and Other Means of Testing	AUS 514
ASA 540	Auditing Accounting Estimates, including Fair Value Accounting Estimates, and Related Disclosures	ISA 540	ASA 540	Audit of Accounting Estimates	AUS 516
N/A	Now part of ASA 540		ASA 545	Auditing Fair Value Measurements and Disclosures	AUS 526
ASA 550	Related Parties	ISA 550	ASA 550	Related Parties	AUS 518
ASA 560	Subsequent Events	ISA 560	ASA 560	Subsequent Events	AUS 706
ASA 570	Going Concern	ISA 570	ASA 570	Going Concern	AUS 708
ASA 580	Written Representations	ISA 580	ASA 580	Management Representations	AUS 520
ASA 600	Special Considerations – Audits of a Group Financial Report (Including the Work of Component Auditors)	ISA 600	ASA 600	Using the Work of Another Auditor	AUS 602
ASA 610	Using the Work of Internal Auditors	ISA 610	ASA 610	Considering the Work of Internal Audit	AUS 604
ASA 620	Using the Work of an Auditor's Expert	ISA 620	ASA 620	Using the Work of an Expert	AUS 606

2009 ASA number (operative 1/1/10)	Title	Current equivalent International Standard	2006 ASA number	Title	Equivalent old AUS series Standard
ASA 700	Forming an Opinion and Reporting on a Financial Report	ISA 700	ASA 700	The Auditor's Report on a General purpose Financial Report	AUS 702
N/A	Split between ASA 705 and ASA 706		ASA 701	Modifications to the Auditor's Report	AUS 702
ASA 705	Modifications to the Opinion in the Independent Auditor's Report	ISA 705			AUS 702
ASA 706	Emphasis of Matter Paragraphs and Other Matter Paragraphs in the Independent Auditor's Report	ISA 706			AUS 702
ASA 710	Comparative Information – Corresponding Figures and Comparative Financial Reports	ISA 710	ASA 710	Comparatives	AUS 704
ASA 720	The Auditor's Responsibilities Relating to Other Information in Documents Containing an Audited Financial Report	ISA 720	ASA 720	Other Information in Documents Containing Audited Financial Reports	AUS 212
ASA 800	Special Considerations – Audits of Financial Reports Prepared in Accordance with Special Purpose Frameworks	ISA 800	ASA 800	The Auditor's Report on Special Purpose Audit Engagements	AUS 802
ASA 805	Special Considerations – Audits of Single Financial Statements and Specific Elements, Accounts or Items of a Financial Statement	ISA 805			
ASA 810	Engagements to Report on Summary Financial Statements	ISA 810			
ASRE 2400	Review of a Financial Report Performed by an Assurance Practitioner Who is Not the Auditor of the Entity	ISRE 2400		Review of Financial Reports	AUS 902
ASRE 2405	Review of Historical Financial Information Other than a Financial Report	ISRE 2400			

2009 ASA number (operative 1/1/10)	Title	Current equivalent International Standard	2006 ASA number	Title	Equivalent old AUS series Standard
ASRE 2410	Review of a Financial Report Performed by the Independent Auditor of the Entity	ISRE 2410	ASRE 2410	Review of an Interim Financial Report Performed by the Independent Auditor of the Entity	
ASRE 2415	Review of a Financial Report – Company Limited by Guarantee				
ASAE 3000	Assurance Engagements other than Audits or Reviews of Historical Financial Information	ISAE 3000		Assurance Engagements other than Audits or Reviews of Historical Information	AUS 110
ASAE 3100	Compliance Engagements				
ASAE 3402	Assurance Reports on Controls at a Service Organisation	ISAE 3402			
ASAE 3410	Assurance on Greenhouse Gas Statements	ISAE 3410			
ASAE 3420	Assurance Engagements to Report on the Compilation of Pro Forma Historical Financial Information included in a Prospectus or other Document				
ASAE 3450	Assurance Engagements involving Corporate Fundraisings and/or Prospective Financial Information			The Audit of Prospective Financial Information	AUS 804
ASAE 3500	Performance Engagements			Performance Auditing Planning Performance Audits	AUS 806 AUS 808
ASRS 4400	Agreed-Upon Procedures Engagements to Report Factual Findings	ISRS 4400	N/A	Engagement to Perform Agreed-Upon Procedures	AUS 904
ASRS 4450	Comfort Letter Engagements				
N/A			N/A	Special Purpose Reports on the Effectiveness of Control Procedures	AUS 810

Understanding Financial Statement Audits: A Guide for Financial Statement Users

(Revised November 2011)

Note from the Institute of Chartered Accountants Australia

This note, prepared by the technical editor, is not part of 'Understanding Financial Statement Audits: A Guide for Financial Statement Users' reproduced below.

Historical development

1990: The International Federation of Accountants, in conjunction with the International Auditing Practices Committee, issued 'Understanding Financial Statements – A Guide for Financial Statements Users'. The publication addressed, in part, the 'audit expectation gap' by explaining the auditor's role in relation to financial statements audits. The major objective of the publication was to explain the meaning of the auditor's report and the level of assurance provided by an auditor's opinion on the financial statements. The booklet contained a detailed review of international auditing guidelines on which Statement of Auditing Practice AUP 3 'Audit on a General Purpose Financial Report' was based.

October 1990: This publication was issued in Australia by the Auditing Standards Board which included comments in the Australian context in Appendix I to the booklet. This booklet was not updated for the IAPC's or the AuSB's Codification and Revision Project.

November 2011: 'Understanding Financial Statement Audits: A Guide for Financial Statement Users' updated by the Institute of Chartered Accountants in Australia to reflect contemporary Australian auditing practice and the 'Clarity' revisions to auditing Standards.

Preface

The first version of this paper, *Understanding Financial Statements – A Guide for Financial Statements Users*, was published in 1990 by the International Federation of Accountants, in conjunction with the International Auditing Practices Committee. Its objective was to explain the meaning of the auditor's report and the level of assurance provided by an auditor's opinion on the financial statements with a view to addressing the 'audit expectation gap' surrounding the auditor's role in financial statement audits.

In the two decades since 1990, there have been many changes in the audit and assurance environment but the issue of managing the expectations of users of audited financial information is as relevant as it ever was. The Institute of Chartered Accountants in Australia has therefore decided to update the paper, with a particular focus on contemporary Australian requirements.

One of the biggest changes that has occurred in this period has been the globalisation of both the world's capital markets, and, in response, the accounting profession. In 1990 globalisation, while perhaps not in its infancy, was less fully developed than it is now. Nevertheless, the growth in international trade and multinational businesses, coupled with the globalisation of the world's capital markets, was already leading to demand for internationally recognised standards for accounting and reporting in both the public and private sectors. The International Federation of Accountants (IFAC) was formed in 1977 in response to these demands.

IFAC's broad objective was to develop and enhance a coordinated worldwide accountancy profession with harmonised standards. In pursuit of this aim, IFAC established the International Auditing and Assurance Standards Board (IAASB) as an independent standard-setting body which served the public interest by setting high-quality international standards for auditing and assurance purposes. It was charged with facilitating the convergence of these international standards with national standards around the world and today its standards are the basis of those used by 125 national standard setters, including the Australian Auditing and Assurance Standards Board (AUASB).

International harmonisation of accounting standards was happening in parallel, with the formation of the International Accounting Standards Committee in 1973, which was reconstituted as the International Accounting Standards Board in 2001 in a move designed to raise the profile of international accounting standards and promote global harmonisation. With the announcement by the EU that listed companies within the EU were to move to International Accounting Standards in 2005, other countries followed suit, including Australia, which converged its standards with those of the IASB from 1 January 2005, reissuing the entire suite of requirements. By 2010, 120 countries had adopted International Financial Reporting Standards (IFRS) and many more announced plans to do so within the following five years.

Convergence on the accounting side has further encouraged convergence of auditing standards. In 2007, the IAASB commenced a major project to improve its standards. This was referred to as the "Clarity" project because its objective was to make the standards clearer to understand and apply. In October 2009, the AUASB reissued its auditing standards in Clarity format, based on the Clarity standards that were issued by the IAASB earlier in 2009. This paper is based on the requirements of the 2009 Clarity reissue of the auditing standards.

A Note on the Scope of this Paper and the Terminology Used

Traditionally in Australia, the term "financial statements" has been used to refer only to the statements of financial position, comprehensive income, changes in equity and cash flows while the term "financial report" has been used to refer to these statements together with the notes to the financial statements and the directors' declaration.[1] Internationally, and in the accounting standards literature, the term "financial statements" is used in the same way as "financial report" is used in Australia. This paper adopts the international terminology and uses the term "financial statements" to refer to the whole document, including notes.

In the technical literature, "audit" is one of a number of assurance services that involves practitioners providing assurance over a range of subject matters that are not limited to financial information; for example, assurance over reports of greenhouse gas emissions. However, the term "audit" is most commonly used in the context of financial information and this paper only deals with that area of assurance services designed to offer reasonable assurance to the users of financial statements. A broader treatment of assurance generally can be found in the IAASB's *Framework for Assurance Engagements* (reissued by the AUASB).

This paper focuses on the audit of general purpose financial statements which are designed for users who cannot demand financial reports tailor made for their specific information needs, such as the shareholders of large companies. Assurance services for special purpose financial information; are beyond the scope of this guide, but interested readers can find out more about these services in ASA 800 *Special Considerations – Audits of Financial Reports Prepared in Accordance with Special Purpose Frameworks*.

Assumed Knowledge

This paper assumes readers have a basic knowledge of the content of financial statements, the purposes for which they are prepared, the terminology used therein, and the accounting principles and practices used in their preparation.[2] Its focus is on explaining the contribution of the audit report to the information these statements contain.

1 *Corporations Act 2001* s. 295.

2 A business library, such as the Institute's Knowledge Centre, can advise on appropriate reference materials.

Contents

Contents continued

Executive Summary

The major objective of this publication is to explain the meaning of the auditor's report and the assurance that is provided by an auditor's opinion on financial statements. It is intended for users of financial statements who want to better understand the message and significance of audit reports. It will also assist students of auditing and preparers of financial statements, including company management, in gaining an understanding of the service an auditor can provide and the limitations on that service.

Financial statements are used for a variety of purposes and decisions. For example, financial statements are used by owners to evaluate management's stewardship, by investors for making decisions about whether to buy or sell securities, by credit rating agencies for making decisions about creditworthiness of entities, and by bankers for making decisions about whether to lend money. Effective use of financial statements requires that the reader understand the roles of those responsible for preparing and auditing them.

Fundamentally, financial statements are the representations of management about what has happened to the entity which they manage. Financial statements are prepared with users in mind and seek to fulfil management's responsibility to be accountable for its use of the entity's resources. When using these statements, the reader must recognise that their preparation requires management to choose those accounting principles and methods that are most appropriate within the framework of generally accepted accounting standards and also make significant accounting estimates and judgments in presenting the information that is recorded.

In contrast, the auditor's responsibility is to express an independent opinion on whether management has fairly presented the information in the financial statements. In an audit, the financial statements are evaluated by the auditor, who is objective and knowledgeable about auditing, accounting, and financial reporting matters. Management of the entity benefits from dialogue with the auditor, whose questioning may hold up a mirror to their business practices, but the auditor remains objective and independent to ensure that the audit opinion provides valuable assurance about the financial report to third parties.

During the audit, the auditor gains an understanding of the business and the environment in which it operates and then collects evidence to obtain reasonable assurance that the amounts and disclosures in the financial statements are free of material misstatement. However, the characteristics of evaluating evidence on a test basis, the fact that accounting estimates are inherently imprecise, and the difficulties associated with detecting misstatements hidden by collusion and careful forgery, prevent the auditor from finding every error or irregularity that may affect a user's decision when relying on the financial statements.

The auditor also evaluates management's assertion about the ability of the entity to continue as a going concern in the foreseeable future. However, readers should recognise that future business performance is uncertain, and neither management nor an auditor can guarantee business success.

Through the audit process, the auditor adds credibility to management's financial statements, which allows owners, investors, bankers, and other creditors to use them with greater confidence.

The auditor expresses his or her assurance on the financial statements in an auditor's report. The report, which follows a standard format for ease of interpretation by the user, conveys the auditor's opinion as to whether the financial statements fairly present the entity's financial position and financial performance. If the auditor has reservations about amounts or disclosures in the statements, he or she modifies the report to describe the reservations.

The auditor's report and management's financial statements are most useful to those who make the effort to understand them. This paper should help you do that.

Chapter 1 – Introduction to Audits and Financial Reporting

In today's economy, information and accountability have assumed a larger role in our society. As a result, the independent audit of an entity's financial statements is a vital service to investors, creditors, and other participants in economic exchanges.

The auditor communicates audit results in a standard report. The auditor's report is based on rigorous work performed by highly trained and skilled professionals. This paper explains the financial statement audit, the assurance provided by the independent auditor's report, and the meaning of the report wording.

Need for Financial Statements

Regardless of the type of entity — whether in the public or private sector, or whether for profit or not — all entities use economic resources to pursue their goals. Financial statements enable an entity's management to provide useful information about its financial position at a particular point in time and the results of its operations and its changes in financial position for a particular period of time. External financial reporting for these entities is directed toward the common interest of various users. Financial statements provide owners with information about the stewardship of management. They also provide a basis for investors' decisions about whether to buy or sell securities; for credit rating services' decisions about the credit worthiness of entities; for bankers' decisions about whether to lend money, and for decisions of other creditors, regulators, and others outside of the entity.[3] The preparation of financial statements may be mandated by legislation, by the entity's constitution or by contract.

The Financial Statement Audit

As with the preparation of financial statements, an audit may be mandated by legislation, regulation, an entity's contitution or by contract. The objective of the financial statement audit is to add credibility to management's financial statements. Access to capital markets, mergers, acquisitions, and investments in an entity depends not only on the information that management provides in financial statements, but also on the level of trust that users are willing to place in those financial statements, itself driven by the degree of assurance provided by the auditor that the financial statements are free of material misstatement whether caused by error or fraud. In the process of providing reasonable assurance that financial statements are fairly presented, an auditor assesses whether:

- Transactions and amounts that should have been recorded are reported in the financial statements – are the financial statements a complete record?
- The assets and liabilities reported in the financial statements existed at the balance sheet date, and the transactions reported in the financial statements occurred during the period covered by the statements.
- Reported assets are owned by the entity and all liabilities owed by the entity at the balance sheet date are reported.
- The financial statement amounts (assets, liabilities, revenues, and expenses) are properly "measured" and appropriately valued in conformity with accounting standards.
- The financial statement amounts are properly classified, described, and disclosed in conformity with accounting standards.

3 For a more elaborate discussion of the objective of financial reporting and users' information needs, refer to the IASB's *Framework for the Preparation and Presentation of Financial Statements* (also issued by the AASB) and the AASB's Statement of Accounting Concepts SAC 2 *Objective of General Purpose Financial Reporting.*

The independent auditor forms an opinion on the overall fairness of the financial statements by testing the above assertions. The opinion is communicated in the auditor's report. The standard auditor's report contains an unmodified opinion, which means that an auditor believes that the financial statements present fairly in all material respects (or give a true and fair view of) the entity's financial position, financial performance and cash flows in conformity with accounting standards. A modified opinion, in contrast, notifies financial statement readers about concerns the auditor has about matters affecting the financial statements (such as the selection of accounting policies or the method of their application or the adequacy of financial statement disclosure) or about limitations in the scope of the auditor's work. Alternatively, it may draw the reader's attention to a particular note in the financial report disclosing significant factors of which, in the auditor's view, the reader should be aware. Therefore, a user should understand the implications of a modified report and read all audit reports very carefully.

Responsibility for Financial Statements

Effective use of financial statements requires that the reader understand the roles of those responsible for preparing, auditing, and using financial statements. Figure 1 depicts the independent auditor's role in auditing management's financial statements.

Management, under the oversight of those charged with governance (for example, the board of directors) is responsible for the content of the financial statements, regardless of an organisation's size or form of ownership. The preparation of these statements requires management to comply with the appropriate financial reporting framework such as the *Corporations Act 2001* and the Australian Accounting Standards. In doing so, management is required to make significant judgments and estimates. Management's responsibility for financial statements is not lessened by having the statements audited, but the quality of management's decision making may be improved by interaction with the auditor.

Figure 1 The various relationships surrounding audited financial information

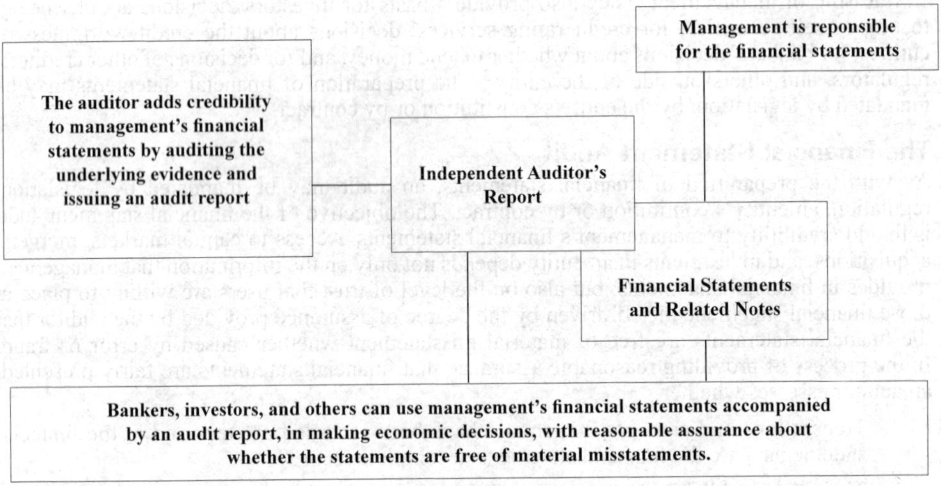

The Independent Audit

An audit allows financial statement users, such as creditors, bankers, analysts, investors, and others to use the financial statements with greater confidence than they would have without the audit. While the audit does not guarantee financial statement accuracy, it provides users with a reasonable assurance that an entity's financial statements give a true and fair view (or present fairly") its financial position, financial performance and cash flows in conformity with accounting standards. An audit enhances users' confidence that financial statements do not contain any material misstatement due to error or fraud that would affect this true and fair view because the auditor is an independent, objective professional who is knowledgeable of the entity's business and financial reporting requirements.

Using Financial Statements

The auditor's report and financial statements presented by management are most useful to those who make the effort to understand them.

Effective use of audited financial statements requires a basic understanding of:

- accounting standards;
- the related concepts of financial measurement and disclosure; and
- the inherent limitations of financial statements caused by the use of accounting estimates, judgments, and various alternative accounting principles and methods.

Knowledgeable use of the auditor's report requires a general understanding of both:

- the audit process; and
- the meaning of the auditor's report.

This paper examines the relationships illustrated in Figure 1 and starts with the benefits of audited financial information for users, while stressing the responsibility of users to understand what they are using. The following chapters of this paper go on to explore the implications of these relationships for preparers and auditors of financial statements.

Chapter 2 – Preparing Financial Statements

Management's Responsibility for Preparing Financial Statements

In this paper, the term "management" is used to indicate those who are running the entity's operations on a day to day basis, whatever their title. "Management"[4] includes the executive directors in the case of a company. Larger entities may also have an oversight tier, for example a Board of Directors that includes non-executive directors. This tier oversees management and is known as "those charged with governance".[5] In smaller entities, the two tiers are often merged.

Management is responsible for establishing an accounting system to identify, measure, record, and adequately disclose an entity's transactions and other events that affect its financial position and financial performance including a system of internal control to ensure that transactions are processed completely and accurately and to safeguard against fraud and error. In addition, management is responsible for selecting accounting principles that appropriately reflect events that occur and for making other accounting estimates and judgments. This responsibility is not lessened by an independent audit. This chapter explains the judgments involved in preparing financial statements in accordance with accounting standards. Figure 2 shows the relationship between management and the financial statements.

4 *Management* is defined in the IAASB and AUASB Glossary as "The person(s) with executive responsibility for the conduct of the entity's operations. For some entities in some jurisdictions, management includes some or all of those charged with governance, for example, executive members of a governance board, or an owner-manager".

5 *Those charged with governance* is defined in the IAASB and AUASB Glossary as "The person(s) or organisation(s) (for example, a corporate trustee) with responsibility for overseeing the strategic direction of the entity and obligations related to the accountability of the entity. This includes overseeing the financial reporting process. For some entities in some jurisdictions, those charged with governance may include management personnel, for example, executive members of a governance board of a private or public sector entity, or an owner-manager".

Figure 2 Management is responsible for the preparation of the financial statements

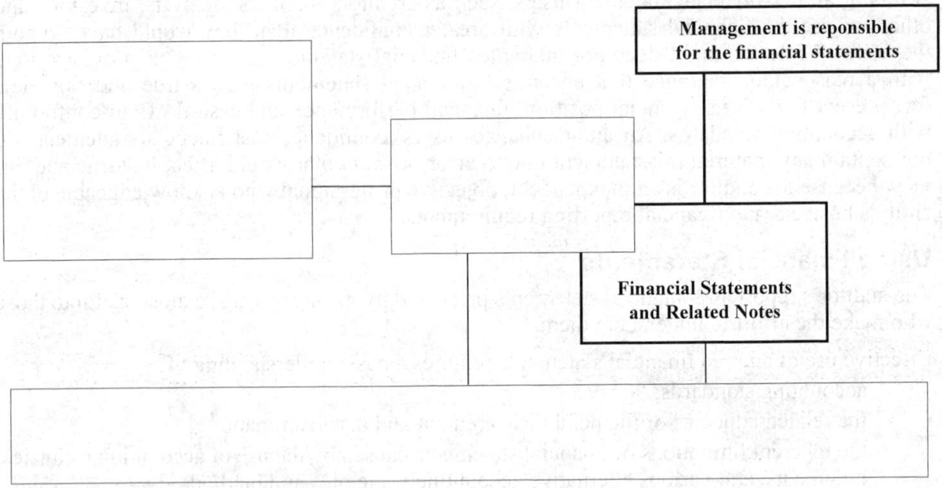

The Role of Internal Control

Management's responsibility for establishing an accounting system that enables the preparation of financial statements that present fairly the entity's financial position and financial performance includes the establishment and maintenance of a system of internal control. The system of internal control provides checks and balances within the accounting system to safeguard against misstatements, both deliberate (fraud) and accidental (error), and ensures that transactions are processed completely and accurately. The larger the organisation, the more complex the system of internal control is likely to be. The auditor's work involves testing these controls to check that they are fulfilling their function and to assess the quality of the information generated by the accounting system.

Objective Versus Judgmental Issues in the Accounting Process

Some transactions, such as the purchase of inventory, can be objectively identified, measured, and recorded when they occur. While the initial recording of a transaction is often straightforward, evaluating the subsequent effects of these transactions on financial position, results of operations, or changes in financial position may require more judgment. For example when inventory is proving unsaleable or has been damaged since its purchase, management may need to estimate the amount of unsold inventory that is obsolete or determine whether its market value is significantly impaired in order to comply with accounting principles. Such applications of accounting principles require significant assumptions, estimates, and professional judgments that are inherently imprecise.

Effects of Accounting Judgments

The judgments management makes on accounting matters affect financial statements in several ways as discussed below.

Financial Measurement

Financial measurement involves measuring the monetary amounts of the effects of events and transactions. Such measurement is not always as easy as determining the amount of a payment. Many financial statement amounts involve significant accounting estimates. For example, what portion of credit sales will be uncollectible? How long will depreciable assets remain in use? What product warranty claims will have to be paid? In current market conditions is this asset still worth what it cost?

Accounting Principles and Methods

Accounting policies encompass the principles, conventions, rules and procedures adopted by management in preparing and presenting financial statements. There may be a variety of different accounting policies in use even in relation to the same subject; judgment is required in determining and applying those that are best suited, in the circumstances, to present properly an entity's financial position and results of operations. For example, there are many acceptable methods for valuing inventory or depreciating fixed assets and so ascertaining the "fair" value of an asset or liability may involve the application of judgment in setting appropriate assumptions.

Management is responsible for determining the accounting principles and methods that are appropriate for the circumstances when preparing financial statements. Once management has determined the initial accounting principle, it must have reasonable justification to change it. Such justifications would include complying with the issue of a new accounting standard or bringing an entity into line with accounting principles used in the rest of a group.

Adequacy of Disclosure

Adequacy of disclosure relates to whether information in the financial statements, including the notes, clearly explains matters that may affect their use and understanding. Accounting standards generally stipulate a minimum level of disclosure, but management also makes decisions about disclosures that concern both the amounts and the usefulness of information in financial statements. Disclosures may be made in the body of the financial statements or in notes to the statements. Notes are considered an integral part of the financial statements. A balance should be achieved between detail and summarisation. Too much disclosure can distract and overburden the user; too little can result in essential information being withheld.

Going Concern

In the preparation of financial statements, an entity's ability to continue as a going concern is assumed. Experience indicates that, in the absence of significant information to the contrary, continuing operation is highly probable for most entities; therefore, the assumption that an entity is a going concern is not discussed in every set of financial statements. If there is doubt about an entity's ability to continue as a going concern in the next year, then management should disclose, in the notes to the financial statements:

- pertinent conditions that raise doubt about the entity's ability to continue as a going concern in the next year;
- the possible effects of such conditions, such as the possibility that the entity may be unable to continue in operation and therefore be unable to realise all of its assets and pay all of its liabilities in the normal course of business.

Relevant Accounting Standards

If management is to fulfil its responsibility for preparing useful financial statements, it must pay careful attention to the quality of its accounting judgments. The choices available to financial statement preparers are governed by accounting standards, also known as financial reporting standards, that deal with financial measurement and disclosure. Such standards, which are referred to simply as accounting standards throughout this paper, set out appropriate accounting treatments for different types of transactions to instruct those who are responsible for preparing financial statements. These technical standards, which have evolved at both national and international levels, provide a benchmark against which the auditor assesses a financial statement presentation.

Within each country, local regulations, legislation[6] and standards also affect, to a greater or lesser degree, the content of financial statements. Such local regulations and standards may include industry specific accounting standards or standards dealing with a particular local issue that are promulgated by the regulatory bodies in the countries concerned.

6 The prime example in Australia is the *Corporations Act 2001*.

Chapter 3 – Auditing Financial Statements

Figure 3 The auditor is responsible for the audit report

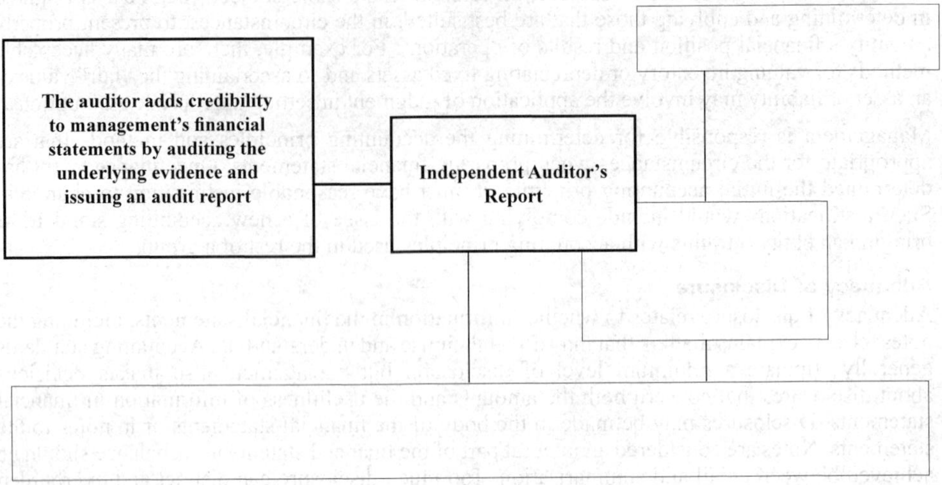

Assurance and Financial Statements

An assurance engagement, such as an audit, has various elements:

- a three-way relationship between the assurance practitioner (auditor), the users of the information and those responsible for preparing the information;
- the information itself, for example, the financial statements;
- suitable criteria against which the information is assessed, for example, the Australian or international accounting standards;
- evidence to support the information being examined; and
- a written assurance report, such as the auditor's report.

The IAASB recognises that an auditor (also known more broadly as an assurance practitioner) can provide assurance over a wide variety of financial and non-financial information. Within the sphere of financial information, it contemplates three levels of service that an assurance practitioner can provide on financial statements:

- an audit;
- a review; and
- a related service using some assurance skills, but not providing assurance to the users (for example, the compilation of a financial report or an agreed-upon procedures engagement).

The principal difference between each level is the degree of assurance about the accuracy of financial information that each type provides, and which in turn is a reflection of the work the auditor has performed in order to be able to provide this level of assurance. The range of alternatives is shown in Figure 4 moving from "audit", which provides a high level of assurance also known as "reasonable assurance", through to a "review", which provides a moderate level of assurance, also known as "limited assurance", and finally to work that provides no assurance at all. Figure 4 also illustrates absolute assurance, but for practical purposes an engagement giving absolute assurance is very rare.

Levels of Assurance

Providing absolute assurance in auditing is generally not considered attainable for a variety of reasons. Financial statements and audit reports need to be timely in order to be of value to users and the time and costs involved in providing a detailed review of every single transaction would make the financial reporting process unworkable. Instead auditors design and use testing to provide the information they require to support their opinion in a more efficient manner.

Even if 100% verification of transactions were practical, factors such as the use by management of judgments and estimates in financial statements (i.e. financial statements contain approximations, not exact amounts), and the fact that most of the evidence available to the auditor is persuasive, rather than conclusive, in nature mean that, at best, it is only possible to provide "reasonable" assurance. However, the procedures that an auditor designs in order to provide this level of assurance do, by definition, have a high probability of detecting any large ("material") errors and misstatements and so allow the auditor to issue his or her opinion with confidence. Lower levels of assurance provide higher levels of risk in this regard and so the opinion given by the auditor differs. Lower levels are chosen for those types of engagements where the users do not need the high level of assurance that audit provides.

The auditing standards set out the types of procedures auditors must undertake in order to ensure they obtain the evidence they need to support the opinion that they issue. The standards require that, in designing procedures to reach a high level of assurance, auditors must understand the risk inherent in the entity, the environment in which it operates and its financial statement preparation process, and respond accordingly.

This paper deals only with the assurance users obtain from an audit, "reasonable assurance", which is the greatest degree of assurance available to users of financial statements.

Figure 4 Illustration of various possible levels of assurance, from no assurance up to absolute assurance

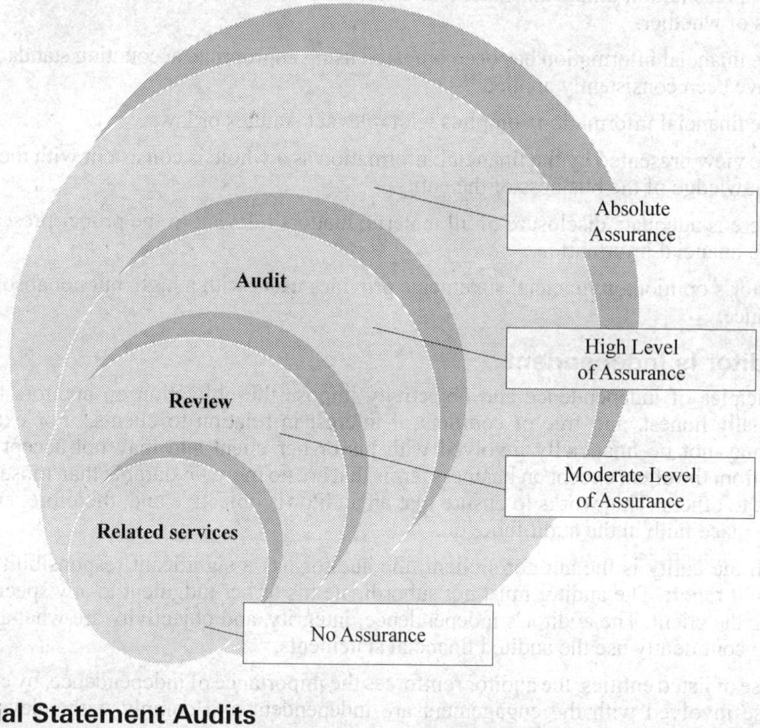

Financial Statement Audits

An audit aims to provide reasonable assurance to users of the financial statements which management has prepared and presented. The auditor provides this assurance by expressing an independent, objective opinion on whether the financial information is presented fairly (or, in the case of companies, gives a true and fair view, to use the *Corporations Act 2001* wording) in conformity with the basis of accounting indicated. The auditor determines and carries out audit procedures that are designed to be able to enable him or her to provide this high level of assurance about the reliability of management's representations in the financial statements.

The auditor tests the data underlying the entity's financial statements and the systems generating that data to obtain evidence that, along with other procedures, provides the basis for the auditor's opinion about whether the financial statements are free of material misstatements.

Financial statement audits fall into two types:

- those where the financial statements are based on a fair presentation framework – that is, they purport to "present fairly" (or, in the case of a company, "give a true and fair view of") the financial position and financial performance of the entity; and
- those where the financial statements are based on a compliance framework, where the auditor opines on whether the financial statements comply with that framework (compliance frameworks are more common in the public sector context where an auditor might need to express an opinion on compliance with set conditions for grant funding, for example).

A fair presentation framework adds an element of judgment to both the preparer's and the auditor's role which is absent in a compliance framework. For example, under a fair presentation framework, management may decide to add additional information[7] beyond that required by accounting standards in order that the financial statements can present fairly the entity's financial position and performance. The auditor then has to form an opinion as to whether this additional information is appropriate.

This paper deals with the financial statement audit of an entity under a fair presentation framework, being the most common scenario encountered in practice; for example, the audit of a company's financial statements.

In a fair presentation financial statement audit, the auditor's overall conclusion embraces questions of whether:

- the financial information has been prepared using appropriate accounting standards, which have been consistently applied;
- the financial information complies with relevant statutes or laws;
- the view presented by the financial information as a whole is consistent with the auditor's knowledge of the business of the entity;
- there is adequate disclosure of all material matters relevant to the proper presentation of the financial information.

The auditor's opinion on financial statements provides users with a high, but not absolute, level of assurance.

An Auditor Is Independent

The principles of independence and objectivity impose the obligation on auditors to be fair, intellectually honest, and free of conflicts of interest in relation to clients.[8] For example, an auditor may not be financially involved with his or her client and may not accept goods or services from the client except on business terms that are no more favourable than those generally available to others. This works to ensure that an auditor is objective and, therefore, enables the public to place faith in the audit function.

Although the entity is the auditor's client, the auditor has a significant responsibility to users of the audit report. The auditor must not subordinate his or her judgment to any specific group, including the client. The auditor's independence, integrity, and objectivity are what allow third parties to confidently use the audited financial statements.

In the case of listed entities, the auditor reinforces the importance of independence, by confirming that those involved with the engagement are independent and comply with relevant ethical requirements.

---

7 In some jurisdictions, it is permissible to override the provisions of an accounting standard if they do not result in information that presents fairly the entity's financial position and performance. However, this course is prevented in Australia by the *Corporations Act 2001* and the preparer's only avenue is to add extra information in order to present fairly the matter in question.

8 APES 110 *Code of Ethics for Professional Accountants* (based on the International Ethics Standards Board for Accountants' code) sets out fundamental ethical principles, including integrity, objectivity, professional competence and care, confidentiality and professional behaviour, and gives guidance as to how these principles should be adhered to in practice.

Auditor's Responsibility for Detecting Material Misstatements

Auditors are responsible for planning and performing an audit to obtain reasonable assurance that the financial statements are free of material misstatements, whether due to fraud or error. The concept of reasonable assurance, however, does not ensure or guarantee the accuracy of the financial statements due to the specific characteristics of an audit that were identified earlier. These specific characteristics are important to understanding the difference between reasonable assurance and a guarantee or absolute assurance and are discussed in more detail below.

Detection of Error or Fraud

The audit opinion on a set of financial statements requires the auditor to state that the statements fairly present the financial results and position of the entity. In order to do this, the auditor must assesses the risk of material error and fraud when planning the audit approach and, accordingly, building on his or her knowledge of the business, designs the audit to provide reasonable assurance of detecting significant errors or fraud. However, some irregularities or frauds are concealed through forgery or collusion (among client personnel or outsiders). Auditors are not specifically trained to detect forgeries, nor will customary audit procedures detect conspiracies. As a result, it is possible that a properly designed and executed audit may not detect material fraud. Therefore, audits can only provide reasonable assurance that financial statements are free of material misstatements and cannot absolutely guarantee the accuracy of financial statements. The primary responsibility for the prevention and detection of fraud rests with management.[9]

Similarly, it is the responsibility of management to ensure that the entity's operations are conducted in accordance with relevant laws and regulations. The auditor may detect some instances of non-compliance during the course of the audit, but should not be expected to detect non-compliance with all laws and regulations.[10]

Audits Involve Tests

Auditors rarely examine 100% of the items in an account or transaction class as this is usually an inefficient and costly way of obtaining the information that they need. Instead, they select and apply procedures to only a portion of those items, also referred to as a sample, and use those results to form an opinion on the individual elements of the financial statements and then ultimately on the financial statements as a whole. The auditor exercises skill and judgment in deciding what evidence to look at, when to look at it, and how much to look at, as well as in interpreting and evaluating results. Depending on the population of items being examined, the auditor may use statistical sampling techniques or a more judgmental method of selection. The aim is to ensure that he or she obtains evidence that is both sufficient and appropriate to support the opinion being issued.

Materiality in the Financial Statements

Although financial statements contain approximations, they must reflect a reasonable degree of accuracy. If an omission or the degree of misstatement is significant enough to influence the decisions of financial statement users, it is considered material. In other words, materiality is the threshold over which the misstatement or omission would matter to a reader.

Materiality is therefore a relative concept. For example, a $100,000 misstatement of sales for a company with a $200,000 profit is material, while that same misstatement for a company with a $50,000,000 profit would prima facie be immaterial in financial terms. However, qualitative characteristics also influence materiality. For example, an error in the financial statements might be small as a percentage of a critical component but this small error could cause an entity to breach a loan agreement, which could result in a misclassification of current and noncurrent debt, which would make it material. An auditor considers both quantitative and qualitative aspects of errors found during the audit.

Auditing Transactions and Accounting Estimates

When an entity engages in transactions with an outside party, documentary evidence of the transaction is usually created. This evidence provides a substantial basis for the auditor to form

9 For further details, see ASA 240 *The Auditor's Responsibilities Relating to Fraud in an Audit of a Financial Report.*

10 For further details, see ASA 250 *Consideration of Laws and Regulations in an Audit of a Financial Report.*

an opinion about whether the transaction occurred and has been accounted for in accordance with relevant accounting standards.

Evidence supporting the fairness of accounting estimates is not as readily available as evidence supporting transactions, because estimates involve the application of assumptions and judgments. While the auditor can design tests to evaluate the reasonableness of management's assumptions and the factors that may influence the accounting estimate, the eventual realised values for these estimates depend on the outcome of future events which are unknown and so the estimation process is inherently imprecise. Common examples of situations where estimation is necessary include assessing the future collectability of receivables or loans, the market values of inventory, the fair value of an asset, or the adequacy of a product warranty liability. The values of these items often depend on economic and market conditions, but economic factors can change quickly. Because estimates are inherently imprecise, the auditor's involvement simply assures their reasonableness at the time of the audit, not their exactness.

Auditor Consideration of Going Concern

Financial reporting assumes that an entity is a going concern in the absence of significant information to the contrary. In the course of planning and performing an audit, the auditor is alert to the possibility that the going concern assumption may not be an appropriate assumption for management's preparation of financial statements. When normal audit procedures raise questions about the appropriateness of the going concern assumption, the auditor obtains information about management's plans for the future. If, after considering management's plans and the reasonableness of those plans, the independent auditor concludes that he or she has serious doubts about the entity's ability to continue as a going concern over the next year, the auditor considers the adequacy of financial statement disclosure about this uncertainty and may include an additional explanatory paragraph in the auditor's report referring to the disclosure of the uncertainty in the notes to the financial statements.

The auditor has a responsibility to consider the ability of the entity to continue as a going concern for the next year[11] based on its current condition. However, the auditor is not responsible for predicting future conditions or events and is unable to do so. For example, the auditor could not be expected to predict a significant drop in commodity prices or other changes in the market for a client's products or services. The absence of a reference, in the report, to the auditor's doubt about the entity's ability to continue in operation should not be viewed as providing assurance that future events will not affect the entity's ability to continue as a going concern. In other words, an unmodified audit report does not guarantee the continued viability of the business.

Reporting Material Error and Fraud

If material error or fraud is discovered and, after being brought to the attention of management, is not corrected in the financial statements, the auditor issues a qualified opinion. See Chapter 6 for examples of modified audit reports.

Reporting Weaknesses in Internal Control

As part of the audit process, the auditor has to gain an understanding of the environment in which the entity operates and the business processes that create its output and generate the information that feeds into the financial report in order to be able to audit those processes and give assurance as to the fair presentation of that information. As part of gaining an understanding of the business, the auditor evaluates the efficacy of the system of internal control so that the audit can be designed to focus on areas of risk.

Where the auditor finds weaknesses in the system of internal control, the audit approach is tailored accordingly. While such weaknesses may not prevent the financial statements from presenting fairly the entity's financial position and performance and therefore may have no impact on the auditor's report on the financial statements, the auditor nevertheless reports them to the appropriate level of management, or, if necessary to those charged with governance, so that the weaknesses can be remedied for the future benefit of the client and its management.

11 ASA 570 *Going Concern* differs from its international counterpart in how it expresses this requirement. ASA 570 para. Aus13.2 expects the auditor to look forward from the date of the audit report for approximately 12 months to the anticipated date of the next audit report.

Is the Auditor's Unqualified Opinion a Clean Bill of Health?

Some financial statement users consider an auditor's unqualified opinion to be a clean bill of health. For example, some users believe that an audit endorses an entity's policy decisions or its use of resources. This is not the objective of a financial statement audit. The auditor's opinion on the financial statements does not pertain to these matters. Other financial statement users believe that an audit provides positive assurance that a business is a safe investment and will not fail. To reiterate, the absence of a reference in the auditor's report to doubt about the entity's ability to continue as a going concern should not be viewed as providing assurance that future events will not affect the entity's ability to continue as a going concern.

An audit enhances users' confidence that financial statements do not contain material misstatements because the auditor is an independent and objective expert who is also knowledgeable of the entity's business and financial reporting requirements.

Communication with Management or Those Charged with Governance

The audit report is not the only means of communication between the auditor and management or those charged with governance. To ensure an effective audit, good two-way communication between management and the auditor is vital. The auditor is dependent on management's explanations of events that have occurred during the year and management needs to understand the responsibilities of the auditor with regard to the financial report and how the auditor plans to execute the audit. When auditor and client management understand each other's role, the audit can progress more smoothly, to mutual benefit. Differences of opinion may be able to be resolved without resorting to modification of the audit report.

The appropriate level for communication varies from client to client. In smaller entities, management and those responsible for governance are one and the same, but in larger entities, management liaises with the auditor on a day to day basis, but the board or audit committee receives formal reports.

During the course of the audit a number of issues may arise that require communication to management or those charged with governance, but do not affect the audit report. Such matters include weaknesses in the system of internal control, aspects of the entity's accounting practices, such as the selection of accounting policies, any difficulties encountered during the audit and any matters that affect the oversight of the financial reporting process.

Chapter 4 – Using Audited Financial Statements

Figure 5 The users are confident to use the financial statements in conjunction with the assurance provided in the auditor's report

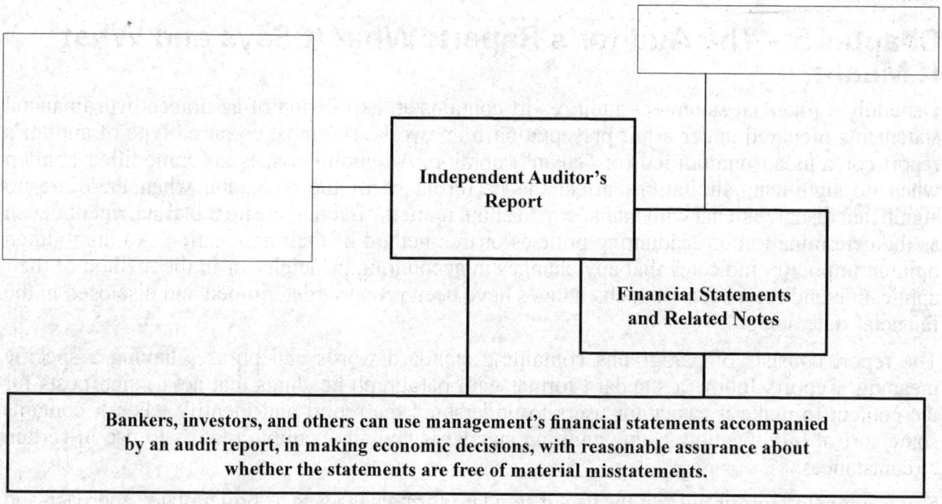

In addition to reading the auditor's report, financial statement users must also evaluate the financial statements in the context of their specific needs. In making that evaluation, users should consider various factors.

Reading the Auditor's Report

The auditor's report provides information about the scope of the independent auditor's work and any material concerns that he or she had about the fairness of presentation of the financial statements in conformity with accounting standards, together with any other issues that the auditor wishes to draw to the reader's attention (Chapters 5, 6 and 7 explain the form of the auditor's report).

Understanding the Accounting Principles Used

The accounting principles determined by management affect the information relevant to the user's decision. An evaluation of the financial statements requires that the user read the notes to the financial statements to ascertain the significant accounting principles used to prepare the statements and any areas on which the preparers have had to exercise significant judgment. These significant accounting issues are generally described at the beginning of the notes to the financial statements.

Evaluating the Financial Stability of the Entity

The evaluation of an entity's financial stability — its financial position, operating results, and changes in financial position — is the user's responsibility. Financial statements provide information helpful in making that evaluation. It is the reader's responsibility to interpret these statements according to his or her interests and concerns.

Evaluating Business Risk, Management, and Management Decisions

Management will take risks with varying degrees of economic potential and uncertainty of results. An audit does not evaluate the wisdom of management's decisions nor indicate the safety or future profitability of investing in the entity. Financial statement users are responsible for deciding whether management has made appropriate decisions. The user must evaluate the quality of past performance and decide whether management has adequate knowledge and experience to successfully guide the entity.

Evaluating the Risk of Financial Involvement with an Entity

Specific decisions about doing business with an entity, such as investing or extending credit, are the responsibility of those contemplating such matters. An audit only adds credibility to management's financial statements that users may consider in evaluating those risks for themselves.

Chapter 5 – The Auditor's Report: What It Says and What It Means

Generally a financial statement audit report contains an expression of assurance over financial statements prepared under a fair presentation framework. The most common type of auditor's report contains an unmodified (or "clean") opinion. An auditor issues an unmodified opinion when no significant limitations affect the performance of the audit and when there are no significant disagreements with management about matters affecting the financial statements, such as the determination of accounting policies or the method of their application. An unmodified opinion implicitly indicates that any changes in accounting principles or in the method of their application and the effects of such changes have been properly determined and disclosed in the financial statements.

The report consists of paragraphs containing standard words and phrases having a specific meaning. Reports follow a standard format with paragraph headings that act as sign posts for the content to make it easier for users to understand the report and identify when it contains some sort of modification. Some auditing standards contain example reports to use in certain circumstances.

Some commentators argue that the use of standard formats leads to a "boiler plate" approach and limits the usefulness of the report by standardising it too much. Standard setters must weigh the ease of use of a standard format to an uninformed reader against the possible benefits of a longer more free-style report more closely tailored to the circumstances of the entity being audited.

Under the current standards, however, an audit report comprises the following elements, which always occur in the same order:

- a title, identifying that it is an independent auditor's report;
- the addressee of the report, for example, "To the members of XYZ Limited";
- an introductory paragraph identifying the entity being audited, the period covered, the financial statements being audited, including the notes and any other explanatory information;
- a paragraph describing management's responsibility for the preparation of the financial report;
- a paragraph stating the auditor's responsibility for forming an opinion on the financial report in accordance with Australian Auditing Standards and describing the audit process in broad terms;
- a statement that the auditor believes that the audit evidence obtained is sufficient to support the opinion;
- a statement that the auditor is independent;
- the auditor's opinion;
- a paragraph covering any other audit reporting responsibilities, for example, in the case of a listed entity, the audit of the Remuneration Report;
- the auditor's signature and address and the date.

The following is an example of an auditor's report containing an unmodified opinion under a fair presentation framework.

Example Audit Report

INDEPENDENT AUDITOR'S REPORT TO THE MEMBERS OF XYZ ENTITY

[Appropriate Addressee]

Report on the Financial Report

We have audited the financial statements of XYZ Entity, which comprise the statement of financial position as at 31 December, 20X1, the statement of comprehensive income, statement of changes in equity and statement of cash flows for the year then ended, notes comprising a summary of significant accounting policies and other explanatory information, and management's assertion statement.

Management's Responsibility for the Financial Statements

Management is responsible for the preparation and fair presentation of the financial statements in accordance with Australian Accounting Standards and [relevant reporting framework] and for such internal control as management determines is necessary to enable the preparation and fair presentation of the financial report that is free from material misstatement, whether due to fraud or error. In Note XX management also states, in accordance with Accounting Standard AASB 101 *Presentation of Financial Statements*, that the financial statements comply with *International Financial Reporting Standards*.

Auditor's Responsibility

Our responsibility is to express an opinion on the financial report based on our audit. We conducted our audit in accordance with Australian Auditing Standards. Those standards require that we comply with relevant ethical requirements relating to audit engagements and plan and perform the audit to obtain reasonable assurance about whether the financial report is free from material misstatement.

An audit involves performing procedures to obtain audit evidence about the amounts and disclosures in the financial report. The procedures selected depend on the auditor's judgment, including the assessment of the risks of material misstatement of the financial report, whether due to fraud or error. In making those risk assessments, the auditor considers internal control relevant to the entity's preparation and fair presentation of the financial report in order to design audit procedures that are appropriate in the circumstances, but not for the purpose of expressing an opinion on the effectiveness of the entity's internal control. An audit also includes evaluating the appropriateness of accounting policies used and the reasonableness of accounting estimates made by management, as well as evaluating the overall presentation of the financial report.

We believe that the audit evidence we have obtained is sufficient and appropriate to provide a basis for our audit opinion.

Opinion

In our opinion:

(a) the financial statements present fairly, in all material respects, the financial position of XYZ Entity at 31 December 20X1, and of its financial performance and its cash flows for the year then ended in accordance with Australian Accounting Standards [and relevant reporting framework].

(b) The financial statements also comply with *International Financial Reporting Standards* as disclosed in Note XX.

Report on Other Legal and Regulatory Requirements

[Form and content of this section of the auditor's report will vary depending on the nature of the auditor's other reporting responsibilities.]

S. Peranto & Co., Auditors
Sydney, Australia
14 February, 20X2

The following paragraph by paragraph discussion explains the specific meaning of the language used in the auditor's unmodified report, reproduced above.

Report Title

The title Independent Auditor's Report helps the reader identify the auditor's report and distinguishes the report from reports that might be issued by others, such as management, the board of directors or an internal auditor.

Report Address

"To the Members of XYZ Entity". The report is addressed to those for whom it has been prepared as required by the circumstances of the engagement and local regulations. Usually, it is addressed to the shareholders or members of the entity whose financial statements are being audited but can also be addressed to those charged with the governance of the entity.

Introductory Paragraph

- "We have audited". This phrase identifies the type of service performed and, therefore, the level of assurance the independent auditor is providing and the corresponding responsibility assumed. An audit is a reasonable assurance engagement, the highest level of assurance that auditors can provide.
- "... the financial statements of XYZ Entity ... as at 31 December 20X1, ...". The auditor's report covers only the financial statements identified in the report including the related notes in those financial statements and any management assertion statement, such as a directors' declaration, for the period identified. The auditor usually identifies the financial statements covered by his or her opinion either by referring to them by name or by making reference to the pages on which such information is included. Any additional information that may also be presented with the financial statements in an annual report but that is not included in this page range has not been audited.

Management's Responsibility

- "Management is responsible for the preparation, …". The auditor is expressing an opinion on the information that management has prepared and for which management takes responsibility.
- "… and fair presentation …". This phrase emphasises to the reader that it is a fair presentation framework. In the company context, the phrase "that give a true and fair view" would be seen here instead. Management is responsible for the fair presentation of the financial statements.
- "… and for such internal control as management determines is necessary to enable the preparation of the financial statements that are free from material misstatement, whether due to fraud or error". This section emphasises management's responsibility for the generation of financial information that is free of material misstatement and implicitly their responsibility for keeping proper books and records.
- "… comply with International Financial Reporting Standards". This phrase tells an international reader that these Australian financial statements also comply with the international standards.

The Auditor's Responsibility

- "Our responsibility is to express an opinion …". The auditor stresses the contrast between the auditor's responsibility and that of management.
- "… in accordance with Australian Auditing Standards." In this sentence, the auditor indicates the auditing standards followed in conducting the audit by including a reference to Australian Auditing Standards. This provides the user with assurance that the audit has been carried out in accordance with established standards or practices. These standards explain how the audit should be performed, the nature and extent of judgments exercised in the audit, and the preparation of the auditor's report. These standards apply equally in any financial statement audit, regardless of the type or size of the entity. Unless otherwise stated in the report, the auditing standards or practices followed are presumed to be those of the country indicated by the auditor's address.
- "These standards require that we comply with relevant ethical requirements …". The requirements referred to here are APES 110 *Code of Ethics for Professional Accountants*, based on the IFAC code of the same name. The *Corporations Act 2001* also contains independence requirements that apply to company audits.
- The next paragraph, starting "An audit involves …" gives a brief description of what an auditor does, including assessing risk, considering relevant parts of the system of internal control, and designing appropriate audit procedures. The report also mentions the auditor's evaluation of management's accounting policies, estimates, and the overall presentation of the financial report.
- "We believe the audit evidence we have obtained is sufficient and appropriate …". The reason for audit testing is so that the auditor obtains sufficient appropriate audit evidence to enable him or her to come to an opinion. This statement confirms that the auditor is satisfied with the evidence obtained. The characteristics of sufficient appropriate audit evidence are described in ASA 500 *Audit Evidence*.

Opinion Paragraph

The auditor's conclusions, as a result of the audit, are described by the following phrases in the opinion paragraph.

- "In our opinion …". This phrase implies that the auditor is reasonably sure of his or her conclusions, that is, giving reasonable assurance; however, the auditor does not express a guarantee. Like a physician or an attorney, an auditor's opinion is based on professional judgment, not absolute certainty.
- "… present fairly …" (or, in the case of a company, "give a true and fair view of"). These financial statements have been prepared under a fair presentation framework, requiring greater use of professional judgment than a report on compliance with regulatory requirements. This framework of concepts has as its goal the fairness of the

financial statements. To express an opinion on the fairness of the presentation, the auditor uses either of two phrases that have equivalent meanings: "give a true and fair view" or "present fairly".

- "... in all material respects ...". The auditor cannot check everything. He or she plans the audit with the expectation of finding material misstatements, not every misstatement.
- "... in accordance with Australian Accounting Standards ...". Financial statements are based upon a framework of concepts and standards developed internationally and adopted by local legislation and by the development of general practice within a country. If an entity is subject to another set of disclosure requirements, for example, the *Corporations Act 2001,* it should be mentioned here. These words indicate the framework of concepts that the auditor used as the basis for the audit opinion and advise the user of the context in which the auditor evaluated the fairness of the financial statements. The addition of the words "in accordance with *International Financial Reporting Standards*" tells the reader that as well as evaluating the financial statements against local standards, the auditor has also evaluated them against international standards.

Report on Other Legal and Regulatory Requirements

The auditor may also be required to give an opinion on whether the financial statements conform with other laws or regulations. The content of this section of the report is dictated by the environment in which the entity operates. An example of a matter that might be included here is the auditor's report under s. 308(3C) of the *Corporations Act 2001* on a Remuneration Report included in the Directors' Report.

Signature and Report Date

The auditor's report is signed in the name of the auditor's firm or the personal name of the auditor, or both, as appropriate in the circumstances. In addition, the auditor's report may disclose the specific location of the auditor's firm that performed the audit. The date of the auditor's report is important because this represents the date that the auditor concluded all significant procedures. If the auditor becomes aware of material transactions and events occurring between the date of his or her report and the date the report is issued, the auditor considers their effect on the financial statements and on the report.[12]

Chapter 6 – Non-Standard Audit Reports: Modifications

If an auditor concludes that the financial statements present fairly (or "give a true and fair view of"), the entity's financial position and results of operations, he or she issues an unmodified opinion on the statements as illustrated in Chapter 5. However, even when expressing an unmodified opinion, certain circumstances may require the auditor to communicate additional information to the user in the report. Circumstances that may cause the auditor to add an additional explanatory paragraph to the report include material uncertainties and going concern problems. An example of an auditor's report with an unmodified opinion and explanatory wording is described in Chapter 7 of this paper.

Circumstances That May Result in a Modified Opinion

Other circumstances may lead the auditor to issue a modified opinion on the financial statements. A modification (also colloquially referred to as a "qualification") is required when the auditor determines, on the basis of the audit evidence obtained, that there are material misstatements in the financial statements or when the auditor is unable to obtain sufficient appropriate evidence to conclude that the financial statements are free of material misstatement.

There are three types of modified opinion:

- a qualified opinion – used when there are material misstatements in the financial statements (i.e. the auditor disagrees with how management has treated a material item or items in the financial statements), or when the auditor is unable to obtain sufficient appropriate audit evidence (also referred to as when there is a limitation of scope) and concludes that the possible effects of undetected misstatements could be material;

12 ASA 560 *Subsequent Events.*

- an adverse opinion – used when there are misstatements that are both material and pervasive to the financial statements. An adverse opinion is rare;
- a disclaimer of opinion – used when the auditor is unable to obtain sufficient appropriate audit evidence and concludes that the possible effects of undetected misstatements could be material and pervasive, or when there are multiple uncertainties surrounding an audit and, in spite of obtaining audit evidence, it is not possible to form an opinion on the financial statements due to the potential interaction of the multiple uncertainties. Again, a disclaimer of opinion is rare.

The wording of the modification is determined by the nature of the matter giving rise to the modification and the extent of its impact on the financial report. Where the matter is pervasive, that is, is not confined to specific accounts or elements, but affects a substantial proportion of the financial report or affects disclosures that are fundamental to a reader's understanding of the financial statements, an adverse opinion or a disclaimer would be contemplated.

The choice of modification is illustrated in Figure 6.

Figure 6 Table from ASA 705 showing the use of the various audit report modifications

Nature of Matter Giving Rise to the Modification	*Auditor's Judgment about the Pervasiveness of the Effects or Possible Effects on the Financial Report*	
	Material but Not Pervasive	*Material and Pervasive*
Financial report is materially misstated	Qualified opinion	Adverse opinion
Inability to obtain sufficient appropriate audit evidence	Qualified opinion	Disclaimer of opinion

Examples of auditors' reports where the opinion on the financial statements is other than unmodified are described below (emphasis provided for modified wording).

Examples of Modified Audit Reports

Qualified Opinion: Material Misstatement in the Financial Statements

INDEPENDENT AUDITOR'S REPORT

[Appropriate Addressee]

Report on the Financial Report

We have audited the accompanying financial report of ABC Entity, which comprises the statement of financial position as at 30 June 20X1, the statement of comprehensive income, statement of changes in equity and statement of cash flows for the year then ended, notes comprising a summary of significant accounting policies and other explanatory information, and management's assertion statement.

Management's Responsibility for the Financial Report

Management is responsible for the preparation and fair presentation of the financial report in accordance with Australian Accounting Standards and [relevant reporting framework], and for such internal control as management determines is necessary to enable the preparation and fair presentation of the financial report that is free from material misstatement, whether due to fraud or error.

Auditor's Responsibility

Our responsibility is to express an opinion on the financial report based on our audit. We conducted our audit in accordance with Australian Auditing Standards. Those standards require that we comply with relevant ethical requirements relating to audit engagements and plan and perform

the audit to obtain reasonable assurance about whether the financial report is free from material misstatement.

An audit involves performing procedures to obtain audit evidence about the amounts and disclosures in the financial report. The procedures selected depend on the auditor's judgment, including the assessment of the risks of material misstatement of the financial report, whether due to fraud or error. In making those risk assessments, the auditor considers internal control relevant to the entity's preparation and fair presentation of the financial report in order to design audit procedures that are appropriate in the circumstances, but not for the purpose of expressing an opinion on the effectiveness of the entity's internal control. An audit also includes evaluating the appropriateness of accounting policies used and the reasonableness of accounting estimates made by management, as well as evaluating the overall presentation of the financial report.

We believe that the audit evidence we have obtained is sufficient and appropriate to provide a basis for our qualified audit opinion.

Basis for Qualified Opinion

The entity's inventories are carried in the statement of financial position at xxx. Management has not stated the inventories at the lower of cost and net realisable value but has stated them solely at cost, which constitutes a departure from Australian Accounting Standards. The entity's records indicate that had management stated the inventories at the lower of cost and net realisable value, an amount of xxx would have been required to write the inventories down to their net realisable value. Accordingly, cost of sales would have been increased by xxx, and income tax, net income and shareholders' equity would have been reduced by xxx, xxx and xxx, respectively.

Qualified Opinion

In our opinion, except for the effects of the matter described in the Basis for Qualified Opinion paragraph, the financial report presents fairly, in all material respects, (or *gives a true and fair view of*) the financial position of ABC Entity as at 30 June 20X1, and (of) its financial performance and its cash flows for the year then ended in accordance with Australian Accounting Standards and [relevant reporting framework].

Report on Other Legal and Regulatory Requirements

[Form and content of this section of the auditor's report will vary depending on the nature of the auditor's other reporting responsibilities.]

[Auditor's signature]

[Date of the auditor's report]

[Auditor's address]

REASON FOR THE QUALIFIED OPINION IN THE AUDITOR'S REPORT

In the example above, the auditor adds an explanatory paragraph because of a disagreement about how the inventory should be accounted for. Management have failed to apply all the requirements of AASB 102 *Inventory*. The report goes on to explain how the correct valuation of inventory would affect cost of sales, income tax, net income and shareholders' equity.

MEANING OF THE QUALIFIED OPINION IN THE AUDITOR'S REPORT

This report contains a modified opinion, which means that, in the auditor's opinion, the financial statements are fairly presented apart from the effects of the incorrect valuation of inventory.

Adverse Opinion: Material Misstatement that is Pervasive

INDEPENDENT AUDITOR'S REPORT

[Appropriate Addressee]

Report on the Financial Report

We have audited the accompanying financial report of ABC Entity, which comprises the statements of financial performance as at 30 June 20X1, the statements of comprehensive income, statements of changes in equity and statements of cash flows for the year then ended, notes comprising a summary of significant accounting policies and other explanatory information, and management's assertion statement of the entity and the consolidated entity comprising the entity and the entities it controlled at the year's end or from time to time during the financial year.

Management's Responsibility for the Financial Report

Management is responsible for the preparation and fair presentation of the financial report in accordance with Australian Accounting Standards and [relevant reporting framework], and for such internal control as management determines is necessary to enable the preparation and fair presentation of the financial report that is free from material misstatement, whether due to fraud or error.

Auditor's Responsibility

Our responsibility is to express an opinion on the financial report based on our audit. We conducted our audit in accordance with Australian Auditing Standards. Those standards require that we comply with relevant ethical requirements relating to audit engagements and plan and perform the audit to obtain reasonable assurance about whether the financial report is free from material misstatement.

An audit involves performing procedures to obtain audit evidence about the amounts and disclosures in the financial report. The procedures selected depend on the auditor's judgment, including the assessment of the risks of material misstatement of the financial report, whether due to fraud or error. In making those risk assessments, the auditor considers internal control relevant to the entity's preparation and fair presentation of the financial report in order to design audit procedures that are appropriate in the circumstances, but not for the purpose of expressing an opinion on the effectiveness of the entity's internal control. An audit also includes evaluating the appropriateness of accounting policies used and the reasonableness of accounting estimates made by management, as well as evaluating the overall presentation of the financial report.

We believe that the audit evidence we have obtained is sufficient and appropriate to provide a basis for our adverse audit opinion.

Basis for Adverse Opinion

As explained in Note X, the entity has not consolidated the financial statements of subsidiary XYZ Entity it acquired during 20X1 because it has not yet been able to ascertain the fair values of certain of the subsidiary's material assets and liabilities at the acquisition date. This investment is therefore accounted for on a cost basis. Under Australian Accounting Standards, the subsidiary should have been consolidated because it is controlled by the entity. Had XYZ been consolidated, many elements in the accompanying financial report would have been materially affected. The effects on the financial report of the failure to consolidate have not been determined.

Adverse Opinion

In our opinion, because of the significance of the matter discussed in the Basis for Adverse Opinion paragraph, the financial report does not present fairly (or *does not give a true and fair view of*) the financial position of ABC Entity and its subsidiaries as at 30 June 20X1, and (of) their financial performance and their cash flows for the year then ended in accordance with Australian Accounting Standards and [relevant reporting framework].

Report on Other Legal and Regulatory Requirements

[Form and content of this section of the auditor's report will vary depending on the nature of the auditor's other reporting responsibilities.]

[Auditor's signature]

[Date of the auditor's report]

[Auditor's address]

REASON FOR THE ADVERSE OPINION IN THE AUDITOR'S REPORT
In the above example, the auditor adds an explanatory paragraph because the financial report is materially misstated. Management decided not to consolidate the results of a recently acquired subsidiary, because fair values of certain of the assets and liabilities acquired had not yet been ascertained. The investment in the subsidiary is of such a size that the misstatement is pervasive.

MEANING OF THE ADVERSE OPINION IN THE AUDITOR'S REPORT
This report contains an adverse opinion, which means that, in the auditor's opinion, the financial statements are not fairly presented because of the impact of accounting for the subsidiary at cost rather than consolidating it.

Note that the modification in this case also affects the statement on audit evidence in the "Auditor's Responsibility" paragraph.

Qualified Opinion: Insufficient Audit Evidence

INDEPENDENT AUDITOR'S REPORT

[Appropriate Addressee]

Report on the Financial Report

We have audited the accompanying financial report of ABC Entity, which comprises the statement of financial position as at 30 June 20X1, the statement of comprehensive income, statement of changes in equity and statement of cash flows for the year then ended, notes comprising a summary of significant accounting policies and other explanatory information, and management's assertion statement.

Management's Responsibility for the Financial Report

Management is responsible for the preparation and fair presentation of the financial report in accordance with Australian Accounting Standards and [relevant reporting framework], and for such internal control as management determines is necessary to enable the preparation and fair presentation of the financial report that is free from material misstatement, whether due to fraud or error.

Auditor's Responsibility

Our responsibility is to express an opinion on the financial report based on our audit. We conducted our audit in accordance with Australian Auditing Standards. Those standards require that we comply with relevant ethical requirements relating to audit engagements and plan and perform the audit to obtain reasonable assurance about whether the financial report is free from material misstatement.

An audit involves performing procedures to obtain audit evidence about the amounts and disclosures in the financial report. The procedures selected depend on the auditor's judgment, including the assessment of the risks of material misstatement of the financial report, whether due to fraud or error. In making those risk assessments, the auditor considers internal control relevant to the entity's preparation and fair presentation of the financial report in order to design audit procedures that are appropriate in the circumstances, but not for the purpose of expressing an opinion on the effectiveness of the entity's internal control. An audit also includes evaluating the appropriateness of accounting policies used and the reasonableness of accounting estimates made by management, as well as evaluating the overall presentation of the financial report.

We believe that the audit evidence we have obtained is sufficient and appropriate to provide a basis for our qualified audit opinion.

Basis for Qualified Opinion

ABC Entity's investment in XYZ Entity, a foreign associate acquired during the year and accounted for by the equity method, is carried at xxx on the statement of financial position as at 30 June 20X1, and ABC's share of XYZ's net income of xxx is included in ABC's statement of comprehensive income for the year then ended. We were unable to obtain sufficient appropriate audit evidence about the carrying amount of ABC's investment in XYZ as at 30 June 20X1 and ABC's share of XYZ's net income for the year because we were denied access to the financial information, management, and the auditors of XYZ. Consequently, we were unable to determine whether any adjustments to these amounts were necessary.

Qualified Opinion

In our opinion, except for the possible effects of the matter described in the Basis for Qualified Opinion paragraph, the financial report presents fairly, in all material respects, (or *gives a true and fair view of*) the financial position of ABC Entity as at 30 June 20X1, and (of) its financial performance and its cash flows for the year then ended in accordance with Australian Accounting Standards and [relevant reporting framework].

Report on Other Legal and Regulatory Requirements

[Form and content of this section of the auditor's report will vary depending on the nature of the auditor's other reporting responsibilities.]

[Auditor's signature]

[Date of the auditor's report]

[Auditor's address]

REASON FOR THE QUALIFIED OPINION IN THE AUDITOR'S REPORT

In the above example, the auditor adds an explanatory paragraph because he or she was unable to obtain sufficient appropriate audit evidence regarding an investment in an overseas associate. Consequently the auditor's ability to audit that aspect of the entity's business was restricted. The investment is material, but not pervasive.

MEANING OF THE QUALIFIED OPINION IN THE AUDITOR'S REPORT

This report contains a modified opinion, which means that, in the auditor's opinion, the financial statements are fairly presented apart from the possible effects of the lack of evidence regarding the associate. If the associate has been sufficiently large such that the impact of being unable to audit it could be considered pervasive, a disclaimer of opinion would have been appropriate.

Disclaimer of Opinion: Insufficient Evidence

INDEPENDENT AUDITOR'S REPORT

[Appropriate Addressee]

Report on the Financial Report

We were engaged to audit the accompanying financial report of ABC Entity, which comprises the statement of financial position as at 30 June 20X1, the statement of comprehensive income, statement of changes in equity and statement of cash flows for the year then ended, notes comprising a summary of significant accounting policies and other explanatory information, and management's assertion statement.

Management's Responsibility for the Financial Report

Management is responsible for the preparation and fair presentation of the financial report in accordance with Australian Accounting Standards and [relevant reporting framework], and for such internal control as management determines is necessary to enable the preparation and fair presentation of the financial report that is free from material misstatement, whether due to fraud or error.

Auditor's Responsibility

Our responsibility is to express an opinion on the financial report based on conducting the audit in accordance with Australian Auditing Standards. Because of the matter described in the Basis for Disclaimer of Opinion paragraph, however, we were not able to obtain sufficient appropriate audit evidence to provide a basis for an audit opinion.

Basis for Disclaimer of Opinion

The entity's investment in its joint venture XYZ (Country X) Entity is carried at xxx on the entity's statement of financial position, which represents over 90% of the entity's net assets as at 30 June 20X1. We were not allowed access to the management and the auditors of XYZ, including XYZ's auditors' audit documentation. As a result, we were unable to determine whether any adjustments were necessary in respect of the entity's proportional share of XYZ's assets that it controls jointly, its proportional share of XYZ's liabilities for which it is jointly responsible, its proportional share of XYZ's income and expenses for the year, and the elements making up the statement of changes in equity and the statement of cash flows.

Disclaimer of Opinion

Because of the significance of the matter described in the Basis for Disclaimer of Opinion paragraph, we have not been able to obtain sufficient appropriate audit evidence to provide a basis for an audit opinion. Accordingly, we do not express an opinion on the financial report.

Report on Other Legal and Regulatory Requirements

[Form and content of this section of the auditor's report will vary depending on the nature of the auditor's other reporting responsibilities.]

[Auditor's signature]

[Date of the auditor's report]

[Auditor's address]

REASON FOR THE DISCLAIMER IN THE AUDITOR'S REPORT

In the above example, the auditor explains that he or she was unable to obtain sufficient appropriate audit evidence regarding an investment in a joint venture that represents over 90% of the entity's net assets. The impact of being unable to audit over 90% of the net assets is so pervasive that the auditor cannot form an opinion on the financial statements.

MEANING OF THE DISCLAIMER IN THE AUDITOR'S REPORT

This report contains a disclaimer of opinion, which means that the auditor was unable to form an opinion. This inability to form an opinion flows through to other areas of the audit report. The introductory paragraph now starts "We were engaged to audit" instead of "We have audited" as the audit was unable to be completed, and the statement relating to audit evidence now reads "we were not able to obtain sufficient appropriate audit evidence to provide a basis for an audit opinion".

Chapter 7 – Non-standard Auditor's Reports: Emphasis of Matter and Other Matter Paragraphs

The other form of a non-standard audit report is one in which additional material is added to an unmodified audit report. This can take two forms:

- an Emphasis of Matter paragraph; or
- an Other Matter paragraph.

Emphasis of Matter Paragraph

An Emphasis of Matter paragraph is a paragraph in the audit report that refers to a matter disclosed in the notes to the financial statements that, in the auditor's view, is of such importance that it is fundamental to users' understanding of the financial statements. Circumstances that may cause the auditor to add such an additional explanatory paragraph to his or her report include material uncertainties and going concern problems.

An Emphasis of Matter is not a modification, because the issue has been treated correctly by means of disclosure. However, the auditor is of the view that the information is so important to users' understanding of the financial statements that he or she wants to draw attention to it.

Other Matter Paragraph

An Other Matter paragraph is used to draw readers' attention to something that is not disclosed in the financial report but is nevertheless relevant to readers' understanding of the audit, the auditor's responsibilities or the auditor's report.

The most common example is where a set of financial statements has been prepared for a specific purpose and distribution is intended to be limited. In this case, the audit report would include a paragraph stating that the auditor's report is intended solely for the nominated users to which it is addressed and should not be distributed to or used by other parties.

Example of Emphasis of Matter: Uncertainty Regarding Pending Litigation

The audit report with an emphasis of matter follows the format for an unmodified report given in Chapter 5, but has an additional paragraph.

INDEPENDENT AUDITOR'S REPORT

[Appropriate Addressee]

Report on the Financial Report

We have audited the accompanying financial report of ABC Entity, which comprises the statement of financial position as at 30 June 20X1, the statement of comprehensive income, statement of changes in equity and statement of cash flows for the year then ended, notes comprising a summary of significant accounting policies and other explanatory information, and management's assertion statement.

Management's Responsibility for the Financial Report

Management is responsible for the preparation and fair presentation of the financial report in accordance with Australian Accounting Standards and [relevant reporting framework], and for such internal control as management determines is necessary to enable the preparation and fair presentation of the financial report that is free from material misstatement, whether due to fraud or error.

Auditor's Responsibility

Our responsibility is to express an opinion on the financial report based on our audit. We conducted our audit in accordance with Australian Auditing Standards. Those standards require that we comply with relevant ethical requirements relating to audit engagements and plan and perform the audit to obtain reasonable assurance about whether the financial report is free from material misstatement.

An audit involves performing procedures to obtain audit evidence about the amounts and disclosures in the financial report. The procedures selected depend on the auditor's judgment, including the assessment of the risks of material misstatement of the financial report, whether due to fraud or error. In making those risk assessments, the auditor considers internal control relevant to the entity's preparation and fair presentation of the financial report in order to design audit procedures that are appropriate in the circumstances, but not for the purpose of expressing an opinion on the effectiveness of the entity's internal control. An audit also includes evaluating the appropriateness of accounting policies used and the reasonableness of accounting estimates made by management, as well as evaluating the overall presentation of the financial report.

We believe that the audit evidence that we have obtained is sufficient and appropriate to provide a basis for our qualified audit opinion.

Qualified Opinion

In our opinion, the financial statements present fairly, in all material respects (or *give a true and fair view of*) the financial position of ABC Entity as at 30 June 20X1, and (of) its financial performance and its cash flows for the year then ended in accordance with Australian Accounting Standards and [relevant reporting framework].

Emphasis of Matter

We draw attention to Note X to the financial statements, which describes the uncertainty related to the outcome of the lawsuit filed against the entity by XYZ Entity. Our opinion is not qualified in respect of this matter.

Report on Other Legal and Regulatory Requirements

[Form and content of this section of the auditor's report will vary depending on the nature of the auditor's other reporting responsibilities.]

[Auditor's signature]

[Date of the auditor's report]

[Auditor's address]

REASON FOR THE EMPHASIS OF MATTER IN THE AUDIT REPORT

In the above example, the entity is involved in litigation, the outcome of which is unknown. This constitutes a material uncertainty.

MEANING OF THE EMPHASIS OF MATTER IN THE AUDIT REPORT

In the auditor's view, knowledge of the pending litigation is essential to a reader's understanding of these financial statements and therefore he or she has inserted the Emphasis of Matter paragraph referring the reader to Note X in which the uncertainty is described.

Conclusion

The purpose of this paper is to explain the nature and significance of the auditor's report that is attached to a set of financial statements by providing an explanation of the processes the auditor undertakes to produce that opinion, and information about what that opinion can and cannot provide to the users of the financial statements. The hope is that this helps clarify what users should reasonably expect the auditor to be able to do and what an audit is able to deliver. It also reconfirms the vital role the audit function has in ensuring the high quality of the financial information on which users are able to rely.

The ongoing challenge for the auditing profession is for assurance services to keep pace with developments in the provision of financial information to users.

Foreword to AUASB Pronouncements

(Reissued November 2012)

Issued by the Auditing and Assurance Standards Board.

Note from the Institute of Chartered Accountants Australia

This note, prepared by the technical editor, is not part of the Foreword to AUASB Pronouncements.

Historical Development

February 1977: First published as Statement C 'Statement of Auditing Standards and Statements of Auditing Practice' effective from date of issue. Reissued without amendment as statement AUS in August 1979.

January 1983: Reissued, after substantial revision, as 'Foreword to Statements of Auditing Standards and Statements of Auditing Practice', operative from date of issue.

February 1988: New para. 10 inserted, subsequent paragraphs being renumbered, and the final paragraph of 'new' para. 19 amended.

February 1989: Paragraph 6 amended. Reference can also be made to the 'Preface to International Auditing Guidelines' issued by IFAC in February 1987 and reissued in July 1989. See also IFAC's 'Framework on International Guidelines on Auditing and Related Services' issued in February 1988.

June 1994: The International Auditing Practices Committee (IAPC) of the International Federation of Accountants (IFAC) approved the issuance of a codified set of International Standards of Auditing (ISAs).

October 1995: The Australian Auditing Standards and Auditing Guidance Statements released. The status of these is explained in APS 1.1 'Conformity With Auditing Standards'. These Standards became operative for the first reporting period commencing on or after 1 July 1996 and later reporting periods, although earlier application was encouraged.

January 2002: AUS 102 reissued to reflect changes in the institutional arrangements for Standard setting, and broadening of the Board's scope to include assurance.

April 2006: A new Foreword was issued to introduce the new 'force of law' ASA Auditing Standards.

December 2009: A new Foreword was issued taking into account the new 'Clarity Project' Standards issued in October 2009.

November 2012: The revised *Foreword* was issued in November 2012, and sets out an overview of the pronouncements and other publications issued by the AUASB. In this revised version, the processes and procedures followed by the AUASB previously summarised under the heading 'Due Process' have been moved to a separate document.

The description of the Board's due process has been expanded and moved to a new document, *AUASB Functions and Processes* also issued in November. It sets out the Board's functions and powers, its relationships with other bodies, such as the Government and the New Zealand Auditing and Assurance Standards Board (NZAuASB) and how it operates and develops Standards and is available from www.auasb.gov.au.

Contents

Preface

Reasons for Issuing the Foreword to AUASB Pronouncements

The Auditing and Assurance Standards Board (AUASB) is an independent statutory committee of the Australian Government, established under section 227A of the *Australian Securities and Investments Commission Act 2001*, as amended (ASIC Act).

The AUASB issues the *Foreword to AUASB Pronouncements* under its powers described in section 227B of the ASIC Act.

Main Features

The *Foreword to AUASB Pronouncements* sets out an overview of the pronouncements and other publications issued by the AUASB.

The *Foreword to AUASB Pronouncements* does not itself establish requirements for the performance of audit, review, other assurance engagements, and related services engagements. Accordingly, the AUASB has not issued the *Foreword to AUASB Pronouncements* for the purposes of the *Corporations Act 2001*.

Authority Statement

The Auditing and Assurance Standards Board (AUASB) formulates the *Foreword to AUASB Pronouncements*, pursuant to section 227B of the *Australian Securities and Investments Commission Act 2001*.

Dated: 30 November 2012

M H Kelsall
Chairman - AUASB

Foreword to AUASB Pronouncements

Introduction

1. The purpose of this *Foreword to AUASB Pronouncements* (the "Foreword") is to set out the range of pronouncements and other publications issued by the Auditing and Assurance Standards Board (the "AUASB").

The Auditing and Assurance Standards Board

Legislative Mandate

2. The AUASB is an independent statutory committee of the Australian Government established under section 227A of the *Australian Securities and Investments Commission Act 2001*, as amended (ASIC Act). Under section 336 of the *Corporations Act 2001*, the AUASB may make Auditing Standards for the purposes of the corporations legislation. These Auditing Standards are legislative instruments under the *Legislative Instruments Act 2003*. The AUASB may also formulate other assurance standards and guidance on audit and assurance matters.

Pronouncements issued by the AUASB

3. The AUASB issues framework pronouncements, standards and guidance statements. Diagrams which illustrate the range of pronouncements issued by the AUASB are contained in the Appendices to this Foreword.

Framework Pronouncements

4. The AUASB issues framework pronouncements to provide information, structure and context to the pronouncements and other publications that it issues. The framework pronouncements comprise:
   - *Foreword to AUASB Pronouncements*;
   - *Framework for Assurance Engagements*; and
   - *AUASB Glossary*.
5. The *Foreword to AUASB Pronouncements* sets out the range of pronouncements and other publications issued by the AUASB.
6. The *Framework for Assurance Engagements* defines and describes the elements and objectives of an assurance engagement, and identifies engagements to which Australian Auditing Standards, Standards on Review Engagements, Standards on Assurance Engagements and Standards on Related Services apply.
7. The *AUASB Glossary* sets out terms that are defined or used in the AUASB Standards.

Standards

8. The AUASB issues the following types of standards:
   (a) Australian Auditing Standards;
   (b) Standards on Review Engagements;
   (c) Standards on Assurance Engagements; and
   (d). Standards on Related Services

   These standards are collectively referred to in this document as the "AUASB Standards".
9. Australian Auditing Standards issued by the AUASB comprise:
   (a) Auditing Standards made under section 336 of the *Corporations Act 2001* which include but are not limited to:
      (i) ASA 100 *Preamble to AUASB Standards*;
      (ii) ASA 101 *Preamble to Australian Auditing Standards* (applicable to engagements for financial reporting periods commencing on or after 1 January 2010);

(iii) ASA 102 *Compliance with Ethical Requirements when Performing Audits, Reviews and Other Assurance Engagements*;

(iv) ASQC 1 *Quality Control for Firms that Perform Audits and Reviews of Financial Reports and Other Financial Information, and Other Assurance Engagements*;

(v) ASRE 2410 *Review of a Financial Report Performed by the Independent Auditor of the Entity*; and

(vi) ASRE 2415 *Review of a Financial Report – Company Limited by Guarantee*; and

(b) ASA 805 Special Considerations—*Audits of Single Financial Statements and Specific Elements, Accounts or Items of a Financial Statement*; and

(c) ASA 810 *Engagements to Report on Summary Financial Statements*.

Australian Auditing Standards, whilst developed in the context of financial report audits, are to be applied also, as appropriate, to all audits of other historical financial information.

10. Standards on Review Engagements are to be applied to the review of a financial report and the review of other historical financial information.

11. Standards on Assurance Engagements are to be applied to assurance engagements dealing with subject matters other than historical financial information.[1]

12. Standards on Related Services are to be applied when an assurance practitioner is engaged to undertake engagements other than assurance engagements covered by Australian Auditing Standards, Standards on Review Engagements or Standards on Assurance Engagements.[2]

Guidance Statements

13. Guidance Statements are issued when the AUASB wishes to provide guidance on procedural matters; or on entity or industry specific matters.

14. Guidance Statements are designed to provide assistance to auditors and assurance practitioners to assist them in fulfilling the objectives of the engagement. Accordingly, Guidance Statements refer to, and are written in the context of:

(a) specified AUASB Standards; and

(b) where relevant, legislation, regulation or other authoritative publication.

15. Guidance Statements, whilst approved and issued by the AUASB, do not establish new principles or amend existing Standards and do not have legal enforceability.

16. Guidance Statements contain a specific clause indicating their operative date. A Guidance Statement remains in force until the operative date of any amendment to the Guidance Statement or until the Guidance Statement is withdrawn by the AUASB. An operative date is one of the features that differentiates a Guidance Statement from an Explanatory Guide.

1 Examples of such subject matters include the efficiency and/or effectiveness of an entity's activities, prospective financial information and the effectiveness of internal controls.

2 Examples of such engagements include: confirming revenue under a lease agreement; assisting management determine if leave provisions have been calculated in accordance with policy; and assisting management determine inventory values and collectability of trade debts.

Other Publications

AUASB – Functions and Processes

17. *AUASB –Functions and Processes* provides information about the AUASB including its functions, mandates, composition, operations and due processes. It is intended to complement the *Foreword to AUASB Pronouncements*.

Explanatory Guides

18. The AUASB issues Explanatory Guides to provide additional information about specific aspects of a standard(s). For example: the *Explanatory Guide to AUASB Standards Applicable to Review Engagements*, explains the historical background to the development of the suite of review standards and when each standard is to be used.

19. Explanatory Guides are *not* Guidance Statements and similarly do not establish or extend requirements for the performance of engagements under the AUASB Standards.

AUASB Bulletins

20. AUASB Bulletins are issued to raise a general awareness of matters that are of interest to auditors and assurance practitioners. They do *not* provide authoritative guidance and do *not* amend existing AUASB Standards or Guidance Statements.

Basis of Conclusions

21. Whenever the AUASB has made decisions on substantive matters relating to the development of a standard, details of the matter, the options considered and the reasons supporting the conclusions made are documented in a *Basis for Conclusions* document.

Other Publications

22. The AUASB may also issue other publications, either in its own right or jointly with other bodies, on the auditing and assurance implications of emerging issues. For example: *Audit Committees: A Guide to Good Practice* (issued jointly with the Australian Institute of Company Directors and The Institute of Internal Auditors Australia).

Compliance

23. Auditing Standards issued by the AUASB under the *Corporations Act 2001,* are legally enforceable by the Australian regulator – the Australian Securities and Investments Commission (ASIC). ASIC conduct regular inspection programmes as an integral part of their enforcement responsibilities.

24. Through the standards issued by the Accounting Professional and Ethical Standards Board (APESB), members of the Australian Professional Accounting Bodies are compelled to comply with the requirements of AUASB Standards.

25. Member compliance is enforced through the inspection programmes of the Professional Accounting Bodies, who are also responsible for member disciplinary action.

Appendix 1

Framework of Pronouncements issued by the AUASB

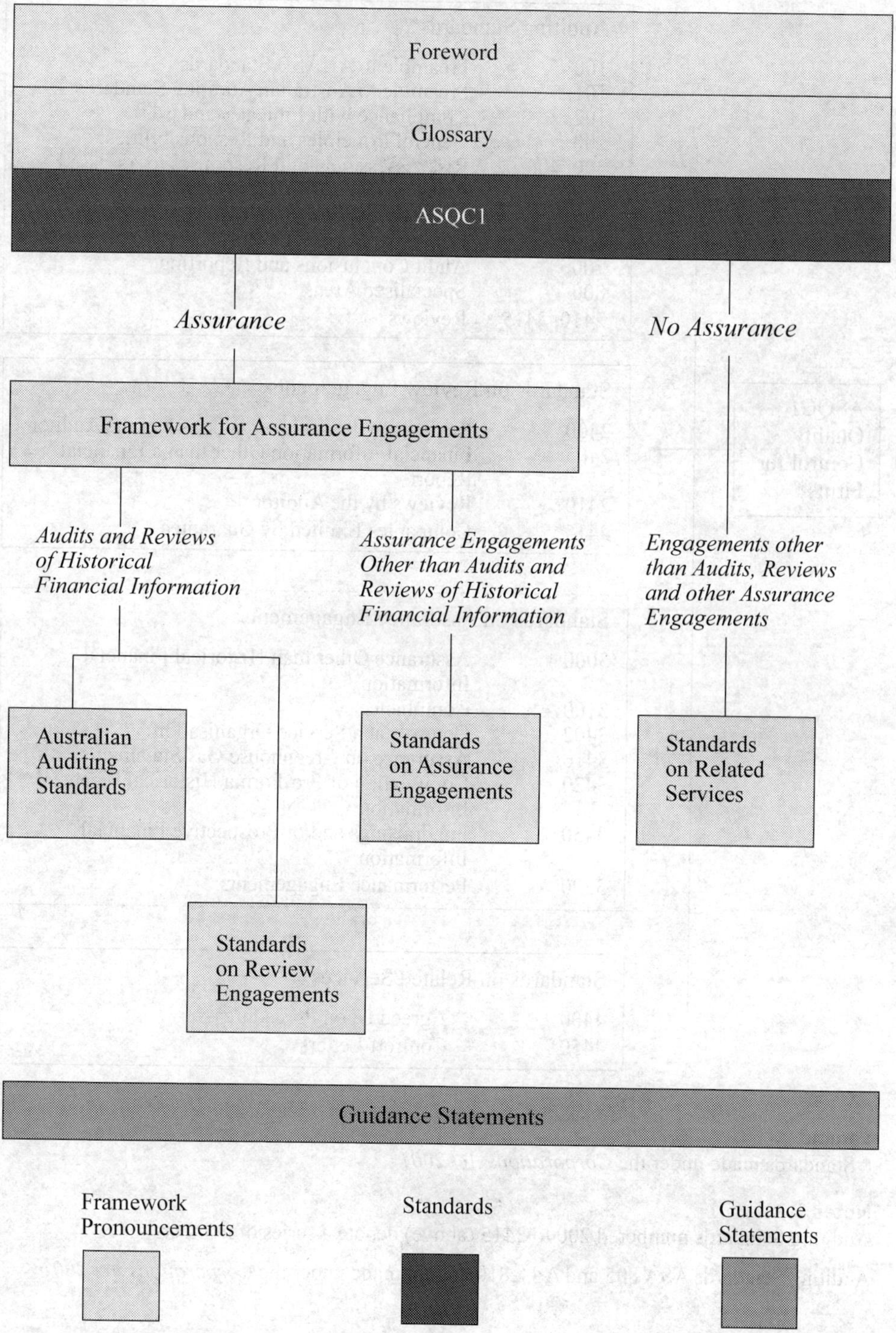

Appendix 2

Overview of Numbering System used in AUASB Standards

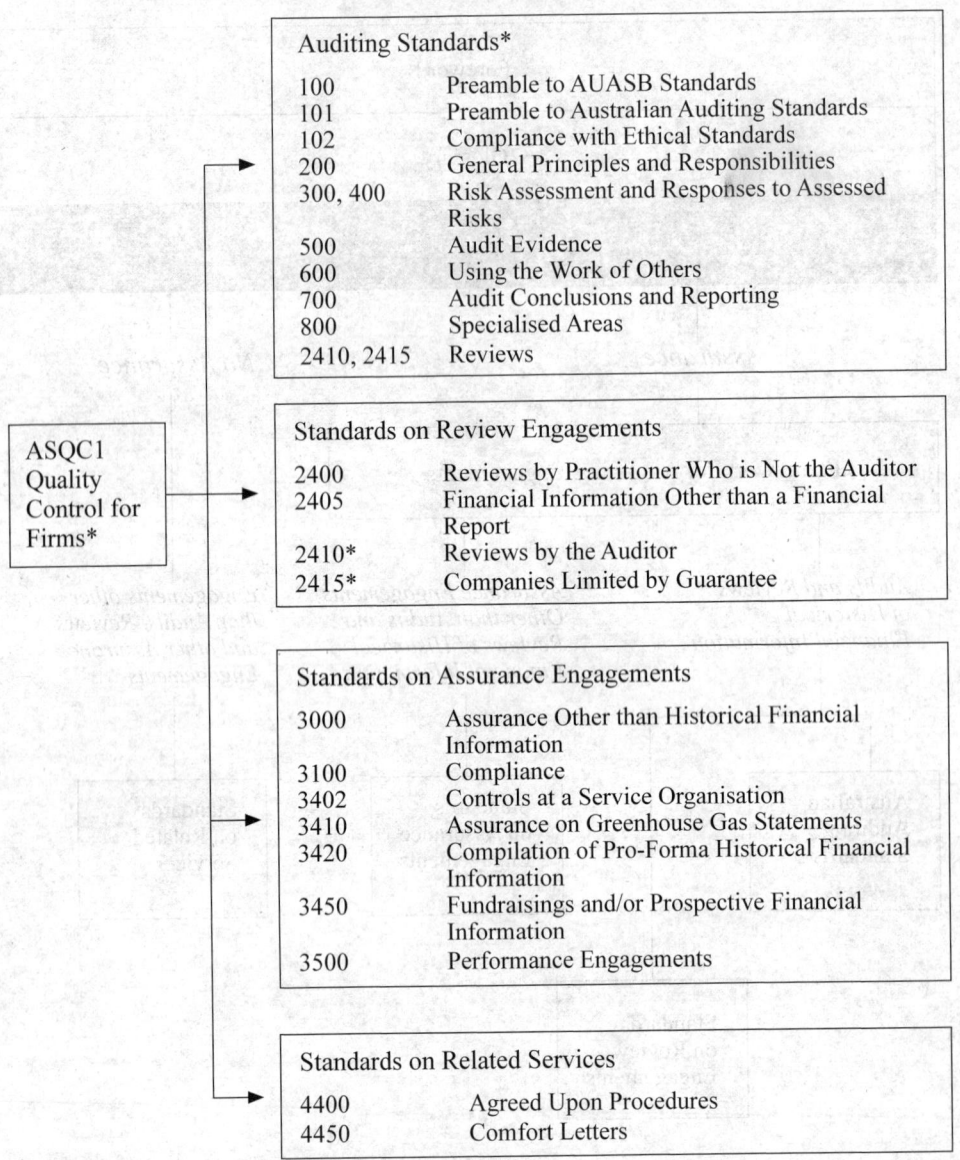

ASQC1 Quality Control for Firms*

Auditing Standards*

100	Preamble to AUASB Standards
101	Preamble to Australian Auditing Standards
102	Compliance with Ethical Standards
200	General Principles and Responsibilities
300, 400	Risk Assessment and Responses to Assessed Risks
500	Audit Evidence
600	Using the Work of Others
700	Audit Conclusions and Reporting
800	Specialised Areas
2410, 2415	Reviews

Standards on Review Engagements

2400	Reviews by Practitioner Who is Not the Auditor
2405	Financial Information Other than a Financial Report
2410*	Reviews by the Auditor
2415*	Companies Limited by Guarantee

Standards on Assurance Engagements

3000	Assurance Other than Historical Financial Information
3100	Compliance
3402	Controls at a Service Organisation
3410	Assurance on Greenhouse Gas Statements
3420	Compilation of Pro-Forma Historical Financial Information
3450	Fundraisings and/or Prospective Financial Information
3500	Performance Engagements

Standards on Related Services

4400	Agreed Upon Procedures
4450	Comfort Letters

Legend

* Standards made under the *Corporations Act 2001*

Notes

Auditing Standards numbered 200 to 2415 (above) denote a series of numbers

Auditing Standards ASA 805 and ASA 810 are not made under the *Corporations Act 2001*

AUASB Glossary

(Issued October 2009)

Issued by the Auditing and Assurance Standards Board.

Note from the Institute of Chartered Accountants Australia

This note, prepared by the technical editor, is not part of the AUASB Glossary.

Historical development

October 1995: The Australian Auditing Standards and Auditing Guidance Statements released. The status of these is explained in APS 1.1 'Conformity With Auditing Standards'. These standards became operative for the first reporting period commencing on or after 1 July 1996 and later reporting periods, although earlier application was encouraged.

July 2002: AUS/AGS Omnibus 3 'Miscellaneous Amendments to AUSs and AGSs' issued by the AuASB. AUS 104 'Glossary of Terms' subsequently reissued to incorporate these amendments. The statement was operative from the date of issue.

April 2006: A new glossary was published with the ASA series of auditing standards.

October 2009: A new glossary was published as part of the Clarity Project.

Contents

Preface

Reasons for Issuing the *AUASB Glossary*

The AUASB is an independent statutory board of the Australian Government established under section 227A of the *Australian Securities and Investments Commission Act 2001*, as amended (ASIC Act).

Under section 227B of the ASIC Act, the AUASB may formulate guidance on auditing and assurance matters. Accordingly, the AUASB issues the *AUASB Glossary* under its powers described in section 227B of the ASIC Act. The AUASB Glossary is not issued under the *Corporations Act 2001*.

Main Features

The *AUASB Glossary* sets out terms defined or used in the AUASB Standards.

The *AUASB Glossary* does not itself establish mandatory requirements for the performance of audit, review, assurance or related service engagements.

The source(s) of terms in this Glossary is (are) indicated beside each term using the alpha-numeric prefix of the source standard(s) only. Where no source is indicated, a term has been retained in the Glossary because it provides useful guidance to the auditor, although it may not be defined in the AUASB Standards.

A term may have more than one definition and should be read in the context of the AUASB Standard to which it applies. Such terms are notated with bracketed words indicating the relevant standard—for example, "(in the context of ASQC 1)".

Operative Date

The AUASB Glossary (October 2009) is operative from 1 January 2010 and from that date replaces the extant AUASB Glossary (April 2006).

The AUASB intends to update the *AUASB Glossary* periodically.

Other Matters

Where accounting terms have not been defined in the AUASB Standards, reference should be made to the *Glossary of Terms* published by the Australian Accounting Standards Board (AASB).

Authority Statement

The Auditing and Assurance Standards Board (AUASB) formulates the *AUASB Glossary* pursuant to section 227B of the *Australian Securities and Investments Commission Act 2001*.

Dated: 27 October 2009

M H Kelsall
Chairman - AUASB

AUASB Glossary

Terms	Source(s)
Accounting estimate means an approximation of a monetary amount in the absence of a precise means of measurement. This term is used for an amount measured at fair value where there is estimation uncertainty, as well as for other amounts that require estimation. Where ASA 540 addresses only accounting estimates involving measurement at fair value, the term *fair value accounting estimates* is used.	ASA 540
Accounting records means the records of initial accounting entries and supporting records, such as cheques and records of electronic fund transfers; invoices; contracts; the general and subsidiary ledgers, journal entries and other adjustments to the financial report that are not reflected in journal entries; and records such as work sheets and spreadsheets supporting cost allocations, computations, reconciliations and disclosures.	ASA 500
Activity (in the context of ASAE 3500) means an action or actions associated with a function or program, including administrative and internal control functions, that are integral to the operations of a business unit or an entity. The economy, efficiency or effectiveness of the activity is the subject matter of a performance engagement.	ASAE 3500
Agreed-upon procedures engagement means an engagement in which an auditor is engaged to carry out those procedures of an audit nature to which the auditor and the entity and any appropriate third parties have agreed and to report on factual findings. The recipients of the report form their own conclusions from the report by the auditor. The report is restricted to those parties that have agreed to the procedures to be performed since others, unaware of the reasons for the procedures may misinterpret the results.	AUS 904
Analytical procedures means evaluations of financial information through analysis of plausible relationships among both financial and non-financial data. Analytical procedures also encompass such investigation as is necessary of identified fluctuations or relationships that are inconsistent with other relevant information or that differ from expected values by a significant amount.	ASA 520
Annual report means a document issued by an entity, ordinarily on an annual basis, which includes its financial report together with the auditor's report thereon.	
Anomaly means a misstatement or deviation that is demonstrably not representative of misstatements or deviations in a population.	ASA 530
Applicable financial reporting framework means the financial reporting framework adopted by management and, where appropriate, those charged with governance in the preparation of the financial report that is acceptable in view of the nature of the entity and the objective of the financial report, or that is required by law or regulation.	ASA 200

The term *fair presentation framework* means a financial reporting framework that requires compliance with the requirements of the framework and:

(a) Acknowledges explicitly or implicitly that, to achieve fair presentation of the financial report, it may be necessary for management to provide disclosures beyond those specifically required by the framework; or

(b) Acknowledges explicitly that it may be necessary for management to depart from a requirement of the framework to achieve fair presentation of the financial report. Such departures are expected to be necessary only in extremely rare circumstances.

The term *compliance framework* means a financial reporting framework that requires compliance with the requirements of the framework, but does not contain the acknowledgements in (a) or (b) above. (see *Fair presentation framework*)

Terms	Source(s)
Applicable financial reporting framework (in the context of ASRE 2410) means a financial reporting framework that is designed to achieve fair presentation.	ASRE 2410
Applied criteria (in the context of ASA 810) means the criteria applied by management in the preparation of the summary financial statements.	ASA 810
Appropriateness (of audit evidence) means the measure of the quality of audit evidence; that is, its relevance and its reliability in providing support for the conclusions on which the auditor's opinion is based.	ASA 200 ASA 500
Arm's length transaction means a transaction conducted on such terms and conditions as between a willing buyer and a willing seller who are unrelated and are acting independently of each other and pursuing their own best interests.	ASA 550
Assertions means representations by management and those charged with governance, explicit or otherwise, that are embodied in the financial report, as used by the auditor to consider the different types of potential misstatements that may occur.	ASA 315
Assertion-based engagement (in the context of ASAE 3100) means a compliance engagement where an entity asserts compliance with requirements as measured by the suitable criteria, and the assurance practitioner evaluates and expresses a conclusion to enhance the intended user's confidence in the entity's assertion.	ASAE 3100
Assertion-based engagement (in the context of ASAE 3500) means a performance engagement where the assurance practitioner reports on assertions prepared by the responsible party regarding the economy, efficiency or effectiveness of the activity.	ASAE 3500
Assess means analyse identified risks to conclude on their significance. "Assess," by convention, is used only in relation to risk. (also see *Evaluate*)	
Assurance engagement means an engagement in which an assurance practitioner expresses a conclusion designed to enhance the degree of confidence of the intended users other than the responsible party about the outcome of the evaluation or measurement of a subject matter against criteria. (see *Reasonable assurance engagement* and *Limited assurance engagement*).	ASQC 1
Assurance engagement risk means the risk that the practitioner expresses an inappropriate conclusion when the subject matter information is materially misstated.	
Assurance practitioner means a person or an organisation, whether in public practice, industry, commerce or the public sector, providing assurance services.	ASQC 1 ASA 220
AUASB Standards means standards issued by the AUASB, comprising: (a) Australian Auditing Standards; (b) Standards on Review Engagements; and (c) Standards on Assurance Engagements.	ASQC 1
Audit documentation means the record of audit procedures performed, relevant audit evidence obtained, and conclusions the auditor reached (terms such as "working papers" or "work papers" are also sometimes used).	ASA 230
Audit engagement (see *Reasonable assurance engagement)*	
Audit evidence means information used by the auditor in arriving at the conclusions on which the auditor's opinion is based. Audit evidence includes both information contained in the accounting records underlying the financial report and other information. (see *Sufficiency (of audit evidence)* and *Appropriateness (of audit evidence)*.)	ASA 200 ASA 500
Audit file means one or more folders or other storage media, in physical or electronic form, containing the records that comprise the audit documentation for a specific engagement.	ASA 230

Terms	Source(s)
Audit firm (see *Firm*)	
Audit opinion (see *Modified opinion* and *Unmodified opinion*)	
Audit risk means the risk that the auditor expresses an inappropriate audit opinion when the financial report is materially misstated. Audit risk is a function of the risks of material misstatement and detection risk.	ASA 200
Audit sampling (sampling) means the application of audit procedures to less than 100% of items within a population of audit relevance such that all sampling units have a chance of selection in order to provide the auditor with a reasonable basis on which to draw conclusions about the entire population.	ASA 530
Audited financial report means a financial report or a complete set of financial statements audited by the auditor in accordance with Australian Auditing Standards, and from which the summary financial statements are derived.	ASA 810
Auditing Standards means auditing standards made under section 336 of the *Corporations Act 2001*, and include: (a) ASQC 1 *Quality Control for Firms that Perform Audits and Reviews of Financial Reports and Other Financial Information, and Other Assurance Engagements*; and (b) ASRE 2410 *Review of a Financial Report Performed by the Independent Auditor of the Entity.* (see *Australian Auditing Standards*)	ASA 101
Auditor means the person or persons conducting the audit, usually the engagement partner or other members of the engagement team, or, as applicable, the firm. Where an Auditing Standard expressly intends that a requirement or responsibility be fulfilled by the engagement partner, the term "engagement partner" rather than "auditor" is used. "Engagement partner" and "firm" are to be read as referring to their public sector equivalents where relevant.	ASA 200
Auditor's expert means an individual or organisation possessing expertise in a field other than accounting or auditing, whose work in that field is used by the auditor to assist the auditor in obtaining sufficient appropriate audit evidence. An auditor's expert may be either an auditor's internal expert (who is a partner or staff, including temporary staff, of the auditor's firm or a network firm), or an auditor's external expert. "Partner" and "firm" should be read as referring to their public sector equivalents where relevant.	ASA 620
Auditor's point estimate or auditor's range means the amount, or range of amounts, respectively, derived from audit evidence for use in evaluating management's point estimate.	ASA 540
Auditor's range (see *Auditor's point estimate*)	
Australian Accounting Standards means the Australian Accounting Standards issued by the Australian Accounting Standards Board.	ASA 700 ASA 805
Australian Auditing Standards means the suite of auditing standards issued by the AUASB, comprising: • Auditing Standards made under section 336 of the *Corporations Act 2001*; • ASA 805 *Special Considerations—Audits of Single Financial Statements and Specific Elements, Accounts or Items of a Financial Statement*; and • ASA 810 *Engagements to Report on Summary Financial Statements.* (see *Australian Auditing Standards*)	ASA 101
Business risk means a risk resulting from significant conditions, events, circumstances, actions or inactions that could adversely affect an entity's ability to achieve its objectives and execute its strategies, or from the setting of inappropriate objectives and strategies.	ASA 315

Terms	Source(s)
Comparative financial report means comparative information where amounts and other disclosures for the prior period are included for comparison with the financial report of the current period but, if audited, are referred to in the auditor's opinion. The level of information included in that comparative financial report is comparable with that of the financial report of the current period.	ASA 710
Comparative information means the amounts and disclosures included in the financial report in respect of one or more prior periods in accordance with the applicable financial reporting framework.	ASA 710
Compilation engagement means an engagement in which accounting expertise, as opposed to auditing expertise, is used to collect, classify and summarise financial information.	
Complementary user entity controls means controls that the service organisation assumes, in the design of its service, will be implemented by user entities, and which, if necessary to achieve control objectives, are identified in the description of its system.	ASA 402
Complete set of financial statements means financial statements and related notes as determined by the requirements of the applicable financial reporting framework. For example, a complete set of financial statements as described in Accounting Standard AASB 101 *Presentation of Financial Statements*[1] includes: (a) a statement of financial position as at the end of the period; (b) a statement of comprehensive income for the period; (c) a statement of changes in equity for the period; (d) a statement of cash flows for the period; and (e) notes, comprising a summary of significant accounting policies and other explanatory information	ASA 200
Compliance means adherence by the entity to the requirements as measured by the suitable criteria.	ASAE 3100
Compliance engagement means an assurance engagement in which an assurance practitioner expresses a conclusion, after evaluating an entity's compliance with the requirements as measured by the suitable criteria.	ASAE 3100
Compliance engagement risk means the risk that the assurance practitioner expresses an inappropriate conclusion when the entity is materially non compliant with the requirements as measured by the suitable criteria.	ASAE 3100
Compliance framework (in the context of ASA 200—relating to financial reporting (see *Applicable financial reporting framework* and *General purpose framework*)	ASA 200
Compliance framework (in the context of ASAE 3100—not relating to financial reporting) means a framework used by the entity, which is designed to ensure that the entity achieves compliance, and includes governance structures, programs, processes, systems, controls and procedures.	ASAE 3100
Component means an entity or business activity for which group or component management prepares financial information that should be included in the group financial report.	ASA 600
Component auditor means an auditor who, at the request of the group engagement team, performs work on financial information related to a component for the group audit.	ASA 600
Component management means management, or those charged with governance, responsible for the preparation of the financial information of a component.	ASA 600
Component materiality means the materiality level for a component determined by the group engagement team.	ASA 600

1 See AASB 101 *Presentation of Financial Statements*, paragraph 10.

Terms **Source(s)**

Concise financial report means a financial report for the year referred to in the *Corporations Act 2001* drawn up in accordance with accounting standard AASB 1039 *Concise Financial Reports.*

Control activities means those policies and procedures that help ensure that management directives are carried out. Control activities are a component of internal control.

Control environment means the governance and management functions and the attitudes, awareness and actions of those charged with governance and management concerning the entity's internal control and its importance in the entity. The control environment is a component of internal control.

Control risk (see *Risk of material misstatement*)

Corporate governance (see *Governance*)

Corresponding figures means comparative information where amounts and other disclosures for the prior period are included as an integral part of the current period financial report, and are intended to be read only in relation to the amounts and other disclosures relating to the current period (referred to as "current period figures"). The level of detail presented in the corresponding amounts and disclosures is dictated primarily by its relevance to the current period figures. — ASA 710

*Criteria (*see *Suitable criteria)*

Criteria means reasonable and acceptable standards of performance against which the extent of economy, efficiency or effectiveness of an activity may be assessed. — ASAE 3500

Suitable criteria have the following characteristics: — ASAE 3500

(a) *relevance*: relevant criteria contribute to conclusions that assist decision-making by the intended users;
(b) *completeness*: criteria are sufficiently complete when relevant factors that could affect the conclusions in the context of the performance engagement circumstances are not omitted. Complete criteria include, where relevant, benchmarks for presentation and disclosure;
(c) *reliability*: reliable criteria allow reasonably consistent evaluation or measurement of the activity, including when used in similar circumstances by similarly qualified assurance practitioners;
(d) *neutrality*: neutral criteria contribute to conclusions that are free from bias; and
(e) *understandability*: understandable criteria contribute to conclusions that are clear, comprehensive, and not subject to significantly different interpretations.

Date of approval of the financial report means the date on which all the statements that comprise the financial report, including the related notes, have been prepared and those with the recognised authority have asserted that they have taken responsibility for that financial report. — ASA 560

Date of report means the date the assurance practitioner signs the report. — ASQC 1

Date of the auditor's report means the date the auditor dates the report on the financial report in accordance with ASA 700. — ASA 560

Date of the financial report means the date of the end of the latest period covered by the financial report. — ASA 560

Date the financial report is issued means the date that the auditor's report and audited financial report are made available to third parties. — ASA 560

Terms	Source(s)
Deficiency in internal control means: (a) A control is designed, implemented or operated in such a way that it is unable to prevent, or detect and correct, misstatements in the financial report on a timely basis; or (b) A control necessary to prevent, or detect and correct, misstatements in the financial report on a timely basis is missing.	ASA 265
Detection risk means the risk that the procedures performed by the auditor to reduce audit risk to an acceptably low level will not detect a misstatement that exists and that could be material, either individually or when aggregated with other misstatements.	ASA 200
Direct reporting engagement (in the context of ASAE 3100) means a compliance engagement where the assurance practitioner directly evaluates an entity's compliance with requirements as measured by the suitable criteria and expresses a conclusion to the intended users in a compliance report.	ASAE 3100
Direct reporting engagement (in the context of ASAE 3500) means performance engagements where the assurance practitioner directly undertakes the evaluation or measurement of the activity to report on the economy, efficiency or effectiveness of the activity.	ASAE 3500
Economy[2] means the acquisition of the appropriate quality and quantity of resources at the appropriate times and at the lowest cost.	ASAE 3500
Efficiency[2] means the use of resources such that output is optimised for any given set of resource inputs, or input is minimised for any given quantity and quality of output.	ASAE 3500
Effectiveness[2] means the achievement of the objectives or other intended effects of activities at a program or entity level.	ASAE 3500
Element (see *Element of a financial statement*)	
Element of a financial statement means an element, account or item of a financial statement.	ASA 805
Emphasis of Matter paragraph means a paragraph included in the auditor's report that refers to a matter appropriately presented or disclosed in the financial report that, in the auditor's judgement, is of such importance that it is fundamental to users' understanding of the financial report.	ASA 706
Engagement documentation means the record of work performed, relevant evidence obtained, and conclusions the assurance practitioner reached (terms such as "working papers" or "work papers" are sometimes used).	ASQC 1
Engagement letter means the written terms of an engagement in the form of a letter.	
Engagement partner (in the context of ASA 220) means the partner or other person in the firm who is responsible for the audit engagement and its performance, and for the auditor's report that is issued on behalf of the firm, and who, where required, has the appropriate authority from a professional, legal or regulatory body. "Engagement partner" should be read as referring to a public sector equivalent where relevant.	ASA 220
Engagement partner (in the context of ASQC 1) means the partner or other person in the firm who is responsible for the assurance engagement and its performance, and for the report that is issued on behalf of the firm, and who, where required, has the appropriate authority from a professional, legal or regulatory body. "Engagement partner" should be read as referring to a public sector equivalent where relevant.	ASQC 1

2 These definitions may have broader application in the public sector and should not be seen as limiting existing legislative arrangements or custom.

Terms	Source(s)
Engagement quality control review (in the context of ASA 220) means a process designed to provide an objective evaluation, on or before the date of the auditor's report, of the significant judgements the engagement team made and the conclusions it reached in formulating the auditor's report. The engagement quality control review process is for audits of financial reports of listed entities and those other audit engagements, if any, for which the firm has determined an engagement quality control review is required.	ASA 220
Engagement quality control review (in the context of ASQC 1) means a process designed to provide an objective evaluation, on or before the date of the report, of the significant judgements the engagement team made and the conclusions it reached in formulating the report. The engagement quality control review process is for audits of financial reports of listed entities and those other engagements, if any, for which the firm has determined an engagement quality control review is required.	ASQC 1
Engagement quality control reviewer (in the context of ASA 220) means a partner, other person in the firm, suitably qualified external person, or a team made up of such individuals, none of whom is part of the engagement team, with sufficient and appropriate experience and authority to objectively evaluate the significant judgements the engagement team made and the conclusions it reached in formulating the auditor's report.	ASA 220
Engagement quality control reviewer (in the context of ASQC 1) means a partner, other person in the firm, suitably qualified external person, or a team made up of such individuals, none of whom is part of the engagement team, with sufficient and appropriate experience and authority to objectively evaluate the significant judgements the engagement team made and the conclusions it reached in formulating the report.	ASQC 1
Engagement team (in the context of ASA 220) means all partners and staff performing the engagement, and any individuals engaged by the firm or a network firm who perform audit procedures on the engagement. This excludes an auditor's external expert engaged by the firm or a network firm. (also see *Auditor's expert*)	ASA 220
Engagement team (in the context of ASQC 1) means all partners and staff performing the engagement, and any individuals engaged by the firm or a network firm who perform procedures on the engagement. This excludes external experts engaged by the firm or a network firm.	ASQC 1
Entity's risk assessment process means a component of internal control that is the entity's process for identifying business risks relevant to financial reporting objectives and deciding about actions to address those risks, and the results thereof.	
Error means an unintentional misstatement in a financial report, including the omission of an amount or a disclosure.	
Estimation uncertainty means the susceptibility of an accounting estimate and related disclosures to an inherent lack of precision in its measurement.	ASA 540
Evaluate means identify and analyse the relevant issues, including performing further procedures as necessary, to come to a specific conclusion on a matter. "Evaluation," by convention, is used only in relation to a range of matters, including evidence, the results of procedures and the effectiveness of management's response to a risk. (also see *Assess*)	
Exception means a response that indicates a difference between information requested to be confirmed, or contained in the entity's records, and information provided by the confirming party.	ASA 505

Terms	Source(s)
Experienced auditor means an individual (whether internal or external to the firm) who has practical audit experience, and a reasonable understanding of: (a) Audit processes; (b) Australian Auditing Standards and applicable legal and regulatory requirements; (c) The business environment in which the entity operates; and (d) Auditing and financial reporting issues relevant to the entity's industry.	ASA 230
Expert (see *Auditor's expert* and *Management's expert*)	
Expertise means skills, knowledge and experience in a particular field.	ASA 620
External confirmation means audit evidence obtained as a direct written response to the auditor from a third party (the confirming party), in paper form, or by electronic or other medium.	ASA 505
Fair presentation framework (see *Applicable financial reporting framework* and *General purpose framework*)	ASA 200
Financial report means, for purposes of the *Corporations Act 2001*, financial statements for the year or the half-year, and notes to the financial statements, and the director's declaration about the statements and notes.[3]	ASA 200 ASA 700
Financial report means, for purposes other than the *Corporations Act 2001*, a complete set of financial statements, including the related notes, and an assertion statement by those responsible for the financial report. The related notes ordinarily comprise a summary of significant accounting policies and other explanatory information. The requirements of the applicable financial reporting framework determine the form and content of the financial report.	
Financial statement means a structured representation of historical financial information, intended to communicate an entity's economic resources or obligations at a point in time or the changes therein for a period of time in accordance with a financial reporting framework. What constitutes a financial statement is determined by the requirements of the applicable financial reporting framework.	ASA 200
Firm means a sole practitioner, partnership or corporation or other entity of assurance practitioners. "Firm" should be read as referring to a public sector equivalent where relevant.	ASQC 1 ASA 220
Forecast means prospective financial information prepared on the basis of assumptions as to future events which management expects to take place and the actions management expects to take as of the date the information is prepared (best-estimate assumptions).	AUS 804
Fraud means an intentional act by one or more individuals among management, those charged with governance, employees, or third parties, involving the use of deception to obtain an unjust or illegal advantage.	ASA 240
Fraud risk factors means events or conditions that indicate an incentive or pressure to commit fraud or provide an opportunity to commit fraud.	ASA 240
Fraudulent financial reporting means financial reporting involving intentional misstatements, including omissions of amounts or disclosures in a financial report, to deceive financial report users.	ASA 240
General purpose financial report means a financial report prepared in accordance with a general purpose framework.	ASA 700
General purpose framework means a financial reporting framework designed to meet the common financial information needs of a wide range of users. The financial reporting framework may be a fair presentation framework or a compliance framework. (see *Applicable financial reporting framework*)	ASA 700

3 See section 295 and section 303 of the *Corporations Act 2001*.

Terms	Source(s)
Governance means the role of person(s) or organisation(s) with responsibility for overseeing the strategic direction of the entity and obligations related to the accountability of the entity.	
Group means all the components whose financial information is included in the group financial report. A group always has more than one component.	ASA 600
Group audit means the audit of a group financial report.	ASA 600
Group audit opinion means the audit opinion on the group financial report.	ASA 600
Group engagement partner means the partner or other person in the firm who is responsible for the group audit engagement and its performance, and for the auditor's report on the group financial report that is issued on behalf of the firm. Where joint auditors conduct the group audit, the joint engagement partners and their engagement teams collectively constitute the group engagement partner and the group engagement team.	ASA 600
Group engagement team means partners, including the group engagement partner, and staff who establish the overall group audit strategy, communicate with component auditors, perform work on the consolidation process, and evaluate the conclusions drawn from the audit evidence as the basis for forming an opinion on the group financial report.	ASA 600
Group financial report means a financial report that includes the financial information of more than one component. The term "group financial report" also refers to combined financial reports aggregating the financial information prepared by components that have no parent but are under common control.	ASA 600
Group management means management, or those charged with governance, responsible for the preparation of the group financial report.	ASA 600
Group-wide controls means controls designed, implemented and maintained by group management over group financial reporting.	ASA 600
Historical financial information means information expressed in financial terms in relation to a particular entity, derived primarily from that entity's accounting system, about economic events occurring in past time periods or about economic conditions or circumstances at points in time in the past.	ASA 200

Historical financial information, other than a financial report (in the context of ASRE 2405) includes:

(a) Specific components, elements, accounts or items of a financial report, such as:
  - (i) A single financial statement, for example, an income statement or balance sheet.
  - (ii) Accounts receivable.
  - (iii) Impairment of asset accounts.
  - (iv) Inventory.
  - (v) The liability for accrued benefits of a defined benefits plan.
  - (vi) The recorded value of identified intangible assets.
  - (vii) Pro-forma historical financial information and adjustments.
  - (viii) The liability for "incurred but not reported" claims in an insurance portfolio, including related explanatory notes.

Terms	Source(s)

(b) Other information derived from financial records, such as:

  (i) A schedule of externally managed assets and income of a private pension plan, including related explanatory notes.

  (ii) A schedule of net tangible assets, including related explanatory notes.

  (iii) A schedule of disbursements in relation to a leased property, including related explanatory notes.

  (iv) A schedule of profit participation or employee bonuses, including related explanatory notes.

(c) Financial statements prepared in accordance with a financial reporting framework that is not designed to achieve fair presentation, such as condensed financial statements and an entity's internal management accounts.

Inconsistency means other information that contradicts information contained in the audited financial report. A material inconsistency may raise doubt about the audit conclusions drawn from audit evidence previously obtained and, possibly, about the basis for the auditor's opinion on the financial report. ASA 720

Information system relevant to financial reporting means a component of internal control that includes the financial reporting system, and consists of the procedures and records established to initiate, record, process and report entity transactions (as well as events and conditions) and to maintain accountability for the related assets, liabilities and equity.

Inherent risk (see *Risk of material misstatement*)

Initial audit engagement means an engagement in which either: ASA 510

(a) The financial report for the prior period was not audited; or

(b) The financial report for the prior period was audited by a predecessor auditor.

Inspection (as an audit procedure) means examining records or documents, whether internal or external, in paper form, electronic form, or other media, or a physical examination of an asset. ASA 500

Inspection (in the context of ASQC 1) means in relation to completed engagements, procedures designed to provide evidence of compliance by engagement teams with the firm's quality control policies and procedures. ASQC 1

Intended users (in the context of ASAE 3100) means the person, persons or class of persons for whom the assurance practitioner prepares the compliance report. The responsible party may be one of the intended users, but not the sole user. ASAE 3100

Intended users (in the context of ASAE 3500) means the person, persons or class of persons for whom the assurance practitioner prepares the assurance report. The responsible party can be one of the intended users, but not the sole user. ASAE 3500

Interim financial report means a financial report that is prepared in accordance with an applicable financial reporting framework[4] for a period that is shorter than the entity's financial year. ASRE 2410

Internal audit function means an appraisal activity established or provided as a service to the entity. Its functions include, amongst other things, examining, evaluating and monitoring the adequacy and effectiveness of internal control. ASA 610

Internal auditors means those individuals who perform the activities of the internal audit function. Internal auditors may belong to an internal audit department or equivalent function. ASA 610

4 See, for example, Accounting Standard AASB 134 *Interim Financial Reporting* and the *Corporations Act 2001*.

Terms	Source(s)
Internal control means the process designed, implemented and maintained by those charged with governance, management and other personnel to provide reasonable assurance about the achievement of an entity's objectives with regard to reliability of financial reporting, effectiveness and efficiency of operations, and compliance with applicable laws and regulations. The term "controls" refers to any aspects of one or more of the components of internal control.	ASA 315
International Financial Reporting Standards means the International Financial Reporting Standards issued by the International Accounting Standards Board.	ASA 700
International Pubic Sector Accounting Standards means the International Public Sector Accounting Standards issued by the International Public Sector Accounting Standards Board.	ASA 700
Investigate means to enquire into matters arising from other procedures to resolve them.	
Limited assurance engagement means an assurance engagement where the assurance practitioner's objective is a reduction in assurance engagement risk to a level that is acceptable in the circumstances of the assurance engagement, but where that risk is greater than for a reasonable assurance engagement, as the basis for a negative form of expression of the assurance practitioner's conclusion. A limited assurance engagement is commonly referred to as a review.	ASQC 1
Listed entity means an entity whose shares, stock or debt are quoted or listed on a recognised stock exchange, or are marketed under the regulations of a recognised stock exchange or other equivalent body.	ASQC 1 ASA 220
Management means the person(s) with executive responsibility for the conduct of the entity's operations. For some entities in some jurisdictions, management includes some or all of those charged with governance, for example, executive members of a governance board, or an owner-manager.	ASA 200 ASA 260
Management bias means a lack of neutrality by management in the preparation of information.	ASA 540
Management's expert means an individual or organisation possessing expertise in a field other than accounting or auditing, whose work in that field is used by the entity to assist the entity in preparing the financial report.	ASA 500 ASA 620
Management's point estimate means the amount selected by management for recognition or disclosure in the financial report as an accounting estimate.	ASA 540
Materiality means, in relation to information, that if information is omitted, misstated or not disclosed, that information has the potential to affect the economic decisions of users of the financial report or the discharge of accountability by management or those charged with governance. (see also *Performance materiality*)	
Misappropriation of assets means the theft of an entity's assets and is often perpetrated by employees in relatively small and immaterial amounts. However, it can also involve management who are usually more capable of disguising or concealing misappropriations in ways that are difficult to detect.	ASA 240
Misstatement means a difference between the amount, classification, presentation, or disclosure of a reported financial report item and the amount, classification, presentation, or disclosure that is required for the item to be in accordance with the applicable financial reporting framework. Misstatements can arise from error or fraud. Where the auditor expresses an opinion on whether the financial report is presented fairly, in all material respects, or gives a true and fair view, misstatements also include those adjustments of amounts, classifications, presentation, or disclosures that, in the auditor's judgement, are necessary for the financial report to be presented fairly, in all material respects, or to give a true and fair view.	ASA 200 ASA 450

Terms	Source(s)
Misstatement of fact means other information that is unrelated to matters appearing in the audited financial report that is incorrectly stated or presented. A material misstatement of fact may undermine the credibility of the document containing the audited financial report.	ASA 720
Modified opinion means a qualified opinion, an adverse opinion or a disclaimer of opinion.	ASA 705
Monitoring means a process comprising an ongoing consideration and evaluation of the firm's system of quality control, including a periodic inspection of a selection of completed engagements, designed to provide the firm with reasonable assurance that its system of quality control is operating effectively.	ASQC 1 ASA 220
Monitoring of controls means a process to assess the effectiveness of internal control performance over time. It includes assessing the design and operation of controls on a timely basis and taking necessary corrective actions modified for changes in conditions. Monitoring of controls is a component of internal control.	
Negative confirmation request means a request that the confirming party respond directly to the auditor only if the confirming party disagrees with the information provided in the request.	ASA 505
Network means a larger structure: (a) That is aimed at cooperation, and (b) That is clearly aimed at profit or cost-sharing or shares common ownership, control or management, common quality control policies and procedures, common business strategy, the use of a common brand name, or a significant part of professional resources.	ASQC 1 ASA 220
Network firm means a firm or entity that belongs to a network.	ASCQ 1 ASA 220
Non-compliance means acts of omission or commission by the entity, either intentional or unintentional, which are contrary to the prevailing laws or regulations. Such acts include transactions entered into by, or in the name of, the entity, or on its behalf, by those charged with governance, management or employees. Non-compliance does not include personal misconduct (unrelated to the business activities of the entity) by those charged with governance, management or employees of the entity.	ASA 250
Non-response means a failure of the confirming party to respond, or fully respond, to a positive confirmation request, or a confirmation request returned undelivered.	ASA 505
Non-sampling risk means the risk that the auditor reaches an erroneous conclusion for any reason not related to sampling risk.	ASA 530
Observation means looking at a process or procedure being performed by others, for example, the auditor's observation of inventory counting by the entity's personnel, or of the performance of control activities.	ASA 500
Opening balances means those account balances that exist at the beginning of the period. Opening balances are based upon the closing balances of the prior period and reflect the effects of transactions and events of prior periods and accounting policies applied in the prior period. Opening balances also include matters requiring disclosure that existed at the beginning of the period, such as contingencies and commitments.	ASA 510
Other financial information means historical financial information and information other than historical financial information (for example prospective financial information)	ASQC 1

Terms	Source(s)
Other information means financial and non-financial information (other than the financial report and the auditor's report thereon) which is included, either by law, regulation, or custom, in a document containing an audited financial report and the auditor's report thereon.	ASA 720
Other Matter paragraph means a paragraph included in the auditor's report that refers to a matter other than those presented or disclosed in the financial report that, in the auditor's judgement, is relevant to users' understanding of the audit, the auditor's responsibilities or the auditor's report.	ASA 706
Outcome of an accounting estimate means the actual monetary amount which results from the resolution of the underlying transaction(s), event(s) or condition(s) addressed by the accounting estimate.	ASA 540
Overall audit strategy means the strategy that sets the scope, timing and direction of the audit, and guides the development of the more detailed audit plan.	ASA 300
Partner (in the context of ASQC 1) means any individual with authority to bind the firm with respect to the performance of an audit, review or other assurance engagement. "Partner" should be read as referring to a public sector equivalent where relevant.	ASQC 1
Partner (in the context of ASA 220) means any individual with authority to bind the firm with respect to the performance of an audit of a financial report or historical financial information. "Partner" should be read as referring to a public sector equivalent where relevant.	ASA 220
Performance audit engagement means a performance engagement where the assurance practitioner provides reasonable assurance.	ASAE 3500
Performance engagement means a performance audit or a performance review of all or a part of the activities of an entity (or entities) to assess economy, efficiency or effectiveness. It includes a *performance audit engagement* or a *performance review engagement* directed to assess: (a) the adequacy of an internal control structure or specific internal controls, in particular those intended to safeguard assets and to ensure due regard for economy, efficiency or effectiveness; (b) the extent to which resources have been managed economically or efficiently; and (c) the extent to which activities have been effective. The terms *performance audit* and *performance review* are predominantly applied in the public sector. In the private sector these audits and reviews are commonly referred to as *operational audits* and *operational reviews*.	ASAE 3500
Performance engagement risk means the risk that the assurance practitioner expresses an inappropriate conclusion when the performance of an activity is not materially economic, efficient or effective. This would arise where the assurance practitioner draws conclusions based on evidence that is not soundly based or that is improper or incomplete as a result of inadequacies in the evidence gathering process, misrepresentation or fraud.	ASAE 3500
Performance materiality means the amount or amounts set by the auditor at less than materiality for the financial report as a whole to reduce to an appropriately low level the probability that the aggregate of uncorrected and undetected misstatements exceeds materiality for the financial report as a whole. If applicable, performance materiality also refers to the amount or amounts set by the auditor at less than the materiality level or levels for particular classes of transactions, account balances or disclosures.	ASA 320
Performance review engagement means a performance engagement where the assurance practitioner provides limited assurance.	ASA 320

Terms	Source(s)
Personnel means partners and staff.	ASA 220 ASQC 1
Pervasive means a term used, in the context of misstatements, to describe the effects on the financial report of misstatements or the possible effects on the financial report of misstatements, if any, that are undetected due to an inability to obtain sufficient appropriate audit evidence. Pervasive effects on the financial report are those that, in the auditor's judgement: (a) Are not confined to specific elements, accounts or items of the financial report; (b) If so confined, represent or could represent a substantial proportion of the financial report; or (c) In relation to disclosures, are fundamental to users' understanding of the financial report.	ASA 705
Population means the entire set of data from which a sample is selected and about which the auditor wishes to draw conclusions.	ASA 530
Positive confirmation request means a request that the confirming party respond directly to the auditor indicating whether the confirming party agrees or disagrees with the information in the request, or providing the requested information.	ASA 505
Preconditions for an audit means the use by management of an acceptable financial reporting framework in the preparation of the financial report and the agreement of management and, where appropriate, those charged with governance to the premise on which an audit is conducted.	ASA 210
Predecessor auditor means the auditor from a different audit firm, who audited the financial report of an entity in the prior period and who has been replaced by the current auditor.	ASA 510
Premise, relating to the responsibilities of management and, where appropriate, those charged with governance, on which an audit is conducted means that management and, where appropriate, those charged with governance have acknowledged and understand that they have the following responsibilities that are fundamental to the conduct of an audit in accordance with Australian Auditing Standards. That is, responsibility: (a) For the preparation of the financial report in accordance with the applicable financial reporting framework; including where relevant their fair presentation; (b) For such internal control as management and, where appropriate, those charged with governance determine is necessary to enable the preparation of the financial report that is free from material misstatement, whether due to fraud or error, and (c) To provide the auditor with: (i) Access to all information of which management and, where appropriate, those charged with governance are aware that is relevant to the preparation of the financial report such as record, documentation and other matters; (ii) Additional information that the auditor may request from management and, where appropriate, those charged with governance, for the purposes of the audit; and (iii) Unrestricted access to persons within the entity from whom the auditor determines it necessary to obtain audit evidence.	ASA 200

Terms	Source(s)
In the case of a fair presentation framework, (a) above may be restated as "for the preparation and *fair* presentation of the financial report in accordance with the financial reporting framework", or "for the preparation of the financial report *that gives a true and fair view* in accordance with the financial reporting framework". The "premise, relating to the responsibilities of management and, where appropriate, those charged with governance, on which an audit is conducted" may also be referred to as the "premise."	
Professional judgement means the application of relevant training, knowledge and experience, within the context provided by auditing, accounting and ethical standards, in making informed decisions about the courses of action that are appropriate in the circumstances of the audit engagement.	ASA 200
Professional scepticism means an attitude that includes a questioning mind, being alert to conditions which may indicate possible misstatement due to error or fraud, and a critical assessment of evidence.	ASA 200
Projection means prospective financial information prepared on the basis of: (a) Hypothetical assumptions about future events and management actions which are not necessarily expected to take place, such as when some entities are in a start-up phase or are considering a major change in the nature of operations; or (b) A mixture of best-estimate and hypothetical assumptions.	AUS 804
Prospective financial information means financial information based on assumptions about events that may occur in the future and possible actions by an entity. It is highly subjective in nature and its preparation requires the exercise of considerable judgement. Prospective financial information can be in the form of a forecast, a projection or a combination of both for example a one year forecast plus a five year projection. (see *Forecast* and *Projection*)	AUS 804
Reasonable assurance means, a high, but not absolute, level of assurance.	ASQC 1 ASA 200 ASAE 3000 ASAE 3100
Reasonable assurance engagement means an assurance engagement where the assurance practitioner's objective is a reduction in assurance engagement risk to an acceptably low level in the circumstances of the assurance engagement as the basis for a positive form of expression of the assurance practitioner's conclusion. A reasonable assurance engagement is commonly referred to as an audit.	
Recalculation means checking the mathematical accuracy of documents or records.	ASA 500
Related party means a party that is either: (a) A related party as defined in the applicable financial reporting framework[5]; or (b) Where the applicable financial reporting framework establishes minimal or no related party requirements: (i) A person or other entity that has control or significant influence, directly or indirectly through one or more intermediaries, over the reporting entity; (ii) Another entity over which the reporting entity has control or significant influence, directly or indirectly through one or more intermediaries; or	ASA 550

5 See also section 228 of the *Corporations Act 2001*.

Terms	Source(s)

(iii) Another entity that is under common control with the reporting entity through having:

a. Common controlling ownership;

b. Owners who are close family members; or

c. Common key management.

However, entities that are under common control by a state (that is, a national, regional or local government) are not considered related unless they engage in significant transactions or share resources to a significant extent with one another.

Related services means agreed-upon procedures and compilations.

Relevant ethical requirements means ethical requirements that apply to the auditor, assurance practitioner, engagement quality control reviewer and firm. In Australia, these include the applicable requirements of APES 110 *Code of Ethics for Professional Accountants* issued by the Accounting Professional and Ethical Standards Board (February 2008), the applicable provisions of the *Corporations Act 2001* and other applicable law or regulation. ASA 102

Reperformance means the auditor's independent execution of procedures or controls that were originally performed as part of the entity's internal control. ASA 500

Report on the description and design of controls at a service organisation (referred to in ASA 402 as a type 1 report) means a report that comprises: ASA 402

(a) A description, prepared by management of the service organisation, of the service organisation's system, control objectives and related controls that have been designed and implemented as at a specified date; and

(b) A report by the service auditor with the objective of conveying reasonable assurance that includes the service auditor's opinion on the description of the service organisation's system, control objectives and related controls and the suitability of the design of the controls to achieve the specified control objectives.

Report on the description, design, and operating effectiveness of controls at a service organisation (referred to in ASA 402 as a type 2 report) means a report that comprises: ASA 402

(a) A description, prepared by management of the service organisation, of the service organisation's system, control objectives and related controls, their design and implementation as at a specified date or throughout a specified period and, in some cases, their operating effectiveness throughout a specified period; and

(b) A report by the service auditor with the objective of conveying reasonable assurance that includes:

(i) The service auditor's opinion on the description of the service organisation's system, control objectives and related controls, the suitability of the design of the controls to achieve the specified control objectives, and the operating effectiveness of the controls; and

(ii) A description of the service auditor's tests of the controls and the results thereof.

Terms	Source(s)
Responsible party (in the context of ASAE 3100) means the person (or persons) who: (a) In a direct reporting engagement, is responsible for the subject matter; or (b) In an assertion-based engagement, is responsible for the subject matter information (the assertion). The responsible party may or may not be the party who engages the practitioner (the engaging party).	ASAE 3100
Responsible Party (in the context of ASAE 3500) means the person (or persons) who: (a) In a direct reporting engagement, is responsible for the activity; and (b) In an assertion-based engagement, is responsible for the assertions or information concerning the performance of the activity and may also be responsible for the activity itself.	ASAE 3500
Review engagement (see *Limited assurance engagement*)	ASRE 2400 ASRE 2405 ASRE 2410 ASAE 3000
Review procedures means the procedures deemed necessary to meet the objective of a review engagement, primarily enquiries of entity personnel and analytical procedures applied to financial data.	ASRE 2410
Risk assessment procedures means the audit procedures performed to obtain an understanding of the entity and its environment, including the entity's internal control, to identify and assess the risks of material misstatement, whether due to fraud or error, at the financial report and assertion levels.	ASA 315
Risk of material misstatement means the risk that the financial report is materially misstated prior to audit. This consists of two components, described as follows at the assertion level: (a) Inherent risk means the susceptibility of an assertion about a class of transaction, account balance or disclosure to a misstatement that could be material, either individually or when aggregated with other misstatements, before consideration of any related controls. (b) Control risk means the risk that a misstatement that could occur in an assertion about a class of transaction, account balance or disclosure and that could be material, either individually or when aggregated with other misstatements, will not be prevented, or detected and corrected, on a timely basis by the entity's internal control.	ASA 200
Sampling (see *Audit sampling*)	ASA 530
Sampling risk means the risk that the auditor's conclusion based on a sample may be different from the conclusion if the entire population were subjected to the same audit procedure. Sampling risk can lead to two types of erroneous conclusions: (a) In the case of a test of controls, that controls are more effective than they actually are, or in the case of a test of details, that a material misstatement does not exist when in fact it does. The auditor is primarily concerned with this type of erroneous conclusion because it affects audit effectiveness and is more likely to lead to an inappropriate audit opinion. (b) In the case of a test of controls, that controls are less effective than they actually are, or in the case of a test of details, that a material misstatement exists when in fact it does not. This type of erroneous conclusion affects audit efficiency as it would usually lead to additional work to establish that initial conclusions were incorrect.	ASA 530

Terms	Source(s)
Sampling unit means the individual items constituting a population.	ASA 530
Service auditor means an auditor who, at the request of the service organisation, provides an assurance report on the controls of a service organisation.	ASA 402
Service organisation means a third-party organisation (or segment of a third-party organisation) that provides services to user entities that are part of those entities' information systems relevant to financial reporting.	ASA 402
Service organisation's system means the policies and procedures designed, implemented and maintained by the service organisation to provide user entities with the services covered by the service auditor's report.	ASA 402
Significance means the relative importance of a matter, taken in context. The significance of a matter is judged by the practitioner in the context in which it is being considered. This might include, for example, the reasonable prospect of its changing or influencing the decisions of intended users of the practitioner's report; or, as another example, where the context is a judgement about whether to report a matter to those charged with governance, whether the matter would be regarded as important by them in relation to their duties. Significance can be considered in the context of quantitative and qualitative factors, such as relative magnitude, the nature and effect on the subject matter and the expressed interests of intended users or recipients.	
Significant component means a component identified by the group engagement team (i) that is of individual financial significance to the group, or (ii) that, due to its specific nature or circumstances, is likely to include significant risks of material misstatement of the group financial report.	ASA 600
Significant deficiency in internal control means a deficiency or combination of deficiencies in internal control that, in the auditor's professional judgement, is of sufficient importance to merit the attention of those charged with governance.	ASA 265
Significant risk means an identified and assessed risk of material misstatement that, in the auditor's judgement, requires special audit consideration.	ASA 315
Single financial statement or specific element of a financial statement includes the related notes. The related notes ordinarily comprise a summary of significant accounting policies and other explanatory information relevant to the financial statement or to the element.	ASA 805

Smaller entity means an entity which typically possesses qualitative characteristics such as:

(a) Concentration of ownership and management in a small number of individuals (often a single individual – either a natural person or another enterprise that owns the entity provided the owner exhibits the relevant qualitative characteristics); and

(b) One or more of the following:

(i) Straightforward or uncomplicated transactions;

(ii) Simple record-keeping;

(iii) Few lines of business and few products within business lines;

(iv) Few internal controls;

(v) Few levels of management with responsibility for a broad range of controls; or

(vi) Few personnel, many having a wide range of duties.

These qualitative characteristics are not exhaustive, they are not exclusive to smaller entities, and smaller entities do not necessarily display all of these characteristics.

Terms	Source(s)
Special purpose financial report means a complete set of financial statements, including the related notes, and an assertion statement by those responsible for the financial report, prepared in accordance with a special purpose framework. The related notes ordinarily comprise a summary of significant accounting policies and other explanatory information. The requirements of the applicable financial reporting framework determine the format and content of a financial report prepared in accordance with a special purpose framework.	ASA 800
Special purpose framework means a financial reporting framework designed to meet the financial information needs of specific users. The financial reporting framework may be a fair presentation framework or a compliance framework. (see *Applicable financial reporting framework*)	ASA 800
Staff means professionals, other than partners, including any experts the firm employs.	ASQC 1 ASA 220
Standards on assurance engagements means standards made by the AUASB which establish requirements and provide explanatory guidance for undertaking and reporting on assurance engagements other than audits or reviews of historical financial information covered by Australian Auditing Standards or Standards on Review Engagements.	
Standards on review engagements means standards made by the AUASB which establish requirements and provide explanatory guidance on the responsibilities of an auditor, or assurance practitioner, when engaged to undertake a review engagement and on the form and content of the auditor's, or assurance practitioner's, review report.	
Statistical sampling means an approach to sampling that has the following characteristics: (a) Random selection of the sample items; and (b) The use of probability theory to evaluate sample results, including measurement of sampling risk. A sampling approach that does not have characteristics (a) and (b) is considered non-statistical sampling.	ASA 530
Stratification means the process of dividing a population into sub-populations, each of which is a group of sampling units which have similar characteristics (often monetary value).	ASA 530
Subject matter information means the outcome of the evaluation or measurement of a subject matter. It is the subject matter information about which the practitioner gathers sufficient appropriate evidence to provide a reasonable basis for expressing a conclusion in an assurance report.	
Subsequent events means events occurring between the date of the financial report and the date of the auditor's report, and facts that become known to the auditor after the date of the auditor's report.	ASA 560
Subservice organisation means a service organisation used by another service organisation to perform some of the services provided to user entities that are part of those user entities' information systems relevant to financial reporting.	ASA 402
Substantive procedure means an audit procedure designed to detect material misstatements at the assertion level. Substantive procedures comprise: (a) Tests of details (of classes of transactions, account balances, and disclosures); and (b) Substantive analytical procedures.	ASA 330
Sufficiency (of audit evidence) means the measure of the quantity of audit evidence. The quantity of the audit evidence needed is affected by the auditor's assessment of the risks of material misstatement and also by the quality of such audit evidence.	ASA 200 ASA 500

Terms	Source(s)
Suitable criteria means the reasonable and acceptable standards of compliance which are subject to the compliance engagement. Suitable criteria have the following characteristics: (a) reliability: reliable criteria allow reasonably consistent evaluation or measurement of the subject matter, when used in similar circumstances by similarly qualified practitioners; (b) neutrality: neutral criteria contribute to conclusions that are free from bias; (c) understandability: understandable criteria contribute to conclusions that are clear, comprehensive, and not subject to significantly different interpretations; (d) relevance: relevant criteria contribute to conclusions that assist decision-making by the intended users; and (e) completeness: criteria are sufficiently complete when relevant factors that could affect the conclusions in the context of the assurance engagement circumstances are not omitted.	ASAE 3100
Suitably qualified external person (in the context of ASQC 1) means an individual outside the firm with the competence and capabilities to act as an engagement partner, for example a partner of another firm, or an employee (with appropriate experience) of either a professional accountancy body whose members may perform audits and reviews of financial reports, or audits and reviews of other financial information, or other assurance engagements, or of an organisation that provides relevant quality control services.	ASQC 1
Suitably qualified external person (in the context of ASA 220) means an individual outside the firm with the competence and capabilities to act as an engagement partner, for example a partner of another firm, or an employee (with ASA 220 appropriate experience) of a professional accountancy body whose members may perform audits of financial reports or audits of other historical financial information, or of an organisation that provides relevant quality control services.	ASA 220
Summary financial statements means historical financial information that is derived from a financial report, but that contains less detail than the financial report, while still providing a structured representation consistent with that provided by the financial report, of the entity's economic resources or obligations at a point in time or the changes therein for a period of time. Summary financial statements may include an assertion by those responsible for the summary financial statements. Different jurisdictions may use different terminology to describe such historical financial information.	ASA 810
Supplementary information means information that is presented together with the financial report that is not required by the applicable financial reporting framework used to prepare the financial report, normally presented in either supplementary schedules or as additional notes.	
Test means the application of procedures to some or all items in a population.	
Test of controls means an audit procedure designed to evaluate the operating effectiveness of controls in preventing, or detecting and correcting, material misstatements at the assertion level.	ASA 330
Those charged with governance means the person(s) or organisation(s) (for example, a corporate trustee) with responsibility for overseeing the strategic direction of the entity and obligations related to the accountability of the entity. This includes overseeing the financial reporting process. For some entities in some jurisdictions, those charged with governance may include management personnel, for example, executive members of a governance board of a private or public sector entity, or an owner-manager.	ASA 200 ASA 260

Terms	Source(s)
Tolerable misstatement means a monetary amount set by the auditor in respect of which the auditor seeks to obtain an appropriate level of assurance that the monetary amount set by the auditor is not exceeded by the actual misstatement in the population.	ASA 530
Tolerable rate of deviation means a rate of deviation from prescribed internal control procedures set by the auditor in respect of which the auditor seeks to obtain an appropriate level of assurance that the rate of deviation set by the auditor is not exceeded by the actual rate of deviation in the population.	ASA 530
Uncertainty means a matter whose outcome depends on future actions or events not under the direct control of the entity but that may affect the financial report.	ASA 570
Uncorrected misstatements means misstatements that the auditor has accumulated during the audit and that have not been corrected.	ASA 450
Unmodified opinion means the opinion expressed by the auditor when the auditor concludes that the financial report is prepared, in all material respects, in accordance with the applicable financial reporting framework.	ASA 700
User auditor means an auditor who audits and reports on the financial reports of a user entity.	ASA 402
User entity means an entity that uses a service organisation and whose financial report is being audited.	ASA 402
Walk-through test means tracing a selected number of transactions through the financial reporting system.	
Written representation means a written statement by management provided to the auditor to confirm certain matters or to support other audit evidence. Written representations in this context do not include the financial report, the assertions therein, or supporting books and records.	ASA 580

Framework for Assurance Engagements

(Reissued April 2010)

Issued by the Auditing and Assurance Standard Board.

Note from the Institute of Chartered Accountants Australia

This note, prepared by the technical editor, is not part of the Framework.

Historical development

October 2001: AUS 108 issued, operative for periods ending on or after 31 December 2001. Based on the International Assurance Standard ASAE 100 'Assurance Engagements'.

June 2004: AUS 108 revised and reissued. Based on the IAASB's International Framework for Assurance Engagements, it defines and describes the features of an assurance engagement but does not set standards.

June 2007: This Statement was revised and reissued as the Framework to reflect the introduction of the legally bonding ASA Auditing Standards. It is now sector-neutral rather than containing a separate section on the public sector perspective. Like its predecessor, AUS 108, it is based on the IAASB's 'International Framework for Assurance Engagements'.

April 2010: This statement was revised and reissued to bring it closer to the IAASB's International Framework for Assurance Engagements, following the Strategic Direction given to the AUASB by the Financial Reporting Council (FRC) to have regard to improvements made by the IAASB to its Standards.

Contents

Preface

Reasons for Issuing the *Framework for Assurance Engagements*

The Auditing and Assurance Standards Board (AUASB) issues *Framework for Assurance Engagements* (Framework) pursuant to the requirements of the legislative provisions explained below.

The AUASB is an independent statutory board of the Australian Government, established under section 227A of the *Australian Securities and Investments Commission Act 2001*, as amended, (ASIC Act). Under 227B of that Act, the AUASB may formulate guidance on auditing and assurance matters. Accordingly, AUASB issues the *Framework for Assurance Engagements* (Framework) under its powers described in section 227B of that Act.

Under the Strategic Direction given to the AUASB by the Financial Reporting Council (FRC), the AUASB is required to have regard to any programme initiated by the International Auditing and Assurance Standards Board (IAASB) for the revision and enhancement of the International Standards on Auditing (ISAs) and to make appropriate consequential amendments to the Australian Auditing Standards. Since issuing this Framework in June 2007, the AUASB has decided to further redraft the Framework, and align it more closely with the *International Framework for Assurance Engagements*, being the equivalent underlying International pronouncement. Footnotes appearing in the *International Framework for Assurance Engagements* have, in some cases, been re-located and appear as "Aus" paragraphs in the Framework.

The Framework does not itself establish requirements for undertaking and reporting on audit, review or other assurance engagements. Accordingly, the AUASB has not issued the *Framework for Assurance Engagements* as an Auditing Standard for the purposes of the *Corporations Act 2001*.

Main Features

The Framework provides a structure for the development of the Australian Auditing Standards, Standards on Review Engagements and Standards on Assurance Engagements (collectively referred to in this Framework as "AUASB Standards"). It defines and describes the elements and objectives of an assurance engagement and identifies engagements to which the AUASB Standards apply.

The Framework also provides a frame of reference for:

1. Assurance practitioners; and
2. Others involved with assurance engagements, including the intended users of an assurance report, and the responsible party.

Authority Statement

The Auditing and Assurance Standards Board (AUASB) formulates the *Framework for Assurance Engagements* pursuant to section 227B of the *Australian Securities and Investments Commission Act 2001*.

Dated: 19 April 2010

M H Kelsall
Chairman - AUASB

Framework for Assurance Engagements

Operative Date

Aus 0.1 This Framework is operative from 19 April 2010 and from that date replaces the existing *Framework for Assurance Engagements* (June 2007).

Introduction

Purpose of this Framework

1. This *Framework for Assurance Engagements* (Framework) defines and describes the elements and objectives of an assurance engagement, and identifies engagements to which Auditing Standards, Standards on Review Engagements and Standards on Assurance Engagements (collectively referred to in this Framework as "AUASB Standards") apply. It provides a frame of reference for:

   (a) assurance practitioners[1];

   (b) others involved with assurance engagements, including the intended users of an assurance report and the responsible party; and

   (c) the AUASB in its development of its pronouncements.

Aus 1.1 The Framework can be applied by assurance practitioners not in public practice who:

   (a) refer to the Framework or the AUASB Standards in their assurance practitioner's report; and/or

   (b) are not independent of the responsible party.

   If the assurance practitioner, members of the assurance team, or the assurance practitioner's employer are not independent of the responsible party in respect of which the assurance engagement is being performed, then the lack of independence and the nature of the relationship(s) with the entity must be prominently disclosed in the assurance practitioner's report. That report must not include the word "independent" in its title, and the purpose and users of the report are to be restricted.

2. This Framework does not itself establish standards or provide requirements for the performance of assurance engagements. The AUASB Standards contain requirements and application and other explanatory material, consistent with the concepts in this Framework, for the performance of assurance engagements. The relationship between the Framework and the AUASB Standards is illustrated in Appendix 1 of the *Foreword to AUASB Pronouncements*.

1 [Footnote deleted by the AUASB and re-located to Aus 1.1]

Overview of the Framework

3. The following is an overview of this Framework:

- *Introduction*: This Framework deals with assurance engagements performed by assurance practitioners. It provides a frame of reference for assurance practitioners and others involved with assurance engagements, such as those engaging an assurance practitioner (the "engaging party").
- *Definitions and Objective of an Assurance Engagement*: This section identifies the two types of assurance engagements an assurance practitioner may perform under this Framework. This Framework describes these two types as reasonable assurance engagements and limited assurance engagements.[2]
- *Scope of the Framework*: This section distinguishes assurance engagements from other engagements, such as consulting engagements.
- *Assurance Engagement Acceptance*: This section sets out characteristics that ought to be exhibited before an assurance practitioner can accept an assurance engagement.
- *Elements of an Assurance Engagement*: This section identifies and discusses five elements assurance engagements performed by an assurance practitioner exhibit: a three party relationship, a subject matter, criteria, evidence and an assurance report. It explains important distinctions between reasonable assurance engagements and limited assurance engagements (also outlined in Appendix 1). This section also discusses, for example, the significant variation in the subject matters of assurance engagements, the characteristics of suitable criteria, the role of risk and materiality in assurance engagements, and how conclusions are expressed in each of the two types of assurance engagement.
- *Inappropriate Use of the Assurance Practitioner's Name*: This section discusses implications of an assurance practitioner's association with a subject matter.
- *Public sector perspective:* This section discusses the relevance of the Framework for assurance practitioners in the public sector.

Ethical Principles and Quality Control Standards

4. In addition to the Framework, practitioners who perform assurance engagements are governed by AUASB Standards, including:
   (a) ASA 102 *Compliance with Ethical Requirements when Performing Audits, Reviews and Other Assurance Engagements*, which requires compliance with relevant ethical principles when conducting assurance engagements; and
   (b) ASQC 1 *Quality Control for Firms that Perform Audits and Reviews of Financial Reports, Other Financial Information, and Other Assurance Engagements*, which establishes standards and provide guidance on a firm's system of quality control.[3]

5. Relevant ethical requirements include the fundamental principles of professional ethics including:
   (a) Integrity;
   (b) Objectivity;
   (c) Professional competence and duty of care;
   (d) Confidentiality; and
   (e) Professional behaviour.

6. [Deleted by the AUASB. Refer Aus 6.1]

Aus 6.1 In addition to this Framework and the AUASB Standards, assurance practitioners who perform assurance engagements may be governed by other applicable law(s),

2 For assurance engagements regarding historical financial information, reasonable assurance engagements are commonly called audits, and limited assurance engagements are commonly called reviews.

3 Additional standards and guidance on quality control procedures for specific types of assurance engagement are set out in individual AUASB Standards.

regulation(s) or professional requirement(s)[#] in respect of relevant ethical requirements.

Aus 6.2 In accordance with ASQC 1[†] a system of quality control is required to be established and maintained by all firms where there are assurance practitioners who perform assurance engagements. Such a system is required to include the following elements:

- Leadership responsibilities for quality within the firm.
- Relevant ethical requirements.
- Acceptance and continuance of client relationships and specific engagements.
- Human resources.
- Engagement performance.
- Monitoring.

Definitions and Objective of an Assurance Engagement

Definitions

7. For purposes of this Framework, the following terms have the meanings attributed below:

Aus 7.1 Assurance engagement means an engagement in which an assurance practitioner expresses a conclusion designed to enhance the degree of confidence of the intended users, other than the responsible party, about the outcome of the evaluation or measurement of a subject matter against criteria.

Aus 7.2 Assurance Practitioner means a person or an organisation, whether in public practice, industry, commerce or the public sector, providing assurance services.

Aus 7.3 AUASB Standards means standards issued by the AUASB, comprising:

(i) Australian Auditing Standards;

(ii) Standards on Review Engagements; and

(iii) Standards on Assurance Engagements.

Aus 7.4 A reasonable assurance engagement means an assurance engagement where the assurance practitioner's objective is a reduction in assurance engagement risk to an acceptably low level in the circumstances of the assurance engagement as the basis for a positive form of expression of the assurance practitioner's conclusion. A reasonable assurance engagement is commonly referred to as an audit.

Aus 7.5 A limited assurance engagement means an assurance engagement where the assurance practitioner's objective is a reduction in assurance engagement risk to a level that is acceptable in the circumstances of the assurance engagement, but where that risk is greater than for a reasonable assurance engagement, as the basis for a negative form of expression of the assurance practitioner's conclusion. A limited assurance engagement is commonly referred to as a review.

Aus 7.6 Professional judgement means the application of relevant training, knowledge and experience, within the context provided by AUASB Standards, in making informed decisions about the courses of action that are appropriate in the circumstances of the assurance engagement.

Aus 7.7 Professional scepticism means where the assurance practitioner makes a critical assessment, with a questioning mind, of the validity of evidence obtained, and is alert to evidence that contradicts or brings into question the reliability of documents and responses to enquiries and other information obtained from management and the responsible party.

Aus 7.8 The AUASB *Glossary* includes definitions of other terms used in the AUASB Standards.

\# Refer APES 210 *Conformity with Auditing and Assurance Standards* (September 2008), issued by the Accounting Professional and Ethical Standards Board. See also the professional requirements arising from membership of the Institute of Chartered Accountants in Australia (ICAA), CPA Australia (CPAA), or the National Institute of Accountants (NIA).

† See ASQC 1, paragraph 16.

Objective

8. The outcome of the evaluation or measurement of a subject matter is the information that results from applying the criteria to the subject matter. For example:

- The recognition, measurement, presentation and disclosure represented in the financial report (outcome) result from applying a financial reporting framework for recognition, measurement, presentation and disclosure, such as Australian Accounting Standards, (criteria) to an entity's financial position, financial performance and cash flows (subject matter).
- An assertion about the effectiveness of internal control (outcome) results from applying a framework for evaluating the effectiveness of internal control, for example, COSO[4] or CoCo,[5] (criteria) to internal control, a process (subject matter).

In the remainder of this Framework, the term "subject matter information" will be used to mean the outcome of the evaluation or measurement of a subject matter. It is the subject matter information about which the assurance practitioner gathers sufficient appropriate evidence to provide a reasonable basis for expressing a conclusion in an assurance report.

9. Subject matter information can fail to be properly expressed in the context of the subject matter and the criteria, and can therefore be misstated, potentially to a material extent. This occurs when the subject matter information does not properly reflect the application of the criteria to the subject matter, for example, when an entity's financial report does not give a true and fair view of (or present fairly, in all material respects) its financial position, financial performance and cash flows in accordance with Australian Accounting Standards, or when an entity's assertion that its internal control is effective is not fairly stated, in all material respects, based on COSO or CoCo.

10. In some assurance engagements, the evaluation or measurement of the subject matter is performed by the responsible party, and the subject matter information is in the form of an assertion by the responsible party that is made available to the intended users. These assurance engagements are called "assertion-based assurance engagements." In other assurance engagements, the assurance practitioner either directly performs the evaluation or measurement of the subject matter, or obtains a representation from the responsible party that has performed the evaluation or measurement that is not available to the intended users. The subject matter information is provided to the intended users in the assurance report. These assurance engagements are called "direct reporting assurance engagements."

11. Under this Framework, there are two types of assurance engagements an assurance practitioner may perform:

(a) A reasonable assurance engagement. The objective of a reasonable assurance engagement is a reduction in assurance engagement risk to an acceptably low level in the circumstances of the assurance engagement as the basis for a positive form of expression of the assurance practitioner's conclusion.

(b) A limited assurance engagement. The objective of a limited assurance engagement is a reduction in assurance engagement risk to a level that is acceptable in the circumstances of the assurance engagement, but where that risk is greater than for a reasonable assurance engagement, as the basis for a negative form of expression of the assurance practitioner's conclusion.

Aus 11.1 Assurance engagement circumstances include:

- the terms of the assurance engagement, including whether it is a reasonable assurance engagement or a limited assurance engagement;
- the characteristics of the subject matter;
- the criteria to be used;
- the needs of the intended users;

4 See *Internal Control – Integrated Framework,* issued by the Committee of Sponsoring Organizations of the Treadway Commission.

5 See *Guidance on Assessing Control – The CoCo Principles,* Criteria of Control Board, issued by the Canadian Institute of Chartered Accountants.

- relevant characteristics of the responsible party and its environment; and
- other matters, for example: events, transactions, conditions and practices, that may have a significant effect on the assurance engagement.

Scope of the Framework

12. Not all engagements performed by assurance practitioners are assurance engagements. Other frequently performed engagements that do not meet the above definition (and therefore are not covered by this Framework) include:
    - Agreed-upon procedures engagements, where they provide no assurance.
    - The preparation of tax returns where no conclusion conveying assurance is expressed, or compilations* of financial or other information.
    - Consulting (or advisory) engagements,[6] such as management and tax consulting.

Aus 12.1 Consulting engagements employ a practitioner's technical skills, education, observations, experiences, and knowledge of the consulting process. The consulting process is an analytical process that typically involves some combination of activities relating to: objective-setting, fact-finding, definition of problems or opportunities, evaluation of alternatives, development of recommendations including actions, communication of results, and sometimes implementation and follow-up. Reports (if issued) are generally written in a narrative (or "long form") style. Generally the work performed is only for the use and benefit of the client. The nature and scope of work is determined by agreement between the practitioner and the client. Any service that meets the definition of an assurance engagement is not a consulting engagement but an assurance engagement.

13. An assurance engagement may be part of a larger engagement, for example, when a business acquisition consulting engagement includes a requirement to convey assurance regarding historical or prospective financial information. In such circumstances, this Framework is relevant only to the assurance portion of the engagement.

14. The following engagements, which may meet the definition in paragraph Aus 7.1 of this Framework, need not be performed in accordance with this Framework:
    - Engagements to testify in legal proceedings regarding accounting, auditing, taxation or other matters.
    - Engagements that include professional opinions, views or wording from which a user may derive some assurance, if all of the following apply:
      (i) Those opinions, views or wording are merely incidental to the overall engagement;
      (ii) Any written report issued is expressly restricted for use by only the intended users specified in the report;
      (iii) Under a written understanding with the specified intended users, the engagement is not intended to be an assurance engagement; and
      (iv) The engagement is not represented as an assurance engagement in the assurance practitioner's report.

Reports on Non-Assurance Engagements

15. An assurance practitioner reporting on an engagement that is not an assurance engagement within the scope of this Framework, clearly distinguishes that report from an assurance report. So as not to confuse users, a report that is not an assurance report avoids, for example:
    - Implying compliance with this Framework or AUASB Standards.
    - Inappropriately using the words "assurance," "audit" or "review".
    - Including a statement that could reasonably be mistaken for a conclusion designed to enhance the degree of confidence of intended users about the outcome of the evaluation or measurement of a subject matter against criteria.

---

* See, for example, guidance contained in APES 315 *Compilation of Financial Information* (July 2008, as amended), issued by the Accounting Professional and Ethical Standards Board.

6 [Footnote deleted by the AUASB and re-located to Aus 12.1]

16. The assurance practitioner and the responsible party may agree to apply the principles of this Framework to an assurance engagement when there are no intended users other than the responsible party but where all other requirements of the AUASB Standards are met. In such cases, the assurance practitioner's report includes a statement restricting the use of the report to the responsible party.

Aus 16.1 Engagements which may meet the definition in paragraph Aus 7.1 of this Framework and are conducted by assurance practitioners who apply this Framework, include internal audit. In these cases, the assurance practitioner should refer to their use of the Framework in the assurance practitioner's report.

Assurance Engagement Acceptance

17. An assurance practitioner accepts an assurance engagement only where the assurance practitioner's preliminary knowledge of the assurance engagement circumstances indicates that:

(a) Relevant ethical requirements, such as independence and professional competence will be satisfied; and

(b) The assurance engagement exhibits all of the following characteristics:

(i) The subject matter is appropriate.

(ii) The criteria to be used are suitable and are available to the intended users.

(iii) The assurance practitioner has access to sufficient appropriate evidence to support the assurance practitioner's conclusion.

(iv) The assurance practitioner's conclusion, in the form appropriate to either a reasonable assurance engagement, or a limited assurance engagement, is to be contained in a written report.

(v) The assurance practitioner is satisfied that there is a rational purpose for the assurance engagement. If there is a significant limitation on the scope of the assurance practitioner's work (see paragraph 55 of this Framework), it may be unlikely that the assurance engagement has a rational purpose. Also, an assurance practitioner may believe the engaging party intends to associate the assurance practitioner's name with the subject matter in an inappropriate manner (see paragraph 61 of this Framework).

Specific AUASB Standards may include additional requirements that need to be satisfied prior to accepting an assurance engagement.

Aus 17.1 For example, Auditing Standards ASA 210 or ASRE 2410* require the assurance practitioner to establish whether the pre-conditions for the assurance engagement are present.

18. When a potential engagement cannot be accepted as an assurance engagement because it does not exhibit all the characteristics in paragraphs 17 and/or Aus 17.1 of this Framework, the engaging party may be able to identify a different engagement that will meet the needs of intended users. For example:

(a) If the original criteria were not suitable, an assurance engagement may still be performed if:

(i) The engaging party can identify an aspect of the original subject matter for which those criteria are suitable, and the assurance practitioner could perform an assurance engagement with respect to that aspect as a subject matter in its own right. In such cases, the assurance report makes it clear that it does not relate to the original subject matter in its entirety; or

(ii) Alternative criteria suitable for the original subject matter can be selected or developed.

(b) The engaging party may request an engagement that is not an assurance engagement, such as a consulting engagement.

---

* See ASA 210 *Agreeing the Terms of Audit Engagements,* paragraph 6, or ASRE 2410 *Review of a Financial Report Performed by the Independent Auditor of the Entity*, paragraph 11.

19. Having accepted an assurance engagement, an assurance practitioner may not change that assurance engagement to a non-assurance engagement, or from a reasonable assurance engagement to a limited assurance engagement without reasonable justification. A change in circumstances that affects the intended users' requirements, or a misunderstanding concerning the nature of the assurance engagement, ordinarily will justify a request for a change in the assurance engagement. If such a change is made, the assurance practitioner does not disregard evidence that was obtained prior to the change.

Aus 19.1 Where law or regulation permits a change in assurance engagement terms, the assurance practitioner agrees such changes with the responsible party and records the new terms in writing.

Aus 19.2 In certain jurisdictions, law or regulation may not permit the assurance practitioner and responsible party to change the nature or terms of certain assurance engagements.

Elements of an Assurance Engagement

20. The following elements of an assurance engagement are discussed in this section:

(a) A three party relationship involving an assurance practitioner, a responsible party, and intended users;

(b) An appropriate subject matter;

(c) Suitable criteria;

(d) Sufficient appropriate evidence; and

(e) A written assurance report in the form appropriate to a reasonable assurance engagement or a limited assurance engagement.

Three Party Relationship

21. Assurance engagements involve three separate parties: an assurance practitioner, a responsible party and intended users.

22. The responsible party and the intended users may be from different entities or the same entity. As an example of the latter case, a governing board may seek assurance about information provided by management of that entity. The relationship between the responsible party and the intended users needs to be viewed within the context of a specific assurance engagement and may differ from more traditionally defined lines of responsibility. For example, an entity's senior management (an intended user) may engage an assurance practitioner to perform an assurance engagement on a particular aspect of the entity's activities that is the immediate responsibility of a lower level of management (the responsible party), but for which senior management is ultimately responsible.

Assurance Practitioner

23. The term "assurance practitioner" as used in this Framework is broader than the term "auditor" as used in certain AUASB Standards, which relate only to assurance practitioners performing audits or certain review engagements with respect to historical financial information.

24. An assurance practitioner may be requested, or decide, to perform assurance engagements on a wide range of subject matters. Some subject matters may require specialised skills and knowledge beyond those ordinarily possessed by an individual assurance practitioner. As noted in paragraph 17(a) of this Framework, an assurance practitioner does not accept an assurance engagement if preliminary knowledge of the assurance engagement circumstances indicates that, inter alia, relevant ethical requirements regarding professional competence will not be satisfied. In some cases this requirement can be satisfied by the assurance practitioner using the work of persons from other professional disciplines, referred to as experts. In such cases, the assurance practitioner needs to be satisfied that those persons carrying out the assurance engagement collectively possess the requisite skills and knowledge, and that the assurance practitioner has an adequate level of involvement in the assurance engagement and understanding of the work for which any expert is used.

Responsible Party

25. The responsible party is the person (or persons) who:

(a) In a direct reporting assurance engagement, is responsible for the subject matter.

(b) In an assertion-based assurance engagement, is responsible for the subject matter information (the assertion), and may be responsible for the subject matter. An example of when the responsible party is responsible for both the subject matter information and the subject matter, is when an entity engages an assurance practitioner to perform an assurance engagement regarding a report it has prepared about its own sustainability practices. An example of when the responsible party is responsible for the subject matter information but not the subject matter, is when a government organisation engages an assurance practitioner to perform an assurance engagement regarding a report about a private company's sustainability practices that the organisation has prepared and is to distribute to intended users.

The responsible party may or may not be the party who engages the assurance practitioner (the engaging party).

26. The responsible party ordinarily provides the assurance practitioner with a written representation that evaluates or measures the subject matter against the identified criteria, whether or not it is to be made available as an assertion to the intended users. In a direct reporting assurance engagement, the assurance practitioner may not be able to obtain such a representation when the engaging party is different from the responsible party.

Intended Users

27. The intended users are the person, persons or class of persons for whom the assurance practitioner prepares the assurance report. The responsible party can be one of the intended users, but not the only one.

28. Whenever practical, the assurance report is addressed to all the intended users, but in some cases there may be other intended users. The assurance practitioner may not be able to identify all those who will read the assurance report, particularly where there are a large number of people who have access to it. In such cases, particularly where possible readers are likely to have a broad range of interests in the subject matter, intended users may be limited to major stakeholders with significant and common interests. Intended users may be identified in different ways, for example, by agreement between the assurance practitioner and the responsible party or engaging party, or by law or regulation.

29. Whenever practical, intended users or their representatives are involved with the assurance practitioner and the responsible party (and the engaging party if different) in determining the requirements of the assurance engagement. Regardless of the involvement of others however, and unlike an agreed-upon procedures engagement (which involves reporting findings based upon the procedures, rather than a conclusion):

(a) the assurance practitioner is responsible for determining the nature, timing and extent of procedures; and

(b) the assurance practitioner ought to pursue any matter the assurance practitioner becomes aware of that leads the assurance practitioner to question whether a material modification ought to be made to the subject matter information.

30. In some cases, intended users (for example, bankers and regulators) impose a requirement on, or request the responsible party (or the engaging party if different) to arrange for, an assurance engagement to be performed for a specific purpose. When assurance engagements are designed for specified intended users or a specific purpose, the assurance practitioner considers including a restriction in the assurance report that limits its use to those users or that purpose.

Subject Matter

31. The subject matter, and subject matter information, of an assurance engagement can take many forms, such as:

- Financial performance or conditions (for example, historical or prospective financial position, financial performance and cash flows) for which the subject matter information may be the recognition, measurement, presentation and disclosure represented in a financial report.

- Non-financial performance or conditions (for example, performance of an entity) for which the subject matter information may be key indicators of efficiency and effectiveness.
- Physical characteristics (for example, capacity of a facility) for which the subject matter information may be a specifications document.
- Systems and processes (for example, an entity's internal control or IT system) for which the subject matter information may be an assertion about effectiveness.
- Behaviour (for example, corporate governance, compliance with regulation, human resource practices) for which the subject matter information may be a statement of compliance or a statement of effectiveness.

32. Subject matters have different characteristics, including the degree to which information about them is qualitative versus quantitative, objective versus subjective, historical versus prospective, and relates to a point in time or covers a period. Such characteristics affect the:

    (a) Precision with which the subject matter can be evaluated or measured against criteria; and

    (b) The persuasiveness of available evidence.

    The assurance report notes characteristics of particular relevance to the intended users.

33. An appropriate subject matter is:

    (a) Identifiable, and capable of consistent evaluation or measurement against the identified criteria; and

    (b) Such that the information about it can be subjected to procedures for gathering sufficient appropriate evidence to support a reasonable assurance or limited assurance conclusion, as appropriate.

Criteria

34. Criteria are the benchmarks used to evaluate or measure the subject matter including, where relevant, benchmarks for presentation and disclosure. Criteria can be formal, for example in the preparation of a financial report, the criteria may be Australian Accounting Standards; when reporting on internal control, the criteria may be an established internal control framework or individual control objectives specifically designed for the assurance engagement; and when reporting on compliance, the criteria may be the applicable law, regulation or contract. Examples of less formal criteria are an internally developed code of conduct or an agreed level of performance (such as the number of times a particular committee is expected to meet in a year).

35. Suitable criteria are preferred for reasonably consistent evaluation or measurement of a subject matter within the context of professional judgement. Without the frame of reference provided by suitable criteria, any conclusion is open to individual interpretation and misunderstanding. Suitable criteria are context-sensitive, that is, relevant to the assurance engagement circumstances. Even for the same subject matter there can be different criteria. For example, one responsible party might select the number of customer complaints resolved to the acknowledged satisfaction of the customer for the subject matter of customer satisfaction; another responsible party might select the number of repeat purchases in the three months following the initial purchase.

36. Suitable criteria exhibit the following characteristics:

    (a) Relevance: relevant criteria contribute to conclusions that assist decision-making by the intended users.

    (b) Completeness: criteria are sufficiently complete when relevant factors that could affect the conclusions in the context of the assurance engagement circumstances are not omitted. Complete criteria include, where relevant, benchmarks for presentation and disclosure.

(c) Reliability: reliable criteria allow reasonably consistent evaluation or measurement of the subject matter including, where relevant, presentation and disclosure, when used in similar circumstances by similarly qualified assurance practitioners.

(d) Neutrality: neutral criteria contribute to conclusions that are free from bias.

(e) Understandability: understandable criteria contribute to conclusions that are clear, comprehensive, and not subject to significantly different interpretations.

The evaluation or measurement of a subject matter on the basis of the assurance practitioner's own expectations, judgements and individual experience would not constitute suitable criteria.

37. The assurance practitioner assesses the suitability of criteria for a particular assurance engagement by considering whether they reflect the above characteristics. The relative importance of each characteristic to a particular assurance engagement is a matter of judgement. Criteria can either be established or specifically developed. Established criteria are those embodied in laws or regulations, or issued by authorised or recognised bodies of experts that follow a transparent due process. Specifically developed criteria are those designed for the purpose of the assurance engagement. Whether criteria are established or specifically developed affects the work that the assurance practitioner carries out to assess their suitability for a particular assurance engagement.

38. Criteria need to be available to the intended users to allow them to understand how the subject matter has been evaluated or measured. Criteria are made available to the intended users in one or more of the following ways:

(a) Publicly.

(b) Through inclusion in a clear manner in the presentation of the subject matter information.

(c) Through inclusion in a clear manner in the assurance report.

(d) By general understanding, for example the criterion for measuring time in hours and minutes.

Criteria may also be available only to specific intended users, for example the terms of a contract, or criteria issued by an industry association that are available only to those in the industry. When identified criteria are available only to specific intended users, or are relevant only to a specific purpose, use of the assurance report is restricted to those users or for that purpose.[7]

Aus 38.1 While an assurance report may be restricted whenever its intended distribution or use is only for specified users or for a specific purpose[*], the absence of a restriction regarding a particular user or purpose, does not itself indicate that a legal responsibility is owed by the assurance practitioner in relation to that user or for that purpose. Whether a legal responsibility is owed will depend on the circumstances of each case and the relevant jurisdiction.

Evidence

39. The assurance practitioner plans and performs an assurance engagement with an attitude of professional scepticism to obtain sufficient appropriate evidence about whether the subject matter information is free of material misstatement. The assurance practitioner considers materiality, assurance engagement risk, and the quantity and quality of available evidence when planning and performing the assurance engagement, in particular when determining the nature, timing and extent of evidence-gathering procedures.

Professional Judgement

Aus 39.1 The assurance practitioner uses professional judgement in performing an assurance engagement. The assurance practitioner exercises professional judgement within the context provided by the AUASB Standards to make informed decisions about

7 [Footnote deleted by the AUASB and re-located to Aus 38.1]

* For example, when the assurance report is in respect of a financial report prepared in accordance with a special purpose framework in accordance with ASA 800 *Special Considerations—Audits of Financial Reports Prepared in Accordance with Special Purpose Frameworks.*

the courses of action that are appropriate based on the facts and circumstances that are known to the assurance practitioner. Such professional judgement is exercised by an assurance practitioner whose training, knowledge and experience have assisted in developing the necessary competencies to achieve reasonable judgements. Consultations on difficult or contentious matters identified during the assurance engagement, both within the engagement team and between the engagement team and others at the appropriate level within or outside the firm, assist the assurance practitioner in making informed and reasonable judgements.

Aus 39.2 Professional judgement is essential to the proper conduct of the assurance engagement and is exercised throughout the assurance engagement by an assurance practitioner. This is because interpretation of the principles-based AUASB Standards and the informed decisions required throughout the assurance engagement cannot be made without the application of relevant knowledge and experience to the facts and circumstances.

Aus 39.3 Professional judgement can be evaluated based on whether the judgement reached reflects a competent application of assurance principles and is appropriate in the light of, and consistent with, the facts and circumstances that were known to the assurance practitioner up to the date of the assurance report.

Aus 39.4 It is important that all significant matters, identified during the assurance engagement and where the assurance practitioner has exercised professional judgement(s) in reaching the conclusion(s), be appropriately documented. Professional judgement should not be used as the justification for decisions that are not otherwise supported by the facts and circumstances of the engagement or sufficient appropriate evidence.

Professional Scepticism

40. The assurance practitioner plans and performs an assurance engagement with an attitude of professional scepticism recognising that circumstances may exist that cause the subject matter information to be materially misstated. An attitude of professional scepticism occurs when the assurance practitioner makes a critical assessment, with a questioning mind, of the validity of evidence obtained and is alert to evidence that contradicts or brings into question the reliability of documents or representations by the responsible party. Professional scepticism also includes consideration of the sufficiency and appropriateness of evidence obtained in the light of the circumstances. For example, an attitude of professional scepticism is necessary throughout the assurance engagement process for the assurance practitioner to reduce the risk of overlooking unusual circumstances, of over generalising when drawing conclusions from observations, and of using inappropriate assumptions in determining the nature, timing and extent of evidence gathering procedures and evaluating the results thereof.

41. An assurance engagement rarely involves the authentication of documentation, nor is the assurance practitioner trained as or expected to be an expert in such authentication. However, the assurance practitioner considers the reliability of the information to be used as evidence, for example photocopies, facsimiles, filmed, digitized or other electronic documents, including consideration of controls over their preparation and maintenance where relevant. In case of doubt about the reliability of information used as evidence, the AUASB Standards require that the assurance practitioner investigate further and determine what modifications or additions to assurance procedures are necessary to resolve the matter.

Sufficiency and Appropriateness of Evidence

42. Sufficiency is the measure of the quantity of evidence. Appropriateness is the measure of the quality of evidence; that is, its relevance and its reliability. The quantity of evidence needed is affected by the risk of the subject matter information being materially misstated (the greater the risk, the more evidence is likely to be required) and also by the quality of such evidence (the higher the quality, the less may be required). Accordingly, the sufficiency and appropriateness of evidence are interrelated. However, merely obtaining more evidence may not compensate for its poor quality.

43. The reliability of evidence is influenced by its source and by its nature, and is dependent on the individual circumstances under which it is obtained. Generalisations about the reliability of various kinds of evidence can be made; however, such generalisations are subject to important exceptions. Even when evidence is obtained from sources external to the entity, circumstances may exist that could affect the reliability of the information obtained. For example, evidence obtained from an independent external source may not be reliable if the source is not knowledgeable. While recognising that exceptions may exist, the following generalisations about the reliability of evidence may be useful:

- Evidence is more reliable when it is obtained from independent sources outside the entity.
- Evidence that is generated internally is more reliable when the related controls are effective.
- Evidence obtained directly by the assurance practitioner (for example, observation of the application of a control) is more reliable than evidence obtained indirectly or by inference (for example, enquiry about the application of a control).
- Evidence is more reliable when it exists in documentary form, whether paper, electronic, or other media (for example, a contemporaneously written record of a meeting is more reliable than a subsequent oral representation of what was discussed).
- Evidence provided by original documents is more reliable than evidence provided by photocopies or facsimiles.

44. The assurance practitioner ordinarily obtains more assurance from consistent evidence obtained from different sources or of a different nature than from items of evidence considered individually. In addition, obtaining evidence from different sources or of a different nature may indicate that an individual item of evidence is not reliable. For example, corroborating information obtained from a source independent of the entity may increase the assurance the assurance practitioner obtains from a representation from the responsible party. Conversely, when evidence obtained from one source is inconsistent with that obtained from another, the assurance practitioner ordinarily determines what additional evidence-gathering procedures are necessary to resolve the inconsistency.

45. In terms of obtaining sufficient appropriate evidence, it is generally more difficult to obtain assurance about subject matter information covering a period than about subject matter information at a point in time. In addition, conclusions provided on processes ordinarily are limited to the period covered by the assurance engagement; the assurance practitioner provides no conclusion about whether the process will continue to function in the specified manner in the future.

46. The assurance practitioner considers the relationship between the cost of obtaining evidence and the usefulness of the information obtained. However, the matter of difficulty or expense involved is not in itself a valid basis for omitting an evidence-gathering procedure for which there is no alternative. The assurance practitioner uses professional judgement and exercises professional scepticism in evaluating the quantity and quality of evidence, and thus its sufficiency and appropriateness, to support the conclusion in the assurance report.

Materiality

47. Materiality is relevant when the assurance practitioner determines the nature, timing and extent of evidence-gathering procedures, and when assessing whether the subject matter information is free of misstatement. When considering materiality, the assurance practitioner understands and assesses what factors might influence the decisions of the intended users. For example, when the identified criteria allow for variations in the presentation of the subject matter information, the assurance practitioner considers how the adopted presentation might influence the decisions of the intended users. Materiality is considered in the context of quantitative and qualitative factors, such as relative magnitude, the nature and extent of the effect of these factors on the evaluation or measurement of the subject matter, and the interests of the intended users. The assessment of materiality and the relative importance of quantitative and qualitative factors in a particular assurance engagement are matters for the assurance practitioner's judgement.

Assurance Engagement Risk

48. Assurance engagement risk is the risk that the assurance practitioner expresses an inappropriate conclusion when the subject matter information is materially misstated.[8] In a reasonable assurance engagement, the assurance practitioner reduces assurance engagement risk to an acceptably low level in the circumstances of the assurance engagement to obtain reasonable assurance as the basis for a positive form of expression of the assurance practitioner's conclusion. The level of assurance engagement risk is higher in a limited assurance engagement than in a reasonable assurance engagement because of the different nature, timing or extent of evidence-gathering procedures. However, in a limited assurance engagement, the combination of the nature, timing and extent of evidence-gathering procedures is at least sufficient for the assurance practitioner to obtain a meaningful level of assurance as the basis for a negative form of expression. To be meaningful, the level of assurance obtained by the assurance practitioner is likely to enhance the intended users' confidence about the subject matter information to a degree that is clearly more than inconsequential.

Aus 48.1 Assurance engagement risk includes the risk, in those direct reporting engagements where the subject matter information is presented only in the assurance practitioner's conclusion, that the practitioner inappropriately concludes that the subject matter does, in all material respects, conform with the criteria, for example: "In our opinion, internal control is effective, in all material respects, based on XYZ criteria."

Aus 48.2 In addition to assurance engagement risk, the assurance practitioner is exposed to and risks through loss from litigation, adverse publicity, or other events arising in connection with a subject matter reported on. These risks are not part of assurance engagement risk.

49. In general, assurance engagement risk can be represented by the following components, although not all of these components will necessarily be present or significant for all assurance engagements:

(a) The risk that the subject matter information is materially misstated, which in turn consists of:

(i) Inherent risk: the susceptibility of the subject matter information to a material misstatement, assuming that there are no related controls.

(ii) Control risk: the risk that a material misstatement that could occur will not be prevented, or detected and corrected, on a timely basis by related internal controls. When control risk is relevant to the subject matter, some control risk will always exist because of the inherent limitations of the design and operation of internal control.

(b) Detection risk: the risk that the assurance practitioner will not detect a material misstatement that exists.

The degree to which the assurance practitioner considers each of these components is affected by the assurance engagement circumstances, in particular by the nature of the subject matter and whether a reasonable assurance engagement or a limited assurance engagement is being performed.

Nature, Timing and Extent of Evidence-Gathering Procedures

50. The exact nature, timing and extent of evidence-gathering procedures will vary from one assurance engagement to the next. In theory, infinite variations in evidence-gathering procedures are possible. In practice, however, these are difficult to communicate clearly and unambiguously. The assurance practitioner attempts to communicate them clearly and unambiguously and uses the form appropriate to a reasonable assurance engagement or a limited assurance engagement.[9]

Aus 50.1 Where the subject matter information comprises a number of aspects, separate conclusions may be provided on each aspect. While not all such conclusions need

8 [Footnote deleted by the AUASB and re-located to Aus 48.1 and Aus 48.2]

9 [Footnote deleted by the AUASB and re-located to Aus 50.1]

to relate to the same level of evidence-gathering procedures, each conclusion is expressed in the form that is appropriate to either a reasonable assurance engagement or a limited assurance engagement.

51. Reasonable assurance is a concept relating to accumulating evidence necessary for the assurance practitioner to conclude in relation to the subject matter information taken as a whole. To be in a position to express a conclusion in the positive form required in a reasonable assurance engagement, it is necessary for the assurance practitioner to obtain sufficient appropriate evidence as part of an iterative, systematic assurance engagement process involving:
    (a) Obtaining an understanding of the subject matter and other assurance engagement circumstances which, depending on the subject matter, includes obtaining an understanding of internal control;
    (b) Based on that understanding, assessing the risks that the subject matter information may be materially misstated;
    (c) Responding to assessed risks, including developing overall responses, and determining the nature, timing and extent of further procedures;
    (d) Performing further evidence-gathering procedures clearly linked to the identified risks, using a combination of inspection, observation, confirmation, re-calculation, re-performance, analytical procedures and enquiry. Such further evidence-gathering procedures involve substantive procedures including, where applicable, obtaining corroborating information from sources independent of the responsible party, and depending on the nature of the subject matter, tests of the operating effectiveness of controls; and
    (e) Evaluating the sufficiency and appropriateness of evidence.

52. Reasonable assurance is less than absolute assurance. Reducing assurance engagement risk to zero is very rarely attainable or cost beneficial as a result of factors such as the following:
    - The use of selective testing.
    - The inherent limitations of internal control.
    - The fact that much of the evidence available to the assurance practitioner is persuasive rather than conclusive.
    - The use of professional judgement in gathering and evaluating evidence and forming conclusions based on that evidence.
    - In some cases, the characteristics of the subject matter when evaluated or measured against the identified criteria.

53. Both reasonable assurance engagements and limited assurance engagements require the application of assurance skills and techniques and the gathering of sufficient appropriate evidence as part of an iterative, systematic process that includes obtaining an understanding of the subject matter and other assurance engagement circumstances. The nature, timing and extent of procedures for gathering sufficient appropriate evidence in a limited assurance engagement are, however, deliberately limited relative to a reasonable assurance engagement. For some subject matters, there may be specific pronouncements that provide requirements and application and other explanatory material on procedures for gathering sufficient appropriate evidence for a limited assurance engagement. For example, ASRE 2410 *Review of a Financial Report Performed by the Independent Auditor of the Entity* establishes that sufficient appropriate evidence for a review of a financial report is obtained primarily through analytical procedures and enquiries. In the absence of a relevant pronouncement, the procedures for gathering sufficient appropriate evidence will vary with the circumstances of the assurance engagement, in particular, the subject matter, and the needs of the intended users and the engaging party, including relevant time and cost constraints. For both reasonable assurance engagements and limited assurance engagements, if the assurance practitioner becomes aware of a matter that leads the assurance practitioner to question whether a material modification ought to be made to the subject matter information, the assurance practitioner pursues the matter by performing other procedures sufficient to enable the assurance practitioner to report.

Quantity and Quality of Available Evidence

54. The quantity or quality of available evidence is affected by:

(a) The characteristics of the subject matter and subject matter information. For example, less objective evidence might be expected when information about the subject matter is future oriented rather than historical (see paragraph 32 of this Framework); and

(b) Circumstances of the assurance engagement other than the characteristics of the subject matter, when evidence that could reasonably be expected to exist is not available because of, for example, the timing of the assurance practitioner's appointment, an entity's document retention policy, or a restriction imposed by the responsible party.

Ordinarily, available evidence will be persuasive rather than conclusive.

55. An unqualified conclusion is not appropriate for either type of assurance engagement in the case of a material limitation on the scope of the assurance practitioner's work, that is, when:

(a) Circumstances prevent the assurance practitioner from obtaining evidence required to reduce assurance engagement risk to the appropriate level; or

(b) The responsible party or the engaging party imposes a restriction that prevents the assurance practitioner from obtaining evidence required to reduce assurance engagement risk to the appropriate level.

Assurance Report

56. The assurance practitioner provides a written report[10] containing a conclusion that conveys the assurance obtained about the subject matter information. AUASB Standards establish basic elements for assurance reports. In addition, the assurance practitioner considers other reporting responsibilities, including communicating with those charged with governance when it is appropriate to do so.

Aus 56.1 In those direct reporting engagements where the subject matter information is presented only in the practitioner's conclusion, and the practitioner concludes that the subject matter does not, in all material respects, conform with the criteria, for example: "In our opinion, except for *[...]*, internal control is effective, in all material respects, based on *XYZ criteria*," such a conclusion would also be considered to be qualified (or adverse as appropriate).

57. In an assertion-based assurance engagement, the assurance practitioner's conclusion can be worded either:

(a) in terms of the responsible party's assertion (for example: "In our opinion the responsible party's assertion that internal control is effective, in all material respects, based on XYZ criteria, is fairly stated"); or

(b) directly in terms of the subject matter and the criteria (for example: "In our opinion internal control is effective, in all material respects, based on XYZ criteria").

In a direct reporting assurance engagement, the assurance practitioner's conclusion is worded directly in terms of the subject matter and the criteria.

58. In a reasonable assurance engagement, the assurance practitioner expresses the conclusion in the positive form, for example: "In our opinion internal control is effective, in all material respects, based on XYZ criteria." This form of expression conveys "reasonable assurance." Having performed evidence-gathering procedures of a nature, timing and extent that were reasonable given the characteristics of the subject matter and other relevant assurance engagement circumstances described in the assurance report, the assurance practitioner has obtained sufficient appropriate evidence to reduce assurance engagement risk to an acceptably low level.

59. In a limited assurance engagement, the assurance practitioner expresses the conclusion in the negative form, for example, "Based on our work described in this report, nothing has come to our attention that causes us to believe that internal control is not effective,

10 [Footnote deleted by the AUASB and re-located to Aus 56.1]

in all material respects, based on XYZ criteria." This form of expression conveys a level of "limited assurance" that is proportional to the level of the assurance practitioner's evidence-gathering procedures given the characteristics of the subject matter and other assurance engagement circumstances described in the assurance report.

60. An assurance practitioner does not express an unqualified conclusion for either type of assurance engagement when the following circumstances exist and, in the assurance practitioner's judgement, the effect of the matter is, or may be, material:

(a) There is a limitation on the scope of the assurance practitioner's work (see paragraph 55 of this Framework). The assurance practitioner expresses a qualified conclusion or a disclaimer of conclusion depending on how material or pervasive the limitation is. In some cases, the assurance practitioner considers withdrawing from the assurance engagement, where practical and possible under applicable law or regulation.

(b) In those cases where:

(i) the assurance practitioner's conclusion is worded in terms of the responsible party's assertion, and that assertion is not fairly stated, in all material respects; or

(ii) the assurance practitioner's conclusion is worded directly in terms of the subject matter and the criteria, and the subject matter information is materially misstated,[11]

the assurance practitioner expresses a qualified or adverse conclusion depending on how material or pervasive the matter is.

(c) When it is discovered after the assurance engagement has been accepted, that the criteria are unsuitable or the subject matter is not appropriate for an assurance engagement, the assurance practitioner expresses:

(i) A qualified conclusion or adverse conclusion depending on how material or pervasive the matter is, when the unsuitable criteria or inappropriate subject matter is likely to mislead the intended users; or

(ii) A qualified conclusion or a disclaimer of conclusion depending on how material or pervasive the matter is, in other cases.

In some cases, and where permitted by law or regulation, the assurance practitioner considers withdrawing from the assurance engagement.

Aus 60.1 AUASB Standards applicable to certain types of assurance engagements require the assurance practitioner to establish that the criteria is suitable and the subject matter is appropriate prior to accepting the assurance engagement. In these circumstances it is inappropriate for the assurance practitioner to express a qualified, adverse, or disclaimer of conclusion due to the materiality and/or pervasive effects of unsuitable criteria or inappropriate subject matter.

Inappropriate Use of the Assurance Practitioner's Name

61. An assurance practitioner is associated with a subject matter when the assurance practitioner reports on information about that subject matter or consents to the use of the assurance practitioner's name in a professional connection with that subject matter. If the assurance practitioner is not associated in this manner, third parties can assume no responsibility of the assurance practitioner. If the assurance practitioner learns that a party is inappropriately using the assurance practitioner's name in association with a subject matter, the assurance practitioner requests the party to cease doing so. The assurance practitioner also considers what other steps may be needed, such as informing any known third party users of the inappropriate use of the assurance practitioner's name or seeking legal advice.

11 [Footnote deleted by the AUASB and re-located to Aus 56.1]

Public Sector Perspective

Aus 61.1 This Framework is relevant to all assurance practitioners in the public sector who are independent of the entity for which they perform assurance engagements. Where assurance practitioners in the public sector are not independent of the entity for which they perform an assurance engagement, the guidance in paragraph Aus 1.1 of this Framework should be adopted.

❖ ❖ ❖

Conformity with International Framework for Assurance Engagements

This *Framework for Assurance Engagements* conforms with the *International Framework for Assurance Engagements* (January 2005), issued by the International Auditing and Assurance Standards Board (IAASB), an independent standing-setting board of the International Federation of Accountants.

Paragraphs that have been added to this Auditing Standard (and do not appear in the text of the equivalent International pronouncement) are identified with the prefix “Aus”. These “Aus” paragraphs include re-located footnotes.

Appendix 1

Differences between Reasonable Assurance Engagements and Limited Assurance Engagements

This Appendix outlines the differences between a reasonable assurance engagement and a limited assurance engagement discussed in the Framework (see in particular the referenced paragraphs).

Type of assurance engagement	Objective	Evidence-gathering procedures[12]	The assurance report
Reasonable assurance engagement	A reduction in assurance engagement risk to an acceptably low level in the circumstances of the assurance engagement, as the basis for a positive form of expression of the assurance practitioner's conclusion. Reasonable assurance means a high, but not absolute, level of assurance. (Ref: Para. 11)	Sufficient appropriate evidence is obtained as part of a systematic assurance engagement process that includes: • Obtaining an understanding of the assurance engagement circumstances; • Assessing risks; • Responding to assessed risks; • Performing further evidence-gathering procedures using a combination of inspection, observation, confirmation, re-calculation, re-performance, analytical procedures and enquiry. Such further evidence-gathering procedures involve substantive procedures, including, where applicable, obtaining corroborating information, and depending on the nature of the subject matter, tests of the operating effectiveness of controls; and • Evaluating the evidence obtained. (Ref: Para. 51-52)	Description of the assurance engagement circumstances, and a positive form of expression of the conclusion. (Ref: Para. 58)
Limited assurance engagement	A reduction in assurance engagement risk to a level that is acceptable in the circumstances of the assurance engagement but where that risk is greater than for a reasonable assurance engagement, as the basis for a negative form of expression of the assurance practitioner's conclusion. (Ref: Para. 11)	Sufficient appropriate evidence is obtained as part of a systematic assurance engagement process that includes obtaining an understanding of the subject matter and other assurance engagement circumstances, but in which evidence-gathering procedures are deliberately limited relative to a reasonable assurance engagement. (Ref: Para. 53)	Description of the assurance engagement circumstances, and a negative form of expression of the conclusion. (Ref: Para. 59)

12 A detailed discussion of evidence-gathering requirements is only possible within AUASB Standards related to specific subject matters.

Principles of Convergence to International Standards of the International Auditing and Assurance Standards Board (IAASB) and Harmonisation with the Standards of the New Zealand Auditing and Assurance Standards Board (NZAuASB)

(Issued November 2012)

Issued by the Auditing and Assurance Standards Board.

Note from the Institute of Chartered Accountants Australia

This note, prepared by the technical editor, is not part of the Principles of Convergence and Harmonisation.

Historical Development

November 2012: 'Principles of Convergence to International Standards of the International Auditing and Assurance Standards Board (IAASB) and Harmonisation with the Standards of the New Zealand Auditing and Assurance Standards Board (NZAuASB)' was issued in November 2012 and applies from July 2012. The document responds to the strategic objective set by the Financial Reporting Council for the AUASB to use ISAs in developing Australian standards, reflected in the AUASB's own twin objectives of adopting international Standards unless there are strong reasons not to and working with the NZAuASB towards the establishment of harmonised Standards across the two countries.

Principles of Convergence to International Standards of the International Auditing and Assurance Standards Board (IAASB) and Harmonisation with the Standards of the New Zealand Auditing and Assurance Standards Board (NZAuASB)

Application Date

1. The policies detailed in this paper apply from 1 July 2012.

Introduction

2. The key strategic objectives set by the Financial Reporting Council (FRC) for the Auditing and Assurance Standards Board (AUASB) include using the International Standards on Auditing (ISAs) to develop Australian Auditing Standards, and modifying the ISAs to conform to the Australian regulatory environment.

Objectives

3. In implementing the FRC's strategic direction, the AUASB has determined the following objectives:
   - to adopt international auditing and assurance standards in Australia unless there are strong reasons not to (which the Board describes as "compelling reasons"); and
   - to work with the New Zealand Auditing and Assurance Standards Board (NZAuASB) towards the establishment of harmonised standards based on international standards.

Policies

4. The AUASB may consider modifying international standards for application in Australia under either of those objectives. The AUASB considers such modifications acceptable provided that they consider the public interest[1], and do not conflict with, or result in lesser requirements than, the international standards.
5. The purpose of this paper is to set out the principles of convergence to international standards and harmonisation with New Zealand standards to be used as the framework for the standard setting process of the AUASB.
6. It is expected that this paper will be revised from time to time to take account of changes to the Australian financial reporting framework.
7. The principles of convergence set out in this paper adhere to the principles set out in the IAASB Policy Position, *Modifications to International Standards of the IAASB - A Guide for National Standard Setters that Adopt IAASB's International Standards but Find it Necessary to Make Limited Modifications* (July 2006).
8. The principles of convergence to the IAASB standards are set out in a flowchart in Appendix 1, and the principles of harmonisation with the New Zealand standards are set out in a flowchart in Appendix 2.

Overarching principles of convergence with International Standards

9. The international standards should be adopted, and should be amended only if there are compelling reasons to do so.

---

1 IFAC defines the public interest as "*The net benefits derived for, and procedural rigor employed on behalf of, all society in relation to any action, decision or policy*". Refer IFAC Policy Position 5 *A Definition of the Public Interest*, June 2012.

10. In the case of an international standard that is being reviewed for the purpose of adoption in Australia, compelling reasons for modifications in the public interest include where:

(1) the international standard does not reflect, or is not consistent with:

a. the Australian regulatory arrangements; or

b. principles and practices that are considered appropriate in Australia (including in the use of significant terminology); and

(2) the standard can be modified so as to result in a standard that:

a. promotes significant improvement in audit quality in the Australian environment; and

b. does not conflict with, or result in lesser requirements than the international standard; and

(3) the relative benefits of making a change outweigh the costs (with costs primarily being compliance costs and benefits primarily relating to audit quality).

Overarching principles of harmonisation with New Zealand Standards

11. When considering harmonisation with a New Zealand standard, compelling reasons for modification of the international standard in the public interest include where:

(1) the New Zealand standard covers a matter not covered in the international standard, and that gap is also relevant in the Australian standard;

(2) the standard can be modified so as to result in a standard that:

a. promotes significant improved audit quality in the Australian environment; and

b. does not conflict with, or result in lesser requirements than the international standard; and

(3) the relative benefits of making a change outweigh the costs (with costs primarily being compliance costs and benefits primarily relating to audit quality).

General

12. When considering developing a standard for which there is no equivalent international standard, compelling reasons for developing the standard are:

a. the standard addresses public interest matters within the Australian environment;

b. the standard will promote significant improved audit quality in the Australian environment; and

c. the benefits of applying the standard will outweigh the costs (with costs primarily being compliance costs and benefits primarily relating to audit quality).

13. The development of an Australian standard should be harmonised with the equivalent New Zealand standard by adopting the New Zealand standard, where applicable. Compelling reasons for differences between Australian and New Zealand standards are where:

a. different regulatory requirements apply; and/or

b. different practices are considered appropriate (including the use of significant terminology).

14. Any deletions from the international standards should be clearly noted, and any additions clearly marked as Australian paragraphs.

15. However, minor wording and spelling changes (as opposed to changes reflecting the use of significant terminology), where the intent remains the same, need not be reflected in the Australian standard as a modification to the international standard.

16. Each AUASB Standard issued prior to 1 July 2012 will be assessed for compliance with the policies in this paper in accordance with the AUASB work program.

Appendix 1: Flowchart to depict the 'compelling reasons test' in the Principles of Convergence with the IAASB standards

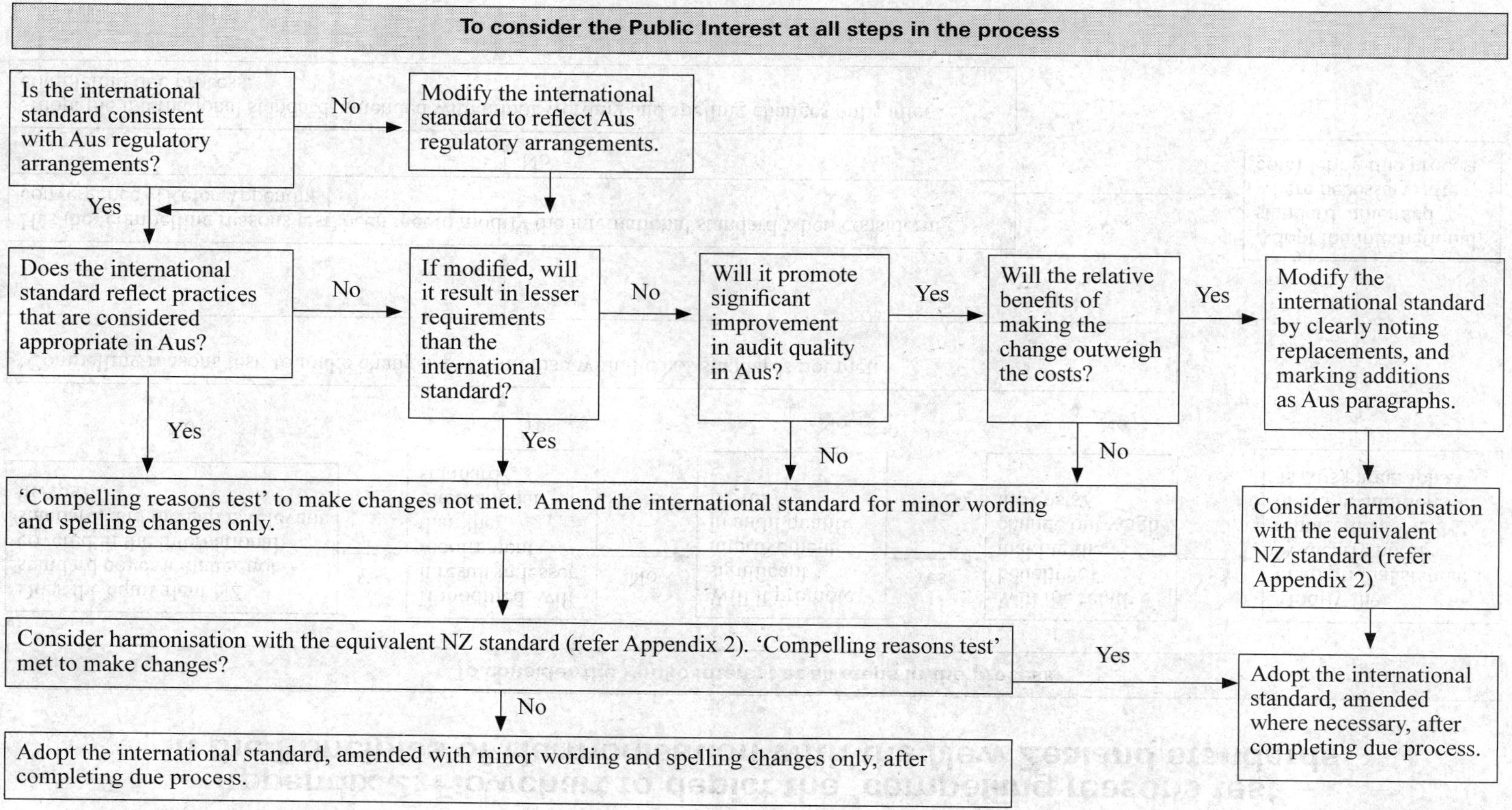

Appendix 2: Flowchart to depict the 'compelling reasons test' in the Principles of Harmonisation with the New Zealand standards

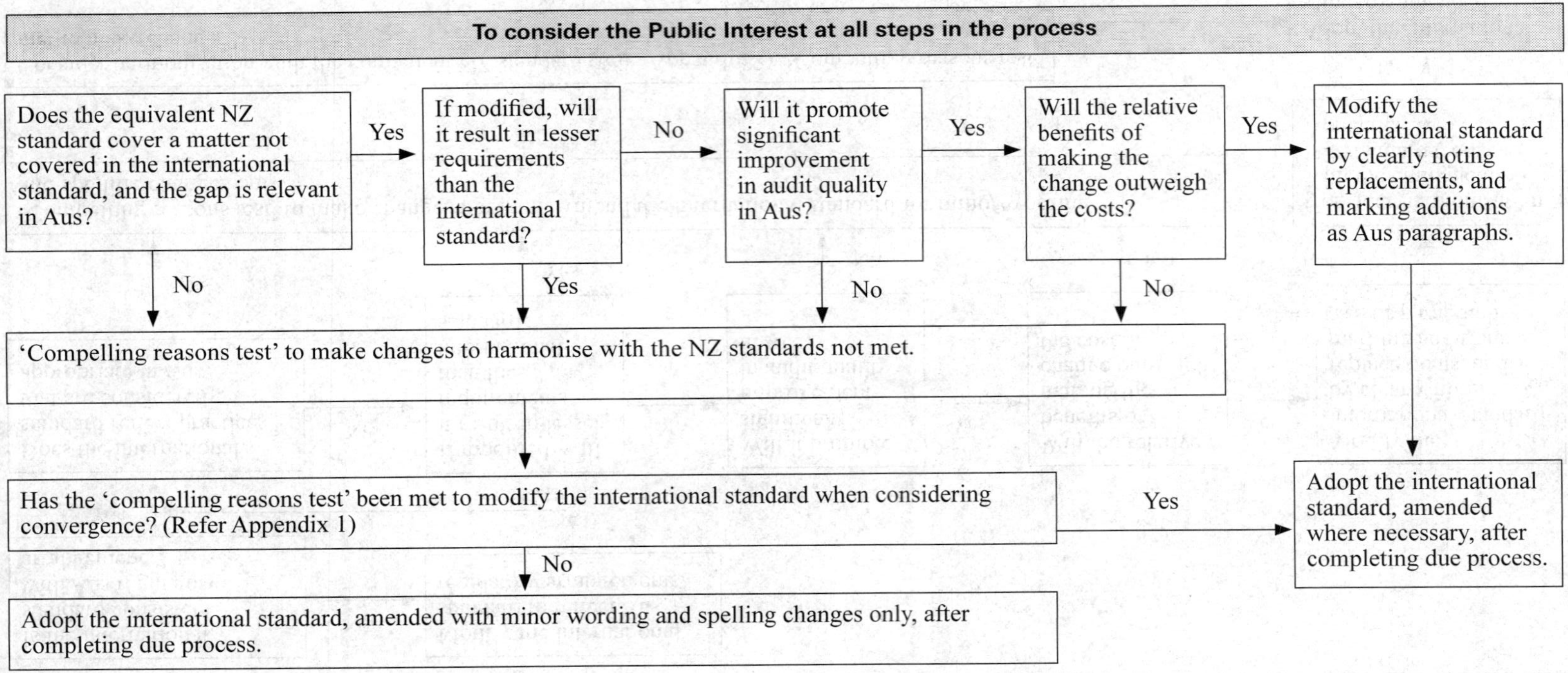

ASQC 1

Quality Control for Firms that Perform Audits and Reviews of Financial Reports and Other Financial Information, and Other Assurance Engagements

(Reissued October 2009: amended and compiled June 2011)

Issued by the Auditing and Assurance Standards Board.

Note from the Institute of Chartered Accountants Australia

This note, prepared by the technical editor, is not part of ASQC 1.

Historical development

October 2009: ASQC 1 issued as part of the AUASB's Clarity Project. It deals with the firm's responsibility for its system of quality control in its assurance practice. While the AUASB has not issued a standard covering this area before, its requirements are similar to those contained in the Accounting Professional and Ethical Standards Board's existing standard APES 320 'Quality Control for Firms'. The issue of ASQC 1 brings these requirements within the suite of auditing standards that are legally enforceable under the Corporations Act. It is based on ISQC 1 of the same name.

June 2011: ASQC 1 updated for editorial amendments contained in ASA 2011-1 'Amendments to Australian Auditing Standards'.

Contents

Compilation Details

Auditing Standard ASQC 1 *Quality Control for Firms that Perform Audits and Reviews of Financial Reports and Other Financial Information, and Other Assurance Engagements* as Amended

This compilation takes into account amendments made up to and including 27 June 2011 and was prepared on 27 June 2011 by the Auditing and Assurance Standards Board (AUASB).

This compilation is not a separate Auditing Standard made by the AUASB. Instead, it is a representation of ASQC 1 (October 2009) as amended by another Auditing Standard which is listed in the Table below.

Table of Standards

Standard	Date made	Operative date
ASQC 1	27 October 2009	1 January 2010
ASA 2011-1	27 June 2011	1 July 2011

Table of Amendments

Paragraph affected	How affected	By … [paragraph]
Aus A63.1	Amended	ASA 2011-1 [11]
Aus 12.12 Footnote *	Amended	ASA 2011-1 [12]
A53 Footnote *	Amended	ASA 2011-1 [13]

Preface

[Preface extracted from the original Auditing Standard issued 27 October 2009]

Reasons for Issuing Auditing Standard ASQC 1 *Quality Control for Firms that Perform Audits and Reviews of Financial Reports and Other Financial Information, and Other Assurance Engagements*

The Auditing and Assurance Standards Board (AUASB) issues Auditing Standard Auditing Standard ASQC 1 *Quality Control for Firms that Perform Audits and Reviews of Financial Reports and Other Financial Information, and Other Assurance Engagements* pursuant to the requirements of the legislative provisions and the Strategic Direction explained below.

The AUASB is an independent statutory board of the Australian Government established under section 227A of the *Australian Securities and Investments Commission Act 2001*, as amended (ASIC Act). Under section 336 of the *Corporations Act 2001*, the AUASB may make Auditing Standards for the purposes of the corporations legislation. These Auditing Standards are legislative instruments under the *Legislative Instruments Act 2003*.

Under the Strategic Direction given to the AUASB by the Financial Reporting Council (FRC), the AUASB is required to have regard to any programme initiated by the International Auditing and Assurance Standards Board (IAASB) for the revision and enhancement of the International Standards on Auditing (ISAs) and to make appropriate consequential amendments to the Australian Auditing Standards. Accordingly, the AUASB has decided to revise and redraft the Australian Auditing Standards using the equivalent redrafted standards of the IAASB.

Main Features

This Auditing Standard establishes requirements and provides application and other explanatory material regarding the firm's responsibilities for its system of quality control for audits and reviews of financial reports and other financial information, and other assurance engagements.

This Auditing Standard:

(a) sets out the firm's responsibilities for applying, and complying, with relevant requirements;

(b) establishes elements of a system of internal control and leadership responsibilities for quality within the firm;

(c) describes relevant ethical requirements;

(d) clarifies the policies and procedures required for the acceptance and continuance of client relationships and specific engagements;

(e) sets out the policies and procedures concerning the firm's allocation of human resources to engagements;

(f) describes the policies and procedures required for the firm's engagement performance, including consultation, quality review processes, resolution of any differences of opinion within the firm concerning the engagement; and the management of and retention of engagement documentation;

(g) requires monitoring processes over the firm's system of quality control, including dealing with any deficiencies identified or any complaints or allegations made; and

(h) sets out the policies and procedures regarding appropriate documentation that provides evidence of the operation of the system of quality control.

Authority Statement

Auditing Standard ASQC 1 *Quality Control for Firms that Perform Audits and Reviews of Financial Reports and Other Financial Information, and Other Assurance Engagements* (as amended at 27 June 2011) is set out in paragraphs 1 to A75.

Dated: 27 June 2011

M H Kelsall
Chairman - AUASB

Auditing Standard ASQC 1

The Auditing and Assurance Standards Board (AUASB) made Auditing Standard ASQC 1 *Quality Control for Firms that Perform Audits and Reviews of Financial Reports and Other Financial Information, and Other Assurance Engagements,* pursuant to section 227B of the *Australian Securities and Investments Commission Act 2001* and section 336 of the *Corporations Act 2001*, on 27 October 2009.

This compiled version of ASQC 1 incorporates subsequent amendments contained in another Auditing Standard made by the AUASB up to and including 27 June 2011 (see Compilation Details).

Auditing Standard ASQC 1

Quality Control for Firms that Perform Audits and Reviews of Financial Reports and Other Financial Information, and Other Assurance Engagements

Application

Aus 0.1 This Auditing Standard applies to a firm that performs:

(a) an audit of a financial report for a financial year, or an audit or review of a financial report for a half-year, in accordance with the *Corporations Act 2001*;

(b) an audit or review of a financial report, or a complete set of financial statements, for any other purpose;

(c) an audit or review of other historical financial information;

(d) an audit or review other than of historical financial information; and

(e) other assurance engagements.

Operative Date

Aus 0.2 Systems of quality control in compliance with this Auditing Standard are required to be established by 1 January 2010.

[Note: For operative dates of paragraphs changed or added by an amending Standard, see Compilation Details.]

Introduction

Scope of this Auditing Standard

1. [Deleted by the AUASB. Refer Aus 1.1]

Aus 1.1 This Auditing Standard, ASQC 1 (the Standard), deals with the firm's responsibilities for its system of quality control for audits and reviews of financial reports, other financial information, and other assurance engagements. This Standard is to be read in conjunction with relevant ethical requirements. Relevant ethical requirements are defined in ASA 102.*

2. Other pronouncements issued by Auditing and Assurance Standards Board (AUASB) set out additional standards and guidance on the responsibilities of firm personnel regarding quality control procedures for specific types of engagements. ASA 220,[1] for example, deals with quality control procedures for an audit of a financial report and other historical financial information.

3. A system of quality control consists of policies designed to achieve the objective set out in paragraph 11 of this Standard and the procedures necessary to implement and monitor compliance with those policies.

Authority of this Auditing Standard

4. [Deleted by the AUASB. Refer Aus 4.1]

Aus 4.1 This Standard applies to all firms of assurance practitioners in respect of audits and reviews of financial reports and other financial information, and other assurance engagements. The nature and extent of the policies and procedures developed by an individual firm to comply with this Standard will depend on various factors such as the size and operating characteristics of the firm, and whether it is part of a network.

Aus 4.2 The requirements of this Standard apply to a firm, not to the individual auditor(s) within the firm.

5. This Standard contains the objective of the firm in following this Standard, and requirements designed to enable the firm to meet that stated objective. In addition, it contains related guidance in the form of application and other explanatory material, as discussed further in paragraph 8 of this Standard, and introductory material that provides context relevant to a proper understanding of this Standard, and definitions.

6. The objective provides the context in which the requirements of this Standard are set, and is intended to assist the firm in:

- Understanding what needs to be accomplished; and
- Deciding whether more needs to be done to achieve the objective.

7. The requirements of this Standard are expressed using "shall."

8. Where necessary, the application and other explanatory material provides further explanation of the requirements and guidance for carrying them out. In particular, it may:

- Explain more precisely what a requirement means or is intended to cover; and
- Include examples of policies and procedures that may be appropriate in the circumstances.

---

* See ASA 102 *Compliance with Ethical Requirements when Performing Audits, Reviews and Other Assurance Engagements.*

1 *See ASA 220 Quality Control for an Audit of a Financial Report and Other Historical Financial Information.*

While such guidance does not in itself impose a requirement, it is relevant to the proper application of the requirements. The application and other explanatory material may also provide background information on matters addressed in this Standard. Where appropriate, additional considerations specific to public sector audit organisations or smaller firms are included within the application and other explanatory material. These additional considerations assist in the application of the requirements in this Standard. They do not, however, limit or reduce the responsibility of the firm to apply and comply with the requirements in this Standard.

9. This Standard includes, under the heading "Definitions," a description of the meanings attributed to certain terms for purposes of this Standard. These are provided to assist in the consistent application and interpretation of this Standard, and are not intended to override definitions that may be established for other purposes, whether in law, regulation or otherwise. The *AUASB Glossary* (October 2009) relating to AUASB Standards, and issued by the AUASB includes the terms defined in this Standard. It also includes descriptions of other terms found in this Standard to assist in common and consistent interpretation and translation.

Effective Date

10. [Deleted by the AUASB. Refer Aus 0.2]

Objective

11. The objective of the firm is to establish and maintain a system of quality control to provide it with reasonable assurance that:

(a) The firm and its personnel comply with AUASB Standards, relevant ethical requirements, and applicable legal and regulatory requirements; and

(b) Reports issued by the firm or engagement partners are appropriate in the circumstances.

Definitions

12. In this Standard, the following terms have the meanings attributed below:

Aus 12.1 Assurance engagement means an engagement in which an assurance practitioner expresses a conclusion designed to enhance the degree of confidence of the intended users, other than the responsible party, about the outcome of the evaluation or measurement of a subject matter against criteria.

Aus 12.2 Assurance practitioner means a person or an organisation, whether in public practice, industry, commerce or the public sector, providing assurance services.

(a) [Deleted by the AUASB. Refer Aus 12.3]

Aus 12.3 Date of report means the date the assurance practitioner signs the report.

(b) [Deleted by the AUASB. Refer Aus 12.4]

Aus 12.4 Engagement documentation means the record of work performed, relevant evidence obtained, and conclusions the assurance practitioner reached (terms such as "working papers" or "workpapers" are sometimes used).

(c) [Deleted by the AUASB. Refer Aus 12.5][2]

Aus 12.5 Engagement partner means the partner or other person in the firm who is responsible for the assurance engagement and its performance, and for the report that is issued on behalf of the firm, and who, where required, has the appropriate authority from a professional, legal or regulatory body. Engagement partner should be read as referring to a public sector equivalent where relevant.

2 [Footnote deleted by the AUASB. Refer Aus 12.5, Aus 12.6 and Aus 12.9]

(d) Engagement quality control review means a process designed to provide an objective evaluation, on or before the date of the report, of the significant judgements the engagement team made and the conclusions it reached in formulating the report. The engagement quality control review process is for audits of financial reports of listed entities, and those other engagements, if any, for which the firm has determined an engagement quality control review is required.

(e) Engagement quality control reviewer means a partner, other person in the firm, suitably qualified external person, or a team made up of such individuals, none of whom is part of the engagement team, with sufficient and appropriate experience and authority to objectively evaluate the significant judgements the engagement team made and the conclusions it reached in formulating the report.

(f) Engagement team means all partners and staff performing the engagement, and any individuals engaged by the firm or a network firm who perform procedures on the engagement. This excludes external experts engaged by the firm or a network firm.

(g) [Deleted by the AUASB. Refer Aus 12.6]

Aus 12.6 Firm means a sole practitioner, partnership or corporation or other entity of assurance practitioners. Firm should be read as referring to a public sector equivalent where relevant.

(h) Inspection means, in relation to completed engagements, procedures designed to provide evidence of compliance by engagement teams with the firm's quality control policies and procedures.

Aus 12.7 Limited assurance engagement means an assurance engagement where the assurance practitioner's objective is a reduction in assurance engagement risk to a level that is acceptable in the circumstances of the assurance engagement, but where that risk is greater than that for a reasonable assurance engagement, as the basis for a negative form of expression of the assurance practitioner's conclusion. A limited assurance engagement is commonly referred to as a review.

(i) Listed entity means an entity whose shares, stock or debt are quoted or listed on a recognised stock exchange, or are marketed under the regulations of a recognised stock exchange or other equivalent body.

(j) Monitoring means a process comprising an ongoing consideration and evaluation of the firm's system of quality control, including a periodic inspection of a selection of completed engagements, designed to provide the firm with reasonable assurance that its system of quality control is operating effectively.

(k) Network firm means a firm or entity that belongs to a network.

(l) Network means a larger structure:

(i) That is aimed at cooperation, and

(ii) That is clearly aimed at profit or cost-sharing or shares common ownership, control or management, common quality control policies and procedures, common business strategy, the use of a common brand name, or a significant part of professional resources.

Aus 12.8 Other financial information means historical financial information and information other than historical financial information (for example, prospective financial information).

(m) [Deleted by the AUASB. Refer Aus 12.9]

Aus 12.9 Partner means any individual with authority to bind the firm with respect to the performance of an audit, review or other assurance engagement. Partner should be read as referring to a public sector equivalent where relevant.

(n) Personnel means partners and staff.

(o) [Deleted by the AUASB. Refer Aus 12.10]

Aus 12.10 AUASB Standards means standards issued by the AUASB, comprising:

(a) Australian Auditing Standards, which means the suite of auditing standards issued by the AUASB, comprising:

- Auditing Standards made under section 336 of the *Corporations Act 2001*;
- ASA 805 *Special Considerations—Audits of Single Financial Statements and Specific Elements, Accounts or Items of a Financial Statement*; and
- ASA 810 *Engagements to Report on Summary Financial Statements*.

(b) Standards on Review Engagements; and

(c) Standards on Assurance Engagements.

(p) Reasonable assurance means a high, but not absolute, level of assurance.

(q) [Deleted by the AUASB. Refer Aus 12.11]

Aus 12.11 Relevant ethical requirements means relevant ethical requirements as defined in ASA 102.

(r) Staff means professionals, other than partners, including any experts the firm employs.

(s) [Deleted by the AUASB. Refer Aus 12.12]

Aus 12.12 Suitably qualified external person means an individual outside the firm with the competence and capabilities to act as an engagement partner. For example:

- a partner of another firm, or
- a member (with appropriate experience) of a professional accountancy body* whose members may perform audits and reviews of financial reports and other financial information, and other assurance engagements, or
- a member (with appropriate experience) of an organisation that provides relevant quality control services.

Requirements

Applying, and Complying with, Relevant Requirements

13. Personnel within the firm responsible for establishing and maintaining the firm's system of quality control shall have an understanding of the entire text of this Standard, including its application and other explanatory material, to understand its objective and to apply its requirements properly.

14. The firm shall comply with each requirement of this Standard unless, in the circumstances of the firm, the requirement is not relevant to the services provided in respect of audits and reviews of financial reports, audits and reviews of other financial information, and other assurance engagements. (Ref: Para. A1-Aus A1.1)

15. The requirements are designed to enable the firm to achieve the objective stated in this Standard. The proper application of the requirements is therefore expected to provide a sufficient basis for the achievement of the objective. However, because circumstances vary widely and all such circumstances cannot be anticipated, the firm shall consider whether there are particular matters or circumstances that require the firm to establish policies and procedures in addition to those required by this Standard to meet the stated objective.

* For example, the Institute of Chartered Accountants in Australia, CPA Australia and the Institute of Public Accountants.

Elements of a System of Quality Control

16. The firm shall establish and maintain a system of quality control that includes policies and procedures that address each of the following elements:
    (a) Leadership responsibilities for quality within the firm.
    (b) Relevant ethical requirements.
    (c) Acceptance and continuance of client relationships and specific engagements.
    (d) Human resources.
    (e) Engagement performance.
    (f) Monitoring.
17. The firm shall document its policies and procedures and communicate them to the firm's personnel. (Ref: Para. A2-A3)

Leadership Responsibilities for Quality within the Firm

18. The firm shall establish policies and procedures designed to promote an internal culture recognising that quality is essential in performing engagements. Such policies and procedures shall require the firm's chief executive officer (or equivalent) or, if appropriate, the firm's managing board of partners (or equivalent) to assume ultimate responsibility for the firm's system of quality control. (Ref: Para. A4-A5)
19. The firm shall establish policies and procedures such that any person or persons assigned operational responsibility for the firm's system of quality control by the firm's chief executive officer or managing board of partners has sufficient and appropriate experience and ability, and the necessary authority, to assume that responsibility.(Ref: Para. A6)

Relevant Ethical Requirements

20. The firm shall establish policies and procedures designed to provide it with reasonable assurance that the firm and its personnel comply with relevant ethical requirements. (Ref: Para. A7-A9)

Independence

21. The firm shall establish policies and procedures designed to provide it with reasonable assurance that the firm, its personnel and, where applicable, others subject to independence requirements (including network firm personnel) maintain independence where required by relevant ethical requirements, laws and regulations. Such policies and procedures shall enable the firm to: (Ref: Para. A10-Aus A10.1)
    (a) Communicate its independence requirements to its personnel and, where applicable, others subject to them; and
    (b) Identify and evaluate circumstances and relationships that create threats to independence, and to take appropriate action to eliminate those threats or reduce them to an acceptable level by applying safeguards, or, if considered appropriate, to withdraw from the engagement, where withdrawal is possible under applicable law or regulation.
22. Such policies and procedures shall require: (Ref: Para. A10-Aus A10.1)
    (a) Engagement partners to provide the firm with relevant information about client engagements, including the scope of services, to enable the firm to evaluate the overall impact, if any, on independence requirements;
    (b) Personnel to promptly notify the firm of circumstances and relationships that create a threat to independence so that appropriate action can be taken; and
    (c) The accumulation and communication of relevant information to appropriate personnel so that:
        (i) The firm and its personnel can readily determine whether they satisfy independence requirements;
        (ii) The firm can maintain and update its records relating to independence; and
        (iii) The firm can take appropriate action regarding identified threats to independence that are not at an acceptable level.

23. The firm shall establish policies and procedures designed to provide it with reasonable assurance that it is notified of breaches of independence requirements, and to enable it to take appropriate actions to resolve such situations. The policies and procedures shall include requirements for: (Ref: Para. A10-Aus A10.1)

    (a) Personnel to promptly notify the firm of independence breaches of which they become aware;

    (b) The firm to promptly communicate identified breaches of these policies and procedures to:

        (i) The engagement partner who, with the firm, needs to address the breach; and

        (ii) Other relevant personnel in the firm and, where appropriate, the network, and those subject to the independence requirements who need to take appropriate action; and

    (c) Prompt communication to the firm, if necessary, by the engagement partner and the other individuals referred to in subparagraph 23(b)(ii) of this Standard, of the actions taken to resolve the matter, so that the firm can determine whether it should take further action.

24. [Deleted by the AUASB. Refer Aus 24.1]

Aus 24.1 At least annually, the firm shall obtain written confirmation of compliance with its policies and procedures on independence from all firm personnel required to be independent by relevant ethical requirements, and applicable legal and regulatory requirements. (Ref: Para. A10-A11)

25. The firm shall establish policies and procedures: (Ref: Para. A10-Aus A10.1)

    (a) Setting out criteria for determining the need for safeguards to reduce the familiarity threat to an acceptable level when using the same senior personnel on an assurance engagement over a long period of time; and

    (b) Requiring, for audits of financial reports of listed entities, the rotation of the engagement partner and the individuals responsible for engagement quality control review, and where applicable, others subject to rotation requirements, after a specified period in compliance with relevant ethical requirements. (Ref: Para. A12-A17)

Acceptance and Continuance of Client Relationships and Specific Engagements

26. The firm shall establish policies and procedures for the acceptance and continuance of client relationships and specific engagements, designed to provide the firm with reasonable assurance that it will only undertake or continue relationships and engagements where the firm:

    (a) Is competent to perform the engagement and has the capabilities, including time and resources, to do so; (Ref: Para. A18, A23)

    (b) Can comply with relevant ethical requirements; and

    (c) Has considered the integrity of the client, and does not have information that would lead it to conclude that the client lacks integrity. (Ref: Para. A19-A20, A23)

27. Such policies and procedures shall require:

    (a) The firm to obtain such information as it considers necessary in the circumstances before accepting an engagement with a new client, when deciding whether to continue an existing engagement, and when considering acceptance of a new engagement with an existing client. (Ref: Para. A21, A23)

    (b) If a potential conflict of interest is identified in accepting an engagement from a new or an existing client, the firm to determine whether it is appropriate to accept the engagement.

    (c) If issues have been identified, and the firm decides to accept or continue the client relationship or a specific engagement, the firm to document how the issues were resolved.

28. The firm shall establish policies and procedures on continuing an engagement and the client relationship, addressing the circumstances where the firm obtains information that would have caused it to decline the engagement had that information been available earlier. Such policies and procedures shall include consideration of:

    (a) The professional and legal responsibilities that apply to the circumstances, including whether there is a requirement for the firm to report to the person or persons who made the appointment or, in some cases, to regulatory authorities; and

    (b) The possibility of withdrawing from the engagement or from both the engagement and the client relationship. (Ref: Para. A22-A23)

Human Resources

29. The firm shall establish policies and procedures designed to provide it with reasonable assurance that it has sufficient personnel with the competence, capabilities, and commitment to ethical principles necessary to:

    (a) Perform engagements in accordance with AUASB Standards, relevant ethical requirements, and applicable legal and regulatory requirements; and

    (b) Enable the firm or engagement partners to issue reports that are appropriate in the circumstances. (Ref: Para. A24-A29)

Assignment of Engagement Teams

30. The firm shall assign responsibility for each engagement to an engagement partner and shall establish policies and procedures requiring that:

    (a) The identity and role of the engagement partner are communicated to key members of client management and those charged with governance;

    (b) The engagement partner has the appropriate competence, capabilities, and authority to perform the role; and

    (c) The responsibilities of the engagement partner are clearly defined and communicated to that partner. (Ref: Para. A30)

31. The firm shall also establish policies and procedures to assign appropriate personnel with the necessary competence, and capabilities to:

    (a) Perform engagements in accordance with AUASB Standards, relevant ethical requirements, and applicable legal and regulatory requirements; and

    (b) Enable the firm or engagement partners to issue reports that are appropriate in the circumstances. (Ref: Para. A31)

Engagement Performance

32. The firm shall establish policies and procedures designed to provide it with reasonable assurance that engagements are performed in accordance with AUASB Standards, relevant ethical requirements, and applicable legal and regulatory requirements, and that the firm or the engagement partner issue reports that are appropriate in the circumstances. Such policies and procedures shall include:

    (a) Matters relevant to promoting consistency in the quality of engagement performance; (Ref: Para. A32-A33)

    (b) Supervision responsibilities; and (Ref: Para. A34)

    (c) Review responsibilities. (Ref: Para. A35)

33. The firm's review responsibility policies and procedures shall be determined on the basis that work of less experienced engagement team members is reviewed by more experienced engagement team members.

Consultation

34. The firm shall establish policies and procedures designed to provide it with reasonable assurance that:

    (a) Appropriate consultation takes place on difficult or contentious matters;

    (b) Sufficient resources are available to enable appropriate consultation to take place;

(c) The nature and scope of, and conclusions resulting from, such consultations are documented and are agreed by both the individual seeking consultation and the individual consulted; and

(d) Conclusions resulting from consultations are implemented; or

Aus 34.1 The reasons alternative courses of action from consultations were undertaken, are documented. (Ref: Para. A36-A40)

Engagement Quality Control Review

35. The firm shall establish policies and procedures requiring, for appropriate engagements, an engagement quality control review that provides an objective evaluation of the significant judgements made by the engagement team and the conclusions reached in formulating the report. Such policies and procedures shall:

(a) Require an engagement quality control review for all audits of financial reports of listed entities;

(b) Set out criteria against which all other audits and reviews of historical financial information and other assurance engagements shall be evaluated to determine whether an engagement quality control review should be performed; and (Ref: Para. A41)

(c) Require an engagement quality control review for all engagements, if any, meeting the criteria established in compliance with subparagraph 35(b) of this Standard.

36. The firm shall establish policies and procedures setting out the nature, timing and extent of an engagement quality control review. Such policies and procedures shall require that the engagement report not be dated until the completion of the engagement quality control review. (Ref: Para. A42-A43)

37. The firm shall establish policies and procedures to require the engagement quality control review to include:

(a) Discussion of significant matters with the engagement partner;

(b) Review of the financial report or other subject matter information and the proposed report;

(c) Review of selected engagement documentation relating to significant judgements the engagement team made and the conclusions it reached; and

(d) Evaluation of the conclusions reached in formulating the report and consideration of whether the proposed report is appropriate. (Ref: Para. A44)

38. For audits of financial reports of listed entities, the firm shall establish policies and procedures to require the engagement quality control review to also include consideration of the following:

(a) The engagement team's evaluation of the firm's independence in relation to the specific engagement;

(b) Whether appropriate consultation has taken place on matters involving differences of opinion or other difficult or contentious matters, and the conclusions arising from those consultations; and

(c) Whether documentation selected for review reflects the work performed in relation to the significant judgements made and supports the conclusions reached. (Ref: Para. A45-A46)

Criteria for the Eligibility of Engagement Quality Control Reviewers

39. The firm shall establish policies and procedures to address the appointment of engagement quality control reviewers and establish their eligibility through:

(a) The technical qualifications required to perform the role, including the necessary experience and authority; and (Ref: Para. A47)

(b) The degree to which an engagement quality control reviewer can be consulted on the engagement without compromising the reviewer's objectivity. (Ref: Para. A48)

40. The firm shall establish policies and procedures designed to maintain the objectivity of the engagement quality control reviewer. (Ref: Para. A49-A51)

41. The firm's policies and procedures shall provide for the replacement of the engagement quality control reviewer where the reviewer's ability to perform an objective review may be impaired.

Documentation of the Engagement Quality Control Review

42. The firm shall establish policies and procedures on documentation of the engagement quality control review which require documentation that:

(a) The procedures required by the firm's policies on engagement quality control review have been performed;

(b) The engagement quality control review has been completed on or before the date of the report; and

(c) The reviewer is not aware of any unresolved matters that would cause the reviewer to believe that the significant judgements the engagement team made and the conclusions it reached were not appropriate.

Differences of Opinion

43. The firm shall establish policies and procedures for dealing with and resolving differences of opinion within the engagement team, with those consulted and, where applicable, between the engagement partner and the engagement quality control reviewer. (Ref: Para. A52-A53)

44. Such policies and procedures shall require that:

(a) Conclusions reached be documented and implemented; and

(b) The date of the report cannot be earlier than the date on which the matter is resolved.

Engagement Documentation

Completion of the Assembly of Final Engagement Files

45. The firm shall establish policies and procedures for engagement teams to complete the assembly of final engagement files on a timely basis after the engagement reports have been finalised. (Ref: Para. A54-A55)

Confidentiality, Safe Custody, Integrity, Accessibility and Retrievability of Engagement Documentation

46. The firm shall establish policies and procedures designed to maintain the confidentiality, safe custody, integrity, accessibility and retrievability of engagement documentation. (Ref: Para. A56-A59)

Retention of Engagement Documentation

47. The firm shall establish policies and procedures for the retention of engagement documentation for a period sufficient to meet the needs of the firm or as required by law or regulation. (Ref: Para. A60-Aus A63.1)

Monitoring

Monitoring the Firm's Quality Control Policies and Procedures

48. The firm shall establish a monitoring process designed to provide it with reasonable assurance that the policies and procedures relating to the system of quality control are relevant, adequate, and operating effectively. This process shall:

(a) Include an ongoing consideration and evaluation of the firm's system of quality control including, on a cyclical basis, inspection of at least one completed engagement for each engagement partner;

(b) Require responsibility for the monitoring process to be assigned to a partner or partners or other persons with sufficient and appropriate experience and authority in the firm to assume that responsibility; and

(c) Require that those performing the engagement or the engagement quality control review are not involved in inspecting the engagements. (Ref: Para. A64-Aus A68.1)

Evaluating, Communicating and Remedying Identified Deficiencies

49. The firm shall evaluate the effect of deficiencies noted as a result of the monitoring process and determine whether they are either:
    (a) Instances that do not necessarily indicate that the firm's system of quality control is insufficient to provide it with reasonable assurance that it complies with AUASB Standards, relevant ethical requirements, and applicable legal and regulatory requirements, and that the reports issued by the firm or engagement partners are appropriate in the circumstances; or
    (b) Systemic, repetitive or other significant deficiencies that require prompt corrective action.

50. The firm shall communicate to relevant engagement partners and other appropriate personnel deficiencies noted as a result of the monitoring process and recommendations for appropriate remedial action. (Ref: Para. A69)

51. Recommendations for appropriate remedial actions for deficiencies noted shall include one or more of the following:
    (a) Taking appropriate remedial action in relation to an individual engagement or member of personnel;
    (b) The communication of the findings to those responsible for training and professional development;
    (c) Changes to the quality control policies and procedures; and
    (d) Disciplinary action against those who fail to comply with the policies and procedures of the firm, especially those who do so repeatedly.

52. The firm shall establish policies and procedures to address cases where the results of the monitoring procedures indicate that a report may be inappropriate or that procedures were omitted during the performance of the engagement. Such policies and procedures shall require the firm to determine what further action is appropriate to comply with relevant AUASB Standards, relevant ethical requirements, and applicable legal and regulatory requirements, and to consider whether to obtain legal advice.

53. The firm shall communicate at least annually the results of the monitoring of its system of quality control to engagement partners and other appropriate individuals within the firm, including the firm's chief executive officer or, if appropriate, its managing board of partners. This communication shall be sufficient to enable the firm and these individuals to take prompt and appropriate action where necessary in accordance with their defined roles and responsibilities. Information communicated shall include the following:
    (a) A description of the monitoring procedures performed.
    (b) The conclusions drawn from the monitoring procedures.
    (c) Where relevant, a description of systemic, repetitive or other significant deficiencies and of the actions taken to resolve or amend those deficiencies.

54. Some firms operate as part of a network and, for consistency, may implement some of their monitoring procedures on a network basis. Where firms within a network operate under common monitoring policies and procedures designed to comply with this Standard, and these firms place reliance on such a monitoring system, the firm's policies and procedures shall require that:
    (a) At least annually, the network communicate the overall scope, extent and results of the monitoring process to appropriate individuals within the network firms; and
    (b) The network communicate promptly any identified deficiencies in the system of quality control to appropriate individuals within the relevant network firm or firms so that the necessary action can be taken,

    in order that engagement partners in the network firms can rely on the results of the monitoring process implemented within the network, unless the firms or the network advise otherwise.

Complaints and Allegations

55. The firm shall establish policies and procedures designed to provide it with reasonable assurance that it deals appropriately with:

    (a) Complaints and allegations that the work performed by the firm fails to comply with AUASB Standards, relevant ethical requirements, and applicable legal and regulatory requirements; and

    (b) Allegations of non-compliance with the firm's system of quality control.

    As part of this process, the firm shall establish clearly defined channels for firm personnel to raise any concerns in a manner that enables them to come forward without fear of reprisals. (Ref: Para. A70)

56. If during the investigations into complaints and allegations, deficiencies in the design or operation of the firm's quality control policies and procedures or non-compliance with the firm's system of quality control by an individual or individuals are identified, the firm shall take appropriate actions as set out in paragraph 51 of this Standard. (Ref: Para. A71-A72)

Documentation of the System of Quality Control

57. The firm shall establish policies and procedures requiring appropriate documentation to provide evidence of the operation of each element of its system of quality control. (Ref: Para. A73-A75)

58. The firm shall establish policies and procedures that require retention of documentation for a period of time sufficient to permit those performing monitoring procedures to evaluate the firm's compliance with its system of quality control, or for a longer period if required by law or regulation.

59. The firm shall establish policies and procedures requiring documentation of complaints and allegations and the responses to them.

❖❖❖

Application and Other Explanatory Material

Applying, and Complying with, Relevant Requirements (Ref: Para. 14)

Considerations Specific to Smaller Firms

A1. This Standard does not call for compliance with requirements that are not relevant, for example, in the circumstances of a sole practitioner with no staff. Requirements in this Standard such as those for policies and procedures for the assignment of appropriate personnel to the engagement team (see paragraph 31), for review responsibilities (see paragraph 33), and for the annual communication of the results of monitoring to assurance practitioners within the firm (see paragraph 53) are not relevant in the case of a sole practitioner where no staff are employed.

Considerations specific to Public Sector Entities

Aus A1.1 For assurance engagements conducted in the public sector by Auditors-General pursuant to legislation, public sector auditors should have regard to the relevant public sector mandate and address any threats in that context. Requirements relating to independence (paragraphs 21-25), acceptance and continuance of client relationships and specific engagements (paragraphs 26-28), and complaints and allegations (paragraphs 55-56) may not be consistent with the Auditors-General legislative mandate in all circumstances.

Elements of a System of Quality Control (Ref: Para. 17)

A2. In general, communication of quality control policies and procedures to firm personnel includes a description of the quality control policies and procedures and the objectives they are designed to achieve, and the message that each individual has a personal responsibility for quality and is expected to comply with these policies and procedures. Encouraging firm personnel to communicate their views or concerns on quality control matters recognises the importance of obtaining feedback on the firm's system of quality control.

Considerations Specific to Smaller Firms

A3. Documentation and communication of policies and procedures for smaller firms may be less formal and less extensive than for larger firms.

Leadership Responsibilities for Quality within the Firm

Promoting an Internal Culture of Quality (Ref: Para. 18)

A4. The firm's leadership and the examples it sets significantly influence the internal culture of the firm. The promotion of a quality-oriented internal culture depends on clear, consistent and frequent actions and messages from all levels of the firm's management that emphasise the firm's quality control policies and procedures, and the requirement to:

(a) perform work that complies with AUASB Standards, relevant ethical requirements, and applicable legal and regulatory requirements; and

(b) issue reports that are appropriate in the circumstances.

Such actions and messages encourage a culture that recognises and rewards high quality work. These actions and messages may be communicated by, but are not limited to, training seminars, meetings, formal or informal dialogue, mission statements, newsletters, or briefing memoranda. They may be incorporated in the firm's internal documentation and training materials, and in partner and staff appraisal procedures such that they will support and reinforce the firm's view on the importance of quality and how, practically, it is to be achieved.

A5. Of particular importance in promoting an internal culture based on quality is the need for the firm's leadership to recognise that the firm's business strategy is subject to the overriding requirement for the firm to achieve quality in all the engagements that the firm performs. Promoting such an internal culture includes:

(a) Establishment of policies and procedures that address performance evaluation, compensation, and promotion (including incentive systems) with regard to its personnel, in order to demonstrate the firm's overriding commitment to quality;

(b) Assignment of management responsibilities so that commercial considerations do not override the quality of work performed; and

(c) Provision of sufficient resources for the development, documentation and support of its quality control policies and procedures.

Assigning Operational Responsibility for the Firm's System of Quality Control (Ref: Para. 19)

A6. Sufficient and appropriate experience and ability enables the person or persons responsible for the firm's system of quality control to identify and understand quality control issues, and to develop appropriate policies and procedures. Necessary authority enables the person or persons to implement those policies and procedures.

Relevant Ethical Requirements

Compliance with Relevant Ethical Requirements (Ref: Para. 20)

A7. [Deleted by the AUASB. Refer Aus A7.1]

Aus A7.1 The firm is required to comply with relevant ethical requirements, including those pertaining to independence, when performing audits, reviews and other assurance engagements, as defined in ASA 102.

A8. [Deleted by the AUASB. Refer ASA 102]

A9. [Deleted by the AUASB. Refer ASA 102]

Definition of "Firm," "Network" and "Network Firm" (Ref: Para. 20-25)

A10. [Deleted by the AUASB. Refer ASA 102][3]

3 [Footnote deleted by the AUASB.]

***Independence** (Ref. Para 21)*

Aus A10.1 Examples of independence requirements that may be applicable are addressed in the *Corporations Act 2001* Part 2M.3 Division 3, and relevant ethical requirements.*

***Written Confirmation** (Ref: Para. Aus 24.1)*

A11. Written confirmation may be in paper or electronic form. By obtaining confirmation and taking appropriate action on information indicating non-compliance, the firm demonstrates the importance that it attaches to independence and makes the issue current for, and visible to, its personnel.

***Familiarity Threat** (Ref: Para. 25)*

A12. [Deleted by the AUASB. Refer Aus A12.1]

Aus A12.1 A familiarity threat may be created by using the same senior personnel on an assurance engagement over a long period of time.

A13. [Deleted by the AUASB. Refer Aus A13.1]

Aus A13.1 Determining appropriate criteria to address familiarity threats may include matters such as:

- The nature of the engagement, including the extent to which it involves a matter of public interest; and
- The length of service of the senior personnel on the engagement.

Examples of safeguards that might be appropriate to address familiarity threats include rotating the senior personnel or requiring an engagement quality control review.

A14. [Deleted by the AUASB. Refer Aus A14.1].

Aus A14.1 A familiarity threat is particularly relevant in the context of financial report audits of listed entities. For these audits, relevant ethical requirements and the *Corporations Act 2001* specify partner rotation requirements.

Considerations specific to public sector audit organisations

A15. Statutory measures may provide safeguards for the independence of public sector auditors. However, threats to independence may still exist regardless of any statutory measures designed to protect it. Therefore, in establishing the policies and procedures required by paragraphs 20-25, the public sector auditor may have regard to the public sector mandate and address any threats to independence in that context.

A16. Listed entities as referred to in paragraphs 25 and A14 are not common in the public sector. However, there may be other public sector entities that are significant due to size, complexity or public interest aspects, and which consequently have a wide range of stakeholders. Therefore, there may be instances when a firm determines, based on its quality control policies and procedures, that a public sector entity is significant for the purposes of expanded quality control procedures.

A17. In the public sector, legislation may establish the appointments and terms of office of the auditor with engagement partner responsibility. As a result, it may not be possible to comply strictly with the engagement partner rotation requirements envisaged for listed entities. Nonetheless, for public sector entities considered significant, as noted in paragraph A16, it may be in the public interest for public sector audit organisations to establish policies and procedures to promote compliance with the spirit of rotation of engagement partner responsibility.

* See ASA 102.

Acceptance and Continuance of Client Relationships and Specific Engagements

Competence, Capabilities, and Resources (Ref: Para. 26(a))

A18. Consideration of whether the firm has the competence, capabilities, and resources to undertake a new engagement from a new or an existing client involves reviewing the specific requirements of the engagement and the existing partner and staff profiles at all relevant levels, and including whether:

- Firm personnel have knowledge of relevant industries or subject matters;
- Firm personnel have experience with relevant regulatory or reporting requirements, or the ability to gain the necessary skills and knowledge effectively;
- The firm has sufficient personnel with the necessary competence and capabilities;
- Experts are available, if needed;
- Individuals meeting the criteria and eligibility requirements to perform engagement quality control review are available, where applicable; and
- The firm is able to complete the engagement within the reporting deadline.

Integrity of Client (Ref: Para. 26(c))

A19. With regard to the integrity of a client, matters to consider include, for example:

- The identity and business reputation of the client's principal owners, key management, and those charged with its governance.
- The nature of the client's operations, including its business practices.
- Information concerning the attitude of the client's principal owners, key management and those charged with its governance towards such matters as aggressive interpretation of Australian Accounting Standards and the internal control environment.
- Whether the client is aggressively concerned with maintaining the firm's fees as low as possible.
- Indications of an inappropriate limitation in the scope of work.
- Indications that the client might be involved in money laundering or other criminal activities.
- The reasons for the proposed appointment of the firm and non-reappointment of the previous firm.
- The identity and business reputation of related parties.

The extent of knowledge a firm will have regarding the integrity of a client will generally grow within the context of an ongoing relationship with that client.

A20. Sources of information on such matters obtained by the firm may include the following:

- Communications with existing or previous providers of professional accountancy services to the client in accordance with relevant ethical requirements, and discussions with other third parties.
- Enquiry of other firm personnel or third parties such as bankers, legal counsel and industry peers.
- Background searches of relevant databases.

Continuance of Client Relationship (Ref: Para. 27(a))

A21. Deciding whether to continue a client relationship includes consideration of significant matters that have arisen during the current or previous engagements, and their implications for continuing the relationship. For example, a client may have started to expand its business operations into an area where the firm does not possess the necessary expertise.

Withdrawal (Ref: Para. 28)

A22. Policies and procedures on withdrawal from an engagement or from both the engagement and the client relationship address issues that include the following:

- Discussing with the appropriate level of the client's management and those charged with its governance the appropriate action that the firm might take based on the relevant facts and circumstances.
- If the firm determines that it is appropriate to withdraw, discussing with the appropriate level of the client's management and those charged with its governance withdrawal from the engagement or from both the engagement and the client relationship, and the reasons for the withdrawal.
- Considering whether there is a professional, legal or regulatory requirement for the firm to remain in place, or for the firm to report the withdrawal from the engagement, or from both the engagement and the client relationship, together with the reasons for the withdrawal, to regulatory authorities.
  - Aus A22.1 For example, the firm may be required to obtain consent from the Australian Securities and Investments Commission (ASIC) prior to resigning from certain audits.*
- Documenting significant matters, consultations, conclusions and the basis for the conclusions.

Considerations Specific to Public Sector Audit Organisations (Ref: Para. 26-28)

A23. In the public sector, auditors may be appointed in accordance with statutory procedures. Accordingly, certain of the requirements and considerations regarding the acceptance and continuance of client relationships and specific engagements as set out paragraphs 26-28 and A18-A22 may not be relevant. Nonetheless, establishing policies and procedures as described may provide valuable information to public sector auditors in performing risk assessments and in carrying out reporting responsibilities.

Human Resources (Ref: Para. 29)

A24. Personnel issues relevant to the firm's policies and procedures related to human resources include, for example:

- Recruitment.
- Performance evaluation.
- Capabilities, including time to perform assignments.
- Competence.
- Career development.
- Promotion.
- Compensation.
- The estimation of personnel needs.

Effective recruitment processes and procedures help the firm select individuals of integrity who have the capacity to develop the competence and capabilities necessary to perform the firm's work and possess the appropriate characteristics to enable them to perform competently.

A25. Competence can be developed through a variety of methods, including the following:

- Professional education.
- Continuing professional development, including training.
- Work experience.
- Coaching by more experienced staff, for example, other members of the engagement team.
- Independence education for personnel who are required to be independent.

* See, for example, ASIC *Regulatory Guide 26 Resignation of Auditors* (June 1992).

A26. The continuing competence of the firm's personnel depends to a significant extent on an appropriate level of continuing professional development so that personnel maintain their knowledge and capabilities. Effective policies and procedures emphasise the need for continuing training for all levels of firm personnel, and provide the necessary training resources and assistance to enable personnel to develop and maintain the required competence and capabilities.

A27. The firm may use a suitably qualified external person, for example, when internal technical and training resources are unavailable.

A28. Performance evaluation, compensation and promotion procedures give due recognition and reward to the development and maintenance of competence and commitment to ethical principles. Steps a firm may take in developing and maintaining competence and commitment to ethical principles include:

- Making personnel aware of the firm's expectations regarding performance and ethical principles;
- Providing personnel with evaluation of, and counselling on, performance, progress and career development; and
- Helping personnel understand that advancement to positions of greater responsibility depends, among other things, upon performance quality and adherence to ethical principles, and that failure to comply with the firm's policies and procedures may result in disciplinary action.

Considerations Specific to Smaller Firms

A29. The size and circumstances of the firm will influence the structure of the firm's performance evaluation process. Smaller firms, in particular, may employ less formal methods of evaluating the performance of their personnel.

Assignment of Engagement Teams

Engagement Partners (Ref: Para. 30)

A30. Policies and procedures may include systems to monitor the workload and availability of engagement partners so as to enable these individuals to have sufficient time to adequately discharge their responsibilities.

Engagement Teams (Ref: Para. 31)

A31. The firm's assignment of engagement teams and the determination of the level of supervision required, include for example, consideration of the engagement team's:

- Understanding of, and practical experience with, engagements of a similar nature and complexity through appropriate training and participation;
- Understanding of AUASB Standards, relevant ethical requirements, and applicable legal and regulatory requirements;
- Technical knowledge and expertise, including knowledge of relevant information technology;
- Knowledge of relevant industries in which the clients operate;
- Ability to apply professional judgement; and
- Understanding of the firm's quality control policies and procedures.

Engagement Performance

Consistency in the Quality of Engagement Performance (Ref: Para. 32(a))

A32. The firm promotes consistency in the quality of engagement performance through its policies and procedures. This is often accomplished through written or electronic manuals, software tools or other forms of standardised documentation, and industry or subject matter-specific guidance materials. Matters addressed may include:

- How engagement teams are briefed on the engagement to obtain an understanding of the objectives of their work.
- Processes for complying with applicable engagement standards.

- Processes of engagement supervision, staff training and coaching.
- Methods of reviewing the work performed, the significant judgements made and the form of report being issued.
- Appropriate documentation of the work performed and of the timing and extent of the review.
- Processes to keep all policies and procedures current.

A33. Appropriate teamwork and training assist less experienced members of the engagement team to clearly understand the objectives of the assigned work.

Supervision (Ref: Para. 32(b))

A34. Engagement supervision includes the following:

- Tracking the progress of the engagement;
- Considering the competence and capabilities of individual members of the engagement team, whether they have sufficient time to carry out their work, whether they understand their instructions and whether the work is being carried out in accordance with the planned approach to the engagement;
- Addressing significant matters arising during the engagement, considering their significance and modifying the planned approach appropriately; and
- Identifying matters for consultation or consideration by more experienced engagement team members during the engagement.

Review (Ref: Para. 32(c))

A35. A review consists of consideration of whether:

- The work has been performed in accordance with AUASB Standards, relevant ethical requirements, and applicable legal and regulatory requirements;
- Significant matters have been raised for further consideration;
- Appropriate consultations have taken place and the resulting conclusions have been documented and implemented;
- There is a need to revise the nature, timing and extent of work performed;
- The work performed supports the conclusions reached and is appropriately documented;
- The evidence obtained is sufficient and appropriate to support the report; and
- The objectives of the engagement procedures have been achieved.

Consultation (Ref: Para. 34-Aus 34.1)

A36. Consultation includes discussion at the appropriate professional level, with individuals within or outside the firm who have specialised expertise.

A37. Consultation uses appropriate research resources as well as the collective experience and technical expertise of the firm. Consultation helps promote quality and improves the application of professional judgement. Appropriate recognition of consultation in the firm's policies and procedures helps promote a culture in which consultation is recognised as a strength and encourages personnel to consult on difficult or contentious matters.

A38. Effective consultation on significant technical, ethical and other matters within the firm, or where applicable, outside the firm can be achieved when those consulted:

- are given all the relevant facts that will enable them to provide informed advice; and
- have appropriate knowledge, seniority and experience,

and when conclusions resulting from consultations are appropriately documented and implemented.

A39. Documentation of consultations with other professionals that involve difficult or contentious matters that is sufficiently complete and detailed contributes to an understanding of:

- The issue on which consultation was sought; and
- The results of the consultation, including any decisions taken, the basis for those decisions and how they were implemented.

Considerations Specific to Smaller Firms

A40. A firm needing to consult externally, for example, a firm without appropriate internal resources, may take advantage of advisory services provided by:

- Other firms;
- Professional and regulatory bodies; or
- Commercial organisations that provide relevant quality control services.

Before contracting for such services, consideration of the competence and capabilities of the external provider helps the firm to determine whether the external provider is suitably qualified for that purpose.

Engagement Quality Control Review

Criteria for an Engagement Quality Control Review (Ref: Para. 35(b))

A41. Criteria for determining which engagements other than audits of financial reports of listed entities are to be subject to an engagement quality control review may include, for example:

- The nature of the engagement, including the extent to which it involves a matter of public interest.
- The identification of unusual circumstances or risks in an engagement or class of engagements.
- Whether laws or regulations require an engagement quality control review.

Nature, Timing and Extent of the Engagement Quality Control Review (Ref: Para. 36-37)

A42. The date of the engagement report cannot be earlier than the date on which the engagement quality control review is completed. However, documentation of the engagement quality control review may be completed after the date of the report.

A43. Conducting the engagement quality control review in a timely manner at appropriate stages during the engagement allows significant matters to be promptly resolved to the engagement quality control reviewer's satisfaction on or before the date of the report.

A44. The extent of the engagement quality control review may depend, among other things, on the complexity of the engagement, whether the entity is a listed entity, and the risk that the report might not be appropriate in the circumstances. The performance of an engagement quality control review does not reduce the responsibilities of the engagement partner.

Engagement Quality Control Review of a Listed Entity (Ref: Para. 38)

A45. Other matters relevant to evaluating the significant judgements made by the engagement team that may be considered in an engagement quality control review of an audit of a financial report of a listed entity include:

- Significant risks identified during the engagement and the responses to those risks.
- Judgements made, particularly with respect to materiality and significant risks.
- The significance and disposition of corrected and uncorrected misstatements identified during the engagement.
- The matters to be communicated to management and those charged with governance and, where applicable, other parties such as regulatory bodies.

These other matters, depending on the circumstances, may also be applicable for engagement quality control reviews for audits of the financial reports of other entities, as well as reviews of financial reports, audits and reviews of other financial information, and other assurance engagements.

Considerations specific to public sector audit organisations

A46. Although not referred to as listed entities, as described in paragraph A16, certain public sector entities may be of sufficient significance to warrant performance of an engagement quality control review.

Criteria for the Eligibility of Engagement Quality Control Reviewers

Sufficient and Appropriate Technical Expertise, Experience and Authority (Ref: Para. 39(a))

A47. What constitutes sufficient and appropriate technical expertise, experience and authority depends on the circumstances of the engagement. For example, the engagement quality control reviewer for an audit of a financial report of a listed entity is likely to be an individual with sufficient and appropriate experience and authority to act as an audit engagement partner on audits of financial reports of listed entities.

Consultation with the Engagement Quality Control Reviewer (Ref: Para. 39(b))

A48. The engagement partner may consult the engagement quality control reviewer during the engagement, for example, to establish that a judgement made by the engagement partner will be acceptable to the engagement quality control reviewer. Such consultation avoids identification of differences of opinion at a late stage of the engagement and need not compromise the engagement quality control reviewer's eligibility to perform the role. Where the nature and extent of the consultations become significant, the reviewer's objectivity may be compromised unless care is taken by both the engagement team and the reviewer to maintain the reviewer's objectivity. Where this is not possible, another individual within the firm or a suitably qualified external person may be appointed to take on the role of either the engagement quality control reviewer or the person to be consulted on the engagement.

Objectivity of the Engagement Quality Control Reviewer (Ref: Para. 40)

A49. The firm is required to establish policies and procedures designed to maintain objectivity of the engagement quality control reviewer. Accordingly, such policies and procedures provide that the engagement quality control reviewer:

- Where practicable, is not selected by the engagement partner;
- Does not otherwise participate in the engagement during the period of review;
- Does not make decisions for the engagement team; and
- Is not subject to other considerations that would threaten the reviewer's objectivity.

Considerations specific to smaller firms

A50. It may not be practicable, in the case of firms with few partners, for the engagement partner not to be involved in selecting the engagement quality control reviewer. Suitably qualified external persons may be contracted where sole practitioners or small firms identify engagements requiring engagement quality control reviews. Alternatively, some sole practitioners or small firms may wish to use other firms to facilitate engagement quality control reviews. Where the firm contracts suitably qualified external persons, the requirements in paragraphs 39-41 and guidance in paragraphs A47-A48 apply.

Considerations specific to public sector audit organisations

A51. In the public sector, a statutorily appointed auditor (for example, an Auditor-General, or other suitably qualified person appointed on behalf of the Auditor-General) may act in a role equivalent to that of engagement partner with overall responsibility for public sector audits. In such circumstances, where applicable, the selection of the engagement quality control reviewer includes consideration of the need for independence from the audited entity and the ability of the engagement quality control reviewer to provide an objective evaluation.

Differences of Opinion (Ref: Para. 43)

A52. Effective procedures encourage identification of differences of opinion at an early stage, provide clear guidelines as to the successive steps to be taken thereafter, and require documentation regarding the resolution of the differences and the implementation of the conclusions reached.

A53. Procedures to resolve such differences may include consulting with another practitioner or firm, or a professional* or regulatory body.

Engagement Documentation

Completion of the Assembly of Final Engagement Files *(Ref: Para. 45)*

A54. Law or regulation may prescribe the time limits by which the assembly of final engagement files for specific types of engagement is to be completed. Where no such time limits are prescribed in law or regulation, paragraph 45 requires the firm to establish time limits that reflect the need to complete the assembly of final engagement files on a timely basis. In the case of an audit, for example, such a time limit would ordinarily not be more than 60 days after the date of the auditor's report.

A55. Where two or more different reports are issued in respect of the same subject matter information of an entity, the firm's policies and procedures relating to time limits for the assembly of final engagement files address each report as if it were for a separate engagement. This may, for example, be the case when the firm issues an auditor's report on a component's financial information for group consolidation purposes and, at a subsequent date, an auditor's report on the same financial information for statutory purposes.

Confidentiality, Safe Custody, Integrity, Accessibility and Retrievability of Engagement Documentation *(Ref: Para. 46)*

A56. Relevant ethical requirements establish an obligation for the firm's personnel to observe at all times the confidentiality of information contained in engagement documentation, unless specific client authority has been given to disclose information, or there is a legal or professional duty to do so. Specific laws or regulations may impose additional obligations on the firm's personnel to maintain client confidentiality, particularly where data of a personal nature are concerned.

A57. Whether engagement documentation is in paper, electronic or other media, the integrity, accessibility or retrievability of the underlying data may be compromised if the documentation could be altered, added to or deleted without the firm's knowledge, or if it could be permanently lost or damaged. Accordingly, controls that the firm designs and implements to avoid unauthorised alteration or loss of engagement documentation may include those that:

- Enable the determination of when and by whom engagement documentation was created, changed or reviewed;
- Protect the integrity of the information at all stages of the engagement, especially when the information is shared within the engagement team or transmitted to other parties via the Internet;
- Prevent unauthorised changes to the engagement documentation; and
- Allow access to the engagement documentation by the engagement team and other authorised parties as necessary to properly discharge their responsibilities.

A58. Controls that the firm designs and implements to maintain the confidentiality, safe custody, integrity, accessibility and retrievability of engagement documentation may include the following:

- The use of a password among engagement team members to restrict access to electronic engagement documentation to authorised users.
- Appropriate back-up routines for electronic engagement documentation at appropriate stages during the engagement.

* For example, the professional accounting bodies in Australia comprises the Institute of Chartered Accountants in Australia, CPA Australia and the Institute of Public Accountants.

- Procedures for properly distributing engagement documentation to the engagement team members at the start of the engagement, processing it during engagement, and collating it at the end of the engagement.
- Procedures for restricting access to, and enabling proper distribution and confidential storage of, hardcopy engagement documentation.

A59. For practical reasons, original paper documentation may be electronically scanned for inclusion in engagement files. In such cases, the firm's procedures designed to maintain the integrity, accessibility, and retrievability of the documentation may include requiring the engagement teams to:

- Generate scanned copies that reflect the entire content of the original paper documentation, including manual signatures, cross-references and annotations;
- Integrate the scanned copies into the engagement files, including indexing and signing off on the scanned copies as necessary; and
- Enable the scanned copies to be retrieved and printed as necessary.

There may be legal, regulatory or other reasons for a firm to retain original paper documentation that has been scanned.

***Retention of Engagement Documentation** (Ref: Para. 47)*

A60. The needs of the firm for retention of engagement documentation, and the period of such retention, will vary with the nature of the engagement and the firm's circumstances, for example, whether the engagement documentation is needed to provide a record of matters of continuing significance to future engagements. The retention period may also depend on other factors, such as whether local law or regulation prescribes specific retention periods for certain types of engagements, or whether there are generally accepted retention periods in the jurisdiction in the absence of specific legal or regulatory requirements.

A61. In the specific case of audit engagements, the retention period would ordinarily be no shorter than five years from the date of the auditor's report, or, if later, the date of the group auditor's report.

Aus A61.1 For audits or reviews of financial reports conducted under the *Corporations Act 2001* (the Act), section 307B of that Act requires an auditor or member of an audit firm to retain all audit working papers prepared by or for, or considered or used by, the auditor in accordance with the requirements of the Australian Auditing Standards until:

(a) The end of seven years after the date of the audit report prepared in relation to the audit or review to which the audit working papers relate; or

(b) An earlier date determined by the Australian Securities and Investments Commission for the audit working papers.

Aus A61.2 Relevant law or regulation, other than the *Corporations Act 2001*, may require the retention of audit working papers for specified periods.

A62. Procedures that the firm adopts for retention of engagement documentation include those that enable the requirements of paragraph 47 to be met during the retention period, for example to:

- Enable the retrieval of, and access to, the engagement documentation during the retention period, particularly in the case of electronic documentation since the underlying technology may be upgraded or changed over time;
- Provide, where necessary, a record of changes made to engagement documentation after the engagement files have been completed; and
- Enable authorised external parties to access and review specific engagement documentation for quality control or other purposes.

Ownership of engagement documentation

A63. [Deleted by the AUASB. Refer Aus A63.1]

Aus A63.1 Unless otherwise specified by law or regulation, engagement documentation remains the property of the firm. The firm may, at its discretion, make portions of, or extracts from, engagement documentation available to clients, provided such disclosure does not undermine the validity of the work performed or the independence of the firm or its personnel.

Monitoring

Monitoring the Firm's Quality Control Policies and Procedures (Ref: Para. 48)

A64. The purpose of monitoring compliance with quality control policies and procedures is to provide an evaluation of:

- Adherence to AUASB Standards, relevant ethical requirements, and applicable legal and regulatory requirements;
- Whether the system of quality control has been appropriately designed and effectively implemented; and
- Whether the firm's quality control policies and procedures have been appropriately applied, so that reports that are issued by the firm or engagement partners are appropriate in the circumstances.

A65. Ongoing consideration and evaluation of the system of quality control include matters such as the following:

- Analysis of:
  - New developments in AUASB Standards, relevant ethical requirements, and applicable legal and regulatory requirements, and how they are reflected in the firm's policies and procedures where appropriate;
  - Written confirmation of compliance with policies and procedures on independence;
  - Continuing professional development, including training; and
  - Decisions related to acceptance and continuance of client relationships and specific engagements.
- Determination of corrective actions to be taken and improvements to be made in the system, including the provision of feedback into the firm's policies and procedures relating to education and training.
- Communication to appropriate firm personnel of weaknesses identified in the system, in the level of understanding of the system, or compliance with it.
- Follow-up by appropriate firm personnel so that necessary modifications are promptly made to the quality control policies and procedures.

A66. Inspection cycle policies and procedures may, for example, specify a cycle that spans three years. The manner in which the inspection cycle is organised, including the timing of selection of individual engagements, depends on many factors, such as the following:

- The size of the firm.
- The number and geographical location of offices.
- The results of previous monitoring procedures.
- The degree of authority both personnel and offices have (for example, whether individual offices are authorised to conduct their own inspections or whether only the head office may conduct them).
- The nature and complexity of the firm's practice and organisation.
- The risks associated with the firm's clients and specific engagements.

A67. The inspection process includes the selection of individual engagements, some of which may be selected without prior notification to the engagement team. In determining the scope of the inspections, the firm may take into account the scope or conclusions of an independent external inspection program. However, an independent external inspection program does not act as a substitute for the firm's own internal monitoring program.

Considerations Specific to Smaller Firms

A68. In the case of small firms, monitoring procedures may need to be performed by individuals who are responsible for the design and implementation of the firm's quality control policies and procedures, or who may be involved in performing the engagement quality control review. A firm with a limited number of persons may choose to use a suitably qualified external person or another firm to carry out engagement inspections and other monitoring procedures. Alternatively, the firm may establish arrangements to share resources with other appropriate organisations to facilitate monitoring activities.

Considerations Specific to Public Sector Organisations

Aus A68.1 In the public sector, an auditor appointed under statute (for example, an Auditor-General) may delegate responsibility for an engagement. The monitoring process needs to include, on a cyclical basis, inspection of at least one completed engagement of each person with delegated responsibility for an engagement and its performance. This includes an external person engaged as the person responsible for an engagement.

Communicating Deficiencies (Ref: Para. 50)

A69. The reporting of identified deficiencies to individuals other than the relevant engagement partners need not include an identification of the specific engagements concerned, although there may be cases where such identification may be necessary for the proper discharge of the responsibilities of the individuals other than the engagement partners.

Complaints and Allegations

Source of Complaints and Allegations (Ref: Para. 55)

A70. Complaints and allegations (which do not include those that are clearly frivolous) may originate from within or outside the firm. They may be made by firm personnel, clients or other third parties. They may be received by engagement team members or other firm personnel.

Investigation Policies and Procedures (Ref: Para. 56)

A71. Policies and procedures established for the investigation of complaints and allegations may include for example, that the partner supervising the investigation:

- Has sufficient and appropriate experience;
- Has authority within the firm; and
- Is otherwise not involved in the engagement.

The partner supervising the investigation may involve legal counsel as necessary.

Considerations specific to smaller firms

A72. It may not be practicable, in the case of firms with few partners, for the partner supervising the investigation not to be involved in the engagement. These small firms and sole practitioners may use the services of a suitably qualified external person or another firm to carry out the investigation into complaints and allegations.

Documentation of the System of Quality Control (Ref: Para. 57)

A73. The form and content of documentation evidencing the operation of each of the elements of the system of quality control is a matter of judgement and depends on a number of factors, including the following:

- The size of the firm and the number of offices.
- The nature and complexity of the firm's practice and organisation

For example, large firms may use electronic databases to document matters such as independence confirmations, performance evaluations and the results of monitoring inspections.

A74. Appropriate documentation relating to monitoring includes, for example:

- Monitoring procedures, including the procedure for selecting completed engagements to be inspected.
- A record of the evaluation of:
  - Adherence to AUASB Standards, relevant ethical requirements, and applicable legal and regulatory requirements;
  - Whether the system of quality control has been appropriately designed and effectively implemented; and
  - Whether the firm's quality control policies and procedures have been appropriately applied, so that reports that are issued by the firm or engagement partners are appropriate in the circumstances.
- Identification of the deficiencies noted, an evaluation of their effect, and the basis for determining whether and what further action is necessary.

Considerations Specific to Smaller Firms

A75. Smaller firms may use more informal methods in the documentation of their systems of quality control such as manual notes, checklists and forms.

❖❖❖

Conformity with International Standards on Quality Control

This Auditing Standard conforms with International Standard on Quality Control ISQC 1 *Quality Control for Firms that Perform Audits and Reviews of Financial Statements, and Other Assurance and Related Services Engagements* issued by the International Auditing and Assurance Standards Board (IAASB), an independent standard-setting board of the International Federation of Accountants (IFAC).

Paragraphs that have been added to this Auditing Standard (and do not appear in the text of the equivalent ISQC 1) are identified with the prefix "Aus".

The following requirements are additional to ISQC 1:

- At least annually, the firm shall obtain written confirmation of compliance with its policies and procedures on independence from all firm personnel required to be independent by relevant ethical requirements, and applicable legal and regulatory requirements. (Ref: Para. Aus 24.1)
- The firm shall establish policies and procedures designed to provide it with reasonable assurance that:
  - Appropriate consultation takes place on difficult or contentious matters;
  - Sufficient resources are available to enable appropriate consultation to take place;
  - The nature and scope of, and conclusions resulting from, such consultations are documented and are agreed by both the individual seeking consultation and the individual consulted; and
  - Conclusions resulting from consultations are implemented; or
  - The reasons alternative courses of action from consultations were undertaken, are documented. (Ref: Para. Aus 34.1)

This Auditing Standard differs in scope from ISQC 1 as it does not apply to related services engagements.

This Auditing Standard incorporates terminology and definitions used in Australia.

The equivalent requirements and related application and other explanatory material included in ISQC 1 in respect of "relevant ethical requirements", have been included in another Auditing Standard, ASA 102 *Compliance with Ethical Requirements when Performing Audits, Reviews and Other Assurance Engagements*. There is no international equivalent to ASA 102.

Compliance with this Auditing Standard enables compliance with ISQC 1, to the extent that ISQC 1 applies to audits and reviews of financial reports and other financial information, and other assurance engagements.

ASA 100
Preamble to AUASB Standards

(Issued April 2006)

Issued by the Auditing and Assurance Standards Board.

Note from the Institute of Chartered Accountants Australia

This note, prepared by the technical editor, is not part of ASA 100.

Historical development

April 2006: The preamble was issued to explain the authority of the new force of law ASA Auditing Standards.

October 2009: ASA 101 issued containing revised interpretive information regarding Auditing Standards. ASA 100 must be read in conjunction with ASA 101 for engagements with financial reporting periods beginning on or after 1 January 2010.

Contents

Preface

Reasons for Issuing Auditing Standard ASA 100 *Preamble to AUASB Standards*

The Auditing and Assurance Standards Board (AUASB) issues Auditing Standard ASA 100 *Preamble to AUASB Standards*, due to the requirements of the legislative provisions explained below.

The *Corporate Law Economic Reform Program (Audit Reform and Corporate Disclosure) Act 2004* (the CLERP 9 Act) established the AUASB as an independent statutory body under section 227A of the *Australian Securities and Investments Commission Act 2001*, as from 1 July 2004. Under section 336 of the *Corporations Act 2001*, the AUASB may make Auditing Standards for the purposes of the corporations legislation. These Auditing Standards are legislative instruments under the *Legislative Instruments Act 2003*.

Main Features

This *Preamble to AUASB Standards* sets out the AUASB's intentions on how AUASB Standards are to be understood, interpreted and applied.

Operative Date

This Auditing Standard is operative for financial reporting periods commencing on or after 1 July 2006.

Authority Statement

The Auditing and Assurance Standards Board (AUASB) makes Auditing Standard ASA 100 *Preamble to AUASB Standards* as set out in paragraphs 1 to 49, pursuant to section 227B of the *Australian Securities and Investments Commission Act 2001* and section 336 of the *Corporations Act 2001*.

This Preamble is to be read in conjunction with AUASB Standards.

Dated 28 April 2006

M H Kelsall
Chairman – AUASB

Auditing Standard ASA 100

Preamble to AUASB Standards

Operative Date

1 **This Auditing Standard is operative for financial reporting periods commencing on or after 1 July 2006.**

Introduction

2 This Preamble sets out the intentions of the Auditing and Assurance Standards Board (AUASB), as to how AUASB Standards are to be understood, interpreted and applied. The AUASB issues AUASB Standards comprising:

(a) Auditing Standards ("ASAs");

(b) Standards on Review Engagements ("ASREs");

(c) Standards on Assurance Engagements ("ASAEs"); and

(d) Standards on Related Services ("ASRSs").

3 **An auditor shall apply AUASB Standards in conjunction with paragraphs 1 to 49 of this Preamble.**

4 The AUASB derives its functions and powers under section 227B of the *Australian Securities and Investments Commission Act 2001*. The AUASB:

(a) makes Auditing Standards under section 336 of the *Corporations Act 2001* (the Act) for the purposes of the corporations legislation; and

(b) formulates auditing and assurance standards for other purposes.

Auditing Standards made under Section 336 of the Act

Application

5 Auditing Standards apply to:

(a) an audit of a financial report for a financial year, or an audit or review[1] of a financial report for a half-year, prepared in accordance with Part 2M.3 of the Act;

(b) an audit of a financial report prepared for any other purpose; or

(c) a review by the independent auditor of the entity, of interim financial reports, prepared for any other purpose.[1]

6 Although Auditing Standards are written mainly in the context of an audit of a financial report, they apply also, as appropriate, to the audit of other financial information.

Enforcement

7 Section 307A of the Act requires auditors to conduct audits and reviews of the financial reports[2] prepared under Part 2M.3 of the Act, in accordance with Auditing Standards. AUASB Standards may have legal enforcement under legislation other than the Act.

---

1 For legislative purposes, ASRE 2410 *Review of an Interim Financial Report Performed by the Independent Auditor of the Entity,* is included in legislation as an "Auditing Standard". ASRE 2410 is to be applied in the review of a half-year financial report prepared under Part 2M.3 of the Act, and a review by the independent auditor of the entity of interim financial reports prepared for any other purpose.

2 Financial Reports required by Part 2M.3 of the Act are:

- the annual financial report; and
- the half-year financial report (for certain entities).

Auditing and Assurance Standards for Other Purposes

8 Auditing and assurance standards for other purposes consist of standards that are designed for subject-specific areas. They include, for example, assurance engagements that relate to:

- reviews (other than a review by the independent auditor of the entity, of interim financial information, including interim financial reports, prepared for other purposes);
- evaluating the efficiency and/or effectiveness of an entity's activities;
- prospective financial information; and
- the effectiveness of internal controls.

Authority of the Paragraphs in AUASB Standards

9 AUASB Standards consist of paragraphs that are either:

(a) mandatory requirements, identified in **bold-type** (black lettering); or

(b) explanatory guidance, identified in normal-type (grey lettering).

The paragraphs in AUASB Standards do not have equal authority.

Mandatory Requirements

10 Within each AUASB Standard, an auditor's obligations are stated as mandatory requirements that are identified in **bold-type**. The mandatory requirements consist of basic principles and essential procedures.

11 An auditor is required to comply with all mandatory requirements except when:

(a) application of the mandatory requirement(s) would relate to classes of transactions, account balances or disclosures that are immaterial;

(b) an auditor, using professional judgement, has chosen not to adopt a particular approach or procedure where the AUASB Standard permits or requires the auditor to choose from alternative approaches or procedures; or

(c) a mandatory requirement(s) is conditional and the condition is not present.

12 When one or more of the exceptions described in paragraph 11 exist, a mandatory requirement is not relevant and the auditor is not required to document the circumstances giving rise to the exception.

13 In the case of an audit engagement, the mandatory requirements of each Auditing Standard are to be applied in conjunction with the mandatory requirements of other relevant Auditing Standards.

14 In the case of a review engagement, the auditor is required to apply the mandatory requirements contained only in the specified standard applicable to that review engagement, in conjunction with this Preamble to AUASB Standards. There is no requirement to apply the mandatory requirements of other AUASB Standards.

Explanatory Guidance

15 Explanatory guidance:

(a) is to be used to improve knowledge and understanding of the scope and application of the basic principles and essential procedures (the mandatory requirements); and

(b) may include practical examples to assist in understanding the application of mandatory requirements.

16 Explanatory Guidance consists of suggested (or typical) audit procedures, practical examples and other explanatory details and procedures that are included for the purposes of understanding and fulfilling mandatory requirements. Explanatory guidance does not include all possible audit procedures that may be used in the application of mandatory requirements. The auditor may consider it necessary to perform alternative procedures to those contained within the explanatory guidance.

17 Explanatory Guidance does not create or extend mandatory requirements or the auditor's obligations under AUASB Standards.

Other Important Elements of AUASB Standards

18 In addition to mandatory requirements (see paragraphs 10 to 14 above), and explanatory guidance (see paragraphs 15 to 17 above), each AUASB Standard contains the following elements that impact on its application:

Authority Statement

19 The purposes of the Authority Statement[3] are to:

(a) link the issuance of each individual AUASB Standard to the mandating legislation;

(b) identify the paragraphs that comprise the AUASB Standard;

(c) set out the requirement to read the AUASB Standard in conjunction with this Preamble; and

(d) identify the mandatory requirements of the AUASB Standard.

Application Paragraphs

20 Each AUASB Standard contains application paragraphs that, in part or in whole, form part of the mandatory requirements.

21 The application paragraphs identify the scope of the AUASB Standard.

22 Auditing Standards made under section 336 of the Act[4] contain mandatory application paragraphs relating to:

(a) an audit of a financial report for a financial year, or an audit of a financial report for a half-year, in accordance with Part 2M.3 of the *Corporations Act 2001*; and

(b) an audit of a financial report for any other purpose.

23 When an Auditing Standard is used for the audit of financial information that is not in the form of a financial report, the application paragraph in that Auditing Standard is excluded from the mandatory requirements.

24 Although the Auditing Standards are written mainly in the context of an external audit of a financial report,[5] they apply also, adapted as necessary, to the audit of other financial information.

Operative Date

25 The operative date stipulates the date from which the AUASB Standard is to be applied. The operative date is stated in relation to the commencement date of the financial reporting period. The requirements of an AUASB Standard remain in force until:

(a) the operative date of any amendment to those requirements;

(b) in relevant circumstances, the early adoption of such amendment; or

(c) the AUASB Standard is withdrawn by the AUASB.

26 When early adoption of an AUASB Standard is allowed, a statement to that effect is included in the operative date paragraph of the AUASB Standard.

Definitions

27 Definitions, contained within AUASB Standards, and/or contained within the *AUASB Glossary*, as issued from time to time, are to be applied in the interpretation of AUASB Standards.

---

3 With the exception of the Authority Statement to this *Preamble to AUASB Standards*, the purpose of which is to link to mandating legislation, to identify the paragraphs comprising the standard and to set out the requirement to read the *Preamble to AUASB Standards* in conjunction with the AUASB Standards.

4 With the exception of ASRE 2410 *Review of an Interim Financial Report Performed by the Independent Auditor of the Entity* and ASA 100 *Preamble to AUASB Standards*.

5 Reference to a 'financial report' includes not only a financial report as defined under Part 2M.3 of the Act, but also a financial report prepared for other purposes.

Conformity Paragraphs

28 The Conformity paragraphs explain the relationship of an AUASB Standard with its equivalent international standard issued by the International Auditing and Assurance Standards Board (IAASB) of the International Federation of Accountants (IFAC). The AUASB takes the position that an AUASB Standard conforms to the equivalent international standard when:

(a) the mandatory requirements of the AUASB Standard correspond with those in the equivalent international standard or the AUASB Standard contains additional mandatory requirements; and

(b) the explanatory guidance is substantially the same as the equivalent international standard or the AUASB Standard contains additional explanatory guidance.

29 The Conformity paragraphs in AUASB Standards include necessary differences from the equivalent international standard relating to terminology, referencing and Australian regulatory requirements.

30 When an AUASB Standard and the equivalent international standard conform, the Conformity paragraphs contain a statement to this effect.

31 When an AUASB Standard and the equivalent international standard are not equivalent, the Conformity paragraphs detail the main differences.

32 The Conformity paragraphs in each AUASB Standard assist the auditor to determine to what extent (if any) compliance with AUASB Standards might enable also the engagement to be conducted in compliance with international standards. It is the responsibility of the auditor to determine which standards apply to the particular engagement and circumstances. Furthermore, where appropriate, the Conformity paragraphs contain the following sentence:

"Compliance with this Standard enables compliance with the equivalent international standard".

Type of Entity

33 AUASB Standards are:

(a) neutral with respect to the audited or reviewed entity's sector and size; and

(b) intended to be applied, as appropriate, to all audit, review, assurance and related service engagements conducted by an external firm in both the public and private sectors.

34 If necessary, entity sector and size considerations are included, and identified, in the body of the relevant AUASB Standard.

35 AUASB Standards do not take into account any specific circumstances affecting entities that are subject to audit or review.

Applying AUASB Standards

Professional Judgement

36 AUASB Standards are principles-based and the auditor is expected to use professional judgement in light of the given circumstances in order to achieve the objectives of the audit, review or other assurance engagement. Professional judgement is exercised:

(a) in applying relevant mandatory requirements;

(b) in determining whether any of the exceptions, described in paragraph 11 of this Preamble, apply; and

(c) in deciding how and whether to carry out procedures or actions, described in explanatory guidance, in light of the circumstances and consistent with the objectives of the Standards.

37 The use of professional judgement is required and applies in particular to:

(a) the determination and application of materiality;

(b) compliance with ethical requirements relevant to audit and review engagements;

(c) the selection and scope of appropriate audit/review procedures;

(d) the assessment and evaluation of available options and results, including the persuasiveness of audit/review evidence; and

(e) the extent of documentation of audit/review plans, procedures, results, conclusions and communications.

Ethics

38 The AUASB takes the view that inclusion in AUASB Standards of references to relevant ethical requirements is important to:

(a) ensure a high level of public confidence in the audit and review functions;

(b) enhance the rigour of AUASB Standards; and

(c) ensure conformity between AUASB Standards and the Standards issued by IAASB.

Accordingly, references to compliance with relevant ethical requirements are included in certain mandatory requirements and explanatory guidance paragraphs in AUASB Standards.

39 The relevant ethical requirements relating to audit engagements referred to in Auditing Standards are contained in the respective codes of professional conduct of the professional accounting bodies in Australia.[6] The codes of professional conduct are aligned with the equivalent international code.[7]

Inability to Comply with Mandatory Requirements

40 Where, in rare and exceptional circumstances, factors outside the auditor's control prevent the auditor from complying with an essential procedure contained in a relevant mandatory requirement, the auditor is required:

(a) if possible, to perform appropriate alternative audit procedures; and

(b) in accordance with ASA 230 *Audit Documentation*, to document in the working papers:

(i) the circumstances surrounding the inability to comply;

(ii) the reasons for the inability to comply; and

(iii) justification of how alternative audit procedures achieve the objective(s) of the mandatory requirement.

When the auditor is unable to perform appropriate alternative audit procedures, the auditor is required to consider the implications for the auditor's report.

Auditing Standards Made Under Section 336 of the *Corporations Act 2001*

41 This Preamble to AUASB Standards is written in the context of the Auditing Standards issued pursuant to section 336 of the Act, and is relevant to understanding and applying AUASB Standards issued for other purposes.

42 The initial Auditing Standards, issued as legislative instruments, are operative for audits and reviews pertaining to financial reporting periods commencing on or after 1 July 2006.

43 In fulfilling its standard-setting function, the AUASB develops Auditing Standards that have a clear public interest focus and are of a high quality. Wherever possible, the AUASB uses, as appropriate, International Standards on Auditing (ISA) as a base from which to develop Auditing Standards. The Auditing Standards are designed to strengthen confidence in the assurance provided by an audit or review.

44 The AUASB has adopted certain drafting principles (see below) in making Auditing Standards under the Australian regulatory environment, wherein the Auditing Standards are legally enforceable and registered as legislative instruments under the *Legislative Instruments Act 2003*.

---

6 In Australia, the codes of conduct of the professional accounting bodies, as issued from time to time, are:

- CPA Australia and The Institute of Chartered Accountants in Australia, *Joint Code of Professional Conduct*; and
- National Institute of Accountants, *Pronouncements of the Board of Directors – Code of Ethics*.

7 See IFAC Code of Ethics for Professional Accountants.

AUASB Drafting Approach

45 The following drafting principles and conventions have been adopted to implement the objectives discussed above:

(a) mandatory requirements and explanatory guidance are shown in separate paragraphs;

(b) paragraphs containing mandatory requirements are shown in **bold-type** text;

(c) the word 'shall' is used within mandatory requirements paragraphs to denote the obligations an auditor is required to comply with in the conduct of an audit or review;

(d) the present tense of verbs is used in the explanatory guidance when it is the best form of expression. Use of the present tense does not create or imply mandatory requirements. The present tense is used in examples and other explanatory guidance that relate to professional judgement and professional scepticism; and

(e) practical examples are used in explanatory guidance. Practical examples do not constitute basic principles or essential procedures (mandatory requirements).

46 The drafting utilised in AUASB Standards reflects the AUASB's intention that:

(a) the auditor is required to exercise professional judgement, as described in paragraph 36, according to the given circumstances; and

(b) explanatory guidance does not extend:

(i) mandatory requirements; or

(ii) the auditor's obligations under AUASB Standards.

47 AUASB Standards, as mentioned above, are based commonly on their ISA-equivalent standard. For each AUASB Standard, obligations implied within the explanatory guidance of the equivalent ISA have been:

(a) when appropriate, elevated to a mandatory requirement (**bold-type**); or

(b) linked to a mandatory requirement(s), thereby demonstrating the AUASB's intention that the explanatory guidance is interpreted in the context of the relevant mandatory requirement; or

(c) prefaced by inserting the word 'ordinarily' as a qualifier (see below).

Words and Phrases

48 The following words and phrases are used in AUASB Standards for the respective stated purposes (alphabetically):

(a) *explanatory guidance* means suggested or typical audit procedures, practical examples and other explanatory details and procedures that are included for the purposes of understanding, and complying with, mandatory requirements. Explanatory guidance does not create or extend mandatory requirements or the auditor's obligations under AUASB Standards.

(b) *'in accordance with...the auditor is required to...'* means explanatory guidance that is directly linked to a mandatory requirement, either in the same AUASB Standard or in another AUASB Standard. The phrase is used only where the wording in the explanatory guidance is identical to that in the mandatory requirement.

(c) *including* means a list of items or examples is provided but the list does not purport to contain all relevant items or examples and intentionally is not exhaustive.

(d) *mandatory requirements* means relevant basic principles and essential procedures that must be applied in order for the audit or review engagement to comply with AUASB Standards.

(e) *ordinarily* means the explanatory guidance indicates practical methods or means by which mandatory requirements may be complied with and is to be read in the following context:

(i) where the word 'ordinarily' is used, the auditor exercises professional judgement in considering:

- whether the noted circumstances apply to the current audit, review or other assurance engagement; and
- if so, whether the suggested procedures are appropriate to perform; or
- where there are alternative procedures which are more appropriate, whether these alternative procedures are to be performed.

(ii) the word 'ordinarily' does not create a rebuttable presumption nor a mandatory requirement.

(f) *shall* means an imperative obligation on auditors when appearing in **bold-type** mandatory requirements. In certain circumstances, imperative obligations are legally binding and enforceable.

(g) *'Under... the auditor needs to...'* means words contained within the explanatory guidance that highlight a linkage between mandatory requirements (**bold-type**) and the relevant explanatory guidance that:

(i) in part, or in whole, restates the meaning of the mandatory requirement; and

(ii) may describe audit or review procedures, more detailed than those contained in the relevant mandatory requirement. However, these described audit or review procedures do not create or extend mandatory requirements.

Furthermore, an auditor may judge it necessary, in order to comply with the relevant mandatory requirement, to:

- perform alternative audit or review procedures in place of some or all of those described in the explanatory guidance; or
- perform some, but not all, of the audit or review procedures described in the explanatory guidance.

The purpose of the linkage between the mandatory requirements and the relevant explanatory guidance is to:

- direct the auditor to the relevant mandatory requirement(s); and
- emphasise that interpretation of the explanatory guidance is to be made in the context of that mandatory requirement.

❖ ❖ ❖

Conformity with International Standards

49 There is no corresponding Standard issued by IAASB.

ASA 101

Preamble to Australian Auditing Standards

(Reissued October 2009: amended and compiled June 2011)

Issued by the Auditing and Assurance Standards Board.

Note from the Institute of Chartered Accountants Australia

This note, prepared by the technical editor, is not part of the Auditing Standards ASA 101.

Historical development

October 2009: ASA 101 issued as part of the AUASB's Clarity Project. It amends ASA 100 'Preamble to AUASB Standards (04/06)' to take into account the Clarity Project and reflects new material issued, such as ASQC 1. It has no international equivalent.

June 2011: ASA 101 updated for editorial amendments contained in ASA 2011-1 'Amendments to Australian Auditing Standards'.

Contents

ASA

Compilation Details

Auditing Standard ASA 101 *Preamble to Australian Auditing Standards* as Amended

This compilation takes into account amendments made up to and including 27 June 2011 and was prepared on 27 June 2011 by the Auditing and Assurance Standards Board (AUASB).

This compilation is not a separate Auditing Standard made by the AUASB. Instead, it is a representation of ASA 101 (October 2009) as amended by another Auditing Standard which is listed in the Table below.

Table of Standards

Standard	Date made	Operative date
ASA 101	27 October 2009	1 January 2010
ASA 2011-1	27 June 2011	1 July 2011

Table of Amendments

Paragraph affected	How affected	By … [paragraph]
Headers - Pages 8-12	Amended	ASA 2011-1 [14]
3	Amended	ASA 2011-1 [15]

Preface

[Preface extracted from the original Auditing Standard issued 27 October 2009]

Reasons for Issuing Auditing Standard ASA 101 *Preamble to Australian Auditing Standards*

The Auditing and Assurance Standards Board (AUASB) issues Auditing Standard ASA 101 *Preamble to Australian Auditing Standards* pursuant to the requirements of the legislative provisions and the Strategic Direction explained below.

The AUASB is an independent statutory board of the Australian Government established under section 227A of the *Australian Securities and Investments Commission Act 2001*, as amended (ASIC Act). Under section 336 of the *Corporations Act 2001*, the AUASB may make Auditing Standards for the purposes of the corporations legislation. These Auditing Standards are legislative instruments under the *Legislative Instruments Act 2003*.

Under the Strategic Direction given to the AUASB by the Financial Reporting Council (FRC), the AUASB is required to have regard to any programme initiated by the International Auditing and Assurance Standards Board (IAASB) for the revision and enhancement of the International Standards on Auditing (ISAs) and to make appropriate consequential amendments to the Australian Auditing Standards. Accordingly, the AUASB has decided to revise and redraft the Australian Auditing Standards using the equivalent redrafted ISAs. The revised Australian Auditing Standards are operative for engagements with financial reporting periods commencing on or after 1 January 2010; and for firms required to establish systems of quality control by 1 January 2010.

ASA 101 *Preamble to Australian Auditing Standards*

As the Australian Auditing Standards are legally enforceable, the AUASB considers it necessary for an interpretive document to form part of the suite of standards. The purpose of ASA 101 *Preamble to Australian Auditing Standards* is to deal with matters that are additional to those dealt with elsewhere in the Australian Auditing Standards.

ASA 101 does not replace or amend ASA 100 *Preamble to AUASB Standards*, which continues to be applicable to all AUASB standards other than:

- the Australian Auditing Standards operative for engagements with financial reporting periods commencing on or after 1 January 2010; and
- the Auditing Standard for firms required to establish systems of quality control by 1 January 2010.

ASA 101 relates to the Australian legislative environment and accordingly, there is no equivalent ISA.

Main Features

This Auditing Standard sets out mandatory components additional to those found elsewhere in the Australian Auditing Standards.

This Auditing Standard:

(a) sets out the authority of paragraphs in Australian Auditing Standards;

(b) lists those parts of the *Corporations Act 2001* to which the "Application" paragraph in each Auditing Standard refers; and

(c) describes the circumstances when an auditor need not document the reasons why a requirement is not relevant.

Authority Statement

Auditing Standard ASA 101 *Preamble to Australian Auditing Standards* (as amended at 27 June 2011) is set out in paragraphs 1 to A2.

This Auditing Standard is to be read in conjunction with the Australian Auditing Standards, operative on and after 1 January 2010.

Dated: 27 June 2011

M H Kelsall
Chairman - AUASB

Auditing Standard 101

The Auditing and Assurance Standards Board (AUASB) made Auditing Standard ASA 101 *Preamble to Australian Auditing Standards,* pursuant to section 227B of the *Australian Securities and Investments Commission Act 2001* and section 336 of the *Corporations Act 2001*, on 27 October 2009.

This compiled version of ASA 101 incorporates subsequent amendments contained in another Auditing Standard made by the AUASB up to and including 27 June 2011 (see Compilation Details).

Auditing Standard ASA 101

Preamble to Australian Auditing Standards

ASA

Application

1. This Auditing Standard applies to:
   (a) an audit of a financial report for a financial year, or an audit or a review of a financial report for a half-year, in accordance with the *Corporations Act 2001*;
   (b) an audit of a financial report, or a complete set of financial statements, for any other purpose;
   (c) a review, by the independent auditor of the entity, of a financial report, or a complete set of financial statements, comprising historical financial information, for any other purpose; and
   (d) a firm[1] required to comply with ASQC 1 *Quality Control for Firms that Perform Audits and Reviews of Financial Reports and Other Financial Information, and Other Assurance Engagements*.
2. This Auditing Standard also applies, as appropriate, to an audit of other historical financial information.

Operative Date

3. This Auditing Standard is operative for engagements with financial reporting periods commencing on or after 1 January 2010, and for firms required to establish systems of quality control in compliance with ASQC 1 by 1 January 2010.
   [Note: For operative dates of paragraphs changed or added by an amending Standard, see Compilation Details.]
4. This Auditing Standard supersedes interpretive information contained in ASA 100 *Preamble to AUASB Standards* to the extent that ASA 100 applies to the Australian Auditing Standards.

Introduction

Scope of this Auditing Standard

5. The purpose of this Auditing Standard is to set out mandatory components additional to those included elsewhere in the Australian Auditing Standards that are operative for:
   - financial reporting periods commencing on or after 1 January 2010; and
   - firms required to establish systems of quality control by 1 January 2010.
6. ASA 100 *Preamble to AUASB Standards* applies to all AUASB Standards other than the Australian Auditing Standards referred to in paragraph 5 of this Auditing Standard.

Objective

7. The objective of the auditor and the firm is to use this Auditing Standard in order to understand, interpret and apply the Australian Auditing Standards that are operative for engagements with financial reporting periods commencing on or after 1 January 2010; and for firms required to establish systems of quality control by 1 January 2010.

1 See ASQC 1 paragraphs Aus 4.1 and 12.6.

Definitions

8. For purposes of the Australian Auditing Standards, the following terms have the meanings attributed below:
   (a) Auditing Standards means auditing standards made under section 336 of the *Corporations Act 2001* (the "Act"), and include:
      (i) ASQC 1 *Quality Control for Firms that Perform Audits and Reviews of Financial Reports and Other Financial Information, and Other Assurance Engagements*; and
      (ii) ASRE 2410 *Review of a Financial Report Performed by the Independent Auditor of the Entity*.
   (b) Australian Auditing Standards means the suite of auditing standards issued by the AUASB, comprising:
      - Auditing Standards made under section 336 of the *Corporations Act 2001*;
      - ASA 805 *Special Considerations—Audits of Single Financial Statements and Specific Elements, Accounts or Items of a Financial Statement;* and
      - ASA 810 *Engagements to Report on Summary Financial Statements*.

Requirements

Authority of the Paragraphs in Australian Auditing Standards

9. The auditor shall apply the mandatory components of the Australian Auditing Standards when conducting an audit or review in accordance with those Standards. The mandatory components are included in each Auditing Standard under the headings listed below:
   (i) Application (paragraph Aus 0.1).
   (ii) Operative Date.
   (iii) Objective(s).
   (iv) Definition(s).
   (v) Requirements.
10. The auditor shall consider the whole text of an Auditing Standard to understand, interpret and apply the mandatory components. The explanatory material is included in each Auditing Standard under the headings listed below:
   (i) Application (paragraph Aus 0.2).
   (ii) Introduction.
   (iii) Application and Other Explanatory Material.
   (iv) Conformity with International Standards on Auditing.
   (v) Appendices.

   Explanatory material does not create or extend mandatory components. (Ref: Para. A1)

Engagements under the *Corporations Act 2001*

11. The "Application" paragraph in each Auditing Standard that refers to audits or reviews conducted in accordance with the *Corporations Act 2001* applies specifically to:
   (a) an audit or a review conducted under Part 2M.3 of the Act; and
   (b) an audit conducted under Part 7.8 of the Act.

Compliance with Requirements

12. When, in the circumstances of the audit, a requirement is not relevant due to the conditions described in ASA 200 *Overall Objectives of the Independent Auditor and the Conduct of an Audit in Accordance with Australian Auditing Standards*, the auditor is not required to document the reason(s) why the requirement is not relevant. (Ref: Para. A2)

❖ ❖ ❖

Application and Other Explanatory Material

Authority of the Paragraphs in Australian Auditing Standards (Ref: Para. 10)

A1. Included within the requirements section of a standard are references to paragraphs in the "Application and Other Explanatory Material" section of the standard. Such references do not extend or create requirements.

Compliance with Requirements (Ref: Para. 12)

A2. Under paragraph 12, an auditor need not document the reasons why a requirement is not relevant. However, where in rare and exceptional circumstances, factors outside the auditor's control prevent the auditor from complying with an essential procedure contained within a relevant requirement, the auditor is required under ASA 230 or ASRE 2410[2], as applicable, to document:

(a) the circumstances surrounding the inability to comply;

(b) the reasons for the inability to comply; and

(c) justification of how alternative procedures achieve the objectives of the requirement.

❖ ❖ ❖

Conformity with International Standards on Auditing

This Auditing Standard relates to the Australian legislative environment and accordingly there is no equivalent International Standard on Auditing (ISA) issued by the International Auditing and Assurance Standards Board (IAASB), an independent standard-setting board of the International Federation of Accountants (IFAC).

Compliance with this Auditing Standard enables compliance with the ISAs.

2 See ASA 230 *Audit Documentation* and ASRE 2410 *Review of a Financial Report Performed by the Independent Auditor of the Entity*.

ASA 102
Compliance with Ethical Requirements when Performing Audits, Reviews and Other Assurance Engagements

(Issued October 2009: amended and compiled June 2011)

Issued by the Auditing and Assurance Standards Board.

Note from the Institute of Chartered Accountants Australia

This note, prepared by the technical editor, is not part of ASA 102.

Historical development

October 2009: ASA 102 issued as part of the AUASB's Clarity Project. The purpose of ASA 102 is to enable references to relevant ethical requirements in other AUASB Standards to remain current and it also provides guidance for auditors and assurance practitioners on the application of APES 110 'Code of Ethics for Professional Accountants'. It has no international equivalent.

June 2011: ASA 102 updated for amendments in ASA 2011-1 'Amendments to Australian Auditing Standards', consequent to the reissue of APES 110 'Code of Ethics for Professional Accountants' in December 2010.

Contents

ASA

Compilation Details

Auditing Standard ASA 102 *Compliance with Ethical Requirements when Performing Audits, Reviews and Other Assurance Engagements*

This compilation takes into account amendments made up to and including 27 June 2011 and was prepared on 27 June 2011 by the Auditing and Assurance Standards Board (AUASB).

This compilation is not a separate Auditing Standard made by the AUASB. Instead, it is a representation of ASA 102 (October 2009) as amended by another Auditing Standard which is listed in the Table below.

Table of Standards

Standard	Date made	Operative date
ASA 102	27 October 2009	1 January 2010
ASA 2011-1	27 June 2011	1 July 2011

Table of Amendments

Paragraph affected	How affected	By … [paragraph]
4(e)	Amended	ASA 2011-1 [9]
A1	Amended	ASA 2011-1 [10]

Preface

[Preface extracted from the original Auditing Standard issued 27 October 2009]

Reasons for Issuing Auditing Standard ASA 102 *Compliance with Ethical Requirements when Performing Audits, Reviews and Other Assurance Engagements*

The Auditing and Assurance Standards Board (AUASB) issues Auditing Standard ASA 102 *Compliance with Ethical Requirements when Performing Audits, Reviews and Other Assurance Engagements* pursuant to the requirements of the legislative provisions and the Strategic Direction explained below.

The AUASB is an independent statutory board of the Australian Government established under section 227A of the *Australian Securities and Investments Commission Act 2001*, as amended (ASIC Act). Under section 336 of the *Corporations Act 2001*, the AUASB may make Australian Auditing Standards for the purposes of the corporations legislation. These Auditing Standards are legislative instruments under the *Legislative Instruments Act 2003*.

Under the Strategic Direction given to the AUASB by the Financial Reporting Council (FRC), the AUASB is required to have regard to any programme initiated by the International Auditing and Assurance Standards Board (IAASB) for the revision and enhancement of the International Standards on Auditing (ISAs) and to make appropriate consequential amendments to the Australian Auditing Standards. Accordingly, the AUASB has decided to revise and redraft the Australian Auditing Standards using the equivalent redrafted ISAs.

ASA 102 is an Auditing Standard made under the *Corporations Act 2001* for Australian legislative purposes. ASA 102 enables references to relevant ethical requirements in other AUASB Standards to remain current as they are explicitly linked to ASA 102. Under ASA 102 the auditor, assurance practitioner, engagement quality control reviewer, and firm are to have regard to the applicable requirements of APES 110 *Code of Ethics for Professional Accountants* issued by the Accounting Professional and Ethical Standards Board (February 2008), which are to be taken into account in determining whether relevant ethical requirements have been met. The AUASB proposes to amend or re-make ASA 102 whenever APES 110 is amended or revised, to ensure that such cross references remain current and to eliminate the need to amend other AUASB Standards.

The requirement and application and other explanatory material in ASA 102 have been drawn from several standards of the IAASB.

The AUASB has made ASA 102 in a format that is consistent with the other Australian Auditing Standards operative for financial reporting periods commencing on or after 1 January 2010 and for firms required to establish systems of quality control in compliance with ASQC 1 *Quality Control for Firms that Perform Audits and Reviews of Financial Reports and Other Financial Information, and Other Assurance Engagements* by 1 January 2010.

Main Features

This Auditing Standard establishes a requirement and provides application and other explanatory material regarding the responsibilities of the auditor, the assurance practitioner, and the firm for compliance with relevant ethical requirements when performing audits, reviews and other assurance engagements.

Authority Statement

Auditing Standard ASA 102 *Compliance with Ethical Requirements when Performing Audits, Reviews and Other Assurance Engagements* (as amended at 27 June 2011) is set out in paragraphs 1 to A7.

This Auditing Standard is to be read in conjunction with ASA 101 *Preamble to Australian Auditing Standards*, which sets out the intentions of the AUASB on how the Australian Auditing Standards, operative for financial reporting periods commencing on or after 1 January 2010, are to be understood, interpreted and applied.

Dated: 27 June 2011

M H Kelsall
Chairman - AUASB

Auditing Standard ASA 102

The Auditing and Assurance Standards Board (AUASB) made Auditing Standard ASA 102 *Compliance with Ethical Requirements when Performing Audits, Reviews and Other Assurance Engagements*, pursuant to section 227B of the *Australian Securities and Investments Commission Act 2001* and section 336 of the *Corporations Act 2001*, on 27 October 2009.

This compiled version of ASA 102 incorporates subsequent amendments contained in another Auditing Standard made by the AUASB up to and including 27 June 2011 (see Compilation Details).

Auditing Standard ASA 102

Compliance with Ethical Requirements when Performing Audits, Reviews and Other Assurance Engagements

Application

1. This Auditing Standard applies to:
   (a) an audit of a financial report for a financial year, or an audit or a review of a financial report for a half-year, in accordance with the *Corporations Act 2001*;
   (b) an audit or review of a financial report, or a complete set of financial statements, for any other purpose;
   (c) an audit or review of other financial information;
   (d) other assurance engagements; and
   (e) a firm required to comply with ASQC 1 *Quality Control for Firms that Perform Audits and Reviews of Financial Reports and Other Financial Information, and Other Assurance Engagements*.

Operative Date

2. This Auditing Standard is operative for engagements with reporting periods commencing on or after 1 January 2010 and for firms required to establish systems of quality control in compliance with ASQC 1 by 1 January 2010.

[Note: For operative dates of paragraphs changed or added by an amending Standard, see Compilation Details.]

Objective

3. The objective of the auditor, assurance practitioner, engagement quality control reviewer and firm is to comply with relevant ethical requirements, including those pertaining to independence, relating to audits, reviews and other assurance engagements.

Definitions

4. The following terms have the meanings attributed below:
   (a) Assurance practitioner means a person or an organisation, whether in public practice, industry, commerce or the public sector, providing assurance services.[1]
   (b) Auditor means the person or persons conducting the audit, usually the engagement partner or other members of the engagement team, or, as applicable, the firm. Where an Auditing Standard expressly intends that a requirement or responsibility be fulfilled by the engagement partner, the term "engagement partner" rather than "auditor" is used. "Engagement partner" and "firm" are to be read as referring to their public sector equivalents where relevant.[2]

1 See ASQC 1.

2 See ASA 200 *Overall Objectives of the Independent Auditor and the Conduct of an Audit in Accordance with Australian Auditing Standards*.

(c) *Engagement quality control reviewer* means a partner, other person in the firm, suitably qualified external person, or a team made up of such individuals, none of whom is part of the engagement team, with sufficient and appropriate experience and authority to objectively evaluate the significant judgements the engagement team made and the conclusions it reached in formulating the auditor's report.

(d) *Firm* means a sole practitioner, partnership or corporation or other entity of assurance practitioners. "Firm" should be read as referring to a public sector equivalent where relevant.[3]

(e) *Relevant ethical requirements* means ethical requirements that apply to the auditor, assurance practitioner, engagement quality control reviewer and firm. In Australia, these include the applicable requirements of APES 110 *Code of Ethics for Professional Accountants* issued by the Accounting Professional and Ethical Standards Board (February 2008 and December 2010 as applicable), the applicable provisions of the *Corporations Act 2001* and other applicable law or regulation.

Requirement

Compliance with Relevant Ethical Requirements (Ref: Para. A1-A7)

5. The auditor, assurance practitioner, engagement quality control reviewer, and firm shall comply with relevant ethical requirements, including those pertaining to independence, when performing audits, reviews and other assurance engagements.

❖ ❖ ❖

Application and Other Explanatory Material

Compliance with Relevant Ethical Requirements (Ref: Para. 5)

A1. The auditor, assurance practitioner, engagement quality control reviewer, and firm are to have regard to the applicable requirements of APES 110 *Code of Ethics for Professional Accountants,* issued by the Accounting Professional and Ethical Standards Board (February 2008 and December 2010 as applicable), which are to be taken into account in determining whether relevant ethical requirements referred to in paragraph 5 of this Auditing Standard have been met. In relation to audits and reviews undertaken in accordance with the *Corporations Act 2001*, the provisions of Division 3 Part 2M.4 of the Act may also apply.

A2. APES 110 establishes the fundamental principles of professional ethics and provides a conceptual framework for applying those principles.

A3. The fundamental principles of professional ethics, as described in APES 110, include:

(a) Integrity;

(b) Objectivity;

(c) Professional competence and due care;

(d) Confidentiality; and

(e) Professional behaviour.

A4. APES 110 illustrates how the conceptual framework is to be applied in specific situations. It provides examples of safeguards that may be appropriate to address threats to compliance with the fundamental principles and also provides examples of situations where safeguards are not available to address the threats.

A5. In the case of an audit engagement, it is in the public interest and required by APES 110, that the auditor be independent of the entity subject to the audit. APES 110 describes independence as comprising both independence of mind and independence in appearance. The auditor's independence from the entity safeguards the auditor's ability to form an audit opinion without being affected by influences that might compromise that opinion. Independence enhances the auditor's ability to act with integrity, to be objective and to maintain an attitude of professional scepticism.

3 See ASQC 1.

A6. The fundamental principles in APES 110 are reinforced in particular by:

- The leadership of the firm;
- Education and training;
- Monitoring; and
- A process for dealing with non-compliance.

A7. The definitions of terms in APES 110 may differ from the definitions of those terms in Australian Auditing Standards, including terms defined in ASQC 1 and ASA 220 *Quality Control for an Audit of a Financial Report and Other Historical Financial Information.*

For example, APES 110 defines the "firm" as:

(a) A sole practitioner, partnership, corporation or other entity of professional accountants;

(b) An entity that controls such parties through ownership, management or other means;

(c) An entity controlled by such parties through ownership, management or other means; and

(d) An auditor-general's office or department.

whereas ASQC 1 defines the "firm" as:

"Firm means a sole practitioner, partnership or corporation or other entity of assurance practitioners. "Firm" should be read as referring to a public sector equivalent where relevant".

APES 110 also provides guidance in relation to the terms "network" and "network firm."

In complying with the requirement of this Auditing Standard, the definitions used in APES 110 apply in so far as is necessary to interpret the ethical requirements of ASQC 1 and ASA 220.

❖ ❖ ❖

Conformity with International Standards on Auditing

This Auditing Standard has been made for Australian legislative purposes and accordingly, there is no single equivalent International Standard on Auditing issued by the International Auditing and Assurance Standards Board (IAASB).

However, the requirement and application and other explanatory material in this Auditing Standard have been drawn from ISQC 1 *Quality Control for Firms that Perform Audits and Reviews of Financial Statements and Other Assurance and Related Services Engagements*, ISA 200 *Overall Objectives of the Independent Auditor and the Conduct of an Audit in Accordance with International Standards on Auditing* and ISA 220 *Quality Control for an Audit of Financial Statements*, as issued by the IAASB (April 2009), as listed in the following table:

ASA 102	International Standards
Paragraph 5 (requirement)	ISA 200 paragraph 14 ISA 220 paragraphs 9-11 ISQC 1 paragraph 20
Paragraph A1	ISQC 200 paragraph A14
Paragraph A2	ISQC 200 paragraph A15
Paragraph A3	ISQC 1 paragraph A7 ISQC 200 paragraph A15 ISQC 220 paragraph A4
Paragraph A4	ISQC 1 paragraph A8

ASA 102	International Standards
Paragraph A5	ISA 200 paragraph A16
Paragraph A6	ISQC 1 paragraph A9
Paragraph A7	ISQC 1 paragraph A10 ISA 220 paragraph A5

Compliance with this Auditing Standard, together with other Australian Auditing Standards, enables compliance with the ISAs and ISQC 1.

ASA 200

Overall Objectives of the Independent Auditor and the Conduct of an Audit in Accordance with Australian Auditing Standards

(Reissued October 2009)

Issued by the Auditing and Assurance Standards Board.

Note from the Institute of Chartered Accountants Australia

This note, prepared by the technical editor, is not part of ASA 200.

Historical development

October 1974: The first publication dealing with Auditing Standards was CS 1 which was issued by The Institute of Chartered Accountants in Australia, effective from date of issue. It was revised and reissued in, and was effective from, February 1977.

August 1979: Reissued, without amendment, as AUS 1. Further minor amendments made in 1980, 1983, 1987, 1989 and 1990.

February 1991: ED 39 'The Audit Report on a General Purpose Financial Report' issued by the AuSB, with comments sought by 30 April 1991. This exposure draft also included a proposed change to AUS 1 which would refine the description of the financial reporting framework within which the auditor's opinion is formed. The proposed change required the auditor to form an overall conclusion as to whether the financial report was prepared in accordance with Statements of Accounting Concepts and Accounting Standards and any relevant regulatory requirements such that the view presented by the financial report as a whole was consistent, in all material respects, with the auditor's understanding of the operations of the entity.

June 1992: ED 47 'The Audit Report on a General Purpose Financial Report' issued by the AuSB. This exposure draft replaced ED 39 'The Audit Report on a General Purpose Financial Report' issued in February 1991, due to a significant change of principle as a result of the comments received on ED 39. The November 1990 version of AUS 1 (para. 28) allowed an auditor, in rare circumstances, to express an unqualified opinion when there had been a departure from an Accounting Standard, or express a qualified opinion because of compliance with an Accounting Standard. ED 47 proposed that a departure from an Accounting Standard should in all cases result in a qualified opinion. ED 47 also proposed that a qualified opinion should be issued when the notes to the financial statements included additional disclosures which indicated that the body of the financial statements was misleading because of the application of an Accounting Standard.

March 1993: ED 45 issued as AUP 12 'Consideration of the Internal Control Structure and its Impact on Risk Assessment in a Financial Report Audit'.

July 1993: ED 47 issued as AUP 3 'The Audit Report on a General Purpose Financial Report'. AUS 1 updated for the consequential changes to auditing standards contained in the revisions to AUP 12 and AUP 3, and reissued in September 1993.

February 1994: AUS 1 'Statement of Auditing Standards' reissued to reflect the removal of the mandatory status of Statements of Accounting Concepts (SACs), effective 31 December 1993.

June 1994: The International Auditing Practices Committee (IAPC) of the International Federation of Accountants (IFAC) approved the issuance of a codified set of International Standards of Auditing (ISAs). The relevant international pronouncement was ISA 200 'Objective and General Principles Governing an Audit of Financial Statements'. The AuASB issued ED 53 'Codification and Revision of Auditing Pronouncements: AUS 202 Objective and General Principles Governing an Audit of a Financial Report (AUS 1)'.

June 1995: AUS 1 reissued. During 1995, Miscellaneous Professional Statement APS 1 was amended and reissued as 'Conformity with Accounting Standards and UIG Consensus Views' to give professional authority to the UIG Consensus Views. As a result of the amendment to APS 1, AUS 1 'Statement of Auditing Standards' and Statement of Auditing Practice AUP 3 'The Audit Report on a General Purpose Financial Report' were revised to reflect the status of UIG Consensus Views.

October 1995: The Australian Auditing Standards and Auditing Guidance Statements released. The status of these is explained in APS 1.1 'Conformity With Auditing Standards'. These Standards became operative for the first reporting period commencing on or after 1 July 1996 and later reporting periods, although earlier application was encouraged. AUS 1 'Statement of Auditing Standards' replaced by AUS 202 'Objective and General Principles Governing an Audit of a Financial Report'.

July 2002: AUS/AGS Omnibus 3 'Miscellaneous Amendments to AUSs and AGSs' issued by the AuASB, operative from date of issue. AUS 202 reissued by the Board to reflect these changes.

February 2004: AUS 202 reissued to include a revised audit risk model. Based on ISA 200 of the same name.

April 2006: ASA 200 was issued as a legally enforceable Standard to replace AUS 202. It is based on ISA 200 of the same name.

June 2007: ASA 200 compiled and republished to reflect the changes to the audit report in ASA 700 introduced by Omnibus ASA 2007-1.

October 2009: ASA 200 reissued as part of the AUASB's Clarity Project. It includes a number of new definitions and expicitly states that an Auditing Standard is relevant to an audit when the circumstances addressed by the standard exist. It establishes the independent auditor's overall responsibilities when conducting an audit of a financial report under Australian Auditing Standards. It is based on the revised ISA 200, 'Overall Objectives of the Independent Auditor and the Conduct of an Audit in Accordance with International Standards on Auditing'.

ASA

Contents

Preface

Reasons for Issuing Auditing Standard ASA 200 *Overall Objectives of the Independent Auditor and the Conduct of an Audit in Accordance with Australian Auditing Standards*

The Auditing and Assurance Standards Board (AUASB) issues Auditing Standard ASA 200 *Overall Objectives of the Independent Auditor and the Conduct of an Audit in Accordance with Australian Auditing Standards* pursuant to the requirements of the legislative provisions and the Strategic Direction explained below.

The AUASB is an independent statutory board of the Australian Government established under section 227A of the *Australian Securities and Investments Commission Act 2001*, as amended (ASIC Act). Under section 336 of the *Corporations Act 2001*, the AUASB may make Auditing Standards for the purposes of the corporations legislation. These Auditing Standards are legislative instruments under the *Legislative Instruments Act 2003*.

Under the Strategic Direction given to the AUASB by the Financial Reporting Council (FRC), the AUASB is required to have regard to any programme initiated by the International Auditing and Assurance Standards Board (IAASB) for the revision and enhancement of the International Standards on Auditing (ISAs) and to make appropriate consequential amendments to the Australian Auditing Standards. Accordingly, the AUASB has decided to revise and redraft the Australian Auditing Standards using the equivalent redrafted ISAs.

Main Features

This Auditing Standard establishes requirements and provides application and other explanatory material regarding the independent auditor's overall responsibilities when conducting an audit of a financial report in accordance with Australian Auditing Standards.

This Auditing Standard:

(a) sets out the overall objectives of the auditor;

(b) explains the nature and scope of an audit designed to assist the auditor in meeting those objectives;

(c) explains the scope, authority and structure of Australian Auditing Standards; and

(d) establishes the general responsibilities of the auditor, applicable in all audits, including the obligation to comply with the Australian Auditing Standards.

Authority Statement

The Auditing and Assurance Standards Board (AUASB) makes this Auditing Standard ASA 200 *Overall Objectives of the Independent Auditor and the Conduct of an Audit in Accordance with Australian Auditing Standards* pursuant to section 227B of the *Australian Securities and Investments Commission Act 2001* and section 336 of the *Corporations Act 2001*.

This Auditing Standard is to be read in conjunction with ASA 101 *Preamble to Australian Auditing Standards*, which sets out the intentions of the AUASB on how the Australian Auditing Standards, operative for financial reporting periods commencing on or after 1 January 2010, are to be understood, interpreted and applied.

Dated: 27 October 2009

M H Kelsall
Chairman - AUASB

Auditing Standard ASA 200

Overall Objectives of the Independent Auditor and the Conduct of an Audit in Accordance with Australian Auditing Standards

Application

Aus 0.1 This Auditing Standard applies to:

(a) an audit of a financial report for a financial year, or an audit of a financial report for a half-year, in accordance with the *Corporations Act 2001*; and

(b) an audit of a financial report, or a complete set of financial statements, for any other purpose.

Aus 0.2 This Auditing Standard also applies, as appropriate, to an audit of other historical financial information.

Operative Date

Aus 0.3 This Auditing Standard is operative for financial reporting periods commencing on or after 1 January 2010.

Introduction

Scope of this Auditing Standard

1. This Auditing Standard deals with the independent auditor's overall responsibilities when conducting an audit of a financial report in accordance with Australian Auditing Standards. Specifically, it sets out the overall objectives of the independent auditor, and explains the nature and scope of an audit designed to enable the independent auditor to meet those objectives. It also explains the scope, authority and structure of the Australian Auditing Standards, and includes requirements establishing the general responsibilities of the independent auditor applicable in all audits, including the obligation to comply with

the Australian Auditing Standards. The independent auditor is referred to as "the auditor" hereafter.

2. Australian Auditing Standards are written in the context of an audit of a financial report by an auditor. They are to be applied as necessary in the circumstances to audits of other historical financial information. Australian Auditing Standards do not address the responsibilities of the auditor that may exist in legislation, regulation or otherwise in connection with, for example, the offering of securities to the public. Such responsibilities may differ from those established in the Australian Auditing Standards. Accordingly, while the auditor may find aspects of the Australian Auditing Standards helpful in such circumstances, it is the responsibility of the auditor to ensure compliance with all relevant legal, regulatory or professional obligations.

An Audit of a Financial Report

3. The purpose of an audit is to enhance the degree of confidence of intended users in the financial report. This is achieved by the expression of an opinion by the auditor on whether the financial report is prepared, in all material respects, in accordance with an applicable financial reporting framework. In the case of most general purpose frameworks, that opinion is on whether the financial report is presented fairly, in all material respects, or gives a true and fair view in accordance with the framework. An audit conducted in accordance with Australian Auditing Standards and relevant ethical requirements enables the auditor to form that opinion. (Ref: Para. A1)

4. The financial report subject to audit is that of the entity, prepared by management of the entity with oversight from those charged with governance. Australian Auditing Standards do not impose responsibilities on management or those charged with governance and do not override laws and regulations that govern their responsibilities. However, an audit in accordance with Australian Auditing Standards is conducted on the premise that management and, where appropriate, those charged with governance have acknowledged certain responsibilities that are fundamental to the conduct of the audit. The audit of the financial report does not relieve management or those charged with governance of their responsibilities. (Ref: Para. A2-A11)

5. As the basis for the auditor's opinion, Australian Auditing Standards require the auditor to obtain reasonable assurance about whether the financial report as a whole is free from material misstatement, whether due to fraud or error. Reasonable assurance is a high level of assurance. It is obtained when the auditor has obtained sufficient appropriate audit evidence to reduce audit risk (that is, the risk that the auditor expresses an inappropriate opinion when the financial report is materially misstated) to an acceptably low level. However, reasonable assurance is not an absolute level of assurance, because there are inherent limitations of an audit which result in most of the audit evidence on which the auditor draws conclusions and bases the auditor's opinion being persuasive rather than conclusive. (Ref: Para. A28-A52)

6. The concept of materiality is applied by the auditor both in planning and performing the audit, and in evaluating the effect of identified misstatements on the audit and of uncorrected misstatements, if any, on the financial report.[1] In general, misstatements, including omissions, are considered to be material if, individually or in the aggregate, they could reasonably be expected to influence the economic decisions of users taken on the basis of the financial report. Judgements about materiality are made in the light of surrounding circumstances, and are affected by the auditor's perception of the financial information needs of users of the financial report, and by the size or nature of a misstatement, or a combination of both. The auditor's opinion deals with the financial report as a whole and therefore, the auditor is not responsible for the detection of misstatements that are not material to the financial report as a whole.

7. The Australian Auditing Standards contain objectives, requirements and application and other explanatory material that are designed to support the auditor in obtaining reasonable assurance. The Australian Auditing Standards require that the auditor exercise

1 See ASA 320 *Materiality in Planning and Performing an Audit*, and ASA 450 *Evaluation of Misstatements Identified during the Audit.*

professional judgement and maintain professional scepticism throughout the planning and performance of the audit and, among other things:

- Identify and assess risks of material misstatement, whether due to fraud or error, based on an understanding of the entity and its environment, including the entity's internal control.
- Obtain sufficient appropriate audit evidence about whether material misstatements exist, through designing and implementing appropriate responses to the assessed risks.
- Form an opinion on the financial report based on conclusions drawn from the audit evidence obtained.

8. The form of opinion expressed by the auditor will depend upon the applicable financial reporting framework and any applicable law or regulation. (Ref: Para. A12-A13)

9. The auditor may also have certain other communication and reporting responsibilities to users, management, those charged with governance, or parties outside the entity, in relation to matters arising from the audit. These may be established by the Australian Auditing Standards or by applicable law or regulation.[2]

Effective Date

10. [Deleted by the AUASB. Refer Aus 0.3]

Overall Objectives of the Auditor

11. In conducting an audit of a financial report, the overall objectives of the auditor are:

(a) To obtain reasonable assurance about whether the financial report as a whole is free from material misstatement, whether due to fraud or error, thereby enabling the auditor to express an opinion on whether the financial report is prepared, in all material respects, in accordance with an applicable financial reporting framework; and

(b) To report on the financial report, and communicate as required by the Australian Auditing Standards, in accordance with the auditor's findings.

12. In all cases when reasonable assurance cannot be obtained and a qualified opinion in the auditor's report is insufficient in the circumstances for purposes of reporting to the intended users of the financial report, the Australian Auditing Standards require that the auditor disclaim an opinion or withdraw (or resign)[3] from the engagement, where withdrawal is possible under applicable law or regulation.

Aus 12.1 In Australian Auditing Standards only the term "withdrawal" is used.

Definitions

13. For purposes of the Australian Auditing Standards, the following terms have the meanings attributed below:

(a) Applicable financial reporting framework means the financial reporting framework adopted by management and, where appropriate, those charged with governance in the preparation of the financial report that is acceptable in view of the nature of the entity and the objective of the financial report, or that is required by law or regulation.

The term "fair presentation framework" means a financial reporting framework that requires compliance with the requirements of the framework and:

(i) Acknowledges explicitly or implicitly that, to achieve fair presentation of the financial report, it may be necessary for management to provide disclosures beyond those specifically required by the framework; or

(ii) Acknowledges explicitly that it may be necessary for management to depart from a requirement of the framework to achieve fair presentation of

---

2 See, for example, ASA 260 *Communication with Those Charged with Governance*; and paragraph 43 of ASA 240 *The Auditor's Responsibilities Relating to Fraud in an Audit of a Financial Report.*

3 [Footnote deleted by the AUASB. Refer Aus 12.1]

the financial report. Such departures are expected to be necessary only in extremely rare circumstances.

The term "compliance framework" means a financial reporting framework that requires compliance with the requirements of the framework, but does not contain the acknowledgements in (i) or (ii) above.

(b) Audit evidence means information used by the auditor in arriving at the conclusions on which the auditor's opinion is based. Audit evidence includes both information contained in the accounting records underlying the financial report and other information. For purposes of the Australian Auditing Standards:

(i) Sufficiency of audit evidence is the measure of the quantity of audit evidence. The quantity of the audit evidence needed is affected by the auditor's assessment of the risks of material misstatement and also by the quality of such audit evidence.

(ii) Appropriateness of audit evidence is the measure of the quality of audit evidence; that is, its relevance and its reliability in providing support for the conclusions on which the auditor's opinion is based.

(c) Audit risk means the risk that the auditor expresses an inappropriate audit opinion when the financial report is materially misstated. Audit risk is a function of the risks of material misstatement and detection risk.

Aus 13.1 A complete set of financial statements means financial statements and related notes as determined by the requirements of the applicable financial reporting framework. For example, a complete set of financial statements as described in Accounting Standard AASB 101* includes:

(a) a statement of financial position as at the end of the period;

(b) a statement of comprehensive income for the period;

(c) a statement of changes in equity for the period;

(d) a statement of cash flows for the period; and

(e) notes, comprising a summary of significant accounting policies and other explanatory information.

(d) Auditor means the person or persons conducting the audit, usually the engagement partner or other members of the engagement team, or, as applicable, the firm. Where an Auditing Standard expressly intends that a requirement or responsibility be fulfilled by the engagement partner, the term "engagement partner" rather than "auditor" is used. "Engagement partner" and "firm" are to be read as referring to their public sector equivalents where relevant.

(e) Detection risk means the risk that the procedures performed by the auditor to reduce audit risk to an acceptably low level will not detect a misstatement that exists and that could be material, either individually or when aggregated with other misstatements.

(f) [Deleted by the AUASB. Refer Aus 13.2]

Aus 13.2 Financial statement means a structured representation of historical financial information, intended to communicate an entity's economic resources or obligations at a point in time or the changes therein for a period of time in accordance with a financial reporting framework. What constitutes a financial statement is determined by the requirements of the applicable financial reporting framework.

Aus 13.3 Financial Report means, for the purpose of the *Corporations Act 2001*,** financial statements for the year or the half-year and notes to the financial statements, and the directors' declaration about the statements and notes.

* See AASB 101 *Presentation of Financial Statements*, paragraph 10.

** See sections 295 and 303 of the *Corporations Act 2001*.

Aus 13.4 Financial Report means, for purposes other than the *Corporations Act 2001*, a complete set of financial statements, including the related notes, and an assertion statement by those responsible for the financial report. The related notes ordinarily comprise a summary of significant accounting policies and other explanatory information. The requirements of the applicable financial reporting framework determine the form and content of the financial report.

(g) Historical financial information means information expressed in financial terms in relation to a particular entity, derived primarily from that entity's accounting system, about economic events occurring in past time periods or about economic conditions or circumstances at points in time in the past.

(h) Management means the person(s) with executive responsibility for the conduct of the entity's operations. For some entities in some jurisdictions, management includes some or all of those charged with governance, for example, executive members of a governance board, or an owner-manager.

(i) Misstatement means a difference between the amount, classification, presentation, or disclosure of a reported financial report item and the amount, classification, presentation, or disclosure that is required for the item to be in accordance with the applicable financial reporting framework. Misstatements can arise from error or fraud.

Where the auditor expresses an opinion on whether the financial report is presented fairly, in all material respects, or gives a true and fair view, misstatements also include those adjustments of amounts, classifications, presentation, or disclosures that, in the auditor's judgement, are necessary for the financial report to be presented fairly, in all material respects, or to give a true and fair view.

(j) Premise, relating to the responsibilities of management and, where appropriate, those charged with governance, on which an audit is conducted means that management and, where appropriate, those charged with governance have acknowledged and understand that they have the following responsibilities that are fundamental to the conduct of an audit in accordance with Australian Auditing Standards. That is, responsibility:

(i) For the preparation of a financial report in accordance with the applicable financial reporting framework, including where relevant, their fair presentation;

(ii) For such internal control as management and, where appropriate, those charged with governance determine is necessary to enable the preparation of a financial report that is free from material misstatement, whether due to fraud or error, and

(iii) To provide the auditor with:

a. Access to all information, of which management and, where appropriate, those charged with governance are aware that is relevant to the preparation of a financial report such as records, documentation and other matters;

b. Additional information that the auditor may request from management and, where appropriate, those charged with governance, for the purpose of the audit; and

c. Unrestricted access to persons within the entity from whom the auditor determines it necessary to obtain audit evidence.

In the case of a fair presentation framework, (i) above may be restated as "for the preparation and *fair* presentation of a financial report in accordance with the financial reporting framework", or "for the preparation of a financial report *that gives a true and fair view* in accordance with the financial reporting framework."

The "premise, relating to the responsibilities of management and, where appropriate, those charged with governance, on which an audit is conducted" may also be referred to as the "premise."

(k) Professional judgement means the application of relevant training, knowledge and experience, within the context provided by auditing, accounting and ethical standards, in making informed decisions about the courses of action that are appropriate in the circumstances of the audit engagement.

(l) Professional scepticism means an attitude that includes a questioning mind, being alert to conditions which may indicate possible misstatement due to error or fraud, and a critical assessment of audit evidence.

(m) Reasonable assurance means, in the context of an audit of a financial report, a high, but not absolute, level of assurance.

(n) Risk of material misstatement means the risk that the financial report is materially misstated prior to audit. This consists of two components, described as follows at the assertion level:

(i) Inherent risk means the susceptibility of an assertion about a class of transaction, account balance or disclosure to a misstatement that could be material, either individually or when aggregated with other misstatements, before consideration of any related controls.

(ii) Control risk means the risk that a misstatement that could occur in an assertion about a class of transaction, account balance or disclosure and that could be material, either individually or when aggregated with other misstatements, will not be prevented, or detected and corrected, on a timely basis by the entity's internal control.

(o) Those charged with governance means the person(s) or organisation(s) (for example, a corporate trustee) with responsibility for overseeing the strategic direction of the entity and obligations related to the accountability of the entity. This includes overseeing the financial reporting process. For some entities in some jurisdictions, those charged with governance may include management personnel, for example, executive members of a governance board of a private or public sector entity, or an owner-manager.

Requirements

Ethical Requirements Relating to an Audit of a Financial Report

14. The auditor shall comply with relevant ethical requirements, including those pertaining to independence, relating to a financial report audit engagement. (Ref: Para. A14-A17)

Professional Scepticism

15. The auditor shall plan and perform an audit with professional scepticism recognising that circumstances may exist that cause the financial report to be materially misstated. (Ref: Para. A18-A22)

Professional Judgement

16. The auditor shall exercise professional judgement in planning and performing an audit of a financial report. (Ref: Para. A23-A27)

Sufficient Appropriate Audit Evidence and Audit Risk

17. To obtain reasonable assurance, the auditor shall obtain sufficient appropriate audit evidence to reduce audit risk to an acceptably low level and thereby enable the auditor to draw reasonable conclusions on which to base the auditor's opinion. (Ref: Para. A28-A52)

Conduct of an Audit in Accordance with Australian Auditing Standards

Complying with Australian Auditing Standards Relevant to the Audit

18. The auditor shall comply with all Australian Auditing Standards relevant to the audit. An Auditing Standard is relevant to the audit when the Auditing Standard is in effect and the circumstances addressed by the Auditing Standard exist. (Ref: Para. A53-A57)

19. The auditor shall have an understanding of the entire text of an Auditing Standard, including its application and other explanatory material, to understand its objectives and to apply its requirements properly. (Ref: Para. A58-A66)

20. The auditor shall not represent compliance with Australian Auditing Standards in the auditor's report unless the auditor has complied with the requirements of this Auditing Standard and all other Australian Auditing Standards relevant to the audit. (Ref: Para. Aus A66.1)

Objectives Stated in Individual Auditing Standards

21. To achieve the overall objectives of the auditor, the auditor shall use the objectives stated in relevant Australian Auditing Standards in planning and performing the audit, having regard to the interrelationships among the Australian Auditing Standards, to: (Ref: Para. A67-A69)

    (a) Determine whether any audit procedures in addition to those required by the Australian Auditing Standards are necessary in pursuance of the objectives stated in the Australian Auditing Standards; and (Ref: Para. A70)

    (b) Evaluate whether sufficient appropriate audit evidence has been obtained. (Ref: Para. A71)

Complying with Relevant Requirements

22. Subject to paragraph Aus 23.1 of this Auditing Standard, the auditor shall comply with each requirement of an Auditing Standard unless, in the circumstances of the audit:

    (a) The entire Auditing Standard is not relevant;

    (b) The requirement is not relevant because it is conditional and the condition does not exist; or (Ref: Para. A72-A73)

    Aus 22.1 Application of the requirement(s) would relate to classes of transactions, account balances or disclosures that the auditor has determined are immaterial.

23. [Deleted by the AUASB. Refer Aus 23.1]

Aus 23.1 Where in rare and exceptional circumstances, factors outside the auditor's control prevent the auditor from complying with an essential procedure contained within a relevant requirement, the auditor shall:

(a) If possible, perform appropriate alternative audit procedures; and

(b) In accordance with ASA 230,* document in the working papers:

(i) The circumstances surrounding the inability to comply;

(ii) The reasons for the inability to comply; and

(iii) Justification of how alternative audit procedures achieve the objectives of the requirement.

When the auditor is unable to perform the appropriate alternative audit procedures, the auditor shall consider the requirement in paragraph 24 of this Auditing Standard. (Ref: Para. A74-Aus A74.1)

Failure to Achieve an Objective

24. If an objective in a relevant Auditing Standard cannot be achieved, the auditor shall evaluate whether this prevents the auditor from achieving the overall objectives of the auditor and thereby requires the auditor, in accordance with Australian Auditing Standards, to modify the auditor's opinion or withdraw from the engagement (where withdrawal is possible under applicable law or regulation). Failure to achieve an objective represents a significant matter requiring documentation in accordance with ASA 230.[4] (Ref: Para. A75-A76)

❖❖❖

* See ASA 230 *Audit Documentation*, paragraph Aus 12.1.

4 See ASA 230 *Audit Documentation*, paragraph 8(c).

Application and Other Explanatory Material

An Audit of a Financial Report

Scope of the Audit (Ref: Para. 3)

A1. The auditor's opinion on the financial report deals with whether the financial report is prepared, in all material respects, in accordance with the applicable financial reporting framework. Such an opinion is common to all audits of financial reports. The auditor's opinion therefore does not assure, for example, the future viability of the entity nor the efficiency or effectiveness with which management has conducted the affairs of the entity. In some jurisdictions, however, applicable law or regulation may require auditors to provide opinions on other specific matters, such as the effectiveness of internal control, or the consistency of a separate management report with the financial report. While the Australian Auditing Standards include requirements and guidance in relation to such matters to the extent that they are relevant to forming an opinion on the financial report, the auditor would be required to undertake further work if the auditor had additional responsibilities to provide such opinions.

ASA

Preparation of the Financial Report (Ref: Para. 4)

A2. Law or regulation may establish the responsibilities of management and, where appropriate, those charged with governance in relation to financial reporting. However, the extent of these responsibilities, or the way in which they are described, may differ across jurisdictions. Despite these differences, an audit in accordance with Australian Auditing Standards is conducted on the premise that management and, where appropriate, those charged with governance have acknowledged and understand that they have responsibility:

(a) For the preparation of a financial report in accordance with the applicable financial reporting framework, including where relevant their fair presentation;

(b) For such internal control as management and, where appropriate, those charged with governance determine is necessary to enable the preparation of a financial report that is free from material misstatement, whether due to fraud or error; and

(c) To provide the auditor with:

(i) Access to all information of which management and, where appropriate, those charged with governance are aware that is relevant to the preparation of the financial report such as records, documentation and other matters;

(ii) Additional information that the auditor may request from management and, where appropriate, those charged with governance for the purpose of the audit; and

(iii) Unrestricted access to persons within the entity from whom the auditor determines it necessary to obtain audit evidence.

A3. The preparation of a financial report by management and, where appropriate, those charged with governance requires:

- The identification of the applicable financial reporting framework, in the context of any relevant laws or regulations.
- The preparation of a financial report in accordance with that framework.
- The inclusion of an adequate description of that framework in the financial report.

The preparation of a financial report requires management to exercise judgement in making accounting estimates that are reasonable in the circumstances, as well as to select and apply appropriate accounting policies. These judgements are made in the context of the applicable financial reporting framework.

A4. The financial report may be prepared in accordance with a financial reporting framework designed to meet:

- The common financial information needs of a wide range of users (that is, a "general purpose financial report"); or
- The financial information needs of specific users (that is, a "special purpose financial report").

A5. The applicable financial reporting framework often encompasses financial reporting standards established by an authorised or recognised standards setting organisation, or legislative or regulatory requirements. In some cases, the financial reporting framework may encompass both financial reporting standards established by an authorised or recognised standards setting organisation and legislative or regulatory requirements. Other sources may provide direction on the application of the applicable financial reporting framework. In some cases, the applicable financial reporting framework may encompass such other sources, or may even consist only of such sources. Such other sources may include:

- The legal and ethical environment, including statutes, regulations, court decisions, and professional ethical obligations in relation to accounting matters;
- Published accounting interpretations of varying authority issued by standards setting, professional or regulatory organisations;
- Published views of varying authority on emerging accounting issues issued by standards setting, professional or regulatory organisations;
- General and industry practices widely recognised and prevalent; and
- Accounting literature.

Where conflicts exist between the financial reporting framework and the sources from which direction on its application may be obtained, or among the sources that encompass the financial reporting framework, the source with the highest authority prevails.

Aus A5.1 An applicable financial reporting framework that may be used in preparing a financial report is represented by the Australian Accounting Standards issued by the Australian Accounting Standards Board (AASB), and relevant law, such as the *Corporations Act 2001* (the Act) for entities covered by that Act, or other relevant law that may be applicable to other entities.

A6. The requirements of the applicable financial reporting framework determine the form and content of a financial report. Although the framework may not specify how to account for or disclose all transactions or events, it ordinarily embodies sufficient broad principles that can serve as a basis for developing and applying accounting policies that are consistent with the concepts underlying the requirements of the framework.

A7. Some financial reporting frameworks are fair presentation frameworks, while others are compliance frameworks. Financial reporting frameworks that encompass primarily the financial reporting standards established by an organisation that is authorised or recognised to promulgate standards to be used by entities for preparing a general purpose financial report are often designed to achieve fair presentation, for example, Australian Accounting Standards issued by the AASB.

A8. The requirements of the applicable financial reporting framework also determine what constitutes a financial report. In the case of many frameworks, a financial report is intended to provide information about the financial position, financial performance and cash flows of an entity. For such frameworks, a financial report* would include a complete set of financial statements,# including the related notes, and an assertion statement by those responsible for the financial report. For some other financial reporting frameworks, a single financial statement and the related notes might constitute a financial report:

- [Deleted by the AUASB. Refer Aus A8.1 and Aus A8.2]
- Other examples of a single financial statement, each of which would include related notes, are a:
  - Balance sheet.
  - Statement of income or statement of operations.
  - Statement of retained earnings.
  - Statement of cash flows.

* See Definitions, paragraphs Aus 13.3 and Aus 13.4, of this Auditing Standard.

\# See Definitions, paragraph Aus 13.1 of this Auditing Standard.

- Statement of assets and liabilities that does not include owner's equity.
- Statement of changes in owners' equity.
- Statement of revenue and expenses.
- Statement of operations by product lines.

Aus A8.1
- Statement of financial position
- Statement of comprehensive income.
- Statement of recognised income and expense.

- Aus A8.2 Under the financial reporting framework defined in the *Corporations Act 2001*[*] and Australian Accounting Standards,[#] a financial report consists of financial statements for the year or the half-year, notes to the financial statements, and the directors' declaration about the statements and notes.

A9. ASA 210 establishes requirements and provides guidance on determining the acceptability of the applicable financial reporting framework.[5] ASA 800 deals with special considerations when the financial report is prepared in accordance with a special purpose framework.[6]

A10. Because of the significance of the premise to the conduct of an audit, the auditor is required to obtain the agreement of management and, where appropriate, those charged with governance that they acknowledge and understand that they have the responsibilities set out in paragraph A2 as a precondition for accepting the audit engagement.[7]

Considerations Specific to Audits in the Public Sector

A11. The mandates for audits of financial reports of public sector entities may be broader than those of other entities. As a result, the premise, relating to management's responsibilities, on which an audit of the financial report of a public sector entity is conducted may include additional responsibilities, such as the responsibility for the execution of transactions and events in accordance with law, regulation or other authority.[8]

Form of the Auditor's Opinion (Ref: Para. 8)

A12. The opinion expressed by the auditor is on whether the financial report is prepared, in all material respects, in accordance with the applicable financial reporting framework. The form of the auditor's opinion, however, will depend upon the applicable financial reporting framework and any applicable law or regulation. Most financial reporting frameworks include requirements relating to the presentation of the financial report; for such frameworks, *preparation* of the financial report in accordance with the applicable financial reporting framework includes *presentation*.

A13. Where the financial reporting framework is a fair presentation framework, as is generally the case for a general purpose financial report, the opinion required by the Australian Auditing Standards is on whether the financial report is presented fairly, in all material respects, or gives a true and fair view. Where the financial reporting framework is a compliance framework, the opinion required is on whether the financial report is prepared, in all material respects, in accordance with the framework. Unless specifically stated otherwise, references in the Australian Auditing Standards to the auditor's opinion cover both forms of opinion.

---

* See sections 295 and 303 of the *Corporations Act 2001*.

\# See AASB 101.

5 See ASA 210 *Agreeing the Terms of Audit Engagements*, paragraph 6(a).

6 See ASA 800 *Special Considerations—Audits of Financial Reports Prepared in Accordance with Special Purpose Frameworks*, paragraph 8.

7 See ASA 210, paragraph 6(b).

8 See paragraph A57 of this Auditing Standard.

Ethical Requirements Relating to an Audit of a Financial Report (Ref: Para. 14)

A14. [Deleted by the AUASB. Refer Aus A14.1]

Aus A14.1 The auditor is subject to relevant ethical requirements, including those pertaining to independence, relating to audit engagements as defined in ASA 102.*

A15. [Deleted by the AUASB. See ASA 102]

A16. [Deleted by the AUASB. See ASA 102]

A17. ASQC 1[9] deals with the firm's responsibilities to establish and maintain its system of quality control for audit engagements.[10] ASQC 1 sets out the responsibilities of the firm for establishing policies and procedures designed to provide it with reasonable assurance that the firm and its personnel comply with relevant ethical requirements, including those pertaining to independence.[11] ASA 220 sets out the engagement partner's responsibilities with respect to relevant ethical requirements. These include remaining alert, through observation and making enquiries as necessary, for evidence of non-compliance with relevant ethical requirements by members of the engagement team, determining the appropriate action if matters come to the engagement partner's attention that indicate that members of the engagement team have not complied with relevant ethical requirements, and forming a conclusion on compliance with independence requirements that apply to the audit engagement.[12] ASA 220 recognises that the engagement team is entitled to rely on a firm's system of quality control in meeting its responsibilities with respect to quality control procedures applicable to the individual audit engagement, unless information provided by the firm or other parties suggests otherwise.

Professional Scepticism (Ref: Para. 15)

A18. Professional scepticism includes being alert to, for example:

- Audit evidence that contradicts other audit evidence obtained.
- Information that brings into question the reliability of documents and responses to enquiries to be used as audit evidence.
- Conditions that may indicate possible fraud.
- Circumstances that suggest the need for audit procedures in addition to those required by the Australian Auditing Standards.

A19. Maintaining professional scepticism throughout the audit is necessary if the auditor is, for example, to reduce the risks of:

- Overlooking unusual circumstances.
- Over-generalising when drawing conclusions from audit observations.
- Using inappropriate assumptions in determining the nature, timing, and extent of the audit procedures and evaluating the results thereof.

A20. Professional scepticism is necessary to the critical assessment of audit evidence. This includes questioning contradictory audit evidence and the reliability of documents and responses to enquiries and other information obtained from management and those charged with governance. It also includes consideration of the sufficiency and appropriateness of audit evidence obtained in the light of the circumstances, for example in the case where fraud risk factors exist and a single document, of a nature that is susceptible to fraud, is the sole supporting evidence for a material financial report amount.

A21. The auditor may accept records and documents as genuine unless the auditor has reason to believe the contrary. Nevertheless, the auditor is required to consider the reliability

---

* See ASA 102 *Compliance with Ethical Requirements when Performing Audits, Reviews and Other Assurance Engagements.*

9 See ASQC 1 *Quality control For Firms that Perform Audits and Reviews of Financial Reports and Other Financial Information, and Other Assurance Engagements.*

10 See ASA 220 *Quality Control for an Audit of a Financial Report and Other Historical Financial Information*, paragraph 2.

11 See ASQC 1, paragraphs 20-25.

12 See ASA 220, paragraphs 9-12.

of information to be used as audit evidence.[13] In cases of doubt about the reliability of information or indications of possible fraud (for example, if conditions identified during the audit cause the auditor to believe that a document may not be authentic or that terms in a document may have been falsified), the Australian Auditing Standards require that the auditor investigate further and determine what modifications or additions to audit procedures are necessary to resolve the matter.[14]

A22. The auditor cannot be expected to disregard past experience of the honesty and integrity of the entity's management and those charged with governance. Nevertheless, a belief that management and those charged with governance are honest and have integrity does not relieve the auditor of the need to maintain professional scepticism or allow the auditor to be satisfied with less-than-persuasive audit evidence when obtaining reasonable assurance.

Professional Judgement (Ref: Para. 16)

A23. Professional judgement is essential to the proper conduct of an audit. This is because interpretation of relevant ethical requirements and the Australian Auditing Standards and the informed decisions required throughout the audit cannot be made without the application of relevant knowledge and experience to the facts and circumstances. Professional judgement is necessary in particular regarding decisions about:

- Materiality and audit risk.
- The nature, timing, and extent of audit procedures used to meet the requirements of the Australian Auditing Standards and gather audit evidence.
- Evaluating whether sufficient appropriate audit evidence has been obtained, and whether more needs to be done to achieve the objectives of the Australian Auditing Standards and thereby, the overall objectives of the auditor.
- The evaluation of management's judgements in applying the entity's applicable financial reporting framework.
- The drawing of conclusions based on the audit evidence obtained, for example, assessing the reasonableness of the estimates made by management in preparing the financial report.

A24. The distinguishing feature of the professional judgement expected of an auditor is that it is exercised by an auditor whose training, knowledge and experience have assisted in developing the necessary competencies to achieve reasonable judgements.

A25. The exercise of professional judgement in any particular case is based on the facts and circumstances that are known by the auditor. Consultation on difficult or contentious matters during the course of the audit, both within the engagement team and between the engagement team and others at the appropriate level within or outside the firm, such as that required by ASA 220,[15] assist the auditor in making informed and reasonable judgements.

A26. Professional judgement can be evaluated based on whether the judgement reached reflects a competent application of auditing and accounting principles and is appropriate in the light of, and consistent with, the facts and circumstances that were known to the auditor up to the date of the auditor's report.

A27. Professional judgement needs to be exercised throughout the audit. It also needs to be appropriately documented. In this regard, the auditor is required to prepare audit documentation sufficient to enable an experienced auditor, having no previous connection with the audit, to understand the significant professional judgements made in reaching conclusions on significant matters arising during the audit.[16] Professional judgement is

13 See ASA 500 *Audit Evidence*, paragraphs 7-9.

14 See ASA 240, paragraph 13; ASA 500, paragraph 11; and ASA 505 *External Confirmations*, paragraphs 10-11 and 16.

15 See ASA 220, paragraph 18.

16 See ASA 230, paragraph 8.

not to be used as the justification for decisions that are not otherwise supported by the facts and circumstances of the engagement or sufficient appropriate audit evidence.

Sufficient Appropriate Audit Evidence and Audit Risk (Ref: Para. 5 and 17)

Sufficiency and Appropriateness of Audit Evidence

A28. Audit evidence is necessary to support the auditor's opinion and report. It is cumulative in nature and is primarily obtained from audit procedures performed during the course of the audit. It may, however, also include information obtained from other sources such as previous audits (provided the auditor has determined whether changes have occurred since the previous audit that may affect its relevance to the current audit[17]) or a firm's quality control procedures for client acceptance and continuance. In addition to other sources inside and outside the entity, the entity's accounting records are an important source of audit evidence. Also, information that may be used as audit evidence may have been prepared by an expert employed or engaged by the entity. Audit evidence comprises both information that supports and corroborates management's assertions, and any information that contradicts such assertions. In addition, in some cases, the absence of information (for example, management's refusal to provide a requested representation) is used by the auditor, and therefore, also constitutes audit evidence. Most of the auditor's work in forming the auditor's opinion consists of obtaining and evaluating audit evidence.

A29. The sufficiency and appropriateness of audit evidence are interrelated. Sufficiency is the measure of the quantity of audit evidence. The quantity of audit evidence needed is affected by the auditor's assessment of the risks of misstatement (the higher the assessed risks, the more audit evidence is likely to be required) and also by the quality of such audit evidence (the higher the quality, the less may be required). Obtaining more audit evidence, however, may not compensate for its poor quality.

A30. Appropriateness is the measure of the quality of audit evidence; that is, its relevance and its reliability in providing support for the conclusions on which the auditor's opinion is based. The reliability of evidence is influenced by its source and by its nature, and is dependent on the individual circumstances under which it is obtained.

A31. Whether sufficient appropriate audit evidence has been obtained to reduce audit risk to an acceptably low level, and thereby enable the auditor to draw reasonable conclusions on which to base the auditor's opinion, is a matter of professional judgement. ASA 500 and other relevant Australian Auditing Standards establish additional requirements and provide further guidance applicable throughout the audit regarding the auditor's considerations in obtaining sufficient appropriate audit evidence.

Audit Risk

A32. Audit risk is a function of the risks of material misstatement and detection risk. The assessment of risks is based on audit procedures to obtain information necessary for that purpose and evidence obtained throughout the audit. The assessment of risks is a matter of professional judgement, rather than a matter capable of precise measurement.

A33. For purposes of the Australian Auditing Standards, audit risk does not include the risk that the auditor might express an opinion that the financial report is materially misstated when they are not. This risk is ordinarily insignificant. Further, audit risk is a technical term related to the process of auditing; it does not refer to the auditor's business risks such as loss from litigation, adverse publicity, or other events arising in connection with the audit of a financial report.

Risks of Material Misstatement

A34. The risks of material misstatement may exist at two levels:

- The overall financial report level; and
- The assertion level for classes of transactions, account balances, and disclosures.

---

17 See ASA 315 *Identifying and Assessing the Risks of Material Misstatement through Understanding the Entity and Its Environment*, paragraph 9.

A35. Risks of material misstatement at the overall financial report level refer to risks of material misstatement that relate pervasively to the financial report as a whole and potentially affect many assertions.

A36. Risks of material misstatement at the assertion level are assessed in order to determine the nature, timing, and extent of further audit procedures necessary to obtain sufficient appropriate audit evidence. This evidence enables the auditor to express an opinion on the financial report at an acceptably low level of audit risk. Auditors use various approaches to accomplish the objective of assessing the risks of material misstatement. For example, the auditor may make use of a model that expresses the general relationship of the components of audit risk in mathematical terms to arrive at an acceptable level of detection risk. Some auditors find such a model to be useful when planning audit procedures.

A37. The risks of material misstatement at the assertion level consist of two components: inherent risk and control risk. Inherent risk and control risk are the entity's risks; they exist independently of the audit of the financial report.

A38. Inherent risk is higher for some assertions and related classes of transactions, account balances, and disclosures than for others. For example, it may be higher for complex calculations or for accounts consisting of amounts derived from accounting estimates that are subject to significant estimation uncertainty. External circumstances giving rise to business risks may also influence inherent risk. For example, technological developments might make a particular product obsolete, thereby causing inventory to be more susceptible to overstatement. Factors in the entity and its environment that relate to several or all of the classes of transactions, account balances, or disclosures may also influence the inherent risk related to a specific assertion. Such factors may include, for example, a lack of sufficient working capital to continue operations or a declining industry characterised by a large number of business failures.

A39. Control risk is a function of the effectiveness of the design, implementation and maintenance of internal control by management, or where applicable, those charged with governance, to address identified risks that threaten the achievement of the entity's objectives relevant to preparation of the entity's financial report. However, internal control, no matter how well designed and operated, can only reduce, but not eliminate, risks of material misstatement in the financial report, because of the inherent limitations of internal control. These include, for example, the possibility of human errors or mistakes, or of controls being circumvented by collusion or inappropriate management override. Accordingly, some control risk will always exist. The Australian Auditing Standards provide the conditions under which the auditor is required to, or may choose to, test the operating effectiveness of controls in determining the nature, timing and extent of substantive procedures to be performed.[18]

A40. The Australian Auditing Standards do not ordinarily refer to inherent risk and control risk separately, but rather to a combined assessment of the "risks of material misstatement." However, the auditor may make separate or combined assessments of inherent and control risk depending on preferred audit techniques or methodologies and practical considerations. The assessment of the risks of material misstatement may be expressed in quantitative terms, such as in percentages, or in non-quantitative terms. In any case, the need for the auditor to make appropriate risk assessments is more important than the different approaches by which they may be made.

A41. ASA 315 establishes requirements and provides guidance on identifying and assessing the risks of material misstatement at the financial report and assertion levels.

Detection Risk

A42. For a given level of audit risk, the acceptable level of detection risk bears an inverse relationship to the assessed risks of material misstatement at the assertion level. For example, the greater the risks of material misstatement the auditor believes exists, the less the detection risk that can be accepted and, accordingly, the more persuasive the audit evidence required by the auditor.

18 See ASA 330 *The Auditor's Responses to Assessed Risks*, paragraphs 7-17.

A43. Detection risk relates to the nature, timing, and extent of the auditor's procedures that are determined by the auditor to reduce audit risk to an acceptably low level. It is therefore a function of the effectiveness of an audit procedure and of its application by the auditor. Matters such as:

- adequate planning;
- proper assignment of personnel to the engagement team;
- the application of professional scepticism; and
- supervision and review of the audit work performed,

assist to enhance the effectiveness of an audit procedure and of its application and reduce the possibility that an auditor might select an inappropriate audit procedure, misapply an appropriate audit procedure, or misinterpret the audit results.

A44. ASA 300[19] and ASA 330 establish requirements and provide guidance on planning an audit of a financial report and the auditor's responses to assessed risks. Detection risk, however, can only be reduced, not eliminated, because of the inherent limitations of an audit. Accordingly, some detection risk will always exist.

Inherent Limitations of an Audit

A45. The auditor is not expected to, and cannot, reduce audit risk to zero and cannot therefore obtain absolute assurance that the financial report is free from material misstatement due to fraud or error. This is because there are inherent limitations of an audit, which result in most of the audit evidence on which the auditor draws conclusions and bases the auditor's opinion being persuasive rather than conclusive. The inherent limitations of an audit arise from:

- The nature of financial reporting;
- The nature of audit procedures; and
- The need for the audit to be conducted within a reasonable period of time and at a reasonable cost.

The Nature of Financial Reporting

A46. The preparation of a financial report involves judgement by management in applying the requirements of the entity's applicable financial reporting framework to the facts and circumstances of the entity. In addition, many financial report items involve subjective decisions or assessments or a degree of uncertainty, and there may be a range of acceptable interpretations or judgements that may be made. Consequently, some financial report items are subject to an inherent level of variability which cannot be eliminated by the application of additional auditing procedures. For example, this is often the case with respect to certain accounting estimates. Nevertheless, the Australian Auditing Standards require the auditor to give specific consideration to whether accounting estimates are reasonable in the context of the applicable financial reporting framework and related disclosures, and to the qualitative aspects of the entity's accounting practices, including indicators of possible bias in management's judgements.[20]

The Nature of Audit Procedures

A47. There are practical and legal limitations on the auditor's ability to obtain audit evidence. For example:

- There is the possibility that management or others may not provide, intentionally or unintentionally, the complete information that is relevant to the preparation of the financial report or that has been requested by the auditor. Accordingly, the auditor cannot be certain of the completeness of information, even though the auditor has performed audit procedures to obtain assurance that all relevant information has been obtained.

---

19 See ASA 300 *Planning an Audit of a Financial Report*.

20 See ASA 540 *Auditing Accounting Estimates, Including Fair Value Accounting Estimates, and Related Disclosures*, and ASA 700 *Forming an Opinion and Reporting on a Financial Report*, paragraph 12.

- Fraud may involve sophisticated and carefully organised schemes designed to conceal it. Therefore, audit procedures used to gather audit evidence may be ineffective for detecting an intentional misstatement that involves, for example, collusion to falsify documentation which may cause the auditor to believe that audit evidence is valid when it is not. The auditor is neither trained as, nor expected to be, an expert in the authentication of documents.
- An audit is not an official investigation into alleged wrongdoing. Accordingly, the auditor is not given specific legal powers, such as the power of search, which may be necessary for such an investigation.

Timeliness of Financial Reporting and the Balance between Benefit and Cost

A48. The matter of difficulty, time, or cost involved is not in itself a valid basis for the auditor to omit an audit procedure for which there is no alternative or to be satisfied with audit evidence that is less than persuasive. Appropriate planning assists in making sufficient time and resources available for the conduct of the audit. Notwithstanding this, the relevance of information, and thereby its value, tends to diminish over time, and there is a balance to be struck between the reliability of information and its cost. This is recognised in certain financial reporting frameworks (see, for example, the AASB's *Framework for the Preparation and Presentation of Financial Statements*).* Therefore, there is an expectation by users of a financial report that the auditor will form an opinion on the financial report within a reasonable period of time and at a reasonable cost, recognising that it is impracticable to address all information that may exist or to pursue every matter exhaustively on the assumption that information is in error or fraudulent until proved otherwise.

A49. Consequently, it is necessary for the auditor to:

- Plan the audit so that it will be performed in an effective manner;
- Direct audit effort to areas most expected to contain risks of material misstatement, whether due to fraud or error, with correspondingly less effort directed at other areas; and
- Use testing and other means of examining populations for misstatements.

A50. In light of the approaches described in paragraph A49, the Australian Auditing Standards contain requirements for the planning and performance of the audit and require the auditor, among other things, to:

- Have a basis for the identification and assessment of risks of material misstatement at the financial report and assertion levels by performing risk assessment procedures and related activities;[21] and
- Use testing and other means of examining populations in a manner that provides a reasonable basis for the auditor to draw conclusions about the population.[22]

Other Matters that Affect the Inherent Limitations of an Audit

A51. In the case of certain assertions or subject matters, the potential effects of the inherent limitations on the auditor's ability to detect material misstatements are particularly significant. Such assertions or subject matters include:

- Fraud, particularly fraud involving senior management or collusion. See ASA 240 for further discussion.
- The existence and completeness of related party relationships and transactions. See ASA 550[23] for further discussion.
- The occurrence of non-compliance with laws and regulations. See ASA 250[24] for further discussion.

* Issued by the Australian Accounting Standards Board, (July 2004).

21 See ASA 315, paragraphs 5-10.

22 See ASA 330; ASA 500; ASA 520 *Analytical Procedures*; and ASA 530 *Audit Sampling*.

23 See ASA 550 *Related Parties*.

24 See ASA 250 *Consideration of Laws and Regulations in an Audit of a Financial Report*.

- Future events or conditions that may cause an entity to cease to continue as a going concern. See ASA 570[25] for further discussion.

Relevant Australian Auditing Standards identify specific audit procedures to assist in mitigating the effect of the inherent limitations.

A52. Because of the inherent limitations of an audit, there is an unavoidable risk that some material misstatements of the financial report may not be detected, even though the audit is properly planned and performed in accordance with Australian Auditing Standards. Accordingly, the subsequent discovery of a material misstatement of the financial report resulting from fraud or error does not by itself indicate a failure to conduct an audit in accordance with Australian Auditing Standards. However, the inherent limitations of an audit are not a justification for the auditor to be satisfied with less-than-persuasive audit evidence. Whether the auditor has performed an audit in accordance with Australian Auditing Standards is determined by the audit procedures performed in the circumstances, the sufficiency and appropriateness of the audit evidence obtained as a result thereof and the suitability of the auditor's report based on an evaluation of that evidence in light of the overall objectives of the auditor.

Conduct of an Audit in Accordance with Australian Auditing Standards

Nature of the Australian Auditing Standards (Ref: Para. 18)

A53. The Australian Auditing Standards, taken together, provide the standards for the auditor's work in fulfilling the overall objectives of the auditor. The Australian Auditing Standards deal with the general responsibilities of the auditor, as well as the auditor's further considerations relevant to the application of those responsibilities to specific topics.

A54. The scope, effective date and any specific limitation of the applicability of a specific Auditing Standard is made clear in the Auditing Standard. Unless otherwise stated in the Auditing Standard, the auditor is not permitted to apply an Auditing Standard before the effective date specified therein.

A55. In performing an audit, the auditor may be required to comply with legal or regulatory requirements in addition to the Australian Auditing Standards. The Australian Auditing Standards do not override law or regulation that governs an audit of a financial report. In the event that such law or regulation differs from the Australian Auditing Standards, an audit conducted only in accordance with law or regulation will not automatically comply with Australian Auditing Standards.

A56. The auditor may also conduct the audit in accordance with both Australian Auditing Standards and auditing standards of a specific jurisdiction or country. In such cases, in addition to complying with each of the Australian Auditing Standards relevant to the audit, it may be necessary for the auditor to perform additional audit procedures in order to comply with the relevant standards of that jurisdiction or country.

Considerations Specific to Audits in the Public Sector

A57. The Australian Auditing Standards are relevant to engagements in the public sector. The public sector auditor's responsibilities, however, may be affected by the audit mandate, or by obligations on public sector entities arising from law, regulation or other authority (such as ministerial directives, government policy requirements, or resolutions of the legislature), which may encompass a broader scope than an audit of a financial report in accordance with the Australian Auditing Standards. These additional responsibilities are not dealt with in the Australian Auditing Standards. They may be dealt with in guidance developed by government audit agencies.

Contents of the Australian Auditing Standards (Ref: Para. 19)

A58. In addition to objectives and requirements (requirements are expressed in the Australian Auditing Standards using "shall"), an Auditing Standard contains related guidance in the form of application and other explanatory material. It may also contain introductory material that provides context relevant to a proper understanding of the Auditing Standard, and definitions. The entire text of an Auditing Standard, therefore, is relevant to an

25 See ASA 570 *Going Concern*.

understanding of the objectives stated in an Auditing Standard and the proper application of the requirements of an Auditing Standard.

A59. Where necessary, the application and other explanatory material provides further explanation of the requirements of an Auditing Standard and guidance for carrying them out. In particular, it may:

- Explain more precisely what a requirement means or is intended to cover.
- Include examples of procedures that may be appropriate in the circumstances.

While such guidance does not in itself impose a requirement, it is relevant to the proper application of the requirements of an Auditing Standard. The application and other explanatory material may also provide background information on matters addressed in an Auditing Standard.

A60. Appendices form part of the application and other explanatory material. The purpose and intended use of an appendix are explained in the body of the related Auditing Standard or within the title and introduction of the appendix itself.

A61. Introductory material may include, as needed, such matters as explanation of:

- The purpose and scope of the Auditing Standard, including how the Auditing Standard relates to other Auditing Standards.
- The subject matter of the Auditing Standard.
- The respective responsibilities of the auditor and others in relation to the subject matter of the Auditing Standard.
- The context in which the Auditing Standard is set.

A62. An Auditing Standard may include, in a separate section under the heading "Definitions," a description of the meanings attributed to certain terms for purposes of the Australian Auditing Standards. These are provided to assist in the consistent application and interpretation of the Australian Auditing Standards, and are not intended to override definitions that may be established for other purposes, whether in law, regulation or otherwise. Unless otherwise indicated, those terms will carry the same meanings throughout the Australian Auditing Standards. The *AUASB Glossary** contains a complete listing of terms defined in the Australian Auditing Standards. It also includes descriptions of other terms found in Australian Auditing Standards to assist in common and consistent interpretation and translation.

A63. When appropriate, additional considerations specific to audits of smaller entities and public sector entities are included within the application and other explanatory material of an Auditing Standard. These additional considerations assist in the application of the requirements of the Auditing Standard in the audit of such entities. They do not, however, limit or reduce the responsibility of the auditor to apply and comply with the requirements of the Australian Auditing Standards.

Considerations Specific to Smaller Entities

A64. For purposes of specifying additional considerations to audits of smaller entities, a "smaller entity" refers to an entity which typically possesses qualitative characteristics such as:

(a) Concentration of ownership and management in a small number of individuals (often a single individual – either a natural person or another enterprise that owns the entity provided the owner exhibits the relevant qualitative characteristics); and

(b) One or more of the following:

(i) Straightforward or uncomplicated transactions;

(ii) Simple record-keeping;

(iii) Few lines of business and few products within business lines;

(iv) Few internal controls;

* Issued by the Auditing and Assurance Standards Board (October 2009).

(v) Few levels of management with responsibility for a broad range of controls; or

(vi) Few personnel, many having a wide range of duties.

These qualitative characteristics are not exhaustive, they are not exclusive to smaller entities, and smaller entities do not necessarily display all of these characteristics.

A65. The considerations specific to smaller entities included in the Australian Auditing Standards have been developed primarily with unlisted entities in mind. Some of the considerations, however, may be helpful in audits of smaller listed entities.

A66. The Australian Auditing Standards refer to the proprietor of a smaller entity who is involved in running the entity on a day-to-day basis as the "owner-manager."

Aus A66.1 When the auditor conducts the audit in accordance with Australian Auditing Standards and International Standards on Auditing ("ISAs"), in accordance with ASA 700 the auditor's report is required to refer to the audit having been conducted in accordance with the Australian Auditing Standards and the ISAs only when the auditor has complied fully with all of the Australian Auditing Standards and ISAs relevant to the audit. (Ref: Para 20)

Objectives Stated in Individual Auditing Standards (Ref: Para. 21)

A67. Each Auditing Standard contains one or more objectives which provide a link between the requirements and the overall objectives of the auditor. The objectives in individual Auditing Standards serve to focus the auditor on the desired outcome of the Auditing Standard, while being specific enough to assist the auditor in:

- Understanding what needs to be accomplished and, where necessary, the appropriate means of doing so; and
- Deciding whether more needs to be done to achieve them in the particular circumstances of the audit.

A68. Objectives are to be understood in the context of the overall objectives of the auditor stated in paragraph 11 of this Auditing Standard. As with the overall objectives of the auditor, the ability to achieve an individual objective is equally subject to the inherent limitations of an audit.

A69. In using the objectives, the auditor is required to have regard to the interrelationships among the Australian Auditing Standards. This is because, as indicated in paragraph A53, the Australian Auditing Standards deal in some cases with general responsibilities and in others, with the application of those responsibilities to specific topics. For example, this Auditing Standard requires the auditor to adopt an attitude of professional scepticism; this is necessary in all aspects of planning and performing an audit but is not repeated as a requirement of each Auditing Standard. At a more detailed level, ASA 315 and ASA 330 contain, among other things, objectives and requirements that deal with the auditor's responsibilities to identify and assess the risks of material misstatement and to design and perform further audit procedures to respond to those assessed risks, respectively; these objectives and requirements apply throughout the audit. An Auditing Standard dealing with specific aspects of the audit (for example, ASA 540) may expand on how the objectives and requirements of such Australian Auditing Standards as ASA 315 and ASA 330 are to be applied in relation to the subject of the Auditing Standard but does not repeat them. Thus, in achieving the objective stated in ASA 540, the auditor has regard to the objectives and requirements of other relevant Australian Auditing Standards.

***Use of Objectives to Determine Need for Additional Audit Procedures** (Ref: Para. 21(a))*

A70. The requirements of the Australian Auditing Standards are designed to enable the auditor to achieve the objectives specified in the Australian Auditing Standards, and thereby the overall objectives of the auditor. The proper application of the requirements of the Australian Auditing Standards by the auditor is therefore expected to provide a sufficient basis for the auditor's achievement of the objectives. However, because the circumstances of audit engagements vary widely and all such circumstances cannot be anticipated in the Australian Auditing Standards, the auditor is responsible for determining the audit procedures necessary to fulfil the requirements of the Australian Auditing Standards and to achieve the objectives. In the circumstances of an engagement, there may be particular matters that require the auditor to perform audit procedures in addition to those required by the Australian Auditing Standards to meet the objectives specified in the Australian Auditing Standards.

Use of Objectives to Evaluate Whether Sufficient Appropriate Audit Evidence Has Been Obtained (Ref: Para. 21(b))

A71. The auditor is required to use the objectives to evaluate whether sufficient appropriate audit evidence has been obtained in the context of the overall objectives of the auditor. If as a result the auditor concludes that the audit evidence is not sufficient and appropriate, then the auditor may follow one or more of the following approaches to meeting the requirement of paragraph 21(b):

- Evaluate whether further relevant audit evidence has been, or will be, obtained as a result of complying with other Australian Auditing Standards;
- Extend the work performed in applying one or more requirements; or
- Perform other procedures judged by the auditor to be necessary in the circumstances.

Where none of the above is expected to be practical or possible in the circumstances, the auditor will not be able to obtain sufficient appropriate audit evidence and is required by Australian Auditing Standards to determine the effect on the auditor's report or on the auditor's ability to complete the engagement.

Complying with Relevant Requirements

Relevant Requirements (Ref: Para. 22)

A72. In some cases, an Auditing Standard (and therefore all of its requirements) may not be relevant in the circumstances. For example, if an entity does not have an internal audit function, nothing in ASA 610[26] is relevant.

A73. Within a relevant Auditing Standard, there may be conditional requirements. Such a requirement is relevant when the circumstances envisioned in the requirement apply and the condition exists. In general, the conditionality of a requirement will either be explicit or implicit, for example:

- The requirement to modify the auditor's opinion if there is limitation of scope[27] represents an explicit conditional requirement.
- The requirement to communicate significant deficiencies in internal control identified during the audit to those charged with governance,[28] which depends on the existence of such identified significant deficiencies; and the requirement to obtain sufficient appropriate audit evidence regarding the presentation and disclosure of segment information in accordance with the applicable financial reporting framework,[29] which depends on that framework requiring or permitting such disclosure, represent implicit conditional requirements.

In some cases, a requirement may be expressed as being conditional on applicable law or regulation. For example, the auditor may be required to withdraw from the audit engagement, *where withdrawal is possible under applicable law or regulation,* or the auditor may be required to do something, *unless prohibited by law or regulation.* Depending on the jurisdiction, the legal or regulatory permission or prohibition may be explicit or implicit.

26 See ASA 610 *Using the Work of Internal Auditors.*

27 See ASA 705 *Modifications to the Opinion in the Independent Auditor's Report*, paragraph 13.

28 See ASA 265 *Communicating Deficiencies in Internal Control to Those Charged with Governance and Management*, paragraph 9.

29 See ASA 501 *Audit Evidence—Specific Considerations for Inventory and Segment Information*, paragraph 13.

***Inability to Comply with a Requirement** (Ref: Para. A23-Aus 23.1)*

A74. ASA 230 establishes documentation requirements in those rare and exceptional circumstances where the auditor is unable to comply with a relevant requirement.[30] Australian Auditing Standards do not call for compliance with a requirement that is not relevant in the circumstances of the audit.

Aus A74.1 Where in rare and exceptional circumstances, factors outside the auditor's control prevent the auditor from complying with an essential procedure contained within a relevant requirement, compliance with Australian Auditing Standards can still be represented provided the auditor has complied with the requirements of paragraph Aus 23.1.

Failure to Achieve an Objective (Ref: Para. 24)

A75. Whether an objective has been achieved is a matter for the auditor's professional judgement. That judgement takes account of the results of audit procedures performed in complying with the requirements of the Australian Auditing Standards, and the auditor's evaluation of whether sufficient appropriate audit evidence has been obtained and whether more needs to be done in the particular circumstances of the audit to achieve the objectives stated in the Australian Auditing Standards. Accordingly, circumstances that may give rise to a failure to achieve an objective include those that:

- Prevent the auditor from complying with the relevant requirements of an Auditing Standard.
- Result in its not being practicable or possible for the auditor to carry out the additional audit procedures or obtain further audit evidence as determined necessary from the use of the objectives in accordance with paragraph 21, for example due to a limitation in the available audit evidence.

A76. Audit documentation that meets the requirements of ASA 230 and the specific documentation requirements of other relevant Australian Auditing Standards provides evidence of the auditor's basis for a conclusion about the achievement of the overall objectives of the auditor. While it is unnecessary for the auditor to document separately (as in a checklist, for example) that individual objectives have been achieved, the documentation of a failure to achieve an objective assists the auditor's evaluation of whether such a failure has prevented the auditor from achieving the overall objectives of the auditor.

❖❖❖

Conformity with International Standards on Auditing

This Auditing Standard conforms with International Standard on Auditing ISA 200 *Overall Objectives of the Independent Auditor and the Conduct of an Audit in Accordance with International Standards on Auditing*, issued by the International Auditing and Assurance Standards Board (IAASB), an independent standard-setting board of the International Federation of Accountants (IFAC).

Paragraphs that have been added to this Auditing Standard (and do not appear in the text of the equivalent ISA) are identified with the prefix "Aus".

The following requirements are additional to ISA 200:

- Subject to paragraph Aus 23.1 of this Auditing Standard, the auditor shall comply with each requirement of an Auditing Standard unless, in the circumstances of the audit:
  - ♦ The entire Auditing Standard is not relevant;
  - ♦ The requirement is not relevant because it is conditional and the condition does not exist; or
  - ♦ Application of the requirement(s) would relate to classes of transactions, account balances or disclosures that the auditor has determined are immaterial. (Ref: Para. Aus 22.1)

30 See ASA 230, paragraph 12.

- Where in rare and exceptional circumstances, factors outside the auditor's control prevent the auditor from complying with an essential procedure contained within a relevant requirement, the auditor shall:
  - If possible, perform appropriate alternative audit procedures; and
  - In accordance with ASA 230, document in the working papers:
    - The circumstances surrounding the inability to comply;
    - The reasons for the inability to comply; and
    - Justification of how alternative audit procedures achieve the objectives of the requirement. (Ref: Para. Aus 23.1)

This Auditing Standard incorporates terminology and definitions used in Australia.

The equivalent requirements and related application and other explanatory material included in ISA 200 in respect of "relevant ethical requirements", have been included in another Auditing Standard, ASA 102 *Compliance with Ethical Requirements when Performing Audits, Reviews and Other Assurance Engagements*. There is no international equivalent to ASA 102.

Compliance with this Auditing Standard enables compliance with ISA 200.

ASA 210
Agreeing the Terms of Audit Engagements

(Reissued October 2009: amended and compiled June 2011)

Issued by the Auditing and Assurance Standards Board.

Note from the Institute of Chartered Accountants Australia

This note, prepared by the technical editor, is not part of ASA 210.

Historical development

January 1983: Statement of Auditing Practice AUP 9, 'Audit Engagement Letters', issued, effective from date of issue. The AuSB did not issue an exposure draft on this topic; however, as noted in para. 14 of the 'Foreword to Statements of Auditing Standards and Statements of Auditing Practice', the AuSB determined that unless noted to the contrary an exposure draft issued by the International Auditing Practice Committee of the International Federation of Accountants is to be regarded as an Australian exposure draft. Such an exposure draft, IAPC ED 2, was issued in May 1979 and was distributed in Australia to subscribers to The Institute of Chartered Accountants in Australia's IASC International Accounting Standards/IFAC Guidelines Handbook and by the Australian Society of Accountants with a request for comments. The statement was based on IAG 2 which was issued in June 1980.

December 1993: ED 53 'Codification and Revision of Auditing Pronouncements: AUS 204 Terms of Audit Engagements (AUP 9)' issued by the AuSB.

June 1994: The International Auditing Practices Committee (IAPC) of the International Federation of Accountants (IFAC) approved the issuance of a codified set of International Standards of Auditing (ISAs). The relevant international pronouncement was ISA 210 'Terms of Audit Engagements'.

October 1995: Australian Auditing Standards and Auditing Guidance Statements released. The status of these was explained in APS 1.1 'Conformity With Auditing Standards'. These Standards become operative for the first reporting period commencing on or after 1 July 1996 and later reporting periods, although earlier application was encouraged. AUP 9 'Audit Engagement Letters' replaced by AUS 204 'Terms of Audit Engagements'.

April 1998: AUS/AGS Omnibus 1 'Miscellaneous Amendments to AUSs and AGSs' issued. AUS 204 subsequently reissued to incorporate these amendments.

September 1999: ED 74 'Terms of Audit Engagements (Revision of AUS 204)' issued by the AuASB, with comments sought by 30 November 1999.

June 2000: AUS 204 reissued by the AuASB, operative for audit engagements beginning on or after 1 January 2001. Superseded the AUS 204 issued in October 1995.

April 2006: ASA 210 was issued as a legally enforceable Standard to replace AUS 204. It is based on ISA 210 of the same name.

June 2007: ASA 210 compiled and republished to reflect the changes to the ASA 700 audit report introduced by Omnibus ASA 2007-1.

October 2009: ASA 210 reissued as part of the AUASB's Clarity Project. As a precondition for an audit, the auditor now has to determine whether the financial reporting framework is acceptable and consider whether there is any limitation on the scope of the audit. It is based on the revised ISA 210 of the same name.

June 2011: ASA 210 updated for editorial amendments contained in ASA 2011-1 'Amendments to Australian Auditing Standards'.

Contents

Compilation Details

Auditing Standard ASA 210 *Agreeing the Terms of Audit Engagements* as Amended

This compilation takes into account amendments made up to and including 27 June 2011 and was prepared on 27 June 2011 by the Auditing and Assurance Standards Board (AUASB).

This compilation is not a separate Auditing Standard made by the AUASB. Instead, it is a representation of ASA 210 (October 2009) as amended by another Auditing Standard which is listed in the Table below.

Table of Standards

Standard	Date made	Operative date
ASA 210	27 October 2009	1 January 2010
ASA 2011-1	27 June 2011	1 July 2011

Table of Amendments

Paragraph affected	How affected	By ... [paragraph]
A4	Amended	ASA 2011-1 [16]
Appendix 2 Para. 4	Amended	ASA 2011-1 [17]
Appendix 1 First Paragraph	Amended	ASA 2011-1 [18]
Appendix 1 Paragraph headed AGM	Amended	ASA 2011-1 [19]

Preface

[Preface extracted from the original Auditing Standard issued 27 October 2009]

Reasons for Issuing Auditing Standard ASA 210 *Agreeing the Terms of Audit Engagements*

The Auditing and Assurance Standards Board (AUASB) issues Auditing Standard ASA 210 *Agreeing the Terms of Audit Engagements* pursuant to the requirements of the legislative provisions and the Strategic Direction explained below.

The AUASB is an independent statutory board of the Australian Government established under section 227A of the *Australian Securities and Investments Commission Act 2001*, as amended (ASIC Act). Under section 336 of the *Corporations Act 2001*, the AUASB may make Auditing Standards for the purposes of the corporations legislation. These Auditing Standards are legislative instruments under the *Legislative Instruments Act 2003*.

Under the Strategic Direction given to the AUASB by the Financial Reporting Council (FRC), the AUASB is required to have regard to any programme initiated by the International Auditing and Assurance Standards Board (IAASB) for the revision and enhancement of the International Standards on Auditing (ISAs) and to make appropriate consequential amendments to the Australian Auditing Standards. Accordingly, the AUASB has decided to revise and redraft the Australian Auditing Standards using the equivalent redrafted ISAs.

Main Features

This Auditing Standard establishes requirements and provides application and other explanatory material regarding the auditor's responsibilities in agreeing the terms of the audit engagement with management and, where appropriate, those charged with governance.

This Auditing Standard:

(a) requires the auditor to establish that the preconditions for an audit are present, including management's use of an acceptable financial reporting framework, and agreement and acknowledgement of its responsibilities in the preparation of the financial report;

(b) prohibits an auditor from accepting, unless required by law or regulation, an audit engagement where management has imposed a limitation in scope that the auditor believes will result in a disclaimer of opinion on the financial report;

(c) requires the auditor to agree the terms of the audit engagement with management or those charged with governance;

(d) requires the auditor to record the terms of engagement in an audit engagement letter or other suitable form of written agreement;

(e) describes the requirements when the auditor has to address a change in the terms of an audit engagement; and

(f) provides direction when:

- the financial reporting standards are supplemented by law or regulation;
- the financial reporting framework is prescribed by law or regulation; and
- the auditor's report is prescribed by law or regulation.

Authority Statement

Auditing Standard ASA 210 *Agreeing the Terms of Audit Engagements* (as amended at 27 June 2011) is set out in paragraphs 1 to A37 and Appendices 1 and 2.

This Auditing Standard is to be read in conjunction with ASA 101 *Preamble to Australian Auditing Standards*, which sets out the intentions of the AUASB on how the Australian Auditing Standards, operative for financial reporting periods commencing on or after 1 January 2010, are to be understood, interpreted and applied. This Auditing Standard is to be read also in conjunction with ASA 200 *Overall Objectives of the Independent Auditor and the Conduct of an Audit in Accordance with Australian Auditing Standards*.

Dated: 27 June 2011

M H Kelsall
Chairman - AUASB

Auditing Standard ASA 210

The Auditing and Assurance Standards Board (AUASB) made Auditing Standard ASA 210 *Agreeing the Terms of Audit Engagements*, pursuant to section 227B of the *Australian Securities and Investments Commission Act 2001* and section 336 of the *Corporations Act 2001*, on 27 October 2009.

This compiled version of ASA 210 incorporates subsequent amendments contained in another Auditing Standard made by the AUASB up to and including 27 June 2011 (see Compilation Details).

ASA

Auditing Standard ASA 210

Agreeing the Terms of Audit Engagements

Application

Aus 0.1 This Auditing Standard applies to:

(a) an audit of a financial report for a financial year, or an audit of a financial report for a half-year, in accordance with the *Corporations Act 2001*; and

(b) an audit of a financial report, or a complete set of financial statements, for any other purpose.

Aus 0.2 This Auditing Standard also applies, as appropriate, to an audit of other historical financial information.

Operative Date

Aus 0.3 This Auditing Standard is operative for financial reporting periods commencing on or after 1 January 2010.

[Note: For operative dates of paragraphs changed or added by an amending Standard, see Compilation Details.]

Introduction

Scope of this Auditing Standard

1. This Auditing Standard deals with the auditor's responsibilities in agreeing the terms of the audit engagement with management and, where appropriate, those charged with governance. This includes establishing that certain preconditions for an audit, responsibility for which rests with management and, where appropriate, those charged with governance, are present. ASA 220[1] deals with those aspects of engagement acceptance that are within the control of the auditor. (Ref: Para. A1)

Effective Date

2. [Deleted by the AUASB. Refer Aus 0.3]

Objective

3. The objective of the auditor is to accept or continue an audit engagement only when the basis upon which it is to be performed has been agreed, through:

(a) Establishing whether the preconditions for an audit are present; and

1 See ASA 220 *Quality Control for an Audit of a Financial Report and Other Historical Financial Information*.

(b) Confirming that there is a common understanding between the auditor and management and, where appropriate, those charged with governance of the terms of the audit engagement.

Definitions

4. For purposes of the Australian Auditing Standards, the following term has the meaning attributed below:

   Preconditions for an audit means the use by management of an acceptable financial reporting framework in the preparation of the financial report and the agreement of management and, where appropriate, those charged with governance to the premise[2] on which an audit is conducted.

5. For the purposes of this Auditing Standard, references to "management" should be read hereafter as "management and, where appropriate, those charged with governance."

Requirements

Preconditions for an Audit

6. In order to establish whether the preconditions for an audit are present, the auditor shall:

   (a) Determine whether the financial reporting framework to be applied in the preparation of the financial report is acceptable; and (Ref: Para. A2-A10)

   (b) Obtain the agreement of management that it acknowledges and understands its responsibility: (Ref: Para. A11-A14, A20-Aus A20.1)

      (i) For the preparation of the financial report in accordance with the applicable financial reporting framework, including where relevant their fair presentation; (Ref: Para. A15)

      (ii) For such internal control as management determines is necessary to enable the preparation of the financial report that is free from material misstatement, whether due to fraud or error; and (Ref: Para. A16-A19)

      (iii) To provide the auditor with:

         a. Access to all information of which management is aware that is relevant to the preparation of the financial report such as records, documentation and other matters;

         b. Additional information that the auditor may request from management for the purpose of the audit; and

         c. Unrestricted access to persons within the entity from whom the auditor determines it necessary to obtain audit evidence.

Limitation on Scope Prior to Audit Engagement Acceptance

7. If management or those charged with governance impose a limitation on the scope of the auditor's work in the terms of a proposed audit engagement such that the auditor believes the limitation will result in the auditor disclaiming an opinion on the financial report, the auditor shall not accept such a limited engagement as an audit engagement, unless required by law or regulation to do so.

Other Factors Affecting Audit Engagement Acceptance

8. If the preconditions for an audit are not present, the auditor shall discuss the matter with management. Unless required by law or regulation to do so, the auditor shall not accept the proposed audit engagement:

   (a) If the auditor has determined that the financial reporting framework to be applied in the preparation of the financial report is unacceptable, except as provided in paragraph 19 of this Auditing Standard; or

   (b) If the agreement referred to in paragraph 6(b) of this Auditing Standard has not been obtained.

---

2 See ASA 200 *Overall Objectives of the Independent Auditor and the Conduct of an Audit in Accordance with Australian Auditing Standards*, paragraph 13.

Agreement on Audit Engagement Terms

9. The auditor shall agree the terms of the audit engagement with management or those charged with governance, as appropriate. (Ref: Para. A21)

10. Subject to paragraph 11 of this Auditing Standard, the agreed terms of the audit engagement shall be recorded in an audit engagement letter or other suitable form of written agreement and shall include: (Ref: Para. A22-A25)
    (a) The objective and scope of the audit of the financial report;
    (b) The responsibilities of the auditor;
    (c) The responsibilities of management;
    (d) Identification of the applicable financial reporting framework for the preparation of the financial report; and
    (e) Reference to the expected form and content of any reports to be issued by the auditor and a statement that there may be circumstances in which a report may differ from its expected form and content.

11. If law or regulation prescribes in sufficient detail the terms of the audit engagement referred to in paragraph 10 of this Auditing Standard, the auditor need not record them in a written agreement, except for the fact that such law or regulation applies and that management acknowledges and understands its responsibilities as set out in paragraph 6(b) of this Auditing Standard. (Ref: Para. A22, A26-A27)

12. If law or regulation prescribes responsibilities of management similar to those described in paragraph 6(b) of this Auditing Standard, the auditor may determine that the law or regulation includes responsibilities that, in the auditor's judgement, are equivalent in effect to those set out in that paragraph. For such responsibilities that are equivalent, the auditor may use the wording of the law or regulation to describe them in the written agreement. For those responsibilities that are not prescribed by law or regulation such that their effect is equivalent, the written agreement shall use the description in paragraph 6(b) of this Auditing Standard. (Ref: Para. A26)

Recurring Audits

13. On recurring audits, the auditor shall assess whether circumstances require the terms of the audit engagement to be revised and whether there is a need to remind the entity of the existing terms of the audit engagement. (Ref: Para. A28)

Acceptance of a Change in the Terms of the Audit Engagement

14. The auditor shall not agree to a change in the terms of the audit engagement where there is no reasonable justification for doing so. (Ref: Para. A29-A31)

15. If, prior to completing the audit engagement, the auditor is requested to change the audit engagement to an engagement that conveys a lower level of assurance, the auditor shall determine whether there is reasonable justification for doing so. (Ref: Para. A32-A33)

16. If the terms of the audit engagement are changed, the auditor and management shall agree on and record the new terms of the engagement in an engagement letter or other suitable form of written agreement.

17. If the auditor is unable to agree to a change of the terms of the audit engagement and is not permitted by management to continue the original audit engagement, the auditor shall:
    (a) Withdraw from the audit engagement where possible under applicable law or regulation; and
    (b) Determine whether there is any obligation, either contractual or otherwise, to report the circumstances to other parties, such as those charged with governance, owners or regulators.

Additional Considerations in Engagement Acceptance

Financial Reporting Standards Supplemented by Law or Regulation

18. If financial reporting standards established by an authorised or recognised standards setting organisation are supplemented by law or regulation, the auditor shall determine whether there are any conflicts between the financial reporting standards and the additional

requirements. If such conflicts exist, the auditor shall discuss with management the nature of the additional requirements and shall agree whether:

(a) The additional requirements can be met through additional disclosures in the financial report; or

(b) The description of the applicable financial reporting framework in the financial report can be amended accordingly.

If neither of the above actions is possible, the auditor shall determine whether it will be necessary to modify the auditor's opinion in accordance with ASA 705.[3] (Ref: Para. A34)

Financial Reporting Framework Prescribed by Law or Regulation—Other Matters Affecting Acceptance

19. If the auditor has determined that the financial reporting framework prescribed by law or regulation would be unacceptable but for the fact that it is prescribed by law or regulation, the auditor shall accept the audit engagement only if the following conditions are present: (Ref: Para. A35)

(a) Management agrees to provide additional disclosures in the financial report required to avoid the financial report being misleading; and

(b) It is recognised in the terms of the audit engagement that:

(i) The auditor's report on the financial report will incorporate an Emphasis of Matter paragraph, drawing users' attention to the additional disclosures, in accordance with ASA 706;[4] and

(ii) Unless the auditor is required by law or regulation to express the auditor's opinion on the financial report by using the phrases "present fairly, in all material respects," or "give a true and fair view" in accordance with the applicable financial reporting framework, the auditor's opinion on the financial report will not include such phrases.

20. If the conditions outlined in paragraph 19 of this Auditing Standard are not present and the auditor is required by law or regulation to undertake the audit engagement, the auditor shall:

(a) Evaluate the effect of the misleading nature of the financial report on the auditor's report; and

(b) Include appropriate reference to this matter in the terms of the audit engagement.

Auditor's Report Prescribed by Law or Regulation

21. In some cases, law or regulation of the relevant jurisdiction prescribes the layout or wording of the auditor's report in a form or in terms that are significantly different from the requirements of the Australian Auditing Standards. In these circumstances, the auditor shall evaluate:

(a) Whether users might misunderstand the assurance obtained from the audit of the financial report and, if so,

(b) Whether additional explanation in the auditor's report can mitigate possible misunderstanding.[5]

If the auditor concludes that additional explanation in the auditor's report cannot mitigate possible misunderstanding, the auditor shall not accept the audit engagement, unless required by law or regulation to do so. An audit conducted in accordance with such law or regulation does not comply with Australian Auditing Standards. Accordingly, the auditor shall not include any reference within the auditor's report to the audit having been conducted in accordance with Australian Auditing Standards.[6] (Ref: Para. A36-A37)

❖ ❖ ❖

3 See ASA 705 *Modifications to the Opinion in the Independent Auditor's Report*.

4 See ASA 706 *Emphasis of Matter Paragraphs and Other Matter Paragraphs in the Independent Auditor's Report*.

5 See ASA 706.

6 See also ASA 700 *Forming an Opinion and Reporting on a Financial Report*, paragraph 43.

Application and Other Explanatory Material

Scope of this Auditing Standard (Ref: Para. 1)

A1. Assurance engagements, which include audit engagements, may only be accepted when the practitioner considers that relevant ethical requirements such as independence and professional competence will be satisfied, and when the engagement exhibits certain characteristics.[7] The auditor's responsibilities in respect of ethical requirements in the context of the acceptance of an audit engagement and in so far as they are within the control of the auditor are dealt with in ASA 220.[8] This Auditing Standard deals with those matters (or preconditions) that are within the control of the entity and upon which it is necessary for the auditor and the entity's management to agree.

Preconditions for an Audit

The Financial Reporting Framework (Ref: Para. 6(a))

A2. A condition for acceptance of an assurance engagement is that the criteria referred to in the definition of an assurance engagement are suitable and available to intended users.[9] Criteria are the benchmarks used to evaluate or measure the subject matter including, where relevant, benchmarks for presentation and disclosure. Suitable criteria enable reasonably consistent evaluation or measurement of a subject matter within the context of professional judgement. For purposes of the Australian Auditing Standards, the applicable financial reporting framework provides the criteria the auditor uses to audit the financial report, including where relevant its fair presentation.

A3. Without an acceptable financial reporting framework, management does not have an appropriate basis for the preparation of the financial report and the auditor does not have suitable criteria for auditing the financial report. In many cases, the auditor may presume that the applicable financial reporting framework is acceptable, as described in paragraphs A8-A9.

Determining the Acceptability of the Financial Reporting Framework

A4. Factors that are relevant to the auditor's determination of the acceptability of the financial reporting framework to be applied in the preparation of the financial report include:

- The nature of the entity (for example, whether it is a business enterprise, a public sector entity or a not-for-profit organisation);
- The purpose of the financial report (for example, whether it is prepared to meet the common financial information needs of a wide range of users or the financial information needs of specific users);
- The nature of the financial statements (for example, whether the financial statements are a complete set of financial statements or a single financial statement); and
- Whether law or regulation prescribes the applicable financial reporting framework.

A5. Many users of financial reports are not in a position to demand financial reports tailored to meet their specific information needs. While all the information needs of specific users cannot be met, there are financial information needs that are common to a wide range of users. Financial reports prepared in accordance with a financial reporting framework designed to meet the common financial information needs of a wide range of users are referred to as general purpose financial reports.

A6. In some cases, the financial report will be prepared in accordance with a financial reporting framework designed to meet the financial information needs of specific users. Such financial reports are referred to as special purpose financial reports. The financial information needs of the intended users will determine the applicable financial reporting

7 See *Framework for Assurance Engagements*.

8 See ASA 220, paragraphs 9-11.

9 See *Framework for Assurance Engagements*.

framework in these circumstances. ASA 800 discusses the acceptability of financial reporting frameworks designed to meet the financial information needs of specific users.[10]

A7. Deficiencies in the applicable financial reporting framework that indicate that the framework is not acceptable may be encountered after the audit engagement has been accepted. When use of that framework is prescribed by law or regulation, the requirements of paragraphs 19-20 apply. When use of that framework is not prescribed by law or regulation, management may decide to adopt another framework that is acceptable. When management does so, as required by paragraph 16, new terms of the audit engagement are agreed to reflect the change in the framework as the previously agreed terms will no longer be accurate.

General purpose frameworks

A8. At present, there is no objective and authoritative basis that has been generally recognised globally for judging the acceptability of general purpose frameworks. In the absence of such a basis, financial reporting standards established by organisations that are authorised or recognised to promulgate standards to be used by certain types of entities are presumed to be acceptable for general purpose financial reports prepared by such entities, provided the organisations follow an established and transparent process involving deliberation and consideration of the views of a wide range of stakeholders. Examples of such financial reporting standards include:

- International Financial Reporting Standards (IFRSs) promulgated by the International Accounting Standards Board;
- International Public Sector Accounting Standards (IPSASs) promulgated by the International Public Sector Accounting Standards Board; and
- Accounting principles promulgated by an authorised or recognised standards setting organisation in a particular jurisdiction,* provided the organisation follows an established and transparent process involving deliberation and consideration of the views of a wide range of stakeholders.

These financial reporting standards are often identified as the applicable financial reporting framework in law or regulation governing the preparation of general purpose financial reports.

Financial reporting frameworks prescribed by law or regulation

A9. In accordance with paragraph 6(a), the auditor is required to determine whether the financial reporting framework, to be applied in the preparation of the financial report, is acceptable. In some jurisdictions, law or regulation may prescribe the financial reporting framework to be used in the preparation of a general purpose financial report for certain types of entities. In the absence of indications to the contrary, such a financial reporting framework is presumed to be acceptable for a general purpose financial report prepared by such entities. In the event that the framework is not considered to be acceptable, paragraphs 19-20 apply.

Jurisdictions that do not have standards setting organisations or prescribed financial reporting frameworks

A10. When an entity is registered or operating in a jurisdiction that does not have an authorised or recognised standards setting organisation, or where use of the financial reporting framework is not prescribed by law or regulation, management identifies a financial reporting framework to be applied in the preparation of the financial report. Appendix 2 contains guidance on determining the acceptability of financial reporting frameworks in such circumstances.

Agreement of the Responsibilities of Management (Ref: Para. 6(b))

A11. An audit in accordance with Australian Auditing Standards is conducted on the premise that management has acknowledged and understands that it has the responsibilities set

* The Australian Accounting Standards Board (AASB) sets accounting standards in Australia.

10 See ASA 800 *Special Considerations—Audits of Financial Reports Prepared in Accordance with Special Purpose Frameworks,* paragraph 8.

out in paragraph 6(b).[11] In certain jurisdictions, such responsibilities may be specified in law or regulation. In others, there may be little or no legal or regulatory definition of such responsibilities. Australian Auditing Standards do not override law or regulation in such matters. However, the concept of an independent audit requires that the auditor's role does not involve taking responsibility for the preparation of the financial report or for the entity's related internal control, and that the auditor has a reasonable expectation of obtaining the information necessary for the audit in so far as management is able to provide or procure it. Accordingly, the premise is fundamental to the conduct of an independent audit. To avoid misunderstanding, agreement is reached with management that it acknowledges and understands that it has such responsibilities as part of agreeing and recording the terms of the audit engagement in paragraphs 9-12.

A12. The way in which the responsibilities for financial reporting are divided between management and those charged with governance will vary according to the resources and structure of the entity and any relevant law or regulation, and the respective roles of management and those charged with governance within the entity. In most cases, management is responsible for execution while those charged with governance have oversight of management. In some cases, those charged with governance will have, or will assume, responsibility for approving the financial report or monitoring the entity's internal control related to financial reporting. In larger or publicly-listed entities, a subgroup of those charged with governance, such as an audit committee, may be charged with certain oversight responsibilities.

A13. ASA 580 requires the auditor to request management to provide written representations that it has fulfilled certain of its responsibilities.[12] It may therefore be appropriate to make management aware that receipt of such written representations will be expected, together with written representations required by other Australian Auditing Standards and, where necessary, written representations to support other audit evidence relevant to the financial report or one or more specific assertions in the financial report.

A14. Where management will not acknowledge its responsibilities, or agree to provide the written representations, the auditor will be unable to obtain sufficient appropriate audit evidence.[13] In such circumstances, it would not be appropriate for the auditor to accept the audit engagement, unless law or regulation requires the auditor to do so. In cases where the auditor is required to accept the audit engagement, the auditor may need to explain to management the importance of these matters, and the implications for the auditor's report.

Preparation of the Financial Report (Ref: Para. 6(b)(i))

A15. Most financial reporting frameworks include requirements relating to the presentation of the financial report; for such frameworks, *preparation* of the financial report in accordance with the financial reporting framework includes *presentation*. In the case of a fair presentation framework the importance of the reporting objective of fair presentation is such that the premise agreed with management includes specific reference to fair presentation, or to the responsibility to ensure that the financial report will "give a true and fair view" in accordance with the financial reporting framework.

Internal Control (Ref: Para. 6(b)(ii))

A16. Management maintains such internal control as it determines is necessary to enable the preparation of the financial report that is free from material misstatement, whether due to fraud or error. Internal control, no matter how effective, can provide an entity with only reasonable assurance about achieving the entity's financial reporting objectives due to the inherent limitations of internal control.[14]

A17. An independent audit conducted in accordance with the Australian Auditing Standards does not act as a substitute for the maintenance of internal control necessary for the preparation of the financial report by management. Accordingly, the auditor is required

11 See ASA 200, paragraph A2.

12 See ASA 580 *Written Representations*, paragraphs 10-11.

13 See ASA 580, paragraphs A26-Aus A26.1.

14 See ASA 315 *Identifying and Assessing the Risks of Material Misstatement through Understanding the Entity and Its Environment*, paragraph A46.

to obtain the agreement of management that it acknowledges and understands its responsibility for internal control. However, the agreement required by paragraph 6(b)(ii) does not imply that the auditor will find that internal control maintained by management has achieved its purpose or will be free of deficiencies.

A18. It is for management to determine what internal control is necessary to enable the preparation of the financial report. The term "internal control" encompasses a wide range of activities within components that may be described as the control environment; the entity's risk assessment process; the information system, including the related business processes relevant to financial reporting, and communication; control activities; and monitoring of controls. This division, however, does not necessarily reflect how a particular entity may design, implement and maintain its internal control, or how it may classify any particular component.[15] An entity's internal control (in particular, its accounting books and records, or accounting systems) will reflect the needs of management, the complexity of the business, the nature of the risks to which the entity is subject, and relevant laws or regulation.

A19. In some jurisdictions, law or regulation may refer to the responsibility of management for the adequacy of accounting books and records, or accounting systems. In some cases, general practice may assume a distinction between accounting books and records or accounting systems on the one hand, and internal control or controls on the other. As accounting books and records, or accounting systems, are an integral part of internal control as referred to in paragraph A18, no specific reference is made to them in paragraph 6(b)(ii) for the description of the responsibility of management. To avoid misunderstanding, it may be appropriate for the auditor to explain to management the scope of this responsibility.

Considerations Relevant to Smaller Entities (Ref: Para. 6(b))

A20. One of the purposes of agreeing the terms of the audit engagement is to avoid misunderstanding about the respective responsibilities of management and the auditor. For example, when a third party has assisted with the preparation of the financial report, it may be useful to remind management that the preparation of the financial report in accordance with the applicable financial reporting framework remains its responsibility.

Management-Imposed Limitation of Scope (Ref: Para. 6(b))

Aus A20.1 Section 312 of the *Corporations Act 2001* (the Act) requires an officer of the entity to allow the auditor access to the books of the entity and give any information, explanation or assistance required under section 310 of the Act. A management-imposed restriction of scope may breach section 312 and trigger the need for a section 311 notice to be provided by the auditor to the Australian Securities and Investments Commission (ASIC).

Agreement on Audit Engagement Terms

Agreeing the Terms of the Audit Engagement (Ref: Para. 9)

A21. The roles of management and those charged with governance in agreeing the terms of the audit engagement for the entity depend on the governance structure of the entity and relevant law or regulation.

Audit Engagement Letter or Other Form of Written Agreement[16] (Ref: Para. 10-11)

A22. It is in the interests of both the entity and the auditor that the auditor sends an audit engagement letter before the commencement of the audit to help avoid misunderstandings with respect to the audit. In some countries, however, the objective and scope of an audit and the responsibilities of management and of the auditor may be sufficiently established by law, that is, they prescribe the matters described in paragraph 10. Although in these circumstances paragraph 11 permits the auditor to include in the engagement letter only reference to the fact that relevant law or regulation applies and that management acknowledges and understands its responsibilities as set out in paragraph 6(b), the auditor

15 See ASA 315, paragraph A51 and Appendix 1.

16 In the paragraphs that follow, any reference to an audit engagement letter is to be taken as a reference to an audit engagement letter or other suitable form of written agreement.

may nevertheless consider it appropriate to include the matters described in paragraph 10 in an engagement letter for the information of management.

Form and Content of the Audit Engagement Letter

A23. The form and content of the audit engagement letter may vary for each entity. Information included in the audit engagement letter on the auditor's responsibilities may be based on ASA 200.[17] Paragraphs 6(b) and 12 of this Auditing Standard deal with the description of the responsibilities of management. In addition to including the matters required by paragraph 10, an audit engagement letter may make reference to, for example:

- Elaboration of the scope of the audit, including reference to applicable legislation, regulations, Australian Auditing Standards, and ethical and other pronouncements of professional bodies to which the auditor adheres.
- The form of any other communication of results of the audit engagement.
- The fact that because of the inherent limitations of an audit, together with the inherent limitations of internal control, there is an unavoidable risk that some material misstatements may not be detected, even though the audit is properly planned and performed in accordance with Australian Auditing Standards.
- Arrangements regarding the planning and performance of the audit, including the composition of the audit team.
- The expectation that management will provide written representations (see also paragraph A13).
- The agreement of management to make available to the auditor a draft financial report and any accompanying other information in time to allow the auditor to complete the audit in accordance with the proposed timetable.
- The agreement of management to inform the auditor of facts that may affect the financial report, of which management may become aware during the period from the date of the auditor's report to the date the financial report is issued.
- The basis on which fees are computed and any billing arrangements.
- A request for management to acknowledge receipt of the audit engagement letter and to agree to the terms of the engagement outlined therein.

A24. When relevant, the following points could also be made in the audit engagement letter:

- Arrangements concerning the involvement of other auditors and experts in some aspects of the audit.
- Arrangements concerning the involvement of internal auditors and other staff of the entity.
- Arrangements to be made with the predecessor auditor, if any, in the case of an initial audit.
- Any restriction of the auditor's liability when such possibility exists.
- A reference to any further agreements between the auditor and the entity.
- Any obligations to provide audit working papers to other parties.

An example of an audit engagement letter is set out in Appendix 1.

Audits of Components

A25. When the auditor of a parent entity is also the auditor of a component,* the factors that may influence the decision whether to send a separate audit engagement letter to the component include the following:

- Who appoints the component auditor;
- Whether a separate auditor's report is to be issued on the component;
- Legal requirements in relation to audit appointments;

17 See ASA 200, paragraphs 3-9.

* See ASA 600 *Special Considerations—Audits of a Group Financial Report (Including the Work of Component Auditors).*

- Degree of ownership by parent; and
- Degree of independence of the component management from the parent entity.

***Responsibilities of Management Prescribed by Law or Regulation** (Ref: Para. 11-12)*

A26. If, in the circumstances described in paragraphs A22 and A27, the auditor concludes that it is not necessary to record certain terms of the audit engagement in an audit engagement letter, the auditor is still required by paragraph 11 to seek the written agreement from management that it acknowledges and understands that it has the responsibilities set out in paragraph 6(b). However, in accordance with paragraph 12, such written agreement may use the wording of the law or regulation if such law or regulation establishes responsibilities for management that are equivalent in effect to those described in paragraph 6(b). The accounting profession, audit standards setter, or audit regulator in a jurisdiction may have provided guidance as to whether the description in law or regulation is equivalent.

Considerations specific to public sector entities

A27. Law or regulation governing the operations of public sector audits generally mandate the appointment of a public sector auditor and commonly set out the public sector auditor's responsibilities and powers, including the power to access an entity's records and other information. When law or regulation prescribes in sufficient detail the terms of the audit engagement, the public sector auditor may nonetheless consider that there are benefits in issuing a fuller audit engagement letter than permitted by paragraph 11.

Recurring Audits (Ref: Para. 13)

A28. The auditor may decide not to send a new audit engagement letter or other written agreement each period. However, the following factors may make it appropriate to revise the terms of the audit engagement or to remind the entity of existing terms:

- Any indication that the entity misunderstands the objective and scope of the audit.
- Any revised or special terms of the audit engagement.
- A recent change of senior management.
- A significant change in ownership.
- A significant change in nature or size of the entity's business.
- A change in legal or regulatory requirements.
- A change in the financial reporting framework adopted in the preparation of the financial report.
- A change in other reporting requirements.

Acceptance of a Change in the Terms of the Audit Engagement

Request to Change the Terms of the Audit Engagement (Ref: Para. 14)

A29. A request from the entity for the auditor to change the terms of the audit engagement may result from a change in circumstances affecting the need for the service, a misunderstanding as to the nature of an audit as originally requested or a restriction on the scope of the audit engagement, whether imposed by management or caused by other circumstances. The auditor, as required by paragraph 14, considers the justification given for the request, particularly the implications of a restriction on the scope of the audit engagement.

A30. A change in circumstances that affects the entity's requirements or a misunderstanding concerning the nature of the service originally requested may be considered a reasonable basis for requesting a change in the audit engagement.

A31. In contrast, a change may not be considered reasonable if it appears that the change relates to information that is incorrect, incomplete or otherwise unsatisfactory. An example might be where the auditor is unable to obtain sufficient appropriate audit evidence regarding receivables and the entity asks for the audit engagement to be changed to a review engagement to avoid a qualified opinion or a disclaimer of opinion.

***Request to Change to a Review or a Related Service** (Ref: Para. 15)*

A32. Before agreeing to change an audit engagement to a review or a related service, an auditor who was engaged to perform an audit in accordance with Australian Auditing Standards may need to assess, in addition to the matters referred to in paragraphs A29-A31 above, any legal or contractual implications of the change.

A33. If the auditor concludes that there is reasonable justification to change the audit engagement to a review or a related service, the audit work performed to the date of change may be relevant to the changed engagement; however, the work required to be performed and the report to be issued would be those appropriate to the revised engagement. In order to avoid confusing the reader, the report on the related service would not include reference to:

(a) The original audit engagement; or

(b) Any procedures that may have been performed in the original audit engagement, except where the audit engagement is changed to an engagement to undertake agreed-upon procedures and thus reference to the procedures performed is a normal part of the report.

Additional Considerations in Engagement Acceptance

Financial Reporting Standards Supplemented by Law or Regulation (Ref: Para. 18)

A34. In some jurisdictions, law or regulation may supplement the financial reporting standards established by an authorised or recognised standards setting organisation with additional requirements relating to the preparation of the financial report. In those jurisdictions, the applicable financial reporting framework for the purposes of applying the Australian Auditing Standards encompasses both the identified financial reporting framework and such additional requirements provided they do not conflict with the identified financial reporting framework. This may, for example, be the case when law or regulation prescribes disclosures in addition to those required by the financial reporting standards or when they narrow the range of acceptable choices that can be made within the financial reporting standards.[18]

Financial Reporting Framework Prescribed by Law or Regulation—Other Matters Affecting Acceptance (Ref: Para. 19)

A35. Law or regulation may prescribe that the wording of the auditor's opinion use the phrases "present fairly, in all material respects" or "give a true and fair view" in a case where the auditor concludes that the applicable financial reporting framework prescribed by law or regulation would otherwise have been unacceptable. In this case, the terms of the prescribed wording of the auditor's report are significantly different from the requirements of Australian Auditing Standards (see paragraph 21).

Auditor's Report Prescribed by Law or Regulation (Ref: Para. 21)

A36. Australian Auditing Standards require that the auditor shall not represent compliance with Australian Auditing Standards unless the auditor has complied with all of the Australian Auditing Standards relevant to the audit.[19] When law or regulation prescribes the layout or wording of the auditor's report in a form or in terms that are significantly different from the requirements of Australian Auditing Standards and the auditor concludes that additional explanation in the auditor's report cannot mitigate possible misunderstanding, the auditor may consider including a statement in the auditor's report that the audit is not conducted in accordance with Australian Auditing Standards. The auditor is, however, encouraged to apply Australian Auditing Standards, including the Australian Auditing Standards that address the auditor's report, to the extent practicable, notwithstanding that the auditor is not permitted to refer to the audit being conducted in accordance with Australian Auditing Standards.

Considerations Specific to Public Sector Entities

A37. In the public sector, specific requirements may exist within the legislation governing the audit mandate; for example, the auditor may be required to report directly to a minister, the legislature or the public if the entity attempts to limit the scope of the audit.

❖ ❖ ❖

18 See ASA 700, paragraph 15, which includes a requirement regarding the evaluation of whether the financial report adequately refers to or describes the applicable financial reporting framework.

19 See ASA 200, paragraph 20.

Conformity with International Standards on Auditing

This Auditing Standard conforms with International Standard on Auditing ISA 210 *Agreeing the Terms of Audit Engagements*, issued by the International Auditing and Assurance Standards Board (IAASB), an independent standard-setting board of the International Federation of Accountants (IFAC).

Paragraphs that have been added to this Auditing Standard (and do not appear in the text of the equivalent ISA) are identified with the prefix "Aus".

Compliance with this Auditing Standard enables compliance with ISA 210.

Appendix 1

(Ref: Para. A23-A24)

Example of an Audit Engagement Letter

The following is an example of an audit engagement letter for an audit of a general purpose financial report prepared in accordance with Australian Accounting Standards and the *Corporations Act 2001*. This letter is not authoritative but is intended only to be a guide that may be used in conjunction with the considerations outlined in this Auditing Standard. It will need to be varied according to individual requirements and circumstances. It is drafted to refer to the audit of a financial report for a single reporting period and would require adaptation if intended or expected to apply to recurring audits (see paragraph 13 of this Auditing Standard). It may be appropriate to seek legal advice that any proposed letter is suitable.

To the appropriate representative of management or those charged with governance of ABC Company:[20]

[The objective and scope of the audit]

You[21] have requested that we audit the financial report of ABC Company which comprises the statement of financial position as at 30 June 20X1 and the statement of comprehensive income, statement of changes in equity and statement of cash flows for the year then ended, and notes comprising a summary of significant accounting policies and other explanatory information, and the directors' declaration. We are pleased to confirm our acceptance and our understanding of this audit engagement by means of this letter. Our audit will be conducted with the objective of expressing an opinion on the financial report.

[The responsibilities of the auditor]

We will conduct our audit in accordance with Australian Auditing Standards. Those standards require that we comply with ethical requirements and plan and perform the audit to obtain reasonable assurance about whether the financial report is free from material misstatement. An audit involves performing procedures to obtain audit evidence about the amounts and disclosures in the financial report. The procedures selected depend on the auditor's judgement, including the assessment of the risks of material misstatement of the financial report, whether due to fraud or error. An audit also includes evaluating the appropriateness of accounting policies used and the reasonableness of accounting estimates made by management, as well as evaluating the overall presentation of the financial report.

Because of the inherent limitations of an audit, together with the inherent limitations of internal control, there is an unavoidable risk that some material misstatements may not be detected, even though the audit is properly planned and performed in accordance with Australian Auditing Standards.

---

20 The addressees and references in the letter would be those that are appropriate in the circumstances of the engagement, including the relevant jurisdiction. It is important to refer to the appropriate persons – see paragraph A21. For an audit under the *Corporations Act 2001*, the appropriate persons are the Directors.

21 Throughout this letter, references to "you," "we," "us," "management," "those charged with governance" and "auditor" would be used or amended as appropriate in the circumstances.

In making our risk assessments, we consider internal control relevant to the entity's preparation of the financial report in order to design audit procedures that are appropriate in the circumstances, but not for the purpose of expressing an opinion on the effectiveness of the entity's internal control. However, we will communicate to you in writing concerning any significant deficiencies in internal control relevant to the audit of the financial report that we have identified during the audit.

[The responsibilities of management and identification of the applicable financial reporting framework (for purposes of this example, it is assumed that the auditor has not determined that the law or regulation prescribes those responsibilities in appropriate terms; the descriptions in paragraph 6(b) of this Auditing Standard are therefore used).]

Our audit will be conducted on the basis that [management and, where appropriate, those charged with governance][22] acknowledge and understand that they have responsibility:

(a) For the preparation of the financial report that gives a true and fair view in accordance with the *Corporations Act 2001* and Australian Accounting Standards;[23]

(b) For such internal control as [management] determines is necessary to enable the preparation of the financial report that is free from material misstatement, whether due to fraud or error; and

(c) To provide us with:

(i) Access to all information of which the directors and management are aware that is relevant to the preparation of the financial report such as records, documentation and other matters;

(ii) Additional information that we may request from the directors and management for the purpose of the audit; and

(iii) Unrestricted access to persons within the entity from whom we determine it necessary to obtain audit evidence.

As part of our audit process, we will request from [management and, where appropriate, those charged with governance], written confirmation concerning representations made to us in connection with the audit.

We look forward to full cooperation from your staff during our audit.

[Other relevant information]

[Insert other information, such as fee arrangements, billings and other specific terms, as appropriate.]

[Reporting]

[Insert appropriate reference to the expected form and content of the auditor's report.]

The form and content of our report may need to be amended in the light of our audit findings.

Other Matters under the *Corporations Act 2001*

Independence

We confirm that, to the best of our knowledge and belief, we currently meet the independence requirements of the *Corporations Act 2001* in relation to the audit of the financial report. In conducting our audit of the financial report, should we become aware that we have contravened the independence requirements of the *Corporations Act 2001*, we shall notify you on a timely basis. As part of our audit process, we shall also provide you with a written independence declaration as required by the *Corporations Act 2001*.

The *Corporations Act 2001* includes specific restrictions on the employment relationships that can exist between the audited entity and its auditors. To assist us in meeting the independence requirements of the *Corporations Act 2001*, and to the extent permitted by law and regulation, we request you discuss with us:

---

22 Use terminology as appropriate in the circumstances. For an audit under the *Corporations Act 2001*, the appropriate terminology is "the Directors".

23 Or, for financial reports not prepared under the *Corporations Act 2001*, "For the preparation and fair presentation of the financial report in accordance with Australian Accounting Standards."

- the provision of services offered to you by [insert firm name] prior to engaging or accepting the service; and
- the prospective employment opportunities of any current or former partner or professional employee of [insert firm name] prior to the commencement of formal employment discussions with the current or former partner or professional employee.

Annual General Meetings

The *Corporations Act 2001* provides that shareholders can submit written questions to the auditor before an Annual General Meeting provided that they relate to the auditor's report or the conduct of the audit. To assist us in meeting this requirement in the *Corporations Act 2001* relating to Annual General Meetings, we request you provide to us written questions submitted to you by shareholders as soon as practicable after the question(s) is received and no later than five business days before the Annual General Meeting, regardless of whether you believe them to be irrelevant. [Applicable only to listed entities]

Presentation of Audited Financial Report on the Internet

It is our understanding that ABC Company intends to publish a hard copy of the audited financial report and auditor's report for members, and to electronically present the audited financial report and auditor's report on its internet web site. When information is presented electronically on a web site, the security and controls over information on the web site should be addressed by the entity to maintain the integrity of the data presented. The examination of the controls over the electronic presentation of audited financial information on the entity's web site is beyond the scope of the audit of the financial report. Responsibility for the electronic presentation of the financial report on the entity's web site is that of the governing body of the entity.

Please sign and return the attached copy of this letter to indicate your acknowledgement of, and agreement with, the arrangements for our audit of the financial report including our respective responsibilities.

Yours faithfully

....

Partner

XYZ & Co.

Acknowledged and agreed on behalf of ABC Company by
(signed)

....

Name and Title

Date

Appendix 2

(Ref: Para. A10)

Determining the Acceptability of General Purpose Frameworks

Jurisdictions that Do Not Have Authorised or Recognised Standards Setting Organisations or Financial Reporting Frameworks Prescribed by Law or Regulation

1. As explained in paragraph A10 of this Auditing Standard, when an entity is registered or operating in a jurisdiction that does not have an authorised or recognised standards setting organisation, or where use of the financial reporting framework is not prescribed by law or regulation, management identifies an applicable financial reporting framework. Practice in such jurisdictions is often to use the financial reporting standards established by one of the organisations described in paragraph A8 of this Auditing Standard.

2. Alternatively, there may be established accounting conventions in a particular jurisdiction that are generally recognised as the financial reporting framework for a general purpose financial report prepared by certain specified entities operating in that jurisdiction. When such a financial reporting framework is adopted, the auditor is required by paragraph 6(a) of this Auditing Standard to determine whether the accounting conventions collectively can be considered to constitute an acceptable financial reporting framework for a general purpose financial report. When the accounting conventions are widely used in a particular jurisdiction, the accounting profession in that jurisdiction may have considered the acceptability of the financial reporting framework on behalf of the auditors. Alternatively, the auditor may make this determination by considering whether the accounting conventions exhibit attributes normally exhibited by acceptable financial reporting frameworks (see paragraph 3 below), or by comparing the accounting conventions to the requirements of an existing financial reporting framework considered to be acceptable (see paragraph 4 below).

3. Acceptable financial reporting frameworks normally exhibit the following attributes that result in information provided in financial reports that is useful to the intended users:

(a) Relevance, in that the information provided in the financial report is relevant to the nature of the entity and the purpose of the financial report. For example, in the case of a business enterprise that prepares a general purpose financial report, relevance is assessed in terms of the information necessary to meet the common financial information needs of a wide range of users in making economic decisions. These needs are ordinarily met by presenting the financial position, financial performance and cash flows of the business enterprise.

(b) Completeness, in that transactions and events, account balances and disclosures that could affect conclusions based on the financial report are not omitted.

(c) Reliability, in that the information provided in the financial report:

(i) Where applicable, reflects the economic substance of events and transactions and not merely their legal form; and

(ii) Results in reasonably consistent evaluation, measurement, presentation and disclosure, when used in similar circumstances.

(d) Neutrality, in that it contributes to information in the financial report that is free from bias.

(e) Understandability, in that the information in the financial report is clear and comprehensive and not subject to significantly different interpretation.

4. The auditor may decide to compare the accounting conventions to the requirements of an existing financial reporting framework considered to be acceptable. For example, the auditor may compare the accounting conventions to IFRSs. For an audit of a small entity, the auditor may decide to compare the accounting conventions to a financial reporting framework specifically developed for such entities by an authorised or recognised standards setting organisation. When the auditor makes such a comparison and differences are identified, the decision as to whether the accounting conventions adopted in the preparation of the financial report constitute an acceptable financial reporting framework includes considering the reasons for the differences and whether application of the accounting conventions, or the description of the financial reporting framework in the financial report, could result in a financial report that is misleading.

5. A conglomeration of accounting conventions devised to suit individual preferences is not an acceptable financial reporting framework for a general purpose financial report. Similarly, a compliance framework will not be an acceptable financial reporting framework, unless it is generally accepted in the particular jurisdictions by preparers and users.

ASA

ASA 220
Quality Control for an Audit of a Financial Report and Other Historical Financial Information

(Reissued October 2009: amended and compiled June 2011)

Issued by the Auditing and Assurance Standards Board.

Note from the Institute of Chartered Accountants Australia

This note, prepared by the technical editor, is not part of ASA 220.

Historical development

January 1983: Statement of Auditing Practice AUP 13, 'Control of the Quality of Audit Work', issued, effective from date of issue. The AuSB did not issue an exposure draft on this topic; however, as noted in para. 14 of the 'Foreword to Statements of Auditing Standards and Statements of Auditing Practice', the AuSB determined that unless noted to the contrary an exposure draft issued by the International Auditing Practice Committee of the International Federation of Accountants is to be regarded as an Australian Exposure Draft. Such an exposure draft, IAPC ED 7, was issued in October 1980 and was distributed in Australia to subscribers to The Institute of Chartered Accountants in Australia's IASC International Accounting Standards/IFAC Guidelines Handbook and by the Australian Society of Accountants with a request for comments. The statement was based on IAG 7 which was issued in September 1981.

May 1994: ED 55 'Codification and Revision of Auditing Pronouncements: AUS 206 Quality Control for Audit Work (AUP 13)' issued by the AuSB.

June 1994: The International Auditing Practices Committee (IAPC) of the International Federation of Accountants (IFAC) approved the issuance of a codified set of International Standards of Auditing (ISAs). The relevant international pronouncement was ISA 220 'Quality Control for Audit Work'.

October 1995: Australian Auditing Standards and Auditing Guidance Statements are released. The status of these was explained in APS 1.1 'Conformity With Auditing Standards'. These Standards become operative for the first reporting period commencing on or after 1 July 1996 and later reporting periods, although earlier application was encouraged. AUP 13 'Control of the Quality of Audit Work' replaced by AUS 206 'Quality Control for Audit Work'.

July 2002: AUS/AGS Omnibus 3 'Miscellaneous Amendments to AUSs and AGSs' issued by the AuASB, operative from date of issue. AUS 206 subsequently reissued by the Board to reflect these changes.

June 2004: AUS 206 reissued to conform with ISA 220, of the same name, but amended for Australian terminology and references. It establishes standards and provides guidance on the responsibilities of firm personnel regarding quality control procedures for audits of historical financial information.

April 2006: ASA 220 'Quality Control for Audits of Historial Financial Information' was issued as a legally enforceable Standard to replace AUS 206. It is based on ISA 220 of the same name.

October 2009: ASA 220 reissued as 'Quality Control for an Audit of a Financial Report and Other Historical Financial Information' as part of the AUASB's Clarity Project referring to the new ASQC 1 'Quality Control for Firms that Perform Audits and Reviews of Financial Reports and Other Financial Information, and Other Assurance Engagements' and requiring documentation of consideration of relevant ethical requirements. It is based on the revised ISA 220 'Quality Control for an Audit of Financial Statements'.

June 2011: ASA 220 updated for editorial amendments contained in ASA 2011-1 'Amendments to Australian Auditing Standards'.

ASA

Contents

Compilation Details

Auditing Standard ASA 220 *Quality Control for an Audit of a Financial Report and Other Historical Financial Information* as Amended

This compilation takes into account amendments made up to and including 27 June 2011 and was prepared on 27 June 2011 by the Auditing and Assurance Standards Board (AUASB).

This compilation is not a separate Auditing Standard made by the AUASB. Instead, it is a representation of ASA 220 (October 2009) as amended by another Auditing Standard which is listed in the Table below.

Table of Standards

Standard	Date made	Operative date
ASA 220	27 October 2009	1 January 2010
ASA 2011-1	27 June 2011	1 July 2011

Table of Amendments

Paragraph affected	How affected	By ... [paragraph]
7(j)(i)	Amended	ASA 2011-1 [20]
7(p) Footnote*	Amended	ASA 2011-1 [21]
A23	Amended	ASA 2011-1 [22]

Preface

[Preface extracted from the original Auditing Standard issued 27 October 2009]

Reasons for Issuing Auditing Standard ASA 220 *Quality Control for an Audit of a Financial Report and Other Historical Financial Information*

The Auditing and Assurance Standards Board (AUASB) issues Auditing Standard ASA 220 *Quality Control for an Audit of a Financial Report and Other Historical Information* pursuant to the requirements of the legislative provisions and the Strategic Direction explained below.

The AUASB is an independent statutory board of the Australian Government established under section 227A of the *Australian Securities and Investments Commission Act 2001*, as amended (ASIC Act). Under section 336 of the *Corporations Act 2001*, the AUASB may make Auditing Standards for the purposes of the corporations legislation. These Auditing Standards are legislative instruments under the *Legislative Instruments Act 2003*.

Under the Strategic Direction given to the AUASB by the Financial Reporting Council (FRC), the AUASB is required to have regard to any programme initiated by the International Auditing and Assurance Standards Board (IAASB) for the revision and enhancement of the International Standards on Auditing (ISAs) and to make appropriate consequential amendments to the Australian Auditing Standards. Accordingly, the AUASB has decided to revise and redraft the Australian Auditing Standards using the equivalent redrafted ISAs.

Main Features

This Auditing Standard establishes requirements and provides application and other explanatory material regarding the auditor's responsibilities in respect of quality control procedures for an audit of a financial report and other historical financial information. It also addresses, where applicable, the responsibilities of the engagement quality control reviewer.

This Auditing Standard:

(a) establishes the leadership responsibilities of the engagement partner for quality on audits;

(b) describes relevant ethical requirements;

(c) sets out the process for the acceptance and continuance of client relationships and audit engagements;

(d) sets out the assignment of an engagement team to the audit engagement;

(e) sets out engagement performance requirements, including direction, supervision, reviews, consultations, and quality control reviews;

(f) explains the monitoring process for compliance with the system of quality control; and

(g) establishes the documentation requirements related to quality control for the audit engagement, including those related to the engagement quality control reviewer.

Authority Statement

Auditing Standard ASA 220 *Quality Control for an Audit of a Financial Report and Other Historical Financial Information* is set out in paragraphs 1 to A35.

This Auditing Standard is to be read in conjunction with ASA 101 *Preamble to Australian Auditing Standards*, which sets out the intentions of the AUASB on how the Australian Auditing Standards, operative for financial reporting periods commencing on or after 1 January 2010, are to be understood, interpreted and applied. This Auditing Standard is to be read also in conjunction with ASA 200 *Overall Objectives of the Independent Auditor and the Conduct of an Audit in Accordance with Australian Auditing Standards*.

Dated: 27 June 2011

M H Kelsall
Chairman - AUASB

Auditing Standard ASA 220

The Auditing and Assurance Standards Board (AUASB) made Auditing Standard ASA 220 *Quality Control for an Audit of a Financial Report and Other Historical Financial Information,* pursuant to section 227B of the *Australian Securities and Investments Commission Act 2001* and section 336 of the *Corporations Act 2001*, on 27 October 2009.

This compiled version of ASA 220 incorporates subsequent amendments contained in another Auditing Standard made by the AUASB up to and including 27 June 2011 (see Compilation Details).

Auditing Standard ASA 220

Quality Control for an Audit of a Financial Report and Other Historical Financial Information

Application

Aus 0.1 This Auditing Standard applies to:

(a) an audit of a financial report for a financial year, or an audit of a financial report for a half-year, in accordance with the *Corporations Act 2001*; and

(b) an audit of a financial report, or a complete set of financial statements, for any other purpose.

Aus 0.2 This Auditing Standard also applies, as appropriate, to an audit of other historical financial information.

Operative Date

Aus 0.3 This Auditing Standard is operative for financial reporting periods commencing on or after 1 January 2010.

[Note: For operative dates of paragraphs changed or added by an amending Standard, see Compilation Details.]

Introduction

Scope of this Auditing Standard

1. This Auditing Standard deals with the specific responsibilities of the auditor regarding quality control procedures for the audit of a financial report and other historical financial information. It also addresses, where applicable, the responsibilities of the engagement quality control reviewer. This Auditing Standard is to be read in conjunction with relevant ethical requirements.

System of Quality Control and Role of Engagement Teams

2. Quality control systems, policies and procedures are the responsibility of the audit firm. Under ASQC 1, the firm has an obligation to establish and maintain a system of quality control to provide it with reasonable assurance that:

(a) The firm and its personnel comply with Australian Auditing Standards, relevant ethical requirements, and applicable legal and regulatory requirements; and

(b) The Reports issued by the firm or engagement partners are appropriate in the circumstances.[1]

This Auditing Standard is premised on the basis that the firm is subject to ASQC 1. (Ref: Para. A1)

3. Within the context of the firm's system of quality control, engagement teams have a responsibility to implement quality control procedures that are applicable to the audit engagement and provide the firm with relevant information to enable the functioning of that part of the firm's system of quality control relating to independence.

4. Engagement teams are entitled to rely on the firm's system of quality control, unless information provided by the firm or other parties suggests otherwise. (Ref: Para. A2-Aus A2.1)

Effective Date

5. [Deleted by the AUASB. Refer Aus 0.3]

Objective

6. The objective of the auditor is to implement quality control procedures at the engagement level that provide the auditor with reasonable assurance that:

(a) The audit complies with Australian Auditing Standards, relevant ethical requirements, and applicable legal and regulatory requirements; and

(b) The auditor's report issued is appropriate in the circumstances.

Definitions

7. For purposes of the Australian Auditing Standards, the following terms have the meanings attributed below:

Aus 7.1 Assurance practitioner means a person or an organisation, whether in public practice, industry, commerce or the public sector, providing assurance services.

(a) Engagement partner[2] means the partner or other person in the firm who is responsible for the audit engagement and its performance, and for the auditor's report that is issued on behalf of the firm, and who, where required, has the appropriate authority from a professional, legal or regulatory body.

Aus 7.2 Engagement partner should be read as referring to a public sector equivalent where relevant.

(b) Engagement quality control review means a process designed to provide an objective evaluation, on or before the date of the auditor's report, of the significant judgements the engagement team made and the conclusions it reached in formulating the auditor's report. The engagement quality control review process is only for audits of financial reports of listed entities and those other audit engagements, if any, for which the firm has determined an engagement quality control review is required.

(c) Engagement quality control reviewer means a partner, other person in the firm, suitably qualified external person, or a team made up of such individuals, none of whom is part of the engagement team, with sufficient and appropriate experience and authority to objectively evaluate the significant judgements the engagement team made and the conclusions it reached in formulating the auditor's report.

(d) Engagement team means all partners and staff performing the engagement, and any individuals engaged by the firm or a network firm who perform audit procedures on the engagement. This excludes an auditor's external expert engaged by the firm or a network firm.[3]

(e) [Deleted by the AUASB. Refer Aus 7.3]

1 See ASQC 1 *Quality Control for Firms that Perform Audits and Reviews of Financial Reports and Other Financial Information, and Other Assurance Engagements*, paragraph 11.

2 [Footnote deleted by the AUASB. Refer Aus 7.2, Aus 7.3 and Aus 7.4.]

3 See ASA 620 *Using the Work of an Auditor's Expert*, paragraph 6(a).

Aus 7.3 Firm means a sole practitioner, partnership, or corporation or other entity of assurance practitioners. Firm should be read as referring to a public sector equivalent where relevant.

(f) Inspection means, in relation to completed audit engagements, procedures designed to provide evidence of compliance by engagement teams with the firm's quality control policies and procedures.

(g) Listed entity means an entity whose shares, stock or debt are quoted or listed on a recognised stock exchange, or are marketed under the regulations of a recognised stock exchange or other equivalent body.

(h) Monitoring means a process comprising an ongoing consideration and evaluation of the firm's system of quality control, including a periodic inspection of a selection of completed engagements, designed to provide the firm with reasonable assurance that its system of quality control is operating effectively.

(i) Network firm means a firm or entity that belongs to a network.

(j) Network means a larger structure:

(i) That is aimed at cooperation; and

(ii) That is clearly aimed at profit or cost-sharing or shares common ownership, control or management, common quality control policies and procedures, common business strategy, the use of a common brand name, or a significant part of professional resources.

(k) [Deleted by the AUASB. Refer Aus 7.4]

Aus 7.4 Partner means any individual with authority to bind the firm with respect to the performance of an audit of a financial report or historical financial information. Partner should be read as referring to a public sector equivalent where relevant.

(l) Personnel means partners and staff.

(m) [Deleted by the AUASB. Refer Aus 7.5]

Aus 7.5 Australian Auditing Standards means the suite of auditing standards issued by the AUASB, and includes ASA 805 *Special Considerations—Audits of Single Financial Statements and Specific Elements, Accounts or Items of a Financial Statement*, and ASA 810 *Engagements to Report on Summary Financial Statements*.

(n) [Deleted by the AUASB. Refer Aus 7.6]

Aus 7.6 Relevant ethical requirements means relevant ethical requirements as defined in ASA 102.*

(o) Staff means professionals, other than partners, including any experts the firm employs.

(p) Suitably qualified external person means an individual outside the firm with the competence and capabilities to act as an engagement partner, for example, a partner of another firm, or an employee (with appropriate experience) of a professional accountancy body# whose members may perform audits of financial reports or audits of other historical financial information, or of an organisation that provides relevant quality control services.

Requirements

Leadership Responsibilities for Quality on Audits

8. The engagement partner shall take responsibility for the overall quality on each audit engagement to which that partner is assigned. (Ref: Para. A3)

---

* See ASA 102 *Compliance with Ethical Requirements when Performing Audits, Reviews and Other Assurance Engagements*.

\# For example, the Institute of Chartered Accountants in Australia, CPA Australia, and the Institute of Public Accountants.

ASA

Relevant Ethical Requirements

9. Throughout the audit engagement, the engagement partner shall remain alert, through observation and making enquiries as necessary, for evidence of non-compliance with relevant ethical requirements by members of the engagement team. (Ref: Para. A4-A5)

10. If matters come to the engagement partner's attention through the firm's system of quality control or otherwise that indicate that members of the engagement team have not complied with relevant ethical requirements, the engagement partner, in consultation with others in the firm, shall determine the appropriate action. (Ref: Para. A5)

Independence

11. The engagement partner shall form a conclusion on compliance with independence requirements that apply to the audit engagement. In doing so, the engagement partner shall: (Ref: Para. A5-Aus A5.1)

    (a) Obtain relevant information from the firm and, where applicable, network firms, to identify and evaluate circumstances and relationships that create threats to independence;

    (b) Evaluate information on identified breaches, if any, of the firm's independence policies and procedures to determine whether they create a threat to independence for the audit engagement; and

    (c) Take appropriate action to eliminate such threats or reduce them to an acceptable level by applying safeguards, or, if considered appropriate, to withdraw from the audit engagement, where withdrawal is possible under applicable law or regulation. The engagement partner shall promptly report to the firm any inability to resolve the matter for appropriate action. (Ref: Para. Aus A5.1, A6-A7)

Acceptance and Continuance of Client Relationships and Audit Engagements

12. The engagement partner shall be satisfied that appropriate procedures regarding the acceptance and continuance of client relationships and audit engagements have been followed, and shall determine that conclusions reached in this regard are appropriate. (Ref: Para. A8-A9)

13. If the engagement partner obtains information that would have caused the firm to decline the audit engagement had that information been available earlier, the engagement partner shall communicate that information promptly to the firm, so that the firm and the engagement partner can take the necessary action. (Ref: Para. A9)

Assignment of Engagement Teams

14. The engagement partner shall be satisfied that the engagement team, and any auditor's experts who are not part of the engagement team, collectively have the appropriate competence and capabilities to:

    (a) Perform the audit engagement in accordance with Australian Auditing Standards, relevant ethical requirements, and applicable legal and regulatory requirements; and

    (b) Enable an auditor's report that is appropriate in the circumstances to be issued. (Ref: Para. A10-A12)

Engagement Performance

Direction, Supervision and Performance

15. The engagement partner shall take responsibility for:

    (a) The direction, supervision and performance of the audit engagement in compliance with Australian Auditing Standards, relevant ethical requirements, and applicable legal and regulatory requirements; and (Ref: Para. A13-A15, A20)

    (b) The auditor's report being appropriate in the circumstances.

Reviews

16. The engagement partner shall take responsibility for reviews being performed in accordance with the firm's review policies and procedures. (Ref: Para. A16-A17, A20)

17. On or before the date of the auditor's report, the engagement partner shall, through a review of the audit documentation and discussion with the engagement team, be satisfied that sufficient appropriate audit evidence has been obtained to support the conclusions reached and for the auditor's report to be issued. (Ref: Para. A18-A20)

Consultation

18. The engagement partner shall:

(a) Take responsibility for the engagement team undertaking appropriate consultation on difficult or contentious matters;

(b) Be satisfied that members of the engagement team have undertaken appropriate consultation during the course of the engagement, both within the engagement team and between the engagement team and others at the appropriate level within or outside the firm;

(c) Be satisfied that the nature and scope of, and conclusions resulting from, such consultations are agreed with the party consulted; and

(d) Determine that conclusions resulting from such consultations have been implemented. (Ref: Para. A21-A22)

Engagement Quality Control Review

19. For audits of financial reports of listed entities, and those other audit engagements, if any, for which the firm has determined that an engagement quality control review is required, the engagement partner shall:

(a) Determine that an engagement quality control reviewer has been appointed;

(b) Discuss significant matters arising during the audit engagement, including those identified during the engagement quality control review, with the engagement quality control reviewer; and

(c) Not date the auditor's report until the completion of the engagement quality control review. (Ref: Para. A23-A25)

20. The engagement quality control reviewer shall perform an objective evaluation of the significant judgements made by the engagement team, and the conclusions reached in formulating the auditor's report. This evaluation shall involve:

(a) Discussion of significant matters with the engagement partner;

(b) Review of the financial reports and the proposed auditor's report;

(c) Review of selected audit documentation relating to the significant judgements the engagement team made and the conclusions it reached; and

(d) Evaluation of the conclusions reached in formulating the auditor's report and consideration of whether the proposed auditor's report is appropriate. (Ref: Para. A26-A27, A29-A31)

21. [Deleted by the AUASB. Refer Aus 21.1]

Aus 21.1 For audits of financial reports of listed entities, and those other audit engagements, if any, for which the firm has determined that an engagement quality control review is required, the engagement quality control reviewer, on performing an engagement quality control review, shall also consider the following:

(a) The engagement team's evaluation of the firm's independence in relation to the audit engagement;

(b) Whether appropriate consultation has taken place on matters involving differences of opinion or other difficult or contentious matters, and the conclusions arising from those consultations; and

(c) Whether audit documentation selected for review reflects the work performed in relation to the significant judgements made and supports the conclusions reached. (Ref: Para. A28-A31)

Differences of Opinion

22. If differences of opinion arise within the engagement team, with those consulted or, where applicable, between the engagement partner and the engagement quality control reviewer, the engagement team shall follow the firm's policies and procedures for dealing with and resolving differences of opinion.

Monitoring

23. An effective system of quality control includes a monitoring process designed to provide the firm with reasonable assurance that its policies and procedures relating to the system of quality control are relevant, adequate, and operating effectively. The engagement partner shall consider the results of the firm's monitoring process as evidenced in the latest information circulated by the firm and, if applicable, other network firms and whether deficiencies noted in that information may affect the audit engagement. (Ref: Para. A32-A34)

Documentation

24. The auditor shall include in the audit documentation:[4]
    (a) Issues identified with respect to compliance with relevant ethical requirements and how they were resolved.
    (b) Conclusions on compliance with independence requirements that apply to the audit engagement, and any relevant discussions with the firm that support these conclusions.
    (c) Conclusions reached regarding the acceptance and continuance of client relationships and audit engagements.
    (d) The nature and scope of, and conclusions resulting from, consultations undertaken during the course of the audit engagement. (Ref: Para. A35)

25. The engagement quality control reviewer shall document, for the audit engagement reviewed, that:
    (a) The procedures required by the firm's policies on engagement quality control review have been performed;
    (b) The engagement quality control review has been completed on or before the date of the auditor's report; and
    (c) The reviewer is not aware of any unresolved matters that would cause the reviewer to believe that the significant judgements the engagement team made and the conclusions it reached were not appropriate.

❖❖❖

Application and Other Explanatory Material

System of Quality Control and Role of Engagement Teams (Ref: Para. 2)

A1. ASQC 1 deals with the firm's responsibilities to establish and maintain its system of quality control for audit engagements. The system of quality control includes policies and procedures that address each of the following elements:

- Leadership responsibilities for quality within the firm;
- Relevant ethical requirements;
- Acceptance and continuance of client relationships and specific engagements;
- Human resources;
- Engagement performance; and
- Monitoring.

4 See ASA 230 *Audit Documentation*, paragraphs 8-11, paragraph Aus 12.1, and paragraph A6.

ASQC 1 contains requirements which are at least as demanding as its international equivalent, ISQC 1 *Quality Control for Firms that Perform Audits and Reviews of Financial Statements, and Other Assurance and Related Services Engagements*[*] , as it addresses all the elements referred to in ISQC 1 and imposes obligations on the firm that achieve the aims of the requirements set out in ISQC 1.

Reliance on the Firm's System of Quality Control (Ref: Para. 4)

A2. Unless information provided by the firm or other parties suggest otherwise, the engagement team may rely on the firm's system of quality control in relation to, for example:

- Competence of personnel through their recruitment and formal training.
- Independence through the accumulation and communication of relevant independence information.
- Maintenance of client relationships through acceptance and continuance systems.
- Adherence to applicable legal and regulatory requirements through the monitoring process.

Aus A2.1 Notwithstanding reliance by the engagement team on the firm's system of quality control, for audits undertaken in accordance with the *Corporations Act 2001* (the Act), the engagement partner is required to comply with the auditing standards under section 307A of that Act.

Leadership Responsibilities for Quality on Audits (Ref: Para. 8)

A3. The actions of the engagement partner and appropriate messages to the other members of the engagement team, in taking responsibility for the overall quality on each audit engagement, emphasise:

(a) The importance to audit quality of:

(i) Performing work that complies with Australian Auditing Standards, relevant ethical requirements, and applicable legal and regulatory requirements;

(ii) Complying with the firm's quality control policies and procedures as applicable;

(iii) Issuing auditor's reports that are appropriate in the circumstances; and

(iv) The engagement team's ability to raise concerns without fear of reprisals; and

(b) The fact that quality is essential in performing audit engagements.

Relevant Ethical Requirements

Compliance with Relevant Ethical Requirements (Ref: Para. 9)

A4. [Deleted by the AUASB. Refer Aus A4.1]

Aus A4.1 The auditor is subject to relevant ethical requirements, including those pertaining to independence, relating to audit engagements as defined in ASA 102.[†]

Definition of "Firm", "Network" and "Network Firm" (Ref: Para. 9-11)

A5. [Deleted by the AUASB. Refer ASA 102]

Independence (Ref: Para. 11)

Aus A5.1 Examples of independence requirements that may be applicable are addressed in the *Corporations Act 2001*, Part 2M.3 Division 3, and relevant ethical requirements.[#]

Threats to Independence (Ref: Para. 11(c))

A6. The engagement partner may identify a threat to independence regarding the audit engagement that safeguards may not be able to eliminate or reduce to an acceptable level.

---

* Issued by the International Auditing and Assurance Standards Board (April 2009).

† See ASA 102 *Compliance with Ethical Requirements when Performing Audits, Reviews and Other Assurance Engagements*.

\# See ASA 102.

In that case, as required by paragraph 11(c), the engagement partner reports to the relevant person(s) within the firm to determine appropriate action, which may include eliminating the activity or interest that creates the threat, or withdrawing from the audit engagement, where withdrawal is possible under applicable law or regulation.

Aus A6.1 The familiarity threat is particularly relevant in the context of financial report audits of listed entities. For these audits, relevant ethical requirements† and the *Corporations Act 2001* specify the partner rotation requirements.

Aus A6.2 The engagement partner may be required to obtain consent from the Australian Securities and Investment Commission (ASIC) prior to resigning from certain audits.

Considerations Specific to Public Sector Entities

A7. Statutory measures may provide safeguards for the independence of public sector auditors. However, public sector auditors or audit firms carrying out public sector audits on behalf of the statutory auditor may, depending on the terms of the mandate in a particular jurisdiction, need to adapt their approach in order to promote compliance with the spirit of paragraph 11. This may include, where the public sector auditor's mandate does not permit withdrawal from the engagement, disclosure through a public report, of circumstances that have arisen that would, if they were in the private sector, lead the auditor to withdraw.

Acceptance and Continuance of Client Relationships and Audit Engagements (Ref: Para. 12)

A8. ASQC 1 requires the firm to obtain information considered necessary in the circumstances before accepting an engagement with a new client, when deciding whether to continue an existing engagement, and when considering acceptance of a new engagement with an existing client.[5] Information such as the following assists the engagement partner in determining whether the conclusions reached regarding the acceptance and continuance of client relationships and audit engagements are appropriate:

- The integrity of the principal owners, key management and those charged with governance of the entity;
- Whether the engagement team is competent to perform the audit engagement and has the necessary capabilities, including time and resources;
- Whether the firm and the engagement team can comply with relevant ethical requirements; and
- Significant matters that have arisen during the current or previous audit engagement, and their implications for continuing the relationship.

Considerations Specific to Public Sector Entities (Ref: Para. 12-13)

A9. In the public sector, auditors may be appointed in accordance with statutory procedures. Accordingly, certain of the requirements and considerations regarding the acceptance and continuance of client relationships and audit engagements as set out in paragraphs 12, 13 and A8 may not be relevant. Nonetheless, information gathered as a result of the process described may be valuable to public sector auditors in performing risk assessments and in carrying out reporting responsibilities.

Assignment of Engagement Teams (Ref: Para. 14)

A10. An engagement team includes a person using expertise in a specialised area of accounting or auditing, whether engaged or employed by the firm, if any, who performs audit procedures on the engagement. However, a person with such expertise is not a member of the engagement team, if that person's involvement with the engagement is only consultation. Consultations are addressed in paragraph 18, and paragraphs A21-A22.

A11. When considering the appropriate competence and capabilities expected of the engagement team as a whole, the engagement partner may take into consideration such matters as the team's:

† See ASA 102.

5 See ASQC 1, paragraph 27(a).

- Understanding of, and practical experience with, audit engagements of a similar nature and complexity through appropriate training and participation.
- Understanding of Australian Auditing Standards, relevant ethical requirements, and applicable legal and regulatory requirements.
- Technical expertise, including expertise with relevant information technology and specialised areas of accounting or auditing.
- Knowledge of relevant industries in which the client operates.
- Ability to apply professional judgement.
- Understanding of the firm's quality control policies and procedures.

Considerations Specific to Public Sector Entities

A12. In the public sector, additional appropriate competence may include skills that are necessary to discharge the terms of the audit mandate in a particular jurisdiction. Such competence may include an understanding of the applicable reporting arrangements, including reporting to the legislature or other governing body or in the public interest. The wider scope of a public sector audit may include, for example, some aspects of performance auditing or a comprehensive assessment of compliance with law, regulation or other authority and preventing and detecting fraud and corruption.

Engagement Performance

Direction, Supervision and Performance (Ref: Para. 15(a))

A13. Direction of the engagement team involves informing the members of the engagement team of matters such as:

- Their responsibilities, including the need to comply with relevant ethical requirements, and to plan and perform an audit with professional scepticism as required by ASA 200.[6]
- Responsibilities of respective partners where more than one partner is involved in the conduct of an audit engagement.
- The objectives of the work to be performed.
- The nature of the entity's business.
- Risk-related issues.
- Problems that may arise.
- The detailed approach to the performance of the engagement.

Discussion among members of the engagement team allows less experienced team members to raise questions with more experienced team members so that appropriate communication can occur within the engagement team.

A14. Appropriate teamwork and training assist less experienced members of the engagement team to clearly understand the objectives of the assigned work.

A15. Supervision includes matters such as:

- Tracking the progress of the audit engagement.
- Considering the competence and capabilities of individual members of the engagement team, including whether they have sufficient time to carry out their work, whether they understand their instructions, and whether the work is being carried out in accordance with the planned approach to the audit engagement.
- Addressing significant matters arising during the audit engagement, considering their significance and modifying the planned approach appropriately.
- Identifying matters for consultation or consideration by more experienced engagement team members during the audit engagement.

6 See ASA 200 *Overall Objectives of the Independent Auditor and the Conduct of an Audit in Accordance with Australian Auditing Standards,* paragraph 15.

Reviews

Review Responsibilities (Ref: Para. 16)

A16. Under ASQC 1, the firm's review responsibility policies and procedures are determined on the basis that work of less experienced engagement team members is reviewed by more experienced engagement team members.[7]

A17. A review consists of consideration whether, for example:

- The work has been performed in accordance with Australian Auditing Standards, relevant ethical requirements, and applicable legal and regulatory requirements;
- Significant matters have been raised for further consideration;
- Appropriate consultations have taken place and the resulting conclusions have been documented and implemented;
- There is a need to revise the nature, timing and extent of work performed;
- The work performed supports the conclusions reached and is appropriately documented;
- The evidence obtained is sufficient and appropriate to support the auditor's report; and
- The objectives of the engagement procedures have been achieved.

The Engagement Partner's Review of Work Performed (Ref: Para. 17)

A18. Timely reviews of the following by the engagement partner at appropriate stages during the engagement allow significant matters to be resolved on a timely basis to the engagement partner's satisfaction on or before the date of the auditor's report:

- Critical areas of judgement, especially those relating to difficult or contentious matters identified during the course of the engagement;
- Significant risks; and
- Other areas the engagement partner considers important.

The engagement partner need not review all audit documentation, but may do so. However, as required by ASA 230, the partner documents the extent and timing of the reviews.[8]

A19. An engagement partner taking over an audit during the engagement may apply the review procedures as described in paragraph A18 to review the work performed to the date when that partner assumes the responsibilities of engagement partner.

Considerations Relevant Where a Member of the Engagement Team with Expertise in a Specialised Area of Accounting or Auditing Is Used (Ref: Para. 15-17)

A20. Where a member of the engagement team with expertise in a specialised area of accounting or auditing is used, direction, supervision and review of that engagement team member's work may include matters such as:

- Agreeing with that member the nature, scope and objectives of that member's work; and the respective roles of, and the nature, timing and extent of communication between that member and other members of the engagement team.
- Evaluating the adequacy of that member's work including the relevance and reasonableness of that member's findings or conclusions and their consistency with other audit evidence.

Consultation (Ref: Para. 18)

A21. Effective consultation on significant technical, ethical, and other matters within the firm or, where applicable, outside the firm can be achieved when those consulted:

- Are given all the relevant facts that will enable them to provide informed advice; and
- Have appropriate knowledge, seniority and experience.

---

7 See ASQC 1, paragraph 33.

8 See ASA 230, paragraph 9(c).

A22. It may be appropriate for the engagement team to consult outside the firm, for example, where the firm lacks appropriate internal resources. They may take advantage of advisory services provided by other firms, professional and regulatory bodies, or commercial organisations that provide relevant quality control services.

Engagement Quality Control Review

Completion of the Engagement Quality Control Review before Dating of the Auditor's Report (Ref: Para. 19(c))

A23. ASA 700 requires the auditor's report to be dated no earlier than the date on which the auditor has obtained sufficient appropriate evidence on which to base the auditor's opinion on the financial report.[9] In the case of an audit of a financial report of a listed entity or when an engagement meets the criteria for an engagement quality control review, such a review assists the auditor in determining whether sufficient appropriate evidence has been obtained.

A24. Conducting the engagement quality control review in a timely manner at appropriate stages during the engagement allows significant matters to be promptly resolved to the engagement quality control reviewer's satisfaction on or before the date of the auditor's report.

A25. Completion of the engagement quality control review means the completion by the engagement quality control reviewer of the requirements in paragraphs 20-Aus 21.1, and where applicable, compliance with paragraph 22. Documentation of the engagement quality control review may be completed after the date of the auditor's report as part of the assembly of the final audit file. ASA 230 establishes requirements and provides guidance in this regard.[10]

Nature, Extent and Timing of Engagement Quality Control Review (Ref: Para. 20)

A26. Remaining alert for changes in circumstances allows the engagement partner to identify situations in which an engagement quality control review is necessary, even though at the start of the engagement, such a review was not required.

A27. The extent of the engagement quality control review may depend, among other things, on the complexity of the audit engagement, whether the entity is a listed entity, and the risk that the auditor's report might not be appropriate in the circumstances. The performance of an engagement quality control review does not reduce the responsibilities of the engagement partner for the audit engagement and its performance.

Engagement Quality Control Review of Listed Entities (Ref: Para. Aus 21.1)

A28. Other matters relevant to evaluating the significant judgements made by the engagement team that may be considered in an engagement quality control review of a listed entity include:

- Significant risks identified during the engagement in accordance with ASA 315,[11] and the responses to those risks in accordance with ASA 330,[12] including the engagement team's assessment of, and response to, the risk of fraud in accordance with ASA 240.[13]
- Judgements made, particularly with respect to materiality and significant risks.
- The significance and disposition of corrected and uncorrected misstatements identified during the audit.
- The matters to be communicated to management and those charged with governance and, where applicable, other parties such as regulatory bodies.

9 See ASA 700 *Forming an Opinion and Reporting on a Financial Report*, paragraph 41.

10 See ASA 230, paragraphs 14-16.

11 See ASA 315 *Identifying and Assessing the Risks of Material Misstatement through Understanding the Entity and Its Environment*.

12 See ASA 330 *The Auditor's Responses to Assessed Risks*.

13 See ASA 240 *The Auditor's Responsibilities Relating to Fraud in an Audit of a Financial Report*.

These other matters, depending on the circumstances, may also be applicable for engagement quality control reviews for audits of financial reports of other entities.

Considerations Specific to Smaller Entities (Ref: Para. 20-Aus 21.1)

A29. In addition to the audits of financial reports of listed entities, an engagement quality control review is required for audit engagements that meet the criteria established by the firm that subjects engagements to an engagement quality control review. In some cases, none of the firm's audit engagements may meet the criteria that would subject them to such a review.

Considerations Specific to Public Sector Entities (Ref: Para. 20-Aus 21.1)

A30. In the public sector, a statutorily appointed auditor (for example, an Auditor-General, or other suitably qualified person appointed on behalf of the Auditor-General), may act in a role equivalent to that of engagement partner with overall responsibility for public sector audits. In such circumstances, where applicable, the selection of the engagement quality control reviewer includes consideration of the need for independence from the audited entity and the ability of the engagement quality control reviewer to provide an objective evaluation.

A31. Listed entities as referred to in paragraphs Aus 21.1 and A28 are not common in the public sector. However, there may be other public sector entities that are significant due to size, complexity or public interest aspects, and which consequently have a wide range of stakeholders. Examples include state owned corporations and public utilities. Ongoing transformations within the public sector may also give rise to new types of significant entities. There are no fixed objective criteria on which the determination of significance is based. Nonetheless, public sector auditors evaluate which entities may be of sufficient significance to warrant performance of an engagement quality control review.

Monitoring (Ref: Para. 23)

A32. ASQC 1 requires the firm to establish a monitoring process designed to provide it with reasonable assurance that the policies and procedures relating to the system of quality control are relevant, adequate and operating effectively.[14]

A33. In considering deficiencies that may affect the audit engagement, the engagement partner may have regard to measures the firm took to rectify the situation that the engagement partner considers are sufficient in the context of that audit.

A34. A deficiency in the firm's system of quality control does not necessarily indicate that a particular audit engagement was not performed in accordance with Australian Auditing Standards, relevant ethical requirements, and applicable legal and regulatory requirements, or that the auditor's report was not appropriate.

Documentation

Documentation of Consultations (Ref: Para. 24(d))

A35. Documentation of consultations with other professionals that involve difficult or contentious matters that is sufficiently complete and detailed contributes to an understanding of:

- The issue on which consultation was sought; and
- The results of the consultation, including any decisions taken, the basis for those decisions and how they were implemented.

❖❖❖

14 See ASQC 1, paragraph 48.

Conformity with International Standards on Auditing

This Auditing Standard conforms with International Standard on Auditing ISA 220 *Quality Control for an Audit of Financial Statements*, issued by the International Auditing and Assurance Standards Board (IAASB), an independent standard-setting board of the International Federation of Accountants (IFAC).

Paragraphs that have been added to this Auditing Standard (and do not appear in the text of the equivalent ISA) are identified with the prefix "Aus".

The following requirement is additional to ISA 220:

- For audits of financial reports of listed entities, and those other audit engagements, if any, for which the firm has determined that an engagement quality control review is required, the engagement quality control reviewer, on performing an engagement quality control review, shall also consider the following:
    - The engagement team's evaluation of the firm's independence in relation to the audit engagement;
    - Whether appropriate consultation has taken place on matters involving differences of opinion or other difficult or contentious matters, and the conclusions arising from those consultations; and
    - Whether audit documentation selected for review reflects the work performed in relation to the significant judgements made and supports the conclusions reached. (Ref: Para. Aus 21.1)

This Auditing Standard incorporates terminology and definitions used in Australia.

The equivalent requirements and related application and other explanatory material included in ISA 220 in respect of "relevant ethical requirements", have been included in another Auditing Standard, ASA 102 *Compliance with Ethical Requirements when Performing Audits, Reviews and Other Assurance Engagements*. There is no international equivalent to ASA 102.

Compliance with this Auditing Standard enables compliance with ISA 220.

ASA 230
Audit Documentation

(Reissued October 2009)

Issued by the Auditing and Assurance Standards Board.

Note from the Institute of Chartered Accountants Australia

This note, prepared by the technical editor, is not part of ASA 230.

Historical development

January 1981: Statement of Auditing Practice AUP 15, 'Documentation' issued. The AuSB did not issue an exposure draft on this topic; however, as noted in para. 14 of the 'Foreword to Statements of Auditing Standards and Statements of Auditing Practice', the AuSB determined that unless noted to the contrary an exposure draft issued by the International Auditing Practice Committee of the International Federation of Accountants is to be regarded as an Australian exposure draft. Such an exposure draft, IAPC ED 9, was issued in February 1981 and was distributed in Australia to subscribers to The Institute of Chartered Accountants in Australia's IASC International Accounting Standards/IFAC Guidelines Handbook and by the Australian Society of Accountants with a request for comments. The statement was based on IAG 9 which was issued in February 1982.

December 1993: ED 53 'Codification and Revision of Auditing Pronouncements: AUS 208 Documentation (AUP 15)' issued by the AuSB.

June 1994: The International Auditing Practices Committee (IAPC) of the International Federation of Accountants (IFAC) approved the issuance of a codified set of International Standards of Auditing (ISAs). The relevant international pronouncement was ISA 230 'Documentation'.

October 1995: Australian Auditing Standards and Auditing Guidance Statements released. The status of these was explained in APS 1.1 'Conformity With Auditing Standards'. These Standards became operative for the first reporting period commencing on or after 1 July 1996 and later reporting periods, although earlier application was encouraged. AUP 15 'Documentation' replaced by AUS 208 'Documentation'.

July 2002: AUS/AGS Omnibus 3 'Miscellaneous Amendments to AUSs and AGSs' issed by the AuASB, operative from date of issue. AUS 208 subsequently reissued by the Board to incorporate these changes.

April 2006: ASA 230 'Audit Documentation' was issued as a legally enforceable Standard to replace AUS 208. It is based on ISA 230 of the same name.

October 2009: ASA 230 reissued as part of the AUASB's Clarity Project based on the redrafted ISA 230 of the same name.

Contents

Preface

Reasons for Issuing Auditing Standard ASA 230 *Audit Documentation*

The Auditing and Assurance Standards Board (AUASB) issues Auditing Standard ASA 230 *Audit Documentation* pursuant to the requirements of the legislative provisions and the Strategic Direction explained below.

The AUASB is an independent statutory board of the Australian Government established under section 227A of the *Australian Securities and Investments Commission Act 2001*, as amended (ASIC Act). Under section 336 of the *Corporations Act 2001*, the AUASB may make Auditing Standards for the purposes of the corporations legislation. These Auditing Standards are legislative instruments under the *Legislative Instruments Act 2003*.

Under the Strategic Direction given to the AUASB by the Financial Reporting Council (FRC), the AUASB is required to have regard to any programme initiated by the International Auditing and Assurance Standards Board (IAASB) for the revision and enhancement of the International Standards on Auditing (ISAs) and to make appropriate consequential amendments to the Australian Auditing Standards. Accordingly, the AUASB has decided to revise and redraft the Australian Auditing Standards using the equivalent redrafted ISAs.

Main Features

This Auditing Standard establishes requirements and provides application and other explanatory material regarding the auditor's responsibility to prepare audit documentation for an audit of a financial report.

This Auditing Standard:

(a) requires the auditor to prepare audit documentation on a timely basis that provides:

  (i) a sufficient appropriate record of the basis for the auditor's report; and

  (ii) evidence that the audit was planned and performed in accordance with Australian Auditing Standards and applicable legal and regulatory requirements;

(b) describes the form, content and extent of audit documentation;

(c) describes the documentation required where, in rare and exceptional circumstances, factors outside the auditor's control prevent the auditor from complying with an essential procedure contained within a relevant requirement;

(d) describes the documentation required where, in exceptional circumstances, the auditor performs new or additional audit procedures or draws new conclusions after the date of the auditor's report;

(e) requires the assembly of the final audit file, including the prohibition of deletions and the permission for certain modifications and additions, on a timely basis after the date of the auditor's report; and

(f) requires the auditor to adopt procedures for maintaining the confidentiality, safe custody, integrity, accessibility and retrievability of audit documentation.

Authority Statement

The Auditing and Assurance Standards Board (AUASB) makes this Auditing Standard ASA 230 *Audit Documentation* pursuant to section 227B of the *Australian Securities and Investments Commission Act 2001* and section 336 of the *Corporations Act 2001*.

This Auditing Standard is to be read in conjunction with ASA 101 *Preamble to Australian Auditing Standards*, which sets out the intentions of the AUASB on how the Australian Auditing Standards, operative for financial reporting periods commencing on or after 1 January 2010, are to be understood, interpreted and applied. This Auditing Standard is to be read also in conjunction with ASA 200 *Overall Objectives of the Independent Auditor and the Conduct of an Audit in Accordance with Australian Auditing Standards*.

Dated: 27 October 2009

M H Kelsall
Chairman - AUASB

Auditing Standard ASA 230

Audit Documentation

Application

Aus 0.1 This Auditing Standard applies to:

(a) an audit of a financial report for a financial year, or an audit of a financial report for a half-year, in accordance with the *Corporations Act 2001*; and

(b) an audit of a financial report, or a complete set of financial statements, for any other purpose.

Aus 0.2 This Auditing Standard also applies, as appropriate, to an audit of other historical financial information.

Operative Date

Aus 0.3 This Auditing Standard is operative for financial reporting periods commencing on or after 1 January 2010.

Introduction

Scope of this Auditing Standard

1. This Auditing Standard deals with the auditor's responsibility to prepare audit documentation for an audit of a financial report. Appendix 1 lists other Auditing Standards that contain specific documentation requirements and guidance. The specific documentation requirements of other Auditing Standards do not limit the application of this Auditing Standard. Law or regulation may establish additional documentation requirements.

Nature and Purpose of Audit Documentation

2. Audit documentation that meets the requirements of this Auditing Standard and the specific documentation requirements of other relevant Australian Auditing Standards provides:

   (a) Evidence of the auditor's basis for a conclusion about the achievement of the overall objective of the auditor;[1] and

   (b) Evidence that the audit was planned and performed in accordance with Australian Auditing Standards and applicable legal and regulatory requirements.

3. Audit documentation serves a number of additional purposes, including the following:

   - Assisting the engagement team to plan and perform the audit.
   - Assisting members of the engagement team responsible for supervision to direct and supervise the audit work, and to discharge their review responsibilities in accordance with ASA 220.[2]
   - Enabling the engagement team to be accountable for its work.
   - Retaining a record of matters of continuing significance to future audits.
   - Enabling the conduct of quality control reviews and inspections in accordance with ASQC 1.[3,4]
   - Enabling the conduct of external inspections in accordance with applicable legal, regulatory or other requirements.

Effective Date

4. [Deleted by the AUASB. Refer Aus 0.3]

Objective

5. The objective of the auditor is to prepare documentation that provides:

   (a) A sufficient and appropriate record of the basis for the auditor's report; and

   (b) Evidence that the audit was planned and performed in accordance with Australian Auditing Standards and applicable legal and regulatory requirements.

Definitions

6. For purposes of the Australian Auditing Standards, the following terms have the meanings attributed below:

   (a) Audit documentation means the record of audit procedures performed, relevant audit evidence obtained, and conclusions the auditor reached (terms such as "working papers" or "workpapers" are also sometimes used).

---

1 See ASA 200 *Overall Objectives of the Independent Auditor and the Conduct of an Audit in Accordance with Australian Auditing Standards*, paragraph 11.

2 See ASA 220 *Quality Control for an Audit of a Financial Report and Other Historical Financial Information*, paragraphs 15-17.

3 See ASQC 1 *Quality Control for Firms that Perform Audits and Reviews of Financial Reports and Other Financial Information, and Other Assurance Engagements*, paragraphs 32-33, 35-38, and 48.

4 [Footnote deleted by the AUASB.]

(b) Audit file means one or more folders or other storage media, in physical or electronic form, containing the records that comprise the audit documentation for a specific engagement.

(c) Experienced auditor means an individual (whether internal or external to the firm) who has practical audit experience, and a reasonable understanding of:

(i) Audit processes;

(ii) Australian Auditing Standards and applicable legal and regulatory requirements;

(iii) The business environment in which the entity operates; and

(iv) Auditing and financial reporting issues relevant to the entity's industry.

Requirements

Timely Preparation of Audit Documentation

7. The auditor shall prepare audit documentation on a timely basis. (Ref: Para. A1)

Documentation of the Audit Procedures Performed and Audit Evidence Obtained

Form, Content and Extent of Audit Documentation

8. The auditor shall prepare audit documentation that is sufficient to enable an experienced auditor, having no previous connection with the audit, to understand: (Ref: Para. A2-A5, A16-A17)

(a) The nature, timing, and extent of the audit procedures performed to comply with the Australian Auditing Standards and applicable legal and regulatory requirements; (Ref: Para. A6-A7)

(b) The results of the audit procedures performed, and the audit evidence obtained; and

(c) Significant matters arising during the audit, the conclusions reached thereon, and significant professional judgements made in reaching those conclusions. (Ref: Para. A8-A11)

9. In documenting the nature, timing and extent of audit procedures performed, the auditor shall record:

(a) The identifying characteristics of the specific items or matters tested; (Ref: Para. A12)

(b) Who performed the audit work and the date such work was completed; and

(c) Who reviewed the audit work performed and the date and extent of such review. (Ref: Para. A13)

10. The auditor shall document discussions of significant matters with management, those charged with governance, and others, including the nature of the significant matters discussed and when and with whom the discussions took place. (Ref: Para. A14)

11. If the auditor identified information that is inconsistent with the auditor's final conclusion regarding a significant matter, the auditor shall document how the auditor addressed the inconsistency. (Ref: Para. A15)

12. [Deleted by the AUASB. Refer Aus 12.1]

Documentation of Inability to Comply with Requirements

Aus 12.1 Where, in rare and exceptional circumstances, factors outside the auditor's control prevent the auditor from complying with an essential procedure contained within a relevant requirement, the auditor shall document: (Ref: Para. A18-A19)

(a) the circumstances surrounding the inability to comply;

(b) the reasons for the inability to comply; and

(c) justification of how alternative audit procedures achieve the objectives of the requirement.

Matters Arising after the Date of the Auditor's Report

13. If, in exceptional circumstances, the auditor performs new or additional audit procedures or draws new conclusions after the date of the auditor's report, the auditor shall document: (Ref: Para. A20)
    (a) The circumstances encountered;
    (b) The new or additional audit procedures performed, audit evidence obtained, and conclusions reached, and their effect on the auditor's report; and
    (c) When and by whom the resulting changes to audit documentation were made and reviewed.

Assembly of the Final Audit File

14. The auditor shall assemble the audit documentation in an audit file and complete the administrative process of assembling the final audit file on a timely basis after the date of the auditor's report. (Ref: Para. A21-A22)
15. After the assembly of the final audit file has been completed, the auditor shall not delete or discard audit documentation of any nature before the end of its retention period. (Ref: Para. A23 - Aus A23.2)
16. In circumstances other than those envisaged in paragraph 13 of this Auditing Standard where the auditor finds it necessary to modify existing audit documentation or add new audit documentation after the assembly of the final audit file has been completed, the auditor shall, regardless of the nature of the modifications or additions, document: (Ref: Para. A24)
    (a) The specific reasons for making them; and
    (b) When and by whom they were made and reviewed.

Confidentiality, Safe Custody, Integrity, Accessibility and Retrievability of the Audit Documentation

Aus 16.1 The auditor shall adopt appropriate procedures for maintaining the confidentiality, safe custody, integrity, accessibility and retrievability of the audit documentation. (Ref: Para. Aus A24.1)

❖ ❖ ❖

Application and Other Explanatory Material

Timely Preparation of Audit Documentation (Ref: Para. 7)

A1. Preparing sufficient and appropriate audit documentation on a timely basis helps to enhance the quality of the audit and facilitates the effective review and evaluation of the audit evidence obtained and conclusions reached before the auditor's report is finalised. Documentation prepared after the audit work has been performed is likely to be less accurate than documentation prepared at the time such work is performed.

Documentation of the Audit Procedures Performed and Audit Evidence Obtained

Form, Content and Extent of Audit Documentation (Ref: Para. 8)

A2. The form, content and extent of audit documentation depend on factors such as:

- The size and complexity of the entity.
- The nature of the audit procedures to be performed.
- The identified risks of material misstatement.
- The significance of the audit evidence obtained.
- The nature and extent of exceptions identified.
- The need to document a conclusion or the basis for a conclusion not readily determinable from the documentation of the work performed or audit evidence obtained.
- The audit methodology and tools used.

A3. Audit documentation may be recorded on paper or on electronic or other media. Examples of audit documentation include:

- Audit programs.
- Analyses.
- Issues memoranda.
- Summaries of significant matters.
- Letters of confirmation and representation.
- Checklists.
- Correspondence (including e-mail) concerning significant matters.

The auditor may include abstracts or copies of the entity's records (for example, significant and specific contracts and agreements) as part of audit documentation. Audit documentation, however, is not a substitute for the entity's accounting records.

A4. The auditor need not include in audit documentation superseded drafts of working papers and financial reports, notes that reflect incomplete or preliminary thinking, previous copies of documents corrected for typographical or other errors, and duplicates of documents.

A5. Oral explanations by the auditor, on their own, do not represent adequate support for the work the auditor performed or conclusions the auditor reached, but may be used to explain or clarify information contained in the audit documentation.

Documentation of Compliance with Australian Auditing Standards *(Ref: Para. 8(a))*

A6. In principle, compliance with the requirements of this Auditing Standard will result in the audit documentation being sufficient and appropriate in the circumstances. Other Australian Auditing Standards contain specific documentation requirements that are intended to clarify the application of this Auditing Standard in the particular circumstances of those other Australian Auditing Standards. The specific documentation requirements of other Australian Auditing Standards do not limit the application of this Auditing Standard. Furthermore, the absence of a documentation requirement in any particular Auditing Standard is not intended to suggest that there is no documentation that will be prepared as a result of complying with that Auditing Standard.

A7. Audit documentation provides evidence that the audit complies with the Australian Auditing Standards. However, it is neither necessary nor practicable for the auditor to document every matter considered, or professional judgement made, in an audit. Further, it is unnecessary for the auditor to document separately (as in a checklist, for example) compliance with matters for which compliance is demonstrated by documents included within the audit file. For example:

- The existence of an adequately documented audit plan demonstrates that the auditor has planned the audit.
- The existence of a signed engagement letter in the audit file demonstrates that the auditor has agreed the terms of the audit engagement with management or, where appropriate, those charged with governance.
- An auditor's report containing an appropriately qualified opinion on the financial report demonstrates that the auditor has complied with the requirement to express a qualified opinion under the circumstances specified in the Australian Auditing Standards.
- In relation to requirements that apply generally throughout the audit, there may be a number of ways in which compliance with them may be demonstrated within the audit file:
    - For example, there may be no single way in which the auditor's professional scepticism is documented. But the audit documentation may nevertheless provide evidence of the auditor's exercise of professional scepticism in accordance with the Australian Auditing Standards. Such evidence may include specific procedures performed to corroborate management's responses to the auditor's enquiries.

- ◦ Similarly, that the engagement partner has taken responsibility for the direction, supervision and performance of the audit in compliance with the Australian Auditing Standards may be evidenced in a number of ways within the audit documentation. This may include documentation of the engagement partner's timely involvement in aspects of the audit, such as participation in the team discussions required by ASA 315.[5]

***Documentation of Significant Matters and Related Significant Professional Judgements** (Ref: Para. 8(c))*

A8. Judging the significance of a matter requires an objective analysis of the facts and circumstances. Examples of significant matters include:

- Matters that give rise to significant risks (as defined in ASA 315).[6]
- Results of audit procedures indicating (a) that the financial report could be materially misstated, or (b) a need to revise the auditor's previous assessment of the risks of material misstatement and the auditor's responses to those risks.
- Circumstances that cause the auditor significant difficulty in applying necessary audit procedures.
- Findings that could result in a modification to the audit opinion or the inclusion of an Emphasis of Matter paragraph in the auditor's report.

A9. An important factor in determining the form, content and extent of audit documentation of significant matters is the extent of professional judgement exercised in performing the work and evaluating the results. Documentation of the professional judgements made, where significant, serves to explain the auditor's conclusions and to reinforce the quality of the judgement. Such matters are of particular interest to those responsible for reviewing audit documentation, including those carrying out subsequent audits when reviewing matters of continuing significance (for example, when performing a retrospective review of accounting estimates).

A10. Some examples of circumstances in which, in accordance with paragraph 8, it is appropriate to prepare audit documentation relating to the use of professional judgement include, where the matters and judgements are significant:

- The rationale for the auditor's conclusion when a requirement provides that the auditor 'shall consider' certain information or factors, and that consideration is significant in the context of the particular engagement.
- The basis for the auditor's conclusion on the reasonableness of areas of subjective judgements (for example, the reasonableness of significant accounting estimates).
- The basis for the auditor's conclusions about the authenticity of a document when further investigation (such as making appropriate use of an expert or of confirmation procedures) is undertaken in response to conditions identified during the audit that caused the auditor to believe that the document may not be authentic.

A11. The auditor may consider it helpful to prepare and retain as part of the audit documentation a summary (sometimes known as a completion memorandum) that describes the significant matters identified during the audit and how they were addressed, or that includes cross-references to other relevant supporting audit documentation that provides such information. Such a summary may facilitate effective and efficient reviews and inspections of the audit documentation, particularly for large and complex audits. Further, the preparation of such a summary may assist the auditor's consideration of the significant matters. It may also help the auditor to consider whether, in light of the audit procedures performed and conclusions reached, there is any individual relevant Auditing Standard objective that the auditor cannot achieve that would prevent the auditor from achieving the overall objectives of the auditor.

---

5 See ASA 315 *Identifying and Assessing the Risks of Material Misstatement through Understanding the Entity and Its Environment*, paragraph 10.

6 See ASA 315, paragraph 4(e).

Identification of Specific Items or Matters Tested, and of the Preparer and Reviewer (Ref: Para. 9)

A12. Recording the identifying characteristics serves a number of purposes. For example, it enables the engagement team to be accountable for its work and facilitates the investigation of exceptions or inconsistencies. Identifying characteristics will vary with the nature of the audit procedure and the item or matter tested. For example:

- For a detailed test of entity-generated purchase orders, the auditor may identify the documents selected for testing by their dates and unique purchase order numbers.
- For a procedure requiring selection or review of all items over a specific amount from a given population, the auditor may record the scope of the procedure and identify the population (for example, all journal entries over a specified amount from the journal register).
- For a procedure requiring systematic sampling from a population of documents, the auditor may identify the documents selected by recording their source, the starting point and the sampling interval (for example, a systematic sample of shipping reports selected from the shipping log for the period from April 1 to September 30, starting with report number 12345 and selecting every 125th report).
- For a procedure requiring enquiries of specific entity personnel, the auditor may record the dates of the enquiries and the names and job designations of the entity personnel.
- For an observation procedure, the auditor may record the process or matter being observed, the relevant individuals, their respective responsibilities, and where and when the observation was carried out.

A13. ASA 220 requires the auditor to review the audit work performed through review of the audit documentation.[7] The requirement to document who reviewed the audit work performed does not imply a need for each specific working paper to include evidence of review. The requirement, however, means documenting what audit work was reviewed, who reviewed such work, and when it was reviewed.

Documentation of Discussions of Significant Matters with Management, Those Charged with Governance, and Others *(Ref: Para. 10)*

A14. The documentation is not limited to records prepared by the auditor but may include other appropriate records such as minutes of meetings prepared by the entity's personnel and agreed by the auditor. Others with whom the auditor may discuss significant matters may include other personnel within the entity, and external parties, such as persons providing professional advice to the entity.

Documentation of How Inconsistencies have been Addressed *(Ref: Para. 11)*

A15. The requirement to document how the auditor addressed inconsistencies in information does not imply that the auditor needs to retain documentation that is incorrect or superseded.

Considerations Specific to Smaller Entities *(Ref. Para. 8)*

A16. The audit documentation for the audit of a smaller entity is generally less extensive than that for the audit of a larger entity. Further, in the case of an audit where the engagement partner performs all the audit work, the documentation will not include matters that might have to be documented solely to inform or instruct members of an engagement team, or to provide evidence of review by other members of the team (for example, there will be no matters to document relating to team discussions or supervision). Nevertheless, the engagement partner complies with the overriding requirement in paragraph 8 to prepare audit documentation that can be understood by an experienced auditor, as the audit documentation may be subject to review by external parties for regulatory or other purposes.

7 See ASA 220, paragraph 17.

A17. When preparing audit documentation, the auditor of a smaller entity may also find it helpful and efficient to record various aspects of the audit together in a single document, with cross-references to supporting working papers as appropriate. Examples of matters that may be documented together in the audit of a smaller entity include the understanding of the entity and its internal control, the overall audit strategy and audit plan, materiality determined in accordance with ASA 320,[8] assessed risks, significant matters noted during the audit, and conclusions reached.

Documentation of Inability to Comply with Relevant Requirements (Ref: Para. Aus 12.1)

A18. The requirements of the Australian Auditing Standards are designed to enable the auditor to achieve the objectives specified in the Australian Auditing Standards, and thereby the overall objectives of the auditor. Accordingly, other than in rare and exceptional circumstances, the Australian Auditing Standards call for compliance with each requirement that is relevant in the circumstances of the audit.

Aus A18.1 ASA 200[*] contains a requirement regarding the situation, where, in rare and exceptional circumstances, factors outside the auditor's control prevent the auditor from complying with an essential procedure contained within a relevant requirement.

A19. The documentation requirement applies only to requirements that are relevant in the circumstances. A requirement is not relevant[9] only in the cases where:

(a) The entire Auditing Standard is not relevant (for example, if an entity does not have an internal audit function, nothing in ASA 610[10] is relevant); or

(b) The requirement is conditional and the condition does not exist (for example, the requirement to modify the auditor's opinion where there is an inability to obtain sufficient appropriate audit evidence, and there is no such inability).

Matters Arising after the Date of the Auditor's Report (Ref: Para. 13)

A20. Examples of exceptional circumstances include facts which become known to the auditor after the date of the auditor's report but which existed at that date and which, if known at that date, might have caused the financial report to be amended or the auditor to modify the opinion in the auditor's report.[11] The resulting changes to the audit documentation are reviewed in accordance with the review responsibilities set out in ASA 220,[12] with the engagement partner taking final responsibility for the changes.

Assembly of the Final Audit File (Ref: Para. 14-16)

A21. ASQC 1 requires firms to establish policies and procedures for the timely completion of the assembly of audit files.[13] An appropriate time limit within which to complete the assembly of the final audit file is ordinarily not more than 60 days after the date of the auditor's report.[14]

A22. The completion of the assembly of the final audit file after the date of the auditor's report is an administrative process that does not involve the performance of new audit procedures or the drawing of new conclusions. Changes may, however, be made to the audit documentation during the final assembly process if they are administrative in nature. Examples of such changes include:

- Deleting or discarding superseded documentation.
- Sorting, collating and cross-referencing working papers.

8 See ASA 320 *Materiality in Planning and Performing an Audit.*

* See ASA 200, paragraph Aus 23.1

9 See ASA 200, paragraph 22.

10 See ASA 610 *Using the Work of Internal Auditors.*

11 See ASA 560 *Subsequent Events*, paragraph 14.

12 See ASA 220, paragraph 16.

13 See ASQC 1, paragraph 45.

14 See ASQC 1, paragraph A54.

- Signing off on completion checklists relating to the file assembly process.
- Documenting audit evidence that the auditor has obtained, discussed and agreed with the relevant members of the engagement team before the date of the auditor's report.

A23. ASQC 1 requires firms to establish policies and procedures for the retention of engagement documentation.[15] The retention period for audit engagements ordinarily is no shorter than five years from the date of the auditor's report, or, if later, the date of the group auditor's report.[16]

Aus A23.1 Under section 307B of the *Corporations Act 2001*, the auditor or member of an audit firm is required to retain all audit working papers prepared by or for, or considered or used by, the auditor in accordance with the requirements of the Australian Auditing Standards until:

(a) The end of seven years after the date of the audit report prepared in relation to the audit or review to which the audit working papers relate; or

(b) An earlier date determined by the Australian Securities and Investments Commission for the audit working papers.

Aus A23.2 Relevant legislation or regulation, other than the *Corporations Act 2001*, may require the retention of audit working papers for specified periods.

A24. An example of a circumstance in which the auditor may find it necessary to modify existing audit documentation or add new audit documentation after file assembly has been completed is the need to clarify existing audit documentation arising from comments received during monitoring inspections performed by internal or external parties.

Confidentiality, Safe Custody, Integrity, Accessibility and Retrievability of the Audit Documentation (Ref: Para. Aus 16.1)

Aus A24.1 Under ASQC 1, firms are required to establish policies and procedures to maintain the confidentiality, safe custody, integrity, accessibility and retrievability of audit documentation.*

❖ ❖ ❖

Conformity with International Standards on Auditing

This Auditing Standard conforms with International Standard on Auditing ISA 230 *Audit Documentation*, issued by the International Auditing and Assurance Standards Board (IAASB), an independent standard-setting board of the International Federation of Accountants (IFAC).

Paragraphs that have been added to this Standard (and do not appear in the text of the equivalent ISA) are identified with the prefix "Aus".

The following requirements are additional to ISA 230:

- Where, in rare and exceptional circumstances, factors outside the auditor's control prevent the auditor from complying with an essential procedure contained within a relevant requirement, the auditor shall document:
  - the circumstances surrounding the inability to comply;
  - the reasons for the inability to comply; and
  - justification of how alternative audit procedures achieve the objectives of the requirement. [Paragraph Aus 12.1]
- The auditor shall adopt appropriate procedures for maintaining the confidentiality, safe custody, integrity, accessibility and retrievability of the audit documentation. [Paragraph Aus 16.1]

Compliance with this Auditing Standard enables compliance with ISA 230.

15 See ASQC 1, paragraph 47.

16 See ASQC 1, paragraph A61.

* See ASQC 1, paragraph 46.

Appendix 1

(Ref: Para. 1)

Specific Audit Documentation Requirements in Other Australian Auditing Standards

This appendix identifies paragraphs in other Australian Auditing Standards in effect for audits of financial reports for periods beginning on or after 1 January 2010 that contain specific documentation requirements. The list is not a substitute for considering the requirements and related application and other explanatory material in Australian Auditing Standards.

- ASA 210 *Agreeing the Terms of Audit Engagements* – paragraphs 10-12
- ASA 220 *Quality Control for an Audit of a Financial Report and Other Historical Financial Information* – paragraphs 24-25
- ASA 240 *The Auditor's Responsibilities Relating to Fraud in an Audit of a Financial Report* – paragraphs 44-47
- ASA 250 *Consideration of Laws and Regulations in an Audit of a Financial Report* – paragraph 29
- ASA 260 *Communication with Those Charged with Governance* – paragraph 23
- ASA 300 *Planning an Audit of a Financial Report* – paragraph 12
- ASA 315 *Identifying and Assessing the Risks of Material Misstatement through Understanding the Entity and Its Environment* – paragraph 32
- ASA 320 *Materiality in Planning and Performing an Audit* – paragraph 14
- ASA 330 *The Auditor's Responses to Assessed Risks* – paragraphs 28-30
- ASA 450 *Evaluation of Misstatements Identified During the Audit* – paragraph 15
- ASA 540 *Auditing Accounting Estimates, Including Fair Value Accounting Estimates, and Related Disclosures* – paragraph 23
- ASA 550 *Related Parties* – paragraph 28
- ASA 600 *Special Considerations—Audits of Group Financial Reports (Including the Work of Component Auditors)* – paragraph 50
- ASA 610 *Using the Work of Internal Auditors* – paragraph 13

ASA

ASA 240

The Auditor's Responsibilities Relating to Fraud in an Audit of a Financial Report

(Reissued October 2009: amended and compiled June 2011)

Issued by the Auditing and Assurance Standards Board.

Note from the Institute of Chartered Accountants Australia

This note, prepared by the technical editor, is not part of ASA 240.

Historical development

June 1983: Statement of Auditing Practice AUP 16 'Fraud and Error' issued, effective from date of issue. The AuSB did not issue an exposure draft on this topic; however, as noted in para. 14 of the 'Foreword to Statements of Auditing Standards and Statements of Auditing Practice' the AuSB has determined that unless noted to the contrary an exposure draft issued by the International Auditing Practice Committee of the International Federation of Accountants is to be regarded as an Australian exposure draft. Such an exposure draft, IPAC ED 11, was issued in October 1981 and was distributed in Australia to subscribers to The Institute of Chartered Accountants in Australia's IASC International Accounting Standards/IFAC Guidelines Handbook and by the Australian Society of Accountants with a request for comments. The statement was based on IAG 11 which was issued in October 1982.

November 1990: Audit Monograph 2 'Auditors' Legal Duties and Liabilities In Australia' issued by the AuSB. The objectives of the monograph were to:

(a) draw together and analyse recent legal decisions to identify the basic principles and legal precedents concerned with the civil and criminal liability of auditors;

(b) provide the AuSB with a legal framework for reviewing existing professional statements and developing future guidance; and

(c) provide auditors and others with a comprehensive reference service about contemporary law concerning civil and criminal liabilities of auditors in Australia.

June 1992: ED 48 'The Auditor's Responsibility for Detecting and Reporting Irregularities including Fraud, Other Illegal Acts and Error' issued by the AuSB.

March 1993: The revised AUP 16 'The Auditor's Responsibility for Detecting and Reporting Irregularities including Fraud, Other Illegal Acts and Error' was issued following the period of exposure of ED 48. The revised AUP 16 provided more detailed and extensive guidance on the auditor's current legal requirements to detect and report irregularities. It emphasised that the auditor's role was not to prevent irregularities; rather it was to exercise skill and care so as to have a reasonable expectation of detecting material misstatements arising from irregularities.

February 1994: ED 54 'Codification and Revision of Auditing Pronouncements: AUS 210 Irregularities Including Fraud, Other Illegal Acts and Error (AUP 16)' issued by the AuSB.

June 1994: The International Auditing Practices Committee (IAPC) of the International Federation of Accountants (IFAC) approved the issuance of a codified set of International Standards of Auditing (ISAs) in June 1994. The relevant international pronouncement was ISA 240 'Fraud and Error'.

October 1995: Australian Auditing Standards and Auditing Guidance Statements released. The status of these was explained in APS 1.1 'Conformity With Auditing Standards'. These Standards became operative for the first reporting period commencing on or after 1 July 1996 and later reporting periods, although earlier application was encouraged. AUP16 'The Auditor's Responsibility for Detecting and Reporting Irregularities including Fraud, Other Illegal Acts and Error' replaced by AUS 210 'Irregularities Including Fraud, Other Illegal Acts and Errors'.

February 1999: AUS/AGS Omnibus 2 'Miscellaneous Amendments to AUSs and AGSs' issued by the AuASB, operative from the date of issue. The Omnibus amended paras.19(a), .31 and .35 of AUS 210.

September 2001: The AuASB issued EDs 77 and 78, which revised AUS 210 and split it into two sections: Consideration of fraud and error, and Consideration of laws and regulations.

January 2002: AUS 210 is reissued in January 2002, dealing with fraud and error only. Laws and regulations addressed in AUS 218 'Consideration of Laws and Regulations in an Audit of a Financial Report'.

June 2004: AUS 210 reissued, dealing only with fraud. This new version expanded on how the risk-based approach in AUSs 402 and 406 applies to fraud. Operative for audits of financial reports for periods beginning on or after 15 December 2004. Based on ISA 240 of the same name.

April 2006: ASA 240 'The Auditor's Responsibility to Consider Fraud in an Audit of a Financial Report' was issued as a legally enforceable Standard to replace AUS 210. It is based on ISA 240 'The Auditor's Responsibility to Consider Fraud in an Audit of Financial Statements'.

October 2009: ASA 240 reissued as 'The Auditor's Responsibilities Relating to Fraud in an Audit of a Financial Report' as part of the AUASB's Clarity Project. It is based on the redrafted ISA 240 'The Auditor's Reponsibilities Relating to Fraud on an Audit of Financial Statements'.

June 2011: ASA 240 updated for editorial amendments contained in ASA 2011-1 'Amendments to Australian Auditing Standards'.

Contents

Compilation Details

Auditing Standard ASA 240 *The Auditor's Responsibilities Relating to Fraud in an Audit of a Financial Report* as Amended

This compilation takes into account amendments made up to and including 27 June 2011 and was prepared on 27 June 2011 by the Auditing and Assurance Standards Board (AUASB).

This compilation is not a separate Auditing Standard made by the AUASB. Instead, it is a representation of ASA 240 (October 2009) as amended by another Auditing Standard which is listed in the Table below.

Table of Standards

Standard	Date made	Operative date
ASA 240	27 October 2009	1 January 2010
ASA 2011-1	27 June 2011	1 July 2011

Table of Amendments

Paragraph affected	How affected	By … [paragraph]
A30	Amended	ASA 2011-1 [23]

Preface

[Preface extracted from the original Auditing Standard issued 27 October 2009]

Reasons for Issuing Auditing Standard ASA 240 *The Auditor's Responsibilities Relating to Fraud in an Audit of a Financial Report*

The Auditing and Assurance Standards Board (AUASB) issues Auditing Standard ASA 240 *The Auditor's Responsibilities Relating to Fraud in an Audit of a Financial Report* pursuant to the requirements of the legislative provisions and the Strategic Direction explained below.

The AUASB is an independent statutory board of the Australian Government under section 227A of the *Australian Securities and Investments Commission Act 2001*, as amended (ASIC Act). Under section 336 of the *Corporations Act 2001*, the AUASB may make Auditing Standards for the purposes of the corporations legislation. These Auditing Standards are legislative instruments under the *Legislative Instruments Act 2003*.

Under the Strategic Direction given to the AUASB by the Financial Reporting Council (FRC), the AUASB is required to have regard to any programme initiated by the International Auditing and Assurance Standards Board (IAASB) for the revision and enhancement of the International Standards on Auditing (ISAs) and to make appropriate consequential amendments to the Australian Auditing Standards. Accordingly, the AUASB has decided to revise and redraft the Australian Auditing Standards using the equivalent redrafted ISAs.

Main Features

This Auditing Standard establishes requirements and provides application and other explanatory material regarding the auditor's responsibilities relating to fraud in an audit of a financial report.

This Auditing Standard:

(a) distinguishes fraud from error and describes the types of fraud relevant to the auditor, that is, misstatements resulting from misappropriation of assets and misstatements resulting from fraudulent financial reporting;

(b) describes the responsibility for the prevention and detection of fraud;

(c) describes the auditor's responsibility for maintaining an attitude of professional scepticism throughout the audit, considering the potential for management override of controls and recognising the fact that audit procedures that are effective for detecting error may not be effective in detecting fraud;

(d) requires the auditor to:

- (i) discuss among the engagement team members how and where the entity's financial report may be susceptible to material misstatement due to fraud, including how fraud might occur;
- (ii) obtain an understanding of the entity and its environment, including the entity's internal control and obtain information for use in identifying the risks of material misstatement due to fraud at the financial report level and at the assertion level; and
- (iii) determine responses to address the assessed risks of material misstatement due to fraud;

(e) requires written representations from management relating to fraud;

(f) requires communications to management and with those charged with governance on matters related to fraud; and

(g) establishes documentation requirements.

Authority Statement

Auditing Standard ASA 240 *The Auditor's Responsibilities Relating to Fraud in an Audit of a Financial Report* (as amended at 27 June 2011) is set out in paragraphs 1 to A67 and Appendices 1 to 3.

This Auditing Standard is to be read in conjunction with ASA 101 *Preamble to Australian Auditing Standards*, which sets out the intentions of the AUASB on how the Australian Auditing Standards, operative for financial reporting periods commencing on or after 1 January 2010, are to be understood, interpreted and applied. This Auditing Standard is to be read also in conjunction with ASA 200 *Overall Objectives of the Independent Auditor and the Conduct of an Audit in Accordance with Australian Auditing Standards*.

Dated: 27 June 2011

M H Kelsall
Chairman - AUASB

Auditing Standard ASA 240

The Auditing and Assurance Standards Board (AUASB) made Auditing Standard ASA 240 *The Auditor's Responsibilities Relating to Frau in an Audit of a Financial Report,* pursuant to section 227B of the *Australian Securities and Investments Commission Act 2001* and section 336 of the *Corporations Act 2001*, on 27 October 2009.

This compiled version of ASA 240 incorporates subsequent amendments contained in another Auditing Standard made by the AUASB up to and including 27 June 2011 (see Compilation Details).

Auditing Standard ASA 240

The Auditor's Responsibilities Relating to Fraud in an Audit of a Financial Report

Application

Aus 0.1 This Auditing Standard applies to:

(a) an audit of a financial report for a financial year, or an audit of a financial report for a half-year, in accordance with the *Corporations Act 2001*; and

(b) an audit of a financial report, or a complete set of financial statements, for any other purpose.

Aus 0.2 This Auditing Standard also applies, as appropriate, to an audit of other historical financial information.

Operative Date

Aus 0.3 This Auditing Standard is operative for financial reporting periods commencing on or after 1 January 2010.

[Note: For operative dates of paragraphs changed or added by an amending Standard, see Compilation Details.]

Introduction

Scope of this Auditing Standard

1. This Auditing Standard deals with the auditor's responsibilities relating to fraud in an audit of a financial report. Specifically, it expands on how ASA 315[1] and ASA 330[2] are to be applied in relation to risks of material misstatement due to fraud.

Characteristics of Fraud

2. Misstatements in the financial report can arise from either fraud or error. The distinguishing factor between fraud and error is whether the underlying action that results in the misstatement of the financial report is intentional or unintentional.

3. Although fraud is a broad legal concept, for the purposes of the Australian Auditing Standards, the auditor is concerned with fraud that causes a material misstatement in the financial report. Two types of intentional misstatements are relevant to the auditor – misstatements resulting from fraudulent financial reporting and misstatements resulting from misappropriation of assets. Although the auditor may suspect or, in rare cases, identify the occurrence of fraud, the auditor does not make legal determinations of whether fraud has actually occurred. (Ref: Para. A1-A6)

Responsibility for the Prevention and Detection of Fraud

4. The primary responsibility for the prevention and detection of fraud rests with both those charged with governance of the entity and management. It is important that management, with the oversight of those charged with governance, place a strong emphasis on fraud prevention, which may reduce opportunities for fraud to take place, and fraud deterrence, which could persuade individuals not to commit fraud because of the likelihood of detection and punishment. This involves a commitment to creating a culture of honesty and ethical behaviour which can be reinforced by an active oversight by those charged with governance. Oversight by those charged with governance includes considering the potential for override of controls or other inappropriate influence over the financial reporting process, such as efforts by management to manage earnings in order to influence the perceptions of analysts as to the entity's performance and profitability.

Responsibilities of the Auditor

5. An auditor conducting an audit in accordance with Australian Auditing Standards is responsible for obtaining reasonable assurance that the financial report taken as a whole is free from material misstatement, whether caused by fraud or error. Owing to the inherent limitations of an audit, there is an unavoidable risk that some material misstatements of the financial report may not be detected, even though the audit is properly planned and performed in accordance with Australian Auditing Standards.[3]

6. As described in ASA 200,[4] the potential effects of inherent limitations are particularly significant in the case of misstatement resulting from fraud. The risk of not detecting a material misstatement resulting from fraud is higher than the risk of not detecting one resulting from error. This is because fraud may involve sophisticated and carefully organised schemes designed to conceal it, such as forgery, deliberate failure to record transactions, or intentional misrepresentations being made to the auditor. Such attempts

---

1 See ASA 315 *Identifying and Assessing the Risks of Material Misstatement through Understanding the Entity and Its Environment.*

2 See ASA 330 *The Auditor's Responses to Assessed Risks.*

3 See ASA 200 *Overall Objectives of the Independent Auditor and the Conduct of an Audit in Accordance with Australian Auditing Standards*, paragraph A51.

4 See ASA 200, paragraph A51.

at concealment may be even more difficult to detect when accompanied by collusion. Collusion may cause the auditor to believe that audit evidence is persuasive when it is, in fact, false. The auditor's ability to detect a fraud depends on factors such as the skilfulness of the perpetrator, the frequency and extent of manipulation, the degree of collusion involved, the relative size of individual amounts manipulated, and the seniority of those individuals involved. While the auditor may be able to identify potential opportunities for fraud to be perpetrated, it is difficult for the auditor to determine whether misstatements in judgement areas such as accounting estimates are caused by fraud or error.

7. Furthermore, the risk of the auditor not detecting a material misstatement resulting from management fraud is greater than for employee fraud, because management is frequently in a position to directly or indirectly manipulate accounting records, present fraudulent financial information or override control procedures designed to prevent similar frauds by other employees.

8. When obtaining reasonable assurance, the auditor is responsible for maintaining professional scepticism throughout the audit, considering the potential for management override of controls and recognising the fact that audit procedures that are effective for detecting error may not be effective in detecting fraud. The requirements in this Auditing Standard are designed to assist the auditor in identifying and assessing the risks of material misstatement due to fraud and in designing procedures to detect such misstatement.

Effective Date

9. [Deleted by the AUASB. Refer Aus 0.3]

Objectives

10. The objectives of the auditor are:

    (a) To identify and assess the risks of material misstatement of the financial report due to fraud;

    (b) To obtain sufficient appropriate audit evidence regarding the assessed risks of material misstatement due to fraud, through designing and implementing appropriate responses; and

    (c) To respond appropriately to fraud or suspected fraud identified during the audit.

Definitions

11. For purposes of the Australian Auditing Standards, the following terms have the meanings attributed below:

    (a) Fraud means an intentional act by one or more individuals among management, those charged with governance, employees, or third parties, involving the use of deception to obtain an unjust or illegal advantage.

    (b) Fraud risk factors means events or conditions that indicate an incentive or pressure to commit fraud or provide an opportunity to commit fraud.

Requirements

Professional Scepticism

12. In accordance with ASA 200, the auditor shall maintain professional scepticism throughout the audit, recognising the possibility that a material misstatement due to fraud could exist, notwithstanding the auditor's past experience of the honesty and integrity of the entity's management and those charged with governance. (Ref: Para. A7- A8)

13. Unless the auditor has reason to believe the contrary, the auditor may accept records and documents as genuine. If conditions identified during the audit cause the auditor to believe that a document may not be authentic or that terms in a document have been modified but not disclosed to the auditor, the auditor shall investigate further. (Ref: Para. A9)

14. Where responses to enquiries of management or those charged with governance are inconsistent, the auditor shall investigate the inconsistencies.

Discussion among the Engagement Team

15. ASA 315 requires a discussion among the engagement team members and a determination by the engagement partner of which matters are to be communicated to those team members not involved in the discussion[5]. This discussion shall place particular emphasis on how and where the entity's financial report may be susceptible to material misstatement due to fraud, including how fraud might occur. The discussion shall occur setting aside beliefs that the engagement team members may have that management and those charged with governance are honest and have integrity. (Ref: Para. A10-A11)

Risk Assessment Procedures and Related Activities

16. When performing risk assessment procedures and related activities to obtain an understanding of the entity and its environment, including the entity's internal control, required by ASA 315[6], the auditor shall perform the procedures in paragraphs 17-24 of this Auditing Standard to obtain information for use in identifying the risks of material misstatement due to fraud.

Management and Others within the Entity

17. The auditor shall make enquiries of management regarding:
   (a) Management's assessment of the risk that the financial report may be materially misstated due to fraud, including the nature, extent and frequency of such assessments; (Ref: Para. A12-A13)
   (b) Management's process for identifying and responding to the risks of fraud in the entity, including any specific risks of fraud that management has identified or that have been brought to its attention, or classes of transactions, account balances, or disclosures for which a risk of fraud is likely to exist; (Ref: Para. A14)
   (c) Management's communication, if any, to those charged with governance regarding its processes for identifying and responding to the risks of fraud in the entity; and
   (d) Management's communication, if any, to employees regarding its views on business practices and ethical behaviour.

18. The auditor shall make enquiries of management, and others within the entity as appropriate, to determine whether they have knowledge of any actual, suspected or alleged fraud affecting the entity. (Ref: Para. A15-A17)

19. For those entities that have an internal audit function, the auditor shall make enquiries of internal audit to determine whether it has knowledge of any actual, suspected or alleged fraud affecting the entity, and to obtain its views about the risks of fraud. (Ref: Para. A18)

Those Charged with Governance

20. Unless all of those charged with governance are involved in managing the entity,[7] the auditor shall obtain an understanding of how those charged with governance exercise oversight of management's processes for identifying and responding to the risks of fraud in the entity and the internal control that management has established to mitigate these risks. (Ref: Para. A19-A21)

21. Unless all of those charged with governance are involved in managing the entity, the auditor shall make enquiries of those charged with governance to determine whether they have knowledge of any actual, suspected or alleged fraud affecting the entity. These enquiries are made in part to corroborate the responses to the enquiries of management.

Unusual or Unexpected Relationships Identified

22. The auditor shall evaluate whether unusual or unexpected relationships that have been identified in performing analytical procedures, including those related to revenue accounts, may indicate risks of material misstatement due to fraud.

---

5 See ASA 315, paragraph 10.

6 See ASA 315, paragraphs 5-24.

7 See ASA 260 *Communication with Those Charged with Governance*, paragraph 13.

Other Information

23. The auditor shall consider whether other information obtained by the auditor indicates risks of material misstatement due to fraud. (Ref: Para. A22)

Evaluation of Fraud Risk Factors

24. The auditor shall evaluate whether the information obtained from the other risk assessment procedures and related activities performed indicates that one or more fraud risk factors are present. While fraud risk factors may not necessarily indicate the existence of fraud, they have often been present in circumstances where frauds have occurred and therefore may indicate risks of material misstatement due to fraud. (Ref: Para. A23-A27)

Identification and Assessment of the Risks of Material Misstatement Due to Fraud

25. In accordance with ASA 315, the auditor shall identify and assess the risks of material misstatement due to fraud at the financial report level, and at the assertion level for classes of transactions, account balances and disclosures.[8]

26. When identifying and assessing the risks of material misstatement due to fraud, the auditor shall, based on a presumption that there are risks of fraud in revenue recognition, evaluate which types of revenue, revenue transactions or assertions give rise to such risks. Paragraph 47 of this Auditing Standard specifies the documentation required where the auditor concludes that the presumption is not applicable in the circumstances of the engagement and, accordingly, has not identified revenue recognition as a risk of material misstatement due to fraud. (Ref: Para. A28-A30)

27. The auditor shall treat those assessed risks of material misstatement due to fraud as significant risks and accordingly, to the extent not already done so, the auditor shall obtain an understanding of the entity's related controls, including control activities, relevant to such risks. (Ref: Para. A31-A32)

Responses to the Assessed Risks of Material Misstatement Due to Fraud

Overall Responses

28. In accordance with ASA 330, the auditor shall determine overall responses to address the assessed risks of material misstatement due to fraud at the financial report level.[9] (Ref: Para. A33)

29. In determining overall responses to address the assessed risks of material misstatement due to fraud at the financial report level, the auditor shall:

    (a) Assign and supervise personnel taking account of the knowledge, skill and ability of the individuals to be given significant engagement responsibilities and the auditor's assessment of the risks of material misstatement due to fraud for the engagement; (Ref: Para. A34-A35)

    (b) Evaluate whether the selection and application of accounting policies by the entity, particularly those related to subjective measurements and complex transactions, may be indicative of fraudulent financial reporting resulting from management's effort to manage earnings; and

    (c) Incorporate an element of unpredictability in the selection of the nature, timing and extent of audit procedures. (Ref: Para. A36)

Audit Procedures Responsive to Assessed Risks of Material Misstatement Due to Fraud at the Assertion Level

30. In accordance with ASA 330, the auditor shall design and perform further audit procedures whose nature, timing and extent are responsive to the assessed risks of material misstatement due to fraud at the assertion level.[10] (Ref: Para. A37-A40)

8 See ASA 315, paragraph 25.

9 See ASA 330, paragraph 5.

10 See ASA 330, paragraph 6.

Audit Procedures Responsive to Risks Related to Management Override of Controls

31. Management is in a unique position to perpetrate fraud because of management's ability to manipulate accounting records and prepare a fraudulent financial report by overriding controls that otherwise appear to be operating effectively. Although the level of risk of management override of controls will vary from entity to entity, the risk is nevertheless present in all entities. Due to the unpredictable way in which such override could occur, it is a risk of material misstatement due to fraud and thus a significant risk.

32. Irrespective of the auditor's assessment of the risks of management override of controls, the auditor shall design and perform audit procedures to:

    (a) Test the appropriateness of journal entries recorded in the general ledger and other adjustments made in the preparation of the financial report. In designing and performing audit procedures for such tests, the auditor shall:

        (i) Make enquiries of individuals involved in the financial reporting process about inappropriate or unusual activity relating to the processing of journal entries and other adjustments;

        (ii) Select journal entries and other adjustments made at the end of a reporting period; and

        (iii) Consider the need to test journal entries and other adjustments throughout the period. (Ref: Para. A41-A44)

    (b) Review accounting estimates for biases and evaluate whether the circumstances producing the bias, if any, represent a risk of material misstatement due to fraud. In performing this review, the auditor shall:

        (i) Evaluate whether the judgements and decisions made by management in making the accounting estimates included in the financial report, even if they are individually reasonable, indicate a possible bias on the part of the entity's management that may represent a risk of material misstatement due to fraud. If so, the auditor shall re-evaluate the accounting estimates taken as a whole; and

        (ii) Perform a retrospective review of management judgements and assumptions related to significant accounting estimates reflected in the financial report of the prior year. (Ref: Para. A45-A47)

    (c) For significant transactions that are outside the normal course of business for the entity, or that otherwise appear to be unusual given the auditor's understanding of the entity and its environment and other information obtained during the audit, evaluate whether the business rationale (or the lack thereof) of the transactions suggests that they may have been entered into to engage in fraudulent financial reporting or to conceal misappropriation of assets. (Ref: Para. A48)

33. The auditor shall determine whether, in order to respond to the identified risks of management override of controls, the auditor needs to perform other audit procedures in addition to those specifically referred to above (that is, where there are specific additional risks of management override that are not covered as part of the procedures performed to address the requirements in paragraph 32 of this Auditing Standard).

Evaluation of Audit Evidence (Ref: Para. A49)

34. The auditor shall evaluate whether analytical procedures that are performed near the end of the audit, when forming an overall conclusion as to whether the financial report is consistent with the auditor's understanding of the entity, indicate a previously unrecognised risk of material misstatement due to fraud. (Ref: Para. A50)

35. If the auditor identifies a misstatement, the auditor shall evaluate whether such a misstatement is indicative of fraud. If there is such an indication, the auditor shall evaluate the implications of the misstatement in relation to other aspects of the audit, particularly the reliability of management representations, recognising that an instance of fraud is unlikely to be an isolated occurrence. (Ref: Para. A51)

36. If the auditor identifies a misstatement, whether material or not, and the auditor has reason to believe that it is or may be the result of fraud and that management (in particular, senior management) is involved, the auditor shall re-evaluate the assessment of the risks of material misstatement due to fraud and its resulting impact on the nature, timing and extent of audit procedures to respond to the assessed risks. The auditor shall also consider whether circumstances or conditions indicate possible collusion involving employees, management or third parties when reconsidering the reliability of evidence previously obtained. (Ref: Para. A52)

37. If the auditor confirms that, or is unable to conclude whether, the financial report is materially misstated as a result of fraud the auditor shall evaluate the implications for the audit. (Ref: Para. A53)

Auditor Unable to Continue the Engagement

38. If, as a result of a misstatement resulting from fraud or suspected fraud, the auditor encounters exceptional circumstances that bring into question the auditor's ability to continue performing the audit, the auditor shall:

(a) Determine the professional and legal responsibilities applicable in the circumstances, including whether there is a requirement for the auditor to report to the person or persons who made the audit appointment or, in some cases, to regulatory authorities;

(b) Consider whether it is appropriate to withdraw from the engagement, where withdrawal is possible under applicable law or regulation; and

(c) If the auditor withdraws:

(i) Discuss with the appropriate level of management and those charged with governance the auditor's withdrawal from the engagement and the reasons for the withdrawal; and

(ii) Determine whether there is a professional or legal requirement to report to the person or persons who made the audit appointment or, in some cases, to regulatory authorities, the auditor's withdrawal from the engagement and the reasons for the withdrawal. (Ref: Para. A54-A57)

Written Representations

39. The auditor shall obtain written representations from management and, where appropriate, those charged with governance that:

(a) They acknowledge their responsibility for the design, implementation and maintenance of internal control to prevent and detect fraud;

(b) They have disclosed to the auditor the results of management's assessment of the risk that the financial report may be materially misstated as a result of fraud;

(c) They have disclosed to the auditor their knowledge of fraud or suspected fraud affecting the entity involving:

(i) Management;

(ii) Employees who have significant roles in internal control; or

(iii) Others where the fraud could have a material effect on the financial report; and

(d) They have disclosed to the auditor their knowledge of any allegations of fraud, or suspected fraud, affecting the entity's financial report communicated by employees, former employees, analysts, regulators or others. (Ref: Para. A58-A59)

Communications to Management and with Those Charged With Governance

40. If the auditor has identified a fraud or has obtained information that indicates that a fraud may exist, the auditor shall communicate these matters on a timely basis to the appropriate level of management in order to inform those with primary responsibility

for the prevention and detection of fraud of matters relevant to their responsibilities. (Ref: Para. A60)

41. Unless all of those charged with governance are involved in managing the entity, if the auditor has identified or suspects fraud involving:

    (a) Management;

    (b) Employees who have significant roles in internal control; or

    (c) Others where the fraud results in a material misstatement in the financial report,

    the auditor shall communicate these matters to those charged with governance on a timely basis. If the auditor suspects fraud involving management, the auditor shall communicate these suspicions to those charged with governance and discuss with them the nature, timing and extent of audit procedures necessary to complete the audit. (Ref: Para. Aus A60.1-A63)

42. The auditor shall communicate with those charged with governance any other matters related to fraud that are, in the auditor's judgement, relevant to their responsibilities. (Ref: Para. A64)

Communications to Regulatory and Enforcement Authorities

43. If the auditor has identified or suspects a fraud, the auditor shall determine whether there is a responsibility to report the occurrence or suspicion to a party outside the entity. Although the auditor's professional duty to maintain the confidentiality of client information may preclude such reporting, the auditor's legal responsibilities may override the duty of confidentiality in some circumstances. (Ref: Para. A65-A67)

Documentation

44. The auditor shall include the following in the audit documentation[11] of the auditor's understanding of the entity and its environment and the assessment of the risks of material misstatement required by ASA 315:[12]

    (a) The significant decisions reached during the discussion among the engagement team regarding the susceptibility of the entity's financial report to material misstatement due to fraud; and

    (b) The identified and assessed risks of material misstatement due to fraud at the financial report level and at the assertion level.

45. The auditor shall include the following in the audit documentation of the auditor's responses to the assessed risks of material misstatement required by ASA 330:[13]

    (a) The overall responses to the assessed risks of material misstatement due to fraud at the financial report level and the nature, timing and extent of audit procedures, and the linkage of those procedures with the assessed risks of material misstatement due to fraud at the assertion level; and

    (b) The results of the audit procedures, including those designed to address the risk of management override of controls.

46. The auditor shall include in the audit documentation communications about fraud made to management, those charged with governance, regulators and others.

47. If the auditor has concluded that the presumption that there is a risk of material misstatement due to fraud related to revenue recognition is not applicable in the circumstances of the engagement, the auditor shall include in the audit documentation the reasons for that conclusion.

❖ ❖ ❖

11 See ASA 230 *Audit Documentation*, paragraphs 8-11 and paragraph A6.

12 See ASA 315, paragraph 32.

13 See ASA 330, paragraph 28.

Application and Other Explanatory Material

Characteristics of Fraud (Ref: Para. 3)

A1. Fraud, whether fraudulent financial reporting or misappropriation of assets, involves incentive or pressure to commit fraud, a perceived opportunity to do so and some rationalisation of the act. For example:

- Incentive or pressure to commit fraudulent financial reporting may exist when management is under pressure, from sources outside or inside the entity, to achieve an expected (and perhaps unrealistic) earnings target or financial outcome – particularly since the consequences to management for failing to meet financial goals can be significant. Similarly, individuals may have an incentive to misappropriate assets, for example, because the individuals are living beyond their means.
- A perceived opportunity to commit fraud may exist when an individual believes internal control can be overridden, for example, because the individual is in a position of trust or has knowledge of specific deficiencies in internal control.
- Individuals may be able to rationalise committing a fraudulent act. Some individuals possess an attitude, character or set of ethical values that allow them knowingly and intentionally to commit a dishonest act. However, even otherwise honest individuals can commit fraud in an environment that imposes sufficient pressure on them.

A2. Fraudulent financial reporting involves intentional misstatements including omissions of amounts or disclosures in the financial report to deceive financial report users. It can be caused by the efforts of management to manage earnings in order to deceive financial report users by influencing their perceptions as to the entity's performance and profitability. Such earnings management may start out with small actions or inappropriate adjustment of assumptions and changes in judgements by management. Pressures and incentives may lead these actions to increase to the extent that they result in fraudulent financial reporting. Such a situation could occur when, due to pressures to meet market expectations or a desire to maximise compensation based on performance, management intentionally takes positions that lead to fraudulent financial reporting by materially misstating the financial report. In some entities, management may be motivated to reduce earnings by a material amount to minimise tax or to inflate earnings to secure bank financing.

A3. Fraudulent financial reporting may be accomplished by the following:

- Manipulation, falsification (including forgery), or alteration of accounting records or supporting documentation from which the financial report is prepared.
- Misrepresentation in, or intentional omission from, the financial report of events, transactions or other significant information.
- Intentional misapplication of accounting principles relating to amounts, classification, manner of presentation, or disclosure.

A4. Fraudulent financial reporting often involves management override of controls that otherwise may appear to be operating effectively. Fraud can be committed by management overriding controls using such techniques as:

- Recording fictitious journal entries, particularly close to the end of an accounting period, to manipulate operating results or achieve other objectives.
- Inappropriately adjusting assumptions and changing judgements used to estimate account balances.
- Omitting, advancing or delaying recognition in the financial report of events and transactions that have occurred during the reporting period.
- Concealing, or not disclosing, facts that could affect the amounts recorded in the financial report.
- Engaging in complex transactions that are structured to misrepresent the financial position or financial performance of the entity.
- Altering records and terms related to significant and unusual transactions.

A5. Misappropriation of assets involves the theft of an entity's assets and is often perpetrated by employees in relatively small and immaterial amounts. However, it can also involve management who are usually more able to disguise or conceal misappropriations in ways that are difficult to detect. Misappropriation of assets can be accomplished in a variety of ways including:

- Embezzling receipts (for example, misappropriating collections on accounts receivable or diverting receipts in respect of written-off accounts to personal bank accounts).
- Stealing physical assets or intellectual property (for example, stealing inventory for personal use or for sale, stealing scrap for resale, colluding with a competitor by disclosing technological data in return for payment).
- Causing an entity to pay for goods and services not received (for example, payments to fictitious vendors, kickbacks paid by vendors to the entity's purchasing agents in return for inflating prices, payments to fictitious employees).
- Using an entity's assets for personal use (for example, using the entity's assets as collateral for a personal loan or a loan to a related party).
- Misappropriation of assets is often accompanied by false or misleading records or documents in order to conceal the fact that the assets are missing or have been pledged without proper authorisation.

Considerations Specific to Public Sector Entities

A6. The public sector auditor's responsibilities relating to fraud may be a result of law, regulation or other authority, applicable to public sector entities or separately covered by the auditor's mandate. Consequently, the public sector auditor's responsibilities may not be limited to consideration of risks of material misstatement of the financial report, but may also include a broader responsibility to consider risks of fraud.

Professional Scepticism (Ref: Para. 12-14)

A7. Maintaining professional scepticism requires an ongoing questioning of whether the information and audit evidence obtained suggests that a material misstatement due to fraud may exist. It includes considering the reliability of the information to be used as audit evidence and the controls over its preparation and maintenance where relevant. Due to the characteristics of fraud, the auditor's professional scepticism is particularly important when considering the risks of material misstatement due to fraud.

A8. Although the auditor cannot be expected to disregard past experience of the honesty and integrity of the entity's management and those charged with governance, the auditor's professional scepticism is particularly important in considering the risks of material misstatement due to fraud because there may have been changes in circumstances.

A9. An audit performed in accordance with Australian Auditing Standards rarely involves the authentication of documents, nor is the auditor trained as or expected to be an expert in such authentication.[14] However, when the auditor identifies conditions that cause the auditor to believe that a document may not be authentic or that terms in a document have been modified but not disclosed to the auditor, possible procedures to investigate further may include:

- Confirming directly with the third party.
- Using the work of an expert to assess the document's authenticity.

Discussion among the Engagement Team (Ref: Para. 15)

A10. Discussing the susceptibility of the entity's financial report to material misstatement due to fraud with the engagement team:

- Provides an opportunity for more experienced engagement team members to share their insights about how and where the financial report may be susceptible to material misstatement due to fraud.

14 See ASA 200, paragraph A47.

- Enables the auditor to consider an appropriate response to such susceptibility and to determine which members of the engagement team will conduct certain audit procedures.
- Permits the auditor to determine how the results of audit procedures will be shared among the engagement team and how to deal with any allegations of fraud that may come to the auditor's attention.

A11. The discussion may include such matters as:

- An exchange of ideas among engagement team members about how and where they believe the entity's financial report may be susceptible to material misstatement due to fraud, how management could perpetrate and conceal fraudulent financial reporting, and how assets of the entity could be misappropriated.
- A consideration of circumstances that might be indicative of earnings management and the practices that might be followed by management to manage earnings that could lead to fraudulent financial reporting.
- A consideration of the known external and internal factors affecting the entity that may create an incentive or pressure for management or others to commit fraud, provide the opportunity for fraud to be perpetrated, and indicate a culture or environment that enables management or others to rationalise committing fraud.
- A consideration of management's involvement in overseeing employees with access to cash or other assets susceptible to misappropriation.
- A consideration of any unusual or unexplained changes in behaviour or lifestyle of management or employees which have come to the attention of the engagement team.
- An emphasis on the importance of maintaining a proper state of mind throughout the audit regarding the potential for material misstatement due to fraud.
- A consideration of the types of circumstances that, if encountered, might indicate the possibility of fraud.
- A consideration of how an element of unpredictability will be incorporated into the nature, timing and extent of the audit procedures to be performed.
- A consideration of the audit procedures that might be selected to respond to the susceptibility of the entity's financial report to material misstatement due to fraud and whether certain types of audit procedures are more effective than others.
- A consideration of any allegations of fraud that have come to the auditor's attention.
- A consideration of the risk of management override of controls.

Risk Assessment Procedures and Related Activities

Enquiries of Management

Management's Assessment of the Risk of Material Misstatement Due to Fraud

(Ref: Para. 17(a))

A12. Management accepts responsibility for the entity's internal control and for the preparation of the entity's financial report. Accordingly, it is appropriate for the auditor to make enquiries of management regarding management's own assessment of the risk of fraud and the controls in place to prevent and detect it. The nature, extent and frequency of management's assessment of such risk and controls may vary from entity to entity. In some entities, management may make detailed assessments on an annual basis or as part of continuous monitoring. In other entities, management's assessment may be less structured and less frequent. The nature, extent and frequency of management's assessment are relevant to the auditor's understanding of the entity's control environment. For example, the fact that management has not made an assessment of the risk of fraud may in some circumstances be indicative of the lack of importance that management places on internal control.

Considerations specific to smaller entities

A13. In some entities, particularly smaller entities, the focus of management's assessment may be on the risks of employee fraud or misappropriation of assets.

Management's Process for Identifying and Responding to the Risks of Fraud (Ref: Para. 17(b))

A14. In the case of entities with multiple locations, management's processes may include different levels of monitoring of operating locations, or business segments. Management may also have identified particular operating locations or business segments for which a risk of fraud may be more likely to exist.

Enquiry of Management and Others within the Entity (Ref: Para. 18)

A15. The auditor's enquiries of management may provide useful information concerning the risks of material misstatements in the financial report resulting from employee fraud. However, such enquiries are unlikely to provide useful information regarding the risks of material misstatement in the financial report resulting from management fraud. Making enquiries of others within the entity may provide individuals with an opportunity to convey information to the auditor that may not otherwise be communicated.

A16. Examples of others within the entity to whom the auditor may direct enquiries about the existence or suspicion of fraud include:

- Operating personnel not directly involved in the financial reporting process.
- Employees with different levels of authority.
- Employees involved in initiating, processing or recording complex or unusual transactions and those who supervise or monitor such employees.
- In-house legal counsel.
- Chief ethics officer or equivalent person.
- The person or persons charged with dealing with allegations of fraud.

A17. Management is often in the best position to perpetrate fraud. Accordingly, when evaluating management's responses to enquiries with an attitude of professional scepticism, the auditor may judge it necessary to corroborate responses to enquiries with other information.

Enquiry of Internal Audit (Ref: Para. 19)

A18. ASA 315 and ASA 610 establish requirements and provide guidance in audits of those entities that have an internal audit function.[15] In carrying out the requirements of those Auditing Standards in the context of fraud, the auditor may enquire about specific internal audit activities including, for example:

- The procedures performed, if any, by the internal auditors during the year to detect fraud.
- Whether management has satisfactorily responded to any findings resulting from those procedures.

Obtaining an Understanding of Oversight Exercised by Those Charged With Governance (Ref: Para. 20)

A19. Those charged with governance of an entity oversee the entity's systems for monitoring risk, financial control and compliance with the law. In many circumstances, corporate governance practices are well developed and those charged with governance play an active role in oversight of the entity's assessment of the risks of fraud and of the relevant internal control. Since the responsibilities of those charged with governance and management may vary by entity and by the circumstances, it is important that the auditor understands their respective responsibilities to enable the auditor to obtain an understanding of the oversight exercised by the appropriate individuals.[16]

15 See ASA 315, paragraph 23 and ASA 610 *Using the Work of Internal Auditors*.

16 See ASA 260, paragraphs A1-A8, that discuss with whom the auditor communicates when the entity's governance structure is not well defined.

A20. An understanding of the oversight exercised by those charged with governance may provide insights regarding the susceptibility of the entity to management fraud, the adequacy of internal control over risks of fraud, and the competency and integrity of management. The auditor may obtain this understanding in a number of ways, such as by attending meetings where such discussions take place, reading the minutes from such meetings or making enquiries of those charged with governance.

Considerations Specific to Smaller Entities

A21. In some cases, all of those charged with governance are involved in managing the entity. This may be the case in a small entity where a single owner manages the entity and no one else has a governance role. In these cases, there is ordinarily no action on the part of the auditor because there is no oversight separate from management.

Consideration of Other Information (Ref: Para. 23)

A22. In addition to information obtained from applying analytical procedures, other information obtained about the entity and its environment may be helpful in identifying the risks of material misstatement due to fraud. The discussion among team members may provide information that is helpful in identifying such risks. In addition, information obtained from the auditor's client acceptance and retention processes, and experience gained on other engagements performed for the entity, for example engagements to review interim financial information, may be relevant in the identification of the risks of material misstatement due to fraud.

Evaluation of Fraud Risk Factors (Ref: Para. 24)

A23. The fact that fraud is usually concealed can make it very difficult to detect. Nevertheless, the auditor may identify events or conditions that indicate an incentive or pressure to commit fraud or provide an opportunity to commit fraud (fraud risk factors). For example:

- The need to meet expectations of third parties to obtain additional equity financing may create pressure to commit fraud;
- The granting of significant bonuses if unrealistic profit targets are met may create an incentive to commit fraud; and
- A control environment that is not effective may create an opportunity to commit fraud.

A24. Fraud risk factors cannot easily be ranked in order of importance. The significance of fraud risk factors varies widely. Some of these factors will be present in entities where the specific conditions do not present risks of material misstatement. Accordingly, the determination of whether a fraud risk factor is present and whether it is to be considered in assessing the risks of material misstatement of the financial report due to fraud requires the exercise of professional judgement.

A25. Examples of fraud risk factors related to fraudulent financial reporting and misappropriation of assets are presented in Appendix 1. These illustrative risk factors are classified based on the three conditions that are generally present when fraud exists:

- An incentive or pressure to commit fraud;
- A perceived opportunity to commit fraud; and
- An ability to rationalise the fraudulent action.

Risk factors reflective of an attitude that permits rationalisation of the fraudulent action may not be susceptible to observation by the auditor. Nevertheless, the auditor may become aware of the existence of such information. Although the fraud risk factors described in Appendix 1 cover a broad range of situations that may be faced by auditors, they are only examples and other risk factors may exist.

A26. The size, complexity, and ownership characteristics of the entity have a significant influence on the consideration of relevant fraud risk factors. For example, in the case of a large entity, there may be factors that generally constrain improper conduct by management, such as:

- Effective oversight by those charged with governance.

- An effective internal audit function.
- The existence and enforcement of a written code of conduct.

Furthermore, fraud risk factors considered at a business segment operating level may provide different insights when compared with those obtained when considered at an entity-wide level.

Considerations Specific to Smaller Entities

A27. In the case of a small entity, some or all of these considerations may be inapplicable or less relevant. For example, a smaller entity may not have a written code of conduct but, instead, may have developed a culture that emphasises the importance of integrity and ethical behaviour through oral communication and by management example. Domination of management by a single individual in a small entity does not generally, in and of itself, indicate a failure by management to display and communicate an appropriate attitude regarding internal control and the financial reporting process. In some entities, the need for management authorisation can compensate for otherwise deficient controls and reduce the risk of employee fraud. However, domination of management by a single individual can be a potential deficiency in internal control since there is an opportunity for management override of controls.

ASA

Identification and Assessment of the Risks of Material Misstatement Due to Fraud

Risks of Fraud in Revenue Recognition (Ref: Para. 26)

A28. Material misstatement due to fraudulent financial reporting relating to revenue recognition often results from an overstatement of revenues through, for example, premature revenue recognition or recording fictitious revenues. It may result also from an understatement of revenues through, for example, improperly shifting revenues to a later period.

A29. The risks of fraud in revenue recognition may be greater in some entities than others. For example, there may be pressures or incentives on management to commit fraudulent financial reporting through inappropriate revenue recognition in the case of listed entities when, for example, performance is measured in terms of year-over-year revenue growth or profit. Similarly, for example, there may be greater risks of fraud in revenue recognition in the case of entities that generate a substantial portion of revenues through cash sales.

A30. The presumption that there are risks of fraud in revenue recognition may be rebutted. For example, the auditor may conclude that there is no risk of material misstatement due to fraud relating to revenue recognition in the case where there is a single type of simple revenue transaction, for example, leasehold revenue from a single unit rental property.

Identifying and Assessing the Risks of Material Misstatement Due to Fraud and Understanding the Entity's Related Controls (Ref: Para. 27)

A31. Management may make judgements on the nature and extent of the controls it chooses to implement, and the nature and extent of the risks it chooses to assume.[17] In determining which controls to implement to prevent and detect fraud, management considers the risks that the financial report may be materially misstated as a result of fraud. As part of this consideration, management may conclude that it is not cost effective to implement and maintain a particular control in relation to the reduction in the risks of material misstatement due to fraud to be achieved.

A32. It is therefore important for the auditor to obtain an understanding of the controls that management has designed, implemented and maintained to prevent and detect fraud. In doing so, the auditor may learn, for example, that management has consciously chosen to accept the risks associated with a lack of segregation of duties. Information from obtaining this understanding may also be useful in identifying fraud risks factors that may affect the auditor's assessment of the risks that the financial report may contain material misstatement due to fraud.

17 See ASA 315, paragraph A48.

Responses to the Assessed Risks of Material Misstatement Due to Fraud

Overall Responses (Ref: Para. 28)

A33. Determining overall responses to address the assessed risks of material misstatement due to fraud generally includes the consideration of how the overall conduct of the audit can reflect increased professional scepticism, for example, through:

- Increased sensitivity in the selection of the nature and extent of documentation to be examined in support of material transactions.
- Increased recognition of the need to corroborate management explanations or representations concerning material matters.

It also involves more general considerations apart from the specific procedures otherwise planned; these considerations include the matters listed in paragraph 29, which are discussed below.

Assignment and Supervision of Personnel (Ref: Para. 29(a))

A34. The auditor may respond to identified risks of material misstatement due to fraud by, for example, assigning additional individuals with specialised skill and knowledge, such as forensic and IT experts, or by assigning more experienced individuals to the engagement.

A35. The extent of supervision reflects the auditor's assessment of risks of material misstatement due to fraud and the competencies of the engagement team members performing the work.

Unpredictability in the Selection of Audit Procedures (Ref: Para. 29(c))

A36. Incorporating an element of unpredictability in the selection of the nature, timing and extent of audit procedures to be performed is important as individuals within the entity who are familiar with the audit procedures normally performed on engagements may be more able to conceal fraudulent financial reporting. This can be achieved by, for example:

- Performing substantive audit procedures on selected account balances and assertions not otherwise tested due to their materiality or risk.
- Adjusting the timing of audit procedures from that otherwise expected.
- Using different sampling methods.
- Performing audit procedures at different locations or at locations on an unannounced basis.

Audit Procedures Responsive to Assessed Risks of Material Misstatement Due to Fraud at the Assertion Level (Ref: Para. 30)

A37. The auditor's responses to address the assessed risks of material misstatement due to fraud at the assertion level may include changing the nature, timing and extent of audit procedures in the following ways:

- The nature of audit procedures to be performed may need to be changed to obtain audit evidence that is more reliable and relevant or to obtain additional corroborative information. This may affect both the type of audit procedures to be performed and their combination. For example:
  - Physical observation or inspection of certain assets may become more important or the auditor may choose to use computer-assisted audit techniques to gather more evidence about data contained in significant accounts or electronic transaction files.
  - The auditor may design procedures to obtain additional corroborative information. For example, if the auditor identifies that management is under pressure to meet earnings expectations, there may be a related risk that management is inflating sales by entering into sales agreements that include terms that preclude revenue recognition or by invoicing sales before delivery. In these circumstances, the auditor may, for example, design external confirmations not only to confirm outstanding amounts, but also to confirm the details of the sales agreements, including date, any rights of return and delivery terms. In addition, the auditor might find it effective

to supplement such external confirmations with enquiries of non-financial personnel in the entity regarding any changes in sales agreements and delivery terms.

- The timing of substantive procedures may need to be modified. The auditor may conclude that performing substantive testing at or near the period end better addresses an assessed risk of material misstatement due to fraud. The auditor may conclude that, given the assessed risks of intentional misstatement or manipulation, audit procedures to extend audit conclusions from an interim date to the period end would not be effective. In contrast, because an intentional misstatement—for example, a misstatement involving improper revenue recognition—may have been initiated in an interim period, the auditor may elect to apply substantive procedures to transactions occurring earlier in or throughout the reporting period.
- The extent of the procedures applied reflects the assessment of the risks of material misstatement due to fraud. For example, increasing sample sizes or performing analytical procedures at a more detailed level may be appropriate. Also, computer-assisted audit techniques may enable more extensive testing of electronic transactions and account files. Such techniques can be used to select sample transactions from key electronic files, to sort transactions with specific characteristics, or to test an entire population instead of a sample.

A38. If the auditor identifies a risk of material misstatement due to fraud that affects inventory quantities, examining the entity's inventory records may help to identify locations or items that require specific attention during or after the physical inventory count. Such a review may lead to a decision to observe inventory counts at certain locations on an unannounced basis or to conduct inventory counts at all locations on the same date.

A39. The auditor may identify a risk of material misstatement due to fraud affecting a number of accounts and assertions. These may include asset valuation, estimates relating to specific transactions (such as acquisitions, restructurings, or disposals of a segment of the business), and other significant accrued liabilities (such as pension or superannuation and other post-employment benefit obligations, or environmental remediation liabilities). The risk may also relate to significant changes in assumptions relating to recurring estimates. Information gathered through obtaining an understanding of the entity and its environment may assist the auditor in evaluating the reasonableness of such management estimates and underlying judgements and assumptions. A retrospective review of similar management judgements and assumptions applied in prior periods may also provide insight about the reasonableness of judgements and assumptions supporting management estimates.

A40. Examples of possible audit procedures to address the assessed risks of material misstatement due to fraud, including those that illustrate the incorporation of an element of unpredictability, are presented in Appendix 2. The appendix includes examples of responses to the auditor's assessment of the risks of material misstatement resulting from both fraudulent financial reporting, including fraudulent financial reporting resulting from revenue recognition, and misappropriation of assets.

Audit Procedures Responsive to Risks Related to Management Override of Controls

Journal Entries and Other Adjustments (Ref: Para. 32(a))

A41. Material misstatement of the financial report due to fraud often involves the manipulation of the financial reporting process by recording inappropriate or unauthorised journal entries. This may occur throughout the year or at period end, or by management making adjustments to amounts reported in the financial report that are not reflected in journal entries, such as through consolidating adjustments and reclassifications.

A42. Further, the auditor's consideration of the risks of material misstatement associated with inappropriate override of controls over journal entries is important since automated processes and controls may reduce the risk of inadvertent error but do not overcome the risk that individuals may inappropriately override such automated processes, for example, by changing the amounts being automatically passed to the general ledger or to the financial reporting system. Furthermore, where IT is used to transfer information automatically, there may be little or no visible evidence of such intervention in the information systems.

A43. When identifying and selecting journal entries and other adjustments for testing and determining the appropriate method of examining the underlying support for the items selected, the following matters are of relevance:

- The *assessment of the risks of material misstatement due to fraud* – the presence of fraud risk factors and other information obtained during the auditor's assessment of the risks of material misstatement due to fraud may assist the auditor to identify specific classes of journal entries and other adjustments for testing.
- *Controls that have been implemented over journal entries and other adjustments* – effective controls over the preparation and posting of journal entries and other adjustments may reduce the extent of substantive testing necessary, provided that the auditor has tested the operating effectiveness of the controls.
- *The entity's financial reporting process and the nature of evidence that can be obtained* – for many entities routine processing of transactions involves a combination of manual and automated steps and procedures. Similarly, the processing of journal entries and other adjustments may involve both manual and automated procedures and controls. When information technology is used in the financial reporting process, journal entries and other adjustments may exist only in electronic form.
- *The characteristics of fraudulent journal entries or other adjustments* – inappropriate journal entries or other adjustments often have unique identifying characteristics. Such characteristics may include entries (a) made to unrelated, unusual, or seldom-used accounts, (b) made by individuals who typically do not make journal entries, (c) recorded at the end of the period or as post-closing entries that have little or no explanation or description, (d) made either before or during the preparation of the financial report that do not have account numbers, or (e) containing round numbers or consistent ending numbers.
- *The nature and complexity of the accounts* – inappropriate journal entries or adjustments may be applied to accounts that (a) contain transactions that are complex or unusual in nature, (b) contain significant estimates and period-end adjustments, (c) have been prone to misstatements in the past, (d) have not been reconciled on a timely basis or contain unreconciled differences, (e) contain inter-company transactions, or (f) are otherwise associated with an identified risk of material misstatement due to fraud. In audits of entities that have several locations or components, consideration is given to the need to select journal entries from multiple locations.
- *Journal entries or other adjustments processed outside the normal course of business* – non standard journal entries may not be subject to the same level of internal control as those journal entries used on a recurring basis to record transactions such as monthly sales, purchases and cash disbursements.

A44. The auditor uses professional judgement in determining the nature, timing and extent of testing of journal entries and other adjustments. However, because fraudulent journal entries and other adjustments are often made at the end of a reporting period, paragraph 32(a)(ii) requires the auditor to select the journal entries and other adjustments made at that time. Further, because material misstatements in the financial report due to fraud can occur throughout the period and may involve extensive efforts to conceal how the fraud is accomplished, paragraph 32(a)(iii) requires the auditor to consider whether there is also a need to test journal entries and other adjustments throughout the period.

Accounting Estimates (Ref: Para. 32(b))

A45. The preparation of the financial report requires management to make a number of judgements or assumptions that affect significant accounting estimates and to monitor the reasonableness of such estimates on an ongoing basis. Fraudulent financial reporting is often accomplished through intentional misstatement of accounting estimates. This may be achieved by, for example, understating or overstating all provisions or reserves in the same fashion so as to be designed either to smooth earnings over two or more accounting periods, or to achieve a designated earnings level in order to deceive financial statement users by influencing their perceptions as to the entity's performance and profitability.

A46. The purpose of performing a retrospective review of management judgements and assumptions related to significant accounting estimates reflected in the financial report of the prior year is to determine whether there is an indication of a possible bias on the part of management. It is not intended to call into question the auditor's professional judgements made in the prior year that were based on information available at the time.

A47. A retrospective review is also required by ASA 540.[18] That review is conducted as a risk assessment procedure to obtain information regarding the effectiveness of management's prior period estimation process, audit evidence about the outcome, or where applicable, the subsequent re-estimation of prior period accounting estimates that is pertinent to making current period accounting estimates, and audit evidence of matters, such as estimation uncertainty, that may be required to be disclosed in the financial report. As a practical matter, the auditor's review of management judgements and assumptions for biases that could represent a risk of material misstatement due to fraud in accordance with this Auditing Standard may be carried out in conjunction with the review required by ASA 540.

Business Rationale for Significant Transactions (Ref: Para. 32(c))

A48. Indicators that may suggest that significant transactions that are outside the normal course of business for the entity, or that otherwise appear to be unusual, may have been entered into to engage in fraudulent financial reporting or to conceal misappropriation of assets include:

- The form of such transactions appears overly complex (for example, the transaction involves multiple entities within a consolidated group or multiple unrelated third parties).
- Management has not discussed the nature of and accounting for such transactions with those charged with governance of the entity, and there is inadequate documentation.
- Management is placing more emphasis on the need for a particular accounting treatment than on the underlying economics of the transaction.
- Transactions that involve non-consolidated related parties, including special purpose entities, have not been properly reviewed or approved by those charged with governance of the entity.
- The transactions involve previously unidentified related parties or parties that do not have the substance or the financial strength to support the transaction without assistance from the entity under audit.

Evaluation of Audit Evidence (Ref: Para. 34-37)

A49. ASA 330 requires the auditor, based on the audit procedures performed and the audit evidence obtained, to evaluate whether the assessments of the risks of material misstatement at the assertion level remain appropriate.[19] This evaluation is primarily a qualitative matter based on the auditor's judgement. Such an evaluation may provide further insight about the risks of material misstatement due to fraud and whether there is a need to perform additional or different audit procedures. Appendix 3 contains examples of circumstances that may indicate the possibility of fraud.

Analytical Procedures Performed Near the End of the Audit in Forming an Overall Conclusion (Ref: Para. 34)

A50. Determining which particular trends and relationships may indicate a risk of material misstatement due to fraud requires professional judgement. Unusual relationships involving year-end revenue and income are particularly relevant. These might include, for example: uncharacteristically large amounts of income being reported in the last few weeks of the reporting period or unusual transactions; or income that is inconsistent with trends in cash flow from operations.

---

18 See ASA 540 *Auditing Accounting Estimates, Including Fair Value Accounting Estimates, and Related Disclosures*, paragraph 9.

19 See ASA 330, paragraph 25.

Consideration of Identified Misstatements (Ref: Para. 35-37)

A51. Since fraud involves incentive or pressure to commit fraud, a perceived opportunity to do so or some rationalisation of the act, an instance of fraud is unlikely to be an isolated occurrence. Accordingly, misstatements, such as numerous misstatements at a specific location even though the cumulative effect is not material, may be indicative of a risk of material misstatement due to fraud.

A52. The implications of identified fraud depend on the circumstances. For example, an otherwise insignificant fraud may be significant if it involves senior management. In such circumstances, the reliability of evidence previously obtained may be called into question, since there may be doubts about the completeness and truthfulness of representations made and about the genuineness of accounting records and documentation. There may also be a possibility of collusion involving employees, management or third parties.

A53. ASA 450[20] and ASA 700[21] establish requirements and provide guidance on the evaluation and disposition of misstatements and the effect on the auditor's opinion in the auditor's report.

Auditor Unable to Continue the Engagement (Ref: Para. 38)

A54. Examples of exceptional circumstances that may arise and that may bring into question the auditor's ability to continue performing the audit include:

- The entity does not take the appropriate action regarding fraud that the auditor considers necessary in the circumstances, even where the fraud is not material to the financial report;
- The auditor's consideration of the risks of material misstatement due to fraud and the results of audit tests indicate a significant risk of material and pervasive fraud; or
- The auditor has significant concern about the competence or integrity of management or those charged with governance.

A55. Because of the variety of the circumstances that may arise, it is not possible to describe definitively when withdrawal from an engagement is appropriate. Factors that affect the auditor's conclusion include the implications of the involvement of a member of management or of those charged with governance (which may affect the reliability of management representations) and the effects on the auditor of a continuing association with the entity.

A56. The auditor has professional and legal responsibilities in such circumstances and these responsibilities may vary according to circumstances. In some circumstances, for example, the auditor may be entitled to, or required to, make a statement or report to the person or persons who made the audit appointment or, in some cases, to regulatory authorities. Given the exceptional nature of the circumstances and the need to consider the legal requirements, the auditor may consider it appropriate to seek legal advice when deciding whether to withdraw from an engagement and in determining an appropriate course of action, including the possibility of reporting to shareholders, regulators or others.[22]

Aus A56.1 For an audit engagement under the *Corporations Act 2001* (the Act), the possibility of withdrawing from the engagement or resigning from the appointment as an auditor can only be made in accordance with the provisions of the Act, including in certain circumstances, obtaining consent to resign from the Australian Securities and Investments Commission (ASIC).

Considerations Specific to Public Sector Entities

A57. In many cases in the public sector, the option of withdrawing from the engagement may not be available to the auditor due to the nature of the mandate or public interest considerations.

20 See ASA 450 *Evaluation of Misstatements Identified during the Audit*.

21 See ASA 700 *Forming an Opinion and Reporting on a Financial Report*.

22 Relevant ethical requirements may provide guidance on communications with a proposed successor auditor. See ASA 102 *Compliance with Ethical Requirements when Performing Audits, Reviews and Other Assurance Engagements*.

Written Representations (Ref: Para. 39)

A58. ASA 580[23] establishes requirements and provides guidance on obtaining appropriate representations from management and, where appropriate, those charged with governance in the audit. In addition to acknowledging that they have fulfilled their responsibility for the preparation of the financial report, it is important that, irrespective of the size of the entity, management and, where appropriate, those charged with governance acknowledge their responsibility for internal control designed, implemented and maintained to prevent and detect fraud.

A59. Because of the nature of fraud and the difficulties encountered by auditors in detecting material misstatements in the financial report resulting from fraud, it is important that the auditor obtain a written representation from management and, where appropriate, those charged with governance confirming that they have disclosed to the auditor:

(a) The results of management's assessment of the risk that the financial report may be materially misstated as a result of fraud; and

(b) Their knowledge of actual, suspected or alleged fraud affecting the entity.

Communications to Management and with Those Charged With Governance

Communication to Management (Ref: Para. 40)

A60. When the auditor has obtained evidence that fraud exists or may exist, it is important that the matter be brought to the attention of the appropriate level of management as soon as practicable. This is so even if the matter might be considered inconsequential (for example, a minor defalcation by an employee at a low level in the entity's organisation). The determination of which level of management is the appropriate one is a matter of professional judgement and is affected by such factors as the likelihood of collusion and the nature and magnitude of the suspected fraud. Ordinarily, the appropriate level of management is at least one level above the persons who appear to be involved with the suspected fraud.

Communication with Those Charged with Governance (Ref: Para. 41)

Aus A60.1 Legislation may require the auditor or a member of the audit team to maintain the confidentiality of information disclosed to the auditor, or a member of the audit team, by a person regarding contraventions or possible contraventions of the law.* In such circumstances, the auditor or a member of the audit team may be prevented from communicating that information to management or those charged with governance in order to protect the identity of the person who has disclosed confidential information that alleges a breach of the law. In such circumstances, the auditor may consider obtaining legal advice to assist in determining the appropriate course of action and may need to consider the implications for the audit engagement.

A61. The auditor's communication with those charged with governance may be made orally or in writing. ASA 260 identifies factors the auditor considers in determining whether to communicate orally or in writing.[24] Due to the nature and sensitivity of fraud involving senior management, or fraud that results in a material misstatement in the financial report, the auditor reports such matters on a timely basis and may consider it necessary to also report such matters in writing.

A62. In some cases, the auditor may consider it appropriate to communicate with those charged with governance when the auditor becomes aware of fraud involving employees other than management that does not result in a material misstatement. Similarly, those charged with governance may wish to be informed of such circumstances. The communication process is assisted if the auditor and those charged with governance agree at an early stage in the audit about the nature and extent of the auditor's communications in this regard.

23 See ASA 580 *Written Representations.*

* See, for example, the *Corporations Act 2001*, Part 9.4AAA Protection for Whistleblowers.

24 See ASA 260, paragraph A38.

A63. In the exceptional circumstances where the auditor has doubts about the integrity or honesty of management or those charged with governance, the auditor may consider it appropriate to obtain legal advice to assist in determining the appropriate course of action.

Other Matters Related to Fraud (Ref: Para. 42)

A64. Other matters related to fraud to be discussed with those charged with governance of the entity may include, for example:

- Concerns about the nature, extent and frequency of management's assessments of the controls in place to prevent and detect fraud and of the risk that the financial report may be misstated.
- A failure by management to appropriately address identified significant deficiencies in internal control, or to appropriately respond to an identified fraud.
- The auditor's evaluation of the entity's control environment, including questions regarding the competence and integrity of management.
- Actions by management that may be indicative of fraudulent financial reporting, such as management's selection and application of accounting policies that may be indicative of management's effort to manage earnings in order to deceive financial statement users by influencing their perceptions as to the entity's performance and profitability.
- Concerns about the adequacy and completeness of the authorisation of transactions that appear to be outside the normal course of business.

Communications to Regulatory and Enforcement Authorities (Ref: Para. 43)

A65. The auditor's professional duty to maintain the confidentiality of client information may preclude reporting fraud to a party outside the client entity. However, the auditor's legal responsibilities vary and, in certain circumstances, the duty of confidentiality may be overridden by statute, the law or courts of law. In some circumstances, the auditor of a financial institution may have a statutory duty to report the occurrence of fraud to supervisory authorities. Also, in some circumstances the auditor may have a duty to report misstatements to authorities in those cases where management and those charged with governance fail to take corrective action.

Aus A65.1 An auditor is required by the Act to notify the Australian Securities and Investments Commission (ASIC) if the auditor is aware of certain circumstances.*

A66. The auditor may consider it appropriate to obtain legal advice to determine the appropriate course of action in the circumstances, the purpose of which is to ascertain the steps necessary in considering the public interest aspects of identified fraud.

Considerations Specific to Public Sector Entities

A67. In the public sector, requirements for reporting fraud, whether or not discovered through the audit process, may be subject to specific provisions of the audit mandate or related law, regulation or other authority.

❖ ❖ ❖

Conformity with International Standards on Auditing

This Auditing Standard conforms with International Standard on Auditing ISA 240 *The Auditor's Responsibilities Relating to Fraud in an Audit of Financial Statements*, issued by the International Auditing and Assurance Standards Board (IAASB), an independent standard-setting board of the International Federation of Accountants (IFAC).

Paragraphs that have been added to this Auditing Standard (and do not appear in the text of the equivalent ISA) are identified with the prefix "Aus".

Compliance with this Auditing Standard enables compliance with ISA 240.

* See ASIC Regulatory Guide 34 *Auditor's obligations: reporting to ASIC* (December 2007), that provides guidance to help auditors comply with their obligations, under sections 311, 601HG and 990K of the Act, to report contraventions and suspected contraventions of the Act to ASIC.

Appendix 1

(Ref: Para. A25)

Examples of Fraud Risk Factors

The fraud risk factors identified in this Appendix are examples of such factors that may be faced by auditors in a broad range of situations. Separately presented are examples relating to the two types of fraud relevant to the auditor's consideration—that is, fraudulent financial reporting and misappropriation of assets. For each of these types of fraud, the risk factors are further classified based on the three conditions generally present when material misstatements due to fraud occur: (a) incentives/pressures, (b) opportunities, and (c) attitudes/rationalisations. Although the risk factors cover a broad range of situations, they are only examples and, accordingly, the auditor may identify additional or different risk factors. Not all of these examples are relevant in all circumstances, and some may be of greater or lesser significance in entities of different size or with different ownership characteristics or circumstances. Also, the order of the examples of risk factors provided is not intended to reflect their relative importance or frequency of occurrence.

Risk Factors Relating to Misstatements Arising from Fraudulent Financial Reporting

The following are examples of risk factors relating to misstatements arising from fraudulent financial reporting.

Incentives/Pressures

Financial stability or profitability is threatened by economic, industry, or entity operating conditions, such as (or as indicated by):

- High degree of competition or market saturation, accompanied by declining margins.
- High vulnerability to rapid changes, such as changes in technology, product obsolescence, or interest rates.
- Significant declines in customer demand and increasing business failures in either the industry or overall economy.
- Operating losses making the threat of bankruptcy, foreclosure, or hostile takeover imminent.
- Recurring negative cash flows from operations or an inability to generate cash flows from operations while reporting earnings and earnings growth.
- Rapid growth or unusual profitability especially compared to that of other companies in the same industry.
- New accounting, statutory, or regulatory requirements.

Excessive pressure exists for management to meet the requirements or expectations of third parties due to the following:

- Profitability or trend level expectations of investment analysts, institutional investors, significant creditors, or other external parties (particularly expectations that are unduly aggressive or unrealistic), including expectations created by management in, for example, overly optimistic press releases or annual report messages.
- Need to obtain additional debt or equity financing to stay competitive—including financing of major research and development or capital expenditures.
- Marginal ability to meet exchange listing requirements or debt repayment or other debt covenant requirements.
- Perceived or real adverse effects of reporting poor financial results on significant pending transactions, such as business combinations or contract awards.

Information available indicates that the personal financial situation of management or those charged with governance is threatened by the entity's financial performance arising from the following:

- Significant financial interests in the entity.

Appendix 1 (continued)

- Significant portions of their compensation (for example, bonuses, share options, and earn-out arrangements) being contingent upon achieving aggressive targets for share price, operating results, financial position, or cash flow.[25]
- Personal guarantees of debts of the entity.

There is excessive pressure on management or operating personnel to meet financial targets established by those charged with governance, including sales or profitability incentive goals.

Opportunities

The nature of the industry or the entity's operations provides opportunities to engage in fraudulent financial reporting that can arise from the following:

- Significant related-party transactions not in the ordinary course of business or with related entities not audited or audited by another firm.
- A strong financial presence or ability to dominate a certain industry sector that allows the entity to dictate terms or conditions to suppliers or customers that may result in inappropriate or non-arm's-length transactions.
- Assets, liabilities, revenues, or expenses based on significant estimates that involve subjective judgements or uncertainties that are difficult to corroborate.
- Significant, unusual, or highly complex transactions, especially those close to period end that pose difficult "substance over form" questions.
- Significant operations located or conducted across international borders in jurisdictions where differing business environments and cultures exist.
- Use of business intermediaries for which there appears to be no clear business justification.
- Significant bank accounts or subsidiary or branch operations in tax-haven jurisdictions for which there appears to be no clear business justification.

The monitoring of management is not effective as a result of the following:

- Domination of management by a single person or small group (in a non owner-managed business) without compensating controls.
- Oversight by those charged with governance over the financial reporting process and internal control is not effective.

There is a complex or unstable organisational structure, as evidenced by the following:

- Difficulty in determining the organisation or individuals that have a controlling interest in the entity.
- Overly complex organisational structure involving unusual legal entities or managerial lines of authority.
- High turnover of senior management, legal counsel, or those charged with governance.

Internal control components are deficient as a result of the following:

- Inadequate monitoring of controls, including automated controls and controls over interim financial reporting (where external reporting is required).
- High turnover rates or employment of accounting, internal audit, or information technology staff that are not effective.
- Accounting and information systems that are not effective, including situations involving significant deficiencies in internal control.

Attitudes/Rationalisations

- Communication, implementation, support, or enforcement of the entity's values or ethical standards by management, or the communication of inappropriate values or ethical standards, that are not effective.

25 Management incentive plans may be contingent upon achieving targets relating only to certain accounts or selected activities of the entity, even though the related accounts or activities may not be material to the entity as a whole.

Appendix 1 (continued)

- Non-financial management's excessive participation in or preoccupation with the selection of accounting policies or the determination of significant estimates.
- Known history of violations of securities laws or other laws and regulations, or claims against the entity, its senior management, or those charged with governance alleging fraud or violations of laws and regulations.
- Excessive interest by management in maintaining or increasing the entity's share price or earnings trend.
- The practice by management of committing to analysts, creditors, and other third parties to achieve aggressive or unrealistic forecasts.
- Management failing to remedy known significant deficiencies in internal control on a timely basis.
- An interest by management in employing inappropriate means to minimise reported earnings for tax-motivated reasons.
- Low morale among senior management.
- The owner-manager makes no distinction between personal and business transactions.
- Dispute between shareholders in a closely held entity.
- Recurring attempts by management to justify marginal or inappropriate accounting on the basis of materiality.
- The relationship between management and the current or predecessor auditor is strained, as exhibited by the following:
  - Frequent disputes with the current or predecessor auditor on accounting, auditing, or reporting matters.
  - Unreasonable demands on the auditor, such as unrealistic time constraints regarding the completion of the audit or the issuance of the auditor's report.
  - Restrictions on the auditor that inappropriately limit access to people or information or the ability to communicate effectively with those charged with governance.
  - Domineering management behaviour in dealing with the auditor, especially involving attempts to influence the scope of the auditor's work or the selection or continuance of personnel assigned to or consulted on the audit engagement.

Risk Factors Relating to Misstatements Arising From Misappropriation of Assets

Risk factors that relate to misstatements arising from misappropriation of assets are also classified according to the three conditions generally present when fraud exists: incentives/pressures, opportunities, and attitudes/rationalisation. Some of the risk factors related to misstatements arising from fraudulent financial reporting also may be present when misstatements arising from misappropriation of assets occur. For example, ineffective monitoring of management and other deficiencies in internal control may be present when misstatements due to either fraudulent financial reporting or misappropriation of assets exist. The following are examples of risk factors related to misstatements arising from misappropriation of assets.

Incentives/Pressures

Personal financial obligations may create pressure on management or employees with access to cash or other assets susceptible to theft to misappropriate those assets.

Adverse relationships between the entity and employees with access to cash or other assets susceptible to theft may motivate those employees to misappropriate those assets. For example, adverse relationships may be created by the following:

- Known or anticipated future employee layoffs.
- Recent or anticipated changes to employee compensation or benefit plans.
- Promotions, compensation, or other rewards inconsistent with expectations.

ASA

Appendix 1 (continued)

Opportunities

Certain characteristics or circumstances may increase the susceptibility of assets to misappropriation. For example, opportunities to misappropriate assets increase when there are the following:

- Large amounts of cash on hand or processed.
- Inventory items that are small in size, of high value, or in high demand.
- Easily convertible assets, such as bearer bonds, diamonds, or computer chips.
- Fixed assets which are small in size, marketable, or lacking observable identification of ownership.

Inadequate internal control over assets may increase the susceptibility of misappropriation of those assets. For example, misappropriation of assets may occur because there is the following:

- Inadequate segregation of duties or independent checks.
- Inadequate oversight of senior management expenditures, such as travel and other reimbursements.
- Inadequate management oversight of employees responsible for assets, for example, inadequate supervision or monitoring of remote locations.
- Inadequate job applicant screening of employees with access to assets.
- Inadequate record keeping with respect to assets.
- Inadequate system of authorisation and approval of transactions (for example, in purchasing).
- Inadequate physical safeguards over cash, investments, inventory, or fixed assets.
- Lack of complete and timely reconciliations of assets.
- Lack of timely and appropriate documentation of transactions, for example, credits for merchandise returns.
- Lack of mandatory holidays for employees performing key control functions.
- Inadequate management understanding of information technology, which enables information technology employees to perpetrate a misappropriation.
- Inadequate access controls over automated records, including controls over and review of computer systems event logs.

Attitudes/Rationalisations

- Disregard for the need for monitoring or reducing risks related to misappropriations of assets.
- Disregard for internal control over misappropriation of assets by overriding existing controls or by failing to take appropriate remedial action on known deficiencies in internal control.
- Behaviour indicating displeasure or dissatisfaction with the entity or its treatment of the employee.
- Changes in behaviour or lifestyle that may indicate assets have been misappropriated.
- Tolerance of petty theft.

Appendix 2

(Ref: Para. A40)

Examples of Possible Audit Procedures to Address the Assessed Risks of Material Misstatement Due to Fraud

The following are examples of possible audit procedures to address the assessed risks of material misstatement due to fraud resulting from both fraudulent financial reporting and misappropriation of assets. Although these procedures cover a broad range of situations, they are only examples and, accordingly they may not be the most appropriate nor necessary in each circumstance. Also the order of the procedures provided is not intended to reflect their relative importance.

Consideration at the Assertion Level

Specific responses to the auditor's assessment of the risks of material misstatement due to fraud will vary depending upon the types or combinations of fraud risk factors or conditions identified, and the classes of transactions, account balances, disclosures and assertions they may affect.

The following are specific examples of responses:

- Visiting locations or performing certain tests on a surprise or unannounced basis. For example, observing inventory at locations where auditor attendance has not been previously announced or counting cash at a particular date on a surprise basis.
- Requesting that inventories be counted at the end of the reporting period or on a date closer to period end to minimise the risk of manipulation of balances in the period between the date of completion of the count and the end of the reporting period.
- Altering the audit approach in the current year. For example, contacting major customers and suppliers orally in addition to sending written confirmation, sending confirmation requests to a specific party within an organisation, or seeking more or different information.
- Performing a detailed review of the entity's month-end or year-end adjusting entries and investigating any that appear unusual as to nature or amount.
- For significant and unusual transactions, particularly those occurring at or near year-end, investigating the possibility of related parties and the sources of financial resources supporting the transactions.
- Performing substantive analytical procedures using disaggregated data. For example, comparing sales and cost of sales by location, line of business or month to expectations developed by the auditor.
- Conducting interviews of personnel involved in areas where a risk of material misstatement due to fraud has been identified, to obtain their insights about the risk and whether, or how, controls address the risk.
- When other independent auditors are auditing the financial report of one or more subsidiaries, divisions or branches, discussing with them the extent of work necessary to be performed to address the assessed risk of material misstatement due to fraud resulting from transactions and activities among these components.
- If the work of an expert becomes particularly significant with respect to a financial statement item for which the assessed risk of misstatement due to fraud is high, performing additional procedures relating to some or all of the expert's assumptions, methods or findings to determine that the findings are not unreasonable, or engaging another expert for that purpose.
- Performing audit procedures to analyse selected opening balance sheet accounts of the previously audited financial report to assess how certain issues involving accounting estimates and judgements, for example, an allowance for sales returns, were resolved with the benefit of hindsight.
- Performing procedures on account or other reconciliations prepared by the entity, including considering reconciliations performed at interim periods.

Appendix 2 (continued)

- Performing computer-assisted techniques, such as data mining to test for anomalies in a population.
- Testing the integrity of computer-produced records and transactions.
- Seeking additional audit evidence from sources outside of the entity being audited.

Specific Responses—Misstatement Resulting from Fraudulent Financial Reporting

Examples of responses to the auditor's assessment of the risks of material misstatement due to fraudulent financial reporting are as follows:

Revenue Recognition

- Performing substantive analytical procedures relating to revenue using disaggregated data, for example, comparing revenue reported by month and by product line or business segment during the current reporting period with comparable prior periods. Computer-assisted audit techniques may be useful in identifying unusual or unexpected revenue relationships or transactions.
- Confirming with customers certain relevant contract terms and the absence of side agreements, because the appropriate accounting often is influenced by such terms or agreements and basis for rebates or the period to which they relate are often poorly documented. For example, acceptance criteria, delivery and payment terms, the absence of future or continuing vendor obligations, the right to return the product, guaranteed resale amounts, and cancellation or refund provisions often are relevant in such circumstances.
- Enquiring of the entity's sales and marketing personnel or in-house legal counsel regarding sales or shipments near the end of the period and their knowledge of any unusual terms or conditions associated with these transactions.
- Being physically present at one or more locations at period end to observe goods being shipped or being readied for shipment (or returns awaiting processing) and performing other appropriate sales and inventory cut-off procedures.
- For those situations for which revenue transactions are electronically initiated, processed, and recorded, testing controls to determine whether they provide assurance that recorded revenue transactions occurred and are properly recorded.

Inventory Quantities

- Examining the entity's inventory records to identify locations or items that require specific attention during or after the physical inventory count.
- Observing inventory counts at certain locations on an unannounced basis or conducting inventory counts at all locations on the same date.
- Conducting inventory counts at or near the end of the reporting period to minimise the risk of inappropriate manipulation during the period between the count and the end of the reporting period.
- Performing additional procedures during the observation of the count, for example, more rigorously examining the contents of boxed items, the manner in which the goods are stacked (for example, hollow squares) or labelled, and the quality (that is, purity, grade, or concentration) of liquid substances such as perfumes or specialty chemicals. Using the work of an expert may be helpful in this regard.
- Comparing the quantities for the current period with prior periods by class or category of inventory, location or other criteria, or comparison of quantities counted with perpetual records.
- Using computer-assisted audit techniques to further test the compilation of the physical inventory counts—for example, sorting by tag number to test tag controls or by item serial number to test the possibility of item omission or duplication.

Appendix 2 (continued)

Management Estimates

- Using an expert to develop an independent estimate for comparison to management's estimate.
- Extending enquiries to individuals outside of management and the accounting department to corroborate management's ability and intent to carry out plans that are relevant to developing the estimate.

Specific Responses—Misstatements Due to Misappropriation of Assets

Differing circumstances would necessarily dictate different responses. Ordinarily, the audit response to an assessed risk of material misstatement due to fraud relating to misappropriation of assets will be directed toward certain account balances and classes of transactions. Although some of the audit responses noted in the two categories above may apply in such circumstances, the scope of the work is to be linked to the specific information about the misappropriation risk that has been identified.

Examples of responses to the auditor's assessment of the risk of material misstatements due to misappropriation of assets are as follows:

- Counting cash or securities at or near year-end.
- Confirming directly with customers the account activity (including credit memo and sales return activity as well as dates payments were made) for the period under audit.
- Analysing recoveries of written-off accounts.
- Analysing inventory shortages by location or product type.
- Comparing key inventory ratios to industry norm.
- Reviewing supporting documentation for reductions to the perpetual inventory records.
- Performing a computerised match of the vendor list with a list of employees to identify matches of addresses or phone numbers.
- Performing a computerised search of payroll records to identify duplicate addresses, employee identification or taxing authority numbers or bank accounts.
- Reviewing personnel files for those that contain little or no evidence of activity, for example, lack of performance evaluations.
- Analysing sales discounts and returns for unusual patterns or trends.
- Confirming specific terms of contracts with third parties.
- Obtaining evidence that contracts are being carried out in accordance with their terms.
- Reviewing the propriety of large and unusual expenses.
- Reviewing the authorisation and carrying value of senior management and related party loans.
- Reviewing the level and propriety of expense reports submitted by senior management.

ASA

Appendix 3

(Ref: Para. A49)

Examples of Circumstances that Indicate the Possibility of Fraud

The following are examples of circumstances that may indicate the possibility that the financial report may contain a material misstatement resulting from fraud.

Discrepancies in the accounting records, including:

- Transactions that are not recorded in a complete or timely manner or are improperly recorded as to amount, accounting period, classification, or entity policy.
- Unsupported or unauthorised balances or transactions.
- Last-minute adjustments that significantly affect financial results.
- Evidence of employees' access to systems and records inconsistent with that necessary to perform their authorised duties.
- Tips or complaints to the auditor about alleged fraud.

Conflicting or missing evidence, including:

- Missing documents.
- Documents that appear to have been altered.
- Unavailability of other than photocopied or electronically transmitted documents when documents in original form are expected to exist.
- Significant unexplained items on reconciliations.
- Unusual balance sheet changes, or changes in trends or important financial statement ratios or relationships – for example receivables growing faster than revenues.
- Inconsistent, vague, or implausible responses from management or employees arising from enquiries or analytical procedures.
- Unusual discrepancies between the entity's records and confirmation replies.
- Large numbers of credit entries and other adjustments made to accounts receivable records.
- Unexplained or inadequately explained differences between the accounts receivable sub-ledger and the control account, or between the customer statements and the accounts receivable sub-ledger.
- Missing or non-existent cancelled cheques in circumstances where cancelled cheques are ordinarily returned to the entity with the bank statement.
- Missing inventory or physical assets of significant magnitude.
- Unavailable or missing electronic evidence, inconsistent with the entity's record retention practices or policies.
- Fewer responses to confirmations than anticipated or a greater number of responses than anticipated.
- Inability to produce evidence of key systems development and program change testing and implementation activities for current-year system changes and deployments.

Problematic or unusual relationships between the auditor and management, including:

- Denial of access to records, facilities, certain employees, customers, vendors, or others from whom audit evidence might be sought.
- Undue time pressures imposed by management to resolve complex or contentious issues.
- Complaints by management about the conduct of the audit or management intimidation of engagement team members, particularly in connection with the auditor's critical assessment of audit evidence or in the resolution of potential disagreements with management.

Appendix 3 (continued)

- Unusual delays by the entity in providing requested information.
- Unwillingness to facilitate auditor access to key electronic files for testing through the use of computer-assisted audit techniques.
- Denial of access to key IT operations staff and facilities, including security, operations, and systems development personnel.
- An unwillingness to add or revise disclosures in the financial report to make them more complete and understandable.
- An unwillingness to address identified deficiencies in internal control on a timely basis.

Other

- Unwillingness by management to permit the auditor to meet privately with those charged with governance.
- Accounting policies that appear to be at variance with industry norms.
- Frequent changes in accounting estimates that do not appear to result from changed circumstances.
- Tolerance of violations of the entity's Code of Conduct.

ASA

ASA 250

Consideration of Laws and Regulations in an Audit of a Financial Report

(Reissued October 2009: amended and compiled June 2011)

Issued by the Auditing and Assurance Standards Board.

Note from the Institute of Chartered Accountants Australia

This note, prepared by the technical editor, is not part of ASA 250.

Historical development

January 2002: AUS 210 'The Auditor's Responsibility to Consider Fraud and Error in an Audit of a Financial Report' and AUS 218 'Consideration of Laws and Regulations in an Audit of a Financial Report' were the two topics originally dealt with in a single AUS 210 'Irregularities, Including Fraud, Other Illegal Acts and Errors'. Following revisions to the International Auditing Standard ISA 240 'The Auditor's Responsibility to Consider Fraud and Error in an Audit of Financial Statements', the guidance in the new AUS 210 was revised and extended.

'Other Illegal Acts' were described as instances of non-compliance with laws and regulations and made the subject of a separate Australian Auditing Standard AUS 218, in line with its International equivalent, ISA 250.

Both AUS 218 and AUS 210 were applicable to reporting periods ending on or after 31 December 2002, but earlier application was encouraged.

April 2006: ASA 250 was issued as a legally enforceable Standard to replace AUS 218. It is based on ISA 250 'Consideration of Laws and Regulations in an Audit of Financial Statements'.

October 2009: ASA 250 reissued as part of the AUASB's Clarity Project. Certain requirements relating to the auditor's need to obtain legal advice have been elevated to the level of mandatory requirements. It is based on the revised ISA 250 'Consideration of Laws and Regulations in an Audit of Financial Statements'.

June 2011: ASA 250 updated for editorial amendments contained in ASA 2011-1 'Amendments to Australian Auditing Standards'.

Contents

Compilation Details

Auditing Standard ASA 250 *Consideration of Laws and Regulations in an Audit of a Financial Report* as Amended

This compilation takes into account amendments made up to and including 27 June 2011 and was prepared on 27 June 2011 by the Auditing and Assurance Standards Board (AUASB).

This compilation is not a separate Auditing Standard made by the AUASB. Instead, it is a representation of ASA 250 (October 2009) as amended by another Auditing Standard which is listed in the Table below.

Table of Standards

Standard	Date made	Operative date
ASA 250	27 October 2009	1 January 2010
ASA 2011-1	27 June 2011	1 July 2011

Table of Amendments

Paragraph affected	How affected	By … [paragraph]
5 Footnote 2	Amended	ASA 2011-1 [24]

Preface

[Preface extracted from the original Auditing Standard issued 27 October 2009]

Reasons for Issuing Auditing Standard ASA 250 *Consideration of Laws and Regulations in an Audit of a Financial Report*

The Auditing and Assurance Standards Board (AUASB) issues Auditing Standard ASA 250 *Consideration of Laws and Regulations in an Audit of a Financial Report* pursuant to the requirements of the legislative provisions and the Strategic Direction explained below.

The AUASB is an independent statutory board of the Australian Government established under section 227A of the *Australian Securities and Investments Commission Act 2001*, as amended (ASIC Act). Under section 336 of the *Corporations Act 2001*, the AUASB may make Auditing Standards for the purposes of the corporations legislation. These Auditing Standards are legislative instruments under the *Legislative Instruments Act 2003*.

Under the Strategic Direction given to the AUASB by the Financial Reporting Council (FRC), the AUASB is required to have regard to any programme initiated by the International Auditing and Assurance Standards Board (IAASB) for the revision and enhancement of the International Standards on Auditing (ISAs) and to make appropriate consequential amendments to the Australian Auditing Standards. Accordingly, the AUASB has decided to revise and redraft the Australian Auditing Standards using the equivalent redrafted ISAs.

Main Features

This Auditing Standard establishes requirements and provides application and other explanatory material regarding the auditor's responsibility to consider laws and regulations when performing an audit of a financial report.

This Auditing Standard:

(a) requires the auditor to obtain audit evidence regarding compliance with those laws and regulations that have a direct effect on the financial report;

(b) requires the auditor to perform audit procedures to help identify non-compliance with other laws and regulations that may have a material effect on the financial report;

(c) requires the auditor to respond appropriately to identified and suspected non-compliance with laws and regulations;

(d) includes specific requirements regarding the auditor's consideration of laws and regulations; and

(e) describes the reporting procedures when non-compliance is discovered or suspected.

Authority Statement

Auditing Standard ASA 250 *Consideration of Laws and Regulations in an Audit of a Financial Report* (as amended at 27 June 2011) is set out in paragraphs 1 to A21.

This Auditing Standard is to be read in conjunction with ASA 101 *Preamble to Australian Auditing Standards*, which sets out the intentions of the AUASB on how the Australian Auditing Standards, operative for financial reporting periods commencing on or after 1 January 2010, are to be understood, interpreted and applied. This Auditing Standard is to be read also in conjunction with ASA 200 *Overall Objectives of the Independent Auditor and the Conduct of an Audit in Accordance with Australian Auditing Standards*.

Dated: 27 June 2011

M H Kelsall
Chairman - AUASB

Auditing Standard ASA 250

The Auditing and Assurance Standards Board (AUASB) made Auditing Standard ASA 250 *Consideration of Laws and Regulations in an Audit of a Financial Report*, pursuant to section 227B of the *Australian Securities and Investments Commission Act 2001* and section 336 of the *Corporations Act 2001*, on 27 October 2009.

This compiled version of ASA 250 incorporates subsequent amendments contained in another Auditing Standard made by the AUASB up to and including 27 June 2011 (see Compilation Details).

Auditing Standard ASA 250

Consideration of Laws and Regulations in an Audit of a Financial Report

Application

Aus 0.1 This Auditing Standard applies to:

(a) an audit of a financial report for a financial year, or an audit of a financial report for a half-year, in accordance with the *Corporations Act 2001*; and

(b) an audit of a financial report, or a complete set of financial statements, for any other purpose.

Aus 0.2 This Auditing Standard also applies, as appropriate, to an audit of other historical financial information.

ASA

Operative Date

Aus 0.3 This Auditing Standard is operative for financial reporting periods commencing on or after 1 January 2010.

[Note: For operative dates of paragraphs changed or added by an amending Standard, see Compilation Details.]

Introduction

Scope of this Auditing Standard

1. This Auditing Standard deals with the auditor's responsibility to consider laws and regulations in an audit of a financial report. This Auditing Standard does not apply to other assurance engagements in which the auditor is specifically engaged to test and report separately on compliance with specific laws or regulations.

Effect of Laws and Regulations

2. The effect on a financial report of laws and regulations varies considerably. Those laws and regulations to which an entity is subject constitute the legal and regulatory framework. The provisions of some laws or regulations have a direct effect on the financial report in that they determine the reported amounts and disclosures in an entity's financial report. Other laws or regulations are to be complied with by management or set the provisions under which the entity is allowed to conduct its business but do not have a direct effect on an entity's financial report. Some entities operate in heavily regulated industries (such as banks and chemical companies). Others are subject only to the many laws and regulations that relate generally to the operating aspects of the business (such as those related to occupational safety and health, and equal employment opportunity). Non-compliance with laws and regulations may result in fines, litigation or other consequences for the entity that may have a material effect on the financial report.

Responsibility for Compliance with Laws and Regulations (Ref: Para. A1-A6)

3. It is the responsibility of management, with the oversight of those charged with governance, to ensure that the entity's operations are conducted in accordance with the provisions of laws and regulations, including compliance with the provisions of laws and regulations that determine the reported amounts and disclosures in an entity's financial report.

Responsibility of the Auditor

4. The requirements in this Auditing Standard are designed to assist the auditor in identifying material misstatement of the financial report due to non-compliance with laws and regulations. However, the auditor is not responsible for preventing non-compliance and cannot be expected to detect non-compliance with all laws and regulations.

5. The auditor is responsible for obtaining reasonable assurance that the financial report, taken as a whole, is free from material misstatement, whether caused by fraud or error.[1] In conducting an audit of a financial report, the auditor takes into account the applicable legal and regulatory framework. Owing to the inherent limitations of an audit, there is an unavoidable risk that some material misstatements in the financial report may not be detected, even though the audit is properly planned and performed in accordance with the Australian Auditing Standards.[2] In the context of laws and regulations, the potential effects of inherent limitations on the auditor's ability to detect material misstatements are greater for such reasons as the following:

- There are many laws and regulations, relating principally to the operating aspects of an entity, that typically do not affect the financial report and are not captured by the entity's information systems relevant to financial reporting.
- Non-compliance may involve conduct designed to conceal it, such as collusion, forgery, deliberate failure to record transactions, management override of controls or intentional misrepresentations being made to the auditor.
- Whether an act constitutes non-compliance is ultimately a matter for legal determination by a court of law.

Ordinarily, the further removed non-compliance is from the events and transactions reflected in the financial report, the less likely the auditor is to become aware of it or to recognise the non-compliance.

6. This Auditing Standard distinguishes the auditor's responsibilities in relation to compliance with two different categories of laws and regulations as follows:

(a) The provisions of those laws and regulations generally recognised to have a direct effect on the determination of material amounts and disclosures in the financial report such as tax and superannuation laws and regulations (see paragraph 13 of this Auditing Standard); and

(b) Other laws and regulations that do not have a direct effect on the determination of the amounts and disclosures in the financial report, but compliance with which may be fundamental to the operating aspects of the business, to an entity's ability to continue its business, or to avoid material penalties (for example, compliance with the terms of an operating license, compliance with regulatory solvency requirements, or compliance with environmental regulations); non-compliance with such laws and regulations may therefore have a material effect on the financial report (see paragraph 14 of this Auditing Standard).

7. In this Auditing Standard, differing requirements are specified for each of the above categories of laws and regulations. For the category referred to in paragraph 6(a) of this Auditing Standard, the auditor's responsibility is to obtain sufficient appropriate audit evidence regarding compliance with the provisions of those laws and regulations. For the category referred to in paragraph 6(b) of this Auditing Standard, the auditor's responsibility is limited to undertaking specified audit procedures to help identify non-compliance with those laws and regulations that may have a material effect on the financial report.

8. The auditor is required by this Auditing Standard to remain alert to the possibility that other audit procedures applied for the purpose of forming an opinion on the financial report may bring instances of identified or suspected non-compliance to the auditor's attention. Maintaining professional scepticism throughout the audit, as required by ASA 200,[3] is important in this context, given the extent of laws and regulations that affect the entity.

Effective Date

9. [Deleted by the AUASB. Refer Aus 0.3]

---

1 See ASA 200, *Overall Objectives of the Independent Auditor and the Conduct of an Audit in Accordance with Australian Auditing Standards*, paragraph 5.

2 See ASA 200, paragraph A51-A52.

3 See ASA 200, paragraph 15.

Objectives

10. The objectives of the auditor are:

    (a) To obtain sufficient appropriate audit evidence regarding compliance with the provisions of those laws and regulations generally recognised to have a direct effect on the determination of material amounts and disclosures in the financial report;

    (b) To perform specified audit procedures to help identify instances of non-compliance with other laws and regulations that may have a material effect on the financial report; and

    (c) To respond appropriately to non-compliance or suspected non-compliance with laws and regulations identified during the audit.

Definition

11. For the purposes of this Auditing Standard, the following term has the meaning attributed below:

    Non-compliance means acts of omission or commission by the entity, either intentional or unintentional, which are contrary to the prevailing laws or regulations. Such acts include transactions entered into by, or in the name of, the entity, or on its behalf, by those charged with governance, management or employees. Non-compliance does not include personal misconduct (unrelated to the business activities of the entity) by those charged with governance, management or employees of the entity.

Requirements

The Auditor's Consideration of Compliance with Laws and Regulations

12. As part of obtaining an understanding of the entity and its environment in accordance with ASA 315,[4] the auditor shall obtain a general understanding of:

    (a) The legal and regulatory framework applicable to the entity and the industry or sector in which the entity operates; and

    (b) How the entity is complying with that framework. (Ref: Para. A7)

13. The auditor shall obtain sufficient appropriate audit evidence regarding compliance with the provisions of those laws and regulations generally recognised to have a direct effect on the determination of material amounts and disclosures in the financial report. (Ref: Para. A8)

14. The auditor shall perform the following audit procedures to help identify instances of non-compliance with other laws and regulations that may have a material effect on the financial report: (Ref: Para. A9-A10)

    (a) Enquiring of management and, where appropriate, those charged with governance, as to whether the entity is in compliance with such laws and regulations; and

    (b) Inspecting correspondence, if any, with the relevant licensing or regulatory authorities.

15. During the audit, the auditor shall remain alert to the possibility that other audit procedures applied may bring instances of non-compliance or suspected non-compliance with laws and regulations to the auditor's attention. (Ref: Para. A11-Aus A11.1)

16. The auditor shall request management and, where appropriate, those charged with governance, to provide written representations that all known instances of non-compliance or suspected non-compliance with laws and regulations whose effects should be considered when preparing the financial report have been disclosed to the auditor. (Ref: Para. A12)

17. In the absence of identified or suspected non-compliance, the auditor is not required to perform audit procedures regarding the entity's compliance with laws and regulations, other than those set out in paragraphs 12-16 of this Auditing Standard.

4 See ASA 315 *Identifying and Assessing the Risks of Material Misstatement through Understanding the Entity and Its Environment*, paragraph 11.

Audit Procedures When Non-Compliance Is Identified or Suspected

18. If the auditor becomes aware of information concerning an instance of non-compliance or suspected non-compliance with laws and regulations, the auditor shall obtain: (Ref: Para. A13)
    (a) An understanding of the nature of the act and the circumstances in which it has occurred; and
    (b) Further information to evaluate the possible effect on the financial report. (Ref: Para. A14)

19. If the auditor suspects there may be non-compliance, the auditor shall discuss the matter with management and, where appropriate, those charged with governance. If management or, as appropriate, those charged with governance do not provide sufficient information that supports that the entity is in compliance with laws and regulations and, in the auditor's judgement, the effect of the suspected non-compliance may be material to the financial report, the auditor shall consider the need to obtain legal advice. (Ref: Para. A15-A16)

20. If sufficient information about suspected non-compliance cannot be obtained, the auditor shall evaluate the effect of the lack of sufficient appropriate audit evidence on the auditor's opinion.

21. The auditor shall evaluate the implications of non-compliance in relation to other aspects of the audit, including the auditor's risk assessment and the reliability of written representations, and take appropriate action. (Ref: Para. A17-A18)

Reporting of Identified or Suspected Non-Compliance

Reporting Non-Compliance to Those Charged with Governance

22. Unless all of those charged with governance are involved in management of the entity, and therefore are aware of matters involving identified or suspected non-compliance already communicated by the auditor,[5] the auditor shall communicate with those charged with governance matters involving non-compliance with laws and regulations that come to the auditor's attention during the course of the audit, other than when the matters are clearly inconsequential.

23. If, in the auditor's judgement, the non-compliance referred to in paragraph 22 of this Auditing Standard is believed to be intentional and material, the auditor shall communicate the matter to those charged with governance as soon as practicable.

24. If the auditor suspects that management or those charged with governance are involved in non-compliance, the auditor shall communicate the matter to the next higher level of authority at the entity, if it exists, such as an audit committee or supervisory board. Where no higher authority exists, or if the auditor believes that the communication may not be acted upon or is unsure as to the person to whom to report, the auditor shall consider the need to obtain legal advice.

Reporting Non-Compliance in the Auditor's Report on the Financial Report

25. If the auditor concludes that the non-compliance has a material effect on the financial report, and has not been adequately reflected in the financial report, the auditor shall, in accordance with ASA 705, express a qualified opinion or an adverse opinion on the financial report.[6] (Ref: Para. A18.1)

26. If the auditor is precluded by management or those charged with governance from obtaining sufficient appropriate audit evidence to evaluate whether non-compliance that may be material to the financial report has, or is likely to have, occurred, the auditor shall express a qualified opinion or disclaim an opinion on the financial report on the basis of a limitation on the scope of the audit in accordance with ASA 705.

27. If the auditor is unable to determine whether non-compliance has occurred because of limitations imposed by the circumstances rather than by management or those charged with governance, the auditor shall evaluate the effect on the auditor's opinion in accordance with ASA 705.

---

5 See ASA 260, *Communication with Those Charged with Governance*, paragraph 13.

6 See ASA 705, *Modifications to the Opinion in the Independent Auditor's Report*, paragraphs 7-8.

Reporting Non-Compliance to Regulatory and Enforcement Authorities

28. If the auditor has identified or suspects non-compliance with laws and regulations, the auditor shall determine whether the auditor has a responsibility to report the identified or suspected non-compliance to parties outside the entity. (Ref: Para. A19-A20)

Documentation

29. The auditor shall include in the audit documentation identified or suspected non-compliance with laws and regulations and the results of discussion with management and, where applicable, those charged with governance and other parties outside the entity.[7] (Ref: Para. A21)

❖❖❖

Application and Other Explanatory Material

Responsibility for Compliance with Laws and Regulations (Ref: Para. 3-8)

A1. It is the responsibility of management, with the oversight of those charged with governance, to ensure that the entity's operations are conducted in accordance with laws and regulations. Laws and regulations may affect an entity's financial report in different ways: for example, most directly, they may affect specific disclosures required of the entity in the financial report or they may prescribe the applicable financial reporting framework. They may also establish certain legal rights and obligations of the entity, some of which will be recognised in the entity's financial report. In addition, laws and regulations may impose penalties in cases of non-compliance.

A2. The following are examples of the types of policies and procedures an entity may implement to assist in the prevention and detection of non-compliance with laws and regulations:

- Monitoring legal requirements and ensuring that operating procedures are designed to meet these requirements.
- Instituting and operating appropriate systems of internal control.
- Developing, publicising and following a code of conduct.
- Ensuring employees are properly trained and understand the code of conduct.
- Monitoring compliance with the code of conduct and acting appropriately to discipline employees who fail to comply with it.
- Engaging legal advisors to assist in monitoring legal requirements.
- Maintaining a register of significant laws and regulations with which the entity has to comply within its particular industry and a record of complaints.

In larger entities, these policies and procedures may be supplemented by assigning appropriate responsibilities to the following:

- An internal audit function.
- An audit committee.
- A compliance function.

Responsibility of the Auditor

A3. Non-compliance by the entity with laws and regulations may result in a material misstatement of the financial report. Detection of non-compliance, regardless of materiality, may affect other aspects of the audit including, for example, the auditor's consideration of the integrity of management or employees.

A4. Whether an act constitutes non-compliance with laws and regulations is a matter for legal determination, which is ordinarily beyond the auditor's professional competence to determine. Nevertheless, the auditor's training, experience and understanding of the entity and its industry or sector may provide a basis to recognise that some acts, coming to the auditor's attention, may constitute non-compliance with laws and regulations.

7 See ASA 230 *Audit Documentation*, paragraphs 8-11, and paragraph A6.

A5. In accordance with specific statutory requirements, the auditor may be specifically required to report, as part of the audit of the financial report, on whether the entity complies with certain provisions of laws or regulations. In these circumstances, ASA 700[8] or ASA 800[9] deal with how these audit responsibilities are addressed in the auditor's report. Furthermore, where there are specific statutory reporting requirements, it may be necessary for the audit plan to include appropriate tests for compliance with these provisions of the laws and regulations.

Considerations Specific to Public Sector Entities

A6. In the public sector, there may be additional audit responsibilities with respect to the consideration of laws and regulations which may relate to the audit of a financial report or may extend to other aspects of the entity's operations.

The Auditor's Consideration of Compliance with Laws and Regulations

Obtaining an Understanding of the Legal and Regulatory Framework (Ref: Para. 12)

A7. To obtain a general understanding of the legal and regulatory framework, and how the entity complies with that framework, the auditor may, for example:

- Use the auditor's existing understanding of the entity's industry, regulatory and other external factors;
- Update the understanding of those laws and regulations that directly determine the reported amounts and disclosures in the financial report;
- Enquire of management as to other laws or regulations that may be expected to have a fundamental effect on the operations of the entity;
- Enquire of management concerning the entity's policies and procedures regarding compliance with laws and regulations; and
- Enquire of management regarding the policies or procedures adopted for identifying, evaluating and accounting for litigation claims.

Laws and Regulations Generally Recognised to Have a Direct Effect on the Determination of Material Amounts and Disclosures in the Financial Report (Ref: Para. 13)

A8. Certain laws and regulations are well-established, known to the entity and within the entity's industry or sector, and relevant to the entity's financial report (as described in paragraph 6(a)). They could include those that relate to, for example:

- The form and content of the financial report;
- Industry-specific financial reporting issues;
- Accounting for transactions under government contracts; or
- The accrual or recognition of expenses for income tax or superannuation costs.

Some provisions in those laws and regulations may be directly relevant to specific assertions in the financial report (for example, the completeness of income tax provisions), while others may be directly relevant to the financial report as a whole (for example, the required statements constituting a complete set of financial statements). The aim of the requirement in paragraph 13 is for the auditor to obtain sufficient appropriate audit evidence regarding the determination of amounts and disclosures in the financial report in compliance with the relevant provisions of those laws and regulations.

Non-compliance with other provisions of such laws and regulations and other laws and regulations may result in fines, litigation or other consequences for the entity, the costs of which may need to be provided for in the financial report, but are not considered to have a direct effect on the financial report as described in paragraph 6(a).

8 See ASA 700 *Forming an Opinion and Reporting on a Financial Report*, paragraph 38.

9 See ASA 800 *Special Considerations — Audits of Financial Reports Prepared in Accordance with Special Purpose Frameworks*, paragraph 11.

Procedures to Identify Instances of Non-Compliance – Other Laws and Regulations (Ref: Para. 14)

A9. Certain other laws and regulations may need particular attention by the auditor because they have a fundamental effect on the operations of the entity (as described in paragraph 6(b)). Non-compliance with laws and regulations that have a fundamental effect on the operations of the entity may cause the entity to cease operations, or call into question the entity's continuance as a going concern. For example, non-compliance with the requirements of the entity's license or other entitlement to perform its operations could have such an impact (for example, for a bank, non-compliance with capital or investment requirements). There are also many laws and regulations relating principally to the operating aspects of the entity that typically do not affect the financial report and are not captured by the entity's information systems relevant to financial reporting.

A10. As the financial reporting consequences of other laws and regulations can vary depending on the entity's operations, the audit procedures required by paragraph 14 are directed to bringing to the auditor's attention instances of non-compliance with laws and regulations that may have a material effect on the financial report.

Non-Compliance Brought to the Auditor's Attention by Other Audit Procedures (Ref: Para. 15)

A11. Audit procedures applied to form an opinion on the financial report may bring instances of non-compliance or suspected non-compliance with laws and regulations to the auditor's attention. For example, such audit procedures may include:

- Reading minutes;
- Enquiring of the entity's management and in-house legal counsel or external legal counsel concerning litigation, claims and assessments; and
- Performing substantive tests of details of classes of transactions, account balances or disclosures; and

Aus A11.1 Review of breach registers and equivalent records (for example, complaints, whistleblower or suspicious matter reports registers).

Written Representations (Ref: Para. 16)

A12. Because the effect on the financial report of laws and regulations can vary considerably, written representations provide necessary audit evidence about management's knowledge of identified or suspected non-compliance with laws and regulations, whose effects may have a material effect on the financial report. However, written representations do not provide sufficient appropriate audit evidence on their own and, accordingly, do not affect the nature and extent of other audit evidence that is to be obtained by the auditor.[10]

Audit Procedures When Non-Compliance Is Identified or Suspected

Indications of Non-Compliance with Laws and Regulations (Ref: Para. 18)

A13. If the auditor becomes aware of the existence of, or information about, the following matters, it may be an indication of non-compliance with laws and regulations:

- Investigations by regulatory organisations and government departments or payment of fines or penalties.
- Payments for unspecified services or loans to consultants, related parties, employees or government employees.
- Sales commissions or agent's fees that appear excessive in relation to those ordinarily paid by the entity or in its industry or to the services actually received.
- Purchasing at prices significantly above or below market price.
- Unusual payments in cash, purchases in the form of cashiers' cheques payable to bearer or transfers to numbered bank accounts.
- Unusual transactions with companies or entities registered in tax havens.

10 See ASA 580 *Written Representations*, paragraph 4.

- Payments for goods or services made other than to the country from which the goods or services originated.
- Payments without proper exchange control documentation.
- Existence of an information system which fails, whether by design or by accident, to provide an adequate audit trail or sufficient evidence.
- Unauthorised transactions or improperly recorded transactions.
- Adverse media comment.

Matters Relevant to the Auditor's Evaluation (Ref: Para. 18(b))

A14. Matters relevant to the auditor's evaluation of the possible effect on the financial report include:

- The potential financial consequences of non-compliance with laws and regulations on the financial report including, for example, the imposition of fines, penalties, damages, threat of expropriation of assets, enforced discontinuation of operations, and litigation.
- Whether the potential financial consequences require disclosure.
- Whether the potential financial consequences are so serious as to call into question the fair presentation of the financial report, or otherwise make the financial report misleading.

Audit Procedures (Ref: Para. 19)

A15. The auditor may discuss the findings with those charged with governance where they may be able to provide additional audit evidence. For example, the auditor may confirm that those charged with governance have the same understanding of the facts and circumstances relevant to transactions or events that have led to the possibility of non-compliance with laws and regulations.

A16. If management or, as appropriate, those charged with governance do not provide sufficient information to the auditor that the entity is in fact in compliance with laws and regulations, the auditor may consider it appropriate to consult with the entity's in-house legal counsel or external legal counsel about the application of the laws and regulations to the circumstances, including the possibility of fraud, and the possible effects on the financial report. If it is not considered appropriate to consult with the entity's legal counsel or if the auditor is not satisfied with the legal counsel's opinion, the auditor may consider it appropriate to consult the auditor's own legal counsel as to whether a contravention of a law or regulation is involved, the possible legal consequences, including the possibility of fraud, and what further action, if any, the auditor would take.

Evaluating the Implications of Non-Compliance (Ref: Para. 21)

A17. As required by paragraph 21, the auditor evaluates the implications of non-compliance in relation to other aspects of the audit, including the auditor's risk assessment and the reliability of written representations. The implications of particular instances of non-compliance identified by the auditor will depend on the relationship of the perpetration and concealment, if any, of the act to specific control activities and the level of management or employees involved, especially implications arising from the involvement of the highest authority within the entity.

A18. In exceptional cases, the auditor may consider whether withdrawal from the engagement, where withdrawal is possible under applicable law or regulation, is necessary when management or those charged with governance do not take the remedial action that the auditor considers appropriate in the circumstances, even when the non-compliance is not material to the financial report. When deciding whether withdrawal from the engagement is necessary, the auditor may consider seeking legal advice. If withdrawal from the engagement is not possible, the auditor may consider alternative actions, including describing the non-compliance in an Other Matter(s) paragraph in the auditor's report.[11]

---

11 See ASA 706 *Emphasis of Matter Paragraphs and Other Matter Paragraphs in the Independent Auditor's Report*, paragraphs 8 and Aus 8.1.

Reporting of Identified or Suspected Non-Compliance

Reporting Non-Compliance in the Auditor's Report on the Financial Report (Ref: Para. 25)

Aus A18.1 If, in the case of an audit conducted under the *Corporations Act 2001*, the auditor identifies non-compliance with an Australian Accounting Standard, defects or irregularities in the financial report or deficiencies, failures or shortcomings in respect of sec 307 of the Act, the auditor's report is to include the information required by the Act.* The auditor needs to consider any other relevant laws and regulations. If the auditor is in doubt as to the proper interpretation of laws or regulations, or whether non-compliance has in fact occurred, the auditor ordinarily seeks legal advice before expressing an opinion on the financial report.

Reporting Non-Compliance to Regulatory and Enforcement Authorities (Ref: Para. 28)

A19. The auditor's professional duty to maintain the confidentiality of client information may preclude reporting identified or suspected non-compliance with laws and regulations to a party outside the entity. However, the auditor's legal responsibilities vary by jurisdiction and, in certain circumstances, the duty of confidentiality may be overridden by statute, the law or courts of law. In some jurisdictions, the auditor of a financial institution has a statutory duty to report the occurrence, or suspected occurrence, of non-compliance with laws and regulations to supervisory authorities. Also, in some jurisdictions, the auditor has a duty to report misstatements to authorities in those cases where management and, where applicable, those charged with governance fail to take corrective action. The auditor may consider it appropriate to obtain legal advice to determine the appropriate course of action.

Aus A19.1 In certain circumstances, the auditor has a statutory responsibility to report instances of non-compliance with laws and regulations. For example, in certain circumstances, the auditor is required under the *Corporations Act 2001*, to report to the Australian Securities and Investments Commission (ASIC).** Establishing the appropriate authority to which such a report would be made in a particular instance will depend on the nature and circumstances of the non-compliance. When in doubt, the auditor would ordinarily seek legal advice.

Considerations Specific to Public Sector Entities

A20. A public sector auditor may be obliged to report on instances of non-compliance to the legislature or other governing body or to report them in the auditor's report.

Documentation (Ref: Para. 29)

A21. The auditor's documentation of findings regarding identified or suspected non-compliance with laws and regulations may include, for example:

- Copies of records or documents.
- Minutes of discussions held with management, those charged with governance or parties outside the entity.

❖ ❖ ❖

Conformity with International Standards on Auditing

This Auditing Standard conforms with International Standard on Auditing ISA 250 *Consideration of Laws and Regulations in an Audit of Financial Statements* (Redrafted), issued by the International Auditing and Assurance Standards Board (IAASB), an independent standard-setting board of the International Federation of Accountants (IFAC).

Paragraphs that have been added to this Auditing Standard (and do not appear in the text of the equivalent ISA) are identified with the prefix "Aus".

Compliance with this Auditing Standard enables compliance with ISA 250.

---

* See sections 308 (2) and (3) of the *Corporations Act 2001*.

** See ASIC Regulatory Guide 34 *Auditors' obligations: reporting to ASIC* (December 2007) that provides guidance to help auditors comply with their obligations, under sections 311, 601HG and 990K of the *Corporations Act 2001*, to report contraventions and suspected contraventions of the Act to ASIC.

ASA 260
Communication with Those Charged with Governance

(Reissued October 2009: amended and compiled June 2011)

Issued by the Auditing and Assurance Standards Board.

Note from the Institute of Chartered Accountants Australia

This note, prepared by the technical editor, is not part of ASA 260.

Historical development

November 1990: ED 35 'Communications with Audit Committees' issued by the AuSB.

May 1991: AUP 31 'Communication with an Audit Committee' issued by the AuSB, operative in relation to the first reporting period ending on or after 1 January 1992, although earlier application encouraged. There was no equivalent IAPC Statement.

March 1993: AUP 35 'Communication to Management on Matters Arising From an Audit' issued following a period of exposure as ED 44. The judgment handed down by Rogers CJ in the Supreme Court of New South Wales regarding the AWA litigation was considered by the AuSB prior to approving AUP 35 for issue. AUP 35 provided guidance regarding communication to management on matters arising from an audit when the objective of the audit was to form an opinion on a financial report. It differentiated between matters that would ordinarily be reported to management, and those that the auditor may consider appropriate to report to management. Guidance was also given on timeliness of the reporting, planning the communication process, and the format of the reports.

June 1994: The International Auditing Practices Committee (IAPC) of the International Federation of Accountants (IFAC) approved the issuance of a codified set of International Standards of Auditing (ISAs). While there was no ISA issued on this area there was an International Statement on Auditing 'Communications with Management'.

October 1995: Australian Auditing Standards and Auditing Guidance Statements released. The status of these was explained in APS 1.1 'Conformity With Auditing Standards'. These Standards became operative for the first reporting period commencing on or after 1 July 1996 and later reporting periods, although earlier application was encouraged. AUP 31 'Communications with an Audit Committee' and AUP 35 'Communication to Management on Matters Arising from an Audit' replaced by AUS 710 'Communication to Management on Matters Arising from an Audit'.

May 1999: AUS 710 'Communicating with Management on Matters Arising from an Audit' reissued, based on the ED 70 proposals, and replaced AUS 710 'Communication to Management on Matters Arising from an Audit', issued in October 1995. ED 70 was issued in July 1998.

April 2006: ASA 260 was issued as a legally enforceable Standard to replace AUS 710. It is based on ISA 260 of the same name.

October 2009: ASA 260 reissued as part of the AUASB's Clarity Project. It includes a new requirement to communicate the auditor's views about significant qualitative aspects of the entity's accounting practices. It is based on the revised ISA 260 of the same name.

June 2011: ASA 260 updated for editorial amendments contained in ASA 2011-1 'Amendments to Australian Auditing Standards'.

Contents

Compilation Details

Auditing Standard ASA 260 *Communication with Those Charged with Governance* as Amended

This compilation takes into account amendments made up to and including 27 June 2011 and was prepared on 27 June 2011 by the Auditing and Assurance Standards Board (AUASB).

This compilation is not a separate Auditing Standard made by the AUASB. Instead, it is a representation of ASA 260 (October 2009) as amended by another Auditing Standard which is listed in the Table below.

Table of Standards

Standard	Date made	Operative date
ASA 260	27 October 2009	1 January 2010
ASA 2011-1	27 June 2011	1 July 2011

Table of Amendments

Paragraph affected	How affected	By … [paragraph]
Aus 0.1(a)	Amended	ASA 2011-1 [25]
Aus 17.1 Footnote *	Amended	ASA 2011-1 [26]

Preface

[Preface extracted from the original Auditing Standard issued 27 October 2009]

Reasons for Issuing Auditing Standard ASA 260 *Communication with Those Charged with Governance*

The Auditing and Assurance Standards Board (AUASB) issues Auditing Standard ASA 260 *Communication of Audit Matters with Those Charged with Governance* pursuant to the requirements of the legislative provisions and the Strategic Direction explained below.

The AUASB is an independent statutory board of the Australian Government established under section 227A of the *Australian Securities and Investments Commission Act 2001*, as amended (ASIC Act). Under section 336 of the *Corporations Act 2001*, the AUASB may make Auditing Standards for the purposes of the corporations legislation. These Auditing Standards are legislative instruments under the *Legislative Instruments Act 2003*.

Under the Strategic Direction given to the AUASB by the Financial Reporting Council (FRC), the AUASB is required to have regard to any programme initiated by the International Auditing and Assurance Standards Board (IAASB) for the revision and enhancement of the International Standards on Auditing (ISAs) and to make appropriate consequential amendments to the Australian Auditing Standards. Accordingly, the AUASB has decided to revise and redraft the Australian Auditing Standards using the equivalent redrafted ISAs.

Main Features

This Auditing Standard establishes requirements and provides application and other explanatory material regarding the auditor's responsibility to communicate with those charged with governance in an audit of a financial report.

This Auditing Standard:

(a) applies irrespective of an entity's governance structure or size;

(b) provides an overarching framework, including key processes, for the auditor's communication with those charged with governance;

(c) distinguishes between 'management' and 'those charged with governance';

(d) identifies specific matters to be communicated by the auditor to those charged with governance;

(e) allows the auditor to communicate other matters, as required by law or regulation;

(f) promotes two-way communication between the auditor and those charged with governance; and

(g) establishes documentation requirements.

Authority Statement

Auditing Standard ASA 260 *Communication with Those Charged with Governance* (as amended at 27 June 2011) is set out in paragraphs 1 to A45 and Appendices 1 and 2.

This Auditing Standard is to be read in conjunction with ASA 101 *Preamble to Australian Auditing Standards*, which sets out the intentions of the AUASB on how the Australian Auditing Standards, operative for financial reporting periods commencing on or after 1 January 2010, are to be understood, interpreted and applied. This Auditing Standard is to be read also in conjunction with ASA 200 *Overall Objectives of the Independent Auditor and the Conduct of an Audit in Accordance with Australian Auditing Standards*.

Dated: 27 June 2011

M H Kelsall
Chairman - AUASB

Auditing Standard ASA 260

The Auditing and Assurance Standards Board (AUASB) made Auditing Standard ASA 260 *Communication with Those Charged with Governance*, pursuant to section 227B of the *Australian Securities and Investments Commission Act 2001* and section 336 of the *Corporations Act 2001*, on 27 October 2009.

This compiled version of ASA 260 incorporates subsequent amendments contained in another Auditing Standard made by the AUASB up to and including 27 June 2011 (see Compilation Details).

Auditing Standard ASA 260

Communication with Those Charged with Governance

Application

Aus 0.1 This Auditing Standard applies to:

(a) an audit of a financial report for a financial year, or an audit of a financial report for a half-year, in accordance with the *Corporations Act 2001*; and

(b) an audit of a financial report, or a complete set of financial statements, for any other purpose.

Aus 0.2 This Auditing Standard also applies, as appropriate, to an audit of other historical financial information.

Operative Date

Aus 0.3 This Auditing Standard is operative for financial reporting periods commencing on or after 1 January 2010.

[Note: For operative dates of paragraphs changed or added by an amending Standard, see Compilation Details.]

Introduction

Scope of this Auditing Standard

1. This Auditing Standard deals with the auditor's responsibility to communicate with those charged with governance in an audit of a financial report. Although this Auditing Standard applies irrespective of an entity's governance structure or size, particular considerations apply where all of those charged with governance are involved in managing an entity, and for entities whose audit is conducted under the *Corporations Act 2001*. This Auditing Standard does not establish requirements regarding the auditor's communication with an entity's management or owners unless they are also charged with a governance role.

2. This Auditing Standard is written in the context of an audit of a financial report, but may also be applicable, adjusted as necessary in the circumstances, to audits of other historical financial information when those charged with governance have a responsibility to oversee the preparation of other historical financial information.

3. Recognising the importance of effective two-way communication in an audit of a financial report, this Auditing Standard provides an overarching framework for the auditor's communication with those charged with governance, and identifies some specific matters to be communicated with them. Additional matters to be communicated, which complement the requirements of this Auditing Standard, are identified in other Auditing Standards (see Appendix 1). In addition, ASA 265[1] establishes specific requirements regarding the communication of significant deficiencies in internal control the auditor has identified during the audit to those charged with governance. Further matters, not required by this or other Auditing Standards, may be required to be communicated by laws or regulations, by agreement with the entity, or by additional requirements applicable to the engagement, for example, the standards of a professional accountancy body. Nothing in this Auditing Standard precludes the auditor from communicating any other matters to those charged with governance. (Ref: Para. A24-A27)

The Role of Communication

4. This Auditing Standard focuses primarily on communications from the auditor to those charged with governance. Nevertheless, effective two-way communication is important in assisting:

1 See ASA 265 *Communicating Deficiencies in Internal Control to Those Charged with Governance and Management*.

(a) The auditor and those charged with governance in understanding matters related to the audit in context, and in developing a constructive working relationship. This relationship is developed while maintaining the auditor's independence and objectivity;

(b) The auditor in obtaining from those charged with governance information relevant to the audit. For example, those charged with governance may assist the auditor in understanding the entity and its environment, in identifying appropriate sources of audit evidence, and in providing information about specific transactions or events; and

(c) Those charged with governance in fulfilling their responsibility to oversee the financial reporting process, thereby reducing the risks of material misstatement of the financial report.

5. Although the auditor is responsible for communicating matters required by this Auditing Standard, management also has a responsibility to communicate matters of governance interest to those charged with governance. Communication by the auditor does not relieve management of this responsibility. Similarly, communication by management with those charged with governance of matters that the auditor is required to communicate does not relieve the auditor of the responsibility to also communicate them. Communication of these matters by management may, however, affect the form or timing of the auditor's communication with those charged with governance.

6. Clear communication of specific matters required to be communicated by Australian Auditing Standards is an integral part of every audit. Australian Auditing Standards do not, however, require the auditor to perform procedures specifically to identify any other matters to communicate with those charged with governance.

7. Law or regulation may restrict the auditor's communication of certain matters with those charged with governance. For example, law or regulation may specifically prohibit a communication, or other action, that might prejudice an investigation by an appropriate authority into an actual, or suspected, illegal act. In some circumstances, potential conflicts between the auditor's obligations of confidentiality and obligations to communicate may be complex. In such cases, the auditor may consider obtaining legal advice.

Effective Date

8. [Deleted by the AUASB. Refer Aus 0.3]

Objectives

9. The objectives of the auditor are:

(a) To communicate clearly with those charged with governance the responsibilities of the auditor in relation to the financial report audit, and an overview of the planned scope and timing of the audit;

(b) To obtain from those charged with governance information relevant to the audit;

(c) To provide those charged with governance with timely observations arising from the audit that are significant and relevant to their responsibility to oversee the financial reporting process; and

(d) To promote effective two-way communication between the auditor and those charged with governance.

Definitions

10. For purposes of the Australian Auditing Standards, the following terms have the meanings attributed below:

(a) Those charged with governance means the person(s) or organisation(s) (for example, a corporate trustee) with responsibility for overseeing the strategic direction of the entity and obligations related to the accountability of the entity. This includes overseeing the financial reporting process. For some entities in some jurisdictions, those charged with governance may include management personnel, for example, executive members of a governance board of a private or public sector entity, or an owner-manager. For discussion of the diversity of governance structures, see paragraphs A1-A8.

(b) Management means the person(s) with executive responsibility for the conduct of the entity's operations. For some entities, in some jurisdictions, management includes some or all of those charged with governance, for example, executive members of a governance board, or an owner-manager.

Requirements

Those Charged with Governance

11. The auditor shall determine the appropriate person(s) within the entity's governance structure with whom to communicate. (Ref: Para. A1-A4)

Communication with a Subgroup of Those Charged with Governance

12. If the auditor communicates with a subgroup of those charged with governance, for example, an audit committee, or an individual, the auditor shall determine whether the auditor also needs to communicate with the governing body. (Ref: Para. A5-A7)

When All of Those Charged with Governance Are Involved in Managing the Entity

13. In some cases, all of those charged with governance are involved in managing the entity, for example, a small business where a single owner manages the entity and no one else has a governance role. In these cases, if matters required by this Auditing Standard are communicated with person(s) with management responsibilities, and those person(s) also have governance responsibilities, the matters need not be communicated again with those same person(s) in their governance role. These matters are noted in paragraph 16(c) of this Auditing Standard. The auditor shall nonetheless be satisfied that communication with person(s) with management responsibilities adequately informs all of those with whom the auditor would otherwise communicate in their governance capacity. (Ref: Para. A8)

Matters to Be Communicated

The Auditor's Responsibilities in Relation to the Financial Report Audit

14. The auditor shall communicate with those charged with governance the responsibilities of the auditor in relation to the financial report audit, including that:

(a) The auditor is responsible for forming and expressing an opinion on the financial report that has been prepared by management with the oversight of those charged with governance; and

(b) The audit of the financial report does not relieve management or those charged with governance of their responsibilities. (Ref: Para. A9-A10)

Planned Scope and Timing of the Audit

15. The auditor shall communicate with those charged with governance an overview of the planned scope and timing of the audit. (Ref: Para. A11-A15)

Significant Findings from the Audit

16. The auditor shall communicate with those charged with governance: (Ref: Para. A16)

(a) The auditor's views about significant qualitative aspects of the entity's accounting practices, including accounting policies, accounting estimates and financial report disclosures. When applicable, the auditor shall explain to those charged with governance why the auditor considers a significant accounting practice, that is acceptable under the applicable financial reporting framework, not to be most appropriate to the particular circumstances of the entity; (Ref: Para. A17)

(b) Significant difficulties, if any, encountered during the audit; (Ref: Para. A18)

(c) Unless all of those charged with governance are involved in managing the entity:

(i) Significant matters, if any, arising from the audit that were discussed, or subject to correspondence with management; and (Ref: Para. A19)

(ii) Written representations the auditor is requesting; and

(d) Other matters, if any, arising from the audit that, in the auditor's professional judgement, are significant to the oversight of the financial reporting process. (Ref: Para. A20)

Auditor Independence

17. In the case of listed entities the auditor shall communicate with those charged with governance:

(a) A statement that the engagement team and others in the firm as appropriate, the firm and, when applicable, network firms have complied with relevant ethical requirements regarding independence;* and

(b) (i) All relationships and other matters between the firm, network firms, and the entity that, in the auditor's professional judgement, may reasonably be thought to bear on independence. This shall include total fees charged during the period covered by the financial report for audit and non-audit services provided by the firm and network firms to the entity and components controlled by the entity. These fees shall be allocated to categories that are appropriate to assist those charged with governance in assessing the effect of services on the independence of the auditor; and

(ii) The related safeguards that have been applied to eliminate identified threats to independence or reduce them to an acceptable level. (Ref: Para. A21-A23)

Aus 17.1 In the case of entities** audited in accordance with the *Corporations Act 2001*, the auditor shall communicate with those charged with governance a statement that the engagement team and others in the firm as appropriate, the firm, and, when applicable network firms, have complied with the independence requirements of section 307C of the *Corporations Act 2001*.

The Communication Process

Establishing the Communication Process

18. The auditor shall communicate with those charged with governance the form, timing and expected general content of communications. (Ref: Para. A28-A36)

Forms of Communication

19. The auditor shall communicate in writing with those charged with governance regarding significant findings from the audit if, in the auditor's professional judgement, oral communication would not be adequate. Written communications need not include all matters that arose during the course of the audit. (Ref: Para. A37-A39)

Aus 19.1 If the auditor is concerned that a written report intended for those charged with governance has not been, or may not be, distributed to all members of that group, the auditor shall endeavour to ensure all members are appropriately informed of the contents of the report.

20. The auditor shall communicate in writing with those charged with governance regarding auditor independence when required by paragraph 17 and Aus 17.1 of this Auditing Standard.

Timing of Communications

21. The auditor shall communicate with those charged with governance on a timely basis. (Ref: Para. A40-A41)

Adequacy of the Communication Process

22. The auditor shall evaluate whether the two-way communication between the auditor and those charged with governance has been adequate for the purpose of the audit. If it has not, the auditor shall evaluate the effect, if any, on the auditor's assessment of the risks of material misstatement and ability to obtain sufficient appropriate audit evidence, and shall take appropriate action. (Ref: Para. A42-A44)

* See ASA 102 *Compliance with Ethical Requirements when Performing Audits, Reviews and Other Assurance Engagements*.

** See, for example, section 292 of the *Corporations Act 2001* for types of entities.

Documentation

23. Where matters required by this Auditing Standard to be communicated are communicated orally, the auditor shall include them in the audit documentation, and when and to whom they were communicated. Where matters have been communicated in writing, the auditor shall retain a copy of the communication as part of the audit documentation.[2] (Ref: Para. A45)

❖ ❖ ❖

Application and Other Explanatory Material

Those Charged with Governance (Ref: Para. 11)

A1. Governance structures vary by entity, reflecting influences such as size and ownership characteristics. For example:

- In some jurisdictions, a supervisory (wholly or mainly non-executive) board exists that is legally separate from an executive (management) board (a two-tier board structure). In other jurisdictions, both the supervisory and executive functions are the legal responsibility of a single, or unitary, board (a one-tier board structure).
- In some entities, those charged with governance hold positions that are an integral part of the entity's legal structure, for example, company directors. In others, for example, some public sector entities, a body that is not part of the entity is charged with governance.
- In some cases, some or all of those charged with governance are involved in managing the entity. In others, those charged with governance and management comprise different persons.
- In some cases, those charged with governance are responsible for approving[3] the entity's financial report (in other cases management has this responsibility).

A2. In most entities, governance is the collective responsibility of a governing body, such as a board of directors, a supervisory board, partners, proprietors, a committee of management, a council of governors, trustees, or equivalent persons. In some smaller entities, however, one person may be charged with governance, for example, the owner-manager where there are no other owners, or a sole trustee. When governance is a collective responsibility, a subgroup such as an audit committee or even an individual, may be charged with specific tasks to assist the governing body in meeting its responsibilities. Alternatively, a subgroup or individual may have specific, legally identified responsibilities that differ from those of the governing body.

A3. Such diversity means that it is not possible for this Auditing Standard to specify for all audits the person(s) with whom the auditor is to communicate particular matters. Also, in some cases the appropriate person(s) with whom to communicate may not be clearly identifiable from the applicable legal framework or other engagement circumstances, for example, entities where the governance structure is not formally defined, such as some owner-managed entities, some not-for-profit organisations, and some public sector entities. In such cases, the auditor may need to discuss and agree with the engaging party the relevant person(s) with whom to communicate. In deciding with whom to communicate, the auditor's understanding of an entity's governance structure and processes obtained in accordance with ASA 315[4] is relevant. The appropriate person(s) with whom to communicate may vary depending on the matter to be communicated.

A4. ASA 600 includes specific matters to be communicated by group auditors with those charged with governance[5]. When the entity is a component of a group, the appropriate person(s) with whom the component auditor communicates depends on the engagement

---

2 See ASA 230 *Audit Documentation*, paragraph 8-11 and paragraph A6.

3 See ASA 700 *Forming an Opinion and Reporting on a Financial Report*, paragraph A40.

4 See ASA 315 *Identifying and Assessing the Risks of Material Misstatement through Understanding the Entity and Its Environment*.

5 See ASA 600 *Special Considerations—Audits of a Group Financial Report (Including the Work of Component Auditors)*, paragraphs 46-49.

ASA

circumstances and the matter to be communicated. In some cases, a number of components may be conducting the same businesses within the same system of internal control and using the same accounting practices. Where those charged with governance of those components are the same (for example, common board of directors), duplication may be avoided by dealing with these components concurrently for the purpose of communication.

Communication with a Subgroup of Those Charged with Governance (Ref: Para. 12)

A5. When considering communicating with a subgroup of those charged with governance, the auditor may take into account such matters as:

- The respective responsibilities of the subgroup and the governing body.
- The nature of the matter to be communicated.
- Relevant legal or regulatory requirements.
- Whether the subgroup has the authority to take action in relation to the information communicated, and can provide further information and explanations the auditor may need.

A6. When deciding whether there is also a need to communicate information, in full or in summary form, with the governing body, the auditor may be influenced by the auditor's assessment of how effectively and appropriately the subgroup communicates relevant information with the governing body. The auditor may make explicit in agreeing the terms of engagement that, unless prohibited by law or regulation, the auditor retains the right to communicate directly with the governing body.

A7. Audit committees (or similar subgroups with different names) exist in many jurisdictions. Although their specific authority and functions may differ, communication with the audit committee, where one exists, has become a key element in the auditor's communication with those charged with governance. Good governance principles suggest that:

- The auditor will be invited to regularly attend meetings of the audit committee.
- The chair of the audit committee and, when relevant, the other members of the audit committee, will liaise with the auditor periodically.
- The audit committee will meet the auditor without management present at least annually.

When All of Those Charged with Governance Are Involved in Managing the Entity (Ref: Para. 13)

A8. In some cases, all of those charged with governance are involved in managing the entity, and the application of communication requirements is modified to recognise this position. In such cases, communication with person(s) with management responsibilities may not adequately inform all of those with whom the auditor would otherwise communicate in their governance capacity. For example, in a company where all directors are involved in managing the entity, some of those directors (for example, one responsible for marketing) may be unaware of significant matters discussed with another director (for example, one responsible for the preparation of the financial report).

Matters to Be Communicated

The Auditor's Responsibilities in Relation to the Financial Report Audit (Ref: Para. 14)

A9. The auditor's responsibilities in relation to the financial report audit are often included in the engagement letter or other suitable form of written agreement that records the agreed terms of the engagement. Providing those charged with governance with a copy of that engagement letter or other suitable form of written agreement may be an appropriate way to communicate with them regarding such matters as:

- The auditor's responsibility for performing the audit in accordance with Australian Auditing Standards, which is directed towards the expression of an opinion on the financial report. The matters that Australian Auditing Standards require to be communicated, therefore, include significant matters arising from the audit of the financial report that are relevant to those charged with governance in taking responsibility for, or overseeing, the financial reporting process.

- The fact that Australian Auditing Standards do not require the auditor to design procedures for the purpose of identifying supplementary matters to communicate with those charged with governance.
- When applicable, the auditor's responsibility for communicating particular matters required by law or regulation, by agreement with the entity or by additional requirements applicable to the engagement, for example, the standards of a professional accountancy body.

A10. Law or regulation, an agreement with the entity or additional requirements applicable to the engagement may provide for broader communication with those charged with governance. For example, (a) an agreement with the entity may provide for particular matters to be communicated when they arise from services provided by a firm or network firm other than the financial report audit; or (b) the mandate of a public sector auditor may provide for matters to be communicated that come to the auditor's attention as a result of other work, such as performance audits.

Planned Scope and Timing of the Audit (Ref: Para. 15)

A11. Communication regarding the planned scope and timing of the audit may:

(a) Assist those charged with governance to understand better the consequences of the auditor's work, to discuss issues of risk and the concept of materiality with the auditor, and to identify any areas in which they may request the auditor to undertake additional procedures; and

(b) Assist the auditor to understand better the entity and its environment.

A12. Care is required when communicating with those charged with governance about the planned scope and timing of the audit so as not to compromise the effectiveness of the audit, particularly where some or all of those charged with governance are involved in managing the entity. For example, communicating the nature and timing of detailed audit procedures may reduce the effectiveness of those procedures by making them too predictable.

A13. Matters communicated may include:

- How the auditor proposes to address the significant risks of material misstatement, whether due to fraud or error.
- The auditor's approach to internal control relevant to the audit.
- The application of the concept of materiality in the context of an audit.[6]

A14. Other planning matters that it may be appropriate to discuss with those charged with governance include:

- Where the entity has an internal audit function, the extent to which the auditor will use the work of internal audit, and how the external and internal auditors can best work together in a constructive and complementary manner.
- The views of those charged with governance of:
  - The appropriate person(s) in the entity's governance structure with whom to communicate.
  - The allocation of responsibilities between those charged with governance and management.
  - The entity's objectives and strategies, and the related business risks that may result in material misstatements.
  - Matters those charged with governance consider warrant particular attention during the audit, and any areas where they request additional procedures to be undertaken.
  - Significant communications with regulators.
  - Other matters those charged with governance consider may influence the audit of the financial report.

6 See ASA 320 *Materiality in Planning and Performing an Audit.*

- The attitudes, awareness, and actions of those charged with governance concerning (a) the entity's internal control and its importance in the entity, including how those charged with governance oversee the effectiveness of internal control, and (b) the detection or possibility of fraud.
- The actions of those charged with governance in response to developments in accounting standards, corporate governance practices, exchange listing rules, and related matters.
- The responses of those charged with governance to previous communications with the auditor.

A15. While communication with those charged with governance may assist the auditor to plan the scope and timing of the audit, it does not change the auditor's sole responsibility to establish the overall audit strategy and the audit plan, including the nature, timing and extent of procedures necessary to obtain sufficient appropriate audit evidence.

Significant Findings from the Audit (Ref: Para. 16)

A16. The communication of findings from the audit may include requesting further information from those charged with governance in order to complete the audit evidence obtained. For example, the auditor may confirm that those charged with governance have the same understanding of the facts and circumstances relevant to specific transactions or events.

Significant Qualitative Aspects of Accounting Practices (Ref: Para. 16(a))

A17. The Financial reporting framework ordinarily allows the entity to make accounting estimates, and judgements about accounting policies and financial report disclosures. Open and constructive communication about significant qualitative aspects of the entity's accounting practices may include comment on the acceptability of significant accounting practices. Appendix 2 identifies matters that may be included in this communication.

Significant Difficulties Encountered During the Audit (Ref: Para. 16(b))

A18. Significant difficulties encountered during the audit may include such matters as:

- Significant delays in management, or those charged with governance providing required information.
- An unnecessarily brief time within which to complete the audit.
- Extensive unexpected effort required to obtain sufficient appropriate audit evidence.
- The unavailability of expected information.
- Restrictions imposed on the auditor by management or those charged with governance.
- Management's, or where appropriate, those charged with governance's, unwillingness to make or extend its assessment of the entity's ability to continue as a going concern when requested.

In some circumstances, such difficulties may constitute a scope limitation that leads to a modification of the auditor's opinion.[7]

Significant Matters Discussed, or Subject to Correspondence with Management (Ref: Para. 16(c) (i))

A19. Significant matters discussed, or subject to correspondence with management may include such matters as:

- Business conditions affecting the entity, and business plans and strategies that may affect the risks of material misstatement.
- Concerns about management's consultations with other accountants on accounting or auditing matters.
- Discussions or correspondence in connection with the initial or recurring appointment of the auditor regarding accounting practices, the application of auditing standards, or fees for audit or other services.

7 See ASA 705 *Modifications to the Opinion in the Independent Auditor's Report.*

Other Significant Matters Relevant to the Financial Reporting Process **(Ref: Para. 16(d))**

A20. Other significant matters arising from the audit that are directly relevant to those charged with governance in their responsibility for, or overseeing, the financial reporting process may include such matters as material misstatements of fact or material inconsistencies in information accompanying the audited financial report that have been corrected.

Auditor Independence (Ref: Para. 17)

A21. The auditor is required to comply with relevant ethical requirements, including those pertaining to independence, relating to an audit of a financial report.[8]

A22. The relationships and other matters, and safeguards to be communicated, vary with the circumstances of the engagement, but generally address:

(a) Threats to independence, which may be categorised as: self-interest threats, self-review threats, advocacy threats, familiarity threats, and intimidation threats; and

(b) Safeguards created by the profession, legislation or regulation, safeguards within the entity, and safeguards within the firm's own systems and procedures.

The communication required by paragraph 17(a) may include an inadvertent violation of relevant ethical requirements as they relate to auditor independence, and any remedial action taken or proposed.

A23. The communication requirements relating to auditor independence that apply in the case of listed entities under paragraph 17 and other entities under paragraph Aus 17.1, may also be relevant in the case of some other entities,* particularly those that may be of significant public interest because, as a result of their business, their size or their corporate status, they have a wide range of stakeholders. Examples of such entities, where the communication of auditor independence may be appropriate or required, include public sector entities, credit institutions, insurance companies, and superannuation funds. On the other hand, there may be situations where communications regarding independence may not be relevant, for example, where all of those charged with governance have been informed of relevant facts through their management activities. This is particularly likely where the entity is owner-managed, and the auditor's firm and network firms have little involvement with the entity beyond a financial report audit.

Supplementary Matters (Ref: Para. 3)

A24. The oversight of management by those charged with governance includes ensuring that the entity designs, implements and maintains appropriate internal control with regard to reliability of financial reporting, effectiveness and efficiency of operations and compliance with applicable laws and regulations.

A25. The auditor may become aware of supplementary matters that do not necessarily relate to the oversight of the financial reporting process but which are, nevertheless, likely to be significant to the responsibilities of those charged with governance in overseeing the strategic direction of the entity or the entity's obligations related to accountability. Such matters may include, for example, significant issues regarding governance structures or processes, and significant decisions or actions by senior management that lack appropriate authorisation.

A26. In determining whether to communicate supplementary matters with those charged with governance, the auditor may discuss matters of this kind of which the auditor has become aware with the appropriate level of management, unless it is inappropriate to do so in the circumstances.

A27. If a supplementary matter is communicated, it may be appropriate for the auditor to make those charged with governance aware that:

(a) Identification and communication of such matters is incidental to the purpose of the audit, which is to form an opinion on the financial report;

8 See ASA 200 *Overall Objectives of the Independent Auditor and the Conduct of an Audit in Accordance with Australian Auditing Standards*, paragraph 14.

* For example, entities which do not have reporting requirements under the *Corporations Act 2001*.

(b) No procedures were carried out with respect to the matter other than any that were necessary to form an opinion on the financial report; and

(c) No procedures were carried out to determine whether other such matters exist.

The Communication Process

Establishing the Communication Process (Ref: Para. 18)

A28. Clear communication of the auditor's responsibilities, the planned scope and timing of the audit, and the expected general content of communications helps establish the basis for effective two-way communication.

A29. Matters that may also contribute to effective two-way communication include discussion of:

- The purpose of communications. When the purpose is clear, the auditor and those charged with governance are better placed to have a mutual understanding of relevant issues and the expected actions arising from the communication process.
- The form in which communications will be made.
- The person(s) in the audit team and amongst those charged with governance who will communicate regarding particular matters.
- The auditor's expectation that communication will be two-way, and that those charged with governance will communicate with the auditor matters they consider relevant to the audit, for example, strategic decisions that may significantly affect the nature, timing, and extent of audit procedures, the suspicion, or the detection of fraud, and concerns with the integrity or competence of senior management.
- The process for taking action and reporting back on matters communicated by the auditor.
- The process for taking action and reporting back on matters communicated by those charged with governance.

A30. The communication process will vary with the circumstances, including the size and governance structure of the entity, how those charged with governance operate, and the auditor's view of the significance of matters to be communicated. Difficulty in establishing effective two-way communication may indicate that the communication between the auditor and those charged with governance is not adequate for the purpose of the audit (see paragraph A44).

Considerations Specific to Smaller Entities

A31. In the case of audits of smaller entities, the auditor may communicate in a less structured manner with those charged with governance than in the case of larger entities.

Communication with Management

A32. Many matters may be discussed with management in the ordinary course of an audit, including matters required by this Auditing Standard to be communicated with those charged with governance. Such discussions recognise management's executive responsibility for the conduct of the entity's operations and, in particular, management's responsibility for the preparation of the financial report.

A33. Before communicating matters with those charged with governance, the auditor may discuss them with management, unless that is inappropriate. For example, it may not be appropriate to discuss questions of management's competence or integrity with management. In addition to recognising management's executive responsibility, these initial discussions may clarify facts and issues, and give management an opportunity to provide further information and explanations. Similarly, when the entity has an internal audit function, the auditor may discuss matters with the internal auditor before communicating with those charged with governance.

Communication with Third Parties

A34. Those charged with governance may wish to provide third parties, for example, bankers or certain regulatory authorities, with copies of a written communication from the auditor. In some cases, disclosure to third parties may be illegal or otherwise inappropriate.

When a written communication prepared for those charged with governance is provided to third parties, it may be important in the circumstances that the third parties be informed that the communication was not prepared with them in mind, for example, by stating in written communications with those charged with governance:

(a) That the communication has been prepared for the sole use of those charged with governance and, where applicable, the group management and the group auditor, and should not be relied upon by third parties;

(b) That no responsibility is assumed by the auditor to third parties; and

(c) Any restrictions on disclosure or distribution to third parties.

A35. In some jurisdictions, the auditor may be required by law or regulation to, for example:

- Notify a regulatory or enforcement body of certain matters communicated with those charged with governance. For example, in some cases the auditor has a duty to report misstatements to authorities where management and those charged with governance fail to take corrective action;

Aus A35.1 An auditor is required under the *Corporations Act 2001* to notify the Australian Securities and Investments Commission (ASIC) if the auditor is aware of certain circumstances;*

- Submit copies of certain reports prepared for those charged with governance to relevant regulatory or funding bodies, or other bodies such as a central authority in the case of some public sector entities; or
- Make reports prepared for those charged with governance publicly available.

A36. Unless required by law or regulation to provide a third party with a copy of the auditor's written communications with those charged with governance, the auditor may need the prior consent of those charged with governance before doing so.

Forms of Communication (Ref: Para. 19-20)

A37. Effective communication may involve structured presentations and written reports as well as less structured communications, including discussions. The auditor may communicate matters other than those identified in paragraphs 19 and 20 either orally or in writing. Written communications may include an engagement letter that is provided to those charged with governance.

A38. In addition to the significance of a particular matter, the form of communication (for example, whether to communicate orally or in writing, the extent of detail or summarisation in the communication, and whether to communicate in a structured or unstructured manner) may be affected by such factors as:

- Whether the matter has been satisfactorily resolved.
- Whether management has previously communicated the matter.
- The size, operating structure, control environment, and legal structure of the entity.
- In the case of an audit of a special purpose financial report, whether the auditor also audits the entity's general purpose financial report.
- Legal requirements. In some jurisdictions, a written communication with those charged with governance may be required in a prescribed form by law.
- The expectations of those charged with governance, including arrangements made for periodic meetings or communications with the auditor.
- The amount of ongoing contact and dialogue the auditor has with those charged with governance.
- Whether there have been significant changes in the membership of a governing body.

A39. When a significant matter is discussed with an individual member of those charged with governance, for example, the chair of an audit committee, it may be appropriate for the

* See ASIC Regulatory Guide 34 *Auditors' Obligations: Reporting to ASIC* (December 2007), which provides guidance to help auditors comply with their obligations under sections 311, 601HG and 990K of the *Corporations Act 2001* to report contraventions and suspected contraventions to ASIC.

ASA

auditor to summarise the matter in later communications so that all of those charged with governance have full and balanced information.

Timing of Communications (Ref: Para. 21)

A40. The appropriate timing for communications will vary with the circumstances of the engagement. Relevant circumstances include the significance and nature of the matter, and the action expected to be taken by those charged with governance. For example:

- Communications regarding planning matters may often be made early in the audit engagement and, for an initial engagement, may be made as part of agreeing the terms of the engagement.
- It may be appropriate to communicate a significant difficulty encountered during the audit as soon as practicable if those charged with governance are able to assist the auditor to overcome the difficulty, or if it is likely to lead to a modified opinion. Similarly, the auditor may communicate orally to those charged with governance as soon as practicable significant deficiencies in internal control that the auditor has identified, prior to communicating these in writing as required by ASA 265.[9] Communications regarding independence may be appropriate whenever significant judgements are made about threats to independence and related safeguards, for example, when accepting an engagement to provide non-audit services, and at a concluding discussion. A concluding discussion may also be an appropriate time to communicate findings from the audit, including the auditor's views about the qualitative aspects of the entity's accounting practices.
- When auditing both general purpose and special purpose financial reports, it may be appropriate to coordinate the timing of communications.

A41. Other factors that may be relevant to the timing of communications include:

- The size, operating structure, control environment, and legal structure of the entity being audited.
- Any legal obligation to communicate certain matters within a specified timeframe.
- The expectations of those charged with governance, including arrangements made for periodic meetings or communications with the auditor.
- The time at which the auditor identifies certain matters, for example, the auditor may not identify a particular matter (for example, non-compliance with a law) in time for preventive action to be taken, but communication of the matter may enable remedial action to be taken.

Adequacy of the Communication Process (Ref: Para. 22)

A42. The auditor need not design specific procedures to support the evaluation of the two-way communication between the auditor and those charged with governance; rather, that evaluation may be based on observations resulting from audit procedures performed for other purposes. Such observations may include:

- The appropriateness and timeliness of actions taken by those charged with governance in response to matters raised by the auditor. Where significant matters raised in previous communications have not been dealt with effectively, it may be appropriate for the auditor to enquire as to why appropriate action has not been taken, and to consider raising the point again. This avoids the risk of giving an impression that the auditor is satisfied that the matter has been adequately addressed or is no longer significant.
- The apparent openness of those charged with governance in their communications with the auditor.
- The willingness and capacity of those charged with governance to meet with the auditor without management present.
- The apparent ability of those charged with governance to fully comprehend matters raised by the auditor, for example, the extent to which those charged with governance probe issues, and question recommendations made to them.

9 See ASA 265, paragraphs 9 and A14.

- Difficulty in establishing with those charged with governance a mutual understanding of the form, timing and expected general content of communications.
- Where all or some of those charged with governance are involved in managing the entity, their apparent awareness of how matters discussed with the auditor affect their broader governance responsibilities, as well as their management responsibilities.
- Whether the two-way communication between the auditor and those charged with governance meets applicable legal and regulatory requirements.

A43. As noted in paragraph 4, effective two-way communication assists both the auditor and those charged with governance. Further, ASA 315 identifies participation by those charged with governance, including their interaction with internal audit, if any, and external auditors, as an element of the entity's control environment.[10] Inadequate two-way communication may indicate an unsatisfactory control environment and influence the auditor's assessment of the risks of material misstatements. There is also a risk that the auditor may not have obtained sufficient appropriate audit evidence to form an opinion on the financial report.

A44. If the two-way communication between the auditor and those charged with governance is not adequate and the situation cannot be resolved, the auditor may take such actions as:

- Modifying the auditor's opinion on the basis of a scope limitation.
- Obtaining legal advice about the consequences of different courses of action.
- Communicating with third parties (for example, a regulator), or a higher authority in the governance structure that is outside the entity, such as the owners of a business (for example, shareholders in a general meeting), or the responsible government minister or parliament in the public sector.
- Withdrawing from the engagement, where withdrawal is possible under applicable law or regulation.

Documentation (Ref: Para. 23)

A45. Documentation of oral communication may include a copy of minutes prepared by the entity retained as part of the audit documentation where those minutes are an appropriate record of the communication.

❖ ❖ ❖

Conformity with International Standards on Auditing

This Auditing Standard conforms with International Standard on Auditing ISA 260 *Communication with Those Charged with Governance* issued by the International Auditing and Assurance Standards Board (IAASB), an independent standard-setting board of the International Federation of Accountants (IFAC).

Paragraphs that have been added to this Auditing Standard (and do not appear in the text of the equivalent ISA) are identified with the prefix "Aus".

The following requirements are additional to ISA 260:

- In the case of entities audited in accordance with the *Corporations Act 2001*, the auditor shall communicate with those charged with governance a statement that the engagement team and others in the firm as appropriate, the firm, and, when applicable network firms, have complied with the independence requirements of section 307C of the *Corporations Act 2001*. [Ref: Para. Aus 17.1]
- If the auditor is concerned that a written report intended for those charged with governance has not been, or may not be, distributed to all members of that group, the auditor shall endeavour to ensure all members are appropriately informed of the contents of the report. [Ref: Para. Aus 19.1].

Compliance with this Auditing Standard enables compliance with ISA 260.

10 See ASA 315, paragraph A70.

Appendix 1
(Ref: Para. 3)

Specific Requirements in ASQC 1 and Other Australian Auditing Standards that Refer to Communications with Those Charged with Governance

This Appendix identifies paragraphs in ASQC 1[11] and other Australian Auditing Standards, in effect for an audit of a financial report, or a complete set of financial statements, for periods commencing on or after 1 January 2010, that require communication of specific matters with those charged with governance. The list is not a substitute for considering the requirements and related application and other explanatory material in the Australian Auditing Standards.

- ASQC 1 *Quality Control for Firms that Perform Audits and Reviews of Financial Reports and Other Financial Information, and Other Assurance Engagements* - paragraph 30(a)
- ASA 240 *The Auditor's Responsibilities Relating to Fraud in an Audit of a Financial Report* - paragraphs 21, 38(c)(i) and 40-42
- ASA 250 *Consideration of Laws and Regulations in an Audit of a Financial Report* - paragraphs 14, 19 and 22-24
- ASA 265 *Communicating Deficiencies in Internal Control to Those Charged with Governance and Management* - paragraph 9
- ASA 450 *Evaluation of Misstatements Identified during the Audit* - paragraphs 12-13
- ASA 505 *External Confirmations* - paragraph 9
- ASA 510 *Initial Audit Engagements—Opening Balances* - paragraph 7
- ASA 550 *Related Parties* - paragraph 27
- ASA 560 *Subsequent Events* - paragraphs 7(b)-(c), 10(a), 13(b), 14(a) and 17
- ASA 570 *Going Concern* - paragraph 23
- ASA 600 *Special Considerations—Audits of a Group Financial Report (Including the Work of Component Auditors)* - paragraph 49
- ASA 705 *Modifications to the Opinion in the Independent Auditor's Report* - paragraphs 12, 14, 19(a) and 28
- ASA 706 *Emphasis of Matter Paragraphs and Other Matter Paragraphs in the Independent Auditor's Report* - paragraph 9
- ASA 710 *Comparative Information—Corresponding Figures and Comparative Financial Reports* - paragraph 18
- ASA 720 *The Auditor's Responsibilities Relating to Other Information in Documents Containing an Audited Financial Report* - paragraphs 10, 13 and 16
- ASRE 2410 *Review of a Financial Report by the Independent Auditor of the Entity* - paragraphs 27, 28, 30 and 31

11 See ASQC 1 *Quality Control for Firms that Perform Audits and Reviews of Financial Reports and Other Financial Information, and Other Assurance Engagements.*

Appendix 2

(Ref: Para. 16 (a) and A17)

Qualitative Aspects of Accounting Practices

The communication required by paragraph 16(a), and discussed in paragraph A17 may include such matters as:

Accounting Policies

- The appropriateness of the accounting policies to the particular circumstances of the entity, having regard to the need to balance the cost of providing information with the likely benefit to users of the entity's financial report. Where acceptable alternative accounting policies exist, the communication may include identification of the financial report items that are affected by the choice of significant accounting policies as well as information on accounting policies used by similar entities.
- The initial selection of, and changes in significant accounting policies, including the application of new accounting pronouncements. The communication may include: the effect of the timing and method of adoption of a change in accounting policy on the current and future earnings of the entity; and the timing of a change in accounting policies in relation to expected new accounting pronouncements.
- The effect of significant accounting policies in controversial or emerging areas (or those unique to an industry, particularly when there is a lack of authoritative guidance or consensus).
- The effect of the timing of transactions in relation to the period in which they are recorded.

Accounting Estimates

- For items for which estimates are significant, issues discussed in ASA 540,[12] including, for example:
  - Management's identification of accounting estimates.
  - Management's process for making accounting estimates.
  - Risks of material misstatement.
  - Indicators of possible management bias.
  - Disclosure of estimation uncertainty in the financial report.

Financial Report Disclosures

- The issues involved, and related judgements made, in formulating particularly sensitive financial report disclosures (for example, disclosures related to revenue recognition, remuneration, going concern, subsequent events, and contingency issues).
- The overall neutrality, consistency, and clarity of the disclosures in the financial report

Related Matters

- The potential effect on the financial report of significant risks, exposures and uncertainties, such as pending litigation, that are disclosed in the financial report.
- The extent to which the financial report is affected by unusual transactions, including non-recurring amounts recognised during the period, and the extent to which such transactions are separately disclosed in the financial report.
- The factors affecting asset and liability carrying values, including the entity's bases for determining useful lives assigned to tangible and intangible assets. The communication may explain how factors affecting carrying values were selected and how alternative selections would have affected the financial report.
- The selective correction of misstatements, for example, correcting misstatements with the effect of increasing reported earnings, but not those that have the effect of decreasing reported earnings.

12 See ASA 540 *Auditing Accounting Estimates, Including Fair Value Accounting Estimates, and Related Disclosures.*

ASA

ASA 265
Communicating Deficiencies in Internal Control to Those Charged with Governance and Management

(Issued October 2009)

Issued by the Auditing and Assurance Standards Board.

Note from the Institute of Chartered Accountants Australia

This note, prepared by the technical editor, is not part of ASA 265.

Historical development

October 2009: ASA 265 issued as part of the AUASB's Clarity Project. ASA 265 deals with the auditor's reponsibility to communicate deficiencies in internal control to management or those charged with governance. Previously this topic was dealt with as part of ASA 260 'Communication of Audit Matters with Those Charged with Governance'. It is based on the international Standard ISA 265 of the same name.

Contents

Preface

Reasons for Issuing Auditing Standard ASA 265 *Communicating Deficiencies in Internal Control to Those Charged with Governance and Management*

The Auditing and Assurance Standards Board (AUASB) issues Auditing Standard ASA 265 *Communicating Deficiencies in Internal Control to Those Charged with Governance and Management* pursuant to the requirements of the legislative provisions and the Strategic Direction explained below.

The AUASB is an independent statutory board of the Australian Government established under section 227A of the *Australian Securities and Investments Commission Act 2001*, as amended (ASIC Act). Under section 336 of the *Corporations Act 2001*, the AUASB may make Australian Auditing Standards for the purposes of the corporations legislation. These Auditing Standards are legislative instruments under the *Legislative Instruments Act 2003*.

Under the Strategic Direction given to the AUASB by the Financial Reporting Council (FRC), the AUASB is required to have regard to any programme initiated by the International Auditing and Assurance Standards Board (IAASB) for the revision and enhancement of the International Standards on Auditing (ISAs) and to make appropriate consequential amendments to the Australian Auditing Standards. Accordingly, the AUASB has decided to revise and redraft the Australian Auditing Standards using the equivalent redrafted ISAs.

Main Features

This Auditing Standard establishes requirements and provides application and other explanatory material regarding the auditor's responsibility to communicate appropriately to those charged with governance and management deficiencies in internal control that the auditor has identified in an audit of a financial report.

This Auditing Standard requires the auditor to:

(a) determine if, on the basis of the work performed, the auditor has identified any deficiencies in internal control;

(b) assess whether identified deficiencies in internal control, individually or in combination, constitute significant deficiencies;

(c) communicate, in writing, all significant deficiencies in internal control and their potential effects to those charged with governance, and where appropriate management;

(d) communicate to management other identified deficiencies in internal control that the auditor considers to be of sufficient importance to merit management's attention; and

(e) explain to those charged with governance, and where appropriate management, that any deficiencies identified and communicated have been identified through the process of auditing the financial report, which does not ordinarily include expressing an opinion on the effectiveness of internal control.

Authority Statement

The Auditing and Assurance Standards Board (AUASB) makes this Auditing Standard ASA 265 *Communicating Deficiencies in Internal Control to Those Charged with Governance and Management* pursuant to section 227B of the *Australian Securities and Investments Commission Act 2001* and section 336 of the *Corporations Act 2001*.

This Auditing Standard is to be read in conjunction with ASA 101 *Preamble to Australian Auditing Standards*, which sets out the intentions of the AUASB on how the Australian Auditing Standards, operative for financial reporting periods commencing on or after 1 January 2010, are to be understood, interpreted and applied. This Auditing Standard is to be read also in conjunction with ASA 200 *Overall Objectives of the Independent Auditor and the Conduct of an Audit in Accordance with Australian Auditing Standards*.

Dated: 27 October 2009

M H Kelsall
Chairman - AUASB

Auditing Standard ASA 265

Communicating Deficiencies in Internal Control to Those Charged with Governance and Management

Application

Aus 0.1 This Auditing Standard applies to:

(a) an audit of a financial report for a financial year, or an audit of a financial report for a half-year, in accordance with the *Corporations Act 2001*; and

(b) an audit of a financial report, or a complete set of financial statements, for any other purpose.

Aus 0.2 This Auditing Standard also applies, as appropriate, to an audit of other historical financial information.

Operative Date

Aus 0.3 This Auditing Standard is operative for financial reporting periods commencing on or after 1 January 2010.

Introduction

Scope of this Auditing Standard

1. This Auditing Standard deals with the auditor's responsibility to communicate appropriately to those charged with governance and management deficiencies in internal control[1] that the auditor has identified in an audit of a financial report. This Auditing Standard does not impose additional responsibilities on the auditor regarding obtaining an understanding of internal control and designing and performing tests of controls over and above the requirements of ASA 315 and ASA 330.[2] ASA 260[3] establishes further requirements and provides guidance regarding the auditor's responsibility to communicate with those charged with governance in relation to the audit.

1 See ASA 315 *Identifying and Assessing the Risks of Material Misstatement through Understanding the Entity and Its Environment*, paragraphs 4 and 12.

2 See ASA 330 *The Auditor's Responses to Assessed Risks*.

3 See ASA 260 *Communication with Those Charged with Governance*.

2. The auditor is required to obtain an understanding of internal control relevant to the audit when identifying and assessing the risks of material misstatement.[4] In making those risk assessments, the auditor considers internal control in order to design audit procedures that are appropriate in the circumstances, but not for the purpose of expressing an opinion on the effectiveness of internal control. The auditor may identify deficiencies in internal control not only during this risk assessment process but also at any other stage of the audit. This Auditing Standard specifies which identified deficiencies the auditor is required to communicate to those charged with governance and management.

3. Nothing in this Auditing Standard precludes the auditor from communicating to those charged with governance and management other internal control matters that the auditor has identified during the audit.

Effective Date

4. [Deleted by the AUASB. Refer Aus 0.3]

Objective

5. The objective of the auditor is to communicate appropriately to those charged with governance and management, deficiencies in internal control that the auditor has identified during the audit and that, in the auditor's professional judgement, are of sufficient importance to merit their respective attentions.

Definitions

6. For purposes of the Australian Auditing Standards, the following terms have the meanings attributed below:
   (a) Deficiency in internal control means:
      (i) A control is designed, implemented or operated in such a way that it is unable to prevent, or detect and correct, misstatements in the financial report on a timely basis; or
      (ii) A control necessary to prevent, or detect and correct, misstatements in the financial report on a timely basis is missing.
   (b) Significant deficiency in internal control means a deficiency or combination of deficiencies in internal control that, in the auditor's professional judgement, is of sufficient importance to merit the attention of those charged with governance. (Ref: Para. A5)

Requirements

7. The auditor shall determine whether, on the basis of the audit work performed, the auditor has identified one or more deficiencies in internal control. (Ref: Para. A1-A4)

8. If the auditor has identified one or more deficiencies in internal control, the auditor shall determine, on the basis of the audit work performed, whether, individually or in combination, they constitute significant deficiencies. (Ref: Para. A5-A11)

9. The auditor shall communicate in writing significant deficiencies in internal control identified during the audit to those charged with governance on a timely basis. (Ref: Para. A12-A18, A27)

10. The auditor shall also communicate to management at an appropriate level of responsibility on a timely basis: (Ref: Para. A19, A27)
   (a) In writing, significant deficiencies in internal control that the auditor has communicated or intends to communicate to those charged with governance, unless it would be inappropriate to communicate directly to management in the circumstances; and (Ref: Para. A14, A20-A21)
   (b) Other deficiencies in internal control identified during the audit that have not been communicated to management by other parties and that, in the auditor's

4 See ASA 315, paragraph 12. Paragraphs A60-A65 provide guidance on controls relevant to the audit.

professional judgement, are of sufficient importance to merit management's attention. (Ref: Para. A22-A26)

11. The auditor shall include in the written communication of significant deficiencies in internal control:

(a) A description of the deficiencies and an explanation of their potential effects; and (Ref: Para. A28)

(b) Sufficient information to enable those charged with governance and management to understand the context of the communication. In particular, the auditor shall explain that: (Ref: Para. A29-A30)

(i) The purpose of the audit was for the auditor to express an opinion on the financial report;

(ii) The audit included consideration of internal control relevant to the preparation of the financial report in order to design audit procedures that are appropriate in the circumstances, but not for the purpose of expressing an opinion on the effectiveness of internal control; or

Aus 11.1 In circumstances when the auditor has a responsibility to express an opinion on the effectiveness of internal control in conjunction with the audit of the financial report, the auditor shall omit the phrase that the auditor's consideration of internal control is not for the purpose of expressing an opinion on the effectiveness of internal control; and

(iii) The matters being reported are limited to those deficiencies that the auditor has identified during the audit and that the auditor has concluded are of sufficient importance to merit being reported to those charged with governance.

❖ ❖ ❖

Application and Other Explanatory Material

Determination of Whether Deficiencies in Internal Control Have Been Identified (Ref: Para. 7)

A1. In determining whether the auditor has identified one or more deficiencies in internal control, the auditor may discuss the relevant facts and circumstances of the auditor's findings with the appropriate level of management. This discussion provides an opportunity for the auditor to alert management on a timely basis to the existence of deficiencies of which management may not have been previously aware. The level of management with whom it is appropriate to discuss the findings is one that is familiar with the internal control area concerned and that has the authority to take remedial action on any identified deficiencies in internal control. In some circumstances, it may not be appropriate for the auditor to discuss the auditor's findings directly with management, for example, if the findings appear to call management's integrity or competence into question (see paragraph A20).

A2. In discussing the facts and circumstances of the auditor's findings with management, the auditor may obtain other relevant information for further consideration, such as:

- Management's understanding of the actual or suspected causes of the deficiencies.
- Exceptions arising from the deficiencies that management may have noted, for example, misstatements that were not prevented by the relevant information technology (IT) controls.
- A preliminary indication from management of its response to the findings.

Considerations Specific to Smaller Entities

A3. While the concepts underlying control activities in smaller entities are likely to be similar to those in larger entities, the formality with which they operate will vary. Further, smaller entities may find that certain types of control activities are not necessary because of controls applied by management. For example, management's sole authority for granting credit to customers and approving significant purchases can provide effective control over important account balances and transactions, lessening or removing the need for more detailed control activities.

A4. Also, smaller entities often have fewer employees which may limit the extent to which segregation of duties is practicable. However, in a small owner-managed entity, the owner-manager may be able to exercise more effective oversight than in a larger entity. This higher level of management oversight needs to be balanced against the greater potential for management override of controls.

Significant Deficiencies in Internal Control (Ref: Para. 6(b), 8)

A5. The significance of a deficiency or a combination of deficiencies in internal control depends not only on whether a misstatement has actually occurred, but also on the likelihood that a misstatement could occur and the potential magnitude of the misstatement. Significant deficiencies may therefore exist even though the auditor has not identified misstatements during the audit.

A6. Examples of matters that the auditor may consider in determining whether a deficiency or combination of deficiencies in internal control constitutes a significant deficiency include:

- The likelihood of the deficiencies leading to material misstatements in the financial report in the future.
- The susceptibility to loss or fraud of the related asset or liability.
- The subjectivity and complexity of determining estimated amounts, such as fair value accounting estimates.
- The financial report amounts exposed to the deficiencies.
- The volume of activity that has occurred or could occur in the account balance or class of transactions exposed to the deficiency or deficiencies.
- The importance of the controls to the financial reporting process; for example:
    - General monitoring controls (such as oversight of management).
    - Controls over the prevention and detection of fraud.
    - Controls over the selection and application of significant accounting policies.
    - Controls over significant transactions with related parties.
    - Controls over significant transactions outside the entity's normal course of business.
    - Controls over the period-end financial reporting process (such as controls over non-recurring journal entries).
- The cause and frequency of the exceptions detected as a result of the deficiencies in the controls.
- The interaction of the deficiency with other deficiencies in internal control.

A7. Indicators of significant deficiencies in internal control include, for example:

- Evidence of ineffective aspects of the control environment, such as:
    - Indications that significant transactions in which management is financially interested are not being appropriately scrutinised by those charged with governance.
    - Identification of management fraud, whether or not material, that was not prevented by the entity's internal control.
    - Management's failure to implement appropriate remedial action on significant deficiencies previously communicated.
- Absence of a risk assessment process within the entity where such a process would ordinarily be expected to have been established.
- Evidence of an ineffective entity risk assessment process, such as management's failure to identify a risk of material misstatement that the auditor would expect the entity's risk assessment process to have identified.

- Evidence of an ineffective response to identified significant risks (for example, absence of controls over such a risk).
- Misstatements detected by the auditor's procedures that were not prevented, or detected and corrected, by the entity's internal control.
- Restatement of a previously issued financial report to reflect the correction of a material misstatement due to error or fraud.
- Evidence of management's inability to oversee the preparation of the financial reports.

A8. Controls may be designed to operate individually or in combination to effectively prevent, or detect and correct, misstatements.[5] For example, controls over accounts receivable may consist of both automated and manual controls designed to operate together to prevent, or detect and correct, misstatements in the account balance. A deficiency in internal control on its own may not be sufficiently important to constitute a significant deficiency. However, a combination of deficiencies affecting the same account balance or disclosure, relevant assertion, or component of internal control may increase the risks of misstatement to such an extent as to give rise to a significant deficiency.

A9. Law or regulation in some jurisdictions may establish a requirement (particularly for audits of listed entities) for the auditor to communicate to those charged with governance or to other relevant parties (such as regulators) one or more specific types of deficiency in internal control that the auditor has identified during the audit. Where law or regulation has established specific terms and definitions for these types of deficiency and requires the auditor to use these terms and definitions for the purpose of the communication, the auditor uses such terms and definitions when communicating in accordance with the legal or regulatory requirement.

A10. Where the jurisdiction has established specific terms for the types of deficiency in internal control to be communicated but has not defined such terms, it may be necessary for the auditor to use judgement to determine the matters to be communicated further to the legal or regulatory requirement. In doing so, the auditor may consider it appropriate to have regard to the requirements and guidance in this Auditing Standard. For example, if the purpose of the legal or regulatory requirement is to bring to the attention of those charged with governance certain internal control matters of which they should be aware, it may be appropriate to regard such matters as being generally equivalent to the significant deficiencies required by this Auditing Standard to be communicated to those charged with governance.

A11. The requirements of this Auditing Standard remain applicable notwithstanding that law or regulation may require the auditor to use specific terms or definitions.

Communication of Deficiencies in Internal Control

Communication of Significant Deficiencies in Internal Control to Those Charged with Governance (Ref: Para. 9)

A12. Communicating significant deficiencies in writing to those charged with governance reflects the importance of these matters, and assists those charged with governance in fulfilling their oversight responsibilities. ASA 260 establishes relevant considerations regarding communication with those charged with governance when all of them are involved in managing the entity.[6]

A13. In determining when to issue the written communication, the auditor may consider whether receipt of such communication would be an important factor in enabling those charged with governance to discharge their oversight responsibilities. In addition, for listed entities in certain jurisdictions, those charged with governance may need to receive the auditor's written communication before the date of approval of the financial report in order to discharge specific responsibilities in relation to internal control for regulatory or other purposes. For other entities, the auditor may issue the written communication at a later date. Nevertheless, in the latter case, as the auditor's written communication

5 See ASA 315, paragraph A66.

6 See ASA 260, paragraph 13.

of significant deficiencies forms part of the final audit file, the written communication is subject to the overriding requirement[7] for the auditor to complete the assembly of the final audit file on a timely basis. ASA 230 states that an appropriate time limit within which to complete the assembly of the final audit file is ordinarily not more than 60 days after the date of the auditor's report.[8]

A14. Regardless of the timing of the written communication of significant deficiencies, the auditor may communicate these orally in the first instance to management and, when appropriate, to those charged with governance to assist them in taking timely remedial action to minimise the risks of material misstatement. Doing so, however, does not relieve the auditor of the responsibility to communicate the significant deficiencies in writing, as this Auditing Standard requires.

A15. The level of detail at which to communicate significant deficiencies is a matter of the auditor's professional judgement in the circumstances. Factors that the auditor may consider in determining an appropriate level of detail for the communication include, for example:

- The nature of the entity. For instance, the communication required for a public interest entity may be different from that for a non-public interest entity.
- The size and complexity of the entity. For instance, the communication required for a complex entity may be different from that for an entity operating a simple business.
- The nature of significant deficiencies that the auditor has identified.
- The entity's governance composition. For instance, more detail may be needed if those charged with governance include members who do not have significant experience in the entity's industry or in the affected areas.
- Legal or regulatory requirements regarding the communication of specific types of deficiency in internal control.

A16. Management and those charged with governance may already be aware of significant deficiencies that the auditor has identified during the audit and may have chosen not to remedy them because of cost or other considerations. The responsibility for evaluating the costs and benefits of implementing remedial action rests with management and those charged with governance. Accordingly, the requirement in paragraph 9 applies regardless of cost or other considerations that management and those charged with governance may consider relevant in determining whether to remedy such deficiencies.

A17. The fact that the auditor communicated a significant deficiency to those charged with governance and management in a previous audit does not eliminate the need for the auditor to repeat the communication if remedial action has not yet been taken. If a previously communicated significant deficiency remains, the current year's communication may repeat the description from the previous communication, or simply reference the previous communication. The auditor may ask management or, where appropriate, those charged with governance, why the significant deficiency has not yet been remedied. A failure to act, in the absence of a rational explanation, may in itself represent a significant deficiency.

Considerations Specific to Smaller Entities

A18. In the case of audits of smaller entities, the auditor may communicate in a less structured manner with those charged with governance than in the case of larger entities.

Communication of Deficiencies in Internal Control to Management (Ref: Para. 10)

A19. Ordinarily, the appropriate level of management is the one that has responsibility and authority to evaluate the deficiencies in internal control and to take the necessary remedial action. For significant deficiencies, the appropriate level is likely to be the chief executive officer or chief financial officer (or equivalent) as these matters are also required to be communicated to those charged with governance. For other deficiencies in internal control,

7 See ASA 230 *Audit Documentation*, paragraph 14.

8 See ASA 230, paragraph A21.

the appropriate level may be operational management with more direct involvement in the control areas affected and with the authority to take appropriate remedial action.

Communication of Significant Deficiencies in Internal Control to Management
(Ref: Para. 10(a))

A20. Certain identified significant deficiencies in internal control may call into question the integrity or competence of management. For example, there may be evidence of fraud or intentional non-compliance with laws and regulations by management, or management may exhibit an inability to oversee the preparation of an adequate financial report that may raise doubt about management's competence. Accordingly, it may not be appropriate to communicate such deficiencies directly to management.

A21. ASA 250 establishes requirements and provides guidance on the reporting of identified or suspected non-compliance with laws and regulations, including when those charged with governance are themselves involved in such non-compliance.[9] ASA 240 establishes requirements and provides guidance regarding communication to those charged with governance when the auditor has identified fraud or suspected fraud involving management.[10]

Communication of Other Deficiencies in Internal Control to Management
(Ref: Para. 10(b))

A22. During the audit, the auditor may identify other deficiencies in internal control that are not significant deficiencies but that may be of sufficient importance to merit management's attention. The determination as to which other deficiencies in internal control merit management's attention is a matter of professional judgement in the circumstances, taking into account the likelihood and potential magnitude of misstatements that may arise in the financial report as a result of those deficiencies.

A23. The communication of other deficiencies in internal control that merit management's attention need not be in writing but may be oral. Where the auditor has discussed the facts and circumstances of the auditor's findings with management, the auditor may consider an oral communication of the other deficiencies to have been made to management at the time of these discussions. Accordingly, a formal communication need not be made subsequently.

A24. If the auditor has communicated deficiencies in internal control other than significant deficiencies to management in a prior period and management has chosen not to remedy them for cost or other reasons, the auditor need not repeat the communication in the current period. The auditor is also not required to repeat information about such deficiencies if it has been previously communicated to management by other parties, such as internal auditors or regulators. It may, however, be appropriate for the auditor to re-communicate these other deficiencies if there has been a change of management, or if new information has come to the auditor's attention that alters the prior understanding of the auditor and management regarding the deficiencies. Nevertheless, the failure of management to remedy other deficiencies in internal control that were previously communicated may become a significant deficiency requiring communication with those charged with governance. Whether this is the case depends on the auditor's professional judgement in the circumstances.

A25. In some circumstances, those charged with governance may wish to be made aware of the details of other deficiencies in internal control the auditor has communicated to management, or be briefly informed of the nature of the other deficiencies. Alternatively, the auditor may consider it appropriate to inform those charged with governance of the communication of the other deficiencies to management. In either case, the auditor may report orally or in writing to those charged with governance as appropriate.

A26. ASA 260 establishes relevant considerations regarding communication with those charged with governance when all of them are involved in managing the entity.[11]

---

9 See ASA 250 *Consideration of Laws and Regulations in an Audit of a Financial Report*, paragraphs 22-28.

10 See ASA 240 *The Auditor's Responsibilities Relating to Fraud in an Audit of a Financial Report*, paragraph 41.

11 See ASA 260, paragraph 13.

Considerations Specific to Public Sector Entities (Ref: Para. 9-10)

A27. Public sector auditors may have additional responsibilities to communicate deficiencies in internal control that the auditor has identified during the audit, in ways, at a level of detail and to parties not envisaged in this Auditing Standard. For example, significant deficiencies may have to be communicated to the legislature or other governing body. Law, regulation or other authority may also mandate that public sector auditors report deficiencies in internal control, irrespective of the significance of the potential effects of those deficiencies. Further, legislation may require public sector auditors to report on broader internal control-related matters than the deficiencies in internal control required to be communicated by this Auditing Standard, for example, controls related to compliance with legislative authorities, regulations, or provisions of contracts or grant agreements.

Content of Written Communication of Significant Deficiencies in Internal Control (Ref: Para. 11)

A28. In explaining the potential effects of the significant deficiencies, the auditor need not quantify those effects. The significant deficiencies may be grouped together for reporting purposes where it is appropriate to do so. The auditor may also include in the written communication suggestions for remedial action on the deficiencies, management's actual or proposed responses, and a statement as to whether or not the auditor has undertaken any steps to verify whether management's responses have been implemented.

A29. The auditor may consider it appropriate to include the following information as additional context for the communication:

- An indication that if the auditor had performed more extensive procedures on internal control, the auditor might have identified more deficiencies to be reported, or concluded that some of the reported deficiencies need not, in fact, have been reported.
- An indication that such communication has been provided for the purposes of those charged with governance, and that it may not be suitable for other purposes.

A30. Law or regulation may require the auditor or management to furnish a copy of the auditor's written communication on significant deficiencies to appropriate regulatory authorities. Where this is the case, the auditor's written communication may identify such regulatory authorities.

❖ ❖ ❖

Conformity with International Standards on Auditing

This Auditing Standard conforms with International Standard on Auditing ISA 265 *Communicating Deficiencies in Internal Control to Those Charged with Governance and Management*, issued by the International Auditing and Assurance Standards Board (IAASB), an independent standard-setting board of the International Federation of Accountants (IFAC).

Paragraphs that have been added to this Auditing Standard (and do not appear in the text of the equivalent ISA) are identified with the prefix "Aus".

Compliance with this Auditing Standard enables compliance with ISA 265.

ASA 300

Planning an Audit of a Financial Report

(Reissued October 2009: amended and compiled June 2011)

Issued by the Auditing and Assurance Standards Board.

Note from the Institute of Chartered Accountants Australia

This note, prepared by the technical editor, is not part of ASA 300.

Historical development

January 1983: Statement of Auditing Practice AUP 10 'Planning' issued, effective from date of issue. The AuSB did not issue an exposure draft on this topic; however, as noted in para. 14 of the 'Foreword to Statements of Auditing Standards and Statements of Auditing Practice', the AuSB determined that unless noted to the contrary an exposure draft issued by the International Auditing Practice Committee of the International Federation of Accountants is to be regarded as an Australian exposure draft. Such an exposure draft, IAPC ED 4, was issued in February 1980 and was distributed in Australia to subscribers to The Institute of Chartered Accountants in Australia's IASC International Accounting Standards/IFAC Guidelines Handbook and by the Australian Society of Accountants with a request for comments. The statement was based on IAG 4, which was issued in February 1981.

December 1993: ED 53 'Codification and Revision of Auditing Pronouncements: AUS 302 Planning (AUP 10)' issued by the AuSB.

June 1994: The International Auditing Practices Committee (IAPC) of the International Federation of Accountants (IFAC) approved the issuance of a codified set of International Standards of Auditing (ISAs). The relevant international pronouncement was ISA 300 'Planning'.

October 1995: Australian Auditing Standards and Auditing Guidance Statements released. The status of these was explained in APS 1.1 'Conformity With Auditing Standards'. These Standards became operative for the first reporting period commencing on or after 1 July 1996 and later reporting periods, although earlier application was encouraged. AUP 10 'Planning' replaced by AUS 302 'Planning'.

April 2006: ASA 300 was issued as a legally enforceable Standard to replace AUS 302. It is based on ISA 300 'Planning an Audit of Financial Statements'.

October 2009: ASA 300 was reissued as part of the AUASB's Clarity Project. It is based on the redrafted ISA 300 'Planning an Audit of Financial Statements'.

June 2011: ASA 300 updated for editorial amendments contained in ASA 2011-1 'Amendments to Australian Auditing Standards'.

Content

Compilation Details

Auditing Standard ASA 300 *Planning an Audit of a Financial Report* as Amended

This compilation takes into account amendments made up to and including 27 June 2011 and was prepared on 27 June 2011 by the Auditing and Assurance Standards Board (AUASB).

This compilation is not a separate Auditing Standard made by the AUASB. Instead, it is a representation of ASA 300 (October 2009) as amended by another Auditing Standard which is listed in the Table below.

Table of Standards

Standard	Date made	Operative date
ASA 300	27 October 2009	1 January 2010
ASA 2011-1	27 June 2011	1 July 2011

Table of Amendments

Paragraph affected	How affected	By … [paragraph]
Appendix 1 Last sub-heading	Amended	ASA 2011-1 [27]

Preface

[Preface extracted from the original Auditing Standard issued 27 October 2009]

Reasons for Issuing Auditing Standard ASA 300 *Planning an Audit of a Financial Report*

The Auditing and Assurance Standards Board (AUASB) issues Auditing Standard ASA 300 *Planning an Audit of a Financial Report* pursuant to the requirements of the legislative provisions and the Strategic Direction explained below.

The AUASB is an independent statutory board of the Australian Government established under section 227A of the *Australian Securities and Investments Commission Act 2001*, as amended (ASIC Act). Under section 336 of the *Corporations Act 2001*, the AUASB may make Auditing Standards for the purposes of the corporations legislation. These Auditing Standards are legislative instruments under the *Legislative Instruments Act 2003*.

Under the Strategic Direction given to the AUASB by the Financial Reporting Council (FRC), the AUASB is required to have regard to any programme initiated by the International Auditing and Assurance Standards Board (IAASB) for the revision and enhancement of the International Standards on Auditing (ISAs) and to make appropriate consequential amendments to the Australian Auditing Standards. Accordingly, the AUASB has decided to revise and redraft the Australian Auditing Standards using the equivalent redrafted ISAs.

Main Features

This Auditing Standard establishes requirements and provides application and other explanatory material regarding the auditor's responsibility to plan an audit of a financial report.

This Auditing Standard:

(a) requires the auditor to plan the audit so that it will be performed in an effective manner;

(b) requires the involvement of key engagement team members in the planning of the audit;

(c) describes the preliminary engagement activities to be performed by the auditor at the beginning of the current audit engagement;

(d) requires the auditor to establish an overall audit strategy and develop an audit plan; and

(e) describes the required audit documentation.

Authority Statement

Auditing Standard ASA 300 *Planning an Audit of a Financial Report* (as amended at 27 June 2011) is set out in paragraphs 1 to A20 and Appendix 1.

This Auditing Standard is to be read in conjunction with ASA 101 *Preamble to Australian Auditing Standards*, which sets out the intentions of the AUASB on how the Australian Auditing Standards, operative for financial reporting periods commencing on or after 1 January 2010, are to be understood, interpreted and applied. This Auditing Standard is to be read also in conjunction with ASA 200 *Overall Objectives of the Independent Auditor and the Conduct of an Audit in Accordance with Australian Auditing Standards*.

Dated: 27 June 2011

M H Kelsall
Chairman - AUASB

Auditing Standard ASA 300

The Auditing and Assurance Standards Board (AUASB) made Auditing Standard ASA 300 *Planning an Audit of a Financial Report*, pursuant to section 227B of the *Australian Securities and Investments Commission Act 2001* and section 336 of the *Corporations Act 2001*, on 27 October 2009.

This compiled version of ASA 300 incorporates subsequent amendments contained in another Auditing Standard made by the AUASB up to and including 27 June 2011 (see Compilation Details).

Auditing Standard ASA 300
Planning an Audit of a Financial Report

Application

Aus 0.1 This Auditing Standard applies to:

(a) an audit of a financial report for a financial year, or an audit of a financial report for a half-year, in accordance with the *Corporations Act 2001*; and

(b) an audit of a financial report, or a complete set of financial statements, for any other purpose.

Aus 0.2 This Auditing Standard also applies, as appropriate, to an audit of other historical financial information.

ASA

Operative Date

Aus 0.3 This Auditing Standard is operative for financial reporting periods commencing on or after 1 January 2010.

[Note: For operative dates of paragraphs changed or added by an amending Standard, see Compilation Details.]

Introduction

Scope of this Auditing Standard

1. This Auditing Standard deals with the auditor's responsibility to plan an audit of a financial report. This Auditing Standard is written in the context of recurring audits. Additional considerations in an initial audit engagement are separately identified.

The Role and Timing of Planning

2. Planning an audit involves establishing the overall audit strategy for the engagement and developing an audit plan. Adequate planning benefits the audit of a financial report in several ways, including the following: (Ref: Para. A1-A3)
   - Helping the auditor to devote appropriate attention to important areas of the audit.
   - Helping the auditor identify and resolve potential problems on a timely basis.
   - Helping the auditor properly organise and manage the audit engagement so that it is performed in an effective and efficient manner.
   - Assisting in the selection of engagement team members with appropriate levels of capabilities and competence to respond to anticipated risks, and the proper assignment of work to them.
   - Facilitating the direction and supervision of engagement team members and the review of their work.
   - Assisting, where applicable, in coordination of work done by auditors of components and experts.

Effective Date

3. [Deleted by the AUASB. Refer Aus 0.3]

Objective

4. The objective of the auditor is to plan the audit so that it will be performed in an effective manner.

Requirements

Involvement of Key Engagement Team Members

5. The engagement partner and other key members of the engagement team shall be involved in planning the audit, including planning and participating in the discussion among engagement team members. (Ref: Para. A4)

Preliminary Engagement Activities

6. The auditor shall undertake the following activities at the beginning of the current audit engagement:
   (a) Performing procedures required by ASA 220 regarding the continuance of the client relationship and the specific audit engagement;[1]
   (b) Evaluating compliance with relevant ethical requirements, including independence, in accordance with ASA 220;[2] and
   (c) Establishing an understanding of the terms of the engagement, as required by ASA 210.[3] (Ref: Para. A5-A7)

Planning Activities

7. The auditor shall establish an overall audit strategy that sets the scope, timing and direction of the audit, and that guides the development of the audit plan.
8. In establishing the overall audit strategy, the auditor shall:
   (a) Identify the characteristics of the engagement that define its scope;
   (b) Ascertain the reporting objectives of the engagement to plan the timing of the audit and the nature of the communications required;
   (c) Consider the factors that, in the auditor's professional judgement, are significant in directing the engagement team's efforts;
   (d) Consider the results of preliminary engagement activities and, where applicable, whether knowledge gained on other engagements performed by the engagement partner for the entity is relevant; and
   (e) Ascertain the nature, timing and extent of resources necessary to perform the engagement. (Ref: Para. A8-A11)
9. The auditor shall develop an audit plan that shall include a description of:
   (a) The nature, timing and extent of planned risk assessment procedures, as determined under ASA 315.[4]
   (b) The nature, timing and extent of planned further audit procedures at the assertion level, as determined under ASA 330.[5]
   (c) Other planned audit procedures that are required to be carried out so that the engagement complies with the Australian Auditing Standards. (Ref: Para. A12)
10. The auditor shall update and change the overall audit strategy and the audit plan as necessary during the course of the audit. (Ref: Para. A13)
11. The auditor shall plan the nature, timing and extent of direction and supervision of engagement team members and the review of their work. (Ref: Para. A14-A15)

Documentation

12. The auditor shall include in the audit documentation:[6]
   (a) The overall audit strategy;
   (b) The audit plan; and
   (c) Any significant changes made during the audit engagement to the overall audit strategy or the audit plan, and the reasons for such changes. (Ref: Para. A16-A19)

---

1 See ASA 220 *Quality Control for an Audit of a Financial Report and Other Historical Financial Information*, paragraphs 12-13.

2 See ASA 220, paragraphs 9-11.

3 See ASA 210 *Agreeing the Terms of Audit Engagements*, paragraphs 9-13.

4 See ASA 315 *Identifying and Assessing the Risks of Material Misstatement through Understanding the Entity and Its Environment*.

5 See ASA 330 *The Auditor's Responses to Assessed Risks*.

6 See ASA 230 *Audit Documentation*, paragraphs 8-11 and paragraph A6.

Additional Considerations in Initial Audit Engagements

13. The auditor shall undertake the following activities prior to starting an initial audit:
    (a) Performing procedures required by ASA 220 regarding the acceptance of the client relationship and the specific audit engagement;[7] and
    (b) Communicating with the predecessor auditor, where there has been a change of auditors, in compliance with relevant ethical requirements. (Ref: Para. A20)

❖ ❖ ❖

Application and Other Explanatory Material

The Role and Timing of Planning (Ref: Para. 2)

A1. The nature and extent of planning activities will vary according to the size and complexity of the entity, the key engagement team members' previous experience with the entity, and changes in circumstances that occur during the audit engagement.

A2. Planning is not a discrete phase of an audit, but rather a continual and iterative process that often begins shortly after (or in connection with) the completion of the previous audit and continues until the completion of the current audit engagement. Planning, however, includes consideration of the timing of certain activities and audit procedures that need to be completed prior to the performance of further audit procedures. For example, planning includes the need to consider, prior to the auditor's identification and assessment of the risks of material misstatement, such matters as:

- The analytical procedures to be applied as risk assessment procedures.
- Obtaining a general understanding of the legal and regulatory framework applicable to the entity and how the entity is complying with that framework.
- The determination of materiality.
- The involvement of experts.
- The performance of other risk assessment procedures.

A3. The auditor may decide to discuss elements of planning with the entity's management, or those charged with governance, to facilitate the conduct and management of the audit engagement (for example, to co-ordinate some of the planned audit procedures with the work of the entity's personnel). Although these discussions often occur, the overall audit strategy and the audit plan remain the auditor's responsibility. When discussing matters included in the overall audit strategy or audit plan, care is required in order not to compromise the effectiveness of the audit. For example, discussing the nature and timing of detailed audit procedures with management, or those charged with governance, may compromise the effectiveness of the audit by making the audit procedures too predictable.

Involvement of Key Engagement Team Members (Ref: Para. 5)

A4. The involvement of the engagement partner and other key members of the engagement team in planning the audit draws on their experience and insight, thereby enhancing the effectiveness and efficiency of the planning process.[8]

Preliminary Engagement Activities (Ref: Para. 6)

A5. Performing the preliminary engagement activities specified in paragraph 6 at the beginning of the current audit engagement assists the auditor in identifying and evaluating events or circumstances that may adversely affect the auditor's ability to plan and perform the audit engagement.

---

7 See ASA 220, paragraphs 12-13.

8 ASA 315, paragraph 10, establishes requirements and provides guidance on the engagement team's discussion of the susceptibility of the entity to material misstatements of the financial report. ASA 240 *The Auditor's Responsibilities Relating to Fraud in an Audit of a Financial Report*, paragraph 15, provides guidance on the emphasis given during this discussion to the susceptibility of the entity's financial report to material misstatement due to fraud.

A6. Performing these preliminary engagement activities enables the auditor to plan an audit engagement for which, for example:

- The auditor maintains the necessary independence and ability to perform the engagement.
- There are no issues with management integrity that may affect the auditor's willingness to continue the engagement.
- There is no misunderstanding with the client as to the terms of the engagement.

A7. The auditor's consideration of client continuance and relevant ethical requirements, including independence,* occurs throughout the audit engagement as conditions and changes in circumstances occur. Performing initial procedures on both client continuance and evaluation of relevant ethical requirements (including independence) at the beginning of the current audit engagement means that they are completed prior to the performance of other significant activities for the current audit engagement. For continuing audit engagements, such initial procedures often occur shortly after (or in connection with) the completion of the previous audit.

Planning Activities

The Overall Audit Strategy (Ref: Para. 7-8)

A8. The process of establishing the overall audit strategy assists the auditor to determine, subject to the completion of the auditor's risk assessment procedures, such matters as:

- The resources to deploy for specific audit areas, such as the use of appropriately experienced team members for high risk areas or the involvement of experts on complex matters;
- The amount of resources to allocate to specific audit areas, such as the number of team members assigned to observe the inventory count at material locations, the extent of review of other auditors' work in the case of group audits, or the audit budget in hours to allocate to high risk areas;
- When these resources are to be deployed, such as whether at an interim audit stage or at key cut-off dates; and
- How such resources are managed, directed and supervised, such as when team briefing and debriefing meetings are expected to be held, how engagement partner and manager reviews are expected to take place (for example, on-site or off-site), and whether to complete engagement quality control reviews.

A9. Appendix 1 lists examples of considerations in establishing the overall audit strategy.

A10. Once the overall audit strategy has been established, an audit plan can be developed to address the various matters identified in the overall audit strategy, taking into account the need to achieve the audit objectives through the efficient use of the auditor's resources. The establishment of the overall audit strategy and the detailed audit plan are not necessarily discrete or sequential processes, but are closely inter-related since changes in one may result in consequential changes to the other.

Considerations Specific to Smaller Entities

A11. In audits of small entities, the entire audit may be conducted by a very small audit team. Many audits of small entities involve the engagement partner (who may be a sole practitioner) working with one engagement team member (or without any engagement team members). With a smaller team, co-ordination of, and communication between, team members are easier. Establishing the overall audit strategy for the audit of a small entity need not be a complex or time-consuming exercise; it varies according to the size of the entity, the complexity of the audit, and the size of the engagement team. For example, a brief memorandum prepared at the completion of the previous audit, based on a review of the working papers and highlighting issues identified in the audit just completed, updated in the current period based on discussions with the owner-manager, can serve as the documented audit strategy for the current audit engagement if it covers the matters noted in paragraph 8.

* See ASA 102 *Compliance with Ethical Requirements when Performing Audits, Reviews and Other Assurance Engagements.*

The Audit Plan (Ref: Para. 9)

A12. The audit plan is more detailed than the overall audit strategy in that it includes the nature, timing and extent of audit procedures to be performed by engagement team members. Planning for these audit procedures takes place over the course of the audit as the audit plan for the engagement develops. For example, planning of the auditor's risk assessment procedures occurs early in the audit process. However, planning the nature, timing and extent of specific further audit procedures depends on the outcome of those risk assessment procedures. In addition, the auditor may begin the execution of further audit procedures for some classes of transactions, account balances and disclosures before planning all remaining further audit procedures.

Changes to Planning Decisions during the Course of the Audit (Ref: Para. 10)

A13. As a result of unexpected events, changes in conditions, or the audit evidence obtained from the results of audit procedures, the auditor may need to modify the overall audit strategy and audit plan and thereby the resulting planned nature, timing and extent of further audit procedures, based on the revised consideration of assessed risks. This may be the case when information comes to the auditor's attention that differs significantly from the information available when the auditor planned the audit procedures. For example, audit evidence obtained through the performance of substantive procedures may contradict the audit evidence obtained through tests of controls.

Direction, Supervision and Review (Ref: Para. 11)

A14. The nature, timing and extent of the direction and supervision of engagement team members and review of their work vary depending on many factors, including:

- The size and complexity of the entity.
- The area of the audit.
- The assessed risks of material misstatement (for example, an increase in the assessed risk of material misstatement for a given area of the audit ordinarily requires a corresponding increase in the extent and timeliness of direction and supervision of engagement team members, and a more detailed review of their work).
- The capabilities and competence of the individual team members performing the audit work.

ASA 220 contains further guidance on the direction, supervision and review of audit work.[9]

Considerations Specific to Smaller Entities

A15. If an audit is carried out entirely by the engagement partner, questions of direction and supervision of engagement team members and review of their work do not arise. In such cases, the engagement partner, having personally conducted all aspects of the work, will be aware of all material issues. Forming an objective view on the appropriateness of the judgements made in the course of the audit can present practical problems when the same individual also performs the entire audit. If particularly complex or unusual issues are involved, and the audit is performed by a sole practitioner, it may be desirable to consult with other suitably experienced auditors or the auditor's professional body.

Documentation (Ref: Para. 12)

A16. The documentation of the overall audit strategy is a record of the key decisions considered necessary to properly plan the audit and to communicate significant matters to the engagement team. For example, the auditor may summarise the overall audit strategy in the form of a memorandum that contains key decisions regarding the overall scope, timing and conduct of the audit.

A17. The documentation of the audit plan is a record of the planned nature, timing and extent of risk assessment procedures and further audit procedures at the assertion level in response to the assessed risks. It also serves as a record of the proper planning of the audit procedures that can be reviewed and approved prior to their performance. The auditor may use standard audit programs or audit completion checklists, tailored as needed to reflect the particular engagement circumstances.

9 See ASA 220, paragraphs 15-17.

A18. A record of the significant changes to the overall audit strategy and the audit plan, and resulting changes to the planned nature, timing and extent of audit procedures, explains why the significant changes were made, and the overall strategy and audit plan finally adopted for the audit. It also reflects the appropriate response to the significant changes occurring during the audit.

Considerations Specific to Smaller Entities

A19. As discussed in paragraph A11, a suitable, brief memorandum may serve as the documented strategy for the audit of a smaller entity. For the audit plan, standard audit programs or checklists (see paragraph A17) drawn up on the assumption of few relevant control activities, as is likely to be the case in a smaller entity, may be used provided that they are tailored to the circumstances of the engagement, including the auditor's risk assessments.

Additional Considerations in Initial Audit Engagements (Ref: Para. 13)

A20. The purpose and objective of planning the audit are the same whether the audit is an initial or recurring engagement. However, for an initial audit, the auditor may need to expand the planning activities because the auditor does not ordinarily have the previous experience with the entity that is considered when planning recurring engagements. For an initial audit engagement, additional matters the auditor may consider in establishing the overall audit strategy and audit plan include the following:

- Unless prohibited by law or regulation, arrangements to be made with the predecessor auditor, for example, to review the predecessor auditor's working papers.
- Any major issues (including the application of accounting principles or of auditing and reporting standards) discussed with management in connection with the initial selection as auditor, the communication of these matters to those charged with governance and how these matters affect the overall audit strategy and audit plan.
- The audit procedures necessary to obtain sufficient appropriate audit evidence regarding opening balances.[10]
- Other procedures required by the firm's system of quality control for initial audit engagements (for example, the firm's system of quality control may require the involvement of another partner or senior individual to review the overall audit strategy prior to commencing significant audit procedures or to review reports prior to their issuance).

❖ ❖ ❖

Conformity with International Standards on Auditing

This Auditing Standard conforms with International Standard on Auditing ISA 300 *Planning an Audit of Financial Statements*, issued by the International Auditing and Assurance Standards Board (IAASB), an independent standard-setting board of the International Federation of Accountants (IFAC).

Paragraphs that have been added to this Standard (and do not appear in the text of the equivalent ISA) are identified with the prefix "Aus".

Compliance with this Auditing Standard enables compliance with ISA 300.

10 See ASA 510 *Initial Audit Engagements—Opening Balances.*

Appendix 1
(Ref: Para. 7-8 and A8-A11)

Considerations in Establishing the Overall Audit Strategy

This appendix provides examples of matters the auditor may consider in establishing the overall audit strategy. Many of these matters will also influence the auditor's detailed audit plan. The examples provided cover a broad range of matters applicable to many engagements. While some of the matters referred to below may be required by other Auditing Standards, not all matters are relevant to every audit engagement and the list is not necessarily complete.

Characteristics of the Engagement

- The financial reporting framework on which the financial information to be audited has been prepared, including any need for reconciliations to another financial reporting framework.
- Industry-specific reporting requirements such as reports mandated by industry regulators.
- The expected audit coverage, including the number and locations of components to be included.
- The nature of the control relationships between a parent and its components that determine how the group is to be consolidated.
- The extent to which components are audited by other auditors.
- The nature of the business segments to be audited, including the need for specialised knowledge.
- The reporting currency to be used, including any need for currency translation for the financial information audited.
- The need for a statutory audit of a stand-alone financial report in addition to an audit for consolidation purposes.
- The availability of the work of internal auditors and the extent of the auditor's potential reliance on such work.
- The entity's use of service organisations and how the auditor may obtain evidence concerning the design or operation of controls performed by them.
- The expected use of audit evidence obtained in previous audits, for example, audit evidence related to risk assessment procedures and tests of controls.
- The effect of information technology on the audit procedures, including the availability of data and the expected use of computer-assisted audit techniques.
- The co-ordination of the expected coverage and timing of the audit work with any reviews of interim financial information and the effect on the audit of the information obtained during such reviews.
- The availability of client personnel and data.

Reporting Objectives, Timing of the Audit, and Nature of Communications

- The entity's timetable for reporting, such as at interim and final stages.
- The organisation of meetings with management and those charged with governance to discuss the nature, timing and extent of the audit work.
- The discussion with management and those charged with governance regarding the expected type and timing of reports to be issued and other communications, both written and oral, including the auditor's report, management letters and communications to those charged with governance.
- The discussion with management regarding the expected communications on the status of audit work throughout the engagement.

- Communication with auditors of components regarding the expected types and timing of reports to be issued and other communications in connection with the audit of components.
- The expected nature and timing of communications among engagement team members, including the nature and timing of team meetings and timing of the review of work performed.
- Whether there are any other expected communications with third parties, including any statutory or contractual reporting responsibilities arising from the audit.

Significant Factors, Preliminary Engagement Activities, and Knowledge Gained on Other Engagements

- The determination of materiality in accordance with ASA 320[11] and, where applicable:
  - The determination of materiality for components and communication thereof to component auditors in accordance with ASA 600.[12]
  - The preliminary identification of significant components and material classes of transactions, account balances and disclosures.
- Preliminary identification of areas where there may be a higher risk of material misstatement.
- The impact of the assessed risk of material misstatement at the overall financial report level on direction, supervision and review.
- The manner in which the auditor emphasises to engagement team members the need to maintain a questioning mind and to exercise professional scepticism in gathering and evaluating audit evidence.
- Results of previous audits that involved evaluating the operating effectiveness of internal control, including the nature of identified deficiencies and action taken to address them.
- The discussion of matters that may affect the audit with firm personnel responsible for performing other services to the entity.
- Evidence of management's commitment to the design, implementation and maintenance of sound internal control, including evidence of appropriate documentation of such internal control.
- Volume of transactions, which may determine whether it is more efficient for the auditor to rely on internal control.
- Importance attached to internal control throughout the entity to the successful operation of the business.
- Significant business developments affecting the entity, including changes in information technology and business processes, changes in key management, and acquisitions, mergers and divestments.
- Significant industry developments such as changes in industry regulations and new reporting requirements.
- Significant changes in the financial reporting framework, such as changes in accounting standards.
- Other significant relevant developments, such as changes in the legal environment affecting the entity.

Nature, Timing and Extent of Resources

- The selection of the engagement team (including, where necessary, the engagement quality control reviewer) and the assignment of audit work to the team members, including the assignment of appropriately experienced team members to areas where there may be higher risks of material misstatement.
- Engagement budgeting, including considering the appropriate amount of time to set aside for areas where there may be higher risks of material misstatement.

---

11 See ASA 320 *Materiality in Planning and Performing an Audit.*

12 See ASA 600 *Special Considerations—Audits of a Group Financial Report (Including the Work of Component Auditors)*, paragraphs 21-23 and 40(c).

ASA 315
Identifying and Assessing the Risks of Material Misstatement through Understanding the Entity and Its Environment

(Reissued October 2009: amended and compiled June 2011)

Issued by the Auditing and Assurance Standards Board.

Note from the Institute of Chartered Accountants Australia

This note, prepared by the technical editor, is not part of ASA 315.

Historical development

February 1977: Statement CP 2: 'Internal Audit as it Affects the External Auditor' prepared by the Audit Standards Committee of the Australian Accounting Research Foundation, and issued by The Institute of Chartered Accountants in Australia and the Australian Society of Accountants.

January 1983: Statement of Auditing Practice AUP 12 'Study and Evaluation of the Accounting System and Related Internal Controls in Connection with an Audit' issued, effective from date of issue. International Auditing Practices Committee ED 6 was issued in June 1980 and distributed in Australia to subscribers to The Institute of Chartered Accountants in Australia's IASC International Accounting Standards/IFAC Guidelines Handbook and by the Australian Society of Accountants with a request for comments. Statement based on IAG 6 which was issued in July 1981.

January 1992: The AuSB issued ED 45 'Consideration of the Internal Control Structure and Its Impact on Risk Assessment in a Financial Report Audit'. ED 45 amalgamated the guidance in AUP 12 with that provided in AUP 30 'Inherent and Control Risk Assessment and Their Impact on Substantive Procedures'.

March 1993: AUP 12 revised and reissued. Superseded the previous AUP 12 and also AUP 30. The statement provided guidance to auditors in considering the impact on audit risk of the internal control structure. Internal control structure defined as the plan of the organisation and all the methods and procedures adopted by the management of an entity to assist in achieving management's objectives. The revised AUP 12 required an auditor to obtain an understanding of the internal control structure sufficient to plan the audit.

February 1994: ED 54 'Codification and Revision of Auditing Pronouncements: AUS 402 Risk Assessments and Internal Controls (AUP 12)' issued by the AuASB.

June 1994: The International Auditing Practices Committee (IAPC) of the International Federation of Accountants (IFAC) approved the issuance of a codified set of International Standards of Auditing (ISAs). The relevant international pronouncement was ISA 400 'Risk Assessments and Internal Control'.

October 1995: Australian Auditing Standards and Auditing Guidance Statements released. The status of these was explained in APS 1.1 'Conformity With Auditing Standards'. These Standards became operative for the first reporting period commencing on or after 1 July 1996 and later reporting periods, although earlier application was encouraged. AUP 12 'Consideration of the Internal Control Structure and its Impact on Risk Assessments in a Financial Report Audit' replaced by AUS 402 'Risk Assessments and Internal Controls'.

July 2002: AUS/AGS Omnibus 3 'Miscellaneous Amendments to AUSs and AGSs' issued by the AuASB, operative from the date of issue. AUS 402 reissued by the Board to reflect these amendments.

February 2004: AUS 402 reissued by the AuASB and renamed 'Understanding the Entity and its Environment and Assessing the Risks of Material Misstatements'. It enhances the requirements relating to understanding internal controls and introduces new requirements for assessing material misstatements. It is based on ISA 315 of the same name.

April 2006: ASA 315 was issued as a legally enforceable Standard to replace AUS 402. It is based on ISA 315 of the same name.

October 2009: ASA 315 reissued as part of the AUASB's Clarity Project. Numerous paragraphs have been elevated from guidance to the status of requirements, including a requirement to identify risks throughout the process of obtaining an understanding of the entity and its environment. It is based on the revised ISA 315 of the same name.

June 2011: ASA 315 updated for editorial amendments contained in ASA 2011-1 'Amendments to Australian Auditing Standards'.

June 2011: ASA 315 updated for editorial amendments contained in ASA 2011-1 'Amendments to Australian Auditing Standards'.

March 2012: The IAASB issued changes to ISA 315 consequent upon revisions to ISA 610 'Using the Work of Internal Auditors'. These changes have not yet been adopted in Australia.

Contents

COMPILATION DETAILS

PREFACE

AUTHORITY STATEMENT

Paragraphs

Compilation Details

Auditing Standard ASA 315 *Identifying and Assessing the Risks of Material Misstatement through Understanding the Entity and Its Environment* as Amended

This compilation takes into account amendments made up to and including 27 June 2011 and was prepared on 27 June 2011 by the Auditing and Assurance Standards Board (AUASB).

This compilation is not a separate Auditing Standard made by the AUASB. Instead, it is a representation of ASA 315 (October 2009) as amended by another Auditing Standard which is listed in the Table below.

Table of Standards

Standard	Date made	Operative date
ASA 315	27 October 2009	1 January 2010
ASA 2011-1	27 June 2011	1 July 2011

Table of Amendments

Paragraph affected	How affected	By ... [paragraph]
A26	Amended	ASA 2011-1 [28]
Appendix 1 Para. 3	Amended	ASA 2011-1 [29]
Appendix 1 Sub-heading above Para. 5	Amended	ASA 2011-1 [30]

Preface

[Preface extracted from the original Auditing Standard issued 27 October 2009]

Reasons for Issuing Auditing Standard ASA 315 *Identifying and Assessing the Risks of Material Misstatement through Understanding the Entity and Its Environment*

The Auditing and Assurance Standards Board (AUASB) issues Auditing Standard ASA 315 *Understanding the Entity and Its Environment and Assessing the Risks of Material Misstatement* pursuant to the requirements of the legislative provisions and the Strategic Direction explained below.

The AUASB is an independent statutory board of the Australian Government established under section 227A of the *Australian Securities and Investments Commission Act 2001*, as amended (ASIC Act). Under section 336 of the *Corporations Act 2001*, the AUASB may make Auditing Standards for the purposes of the corporations legislation. These Auditing Standards are legislative instruments under the *Legislative Instruments Act 2003*.

Under the Strategic Direction given to the AUASB by the Financial Reporting Council (FRC), the AUASB is required to have regard to any programme initiated by the International Auditing and Assurance Standards Board (IAASB) for the revision and enhancement of the International Standards on Auditing (ISAs) and to make appropriate consequential amendments to the Australian Auditing Standards. Accordingly, the AUASB has decided to revise and redraft the Australian Auditing Standards using the equivalent redrafted ISAs.

Main Features

This Auditing Standard establishes requirements and provides application and other explanatory material regarding the auditor's responsibility to identify and assess the risks of material misstatement in the financial report, through understanding the entity and its environment, including the entity's internal control.

This Auditing Standard requires the auditor to:

(a) perform risk assessment procedures to obtain an understanding of the entity and its environment, and the entity's internal control relevant to the audit;

(b) discuss with the engagement team, the susceptibility of the entity's financial report to material misstatements, including those due to fraud or error;

(c) obtain an understanding of the entity's internal audit function, where the entity has that function, to determine whether the function has relevance to the audit process;

(d) identify and assess the risk of material misstatement at the financial report and assertion levels;

(e) use professional judgement in determining whether any of the risks identified represent a significant risk;

(f) obtain an understanding of the entity's internal controls relevant to the assessed risk, where the risk of misstatement is significant, or substantive procedures alone do not provide sufficient appropriate audit evidence in respect of an identified risk;

(g) design, implement, and where appropriate revise, their response to the assessed risks of material misstatement; and

(h) follow the documentation requirements.

Authority Statement

Auditing Standard ASA 315 *Identifying and Assessing the Risks of Material Misstatement through Understanding the Entity and Its Environment* (as amended at 27 June 2011) is set out in paragraphs 1 to A134 and Appendices 1 and 2.

This Auditing Standard is to be read in conjunction with ASA 101 *Preamble to Australian Auditing Standards*, which sets out the intentions of the AUASB on how the Australian Auditing Standards, operative for financial reporting periods commencing on or after 1 January 2010, are to be understood, interpreted and applied. This Auditing Standard is to be read also in conjunction with ASA 200 *Overall Objectives of the Independent Auditor and the Conduct of an Audit in Accordance with Australian Auditing Standards.*

Dated: 27 June 2011

M H Kelsall
Chairman - AUASB

Auditing Standard ASA 315

The Auditing and Assurance Standards Board (AUASB) made Auditing Standard ASA 315 *Identifying and Assessing the Risks of Material Misstatement through Understanding the Entity and Its Environment,* pursuant to section 227B of the *Australian Securities and Investments Commission Act 2001* and section 336 of the *Corporations Act 2001*, on 27 October 2009.

This compiled version of ASA 315 incorporates subsequent amendments contained in another Auditing Standard made by the AUASB up to and including 27 June 2011 (see Compilation Details).

Auditing Standard ASA 315

Identifying and Assessing the Risks of Material Misstatement through Understanding the Entity and Its Environment

Application

Aus 0.1 This Auditing Standard applies to:

(a) an audit of a financial report for a financial year, or an audit of a financial report for a half-year, in accordance with the *Corporations Act 2001*; and

(b) an audit of a financial report, or a complete set of financial statements, for any other purpose.

Aus 0.2 This Auditing Standard also applies, as appropriate, to an audit of other historical financial information.

Operative Date

Aus 0.3 This Auditing Standard is operative for financial reporting periods commencing on or after 1 January 2010.

[Note: For operative dates of paragraphs changed or added by an amending Standard, see Compilation Details.]

Introduction

Scope of this Auditing Standard

1. This Auditing Standard deals with the auditor's responsibility to identify and assess the risks of material misstatement in the financial report, through understanding the entity and its environment, including the entity's internal control.

Effective Date

2. [Deleted by the AUASB. Refer Aus 0.3]

Objective

3. The objective of the auditor is to identify and assess the risks of material misstatement, whether due to fraud or error, at the financial report and assertion levels, through understanding the entity and its environment, including the entity's internal control,

thereby providing a basis for designing and implementing responses to the assessed risks of material misstatement.

Definitions

4. For purposes of the Australian Auditing Standards, the following terms have the meanings attributed below:

   (a) Assertions means representations by management and those charged with governance, explicit or otherwise, that are embodied in the financial report, as used by the auditor to consider the different types of potential misstatements that may occur.

   (b) Business risk means a risk resulting from significant conditions, events, circumstances, actions or inactions that could adversely affect an entity's ability to achieve its objectives and execute its strategies, or from the setting of inappropriate objectives and strategies.

   (c) Internal control means the process designed, implemented and maintained by those charged with governance, management and other personnel to provide reasonable assurance about the achievement of an entity's objectives with regard to reliability of financial reporting, effectiveness and efficiency of operations, and compliance with applicable laws and regulations. The term "controls" refers to any aspects of one or more of the components of internal control.

   (d) Risk assessment procedures means the audit procedures performed to obtain an understanding of the entity and its environment, including the entity's internal control, to identify and assess the risks of material misstatement, whether due to fraud or error, at the financial report and assertion levels.

   (e) Significant risk means an identified and assessed risk of material misstatement that, in the auditor's judgement, requires special audit consideration.

Requirements

Risk Assessment Procedures and Related Activities

5. The auditor shall perform risk assessment procedures to provide a basis for the identification and assessment of risks of material misstatement at the financial report and assertion levels. Risk assessment procedures by themselves, however, do not provide sufficient appropriate audit evidence on which to base the audit opinion. (Ref: Para. A1-A5)

6. The risk assessment procedures shall include the following:

   (a) Enquiries of management, and of others within the entity who in the auditor's judgement may have information that is likely to assist in identifying risks of material misstatement due to fraud or error. (Ref: Para. A6)

   (b) Analytical procedures. (Ref: Para. A7-A10)

   (c) Observation and inspection. (Ref: Para. A11)

7. The auditor shall consider whether information obtained from the auditor's client acceptance or continuance process is relevant to identifying risks of material misstatement.

8. If the engagement partner has performed other engagements for the entity, the engagement partner shall consider whether information obtained is relevant to identifying risks of material misstatement.

9. Where the auditor intends to use information obtained from the auditor's previous experience with the entity and from audit procedures performed in previous audits, the auditor shall determine whether changes have occurred since the previous audit that may affect its relevance to the current audit. (Ref: Para. A12-A13)

10. The engagement partner and other key engagement team members shall discuss the susceptibility of the entity's financial report to material misstatement, and the application of the applicable financial reporting framework to the entity's facts and circumstances. The engagement partner shall determine which matters are to be communicated to engagement team members not involved in the discussion. (Ref: Para. A14-A16)

The Required Understanding of the Entity and its Environment, Including the Entity's Internal Control

The Entity and Its Environment

11. The auditor shall obtain an understanding of the following:

(a) Relevant industry, regulatory, and other external factors and the applicable financial reporting framework. (Ref: Para. A17-A22)

(b) The nature of the entity, including:

(i) its operations;

(ii) its ownership and governance structures;

(iii) the types of investments that the entity is making and plans to make, including investments in special-purpose entities; and

(iv) the way that the entity is structured and how it is financed

to enable the auditor to understand the classes of transactions, account balances, and disclosures to be expected in the financial report. (Ref: Para. A23-A27)

(c) The entity's selection and application of accounting policies, including the reasons for changes thereto. The auditor shall evaluate whether the entity's accounting policies are appropriate for its business and consistent with the applicable financial reporting framework and accounting policies used in the relevant industry. (Ref: Para. A28)

(d) The entity's objectives and strategies, and those related business risks that may result in risks of material misstatement. (Ref: Para. A29-A35)

(e) The measurement and review of the entity's financial performance. (Ref: Para. A36-A41)

The Entity's Internal Control

12. The auditor shall obtain an understanding of internal control relevant to the audit. Although most controls relevant to the audit are likely to relate to financial reporting, not all controls that relate to financial reporting are relevant to the audit. It is a matter of the auditor's professional judgement whether a control, individually or in combination with others, is relevant to the audit. (Ref: Para. A42-A65)

Nature and Extent of the Understanding of Relevant Controls

13. When obtaining an understanding of controls that are relevant to the audit, the auditor shall evaluate the design of those controls and determine whether they have been implemented, by performing procedures in addition to enquiry of the entity's personnel. (Ref: Para. A66-A68)

Components of Internal Control

Control environment

14. The auditor shall obtain an understanding of the control environment. As part of obtaining this understanding, the auditor shall evaluate whether:

(a) Management, with the oversight of those charged with governance, has created and maintained a culture of honesty and ethical behaviour; and

(b) The strengths in the control environment elements collectively provide an appropriate foundation for the other components of internal control, and whether those other components are not undermined by control environment weaknesses. (Ref: Para. A69-A78)

The entity's risk assessment process

15. The auditor shall obtain an understanding of whether the entity has a process for:

(a) Identifying business risks relevant to financial reporting objectives;

(b) Estimating the significance of the risks;

(c) Assessing the likelihood of their occurrence; and

(d) Deciding about actions to address those risks. (Ref: Para. A79)

ASA

16. If the entity has established such a process (referred to hereafter as the "entity's risk assessment process"), the auditor shall obtain an understanding of it, and the results thereof. If the auditor identifies risks of material misstatement that management failed to identify, the auditor shall evaluate whether there was an underlying risk of a kind that the auditor expects would have been identified by the entity's risk assessment process. If there is such a risk, the auditor shall obtain an understanding of why that process failed to identify it, and evaluate whether the process is appropriate to its circumstances or determine if there is a significant deficiency in internal control with regard to the entity's risk assessment process.

17. If the entity has not established such a process or has an ad hoc undocumented process, the auditor shall discuss with management whether business risks relevant to financial reporting objectives have been identified and how they have been addressed. The auditor shall evaluate whether the absence of a documented risk assessment process is appropriate in the circumstances, or determine whether it represents a significant deficiency in internal control. (Ref: Para. A80)

The information system, including the related business processes, relevant to financial reporting, and communication

18. The auditor shall obtain an understanding of the information system, including the related business processes, relevant to financial reporting, including the following areas:
    (a) The classes of transactions in the entity's operations that are significant to the financial report;
    (b) The procedures, within both information technology (IT) and manual systems, by which those transactions are initiated, recorded, processed, corrected as necessary, transferred to the general ledger and reported in the financial report;
    (c) The related accounting records, supporting information and specific accounts in the financial report that are used to initiate, record, process and report transactions; this includes the correction of incorrect information and how information is transferred to the general ledger. The records may be in either manual or electronic form;
    (d) How the information system captures events and conditions, other than transactions, that are significant to the financial report;
    (e) The financial reporting process used to prepare the entity's financial report, including significant accounting estimates and disclosures; and
    (f) Controls surrounding journal entries, including non-standard journal entries used to record non-recurring, unusual transactions or adjustments. (Ref: Para. A81-A85)

19. The auditor shall obtain an understanding of how the entity communicates financial reporting roles and responsibilities and significant matters relating to financial reporting, including: (Ref: Para. A86-A87)
    (a) Communications between management and those charged with governance; and
    (b) External communications, such as those with regulatory authorities.

Control activities relevant to the audit

20. The auditor shall obtain an understanding of control activities relevant to the audit, being those the auditor judges it necessary to understand in order to assess the risks of material misstatement at the assertion level and design further audit procedures responsive to assessed risks. An audit does not require an understanding of all the control activities related to each significant class of transactions, account balance, and disclosure in the financial report or to every assertion relevant to them. (Ref: Para. A88-A94)

21. In understanding the entity's control activities, the auditor shall obtain an understanding of how the entity has responded to risks arising from IT. (Ref: Para. A95-A97)

Monitoring of controls

22. The auditor shall obtain an understanding of the major activities that the entity uses to monitor internal control over financial reporting, including those related to those control activities relevant to the audit, and how the entity initiates remedial actions to address deficiencies in its controls. (Ref: Para. A98-A100)

23. If the entity has an internal audit function,[1] the auditor shall obtain an understanding of the following in order to determine whether the internal audit function is likely to be relevant to the audit:
    (a) The nature of the internal audit function's responsibilities and how the internal audit function fits in the entity's organisational structure; and
    (b) The activities performed, or to be performed, by the internal audit function. (Ref Para. A101-A103)

24. The auditor shall obtain an understanding of the sources of the information used in the entity's monitoring activities, and the basis upon which management considers the information to be sufficiently reliable for the purpose. (Ref: Para. A104)

Identifying and Assessing the Risks of Material Misstatement

25. The auditor shall identify and assess the risks of material misstatement at:
    (a) the financial report level; and (Ref: Para. A105-A108)
    (b) the assertion level for classes of transactions, account balances, and disclosures (Ref: Para. A109-A113)

    to provide a basis for designing and performing further audit procedures.

26. For this purpose, the auditor shall:
    (a) Identify risks throughout the process of obtaining an understanding of the entity and its environment, including relevant controls that relate to the risks, and by considering the classes of transactions, account balances, and disclosures in the financial report; (Ref: Para. A114-A115)
    (b) Assess the identified risks, and evaluate whether they relate more pervasively to the financial report as a whole and potentially affect many assertions;
    (c) Relate the identified risks to what can go wrong at the assertion level, taking account of relevant controls that the auditor intends to test; and (Ref: Para. A116-A118)
    (d) Consider the likelihood of misstatement, including the possibility of multiple misstatements, and whether the potential misstatement is of a magnitude that could result in a material misstatement.

Risks that Require Special Audit Consideration

27. As part of the risk assessment as described in paragraph 25 of this Auditing Standard, the auditor shall determine whether any of the risks identified are, in the auditor's judgement, a significant risk. In exercising this judgement, the auditor shall exclude the effects of identified controls related to the risk.

28. In exercising judgement as to which risks are significant risks, the auditor shall consider at least the following:
    (a) Whether the risk is a risk of fraud;
    (b) Whether the risk is related to recent significant economic, accounting or other developments and, therefore, requires specific attention;
    (c) The complexity of transactions;
    (d) Whether the risk involves significant transactions with related parties;
    (e) The degree of subjectivity in the measurement of financial information related to the risk, especially those measurements involving a wide range of measurement uncertainty; and
    (f) Whether the risk involves significant transactions that are outside the normal course of business for the entity, or that otherwise appear to be unusual. (Ref: Para. A119-A123)

29. If the auditor has determined that a significant risk exists, the auditor shall obtain an understanding of the entity's controls, including control activities, relevant to that risk. (Ref: Para. A124-A126)

---

1 See ASA 610 *Using the Work of Internal Auditors*, paragraph 7(a).

ASA

Risks for Which Substantive Procedures Alone Do Not Provide Sufficient Appropriate Audit Evidence

30. In respect of some risks, the auditor may judge that it is not possible or practicable to obtain sufficient appropriate audit evidence only from substantive procedures. Such risks may relate to the inaccurate or incomplete recording of routine and significant classes of transactions or account balances, the characteristics of which often permit highly automated processing with little or no manual intervention. In such cases, the entity's controls over such risks are relevant to the audit and the auditor shall obtain an understanding of them. (Ref: Para. A127-A129)

Revision of Risk Assessment

31. The auditor's assessment of the risks of material misstatement at the assertion level may change during the course of the audit as additional audit evidence is obtained. In circumstances where the auditor obtains audit evidence from performing further audit procedures, or if new information is obtained, either of which is inconsistent with the audit evidence on which the auditor originally based the assessment, the auditor shall revise the assessment and modify the further planned audit procedures accordingly. (Ref: Para. A130)

Documentation

32. The auditor shall include in the audit documentation:[2]
    (a) The discussion among the engagement team where required by paragraph 10 of this Auditing Standard, and the significant decisions reached;
    (b) Key elements of the understanding obtained regarding each of the aspects of the entity and its environment specified in paragraph 11 of this Auditing Standard and of each of the internal control components specified in paragraphs 14-24 of this Auditing Standard; the sources of information from which the understanding was obtained; and the risk assessment procedures performed;
    (c) The identified and assessed risks of material misstatement at the financial report level and at the assertion level as required by paragraph 25 of this Auditing Standard; and
    (d) The risks identified, and related controls about which the auditor has obtained an understanding, as a result of the requirements in paragraphs 27-30 of this Auditing Standard. (Ref: Para. A131-A134)

❖ ❖ ❖

Application and Other Explanatory Material

Risk Assessment Procedures and Related Activities (Ref: Para. 5)

A1. Obtaining an understanding of the entity and its environment, including the entity's internal control (referred to hereafter as an "understanding of the entity"), is a continuous, dynamic process of gathering, updating and analysing information throughout the audit. The understanding establishes a frame of reference within which the auditor plans the audit and exercises professional judgement throughout the audit, for example, when:

- Assessing risks of material misstatement of the financial report;
- Determining materiality in accordance with ASA 320;[3]
- Considering the appropriateness of the selection and application of accounting policies, and the adequacy of financial report disclosures;
- Identifying areas where special audit consideration may be necessary, for example, related party transactions, the appropriateness of management's use of the going concern assumption, or considering the business purpose of transactions;
- Developing expectations for use when performing analytical procedures;

2 See ASA 230 *Audit Documentation*, paragraphs 8-11 and paragraph A6.

3 See ASA 320 *Materiality in Planning and Performing an Audit*.

- Responding to the assessed risks of material misstatement, including designing and performing further audit procedures to obtain sufficient appropriate audit evidence; and
- Evaluating the sufficiency and appropriateness of audit evidence obtained, such as the appropriateness of assumptions and of management's oral and written representations.

A2. Information obtained by performing risk assessment procedures and related activities may be used by the auditor as audit evidence to support assessments of the risks of material misstatement. In addition, the auditor may obtain audit evidence about classes of transactions, account balances, or disclosures and related assertions and about the operating effectiveness of controls, even though such procedures were not specifically planned as substantive procedures or as tests of controls. The auditor also may choose to perform substantive procedures or tests of controls concurrently with risk assessment procedures because it is efficient to do so.

A3. The auditor uses professional judgement to determine the extent of the understanding required. The auditor's primary consideration is whether the understanding that has been obtained is sufficient to meet the objective stated in this Auditing Standard. The depth of the overall understanding that is required by the auditor is less than that possessed by management in managing the entity.

A4. The risks to be assessed include both those due to error and those due to fraud, and both are covered by this Auditing Standard. However, the significance of fraud is such that further requirements and guidance are included in ASA 240, in relation to risk assessment procedures and related activities to obtain information that is used to identify the risks of material misstatement due to fraud.[4]

A5. Although the auditor is required to perform all the risk assessment procedures described in paragraph 6 in the course of obtaining the required understanding of the entity (see paragraphs 11-24), the auditor is not required to perform all of them for each aspect of that understanding. Other procedures may be performed where the information to be obtained therefrom may be helpful in identifying risks of material misstatement. Examples of such procedures include:

- Reviewing information obtained from external sources such as trade and economic journals; reports by analysts, banks, or rating agencies; or regulatory or financial publications.
- Making enquiries of the entity's external legal counsel or of valuation experts that the entity has used.

Enquiries of Management and Others within the Entity (Ref: Para. 6(a))

A6. Much of the information obtained by the auditor's enquiries is obtained from management and those responsible for financial reporting. However, the auditor may also obtain information, or a different perspective in identifying risks of material misstatement, through enquiries of others within the entity and other employees with different levels of authority. For example:

- Enquiries directed towards those charged with governance may help the auditor understand the environment in which the financial report is prepared.
- Enquiries directed toward internal audit personnel may provide information about internal audit procedures performed during the year relating to the design and effectiveness of the entity's internal control and whether management has satisfactorily responded to findings from those procedures.
- Enquiries of employees involved in initiating, processing, or recording complex or unusual transactions may help the auditor to evaluate the appropriateness of the selection and application of certain accounting policies.

4 See ASA 240 *The Auditor's Responsibilities Relating to Fraud in an Audit of a Financial Report*, paragraphs 12-24.

- Enquiries directed toward in-house legal counsel may provide information about such matters as litigation, compliance with laws and regulations, knowledge of fraud or suspected fraud affecting the entity, warranties, post-sales obligations, arrangements (such as joint ventures) with business partners and the meaning of contract terms.
- Enquiries directed towards marketing or sales personnel may provide information about changes in the entity's marketing strategies, sales trends, or contractual arrangements with its customers.

Analytical Procedures (Ref: Para. 6(b))

A7. Analytical procedures performed as risk assessment procedures may identify aspects of the entity of which the auditor was unaware and may assist in assessing the risks of material misstatement in order to provide a basis for designing and implementing responses to the assessed risks. Analytical procedures performed as risk assessment procedures may include both financial and non-financial information, for example, the relationship between sales and square footage of selling space or volume of goods sold.

A8. Analytical procedures may help identify the existence of unusual transactions or events, and amounts, ratios, and trends that might indicate matters that have audit implications. Unusual or unexpected relationships that are identified may assist the auditor in identifying risks of material misstatement, especially risks of material misstatement due to fraud.

A9. However, when such analytical procedures use data aggregated at a high level (which may be the situation with analytical procedures performed as risk assessment procedures), the results of those analytical procedures only provide a broad initial indication about whether a material misstatement may exist. Accordingly, in such cases, consideration of other information that has been gathered when identifying the risks of material misstatement together with the results of such analytical procedures may assist the auditor in understanding and evaluating the results of the analytical procedures.

Considerations Specific to Smaller Entities

A10. Some smaller entities may not have interim or monthly financial information that can be used for purposes of analytical procedures. In these circumstances, although the auditor may be able to perform limited analytical procedures for purposes of planning the audit or obtain some information through enquiry, the auditor may need to plan to perform analytical procedures to identify and assess the risks of material misstatement when an early draft of the entity's financial report is available.

Observation and Inspection (Ref: Para. 6(c))

A11. Observation and inspection may support enquiries of management and others, and may also provide information about the entity and its environment. Examples of such audit procedures include observation or inspection of the following:

- The entity's operations.
- Documents (such as business plans and strategies), records, and internal control manuals.
- Reports prepared by management (such as quarterly management reports and interim financial reports) and those charged with governance (such as minutes of board of directors' meetings).
- The entity's premises and plant facilities.

Information Obtained in Prior Periods (Ref: Para. 9)

A12. The auditor's previous experience with the entity and audit procedures performed in previous audits may provide the auditor with information about such matters as:

- Past misstatements and whether they were corrected on a timely basis.
- The nature of the entity and its environment, and the entity's internal control (including deficiencies in internal control).
- Significant changes that the entity or its operations may have undergone since the prior financial period, which may assist the auditor in gaining a sufficient understanding of the entity to identify and assess risks of material misstatement.

A13. The auditor is required to determine whether information obtained in prior periods remains relevant, if the auditor intends to use that information for the purposes of the current audit. This is because changes in the control environment, for example, may affect the relevance of information obtained in the prior year. To determine whether changes have occurred that may affect the relevance of such information, the auditor may make enquiries and perform other appropriate audit procedures, such as walk-throughs of relevant systems.

Discussion among the Engagement Team (Ref: Para. 10)

A14. The discussion among the engagement team about the susceptibility of the entity's financial report to material misstatement:

- Provides an opportunity for more experienced engagement team members, including the engagement partner, to share their insights based on their knowledge of the entity.
- Allows the engagement team members to exchange information about the business risks to which the entity is subject and about how and where the financial report might be susceptible to material misstatement due to fraud or error.
- Assists the engagement team members to gain a better understanding of the potential for material misstatement of the financial report in the specific areas assigned to them, and to understand how the results of the audit procedures that they perform may affect other aspects of the audit including the decisions about the nature, timing, and extent of further audit procedures.
- Provides a basis upon which engagement team members communicate and share new information obtained throughout the audit that may affect the assessment of risks of material misstatement or the audit procedures performed to address these risks.

ASA 240 provides further requirements and guidance in relation to the discussion among the engagement team about the risks of fraud.[5]

A15. It is not always necessary or practical for the discussion to include all members in a single discussion (as, for example, in a multi-location audit), nor is it necessary for all of the members of the engagement team to be informed of all of the decisions reached in the discussion. The engagement partner may discuss matters with key members of the engagement team including, if considered appropriate, specialists and those responsible for the audits of components, while delegating discussion with others, taking account of the extent of communication considered necessary throughout the engagement team. A communications plan, agreed by the engagement partner, may be useful.

Considerations Specific to Smaller Entities

A16. Many small audits are carried out entirely by the engagement partner (who may be a sole practitioner). In such situations, it is the engagement partner who, having personally conducted the planning of the audit, would be responsible for considering the susceptibility of the entity's financial report to material misstatement due to fraud or error.

The Required Understanding of the Entity and Its Environment, Including the Entity's Internal Control

The Entity and Its Environment

Industry, Regulatory and Other External Factors (Ref: Para. 11(a))

Industry Factors

A17. Relevant industry factors include industry conditions such as the competitive environment, supplier and customer relationships, and technological developments. Examples of matters the auditor may consider include:

- The market and competition, including demand, capacity, and price competition.
- Cyclical or seasonal activity.
- Product technology relating to the entity's products.
- Energy supply and cost.

5 See ASA 240, paragraph 15.

A18. The industry in which the entity operates may give rise to specific risks of material misstatement arising from the nature of the business or the degree of regulation. For example, long-term contracts may involve significant estimates of revenues and expenses that give rise to risks of material misstatement. In such cases, it is important that the engagement team include members with sufficient relevant knowledge and experience, as required by ASA 220.[6]

Regulatory Factors

A19. Relevant regulatory factors include the regulatory environment. The regulatory environment encompasses, among other matters, the applicable financial reporting framework and the legal and political environment. Examples of matters the auditor may consider include:

- Accounting principles and industry specific practices.
- Regulatory framework for a regulated industry.
- Legislation and regulation that significantly affect the entity's operations, including direct supervisory activities.
- Taxation (corporate and other).
- Government policies currently affecting the conduct of the entity's business, such as monetary, including foreign exchange controls, fiscal, financial incentives (for example, government aid programs), and tariffs or trade restrictions policies.
- Environmental requirements affecting the industry and the entity's business.

A20. ASA 250 includes some specific requirements related to the legal and regulatory framework applicable to the entity and the industry or sector in which the entity operates.[7]

Considerations specific to public sector entities

A21. For the audits of public sector entities, law, regulation or other authority may affect the entity's operations. Such elements are essential to consider when obtaining an understanding of the entity and its environment.

Other External Factors

A22. Examples of other external factors affecting the entity that the auditor may consider include the general economic conditions, interest rates and availability of financing, and inflation or currency revaluation.

Nature of the Entity (Ref: Para. 11(b))

A23. An understanding of the nature of an entity enables the auditor to understand such matters as:

- Whether the entity has a complex structure, for example with subsidiaries or other components in multiple locations. Complex structures often introduce issues that may give rise to risks of material misstatement. Such issues may include whether goodwill, joint ventures, investments, or special-purpose entities are accounted for appropriately.
- The ownership, and relations between owners and other people or entities. This understanding assists in determining whether related party transactions have been identified and accounted for appropriately. ASA 550[8] establishes requirements and provides guidance on the auditor's considerations relevant to related parties.

A24. Examples of matters that the auditor may consider when obtaining an understanding of the nature of the entity include:

- Business operations such as:
  - Nature of revenue sources, products or services, and markets, including involvement in electronic commerce such as Internet sales and marketing activities.

6 See ASA 220 *Quality Control for an Audit of a Financial Report and Other Historical Financial Information*, paragraph 14.

7 See ASA 250 *Consideration of Laws and Regulations in the Audit of a Financial Report*, paragraph 12.

8 See ASA 550 *Related Parties*.

- Conduct of operations (for example, stages and methods of production, or activities exposed to environmental risks).
- Alliances, joint ventures, and outsourcing activities.
- Geographic dispersion and industry segmentation.
- Location of production facilities, warehouses, and offices, and location and quantities of inventories.
- Key customers and important suppliers of goods and services, employment arrangements (including the existence of union contracts, superannuation and other post employment benefits, share option or incentive bonus arrangements, and government regulation related to employment matters).
- Research and development activities and expenditures.
- Transactions with related parties.

- Investments and investment activities such as:
  - Planned or recently executed acquisitions or divestitures.
  - Investments and dispositions of securities and loans.
  - Capital investment activities.
  - Investments in non-consolidated entities, including partnerships, joint ventures and special-purpose entities.
- Financing and financing activities such as:
  - Major subsidiaries and associated entities, including consolidated and non-consolidated structures.
  - Debt structure and related terms, including off-balance-sheet financing arrangements and leasing arrangements.
  - Beneficial owners (local, foreign, business reputation and experience) and related parties.
  - Use of derivative financial instruments.
- Financial reporting such as:
  - Accounting principles and industry specific practices, including industry-specific significant categories (for example, loans and investments for banks, or research and development for pharmaceuticals).
  - Revenue recognition practices.
  - Accounting for fair values.
  - Foreign currency assets, liabilities and transactions.
  - Accounting for unusual or complex transactions including those in controversial or emerging areas (for example, accounting for share-based compensation).

Aus A24.1 Ownership and Governance arrangements such as:

- The role of the board of directors and those charged with governance in determining policies for the levels of risk that the entity is willing to accept in its daily operations.
- The role of senior management in designing, implementing, and monitoring effective risk management systems to implement the policies prescribed by the board of directors.
- The presence of non-executive directors on the board and an independent compensation committee that reviews incentive plans, including commissions, discretionary bonuses, directors' service contracts, and profit-sharing plans.
- The role of line management in carrying out the prescribed procedures and control activities.

ASA

- ◦ The strength of the internal audit function and the audit committee and their role as an independent appraisal function.
- ◦ The strength of other significant committees, for example, risk management committee, asset and liability management committee, or general management committee.
- ◦ The adequacy of segregation of duties.
- ◦ Prior period financial reporting disclosures include the form, classification, terminology, basis of amounts and level of detail provided.

A25. Significant changes in the entity from prior periods may give rise to, or change, risks of material misstatement.

Nature of Special-Purpose Entities

A26. A special-purpose entity (sometimes referred to as a special purpose vehicle) is an entity that is generally established for a narrow and well-defined purpose, such as to effect a lease or a securitisation of financial assets, or to carry out research and development activities. It may take the form of a corporation, trust, partnership, or unincorporated entity. The entity on behalf of which the special-purpose entity has been created may often transfer assets to the latter (for example, as part of a derecognition transaction involving financial assets), obtain the right to use the latter's assets, or perform services for the later, while other parties may provide the funding to the latter. As ASA 550 indicates, in some circumstances, a special-purpose entity may be a related party of the entity.[9]

A27. Financial reporting frameworks often specify detailed conditions that are deemed to amount to control, or circumstances under which the special-purpose entity should be considered for consolidation. The interpretation of the requirements of such frameworks often demands a detailed knowledge of the relevant agreements involving the special-purpose entity.

The Entity's Selection and Application of Accounting Policies (Ref: Para.11(c))

A28. An understanding of the entity's selection and application of accounting policies may encompass such matters as:

- The methods the entity uses to account for significant and unusual transactions.
- The effect of significant accounting policies in controversial or emerging areas for which there is a lack of authoritative guidance or consensus.
- Changes in the entity's accounting policies.
- Financial reporting standards and laws and regulations that are new to the entity and when and how the entity will adopt such requirements.

Objectives and Strategies and Related Business Risks (Ref: Para.11(d))

A29. The entity conducts its business in the context of industry, regulatory and other internal and external factors. To respond to these factors, the entity's management or those charged with governance define objectives, which are the overall plans for the entity. Strategies are the approaches by which management intends to achieve its objectives. The entity's objectives and strategies may change over time.

A30. Business risk is broader than the risk of material misstatement of the financial report, though it includes the latter. Business risk may arise from change or complexity. A failure to recognise the need for change may also give rise to business risk. Business risk may arise, for example, from:

- The development of new products or services that may fail;
- A market which, even if successfully developed, is inadequate to support a product or service; or
- Flaws in a product or service that may result in liabilities and reputational risk.

9 See ASA 550, paragraph A7.

A31. An understanding of the business risks facing the entity increases the likelihood of identifying risks of material misstatement, since most business risks will eventually have financial consequences and, therefore, an effect on the financial report. However, the auditor does not have a responsibility to identify or assess all business risks because not all business risks give rise to risks of material misstatement.

A32. Examples of matters that the auditor may consider when obtaining an understanding of the entity's objectives, strategies and related business risks that may result in a risk of material misstatement of the financial report include:

- Industry developments (a potential related business risk might be, for example, that the entity does not have the personnel or expertise to deal with the changes in the industry).
- New products and services (a potential related business risk might be, for example, that there is increased product liability).
- Expansion of the business (a potential related business risk might be, for example, that the demand has not been accurately estimated).
- New accounting requirements (a potential related business risk might be, for example, incomplete or improper implementation, or increased costs).
- Regulatory requirements (a potential related business risk might be, for example, that there is increased legal exposure).
- Current and prospective financing requirements (a potential related business risk might be, for example, the loss of financing due to the entity's inability to meet requirements).
- Use of IT (a potential related business risk might be, for example, that systems and processes are incompatible).
- The effects of implementing a strategy, particularly any effects that will lead to new accounting requirements (a potential related business risk might be, for example, incomplete or improper implementation).

A33. A business risk may have an immediate consequence for the risk of material misstatement for classes of transactions, account balances, and disclosures at the assertion level or the financial report level. For example, the business risk arising from a contracting customer base may increase the risk of material misstatement associated with the valuation of receivables. However, the same risk, particularly in combination with a contracting economy, may also have a longer-term consequence, which the auditor considers when assessing the appropriateness of the going concern assumption. Whether a business risk may result in a risk of material misstatement is, therefore, considered in light of the entity's circumstances. Examples of conditions and events that may indicate risks of material misstatement are indicated in Appendix 2.

A34. Usually, management identifies business risks and develops approaches to address them. Such a risk assessment process is part of internal control and is discussed in paragraph 15 and paragraphs A79-A80.

Considerations Specific to Public Sector Entities

A35. For the audits of public sector entities, "management objectives" may be influenced by concerns regarding public accountability and may include objectives which have their source in law, regulation, or other authority.

Measurement and Review of the Entity's Financial Performance (Ref: Para. 11(e))

A36. Management and others will measure and review those things they regard as important. Performance measures, whether external or internal, create pressures on the entity. These pressures, in turn, may motivate management to take action to improve the business performance or to misstate the financial report. Accordingly, an understanding of the entity's performance measures assists the auditor in considering whether pressures to achieve performance targets may result in management actions that increase the risks of material misstatement, including those due to fraud. See ASA 240 for requirements and guidance in relation to the risks of fraud.

A37. The measurement and review of financial performance is not the same as the monitoring of controls (discussed as a component of internal control in paragraphs A98-A104), though their purposes may overlap:

- The measurement and review of performance is directed at whether business performance is meeting the objectives set by management (or third parties).
- Monitoring of controls is specifically concerned with the effective operation of internal control.

In some cases, however, performance indicators also provide information that enables management to identify deficiencies in internal control.

A38. Examples of internally-generated information used by management for measuring and reviewing financial performance, and which the auditor may consider, include:

- Key performance indicators (financial and non-financial) and key ratios, trends and operating statistics.
- Period-on-period financial performance analyses.
- Budgets, forecasts, variance analyses, segment information and divisional, departmental or other level performance reports.
- Employee performance measures and incentive compensation policies.
- Comparisons of an entity's performance with that of competitors.

A39. External parties may also measure and review the entity's financial performance. For example, external information such as analysts' reports and credit rating agency reports may represent useful information for the auditor. Such reports can often be obtained from the entity being audited.

A40. Internal measures may highlight unexpected results or trends requiring management to determine their cause and take corrective action (including, in some cases, the detection and correction of misstatements on a timely basis). Performance measures may also indicate to the auditor that risks of misstatement of related financial report information do exist. For example, performance measures may indicate that the entity has unusually rapid growth or profitability when compared to that of other entities in the same industry. Such information, particularly if combined with other factors such as performance-based bonus or incentive remuneration, may indicate the potential risk of management bias in the preparation of the financial report.

Considerations Specific to Smaller Entities

A41. Smaller entities often do not have processes to measure and review financial performance. Enquiry of management may reveal that it relies on certain key indicators for evaluating financial performance and taking appropriate action. If such enquiry indicates an absence of performance measurement or review, there may be an increased risk of misstatements not being detected and corrected.

The Entity's Internal Control (Ref: Para. 12)

A42. An understanding of internal control assists the auditor in identifying types of potential misstatements and factors that affect the risks of material misstatement, and in designing the nature, timing, and extent of further audit procedures.

A43. The following application material on internal control is presented in four sections, as follows:

- General Nature and Characteristics of Internal Control.
- Controls Relevant to the Audit.
- Nature and Extent of the Understanding of Relevant Controls.
- Components of Internal Control.

General Nature and Characteristics of Internal Control

Purpose of Internal Control

A44. Internal control is designed, implemented and maintained to address identified business risks that threaten the achievement of any of the entity's objectives that concern:

- The reliability of the entity's financial reporting;
- The effectiveness and efficiency of its operations; and
- Its compliance with applicable laws and regulations.

The way in which internal control is designed, implemented and maintained varies with an entity's size and complexity.

Considerations specific to smaller entities

A45. Smaller entities may use less structured means and simpler processes and procedures to achieve their objectives.

Limitations of Internal Control

A46. Internal control, no matter how effective, can provide an entity with only reasonable assurance about achieving the entity's financial reporting objectives. The likelihood of their achievement is affected by the inherent limitations of internal control. These include the realities that human judgement in decision-making can be faulty and that breakdowns in internal control can occur because of human error. For example, there may be an error in the design of, or in the change to, a control. Equally, the operation of a control may not be effective, such as where information produced for the purposes of internal control (for example, an exception report) is not effectively used because the individual responsible for reviewing the information does not understand its purpose or fails to take appropriate action.

A47. Additionally, controls can be circumvented by the collusion of two or more people or inappropriate management override of internal control. For example, management may enter into side agreements with customers that alter the terms and conditions of the entity's standard sales contracts, which may result in improper revenue recognition. Also, edit checks in a software program that are designed to identify and report transactions that exceed specified credit limits may be overridden or disabled.

A48. Further, in designing and implementing controls, management may make judgements on the nature and extent of the controls it chooses to implement, and the nature and extent of the risks it chooses to assume.

Considerations specific to smaller entities

A49. Smaller entities often have fewer employees which may limit the extent to which segregation of duties is practicable. However, in a small owner-managed entity, the owner-manager may be able to exercise more effective oversight than in a larger entity. This oversight may compensate for the generally more limited opportunities for segregation of duties.

A50. On the other hand, the owner-manager may be more able to override controls because the system of internal control is less structured. This is taken into account by the auditor when identifying the risks of material misstatement due to fraud.

Division of Internal Control into Components

A51. The division of internal control into the following five components, for purposes of Australian Auditing Standards, provides a useful framework for auditors to consider how different aspects of an entity's internal control may affect the audit:

(a) The control environment;

(b) The entity's risk assessment process;

(c) The information system, including the related business processes, relevant to financial reporting, and communication;

(d) Control activities; and

(e) Monitoring of controls.

The division does not necessarily reflect how an entity designs, implements and maintains internal control, or how it may classify any particular component. Auditors may use different terminology or frameworks to describe the various aspects of internal control, and their effect on the audit than those used in this Auditing Standard, provided all the components described in this Auditing Standard are addressed.

A52. Application material relating to the five components of internal control as they relate to a financial report audit is set out in paragraphs A69-A104 below. Appendix 1 provides further explanation of these components of internal control.

Characteristics of Manual and Automated Elements of Internal Control Relevant to the Auditor's Risk Assessment

A53. An entity's system of internal control contains manual elements and often contains automated elements. The characteristics of manual or automated elements are relevant to the auditor's risk assessment and further audit procedures based thereon.

A54. The use of manual or automated elements in internal control also affects the manner in which transactions are initiated, recorded, processed, and reported:

- Controls in a manual system may include such procedures as approvals and reviews of transactions, and reconciliations and follow-up of reconciling items. Alternatively, an entity may use automated procedures to initiate, record, process, and report transactions, in which case records in electronic format replace paper documents.
- Controls in IT systems consist of a combination of automated controls (for example, controls embedded in computer programs) and manual controls. Further, manual controls may be independent of IT, may use information produced by IT, or may be limited to monitoring the effective functioning of IT and of automated controls, and to handling exceptions. When IT is used to initiate, record, process or report transactions, or other financial data for inclusion in the financial report, the systems and programs may include controls related to the corresponding assertions for material accounts or may be critical to the effective functioning of manual controls that depend on IT.

An entity's mix of manual and automated elements in internal control varies with the nature and complexity of the entity's use of IT.

A55. Generally, IT benefits an entity's internal control by enabling an entity to:

- Consistently apply predefined business rules and perform complex calculations in processing large volumes of transactions or data;
- Enhance the timeliness, availability, and accuracy of information;
- Facilitate the additional analysis of information;
- Enhance the ability to monitor the performance of the entity's activities and its policies and procedures;
- Reduce the risk that controls will be circumvented; and
- Enhance the ability to achieve effective segregation of duties by implementing security controls in applications, databases, and operating systems.

A56. IT also poses specific risks to an entity's internal control, including, for example:

- Reliance on systems or programs that are inaccurately processing data, processing inaccurate data, or both.
- Unauthorised access to data that may result in destruction of data or improper changes to data, including the recording of unauthorised or non-existent transactions, or inaccurate recording of transactions. Particular risks may arise where multiple users access a common database.
- The possibility of IT personnel gaining access privileges beyond those necessary to perform their assigned duties thereby breaking down segregation of duties.
- Unauthorised changes to data in master files.
- Unauthorised changes to systems or programs.

- Failure to make necessary changes to systems or programs.
- Inappropriate manual intervention.
- Potential loss of data or inability to access data as required.

A57. Manual elements in internal control may be more suitable where judgement and discretion are required such as for the following circumstances:

- Large, unusual or non-recurring transactions.
- Circumstances where errors are difficult to define, anticipate or predict.
- In changing circumstances that require a control response outside the scope of an existing automated control.
- In monitoring the effectiveness of automated controls.

A58. Manual elements in internal control may be less reliable than automated elements because they can be more easily bypassed, ignored, or overridden and they are also more prone to simple errors and mistakes. Consistency of application of a manual control element cannot therefore be assumed. Manual control elements may be less suitable for the following circumstances:

- High volume or recurring transactions, or in situations where errors that can be anticipated or predicted can be prevented, or detected and corrected, by control parameters that are automated.
- Control activities where the specific ways to perform the control can be adequately designed and automated.

A59. The extent and nature of the risks to internal control vary depending on the nature and characteristics of the entity's information system. The entity responds to the risks arising from the use of IT or from use of manual elements in internal control by establishing effective controls in light of the characteristics of the entity's information system.

Controls Relevant to the Audit

A60. There is a direct relationship between an entity's objectives and the controls it implements to provide reasonable assurance about their achievement. The entity's objectives, and therefore controls, relate to financial reporting, operations and compliance; however, not all of these objectives and controls are relevant to the auditor's risk assessment.

A61. Factors relevant to the auditor's judgement about whether a control, individually or in combination with others, is relevant to the audit may include such matters as the following:

- Materiality.
- The significance of the related risk.
- The size of the entity.
- The nature of the entity's business, including its organisation and ownership characteristics.
- The diversity and complexity of the entity's operations.
- Applicable legal and regulatory requirements.
- The circumstances and the applicable component of internal control.
- The nature and complexity of the systems that are part of the entity's internal control, including the use of service organisations.
- Whether, and how, a specific control, individually or in combination with others, prevents, or detects and corrects, material misstatement.

A62. Controls over the completeness and accuracy of information produced by the entity may be relevant to the audit if the auditor intends to make use of the information in designing and performing further audit procedures. Controls relating to operations and compliance objectives may also be relevant to an audit if they relate to data the auditor evaluates or uses in applying audit procedures.

A63. Internal control over safeguarding of assets against unauthorised acquisition, use, or disposition may include controls relating to both financial reporting and operations objectives. The auditor's consideration of such controls is generally limited to those relevant to the reliability of financial reporting.

A64. An entity generally has controls relating to objectives that are not relevant to an audit and therefore need not be considered. For example, an entity may rely on a sophisticated system of automated controls to provide efficient and effective operations (such as an airline's system of automated controls to maintain flight schedules), but these controls ordinarily would not be relevant to the audit. Further, although internal control applies to the entire entity or to any of its operating units or business processes, an understanding of internal control relating to each of the entity's operating units and business processes may not be relevant to the audit.

Considerations Specific to Public Sector Entities

A65. Public sector auditors often have additional responsibilities with respect to internal control, for example to report on compliance with an established Code of Practice. Public sector auditors can also have responsibilities to report on the compliance with law, regulation or other authority. As a result, their review of internal control may be broader and more detailed.

Nature and Extent of the Understanding of Relevant Controls (Ref: Para. 13)

A66. Evaluating the design of a control involves considering whether the control, individually or in combination with other controls, is capable of effectively preventing, or detecting and correcting, material misstatements. Implementation of a control means that the control exists and that the entity is using it. There is little point in assessing the implementation of a control that is not effective, and so the design of a control is considered first. An improperly designed control may represent a significant deficiency in internal control.

A67. Risk assessment procedures to obtain audit evidence about the design and implementation of relevant controls may include:

- Enquiring of entity personnel.
- Observing the application of specific controls.
- Inspecting documents and reports.
- Tracing transactions through the information system relevant to financial reporting.

Enquiry alone, however, is not sufficient for such purposes.

A68. Obtaining an understanding of an entity's controls is not sufficient to test their operating effectiveness, unless there is some automation that provides for the consistent operation of the controls. For example, obtaining audit evidence about the implementation of a manual control at a point in time does not provide audit evidence about the operating effectiveness of the control at other times during the period under audit. However, because of the inherent consistency of IT processing (see paragraph A55), performing audit procedures to determine whether an automated control has been implemented may serve as a test of that control's operating effectiveness, depending on the auditor's assessment and testing of controls such as those over program changes. Tests of the operating effectiveness of controls are further described in ASA 330.[10]

Components of Internal Control—Control Environment (Ref: Para. 14)

A69. The control environment includes the governance and management functions and the attitudes, awareness, and actions of those charged with governance and management concerning the entity's internal control and its importance in the entity. The control environment sets the tone of an organisation, influencing the control consciousness of its people.

A70. Elements of the control environment that may be relevant when obtaining an understanding of the control environment include the following:

(a) *Communication and enforcement of integrity and ethical values* – These are essential elements that influence the effectiveness of the design, administration and monitoring of controls.

10 See ASA 330 *The Auditor's Responses to Assessed Risks.*

(b) *Commitment to competence* – Matters such as management's consideration of the competence levels for particular jobs and how those levels translate into requisite skills and knowledge.

(c) *Participation by those charged with governance* – Attributes of those charged with governance such as:

- Their independence from management.
- Their experience and stature.
- The extent of their involvement and the information they receive, and the scrutiny of activities.
- The appropriateness of their actions, including the degree to which difficult questions are raised and pursued with management, and their interaction with internal and external auditors.

(d) *Management's philosophy and operating style* – Characteristics such as management's:

- Approach to taking and managing business risks.
- Attitudes and actions toward financial reporting.
- Attitudes toward information processing and accounting functions and personnel.

(e) *Organisational structure* – The framework within which an entity's activities for achieving its objectives are planned, executed, controlled, and reviewed.

(f) *Assignment of authority and responsibility* – Matters such as how authority and responsibility for operating activities are assigned and how reporting relationships and authorisation hierarchies are established.

(g) *Human resource policies and practices* – Policies and practices that relate to, for example, recruitment, orientation, training, evaluation, counselling, promotion, compensation, and remedial actions.

Audit Evidence for Elements of the Control Environment

A71. Relevant audit evidence may be obtained through a combination of enquiries and other risk assessment procedures such as corroborating enquiries through observation or inspection of documents. For example, through enquiries of management and employees, the auditor may obtain an understanding of how management communicates to employees its views on business practices and ethical behaviour. The auditor may then determine whether relevant controls have been implemented by considering, for example, whether management has a written code of conduct and whether it acts in a manner that supports the code.

Effect of the Control Environment on the Assessment of the Risks of Material Misstatement

A72. Some elements of an entity's control environment have a pervasive effect on assessing the risks of material misstatement. For example, an entity's control consciousness is influenced significantly by those charged with governance, because one of their roles is to counterbalance pressures on management in relation to financial reporting that may arise from market demands or remuneration schemes. The effectiveness of the design of the control environment in relation to participation by those charged with governance is therefore influenced by such matters as:

- Their independence from management and their ability to evaluate the actions of management.
- Whether they understand the entity's business transactions.
- The extent to which they evaluate whether the financial report is prepared in accordance with the applicable financial reporting framework.

A73. An active and independent board of directors may influence the philosophy and operating style of senior management. However, other elements may be more limited in their effect. For example, although human resource policies and practices directed toward hiring competent financial, accounting, and IT personnel may reduce the risk of errors in

ASA

processing financial information, they may not mitigate a strong bias by top management to overstate earnings.

A74. The existence of a satisfactory control environment can be a positive factor when the auditor assesses the risks of material misstatement. However, although it may help reduce the risk of fraud, a satisfactory control environment is not an absolute deterrent to fraud. Conversely, deficiencies in the control environment may undermine the effectiveness of controls, in particular in relation to fraud. For example, management's failure to commit sufficient resources to address IT security risks may adversely affect internal control by allowing improper changes to be made to computer programs or to data, or unauthorised transactions to be processed. As explained in ASA 330, the control environment also influences the nature, timing, and extent of the auditor's further procedures.[11]

A75. The control environment in itself does not prevent, or detect and correct, a material misstatement. It may, however, influence the auditor's evaluation of the effectiveness of other controls (for example, the monitoring of controls and the operation of specific control activities) and thereby, the auditor's assessment of the risks of material misstatement.

Considerations Specific to Smaller Entities

A76. The control environment within small entities is likely to differ from larger entities. For example, those charged with governance in small entities may not include an independent or outside member, and the role of governance may be undertaken directly by the owner-manager where there are no other owners. The nature of the control environment may also influence the significance of other controls, or their absence. For example, the active involvement of an owner-manager may mitigate certain of the risks arising from a lack of segregation of duties in a small business; it may, however, increase other risks, for example, the risk of override of controls.

A77. In addition, audit evidence for elements of the control environment in smaller entities may not be available in documentary form, in particular where communication between management and other personnel may be informal, yet effective. For example, small entities might not have a written code of conduct but, instead, develop a culture that emphasises the importance of integrity and ethical behaviour through oral communication and by management example.

A78. Consequently, the attitudes, awareness and actions of management or the owner-manager are of particular importance to the auditor's understanding of a smaller entity's control environment.

Components of Internal Control—The Entity's Risk Assessment Process (Ref: Para. 15)

A79. The entity's risk assessment process forms the basis for how management determines the risks to be managed. If that process is appropriate to the circumstances, including the nature, size and complexity of the entity, it assists the auditor in identifying risks of material misstatement. Whether the entity's risk assessment process is appropriate to the circumstances is a matter of judgement.

Considerations Specific to Smaller Entities (Ref: Para. 17)

A80. There is unlikely to be an established risk assessment process in a small entity. In such cases, it is likely that management will identify risks through direct personal involvement in the business. Irrespective of the circumstances, however, enquiry about identified risks and how they are addressed by management is still necessary.

Components of Internal Control—The Information System, Including the Related Business Processes, Relevant to Financial Reporting, and Communication

The Information System, Including Related Business Processes, Relevant to Financial Reporting (Ref: Para. 18)

A81. The information system relevant to financial reporting objectives, which includes the accounting system, consists of the procedures and records designed and established to:

- Initiate, record, process, and report entity transactions (as well as events and conditions) and to maintain accountability for the related assets, liabilities, and equity;

11 See ASA 330, paragraphs A2-A3.

- Resolve incorrect processing of transactions, for example, automated suspense files and procedures followed to clear suspense items out on a timely basis;
- Process and account for system overrides or bypasses to controls;
- Transfer information from transaction processing systems to the general ledger;
- Capture information relevant to financial reporting for events and conditions other than transactions, such as the depreciation and amortisation of assets and changes in the recoverability of accounts receivables; and
- Ensure information required to be disclosed by the applicable financial reporting framework is accumulated, recorded, processed, summarised and appropriately reported in the financial report.

Journal entries

A82. An entity's information system typically includes the use of standard journal entries that are required on a recurring basis to record transactions. Examples might be journal entries to record sales, purchases, and cash disbursements in the general ledger, or to record accounting estimates that are periodically made by management, such as changes in the estimate of uncollectible accounts receivable.

A83. An entity's financial reporting process also includes the use of non-standard journal entries to record non-recurring, unusual transactions or adjustments. Examples of such entries include consolidating adjustments and entries for a business combination or disposal or non-recurring estimates such as the impairment of an asset. In manual general ledger systems, non-standard journal entries may be identified through inspection of ledgers, journals, and supporting documentation. When automated procedures are used to maintain the general ledger and prepare a financial report, such entries may exist only in electronic form and may therefore be more easily identified through the use of computer-assisted audit techniques.

Related business processes

A84. An entity's business processes are the activities designed to:

- Develop, purchase, produce, sell and distribute an entity's products and services;
- Ensure compliance with laws and regulations; and
- Record information, including accounting and financial reporting information.

Business processes result in the transactions that are recorded, processed and reported by the information system. Obtaining an understanding of the entity's business processes, which include how transactions are originated, assists the auditor obtain an understanding of the entity's information system relevant to financial reporting in a manner that is appropriate to the entity's circumstances.

Considerations specific to smaller entities

A85. Information systems and related business processes relevant to financial reporting in small entities are likely to be less sophisticated than in larger entities, but their role is just as significant. Small entities with active management involvement may not need extensive descriptions of accounting procedures, sophisticated accounting records, or written policies. Understanding the entity's systems and processes may therefore be easier in an audit of smaller entities, and may be more dependent on enquiry than on review of documentation. The need to obtain an understanding, however, remains important.

Communication (Ref: Para. 19)

A86. Communication by the entity of the financial reporting roles and responsibilities and of significant matters relating to financial reporting involves providing an understanding of individual roles and responsibilities pertaining to internal control over financial reporting. It includes such matters as the extent to which personnel understand how their activities in the financial reporting information system relate to the work of others and the means of reporting exceptions to an appropriate higher level within the entity. Communication may take such forms as policy manuals and financial reporting manuals. Open communication channels help ensure that exceptions are reported and acted on.

Considerations specific to smaller entities

A87. Communication may be less structured and easier to achieve in a small entity than in a larger entity due to fewer levels of responsibility and management's greater visibility and availability.

Components of Internal Control—Control Activities (Ref: Para. 20)

A88. Control activities are the policies and procedures that help ensure that management directives are carried out. Control activities, whether within IT or manual systems, have various objectives and are applied at various organisational and functional levels. Examples of specific control activities include those relating to the following:

- Authorisation.
- Performance reviews.
- Information processing.
- Physical controls.
- Segregation of duties.

A89. Control activities that are relevant to the audit are:

- Those that are required to be treated as such, being control activities that relate to significant risks and those that relate to risks for which substantive procedures alone do not provide sufficient appropriate audit evidence, as required by paragraphs 29 and 30, respectively; or
- Those that are considered to be relevant in the judgement of the auditor.

A90. The auditor's judgement about whether a control activity is relevant to the audit is influenced by the risk that the auditor has identified that may give rise to a material misstatement and whether the auditor thinks it is likely to be appropriate to test the operating effectiveness of the control in determining the extent of substantive testing.

A91. The auditor's emphasis may be on identifying and obtaining an understanding of control activities that address the areas where the auditor considers that risks of material misstatement are likely to be higher. When multiple control activities each achieve the same objective, it is unnecessary to obtain an understanding of each of the control activities related to such objective.

A92. The auditor's knowledge about the presence or absence of control activities obtained from the understanding of the other components of internal control assists the auditor in determining whether it is necessary to devote additional attention to obtaining an understanding of control activities.

Considerations Specific to Smaller Entities

A93. The concepts underlying control activities in small entities are likely to be similar to those in larger entities, but the formality with which they operate may vary. Further, small entities may find that certain types of control activities are not relevant because of controls applied by management. For example, management's sole authority for granting credit to customers and approving significant purchases can provide strong control over important account balances and transactions, lessening or removing the need for more detailed control activities.

A94. Control activities relevant to the audit of a smaller entity are likely to relate to the main transaction cycles such as revenues, purchases and employment expenses.

Risks Arising From IT *(Ref: Para. 21)*

A95. The use of IT affects the way that control activities are implemented. From the auditor's perspective, controls over IT systems are effective when they maintain the integrity of information and the security of the data such systems process, and include effective general IT-controls and application controls.

A96. General IT-controls are policies and procedures that relate to many applications and support the effective functioning of application controls. They apply to mainframe, miniframe, and end-user environments. General IT-controls that maintain the integrity of information and security of data commonly include controls over the following:

- Data centre and network operations.
- System software acquisition, change and maintenance.
- Program change.
- Access security.
- Application system acquisition, development, and maintenance.

They are generally implemented to deal with the risks referred to in paragraph A56 above.

A97. Application controls are manual or automated procedures that typically operate at a business process level and apply to the processing of transactions by individual applications. Application controls can be preventive or detective in nature and are designed to ensure the integrity of the accounting records. Accordingly, application controls relate to procedures used to initiate, record, process and report transactions or other financial data. These controls help ensure that transactions occurred, are authorised, and are completely and accurately recorded and processed. Examples include edit checks of input data, and numerical sequence checks with manual follow-up of exception reports or correction at the point of data entry.

Components of Internal Control—Monitoring of Controls (Ref: Para. 22)

A98. Monitoring of controls is a process to assess the effectiveness of internal control performance over time. It involves assessing the effectiveness of controls on a timely basis and taking necessary remedial actions. Management accomplishes monitoring of controls through ongoing activities, separate evaluations, or a combination of the two. Ongoing monitoring activities are often built into the normal recurring activities of an entity and include regular management and supervisory activities.

A99. Management's monitoring activities may also include using information from communications from external parties such as customer complaints and regulator comments that may indicate problems or highlight areas in need of improvement.

Considerations Specific to Smaller Entities

A100. Management's monitoring of control is often accomplished by management's or the owner-manager's close involvement in operations. This involvement often will identify significant variances from expectations and inaccuracies in financial data leading to remedial action to the control.

Internal Audit Functions (Ref: Para 23)

A101. The entity's internal audit function is likely to be relevant to the audit if the nature of the internal audit function's responsibilities and activities are related to the entity's financial reporting, and the auditor expects to use the work of the internal auditors to modify the nature or timing, or reduce the extent, of audit procedures to be performed. If the auditor determines that the internal audit function is likely to be relevant to the audit, ASA 610 applies.

A102. The objectives of an internal audit function, and therefore the nature of its responsibilities and its status within the organisation, vary widely and depend on the size and structure of the entity and the requirements of management and, where applicable, those charged with governance. The responsibilities of an internal audit function may include, for example, monitoring of internal control, risk management, and review of compliance with laws and regulations. On the other hand, the responsibilities of the internal audit function may be limited to the review of the economy, efficiency and effectiveness of operations, for example, and accordingly, may not relate to the entity's financial reporting.

A103. If the nature of the internal audit function's responsibilities are related to the entity's financial reporting, the external auditor's consideration of the activities performed, or to be performed by, the internal audit function may include review of the internal audit function's audit plan for the period, if any, and discussion of that plan with the internal auditors.

Sources of Information (Ref: Para. 24)

A104. Much of the information used in monitoring may be produced by the entity's information system. If management assumes that data used for monitoring are accurate without having a basis for that assumption, errors that may exist in the information could potentially lead management to incorrect conclusions from its monitoring activities. Accordingly, an understanding of:

- the sources of the information related to the entity's monitoring activities; and
- the basis upon which management considers the information to be sufficiently reliable for the purpose

is required as part of the auditor's understanding of the entity's monitoring activities as a component of internal control.

Identifying and Assessing the Risks of Material Misstatement

Assessment of Risks of Material Misstatement at the Financial Report Level (Ref: Para. 25 (a))

A105. Risks of material misstatement at the financial report level refer to risks that relate pervasively to the financial report as a whole and potentially affect many assertions. Risks of this nature are not necessarily risks identifiable with specific assertions at the class of transactions, account balance, or disclosure level. Rather, they represent circumstances that may increase the risks of material misstatement at the assertion level, for example, through management override of internal control. Financial report level risks may be especially relevant to the auditor's consideration of the risks of material misstatement arising from fraud.

A106. Risks at the financial report level may derive in particular from a deficient control environment (although these risks may also relate to other factors, such as declining economic conditions). For example, deficiencies such as management's lack of competence may have a more pervasive effect on the financial report and may require an overall response by the auditor.

A107. The auditor's understanding of internal control may raise doubts about the auditability of an entity's financial report. For example:

- Concerns about the integrity of the entity's management may be so serious as to cause the auditor to conclude that the risk of management misrepresentation in the financial report is such that an audit cannot be conducted.
- Concerns about the condition and reliability of an entity's records may cause the auditor to conclude that it is unlikely that sufficient appropriate audit evidence will be available to support an unqualified opinion on the financial report.

A108. ASA 705[12] establishes requirements and provides guidance in determining whether there is a need for the auditor to express a qualified opinion or disclaim an opinion or, as may be required in some cases, to withdraw from the engagement where withdrawal is possible under applicable law or regulation.

Assessment of Risks of Material Misstatement at the Assertion Level (Ref: Para. 25(b))

A109. Risks of material misstatement at the assertion level for classes of transactions, account balances, and disclosures need to be considered because such consideration directly assists in determining the nature, timing, and extent of further audit procedures at the assertion level necessary to obtain sufficient appropriate audit evidence. In identifying and assessing risks of material misstatement at the assertion level, the auditor may conclude that the identified risks relate more pervasively to the financial report as a whole and potentially affect many assertions.

The Use of Assertions

A110. In representing that the financial report is in accordance with the applicable financial reporting framework, management or where appropriate those charged with governance implicitly

12 See ASA 705 *Modifications to the Opinion in the Independent Auditor's Report.*

or explicitly makes assertions regarding the recognition, measurement, presentation and disclosure of the various elements of the financial report and related disclosures.

A111. Assertions used by the auditor to consider the different types of potential misstatements that may occur fall into the following three categories and may take the following forms:

(a) Assertions about classes of transactions and events for the period under audit:

(i) Occurrence—transactions and events that have been recorded have occurred and pertain to the entity.

(ii) Completeness—all transactions and events that should have been recorded have been recorded.

(iii) Accuracy—amounts and other data relating to recorded transactions and events have been recorded appropriately.

(iv) Cut-off—transactions and events have been recorded in the correct accounting period.

(v) Classification—transactions and events have been recorded in the proper accounts.

(b) Assertions about account balances at the period end:

(i) Existence—assets, liabilities, and equity interests exist.

(ii) Rights and obligations—the entity holds or controls the rights to assets, and liabilities are the obligations of the entity.

(iii) Completeness—all assets, liabilities and equity interests that should have been recorded have been recorded.

(iv) Valuation and allocation—assets, liabilities, and equity interests are included in the financial report at appropriate amounts and any resulting valuation or allocation adjustments are appropriately recorded.

(c) Assertions about presentation and disclosure:

(i) Occurrence and rights and obligations—disclosed events, transactions, and other matters have occurred and pertain to the entity.

(ii) Completeness—all disclosures that should have been included in the financial report have been included.

(iii) Classification and understandability—financial information is appropriately presented and described, and disclosures are clearly expressed.

(iv) Accuracy and valuation—financial and other information are disclosed fairly and at appropriate amounts.

A112. The auditor may use the assertions as described above or may express them differently provided all aspects described above have been covered. For example, the auditor may choose to combine the assertions about transactions and events with the assertions about account balances.

Considerations specific to public sector entities

A113. When making assertions about the financial report of public sector entities, in addition to those assertions set out in paragraph A111, management or those charged with governance may often assert that transactions and events have been carried out in accordance with law, regulation or other authority. Such assertions may fall within the scope of the financial report audit.

Process of Identifying Risks of Material Misstatement (Ref: Para. 26(a))

A114. Information gathered by performing risk assessment procedures, including the audit evidence obtained in evaluating the design of controls and determining whether they have been implemented, is used as audit evidence to support the risk assessment. The risk assessment determines the nature, timing, and extent of further audit procedures to be performed.

A115. Appendix 2 provides examples of conditions and events that may indicate the existence of risks of material misstatement.

Relating Controls to Assertions (Ref: Para. 26(c))

A116. In making risk assessments, the auditor may identify the controls that are likely to prevent, or detect and correct, material misstatement in specific assertions. Generally, it is useful to obtain an understanding of controls and relate them to assertions in the context of processes and systems in which they exist because individual control activities often do not in themselves address a risk. Often, only multiple control activities, together with other components of internal control, will be sufficient to address a risk.

A117. Conversely, some control activities may have a specific effect on an individual assertion embodied in a particular class of transactions or account balance. For example, the control activities that an entity established to ensure that its personnel are properly counting and recording the annual physical inventory relate directly to the existence and completeness assertions for the inventory account balance.

A118. Controls can be either directly or indirectly related to an assertion. The more indirect the relationship, the less effective that control may be in preventing, or detecting and correcting, misstatements in that assertion. For example, a sales manager's review of a summary of sales activity for specific stores by region ordinarily is only indirectly related to the completeness assertion for sales revenue. Accordingly, it may be less effective in reducing risk for that assertion than controls more directly related to that assertion, such as matching shipping documents with billing documents.

Significant Risks

Identifying Significant Risks (Ref: Para. 28)

A119. Significant risks often relate to significant non-routine transactions or judgemental matters. Non-routine transactions are transactions that are unusual, due to either size or nature, and that therefore occur infrequently. Judgemental matters may include the development of accounting estimates for which there is significant measurement uncertainty. Routine, non-complex transactions that are subject to systematic processing are less likely to give rise to significant risks.

A120. Risks of material misstatement may be greater for significant non-routine transactions arising from matters such as the following:

- Greater management intervention to specify the accounting treatment.
- Greater manual intervention for data collection and processing.
- Complex calculations or accounting principles.
- The nature of non-routine transactions, which may make it difficult for the entity to implement effective controls over the risks.

A121. Risks of material misstatement may be greater for significant judgemental matters that require the development of accounting estimates, arising from matters such as the following:

- Accounting principles for accounting estimates or revenue recognition may be subject to differing interpretation.
- Required judgement may be subjective or complex, or require assumptions about the effects of future events, for example, judgement about fair value.

A122. ASA 330 describes the consequences for further audit procedures of identifying a risk as significant.[13]

Significant risks relating to the risks of material misstatement due to fraud

A123. ASA 240 provides further requirements and guidance in relation to the identification and assessment of the risks of material misstatement due to fraud.[14]

13 See ASA 330, paragraphs 15 and 21.

14 See ASA 240, paragraphs 25-27.

Understanding Controls Related to Significant Risks (Ref: Para. 29)

A124. Although risks relating to significant non-routine or judgemental matters are often less likely to be subject to routine controls, management may have other responses intended to deal with such risks. Accordingly, the auditor's understanding of whether the entity has designed and implemented controls for significant risks arising from non-routine or judgemental matters includes whether and how management responds to the risks. Such responses might include:

- Control activities such as a review of assumptions by senior management or experts.
- Documented processes for estimations.
- Approval by those charged with governance.

A125. For example, where there are one-off events such as the receipt of notice of a significant lawsuit, consideration of the entity's response may include such matters as whether it has been referred to appropriate experts (such as internal or external legal counsel), whether an assessment has been made of the potential effect, and how it is proposed that the circumstances are to be disclosed in the financial report.

A126. In some cases, management may not have appropriately responded to significant risks of material misstatement by implementing controls over these significant risks. Failure by management to implement such controls is an indicator of a significant deficiency in internal control.[15]

Risks for Which Substantive Procedures Alone Do Not Provide Sufficient Appropriate Audit Evidence (Ref: Para. 30)

A127. Risks of material misstatement may relate directly to the recording of routine classes of transactions or account balances, and the preparation of a reliable financial report. Such risks may include risks of inaccurate or incomplete processing for routine and significant classes of transactions such as an entity's revenue, purchases, and cash receipts or cash payments.

A128. Where such routine business transactions are subject to highly automated processing with little or no manual intervention, it may not be possible to perform only substantive procedures in relation to the risk. For example, the auditor may consider this to be the case in circumstances where a significant amount of an entity's information is initiated, recorded, processed, or reported only in electronic form such as in an integrated system. In such cases:

- Audit evidence may be available only in electronic form, and its sufficiency and appropriateness usually depend on the effectiveness of controls over its accuracy and completeness.
- The potential for improper initiation or alteration of information to occur and not be detected may be greater if appropriate controls are not operating effectively.

A129. The consequences for further audit procedures of identifying such risks are described in ASA 330.[16]

Revision of Risk Assessment (Ref: Para. 31)

A130. During the audit, information may come to the auditor's attention that differs significantly from the information on which the risk assessment was based. For example, the risk assessment may be based on an expectation that certain controls are operating effectively. In performing tests of those controls, the auditor may obtain audit evidence that they were not operating effectively at relevant times during the audit. Similarly, in performing substantive procedures the auditor may detect misstatements in amounts or frequency greater than is consistent with the auditor's risk assessments. In such circumstances, the risk assessment may not appropriately reflect the true circumstances of the entity and the further planned audit procedures may not be effective in detecting material misstatements. See ASA 330 for further guidance.

---

15 See ASA 265 *Communicating Deficiencies in Internal Control to Those Charged with Governance and Management*, paragraph A7.

16 See ASA 330, paragraph 8.

Documentation (Ref: Para. 32)

A131. The manner in which the requirements of paragraph 32 are documented is for the auditor to determine using professional judgement. For example, in audits of small entities the documentation may be incorporated in the auditor's documentation of the overall strategy and audit plan.[17] Similarly, for example, the results of the risk assessment may be documented separately, or may be documented as part of the auditor's documentation of further procedures.[18] The form and extent of the documentation is influenced by the nature, size and complexity of the entity and its internal control, availability of information from the entity and the audit methodology and technology used in the course of the audit.

A132. For entities that have uncomplicated businesses and processes relevant to financial reporting, the documentation may be simple in form and relatively brief. It is not necessary to document the entirety of the auditor's understanding of the entity and matters related to it. Key elements of understanding documented by the auditor include those on which the auditor based the assessment of the risks of material misstatement.

A133. The extent of documentation may also reflect the experience and capabilities of the members of the audit engagement team. Provided the requirements of ASA 230, are always met, an audit undertaken by an engagement team comprising less experienced individuals may require more detailed documentation to assist them to obtain an appropriate understanding of the entity than one that includes experienced individuals.

A134. For recurring audits, certain documentation may be carried forward, updated as necessary to reflect changes in the entity's business or processes.

❖ ❖ ❖

Conformity with International Standards on Auditing

This Auditing Standard conforms with International Standard on Auditing ISA 315 *Identifying and Assessing the Risks of Material Misstatement through Understanding the Entity and its Environment*, issued by the International Auditing and Assurance Standards Board (IAASB), an independent standard-setting board of the International Federation of Accountants (IFAC).

Paragraphs that have been added to this Auditing Standard (and do not appear in the text of the equivalent ISA) are identified with the prefix "Aus".

Compliance with this Auditing Standard enables compliance with ISA 315.

Appendix 1

(Ref: Para. 4(c), 14-24 and A69-A104)

Internal Control Components

1. This appendix further explains the components of internal control, as set out in paragraphs 4(c), 14-24 and A69-A104 as they relate to a financial report audit.

Control Environment

2. The control environment encompasses the following elements:

   (a) *Communication and enforcement of integrity and ethical values.* The effectiveness of controls cannot rise above the integrity and ethical values of the people who create, administer, and monitor them. Integrity and ethical behaviour are the product of the entity's ethical and behavioural standards, how they are communicated, and how they are reinforced in practice. The enforcement of integrity and ethical values includes, for example, management actions to eliminate or mitigate incentives or temptations that might prompt personnel to engage in dishonest, illegal, or unethical acts. The communication of entity policies on integrity and ethical values may include the communication of behavioural standards to personnel through policy statements and codes of conduct and by example.

17 See ASA 300 *Planning an Audit of a Financial Report*, paragraphs 7 and 9.

18 See ASA 330, paragraph 28.

(b) *Commitment to competence.* Competence is the knowledge and skills necessary to accomplish tasks that define the individual's job.

(c) *Participation by those charged with governance.* An entity's control consciousness is influenced significantly by those charged with governance. The importance of the responsibilities of those charged with governance is recognised in codes of practice and other laws and regulations or guidance produced for the benefit of those charged with governance. Other responsibilities of those charged with governance include oversight of the design and effective operation of whistle blower procedures and the process for reviewing the effectiveness of the entity's internal control.

(d) *Management's philosophy and operating style.* Management's philosophy and operating style encompass a broad range of characteristics. For example, management's attitudes and actions toward financial reporting may manifest themselves through conservative or aggressive selection from available alternative accounting principles, or conscientiousness and conservatism with which accounting estimates are developed.

(e) *Organisational structure.* Establishing a relevant organisational structure includes considering key areas of authority and responsibility and appropriate lines of reporting. The appropriateness of an entity's organisational structure depends, in part, on its size and the nature of its activities.

(f) *Assignment of authority and responsibility.* The assignment of authority and responsibility may include policies relating to appropriate business practices, knowledge and experience of key personnel, and resources provided for carrying out duties. In addition, it may include policies and communications directed at ensuring that all personnel understand the entity's objectives, know how their individual actions interrelate and contribute to those objectives, and recognise how and for what they will be held accountable.

(g) *Human resource policies and practices.* Human resource policies and practices often demonstrate important matters in relation to the control consciousness of an entity. For example, standards for recruiting the most qualified individuals – with emphasis on educational background, prior work experience, past accomplishments, and evidence of integrity and ethical behaviour – demonstrate an entity's commitment to competent and trustworthy people. Training policies that communicate prospective roles and responsibilities and include practices such as training schools and seminars illustrate expected levels of performance and behaviour. Promotions driven by periodic performance appraisals demonstrate the entity's commitment to the advancement of qualified personnel to higher levels of responsibility.

Entity's Risk Assessment Process

3. For financial reporting purposes, the entity's risk assessment process includes how management identifies business risks relevant to the preparation of the financial report in accordance with the entity's applicable financial reporting framework, estimates their significance, assesses the likelihood of their occurrence, and decides upon actions to respond to and manage them and the results thereof. For example, the entity's risk assessment process may address how the entity considers the possibility of unrecorded transactions or identifies and analyses significant estimates recorded in the financial report.

4. Risks relevant to reliable financial reporting include external and internal events, transactions or circumstances that may occur and adversely affect an entity's ability to initiate, record, process, and report financial data consistent with the assertions of management in the financial report. Management may initiate plans, programs, or actions to address specific risks or it may decide to accept a risk because of cost or other considerations. Risks can arise or change due to circumstances such as the following:

- *Changes in operating environment.* Changes in the regulatory or operating environment can result in changes in competitive pressures and significantly different risks.
- *New personnel.* New personnel may have a different focus on or understanding of internal control.

- *New or revamped information systems.* Significant and rapid changes in information systems can change the risk relating to internal control.
- *Rapid growth.* Significant and rapid expansion of operations can strain controls and increase the risk of a breakdown in controls.
- *New technology.* Incorporating new technologies into production processes or information systems may change the risk associated with internal control.
- *New business models, products, or activities.* Entering into business areas or transactions with which an entity has little experience may introduce new risks associated with internal control.
- *Corporate restructurings.* Restructurings may be accompanied by staff reductions and changes in supervision and segregation of duties that may change the risk associated with internal control.
- *Expanded foreign operations.* The expansion or acquisition of foreign operations carries new and often unique risks that may affect internal control, for example, additional or changed risks from foreign currency transactions.
- *New accounting pronouncements.* Adoption of new accounting principles or changing accounting principles may affect risks in preparing the financial report.

Information System, Including the Related Business Processes, Relevant to Financial Reporting, and Communication

5. An information system consists of infrastructure (physical and hardware components), software, people, procedures, and data. Many information systems make extensive use of information technology (IT).

6. The information system relevant to financial reporting objectives, which includes the financial reporting system, encompasses methods and records that:
   - Identify and record all valid transactions.
   - Describe on a timely basis the transactions in sufficient detail to permit proper classification of transactions for financial reporting.
   - Measure the value of transactions in a manner that permits recording their proper monetary value in the financial report.
   - Determine the time period in which transactions occurred to permit recording of transactions in the proper accounting period.
   - Present properly the transactions and related disclosures in the financial report.

7. The quality of system-generated information affects management's ability to make appropriate decisions in managing and controlling the entity's activities and to prepare reliable financial reports.

8. Communication, which involves providing an understanding of individual roles and responsibilities pertaining to internal control over financial reporting, may take such forms as policy manuals, accounting and financial reporting manuals, and memoranda. Communication also can be made electronically, orally, and through the actions of management.

Control Activities

9. Generally, control activities that may be relevant to an audit may be categorised as policies and procedures that pertain to the following:
   - *Performance reviews.* These control activities include reviews and analyses of actual performance versus budgets, forecasts, and prior period performance; relating different sets of data – operating or financial – to one another, together with analyses of the relationships and investigative and corrective actions; comparing internal data with external sources of information; and review of functional or activity performance.

- *Information processing.* The two broad groupings of information systems control activities are application controls, which apply to the processing of individual applications, and general IT-controls, which are policies and procedures that relate to many applications and support the effective functioning of application controls by helping to ensure the continued proper operation of information systems. Examples of application controls include checking the arithmetical accuracy of records, maintaining and reviewing accounts and trial balances, automated controls such as edit checks of input data and numerical sequence checks, and manual follow-up of exception reports. Examples of general IT-controls are program change controls, controls that restrict access to programs or data, controls over the implementation of new releases of packaged software applications, and controls over system software that restrict access to or monitor the use of system utilities that could change financial data or records without leaving an audit trail.
- *Physical controls.* Controls that encompass:
  - The physical security of assets, including adequate safeguards such as secured facilities over access to assets and records.
  - The authorisation for access to computer programs and data files.
  - The periodic counting and comparison with amounts shown on control records (for example comparing the results of cash, security and inventory counts with accounting records).

  The extent to which physical controls intended to prevent theft of assets are relevant to the reliability of financial report preparation, and therefore the audit, depends on circumstances such as when assets are highly susceptible to misappropriation.
- *Segregation of duties.* Assigning different people the responsibilities of authorising transactions, recording transactions, and maintaining custody of assets. Segregation of duties is intended to reduce the opportunities to allow any person to be in a position to both perpetrate and conceal errors or fraud in the normal course of the person's duties.

10. Certain control activities may depend on the existence of appropriate higher level policies established by management or those charged with governance. For example, authorisation controls may be delegated under established guidelines, such as investment criteria set by those charged with governance; alternatively, non-routine transactions such as major acquisitions or divestments may require specific high level approval, including in some cases that of shareholders.

Monitoring of Controls

11. An important management responsibility is to establish and maintain internal control on an ongoing basis. Management's monitoring of controls includes considering whether they are operating as intended and that they are modified as appropriate for changes in conditions. Monitoring of controls may include activities such as management's review of whether bank reconciliations are being prepared on a timely basis, internal auditors' evaluation of sales personnel's compliance with the entity's policies on terms of sales contracts, and a legal department's oversight of compliance with the entity's ethical or business practice policies. Monitoring is done also to ensure that controls continue to operate effectively over time. For example, if the timeliness and accuracy of bank reconciliations are not monitored, personnel are likely to stop preparing them.

12. Internal auditors or personnel performing similar functions may contribute to the monitoring of an entity's controls through separate evaluations. Ordinarily, they regularly provide information about the functioning of internal control, focusing considerable attention on evaluating the effectiveness of internal control, and communicate information about strengths and deficiencies in internal control and recommendations for improving internal control.

13. Monitoring activities may include using information from communications from external parties that may indicate problems or highlight areas in need of improvement. Customers implicitly corroborate billing data by paying their invoices or complaining about their charges. In addition, regulators may communicate with the entity concerning

matters that affect the functioning of internal control, for example, communications concerning examinations by bank regulatory agencies. Also, management may consider communications relating to internal control from external auditors in performing monitoring activities.

Appendix 2

(Ref: Para. A33 and A115)

Conditions and Events That May Indicate Risks of Material Misstatement

The following are examples of conditions and events that may indicate the existence of risks of material misstatement. The examples provided cover a broad range of conditions and events; however, not all conditions and events are relevant to every audit engagement and the list of examples is not necessarily complete.

- Operations in regions that are economically unstable, for example, countries with significant currency devaluation or highly inflationary economies.
- Operations exposed to volatile markets, for example, futures trading.
- Operations that are subject to a high degree of complex regulation.
- Going concern and liquidity issues including loss of significant customers.
- Constraints on the availability of capital and credit.
- Changes in the industry in which the entity operates.
- Changes in the supply chain.
- Developing or offering new products or services, or moving into new lines of business.
- Expanding into new locations.
- Changes in the entity such as large acquisitions or reorganisations or other unusual events.
- Entities or business segments likely to be sold.
- The existence of complex alliances and joint ventures.
- Use of off-balance-sheet finance, special-purpose entities, and other complex financing arrangements.
- Significant transactions with related parties.
- Lack of personnel with appropriate accounting and financial reporting skills.
- Changes in key personnel including departure of key executives.
- Deficiencies in internal control, especially those not addressed by management.
- Inconsistencies between the entity's IT strategy and its business strategies.
- Changes in the IT environment.
- Installation of significant new IT systems related to financial reporting.
- Enquiries into the entity's operations or financial results by regulatory or government bodies.
- Past misstatements, history of errors or a significant amount of adjustments at period end.
- Significant amount of non-routine or non-systematic transactions including intercompany transactions and large revenue transactions at period end.
- Transactions that are recorded based on management's intent, for example, debt refinancing, assets to be sold and classification of marketable securities.
- Application of new accounting pronouncements.
- Accounting measurements that involve complex processes.
- Events or transactions that involve significant measurement uncertainty, including accounting estimates.
- Pending litigation and contingent liabilities, for example, sales warranties, financial guarantees and environmental remediation.

ASA 320

Materiality in Planning and Performing an Audit

(Reissued October 2009: amended and compiled June 2011)

Issued by the Auditing and Assurance Standards Board.

Note from the Institute of Chartered Accountants Australia

This note, prepared by the technical editor, is not part of ASA 320.

Historical development

February 1988: Statement of Auditing Practice AUP 27 'Materiality and Audit Risk' issued, effective from date of issue, following the issue of ED 24 (IAPC ED 25) in July 1986.

June 1994: The International Auditing Practices Committee (IAPC) of the International Federation of Accountants (IFAC) approved the issuance of a codified set of International Standards of Auditing (ISAs). The relevant international pronouncement is ISA 320 'Audit Materiality'.

October 1995: Australian Auditing Standards and Auditing Guidance Statements released. The status of these was explained in APS 1.1 'Conformity With Auditing Standards'. These Standards became operative for the first reporting period commencing on or after 1 July 1996 and later reporting periods, although earlier application was encouraged. AUP 27 'Materiality and Audit Risk' replaced by AUS 306 'Materiality'.

June 2001: AUS 306 revised to clarify existing practice regarding the auditor's consideration of materiality in planning an audit and evaluating audit evidence. Operative from the date of issue.

April 2006: ASA 320 was issued as a legally enforceable Standard to replace AUS 306. It is based on ISA 320 'Audit Materiality'.

October 2009: ASA 320 reissued as part of the AUASB's Clarity Project. It includes a new Introduction discussing the nature of materiality in the context of the audit. It is based on the revised ISA 320 of the same name.

June 2011: ASA 320 updated for editorial amendments contained in ASA 2011-1 'Amendments to Australian Auditing Standards'.

Contents

Compilation Details

Auditing Standard ASA 320 *Materiality in Planning and Performing an Audit* as Amended

This compilation takes into account amendments made up to and including 27 June 2011 and was prepared on 27 June 2011 by the Auditing and Assurance Standards Board (AUASB).

This compilation is not a separate Auditing Standard made by the AUASB. Instead, it is a representation of ASA 320 (October 2009) as amended by another Auditing Standard which is listed in the Table below.

Table of Standards

Standard	Date made	Operative date
ASA 320	27 October 2009	1 January 2010
ASA 2011-1	27 June 2011	1 July 2011

Table of Amendments

Paragraph affected	How affected	By … [paragraph]
Title Page	Amended	ASA 2011-1 [31]

Preface

[Preface extracted from the original Auditing Standard issued 27 October 2009]

Reasons for Issuing Auditing Standard ASA 320 *Materiality in Planning and Performing an Audit*

The Auditing and Assurance Standards Board (AUASB) issues Auditing Standard ASA 320 *Materiality in Planning and Performing an Audit* pursuant to the requirements of the legislative provisions and the Strategic Direction explained below.

The AUASB is an independent statutory board of the Australian Government under section 227A of the *Australian Securities and Investments Commission Act 2001*, as amended (ASIC Act). Under section 336 of the *Corporations Act 2001*, the AUASB may make Auditing Standards for the purposes of the corporations legislation. These Auditing Standards are legislative instruments under the *Legislative Instruments Act 2003*.

Under the Strategic Direction given to the AUASB by the Financial Reporting Council (FRC), the AUASB is required to have regard to any programme initiated by the International Auditing and Assurance Standards Board (IAASB) for the revision and enhancement of the International Standards on Auditing (ISAs) and to make appropriate consequential amendments to the Australian Auditing Standards. Accordingly, the AUASB has decided to revise and redraft the Australian Auditing Standards using the equivalent redrafted ISAs.

Main Features

This Auditing Standard establishes requirements and provides application and other explanatory material regarding the auditor's responsibility to apply the concept of materiality in planning and performing an audit of a financial report.

This Auditing Standard requires the auditor to:

(a) exercise professional judgement to determine materiality (including performance materiality) when planning the audit;

(b) revise materiality as the audit progresses if the auditor considers it necessary; and

(c) document the factors used by the auditor in determining or revising materiality.

Authority Statement

Auditing Standard ASA 320 *Materiality in Planning and Performing an Audit* (as amended at 27 June 2011) is set out in paragraphs 1 to A13.

This Auditing Standard is to be read in conjunction with ASA 101 *Preamble to Australian Auditing Standards*, which sets out the intentions of the AUASB on how the Australian Auditing Standards, operative for financial reporting periods commencing on or after 1 January 2010, are to be understood, interpreted and applied. This Auditing Standard is to be read also in conjunction with ASA 200 *Overall Objectives of the Independent Auditor and the Conduct of an Audit in Accordance with Australian Auditing Standards*.

Dated: 27 June 2011

M H Kelsall
Chairman - AUASB

Auditing Standard ASA 320

The Auditing and Assurance Standards Board (AUASB) made Auditing Standard ASA 320 *Materiality in Planning and Performing an Audit,* pursuant to section 227B of the *Australian Securities and Investments Commission Act 2001* and section 336 of the *Corporations Act 2001*, on 27 October 2009.

This compiled version of ASA 320 incorporates subsequent amendments contained in another Auditing Standard made by the AUASB up to and including 27 June 2011 (see Compilation Details).

Auditing Standard ASA 320

Materiality in Planning and Performing an Audit

Application

Aus 0.1 This Auditing Standard applies to:

(a) an audit of a financial report for a financial year, or an audit of a financial report for a half-year, in accordance with the *Corporations Act 2001*; and

(b) an audit of a financial report, or a complete set of financial statements, for any other purpose.

Aus 0.2 This Auditing Standard also applies, as appropriate, to an audit of other historical financial information.

Operative Date

Aus 0.3 This Auditing Standard is operative for financial reporting periods commencing on or after 1 January 2010.

[Note: For operative dates of paragraphs changed or added by an amending Standard, see Compilation Details.]

Introduction

Scope of this Auditing Standard

1. This Auditing Standard deals with the auditor's responsibility to apply the concept of materiality in planning and performing an audit[1] of a financial report. ASA 450[1] explains how materiality is applied in evaluating the effect of identified misstatements on the audit and of uncorrected misstatements, if any, on the financial report.

Materiality in the Context of an Audit

2. Financial reporting frameworks often discuss the concept of materiality in the context of the preparation and presentation of a financial report. Although financial reporting frameworks may discuss materiality in different terms, they generally explain that:

- Misstatements, including omissions, are considered to be material if they, individually or in the aggregate, could reasonably be expected to influence the economic decisions of users taken on the basis of the financial report;
- Judgements about materiality are made in light of surrounding circumstances, and are affected by the size or nature of a misstatement, or a combination of both; and
- Judgements about matters that are material to users of the financial report are based on a consideration of the common financial information needs of users as a group.[2] The possible effect of misstatements on specific individual users, whose needs may vary widely, is not considered.

3. Such a discussion, if present in the applicable financial reporting framework, provides a frame of reference to the auditor in determining materiality for the audit. If the applicable financial reporting framework does not include a discussion of the concept of materiality, the characteristics referred to in paragraph 2 of this Auditing Standard provide the auditor with such a frame of reference.

4. The auditor's determination of materiality is a matter of professional judgement, and is affected by the auditor's perception of the financial information needs of users of the financial report. In this context, it is reasonable for the auditor to assume that users:

(a) Have a reasonable knowledge of business and economic activities and accounting and a willingness to study the information in the financial report with reasonable diligence;

1 See ASA 450 *Evaluation of Misstatements Identified during the Audit*.

2 See, for example, the AASB's *Framework for the Preparation and Presentation of Financial Statements* (July 2004).

(b) Understand that the financial report is prepared, presented and audited to levels of materiality;

(c) Recognise the uncertainties inherent in the measurement of amounts based on the use of estimates, judgement and the consideration of future events; and

(d) Make reasonable economic decisions on the basis of the information in the financial report.

5. The concept of materiality is applied by the auditor both in planning and performing the audit, and in evaluating the effect of identified misstatements on the audit and of uncorrected misstatements, if any, on the financial report and in forming the opinion in the auditor's report. (Ref: Para. A1)

6. In planning the audit, the auditor makes judgements about the size of misstatements that will be considered material. These judgements provide a basis for:

(a) Determining the nature, timing and extent of risk assessment procedures;

(b) Identifying and assessing the risks of material misstatement; and

(c) Determining the nature, timing and extent of further audit procedures.

The materiality determined when planning the audit does not necessarily establish an amount below which uncorrected misstatements, individually or in the aggregate, will always be evaluated as immaterial. The circumstances related to some misstatements may cause the auditor to evaluate them as material even if they are below materiality. Although it is not practicable to design audit procedures to detect misstatements that could be material solely because of their nature, the auditor considers not only the size but also the nature of uncorrected misstatements, and the particular circumstances of their occurrence, when evaluating their effect on the financial report.[3]

Effective Date

7. [Deleted by the AUASB. Refer Aus 0.3]

Objective

8. The objective of the auditor is to apply the concept of materiality appropriately in planning and performing the audit.

Definition

9. For purposes of the Australian Auditing Standards, performance materiality means the amount or amounts set by the auditor at less than materiality for the financial report as a whole to reduce to an appropriately low level the probability that the aggregate of uncorrected and undetected misstatements exceeds materiality for the financial report as a whole. If applicable, performance materiality also refers to the amount or amounts set by the auditor at less than the materiality level or levels for particular classes of transactions, account balances or disclosures.

Requirements

Determining Materiality and Performance Materiality When Planning the Audit

10. When establishing the overall audit strategy, the auditor shall determine materiality for the financial report as a whole. If, in the specific circumstances of the entity, there is one or more particular classes of transactions, account balances or disclosures for which misstatements of lesser amounts than materiality for the financial report as a whole could reasonably be expected to influence the economic decisions of users taken on the basis of the financial report, the auditor shall also determine the materiality level or levels to be applied to those particular classes of transactions, account balances or disclosures. (Ref: Para. A2-A11)

3 See ASA 450, paragraph A16.

11. The auditor shall determine performance materiality for purposes of assessing the risks of material misstatement and determining the nature, timing and extent of further audit procedures. (Ref: Para. A12)

Revision as the Audit Progresses

12. The auditor shall revise materiality for the financial report as a whole (and, if applicable, the materiality level or levels for particular classes of transactions, account balances or disclosures) in the event of becoming aware of information during the audit that would have caused the auditor to have determined a different amount (or amounts) initially. (Ref: Para. A13)

13. If the auditor concludes that a lower materiality for the financial report as a whole (and, if applicable, materiality level or levels for particular classes of transactions, account balances or disclosures) than that initially determined is appropriate, the auditor shall determine whether it is necessary to revise performance materiality, and whether the nature, timing and extent of the further audit procedures remain appropriate.

Documentation

14. The auditor shall include in the audit documentation the following amounts and the factors considered in their determination[4]:

    (a) Materiality for the financial report as a whole (see paragraph 10 of this Auditing Standard);

    (b) If applicable, the materiality level or levels for particular classes of transactions, account balances or disclosures (see paragraph 10 of this Auditing Standard);

    (c) Performance materiality (see paragraph 11 of this Auditing Standard); and

    (d) Any revision of (a)-(c) as the audit progressed (see paragraphs 12-13 of this Auditing Standard).

❖ ❖ ❖

Application and Other Explanatory Material

Materiality and Audit Risk (Ref: Para. 5)

A1. In conducting an audit of a financial report, the overall objectives of the auditor are to obtain reasonable assurance about whether the financial report as a whole is free from material misstatement, whether due to fraud or error, thereby enabling the auditor to express an opinion on whether the financial report is prepared, in all material respects, in accordance with an applicable financial reporting framework; and to report on the financial report, and communicate as required by the Australian Auditing Standards, in accordance with the auditor's findings.[5] The auditor obtains reasonable assurance by obtaining sufficient appropriate audit evidence to reduce audit risk to an acceptably low level.[6] Audit risk is the risk that the auditor expresses an inappropriate audit opinion when the financial report is materially misstated. Audit risk is a function of the risks of material misstatement and detection risk.[7] Materiality and audit risk are considered throughout the audit, in particular, when:

    (a) Identifying and assessing the risks of material misstatement;[8]

    (b) Determining the nature, timing and extent of further audit procedures;[9] and

---

4 See ASA 230 *Audit Documentation*, paragraphs 8-11 and paragraph A6.

5 See ASA 200 *Overall Objectives of the Independent Auditor and the Conduct of an Audit in Accordance with Australian Auditing Standards*, paragraph 11.

6 See ASA 200, paragraph 17.

7 See ASA 200, paragraph 13(c).

8 See ASA 315 *Identifying and Assessing the Risks of Material Misstatement through Understanding the Entity and Its Environment.*

9 See ASA 330 *The Auditor's Responses to Assessed Risks.*

(c) Evaluating the effect of uncorrected misstatements, if any, on the financial report[10] and in forming the opinion in the auditor's report.[11]

Aus A1.1 Australian Accounting Standards* explain the role of materiality in making judgements in the preparation and presentation of a financial report by the entity.

Determining Materiality and Performance Materiality When Planning the Audit

Considerations Specific to Public Sector Entities (Ref: Para. 10)

A2. In the case of a public sector entity, legislators and regulators are often the primary users of its financial report. Furthermore, the financial report may be used to make decisions other than economic decisions. The determination of materiality for the financial report as a whole (and, if applicable, materiality level or levels for particular classes of transactions, account balances or disclosures) in an audit of the financial report of a public sector entity is therefore influenced by law, regulation or other authority, and by the financial information needs of legislators and the public in relation to public sector programs.

Use of Benchmarks in Determining Materiality for the Financial Report as a Whole (Ref: Para. 10)

A3. Determining materiality involves the exercise of professional judgement. A percentage is often applied to a chosen benchmark as a starting point in determining materiality for the financial report as a whole. Factors that may affect the identification of an appropriate benchmark include the following:

- The elements of the financial report (for example, assets, liabilities, equity, revenue, expenses);
- Whether there are items on which the attention of the users of the particular entity's financial report tends to be focused (for example, for the purpose of evaluating financial performance users may tend to focus on profit, revenue or net assets);
- The nature of the entity, where the entity is in its life cycle, and the industry and economic environment in which the entity operates;
- The entity's ownership structure and the way it is financed (for example, if an entity is financed solely by debt rather than equity, users may put more emphasis on assets, and claims on them, than on the entity's earnings); and
- The relative volatility of the benchmark.

A4. Examples of benchmarks that may be appropriate, depending on the circumstances of the entity, include categories of reported income such as profit before tax, total revenue, gross profit and total expenses, total equity or net asset value. Profit before tax from continuing operations is often used for profit-oriented entities. When profit before tax from continuing operations is volatile, other benchmarks may be more appropriate, such as gross profit or total revenues.

A5. In relation to the chosen benchmark, relevant financial data ordinarily includes prior periods' financial results and financial positions, the period-to-date financial results and financial position, and budgets or forecasts for the current period, adjusted for significant changes in the circumstances of the entity (for example, a significant business acquisition) and relevant changes of conditions in the industry or economic environment in which the entity operates. For example, when, as a starting point, materiality for the financial report as a whole is determined for a particular entity based on a percentage of profit before tax from continuing operations, circumstances that give rise to an exceptional decrease or increase in such profit may lead the auditor to conclude that materiality for the financial report as a whole is more appropriately determined using a normalised profit before tax from continuing operations figure based on past results.

---

10 See ASA 450.

11 See ASA 700 *Forming an Opinion and Reporting on a Financial Report.*

* See Accounting Standard AASB 1031 *Materiality*.

A6. Materiality relates to the financial report on which the auditor is reporting. Where the financial report is prepared for a financial reporting period of more or less than twelve months, such as may be the case for a new entity or a change in the financial reporting period, materiality relates to the financial report prepared for that financial reporting period.

A7. Determining a percentage to be applied to a chosen benchmark involves the exercise of professional judgement. There is a relationship between the percentage and the chosen benchmark, such that a percentage applied to profit before tax from continuing operations will normally be higher than a percentage applied to total revenue. For example, the auditor may consider five percent of profit before tax from continuing operations to be appropriate for a profit-oriented entity in a manufacturing industry, while the auditor may consider one percent of total revenues or total expenses to be appropriate for a not-for-profit entity. Higher or lower percentages, however, may be deemed appropriate in the circumstances.

Considerations Specific to Small Entities

A8. When an entity's profit before tax from continuing operations is consistently nominal, as might be the case for an owner-managed business where the owner takes much of the profit before tax in the form of remuneration, a benchmark such as profit before remuneration and tax may be more relevant.

Considerations Specific to Public Sector Entities

A9. In an audit of a public sector entity, total cost or net cost (expenses less revenues or expenditure less receipts) may be appropriate benchmarks for program activities. Where a public sector entity has custody of public assets, assets may be an appropriate benchmark.

Materiality Level or Levels for Particular Classes of Transactions, Account Balances or Disclosures (Ref: Para. 10)

A10. Factors that may indicate the existence of one or more particular classes of transactions, account balances or disclosures for which misstatements of lesser amounts than materiality for the financial report as a whole could reasonably be expected to influence the economic decisions of users taken on the basis of the financial report include the following:

- Whether law, regulation or the applicable financial reporting framework affect users' expectations regarding the measurement or disclosure of certain items (for example, related party transactions, and the remuneration of management and those charged with governance).
- The key disclosures in relation to the industry in which the entity operates (for example, research and development costs for a pharmaceutical company).
- Whether attention is focused on a particular aspect of the entity's business that is separately disclosed in the financial report (for example, a newly acquired business).

Aus A10.1 In certain circumstances, an entity may be required to make disclosures in the financial report that are not subject to materiality.*

A11. In considering whether, in the specific circumstances of the entity, such classes of transactions, account balances or disclosures exist, the auditor may find it useful to obtain an understanding of the views and expectations of those charged with governance and management.

Performance Materiality (Ref: Para. 11)

A12. Planning the audit solely to detect individually material misstatements overlooks the fact that the aggregate of individually immaterial misstatements may cause the financial report to be materially misstated, and leaves no margin for possible undetected misstatements. Performance materiality (which, as defined, is one or more amounts) is set to reduce to an appropriately low level the probability that the aggregate of uncorrected and undetected misstatements in the financial report exceeds materiality for the financial report as a whole. Similarly, performance materiality relating to a materiality level

* See, for example, sections 300 and 300A of the *Corporations Act 2001* and Australian Accounting Standards.

determined for a particular class of transactions, account balance or disclosure is set to reduce to an appropriately low level the probability that the aggregate of uncorrected and undetected misstatements in that particular class of transactions, account balance or disclosure exceeds the materiality level for that particular class of transactions, account balance or disclosure. The determination of performance materiality is not a simple mechanical calculation and involves the exercise of professional judgement. It is affected by the auditor's understanding of the entity, updated during the performance of the risk assessment procedures; and the nature and extent of misstatements identified in previous audits and thereby the auditor's expectations in relation to misstatements in the current period.

Revision as the Audit Progresses (Ref: Para. 12)

A13. Materiality for the financial report as a whole (and, if applicable, the materiality level or levels for particular classes of transactions, account balances or disclosures) may need to be revised as a result of a change in circumstances that occurred during the audit (for example, a decision to dispose of a major part of the entity's business), new information, or a change in the auditor's understanding of the entity and its operations as a result of performing further audit procedures. For example, if during the audit it appears as though actual financial results are likely to be substantially different from the anticipated period end financial results that were used initially to determine materiality for the financial report as a whole, the auditor revises that materiality.

❖ ❖ ❖

Conformity with International Standards on Auditing

This Auditing Standard conforms with International Standard on Auditing ISA 320 *Materiality in Planning and Performing* an Audit, issued by the International Auditing and Assurance Standards Board (IAASB), an independent standard-setting board of the International Federation of Accountants (IFAC).

Paragraphs that have been added to this Auditing Standard (and do not appear in the text of the equivalent ISA) are identified with the prefix "Aus".

Compliance with this Auditing Standard enables compliance with ISA 320.

ASA 330
The Auditor's Responses to Assessed Risks

(Reissued October 2009)

Issued by the Auditing and Assurance Standards Board.

Note from the Institute of Chartered Accountants Australia

This note, prepared by the technical editor, is not part of ASA 330.

Historical development

February 2004: Auditing Standard AUS 406 'The Auditor's Procedures in Response to Assessed Risks' is issued, based on the international ISA 300, of the same name. It discusses how auditors should determine their overall responses to assessed risks, and gives guidance on appropriate precedures. It is applicable for reporting periods beginning on or after 15 December 2004, but earlier application is encouraged.

April 2006: ASA 330 was issued as a legally enforceable Standard to replace AUS 406. It is based on ISA 330 of the same name.

October 2009: ASA 330 reissued as part of the AUASB's Clarity Project. It is based on the redrafted ISA 330 of the same name.

Contents

Preface

Reasons for Issuing Auditing Standard ASA 330 *The Auditor's Responses to Assessed Risks*

The Auditing and Assurance Standards Board (AUASB) issues Auditing Standard ASA 330 *The Auditor's Responses to Assessed Risks* pursuant to the requirements of the legislative provisions and the Strategic Direction explained below.

The AUASB is an independent statutory board of the Australian Government established under section 227A of the *Australian Securities and Investments Commission Act 2001*, as amended (ASIC Act). Under section 336 of the *Corporations Act 2001*, the AUASB may make Auditing Standards for the purposes of the corporations legislation. These Auditing Standards are legislative instruments under the *Legislative Instruments Act 2003*.

Under the Strategic Direction given to the AUASB by the Financial Reporting Council (FRC), the AUASB is required to have regard to any programme initiated by the International Auditing and Assurance Standards Board (IAASB) for the revision and enhancement of the International Standards on Auditing (ISAs) and to make appropriate consequential amendments to the Australian Auditing Standards. Accordingly, the AUASB has decided to revise and redraft the Australian Auditing Standards using the equivalent redrafted ISAs.

Main Features

This Auditing Standard establishes requirements and provides application and other explanatory material regarding the auditor's responsibility to design and implement responses to the assessed risks of material misstatement in a financial report audit.

This Auditing Standard requires the auditor to:

(a) determine overall responses to address the assessed risks of material misstatement at the financial report level;

(b) design and perform further audit procedures to respond to the assessed risks of material misstatement at the assertion level;

(c) test controls if:

- the auditor's assessment of risk includes an expectation that controls are operating effectively; and
- substantive procedures alone cannot provide sufficient appropriate audit evidence;

(d) design and perform substantive procedures for:

- each material class of transaction, account balance and disclosure;
- the financial report closing process; and
- any identified significant risks;

(e) assess whether the overall presentation of the financial report is in accordance with the applicable financial reporting framework;

(f) evaluate the sufficiency and appropriateness of audit evidence obtained; and

(g) document certain matters in respect of procedures performed in response to assessed risks.

Authority Statement

The Auditing and Assurance Standards Board (AUASB) makes this Auditing Standard ASA 330 *The Auditor's Responses to Assessed Risks* pursuant to section 227B of the *Australian Securities and Investments Commission Act 2001* and section 336 of the *Corporations Act 2001*.

This Auditing Standard is to be read in conjunction with ASA 101 *Preamble to Australian Auditing Standards*, which sets out the intentions of the AUASB on how Australian Auditing Standards, operative for financial reporting periods commencing on or after 1 January 2010, are to be understood, interpreted and applied. This Auditing Standard is to be read also in conjunction with ASA 200 *Overall Objectives of the Independent Auditor and the Conduct of an Audit in Accordance with Australian Auditing Standards*.

Dated: 27 October 2009

M H Kelsall
Chairman - AUASB

Auditing Standard ASA 330

The Auditor's Responses to Assessed Risks

Application

Aus 0.1 This Auditing Standard applies to:

(a) an audit of a financial report for a financial year, or an audit of a financial report for a half-year, in accordance with the *Corporations Act 2001*; and

(b) an audit of a financial report, or a complete set of financial statements, for any other purpose.

Aus 0.2 This Auditing Standard also applies, as appropriate, to an audit of other historical financial information.

Operative Date

Aus 0.3 This Auditing Standard is operative for financial reporting periods commencing on or after 1 January 2010.

Introduction

Scope of this Auditing Standard

1. This Auditing Standard deals with the auditor's responsibility to design and implement responses to the risks of material misstatement identified and assessed by the auditor in accordance with ASA 315[1] in an audit of a financial report.

Effective Date

2. [Deleted by the AUASB. Refer Aus 0.3]

Objective

3. The objective of the auditor is to obtain sufficient appropriate audit evidence regarding the assessed risks of material misstatement, through designing and implementing appropriate responses to those risks.

Definitions

4. For purposes of the Australian Auditing Standards, the following terms have the meanings attributed below:
   (a) Substantive procedure means an audit procedure designed to detect material misstatements at the assertion level. Substantive procedures comprise:
      (i) Tests of details (of classes of transactions, account balances, and disclosures); and
      (ii) Substantive analytical procedures.
   (b) Test of controls means an audit procedure designed to evaluate the operating effectiveness of controls in preventing, or detecting and correcting, material misstatements at the assertion level.

Requirements

Overall Responses

5. The auditor shall design and implement overall responses to address the assessed risks of material misstatement at the financial report level. (Ref: Para. A1-A3)

Audit Procedures Responsive to the Assessed Risks of Material Misstatement at the Assertion Level

6. The auditor shall design and perform further audit procedures whose nature, timing, and extent are based on and are responsive to the assessed risks of material misstatement at the assertion level. (Ref: Para. A4-A8)

7. In designing the further audit procedures to be performed, the auditor shall:
   (a) Consider the reasons for the assessment given to the risk of material misstatement at the assertion level for each class of transactions, account balance, and disclosure, including:
      (i) The likelihood of material misstatement due to the particular characteristics of the relevant class of transactions, account balance, or disclosure (that is, the inherent risk); and
      (ii) Whether the risk assessment takes account of relevant controls (that is, the control risk), thereby requiring the auditor to obtain audit evidence to determine whether the controls are operating effectively (that is, the auditor

1 See ASA 315 *Identifying and Assessing the Risks of Material Misstatement through Understanding the Entity and Its Environment.*

intends to rely on the operating effectiveness of controls in determining the nature, timing and extent of substantive procedures); and (Ref: Para. A9-A18)

(b) Obtain more persuasive audit evidence the higher the auditor's assessment of risk. (Ref: Para. A19)

Tests of Controls

8. The auditor shall design and perform tests of controls to obtain sufficient appropriate audit evidence as to the operating effectiveness of relevant controls if:
   (a) The auditor's assessment of risks of material misstatement at the assertion level includes an expectation that the controls are operating effectively (that is, the auditor intends to rely on the operating effectiveness of controls in determining the nature, timing and extent of substantive procedures); or
   (b) Substantive procedures alone cannot provide sufficient appropriate audit evidence at the assertion level. (Ref: Para. A20-A24)

9. In designing and performing tests of controls, the auditor shall obtain more persuasive audit evidence the greater the reliance the auditor places on the effectiveness of a control. (Ref: Para. A25)

Nature and Extent of Tests of Controls

10. In designing and performing tests of controls, the auditor shall:
    (a) Perform other audit procedures in combination with enquiry to obtain audit evidence about the operating effectiveness of the controls, including:
        (i) How the controls were applied at relevant times during the period under audit;
        (ii) The consistency with which they were applied; and
        (iii) By whom or by what means they were applied. (Ref: Para. A26-A29)
    (b) Determine whether the controls to be tested depend upon other controls (indirect controls), and if so, whether it is necessary to obtain audit evidence supporting the effective operation of those indirect controls. (Ref: Para. A30-A31)

Timing of Tests of Controls

11. The auditor shall test controls for the particular time, or throughout the period, for which the auditor intends to rely on those controls, subject to paragraphs 12 and 15 of this Auditing Standard, in order to provide an appropriate basis for the auditor's intended reliance. (Ref: Para. A32)

Using audit evidence obtained during an interim period

12. If the auditor obtains audit evidence about the operating effectiveness of controls during an interim period, the auditor shall:
    (a) Obtain audit evidence about significant changes to those controls subsequent to the interim period; and
    (b) Determine the additional audit evidence to be obtained for the remaining period. (Ref: Para. A33-A34)

Using audit evidence obtained in previous audits

13. In determining whether it is appropriate to use audit evidence about the operating effectiveness of controls obtained in previous audits, and, if so, the length of the time period that may elapse before retesting a control, the auditor shall consider the following:
    (a) The effectiveness of other elements of internal control, including the control environment, the entity's monitoring of controls, and the entity's risk assessment process;
    (b) The risks arising from the characteristics of the control, including whether it is manual or automated;
    (c) The effectiveness of general IT-controls;
    (d) The effectiveness of the control and its application by the entity, including the nature and extent of deviations in the application of the control noted in previous

audits, and whether there have been personnel changes that significantly affect the application of the control;

(e) Whether the lack of a change in a particular control poses a risk due to changing circumstances; and

(f) The risks of material misstatement and the extent of reliance on the control. (Ref:Para. A35)

14. If the auditor plans to use audit evidence from a previous audit about the operating effectiveness of specific controls, the auditor shall establish the continuing relevance of that evidence by obtaining audit evidence about whether significant changes in those controls have occurred subsequent to the previous audit. The auditor shall obtain this evidence by performing enquiry combined with observation or inspection, to confirm the understanding of those specific controls, and:

(a) If there have been changes that affect the continuing relevance of the audit evidence from the previous audit, the auditor shall test the controls in the current audit. (Ref: Para. A36)

(b) If there have not been such changes, the auditor shall test the controls at least once in every third audit, and shall test some controls each audit to avoid the possibility of testing all the controls on which the auditor intends to rely in a single audit period with no testing of controls in the subsequent two audit periods. (Ref: Para. A37-A39)

ASA

Controls over significant risks

15. If the auditor plans to rely on controls over a risk the auditor has determined to be a significant risk, the auditor shall test those controls in the current period.

Evaluating the Operating Effectiveness of Controls

16. When evaluating the operating effectiveness of relevant controls, the auditor shall evaluate whether misstatements that have been detected by substantive procedures indicate that controls are not operating effectively. The absence of misstatements detected by substantive procedures, however, does not provide audit evidence that controls related to the assertion being tested are effective. (Ref: Para. A40)

17. If deviations from controls upon which the auditor intends to rely are detected, the auditor shall make specific enquiries to understand these matters and their potential consequences, and shall determine whether: (Ref: Para. A41)

(a) The tests of controls that have been performed provide an appropriate basis for reliance on the controls;

(b) Additional tests of controls are necessary; or

(c) The potential risks of misstatement need to be addressed using substantive procedures.

Substantive Procedures

18. Irrespective of the assessed risks of material misstatement, the auditor shall design and perform substantive procedures for each material class of transactions, account balance, and disclosure. (Ref: Para. A42-A47)

19. The auditor shall consider whether external confirmation procedures are to be performed as substantive audit procedures. (Ref: Para. A48-A51)

Substantive Procedures Related to the Financial Report Closing Process

20. The auditor's substantive procedures shall include the following audit procedures related to the financial report closing process:

(a) Agreeing or reconciling the financial report with the underlying accounting records; and

(b) Examining material journal entries and other adjustments made during the course of preparing the financial report. (Ref: Para. A52)

Substantive Procedures Responsive to Significant Risks

21. If the auditor has determined that an assessed risk of material misstatement at the assertion level is a significant risk, the auditor shall perform substantive procedures that are

specifically responsive to that risk. When the approach to a significant risk consists only of substantive procedures, those procedures shall include tests of details. (Ref: Para. A53)

Timing of Substantive Procedures

Aus 21.1 Where the auditor plans to use audit evidence from the performance of substantive procedures in a prior audit, the auditor shall perform audit procedures during the current period to establish the continuing relevance of the audit evidence. (Ref: Para. A54)

22. If substantive procedures are performed at an interim date, the auditor shall cover the remaining period by performing:

    (a) substantive procedures, combined with tests of controls for the intervening period; or

    (b) if the auditor determines that it is sufficient, further substantive procedures only,

    that provide a reasonable basis for extending the audit conclusions from the interim date to the period end. (Ref: Para. A54-A57)

23. If misstatements that the auditor did not expect when assessing the risks of material misstatement are detected at an interim date, the auditor shall evaluate whether the related assessment of risk and the planned nature, timing, or extent of substantive procedures covering the remaining period need to be modified. (Ref: Para. A58)

Adequacy of Presentation and Disclosure

24. The auditor shall perform audit procedures to evaluate whether the overall presentation of the financial report, including the related disclosures, is in accordance with the applicable financial reporting framework. (Ref: Para. A59)

Evaluating the Sufficiency and Appropriateness of Audit Evidence

25. Based on the audit procedures performed and the audit evidence obtained, the auditor shall evaluate before the conclusion of the audit whether the assessments of the risks of material misstatement at the assertion level remain appropriate. (Ref: Para. A60-A61)

26. The auditor shall conclude whether sufficient appropriate audit evidence has been obtained. In forming an opinion, the auditor shall consider all relevant audit evidence, regardless of whether it appears to corroborate or to contradict the assertions in the financial report. (Ref: Para. A62)

27. If the auditor has not obtained sufficient appropriate audit evidence as to a material financial report assertion, the auditor shall attempt to obtain further audit evidence. If the auditor is unable to obtain sufficient appropriate audit evidence, the auditor shall express a qualified opinion or disclaim an opinion on the financial report.

Documentation

28. The auditor shall include in the audit documentation:[2]

    (a) The overall responses to address the assessed risks of material misstatement at the financial report level, and the nature, timing, and extent of the further audit procedures performed;

    (b) The linkage of those procedures with the assessed risks at the assertion level; and

    (c) The results of the audit procedures, including the conclusions where these are not otherwise clear. (Ref: Para. A63)

29. If the auditor plans to use audit evidence about the operating effectiveness of controls obtained in previous audits, the auditor shall include in the audit documentation the conclusions reached about relying on such controls that were tested in a previous audit.

30. The auditor's documentation shall demonstrate that the financial report agrees or reconciles with the underlying accounting records.

❖ ❖ ❖

2 ASA 230 *Audit Documentation*, paragraphs 8-11 and paragraph A6.

Application and Other Explanatory Material

Overall Responses (Ref: Para. 5)

A1. Overall responses to address the assessed risks of material misstatement at the financial report level may include:

- Emphasising to the audit team the need to maintain professional scepticism.
- Assigning more experienced staff or those with special skills or using experts.
- Providing more supervision.
- Incorporating additional elements of unpredictability in the selection of further audit procedures to be performed.
- Making general changes to the nature, timing, or extent of audit procedures, for example: performing substantive procedures at the period end instead of at an interim date; or modifying the nature of audit procedures to obtain more persuasive audit evidence.

A2. The assessment of the risks of material misstatement at the financial report level, and thereby the auditor's overall responses, is affected by the auditor's understanding of the control environment. An effective control environment may allow the auditor to have more confidence in internal control and the reliability of audit evidence generated internally within the entity and thus, for example, allow the auditor to conduct some audit procedures at an interim date rather than at the period end. Deficiencies in the control environment, however, have the opposite effect; for example, the auditor may respond to an ineffective control environment by:

- Conducting more audit procedures as of the period end rather than at an interim date.
- Obtaining more extensive audit evidence from substantive procedures.
- Increasing the number of locations to be included in the audit scope.

A3. Such considerations, therefore, have a significant bearing on the auditor's general approach, for example, an emphasis on substantive procedures (substantive approach), or an approach that uses tests of controls as well as substantive procedures (combined approach).

Audit Procedures Responsive to the Assessed Risks of Material Misstatement at the Assertion Level

The Nature, Timing, and Extent of Further Audit Procedures (Ref: Para. 6)

A4. The auditor's assessment of the identified risks at the assertion level provides a basis for considering the appropriate audit approach for designing and performing further audit procedures. For example, the auditor may determine that:

(a) Only by performing tests of controls may the auditor achieve an effective response to the assessed risk of material misstatement for a particular assertion;

(b) Performing only substantive procedures is appropriate for particular assertions and, therefore, the auditor excludes the effect of controls from the relevant risk assessment. This may be because the auditor's risk assessment procedures have not identified any effective controls relevant to the assertion, or because testing controls would be inefficient and therefore the auditor does not intend to rely on the operating effectiveness of controls in determining the nature, timing and extent of substantive procedures; or

(c) A combined approach using both tests of controls and substantive procedures is an effective approach.

However, as required by paragraph 18, irrespective of the approach selected, the auditor designs and performs substantive procedures for each material class of transactions, account balance, and disclosure.

A5. The nature of an audit procedure refers to its purpose (that is, test of controls or substantive procedure) and its type (that is, inspection, observation, enquiry, confirmation,

ASA

recalculation, re-performance, or analytical procedure). The nature of the audit procedures is of most importance in responding to the assessed risks.

A6. Timing of an audit procedure refers to when it is performed, or the period or date to which the audit evidence applies.

A7. Extent of an audit procedure refers to the quantity to be performed, for example, a sample size or the number of observations of a control activity.

A8. Designing and performing further audit procedures whose nature, timing, and extent are based on and are responsive to the assessed risks of material misstatement at the assertion level provides a clear linkage between the auditor's further audit procedures and the risk assessment.

Responding to the Assessed Risks at the Assertion Level (Ref: Para. 7(a))

Nature

A9. The auditor's assessed risks may affect both the types of audit procedures to be performed and their combination. For example, when an assessed risk is high, the auditor may confirm the completeness of the terms of a contract with the counterparty, in addition to inspecting the document. Further, certain audit procedures may be more appropriate for some assertions than others. For example, in relation to revenue, tests of controls may be most responsive to the assessed risk of misstatement of the completeness assertion, whereas substantive procedures may be most responsive to the assessed risk of misstatement of the occurrence assertion.

A10. The reasons for the assessment given to a risk are relevant in determining the nature of audit procedures. For example, if an assessed risk is lower because of the particular characteristics of a class of transactions without consideration of the related controls, then the auditor may determine that substantive analytical procedures alone provide sufficient appropriate audit evidence. On the other hand, if the assessed risk is lower because of internal controls, and the auditor intends to base the substantive procedures on that low assessment, then the auditor performs tests of those controls, as required by paragraph 8(a). This may be the case, for example, for a class of transactions of reasonably uniform, non-complex characteristics that are routinely processed and controlled by the entity's information system.

Timing

A11. The auditor may perform tests of controls or substantive procedures at an interim date or at the period end. The higher the risk of material misstatement, the more likely it is that the auditor may decide it is more effective to perform substantive procedures nearer to, or at, the period end rather than at an earlier date, or to perform audit procedures unannounced or at unpredictable times (for example, performing audit procedures at selected locations on an unannounced basis). This is particularly relevant when considering the response to the risks of fraud. For example, the auditor may conclude that, when the risks of intentional misstatement or manipulation have been identified, audit procedures to extend audit conclusions from interim date to the period end would not be effective.

A12. On the other hand, performing audit procedures before the period end may assist the auditor in identifying significant matters at an early stage of the audit, and consequently resolving them with the assistance of management or developing an effective audit approach to address such matters.

A13. In addition, certain audit procedures can be performed only at or after the period end, for example:

- Agreeing the financial report to the accounting records;
- Examining adjustments made during the course of preparing the financial report; and
- Procedures to respond to a risk that, at the period end, the entity may have entered into improper sales contracts, or transactions may not have been finalised.

A14. Further relevant factors that influence the auditor's consideration of when to perform audit procedures include the following:

- The control environment.
- When relevant information is available (for example, electronic files may subsequently be overwritten, or procedures to be observed may occur only at certain times).
- The nature of the risk (for example, if there is a risk of inflated revenues to meet earnings expectations by subsequent creation of false sales agreements, the auditor may wish to examine contracts available on the date of the period end).
- The period or date to which the audit evidence relates.

Extent

A15. The extent of an audit procedure judged necessary is determined after considering the materiality, the assessed risk, and the degree of assurance the auditor plans to obtain. When a single purpose is met by a combination of procedures, the extent of each procedure is considered separately. In general, the extent of audit procedures increases as the risk of material misstatement increases. For example, in response to the assessed risk of material misstatement due to fraud, increasing sample sizes or performing substantive analytical procedures at a more detailed level may be appropriate. However, increasing the extent of an audit procedure is effective only if the audit procedure itself is relevant to the specific risk.

A16. The use of computer-assisted audit techniques (CAATs) may enable more extensive testing of electronic transactions and account files, which may be useful when the auditor decides to modify the extent of testing, for example, in responding to the risks of material misstatement due to fraud. Such techniques can be used to select sample transactions from key electronic files, to sort transactions with specific characteristics, or to test an entire population instead of a sample.

Considerations specific to public sector entities

A17. For the audits of public sector entities, the audit mandate and any other special auditing requirements may affect the auditor's consideration of the nature, timing and extent of further audit procedures.

Considerations specific to smaller entities

A18. In the case of smaller entities, there may not be many control activities that could be identified by the auditor, or the extent to which their existence or operation have been documented by the entity may be limited. In such cases, it may be more efficient for the auditor to perform further audit procedures that are primarily substantive procedures. In some rare cases, however, the absence of control activities or of other components of control may make it impossible to obtain sufficient appropriate audit evidence.

***Higher Assessments of Risk** (Ref: Para 7(b))*

A19. When obtaining more persuasive audit evidence because of a higher assessment of risk, the auditor may increase the quantity of the evidence, or obtain evidence that is more relevant or reliable, for example, by placing more emphasis on obtaining third party evidence or by obtaining corroborating evidence from a number of independent sources.

Tests of Controls

***Designing and Performing Tests of Controls** (Ref: Para. 8)*

A20. Tests of controls are performed only on those controls that the auditor has determined are suitably designed to prevent, or detect and correct, a material misstatement in an assertion. If substantially different controls were used at different times during the period under audit, each is considered separately.

A21. Testing the operating effectiveness of controls is different from obtaining an understanding of and evaluating the design and implementation of controls. However, the same types of audit procedures are used. The auditor may, therefore, decide it is efficient to test the operating effectiveness of controls at the same time as evaluating their design and determining that they have been implemented.

A22. Further, although some risk assessment procedures may not have been specifically designed as tests of controls, they may nevertheless provide audit evidence about the operating effectiveness of the controls and, consequently, serve as tests of controls. For example, the auditor's risk assessment procedures may have included:

- Enquiring about management's use of budgets.
- Observing management's comparison of monthly budgeted and actual expenses.
- Inspecting reports pertaining to the investigation of variances between budgeted and actual amounts.

These audit procedures provide knowledge about the design of the entity's budgeting policies and whether they have been implemented, but may also provide audit evidence about the effectiveness of the operation of budgeting policies in preventing or detecting material misstatements in the classification of expenses.

A23. In addition, the auditor may design a test of controls to be performed concurrently with a test of details on the same transaction. Although the purpose of a test of controls is different from the purpose of a test of details, both may be accomplished concurrently by performing a test of controls and a test of details on the same transaction, also known as a dual-purpose test. For example, the auditor may design, and evaluate the results of, a test to examine an invoice to determine whether it has been approved and to provide substantive audit evidence of a transaction. A dual-purpose test is designed and evaluated by considering each purpose of the test separately.

A24. In some cases, as discussed in ASA 315, the auditor may find it impossible to design effective substantive procedures that by themselves provide sufficient appropriate audit evidence at the assertion level.[3] This may occur when an entity conducts its business using IT and no documentation of transactions is produced or maintained, other than through the IT system. In such cases, paragraph 8(b) requires the auditor to perform tests of relevant controls.

Audit Evidence and Intended Reliance (Ref: Para. 9)

A25. A higher level of assurance may be sought about the operating effectiveness of controls when the approach adopted consists primarily of tests of controls, in particular where it is not possible or practicable to obtain sufficient appropriate audit evidence only from substantive procedures.

Nature and Extent of Tests of Controls

Other audit procedures in combination with enquiry (Ref: Para. 10(a))

A26. Enquiry alone is not sufficient to test the operating effectiveness of controls. Accordingly, other audit procedures are performed in combination with enquiry. In this regard, enquiry combined with inspection or re-performance may provide more assurance than enquiry and observation, since an observation is pertinent only at the point in time at which it is made.

A27. The nature of the particular control influences the type of procedure required to obtain audit evidence about whether the control was operating effectively. For example, if operating effectiveness is evidenced by documentation, the auditor may decide to inspect it to obtain audit evidence about operating effectiveness. For other controls, however, documentation may not be available or relevant.

For example, documentation of operation may not exist for some factors in the control environment, such as assignment of authority and responsibility, or for some types of control activities, such as control activities performed by a computer. In such circumstances, audit evidence about operating effectiveness may be obtained through enquiry in combination with other audit procedures such as observation or the use of CAATs.

Extent of tests of controls

A28. When more persuasive audit evidence is needed regarding the effectiveness of a control, it may be appropriate to increase the extent of testing of the control. As well as the degree

3 See ASA 315, paragraph 30.

of reliance on controls, matters the auditor may consider in determining the extent of tests of controls include the following:

- The frequency of the performance of the control by the entity during the period.
- The length of time during the audit period that the auditor is relying on the operating effectiveness of the control.
- The expected rate of deviation from a control.
- The relevance and reliability of the audit evidence to be obtained regarding the operating effectiveness of the control at the assertion level.
- The extent to which audit evidence is obtained from tests of other controls related to the assertion.

ASA 530[4] contains further guidance on the extent of testing.

A29. Because of the inherent consistency of IT processing, it may not be necessary to increase the extent of testing of an automated control. An automated control can be expected to function consistently unless the program (including the tables, files, or other permanent data used by the program) is changed. Once the auditor determines that an automated control is functioning as intended (which could be done at the time the control is initially implemented or at some other date), the auditor may consider performing tests to determine that the control continues to function effectively. Such tests might include determining that:

- Changes to the program are not made without being subject to the appropriate program change controls,
- The authorised version of the program is used for processing transactions, and
- Other relevant general controls are effective.

Such tests also might include determining that changes to the programs have not been made, as may be the case when the entity uses packaged software applications without modifying or maintaining them. For example, the auditor may inspect the record of the administration of IT security to obtain audit evidence that unauthorised access has not occurred during the period.

Testing of indirect controls (Ref: Para. 10(b))

A30. In some circumstances, it may be necessary to obtain audit evidence supporting the effective operation of indirect controls. For example, when the auditor decides to test the effectiveness of a user review of exception reports detailing sales in excess of authorised credit limits, the user review and related follow up is the control that is directly of relevance to the auditor. Controls over the accuracy of the information in the reports (for example, the general IT-controls) are described as 'indirect' controls.

A31. Because of the inherent consistency of IT processing, audit evidence about the implementation of an automated application control, when considered in combination with audit evidence about the operating effectiveness of the entity's general controls (in particular, change controls), may also provide substantial audit evidence about its operating effectiveness.

Timing of Tests of Controls

Intended period of reliance (Ref: Para. 11)

A32. Audit evidence pertaining only to a point in time may be sufficient for the auditor's purpose, for example, when testing controls over the entity's physical inventory counting at the period end. If, on the other hand, the auditor intends to rely on a control over a period, tests that are capable of providing audit evidence that the control operated effectively at relevant times during that period are appropriate. Such tests may include tests of the entity's monitoring of controls.

4 See ASA 530 *Audit Sampling.*

***Using audit evidence obtained during an interim period** (Ref: Para. 12(b))*

A33. Relevant factors in determining what additional audit evidence to obtain about controls that were operating during the period remaining after an interim period, include:

- The significance of the assessed risks of material misstatement at the assertion level.
- The specific controls that were tested during the interim period, and significant changes to them since they were tested, including changes in the information system, processes, and personnel.
- The degree to which audit evidence about the operating effectiveness of those controls was obtained.
- The length of the remaining period.
- The extent to which the auditor intends to reduce further substantive procedures based on the reliance of controls.
- The control environment.

A34. Additional audit evidence may be obtained, for example, by extending tests of controls over the remaining period or testing the entity's monitoring of controls.

***Using audit evidence obtained in previous audits** (Ref: Para. 13)*

A35. In certain circumstances, audit evidence obtained from previous audits may provide audit evidence where the auditor performs audit procedures to establish its continuing relevance. For example, in performing a previous audit, the auditor may have determined that an automated control was functioning as intended. The auditor may obtain audit evidence to determine whether changes to the automated control have been made that affect its continued effective functioning through, for example, enquiries of management and the inspection of logs to indicate what controls have been changed. Consideration of audit evidence about these changes may support either increasing or decreasing the expected audit evidence to be obtained in the current period about the operating effectiveness of the controls.

***Controls that have changed from previous audits** (Ref: Para. 14(a))*

A36. Changes may affect the relevance of the audit evidence obtained in previous audits such that there may no longer be a basis for continued reliance. For example, changes in a system that enable an entity to receive a new report from the system probably do not affect the relevance of audit evidence from a previous audit, however, a change that causes data to be accumulated or calculated differently does affect it.

***Controls that have not changed from previous audits** (Ref: Para. 14(b))*

A37. The auditor's decision on whether to rely on audit evidence obtained in previous audits for controls that:

(a) have not changed since they were last tested; and

(b) are not controls that mitigate a significant risk,

is a matter of professional judgement. In addition, the length of time between retesting such controls is also a matter of professional judgement, but is required by paragraph 14(b) to be at least once in every third year.

A38. In general, the higher the risk of material misstatement, or the greater the reliance on controls, the shorter the time period elapsed, if any, is likely to be. Factors that may decrease the period for retesting a control, or result in not relying on audit evidence obtained in previous audits at all, include the following:

- A deficient control environment.
- Deficient monitoring of controls.
- A significant manual element to the relevant controls.
- Personnel changes that significantly affect the application of the control.
- Changing circumstances that indicate the need for changes in the control.
- Deficient general IT-controls.

A39. When there are a number of controls for which the auditor intends to rely on audit evidence obtained in previous audits, testing some of those controls in each audit provides corroborating information about the continuing effectiveness of the control environment. This contributes to the auditor's decision about whether it is appropriate to rely on audit evidence obtained in previous audits.

Evaluating the Operating Effectiveness of Controls (Ref: Para. 16-17)

A40. A material misstatement detected by the auditor's procedures is a strong indicator of the existence of a significant deficiency in internal control.

A41. The concept of effectiveness of the operation of controls recognises that some deviations in the way controls are applied by the entity may occur. Deviations from prescribed controls may be caused by such factors as changes in key personnel, significant seasonal fluctuations in volume of transactions and human error. The detected rate of deviation, in particular in comparison with the expected rate, may indicate that the control cannot be relied on to reduce risk at the assertion level to that assessed by the auditor.

Substantive Procedures (Ref: Para. 18)

A42. Paragraph 18 requires the auditor to design and perform substantive procedures for each material class of transactions, account balance, and disclosure, irrespective of the assessed risks of material misstatement. This requirement reflects the facts that: (i) the auditor's assessment of risk is judgemental and so may not identify all risks of material misstatement; and (ii) there are inherent limitations to internal control, including management override.

Nature and Extent of Substantive Procedures

A43. Depending on the circumstances, the auditor may determine that:

- Performing only substantive analytical procedures will be sufficient to reduce audit risk to an acceptably low level. For example, where the auditor's assessment of risk is supported by audit evidence from tests of controls.
- Only tests of details are appropriate.
- A combination of substantive analytical procedures and tests of details are most responsive to the assessed risks.

A44. Substantive analytical procedures are generally more applicable to large volumes of transactions that tend to be predictable over time. ASA 520[5] establishes requirements and provides guidance on the application of analytical procedures during an audit.

A45. The nature of the risk and assertion is relevant to the design of tests of details. For example, tests of details related to the existence or occurrence assertion may involve selecting from items contained in a financial report amount and obtaining the relevant audit evidence. On the other hand, tests of details related to the completeness assertion may involve selecting from items that are expected to be included in the relevant financial statement amount and investigating whether they are included.

A46. Because the assessment of the risk of material misstatement takes account of internal control, the extent of substantive procedures may need to be increased when the results from tests of controls are unsatisfactory. However, increasing the extent of an audit procedure is appropriate only if the audit procedure itself is relevant to the specific risk.

A47. In designing tests of details, the extent of testing is ordinarily thought of in terms of the sample size. However, other matters are also relevant, including whether it is more effective to use other selective means of testing. See ASA 500.[6]

Considering Whether External Confirmation Procedures Are to Be Performed (Ref: Para. 19)

A48. External confirmation procedures frequently are relevant when addressing assertions associated with account balances and their elements, but need not be restricted to these items. For example, the auditor may request external confirmation of the terms of agreements, contracts, or transactions between an entity and other parties. External

5 See ASA 520 *Analytical Procedures.*

6 See ASA 500 *Audit Evidence*, paragraph 10.

confirmation procedures also may be performed to obtain audit evidence about the absence of certain conditions. For example, a request may specifically seek confirmation that no "side agreement" exists that may be relevant to an entity's revenue cut-off assertion. Other situations where external confirmation procedures may provide relevant audit evidence in responding to assessed risks of material misstatement include:

- Bank balances and other information relevant to banking relationships.
- Accounts receivable balances and terms.
- Inventories held by third parties at bonded warehouses for processing or on consignment.
- Property title deeds held by lawyers or financiers for safe custody or as security.
- Investments held for safekeeping by third parties, or purchased from stockbrokers but not delivered at the balance sheet date.
- Amounts due to lenders, including relevant terms of repayment and restrictive covenants.
- Accounts payable balances and terms.

A49. Although external confirmations may provide relevant audit evidence relating to certain assertions, there are some assertions for which external confirmations provide less relevant audit evidence. For example, external confirmations provide less relevant audit evidence relating to the recoverability of accounts receivable balances, than they do of their existence.

A50. The auditor may determine that external confirmation procedures performed for one purpose provide an opportunity to obtain audit evidence about other matters. For example, confirmation requests for bank balances often include requests for information relevant to other financial report assertions. Such considerations may influence the auditor's decision about whether to perform external confirmation procedures.

A51. Factors that may assist the auditor in determining whether external confirmation procedures are to be performed as substantive audit procedures include:

- The confirming party's knowledge of the subject matter – responses may be more reliable if provided by a person at the confirming party who has the requisite knowledge about the information being confirmed.
- The ability or willingness of the intended confirming party to respond – for example, the confirming party:
  - May not accept responsibility for responding to a confirmation request;
  - May consider responding too costly or time consuming;
  - May have concerns about the potential legal liability resulting from responding;
  - May account for transactions in different currencies; or
  - May operate in an environment where responding to confirmation requests is not a significant aspect of day-to-day operations.

  In such situations, confirming parties may not respond, may respond in a casual manner or may attempt to restrict the reliance placed on the response.
- The objectivity of the intended confirming party – if the confirming party is a related party of the entity, responses to confirmation requests may be less reliable.

Substantive Procedures Related to the Financial Report Closing Process
(Ref: Para. 20(b))

A52. The nature, and also the extent, of the auditor's examination of journal entries and other adjustments depends on the nature and complexity of the entity's financial reporting process and the related risks of material misstatement.

***Substantive Procedures Responsive to Significant Risks** (Ref: Para. 21)*

A53. Paragraph 21 of this Auditing Standard requires the auditor to perform substantive procedures that are specifically responsive to risks the auditor has determined to be significant risks. Audit evidence in the form of external confirmations received directly by the auditor from appropriate confirming parties may assist the auditor in obtaining audit evidence with the high level of reliability that the auditor requires to respond to significant risks of material misstatement, whether due to fraud or error. For example, if the auditor identifies that management is under pressure to meet earnings expectations, there may be a risk that management is inflating sales by improperly recognising revenue related to sales agreements with terms that preclude revenue recognition or by invoicing sales before shipment. In these circumstances, the auditor may, for example, design external confirmation procedures not only to confirm outstanding amounts, but also to confirm the details of the sales agreements, including date, any rights of return and delivery terms. In addition, the auditor may find it effective to supplement such external confirmation procedures with enquiries of non-financial personnel in the entity regarding any changes in sales agreements and delivery terms.

***Timing of Substantive Procedures** (Ref: Para. Aus 21.1-23)*

A54. In most cases, audit evidence from a previous audit's substantive procedures provides little or no audit evidence for the current period. There are, however, exceptions, for example, a legal opinion obtained in a previous audit related to the structure of a securitisation to which no changes have occurred, may be relevant in the current period. In such cases, it may be appropriate to use audit evidence from a previous audit's substantive procedures if that evidence and the related subject matter have not fundamentally changed, and audit procedures have been performed during the current period to establish its continuing relevance.

***Using audit evidence obtained during an interim period** (Ref: Para. 22)*

A55. In some circumstances, the auditor may determine that it is effective to perform substantive procedures at an interim date, and to compare and reconcile information concerning the balance at the period end with the comparable information at the interim date to:

(a) Identify amounts that appear unusual,

(b) Investigate any such amounts, and

(c) Perform substantive analytical procedures or tests of details to test the intervening period.

A56. Performing substantive procedures at an interim date without undertaking additional procedures at a later date increases the risk that the auditor will not detect misstatements that may exist at the period end. This risk increases as the remaining period is lengthened. Factors such as the following may influence whether to perform substantive procedures at an interim date:

- The control environment and other relevant controls.
- The availability at a later date of information necessary for the auditor's procedures.
- The purpose of the substantive procedure.
- The assessed risk of material misstatement.
- The nature of the class of transactions or account balance and related assertions.
- The ability of the auditor to perform appropriate substantive procedures or substantive procedures combined with tests of controls to cover the remaining period in order to reduce the risk that misstatements that may exist at the period end will not be detected.

A57. Factors such as the following may influence whether to perform substantive analytical procedures with respect to the period between the interim date and the period end:

- Whether the period end balances of the particular classes of transactions or account balances are reasonably predictable with respect to amount, relative significance, and composition.

- Whether the entity's procedures for analysing and adjusting such classes of transactions or account balances at interim dates and for establishing proper accounting cut-offs are appropriate.
- Whether the information system relevant to financial reporting will provide information concerning the balances at the period end and the transactions in the remaining period that is sufficient to permit investigation of:
  - (a) Significant unusual transactions or entries (including those at or near the period end);
  - (b) Other causes of significant fluctuations, or expected fluctuations that did not occur; and
  - (c) Changes in the composition of the classes of transactions or account balances.

Misstatements detected at an interim date ***(Ref: Para. 23)***

A58. When the auditor concludes that the planned nature, timing, or extent of substantive procedures covering the remaining period need to be modified as a result of unexpected misstatements detected at an interim date, such modification may include extending or repeating the procedures performed at the interim date at the period end.

Adequacy of Presentation and Disclosure (Ref: Para. 24)

A59. Evaluating the overall presentation of the financial report, including the related disclosures, relates to whether the individual financial statements are presented in a manner that reflects the appropriate classification and description of financial information, and the form, arrangement, and content of the financial statements and their appended notes. This includes, for example, the terminology used, the amount of detail given, the classification of items in the report, and the basis of amounts set forth.

Evaluating the Sufficiency and Appropriateness of Audit Evidence (Ref: Para. 25-27)

A60. An audit of a financial report is a cumulative and iterative process. As the auditor performs planned audit procedures, the audit evidence obtained may cause the auditor to modify the nature, timing or extent of other planned audit procedures. Information may come to the auditor's attention that differs significantly from the information on which the risk assessment was based. For example:

- The extent of misstatements that the auditor detects by performing substantive procedures may alter the auditor's judgement about the risk assessments and may indicate a significant deficiency in internal control.
- The auditor may become aware of discrepancies in accounting records, or conflicting or missing evidence.
- Analytical procedures performed at the overall review stage of the audit may indicate a previously unrecognised risk of material misstatement.

In such circumstances, the auditor may need to re-evaluate the planned audit procedures, based on the revised consideration of assessed risks for all or some of the classes of transactions, account balances, or disclosures and related assertions. ASA 315 contains further guidance on revising the auditor's risk assessment.[7]

A61. The auditor cannot assume that an instance of fraud or error is an isolated occurrence. Therefore, the consideration of how the detection of a misstatement affects the assessed risks of material misstatement is important in determining whether the assessment remains appropriate.

7 See ASA 315, paragraph 31.

A62. The auditor's judgement as to what constitutes sufficient appropriate audit evidence is influenced by such factors as the following:

- Significance of the potential misstatement in the assertion and the likelihood of its having a material effect, individually or aggregated with other potential misstatements, on the financial report.
- Effectiveness of management's responses and controls to address the risks.
- Experience gained during previous audits with respect to similar potential misstatements.
- Results of audit procedures performed, including whether such audit procedures identified specific instances of fraud or error.
- Source and reliability of the available information.
- Persuasiveness of the audit evidence.
- Understanding of the entity and its environment, including the entity's internal control.

Documentation (Ref: Para. 28)

A63. The form and extent of audit documentation is a matter of professional judgement, and is influenced by the nature, size and complexity of the entity and its internal control, availability of information from the entity and the audit methodology and technology used in the audit.

❖ ❖ ❖

Conformity with International Standards on Auditing

This Auditing Standard conforms with International Standard on Auditing ISA 330 *The Auditor's Responses to Assessed Risks*, issued by the International Auditing and Assurance Standards Board (IAASB), an independent standard-setting board of the International Federation of Accountants (IFAC).

Paragraphs that have been added to this Standard (and do not appear in the text of the equivalent ISA) are identified with the prefix "Aus."

The following requirement is additional to ISA 330:

- Where the auditor plans to use audit evidence from the performance of substantive procedures in a prior audit, the auditor shall perform audit procedures during the current period to establish the continuing relevance of the audit evidence. [Paragraph Aus 21.1]

Compliance with this Auditing Standard enables compliance with ISA 330.

ASA 402

Audit Considerations Relating to an Entity Using a Service Organisation

(Reissued October 2009: amended and compiled June 2011)

Issued by the Auditing and Assurance Standards Board.

Note from the Institute of Chartered Accountants Australia

This note, prepared by the technical editor, is not part of ASA 402.

Historical development

February 1989: Statement of Auditing Practice AUP 20 'Audit Evidence Implications of Using a Service Entity' issued, effective from date of issue. Followed the issue of ED 23 in May 1986.

June 1994: The International Auditing Practices Committee (IAPC) of the International Federation of Accountants (IFAC) approved the issuance of a codified set of International Standards of Auditing (ISAs). The relevant international pronouncement was ISA 402 'Audit Considerations relating to Entities Using Service Organisations'.

October 1995: Australian Auditing Standards and Auditing Guidance Statements released. The status of the guidance was explained in APS 1.1 'Conformity With Auditing Standards'. These Standards became operative for the first reporting period commencing on or after 1 July 1996 and later reporting periods, although earlier application was encouraged. AUP 20 'Audit Evidence Implications of Using a Service Entity' replaced by AUS 404 'Audit Implications Relating to Entities Using a Service Entity'.

February 1999: AUS/AGS Omnibus 2 'Miscellaneous Amendments to AUSs and AGSs' issued by the AuASB, operative from the date of issue. The Omnibus amended para. 12 of AUS 404.

July 2002: AUS/AGS Omnibus 3 'Miscellaneous Amendments to AUSs and AGSs' issued by the AuASB, operative from date of issue. AUS 404 now reissued by the Board to reflect these amendments.

April 2006: ASA 402 was issued as a legally enforceable Standard to replace AUS 404. It is based on ISA 402 of the same name.

October 2009: ASA 402 reissued as part of the AUASB's Clarity Project. It contains new definitions and new requirements regarding the integration of the report on the service organisation into the audit. It is based on the revised ISA 402 of the same name.

June 2011: ASA 402 updated for editorial amendments contained in ASA 2011-1 'Amendments to Australian Auditing Standards'.

Contents

Compilation Details

Auditing Standard ASA 402 *Audit Considerations Relating to an Entity Using a Service Organisation* as Amended

This compilation takes into account amendments made up to and including 27 June 2011 and was prepared on 27 June 2011 by the Auditing and Assurance Standards Board (AUASB).

This compilation is not a separate Auditing Standard made by the AUASB. Instead, it is a representation of ASA 402 (October 2009) as amended by another Auditing Standard which is listed in the Table below.

Table of Standards

Standard	Date made	Operative date
ASA 402	27 October 2009	1 January 2010
ASA 2011-1	27 June 2011	1 July 2011

Table of Amendments

Paragraph affected	How affected	By ... [paragraph]
A19	Amended	ASA 2011-1 [32]

Preface

[Preface extracted from the original Auditing Standard issued 27 October 2009]

Reasons for Issuing Auditing Standard ASA 402 *Audit Considerations Relating to an Entity Using a Service Organisation*

The Auditing and Assurance Standards Board (AUASB) issues Auditing Standard ASA 402 *Audit Considerations Relating to an Entity Using a Service Organisation* pursuant to the requirements of the legislative provisions and the Strategic Direction explained below.

The AUASB is an independent statutory board of the Australian Government established under section 227A of the *Australian Securities and Investments Commission Act 2001*, as amended (ASIC Act). Under section 336 of the *Corporations Act 2001*, the AUASB may make Auditing Standards for the purposes of the corporations legislation. These Auditing Standards are legislative instruments under the *Legislative Instruments Act 2003*.

Under the Strategic Direction given to the AUASB by the Financial Reporting Council (FRC), the AUASB is required to have regard to any programme initiated by the International Auditing and Assurance Standards Board (IAASB) for the revision and enhancement of the International Standards on Auditing (ISAs) and to make appropriate consequential amendments to the Australian Auditing Standards. Accordingly, the AUASB has decided to revise and redraft the Australian Auditing Standards using the equivalent redrafted ISAs.

Main Features

This Auditing Standard establishes requirements and provides application and other explanatory material regarding the auditor's responsibility to obtain sufficient appropriate audit evidence when a user entity uses the services of one or more service organisations.

This Auditing Standard:

(a) specifically expands on how the user auditor applies ASA 315 and ASA 330 in relation to the user entity;

(b) provides relevant definitions;

(c) requires the auditor to obtain an understanding of the services provided by a service organisation, including internal controls;

(d) describes how type 1 and type 2 reports are to be used;

(e) provides requirements on responding to assessed risks of material misstatement, including the tests of controls; and

(f) provides requirements on reporting by the user auditor.

Authority Statement

Auditing Standard ASA 402 *Audit Considerations Relating to an Entity Using a Service Organisation* (as amended at 27 June 2011) is set out in paragraphs 1 to A44.

This Auditing Standard is to be read in conjunction with ASA 101 *Preamble to Australian Auditing Standards*, which sets out the intentions of the AUASB on how the Australian Auditing Standards, operative for financial reporting periods commencing on or after 1 January 2010, are to be understood, interpreted and applied. This Auditing Standard is to be read also in conjunction with ASA 200 *Overall Objectives of the Independent Auditor and the Conduct of an Audit in Accordance with Australian Auditing Standards*.

Dated: 27 June 2011

M H Kelsall
Chairman - AUASB

Auditing Standard ASA 402

The Auditing and Assurance Standards Board (AUASB) made Auditing Standard ASA 402 *Audit Considerations Relating to an Entity Using a Service Organisation,* pursuant to section 227B of the *Australian Securities and Investments Commission Act 2001* and section 336 of the *Corporations Act 2001*, on 27 October 2009.

This compiled version of ASA 402 incorporates subsequent amendments contained in another Auditing Standard made by the AUASB up to and including 27 June 2011 (see Compilation Details).

Auditing Standard ASA 402

Audit Considerations Relating to an Entity Using a Service Organisation

Application

Aus 0.1 This Auditing Standard applies to:

(a) an audit of a financial report for a financial year, or an audit of a financial report for a half-year, in accordance with the *Corporations Act 2001*; and

(b) an audit of a financial report, or a complete set of financial statements, for any other purpose.

Aus 0.2 This Auditing Standard also applies, as appropriate, to an audit of other historical financial information.

Operative Date

Aus 0.3 This Auditing Standard is operative for financial reporting periods commencing on or after 1 January 2010.

[Note: For operative dates of paragraphs changed or added by an amending Standard, see Compilation Details.]

Introduction

Scope of this Auditing Standard

1. This Auditing Standard deals with the user auditor's responsibility to obtain sufficient appropriate audit evidence when a user entity uses the services of one or more service organisations. Specifically, it expands on how the user auditor applies ASA 315[1] and ASA 330[2] in obtaining an understanding of the user entity, including internal control relevant to the audit, sufficient to identify and assess the risks of material misstatement and in designing and performing further audit procedures responsive to those risks.

2. Many entities outsource aspects of their business to organisations that provide services ranging from performing a specific task under the direction of an entity to replacing an entity's entire business units or functions, such as the tax compliance function. Many of the services provided by such organisations are integral to the entity's business operations; however, not all those services are relevant to the audit.

3. Services provided by a service organisation are relevant to the audit of a user entity's financial report when those services, and the controls over them, are part of the user entity's information system, including related business processes, relevant to financial reporting. Although most controls at the service organisation are likely to relate to financial reporting, there may be other controls that may also be relevant to the audit, such as controls over the safeguarding of assets. A service organisation's services are part of a user entity's information system, including related business processes, relevant to financial reporting if these services affect any of the following:

   (a) The classes of transactions in the user entity's operations that are significant to the user entity's financial report;

1 See ASA 315 *Identifying and Assessing the Risks of Material Misstatement through Understanding the Entity and Its Environment.*

2 See ASA 330 *The Auditor's Responses to Assessed Risks.*

(b) The procedures, within both information technology (IT) and manual systems, by which the user entity's transactions are initiated, recorded, processed, corrected as necessary, transferred to the general ledger and reported in the financial report;

(c) The related accounting records, either in electronic or manual form, supporting information and specific accounts in the user entity's financial report that are used to initiate, record, process and report the user entity's transactions; this includes the correction of incorrect information and how information is transferred to the general ledger;

(d) How the user entity's information system captures events and conditions, other than transactions, that are significant to the financial report;

(e) The financial reporting process used to prepare the user entity's financial report, including significant accounting estimates and disclosures; and

(f) Controls surrounding journal entries, including non-standard journal entries used to record non-recurring, unusual transactions or adjustments.

4. The nature and extent of work to be performed by the user auditor regarding the services provided by a service organisation depend on the nature and significance of those services to the user entity and the relevance of those services to the audit.

5. This Auditing Standard does not apply to services provided by financial institutions that are limited to processing, for an entity's account held at the financial institution, transactions that are specifically authorised by the entity, such as the processing of cheque account transactions by a bank or the processing of securities transactions by a broker. In addition, this Auditing Standard does not apply to the audit of transactions arising from proprietary financial interests in other entities, such as partnerships, corporations and joint ventures, when proprietary interests are accounted for and reported to interest holders.

Aus 5.1 An auditor appointed to provide an opinion on an entity's financial report may also have additional statutory or regulatory responsibilities, which may be affected by the entity's use of a service organisation. For example, sections 307(c) and 307(d) of the *Corporations Act 2001* (the Act) require the auditor to form an opinion on whether the entity has kept proper financial records, and other records and registers as required by that Act.

Effective Date

6. [Deleted by the AUASB. Refer Aus 0.3]

Objectives

7. The objectives of the user auditor, when the user entity uses the services of a service organisation, are:

(a) To obtain an understanding of the nature and significance of the services provided by the service organisation and their effect on the user entity's internal control relevant to the audit, sufficient to identify and assess the risks of material misstatement; and

(b) To design and perform audit procedures responsive to those risks.

Definitions

8. For purposes of the Australian Auditing Standards, the following terms have the meanings attributed below:

(a) Complementary user entity controls means controls that the service organisation assumes, in the design of its service, will be implemented by user entities, and which, if necessary to achieve control objectives, are identified in the description of its system.

(b) Report on the description and design of controls at a service organisation (referred to in this Auditing Standard as a type 1 report) means a report that comprises:

(i) A description, prepared by management of the service organisation, of the service organisation's system, control objectives and related controls that have been designed and implemented as at a specified date; and

(ii) A report by the service auditor with the objective of conveying reasonable assurance that includes the service auditor's opinion on the description of the service organisation's system, control objectives and related controls and the suitability of the design of the controls to achieve the specified control objectives.

(c) Report on the description, design, and operating effectiveness of controls at a service organisation (referred to in this Auditing Standard as a type 2 report) means a report that comprises:

(i) A description, prepared by management of the service organisation, of the service organisation's system, control objectives and related controls, their design and implementation as at a specified date or throughout a specified period and, in some cases, their operating effectiveness throughout a specified period; and

(ii) A report by the service auditor with the objective of conveying reasonable assurance that includes:

a. The service auditor's opinion on the description of the service organisation's system, control objectives and related controls, the suitability of the design of the controls to achieve the specified control objectives, and the operating effectiveness of the controls; and

b. A description of the service auditor's tests of the controls and the results thereof.

(d) Service auditor means an auditor who, at the request of the service organisation, provides an assurance report on the controls of a service organisation.

(e) Service organisation means a third-party organisation (or segment of a third-party organisation) that provides services to user entities that are part of those entities' information systems relevant to financial reporting.

(f) Service organisation's system means the policies and procedures designed, implemented and maintained by the service organisation to provide user entities with the services covered by the service auditor's report.

(g) Subservice organisation means a service organisation used by another service organisation to perform some of the services provided to user entities that are part of those user entities' information systems relevant to financial reporting.

(h) User auditor means an auditor who audits and reports on the financial report of a user entity.

(i) User entity means an entity that uses a service organisation and whose financial report is being audited.

Requirements

Obtaining an Understanding of the Services Provided by a Service Organisation, Including Internal Control

9. When obtaining an understanding of the user entity in accordance with ASA 315,[3] the user auditor shall obtain an understanding of how a user entity uses the services of a service organisation in the user entity's operations, including: (Ref: Para. A1-A2)

(a) The nature of the services provided by the service organisation and the significance of those services to the user entity, including the effect thereof on the user entity's internal control; (Ref: Para. A3-A5)

(b) The nature and materiality of the transactions processed or accounts or financial reporting processes affected by the service organisation; (Ref: Para. A6)

(c) The degree of interaction between the activities of the service organisation and those of the user entity; and (Ref: Para. A7)

3 See ASA 315, paragraph 11.

ASA

(d) The nature of the relationship between the user entity and the service organisation, including the relevant contractual terms for the activities undertaken by the service organisation. (Ref: Para. A8-A11)

10. When obtaining an understanding of internal control relevant to the audit in accordance with ASA 315,[4] the user auditor shall evaluate the design and implementation of relevant controls at the user entity that relate to the services provided by the service organisation, including those that are applied to the transactions processed by the service organisation. (Ref: Para. A12-A14)

11. The user auditor shall determine whether a sufficient understanding of the nature and significance of the services provided by the service organisation and their effect on the user entity's internal control relevant to the audit has been obtained to provide a basis for the identification and assessment of risks of material misstatement.

12. If the user auditor is unable to obtain a sufficient understanding from the user entity, the user auditor shall obtain that understanding from one or more of the following procedures:

(a) Obtaining a type 1 or type 2 report, if available;

(b) Contacting the service organisation, through the user entity, to obtain specific information;

(c) Visiting the service organisation and performing procedures that will provide the necessary information about the relevant controls at the service organisation; or

(d) Using another auditor to perform procedures that will provide the necessary information about the relevant controls at the service organisation. (Ref: Para. A15-A20)

Using a Type 1 or Type 2 Report to Support the User Auditor's Understanding of the Service Organisation

13. In determining the sufficiency and appropriateness of the audit evidence provided by a type 1 or type 2 report, the user auditor shall be satisfied as to:

(a) The service auditor's professional competence and independence from the service organisation; and

(b) The adequacy of the standards under which the type 1 or type 2 report was issued. (Ref: Para. A21)

14. If the user auditor plans to use a type 1 or type 2 report as audit evidence to support the user auditor's understanding about the design and implementation of controls at the service organisation, the user auditor shall:

(a) Evaluate whether the description and design of controls at the service organisation is at a date or for a period that is appropriate for the user auditor's purposes;

(b) Evaluate the sufficiency and appropriateness of the evidence provided by the report for the understanding of the user entity's internal control relevant to the audit; and

(c) Determine whether complementary user entity controls identified by the service organisation are relevant to the user entity and, if so, obtain an understanding of whether the user entity has designed and implemented such controls. (Ref: Para. A22-A23)

Responding to the Assessed Risks of Material Misstatement

15. In responding to assessed risks in accordance with ASA 330, the user auditor shall:

(a) Determine whether sufficient appropriate audit evidence concerning the relevant financial report assertions is available from records held at the user entity; and, if not,

(b) Perform further audit procedures to obtain sufficient appropriate audit evidence or use another auditor to perform those procedures at the service organisation on the user auditor's behalf. (Ref: Para. A24-A28)

4 See ASA 315, paragraph 12.

Tests of Controls

16. When the user auditor's risk assessment includes an expectation that controls at the service organisation are operating effectively, the user auditor shall obtain audit evidence about the operating effectiveness of those controls from one or more of the following procedures:
    (a) Obtaining a type 2 report, if available;
    (b) Performing appropriate tests of controls at the service organisation; or
    (c) Using another auditor to perform tests of controls at the service organisation on behalf of the user auditor. (Ref: Para. A29-A30)

Using a Type 2 Report as Audit Evidence that Controls at the Service Organisation Are Operating Effectively

17. If, in accordance with paragraph 16(a) of this Auditing Standard, the user auditor plans to use a type 2 report as audit evidence that controls at the service organisation are operating effectively, the user auditor shall determine whether the service auditor's report provides sufficient appropriate audit evidence about the effectiveness of the controls to support the user auditor's risk assessment by:
    (a) Evaluating whether the description, design and operating effectiveness of controls at the service organisation is at a date or for a period that is appropriate for the user auditor's purposes;
    (b) Determining whether complementary user entity controls identified by the service organisation are relevant to the user entity and, if so, obtaining an understanding of whether the user entity has designed and implemented such controls and, if so, testing their operating effectiveness;
    (c) Evaluating the adequacy of the time period covered by the tests of controls and the time elapsed since the performance of the tests of controls; and
    (d) Evaluating whether the tests of controls performed by the service auditor and the results thereof, as described in the service auditor's report, are relevant to the assertions in the user entity's financial report and provide sufficient appropriate audit evidence to support the user auditor's risk assessment. (Ref: Para. A31-A39)

Type 1 and Type 2 Reports that Exclude the Services of a Subservice Organisation

18. If the user auditor plans to use a type 1 or a type 2 report that excludes the services provided by a subservice organisation and those services are relevant to the audit of the user entity's financial report, the user auditor shall apply the requirements of this Auditing Standard with respect to the services provided by the subservice organisation. (Ref: Para. A40)

Fraud, Non-Compliance with Laws and Regulations and Uncorrected Misstatements in Relation to Activities at the Service Organisation

19. The user auditor shall enquire of management of the user entity whether the service organisation has reported to the user entity, or whether the user entity is otherwise aware of, any fraud, non-compliance with laws and regulations or uncorrected misstatements affecting the financial report of the user entity. The user auditor shall evaluate how such matters affect the nature, timing and extent of the user auditor's further audit procedures, including the effect on the user auditor's conclusions and user auditor's report. (Ref: Para. A41)

Reporting by the User Auditor

20. The user auditor shall modify the opinion in the user auditor's report in accordance with ASA 705[5] if the user auditor is unable to obtain sufficient appropriate audit evidence regarding the services provided by the service organisation relevant to the audit of the user entity's financial report. (Ref: Para. A42)

21. The user auditor shall not refer to the work of a service auditor in the user auditor's report containing an unmodified opinion unless required by law or regulation to do so. If such reference is required by law or regulation, the user auditor's report shall indicate that

5 See ASA 705 *Modifications to the Opinion in the Independent Auditor's Report*, paragraph 6.

the reference does not diminish the user auditor's responsibility for the audit opinion. (Ref: Para. A43)

22. If reference to the work of a service auditor is relevant to an understanding of a modification to the user auditor's opinion, the user auditor's report shall indicate that such reference does not diminish the user auditor's responsibility for that opinion. (Ref: Para. A44)

❖❖❖

Application and Other Explanatory Material

Obtaining an Understanding of the Services Provided by a Service Organisation, Including Internal Control

Sources of Information (Ref: Para. 9)

A1. Information on the nature of the services provided by a service organisation may be available from a wide variety of sources, such as:

- User manuals.
- System overviews.
- Technical manuals.
- The contract or service level agreement between the user entity and the service organisation.
- Reports by service organisations, internal auditors or regulatory authorities on controls at the service organisation.
- Reports by the service auditor, including management letters, if available.

A2. Knowledge obtained through the user auditor's experience with the service organisation, for example through experience with other audit engagements, may also be helpful in obtaining an understanding of the nature of the services provided by the service organisation. This may be particularly helpful if the services and controls at the service organisation over those services are highly standardised.

Nature of the Services Provided by the Service Organisation (Ref: Para. 9(a))

A3. A user entity may use a service organisation such as one that processes transactions and maintains related accountability, or records transactions and processes related data. Service organisations that provide such services include, for example, bank trust departments that invest and service assets for employee benefit plans or for others; mortgage bankers that service mortgages for others; and application service providers that provide packaged software applications and a technology environment that enables customers to process financial and operational transactions.

A4. Examples of service organisation services that are relevant to the audit include:

- Maintenance of the user entity's accounting records.
- Management of assets.
- Initiating, recording or processing transactions as agent of the user entity.

Considerations Specific to Smaller Entities

A5. Smaller entities may use external bookkeeping services ranging from the processing of certain transactions (for example, payment of payroll taxes) and maintenance of their accounting records, to the preparation of their financial report. The use of such a service organisation for the preparation of its financial report does not relieve management of the smaller entity and, where appropriate, those charged with governance, of their responsibilities for the financial report.[6]

6 See ASA 200 *Overall Objectives of the Independent Auditor and the Conduct of an Audit in Accordance with Australian Auditing Standards*, paragraphs 4 and A2-A3.

Nature and Materiality of Transactions Processed by the Service Organisation (Ref: Para. 9(b))

A6. A service organisation may establish policies and procedures that affect the user entity's internal control. These policies and procedures are at least in part physically and operationally separate from the user entity. The significance of the controls of the service organisation to those of the user entity depends on the nature of the services provided by the service organisation, including the nature and materiality of the transactions it processes for the user entity. In certain situations, the transactions processed and the accounts affected by the service organisation may not appear to be material to the user entity's financial report, but the nature of the transactions processed may be significant and the user auditor may determine that an understanding of those controls is necessary in the circumstances.

The Degree of Interaction between the Activities of the Service Organisation and the User Entity (Ref: Para. 9(c))

A7. The significance of the controls of the service organisation to those of the user entity also depends on the degree of interaction between its activities and those of the user entity. The degree of interaction refers to the extent to which a user entity is able to and elects to implement effective controls over the processing performed by the service organisation. For example, a high degree of interaction exists between the activities of the user entity and those at the service organisation when the user entity authorises transactions and the service organisation processes and does the accounting for those transactions. In these circumstances, it may be practicable for the user entity to implement effective controls over those transactions. On the other hand, when the service organisation initiates or initially records, processes, and does the accounting for the user entity's transactions, there is a lower degree of interaction between the two organisations. In these circumstances, the user entity may be unable to, or may elect not to, implement effective controls over these transactions at the user entity and may rely on controls at the service organisation.

Nature of the Relationship between the User Entity and the Service Organisation (Ref: Para. 9(d))

A8. The contract or service level agreement between the user entity and the service organisation may provide for matters such as:

- The information to be provided to the user entity and responsibilities for initiating transactions relating to the activities undertaken by the service organisation;
- The application of requirements of regulatory bodies concerning the form of records to be maintained, or access to them;
- The indemnification, if any, to be provided to the user entity in the event of a performance failure;
- Whether the service organisation will provide a report on its controls and, if so, whether such report would be a type 1 or type 2 report;
- Whether the user auditor has rights of access to the accounting records of the user entity maintained by the service organisation and other information necessary for the conduct of the audit; and
- Whether the agreement allows for direct communication between the user auditor and the service auditor.

A9. There is a direct relationship between the service organisation and the user entity and between the service organisation and the service auditor. These relationships do not necessarily create a direct relationship between the user auditor and the service auditor. When there is no direct relationship between the user auditor and the service auditor, communications between the user auditor and the service auditor are usually conducted through the user entity and the service organisation. A direct relationship may also be created between a user auditor and a service auditor, taking into account the relevant ethical and confidentiality considerations. A user auditor, for example, may use a service auditor to perform procedures on the user auditor's behalf, such as:

(a) Tests of controls at the service organisation; or

(b) Substantive procedures on the user entity's financial report transactions and balances maintained by a service organisation.

Considerations Specific to Public Sector Entities

A10. Public sector auditors generally have broad rights of access established by legislation. However, there may be situations where such rights of access are not available, for example when the service organisation is located in a different jurisdiction. In such cases, a public sector auditor may need to obtain an understanding of the legislation applicable in the different jurisdiction to determine whether appropriate access rights can be obtained. A public sector auditor may also obtain or ask the user entity to incorporate rights of access in any contractual arrangements between the user entity and the service organisation.

A11. Public sector auditors may also use another auditor to perform tests of controls or substantive procedures in relation to compliance with law, regulation or other authority.

Understanding the Controls Relating to Services Provided by the Service Organisation (Ref: Para. 10)

A12. The user entity may establish controls over the service organisation's services that may be tested by the user auditor and that may enable the user auditor to conclude that the user entity's controls are operating effectively for some or all of the related assertions, regardless of the controls in place at the service organisation. If a user entity, for example, uses a service organisation to process its payroll transactions, the user entity may establish controls over the submission and receipt of payroll information that could prevent or detect material misstatements. These controls may include:

- Comparing the data submitted to the service organisation with reports of information received from the service organisation after the data has been processed.
- Recomputing a sample of the payroll amounts for clerical accuracy and reviewing the total amount of the payroll for reasonableness.

A13. In this situation, the user auditor may perform tests of the user entity's controls over payroll processing that would provide a basis for the user auditor to conclude that the user entity's controls are operating effectively for the assertions related to payroll transactions.

A14. As noted in ASA 315,[7] in respect of some risks, the user auditor may judge that it is not possible or practicable to obtain sufficient appropriate audit evidence only from substantive procedures. Such risks may relate to the inaccurate or incomplete recording of routine and significant classes of transactions and account balances, the characteristics of which often permit highly automated processing with little or no manual intervention. Such automated processing characteristics may be particularly present when the user entity uses service organisations. In such cases, the user entity's controls over such risks are relevant to the audit and the user auditor is required to obtain an understanding of, and to evaluate, such controls in accordance with paragraphs 9 and 10 of this Auditing Standard.

Further Procedures When a Sufficient Understanding Cannot Be Obtained from the User Entity (Ref: Para. 12)

A15. The user auditor's decision as to which procedure, individually or in combination, in paragraph 12 to undertake, in order to obtain the information necessary to provide a basis for the identification and assessment of the risks of material misstatement in relation to the user entity's use of the service organisation, may be influenced by such matters as:

- The size of both the user entity and the service organisation;
- The complexity of the transactions at the user entity and the complexity of the services provided by the service organisation;
- The location of the service organisation (for example, the user auditor may decide to use another auditor to perform procedures at the service organisation on the user auditor's behalf if the service organisation is in a remote location);
- Whether the procedure(s) is expected to effectively provide the user auditor with sufficient appropriate audit evidence; and
- The nature of the relationship between the user entity and the service organisation.

7 See ASA 315, paragraph 30.

A16. [Deleted by the AUASB. Refer Aus A16.1].[8]

Aus A16.1 A service organisation may engage a service auditor to report on the description and design of its controls (type 1 report) or on the description and design of its controls and their operating effectiveness (type 2 report).

A17. The availability of a type 1 or type 2 report will generally depend on whether the contract between a service organisation and a user entity includes the provision of such a report by the service organisation. A service organisation may also elect, for practical reasons, to make a type 1 or type 2 report available to the user entities. However, in some cases, a type 1 or type 2 report may not be available to user entities.

A18. In some circumstances, a user entity may outsource one or more significant business units or functions, such as its entire tax planning and compliance functions, or finance and accounting or the control function to one or more service organisations. As a report on controls at the service organisation may not be available in these circumstances, visiting the service organisation may be the most effective procedure for the user auditor to gain an understanding of controls at the service organisation, as there is likely to be direct interaction of management of the user entity with management at the service organisation.

A19. Another auditor may be used to perform procedures that will provide the necessary information about the relevant controls at the service organisation. If a type 1 or type 2 report has been issued, the user auditor may use the service auditor to perform these procedures as the service auditor has an existing relationship with the service organisation. The user auditor, using the work of another auditor, may find the guidance in ASA 600[9] useful as it relates to understanding another auditor (including that auditor's independence and professional competence), involvement in the work of another auditor in planning the nature, timing and extent of such work, and in evaluating the sufficiency and appropriateness of the audit evidence obtained.

A20. A user entity may use a service organisation that in turn uses a subservice organisation to provide some of the services provided to a user entity that are part of the user entity's information system relevant to financial reporting. The subservice organisation may be a separate entity from the service organisation or may be related to the service organisation. A user auditor may need to consider controls at the subservice organisation. In situations where one or more subservice organisations are used, the interaction between the activities of the user entity and those of the service organisation is expanded to include the interaction between the user entity, the service organisation and the subservice organisations. The degree of this interaction, as well as the nature and materiality of the transactions processed by the service organisation and the subservice organisations are the most important factors for the user auditor to consider in determining the significance of the service organisation's and subservice organisation's controls to the user entity's controls.

Using a Type 1 or Type 2 Report to Support the User Auditor's Understanding of the Service Organisation (Ref: Para. 13-14)

A21. The user auditor may make enquiries about the service auditor to the service auditor's professional organisation or other practitioners and enquire whether the service auditor is subject to regulatory oversight. The service auditor may be practicing in a jurisdiction where different standards are followed in respect of reports on controls at a service organisation, and the user auditor may obtain information about the standards used by the service auditor from the standard setting organisation.

A22. A type 1 or type 2 report, along with information about the user entity, may assist the user auditor in obtaining an understanding of:

(a) The aspects of controls at the service organisation that may affect the processing of the user entity's transactions, including the use of subservice organisations;

8 [Footnote deleted by the AUASB. Refer Aus A16.1]

9 See ASA 600 *Special Considerations—Audits of a Group Financial Report (Including the Work of Component Auditors)*, paragraphs 2 and 19.

(b) The flow of significant transactions through the service organisation to determine the points in the transaction flow where material misstatements in the user entity's financial report could occur;

(c) The control objectives at the service organisation that are relevant to the user entity's financial report assertions; and

(d) Whether controls at the service organisation are suitably designed and implemented to prevent or detect processing errors that could result in material misstatements in the user entity's financial report.

A type 1 or type 2 report may assist the user auditor in obtaining a sufficient understanding to identify and assess the risks of material misstatement. A type 1 report, however, does not provide any evidence of the operating effectiveness of the relevant controls.

A23. A type 1 or type 2 report that is as of a date or for a period that is outside of the reporting period of a user entity may assist the user auditor in obtaining a preliminary understanding of the controls implemented at the service organisation if the report is supplemented by additional current information from other sources. If the service organisation's description of controls is as of a date or for a period that precedes the beginning of the period under audit, the user auditor may perform procedures to update the information in a type 1 or type 2 report, such as:

- Discussing the changes at the service organisation with user entity personnel who would be in a position to know of such changes;
- Reviewing current documentation and correspondence issued by the service organisation; or
- Discussing the changes with service organisation personnel.

Responding to the Assessed Risks of Material Misstatement (Ref: Para. 15)

A24. Whether the use of a service organisation increases a user entity's risk of material misstatement depends on the nature of the services provided and the controls over these services; in some cases, the use of a service organisation may decrease a user entity's risk of material misstatement, particularly if the user entity itself does not possess the expertise necessary to undertake particular activities, such as initiating, processing, and recording transactions, or does not have adequate resources (for example, an IT system).

A25. When the service organisation maintains material elements of the accounting records of the user entity, direct access to those records may be necessary in order for the user auditor to obtain sufficient appropriate audit evidence relating to the operations of controls over those records or to substantiate transactions and balances recorded in them, or both. Such access may involve either physical inspection of records at the service organisation's premises or interrogation of records maintained electronically from the user entity or another location, or both. Where direct access is achieved electronically, the user auditor may thereby obtain evidence as to the adequacy of controls operated by the service organisation over the completeness and integrity of the user entity's data for which the service organisation is responsible.

A26. In determining the nature and extent of audit evidence to be obtained in relation to balances representing assets held or transactions undertaken by a service organisation on behalf of the user entity, the following procedures may be considered by the user auditor:

(a) Inspecting records and documents held by the user entity: the reliability of this source of evidence is determined by the nature and extent of the accounting records and supporting documentation retained by the user entity. In some cases, the user entity may not maintain independent detailed records or documentation of specific transactions undertaken on its behalf.

(b) Inspecting records and documents held by the service organisation: the user auditor's access to the records of the service organisation may be established as part of the contractual arrangements between the user entity and the service organisation. The user auditor may also use another auditor, on its behalf, to gain access to the user entity's records maintained by the service organisation.

(c) Obtaining confirmations of balances and transactions from the service organisation: where the user entity maintains independent records of balances and transactions, confirmation from the service organisation corroborating the user entity's records may constitute reliable audit evidence concerning the existence of the transactions and assets concerned. For example, when multiple service organisations are used, such as an investment manager and a custodian, and these service organisations maintain independent records, the user auditor may confirm balances with these organisations in order to compare this information with the independent records of the user entity.

If the user entity does not maintain independent records, information obtained in confirmations from the service organisation is merely a statement of what is reflected in the records maintained by the service organisation. Therefore, such confirmations do not, taken alone, constitute reliable audit evidence. In these circumstances, the user auditor may consider whether an alternative source of independent evidence can be identified.

(d) Performing analytical procedures on the records maintained by the user entity or on the reports received from the service organisation: the effectiveness of analytical procedures is likely to vary by assertion and will be affected by the extent and detail of information available.

A27. Another auditor may perform procedures that are substantive in nature for the benefit of user auditors. Such an engagement may involve the performance, by another auditor, of procedures agreed upon by the user entity and its user auditor and by the service organisation and its service auditor. The findings resulting from the procedures performed by another auditor are reviewed by the user auditor to determine whether they constitute sufficient appropriate audit evidence. In addition, there may be requirements imposed by governmental authorities or through contractual arrangements whereby a service auditor performs designated procedures that are substantive in nature. The results of the application of the required procedures to balances and transactions processed by the service organisation may be used by user auditors as part of the evidence necessary to support their audit opinions. In these circumstances, it may be useful for the user auditor and the service auditor to agree, prior to the performance of the procedures, to the audit documentation or access to audit documentation that will be provided to the user auditor.

A28. In certain circumstances, in particular when a user entity outsources some or all of its finance function to a service organisation, the user auditor may face a situation where a significant portion of the audit evidence resides at the service organisation. Substantive procedures may need to be performed at the service organisation by the user auditor or another auditor on its behalf. A service auditor may provide a type 2 report and, in addition, may perform substantive procedures on behalf of the user auditor. The involvement of another auditor does not alter the user auditor's responsibility to obtain sufficient appropriate audit evidence to afford a reasonable basis to support the user auditor's opinion. Accordingly, the user auditor's consideration of whether sufficient appropriate audit evidence has been obtained and whether the user auditor needs to perform further substantive procedures includes the user auditor's involvement with, or evidence of, the direction, supervision and performance of the substantive procedures performed by another auditor.

Tests of Controls (Ref: Para. 16)

A29. The user auditor is required by ASA 330[10] to design and perform tests of controls to obtain sufficient appropriate audit evidence as to the operating effectiveness of relevant controls in certain circumstances. In the context of a service organisation, this requirement applies when:

(a) The user auditor's assessment of risks of material misstatement includes an expectation that the controls at the service organisation are operating effectively (that is, the user auditor intends to rely on the operating effectiveness of controls at the service organisation in determining the nature, timing and extent of substantive procedures); or

10 See ASA 330, paragraph 8.

(b) Substantive procedures alone, or in combination with tests of the operating effectiveness of controls at the user entity, cannot provide sufficient appropriate audit evidence at the assertion level.

A30. If a type 2 report is not available, a user auditor may contact the service organisation, through the user entity, to request that a service auditor be engaged to provide a type 2 report that includes tests of the operating effectiveness of the relevant controls or the user auditor may use another auditor to perform procedures at the service organisation that test the operating effectiveness of those controls. A user auditor may also visit the service organisation and perform tests of relevant controls if the service organisation agrees to it. The user auditor's risk assessments are based on the combined evidence provided by the work of another auditor and the user auditor's own procedures.

Using a Type 2 Report as Audit Evidence that Controls at the Service Organisation Are Operating Effectively (Ref: Para. 17)

A31. A type 2 report may be intended to satisfy the needs of several different user auditors; therefore tests of controls and results described in the service auditor's report may not be relevant to assertions that are significant in the user entity's financial report. The relevant tests of controls and results are evaluated to determine that the service auditor's report provides sufficient appropriate audit evidence about the effectiveness of the controls to support the user auditor's risk assessment. In doing so, the user auditor may consider the following factors:

(a) The time period covered by the tests of controls and the time elapsed since the performance of the tests of controls;

(b) The scope of the service auditor's work and the services and processes covered, the controls tested and tests that were performed, and the way in which tested controls relate to the user entity's controls; and

(c) The results of those tests of controls and the service auditor's opinion on the operating effectiveness of the controls.

A32. For certain assertions, the shorter the period covered by a specific test and the longer the time elapsed since the performance of the test, the less audit evidence the test may provide. In comparing the period covered by the type 2 report to the user entity's financial reporting period, the user auditor may conclude that the type 2 report offers less audit evidence if there is little overlap between the period covered by the type 2 report and the period for which the user auditor intends to rely on the report. When this is the case, a type 2 report covering a preceding or subsequent period may provide additional audit evidence. In other cases, the user auditor may determine it is necessary to perform, or use another auditor to perform, tests of controls at the service organisation in order to obtain sufficient appropriate audit evidence about the operating effectiveness of those controls.

A33. It may also be necessary for the user auditor to obtain additional evidence about significant changes to the relevant controls at the service organisation outside of the period covered by the type 2 report or determine additional audit procedures to be performed. Relevant factors in determining what additional audit evidence to obtain about controls at the service organisation that were operating outside of the period covered by the service auditor's report may include:

- The significance of the assessed risks of material misstatement at the assertion level;
- The specific controls that were tested during the interim period, and significant changes to them since they were tested, including changes in the information system, processes, and personnel;
- The degree to which audit evidence about the operating effectiveness of those controls was obtained;
- The length of the remaining period;
- The extent to which the user auditor intends to reduce further substantive procedures based on the reliance on controls; and
- The effectiveness of the control environment and monitoring of controls at the user entity.

A34. Additional audit evidence may be obtained, for example, by extending tests of controls over the remaining period or testing the user entity's monitoring of controls.

A35. If the service auditor's testing period is completely outside the user entity's financial reporting period, the user auditor will be unable to rely on such tests for the user auditor to conclude that the user entity's controls are operating effectively because they do not provide current audit period evidence of the effectiveness of the controls, unless other procedures are performed.

A36. In certain circumstances, a service provided by the service organisation may be designed with the assumption that certain controls will be implemented by the user entity. For example, the service may be designed with the assumption that the user entity will have controls in place for authorising transactions before they are sent to the service organisation for processing. In such a situation, the service organisation's description of controls may include a description of those complementary user entity controls. The user auditor considers whether those complementary user entity controls are relevant to the service provided to the user entity.

A37. If the user auditor believes that the service auditor's report may not provide sufficient appropriate audit evidence, for example, if a service auditor's report does not contain a description of the service auditor's tests of controls and results thereon, the user auditor may supplement the understanding of the service auditor's procedures and conclusions by contacting the service organisation, through the user entity, to request a discussion with the service auditor about the scope and results of the service auditor's work. Also, if the user auditor believes it is necessary, the user auditor may contact the service organisation, through the user entity, to request that the service auditor perform procedures at the service organisation. Alternatively, the user auditor, or another auditor at the request of the user auditor, may perform such procedures.

A38. The service auditor's type 2 report identifies results of tests, including exceptions and other information that could affect the user auditor's conclusions. Exceptions noted by the service auditor or a modified opinion in the service auditor's type 2 report do not automatically mean that the service auditor's type 2 report will not be useful for the audit of the user entity's financial report in assessing the risks of material misstatement. Rather, the exceptions and the matter giving rise to a modified opinion in the service auditor's type 2 report are considered in the user auditor's assessment of the testing of controls performed by the service auditor. In considering the exceptions and matters giving rise to a modified opinion, the user auditor may discuss such matters with the service auditor. Such communication is dependent upon the user entity contacting the service organisation, and obtaining the service organisation's approval for the communication to take place.

Communication of deficiencies in internal control identified during the audit

A39. The user auditor is required to communicate in writing significant deficiencies identified during the audit to both management and those charged with governance on a timely basis.[11] The user auditor is also required to communicate to management at an appropriate level of responsibility on a timely basis other deficiencies in internal control identified during the audit that, in the user auditor's professional judgement, are of sufficient importance to merit management's attention.[12] Matters that the user auditor may identify during the audit and may communicate to management and those charged with governance of the user entity include:

- Any monitoring of controls that could be implemented by the user entity, including those identified as a result of obtaining a type 1 or type 2 report;
- Instances where complementary user entity controls are noted in the type 1 or type 2 report and are not implemented at the user entity; and
- Controls that may be needed at the service organisation that do not appear to have been implemented or that are not specifically covered by a type 2 report.

11 See ASA 265 *Communicating Deficiencies in Internal Control to Those Charged with Governance and Management*, paragraphs 9-10.

12 See ASA 265, paragraph 10.

Type 1 and Type 2 Reports that Exclude the Services of a Subservice Organisation (Ref: Para. 18)

A40. If a service organisation uses a subservice organisation, the service auditor's report may either include or exclude the subservice organisation's relevant control objectives and related controls in the service organisation's description of its system and in the scope of the service auditor's engagement. These two methods of reporting are known as the inclusive method and the carve-out method, respectively. If the type 1 or type 2 report excludes the controls at a subservice organisation, and the services provided by the subservice organisation are relevant to the audit of the user entity's financial report, the user auditor is required to apply the requirements of this Auditing Standard in respect of the subservice organisation. The nature and extent of work to be performed by the user auditor regarding the services provided by a subservice organisation depend on the nature and significance of those services to the user entity and the relevance of those services to the audit. The application of the requirement in paragraph 9 assists the user auditor in determining the effect of the subservice organisation and the nature and extent of work to be performed.

Fraud, Non-Compliance with Laws and Regulations and Uncorrected Misstatements in Relation to Activities at the Service Organisation (Ref: Para. 19)

A41. A service organisation may be required under the terms of the contract with user entities to disclose to affected user entities any fraud, non-compliance with laws and regulations or uncorrected misstatements attributable to the service organisation's management or employees. As required by paragraph 19, the user auditor makes enquiries of the user entity management regarding whether the service organisation has reported any such matters and evaluates whether any matters reported by the service organisation affect the nature, timing and extent of the user auditor's further audit procedures. In certain circumstances, the user auditor may require additional information to perform this evaluation, and may request the user entity to contact the service organisation to obtain the necessary information.

Reporting by the User Auditor (Ref: Para. 20)

A42. When a user auditor is unable to obtain sufficient appropriate audit evidence regarding the services provided by the service organisation relevant to the audit of the user entity's financial report, a limitation on the scope of the audit exists. This may be the case when:

- The user auditor is unable to obtain a sufficient understanding of the services provided by the service organisation and does not have a basis for the identification and assessment of the risks of material misstatement;
- A user auditor's risk assessment includes an expectation that controls at the service organisation are operating effectively and the user auditor is unable to obtain sufficient appropriate audit evidence about the operating effectiveness of these controls; or
- Sufficient appropriate audit evidence is only available from records held at the service organisation, and the user auditor is unable to obtain direct access to these records.

Whether the user auditor expresses a qualified opinion or disclaims an opinion depends on the user auditor's conclusion as to whether the possible effects on the financial report are material or pervasive.

Reference to the Work of a Service Auditor (Ref: Para. 21-22)

A43. In some cases, law or regulation may require a reference to the work of a service auditor in the user auditor's report, for example, for the purposes of transparency in the public sector. In such circumstances, the user auditor may need the consent of the service auditor before making such a reference.

A44. The fact that a user entity uses a service organisation does not alter the user auditor's responsibility under the Australian Auditing Standards to obtain sufficient appropriate audit evidence to afford a reasonable basis to support the user auditor's opinion. Therefore, the user auditor does not make reference to the service auditor's report as a basis, in part, for the user auditor's opinion on the user entity's financial report. However, when the user auditor expresses a modified opinion because of a modified opinion in a service auditor's report, the user auditor is not precluded from referring to the service auditor's report if such reference assists in explaining the reason for the user auditor's modified opinion. In such circumstances, the user auditor may need the consent of the service auditor before making such a reference.

❖ ❖ ❖

Conformity with International Standards on Auditing

This Auditing Standard conforms with International Standard on Auditing ISA 402 *Audit Considerations Relating to an Entity Using a Service Organization*, issued by the International Auditing and Assurance Standards Board (IAASB), an independent standard-setting board of the International Federation of Accountants (IFAC).

Paragraphs that have been added to this Auditing Standard (and do not appear in the text of the equivalent ISA) are identified with the prefix "Aus".

Compliance with this Auditing Standard enables compliance with ISA 402.

ASA

ASA 450

Evaluation of Misstatements Identified during the Audit

(Issued October 2009)

Issued by the Auditing and Assurance Standards Board.

Note from the Institute of Chartered Accountants Australia

This note, prepared by the technical editor, is not part of ASA 450.

Historical development

October 2009: ASA 450 issued as part of the AUASB's Clarity Project. ASA 450 deals with the auditor's responsibility to evaluate the effect of identified misstatements on the audit and the effect of any uncorrected misstatements on the financial report. Previously this topic was dealt with as part of ASA 320 'Materiality and Audit Adjustments'. It is based on the international Standard ISA 450 of the same name.

ASA

Contents

Preface

Reasons for Issuing Auditing Standard ASA 450 *Evaluation of Misstatements Identified during the Audit*

The Auditing and Assurance Standards Board (AUASB) issues Auditing Standard ASA 450 *Evaluation of Misstatements Identified during the Audit* pursuant to the requirements of the legislative provisions and the Strategic Direction explained below.

The AUASB is an independent statutory board of the Australian Government established under section 227A of the *Australian Securities and Investments Commission Act 2001*, as amended (ASIC Act). Under section 336 of the *Corporations Act 2001*, the AUASB may make Australian Auditing Standards for the purposes of the corporations legislation. These Auditing Standards are legislative instruments under the *Legislative Instruments Act 2003*.

Under the Strategic Direction given to the AUASB by the Financial Reporting Council (FRC), the AUASB is required to have regard to any programme initiated by the International Auditing and Assurance Standards Board (IAASB) for the revision and enhancement of the International Standards on Auditing (ISAs) and to make appropriate consequential amendments to the Australian Auditing Standards. Accordingly, the AUASB has decided to revise and redraft the Australian Auditing Standards using the equivalent redrafted ISAs.

Main Features

This Auditing Standard establishes requirements and provides application and other explanatory material regarding the auditor's responsibility to evaluate the effect of identified misstatements on the audit and of uncorrected misstatements, if any, on the financial report.

This Auditing Standard:

(a) requires the identification, accumulation and consideration of identified misstatements during the audit;

(b) requires communication of identified misstatements to management for correction;

(c) requires evaluation of uncorrected misstatements and communication of such misstatements to those charged with governance;

(d) directs the auditor to obtain a written representation from management, and where appropriate, those charged with governance, regarding the effects of any uncorrected misstatements; and

(e) describes the required audit documentation.

Authority Statement

The Auditing and Assurance Standards Board (AUASB) makes this Auditing Standard ASA 450 *Evaluation of Misstatements Identified during the Audit* pursuant to section 227B of the *Australian Securities and Investments Commission Act 2001* and section 336 of the *Corporations Act 2001*.

This Auditing Standard is to be read in conjunction with ASA 101 *Preamble to Australian Auditing Standards*, which sets out the intentions of the AUASB on how the Australian Auditing Standards, operative for financial reporting periods commencing on or after 1 January 2010, are to be understood, interpreted and applied. This Auditing Standard is to be read also in conjunction with ASA 200 *Overall Objectives of the Independent Auditor and the Conduct of an Audit in Accordance with Australian Auditing Standards*.

Dated: 27 October 2009

M H Kelsall
Chairman - AUASB

Auditing Standard ASA 450

Evaluation of Misstatements Identified during the Audit

Application

Aus 0.1 This Auditing Standard applies to:

(a) an audit of a financial report for a financial year, or an audit of a financial report for a half-year, in accordance with the *Corporations Act 2001*; and

(b) an audit of a financial report or a complete set of financial statements for any other purpose.

Aus 0.2 This Auditing Standard also applies, as appropriate, to an audit of other historical financial information.

Operative Date

Aus 0.3 This Auditing Standard is operative for financial reporting periods commencing on or after 1 January 2010.

Introduction

Scope of this Auditing Standard

1. This Auditing Standard deals with the auditor's responsibility to evaluate the effect of identified misstatements on the audit and of uncorrected misstatements, if any, on the financial report. ASA 700 deals with the auditor's responsibility, in forming an opinion on the financial report, to conclude whether reasonable assurance has been obtained about whether the financial report as a whole is free from material misstatement. The auditor's

conclusion required by ASA 700 takes into account the auditor's evaluation of uncorrected misstatements, if any, on the financial report, in accordance with this Auditing Standard.[1] ASA 320[2] deals with the auditor's responsibility to apply the concept of materiality appropriately in planning and performing an audit of a financial report.

Effective Date

2. [Deleted by the AUASB. Refer Aus 0.3]

Objective

3. The objective of the auditor is to evaluate:

   (a) The effect of identified misstatements on the audit; and

   (b) The effect of uncorrected misstatements, if any, on the financial report.

Definitions

4. For purposes of the Australian Auditing Standards, the following terms have the meanings attributed below:

   (a) Misstatement means a difference between the amount, classification, presentation, or disclosure of a reported financial report item and the amount, classification, presentation, or disclosure that is required for the item to be in accordance with the applicable financial reporting framework. Misstatements can arise from error or fraud. (Ref: Para. A1)

   When the auditor expresses an opinion on whether the financial report is presented fairly, in all material respects, or gives a true and fair view, misstatements also include those adjustments of amounts, classifications, presentation, or disclosures that, in the auditor's judgement, are necessary for the financial report to be presented fairly, in all material respects, or to give a true and fair view.

   (b) Uncorrected misstatements means misstatements that the auditor has accumulated during the audit and that have not been corrected.

Requirements

Accumulation of Identified Misstatements

5. The auditor shall accumulate misstatements identified during the audit, other than those that are clearly trivial. (Ref: Para. A2-A3)

Consideration of Identified Misstatements as the Audit Progresses

6. The auditor shall determine whether the overall audit strategy and audit plan need to be revised if:

   (a) The nature of identified misstatements and the circumstances of their occurrence indicate that other misstatements may exist that, when aggregated with misstatements accumulated during the audit, could be material; or (Ref: Para. A4)

   (b) The aggregate of misstatements accumulated during the audit approaches materiality determined in accordance with ASA 320. (Ref: Para. A5)

7. If, at the auditor's request, management has examined a class of transactions, account balances or disclosures and corrected misstatements that were detected, the auditor shall perform additional audit procedures to determine whether misstatements remain. (Ref: Para. A6)

1 See ASA 700 *Forming an Opinion and Reporting on a Financial Report*, paragraphs 10-11.

2 See ASA 320 *Materiality in Planning and Performing an Audit*.

Communication and Correction of Misstatements

8. The auditor shall communicate on a timely basis all misstatements accumulated during the audit with the appropriate level of management, unless prohibited by law or regulation.[3] The auditor shall request management to correct those misstatements. (Ref: Para. A7-A9)

9. If management refuses to correct some or all of the misstatements communicated by the auditor, the auditor shall obtain an understanding of management's reasons for not making the corrections and shall take that understanding into account when evaluating whether the financial report as a whole is free from material misstatement. (Ref: Para A10)

Evaluating the Effect of Uncorrected Misstatements

10. Prior to evaluating the effect of uncorrected misstatements, the auditor shall reassess materiality determined in accordance with ASA 320 to confirm whether it remains appropriate in the context of the entity's actual financial results. (Ref: Para. A11-A12)

11. The auditor shall determine whether uncorrected misstatements are material, individually or in aggregate. In making this determination, the auditor shall consider:

    (a) The size and nature of the misstatements, both in relation to particular classes of transactions, account balances or disclosures and the financial report as a whole, and the particular circumstances of their occurrence; and (Ref: Para. A13-A17, A19-A20)

    (b) The effect of uncorrected misstatements related to prior periods on the relevant classes of transactions, account balances or disclosures, and the financial report as a whole. (Ref: Para. A18)

Communication with Those Charged with Governance

12. The auditor shall communicate with those charged with governance uncorrected misstatements and the effect that they, individually or in aggregate, may have on the opinion in the auditor's report, unless prohibited by law or regulation.[4] The auditor's communication shall identify material uncorrected misstatements individually. The auditor shall request that uncorrected misstatements be corrected. (Ref: Para. A21-A23)

13. The auditor shall also communicate with those charged with governance the effect of uncorrected misstatements related to prior periods on the relevant classes of transactions, account balances or disclosures, and the financial report as a whole.

Written Representation

14. The auditor shall request a written representation from management and, where appropriate, those charged with governance whether they believe the effects of uncorrected misstatements are immaterial, individually and in aggregate, to the financial report as a whole. A summary of such items shall be included in or attached to the written representation. (Ref: Para. A24)

Documentation

15. The auditor shall include in the audit documentation:[5] (Ref: Para. A25)

    (a) The amount below which misstatements would be regarded as clearly trivial (see paragraph 5 of this Auditing Standard);

    (b) All misstatements accumulated during the audit and whether they have been corrected (see paragraphs 5, 8 and 12 of this Auditing Standard); and

    (c) The auditor's conclusion as to whether uncorrected misstatements are material, individually or in aggregate, and the basis for that conclusion (see paragraph 11 of this Auditing Standard).

❖ ❖ ❖

3 See ASA 260 *Communication with Those Charged with Governance*, paragraph 7.

4 See footnote 3.

5 ASA 230 *Audit Documentation*, paragraphs 8-11 and paragraph A6.

Application and Other Explanatory Material

Definition of Misstatement (Ref: Para. 4(a))

A1. Misstatements may result from:

(a) An inaccuracy in gathering or processing data from which the financial report is prepared;

(b) An omission of an amount or disclosure;

(c) An incorrect accounting estimate arising from overlooking, or clear misinterpretation of, facts; and

(d) Judgements of management concerning accounting estimates that the auditor considers unreasonable or the selection and application of accounting policies that the auditor considers inappropriate.

Examples of misstatements arising from fraud are provided in ASA 240.[6]

Aus A1.1 The Australian Accounting Standards[*] explain the role of materiality in making judgements in the preparation and presentation of financial reports by the entity.

ASA

Accumulation of Identified Misstatements (Ref: Para. 5)

A2. The auditor may designate an amount below which misstatements would be clearly trivial and would not need to be accumulated because the auditor expects that the accumulation of such amounts clearly would not have a material effect on the financial report. "Clearly trivial" is not another expression for "not material." Matters that are clearly trivial will be of a wholly different (smaller) order of magnitude than materiality determined in accordance with ASA 320, and will be matters that are clearly inconsequential, whether taken individually or in aggregate and whether judged by any criteria of size, nature or circumstances. When there is any uncertainty about whether one or more items are clearly trivial, the matter is considered not to be clearly trivial.

A3. To assist the auditor in evaluating the effect of misstatements accumulated during the audit and in communicating misstatements to management and those charged with governance, it may be useful to distinguish between factual misstatements, judgemental misstatements and projected misstatements.

- Factual misstatements are misstatements about which there is no doubt.
- Judgemental misstatements are differences arising from the judgements of management concerning accounting estimates that the auditor considers unreasonable, or the selection or application of accounting policies that the auditor considers inappropriate.
- Projected misstatements are the auditor's best estimate of misstatements in populations, involving the projection of misstatements identified in audit samples to the entire populations from which the samples were drawn. Guidance on the determination of projected misstatements and evaluation of the results is set out in ASA 530.[7]

Consideration of Identified Misstatements as the Audit Progresses (Ref: Para. 6-7)

A4. A misstatement may not be an isolated occurrence. Evidence that other misstatements may exist include, for example, where the auditor identifies that a misstatement arose from a breakdown in internal control or from inappropriate assumptions or valuation methods that have been widely applied by the entity.

A5. If the aggregate of misstatements accumulated during the audit approaches materiality determined in accordance with ASA 320, there may be a greater than acceptably low

6 See ASA 240 *The Auditor's Responsibilities Relating to Fraud in an Audit of a Financial Report*, paragraphs A1-A6.

* See AASB 1031 *Materiality.*

7 See ASA 530 *Audit Sampling*, paragraphs 14-15.

level of risk that possible undetected misstatements, when taken with the aggregate of misstatements accumulated during the audit, could exceed materiality. Undetected misstatements could exist because of the presence of sampling risk and non-sampling risk.[8]

A6. The auditor may request management to examine a class of transactions, account balances or disclosures in order for management to understand the cause of a misstatement identified by the auditor, perform procedures to determine the amount of the actual misstatement in the class of transactions, account balance or disclosure, and to make appropriate adjustments to the financial report. Such a request may be made, for example, based on the auditor's projection of misstatements identified in an audit sample to the entire population from which it was drawn.

Communication and Correction of Misstatements (Ref: Para. 8-9)

A7. Timely communication of misstatements to the appropriate level of management is important as it enables management to evaluate whether the items are misstatements, inform the auditor if it disagrees, and take action as necessary. Ordinarily, the appropriate level of management is the one that has responsibility and authority to evaluate the misstatements and to take the necessary action.

A8. Law or regulation may restrict the auditor's communication of certain misstatements to management, or others, within the entity. For example, laws or regulations may specifically prohibit a communication, or other action, that might prejudice an investigation by an appropriate authority into an actual, or suspected, illegal act. In some circumstances, potential conflicts between the auditor's obligations of confidentiality and obligations to communicate may be complex.* In such cases, the auditor may consider seeking legal advice.

A9. The correction by management of all misstatements, including those communicated by the auditor, enables management to maintain accurate accounting books and records and reduces the risks of material misstatement of future financial reports because of the cumulative effect of immaterial uncorrected misstatements related to prior periods.

A10. ASA 700 requires the auditor to evaluate whether the financial report is prepared and presented, in all material respects, in accordance with the requirements of the applicable financial reporting framework. This evaluation includes consideration of the qualitative aspects of the entity's accounting practices, including indicators of possible bias in management's judgements,[9] which may be affected by the auditor's understanding of management's reasons for not making the corrections.

Evaluating the Effect of Uncorrected Misstatements (Ref: Para. 10-11)

A11. The auditor's determination of materiality in accordance with ASA 320 is often based on estimates of the entity's financial results, because the actual financial results may not yet be known. Therefore, prior to the auditor's evaluation of the effect of uncorrected misstatements, it may be necessary to revise materiality determined in accordance with ASA 320 based on the actual financial results.

A12. ASA 320 explains that, as the audit progresses, materiality for the financial report as a whole (and, if applicable, the materiality level or levels for particular classes of transactions, account balances or disclosures) is revised in the event of the auditor becoming aware of information during the audit that would have caused the auditor to have determined a different amount (or amounts) initially.[10] Thus, any significant revision is likely to have been made before the auditor evaluates the effect of uncorrected misstatements. However, if the auditor's reassessment of materiality determined in accordance with ASA 320 (see paragraph 10 of this Auditing Standard) gives rise to a lower amount (or amounts), then performance materiality and the appropriateness of the nature, timing and extent of the

---

8 See ASA 530, paragraph 5(c)-(d).

* See, for example, Part 9.4AAA of the *Corporations Act 2001*.

9 See ASA 700, paragraph 12.

10 See ASA 320, paragraph 12.

further audit procedures are reconsidered so as to obtain sufficient appropriate audit evidence on which to base the audit opinion.

A13. Each individual misstatement is considered to evaluate its effect on the relevant classes of transactions, account balances or disclosures, including whether the materiality level for that particular class of transactions, account balance or disclosure, if any, has been exceeded.

A14. If an individual misstatement is judged to be material, it is unlikely that it can be offset by other misstatements. For example, if revenue has been materially overstated, the financial report as a whole will be materially misstated, even if the effect of the misstatement on earnings is completely offset by an equivalent overstatement of expenses. It may be appropriate to offset misstatements within the same account balance or class of transactions; however, the risk that further undetected misstatements may exist is considered before concluding that offsetting even immaterial misstatements is appropriate.[11]

A15. Determining whether a classification misstatement is material involves the evaluation of qualitative considerations, such as the effect of the classification misstatement on debt or other contractual covenants, the effect on individual line items or sub-totals, or the effect on key ratios. There may be circumstances where the auditor concludes that a classification misstatement is not material in the context of the financial report as a whole, even though it may exceed the materiality level or levels applied in evaluating other misstatements. For example, a misclassification between balance sheet line items may not be considered material in the context of the financial report as a whole when the amount of the misclassification is small in relation to the size of the related balance sheet line items and the misclassification does not affect the income statement or any key ratios.

A16. The circumstances related to some misstatements may cause the auditor to evaluate them as material, individually or when considered together with other misstatements accumulated during the audit, even if they are lower than materiality for the financial report as a whole. Circumstances that may affect the evaluation include the extent to which the misstatement:

- Affects compliance with regulatory requirements;
- Affects compliance with debt covenants or other contractual requirements;
- Relates to the incorrect selection or application of an accounting policy that has an immaterial effect on the current period's financial report but is likely to have a material effect on future periods' financial reports;
- Masks a change in earnings or other trends, especially in the context of general economic and industry conditions;
- Affects ratios used to evaluate the entity's financial position, results of operations or cash flows;
- Affects segment information presented in the financial report (for example, the significance of the matter to a segment or other portion of the entity's business that has been identified as playing a significant role in the entity's operations or profitability);
- Has the effect of increasing management compensation, for example, by ensuring that the requirements for the award of bonuses or other incentives are satisfied;
- Is significant having regard to the auditor's understanding of known previous communications to users, for example, in relation to forecast earnings;
- Relates to items involving particular parties (for example, whether external parties to the transaction are related to members of the entity's management);
- Is an omission of information not specifically required by the applicable financial reporting framework but which, in the judgement of the auditor, is important to the users' understanding of the financial position, financial performance or cash flows of the entity; or

11 The identification of a number of immaterial misstatements within the same account balance or class of transactions may require the auditor to reassess the risk of material misstatement for that account balance or class of transactions.

ASA

- Affects other information that will be communicated in documents containing the audited financial report (for example, information to be included in a "Management Discussion and Analysis" or an "Operating and Financial Review") that may reasonably be expected to influence the economic decisions of the users of the financial report. ASA 720[12] deals with the auditor's consideration of other information, on which the auditor has no obligation to report, in documents containing audited financial reports.

These circumstances are only examples; not all are likely to be present in all audits nor is the list necessarily complete. The existence of any circumstances such as these does not necessarily lead to a conclusion that the misstatement is material.

A17. ASA 240[13] explains how the implications of a misstatement that is, or may be, the result of fraud ought to be considered in relation to other aspects of the audit, even if the size of the misstatement is not material in relation to the financial report.

A18. The cumulative effect of immaterial uncorrected misstatements related to prior periods may have a material effect on the current period's financial report. There are different acceptable approaches to the auditor's evaluation of such uncorrected misstatements on the current period's financial report. Using the same evaluation approach provides consistency from period to period.

Considerations Specific to Public Sector Entities (Ref: Para 11(a))

A19. In the case of an audit of a public sector entity, the evaluation whether a misstatement is material may also be affected by the auditor's responsibilities established by law, regulation or other authority to report specific matters, including, for example, fraud.

A20. Furthermore, issues such as public interest, accountability, probity and ensuring effective legislative oversight, in particular, may affect the assessment whether an item is material by virtue of its nature. This is particularly so for items that relate to compliance with law, regulation, or other authority.

Communication with Those Charged with Governance (Ref: Para. 12)

A21. If uncorrected misstatements have been communicated with person(s) with management responsibilities, and those person(s) also have governance responsibilities, they need not be communicated again with those same person(s) in their governance role. The auditor nonetheless has to be satisfied that communication with person(s) with management responsibilities adequately informs all of those with whom the auditor would otherwise communicate in their governance capacity.[14]

A22. Where there is a large number of individual immaterial uncorrected misstatements, the auditor may communicate the number and overall monetary effect of the uncorrected misstatements, rather than the details of each individual uncorrected misstatement.

A23. ASA 260 requires the auditor to communicate with those charged with governance the written representations the auditor is requesting (see paragraph 14 of this Auditing Standard).[15] The auditor may discuss with those charged with governance the reasons for, and the implications of, a failure to correct misstatements, having regard to the size and nature of the misstatement judged in the surrounding circumstances, and possible implications in relation to a future financial report.

Written Representation (Ref: Para. 14)

A24. Because the preparation of the financial report requires management and, where appropriate, those charged with governance to adjust the financial report to correct material misstatements, the auditor is required to request them to provide a written representation about uncorrected misstatements.* In some circumstances, management

12 See ASA 720 *The Auditor's Responsibilities Relating to Other Information in Documents Containing an Audited Financial Report.*

13 See ASA 240, paragraph 35.

14 See ASA 260, paragraph 13.

15 See ASA 260, paragraph 16(c)(ii).

* See ASA 580 *Written Representations*, Appendix 2, Illustrative Representation Letter.

and, where appropriate, those charged with governance may not believe that certain uncorrected misstatements are misstatements. For that reason, they may want to add to their written representation words such as: "We do not agree that items … and … constitute misstatements because [description of reasons]." Obtaining this representation does not, however, relieve the auditor of the need to form a conclusion on the effect of uncorrected misstatements.

Documentation (Ref: Para. 15)

A25. The auditor's documentation of uncorrected misstatements may take into account:

(a) The consideration of the aggregate effect of uncorrected misstatements;

(b) The evaluation of whether the materiality level or levels for particular classes of transactions, account balances or disclosures, if any, have been exceeded; and

(c) The evaluation of the effect of uncorrected misstatements on key ratios or trends, and compliance with legal, regulatory and contractual requirements (for example, debt covenants).

❖ ❖ ❖

Conformity with International Standards on Auditing

This Auditing Standard conforms with International Standard on Auditing ISA 450 *Evaluation of Misstatements Identified during the Audit*, issued by the International Auditing and Assurance Standards Board (IAASB), an independent standard-setting board of the International Federation of Accountants (IFAC).

Paragraphs that have been added to this Auditing Standard (and do not appear in the text of the equivalent ISA) are identified with the prefix "Aus".

Compliance with this Auditing Standard enables compliance with ISA 450.

ASA 500
Audit Evidence
(Reissued October 2009: amended and compiled June 2011)

Issued by the Auditing and Assurance Standards Board.

Note from the Institute of Chartered Accountants Australia

This note, prepared by the technical editor, is not part of ASA 500.

Historical development

January 1983: Statement of Auditing Practice AUP 14 'Audit Evidence' issued, effective January 1983. Based on International Auditing Practices Committee ED 8, issued and distributed in Australia in February 1981 to subscribers to The Institute of Chartered Accountants in Australia's IASC International Accounting Standards/IFAC Guidelines Handbook and by the Australian Society of Accountants with a request for comments.

March 1992: ED 46 'Audit Evidence — Confirmation of Receivables' issued by the AuSB. The relevant IAPC publication was IAG 8 'Audit Evidence' and its Addendum 1 'Additional Guidance on the Observation of Inventory, Confirmation of Accounts Receivable and Inquiry Regarding Litigation and Claims'.

February 1994: ED 54 'Codification and Revision of Auditing Pronouncements: AUS 502 Audit Evidence (AUP 14)' issued by the AuSB.

June 1994: The International Auditing Practices Committee (IAPC) of the International Federation of Accountants (IFAC) approved the issuance of a codified set of International Standards of Auditing (ISAs). The relevant international pronouncement was ISA 500 'Audit Evidence'.

October 1995: Australian Auditing Standards and Auditing Guidance Statements released. The status of these was explained in APS 1.1 'Conformity With Auditing Standards'. These Standards became operative for the first reporting period commencing on or after 1 July 1996 and later reporting periods, although earlier application was encouraged.

February 2004: AUS 502 reissued by the AuASB to provide improved guidance on the meaning of the term 'sufficient appropriate audit evidence'. Based on ISA 500 of the same name.

April 2006: ASA 500 was issued as a legally enforceable Standard to replace AUS 502. It is based on ISA 500 of the same name.

October 2009: ASA 500 reissued as part of the AUASB's Clarity Project. It is based on the redrafted ISA 500 of the same name and contains new material relating to the auditor's use of work by management's experts.

June 2011: ASA 500 updated for editorial amendments contained in ASA 2011-1 'Amendments to Australian Auditing Standards'.

Contents

Compilation Details

Auditing Standard ASA 500 *Audit Evidence* as Amended

This compilation takes into account amendments made up to and including 27 June 2011 and was prepared on 27 June 2011 by the Auditing and Assurance Standards Board (AUASB).

This compilation is not a separate Auditing Standard made by the AUASB. Instead, it is a representation of ASA 500 (October 2009) as amended by another Auditing Standard which is listed in the Table below.

Table of Standards

Standard	Date made	Operative date
ASA 500	27 October 2009	1 January 2010
ASA 2011-1	27 June 2011	1 July 2011

Table of Amendments

Paragraph affected	How affected	By … [paragraph]
A45 Last bullet point	Amended	ASA 2011-1 [33]

Preface

[Preface extracted from the original Auditing Standard issued 27 October 2009]

Reasons for Issuing Auditing Standard ASA 500 *Audit Evidence*

The Auditing and Assurance Standards Board (AUASB) issues Auditing Standard ASA 500 *Audit Evidence* pursuant to the requirements of the legislative provisions and the Strategic Direction explained below.

The AUASB is an independent statutory board of the Australian Government established under section 227A of the *Australian Securities and Investments Commission Act 2001*, as amended (ASIC Act). Under section 336 of the *Corporations Act 2001*, the AUASB may make Australian Auditing Standards for the purposes of the corporations legislation. These Auditing Standards are legislative instruments under the *Legislative Instruments Act 2003*.

Under the Strategic Direction given to the AUASB by the Financial Reporting Council (FRC), the AUASB is required to have regard to any programme initiated by the International Auditing and Assurance Standards Board (IAASB) for the revision and enhancement of the International Standards on Auditing (ISAs) and to make appropriate consequential amendments to the Australian Auditing Standards. Accordingly, the AUASB has decided to revise and redraft the Australian Auditing Standards using the equivalent redrafted ISAs.

Main Features

This Auditing Standard establishes requirements and provides application and other explanatory material regarding what constitutes audit evidence in an audit of a financial report, and deals with the auditor's responsibility to design and perform audit procedures to obtain sufficient appropriate audit evidence to be able to draw reasonable conclusions on which to base the auditor's opinion.

This Auditing Standard:

(a) requires the auditor to consider the relevance and reliability of the information to be used as audit evidence;

(b) describes the responsibilities of the auditor when the information to be used as audit evidence has been prepared using the work of a management's expert;

(c) describes the responsibilities of the auditor when the information to be used as audit evidence has been produced by the entity;

(d) describes requirements for selecting items for testing to obtain audit evidence; and

(e) describes the auditor's responsibilities when there is inconsistency in audit evidence obtained from different sources or doubts over the reliability of information to be used as audit evidence.

Authority Statement

Auditing Standard ASA 500 *Audit Evidence* (as amended at 27 June 2011) is set out in paragraphs 1 to A57.

This Auditing Standard is to be read in conjunction with ASA 101 *Preamble to Australian Auditing Standards*, which sets out the intentions of the AUASB on how the Australian Auditing Standards operative for financial reporting periods commencing on or after 1 January 2010 are to be understood, interpreted and applied. This Auditing Standard is to be read also in conjunction with ASA 200 *Overall Objectives of the Independent Auditor and the Conduct of an Audit in Accordance with Australian Auditing Standards*.

Dated: 27 June 2011

M H Kelsall
Chairman - AUASB

Auditing Standard ASA 500

The Auditing and Assurance Standards Board (AUASB) made Auditing Standard ASA 500 *Audit Evidence*, pursuant to section 227B of the *Australian Securities and Investments Commission Act 2001* and section 336 of the *Corporations Act 2001*, on 27 October 2009.

This compiled version of ASA 500 incorporates subsequent amendments contained in another Auditing Standard made by the AUASB up to and including 27 June 2011 (see Compilation Details).

Auditing Standard ASA 500
Audit Evidence

Application

Aus 0.1 This Auditing Standard applies to:

(a) an audit of a financial report for a financial year, or an audit of a financial report for a half-year, in accordance with the *Corporations Act 2001*; and

(b) an audit of a financial report, or a complete set of financial statements, for any other purpose.

Aus 0.2 This Auditing Standard also applies, as appropriate, to an audit of other historical financial information.

Operative Date

Aus 0.3 This Auditing Standard is operative for financial reporting periods commencing on or after 1 January 2010.

[Note: For operative dates of paragraphs changed or added by an amending Standard, see Compilation Details.]

Introduction

Scope of this Auditing Standard

1. This Auditing Standard explains what constitutes audit evidence in an audit of a financial report, and deals with the auditor's responsibility to design and perform audit procedures to obtain sufficient appropriate audit evidence to be able to draw reasonable conclusions on which to base the auditor's opinion.

2. This Auditing Standard is applicable to all the audit evidence obtained during the course of the audit. Other Auditing Standards deal with specific aspects of the audit (for example, ASA 315[1]), the audit evidence to be obtained in relation to a particular topic (for example, ASA 570[2]), specific procedures to obtain audit evidence (for example, ASA 520[3]), and the evaluation of whether sufficient appropriate audit evidence has been obtained (ASA 200[4] and ASA 330[5]).

Effective Date

3. [Deleted by the AUASB. Refer Aus 0.3]

Objective

4. The objective of the auditor is to design and perform audit procedures in such a way as to enable the auditor to obtain sufficient appropriate audit evidence to be able to draw reasonable conclusions on which to base the auditor's opinion.

Definitions

5. For purposes of the Australian Auditing Standards, the following terms have the meanings attributed below:

(a) Accounting records means the records of initial accounting entries and supporting records, such as cheques and records of electronic fund transfers; invoices; contracts; the general and subsidiary ledgers, journal entries and other adjustments to the financial report that are not reflected in journal entries; and records such

---

1 See ASA 315 *Identifying and Assessing the Risks of Material Misstatement through Understanding the Entity and Its Environment*.

2 See ASA 570 *Going Concern*.

3 See ASA 520 *Analytical Procedures*.

4 See ASA 200 *Overall Objectives of the Independent Auditor and the Conduct of an Audit in Accordance with Australian Auditing Standards*.

5 See ASA 330 *The Auditor's Responses to Assessed Risks*.

as work sheets and spreadsheets supporting cost allocations, computations, reconciliations and disclosures.

(b) Appropriateness (of audit evidence) means the measure of the quality of audit evidence; that is, its relevance and its reliability in providing support for the conclusions on which the auditor's opinion is based.

(c) Audit evidence means information used by the auditor in arriving at the conclusions on which the auditor's opinion is based. Audit evidence includes both information contained in the accounting records underlying the financial report and other information.

(d) Management's expert means an individual or organisation possessing expertise in a field other than accounting or auditing, whose work in that field is used by the entity to assist the entity in preparing the financial report.

(e) Sufficiency (of audit evidence) means the measure of the quantity of audit evidence. The quantity of the audit evidence needed is affected by the auditor's assessment of the risks of material misstatement and also by the quality of such audit evidence.

Requirements

Sufficient Appropriate Audit Evidence

6. The auditor shall design and perform audit procedures that are appropriate in the circumstances for the purpose of obtaining sufficient appropriate audit evidence. (Ref: Para. A1-A25)

Information to Be Used as Audit Evidence

7. When designing and performing audit procedures, the auditor shall consider the relevance and reliability of the information to be used as audit evidence. (Ref: Para. A26-A33)

8. If information to be used as audit evidence has been prepared using the work of a management's expert, the auditor shall, to the extent necessary, having regard to the significance of that expert's work for the auditor's purposes: (Ref: Para. A34-A36)

   (a) Evaluate the competence, capabilities and objectivity of that expert; (Ref: Para. A37-A43)

   (b) Obtain an understanding of the work of that expert; and (Ref: Para. A44-A47)

   (c) Evaluate the appropriateness of that expert's work as audit evidence for the relevant assertion. (Ref: Para. A48)

9. When using information produced by the entity, the auditor shall evaluate whether the information is sufficiently reliable for the auditor's purposes, including as necessary in the circumstances:

   (a) Obtaining audit evidence about the accuracy and completeness of the information; and (Ref: Para. A49-A50)

   (b) Evaluating whether the information is sufficiently precise and detailed for the auditor's purposes. (Ref: Para. A51)

Selecting Items for Testing to Obtain Audit Evidence

10. When designing tests of controls and tests of details, the auditor shall determine means of selecting items for testing that are effective in meeting the purpose of the audit procedure. (Ref: Para. A52-A56)

Inconsistency in, or Doubts over Reliability of, Audit Evidence

11. If:

   (a) audit evidence obtained from one source is inconsistent with that obtained from another; or

   (b) the auditor has doubts over the reliability of information to be used as audit evidence,

   the auditor shall determine what modifications or additions to audit procedures are necessary to resolve the matter, and shall consider the effect of the matter, if any, on other aspects of the audit. (Ref: Para. A57)

❖ ❖ ❖

Application and Other Explanatory Material

Sufficient Appropriate Audit Evidence (Ref: Para. 6)

A1. Audit evidence is necessary to support the auditor's opinion and report. It is cumulative in nature and is primarily obtained from audit procedures performed during the course of the audit. It may, however, also include information obtained from other sources such as previous audits (provided the auditor has determined whether changes have occurred since the previous audit that may affect its relevance to the current audit)[6] or a firm's quality control procedures for client acceptance and continuance. In addition to other sources inside and outside the entity, the entity's accounting records are an important source of audit evidence. Also, information that may be used as audit evidence may have been prepared using the work of a management's expert. Audit evidence comprises both information that supports and corroborates management's assertions, and any information that contradicts such assertions. In addition, in some cases the absence of information (for example, management's refusal to provide a requested representation) is used by the auditor, and therefore, also constitutes audit evidence.

ASA

A2. Most of the auditor's work in forming the auditor's opinion consists of obtaining and evaluating audit evidence. Audit procedures to obtain audit evidence can include inspection, observation, confirmation, re-calculation, re-performance and analytical procedures, often in some combination, in addition to enquiry. Although enquiry may provide important audit evidence, and may even produce evidence of a misstatement, enquiry alone ordinarily does not provide sufficient audit evidence of the absence of a material misstatement at the assertion level, nor of the operating effectiveness of controls.

A3. As explained in ASA 200,[7] reasonable assurance is obtained when the auditor has obtained sufficient appropriate audit evidence to reduce audit risk (that is, the risk that the auditor expresses an inappropriate opinion when the financial report is materially misstated) to an acceptably low level.

A4. The sufficiency and appropriateness of audit evidence are interrelated. Sufficiency is the measure of the quantity of audit evidence. The quantity of audit evidence needed is affected by the auditor's assessment of the risks of misstatement (the higher the assessed risks, the more audit evidence is likely to be required) and also by the quality of such audit evidence (the higher the quality, the less may be required). Obtaining more audit evidence, however, may not compensate for its poor quality.

A5. Appropriateness is the measure of the quality of audit evidence; that is, its relevance and its reliability in providing support for the conclusions on which the auditor's opinion is based. The reliability of evidence is influenced by its source and by its nature, and is dependent on the individual circumstances under which it is obtained.

A6. ASA 330 requires the auditor to conclude whether sufficient appropriate audit evidence has been obtained.[8] Whether sufficient appropriate audit evidence has been obtained to reduce audit risk to an acceptably low level, and thereby enable the auditor to draw reasonable conclusions on which to base the auditor's opinion, is a matter of professional judgement. ASA 200 contains discussion of such matters as the nature of audit procedures, the timeliness of financial reporting, and the balance between benefit and cost, which are relevant factors when the auditor exercises professional judgement regarding whether sufficient appropriate audit evidence has been obtained.

Sources of Audit Evidence

A7. Some audit evidence is obtained by performing audit procedures to test the accounting records, for example, through analysis and review, reperforming procedures followed in the financial reporting process, and reconciling related types and applications of the same information. Through the performance of such audit procedures, the auditor may determine that the accounting records are internally consistent and agree to the financial report.

6 See ASA 315, paragraph 9.

7 See ASA 200, paragraph 5.

8 See ASA 330, paragraph 26.

A8. More assurance is ordinarily obtained from consistent audit evidence obtained from different sources or of a different nature than from items of audit evidence considered individually. For example, corroborating information obtained from a source independent of the entity may increase the assurance the auditor obtains from audit evidence that is generated internally, such as evidence existing within the accounting records, minutes of meetings, or a management representation.

A9. Information from sources independent of the entity that the auditor may use as audit evidence may include confirmations from third parties, analysts' reports, and comparable data about competitors (benchmarking data).

Audit Procedures for Obtaining Audit Evidence

A10. As required by, and explained further in, ASA 315 and ASA 330, audit evidence to draw reasonable conclusions on which to base the auditor's opinion is obtained by performing:

(a) Risk assessment procedures; and

(b) Further audit procedures, which comprise:

  (i) Tests of controls, when required by the Australian Auditing Standards or when the auditor has chosen to do so; and

  (ii) Substantive procedures, including tests of details and substantive analytical procedures.

A11. The audit procedures described in paragraphs A14-A25 below may be used as risk assessment procedures, tests of controls or substantive procedures, depending on the context in which they are applied by the auditor. As explained in ASA 330, audit evidence obtained from previous audits may, in certain circumstances, provide appropriate audit evidence where the auditor performs audit procedures to establish its continuing relevance.[9]

A12. The nature and timing of the audit procedures to be used may be affected by the fact that some of the accounting data and other information may be available only in electronic form or only at certain points or periods in time. For example, source documents, such as purchase orders and invoices, may exist only in electronic form when an entity uses electronic commerce, or may be discarded after scanning when an entity uses image processing systems to facilitate storage and reference.

A13. Certain electronic information may not be retrievable after a specified period of time, for example, if files are changed and if backup files do not exist. Accordingly, the auditor may find it necessary as a result of an entity's data retention policies to request retention of some information for the auditor's review or to perform audit procedures at a time when the information is available.

Inspection

A14. Inspection involves examining records or documents, whether internal or external, in paper form, electronic form, or other media, or a physical examination of an asset. Inspection of records and documents provides audit evidence of varying degrees of reliability, depending on their nature and source and, in the case of internal records and documents, on the effectiveness of the controls over their production. An example of inspection used as a test of controls is inspection of records for evidence of authorisation.

A15. Some documents represent direct audit evidence of the existence of an asset, for example, a document constituting a financial instrument such as a share or bond. Inspection of such documents may not necessarily provide audit evidence about ownership or value. In addition, inspecting an executed contract may provide audit evidence relevant to the entity's application of accounting policies, such as revenue recognition.

A16. Inspection of tangible assets may provide reliable audit evidence with respect to their existence, but not necessarily about the entity's rights and obligations or the valuation of the assets. Inspection of individual inventory items may accompany the observation of inventory counting.

---

9 See ASA 330, paragraph A35.

Observation

A17. Observation consists of looking at a process or procedure being performed by others, for example, the auditor's observation of inventory counting by the entity's personnel, or of the performance of control activities. Observation provides audit evidence about the performance of a process or procedure, but is limited to the point in time at which the observation takes place, and by the fact that the act of being observed may affect how the process or procedure is performed. See ASA 501 for further guidance on observation of the counting of inventory.[10]

External Confirmation

A18. An external confirmation represents audit evidence obtained by the auditor as a direct written response to the auditor from a third party (the confirming party), in paper form, or by electronic or other medium. External confirmation procedures frequently are relevant when addressing assertions associated with certain account balances and their elements. However, external confirmations need not be restricted to account balances only. For example, the auditor may request confirmation of the terms of agreements or transactions an entity has with third parties; the confirmation request may be designed to ask if any modifications have been made to the agreement and, if so, what the relevant details are. External confirmation procedures also are used to obtain audit evidence about the absence of certain conditions, for example, the absence of a "side agreement" that may influence revenue recognition. See ASA 505 for further guidance.[11]

Re-calculation

A19. Re-calculation consists of checking the mathematical accuracy of documents or records. Re-calculation may be performed manually or electronically.

Re-performance

A20. Re-performance involves the auditor's independent execution of procedures or controls that were originally performed as part of the entity's internal control.

Analytical Procedures

A21. Analytical procedures consist of evaluations of financial information through analysis of plausible relationships among both financial and non-financial data. Analytical procedures also encompass such investigation as is necessary of identified fluctuations or relationships that are inconsistent with other relevant information or that differ from expected values by a significant amount. See ASA 520 for further guidance.

Enquiry

A22. Enquiry consists of seeking information of knowledgeable persons, both financial and non-financial, within the entity or outside the entity. Enquiry is used extensively throughout the audit in addition to other audit procedures. Enquiries may range from formal written enquiries to informal oral enquiries. Evaluating responses to enquiries is an integral part of the enquiry process.

A23. Responses to enquiries may provide the auditor with information not previously possessed or with corroborative audit evidence. Alternatively, responses might provide information that differs significantly from other information that the auditor has obtained, for example, information regarding the possibility of management override of controls. In some cases, responses to enquiries provide a basis for the auditor to modify or perform additional audit procedures.

A24. Although corroboration of evidence obtained through enquiry is often of particular importance, in the case of enquiries about management intent, the information available to support management's intent may be limited. In these cases, understanding management's past history of carrying out its stated intentions, management's stated reasons for choosing a particular course of action, and management's ability to pursue a specific course of action may provide relevant information to corroborate the evidence obtained through enquiry.

---

10 See ASA 501 *Audit Evidence—Specific Considerations for Inventory and Segment Information.*

11 See ASA 505 *External Confirmations.*

A25. In respect of some matters, the auditor may consider it necessary to obtain written representations from management and, where appropriate, those charged with governance to confirm responses to oral enquiries. See ASA 580 for further guidance.[12]

Information to Be Used as Audit Evidence

Relevance and Reliability (Ref: Para. 7)

A26. As noted in paragraph A1, while audit evidence is primarily obtained from audit procedures performed during the course of the audit, it may also include information obtained from other sources such as, for example, previous audits, in certain circumstances, and a firm's quality control procedures for client acceptance and continuance. The quality of all audit evidence is affected by the relevance and reliability of the information upon which it is based.

Relevance

A27. Relevance deals with the logical connection with, or bearing upon, the purpose of the audit procedure and, where appropriate, the assertion under consideration. The relevance of information to be used as audit evidence may be affected by the direction of testing. For example, if the purpose of an audit procedure is to test for overstatement in the existence or valuation of accounts payable, testing the recorded accounts payable may be a relevant audit procedure. On the other hand, when testing for understatement in the existence or valuation of accounts payable, testing the recorded accounts payable would not be relevant, but testing such information as subsequent disbursements, unpaid invoices, suppliers' statements, and unmatched receiving reports may be relevant.

A28. A given set of audit procedures may provide audit evidence that is relevant to certain assertions, but not others. For example, inspection of documents related to the collection of receivables after the period end may provide audit evidence regarding existence and valuation, but not necessarily cut-off. Similarly, obtaining audit evidence regarding a particular assertion, for example, the existence of inventory, is not a substitute for obtaining audit evidence regarding another assertion, for example, the valuation of that inventory. On the other hand, audit evidence from different sources or of a different nature may often be relevant to the same assertion.

A29. Tests of controls are designed to evaluate the operating effectiveness of controls in preventing, or detecting and correcting, material misstatements at the assertion level. Designing tests of controls to obtain relevant audit evidence includes identifying conditions (characteristics or attributes) that indicate performance of a control, and deviation conditions which indicate departures from adequate performance. The presence or absence of those conditions can then be tested by the auditor.

A30. Substantive procedures are designed to detect material misstatements at the assertion level. They comprise tests of details and substantive analytical procedures. Designing substantive procedures includes identifying conditions relevant to the purpose of the test that constitute a misstatement in the relevant assertion.

Reliability

A31. The reliability of information to be used as audit evidence, and therefore of the audit evidence itself, is influenced by its source and its nature, and the circumstances under which it is obtained, including the controls over its preparation and maintenance where relevant. Therefore, generalisations about the reliability of various kinds of audit evidence are subject to important exceptions. Even when information to be used as audit evidence is obtained from sources external to the entity, circumstances may exist that could affect its reliability. For example, information obtained from an independent external source may not be reliable if the source is not knowledgeable, or a management's expert may lack objectivity. While recognising that exceptions may exist, the following generalisations about the reliability of audit evidence may be useful:

- The reliability of audit evidence is increased when it is obtained from independent sources outside the entity.

12 See ASA 580 *Written Representations*.

- The reliability of audit evidence that is generated internally is increased when the related controls, including those over its preparation and maintenance, imposed by the entity are effective.
- Audit evidence obtained directly by the auditor (for example, observation of the application of a control) is more reliable than audit evidence obtained indirectly or by inference (for example, enquiry about the application of a control).
- Audit evidence in documentary form, whether paper, electronic, or other medium, is more reliable than evidence obtained orally (for example, a contemporaneously written record of a meeting is more reliable than a subsequent oral representation of the matters discussed).
- Audit evidence provided by original documents is more reliable than audit evidence provided by photocopies or facsimiles, or documents that have been filmed, digitised or otherwise transformed into electronic form, the reliability of which may depend on the controls over their preparation and maintenance.

A32. ASA 520 provides further guidance regarding the reliability of data used for purposes of designing analytical procedures as substantive procedures.[13]

A33. ASA 240 deals with circumstances where the auditor has reason to believe that a document may not be authentic, or may have been modified without that modification having been disclosed to the auditor.[14]

Reliability of Information Produced by a Management's Expert (Ref: Para. 8)

A34. The preparation of an entity's financial report may require expertise in a field other than accounting or auditing, such as actuarial calculations, valuations, or engineering data. The entity may employ or engage experts in these fields to obtain the needed expertise to prepare the financial report. Failure to do so when such expertise is necessary increases the risks of material misstatement.

A35. When information to be used as audit evidence has been prepared using the work of a management's expert, the requirement in paragraph 8 of this Auditing Standard applies. For example, an individual or organisation may possess expertise in the application of models to estimate the fair value of securities for which there is no observable market. If the individual or organisation applies that expertise in making an estimate which the entity uses in preparing its financial report, the individual or organisation is a management's expert and paragraph 8 applies. If, on the other hand, that individual or organisation merely provides price data regarding private transactions not otherwise available to the entity which the entity uses in its own estimation methods, such information, if used as audit evidence, is subject to paragraph 7 of this Auditing Standard, but is not the use of a management's expert by the entity.

A36. The nature, timing and extent of audit procedures in relation to the requirement in paragraph 8 of this Auditing Standard, may be affected by such matters as:

- The nature and complexity of the matter to which the management's expert relates.
- The risks of material misstatement in the matter.
- The availability of alternative sources of audit evidence.
- The nature, scope and objectives of the management's expert's work.
- Whether the management's expert is employed by the entity, or is a party engaged by it to provide relevant services.
- The extent to which management can exercise control or influence over the work of the management's expert.
- Whether the management's expert is subject to technical performance standards or other professional or industry requirements.
- The nature and extent of any controls within the entity over the management's expert's work.

13 See ASA 520, paragraph 5(a).

14 See ASA 240 *The Auditor's Responsibilities Relating to Fraud in an Audit of a Financial Report*, paragraph 13.

- The auditor's knowledge and experience of the management's expert's field of expertise.
- The auditor's previous experience of the work of that expert.

The Competence, Capabilities and Objectivity of a Management's Expert *(Ref: Para. 8(a))*

A37. Competence relates to the nature and level of expertise of the management's expert. Capability relates to the ability of the management's expert to exercise that competence in the circumstances. Factors that influence capability may include, for example, geographic location, and the availability of time and resources. Objectivity relates to the possible effects that bias, conflict of interest or the influence of others may have on the professional or business judgement of the management's expert. The competence, capabilities and objectivity of a management's expert, and any controls within the entity over that expert's work, are important factors in relation to the reliability of any information produced by a management's expert.

A38. Information regarding the competence, capabilities and objectivity of a management's expert may come from a variety of sources, such as:

- Personal experience with previous work of that expert.
- Discussions with that expert.
- Discussions with others who are familiar with that expert's work.
- Knowledge of that expert's qualifications, membership of a professional body or industry association, license to practice, or other forms of external recognition.
- Published papers or books written by that expert.
- An auditor's expert, if any, who assists the auditor in obtaining sufficient appropriate audit evidence with respect to information produced by the management's expert.

A39. Matters relevant to evaluating the competence, capabilities and objectivity of a management's expert include whether that expert's work is subject to technical performance standards or other professional or industry requirements, for example, ethical standards and other membership requirements of a professional body or industry association, accreditation standards of a licensing body, or requirements imposed by law or regulation.

A40. Other matters that may be relevant include:

- The relevance of the management's expert's competence to the matter for which that expert's work will be used, including any areas of specialty within that expert's field. For example, a particular actuary may specialise in property and casualty insurance, but have limited expertise regarding pension calculations.
- The management's expert's competence with respect to relevant accounting requirements, for example, knowledge of assumptions and methods, including models where applicable, that are consistent with the applicable financial reporting framework.
- Whether unexpected events, changes in conditions, or the audit evidence obtained from the results of audit procedures indicate that it may be necessary to reconsider the initial evaluation of the competence, capabilities and objectivity of the management's expert as the audit progresses.

A41. A broad range of circumstances may threaten objectivity, for example, self-interest threats, advocacy threats, familiarity threats, self-review threats and intimidation threats. Safeguards may reduce such threats, and may be created either by external structures (for example, the management's expert's profession, legislation or regulation), or by the management's expert's work environment (for example, quality control policies and procedures).

A42. Although safeguards cannot eliminate all threats to a management's expert's objectivity, threats such as intimidation threats may be of less significance to an expert engaged by the entity than to an expert employed by the entity, and the effectiveness of safeguards such as quality control policies and procedures may be greater. Because the threat to objectivity created by being an employee of the entity will always be present, an expert employed by the entity cannot ordinarily be regarded as being more likely to be objective than other employees of the entity.

A43. When evaluating the objectivity of an expert engaged by the entity, it may be relevant to discuss with management and that expert any interests and relationships that may create threats to the expert's objectivity, and any applicable safeguards, including any professional requirements that apply to the expert; and to evaluate whether the safeguards are adequate. Interests and relationships creating threats may include:

- Financial interests.
- Business and personal relationships.
- Provision of other services.

Obtaining an Understanding of the Work of the Management's Expert (Ref: Para. 8(b))

A44. An understanding of the work of the management's expert includes an understanding of the relevant field of expertise. An understanding of the relevant field of expertise may be obtained in conjunction with the auditor's determination of whether the auditor has the expertise to evaluate the work of the management's expert, or whether the auditor needs an auditor's expert for this purpose.[15]

A45. Aspects of the management's expert's field relevant to the auditor's understanding may include:

- Whether that expert's field has areas of specialty within it that are relevant to the audit.
- Whether any professional or other standards, and regulatory or legal requirements apply.
- What assumptions and methods are used by the management's expert, and whether they are generally accepted within that expert's field and appropriate for financial reporting purposes.
- The nature of internal and external data or information the management's expert uses.

A46. In the case of a management's expert engaged by the entity, there will ordinarily be an engagement letter or other written form of agreement between the entity and that expert. Evaluating that agreement when obtaining an understanding of the work of the management's expert may assist the auditor in determining the appropriateness of the following for the auditor's purposes:

- The nature, scope and objectives of that expert's work;
- The respective roles and responsibilities of management and that expert; and
- The nature, timing and extent of communication between management and that expert, including the form of any report to be provided by that expert.

A47. In the case of a management's expert employed by the entity, it is less likely there will be a written agreement of this kind. Enquiry of the expert and other members of management may be the most appropriate way for the auditor to obtain the necessary understanding.

Evaluating the Appropriateness of the Management's Expert's Work (Ref: Para. 8(c))

A48. Considerations when evaluating the appropriateness of the management's expert's work as audit evidence for the relevant assertion may include:

- The relevance and reasonableness of that expert's findings or conclusions, their consistency with other audit evidence, and whether they have been appropriately reflected in the financial report;
- If that expert's work involves use of significant assumptions and methods, the relevance and reasonableness of those assumptions and methods; and
- If that expert's work involves significant use of source data, the relevance, completeness, and accuracy of that source data.

15 See ASA 620 *Using the Work of an Auditor's Expert*, paragraph 7.

ASA

Information Produced by the Entity and Used for the Auditor's Purposes (Ref: Para. 9(a)-(b))

A49. In order for the auditor to obtain reliable audit evidence, information produced by the entity that is used for performing audit procedures needs to be sufficiently complete and accurate. For example, the effectiveness of auditing revenue by applying standard prices to records of sales volume is affected by the accuracy of the price information and the completeness and accuracy of the sales volume data. Similarly, if the auditor intends to test a population (for example, payments) for a certain characteristic (for example, authorisation), the results of the test will be less reliable if the population from which items are selected for testing is not complete.

A50. Obtaining audit evidence about the accuracy and completeness of such information may be performed concurrently with the actual audit procedure applied to the information when obtaining such audit evidence is an integral part of the audit procedure itself. In other situations, the auditor may have obtained audit evidence of the accuracy and completeness of such information by testing controls over the preparation and maintenance of the information. In some situations, however, the auditor may determine that additional audit procedures are needed.

A51. In some cases, the auditor may intend to use information produced by the entity for other audit purposes. For example, the auditor may intend to make use of the entity's performance measures for the purpose of analytical procedures, or to make use of the entity's information produced for monitoring activities, such as internal auditor's reports. In such cases, the appropriateness of the audit evidence obtained is affected by whether the information is sufficiently precise or detailed for the auditor's purposes. For example, performance measures used by management may not be precise enough to detect material misstatements.

Selecting Items for Testing to Obtain Audit Evidence (Ref: Para. 10)

A52. An effective test provides appropriate audit evidence to an extent that, taken with other audit evidence obtained or to be obtained, will be sufficient for the auditor's purposes. In selecting items for testing, the auditor is required by paragraph 7 to determine the relevance and reliability of information to be used as audit evidence; the other aspect of effectiveness (sufficiency) is an important consideration in selecting items to test. The means available to the auditor for selecting items for testing are:

(a) Selecting all items (100% examination);

(b) Selecting specific items; and

(c) Audit sampling.

The application of any one or combination of these means may be appropriate depending on the particular circumstances, for example, the risks of material misstatement related to the assertion being tested, and the practicality and efficiency of the different means.

Selecting All Items

A53. The auditor may decide that it will be most appropriate to examine the entire population of items that make up a class of transactions or account balance (or a stratum within that population). 100% examination is unlikely in the case of tests of controls; however, it is more common for tests of details. 100% examination may be appropriate when, for example:

- The population constitutes a small number of large value items;
- There is a significant risk and other means do not provide sufficient appropriate audit evidence; or
- The repetitive nature of a calculation or other process performed automatically by an information system makes a 100% examination cost effective.

Selecting Specific Items

A54. The auditor may decide to select specific items from a population. In making this decision, factors that may be relevant include the auditor's understanding of the entity, the assessed risks of material misstatement and the characteristics of the population being tested. The judgemental selection of specific items is subject to non-sampling risk. Specific items selected may include:

- *High value or key items.* The auditor may decide to select specific items within a population because they are of high value, or exhibit some other characteristic, for example, items that are suspicious, unusual, particularly risk-prone or that have a history of error.
- *All items over a certain amount.* The auditor may decide to examine items whose recorded values exceed a certain amount so as to verify a large proportion of the total amount of a class of transactions or account balance.
- *Items to obtain information.* The auditor may examine items to obtain information about matters such as the nature of the entity or the nature of transactions.

A55. While selective examination of specific items from a class of transactions or account balance will often be an efficient means of obtaining audit evidence, it does not constitute audit sampling. The results of audit procedures applied to items selected in this way cannot be projected to the entire population; accordingly, selective examination of specific items does not provide audit evidence concerning the remainder of the population.

ASA

Audit Sampling

A56. Audit sampling is designed to enable conclusions to be drawn about an entire population on the basis of testing a sample drawn from it. Audit sampling is discussed in ASA 530.[16]

Inconsistency in, or Doubts over Reliability of, Audit Evidence (Ref: Para. 11)

A57. Obtaining audit evidence from different sources or of a different nature may indicate that an individual item of audit evidence is not reliable, such as when audit evidence obtained from one source is inconsistent with that obtained from another. This may be the case when, for example, responses to enquiries of management, internal audit, and others are inconsistent, or when responses to enquiries of those charged with governance made to corroborate the responses to enquiries of management are inconsistent with the response by management. ASA 230 includes a specific documentation requirement if the auditor identified information that is inconsistent with the auditor's final conclusion regarding a significant matter.[17]

❖ ❖ ❖

Conformity with International Standards on Auditing

This Auditing Standard conforms with International Standard on Auditing ISA 500 *Audit Evidence*, issued by the International Auditing and Assurance Standards Board (IAASB), an independent standard-setting board of the International Federation of Accountants (IFAC).

Paragraphs that have been added to this Auditing Standard (and do not appear in the text of the equivalent ISA) are identified with the prefix "Aus".

Compliance with this Auditing Standard enables compliance with ISA 500.

16 See ASA 530 *Audit Sampling*.

17 See ASA 230 *Audit Documentation*, paragraph 11.

ASA 501
Audit Evidence—Specific Considerations for Inventory and Segment Information

(Reissued October 2009: amended and compiled June 2011)

Issued by the Auditing and Assurance Standards Board.

Note from the Institute of Chartered Accountants Australia

This note, prepared by the technical editor, is not part of ASA 501.

Historical development

February 1978: Auditing Statement CP 5, 'Existence and Valuation of Inventories in the Context of Historical Cost' issued in, and effective from, February 1978. Reissued, without amendment, as AUP 5 in August 1979.

February 1994: ED 54 'Codification and Revision of Auditing Pronouncements: AUS 508 Existence and Valuation of Inventories (AUP 5)' issued by the AuSB.

June 1994: The International Auditing Practices Committee (IAPC) of the International Federation of Accountants (IFAC) approved the issuance of a codified set of International Standards of Auditing (ISAs). The relevant international pronouncement was ISA 501 'Audit Evidence—Additional Considerations for Specific Items (Part A)'.

October 1995: Australian Auditing Standards and Auditing Guidance Statements released. The status of these was explained in APS 1.1 'Conformity With Auditing Standards'. These Standards became operative for the first reporting period commencing on or after 1 July 1996 and later reporting periods, although earlier application was encouraged. AUP 5 'Existence and Valuation of Inventories in the Context of the Historical Cost System' replaced by AUS 506 'Existence and Valuation of Inventory'.

July 2002: AUS/AGS Omnibus 3 'Miscellaneous Amendments to AUSs and AGSs' issued by the AuASB, operative from date of issue. AUS 506 now reissued by the Board to incorporate these amendments.

April 2006: ASA 501 was issued as a legally enforceable Standard to replace AUS 506. It is based on ISA 501 'Audit Evidence—Additional Considerations for Specific Items (Part A) Attendance or Physical Inventory Counting'.

October 2009: ASA 501 reissued as part of the AUASB's Clarity Project. It includes new requirements relating to the audit of segment information. It is based on ISA 501, 'Audit Evidence Specific Considerations for Selected Items'.

June 2011: ASA 501 updated for editorial amendments contained in ASA 2011-1 'Amendments to Australian Auditing Standards.'

Contents

Compilation Details

Auditing Standard ASA 501 *Audit Evidence – Specific Considerations for Inventory and Segment Information* as Amended

This compilation takes into account amendments made up to and including 27 June 2011 and was prepared on 27 June 2011 by the Auditing and Assurance Standards Board (AUASB).

This compilation is not a separate Auditing Standard made by the AUASB. Instead, it is a representation of ASA 501 (October 2009) as amended by another Auditing Standard which is listed in the Table below.

Table of Standards

Standard	Date made	Operative date
ASA 501	27 October 2009	1 January 2010
ASA 2011-1	27 June 2011	1 July 2011

Table of Amendments

Paragraph affected	How affected	By ... [paragraph]
Aus 0.1(a)	Amended	ASA 2011-1 [34]

Preface

[Preface extracted from the original Auditing Standard issued 27 October 2009]

Reasons for Issuing Auditing Standard ASA 501 *Audit Evidence—Specific Considerations for Inventory and Segment Information*

The Auditing and Assurance Standards Board (AUASB) issues Auditing Standard ASA 501 *Audit Evidence—Specific Considerations for Inventory and Segment Information* pursuant to the requirements of the legislative provisions and the Strategic Direction explained below.

The AUASB is an independent statutory board of the Australian Government established under section 227A of the *Australian Securities and Investments Commission Act 2001*, as amended (ASIC Act). Under section 336 of the *Corporations Act 2001*, the AUASB may make Australian Auditing Standards for the purposes of the corporations legislation. These Auditing Standards are legislative instruments under the *Legislative Instruments Act 2003*.

Under the Strategic Direction given to the AUASB by the Financial Reporting Council (FRC), the AUASB is required to have regard to any programme initiated by the International Auditing and Assurance Standards Board (IAASB) for the revision and enhancement of the International Standards on Auditing (ISAs) and to make appropriate consequential amendments to the Australian Auditing Standards. Accordingly, the AUASB has decided to revise and redraft the Australian Auditing Standards using the equivalent redrafted ISAs.

The equivalent international standard is ISA 501 *Audit Evidence—Specific Considerations for Selected Items*, issued by the IAASB as a composite standard containing sections on Inventory, Litigation and Claims, and Segment Information.

The AUASB has decided to continue to issue ASA 502 *Audit Evidence—Specific Considerations for Litigation and Claims* as a separate Auditing Standard, in the same way that the previous standard, ASA 508 *Enquiry Regarding Litigation and Claims* (April 2006), is a separate standard. ASA 508 contains requirements and guidance that the AUASB considers important to carry forward in the Australian Auditing Standards, and as a result, the revised standard is better suited to presentation as a separate standard. Accordingly, ASA 502 deals with Litigation and Claims, while ASA 501 deals with Inventory and Segment Information.

Main Features

This Auditing Standard establishes requirements and provides application and other explanatory material regarding specific considerations by the auditor in obtaining sufficient appropriate audit evidence relating to certain aspects of inventory and segment information in an audit of a financial report.

This Auditing Standard describes the:

(a) procedures to be performed by the auditor when inventory is material to the financial report, to obtain sufficient appropriate audit evidence regarding the existence and condition of inventory;

(b) auditor's responsibilities in relation to attendance at physical inventory counting;

(c) auditor's responsibilities when inventory under the custody and control of a third party is material to the financial report; and

(d) requirements in respect of obtaining sufficient appropriate audit evidence regarding the presentation and disclosure of segment information in accordance with the applicable financial reporting framework.

Authority Statement

Auditing Standard ASA 501 *Audit Evidence—Specific Considerations for Inventory and Segment Information* (as amended at 27 June 2011) is set out in paragraphs 1 to A27.

This Auditing Standard is to be read in conjunction with ASA 101 *Preamble to Australian Auditing Standards*, which sets out the intentions of the AUASB on how the Australian Auditing Standards, operative for financial reporting periods commencing on or after 1 January 2010, are to be understood, interpreted and applied. This Auditing Standard is to be read also in conjunction with ASA 200 *Overall Objectives of the Independent Auditor and the Conduct of an Audit in Accordance with Australian Auditing Standards*.

Dated: 27 June 2011

M H Kelsall
Chairman - AUASB

Auditing Standard ASA 501

The Auditing and Assurance Standards Board (AUASB) made Auditing Standard ASA 501 *Audit Evidence—Specific Considerations for Inventory and Segment Information,* pursuant to section 227B of the *Australian Securities and Investments Commission Act 2001* and section 336 of the *Corporations Act 2001*, on 27 October 2009.

This compiled version of ASA 501 incorporates subsequent amendments contained in another Auditing Standard made by the AUASB up to and including 27 June 2011 (see Compilation Details).

Auditing Standard ASA 501

Audit Evidence—Specific Considerations for Inventory and Segment Information

Application

Aus 0.1 This Auditing Standard applies to:

(a) an audit of a financial report for a financial year, or an audit of a financial report for a half-year, in accordance with the *Corporations Act 2001*; and

(b) an audit of a financial report, or a complete set of financial statements, for any other purpose.

Aus 0.2 This Auditing Standard also applies, as appropriate, to an audit of other historical financial information.

Operative Date

Aus 0.3 This Auditing Standard is operative for financial reporting periods commencing on or after 1 January 2010.

[Note: For operative dates of paragraphs changed or added by an amending Standard, see Compilation Details.]

Introduction

Scope of this Auditing Standard

1. This Auditing Standard deals with specific considerations by the auditor in obtaining sufficient appropriate audit evidence in accordance with ASA 330,[1] ASA 500[2] and other relevant Australian Auditing Standards, with respect to certain aspects of inventory and segment information in an audit of a financial report.

Effective Date

2. [Deleted by the AUASB. Refer Aus 0.3]

1 See ASA 330 *The Auditor's Responses to Assessed Risks.*

2 See ASA 500 *Audit Evidence.*

Objective

3. The objective of the auditor is to obtain sufficient appropriate audit evidence regarding the:

   (a) Existence and condition of inventory; and

   (b) [Deleted by the AUASB. Refer ASA 502 *Audit Evidence—Specific Considerations for Litigation and Claims*]

   (c) Presentation and disclosure of segment information in accordance with the applicable financial reporting framework.

Requirements

Inventory

4. If inventory is material to the financial report, the auditor shall obtain sufficient appropriate audit evidence regarding the existence and condition of inventory by:

   (a) Attendance at physical inventory counting, unless impracticable, to: (Ref: Para. A1-A3)

      (i) Evaluate management's instructions and procedures for recording and controlling the results of the entity's physical inventory counting; (Ref: Para. A4)

      (ii) Observe the performance of management's count procedures; (Ref: Para. A5)

      (iii) Inspect the inventory; and (Ref: Para. A6)

      (iv) Perform test counts; and (Ref: Para. A7-A8)

   (b) Performing audit procedures over the entity's final inventory records to determine whether they accurately reflect actual inventory count results.

5. If physical inventory counting is conducted at a date other than the date of the financial report, the auditor shall, in addition to the procedures required by paragraph 4 of this Auditing Standard, perform audit procedures to obtain audit evidence about whether changes in inventory between the count date and the date of the financial report are properly recorded. (Ref: Para. A9-A11)

6. If the auditor is unable to attend physical inventory counting due to unforeseen circumstances, the auditor shall make or observe some physical counts on an alternative date, and perform audit procedures on intervening transactions.

7. If attendance at physical inventory counting is impracticable, the auditor shall perform alternative audit procedures to obtain sufficient appropriate audit evidence regarding the existence and condition of inventory. If it is not possible to do so, the auditor shall modify the opinion in the auditor's report in accordance with ASA 705.[3] (Ref: Para. A12-A14)

8. If inventory under the custody and control of a third party is material to the financial report, the auditor shall obtain sufficient appropriate audit evidence regarding the existence and condition of that inventory by performing one or both of the following:

   (a) Request confirmation from the third party as to the quantities and condition of inventory held on behalf of the entity. (Ref: Para. A15)

   (b) Perform inspection or other audit procedures appropriate in the circumstances. (Ref: Para. A16)

Litigation and Claims

9.-12. [Deleted by the AUASB. Refer ASA 502 *Audit Evidence—Specific Considerations for Litigation and Claims*]

Segment Information

13. The auditor shall obtain sufficient appropriate audit evidence regarding the presentation and disclosure of segment information in accordance with the applicable financial reporting framework by: (Ref: Para. A26)

3 See ASA 705 *Modifications to the Opinion in the Independent Auditor's Report*.

(a) Obtaining an understanding of the methods used by management in determining segment information, and: (Ref: Para. A27)

(i) Evaluating whether such methods are likely to result in disclosure in accordance with the applicable financial reporting framework; and

(ii) Where appropriate, testing the application of such methods; and

(b) Performing analytical procedures or other audit procedures appropriate in the circumstances.

❖ ❖ ❖

Application and Other Explanatory Material

Inventory

Attendance at Physical Inventory Counting (Ref: Para. 4(a))

A1. Management ordinarily establishes procedures under which inventory is physically counted at least once a year to serve as a basis for the preparation of the financial report and, if applicable, to ascertain the reliability of the entity's perpetual inventory system.

A2. Attendance at physical inventory counting involves:

- Inspecting the inventory to ascertain its existence and evaluate its condition, and performing test counts;
- Observing compliance with management's instructions and the performance of procedures for recording and controlling the results of the physical inventory count; and
- Obtaining audit evidence as to the reliability of management's count procedures.

These procedures may serve as test of controls or substantive procedures depending on the auditor's risk assessment, planned approach and the specific procedures carried out.

A3. Matters relevant in planning attendance at physical inventory counting (or in designing and performing audit procedures pursuant to paragraphs 4-8 of this Auditing Standard) include, for example:

- The risks of material misstatement related to inventory.
- The nature of the internal control related to inventory.
- Whether adequate procedures are expected to be established and proper instructions issued for physical inventory counting.
- The timing of physical inventory counting.
- Whether the entity maintains a perpetual inventory system.
- The locations at which inventory is held, including the materiality of the inventory and the risks of material misstatement at different locations, in deciding at which locations attendance is appropriate. ASA 600[4] deals with the involvement of other auditors and accordingly may be relevant if such involvement is with regards to attendance of physical inventory counting at a remote location.
- Whether the assistance of an auditor's expert is needed. ASA 620[5] deals with the use of an auditor's expert to assist the auditor to obtain sufficient appropriate audit evidence.

---

4 See ASA 600 *Special Considerations—Audits of a Group Financial Report (Including the Work of Component Auditors).*

5 See ASA 620 *Using the Work of an Auditor's Expert.*

***Evaluate Management's Instructions and Procedures** (Ref: Para. 4(a)(i))*

A4. Matters relevant in evaluating management's instructions and procedures for recording and controlling the physical inventory counting include whether they address, for example:

- The application of appropriate control activities, for example, collection of used physical inventory count records, accounting for unused physical inventory count records, and count and re-count procedures.
- The accurate identification of the stage of completion of work in progress, of slow moving, obsolete or damaged items and of inventory owned by a third party, for example, on consignment.
- The procedures used to estimate physical quantities, where applicable, such as may be needed in estimating the physical quantity of a coal pile.
- Control over the movement of inventory between areas and the shipping and receipt of inventory before and after the cut-off date.

***Observe the Performance of Management's Count Procedures** (Ref: Para. 4(a)(ii))*

A5. Observing the performance of management's count procedures, for example those relating to control over the movement of inventory before, during and after the count, assists the auditor in obtaining audit evidence that management's instructions and count procedures are adequately designed and implemented. In addition, the auditor may obtain copies of cut-off information, such as details of the movement of inventory, to assist the auditor in performing audit procedures over the accounting for such movements at a later date.

***Inspect the Inventory** (Ref: Para. 4(a)(iii))*

A6. Inspecting inventory when attending physical inventory counting assists the auditor in ascertaining the existence of the inventory (though not necessarily its ownership), and in identifying, for example, obsolete, damaged or ageing inventory.

***Perform Test Counts** (Ref: Para. 4(a)(iv))*

A7. Performing test counts, for example by tracing items selected from management's count records to the physical inventory and tracing items selected from the physical inventory to management's count records, provides audit evidence about the completeness and the accuracy of those records.

A8. In addition to recording the auditor's test counts, obtaining copies of management's completed physical inventory count records assists the auditor in performing subsequent audit procedures to determine whether the entity's final inventory records accurately reflect actual inventory count results.

Physical Inventory Counting Conducted Other than At the Date of the Financial Report (Ref: Para. 5)

A9. For practical reasons, the physical inventory counting may be conducted at a date, or dates, other than the date of the financial report. This may be done irrespective of whether management determines inventory quantities by an annual physical inventory counting or maintains a perpetual inventory system. In either case, the effectiveness of the design, implementation and maintenance of controls over changes in inventory determines whether the conduct of physical inventory counting at a date, or dates, other than the date of the financial report is appropriate for audit purposes. ASA 330 establishes requirements and provides guidance on substantive procedures performed at an interim date.[6]

A10. Where a perpetual inventory system is maintained, management may perform physical counts or other tests to ascertain the reliability of inventory quantity information included in the entity's perpetual inventory records. In some cases, management or the auditor may identify differences between the perpetual inventory records and actual physical inventory quantities on hand; this may indicate that the controls over changes in inventory are not operating effectively.

6 See ASA 330, paragraphs 22-23.

A11. Relevant matters for consideration when designing audit procedures to obtain audit evidence about whether changes in inventory amounts between the count date, or dates, and the final inventory records are properly recorded include:

- Whether the perpetual inventory records are properly adjusted.
- Reliability of the entity's perpetual inventory records.
- Reasons for significant differences between the information obtained during the physical count and the perpetual inventory records.

Attendance at Physical Inventory Counting Is Impracticable (Ref: Para. 7)

A12. In some cases, attendance at physical inventory counting may be impracticable. This may be due to factors such as the nature and location of the inventory, for example, where inventory is held in a location that may pose threats to the safety of the auditor. The matter of general inconvenience to the auditor, however, is not sufficient to support a decision by the auditor that attendance is impracticable. Further as explained in ASA 200,[7] the matter of difficulty, time, or cost involved is not in itself a valid basis for the auditor to omit an audit procedure for which there is no alternative or to be satisfied with audit evidence that is less than persuasive.

A13. In some cases where attendance is impracticable, alternative audit procedures, for example inspection of documentation of the subsequent sale of specific inventory items acquired or purchased prior to the physical inventory counting, may provide sufficient appropriate audit evidence about the existence and condition of inventory.

A14. In other cases, however, it may not be possible to obtain sufficient appropriate audit evidence regarding the existence and condition of inventory by performing alternative audit procedures. In such cases, ASA 705 requires the auditor to modify the opinion in the auditor's report as a result of the scope limitation.[8]

Inventory under the Custody and Control of a Third Party

Confirmation (Ref: Para. 8(a))

A15. ASA 505[9] establishes requirements and provides guidance for performing external confirmation procedures.

Other Audit Procedures (Ref: Para. 8(b))

A16. Depending on the circumstances, for example where information is obtained that raises doubt about the integrity and objectivity of the third party, the auditor may consider it appropriate to perform other audit procedures instead of, or in addition to, confirmation with the third party. Examples of other audit procedures include:

- Attending, or arranging for another auditor to attend, the third party's physical counting of inventory, if practicable.
- Obtaining another auditor's report, or a service auditor's report, on the adequacy of the third party's internal control for ensuring that inventory is properly counted and adequately safeguarded.
- Inspecting documentation regarding inventory held by third parties, for example, warehouse receipts.
- Requesting confirmation from other parties when inventory has been pledged as collateral.

Litigation and Claims

A17.-A25. [Deleted by the AUASB. Refer ASA 502 *Audit Evidence—Specific Considerations for Litigation and Claims*]

7 See ASA 200 *Overall Objectives of the Independent Auditor and the Conduct of an Audit in Accordance with Australian Auditing Standards*, paragraph A48.

8 See ASA 705, paragraph 13.

9 See ASA 505 *External Confirmations*.

Segment Information (Ref: Para. 13)

A26. Depending on the applicable financial reporting framework, the entity may be required or permitted to disclose segment information in the financial report. The auditor's responsibility regarding the presentation and disclosure of segment information is in relation to the financial report taken as a whole. Accordingly, the auditor is not required to perform audit procedures that would be necessary to express an opinion on the segment information presented on a stand-alone basis.

Understanding of the Methods Used by Management (Ref: Para. 13(a))

A27. Depending on the circumstances, example of matters that may be relevant when obtaining an understanding of the methods used by management in determining segment information and whether such methods are likely to result in disclosure in accordance with the applicable financial reporting framework include:

- Sales, transfers and charges between segments, and elimination of inter-segment amounts.
- Comparisons with budgets and other expected results, for example, operating profits as a percentage of sales.
- The allocation of assets and costs among segments.
- Consistency with prior periods, and the adequacy of the disclosures with respect to inconsistencies.

❖ ❖ ❖

Conformity with International Standards on Auditing

This Auditing Standard conforms with the Inventory and Segment Information sections (paragraphs 1-8, 13, A1-A16 and A26-A27) of International Standard on Auditing ISA 501 *Audit Evidence—Specific Considerations for Selected Items*, issued by the International Auditing and Assurance Standards Board (IAASB), an independent standard-setting board of the International Federation of Accountants (IFAC).

The other paragraphs of ISA 501 relating to Litigation and Claims (paragraphs 9-12 and A17-A25) are incorporated into ASA 502 *Audit Evidence—Specific Considerations for Litigation and Claims*.

The AUASB has decided to continue to issue ASA 502 as a separate Auditing Standard, in the same way that the previous standard, ASA 508 *Enquiry Regarding Litigation and Claims* (April 2006), is a separate standard. ASA 508 contains requirements and guidance that the AUASB considers important to carry forward in the Australian Auditing Standards, and as a result, the revised standard is better suited to presentation as a separate standard.

This Auditing Standard, ASA 501, contains all the requirements and guidance contained in ISA 501 relating to Inventory and Segment Information. Paragraphs that have been added to this Auditing Standard (and do not appear in the text of the equivalent ISA) are identified with the prefix "Aus".

Compliance with this Auditing Standard, in conjunction with ASA 502, enables compliance with ISA 501.

ASA 502

Audit Evidence—Specific Considerations for Litigation and Claims

(Reissued October 2009: amended and compiled June 2011)

Issued by the Auditing and Assurance Standards Board.

Note from the Institute of Chartered Accountants Australia

This note, prepared by the technical editor, is not part of ASA 502.

Historical development

July 1974: Statement of Auditing Practice CS 5 'Solicitors' Representation Letters' issued.

August 1979: Reissued without amendment as AUP 6 in August 1979.

October 1990: ED 33 'Solicitors' Representation Letters' issued by the AuSB with comments due by 31 January 1991.

May 1991: AUP 6 'Solicitors' Representation Letters' reissued, operative for the first financial reporting period ending on or after 1 January 1992, although earlier application was encouraged. The major changes to AUP 6 as a result of the reissue were the provision of guidance on the implications of legal matters, the audit evidence implications of solicitors' representations, the use of employee-solicitors, and amendments to the example Solicitor's Representation Letter.

February 1994: ED 54 'Codification and Revision of Auditing Pronouncements: AUS 510 Inquiry Regarding Litigation and Claims (AUP 6)' issued by the AuSB.

June 1994: The International Auditing Practices Committee (IAPC) of the International Federation of Accountants (IFAC) approved the issuance of a codified set of International Standards of Auditing (ISAs). The relevant international pronouncement was ISA 501 'Audit Evidence—Additional Considerations for Specific Items (Part C)'.

October 1995: Australian Auditing Standards and Auditing Guidance Statements released. The status of these was explained in APS 1.1 'Conformity With Auditing Standards'. These Standards became operative for the first reporting period commencing on or after 1 July 1996 and later reporting periods, although earlier application was encouraged. AUP 6 'Solicitors' Representation Letters' replaced by AUS 508 'Inquiry Regarding Litigation and Claims'.

February 1999: AUS/AGS Omnibus 2 'Miscellaneous Amendments to AUSs and AGSs' issued by AuASB, operative from the date of issue. The Omnibus amended para. .24 of AUS 508.

July 2002: AUS/AGS Omnibus 3 'Miscellaneous Amendments to AUSs and AGSs' issued by the AuASB, operative from date of issue. AUS 508 now reissued by the Board to incorporate these amendments.

April 2006: ASA 508 was issued as a legally enforceable Standard to replace AUS 508. It was based on ISA 501 'Audit Evidence—Additional Considerations for Specific Items (Part C): Procedures Regarding Litigation and Claims'.

October 2009: ASA 502 issued as part of the AUASB's Clarity Project to replace ASA 508. It is based on ISA 501 'Audit Evidence—Specific Considerations for Selected Items'.

June 2011: ASA 502 updated for editorial amendments contained in ASA 2011-1 'Amendments to Australian Auditing Standards'.

Contents

Compilation Details

Auditing Standard ASA 502 *Audit Evidence – Specific Considerations for Litigation and Claims* as Amended

This compilation takes into account amendments made up to and including 27 June 2011 and was prepared on 27 June 2011 by the Auditing and Assurance Standards Board (AUASB).

This compilation is not a separate Auditing Standard made by the AUASB. Instead, it is a representation of ASA 502 (October 2009) as amended by another Auditing Standard which is listed in the Table below.

Table of Standards

Standard	Date made	Operative date
ASA 502	27 October 2009	1 January 2010
ASA 2011-1	27 June 2011	1 July 2011

Table of Amendments

Paragraph affected	How affected	By … [paragraph]
Sub-heading above Para. A4	Amended	ASA 2011-1 [36]

Preface

[Preface extracted from the original Auditing Standard issued 27 October 2009]

Reasons for Issuing Auditing Standard ASA 502 *Audit Evidence—Specific Considerations for Litigation and Claims*

The Auditing and Assurance Standards Board (AUASB) issues Auditing Standard ASA 502 *Audit Evidence—Specific Considerations for Litigation and Claims* pursuant to the requirements of the legislative provisions and the Strategic Direction explained below.

The AUASB is an independent statutory board of the Australian Government established under section 227A of the *Australian Securities and Investments Commission Act 2001*, as amended (ASIC Act). Under section 336 of the *Corporations Act 2001*, the AUASB may make Australian Auditing Standards for the purposes of the corporations legislation. These Auditing Standards are legislative instruments under the *Legislative Instruments Act 2003*.

Under the Strategic Direction given to the AUASB by the Financial Reporting Council (FRC), the AUASB is required to have regard to any programme initiated by the International Auditing and Assurance Standards Board (IAASB) for the revision and enhancement of the International Standards on Auditing (ISAs) and to make appropriate consequential amendments to the Australian Auditing Standards. Accordingly, the AUASB has decided to revise and redraft the Australian Auditing Standards using the equivalent redrafted ISAs.

The equivalent international standard is ISA 501 *Audit Evidence—Specific Considerations for Selected Items*, issued by the IAASB as a composite standard containing sections on Inventory, Litigation and Claims, and Segment Information.

The AUASB has decided to continue to issue ASA 502 as a separate Auditing Standard, in the same way that the previous standard, ASA 508 *Enquiry Regarding Litigation and Claims*, is a separate standard. ASA 508 contains requirements and guidance that the AUASB considers important to carry forward in the Australian Auditing Standards, and as a result, the revised standard is better suited to presentation as a separate standard. Accordingly, ASA 502 deals with Litigation and Claims, while ASA 501 *Audit Evidence—Specific Considerations* for *Inventory and Segment Information* deals with Inventory and Segment Information.

Main Features

This Auditing Standard establishes requirements and provides application and other explanatory material regarding specific considerations by the auditor in obtaining sufficient appropriate audit evidence relating to certain aspects of litigation and claims.

This Auditing Standard:

(a) sets out the procedures the auditor should include when designing and performing audit procedures to identify litigation and claims involving the entity which may give rise to a risk of material misstatement;

(b) requires the auditor to endeavour to communicate in writing with the entity's external legal counsel, if a risk of material misstatement regarding litigation and claims is identified, or where audit procedures performed indicate that other material litigation and claims may exist;

(c) requires the auditor to endeavour to communicate in writing with the entity's internal legal counsel, if in-house legal counsel has the primary responsibility for litigation and claims involving both in-house and external legal counsel;

(d) describes the written representations that the auditor must request from management and, where appropriate, those changed with governance; and

(e) describes the auditor's responsibilities:

  (i) when the response from legal counsel contains a material disagreement with management's original evaluation of a particular matter; and

  (ii) when management refuses to give the auditor permission to communicate with legal counsel, or legal counsel refuses to respond appropriately and the auditor is unable to obtain sufficient appropriate audit evidence by performing alternative audit procedures.

Authority Statement

Auditing Standard ASA 502 *Audit Evidence—Specific Considerations for Litigation and Claims* (as amended at 27 June 2011) is set out in paragraphs 1 to Aus A9.3 and [Aus] Appendix 1.

This Auditing Standard is to be read in conjunction with ASA 101 *Preamble to Australian Auditing Standards*, which sets out the intentions of the AUASB on how the Australian Auditing Standards, operative for financial reporting periods commencing on or after 1 January 2010, are to be understood, interpreted and applied. This Auditing Standard is to be read also in conjunction with ASA 200 *Overall Objectives of the Independent Auditor and the Conduct of an Audit in Accordance with Australian Auditing Standards*.

Dated: 27 June 2011

M H Kelsall
Chairman - AUASB

Auditing Standard ASA 502

The Auditing and Assurance Standards Board (AUASB) made Auditing Standard ASA 502 *Audit Evidence—Specific Considerations for Litigation and Claims,* pursuant to section 227B of the *Australian Securities and Investments Commission Act 2001* and section 336 of the *Corporations Act 2001*, on 27 October 2009.

This compiled version of ASA 502 incorporates subsequent amendments contained in another Auditing Standard made by the AUASB up to and including 27 June 2011 (see Compilation Details).

Auditing Standard ASA 502

Audit Evidence—Specific Considerations for Litigation and Claims

Application

Aus 0.1 This Auditing Standard applies to:

(a) an audit of a financial report for a financial year, or an audit of a financial report for a half-year, in accordance with the *Corporations Act 2001*; and

(b) an audit of a financial report, or a complete set of financial statements, for any other purpose.

Aus 0.2 This Auditing Standard also applies, as appropriate, to an audit of other historical financial information.

Operative Date

Aus 0.3 This Auditing Standard is operative for financial reporting periods commencing on or after 1 January 2010.

[Note: For operative dates of paragraphs changed or added by an amending Standard, see Compilation Details.]

Introduction

Scope of this Auditing Standard

1. This Auditing Standard deals with specific considerations by the auditor in obtaining sufficient appropriate audit evidence in accordance with ASA 330,[1] ASA 500[2] and other relevant Australian Auditing Standards, with respect to litigation and claims involving the entity in an audit of a financial report.

Effective Date

1. [Deleted by the AUASB. Refer Aus 0.3]

Objective

2. The objective of the auditor is to obtain sufficient appropriate audit evidence regarding the completeness of litigation and claims involving the entity.

1 See ASA 330 *The Auditor's Responses to Assessed Risks.*

2 See ASA 500 *Audit Evidence.*

Requirements

Completeness of Litigation and Claims

3. The auditor shall design and perform audit procedures in order to identify litigation and claims involving the entity which may give rise to a risk of material misstatement, including: (Ref: Para. A1-Aus A4.1)
   (a) Enquiry of management and, where applicable, others within the entity, including in-house legal counsel;
   (b) Reviewing minutes of meetings of those charged with governance and correspondence between the entity and its external legal counsel; and
   (c) Reviewing legal expense accounts. (Ref: Para. A4)

Communication with the Entity's Legal Counsel

External Legal Counsel

4. If the auditor assesses a risk of material misstatement regarding litigation or claims that have been identified, or when audit procedures performed indicate that other material litigation or claims may exist, the auditor shall endeavour to, in addition to the procedures required by other Australian Auditing Standards, seek direct communication with the entity's external legal counsel. The auditor shall do so through a letter of enquiry, prepared by management and sent by the auditor, requesting the entity's external legal counsel to communicate directly with the auditor. If law, regulation or the respective legal professional body prohibits the entity's external legal counsel from communicating directly with the auditor, the auditor shall perform alternative audit procedures. (Ref: Para. A5-A8)

In-house and/or External Legal Counsel

Aus 5.1 Where in-house legal counsel has the primary responsibility for litigation and claims and is in the best position to corroborate management's representations, the auditor shall endeavour to obtain a representation letter from the in-house legal counsel, seeking information similar to that sought from the entity's external legal counsel. (Ref: Para. Aus A8.1-Aus A8.2)

Legal Counsel's Response

Aus 5.2 If a response from the entity's external or internal legal counsel contains a material disagreement with management's original evaluation of a particular matter, the auditor shall seek discussions with management and the entity's legal counsel, unless management subsequently agrees with the legal counsel's evaluation. (Ref: Para. Aus A8.3-Aus A8.6)

5. If:
   (a) management refuses to give the auditor permission to communicate or meet with the entity's external legal counsel, or the entity's external legal counsel refuses to respond appropriately to the letter of enquiry, or is prohibited from responding; and (Ref: Para. Aus 8.7-Aus 8.8)
   (b) the auditor is unable to obtain sufficient appropriate audit evidence by performing alternative audit procedures, (Ref: Para. Aus A8.9-Aus A8.10)

   the auditor shall modify the opinion in the auditor's report in accordance with ASA 705 *Modifications to the Opinion in the Independent Auditor's Report*. (Ref: Para. Aus A8.11)

Written Representations

6. The auditor shall request management and, where appropriate, those charged with governance, to provide written representations that all known actual or possible litigation and claims whose effects should be considered when preparing the financial report have been disclosed to the auditor and accounted for and disclosed in accordance with the applicable financial reporting framework. (Ref: Para. Aus A8.12-Aus A8.13)

Related Procedures

Aus 6.1 The auditor shall enquire of management about new litigation and claims referred to the entity's legal counsel subsequent to the date of the request for a letter of enquiry to the entity's legal counsel and prior to signing the auditor's report. (Ref: Para. A9-Aus A9.1)

Aus 6.2 If audit procedures lead to the discovery of matters of a legal nature not previously identified by management, the auditor shall consider the impact of each of the matters on the financial report. (Ref: Para. Aus A9.2-Aus A9.3)

❖ ❖ ❖

Application and Other Explanatory Material

Completeness of Litigation and Claims (Ref: Para. 4)

A1. Litigation and claims involving the entity may have a material effect on the financial report and thus may be required to be disclosed or accounted for in the financial report.

Aus A1.1 It is the responsibility of those charged with governance of an entity to adopt policies and procedures to identify, evaluate, record and report on the outcome of any material litigation and claims. However, since the factors that would be considered in the accounting for and reporting of litigation and claims are within the direct knowledge and control of the management of an entity, management is the primary source of information. Ordinarily, the auditor would seek audit evidence from different sources to corroborate management's assertions.

A2. In addition to the procedures identified in paragraph 4, other relevant procedures include, for example, using information obtained through risk assessment procedures carried out as part of obtaining an understanding of the entity and its environment to assist the auditor to become aware of litigation and claims involving the entity.

Aus A2.1 The procedures identified in paragraphs 4 and A2 would ordinarily include the following:

- reviewing and discussing with management the procedures within the entity's internal control structure for identifying and recording litigation and claims and bringing them to the attention of management;
- reviewing and discussing with management the procedures within the entity's internal control structure for the identification, control and recording of litigation and claims and associated revenues and expenses in appropriate accounts; and
- obtaining and discussing with management:
  - (i) a list of litigation and claims, including a description of the matters and an estimate of their likely financial consequences; and
  - (ii) an analysis identifying litigation and claims.

Aus A2.2 Audit procedures that are undertaken for different purposes might also identify litigation and claims. Such procedures include:

- examining contracts, loan agreements, leases, insurance policies and claims, and other correspondence;
- reading minutes of meetings of the audit committee, shareholders and appropriate committees;
- obtaining information concerning guarantees from bank confirmations; and
- enquiries of management and other employees of the entity.

A3. Audit evidence obtained for purposes of identifying litigation and claims that may give rise to a risk of material misstatement also may provide audit evidence regarding other relevant considerations, such as valuation or measurement, regarding litigation and claims.

ASA 540* establishes requirements and provides guidance relevant to the auditor's consideration of litigation and claims requiring accounting estimates or related disclosures in the financial report.

Reviewing Legal Expense Accounts (Ref: Para. 4(c))

A4. Depending on the circumstances, the auditor may judge it appropriate to examine related source documents, such as invoices for legal expenses, as part of the auditor's review of legal expense accounts.

Outcome of Litigation and Claims (Ref: Para. 4)

Aus A4.1 The procedures outlined in paragraphs A1-A4 are methods whereby the auditor can identify both material litigation and claims and legal counsel who have been consulted by the entity. However, these procedures may not necessarily provide the auditor with sufficient appropriate audit evidence concerning the likely outcome of litigation and claims. Furthermore, the auditor ordinarily does not possess the skills necessary and is not in a position to make legal judgements concerning the likely outcome of litigation and claims.

Communication with the Entity's Legal Counsel (Ref: Para. 5-6)

External Legal Counsel (Ref: Para. 5)

A5. Direct communication with the entity's external legal counsel assists the auditor in obtaining sufficient appropriate audit evidence as to whether potentially material litigation and claims are known and management's estimates of the financial implications, including costs, are reasonable.

A6. In some cases, the auditor may seek direct communication with the entity's external legal counsel through a letter of general enquiry. For this purpose, a letter of general enquiry requests the entity's external legal counsel to inform the auditor of any litigation and claims that the counsel is aware of, together with an assessment of the outcome of the litigation and claims, and an estimate of the financial implications, including costs involved.

A7. If it is considered unlikely that the entity's external legal counsel will respond appropriately to a letter of general enquiry, for example if the professional body to which the external legal counsel belongs prohibits response to such a letter, the auditor may seek direct communication through a letter of specific enquiry. For this purpose, a letter of specific enquiry includes:

(a) A list of litigation and claims;

(b) Where available, management's assessment of the outcome of each of the identified litigation and claims and its estimate of the financial implications, including costs involved; and

(c) A request that the entity's external legal counsel confirm the reasonableness of management's assessments and provide the auditor with further information if the list is considered by the entity's external legal counsel to be incomplete or incorrect.

Aus A7.1 An example of a letter of specific enquiry is included in [Aus] Appendix 1.

Aus A7.2 An auditor may in some cases request that management send a letter of enquiry to the entity's legal counsel who are not identified as currently handling the entity's litigation and claims. For example when the entity has changed legal counsel on a particular matter, or when legal counsel engaged by the entity has resigned, the auditor would consider the need for enquiries concerning the reasons for the change or resignation.

A8. In certain circumstances, the auditor also may judge it necessary to meet with the entity's external legal counsel to discuss the likely outcome of the litigation or claims. This may be the case, for example, where:

- The auditor determines that the matter is a significant risk.

* See ASA 540 *Auditing Accounting Estimates, Including Fair Value Accounting Estimates, and Related Disclosures.*

- The matter is complex.
- There is disagreement between management and the entity's external legal counsel.

Ordinarily, such meetings require management's permission and are held with a representative of management in attendance.

In-house and/or External Legal Counsel (Ref: Para. Aus 5.1)

Aus A8.1 If both in-house and external legal counsel are involved in advising the entity on the same litigation and claims, the auditor would ordinarily seek a letter of enquiry from the legal counsel with the primary responsibility for that matter. However, there may be circumstances where the in-house legal counsel has primary responsibility, but the matter has involved substantial participation by an external legal counsel, and is of such significance that the auditor would consider obtaining a letter of enquiry from the external legal counsel to determine that their opinion does not differ materially from that of the in-house legal counsel.

Aus A8.2 In circumstances where both in-house and external legal counsel have devoted substantial attention to litigation and claims involving the entity and primary responsibility rests with the external legal counsel, evidence obtained from an in-house legal counsel is not an adequate substitute for any information that the external legal counsel may refuse to furnish.

Legal Counsel's Response

Aus A8.3 Before relying on the opinion of either in-house legal counsel or external legal counsel, care should be exercised to ensure that conditions prevail which would make such reliance reasonable.*

Aus A8.4 If a disagreement between management and legal counsel is resolved after discussions, the auditor would ordinarily request the entity's legal counsel to confirm the details in writing to the auditor. (Ref: Para. Aus 5.2)

Aus A8.5 If the disagreement is not resolved, the auditor would ordinarily prepare a memorandum of the discussion and seek written confirmation from management and the entity's legal counsel that it is an accurate record of the discussion. In conjunction with evidence from other audit procedures, the auditor, under ASA 705, needs to consider the effect of such disagreement on the auditor's report.

Aus A8.6 If the response from the entity's legal counsel contains information that requires clarification, the auditor would ordinarily make further enquiries of management and the entity's legal counsel, as appropriate, and request clarification in writing.

Legal Counsel's Inability to Respond Comprehensively or Limitations in a Response (Ref: Para. 6(a))

Aus A8.7 If a response is not received from the entity's legal counsel, or the response received is incomplete, the auditor would ordinarily consider:

(a) requesting management to contact the entity's legal counsel to either seek a complete answer to the original request, or an explanation for the lack of, or limitation in, a response, which ought to be sent directly to the auditor; or

(b) making arrangements to discuss with management or the entity's legal counsel the reasons for the lack of, or limitation in, a response.

Aus A8.8 Due to the following circumstances it may be difficult to either obtain a response to a letter of enquiry or be provided with information about litigation and claims from the entity's legal counsel:

(a) If the entity is involved in litigation, or litigation is anticipated or contemplated, relevant information about legal matters may be subject to legal professional privilege. Disclosure of this information in the letter of enquiry, directly to the auditor for the purposes of the audit of the entity's financial report, is not privileged. This may cause legal professional privilege attaching to the entity's communications with its legal counsel

* See ASA 500 for the applicable requirements and guidance on using the work of a management's expert.

to be compromised, as information in the letter of enquiry might become discoverable in litigation proceedings.

(b) Factors influencing the outcome of a legal matter may sometimes not be within the legal counsel's competence to judge, for example where there is no relevant or historical experience of the entity or other entities in similar matters, or where the litigation is at an early stage.

(c) Due to material uncertainties, the entity's legal counsel may be unable to form a conclusion to corroborate management's representations regarding outstanding litigation and claims.

Alternative Audit Procedures (Ref: Para. 6(b))

Aus A8.9 Where the auditor has not obtained sufficient appropriate audit evidence as to a material financial report assertion regarding litigation and claims, under ASA 330, the auditor needs to consider whether alternative audit procedures can provide further audit evidence. Alternative audit procedures may include:

(a) further enquiries of management or those charged with governance, about for instance the processes, procedures and assumptions they implement, adopt or make to ensure litigation and claims are recognised and disclosed in accordance with the applicable financial reporting framework;

(b) where possible, making arrangements to discuss litigation and claims with management and the entity's legal counsel;

(c) further review of documents in management's possession concerning litigation and claims, including the entity's board minutes; and

(d) further examination of accounts rendered by the entity's external legal counsel.

Aus A8.10 The auditor may also consider any relevant legislation to assist in obtaining information about litigation and claims, including, for example:

- Section 310 of the *Corporations Act 2001* which entitles the auditor to a right of access at all reasonable times to the books of a company, registered scheme or disclosing entity, and to require from any officer information, explanations or other assistance for the purposes of the audit or review.
- When the entity is a disclosing entity, whether disclosure of any litigation and claims has been made in accordance with the continuous disclosure requirements under sections 674 or 675 of the *Corporations Act 2001*.

Other Audit Reporting Considerations (Ref: Para. 6)

Aus A8.11 In those circumstances where, due to uncertainties, the entity's legal counsel is unable to form a conclusion to corroborate management's representation, the auditor needs to consider the effect on the auditor's report arising from the extent of disclosure of the uncertainty in the financial report:

(a) where the auditor considers that the disclosure of the uncertainty in the financial report is adequate, the auditor needs to consider including an Emphasis of Matter paragraph; in accordance with ASA 706,* or

(b) if in the auditor's opinion the disclosure of the uncertainty is inadequate or unreliable, a modified opinion needs to be expressed in accordance with ASA 705.

Written Representations (Ref: Para.7)

Aus A8.12 ASA 580# deals with the auditor's responsibility to obtain written representations from management and, where appropriate, those charged with governance, in an audit of a financial report. Appendix 2 of that Standard provides an illustrative example of a representation letter.

---

* See ASA 706 *Emphasis of Matter Paragraphs and Other Matter Paragraphs in the Independent Auditor's Report.*

\# See ASA 580 *Written Representations.*

Aus A8.13 As management is the primary source of information regarding litigation and claims, the auditor is required to request management to provide written representations about such matters. Written representations from management provide audit evidence regarding litigation and claims that may have a material effect on the financial report.

Related Procedures (Ref: Para. Aus 7.1-Aus 7.2)

A9. In accordance with ASA 700,[†] the auditor is required to date the auditor's report no earlier than the date on which the auditor has obtained sufficient appropriate audit evidence on which to base the auditor's opinion on the financial report. Audit evidence about the status of litigation and claims up to the date of the auditor's report may be obtained by enquiry of management, including in-house legal counsel, responsible for dealing with the relevant matters. In some instances, the auditor may need to obtain updated information from the entity's external legal counsel.

Aus A9.1 When new litigation or claims, which may have a material effect on the financial report, have been referred to the entity's legal counsel subsequent to sending the letter of enquiry to the entity's legal counsel and prior to signing the auditor's report, the auditor would ordinarily request management to prepare an additional letter of enquiry to the legal counsel regarding the new litigation or claims.

Aus A9.2 When litigation and claims matters, which may have a material effect on the financial report, are discovered, which were not previously identified by management, the auditor would ordinarily inform management and request management to address further enquiries to, or arrange a meeting with, the entity's legal counsel or other relevant experts, at which the auditor would be present. In addition, the auditor needs to extend the auditor's audit procedures to ensure that sufficient appropriate audit evidence on which to form an opinion has been obtained. If, however, having regard to all the circumstances, the auditor is unable to obtain satisfaction that all the information required for the purposes of the audit has been received, the auditor considers the effect on the auditor's report.*

Aus A9.3 If information comes to the auditor's attention that may indicate the existence of material liabilities resulting from litigation and claims on which management has not sought advice, the auditor ordinarily discusses the matter with those charged with governance. Depending on the circumstances, refusal by management to seek advice may be considered to be a limitation in the scope of the auditor's work.

❖❖❖

Conformity with International Standards on Auditing

This Auditing Standard conforms with the Litigation and Claims sections (paragraphs 1-3, 9-12 and A17-A25) of International Standard on Auditing ISA 501 *Audit Evidence—Specific Considerations for Selected Items*, issued by the International Auditing and Assurance Standards Board (IAASB), an independent standard-setting board of the International Federation of Accountants (IFAC).

The other paragraphs of ISA 501 relating to Inventory and Segment Information (paragraphs 4-8, 13, A1-A16 and A26-A27) are incorporated into ASA 501 *Audit Evidence—Specific Considerations for Inventory and Segment Information*.

The AUASB has decided to continue to issue ASA 502 as a separate Auditing Standard, in the same way that the previous standard, ASA 508 *Enquiry Regarding Litigation and Claims*, is a separate standard. ASA 508 contains requirements and guidance that the AUASB considers important to carry forward in the Australian Auditing Standards, and as a result, the revised standard is better suited to presentation as a separate standard.

This Auditing Standard contains all the requirements and guidance contained in ISA 501 relating to Litigation and Claims, as well as additional requirements and guidance that are contained in ASA 508. Paragraphs in this Auditing Standard that do not appear in the text of ISA 501 are identified with the prefix "Aus".

† See ASA 700 *Forming an Opinion and Reporting on a Financial Report*.

* See ASA 705.

Compliance with this Auditing Standard, in conjunction with ASA 501, enables compliance with ISA 501.

Table 1, following, shows how paragraphs in this Auditing Standard have been re-numbered, compared to the equivalent paragraphs in ISA 501:

Table 1: Paragraph Re-numbering in ASA 502

Description	ISA 501	ASA 502	
	Para. #	Para. #	"Aus" Para. #
Requirements			
Litigation and Claims	9	4	
	10	5	Aus 5.1-Aus 5.2
	11	6	
	12	7	Aus 7.1-Aus 7.2
Application and Other Explanatory Material			
Litigation and Claims	A17	A1	Aus A1.1
	A18	A2	Aus A2.1-Aus A2.2
	A19	A3	
	A20	A4	Aus A 4.1
	A21	A5	
	A22	A6	
	A23	A7	Aus A7.1-Aus A7.2
	A24	A8	Aus A8.1-Aus A8.13
	A25	A9	Aus A9.1-Aus A9.3
	Footnote 10	*	
	Footnote 11	*	

ASA

[Aus] Appendix 1

(Ref: Para. 5 and A7)

This example letter relates to specific enquiry directed to the entity's external legal counsel, but may be adapted, as appropriate, to specific enquiry directed to the entity's internal legal counsel.

Example of a Letter of Specific Enquiry to External Legal Counsel (For an Audit Client)

(Client Letterhead)

(Date)

(Name and Address of External Legal Counsel)

Dear ...

In connection with the preparation and audit of the financial report of (name of company) (and the following subsidiaries and/or divisions) for the reporting period ended (date) we request that you provide to this company, at our cost, the following information:

1 Confirmation that you are acting for the company (and the above-named subsidiaries and/or divisions) in relation to the matters mentioned below and that the directors'

description and estimates of the amounts of the financial settlement (including costs and disbursements) which might arise in relation to those matters are in your opinion reasonable.

Name of Company (subsidiary or division)	Directors' Description of Matter (including current status)	Directors' Estimate of the Financial Settlement (inclusive of costs and disbursements)

2 Should you disagree with any of the information included in 1 above, please comment on the nature of your disagreement.

3 In addition to the above, a list of open files that you maintain in relation to the company (and the above mentioned subsidiaries and/or divisions).

4 In relation to the matters identified under 2 and 3 above, we authorise you to discuss these matters with our auditor (name and address), if requested, and at our cost.

It is understood that:

(a) the company (and the above-named subsidiaries and/or divisions) may have used other legal counsel in certain matters;

(b) the information sought relates only to information relating to litigation and claims referred to your firm (including branches or subsidiaries) which were current at any time during the above-mentioned reporting period, or have arisen since the end of the reporting period and up to the date of your response;

(c) unless separately requested in writing, you are not responsible for keeping the auditors advised of any changes after the date of your reply;

(d) you are only required to respond on matters referred to you as legal counsel for the company (and the above-mentioned subsidiaries and/or divisions), not on those within your knowledge solely because of the holding of any office as director, secretary or otherwise of the company (and the above-mentioned subsidiaries and/or divisions) by a consultant, partner or employee of your firm; and

(e) your reply is sought solely for the information of, and assistance to, this company in connection with the audit of, and report with respect to, the financial report of the company (and the above-mentioned subsidiaries and/or divisions) and will not be quoted or otherwise referred to in any financial report or related documents of the company (and the above-mentioned subsidiaries and/or divisions) nor will it be furnished to any governmental agency or other person, subject to specific legislative requirements, without the prior written consent of your firm.

Your prompt assistance in this matter will be appreciated. If you are unable to confirm or provide the information requested above, please advise us and our auditor the reasons for any limitation or impediment to fulfilling this request.

Please forward a signed copy of your reply directly to our auditors, (name) at (address), by (date).

Yours faithfully,

(Signature and Title of client)

ASA 505

External Confirmations

(Reissued October 2009)

Issued by the Auditing and Assurance Standards Board.

Note from the Institute of Chartered Accountants Australia

This note, prepared by the technical editor, is not part of ASA 505.

Historical development

December 1992: AUP 14 Supplement 1 'Audit Evidence — Confirmation of Receivables' issued following a period of exposure as ED 46. The Supplementary Statement included guidance on sample design and selection considerations. It also discussed the effect that the assessment of control risk has on the decision as to the use of the positive or negative form of confirmation request.

June 1994: The International Auditing Practices Committee (IAPC) of the International Federation of Accountants (IFAC) approved the issuance of a codified set of International Standards of Auditing (ISAs). The relevant international pronouncement is ISA 501 'Audit Evidence — Additional Considerations for Specific Items (Part B)'.

October 1995: Australian Auditing Standards and Auditing Guidance Statements released. The status of these was explained in APS 1.1 'Conformity With Auditing Standards'. These Standards became operative for the first reporting period commencing on or after 1 July 1996 and later reporting periods, although earlier application was encouraged. AUP 14 Supplement 1 'Audit Evidence–Confirmation of Receivables' replaced by AUS 504 'Confirmation of Receivables'.

February 2000: AUS 504 'External Confirmations' reissued by the AuASB, operative for reporting periods beginning on or after 1 July 2000. Based on ED 71 with the same title and superseded AUS 504 'Confirmation of Receivables', previously issued in October 1995, which addressed only confirmation of accounts receivable.

July 2002: AUS/AGS Omnibus 3 'Miscellaneous Amendments to AUSs and AGSs' issued by the AuASB, operative from date of issue. AUS 504 now reissued by the Board to incorporate these amendments.

April 2006: ASA 505 was issued as a legally enforceable Standard to replace AUS 504. It is based on ISA 505 of the same name.

October 2009: ASA 505 reissued as part of the AUSASB's Clarity Project. It is based on ISA 505 of the same name.

Contents

Preface

Reasons for Issuing Auditing Standard ASA 505 *External Confirmations*

The Auditing and Assurance Standards Board (AUASB) issues Auditing Standard ASA 505 *External Confirmations* pursuant to the requirements of the legislative provisions and the Strategic Direction explained below.

The AUASB is an independent statutory board of the Australian Government established under section 227A of the *Australian Securities and Investments Commission Act 2001*, as amended (ASIC Act). Under section 336 of the *Corporations Act 2001*, the AUASB may make Australian Auditing Standards for the purposes of the corporations legislation. These Auditing Standards are legislative instruments under the *Legislative Instruments Act 2003*.

Under the Strategic Direction given to the AUASB by the Financial Reporting Council (FRC), the AUASB is required to have regard to any programme initiated by the International Auditing and Assurance Standards Board (IAASB) for the revision and enhancement of the International Standards on Auditing (ISAs) and to make appropriate consequential amendments to the Australian Auditing Standards. Accordingly, the AUASB has decided to revise and redraft the Australian Auditing Standards using the equivalent redrafted ISAs.

Main Features

This Auditing Standard establishes requirements and provides application and other explanatory material regarding the auditor's use of external confirmation procedures to obtain audit evidence.

This Auditing Standard:

(a) describes the procedures the auditor shall follow to maintain control over external confirmation requests;

(b) describes the requirements of the auditor when management refuses to allow the auditor to send a confirmation request; and

(c) details the requirements relating to the results of external confirmation procedures.

Authority Statement

The Auditing and Assurance Standards Board (AUASB) makes this Auditing Standard ASA 505 *External Confirmations* pursuant to section 227B of the *Australian Securities and Investments Commission Act 2001* and section 336 of the *Corporations Act 2001*.

This Auditing Standard is to be read in conjunction with ASA 101 *Preamble to Australian Auditing Standards*, which sets out the intentions of the AUASB on how the Australian Auditing Standards operative for financial reporting periods commencing on or after 1 January 2010 are to be understood, interpreted and applied. This Auditing Standard is to be read also in conjunction with ASA 200 *Overall Objectives of the Independent Auditor and the Conduct of an Audit in Accordance with Australian Auditing Standards*.

Dated: 27 October 2009

M H Kelsall
Chairman - AUASB

ASA

Auditing Standard ASA 505

External Confirmations

Application

Aus 0.1 This Auditing Standard applies to:

(a) an audit of a financial report for a financial year, or an audit of a financial report for a half-year, in accordance with the *Corporations Act 2001*; and

(b) an audit of a financial report, or a complete set of financial statements, for any other purpose.

Aus 0.2 This Auditing Standard also applies, as appropriate, to an audit of other historical financial information.

Operative Date

Aus 0.3 This Auditing Standard is operative for financial reporting periods commencing on or after 1 January 2010.

Introduction

Scope of this Auditing Standard

1. This Auditing Standard deals with the auditor's use of external confirmation procedures to obtain audit evidence in accordance with the requirements of ASA 330[1] and ASA 500.[2] It does not address enquiries regarding litigation and claims, which are dealt with in ASA 502.[3]

External Confirmation Procedures to Obtain Audit Evidence

2. ASA 500 indicates that the reliability of audit evidence is influenced by its source and by its nature, and is dependent on the individual circumstances under which it is obtained.[4]

1 See ASA 330 *The Auditor's Responses to Assessed Risks*.

2 See ASA 500 *Audit Evidence*.

3 See ASA 502 *Audit Evidence—Specific Considerations for Litigation and Claims*.

4 See ASA 500, paragraph A5.

That Auditing Standard also includes the following generalisations applicable to audit evidence:[5]

- Audit evidence is more reliable when it is obtained from independent sources outside the entity.
- Audit evidence obtained directly by the auditor is more reliable than audit evidence obtained indirectly or by inference.
- Audit evidence is more reliable when it exists in documentary form, whether paper, electronic or other medium.

Accordingly, depending on the circumstances of the audit, audit evidence in the form of external confirmations received directly by the auditor from confirming parties may be more reliable than evidence generated internally by the entity. This Auditing Standard is intended to assist the auditor in designing and performing external confirmation procedures to obtain relevant and reliable audit evidence.

3. Other Auditing Standards recognise the importance of external confirmations as audit evidence, for example:

- ASA 330 discusses the auditor's responsibility to design and implement overall responses to address the assessed risks of material misstatement at the financial statement level, and to design and perform further audit procedures whose nature, timing and extent are based on, and are responsive to, the assessed risks of material misstatement at the assertion level.[6] In addition, ASA 330 requires that, irrespective of the assessed risks of material misstatement, the auditor designs and performs substantive procedures for each material class of transactions, account balance, and disclosure. The auditor is also required to consider whether external confirmation procedures are to be performed as substantive audit procedures.[7]
- ASA 330 requires that the auditor obtain more persuasive audit evidence the higher the auditor's assessment of risk.[8]

  To do this, the auditor may increase the quantity of the evidence or obtain evidence that is more relevant or reliable, or both. For example, the auditor may place more emphasis on obtaining evidence directly from third parties or obtaining corroborating evidence from a number of independent sources. ASA 330 also indicates that external confirmation procedures may assist the auditor in obtaining audit evidence with the high level of reliability that the auditor requires to respond to significant risks of material misstatement, whether due to fraud or error.[9]
- ASA 240 indicates that the auditor may design confirmation requests to obtain additional corroborative information as a response to address the assessed risks of material misstatement due to fraud at the assertion level.[10]
- ASA 500 indicates that corroborating information obtained from a source independent of the entity, such as external confirmations, may increase the assurance the auditor obtains from evidence existing within the accounting records or from representations made by management.[11]

Effective Date

4. [Deleted by the AUASB. Refer Aus 0.3]

5 See ASA 500, paragraph A31.

6 See ASA 330, paragraphs 5-6.

7 See ASA 330, paragraphs 18-19.

8 See ASA 330, paragraph 7(b).

9 See ASA 330, paragraph A53.

10 See ASA 240 *The Auditor's Responsibilities Relating to Fraud in an Audit of a Financial Report*, paragraph A37.

11 See ASA 500, paragraphs A8-A9.

Objective

5. The objective of the auditor, when using external confirmation procedures, is to design and perform such procedures to obtain relevant and reliable audit evidence.

Definitions

6. For purposes of the Australian Auditing Standards, the following terms have the meanings attributed below:

   (a) External confirmation means audit evidence obtained as a direct written response to the auditor from a third party (the confirming party), in paper form, or by electronic or other medium.

   (b) Positive confirmation request means a request that the confirming party respond directly to the auditor indicating whether the confirming party agrees or disagrees with the information in the request, or providing the requested information.

   (c) Negative confirmation request means a request that the confirming party respond directly to the auditor only if the confirming party disagrees with the information provided in the request.

   (d) Non-response means a failure of the confirming party to respond, or fully respond, to a positive confirmation request, or a confirmation request returned undelivered.

   (e) Exception means a response that indicates a difference between information requested to be confirmed, or contained in the entity's records, and information provided by the confirming party.

Requirements

External Confirmation Procedures

7. When using external confirmation procedures, the auditor shall maintain control over external confirmation requests, including:

   (a) Determining the information to be confirmed or requested; (Ref: Para. A1)

   (b) Selecting the appropriate confirming party; (Ref: Para. A2)

   (c) Designing the confirmation requests, including determining that requests are properly addressed and contain return information for responses to be sent directly to the auditor; and (Ref: Para. A3-A6)

   (d) Sending the requests, including follow-up requests when applicable, to the confirming party. (Ref: Para. A7)

Management's Refusal to Allow the Auditor to Send a Confirmation Request

8. If management refuses to allow the auditor to send a confirmation request, the auditor shall:

   (a) Enquire as to management's reasons for the refusal, and seek audit evidence as to their validity and reasonableness; (Ref: Para. A8)

   (b) Evaluate the implications of management's refusal on the auditor's assessment of the relevant risks of material misstatement, including the risk of fraud, and on the nature, timing and extent of other audit procedures; and (Ref: Para. A9)

   (c) Perform alternative audit procedures designed to obtain relevant and reliable audit evidence. (Ref: Para. A10)

9. If the auditor concludes that management's refusal to allow the auditor to send a confirmation request is unreasonable, or the auditor is unable to obtain relevant and reliable audit evidence from alternative audit procedures, the auditor shall communicate with those charged with governance in accordance with ASA 260.[12] The auditor also

12 See ASA 260 *Communication with Those Charged with Governance*, paragraph 16.

shall determine the implications for the audit and the auditor's opinion in accordance with ASA 705.[13]

Results of the External Confirmation Procedures

Reliability of Responses to Confirmation Requests

10. If the auditor identifies factors that give rise to doubts about the reliability of the response to a confirmation request, the auditor shall obtain further audit evidence to resolve those doubts. (Ref: Para. A11-A16)

11. If the auditor determines that a response to a confirmation request is not reliable, the auditor shall evaluate the implications on the assessment of the relevant risks of material misstatement, including the risk of fraud, and on the related nature, timing and extent of other audit procedures. (Ref: Para. A17)

Non-Responses

12. In the case of each non-response, the auditor shall perform alternative audit procedures to obtain relevant and reliable audit evidence. (Ref: Para A18-A19)

When a Response to a Positive Confirmation Request Is Necessary to Obtain Sufficient Appropriate Audit Evidence

13. If the auditor has determined that a response to a positive confirmation request is necessary to obtain sufficient appropriate audit evidence, alternative audit procedures will not provide the audit evidence the auditor requires. If the auditor does not obtain such confirmation, the auditor shall determine the implications for the audit and the auditor's opinion in accordance with ASA 705. (Ref: Para A20)

Exceptions

14. The auditor shall investigate exceptions to determine whether or not they are indicative of misstatements. (Ref: Para. A21-A22)

Negative Confirmations

15. Negative confirmations provide less persuasive audit evidence than positive confirmations. Accordingly, the auditor shall not use negative confirmation requests as the sole substantive audit procedure to address an assessed risk of material misstatement at the assertion level unless all of the following are present: (Ref: Para. A23)
    (a) The auditor has assessed the risk of material misstatement as low and has obtained sufficient appropriate audit evidence regarding the operating effectiveness of controls relevant to the assertion;
    (b) The population of items subject to negative confirmation procedures comprises a large number of small, homogeneous, account balances, transactions or conditions;
    (c) A very low exception rate is expected; and
    (d) The auditor is not aware of circumstances or conditions that would cause recipients of negative confirmation requests to disregard such requests.

Evaluating the Evidence Obtained

16. The auditor shall evaluate whether the results of the external confirmation procedures provide relevant and reliable audit evidence, or whether further audit evidence is necessary. (Ref: Para A24-A25)

❖ ❖ ❖

Application and Other Explanatory Material

External Confirmation Procedures

Determining the Information to Be Confirmed or Requested (Ref: Para. 7(a))

A1. External confirmation procedures frequently are performed to confirm or request information regarding account balances and their elements. They may also be used to

13 See ASA 705 *Modifications to the Opinion in the Independent Auditor's Report.*

confirm terms of agreements, contracts, or transactions between an entity and other parties, or to confirm the absence of certain conditions, such as a "side agreement."

Selecting the Appropriate Confirming Party (Ref: Para. 7(b))

A2. Responses to confirmation requests provide more relevant and reliable audit evidence when confirmation requests are sent to a confirming party the auditor believes is knowledgeable about the information to be confirmed. For example, a financial institution official who is knowledgeable about the transactions or arrangements for which confirmation is requested may be the most appropriate person at the financial institution from whom to request confirmation.

Designing Confirmation Requests (Ref: Para. 7(c))

A3. The design of a confirmation request may directly affect the confirmation response rate, and the reliability and the nature of the audit evidence obtained from responses.

A4. Factors to consider when designing confirmation requests include:

- The assertions being addressed.
- Specific identified risks of material misstatement, including fraud risks.
- The layout and presentation of the confirmation request.
- Prior experience on the audit or similar engagements.
- The method of communication (for example, in paper form, or by electronic or other medium).
- Management's authorisation or encouragement to the confirming parties to respond to the auditor. Confirming parties may only be willing to respond to a confirmation request containing management's authorisation.
- The ability of the intended confirming party to confirm or provide the requested information (for example, individual invoice amount versus total balance).

A5. A positive external confirmation request asks the confirming party to reply to the auditor in all cases, either by indicating the confirming party's agreement with the given information, or by asking the confirming party to provide information. A response to a positive confirmation request ordinarily is expected to provide reliable audit evidence. There is a risk, however, that a confirming party may reply to the confirmation request without verifying that the information is correct. The auditor may reduce this risk by using positive confirmation requests that do not state the amount (or other information) on the confirmation request, and ask the confirming party to fill in the amount or furnish other information. On the other hand, use of this type of "blank" confirmation request may result in lower response rates because additional effort is required of the confirming parties.

A6. Determining that requests are properly addressed includes testing the validity of some or all of the addresses on confirmation requests before they are sent out.

Follow-Up on Confirmation Requests (Ref: Para. 7(d))

A7. The auditor may send an additional confirmation request when a reply to a previous request has not been received within a reasonable time. For example, the auditor may, having re-verified the accuracy of the original address, send an additional or follow-up request.

Management's Refusal to Allow the Auditor to Send a Confirmation Request

Reasonableness of Management's Refusal (Ref: Para. 8(a))

A8. A refusal by management to allow the auditor to send a confirmation request is a limitation on the audit evidence the auditor may wish to obtain. The auditor is therefore required to enquire as to the reasons for the limitation. A common reason advanced is the existence of a legal dispute or ongoing negotiation with the intended confirming party, the resolution of which may be affected by an untimely confirmation request. The auditor is required to seek audit evidence as to the validity and reasonableness of the reasons because of the risk that management may be attempting to deny the auditor access to audit evidence that may reveal fraud or error.

Implications for the Assessment of Risks of Material Misstatement (Ref: Para. 8(b))

A9. The auditor may conclude from the evaluation in paragraph 8(b) that it would be appropriate to revise the assessment of the risks of material misstatement at the assertion level and modify planned audit procedures in accordance with ASA 315.[14] For example, if management's request to not confirm is unreasonable, this may indicate a fraud risk factor that requires evaluation in accordance with ASA 240.[15]

Alternative Audit Procedures (Ref: Para. 8(c))

A10. The alternative audit procedures performed may be similar to those appropriate for a non-response as set out in paragraphs A18-A19 of this Auditing Standard. Such procedures also would take account of the results of the auditor's evaluation in paragraph 8(b) of this Auditing Standard.

Results of the External Confirmation Procedures

Reliability of Responses to Confirmation Requests (Ref: Para. 10)

A11. ASA 500 indicates that even when audit evidence is obtained from sources external to the entity, circumstances may exist that affect its reliability.[16] All responses carry some risk of interception, alteration or fraud. Such risk exists regardless of whether a response is obtained in paper form, or by electronic or other medium. Factors that may indicate doubts about the reliability of a response include that it:

- Was received by the auditor indirectly; or
- Appeared not to come from the originally intended confirming party.

A12. Responses received electronically, for example by facsimile or electronic mail, involve risks as to reliability because proof of origin and authority of the respondent may be difficult to establish, and alterations may be difficult to detect. A process used by the auditor and the respondent that creates a secure environment for responses received electronically may mitigate these risks. If the auditor is satisfied that such a process is secure and properly controlled, the reliability of the related responses is enhanced. An electronic confirmation process might incorporate various techniques for validating the identity of a sender of information in electronic form, for example, through the use of encryption, electronic digital signatures, and procedures to verify web site authenticity.

A13. If a confirming party uses a third party to coordinate and provide responses to confirmation requests, the auditor may perform procedures to address the risks that:

(a) The response may not be from the proper source;

(b) A respondent may not be authorised to respond; and

(c) The integrity of the transmission may have been compromised.

A14. The auditor is required by ASA 500 to determine whether to modify or add procedures to resolve doubts over the reliability of information to be used as audit evidence.[17] The auditor may choose to verify the source and contents of a response to a confirmation request by contacting the confirming party. For example, when a confirming party responds by electronic mail, the auditor may telephone the confirming party to determine whether the confirming party did, in fact, send the response. When a response has been returned to the auditor indirectly (for example, because the confirming party incorrectly addressed it to the entity rather than to the auditor), the auditor may request the confirming party to respond in writing directly to the auditor.

A15. On its own, an oral response to a confirmation request does not meet the definition of an external confirmation because it is not a direct written response to the auditor.

---

14 See ASA 315 *Identifying and Assessing the Risks of Material Misstatement through Understanding the Entity and Its Environment*, paragraph 31.

15 See ASA 240, paragraph 24.

16 See ASA 500, paragraph A31.

17 See ASA 500, paragraph 11.

However, upon obtaining an oral response to a confirmation request, the auditor may, depending on the circumstances, request the confirming party to respond in writing directly to the auditor. If no such response is received, in accordance with paragraph 12, the auditor seeks other audit evidence to support the information in the oral response.

A16. A response to a confirmation request may contain restrictive language regarding its use. Such restrictions do not necessarily invalidate the reliability of the response as audit evidence.

Unreliable Responses (Ref: Para. 11)

A17. When the auditor concludes that a response is unreliable, the auditor may need to revise the assessment of the risks of material misstatement at the assertion level and modify planned audit procedures accordingly, in accordance with ASA 315.[18] For example, an unreliable response may indicate a fraud risk factor that requires evaluation in accordance with ASA 240.[19]

Non-Responses (Ref: Para. 12)

A18. Examples of alternative audit procedures the auditor may perform include:

- For accounts receivable balances – examining specific subsequent cash receipts, shipping documentation, and sales near the period-end.
- For accounts payable balances – examining subsequent cash disbursements or correspondence from third parties, and other records, such as goods received notes.

A19. The nature and extent of alternative audit procedures are affected by the account and assertion in question. A non-response to a confirmation request may indicate a previously unidentified risk of material misstatement. In such situations, the auditor may need to revise the assessed risk of material misstatement at the assertion level, and modify planned audit procedures, in accordance with ASA 315.[20] For example, fewer responses to confirmation requests than anticipated, or a greater number of responses than anticipated, may indicate a previously unidentified fraud risk factor that requires evaluation in accordance with ASA 240.[21]

When a Response to a Positive Confirmation Request Is Necessary to Obtain Sufficient Appropriate Audit Evidence (Ref: Para. 13)

A20. In certain circumstances, the auditor may identify an assessed risk of material misstatement at the assertion level for which a response to a positive confirmation request is necessary to obtain sufficient appropriate audit evidence. Such circumstances may include where:

- The information available to corroborate management's assertion(s) is only available outside the entity.
- Specific fraud risk factors, such as the risk of management override of controls, or the risk of collusion which can involve employee(s) and/or management, prevent the auditor from relying on evidence from the entity.

Exceptions (Ref: Para. 14)

A21. Exceptions noted in responses to confirmation requests may indicate misstatements or potential misstatements in the financial statements. When a misstatement is identified, the auditor is required by ASA 240 to evaluate whether such misstatement is indicative of fraud.[22] Exceptions may provide a guide to the quality of responses from similar confirming parties or for similar accounts. Exceptions also may indicate a deficiency, or deficiencies, in the entity's internal control over financial reporting.

A22. Some exceptions do not represent misstatements. For example, the auditor may conclude that differences in responses to confirmation requests are due to timing, measurement, or clerical errors in the external confirmation procedures.

---

18 See ASA 315, paragraph 31.

19 See ASA 240, paragraph 24.

20 See ASA 315, paragraph 31.

21 See ASA 240, paragraph 24.

22 See ASA 240, paragraph 35.

Negative Confirmations (Ref: Para. 15)

A23. The failure to receive a response to a negative confirmation request does not explicitly indicate receipt by the intended confirming party of the confirmation request or verification of the accuracy of the information contained in the request. Accordingly, a failure of a confirming party to respond to a negative confirmation request provides significantly less persuasive audit evidence than does a response to a positive confirmation request. Confirming parties also may be more likely to respond indicating their disagreement with a confirmation request when the information in the request is not in their favour, and less likely to respond otherwise. For example, holders of bank deposit accounts may be more likely to respond if they believe that the balance in their account is understated in the confirmation request, but may be less likely to respond when they believe the balance is overstated. Therefore, sending negative confirmation requests to holders of bank deposit accounts may be a useful procedure in considering whether such balances may be understated, but is unlikely to be effective if the auditor is seeking evidence regarding overstatement.

Evaluating the Evidence Obtained (Ref: Para. 16)

A24. When evaluating the results of individual external confirmation requests, the auditor may categorise such results as follows:

(a) A response by the appropriate confirming party indicating agreement with the information provided in the confirmation request, or providing requested information without exception;

(b) A response deemed unreliable;

(c) A non-response; or

(d) A response indicating an exception.

A25. The auditor's evaluation, when taken into account with other audit procedures the auditor may have performed, may assist the auditor in concluding whether sufficient appropriate audit evidence has been obtained or whether further audit evidence is necessary, as required by ASA 330.[23]

❖❖❖

Conformity with International Standards on Auditing

This Auditing Standard conforms with International Standard on Auditing ISA 505 *External Confirmations*, issued by the International Auditing and Assurance Standards Board (IAASB), an independent standard-setting board of the International Federation of Accountants (IFAC).

Paragraphs that have been added to this Auditing Standard (and do not appear in the text of the equivalent ISA) are identified with the prefix "Aus".

Compliance with this Auditing Standard enables compliance with ISA 505.

23 See ASA 330, paragraphs 26-27.

ASA 510

Initial Audit Engagements—Opening Balances

(Reissued October 2009)

Issued by the Auditing and Assurance Standards Board.

Note from the Institute of Chartered Accountants Australia

This note, prepared by the technical editor, is not part of ASA 510.

Historical development

July 1990: Statement of Auditing Practice AUP 29 'First Year Audit Consideration Opening Balance' issued following the issue of IAG 28 in July 1990, which in turn was based on IPAC ED 30 (October 1988). Apparently the AuSB did not consider it appropriate to issue an exposure draft on this topic. However, copies of IAPC ED 30 were distributed to subscribers to IASC International Accounting Standards IAPC Guidelines Handbook.

May 1994: ED 55 'Codification and Revision of Auditing Pronouncements: AUS 512 Initial Engagements–Opening Balances (AUP 29)' issued by the AuSB.

June 1994: The International Auditing Practices Committee (IAPC) of the International Federation of Accountants (IFAC) approved the issuance of a codified set of International Standards of Auditing (ISAs). The relevant international pronouncement is ISA 510 'Initial Engagements — Opening Balances'.

October 1995: Australian Auditing Standards and Auditing Guidance Statements released. The status of these was explained in APS 1.1 'Conformity With Auditing Standards'. These Standards became operative for the first reporting period commencing on or after 1 July 1996 and later reporting periods, although earlier application was encouraged. AUP 29 'First Year Audit Considerations — Opening Balances' replaced by AUS 510 'Initial Engagements — Opening Balances'.

April 1998: AUS/AGS Omnibus 1 'Miscellaneous Amendments to AUSs and AGSs' issued. The changes to AUS 510 embodied in Omnibus 1 were incorporated in this version of AUS 510.

July 2002: AUS/AGS Omnibus 3 'Miscellaneous Amendments to AUSs and AGSs' issued by the AuASB, operative from date of issue. AUS 510 now reissued by the Board to incorporate these amendments.

April 2006: ASA 510 was issued as a legally enforceable Standard to replace AUS 510. It is based on ISA 510 of the same name.

June 2007: ASA 510 compiled and republished to reflect the changes to the Audit Report in ASA 700 introduced by Omnibus ASA 2007-1.

October 2009: ASA 510 reissued as part of the AUASB's Clarity Project. It now contains an explicit requirement to read the most recent financial report and audit report to look for information relating to opening balances, including disclosures. It is based on the revised ISA 510 of the same name.

May 2012: 'Explanatory Guide: Opening Balances' issued by the AUASB to explain how to apply ASA 510 in the context of the Corporations Act requirement in Section 307 to express an opinion on the financial report as a whole.

Contents

Preface

Reasons for Issuing Auditing Standard ASA 510 *Initial Audit Engagements—Opening Balances*

The Auditing and Assurance Standards Board (AUASB) issues Auditing Standard ASA 510 *Initial Audit Engagements—Opening Balances* pursuant to the requirements of the legislative provisions and the Strategic Direction explained below.

The AUASB is an independent statutory board of the Australian Government established under section 227A of the *Australian Securities and Investments Commission Act 2001*, as amended (ASIC Act). Under section 336 of the *Corporations Act 2001*, the AUASB may make Australian Auditing Standards for the purposes of the corporations legislation. These Auditing Standards are legislative instruments under the *Legislative Instruments Act 2003*.

Under the Strategic Direction given to the AUASB by the Financial Reporting Council (FRC), the AUASB is required to have regard to any programme initiated by the International Auditing and Assurance Standards Board (IAASB) for the revision and enhancement of the International Standards on Auditing (ISAs) and to make appropriate consequential amendments to the Australian Auditing Standards. Accordingly, the AUASB has decided to revise and redraft the Australian Auditing Standards using the equivalent redrafted ISAs.

Main Features

This Auditing Standard establishes requirements and provides application and other explanatory material regarding the auditor's responsibilities relating to opening balances in an initial audit engagement.

This Auditing Standard:

(a) establishes requirements and provides guidance regarding opening balances when the financial report for the prior period was not audited, or the financial report for the prior period was audited by a predecessor auditor;

(b) provides audit procedures for the auditor to obtain audit evidence about:
- whether the opening balances contain misstatements;
- whether the accounting policies reflected in the opening balances have been consistently applied in the current period's financial report; and
- whether changes in the accounting policies have been properly accounted for and adequately presented and disclosed; and

(c) establishes requirements and provides guidance on audit conclusions and the auditor's report.

Authority Statement

The Auditing and Assurance Standards Board (AUASB) makes this Auditing Standard ASA 510 *Initial Audit Engagements—Opening Balances* pursuant to section 227B of the *Australian Securities and Investments Commission Act 2001* and section 336 of the *Corporations Act 2001*.

This Auditing Standard is to be read in conjunction with ASA 101 *Preamble to Australian Auditing Standards*, which sets out the intentions of the AUASB on how the Australian Auditing Standards, operative for financial reporting periods commencing on or after 1 January 2010, are to be understood, interpreted and applied. This Auditing Standard is to be read also in conjunction with ASA 200 *Overall Objectives of the Independent Auditor and the Conduct of an Audit in Accordance with Australian Auditing Standards*.

Dated: 27 October 2009

M H Kelsall
Chairman - AUASB

ASA

Auditing Standard ASA 510

Initial Audit Engagements—Opening Balances

Application

Aus 0.1 This Auditing Standard applies to:

(a) an audit of a financial report for a financial year, or an audit of a financial report for a half-year, in accordance with the *Corporations Act 2001*; and

(b) an audit of a financial report, or a complete set of financial statements, for any other purpose.

Aus 0.2 This Auditing Standard also applies, as appropriate, to an audit of other historical financial information.

Operative Date

Aus 0.3 This Auditing Standard is operative for financial reporting periods commencing on or after 1 January 2010.

Introduction

Scope of this Auditing Standard

1. This Auditing Standard deals with the auditor's responsibilities relating to opening balances in an initial audit engagement. In addition to financial statement amounts, opening balances include matters requiring disclosure that existed at the beginning of the period, such as contingencies and commitments. When the financial report includes comparative financial information, the requirements and guidance in ASA 710[1] also apply. ASA 300[2] includes additional requirements and guidance regarding activities prior to starting an initial audit.

Effective Date

2. [Deleted by the AUASB. Refer Aus 0.3]

1 See ASA 710 *Comparative Information—Corresponding Figures and Comparative Financial Reports*.

2 See ASA 300 *Planning an Audit of a Financial Report*.

Objective

3. In conducting an initial audit engagement, the objective of the auditor is to obtain sufficient appropriate audit evidence about whether:
   (a) Opening balances contain misstatements that materially affect the current period's financial report; and
   (b) Appropriate accounting policies reflected in the opening balances have been consistently applied in the current period's financial report, or changes thereto are appropriately accounted for and adequately presented and disclosed in accordance with the applicable financial reporting framework.

Definitions

4. For purposes of the Australian Auditing Standards, the following terms have the meanings attributed below:
   (a) Initial audit engagement means an engagement in which either:
      (i) The financial report for the prior period was not audited; or
      (ii) The financial report for the prior period was audited by a predecessor auditor.
   (b) Opening balances means those account balances that exist at the beginning of the period. Opening balances are based upon the closing balances of the prior period and reflect the effects of transactions and events of prior periods and accounting policies applied in the prior period. Opening balances also include matters requiring disclosure that existed at the beginning of the period, such as contingencies and commitments.
   (c) Predecessor auditor means the auditor from a different audit firm, who audited the financial report of an entity in the prior period and who has been replaced by the current auditor.

Requirements

Audit Procedures

Opening Balances

5. The auditor shall read the most recent financial report, if any, and the predecessor auditor's report thereon, if any, for information relevant to opening balances, including disclosures.
6. The auditor shall obtain sufficient appropriate audit evidence about whether the opening balances contain misstatements that materially affect the current period's financial report by: (Ref: Para. A1-A2)
   (a) Determining whether the prior period's closing balances have been correctly brought forward to the current period or, when appropriate, have been restated;
   (b) Determining whether the opening balances reflect the application of appropriate accounting policies; and
   (c) Performing one or more of the following: (Ref: Para. A3-A7)
      (i) Where the prior year financial report was audited, reviewing the predecessor auditor's working papers to obtain evidence regarding the opening balances;
      (ii) Evaluating whether audit procedures performed in the current period provide evidence relevant to the opening balances; or
      (iii) Performing specific audit procedures to obtain evidence regarding the opening balances.
7. If the auditor obtains audit evidence that the opening balances contain misstatements that could materially affect the current period's financial report, the auditor shall perform such additional audit procedures as are appropriate in the circumstances to determine the effect on the current period's financial report. If the auditor concludes that such misstatements exist in the current period's financial report, the auditor shall communicate

the misstatements with the appropriate level of management and those charged with governance in accordance with ASA 450.[3]

Consistency of Accounting Policies

8. The auditor shall obtain sufficient appropriate audit evidence about whether the accounting policies reflected in the opening balances have been consistently applied in the current period's financial report, and whether changes in the accounting policies have been appropriately accounted for and adequately presented and disclosed in accordance with the applicable financial reporting framework.

Relevant Information in the Predecessor Auditor's Report

9. If the prior period's financial report was audited by a predecessor auditor and there was a modification to the opinion, the auditor shall evaluate the effect of the matter giving rise to the modification in assessing the risks of material misstatement in the current period's financial report in accordance with ASA 315.[4]

Audit Conclusions and Reporting

Opening Balances

10. If the auditor is unable to obtain sufficient appropriate audit evidence regarding the opening balances, the auditor shall express a qualified opinion or disclaim an opinion on the financial report, as appropriate, in accordance with ASA 705.[5] (Ref: Para. A8)

11. If the auditor concludes that the opening balances contain a misstatement that materially affects the current period's financial report, and the effect of the misstatement is not appropriately accounted for or not adequately presented or disclosed, the auditor shall express a qualified opinion or an adverse opinion, as appropriate, in accordance with ASA 705.

Consistency of Accounting Policies

12. If the auditor concludes that:

    (a) the current period's accounting policies are not consistently applied in relation to opening balances in accordance with the applicable financial reporting framework; or

    (b) a change in accounting policies is not appropriately accounted for or not adequately presented or disclosed in accordance with the applicable financial reporting framework,

    the auditor shall express a qualified opinion or an adverse opinion as appropriate in accordance with ASA 705.

Modification to the Opinion in the Predecessor Auditor's Report

13. If the predecessor auditor's opinion regarding the prior period's financial report included a modification to the auditor's opinion that remains relevant and material to the current period's financial report, the auditor shall modify the auditor's opinion on the current period's financial report in accordance with ASA 705 and ASA 710. (Ref: Para. A9)

❖ ❖ ❖

Application and Other Explanatory Material

Audit Procedures

Considerations Specific to Public Sector Entities (Ref: Para. 6)

A1. In the public sector, there may be legal or regulatory limitations on the information that the current auditor can obtain from a predecessor auditor. For example, if a public sector entity that has previously been audited by a statutorily appointed auditor (for example, an Auditor-General, or other suitably qualified person appointed on behalf of the Auditor-

3 See ASA 450 *Evaluation of Misstatements Identified during the Audit*, paragraphs 8 and 12.

4 See ASA 315 *Identifying and Assessing the Risks of Material Misstatement through Understanding the Entity and Its Environment*.

5 See ASA 705 *Modifications to the Opinion in the Independent Auditor's Report*.

General) is privatised, the amount of access to working papers or other information that the statutorily appointed auditor can provide a newly appointed auditor that is in the private sector may be constrained by privacy laws or regulations. In situations where such communications are constrained, audit evidence may need to be obtained through other means and, if sufficient appropriate audit evidence cannot be obtained, consideration given to the effect on the auditor's opinion.

A2. If the statutorily appointed auditor outsources an audit of a public sector entity to a private sector audit firm, and the statutorily appointed auditor appoints an audit firm other than the firm that audited the financial report of the public sector entity in the prior period, this is not usually regarded as a change in auditors for the statutorily appointed auditor. Depending on the nature of the outsourcing arrangement, however, the audit engagement may be considered an initial audit engagement from the perspective of the private sector auditor in fulfilling their responsibilities, and therefore this Auditing Standard applies.

Opening Balances (Ref: Para. 6(c))

A3. The nature and extent of audit procedures necessary to obtain sufficient appropriate audit evidence regarding opening balances depend on such matters as:

- The accounting policies followed by the entity.
- The nature of the account balances, classes of transactions and disclosures and the risks of material misstatement in the current period's financial report.
- The significance of the opening balances relative to the current period's financial report.
- Whether the prior period's financial report was audited and, if so, whether the predecessor auditor's opinion was modified.

A4. If the prior period's financial report was audited by a predecessor auditor, the auditor may be able to obtain sufficient appropriate audit evidence regarding the opening balances by reviewing the predecessor auditor's working papers. Whether such a review provides sufficient appropriate audit evidence is influenced by the professional competence and independence of the predecessor auditor.

A5. Relevant ethical and professional requirements* guide the current auditor's communications with the predecessor auditor.

A6. For current assets and liabilities, some audit evidence about opening balances may be obtained as part of the current period's audit procedures. For example, the collection (payment) of opening accounts receivable (accounts payable) during the current period will provide some audit evidence of their existence, rights and obligations, completeness and valuation at the beginning of the period. In the case of inventories, however, the current period's audit procedures on the closing inventory balance provide little audit evidence regarding inventory on hand at the beginning of the period. Therefore, additional audit procedures may be necessary, and one or more of the following may provide sufficient appropriate audit evidence:

- Observing a current physical inventory count and reconciling it to the opening inventory quantities.
- Performing audit procedures on the valuation of the opening inventory items.
- Performing audit procedures on gross profit and cut-off.

A7. For non-current assets and liabilities, such as property, plant and equipment, investments and long-term debt, some audit evidence may be obtained by examining the accounting records and other information underlying the opening balances. In certain cases, the auditor may be able to obtain some audit evidence regarding opening balances through confirmation with third parties, for example, for long-term debt and investments. In other cases, the auditor may need to carry out additional audit procedures.

* See ASA 102 *Compliance with Ethical Requirements when Performing Audits, Reviews and Other Assurance Engagements.*

Audit Conclusions and Reporting

Opening Balances (Ref: Para. 10)

A8. ASA 705 establishes requirements and provides guidance on circumstances that may result in a modification to the auditor's opinion on the financial report, the type of opinion appropriate in the circumstances, and the content of the auditor's report when the auditor's opinion is modified. The inability of the auditor to obtain sufficient appropriate audit evidence regarding opening balances may result in the following modifications to the opinion in the auditor's report:

(a) A qualified opinion or a disclaimer of opinion, as is appropriate in the circumstances.

(b) [Deleted by the AUASB. Refer Illustration 2]

Appendix 1 includes illustrative auditors' reports.

Modification to the Opinion in the Predecessor Auditor's Report (Ref: Para. 13)

A9. In some situations, a modification to the predecessor auditor's opinion may not be relevant and material to the opinion on the current period's financial report. This may be the case where, for example, there was a scope limitation in the prior period, but the matter giving rise to the scope limitation has been resolved in the current period.

❖ ❖ ❖

Conformity with International Standards on Auditing

This Auditing Standard conforms with International Standard on Auditing ISA 510 *Initial Audit Engagements—Opening Balances*, issued by the International Auditing and Assurance Standards Board (IAASB), an independent standard-setting board of the International Federation of Accountants (IFAC).

Paragraphs that have been added to this Auditing Standard (and do not appear in the text of the equivalent ISA) are identified with the prefix "Aus".

Compliance with this Auditing Standard enables compliance with ISA 510.

Appendix 1

(Ref: Para. A8)

Illustrations of Auditors' Reports with Modified Opinions

- Illustration 1: An auditor's report containing a qualified opinion due to the inability of the auditor to obtain sufficient appropriate audit evidence regarding opening balances—the financial report is not prepared under the *Corporations Act 2001*.
- Illustration 2: [Example Auditor's Report deleted by the AUASB—not applicable in Australia.]
- [Aus] Illustration 2A: An auditor's report containing a qualified opinion due to the inability of the auditor to obtain sufficient appropriate audit evidence regarding opening balances—the financial report is prepared under the *Corporations Act 2001*.

Example Auditor's Report
Qualified Opinion—Jurisdiction Prohibits a Qualified Opinion on Performance and Cash Flows and an Unmodified Opinion on Financial Position

Illustration 1:

Circumstances described in paragraph A8(a) include the following:

- **The auditor did not observe the counting of the physical inventory at the beginning of the current period and was unable to obtain sufficient appropriate audit evidence regarding the opening balances of inventory.**
- **The possible effects of the inability to obtain sufficient appropriate audit evidence regarding opening balances of inventory are deemed to be material but not pervasive to the entity's financial performance and cash flows.[6]**
- **The financial position at year end is fairly presented.**
- **In this jurisdiction, law and regulation prohibit the auditor from giving an opinion which is qualified regarding the financial performance and cash flows and unmodified regarding financial position.**
- **The financial report is not prepared under the *Corporations Act 2001*.**

INDEPENDENT AUDITOR'S REPORT

[Appropriate Addressee]

Report on the Financial Report[7]

We have audited the accompanying financial report of ABC Entity, which comprises the statement of financial position as at 30 June 20X1, the statement of comprehensive income, statement of changes in equity and statement of cash flows for the year then ended, notes comprising a summary of significant accounting policies and other explanatory information, and management's assertion statement.*

Management's[8] Responsibility for the Financial Report

Management is responsible for the preparation and fair presentation[9] of the financial report in accordance with Australian Accounting Standards, and for such internal control as management determines is necessary to enable the preparation of the financial report that is free from material misstatement, whether due to fraud or error.

Auditor's Responsibility

Our responsibility is to express an opinion on the financial report based on our audit. We conducted our audit in accordance with Australian Auditing Standards. Those standards require that we comply with relevant ethical requirements relating to audit engagements and plan and perform the audit to obtain reasonable assurance about whether the financial report is free from material misstatement.

An audit involves performing procedures to obtain audit evidence about the amounts and disclosures in the financial report. The procedures selected depend on the auditor's judgement, including the assessment of the risks of material misstatement of the financial report, whether due to fraud or error. In making those risk assessments, the auditor considers internal control

6 [Footnote deleted by the AUASB—not applicable in Australia.]

7 The sub-title "Report on the Financial Report" is unnecessary in circumstances when the second sub-title "Report on Other Legal and Regulatory Requirements" is not applicable.

* Or other appropriate term.

8 Or other term that is appropriate in the context of the legal framework in the particular jurisdiction.

9 Where management's responsibility is to prepare a financial report that give a true and fair view, this may read: "Management is responsible for the preparation of the financial report that gives a true and fair view in accordance with Australian Accounting Standards, and for such ..."

relevant to the entity's preparation and fair presentation[10] of the financial report in order to design audit procedures that are appropriate in the circumstances, but not for the purpose of expressing an opinion on the effectiveness of the entity's internal control.[11] An audit also includes evaluating the appropriateness of accounting policies used and the reasonableness of accounting estimates made by management, as well as evaluating the overall presentation of the financial report.

We believe that the audit evidence we have obtained is sufficient and appropriate to provide a basis for our qualified audit opinion.

Basis for Qualified Opinion

We were appointed as auditors of the entity on 31 December 20X0 and thus did not observe the counting of the physical inventories at the beginning of the year. We were unable to satisfy ourselves by alternative means concerning inventory quantities held at 30 June 20X0. Since opening inventories enter into the determination of the financial performance and cash flows, we were unable to determine whether adjustments might have been necessary in respect of the income for the year reported in the statement of comprehensive income and the net cash flows from operating activities reported in the statement of cash flows.

Qualified Opinion

In our opinion, except for the possible effects of the matter described in the Basis for Qualified Opinion paragraph, the financial report presents fairly, in all material respects, (or *gives a true and fair view of*) the financial position of ABC Entity as at 30 June 20X1 and (*of*) its financial performance and its cash flows for the year then ended in accordance with Australian Accounting Standards.

Other Matter

The financial report of ABC Entity for the year ended 30 June 20X0 was audited by another auditor who expressed an unmodified opinion on the financial report on 30 September 20X0.

Report on Other Legal and Regulatory Requirements

[Form and content of this section of the auditor's report will vary depending on the nature of the auditor's other reporting responsibilities.]

[Auditor's signature]*

[Date of the auditor's report]#

[Auditor's address]

10 In the case of footnote 9, this may read: "In making those risk assessments, the auditor considers internal control relevant to the entity's preparation of the financial report that gives a true and fair view in order to design audit procedures that are appropriate in the circumstances, but not for the purpose of expressing an opinion on the effectiveness of the entity's internal control."

11 In circumstances when the auditor also has responsibility to express an opinion on the effectiveness of internal control in conjunction with the audit of the financial report, this sentence would be worded as follows: "In making those risk assessments, the auditor considers internal control relevant to the entity's preparation and fair presentation of the financial report in order to design audit procedures that are appropriate in the circumstances." In the case of footnote 9, this may read: "In making those risk assessments, the auditor considers internal control relevant to the entity's preparation of the financial report that gives a true and fair view in order to design audit procedures that are appropriate in the circumstances."

* The auditor's report needs to be signed in one or more of the following ways: name of the audit firm, the name of the audit company or the personal name of the auditor as appropriate.

\# The date of the auditor's report is the date the auditor signs the report.

Example Auditor's Report
An Opinion that is Qualified Regarding the Financial Performance and Cash Flows and Unmodified Regarding Financial Position

Illustration 2:

[Example Auditor's Report deleted by the AUASB—not applicable in Australia.

Refer ASA 200 *Overall Objectives of the Independent Auditor and the Conduct of an Audit in Accordance with Australian Auditing Standards*, paragraph 11(a).

The *Corporation Act 2001* does not provide for split opinions.][12-17]

Example Auditor's Report
Qualified Opinion—Jurisdiction Prohibits a Qualified Opinion on Performance and Cash Flows and an Unmodified Opinion on Financial Position—*Corporations Act 2001*

[Aus] Illustration 2A:

Circumstances described in paragraph A8(a) include the following:

- **The auditor did not observe the counting of the physical inventory at the beginning of the current period and was unable to obtain sufficient appropriate audit evidence regarding the opening balances of inventory.**
- **The possible effects of the inability to obtain sufficient appropriate audit evidence regarding opening balances of inventory are deemed to be material but not pervasive to the entity's financial performance and cash flows.**
- **The financial position at year end is fairly presented.**
- **In this jurisdiction, law and regulation prohibit the auditor from giving an opinion which is qualified regarding the financial performance and cash flows and unmodified regarding financial position.**
- **The financial report is prepared under the *Corporations Act 2001*.**

INDEPENDENT AUDITOR'S REPORT

[Appropriate Addressee]

Report on the Financial Report*

We have audited the accompanying financial report of ABC Company Ltd., which comprises the statement of financial position as at 30 June 20X1, the statement of comprehensive income, statement of changes in equity and statement of cash flows for the year then ended, notes comprising a summary of significant accounting policies and other explanatory information, and the directors' declaration.

Directors' Responsibility for the Financial Report

The directors of the company [registered scheme/disclosing entity] are responsible for the preparation of the financial report that gives a true and fair view in accordance with Australian Accounting Standards and the *Corporations Act 2001*, and for such internal control as the directors determine is necessary to enable the preparation of the financial report that is free from material misstatement, whether due to fraud or error.

12-17 [Footnotes deleted by the AUASB. Refer text box above.]

* The sub-title "Report on the Financial Report" is unnecessary in circumstances when the second sub-title "Report on Other Legal and Regulatory Requirements", or other appropriate sub-title, is not applicable.

Auditor's Responsibility

Our responsibility is to express an opinion on the financial report based on our audit. We conducted our audit in accordance with Australian Auditing Standards. Those standards require that we comply with relevant ethical requirements relating to audit engagements and plan and perform the audit to obtain reasonable assurance about whether the financial report is free from material misstatement.

An audit involves performing procedures to obtain audit evidence about the amounts and disclosures in the financial report. The procedures selected depend on the auditor's judgement, including the assessment of the risks of material misstatement of the financial report, whether due to fraud or error. In making those risk assessments, the auditor considers internal control relevant to the company's preparation of the financial report that gives a true and fair view in order to design audit procedures that are appropriate in the circumstances, but not for the purpose of expressing an opinion on the effectiveness of the company's internal control. An audit also includes evaluating the appropriateness of accounting policies used and the reasonableness of accounting estimates made by the directors, as well as evaluating the overall presentation of the financial report.

We believe that the audit evidence we have obtained is sufficient and appropriate to provide a basis for our qualified audit opinion.

Independence

In conducting our audit, we have complied with the independence requirements of the *Corporations Act 2001*. We confirm that the independence declaration required by the *Corporations Act 2001*, which has been given to the directors of ABC Company Ltd., would be in the same terms if given to the directors as at the time of this auditor's report.†

Basis for Qualified Opinion

We were appointed as auditors of the company on 31 December 20X0 and thus did not observe the counting of the physical inventories at the beginning of the year. We were unable to satisfy ourselves by alternative means concerning inventory quantities held at 30 June 20X0. Since opening inventories enter into the determination of the financial performance and cash flows, we were unable to determine whether adjustments might have been necessary in respect of the income for the year reported in the statement of comprehensive income and the net cash flows from operating activities reported in the statement of cash flows.

Qualified Opinion

In our opinion, except for the possible effects of the matter described in the Basis for Qualified Opinion paragraph, the financial report of ABC Company Ltd. is in accordance with the *Corporations Act 2001*, including:

(a) giving a true and fair view of the company's [registered scheme/disclosing entity]'s financial position as at 30 June 20X1 and of its performance for the year ended on that date; and

(b) complying with Australian Accounting Standards and the *Corporations Regulations 2001*.

Other Matter

The financial report of ABC Company Ltd. for the year ended 30 June 20X0 was audited by another auditor who expressed an unmodified opinion on the financial report on 30 September 20X0.

† Or, alternatively, include statements (a) to the effect that circumstances have changed since the declaration was given to the relevant directors; and (b) setting out how the declaration would differ if it had been given to the relevant directors at the time the auditor's report was made.

Report on the Remuneration Report*

We have audited the Remuneration Report included in [paragraphs a to b or pages x to y] of the directors' report for the [period] ended 30 June 20X1. The directors of the company are responsible for the preparation and presentation of the Remuneration Report in accordance with section 300A of the *Corporations Act 2001*. Our responsibility is to express an opinion on the Remuneration Report, based on our audit conducted in accordance with Australian Auditing Standards.

Opinion

In our opinion the Remuneration Report of ABC Company Ltd. for the year [period] ended 30 June 20X1, complies with section 300A of the *Corporations Act 2001*.

[Auditor's signature]#

[Date of the auditor's report] †

[Auditor's address]

---

* The Report on the Remuneration Report is an example of "other reporting responsibilities". Any additional "other reporting responsibilities" that the auditor needs to address, will also be included in a separate section of the auditor's report following the opinion paragraph on the financial report. Under paragraph 38 of ASA 700, the sub-title "Report on Other Legal and Regulatory Requirements" or other sub-title as appropriate to the section, is used.

\# The auditor's report needs to be signed in one or more of the following ways: name of the audit firm, the name of the audit company or the personal name of the auditor as appropriate.

† The date of the auditor's report is the date the auditor signs the report.

Explanatory Guide: Opening Balances

(Issued May 2012)

Issued by the Auditing and Assurance Standards Board.

Note from the Institute of Chartered Accountants Australia

This note, prepared by the technical editor, is not part of the Explanatory Guide.

Historical development

May 2012: The 'Explanatory Guide: Opening Balances' was issued to support ASA 510 'Initial Audit Engagements – Opening Balances'. It gives guidance on the application of ASA 510 in the first and second periods of a new audit.

ASA

This Explanatory Guide *Opening Balances* is issued by the Auditing and Assurance Standards Board (AUASB).

This Explanatory Guide:

1. is not an AUASB *Guidance Statement* that provides guidance to assist auditors and assurance practitioners to fulfil the objectives of the audit or assurance engagement; and
2. does not itself establish or extend requirements for the performance of audit, review, or other assurance engagements under the AUASB Standards.

Contents

Explanatory Guide

Opening Balances

Purpose

1. The purpose of this Explanatory Guide is to provide information to auditors who are required under Australian Auditing Standards to modify their audit opinions in relation to opening balances in an initial audit engagement.
2. Auditors reporting other than under Australian Auditing Standards should clarify their reporting responsibilities. For example, an overseas jurisdiction may specifically require a separate audit opinion on each element of a financial report rather than the financial report taken as a whole as commented on in paragraph 5 below.

Introduction

3. The information in this explanatory guide relates primarily to reporting under ASA 510 *Initial Audit Engagements – Opening Balances* and ASA 705 *Modifications to the Opinion in the Independent Auditor's Report*. Where applicable, reference is also made to ASA 710 *Comparative Information – Corresponding Figures and Comparative Financial Reports*.
4. In performing an initial audit engagement, it is not uncommon for the auditor to be faced with difficulties in obtaining sufficient appropriate audit evidence in relation to opening balances. Such difficulties may be due to the following circumstances:
   (a) The auditor was appointed after the commencement of the current financial reporting period and accordingly was unable to attend the physical counting and inspection of inventory or other assets.

   (b) The prior financial reporting period was not audited.

(c) The prior financial reporting period was audited and the predecessor auditor:
   (i) qualified the opinion; or
   (ii) issued an adverse opinion; or
   (iii) disclaimed an opinion.

(d) The predecessor auditor does not, or cannot, provide access to the audit working papers for the previous reporting period.

(e) The auditor cannot obtain sufficient appropriate audit evidence through:
   (i) audit procedures performed in the current year; or
   (ii) specific procedures designed to obtain audit evidence regarding opening balances.

5. Under the Auditing Standards,[1] the overall objectives of the auditor include obtaining reasonable assurance about whether the financial report *as a whole* is free from material misstatement. Accordingly, where the auditor is faced with any of the circumstances listed in paragraph 4 above, the auditor is required to determine the effect that the issue has on the financial report *as a whole*. The auditor then expresses an opinion on the financial report *as a whole*. The auditor cannot express separate opinions on each element of the financial report.

6. It is important to emphasise that:

(a) The current period audit engagement is to form, and express, an opinion on:
   (i) the financial performance for the current reporting period; and
   (ii) the financial position at the end of the current reporting period.

(b) The fundamental audit requirements are prescribed under ASA 510, paragraph 6:

The auditor shall obtain sufficient appropriate audit evidence about whether the opening balances contain misstatements that materially affect the current period's financial report by:
   (i) *Determining whether the prior period's closing balances have been correctly brought forward to the current period or, when appropriate, have been restated*;
   (ii) *Determining whether the opening balances reflect the application of appropriate accounting policies*; ***and*** (emphasis added)
   (iii) *Performing one or more of the following*:
   - *Where the prior year financial report was audited, reviewing the predecessor auditor's working papers to obtain evidence regarding the opening balances*;
   - *Evaluating whether audit procedures performed in the current period provide evidence relevant to the opening balances*; or
   - *Performing specific audit procedures to obtain evidence regarding the opening balances.*

(c) Under the *Corporations Act 2001*[2] an auditor is required to form and express an opinion on whether the financial report complies with Accounting Standards and presents a true and fair view.

(d) The inclusion of comparative figures in a financial report is required by the Accounting Standards.[3]

1 See ASA 200 *Overall Objectives of the Independent Auditor and the Conduct of an Audit in Accordance with Australian Auditing Standards.*

2 See sections 307 and 308.

3 See AASB 101 *Presentation of Financial Statements,* issued by the Australian Accounting Standards Board.

Audit Requirements

7. When the opening balances have not been previously audited or the previous auditor has issued a disclaimer of opinion, the auditor is still required to comply with ASA 510, paragraph 6. The supporting application and other explanatory material contained in the standard, especially from paragraphs A3 to A7, provide useful suggestions on the audit procedures that an auditor may undertake.

8. It is incumbent on the auditor to exercise professional judgement and to explore all reasonable avenues in obtaining sufficient appropriate audit evidence as to whether the opening balances contain misstatements that materially affect the current period's financial report.

9. It is important to remember that all relevant requirements in the Auditing Standards are also to be complied with in conducting the initial engagement. It is not appropriate for an auditor to by-pass the relevant requirements of the Auditing Standards and rely only on a modified opinion or disclaimer of opinion in relation to opening balances, as constituting compliance with the Auditing Standards.

Modifications to the Auditor's Opinion

10. When the auditor is unable to obtain sufficient appropriate audit evidence as required by ASA 510, paragraph 6, a qualified opinion or disclaimer of opinion in relation to the opening balances is required in accordance with ASA 705.[4]

11. If the auditor concludes that the opening balances contain a misstatement that materially affects the current period's financial report, and which has not been appropriately accounted for or presented or disclosed, the auditor shall express a qualified opinion or adverse opinion as appropriate, in accordance with ASA 705.[5]

12. The type of modification to the auditor's opinion under the Australian Auditing Standards (particularly ASA 705), is a direct result of the specific circumstances of the engagement and the audit evidence obtained by the auditor.

Examples

13. The appendices to this explanatory guide provide illustrative examples of audit reports relating to opening balances. The examples have been based on the standardised formats of modified auditor's reports prepared under the Act (see examples in ASA 705). For the sake of brevity, not all elements of the ASA 705 examples have been included, such as the auditor's opinion on IFRS.

14. Example auditor's reports that are modified in regard to opening balances, are set out in the appendices as shown in the following table:

Appendix 1	**Illustrations of Auditor's Reports with Qualified Opinions**
Example 1	Previous auditor issued an unmodified opinion
Example 2	Previous auditor issued a qualified opinion
Appendix 2	**Illustration of an Auditor's Report with Adverse Opinion**
Example 3	Previous auditor issued an adverse opinion
Appendix 3	**Illustrations of Auditor's Reports with a Disclaimer of Opinion**
Example 4	Previous auditor issued a disclaimer of opinion
Example 5	No previous audit (and opening balances not otherwise able to be audited)

Following each example report in the appendices, there is a brief commentary and description of the type of auditor's report that would ordinarily be issued in the subsequent reporting period (Period 2).

4 See ASA 510, paragraph 10.

5 See ASA 510, paragraph 11.

Appendix 1

Example 1: Qualified Opinion

[Previous auditor issued an unmodified opinion]

PERIOD 1: INITIAL ENGAGEMENT

Circumstances:

- Previous auditor issued an unmodified opinion.
- Auditor appointed *after* commencement of current reporting period.
- The auditor did not observe the counting of the physical inventory at the beginning of the current period and was unable to obtain sufficient appropriate audit evidence regarding the opening balances of inventory.
- The possible effects of the inability to obtain sufficient appropriate audit evidence regarding opening balances of inventory are deemed to be material but not pervasive to the entity's financial report.
- With the exception of the matter described above, the financial report presents fairly.
- The auditor decides to refer to the previous auditor's report in an Other Matter Paragraph (ASA 710, paragraph 13).
- The financial report is prepared under the *Corporations Act 2001*.

Audit Work Performed:

- Audit conducted in accordance with Auditing Standards. Opening balances audited in accordance with ASA 510. Sufficient appropriate audit evidence obtained with the exception of opening inventory quantities (see qualification).

ASA

INDEPENDENT AUDITOR'S REPORT

[Appropriate Addressee]

Report on the Financial Report

We have audited the accompanying financial report of ABC Company Ltd., which comprises the statement of financial position as at 30 June 20X1, the statement of comprehensive income, statement of changes in equity and statement of cash flows for the year then ended, notes comprising a summary of significant accounting policies and other explanatory information, and the directors' declaration.

Directors' Responsibility for the Financial Report

The directors of the company [registered scheme/disclosing entity] are responsible for the preparation of the financial report that gives a true and fair view in accordance with Australian Accounting Standards and the *Corporations Act 2001*, and for such internal control as the directors determine is necessary to enable the preparation of the financial report that gives a true and fair view and is free from material misstatement, whether due to fraud or error.

Auditor's Responsibility

Our responsibility is to express an opinion on the financial report based on our audit. We conducted our audit in accordance with Australian Auditing Standards. Those standards require that we comply with relevant ethical requirements relating to audit engagements and plan and perform the audit to obtain reasonable assurance about whether the financial report is free from material misstatement.

An audit involves performing procedures to obtain audit evidence about the amounts and disclosures in the financial report. The procedures selected depend on the auditor's judgement, including the assessment of the risks of material misstatement of the financial report, whether due to fraud or error. In making those risk assessments, the auditor considers internal control relevant to the company's preparation of the financial report that gives a true and fair view in order to design audit procedures that are appropriate in the circumstances, but not for the purpose of expressing an opinion on the effectiveness of the company's internal control. An audit also includes evaluating the appropriateness of accounting policies used and the reasonableness of accounting estimates made by the directors, as well as evaluating the overall presentation of the financial report.

We believe that the audit evidence we have obtained is sufficient and appropriate to provide a basis for our qualified audit opinion.

Independence

In conducting our audit, we have complied with the independence requirements of the *Corporations Act 2001*. We confirm that the independence declaration required by the *Corporations Act 2001*, which has been given to the directors of ABC Company Ltd., would be in the same terms if given to the directors as at the time of this auditor's report.

Basis for Qualified Opinion

We were appointed as auditors of the company on 31 December 20X0 and thus did not observe the counting of the physical inventories at the beginning of the year. We were unable to satisfy ourselves by alternative means concerning inventory quantities held at 30 June 20X0. Since opening inventories enter into the determination of the financial performance and cash flows, we were unable to determine whether adjustments might have been necessary in respect of the income for the year reported in the statement of comprehensive income and the net cash flows from operating activities reported in the statement of cash flows.

Qualified Opinion

In our opinion, except for the possible effects of the matter described in the Basis for Qualified Opinion paragraph, the financial report of ABC Company Ltd. is in accordance with the *Corporations Act 2001*, including:

(a) giving a true and fair view of the company's [registered scheme's/disclosing entity's] financial position as at 30 June 20X1 and of its performance for the year ended on that date; and

(b) complying with Australian Accounting Standards and the *Corporations Regulations 2001*.

Other Matter

The financial report of ABC Company Ltd. for the year ended 30 June 20X0 was audited by another auditor who expressed an unmodified opinion on that financial report on 30 September 20X0.

Report on the Remuneration Report

We have audited the Remuneration Report included in [paragraphs a to b or pages x to y] of the directors' report for the year ended 30 June 20X1. The directors of the company are responsible for the preparation and presentation of the Remuneration Report in accordance with section 300A of the *Corporations Act 2001*. Our responsibility is to express an opinion on the Remuneration Report, based on our audit conducted in accordance with Australian Auditing Standards.

Opinion

In our opinion the Remuneration Report of ABC Company Ltd. for the year ended 30 June 20X1, complies with section 300A of the *Corporations Act 2001*.

[Auditor's signature]

[Date of the auditor's report]

[Auditor's address]

PERIOD 2

Circumstances:

- The auditor did not observe the counting of the physical inventory at the beginning of the initial engagement [i.e. the *prior* period (Period 1)] and issued a qualified auditor's report. [See above]
- With this exception, the financial report for the initial engagement (Period 1) was fairly presented.
- No other matters required modification to the opinion.

Audit Work Performed:

- Audit of Period 2 conducted in accordance with Auditing Standards. Sufficient appropriate audit evidence obtained.
- Under ASA 510 and ASA 710, the auditor determines if comparatives include a misstatement that affects the current period. As the auditor attended the inventory count at the end of Period 1, the auditor concludes that the basis for qualification in Period 1 does not result in an unacceptable risk of material misstatement in Period 2.

Period 2 Auditor's Report:

- Unmodified opinion.
- There is no requirement for an Other Matter Paragraph in respect of the prior period audit report.

Example 2: Qualified Opinion

[Previous auditor issued an qualified opinion]

PERIOD 1: INITIAL ENGAGEMENT

Circumstances:

- Same as in Example 1, however, previous auditor issued a qualified opinion - qualification *not* related to inventory.

Audit Work Performed:

- Audit conducted in accordance with Auditing Standards. Opening balances audited in accordance with ASA 510.
- Auditor obtains sufficient appropriate evidence to determine the effect, if any, that the matter causing the previous auditor to qualify has on the Period 1 (initial engagement) financial report.

Auditor's Report:

- If the matter causing the previous auditor to qualify is *not* resolved and the auditor determines that the matter affects the Period 1 financial performance or position, the auditor must decide (in accordance with ASA 705) whether to:
  - repeat the qualification; or
  - issue an adverse opinion or a disclaimer of opinion, depending on the circumstances and taking into consideration the additional qualification arising from non-attendance at the physical count of inventories; or
- If the matter causing the previous auditor to qualify *is* resolved, the auditor qualifies only on non-attendance at the physical count of inventories (as per Example 1); and
- The auditor considers inclusion of an Emphasis of Matter Paragraph where the financial report contains disclosures of the resolution of the matter.

PERIOD 2

Audit Work Performed:

- Audit of Period 2 conducted in accordance with Auditing Standards. Sufficient appropriate audit evidence obtained.
- Under ASA 510 and ASA 710, the auditor determines if comparatives include a misstatement that affects the current period. As the auditor attended the inventory count at the e\nd of Period 1, the auditor concludes that the basis for qualification in Period 1 does not result in an unacceptable risk of material misstatement in Period 2.
- The auditor determines the status of the matter causing the previous auditor to qualify and which was *not* resolved in the initial engagement and resulted in a modification to the auditor's report in Period 1.

Period 2 Auditor's Report:

- Unmodified opinion; or
- Modified opinion under ASA 705 - dependent on the status of the unresolved matter(s) carried over from Period 1.

Appendix 2

Example 3: Adverse Opinion

[Previous auditor issued an adverse opinion]

PERIOD 1: INITIAL ENGAGEMENT

Circumstances:

- Previous auditor issued an adverse opinion due to a departure from Australian Accounting Standard requirements.
- The matter that caused the previous auditor to issue an adverse opinion remains unresolved.
- The auditor determines that the unresolved matter in the opening balances is a misstatement that materially affects the current period (Period 1) financial report.
- The auditor decides to refer to the previous auditor's report in an Other Matter Paragraph (ASA 710, paragraph 13).
- The financial report is prepared under the *Corporations Act 2001*.

Audit Work Performed:

- Audit conducted in accordance with Auditing Standards. Opening balances audited in accordance with ASA 510. Sufficient appropriate audit evidence obtained to support the auditor's expression of an adverse opinion.

INDEPENDENT AUDITOR'S REPORT

[Appropriate Addressee]

Report on the Financial Report

We have audited the accompanying financial report of ABC Company Ltd., which comprises the statements of financial position as at 30 June 20X1, the statements of comprehensive income, statements of changes in equity and the statements of cash flows for the year then ended, notes comprising a summary of significant accounting policies and other explanatory information, and the directors' declaration of the company [registered scheme/disclosing entity] and the consolidated entity comprising the company [registered scheme/disclosing entity]and the entities it controlled at the year's end or from time to time during the financial year.

Directors' Responsibility for the Financial Report

The directors of the company [registered scheme/disclosing entity] are responsible for the preparation of the financial report that gives a true and fair view in accordance with Australian Accounting Standards and the *Corporations Act 2001* and for such internal control as the directors determine is necessary to enable the preparation of the financial report that gives a true and fair view and is free from material misstatement, whether due to fraud or error.

Auditor's Responsibility

Our responsibility is to express an opinion on the financial report based on our audit. We conducted our audit in accordance with Australian Auditing Standards. Those standards require that we comply with relevant ethical requirements relating to audit engagements and plan and perform the audit to obtain reasonable assurance about whether the financial report is free from material misstatement.

An audit involves performing procedures to obtain audit evidence about the amounts and disclosures in the financial report. The procedures selected depend on the auditor's judgement, including the assessment of the risks of material misstatement of the financial report, whether due to fraud or error. In making those risk assessments, the auditor considers internal control relevant to the entity's preparation of the financial report that gives a true and fair view in order to design audit procedures that are appropriate in the circumstances, but not for the purpose of expressing an opinion on the effectiveness of the company's internal control. An audit also includes evaluating the appropriateness of accounting policies used and the reasonableness of accounting estimates made by the directors, as well as evaluating the overall presentation of the financial report.

We believe that the audit evidence we have obtained is sufficient and appropriate to provide a basis for our adverse audit opinion.

Independence

In conducting our audit, we have complied with the independence requirements of the *Corporations Act 2001*. We confirm that the independence declaration required by the *Corporations Act 2001*, which has been given to the directors of ABC Company Ltd., would be in the same terms if given to the directors as at the time of this auditor's report.

Basis for Adverse Opinion

As explained in Note X, the entity has not consolidated the financial statements of subsidiary XYZ Company it acquired during the previous financial year to 30 June 20X0, because it has not yet been able to ascertain the fair values of certain of the subsidiary's material assets and liabilities at the acquisition date. This investment is therefore accounted for on a cost basis. Under Australian Accounting Standards, the subsidiary should have been consolidated because it is controlled by the company. Had XYZ Company been consolidated, many elements in the accompanying financial report would have been materially affected. The effects on the financial report of the failure to consolidate have not been determined.

Adverse Opinion

In our opinion, because of the significance of the matter discussed in the Basis for Adverse Opinion paragraph, the financial report is not in accordance with the *Corporations Act 2001* including:

(i) giving a true and fair view of the company's [registered scheme's/disclosing entity's]and consolidated entity's financial positions as at 30 June 20X1 and of their performance for the year ended on that date; and

(ii) complying with Australian Accounting Standards and the *Corporations Regulations 2001*.

Other Matter

The financial report of ABC Company Ltd. for the year ended 30 June 20X0 was audited by another auditor who expressed an adverse opinion on that financial report on 30 September 20X0.

Report on the Remuneration Report

We have audited the Remuneration Report included in [paragraphs a to b or pages x to y] of the directors' report for the year ended 30 June 20X1. The directors of the company are responsible for the preparation and presentation of the Remuneration Report in accordance with section 300A of the *Corporations Act 2001*. Our responsibility is to express an opinion on the Remuneration Report, based on our audit conducted in accordance with Australian Auditing Standards.

Opinion

In our opinion, the Remuneration Report of ABC Company Ltd. for the year ended 30 June 20X1, complies with section 300A of the *Corporations Act 2001*.

[Auditor's signature]

[Date of the auditor's report]

[Auditor's address]

PERIOD 2

Audit Work Performed:

- The auditor determines the status of the matter causing the adverse opinion in the prior period.
- Audit of Period 2 conducted in accordance with Auditing Standards.

Period 2 Auditor's Report:

- If the matter causing the auditor to issue an adverse opinion in the previous period is *not* resolved, the auditor issues an adverse opinion; or
- If the matter causing the auditor to issue an adverse opinion in Period 1 *is* resolved; and there are no other unresolved matters arising from the Period 2 audit, the auditor issues an unmodified opinion; and
- The auditor considers including an Emphasis of Matter Paragraph where the financial report contains disclosures of the resolution of the matter.
- There is no requirement for an Other Mater Paragraph in respect of the prior period audit report.

Appendix 3

Example 4: Disclaimer of Opinion

[Previous auditor issued a disclaimer of opinion]

PERIOD 1: INITIAL ENGAGEMENT

Circumstances:

- Previous auditor issued a disclaimer of opinion. The reasons given were accidental loss of accounting records and difficulties with the completeness and accuracy of subsequent processing under a new accounting system.
- The possible effects of the inability to obtain sufficient appropriate audit evidence regarding opening balances are considered by the auditor to be material and pervasive to the entity's current financial report.
- In addition, the auditor is unable to obtain sufficient appropriate audit evidence regarding the collectability of overseas debts.
- The auditor decides to refer to the previous auditor's report in an Other Matter Paragraph (ASA 710, paragraph 13).
- The financial report is prepared under the *Corporations Act 2001*.

Audit Work Performed:

- Auditor engaged to, and, conducts an audit in accordance with Auditing Standards. Opening balances audited in accordance with ASA 510. Current year transactions and balances audited.
- Following ASA 510, paragraph 6 and determining the status of the matter(s) causing the disclaimer of opinion given by the previous auditor, the auditor exercises professional judgement in endeavouring to obtain sufficient appropriate audit evidence as to whether the opening balances contain misstatements that materially affect the current period's financial report.
- Auditor's endeavours are *unsuccessful* and the auditor is therefore unable to obtain sufficient appropriate audit evidence on the opening balances.

Auditor's Report:

- As the auditor is unable to obtain sufficient appropriate audit evidence over all, or a significant number of, opening balances, a disclaimer of opinion is appropriate.
- Under ASA 705, paragraph 21, even when the auditor has expressed a disclaimer of opinion, the auditor is required to describe the reasons for any other matter of which the auditor is aware that would have required a modification to the opinion. In this case, the auditor is unable to obtain sufficient appropriate audit evidence over the collectability of material export debts from customers in a country experiencing civil war.

INDEPENDENT AUDITOR'S REPORT

[Appropriate Addressee]

Report on the Financial Report

We were engaged to audit the accompanying financial report of ABC Company Ltd., which comprises the statement of financial position as at 30 June 20X1, the statement of comprehensive income, statement of changes in equity and statement of cash flows for the year then ended, notes comprising a summary of significant accounting policies and other explanatory information, and the directors' declaration.

The Directors' Responsibility for the Financial Report

The Directors of the company [registered scheme/disclosing entity] are responsible for the preparation of the financial report that presents a true and fair view in accordance with Australian Accounting Standards and the *Corporations Act 2001*, and for such internal control as the directors determine is necessary to enable the preparation of the financial report that gives a true and fair view and is free from material misstatement, whether due to fraud or error.

Auditor's Responsibility

Our responsibility is to express an opinion on the financial report based on our audit. We conducted our audit in accordance with Australian Auditing Standards. Because of the matter(s) described in the Basis for Disclaimer of Opinion paragraph, however, we were not able to obtain sufficient appropriate audit evidence to provide a basis for an audit opinion.

Independence

In conducting our audit, we have complied with the independence requirements of the *Corporations Act 2001*. We confirm that the independence declaration required by the *Corporations Act 2001*, which has been given to the directors of ABC Company Ltd., would be in the same terms if given to the directors as at the time of this auditor's report.

Basis for Disclaimer of Opinion

Due to the accidental destruction of financial records and the subsequent introduction of a new computerised system in the previous financial year to 30 June 20X0, we were unable to obtain sufficient appropriate audit evidence in regard to opening balances. We were unable to satisfy ourselves by alternative means concerning a number of opening balances disclosed in the statements of financial performance and cash flows and the statement of financial position as at that date. Accordingly, we were unable to determine whether adjustments might have been necessary in respect of the financial performance, cash flows and financial position for the year to 30 June 20X1. Whilst we were satisfied with the material accuracy of amounts recorded in the statement of financial position at 30 June 20X1, the impact of opening balances on the current period financial performance and cash flows prevents us from forming an opinion on the financial report taken as a whole.

In addition, we were unable to obtain sufficient appropriate audit evidence regarding the collectability of export debts to customers in the Republic of XXXX, a country currently suffering from civil war. These debts are included in Trade Receivables at 30 June 20X1 in the amount of $zzzzz. We were unable to determine whether any adjustments to these amounts were necessary.

Disclaimer of Opinion

Because of the significance of the matters described in the Basis for Disclaimer of Opinion paragraph, we have not been able to obtain sufficient appropriate audit evidence to provide a basis for an audit opinion. Accordingly, we do not express an opinion on the financial report.

Other Matter

The financial report of ABC Company Ltd. for the year ended 30 June 20X0 was audited by another auditor who disclaimed an opinion on that financial report on 30 September 20X0.

Report on the Remuneration Report

We have audited the Remuneration Report included in [paragraphs a to b or pages x to y] of the directors' report for the year ended 30 June 20X1. The directors of the company are responsible for the preparation and presentation of the Remuneration Report in accordance with section 300A of the *Corporations Act 2001*. Our responsibility is to express an opinion on the Remuneration Report, based on our audit conducted in accordance with Australian Auditing Standards.

Opinion

In our opinion the Remuneration Report of ABC Company Ltd. for the year ended 30 June 20X1, complies with section 300A of the *Corporations Act 2001*.

[Auditor's signature]

[Date of the auditor's report]

[Auditor's address]

PERIOD 2

Audit Work Performed:

- The auditor determines the status of the matter(s) causing the disclaimer of opinion in the prior period (Period 1).
- Audit of Period 2 conducted in accordance with Auditing Standards. In particular, if the auditor becomes aware of a possible misstatement in the comparative information while performing the current year audit, the auditor is required to obtain sufficient appropriate audit evidence to determine whether a material misstatement exists (ASA 710 paragraph 8).

Period 2 Auditor's Report:

- If the matters causing the auditor to issue a disclaimer of opinion in the previous period (Period 1) are *not* resolved, the auditor issues a disclaimer of opinion; or
- If one of the matters (say the issues around the destruction of financial records in the year to 30 June 20X0) causing the auditor to issue a disclaimer of opinion in Period 1 *is* resolved but the matter that would have resulted in a modification to the opinion (in this case, the collectability of overseas debts) remains, the auditor issues a modified opinion (in this case a *qualification* over the continuing issue of collectability of overseas debts); or
- If the matters causing the auditor to issue a disclaimer of opinion in Period 1 *is* resolved; and there are no other unresolved matters arising from the Period 2 audit, the auditor issues an unmodified opinion; and
- The auditor considers including an Emphasis of Matter Paragraph where the financial report contains disclosures of the resolution of the matter.
- There is no requirement for an Other Matter Paragraph in respect of the prior period audit report.

Example 5: Disclaimer of Opinion

[No previous audit]

PERIOD 1: INITIAL ENGAGEMENT

Circumstances:

- No previous audit and opening balances not otherwise able to be audited.
- The possible effects of the inability to obtain sufficient appropriate audit evidence regarding opening balances are considered by the auditor to be material and pervasive to the entity's financial report.
- The financial report is prepared under the *Corporations Act 2001*.

Audit Work Performed:

- Audit conducted in accordance with Auditing Standards. Opening balances audited in accordance with ASA 510. Current year transactions and balances audited.
- In accordance with ASA 510, paragraph 6, the auditor seeks to obtain sufficient appropriate evidence to determine whether the opening balances contain misstatements.
- The auditor exercises professional judgement in endeavouring to obtain sufficient appropriate audit evidence as to whether the opening balances contain misstatements that materially affect the current period's financial report.
- Auditor's endeavours are *un*successful and the auditor is therefore unable to obtain sufficient appropriate audit evidence on the opening balances (financial performance **and** financial position).

Auditor's Report:

- The auditor issues a disclaimer of opinion – note second bullet point in "circumstances" above.

  [If, on the other hand, the opening balances are not considered by the auditor to be pervasive to the entity's financial report for the current period, then a *qualified* opinion is required by ASA 510, paragraph 10.]
- As the previous financial report was not audited, ASA 710, paragraph 14 requires the auditor to include an Other Matter Paragraph stating that the corresponding figures are unaudited.

INDEPENDENT AUDITOR'S REPORT
[Appropriate Addressee]

Report on the Financial Report

We were engaged to audit the accompanying financial report of ABC Company Ltd., which comprises the statement of financial position as at 30 June 20X1, the statement of comprehensive income, statement of changes in equity and statement of cash flows for the year then ended, notes comprising a summary of significant accounting policies and other explanatory information, and the directors' declaration.

The Directors' Responsibility for the Financial Report

The Directors of the company [registered scheme/disclosing entity] are responsible for the preparation of the financial report that gives a true and fair view in accordance with Australian Accounting Standards and the *Corporations Act 2001* and for such internal control as the directors determine is necessary to enable the preparation of the financial report that gives a true and fair view and is free from material misstatement, whether due to fraud or error.

Auditor's Responsibility

Our responsibility is to express an opinion on the financial report based on conducting the audit in accordance with Australian Auditing Standards. Because of the matter(s) described in the Basis for Disclaimer of Opinion paragraph, however, we were not able to obtain sufficient appropriate audit evidence to provide a basis for an audit opinion.

Independence

In conducting our audit, we have complied with the independence requirements of the *Corporations Act 2001*. We confirm that the independence declaration required by the *Corporations Act 2001*, which has been given to the directors of ABC Company Ltd., would be in the same terms if given to the directors as at the time of this auditor's report.

Basis for Disclaimer of Opinion

The previous financial report was not audited. We were unable to satisfy ourselves by alternative means concerning a number of opening balances disclosed in the statements of financial performance and cash flows and the statement of financial position, as comparative figures. Whilst we were satisfied with the material accuracy of amounts recorded in the statement of financial position at 30 June 20X1, the impact of opening balances on the current period financial performance and cash flows prevents us from forming an opinion on the financial report taken as a whole.

Disclaimer of Opinion

Because of the significance of the matter(s) described in the Basis for Disclaimer of Opinion paragraph, we have not been able to obtain sufficient appropriate audit evidence to provide a basis for an audit opinion. Accordingly, we do not express an opinion on the financial report.

Report on the Remuneration Report

We have audited the Remuneration Report included in [paragraphs a to b or pages x to y] of the directors' report for the year ended 30 June 20X1. The directors of the company are responsible for the preparation and presentation of the Remuneration Report in accordance with section 300A of the *Corporations Act 2001*. Our responsibility is to express an opinion on the Remuneration Report, based on our audit conducted in accordance with Australian Auditing Standards.

Opinion

In our opinion the Remuneration Report of ABC Company Ltd. for the year ended 30 June 20X1 complies with section 300A of the *Corporations Act 2001*.

[Auditor's signature]

[Date of the auditor's report]

[Auditor's address]

PERIOD 2

Audit Work Performed:

- The auditor conducted an audit of Period 1 in accordance with Auditing Standards and disclaimed on the opening balances.
- The auditor determines the status of the matter(s) causing the disclaimer of opinion in the prior period.
- The audit of Period 2 is conducted in accordance with Auditing Standards. If the auditor becomes aware of a possible misstatement in the comparative information while performing the current year audit, the auditor is required to obtain sufficient appropriate audit evidence to determine whether a material misstatement exists (ASA 710, paragraph 8).

Period 2 Auditor's Report:

- In the absence of identified material misstatements, the auditor issues an unmodified opinion because Period 1 has been audited. Balances and transactions have been audited and the disclaimer was due only to the inability to obtain sufficient appropriate audit evidence regarding the prior period opening balances.
- The Period 1 profit and loss transactions have been audited as well as the balance sheet, including the closing inventory. Accordingly, the risk of a material misstatement in the Period 1 comparatives shown in the Period 2 financial report is likely to be assessed by the auditor as low and therefore the auditor will issue an unmodified opinion for Period 2.
- There is no requirement for an Other Matter Paragraph in respect of the prior period audit report.

ASA 520
Analytical Procedures

(Reissued October 2009)

Issued by the Auditing and Assurance Standards Board.

Note from the Institute of Chartered Accountants Australia

This note, prepared by the technical editor, is not part of ASA 520.

Historical development

November 1989: ED 31 'Analytical Procedures', based on the IAPC ED 35 of the same name, issued by the AuSB.

June 1990: Audit Monograph No. 1 'Analytical Review' published.

January 1991: AUP 17 'Analytical Procedures' issued by the AuSB, operative from 1 July 1991. The Appendix to AUP 17 was additional to IAG 12.

June 1994: The International Auditing Practices Committee (IAPC) of the International Federation of Accountants (IFAC) approved the issuance of a codified set of International Standards of Auditing (ISAs). The relevant international pronouncement was ISA 520 'Analytical Procedures'.

October 1995: Australian Auditing Standards and Auditing Guidance Statements released. The status of these was explained in APS 1.1 'Conformity With Auditing Standards'. These Standards became operative for the first reporting period commencing on or after 1 July 1996 and later reporting periods, although earlier application was encouraged. AUP 17 'Analytical Procedures' replaced by AUS 512 'Analytical Procedures'.

April 2006: ASA 520 was issued as a legally enforceable Standard to replace AUS 512. It is based on ISA 520 of the same name.

October 2009: ASA 520 reissued as part of the AUASB's Clarity Project. It is based on the redrafted ISA 520 of the same name.

ASA

Contents

Preface

Reasons for Issuing Auditing Standard ASA 520 *Analytical Procedures*

The Auditing and Assurance Standards Board (AUASB) issues Auditing Standard ASA 520 *Analytical Procedures* pursuant to the requirements of the legislative provisions and the Strategic Direction explained below.

The AUASB is an independent statutory board of the Australian Government established under section 227A of the *Australian Securities and Investments Commission Act 2001*, as amended (ASIC Act). Under section 336 of the *Corporations Act 2001*, the AUASB may make Auditing Standards for the purposes of the corporations legislation. These Auditing Standards are legislative instruments under the *Legislative Instruments Act 2003*.

Under the Strategic Direction given to the AUASB by the Financial Reporting Council (FRC), the AUASB is required to have regard to any programme initiated by the International Auditing and Assurance Standards Board (IAASB) for the revision and enhancement of the International Standards on Auditing (ISAs) and to make appropriate consequential amendments to the Australian Auditing Standards. Accordingly, the AUASB has decided to revise and redraft the Australian Auditing Standards using the equivalent redrafted ISAs.

Main Features

This Auditing Standard establishes requirements and provides application and other explanatory material regarding the auditor's use of analytical procedures as substantive procedures ("substantive analytical procedures"). It also deals with the auditor's responsibility to perform analytical procedures near the end of the audit that assist the auditor when forming an overall conclusion on the financial report.

This Auditing Standard:

(a) sets out the procedures an auditor is to undertake when designing and performing substantive analytical procedures;

(b) requires the auditor to design and perform analytical procedures near the end of the audit that assist the auditor when forming an overall conclusion on the financial report; and

(c) requires the auditor to investigate fluctuations or relationships that are inconsistent with other relevant information or that differ from expected values by a significant amount.

Authority Statement

The Auditing and Assurance Standards Board (AUASB) makes this Auditing Standard ASA 520 *Analytical Procedures* pursuant to section 227B of the *Australian Securities and Investments Commission Act 2001* and section 336 of the *Corporations Act 2001*.

This Auditing Standard is to be read in conjunction with ASA 101 *Preamble to Australian Auditing Standards*, which sets out the intentions of the AUASB on how the Australian Auditing Standards, operative for financial reporting periods commencing on or after 1 January 2010, are to be understood, interpreted and applied. This Auditing Standard is to be read also in conjunction with ASA 200 *Overall Objectives of the Independent Auditor and the Conduct of an Audit in Accordance with Australian Auditing Standards*.

Dated: 27 October 2009

M H Kelsall
Chairman - AUASB

Auditing Standard ASA 520

Analytical Procedures

Application

Aus 0.1 This Auditing Standard applies to:

(a) an audit of a financial report for a financial year, or an audit of a financial report for a half-year, in accordance with the *Corporations Act 2001*; and

(b) an audit of a financial report, or a complete set of financial statements, for any other purpose.

Aus 0.2 This Auditing Standard also applies, as appropriate, to an audit of other historical financial information.

Operative Date

Aus 0.3 This Auditing Standard is operative for financial reporting periods commencing on or after 1 January 2010.

Introduction

Scope of this Auditing Standard

1. This Auditing Standard deals with the auditor's use of analytical procedures as substantive procedures ("substantive analytical procedures"). It also deals with the auditor's responsibility to perform analytical procedures near the end of the audit that assist the auditor when forming an overall conclusion on the financial report. ASA 315[1] deals with the use of analytical procedures as risk assessment procedures. ASA 330 includes requirements and guidance regarding the nature, timing and extent of audit procedures in response to assessed risks; these audit procedures may include substantive analytical procedures.[2]

Effective Date

2. [Deleted by the AUASB. Refer Aus 0.3]

1 See ASA 315 *Identifying and Assessing the Risks of Material Misstatement through Understanding the Entity and Its Environment*, paragraph 6(b).

2 See ASA 330 *The Auditor's Responses to Assessed Risks*, paragraphs 6 and 18.

Objectives

3. The objectives of the auditor are:

   (a) To obtain relevant and reliable audit evidence when using substantive analytical procedures; and

   (b) To design and perform analytical procedures near the end of the audit that assist the auditor when forming an overall conclusion as to whether the financial report is consistent with the auditor's understanding of the entity.

Definition

4. For purposes of the Australian Auditing Standards, the term "analytical procedures" means evaluations of financial information through analysis of plausible relationships among both financial and non-financial data. Analytical procedures also encompass such investigation as is necessary of identified fluctuations or relationships that are inconsistent with other relevant information or that differ from expected values by a significant amount. (Ref: Para. A1-A3)

Requirements

Substantive Analytical Procedures

5. When designing and performing substantive analytical procedures, either alone or in combination with tests of details, as substantive procedures in accordance with ASA 330,[3] the auditor shall: (Ref: Para. A4-A5)

   (a) Determine the suitability of particular substantive analytical procedures for given assertions, taking account of the assessed risks of material misstatement and tests of details, if any, for these assertions; (Ref: Para. A6-A11)

   (b) Evaluate the reliability of data from which the auditor's expectation of recorded amounts or ratios is developed, taking account of source, comparability, and nature and relevance of information available, and controls over preparation; (Ref: Para. A12-A14)

   (c) Develop an expectation of recorded amounts or ratios and evaluate whether the expectation is sufficiently precise to identify a misstatement that, individually or when aggregated with other misstatements, may cause the financial report to be materially misstated; and (Ref: Para. A15)

   (d) Determine the amount of any difference of recorded amounts from expected values that is acceptable without further investigation as required by paragraph 7 of this Auditing Standard. (Ref: Para. A16)

Analytical Procedures that Assist When Forming an Overall Conclusion

6. The auditor shall design and perform analytical procedures near the end of the audit that assist the auditor when forming an overall conclusion as to whether the financial report is consistent with the auditor's understanding of the entity. (Ref: Para. A17-A19)

Investigating Results of Analytical Procedures

7. If analytical procedures performed in accordance with this Auditing Standard identify fluctuations or relationships that are inconsistent with other relevant information or that differ from expected values by a significant amount, the auditor shall investigate such differences by:

   (a) Enquiring of management and obtaining appropriate audit evidence relevant to management's responses; and

   (b) Performing other audit procedures as necessary in the circumstances. (Ref: Para. A20-A21)

❖ ❖ ❖

3 See ASA 330, paragraph 18.

Application and Other Explanatory Material

Definition of Analytical Procedures (Ref: Para. 4)

A1. Analytical procedures include the consideration of comparisons of the entity's financial information with, for example:

- Comparable information for prior periods.
- Anticipated results of the entity, such as budgets or forecasts, or expectations of the auditor, such as an estimation of depreciation.
- Similar industry information, such as a comparison of the entity's ratio of sales to accounts receivable with industry averages or with other entities of comparable size in the same industry.

A2. Analytical procedures also include consideration of relationships, for example:

- Among elements of financial information that would be expected to conform to a predictable pattern based on the entity's experience, such as gross margin percentages.
- Between financial information and relevant non-financial information, such as payroll costs to number of employees.

A3. Various methods may be used to perform analytical procedures. These methods range from performing simple comparisons to performing complex analyses using advanced statistical techniques. Analytical procedures may be applied to a consolidated financial report, components and individual elements of information.

Substantive Analytical Procedures (Ref: Para. 5)

A4. The auditor's substantive procedures at the assertion level may be tests of details, substantive analytical procedures, or a combination of both. The decision about which audit procedures to perform, including whether to use substantive analytical procedures, is based on the auditor's judgement about the expected effectiveness and efficiency of the available audit procedures to reduce audit risk at the assertion level to an acceptably low level.

A5. The auditor may enquire of management as to the availability and reliability of information needed to apply substantive analytical procedures, and the results of any such analytical procedures performed by the entity. It may be effective to use analytical data prepared by management, provided the auditor is satisfied that such data is properly prepared.

Suitability of Particular Analytical Procedures for Given Assertions (Ref: Para. 5(a))

A6. Substantive analytical procedures are generally more applicable to large volumes of transactions that tend to be predictable over time. The application of planned analytical procedures is based on the expectation that relationships among data exist and continue in the absence of known conditions to the contrary. However, the suitability of a particular analytical procedure will depend upon the auditor's assessment of how effective it will be in detecting a misstatement that, individually or when aggregated with other misstatements, may cause the financial report to be materially misstated.

A7. In some cases, even an unsophisticated predictive model may be effective as an analytical procedure. For example, where an entity has a known number of employees at fixed rates of pay throughout the period, it may be possible for the auditor to use this data to estimate the total payroll costs for the period with a high degree of accuracy, thereby providing audit evidence for a significant item in the financial report and reducing the need to perform tests of details on the payroll. The use of widely recognised trade ratios (such as profit margins for different types of retail entities) can often be used effectively in substantive analytical procedures to provide evidence to support the reasonableness of recorded amounts.

A8. Different types of analytical procedures provide different levels of assurance. Analytical procedures involving, for example, the prediction of total rental income on a building divided into apartments, taking the rental rates, the number of apartments and vacancy rates into consideration, can provide persuasive evidence and may eliminate the need for further verification by means of tests of details, provided the elements are appropriately verified. In contrast, calculation and comparison of gross margin percentages as a means of confirming a revenue figure may provide less persuasive evidence, but may provide useful corroboration if used in combination with other audit procedures.

A9. The determination of the suitability of particular substantive analytical procedures is influenced by the nature of the assertion and the auditor's assessment of the risk of material misstatement. For example, if controls over sales order processing are deficient, the auditor may place more reliance on tests of details rather than on substantive analytical procedures for assertions related to receivables.

A10. Particular substantive analytical procedures may also be considered suitable when tests of details are performed on the same assertion. For example, when obtaining audit evidence regarding the valuation assertion for accounts receivable balances, the auditor may apply analytical procedures to an ageing of customers' accounts in addition to performing tests of details on subsequent cash receipts to determine the collectability of the receivables.

Considerations Specific to Public Sector Entities

A11. The relationships between individual financial report items traditionally considered in the audit of business entities may not always be relevant in the audit of governments or other non-business public sector entities; for example, in many public sector entities there may be little direct relationship between revenue and expenditure. In addition, because expenditure on the acquisition of assets may not be capitalised, there may be no relationship between expenditures on, for example, inventories and fixed assets and the amount of those assets reported in the financial report. Also, industry data or statistics for comparative purposes may not be available in the public sector. However, other relationships may be relevant, for example, variations in the cost per kilometre of road construction or the number of vehicles acquired compared with vehicles retired.

The Reliability of the Data (Ref: Para. 5(b))

A12. The reliability of data is influenced by its source and nature and is dependent on the circumstances under which it is obtained. Accordingly, the following are relevant when determining whether data is reliable for purposes of designing substantive analytical procedures:

(a) Source of the information available. For example, information may be more reliable when it is obtained from independent sources outside the entity;[4]

(b) Comparability of the information available. For example, broad industry data may need to be supplemented to be comparable to that of an entity that produces and sells specialised products;

(c) Nature and relevance of the information available. For example, whether budgets have been established as results to be expected rather than as goals to be achieved; and

(d) Controls over the preparation of the information that are designed to ensure its completeness, accuracy and validity. For example, controls over the preparation, review and maintenance of budgets.

A13. The auditor may consider testing the operating effectiveness of controls, if any, over the entity's preparation of information used by the auditor in performing substantive analytical procedures in response to assessed risks. When such controls are effective, the auditor generally has greater confidence in the reliability of the information and, therefore, in the results of analytical procedures. The operating effectiveness of controls over non-financial information may often be tested in conjunction with other tests of controls. For example, in establishing controls over the processing of sales invoices, an entity may include controls over the recording of unit sales. In these circumstances, the auditor may test the operating effectiveness of controls over the recording of unit sales in conjunction with tests of the operating effectiveness of controls over the processing of sales invoices. Alternatively, the auditor may consider whether the information was subjected to audit testing. ASA 500 establishes requirements and provides guidance in determining the audit procedures to be performed on the information to be used for substantive analytical procedures.[5]

4 See ASA 500 *Audit Evidence*, paragraph A31.

5 See ASA 500, paragraph 10.

A14. The matters discussed in paragraphs A12(a)-A12(d) are relevant irrespective of whether the auditor performs substantive analytical procedures on the entity's period end financial report, or at an interim date and plans to perform substantive analytical procedures for the remaining period. ASA 330 establishes requirements and provides guidance on substantive procedures performed at an interim date.[6]

Evaluation Whether the Expectation Is Sufficiently Precise (Ref: Para. 5(c))

A15. Matters relevant to the auditor's evaluation of whether the expectation can be developed sufficiently precisely to identify a misstatement that, when aggregated with other misstatements, may cause the financial report to be materially misstated, include:

- The accuracy with which the expected results of substantive analytical procedures can be predicted. For example, the auditor may expect greater consistency in comparing gross profit margins from one period to another than in comparing discretionary expenses, such as research or advertising.
- The degree to which information can be disaggregated. For example, substantive analytical procedures may be more effective when applied to financial information on individual sections of an operation or to financial reports of components of a diversified entity, than when applied to the financial report of the entity as a whole.
- The availability of the information, both financial and non-financial. For example, the auditor may consider whether financial information, such as budgets or forecasts, and non-financial information, such as the number of units produced or sold, is available to design substantive analytical procedures. If the information is available, the auditor may also consider the reliability of the information as discussed in paragraphs A12-A13 above.

Amount of Difference of Recorded Amounts from Expected Values that Is Acceptable (Ref: Para. 5(d))

A16. The auditor's determination of the amount of difference from the expectation that can be accepted without further investigation is influenced by materiality[7] and the consistency with the desired level of assurance, taking account of the possibility that a misstatement, individually or when aggregated with other misstatements, may cause the financial report to be materially misstated. ASA 330 requires the auditor to obtain more persuasive audit evidence the higher the auditor's assessment of risk.[8] Accordingly, as the assessed risk increases, the amount of difference considered acceptable without investigation decreases in order to achieve the desired level of persuasive evidence.[9]

Analytical Procedures that Assist When Forming an Overall Conclusion (Ref: Para. 6)

A17. The conclusions drawn from the results of analytical procedures designed and performed in accordance with paragraph 6 are intended to corroborate conclusions formed during the audit of individual components or elements of the financial report. This assists the auditor to draw reasonable conclusions on which to base the auditor's opinion.

A18. The results of such analytical procedures may identify a previously unrecognised risk of material misstatement. In such circumstances, ASA 315 requires the auditor to revise the auditor's assessment of the risks of material misstatement and modify the further planned audit procedures accordingly.[10]

A19. The analytical procedures performed in accordance with paragraph 6 may be similar to those that would be used as risk assessment procedures.

6 See ASA 330, paragraphs 22-23.

7 See ASA 320 *Materiality in Planning and Performing an Audit*, paragraph A13.

8 See ASA 330, paragraph 7(b).

9 See ASA 330, paragraph A19.

10 See ASA 315, paragraph 31.

Investigating Results of Analytical Procedures (Ref: Para. 7)

A20. Audit evidence relevant to management's responses may be obtained by evaluating those responses taking into account the auditor's understanding of the entity and its environment, and with other audit evidence obtained during the course of the audit.

A21. The need to perform other audit procedures may arise when, for example, management is unable to provide an explanation, or the explanation, together with the audit evidence obtained relevant to management's response, is not considered adequate.

❖ ❖ ❖

Conformity with International Standards on Auditing

This Auditing Standard conforms with International Standard on Auditing ISA 520 *Analytical Procedures*, issued by the International Auditing and Assurance Standards Board (IAASB), an independent standard-setting board of the International Federation of Accountants (IFAC).

Paragraphs that have been added to this Auditing Standard (and do not appear in the text of the equivalent ISA) are identified with the prefix "Aus".

Compliance with this Auditing Standard enables compliance with ISA 520.

ASA 530

Audit Sampling

(Reissued October 2009)

Issued by the Auditing and Assurance Standards Board.

Note from the Institute of Chartered Accountants Australia

This note, prepared by the technical editor, is not part of ASA 530.

Historical development

1983: Audit Guide No. 1 'Audit Sampling' published by AARF who developed it from a guide prepared by the Statistical Sampling Subcommittee of the American Institute of Certified Public Accountants.

June 1985: Statement of Auditing Practice AUP 24 'Audit Sampling' issued following the issue of ED 13 (IAPC ED 20) in October 1983. The relevant IAPC publication was IAG 19 which was issued in February 1985.

June 1994: The International Auditing Practices Committee (IAPC) of the International Federation of Accountants (IFAC) approved the issue of a codified set of International Standards of Auditing (ISAs). The relevant international pronouncement was ISA 530 'Audit Sampling'.

December 1994: ED 63 'Codification and Revision of Auditing Pronouncements: AUS 516 Audit Sampling (AUP 20)' issued by AuSB.

October 1995: Australian Auditing Standards and Auditing Guidance Statements released. The status of these was explained in APS 1.1 'Conformity with Auditing Standards'. These Standards became operative for the first reporting period commencing on or after 1 July 1996 and later reporting periods, although earlier application was encouraged. AUS 514 'Audit Sampling' replaced AUP 24 of the same name.

April 1998: AUS 514 'Audit Sampling and Other Selective Testing Procedures' reissued by the AuSB.

April 2006: ASA 530 'Audit Sampling and Other Means of Testing' was issued as a legally enforceable Standard to replace AUS 514. It is based on ISA 530 of the same name.

October 2009: ASA 530 reissued as 'Audit Sampling' as part of the AUASB's Clarity Project. It is based on the redrafted ISA 530 of the same name.

Contents

Preface

Reasons for Issuing Auditing Standard ASA 530 *Audit Sampling*

The Auditing and Assurance Standards Board (AUASB) issues Auditing Standard ASA 530 *Audit Sampling* pursuant to the requirements of the legislative provisions and the Strategic Direction explained below.

The AUASB is an independent statutory board of the Australian Government established under section 227A of the *Australian Securities and Investments Commission Act 2001*, as amended (ASIC Act). Under section 336 of the *Corporations Act 2001*, the AUASB may make Australian Auditing Standards for the purposes of the corporations legislation. These Auditing Standards are legislative instruments under the *Legislative Instruments Act 2003*.

Under the Strategic Direction given to the AUASB by the Financial Reporting Council (FRC), the AUASB is required to have regard to any programme initiated by the International Auditing and Assurance Standards Board (IAASB) for the revision and enhancement of the International Standards on Auditing (ISAs) and to make appropriate consequential amendments to the

Australian Auditing Standards. Accordingly, the AUASB has decided to revise and redraft the Australian Auditing Standards using the equivalent redrafted ISAs.

Main Features

This Auditing Standard establishes requirements and provides application and other explanatory material when the auditor has decided to use audit sampling in performing audit procedures.

This Auditing Standard requires the auditor to:

(a) consider the purpose of the audit procedure and the characteristics of the population from which the sample will be drawn when designing an audit sample;

(b) perform audit procedures, appropriate to the purpose, on each item selected; and

(c) evaluate the results of the sample and whether the use of audit sampling has provided a reasonable basis for conclusions about the population that has been tested.

Authority Statement

The Auditing and Assurance Standards Board (AUASB) makes this Auditing Standard ASA 530 *Audit Sampling* pursuant to section 227B of the *Australian Securities and Investments Commission Act 2001* and section 336 of the *Corporations Act 2001.*

This Auditing Standard is to be read in conjunction with ASA 101 *Preamble to Australian Auditing Standards*, which sets out the intentions of the AUASB on how the Australian Auditing Standards operative for financial reporting periods commencing on or after 1 January 2010 are to be understood, interpreted and applied. This Auditing Standard is to be read also in conjunction with ASA 200 *Overall Objectives of the Independent Auditor and the Conduct of an Audit in Accordance with Australian Auditing Standards.*

Dated: 27 October 2009

M H Kelsall
Chairman - AUASB

Auditing Standard ASA 530

Audit Sampling

Application

Aus 0.1 This Auditing Standard applies to:

(a) an audit of a financial report for a financial year, or an audit of a financial report for a half-year, in accordance with the *Corporations Act 2001*; and

(b) an audit of a financial report, or a complete set of financial statements, for any other purpose.

Aus 0.2 This Auditing Standard also applies, as appropriate, to an audit of other historical financial information.

Operative Date

Aus 0.3 This Auditing Standard is operative for financial reporting periods commencing on or after 1 January 2010.

Introduction

Scope of this Auditing Standard

1. This Auditing Standard applies when the auditor has decided to use audit sampling in performing audit procedures. It deals with the auditor's use of statistical and non-statistical sampling when designing and selecting the audit sample, performing tests of controls and tests of details, and evaluating the results from the sample.

2. This Auditing Standard complements ASA 500,[1] which deals with the auditor's responsibility to design and perform audit procedures to obtain sufficient appropriate audit evidence to

1 See ASA 500 *Audit Evidence.*

be able to draw reasonable conclusions on which to base the auditor's opinion. ASA 500 provides guidance on the means available to the auditor for selecting items for testing, of which audit sampling is one means.

Effective Date

3. [Deleted by the AUASB. Refer Aus 0.3]

Objective

4. The objective of the auditor, when using audit sampling, is to provide a reasonable basis for the auditor to draw conclusions about the population from which the sample is selected.

Definitions

5. For the purposes of the Australian Auditing Standards, the following terms have the meanings attributed below:

   (a) Audit sampling (sampling) means the application of audit procedures to less than 100% of items within a population of audit relevance such that all sampling units have a chance of selection in order to provide the auditor with a reasonable basis on which to draw conclusions about the entire population.

   (b) Population means the entire set of data from which a sample is selected and about which the auditor wishes to draw conclusions.

   (c) Sampling risk means the risk that the auditor's conclusion based on a sample may be different from the conclusion if the entire population were subjected to the same audit procedure. Sampling risk can lead to two types of erroneous conclusions:

      (i) In the case of a test of controls, that controls are more effective than they actually are, or in the case of a test of details, that a material misstatement does not exist when in fact it does. The auditor is primarily concerned with this type of erroneous conclusion because it affects audit effectiveness and is more likely to lead to an inappropriate audit opinion.

      (ii) In the case of a test of controls, that controls are less effective than they actually are, or in the case of a test of details, that a material misstatement exists when in fact it does not. This type of erroneous conclusion affects audit efficiency as it would usually lead to additional work to establish that initial conclusions were incorrect.

   (d) Non-sampling risk means the risk that the auditor reaches an erroneous conclusion for any reason not related to sampling risk. (Ref: Para. A1)

   (e) Anomaly means a misstatement or deviation that is demonstrably not representative of misstatements or deviations in a population.

   (f) Sampling unit means the individual items constituting a population. (Ref: Para. A2)

   (g) Statistical sampling means an approach to sampling that has the following characteristics:

      (i) Random selection of the sample items; and

      (ii) The use of probability theory to evaluate sample results, including measurement of sampling risk.

   A sampling approach that does not have characteristics (i) and (ii) is considered non-statistical sampling.

   (h) Stratification means the process of dividing a population into sub-populations, each of which is a group of sampling units which have similar characteristics (often monetary value).

   (i) Tolerable misstatement means a monetary amount set by the auditor in respect of which the auditor seeks to obtain an appropriate level of assurance that the monetary amount set by the auditor is not exceeded by the actual misstatement in the population. (Ref: Para. A3)

(j) Tolerable rate of deviation means a rate of deviation from prescribed internal control procedures set by the auditor in respect of which the auditor seeks to obtain an appropriate level of assurance that the rate of deviation set by the auditor is not exceeded by the actual rate of deviation in the population.

Requirements

Sample Design, Size and Selection of Items for Testing

6. When designing an audit sample, the auditor shall consider the purpose of the audit procedure and the characteristics of the population from which the sample will be drawn. (Ref: Para. A4-A9)

7. The auditor shall determine a sample size sufficient to reduce sampling risk to an acceptably low level. (Ref: Para. A10-A11)

8. The auditor shall select items for the sample in such a way that each sampling unit in the population has a chance of selection. (Ref: Para. A12-A13)

Performing Audit Procedures

9. The auditor shall perform audit procedures, appropriate to the purpose, on each item selected.

10. If the audit procedure is not applicable to the selected item, the auditor shall perform the procedure on a replacement item. (Ref: Para. A14)

11. If the auditor is unable to apply the designed audit procedures, or suitable alternative procedures, to a selected item, the auditor shall treat that item as a deviation from the prescribed control, in the case of tests of controls, or a misstatement, in the case of tests of details. (Ref: Para. A15-A16)

Nature and Cause of Deviations and Misstatements

12. The auditor shall investigate the nature and cause of any deviations or misstatements identified, and evaluate their possible effect on the purpose of the audit procedure and on other areas of the audit. (Ref: Para. A17)

13. In the extremely rare circumstances when the auditor considers a misstatement or deviation discovered in a sample to be an anomaly, the auditor shall obtain a high degree of certainty that such misstatement or deviation is not representative of the population. The auditor shall obtain this degree of certainty by performing additional audit procedures to obtain sufficient appropriate audit evidence that the misstatement or deviation does not affect the remainder of the population.

Projecting Misstatements

14. For tests of details, the auditor shall project misstatements found in the sample to the population. (Ref: Para. A18-A20)

Evaluating Results of Audit Sampling

15. The auditor shall evaluate:

    (a) The results of the sample; and (Ref: Para. A21-A22)

    (b) Whether the use of audit sampling has provided a reasonable basis for conclusions about the population that has been tested. (Ref: Para. A23)

❖ ❖ ❖

Application and Other Explanatory Material

Definitions

Non-Sampling Risk (Ref: Para. 5(d))

A1. Examples of non-sampling risk include use of inappropriate audit procedures, or misinterpretation of audit evidence and failure to recognise a misstatement or deviation.

Sampling Unit (Ref: Para. 5(f))

A2. The sampling units might be physical items (for example, cheques listed on deposit slips, credit entries on bank statements, sales invoices or debtors' balances) or monetary units.

Tolerable Misstatement (Ref: Para. 5(i))

A3. When designing a sample, the auditor determines tolerable misstatement in order to address the risk that the aggregate of individually immaterial misstatements may cause the financial report to be materially misstated and provide a margin for possible undetected misstatements. Tolerable misstatement is the application of performance materiality, as defined in ASA 320,[2] to a particular sampling procedure. Tolerable misstatement may be the same amount or an amount lower than performance materiality.

Sample Design, Size and Selection of Items for Testing

Sample Design (Ref: Para. 6)

A4. Audit sampling enables the auditor to obtain and evaluate audit evidence about some characteristic of the items selected in order to form or assist in forming a conclusion concerning the population from which the sample is drawn. Audit sampling can be applied using either non-statistical or statistical sampling approaches.

A5. When designing an audit sample, the auditor's consideration includes the specific purpose to be achieved and the combination of audit procedures that is likely to best achieve that purpose. Consideration of the nature of the audit evidence sought and possible deviation or misstatement conditions or other characteristics relating to that audit evidence will assist the auditor in defining what constitutes a deviation or misstatement and what population to use for sampling. In fulfilling the requirement of paragraph 10 of ASA 500, when performing audit sampling, the auditor performs audit procedures to obtain evidence that the population from which the audit sample is drawn is complete.

A6. The auditor's consideration of the purpose of the audit procedure, as required by paragraph 6, includes a clear understanding of what constitutes a deviation or misstatement so that all, and only, those conditions that are relevant to the purpose of the audit procedure are included in the evaluation of deviations or projection of misstatements. For example, in a test of details relating to the existence of accounts receivable, such as confirmation, payments made by the customer before the confirmation date but received shortly after that date by the client, are not considered a misstatement. Also, a misposting between customer accounts does not affect the total accounts receivable balance. Therefore, it may not be appropriate to consider this a misstatement in evaluating the sample results of this particular audit procedure, even though it may have an important effect on other areas of the audit, such as the assessment of the risk of fraud or the adequacy of the allowance for doubtful accounts.

A7. In considering the characteristics of a population, for tests of controls, the auditor makes an assessment of the expected rate of deviation based on the auditor's understanding of the relevant controls or on the examination of a small number of items from the population. This assessment is made in order to design an audit sample and to determine sample size. For example, if the expected rate of deviation is unacceptably high, the auditor will ordinarily decide not to perform tests of controls. Similarly, for tests of details, the auditor makes an assessment of the expected misstatement in the population. If the expected misstatement is high, 100% examination or use of a large sample size may be appropriate when performing tests of details.

2 See ASA 320 *Materiality in Planning and Performing an Audit*, paragraph 9.

A8. In considering the characteristics of the population from which the sample will be drawn, the auditor may determine that stratification or value-weighted selection is appropriate. Appendix 1 provides further discussion on stratification and value-weighted selection.

A9. The decision whether to use a statistical or non-statistical sampling approach is a matter for the auditor's judgement, however, sample size is not a valid criterion to distinguish between statistical and non-statistical approaches.

Sample Size (Ref: Para. 7)

A10. The level of sampling risk that the auditor is willing to accept affects the sample size required. The lower the risk the auditor is willing to accept, the greater the sample size will need to be.

A11. The sample size can be determined by the application of a statistically-based formula or through the exercise of professional judgement. Appendices 2 and 3 indicate the influences that various factors typically have on the determination of sample size. When circumstances are similar, the effect on sample size of factors such as those identified in Appendices 2 and 3 will be similar regardless of whether a statistical or non-statistical approach is chosen.

Selection of Items for Testing (Ref: Para. 8)

A12. With statistical sampling, sample items are selected in a way that each sampling unit has a known probability of being selected. With non-statistical sampling, judgement is used to select sample items. Because the purpose of sampling is to provide a reasonable basis for the auditor to draw conclusions about the population from which the sample is selected, it is important that the auditor selects a representative sample, so that bias is avoided, by choosing sample items which have characteristics typical of the population.

A13. The principal methods of selecting samples are the use of random selection, systematic selection and haphazard selection. Each of these methods is discussed in Appendix 4.

Performing Audit Procedures (Ref: Para. 10-11)

A14. An example of when it is necessary to perform the procedure on a replacement item is when a voided cheque is selected while testing for evidence of payment authorisation. If the auditor is satisfied that the cheque has been properly voided such that it does not constitute a deviation, an appropriately chosen replacement is examined.

A15. An example of when the auditor is unable to apply the designed audit procedures to a selected item is when documentation relating to that item has been lost.

A16. An example of a suitable alternative procedure might be the examination of subsequent cash receipts together with evidence of their source and the items they are intended to settle when no reply has been received in response to a positive confirmation request.

Nature and Cause of Deviations and Misstatements (Ref: Para. 12)

A17. In analysing the deviations and misstatements identified, the auditor may observe that many have a common feature, for example, type of transaction, location, product line or period of time. In such circumstances, the auditor may decide to identify all items in the population that possess the common feature, and extend audit procedures to those items. In addition, such deviations or misstatements may be intentional, and may indicate the possibility of fraud.

Projecting Misstatements (Ref: Para. 14)

A18. The auditor is required to project misstatements for the population to obtain a broad view of the scale of misstatement but this projection may not be sufficient to determine an amount to be recorded.

A19. When a misstatement has been established as an anomaly, it may be excluded when projecting misstatements to the population. However, the effect of any such misstatement, if uncorrected, still needs to be considered in addition to the projection of the non-anomalous misstatements.

A20. For tests of controls, no explicit projection of deviations is necessary since the sample deviation rate is also the projected deviation rate for the population as a whole. ASA 330[3] provides guidance when deviations from controls upon which the auditor intends to rely are detected.

Evaluating Results of Audit Sampling (Ref: Para. 15)

A21. For tests of controls, an unexpectedly high sample deviation rate may lead to an increase in the assessed risk of material misstatement, unless further audit evidence substantiating the initial assessment is obtained. For tests of details, an unexpectedly high misstatement amount in a sample may cause the auditor to believe that a class of transactions or account balance is materially misstated, in the absence of further audit evidence that no material misstatement exists.

A22. In the case of tests of details, the projected misstatement plus anomalous misstatement, if any, is the auditor's best estimate of misstatement in the population. When the projected misstatement plus anomalous misstatement, if any, exceeds tolerable misstatement, the sample does not provide a reasonable basis for conclusions about the population that has been tested. The closer the projected misstatement plus anomalous misstatement is to tolerable misstatement, the more likely that actual misstatement in the population may exceed tolerable misstatement. Also, if the projected misstatement is greater than the auditor's expectations of misstatement used to determine the sample size, the auditor may conclude that there is an unacceptable sampling risk that the actual misstatement in the population exceeds the tolerable misstatement. Considering the results of other audit procedures helps the auditor to assess the risk that actual misstatement in the population exceeds tolerable misstatement, and the risk may be reduced if additional audit evidence is obtained.

A23. If the auditor concludes that audit sampling has not provided a reasonable basis for conclusions about the population that has been tested, the auditor may:

- Request management to investigate misstatements that have been identified and the potential for further misstatements and to make any necessary adjustments; or
- Tailor the nature, timing and extent of those further audit procedures to best achieve the required assurance. For example, in the case of tests of controls, the auditor might extend the sample size, test an alternative control or modify related substantive procedures.

❖ ❖ ❖

Conformity with International Standards on Auditing

This Auditing Standard conforms with International Standard on Auditing ISA 530 *Audit Sampling*, issued by the International Auditing and Assurance Standards Board (IAASB), an independent standard-setting board of the International Federation of Accountants (IFAC).

Paragraphs that have been added to this Auditing Standard (and do not appear in the text of the equivalent ISA) are identified with the prefix "Aus".

Compliance with this Auditing Standard enables compliance with ISA 530.

3 See ASA 330 *The Auditor's Responses to Assessed Risks*, paragraph 17.

Appendix 1
(Ref: Para. A8)

Stratification and Value-Weighted Selection

In considering the characteristics of the population from which the sample will be drawn, the auditor may determine that stratification or value-weighted selection is appropriate. This Appendix provides guidance to the auditor on the use of stratification and value-weighted sampling techniques.

Stratification

1. Audit efficiency may be improved if the auditor stratifies a population by dividing it into discrete sub-populations which have an identifying characteristic. The objective of stratification is to reduce the variability of items within each stratum and therefore allow sample size to be reduced without increasing sampling risk.
2. When performing tests of details, the population is often stratified by monetary value. This allows greater audit effort to be directed to the larger value items, as these items may contain the greatest potential misstatement in terms of overstatement. Similarly, a population may be stratified according to a particular characteristic that indicates a higher risk of misstatement, for example, when testing the allowance for doubtful accounts in the valuation of accounts receivable, balances may be stratified by age.
3. The results of audit procedures applied to a sample of items within a stratum can only be projected to the items that make up that stratum. To draw a conclusion on the entire population, the auditor will need to consider the risk of material misstatement in relation to whatever other strata make up the entire population. For example, 20% of the items in a population may make up 90% of the value of an account balance. The auditor may decide to examine a sample of these items. The auditor evaluates the results of this sample and reaches a conclusion on the 90% of value separately from the remaining 10% (on which a further sample or other means of gathering audit evidence will be used, or which may be considered immaterial).
4. If a class of transactions or account balance has been divided into strata, the misstatement is projected for each stratum separately. Projected misstatements for each stratum are then combined when considering the possible effect of misstatements on the total class of transactions or account balance.

Value-Weighted Selection

5. When performing tests of details it may be efficient to identify the sampling unit as the individual monetary units that make up the population. Having selected specific monetary units from within the population, for example, the accounts receivable balance, the auditor may then examine the particular items, for example, individual balances, that contain those monetary units. One benefit of this approach to defining the sampling unit is that audit effort is directed to the larger value items because they have a greater chance of selection, and can result in smaller sample sizes. This approach may be used in conjunction with the systematic method of sample selection (described in Appendix 4) and is most efficient when selecting items using random selection.

Appendix 2

(Ref: Para. A11)

Examples of Factors Influencing Sample Size for Tests of Controls

The following are factors that the auditor may consider when determining the sample size for tests of controls. These factors, which need to be considered together, assume the auditor does not modify the nature or timing of tests of controls or otherwise modify the approach to substantive procedures in response to assessed risks.

FACTOR	EFFECT ON SAMPLE SIZE	
1. An increase in the extent to which the auditor's risk assessment takes into account relevant controls	Increase	The more assurance the auditor intends to obtain from the operating effectiveness of controls, the lower the auditor's assessment of the risk of material misstatement will be, and the larger the sample size will need to be. When the auditor's assessment of the risk of material misstatement at the assertion level includes an expectation of the operating effectiveness of controls, the auditor is required to perform tests of controls. Other things being equal, the greater the reliance the auditor places on the operating effectiveness of controls in the risk assessment, the greater is the extent of the auditor's tests of controls (and therefore, the sample size is increased).
2. An increase in the tolerable rate of deviation	Decrease	The lower the tolerable rate of deviation, the larger the sample size needs to be.
3. An increase in the expected rate of deviation of the population to be tested	Increase	The higher the expected rate of deviation, the larger the sample size needs to be so that the auditor is in a position to make a reasonable estimate of the actual rate of deviation. Factors relevant to the auditor's consideration of the expected rate of deviation include the auditor's understanding of the business (in particular, risk assessment procedures undertaken to obtain an understanding of internal control), changes in personnel or in internal control, the results of audit procedures applied in prior periods and the results of other audit procedures. High expected control deviation rates ordinarily warrant little, if any, reduction of the assessed risk of material misstatement.
4. An increase in the auditor's desired level of assurance that the tolerable rate of deviation is not exceeded by the actual rate of deviation in the population	Increase	The greater the level of assurance that the auditor desires that the results of the sample are in fact indicative of the actual incidence of deviation in the population, the larger the sample size needs to be.
5. An increase in the number of sampling units in the population	Negligible effect	For large populations, the actual size of the population has little, if any, effect on sample size. For small populations however, audit sampling may not be as efficient as alternative means of obtaining sufficient appropriate audit evidence.

Appendix 3
(Ref: Para. A11)

Examples of Factors Influencing Sample Size for Tests of Details

The following are factors that the auditor may consider when determining the sample size for tests of details. These factors, which need to be considered together, assume the auditor does not modify the approach to tests of controls or otherwise modify the nature or timing of substantive procedures in response to the assessed risks.

FACTOR	EFFECT ON SAMPLE SIZE	
1. An increase in the auditor's assessment of the risk of material misstatement	Increase	The higher the auditor's assessment of the risk of material misstatement, the larger the sample size needs to be. The auditor's assessment of the risk of material misstatement is affected by inherent risk and control risk. For example, if the auditor does not perform tests of controls, the auditor's risk assessment cannot be reduced for the effective operation of internal controls with respect to the particular assertion. Therefore, in order to reduce audit risk to an acceptably low level, the auditor needs a low detection risk and will rely more on substantive procedures. The more audit evidence that is obtained from tests of details (that is, the lower the detection risk), the larger the sample size will need to be.
2. An increase in the use of other substantive procedures directed at the same assertion	Decrease	The more the auditor is relying on other substantive procedures (tests of details or substantive analytical procedures) to reduce to an acceptable level the detection risk regarding a particular population, the less assurance the auditor will require from sampling and, therefore, the smaller the sample size can be.
3. An increase in the auditor's desired level of assurance that tolerable misstatement is not exceeded by actual misstatement in the population	Increase	The greater the level of assurance that the auditor requires that the results of the sample are in fact indicative of the actual amount of misstatement in the population, the larger the sample size needs to be.
4. An increase in tolerable misstatement	Decrease	The lower the tolerable misstatement, the larger the sample size needs to be.
5. An increase in the amount of misstatement the auditor expects to find in the population	Increase	The greater the amount of misstatement the auditor expects to find in the population, the larger the sample size needs to be in order to make a reasonable estimate of the actual amount of misstatement in the population. Factors relevant to the auditor's consideration of the expected misstatement amount include the extent to which item values are determined subjectively, the results of risk assessment procedures, the results of tests of control, the results of audit procedures applied in prior periods, and the results of other substantive procedures.

ASA

FACTOR	EFFECT ON SAMPLE SIZE	
6. Stratification of the population when appropriate	Decrease	When there is a wide range (variability) in the monetary size of items in the population, it may be useful to stratify the population. When a population can be appropriately stratified, the aggregate of the sample sizes from the strata generally will be less than the sample size that would have been required to attain a given level of sampling risk, had one sample been drawn from the whole population.
7. The number of sampling units in the population	Negligible effect	For large populations, the actual size of the population has little, if any, effect on sample size. Thus, for small populations, audit sampling is often not as efficient as alternative means of obtaining sufficient appropriate audit evidence. (However, when using monetary unit sampling, an increase in the monetary value of the population increases sample size, unless this is offset by a proportional increase in materiality for the financial report as a whole [and, if applicable, materiality level or levels for particular classes of transactions, account balances or disclosures]).

Appendix 4

(Ref: Para. A13)

Sample Selection Methods

There are many methods of selecting samples. The principal methods are as follows:

(a) Random selection (applied through random number generators, for example, random number tables).

(b) Systematic selection, in which the number of sampling units in the population is divided by the sample size to give a sampling interval, for example 50, and having determined a starting point within the first 50, each 50th sampling unit thereafter is selected. Although the starting point may be determined haphazardly, the sample is more likely to be truly random if it is determined by use of a computerised random number generator or random number tables. When using systematic selection, the auditor would need to determine that sampling units within the population are not structured in such a way that the sampling interval corresponds with a particular pattern in the population.

(c) Monetary Unit Sampling is a type of value-weighted selection (as described in Appendix 1) in which sample size, selection and evaluation results in a conclusion in monetary amounts.

(d) Haphazard selection, in which the auditor selects the sample without following a structured technique. Although no structured technique is used, the auditor would nonetheless avoid any conscious bias or predictability (for example, avoiding difficult to locate items, or always choosing or avoiding the first or last entries on a page) and thus attempt to ensure that all items in the population have a chance of selection. Haphazard selection is not appropriate when using statistical sampling.

(e) Block selection involves selection of a block(s) of contiguous items from within the population. Block selection cannot ordinarily be used in audit sampling because most populations are structured such that items in a sequence can be expected to have similar characteristics to each other, but different characteristics from items elsewhere in the population. Although in some circumstances it may be an appropriate audit procedure to examine a block of items, it would rarely be an appropriate sample selection technique when the auditor intends to draw valid inferences about the entire population based on the sample.

ASA 540

Auditing Accounting Estimates, Including Fair Value Accounting Estimates, and Related Disclosures

(Reissued October 2009: amended and compiled June 2011)

Issued by the Auditing and Assurance Standards Board.

Note from the Institute of Chartered Accountants Australia

This note, prepared by the technical editor, is not part of ASA 540.

Historical development

February 1988: Statement of Auditing Practice AUP 28 'Audit of Accounting Estimates' issued in, and effective from, February 1988 following the issue of ED 25 (IAPC ED 26) in July 1986.

May 1994: ED 55 'Codification and Revision of Auditing Pronouncements: AUS 518 Audit of Accounting Estimates (AUP 28)' issued by the AuSB.

June 1994: The International Auditing Practices Committee (IAPC) of the International Federation of Accountants (IFAC) approved the issuance of a codified set of International Standards of Auditing (ISAs). The relevant international pronouncement was ISA 540 'Audit of Accounting Estimates'.

October 1995: Australian Auditing Standards and Auditing Guidance Statements released. The status of these was explained in APS 1.1 'Conformity With Auditing Standards'. These Standards became operative for the first reporting period commencing on or after 1 July 1996 and later reporting periods, although earlier application was encouraged. AUP 28 'Audit of Accounting Estimates' replaced by AUS 516 'Audit of Accounting Estimates'.

April 2006: ASA 540 was issued as a legally enforceable Standard to replace AUS 516. It is based on ISA 540 of the same name.

October 2009: ASA 540 reissued as 'Auditing Accounting Estimates, Including Fair Value Accounting Estimates, and Related Disclosures' as part of the AUASB's Clarity Project. It now includes material that used to be in ASA 545 'Auditing Fair Value Measurements and Disclosures' as fair value measurements are a type of estimate. It contains new material on risk assessment and obtaining an understanding of the entity in the context of accounting estimates. It is based on the revised ISA 540 of the same name.

June 2011: ASA 540 updated for editorial amendments contained in ASA 2011-1 'Amendments to Australian Auditing Standards'.

Contents

Compilation Details

Auditing Standard ASA 540 *Auditing Accounting Estimates, Including Fair Value Accounting Estimates, and Related Disclosures* as Amended

This compilation takes into account amendments made up to and including 27 June 2011 and was prepared on 27 June 2011 by the Auditing and Assurance Standards Board (AUASB).

This compilation is not a separate Auditing Standard made by the AUASB. Instead, it is a representation of ASA 540 (October 2009) as amended by another Auditing Standard which is listed in the Table below.

Table of Standards

Standard	Date made	Operative date
ASA 540	27 October 2009	1 January 2010
ASA 2011-1	27 June 2011	1 July 2011

Table of Amendments

Paragraph affected	How affected	By … [paragraph]
A87	Amended	ASA 2011-1 [37]
Conformity Paragraph	Amended	ASA 2011-1 [38]

Preface

[Preface extracted from the original Auditing Standard issued 27 October 2009]

Reasons for Issuing Auditing Standard ASA 540 *Auditing Accounting Estimates, Including Fair Value Accounting Estimates, and Related Disclosures*

The Auditing and Assurance Standards Board (AUASB) issues Auditing Standards ASA 540 *Auditing Accounting Estimates, Including Fair Value Accounting Estimates, and Related Disclosures* and ASA 545 *Auditing Fair Value Measurements and Disclosures* as one Auditing Standard, pursuant to the requirements of the legislative provisions and the Strategic Direction explained below.

The AUASB is an independent statutory board of the Australian Government established under section 227A of the *Australian Securities and Investments Commission Act 2001*, as amended (ASIC Act). Under section 336 of the *Corporations Act 2001*, the AUASB may make Auditing Standards for the purposes of the corporations legislation. These Auditing Standards are legislative instruments under the *Legislative Instruments Act 2003*.

Under the Strategic Direction given to the AUASB by the Financial Reporting Council (FRC), the AUASB is required to have regard to any programme initiated by the International Auditing and Assurance Standards Board (IAASB) for the revision and enhancement of the International Standards on Auditing (ISAs) and to make appropriate consequential amendments to the Australian Auditing Standards. Accordingly, the AUASB has decided to revise and redraft the Australian Auditing Standards using the equivalent redrafted ISAs.

Main Features

This Auditing Standard establishes requirements and provides application and other explanatory material regarding the auditor's responsibilities regarding accounting estimates including fair value accounting estimates and related disclosures in an audit of a financial report.

This Auditing Standard requires the auditor to:

(a) obtain an understanding of the entity and its environment to provide a basis for the identification and assessment of the risks of material misstatement for accounting estimates;

(b) design and perform audit procedures to respond to the assessed risks of material misstatement of an entity's accounting estimates;

(c) perform further substantive procedures in response to any identified significant risks;

(d) evaluate the reasonableness of accounting estimates, and their disclosure in the financial report; and

(e) obtain written representations from management about the reasonableness of significant assumptions used by it in making accounting estimates.

Authority Statement

Auditing Standard ASA 540 *Auditing Accounting Estimates, Including Fair Value Accounting Estimates, and Related Disclosures* (as amended as at June 2011) is set out in paragtraphs 1 to A128 and Appendix 1.

This Auditing Standard is to be read in conjunction with ASA 101 *Preamble to Australian Auditing Standards*, which sets out the intentions of the AUASB on how the Australian Auditing Standards, operative for financial reporting periods commencing on or after 1 January 2010, are to be understood, interpreted and applied. This Auditing Standard is to be read also in conjunction with ASA 200 *Overall Objectives of the Independent Auditor and the Conduct of an Audit in Accordance with Australian Auditing Standards*.

Dated: 27 June 2011

M H Kelsall
Chairman - AUASB

Auditing Standard ASA 540

The Auditing and Assurance Standards Board (AUASB) made Auditing Standard ASA 540 *Auditing Accounting Estimates, Including Fair Value Accounting Estimates, and Related Disclosures,* pursuant to section 227B of the *Australian Securities and Investments Commission Act 2001* and section 336 of the *Corporations Act 2001*, on 27 October 2009.

This compiled version of ASA 540 incorporates subsequent amendments contained in another Auditing Standard made by the AUASB up to and including 27 June 2011 (see Compilation Details).

Auditing Standard ASA 540

Auditing Accounting Estimates, Including Fair Value Accounting Estimates, and Related Disclosures

Application

Aus 0.1 This Auditing Standard applies to:

(a) an audit of a financial report for a financial year, or an audit of a financial report for a half-year, in accordance with the *Corporations Act 2001*; and

(b) an audit of a financial report, or a complete set of financial statements, for any other purpose.

Aus 0.2 This Auditing Standard also applies, as appropriate, to an audit of other historical financial information.

Operative Date

Aus 0.3 This Auditing Standard is operative for financial reporting periods commencing on or after 1 January 2010.

[Note: For operative dates of paragraphs changed or added by an amending Standard, see Compilation Details.]

Introduction

Scope of this Auditing Standard

1. This Auditing Standard deals with the auditor's responsibilities relating to accounting estimates, including fair value accounting estimates, and related disclosures in an audit of a financial report. Specifically, it expands on how ASA 315[1] and ASA 330[2] and other relevant Auditing Standards are to be applied in relation to accounting estimates. It also includes requirements and guidance on misstatements of individual accounting estimates, and indicators of possible management bias.

Nature of Accounting Estimates

2. Some financial report items cannot be measured precisely, but can only be estimated. For purposes of this Auditing Standard, such financial report items are referred to as accounting estimates. The nature and reliability of information available to management to support the making of an accounting estimate varies widely, which thereby affects the degree of estimation uncertainty associated with accounting estimates. The degree of estimation uncertainty affects, in turn, the risks of material misstatement of accounting estimates, including their susceptibility to unintentional or intentional management bias. (Ref: Para. A1-A11)

3. The measurement objective of accounting estimates can vary depending on the applicable financial reporting framework and the financial item being reported. The measurement objective for some accounting estimates is to forecast the outcome of one or more transactions, events or conditions giving rise to the need for the accounting estimate. For other accounting estimates, including many fair value accounting estimates, the measurement objective is different, and is expressed in terms of the value of a current transaction or financial report item based on conditions prevalent at the measurement date, such as estimated market price for a particular type of asset or liability. For example, the applicable financial reporting framework may require fair value measurement based on an assumed hypothetical current transaction between knowledgeable, willing parties (sometimes referred to as "marketplace participants" or equivalent) in an arm's length transaction, rather than the settlement of a transaction at some past or future date.[3]

4. A difference between the outcome of an accounting estimate and the amount originally recognised or disclosed in the financial report does not necessarily represent a misstatement of the financial report. This is particularly the case for fair value accounting estimates, as any observed outcome is invariably affected by events or conditions subsequent to the date at which the measurement is estimated for purposes of the financial report.

Effective Date

5. [Deleted by the AUASB. Refer Aus 0.3]

Objective

6. The objective of the auditor is to obtain sufficient appropriate audit evidence about whether:

   (a) accounting estimates, including fair value accounting estimates, in the financial report, whether recognised or disclosed, are reasonable; and

   (b) related disclosures in the financial report are adequate,

   in the context of the applicable financial reporting framework.

---

1 See ASA 315 *Identifying and Assessing the Risks of Material Misstatement through Understanding the Entity and Its Environment.*

2 See ASA 330 *The Auditor's Responses to Assessed Risks.*

3 Different definitions of fair value may exist in financial reporting frameworks.

Definitions

7. For purposes of the Australian Auditing Standards, the following terms have the meanings attributed below:
   (a) Accounting estimate means an approximation of a monetary amount in the absence of a precise means of measurement. This term is used for an amount measured at fair value where there is estimation uncertainty, as well as for other amounts that require estimation. Where this Auditing Standard addresses only accounting estimates involving measurement at fair value, the term "fair value accounting estimates" is used.
   (b) Auditor's point estimate or auditor's range means the amount, or range of amounts, respectively, derived from audit evidence for use in evaluating management's point estimate.
   (c) Estimation uncertainty means the susceptibility of an accounting estimate and related disclosures to an inherent lack of precision in its measurement.
   (d) Management bias means a lack of neutrality by management in the preparation of information.
   (e) Management's point estimate means the amount selected by management for recognition or disclosure in the financial report as an accounting estimate.
   (f) Outcome of an accounting estimate means the actual monetary amount which results from the resolution of the underlying transaction(s), event(s) or condition(s) addressed by the accounting estimate.

Requirements

Risk Assessment Procedures and Related Activities

8. When performing risk assessment procedures and related activities to obtain an understanding of the entity and its environment, including the entity's internal control, as required by ASA 315,[4] the auditor shall obtain an understanding of the following in order to provide a basis for the identification and assessment of the risks of material misstatement for accounting estimates: (Ref: Para. A12)
   (a) The requirements of the applicable financial reporting framework relevant to accounting estimates, including related disclosures. (Ref: Para. A13-A15)
   (b) How management identifies those transactions, events and conditions that may give rise to the need for accounting estimates to be recognised or disclosed in the financial report. In obtaining this understanding, the auditor shall make enquiries of management about changes in circumstances that may give rise to new, or the need to revise existing, accounting estimates. (Ref: Para. A16-A21)
   (c) How management makes the accounting estimates, and an understanding of the data on which they are based, including: (Ref: Para. A22-A23)
      (i) The method, including where applicable the model, used in making the accounting estimate; (Ref: Para. A24-A26)
      (ii) Relevant controls; (Ref: Para. A27-A28)
      (iii) Whether management has used an expert; (Ref: Para. A29-A30)
      (iv) The assumptions underlying the accounting estimates; (Ref: Para. A31-A36)
      (v) Whether there has been or ought to have been a change from the prior period in the methods for making the accounting estimates, and if so, why; and (Ref: Para. A37)
      (vi) Whether and, if so, how management has assessed the effect of estimation uncertainty. (Ref: Para. A38)

9. The auditor shall review the outcome of accounting estimates included in the prior period financial report, or, where applicable, their subsequent re-estimation for the purpose

4 See ASA 315, paragraphs 5-6 and 11-12.

of the current period. The nature and extent of the auditor's review takes account of the nature of the accounting estimates, and whether the information obtained from the review would be relevant to identifying and assessing risks of material misstatement of accounting estimates made in the current period financial report. However, the review is not intended to call into question the judgements made in the prior periods that were based on information available at the time. (Ref: Para. A39-A44)

Identifying and Assessing the Risks of Material Misstatement

10. In identifying and assessing the risks of material misstatement, as required by ASA 315,[5] the auditor shall evaluate the degree of estimation uncertainty associated with an accounting estimate. (Ref: Para. A45-A46)

11. The auditor shall determine whether, in the auditor's judgement, any of those accounting estimates that have been identified as having high estimation uncertainty give rise to significant risks. (Ref: Para. A47-A51)

Responses to the Assessed Risks of Material Misstatement

12. Based on the assessed risks of material misstatement, the auditor shall determine: (Ref: Para. A52)
    - (a) Whether management has appropriately applied the requirements of the applicable financial reporting framework relevant to the accounting estimate; and (Ref: Para. A53-A56)
    - (b) Whether the methods for making the accounting estimates are appropriate and have been applied consistently, and whether changes, if any, in accounting estimates or in the method for making them from the prior period are appropriate in the circumstances. (Ref: Para. A57-A58)

13. In responding to the assessed risks of material misstatement, as required by ASA 330,[6] the auditor shall undertake one or more of the following, taking account of the nature of the accounting estimate: (Ref: Para. A59-A61)
    - (a) Determine whether events occurring up to the date of the auditor's report provide audit evidence regarding the accounting estimate. (Ref: Para. A62-A67)
    - (b) Test how management made the accounting estimate and the data on which it is based. In doing so, the auditor shall evaluate whether: (Ref: Para. A68-A70)
        - (i) The method of measurement used is appropriate in the circumstances; and (Ref: Para. A71-A76)
        - (ii) The assumptions used by management are reasonable in light of the measurement objectives of the applicable financial reporting framework. (Ref: Para. A77-A83)
    - (c) Test the operating effectiveness of the controls over how management made the accounting estimate, together with appropriate substantive procedures (Ref: Para. A84-A86)
    - (d) Develop a point estimate or a range to evaluate management's point estimate. For this purpose: (Ref: Para. A87-A91)
        - (i) If the auditor uses assumptions or methods that differ from management's, the auditor shall obtain an understanding of management's assumptions or methods sufficient to establish that the auditor's point estimate or range takes into account relevant variables and to evaluate any significant differences from management's point estimate. (Ref: Para. A92)
        - (ii) If the auditor concludes that it is appropriate to use a range, the auditor shall narrow the range, based on audit evidence available, until all outcomes within the range are considered reasonable. (Ref: Para. A93-A95)

5 See ASA 315, paragraph 25.

6 See ASA 330, paragraph 5.

14. In determining the matters identified in paragraph 12 of this Auditing Standard or in responding to the assessed risks of material misstatement in accordance with paragraph 13 of this Auditing Standard, the auditor shall consider whether specialised skills or knowledge in relation to one or more aspects of the accounting estimates are required in order to obtain sufficient appropriate audit evidence. (Ref: Para. A96-A101)

Further Substantive Procedures to Respond to Significant Risks

Estimation Uncertainty

15. For accounting estimates that give rise to significant risks, in addition to other substantive procedures performed to meet the requirements of ASA 330,[7] the auditor shall evaluate the following: (Ref: Para. A102)
    (a) How management has considered alternative assumptions or outcomes, and why it has rejected them, or how management has otherwise addressed estimation uncertainty in making the accounting estimate. (Ref: Para. A103-A106)
    (b) Whether the significant assumptions used by management are reasonable (Ref: Para. A107-A109)
    (c) Where relevant to the reasonableness of the significant assumptions used by management or the appropriate application of the applicable financial reporting framework, management's intent to carry out specific courses of action and its ability to do so. (Ref: Para. A110)

16. If, in the auditor's judgement, management has not adequately addressed the effects of estimation uncertainty on the accounting estimates that give rise to significant risks, the auditor shall, if considered necessary, develop a range with which to evaluate the reasonableness of the accounting estimate. (Ref: Para. A111-A112)

Recognition and Measurement Criteria

17. For accounting estimates that give rise to significant risks, the auditor shall obtain sufficient appropriate audit evidence about whether:
    (a) management's decision to recognise, or to not recognise, the accounting estimates in the financial report; and (Ref: Para. A113-A114)
    (b) the selected measurement basis for the accounting estimates, (Ref: Para. A115)

    are in accordance with the requirements of the applicable financial reporting framework.

Evaluating the Reasonableness of the Accounting Estimates, and Determining Misstatements

18. The auditor shall evaluate, based on the audit evidence, whether the accounting estimates in the financial report are either reasonable in the context of the applicable financial reporting framework, or are misstated. (Ref: Para. A116-A119)

Disclosures Related to Accounting Estimates

19. The auditor shall obtain sufficient appropriate audit evidence about whether the disclosures in the financial report related to accounting estimates are in accordance with the requirements of the applicable financial reporting framework. (Ref: Para. A120-A121)

20. For accounting estimates that give rise to significant risks, the auditor shall also evaluate the adequacy of the disclosure of their estimation uncertainty in the financial report in the context of the applicable financial reporting framework. (Ref: Para. A122-A123)

Indicators of Possible Management Bias

21. The auditor shall review the judgements and decisions made by management in the making of accounting estimates to identify whether there are indicators of possible management bias. Indicators of possible management bias do not themselves constitute misstatements for the purposes of drawing conclusions on the reasonableness of individual accounting estimates. (Ref: Para. A124-A125)

7 See ASA 330, paragraph 18.

Written Representations

22. The auditor shall obtain written representations from management and, where appropriate, those charged with governance whether they believe significant assumptions used in making accounting estimates are reasonable. (Ref: Para. A126-A127)

Documentation

23. The auditor shall include in the audit documentation:[8]

(a) The basis for the auditor's conclusions about the reasonableness of accounting estimates and their disclosure that give rise to significant risks;

(b) Indicators of possible management bias, if any (Ref: Para. A128); and

Aus 23.1. The auditor's evaluation of any indicators of possible management bias in making accounting estimates, including whether the circumstances giving rise to the indicators of bias represent a risk of material misstatement due to fraud. (Ref: Para. A128)

❖ ❖ ❖

Application and Other Explanatory Material

Nature of Accounting Estimates (Ref: Para. 2)

A1. Because of the uncertainties inherent in business activities, some financial report items can only be estimated. Further, the specific characteristics of an asset, liability or component of equity, or the basis of or method of measurement prescribed by the financial reporting framework, may give rise to the need to estimate a financial report item. Some financial reporting frameworks prescribe specific methods of measurement and the disclosures that are required to be made in the financial report, while other financial reporting frameworks are less specific. Appendix 1 to this Auditing Standard discusses fair value measurements and disclosures under different financial reporting frameworks.

A2. Some accounting estimates involve relatively low estimation uncertainty and may give rise to lower risks of material misstatements, for example:

- Accounting estimates arising in entities that engage in business activities that are not complex.
- Accounting estimates that are frequently made and updated because they relate to routine transactions.
- Accounting estimates derived from data that is readily available, such as published interest rate data or exchange-traded prices of securities. Such data may be referred to as "observable" in the context of a fair value accounting estimate.
- Fair value accounting estimates where the method of measurement prescribed by the applicable financial reporting framework is simple and applied easily to the asset or liability requiring measurement at fair value.
- Fair value accounting estimates where the model used to measure the accounting estimate is well-known or generally accepted, provided that the assumptions or inputs to the model are observable.

A3. For some accounting estimates, however, there may be relatively high estimation uncertainty, particularly where they are based on significant assumptions, for example:

- Accounting estimates relating to the outcome of litigation.
- Fair value accounting estimates for derivative financial instruments not publicly traded.
- Fair value accounting estimates for which a highly specialised entity-developed model is used or for which there are assumptions or inputs that cannot be observed in the marketplace.

A4. The degree of estimation uncertainty varies based on the nature of the accounting estimate, the extent to which there is a generally accepted method or model used to

8 See ASA 230 *Audit Documentation*, paragraphs 8-11 and paragraph A6.

make the accounting estimate, and the subjectivity of the assumptions used to make the accounting estimate. In some cases, estimation uncertainty associated with an accounting estimate may be so great that the recognition criteria in the applicable financial reporting framework are not met and the accounting estimate cannot be made.

A5. Not all financial report items requiring measurement at fair value, involve estimation uncertainty. For example, this may be the case for some financial report items where there is an active and open market that provides readily available and reliable information on the prices at which actual exchanges occur, in which case the existence of published price quotations ordinarily are the best audit evidence of fair value. However, estimation uncertainty may exist even when the valuation method and data are well defined. For example, valuation of securities quoted on an active and open market at the listed market price may require adjustment if the holding is significant in relation to the market or is subject to restrictions in marketability. In addition, general economic circumstances prevailing at the time, for example, illiquidity in a particular market, may impact estimation uncertainty.

A6. Additional examples of situations where accounting estimates, other than fair value accounting estimates, may be required include:

- Allowance for doubtful accounts.
- Inventory obsolescence.
- Warranty obligations.
- Depreciation method or asset useful life.
- Provision against the carrying amount of an investment where there is uncertainty regarding its recoverability.
- Outcome of long term contracts.
- Costs arising from litigation settlements and judgements.

A7. Additional examples of situations where fair value accounting estimates may be required include:

- Complex financial instruments, which are not traded in an active and open market.
- Share-based payments.
- Property or equipment held for disposal.
- Certain assets or liabilities acquired in a business combination, including goodwill and intangible assets.
- Transactions involving the exchange of assets or liabilities between independent parties without monetary consideration, for example, a non-monetary exchange of plant facilities in different lines of business.

Aus A7.1 Impairment testing of assets.

A8. Estimation involves judgements based on information available when the financial report is prepared. For many accounting estimates, these include making assumptions about matters that are uncertain at the time of estimation. The auditor is not responsible for predicting future conditions, transactions or events that, if known at the time of the audit, might have significantly affected management's actions or the assumptions used by management.

Management Bias

A9. Financial reporting frameworks often call for neutrality, that is, freedom from bias. Accounting estimates are imprecise, however, and can be influenced by management judgement. Such judgement may involve unintentional or intentional management bias (for example, as a result of motivation to achieve a desired result). The susceptibility of an accounting estimate to management bias increases with the subjectivity involved in making it. Unintentional management bias and the potential for intentional management bias are inherent in subjective decisions that are often required in making an accounting estimate. For continuing audits, indicators of possible management bias identified during the audit of the preceding periods influence the planning and risk identification and assessment activities of the auditor in the current period.

A10. Management bias can be difficult to detect at an account level. It may only be identified when considered in the aggregate of groups of accounting estimates or all accounting estimates, or when observed over a number of accounting periods. Although some form of management bias is inherent in subjective decisions, in making such judgements there may be no intention by management to mislead the users of the financial report. Where, however, there is intention to mislead, management bias is fraudulent in nature.

Considerations Specific to Public Sector Entities

A11. Public sector entities may have significant holdings of specialised assets for which there are no readily available and reliable sources of information for purposes of measurement at fair value or other current value bases, or a combination of both. Often specialised assets held do not generate cash flows and do not have an active market. Measurement at fair value therefore ordinarily requires estimation and may be complex, and in some rare cases may not be possible at all.

Risk Assessment Procedures and Related Activities (Ref: Para. 8)

A12. The risk assessment procedures and related activities required by paragraph 8 of this Auditing Standard assist the auditor in developing an expectation of the nature and type of accounting estimates that an entity may have. The auditor's primary consideration is whether the understanding that has been obtained is sufficient to identify and assess the risks of material misstatement in relation to accounting estimates, and to plan the nature, timing and extent of further audit procedures.

Obtaining an Understanding of the Requirements of the Applicable Financial Reporting Framework (Ref: Para. 8(a))

A13. Obtaining an understanding of the requirements of the applicable financial reporting framework assists the auditor in determining whether it, for example:

- Prescribes certain conditions for the recognition,[9] or methods for the measurement, of accounting estimates.
- Specifies certain conditions that permit or require measurement at a fair value, for example, by referring to management's intentions to carry out certain courses of action with respect to an asset or liability.
- Specifies required or permitted disclosures.

Obtaining this understanding also provides the auditor with a basis for discussion with management about how management has applied those requirements relevant to the accounting estimate, and the auditor's determination of whether they have been applied appropriately.

A14. Financial reporting frameworks may provide guidance for management on determining point estimates where alternatives exist. Some financial reporting frameworks, for example, require that the point estimate selected be the alternative that reflects management's judgement of the most likely outcome.[10] Others may require, for example, use of a discounted probability-weighted expected value. In some cases, management may be able to make a point estimate directly. In other cases, management may be able to make a reliable point estimate only after considering alternative assumptions or outcomes from which it is able to determine a point estimate.

A15. Financial reporting frameworks may require the disclosure of information concerning the significant assumptions to which the accounting estimate is particularly sensitive. Furthermore, where there is a high degree of estimation uncertainty, some financial reporting frameworks do not permit an accounting estimate to be recognised in the financial report, but certain disclosures may be required in the notes to the financial report.

---

9 Most financial reporting frameworks require incorporation in the balance sheet or income statement of items that satisfy their criteria for recognition. Disclosure of accounting policies or adding notes to the financial report does not rectify a failure to recognise such items, including accounting estimates.

10 Different financial reporting frameworks may use different terminology to describe point estimates determined in this way.

Obtaining an Understanding of How Management Identifies the Need for Accounting Estimates (Ref: Para. 8(b))

A16. The preparation of the financial report requires management to determine whether a transaction, event or condition gives rise to the need to make an accounting estimate, and that all necessary accounting estimates have been recognised, measured and disclosed in the financial report in accordance with the applicable financial reporting framework.

A17. Management's identification of transactions, events and conditions that give rise to the need for accounting estimates is likely to be based on:

- Management's knowledge of the entity's business and the industry in which it operates.
- Management's knowledge of the implementation of business strategies in the current period.
- Where applicable, management's cumulative experience of preparing the entity's financial report in prior periods.

In such cases, the auditor may obtain an understanding of how management identifies the need for accounting estimates primarily through enquiry of management. In other cases, where management's process is more structured, for example, when management has a formal risk management function, the auditor may perform risk assessment procedures directed at the methods and practices followed by management for periodically reviewing the circumstances that give rise to the accounting estimates and re-estimating the accounting estimates as necessary. The completeness of accounting estimates is often an important consideration of the auditor, particularly accounting estimates relating to liabilities.

A18. The auditor's understanding of the entity and its environment obtained during the performance of risk assessment procedures, together with other audit evidence obtained during the course of the audit, assist the auditor in identifying circumstances, or changes in circumstances, that may give rise to the need for an accounting estimate.

A19. Enquiries of management about changes in circumstances may include, for example, enquiries about whether:

- The entity has engaged in new types of transactions that may give rise to accounting estimates.
- Terms of transactions that gave rise to accounting estimates have changed.
- Accounting policies relating to accounting estimates have changed, as a result of changes to the requirements of the applicable financial reporting framework or otherwise.
- Regulatory or other changes outside the control of management have occurred that may require management to revise, or make new, accounting estimates.
- New conditions or events have occurred that may give rise to the need for new or revised accounting estimates.

A20. During the audit, the auditor may identify transactions, events and conditions that give rise to the need for accounting estimates that management failed to identify. ASA 315 deals with circumstances where the auditor identifies risks of material misstatement that management failed to identify, including determining whether there is a significant deficiency in internal control with regard to the entity's risk assessment processes.[11]

Considerations Specific to Smaller Entities

A21. Obtaining this understanding for smaller entities is often less complex as their business activities are often limited and transactions are less complex. Further, often a single person, for example the owner-manager, identifies the need to make an accounting estimate and the auditor may focus enquiries accordingly.

11 See ASA 315, paragraph 16.

Obtaining an Understanding of How Management Makes the Accounting Estimates (Ref: Para. 8(c))

A22. The preparation of the financial report also requires management to establish financial reporting processes for making accounting estimates, including adequate internal control. Such processes include the following:

- Selecting appropriate accounting policies and prescribing estimation processes, including appropriate estimation or valuation methods, including, where applicable, models.
- Developing or identifying relevant data and assumptions that affect accounting estimates.
- Periodically reviewing the circumstances that give rise to the accounting estimates and re-estimating the accounting estimates as necessary.

A23. Matters that the auditor may consider in obtaining an understanding of how management makes the accounting estimates include, for example:

- The types of accounts or transactions to which the accounting estimates relate (for example, whether the accounting estimates arise from the recording of routine and recurring transactions or whether they arise from non-recurring or unusual transactions).
- Whether and, if so, how management has used recognised measurement techniques for making particular accounting estimates.
- Whether the accounting estimates were made based on data available at an interim date and, if so, whether and how management has taken into account the effect of events, transactions and changes in circumstances occurring between that date and the period end.

Method of Measurement, Including the Use of Models (Ref: Para. 8(c)(i))

A24. In some cases, the applicable financial reporting framework may prescribe the method of measurement for an accounting estimate, for example, a particular model that is to be used in measuring a fair value estimate. In many cases, however, the applicable financial reporting framework does not prescribe the method of measurement, or may specify alternative methods for measurement.

A25. When the applicable financial reporting framework does not prescribe a particular method to be used in the circumstances, matters that the auditor may consider in obtaining an understanding of the method or, where applicable the model, used to make accounting estimates include, for example:

- How management considered the nature of the asset or liability being estimated when selecting a particular method.
- Whether the entity operates in a particular business, industry or environment in which there are methods commonly used to make the particular type of accounting estimate.

A26. There may be greater risks of material misstatement, for example, in cases when management has internally developed a model to be used to make the accounting estimate or is departing from a method commonly used in a particular industry or environment.

Relevant Controls (Ref: Para. 8(c)(ii))

A27. Matters that the auditor may consider in obtaining an understanding of relevant controls include, for example, the experience and competence of those who make the accounting estimates, and controls related to:

- How management determines the completeness, relevance and accuracy of the data used to develop accounting estimates.
- The review and approval of accounting estimates, including the assumptions or inputs used in their development, by appropriate levels of management and, where appropriate, those charged with governance.

- The segregation of duties between those committing the entity to the underlying transactions and those responsible for making the accounting estimates, including whether the assignment of responsibilities appropriately takes account of the nature of the entity and its products or services (for example, in the case of a large financial institution, relevant segregation of duties may include an independent function responsible for estimation and validation of fair value pricing of the entity's proprietary financial products staffed by individuals whose remuneration is not tied to such products).

A28. Other controls may be relevant to making the accounting estimates depending on the circumstances. For example, if the entity uses specific models for making accounting estimates, management may put into place specific policies and procedures around such models. Relevant controls may include, for example, those established over:

- The design and development, or selection, of a particular model for a particular purpose.
- The use of the model.
- The maintenance and periodic validation of the integrity of the model.

Management's Use of Experts (Ref: Para. 8(c)(iii))

A29. Management may have, or the entity may employ individuals with, the experience and competence necessary to make the required point estimates. In some cases, however, management may need to engage an expert to make, or assist in making, them. This need may arise because of, for example:

- The specialised nature of the matter requiring estimation, for example, the measurement of mineral or hydrocarbon reserves in extractive industries.
- The technical nature of the models required to meet the relevant requirements of the applicable financial reporting framework, as may be the case in certain measurements at fair value.
- The unusual or infrequent nature of the condition, transaction or event requiring an accounting estimate.

Considerations specific to smaller entities

A30. In smaller entities, the circumstances requiring an accounting estimate often are such that the owner-manager is capable of making the required point estimate. In some cases, however, an expert will be needed. Discussion with the owner-manager early in the audit process about the nature of any accounting estimates, the completeness of the required accounting estimates, and the adequacy of the estimating process may assist the owner-manager in determining the need to use an expert.

Assumptions (Ref: Para. 8(c)(iv))

A31. Assumptions are integral components of accounting estimates. Matters that the auditor may consider in obtaining an understanding of the assumptions underlying the accounting estimates include, for example:

- The nature of the assumptions, including which of the assumptions are likely to be significant assumptions.
- How management assesses whether the assumptions are relevant and complete (that is, that all relevant variables have been taken into account).
- Where applicable, how management determines that the assumptions used are internally consistent.
- Whether the assumptions relate to matters within the control of management (for example, assumptions about the maintenance programs that may affect the estimation of an asset's useful life), and how they conform to the entity's business plans and the external environment, or to matters that are outside its control (for example, assumptions about interest rates, mortality rates, potential judicial or regulatory actions, or the variability and the timing of future cash flows).
- The nature and extent of documentation, if any, supporting the assumptions.

Assumptions may be made or identified by an expert to assist management in making the accounting estimates. Such assumptions, when used by management, become management's assumptions.

A32. In some cases, assumptions may be referred to as inputs, for example, where management uses a model to make an accounting estimate, though the term inputs may also be used to refer to the underlying data to which specific assumptions are applied.

A33. Management may support assumptions with different types of information drawn from internal and external sources, the relevance and reliability of which will vary. In some cases, an assumption may be reliably based on applicable information from either external sources (for example, published interest rate or other statistical data) or internal sources (for example, historical information or previous conditions experienced by the entity). In other cases, an assumption may be more subjective, for example, where the entity has no experience or external sources from which to draw.

A34. In the case of fair value accounting estimates, assumptions reflect, or are consistent with, what knowledgeable, willing arm's length parties (sometimes referred to as "marketplace participants" or equivalent) would use in determining fair value when exchanging an asset or settling a liability. Specific assumptions will also vary with the characteristics of the asset or liability being valued, the valuation method used (for example, a market approach, or an income approach) and the requirements of the applicable financial reporting framework.

A35. With respect to fair value accounting estimates, assumptions or inputs vary in terms of their source and bases, as follows:

(a) Those that reflect what marketplace participants would use in pricing an asset or liability developed based on market data obtained from sources independent of the reporting entity (sometimes referred to as "observable inputs" or equivalent).

(b) Those that reflect the entity's own judgements about what assumptions marketplace participants would use in pricing the asset or liability developed based on the best information available in the circumstances (sometimes referred to as "unobservable inputs" or equivalent).

In practice, however, the distinction between (a) and (b) is not always apparent. Further, it may be necessary for management to select from a number of different assumptions used by different marketplace participants.

A36. The extent of subjectivity, such as whether an assumption or input is observable, influences the degree of estimation uncertainty and thereby the auditor's assessment of the risks of material misstatement for a particular accounting estimate.

Changes in Methods for Making Accounting Estimates (Ref: Para. 8(c)(v))

A37. In evaluating how management makes the accounting estimates, the auditor is required to understand whether there has been or ought to have been a change from the prior period in the methods for making the accounting estimates. A specific estimation method may need to be changed in response to changes in the environment or circumstances affecting the entity or in the requirements of the applicable financial reporting framework. If management has changed the method for making an accounting estimate, it is important that management can demonstrate that the new method is more appropriate, or is itself a response to such changes. For example, if management changes the basis of making an accounting estimate from a mark-to-market approach to using a model, the auditor challenges whether management's assumptions about the marketplace are reasonable in light of economic circumstances.

Estimation Uncertainty (Ref: Para. 8(c)(vi))

A38. Matters that the auditor may consider in obtaining an understanding of whether and, if so, how management has assessed the effect of estimation uncertainty include, for example:

- Whether and, if so, how management has considered alternative assumptions or outcomes by, for example, performing a sensitivity analysis to determine the effect of changes in the assumptions on an accounting estimate.

- How management determines the accounting estimate when analysis indicates a number of outcome scenarios.
- Whether management monitors the outcome of accounting estimates made in the prior period, and whether management has appropriately responded to the outcome of that monitoring procedure.

Reviewing Prior Period Accounting Estimates (Ref: Para. 9)

A39. The outcome of an accounting estimate will often differ from the accounting estimate recognised in the prior period financial report. By performing risk assessment procedures to identify and understand the reasons for such differences, the auditor may obtain:

- Information regarding the effectiveness of management's prior period estimation process, from which the auditor can judge the likely effectiveness of management's current process.
- Audit evidence that is pertinent to the re-estimation, in the current period, of prior period accounting estimates.
- Audit evidence of matters, such as estimation uncertainty, that may be required to be disclosed in the financial report.

A40. The review of prior period accounting estimates may also assist the auditor, in the current period, in identifying circumstances or conditions that increase the susceptibility of accounting estimates to, or indicate the presence of, possible management bias. The auditor's professional scepticism assists in identifying such circumstances or conditions and in determining the nature, timing and extent of further audit procedures.

A41. A retrospective review of management judgements and assumptions related to significant accounting estimates is also required by ASA 240.[12] That review is conducted as part of the requirement for the auditor to design and perform procedures to review accounting estimates for biases that could represent a risk of material misstatement due to fraud, in response to the risks of management override of controls. As a practical matter, the auditor's review of prior period accounting estimates as a risk assessment procedure in accordance with this Auditing Standard may be carried out in conjunction with the review required by ASA 240.

A42. The auditor may judge that a more detailed review is required for those accounting estimates that were identified during the prior period audit as having high estimation uncertainty, or for those accounting estimates that have changed significantly from the prior period. On the other hand, for example, for accounting estimates that arise from the recording of routine and recurring transactions, the auditor may judge that the application of analytical procedures as risk assessment procedures is sufficient for purposes of the review.

A43. For fair value accounting estimates and other accounting estimates based on current conditions at the measurement date, more variation may exist between the fair value amount recognised in the prior period financial reports and the outcome or the amount re-estimated for the purpose of the current period. This is because the measurement objective for such accounting estimates deals with perceptions about value at a point in time, which may change significantly and rapidly as the environment in which the entity operates changes. The auditor may therefore focus the review on obtaining information that would be relevant to identifying and assessing risks of material misstatement. For example, in some cases obtaining an understanding of changes in marketplace participant assumptions which affected the outcome of a prior period fair value accounting estimate may be unlikely to provide relevant information for audit purposes. If so, then the auditor's consideration of the outcome of prior period fair value accounting estimates may be directed more towards understanding the effectiveness of management's prior estimation process, that is, management's track record, from which the auditor can judge the likely effectiveness of management's current process.

12 See ASA 240 *The Auditor's Responsibilities Relating to Fraud in an Audit of a Financial Report*, paragraph 32(b)(ii).

A44. A difference between the outcome of an accounting estimate and the amount recognised in the prior period financial report does not necessarily represent a misstatement of the prior period financial report. However, it may do so if, for example, the difference arises from information that was available to management when the prior period's financial report was finalised, or that could reasonably be expected to have been obtained and taken into account in the preparation of that financial report. Many financial reporting frameworks contain guidance on distinguishing between changes in accounting estimates that constitute misstatements and changes that do not, and the accounting treatment required to be followed.

Identifying and Assessing the Risks of Material Misstatement

Estimation Uncertainty (Ref: Para. 10)

A45. The degree of estimation uncertainty associated with an accounting estimate may be influenced by factors such as:

- The extent to which the accounting estimate depends on judgement.
- The sensitivity of the accounting estimate to changes in assumptions.
- The existence of recognised measurement techniques that may mitigate the estimation uncertainty (though the subjectivity of the assumptions used as inputs may nevertheless give rise to estimation uncertainty).
- The length of the forecast period, and the relevance of data drawn from past events to forecast future events.
- The availability of reliable data from external sources.
- The extent to which the accounting estimate is based on observable or unobservable inputs.

The degree of estimation uncertainty associated with an accounting estimate may influence the estimate's susceptibility to bias.

A46. Matters that the auditor considers in assessing the risks of material misstatement may also include:

- The actual or expected magnitude of an accounting estimate.
- The recorded amount of the accounting estimate (that is, management's point estimate) in relation to the amount expected by the auditor to be recorded.
- Whether management has used an expert in making the accounting estimate.
- The outcome of the review of prior period accounting estimates.

High Estimation Uncertainty and Significant Risks (Ref: Para. 11)

A47. Examples of accounting estimates that may have high estimation uncertainty include the following:

- Accounting estimates that are highly dependent upon judgement, for example, judgements about the outcome of pending litigation or the amount and timing of future cash flows dependent on uncertain events many years in the future.
- Accounting estimates that are not calculated using recognised measurement techniques.
- Accounting estimates where the results of the auditor's review of similar accounting estimates made in the prior period financial report indicate a substantial difference between the original accounting estimate and the actual outcome.
- Fair value accounting estimates for which a highly specialised entity-developed model is used or for which there are no observable inputs.

A48. A seemingly immaterial accounting estimate may have the potential to result in a material misstatement due to the estimation uncertainty associated with the estimation; that is, the size of the amount recognised or disclosed in the financial report for an accounting estimate may not be an indicator of its estimation uncertainty.

A49. In some circumstances, the estimation uncertainty is so high that a reasonable accounting estimate cannot be made. The applicable financial reporting framework may, therefore, preclude recognition of the item in the financial report, or its measurement at fair value. In such cases, the significant risks relate not only to whether an accounting estimate should be recognised, or whether it should be measured at fair value, but also to the adequacy of the disclosures. With respect to such accounting estimates, the applicable financial reporting framework may require disclosure of the accounting estimates and the high estimation uncertainty associated with them (see paragraphs A120-A123).

A50. If the auditor determines that an accounting estimate gives rise to a significant risk, the auditor is required to obtain an understanding of the entity's controls, including control activities.[13]

A51. In some cases, the estimation uncertainty of an accounting estimate may cast significant doubt about the entity's ability to continue as a going concern. ASA 570[14] establishes requirements and provides guidance in such circumstances.

Responses to the Assessed Risks of Material Misstatement (Ref: Para. 12)

A52. ASA 330 requires the auditor to design and perform audit procedures whose nature, timing and extent are responsive to the assessed risks of material misstatement in relation to accounting estimates at both the financial report and assertion levels.[15] Paragraphs A53-A116 focus on specific responses at the assertion level only.

Application of the Requirements of the Applicable Financial Reporting Framework (Ref: Para. 12(a))

A53. Many financial reporting frameworks prescribe certain conditions for the recognition of accounting estimates and specify the methods for making them and required disclosures. Such requirements may be complex and require the application of judgement. Based on the understanding obtained in performing risk assessment procedures, the requirements of the applicable financial reporting framework that may be susceptible to misapplication or differing interpretations become the focus of the auditor's attention.

A54. Determining whether management has appropriately applied the requirements of the applicable financial reporting framework is based, in part, on the auditor's understanding of the entity and its environment. For example, the measurement of the fair value of some items, such as intangible assets acquired in a business combination, may involve special considerations that are affected by the nature of the entity and its operations.

A55. In some situations, additional audit procedures, such as the inspection by the auditor of the current physical condition of an asset, may be necessary to determine whether management has appropriately applied the requirements of the applicable financial reporting framework.

A56. The application of the requirements of the applicable financial reporting framework requires management to consider changes in the environment or circumstances that affect the entity. For example, the introduction of an active market for a particular class of asset or liability may indicate that the use of discounted cash flows to estimate the fair value of such asset or liability is no longer appropriate.

Consistency in Methods and Basis for Changes (Ref: Para. 12(b))

A57. The auditor's consideration of a change in an accounting estimate, or in the method for making it from the prior period, is important because a change that is not based on a change in circumstances or new information is considered arbitrary. Arbitrary changes in an accounting estimate result in an inconsistent financial report over time and may give rise to a financial report misstatement or be an indicator of possible management bias.

A58. Management often is able to demonstrate good reason for a change in an accounting estimate or the method for making an accounting estimate from one period to another based on a change in circumstances. What constitutes a good reason, and the adequacy

13 See ASA 315, paragraph 29.

14 See ASA 570 *Going Concern.*

15 See ASA 330, paragraphs 5-6.

of support for management's contention that there has been a change in circumstances that warrants a change in an accounting estimate or the method for making an accounting estimate, are matters of judgement.

Responses to the Assessed Risks of Material Misstatements (Ref: Para. 13)

A59. The auditor's decision as to which response, individually or in combination, in paragraph 13 to undertake to respond to the risks of material misstatement may be influenced by such matters as:

- The nature of the accounting estimate, including whether it arises from routine or non-routine transactions.
- Whether the procedure(s) is expected to effectively provide the auditor with sufficient appropriate audit evidence.
- The assessed risk of material misstatement, including whether the assessed risk is a significant risk.

A60. For example, when evaluating the reasonableness of the allowance for doubtful accounts, an effective procedure for the auditor may be to review subsequent cash collections in combination with other procedures. Where the estimation uncertainty associated with an accounting estimate is high, for example, an accounting estimate based on a proprietary model for which there are unobservable inputs, it may be that a combination of the responses to assessed risks in paragraph 13 is necessary in order to obtain sufficient appropriate audit evidence.

A61. Additional guidance explaining the circumstances in which each of the responses may be appropriate is provided in paragraphs A62-A95.

Events Occurring Up to the Date of the Auditor's Report (Ref: Para. 13(a))

A62. Determining whether events occurring up to the date of the auditor's report provide audit evidence regarding the accounting estimate may be an appropriate response when such events are expected to:

- Occur; and
- Provide audit evidence that confirms or contradicts the accounting estimate.

A63. Events occurring up to the date of the auditor's report may sometimes provide sufficient appropriate audit evidence about an accounting estimate. For example, sale of the complete inventory of a superseded product shortly after the period end may provide audit evidence relating to the estimate of its net realisable value. In such cases, there may be no need to perform additional audit procedures on the accounting estimate, provided that sufficient appropriate evidence about the events is obtained.

A64. For some accounting estimates, events occurring up to the date of the auditor's report are unlikely to provide audit evidence regarding the accounting estimate. For example, the conditions or events relating to some accounting estimates develop only over an extended period. Also, because of the measurement objective of fair value accounting estimates, information after the period-end may not reflect the events or conditions existing at the balance sheet date and therefore may not be relevant to the measurement of the fair value accounting estimate. Paragraph 13 identifies other responses to the risks of material misstatement that the auditor may undertake.

A65. In some cases, events that contradict the accounting estimate may indicate that management has ineffective processes for making accounting estimates, or that there is management bias in the making of accounting estimates.

A66. Even though the auditor may decide not to undertake this approach in respect of specific accounting estimates, the auditor is required to comply with ASA 560.[16] The auditor is required to perform audit procedures designed to obtain sufficient appropriate audit evidence that all events occurring between the date of the financial report and the date of the auditor's report that require adjustment of, or disclosure in, the financial report

16 See ASA 560 *Subsequent Events.*

have been identified[17] and appropriately reflected in the financial report.[18] Because the measurement of many accounting estimates, other than fair value accounting estimates, usually depends on the outcome of future conditions, transactions or events, the auditor's work under ASA 560 is particularly relevant.

Considerations specific to smaller entities

A67. When there is a longer period between the balance sheet date and the date of the auditor's report, the auditor's review of events in this period may be an effective response for accounting estimates other than fair value accounting estimates. This may particularly be the case in some smaller owner-managed entities, especially when management does not have formalised control procedures over accounting estimates.

Testing How Management Made the Accounting Estimate (Ref: Para. 13(b))

A68. Testing how management made the accounting estimate and the data on which it is based may be an appropriate response when the accounting estimate is a fair value accounting estimate developed on a model that uses observable and unobservable inputs. It may also be appropriate when, for example:

- The accounting estimate is derived from the routine processing of data by the entity's accounting system.
- The auditor's review of similar accounting estimates made in the prior period financial report suggests that management's current period process is likely to be effective.
- The accounting estimate is based on a large population of items of a similar nature that individually are not significant.

A69. Testing how management made the accounting estimate may involve, for example:

- Testing the extent to which data on which the accounting estimate is based is accurate, complete and relevant, and whether the accounting estimate has been properly determined using such data and management assumptions.
- Considering the source, relevance and reliability of external data or information, including that received from external experts engaged by management to assist in making an accounting estimate.
- Recalculating the accounting estimate, and reviewing information about an accounting estimate for internal consistency.
- Considering management's review and approval processes.

Considerations specific to smaller entities

A70. In smaller entities, the process for making accounting estimates is likely to be less structured than in larger entities. Smaller entities with active management involvement may not have extensive descriptions of accounting procedures, sophisticated accounting records, or written policies. Even if the entity has no formal established process, it does not mean that management is not able to provide a basis upon which the auditor can test the accounting estimate.

Evaluating the method of measurement (Ref: Para. 13(b)(i))

A71. When the applicable financial reporting framework does not prescribe the method of measurement, evaluating whether the method used, including any applicable model, is appropriate in the circumstances is a matter of professional judgement.

A72. For this purpose, matters that the auditor may consider include, for example, whether:

- Management's rationale for the method selected is reasonable.
- Management has sufficiently evaluated and appropriately applied the criteria, if any, provided in the applicable financial reporting framework to support the selected method.

17 See ASA 560, paragraph 6.

18 See ASA 560, paragraph 8.

- The method is appropriate in the circumstances given the nature of the asset or liability being estimated and the requirements of the applicable financial reporting framework relevant to accounting estimates.
- The method is appropriate in relation to the business, industry and environment in which the entity operates.

A73. In some cases, management may have determined that different methods result in a range of significantly different estimates. In such cases, obtaining an understanding of how the entity has investigated the reasons for these differences may assist the auditor in evaluating the appropriateness of the method selected.

Evaluating the use of models

A74. In some cases, particularly when making fair value accounting estimates, management may use a model. Whether the model used is appropriate in the circumstances may depend on a number of factors, such as the nature of the entity and its environment, including the industry in which it operates, and the specific asset or liability being measured.

ASA

A75. The extent to which the following considerations are relevant depends on the circumstances, including whether the model is one that is commercially available for use in a particular sector or industry, or a proprietary model. In some cases, an entity may use an expert to develop and test a model.

A76. Depending on the circumstances, matters that the auditor may also consider in testing the model include, for example, whether:

- The model is validated prior to usage, with periodic reviews to ensure it is still suitable for its intended use. The entity's validation process may include evaluation of:
  - The model's theoretical soundness and mathematical integrity, including the appropriateness of model parameters.
  - The consistency and completeness of the model's inputs with market practices.
  - The model's output as compared to actual transactions.
- Appropriate change control policies and procedures exist.
- The model is periodically calibrated and tested for validity, particularly when inputs are subjective.
- Adjustments are made to the output of the model, including in the case of fair value accounting estimates, whether such adjustments reflect the assumptions marketplace participants would use in similar circumstances.
- The model is adequately documented, including the model's intended applications and limitations and its key parameters, required inputs, and results of any validation analysis performed.

***Assumptions used by management** (Ref: Para. 13(b)(ii))*

A77. The auditor's evaluation of the assumptions used by management is based only on information available to the auditor at the time of the audit. Audit procedures dealing with management assumptions are performed in the context of the audit of the entity's financial report, and not for the purpose of providing an opinion on assumptions themselves.

A78. Matters that the auditor may consider in evaluating the reasonableness of the assumptions used by management include, for example:

- Whether individual assumptions appear reasonable.
- Whether the assumptions are interdependent and internally consistent.
- Whether the assumptions appear reasonable when considered collectively or in conjunction with other assumptions, either for that accounting estimate or for other accounting estimates.
- In the case of fair value accounting estimates, whether the assumptions appropriately reflect observable marketplace assumptions.

A79. The assumptions on which accounting estimates are based may reflect what management expects will be the outcome of specific objectives and strategies. In such cases, the auditor may perform audit procedures to evaluate the reasonableness of such assumptions by considering, for example, whether the assumptions are consistent with:

- The general economic environment and the entity's economic circumstances.
- The plans of the entity.
- Assumptions made in prior periods, if relevant.
- Experience of, or previous conditions experienced by, the entity, to the extent this historical information may be considered representative of future conditions or events.
- Other assumptions used by management relating to the financial report.

A80. The reasonableness of the assumptions used may depend on management's intent and ability to carry out certain courses of action. Management often documents plans and intentions relevant to specific assets or liabilities and the financial reporting framework may require it to do so. Although the extent of audit evidence to be obtained about management's intent and ability is a matter of professional judgement, the auditor's procedures may include the following:

- Review of management's history of carrying out its stated intentions.
- Review of written plans and other documentation, including, where applicable, formally approved budgets, authorisations or minutes.
- Enquiry of management about its reasons for a particular course of action.
- Review of events occurring subsequent to the date of the financial report and up to the date of the auditor's report.
- Evaluation of the entity's ability to carry out a particular course of action given the entity's economic circumstances, including the implications of its existing commitments.

Certain financial reporting frameworks, however, may not permit management's intentions or plans to be taken into account when making an accounting estimate. This is often the case for fair value accounting estimates because their measurement objective requires that assumptions reflect those used by marketplace participants.

A81. Matters that the auditor may consider in evaluating the reasonableness of assumptions used by management underlying fair value accounting estimates, in addition to those discussed above where applicable, may include, for example:

- Where relevant, whether and, if so, how management has incorporated market-specific inputs into the development of assumptions.
- Whether the assumptions are consistent with observable market conditions, and the characteristics of the asset or liability being measured at fair value.
- Whether the sources of market-participant assumptions are relevant and reliable, and how management has selected the assumptions to use when a number of different market participant assumptions exist.
- Where appropriate, whether and, if so, how management considered assumptions used in, or information about, comparable transactions, assets or liabilities.

A82. Further, fair value accounting estimates may comprise observable inputs as well as unobservable inputs. Where fair value accounting estimates are based on unobservable inputs, matters that the auditor may consider include, for example, how management supports the following:

- The identification of the characteristics of marketplace participants relevant to the accounting estimate.
- Modifications it has made to its own assumptions to reflect its view of assumptions marketplace participants would use.
- Whether it has incorporated the best information available in the circumstances.
- Where applicable, how its assumptions take account of comparable transactions, assets or liabilities.

If there are unobservable inputs, it is more likely that the auditor's evaluation of the assumptions will need to be combined with other responses to assessed risks in paragraph 13 in order to obtain sufficient appropriate audit evidence. In such cases, it may be necessary for the auditor to perform other audit procedures, for example, examining documentation supporting the review and approval of the accounting estimate by appropriate levels of management and, where appropriate, by those charged with governance.

A83. In evaluating the reasonableness of the assumptions supporting an accounting estimate, the auditor may identify one or more significant assumptions. If so, it may indicate that the accounting estimate has high estimation uncertainty and may, therefore, give rise to a significant risk. Additional responses to significant risks are described in paragraphs A102-A115.

Testing the Operating Effectiveness of Controls (Ref: Para. 13(c))

A84. Testing the operating effectiveness of the controls over how management made the accounting estimate may be an appropriate response when management's process has been well-designed, implemented and maintained, for example:

- Controls exist for the review and approval of the accounting estimates by appropriate levels of management and, where appropriate, by those charged with governance.
- The accounting estimate is derived from the routine processing of data by the entity's accounting system.

A85. Testing the operating effectiveness of the controls is required when:

(a) The auditor's assessment of risks of material misstatement at the assertion level includes an expectation that controls over the process are operating effectively; or

(b) Substantive procedures alone do not provide sufficient appropriate audit evidence at the assertion level.[19]

Considerations specific to smaller entities

A86. Controls over the process to make an accounting estimate may exist in smaller entities, but the formality with which they operate varies. Further, smaller entities may determine that certain types of controls are not necessary because of active management involvement in the financial reporting process. In the case of very small entities, however, there may not be many controls that the auditor can identify. For this reason, the auditor's response to the assessed risks is likely to be substantive in nature, with the auditor performing one or more of the other responses in paragraph 13.

Developing a Point Estimate or Range (Ref: Para. 13(d))

A87. Developing a point estimate or a range to evaluate management's point estimate may be an appropriate response where, for example:

- An accounting estimate is not derived from the routine processing of data by the accounting system.
- The auditor's review of similar accounting estimates made in the prior period financial report suggests that management's current period process is unlikely to be effective.
- The entity's controls within and over management's processes for determining accounting estimates are not well designed or properly implemented.
- Events or transactions between the period end and the date of the auditor's report contradict management's point estimate.
- There are alternative sources of relevant data available to the auditor which can be used in developing a point estimate or a range.

A88. Even where the entity's controls are well designed and properly implemented, developing a point estimate or a range may be an effective or efficient response to the assessed risks. In other situations, the auditor may consider this approach as part of determining whether further procedures are necessary and, if so, their nature and extent.

---

19 See ASA 330, paragraph 8.

A89. The approach taken by the auditor in developing either a point estimate or a range may vary based on what is considered most effective in the circumstances. For example, the auditor may initially develop a preliminary point estimate, and then assess its sensitivity to changes in assumptions to ascertain a range with which to evaluate management's point estimate. Alternatively, the auditor may begin by developing a range for purposes of determining, where possible, a point estimate.

A90. The ability of the auditor to make a point estimate, as opposed to a range, depends on several factors, including the model used, the nature and extent of data available and the estimation uncertainty involved with the accounting estimate. Further, the decision to develop a point estimate or range may be influenced by the applicable financial reporting framework, which may prescribe the point estimate that is to be used after consideration of the alternative outcomes and assumptions, or prescribe a specific measurement method (for example, the use of a discounted probability-weighted expected value).

A91. The auditor may develop a point estimate or a range in a number of ways, for example, by:

- Using a model, for example, one that is commercially available for use in a particular sector or industry, or a proprietary or auditor-developed model.
- Further developing management's consideration of alternative assumptions or outcomes, for example, by introducing a different set of assumptions.
- Employing or engaging a person with specialised expertise to develop or execute the model, or to provide relevant assumptions.
- Making reference to other comparable conditions, transactions or events, or, where relevant, markets for comparable assets or liabilities.

Understanding Management's Assumptions or Method *(Ref: Para. 13(d)(i))*

A92. When the auditor makes a point estimate or a range and uses assumptions or a method different from those used by management, paragraph 13(d)(i) requires the auditor to obtain a sufficient understanding of the assumptions or method used by management in making the accounting estimate. This understanding provides the auditor with information that may be relevant to the auditor's development of an appropriate point estimate or range. Further, it assists the auditor to understand and evaluate any significant differences from management's point estimate. For example, a difference may arise because the auditor used different, but equally valid, assumptions as compared with those used by management. This may reveal that the accounting estimate is highly sensitive to certain assumptions and therefore subject to high estimation uncertainty, indicating that the accounting estimate may be a significant risk. Alternatively, a difference may arise as a result of a factual error made by management. Depending on the circumstances, the auditor may find it helpful in drawing conclusions to discuss with management the basis for the assumptions used and their validity, and the difference, if any, in the approach taken to making the accounting estimate.

Narrowing a Range *(Ref: Para. 13(d)(ii))*

A93. When the auditor concludes that it is appropriate to use a range to evaluate the reasonableness of management's point estimate (the auditor's range), paragraph 13(d)(ii) requires that range to encompass all "reasonable outcomes" rather than all possible outcomes. The range cannot be one that comprises all possible outcomes if it is to be useful, as such a range would be too wide to be effective for purposes of the audit. The auditor's range is useful and effective when it is sufficiently narrow to enable the auditor to conclude whether the accounting estimate is misstated.

A94. Ordinarily, a range that has been narrowed to be equal to or less than performance materiality is adequate for the purposes of evaluating the reasonableness of management's point estimate. However, particularly in certain industries, it may not be possible to narrow the range to below such an amount. This does not necessarily preclude recognition of the accounting estimate. It may indicate, however, that the estimation uncertainty associated with the accounting estimate is such that it gives rise to a significant risk. Additional responses to significant risks are described in paragraphs A102-A115.

A95. Narrowing the range to a position where all outcomes within the range are considered reasonable may be achieved by:

(a) Eliminating from the range those outcomes at the extremities of the range judged by the auditor to be unlikely to occur; and

(b) Continuing to narrow the range, based on audit evidence available, until the auditor concludes that all outcomes within the range are considered reasonable. In some rare cases, the auditor may be able to narrow the range until the audit evidence indicates a point estimate.

Considering whether Specialised Skills or Knowledge Are Required *(Ref: Para. 14)*

A96. In planning the audit, the auditor is required to ascertain the nature, timing and extent of resources necessary to perform the audit engagement.[20] This may include, as necessary, the involvement of those with specialised skills or knowledge. In addition, ASA 220 requires the engagement partner to be satisfied that the engagement team, and any auditor's external experts who are not part of the engagement team, collectively have the appropriate competence and capabilities to perform the audit engagement.[21] During the course of the audit of accounting estimates the auditor may identify, in light of the experience of the auditor and the circumstances of the engagement, the need for specialised skills or knowledge to be applied in relation to one or more aspects of the accounting estimates.

A97. Matters that may affect the auditor's consideration of whether specialised skills or knowledge is required include, for example:

- The nature of the underlying asset, liability or component of equity in a particular business or industry (for example, mineral deposits, agricultural assets, complex financial instruments).
- A high degree of estimation uncertainty.
- Complex calculations or specialised models are involved, for example, when estimating fair values when there is no observable market.
- The complexity of the requirements of the applicable financial reporting framework relevant to accounting estimates, including whether there are areas known to be subject to differing interpretation or practice is inconsistent or developing.
- The procedures the auditor intends to undertake in responding to assessed risks.

A98. For the majority of accounting estimates, even when there is estimation uncertainty, it is unlikely that specialised skills or knowledge will be required. For example, it is unlikely that specialised skills or knowledge would be necessary for an auditor to evaluate an allowance for doubtful accounts.

A99. However, the auditor may not possess the specialised skills or knowledge required when the matter involved is in a field other than accounting or auditing and may need to obtain it from an auditor's expert. ASA 620[22] establishes requirements and provides guidance in determining the need to employ or engage an auditor's expert and the auditor's responsibilities when using the work of an auditor's expert.

A100. Further, in some cases, the auditor may conclude that it is necessary to obtain specialised skills or knowledge related to specific areas of accounting or auditing. Individuals with such skills or knowledge may be employed by the auditor's firm or engaged from an external organisation outside of the auditor's firm. Where such individuals perform audit procedures on the engagement, they are part of the engagement team and accordingly, they are subject to the requirements in ASA 220.

A101. Depending on the auditor's understanding and experience of working with the auditor's expert or those other individuals with specialised skills or knowledge, the auditor may consider it appropriate to discuss matters such as the requirements of the applicable financial reporting framework with the individuals involved to establish that their work is relevant for audit purposes.

20 See ASA 300 *Planning an Audit of a Financial Report*, paragraph 8(e).

21 See ASA 220 *Quality Control for an Audit of a Financial Report and Other Historical Financial Information*, paragraph 14.

22 See ASA 620 *Using the Work of an Auditor's Expert*.

Further Substantive Procedures to Respond to Significant Risks

(Ref: Para. 15)

A102. In auditing accounting estimates that give rise to significant risks, the auditor's further substantive procedures are focused on the evaluation of:

(a) How management has assessed the effect of estimation uncertainty on the accounting estimate, and the effect such uncertainty may have on the appropriateness of the recognition of the accounting estimate in the financial report; and

(b) The adequacy of related disclosures.

Estimation Uncertainty

***Management's Consideration of Estimation Uncertainty** (Ref: Para. 15(a))*

A103. Management may evaluate alternative assumptions or outcomes of the accounting estimates through a number of methods, depending on the circumstances. One possible method used by management is to undertake a sensitivity analysis. This might involve determining how the monetary amount of an accounting estimate varies with different assumptions. Even for accounting estimates measured at fair value there can be variation because different market participants will use different assumptions. A sensitivity analysis could lead to the development of a number of outcome scenarios, sometimes characterised as a range of outcomes by management, such as "pessimistic" and "optimistic" scenarios.

A104. A sensitivity analysis may demonstrate that an accounting estimate is not sensitive to changes in particular assumptions. Alternatively, it may demonstrate that the accounting estimate is sensitive to one or more assumptions that then become the focus of the auditor's attention.

A105. This is not intended to suggest that one particular method of addressing estimation uncertainty (such as sensitivity analysis) is more suitable than another, or that management's consideration of alternative assumptions or outcomes needs to be conducted through a detailed process supported by extensive documentation. Rather, it is whether management has assessed how estimation uncertainty may affect the accounting estimate that is important, not the specific manner in which it is done. Accordingly, where management has not considered alternative assumptions or outcomes, it may be necessary for the auditor to discuss with management, and request support for, how it has addressed the effects of estimation uncertainty on the accounting estimate.

Considerations specific to smaller entities

A106. Smaller entities may use simple means to assess the estimation uncertainty. In addition to the auditor's review of available documentation, the auditor may obtain other audit evidence of management consideration of alternative assumptions or outcomes by enquiry of management. In addition, management may not have the expertise to consider alternative outcomes or otherwise address the estimation uncertainty of the accounting estimate. In such cases, the auditor may explain to management the process or the different methods available for doing so, and the documentation thereof. This would not, however, change the responsibilities of management for the preparation of the financial report.

***Significant Assumptions** (Ref: Para. 15(b))*

A107. An assumption used in making an accounting estimate may be deemed to be significant if a reasonable variation in the assumption would materially affect the measurement of the accounting estimate.

A108. Support for significant assumptions derived from management's knowledge may be obtained from management's continuing processes of strategic analysis and risk management. Even without formal established processes, such as may be the case in smaller entities, the auditor may be able to evaluate the assumptions through enquiries of and discussions with management, along with other audit procedures in order to obtain sufficient appropriate audit evidence.

A109. The auditor's considerations in evaluating assumptions made by management are described in paragraphs A77-A83.

Management Intent and Ability (Ref: Para. 15(c))

A110. The auditor's considerations in relation to assumptions made by management and management's intent and ability are described in paragraphs A13 and A80.

Development of a Range (Ref: Para. 16)

A111. In preparing the financial report, management may be satisfied that it has adequately addressed the effects of estimation uncertainty on the accounting estimates that give rise to significant risks. In some circumstances, however, the auditor may view the efforts of management as inadequate. This may be the case, for example, where, in the auditor's judgement:

- Sufficient appropriate audit evidence could not be obtained through the auditor's evaluation of how management has addressed the effects of estimation uncertainty.
- It is necessary to explore further the degree of estimation uncertainty associated with an accounting estimate, for example, where the auditor is aware of wide variation in outcomes for similar accounting estimates in similar circumstances.
- It is unlikely that other audit evidence can be obtained, for example, through the review of events occurring up to the date of the auditor's report.
- Indicators of management bias in the making of accounting estimates may exist.

A112. The auditor's considerations in determining a range for this purpose are described in paragraphs A87-A95.

Recognition and Measurement Criteria

Recognition of the Accounting Estimates in the Financial Report (Ref: Para. 17(a))

A113. Where management has recognised an accounting estimate in the financial report, the focus of the auditor's evaluation is on whether the measurement of the accounting estimate is sufficiently reliable to meet the recognition criteria of the applicable financial reporting framework.

A114. With respect to accounting estimates that have not been recognised, the focus of the auditor's evaluation is on whether the recognition criteria of the applicable financial reporting framework have in fact been met. Even where an accounting estimate has not been recognised, and the auditor concludes that this treatment is appropriate, there may be a need for disclosure of the circumstances in the notes to the financial report. The auditor may also determine that there is a need to draw the reader's attention to a significant uncertainty by adding an Emphasis of Matter paragraph to the auditor's report. ASA 706[23] establishes requirements and provides guidance concerning such paragraphs.

Measurement Basis for the Accounting Estimates (Ref: Para. 17(b))

A115. With respect to fair value accounting estimates, some financial reporting frameworks presume that fair value can be measured reliably as a prerequisite to either requiring or permitting fair value measurements and disclosures. In some cases, this presumption may be overcome when, for example, there is no appropriate method or basis for measurement. In such cases, the focus of the auditor's evaluation is on whether management's basis for overcoming the presumption relating to the use of fair value set forth under the applicable financial reporting framework is appropriate.

Evaluating the Reasonableness of the Accounting Estimates, and Determining Misstatements (Ref: Para. 18)

A116. Based on the audit evidence obtained, the auditor may conclude that the evidence points to an accounting estimate that differs from management's point estimate. Where the audit evidence supports a point estimate, the difference between the auditor's point estimate and management's point estimate constitutes a misstatement. Where the auditor has concluded that using the auditor's range provides sufficient appropriate audit evidence, a management point estimate that lies outside the auditor's range would not be supported by audit evidence. In such cases, the misstatement is no less than the difference between management's point estimate and the nearest point of the auditor's range.

---

23 See ASA 706 *Emphasis of Matter Paragraphs and Other Matter Paragraphs in the Independent Auditor's Report.*

A117. Where management has changed an accounting estimate, or the method in making it, from the prior period based on a subjective assessment that there has been a change in circumstances, the auditor may conclude based on the audit evidence that the accounting estimate is misstated as a result of an arbitrary change by management, or may regard it as an indicator of possible management bias (see paragraphs A124-A125).

A118. ASA 450[24] provides guidance on distinguishing misstatements for purposes of the auditor's evaluation of the effect of uncorrected misstatements on the financial report. In relation to accounting estimates, a misstatement, whether caused by fraud or error, may arise as a result of:

- Misstatements about which there is no doubt (factual misstatements).
- Differences arising from management's judgements concerning accounting estimates that the auditor considers unreasonable, or the selection or application of accounting policies that the auditor considers inappropriate (judgemental misstatements).
- The auditor's best estimate of misstatements in populations, involving the projection of misstatements identified in audit samples to the entire populations from which the samples were drawn (projected misstatements).

In some cases involving accounting estimates, a misstatement could arise as a result of a combination of these circumstances, making separate identification difficult or impossible.

A119. Evaluating the reasonableness of accounting estimates and related disclosures included in the notes to the financial report, whether required by the applicable financial reporting framework or disclosed voluntarily, involves essentially the same types of considerations applied when auditing an accounting estimate recognised in the financial report.

Disclosures Related to Accounting Estimates

Disclosures in Accordance with the Applicable Financial Reporting Framework

(Ref: Para. 19)

A120. The presentation of the financial report in accordance with the applicable financial reporting framework includes adequate disclosure of material matters. The applicable financial reporting framework may permit, or prescribe, disclosures related to accounting estimates, and some entities may disclose voluntarily additional information in the notes to the financial report. These disclosures may include, for example:

- The assumptions used.
- The method of estimation used, including any applicable model.
- The basis for the selection of the method of estimation.
- The effect of any changes to the method of estimation from the prior period.
- The sources and implications of estimation uncertainty.

Such disclosures are relevant to users in understanding the accounting estimates recognised or disclosed in the financial report, and sufficient appropriate audit evidence needs to be obtained about whether the disclosures are in accordance with the requirements of the applicable financial reporting framework.

A121. In some cases, the applicable financial reporting framework may require specific disclosures regarding uncertainties. For example, some financial reporting frameworks prescribe:

- The disclosure of key assumptions and other sources of estimation uncertainty that have a significant risk of causing a material adjustment to the carrying amounts of assets and liabilities. Such requirements may be described using terms such as "Key Sources of Estimation Uncertainty" or "Critical Accounting Estimates".
- The disclosure of the range of possible outcomes, and the assumptions used in determining the range.

24 See ASA 450 *Evaluation of Misstatements Identified during the Audit.*

- The disclosure of information regarding the significance of fair value accounting estimates to the entity's financial position and performance.
- Qualitative disclosures such as the exposures to risk and how they arise, the entity's objectives, policies and procedures for managing the risk and the methods used to measure the risk and any changes from the previous period of these qualitative concepts.
- Quantitative disclosures such as the extent to which the entity is exposed to risk, based on information provided internally to the entity's key management personnel, including credit risk, liquidity risk and market risk.

Disclosures of Estimation Uncertainty for Accounting Estimates that Give Rise to Significant Risks (Ref: Para. 20)

A122. In relation to accounting estimates having significant risk, even where the disclosures are in accordance with the applicable financial reporting framework, the auditor may conclude that the disclosure of estimation uncertainty is inadequate in light of the circumstances and facts involved. The auditor's evaluation of the adequacy of disclosure of estimation uncertainty increases in importance the greater the range of possible outcomes of the accounting estimate is in relation to materiality (see related discussion in paragraph A94).

A123. In some cases, the auditor may consider it appropriate to encourage management to describe, in the notes to the financial report, the circumstances relating to the estimation uncertainty. ASA 705[25] provides guidance on the implications for the auditor's opinion when the auditor believes that management's disclosure of estimation uncertainty in the financial report is inadequate or misleading.

Indicators of Possible Management Bias (Ref: Para. 21)

A124. During the audit, the auditor may become aware of judgements and decisions made by management which give rise to indicators of possible management bias. Such indicators may affect the auditor's conclusion as to whether the auditor's risk assessment and related responses remain appropriate, and the auditor may need to consider the implications for the rest of the audit. Further, they may affect the auditor's evaluation of whether the financial report as a whole is free from material misstatement, as discussed in ASA 700.[26]

Aus A124.1 Indicators of possible management bias affecting accounting estimates may represent a risk of material misstatement due to fraud as discussed in ASA 240.[*]

A125. Examples of indicators of possible management bias with respect to accounting estimates include:

- Changes in an accounting estimate, or the method for making it, where management has made a subjective assessment that there has been a change in circumstances.
- Use of an entity's own assumptions for fair value accounting estimates when they are inconsistent with observable marketplace assumptions.
- Selection or construction of significant assumptions that yield a point estimate favourable for management objectives.
- Selection of a point estimate that may indicate a pattern of optimism or pessimism.

25 See ASA 705 *Modifications to the Opinion in the Independent Auditor's Report.*

26 See ASA 700 *Forming an Opinion and Reporting on a Financial Report.*

* See ASA 240, para 32 (b)(i).

Written Representations (Ref: Para. 22)

A126. ASA 580[27] discusses the use of written representations. Depending on the nature, materiality and extent of estimation uncertainty, written representations about accounting estimates recognised or disclosed in the financial report may include representations:

- About the appropriateness of the measurement processes, including related assumptions and models, used by management in determining accounting estimates in the context of the applicable financial reporting framework, and the consistency in application of the processes.
- That the assumptions appropriately reflect management's intent and ability to carry out specific courses of action on behalf of the entity, where relevant to the accounting estimates and disclosures.
- That disclosures related to accounting estimates are complete and appropriate under the applicable financial reporting framework.
- That no subsequent event requires adjustment to the accounting estimates and disclosures included in the financial report.

A127. For those accounting estimates not recognised or disclosed in the financial report, written representations may also include representations about:

- The appropriateness of the basis used by management for determining that the recognition or disclosure criteria of the applicable financial reporting framework have not been met (see paragraph A114).
- The appropriateness of the basis used by management to overcome the presumption relating to the use of fair value set forth under the entity's applicable financial reporting framework, for those accounting estimates not measured or disclosed at fair value (see paragraph A115).

Documentation (Ref: Para. 23)

A128. Documentation of indicators of possible management bias identified during the audit assists the auditor in concluding whether the auditor's risk assessment and related responses remain appropriate, and in evaluating whether the financial report as a whole is free from material misstatement. See paragraph A125 for examples of indicators of possible management bias.

❖ ❖ ❖

Conformity with International Standards on Auditing

This Auditing Standard conforms with International Standard on Auditing ISA 540 *Auditing Accounting Estimates, Including Fair Value Accounting Estimates, and Related Disclosures*, issued by the International Auditing and Assurance Standards Board (IAASB), an independent standard-setting board of the International Federation of Accountants (IFAC).

Paragraphs that have been added to this Auditing Standard (and do not appear in the text of the equivalent ISA) are identified with the prefix "Aus".

The following requirement is additional to ISA 540:

- The auditor shall include in the audit documentation:
  - ♦ The auditor's evaluation of any indicators of possible management bias in making accounting estimates, including whether the circumstances giving rise to the indicators of bias represent a risk of material misstatement due to fraud. [Ref: Para. Aus 23.1]

Compliance with this Auditing Standard enables compliance with ISA 540.

27 See ASA 580 *Written Representations.*

Appendix 1

(Ref: Para. A1)

Fair Value Measurements and Disclosures Under Different Financial Reporting Frameworks

The purpose of this appendix is only to provide a general discussion of fair value measurements and disclosures under different financial reporting frameworks, for background and context.

1. Different financial reporting frameworks require or permit a variety of fair value measurements and disclosures in the financial report. They also vary in the level of guidance that they provide on the basis for measuring assets and liabilities or the related disclosures. Some financial reporting frameworks give prescriptive guidance, others give general guidance, and some give no guidance at all. In addition, certain industry-specific measurement and disclosure practices for fair values also exist.

2. Definitions of fair value may differ among financial reporting frameworks, or for different assets, liabilities or disclosures within a particular framework. For example, Australian Accounting Standards[28] define fair value as "the amount for which an asset could be exchanged, or a liability settled, between knowledgeable, willing parties in an arm's length transaction." The concept of fair value ordinarily assumes a current transaction, rather than settlement at some past or future date. Accordingly, the process of measuring fair value would be a search for the estimated price at which that transaction would occur. Additionally, different financial reporting frameworks may use such terms as "entity-specific value," "value in use," or similar terms, but may still fall within the concept of fair value in this Auditing Standard.

3. Financial reporting frameworks may treat changes in fair value measurements that occur over time in different ways. For example, a particular financial reporting framework may require that changes in fair value measurements of certain assets or liabilities be reflected directly in equity, while such changes might be reflected in income under another framework. In some frameworks, the determination of whether to use fair value accounting or how it is applied is influenced by management's intent to carry out certain courses of action with respect to the specific asset or liability.

4. Different financial reporting frameworks may require certain specific fair value measurements and disclosures in the financial report and prescribe or permit them in varying degrees. The financial reporting frameworks may:

   - Prescribe measurement, presentation and disclosure requirements for certain information included in the financial report or for information disclosed in the notes to financial report or presented as supplementary information;
   - Permit certain measurements using fair values at the option of an entity or only when certain criteria have been met;
   - Prescribe a specific method for determining fair value, for example, through the use of an independent appraisal or specified ways of using discounted cash flows;
   - Permit a choice of method for determining fair value from among several alternative methods (the criteria for selection may or may not be provided by the financial reporting framework); or
   - Provide no guidance on the fair value measurements or disclosures of fair value other than their use being evident through custom or practice, for example, an industry practice.

5. Some financial reporting frameworks presume that fair value can be measured reliably for assets or liabilities as a prerequisite to either requiring or permitting fair value measurements or disclosures. In some cases, this presumption may be overcome when an asset or liability does not have a quoted market price in an active market and for which other methods of reasonably estimating fair value are clearly inappropriate or unworkable.

28 See AASB 139 *Financial Instruments: Recognition and Measurement.*

Some financial reporting frameworks may specify a fair value hierarchy that distinguishes inputs for use in arriving at fair values ranging from those that involve clearly "observable inputs" based on quoted prices and active markets and those "unobservable inputs" that involve an entity's own judgements about assumptions that marketplace participants would use.

6. Some financial reporting frameworks require certain specified adjustments or modifications to valuation information, or other considerations unique to a particular asset or liability. For example, accounting for investment properties may require adjustments to be made to an appraised market value, such as adjustments for estimated closing costs on sale, adjustments related to the property's condition and location, and other matters. Similarly, if the market for a particular asset is not an active market, published price quotations may have to be adjusted or modified to arrive at a more suitable measure of fair value. For example, quoted market prices may not be indicative of fair value if there is infrequent activity in the market, the market is not well established, or small volumes of units are traded relative to the aggregate number of trading units in existence. Accordingly, such market prices may have to be adjusted or modified. Alternative sources of market information may be needed to make such adjustments or modifications. Further, in some cases, collateral assigned (for example, when collateral is assigned for certain types of investment in debt) may need to be considered in determining the fair value or possible impairment of an asset or liability.

7. In most financial reporting frameworks, underlying the concept of fair value measurements is a presumption that the entity is a going concern without any intention or need to liquidate, curtail materially the scale of its operations, or undertake a transaction on adverse terms. Therefore, in this case, fair value would not be the amount that an entity would receive or pay in a forced transaction, involuntary liquidation, or distress sale. On the other hand, general economic conditions or economic conditions specific to certain industries may cause illiquidity in the marketplace and require fair values to be predicated upon depressed prices, potentially significantly depressed prices. An entity, however, may need to take its current economic or operating situation into account in determining the fair values of its assets and liabilities if prescribed or permitted to do so by its financial reporting framework and such framework may or may not specify how that is done. For example, management's plan to dispose of an asset on an accelerated basis to meet specific business objectives may be relevant to the determination of the fair value of that asset.

Prevalence of Fair Value Measurements

8. Measurements and disclosures based on fair value are becoming increasingly prevalent in financial reporting frameworks. Fair values may occur in, and affect the determination of, the financial report in a number of ways, including the measurement at fair value of the following:

- Specific assets or liabilities, such as marketable securities or liabilities to settle an obligation under a financial instrument, routinely or periodically "marked-to-market".
- Specific components of equity, for example when accounting for the recognition, measurement and presentation of certain financial instruments with equity features, such as a bond convertible by the holder into common shares of the issuer.
- Specific assets or liabilities acquired in a business combination. For example, the initial determination of goodwill arising on the purchase of an entity in a business combination usually is based on the fair value measurement of the identifiable assets and liabilities acquired and the fair value of the consideration given.
- Specific assets or liabilities adjusted to fair value on a one-time basis. Some financial reporting frameworks may require the use of a fair value measurement to quantify an adjustment to an asset or a group of assets as part of an asset impairment determination, for example, a test of impairment of goodwill acquired in a business combination based on the fair value of a defined operating entity or reporting unit, the value of which is then allocated among the entity's or unit's group of assets and

liabilities in order to derive an implied goodwill for comparison to the recorded goodwill.

- Aggregations of assets and liabilities. In some circumstances, the measurement of a class or group of assets or liabilities calls for an aggregation of fair values of some of the individual assets or liabilities in such class or group. For example, under an entity's applicable financial reporting framework, the measurement of a diversified loan portfolio might be determined based on the fair value of some categories of loans comprising the portfolio.
- Information disclosed in the notes to financial report or presented as supplementary information, but not recognised in the financial report.

ASA 550

Related Parties

(Reissued October 2009: amended and compiled June 2011)

Issued by the Auditing and Assurance Standards Board.

Note from the Institute of Chartered Accountants Australia

This note, prepared by the technical editor, is not part of ASA 550.

Historical development

April 1986: Statement of Auditing Practice AUP 26, 'Related Parties' is issued in, and effective from, April 1986, following the issue of ED 10 (IAPC ED 18) in July 1983. The relevant IAPC publication was IAG 17 which was issued in October 1984.

December 1991: AUP 26 'Related Parties' reissued by the AuASB, revised to reflect the accounting standards issued on related parties, i.e. AAS 22 'Related Party Disclosures' and AASB 1017 of the same name.

December 1993: ED 53 'Codification and Revision of Auditing Pronouncements: AUS 520 Related Parties (AUP 26)' issued by the AuSB.

June 1994: The International Auditing Practices Committee (IAPC) of the International Federation of Accountants (IFAC) approved the issuance of a codified set of International Standards of Auditing (ISAs). The relevant international pronouncement was ISA 550 'Related Parties'.

October 1995: Australian Auditing Standards and Auditing Guidance Statements released. The status of these was explained in APS 1.1 'Conformity With Auditing Standards'. These Standards became operative for the first reporting period commencing on or after 1 July 1996 and later reporting periods, although earlier application was encouraged. AUP 26 'Related Parties' replaced by AUS 518 'Related Parties'.

February 2000: AUS 518 'Related Parties' reissued by the AuASB, operative for reporting periods commencing on or after 1 July 2000. AUS 518 was based on ED 73 of the same title.

July 2002: AUS/AGS Omnibus 3 'Miscellaneous Amendments to AUSs and AGSs' issued by the AuASB, operative from the date of issue. AUS 518 since reissued by the Board to incorporate these amendments.

April 2006: ASA 550 was issued as a legally enforceable Standard to replace AUS 518. It is based on ISA 550 of the same name.

October 2006: ASA 550 was reissued to correct a typographical error.

October 2009: ASA 550 reissued as part of the AUASB's Clarity Project. It has been considerably strengthened and includes new requirements for the audit team to consider whether the notes associated with related parties are significant, and in certain circumstances to inspect significant related party agreements. It is based on the revised ISA 550 of the same name.

June 2011: ASA 550 updated for editorial amendments contained in ASA 2011-1 'Amendments to Australian Auditing Standards'.

Contents

Compilation Details

Auditing Standard ASA 550 *Related Parties* as Amended

This compilation takes into account amendments made up to and including 27 June 2011 and was prepared on 27 June 2011 by the Auditing and Assurance Standards Board (AUASB).

This compilation is not a separate Auditing Standard made by the AUASB. Instead, it is a representation of ASA 550 (October 2009) as amended by another Auditing Standard which is listed in the Table below.

Table of Standards

Standard	Date made	Operative date
ASA 550	27 October 2009	1 January 2010
ASA 2011-1	27 June 2011	1 July 2011

Table of Amendments

Paragraph affected	How affected	By … [paragraph]
11 Footnote 7	Amended	ASA 2011-1 [39]
Subheading above Paragraph A23	Amended	ASA 2011-1 [40]

Preface

[Preface extracted from the original Auditing Standard issued 27 October 2009]

Reasons for Issuing Auditing Standard ASA 550 *Related Parties*

The Auditing and Assurance Standards Board (AUASB) issues Auditing Standard ASA 550 *Related Parties* pursuant to the requirements of the legislative provisions and the Strategic Direction explained below.

The AUASB is an independent statutory board of the Australian Government established under section 227A of the *Australian Securities and Investments Commission Act 2001*, as amended (ASIC Act). Under section 336 of the *Corporations Act 2001*, the AUASB may make Auditing Standards for the purposes of the corporations legislation. These Auditing Standards are legislative instruments under the *Legislative Instruments Act 2003*.

Under the Strategic Direction given to the AUASB by the Financial Reporting Council (FRC), the AUASB is required to have regard to any programme initiated by the International Auditing and Assurance Standards Board for the revision and enhancement of the International Standards on Auditing (ISAs) and to make appropriate consequential amendments to the Australian Auditing Standards. Accordingly, the AUASB has decided to revise and redraft the Australian Auditing Standards using the equivalent redrafted ISAs.

Main Features

This Auditing Standard establishes requirements and provides application and other explanatory material regarding the auditor's responsibilities relating to related party relationships and transactions when performing an audit of a financial report.

This Auditing Standard:

(a) requires the auditor to gain an understanding of related party relationships and transactions and to obtain information relevant to identifying the risks of material misstatement associated with related party relationships and transactions;

(b) describes risk assessment procedures and responses to assessed risks;

(c) requires the auditor to evaluate the accounting and disclosure of related party relationships and transactions;

(d) when relevant, requires the auditor to obtain written representations; and

(e) requires the auditor to communicate significant matters to those charged with governance.

Authority Statement

Auditing Standard ASA 550 *Related Parties* (as amended at 27 June 2011) is set out in paragraphs 1 to A50.

This Auditing Standard is to be read in conjunction with ASA 101 *Preamble to Australian Auditing Standards* which sets out the intentions of the AUASB on how the Australian Auditing Standards, operative for financial reporting periods commencing on or after 1 January 2010, are to be understood, interpreted and applied. This Auditing Standard is to be read also in conjunction with ASA 200 *Overall Objectives of the Independent Auditor and the Conduct of an Audit in Accordance with Australian Auditing Standards*.

Dated: 27 June 2011

M H Kelsall
Chairman - AUASB

Auditing Standard ASA 550

The Auditing and Assurance Standards Board (AUASB) made Auditing Standard ASA 550 *Related Parties*, pursuant to section 227B of the *Australian Securities and Investments Commission Act 2001* and section 336 of the *Corporations Act 2001*, on 27 October 2009.

This compiled version of ASA 550 incorporates subsequent amendments contained in another Auditing Standard made by the AUASB up to and including 27 June 2011 (see Compilation Details).

Auditing Standard ASA 550

Related Parties

Application

Aus 0.1 This Auditing Standard applies to:

(a) an audit of a financial report for a financial year, or an audit of a financial report for a half-year, in accordance with the *Corporations Act 2001*; and

(b) an audit of a financial report, or a complete set of financial statements, for any other purpose.

Aus 0.2 This Auditing Standard also applies, as appropriate, to an audit of other historical financial information.

Operative Date

Aus 0.3 This Auditing Standard is operative for financial reporting periods commencing on or after 1 January 2010.

[Note: For operative dates of paragraphs changed or added by an amending Standard, see Compilation Details.]

Introduction

Scope of this Auditing Standard

1. This Auditing Standard deals with the auditor's responsibilities relating to related party relationships and transactions in an audit of a financial report. Specifically, it expands on how ASA 315,[1] ASA 330,[2] and ASA 240[3] are to be applied in relation to risks of material misstatement associated with related party relationships and transactions.

Nature of Related Party Relationships and Transactions

2. Many related party transactions are in the normal course of business. In such circumstances, they may carry no higher risk of material misstatement of the financial report than similar

1 See ASA 315 *Identifying and Assessing the Risks of Material Misstatement through Understanding the Entity and Its Environment*.

2 See ASA 330 *The Auditor's Responses to Assessed Risks*.

3 See ASA 240 *The Auditor's Responsibilities Relating to Fraud in an Audit of a Financial Report*.

transactions with unrelated parties. However, the nature of related party relationships and transactions may, in some circumstances, give rise to higher risks of material misstatement of the financial report than transactions with unrelated parties. For example:

- Related parties may operate through an extensive and complex range of relationships and structures, with a corresponding increase in the complexity of related party transactions.
- Information systems may be ineffective at identifying or summarising transactions and outstanding balances between an entity and its related parties.
- Related party transactions may not be conducted under normal market terms and conditions; for example, some related party transactions may be conducted with no exchange of consideration.

Responsibilities of the Auditor

3. Because related parties are not independent of each other, many financial reporting frameworks establish specific accounting and disclosure requirements for related party relationships, transactions and balances to enable users of the financial report to understand their nature and actual or potential effects on the financial report. Where the applicable financial reporting framework establishes such requirements, the auditor has a responsibility to perform audit procedures to identify, assess and respond to the risks of material misstatement arising from the entity's failure to appropriately account for or disclose related party relationships, transactions or balances in accordance with the requirements of the framework.

4. Even if the applicable financial reporting framework establishes minimal or no related party requirements, the auditor nevertheless needs to obtain an understanding of the entity's related party relationships and transactions sufficient to be able to conclude whether the financial report, insofar as it is affected by those relationships and transactions: (Ref: Para. A1)

   (a) Achieves fair presentation (for fair presentation frameworks); or (Ref: Para. A2)

   (b) Is not misleading (for compliance frameworks). (Ref: Para. A3)

5. In addition, an understanding of the entity's related party relationships and transactions is relevant to the auditor's evaluation of whether one or more fraud risk factors are present as required by ASA 240,[4] because fraud may be more easily committed through related parties.

6. Owing to the inherent limitations of an audit, there is an unavoidable risk that some material misstatements of the financial report may not be detected, even though the audit is properly planned and performed in accordance with the Australian Auditing Standards.[5] In the context of related parties, the potential effects of inherent limitations on the auditor's ability to detect material misstatements are greater for such reasons as the following:

   - Management may be unaware of the existence of all related party relationships and transactions, particularly if the applicable financial reporting framework does not establish related party requirements.
   - Related party relationships may present a greater opportunity for collusion, concealment or manipulation by management.

7. Planning and performing the audit with professional scepticism as required by ASA 200[6] is therefore particularly important in this context, given the potential for undisclosed related party relationships and transactions. The requirements in this Auditing Standard are designed to assist the auditor in identifying and assessing the risks of material misstatement associated with related party relationships and transactions, and in designing audit procedures to respond to the assessed risks.

---

4 See ASA 240, paragraph 24.

5 See ASA 200 *Overall Objectives of the Independent Auditor and the Conduct of an Audit in Accordance with Australian Auditing Standards*, paragraph A52.

6 See ASA 200, paragraph 15.

Effective Date

8. [Deleted by the AUASB. Refer Aus 0.3]

Objectives

9. The objectives of the auditor are:
   (a) Irrespective of whether the applicable financial reporting framework establishes related party requirements, to obtain an understanding of related party relationships and transactions sufficient to be able:
      (i) To recognise fraud risk factors, if any, arising from related party relationships and transactions that are relevant to the identification and assessment of the risks of material misstatement due to fraud; and
      (ii) To conclude, based on the audit evidence obtained, whether the financial report, insofar as it is affected by those relationships and transactions:
         a. Achieves fair presentation (for fair presentation frameworks); or
         b. Are not misleading (for compliance frameworks); and
   (b) In addition, where the applicable financial reporting framework establishes related party requirements, to obtain sufficient appropriate audit evidence about whether related party relationships and transactions have been appropriately identified, accounted for and disclosed in the financial report in accordance with the framework.

Definitions

10. For purposes of the Australian Auditing Standards, the following terms have the meanings attributed below:
   (a) Arm's length transaction means a transaction conducted on such terms and conditions as between a willing buyer and a willing seller who are unrelated and are acting independently of each other and pursuing their own best interests.
   (b) Related party means a party that is either: (Ref: Para. A4-A7)
      (i) A related party as defined in the applicable financial reporting framework*; or
      (ii) Where the applicable financial reporting framework establishes minimal or no related party requirements:
         a. A person or other entity that has control or significant influence, directly or indirectly through one or more intermediaries, over the reporting entity;
         b. Another entity over which the reporting entity has control or significant influence, directly or indirectly through one or more intermediaries; or
         c. Another entity that is under common control with the reporting entity through having:
            i. Common controlling ownership;
            ii. Owners who are close family members; or
            iii. Common key management.

      However, entities that are under common control by a state (that is, a national, regional or local government) are not considered related unless they engage in significant transactions or share resources to a significant extent with one another.

* See, for example, section 228 of the *Corporations Act 2001*.

Requirements

Risk Assessment Procedures and Related Activities

11. As part of the risk assessment procedures and related activities that ASA 315 and ASA 240 require the auditor to perform during the audit,[7] the auditor shall perform the audit procedures and related activities set out in paragraphs 12-17 of this Auditing Standard, to obtain information relevant to identifying the risks of material misstatement associated with related party relationships and transactions. (Ref: Para. A8)

Understanding the Entity's Related Party Relationships and Transactions

12. The engagement team discussion that ASA 315 and ASA 240 require[8] shall include specific consideration of the susceptibility of the financial report to material misstatement due to fraud or error that could result from the entity's related party relationships and transactions. (Ref: Para. A9-A10)

13. The auditor shall enquire of management regarding:
    (a) The identity of the entity's related parties, including changes from the prior period; (Ref: Para. A11-A14)
    (b) The nature of the relationships between the entity and these related parties; and
    (c) Whether the entity entered into any transactions with these related parties during the period and, if so, the type and purpose of the transactions.

14. The auditor shall enquire of management and others within the entity, and perform other risk assessment procedures considered appropriate, to obtain an understanding of the controls, if any, that management has established to: (Ref: Para. A15-A20)
    (a) Identify, account for, and disclose related party relationships and transactions in accordance with the applicable financial reporting framework;
    (b) Authorise and approve significant transactions and arrangements with related parties; and (Ref: Para. A21)
    (c) Authorise and approve significant transactions and arrangements outside the normal course of business.

Maintaining Alertness for Related Party Information When Reviewing Records or Documents

15. During the audit, the auditor shall remain alert, when inspecting records or documents, for arrangements or other information that may indicate the existence of related party relationships or transactions that management has not previously identified or disclosed to the auditor. (Ref: Para. A22-A23)

    In particular, the auditor shall inspect the following for indications of the existence of related party relationships or transactions that management has not previously identified or disclosed to the auditor:
    (a) Bank and legal confirmations obtained as part of the auditor's procedures;
    (b) Minutes of meetings of shareholders and of those charged with governance; and
    (c) Such other records or documents as the auditor considers necessary in the circumstances of the entity.

16. If the auditor identifies significant transactions outside the entity's normal course of business when performing the audit procedures required by paragraph 15 of this Auditing Standard or through other audit procedures, the auditor shall enquire of management about: (Ref: Para. A24-A25)
    (a) The nature of these transactions; and (Ref: Para. A26)
    (b) Whether related parties could be involved. (Ref: Para. A27)

---

7 See ASA 315, paragraph 5; and ASA 240, paragraph 16.

8 See ASA 315, paragraph 10; and ASA 240, paragraph 15.

Sharing Related Party Information with the Engagement Team

17. The auditor shall share relevant information obtained about the entity's related parties with the other members of the engagement team. (Ref: Para. A28)

Identification and Assessment of the Risks of Material Misstatement Associated with Related Party Relationships and Transactions

18. In meeting the ASA 315 requirement to identify and assess the risks of material misstatement,[9] the auditor shall identify and assess the risks of material misstatement associated with related party relationships and transactions and determine whether any of those risks are significant risks. In making this determination, the auditor shall treat identified significant related party transactions outside the entity's normal course of business as giving rise to significant risks.

19. If the auditor identifies fraud risk factors (including circumstances relating to the existence of a related party with dominant influence) when performing the risk assessment procedures and related activities in connection with related parties, the auditor shall consider such information when identifying and assessing the risks of material misstatement due to fraud in accordance with ASA 240. (Ref: Para. A6 and A29-A30)

Responses to the Risks of Material Misstatement Associated with Related Party Relationships and Transactions

20. As part of the ASA 330 requirement that the auditor respond to assessed risks,[10] the auditor designs and performs further audit procedures to obtain sufficient appropriate audit evidence about the assessed risks of material misstatement associated with related party relationships and transactions. These audit procedures shall include those required by paragraphs 21-24 of this Auditing Standard. (Ref: Para. A31-A34)

Identification of Previously Unidentified or Undisclosed Related Parties or Significant Related Party Transactions

21. If the auditor identifies arrangements or information that suggests the existence of related party relationships or transactions that management has not previously identified or disclosed to the auditor, the auditor shall determine whether the underlying circumstances confirm the existence of those relationships or transactions. (Ref: Para. Aus A34.1)

22. If the auditor identifies related parties or significant related party transactions that management has not previously identified or disclosed to the auditor, the auditor shall:

    (a) Promptly communicate the relevant information to the other members of the engagement team; (Ref: Para. A35)

    (b) Where the applicable financial reporting framework establishes related party requirements:

        (i) Request management to identify all transactions with the newly identified related parties for the auditor's further evaluation; and

        (ii) Enquire as to why the entity's controls over related party relationships and transactions failed to enable the identification or disclosure of the related party relationships or transactions;

    (c) Perform appropriate substantive audit procedures relating to such newly identified related parties or significant related party transactions; (Ref: Para. A36)

    (d) Reconsider the risk that other related parties or significant related party transactions may exist that management has not previously identified or disclosed to the auditor, and perform additional audit procedures as necessary; and

    (e) If the non-disclosure by management appears intentional (and therefore indicative of a risk of material misstatement due to fraud), evaluate the implications for the audit. (Ref: Para. A37)

9 See ASA 315, paragraph 25.

10 See ASA 330, paragraph 5-6.

Identified Significant Related Party Transactions outside the Entity's Normal Course of Business

23. For identified significant related party transactions outside the entity's normal course of business, the auditor shall:

    (a) Inspect the underlying contracts or agreements, if any, and evaluate whether:

        (i) The business rationale (or lack thereof) of the transactions suggests that they may have been entered into to engage in fraudulent financial reporting or to conceal misappropriation of assets;[11] (Ref: Para. A38-A39)

        (ii) The terms of the transactions are consistent with management's explanations; and

        (iii) The transactions have been appropriately accounted for and disclosed in accordance with the applicable financial reporting framework; and

    (b) Obtain audit evidence that the transactions have been appropriately authorised and approved. (Ref: Para. A40-A41)

Assertions That Related Party Transactions Were Conducted on Terms Equivalent to Those Prevailing in an Arm's Length Transaction

24. If management has made an assertion in the financial report to the effect that a related party transaction was conducted on terms equivalent to those prevailing in an arm's length transaction, the auditor shall obtain sufficient appropriate audit evidence about the assertion. (Ref: Para. A42-A45)

Evaluation of the Accounting for and Disclosure of Identified Related Party Relationships and Transactions

25. In forming an opinion on the financial report in accordance with ASA 700,[12] the auditor shall evaluate: (Ref: Para. A46)

    (a) Whether the identified related party relationships and transactions have been appropriately accounted for and disclosed in accordance with the applicable financial reporting framework; and (Ref: Para. A47)

    (b) Whether the effects of the related party relationships and transactions:

        (i) Prevent the financial report from achieving fair presentation (for fair presentation frameworks); or

        (ii) Cause the financial report to be misleading (for compliance frameworks).

Written Representations

26. Where the applicable financial reporting framework establishes related party requirements, the auditor shall obtain written representations from management and, where appropriate, those charged with governance that: (Ref: Para. A48-A49)

    (a) They have disclosed to the auditor the identity of the entity's related parties and all the related party relationships and transactions of which they are aware; and

    (b) They have appropriately accounted for and disclosed such relationships and transactions in accordance with the requirements of the framework.

Communication with Those Charged with Governance

27. Unless all of those charged with governance are involved in managing the entity,[13] the auditor shall communicate with those charged with governance significant matters arising during the audit in connection with the entity's related parties. (Ref: Para. A50)

---

11 See ASA 240, paragraph 32(c).

12 See ASA 700 *Forming an Opinion and Reporting on a Financial Report*, paragraphs 10-15.

13 See ASA 260 *Communication with Those Charged with Governance*, paragraph 13.

Reporting Considerations

Aus 27.1 If the auditor is unable to:

(a) obtain sufficient appropriate audit evidence regarding related parties and related party transactions; or

(b) form a conclusion as to the completeness of the disclosure of related party relationships and transactions in accordance with the applicable financial reporting framework;

the auditor shall modify the auditor's opinion in accordance with ASA 705.*

Aus 27.2 If the auditor concludes that the related party disclosures in the financial report do not satisfy the requirements of the applicable financial reporting framework, the auditor shall modify the auditor's opinion in accordance with ASA 705.

Documentation

28. The auditor shall include in the audit documentation the names of the identified related parties and the nature of the related party relationships.[14]

❖❖❖

Application and Other Explanatory Material

Responsibilities of the Auditor

Financial Reporting Frameworks That Establish Minimal Related Party Requirements (Ref: Para. 4)

A1. An applicable financial reporting framework that establishes minimal related party requirements is one that defines the meaning of a related party but that definition has a substantially narrower scope than the definition set out in paragraph 10(b)(ii) of this Auditing Standard, so that a requirement in the framework to disclose related party relationships and transactions would apply to substantially fewer related party relationships and transactions.

Fair Presentation Frameworks (Ref: Para. 4(a))

A2. In the context of a fair presentation framework,[15] related party relationships and transactions may cause the financial report to fail to achieve fair presentation if, for example, the economic reality of such relationships and transactions is not appropriately reflected in the financial report. For instance, fair presentation may not be achieved if the sale of a property by the entity to a controlling shareholder at a price above or below fair market value has been accounted for as a transaction involving a profit or loss for the entity when it may constitute a contribution or return of capital or the payment of a dividend.

Compliance Frameworks (Ref: Para. 4(b))

A3. In the context of a compliance framework, whether related party relationships and transactions cause the financial report to be misleading as discussed in ASA 700 depends upon the particular circumstances of the engagement. For example, even if non-disclosure of related party transactions in the financial report is in compliance with the framework and applicable law or regulation, the financial report could be misleading if the entity derives a very substantial portion of its revenue from transactions with related parties, and that fact is not disclosed. However, it will be extremely rare for the auditor to consider a financial report that is prepared and presented in accordance with a compliance framework to be misleading if in accordance with ASA 210[16] the auditor determined that the framework is acceptable.[17]

---

* See ASA 705 *Modifications to the Opinion in the Independent Auditor's Report*.

14 See ASA 230 *Audit Documentation*, paragraphs 8-11, and paragraph A6.

15 See ASA 200, paragraph 13(a), which defines the meaning of fair presentation and compliance frameworks.

16 See ASA 210 *Agreeing the Terms of Audit Engagements*, paragraph 6(a).

17 See ASA 700, paragraph A12.

ASA

Definition of a Related Party (Ref: Para. 10(b))

A4. Many financial reporting frameworks discuss the concepts of control and significant influence. Although they may discuss these concepts using different terms, they generally explain that:

(a) Control is the power to govern the financial and operating policies of an entity so as to obtain benefits from its activities; and

(b) Significant influence (which may be gained by share ownership, statute or agreement) is the power to participate in the financial and operating policy decisions of an entity, but is not control over those policies.

A5. The existence of the following relationships may indicate the presence of control or significant influence:

(a) Direct or indirect equity holdings or other financial interests in the entity.

(b) The entity's holdings of direct or indirect equity or other financial interests in other entities.

(c) Being part of those charged with governance or key management (that is, those members of management who have the authority and responsibility for planning, directing and controlling the activities of the entity).

(d) Being a close family member of any person referred to in subparagraph (c).

(e) Having a significant business relationship with any person referred to in subparagraph (c).

Related Parties with Dominant Influence (Ref: Para. 19)

A6. Related parties, by virtue of their ability to exert control or significant influence, may be in a position to exert dominant influence over the entity or its management. Consideration of such behaviour is relevant when identifying and assessing the risks of material misstatement due to fraud, as further explained in paragraphs A29-A30.

Special-Purpose Entities as Related Parties

A7. In some circumstances, a special-purpose entity[18] may be a related party of the entity because the entity may in substance control it, even if the entity owns little or none of the special-purpose entity's equity.

Risk Assessment Procedures and Related Activities

Risks of Material Misstatement Associated with Related Party Relationships and Transactions (Ref: Para. 11)

Considerations Specific to Public Sector Entities

A8. The public sector auditor's responsibilities regarding related party relationships and transactions may be affected by the audit mandate, or by obligations on public sector entities arising from law, regulation or other authority. Consequently, the public sector auditor's responsibilities may not be limited to addressing the risks of material misstatement associated with related party relationships and transactions, but may also include a broader responsibility to address the risks of non-compliance with law, regulation and other authority governing public sector bodies that lay down specific requirements in the conduct of business with related parties. Further, the public sector auditor may need to have regard to public sector financial reporting requirements for related party relationships and transactions that may differ from those in the private sector.

Understanding the Entity's Related Party Relationships and Transactions

Discussion among the Engagement Team (Ref: Para. 12)

A9. Matters that may be addressed in the discussion among the engagement team include:

- The nature and extent of the entity's relationships and transactions with related parties (using, for example, the auditor's record of identified related parties updated after each audit).

18 See ASA 315, paragraphs A26-A27, which provide guidance regarding the nature of a special-purpose entity.

- An emphasis on the importance of maintaining professional scepticism throughout the audit regarding the potential for material misstatement associated with related party relationships and transactions.
- The circumstances or conditions of the entity that may indicate the existence of related party relationships or transactions that management has not identified or disclosed to the auditor (for example, a complex organisational structure, use of special-purpose entities for off-balance sheet transactions, or an inadequate information system).
- The records or documents that may indicate the existence of related party relationships or transactions.
- The importance that management and those charged with governance attach to the identification, appropriate accounting for, and disclosure of related party relationships and transactions (if the applicable financial reporting framework establishes related party requirements), and the related risk of management override of relevant controls.

A10. In addition, the discussion in the context of fraud may include specific consideration of how related parties may be involved in fraud. For example:

- How special-purpose entities controlled by management might be used to facilitate earnings management.
- How transactions between the entity and a known business partner of a key member of management could be arranged to facilitate misappropriation of the entity's assets.

The Identity of the Entity's Related Parties *(Ref: Para. 13(a))*

A11. Where the applicable financial reporting framework establishes related party requirements, information regarding the identity of the entity's related parties is likely to be readily available to management because the entity's information systems will need to record, process and summarise related party relationships and transactions to enable the entity to meet the accounting and disclosure requirements of the framework. Management is therefore likely to have a comprehensive list of related parties and changes from the prior period. For recurring engagements, making the enquiries provides a basis for comparing the information supplied by management with the auditor's record of related parties noted in previous audits.

A12. However, where the framework does not establish related party requirements, the entity may not have such information systems in place. Under such circumstances, it is possible that management may not be aware of the existence of all related parties. Nevertheless, the requirement to make the enquiries specified by paragraph 13 still applies because management may be aware of parties that meet the related party definition set out in this Auditing Standard. In such a case, however, the auditor's enquiries regarding the identity of the entity's related parties are likely to form part of the auditor's risk assessment procedures and related activities performed in accordance with ASA 315 to obtain information regarding:

- The entity's ownership and governance structures;
- The types of investments that the entity is making and plans to make; and
- The way the entity is structured and how it is financed.

In the particular case of common control relationships, as management is more likely to be aware of such relationships if they have economic significance to the entity, the auditor's enquiries are likely to be more effective if they are focused on whether parties with which the entity engages in significant transactions, or shares resources to a significant degree, are related parties.

A13. In the context of a group audit, ASA 600 requires the group engagement team to provide each component auditor with a list of related parties prepared by group management and any other related parties of which the group engagement team is aware.[19] Where the entity

19 See ASA 600 *Special Considerations—Audits of a Group Financial Report (Including the Work of Component Auditors)*, paragraph 40(e).

is a component within a group, this information provides a useful basis for the auditor's enquiries of management regarding the identity of the entity's related parties.

A14. The auditor may also obtain some information regarding the identity of the entity's related parties through enquiries of management during the engagement acceptance or continuance process.

***The Entity's Controls over Related Party Relationships and Transactions** (Ref: Para. 14)*

A15. Others within the entity are those considered likely to have knowledge of the entity's related party relationships and transactions, and the entity's controls over such relationships and transactions. These may include, to the extent that they do not form part of management:

- Those charged with governance;
- Personnel in a position to initiate, process, or record transactions that are both significant and outside the entity's normal course of business, and those who supervise or monitor such personnel;
- Internal auditors;
- In-house legal counsel; and
- The chief ethics officer or equivalent person.

A16. The audit is conducted on the premise that management and, where appropriate, those charged with governance have acknowledged and understand that they have responsibility for the preparation of the financial report in accordance with the applicable financial reporting framework, including where relevant their fair presentation, and for such internal control as management and, where appropriate, those charged with governance determine is necessary to enable the preparation of the financial report that is free from material misstatement, whether due to fraud or error.[20] Accordingly, where the framework establishes related party requirements, the preparation of the financial report requires management, with oversight from those charged with governance, to design, implement and maintain adequate controls over related party relationships and transactions so that these are identified and appropriately accounted for and disclosed in accordance with the framework. In their oversight role, those charged with governance monitor how management is discharging its responsibility for such controls. Regardless of any related party requirements the framework may establish, those charged with governance may, in their oversight role, obtain information from management to enable them to understand the nature and business rationale of the entity's related party relationships and transactions.

A17. In meeting the ASA 315 requirement to obtain an understanding of the control environment,[21] the auditor may consider features of the control environment relevant to mitigating the risks of material misstatement associated with related party relationships and transactions, such as:

- Internal ethical codes, appropriately communicated to the entity's personnel and enforced, governing the circumstances in which the entity may enter into specific types of related party transactions.
- Policies and procedures for open and timely disclosure of the interests that management and those charged with governance have in related party transactions.
- The assignment of responsibilities within the entity for identifying, recording, summarising, and disclosing related party transactions.
- Timely disclosure and discussion between management and those charged with governance of significant related party transactions outside the entity's normal course of business, including whether those charged with governance have appropriately challenged the business rationale of such transactions (for example, by seeking advice from external professional advisors).
- Clear guidelines for the approval of related party transactions involving actual or perceived conflicts of interest, such as approval by a subcommittee of those charged with governance comprising individuals independent of management.

20 See ASA 200, paragraph A2.

21 See ASA 315, paragraph 14.

- Periodic reviews by internal auditors, where applicable.
- Proactive action taken by management to resolve related party disclosure issues, such as by seeking advice from the auditor or external legal counsel.
- The existence of whistle-blowing policies and procedures, where applicable.

A18. Controls over related party relationships and transactions within some entities may be deficient or non-existent for a number of reasons, such as:

- The low importance attached by management to identifying and disclosing related party relationships and transactions.
- The lack of appropriate oversight by those charged with governance.
- An intentional disregard for such controls because related party disclosures may reveal information that management considers sensitive, for example, the existence of transactions involving family members of management.
- An insufficient understanding by management of the related party requirements of the applicable financial reporting framework.
- The absence of disclosure requirements under the applicable financial reporting framework.

Where such controls are ineffective or non-existent, the auditor may be unable to obtain sufficient appropriate audit evidence about related party relationships and transactions. If this were the case, the auditor would, in accordance with ASA 705,[22] consider the implications for the audit, including the opinion in the auditor's report.

A19. Fraudulent financial reporting often involves management override of controls that otherwise may appear to be operating effectively.[23] The risk of management override of controls is higher if management has relationships that involve control or significant influence with parties with which the entity does business because these relationships may present management with greater incentives and opportunities to perpetrate fraud. For example, management's financial interests in certain related parties may provide incentives for management to override controls by (a) directing the entity, against its interests, to conclude transactions for the benefit of these parties, or (b) colluding with such parties or controlling their actions. Examples of possible fraud include:

- Creating fictitious terms of transactions with related parties designed to misrepresent the business rationale of these transactions.
- Fraudulently organising the transfer of assets from or to management or others at amounts significantly above or below market value.
- Engaging in complex transactions with related parties, such as special-purpose entities, that are structured to misrepresent the financial position or financial performance of the entity.

Considerations specific to smaller entities

A20. Control activities in smaller entities are likely to be less formal and smaller entities may have no documented processes for dealing with related party relationships and transactions. An owner-manager may mitigate some of the risks arising from related party transactions, or potentially increase those risks, through active involvement in all the main aspects of the transactions. For such entities, the auditor may obtain an understanding of the related party relationships and transactions, and any controls that may exist over these, through enquiry of management combined with other procedures, such as observation of management's oversight and review activities, and inspection of available relevant documentation.

Authorisation and approval of significant transactions and arrangements (Ref: Para. 14(b))

A21. Authorisation involves the granting of permission by a party or parties with the appropriate authority (whether management, those charged with governance or the entity's shareholders) for the entity to enter into specific transactions in accordance with pre-determined criteria, whether judgemental or not. Approval involves those parties'

22 See ASA 705 *Modifications to the Opinion in the Independent Auditor's Report.*

23 See ASA 240, paragraphs 31 and A4.

acceptance of the transactions the entity has entered into as having satisfied the criteria on which authorisation was granted. Examples of controls the entity may have established to authorise and approve significant transactions and arrangements with related parties or significant transactions and arrangements outside the normal course of business include:

- Monitoring controls to identify such transactions and arrangements for authorisation and approval.
- Approval of the terms and conditions of the transactions and arrangements by management, those charged with governance or, where applicable, shareholders.

Maintaining Alertness for Related Party Information When Reviewing Records or Documents

Records or Documents That the Auditor May Inspect (Ref: Para. 15)

A22. During the audit, the auditor may inspect records or documents that may provide information about related party relationships and transactions, for example:

- Third-party confirmations obtained by the auditor (in addition to bank and legal confirmations).
- Entity income tax returns.
- Information supplied by the entity to regulatory authorities.
- Shareholder registers to identify the entity's principal shareholders.
- Statements of conflicts of interest from management and those charged with governance.
- Records of the entity's investments and those of its superannuation plans.
- Contracts and agreements with key management or those charged with governance.
- Significant contracts and agreements not in the entity's ordinary course of business.
- Specific invoices and correspondence from the entity's professional advisors.
- Life insurance policies acquired by the entity.
- Significant contracts re-negotiated by the entity during the period.
- Internal auditors' reports.
- Documents associated with the entity's filings with a securities regulator (for example, prospectuses).

Arrangements that may indicate the existence of previously unidentified or undisclosed related party relationships or transactions (Ref: Para. 15)

A23. An arrangement involves a formal or informal agreement between the entity and one or more other parties for such purposes as:

- The establishment of a business relationship through appropriate vehicles or structures.
- The conduct of certain types of transactions under specific terms and conditions.
- The provision of designated services or financial support.

Examples of arrangements that may indicate the existence of related party relationships or transactions that management has not previously identified or disclosed to the auditor include:

- Participation in unincorporated partnerships with other parties.
- Agreements for the provision of services to certain parties under terms and conditions that are outside the entity's normal course of business.
- Guarantees and guarantor relationships.

Identification of Significant Transactions outside the Normal Course of Business (Ref: Para. 16)

A24. Obtaining further information on significant transactions outside the entity's normal course of business enables the auditor to evaluate whether fraud risk factors, if any, are present and, where the applicable financial reporting framework establishes related party requirements, to identify the risks of material misstatement.

A25. Examples of transactions outside the entity's normal course of business may include:

- Complex equity transactions, such as corporate restructurings or acquisitions.
- Transactions with offshore entities in jurisdictions with weak corporate laws.
- The leasing of premises or the rendering of management services by the entity to another party if no consideration is exchanged.
- Sales transactions with unusually large discounts or returns.
- Transactions with circular arrangements, for example, sales with a commitment to repurchase.
- Transactions under contracts whose terms are changed before expiry.

Understanding the nature of significant transactions outside the normal course of business *(Ref: Para. 16(a))*

A26. Enquiring into the nature of the significant transactions outside the entity's normal course of business involves obtaining an understanding of the business rationale of the transactions, and the terms and conditions under which these have been entered into.

Enquiring into whether related parties could be involved *(Ref: Para. 16(b))*

A27. A related party could be involved in a significant transaction outside the entity's normal course of business not only by directly influencing the transaction through being a party to the transaction, but also by indirectly influencing it through an intermediary. Such influence may indicate the presence of a fraud risk factor.

Sharing Related Party Information with the Engagement Team (Ref: Para. 17)

A28. Relevant related party information that may be shared among the engagement team members includes, for example:

- The identity of the entity's related parties.
- The nature of the related party relationships and transactions.
- Significant or complex related party relationships or transactions that may require special audit consideration, in particular transactions in which management or those charged with governance are financially involved.

Identification and Assessment of the Risks of Material Misstatement Associated with Related Party Relationships and Transactions

Fraud Risk Factors Associated with a Related Party with Dominant Influence (Ref: Para. 19)

A29. Domination of management by a single person or small group of persons without compensating controls is a fraud risk factor.[24] Indicators of dominant influence exerted by a related party include:

- The related party has vetoed significant business decisions taken by management or those charged with governance.
- Significant transactions are referred to the related party for final approval.
- There is little or no debate among management and those charged with governance regarding business proposals initiated by the related party.
- Transactions involving the related party (or a close family member of the related party) are rarely independently reviewed and approved.

Dominant influence may also exist in some cases if the related party has played a leading role in founding the entity and continues to play a leading role in managing the entity.

24 See ASA 240, Appendix 1.

A30. In the presence of other risk factors, the existence of a related party with dominant influence may indicate significant risks of material misstatement due to fraud. For example:

- An unusually high turnover of senior management or professional advisors may suggest unethical or fraudulent business practices that serve the related party's purposes.
- The use of business intermediaries for significant transactions for which there appears to be no clear business justification may suggest that the related party could have an interest in such transactions through control of such intermediaries for fraudulent purposes.
- Evidence of the related party's excessive participation in or preoccupation with the selection of accounting policies or the determination of significant estimates may suggest the possibility of fraudulent financial reporting.

Responses to the Risks of Material Misstatement Associated with Related Party Relationships and Transactions (Ref: Para. 20)

A31. The nature, timing and extent of the further audit procedures that the auditor may select to respond to the assessed risks of material misstatement associated with related party relationships and transactions depend upon the nature of those risks and the circumstances of the entity.[25]

A32. Examples of substantive audit procedures that the auditor may perform when the auditor has assessed a significant risk that management has not appropriately accounted for or disclosed specific related party transactions in accordance with the applicable financial reporting framework (whether due to fraud or error) include:

- Confirming or discussing specific aspects of the transactions with intermediaries such as banks, law firms, guarantors, or agents, where practicable and not prohibited by law, regulation or ethical rules.
- Confirming the purposes, specific terms or amounts of the transactions with the related parties (this audit procedure may be less effective where the auditor judges that the entity is likely to influence the related parties in their responses to the auditor).
- Where applicable, reading the financial report(s) or other relevant financial information, if available, of the related parties for evidence of the accounting of the transactions in the related parties' accounting records.

A33. If the auditor has assessed a significant risk of material misstatement due to fraud as a result of the presence of a related party with dominant influence, the auditor may, in addition to the general requirements of ASA 240, perform audit procedures such as the following to obtain an understanding of the business relationships that such a related party may have established directly or indirectly with the entity and to determine the need for further appropriate substantive audit procedures:

- Enquiries of, and discussion with, management and those charged with governance.
- Enquiries of the related party.
- Inspection of significant contracts with the related party.
- Appropriate background research, such as through the Internet or specific external business information databases.
- Review of employee whistle-blowing reports where these are retained.

A34. Depending upon the results of the auditor's risk assessment procedures, the auditor may consider it appropriate to obtain audit evidence without testing the entity's controls over related party relationships and transactions. In some circumstances, however, it may not be possible to obtain sufficient appropriate audit evidence from substantive audit procedures alone in relation to the risks of material misstatement associated with related party relationships and transactions. For example, where intra-group transactions between

25 See ASA 330 which provides further guidance on considering the nature, timing and extent of further audit procedures. ASA 240 establishes requirements and provides guidance on appropriate responses to assessed risks of material misstatement due to fraud.

the entity and its components are numerous and a significant amount of information regarding these transactions is initiated, recorded, processed or reported electronically in an integrated system, the auditor may determine that it is not possible to design effective substantive audit procedures that by themselves would reduce the risks of material misstatement associated with these transactions to an acceptably low level. In such a case, in meeting the ASA 330 requirement to obtain sufficient appropriate audit evidence as to the operating effectiveness of relevant controls,[26] the auditor is required to test the entity's controls over the completeness and accuracy of the recording of the related party relationships and transactions.

Identification of Previously Unidentified or Undisclosed Related Parties or Significant Related Party Transactions

Existence of Related Parties (Ref: Para. 21)

Aus A34.1 In determining whether underlying circumstances confirm the existence of related party relationships or transactions, the auditor may consider the Australian Accounting Standards,[*] including consideration of the substance of the relationship and/or transaction and not merely the legal form.

Communicating Newly Identified Related Party Information to the Engagement Team (Ref: Para. 22(a))

A35. Communicating promptly any newly identified related parties to the other members of the engagement team assists them in determining whether this information affects the results of, and conclusions drawn from, risk assessment procedures already performed, including whether the risks of material misstatement need to be reassessed.

Substantive Procedures Relating to Newly Identified Related Parties or Significant Related Party Transactions (Ref: Para. 22(c))

A36. Examples of substantive audit procedures that the auditor may perform relating to newly identified related parties or significant related party transactions include:

- Making enquiries regarding the nature of the entity's relationships with the newly identified related parties, including (where appropriate and not prohibited by law, regulation or ethical rules) enquiring of parties outside the entity who are presumed to have significant knowledge of the entity and its business, such as legal counsel, principal agents, major representatives, consultants, guarantors, or other close business partners.
- Conducting an analysis of accounting records for transactions with the newly identified related parties. Such an analysis may be facilitated using computer-assisted audit techniques.
- Verifying the terms and conditions of the newly identified related party transactions, and evaluating whether the transactions have been appropriately accounted for and disclosed in accordance with the applicable financial reporting framework.

Intentional Non-Disclosure by Management (Ref: Para. 22(e))

A37. The requirements and guidance in ASA 240 regarding the auditor's responsibilities relating to fraud in an audit of a financial report are relevant where management appears to have intentionally failed to disclose related parties or significant related party transactions to the auditor. The auditor may also consider whether it is necessary to re-evaluate the reliability of management's responses to the auditor's enquiries and management's representations to the auditor.

---

26 See ASA 330, paragraph 8(b).

* See, in particular, *Framework for the Preparation and Presentation of Financial Statements* (July 2004) and AASB 124 *Related Party Disclosures*.

Identified Significant Related Party Transactions outside the Entity's Normal Course of Business

Evaluating the Business Rationale of Significant Related Party Transactions (Ref: Para. 23(a))

A38. In evaluating the business rationale of a significant related party transaction outside the entity's normal course of business, the auditor may consider the following:

- Whether the transaction:
  - Is overly complex (for example, it may involve multiple related parties within a consolidated group).
  - Has unusual terms of trade, such as unusual prices, interest rates, guarantees and repayment terms.
  - Lacks an apparent logical business reason for its occurrence.
  - Involves previously unidentified related parties.
  - Is processed in an unusual manner.
- Whether management has discussed the nature of, and accounting for, such a transaction with those charged with governance.
- Whether management is placing more emphasis on a particular accounting treatment rather than giving due regard to the underlying economics of the transaction.

If management's explanations are materially inconsistent with the terms of the related party transaction, the auditor is required, in accordance with ASA 500,[27] to consider the reliability of management's explanations and representations on other significant matters.

A39. The auditor may also seek to understand the business rationale of such a transaction from the related party's perspective, as this may help the auditor to better understand the economic reality of the transaction and why it was carried out. A business rationale from the related party's perspective that appears inconsistent with the nature of its business may represent a fraud risk factor.

Authorisation and Approval of Significant Related Party Transactions (Ref: Para. 23(b))

A40. Authorisation and approval by management, those charged with governance, or, where applicable, the shareholders of significant related party transactions outside the entity's normal course of business may provide audit evidence that these have been duly considered at the appropriate levels within the entity and that their terms and conditions have been appropriately reflected in the financial report. The existence of transactions of this nature that were not subject to such authorisation and approval, in the absence of rational explanations based on discussion with management or those charged with governance, may indicate risks of material misstatement due to error or fraud. In these circumstances, the auditor may need to be alert for other transactions of a similar nature. Authorisation and approval alone, however, may not be sufficient in concluding whether risks of material misstatement due to fraud are absent because authorisation and approval may be ineffective if there has been collusion between the related parties or if the entity is subject to the dominant influence of a related party.

Considerations specific to smaller entities

A41. A smaller entity may not have the same controls provided by different levels of authority and approval that may exist in a larger entity. Accordingly, when auditing a smaller entity, the auditor may rely to a lesser degree on authorisation and approval for audit evidence regarding the validity of significant related party transactions outside the entity's normal course of business. Instead, the auditor may consider performing other audit procedures such as inspecting relevant documents, confirming specific aspects of the transactions with relevant parties, or observing the owner-manager's involvement with the transactions.

27 See ASA 500 *Audit Evidence*, paragraph 11.

Assertions That Related Party Transactions Were Conducted on Terms Equivalent to Those Prevailing in an Arm's Length Transaction (Ref: Para. 24)

A42. Although audit evidence may be readily available regarding how the price of a related party transaction compares to that of a similar arm's length transaction, there are ordinarily practical difficulties that limit the auditor's ability to obtain audit evidence that all other aspects of the transaction are equivalent to those of the arm's length transaction. For example, although the auditor may be able to confirm that a related party transaction has been conducted at a market price, it may be impracticable to confirm whether other terms and conditions of the transaction (such as credit terms, contingencies and specific charges) are equivalent to those that would ordinarily be agreed between independent parties. Accordingly, there may be a risk that management's assertion that a related party transaction was conducted on terms equivalent to those prevailing in an arm's length transaction may be materially misstated.

A43. The preparation of the financial report requires management to substantiate an assertion that a related party transaction was conducted on terms equivalent to those prevailing in an arm's length transaction. Management's support for the assertion may include:

- Comparing the terms of the related party transaction to those of an identical or similar transaction with one or more unrelated parties.
- Engaging an external expert to determine a market value and to confirm market terms and conditions for the transaction.
- Comparing the terms of the transaction to known market terms for broadly similar transactions on an open market.

A44. Evaluating management's support for this assertion may involve one or more of the following:

- Considering the appropriateness of management's process for supporting the assertion.
- Verifying the source of the internal or external data supporting the assertion, and testing the data to determine their accuracy, completeness and relevance.
- Evaluating the reasonableness of any significant assumptions on which the assertion is based.

A45. Some financial reporting frameworks require the disclosure of related party transactions not conducted on terms equivalent to those prevailing in arm's length transactions. In these circumstances, if management has not disclosed a related party transaction in the financial report, there may be an implicit assertion that the transaction was conducted on terms equivalent to those prevailing in an arm's length transaction.

Evaluation of the Accounting for and Disclosure of Identified Related Party Relationships and Transactions

Materiality Considerations in Evaluating Misstatements (Ref: Para. 25)

A46. ASA 450 requires the auditor to consider both the size and the nature of a misstatement, and the particular circumstances of its occurrence, when evaluating whether the misstatement is material.[28] The significance of the transaction to the financial report users may not depend solely on the recorded amount of the transaction but also on other specific relevant factors, such as the nature of the related party relationship.

Evaluation of Related Party Disclosures (Ref: Para. 25(a))

A47. Evaluating the related party disclosures in the context of the disclosure requirements of the applicable financial reporting framework means considering whether the facts and circumstances of the entity's related party relationships and transactions have been appropriately summarised and presented so that the disclosures are understandable.

28 See ASA 450 *Evaluation of Misstatements Identified during the Audit*, paragraph 11(a). Paragraph A16 of ASA 450 provides guidance on the circumstances that may affect the evaluation of a misstatement.

Disclosures of related party transactions may not be understandable if:

(a) The business rationale and the effects of the transactions on the financial report are unclear or misstated; or

(b) Key terms, conditions, or other important elements of the transactions necessary for understanding them are not appropriately disclosed.

Written Representations (Ref: Para. 26)

A48. Circumstances in which it may be appropriate to obtain written representations from those charged with governance include:

- When they have approved specific related party transactions that (a) materially affect the financial report, or (b) involve management.
- When they have made specific oral representations to the auditor on details of certain related party transactions.
- When they have financial or other interests in the related parties or the related party transactions.

A49. The auditor may also decide to obtain written representations regarding specific assertions that management may have made, such as a representation that specific related party transactions do not involve undisclosed side agreements.

Communication with Those Charged with Governance (Ref: Para. 27)

A50. Communicating significant matters arising during the audit[29] in connection with the entity's related parties helps the auditor to establish a common understanding with those charged with governance of the nature and resolution of these matters. Examples of significant related party matters include:

- Non-disclosure (whether intentional or not) by management to the auditor of related parties or significant related party transactions, which may alert those charged with governance to significant related party relationships and transactions of which they may not have been previously aware.
- The identification of significant related party transactions that have not been appropriately authorised and approved, which may give rise to suspected fraud.
- Disagreement with management regarding the accounting for and disclosure of significant related party transactions in accordance with the applicable financial reporting framework.
- Non-compliance with applicable law or regulation prohibiting or restricting specific types of related party transactions.
- Difficulties in identifying the party that ultimately controls the entity.

❖ ❖ ❖

29 See ASA 230, paragraph A8, which provides further guidance on the nature of significant matters arising during the audit.

Conformity with International Standards on Auditing

This Auditing Standard conforms with International Standard on Auditing ISA 550 *Related Parties*, issued by the International Auditing and Assurance Standards Board (IAASB), an independent standard-setting board of the International Federation of Accountants (IFAC).

Paragraphs that have been added to this Auditing Standard (and do not appear in the text of the equivalent ISA) are identified with the prefix "Aus".

The following requirements are additional to ISA 550:

- If the auditor is unable to:
  - obtain sufficient appropriate audit evidence regarding related parties and related party transactions; or
  - form a conclusion as to the completeness of the disclosure of related party relationships and transactions in accordance with the applicable financial reporting framework;

  the auditor shall modify the auditor's opinion in accordance with ASA 705. (Ref: Para. Aus 27.1)
- If the auditor concludes that the related party disclosures in the financial report do not satisfy the requirements of the applicable financial reporting framework, the auditor shall modify the auditor's opinion in accordance with ASA 705. (Ref: Para. Aus 27.2)

Compliance with this Auditing Standard enables compliance with ISA 550.

ASA 560
Subsequent Events

(Reissued October 2009: amended and compiled June 2011)

Issued by the Auditing and Assurance Standards Board.

Note from the Institute of Chartered Accountants Australia

This note, prepared by the technical editor, is not part of ASA 560.

Historical development

September 1981: Statement of Auditing Practice AUP 8 'Audit Implications of Events Occurring after Balance Date' was issued in, and effective from, September 1981. It was substantially revised and reissued in, and effective from, April 1986 following the issue of ED 6 (IAPC ED 16) in January 1983 and ED15 (IAPC re-exposure draft ED 16) in June 1984.

February 1994: ED 54 'Codification and Revision of Auditing Pronouncements: AUS 708 Subsequent Events (AUP 8)' issued by the AuSB.

June 1994: The International Auditing Practices Committee (IAPC) of the International Federation of Accountants (IFAC) approved the issuance of a codified set of International Standards of Auditing (ISAs) in June 1994. The relevant international pronouncement was ISA 560 'Subsequent Events'.

October 1995: Australian Auditing Standards and Auditing Guidance Statements released. The status of these was explained in APS 1.1 'Conformity With Auditing Standards'. These Standards became operative for the first reporting period commencing on or after 1 July 1996 and later reporting periods, although earlier application was encouraged. AUP 8 'Audit Implications of Events Occurring After Balance Date' was replaced by AUS 706 'Subsequent Events'.

April 2006: ASA 560 was issued as a legally enforceable Standard to replace AUS 706. It is based on ISA 560 of the same name.

October 2009: ASA 560 reissued as part of the AUASB's Clarity Project. It is based on the redrafted ISA 560 of the same name.

June 2011: ASA 560 updated for editorial amendments contained in ASA 2011-1 'Amendments to Australian Auditing Standards'.

Contents

Compilation Details

Auditing Standard ASA 560 *Subsequent Events* as Amended

This compilation takes into account amendments made up to and including 27 June 2011 and was prepared on 27 June 2011 by the Auditing and Assurance Standards Board (AUASB).

This compilation is not a separate Auditing Standard made by the AUASB. Instead, it is a representation of ASA 560 (October 2009) as amended by another Auditing Standard which is listed in the Table below.

Table of Standards

Standard	Date made	Operative date
ASA 560	27 October 2009	1 January 2010
ASA 2011-1	27 June 2011	1 July 2011

Table of Amendments

Paragraph affected	How affected	By ... [paragraph]
10(b)	Amended	ASA 2011-1 [41]

Preface

[Preface extracted from the original Auditing Standard issued 27 October 2009]

Reasons for Issuing Auditing Standard ASA 560 *Subsequent Events*

The Auditing and Assurance Standards Board (AUASB) issues Auditing Standard ASA 560 *Subsequent Events* pursuant to the requirements of the legislative provisions and the Strategic Direction explained below.

The AUASB is an independent statutory board of the Australian Government under section 227A of the *Australian Securities and Investments Commission Act 2001*, as amended (ASIC Act). Under section 336 of the *Corporations Act 2001*, the AUASB may make Auditing Standards for the purposes of the corporations legislation. These Auditing Standards are legislative instruments under the *Legislative Instruments Act 2003*.

Under the Strategic Direction given to the AUASB by the Financial Reporting Council (FRC), the AUASB is required to have regard to any programme initiated by the International Auditing and Assurance Standards Board (IAASB) for the revision and enhancement of the International Standards on Auditing (ISAs) and to make appropriate consequential amendments to the Australian Auditing Standards. Accordingly, the AUASB has decided to revise and redraft the Australian Auditing Standards using the equivalent redrafted ISAs.

Main Features

This Auditing Standard establishes requirements and provides application and other explanatory material regarding the auditor's responsibilities relating to subsequent events in an audit of a financial report.

This Auditing Standard:

(a) requires the auditor to consider the effect of subsequent events on the financial report and on the auditor's report;

(b) establishes the auditor's responsibilities regarding events occurring between the date of the financial report and the date of the auditor's report;

(c) establishes the auditor's responsibilities regarding facts which became known to the auditor after the date of the auditor's report but before the financial report is issued; and

(d) establishes the auditor's responsibilities regarding facts which became known to the auditor after the financial report is issued.

Authority Statement

Auditing Standard ASA 560 *Subsequent Events* (as amended at 27 June 2011) is set out in paragraphs 1 to A18.

This Auditing Standard is to be read in conjunction with ASA 101 *Preamble to Australian Auditing Standards* which sets out the intentions of the AUASB on how the Australian Auditing Standards, operative for financial reporting periods commencing on or after 1 January 2010, are to be understood, interpreted and applied. This Auditing Standard is to be read also in conjunction with ASA 200 *Overall Objectives of the Independent Auditor and the Conduct of an Audit in Accordance with Australian Auditing Standards*.

Dated: 27 June 2011

M H Kelsall
Chairman - AUASB

Auditing Standard ASA 560

The Auditing and Assurance Standards Board (AUASB) made Auditing Standard ASA 560 *Subsequent Events*, pursuant to section 227B of the *Australian Securities and Investments Commission Act 2001* and section 336 of the *Corporations Act 2001*, on 27 October 2009.

This compiled version of ASA 560 incorporates subsequent amendments contained in another Auditing Standard made by the AUASB up to and including 27 June 2011 (see Compilation Details).

Auditing Standard ASA 560

Subsequent Events

Application

Aus 0.1 This Auditing Standard applies to:

(a) an audit of a financial report for a financial year, or an audit of a financial report for a half-year, in accordance with the *Corporations Act 2001*; and

(b) an audit of a financial report, or a complete set of financial statements, for any other purpose.

Aus 0.2 This Auditing Standard also applies, as appropriate, to an audit of other historical financial information.

Operative Date

Aus 0.3 This Auditing Standard is operative for financial reporting periods commencing on or after 1 January 2010.

[Note: For operative dates of paragraphs changed or added by an amending Standard, see Compilation Details.]

Introduction

Scope of this Auditing Standard

1. This Auditing Standard deals with the auditor's responsibilities relating to subsequent events in an audit of a financial report. (Ref: Para. A1)

Subsequent Events

2. A financial report may be affected by certain events that occur after the date of the financial report. Many financial reporting frameworks specifically refer to such events.[1] Such financial reporting frameworks ordinarily identify two types of events:

(a) Those that provide evidence of conditions that existed at the date of the financial report; and

(b) Those that provide evidence of conditions that arose after the date of the financial report.

ASA 700 explains that the date of the auditor's report informs the reader that the auditor has considered the effect of events and transactions of which the auditor becomes aware and that occurred up to that date.[2]

Effective Date

3. [Deleted by the AUASB. Refer Aus 0.3]

Objectives

4. The objectives of the auditor are:

(a) To obtain sufficient appropriate audit evidence about whether events occurring between the date of the financial report and the date of the auditor's report that require

1 See, for example, Accounting Standard AASB 110 *Events After the Reporting Date.*

2 See ASA 700 *Forming an Opinion and Reporting on a Financial Report*, paragraph A38.

ASA

adjustment of, or disclosure in, the financial report are appropriately reflected in that financial report in accordance with the applicable financial reporting framework; and

(b) To respond appropriately to facts that become known to the auditor after the date of the auditor's report, that, had they been known to the auditor at that date, may have caused the auditor to amend the auditor's report.

Definitions

5. For purposes of the Australian Auditing Standards, the following terms have the meanings attributed below:

(a) Date of the financial report means the date of the end of the latest period covered by the financial report. Date of approval of the financial report means the date on which all the financial statements that comprise the financial report, including the related notes, have been prepared and those with the recognised authority have asserted that they have taken responsibility for that financial report. (Ref: Para. A2)

(b) Date of the auditor's report means the date the auditor dates the report on the financial report in accordance with ASA 700. (Ref: Para. A3-Aus A3.1)

(c) Date the financial report is issued means the date that the auditor's report and audited financial report are made available to third parties. (Ref: Para. A4-A5)

(d) Subsequent events means events occurring between the date of the financial report and the date of the auditor's report, and facts that become known to the auditor after the date of the auditor's report.

Requirements

Events Occurring between the Date of the Financial Report and the Date of the Auditor's Report

6. The auditor shall perform audit procedures designed to obtain sufficient appropriate audit evidence that all events occurring between the date of the financial report and the date of the auditor's report that require adjustment of, or disclosure in, the financial report have been identified. The auditor is not, however, expected to perform additional audit procedures on matters to which previously applied audit procedures have provided satisfactory conclusions. (Ref: Para. A6)

7. The auditor shall perform the procedures required by paragraph 6 of this Auditing Standard so that they cover the period from the date of the financial report to the date of the auditor's report, or as near as practicable thereto. The auditor shall take into account the auditor's risk assessment in determining the nature and extent of such audit procedures, which shall include the following: (Ref: Para. A7-A8)

(a) Obtaining an understanding of any procedures management has established to ensure that subsequent events are identified.

(b) Enquiring of management and, where appropriate, those charged with governance, as to whether any subsequent events have occurred which might affect the financial report. (Ref: Para. A9)

(c) Reading minutes, if any, of the meetings, of the entity's owners, management and those charged with governance, that have been held after the date of the financial report and enquiring about matters discussed at any such meetings for which minutes are not yet available. (Ref: Para. A10)

(d) Reading the entity's latest subsequent interim financial report, if any.

8. If, as a result of the procedures performed as required by paragraphs 6 and 7 of this Auditing Standard, the auditor identifies events that require adjustment of, or disclosure in, the financial report, the auditor shall determine whether each such event is appropriately reflected in that financial report in accordance with the applicable financial reporting framework.

Written Representations

9. The auditor shall request management and, where appropriate, those charged with governance, to provide a written representation in accordance with ASA 580[3] that all events occurring subsequent to the date of the financial report and for which the applicable financial reporting framework requires adjustment or disclosure have been adjusted or disclosed.

Facts Which Become Known to the Auditor after the Date of the Auditor's Report but before the Date the Financial Report is Issued

10. The auditor has no obligation to perform any audit procedures regarding the financial report after the date of the auditor's report. However, if, after the date of the auditor's report but before the date the financial report is issued, a fact becomes known to the auditor that, had it been known to the auditor at the date of the auditor's report, may have caused the auditor to amend the auditor's report, the auditor shall: (Ref: Para. A11)
   (a) Discuss the matter with management and, where appropriate, those charged with governance.
   (b) Determine whether the financial report needs amendment; and if so,
   (c) Enquire how management intends to address the matter in the financial report.

11. If management amends the financial report, the auditor shall:
   (a) Carry out the audit procedures necessary in the circumstances on the amendment.
   (b) Unless the circumstances in paragraph 12 of this Auditing Standard apply:
      (i) Extend the audit procedures referred to in paragraphs 6 and 7 of this Auditing Standard to the date of the new auditor's report; and
      (ii) Provide a new auditor's report on the amended financial report. The new auditor's report shall not be dated earlier than the date of approval of the amended financial report.

12. Where law, regulation or the financial reporting framework does not prohibit management from restricting the amendment of the financial report to the effects of the subsequent event, or events causing that amendment, and those responsible for approving the financial report are not prohibited from restricting their approval to that amendment, the auditor is permitted to restrict the audit procedures on subsequent events required in paragraph 11(b)(i) of this Auditing Standard to that amendment. In such cases, the auditor shall either:
   (a) Amend the auditor's report to include an additional date restricted to that amendment that thereby indicates that the auditor's procedures on subsequent events are restricted solely to the amendment of the financial report described in the relevant note to the financial report; or (Ref: Para. A12)
   (b) Provide a new or amended auditor's report that includes a statement in an Emphasis of Matter paragraph[4] or Other Matter paragraph that conveys that the auditor's procedures on subsequent events are restricted solely to the amendment of the financial report as described in the relevant note to the financial report.

Aus 12.1 For an audit engagement conducted under the *Corporations Act 2001*, management, and those charged with governance, are prohibited from restricting an amendment of the financial report to the effects of the subsequent event or events causing that amendment. Consequently, the auditor is prohibited from restricting audit procedures as required under paragraph 11(b)(i) of this Auditing Standard to such an amendment.

13. In some jurisdictions, management may not be required by law, regulation or the financial reporting framework to issue an amended financial report and, accordingly, the auditor need not provide an amended or new auditor's report. However, if management does not amend the financial report in circumstances where the auditor believes it needs to be amended, then: (Ref: Para. A13-A14)

---

3 See ASA 580 *Written Representations.*

4 See ASA 706 *Emphasis of Matter Paragraphs and Other Matter Paragraphs in the Independent Auditor's Report.*

(a) If the auditor's report has not yet been provided to the entity, the auditor shall modify the opinion as required by ASA 705[5] and then provide the auditor's report; or

(b) If the auditor's report has already been provided to the entity, the auditor shall notify management and, unless all of those charged with governance are involved in managing the entity, those charged with governance, not to issue the financial report to third parties before the necessary amendments have been made. If the financial report is nevertheless subsequently issued without the necessary amendments, the auditor shall take appropriate action, to seek to prevent reliance on the auditor's report. (Ref. Para: A15-A16)

Facts Which Become Known to the Auditor after the Financial Report Has Been Issued

14. After the financial report has been issued, the auditor has no obligation to perform any audit procedures regarding such financial report. However, if, after the financial report has been issued, a fact becomes known to the auditor that, had it been known to the auditor at the date of the auditor's report, may have caused the auditor to amend the auditor's report, the auditor shall:

(a) Discuss the matter with management and, where appropriate, those charged with governance;

(b) Determine whether the financial report needs amendment and; if so,

(c) Enquire how management intends to address the matter in the financial report.

15. If management amends the financial report, the auditor shall: (Ref: Para. A17)

(a) Carry out the audit procedures necessary in the circumstances on the amendment.

(b) Review the steps taken by management to ensure that anyone in receipt of the previously issued financial report together with the auditor's report thereon is informed of the situation.

(c) Unless the circumstances in paragraph 12 of this Auditing Standard apply:

(i) Extend the audit procedures referred to in paragraphs 6 and 7 of this Auditing Standard to the date of the new auditor's report, and date the new auditor's report no earlier than the date of approval of the amended financial report; and

(ii) Provide a new auditor's report on the amended financial report.

(d) When the circumstances in paragraph 12 of this Auditing Standard apply, amend the auditor's report, or provide a new auditor's report as required by paragraph 12 of this Auditing Standard.

16. The auditor shall include in the new or amended auditor's report an Emphasis of Matter paragraph or Other Matter(s) paragraph referring to a note in the financial report that more extensively discusses the reason for the amendment of the previously issued financial report and to the earlier report provided by the auditor.

17. If management, or those charged with governance, do not take the necessary steps to ensure that anyone in receipt of the previously issued financial report is informed of the situation and does not amend the financial report in circumstances where the auditor believes they need to be amended, the auditor shall notify management and, unless all of those charged with governance are involved in managing the entity,[6] those charged with governance, that the auditor will seek to prevent future reliance on the auditor's report. If, despite such notification, management or those charged with governance do not take these necessary steps, the auditor shall take appropriate action to seek to prevent reliance on the auditor's report. (Ref: Para. A18)

❖ ❖ ❖

5 See ASA 705 *Modifications to the Opinion in the Independent Auditor's Report.*

6 See ASA 260 *Communication with Those Charged with Governance,* paragraph 13.

Application and Other Explanatory Material

Scope of this Auditing Standard (Ref: Para. 1)

A1. When the audited financial report is included in other documents subsequent to the issuance of the financial report, the auditor may have additional responsibilities relating to subsequent events that the auditor may need to consider, such as legal or regulatory requirements involving the offering of securities to the public in jurisdictions in which the securities are being offered. For example, the auditor may be required to perform additional audit procedures to the date of the final offering document. These procedures may include those referred to in paragraphs 6 and 7 performed up to a date at or near the effective date of the final offering document, and reading the offering document to assess whether the other information in the offering document is consistent with the financial information with which the auditor is associated.[7]

Definitions

Date of Approval of the Financial Report (Ref: Para. 5(a))

A2. In some jurisdictions, law or regulation identifies the individuals or bodies (for example, management or those charged with governance) that are responsible for concluding that all the financial statements that comprise the financial report, including the related notes, have been prepared, and specifies the necessary approval process. In other jurisdictions, the approval process is not prescribed in law or regulation and the entity follows its own procedures in preparing and finalising its financial report in view of its management and governance structures. In some jurisdictions, final approval of the financial report by shareholders is required. In these jurisdictions, final approval by shareholders is not necessary for the auditor to conclude that sufficient appropriate audit evidence on which to base the auditor's opinion on the financial report has been obtained. The date of approval of the financial report for the purposes of the Australian Auditing Standards is the earlier date on which those with the recognised authority determine that all the financial statements that comprise the financial report, including the related notes, have been prepared and that those with the recognised authority have asserted that they have taken responsibility for that financial report.

Date of the Auditor's Report (Ref: Para. 5(b))

A3. The auditor's report cannot be dated earlier than the date on which the auditor has obtained sufficient appropriate audit evidence on which to base the opinion on the financial report including evidence that all the financial statements that comprise the financial report, including the related notes, have been prepared and that those with the recognised authority have asserted that they have taken responsibility for that financial report.[8] Consequently, the date of the auditor's report cannot be earlier than the date of approval of the financial report as defined in paragraph 5(b). A time period may elapse due to administrative issues between the date of the auditor's report as defined in paragraph 5(c) and the date the auditor's report is provided to the entity.

Aus A3.1 In some cases, law or regulation may identify the point in the financial reporting process at which the audit is expected to be complete.

Date the Financial Report Is Issued (Ref: Para. 5(c))

A4. The date the financial report is issued generally depends on the regulatory environment of the entity. In some circumstances, the date the financial report is issued may be the date that they are filed with a regulatory authority. Since an audited financial report cannot be issued without an auditor's report, the date that the audited financial report is issued must not only be at or later than the date of the auditor's report, but must also be at or later than the date the auditor's report is provided to the entity.

---

7 See ASA 200 *Overall Objectives of the Independent Auditor and the Conduct of an Audit in Accordance with Australian Auditing Standards*, paragraph 2.

8 See ASA 700, paragraphs Aus 40.1 and 41.

Considerations Specific to Public Sector Entities

A5. In the case of the public sector, the date the financial report is issued may be the date the audited financial report and the auditor's report thereon are presented to the legislature or otherwise made public.

Events Occurring between the Date of the Financial Report and the Date of the Auditor's Report (Ref: Para. 6-9)

A6. Depending on the auditor's risk assessment, the audit procedures required by paragraph 6 may include procedures, necessary to obtain sufficient appropriate audit evidence, involving the review or testing of accounting records or transactions occurring between the date of the financial report and the date of the auditor's report. The audit procedures required by paragraphs 6 and 7 are in addition to procedures that the auditor may perform for other purposes that, nevertheless, may provide evidence about subsequent events (for example, to obtain audit evidence for account balances as at the date of the financial report, such as cut-off procedures or procedures in relation to subsequent receipts of accounts receivable).

A7. Paragraph 7 stipulates certain audit procedures in this context that the auditor is required to perform pursuant to paragraph 6. The subsequent events procedures that the auditor performs may, however, depend on the information that is available and, in particular, the extent to which the accounting records have been prepared since the date of the financial report. Where the accounting records are not up-to-date, and accordingly no interim financial report (whether for internal or external purposes) has been prepared, or minutes of meetings of management or those charged with governance have not been prepared, relevant audit procedures may take the form of inspection of available books and records, including bank statements. Paragraph A8 gives examples of some of the additional matters that the auditor may consider in the course of these enquiries.

A8. In addition to the audit procedures required by paragraph 7, the auditor may consider it necessary and appropriate to:

- Read the entity's latest available budgets, cash flow forecasts and other related management reports for periods after the date of the financial report;
- Enquire, or extend previous oral or written enquiries, of the entity's legal counsel concerning litigation and claims; or
- Consider whether written representations covering particular subsequent events may be necessary to support other audit evidence and thereby obtain sufficient appropriate audit evidence.

Enquiry (Ref. Para. 7(b))

A9. In enquiring of management and, where appropriate, those charged with governance, as to whether any subsequent events have occurred that might affect the financial report, the auditor may enquire as to the current status of items that were accounted for on the basis of preliminary or inconclusive data and may make specific enquiries about the following matters:

- Whether new commitments, borrowings or guarantees have been entered into.
- Whether sales or acquisitions of assets have occurred or are planned.
- Whether there have been increases in capital or issuance of debt instruments, such as the issue of new shares or debentures, or an agreement to merge or liquidate has been made or is planned.
- Whether any assets have been appropriated by government or destroyed, for example, by fire or flood.
- Whether there have been any developments regarding contingencies.
- Whether any unusual accounting adjustments have been made or are contemplated.
- Whether any events have occurred or are likely to occur that will bring into question the appropriateness of accounting policies used in the financial report, as would be the case, for example, if such events call into question the validity of the going concern assumption.

- Whether any events have occurred that are relevant to the measurement of estimates or provisions made in the financial report.
- Whether any events have occurred that are relevant to the recoverability of assets.

Reading Minutes (Ref. Para. 7(c))

Considerations Specific to Public Sector Entities

A10. In the public sector, the auditor may read the official records of relevant proceedings of the legislature and enquire about matters addressed in proceedings for which official records are not yet available.

Facts Which Become Known to the Auditor after the Date of the Auditor's Report but before the Date the Financial Report Is Issued

Management Responsibility Towards Auditor (Ref: Para. 10)

A11. As explained in ASA 210, the terms of the audit engagement include the agreement of management to inform the auditor of facts that may affect the financial report, of which management may become aware during the period from the date of the auditor's report to the date the financial report is issued.[9]

Dual Dating (Ref: Para. 12(a))

A12. When, in the circumstances described in paragraph 12(a), the auditor amends the auditor's report to include an additional date restricted to that amendment, the date of the auditor's report on the financial report prior to their subsequent amendment by management remains unchanged because this date informs the reader as to when the audit work on that financial report was completed. However, an additional date is included in the auditor's report to inform users that the auditor's procedures subsequent to that date were restricted to the subsequent amendment of the financial report. The following is an illustration of such an additional date:

"(Date of auditor's report), except as to Note Y, which is as of (date of completion of audit procedures restricted to amendment described in Note Y)."

No Amendment of the Financial Report by Management (Ref: Para. 13)

A13. In some jurisdictions, management may not be required by law, regulation or the financial reporting framework to issue an amended financial report. This is often the case when issuance of the financial report for the following period is imminent, provided appropriate disclosures are made in such a report.

Considerations Specific to Public Sector Entities

A14. In the public sector, the actions taken in accordance with paragraph 13 when management does not amend the financial report may also include reporting separately to the legislature, or other relevant body in the reporting hierarchy, on the implications of the subsequent event for the financial report and the auditor's report.

Auditor Action to Seek to Prevent Reliance on Auditor's Report (Ref: Para. 13(b))

A15. The auditor may need to fulfil additional legal obligations even when the auditor has notified management not to issue the financial report and management has agreed to this request.

A16. Where management has issued the financial report despite the auditor's notification not to issue the financial report to third parties, the auditor's course of action to prevent reliance on the auditor's report on the financial report depends upon the auditor's legal rights and obligations. Consequently, the auditor may consider it appropriate to seek legal advice.

---

9 See ASA 210 *Agreeing the Terms of Audit Engagements*, paragraph A23.

Facts Which Become Known to the Auditor after the Financial Report Has Been Issued

No Amendment of the Financial Report by Management (Ref: Para. 15)

Considerations Specific to Public Sector Entities

A17. In some jurisdictions, entities in the public sector may be prohibited from issuing an amended financial report by law or regulation. In such circumstances, the appropriate course of action for the auditor may be to report to the appropriate statutory body.

Auditor Action to Seek to Prevent Reliance on Auditor's Report (Ref: Para. 17)

A18. Where the auditor believes that management, or those charged with governance, have failed to take the necessary steps to prevent reliance on the auditor's report on the financial report previously issued by the entity despite the auditor's prior notification that the auditor will take action to seek to prevent such reliance, the auditor's course of action depends upon the auditor's legal rights and obligations. Consequently, the auditor may consider it appropriate to seek legal advice.

❖ ❖ ❖

Conformity with International Standards on Auditing

This Auditing Standard conforms with International Standard on Auditing ISA 560 *Subsequent Events*, issued by the International Auditing and Assurance Standards Board (IAASB), an independent standard-setting board of the International Federation of Accountants (IFAC).

Paragraphs that have been added to this Auditing Standard (and do not appear in the text of the equivalent ISA) are identified with the prefix "Aus".

The following requirement is additional to ISA 560:

- For an audit engagement conducted under the *Corporations Act 2001*, management, and those charged with governance, are prohibited from restricting an amendment of the financial report to the effects of the subsequent event or events causing that amendment. Consequently, the auditor is prohibited from restricting audit procedures as required under paragraph 11(b)(i) of this Auditing Standard to such an amendment. [Ref: Para. Aus 12.1]

Compliance with this Auditing Standard enables compliance with ISA 560.

ASA 570

Going Concern

(Reissued October 2009: amended and compiled July 2012)

Issued by the Auditing and Assurance Standards Board.

ASA

Note from the Institute of Chartered Accountants Australia

This note, prepared by the technical editor, is not part of ASA 570.

Historical development

June 1981: AUP 7 'Going Concern' issued in, and effective from, June 1981 following the issue of ED 2 in August 1980.

August 1986: Substantially revised and reissued in, and effective from, August 1986 following the issue of ED 20 (IAPC ED23) in November 1984.

October 1990: ED 36 'Going Concern' issued by the AuSB, with comments due by 31 January 1991.

May 1991: AUP 7 'Going Concern' reissued, operative for the first financial reporting period ending on or after 1 January 1992. The major changes to AUP 7 as a result of the reissue were clarification of the auditor's role in relation to the going concern basis, the redefinition of foreseeable future, the provision of guidance on 'comfort letters', identification of additional examples of going concern problems and changes to the audit reporting provisions.

June 1994: The International Auditing Practices Committee (IAPC) of the International Federation of Accountants (IFAC) approved the issuance of a codified set of International Standards of Auditing (ISAs) in June 1994. The relevant international pronouncement was ISA 570 'Going Concern'.

September 1994: ED 62 'Codification and Revision of Auditing Pronouncements: AUS 710 Going Concern (AUP 7)' issued by the AuSB.

October 1995: Australian Auditing Standards and Auditing Guidance Statements released. The status of the guidance was explained in APS 1.1 'Conformity With Auditing Standards'. These Standards became operative for the first reporting period commencing on or after 1 July 1996 and later reporting periods, although earlier application was encouraged. AUP 7 'Going Concern' replaced by AUS 708 'Going Concern'.

March 1996: The AuSB published ED 64 'Going Concern (AUS 708)' and a brief guide to ED 64. The exposure draft reflected the audit implications of the revised definition of going concern in the reissued Accounting Standards AAS 6 and AASB 1001 'Accounting Policies'. Key features discussed in ED 64 include half-year accounts, audit procedures and the 'relevant period'.

September 1996: AUS 708 'Going Concern' reissued by the AuSB, based on ED 64 of the same name. The revised Standard was operative from the date of issue.

April 1998: ED 67 'Amendments to AUS 702 The Audit Report on a General Purpose Financial Report' and AUS 708 'Going Concern' were released, with comments sought by 30 June 1998. AUS/AGS Omnibus 1 'Miscellaneous Amendments to AUSs and AGSs' issued making minor changes to AUS 708.

October 1998: AUS 708 'Going Concern' reissued, based on the proposals in ED 67 'Amendments to AUS 702 The Audit Report on a General Purpose Financial Report' and AUS 708 'Going Concern'.

July 2002: AUS/AGS Omnibus 3 'Miscellaneous Amendments to AUSs and AGSs' issued by the AuASB, operative from the date of issue. AUS 708 'Going Concern' since reissued by the Board to incorporate these amendments.

April 2006: ASA 570 was issued as a legally enforcable Standard to replace AUS 708. It is based on ISA 570 of the same name.

June 2007: ASA 570 compiled and republished to reflect changes to the ASA 700 Audit Report made in Omnibus ASA 2007-1.

October 2009: ASA 570 reissued as part of the AUASB's Clarity Project. It is based on the redrafted ISA 570 of the same name.

June 2011: ASA 570 updated for editorial amendments contained in ASA 2011-1 'Amendments to Australian Auditing Standards'.

July 2012: ASA 570 updated for amendments to the flowchart in Appendix 1 contained in ASA 2012-1 'Amending Standard to ASA 570 Going Concern'. The amendments improve the diagram's clarity, but do not add to or change the existing requirements. The diagram is not in the underlying international Standard.

Contents

ASA

Compilation details

Auditing Standard ASA 570 *Going Concern* as Amended

This compilation takes into account amendments made up to and including 31 July 2012 and was prepared on 31 July 2012 by the Auditing and Assurance Standards Board (AUASB).

This compilation is not a separate Auditing Standard made by the AUASB. Instead, it is a representation of ASA 570 (October 2009) as amended by other Auditing Standards which are listed in the Table below.

Table of Standards

Standard		Date made	Operative Date
ASA 570	[A]	27 October 2009	financial reporting periods commencing on or after 1 January 2010
ASA 2011-1	[B]	27 June 2011	financial reporting periods commencing on or after 1 July 2011. Early adoption permitted.
ASA 2012-1	[C]	31 July 2012	financial reporting periods commencing on or after 1 July 2012

Table of Amendments

Paragraph affected	How affected	By … [paragraph]
A8	Amended	ASA 2011-1 [42]
A12	Amended	ASA 2011-1 [43]
[Aus] Appendix 2	Amended	ASA 2011-1 [44]
[Aus] Appendix 2 and [Aus] Appendix 3	Amended	ASA 2011-1 [45]
[Aus] Appendix 2 and [Aus] Appendix 3	Amended	ASA 2011-1 [46]
[Aus] Appendix 3	Amended	ASA 2011-1 [47]
[Aus] Appendix 2 and [Aus] Appendix 3	Amended	ASA 2011-1 [48]
[Aus] Appendix 2 and [Aus] Appendix 3	Amended	ASA 2011-1 [49]
[Aus] Appendix 1	Replaced	ASA 2012-1 [4]

[A] Federal Register of Legislative Instruments – registration number F2009L04095, issued 13 November 2009

[B] Federal Register of Legislative Instruments – registration number F2011L01379, issued 30 June 2011

[C] Federal Register of Legislative Instruments – registration number F2012L01671, issued 10 August 2012.

Authority Statement

Auditing Standard ASA 570 *Going Concern* (as amended by ASA 2012-1 and ASA 2011-1, amendments up to 31 July 2012) is set out in paragraphs Aus 0.1 to Aus A27.2 and [Aus] Appendices 1, 2 and 3.

This Auditing Standard is to be read in conjunction with ASA 101 *Preamble to Australian Auditing Standards*, which sets out the intentions of the AUASB on how the Australian Auditing Standards, operative for financial reporting periods commencing on or after 1 January 2010, are to be understood, interpreted and applied. This Auditing Standard is to be read also in conjunction with ASA 200 *Overall Objectives of the Independent Auditor and the Conduct of an Audit in Accordance with Australian Auditing Standards.*

Dated: 31 July 2012

Auditing Standard ASA 570

The Auditing and Assurance Standards Board (AUASB) made Auditing Standard ASA 570 *Going Concern*, pursuant to section 227B of the *Australian Securities and Investments Commission Act 2001* and section 336 of the *Corporations Act 2001*, on 27 October 2009.

This compiled version of ASA 570 incorporates subsequent amendments contained in other Auditing Standards made by the AUASB up to and including 31 July 2012 (see Compilation Details).

Preface

[Preface extracted from the original Auditing Standard issued 27 October 2009]

Reasons for Issuing Auditing Standard ASA 570 *Going Concern*

The Auditing and Assurance Standards Board (AUASB) issues Auditing Standard ASA 570 *Going Concern* pursuant to the requirements of the legislative provisions and the Strategic Direction explained below.

The AUASB is an independent statutory board of the Australian Government established under section 227A of the *Australian Securities and Investments Commission Act 2001*, as amended (ASIC Act). Under section 336 of the *Corporations Act 2001*, the AUASB may make Auditing Standards for the purposes of the corporations legislation. These Auditing Standards are legislative instruments under the *Legislative Instruments Act 2003*.

Under the Strategic Direction given to the AUASB by the Financial Reporting Council (FRC), the AUASB is required to have regard to any programme initiated by the International Auditing and Assurance Standards Board (IAASB) for the revision and enhancement of the International Standards on Auditing (ISAs) and to make appropriate consequential amendments to the Australian Auditing Standards. Accordingly, the AUASB has decided to revise and redraft the Australian Auditing Standards using the equivalent redrafted ISAs.

Main Features

This Auditing Standard establishes requirements and provides application and other explanatory material regarding the auditor's responsibilities in the audit of a financial report relating to management's use of the going concern assumption in the preparation of the financial report.

This Auditing Standard requires the auditor to:

(a) plan and perform risk assessment procedures to determine if there are events or conditions that may cast significant doubt on the entity's ability to continue as a going concern;

(b) evaluate management's assessment of the entity's ability to continue as a going concern;

(c) use professional judgement to determine if a material uncertainty exists that may cast significant doubt on the entity's ability to continue as a going concern;

(d) perform additional audit procedures when events or conditions are identified that may cast significant doubt on the entity's ability to continue as a going concern;

(e) determine if adequate disclosure is made in the financial report regarding the entity's going concern position and to consider the implications of such disclosure on the auditor's opinion; and

(f) communicate with management, and where appropriate, those charged with governance, any events or conditions identified that may cast significant doubt on the entity's ability to continue as a going concern.

Auditing Standard ASA 570
Going Concern

Application

Aus 0.1 This Auditing Standard applies to:

(a) an audit of a financial report for a financial year, or an audit of a financial report for a half-year, in accordance with the *Corporations Act 2001*; and

(b) an audit of a financial report, or a complete set of financial statements, for any other purpose.

Aus 0.2 This Auditing Standard also applies, as appropriate, to an audit of other historical financial information.

Operative Date

Aus 0.3 This Auditing Standard is operative for financial reporting periods commencing on or after financial reporting period commencing on or after 1 January 2010.

[Note: For operative dates of paragraphs changed or added by an Amending Standard, see Compilation Details.]

Introduction

Scope of this Auditing Standard

1. This Auditing Standard deals with the auditor's responsibilities in the audit of a financial report relating to management's use of the going concern assumption in the preparation of the financial report.

Aus 1.1 For the purposes of this Auditing Standard, a reference to management is taken to mean "management, and where appropriate, those charged with governance".

Going Concern Assumption

2. Under the going concern assumption, an entity is viewed as continuing in business for the foreseeable future. A general purpose financial report is prepared on a going concern basis, unless management either intends to liquidate the entity or to cease operations, or has no realistic alternative but to do so. A special purpose financial report may or may not be prepared in accordance with a financial reporting framework for which the going concern basis is relevant (for example, the going concern basis is not relevant for some financial reports prepared on a tax basis in particular jurisdictions). When the use of the going concern assumption is appropriate, assets and liabilities are recorded on the basis that the entity will be able to realise its assets and discharge its liabilities in the normal course of business. (Ref: Para. A1)

Responsibility for Assessment of the Entity's Ability to Continue as a Going Concern

3. Some financial reporting frameworks contain an explicit requirement for management to make a specific assessment of the entity's ability to continue as a going concern, and standards regarding matters to be considered and disclosures to be made in connection with going concern.[1] The detailed requirements regarding management's responsibility to assess the entity's ability to continue as a going concern and related financial report disclosures may also be set out in law or regulation.

Aus 3.1 Australian Accounting Standards[*] require management to make an assessment of an entity's ability to continue as a going concern. In addition, certain legislation, such as the *Corporations Act 2001*,[#] requires a formal statement as to the solvency

1 [Footnote deleted by the AUASB. Refer Aus 3.1]

* See AASB 101 *Presentation of Financial Statements.*

See, for example, section 295(4) of the *Corporations Act 2001.*

of the entity to be made by those charged with governance and included as part of the financial report upon which the auditor's opinion is expressed.

4. In other financial reporting frameworks, there may be no explicit requirement for management to make a specific assessment of the entity's ability to continue as a going concern. Nevertheless, since the going concern assumption is a fundamental principle in the preparation of a financial report as discussed in paragraph 2 of this Auditing Standard, the preparation of the financial report requires management to assess the entity's ability to continue as a going concern even if the financial reporting framework does not include an explicit requirement to do so.

5. Management's assessment of the entity's ability to continue as a going concern involves making a judgement, at a particular point in time, about inherently uncertain future outcomes of events or conditions. The following factors are relevant to that judgement:

- The degree of uncertainty associated with the outcome of an event or condition increases significantly the further into the future an event or condition or the outcome occurs. For that reason, most financial reporting frameworks that require an explicit management assessment specify the period for which management is required to take into account all available information.
- The size and complexity of the entity, the nature and condition of its business and the degree to which it is affected by external factors affect the judgement regarding the outcome of events or conditions.
- Any judgement about the future is based on information available at the time at which the judgement is made. Subsequent events may result in outcomes that are inconsistent with judgements that were reasonable at the time they were made.

Responsibilities of the Auditor

6. The auditor's responsibility is to obtain sufficient appropriate audit evidence about the appropriateness of management's use of the going concern assumption in the preparation and presentation of the financial report and to conclude whether there is a material uncertainty about the entity's ability to continue as a going concern. This responsibility exists even if the financial reporting framework used in the preparation of the financial report does not include an explicit requirement for management to make a specific assessment of the entity's ability to continue as a going concern.

7. However, as described in ASA 200,[2] the potential effects of inherent limitations on the auditor's ability to detect material misstatements are greater for future events or conditions that may cause an entity to cease to continue as a going concern. The auditor cannot predict such future events or conditions. Accordingly, the absence of any reference to going concern uncertainty in an auditor's report cannot be viewed as a guarantee as to the entity's ability to continue as a going concern.

Effective Date

8. [Deleted by the AUASB. Refer AUS 0.3]

Objectives

9. The objectives of the auditor are:
   (a) To obtain sufficient appropriate audit evidence regarding the appropriateness of management's use of the going concern assumption in the preparation of the financial report;
   (b) To conclude, based on the audit evidence obtained, whether a material uncertainty exists related to events or conditions that may cast significant doubt on the entity's ability to continue as a going concern; and
   (c) To determine the implications for the auditor's report.

2 See ASA 200 *Overall Objectives of the Independent Auditor and the Conduct of an Audit in Accordance with Australian Auditing Standards.*

Requirements

Risk Assessment Procedures and Related Activities

10. When performing risk assessment procedures as required by ASA 315[3] the auditor shall consider whether there are events or conditions that may cast significant doubt on the entity's ability to continue as a going concern. In so doing, the auditor shall determine whether management has already performed a preliminary assessment of the entity's ability to continue as a going concern, and: (Ref: Para. A2-A5)

    (a) If such an assessment has been performed, the auditor shall discuss the assessment with management and determine whether management has identified events or conditions that, individually or collectively, may cast significant doubt on the entity's ability to continue as a going concern and, if so, management's plans to address them; or

    (b) If such an assessment has not yet been performed, the auditor shall discuss with management the basis for the intended use of the going concern assumption, and enquire of management whether events or conditions exist that, individually or collectively, may cast significant doubt on the entity's ability to continue as a going concern.

11. The auditor shall remain alert throughout the audit for audit evidence of events or conditions that may cast significant doubt on the entity's ability to continue as a going concern. (Ref: Para. A6)

Evaluating Management's Assessment

12. The auditor shall evaluate management's assessment of the entity's ability to continue as a going concern. (Ref: Para. A7-A9; A11-A12)

13. [Deleted by the AUASB. Refer Aus 13.1[4]]

Aus 13.1 In evaluating management's assessment of the entity's ability to continue as a going concern, the auditor shall consider the relevant period, which may be the same or may differ from that used by management to make its assessment as required by the applicable financial reporting framework. If management's assessment of the entity's ability to continue as a going concern covers less than the relevant period, the auditor shall request management to correspond to the relevant period used by the auditor. (Ref: Para. A10-A12)

Aus 13.2 Relevant period means the period of approximately 12 months from the date of the auditor's current report to the expected date of the auditor's report for:

(a) the next annual reporting period in the case of an annual financial report; or

(b) the corresponding reporting period for the following year in the case of an interim reporting period.

14. In evaluating management's assessment, the auditor shall consider whether management's assessment includes all relevant information of which the auditor is aware as a result of the audit.

Period beyond Management's Assessment

15. The auditor shall enquire of management as to its knowledge of events or conditions beyond the period of management's assessment that may cast significant doubt on the entity's ability to continue as a going concern. (Ref: Para. A13-A14)

Additional Audit Procedures When Events or Conditions Are Identified

16. If events or conditions have been identified that may cast significant doubt on the entity's ability to continue as a going concern, the auditor shall obtain sufficient appropriate audit evidence to determine whether or not a material uncertainty exists through performing

3 See ASA 315 *Identifying and Assessing the Risks of Material Misstatement through Understanding the Entity and Its Environment,* paragraph 5.

4 [Footnote deleted by the AUASB. Refer Aus 13.1 and Aus 13.2]

additional audit procedures, including consideration of mitigating factors. These procedures shall include: (Ref: Para. A15)

(a) Where management has not yet performed an assessment of the entity's ability to continue as a going concern, requesting management to make its assessment.

(b) Evaluating management's plans for future actions in relation to its going concern assessment, whether the outcome of these plans is likely to improve the situation and whether management's plans are feasible in the circumstances. (Ref: Para. A16)

(c) Where the entity has prepared a cash flow forecast, and analysis of the forecast is a significant factor in considering the future outcome of events or conditions in the evaluation of management's plans for future action: (Ref: Para. A17-A18)

(i) Evaluating the reliability of the underlying data generated to prepare the forecast; and

(ii) Determining whether there is adequate support for the assumptions underlying the forecast.

(d) Considering whether any additional facts or information have become available since the date on which management made its assessment.

(e) Requesting written representations from management and, where appropriate, those charged with governance, regarding their plans for future action and the feasibility of these plans.

Aus 16.1 If such events or conditions are identified, the auditor shall consider whether they affect the auditor's assessment of the risks of material misstatement in accordance with ASA 315.*

Audit Conclusions and Reporting

17. Based on the audit evidence obtained, the auditor shall conclude whether, in the auditor's judgement, a material uncertainty exists related to events or conditions that, individually or collectively, may cast significant doubt on the entity's ability to continue as a going concern. A material uncertainty exists when the magnitude of its potential impact and likelihood of occurrence is such that, in the auditor's judgement, appropriate disclosure of the nature and implications of the uncertainty is necessary for: (Ref: Para. A19-Aus A19.1)

(a) In the case of a fair presentation financial reporting framework, the fair presentation of the financial report, or

(b) In the case of a compliance framework, the financial report not to be misleading.

Use of Going Concern Assumption Appropriate but a Material Uncertainty Exists

18. If the auditor concludes that the use of the going concern assumption is appropriate in the circumstances but a material uncertainty exists, the auditor shall determine whether the financial report:

(a) Adequately describes the principal events or conditions that may cast significant doubt on the entity's ability to continue as a going concern and management's plans to deal with these events or conditions; and

(b) Discloses clearly that there is a material uncertainty related to events or conditions that may cast significant doubt on the entity's ability to continue as a going concern and, therefore, that it may be unable to realise its assets and discharge its liabilities in the normal course of business. (Ref: Para. A20)

19. If adequate disclosure is made in the financial report, the auditor shall express an unmodified opinion and include an Emphasis of Matter paragraph in the auditor's report to:

(a) Highlight the existence of a material uncertainty relating to the event or condition that may cast significant doubt on the entity's ability to continue as a going concern; and

---

* See ASA 315, paragraph 31.

ASA

(b) Draw attention to the note in the financial report that discloses the matters set out in paragraph 18 of this Auditing Standard.[5] (Ref: Para. A21-A22)

20. If adequate disclosure is not made in the financial report, the auditor shall express a qualified opinion or adverse opinion, as appropriate in accordance with ASA 705.[6] The auditor shall state in the auditor's report that there is a material uncertainty that may cast significant doubt about the entity's ability to continue as a going concern. (Ref: Para. A23-Aus A24.2)

Use of Going Concern Assumption Inappropriate

21. If the financial report has been prepared on a going concern basis but, in the auditor's judgement, management's use of the going concern assumption in the financial report is inappropriate, the auditor shall express an adverse opinion. (Ref: Para. A25-A26)

Management Unwilling to Make or Extend Its Assessment

22. If management is unwilling to make or extend its assessment when requested to do so by the auditor, the auditor shall consider the implications for the auditor's report. (Ref: Para. A27-Aus A27.2)

Communication with Those Charged with Governance

23. Unless all those charged with governance are involved in managing the entity,[7] the auditor shall communicate with those charged with governance events or conditions identified that may cast significant doubt on the entity's ability to continue as a going concern. Such communication with those charged with governance shall include the following:

(a) Whether the events or conditions constitute a material uncertainty;

(b) Whether the use of the going concern assumption is appropriate in the preparation and presentation of the financial report;

(c) The adequacy of related disclosures in the financial report; and

Aus 23.1 Whether management is unwilling to make or extend its assessment as described in paragraph 22 of this Auditing Standard.

Significant Delay in the Approval of the Financial Report

24. If there is significant delay in the approval of the financial report by management or those charged with governance after the date of the financial report, the auditor shall enquire as to the reasons for the delay. If the auditor believes that the delay could be related to events or conditions relating to the going concern assessment, the auditor shall perform those additional audit procedures necessary, as described in paragraph 16 of this Auditing Standard, as well as consider the effect on the auditor's conclusion regarding the existence of a material uncertainty, as described in paragraph 17 of this Auditing Standard.

❖❖❖

Application and Other Explanatory Material

Going Concern Assumption (Ref: Para. 2)

Considerations Specific to Public Sector Entities

A1. Management's use of the going concern assumption is also relevant to public sector entities.[8] Going concern risks may arise, but are not limited to, situations where public sector entities operate on a for-profit basis, where government support may be reduced or withdrawn, or in the case of privatisation. Events or conditions that may cast significant doubt on an entity's ability to continue as a going concern in the public sector may include

5 See ASA 706 *Emphasis of Matter Paragraphs and Other Matter Paragraphs in the Independent Auditor's Report.*

6 See ASA 705 *Modifications to the Opinion in the Independent Auditor's Report,* paragraphs 7-8.

7 See ASA 260 *Communication with Those Charged with Governance*, paragraph 13.

8 [Footnote deleted by the AUASB as not applicable in Australia.]

situations where the public sector entity lacks funding for its continued existence or when policy decisions are made that affect the services provided by the public sector entity.

Risk Assessment Procedures and Related Activities

Events or Conditions That May Cast Doubt about Going Concern Assumption (Ref: Para. 10)

A2. The following are examples of events or conditions that, individually or collectively, may cast significant doubt about the going concern assumption. This listing is not all-inclusive nor does the existence of one or more of the items always signify that a material uncertainty exists.

Financial

- Net liability or net current liability position.
- Fixed-term borrowings approaching maturity without realistic prospects of renewal or repayment; or excessive reliance on short-term borrowings to finance long-term assets.
- Indications of withdrawal of financial support by creditors.
- Negative operating cash flows indicated by historical or prospective financial report.
- Adverse key financial ratios.
- Substantial operating losses or significant deterioration in the value of assets used to generate cash flows.
- Arrears or discontinuance of dividends.
- Inability to pay creditors on due dates.
- Inability to comply with the terms of loan agreements.
- Change from credit to cash-on-delivery transactions with suppliers.
- Inability to obtain financing for essential new product development or other essential investments.

Operating

- Management intentions to liquidate the entity or to cease operations.
- Loss of key management without replacement.
- Loss of a major market, key customer(s), franchise, licence, or principal supplier(s).
- Labour difficulties.
- Shortages of important supplies.
- Emergence of a highly successful competitor.

Other

- Non-compliance with capital or other statutory requirements.
- Pending legal or regulatory proceedings against the entity that may, if successful, result in claims that the entity is unlikely to be able to satisfy.
- Changes in law or regulation or government policy expected to adversely affect the entity.
- Uninsured or underinsured catastrophes when they occur.

The significance of such events or conditions often can be mitigated by other factors. For example, the effect of an entity being unable to make its normal debt repayments may be counter-balanced by management's plans to maintain adequate cash flows by alternative means, such as by disposing of assets, rescheduling loan repayments, or obtaining additional capital. Similarly, the loss of a principal supplier may be mitigated by the availability of a suitable alternative source of supply.

A3. The risk assessment procedures required by paragraph 10 help the auditor to determine whether management's use of the going concern assumption is likely to be an important issue and its impact on planning the audit. These procedures also allow for more timely discussions with management, including a discussion of management's plans and resolution of any identified going concern issues.

Considerations Specific to Smaller Entities

A4. The size of an entity may affect its ability to withstand adverse conditions. Small entities may be able to respond quickly to exploit opportunities, but may lack reserves to sustain operations.

A5. Conditions of particular relevance to small entities include the risk that banks and other lenders may cease to support the entity, as well as the possible loss of a principal supplier, major customer, key employee, or the right to operate under a license, franchise or other legal agreement.

Remaining Alert throughout the Audit for Audit Evidence about Events or Conditions (Ref: Para. 11)

A6. ASA 315 requires the auditor to revise the auditor's risk assessment and modify the further planned audit procedures accordingly when additional audit evidence is obtained during the course of the audit that affects the auditor's assessment of risk.[9] If events or conditions that may cast significant doubt on the entity's ability to continue as a going concern are identified after the auditor's risk assessments are made, in addition to performing the procedures in paragraph 16, the auditor's assessment of the risks of material misstatement may need to be revised. The existence of such events or conditions may also affect the nature, timing and extent of the auditor's further procedures in response to the assessed risks. ASA 330[10] establishes requirements and provides guidance on this issue.

Evaluating Management's Assessment

Management's Assessment and Supporting Analysis and the Auditor's Evaluation (Ref: Para. 12)

A7. Management's assessment of the entity's ability to continue as a going concern is a key part of the auditor's consideration of management's use of the going concern assumption.

A8. It is not the auditor's responsibility to rectify the lack of analysis by management. In some circumstances, however, the lack of detailed analysis by management to support its assessment may not prevent the auditor from concluding whether management's use of the going concern assumption is appropriate in the circumstances. For example, when there is a history of profitable operations and a ready access to financial resources, management may make its assessment without detailed analysis. In this case, the auditor's evaluation of the appropriateness of management's assessment may be made without performing detailed evaluation procedures if the auditor's other audit procedures are sufficient to enable the auditor to conclude whether management's use of the going concern assumption in the preparation of the financial report is appropriate in the circumstances.

A9. In other circumstances, evaluating management's assessment of the entity's ability to continue as a going concern, as required by paragraph 12, may include an evaluation of the process management followed to make its assessment, the assumptions on which the assessment is based and management's plans for future action and whether management's plans are feasible in the circumstances.

The Period of Management's Assessment (Ref: Para. Aus 13.1-Aus 13.2)

A10. Most financial reporting frameworks requiring an explicit management assessment specify the period for which management is required to take into account all available information.[11]

Considerations Specific to Smaller Entities (Ref: Para. 12-13)

A11. In many cases, the management of smaller entities may not have prepared a detailed assessment of the entity's ability to continue as a going concern, but instead may rely

9 See ASA 315, paragraph 31.

10 See ASA 330 *The Auditor's Responses to Assessed Risks.*

11 See AASB 101, paragraphs 25 and 26.

on in-depth knowledge of the business and anticipated future prospects. Nevertheless, in accordance with the requirements of this Auditing Standard, the auditor needs to evaluate management's assessment of the entity's ability to continue as a going concern. For smaller entities, it may be appropriate to discuss the medium and long-term financing of the entity with management, provided that management's contentions can be corroborated by sufficient documentary evidence and are not inconsistent with the auditor's understanding of the entity. Therefore, the requirement in paragraph Aus 13.1 for the auditor to request management to extend its assessment may, for example, be satisfied by discussion, enquiry and inspection of supporting documentation, for example, orders received for future supply, evaluated as to their feasibility or otherwise substantiated.

A12. Continued support by owner-managers is often important to smaller entities' ability to continue as a going concern. Where a small entity is largely financed by a loan from the owner-manager, it may be important that these funds are not withdrawn. For example, the continuance of a small entity in financial difficulty may be dependent on the owner-manager subordinating a loan to the entity in favour of banks or other creditors, or the owner-manager supporting a loan for the entity by providing a guarantee with the owner-manager's personal assets as collateral. In such circumstances, the auditor may obtain appropriate documentary evidence of the subordination of the owner-manager's loan or of the guarantee. Where an entity is dependent on additional support from the owner-manager, the auditor may evaluate the owner-manager's ability to meet the obligation under the support arrangement. In addition, the auditor may request written confirmation of the terms and conditions attaching to such support and the owner-manager's intention or understanding.

ASA

Period beyond Management's Assessment (Ref: Para. 15)

A13. As required by paragraph 11, the auditor remains alert to the possibility that there may be known events, scheduled or otherwise, or conditions that will occur beyond the period of assessment used by management that may bring into question the appropriateness of management's use of the going concern assumption in preparing the financial report. Since the degree of uncertainty associated with the outcome of an event or condition increases as the event or condition is further into the future, in considering events or conditions further in the future, the indications of going concern issues need to be significant before the auditor needs to consider taking further action. If such events or conditions are identified, the auditor may need to request management to evaluate the potential significance of the event or condition on its assessment of the entity's ability to continue as a going concern. In these circumstances the procedures in paragraph 16 apply.

A14. [Deleted by the AUASB. Refer Aus A14.1]

Aus A14.1 Other than enquiry of management, the auditor does not have a responsibility to perform any other audit procedures to identify events or conditions that may cast significant doubt on the entity's ability to continue as a going concern beyond the relevant period, which, as discussed in paragraph Aus 13.2, is approximately twelve months from the date of the auditor's report on the current financial report.

Additional Audit Procedures When Events or Conditions Are Identified (Ref: Para. 16)

A15. Audit procedures that are relevant to the requirement in paragraph 16 may include the following:

- Analysing and discussing cash flow, profit and other relevant forecasts with management.
- Analysing and discussing the entity's latest available interim financial report.
- Reading the terms of debentures and loan agreements and determining whether any have been breached.
- Reading minutes of the meetings of shareholders, those charged with governance and relevant committees for reference to financing difficulties.

- Enquiring of the entity's legal counsel regarding the existence of litigation and claims and the reasonableness of management's assessments of their outcome and the estimate of their financial implications.
- Confirming the existence, legality and enforceability of arrangements to provide or maintain financial support with related and third parties and assessing the financial ability of such parties to provide additional funds.
- Evaluating the entity's plans to deal with unfilled customer orders.
- Performing audit procedures regarding subsequent events to identify those that either mitigate or otherwise affect the entity's ability to continue as a going concern.
- Confirming the existence, terms and adequacy of borrowing facilities.
- Obtaining and reviewing reports of regulatory actions.
- Determining the adequacy of support for any planned disposals of assets.

Evaluating Management's Plans for Future Actions (Ref: Para. 16(b))

A16. Evaluating management's plans for future actions may include enquiries of management as to its plans for future action, including, for example, its plans to liquidate assets, borrow money or restructure debt, reduce or delay expenditures, or increase capital.

The Period of Management's Assessment (Ref: Para. 16(c))

A17. In addition to the procedures required in paragraph 16(c), the auditor may compare:

- The prospective financial information for recent prior periods with historical results; and
- The prospective financial information for the current period with results achieved to date.

A18. Where management's assumptions include continued support by third parties, whether through the subordination of loans, commitments to maintain or provide additional funding, or guarantees, and such support is important to an entity's ability to continue as a going concern, the auditor may need to consider requesting written confirmation (including of terms and conditions) from those third parties and to obtain evidence of their ability to provide such support.

Audit Conclusions and Reporting (Ref: Para. 17)

A19. The phrase "material uncertainty" is used in Australian Accounting Standards* in discussing the uncertainties related to events or conditions which may cast significant doubt on the entity's ability to continue as a going concern that should be disclosed in the financial report. In some other financial reporting frameworks, the phrase "significant uncertainty" is used in similar circumstances.

Aus A19.1 Refer to [Aus] Appendix 1 for a diagrammatic illustration of the links between going concern considerations and the types of audit opinions.

Use of Going Concern Assumption Appropriate but a Material Uncertainty Exists

Adequacy of Disclosure of Material Uncertainty (Ref: Para. 18)

A20. The determination of the adequacy of the financial report disclosure may involve determining whether the information explicitly draws the reader's attention to the possibility that the entity may be unable to continue realising its assets and discharging its liabilities in the normal course of business.

Audit Reporting When Disclosure of Material Uncertainty Is Adequate (Ref: Para. 19)

A21. The following is an illustration of an Emphasis of Matter paragraph when the auditor is satisfied as to the adequacy of the note disclosure:

Emphasis of Matter

Without qualifying our opinion, we draw attention to Note X in the financial report which indicates that the entity incurred a net loss of ZZZ during the year ended 30 June 20X1 and, as of that date, the entity's current liabilities exceeded its total assets by YYY.

* See AASB 101.

These conditions, along with other matters as set forth in Note X, indicate the existence of a material uncertainty that may cast significant doubt about the entity's ability to continue as a going concern and therefore the entity may be unable to realise its assets and discharge its liabilities in the normal course of business.

Aus A21.1 Refer to [Aus] Appendix 3 for an Illustrative Auditor's Report that contains an unqualified opinion with an Emphasis of Matter paragraph.

A22. In situations involving multiple material uncertainties that are significant to the financial report as a whole, the auditor may consider it appropriate in extremely rare cases to express a disclaimer of opinion instead of adding an Emphasis of Matter paragraph. ASA 705 provides guidance on this issue.

Audit Reporting When Disclosure of Material Uncertainty Is Inadequate (Ref: Para. 20)

A23. The following is an illustration of the relevant paragraphs when a qualified opinion is to be expressed:

Basis for Qualified Opinion

The company's financing arrangements expire and amounts outstanding are payable on 19 September 20X1. The company has been unable to re-negotiate or obtain replacement financing. This situation indicates the existence of a material uncertainty that may cast significant doubt on the company's ability to continue as a going concern and therefore the company may be unable to realise its assets and discharge its liabilities in the normal course of business. The financial report does not fully disclose this fact.

Qualified Opinion

[Deleted by the AUASB. Refer Aus A23.1]

Qualified Opinion

Aus A23.1 In our opinion, except for the incomplete disclosure of the information referred to in the Basis for Qualified Opinion paragraph, the financial report of ABC Company Ltd. is in accordance with the *Corporations Act 2001*, including:

(a) giving a true and fair view of the company's financial position as at 30 June 20X1 and of its performance for the year then ended; and

(b) complying with Australian Accounting Standards and the *Corporations Regulations 2001.*

Aus A23.2 Refer to [Aus] Appendix 2 for an Illustrative Auditor's Report that contains a qualified opinion.

A24. The following is an illustration of the relevant paragraphs when an adverse opinion is to be expressed:

Basis for Adverse Opinion

The company's financing arrangements expired and the amount outstanding was payable on 30 June 20X1. The company has been unable to re-negotiate or obtain replacement financing and is considering filing for bankruptcy. These events indicate a material uncertainty that may cast significant doubt on the company's ability to continue as a going concern and therefore it may be unable to realise its assets and discharge its liabilities in the normal course of business. The financial report does not disclose this fact.

Adverse Opinion

[Deleted by the AUASB. Refer Aus A24.1]

ASA

Adverse Opinion

Aus A24.1 In our opinion, because of the omission of the information described in the Basis for Adverse Opinion paragraph, the financial report of ABC Company Ltd. is not in accordance with the *Corporations Act 2001*, and does not:

(a) give a true and fair view of the financial position of the company as at 30 June 20X1, and of its performance for the year then ended; and

(b) comply with Australian Accounting Standards and the *Corporations Regulations 2001*.

Aus A24.2 Refer to [Aus] Appendix 2 for an Illustrative Auditor's Report that contains an adverse opinion.

Use of Going Concern Assumption Inappropriate (Ref: Para. 21)

A25. If the financial report has been prepared on a going concern basis but, in the auditor's judgement, management's use of the going concern assumption in the financial report is inappropriate, the requirement of paragraph 21 for the auditor to express an adverse opinion applies regardless of whether or not the financial report includes disclosure of the inappropriateness of management's use of the going concern assumption.

A26. If the entity's management is required, or elects, to prepare the financial report when the use of the going concern assumption is not appropriate in the circumstances, the financial report is prepared on an alternative basis (for example, liquidation basis). The auditor may be able to perform an audit of that financial report provided that the auditor determines that the alternative basis is an acceptable financial reporting framework in the circumstances. The auditor may be able to express an unmodified opinion on that financial report, provided there is adequate disclosure therein but may consider it appropriate or necessary to include an Emphasis of Matter paragraph in the auditor's report to draw the user's attention to that alternative basis and the reasons for its use.

Management Unwilling to Make or Extend Its Assessment (Ref: Para. 22)

A27. In certain circumstances, the auditor may believe it necessary to request management to make or extend its assessment. If management is unwilling to do so, a qualified opinion or a disclaimer of opinion in the auditor's report may be appropriate, because it may not be possible for the auditor to obtain sufficient appropriate audit evidence regarding the use of the going concern assumption in the preparation of the financial report, such as audit evidence regarding the existence of plans management has put in place or the existence of other mitigating factors.

Aus A27.1 Refer to [Aus] Appendix 2 for an Illustrative Auditor's Report that contains a disclaimer of opinion.

Other Considerations (Ref: Para. 22)

Aus A27.2 An auditor is required under the *Corporations Act 2001*[*] (the Act) to notify the Australian Securities and Investments Commission (ASIC) if the auditor, when conducting an audit, becomes aware of certain circumstances specified in the Act. ASIC[#] provides guidance to help auditors comply with their obligations under the *Corporations Act 2001*, such as reporting suspected insolvent trading.

Conformity with International Standards on Auditing

This Auditing Standard conforms with International Standard on Auditing ISA 570 *Going Concern* issued by the International Auditing and Assurance Standards Board (IAASB), an independent standard-setting board of the International Federation of Accountants (IFAC).

Paragraphs that have been added to this Auditing Standard (and do not appear in the text of the equivalent ISA) are identified with the prefix "Aus".

The following requirements are additional to ISA 570:

- If such events or conditions are identified, the auditor shall consider whether they affect the auditor's assessment of the risks of material misstatement in accordance with ASA 315. (Ref: Para. Aus 16.1)
- Whether management is unwilling to make or extend its assessment as described in paragraph 22 of this Auditing Standard. (Ref: Para. Aus 23.1)

This Auditing Standard requires the auditor to assess the appropriateness of the going concern assumption for the relevant period, which is approximately 12 months from the date of the auditor's current report to the expected date of the auditor's report for the next reporting period. However, ISA 570 requires the auditor to consider the appropriateness of the going concern assumption for a period of at least, but not limited to, twelve months from the balance sheet date. (Ref: Para. Aus 13.1-13.2)

The following application and other explanatory material is additional to ISA 570:

- [Aus] Appendix 1 contains an explanatory diagram mapping going concern considerations and types of audit opinions.
- [Aus] Appendix 2 contains illustrations of auditors' reports modified due to going concern considerations.
- [Aus] Appendix 3 contains an illustration of an auditor's report with an Emphasis of Matter paragraph due to material uncertainties on the going concern basis.

Compliance with this Auditing Standard enables compliance with ISA 570.

[Aus] Appendix 1 (Ref: Para. Aus A19.1)

Linking Going Concern Considerations and Types of Audit Opinions

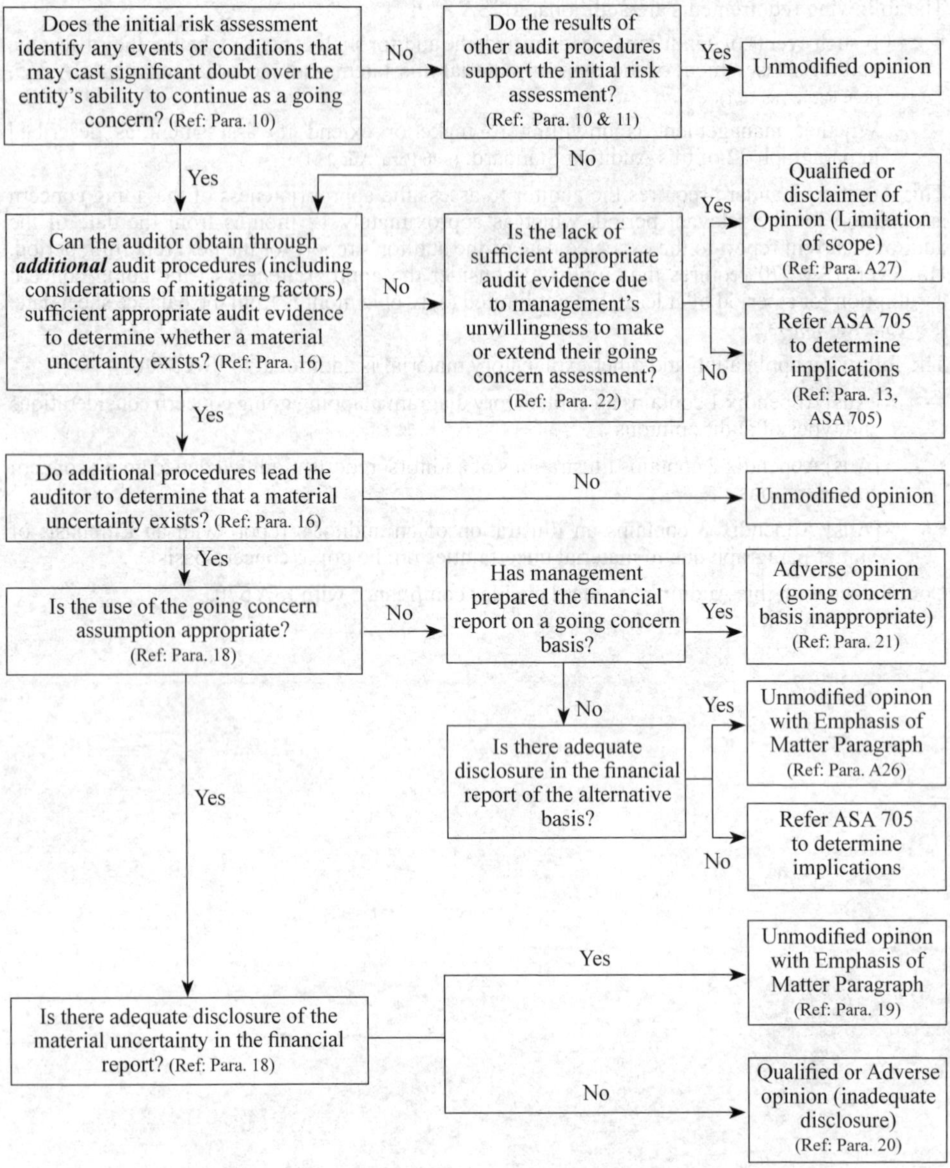

Note: Audit opinions referred to in this diagram must comply, as appropriate, with:

- ASA 700 *Forming an Opinion and Reporting on a Financial Report.*
- ASA 705 *Modifications to the Opinion in the Independent Auditor's Report*
- ASA 706 *Emphasis of Matter Paragraphs and Other Matter Paragraphs in the Independent Auditor's Report*

[Aus] Appendix 2

(Ref: Para. A23-Aus A27.1)

Illustrations of Auditors' Reports on a General Purpose Financial Report—Modified Opinions due to Going Concern Considerations (Fair Presentation Framework)

- [Aus] Illustration 1: An auditor's report on a financial report containing a qualified opinion due to inadequate disclosure of a material uncertainty in the financial report (under the *Corporations Act 2001*). (Ref: Para. A23-Aus A23.2)
- [Aus] Illustration 2: An auditor's report on a financial report containing an adverse opinion due to inadequate disclosure of a material uncertainty in the financial report. (under the *Corporations Act 2001*). (Ref: Para. A24-Aus A24.2)
- [Aus] Illustration 3: An auditor's report on a financial report containing a disclaimer of opinion due to a limitation of scope on the auditor (under the *Corporations Act 2001*). (Ref: Para. A27-Aus A27.1)

See ASA 700* for applicable wording in the auditor's report when the company makes a statement on compliance with *International Financial Reporting Standards* (IFRSs) and/or includes a Remuneration Report in the Directors' Report.

Example Auditor's Report
General Purpose Financial Report
Qualified Opinion due to inadequate disclosures
Corporations Act 2001
(Fair Presentation Framework)

[Aus] Illustration 1:

Circumstances include the following:

- **Audit of a single company's financial report.**
- **The financial report has been prepared under the *Corporations Act 2001*.**
- **The terms of the audit engagement reflect the description of management's responsibility for the financial report in ASA 210.**
- **There is a material uncertainty which has not been adequately disclosed in the financial report. It relates to the company's ability to re-negotiate, or obtain replacement financing facilities for its existing facilities.**

INDEPENDENT AUDITOR'S REPORT

[Appropriate Addressee]

Report on the Financial Report†

We have audited the accompanying financial report of ABC Company Ltd., which comprises the statement of financial position as at 30 June 20X1, the statement of comprehensive income, statement of changes in equity and statement of cash flows for the year then ended, notes comprising a summary of significant accounting policies and other explanatory information, and the directors' declaration.

Directors' Responsibility for the Financial Report

The directors of the company are responsible for the preparation of the financial report that gives a true and fair view in accordance with Australian Accounting Standards, and the *Corporations*

* See ASA 700 *Forming an Opinion and Reporting on a Financial Report.*

† The sub-title "Report on the Financial Report" is unnecessary in circumstances when the second sub-title "Report on Other Legal and Regulatory Requirements", or other appropriate sub-title, is not applicable.

Act 2001, and for such internal control as the directors determine is necessary to enable the preparation of a financial report that is free from material misstatement, whether due to fraud or error.

Auditor's Responsibility

Our responsibility is to express an opinion on the financial report based on our audit. We conducted our audit in accordance with Australian Auditing Standards. Those standards require that we comply with relevant ethical requirements relating to audit engagements and plan and perform the audit to obtain reasonable assurance about whether the financial report is free from material misstatement.

An audit involves performing procedures to obtain audit evidence about the amounts and disclosures in the financial report. The procedures selected depend on the auditor's judgement, including the assessment of the risks of material misstatement of the financial report, whether due to fraud or error. In making those risk assessments, the auditor considers internal control relevant to the company's preparation of the financial report that gives a true and fair view in order to design audit procedures that are appropriate in the circumstances, but not for the purpose of expressing an opinion on the effectiveness of the company's internal control. An audit also includes evaluating the appropriateness of accounting policies used and the reasonableness of accounting estimates made by the directors, as well as evaluating the overall presentation of the financial report.

We believe that the audit evidence that we have obtained is sufficient and appropriate to provide a basis for our qualified audit opinion.

Independence

In conducting our audit, we have complied with the independence requirements of the *Corporations Act 2001*. We confirm that the independence declaration required by the *Corporations Act 2001*, which has been given to the directors of ABC Company Ltd., would be in the same terms if given to the directors as at the time of the auditor's report.*

Basis for Qualified Opinion

ABC Company Ltd.'s financing arrangements expire within the next financial year. The company has been unable to re-negotiate or obtain replacement financing. This situation indicates the existence of a material uncertainty that may cast significant doubt on the company's ability to continue as a going concern and therefore, the company may be unable to realise its assets and discharge its liabilities in the normal course of business. The financial report does not fully disclose this fact.

Qualified Opinion

In our opinion, except for the incomplete disclosure of the information referred to in the Basis for Qualified Opinion paragraph, the financial report of ABC Company Ltd. is in accordance with the *Corporations Act 2001*, including:

(a) giving a true and fair view of the company's financial position as at 30 June 20X1 and of its performance for the year ended on that date; and

(c) complying with Australian Accounting Standards and the *Corporations Regulations 2001*.

Report on Other Legal and Regulatory Requirements

[Form and content of this section of the auditor's report will vary depending on the nature of the auditor's other reporting responsibilities.]

[Auditor's signature]#

[Date of the auditor's report]†

[Auditor's address]

---

* Or, alternatively, include statements (a) to the effect that circumstances have changed since the declaration was given to the relevant directors; and (b) setting out how the declaration would differ if it had been given to the relevant directors at the time the auditor's report was made.

\# The auditor's report needs to be signed in one or more of the following ways: name of the audit firm, the name of the audit company or the personal name of the auditor as appropriate.

† The date of the auditor's report is the date the auditor signs the report.

Example Auditor's Report
General Purpose Financial Report
Adverse Opinion due to inadequate disclosures
Corporations Act 2001
(Fair Presentation Framework)

[Aus] Illustration 2:

Audit of a single company's financial report.

- **The financial report has been prepared under the *Corporations Act 2001*.**
- **The terms of the audit engagement reflect the description of management's responsibility for the financial report in ASA 210.**
- **The company is unable to negotiate or obtain replacement financing arrangements and is considering bankruptcy, which has not been adequately disclosed in the financial report.**

INDEPENDENT AUDITOR'S REPORT

[Appropriate Addressee]

Report on the Financial Report†

We have audited the accompanying financial report of ABC Company Ltd., which comprises the statement of financial position as at 30 June 20X1, the statement of comprehensive income, statement of changes in equity and statement of cash flows for the year then ended, notes comprising a summary of significant accounting policies and other explanatory information, and the directors' declaration.

Directors' Responsibility for the Financial Report

The directors of the company are responsible for the preparation of the financial report that gives a true and fair view in accordance with Australian Accounting Standards, and the *Corporations Act 2001*, and for such internal control as the directors determine is necessary to enable the preparation of a financial report that is free from material misstatement, whether due to fraud or error.

Auditor's Responsibility

Our responsibility is to express an opinion on the financial report based on our audit. We conducted our audit in accordance with Australian Auditing Standards. Those standards require that we comply with relevant ethical requirements relating to audit engagements and plan and perform the audit to obtain reasonable assurance about whether the financial report is free from material misstatement.

An audit involves performing procedures to obtain audit evidence about the amounts and disclosures in the financial report. The procedures selected depend on the auditor's judgement, including the assessment of the risks of material misstatement of the financial report, whether due to fraud or error. In making those risk assessments, the auditor considers internal control relevant to the company's preparation of the financial report that gives a true and fair view in order to design audit procedures that are appropriate in the circumstances, but not for the purpose of expressing an opinion on the effectiveness of the company's internal control. An audit also includes evaluating the appropriateness of accounting policies used and the reasonableness of accounting estimates made by the directors, as well as evaluating the overall presentation of the financial report.

We believe that the audit evidence that we have obtained is sufficient and appropriate to provide a basis for our adverse audit opinion.

† The sub-title "Report on the Financial Report" is unnecessary in circumstances when the second sub-title "Report on Other Legal and Regulatory Requirements", or other appropriate sub-title, is not applicable.

Independence

In conducting our audit, we have complied with the independence requirements of the *Corporations Act 2001.* We confirm that the independence declaration required by the *Corporations Act 2001*, which has been given to the directors of ABC Company Ltd., would be in the same terms if given to the directors as at the time of the auditor's report.*

Basis for Adverse Opinion

The company's financing arrangements expired and the amount outstanding was payable on 30 June 20X1. The company has been unable to re-negotiate or obtain replacement financing and is considering filing for bankruptcy. These events indicate a material uncertainty that may cast significant doubt on the company's ability to continue as a going concern and therefore, it may be unable to realise its assets and discharge its liabilities in the normal course of business. The financial report does not disclose this fact.

Adverse Opinion

In our opinion, because of the omission of the information described in the Basis for Adverse Opinion paragraph, the financial report of ABC Company Ltd. is not in accordance with the *Corporations Act 2001*, and does not:

(a) give a true and fair view of the financial position of the company as at 30 June 20X1, and of its performance for the year then ended; and

(b) comply with Australian Accounting Standards and the *Corporations Regulations 2001*.

Report on Other Legal and Regulatory Requirements

[Form and content of this section of the auditor's report will vary depending on the nature of the auditor's other reporting responsibilities.]

[Auditor's signature]#

[Date of the auditor's report]†

[Auditor's address]

Example Auditor's Report
General Purpose Financial Report
Disclaimer of Opinion (due to limitation of scope)
Corporations Act 2001
(Fair Presentation Framework)

[Aus] Illustration 3:

- **Audit of a single company's financial report.**
- **The financial report has been prepared under the *Corporations Act 2001.***
- **The terms of the audit engagement reflect the description of management's responsibility for the financial report in ASA 210.**
- **The auditor is unable to obtain sufficient appropriate audit evidence about the company's ability to continue as a going concern as the directors have refused to extend their going concern assessment up to the relevant period.**

* Or, alternatively, include statements (a) to the effect that circumstances have changed since the declaration was given to the relevant directors; and (b) setting out how the declaration would differ if it had been given to the relevant directors at the time the auditor's report was made.

The auditor's report needs to be signed in one or more of the following ways: name of the audit firm, the name of the audit company or the personal name of the auditor as appropriate.

† The date of the auditor's report is the date the auditor signs the report.

INDEPENDENT AUDITOR'S REPORT

[Appropriate Addressee]

Report on the Financial Report†

We have audited the accompanying financial report of ABC Company Ltd., which comprises the statement of financial position as at 30 June 20X1, the statement of comprehensive income, statement of changes in equity and statement of cash flows for the year then ended, notes comprising a summary of significant accounting policies and other explanatory information, and the directors' declaration.

Directors' Responsibility for the Financial Report

The directors of the company are responsible for the preparation of the financial report that gives a true and fair view in accordance with Australian Accounting Standards and the *Corporations Act 2001*, and for such internal control as the directors determine is necessary to enable the preparation of a financial report that is free from material misstatement, whether due to fraud or error.

Auditor's Responsibility

Our responsibility is to express an opinion on the financial report based on conducting the audit in accordance with Australian Auditing Standards. Because of the matter described in the Basis for Disclaimer of Opinion paragraph, however, we were not able to obtain sufficient appropriate audit evidence to provide a basis for an audit opinion.

Independence

In conducting our audit, we have complied with the independence requirements of the *Corporations Act 2001*. We confirm that the independence declaration required by the *Corporations Act 2001*, which has been given to the directors of ABC Company Ltd., would be in the same terms if given to the directors as at the time of the auditor's report.*

Basis for Disclaimer of Opinion

The company's financing arrangements expired and the amount outstanding was payable on 30 June 20X1. The company has been unable to re-negotiate or obtain replacement financing. The directors have refused to extend their assessment of the company's ability to continue as a going concern beyond 30 September 20X1 given the uncertainty of obtaining suitable replacement financing. We have been unable to obtain alternative evidence which would provide sufficient appropriate audit evidence as to whether the company may be able to obtain such financing, and hence remove significant doubt of its ability to continue as a going concern within 12 months of the date of this auditor's report.

Disclaimer of Opinion

Because of the significance of the matter described in the Basis for Disclaimer of Opinion paragraph, we have not been able to obtain sufficient appropriate audit evidence to provide a basis for an audit opinion. Accordingly, we do not express an opinion on the financial report.

Report on Other Legal and Regulatory Requirements

[Form and content of this section of the auditor's report will vary depending on the nature of the auditor's other reporting responsibilities.]

[Auditor's signature]**

[Date of the auditor's report]#

[Auditor's address]

† The sub-title "Report on the Financial Report" is unnecessary in circumstances when the second sub-title "Report on Other Legal and Regulatory Requirements", or other appropriate sub-title, is not applicable.

* Or, alternatively, include statements (a) to the effect that circumstances have changed since the declaration was given to the relevant directors; and (b) setting out how the declaration would differ if it had been given to the relevant directors at the time the auditor's report was made.

** The auditor's report needs to be signed in one or more of the following ways: name of the audit firm, the name of the audit company or the personal name of the auditor as appropriate.

The date of the auditor's report is the date the auditor signs the report.

[Aus] Appendix 3

(Ref: Para. A21-A22)

Illustration of an Auditor's Report on a General Purpose Financial Report—Emphasis of Matter Paragraph due to a Material Uncertainty regarding Going Concern

- [Aus] Illustration 1: An auditor's report on a financial report containing an Emphasis of Matter paragraph due to a material uncertainty in the financial report (prepared under the *Corporations Act 2001*).

See ASA 700* for applicable wording in the auditor's report when the company makes a statement on compliance with *International Financial Reporting Standards* (IFRSs) and/or includes a Remuneration Report in the Directors' Report.

Example Auditor's Report General Purpose Financial Report Unmodified Opinion, Emphasis of Matter paragraph *Corporations Act 2001* (Fair Presentation Framework)

[Aus] Illustration 1:

Audit of a single company financial report.

- **The financial report is prepared under the *Corporations Act 2001*.**
- **The terms of the audit engagement reflect the description of management's responsibility for the financial report in ASA 210.**
- **There is uncertainty resulting from a net loss for the year and net liabilities exceeding net assets.**

INDEPENDENT AUDITOR'S REPORT

[Appropriate Addressee]

Report on the Financial Report†

We have audited the accompanying financial report of ABC Company Ltd., which comprises the statement of financial position as at 30 June 20X1, the statement of comprehensive income, statement of changes in equity and statement of cash flows for the year then ended, notes comprising a summary of significant accounting policies and other explanatory information, and the directors' declaration.

Directors' Responsibility for the Financial Report

The directors of the company are responsible for the preparation of the financial report that gives a true and fair view in accordance with Australian Accounting Standards and the *Corporations Act 2001*, and for such internal control as the directors determine is necessary to enable the preparation of a financial report that is free from material misstatement, whether due to fraud or error.

Auditor's Responsibility

Our responsibility is to express an opinion on the financial report based on our audit. We conducted our audit in accordance with Australian Auditing Standards. Those standards require that we comply with relevant ethical requirements relating to audit engagements and plan and perform the audit to obtain reasonable assurance about whether the financial report is free from material misstatement.

* See ASA 700 *Forming an Opinion and Reporting on a Financial Report.*

† The sub-title "Report on the Financial Report" is unnecessary in circumstances when the second sub-title "Report on Other Legal and Regulatory Requirements", or other appropriate sub-title, is not applicable.

An audit involves performing procedures to obtain audit evidence about the amounts and disclosures in the financial report. The procedures selected depend on the auditor's judgement, including the assessment of the risks of material misstatement of the financial report, whether due to fraud or error. In making those risk assessments, the auditor considers internal control relevant to the company's preparation of the financial report that gives a true and fair view in order to design audit procedures that are appropriate in the circumstances, but not for the purpose of expressing an opinion on the effectiveness of the company's internal control. An audit also includes evaluating the appropriateness of accounting policies used and the reasonableness of accounting estimates made by the directors, as well as evaluating the overall presentation of the financial report.

We believe that the audit evidence that we have obtained is sufficient and appropriate to provide a basis for our qualified audit opinion.

Independence

In conducting our audit, we have complied with the independence requirements of the *Corporations Act 2001*. We confirm that the independence declaration required by the *Corporations Act 2001*, which has been given to the directors of ABC Company Ltd., would be in the same terms if given to the directors as at the time of this auditor's report.*

Opinion

In our opinion the financial report of ABC Company Ltd. is in accordance with the *Corporations Act 2001*, including:

(a) giving a true and fair view of the company's financial position as at 30 June 20X1 and of its performance for the year ended on that date; and

(b) complying with Australian Accounting Standards and the *Corporations Regulations 2001*.

Emphasis of Matter

Without modifying our opinion, we draw attention to Note X in the financial report, which indicates that the company incurred a net loss of ZZZ during the year ended 30 June 20X1 and, as of that date, the company's current liabilities exceeded its total assets by YYY. These conditions, along with other matters as set forth in Note X, indicate the existence of a material uncertainty that may cast significant doubt about the company's ability to continue as a going concern and therefore, the company may be unable to realise its assets and discharge its liabilities in the normal course of business.

Report on Other Legal and Regulatory Requirements

[Form and content of this section of the auditor's report will vary depending on the nature of the auditor's other reporting responsibilities.]

[Auditor's signature]#

[Date of the auditor's report]†

[Auditor's address]

* Or, alternatively, include statements (a) to the effect that circumstances have changed since the declaration was given to the relevant directors; and (b) setting out how the declaration would differ if it had been given to the relevant directors at the time the auditor's report was made.

\# The auditor's report needs to be signed in one or more of the following ways: name of the audit firm, the name of the audit company or the personal name of the auditor as appropriate.

† The date of the auditor's report is the date the auditor signs the report.

ASA 580
Written Representations

(Reissued October 2009: amended and compiled June 2011)

Issued by the Auditing and Assurance Standards Board.

Note from the Institute of Chartered Accountants Australia

This note, prepared by the technical editor, is not part of ASA 580.

Historical development

December 1985: Statement of Auditing Practice AUP 25 'Representations by Management' issued in, and effective from, December 1985 following the issue of ED 17 (IAPC ED 22) in June 1984.

May 1994: ED 55 'Codification and Revision of Auditing Pronouncements: AUS 522 Management Representations (AUP 25)' issued by the AuSB.

June 1994: The International Auditing Practices Committee (IAPC) of the International Federation of Accountants (IFAC) approved the issuance of a codified set of International Standards of Auditing (ISAs). The relevant international pronouncement was ISA 580 'Management Representations'.

October 1995: Australian Auditing Standards and Auditing Guidance Statements released. The status of these was explained in APS 1.1 'Conformity With Auditing Standards'. These Standards became operative for the first reporting period commencing on or after 1 July 1996 and later reporting periods, although earlier application was encouraged. AUP 25 'Representations by Management' replaced by AUS 520 'Management Representations'.

February 1999: AUS/AGS Omnibus 2 'Miscellaneous Amendments to AUSs and AGSs' issued by the AuASB, operative from the date of issue. The Omnibus amended paras .03 and .16(b) and (c) of AUS 520.

August 1999: AUS 520 'Management Representations' reissued to take into account changes in standards in other countries. Operative as at 31 December 1999.

July 2002: AUS/AGS Omnibus 3 'Miscellaneous Amendments to AUSs and AGSs' issued by the AuASB, operative from the date of issue. AUS 520 since reissued by the Board to incorporate these amendments.

April 2006: ASA 580 'Management Representations' was issued as a legally enforceable Standard to replace AUS 520. It is based on ISA 580 of the same name.

October 2009: ASA 580 reissued as 'Written Representations' as part of the AUASB's Clarity Project. Its requirements have been strengthened and 'management' is now deemed to mean 'management, and, where appropriate, those charged with governance'. Where management decline to provide representations or those provided are inconsistent with other evidence, the auditor must re-evaluate management's integrity and consider the effect on the audit report. It is based on the revised ISA 580 of the same name.

June 2011: ASA 580 updated for editorial amendments contained in ASA 2011-1 'Amendments to Australian Auditing Standards'.

Contents

ASA

Compilation Details

Auditing Standard ASA 580 *Written Representations* as Amended

This compilation takes into account amendments made up to and including 27 June 2011 and was prepared on 27 June 2011 by the Auditing and Assurance Standards Board (AUASB).

This compilation is not a separate Auditing Standard made by the AUASB. Instead, it is a representation of ASA 580 (October 2009) as amended by another Auditing Standard which is listed in the Table below.

Table of Standards

Standard	Date made	Operative date
ASA 580	27 October 2009	1 January 2010
ASA 2011-1	27 June 2011	1 July 2011

Table of Amendments

Paragraph affected	How affected	By … [paragraph]
Appendix 2 First Paragraph	Amended	ASA 2011-1 [50]
Appendix 2 Footnote 10	Amended	ASA 2011-1 [51]
Appendix 2 Second Paragraph	Amended	ASA 2011-1 [52]
Appendix 2 Fourth Paragraph	Amended	ASA 2011-1 [53]
Appendix 2 Third bullet point	Amended	ASA 2011-1 [54]
Appendix 2 Eighth bullet point	Amended	ASA 2011-1 [55]

Preface

[Preface extracted from the original Auditing Standard issued 27 October 2009]

Reasons for Issuing Auditing Standard ASA 580 *Written Representations*

The Auditing and Assurance Standards Board (AUASB) issues Auditing Standard ASA 580 *Written Representations* pursuant to the requirements of the legislative provisions and the Strategic Direction explained below.

The AUASB is an independent statutory board of the Australian Government established under section 227A of the *Australian Securities and Investments Commission Act 2001*, as amended (ASIC Act). Under section 336 of the *Corporations Act 2001*, the AUASB may make Auditing Standards for the purposes of the corporations legislation. These Auditing Standards are legislative instruments under the *Legislative Instruments Act 2003*.

Under the Strategic Direction given to the AUASB by the Financial Reporting Council (FRC), the AUASB is required to have regard to any programme initiated by the International Auditing and Assurance Standards Board (IAASB) for the revision and enhancement of the International Standards on Auditing (ISAs) and to make appropriate consequential amendments to the Australian Auditing Standards. Accordingly, the AUASB has decided to revise and redraft the Australian Auditing Standards using the equivalent redrafted ISAs.

Main Features

This Auditing Standard establishes requirements and provides application and other explanatory material regarding the auditor's responsibility to obtain written representations from management and, where appropriate, those charged with governance in an audit of a financial report.

This Auditing Standard:

(a) establishes the requirements and related guidance for the auditor to obtain written representations from management, and where appropriate, those charged with governance as part of their audit evidence;

(b) establishes the nature of the information to be included in written representations;

(c) references to other written representations that may be required by other Auditing Standards; and

(d) identifies the action(s) to take if management do not provide the written representations requested.

Authority Statement

Auditing Standard ASA 580 *Written Representations* (as amended at 27 June 2011) is set out in paragraphs 1 to A27 and Appendices 1 and 2.

This Auditing Standard is to be read in conjunction with ASA 101 *Preamble to Australian Auditing Standards*, which sets out the intentions of the AUASB on how the Australian Auditing Standards, operative for financial reporting periods commencing on or after 1 January 2010, are to be understood, interpreted and applied. This Auditing Standard is to be read also in conjunction with ASA 200 *Overall Objectives of the Independent Auditor and the Conduct of the Audit in Accordance with Australian Auditing Standards*.

Dated: 27 June 2011

M H Kelsall
Chairman - AUASB

Auditing Standard ASA 580

The Auditing and Assurance Standards Board (AUASB) made Auditing Standard ASA 580 *Written Representations,* pursuant to section 227B of the *Australian Securities and Investments Commission Act 2001* and section 336 of the *Corporations Act 2001*, on 27 October 2009.

This compiled version of ASA 580 incorporates subsequent amendments contained in another Auditing Standard made by the AUASB up to and including 27 June 2011 (see Compilation Details).

Auditing Standard ASA 580

Written Representations

Application

Aus 0.1 This Auditing Standard applies to:

(a) an audit of a financial report for a financial year, or an audit of a financial report for a half-year, in accordance with the *Corporations Act 2001*; and

(b) an audit of a financial report, or a complete set of financial statements, for any other purpose.

Aus 0.2 This Auditing Standard also applies, as appropriate, to an audit of other historical financial information.

Operative Date

Aus 0.3 This Auditing Standard is operative for financial reporting periods commencing on or after 1 January 2010.

[Note: For operative dates of paragraphs changed or added by an amending Standard, see Compilation Details.]

Introduction

Scope of this Auditing Standard

1. This Auditing Standard deals with the auditor's responsibility to obtain written representations from management and, where appropriate, those charged with governance in an audit of a financial report.

2. Appendix 1 lists other Australian Auditing Standards containing subject-matter specific requirements for written representations. The specific requirements for written

representations of other Australian Auditing Standards do not limit the application of this Auditing Standard.

Written Representations as Audit Evidence

3. Audit evidence is the information used by the auditor in arriving at the conclusions on which the auditor's opinion is based.[1] Written representations are necessary information that the auditor requires in connection with the audit of the entity's financial report. Accordingly, similar to responses to enquiries, written representations are audit evidence. (Ref: Para. A1)

4. Although written representations provide necessary audit evidence, they do not provide sufficient appropriate audit evidence on their own about any of the matters with which they deal. Furthermore, the fact that management has provided reliable written representations does not affect the nature or extent of other audit evidence that the auditor obtains about the fulfilment of management's responsibilities, or about specific assertions.

Effective Date

5. [Deleted by the AUASB. Refer Aus 0.3]

Objectives

6. The objectives of the auditor are:
   (a) To obtain written representations from management and, where appropriate, those charged with governance that they believe that they have fulfilled their responsibility for the preparation of the financial report and for the completeness of the information provided to the auditor;
   (b) To support other audit evidence relevant to the financial report or specific assertions in the financial report by means of written representations if determined necessary by the auditor or required by other Australian Auditing Standards; and
   (c) To respond appropriately to written representations provided by management and, where appropriate, those charged with governance, or if management or, where appropriate, those charged with governance do not provide the written representations requested by the auditor.

Definitions

7. For purposes of the Australian Auditing Standards, the following term has the meaning attributed below:

   Written representation means a written statement by management provided to the auditor to confirm certain matters or to support other audit evidence. Written representations in this context do not include the financial report, the assertions therein, or supporting books and records.

8. For purposes of this Auditing Standard, references to "management" should be read as "management and, where appropriate, those charged with governance." Furthermore, in the case of a fair presentation framework, management is responsible for the preparation and *fair* presentation of the financial report in accordance with the applicable financial reporting framework; or the preparation of a financial report that gives *a true and fair view* in accordance with the applicable financial reporting framework.

Requirements

Management from whom Written Representations are Requested

9. The auditor shall request written representations from management with appropriate responsibilities for the financial report and knowledge of the matters concerned. (Ref: Para. A2-A6)

1 See ASA 500 *Audit Evidence*, paragraph 5(c).

Written Representations about Management's Responsibilities

Preparation of the Financial report

10. The auditor shall request management to provide a written representation that it has fulfilled its responsibility for the preparation of the financial report in accordance with the applicable financial reporting framework, including where relevant their fair presentation, as set out in the terms of the audit engagement.[2] (Ref: Para. A7-A9, A14, A22)

Information Provided and Completeness of Transactions

11. The auditor shall request management to provide a written representation that:

    (a) It has provided the auditor with all relevant information and access as agreed in the terms of the audit engagement;[3] and

    (b) All transactions have been recorded and are reflected in the financial report. (Ref: Para. A7-A9, A14, A22)

Description of Management's Responsibilities in the Written Representations

12. Management's responsibilities shall be described in the written representations required by paragraphs 10 and 11 of this Auditing Standard in the manner in which these responsibilities are described in the terms of the audit engagement.

Other Written Representations

13. Other Auditing Standards require the auditor to request written representations. If, in addition to such required representations, the auditor determines that it is necessary to obtain one or more written representations to support other audit evidence relevant to the financial report or one or more specific assertions in the financial report, the auditor shall request such other written representations. (Ref: Para. A10-A14, A22)

Date of and Period(s) Covered by Written Representations

14. The date of the written representations shall be as near as practicable to, but not after, the date of the auditor's report on the financial report. The written representations shall be for all the financial report(s) and period(s) referred to in the auditor's report. (Ref: Para. A15-A18)

Form of Written Representations

15. The written representations shall be in the form of a representation letter addressed to the auditor. If law or regulation requires management to make written public statements about its responsibilities, and the auditor determines that such statements provide some or all of the representations required by paragraphs 10 or 11 of this Auditing Standard, the relevant matters covered by such statements need not be included in the representation letter. (Ref: Para. A19-A21)

Doubt as to the Reliability of Written Representations and Requested Written Representations Not Provided

Doubt as to the Reliability of Written Representations

16. If the auditor has concerns about the competence, integrity, ethical values or diligence of management, or about its commitment to or enforcement of these, the auditor shall determine the effect that such concerns may have on the reliability of representations (oral or written) and audit evidence in general. (Ref: Para. A24-A25)

17. In particular, if written representations are inconsistent with other audit evidence, the auditor shall perform audit procedures to attempt to resolve the matter. If the matter remains unresolved, the auditor shall reconsider the assessment of the competence, integrity, ethical values or diligence of management, or of its commitment to or enforcement of these, and shall determine the effect that this may have on the reliability of representations (oral or written) and audit evidence in general. (Ref: Para. A23)

---

2 See ASA 210 *Agreement the terms of Audit Engagements*, paragraph 6(b)(i).

3 See ASA 210, paragraph 6(b)(iii).

18. If the auditor concludes that the written representations are not reliable, the auditor shall take appropriate actions, including determining the possible effect on the opinion in the auditor's report in accordance with ASA 705,[4] having regard to the requirement in paragraph 20 of this Auditing Standard.

Requested Written Representations Not Provided

19. If management does not provide one or more of the requested written representations, the auditor shall:
    (a) Discuss the matter with management;
    (b) Re-evaluate the integrity of management and evaluate the effect that this may have on the reliability of representations (oral or written) and audit evidence in general; and
    (c) Take appropriate actions, including determining the possible effect on the opinion in the auditor's report in accordance with ASA 705, having regard to the requirement in paragraph 20 of this Auditing Standard.

Written Representations about Management's Responsibilities

20. The auditor shall disclaim an opinion on the financial report in accordance with ASA 705 if:
    (a) The auditor concludes that there is sufficient doubt about the integrity of management such that the written representations required by paragraphs 10 and 11 of this Auditing Standard are not reliable; or
    (b) Management does not provide the written representations required by paragraphs 10 and 11 of this Auditing Standard. (Ref: Para. A26-A27)

❖ ❖ ❖

Application and Other Explanatory Material

Written Representations as Audit Evidence (Ref: Para. 3)

A1. Written representations are an important source of audit evidence. If management modifies or does not provide the requested written representations, it may alert the auditor to the possibility that one or more significant issues may exist. Further, a request for written, rather than oral, representations in many cases may prompt management to consider such matters more rigorously, thereby enhancing the quality of the representations.

Management from whom Written Representations are Requested (Ref: Para. 9)

A2. Written representations are requested from those responsible for the preparation of the financial report. Those individuals may vary depending on the governance structure of the entity, and relevant law or regulation; however, management (rather than those charged with governance) is often the responsible party. Written representations may therefore be requested from the entity's chief executive officer and chief financial officer, or other equivalent persons in entities that do not use such titles. In some circumstances, however, other parties, such as those charged with governance, are also responsible for the preparation of the financial report.

A3. Due to its responsibility for the preparation of the financial report, and its responsibilities for the conduct of the entity's business, management would be expected to have sufficient knowledge of the process followed by the entity in preparing and presenting the financial report and the assertions therein on which to base the written representations.

A4. In some cases, however, management may decide to make enquiries of others who participate in preparing and presenting the financial report and assertions therein,

4 See ASA 705 *Modifications to the Opinion in the Independent Auditor's Report.*

including individuals who have specialised knowledge relating to the matters about which written representations are requested. Such individuals may include:

- An actuary responsible for actuarially determined accounting measurements.
- Staff engineers who may have responsibility for and specialised knowledge about environmental liability measurements.
- Internal counsel who may provide information essential to provisions for legal claims.

A5. In some cases, management may include in the written representations qualifying language to the effect that representations are made to the best of its knowledge and belief. It is reasonable for the auditor to accept such wording if the auditor is satisfied that the representations are being made by those with appropriate responsibilities and knowledge of the matters included in the representations.

A6. To reinforce the need for management to make informed representations, the auditor may request that management include in the written representations confirmation that it has made such enquiries as it considered appropriate to place it in the position to be able to make the requested written representations. It is not expected that such enquiries would usually require a formal internal process beyond those already established by the entity.

ASA

Written Representations about Management's Responsibilities

(Ref: Para. 10-11)

A7. Audit evidence obtained during the audit that management has fulfilled the responsibilities referred to in paragraphs 10 and 11 is not sufficient without obtaining confirmation from management that it believes that it has fulfilled those responsibilities. This is because the auditor is not able to judge solely on other audit evidence whether management has prepared and presented the financial report and provided information to the auditor on the basis of the agreed acknowledgement and understanding of its responsibilities. For example, the auditor could not conclude that management has provided the auditor with all relevant information agreed in the terms of the audit engagement without asking it whether, and receiving confirmation that, such information has been provided.

A8. The written representations required by paragraphs 10 and 11 draw on the agreed acknowledgement and understanding of management of its responsibilities in the terms of the audit engagement by requesting confirmation that it has fulfilled them. The auditor may also ask management to reconfirm its acknowledgement and understanding of those responsibilities in written representations.

This is common in certain jurisdictions, but in any event may be particularly appropriate when:

- Those who signed the terms of the audit engagement on behalf of the entity no longer have the relevant responsibilities;
- The terms of the audit engagement were prepared in a previous year;
- There is any indication that management misunderstands those responsibilities; or
- Changes in circumstances make it appropriate to do so.

Consistent with the requirement of ASA 210,[5] such reconfirmation of management's acknowledgement and understanding of its responsibilities is not made subject to the best of management's knowledge and belief (as discussed in paragraph A5).

Considerations Specific to Public Sector Entities

A9. The mandates for audits of financial reports of public sector entities may be broader than those of other entities. As a result, the premise, relating to management's responsibilities, on which an audit of the financial report of a public sector entity is conducted may give rise to additional written representations. These may include written representations confirming that transactions and events have been carried out in accordance with law, regulation or other authority.

5 See ASA 210, paragraph 6(b).

Other Written Representations (Ref: Para. 13)

Additional Written Representations about the Financial Report

A10. In addition to the written representation required by paragraph 10, the auditor may consider it necessary to request other written representations about the financial report. Such written representations may supplement, but do not form part of, the written representation required by paragraph 10. They may include representations about the following:

- Whether the selection and application of accounting policies are appropriate; and
- Whether matters such as the following, where relevant under the applicable financial reporting framework, have been recognised, measured, presented or disclosed in accordance with that framework:
  - Plans or intentions that may affect the carrying value or classification of assets and liabilities;
  - Liabilities, both actual and contingent;
  - Title to, or control over, assets, the liens or encumbrances on assets, and assets pledged as collateral; and
  - Aspects of laws, regulations and contractual agreements that may affect the financial report, including non-compliance.

Additional Written Representations about Information Provided to the Auditor

A11. In addition to the written representation required by paragraph 11, the auditor may consider it necessary to request management to provide a written representation that it has communicated to the auditor all deficiencies in internal control of which management is aware.

Written Representations about Specific Assertions

A12. When obtaining evidence about, or evaluating, judgements and intentions, the auditor may consider one or more of the following:

- The entity's past history in carrying out its stated intentions.
- The entity's reasons for choosing a particular course of action.
- The entity's ability to pursue a specific course of action.
- The existence or lack of any other information that might have been obtained during the course of the audit that may be inconsistent with management's judgement or intent.

A13. In addition, the auditor may consider it necessary to request management to provide written representations about specific assertions in the financial report; in particular, to support an understanding that the auditor has obtained from other audit evidence of management's judgement or intent in relation to, or the completeness of, a specific assertion. For example, if the intent of management is important to the valuation basis for investments, it may not be possible to obtain sufficient appropriate audit evidence without a written representation from management about its intentions. Although such written representations provide necessary audit evidence, they do not provide sufficient appropriate audit evidence on their own for that assertion.

Communicating a Threshold Amount (Ref: Para. 10-11, 13)

A14. ASA 450 requires the auditor to accumulate misstatements identified during the audit, other than those that are clearly trivial.[6] The auditor may determine a threshold above which misstatements cannot be regarded as clearly trivial. In the same way, the auditor may consider communicating to management a threshold for purposes of the requested written representations.

6 See ASA 450 *Evaluation of Misstatements Identified during the Audit,* paragraph 5.

Date of and Period(s) Covered by Written Representations (Ref: Para. 14)

A15. Because written representations are necessary audit evidence, the auditor's opinion cannot be expressed, and the auditor's report cannot be dated, before the date of the written representations. Furthermore, because the auditor is concerned with events occurring up to the date of the auditor's report that may require adjustment to or disclosure in the financial report, the written representations are dated as near as practicable to, but not after, the date of the auditor's report on the financial report.

A16. In some circumstances, it may be appropriate for the auditor to obtain a written representation about a specific assertion in the financial report during the course of the audit. Where this is the case, it may be necessary to request an updated written representation.

A17. The written representations are for all periods referred to in the auditor's report because management needs to reaffirm that the written representations it previously made with respect to the prior periods remain appropriate. The auditor and management may agree to a form of written representation that updates written representations relating to the prior periods by addressing whether there are any changes to such written representations and, if so, what they are.

A18. Situations may arise where current management were not present during all periods referred to in the auditor's report. Such persons may assert that they are not in a position to provide some or all of the written representations because they were not in place during the period. This fact, however, does not diminish such persons' responsibilities for the financial report as a whole. Accordingly, the requirement for the auditor to request from them written representations that cover the whole of the relevant period(s) still applies.

Form of Written Representations (Ref: Para. 15)

A19. Written representations are required to be included in a representation letter addressed to the auditor. In some jurisdictions, however, management may be required by law or regulation to make a written public statement about its responsibilities. Although such a statement is a representation to the users of the financial report, or to relevant authorities, the auditor may determine that it is an appropriate form of written representation in respect of some or all of the representations required by paragraph 10 or 11. Consequently, the relevant matters covered by such a statement need not be included in the representation letter. Factors that may affect the auditor's determination include:

- Whether the statement includes confirmation of the fulfilment of the responsibilities referred to in paragraphs 10 and 11.
- Whether the statement has been given or approved by those from whom the auditor requests the relevant written representations.
- Whether a copy of the statement is provided to the auditor as near as practicable to, but not after, the date of the auditor's report on the financial report (see paragraph 14).

A20. A formal statement of compliance with law or regulation, or of approval of the financial report, would not contain sufficient information for the auditor to be satisfied that all necessary representations have been consciously made. The expression of management's responsibilities in law or regulation is also not a substitute for the requested written representations.

Aus A20.1 If the auditor intends to rely on some, or all, of the written representations made by management in a written public statement, the auditor ordinarily communicates their intention to place such reliance.

A21. Appendix 2 provides an illustrative example of a representation letter.

Communication with Those Charged with Governance (Ref: Para. 10-11, 13)

A22. ASA 260 requires the auditor to communicate with those charged with governance the written representations which the auditor has requested from management.[7]

7 See ASA 260 *Communication with Those Charged with Governance*, paragraph 16(c)(ii).

ASA

Doubt as to the Reliability of Written Representations and Requested Written Representations Not Provided

Doubt as to the Reliability of Written Representations (Ref: Para. 16-17)

A23. In the case of identified inconsistencies between one or more written representations and audit evidence obtained from another source, the auditor may consider whether the risk assessment remains appropriate and, if not, revise the risk assessment and determine the nature, timing and extent of further audit procedures to respond to the assessed risks.

A24. Concerns about the competence, integrity, ethical values or diligence of management, or about its commitment to or enforcement of these, may cause the auditor to conclude that the risk of management misrepresentation in the financial report is such that an audit cannot be conducted. In such a case, the auditor may consider withdrawing from the engagement, where withdrawal is possible under applicable law or regulation, unless those charged with governance put in place appropriate corrective measures. Such measures, however, may not be sufficient to enable the auditor to issue an unmodified audit opinion.

A25. ASA 230 requires the auditor to document significant matters arising during the audit, the conclusions reached thereon, and significant professional judgements made in reaching those conclusions.[8] The auditor may have identified significant issues relating to the competence, integrity, ethical values or diligence of management, or about its commitment to or enforcement of these, but concluded that the written representations are nevertheless reliable. In such a case, this significant matter is documented in accordance with ASA 230.

Written Representations about Management's Responsibilities (Ref: Para. 20)

A26. As explained in paragraph A7, the auditor is not able to judge solely on other audit evidence whether management has fulfilled the responsibilities referred to in paragraphs 10 and 11. Therefore, if, as described in paragraph 20(a), the auditor concludes that the written representations about these matters are unreliable, or if management does not provide those written representations, the auditor is unable to obtain sufficient appropriate audit evidence. The possible effects on the financial report of such inability are not confined to specific elements, accounts or items of the financial report and are hence pervasive. ASA 705 requires the auditor to disclaim an opinion on the financial report in such circumstances.[9]

If Management do not Provide Written Representations

Aus A26.1 If management do not provide written representations, the auditor would ordinarily:

(a) draw to the attention of those charged with governance any relevant regulatory requirements which give the auditor a right of access to any requested information, explanations or assistance for the purposes of the audit;[*]

(b) consider any other implications of the refusal that may have any effect on the auditor's report;[#] and

(c) consider whether the auditor has any regulatory obligation to report that management has not provided a written representation.[†]

A27. A written representation that has been modified from that requested by the auditor does not necessarily mean that management did not provide the written representation. However, the underlying reason for such modification may affect the opinion in the auditor's report. For example:

- The written representation about management's fulfilment of its responsibility for the preparation of the financial report may state that management believes that,

---

8 See ASA 230 *Audit Documentation*, paragraphs 8(c) and 10.

9 See ASA 705, paragraph 9.

* See, for example, section 310 of the *Corporations Act 2001*.

\# See, for example, section 307(b) and section 308(3)(b) of the *Corporations Act 2001*.

† See, for example, sections 310-312, section 601HG, or section 990K of the *Corporations Act 2001*.

except for material non-compliance with a particular requirement of the applicable financial reporting framework, the financial report is prepared in accordance with that framework. The requirement in paragraph 20 does not apply because the auditor concluded that management has provided reliable written representations. However, the auditor is required to consider the effect of the non-compliance on the opinion in the auditor's report in accordance with ASA 705.

- The written representation about the responsibility of management to provide the auditor with all relevant information agreed in the terms of the audit engagement may state that management believes that, except for information destroyed in a fire, it has provided the auditor with such information. The requirement in paragraph 20 does not apply because the auditor concluded that management has provided reliable written representations. However, the auditor is required to consider the effects of the pervasiveness of the information destroyed in the fire on the financial report and the effect thereof on the opinion in the auditor's report in accordance with ASA 705.

❖ ❖ ❖

Conformity with International Standards on Auditing

This Auditing Standard conforms with International Standard on Auditing ISA 580 *Written Representations*, issued by the International Auditing and Assurance Standards Board (IAASB), an independent standard-setting board of the International Federation of Accountants (IFAC).

Paragraphs that have been added to this Auditing Standard (and do not appear in the text of the equivalent ISA) are identified with the prefix "Aus".

Compliance with this Auditing Standard enables compliance with ISA 580.

Appendix 1

(Ref: Para. 2)

List of Australian Auditing Standards Containing Requirements for Written Representations

This appendix identifies paragraphs in other Auditing Standards, in effect for audits of financial reports for periods beginning on or after 1 January 2010, that require subject-matter specific written representations. The list is not a substitute for considering the requirements and related application and other explanatory material in the Australian Auditing Standards.

ASA 240 *The Auditor's Responsibilities Relating to Fraud in an Audit of the Financial Report* – paragraph 39

ASA 250 *Consideration of Laws and Regulations in an Audit of a Financial Report* – paragraph 16

ASA 450 *Evaluation of Misstatements Identified during the Audit* – paragraph 14

ASA 502 *Audit Evidence—Specific Considerations for Litigation and Claims* – paragraph 7

ASA 540 *Auditing Accounting Estimates, Including Fair Value Accounting Estimates, and Related Disclosures* – paragraph 22

ASA 550 *Related Parties* – paragraph 26

ASA 560 *Subsequent Events* – paragraph 9

ASA 570 *Going Concern* – paragraph 16(e)

ASA 710 *Comparative Information—Corresponding Figures and Comparative Financial Reports* – paragraph 9

Appendix 2

(Ref: Para. A21)

Illustrative Representation Letter

The following illustrative letter includes written representations that are required by this and other Auditing Standards, in effect for audits of financial reports for periods beginning on or after 1 January 2010. It is assumed in this illustration that the applicable financial reporting framework is the Australian Accounting Standards and the *Corporations Act 2001*; the requirement of ASA 570[10] and ASA 710[#] to obtain a written representation is not relevant; and that there are no exceptions to the requested written representations. If there were exceptions, the representations would need to be modified to reflect the exceptions.

(Entity Letterhead)

(To Auditor) (Date)

This representation letter is provided in connection with your audit of the financial report of ABC Company Limited for the year ended 30 June 20XX[11] [or period covered by the auditor's report] for the purpose of expressing an opinion as to whether the financial report gives a true and fair view in accordance with the Australian Accounting Standards and the *Corporations Act 2001.*

We confirm that *(to the best of our knowledge and belief, having made such enquiries as we considered necessary for the purpose of appropriately informing ourselves)*:

Financial Report

- We have fulfilled our responsibilities, as set out in the terms of the audit engagement dated [insert date], for the preparation of the financial report in accordance with Australian Accounting Standards and the *Corporations Act 2001*; in particular the financial report gives a true and fair view in accordance therewith.
- Significant assumptions used by us in making accounting estimates, including those measured at fair value, are reasonable. (ASA 540)
- Related party relationships and transactions have been appropriately accounted for and disclosed in accordance with the requirements of Australian Accounting Standards. (ASA 550)
- All events subsequent to the date of the financial report and for which Australian Accounting Standards require adjustment or disclosure have been adjusted or disclosed. (ASA 560)
- The effects of uncorrected misstatements are immaterial, both individually and in the aggregate, to the financial report as a whole. A list of the uncorrected misstatements is attached to the representation letter. (ASA 450)
- [Any other matters that the auditor may consider appropriate (see paragraph A10 of this Auditing Standard).]

Information Provided

- We have provided you with:
  - Access to all information of which we are aware that is relevant to the preparation of the financial report such as records, documentation and other matters;
  - Additional information that you have requested from us for the purpose of the audit; and
  - Unrestricted access to persons within the entity from whom you determined it necessary to obtain audit evidence.

10 See ASA 570 *Going Concern.*

See ASA 710 *Comparative Information – Corresponding Figures and Comparative Financial Reports.*

11 [Footnote deleted by the AUASB as not applicable in Australia.]

- All transactions have been recorded in the accounting records and are reflected in the financial report.
- We acknowledge our responsibility for the design, implementation and maintenance of internal control to prevent and detect fraud.
- We have disclosed to you the results of our assessment of the risk that the financial report may be materially misstated as a result of fraud. (ASA 240)
- We have disclosed to you all information in relation to fraud or suspected fraud that we are aware of and that affects the entity and involves:
    - Management;
    - Employees who have significant roles in internal control; or
    - Others where the fraud could have a material effect on the financial report. (ASA 240)
- We have disclosed to you all information in relation to allegations of fraud, or suspected fraud, affecting the entity's financial report communicated by employees, former employees, analysts, regulators or others. (ASA 240)
- We have disclosed to you all known instances of non-compliance or suspected non-compliance with laws and regulations whose effects should be considered when preparing the financial report. (ASA 250)
- We have disclosed to you all known actual or possible litigation and claims whose effects should be considered when preparing the financial report; and accounted for and disclosed in accordance with [the applicable financial reporting framework]. (ASA 502)
- We have disclosed to you the identity of the entity's related parties and all the related party relationships and transactions of which we are aware. (ASA 550)
- [Any other matters that the auditor may consider necessary (see paragraph A11 of this Auditing Standard).]
- Aus We have provided you with all requested information, explanations and assistance for the purposes of the audit.*
- Aus We have provided you with all information required by the *Corporations Act 2001* [where applicable].#

Management	Management

* There may be a regulatory requirement for particular information to be provided. For example, see section 312 of the *Corporations Act 2001*.

See, for example, sections 300A and 295A of the *Corporations Act 2001*.

ASA 600

Special Considerations—Audits of a Group Financial Report (Including the Work of Component Auditors)

(Reissued October 2009)

Issued by the Auditing and Assurance Standards Board.

Note from the Institute of Chartered Accountants Australia

This note, prepared by the technical editor, is not part of ASA 600.

Historical development

January 1983: Statement of Auditing Practice AUP 11 'Using the Work of Another Auditor', issued in, and effective from, January 1983.

May 1985: Statement amended when para. 14 inserted. IAPC ED 5 issued in June 1980 and distributed in Australia to subscribers to The Institute of Chartered Accountants in Australia's IASC International Accounting Standards/IFAC Guidelines Handbook and by the Australian Society of Accountants with a request for comments. The statement was based on IAG 5 which was issued in July 1981. Amendments were made in May 1985 by introducing the heading prior to para. 11 and adding para. 14.

December 1993: ED 53 'Codification and Revision of Auditing Pronouncements: AUS 602 Using the Work of Another Auditor (AUP 11)' issued by the AuSB.

June 1994: The International Auditing Practices Committee (IAPC) of the International Federation of Accountants (IFAC) approved the issuance of a codified set of International Standards of Auditing (ISAs). The relevant international pronouncement was ISA 600 'Using the Work of Another Auditor'.

October 1995: Australian Auditing Standards and Auditing Guidance Statements released. The status of these was explained in APS 1.1 'Conformity With Auditing Standards'. These Standards became operative for the first reporting period commencing on or after 1 July 1996 and later reporting periods, although earlier application was encouraged. AUP 11 'Using the Work of Another Auditor' replaced by AUS 602 'Using the Work of Another Auditor'.

July 2002: AUS/AGS Omnibus 3 'Miscellaneous Amendments to AUSs and AGSs' issued by the AuASB, operative from the date of issue. AUS 602 since reissued by the Board to incorporate these amendments.

April 2006: ASA 600 was issued as a legally enforceable Standard to replace AUS 602. It is based on ISA 600 of the same name.

October 2009: ASA 600 was reissued with a new name 'Special Considerations–Audits of a Group Financial Report (Including the Work of Component Auditors)' as part of the AUASB's Clarity Project. This revision has resulted in substantial changes to the form and content of the Standard but there is no reduction in the auditor's obligations. It is based on ISA 600 'Special Considerations–Audits of Group Financial Statements (Including the work of Component Auditors)'.

Contents

PREFACE

AUTHORITY STATEMENT

ASA

Preface

Reasons for Issuing Auditing Standard ASA 600 *Special Considerations—Audits of a Group Financial Report (Including the Work of Component Auditors)*

The Auditing and Assurance Standards Board (AUASB) issues Auditing Standard ASA 600 *Special Considerations—Audits of a Group Financial Report (Including the Work of Component Auditors)* pursuant to the requirements of the legislative provisions and the Strategic Direction explained below.

The AUASB is an independent statutory board of the Australian Government established under section 227A of the *Australian Securities and Investments Commission Act 2001*, as amended (ASIC Act). Under section 336 of the *Corporations Act 2001*, the AUASB may make Auditing Standards for the purposes of the corporations legislation. These Auditing Standards are legislative instruments under the *Legislative Instruments Act 2003*.

Under the Strategic Direction given to the AUASB by the Financial Reporting Council (FRC), the AUASB is required to have regard to any programme initiated by the International Auditing and Assurance Standards Board (IAASB) for the revision and enhancement of the International Standards on Auditing (ISAs) and to make appropriate consequential amendments to the Australian Auditing Standards. Accordingly, the AUASB has decided to revise and redraft the Australian Auditing Standards using the equivalent redrafted ISAs.

Main Features

This Auditing Standard establishes requirements and provides application and other explanatory material regarding the special considerations that apply to group audits, including those that involve component auditors.

This Auditing Standard:

(a) describes the responsibilities of the group engagement partner;

(b) describes acceptance and continuance requirements;

(c) requires an overall audit strategy to be established and an audit plan to be developed;

(d) requires the auditor to identify and assess the risks of material misstatement through obtaining an understanding of the entity and its environment;

(e) details the requirements in responding to assessed risks;

(f) details the requirements in communicating with component auditors, group management and those charged with governance of the group; and

(g) describes specific documentation requirements.

Authority Statement

The Auditing and Assurance Standards Board (AUASB) makes this Auditing Standard ASA 600 *Special Considerations—Audits of a Group Financial Report (Including the Work of Component Auditors)* pursuant to section 227B of the *Australian Securities and Investments Commission Act 2001* and section 336 of the *Corporations Act 2001*.

This Auditing Standard is to be read in conjunction with ASA 101 *Preamble to Australian Auditing Standards*, which sets out the intentions of the AUASB on how the Australian Auditing Standards, operative for financial reporting periods commencing on or after 1 January 2010, are to be understood, interpreted and applied. This Auditing Standard is to be read also in conjunction with ASA 200 *Overall Objectives of the Independent Auditor and the Conduct of an Audit in Accordance with Australian Auditing Standards*.

Dated: 27 October 2009

M H Kelsall
Chairman - AUASB

ASA

Auditing Standard ASA 600

Special Considerations—Audits of a Group Financial Report (Including the Work of Component Auditors)

Application

Aus 0.1 This Auditing Standard applies to:

(a) an audit of a financial report for a financial year, or an audit of a financial report for a half-year, in accordance with the *Corporations Act 2001*; and

(b) an audit of a financial report, or a complete set of financial statements, for any other purpose.

Aus 0.2 This Auditing Standard also applies, as appropriate, to an audit of other historical financial information.

Operative Date

Aus 0.3 This Auditing Standard is operative for financial reporting periods commencing on or after 1 January 2010.

Introduction

Scope of this Auditing Standard

1. The Australian Auditing Standards apply to group audits. This Auditing Standard deals with special considerations that apply to group audits, in particular those that involve component auditors.

2. This Auditing Standard also applies, as appropriate, when the auditor involves other auditors in the audit of financial reports that are not group financial reports. For example, an auditor may involve another auditor to observe the inventory count or inspect physical fixed assets at a remote location.

3. A component auditor may be required by statute, regulation or for another reason, to express an audit opinion on the financial report of a component. The group engagement team may decide to use the audit evidence on which the audit opinion on the financial report of the component is based to provide audit evidence for the group audit, but the requirements of this Auditing Standard nevertheless apply. (Ref: Para. A1)

4. In accordance with ASA 220,[1] the group engagement partner is required to be satisfied that those performing the group audit engagement, including component auditors, collectively have the appropriate competence and capabilities. The group engagement partner is also responsible for the direction, supervision and performance of the group audit engagement.

1 See ASA 220 *Quality Control for an Audit of a Financial Report*, paragraphs 14 and 15.

5. The group engagement partner applies the requirements of ASA 220 regardless of whether the group engagement team or a component auditor performs the work on the financial information of a component. This Auditing Standard assists the group engagement partner to meet the requirements of ASA 220 where component auditors perform work on the financial information of components.

6. Audit risk is a function of the risk of material misstatement of the financial report and the risk that the auditor will not detect such misstatements.[2] In a group audit, this includes the risk that the component auditor may not detect a misstatement in the financial information of the component that could cause a material misstatement of the group financial report, and the risk that the group engagement team may not detect this misstatement. This Auditing Standard explains the matters that the group engagement team considers when determining the nature, timing and extent of its involvement in the risk assessment procedures and further audit procedures performed by the component auditors on the financial information of the components. The purpose of this involvement is to obtain sufficient appropriate audit evidence on which to base the audit opinion on the group financial report.

Effective Date

7. [Deleted by the AUASB. Refer Aus 0.3]

Objectives

8. The objectives of the auditor are:

    (a) To determine whether to act as the auditor of the group financial report; and

    (b) If acting as the auditor of the group financial report:

        (i) To communicate clearly with component auditors about the scope and timing of their work on financial information related to components and their findings; and

        (ii) To obtain sufficient appropriate audit evidence regarding the financial information of the components and the consolidation process to express an opinion on whether the group financial report is prepared, in all material respects, in accordance with the applicable financial reporting framework.

Definitions

9. For purposes of the Australian Auditing Standards, the following terms have the meanings attributed below:

    (a) Component means an entity or business activity for which group or component management prepares financial information that should be included in the group financial report. (Ref: Para. A2-A4)

    (b) Component auditor means an auditor who, at the request of the group engagement team, performs work on financial information related to a component for the group audit. (Ref: Para. A7)

    (c) Component management means management, or those charged with governance, responsible for the preparation of the financial information of a component.

    (d) Component materiality means the materiality for a component determined by the group engagement team.

    (e) Group means all the components whose financial information is included in the group financial report. A group always has more than one component.

    (f) Group audit means the audit of a group financial report.

    (g) Group audit opinion means the audit opinion on the group financial report.

    (h) Group engagement partner means the partner or other person in the firm who is responsible for the group audit engagement and its performance, and for the auditor's report on the group financial report that is issued on behalf of the firm. Where joint auditors conduct the group audit, the joint engagement partners and their engagement

2 See ASA 200 *Overall Objectives of the Independent Auditor, and the Conduct of an Audit in Accordance with Australian Auditing Standards*, paragraph A32.

teams collectively constitute the group engagement partner and the group engagement team. This Auditing Standard does not, however, deal with the relationship between joint auditors or the work that one joint auditor performs in relation to the work of the other joint auditor.

(i) Group engagement team means partners, including the group engagement partner, and staff who establish the overall group audit strategy, communicate with component auditors, perform work on the consolidation process, and evaluate the conclusions drawn from the audit evidence as the basis for forming an opinion on the group financial report.

(j) Group financial report means a financial report that includes the financial information of more than one component. The term "group financial report" also refers to combined financial reports aggregating the financial information prepared by components that have no parent but are under common control.

(k) Group management means management, or those charged with governance, responsible for the preparation of the group financial report.

(l) Group-wide controls means controls designed, implemented and maintained by group management over group financial reporting.

(m) Significant component means a component identified by the group engagement team (i) that is of individual financial significance to the group, or (ii) that, due to its specific nature or circumstances, is likely to include significant risks of material misstatement of the group financial report. (Ref: Para. A5-A6)

10. Reference to "the applicable financial reporting framework" means the financial reporting framework that applies to the group financial report. Reference to "the consolidation process" includes:

(a) The recognition, measurement, presentation, and disclosure of the financial information of the components in the group financial report by way of consolidation, proportionate consolidation, or the equity or cost methods of accounting; and

(b) The aggregation in combined financial reports of the financial information of components that have no parent but are under common control.

Requirements

Responsibility

11. The group engagement partner is responsible for the direction, supervision and performance of the group audit engagement in compliance with professional standards and applicable legal and regulatory requirements, and whether the auditor's report that is issued is appropriate in the circumstances.[3] As a result, the auditor's report on the group financial reports shall not refer to a component auditor, unless required by law or regulation to include such reference. If such reference is required by law or regulation, the auditor's report shall indicate that the reference does not diminish the group engagement partner's or the group engagement partner's firm's responsibility for the group audit opinion. (Ref: Para. A8-A9)

Acceptance and Continuance

12. In applying ASA 220, the group engagement partner shall determine whether sufficient appropriate audit evidence can reasonably be expected to be obtained in relation to the consolidation process and the financial information of the components on which to base the group audit opinion. For this purpose, the group engagement team shall obtain an understanding of the group, its components, and their environments that is sufficient to identify components that are likely to be significant components. Where component auditors will perform work on the financial information of such components, the group engagement partner shall evaluate whether the group engagement team will be able to be involved in the work of those component auditors to the extent necessary to obtain sufficient appropriate audit evidence. (Ref: Para. A10-A12)

3 See ASA 220, paragraph 15.

13. If the group engagement partner concludes that:
    (a) it will not be possible for the group engagement team to obtain sufficient appropriate audit evidence due to restrictions imposed by group management; and
    (b) the possible effect of this inability will result in a disclaimer of opinion on the group financial report,[4]

    the group engagement partner shall either:
    - in the case of a new engagement, not accept the engagement, or, in the case of a continuing engagement, withdraw from the engagement, where withdrawal is possible under applicable law or regulation; or
    - where law or regulation prohibits an auditor from declining an engagement or where withdrawal from an engagement is not otherwise possible, having performed the audit of the group financial report to the extent possible, disclaim an opinion on the group financial report. (Ref: Para. A13-A19)

Terms of Engagement

14. The group engagement partner shall agree on the terms of the group audit engagement in accordance with ASA 210.[5] (Ref: Para. A20-A21)

Overall Audit Strategy and Audit Plan

15. The group engagement team shall establish an overall group audit strategy and shall develop a group audit plan in accordance with ASA 300.[6]
16. The group engagement partner shall review the overall group audit strategy and group audit plan. (Ref: Para. A22)

Understanding the Group, Its Components and Their Environments

17. The auditor is required to identify and assess the risks of material misstatement through obtaining an understanding of the entity and its environment.[7] The group engagement team shall:
    (a) Enhance its understanding of the group, its components, and their environments, including group-wide controls, obtained during the acceptance or continuance stage; and
    (b) Obtain an understanding of the consolidation process, including the instructions issued by group management to components. (Ref: Para. A23-A29)
18. The group engagement team shall obtain an understanding that is sufficient to:
    (a) Confirm or revise its initial identification of components that are likely to be significant; and
    (b) Assess the risks of material misstatement of the group financial report, whether due to fraud or error.[8] (Ref: Para. A30-A31)

Understanding the Component Auditors

19. If the group engagement team plans to request a component auditor to perform work on the financial information of a component, the group engagement team shall obtain an understanding of the following: (Ref: Para. A32-A35)
    (a) Whether the component auditor understands and will comply with the ethical requirements that are relevant to the group audit and, in particular, is independent. (Ref: Para. A37)
    (b) The component auditor's professional competence. (Ref: Para. A38)

---

4 See ASA 705 *Modifications to the Opinion in the Independent Auditor's Report*.

5 See ASA 210 *Agreeing the Terms of Audit Engagements*.

6 See ASA 300 *Planning an Audit of a Financial Report*, paragraphs 7-12.

7 See ASA 315 *Identifying and Assessing the Risks of Material Misstatement through Understanding the Entity and Its Environment*.

8 See ASA 315.

(c) Whether the group engagement team will be able to be involved in the work of the component auditor to the extent necessary to obtain sufficient appropriate audit evidence.

(d) Whether the component auditor operates in a regulatory environment that actively oversees auditors. (Ref: Para. A36)

20. If a component auditor does not meet the independence requirements that are relevant to the group audit, or the group engagement team has serious concerns about the other matters listed in paragraph 19(a)-(c) of this Auditing Standard, the group engagement team shall obtain sufficient appropriate audit evidence relating to the financial information of the component without requesting that component auditor to perform work on the financial information of that component. (Ref: Para. A39-A41)

Materiality

21. The group engagement team shall determine the following: (Ref: Para. A42)

(a) Materiality for the group financial report as a whole when establishing the overall group audit strategy.

(b) If, in the specific circumstances of the group, there are particular classes of transactions, account balances or disclosures in the group financial report for which misstatements of lesser amounts than materiality for the group financial report as a whole could reasonably be expected to influence the economic decisions of users taken on the basis of the group financial report, the materiality level or levels to be applied to those particular classes of transactions, account balances or disclosures.

(c) Component materiality for those components where component auditors will perform an audit or a review for purposes of the group audit. To reduce to an appropriately low level the probability that the aggregate of uncorrected and undetected misstatements in the group financial report exceeds materiality for the group financial report as a whole, component materiality shall be lower than materiality for the group financial report as a whole. (Ref: Para. A43-A44)

(d) The threshold above which misstatements cannot be regarded as clearly trivial to the group financial report. (Ref: Para. A45)

22. Where component auditors will perform an audit for purposes of the group audit, the group engagement team shall evaluate the appropriateness of performance materiality determined at the component level. (Ref: Para. A46)

23. If a component is subject to audit by statute, regulation or other reason, and the group engagement team decides to use that audit to provide audit evidence for the group audit, the group engagement team shall determine whether:

(a) materiality for the component financial report as a whole; and

(b) performance materiality at the component level

meet the requirements of this Auditing Standard.

Responding to Assessed Risks

24. The auditor is required to design and implement appropriate responses to address the assessed risks of material misstatement of the financial report.[9] The group engagement team shall determine the type of work to be performed by the group engagement team, or the component auditors on its behalf, on the financial information of the components, see paragraphs 26-29 of this Auditing Standard. The group engagement team shall also determine the nature, timing and extent of its involvement in the work of the component auditors, see paragraphs 30-31 of this Auditing Standard.

25. If the nature, timing and extent of the work to be performed on the consolidation process or the financial information of the components are based on an expectation that group-wide controls are operating effectively, or if substantive procedures alone cannot provide sufficient appropriate audit evidence at the assertion level, the group engagement team shall test, or request a component auditor to test, the operating effectiveness of those controls.

9 See ASA 330 *The Auditor's Responses to Assessed Risks.*

Determining the Type of Work to Be Performed on the Financial Information of Components (Ref: Para. A47)

Significant Components

26. For a component that is significant due to its individual financial significance to the group, the group engagement team, or a component auditor on its behalf, shall perform an audit of the financial information of the component using component materiality.

27. For a component that is significant because it is likely to include significant risks of material misstatement of the group financial report due to its specific nature or circumstances, the group engagement team, or a component auditor on its behalf, shall perform one or more of the following:

    (a) An audit of the financial information of the component using component materiality.

    (b) An audit of one or more account balances, classes of transactions or disclosures relating to the likely significant risks of material misstatement of the group financial report. (Ref: Para. A48)

    (c) Specified audit procedures relating to the likely significant risks of material misstatement of the group financial report. (Ref: Para. A49)

Components that Are Not Significant Components

28. For components that are not significant components, the group engagement team shall perform analytical procedures at group level. (Ref: Para. A50)

29. If the group engagement team does not consider that sufficient appropriate audit evidence on which to base the group audit opinion will be obtained from:

    (a) the work performed on the financial information of significant components;

    (b) the work performed on group-wide controls and the consolidation process; and

    (c) the analytical procedures performed at group level,

    the group engagement team shall select components that are not significant components and shall perform, or request a component auditor to perform, one or more of the following on the financial information of the individual components selected: (Ref: Para. A51-A53)

    - An audit of the financial information of the component using component materiality.
    - An audit of one or more account balances, classes of transactions or disclosures.
    - A review of the financial information of the component using component materiality.
    - Specified procedures.

    The group engagement team shall vary the selection of components over a period of time.

Involvement in the Work Performed by Component Auditors (Ref: Para. A54-A55)

Significant Components—Risk Assessment

30. If a component auditor performs an audit of the financial information of a significant component, the group engagement team shall be involved in the component auditor's risk assessment to identify significant risks of material misstatement of the group financial report. The nature, timing and extent of this involvement are affected by the group engagement team's understanding of the component auditor, but at a minimum shall include:

    (a) Discussing with the component auditor or component management those of the component's business activities that are significant to the group;

    (b) Discussing with the component auditor the susceptibility of the component to material misstatement of the financial information due to fraud or error; and

    (c) Reviewing the component auditor's documentation of identified significant risks of material misstatement of the group financial report. Such documentation may take the form of a memorandum that reflects the component auditor's conclusion with regard to the identified significant risks.

Identified Significant Risks of Material Misstatement of the Group Financial Report—Further Audit Procedures

31. If significant risks of material misstatement of the group financial report have been identified in a component on which a component auditor performs the work, the group engagement team shall evaluate the appropriateness of the further audit procedures to be performed to respond to the identified significant risks of material misstatement of the group financial report. Based on its understanding of the component auditor, the group engagement team shall determine whether it is necessary to be involved in the further audit procedures.

Consolidation Process

32. In accordance with paragraph 17 of this Auditing Standard, the group engagement team obtains an understanding of group-wide controls and the consolidation process, including the instructions issued by group management to components. In accordance with paragraph 25 of this Auditing Standard, the group engagement team, or component auditor at the request of the group engagement team, tests the operating effectiveness of group-wide controls if the nature, timing and extent of the work to be performed on the consolidation process are based on an expectation that group-wide controls are operating effectively, or if substantive procedures alone cannot provide sufficient appropriate audit evidence at the assertion level.
33. The group engagement team shall design and perform further audit procedures on the consolidation process to respond to the assessed risks of material misstatement of the group financial report arising from the consolidation process. This shall include evaluating whether all components have been included in the group financial report.
34. The group engagement team shall evaluate the appropriateness, completeness and accuracy of consolidation adjustments and reclassifications, and shall evaluate whether any fraud risk factors or indicators of possible management bias exist. (Ref: Para. A56)
35. If the financial information of a component has not been prepared in accordance with the same accounting policies applied to the group financial report, the group engagement team shall evaluate whether the financial information of that component has been appropriately adjusted for purposes of preparing and presenting the group financial report.
36. The group engagement team shall determine whether the financial information identified in the component auditor's communication, see paragraph 41(c) of this Auditing Standard, is the financial information that is incorporated in the group financial report.
37. If the group financial report includes the financial report of a component with a financial reporting period-end that differs from that of the group, the group engagement team shall evaluate whether appropriate adjustments have been made to the financial report in accordance with the applicable financial reporting framework.

Subsequent Events

38. Where the group engagement team or component auditors perform audits on the financial information of components, the group engagement team or the component auditors shall perform procedures designed to identify events at those components that occur between the dates of the financial information of the components and the date of the auditor's report on the group financial report, and that may require adjustment to or disclosure in the group financial report.
39. Where component auditors perform work other than audits of the financial information of components, the group engagement team shall request the component auditors to notify the group engagement team if they become aware of subsequent events that may require an adjustment to or disclosure in the group financial report.

Communication with the Component Auditor

40. The group engagement team shall communicate its requirements to the component auditor on a timely basis. This communication shall set out the work to be performed, the use to be

made of that work, and the form and content of the component auditor's communication with the group engagement team. It shall also include the following: (Ref: Para. A57, A58, A60)

(a) A request that the component auditor, knowing the context in which the group engagement team will use the work of the component auditor, confirms that the component auditor will cooperate with the group engagement team. (Ref: Para. A59)

(b) The ethical requirements that are relevant to the group audit and, in particular, the independence requirements.

(c) In the case of an audit or review of the financial information of the component, component materiality (and, if applicable, the materiality level or levels for particular classes of transactions, account balances or disclosures) and the threshold above which misstatements cannot be regarded as clearly trivial to the group financial report.

(d) Identified significant risks of material misstatement of the group financial report, due to fraud or error, that are relevant to the work of the component auditor. The group engagement team shall request the component auditor to communicate on a timely basis any other identified significant risks of material misstatement of the group financial report, due to fraud or error, in the component, and the component auditor's responses to such risks.

(e) A list of related parties prepared by group management, and any other related parties of which the group engagement team is aware. The group engagement team shall request the component auditor to communicate on a timely basis related parties not previously identified by group management or the group engagement team. The group engagement team shall determine whether to identify such additional related parties to other component auditors.

41. The group engagement team shall request the component auditor to communicate matters relevant to the group engagement team's conclusion with regard to the group audit. Such communication shall include: (Ref: Para. A60)

(a) Whether the component auditor has complied with ethical requirements that are relevant to the group audit, including independence and professional competence;

(b) Whether the component auditor has complied with the group engagement team's requirements;

(c) Identification of the financial information of the component on which the component auditor is reporting;

(d) Information on instances of non-compliance with laws or regulations that could give rise to a material misstatement of the group financial report;

(e) A list of uncorrected misstatements of the financial information of the component (the list need not include misstatements that are below the threshold for clearly trivial misstatements communicated by the group engagement team, see paragraph 40(c) of this Auditing Standard);

(f) Indicators of possible management bias;

(g) Description of any identified significant deficiencies in internal control at the component level;

(h) Other significant matters that the component auditor communicated or expects to communicate to those charged with governance of the component, including fraud or suspected fraud involving component management, employees who have significant roles in internal control at the component level or others where the fraud resulted in a material misstatement of the financial information of the component;

(i) Any other matters that may be relevant to the group audit, or that the component auditor wishes to draw to the attention of the group engagement team, including exceptions noted in the written representations that the component auditor requested from component management; and

(j) The component auditor's overall findings, conclusions or opinion.

Evaluating the Sufficiency and Appropriateness of Audit Evidence Obtained

Evaluating the Component Auditors' Communication and Adequacy of their Work

42. The group engagement team shall evaluate the component auditor's communication, see paragraph 41 of this Auditing Standard. The group engagement team shall:
    (a) Discuss significant matters arising from that evaluation with the component auditor, component management or group management, as appropriate; and
    (b) Determine whether it is necessary to review other relevant parts of the component auditor's audit documentation. (Ref: Para. A61)
43. If the group engagement team concludes that the work of the component auditor is insufficient, the group engagement team shall determine what additional procedures are to be performed, and whether they are to be performed by the component auditor or by the group engagement team.

Sufficiency and Appropriateness of Audit Evidence

44. The auditor is required to obtain sufficient appropriate audit evidence to reduce audit risk to an acceptably low level and thereby enable the auditor to draw reasonable conclusions on which to base the auditor's opinion.[10] The group engagement team shall evaluate whether sufficient appropriate audit evidence has been obtained from the audit procedures performed on the consolidation process and the work performed by the group engagement team and the component auditors on the financial information of the components, on which to base the group audit opinion. (Ref: Para. A62)
45. The group engagement partner shall evaluate the effect on the group audit opinion of any uncorrected misstatements (either identified by the group engagement team or communicated by component auditors) and any instances where there has been an inability to obtain sufficient appropriate audit evidence. (Ref: Para. A63)

Communication with Group Management and Those Charged with Governance of the Group

Communication with Group Management

46. The group engagement team shall determine which identified deficiencies in internal control to communicate to those charged with governance and group management in accordance with ASA 265.[11] In making this determination, the group engagement team shall consider:
    (a) Deficiencies in group-wide internal control that the group engagement team has identified;
    (b) Deficiencies in internal control that the group engagement team has identified in internal controls at components; and
    (c) Deficiencies in internal control that component auditors have brought to the attention of the group engagement team.
47. If fraud has been identified by the group engagement team or brought to its attention by a component auditor, see paragraph 41(h) of this Auditing Standard, or information indicates that a fraud may exist, the group engagement team shall communicate this on a timely basis to the appropriate level of group management in order to inform those with primary responsibility for the prevention and detection of fraud of matters relevant to their responsibilities. (Ref. Para. A64)
48. A component auditor may be required by statute, regulation or for another reason, to express an audit opinion on the financial report of a component. In that case, the group engagement team shall request group management to inform component management of any matter of which the group engagement team becomes aware that may be significant to the financial report of the component, but of which component management may be unaware. If group management refuses to communicate the matter to component management, the group

10 See ASA 200, paragraph 17.

11 See ASA 265 *Communicating Deficiencies in Internal Control to Those Charged with Governance and Management.*

ASA

engagement team shall discuss the matter with those charged with governance of the group. If the matter remains unresolved, the group engagement team, subject to legal and professional confidentiality considerations, shall consider whether to advise the component auditor not to issue the auditor's report on the financial report of the component until the matter is resolved. (Ref: Para. A65)

Communication with Those Charged with Governance of the Group

49. The group engagement team shall communicate the following matters with those charged with governance of the group, in addition to those required by ASA 260[12] and other Auditing Standards: (Ref: Para. A66)

   (a) An overview of the type of work to be performed on the financial information of the components.

   (b) An overview of the nature of the group engagement team's planned involvement in the work to be performed by the component auditors on the financial information of significant components.

   (c) Instances where the group engagement team's evaluation of the work of a component auditor gave rise to a concern about the quality of that auditor's work.

   (d) Any limitations on the group audit, for example, where the group engagement team's access to information may have been restricted.

   (e) Fraud or suspected fraud involving group management, component management, employees who have significant roles in group-wide controls or others where the fraud resulted in a material misstatement of the group financial report.

Reporting Considerations

Aus 49.1 Where a component auditor issues, or intends to issue, a modified auditor's report, the group engagement partner shall consider:

   (a) the nature and significance of the modification, in relation to the financial report of the entity on which the group engagement partner is reporting; and

   (b) whether a modification is also required to the group engagement partner's audit report, under ASA 705.[*]

Documentation

50. The group engagement team shall include in the audit documentation the following matters:[13]

   (a) An analysis of components, indicating those that are significant, and the type of work performed on the financial information of the components.

   (b) The nature, timing and extent of the group engagement team's involvement in the work performed by the component auditors on significant components including, where applicable, the group engagement team's review of relevant parts of the component auditors' audit documentation and conclusions thereon.

   (c) Written communications between the group engagement team and the component auditors about the group engagement team's requirements.

❖ ❖ ❖

12 See ASA 260 *Communication with Those Charged with Governance.*

* See ASA 705 *Modifications to the Opinion in the Independent Auditor's Report.*

13 See ASA 230 *Audit Documentation*, paragraphs 8-11, and paragraph A6.

Application and Other Explanatory Material

Components Subject to Audit by Statute, Regulation or Other Reason

(Ref: Para. 3)

A1. Factors that may affect the group engagement team's decision whether to use an audit required by statute, regulation or for another reason to provide audit evidence for the group audit include the following:

- Differences in the financial reporting framework applied in preparing the financial report of the component and that applied in preparing the group financial report.
- Differences in the auditing and other standards applied by the component auditor and those applied in the audit of the group financial report.
- Whether the audit of the financial report of the component will be completed in time to meet the group reporting timetable.

Definitions

Component (Ref: Para. 9(a))

A2. The structure of a group affects how components are identified. For example, the group financial reporting system may be based on an organisational structure that provides for financial information to be prepared by a parent and one or more subsidiaries, joint ventures, or investees accounted for by the equity or cost methods of accounting; by a head office and one or more divisions or branches; or by a combination of both. Some groups, however, may organise their financial reporting system by function, process, product or service (or by groups of products or services), or geographical locations. In these cases, the entity or business activity for which group or component management prepares financial information that is included in the group financial report may be a function, process, product or service (or group of products or services), or geographical location.

A3. Various levels of components may exist within the group financial reporting system, in which case it may be more appropriate to identify components at certain levels of aggregation rather than individually.

A4. Components aggregated at a certain level may constitute a component for purposes of the group audit; however, such a component may also prepare a group financial report that incorporate the financial information of the components it encompasses (that is, a subgroup). This Auditing Standard may therefore be applied by different group engagement partners and teams for different subgroups within a larger group.

Significant Component (Ref: Para. 9(m))

A5. As the individual financial significance of a component increases, the risks of material misstatement of the group financial report ordinarily increase. The group engagement team may apply a percentage to a chosen benchmark as an aid to identify components that are of individual financial significance. Identifying a benchmark and determining a percentage to be applied to it involve the exercise of professional judgement. Depending on the nature and circumstances of the group, appropriate benchmarks might include group assets, liabilities, cash flows, profit or turnover. For example, the group engagement team may consider that components exceeding 15% of the chosen benchmark are significant components. A higher or lower percentage may, however, be deemed appropriate in the circumstances.

A6. The group engagement team may also identify a component as likely to include significant risks of material misstatement of the group financial report due to its specific nature or circumstances (that is, risks that require special audit consideration[14]). For example, a component could be responsible for foreign exchange trading and thus expose the group to a significant risk of material misstatement, even though the component is not otherwise of individual financial significance to the group.

Component Auditor (Ref: Para. 9(b))

A7. A member of the group engagement team may perform work on the financial information of a component for the group audit at the request of the group engagement team. Where this is the case, such a member of the engagement team is also a component auditor.

14 See ASA 315 , paragraphs 27-29.

Responsibility (Ref: Para. 11)

A8. Although component auditors may perform work on the financial information of the components for the group audit and as such are responsible for their overall findings, conclusions or opinions, the group engagement partner or the group engagement partner's firm is responsible for the group audit opinion.

A9. When the group audit opinion is modified because the group engagement team was unable to obtain sufficient appropriate audit evidence in relation to the financial information of one or more components, the Basis for Modification paragraph in the auditor's report on the group financial report describes the reasons for that inability without referring to the component auditor, unless such a reference is necessary for an adequate explanation of the circumstances.[15]

Acceptance and Continuance

Obtaining an Understanding at the Acceptance or Continuance Stage (Ref: Para. 12)

A10. In the case of a new engagement, the group engagement team's understanding of the group, its components, and their environments may be obtained from:

- Information provided by group management;
- Communication with group management; and
- Where applicable, communication with the previous group engagement team, component management, or component auditors.

A11. The group engagement team's understanding may include matters such as the following:

- The group structure, including both the legal and organisational structure (that is, how the group financial reporting system is organised).
- Components' business activities that are significant to the group, including the industry and regulatory, economic and political environments in which those activities take place.
- The use of service organisations, including shared service centres.
- A description of group-wide controls.
- The complexity of the consolidation process.
- Whether component auditors that are not from the group engagement partner's firm or network will perform work on the financial information of any of the components, and group management's rationale for appointing more than one auditor.
- Whether the group engagement team:
  - Will have unrestricted access to those charged with governance of the group, group management, those charged with governance of the component, component management, component information, and the component auditors (including relevant audit documentation sought by the group engagement team); and
  - Will be able to perform necessary work on the financial information of the components.

A12. In the case of a continuing engagement, the group engagement team's ability to obtain sufficient appropriate audit evidence may be affected by significant changes, for example:

- Changes in the group structure (for example, acquisitions, disposals, reorganisations, or changes in how the group financial reporting system is organised).
- Changes in components' business activities that are significant to the group.
- Changes in the composition of those charged with governance of the group, group management, or key management of significant components.
- Concerns the group engagement team has with regard to the integrity and competence of group or component management.
- Changes in group-wide controls.
- Changes in the applicable financial reporting framework.

15 See ASA 705, paragraph 20.

Aus A12.1 Section 323B of the *Corporations Act 2001* (the Act) requires the auditor of a controlled (component) entity to give the principal (group) auditor any information, explanation or assistance required under section 323A of the Act.

Expectation to Obtain Sufficient Appropriate Audit Evidence (Ref: Para. 13)

A13. A group may consist only of components not considered significant components. In these circumstances, the group engagement partner can reasonably expect to obtain sufficient appropriate audit evidence on which to base the group audit opinion if the group engagement team will be able to:

(a) Perform the work on the financial information of some of these components; and

(b) Be involved in the work performed by component auditors on the financial information of other components to the extent necessary to obtain sufficient appropriate audit evidence.

Access to Information (Ref: Para. 13)

A14. The group engagement team's access to information may be restricted by circumstances that cannot be overcome by group management, for example laws relating to confidentiality and data privacy, or denial by the component auditor of access to relevant audit documentation sought by the group engagement team. It may also be restricted by group management.

A15. Where access to information is restricted by circumstances, the group engagement team may still be able to obtain sufficient appropriate audit evidence; however, this is less likely as the significance of the component increases. For example, the group engagement team may not have access to those charged with governance, management, or the auditor (including relevant audit documentation sought by the group engagement team) of a component that is accounted for by the equity method of accounting. If the component is not a significant component, and the group engagement team has a financial report of the component, including the auditor's report thereon, and has access to information kept by group management in relation to that component, the group engagement team may conclude that this information constitutes sufficient appropriate audit evidence in relation to that component. If the component is a significant component, however, the group engagement team will not be able to comply with the requirements of this Auditing Standard relevant in the circumstances of the group audit. For example, the group engagement team will not be able to comply with the requirements in paragraphs 30-31 to be involved in the work of the component auditor. The group engagement team will not, therefore, be able to obtain sufficient appropriate audit evidence in relation to that component. The effect of the group engagement team's inability to obtain sufficient appropriate audit evidence is considered in terms of ASA 705.

A16. The group engagement team will not be able to obtain sufficient appropriate audit evidence if group management restricts the access of the group engagement team or a component auditor to the information of a significant component.

A17. Although the group engagement team may be able to obtain sufficient appropriate audit evidence if such restriction relates to a component considered not a significant component, the reason for the restriction may affect the group audit opinion. For example, it may affect the reliability of group management's responses to the group engagement team's enquiries and group management's representations to the group engagement team.

A18. Law or regulation may prohibit the group engagement partner from declining or withdrawing from an engagement. For example, in some jurisdictions the auditor is appointed for a specified period of time and is prohibited from withdrawing before the end of that period. Also, in the public sector, the option of declining or withdrawing from an engagement may not be available to the auditor due to the nature of the mandate or public interest considerations. In these circumstances, this Auditing Standard still applies to the group audit, and the effect of the group engagement team's inability to obtain sufficient appropriate audit evidence is considered in terms of ASA 705.

A19. Appendix 1 contains an example of an auditor's report containing a qualified opinion based on the group engagement team's inability to obtain sufficient appropriate audit evidence in relation to a significant component accounted for by the equity method of accounting, but where, in the group engagement team's judgement, the effect is material but not pervasive.

Terms of Engagement (Ref: Para. 14)

A20. The terms of engagement identify the applicable financial reporting framework.[16] Additional matters may be included in the terms of a group audit engagement, such as the fact that:

- The communication between the group engagement team and the component auditors should be unrestricted to the extent possible under law or regulation;
- Important communications between the component auditors, those charged with governance of the component, and component management, including communications on significant deficiencies in internal control, should be communicated as well to the group engagement team;
- Important communications between regulatory authorities and components related to financial reporting matters should be communicated to the group engagement team; and
- To the extent the group engagement team considers necessary, it should be permitted:
    - Access to component information, those charged with governance of components, component management, and the component auditors (including relevant audit documentation sought by the group engagement team); and
    - To perform work or request a component auditor to perform work on the financial information of the components.

A21. Restrictions imposed on:

- the group engagement team's access to component information, those charged with governance of components, component management, or the component auditors (including relevant audit documentation sought by the group engagement team); or
- the work to be performed on the financial information of the components,

after the group engagement partner's acceptance of the group audit engagement, constitute an inability to obtain sufficient appropriate audit evidence that may affect the group audit opinion. In exceptional circumstances it may even lead to withdrawal from the engagement where withdrawal is possible under applicable law or regulation.

Overall Audit Strategy and Audit Plan (Ref: Para. 16)

A22. The group engagement partner's review of the overall group audit strategy and group audit plan is an important part of fulfilling the group engagement partner's responsibility for the direction of the group audit engagement.

Understanding the Group, Its Components and Their Environments

Matters about Which the Group Engagement Team Obtains an Understanding (Ref: Para. 17)

A23. ASA 315 contains guidance on matters the auditor may consider when obtaining an understanding of the industry, regulatory, and other external factors that affect the entity, including the applicable financial reporting framework; the nature of the entity; objectives and strategies and related business risks; and measurement and review of the entity's financial performance.[17] Appendix 2 of this Auditing Standard contains guidance on matters specific to a group, including the consolidation process.

Instructions Issued by Group Management to Components (Ref: Para. 17)

A24. To achieve uniformity and comparability of financial information, group management ordinarily issues instructions to components. Such instructions specify the requirements for financial information of the components to be included in the group financial report and often include financial reporting procedures manuals and a reporting package. A reporting package ordinarily consists of standard formats for providing financial information for

16 See ASA 210, paragraph 8.

17 See ASA 315, paragraphs A17-A41.

incorporation in the group financial report. Reporting packages generally do not, however, take the form of a financial report prepared and presented in accordance with the applicable financial reporting framework.

A25. The instructions ordinarily cover:

- The accounting policies to be applied;
- Statutory and other disclosure requirements applicable to the group financial report, including:
  - The identification and reporting of segments;
  - Related party relationships and transactions;
  - Intra-group transactions and unrealised profits;
  - Intra-group account balances; and
- A reporting timetable.

A26. The group engagement team's understanding of the instructions may include the following:

- The clarity and practicality of the instructions for completing the reporting package.
- Whether the instructions:
  - Adequately describe the characteristics of the applicable financial reporting framework;
  - Provide for disclosures that are sufficient to comply with the requirements of the applicable financial reporting framework, for example disclosure of related party relationships and transactions, and segment information;
  - Provide for the identification of consolidation adjustments, for example intra-group transactions and unrealised profits, and intra-group account balances; and
  - Provide for the approval of the financial information by component management.

Fraud (Ref: Para. 17)

A27. The auditor is required to identify and assess the risks of material misstatement of the financial report due to fraud, and to design and implement appropriate responses to the assessed risks.[18] Information used to identify the risks of material misstatement of the group financial report due to fraud may include the following:

- Group management's assessment of the risks that the group financial report may be materially misstated as a result of fraud.
- Group management's process for identifying and responding to the risks of fraud in the group, including any specific fraud risks identified by group management, or account balances, classes of transactions, or disclosures for which a risk of fraud is likely.
- Whether there are particular components for which a risk of fraud is likely.
- How those charged with governance of the group monitor group management's processes for identifying and responding to the risks of fraud in the group, and the controls group management has established to mitigate these risks.
- Responses of those charged with governance of the group, group management, internal audit (and if considered appropriate, component management, the component auditors, and others) to the group engagement team's enquiry whether they have knowledge of any actual, suspected, or alleged fraud affecting a component or the group.

Discussion among Group Engagement Team Members and Component Auditors Regarding the Risks of Material Misstatement of the Group Financial Report, Including Risks of Fraud (Ref: Para. 17)

A28. The key members of the engagement team are required to discuss the susceptibility of an entity to material misstatement of the financial reports due to fraud or error, specifically

18 See ASA 240 *The Auditor's Responsibilities Relating to Fraud in an Audit of a Financial Report.*

emphasising the risks due to fraud. In a group audit, these discussions may also include the component auditors.[19] The group engagement partner's determination of who to include in the discussions, how and when they occur, and their extent, is affected by factors such as prior experience with the group.

A29. The discussions provide an opportunity to:

- Share knowledge of the components and their environments, including group-wide controls.
- Exchange information about the business risks of the components or the group.
- Exchange ideas about how and where the group financial report may be susceptible to material misstatement due to fraud or error, how group management and component management could perpetrate and conceal fraudulent financial reporting, and how assets of the components could be misappropriated.
- Identify practices followed by group or component management that may be biased or designed to manage earnings that could lead to fraudulent financial reporting, for example revenue recognition practices that do not comply with the applicable financial reporting framework.
- Consider known external and internal factors affecting the group that may create an incentive or pressure for group management, component management, or others to commit fraud, provide the opportunity for fraud to be perpetrated, or indicate a culture or environment that enables group management, component management, or others to rationalise committing fraud.
- Consider the risk that group or component management may override controls.
- Consider whether uniform accounting policies are used to prepare the financial information of the components for the group financial reports and, where not, how differences in accounting policies are identified and adjusted (where required by the applicable financial reporting framework).
- Discuss fraud that has been identified in components, or information that indicates existence of a fraud in a component.
- Share information that may indicate non-compliance with national laws or regulations, for example payments of bribes and improper transfer pricing practices.

Risk Factors (Ref: Para. 18)

A30. Appendix 3 sets out examples of conditions or events that, individually or together, may indicate risks of material misstatement of the group financial report, including risks due to fraud.

Risk Assessment (Ref: Para. 18)

A31. The group engagement team's assessment at group level of the risks of material misstatement of the group financial report is based on information such as the following:

- Information obtained from the understanding of the group, its components, and their environments, and of the consolidation process, including audit evidence obtained in evaluating the design and implementation of group-wide controls and controls that are relevant to the consolidation.
- Information obtained from the component auditors.

Understanding the Component Auditors (Ref: Para. 19)

A32. The group engagement team obtains an understanding of a component auditor only when it plans to request the component auditor to perform work on the financial information of a component for the group audit. For example, it will not be necessary to obtain an understanding of the auditors of those components for which the group engagement team plans to perform analytical procedures at group level only.

19 See ASA 240, paragraph 15; and ASA 315, paragraph 10.

Group Engagement Team's Procedures to Obtain an Understanding of the Component Auditor and Sources of Audit Evidence (Ref: Para. 19)

A33. The nature, timing and extent of the group engagement team's procedures to obtain an understanding of the component auditor are affected by factors such as previous experience with or knowledge of the component auditor, and the degree to which the group engagement team and the component auditor are subject to common policies and procedures, for example:

- Whether the group engagement team and a component auditor share:
  - Common policies and audit procedures for performing the work (for example, audit methodologies);
  - Common quality control policies and procedures; or
  - Common monitoring policies and procedures.
- The consistency or similarity of:
  - Laws and regulations or legal system;
  - Professional oversight, discipline, and external quality assurance;
  - Education and training;
  - Professional organisations and standards; and
  - Language and culture.

A34. These factors interact and are not mutually exclusive. For example, the extent of the group engagement team's procedures to obtain an understanding of Component Auditor A, who consistently applies common quality control and monitoring policies and procedures and a common audit methodology or operates in the same jurisdiction as the group engagement partner, may be less than the extent of the group engagement team's procedures to obtain an understanding of Component Auditor B, who is not consistently applying common quality control and monitoring policies and procedures and a common audit methodology or operates in a foreign jurisdiction. The nature of the procedures performed in relation to Component Auditors A and B may also be different.

A35. The group engagement team may obtain an understanding of the component auditor in a number of ways. In the first year of involving a component auditor, the group engagement team may, for example:

- Evaluate the results of the quality control monitoring system where the group engagement team and component auditor are from a firm or network that operates under and complies with common monitoring policies and procedures;[20]
- Visit the component auditor to discuss the matters in paragraph 19(a)-(c);
- Request the component auditor to confirm the matters referred to in paragraph 19(a)-(c) in writing. Appendix 4 contains an example of written confirmations by a component auditor;
- Request the component auditor to complete questionnaires about the matters in paragraph 19(a)-(c);
- Discuss the component auditor with colleagues in the group engagement partner's firm, or with a reputable third party that has knowledge of the component auditor; or
- Obtain, where possible under applicable law or regulation, confirmations of credentials, such as confirmation of membership of a professional body, from the professional body or bodies to which the component auditor belongs, the authorities by which the component auditor is licensed, or other third parties.

In subsequent years, the understanding of the component auditor may be based on the group engagement team's previous experience with the component auditor.

20 See ASQC 1 *Quality Control for Firms that Perform Audits and Reviews of Financial Reports and Other Financial Information, and Other Assurance Engagements,* paragraph 54.

The group engagement team may request the component auditor to confirm whether anything in relation to the matters listed in paragraph 19(a)-(c) has changed since the previous year.

A36. Where independent oversight bodies have been established to oversee the auditing profession and monitor the quality of audits, awareness of the regulatory environment may assist the group engagement team in evaluating the independence and competence of the component auditor. Information about the regulatory environment may be obtained from the component auditor or information provided by the independent oversight bodies.

Ethical Requirements that Are Relevant to the Group Audit (Ref: Para. 19(a))

A37. When performing work on the financial information of a component for a group audit, the component auditor is subject to ethical requirements that are relevant to the group audit. Such requirements may be different or in addition to those applying to the component auditor when performing a statutory audit in the component auditor's jurisdiction. The group engagement team therefore obtains an understanding whether the component auditor understands and will comply with the ethical requirements that are relevant to the group audit, sufficient to fulfil the component auditor's responsibilities in the group audit.

The Component Auditor's Professional Competence (Ref: Para. 19(b))

A38. The group engagement team's understanding of the component auditor's professional competence may include whether the component auditor:

- Possesses an understanding of auditing and other standards applicable to the group audit that is sufficient to fulfill the component auditor's responsibilities in the group audit;
- Possesses the special skills (for example, industry specific knowledge) necessary to perform the work on the financial information of the particular component; and
- Where relevant, possesses an understanding of the applicable financial reporting framework that is sufficient to fulfill the component auditor's responsibilities in the group audit (instructions issued by group management to components often describe the characteristics of the applicable financial reporting framework).

Application of the Group Engagement Team's Understanding of a Component Auditor (Ref: Para. 20)

A39. The group engagement team cannot overcome the fact that a component auditor is not independent by being involved in the work of the component auditor or by performing additional risk assessment or further audit procedures on the financial information of the component.

A40. However, the group engagement team may be able to overcome less than serious concerns about the component auditor's professional competency (for example, lack of industry specific knowledge), or the fact that the component auditor does not operate in an environment that actively oversees auditors, by being involved in the work of the component auditor or by performing additional risk assessment or further audit procedures on the financial information of the component.

A41. Where law or regulation prohibits access to relevant parts of the audit documentation of the component auditor, the group engagement team may request the component auditor to overcome this by preparing a memorandum that covers the relevant information.

Materiality (Ref: Para. 21-23)

A42. The auditor is required:[21]

(a) When establishing the overall audit strategy, to determine:

(i) Materiality for the financial report as a whole; and

(ii) If, in the specific circumstances of the entity, there are particular classes of transactions, account balances or disclosures for which misstatements of lesser amounts than materiality for the financial report as a whole could reasonably be expected to influence the economic decisions of users taken on the basis of

21 See ASA 320 *Materiality in Planning and Performing an Audit*, paragraphs 10-11.

the financial report, the materiality level or levels to be applied to those particular classes of transactions, account balances or disclosures; and

(b) To determine performance materiality.

In the context of a group audit, materiality is established for both the group financial report as a whole, and for the financial information of the components. Materiality for the group financial report as a whole is used when establishing the overall group audit strategy.

A43. To reduce to an appropriately low level the probability that the aggregate of uncorrected and undetected misstatements in the group financial report exceeds materiality for the group financial report as a whole, component materiality is set lower than materiality for the group financial report as a whole. Different component materiality may be established for different components. Component materiality need not be an arithmetical portion of materiality for the group financial report as a whole and, consequently, the aggregate of component materiality for the different components may exceed the materiality for the group financial report as a whole. Component materiality is used when establishing the overall audit strategy for a component.

A44. Component materiality is determined for those components whose financial information will be audited or reviewed as part of the group audit in accordance with paragraphs 26, 27(a) and 29. Component materiality is used by the component auditor to evaluate whether uncorrected detected misstatements are material, individually or in the aggregate.

A45. A threshold for misstatements is determined in addition to component materiality. Misstatements identified in the financial information of the component that are above the threshold for misstatements are communicated to the group engagement team.

A46. In the case of an audit of the financial information of a component, the component auditor (or group engagement team) determines performance materiality at the component level. This is necessary to reduce to an appropriately low level the probability that the aggregate of uncorrected and undetected misstatements in the financial information of the component exceeds component materiality. In practice, the group engagement team may set component materiality at this lower level. Where this is the case, the component auditor uses component materiality for purposes of assessing the risks of material misstatement of the financial information of the component and to design further audit procedures in response to assessed risks as well as for evaluating whether detected misstatements are material individually or in the aggregate.

Responding to Assessed Risks

Determining the Type of Work to Be Performed on the Financial Information of Components (Ref: Para. 26-27)

A47. The group engagement team's determination of the type of work to be performed on the financial information of a component and its involvement in the work of the component auditor is affected by:

(a) The significance of the component;

(b) The identified significant risks of material misstatement of the group financial report;

(c) The group engagement team's evaluation of the design of group-wide controls and determination whether they have been implemented; and

(d) The group engagement team's understanding of the component auditor.

The following diagram shows how the significance of the component affects the group engagement team's determination of the type of work to be performed on the financial information of the component.

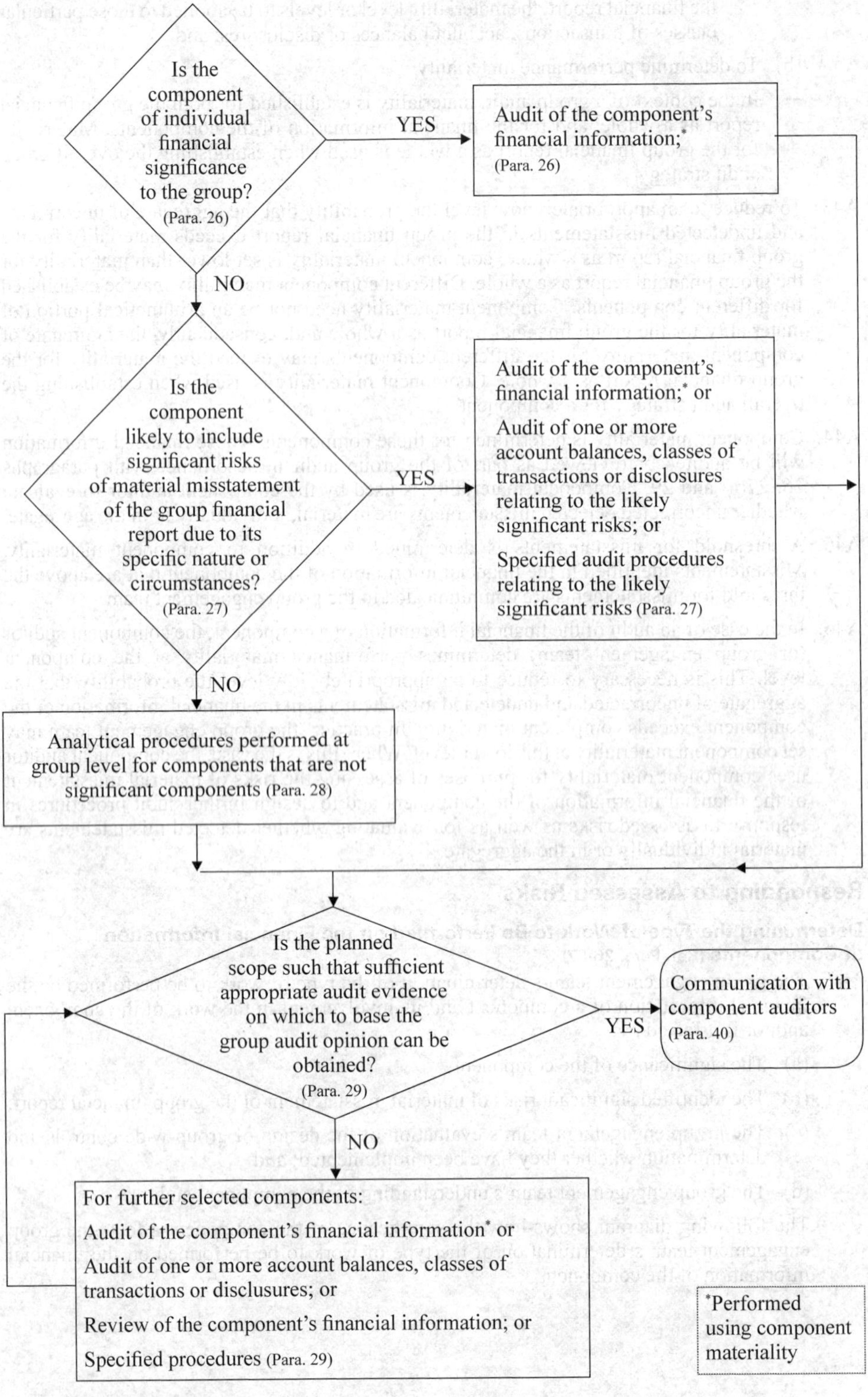
Is the component of individual financial significance to the group? (Para. 26)
YES
Audit of the component's financial information;* (Para. 26)
NO
Is the component likely to include significant risks of material misstatement of the group financial report due to its specific nature or circumstances? (Para. 27)
YES
Audit of the component's financial information;* or
Audit of one or more account balances, classes of transactions or disclosures relating to the likely significant risks; or
Specified audit procedures relating to the likely significant risks (Para. 27)
NO
Analytical procedures performed at group level for components that are not significant components (Para. 28)
Is the planned scope such that sufficient appropriate audit evidence on which to base the group audit opinion can be obtained? (Para. 29)
YES
Communication with component auditors (Para. 40)
NO
For further selected components:
Audit of the component's financial information* or
Audit of one or more account balances, classes of transactions or disclosures; or
Review of the component's financial information; or
Specified procedures (Para. 29)
*Performed using component materiality

Significant Components *(Ref: Para. 27(b)-(c))*

A48. The group engagement team may identify a component as a significant component because that component is likely to include significant risks of material misstatement of the group financial report due to its specific nature or circumstances. In that case, the group engagement team may be able to identify the account balances, classes of transactions or disclosures affected by the likely significant risks. Where this is the case, the group engagement team may decide to perform, or request a component auditor to perform, an audit of only those account balances, classes of transactions or disclosures. For example, in the situation described in paragraph A6, the work on the financial information of the component may be limited to an audit of the account balances, classes of transactions and disclosures affected by the foreign exchange trading of that component. Where the group engagement team requests a component auditor to perform an audit of one or more specific account balances, classes of transactions or disclosures, the communication of the group engagement team (see paragraph 40) takes account of the fact that many financial report items are interrelated.

A49. The group engagement team may design audit procedures that respond to a likely significant risk of material misstatement of the group financial report. For example, in the case of a likely significant risk of inventory obsolescence, the group engagement team may perform, or request a component auditor to perform, specified audit procedures on the valuation of inventory at a component that holds a large volume of potentially obsolete inventory, but that is not otherwise significant.

Components that Are Not Significant Components *(Ref: Para. 28-29)*

A50. Depending on the circumstances of the engagement, the financial information of the components may be aggregated at various levels for purposes of the analytical procedures. The results of the analytical procedures corroborate the group engagement team's conclusions that there are no significant risks of material misstatement of the aggregated financial information of components that are not significant components.

A51. The group engagement team's decision as to how many components to select in accordance with paragraph 29, which components to select, and the type of work to be performed on the financial information of the individual components selected may be affected by factors such as the following:

- The extent of audit evidence expected to be obtained on the financial information of the significant components.
- Whether the component has been newly formed or acquired.
- Whether significant changes have taken place in the component.
- Whether internal audit has performed work at the component and any effect of that work on the group audit.
- Whether the components apply common systems and processes.
- The operating effectiveness of group-wide controls.
- Abnormal fluctuations identified by analytical procedures performed at group level.
- The individual financial significance of, or the risk posed by, the component in comparison with other components within this category.
- Whether the component is subject to audit required by statute, regulation or for another reason.

Including an element of unpredictability in selecting components in this category may increase the likelihood of identifying material misstatement of the components' financial information. The selection of components is often varied on a cyclical basis.

A52. A review of the financial information of a component may be performed in accordance with ASRE 2410[22, 23]. The group engagement team may also specify additional audit procedures to supplement this work.

A53. As explained in paragraph A13, a group may consist only of components that are not significant components. In these circumstances, the group engagement team can obtain sufficient appropriate audit evidence on which to base the group audit opinion by determining the type of work to be performed on the financial information of the components in accordance with paragraph 29. It is unlikely that the group engagement team will obtain sufficient appropriate audit evidence on which to base the group audit opinion if the group engagement team, or a component auditor, only tests group-wide controls and performs analytical procedures on the financial information of the components.

Involvement in the Work Performed by Component Auditors (Ref: Para. 30-31)

A54. Factors that may affect the group engagement team's involvement in the work of the component auditor include:

(a) The significance of the component;

(b) The identified significant risks of material misstatement of the group financial report; and

(c) The group engagement team's understanding of the component auditor.

In the case of a significant component or identified significant risks, the group engagement team performs the procedures described in paragraphs 30-31. In the case of a component that is not a significant component, the nature, timing and extent of the group engagement team's involvement in the work of the component auditor will vary based on the group engagement team's understanding of that component auditor. The fact that the component is not a significant component becomes secondary. For example, even though a component is not considered a significant component, the group engagement team nevertheless may decide to be involved in the component auditor's risk assessment, because it has less than serious concerns about the component auditor's professional competency (for example, lack of industry specific knowledge), or the component auditor does not operate in an environment that actively oversees auditors.

A55. Forms of involvement in the work of a component auditor other than those described in paragraphs 30-31 and 42 may, based on the group engagement team's understanding of the component auditor, include one or more of the following:

(a) Meeting with component management or the component auditors to obtain an understanding of the component and its environment.

(b) Reviewing the component auditors' overall audit strategy and audit plan.

(c) Performing risk assessment procedures to identify and assess the risks of material misstatement at the component level. These may be performed with the component auditors, or by the group engagement team.

(d) Designing and performing further audit procedures. These may be designed and performed with the component auditors, or by the group engagement team.

(e) Participating in the closing and other key meetings between the component auditors and component management.

(f) Reviewing other relevant parts of the component auditors' audit documentation.

---

22 [Deleted by the AUASB].

23 See ASRE 2410 *Review of a Financial Report Performed by the Independent Auditor of the Entity.* See also ASRE 2400 *Review of a Financial Report Performed by an Assurance Practitioner Who is Not the Auditor of the Entity* and ASRE 2405 *Review of Historical Financial Information Other than a Financial Report.*

Consolidation Process

Consolidation Adjustments and Reclassifications (Ref: Para. 34)

A56. The consolidation process may require adjustments to amounts reported in the group financial report that do not pass through the usual transaction processing systems, and may not be subject to the same internal controls to which other financial information is subject. The group engagement team's evaluation of the appropriateness, completeness and accuracy of the adjustments may include:

- Evaluating whether significant adjustments appropriately reflect the events and transactions underlying them;
- Determining whether significant adjustments have been correctly calculated, processed and authorised by group management and, where applicable, by component management;
- Determining whether significant adjustments are properly supported and sufficiently documented; and
- Checking the reconciliation and elimination of intra-group transactions and unrealised profits, and intra-group account balances.

Communication with the Component Auditor (Ref: Para. 40-41)

A57. If effective two-way communication between the group engagement team and the component auditors does not exist, there is a risk that the group engagement team may not obtain sufficient appropriate audit evidence on which to base the group audit opinion. Clear and timely communication of the group engagement team's requirements forms the basis of effective two-way communication between the group engagement team and the component auditor(s).

A58. The group engagement team's requirements are often communicated in a letter of instruction. Appendix 5 contains guidance on required and additional matters that may be included in such a letter of instruction. The component auditor's communication with the group engagement team often takes the form of a memorandum or report of work performed. Communication between the group engagement team and the component auditor, however, may not necessarily be in writing. For example, the group engagement team may visit the component auditor to discuss identified significant risks or review relevant parts of the component auditor's audit documentation. Nevertheless, the documentation requirements of this and other Auditing Standards apply.

A59. In cooperating with the group engagement team, the component auditor(s), for example, would provide the group engagement team with access to relevant audit documentation if not prohibited by law or regulation.

A60. Where a member of the group engagement team is also a component auditor, the objective for the group engagement team to communicate clearly with the component auditor can often be achieved by means other than specific written communication. For example:

- Access by the component auditor to the overall audit strategy and audit plan may be sufficient to communicate the group engagement team's requirements set out in paragraph 40; and
- A review of the component auditor's audit documentation by the group engagement team may be sufficient to communicate matters relevant to the group engagement team's conclusion set out in paragraph 41.

Evaluating the Sufficiency and Appropriateness of Audit Evidence Obtained

Reviewing the Component Auditor's Audit Documentation (Ref: Para. 42(b))

A61. What parts of the audit documentation of the component auditor will be relevant to the group audit may vary depending on the circumstances. Often the focus is on audit documentation that is relevant to the significant risks of material misstatement of the group financial report. The extent of the review may be affected by the fact that the component auditor's audit documentation has been subjected to the component auditor's firm's review procedures.

Sufficiency and Appropriateness of Audit Evidence (Ref: Para. 44-45)

A62. If the group engagement team concludes that sufficient appropriate audit evidence on which to base the group audit opinion has not been obtained, the group engagement team may request the component auditor to perform additional procedures. If this is not feasible, the group engagement team may perform its own procedures on the financial information of the component.

A63. The group engagement partner's evaluation of the aggregate effect of any misstatements (either identified by the group engagement team or communicated by component auditors) allows the group engagement partner to determine whether the group financial report as a whole is materially misstated.

Communication with Group Management and Those Charged with Governance of the Group

Communication with Group Management (Ref: Para. 46-48)

A64. ASA 240 contains requirements and guidance on communication of fraud to management and, where management may be involved in the fraud, to those charged with governance.[24]

A65. Group management may need to keep certain material sensitive information confidential. Examples of matters that may be significant to the financial report of the component of which component management may be unaware include the following:

- Potential litigation.
- Plans for abandonment of material operating assets.
- Subsequent events.
- Significant legal agreements.

Aus A65.1 In the public sector, group management may not always be readily identifiable at the whole of government level. Furthermore, responsibility for internal control may remain at individual entity level only. In such cases, the auditor determines the appropriate level of management with whom to communicate.

Communication with Those Charged with Governance of the Group (Ref: Para. 49)

A66. The matters the group engagement team communicates to those charged with governance of the group may include those brought to the attention of the group engagement team by component auditors that the group engagement team judges to be significant to the responsibilities of those charged with governance of the group. Communication with those charged with governance of the group takes place at various times during the group audit. For example, the matters referred to in paragraph 49(a)-(b) may be communicated after the group engagement team has determined the work to be performed on the financial information of the components. On the other hand, the matter referred to in paragraph 49(c) may be communicated at the end of the audit, and the matters referred to in paragraph 49(d)-(e) may be communicated when they occur.

❖ ❖ ❖

Conformity with International Standards on Auditing

This Auditing Standard conforms with International Standard on Auditing ISA 600 *Special Considerations—Audits of Group Financial Statements (Including the Work of Component Auditors)* issued by the International Auditing and Assurance Standards Board (IAASB), an independent standard-setting board of the International Federation of Accountants (IFAC).

Paragraphs that have been added to this Auditing Standard (and do not appear in the text of the equivalent ISA) are identified with the prefix "Aus".

Compliance with this Auditing Standard enables compliance with ISA 600.

24 See ASA 240, paragraphs 40-42.

Appendix 1

(Ref: Para. A19)

Illustrations of Auditors' Reports with Modifications to the Opinion—General Purpose Financial Reports

- Illustration 1: An auditor's report containing a qualified opinion due to the auditor's inability to obtain sufficient appropriate audit evidence.
- Illustration 1A: An auditor's report containing a qualified opinion due to the auditor's inability to obtain sufficient appropriate audit evidence (under the *Corporations Act 2001*).

Example Auditor's Report General Purpose Financial Report—Qualified Opinion The group engagement team is not able to obtain sufficient appropriate audit evidence on which to base the group audit opinion

Illustration 1:

Circumstances include the following:

- **Audit of a general purpose financial report prepared by management of the entity—the financial statements are prepared in accordance with Australian Accounting Standards.**
- **The financial report is not prepared under the *Corporations Act 2001*.**
- **In this example, the group engagement team is unable to obtain sufficient appropriate audit evidence relating to a significant component accounted for by the equity method (recognised at $15 million in the balance sheet, which reflects total assets of $60 million) because the group engagement team did not have access to the accounting records, management, or auditor of the component.**
- **The group engagement team has read the audited financial report of the component as of 30 June 20X1, including the auditor's report thereon, and considered related financial information kept by group management in relation to the component.**
- **In the group engagement partner's judgement, the effect on the group financial report of this inability to obtain sufficient appropriate audit evidence is material but not pervasive.**

INDEPENDENT AUDITOR'S REPORT

[Appropriate Addressee]

Report on the Financial Report[25]

We have audited the accompanying financial report of ABC Entity, which comprises the statements of financial position as at 30 June 20X1, the statements of comprehensive income, the statements of changes in equity and the statements of cash flows for the year then ended, notes comprising a summary of significant accounting policies and other explanatory information and management's assertion statement* of the entity and the consolidated entity comprising the entity and the entities it controlled at the year's end or from time to time during the financial year.

25 The sub-title "Report on the Financial Report" is unnecessary in circumstances when the second sub-title "Report on Other Legal and Regulatory Requirements", or other appropriate sub-title, is not applicable.

* Or other appropriate term.

Management's[26] Responsibility for the Financial Report

Management is responsible for the preparation and fair presentation of the financial report in accordance with Australian Accounting Standards and [relevant reporting framework],[27] and for such internal control as management determines is necessary to enable the preparation of the financial report that is free from material misstatement, whether due to fraud or error.

Auditor's Responsibility

Our responsibility is to express an opinion on the financial report based on our audit. We conducted our audit in accordance with Australian Auditing Standards. Those standards require that we comply with relevant ethical requirements relating to audit engagements and plan and perform the audit to obtain reasonable assurance about whether the financial report is free from material misstatement.

An audit involves performing procedures to obtain audit evidence about the amounts and disclosures in the financial report. The procedures selected depend on the auditor's judgement, including the assessment of the risks of material misstatement of the financial report, whether due to fraud or error. In making those risk assessments, the auditor considers internal control relevant to the entity's preparation and fair presentation[28] of the financial report in order to design audit procedures that are appropriate in the circumstances, but not for the purpose of expressing an opinion on the effectiveness of the entity's internal control.[29] An audit also includes evaluating the appropriateness of accounting policies used and the reasonableness of accounting estimates made by management, as well as evaluating the overall presentation of the financial report.

We believe that the audit evidence we have obtained is sufficient and appropriate to provide a basis for our qualified audit opinion.

Basis for Qualified Opinion

ABC Entity's investment in XYZ Entity, a foreign associate acquired during the year and accounted for by the equity method, is carried at $15 million on the consolidated statement of financial position as at 30 June 20X1, and ABC's share of XYZ's profit of $1 million is included in the consolidated statement of comprehensive income for the year then ended. We were unable to obtain sufficient appropriate audit evidence about the carrying amount of ABC's investment in XYZ as at 30 June 20X1 and ABC's share of XYZ's profit for the year because we were denied access to the financial information, management, and the auditors of XYZ. Consequently, we were unable to determine whether any adjustments to these amounts were necessary.

Qualified Opinion

In our opinion, except for the possible effects of the matter described in the Basis for Qualified Opinion paragraph, the financial report presents fairly, in all material respects, (or "*gives a true and fair view of*") the financial position of ABC Entity and its subsidiaries as at 30 June 20X1, and (of) their financial performance and cash flows for the year then ended in accordance with Australian Accounting Standards and [relevant reporting framework].

Report on Other Legal and Regulatory Requirements

[Form and content of this section of the auditor's report will vary depending on the nature of the auditor's other reporting responsibilities.]

---

26 Or other term that is appropriate in the context of the legal framework in the particular jurisdiction.

27 Where management's responsibility is to prepare a financial report that gives a true and fair view, this may read: "Management is responsible for the preparation and presentation of the financial report that gives a true and fair view in accordance with Australian Accounting Standards, and for such…"

28 In the case of footnote 27, this may read: "In making those risk assessments, the auditor considers internal control relevant to the entity's preparation of the financial report that gives a true and fair view in order to design audit procedures that are appropriate in the circumstances, but not for the purpose of expressing an opinion on the effectiveness of the entity's internal control."

29 In circumstances when the auditor also has responsibility to express an opinion on the effectiveness of internal control in conjunction with the audit of the financial report, this sentence would be worded as follows: "In making those risk assessments, the auditor considers internal control relevant to the entity's preparation and fair presentation of the financial report in order to design audit procedures that are appropriate in the circumstances." In the case of footnote 27, this may read: "In making those risk assessments, the auditor considers internal control relevant to the entity's preparation of the financial report that gives a true and fair view in order to design audit procedures that are appropriate in the circumstances."

[Auditor's signature]*

[Date of the auditor's report]#

[Auditor's address]

If, in the group engagement partner's judgement, the effect on the group financial report of the inability to obtain sufficient appropriate audit evidence is material and pervasive, the group engagement partner would disclaim an opinion in accordance with ASA 705.

Example Auditor's Report General Purpose Financial Report— Qualified Opinion *Corporations Act 2001* The group engagement team is not able to obtain sufficient appropriate audit evidence on which to base the group audit opinion

Illustration 1A:

Circumstances include the following:

- **Audit of a general purpose financial report prepared by management of the entity—the financial statements are prepared in accordance with Australian Accounting Standards.**
- **The financial report is prepared under the *Corporations Act 2001*.**
- **In this example, the group engagement team is unable to obtain sufficient appropriate audit evidence relating to a significant component accounted for by the equity method (recognised at $15 million in the balance sheet, which reflects total assets of $60 million) because the group engagement team did not have access to the accounting records, management, or auditor of the component.**
- **The group engagement team has read the audited financial report of the component as of 30June 20X1, including the auditor's report thereon, and considered related financial information kept by group management in relation to the component.**
- **In the group engagement partner's judgement, the effect on the group financial report of this inability to obtain sufficient appropriate audit evidence is material but not pervasive.**
- **In addition to the audit of the financial report, the auditor has other reporting responsibilities under section 308(3C) of the *Corporations Act 2001*.**

INDEPENDENT AUDITOR'S REPORT

[Appropriate Addressee]

Report on the Financial Report**

We have audited the accompanying financial report of ABC Company Ltd., which comprises the statements of financial position as at 30 June 20X1, the statements of comprehensive income, the statements of changes in equity and the statements of cash flows for the year then ended, notes comprising a summary of significant accounting policies and other explanatory information, and the directors' declaration of the company and the consolidated entity comprising the company [registered scheme/disclosing entity] and the entities it controlled at the year's end or from time to time during the financial year.

* The auditor's report needs to be signed in one or more of the following ways: name of the audit firm, the name of the audit company or the personal name of the auditor as appropriate.

\# The date of the auditor's report is the date the auditor signs the report.

** The sub-title "Report on the Financial Report" is unnecessary in circumstances when the second sub-title "Report on Other Legal and Regulatory Requirements", or other appropriate sub-title, is not applicable.

Directors' Responsibility for the Financial Report

The directors of the company [registered scheme/disclosing entity] are responsible for the preparation of the financial report that gives a true and fair view in accordance with Australian Accounting Standards and the *Corporations Act 2001* and for such internal control as the directors determine is necessary to enable the preparation of the financial report that is free from material misstatement, whether due to fraud or error.

Auditor's Responsibility

Our responsibility is to express an opinion on the financial report based on our audit. We conducted our audit in accordance with Australian Auditing Standards. Those standards require that we comply with relevant ethical requirements relating to audit engagements and plan and perform the audit to obtain reasonable assurance about whether the financial report is free from material misstatement.

An audit involves performing procedures to obtain audit evidence about the amounts and disclosures in the financial report. The procedures selected depend on the auditor's judgement, including the assessment of the risks of material misstatement of the financial report, whether due to fraud or error. In making those risk assessments, the auditor considers internal control relevant to the company's preparation and fair presentation of the financial report in order to design audit procedures that are appropriate in the circumstances, but not for the purpose of expressing an opinion on the effectiveness of the company's internal control. An audit also includes evaluating the appropriateness of accounting policies used and the reasonableness of accounting estimates made by the directors, as well as evaluating the overall presentation of the financial report.

We believe that the audit evidence we have obtained is sufficient and appropriate to provide a basis for our audit opinion.

Independence

In conducting our audit, we have complied with the independence requirements of the *Corporations Act 2001*. We confirm that the independence declaration required by the *Corporations Act 2001*, which has been given to the directors of ABC Company Ltd., would be in the same terms if given to the directors as at the time of this auditor's report.*

Basis for Qualified Opinion

ABC Company Ltd's investment in XYZ Entity, a foreign associate acquired during the year and accounted for by the equity method, is carried at $15 million on the consolidated statement of financial position as at 30 June 20X1, and ABC's share of XYZ's profit of $1 million is included in the consolidated statement of comprehensive income for the year then ended. We were unable to obtain sufficient appropriate audit evidence about the carrying amount of ABC's investment in XYZ as at 30 June 20X1 and ABC's share of XYZ's profit for the year because we were denied access to the financial information, management, and the auditors of XYZ. Consequently, we were unable to determine whether any adjustments to these amounts were necessary.

Qualified Opinion

In our opinion, except for the possible effects of the matter described in the Basis for Qualified Opinion paragraph, the financial report of ABC Company Ltd. is in accordance with the *Corporations Act 2001*, including:

(a) giving a true and fair view of the company's [registered scheme's / disclosing entity's] financial position as at 30 June 20X1 and of its performance for the year ended on that date; and

(b) complying with Australian Accounting Standards and the *Corporations Regulations 2001*.

---

* Or, alternatively, include statements (a) to the effect that circumstances have changed since the declaration was given to the relevant directors; and (b) setting out how the declaration would differ if it had been given to the relevant directors at the time the auditor's report was made.

Report on the Remuneration Report*

We have audited the Remuneration Report included in [paragraphs a to b or pages x to y] of the directors' report for the year [period] ended 30 June 20X1. The directors of the company are responsible for the preparation and presentation of the Remuneration Report in accordance with section 300A of the *Corporations Act 2001*. Our responsibility is to express an opinion on the Remuneration Report, based on our audit conducted in accordance with Australian Auditing Standards.

Opinion

In our opinion the Remuneration Report of ABC Company Ltd. for the year [period] ended 30 June 20X1, complies with section 300A of the *Corporations Act 2001*.

[Auditor's signature]#

[Date of the auditor's report]†

[Auditor's address]

ASA

Appendix 2

(Ref: Para. A23)

Examples of Matters about Which the Group Engagement Team Obtains an Understanding

The examples provided cover a broad range of matters; however, not all matters are relevant to every group audit engagement and the list of examples is not exhaustive.

Group-Wide Controls

1. Group-wide controls may include a combination of the following:
   - Regular meetings between group and component management to discuss business developments and to review performance.
   - Monitoring of components' operations and their financial results, including regular reporting routines, which enables group management to monitor components' performance against budgets, and to take appropriate action.
   - Group management's risk assessment process, that is, the process for identifying, analysing and managing business risks, including the risk of fraud, that may result in material misstatement of the group financial report.
   - Monitoring, controlling, reconciling, and eliminating intra-group transactions and unrealised profits, and intra-group account balances at group level.
   - A process for monitoring the timeliness and assessing the accuracy and completeness of financial information received from components.
   - A central IT system controlled by the same general IT controls for all or part of the group.
   - Control activities within an IT system that is common for all or some components.
   - Monitoring of controls, including activities of internal audit and self-assessment programs.

* The Report on the Remuneration Report is an example of "other reporting responsibilities"—see ASA 700, paragraphs 38 and 39. Any additional "other reporting responsibilities" that the auditor needs to address, will also be included in a separate section of the auditor's report following the opinion paragraph on the financial report. Under ASA 700, paragraph 38, the sub-title "Report on Other Legal and Regulatory Requirements" or other sub-title as appropriate to the section, is used.

\# The auditor's report needs to be signed in one or more of the following ways: name of the audit firm, the name of the audit company or the personal name of the auditor as appropriate.

† The date of the auditor's report is the date the auditor signs the report.

- Consistent policies and procedures, including a group financial reporting procedures manual.
- Group-wide programs, such as codes of conduct and fraud prevention programs.
- Arrangements for assigning authority and responsibility to component management.

2. Internal audit may be regarded as part of group-wide controls, for example, when the internal audit function is centralised. ASA 610[30] deals with the group engagement team's evaluation of the competence and objectivity of the internal auditors where it plans to use their work.

Consolidation Process

3. The group engagement team's understanding of the consolidation process may include matters such as the following:

   Matters relating to the applicable financial reporting framework:

   - The extent to which component management has an understanding of the applicable financial reporting framework.
   - The process for identifying and accounting for components in accordance with the applicable financial reporting framework.
   - The process for identifying reportable segments for segment reporting in accordance with the applicable financial reporting framework.
   - The process for identifying related party relationships and related party transactions for reporting in accordance with the applicable financial reporting framework.
   - The accounting policies applied to the group financial report, changes from those of the previous financial year, and changes resulting from new or revised standards under the applicable financial reporting framework.
   - The procedures for dealing with components with financial year-ends different from the group's year-end.

   Matters relating to the consolidation process:

   - Group management's process for obtaining an understanding of the accounting policies used by components, and, where applicable, ensuring that uniform accounting policies are used to prepare the financial information of the components for the group financial report, and that differences in accounting policies are identified, and adjusted where required in terms of the applicable financial reporting framework. Uniform accounting policies are the specific principles, bases, conventions, rules, and practices adopted by the group, based on the applicable financial reporting framework, that the components use to report similar transactions consistently. These policies are ordinarily described in the financial reporting procedures manual and reporting package issued by group management.
   - Group management's process for ensuring complete, accurate and timely financial reporting by the components for the consolidation.
   - The process for translating the financial information of foreign components into the currency of the group financial report.
   - How IT is organised for the consolidation, including the manual and automated stages of the process, and the manual and programmed controls in place at various stages of the consolidation process.
   - Group management's process for obtaining information on subsequent events.

   Matters relating to consolidation adjustments:

   - The process for recording consolidation adjustments, including the preparation, authorisation and processing of related journal entries, and the experience of personnel responsible for the consolidation.

30 See ASA 610 *Using the Work of Internal Auditors*, paragraph 9.

- The consolidation adjustments required by the applicable financial reporting framework.
- Business rationale for the events and transactions that gave rise to the consolidation adjustments.
- Frequency, nature and size of transactions between components.
- Procedures for monitoring, controlling, reconciling and eliminating intra-group transactions and unrealised profits, and intra-group account balances.
- Steps taken to arrive at the fair value of acquired assets and liabilities, procedures for amortising goodwill (where applicable), and impairment testing of goodwill, in accordance with the applicable financial reporting framework.
- Arrangements with a majority owner or minority interests regarding losses incurred by a component (for example, an obligation of the minority interest to make good such losses).

Appendix 3

(Ref: Para. A30)

Examples of Conditions or Events that May Indicate Risks of Material Misstatement of the Group Financial Report

The examples provided cover a broad range of conditions or events; however, not all conditions or events are relevant to every group audit engagement and the list of examples is not exhaustive.

- A complex group structure, especially where there are frequent acquisitions, disposals or reorganisations.
- Poor corporate governance structures, including decision-making processes, that are not transparent.
- Non-existent or ineffective group-wide controls, including inadequate group management information on monitoring of components' operations and their results.
- Components operating in foreign jurisdictions that may be exposed to factors such as unusual government intervention in areas such as trade and fiscal policy, and restrictions on currency and dividend movements; and fluctuations in exchange rates.
- Business activities of components that involve high risk, such as long-term contracts or trading in innovative or complex financial instruments.
- Uncertainties regarding which components' financial information require incorporation in the group financial report in accordance with the applicable financial reporting framework, for example whether any special-purpose entities or non-trading entities exist and require incorporation.
- Unusual related party relationships and transactions.
- Prior occurrences of intra-group account balances that did not balance or reconcile on consolidation.
- The existence of complex transactions that are accounted for in more than one component.
- Components' application of accounting policies that differ from those applied to the group financial report.
- Components with different financial year-ends, which may be utilised to manipulate the timing of transactions.
- Prior occurrences of unauthorised or incomplete consolidation adjustments.
- Aggressive tax planning within the group, or large cash transactions with entities in tax havens.
- Frequent changes of auditors engaged to audit the financial report of components.

Appendix 4
(Ref: Para. A35)

Examples of a Component Auditor's Confirmations

The following is not intended to be a standard letter. Confirmations may vary from one component auditor to another and from one period to the next.

Confirmations often are obtained before work on the financial information of the component commences.

[Component Auditor Letterhead]

[Date]

[To Group Engagement Partner]

This letter is provided in connection with your audit of the group financial report of [name of parent] for the year ended [date] for the purpose of expressing an opinion on whether the group financial report presents fairly, in all material respects (or *gives a true and fair view of*) the financial position of the group as of [date] and [*of*] its financial performance and cash flows for the year then ended in accordance with [indicate applicable financial reporting framework].

We acknowledge receipt of your instructions dated [date], requesting us to perform the specified work on the financial information of [name of component] for the year ended [date].

We confirm that:

1. We will be able to comply with the instructions. / We advise you that we will not be able to comply with the following instructions [specify instructions] for the following reasons [specify reasons].
2. The instructions are clear and we understand them. / We would appreciate it if you could clarify the following instructions [specify instructions].
3. We will co-operate with you and provide you with access to relevant audit documentation.

We acknowledge that:

1. The financial information of [name of component] will be included in the group financial report of [name of parent].
2. You may consider it necessary to be involved in the work you have requested us to perform on the financial information of [name of component] for the year ended [date].
3. You intend to evaluate and, if considered appropriate, use our work for the audit of the group financial report of [name of parent].

In connection with the work that we will perform on the financial information of [name of component], a [describe component, for example, wholly-owned subsidiary, subsidiary, joint venture, investee accounted for by the equity or cost methods of accounting] of [name of parent], we confirm the following:

1. We have an understanding of [indicate relevant ethical requirements] that is sufficient to fulfill our responsibilities in the audit of the group financial reports, and will comply therewith. In particular, and with respect to [name of parent] and the other components in the group, we are independent within the meaning of [indicate relevant ethical requirements] and comply with the applicable requirements of [refer to rules] promulgated by [name of regulatory agency].
2. We have an understanding of Australian Auditing Standards and [indicate other national standards applicable to the audit of the group financial report] that is sufficient to fulfill our responsibilities in the audit of the group financial report and will conduct our work on the financial information of [name of component] for the year ended [date] in accordance with those standards.

3. We possess the special skills (for example, industry specific knowledge) necessary to perform the work on the financial information of the particular component.
4. We have an understanding of [indicate applicable financial reporting framework or group financial reporting procedures manual] that is sufficient to fulfill our responsibilities in the audit of the group financial report.

We will inform you of any changes in the above representations during the course of our work on the financial information of [name of component].

[Auditor's signature]

[Date]

[Auditor's address]

Appendix 5

(Ref: Para. A58)

Required and Additional Matters Included in the Group Engagement Team's Letter of Instruction

Matters required by this Auditing Standard to be communicated to the component auditor are shown in italicised text.

Matters that are relevant to the planning of the work of the component auditor:

- *A request for the component auditor, knowing the context in which the group engagement team will use the work of the component auditor, to confirm that the component auditor will co-operate with the group engagement team.*
- The timetable for completing the audit.
- Dates of planned visits by group management and the group engagement team, and dates of planned meetings with component management and the component auditor.
- A list of key contacts.
- *The work to be performed by the component auditor, the use to be made of that work,* and arrangements for coordinating efforts at the initial stage of and during the audit, including the group engagement team's planned involvement in the work of the component auditor.
- *The ethical requirements that are relevant to the group audit and, in particular, the independence requirements.*
- *In the case of an audit or review of the financial information of the component, component materiality (and, if applicable, the materiality level or levels for particular classes of transactions, account balances or disclosures), and the threshold above which misstatements cannot be regarded as clearly trivial to the group financial report.*
- *A list of related parties prepared by group management, and any other related parties that the group engagement team is aware of, and a request that the component auditor communicates on a timely basis to the group engagement team related parties not previously identified by group management or the group engagement team.*
- Work to be performed on intra-group transactions and unrealised profits and intra-group account balances.
- Guidance on other statutory reporting responsibilities, for example reporting on group management's assertion on the effectiveness of internal control.
- Where time lag between completion of the work on the financial information of the components and the group engagement team's conclusion on the group financial report is likely, specific instructions for a subsequent events review.

Matters that are relevant to the conduct of the work of the component auditor:

- The findings of the group engagement team's tests of control activities of a processing system that is common for all or some components, and tests of controls to be performed by the component auditor.
- *Identified significant risks of material misstatement of the group financial report, due to fraud or error, that are relevant to the work of the component auditor, and a request that the component auditor communicates on a timely basis any other significant risks of material misstatement of the group financial report, due to fraud or error, identified in the component and the component auditor's response to such risks.*
- The findings of internal audit, based on work performed on controls at or relevant to components.
- A request for timely communication of audit evidence obtained from performing work on the financial information of the components that contradicts the audit evidence on which the group engagement team originally based the risk assessment performed at group level.
- A request for a written representation on component management's compliance with the applicable financial reporting framework, or a statement that differences between the accounting policies applied to the financial information of the component and those applied to the group financial report have been disclosed.
- Matters to be documented by the component auditor.

Other information

- A request that the following be reported to the group engagement team on a timely basis:
  - Significant accounting, financial reporting and auditing matters, including accounting estimates and related judgements.
  - Matters relating to the going concern status of the component.
  - Matters relating to litigation and claims.
  - Significant deficiencies in internal in control that the component auditor has identified during the performance of the work on the financial information of the component, and information that indicates the existence of fraud.
- A request that the group engagement team be notified of any significant or unusual events as early as possible.
- *A request that the matters listed in paragraph 41 be communicated to the group engagement team when the work on the financial information of the component is completed.*

ASA 610

Using the Work of Internal Auditors

(Reissued October 2009)

Issued by the Auditing and Assurance Standards Board.

Note from the Institute of Chartered Accountants Australia

This note, prepared by the technical editor, is not part of ASA 610.

Historical development

February 1977: Statement of Auditing Practice AUP 2 first issued in, and effective from, February 1977 as CP 2 'Internal Audit as it Affects the External Auditor'. Reissued, without amendment, as AUP 2 in August 1979.

January 1983: Reissued, following extensive revisions, as AUP 2 'Using the Work of an Internal Auditor', effective from date of issue. The relevant IFAC publication was IAG 10 which was issued in July 1982.

December 1993: ED 53 'Codification and Revision of Auditing Pronouncements: AUS 604 Considering the Work of Internal Audit (AUP 2)' issued by the AuSB.

June 1994: The International Auditing Practices Committee (IAPC) of the International Federation of Accountants (IFAC) approved the issuance of a codified set of International Standards of Auditing (ISAs). The relevant international pronouncement was ISA 610 'Considering the Work of Internal Auditing'.

October 1995: Australian Auditing Standards and Auditing Guidance Statements released. The status of these was explained in APS 1.1 'Conformity With Auditing Standards'. These Standards became operative for the first reporting period commencing on or after 1 July 1996 and later reporting periods, although earlier application was encouraged. AUP 2 'Using the Work of an Internal Auditor' replaced by AUS 604 'Considering the Work of Internal Auditing'.

April 2006: ASA 610 'Considering the Work of Internal Audit' was issued as a legally enforceable Standard to replace AUS 604. It is based on ISA 610 of the same name.

October 2009: ASA 610 'Using the Work of Internal Auditors' reissued as part of the AUASB's Clarity Project. It is based on the redrafted ISA 610 of the same name.

March 2012: ISA 610 'Using the Work of Internal Auditors' reissued. These changes have not been adopted in Australia, pending the International Ethical Standards Board for Accountants' deliberations on internal auditors providing direct assistance during the audit.

Contents

Preface

Reasons for Issuing Auditing Standard ASA 610 *Using the Work of Internal Auditors*

The Auditing and Assurance Standards Board (AUASB) issues Auditing Standard ASA 610 *Using the Work of Internal Auditors* pursuant to the requirements of the legislative provisions and the Strategic Direction explained below.

The AUASB is an independent statutory board of the Australian Government established under section 227A of the *Australian Securities and Investments Commission Act 2001*, as amended (ASIC Act). Under section 336 of the *Corporations Act 2001*, the AUASB may make Auditing Standards for the purposes of the corporations legislation. These Auditing Standards are legislative instruments under the *Legislative Instruments Act 2003*.

Under the Strategic Direction given to the AUASB by the Financial Reporting Council (FRC), the AUASB is required to have regard to any programme initiated by the International Auditing and Assurance Standards Board (IAASB) for the revision and enhancement of the International Standards on Auditing (ISAs) and to make appropriate consequential amendments to the Australian Auditing Standards. Accordingly, the AUASB has decided to revise and redraft the Australian Auditing Standards using the equivalent redrafted ISAs.

Main Features

This Auditing Standard establishes requirements and provides application and other explanatory material relating to the auditor's responsibilities in respect of the work of internal auditors where they have determined it is relevant to the external auditor.

This Auditing Standard:

(a) describes the relationship between the internal audit function and external audit;

(b) requires the external auditor to assess the internal audit function, and to determine the extent of planned reliance on the work performed; and

(c) requires the external auditor to document the conclusions reached on the work of internal audit, and the audit procedures performed by the external auditor on that work.

Authority Statement

The Auditing and Assurance Standards Board (AUASB) makes this Auditing Standard ASA 610 *Using the Work of Internal Auditors* pursuant to section 227B of the *Australian Securities and Investments Commission Act 2001* and section 336 of the *Corporations Act 2001*.

This Auditing Standard is to be read in conjunction with ASA 101 *Preamble to Australian Auditing Standards*, which sets out the intentions of the AUASB on how the Australian Auditing Standards, operative for financial reporting periods commencing, on or after 1 January 2010, are to be understood, interpreted and applied. This Auditing Standard is to be read also in conjunction with ASA 200 *Overall Objectives of the Independent Auditor and the Conduct of the Audit in Accordance with Australian Auditing Standards*.

Dated: 27 October 2009

M H Kelsall
Chairman - AUASB

Auditing Standard ASA 610
Using the Work of Internal Auditors

Application

Aus 0.1 This Auditing Standard applies to:

(a) an audit of a financial report for a financial year, or an audit of a financial report for a half-year, in accordance with the *Corporations Act 2001*; and

(b) an audit of a financial report, or a complete set of financial statements, for any other purpose.

Aus 0.2 This Auditing Standard also applies, as appropriate, to an audit of other historical financial information.

Operative Date

Aus 0.3 This Auditing Standard is operative for financial reporting periods commencing on or after 1 January 2010.

Introduction

Scope of this Auditing Standard

1. This Auditing Standard deals with the auditor's responsibilities relating to the work of internal auditors when the external auditor has determined, in accordance with ASA 315,[1] that the internal audit function is likely to be relevant to the audit. (Ref: Para. A1-A2)

2. This Auditing Standard does not deal with instances when individual internal auditors provide direct assistance to the external auditor in carrying out audit procedures.

Relationship between the Internal Audit Function and the External Auditor

3. The objectives of the internal audit function are determined by management and, where applicable, those charged with governance.

While the objectives of the internal audit function and the external auditor are different, some of the ways in which the internal audit function and the external auditor achieve their respective objectives may be similar. (Ref: Para. A3)

1 See ASA 315 *Identifying and Assessing the Risks of Material Misstatement through Understanding the Entity and Its Environment*, paragraph 23.

4. Irrespective of the degree of autonomy and objectivity of the internal audit function, such function is not independent of the entity as is required of the external auditor when expressing an opinion on the financial report. The external auditor has sole responsibility for the audit opinion expressed, and that responsibility is not reduced by the external auditor's use of the work of the internal auditors.

Effective Date

5. [Deleted by the AUASB. Refer Aus 0.3]

Objectives

6. The objectives of the external auditor, where the entity has an internal audit function that the external auditor has determined is likely to be relevant to the audit are:

   (a) To determine whether, and to what extent, to use specific work of the internal auditors; and

   (b) If using the specific work of the internal auditors, to determine whether that work is adequate for the purposes of the audit.

Definitions

7. For purposes of the Australian Auditing Standards, the following terms have the meanings attributed below:

   (a) Internal audit function means an appraisal activity established or provided as a service to the entity. Its functions include, amongst other things, examining, evaluating and monitoring the adequacy and effectiveness of internal control.

   (b) Internal auditors means those individuals who perform the activities of the internal audit function. Internal auditors may belong to an internal audit department or equivalent function.

Requirements

Determining Whether and to What Extent to Use the Work of the Internal Auditors

8. The external auditor shall determine:

   (a) Whether the work of the internal auditors is likely to be adequate for purposes of the audit; and

   (b) If so, the planned effect of the work of the internal auditors on the nature, timing or extent of the external auditor's procedures.

9. In determining whether the work of the internal auditors is likely to be adequate for purposes of the audit, the external auditor shall evaluate:

   (a) The objectivity of the internal audit function;

   (b) The technical competence of the internal auditors;

   (c) Whether the work of the internal auditors is likely to be carried out with due professional care; and

   (d) Whether there is likely to be effective communication between the internal auditors and the external auditor. (Ref: Para. A4)

10. In determining the planned effect of the work of the internal auditors on the nature, timing or extent of the external auditor's procedures, the external auditor shall consider:

   (a) The nature and scope of specific work performed, or to be performed, by the internal auditors;

   (b) The assessed risks of material misstatement at the assertion level for particular classes of transactions, account balances, and disclosures; and

   (c) The degree of subjectivity involved in the evaluation of the audit evidence gathered by the internal auditors in support of the relevant assertions. (Ref: Para. A5)

Using Specific Work of the Internal Auditors

11. In order for the external auditor to use specific work of the internal auditors, the external auditor shall evaluate and perform audit procedures on that work to determine its adequacy for the external auditor's purposes. (Ref: Para. A6)

12. To determine the adequacy of specific work performed by the internal auditors for the external auditor's purposes, the external auditor shall evaluate whether:

    (a) The work was performed by internal auditors having adequate technical training and proficiency;

    (b) The work was properly supervised, reviewed and documented;

    (c) Adequate audit evidence has been obtained to enable the internal auditors to draw reasonable conclusions;

    (d) Conclusions reached are appropriate in the circumstances and any reports prepared by the internal auditors are consistent with the results of the work performed; and

    (e) Any exceptions or unusual matters disclosed by the internal auditors are properly resolved.

Documentation

13. If the external auditor uses specific work of the internal auditors, the external auditor shall include in the audit documentation the conclusions reached regarding the evaluation of the adequacy of the work of the internal auditors, and the audit procedures performed by the external auditor on that work, in accordance with paragraph 11 of this Auditing Standard.[2]

❖ ❖ ❖

Application and Other Explanatory Material

Scope of this Auditing Standard (Ref: Para. 1)

A1. As described in ASA 315,[3] the entity's internal audit function is likely to be relevant to the audit if the nature of the internal audit function's responsibilities and activities are related to the entity's financial reporting, and the auditor expects to use the work of the internal auditors to modify the nature or timing, or reduce the extent, of audit procedures to be performed.

A2. Carrying out procedures in accordance with this Auditing Standard may cause the external auditor to re-evaluate the external auditor's assessment of the risks of material misstatement. Consequently, this may affect the external auditor's determination of the relevance of the internal audit function to the audit. Similarly, the external auditor may decide not to otherwise use the work of the internal auditors to affect the nature, timing or extent of the external auditor's procedures. In such circumstances, the external auditor's further application of this Auditing Standard may not be necessary.

Objectives of the Internal Audit Function (Ref: Para. 3)

A3. The objectives of internal audit functions vary widely and depend on the size and structure of the entity and the requirements of management and, where applicable, those charged with governance. The activities of the internal audit function may include one or more of the following:

- Monitoring of internal control. The internal audit function may be assigned specific responsibility for reviewing controls, monitoring their operation and recommending improvements thereto.
- Examination of financial and operating information. The internal audit function may be assigned to review the means used to identify, measure, classify and report financial and operating information, and to make specific enquiry into individual items, including detailed testing of transactions, balances and procedures.

2 See ASA 230 *Audit Documentation*, paragraphs 8-11 and paragraph A6.

3 See ASA 315, paragraph A101.

- Review of operating activities. The internal audit function may be assigned to review the economy, efficiency and effectiveness of operating activities, including non-financial activities of an entity.
- Review of compliance with laws and regulations. The internal audit function may be assigned to review compliance with laws, regulations and other external requirements, and with management policies and directives and other internal requirements.
- Risk management. The internal audit function may assist the organisation by identifying and evaluating significant exposures to risk and contributing to the improvement of risk management and control systems.
- Governance. The internal audit function may assess the governance process in its accomplishment of objectives on ethics and values, performance management and accountability, communicating risk and control information to appropriate areas of the organisation and effectiveness of communication among those charged with governance, external and internal auditors, and management.

Determining Whether and to What Extent to Use the Work of the Internal Auditors

Whether the Work of the Internal Auditors Is Likely to Be Adequate for Purposes of the Audit (Ref: Para. 9)

A4. Factors that may affect the external auditor's determination of whether the work of the internal auditors is likely to be adequate for the purposes of the audit include:

Objectivity

- The status of the internal audit function within the entity and the effect such status has on the ability of the internal auditors to be objective.
- Whether the internal audit function reports to those charged with governance or an officer with appropriate authority, and whether the internal auditors have direct access to those charged with governance.
- Whether the internal auditors are free of any conflicting responsibilities.
- Whether those charged with governance oversee employment decisions related to the internal audit function.
- Whether there are any constraints or restrictions placed on the internal audit function by management or those charged with governance.
- Whether, and to what extent, management acts on the recommendations of the internal audit function, and how such action is evidenced.

Technical competence

- Whether the internal auditors are members of relevant professional bodies.
- Whether the internal auditors have adequate technical training and proficiency as internal auditors.
- Whether there are established policies for hiring and training internal auditors.

Due professional care

- Whether activities of the internal audit function are properly planned, supervised, reviewed and documented.
- The existence and adequacy of audit manuals or other similar documents, work programs and internal audit documentation.

Communication

Communication between the external auditor and the internal auditors may be most effective when the internal auditors are free to communicate openly with the external auditors, and:

- Meetings are held at appropriate intervals throughout the period;
- The external auditor is advised of, and has access to, relevant internal audit reports and is informed of any significant matters that come to the attention of the internal auditors when such matters may affect the work of the external auditor; and

- The external auditor informs the internal auditors of any significant matters that may affect the internal audit function.

Aus A4.1 An illustrative example questionnaire is included in [Aus] Appendix 1, to assist the external auditor in obtaining an understanding and making a preliminary assessment of the internal audit function.

Planned Effect of the Work of the Internal Auditors on the Nature, Timing or Extent of the External Auditor's Procedures (Ref: Para. 10)

A5. Where the work of the internal auditors is to be a factor in determining the nature, timing or extent of the external auditor's procedures, it may be useful to agree in advance the following matters with the internal auditors:

- The timing of such work;
- The extent of audit coverage;
- Materiality for the financial report as a whole (and, if applicable, materiality level or levels for particular classes of transactions, account balances or disclosures), and performance materiality;
- Proposed methods of item selection;
- Documentation of the work performed; and
- Review and reporting procedures.

Using Specific Work of the Internal Auditors (Ref: Para. 11)

A6. The nature, timing and extent of the audit procedures performed on specific work of the internal auditors will depend on the external auditor's assessment of the risk of material misstatement, the evaluation of the internal audit function, and the evaluation of the specific work of the internal auditors. Such audit procedures may include:

- *Examination of items already examined by the internal auditors;*
- *Examination of other similar items; and*
- *Observation of procedures performed by the internal auditors.*

❖ ❖ ❖

Conformity with International Standards on Auditing

This Auditing Standard conforms with International Standard on Auditing ISA 610 *Using the Work of Internal Auditors*, issued by the International Auditing and Assurance Standards Board (IAASB), an independent standard-setting board of the International Federation of Accountants (IFAC).

Paragraphs that have been added to this Auditing Standard (and do not appear in the text of the equivalent ISA) are identified with the prefix "Aus".

Compliance with this Auditing Standard enables compliance with ISA 610.

[Aus] Appendix 1

(Ref: Para. Aus A4.1)

Illustrative Example Questionnaire – Obtaining an understanding of, and making a preliminary assessment of, the internal audit function

The following illustrative questionnaire provides a broad range of questions related to the external auditor obtaining an understanding of, and making a preliminary assessment of, the internal audit function. Not all questions are necessarily relevant to every audit or review engagement, and the questionnaire is not intended to be exhaustive.

The answers to the following questions may assist in obtaining an understanding and making a preliminary assessment of the internal audit function.

Questionnaire	Yes	No	N/A
Organisational Status			
1. To whom does the head of internal audit report, and is this appropriate?			
2. Do those charged with governance and/or management's view of internal audit appear not to limit internal audit?			
3. Is the head of internal audit free from:			
(a) The influences of operational management which would impact on the head of internal audit's objectivity?			
(b) Any operating responsibility?			
4. Does the head of internal audit have:			
(a) Direct access (as required) to:			
(i) The governing body?			
(ii) The chairman of the governing body?			
(iii) The chief executive?			
(iv) The audit committee (if applicable)?			
(b) Freedom/flexibility from direct instruction from those charged with governance as to the scope and direction of audit activity?			
(c) Freedom to communicate with the external auditor on relevant matters on a regular basis?			
(If the answer to any of questions 3(a) to (b), or 4(a) to (c) is negative, describe how objectivity is achieved and maintained).			
Scope of Function			
5. (a) Does internal audit regularly examine the controls over all significant accounting operations which affect the financial report? (If not, describe the areas not covered by internal audit).			
(b) Does the head of internal audit have flexibility to act using discretion on suggestions made by the external auditor as to areas to be included in the internal audit program?			
(c) Do internal audit reports and working papers indicate that internal audit applies a professional approach to audit assignments?			
(d) Has past experience shown that internal audit has been able to complete previous internal audit programs?			

Questionnaire	Yes	No	N/A
6. (a) (i) Do internal audit reports identify weaknesses or problems, and contain recommendations for improvements?			
(ii) Are such reports addressed to the appropriate level of those charged with governance who are capable and able to achieve satisfactory audit results?			
(iii) Are copies of all reports forwarded to:			
• the chairman of the governing body or chief executive? and/or			
• the audit committee (if applicable)?			
(b) Are copies of all reports relating to accounting and associated records available to the external auditor?			
(If 6(a) or (b) are answered in the negative, describe the method of reporting).			
7. (a) Is there evidence, for example in the minutes of governing body and/or audit committee meetings, that internal audit reports have been considered?			
(b) Is there evidence that a person of senior authority, for example the chief executive, has taken action to see that internal audit recommendations are properly considered?			
(If the answer to 7(a) or (b) is negative, describe the process for ensuring that consideration is given to internal audit reports and recommendations).			
Technical Competence			
8. Is the head of internal audit a professionally trained auditor? (If not, describe qualifications by training and by experience for the position held).			
9. (a) Do the entity's hiring and/or internal promotion/transfer policies for internal audit require:			
(i) Tertiary qualifications?			
(ii) Formal professional qualifications?			
(iii) Previous internal audit experience?			
(b) Does the entity provide internal audit staff with the opportunity to maintain professional competence, for example by encouraging:			
(i) Internal staff training?			
(ii) Attendance at external training and professional courses?			
10. Do assignments undertaken reflect that those charged with governance have confidence in internal audit, and provide experience in audit related work?			
11. Do the reports prepared by internal audit reflect a clear understanding of the audit task undertaken and the expression of valid conclusions?			
12. If the entity has a large internal audit function, does it contain an adequate proportion of professionally trained/experienced auditors?			

ASA

Questionnaire	Yes	No	N/A
Due Professional Care			
13. (a) Does internal audit have a procedures manual clearly describing staff responsibilities and audit procedures concerning documentation?			
(b) Is the work of internal audit controlled and supervised through managers or supervisors responsible to the head of the department, each of whom supervises the work of staff allocated?			
14. (a) Does internal audit use written audit programs prepared in conformity with appropriate professional standards and practice?			
(b) Are comprehensive audit programs prepared for all internal audit engagements?			
15. (a) Does internal audit prepare working papers to record work done and conclusions drawn?			
(b) Are the working papers reviewed by appropriate internal audit staff?			
16. Where the internal audit activity is co-sourced or fully outsourced, is the relationship between the entity and the third party provider appropriate and well managed?			

(If the answer to any of questions 13 to 16 is negative describe the process used for planning, supervising, reviewing and documenting internal audit work).

ASA 620

Using the Work of an Auditor's Expert

(Reissued October 2009)

Issued by the Auditing and Assurance Standards Board.

Note from the Institute of Chartered Accountants Australia

This note, prepared by the technical editor, is not part of ASA 620.

Historical development

June 1985: Statement of Auditing Practice AUP 22 'Using the Work of an Expert' issued in, and effective from, June 1985 following the issue of ED 11 (IAPC ED 19) in July 1983 and ED 16 in June 1984. The Appendix to AUP 22 was, however, additional to IAG 18. The relevant IAPC publication was IAG 18 which was issued in February 1985.

May 1994: ED 55 'Codification and Revision of Auditing Pronouncements: AUS 606 Using the Work of an Expert (AUP 22)' issued by the AuSB.

June 1994: The International Auditing Practices Committee (IAPC) of the International Federation of Accountants (IFAC) approved the issuance of a codified set of International Standards of Auditing (ISAs) in June 1994. The relevant international pronouncement was ISA 620 'Using the Work of an Expert'.

October 1995: Australian Auditing Standards and Auditing Guidance Statements released. The status of these was explained in APS 1.1 'Conformity With Auditing Standards'. These Standards became operative for the first reporting period commencing on or after 1 July 1996 and later reporting periods, although earlier application was encouraged. AUP 22 'Using the Work of an Expert' replaced by AUS 606 'Using the Work of an Expert'.

July 2002: AUS/AGS Omnibus 3 'Miscellaneous Amendments to AUSs and AGSs' issued by the AuASB, operative from the date of issue. AUS 606 since reissued by the Board to incorporate these amendments.

April 2006: ASA 620 was issued as a legally enforceable Standard to replace AUS 606. It is based on ISA 620 of the same name.

October 2009: ASA 620 reissued as part of the AUASB's Clarity Project. For the first time the Standard differentiates between the auditor's expert and management's expert. It is based on the revised ISA 620 of the same name.

Contents

Preface

Reasons for Issuing Auditing Standard ASA 620 *Using the Work of an Auditor's Expert*

The Auditing and Assurance Standards Board (AUASB) is proposing to re-issue Auditing Standard ASA 620 *Using the Work of an Auditor's Expert* pursuant to the requirements of the legislative provisions and the Strategic Direction explained below.

The AUASB is an independent statutory board of the Australian Government established under section 227A of the *Australian Securities and Investments Commission Act 2001*, as amended (ASIC Act). Under section 336 of the *Corporations Act 2001*, the AUASB may make Australian Auditing Standards for the purposes of the corporations legislation. These Auditing Standards are legislative instruments under the *Legislative Instruments Act 2003*.

Under the Strategic Direction given to the AUASB by the Financial Reporting Council (FRC), the AUASB is required to have regard to any programme initiated by the International Auditing and Assurance Standards Board (IAASB) for the revision and enhancement of the International Standards on Auditing (ISAs) and to make appropriate consequential amendments to the Australian Auditing Standards. Accordingly, the AUASB has decided to revise and redraft the Australian Auditing Standards using the equivalent redrafted ISAs.

Main Features

This Auditing Standard establishes requirements and provides application and other explanatory material relating to the work of an individual or organisation in a field of expertise other than accounting or auditing, when that work is used to assist the auditor in obtaining sufficient appropriate audit evidence.

This Auditing Standard requires the auditor to determine whether to use the work of an auditor's expert, where such expertise is necessary to obtain sufficient appropriate audit evidence, and:

(a) describes how the nature, timing and extent of audit procedures performed will vary depending on the circumstances of the audit engagement;

(b) requires the auditor to evaluate whether the auditor's expert has the necessary competence, capabilities and objectivity for the auditor's purposes;

(c) requires the auditor to obtain a sufficient understanding of the field of expertise of the auditor's expert to enable the auditor to:

  (i) determine the work to be performed by the expert; and

  (ii) evaluate the adequacy of that work for the auditor's purposes;

(d) requires the auditor to agree certain matters with the auditor's expert in respect of the work to be performed;

(e) requires the auditor to evaluate the adequacy of specific aspects of the expert's work; and

(f) describes the auditor's responsibilities when referring to the auditor's expert in the auditor's report.

Authority Statement

The Auditing and Assurance Standards Board (AUASB) makes this Auditing Standard ASA 620 *Using the Work of an Auditor's Expert* pursuant to section 227B of the *Australian Securities and Investments Commission Act 2001* and section 336 of the *Corporations Act 2001*.

This Auditing Standard is to be read in conjunction with ASA 101 *Preamble to Australian Auditing Standards*, which sets out the intentions of the AUASB on how the Australian Auditing Standards, operative for financial reporting periods commencing on or after 1 January 2010, are to be understood, interpreted and applied. This Auditing Standard is to be read also in conjunction with ASA 200 *Overall Objectives of the Independent Auditor and the Conduct of an Audit in Accordance with Australian Auditing Standards*.

Dated: 27 October 2009

M H Kelsall
Chairman - AUASB

Auditing Standard ASA 620

Using the Work of an Auditor's Expert

Application

Aus 0.1 This Auditing Standard applies to:

(a) an audit of a financial report for a financial year, or an audit of a financial report for a half-year, in accordance with the *Corporations Act 2001*; and

(b) an audit of a financial report, or a complete set of financial statements, for any other purpose.

Aus 0.2 This Auditing Standard also applies, as appropriate, to an audit of other historical financial information.

Operative Date

Aus 0.3 This Auditing Standard is operative for financial reporting periods commencing on or after 1 January 2010.

Introduction

Scope of this Auditing Standard

1. This Auditing Standard deals with the auditor's responsibilities relating to the work of an individual or organisation in a field of expertise other than accounting or auditing, when that work is used to assist the auditor in obtaining sufficient appropriate audit evidence.

2. This Auditing Standard does not deal with:

   (a) Situations where the engagement team includes a member, or consults an individual or organisation, with expertise in a specialised area of accounting or auditing, which are dealt with in ASA 220;[1] or

   (b) The auditor's use of the work of an individual or organisation possessing expertise in a field other than accounting or auditing, whose work in that field is used by the entity to assist the entity in preparing the financial report (a management's expert), which is dealt with in ASA 500.[2]

The Auditor's Responsibility for the Audit Opinion

3. The auditor has sole responsibility for the audit opinion expressed, and that responsibility is not reduced by the auditor's use of the work of an auditor's expert. Nonetheless, if the auditor using the work of an auditor's expert, having followed this Auditing Standard, concludes that the work of that expert is adequate for the auditor's purposes, the auditor may accept that expert's findings or conclusions in the expert's field as appropriate audit evidence.

Effective Date

4. [Deleted by the AUASB. Refer Aus 0.3]

Objectives

5. The objectives of the auditor are:

   (a) To determine whether to use the work of an auditor's expert; and

   (b) If using the work of an auditor's expert, to determine whether that work is adequate for the auditor's purposes.

Definitions

6. For purposes of the Australian Auditing Standards, the following terms have the meanings attributed below:

   (a) Auditor's expert means an individual or organisation possessing expertise in a field other than accounting or auditing, whose work in that field is used by the auditor to assist the auditor in obtaining sufficient appropriate audit evidence. An auditor's expert may be either an auditor's internal expert (who is a partner[3] or staff, including temporary staff, of the auditor's firm or a network firm), or an auditor's external expert. (Ref: Para. A1-A3)

Aus 6.1 "Partner" and "firm" should be read as referring to their public sector equivalents where relevant.

   (b) Expertise means skills, knowledge and experience in a particular field.

   (c) Management's expert means an individual or organisation possessing expertise in a field other than accounting or auditing, whose work in that field is used by the entity to assist the entity in preparing the financial report.

---

1 See ASA 220 *Quality Control for an Audit of a Financial Report and Other Historical Financial Information*, paragraphs A10, A20-A22.

2 See ASA 500 *Audit Evidence*, paragraphs A34-A48.

3 [Footnote deleted by the AUASB. Refer Aus 6.1]

Requirements

Determining the Need for an Auditor's Expert

7. If expertise in a field other than accounting or auditing is necessary to obtain sufficient appropriate audit evidence, the auditor shall determine whether to use the work of an auditor's expert. (Ref: Para. A4-A9)

Nature, Timing and Extent of Audit Procedures

8. The nature, timing and extent of the auditor's procedures with respect to the requirements in paragraphs 9-13 of this Auditing Standard will vary depending on the circumstances. In determining the nature, timing and extent of those procedures, the auditor shall consider matters including: (Ref: Para. A10)
   (a) The nature of the matter to which that expert's work relates;
   (b) The risks of material misstatement in the matter to which that expert's work relates;
   (c) The significance of that expert's work in the context of the audit;
   (d) The auditor's knowledge of and experience with previous work performed by that expert; and
   (e) Whether that expert is subject to the auditor's firm's quality control policies and procedures. (Ref: Para. A11-A13)

ASA

The Competence, Capabilities and Objectivity of the Auditor's Expert

9. The auditor shall evaluate whether the auditor's expert has the necessary competence, capabilities and objectivity for the auditor's purposes. In the case of an auditor's external expert, the evaluation of objectivity shall include enquiry regarding interests and relationships that may create a threat to that expert's objectivity. (Ref: Para. A14-A20)

Obtaining an Understanding of the Field of Expertise of the Auditor's Expert

10. The auditor shall obtain a sufficient understanding of the field of expertise of the auditor's expert to enable the auditor to: (Ref: Para. A21-A22)
    (a) Determine the nature, scope and objectives of that expert's work for the auditor's purposes; and
    (b) Evaluate the adequacy of that work for the auditor's purposes.

Agreement with the Auditor's Expert

11. The auditor shall agree, in writing when appropriate, on the following matters with the auditor's expert: (Ref: Para. A23-A26)
    (a) The nature, scope and objectives of that expert's work; (Ref: Para. A27)
    (b) The respective roles and responsibilities of the auditor and that expert; (Ref: Para. A28-A29)
    (c) The nature, timing and extent of communication between the auditor and that expert, including the form of any report to be provided by that expert; and (Ref: Para. A30)
    (d) The need for the auditor's expert to observe confidentiality requirements.(Ref: Para. A31)

Evaluating the Adequacy of the Auditor's Expert's Work

12. The auditor shall evaluate the adequacy of the auditor's expert's work for the auditor's purposes, including: (Ref: Para. A32)
    (a) The relevance and reasonableness of that expert's findings or conclusions, and their consistency with other audit evidence; (Ref: Para. A33-A34)
    (b) If that expert's work involves use of significant assumptions and methods, the relevance and reasonableness of those assumptions and methods in the circumstances; and (Ref: Para. A35-A37)
    (c) If that expert's work involves the use of source data that is significant to that expert's work, the relevance, completeness, and accuracy of that source data (Ref: Para. A38-A39)

13. If the auditor determines that the work of the auditor's expert is not adequate for the auditor's purposes, the auditor shall: (Ref: Para. A40)
    (a) Agree with that expert on the nature and extent of further work to be performed by that expert; or
    (b) Perform additional audit procedures appropriate to the circumstances.

Reference to the Auditor's Expert in the Auditor's Report

14. The auditor shall not refer to the work of an auditor's expert in an auditor's report containing an unmodified opinion unless required by law or regulation to do so. If such reference is required by law or regulation, the auditor shall indicate in the auditor's report that the reference does not reduce the auditor's responsibility for the auditor's opinion. (Ref: Para. A41)

15. If the auditor makes reference to the work of an auditor's expert in the auditor's report because such reference is relevant to an understanding of a modification to the auditor's opinion, the auditor shall indicate in the auditor's report that such reference does not reduce the auditor's responsibility for that opinion. (Ref: Para. A42)

❖❖❖

Application and Other Explanatory Material

Definition of an Auditor's Expert (Ref: Para. 6(a))

A1. Expertise in a field other than accounting or auditing may include expertise in relation to such matters as:
- The valuation of complex financial instruments, land and buildings, plant and machinery, jewellery, works of art, antiques, intangible assets, assets acquired and liabilities assumed in business combinations and assets that may have been impaired.
- The actuarial calculation of liabilities associated with insurance contracts or employee benefit plans.
- The estimation of oil and gas reserves.
- The valuation of environmental liabilities, and site clean-up costs.
- The interpretation of contracts, laws and regulations.
- The analysis of complex or unusual tax compliance issues.

A2. In many cases, distinguishing between expertise in accounting or auditing, and expertise in another field, will be straightforward, even where this involves a specialised area of accounting or auditing. For example, an individual with expertise in applying methods of accounting for deferred income tax can often be easily distinguished from an expert in taxation law. The former is not an expert for the purposes of this Auditing Standard as this constitutes accounting expertise; the latter is an expert for the purposes of this Auditing Standard as this constitutes legal expertise. Similar distinctions may also be able to be made in other areas, for example, between expertise in methods of accounting for financial instruments, and expertise in complex modelling for the purpose of valuing financial instruments. In some cases, however, particularly those involving an emerging area of accounting or auditing expertise, distinguishing between specialised areas of accounting or auditing, and expertise in another field, will be a matter of professional judgement. Applicable professional rules and standards regarding education and competency requirements for accountants and auditors may assist the auditor in exercising that judgement.[4]

A3. It is necessary to apply judgement when considering how the requirements of this Auditing Standard are affected by the fact that an auditor's expert may be either an individual or an organisation. For example, when evaluating the competence, capabilities and objectivity of an auditor's expert, it may be that the expert is an organisation the auditor has previously used, but the auditor has no prior experience of the individual expert assigned by the organisation for the particular engagement; or it may be the reverse, that is, the auditor may be familiar with the work of an individual expert but not with the organisation that expert has joined.

4 [Footnote deleted by the AUASB, as not applicable in Australia]

In either case, both the personal attributes of the individual and the managerial attributes of the organisation (such as systems of quality control the organisation implements) may be relevant to the auditor's evaluation.

Determining the Need for an Auditor's Expert (Ref: Para. 7)

A4. An auditor's expert may be needed to assist the auditor in one or more of the following:

- Obtaining an understanding of the entity and its environment, including its internal control.
- Identifying and assessing the risks of material misstatement.
- Determining and implementing overall responses to assessed risks at the financial statement level.
- Designing and performing further audit procedures to respond to assessed risks at the assertion level, comprising tests of controls or substantive procedures.
- Evaluating the sufficiency and appropriateness of audit evidence obtained in forming an opinion on the financial report.

A5. The risks of material misstatement may increase when expertise in a field other than accounting is needed for management to prepare the financial report, for example, because this may indicate some complexity, or because management may not possess knowledge of the field of expertise. If in preparing the financial report management does not possess the necessary expertise, a management's expert may be used in addressing those risks. Relevant controls, including controls that relate to the work of a management's expert, if any, may also reduce the risks of material misstatement.

A6. If the preparation of the financial report involves the use of expertise in a field other than accounting, the auditor, who is skilled in accounting and auditing, may not possess the necessary expertise to audit that financial report. The engagement partner is required to be satisfied that the engagement team, and any auditor's experts who are not part of the engagement team, collectively have the appropriate competence and capabilities to perform the audit engagement.[5] Further, the auditor is required to ascertain the nature, timing and extent of resources necessary to perform the engagement.[6] The auditor's determination of whether to use the work of an auditor's expert, and if so when and to what extent, assists the auditor in meeting these requirements. As the audit progresses, or as circumstances change, the auditor may need to revise earlier decisions about using the work of an auditor's expert.

A7. An auditor who is not an expert in a relevant field other than accounting or auditing may nevertheless be able to obtain a sufficient understanding of that field to perform the audit without an auditor's expert. This understanding may be obtained through, for example:

- Experience in auditing entities that require such expertise in the preparation of their financial report.
- Education or professional development in the particular field. This may include formal courses or discussion with individuals possessing expertise in the relevant field for the purpose of enhancing the auditor's own capacity to deal with matters in that field. Such discussion differs from consultation with an auditor's expert regarding a specific set of circumstances encountered on the engagement where that expert is given all the relevant facts that will enable the expert to provide informed advice about the particular matter.[7]
- Discussion with auditors who have performed similar engagements.

A8. In other cases, however, the auditor may determine that it is necessary, or may choose, to use an auditor's expert to assist in obtaining sufficient appropriate audit evidence. Considerations when deciding whether to use an auditor's expert may include:

- Whether management has used a management's expert in preparing the financial report (see paragraph A9).

5 See ASA 220, paragraph 14.

6 See ASA 300 *Planning an Audit of a Financial Report*, paragraph 8(e).

7 See ASA 220, paragraph A21.

- The nature and significance of the matter, including its complexity.
- The risks of material misstatement in the matter.
- The expected nature of procedures to respond to identified risks, including the auditor's knowledge of and experience with the work of experts in relation to such matters; and the availability of alternative sources of audit evidence.

A9. When management has used a management's expert in preparing the financial report, the auditor's decision on whether to use an auditor's expert may also be influenced by such factors as:

- The nature, scope and objectives of the management's expert's work.
- Whether the management's expert is employed by the entity, or is a party engaged by it to provide relevant services.
- The extent to which management can exercise control or influence over the work of the management's expert.
- The management's expert's competence and capabilities.
- Whether the management's expert is subject to technical performance standards or other professional or industry requirements.
- Any controls within the entity over the management's expert's work.

ASA 500[8] includes requirements and guidance regarding the effect of the competence, capabilities and objectivity of management's experts on the reliability of audit evidence.

Nature, Timing and Extent of Audit Procedures (Ref: Para. 8)

A10. The nature, timing and extent of audit procedures with respect to the requirements in paragraphs 9-13 of this Auditing Standard will vary depending on the circumstances. For example, the following factors may suggest the need for different or more extensive procedures than would otherwise be the case:

- The work of the auditor's expert relates to a significant matter that involves subjective and complex judgements.
- The auditor has not previously used the work of the auditor's expert, and has no prior knowledge of that expert's competence, capabilities and objectivity.
- The auditor's expert is performing procedures that are integral to the audit, rather than being consulted to provide advice on an individual matter.
- The expert is an auditor's external expert and is not, therefore, subject to the firm's quality control policies and procedures.

The Auditor's Firm's Quality Control Policies and Procedures (Ref: Para. 8(e))

A11. An auditor's internal expert may be a partner or staff, including temporary staff, of the auditor's firm, and therefore subject to the quality control policies and procedures of that firm in accordance with ASQC 1.[9, 10] Alternatively, an auditor's internal expert may be a partner or staff, including temporary staff, of a network firm, which may share common quality control policies and procedures with the auditor's firm.

A12. An auditor's external expert is not a member of the engagement team and is not subject to quality control policies and procedures in accordance with ASQC 1.[11] In some jurisdictions, however, law or regulation may require that an auditor's external expert be treated as a member of the engagement team, and may therefore be subject to relevant ethical requirements, including those pertaining to independence, and other professional requirements, as determined by that law or regulation.

8 See ASA 500, paragraph 8.

9 See ASQC 1 *Quality Control for Firms that Perform Audits and Reviews of Financial Reports and Other Financial Information, and Other Assurance Engagements*, paragraph 12(f).

10 See ASA 220, paragraphs 2 and A1.

11 See ASQC 1, paragraph 12(f).

A13. Engagement teams are entitled to rely on the firm's system of quality control, unless information provided by the firm or other parties suggests otherwise.[12] The extent of that reliance will vary with the circumstances, and may affect the nature, timing and extent of the auditor's procedures with respect to such matters as:

- Competence and capabilities, through recruitment and training programs.
- Objectivity. Auditor's internal experts are subject to relevant ethical requirements, including those pertaining to independence.
- The auditor's evaluation of the adequacy of the auditor's expert's work. For example, the firm's training programs may provide auditor's internal experts with an appropriate understanding of the interrelationship of their expertise with the audit process. Reliance on such training and other firm processes, such as protocols for scoping the work of auditor's internal experts, may affect the nature, timing and extent of the auditor's procedures to evaluate the adequacy of the auditor's expert's work.
- Adherence to regulatory and legal requirements, through monitoring processes.
- Agreement with the auditor's expert.

Such reliance does not reduce the auditor's responsibility to meet the requirements of this Auditing Standard.

ASA

The Competence, Capabilities and Objectivity of the Auditor's Expert

(Ref: Para. 9)

A14. The competence, capabilities and objectivity of an auditor's expert are factors that significantly affect whether the work of the auditor's expert will be adequate for the auditor's purposes. Competence relates to the nature and level of expertise of the auditor's expert. Capability relates to the ability of the auditor's expert to exercise that competence in the circumstances of the engagement. Factors that influence capability may include, for example, geographic location, and the availability of time and resources. Objectivity relates to the possible effects that bias, conflict of interest, or the influence of others may have on the professional or business judgement of the auditor's expert.

A15. Information regarding the competence, capabilities and objectivity of an auditor's expert may come from a variety of sources, such as:

- Personal experience with previous work of that expert.
- Discussions with that expert.
- Discussions with other auditors or others who are familiar with that expert's work.
- Knowledge of that expert's qualifications, membership of a professional body or industry association, licence to practice, or other forms of external recognition.
- Published papers or books written by that expert.
- The auditor's firm's quality control policies and procedures (see paragraphs A11-A13).

A16. Matters relevant to evaluating the competence, capabilities and objectivity of the auditor's expert include whether that expert's work is subject to technical performance standards or other professional or industry requirements, for example, ethical standards and other membership requirements of a professional body or industry association, accreditation standards of a licensing body, or requirements imposed by law or regulation.

A17. Other matters that may be relevant include:

- The relevance of the auditor's expert's competence to the matter for which that expert's work will be used, including any areas of specialty within that expert's field. For example, a particular actuary may specialise in property and casualty insurance, but have limited expertise regarding pension calculations.
- The auditor's expert's competence with respect to relevant accounting and auditing requirements, for example, knowledge of assumptions and methods, including models where applicable, that are consistent with the applicable financial reporting framework.

12 See ASA 220, paragraph 4.

- Whether unexpected events, changes in conditions, or the audit evidence obtained from the results of audit procedures indicate that it may be necessary to reconsider the initial evaluation of the competence, capabilities and objectivity of the auditor's expert as the audit progresses.

A18. A broad range of circumstances may threaten objectivity, for example, self-interest threats, advocacy threats, familiarity threats, self-review threats, and intimidation threats. Safeguards may eliminate or reduce such threats, and may be created by external structures (for example, the auditor's expert's profession, legislation or regulation), or by the auditor's expert's work environment (for example, quality control policies and procedures). There may also be safeguards specific to the audit engagement.

A19. The evaluation of the significance of threats to objectivity and of whether there is a need for safeguards may depend upon the role of the auditor's expert and the significance of the expert's work in the context of the audit. There may be some circumstances in which safeguards cannot reduce threats to an acceptable level, for example, if a proposed auditor's expert is an individual who has played a significant role in preparing the information that is being audited, that is, if the auditor's expert is a management's expert.

A20. When evaluating the objectivity of an auditor's external expert, it may be relevant to:

(a) Enquire of the entity about any known interests or relationships that the entity has with the auditor's external expert that may affect that expert's objectivity.

(b) Discuss with that expert any applicable safeguards, including any professional requirements that apply to that expert; and evaluate whether the safeguards are adequate to reduce threats to an acceptable level. Interests and relationships that may be relevant to discuss with the auditor's expert include:

- Financial interests.
- Business and personal relationships.
- Provision of other services by the expert, including by the organisation in the case of an external expert that is an organisation.

In some cases, it may also be appropriate for the auditor to obtain a written representation from the auditor's external expert about any interests or relationships with the entity of which that expert is aware.

Obtaining an Understanding of the Field of Expertise of the Auditor's Expert (Ref: Para. 10)

A21. The auditor may obtain an understanding of the auditor's expert's field of expertise through the means described in paragraph A7, or through discussion with that expert.

A22. Aspects of the auditor's expert's field relevant to the auditor's understanding may include:

- Whether that expert's field has areas of specialty within it that are relevant to the audit (see paragraph A17).
- Whether any professional or other standards and regulatory or legal requirements apply.
- What assumptions and methods, including models where applicable, are used by the auditor's expert, and whether they are generally accepted within that expert's field and appropriate for financial reporting purposes.
- The nature of internal and external data or information the auditor's expert uses.

Agreement with the Auditor's Expert (Ref: Para. 11)

A23. The nature, scope and objectives of the auditor's expert's work may vary considerably with the circumstances, as may the respective roles and responsibilities of the auditor and the auditor's expert, and the nature, timing and extent of communication between the auditor and the auditor's expert. It is therefore required that these matters are agreed between the auditor and the auditor's expert regardless of whether the expert is an auditor's external expert or an auditor's internal expert.

A24. The matters noted in paragraph 8 may affect the level of detail and formality of the agreement between the auditor and the auditor's expert, including whether it is appropriate that the agreement be in writing. For example, the following factors may suggest the need for more a detailed agreement than would otherwise be the case, or for the agreement to be set out in writing:

- The auditor's expert will have access to sensitive or confidential entity information.
- The respective roles or responsibilities of the auditor and the auditor's expert are different from those normally expected.
- Multi-jurisdictional legal or regulatory requirements apply.
- The matter to which the auditor's expert's work relates is highly complex.
- The auditor has not previously used work performed by that expert.
- The greater the extent of the auditor's expert's work, and its significance in the context of the audit.

A25. The agreement between the auditor and an auditor's external expert is often in the form of an engagement letter. Appendix 1 lists matters that the auditor may consider for inclusion in such an engagement letter, or in any other form of agreement with an auditor's external expert.

A26. When there is no written agreement between the auditor and the auditor's expert, evidence of the agreement may be included in, for example:

- Planning memoranda, or related working papers such as the audit program.
- The policies and procedures of the auditor's firm. In the case of an auditor's internal expert, the established policies and procedures to which that expert is subject may include particular policies and procedures in relation to that expert's work. The extent of documentation in the auditor's working papers depends on the nature of such policies and procedures. For example, no documentation may be required in the auditor's working papers if the auditor's firm has detailed protocols covering the circumstances in which the work of such an expert is used.

Nature, Scope and Objectives of Work (Ref: Para. 11(a))

A27. It may often be relevant when agreeing on the nature, scope and objectives of the auditor's expert's work to include discussion of any relevant technical performance standards or other professional or industry requirements that the expert will follow.

Respective Roles and Responsibilities (Ref: Para. 11(b))

A28. Agreement on the respective roles and responsibilities of the auditor and the auditor's expert may include:

- Whether the auditor or the auditor's expert will perform detailed testing of source data.
- Consent for the auditor to discuss the auditor's expert's findings or conclusions with the entity and others, and to include details of that expert's findings or conclusions in the basis for a modified opinion in the auditor's report, if necessary (see paragraph A42).
- Any agreement to inform the auditor's expert of the auditor's conclusions concerning that expert's work.

Working Papers

A29. Agreement on the respective roles and responsibilities of the auditor and the auditor's expert may also include agreement about access to, and retention of, each other's working papers. When the auditor's expert is a member of the engagement team, that expert's working papers form part of the audit documentation. Subject to any agreement to the contrary, auditor's external experts' working papers are their own and do not form part of the audit documentation.

Communication (Ref: Para. 11(c))

A30. Effective two-way communication facilitates the proper integration of the nature, timing and extent of the auditor's expert's procedures with other work on the audit, and appropriate modification of the auditor's expert's objectives during the course of the audit. For example, when the work of the auditor's expert relates to the auditor's conclusions regarding a significant risk, both a formal written report at the conclusion of that expert's work, and oral reports as the work progresses, may be appropriate. Identification of specific partners or staff who will liaise with the auditor's expert, and procedures for communication between that expert and the entity, assists timely and effective communication, particularly on larger engagements.

Confidentiality (Ref: Para. 11(d))

A31. It is necessary for the confidentiality provisions of relevant ethical requirements that apply to the auditor also to apply to the auditor's expert. Additional requirements may be imposed by law or regulation. The entity may also have requested that specific confidentiality provisions be agreed with auditor's external experts.

Evaluating the Adequacy of the Auditor's Expert's Work (Ref: Para. 12)

A32. The auditor's evaluation of the auditor's expert's competence, capabilities and objectivity, the auditor's familiarity with the auditor's expert's field of expertise, and the nature of the work performed by the auditor's expert affect the nature, timing and extent of audit procedures to evaluate the adequacy of that expert's work for the auditor's purposes.

The Findings and Conclusions of the Auditor's Expert (Ref: Para. 12(a))

A33. Specific procedures to evaluate the adequacy of the auditor's expert's work for the auditor's purposes may include:

- Enquiries of the auditor's expert.
- Reviewing the auditor's expert's working papers and reports.
- Corroborative procedures, such as:
  - Observing the auditor's expert's work;
  - Examining published data, such as statistical reports from reputable, authoritative sources;
  - Confirming relevant matters with third parties;
  - Performing detailed analytical procedures; and
  - Re-performing calculations.
- Discussion with another expert with relevant expertise when, for example, the findings or conclusions of the auditor's expert are not consistent with other audit evidence.
- Discussing the auditor's expert's report with management.

A34. Relevant factors when evaluating the relevance and reasonableness of the findings or conclusions of the auditor's expert, whether in a report or other form, may include whether they are:

- Presented in a manner that is consistent with any standards of the auditor's expert's profession or industry;
- Clearly expressed, including reference to the objectives agreed with the auditor, the scope of the work performed and standards applied;
- Based on an appropriate period and take into account subsequent events, where relevant;
- Subject to any reservation, limitation or restriction on use, and if so, whether this has implications for the auditor; and
- Based on appropriate consideration of errors or deviations encountered by the auditor's expert.

Assumptions, Methods and Source Data

Assumptions and Methods (Ref: Para. 12(b))

A35. When the auditor's expert's work is to evaluate underlying assumptions and methods, including models where applicable, used by management in developing an accounting estimate, the auditor's procedures are likely to be primarily directed to evaluating whether the auditor's expert has adequately reviewed those assumptions and methods. When the auditor's expert's work is to develop an auditor's point estimate or an auditor's range for comparison with management's point estimate, the auditor's procedures may be primarily directed to evaluating the assumptions and methods, including models where appropriate, used by the auditor's expert.

A36. ASA 540[13] discusses the assumptions and methods used by management in making accounting estimates, including the use in some cases of highly specialised, entity-developed models. Although that discussion is written in the context of the auditor obtaining sufficient appropriate audit evidence regarding management's assumptions and methods, it may also assist the auditor when evaluating an auditor's expert's assumptions and methods.

A37. When an auditor's expert's work involves the use of significant assumptions and methods, factors relevant to the auditor's evaluation of those assumptions and methods include whether they are:

- Generally accepted within the auditor's expert's field;
- Consistent with the requirements of the applicable financial reporting framework;
- Dependent on the use of specialised models; and
- Consistent with those of management, and if not, the reason for, and effects of, the differences.

Source Data Used by the Auditor's Expert (Ref: Para. 12(c))

A38. When an auditor's expert's work involves the use of source data that is significant to that expert's work, procedures such as the following may be used to test that data:

- Verifying the origin of the data, including obtaining an understanding of, and where applicable testing, the internal controls over the data and, where relevant, its transmission to the expert.
- Reviewing the data for completeness and internal consistency.

A39. In many cases, the auditor may test source data. However, in other cases, when the nature of the source data used by an auditor's expert is highly technical in relation to the expert's field, that expert may test the source data. If the auditor's expert has tested the source data, enquiry of that expert by the auditor, or supervision or review of that expert's tests may be an appropriate way for the auditor to evaluate that data's relevance, completeness, and accuracy.

Inadequate Work (Ref: Para. 13)

A40. If the auditor concludes that the work of the auditor's expert is not adequate for the auditor's purposes and the auditor cannot resolve the matter through the additional audit procedures required by paragraph 13, which may involve further work being performed by both the expert and the auditor, or include employing or engaging another expert, it may be necessary to express a modified opinion in the auditor's report in accordance with ASA 705 because the auditor has not obtained sufficient appropriate audit evidence.[14]

Reference to the Auditor's Expert in the Auditor's Report (Ref: Para. 14-15)

A41. In some cases, law or regulation may require a reference to the work of an auditor's expert, for example, for the purposes of transparency in the public sector.

A42. It may be appropriate in some circumstances to refer to the auditor's expert in an auditor's report containing a modified opinion, to explain the nature of the modification. In such circumstances, the auditor may need the permission of the auditor's expert before making such a reference.

❖ ❖ ❖

---

13 See ASA 540 *Auditing Accounting Estimates, Including Fair Value Accounting Estimates, and Related Disclosures*, paragraphs 8, 13 and 15.

14 See ASA 705 *Modifications to the Opinion in the Independent Auditor's Report*, paragraph 6(b).

Conformity with International Standards on Auditing

This Auditing Standard conforms with International Standard on Auditing ISA 620 *Using the Work of an Auditor's Expert*, issued by the International Auditing and Assurance Standards Board (IAASB), an independent standard-setting board of the International Federation of Accountants (IFAC).

Paragraphs that have been added to this Auditing Standard (and do not appear in the text of the equivalent ISA) are identified with the prefix "Aus".

Compliance with this Auditing Standard enables compliance with ISA 620.

Appendix 1

(Ref: Para. A25)

Considerations for Agreement between the Auditor and an Auditor's External Expert

This Appendix lists matters that the auditor may consider for inclusion in any agreement with an auditor's external expert. The following list is illustrative and is not exhaustive; it is intended only to be a guide that may be used in conjunction with the considerations outlined in this Auditing Standard. Whether to include particular matters in the agreement depends on the circumstances of the engagement. The list may also be of assistance in considering the matters to be included in an agreement with an auditor's internal expert.

Nature, Scope and Objectives of the Auditor's External Expert's Work

- The nature and scope of the procedures to be performed by the auditor's external expert.
- The objectives of the auditor's external expert's work in the context of materiality and risk considerations concerning the matter to which the auditor's external expert's work relates, and, when relevant, the applicable financial reporting framework.
- Any relevant technical performance standards or other professional or industry requirements the auditor's external expert will follow.
- The assumptions and methods, including models where applicable, the auditor's external expert will use, and their authority.
- The effective date of, or when applicable the testing period for, the subject matter of the auditor's external expert's work, and requirements regarding subsequent events.

The Respective Roles and Responsibilities of the Auditor and the Auditor's External Expert

- Relevant auditing and accounting standards, and relevant regulatory or legal requirements.
- The auditor's external expert's consent to the auditor's intended use of that expert's report, including any reference to it, or disclosure of it, to others, for example reference to it in the basis for a modified opinion in the auditor's report, if necessary, or disclosure of it to management or an audit committee.
- The nature and extent of the auditor's review of the auditor's external expert's work.
- Whether the auditor or the auditor's external expert will test source data.
- The auditor's external expert's access to the entity's records, files, personnel and to experts engaged by the entity.
- Procedures for communication between the auditor's external expert and the entity.
- The auditor's and the auditor's external expert's access to each other's working papers.
- Ownership and control of working papers during and after the engagement, including any file retention requirements.
- The auditor's external expert's responsibility to perform work with due skill and care.

- The auditor's external expert's competence and capability to perform the work.
- The expectation that the auditor's external expert will use all knowledge that expert has that is relevant to the audit or, if not, will inform the auditor.
- Any restriction on the auditor's external expert's association with the auditor's report.
- Any agreement to inform the auditor's external expert of the auditor's conclusions concerning that expert's work.

Communications and Reporting

- Methods and frequency of communications, including:
  - How the auditor's external expert's findings or conclusions will be reported (for example, written report, oral report, ongoing input to the engagement team).
  - Identification of specific persons within the engagement team who will liaise with the auditor's external expert.
- When the auditor's external expert will complete the work and report findings or conclusions to the auditor.
- The auditor's external expert's responsibility to communicate promptly any potential delay in completing the work, and any potential reservation or limitation on that expert's findings or conclusions.
- The auditor's external expert's responsibility to communicate promptly instances in which the entity restricts that expert's access to records, files, personnel or experts engaged by the entity.
- The auditor's external expert's responsibility to communicate to the auditor all information that expert believes may be relevant to the audit, including any changes in circumstances previously communicated.
- The auditor's external expert's responsibility to communicate circumstances that may create threats to that expert's objectivity, and any relevant safeguards that may eliminate or reduce such threats to an acceptable level.

Confidentiality

- The need for the auditor's expert to observe confidentiality requirements, including:
  - The confidentiality provisions of relevant ethical requirements that apply to the auditor.
  - Additional requirements that may be imposed by law or regulation, if any.
  - Specific confidentiality provisions requested by the entity, if any.

Explanatory Guide: Auditor's Reports

(Reissued February 2010)

Issued by the Auditing and Assurance Standards Board.

Note from the Institute of Chartered Accountants Australia

This note, prepared by the technical editor, is not part of the Explanatory Guide.

Historical Development

March 2009: The 'Explanatory Guide: Auditors Reports' was issued when the audit reporting Standards ASAs 700, 705, 706, 800, 805 and 810 were at exposure draft stage to explain how the Standards fit together and when each should be used.

Although the fundamental principles governing auditors' reporting responsibilities are unchanged by the Clarity project, the Standards have been revised extensively. This Guide is an aid to understanding how these new Standards interact. It has no international equivalent.

February 2010: The Explanatory Guide was reissued following the final issue of the relevant Standards – Clarity Format.

This *Explanatory Guide: Auditor's Reports* is issued by the Auditing and Assurance Standards Board (AUASB).

This *Explanatory Guide*:

(1) is not an AUASB Guidance Statement that provides guidance to assist auditors and assurance practitioners to fulfil the objectives of the audit or assurance engagement; and

(2) does not itself establish or extend requirements for the performance of audit, review, or assurance engagements under the AUASB Standards.

ASA

Contents

Explanatory Guide: Auditor's Reports

Purpose

The purpose of this *Explanatory Guide* is to provide information to auditors on the suite of reporting standards, covering historical financial information, that form part of the *Australian Auditing Standards* (the "Standards") operative for financial reporting periods commencing on or after 1 January 2010.

Introduction

In October 2007, the AUASB decided to revise and redraft the pre-existing Auditing Standards using the equivalent "clarity" versions of the International Standards on Auditing (ISAs) as the underlying standards. The exception was ASRE 2410 *Review of a Financial Report Performed by the Independent Auditor of the Entity*, which was to be based on pre-existing ASRE 2410 (August 2008).

The new Auditing Standards were approved by the AUASB in October 2009. Unless otherwise stated, a reference to "Standards" in this *Explanatory Guide* refers to the revised and redrafted *Australian Auditing Standards* applicable from 1 January 2010.

Although the fundamental principles governing an auditor's reporting responsibilities remain unchanged, the pre-existing Standards have been subject to extensive revision. Accordingly, this *Explanatory Guide* illustrates the main features of the new suite of Standards that relate to reporting, and describes some of the key changes from the pre-existing Standards.

Auditors and other assurance practitioners are reminded that requirements and related application and other explanatory material (referred to as "guidance material" hereafter) are found in the *Australian Auditing Standards*, the texts of which alone are authoritative, and that this *Explanatory Guide* (which is not exhaustive) is merely an aid to understanding these Standards, and should not be considered as a substitute for the Standards.

Requirements and guidance material are described only, and are not reproduced from the relevant Auditing Standards.

Definitions of Key Reporting Terms used in the Standards

The following definitions refer to terms used throughout this *Explanatory Guide*, and the Standards, and are reproduced here to assist readers.

"A complete set of financial statements" means financial statements and related notes as determined by the requirements of the applicable financial reporting framework. For example, a complete set of financial statements as described in Accounting Standard AASB 101 *Presentation of Financial Statements* includes:

(a) a statement of financial position as at the end of the period;

(b) a statement of comprehensive income for the period;

(c) a statement of changes in equity for the period;

(d) a statement of cash flows for the period; and

(e) notes, comprising a summary of significant accounting policies and other explanatory information. [Refer ASA 200, Para. 13]

"Element of a financial statement" means an element, account or item of a financial statement. [Refer ASA 805, Para. 6(a)]

"Financial Report" means, for the purpose of the *Corporations Act 2001*, financial statements for the year or the half-year and notes to the financial statements, and the director's declaration about the statements and notes [Refer ASA 200, Para. Aus 13.3]

"Financial Report" means, for purposes other than the *Corporations Act 2001*, a complete set of financial statements, including the related notes, and an assertion statement by those responsible for the financial report. The related notes ordinarily comprise a summary of significant accounting policies and other explanatory information. The requirements of the applicable financial reporting framework determine the form and content of the financial report. [Refer ASA 200, Para. Aus 13.4]

"Financial Statement" means a structured representation of historical financial information, intended to communicate an entity's economic resources or obligations at a point in time or the changes therein for a period of time in accordance with a financial reporting framework. What constitutes a financial statement is determined by the requirements of the applicable financial reporting framework. [Refer ASA 200, Para. Aus 13.2]

"Historical financial information" means information expressed in financial terms in relation to a particular entity, derived primarily from that entity's accounting system, about economic events occurring in past time periods or about economic conditions or circumstances at points in time in the past. [Refer ASA 200, Para. 13(g)]

"Interim financial report" means a financial report that is prepared in accordance with an applicable financial reporting framework for a period that is shorter than the entity's financial year. [Refer ASRE 2410, Para. 5]

"Single financial statement" or a specific element of a financial statement includes the related notes. The related notes ordinarily comprise a summary of significant accounting policies and other explanatory information relevant to the financial statement or to the element. [Refer ASA 805, Para. 6(c)]

"Summary financial statements" means historical financial information that is derived from an financial report, but that contains less detail than the financial report, while still providing a structured representation consistent with that provided by the financial report, of the entity's economic resources or obligations at a point in time or the changes therein for a period of time. Summary financial statements may include an assertion by those responsible for the summary financial statements. Different jurisdictions may use different terminology to describe such historical financial information. [Refer ASA 810, Para. Aus 4.1]

The New Reporting Standards

The following table lists the relevant new reporting Standards that are operative for financial reporting periods commencing on or after 1 January 2010:

Standard No.	Standard Name
ASA 700	*Forming an Opinion and Reporting on a Financial Report*
ASA 705	*Modifications to the Opinion in the Independent Auditor's Report*
ASA 706	*Emphasis of Matter Paragraphs and Other Matter Paragraphs in the Independent Auditor's Report*
ASA 800	*Special Considerations–Audits of Financial Reports Prepared in Accordance with Special Purpose Frameworks*
ASA 805*	*Special Considerations–Audits of Single Financial Statements and Specific Elements, Accounts or Items of a Financial Statement*
ASA 810*	*Engagements to Report on Summary Financial Statements*
ASRE 2410	*Review of a Financial Report Performed by the Independent Auditor of the Entity*

* These Auditing Standards do not apply to *Corporations Act 2001* (the Act) audit engagements and therefore are not made under that Act.

Comparative Table

The following table lists the new reporting Standards that will replace the pre-existing reporting Standards for financial reporting periods commencing on or after 1 January 2010.

Pre-existing Standard	Issue Date		New Standard	Issued
ASA 700 *The Auditor's Report on a General Purpose Financial Report*	6/07	→	ASA 700 *Forming an Opinion and Reporting on a Financial Report*	10/09
ASA 701 *Modifications to the Auditor's Report*	6/07	→	ASA 705 *Modifications to the Opinion in the Independent Auditor's Report* and ASA 706 *Emphasis of Matter Paragraphs and Other Matter Paragraphs in the Independent Auditor's Report*	10/09 10/09
ASA 800 *The Auditor's Report on Special Purpose Audit Engagements*	6/07	→	ASA 800 *Special Considerations–Audits of Financial Reports Prepared in Accordance with Special Purpose Frameworks* and ASA 805 *Special Considerations–Audits of Single Financial Statements and Specific Elements, Accounts or Items of a Financial Statement* and ASA 810 *Engagements to Report on Summary Financial Statements*	10/09 10/09 10/09
ASRE 2410 *Review of Interim and Other Financial Reports Performed by the Independent Auditor of the Entity*	8/08	→	ASRE 2410 *Review of Financial Reports Performed by the Independent Auditor of the Entity*	10/09

Scope

The reporting Standards deal with forming an opinion and the form and content of the auditor's report issued as a result of an audit or review of historical financial information.

Depending on the financial reporting framework adopted, historical financial information can be presented in the following forms:

- a financial report (under the *Corporations Act 2001*);
- a financial report (not under the *Corporations Act 2001*);
- interim financial report (under the *Corporations Act 2001*);
- interim financial report (not under the *Corporations Act 2001*);
- a financial report, or interim financial report (under other legislation);
- a complete set of financial statements;
- a single financial statement;
- a specific element, account or item of a financial statement; and
- summary financial statements (derived from an audited financial report).

The financial reporting framework (described below) is determined by the requirements of applicable law and regulation; Accounting Standards; or the information needs of the entity's users.

The new suite of reporting Standards is organised so as to differentiate reporting requirements for a financial report/complete set of financial statements [ASAs 700, 705, 706, 800 and ASRE 2410] from reporting requirements of other historical financial information [ASAs 805 and 810].

ASA 700 is an overarching Standard on forming an opinion and reporting on an audit of a financial report/complete set of financial statements. It is also relevant to a single financial statement/element. Accordingly, the requirements in the Standard are to be applied by the auditor regardless of whether the financial report audited is "general purpose" *or* "special purpose".

ASA 800 deals with special considerations when a financial report is prepared in accordance with a special purpose framework. In situations requiring a modification to the auditor's opinion, refer ASA 705; or in situations where the auditor needs to draw users' attention to certain matters, refer ASA 706.

Reporting Frameworks

Applicable Financial Reporting Frameworks

The financial reporting framework may be prescribed by law or regulation or may be selected by management of an entity as the basis of preparation of the financial report. It is based on the financial information needs of the users of the financial report.

The framework selected also provides the auditor with the criteria to use for auditing the financial report. The terms of the audit engagement will determine the auditor's objective in their audit, and therefore assist them in determining the acceptability of the framework chosen by management. The auditor also uses professional judgement and considers the nature of the entity, purpose of the financial report and whether any law/regulation prescribes the applicable framework. [Refer ASA 210 *Terms of Engagement* for further information.] Refer Australian Accounting Standards Board (AASB) pronouncements for an explanation of the different types of reporting entities.

"Financial reporting frameworks" are classified in both the pre-existing and the new Standards as either:

a. A general purpose framework—designed to meet the common financial information needs of a wide range of users; *or*

b. A special purpose framework—designed to meet the financial information needs of specific users.

References to an "applicable financial reporting framework" in the Standards means the financial reporting framework that is applicable (relevant) in the circumstances of the reporting entity.

Further Classification of Financial Reporting Frameworks as either "Fair Presentation" or "Compliance"

General or special purpose frameworks are further classified in ASA 200 *Overall Objectives of the Independent Auditor and the Conduct of an Audit in Accordance with Australian Auditing Standards* as either "fair presentation" *or* "compliance" in nature.

The term "fair presentation framework" means a financial reporting framework that requires compliance with the requirements of the framework and:

(i) Acknowledges explicitly or implicitly that, to achieve fair presentation of the financial report/statements, it may be necessary for management to provide disclosures beyond those specifically required by the framework; or

(ii) Acknowledges explicitly that it may be necessary for management to depart from a requirement of the framework to achieve fair presentation of the financial report/statements. Such departures are expected to be necessary only in extremely rare circumstances.

The term "compliance framework" means a financial reporting framework that requires compliance with the requirements of that framework, but does *not* contain the acknowledgements in (i) or (ii) above. A compliance framework requires compliance with the requirements of the framework; however, it does <u>not</u> provide scope for additional disclosure or departures from the requirements in order for the financial report to achieve compliance.

Framework Diagram

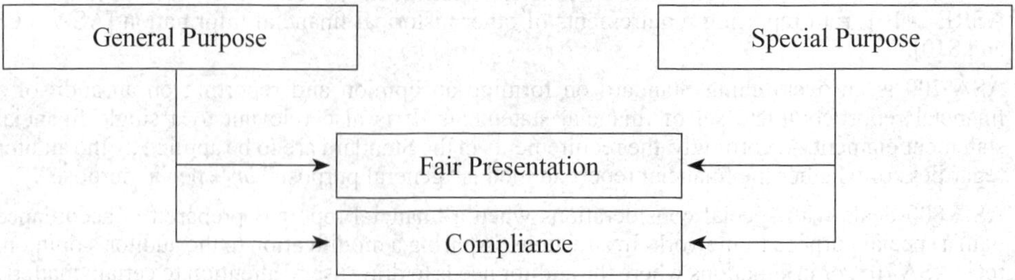

Engagements including Assurance on non-financial information

The terms of the auditor's engagement with the entity may require the auditor to opine on more than assurance on a financial report prepared in accordance with a fair presentation *or* compliance framework. For example, the auditor may also be requested to provide assurance on non-financial criteria under ASAE 3100 *Compliance Engagements* (e.g. compliance with stated terms of a contract).

In this case, the auditor has a choice of including in their auditor's report on financial information, the additional reporting requirements from ASAE 3100 *or* to issue two separate auditor's reports covering both types of engagements.

Note: It is important to remember that the requirements of the applicable financial reporting framework determine the form and content of the historical financial information (whether it is a financial report, complete set of financial statements, single financial statement, or summary financial statements) and therefore what constitutes that historical financial information.

Types of Historical Financial Information

Financial report/complete set of financial statements

A financial report/complete set of financial statements may be prepared in accordance with a general or special purpose framework, and can be either fair presentation or compliance in nature. A financial report differs from a complete set of financial statements as it includes a directors' declaration *or* an assertion statement by those responsible for the financial report, about the financial statements and notes. The directors' declaration, or assertion statement, forms part of the auditor's subject matter. Hereafter references to a "financial report" in this document are taken to include a complete set of financial statements.

Other Historical Financial Information

Other historical financial information, such as a single financial statement, or a specific element, account or item of a financial statement, may be prepared in accordance with a general or special purpose framework, and can be either fair presentation or compliance in nature. The financial information may be accompanied by an assertion statement, which will form part of the auditor's subject matter.

The reporting Standard ASA 805 contemplates (but does not require) that the single financial statement be derived from a financial report already audited by the same auditor. Hereafter references to a single financial statement are taken to include a specific element, account, or item of a financial statement.

Summary Financial Statements

Summary financial statements can only be prepared under a compliance framework. They may be accompanied by an assertion statement, which forms part of the auditor's subject matter. Summary financial statements contain less detail than the audited financial report. The reporting Standard (ASA 810) requires summary financial statements to be derived from a financial report that has been audited by the same auditor.

Concise Financial Reports

A concise financial report is prepared in certain circumstances under the *Corporations Act 2001*, and in compliance with the requirements of AASB 1039 *Concise Financial Reports*. It is a particular example of summary financial statements. AASB 1039 is silent on the nature of the financial reporting framework applicable to a concise financial report (i.e. general or special purpose), as well as its format; however, it does contain minimum information requirements for the concise financial report. AUASB Guidance Statement GS 001 *Concise Financial Reports* (as amended) provides specific guidance material on the auditor's report on a concise financial report.

Form of Auditor's Opinion

The form of an auditor's opinion is determined by reference to the:

(a) applicable financial reporting framework (i.e. fair presentation or compliance); and, where applicable

(b) law/regulation (prescribed reporting).

Auditor's Opinion – Fair Presentation

When expressing an unmodified opinion on historical financial information prepared in accordance with a fair presentation framework, the opinion will include one of the following phrases, which are regarded as being equal:

a. The financial report present(s) fairly, in all material respects, …… in accordance with [the applicable financial reporting framework]; *or*

b. The financial report give(s) a true and fair view of …… in accordance with [the applicable financial reporting framework].

Auditor's Review Conclusion – Fair Presentation

When expressing an unmodified review conclusion on a financial report prepared in accordance with a fair presentation framework, the form of the review report depends on the applicable financial reporting framework.

The auditor's conclusion broadly takes the following form: Based on our review, which is not an audit, nothing has come to our attention that causes us to believe that the [period financial report] of [name of entity] does not present fairly, in all material respects [*or gives a true and fair view of*] the …………in accordance with the [applicable financial reporting framework] ……….

Auditor's Opinion – Compliance

Financial Report

When expressing an unmodified opinion on a financial report prepared in accordance with a compliance framework, the auditor's opinion broadly takes the following form: that the financial report is prepared, in all material respects, in accordance with [the applicable financial reporting framework].

Summary Financial Statements

Due to the nature of summary financial statement engagements, the auditor's opinion differs from the above framework opinions. Other than when prescribed by law or regulation, when expressing an unmodified opinion on summary financial statements, the opinion will use one of the following phrases, which are regarded as being equal:

a. The summary financial statements derived from the audited financial report of [name of entity] for the year ended [date] are consistent, in all material respects, with that audited financial report, in accordance with [the applied criteria]; <u>or</u>

b. The summary financial statements derived from the audited financial report of [name of entity] for the year ended [date] are a fair summary of that audited financial report in accordance with [the applied criteria].

Concise Financial Report

As noted above, a concise financial report is a particular type of summary financial statement where the auditors reporting obligations are compliance in nature. These reporting obligations are specified under the *Corporations Act 2001*, with reference to AASB 1039. The auditor's opinion takes the form: the concise financial report of [name of entity] for the year ended [date] complies with Accounting Standard AASB 1039.

Auditor's Report Prescribed by Law or Regulation

In some cases, law or regulation prescribes the layout or wording of the auditor's report in a form, or in terms that are significantly different from the requirements of Australian Auditing Standards. There are two Standards which specifically address this issue:

1. ASA 210 *Agreeing the Terms of Audit Engagements*

This Standard deals with the situation where the prescribed wording of the auditor's report is in terms that are significantly different from the requirements of the Australian Auditing Standards. In such cases, the auditor is required by the Standard, to evaluate:

(a) Whether users might misunderstand the assurance obtained from the audit of the financial report, if so,

(b) Whether additional explanation in the auditor's report can mitigate possible misunderstanding.

The Standard provides further requirements and guidance material relating to this evaluation. [Refer ASA 210, Para. 21]

2. ASA 700 *Forming an Opinion and Reporting on a Financial Report*

Where the specific layout or wording of the auditor's report is prescribed by law or regulation, this Standard permits a reference to the Australian Auditing Standards only when specific elements, set out in paragraph 43 of the Standard, are included in the auditor's report. [Refer ASA 700, Para. 43]

Examples

Examples of the applicability of each of the reporting Standards to various forms of historical financial information are included in the following tables:

Entity and Information Type	Framework	Form of Opinion
ASA 700: General Purpose—*Fair Presentation*		
Disclosing entity (e.g. listed company) — financial report	• *Corporations Act 2001.* • Australian Accounting Standards (Accounting Standards).*	"True and fair" **and** "in accordance with Accounting Standards"
Government department (reporting entity) — financial report	• Sector-specific Accounting Standards.	"Presents fairly in all material respects" **or** "true and fair"
Reporting entity or Non-reporting entity — financial report	• Accounting Standards.	"Presents fairly in all material respects" **or** "true and fair"

ASA 700: General Purpose—*Compliance*		
Entity funded with public money — financial report	• Reporting requirements specified by applicable regulation.	"Prepared in all material respects"

ASRE 2410: General Purpose—*Fair Presentation*		
Disclosing entity (e.g. listed company)— half-year financial report	• *Corporations Act 2001.* • Accounting Standards.	[Negative form] "Not aware of any matter… believe… does not present a true and fair view of ….in accordance with…"

* see AASB 101 *Presentation of Financial Statements.*

Entity and Information Type	Framework	Form of Opinion
ASA 800: Special Purpose—*Fair Presentation*		
Non-reporting entity — complete set of financial statements	• Accounting Standards. • Reporting requirements specified by Management.	"Presents fairly in all material respects" **or** "true and fair"
Incorporated Association subject to audit — complete set of financial statements	• Requirements of applicable Act.	"True and fair"
Financial Services Licensee — complete set of financial statements	• Accounting Standards. • Reporting requirements specified by regulator.	"Presents fairly in all material respects" **or** "true and fair"
Any entity type— financial report for borrowing covenant reporting purposes	• Accounting Standards. • Reporting requirements specified by borrowings agreement.	"Presents fairly in all material respects" **or** "true and fair"

ASA 800: Special Purpose—*Compliance*		
Joint venture — complete set of financial statements	• Reporting provisions of a joint venture agreement.	"Prepared in all material respects"
Listed entity — borrowing covenant reporting	• Reporting requirements specified by borrowing agreement.	"Prepared in all material respects"

ASA 805: General or Special Purpose—*Fair Presentation*		
Small company — single balance sheet (incl. related notes)	• Accounting Standards.	"Presents fairly in all material respects"
Large proprietary company — debtors balance audit at year end	• Accounting Standards. • Reporting requirements specified by Management.	"Presents fairly in all material respects"
Small company — statement of cash receipts and payments, with related notes	• Cash basis of accounting.	"Presents fairly in all material respects"

ASA 805: General or Special Purpose—*Compliance*		
Insurance company— statement of liability for claims incurred but not reported	• Reporting requirements specified by regulation.	"Prepared in all material respects"
Financial Services License — financial return	• Reporting requirements specified by regulation.	"Prepared in all material respects"
Small company— statement of cash receipts and payments for a grant received by Government Agency	• Reporting requirements determined by grant agreement (not fair presentation framework).	"Prepared in all material respects"
Authorised Deposit-Taking Institution — APRA reporting forms	• APRA Prudential and Reporting Standards.	"Prepared in all material respects"

ASA 810: Summary Financial Statements		
Large proprietary company — summary financial statements	• Reporting requirements specified by Management.	"Consistent, in all material respects with"; **or** "a fair summary of"
Listed disclosing entity— concise financial report	• *Corporations Act 2001*. • AASB 1039.	"Complies with AASB 1039…"

ASA

Other Reporting Responsibilities

Report on Other Legal and Regulatory Requirements

The auditor may have additional responsibilities to report on other matters that are supplementary to the auditor's reporting responsibilities for the financial report. For example, the auditor may be required or requested to report on certain matters that come to the auditor's attention during the course of the audit of the financial report. Alternatively, the auditor may be required or requested to perform, and report on, additional specified procedures, or to express an opinion on specific matters, such as the adequacy of accounting books and records.

Such other reporting responsibilities are addressed in a separate section of the auditor's report in order to clearly distinguish them from the auditor's responsibility under the Standards to report on the financial report. The separate section in the auditor's report is sub-titled "Report on Other Legal and Regulatory Requirements" (or other heading, as appropriate). Where relevant, this section may also contain sub-heading(s) that describe(s) the content of the other reporting responsibility paragraph(s). [Refer ASA 700, Para. 38-39]

Other Matter Paragraph

An "Other Matter Paragraph" (OMP) in the auditor's report is used if the auditor considers it necessary to communicate a matter, other than those that are presented or disclosed in the financial report that in the auditor's professional judgement is relevant to the users' understanding of the audit, the auditor's responsibilities, or the auditor's report. The paragraph is sub-titled "Other Matter," or other appropriate heading. [See ASA 706, Para. 8]

Note: An "Other Matter Paragraph" is *not* used for other reporting responsibilities under ASA 700, Para. 38-39 (discussed above).

Main Features of the New Reporting Standards

ASA 700—*Unmodified opinions, General Purpose*

Features	
1	Covers both financial reporting frameworks: • Fair presentation; and • Compliance (new requirements and guidance material). Appendix 1 includes examples of both types.
2	The auditor must evaluate whether the financial report is prepared in accordance with the financial reporting framework, and adequately refers to, or describes the framework.
3	Auditor's report no longer needs to refer to: • Those charged with governance being responsible for "selecting and applying appropriate accounting policies"; and • *Australian Accounting Interpretations.* There are also changes to the wording of management's responsibilities in relation to internal control.
4	If the auditor is required by law or regulation to use a prescribed layout or wording in the auditor's report, the auditor can only refer to the Australian Auditing Standards when the report contains certain elements set out in the Standard.

ASA 705—*Modified Opinions*

Features	
1	Covers only modifications to the opinion, whereas the pre-existing Standard (ASA 701) also included requirements and guidance material relating to an Emphasis of Matter paragraph (EOM) – now covered in ASA 706.
2	The Standard emphasises that the form of opinion is based on whether or not sufficient appropriate audit evidence has been obtained.
3	When expressing an adverse opinion or disclaimer of opinion, the description of the auditor's responsibilities in the auditor's report must be amended.
4	The auditor is required to communicate with those charged with governance when there is going to be any modification wording included in the auditor's report and modifications to the auditor's opinion.
5	Appendix 1 contains illustrations of auditor's reports containing modified opinions for general purpose financial reports.

ASA 706—*Emphasis of Matter Paragraph (EOM) and Other Matter Paragraph* (OMP)

Features	
1	Does not include requirements and guidance material relating to modifications to the opinion (now covered by ASA 705).
2	Contains new requirements and guidance material on "Other Matter Paragraphs".
3	No longer prescribes the circumstances requiring an EOM but contains lists of other Standards that require an EOM or OMP (see Appendices 1 & 2). ASA 706 provides requirements on the form and placement of such paragraphs.
4	The auditor must use professional judgement to determine what is *fundamental* to users': • understanding of the financial report; *or* • relevant to users' understanding of the audit, the auditor's responsibilities, or the auditor's report.
5	An EOM draws users' attention to a matter that is disclosed/presented in the financial report, that the auditor considers fundamental to users' understanding of the financial report.
6	An OMP is used for the communication of a matter other than which is disclosed/presented in the financial report, that the auditor considers relevant to users' understanding of the audit, the auditor's responsibilities, or the auditor's report.
7	The auditor is required to communicate with those charged with governance when there is going to be any EOM and/or OMP included in the auditor's report.
8	Appendix 3 contains illustrations of auditor's reports containing an EOM and/or OMP for general purpose financial reports.
9	When a general purpose framework has been used for a specific purpose because it meets the users' special information needs, the auditor may use an OMP to restrict distribution or use of the auditor's report.
10	Paragraphs 15 and 34 in the pre-existing Standard deal with additional information in the financial report so as to achieve fair presentation. In the new Standard, these two paragraphs have been combined and reworded so as to remove reference to modifications to the opinion (now covered by ASA 705).

ASA 800—*Unmodified, Special Purpose*

Features	
1	Covers only auditors reporting in relation to a financial report. Pre-existing ASA 800 includes requirements and guidance material on other historical financial information (now covered in ASA 805 and ASA 810).
2	Clarifies that ASA 101 to ASA 700 apply to the audit of a financial report, and that ASA 800 deals with "*...special considerations in the application of those Auditing Standards to an audit of a financial report prepared in accordance with a <u>special purpose framework</u>*". (Note: underlined words – emphasis added)
3	The auditor must evaluate whether the financial report is prepared in accordance with the financial reporting framework, and adequately refers to, or describes the framework.
4	Reference is made to ASA 700 for the auditor's report format and content, with ASA 800 providing additional requirements in respect of the purpose of the financial report and management's choice of the applicable financial reporting framework. Accordingly, modifications, EOM and OMP in relation to special purpose reporting are now covered by ASAs 705 and 706. Pre-existing ASA 800 prescribes the basic elements of the report.
5	An EOM in the auditor's report is now used to alert users that the financial report is prepared in accordance with a special purpose framework and accordingly may not be suitable for other purposes. Previously this was included in the Scope section of the auditor's report.
6	Financial reporting requirements under the *Corporations Act 2001* (the Act) are no longer included in the Appendices.
7	Appendix 1 contains illustrations of auditor's reports for special purpose financial reports.

ASA 805—*Single Financial Statements and their Specific Elements, Accounts and Items*

Features	
1	The new Standard (carved out from pre-existing ASA 800) covers auditor's reporting only in relation to "*...special considerations in the application of the Australian Auditing Standards to an audit of a single financial statement or of a specific element, account, or item of a financial statement*".
2	The Standard is <u>not</u> "made" under the Act because there is no requirement to audit a single financial statement under the Act. It is not considered a stand-alone Standard and should be read in conjunction with the other Standards (including ASA 800, where the single financial statement is prepared using a special purpose framework).

Features	
3	The auditor must evaluate whether the single financial statement is prepared in accordance with the financial reporting framework, and adequately refers to, or describes the framework.
4	Reference is made to ASA 700 for the auditor's reporting format and content, which is then tailored to the engagement circumstances.
5	The Standard contemplates (but does not require) that the auditor has already performed the audit of the financial report from which the single financial statement has been derived. If the auditor has not already audited the financial report, the auditor has to determine if the audit of a single financial statement is practical.
6	The auditor is not to issue the auditor's report containing the opinion on the single financial statement or on the specific element of a financial statement unless satisfied the report is adequately differentiated from the auditor's report on the financial report.
7	If the opinion in the auditor's report on the financial report is modified or includes an EOM and/or OMP, the auditor must determine what effect this has on the auditor's report on a single financial statement.
8	The auditor must not express an unmodified opinion on a single financial statement if the auditor has expressed an adverse opinion or disclaimed an opinion on the financial report.
9	Appendix 2 contains illustrations of auditor's reports for single financial statements and their elements, accounts or items.

ASA 810—*Summary Financial Statements*

Features	
1	The new Standard (carved out from pre-existing ASA 800) applies to summary financial statements derived from a financial report audited by the same auditor.
2	The Standard is not "made" under the Act because there is no requirement to audit summary financial statements under the Act. It is considered a stand-alone Standard, covering all aspects of the audit engagement. Its principles and procedures are consistent with the other Standards.
3	The auditor must determine the acceptability of the criteria used by management in the preparation of the summary financial statements.
4	The auditor's report refers only to an audit conducted in accordance with ASA 810 (not the Australian Auditing Standards as in the pre-existing Standards).
5	The Standard details the procedures (not those in other Standards) required to be performed by the auditor in order to form a conclusion on summary financial statements.
6	The Standard provides the format and content of the auditor's report (i.e. no reference is made to ASA 700).
7	Any restrictions, modifications, EOM or OMP contained in the auditor's report on the financial report from which the summary financial statements were derived must be reflected in the auditor's report on the summary financial statements.
8	The Standard applies to a concise financial report; to the extent it is applicable in meeting the objectives of the audit of the concise report. (see also GS 001)
9	Appendix 1 contains illustrations of auditor's reports for summary financial statements.

ASRE 2410—*Review of a Financial Report Performed by the Independent Auditor of the Entity*

Features	
1	Covers only a review of a financial report by an independent auditor.
2	The auditor must evaluate whether the financial report is prepared in accordance with a fair presentation financial reporting framework, and adequately refers to, or describes, the framework.
3	The auditor must determine the preconditions for the review.
4	Consistent with the principles in ASA 706, where there is significant uncertainty adequately disclosed in the financial report (not related to going concern), the auditor is required to consider including an EOM in the auditor's report. An EOM is mandated in the pre-existing Standard.
5	Appendix 3 contains illustrations of review reports.

This *Explanatory Guide* should be read in conjunction with:

- the AUASB pronouncements mentioned in this *Explanatory Guide*;
- ASA 101 *Preamble to Australian Auditing Standards*; and
- ASA 200 *Overall Objectives of the Independent Auditor and the Conduct of an Audit in Accordance with Australian Auditing Standards.*

Appendix

Overview of the Reporting Standards – Audit

The following diagram is a broad illustration of the Standards in the ASA 700 and 800 series, which relate to the auditor's reporting on historical financial information (reporting Standards). Whilst the Standards listed are the primary Standards applicable to reporting for the particular audit engagement types listed, readers are reminded that they do not represent the *only* Standards that may be applicable to forming an opinion and reporting on an audit of a financial report/single financial statement. Where appropriate, the Standards contain cross references to other Standards (including other reporting Standards) that *may* be applicable in the circumstances of the audit.

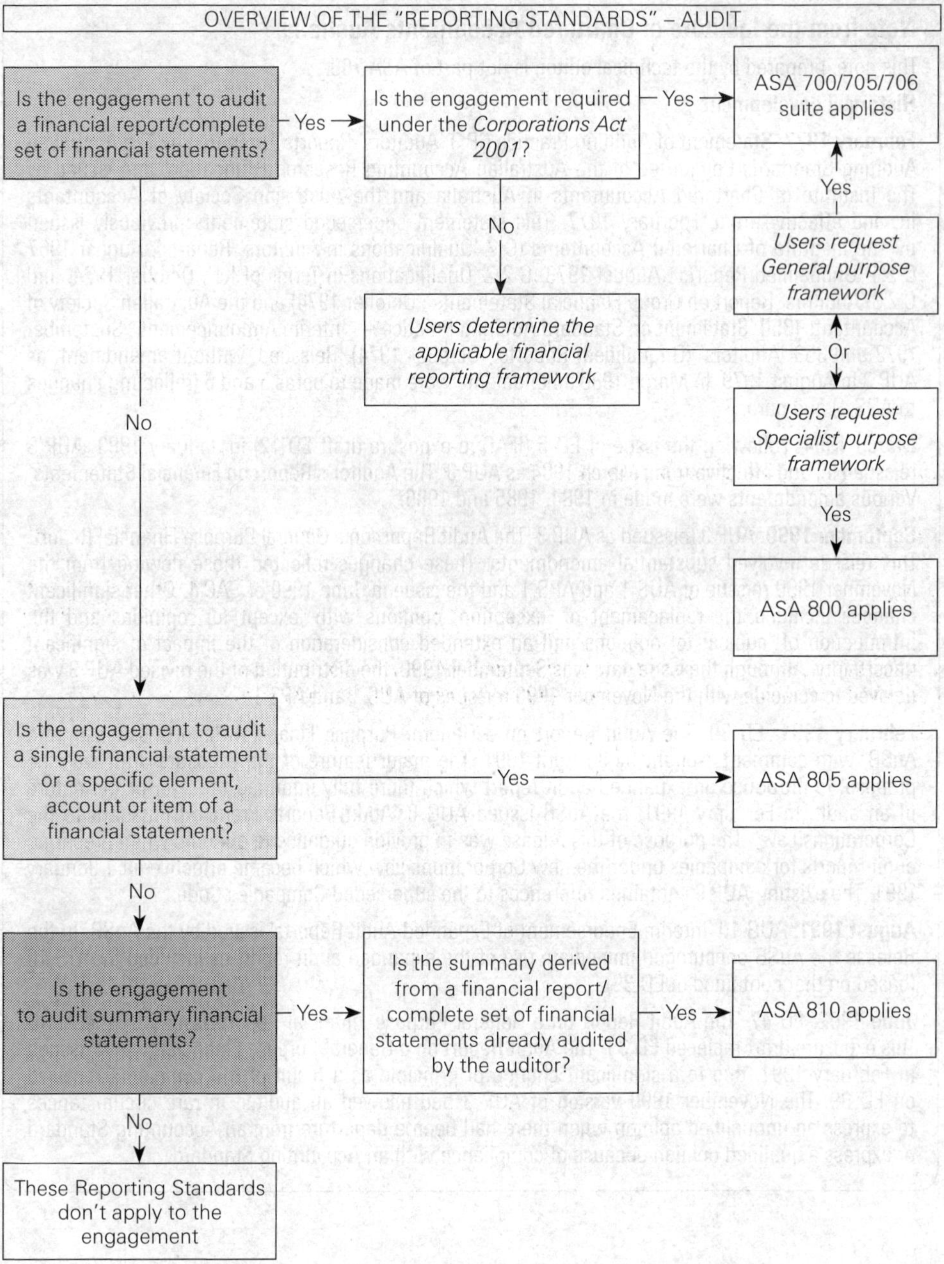

ASA 700

Forming an Opinion and Reporting on a Financial Report

(Reissued October 2009: amended and compiled June 2011)

Issued by the Auditing and Assurance Standards Board.

Note from the Institute of Chartered Accountants Australia

This note, prepared by the technical editor, is not part of ASA 700.

Historical development

February 1977: Statement of Auditing Practice CP 3 'Auditors' Reports', prepared by The Australian Auditing Standards Committee of the Australian Accounting Research Foundation, and issued by The Institute of Chartered Accountants in Australia and the Australian Society of Accountants in, and effective from, February 1977. This statement superseded statements previously issued by The Institute of Chartered Accountants (C 2 'Qualifications in Auditors' Reports', August 1967, C 2.1 'Unqualified Reports', August 1973, C 2.2 'Qualifications in Terms of K1', October 1974, and C 2.3 'Auditors' Report on Group Financial Statements', October 1974) and the Australian Society of Accountants (350 'Statement on Standard Auditing Practice — Interim Announcement', September 1973 and 353 'Auditors' (Unqualified) Reports', October 1974). Reissued, without amendment, as AUP 3 in August 1979. In March 1980 amendments were made to paras 5 and 6 (reflecting changes to AUS 1) and para. 8.

March 1984: Following the issue of ED 5 (IFAC re-exposure draft ED 12) in January 1983, AUP 3 reissued in, and effective from, March 1984 as AUP 3 'The Auditor's Report on Financial Statements'. Various amendments were made in 1984, 1985 and 1986.

September 1990: AUP 3 reissued as AUP 3 'The Audit Report on a General Purpose Financial Report'. This reissue involved substantial amendments. These changes reflected those flowing from the November 1990 reissue of AUS 1 and APS 1 and the issue in June 1990 of SAC 1. Other significant changes included the replacement of 'exception' opinions with 'except for' opinions and the introduction of 'subject to' opinions and an extended consideration of the impact of significant uncertainty. Although the issue date was September 1990, the distribution of the revised AUP 3 was delayed to coincide with the November 1990 reissues of AUS 1 and APS 1.

February 1991: ED 39 'The Audit Report on a General Purpose Financial Report' issued by the AuSB, with comments sought by 30 April 1991. The major feature of the exposure draft was the proposal to introduce an expanded audit report which more fully informed the user of the nature of an audit. In February 1991, the AuSB issued AUG 8 'Audit Reports Prepared Pursuant to the Corporations Law'. The purpose of this release was to provide guidance to auditors when preparing audit reports for companies under the new Corporations Law which became effective on 1 January 1991. The existing AUP 3 contained references to the superseded Companies Code.

August 1991: AUG 10 'Interim Endorsement of Expanded Audit Reports' issued by the AuSB. In the Release the AuSB encouraged immediate use of the expanded audit report as included in AUG 10 (based on that contained in ED 39).

June 1992: ED 47 'The Audit Report on a General Purpose Financial Report' issued by the AuSB. This exposure draft replaced ED 39 'The Audit Report on a General Purpose Financial Report' issued in February 1991, due to a significant change of principle as a result of the comments received on ED 39. The November 1990 version of AUP 3 had allowed an auditor, in rare circumstances, to express an unqualified opinion when there had been a departure from an Accounting Standard, or express a qualified opinion because of compliance with an Accounting Standard.

July 1993: ED 47 issued as AUP 3 'The Audit Report on a General Purpose Financial Report'. AUP 3 applied to audits of general purpose financial reports in relation to financial reporting periods ending on or after 30 June 1993. The revised AUP 3 required that a departure from an Accounting Standard results, in all cases, in a qualified audit opinion. AUP 3 further required a qualified opinion to be given when additional disclosures had been made in the financial report on the basis that application of a particular Accounting Standard had resulted in the financial report being potentially misleading. Exceptions were permitted only in the rare circumstances outlined in para. 32.

February 1994: AUP 3 reissued by the AuSB. AUP 3 provided authoritative guidance on the application of Standards in AUS 1 'Statement of Auditing Standards'. As a result of the changes to AUS 1 references to SACs, including references in the 'scope' and 'opinion' sections of the example audit reports in the Appendices were removed. In addition, para. 47 of the July 1993 version of AUP 3 was deleted. This paragraph provided guidance as to when it was appropriate to refer to a prior period's qualified report in the current period's audit report. The AuSB advised that guidance on this issue was now dealt with in Statement of Auditing Practice AUP 37 'Audit Implications of Comparatives'.

May 1994: ED 56 'Codification and Revision of Auditing Pronouncements: AUS 702 The Audit Report on a General Purpose Financial Report (AUP 3)' issued by the AuSB.

June 1994: The International Auditing Practices Committee (IAPC) of the International Federation of Accountants (IFAC) approved the issuance of a codified set of International Standards of Auditing (ISAs). The relevant international pronouncement was ISA 700 'The Auditor's Report on Financial Statements'.

June 1995: AUP 3 'The Audit Report on a General Purpose Financial Report' revised. During 1995 Miscellaneous Professional Statement APS 1 was amended and reissued under the title 'Conformity with Accounting Standards and UIG Consensus Views' to give professional authority to the consensus views of the Urgent Issues Group (UIG). As a result of the amendment to APS 1, AUS 1 'Statement of Auditing Standards' and Statement of Auditing Practice AUP 3 'The Audit Report on a General Purpose Financial Report' were revised to reflect the status of UIG Consensus Views.

October 1995: Australian Auditing Standards and Auditing Guidance Statements released. The status of these was explained in APS 1.1 'Conformity With Auditing' Standards. AUS 702 became operative in relation to audit reports dated on or after 1 January 1997 and later reporting periods, although earlier application was encouraged. AUP 3 'The Audit Report on a General Purpose Financial Report' replaced by AUS 702 'The Audit Report on a General Purpose Financial Report'.

April 1998: AUS/AGS Omnibus 1 'Miscellaneous Amendments to AUSs and AGSs' issued, with minor amendments to AUS 702. Also, ED 67 'Amendments to AUS 702 The Audit Report on a General Purpose Financial Report' and AUS 708 'Going Concern' were released, with comments sought by 30 June 1998.

October 1998: AUS 702 'The Audit Report on a General Purpose Financial Report' reissued, based on the ED 67 proposals. It replaced AUS 702 of the same title issued in October 1995.

February 1999: AUS 702 'The Audit Report on a General Purpose Financial Report' reissued operative from the date of issue.

May 2002: AUS 702 revised by ED 79 which was issued in October 2001. These changes require entities to specify Australia as the country of origin of the financial reporting framework on which the report is based. These changes are reflected in the version of AUS 702 issued in May 2002.

July 2003: Guidance note: Improving Communication Between Auditors and Shareholders issued. The guidance note (also included in this Handbook) contains an optional alternative format for the audit report.

April 2006: The material in AUS 702 has been split between ASA 700 'The Auditor's Report on a General Purpose Financial Report' and ASA 701 'Modifications to the Auditor's Report'. ASA 700 is a legally enforceable Standard based on ISA 700 'The Independent Auditor's Report on a Complete Set of General Purpose Financial Statements'.

June 2007: ASA 700 was amended by Omnibus ASA 2007-1 which introduced a statement in the Audit Report on an entity's compliance with International Financial Reporting Standards. It also clarified the description of the responsibility of those charged with the entity's governance in respect of internal controls in the audit report.

October 2009: ASA 700 reissued as part of the AUASB's Clarity Project with a new title 'Forming an Opinion and Reporting on a Financial Report'. It differentiates between reporting under a 'compliance framework' as opposed to a 'fair presentation framework', and requires the auditor to evaluate whether the financial report adequately describes its financial reporting framework. It is based on ISA 700, 'Forming an Opinion and Reporting on Financial Statements'.

June 2011: ASA 700 updated for editorial amendments contained in ASA 2011-1 'Amendments to Australian Auditing Standards'.

Contents

Compilation Details

Auditing Standard ASA 700 *Forming an Opinion and Reporting on a Financial Report* as Amended

This compilation takes into account amendments made up to and including 27 June 2011 and was prepared on 27 June 2011 by the Auditing and Assurance Standards Board (AUASB).

This compilation is not a separate Auditing Standard made by the AUASB. Instead, it is a representation of ASA 700 (October 2009) as amended by another Auditing Standard which is listed in the Table below.

Table of Standards

Standard	Date made	Operative date
ASA 700	27 October 2009	1 January 2010
ASA 2011-1	27 June 2011	1 July 2011

Table of Amendments

Paragraph affected	How affected	By ... [paragraph]
Appendix 1 Illustrations 1 and 3	Amended	ASA 2011-1 [56]
Appendix 1 Illustrations 1A and 3A	Amended	ASA 2011-1 [57]
Appendix 1 Illustration 2	Amended	ASA 2011-1 [58]
Appendix 1 [Aus] Illustration 1A	Amended	ASA 2011-1 [59]
Appendix 1 [Aus] Illustration 3A	Amended	ASA 2011-1 [60]

Preface

[Preface extracted from the original Auditing Standard issued 27 October 2009]

Reasons for Issuing Auditing Standard ASA 700 *Forming an Opinion and Reporting on a Financial Report*

The Auditing and Assurance Standards Board (AUASB) issues Auditing Standard ASA 700 *Forming an Opinion and Reporting on a Financial Report* pursuant to the requirements of the legislative provisions and the Strategic Direction explained below.

The AUASB is an independent statutory board of the Australian Government established under section 227A of the *Australian Securities and Investments Commission Act 2001*, as amended (ASIC Act). Under section 336 of the *Corporations Act 2001*, the AUASB may make Australian Auditing Standards for the purposes of the corporations legislation. These Auditing Standards are legislative instruments under the *Legislative Instruments Act 2003*.

Under the Strategic Direction given to the AUASB by the Financial Reporting Council (FRC), the AUASB is required to have regard to any programme initiated by the International Auditing and Assurance Standards Board (IAASB) for the revision and enhancement of the International Standards on Auditing (ISAs) and to make appropriate consequential amendments to the Australian Auditing Standards. Accordingly, the AUASB has decided to revise and redraft the Australian Auditing Standards using the equivalent redrafted ISAs.

Main Features

This Auditing Standard establishes requirements and provides application and other explanatory material regarding the auditor's responsibility to form an opinion on the financial report. It also deals with the form and content of the auditor's report issued as a result of an audit of a financial report.

This Auditing Standard:

(a) defines a general purpose financial report;

(b) describes the terms "fair presentation framework" and "compliance framework";

(c) requires the auditor to form an opinion having concluded on whether the auditor has obtained reasonable assurance;

(d) requires the auditor to evaluate whether the financial report is prepared, in all material respects, in accordance with the applicable financial reporting framework;

(e) describes the form of opinion and the circumstances under which each form of opinion is required; and

(f) describes the required content of the independent auditor's report.

Authority Statement

Auditing Standard ASA 700 *Forming an Opinion and Reporting on a Financial Report* (as amended at 27 June 2011) is set out in paragraphs 1 to A51 and Appendix 1.

This Auditing Standard is to be read in conjunction with ASA 101 *Preamble to Australian Auditing Standards*, which sets out the intentions of the AUASB on how the Australian Auditing Standards, operative for financial reporting periods commencing on or after 1 January 2010, are to be understood, interpreted and applied. This Auditing Standard is to be read also in conjunction with ASA 200 *Overall Objectives of the Independent Auditor and the Conduct of an Audit in Accordance with Australian Auditing Standards*.

Dated: 27 June 2011

M H Kelsall
Chairman - AUASB

Auditing Standard ASA 700

The Auditing and Assurance Standards Board (AUASB) made Auditing Standard ASA 700 *Forming an Opinion and Reporting on a Financial Report,* pursuant to section 227B of the *Australian Securities and Investments Commission Act 2001* and section 336 of the *Corporations Act 2001*, on 27 October 2009.

This compiled version of ASA 700 incorporates subsequent amendments contained in another Auditing Standard made by the AUASB up to and including 27 June 2011 (see Compilation Details).

Auditing Standard ASA 700

Forming an Opinion and Reporting on a Financial Report

ASA

Application

Aus 0.1 This Auditing Standard applies to:

(a) an audit of a financial report for a financial year, or an audit of a financial report for a half-year, in accordance with the *Corporations Act 2001*; and

(b) an audit of a financial report, or a complete set of financial statements, for any other purpose.

Aus 0.2 This Auditing Standard also applies, as appropriate, to an audit of other historical financial information.

Operative Date

Aus 0.3 This Auditing Standard is operative for financial reporting periods commencing on or after 1 January 2010. [Note: For operative dates of paragraphs changed or added by an amending Standard, see Compilation Details.]

Introduction

Scope of this Auditing Standard

1. This Auditing Standard deals with the auditor's responsibility to form an opinion on the financial report. It also deals with the form and content of the auditor's report issued as a result of an audit of a financial report.

2. ASA 705[1] and ASA 706[2] deal with how the form and content of the auditor's report are affected when the auditor expresses a modified opinion or includes an Emphasis of Matter paragraph or an Other Matter paragraph in the auditor's report.

3. This Auditing Standard is written in the context of a general purpose financial report. ASA 800[3] deals with special considerations when a financial report is prepared in accordance with a special purpose framework. ASA 805[4] deals with special considerations relevant to an audit of a single financial statement or of a specific element, account or item of a financial statement.

4. This Auditing Standard promotes consistency in the auditor's report. Consistency in the auditor's report, when the audit has been conducted in accordance with the Australian Auditing Standards, which use the International Standards on Auditing (ISAs) as the underlying auditing standards, promotes credibility in the global marketplace by making more readily identifiable those audits that have been conducted in accordance with globally recognised standards. It also helps to promote the user's understanding and to identify unusual circumstances when they occur.

---

1 See ASA 705 *Modifications to the Opinion in the Independent Auditor's Report.*

2 See ASA 706 *Emphasis of Matter Paragraphs and Other Matter Paragraphs in the Independent Auditor's Report.*

3 See ASA 800 *Special Considerations—Audits of Financial Reports Prepared in Accordance with Special Purpose Frameworks.*

4 See ASA 805 *Special Considerations—Audits of Single Financial Statements and Specific Elements, Accounts or Items of a Financial Statement.*

Effective Date

5. [Deleted by the AUASB. Refer Aus 0.3]

Objectives

6. The objectives of the auditor are:

(a) To form an opinion on the financial report based on an evaluation of the conclusions drawn from the audit evidence obtained; and

(b) To express clearly that opinion through a written report that also describes the basis for that opinion.

Definitions

7. For purposes of the Australian Auditing Standards, the following terms have the meanings attributed below:

(a) General purpose financial report means a financial report prepared in accordance with a general purpose framework.

(b) General purpose framework means a financial reporting framework designed to meet the common financial information needs of a wide range of users. The financial reporting framework may be a fair presentation framework or a compliance framework.

The term "fair presentation framework" is used to refer to a financial reporting framework that requires compliance with the requirements of the framework and:

(i) Acknowledges explicitly or implicitly that, to achieve fair presentation of the financial report, it may be necessary for management to provide disclosures beyond those specifically required by the framework; or

(ii) Acknowledges explicitly that it may be necessary for management to depart from a requirement of the framework to achieve fair presentation of the financial report. Such departures are expected to be necessary only in extremely rare circumstances.

The term "compliance framework" is used to refer to a financial reporting framework that requires compliance with the requirements of the framework, but does not contain the acknowledgements in (i) or (ii) above.[5]

(c) Unmodified opinion means the opinion expressed by the auditor when the auditor concludes that the financial report is prepared, in all material respects, in accordance with the applicable financial reporting framework.[6]

8. Reference to "a financial report" in this Auditing Standard means "a complete set of general purpose financial statements, including the related notes and an assertion statement by those responsible for the financial report." The related notes ordinarily comprise a summary of significant accounting policies and other explanatory information. The requirements of the applicable financial reporting framework[*] determine the form and content of the financial report.[#]

9. [Deleted by the AUASB. Refer Aus 9.1]

Aus 9.1 Reference to "Australian Accounting Standards" in this Auditing Standard means the Australian Accounting Standards issued by the Australian Accounting Standards Board, and reference to "International Financial Reporting Standards" means the International Financial Reporting Standards issued by the International Accounting Standards Board.

5 See ASA 200 *Overall Objectives of the Independent Auditor and the Conduct of an Audit in Accordance with Australian Auditing Standards*, paragraph 13(a).

6 Paragraphs 35-36 of this Auditing Standard deal with the phrases used to express this opinion in the case of a fair presentation framework and a compliance framework, respectively.

* See, for example, Australian Accounting Standards and the *Corporations Act 2001*.

See ASA 200, paragraphs Aus 13.3 and Aus 13.4.

Requirements

Forming an Opinion on the Financial Report

10. The auditor shall form an opinion on whether the financial report is prepared, in all material respects, in accordance with the applicable financial reporting framework.[7, 8]

11. In order to form that opinion, the auditor shall conclude as to whether the auditor has obtained reasonable assurance about whether the financial report as a whole is free from material misstatement, whether due to fraud or error. That conclusion shall take into account:
    (a) The auditor's conclusion, in accordance with ASA 330, whether sufficient appropriate audit evidence has been obtained;[9]
    (b) The auditor's conclusion, in accordance with ASA 450, whether uncorrected misstatements are material, individually or in aggregate;[10] and
    (c) The evaluations required by paragraphs 12-15 of this Auditing Standard.

12. The auditor shall evaluate whether the financial report is prepared, in all material respects, in accordance with the requirements of the applicable financial reporting framework. This evaluation shall include consideration of the qualitative aspects of the entity's accounting practices, including indicators of possible bias in management's judgements. (Ref: Para. A1-A3)

13. In particular, the auditor shall evaluate whether, in view of the requirements of the applicable financial reporting framework:
    (a) The financial report adequately discloses the significant accounting policies selected and applied;
    (b) The accounting policies selected and applied are consistent with the applicable financial reporting framework and are appropriate;
    (c) The accounting estimates made by management are reasonable;
    (d) The information presented in the financial report is relevant, reliable, comparable and understandable;
    (e) The financial report provides adequate disclosures to enable the intended users to understand the effect of material transactions and events on the information conveyed in the financial report; and (Ref: Para. A4)
    (f) The terminology used in the financial report, including the title of each financial statement, is appropriate.

14. When the financial report is prepared in accordance with a fair presentation framework, the evaluation required by paragraphs 12-13 of this Auditing Standard shall also include whether the financial report achieves fair presentation. The auditor's evaluation as to whether the financial report achieves fair presentation shall include consideration of:
    (a) The overall presentation, structure and content of the financial report; and
    (b) Whether the financial report, including the related notes, represents the underlying transactions and events in a manner that achieves fair presentation.

15. The auditor shall evaluate whether the financial report adequately refers to or describes the applicable financial reporting framework. (Ref: Para. A5-A10)

Form of Opinion

16. The auditor shall express an unmodified opinion when the auditor concludes that the financial report is prepared, in all material respects, in accordance with the applicable financial reporting framework.

---

7 See ASA 200, paragraph 11.

8 See paragraphs 35-36 of this Auditing Standard for phrases used to express this opinion in the case of a fair presentation framework and a compliance framework, respectively.

9 See ASA 330 *The Auditor's Responses to Assessed Risks*, paragraph 26.

10 See ASA 450 *Evaluation of Misstatements Identified during the Audit*, paragraph 11.

17. If the auditor:

    (a) concludes that, based on the audit evidence obtained, the financial report as a whole is not free from material misstatement; or

    (b) is unable to obtain sufficient appropriate audit evidence to conclude that the financial report as a whole is free from material misstatement,

    the auditor shall modify the opinion in the auditor's report in accordance with ASA 705.

18. If the financial report prepared in accordance with the requirements of a fair presentation framework does not achieve fair presentation, the auditor shall discuss the matter with management and, depending on the requirements of the applicable financial reporting framework and how the matter is resolved, shall determine whether it is necessary to modify the opinion in the auditor's report in accordance with ASA 705. (Ref: Para. A11)

19. When the financial report is prepared in accordance with a compliance framework, the auditor is not required to evaluate whether the financial report achieves fair presentation. However, if in extremely rare circumstances the auditor concludes that such financial report is misleading, the auditor shall discuss the matter with management and, depending on how it is resolved, shall determine whether, and how, to communicate it in the auditor's report. (Ref: Para. A12)

Auditor's Report

20. The auditor's report shall be in writing. (Ref: Para. A13-A14)

Auditor's Report for Audits Conducted in Accordance with Australian Auditing Standards

Title

21. The auditor's report shall have a title that clearly indicates that it is the report of an independent auditor. (Ref: Para. A15)

Addressee

22. The auditor's report shall be addressed as required by the circumstances of the engagement. (Ref: Para. A16)

Introductory Paragraph

23. The introductory paragraph in the auditor's report shall: (Ref: Para. A17-A19)

    (a) Identify the entity whose financial report has been audited;

    (b) State that the financial report has been audited;

    (c) Identify the title of each statement that comprises the financial report;

    (d) Refer to the summary of significant accounting policies and other explanatory information; and

    (e) Specify the date or period covered by each financial statement comprising the financial report.

Management's Responsibility for the Financial Report

24. This section of the auditor's report describes the responsibilities of those in the organisation who are responsible for the preparation of the financial report. The auditor's report need not refer specifically to "management," but shall use the term that is appropriate in the context of the legal framework in the particular jurisdiction. In some jurisdictions, the appropriate reference may be to those charged with governance.

25. The auditor's report shall include a section with the heading "Management's [or other appropriate term] Responsibility for the Financial Report."

26. The auditor's report shall describe management's responsibility for the preparation of the financial report. The description shall include an explanation that management is responsible for the preparation of the financial report in accordance with the applicable financial reporting framework, and for such internal control as it determines is necessary to enable the preparation of the financial report that is free from material misstatement, whether due to fraud or error. (Ref: Para. A20-A23)

27. Where the financial report is prepared in accordance with a fair presentation framework, the explanation of management's responsibility for the financial report in the auditor's report shall refer to "the preparation and fair presentation of the financial report" or "the preparation of the financial report that gives a true and fair view," as appropriate in the circumstances.

Auditor's Responsibility

28. The auditor's report shall include a section with the heading "Auditor's Responsibility."

29. The auditor's report shall state that the responsibility of the auditor is to express an opinion on the financial report based on the audit. (Ref: Para. A24)

30. The auditor's report shall state that the audit was conducted in accordance with Australian Auditing Standards. The auditor's report shall also explain that those standards require that the auditor comply with relevant ethical requirements and that the auditor plan and perform the audit to obtain reasonable assurance about whether the financial report is free from material misstatement. (Ref: Para. A25-A26)

31. The auditor's report shall describe an audit by stating that:
    (a) An audit involves performing procedures to obtain audit evidence about the amounts and disclosures in the financial report;
    (b) The procedures selected depend on the auditor's judgement, including the assessment of the risks of material misstatement of the financial report, whether due to fraud or error. In making those risk assessments, the auditor considers internal control relevant to the entity's preparation of the financial report in order to design audit procedures that are appropriate in the circumstances, but not for the purpose of expressing an opinion on the effectiveness of the entity's internal control. In circumstances when the auditor also has a responsibility to express an opinion on the effectiveness of internal control in conjunction with the audit of the financial report, the auditor shall omit the phrase that the auditor's consideration of internal control is not for the purpose of expressing an opinion on the effectiveness of internal control; and
    (c) An audit also includes evaluating the appropriateness of the accounting policies used and the reasonableness of accounting estimates made by management, as well as the overall presentation of the financial report.

32. Where the financial report is prepared in accordance with a fair presentation framework, the description of the audit in the auditor's report shall refer to "the entity's preparation and fair presentation of the financial report" or "the entity's preparation of the financial report that gives a true and fair view," as appropriate in the circumstances.

33. The auditor's report shall state whether the auditor believes that the audit evidence the auditor has obtained is sufficient and appropriate to provide a basis for the auditor's opinion.

Auditor's Opinion

34. The auditor's report shall include a section with the heading "Opinion."

35. When expressing an unmodified opinion on the financial report prepared in accordance with a fair presentation framework, the auditor's opinion shall, unless otherwise required by law or regulation, use one of the following phrases, which are regarded as being equivalent:
    (a) The financial report presents fairly, in all material respects, … in accordance with [the applicable financial reporting framework]; or
    (b) The financial report gives a true and fair view of … in accordance with [the applicable financial reporting framework]. (Ref: Para. A27-A33)

36. When expressing an unmodified opinion on the financial report prepared in accordance with a compliance framework, the auditor's opinion shall be that the financial report is prepared, in all material respects, in accordance with [the applicable financial reporting framework]. (Ref: Para. A27, A29-A33)

37. If the reference to the applicable financial reporting framework in the auditor's opinion is not to Australian Accounting Standards, and, where applicable, Australian law or regulation, the auditor's opinion shall identify the jurisdiction of origin of the framework.

Aus 37.1 When an entity, in accordance with Accounting Standard AASB 101 *Presentation of Financial Statements*, has included in the notes to the financial statements an explicit and unreserved statement of compliance with *International Financial Reporting Standards* (IFRSs), and the auditor agrees with the entity's statement of compliance, the auditor shall state that in the auditor's opinion, the financial report complies with IFRSs. (Ref: Para. Aus A33.1-Aus A33.2)

Other Reporting Responsibilities

38. If the auditor addresses other reporting responsibilities in the auditor's report on the financial report that are in addition to the auditor's responsibility under the Australian Auditing Standards to report on the financial report, these other reporting responsibilities shall be addressed in a separate section in the auditor's report that shall be sub-titled "Report on Other Legal and Regulatory Requirements," or otherwise as appropriate to the content of the section. (Ref: Para. A34-A35)

39. If the auditor's report contains a separate section on other reporting responsibilities, the headings, statements and explanations referred to in paragraphs 23-37 of this Auditing Standard shall be under the sub-title "Report on the Financial Report." The "Report on Other Legal and Regulatory Requirements" shall follow the "Report on the Financial Report." (Ref: Para. A36 and Aus A36.1)

Signature of the Auditor

40. The auditor's report shall be signed. (Ref: Para. A37 and Aus A37.1)

Date of the Auditor's Report (Ref: Para. A38-A41)

Aus 40.1 The auditor's report shall be dated as of the date the auditor signs that report.

41. The auditor's report shall be dated no earlier than the date on which the auditor has obtained sufficient appropriate audit evidence on which to base the auditor's opinion on the financial report, including evidence that:

(a) All the statements that comprise the financial report, including the related notes, have been prepared; and

(b) Those with the recognised authority have asserted that they have taken responsibility for the financial report.

Auditor's Address

42. The auditor's report shall name the location in the jurisdiction where the auditor practices.

Auditor's Report Prescribed by Law or Regulation

43. If the auditor is required by law or regulation of a specific jurisdiction to use a specific layout or wording of the auditor's report, the auditor's report shall refer to Australian Auditing Standards only if the auditor's report includes, at a minimum, each of the following elements: (Ref: Para. A42)

(a) A title;

(b) An addressee, as required by the circumstances of the engagement;

(c) An introductory paragraph that identifies the financial report audited;

(d) A description of the responsibility of management (or other appropriate term, see paragraph 24 of this Auditing Standard) for the preparation of the financial report;

(e) A description of the auditor's responsibility to express an opinion on the financial report and the scope of the audit, that includes:

- A reference to Australian Auditing Standards and the law or regulation; and
- A description of an audit in accordance with those standards;

(f) An opinion paragraph containing an expression of opinion on the financial report and a reference to the applicable financial reporting framework used to prepare the financial report (including identifying the jurisdiction of origin of the financial reporting framework that is not Australian Accounting Standards and, where applicable, Australian law or regulation);

(g) The auditor's signature;

(h) The date of the auditor's report; and

(i) The auditor's address.

Auditor's Report for Audits Conducted in Accordance with Both Auditing Standards of a Specific Jurisdiction and Australian Auditing Standards

44. An auditor may be required to conduct an audit in accordance with the auditing standards of a specific jurisdiction ("other auditing standards"), but may additionally have complied with the Australian Auditing Standards in the conduct of the audit. If this is the case, the auditor's report may refer to Australian Auditing Standards in addition to the other auditing standards, but the auditor shall do so only if: (Ref: Para. A43-A44)

(a) There is no conflict between the requirements in the other auditing standards and those in the Australian Auditing Standards that would lead the auditor (i) to form a different opinion, or (ii) not to include an Emphasis of Matter paragraph that, in the particular circumstances, is required by Australian Auditing Standards; and

(b) The auditor's report includes, at a minimum, each of the elements set out in paragraph 43(a)-(i) of this Auditing Standard when the auditor uses the layout or wording specified by the other auditing standards. Reference to law or regulation in paragraph 43(e) of this Auditing Standard shall be read as reference to the other auditing standards. The auditor's report shall thereby identify such other auditing standards.

45. When the auditor's report refers to both the other auditing standards and Australian Auditing Standards, the auditor's report shall identify the jurisdiction of origin of the other auditing standards.

Supplementary Information Presented with the Financial Report

(Ref: Para. A45-A51)

46. If supplementary information that is not required by the applicable financial reporting framework is presented with the audited financial report, the auditor shall evaluate whether such supplementary information is clearly differentiated from the audited financial report. If such supplementary information is not clearly differentiated from the audited financial report, the auditor shall ask management to change how the unaudited supplementary information is presented. If management refuses to do so, the auditor shall explain in the auditor's report that such supplementary information has not been audited.

47. Supplementary information that is not required by the applicable financial reporting framework, but is nevertheless an integral part of the financial report because it cannot be clearly differentiated from the audited financial report due to its nature and how it is presented, shall be covered by the auditor's opinion.

❖ ❖ ❖

Application and Other Explanatory Material

Qualitative Aspects of the Entity's Accounting Practices (Ref: Para. 12)

A1. Management makes a number of judgements about the amounts and disclosures in the financial report.

A2. ASA 260 contains a discussion of the qualitative aspects of accounting practices.[11] In considering the qualitative aspects of the entity's accounting practices, the auditor may become aware of possible bias in management's judgements. The auditor may conclude that the cumulative effect of a lack of neutrality, together with the effect of uncorrected misstatements, causes the financial report as a whole to be materially misstated. Indicators

11 See ASA 260 *Communication with Those Charged with Governance*, Appendix 2.

of a lack of neutrality that may affect the auditor's evaluation of whether the financial report as a whole is materially misstated include the following:

- The selective correction of misstatements brought to management's attention during the audit (for example, correcting misstatements with the effect of increasing reported earnings, but not correcting misstatements that have the effect of decreasing reported earnings).
- Possible management bias in the making of accounting estimates.

A3. ASA 540 addresses possible management bias in making accounting estimates.[12] Indicators of possible management bias do not constitute misstatements for purposes of drawing conclusions on the reasonableness of individual accounting estimates. They may, however, affect the auditor's evaluation of whether the financial report as a whole is free from material misstatement.

Disclosure of the Effect of Material Transactions and Events on the Information Conveyed in the Financial Report (Ref: Para. 13(e))

A4. It is common for a financial report prepared in accordance with a general purpose framework to present an entity's financial position, financial performance and cash flows. In such circumstances, the auditor evaluates whether the financial report provides adequate disclosures to enable the intended users to understand the effect of material transactions and events on the entity's financial position, financial performance and cash flows.

Description of the Applicable Financial Reporting Framework (Ref: Para. 15)

A5. As explained in ASA 200, the preparation of the financial report by management and, where appropriate, those charged with governance requires the inclusion of an adequate description of the applicable financial reporting framework in the financial report.[13] That description is important because it advises users of the financial report of the framework on which the financial report is based.

A6. A description that the financial report is prepared in accordance with a particular applicable financial reporting framework is appropriate only if the financial report complies with all the requirements of that framework that is effective during the period covered by the financial report.

A7. A description of the applicable financial reporting framework that contains imprecise, qualifying or limiting language (for example, "the financial report is in substantial compliance with Australian Accounting Standards") is not an adequate description of that framework as it may mislead users of the financial report.[*]

Reference to More than One Financial Reporting Framework

A8. In some cases, the financial report may represent that it is prepared in accordance with two financial reporting frameworks (for example, Australian Accounting Standards and International Financial Reporting Standards). This may be because management is required, or has chosen, to prepare the financial report in accordance with both frameworks, in which case both are applicable financial reporting frameworks. Such description is appropriate only if the financial report complies with each of the frameworks individually. To be regarded as being prepared in accordance with both frameworks, the financial report needs to comply with both frameworks simultaneously and without any need for reconciling statements. In practice, simultaneous compliance is unlikely unless the jurisdiction has adopted the other framework or has eliminated all barriers to compliance with the other framework.

A9. A financial report that is prepared in accordance with one financial reporting framework and that contains a note or supplementary statement reconciling the results to those that would be shown under another framework, is not prepared in accordance with that other

12 See ASA 540 *Auditing Accounting Estimates, Including Fair Value Accounting Estimates, and Related Disclosures,* paragraph 21.

13 See ASA 200, paragraphs A2-A3.

* See also AASB 101 *Presentation of Financial Statements*.

framework. This is because the financial report does not include all the information in the manner required by that other framework.

A10. The financial report may, however, be prepared in accordance with one applicable financial reporting framework and, in addition, describe in the notes to the financial statements the extent to which the financial report complies with another framework (for example, a financial report prepared in accordance with the Australian Accounting Standards that also describes the extent to which it complies with other financial reporting standards). Such description is supplementary financial information and, as discussed in paragraph 47, is considered an integral part of the financial report and, accordingly, is covered by the auditor's opinion.

Form of Opinion (Ref: Para. 18-19)

A11. There may be cases where the financial report, although prepared in accordance with the requirements of a fair presentation framework, does not achieve fair presentation. Where this is the case, it may be possible for management to include additional disclosures in the financial report beyond those specifically required by the framework or, in extremely rare circumstances, to depart from a requirement in the framework in order to achieve fair presentation of the financial report.*

A12. It will be extremely rare for the auditor to consider a financial report that is prepared in accordance with a compliance framework to be misleading if, in accordance with ASA 210, the auditor determined that the framework is acceptable.[14]

Auditor's Report (Ref: Para. 20)

A13. A written report encompasses reports issued in hard copy format and those using an electronic medium.

A14. Appendix 1 contains illustrations of auditors' reports on a financial report, incorporating the elements set forth in paragraphs 21-42.

Auditor's Report for Audits Conducted in Accordance with Australian Auditing Standards

Title (Ref: Para. 21)

A15. A title indicating the report is the report of an independent auditor, for example, "Independent Auditor's Report," affirms that the auditor has met all of the relevant ethical requirements regarding independence and, therefore, distinguishes the independent auditor's report from reports issued by others.

Addressee (Ref: Para. 22)

A16. Law or regulation often specifies to whom the auditor's report is to be addressed in that particular jurisdiction. The auditor's report is normally addressed to those for whom the report is prepared, often either to the shareholders or to those charged with governance of the entity whose financial report is being audited.

Introductory Paragraph (Ref: Para. 23)

A17. The introductory paragraph states, for example, that the auditor has audited the accompanying financial report of the entity, which comprises [state the title of each financial statement comprising the financial report required by the applicable financial reporting framework, specifying the date or period covered by each financial statement] and the summary of significant accounting policies and other explanatory information.

A18. When the auditor is aware that the audited financial report will be included in a document that contains other information, such as an annual report, the auditor may consider, if the form of presentation allows, identifying the page numbers on which the audited financial report is presented. This helps users to identify the financial report to which the auditor's report relates.

A19. The auditor's opinion covers the financial report as defined by the applicable financial reporting framework. For example, in the case of many general purpose frameworks, the

* See the *Corporations Act 2001*.

14 See ASA 210 *Agreeing the Terms of Audit Engagements,* paragraph 6(a).

financial report includes: a statement of financial position, a statement of comprehensive income, a statement of changes in equity, a statement of cash flows, notes comprising a summary of significant accounting policies and other explanatory information, and an assertion by those responsible for the financial report. In some jurisdictions additional information might also be considered to be an integral part of the financial report.

Management's Responsibility for the Financial Report (Ref: Para. 26)

A20. ASA 200 explains the premise, relating to the responsibilities of management and, where appropriate, those charged with governance, on which an audit in accordance with Australian Auditing Standards is conducted.[15] Management and, where appropriate, those charged with governance accept responsibility for the preparation of the financial report in accordance with the applicable financial reporting framework, including where relevant its fair presentation. Management also accepts responsibility for such internal control as it deems necessary to enable the preparation of the financial report that is free from material misstatement, whether due to fraud or error. The description of management's responsibilities in the auditor's report includes reference to both responsibilities as it helps to explain to users the premise on which an audit is conducted.

A21. There may be circumstances when it is appropriate for the auditor to add to the description of management's responsibility in paragraph 26 to reflect additional responsibilities that are relevant to the preparation of the financial report in the context of the particular jurisdiction or the nature of the entity.

A22. Paragraph 26 is consistent with the form in which the responsibilities are agreed in the engagement letter or other suitable form of written agreement, as required by ASA 210.[16] ASA 210 provides some flexibility by explaining that, if law or regulation prescribes the responsibilities of management and, where appropriate, those charged with governance in relation to financial reporting, the auditor may determine that the law or regulation includes responsibilities that, in the auditor's judgement, are equivalent in effect to those set out in ASA 210. For such responsibilities that are equivalent, the auditor may use the wording of the law or regulation to describe them in the engagement letter or other suitable form of written agreement. In such cases, this wording may also be used in the auditor's report to describe management's responsibilities as required by paragraph 26. In other circumstances, including where the auditor decides not to use the wording of law or regulation as incorporated in the engagement letter, the wording of paragraph 26 is used.

A23. In some jurisdictions, law or regulation prescribing management's responsibilities may specifically refer to a responsibility for the adequacy of accounting books and records, or accounting system. As books, records and systems are an integral part of internal control (as defined in ASA 315[17]), the descriptions in ASA 210 and in paragraph 26 do not make specific reference to them.

Auditor's Responsibility (Ref: Para. 29-30)

A24. The auditor's report states that the auditor's responsibility is to express an opinion on the financial report based on the audit in order to contrast it to management's responsibility for the preparation of the financial report.

A25. The reference to the standards used conveys to the users of the auditor's report that the audit has been conducted in accordance with established standards.

A26. In accordance with ASA 200, the auditor does not represent compliance with the Australian Auditing Standards in the auditor's report unless the auditor has complied with the requirements of ASA 200 and all other Australian Auditing Standards relevant to the audit.[18]

---

15 See ASA 200, paragraph 13(j).

16 See ASA 210, paragraph 6(b)(i)-(ii).

17 See ASA 315 *Identifying and Assessing Risks of Material Misstatement through Understanding the Entity and Its Environment*, paragraph 4(c).

18 See ASA 200, paragraph 20.

Auditor's Opinion (Ref: Para. 35-37)

Wording of the auditor's opinion prescribed by law or regulation

A27. ASA 210 explains that, in some cases, law or regulation of the relevant jurisdiction prescribes the wording of the auditor's report (which in particular includes the auditor's opinion) in terms that are significantly different from the requirements of the Australian Auditing Standards. In these circumstances, ASA 210 requires the auditor to evaluate:

(a) Whether users might misunderstand the assurance obtained from the audit of the financial report and, if so,

(b) Whether additional explanation in the auditor's report can mitigate possible misunderstanding.

If the auditor concludes that additional explanation in the auditor's report cannot mitigate possible misunderstanding, ASA 210 requires the auditor not to accept the audit engagement, unless required by law or regulation to do so. In accordance with ASA 210, an audit conducted in accordance with such law or regulation does not comply with the Australian Auditing Standards. Accordingly, the auditor does not include any reference in the auditor's report to the audit having been conducted in accordance with Australian Auditing Standards.[19]

ASA

"Presents fairly, in all material respects" or "gives a true and fair view"

A28. Whether the phrase "presents fairly, in all material respects," or the phrase "gives a true and fair view" is used in any particular jurisdiction is determined by the law or regulation governing the audit of a financial report in that jurisdiction, or by generally accepted practice in that jurisdiction. Where law or regulation requires the use of different wording, this does not affect the requirement in paragraph 14 of this Auditing Standard for the auditor to evaluate the fair presentation of the financial report prepared in accordance with a fair presentation framework.

Description of information that the financial report presents

A29. In the case of a financial report prepared in accordance with a fair presentation framework, the auditor's opinion states that the financial report presents fairly, in all material respects, or gives a true and fair view of the information that the financial report is designed to present, for example, in the case of many general purpose frameworks, the financial position of the entity as at the end of the period and the entity's financial performance and cash flows for the period then ended.

Description of the applicable financial reporting framework and how it may affect the auditor's opinion

A30. The identification of the applicable financial reporting framework in the auditor's opinion is intended to advise users of the auditor's report of the context in which the auditor's opinion is expressed; it is not intended to limit the evaluation required in paragraph 14. The applicable financial reporting framework is identified in such terms as:

"… in accordance with Australian Accounting Standards" or

"… in accordance with accounting principles generally accepted in Jurisdiction X …"

A31. When the applicable financial reporting framework encompasses financial reporting standards and legal or regulatory requirements, the framework is identified in such terms as "… in accordance with Australian Accounting Standards, the requirements of the *Corporations Act 2001* and the *Corporations Regulations 2001*." ASA 210 deals with circumstances where there are conflicts between the financial reporting standards and the legislative or regulatory requirements.[20]

A32. As indicated in paragraph A8, the financial report may be prepared in accordance with two financial reporting frameworks, which are therefore both applicable financial reporting frameworks. Accordingly, each framework is considered separately when forming the

19 See ASA 210, paragraph 21.

20 See ASA 210, paragraph 18.

auditor's opinion on the financial report, and the auditor's opinion in accordance with paragraphs 35-36 refers to both frameworks as follows:

(a) If the financial report complies with each of the frameworks individually, two opinions are expressed: that is, that the financial report is prepared in accordance with one of the applicable financial reporting frameworks (for example, Australian Accounting Standards) and an opinion that the financial report is prepared in accordance with the other applicable financial reporting framework (for example, International Financial Reporting Standards). These opinions may be expressed separately or in a single sentence (for example, the financial report is presented fairly, in all material respects, in accordance with Australian Accounting Standards and with International Financial Reporting Standards).

(b) If the financial report complies with one of the frameworks but fails to comply with the other framework, an unmodified opinion can be given that the financial report is prepared in accordance with the one framework (for example, Australian Accounting Standards) but a modified opinion given with regard to the other framework (for example, International Financial Reporting Standards) in accordance with ASA 705.

A33. As indicated in paragraph A10, the financial report may represent compliance with the applicable financial reporting framework and, in addition, disclose the extent of compliance with another financial reporting framework. As explained in paragraph A46, such supplementary information is covered by the auditor's opinion as it cannot be clearly differentiated from the financial report.

(a) If the disclosure as to the compliance with the other framework is misleading, a modified opinion is expressed in accordance with ASA 705.

(b) If the disclosure is not misleading, but the auditor judges it to be of such importance that it is fundamental to the users' understanding of the financial report, an Emphasis of Matter paragraph is added in accordance with ASA 706, drawing attention to the disclosure.

Aus A33.1 With respect to the requirement in paragraph Aus 37.1, Appendix 1 provides illustrations of auditors' reports, see:

- [Aus] Illustration 1A: Example Auditor's Report Single Company—*Corporations Act 2001*; and
- [Aus] Illustration 3A: Example Auditor's Report Consolidated Entity—*Corporations Act 2001*.

Aus A33.2 ASA 705 provides requirements and guidance when the auditor disagrees with those charged with governance in relation to compliance with the requirements of Australian Accounting Standards, and this applies to, and includes, AASB 101 requirements. (Ref: Para. Aus 37.1)

***Other Reporting Responsibilities** (Ref: Para. 38-39)*

A34. In some jurisdictions, the auditor may have additional responsibilities to report on other matters that are supplementary to the auditor's responsibility under the Australian Auditing Standards to report on the financial report. For example, the auditor may be asked to report certain matters if they come to the auditor's attention during the course of the audit of the financial report. Alternatively, the auditor may be asked to perform and report on additional specified procedures, or to express an opinion on specific matters, such as the adequacy of accounting books and records. Auditing standards in the specific jurisdiction often provide guidance on the auditor's responsibilities with respect to specific additional reporting responsibilities in that jurisdiction.

Aus A34.1 When the audit of a financial report is conducted in accordance with the *Corporations Act 2001* (the "Act"), section 308(3)(b) of that Act requires the auditor to describe in the auditor's report any deficiency, failure or shortcoming in respect of certain matters referred to in section 307(b), (c) or (d) of that Act.

A35. In some cases, the relevant law or regulation may require or permit the auditor to report on these other responsibilities within the auditor's report on the financial report. In other cases, the auditor may be required or permitted to report on them in a separate report.

A36. These other reporting responsibilities are addressed in a separate section of the auditor's report in order to clearly distinguish them from the auditor's responsibility under the Australian Auditing Standards to report on the financial report. Where relevant, this section may contain a sub-heading(s) that describe(s) the content of the other reporting responsibility paragraph(s).

Aus A36.1 An example of "other reporting responsibilities" is where a remuneration report is included in a directors' report and the auditor is required to report in accordance with section 308(3C) of the *Corporations Act 2001*.*

Signature of the Auditor *(Ref: Para. 40)*

A37. The auditor's signature is either in the name of the audit firm, the personal name of the auditor or both, as appropriate for the particular jurisdiction. In addition to the auditor's signature, in certain jurisdictions, the auditor may be required to declare in the auditor's report the auditor's professional accountancy designation or the fact that the auditor or firm, as appropriate, has been recognised by the appropriate licensing authority in that jurisdiction.

Aus A37.1 Under the *Corporations Act 2001*, the auditor of a company or registered scheme is required to sign the auditor's report in both their own name and the name of their firm [section 324AB(3)] or the name of the audit company [section 324AD(1)], as applicable.

Date of the Auditor's Report *(Ref: Para. Aus 40.1 and 41)*

A38. The date of the auditor's report informs the user of the auditor's report that the auditor has considered the effect of events and transactions of which the auditor became aware and that occurred up to that date. The auditor's responsibility for events and transactions after the date of the auditor's report is addressed in ASA 560.[21]

A39. Since the auditor's opinion is provided on the financial report and the financial report is the responsibility of management, the auditor is not in a position to conclude that sufficient appropriate audit evidence has been obtained until evidence is obtained that all the statements that comprise the financial report, including the related notes, have been prepared and management has accepted responsibility for them.

A40. In some jurisdictions, the law or regulation identifies the individuals or bodies (for example, the directors) that are responsible for concluding that all the statements that comprise the financial report, including the related notes, have been prepared, and specifies the necessary approval process. In such cases, evidence is obtained of that approval before dating the report on the financial report. In other jurisdictions, however, the approval process is not prescribed in law or regulation. In such cases, the procedures the entity follows in preparing and finalising its financial report in view of its management and governance structures are considered in order to identify the individuals or body with the authority to conclude that all the statements that comprise the financial report, including the related notes, have been prepared. In some cases, law or regulation identifies the point in the financial reporting process at which the audit is expected to be complete.

A41. In some jurisdictions, final approval of the financial report by shareholders is required before the financial report is issued publicly. In these jurisdictions, final approval by shareholders is not necessary for the auditor to conclude that sufficient appropriate audit evidence has been obtained. The date of approval of the financial report for purposes of the Australian Auditing Standards is the earlier date on which those with the recognised authority determine that all the statements that comprise the financial report, including the related notes, have been prepared and that those with the recognised authority have asserted that they have taken responsibility for them.

---

* See also AUASB Guidance Statement GS 008 *The Auditor's Report on a Remuneration Report Pursuant to Section 307A of the Corporations Act 2001.* (June 2008).

21 See ASA 560 *Subsequent Events*, paragraphs 10-17.

Auditor's Report Prescribed by Law or Regulation (Ref: Para. 43)

A42. ASA 200 explains that the auditor may be required to comply with legal or regulatory requirements in addition to Australian Auditing Standards.[22] Where this is the case, the auditor may be obliged to use a layout or wording in the auditor's report that differs from that described in this Auditing Standard. As explained in paragraph 4, consistency in the auditor's report, when the audit has been conducted in accordance with the Australian Auditing Standards, which use the ISAs as the underlying auditing standards, promotes credibility in the global marketplace by making more readily identifiable those audits that have been conducted in accordance with globally recognised standards. When the differences between the legal or regulatory requirements and the Australian Auditing Standards relate only to the layout and wording of the auditor's report and, at a minimum, each of the elements identified in paragraph 43(a)-(i) are included in the auditor's report, the auditor's report may refer to Australian Auditing Standards. Accordingly, in such circumstances the auditor is considered to have complied with the requirements of the Australian Auditing Standards, even when the layout and wording used in the auditor's report are specified by legal or regulatory reporting requirements. Where specific requirements in a particular jurisdiction do not conflict with Australian Auditing Standards, adoption of the layout and wording used in this Auditing Standard assists users of the auditor's report more readily to recognise the auditor's report as a report on an audit conducted in accordance with the Australian Auditing Standards. ASA 210 deals with circumstances where law or regulation prescribes the layout or wording of the auditor's report in terms that are significantly different from the requirements of Australian Auditing Standards.

Auditor's Report for Audits Conducted in Accordance with Both Auditing Standards of a Specific Jurisdiction and Australian Auditing Standards (Ref: Para. 44)

A43. The auditor may refer in the auditor's report to the audit having been conducted in accordance with both Australian Auditing Standards as well as other auditing standards when, in addition to complying with the relevant other auditing standards, the auditor complies with each of the Australian Auditing Standards relevant to the audit.[23]

A44. A reference to both Australian Auditing Standards and other auditing standards is not appropriate if there is a conflict between the requirements in the Australian Auditing Standards and those in the other auditing standards that would lead the auditor to form a different opinion or not to include an Emphasis of Matter paragraph that, in the particular circumstances, is required by the Australian Auditing Standards. For example, some other auditing standards prohibit the auditor from including an Emphasis of Matter paragraph to highlight a going concern problem, whereas ASA 570 requires the auditor to add an Emphasis of Matter paragraph in such circumstances.[24] In such a case, the auditor's report refers only to the auditing standards (either Australian Auditing Standards or the other auditing standards) in accordance with which the auditor's report has been prepared.

Supplementary Information Presented with the Financial Report

(Ref: Para. 46-47)

A45. In some circumstances, the entity may be required by law, regulation or standards, or may voluntarily choose, to present together with the financial report supplementary information that is not required by the applicable financial reporting framework. For example, supplementary information might be presented to enhance a user's understanding of the applicable financial reporting framework or to provide further explanation of specific financial statement items. Such information is normally presented in either supplementary schedules or as additional notes.

A46. The auditor's opinion covers supplementary information that cannot be clearly differentiated from the financial report because of its nature and how it is presented. For example, this would be the case when the notes to the financial statements include an explanation of the extent to which the financial report complies with another financial reporting framework. The auditor's opinion would also cover notes or supplementary schedules that are cross-referenced from the financial report.

22 See ASA 200, paragraph A55.

23 See ASA 200, paragraph A56.

24 See ASA 570 *Going Concern,* paragraph 19.

A47. Supplementary information that is covered by the auditor's opinion does not need to be specifically referred to in the introductory paragraph of the auditor's report when the reference to the notes in the description of the statements that comprise the financial report in the introductory paragraph is sufficient.

A48. Law or regulation may not require that the supplementary information be audited, and management may decide not to ask the auditor to include the supplementary information within the scope of the audit of the financial report.

A49. The auditor's evaluation whether unaudited supplementary information is presented in a manner that could be construed as being covered by the auditor's opinion includes, for example, where that information is presented in relation to the financial report and any audited supplementary information, and whether it is clearly labelled as "unaudited."

A50. Management could change the presentation of unaudited supplementary information that could be construed as being covered by the auditor's opinion, for example, by:

- Removing any cross references from the financial report to unaudited supplementary schedules or unaudited notes so that the demarcation between the audited and unaudited information is sufficiently clear.
- Placing the unaudited supplementary information outside of the financial report or, if that is not possible in the circumstances, at a minimum place the unaudited notes together at the end of the required notes to the financial statements and clearly label them as unaudited. Unaudited notes that are intermingled with the audited notes can be misinterpreted as being audited.

A51. The fact that supplementary information is unaudited does not relieve the auditor of the responsibility to read that information to identify material inconsistencies with the audited financial report. The auditor's responsibilities with respect to unaudited supplementary information are consistent with those described in ASA 720.[25]

❖ ❖ ❖

Conformity with International Standards on Auditing

This Auditing Standard conforms with International Standard on Auditing ISA 700 *Forming an Opinion and Reporting on Financial Statements*, issued by the International Auditing and Assurance Standards Board (IAASB), an independent standard-setting board of the International Federation of Accountants (IFAC).

Paragraphs that have been added to this Auditing Standard (and do not appear in the text of the equivalent ISA) are identified with the prefix "Aus".

The following requirements are additional to ISA 700:

- When an entity, in accordance with Accounting Standard AASB 101 *Presentation of Financial Statements* has included in the notes to the financial statements, an explicit and unreserved statement of compliance with *International Financial Reporting Standards* (IFRSs), and the auditor agrees with the entity's statement of compliance, the auditor shall state that in the auditor's opinion, the financial report complies with IFRSs. (Ref: Para. Aus 37.1)
- The auditor's report shall be dated as of the date the auditor signs that report. (Ref: Para. Aus 40.1)

Compliance with this Auditing Standard enables compliance with ISA 700.

25 See ASA 720 *The Auditor's Responsibilities Relating to Other Information in Documents Containing an Audited Financial Report.*

Appendix 1
(Ref: Para. A14)

Illustrations of Auditors' Reports on a General Purpose Financial Report—Unmodified Opinions

- Illustration 1: An auditor's report on a financial report prepared in accordance with a fair presentation framework designed to meet the common financial information needs of a wide range of users (for example, financial statements prepared in accordance with Australian Accounting Standards).
- [Aus] Illustration 1A: An auditor's report on a single entity's financial report prepared in accordance with a fair presentation framework designed to meet the common financial information needs of a wide range of users (under the *Corporations Act 2001*).
- Illustration 2: An auditor's report on a complete set of financial statements prepared in accordance with a compliance framework designed to meet the common financial information needs of a wide range of users.
- Illustration 3: An auditor's report on a consolidated entity's financial report prepared in accordance with a fair presentation framework designed to meet the common financial information needs of a wide range of users (for example, financial statements prepared in accordance with Australian Accounting Standards).
- [Aus] Illustration 3A: An auditor's report on a consolidated entity's financial report prepared in accordance with a fair presentation framework designed to meet the common financial information needs of a wide range of users (under the *Corporations Act 2001*).

Example Auditor's Report
General Purpose Financial Report
(Fair Presentation Framework)

Illustration 1:

Circumstances include the following:

- **Audit of a financial report.**
- **The financial report is prepared for a general purpose by management of the entity—the financial statements are prepared in accordance with Australian Accounting Standards.**
- **The financial report is *not* prepared under the *Corporations Act 2001*.**
- **The financial report includes a statement that the financial statements comply with *International Financial Reporting Standards (IFRSs)*.**
- **The terms of the audit engagement reflect the description of management's responsibility for the financial report in ASA 210.**
- **In addition to the audit of the financial report, the auditor has other reporting responsibilities required under local law.**

INDEPENDENT AUDITOR'S REPORT

[Appropriate Addressee]

Report on the Financial Report[26]

We have audited the accompanying financial report of ABC Entity, which comprises the statement of financial position as at 30 June 20X1, the statement of comprehensive income, statement of changes in equity and statement of cash flows for the year then ended, notes comprising a summary of significant accounting policies and other explanatory information, and management's assertion statement.*

26 The sub-title "Report on the Financial Report" is unnecessary in circumstances when the second sub-title "Report on Other Legal and Regulatory Requirements", or other appropriate sub-title, is not applicable.

* Or other appropriate term.

Management's[27] Responsibility for the Financial Report

Management is responsible for the preparation and fair presentation of the financial report in accordance with Australian Accounting Standards and [relevant reporting framework],[28] and for such internal control as management determines is necessary to enable the preparation and fair presentation of the financial report that is free from material misstatement, whether due to fraud or error. In Note XX, management also states, in accordance with Accounting Standard AASB 101 *Presentation of Financial Statements*, that the financial statements comply with *International Financial Reporting Standards*.[#]

Auditor's Responsibility

Our responsibility is to express an opinion on the financial report based on our audit. We conducted our audit in accordance with Australian Auditing Standards. Those standards require that we comply with relevant ethical requirements relating to audit engagements and plan and perform the audit to obtain reasonable assurance about whether the financial report is free from material misstatement.

An audit involves performing procedures to obtain audit evidence about the amounts and disclosures in the financial report. The procedures selected depend on the auditor's judgement, including the assessment of the risks of material misstatement of the financial report, whether due to fraud or error. In making those risk assessments, the auditor considers internal control relevant to the entity's preparation and fair presentation[29] of the financial report in order to design audit procedures that are appropriate in the circumstances, but not for the purpose of expressing an opinion on the effectiveness of the entity's internal control.[30] An audit also includes evaluating the appropriateness of accounting policies used and the reasonableness of accounting estimates made by management, as well as evaluating the overall presentation of the financial report.

We believe that the audit evidence we have obtained is sufficient and appropriate to provide a basis for our audit opinion.

Opinion

In our opinion:

(a) the financial report presents fairly, in all material respects, (or *gives a true and fair view of*) the financial position of ABC Entity as at 30 June 20X1, and (*of*) its financial performance and its cash flows for the year then ended in accordance with Australian Accounting Standards and [relevant reporting framework]; and

(b) the financial report also complies with *International Financial Reporting Standards* as disclosed in Note XX.[†]

---

27 Or other term that is appropriate in the context of the legal framework in the particular jurisdiction.

28 Where management's responsibility is to prepare the financial report that gives a true and fair view, this may read: "Management is responsible for the preparation of the financial report that gives a true and fair view in accordance with [relevant financial reporting framework] and for such…"

\# Insert only where the entity has included in the notes to the financial statements an explicit and unreserved statement of compliance with *International Financial Reporting Standards* in accordance with AASB 101.

29 In the case of footnote 28, this may read: "In making those risk assessments, the auditor considers internal control relevant to the entity's preparation of the financial report that gives a true and fair view in order to design audit procedures that are appropriate in the circumstances, but not for the purpose of expressing an opinion on the effectiveness of the entity's internal control."

30 In circumstances when the auditor also has responsibility to express an opinion on the effectiveness of internal control in conjunction with the audit of the financial report, this sentence would be worded as follows: "In making those risk assessments, the auditor considers internal control relevant to the entity's preparation and fair presentation of the financial report in order to design audit procedures that are appropriate in the circumstances." In the case of footnote 28, this may read: "In making those risk assessments, the auditor considers internal control relevant to the entity's preparation of the financial report that gives a true and fair view in order to design audit procedures that are appropriate in the circumstances."

† Insert only where the entity has included in the notes to the financial statements an explicit and unreserved statement of compliance with *International Financial Reporting Standards* in accordance with AASB 101 and the auditor agrees with the entity's statement. If the auditor does not agree with the statement, the auditor refers to ASA 705.

Report on Other Legal and Regulatory Requirements

[Form and content of this section of the auditor's report will vary depending on the nature of the auditor's other reporting responsibilities.]

[Auditor's signature]*

[Date of the auditor's report]#

[Auditor's address]

Example Auditor's Report Single Company—*Corporations Act 2001* (Fair Presentation Framework)

[Aus] Illustration 1A:

Circumstances include the following:

- **Audit of a single company's financial report.**
- **The financial report is prepared for a general purpose under the *Corporations Act 2001*.**
- **The financial report includes a statement that the financial statements comply with *International Financial Reporting Standards* (IFRSs).**
- **The terms of the audit engagement reflect the description of management's responsibility for the financial report in ASA 210.**
- **In addition to the audit of the financial report, the auditor has other reporting responsibilities required under section 308(3C) of the *Corporations Act 2001*.** (Ref: Para. 38 and 39)

INDEPENDENT AUDITOR'S REPORT

[Appropriate Addressee]

Report on the Financial Report**

We have audited the accompanying financial report of ABC Company Ltd., which comprises the statement of financial position as at 30 June 20X1, the statement of comprehensive income, statement of changes in equity and statement of cash flows for the year then ended, notes comprising a summary of significant accounting policies and other explanatory information, and the directors' declaration.

Directors' Responsibility for the Financial Report

The directors of the company [registered scheme/disclosing entity] are responsible for the preparation of the financial report that gives a true and fair view in accordance with Australian Accounting Standards and the *Corporations Act 2001* and for such internal control as the directors determine is necessary to enable the preparation of the financial report that gives a fair and true view and is free from material misstatement, whether due to fraud or error. In Note XX, the directors also state, in accordance with Accounting Standard AASB 101 *Presentation of Financial Statements*, that the financial statements comply with *International Financial Reporting Standards*.***

Auditor's Responsibility

Our responsibility is to express an opinion on the financial report based on our audit. We conducted our audit in accordance with Australian Auditing Standards. Those standards require that we comply with relevant ethical requirements relating to audit engagements and plan and perform the audit to obtain reasonable assurance about whether the financial report is free from material misstatement.

---

* The auditor's report needs to be signed in one or more of the following ways: name of the audit firm, the name of the audit company or the personal name of the auditor as appropriate.

\# The date of the auditor's report is the date the auditor signs the report.

** The sub-title "Report on the Financial Report" is unnecessary in circumstances when the second sub-title "Report on Other Legal and Regulatory Requirements", or other appropriate sub-title, is not applicable.

*** Insert only where the entity has included in the notes to the financial statements an explicit and unreserved statement of compliance with *International Financial Reporting Standards* in accordance with AASB 101.

An audit involves performing procedures to obtain audit evidence about the amounts and disclosures in the financial report. The procedures selected depend on the auditor's judgement, including the assessment of the risks of material misstatement of the financial report, whether due to fraud or error. In making those risk assessments, the auditor considers internal control relevant to the company's preparation of the financial report that gives a true and fair view in order to design audit procedures that are appropriate in the circumstances, but not for the purpose of expressing an opinion on the effectiveness of the company's internal control. An audit also includes evaluating the appropriateness of accounting policies used and the reasonableness of accounting estimates made by the directors, as well as evaluating the overall presentation of the financial report.

We believe that the audit evidence we have obtained is sufficient and appropriate to provide a basis for our audit opinion.

Independence

In conducting our audit, we have complied with the independence requirements of the *Corporations Act 2001*. We confirm that the independence declaration required by the *Corporations Act 2001*, which has been given to the directors of ABC Company Ltd., would be in the same terms if given to the directors as at the time of this auditor's report.*

Opinion

In our opinion:

(a) the financial report of ABC Company Ltd. is in accordance with the *Corporations Act 2001*, including:

 (i) giving a true and fair view of the company's [registered scheme's/disclosing entity's] financial position as at 30 June 20X1 and of its performance for the year ended on that date; and

 (ii) complying with Australian Accounting Standards and the *Corporations Regulations 2001*; and

(b) the financial report also complies with *International Financial Reporting Standards* as disclosed in Note XX.†

Report on the Remuneration Report§

We have audited the Remuneration Report included in [paragraphs a to b or pages x to y] of the directors' report for the year ended 30 June 20X1. The directors of the company are responsible for the preparation and presentation of the Remuneration Report in accordance with section 300A of the *Corporations Act 2001*. Our responsibility is to express an opinion on the Remuneration Report, based on our audit conducted in accordance with Australian Auditing Standards.

* Or, alternatively, include statements (a) to the effect that circumstances have changed since the declaration was given to the relevant directors; and (b) setting out how the declaration would differ if it had been given to the relevant directors at the time the auditor's report was made.

† Insert only where the entity has included in the notes to the financial statements an explicit and unreserved statement of compliance with I*nternational Financial Reporting Standards* in accordance with AASB 101 and the auditor agrees with the entity's statement. If the auditor does not agree with the statement, the auditor refers to ASA 705.

§ The Report on the Remuneration Report is an example of "Other Reporting Responsibilities"—refer paragraphs 38 and 39. Any additional "Other Reporting Responsibilities" that the auditor needs to address will also be included in a separate section of the auditor's report following the opinion paragraph on the financial report. Under paragraph 38, the sub-title "Report on Other Legal and Regulatory Requirements" or other sub-title as appropriate to the section is used.

Opinion

In our opinion, the Remuneration Report of ABC Company Ltd. for the year [period] ended 30 June 20X1 complies with section 300A of the *Corporations Act 2001*.

[Auditor's signature]**

[Date of the auditor's report]#

[Auditor's address]

Example Auditor's Report General Purpose Financial Report—XYZ Law of Jurisdiction X (Compliance Framework)

Illustration 2:

Circumstances include the following:

- **Audit of a complete set of financial statements required by law or regulation.**
- **The financial statements are prepared for a general purpose by management of the entity in accordance with the Financial Reporting Framework (XYZ Law) of Jurisdiction X (that is, a financial reporting framework, encompassing law or regulation, designed to meet the common financial information needs of a wide range of users, but which is not a fair presentation framework).**
- **The financial statements are *not* prepared under the *Corporations Act 2001*.**
- **The terms of the audit engagement reflect the description of management's responsibility for the financial statements in ASA 210.**

INDEPENDENT AUDITOR'S REPORT

[Appropriate Addressee]

We have audited the accompanying financial statements of ABC Entity, which comprise the statement of financial position as at 30 June 20X1, the statement of comprehensive income, statement of changes in equity and statement of cash flows for the year then ended, and notes comprising a summary of significant accounting policies and other explanatory information.

Management's[31] Responsibility for the Financial Statements

Management is responsible for the preparation of the financial statements in accordance with XYZ Law of Jurisdiction X, and for such internal control as management determines is necessary to enable the preparation of the financial statements that are free from material misstatement, whether due to fraud or error.

Auditor's Responsibility

Our responsibility is to express an opinion on the financial statements based on our audit. We conducted our audit in accordance with Australian Auditing Standards. Those standards require that we comply with relevant ethical requirements relating to audit engagements and plan and perform the audit to obtain reasonable assurance about whether the financial statements are free from material misstatement.

An audit involves performing procedures to obtain audit evidence about the amounts and disclosures in the financial statements. The procedures selected depend on the auditor's judgement, including the assessment of the risks of material misstatement of the financial statements, whether due to fraud or error. In making those risk assessments, the auditor considers internal control relevant to the entity's preparation of the financial statements in order to design audit procedures that are appropriate in the circumstances, but not for the purpose of expressing

** The auditor's report needs to be signed in one or more of the following ways: name of the audit firm, the name of the audit company or the personal name of the auditor as appropriate.

The date of the auditor's report is the date the auditor signs the report.

31 Or other term that is appropriate in the context of the legal framework in the particular jurisdiction.

an opinion on the effectiveness of the entity's internal control.[32] An audit also includes evaluating the appropriateness of accounting policies used and the reasonableness of accounting estimates made by management, as well as evaluating the presentation of the financial statements.

We believe that the audit evidence we have obtained is sufficient and appropriate to provide a basis for our audit opinion.

Opinion

In our opinion, the financial statements of ABC Entity for the year ended 30 June 20X1 are prepared, in all material respects, in accordance with XYZ Law of Jurisdiction X.

[Auditor's signature]*

[Date of the auditor's report]#

[Auditor's address]

Example Auditor's Report Consolidated Entity (Fair Presentation Framework)

Illustration 3:

Circumstances include the following:

- **Audit of a consolidated entity's financial report prepared for a general purpose by management of the parent—the financial statements are prepared in accordance with Australian Accounting Standards.**
- **The financial report is *not* prepared under the *Corporations Act 2001*.**
- **The financial report includes a statement that the financial statements comply with *International Financial Reporting Standards* (IFRSs).**
- **The terms of the group audit engagement reflect the description of management's responsibility for the financial report in ASA 210.**
- **In addition to the audit of the group financial report, the auditor has other reporting responsibilities required under local law.**

INDEPENDENT AUDITOR'S REPORT

[Appropriate Addressee]

Report on the Financial Report[33]

We have audited the accompanying financial report of ABC Entity, which comprises the statements of financial position as at 30 June 20X1, the statements of comprehensive income, the statements of changes in equity and the statements of cash flows for the year then ended, notes comprising a summary of significant accounting policies and other explanatory information, and management's assertion statement** of the entity and the consolidated entity comprising the entity and the entities it controlled at the year's end or from time to time during the financial year.

32 In circumstances when the auditor also has responsibility to express an opinion on the effectiveness of internal control in conjunction with the audit of the financial statements, this sentence would be worded as follows: "In making those risk assessments, the auditor considers internal control relevant to the entity's preparation of the financial statements in order to design audit procedures that are appropriate in the circumstances."

* The auditor's report needs to be signed in one or more of the following ways: name of the audit firm, the name of the audit company or the personal name of the auditor, as appropriate.

\# The date of the auditor's report is the date the auditor signs the report.

33 The sub-title "Report on the Financial Report" is unnecessary in circumstances when the second sub-title "Report on Other Legal and Regulatory Requirements", or other appropriate sub-title, is not applicable.

** Or other appropriate term.

Management's[34] Responsibility for the Financial Report

Management is responsible for the preparation and fair presentation of the financial report in accordance with Australian Accounting Standards and [relevant reporting framework],[35] and for such internal control as management determines is necessary to enable the preparation and fair presentation of the financial report that is free from material misstatement, whether due to fraud or error. In Note XX, management also states, in accordance with Accounting Standard AASB 101 *Presentation of Financial Statements*, that the financial statements comply with *International Financial Reporting Standards*.[#]

Auditor's Responsibility

Our responsibility is to express an opinion on the financial report based on our audit. We conducted our audit in accordance with Australian Auditing Standards. Those standards require that we comply with relevant ethical requirements relating to audit engagements and plan and perform the audit to obtain reasonable assurance about whether the financial report is free from material misstatement.

An audit involves performing procedures to obtain audit evidence about the amounts and disclosures in the financial report. The procedures selected depend on the auditor's judgement, including the assessment of the risks of material misstatement of the financial report, whether due to fraud or error. In making those risk assessments, the auditor considers internal control relevant to the entity's preparation and fair presentation[36] of the financial report in order to design audit procedures that are appropriate in the circumstances, but not for the purpose of expressing an opinion on the effectiveness of the entity's internal control.[37] An audit also includes evaluating the appropriateness of accounting policies used and the reasonableness of accounting estimates made by management, as well as evaluating the overall presentation of the financial report.

We believe that the audit evidence we have obtained is sufficient and appropriate to provide a basis for our audit opinion.

Opinion

In our opinion:

(a) the financial report presents fairly, in all material respects, (or *gives a true and fair view of*) the financial position of ABC Entity and its subsidiaries, as at 30 June 20X1, and (*of*) their financial performance and cash flows for the year then ended in accordance with Australian Accounting Standards and [relevant reporting framework]; and

(b) the [consolidated/parent financial statements and notes or financial report[††]] also comply [complies] with International Financial Reporting Standards as disclosed in Note XX.[†††]

---

34 Or other term that is appropriate in the context of the legal framework in the particular jurisdiction.

35 Where management's responsibility is to prepare a financial report that gives a true and fair view, this may read: "Management is responsible for the preparation of the financial report that gives a true and fair view in accordance with [relevant financial reporting framework], and for such …"

Insert only where the entity has included in the notes to the financial statements an explicit and unreserved statement of compliance with International Financial Reporting Standards in accordance with AASB 101.

36 In the case of footnote 35, this may read: "In making those risk assessments, the auditor considers internal control relevant to the entity's preparation of the financial report that gives a true and fair view in order to design audit procedures that are appropriate in the circumstances, but not for the purpose of expressing an opinion on the effectiveness of the entity's internal control."

37 In circumstances when the auditor also has responsibility to express an opinion on the effectiveness of internal control in conjunction with the audit of the financial report, this sentence would be worded as follows: "In making those risk assessments, the auditor considers internal control relevant to the entity's preparation and fair presentation of the financial report in order to design audit procedures that are appropriate in the circumstances." In the case of footnote 35, this may read: "In making those risk assessments, the auditor considers internal control relevant to the entity's preparation of the financial report that gives a true and fair view in order to design audit procedures that are appropriate in the circumstances."

†† Use "consolidated" or "parent" as appropriate where the entity has made the statement of compliance under AASB 101, paragraph Aus 16.1(a) or paragraph Aus 16.1(b). Where the entity states that both the parent and consolidated financial statements and notes comply with IFRSs, use the term "financial report".

††† Insert only where the entity has included in the notes to the financial statements an explicit and unreserved statement of compliance with *International Financial Reporting Standards* in accordance with AASB 101 and the auditor agrees with the entity's statement. If the auditor does not agree with the statement, the auditor refers to ASA 705.

Report on Other Legal and Regulatory Requirements

[Form and content of this section of the auditor's report will vary depending on the nature of the auditor's other reporting responsibilities.]

[Auditor's signature]*

[Date of the auditor's report]#

[Auditor's address]

Example Auditor's Report Consolidated Entity—*Corporations Act 2001* (Fair Presentation Framework)

[Aus] Illustration 3A:

Circumstances include the following:

- **Audit of a consolidated entity's financial report.**
- **The financial report is prepared for a general purpose under the *Corporations Act 2001.***
- **The financial report includes a statement that the financial statements comply with *International Financial Reporting Standards* (IFRSs).**
- **The terms of the audit engagement reflect the description of management's responsibility for the financial report in ASA 210.**
- **In addition to the audit of the financial report, the auditor has other reporting responsibilities required under section 308(3C) of the *Corporations Act 2001.*** **(Ref: Para. 38 and 39)**

INDEPENDENT AUDITOR'S REPORT

[Appropriate Addressee]

Report on the Financial Report**

We have audited the accompanying financial report of ABC Company Ltd., which comprises the statements of financial position as at 30 June 20X1, the statements of comprehensive income, the statements of changes in equity and the statements of cash flows for the year then ended, notes comprising a summary of significant accounting policies and other explanatory information, and the directors' declaration of the company and the consolidated entity comprising the company [registered scheme/disclosing entity] and the entities it controlled at the year's end or from time to time during the financial year.

Directors' Responsibility for the Financial Report

The directors of the company [registered scheme/disclosing entity] are responsible for the preparation of the financial report that gives a true and fair view in accordance with Australian Accounting Standards and the *Corporations Act 2001* and for such internal control as the directors determine is necessary to enable the preparation of the financial report that gives a true and fair view and is free from material misstatement, whether due to fraud or error. In Note XX, the directors also state, in accordance with Accounting Standard AASB 101 *Presentation of Financial Statements*, that the financial statements comply with *International Financial Reporting Standards.****

* The auditor's report needs to besigned in one or more of the following ways: name of the audit firm, the name of the audit company or the personal name of the auditor, as appropriate.

\# The date of the auditor's report is the date the auditor signs the report.

** The sub-title "Report on the Financial Report" is unnecessary in circumstances when the second sub-title "Report on Other Legal and Regulatory Requirements", or other appropriate sub-title, is not applicable.

*** Insert only where the entity has included in the notes to the financial statements an explicit and unreserved statement of compliance with *International Financial Reporting Standards* in accordance with AASB 101.

Auditor's Responsibility

Our responsibility is to express an opinion on the financial report based on our audit. We conducted our audit in accordance with Australian Auditing Standards. Those standards require that we comply with relevant ethical requirements relating to audit engagements and plan and perform the audit to obtain reasonable assurance about whether the financial report is free from material misstatement.

An audit involves performing procedures to obtain audit evidence about the amounts and disclosures in the financial report. The procedures selected depend on the auditor's judgement, including the assessment of the risks of material misstatement of the financial report, whether due to fraud or error. In making those risk assessments, the auditor considers internal control relevant to the company's preparation of the financial report that gives a true and fair view in order to design audit procedures that are appropriate in the circumstances, but not for the purpose of expressing an opinion on the effectiveness of the company's internal control. An audit also includes evaluating the appropriateness of accounting policies used and the reasonableness of accounting estimates made by the directors, as well as evaluating the overall presentation of the financial report.

We believe that the audit evidence we have obtained is sufficient and appropriate to provide a basis for our audit opinion.

Independence

In conducting our audit, we have complied with the independence requirements of the *Corporations Act 2001*. We confirm that the independence declaration required by the *Corporations Act 2001*, which has been given to the directors of ABC Company Ltd., would be in the same terms if given to the directors as at the time of this auditor's report.**

Opinion

In our opinion:

(a) the financial report of ABC Company Ltd. is in accordance with the *Corporations Act 2001*, including:

  (i) giving a true and fair view of the company's [registered scheme's/disclosing entity's] and consolidated entity's financial positions as at 30 June 20X1 and of their performance for the year ended on that date; and

  (ii) complying with Australian Accounting Standards and the *Corporations Regulations 2001*; and

(b) the [consolidated/parent financial statements and notes or financial report††] also comply [complies] with *International Financial Reporting Standards* as disclosed in Note XX.†††

Report on the Remuneration Report§

We have audited the Remuneration Report included in [paragraphs a to b or pages x to y] of the directors' report for the year [period] ended 30 June 20X1. The directors of the company are responsible for the preparation and presentation of the Remuneration Report in accordance with section 300A of the *Corporations Act 2001*. Our responsibility is to express an opinion on the Remuneration Report, based on our audit conducted in accordance with Australian Auditing Standards.

** Or, alternatively, include statements (a) to the effect that circumstances have changed since the declaration was given to the relevant directors; and (b) setting out how the declaration would differ if it had been given to the relevant directors at the time the auditor's report was made.

†† Use "consolidated" or "parent" as appropriate where the entity has made the statement of compliance under AASB 101, paragraph Aus 16.1(a) or paragraph Aus 16.1(b). Where the entity states that both the parent and consolidated financial statements and notes comply with IFRSs, use the term "financial report".

††† Insert only where the entity has included in the notes to the financial statements an explicit and unreserved statement of compliance with *International Financial Reporting Standards* in accordance with AASB 101 <u>and</u> the auditor agrees with the entity's statement. If the auditor does not agree with the statement, the auditor refers to ASA 705.

§ The Report on the Remuneration Report is an example of "Other Reporting Responsibilities"—refer paragraphs 38 and 39. Any additional "Other Reporting Responsibilities" that the auditor needs to address, will also be included in a separate section of the auditor's report following the opinion paragraph on the financial report. Under paragraph 38, the sub-title "Report on Other Legal and Regulatory Requirements" or other sub-title as appropriate to the section is used.

Opinion

In our opinion, the Remuneration Report of ABC Company Ltd. for the year [period] ended 30 June 20X1, complies with section 300A of the *Corporations Act 2001*.

[Auditor's signature]*

[Date of the auditor's report]#

[Auditor's address]

* The auditor's report needs to be signed in one or more of the following ways: name of the audit firm, the name of the audit company or the personal name of the auditor, as appropriate.

\# The date of the auditor's report is the date the auditor signs the report.

ASA 705
Modifications to the Opinion in the Independent Auditor's Report

(Reissued October 2009: amended and compiled June 2011)

Issued by the Auditing and Assurance Standards Board.

Note from the Institute of Chartered Accountants Australia

This note, prepared by the technical editor, is not part of ASA 705.

Historical development

April 2006: ASA 701 'Modifications to the Auditor's Report' was issued as a legally enforceable auditing Standard. It is based on ISA 701 of the same name. The material was previously included in AUS 702 together with the subject matter of ASA 700 'The Auditor's Report on a General Purpose Financial Report'.

June 2007: ASA 701 compiled and republished to reflect changes to ASA 700 'The Auditor's Report in a General Purpose Financial Report' introduced by Omnibus ASA 2007-1.

October 2009: Under the AUASB's Clarity Project, the material in ASA 701 was split and the Standard replaced by two new standards, ASA 705 'Modifications to the Opinion in the Independent Auditor's Report' and ASA 706 'Emphasis of Matter Paragraphs and Other Matter Paragraphs in the Independent Auditor's Report'. ASAs 705 and 706 are based on ISAs 705 and 706 of the same names.

June 2011: ASA 705 updated for editorial amendments contained in ASA 2011-1 'Amendments to Australian Auditing Standards'.

Contents

ASA

Compilation Details

Auditing Standard ASA 705 *Modifications to the Opinion in the Independent Auditor's Report* as Amended

This compilation takes into account amendments made up to and including 27 June 2011 and was prepared on 27 June 2011 by the Auditing and Assurance Standards Board (AUASB).

This compilation is not a separate Auditing Standard made by the AUASB. Instead, it is a representation of ASA 705 (October 2009) as amended by another Auditing Standard which is listed in the Table below.

Table of Standards

Standard	Date made	Operative date
ASA 705	27 October 2009	1 January 2010
ASA 2011-1	27 June 2011	1 July 2011

Table of Amendments

Paragraph affected	How affected	By ... [paragraph]
A24	Amended	ASA 2011-1 [61]
Appendix 1 Illustrations 1,2,3,4 & 5	Amended	ASA 2011-1 [62]
Appendix 1 Illustration 3A	Amended	ASA 2011-1 [63]

Preface

[Preface extracted from the original Auditing Standard issued 27 October 2009]

Reasons for Issuing Auditing Standard ASA 705 *Modifications to the Opinion in the Independent Auditor's Report*

The Auditing and Assurance Standards Board (AUASB) issues Auditing Standard ASA 705 *Modifications to the Opinion in the Independent Auditor's Report* pursuant to the requirements of the legislative provisions and the Strategic Direction explained below.

The AUASB is an independent statutory board of the Australian Government established under section 227A of the *Australian Securities and Investments Commission Act 2001*, as amended (ASIC Act). Under section 336 of the *Corporations Act 2001*, the AUASB may make Australian Auditing Standards for the purposes of the corporations legislation. These Auditing Standards are legislative instruments under the *Legislative Instruments Act 2003*.

Under the Strategic Direction given to the AUASB by the Financial Reporting Council (FRC), the AUASB is required to have regard to any programme initiated by the International Auditing and Assurance Standards Board (IAASB) for the revision and enhancement of the International Standards on Auditing (ISAs) and to make appropriate consequential amendments to the Australian Auditing Standards. Accordingly, the AUASB has decided to revise and redraft the Australian Auditing Standards using the equivalent redrafted ISAs.

Main Features

This Auditing Standard establishes requirements and provides application and other explanatory material regarding the auditor's responsibility to modify the auditor's opinion on the financial report when the auditor concludes the financial report is not free from material misstatement or the auditor is unable to obtain sufficient appropriate audit evidence to conclude the financial report is free from material misstatement.

This Auditing Standard:

(a) defines the circumstances when an auditor is required to modify the auditor's opinion;

(b) describes how the auditor determines the appropriate type of modification to the auditor's opinion;

(c) describes the form and content of the auditor's report when the opinion is modified; and

(d) requires the auditor to communicate with those charged with governance when the auditor expects to modify the opinion in the auditor's report.

Authority Statement

Auditing Standard ASA 705 *Modifications to the Opinion in the Independent Auditor's Report* (as amended at 27 June 2011) is set out in paragraphs 1 to A25 and Appendix 1.

This Auditing Standard is to be read in conjunction with ASA 101 *Preamble to Australian Auditing Standards*, which sets out the intentions of the AUASB on how the Australian Auditing Standards, operative for financial reporting periods commencing on or after 1 January 2010, are to be understood, interpreted and applied. This Auditing Standard is to be read also in conjunction with ASA 200 *Overall Objectives of the Independent Auditor and the Conduct of an Audit in Accordance with Australian Auditing Standards*.

Dated: 27 June 2011

M H Kelsall
Chairman - AUASB

Auditing Standard ASA 705

The Auditing and Assurance Standards Board (AUASB) made Auditing Standard ASA 705 *Modifications to the Opinion in the Independent Auditor's Report*, pursuant to section 227B of the *Australian Securities and Investments Commission Act 2001* and section 336 of the *Corporations Act 2001*, on 27 October 2009.

This compiled version of ASA 705 incorporates subsequent amendments contained in another Auditing Standard made by the AUASB up to and including 27 June 2011 (see Compilation Details).

Auditing Standard ASA 705

Modifications to the Opinion in the Independent Auditor's Report

Application

Aus 0.1 This Auditing Standard applies to:

(a) an audit of a financial report for a financial year, or an audit of a financial report for a half-year, in accordance with the *Corporations Act 2001*; and

(b) an audit of a financial report, or a complete set of financial statements, for any other purpose.

Aus 0.2 This Auditing Standard also applies, as appropriate, to an audit of other historical financial information.

Operative Date

Aus 0.3 This Auditing Standard is operative for financial reporting periods commencing on or after 1 January 2010.

[Note: For operative dates of paragraphs changed or added by an amending Standard, see Compilation Details.]

Introduction

Scope of this Auditing Standard

1. This Auditing Standard deals with the auditor's responsibility to issue an appropriate report in circumstances when, in forming an opinion in accordance with ASA 700,[1] the auditor concludes that a modification to the auditor's opinion on the financial report is necessary.

1 See ASA 700 *Forming an Opinion and Reporting on a Financial Report*.

ASA

Types of Modified Opinions

2. This Auditing Standard establishes three types of modified opinions, namely, a qualified opinion, an adverse opinion, and a disclaimer of opinion. The decision regarding which type of modified opinion is appropriate depends upon:
   (a) The nature of the matter giving rise to the modification, that is, whether the financial report is materially misstated or, in the case of an inability to obtain sufficient appropriate audit evidence, may be materially misstated; and
   (b) The auditor's judgement about the pervasiveness of the effects or possible effects of the matter on the financial report. (Ref: Para. A1)

Effective Date

3. [Deleted by the AUASB. Refer Aus 0.3]

Objective

4. The objective of the auditor is to express clearly an appropriately modified opinion on the financial report that is necessary when:
   (a) The auditor concludes, based on the audit evidence obtained, that the financial report as a whole is not free from material misstatement; or
   (b) The auditor is unable to obtain sufficient appropriate audit evidence to conclude that the financial report as a whole is free from material misstatement.

Definitions

5. For purposes of the Australian Auditing Standards, the following terms have the meanings attributed below:
   (a) Pervasive means a term used, in the context of misstatements, to describe the effects on the financial report of misstatements or the possible effects on the financial report of misstatements, if any, that are undetected due to an inability to obtain sufficient appropriate audit evidence. Pervasive effects on the financial report are those that, in the auditor's judgement:
      (i) Are not confined to specific elements, accounts or items of the financial report;
      (ii) If so confined, represent or could represent a substantial proportion of the financial report; or
      (iii) In relation to disclosures, are fundamental to users' understanding of the financial report.
   (b) Modified opinion means a qualified opinion, an adverse opinion or a disclaimer of opinion.

Requirements

Circumstances When a Modification to the Auditor's Opinion is Required

6. The auditor shall modify the opinion in the auditor's report when:
   (a) The auditor concludes that, based on the audit evidence obtained, the financial report as a whole is not free from material misstatement; or (Ref: Para. A2-A7)
   (b) The auditor is unable to obtain sufficient appropriate audit evidence to conclude that the financial report as a whole is free from material misstatement. (Ref: Para. A8-A12)

Determining the Type of Modification to the Auditor's Opinion

Qualified Opinion

7. The auditor shall express a qualified opinion when:
   (a) The auditor, having obtained sufficient appropriate audit evidence, concludes that misstatements, individually or in the aggregate, are material, but not pervasive, to the financial report; or

(b) The auditor is unable to obtain sufficient appropriate audit evidence on which to base the opinion, but the auditor concludes that the possible effects on the financial report of undetected misstatements, if any, could be material but not pervasive.

Adverse Opinion

8. The auditor shall express an adverse opinion when the auditor, having obtained sufficient appropriate audit evidence, concludes that misstatements, individually or in the aggregate, are both material and pervasive to the financial report.

Disclaimer of Opinion

9. The auditor shall disclaim an opinion when the auditor is unable to obtain sufficient appropriate audit evidence on which to base the opinion, and the auditor concludes that the possible effects on the financial report of undetected misstatements, if any, could be both material and pervasive.

10. The auditor shall disclaim an opinion when, in extremely rare circumstances involving multiple uncertainties, the auditor concludes that, notwithstanding having obtained sufficient appropriate audit evidence regarding each of the individual uncertainties, it is not possible to form an opinion on the financial report due to the potential interaction of the uncertainties and their possible cumulative effect on the financial report.

ASA

Consequence of an Inability to Obtain Sufficient Appropriate Audit Evidence Due to a Management-Imposed Limitation after the Auditor Has Accepted the Engagement

11. If, after accepting the engagement, the auditor becomes aware that management has imposed a limitation on the scope of the audit that the auditor considers likely to result in the need to express a qualified opinion or to disclaim an opinion on the financial report, the auditor shall request that management remove the limitation.

12. If management refuses to remove the limitation referred to in paragraph 11 of this Auditing Standard, the auditor shall communicate the matter to those charged with governance, unless all of those charged with governance are involved in managing the entity,[2] and determine whether it is possible to perform alternative procedures to obtain sufficient appropriate audit evidence.

13. If the auditor is unable to obtain sufficient appropriate audit evidence, the auditor shall determine the implications as follows:

(a) If the auditor concludes that the possible effects on the financial report of undetected misstatements, if any, could be material but not pervasive, the auditor shall qualify the opinion; or

(b) If the auditor concludes that the possible effects on the financial report of undetected misstatements, if any, could be both material and pervasive so that a qualification of the opinion would be inadequate to communicate the gravity of the situation, the auditor shall:

(i) Withdraw from the audit, where practicable and possible under applicable law or regulation; or (Ref: Para. Aus A12.1-A14)

(ii) If withdrawal from the audit before issuing the auditor's report is not practicable or possible, disclaim an opinion on the financial report.

14. If the auditor withdraws as contemplated by paragraph 13(b)(i) of this Auditing Standard, before withdrawing, the auditor shall communicate to those charged with governance any matters regarding misstatements identified during the audit that would have given rise to a modification of the opinion. (Ref: Para. A15- Aus A15.1)

Other Considerations Relating to an Adverse Opinion or Disclaimer of Opinion

15. When the auditor considers it necessary to express an adverse opinion or disclaim an opinion on the financial report as a whole, the auditor's report shall not also include an unmodified opinion with respect to the same financial reporting framework on a single financial statement or one or more specific elements, accounts or items of a financial

2 See ASA 260 *Communication with Those Charged with Governance*, paragraph 13.

statement. To include such an unmodified opinion in the same report[3] in these circumstances would contradict the auditor's adverse opinion or disclaimer of opinion on the financial report as a whole. (Ref: Para. A16)

Form and Content of the Auditor's Report When the Opinion Is Modified

Basis for Modification Paragraph

16. When the auditor modifies the opinion on the financial report, the auditor shall, in addition to the specific elements required by ASA 700, include a paragraph in the auditor's report that provides a description of the matter giving rise to the modification. The auditor shall place this paragraph immediately before the opinion paragraph in the auditor's report and use the heading "Basis for Qualified Opinion," "Basis for Adverse Opinion," or "Basis for Disclaimer of Opinion," as appropriate. (Ref: Para. A17)

17. If there is a material misstatement of the financial report that relates to specific amounts in the financial report (including quantitative disclosures), the auditor shall include in the basis for modification paragraph a description and quantification of the financial effects of the misstatement, unless impracticable. If it is not practicable to quantify the financial effects, the auditor shall so state in the basis for modification paragraph. (Ref: Para. A18)

18. If there is a material misstatement of the financial report that relates to narrative disclosures, the auditor shall include in the basis for modification paragraph an explanation of how the disclosures are misstated.

19. If there is a material misstatement of the financial report that relates to the non-disclosure of information required to be disclosed, the auditor shall:

    (a) Discuss the non-disclosure with those charged with governance;

    Aus 19.1 Request management and/or those charged with governance to correct the non-disclosure in the financial report; (Ref: Para. Aus A19.1)

    (b) Describe in the basis for modification paragraph the nature of the omitted information; and

    (c) Unless prohibited by law or regulation, include the omitted disclosures, provided it is practicable to do so and the auditor has obtained sufficient appropriate audit evidence about the omitted information. (Ref: Para. A19)

    Aus 19.2 Where, under paragraph 19(c) of this Auditing Standard, the omitted disclosures are not included in the basis of modification paragraph, the auditor shall include the reasons for the omission from the basis of modification paragraph.

20. If the modification results from an inability to obtain sufficient appropriate audit evidence, the auditor shall include in the basis for modification paragraph the reasons for that inability.

21. Even if the auditor has expressed an adverse opinion or disclaimed an opinion on the financial report, the auditor shall describe in the basis for modification paragraph the reasons for any other matters of which the auditor is aware that would have required a modification to the opinion, and the effects thereof. (Ref: Para. A20)

Opinion Paragraph

22. When the auditor modifies the audit opinion, the auditor shall use the heading "Qualified Opinion," "Adverse Opinion," or "Disclaimer of Opinion," as appropriate, for the opinion paragraph. (Ref: Para. A21, A23-A24)

23. When the auditor expresses a qualified opinion due to a material misstatement in the financial report, the auditor shall state in the opinion paragraph that, in the auditor's opinion, except for the effects of the matter(s) described in the Basis for Qualified Opinion paragraph:

3 See ASA 805 *Special Considerations—Audits of Single Financial Statements and Specific Elements, Accounts or Items of a Financial Statement*, which deals with circumstances where the auditor is engaged to express a separate opinion on one or more specific elements, accounts or items of a financial statement.

(a) The financial report presents fairly, in all material respects (or gives a true and fair view) in accordance with the applicable financial reporting framework when reporting in accordance with a fair presentation framework; or

(b) The financial report has been prepared, in all material respects, in accordance with the applicable financial reporting framework when reporting in accordance with a compliance framework.

When the modification arises from an inability to obtain sufficient appropriate audit evidence, the auditor shall use the corresponding phrase "except for the possible effects of the matter(s) ..." for the modified opinion. (Ref: Para. A22)

24. When the auditor expresses an adverse opinion, the auditor shall state in the opinion paragraph that, in the auditor's opinion, because of the significance of the matter(s) described in the Basis for Adverse Opinion paragraph:

(a) The financial report does not present fairly (or give a true and fair view) in accordance with the applicable financial reporting framework when reporting in accordance with a fair presentation framework; or

(b) The financial report has not been prepared, in all material respects, in accordance with the applicable financial reporting framework when reporting in accordance with a compliance framework.

25. When the auditor disclaims an opinion due to an inability to obtain sufficient appropriate audit evidence, the auditor shall state in the opinion paragraph that:

(a) Because of the significance of the matter(s) described in the Basis for Disclaimer of Opinion paragraph, the auditor has not been able to obtain sufficient appropriate audit evidence to provide a basis for an audit opinion; and, accordingly,

(b) The auditor does not express an opinion on the financial report.

Description of Auditor's Responsibility When the Auditor Expresses a Qualified or Adverse Opinion

26. When the auditor expresses a qualified or adverse opinion, the auditor shall amend the description of the auditor's responsibility to state that the auditor believes that the audit evidence the auditor has obtained is sufficient and appropriate to provide a basis for the auditor's modified audit opinion.

Description of Auditor's Responsibility When the Auditor Disclaims an Opinion

27. When the auditor disclaims an opinion due to an inability to obtain sufficient appropriate audit evidence, the auditor shall amend the introductory paragraph of the auditor's report to state that the auditor was engaged to audit the financial report. The auditor shall also amend the description of the auditor's responsibility and the description of the scope of the audit to state only the following: "Our responsibility is to express an opinion on the financial report based on conducting the audit in accordance with Australian Auditing Standards. Because of the matter(s) described in the Basis for Disclaimer of Opinion paragraph, however, we were not able to obtain sufficient appropriate audit evidence to provide a basis for an audit opinion."

Communication with Those Charged with Governance

28. When the auditor expects to modify the opinion in the auditor's report, the auditor shall communicate with those charged with governance the circumstances that led to the expected modification and the proposed wording of the modification. (Ref: Para. A25)

❖ ❖ ❖

Application and Other Explanatory Material

Types of Modified Opinions (Ref: Para. 2)

A1. The table below illustrates how the auditor's judgement about the nature of the matter giving rise to the modification, and the pervasiveness of its effects or possible effects on the financial report affects the type of opinion to be expressed.

Nature of Matter Giving Rise to the Modification	*Auditor's Judgement about the Pervasiveness of the Effects or Possible Effects on the Financial Report*	
	Material but Not Pervasive	*Material and Pervasive*
Financial report is materially misstated	Qualified opinion [Illustration 1]	Adverse opinion [Illustration 2]
Inability to obtain sufficient appropriate audit evidence	Qualified opinion [Illustrations 3 and 3A]	Disclaimer of opinion [Illustrations 4 and 5]

Nature of Material Misstatements (Ref: Para. 6(a))

A2. ASA 700 requires the auditor, in order to form an opinion on the financial report, to conclude as to whether reasonable assurance has been obtained about whether the financial report as a whole is free from material misstatement.[4] This conclusion takes into account the auditor's evaluation of uncorrected misstatements, if any, on the financial report in accordance with ASA 450.[5]

A3. ASA 450 defines a misstatement as a difference between the amount, classification, presentation, or disclosure of a reported financial report item and the amount, classification, presentation, or disclosure that is required for the item to be in accordance with the applicable financial reporting framework. Accordingly, a material misstatement of the financial report may arise in relation to:

(a) The appropriateness of the selected accounting policies;

(b) The application of the selected accounting policies; or

(c) The appropriateness or adequacy of disclosures in the financial report.

Appropriateness of the Selected Accounting Policies

A4. In relation to the appropriateness of the accounting policies management has selected, material misstatements of the financial report may arise when:

(a) The selected accounting policies are not consistent with the applicable financial reporting framework; or

(b) The financial statements, including the related notes, do not represent the underlying transactions and events in a manner that achieves fair presentation.

A5. Financial reporting frameworks often contain requirements for the accounting for, and disclosure of, changes in accounting policies. Where the entity has changed its selection of significant accounting policies, a material misstatement of the financial report may arise when the entity has not complied with these requirements.

Application of the Selected Accounting Policies

A6. In relation to the application of the selected accounting policies, material misstatements of the financial report may arise:

(a) When management has not applied the selected accounting policies consistently with the financial reporting framework, including when management has not applied the selected accounting policies consistently between periods or to similar transactions and events (consistency in application); or

(b) Due to the method of application of the selected accounting policies (such as an unintentional error in application).

4 See ASA 700, paragraph 11.

5 See ASA 450 *Evaluation of Misstatements Identified during the Audit*, paragraph 4(a).

Appropriateness or Adequacy of Disclosures in the Financial Report

A7. In relation to the appropriateness or adequacy of disclosures in the financial report, material misstatements of the financial report may arise when:

(a) The financial report does not include all of the disclosures required by the applicable financial reporting framework;

(b) The disclosures in the financial report are not presented in accordance with the applicable financial reporting framework; or

(c) The financial report does not provide the disclosures necessary to achieve fair presentation.

Nature of an Inability to Obtain Sufficient Appropriate Audit Evidence

(Ref: Para. 6(b))

A8. The auditor's inability to obtain sufficient appropriate audit evidence (also referred to as a limitation on the scope of the audit) may arise from:

(a) Circumstances beyond the control of the entity;

(b) Circumstances relating to the nature or timing of the auditor's work; or

(c) Limitations imposed by management.

A9. An inability to perform a specific procedure does not constitute a limitation on the scope of the audit if the auditor is able to obtain sufficient appropriate audit evidence by performing alternative procedures. If this is not possible, the requirements of paragraphs 7(b) and 10 apply as appropriate. Limitations imposed by management may have other implications for the audit, such as for the auditor's assessment of fraud risks and consideration of engagement continuance.

A10. Examples of circumstances beyond the control of the entity include when:

- The entity's accounting records have been destroyed.
- The accounting records of a significant component have been seized indefinitely by governmental authorities.

A11. Examples of circumstances relating to the nature or timing of the auditor's work include when:

- The entity is required to use the equity method of accounting for an associated entity, and the auditor is unable to obtain sufficient appropriate audit evidence about the latter's financial information to evaluate whether the equity method has been appropriately applied.
- The timing of the auditor's appointment is such that the auditor is unable to observe the counting of the physical inventories.
- The auditor determines that performing substantive procedures alone is not sufficient, but the entity's controls are not effective.

A12. Examples of an inability to obtain sufficient appropriate audit evidence arising from a limitation on the scope of the audit imposed by management include when:

- Management prevents the auditor from observing the counting of the physical inventory.
- Management prevents the auditor from requesting external confirmation of specific account balances.

Consequence of an Inability to Obtain Sufficient Appropriate Audit Evidence Due to a Management-Imposed Limitation after the Auditor Has Accepted the Engagement (Ref: Para. 13(b)-14)

Aus A12.1 An inability to obtain sufficient appropriate audit evidence due to a management-imposed limitation may be a matter that the auditor is required to report to the Australian Securities and Investments Commission (ASIC) under sections 311, 601HG or 990K of the *Corporations Act 2001* (the Act). Particular attention should be given to section 312 of the Act which deals with assisting an auditor.

A13. The practicality of withdrawing from the audit may depend on the stage of completion of the engagement at the time that management imposes the scope limitation. If the auditor has substantially completed the audit, the auditor may decide to complete the audit to the extent possible, disclaim an opinion and explain the scope limitation in the Basis for Disclaimer of Opinion paragraph prior to withdrawing.

A14. In certain circumstances, withdrawal from the audit may not be possible if the auditor is required by law or regulation to continue the audit engagement. This may be the case for an auditor that is appointed to audit the financial report of public sector entities. It may also be the case in jurisdictions where the auditor is appointed to audit the financial report covering a specific period, or appointed for a specific period and is prohibited from withdrawing before the completion of the audit of that financial report or before the end of that period, respectively. The auditor may also consider it necessary to include an Other Matter paragraph in the auditor's report.[6]

A15. When the auditor concludes that withdrawal from the audit is necessary because of a scope limitation, there may be a professional, legal or regulatory requirement for the auditor to communicate matters relating to the withdrawal from the engagement to regulators or the entity's owners.

Aus A15.1 Under the *Corporations Act 2001*, the removal and resignation of auditors is covered by sections 329 and 331AC.[*]

Other Considerations Relating to an Adverse Opinion or Disclaimer of Opinion (Ref: Para. 15)

A16. The following is an example of reporting circumstances that would not contradict the auditor's adverse opinion or disclaimer of opinion:

- The expression of an unmodified opinion on a financial report prepared under a given financial reporting framework and, within the same report, the expression of an adverse opinion on the same financial report under a different financial reporting framework.[7]
- [Deleted by the AUASB.][8]

Form and Content of the Auditor's Report When the Opinion is Modified

Basis for Modification Paragraph (Ref: Para. 16-17, 19, 21)

A17. Consistency in the auditor's report helps to promote users' understanding and to identify unusual circumstances when they occur. Accordingly, although uniformity in the wording of a modified opinion and in the description of the basis for the modification may not be possible, consistency in both the form and content of the auditor's report is desirable.

A18. An example of the financial effects of material misstatements that the auditor may describe in the basis for modification paragraph in the auditor's report is the quantification of the effects on income tax, income before taxes, net income and equity if inventory is overstated.

A19. Disclosing the omitted information in the basis for modification paragraph would not be practicable if:

(a) The disclosures have not been prepared by management or the disclosures are otherwise not readily available to the auditor; or

(b) In the auditor's judgement, the disclosures would be unduly voluminous in relation to the auditor's report.

Aus A19.1 Where an audit is conducted under the *Corporations Act 2001* (the Act) and there is a material misstatement of the financial report that relates to the non-disclosure of required information, the auditor needs to consider reporting obligations under the Act. (Ref: Para. Aus 19.1)

6 See ASA 706 *Emphasis of Matter Paragraphs and Other Matter Paragraphs in the Independent Auditor's Report*, paragraph A5.

* See also ASIC Regulatory Guide 26 *Resignation of Auditors* (June 1992).

7 See paragraph A32 of ASA 700 for a description of this circumstance.

8 [Footnote deleted by the AUASB as not applicable in Australia. See ASA 510, *Initial Audit Engagements—Opening Balances*, Appendix 1, Illustration 2].

A20. An adverse opinion or a disclaimer of opinion relating to a specific matter described in the basis for qualification paragraph does not justify the omission of a description of other identified matters that would have otherwise required a modification of the auditor's opinion. In such cases, the disclosure of such other matters of which the auditor is aware may be relevant to users of the financial report.

Opinion Paragraph (Ref: Para. 22-23)

A21. Inclusion of this paragraph heading makes it clear to the user that the auditor's opinion is modified and indicates the type of modification.

A22. When the auditor expresses a qualified opinion, it would not be appropriate to use phrases such as "with the foregoing explanation" or "subject to" in the opinion paragraph as these are not sufficiently clear or forceful.

Illustrative Auditors' Reports

A23. Illustrations 1 and 2 in Appendix 1 contain auditors' reports with qualified and adverse opinions, respectively, as the financial report is materially misstated.

A24. Illustrations 3 and 3A in Appendix 1 contain an auditor's report with a qualified opinion as the auditor is unable to obtain sufficient appropriate audit evidence. Illustration 4 contains a disclaimer of opinion due to an inability to obtain sufficient appropriate audit evidence about a single element of the financial report. Illustration 5 contains a disclaimer of opinion due to an inability to obtain sufficient appropriate audit evidence about multiple elements of the financial report. In each of the latter two cases, the possible effects on the financial report of the inability are both material and pervasive.

Communication with Those Charged with Governance (Ref: Para. 28)

A25. Communicating with those charged with governance the circumstances that led to an expected modification to the auditor's opinion and the proposed wording of the modification enables:

(a) The auditor to give notice to those charged with governance of the intended modification(s) and the reasons (or circumstances) for the modification(s);

(b) The auditor to seek the concurrence of those charged with governance regarding the facts of the matter(s) giving rise to the expected modification(s), or to confirm matters of disagreement with management as such; and

(c) Those charged with governance to have an opportunity, where appropriate, to provide the auditor with further information and explanations in respect of the matter(s) giving rise to the expected modification(s).

❖ ❖ ❖

Conformity with International Standards on Auditing

This Auditing Standard conforms with International Standard on Auditing ISA 705 *Modifications to the Opinion in the Independent Auditor's Report*, issued by the International Auditing and Assurance Standards Board (IAASB), an independent standard-setting board of the International Federation of Accountants (IFAC).

Paragraphs that have been added to this Auditing Standard (and do not appear in the text of the equivalent ISA) are identified with the prefix "Aus".

The following requirements are additional to ISA 705:

- If there is a material misstatement of the financial report that relates to the non-disclosure of information required to be disclosed, the auditor shall:
  - Request management and/or those charged with governance to correct the non-disclosure in the financial report. (Ref: Para. Aus 19.1)
  - Where, under paragraph 19(c) of this Auditing Standard, the omitted disclosures are not included in the basis of modification paragraph, the auditor shall include the reasons for the omission from the basis of modification paragraph. (Ref: Para. Aus 19.2)

Compliance with this Auditing Standard enables compliance with ISA 705.

Appendix 1

(Ref: Para. A23-24 and A1)

Illustrations of Auditors' Reports with Modifications to the Opinion—General Purpose Financial Reports

- Illustration 1: An auditor's report containing a qualified opinion due to a material misstatement of the financial report.
- Illustration 2: An auditor's report containing an adverse opinion due to a material misstatement of the financial report.
- Illustration 3: An auditor's report containing a qualified opinion due to the auditor's inability to obtain sufficient appropriate audit evidence.
- [Aus] Illustration 3A: An auditor's report containing a qualified opinion due to the auditor's inability to obtain sufficient appropriate audit evidence (under the *Corporations Act 2001*)
- Illustration 4: An auditor's report containing a disclaimer of opinion due to the auditor's inability to obtain sufficient appropriate audit evidence about a single element of the financial report.
- Illustration 5: An auditor's report containing a disclaimer of opinion due to the auditor's inability to obtain sufficient appropriate audit evidence about multiple elements of the financial report.

Example Auditor's Report General Purpose Financial Report—Qualified Opinion (material misstatement)

Illustration 1:

Circumstances include the following:

- **Audit of a general purpose financial report prepared by management of the entity—the financial statements are prepared in accordance with Australian Accounting Standards.**
- **The financial report is *not* prepared under the *Corporations Act 2001*.**
- **The terms of the audit engagement reflect the description of management's responsibility for the financial report in ASA 210.[9]**
- **Inventories are misstated. The misstatement is deemed to be material but not pervasive to the financial report.**
- **In addition to the audit of the financial report, the auditor has other reporting responsibilities required under local law.**

INDEPENDENT AUDITOR'S REPORT

[Appropriate Addressee]

Report on the Financial Report[10]

We have audited the accompanying financial report of ABC Entity, which comprises the statement of financial position as at 30 June 20X1, the statement of comprehensive income, statement of changes in equity and statement of cash flows for the year then ended, notes comprising a summary of significant accounting policies and other explanatory information, and management's assertion statement*.

9 See ASA 210 Agreeing the *Terms of Audit Engagements*.

10 The sub-title "Report on the Financial Report" is unnecessary in circumstances when the second sub-title "Report on Other Legal and Regulatory Requirements", or other appropriate sub-title, is not applicable.

* Or other appropriate term.

Management's[11] *Responsibility for the Financial Report*

Management is responsible for the preparation and fair presentation of the financial report in accordance with Australian Accounting Standards and [relevant reporting framework],[12] and for such internal control as management determines is necessary to enable the preparation and fair presentation of the financial report that is free from material misstatement, whether due to fraud or error.

Auditor's Responsibility

Our responsibility is to express an opinion on the financial report based on our audit. We conducted our audit in accordance with Australian Auditing Standards. Those standards require that we comply with relevant ethical requirements relating to audit engagements and plan and perform the audit to obtain reasonable assurance about whether the financial report is free from material misstatement.

An audit involves performing procedures to obtain audit evidence about the amounts and disclosures in the financial report. The procedures selected depend on the auditor's judgement, including the assessment of the risks of material misstatement of the financial report, whether due to fraud or error. In making those risk assessments, the auditor considers internal control relevant to the entity's preparation and fair presentation[13] of the financial report in order to design audit procedures that are appropriate in the circumstances, but not for the purpose of expressing an opinion on the effectiveness of the entity's internal control.[14] An audit also includes evaluating the appropriateness of accounting policies used and thereasonableness of accounting estimates made by management, as well as evaluating the overall presentation of the financial report.

We believe that the audit evidence we have obtained is sufficient and appropriate to provide a basis for our qualified audit opinion.

Basis for Qualified Opinion

The entity's inventories are carried in the statement of financial position at xxx. Management has not stated the inventories at the lower of cost and net realisable value but has stated them solely at cost, which constitutes a departure from Australian Accounting Standards. The entity's records indicate that had management stated the inventories at the lower of cost and net realisable value, an amount of xxx would have been required to write the inventories down to their net realisable value. Accordingly, cost of sales would have been increased by xxx, and income tax, net income and shareholders' equity would have been reduced by xxx, xxx and xxx, respectively.

Qualified Opinion

In our opinion, except for the effects of the matter described in the Basis for Qualified Opinion paragraph, the financial report presents fairly, in all material respects, (or *gives a true and fair view of*) the financial position of ABC Entity as at 30 June 20X1, and (*of*) its financial performance and its cash flows for the year then ended in accordance with Australian Accounting Standards and [relevant reporting framework].

Report on Other Legal and Regulatory Requirements

[Form and content of this section of the auditor's report will vary depending on the nature of the auditor's other reporting responsibilities.]

---

11 Or other term that is appropriate in the context of the legal framework in the particular jurisdiction.

12 Where management's responsibility is to prepare a financial report that gives a true and fair view, this may read: "Management is responsible for the preparation of the financial report that gives a true and fair view in accordance with Australian Accounting Standards, and for such..."

13 In the case of footnote 12, this may read: "In making those risk assessments, the auditor considers internal control relevant to the entity's preparation of the financial report that gives a true and fair view in order to design audit procedures that are appropriate in the circumstances, but not for the purpose of expressing an opinion on the effectiveness of the entity's internal control."

14 In circumstances when the auditor also has responsibility to express an opinion on the effectiveness of internal control in conjunction with the audit of the financial report, this sentence would be worded as follows: "In making those risk assessments, the auditor considers internal control relevant to the entity's preparation and fair presentation of the financial report in order to design audit procedures that are appropriate in the circumstances." In the case of footnote 12, this may read: "In making those risk assessments, the auditor considers internal control relevant to the entity's preparation of the financial report that gives a true and fair view in order to design audit procedures that are appropriate in the circumstances."

[Auditor's signature]*

[Date of the auditor's report]#

[Auditor's address]

Example Auditor's Report General Purpose Financial Report—Adverse Opinion (material misstatement)

Illustration 2:

Circumstances include the following:

- **Audit of a consolidated entity's general purpose financial report prepared by management of the parent—the financial statements are prepared in accordance with Australian Accounting Standards.**
- **The financial report is *not* prepared under the *Corporations Act 2001*.**
- **The terms of the audit engagement reflect the description of management's responsibility for the financial report in ASA 210.**
- **The financial report is materially misstated due to the non-consolidation of a subsidiary. The material misstatement is deemed to be pervasive to the financial report. The effects of the misstatement on the financial report have not been determined because it was not practicable to do so.**
- **In addition to the audit of the consolidated entity's financial report, the auditor has other reporting responsibilities required under local law.**

INDEPENDENT AUDITOR'S REPORT

[Appropriate Addressee]

Report on the Financial Report[15]

We have audited the accompanying financial report of ABC Entity, which comprises the statements of financial performance as at 30 June 20X1, the statements of comprehensive income, statements of changes in equity and statements of cash flows for the year then ended, notes comprising a summary of significant accounting policies and other explanatory information, and management's assertion statement* of the entity and the consolidated entity comprising the entity and the entities it controlled at the year's end or from time to time during the financial year.

Management's[16] Responsibility for the Financial Report

Management is responsible for the preparation and fair presentation of the financial report in accordance with Australian Accounting Standards and [relevant reporting framework],[17] and for such internal control as management determines is necessary to enable the preparation and fair presentation of the financial report that is free from material misstatement, whether due to fraud or error.

Auditor's Responsibility

Our responsibility is to express an opinion on the financial report based on our audit. We conducted our audit in accordance with Australian Auditing Standards. Those standards require that we comply with relevant ethical requirements relating to audit engagements and plan and perform

* The auditor's report needs to be signed in one or more of the following ways: name of the audit firm, the name of the audit company or the personal name of the auditor, as appropriate.

\# The date of the auditor's report is the date the auditor signs the report.

15 The sub-title "Report on the Financial Report" is unnecessary in circumstances when the second sub-title "Report on Other Legal and Regulatory Requirements", or other appropriate sub-title, is not applicable.

* Or other appropriate term.

16 Or other term that is appropriate in the context of the legal framework in the particular jurisdiction.

17 Where management's responsibility is to prepare a financial report that gives a true and fair view, this may read: "Management is responsible for the preparation of the financial report that gives a true and fair view in accordance with Australian Accounting Standards, and for such..."

the audit to obtain reasonable assurance about whether the financial report is free from material misstatement.

An audit involves performing procedures to obtain audit evidence about the amounts and disclosures in the financial report. The procedures selected depend on the auditor's judgement, including the assessment of the risks of material misstatement of the financial report, whether due to fraud or error. In making those risk assessments, the auditor considers internal control relevant to the entity's preparation and fair presentation[18] of the financial report in order to design audit procedures that are appropriate in the circumstances, but not for the purpose of expressing an opinion on the effectiveness of the entity's internal control.[19] An audit also includes evaluating the appropriateness of accounting policies used and the reasonableness of accounting estimates made by management, as well as evaluating the overall presentation of the financial report.

We believe that the audit evidence we have obtained is sufficient and appropriate to provide a basis for our adverse audit opinion.

Basis for Adverse Opinion

As explained in Note X, the entity has not consolidated the financial statements of subsidiary XYZ Entity it acquired during 20X1 because it has not yet been able to ascertain the fair values of certain of the subsidiary's material assets and liabilities at the acquisition date. This investment is therefore accounted for on a cost basis. Under Australian Accounting Standards, the subsidiary should have been consolidated because it is controlled by the entity. Had XYZ been consolidated, many elements in the accompanying financial report would have been materially affected. The effects on the financial report of the failure to consolidate have not been determined.

Adverse Opinion

In our opinion, because of the significance of the matter discussed in the Basis for Adverse Opinion paragraph, the financial report does not present fairly (or *does not give a true and fair view of*) the financial position of ABC Entity and its subsidiaries as at 30 June 20X1, and (of) their financial performance and their cash flows for the year then ended in accordance with Australian Accounting Standards and [relevant reporting framework].

Report on Other Legal and Regulatory Requirements

[Form and content of this section of the auditor's report will vary depending on the nature of the auditor's other reporting responsibilities.]

[Auditor's signature]*

[Date of the auditor's report]#

[Auditor's address]

18 In the case of footnote 17, this may read: "In making those risk assessments, the auditor considers internal control relevant to the entity's preparation of the financial report that gives a true and fair view in order to design audit procedures that are appropriate in the circumstances, but not for the purpose of expressing an opinion on the effectiveness of the entity's internal control."

19 In circumstances when the auditor also has responsibility to express an opinion on the effectiveness of internal control in conjunction with the audit of the financial report, this sentence would be worded as follows: "In making those risk assessments, the auditor considers internal control relevant to the entity's preparation and fair presentation of the financial report in order to design audit procedures that are appropriate in the circumstances." In the case of footnote 17, this may read: "In making those risk assessments, the auditor considers internal control relevant to the entity's preparation of the financial report that gives a true and fair view in order to design audit procedures that are appropriate in the circumstances."

* The auditor's report needs to be signed in one or more of the following ways: name of the audit firm, the name of the audit company or the personal name of the auditor, as appropriate.

\# The date of the auditor's report is the date the auditor signs the report.

Example Auditor's Report
General Purpose Financial Report—Qualified Opinion (insufficient evidence)

Illustration 3:

Circumstances include the following:

- **Audit of a general purpose financial report prepared by management of the entity—the financial statements are prepared in accordance with Australian Accounting Standards.**
- **The financial report is *not* prepared under the *Corporations Act 2001*.**
- **The terms of the audit engagement reflect the description of management's responsibility for the financial report in ASA 210.**
- **The auditor was unable to obtain sufficient appropriate audit evidence regarding an investment in a foreign affiliate. The possible effects of the inability to obtain sufficient appropriate audit evidence are deemed to be material but not pervasive to the financial report.**
- **In addition to the audit of the financial report, the auditor has other reporting responsibilities required under local law.**

INDEPENDENT AUDITOR'S REPORT

[Appropriate Addressee]

Report on the Financial Report[20]

We have audited the accompanying financial report of ABC Entity, which comprises the statement of financial position as at 30 June 20X1, the statement of comprehensive income, statement of changes in equity and statement of cash flows for the year then ended, notes comprising a summary of significant accounting policies and other explanatory information, and management's assertion statement[**].

Management's[21] Responsibility for the Financial Report

Management is responsible for the preparation and fair presentation of the financial report in accordance with Australian Accounting Standards and [relevant reporting framework],[22] and for such internal control as management determines is necessary to enable the preparation and fair presentation of financial report that is free from material misstatement, whether due to fraud or error.

Auditor's Responsibility

Our responsibility is to express an opinion on the financial report based on our audit. We conducted our audit in accordance with Australian Auditing Standards. Those standards require that we comply with relevant ethical requirements relating to audit engagements and plan and perform the audit to obtain reasonable assurance about whether the financial report is free from material misstatement.

An audit involves performing procedures to obtain audit evidence about the amounts and disclosures in the financial report. The procedures selected depend on the auditor's judgement, including the assessment of the risks of material misstatement of the financial report, whether due to fraud or error. In making those risk assessments, the auditor considers internal control

20 The sub-title "Report on the Financial Report" is unnecessary in circumstances when the second sub-title "Report on Other Legal and Regulatory Requirements", or other appropriate sub-title, is not applicable.

** Or other appropriate term.

21 Or other term that is appropriate in the context of the legal framework in the particular jurisdiction.

22 Where management's responsibility is to prepare the financial report that gives a true and fair view, this may read: "Management is responsible for the preparation of the financial report that gives a true and fair view in accordance with Australian Accounting Standards, and for such..."

relevant to the entity's preparation and fair presentation[23] of the financial report in order to design audit procedures that are appropriate in the circumstances, but not for the purpose of expressing an opinion on the effectiveness of the entity's internal control.[24] An audit also includes evaluating the appropriateness of accounting policies used and the reasonableness of accounting estimates made by management, as well as evaluating the overall presentation of the financial report.

We believe that the audit evidence we have obtained is sufficient and appropriate to provide a basis for our qualified audit opinion.

Basis for Qualified Opinion

ABC Entity's investment in XYZ Entity, a foreign associate acquired during the year and accounted for by the equity method, is carried at xxx on the statement of financial position as at 30 June 20X1, and ABC's share of XYZ's net income of xxx is included in ABC's statement of comprehensive income for the year then ended. We were unable to obtain sufficient appropriate audit evidence about the carrying amount of ABC's investment in XYZ as at 30 June 20X1 and ABC's share of XYZ's net income for the year because we were denied access to the financial information, management, and the auditors of XYZ. Consequently, we were unable to determine whether any adjustments to these amounts were necessary.

Qualified Opinion

In our opinion, except for the possible effects of the matter described in the Basis for Qualified Opinion paragraph, the financial report presents fairly, in all material respects, (or *gives a true and fair view of*) the financial position of ABC Entity as at 30 June 20X1, and (*of*) its financial performance and its cash flows for the year then ended in accordance with Australian Accounting Standards and [relevant reporting framework].

Report on Other Legal and Regulatory Requirements

[Form and content of this section of the auditor's report will vary depending on the nature of the auditor's other reporting responsibilities.]

[Auditor's signature]*

[Date of the auditor's report]#

[Auditor's address]

23 In the case of footnote 22, this may read: "In making those risk assessments, the auditor considers internal control relevant to the entity's preparation of the financial report that gives a true and fair view in order to design audit procedures that are appropriate in the circumstances, but not for the purpose of expressing an opinion on the effectiveness of the entity's internal control."

24 In circumstances when the auditor also has responsibility to express an opinion on the effectiveness of internal control in conjunction with the audit of the financial report, this sentence would be worded as follows: "In making those risk assessments, the auditor considers internal control relevant to the entity's preparation and fair presentation of the financial report in order to design audit procedures that are appropriate in the circumstances." In the case of footnote 22, this may read: "In making those risk assessments, the auditor considers internal control relevant to the entity's preparation of the financial report that gives a true and fair view in order to design audit procedures that are appropriate in the circumstances."

* The auditor's report needs to be signed in one or more of the following ways: name of the audit firm, the name of the audit company or the personal name of the auditor, as appropriate.

\# The date of the auditor's report is the date the auditor signs the report.

Example Auditor's Report
General Purpose Financial Report—Qualified Opinion (insufficient evidence)
Single Company—*Corporations Act 2001*

[Aus] Illustration 3A:

Circumstances include the following:

- **Audit of a single entity's financial report.**
- **The financial report is prepared by management of the entity under the *Corporations Act 2001*.**
- **The terms of the audit engagement reflect the description of management's responsibility for the financial report in ASA 210.**
- **The auditor was unable to obtain sufficient appropriate audit evidence regarding an investment in a foreign affiliate. The possible effects of the inability to obtain sufficient appropriate audit evidence are deemed to be material but not pervasive to the financial report.**
- **In addition to the audit of the financial report, the auditor has other reporting responsibilities required under section 308(3C) of the *Corporations Act 2001*.**

INDEPENDENT AUDITOR'S REPORT

[Appropriate Addressee]

Report on the Financial Report†

We have audited the accompanying financial report of ABC Company Ltd., which comprises the statement of financial position as at 30 June 20X1, the statement of comprehensive income, statement of changes in equity and statement of cash flows for the year then ended, notes comprising a summary of significant accounting policies and other explanatory information, and the directors' declaration.

Directors' Responsibility for the Financial Report

The directors of the company [registered scheme/disclosing entity] are responsible for the preparation of the financial report that gives a true and fair view in accordance with Australian Accounting Standards and the *Corporations Act 2001*, and for such internal control as the directors determine is necessary to enable the preparation of the financial report that gives a true and fair view and is free from material misstatement, whether due to fraud or error.

Auditor's Responsibility

Our responsibility is to express an opinion on the financial report based on our audit. We conducted our audit in accordance with Australian Auditing Standards. Those standards require that we comply with relevant ethical requirements relating to audit engagements and plan and perform the audit to obtain reasonable assurance about whether the financial report is free from material misstatement.

An audit involves performing procedures to obtain audit evidence about the amounts and disclosures in the financial report. The procedures selected depend on the auditor's judgement, including the assessment of the risks of material misstatement of the financial report, whether due to fraud or error. In making those risk assessments, the auditor considers internal control relevant to the entity's preparation of the financial report that gives a true and fair view in order to design audit procedures that are appropriate in the circumstances, but not for the purpose of expressing an opinion on the effectiveness of the entity's internal control. An audit also includes evaluating the appropriateness of accounting policies used and the reasonableness of accounting estimates made by the directors, as well as evaluating the overall presentation of the financial report.

We believe that the audit evidence we have obtained is sufficient and appropriate to provide a basis for our qualified audit opinion.

† The sub-title "Report on the Financial Report" is unnecessary in circumstances when the second sub-title "Report on Other Legal and Regulatory Requirements", or other appropriate sub-title, is not applicable.

Independence

In conducting our audit, we have complied with the independence requirements of the *Corporations Act 2001*. We confirm that the independence declaration required by the *Corporations Act 2001*, which has been given to the directors of ABC Company Ltd., would be in the same terms if given to the directors as at the time of this auditor's report.*

Basis for Qualified Opinion

ABC Company Ltd.'s investment in XYZ Entity, a foreign associate acquired during the year and accounted for by the equity method, is carried at xxx on the statement of financial position as at 30 June 20X1, and ABC's share of XYZ's net income of xxx is included in ABC's statement of comprehensive income for the year then ended. We were unable to obtain sufficient appropriate audit evidence about the carrying amount of ABC's investment in XYZ as at 30 June 20X1 and ABC's share of XYZ's net income for the year because we were denied access to the financial information, management, and the auditors of XYZ. Consequently, we were unable to determine whether any adjustments to these amounts were necessary.

Qualified Opinion

In our opinion, except for the possible effects of the matter described in the Basis for Qualified Opinion paragraph, the financial report of ABC Company Ltd. is in accordance with the *Corporations Act 2001*, including:

(a) giving a true and fair view of the company's [registered scheme's/disclosing entity's] financial position as at 30 June 20X1 and of its performance for the year ended on that date; and

(b) complying with Australian Accounting Standards and the *Corporations Regulations 2001*.

Report on the Remuneration Report**

We have audited the Remuneration Report included in [paragraphs a to b or pages x to y] of the directors' report for the year ended 30 June 20X1. The directors of the company are responsible for the preparation and presentation of the Remuneration Report in accordance with section 300A of the *Corporations Act 2001*. Our responsibility is to express an opinion on the Remuneration Report, based on our audit conducted in accordance with Australian Auditing Standards.

Opinion

In our opinion, the Remuneration Report of ABC Company Ltd. for the year ended 30 June 20X1 complies with section 300A of the *Corporations Act 2001*.

[Auditor's signature]#

[Date of the auditor's report]†

[Auditor's address]

* Or, alternatively, include statements (a) to the effect that circumstances have changed since the declaration was given to the relevant directors; and (b) setting out how the declaration would differ if it had been given to the relevant directors at the time the auditor's report was made.

** The Report on the Remuneration Report is an example of "Other Reporting Responsibilities" (see ASA 700, paragraphs 38 and 39). Any additional "other reporting responsibilities" that the auditor needs to address, will also be included in a separate section of the auditor's report following the opinion paragraph on the financial report. Under paragraph 38 of ASA 700, the sub-title "Report on Other Legal and Regulatory Requirements" or other sub-title as appropriate to the section is used.

\# The auditor's report needs to be signed in one or more of the following ways: name of the audit firm, the name of the audit company or the personal name of the auditor, as appropriate.

† The date of the auditor's report is the date the auditor signs the report.

Example Auditor's Report
General Purpose Financial Report—Disclaimer of Opinion (insufficient evidence: single element)

Illustration 4:

Circumstances include the following:

- **Audit of a general purpose financial report prepared by management of the entity—the financial statements are prepared in accordance with Australian Accounting Standards.**
- **The financial report is *not* prepared under the *Corporations Act 2001*.**
- **The terms of the audit engagement reflect the description of management's responsibility for the financial report in ASA 210.**
- **The auditor was unable to obtain sufficient appropriate audit evidence about a single element of the financial report. That is, the auditor was unable to obtain audit evidence about the financial information of a joint venture investment that represents over 90% of the entity's net assets. The possible effects of this inability to obtain sufficient appropriate audit evidence are deemed to be both material and pervasive to the financial report.**
- **In addition to the audit of the financial report, the auditor has other reporting responsibilities required under local law.**

INDEPENDENT AUDITOR'S REPORT

[Appropriate Addressee]

Report on the Financial Report[25]

We were engaged to audit the accompanying financial report of ABC Entity, which comprises the statement of financial position as at 30 June 20X1, the statement of comprehensive income, statement of changes in equity and statement of cash flows for the year then ended, notes comprising a summary of significant accounting policies and other explanatory information, and management's assertion statement[*].

Management's[26] *Responsibility for the Financial Report*

Management is responsible for the preparation and fair presentation of the financial report in accordance with Australian Accounting Standards and [relevant reporting framework],[27] and for such internal control as management determines is necessary to enable the preparation and fair presentation of the financial report that is free from material misstatement, whether due to fraud or error.

Auditor's Responsibility

Our responsibility is to express an opinion on the financial report based on conducting the audit in accordance with Australian Auditing Standards. Because of the matter described in the Basis for Disclaimer of Opinion paragraph, however, we were not able to obtain sufficient appropriate audit evidence to provide a basis for an audit opinion.

Basis for Disclaimer of Opinion

The entity's investment in its joint venture XYZ (Country X) Entity is carried at xxx on the entity's statement of financial position, which represents over 90% of the entity's net assets as at 30 June 20X1. We were not allowed access to the management and the auditors of XYZ, including XYZ's auditors' audit documentation. As a result, we were unable to determine

25 The sub-title "Report on the Financial Report" is unnecessary in circumstances when the second sub-title "Report on Other Legal and Regulatory Requirements", or other appropriate sub-title, is not applicable.

* Or other appropriate term.

26 Or other term that is appropriate in the context of the legal framework in the particular jurisdiction.

27 Where management's responsibility is to prepare the financial report that gives a true and fair view, this may read: "Management is responsible for the preparation of the financial report that gives a true and fair view in accordance with Australian Accounting Standards, and for such..."

whether any adjustments were necessary in respect of the entity's proportional share of XYZ's assets that it controls jointly, its proportional share of XYZ's liabilities for which it is jointly responsible, its proportional share of XYZ's income and expenses for the year, and the elements making up the statement of changes in equity and the statement of cash flows.

Disclaimer of Opinion

Because of the significance of the matter described in the Basis for Disclaimer of Opinion paragraph, we have not been able to obtain sufficient appropriate audit evidence to provide a basis for an audit opinion. Accordingly, we do not express an opinion on the financial report.

Report on Other Legal and Regulatory Requirements

[Form and content of this section of the auditor's report will vary depending on the nature of the auditor's other reporting responsibilities.]

[Auditor's signature]†

[Date of the auditor's report]#

[Auditor's address]

Example Auditor's Report General Purpose Financial Report—Disclaimer of Opinion (insufficient evidence: multiple elements)

Illustration 5:

Circumstances include the following:

- **Audit of a general purpose financial report prepared by management of the entity—the financial statements are prepared in accordance with Australian Accounting Standards.**
- **The financial report is *not* prepared under the *Corporations Act 2001*.**
- **The terms of the audit engagement reflect the description of management's responsibility for the financial report in ASA 210.**
- **The auditor was unable to obtain sufficient appropriate audit evidence about multiple elements of the financial report. That is, the auditor was unable to obtain audit evidence about the entity's inventories and accounts receivable. The possible effects of this inability to obtain sufficient appropriate audit evidence are deemed to be both material and pervasive to the financial report.**
- **In addition to the audit of the financial report, the auditor has other reporting responsibilities required under local law.**

INDEPENDENT AUDITOR'S REPORT

[Appropriate Addressee]

Report on the Financial Report[28]

We were engaged to audit the accompanying financial report of ABC Entity, which comprises the statement of financial position as at 30 June 20X1, the statement of comprehensive income, statement of changes in equity and statement of cash flows for the year then ended, notes comprising a summary of significant accounting policies and other explanatory information, and management's assertion statement*.

† The auditor's report needs to be signed in one or more of the following ways: name of the audit firm, the name of the audit company or the personal name of the auditor, as appropriate.

The date of the auditor's report is the date the auditor signs the report.

28 The sub-title "Report on the Financial Report" is unnecessary in circumstances when the second sub-title "Report on Other Legal and Regulatory Requirements", or other appropriate sub-title, is not applicable.

* Or other appropriate term.

Management's[29] Responsibility for the Financial Report

Management is responsible for the preparation and fair presentation of the financial report in accordance with Australian Accounting Standards and [relevant reporting framework],[30] and for such internal control as management determines is necessary to enable the preparation and fair presentation of the financial report that is free from material misstatement, whether due to fraud or error.

Auditor's Responsibility

Our responsibility is to express an opinion on the financial report based on conducting the audit in accordance with Australian Auditing Standards. Because of the matters described in the Basis for Disclaimer of Opinion paragraph, however, we were not able to obtain sufficient appropriate audit evidence to provide a basis for an audit opinion.

Basis for Disclaimer of Opinion

We were not appointed as auditors of the entity until after 30 June 20X1 and thus did not observe the counting of physical inventories at the beginning and end of the year. We were unable to satisfy ourselves by alternative means concerning the inventory quantities held at 30 June 20X0 and 20X1 which are stated in the statement of financial position at xxx and xxx, respectively. In addition, the introduction of a new computerised accounts receivable system in March 20X1 resulted in numerous errors in accounts receivable. As of the date of our audit report, management was still in the process of rectifying the system deficiencies and correcting the errors. We were unable to confirm or verify by alternative means accounts receivable included in the statement of financial position at a total amount of xxx as at 30 June 20X1. As a result of these matters, we were unable to determine whether any adjustments might have been found necessary in respect of recorded or unrecorded inventories and accounts receivable, and the elements making up the statement of comprehensive income, statement of changes in equity and statement of cash flows.

Disclaimer of Opinion

Because of the significance of the matters described in the Basis for Disclaimer of Opinion paragraph, we have not been able to obtain sufficient appropriate audit evidence to provide a basis for an audit opinion. Accordingly, we do not express an opinion on the financial report.

Report on Other Legal and Regulatory Requirements

[Form and content of this section of the auditor's report will vary depending on the nature of the auditor's other reporting responsibilities.]

[Auditor's signature]*

[Date of the auditor's report]#

[Auditor's address]

29 Or other term that is appropriate in the context of the legal framework in the particular jurisdiction.

30 Where management's responsibility is to prepare the financial report that gives a true and fair view, this may read: "Management is responsible for the preparation of the financial report that gives a true and fair view in accordance with Australian Accounting Standards, and for such..."

* The auditor's report needs to be signed in one or more of the following ways: name of the audit firm, the name of the audit company or the personal name of the auditor, as appropriate.

\# The date of the auditor's report is the date the auditor signs the report.

ASA 706

Emphasis of Matter Paragraphs and Other Matter Paragraphs in the Independent Auditor's Report

(Reissued October 2009: amended and compiled June 2011)

Issued by the Auditing and Assurance Standards Board.

ASA

Note from the Institute of Chartered Accountants Australia

This note, prepared by the technical editor, is not part of ASA 706.

Historical development

April 2006: ASA 701 'Modifications to the Auditor's Report' was issued as a legally enforecable auditing standard. It is based on ISA 701 of the same name. The material was previously included in AUS 702 together with the subject matter of ASA 700 'The Auditor's Report on a General Purpose Financial Report'.

June 2007: ASA 701 compiled and republished to reflect changes to ASA 700 'The Auditor's Report in a General Purpose Financial Report' introduced by Omnibus ASA 2007-1.

October 2009: Under the AUASB's Clarity Project, the material in ASA 701 was split and the standard replaced by two new standards, ASA 705 'Modifications to the Opinion in the Independent Auditor's Report' and ASA 706 ' Emphasis of Matter Paragraphs and other Matter Paragraphs in the Independent Auditor's Report'. ASA 706 introduces the concept of an 'Other Matter' paragraph. ASAs 705 and 706 are based on ISAs 705 and 706 of the same names.

June 2011: ASA 706 updated for editorial amendments contained in ASA 2011-1 'Amendments to Australian Auditing Standards'.

Contents

Compilation Details

Auditing Standard ASA 706 *Emphasis of Matter Paragraphs and Other Matter Paragraphs in the Independent Auditor's Report* as Amended

This compilation takes into account amendments made up to and including 27 June 2011 and was prepared on 27 June 2011 by the Auditing and Assurance Standards Board (AUASB).

This compilation is not a separate Auditing Standard made by the AUASB. Instead, it is a representation of ASA 706 (October 2009) as amended by another Auditing Standard which is listed in the Table below.

Table of Standards

Standard	Date made	Operative date
ASA 706	27 October 2009	1 January 2010
ASA 2011-1	27 June 2011	1 July 2011

Table of Amendments

Paragraph affected	How affected	By ... [paragraph]
Aus A1.1	Amended	ASA 2011-1 [64]
Appendix 3: [Aus] Illustration 1A	Amended	ASA 2011-1 [65]
Appendix 3: Illustration 1	Amended	ASA 2011-1 [66]
Appendix 3: [Aus] Illustration 1A	Amended	ASA 2011-1 [67]
Appendix 3: Illustration 1A	Amended	ASA 2011-1 [68]
Appendix 3: Illustration 1 and [Aus] Illustration 1A	Amended	ASA 2011-1 [69]

Preface

[Preface extracted from the original Auditing Standard issued 27 October 2009]

Reasons for Issuing Auditing Standard ASA 706 *Emphasis of Matter Paragraphs and Other Matter Paragraphs in the Independent Auditor's Report*

The Auditing and Assurance Standards Board (AUASB) issues Auditing Standard ASA 706 *Emphasis of Matter Paragraphs and Other Matter Paragraphs in the Independent Auditor's Report* pursuant to the requirements of the legislative provisions and the Strategic Direction explained below.

The AUASB is an independent statutory board of the Australian Government established under section 227A of the *Australian Securities and Investments Commission Act 2001*, as amended (ASIC Act). Under section 336 of the *Corporations Act 2001*, the AUASB may make Australian Auditing Standards for the purposes of the corporations legislation. These Auditing Standards are legislative instruments under the *Legislative Instruments Act 2003*.

Under the Strategic Direction given to the AUASB by the Financial Reporting Council (FRC), the AUASB is required to have regard to any programme initiated by the International Auditing and Assurance Standards Board (IAASB) for the revision and enhancement of the International Standards on Auditing (ISAs) and to make appropriate consequential amendments to the Australian Auditing Standards. Accordingly, the AUASB has decided to revise and redraft the Australian Auditing Standards using the equivalent redrafted ISAs.

Main Features

This Auditing Standard establishes requirements and provides application and other explanatory material regarding the auditor's responsibility to draw user's attention to a matter in the financial report that is of such importance that it is fundamental to the user's understanding of the financial report, or to any other matter that is relevant to the user's understanding of the audit, the auditor's responsibilities or the auditor's report.

This Auditing Standard:

(a) defines, and distinguishes between, an "Emphasis of Matter" paragraph and an "Other Matter" paragraph;

(b) describes the circumstances when an Emphasis of Matter paragraph is used and the form and content of such a paragraph;

(c) describes the circumstances when an Other Matter paragraph is used and the form and content of such a paragraph;

(d) requires the auditor to communicate with those charged with governance when the auditor expects to include an Emphasis of Matter paragraph and/or an Other Matter paragraph in the auditor's report; and

(e) identifies other Auditing Standards containing requirements for Emphasis of Matter paragraphs and Other Matter paragraphs.

Authority Statement

Auditing Standard ASA 706 *Emphasis of Matter Paragraphs and Other Matter Paragraphs in the Independent Auditor's Report* (as amended at 27 June 2011) is set out in paragraphs 1 to A12 and Appendices 1 to 3.

This Auditing Standard is to be read in conjunction with ASA 101 *Preamble to Australian Auditing Standards*, which sets out the intentions of the AUASB on how the Australian Auditing Standards, operative for financial reporting periods commencing on or after 1 January 2010, are to be understood, interpreted and applied. This Auditing Standard is to be read also in conjunction with ASA 200 *Overall Objectives of the Independent Auditor and the Conduct of an Audit in Accordance with Australian Auditing Standards.*

Dated: 27 June 2011

M H Kelsall
Chairman - AUASB

Auditing Standard ASA 706

The Auditing and Assurance Standards Board (AUASB) made Auditing Standard ASA 706 *Emphasis of Matter Paragraphs and Other Matter Paragraphs in the Independent Auditor's Report,* pursuant to section 227B of the *Australian Securities and Investments Commission Act 2001* and section 336 of the *Corporations Act 2001*, on 27 October 2009.

This compiled version of ASA 706 incorporates subsequent amendments contained in another Auditing Standard made by the AUASB up to and including 27 June 2011 (see Compilation Details).

Auditing Standard ASA 706

Emphasis of Matter Paragraphs and Other Matter Paragraphs in the Independent Auditor's Report

Application

Aus 0.1 This Auditing Standard applies to:

(a) an audit of a financial report for a financial year, or an audit of a financial report for a half-year, in accordance with the *Corporations Act 2001*; and

(b) an audit of a financial report, or a complete set of financial statements, for any other purpose.

Aus 0.2 This Auditing Standard also applies, as appropriate, to an audit of other historical financial information.

Operative Date

Aus 0.3 This Auditing Standard is operative for financial reporting periods commencing on or after 1 January 2010.

[Note: For operative dates of paragraphs changed or added by an amending Standard, see Compilation Details.]

Introduction

Scope of this Auditing Standard

1. This Auditing Standard deals with the auditor's responsibility regarding additional communication in the auditor's report when the auditor considers it necessary to:

(a) Draw users' attention to a matter or matters presented or disclosed in the financial report that are of such importance that they are fundamental to users' understanding of the financial report; or

(b) Draw users' attention to any matter or matters other than those presented or disclosed in the financial report that are relevant to users' understanding of the audit, the auditor's responsibilities or the auditor's report.

2. Appendices 1 and 2 identify Auditing Standards that contain specific requirements for the auditor to include Emphasis of Matter paragraphs or Other Matter paragraphs in the auditor's report. In those circumstances, the requirements in this Auditing Standard regarding the form and placement of such paragraphs apply.

Effective Date

3. [Deleted by the AUASB. Refer Aus 0.3]

Objective

4. The objective of the auditor, having formed an opinion on the financial report, is to draw users' attention, when in the auditor's judgement it is necessary to do so, by way of clear additional communication in the auditor's report, to:
   (a) A matter, although appropriately presented or disclosed in the financial report, that is of such importance that it is fundamental to users' understanding of the financial report; or
   (b) As appropriate, any other matter that is relevant to users' understanding of the audit, the auditor's responsibilities or the auditor's report.

Definitions

5. For purposes of the Australian Auditing Standards, the following terms have the meanings attributed below:
   (a) Emphasis of Matter paragraph means a paragraph included in the auditor's report that refers to a matter appropriately presented or disclosed in the financial report that, in the auditor's judgement, is of such importance that it is fundamental to users' understanding of the financial report.
   (b) Other Matter paragraph means a paragraph included in the auditor's report that refers to a matter other than those presented or disclosed in the financial report that, in the auditor's judgement, is relevant to users' understanding of the audit, the auditor's responsibilities or the auditor's report.

Requirements

Emphasis of Matter Paragraphs in the Auditor's Report

6. If the auditor considers it necessary to draw users' attention to a matter presented or disclosed in the financial report that, in the auditor's judgement, is of such importance that it is fundamental to users' understanding of the financial report, the auditor shall include an Emphasis of Matter paragraph in the auditor's report provided the auditor has obtained sufficient appropriate audit evidence that the matter is not materially misstated in the financial report. Such a paragraph shall refer only to information presented or disclosed in the financial report. (Ref: Para. A1-Aus 2.1)

Aus 6.1 In addition to the requirements in paragraph 6 of this Auditing Standard, the auditor shall include an Emphasis of Matter paragraph in the auditor's report where required by other Auditing Standards. (Ref: Appendix 1)

7. When the auditor includes an Emphasis of Matter paragraph in the auditor's report, the auditor shall:
   (a) Include it immediately after the Opinion paragraph in the auditor's report;
   (b) Use the heading "Emphasis of Matter," or other appropriate heading;
   (c) Include in the paragraph a clear reference to the matter being emphasised and to where relevant disclosures that fully describe the matter can be found in the financial report; and
   (d) Indicate that the auditor's opinion is not modified in respect of the matter emphasised. (Ref: Para. A3-A4)

Aus 7.1 When the financial report has been prepared in accordance with Australian Accounting Standards but additional disclosures have been made in the financial report:
   - on the basis that, or which imply that, application of a particular Accounting Standard has resulted in the financial report being potentially misleading; or
   - that, in the opinion of those charged with governance, are necessary to present a true and fair view;

and the auditor is of the opinion that:

(a) it is likely, in the absence of the additional disclosures, that users would be misled when making evaluations or decisions about the allocation of scarce resources; and

(b) the additional disclosures contain all, and only, relevant and reliable information, and are presented in such a manner as to ensure the financial report as a whole is comparable and understandable in meeting the objectives of the financial report,

the auditor shall include in the auditor's report an Emphasis of Matter paragraph headed "Application of Australian Accounting Standard AASB ..." or an appropriate alternative which:

(i) draws attention to the additional disclosures;

(ii) where relevant, states that in the auditor's opinion application of the particular Accounting Standard has, in this instance, resulted in the financial report being potentially misleading;

(iii) states the specific reasons why the auditor believes the additional disclosures are necessary to ensure the financial report as a whole is not misleading (the auditor's reasons are to be stated in the auditor's report itself rather than only by reference to the reasons included in the financial report); and

(iv) states that, in the auditor's opinion, the additional disclosures are relevant and reliable in meeting the objectives of the financial report. (Ref: Para. Aus A4.1)

Other Matter Paragraphs in the Auditor's Report (Ref: Para. A5-A11)

8. If the auditor considers it necessary to communicate a matter other than those that are presented or disclosed in the financial report that, in the auditor's judgement, is relevant to users' understanding of the audit, the auditor's responsibilities or the auditor's report and this is not prohibited by law or regulation, the auditor shall do so in a paragraph in the auditor's report, with the heading "Other Matter," or other appropriate heading. The auditor shall include this paragraph immediately after the Opinion paragraph and any Emphasis of Matter paragraph, or elsewhere in the auditor's report if the content of the Other Matter paragraph is relevant to the Other Reporting Responsibilities section.

Aus 8.1 In addition to the requirements in paragraph 8 of this Auditing Standard, the auditor shall include an Other Matter paragraph in the auditor's report where required by other Auditing Standards. (Ref: Appendix 2)

Communication with Those Charged with Governance

9. If the auditor expects to include an Emphasis of Matter or an Other Matter paragraph in the auditor's report, the auditor shall communicate with those charged with governance regarding this expectation and the proposed wording of this paragraph. (Ref: Para. A12)

❖ ❖ ❖

Application and Other Explanatory Material

Emphasis of Matter Paragraphs in the Auditor's Report

Circumstances in Which an Emphasis of Matter Paragraph May Be Necessary (Ref: Para. 6-Aus 6.1 and Aus 7.1)

A1. Examples of circumstances where the auditor may consider it necessary to include an Emphasis of Matter paragraph are:

- An uncertainty relating to the future outcome of exceptional litigation or regulatory action.
- Early application (where permitted) of a new accounting standard (for example, a new Australian Accounting Standard) that has a pervasive effect on the financial report in advance of its effective date.

- A major catastrophe that has had, or continues to have, a significant effect on the entity's financial position.

Aus A1.1 Ordinarily, an uncertainty, the resolution of which may materially affect the financial report, would warrant an Emphasis of Matter paragraph in the auditor's report.

A2. A widespread use of Emphasis of Matter paragraphs diminishes the effectiveness of the auditor's communication of such matters. Additionally, to include more information in an Emphasis of Matter paragraph than is presented or disclosed in the financial report may imply that the matter has not been appropriately presented or disclosed; accordingly, paragraph 6 limits the use of an Emphasis of Matter paragraph to matters presented or disclosed in the financial report.

Aus A2.1 Accounting estimates are ordinarily made in connection with amounts and other disclosures appearing in the financial report. In most cases the auditor is able to be satisfied regarding the reasonableness of an accounting estimate. Requirements and application and other explanatory material on this matter are contained in ASA 540 *Auditing Accounting Estimates, Including Fair Value Accounting Estimates, and Related Disclosures*. Such an accounting estimate will not ordinarily be regarded as a significant uncertainty for the purposes of this Auditing Standard.

ASA

Including an Emphasis of Matter Paragraph in the Auditor's Report (Ref: Para. 7)

A3. The inclusion of an Emphasis of Matter paragraph in the auditor's report does not affect the auditor's opinion. An Emphasis of Matter paragraph is not a substitute for either:

(a) The auditor expressing a qualified opinion or an adverse opinion, or disclaiming an opinion, when required by the circumstances of a specific audit engagement (see ASA 705[1]); or

(b) Disclosures in the financial report that the applicable financial reporting framework requires management to make.

A4. The illustrative report (example 1) in Appendix 3 includes an Emphasis of Matter paragraph in an auditor's report that contains a qualified opinion.

Aus A4.1 When an auditor's report is prepared on a financial report prepared under the *Corporations Act 2001* (the Act), section 308(3B) of the Act requires that if the financial report includes additional information under paragraph 295(3)(c) (additional information included to give a true and fair view of the entity's financial position and performance), the auditor's report includes the auditor's opinion on whether the additional information was necessary to give a true and fair view. (Ref: Para. Aus 7.1)

Other Matter Paragraphs in the Auditor's Report (Ref: Para. 8 – Aus 8.1)

Circumstances in Which an Other Matter Paragraph May Be Necessary

Relevant to Users' Understanding of the Audit

A5. In the rare circumstance where the auditor is unable to withdraw from an engagement even though the possible effect of an inability to obtain sufficient appropriate audit evidence due to a limitation on the scope of the audit imposed by management is pervasive,[2] the auditor may consider it necessary to include an Other Matter paragraph in the auditor's report to explain why it is not possible for the auditor to withdraw from the engagement.

Relevant to Users' Understanding of the Auditor's Responsibilities or the Auditor's Report

A6. Law, regulation or generally accepted practice in a jurisdiction may require or permit the auditor to elaborate on matters that provide further explanation of the auditor's responsibilities in the audit of the financial report or of the auditor's report thereon. Where relevant, one or more sub-headings may be used that describe the content of the Other Matter paragraph.

---

1 See ASA 705 *Modifications to the Opinion in the Independent Auditor's Report.*

2 See ASA 705, paragraph 13(b)(ii) for a discussion of this circumstance.

A7. An Other Matter paragraph does not deal with circumstances where the auditor has other reporting responsibilities that are in addition to the auditor's responsibility under the Australian Auditing Standards to report on the financial report (see "Other Reporting Responsibilities" section in ASA 700[3]), or where the auditor has been asked to perform and report on additional specified procedures, or to express an opinion on specific matters.

Reporting on more than one financial report

A8. An entity may prepare one financial report in accordance with a general purpose framework (for example, the Australian Accounting Standards) and another financial report in accordance with another general purpose framework (for example, International Financial Reporting Standards), and engage the auditor to report on both financial reports. If the auditor has determined that the frameworks are acceptable in the respective circumstances, the auditor may include an Other Matter paragraph in the auditor's report, referring to the fact that another financial report has been prepared by the same entity in accordance with another general purpose framework and that the auditor has issued a report on that financial report.

Restriction on distribution or use of the auditor's report

A9. A financial report prepared for a specific purpose may be prepared in accordance with a general purpose framework because the intended users have determined that such a general purpose financial report meets their financial information needs. Since the auditor's report is intended for specific users, the auditor may consider it necessary in the circumstances to include an Other Matter paragraph, stating that the auditor's report is intended solely for the intended users, and should not be distributed to or used by other parties.

Including an Other Matter Paragraph in the Auditor's Report

A10. The content of an Other Matter paragraph reflects clearly that such other matter is not required to be presented and disclosed in the financial report. An Other Matter paragraph does not include information that the auditor is prohibited from providing by law, regulation or other professional standards, for example, ethical standards relating to confidentiality of information. An Other Matter paragraph also does not include information that is required to be provided by management.

Aus A10.1 The inclusion of an Other Matter paragraph in the auditor's report does not affect the auditor's opinion. An auditor needs to consider whether, in the circumstances, it is appropriate to indicate that the auditor's opinion is not modified in respect of the Other Matter paragraph.

A11. The placement of an Other Matter paragraph depends on the nature of the information to be communicated. When an Other Matter paragraph is included to draw users' attention to a matter relevant to their understanding of the audit of the financial report, the paragraph is included immediately after the Opinion paragraph and any Emphasis of Matter paragraph. When an Other Matter paragraph is included to draw users' attention to a matter relating to Other Reporting Responsibilities addressed in the auditor's report, the paragraph may be included in the section sub-titled "Report on Other Legal and Regulatory Requirements." Alternatively, when relevant to all the auditor's responsibilities or users' understanding of the auditor's report, the Other Matter paragraph may be included as a separate section following the Report on the Financial Report and the Report on Other Legal and Regulatory Requirements.

Communication with Those Charged with Governance (Ref: Para. 9)

A12. Such communication enables those charged with governance to be made aware of the nature of any specific matters that the auditor intends to highlight in the auditor's report, and provides them with an opportunity to obtain further clarification from the auditor where necessary. Where the inclusion of an Other Matter paragraph on a particular matter in the auditor's report recurs on each successive engagement, the auditor may determine that it is unnecessary to repeat the communication on each engagement.

❖ ❖ ❖

3 See ASA 700 *Forming an Opinion and Reporting on a Financial Report,* paragraphs 38-39.

Conformity with International Standards on Auditing

This Auditing Standard conforms with International Standard on Auditing ISA 706 *Emphasis of Matter Paragraphs and Other Matter Paragraphs in the Independent Auditor's Report*, issued by the International Auditing and Assurance Standards Board (IAASB), an independent standard-setting board of the International Federation of Accountants (IFAC).

Paragraphs that have been added to this Auditing Standard (and do not appear in the text of the equivalent ISA) are identified with the prefix "Aus".

The following requirements are additional to ISA 706:

- In addition to the requirements in paragraph 6 of this Auditing Standard, the auditor shall include an Emphasis of Matter paragraph in the auditor's report where required by other Auditing Standards. (Ref: Para. Aus 6.1)
- When the financial report has been prepared in accordance with Australian Accounting Standards but additional disclosures have been made in the financial report:
  - ♦ on the basis that, or which imply that, application of a particular Accounting Standard has resulted in the financial report being potentially misleading; or
  - ♦ that, in the opinion of those charged with governance, are necessary to present a true and fair view;

  and the auditor is of the opinion that:

  - ♦ it is likely, in the absence of the additional disclosures, that users would be misled when making evaluations or decisions about the allocation of scarce resources; and
  - ♦ the additional disclosures contain all, and only, relevant and reliable information, and are presented in such a manner as to ensure the financial report as a whole is comparable and understandable in meeting the objectives of the financial report,

  the auditor shall include in the auditor's report an Emphasis of Matter paragraph headed "Application of Australian Accounting Standard AASB ..." or an appropriate alternative which:

  - ♦ draws attention to the additional disclosures;
  - ♦ where relevant, states that in the auditor's opinion application of the particular Accounting Standard has, in this instance, resulted in the financial report being potentially misleading;
  - ♦ states the specific reasons why the auditor believes the additional disclosures are necessary to ensure the financial report as a whole is not misleading (the auditor's reasons are to be stated in the auditor's report itself rather than only by reference to the reasons included in the financial report); and
  - ♦ states that, in the auditor's opinion, the additional disclosures are relevant and reliable in meeting the objectives of the financial report. (Ref: Para Aus 7.1)
- In addition to the requirements in paragraph 8 of this Auditing Standard, the auditor shall include an Other Matter paragraph in the auditor's report where required by other Auditing Standards. (Ref: Para. Aus 8.1)

Compliance with this Auditing Standard enables compliance with ISA 706.

Appendix 1

(Ref: Para. 2 and Aus 6.1)

List of Auditing Standards Containing Requirements for Emphasis of Matter Paragraphs

This appendix identifies paragraphs in other Auditing Standards in effect for audits of financial reports for financial reporting periods commencing on or after 1 January 2010, that require the auditor to include an Emphasis of Matter paragraph in the auditor's report in certain circumstances. The list is not a substitute for considering the requirements and related application and other explanatory material in the Australian Auditing Standards.

- ASA 210 *Agreeing the Terms of Audit Engagements* – paragraph 19(b)
- ASA 560 *Subsequent Events* – paragraphs 12(b) and 16
- ASA 570 *Going Concern* – paragraph 19
- ASA 800 *Special Considerations—Audits of Financial Reports Prepared in Accordance with Special Purpose Frameworks* – paragraph 14

Appendix 2

(Ref: Para. 2 and Aus 8.1)

List of Auditing Standards Containing Requirements for Other Matter Paragraphs

This appendix identifies paragraphs in other Auditing Standards in effect for audits of financial reports for financial reporting periods commencing on or after 1 January 2010, that require the auditor to include an Other Matter paragraph in the auditor's report in certain circumstances. The list is not a substitute for considering the requirements and related application and other explanatory material in the Australian Auditing Standards.

- ASA 560 *Subsequent Events* – paragraphs 12(b) and 16
- ASA 710 *Comparative Information—Corresponding Figures and Comparative Financial Reports* – paragraphs 13-14, 16-17 and 19
- ASA 720 *The Auditor's Responsibilities Relating to Other Information in Documents Containing an Audited Financial Report* – paragraph 10(a)

Appendix 3

Illustrations of an Auditor's Report that Includes an Emphasis of Matter Paragraph

- Illustration 1: An auditor's report containing a qualified opinion and an Emphasis of Matter paragraph – general purpose financial report. (Ref: Para. A4)
- [Aus] Illustration 1A: A general purpose financial report prepared under the *Corporations Act 2001*. The auditor's report contains:
  - an unmodified opinion;
  - an Emphasis of Matter paragraph;
  - an Other Reporting Responsibility paragraph; and
  - an Other Matter paragraph.

Example Auditor's Report
General Purpose Financial Report
Qualified Opinion and Emphasis of Matter

Illustration 1:

Circumstances include the following:

- **Audit of a general purpose financial report prepared by management of the entity—the financial statements are prepared in accordance with Australian Accounting Standards.**
- **The financial report is not prepared under the *Corporations Act 2001*.**
- **The terms of the audit engagement reflect the description of management's responsibility for the financial report in ASA 210.[4]**
- **There is uncertainty relating to a pending exceptional litigation matter.**
- **A departure from the applicable financial reporting framework resulted in a qualified opinion.**
- **In addition to the audit of the financial report, the auditor has other reporting responsibilities required under local law.**

ASA

INDEPENDENT AUDITOR'S REPORT

[Appropriate Addressee]

Report on the Financial Report[5]

We have audited the accompanying financial report of ABC Entity, which comprises the statement of financial position as at 30 June 20X1, the statement of comprehensive income, statement of changes in equity and statement of cash flows for the year then ended, notes comprising a summary of significant accounting policies and other explanatory information, and management's assertion statement.[*]

Management's[6] Responsibility for the Financial Report

Management is responsible for the preparation and fair presentation of the financial report in accordance with Australian Accounting Standards and [relevant reporting framework],[7] and for such internal control as management determines is necessary to enable the preparation and fair presentation of the financial report that is free from material misstatement, whether due to fraud or error.

Auditor's Responsibility

Our responsibility is to express an opinion on the financial report based on our audit. We conducted our audit in accordance with Australian Auditing Standards. Those standards require that we comply with relevant ethical requirements relating to audit engagements and plan and perform the audit to obtain reasonable assurance about whether the financial report is free from material misstatement.

An audit involves performing procedures to obtain audit evidence about the amounts and disclosures in the financial report. The procedures selected depend on the auditor's judgement, including the assessment of the risks of material misstatement of the financial report, whether due to fraud or error. In making those risk assessments, the auditor considers internal control

4 See ASA 210 *Agreeing the Term of Audit Engagements*.

5 The sub-title "Report on the Financial Report" is unnecessary in circumstances when the second sub-title "Report on Other Legal and Regulatory Requirements", or other appropriate sub-title, is not applicable.

* Or other appropriate term.

6 Or other term that is appropriate in the context of the legal framework in the particular jurisdiction.

7 Where management's responsibility is to prepare the financial report that gives a true and fair view, this may read: "Management is responsible for the preparation of the financial report that gives a true and fair view in accordance with Australian Accounting Standards, and for such..."

relevant to the entity's preparation and fair presentation[8] of the financial report in order to design audit procedures that are appropriate in the circumstances, but not for the purpose of expressing an opinion on the effectiveness of the entity's internal control.[9] An audit also includes evaluating the appropriateness of accounting policies used and the reasonableness of accounting estimates made by management, as well as evaluating the overall presentation of the financial report.

We believe that the audit evidence that we have obtained is sufficient and appropriate to provide a basis for our qualified audit opinion.

Basis for Qualified Opinion

The entity's short-term marketable securities are carried in the statement of financial position at xxx. Management has not marked these securities to market but has instead stated them at cost, which constitutes a departure from Australian Accounting Standards. The entity's records indicate that had management marked the marketable securities to market, the entity would have recognised an unrealised loss of xxx in the statement of comprehensive income for the year. The carrying amount of the securities in the statement of financial position would have been reduced by the same amount at 30 June 20X1, and income tax, net income and shareholders' equity would have been reduced by xxx, xxx and xxx, respectively.

Qualified Opinion

In our opinion, except for the effects of the matter described in the Basis for Qualified Opinion paragraph, the financial report presents fairly, in all material respects (or *give a true and fair view of*) the financial position of ABC Entity as at 30 June 20X1, and (*of*) its financial performance and its cash flows for the year then ended in accordance with Australian Accounting Standards and [relevant reporting framework].

Emphasis of Matter

We draw attention to Note X to the financial statements which describes the uncertainty[10] related to the outcome of the lawsuit filed against the entity by XYZ Entity. Our opinion is not modified in respect of this matter.

Report on Other Legal and Regulatory Requirements

[Form and content of this section of the auditor's report will vary depending on the nature of the auditor's other reporting responsibilities.]

[Auditor's signature][*]

[Date of the auditor's report][#]

[Auditor's address]

8 In the case of footnote 7, this may read: "In making those risk assessments, the auditor considers internal control relevant to the entity's preparation of the financial report that gives a true and fair view in order to design audit procedures that are appropriate in the circumstances, but nor for the purpose of expressing an opinion on the effectiveness of the entity's internal control."

9 In circumstances when the auditor also has responsibility to express an opinion on the effectiveness of internal control in conjunction with the audit of the financial report, this sentence would be worded as follows: "In making those risk assessments, the auditor considers internal control relevant to the entity's preparation and fair presentation of the financial report in order to design audit procedures that are appropriate in the circumstances." In the case of footnote 7, this may read: "In making those risk assessments, the auditor considers internal control relevant to the entity's preparation of the financial report that gives a true and fair view in order to design audit procedures that are appropriate in the circumstances."

10 In highlighting the uncertainty, the auditor uses the same terminology that is used in the note to the financial statements.

* The auditor's report needs to be signed in one or more of the following ways: the name of the audit firm, the name of the audit company or the personal name of the auditor, as appropriate.

\# The date of the auditor's report is the date the auditor signs the report.

Example Auditor's Report
General Purpose Financial Report
Unmodified Opinion, Emphasis of Matter and Other Matter—*Corporations Act 2001*

[Aus] Illustration 1A:

Circumstances include the following:

- **Audit of a single company's financial report.**
- **The financial report is prepared for a general purpose by management of the entity under the *Corporations Act 2001.***
- **The financial report includes a statement that the financial statements comply with International Financial Reporting Standards (IFRSs).**
- **The terms of the audit engagement reflect the description of management's responsibility for the financial report in ASA 210.**
- **There is uncertainty relating to a pending exceptional litigation matter.**
- **In addition to the audit of the financial report, the auditor has other reporting responsibilities required under section 308(3C) of the *Corporations Act 2001.***
- **The auditor has decided to include an Other Matter paragraph.**

INDEPENDENT AUDITOR'S REPORT [Appropriate Addressee]

Report on the Financial Report*

We have audited the accompanying financial report of ABC Company Ltd., which comprises the statement of financial position as at 30 June 20X1, the statement of comprehensive income, statement of changes in equity and statement of cash flows for the year then ended, notes comprising a summary of significant accounting policies and other explanatory information, and the directors' declaration.

Directors' Responsibility for the Financial Report

The directors of the company [registered scheme/disclosing entity] are responsible for the preparation of the financial report that gives a true and fair view in accordance with Australian Accounting Standards and the *Corporations Act 2001*, and for such internal control as the directors determine is necessary to enable the preparation of the financial report that gives a true and fair view and is free from material misstatement, whether due to fraud or error. In Note XX, the directors also state, in accordance with Accounting Standard AASB 101 *Presentation of Financial Statements,* that the financial statements comply with *International Financial Reporting Standards.***

Auditor's Responsibility

Our responsibility is to express an opinion on the financial report based on our audit. We conducted our audit in accordance with Australian Auditing Standards. Those standards require that we comply with relevant ethical requirements relating to audit engagements and plan and perform the audit to obtain reasonable assurance about whether the financial report is free from material misstatement.

An audit involves performing procedures to obtain audit evidence about the amounts and disclosures in the financial report. The procedures selected depend on the auditor's judgement, including the assessment of the risks of material misstatement of the financial report, whether due to fraud or error. In making those risk assessments, the auditor considers internal control

* The sub-title "Report on the Financial Report" is unnecessary in circumstances when the second sub-title "Report on Other Legal and Regulatory Requirements", or other appropriate sub-title, is not applicable.

** Insert only where the entity has included in the notes to the financial statements an explicit and unreserved statement of compliance with *International Financial Reporting Standards* in accordance with AASB 101.

relevant to the company's preparation of the financial report that gives a true and fair view in order to design audit procedures that are appropriate in the circumstances, but not for the purpose of expressing an opinion on the effectiveness of the company's internal control. An audit also includes evaluating the appropriateness of accounting policies used and the reasonableness of accounting estimates made by the directors, as well as evaluating the overall presentation of the financial report.

We believe that the audit evidence we have obtained is sufficient and appropriate to provide a basis for our audit opinion.

Independence

In conducting our audit, we have complied with the independence requirements of the *Corporations Act 2001*. We confirm that the independence declaration required by the *Corporations Act 2001*, which has been given to the directors of ABC Company Ltd., would be in the same terms if given to the directors as at the time of this auditor's report.*

Opinion

In our opinion:

(a) the financial report of ABC Company Ltd. is in accordance with the *Corporations Act 2001*, including:

 (i) giving a true and fair view of the company's [registered scheme's/disclosing entity's] financial position as at 30 June 20X1 and of its performance for the year ended on that date; and

 (ii) complying with Australian Accounting Standards and the *Corporations Regulations 2001*; and

(b) the financial report also complies with *International Financial Reporting Standards* as disclosed in Note XX.#

Emphasis of Matter

We draw attention to Note X to the financial statements which describes the uncertainty† related to the outcome of the lawsuit filed against the company by XYZ Entity. Our opinion is not modified in respect of this matter.

Report on the Remuneration Report**

We have audited the Remuneration Report included in [paragraphs a to b or pages x to y] of the directors' report for the year [period] ended 30 June 20X1. The directors of the company are responsible for the preparation and presentation of the Remuneration Report in accordance with section 300A of the *Corporations Act 2001*. Our responsibility is to express an opinion on the Remuneration Report, based on our audit conducted in accordance with Australian Auditing Standards.

---

* Or, alternatively, include statements (a) to the effect that circumstances have changed since the declaration was given to the relevant directors; and (b) setting out how the declaration would differ if it had been given to the relevant directors at the time the auditor's report was made.

Insert only where the entity has included in the notes to the financial statements an explicit and unreserved statement of compliance with *International Financial Reporting Standards* in accordance with AASB 101 and the auditor agrees with the entity's statement. If the auditor does not agree with the statement, the auditor refers to ASA 705.

† In highlighting the uncertainty, the auditor uses the same terminology that is used in the note to the financial statements.

** The Report on the Remuneration Report is an example of "Other Reporting responsibilities"(see ASA 700, paragraphs 38 and 39). Any additional "other reporting responsibilities" that the auditor needs to address, will also be included in a separate section of the auditor's report following the opinion paragraph on the financial report. Under ASA 700, paragraph 38, the sub-title "Report on Other Legal and Regulatory Requirements" or other sub-title as appropriate to the section is used.

Opinion

In our opinion the Remuneration Report of ABC Company Ltd. for the year [period] ended 30 June 20X1, complies with section 300A of the *Corporations Act 2001*.

Other Matter

ABC Company Ltd. has prepared a separate financial report for the year ended 30 June 20X1 in accordance with the [name of country] Financial Reporting Standards on which we issued a separate auditor's report to the shareholders of ABC Company Ltd. dated 30 September 20X1.

[Auditor's signature][#]

[Date of the auditor's report][†]

[Auditor's address]

\# The auditor's report needs to be signed in one or more of the following ways: name of the audit firm, the name of the audit company or the personal name of the auditor, as appropriate.

† The date of the auditor's report is the date the auditor signs the report.

ASA 710
Comparative Information—Corresponding Figures and Comparative Financial Reports

(Reissued October 2009: amended and compiled June 2011)

Issued by the Auditing and Assurance Standards Board.

Note from the Institute of Chartered Accountants Australia

This note, prepared by the technical editor, is not part of ASA 710.

Historical development

September 1994: ED 62 'Codification and Revision of Auditing Pronouncements: AUS 704 Comparatives (AUP 37)' issued by the AuSB.

October 1995: Australian Auditing Standards and Auditing Guidance Statements released. The status of these was explained in APS 1.1 'Conformity with Auditing Standards'. These Standards became operative for the first reporting period commencing on or after 1 July 1996 and later reporting periods, although earlier application was encouraged. AUP 37 'Audit Implications of Comparatives' replaced by AUS 704 'Comparatives'.

April 1996: The International Auditing Practices Committee (IAPC) of the International Federation of Accountants (IFAC) approved the issuance of a codified set of International Standards of Auditing (ISAs). The relevant international pronouncement was ISA 710 'Comparatives'.

October 1996: AUS 704 'Comparatives' reissued by the AuSB, with amendments made to the Compatibility with International Standards on Auditing section of the Standard.

April 1998: AUS/AGS Omnibus 1 'Miscellaneous Amendments to AUSs and AGSs' issued. The changes to AUS 704 embodied in Omnibus 1 were incorporated into this version of AUS 704.

February 1999: AUS/AGS Omnibus 2 'Miscellaneous Amendments to AUSs and AGSs' issued by the AuASB, operative from the date of issue. The Omnibus amended para. .04 of AUS 704.

July 2002: AUS/AGS Omnibus 3 'Miscellaneous Amendments to AUSs and AGSs' issued by the AuASB, operative from the date of issue. AUS 704 since reissued by the Board to incorporate these amendments.

April 2006: ASA 710 'Comparatives' was issued as a legally enforceable Standard to replace AUS 704. It is based on ISA 710 of the same name.

June 2007: ASA 710 compiled and republished to reflect changes to ASA 710 'Comparatives' introduced by Omnibus ASA 2007-1.

October 2009: ASA 710 reissued as part of the AUASB's Clarity Project, entitled 'Comparative Information—Corresponding Figures and Comparative Financial Statements'. It is based on ISA 710 'Comparative Information—Corresponding Figures and Comparative Financial Statements'.

June 2011: ASA 710 updated for editorial amendments contained in ASA 2011-1 'Amendments to Australian Auditing Standards'.

Contents

Compilation Details

Auditing Standard ASA 710 *Comparative Information – Corresponding Figures and Comparative Financial Reports* as Amended

This compilation takes into account amendments made up to and including 27 June 2011 and was prepared on 27 June 2011 by the Auditing and Assurance Standards Board (AUASB).

This compilation is not a separate Auditing Standard made by the AUASB. Instead, it is a representation of ASA 710 (October 2009) as amended by another Auditing Standard which is listed in the Table below.

Table of Standards

Standard	Date made	Operative date
ASA 710	27 October 2009	1 January 2010
ASA 2011-1	27 June 2011	1 July 2011

Table of Amendments

Paragraph affected	How affected	By … [paragraph]
Appendix 1: Illustrations 1A and 2A	Amended	ASA 2011-1 [70]
Appendix 1: [Aus] Illustration 1A	Amended	ASA 2011-1 [71]
Appendix 1: [Aus] Illustration 2A	Amended	ASA 2011-1 [72]
Appendix 1: [Aus] Illustration 2A		ASA 2011-1 [73]

Paragraph affected	How affected	By … [paragraph]
Appendix 1: Illustration 1, 2, 3 and 4	Amended	ASA 2011-1 [74]
Appendix 1: Illustrations 1, 2, 3, 4 and [Aus] Illustrations 1A and 2A	Amended	ASA 2011-1 [75]

Preface

[Preface extracted from the original Auditing Standard issued 27 October 2009]

Reasons for Issuing Auditing Standard ASA 710 *Comparative Information—Corresponding Figures and Comparative Financial Reports*

The Auditing and Assurance Standards Board (AUASB) issues Auditing Standard ASA 710 *Comparative Information—Corresponding Figures and Comparative Financial Reports* pursuant to the requirements of the legislative provisions and the Strategic Direction explained below.

The AUASB is an independent statutory board of the Australian Government established under section 227A of the *Australian Securities and Investments Commission Act 2001*, as amended (ASIC Act). Under section 336 of the *Corporations Act 2001*, the AUASB may make Auditing Standards for the purposes of the corporations legislation. These Auditing Standards are legislative instruments under the *Legislative Instruments Act 2003*.

Under the Strategic Direction given to the AUASB by the Financial Reporting Council (FRC), the AUASB is required to have regard to any programme initiated by the International Auditing and Assurance Standards Board (IAASB) for the revision and enhancement of the International Standards on Auditing (ISAs) and to make appropriate consequential amendments to the Australian Auditing Standards. Accordingly, the AUASB has decided to revise and redraft the Australian Auditing Standards using the equivalent redrafted ISAs.

Main Features

This Auditing Standard establishes requirements and provides application and other explanatory material regarding the auditor's responsibilities relating to comparative information in an audit of a financial report.

This Auditing Standard:

(a) describes the nature of comparative information as being either in the form of corresponding figures or comparative financial reports;

(b) sets out the audit procedures the auditor is required to conduct in respect of each type of comparative information; and

(c) sets out the reporting obligations of the auditor in respect of comparative information.

Authority Statement

Auditing Standard ASA 710 *Comparative Information—Corresponding Figures and Comparative Financial Reports* (as amended at 27 June 2011) is set out in paragraphs 1 to A11 and Appendix 1.

This Auditing Standard is to be read in conjunction with ASA 101 *Preamble to Australian Auditing Standards*, which sets out the intentions of the AUASB on how the Australian Auditing Standards, operative for financial reporting periods commencing on or after 1 January 2010, are to be understood, interpreted and applied. This Auditing Standard is to be read also in conjunction with ASA 200 *Objectives of the Independent Auditor and the Conduct of an Audit in Accordance with Australian Auditing Standards.*

Dated: 27 June 2011

M H Kelsall
Chairman - AUASB

Auditing Standard ASA 710

The Auditing and Assurance Standards Board (AUASB) made Auditing Standard ASA 710 *Comparative Information—Corresponding Figures and Comparative Financial Reports* pursuant to section 227B of the *Australian Securities and Investments Commission Act 2001* and section 336 of the *Corporations Act 2001*, on 27 October 2009.

This compiled version of ASA 710 incorporates subsequent amendments contained in another Auditing Standard made by the AUASB up to and including 27 June 2011 (see Compilation Details).

ASA

Auditing Standard ASA 710

Comparative Information—Corresponding Figures and Comparative Financial Reports

Application

Aus 0.1 This Auditing Standard applies to:

(a) an audit of a financial report for a financial year, or an audit of a financial report for a half-year, in accordance with the *Corporations Act 2001*; and

(b) an audit of a financial report, or a complete set of financial statements, for any other purpose.

Aus 0.2 This Auditing Standard also applies, as appropriate, to an audit of other historical financial information.

Operative Date

Aus 0.3 This Auditing Standard is operative for financial reporting periods commencing on or after 1 January 2010.

[Note: For operative dates of paragraphs changed or added by an amending Standard, see Compilation Details.]

Introduction

Scope of this Auditing Standard

1. This Auditing Standard deals with the auditor's responsibilities relating to comparative information in an audit of a financial report. When the financial report of the prior period has been audited by a predecessor auditor or was not audited, the requirements and guidance in ASA 510[1] regarding opening balances also apply.

The Nature of Comparative Information

2. The nature of the comparative information that is presented in an entity's financial report depends on the requirements of the applicable financial reporting framework. There are two different broad approaches to the auditor's reporting responsibilities in respect of such comparative information: corresponding figures and comparative financial reports. The approach to be adopted is often specified by law or regulation but may also be specified in the terms of engagement.

3. The essential audit reporting differences between the approaches are:

(a) For corresponding figures, the auditor's opinion on the financial report refers to the current period only; whereas

(b) For comparative financial reports, the auditor's opinion refers to each period for which a financial report is presented.

This Auditing Standard addresses separately the auditor's reporting requirements for each approach.

1 See ASA 510 *Initial Audit Engagements—Opening Balances*.

Effective Date

4. [Deleted by the AUASB. Refer Aus 0.3]

Objectives

5. The objectives of the auditor are:

   (a) To obtain sufficient appropriate audit evidence about whether the comparative information included in the financial report has been presented, in all material respects, in accordance with the requirements for comparative information in the applicable financial reporting framework; and

   (b) To report in accordance with the auditor's reporting responsibilities.

Definitions

6. For purposes of the Australian Auditing Standards, the following terms have the meanings attributed below:

   (a) Comparative information means the amounts and disclosures included in the financial report in respect of one or more prior periods in accordance with the applicable financial reporting framework.

   (b) Corresponding figures mean comparative information where amounts and other disclosures for the prior period are included as an integral part of the current period financial report, and are intended to be read only in relation to the amounts and other disclosures relating to the current period (referred to as "current period figures"). The level of detail presented in the corresponding amounts and disclosures is dictated primarily by its relevance to the current period figures.

   (c) Comparative financial reports means comparative information where amounts and other disclosures for the prior period are included for comparison with the financial report of the current period but, if audited, are referred to in the auditor's opinion. The level of information included in those comparative financial reports is comparable with that of the financial report of the current period.

Aus 6.1 In accordance with the applicable financial reporting framework of the *Corporations Act 2001* and Australian Accounting Standards, comparative information refers to corresponding figures.

For purposes of this Auditing Standard, references to "prior period" should be read as "prior periods" when the comparative information includes amounts and disclosures for more than one period.

Requirements

Audit Procedures

7. The auditor shall determine whether the financial report includes the comparative information required by the applicable financial reporting framework and whether such information is appropriately classified. For this purpose, the auditor shall evaluate whether:

   (a) The comparative information agrees with the amounts and other disclosures presented in the prior period or, when appropriate, have been restated; and

   (b) The accounting policies reflected in the comparative information are consistent with those applied in the current period or, if there have been changes in accounting policies, whether those changes have been properly accounted for and adequately presented and disclosed.

8. If the auditor becomes aware of a possible material misstatement in the comparative information while performing the current period audit, the auditor shall perform such additional audit procedures as are necessary in the circumstances to obtain sufficient appropriate audit evidence to determine whether a material misstatement exists. If the auditor had audited the prior period's financial report, the auditor shall also follow the

relevant requirements of ASA 560.[2] If the prior period financial report is amended, the auditor shall determine that the comparative information agrees with the amended financial report.

9. As required by ASA 580,[3] the auditor shall request written representations for all periods referred to in the auditor's opinion. The auditor shall also obtain a specific written representation regarding any restatement made to correct a material misstatement in the prior period financial report that affects the comparative information. (Ref: Para. A1)

Audit Reporting

Corresponding Figures

10. When corresponding figures are presented, the auditor's opinion shall not refer to the corresponding figures except in the circumstances described in paragraphs 11, 12, and 14 of this Auditing Standard. (Ref: Para. A2)

11. If the auditor's report on the prior period, as previously issued, included a qualified opinion, a disclaimer of opinion, or an adverse opinion and the matter which gave rise to the modification is unresolved, the auditor shall modify the auditor's opinion on the current period's financial report. In the Basis for Modification paragraph in the auditor's report, the auditor shall either:

    (a) Refer to both the current period's figures and the corresponding figures in the description of the matter giving rise to the modification when the effects or possible effects of the matter on the current period's figures are material; or

    (b) In other cases, explain that the audit opinion has been modified because of the effects or possible effects of the unresolved matter on the comparability of the current period's figures and the corresponding figures. (Ref: Para. A3-A5)

12. If the auditor obtains audit evidence that a material misstatement exists in the prior period financial report on which an unmodified opinion has been previously issued, and the corresponding figures have not been properly restated or appropriate disclosures have not been made, the auditor shall express a qualified opinion or an adverse opinion in the auditor's report on the current period financial report, modified with respect to the corresponding figures included therein. (Ref: Para. A6)

Prior Period Financial Report Audited by a Predecessor Auditor

13. If the financial report of the prior period was audited by a predecessor auditor and the auditor is not prohibited by law or regulation from referring to the predecessor auditor's report on the corresponding figures and decides to do so, the auditor shall state in an Other Matter paragraph in the auditor's report:

    (a) That the financial report of the prior period was audited by the predecessor auditor;

    (b) The type of opinion expressed by the predecessor auditor and, if the opinion was modified, the reasons therefore; and

    (c) The date of that report. (Ref: Para. A7-Aus A7.1)

Prior Period Financial Report Not Audited

14. If the prior period financial report was not audited, the auditor shall state in an Other Matter paragraph in the auditor's report that the corresponding figures are unaudited. Such a statement does not, however, relieve the auditor of the requirement to obtain sufficient appropriate audit evidence that the opening balances do not contain misstatements that materially affect the current period's financial report.[4]

Comparative Financial Reports

15. When comparative financial reports are presented, the auditor's opinion shall refer to each period for which a financial report is presented and on which an audit opinion is expressed. (Ref: Para. Aus A7.2-A9)

---

2 See ASA 560 *Subsequent Events*, paragraphs 14-17.

3 See ASA 580 *Written Representations*, paragraph 14.

4 See ASA 510, paragraph 6.

16. When reporting on a prior period financial report in connection with the current period's audit, if the auditor's opinion on such a prior period financial report differs from the opinion the auditor previously expressed, the auditor shall disclose the substantive reasons for the different opinion in an Other Matter paragraph in accordance with ASA 706.[5] (Ref: Para. Aus A7.2, A10)

Prior Period Financial Report Audited by a Predecessor Auditor

17. If the financial report of the prior period was audited by a predecessor auditor, in addition to expressing an opinion on the current period's financial report, the auditor shall state in an Other Matter paragraph:

    (a) that the financial report of the prior period was audited by a predecessor auditor;

    (b) the type of opinion expressed by the predecessor auditor and, if the opinion was modified, the reasons therefore; and

    (c) the date of that report,

    unless the predecessor auditor's report on the prior period's financial report is reissued with the financial report. (Ref: Para. Aus A7.2)

18. If the auditor concludes that a material misstatement exists that affects the prior period financial report on which the predecessor auditor had previously reported without modification, the auditor shall communicate the misstatement with the appropriate level of management and, and unless all of those charged with governance are involved in managing the entity,[6] those charged with governance and request that the predecessor auditor be informed. If the prior period financial report is amended, and the predecessor auditor agrees to issue a new auditor's report on the amended financial report of the prior period, the auditor shall report only on the current period. (Ref: Para. Aus A7.2, Aus A10.1-A11)

Prior Period Financial Report Not Audited

19. If the prior period financial report was not audited, the auditor shall state in an Other Matter paragraph that the comparative financial report is unaudited. Such a statement does not, however, relieve the auditor of the requirement to obtain sufficient appropriate audit evidence that the opening balances do not contain misstatements that materially affect the current period's financial report.[7] (Ref: Para. Aus A7.2)

Application and Other Explanatory Material

Audit Procedures

Written Representations (Ref: Para. 9)

A1. In the case of a comparative financial report, the written representations are requested for all periods referred to in the auditor's opinion because management needs to reaffirm that the written representations it previously made with respect to the prior period remain appropriate. In the case of corresponding figures, the written representations are requested for the financial report of the current period only because the auditor's opinion is on that financial report, which includes the corresponding figures. However, the auditor requests a specific written representation regarding any restatement made to correct a material misstatement in the prior period financial report that affects the comparative information.

Audit Reporting

Corresponding Figures

No Reference in Auditor's Opinion (Ref: Para. 10)

A2. The auditor's opinion does not refer to the corresponding figures because the auditor's opinion is on the current period financial report as a whole, including the corresponding figures.

5 See ASA 706 *Emphasis of Matter Paragraphs and Other Matter Paragraphs in the Independent Auditor's Report*, paragraphs 8 and Aus 8.1.

6 See ASA 260 *Communication with Those Charged with Governance*, paragraph 13.

7 See ASA 510, paragraph 6.

Modification in Auditor's Report on the Prior Period Unresolved (Ref: Para. 11)

A3. When the auditor's report on the prior period, as previously issued, included a qualified opinion, a disclaimer of opinion, or an adverse opinion and the matter which gave rise to the modified opinion is resolved and properly accounted for or disclosed in the financial report in accordance with the applicable financial reporting framework, the auditor's opinion on the current period need not refer to the previous modification.

A4. When the auditor's opinion on the prior period, as previously expressed, was modified, the unresolved matter that gave rise to the modification may not be relevant to the current period figures. Nevertheless, a qualified opinion, a disclaimer of opinion, or an adverse opinion (as applicable) may be required on the current period's financial report because of the effects or possible effects of the unresolved matter on the comparability of the current and corresponding figures.

A5. Illustrative examples of the auditor's report if the auditor's report on the prior period included a modified opinion and the matter giving rise to the modification is unresolved are contained in Illustrations 1, 1A, 2 and 2A of Appendix 1.

Misstatement in Prior Period Financial Report (Ref: Para. 12)

A6. When a prior period financial report that is misstated has not been amended and an auditor's report has not been reissued, but the corresponding figures have been properly restated or appropriate disclosures have been made in the current period financial report, the auditor's report may include an Emphasis of Matter paragraph describing the circumstances and referring to, where relevant, disclosures that fully describe the matter that can be found in the financial report (see ASA 706).

Prior Period Financial Report Audited by a Predecessor Auditor (Ref: Para. 13)

A7. An illustrative example of the auditor's report if the prior period financial report was audited by a predecessor auditor and the auditor is not prohibited by law or regulation from referring to the predecessor auditor's report on the corresponding figures is contained in Illustration 3 of Appendix 1.

Aus A7.1 When the prior period's financial report was audited by a predecessor auditor, and the audit opinion was unmodified, the auditor would not ordinarily include a reference to that predecessor auditor's opinion in the auditor's report. If the predecessor auditor's report was modified, the auditor considers the appropriateness of including a reference to that predecessor auditor's opinion in the auditor's report.

Comparative Financial Reports

Aus A7.2 In respect of audit engagements conducted under the *Corporations Act 2001*, the auditor's opinion refers to a financial report for the current period, which include corresponding figures, and not to comparative financial report(s). Consequently, paragraphs 15, 16, 17, 18 and 19, and related paragraphs A8, A9, A10, and A11 have no application to audit engagements under the *Corporations Act 2001*.

Reference in Auditor's Opinion (Ref: Para. 15)

A8. Because the auditor's report on comparative financial reports applies to the financial report for each of the periods presented, the auditor may express a qualified opinion or an adverse opinion, disclaim an opinion, or include an Emphasis of Matter paragraph with respect to one or more periods, while expressing a different auditor's opinion on the financial report of the other period.

A9. An illustrative example of the auditor's report if the auditor is required to report on both the current and the prior period financial reports in connection with the current year's audit and the prior period included a modified opinion and the matter giving rise to the modification is unresolved, is contained in Illustration 4 of Appendix 1.

Opinion on the Prior Period Financial Report Different from Previous Opinion (Ref: Para. 16)

A10. When reporting on the prior period financial report in connection with the current period's audit, the opinion expressed on the prior period financial report may be different from the opinion previously expressed if the auditor becomes aware of circumstances or events that materially affect the financial report of a prior period during the course of the audit of the current period. In some jurisdictions, the auditor may have additional reporting responsibilities designed to prevent future reliance on the auditor's previously issued report on the prior period financial report.

***Prior Period Financial Report Audited by a Predecessor Auditor** (Ref: Para. 18)*

Aus A10.1 In respect of audit engagements conducted under the *Corporations Act 2001*, if the prior period auditor's report on the prior period financial report is amended by a predecessor auditor during the current financial year, the auditor is unable to express an opinion in the current period auditor's report in respect of that amendment.

A11. The predecessor auditor may be unable or unwilling to reissue the auditor's report on the prior period financial report. An Other Matter paragraph of the auditor's report may indicate that the predecessor auditor reported on the financial report of the prior period before amendment.

In addition, if the auditor is engaged to audit and obtains sufficient appropriate audit evidence to be satisfied as to the appropriateness of the amendment, the auditor's report may also include the following paragraph:

> As part of our audit of the 20X2 financial report, we also audited the adjustments described in Note X that were applied to amend the 20X1 financial report. In our opinion, such adjustments are appropriate and have been properly applied. We were not engaged to audit, review, or apply any procedures to the 20X1 financial report of the entity other than with respect to the adjustments and, accordingly, we do not express an opinion or any other form of assurance on the 20X1 financial report taken as a whole.

❖❖❖

Conformity with International Standards on Auditing

This Auditing Standard conforms with International Standard on Auditing ISA 710 *Comparative Information—Corresponding Figures and Comparative Financial Statements*, issued by the International Auditing and Assurance Standards Board (IAASB), an independent standard-setting board of the International Federation of Accountants (IFAC).

Paragraphs that have been added to this Auditing Standard (and do not appear in the text of the equivalent ISA) are identified with the prefix "Aus".

Compliance with this Auditing Standard enables compliance with ISA 710.

Appendix 1

(Ref: Para. A5, A7, A9)

Illustrations of Auditors' Reports on a General Purpose Financial Report—Corresponding Figures and Comparative Financial Reports (Fair Presentation Framework)

- Illustration 1: An auditor's report on a financial report, containing a qualified opinion due to a material misstatement of prior period corresponding figures, which impact the current period's financial report.
- [Aus] Illustration 1A: An auditor's report on a financial report, containing a qualified opinion due to a material misstatement of prior period corresponding figures, which impact the current period's financial report. (under the *Corporations Act 2001*).
- Illustration 2: An auditor's report on a current period financial report, containing a qualified opinion due to a material misstatement of the prior period corresponding figures, which impact the comparability of the financial report.

- [Aus] Illustration 2A: An auditor's report on a current period financial report, containing a qualified opinion due to a material misstatement of the prior period corresponding figures, which impact the comparability of the financial report. (under the *Corporations Act 2001*).
- Illustration 3: An auditor's report on a financial report, contains a reference to the predecessor auditor's prior period auditor's report.
- Illustration 4: An auditor's report on the current period and prior period's financial reports, containing a qualified opinion due to a material misstatement of the prior period financial report, which impact the current period's financial report.

See ASA 700* for applicable wording in the auditor's report when the company makes a statement on compliance with *International Financial Reporting Standards* (IFRSs) and/or includes a Remuneration Report in the Directors' Report.

Example Auditor's Report General Purpose Financial Report Corresponding Figures

Qualified Opinion on prior year, which materially affects current year financial report (Fair Presentation Framework)

Illustration 1 - Corresponding Figures (Ref: Para. A5)

Report illustrative of the circumstances described in paragraph 11(a), as follows:

- **The auditor's report on the prior period, as previously issued, included a qualified opinion.**
- **The matter giving rise to the modification is unresolved.**
- **The effects or possible effects of the matter on the current period's figures are material and require a modification to the auditor's opinion regarding the current period figures.**
- **The financial report is not prepared under the *Corporations Act 2001*.**

INDEPENDENT AUDITOR'S REPORT [Appropriate Addressee]

Report on the Financial Report[8]

We have audited the accompanying financial report of ABC Entity, which comprises the statement of financial position as at 30 June 20X1, statement of comprehensive income, statement of changes in equity and statement of cash flows for the year then ended, notes comprising a summary of significant accounting policies and other explanatory information, and management's assertion statement.*

Management's[9] *Responsibility for the Financial Report*

Management is responsible for the preparation and fair presentation of the financial report in accordance with Australian Accounting Standards and [relevant reporting framework],[10] and for such internal control as management determines is necessary to enable the preparation and fair presentation of a financial report that is free from material misstatement, whether due to fraud or error.

* See ASA 700 *Forming an Opinion and Reporting on a Financial Report.*

8 The sub-title "Report on the Financial Report" is unnecessary in circumstances when the second sub-title "Report on Other Legal and Regulatory Requirements", or other appropriate sub-title, is not applicable.

* Or other appropriate term.

9 Or other term that is appropriate in the context of the legal framework in the particular jurisdiction.

10 Where management's responsibility is to prepare a financial report that gives a true and fair view, this may read: "Management is responsible for the preparation of the financial report that gives a true and fair view in accordance with Australian Accounting Standards, and for such……

Auditor's Responsibility

Our responsibility is to express an opinion on the financial report based on our audit. We conducted our audit in accordance with Australian Auditing Standards. Those standards require that we comply with relevant ethical requirements relating to audit engagements and plan and perform the audit to obtain reasonable assurance about whether the financial report is free from material misstatement.

An audit involves performing procedures to obtain audit evidence about the amounts and disclosures in the financial report. The procedures selected depend on the auditor's judgement, including the assessment of the risks of material misstatement of the financial report, whether due to fraud or error. In making those risk assessments, the auditor considers internal control relevant to the entity's preparation and fair presentation[11] of the financial report in order to design audit procedures that are appropriate in the circumstances, but not for the purpose of expressing an opinion on the effectiveness of the entity's internal control.[12] An audit also includes evaluating the appropriateness of accounting policies used and the reasonableness of accounting estimates made by management, as well as evaluating the overall presentation of the financial report.

We believe that the audit evidence we have obtained is sufficient and appropriate to provide a basis for our qualified audit opinion.

Basis for Qualified Opinion

As discussed in Note X to the financial report, no depreciation has been provided in the financial report which constitutes a departure from Australian Accounting Standards. This is the result of a decision taken by management at the start of the preceding financial year and caused us to qualify our audit opinion on the financial report relating to that year. Based on the straight-line method of depreciation and annual rates of 5% for the building and 20% for the equipment, the loss for the year should be increased by xxx in 20X1 and xxx in 20X0, property, plant and equipment should be reduced by accumulated depreciation of xxx in 20X1 and xxx in 20X0, and the accumulated loss should be increased by xxx in 20X1 and xxx in 20X0.

Qualified Opinion

In our opinion, except for the effects of the matter described in the Basis for Qualified Opinion paragraph, the financial report presents fairly, in all material respects, (or *gives a true and fair view of*) the financial position of ABC Entity as at 30 June 20X1, and (*of*) its financial performance and its cash flows for the year then ended in accordance with Australian Accounting Standards and [relevant reporting framework].

Report on Other Legal and Regulatory Requirements

[Form and content of this section of the auditor's report will vary depending on the nature of the auditor's other reporting responsibilities.]

[Auditor's signature]*

[Date of the auditor's report]#

[Auditor's address]

11 In the case of footnote 10, this may read: "In making those risk assessments, the auditor considers internal control relevant to the entity's preparation of the financial report that gives a true and fair view in order to design audit procedures that are appropriate in the circumstances, but not for the purpose of expressing an opinion on the effectiveness of the entity's internal control."

12 In circumstances when the auditor also has responsibility to express an opinion on the effectiveness of internal control in conjunction with the audit of the financial report, this sentence would be worded as follows: "In making those risk assessments, the auditor considers internal control relevant to the entity's preparation and fair presentation of the financial report in order to design audit procedures that are appropriate in the circumstances." In the case of footnote 10, this may read: "In making those risk assessments, the auditor considers internal control relevant to the entity's preparation of the financial report that gives a true and fair view in order to design audit procedures that are appropriate in the circumstances."

* The auditor's report needs to be signed in one or more of the following ways: name of the audit firm, the name of the audit company or the personal name of the auditor as appropriate.

\# The date of the auditor's report is the date the auditor signs the report.

Example Auditor's Report
General Purpose Financial Report
Corresponding Figures
Qualified opinion on prior year, which materially affects current year financial report—*Corporations Act 2001*
(Fair Presentation Framework)

[Aus] Illustration 1A - Corresponding Figures (Ref: Para. A5)

Report illustrative of the circumstances described in paragraph 11(a), as follows:

- **The auditor's report on the prior period, as previously issued, included a qualified opinion.**
- **The matter giving rise to the modification is unresolved.**
- **The effects or possible effects of the matter on the current period's figures are material and require a modification to the auditor's opinion regarding the current period figures.**
- **The financial report is prepared under the *Corporations Act 2001*.**

INDEPENDENT AUDITOR'S REPORT

[Appropriate Addressee]

Report on the Financial Report*

We have audited the accompanying financial report of ABC Company Ltd., which comprises the statement of financial position as at 30 June 20X1, the statement of comprehensive income, statement of changes in equity and statement of cash flows for the year then ended, notes comprising a summary of significant accounting policies and other explanatory information, and directors' declaration.

Directors' Responsibility for the Financial Report

The directors of the company are responsible for the preparation of the financial report that gives a true and fair view in accordance with Australian Accounting Standards and *Corporations Act 2001*, and for such internal control as the directors determine is necessary to enable the preparation of a financial report that gives a true and fair view and is free from material misstatement, whether due to fraud or error.

Auditor's Responsibility

Our responsibility is to express an opinion on the financial report based on our audit. We conducted our audit in accordance with Australian Auditing Standards. Those standards require that we comply with relevant ethical requirements relating to audit engagements and plan and perform the audit to obtain reasonable assurance about whether the financial report is free from material misstatement.

An audit involves performing procedures to obtain audit evidence about the amounts and disclosures in the financial report. The procedures selected depend on the auditor's judgement, including the assessment of the risks of material misstatement of the financial report, whether due to fraud or error. In making those risk assessments, the auditor considers internal control relevant to the company's preparation of the financial report that gives a true and fair view in order to design audit procedures that are appropriate in the circumstances, but not for the purpose of expressing an opinion on the effectiveness of the company's internal control. An audit also includes evaluating the appropriateness of accounting policies used and the reasonableness of accounting estimates made by the directors, as well as evaluating the overall presentation of the financial report.

We believe that the audit evidence we have obtained is sufficient and appropriate to provide a basis for our qualified audit opinion.

---

* The sub-title "Report on the Financial Report" is unnecessary in circumstances when the second sub-title "Report on Other Legal and Regulatory Requirements", or other appropriate sub-title, is not applicable.

Independence

In conducting our audit, we have complied with the independence requirements of the *Corporations Act 2001*. We confirm that the independence declaration required by the *Corporations Act 2001*, which has been given to the directors of ABC Company Ltd., would be in the same terms if given to the directors as at the time of this auditor's report.*

Basis for Qualified Opinion

As discussed in Note X to the financial report, no depreciation has been provided in the financial report which constitutes a departure from Australian Accounting Standards. This is the result of a decision taken by the directors at the start of the preceding financial year and caused us to qualify our audit opinion on the financial report relating to that year. Based on the straight-line method of depreciation and annual rates of 5% for the building and 20% for the equipment, the loss for the year should be increased by xxx in 20X1 and xxx in 20X0, property, plant and equipment should be reduced by accumulated depreciation of xxx in 20X1 and xxx in 20X0, and the accumulated loss should be increased by xxx in 20X1 and xxx in 20X0.

Qualified Opinion

In our opinion, except for the effects of the matter described in the Basis for Qualified Opinion paragraph, the financial report of ABC Company Ltd. is in accordance with the *Corporations Act 2001*, including:

(a) giving a true and fair view of the company's financial position as at 30 June 20X1, and of its performance for the year ended on that date; and

(b) complying with Australian Accounting Standards and the *Corporations Regulations 2001*.

Report on Other Legal and Regulatory Requirements

[Form and content of this section of the auditor's report will vary depending on the nature of the auditor's other reporting responsibilities.]

[Auditor's signature]**

[Date of the auditor's report]#

[Auditor's address]

Example Auditor's Report
General Purpose Financial Report
Corresponding Figures

Qualified opinion on prior year, which affects the comparability of the current year financial report (Fair Presentation Framework)

Illustration 2 – Corresponding Figures (Ref: Para. A5)

Report illustrative of the circumstances described in paragraph 11(b), as follows:

- **The auditor's report on the prior period, as previously issued, included a qualified opinion.**
- **The matter giving rise to the modification is unresolved.**
- **The effects or possible effects of the matter on the current period's figures are immaterial but require a modification to the auditor's opinion because of the effects or possible effects of the unresolved matter on the comparability of the current period's figures and the corresponding figures.**
- **The financial report is *not* prepared under the *Corporations Act 2001*.**

* Or, alternatively, include statements (a) to the effect that circumstances have changed since the declaration was given to the relevant directors; and (b) setting out how the declaration would differ if it had been given to the relevant directors at the time the auditor's report was made.

** The auditor's report needs to be signed in one or more of the following ways: name of the audit firm, the name of the audit company or the personal name of the auditor as appropriate.

The date of the auditor's report is the date the auditor signs the report.

INDEPENDENT AUDITOR'S REPORT

[Appropriate Addressee]

Report on the Financial Report[13]

We have audited the accompanying financial report of ABC Entity, which comprises the statement of financial position as at 30 June 20X1, statement of comprehensive income, statement of changes in equity and statement of cash flows for the year then ended, notes comprising a summary of significant accounting policies and other explanatory information, and management's assertion statement.*

Management's[14] *Responsibility for the Financial Report*

Management is responsible for the preparation and fair presentation of the financial report in accordance with Australian Accounting Standards, and [relevant reporting framework],[15] and for such internal control as management determines is necessary to enable the preparation and fair presentation of a financial report that is free from material misstatement, whether due to fraud or error.

Auditor's Responsibility

Our responsibility is to express an opinion on the financial report based on our audit. We conducted our audit in accordance with Australian Auditing Standards. Those standards require that we comply with relevant ethical requirements relating to audit engagements and plan and perform the audit to obtain reasonable assurance about whether the financial report is free from material misstatement.

An audit involves performing procedures to obtain audit evidence about the amounts and disclosures in the financial report. The procedures selected depend on the auditor's judgement, including the assessment of the risks of material misstatement of the financial report, whether due to fraud or error. In making those risk assessments, the auditor considers internal control relevant to the entity's preparation and fair presentation[16] of the financial report in order to design audit procedures that are appropriate in the circumstances, but not for the purpose of expressing an opinion on the effectiveness of the entity's internal control.[17] An audit also includes evaluating the appropriateness of accounting policies used and the reasonableness of accounting estimates made by management, as well as evaluating the overall presentation of the financial report.

We believe that the audit evidence we have obtained is sufficient and appropriate to provide a basis for our qualified audit opinion.

Basis for Qualified Opinion

Because we were appointed auditors of ABC Entity during 20X0, we were not able to observe the counting of the physical inventories at the beginning of that period or satisfy ourselves concerning those inventory quantities by alternative means. Since opening inventories affect the determination of the results of operations, we were unable to determine whether adjustments to

---

13 The sub-title "Report on the Financial Report" is unnecessary in circumstances when the second sub-title "Report on Other Legal and Regulatory Requirements", or other appropriate sub-title, is not applicable.

* Or other appropriate term.

14 Or other term that is appropriate in the context of the legal framework in the particular jurisdiction.

15 Where management's responsibility is to prepare a financial report that gives a true and fair view, this may read: "Management is responsible for the preparation of the financial report that gives a true and fair view in accordance with Australian Accounting Standards, and for such……"

16 In the case of footnote 15, this may read: "In making those risk assessments, the auditor considers internal control relevant to the entity's preparation of the financial report that gives a true and fair view in order to design audit procedures that are appropriate in the circumstances, but not for the purpose of expressing an opinion on the effectiveness of the entity's internal control."

17 In circumstances when the auditor also has responsibility to express an opinion on the effectiveness of internal control in conjunction with the audit of the financial report, this sentence would be worded as follows: "In making those risk assessments, the auditor considers internal control relevant to the entity's preparation and fair presentation of the financial report in order to design audit procedures that are appropriate in the circumstances." In the case of footnote 15, this may read: "In making those risk assessments, the auditor considers internal control relevant to the entity's preparation of the financial report that gives a true and fair view in order to design audit procedures that are appropriate in the circumstances."

the results of operations and opening retained earnings might be necessary for 20X0. Our audit opinion on the financial report for the period ended 30 June 20X0 was modified accordingly. Our opinion on the current period's financial report is also modified because of the possible effect of this matter on the comparability of the current period's figures and the corresponding figures.

Qualified Opinion

In our opinion, except for the possible effects on the corresponding figures of the matter described in the Basis for Qualified Opinion paragraph, the financial report presents fairly, in all material respects, (or gives a true and fair view of) the financial position of ABC Entity as at 30 June 20X1, and (of) its financial performance and its cash flows for the year then ended in accordance with Australian Accounting Standards and [relevant reporting framework].

Report on Other Legal and Regulatory Requirements

[Form and content of this section of the auditor's report will vary depending on the nature of the auditor's other reporting responsibilities.]

[Auditor's signature]*

[Date of the auditor's report]#

[Auditor's address]

Example Auditor's Report General Purpose Financial Report Corresponding Figures

Qualified opinion on prior year, which affects the comparability of the current year financial report—*Corporations Act 2001* (Fair Presentation Framework)

[Aus] Illustration 2A – Corresponding Figures (Ref: Para. A5)

Report illustrative of the circumstances described in paragraph 11(b), as follows:

- **The auditor's report on the prior period, as previously issued, included a qualified opinion.**
- **The matter giving rise to the modification is unresolved.**
- **The effects or possible effects of the matter on the current period's figures are immaterial but require a modification to the auditor's opinion because of the effects or possible effects of the unresolved matter on the comparability of the current period's figures and the corresponding figures.**
- **The financial report is prepared under the *Corporations Act 2001*.**

INDEPENDENT AUDITOR'S REPORT

[Appropriate Addressee]

Report on the Financial Report**

We have audited the accompanying financial report of ABC Company Ltd., which comprises the statement of financial position as at 30 June 20X1, statement of comprehensive income, statement of changes in equity, statement of cash flows for the year then ended, notes comprising a summary of significant accounting policies and other explanatory information, and the directors' declaration.

* The auditor's report needs to be signed in one or more of the following ways: name of the audit firm, the name of the audit company or the personal name of the auditor as appropriate.

\# The date of the auditor's report is the date the auditor signs the report.

** The sub-title "Report on the Financial Report" is unnecessary in circumstances when the second sub-title "Report on Other Legal and Regulatory Requirements", or other appropriate sub-title, is not applicable.

Directors' Responsibility for the Financial Report

The directors of the company are responsible for the preparation of the financial report that gives a true and fair view in accordance with Australian Accounting Standards and the *Corporations Act 2001*, and for such internal control as the directors determine is necessary to enable the preparation of a financial report that gives a true and fair view and is free from material misstatement, whether due to fraud or error.

Auditor's Responsibility

Our responsibility is to express an opinion on the financial report based on our audit. We conducted our audit in accordance with Australian Auditing Standards. Those standards require that we comply with relevant ethical requirements relating to audit engagements and plan and perform the audit to obtain reasonable assurance about whether the financial report is free from material misstatement.

An audit involves performing procedures to obtain audit evidence about the amounts and disclosures in the financial report. The procedures selected depend on the auditor's judgement, including the assessment of the risks of material misstatement of the financial report, whether due to fraud or error. In making those risk assessments, the auditor considers internal control relevant to the company's preparation of the financial report that gives a true and fair view in order to design audit procedures that are appropriate in the circumstances, but not for the purpose of expressing an opinion on the effectiveness of the company's internal control. An audit also includes evaluating the appropriateness of accounting policies used and the reasonableness of accounting estimates made by the directors, as well as evaluating the overall presentation of the financial report.

We believe that the audit evidence we have obtained is sufficient and appropriate to provide a basis for our qualified audit opinion.

Independence

In conducting our audit, we have complied with the independence requirements of the *Corporations Act 2001*. We confirm that the independence declaration required by the *Corporations Act 2001*, which has been given to the directors of ABC Company Ltd., would be in the same terms if given to the directors as at the time of this auditor's report.*

Basis for Qualified Opinion

Because we were appointed auditors of ABC Company Ltd. during 20X0, we were not able to observe the counting of the physical inventories at the beginning of that period or satisfy ourselves concerning those inventory quantities by alternative means. Since opening inventories affect the determination of the results of operations, we were unable to determine whether adjustments to the results of operations and opening retained earnings might be necessary for 20X0. Our audit opinion on the financial report for the period ended 30 June 20X0 was modified accordingly. Our opinion on the current period's financial report is also modified because of the possible effect of this matter on the comparability of the current period's figures and the corresponding figures.

Qualified Opinion

In our opinion, except for the effects of the matter described in the Basis for Qualified Opinion paragraph, the financial report of ABC Company Ltd. is in accordance with the *Corporations Act 2001*, including:

(a) giving a true and fair view of the company's financial position as at 30 June 20X1, and of its performance for the year ended on that date; and

(b) complying with Australian Accounting Standards and the *Corporations Regulations 2001*.

Report on Other Legal and Regulatory Requirements

[Form and content of this section of the auditor's report will vary depending on the nature of the auditor's other reporting responsibilities.]

---

* Or, alternatively, include statements (a) to the effect that circumstances have changed since the declaration was given to the relevant directors; and (b) setting out how the declaration would differ if it had been given to the relevant directors at the time the auditor's report was made.

[Auditor's signature]**

[Date of the auditor's report]#

[Auditor's address]

Example Auditor's Report
General Purpose Financial Report Corresponding Figures

Prior year financial report audited by a predecessor auditor, and is referred to in the auditor's report on the current year financial report (Fair Presentation Framework)

Illustration 3 - Corresponding Figures (Ref: Para. A7)

Report illustrative of the circumstances described in paragraph 13, as follows:

- **The prior period's financial report was audited by a predecessor auditor.**
- **The auditor is not prohibited by law or regulation from referring to the predecessor auditor's report on the corresponding figures and decides to do so.**
- **The financial report is not prepared under the *Corporations Act 2001*.**

INDEPENDENT AUDITOR'S REPORT

[Appropriate Addressee]

Report on the Financial Report[18]

We have audited the accompanying financial report of ABC Entity, which comprises the statement of financial position as at 30 June 20X1, statement of comprehensive income, statement of changes in equity, statement of cash flows for the year then ended, notes comprising a summary of significant accounting policies and other explanatory information, and management's assertion statement.*

Management's[19] *Responsibility for the Financial Report*

Management is responsible for the preparation and fair presentation of the financial report in accordance with Australian Accounting Standards and [relevant reporting framework],[20] and for such internal control as management determines is necessary to enable the preparation and fair presentation of a financial report that is free from material misstatement, whether due to fraud or error.

Auditor's Responsibility

Our responsibility is to express an opinion on the financial report based on our audit. We conducted our audit in accordance with Australian Auditing Standards. Those standards require that we comply with relevant ethical requirements relating to audit engagements and plan and perform the audit to obtain reasonable assurance about whether the financial report is free from material misstatement.

An audit involves performing procedures to obtain audit evidence about the amounts and disclosures in the financial report. The procedures selected depend on the auditor's judgement,

** The auditor's report needs to be signed in one or more of the following ways: name of the audit firm, the name of the audit company or the personal name of the auditor as appropriate.

The date of the auditor's report is the date the auditor signs the report.

18 The sub-title "Report on the Financial Report" is unnecessary in circumstances when the second sub-title "Report on Other Legal and Regulatory Requirements", or other appropriate sub-title, is not applicable.

* Or other appropriate term.

19 Or other term that is appropriate in the context of the legal framework in the particular jurisdiction.

20 Where management's responsibility is to prepare a financial report that gives a true and fair view, this may read: "Management is responsible for the preparation of the financial report that gives a true and fair view in accordance with Australian Accounting Standards, and for such….."

including the assessment of the risks of material misstatement of the financial report, whether due to fraud or error. In making those risk assessments, the auditor considers internal control relevant to the entity's preparation and fair presentation[21] of the financial report in order to design audit procedures that are appropriate in the circumstances, but not for the purpose of expressing an opinion on the effectiveness of the entity's internal control.[22] An audit also includes evaluating the appropriateness of accounting policies used and the reasonableness of accounting estimates made by management, as well as evaluating the overall presentation of the financial report.

We believe that the audit evidence we have obtained is sufficient and appropriate to provide a basis for our audit opinion.

Opinion

In our opinion, the financial report presents fairly, in all material respects, (or *gives a true and fair view of*) the financial position of ABC Entity as at 30 June 20X1, and (*of*) its financial performance and its cash flows for the year then ended in accordance with Australian Accounting Standards and [relevant reporting framework].

Other Matters

The financial report of ABC Entity for the year ended 30 June 20X0 was audited by another auditor who expressed an unmodified opinion on that financial report on 31 August 20X0.

Report on Other Legal and Regulatory Requirements

[Form and content of this section of the auditor's report will vary depending on the nature of the auditor's other reporting responsibilities.]

[Auditor's signature]*

[Date of the auditor's report]#

[Auditor's address]

21 In the case of footnote 20, this may read: "In making those risk assessments, the auditor considers internal control relevant to the entity's preparation of the financial report that gives a true and fair view in order to design audit procedures that are appropriate in the circumstances, but not for the purpose of expressing an opinion on the effectiveness of the entity's internal control."

22 In circumstances when the auditor also has responsibility to express an opinion on the effectiveness of internal control in conjunction with the audit of the financial report, this sentence would be worded as follows: "In making those risk assessments, the auditor considers internal control relevant to the entity's preparation and fair presentation of the financial report in order to design audit procedures that are appropriate in the circumstances." In the case of footnote 20, this may read: "In making those risk assessments, the auditor considers internal control relevant to the entity's preparation of the financial report that gives a true and fair view in order to design audit procedures that are appropriate in the circumstances."

* The auditor's report needs to be signed in one or more of the following ways: name of the audit firm, the name of the audit company or the personal name of the auditor as appropriate.

\# The date of the auditor's report is the date the auditor signs the report.

Example Auditor's Report
General Purpose Financial Report
Comparative Financial Reports

Qualified opinion on prior year financial report, which materially affects current year financial report (Fair Presentation Framework)

Illustration 4 - Comparative Financial Reports (Ref: Para. A9)

Report illustrative of the circumstances described in paragraph 15, as follows:

- **Auditor is required to report on both the current period financial report and the prior period financial report in connection with the current year's audit.**
- **The auditor's report on the prior period, as previously issued, included a qualified opinion.**
- **The matter giving rise to the modification is unresolved.**
- **The effects or possible effects of the matter on the current period's figures are material to both the current period financial report and prior period financial reports, and require a modification to the auditor's opinion.**
- **The financial report is not prepared under the *Corporations Act 2001*.**

INDEPENDENT AUDITOR'S REPORT

[Appropriate Addressee]

Report on the Financial Report[23]

We have audited the accompanying financial report of ABC Entity, which comprises the statements of financial position as at 30 June 20X1 and 20X0, statements of comprehensive income, statements of changes in equity, statement of cash flows for the years then ended, notes comprising a summary of significant accounting policies and other explanatory information, and management's assertion statement.*

Management's[24] Responsibility for the Financial Report

Management is responsible for the preparation and fair presentation of the financial report in accordance with Australian Accounting Standards and [relevant reporting framework],[25] and for such internal control as management determines is necessary to enable the preparation and fair presentation of a financial report that is free from material misstatement, whether due to fraud or error.

Auditor's Responsibility

Our responsibility is to express an opinion on the financial report based on our audits. We conducted our audits in accordance with Australian Auditing Standards. Those standards require that we comply with relevant ethical requirements relating to audit engagements and plan and perform the audit to obtain reasonable assurance about whether the financial report is free from material misstatement.

An audit involves performing procedures to obtain audit evidence about the amounts and disclosures in the financial report. The procedures selected depend on the auditor's judgement, including the assessment of the risks of material misstatement of the financial report, whether due to fraud or error. In making those risk assessments, the auditor considers internal control

23 The sub-title "Report on the Financial Report" is unnecessary in circumstances when the second sub-title "Report on Other Legal and Regulatory Requirements", or other appropriate sub-title, is not applicable.

* Or other appropriate term.

24 Or other term that is appropriate in the context of the legal framework in the particular jurisdiction.

25 Where management's responsibility is to prepare a financial report that gives a true and fair view, this may read: "Management is responsible for the preparation of the financial report that gives a true and fair view in accordance with Australian Accounting Standards, and for such….."

relevant to the entity's preparation and fair presentation[26] of the financial report in order to design audit procedures that are appropriate in the circumstances, but not for the purpose of expressing an opinion on the effectiveness of the entity's internal control.[27] An audit also includes evaluating the appropriateness of accounting policies used and the reasonableness of accounting estimates made by management, as well as evaluating the overall presentation of the financial report.

We believe that the audit evidence we have obtained in our audits is sufficient and appropriate to provide a basis for our qualified audit opinion.

Basis for Qualified Opinion

As discussed in Note X to the financial report, no depreciation has been provided in the financial report which constitutes a departure from Australian Accounting Standards. Based on the straight-line method of depreciation and annual rates of 5% for the building and 20% for the equipment, the loss for the year should be increased by xxx in 20X1 and xxx in 20X0, property, plant and equipment should be reduced by accumulated depreciation of xxx in 20X1 and xxx in 20X0, and the accumulated loss should be increased by xxx in 20X1 and xxx in 20X0.

Qualified Opinion

In our opinion, except for the effects of the matter described in the Basis for Qualified Opinion paragraph, the financial report presents fairly, in all material respects, (or gives a true and fair view of) the financial position of ABC Entity as at 30 June 20X1 and 20X0 and (of) its financial performance and its cash flows for the years then ended in accordance with Australian Accounting Standards and [relevant reporting framework].

Report on Other Legal and Regulatory Requirements

[Form and content of this section of the auditor's report will vary depending on the nature of the auditor's other reporting responsibilities.]

[Auditor's signature]*

[Date of the auditor's report]#

[Auditor's address]

ASA

26 In the case of footnote 25, this may read: "In making those risk assessments, the auditor considers internal control relevant to the entity's preparation of the financial report that gives a true and fair view in order to design audit procedures that are appropriate in the circumstances, but not for the purpose of expressing an opinion on the effectiveness of the entity's internal control."

27 In circumstances when the auditor also has responsibility to express an opinion on the effectiveness of internal control in conjunction with the audit of the financial report, this sentence would be worded as follows: "In making those risk assessments, the auditor considers internal control relevant to the entity's preparation and fair presentation of the financial report in order to design audit procedures that are appropriate in the circumstances." In the case of footnote 25, this may read: "In making those risk assessments, the auditor considers internal control relevant to the entity's preparation of the financial report that gives a true and fair view in order to design audit procedures that are appropriate in the circumstances."

* The auditor's report needs to be signed in one or more of the following ways: name of the audit firm, the name of the audit company or the personal name of the auditor as appropriate.

\# The date of the auditor's report is the date the auditor signs the report.

ASA 720

The Auditor's Responsibilities Relating to Other Information in Documents Containing an Audited Financial Report

(Reissued October 2009)

Issued by the Auditing and Assurance Standards Board.

Note from the Institute of Chartered Accountants Australia

This note, prepared by the technical editor, is not part of ASA 720.

Historical development

June 1984: Statement of Auditing Practice AUP 19 'Other Information in Documents Containing Audited Financial Statements' issued, effective from date of issue, following the issue of ED 4 (IAPC ED 14) in October 1982.

May 1994: ED 55 'Codification and Revision of Auditing Pronouncements: AUS 706 Other Information in Documents Containing Audited Financial Reports (AUP 19)' issued by the AuSB.

June 1994: The International Auditing Practices Committee (IAPC) of the International Federation of Accountants (IFAC) approved the issuance of a codified set of International Standards of Auditing (ISAs). The relevant international pronouncement was ISA 720 'Other Information in Documents Containing Audited Financial Statements'.

October 1995: Australian Auditing Standards and Auditing Guidance Statements released. The status of these was explained in APS 1.1 'Conformity With Auditing Standards'. These Standards became operative for the first reporting period commencing on or after 1 July 1996 and later reporting periods, although earlier application was encouraged. AUP 19 'Other Information in Documents Containing Audited Financial Statements' replaced by AUS 212 'Other Information in Documents Containing Audited Financial Reports'.

April 2006: ASA 720 was issued as a legally enforceable Standard to replace AUS 212. It is based on ISA 720 of the same name.

October 2009: ASA 720 reissued as part of the AUASB's Clarity Project. It is based on the redrafted ISA 720 'The Auditor's Responsibilities Relating to Other Information in Documents Containing Audited Financial Statements'.

Contents

ASA

Preface

Reasons for Issuing Auditing Standard ASA 720 *The Auditor's Responsibilities Relating to Other Information in Documents Containing an Audited Financial Report*

The Auditing and Assurance Standards Board (AUASB) issues Auditing Standard ASA 720 *The Auditor's Responsibilities Relating to Other Information in Documents Containing an Audited Financial Report* pursuant to the requirements of the legislative provisions and the Strategic Direction explained below.

The AUASB is an independent statutory board of the Australian Government established under section 227A of the *Australian Securities and Investments Commission Act 2001*, as amended (ASIC Act). Under section 336 of the *Corporations Act 2001*, the AUASB may make Australian Auditing Standards for the purposes of the corporations legislation. These Auditing Standards are legislative instruments under the *Legislative Instruments Act 2003*.

Under the Strategic Direction given to the AUASB by the Financial Reporting Council (FRC), the AUASB is required to have regard to any programme initiated by the International Auditing and Assurance Standards Board (IAASB) for the revision and enhancement of the International Standards on Auditing (ISAs) and to make appropriate consequential amendments to the Australian Auditing Standards. Accordingly, the AUASB has decided to revise and redraft the Australian Auditing Standards using the equivalent redrafted ISAs.

Main Features

This Auditing Standard establishes requirements and provides application and other explanatory material regarding the auditor's responsibilities relating to other information in documents containing an audited financial report and the auditor's report thereon.

This Auditing Standard:

(a) requires the auditor to read the other information to identify material inconsistencies, if any, with the audited financial report;

(b) requires the auditor to make appropriate arrangements with management to obtain the other information prior to the date of the auditor's report;

(c) requires the auditor to determine whether the audited financial report or the other information needs to be revised when material inconsistencies are identified; and

(d) describes the auditor's responsibilities when material inconsistencies are identified.

Authority Statement

The Auditing and Assurance Standards Board (AUASB) makes this Auditing Standard ASA 720 *The Auditor's Responsibilities Relating to Other Information in Documents Containing an Audited Financial Report* pursuant to section 227B of the *Australian Securities and Investments Commission Act 2001* and section 336 of the *Corporations Act 2001*.

This Auditing Standard is to be read in conjunction with ASA 101 *Preamble to Australian Auditing Standards*, which sets out the intentions of the AUASB on how the Australian Auditing Standards, operative for financial reporting periods commencing on or after 1 January 2010, are to be understood, interpreted and applied. This Auditing Standard is to be read also in conjunction with ASA 200 *Overall Objectives of the Independent Auditor and the Conduct of an Audit in Accordance with Australian Auditing Standards*.

Dated: 27 October 2009

M H Kelsall
Chairman - AUASB

Auditing Standard ASA 720

The Auditor's Responsibilities Relating to Other Information in Documents Containing an Audited Financial Report

Application

Aus 0.1 This Auditing Standard applies to:

(a) an audit of a financial report for a financial year, or an audit of a financial report for a half-year, in accordance with the *Corporations Act 2001*; and

(b) an audit of a financial report, or a complete set of financial statements, for any other purpose.

Aus 0.2 This Auditing Standard also applies, as appropriate, to an audit of other historical financial information.

Operative Date

Aus 0.3 This Auditing Standard is operative for financial reporting periods commencing on or after 1 January 2010.

Introduction

Scope of this Auditing Standard

1. This Auditing Standard deals with the auditor's responsibilities relating to other information in documents containing an audited financial report and the auditor's report thereon. In the absence of any separate requirement in the particular circumstances of the engagement, the auditor's opinion does not cover other information and the auditor has no specific responsibility for determining whether or not other information is properly stated. However, the auditor reads the other information because the credibility of the audited financial report may be undermined by material inconsistencies between the audited financial report and other information. (Ref: Para. A1)

2. In this Auditing Standard "documents containing an audited financial report" refers to annual reports (or similar documents), that are issued to owners (or similar stakeholders), containing

an audited financial report and the auditor's report thereon. This Auditing Standard may also be applied, as necessary in the circumstances, to other documents containing an audited financial report, such as those used in securities offerings.[1] (Ref: Para. A2)

Effective Date

3. [Deleted by the AUASB. Refer Aus 0.3]

Objective

4. The objective of the auditor is to respond appropriately when documents containing an audited financial report and the auditor's report thereon include other information that could undermine the credibility of that financial report and the auditor's report.

Definitions

5. For purposes of the Australian Auditing Standards, the following terms have the meanings attributed below:

   (a) Other information means financial and non-financial information (other than the financial report and the auditor's report thereon) which is included, either by law, regulation or custom, in a document containing an audited financial report and the auditor's report thereon. (Ref: Para. A3-A4)

   (b) Inconsistency means other information that contradicts information contained in the audited financial report. A material inconsistency may raise doubt about the audit conclusions drawn from audit evidence previously obtained and, possibly, about the basis for the auditor's opinion on the financial report.

   (c) Misstatement of fact means other information that is unrelated to matters appearing in the audited financial report that is incorrectly stated or presented. A material misstatement of fact may undermine the credibility of the document containing the audited financial report.

Requirements

Reading Other Information

6. The auditor shall read the other information to identify material inconsistencies, if any, with the audited financial report.

7. The auditor shall make appropriate arrangements with management or those charged with governance to obtain the other information prior to the date of the auditor's report. If it is not possible to obtain all the other information prior to the date of the auditor's report, the auditor shall read such other information as soon as practicable. (Ref: Para. A5)

Material Inconsistencies

8. If, on reading the other information, the auditor identifies a material inconsistency, the auditor shall determine whether the audited financial report or the other information needs to be revised.

Material Inconsistencies Identified in Other Information Obtained Prior to the Date of the Auditor's Report

9. If revision of the audited financial report is necessary and management refuses to make the revision, the auditor shall modify the opinion in the auditor's report in accordance with ASA 705.[2]

10. If revision of the other information is necessary and management refuses to make the revision, the auditor shall communicate this matter to those charged with governance, unless all of those charged with governance are involved in managing the entity;[3] and

1 See ASA 200 *Overall Objectives of the Independent Auditor and the Conduct of an Audit in Accordance with Australian Auditing Standards*, paragraph 2.

2 See ASA 705 *Modifications to the Opinion in the Independent Auditor's Report.*

3 See ASA 260 *Communication with Those Charged with Governance*, paragraph 13.

(a) Include in the auditor's report an Other Matter(s) paragraph describing the material inconsistency in accordance with ASA 706;[4] or

(b) Withhold the auditor's report; or

(c) Withdraw from the engagements, where withdrawal is possible under applicable law or regulation. (Ref: Para. A6-A7)

Aus 10.1 Withholding the auditor's report is not permitted under the *Corporations Act 2001.*

Material Inconsistencies Identified in Other Information Obtained Subsequent to the Date of the Auditor's Report

11. If revision of the audited financial report is necessary, the auditor shall follow the relevant requirements in ASA 560.[5]

12. If revision of the other information is necessary and management agrees to make the revision, the auditor shall carry out the procedures necessary under the circumstances. (Ref: Para. A8)

13. If revision of the other information is necessary, but management refuses to make the revision, the auditor shall notify those charged with governance, unless all of those charged with governance are involved in managing the entity, of the auditor's concern regarding the other information and take any further appropriate action. (Ref: Para. A9)

Material Misstatements of Fact

14. If, on reading the other information for the purpose of identifying material inconsistencies, the auditor becomes aware of an apparent material misstatement of fact, the auditor shall discuss the matter with management. (Ref: Para. A10)

15. If, following such discussions, the auditor still considers that there is an apparent material misstatement of fact, the auditor shall request management to consult with a qualified third party, such as the entity's legal counsel, and the auditor shall consider the advice received.

16. If the auditor concludes that there is a material misstatement of fact in the other information which management refuses to correct, the auditor shall notify those charged with governance, unless all of those charged with governance are involved in managing the entity, of the auditor's concern regarding the other information and take any further appropriate action. (Ref: Para. A11)

❖❖❖

Application and Other Explanatory Material

Scope of this Auditing Standard

Additional Responsibilities, through Statutory or Other Regulatory Requirements, in Relation to Other Information (Ref: Para. 1)

A1. The auditor may have additional responsibilities, through statutory or other regulatory requirements,* in relation to other information that are beyond the scope of this Auditing Standard. For example, some jurisdictions may require the auditor to apply specific procedures to certain of the other information such as required supplementary data or to express an opinion on the reliability of performance indicators described in the other information. Where there are such obligations, the auditor's additional responsibilities are determined by the nature of the engagement and by law, regulation and professional standards. If such other information is omitted or contains deficiencies, the auditor may be required by law or regulation to refer to the matter in the auditor's report.

---

4 See ASA 706 *Emphasis of Matter Paragraphs and Other Matter Paragraphs in the Independent Auditor's Report*, paragraph 8.

5 See ASA 560 *Subsequent Events*, paragraphs 10-17.

* See, for example, ASIC Regulatory Guide 34 *Auditors' obligations: reporting to ASIC* (December 2007), which provides guidance on the auditor's responsibilities under sections 311, 601HG and 990K of the *Corporations Act 2001.*

Documents Containing an Audited Financial Report (Ref: Para. 2)

Considerations Specific to Smaller Entities

A2. Unless required by law or regulation, smaller entities are less likely to issue documents containing an audited financial report. However, an example of such a document would be where a legal requirement exists for an accompanying report by those charged with governance. Examples of other information that may be included in a document containing the audited financial report of a smaller entity are a detailed income statement and a management report.

Definition of Other Information (Ref: Para. 5(a))

A3. Other information may comprise, for example:

- A report by management or those charged with governance on operations.
- Financial summaries or highlights.
- Employment data.
- Planned capital expenditures.
- Financial ratios.
- Names of officers and directors.
- Selected quarterly data.

A4. For purposes of the Australian Auditing Standards, other information does not encompass, for example:

- A press release or a transmittal memorandum, such as a covering letter, accompanying the document containing the audited financial report and the auditor's report thereon.
- Information contained in analyst briefings.
- Information contained on the entity's website.

Reading Other Information (Ref: Para. 7)

A5. Obtaining the other information prior to the date of the auditor's report enables the auditor to resolve possible material inconsistencies and apparent material misstatements of fact with management on a timely basis. An agreement with management as to when the other information will be available may be helpful.

Material Inconsistencies

Material Inconsistencies Identified in Other Information Obtained Prior to the Date of the Auditor's Report (Ref: Para. 10-Aus 10.1)

A6. When management refuses to revise the other information, the auditor may base any decision on what further action to take on advice from the auditor's legal counsel.

Aus A6.1 For example, the auditor may be required to obtain consent from the Australian Securities and Investments Commission (ASIC) prior to resigning from certain audits.*

Considerations Specific to Public Sector Entities

A7. In the public sector, withdrawal from the engagement or withholding the auditor's report may not be options. In such cases, the auditor may issue a report to the appropriate statutory body giving details of the inconsistency.

* See, for example, ASIC Regulatory Guide 26 *Resignation of Auditors* (June 1992).

Material Inconsistencies Identified in Other Information Obtained Subsequent to the Date of the Auditor's Report (Ref: Para. 12-13)

A8. When management agrees to revise the other information, the auditor's procedures may include reviewing the steps taken by management to ensure that individuals in receipt of the previously issued financial report, the auditor's report thereon, and the other information are informed of the revision.

A9. When management refuses to make the revision of such other information that the auditor concludes is necessary, appropriate further actions by the auditor may include obtaining advice from the auditor's legal counsel.

Material Misstatements of Fact (Ref: Para. 14-16)

A10. When discussing an apparent material misstatement of fact with management, the auditor may not be able to evaluate the validity of some disclosures included within the other information and management's responses to the auditor's enquiries, and may conclude that valid differences of judgement or opinion exist.

A11. When the auditor concludes that there is a material misstatement of fact that management refuses to correct, appropriate further actions by the auditor may include obtaining advice from the auditor's legal counsel.

❖ ❖ ❖

Conformity with International Standards on Auditing

This Auditing Standard conforms with International Standard on Auditing ISA 720 *The Auditor's Responsibilities Relating to Other Information in Documents Containing Audited Financial Statements*, issued by the International Auditing and Assurance Standards Board (IAASB), an independent standard-setting board of the International Federation of Accountants (IFAC).

Paragraphs that have been added to this Auditing Standard (and do not appear in the text of the equivalent ISA) are identified with the prefix "Aus".

The following requirement is additional to ISA 720:

- Withholding the auditor's report is not permitted under the *Corporations Act 2001*. [Paragraph Aus 10.1]

Compliance with this Auditing Standard enables compliance with ISA 720.

ASA 800

Special Considerations—Audits of Financial Reports Prepared in Accordance with Special Purpose Frameworks

(Reissued October 2009: amended and compiled June 2011)

Issued by the Auditing and Assurance Standards Board.

Note from the Institute of Chartered Accountants Australia

This note, prepared by the technical editor, is not part of ASA 800.

Historical development

March 1985: ED 21 (IAPC ED 21) issued.

October 1986: Statement of Auditing Practice AUP 3.2 'Special Purpose Auditors Reports' issued, effective from date of issue.

August 1992: ED 50 'The Audit Report on Information Other Than a General Purpose Financial Report' issued by the AuSB.

March 1993: AUP 3.2 'The Audit Report on Financial Information Other Than a General Purpose Financial Report' issued. This revision of AUP 3.2 dealt with audit reporting for special purpose financial reports, for other financial information which does not constitute a financial report, and for summarised financial reports. Appendix 4 also provided guidance on the effect of the reporting entity concept on audit reports prepared pursuant to the Corporations Law for companies that are not reporting entities. The relevant International Standard on Auditing was ISA 24 'Special Purpose Auditor's Reports'. However, there were some areas of difference.

May 1994: ED 57 'Codification and Revision of Auditing Pronouncements: AUS 802 The Audit Report on Financial Information Other Than a General Purpose Financial Report' issued by the AuSB.

June 1994: The International Auditing Practices Committee (IAPC) of the International Federation of Accountants (IFAC) approved the issuance of a codified set of International Standards of Auditing (ISAs). The relevant International pronouncement was ISA 800 'The Auditor's Report on Special Purpose Audit Engagements'.

October 1995: The codified Australian Auditing Standards and Auditing Guidance Statements released. The status of these was explained in APS 1.1 'Conformity With Auditing Standards'. These Standards became operative for the first reporting period commencing on or after 1 July 1996. AUP 3.2 'The Audit Report on Financial Information Other Than a General Purpose Financial Report' replaced by AUS 802 'The Audit Report on Financial Information Other Than a General Purpose Financial Report'.

May 2002: AUS 802 reissued to reflect the new Corporations Act and changes to ASIC guidance.

April 2006: ASA 800 was issued as a legally enforceable Standard to replace AUS 802. It is based on ISA 800 of the same name.

June 2007: ASA 800 compiled and republished to reflect changes to ASA 700 'The Auditor's Report on a General Purpose Financial Report' introduced by Omnibus ASA 2007-1.

October 2009: ASA 800 reissued as part of the AUASB's Clarity Project, with a new title 'Special Considerations—Audits of Financial Reports Prepared in Accordance with Special Purpose Frameworks'. The scope differs from the previous version of ASA 800 in that it only deals with financial statements prepared under a special purpose framework and it contains a new requirement that the auditor's report on a special purpose financial report shall include an Emphasis of Matter paragraph. It is based on ISA 800. Requirements relating to the audit of a single financial statement or an element of a financial statement have been moved to ASA 805.

June 2011: ASA 800 updated for editorial amendments contained in ASA 2011-1 'Amendments to Australian Auditing Standards'.

Contents

Compilation Details

Auditing Standard ASA 800 *Special Considerations – Audits of Financial Reports Prepared in Accordance with Special Purpose Frameworks* as Amended

This compilation takes into account amendments made up to and including 27 June 2011 and was prepared on 27 June 2011 by the Auditing and Assurance Standards Board (AUASB).

This compilation is not a separate Auditing Standard made by the AUASB. Instead, it is a representation of ASA 800 (October 2009) as amended by another Auditing Standard which is listed in the Table below.

Table of Standards

Standard	Date made	Operative date
ASA 800	27 October 2009	1 January 2010
ASA 2011-1	27 June 2011	1 July 2011

Table of Amendments

Paragraph affected	How affected	By … [paragraph]
Appendix 1 Illustration 3	Amended	ASA 2011-1 [76]
Appendix 1 [Aus] Illustration 4	Amended	ASA 2011-1 [77]
Appendix 1 [Aus] Illustration 4	Amended	ASA 2011-1 [78]
Appendix 1 [Aus] Illustration 4	Amended	ASA 2011-1 [79]

Paragraph affected	How affected	By ... [paragraph]
Appendix 1 [Aus] Illustration 4	Amended	ASA 2011-1 [80]
Appendix 1 [Aus] Illustration 5	Amended	ASA 2011-1 [81]
Appendix 1 [Aus] Illustration 5	Amended	ASA 2011-1 [82]
Appendix 1 [Aus] Illustration 5	Amended	ASA 2011-1 [83]
Appendix 1 [Aus] Illustration 5	Amended	ASA 2011-1 [84]
Appendix 1 Illustration 1, 2 and 3	Amended	ASA 2011-1 [85]
Appendix 1 Illustrations 1, 2 and 3 [Aus] Illustration 4 [Aus] Illustration 5	Amended	ASA 2011-1 [86]

ASA

Preface

[Preface extracted from the original Auditing Standard issued 27 October 2009

Reasons for Issuing Auditing Standard ASA 800 *Special Considerations—Audits of Financial Reports Prepared in Accordance with Special Purpose Frameworks*

The Auditing and Assurance Standards Board (AUASB) issues Auditing Standard ASA 800 *Special Considerations—Audits of Financial Reports Prepared in Accordance with Special Purpose Frameworks* pursuant to the requirements of the legislative provisions and the Strategic Direction explained below.

The AUASB is an independent statutory board of the Australian Government established under section 227A of the *Australian Securities and Investments Commission Act 2001*, as amended (ASIC Act). Under section 336 of the *Corporations Act 2001*, the AUASB may make Auditing Standards for the purposes of the corporations legislation. These Auditing Standards are legislative instruments under the *Legislative Instruments Act 2003*.

Under the Strategic Direction given to the AUASB by the Financial Reporting Council (FRC), the AUASB is required to have regard to any programme initiated by the International Auditing and Assurance Board (IAASB) for the revision and enhancement of the International Standards on Auditing (ISAs) and to make appropriate consequential amendments to the Australian Auditing Standards. Accordingly, the AUASB has decided to revise and redraft the Australian Auditing Standards using the equivalent redrafted ISAs.

Main Features

This Auditing Standard establishes requirements and provides application and other explanatory material regarding special considerations in the application of Australian Auditing Standards to an audit of a financial report prepared in accordance with a special purpose framework.

This Auditing Standard:

(a) details the auditor's considerations when accepting the engagement and planning and performing the audit;

(b) requires the auditor to apply the requirements in ASA 700 *Forming an Opinion and Reporting on a Financial Report* when forming an opinion, and reporting on, a special purpose financial report; and

(c) requires the auditor to include in the auditor's report an Emphasis of Matter paragraph to alert readers of the financial report that it is prepared in accordance with a special purpose framework.

Authority Statement

Auditing Standard ASA 800 *Special Considerations—Audits of Financial Reports Prepared in Accordance with Special Purpose Frameworks* (as amended at 27 June 2011) is set out in paragraphs 1 to A15 and Appendix 1.

This Auditing Standard is to be read in conjunction with ASA 101 *Preamble to Australian Auditing Standards*, which sets out the intentions of the AUASB on how the Australian Auditing Standards, operative for financial reporting periods commencing on or after 1 January 2010, are to be understood, interpreted and applied. This Standard is to be read also in conjunction with ASA 200 *Overall Objectives of the Independent Auditor and the Conduct of an Audit in Accordance with Australian Accounting Standards*.

Dated: 27 June 2011

M H Kelsall
Chairman - AUASB

Auditing Standard ASA 800

The Auditing and Assurance Standards Board (AUASB) made Auditing Standard ASA 800 *Special Considerations—Audits of Financial Reports Prepared in Accordance with Special Purpose Frameworks*, pursuant to section 227B of the *Australian Securities and Investments Commission Act 2001* and section 336 of the *Corporations Act 2001*, on 27 October 2009.

This compiled version of ASA 800 incorporates subsequent amendments contained in another Auditing Standard made by the AUASB up to and including 27 June 2011 (see Compilation Details).

Auditing Standard ASA 800

Special Considerations—Audits of Financial Reports Prepared in Accordance with Special Purpose Frameworks

Application

Aus 0.1 This Auditing Standard applies to:

(a) an audit of a financial report prepared in accordance with a special purpose framework for a financial year, under the *Corporations Act 2001*; and

(b) an audit of a financial report, or a complete set of financial statements, prepared in accordance with a special purpose framework, for any other special purpose.

Aus 0.2 This Auditing Standard also applies, as appropriate, to an audit of other historical financial information prepared in accordance with a special purpose framework.

Operative Date

Aus 0.3 This Auditing Standard is operative for financial reporting periods commencing on or after 1 January 2010.

[Note: For operative dates of paragraphs changed or added by an amending Standard, see Compilation Details.]

Introduction

Scope of this Auditing Standard

1. The Australian Auditing Standards in the ASA 100 - ASA 700 series apply to an audit of a financial report. This Auditing Standard deals with special considerations in the application of those Australian Auditing Standards to an audit of a financial report prepared in accordance with a special purpose framework.

2. This Auditing Standard is written in the context of a financial report prepared in accordance with a special purpose framework. ASA 805[1] deals with special considerations relevant

1 See ASA 805 *Special Considerations—Audits of Single Financial Statements and Specific Elements, Accounts or Items of a Financial Statement*.

to an audit of a single financial statement or of a specific element, account, or item of a financial statement.

3. This Auditing Standard does not override the requirements of the other Auditing Standards; nor does it purport to deal with all special considerations that may be relevant in the circumstances of the engagement.

Effective Date

4. [Deleted by the AUASB. Refer Aus 0.3]

Objective

5. The objective of the auditor, when applying Australian Auditing Standards in an audit of a financial report prepared in accordance with a special purpose framework, is to address appropriately the special considerations that are relevant to:
   (a) The acceptance of the engagement;
   (b) The planning and performance of that engagement; and
   (c) Forming an opinion and reporting on the financial report.

Definitions

6. For purposes of the Australian Auditing Standards, the following terms have the meanings attributed below:
   (a) [Deleted by the AUASB. Refer Aus 6.1]
   (b) Special purpose framework means a financial reporting framework designed to meet the financial information needs of specific users. The financial reporting framework may be a fair presentation framework or a compliance framework.[2] (Ref: Para. A1-A4)

Aus 6.1 Special purpose financial report means a complete set of financial statements,[*] including the related notes and an assertion statement by those responsible for the financial report, prepared in accordance with a special purpose framework. The related notes ordinarily comprise a summary of significant accounting policies and other explanatory information. The requirements of the applicable financial reporting framework[#] determine the form and content of a financial report[†] prepared in accordance with a special purpose framework. (Ref: Para A4)

7. [Deleted by the AUASB. Refer Aus 6.1]

Requirements

Considerations When Accepting the Engagement

Acceptability of the Financial Reporting Framework

8. ASA 210 requires the auditor to determine the acceptability of the financial reporting framework applied in the preparation of the financial report.[3] In an audit of a special purpose financial report, the auditor shall obtain an understanding of:
   (a) The purpose for which the financial report is prepared;
   (b) The intended users; and
   (c) The steps taken by management to determine that the applicable financial reporting framework is acceptable in the circumstances. (Ref: Para. A5-A8)

2 See ASA 200 *Overall Objectives of the Independent Auditor and the Conduct of an Audit in Accordance with Australian Auditing Standards*, paragraph 13(a).

* See ASA 200, paragraph Aus 13.1.

\# See, for example, the Australian Accounting Standards and the *Corporations Act 2001*.

† See ASA 200, paragraphs Aus 13.3 and Aus 13.4.

3 See ASA 210 *Agreeing the Terms of Audit Engagements,* paragraph 6(a).

Considerations When Planning and Performing the Audit

9. ASA 200 requires the auditor to comply with all Australian Auditing Standards relevant to the audit.[4] In planning and performing an audit of a special purpose financial report, the auditor shall determine whether application of the Australian Auditing Standards requires special consideration in the circumstances of the engagement. (Ref: Para. A9-A12)

10. ASA 315 requires the auditor to obtain an understanding of the entity's selection and application of accounting policies.[5] In the case of a financial report prepared in accordance with the provisions of a contract, the auditor shall obtain an understanding of any significant interpretations of the contract that management made in the preparation of that financial report. An interpretation is significant when adoption of another reasonable interpretation would have produced a material difference in the information presented in the financial report.

Forming an Opinion and Reporting Considerations

11. When forming an opinion and reporting on a special purpose financial report, the auditor shall apply the requirements in ASA 700.[6] (Ref: Para. A13)

Description of the Applicable Financial Reporting Framework

12. ASA 700 requires the auditor to evaluate whether the financial report adequately refers to, or describes the applicable financial reporting framework.[7] In the case of a financial report prepared in accordance with the provisions of a contract, the auditor shall evaluate whether the financial report adequately describes any significant interpretations of the contract on which the financial report is based.

13. ASA 700 deals with the form and content of the auditor's report. In the case of an auditor's report on a special purpose financial report:

    (a) The auditor's report shall also describe the purpose for which the financial report is prepared and, if necessary, the intended users, or refer to a note in the special purpose financial report that contains that information; and

    (b) If management has a choice of financial reporting frameworks in the preparation of such a financial report, the explanation of management's[8] responsibility for the financial report shall also make reference to its responsibility for determining that the applicable financial reporting framework is acceptable in the circumstances.

Alerting Readers that the Financial Report is Prepared in Accordance with a Special Purpose Framework

14. The auditor's report on the special purpose financial report shall include an Emphasis of Matter paragraph alerting users of the auditor's report that the financial report is prepared in accordance with a special purpose framework and that, as a result, the financial report may not be suitable for another purpose. The auditor shall include this paragraph under an appropriate heading. (Ref: Para. A14-A15)

❖ ❖ ❖

Application and Other Explanatory Material

Definition of Special Purpose Framework (Ref: Para. 6-Aus 6.1)

A1. Examples of special purpose frameworks are:

- A tax basis of accounting for a financial report that accompanies an entity's tax return;
- The cash receipts and disbursements basis of accounting for cash flow information that an entity may be requested to prepare for creditors;

4 See ASA 200, paragraph 18.

5 See ASA 315 *Identifying and Assessing the Risks of Material Misstatement through Understanding the Entity and Its Environment*, paragraph 11(c).

6 See ASA 700 *Forming an Opinion and Reporting on a Financial Report*.

7 See ASA 700, paragraph 15.

8 Or other term that is appropriate in the context of the legal framework in the particular jurisdiction.

- The financial reporting provisions established by a regulator to meet the requirements of that regulator; or
- The financial reporting provisions of a contract, such as a bond indenture, a loan agreement, or a project grant.

Aus A1.1 The *Corporations Act 2001*,* Australian Accounting Standards,# other applicable law or regulation, or specific users of the financial report, may determine if a financial report is required to be prepared. Australian Accounting Standards provide the applicable financial reporting framework for determining if the entity is a "reporting entity"† or a "non-reporting entity" and consequently if the financial report is required to be general purpose or special purpose. For "reporting entities" preparing a financial report under the *Corporations Act 2001*, the applicable framework is general purpose. For "non-reporting entities" preparing a financial report under the *Corporations Act 2001*, the applicable framework may be general purpose or special purpose.§

A2. There may be circumstances where a special purpose framework is based on a financial reporting framework established by an authorised or recognised standards setting organisation or by law or regulation, but does not comply with all the requirements of that framework. An example is a contract that requires a financial report to be prepared in accordance with most, but not all, of the Australian Accounting Standards. When this is acceptable in the circumstances of the engagement, it is inappropriate for the description of the applicable financial reporting framework in the special purpose financial report to imply full compliance with the financial reporting framework established by the authorised or recognised standards setting organisation or by law or regulation. In the above example of the contract, the description of the applicable financial reporting framework may refer to the financial reporting provisions of the contract, rather than make any reference to the Australian Accounting Standards.

A3. In the circumstances described in paragraph A2, the special purpose framework may not be a fair presentation framework even if the financial reporting framework on which it is based is a fair presentation framework. This is because the special purpose framework may not comply with all the requirements of the financial reporting framework established by the authorised or recognised standards setting organisation or by law or regulation that are necessary to achieve fair presentation of the financial report.

A4. A financial report prepared in accordance with a special purpose framework may be the only financial report an entity prepares. In such circumstances, that financial report may be used by users other than those for whom the financial reporting framework is designed. Despite the broad distribution of the financial report in those circumstances, it is still considered to be a financial report prepared in accordance with a special purpose framework under Australian Auditing Standards. The requirements in paragraphs 13-14 are designed to avoid misunderstandings about the purpose for which the financial report is prepared.

Considerations When Accepting the Engagement

Acceptability of the Financial Reporting Framework (Ref: Para. 8)

A5. In the case of a special purpose financial report, the financial information needs of the intended users are a key factor in determining the acceptability of the financial reporting framework applied in the preparation of the financial report.

A6. The applicable financial reporting framework may encompass the financial reporting standards established by an organisation that is authorised or recognised to promulgate

* See, for example, Division 1 of Part 2M.3 of the *Corporations Act 2001*.

\# See, for example, Accounting Standard AASB 101 *Presentation of Financial Statements*.

† See, for example, *Glossary of Defined Terms* (June 2009) or Statement of Accounting Concepts 1 *Definition of the Reporting Entity* (August 1990) issued by the AASB.

§ See, for example, ASIC Regulatory Guide 85 *Reporting Requirements for non-reporting entities* (July 2005).

standards for a special purpose financial report. In that case, those standards will be presumed acceptable for that purpose if the organisation follows an established and transparent process involving deliberation and consideration of the views of relevant stakeholders. In some jurisdictions, law or regulation may prescribe the financial reporting framework to be used by management in the preparation of a special purpose financial report for a certain type of entity. For example, a regulator may establish financial reporting provisions to meet the requirements of that regulator. In the absence of indications to the contrary, such a financial reporting framework is presumed acceptable for a special purpose financial report prepared by such entity.

A7. Where the financial reporting standards referred to in paragraph A6 are supplemented by legislative or regulatory requirements, ASA 210 requires the auditor to determine whether any conflicts between the financial reporting standards and the additional requirements exist, and prescribes actions to be taken by the auditor if such conflicts exist.[9]

A8. The applicable financial reporting framework may encompass the financial reporting provisions of a contract, or sources other than those described in paragraphs A6 and A7. In that case, the acceptability of the financial reporting framework in the circumstances of the engagement is determined by considering whether the framework exhibits attributes normally exhibited by acceptable financial reporting frameworks as described in Appendix 2 of ASA 210. In the case of a special purpose framework, the relative importance to a particular engagement of each of the attributes normally exhibited by acceptable financial reporting frameworks is a matter of professional judgement. For example, for purposes of establishing the value of net assets of an entity at the date of its sale, the vendor and the purchaser may have agreed that very prudent estimates of allowances for uncollectible accounts receivable are appropriate for their needs, even though such financial information is not neutral when compared with financial information prepared in accordance with a general purpose framework.

Considerations When Planning and Performing the Audit (Ref: Para. 9)

A9. [Deleted by the AUASB. Refer Aus A9.1]

Aus A9.1 ASA 200 requires the auditor to comply with (a) relevant ethical requirements, including those pertaining to independence, relating to financial report audit engagements, and (b) all Australian Auditing Standards relevant to the audit. It also requires the auditor to comply with each requirement of an Australian Auditing Standard unless, in the circumstances of the audit, the entire Auditing Standard is not relevant or the requirement is not relevant because it is conditional and the condition does not exist; or application of the requirement(s) would relate to classes of transactions, account balances or disclosures that the auditor has determined are immaterial. In rare and exceptional circumstances, when there are factors outside the auditor's control that prevent the auditor from complying with a requirement, the auditor where possible, performs appropriate alternative audit procedures.[10]

A10. Application of some of the requirements of the Auditing Standards in an audit of a special purpose financial report may require special consideration by the auditor. For example, in ASA 320, judgements about matters that are material to users of the financial report are based on a consideration of the common financial information needs of users as a group.[11] In the case of an audit of a special purpose financial report, however, those judgements are based on a consideration of the financial information needs of the intended users.

A11. In the case of a special purpose financial report, such as those prepared in accordance with the requirements of a contract, management may agree with the intended users on a threshold below which misstatements identified during the audit will not be corrected or otherwise adjusted. The existence of such a threshold does not relieve the auditor from the requirement to determine materiality in accordance with ASA 320 for purposes of planning and performing the audit of the special purpose financial report.

9 See ASA 210, paragraph 18.

10 See ASA 200, paragraphs 14, 18, Aus 22.1 and Aus 23.1.

11 See ASA 320 *Materiality in Planning and Performing an Audit*, paragraph 2.

A12. Communication with those charged with governance in accordance with Australian Auditing Standards is based on the relationship between those charged with governance and the financial report subject to audit, in particular, whether those charged with governance are responsible for overseeing the preparation of that financial report. In the case of a special purpose financial report, those charged with governance may not have such a responsibility; for example, when the financial information is prepared solely for management's use. In such cases, the requirements of ASA 260[12] may not be relevant to the audit of the special purpose financial report, except when the auditor is also responsible for the audit of the entity's general purpose financial report or, for example, has agreed with those charged with governance of the entity to communicate to them relevant matters identified during the audit of the special purpose financial report.

Forming an Opinion and Reporting Considerations (Ref: Para. 11)

A13. Appendix 1 to this Auditing Standard contains illustrations of auditors' reports on special purpose financial reports.

Alerting Readers that the Financial Report is Prepared in Accordance with a Special Purpose Framework (Ref: Para. 14)

A14. The special purpose financial report may be used for purposes other than that for which it was intended. For example, a regulator may require certain entities to place the special purpose financial report on public record. To avoid misunderstandings, the auditor alerts users of the auditor's report that the financial report is prepared in accordance with a special purpose framework and, therefore, may not be suitable for another purpose.

Restriction on Distribution or Use (Ref: Para. 14)

A15. In addition to the alert required by paragraph 14, the auditor may consider it appropriate to indicate that the auditor's report is intended solely for the specific users. Depending on the law or regulation of the particular jurisdiction, this may be achieved by restricting the distribution or use of the auditor's report. In these circumstances, the paragraph referred to in paragraph 14 may be expanded to include these other matters, and the heading modified accordingly.

❖❖❖

Conformity with International Standards on Auditing

This Auditing Standard conforms with International Standard on Auditing ISA 800 *Special Considerations—Audits of Financial Statements Prepared in Accordance with Special Purpose Frameworks*, issued by the International Auditing and Assurance Standards Board (IAASB), an independent standard-setting board of the International Federation of Accountants (IFAC).

Paragraphs that have been added to this Auditing Standard (and do not appear in the text of the equivalent ISA) are identified with the prefix "Aus".

Compliance with this Auditing Standard enables compliance with ISA 800.

Appendix 1

(Ref: Para. A13)

Illustrations of Auditors' Reports on Special Purpose Financial Reports

- Illustration 1: An auditor's report on a financial report prepared in accordance with the financial reporting provisions of a contract (for purposes of this illustration, a compliance framework).
- Illustration 2: An auditor's report on a financial report prepared in accordance with the tax basis of accounting (for purposes of this illustration, a compliance framework).

12 See ASA 260 *Communication with Those Charged with Governance*.

- Illustration 3: An auditor's report on a financial report prepared in accordance with the financial reporting provisions established by a regulatory authority (for purposes of this illustration, a fair presentation framework).
- [Aus] Illustration 4: An auditor's report on a financial report prepared by a non-reporting entity under the *Corporations Act 2001* (for purposes of this illustration, a fair presentation framework).
- [Aus] Illustration 5: An auditor's report on a financial report prepared by a not-for-profit incorporated association in accordance with the financial reporting provisions of the *Applicable State Act* (for purposes of this illustration, a fair presentation framework).

See ASA 700* for applicable wording in the auditor's report, when the company has made a statement on compliance with *International Financial Reporting Standards* (IFRSs) and/or includes a Remuneration Report in the Directors' Report.

Example Auditor's Report Special Purpose Financial Report—Compliance with a Contract (Compliance Framework)

Illustration 1:

Circumstances include the following:

- **The financial report has been prepared by management of the entity in accordance with the financial reporting provisions of a contract (that is, a special purpose framework) to comply with the provisions of that contract. Management does not have a choice of financial reporting frameworks.**
- **The applicable financial reporting framework is a compliance framework.**
- **The financial report is *not* prepared under the *Corporations Act 2001.***
- **The terms of the audit engagement reflect the description of management's responsibility for the financial report in ASA 210.**
- **Distribution and use of the auditor's report is restricted.**

INDEPENDENT AUDITOR'S REPORT

[Appropriate Addressee]

We have audited the accompanying financial report of ABC Entity, which comprises the statement of financial position as at 30 June 20X1, the statement of comprehensive income, statement of changes in equity and statement of cash flows for the year then ended, notes comprising a summary of significant accounting policies and other explanatory information, and management's assertion statement.† The financial report has been prepared by the management of ABC Entity based on the financial reporting provisions of Section Z of the contract dated 1 July 20X0 between ABC Entity and DEF Company ("the contract").

Management's[13] Responsibility for the Financial Report

Management is responsible for the preparation of the financial report in accordance with the financial reporting provisions of Section Z of the contract; and for such internal control as management determines is necessary to enable the preparation of a financial report that is free from material misstatement, whether due to fraud or error.

* See ASA 700 *Forming an Opinion and Reporting on a Financial Report.*

† Or other appropriate term.

13 Or another term that is appropriate in the context of the legal framework in the particular jurisdiction.

Auditor's Responsibility

Our responsibility is to express an opinion on the financial report based on our audit. We conducted our audit in accordance with Australian Auditing Standards. Those standards require that we comply with relevant ethical requirements relating to audit engagements and plan and perform the audit to obtain reasonable assurance about whether the financial report is free from material misstatement.

An audit involves performing procedures to obtain audit evidence about the amounts and disclosures in the financial report. The procedures selected depend on the auditor's judgement, including the assessment of the risks of material misstatement of the financial report, whether due to fraud or error. In making those risk assessments, the auditor considers internal control relevant to the entity's preparation of the financial report in order to design audit procedures that are appropriate in the circumstances, but not for the purpose of expressing an opinion on the effectiveness of the entity's internal control. An audit also includes evaluating the appropriateness of accounting policies used and the reasonableness of accounting estimates made by management, as well as evaluating the overall presentation of the financial report.

We believe that the audit evidence we have obtained is sufficient and appropriate to provide a basis for our audit opinion.

Opinion

In our opinion, the financial report of ABC Entity for the year ended 30 June 20X1 is prepared, in all material respects, in accordance with the financial reporting provisions of Section Z of the contract.

Basis of Accounting and Restriction on Distribution and Use

Without modifying our opinion, we draw attention to Note X to the financial report, which describes the basis of accounting. The financial report is prepared to assist ABC Entity to comply with the financial reporting provisions of the contract referred to above. As a result, the financial report may not be suitable for another purpose. Our report is intended solely for ABC Entity and DEF Company and should not be distributed to or used by parties other than ABC Entity or DEF Company.

[Auditor's signature]*

[Date of the auditor's report]#

[Auditor's address]

Example Auditor's Report
Special Purpose Financial Report—Tax Basis of Accounting (Compliance Framework)

Illustration 2:

Circumstances include the following:

- **The financial report has been prepared by management of a partnership in accordance with the tax basis of accounting (that is, a special purpose framework) to assist the partners in preparing their individual income tax returns. Management does not have a choice of financial reporting frameworks.**
- **The applicable financial reporting framework is a compliance framework.**
- **The financial report is *not* prepared under the *Corporations Act 2001*.**
- **The terms of the audit engagement reflect the description of management's responsibility for the financial report in ASA 210.**
- **Distribution and use of the auditor's report is restricted.**

* The auditor's report needs to be signed in one or more of the following ways: name of the audit firm, the name of the audit company or the personal name of the auditor as appropriate.

\# The date of the auditor's report is the date the auditor signs the report.

INDEPENDENT AUDITOR'S REPORT

[Appropriate Addressee]

We have audited the accompanying financial report of ABC Partnership, which comprises the statement of financial position as at 30 June 20X1, the statement of comprehensive income for the year then ended, notes comprising a summary of significant accounting policies and other explanatory information, and management's assertion statement.** The financial report has been prepared by management using the tax basis of accounting.

Management's[14] Responsibility for the Financial Report

Management is responsible for the preparation of the financial report in accordance with the tax basis of accounting; and for such internal control as management determines is necessary to enable the preparation of a financial report that is free from material misstatement, whether due to fraud or error.

Auditor's Responsibility

Our responsibility is to express an opinion on the financial report based on our audit. We conducted our audit in accordance with Australian Auditing Standards. Those standards require that we comply with relevant ethical requirements relating to audit engagements and plan and perform the audit to obtain reasonable assurance about whether the financial report is free from material misstatement.

An audit involves performing procedures to obtain audit evidence about the amounts and disclosures in the financial report. The procedures selected depend on the auditor's judgement, including the assessment of the risks of material misstatement of the financial report, whether due to fraud or error. In making those risk assessments, the auditor considers internal control relevant to the partnership's preparation of the financial report in order to design audit procedures that are appropriate in the circumstances, but not for the purpose of expressing an opinion on the effectiveness of the partnership's internal control. An audit also includes evaluating the appropriateness of accounting policies used and the reasonableness of accounting estimates made by management, as well as evaluating the overall presentation of the financial report.

We believe that the audit evidence we have obtained is sufficient and appropriate to provide a basis for our audit opinion.

Opinion

In our opinion, the financial report of ABC Partnership for the year ended 30 June 20X1 is prepared, in all material respects, in accordance with [describe the applicable income tax law].

Basis of Accounting and Restriction on Distribution

Without modifying our opinion, we draw attention to Note X to the financial report, which describes the basis of accounting. The financial report is prepared to assist the partners of ABC Partnership in preparing their individual income tax returns. As a result, the financial report may not be suitable for another purpose. Our report is intended solely for ABC Partnership and its partners and should not be distributed to parties other than ABC Partnership or its partners.

[Auditor's signature]†

[Date of the auditor's report]#

[Auditor's address]

** Or other appropriate term.

14 Or another term that is appropriate in the context of the legal framework in the particular jurisdiction.

† The auditor's report needs to be signed in one or more of the following ways: name of the audit firm, the name of the audit company or the personal name of the auditor as appropriate.

The date of the auditor's report is the date the auditor signs the report.

Example Auditor's Report
Special Purpose Financial Report—Regulatory Authority Requirements
(Fair Presentation Framework)

Illustration 3:

Circumstances include the following:

- **The financial report has been prepared by management of the entity in accordance with the financial reporting provisions established by a regulatory authority (that is, a special purpose framework) to meet the requirements of that authority. Management does not have a choice of financial reporting frameworks.**
- **The applicable financial reporting framework is a fair presentation framework.**
- **The financial report is *not* prepared under the *Corporations Act 2001*.**
- **The terms of the audit engagement reflect the description of management's responsibility for the financial report in ASA 210.**
- **The Other Matter paragraph refers to the fact that the auditor has also issued an auditor's report on the financial report prepared by ABC Entity for the same period in accordance with a general purpose framework.**
- **Distribution or use of the auditor's report is not restricted.**

ASA

INDEPENDENT AUDITOR'S REPORT

[Appropriate Addressee]

We have audited the accompanying financial report of ABC Entity, which comprises the statement of financial position as at 30 June 20X1, the statement of comprehensive income, statement of changes in equity and statement of cash flows for the year then ended, notes comprising a summary of significant accounting policies and other explanatory information, and management's assertion statement.* The financial report has been prepared by management based on the [financial reporting provisions of Section Y of Regulation Z].

Management's[15] Responsibility for the Financial Report

Management is responsible for the preparation[16] and fair presentation of the financial report in accordance with the [financial reporting provisions of Section Y of Regulation Z,] and for such internal control as management determines is necessary to enable the preparation and fair presentation of a financial report that is free from material misstatement, whether due to fraud or error.

Auditor's Responsibility

Our responsibility is to express an opinion on the financial report based on our audit. We conducted our audit in accordance with Australian Auditing Standards. Those standards require that we comply with relevant ethical requirements relating to audit engagements and plan and perform the audit to obtain reasonable assurance about whether the financial report is free from material misstatement.

An audit involves performing procedures to obtain audit evidence about the amounts and disclosures in the financial report. The procedures selected depend on the auditor's judgement, including the assessment of the risks of material misstatement of the financial report, whether due to fraud or error. In making those risk assessments, the auditor considers internal control

* Or other appropriate term.

15 Or another term that is appropriate in the context of the legal framework in the particular jurisdiction.

16 Where management's responsibility is to prepare a financial report that gives a true and fair view, this may read: "Management is responsible for the preparation of the financial report that gives a true and fair view in accordance with the financial reporting provisions of section Y of Regulation Z, and for such…"

relevant to the entity's preparation and fair presentation[17] of the financial report in order to design audit procedures that are appropriate in the circumstances, but not for the purpose of expressing an opinion on the effectiveness of the entity's internal control.[18] An audit also includes evaluating the appropriateness of accounting policies used and the reasonableness of accounting estimates made by management, as well as evaluating the overall presentation of the financial report.

We believe that the audit evidence we have obtained is sufficient and appropriate to provide a basis for our audit opinion.

Opinion

In our opinion, the financial report presents fairly, in all material respects, (or *gives a true and fair view of*) the financial position of ABC Entity as at 30 June, 20X1, and (*of*) its financial performance and its cash flows for the year then ended in accordance with [the financial reporting provisions of Section Y of Regulation Z].

Basis of Accounting

Without modifying our opinion, we draw attention to Note X to the financial report, which describes the basis of accounting. The financial report is prepared to assist ABC Entity to meet the requirements of Regulatory Authority DEF. As a result, the financial report may not be suitable for another purpose.

Other Matter

ABC Entity has prepared a separate financial report for the year ended 30 June 20X1 in accordance with Australian Accounting Standards on which we issued a separate auditor's report to the shareholders of ABC Entity dated 30 September 20X1.

[Auditor's signature]*

[Date of the auditor's report]#

[Auditor's address]

17 In the case of footnote 16, this sentence may read: "In making those risk assessments, the auditor considers internal control relevant to the entity's preparation of the financial report that gives a true and fair view in order to design audit procedures that are appropriate in the circumstances, but not for the purpose of expressing an opinion on the effectiveness of the entity's internal control."

18 In circumstances when the auditor also has responsibility to express an opinion on the effectiveness of internal control in conjunction with the audit of the financial report, this sentence would be worded as follows: "In making those risk assessments, the auditor considers internal control relevant to the entity's preparation and fair presentation of the financial report in order to design audit procedures that are appropriate in the circumstances." In the case of footnote 16, this may read: "In making those risk assessments, the auditor considers internal control relevant to the entity's preparation of the financial report that gives a true and fair view in order to design audit procedures that are appropriate in the circumstances."

* The auditor's report needs to be signed in one or more of the following ways: name of the audit firm, the name of the audit company or the personal name of the auditor as appropriate.

\# The date of the auditor's report is the date the auditor signs the report.

Example Auditor's Report
Special Purpose Financial Report—*Corporations Act 2001* (Fair Presentation Framework)

[Aus] Illustration 4:

Circumstances include the following:

- **The entity is a small proprietary company controlled by a foreign company and is required to lodge a financial report with the Australian Securities and Investments Commission (ASIC) under the *Corporations Act 2001*. The entity is a non-reporting entity.**
- **The financial report is prepared under the *Corporations Act 2001*.**
- **The applicable financial reporting framework is a fair presentation framework.**
- **The terms of the audit engagement reflect the description of management's responsibility for the financial report in ASA 210.**
- **Distribution or use of the auditor's report is not restricted.**

INDEPENDENT AUDITOR'S REPORT

[Appropriate addressee]

Report on the Financial Report†

We have audited the accompanying financial report, being a special purpose financial report of ABC Company Ltd., which comprises the statement of financial position as at 30 June 20X1, the statement of comprehensive income, statement of changes in equity and statement of cash flows for the year then ended, notes comprising a summary of significant accounting policies and other explanatory information, and the directors' declaration.

Directors' Responsibility for the Financial Report

The directors of the company are responsible for the preparation of the financial report that gives a true and fair view and have determined that the basis of preparation described in Note X to the financial report is appropriate to meet the requirements of the *Corporations Act 2001* and is appropriate to meet the needs of the members. The directors' responsibility also includes such internal control as the directors determine is necessary to enable the preparation of a financial report that gives a true and fair view and is free from material misstatement, whether due to fraud or error.

Auditor's Responsibility

Our responsibility is to express an opinion on the financial report based on our audit. We have conducted our audit in accordance with Australian Auditing Standards. Those standards require that we comply with relevant ethical requirements relating to audit engagements and plan and perform the audit to obtain reasonable assurance whether the financial report is free from material misstatement.

An audit involves performing procedures to obtain audit evidence about the amounts and disclosures in the financial report. The procedures selected depend on the auditor's judgement, including the assessment of the risks of material misstatement of the financial report, whether due to fraud or error. In making those risk assessments, the auditor considers internal control relevant to the entity's preparation of the financial report that gives a true and fair view in order to design audit procedures that are appropriate in the circumstances, but not for the purpose of expressing an opinion on the effectiveness of the entity's internal control. An audit also includes evaluating the appropriateness of accounting policies used and the reasonableness of accounting estimates made by the directors, as well as evaluating the overall presentation of the financial report.

We believe that the audit evidence we have obtained is sufficient and appropriate to provide a basis for our audit opinion.

† The sub-title "Report on the Financial Report" is unnecessary in circumstances when the second sub-title "Report on Other Legal and Regulatory Requirements", or other appropriate sub-title, is not applicable.

Independence

In conducting our audit, we have complied with the independence requirements of the *Corporations Act 2001*. We confirm that the independence declaration required by the *Corporations Act 2001*, which has been given to the directors of ABC Company Ltd., would be in the same terms if given to the directors as at the time of the auditor's report.*

Opinion

In our opinion the financial report of ABC Company Ltd. is in accordance with the *Corporations Act 2001*, including:

(a) giving a true and fair view of the company's financial position as at 30 June 20X1 and of its performance for the year ended on that date; and

(b) complying with Australian Accounting Standards to the extent described in Note X, and the *Corporations Regulations 2001*.

Basis of Accounting

Without modifying our opinion, we draw attention to Note X to the financial report, which describes the basis of accounting. The financial report has been prepared for the purpose of fulfilling the directors' financial reporting responsibilities under the *Corporations Act 2001*. As a result, the financial report may not be suitable for another purpose.

Report on Other Legal and Regulatory Standards

[Auditor's signature]#

[Date of the auditor's report]†

[Auditor's address]

Example Auditor's Report
Special Purpose Financial Report—*Applicable State Act (Year)*
(Fair Presentation Framework)

[Aus] Illustration 5:

Circumstances include the following:

- **The financial report is prepared by a not-for-profit incorporated association to meet the financial reporting requirements of the *Applicable State Act (Year)*.**
- **The applicable financial reporting framework is a fair presentation framework.**
- **The financial report is *not* prepared under the *Corporations Act 2001*.**
- **The terms of the audit engagement reflect the description of management's responsibility for the financial report in ASA 210.**
- **Distribution or use of the auditor's report is not restricted.**

* Or, alternatively, include statements (a) to the effect that circumstances have changed since the declaration was given to the relevant directors; and (b) setting out how the declaration would differ if it had been given to the relevant directors at the time the auditor's report was made.

\# The auditor's report needs to be signed in one or more of the following ways: name of the audit firm, the name of the audit company or the personal name of the auditor as appropriate.

† The date of the auditor's report is the date the auditor signs the report.

INDEPENDENT AUDITOR'S REPORT

[Appropriate Addressee]

We have audited the accompanying financial report, being a special purpose financial report, of ABC Not-for-Profit Incorporated, which comprises the statement of financial position as at 30 June 20X1, the statement of comprehensive income and statement of cash flows for the year then ended, notes comprising a summary of significant accounting policies and other explanatory information, and the officers' assertion statement.*

Officers'† Responsibility for the Financial Report

The officers of ABC Not-for-Profit Incorporated are responsible for the preparation and fair presentation of the financial report, and have determined that the basis of preparation described in Note X, is appropriate to meet the requirements of the *Applicable State Act*# and is appropriate to meet the needs of the members. The officers' responsibility also includes such internal control as the officers determine is necessary to enable the preparation and fair presentation of a financial report that is free from material misstatement, whether due to fraud or error.

Auditor's Responsibility

Our responsibility is to express an opinion on the financial report based on our audit. We have conducted our audit in accordance with Australian Auditing Standards. Those standards require that we comply with relevant ethical requirements relating to audit engagements and plan and perform the audit to obtain reasonable assurance whether the financial report is free from material misstatement.

An audit involves performing procedures to obtain audit evidence about the amounts and disclosures in the financial report. The procedures selected depend on the auditor's judgement, including the assessment of the risks of material misstatement of the financial report, whether due to fraud or error. In making those risk assessments, the auditor considers internal control relevant to the association's preparation and fair presentation of the financial report in order to design audit procedures that are appropriate in the circumstances, but not for the purpose of expressing an opinion on the effectiveness of the association's internal control. An audit also includes evaluating the appropriateness of accounting policies used and the reasonableness of accounting estimates made by the officers, as well as evaluating the overall presentation of the financial report.

We believe that the audit evidence we have obtained is sufficient and appropriate to provide a basis for our audit opinion.

Opinion

In our opinion, the financial report presents fairly, in all material respects, (or *gives a true and fair view of*) the financial position of ABC Not-for-Profit Incorporated as at 30 June 20X1, and (*of*) its financial performance and its cash flows for the year then ended in accordance with [the financial reporting requirements of *Applicable State Act* (Year)].

Basis of Accounting

Without modifying our opinion, we draw attention to Note X to the financial report, which describes the basis of accounting. The financial report has been prepared to assist ABC Not-for-Profit Incorporated to meet the requirements of the *Applicable State Act*. As a result, the financial report may not be suitable for another purpose.

[Auditor's signature]**

[Date of the auditor's report]##

[Auditor's address]

* Or other appropriate term.

† Or other term that is appropriate in the context of the legal framework in the particular jurisdiction.

\# Insert reference to appropriate framework.

** The auditor's report needs to be signed in one or more of the following ways: name of the audit firm, the name of the audit company or the personal name of the auditor as appropriate.

\## The date of the auditor's report is the date the auditor signs the report.

ASA

ASA 805

Special Considerations—Audits of Single Financial Statements and Specific Elements, Accounts or Items of a Financial Statement

(Issued October 2009)

Issued by the Auditing and Assurance Standards Board.

Note from the Institute of Chartered Accountants Australia

This note, prepared by the technical editor, is not part of ASA 805.

Historical development

October 2009: ASA 805 issued as part of the AUASB's Clarity Project. ASA 805 deals with the auditor's responsibilities in connection with the audit of a single financial statement, such as a balance sheet, or a specific element, account or item of a financial statement, such as a schedule of accounts receivable, prepared in accordance with a special purpose framework. It is based on ISA 805 of the same name. Requirements covering these engagements were previously included in ASA 800 'The Auditor's Report on Special Purpose Audit Engagements'.

Contents

PREFACE

AUTHORITY STATEMENT

Preface

Reasons for Issuing Auditing Standard ASA 805 *Special Considerations—Audits of Single Financial Statements and Specific Elements, Accounts or Items of a Financial Statement*

The Auditing and Assurance Standards Board (AUASB) issues Auditing Standard ASA 805 *Special Considerations—Audits of Single Financial Statements and Specific Elements, Accounts or Items of a Financial Statement* pursuant to the requirements of the legislative provisions and the Strategic Direction explained below.

The AUASB is an independent statutory board of the Australian Government established under section 227A of the *Australian Securities and Investments Commission Act 2001*, as amended (ASIC Act). Under section 227B of the ASIC Act, the AUASB may formulate Auditing Standards for other purposes.

Under the Strategic Direction given to the AUASB by the Financial Reporting Council (FRC), the AUASB is required to have regard to any programme initiated by the International Auditing and Assurance Standards Board (IAASB) for the revision and enhancement of the International Standards on Auditing (ISAs) and to make appropriate consequential amendments to the Australian Auditing Standards. Accordingly, the AUASB has decided to revise and redraft the Australian Auditing Standards using the equivalent redrafted ISAs.

Main Features

This Auditing Standard establishes requirements and provides application and other explanatory material to auditors regarding special considerations in the application of Australian Auditing Standards to an audit of a single financial statement or of a specific element, account or item of a financial statement.

This Auditing Standard:

(a) describes the auditor's considerations in accepting an engagement covered by this Standard;

(b) requires the auditor to consider the practicalities of accepting an engagement to audit a single financial statement, or a specific element, account or item of a financial statement, if the auditor is not already engaged to audit the financial report from which that single financial statement, or a specific element, account or item of a financial statement is derived;

(c) requires the auditor to apply the Australian Auditing Standards as appropriate when planning and performing the audit;

(d) requires the auditor to form an opinion and report on the single financial statement, or a specific element, account or item of a financial statement by applying, as appropriate, the requirements of ASA 700 *Forming an Opinion and Reporting on a Financial Report*; and

(e) requires the auditor to consider the type of audit opinion expressed on the financial report from which the single financial statement, or a specific element, account or item of a financial statement, is derived.

Authority Statement

The Auditing and Assurance Standards Board (AUASB) formulates this Auditing Standard ASA 805 *Special Considerations—Audits of Single Financial Statements and Specific Elements, Accounts or Items of a Financial Statement* pursuant to section 227B of the *Australian Securities and Investments Commission Act 2001*.

This Auditing Standard is to be read in conjunction with ASA 101 *Preamble to Australian Auditing Standards*, which sets out the intentions of the AUASB on how the Australian Auditing Standards, operative for financial reporting periods commencing on or after 1 January 2010, are to be understood, interpreted and applied. This Auditing Standard is to be read also in conjunction with ASA 200 *Overall Objectives of the Independent Auditor and the Conduct of the Audit in Accordance with Australian Auditing Standards*.

Dated: 27 October 2009

M H Kelsall
Chairman - AUASB

Auditing Standard ASA 805

Special Considerations—Audits of Single Financial Statements and Specific Elements, Accounts or Items of a Financial Statement

Application

Aus 0.1 This Auditing Standard applies to an audit of a single financial statement, or a specific element, account, or item of a financial statement.

Aus 0.2 This Auditing Standard also applies, as appropriate, to an audit of other historical financial information.

Operative Date

Aus 0.3 This Auditing Standard is operative for financial reporting periods commencing on or after 1 January 2010.

Introduction

Scope of this Auditing Standard

1. The Auditing Standards in the ASA 100 - ASA 700 series relate to an audit of a financial report and are to be applied as necessary in the circumstances of an audit of other historical financial information. This Auditing Standard deals with special considerations in the application of those Australian Auditing Standards to an audit of a single financial statement or of a specific element, account or item of a financial statement. The single financial statement or the specific element, account or item of a financial statement may be prepared in accordance with a general or special purpose framework. If prepared in accordance with a special purpose framework, ASA 800[1] also applies to the audit. (Ref: Para. A1-A4)
2. This Auditing Standard does not apply to the report of a component auditor, issued as a result of work performed on the financial information of a component at the request of a group engagement team for purposes of an audit of a group financial report (see ASA 600[2]).
3. This Auditing Standard does not override the requirements of other Auditing Standards; nor does it purport to deal with all special considerations that may be relevant in the circumstances of the engagement.

ASA

Effective Date

4. [Deleted by the AUASB. Refer Aus 0.3]

Objective

5. The objective of the auditor, when applying Australian Auditing Standards in an audit of a single financial statement or of a specific element, account or item of a financial statement, is to address appropriately the special considerations that are relevant to:
   (a) The acceptance of the engagement;
   (b) The planning and performance of that engagement; and
   (c) Forming an opinion and reporting on the single financial statement or on the specific element, account or item of a financial statement.

Definitions

6. For purposes of this Auditing Standard, the following terms have the meanings attributed below:
   (a) Element of a financial statement or element means an element, account or item of a financial statement;
   (b) Australian Accounting Standards means the Australian Accounting Standards issued by the Australian Accounting Standards Board; and
   (c) A single financial statement or a specific element of a financial statement includes the related notes. The related notes ordinarily comprise a summary of significant accounting policies and other explanatory information relevant to the financial statement or to the element.

Requirements

Considerations When Accepting the Engagement

Application of Australian Auditing Standards

7. ASA 200 requires the auditor to comply with all Australian Auditing Standards relevant to the audit.[3] In the case of an audit of a single financial statement or of a specific element

1 See ASA 800 *Special Considerations—Audits of Financial Reports Prepared in Accordance with Special Purpose Frameworks.*

2 See ASA 600 *Special Considerations—Audits of a Group Financial Report (Including the Work of Component Auditors).*

3 See ASA 200 *Overall Objectives of the Independent Auditor and the Conduct of an Audit in Accordance with Australian Auditing Standards*, paragraph 18.

of a financial statement, this requirement applies irrespective of whether the auditor is also engaged to audit the entity's financial report. If the auditor is not also engaged to audit the entity's financial report, the auditor shall determine whether the audit of a single financial statement or of a specific element of the financial statements in accordance with Australian Auditing Standards is practicable. (Ref: Para. A5-A6)

Acceptability of the Financial Reporting Framework

8. ASA 210 requires the auditor to determine the acceptability of the financial reporting framework applied in the preparation of the financial report.[4] In the case of an audit of a single financial statement or of a specific element of a financial statement, this shall include whether application of the financial reporting framework will result in a presentation that provides adequate disclosures to enable the intended users to understand the information conveyed in the financial statement or the element, and the effect of material transactions and events on the information conveyed in the financial statement or the element. (Ref: Para. A7)

Form of Opinion

9. ASA 210 requires that the agreed terms of the audit engagement include the expected form of any reports to be issued by the auditor.[5] In the case of an audit of a single financial statement or of a specific element of a financial statement, the auditor shall consider whether the expected form of opinion is appropriate in the circumstances. (Ref: Para. A8-A9)

Considerations When Planning and Performing the Audit

10. ASA 200 states that Australian Auditing Standards are written in the context of an audit of a financial report; they are to be applied as necessary in the circumstances of an audit of other historical financial information.[6] [7] In planning and performing the audit of a single financial statement or of a specific element of a financial statement, the auditor shall apply all Australian Auditing Standards relevant to the audit as necessary in the circumstances of the engagement. (Ref: Para. A10-A14)

Forming an Opinion and Reporting Considerations

11. When forming an opinion and reporting on a single financial statement or on a specific element of a financial statement, the auditor shall apply the requirements in ASA 700,[8] as necessary in the circumstances of the engagement. (Ref: Para. A15-A16)

Reporting on the Entity's Financial Report and on a Single Financial Statement or on a Specific Element of that Financial Statement

12. If the auditor undertakes an engagement to report on a single financial statement or on a specific element of a financial statement in conjunction with an engagement to audit the entity's financial report, the auditor shall express a separate opinion for each engagement.

13. An audited single financial statement or an audited specific element of a financial statement may be published together with the entity's audited financial report. If the auditor concludes that the presentation of the single financial statement or of the specific element of a financial statement does not differentiate it sufficiently from the financial report, the auditor shall ask management to rectify the situation. Subject to paragraphs 15 and 16 of this Auditing Standard, the auditor shall also differentiate the opinion on the single financial statement or on the specific element of a financial statement from the opinion on the financial report. The auditor shall not issue the auditor's report containing the opinion on the single financial statement or on the specific element of a financial statement until satisfied with the differentiation.

4 See ASA 210 *Agreeing the Terms of Audit Engagements*, paragraph 6(a).

5 See ASA 210, paragraph 10(e).

6 See ASA 200, paragraph 2.

7 See ASA 200, paragraphs Aus 13.1, Aus 13.2, Aus 13.3 and Aus 13.4.

8 See ASA 700 *Forming an Opinion and Reporting on a Financial Report.*

Modified Opinion, Emphasis of Matter Paragraph or Other Matter Paragraph in the Auditor's Report on the Entity's Financial Report

14. If the opinion in the auditor's report on an entity's financial report is modified, or that report includes an Emphasis of Matter paragraph or an Other Matter paragraph, the auditor shall determine the effect that this may have on the auditor's report on a single financial statement or on a specific element of those financial statements. When deemed appropriate, the auditor shall modify the opinion on the single financial statement or on the specific element of a financial statement, or include an Emphasis of Matter paragraph or an Other Matter paragraph in the auditor's report, accordingly. (Ref: Para. A15, A17)

15. If the auditor concludes that it is necessary to express an adverse opinion or disclaim an opinion on the entity's financial report, ASA 705 does not permit the auditor to include in the same auditor's report an unmodified opinion on a single financial statement that forms part of that financial report or on a specific element that forms part of that financial report.[9] This is because such an unmodified opinion would contradict the adverse opinion or disclaimer of opinion on the entity's financial report. (Ref: Para. A18)

16. If the auditor concludes that it is necessary to express an adverse opinion or disclaim an opinion on the entity's financial report as a whole but, in the context of a separate audit of a specific element that is included in that financial report, the auditor nevertheless considers it appropriate to express an unmodified opinion on that element, the auditor shall only do so if:

    (a) The auditor is not prohibited by law or regulation from doing so;

    (b) That opinion is expressed in an auditor's report that is not published together with the auditor's report containing the adverse opinion or disclaimer of opinion; and

    (c) The specific element does not constitute a major portion of the entity's financial report.

17. The auditor shall not express an unmodified opinion on a single financial statement that forms part of a financial report if the auditor has expressed an adverse opinion or disclaimed an opinion on the financial report. This is the case even if the auditor's report on the single financial statement is not published together with the auditor's report containing the adverse opinion or disclaimer of opinion. This is because a single financial statement is deemed to constitute a major portion of that financial report.

❖ ❖ ❖

Application and Other Explanatory Material

Scope of this Auditing Standard (Ref: Para. 1)

A1. ASA 200 defines the term "historical financial information" as information expressed in financial terms in relation to a particular entity, derived primarily from that entity's accounting system, about economic events occurring in past time periods or about economic conditions or circumstances at points in time in the past.[10]

A2. [Deleted by the AUASB. Refer Aus A2.1]

Aus A2.1 ASA 200 defines the term "financial statement" as a structured representation of historical financial information, intended to communicate an entity's economic resources or obligations at a point in time or the changes therein for a period of time in accordance with a financial reporting framework. What constitutes a financial statement is determined by the requirements of the applicable financial reporting framework.[11] In the context of this Auditing Standard, a single financial statement includes the related notes.

A3. Australian Auditing Standards are written in the context of an audit of a financial report;[12] they are to be applied as necessary in the circumstances when applied to an audit of other

9 See ASA 705 *Modification to the Opinion in the Independent Auditor's Report*, paragraph 15.

10 See ASA 200, paragraph 13(g).

11 See ASA 200, paragraph Aus 13.2.

12 See ASA 200, paragraph 2.

historical financial information, such as a single financial statement or a specific element of a financial statement. This Auditing Standard assists in this regard. (Appendix 1 lists examples of such other historical financial information.)

A4. A reasonable assurance engagement other than an audit of historical financial information is performed in accordance with Australian Standard on Assurance Engagements ASAE 3000.[13]

Considerations When Accepting the Engagement

Application of Australian Auditing Standards (Ref: Para. 7)

A5. [Deleted by the AUASB. Refer Aus A5.1]

Aus A5.1 ASA 200 requires the auditor to comply with (a) relevant ethical requirements, including those pertaining to independence, relating to financial report audit engagements, and (b) all Australian Auditing Standards relevant to the audit. It also requires the auditor to comply with each requirement of an Australian Auditing Standard unless, in the circumstances of the audit, the entire Auditing Standard is not relevant or the requirement is not relevant because it is conditional and the condition does not exist, or application of the requirement(s) would relate to classes of transactions, account balances or disclosures that the auditor has determined are immaterial. In rare and exceptional circumstances, when there are factors outside the auditor's control that prevent the auditor from complying with a requirement, the auditor, where possible, performs appropriate alternative audit procedures.[14]

A6. Compliance with the requirements of Australian Auditing Standards relevant to the audit of a single financial statement or of a specific element of a financial statement may not be practicable when the auditor is not also engaged to audit the entity's financial report. In such cases, the auditor often does not have the same understanding of the entity and its environment, including its internal control, as an auditor who also audits the entity's financial report. The auditor also does not have the audit evidence about the general quality of the accounting records or other accounting information that would be acquired in an audit of the entity's financial report. Accordingly, the auditor may need further evidence to corroborate audit evidence acquired from the accounting records. In the case of an audit of a specific element of a financial statement, certain Australian Auditing Standards require audit work that may be disproportionate to the element being audited. For example, although the requirements of ASA 570[15] are likely to be relevant in the circumstances of an audit of a schedule of accounts receivable, complying with those requirements may not be practicable because of the audit effort required. If the auditor concludes that an audit of a single financial statement or of a specific element of a financial statement in accordance with Australian Auditing Standards may not be practicable, the auditor may discuss with management whether another type of engagement might be more practicable.[*]

Acceptability of the Financial Reporting Framework (Ref: Para. 8)

A7. A single financial statement or a specific element of a financial statement may be prepared in accordance with an applicable financial reporting framework that is based on a financial reporting framework established by an authorised or recognised standards setting organisation for the preparation of a financial report (for example, Australian Accounting Standards). If this is the case, determination of the acceptability of the applicable framework may involve considering whether that framework includes all the requirements of the framework on which it is based that are relevant to the presentation of a single financial statement or of a specific element of a financial statement that provides adequate disclosures.

13 See ASAE 3000 *Assurance Engagements Other than Audits or Reviews of Historical Financial Information* (July 2007).

14 See ASA 200, paragraphs 14, 18, 22, Aus 22.1, 23 and Aus 23.1.

15 See ASA 570 *Going Concern.*

* See, for example, ASAE 3100 *Compliance Engagements* (September 2008) or ASRE 2405 *Review of Historical Financial Information Other than a Financial Report* (August 2008).

Form of Opinion (Ref: Para. 9)

A8. The form of opinion to be expressed by the auditor depends on the applicable financial reporting framework and any applicable laws or regulations.[16] In accordance with ASA 700:[17]

(a) When expressing an unmodified opinion on a financial report prepared in accordance with a fair presentation framework, the auditor's opinion, unless otherwise required by law or regulation, uses one of the following phrases: (i) the financial report presents fairly, in all material respects, in accordance with [the applicable financial reporting framework]; or (ii) the financial report gives a true and fair view in accordance with [the applicable financial reporting framework]; and

(b) When expressing an unmodified opinion on a financial report prepared in accordance with a compliance framework, the auditor's opinion states that the financial report is prepared, in all material respects, in accordance with [the applicable financial reporting framework].

A9. In the case of a single financial statement or of a specific element of a financial statement, the applicable financial reporting framework may not explicitly address the presentation of the financial statement or of the element. This may be the case when the applicable financial reporting framework is based on a financial reporting framework established by an authorised or recognised standards setting organisation for the preparation of a complete set of financial statements (for example, Australian Accounting Standards). The auditor therefore considers whether the expected form of opinion is appropriate in the light of the applicable financial reporting framework. Factors that may affect the auditor's consideration as to whether to use the phrases "presents fairly, in all material respects," or "gives a true and fair view" in the auditor's opinion include:

- Whether the applicable financial reporting framework is explicitly or implicitly restricted to the preparation of a financial report.
- Whether the single financial statement or the specific element of a financial statement will:
  - Comply fully with each of those requirements of the framework relevant to the particular financial statement or the particular element, and the presentation of the financial statement or the element include the related notes.
  - If necessary to achieve fair presentation, provide disclosures beyond those specifically required by the framework or, in exceptional circumstances, depart from a requirement of the framework.

The auditor's decision as to the expected form of opinion is a matter of professional judgement. It may be affected by whether use of the phrases "presents fairly, in all material respects," or "gives a true and fair view", in the auditor's opinion on a single financial statement or on a specific element of a financial statement prepared in accordance with a fair presentation framework, is generally accepted in the particular jurisdiction.

Considerations When Planning and Performing the Audit (Ref: Para. 10)

A10. The relevance of each of the Australian Auditing Standards requires careful consideration. Even when only a specific element of a financial statement is the subject of the audit, Australian Auditing Standards such as ASA 240,[18] ASA 550,[19] and ASA 570 are, in principle, relevant. This is because the element could be misstated as a result of fraud, the effect of related party transactions, or the incorrect application of the going concern assumption under the applicable financial reporting framework.

A11. Furthermore, Australian Auditing Standards are written in the context of an audit of a financial report they are to be applied as necessary in the circumstances to the audit of

16 See ASA 200, paragraph 8.

17 See ASA 700, paragraphs 35-36.

18 See ASA 240 *The Auditor's Responsibilities Relating to Fraud in an Audit of a Financial Report.*

19 See ASA 550 *Related Parties.*

a single financial statement or of a specific element of a financial statement.[20] For example, written representations from management, and where appropriate, those charged with governance, about the financial report would be replaced by written representations about the presentation of the financial statement or the element in accordance with the applicable financial reporting framework.

A12. When auditing a single financial statement or a specific element of a financial statement in conjunction with the audit of the entity's financial report, the auditor may be able to use audit evidence obtained as part of the audit of the entity's financial report in the audit of the financial statement or the element. Australian Auditing Standards, however, require the auditor to plan and perform the audit of the financial statement or element to obtain sufficient appropriate audit evidence on which to base the opinion on the financial statement or on the element.

A13. The individual financial statements that comprise a financial report, and many of the elements of that financial report, including their related notes, are interrelated. Accordingly, when auditing a single financial statement or a specific element of a financial statement, the auditor may not be able to consider the financial statement or the element in isolation. Consequently, the auditor may need to perform procedures in relation to the interrelated items to meet the objective of the audit.

A14. Furthermore, the materiality determined for a single financial statement or for a specific element of a financial statement may be lower than the materiality determined for the entity's financial report; this will affect the nature, timing and extent of the audit procedures and the evaluation of uncorrected misstatements.

Forming an Opinion and Reporting Considerations (Ref: Para. 11)

A15. ASA 700 requires the auditor, in forming an opinion, to evaluate whether the financial report provides adequate disclosures to enable the intended users to understand the effect of material transactions and events on the information conveyed in the financial report.[21] In the case of a single financial statement or of a specific element of a financial statement, it is important that the financial statement or the element, including the related notes, in view of the requirements of the applicable financial reporting framework, provides adequate disclosures to enable the intended users to understand the information conveyed in the financial statement or the element, and the effect of material transactions and events on the information conveyed in the financial statement or the element.

A16. Appendix 2 of this Auditing Standard contains illustrations of auditors' reports on a single financial statement and on a specific element of a financial statement.

Modified Opinion, Emphasis of Matter Paragraph or Other Matter Paragraph in the Auditor's Report on the Entity's Financial Report (Ref: Para. 14-15)

A17. Even when the modified opinion on the entity's financial report, Emphasis of Matter paragraph or Other Matter paragraph does not relate to the audited financial statement or the audited element, the auditor may still deem it appropriate to refer to the modification in an Other Matter paragraph in an auditor's report on the financial statement or on the element because the auditor judges it to be relevant to the users' understanding of the audited financial statement or the audited element or the related auditor's report (see ASA 706).[22]

A18. [Deleted by the AUASB as not applicable in Australia.][23]

❖❖❖

20 See ASA 200, paragraph 2.

21 See ASA 700, paragraph 13(e).

22 See ASA 706 *Emphasis of Matter Paragraphs and Other Matter Paragraphs in the Independent Auditor's Report*, paragraph 6.

23 See ASA 510 *Initial Audit Engagements—Opening Balances*, Appendix 1, Illustration 2, and ASA 705, paragraph A16.

Conformity with International Standards on Auditing

This Auditing Standard conforms with International Standard on Auditing ISA 805 *Special Considerations—Audits of Single Financial Statements and Specific Elements, Accounts or Items of a Financial Statement* issued by the International Auditing and Assurance Standards Board (IAASB), an independent standard-setting board of the International Federation of Accountants (IFAC).

Paragraphs that have been added to this Auditing Standard (and do not appear in the text of the equivalent ISA) are identified with the prefix "Aus".

Compliance with this Auditing Standard enables compliance with ISA 805.

Appendix 1

(Ref: Para. A3)

Examples of Specific Elements, Accounts or Items of a Financial Statement

- Accounts receivable, allowance for doubtful accounts receivable, inventory, the liability for accrued benefits of a superannuation fund, the recorded value of identified intangible assets, or the liability for "incurred but not reported" claims in an insurance portfolio, including related notes.
- A schedule of externally managed assets and income of a private superannuation fund, including related notes.
- A schedule of net tangible assets, including related notes.
- A schedule of disbursements in relation to a lease property, including explanatory notes.
- A schedule of profit participation or employee bonuses, including explanatory notes.

Appendix 2

(Ref: Para. A16)

Illustrations of Auditors' Reports on a Single Financial Statement and on a Specific Element of a Financial Statement

- Illustration 1: An auditor's report on a single financial statement prepared in accordance with a general purpose framework (for purposes of this illustration, a fair presentation framework).
- Illustration 2: An auditor's report on a single financial statement prepared in accordance with a special purpose framework (for purposes of this illustration, a fair presentation framework).
- Illustration 3: An auditor's report on a specific element, account or item of a financial statement prepared in accordance with a special purpose framework (for purposes of this illustration, a compliance framework).

Example Auditor's Report General Purpose Financial Statement—Statement of Financial Position (Fair Presentation Framework)

Illustration 1:

Circumstances include the following:

- **Audit of a statement of financial position (that is, a single financial statement).**
- **The statement of financial position has been prepared by management of the entity in accordance with the requirements of the Financial Reporting Framework of Jurisdiction X using the basis of preparation described in Note X to the statement of financial position.**
- **The applicable financial reporting framework is a fair presentation framework designed to meet the common financial information needs of a wide range of users.**
- **The single financial statement is *not* prepared under the *Corporations Act 2001*.**
- **The terms of the audit engagement reflect the description of management's responsibility for the single financial statement in ASA 210.**
- **The auditor has determined that it is appropriate to use the phrase "presents fairly, in all material respects", in the auditor's opinion.**

INDEPENDENT AUDITOR'S REPORT

[Appropriate Addressee]

We have audited the accompanying statement of financial position of ABC Entity as at 30 June 20X1, a summary of significant accounting policies and other explanatory information, and management's assertion statement* (together "the financial statement"). The financial statement has been prepared by management using the basis of preparation described in Note X.

Management's[24] Responsibility for the Financial Statement

Management is responsible for the preparation and fair presentation of the financial statement in accordance with the basis of accounting described in Note X, and for such internal control as management determines is necessary to enable the preparation of the financial statement that is free from material misstatement, whether due to fraud or error.

Auditor's Responsibility

Our responsibility is to express an opinion on the financial statement based on our audit. We conducted our audit in accordance with Australian Auditing Standards. Those standards require that we comply with relevant ethical requirements and plan and perform the audit to obtain reasonable assurance about whether the financial statement is free from material misstatement.

An audit involves performing procedures to obtain audit evidence about the amounts and disclosures in the financial statement. The procedures selected depend on the auditor's judgement, including the assessment of the risks of material misstatement of the financial statement, whether due to fraud or error. In making those risk assessments, the auditor considers internal control relevant to the entity's preparation and fair presentation of the financial statement in order to design audit procedures that are appropriate in the circumstances, but not for the purpose of

* Or other appropriate term.

24 Or other term that is appropriate in the context of the legal framework in the particular jurisdiction.

expressing an opinion on the effectiveness of the entity's internal control.[25] An audit also includes evaluating the appropriateness of accounting policies used and the reasonableness of accounting estimates, if any, made by management, as well as evaluating the overall presentation of the financial statement.

We believe that the audit evidence we have obtained is sufficient and appropriate to provide a basis for our audit opinion.

Opinion

In our opinion, the financial statement presents fairly, in all material respects, the financial position of ABC Entity as at 30 June 20X1 in accordance with the basis of preparation described in Note X.

[Auditor's signature]*

[Date of the auditor's report]#

[Auditor's address]

ASA

Example Auditor's Report
Special Purpose Financial Statement—Statement of Cash Receipts and Disbursements (Fair Presentation Framework)

Illustration 2:

Circumstances include the following:

- **Audit of a statement of cash receipts and disbursements (that is, a single financial statement).**
- **The financial statement has been prepared by management of the entity in accordance with the cash receipts and disbursements basis of accounting to respond to a request for cash flow information received from a creditor. Management has a choice of financial reporting frameworks.**
- **The applicable financial reporting framework is a fair presentation framework designed to meet the financial information needs of specific users.[26]**
- **The single financial statement is *not* prepared under the *Corporations Act 2001*.**
- **The auditor has determined that it is appropriate to use the phrase "presents fairly, in all material respects", in the auditor's opinion.**
- **Distribution or use of the auditor's report is not restricted.**

INDEPENDENT AUDITOR'S REPORT

[Appropriate Addressee]

We have audited the accompanying statement of cash receipts and disbursements of ABC Entity for the year ended 30 June 20X1, a summary of significant accounting policies and other explanatory information, and management's assertion statement** (together "the financial statement"). The financial statement has been prepared by management using the cash receipts and disbursements basis of accounting described in Note X.

---

25 In circumstances when the auditor also has responsibility to express an opinion on the effectiveness of internal control in conjunction with the audit of the financial statement, this sentence would be worded as follows: "In making those risk assessments, the auditor considers internal control relevant to the entity's preparation and fair presentation of the financial statement in order to design audit procedures that are appropriate in the circumstances."

* The auditor's report needs to be signed in one or more of the following ways: name of the audit firm, the name of the audit company or the personal name of the auditor as appropriate.

\# The date of the auditor's report is the date the auditor signs the report.

26 See ASA 800, which contains requirements and guidance on the form and content of an auditor's report prepared in accordance with a special purpose framework.

** Or other appropriate term.

Management's[27] Responsibility for the Financial Statement

Management is responsible for the preparation and fair presentation of the financial statement in accordance basis of accounting described in Note X; this includes determining that the cash receipts and disbursements basis of accounting is an acceptable basis for the preparation of the financial statement in the circumstances, and for such internal control as management determines is necessary to enable the preparation of a financial statement that is free from material misstatement, whether due to fraud or error.

Auditor's Responsibility

Our responsibility is to express an opinion on the financial statement based on our audit. We conducted our audit in accordance with Australian Auditing Standards. Those standards require that we comply with relevant ethical requirements and plan and perform the audit to obtain reasonable assurance about whether the financial statement is free from material misstatement.

An audit involves performing procedures to obtain audit evidence about the amounts and disclosures in the financial statement. The procedures selected depend on the auditor's judgement, including the assessment of the risks of material misstatement of the financial statement, whether due to fraud or error. In making those risk assessments, the auditor considers internal control relevant to the entity's preparation and fair presentation of the financial statement in order to design audit procedures that are appropriate in the circumstances, but not for the purpose of expressing an opinion on the effectiveness of the entity's internal control. An audit also includes evaluating the appropriateness of accounting policies used and the reasonableness of accounting estimates, if any, made by management, as well as evaluating the overall presentation of the financial statement.

We believe that the audit evidence we have obtained is sufficient and appropriate to provide a basis for our audit opinion.

Opinion

In our opinion, the financial statement presents fairly, in all material respects, the cash receipts and disbursements of ABC Entity for the year ended 30 June 20X1 in accordance with the cash receipts and disbursements basis of accounting described in Note X.

Basis of Accounting

Without modifying our opinion, we draw attention to Note X to the financial statement, which describes the basis of accounting. The financial statement is prepared to provide information to XYZ Creditor. As a result, the financial statement may not be suitable for another purpose.

[Auditor's signature]†

[Date of the auditor's report]#

[Auditor's address]

27 Or other term that is appropriate in the context of the legal framework in the particular jurisdiction.

† The auditor's report needs to be signed in one or more of the following ways: name of the audit firm, the name of the audit company or the personal name of the auditor as appropriate.

The date of the auditor's report is the date the auditor signs the report.

Example Auditor's Report Special Purpose Financial Statement—Liability Incurred but Not Reported Schedule (Compliance Framework)

Illustration 3:

Circumstances include the following:

- **Audit of the liability for "incurred but not reported" claims in an insurance portfolio (that is, an element, account or item of a financial statement).**
- **The financial information has been prepared by management of the entity in accordance with the financial reporting provisions established by a regulatory authority to meet the requirements of that authority. Management does not have a choice of financial reporting frameworks.**
- **The applicable financial reporting framework is a compliance framework designed to meet the financial information needs of specific users.[28]**
- **The schedule is *not* prepared under the *Corporations Act 2001*.**
- **The terms of the audit engagement reflect the description of management's responsibility for the financial statement in ASA 210.**
- **Distribution or use of the auditor's report is restricted.**

INDEPENDENT AUDITOR'S REPORT

[Appropriate Addressee]

We have audited the accompanying schedule of the liability for "incurred but not reported" claims of ABC Insurance Company as at 30 June 20X1, and management's assertion statement* ("the schedule"). The schedule has been prepared by management based on [describe the financial reporting provisions established by the regulatory authority].

Management's[29] Responsibility for the Schedule

Management is responsible for the preparation of the schedule in accordance with [describe the financial reporting provisions established by the regulatory authority], and for such internal control as management determines is necessary to enable the preparation of the schedule that is free from material misstatement, whether due to fraud or error.

Auditor's Responsibility

Our responsibility is to express an opinion on the schedule based on our audit. We conducted our audit in accordance with Australian Auditing Standards. Those standards require that we comply with relevant ethical requirements and plan and perform the audit to obtain reasonable assurance about whether the schedule is free from material misstatement.

An audit involves performing procedures to obtain audit evidence about the amounts and disclosures in the schedule. The procedures selected depend on the auditor's judgement, including the assessment of the risks of material misstatement of the schedule, whether due to fraud or error. In making those risk assessments, the auditor considers internal control relevant to the company's preparation of the schedule in order to design audit procedures that are appropriate in the circumstances, but not for the purpose of expressing an opinion on the effectiveness of the company's internal control. An audit also includes evaluating the appropriateness of accounting policies used and the reasonableness of accounting estimates made by management, as well as evaluating the overall presentation of the schedule.

We believe that the audit evidence we have obtained is sufficient and appropriate to provide a basis for our audit opinion.

28 See ASA 800, which contains requirements and guidance on the form and content of an auditor's report prepared in accordance with a special purpose framework.

* Or other appropriate term.

29 Or other term that is appropriate in the context of the legal framework in the particular jurisdiction.

Opinion

In our opinion, the financial information in the schedule of the liability for "incurred but not reported" claims of ABC Insurance Company as at 30 June 20X1 is prepared, in all material respects, in accordance with [describe the financial reporting provisions established by the regulatory authority].

Basis of Accounting and Restriction on Distribution

Without modifying our opinion, we draw attention to Note X to the schedule, which describes the basis of accounting. The schedule is prepared to assist ABC Insurance Company to meet the requirements of Regulator DEF. As a result, the schedule may not be suitable for another purpose. Our report is intended solely for ABC Insurance Company and Regulator DEF and should not be distributed to parties other than ABC Insurance Company or Regulator DEF.

[Auditor's signature]*

[Date of the auditor's report]#

[Auditor's address]

* The auditor's report needs to be signed in one or more of the following ways: name of the audit firm, the name of the audit company or the personal name of the auditor as appropriate.

The date of the auditor's report is the date the auditor signs the report.

ASA 810

Engagements to Report on Summary Financial Statements

(Issued October 2009)

Issued by the Auditing and Assurance Standards Board.

Note from the Institute of Chartered Accountants Australia

This note, prepared by the technical editor, is not part of ASA 805.

Historical development

October 2009: ASA 810 issued as part of the AUASB's Clarity Project. ASA 810 deals with the auditor's responsibilities in connection with a report on summary financial statements derived from a full financial report he or she has already audited. It is based on ISA 810 of the same name. Requirements covering these engagements were previously included in ASA 800, 'The Auditor's Report on Special Purpose Audit Engagements'.

Contents

Preface

Reasons for Issuing Auditing Standard ASA 810 *Engagements to Report on Summary Financial Statements*

The Auditing and Assurance Standards Board (AUASB) issues Auditing Standard ASA 810 *Engagements to Report on Summary Financial Statements* pursuant to the requirements of the legislative provisions and the Strategic Direction explained below.

The AUASB is an independent statutory board of the Australian Government established under section 227A of the *Australian Securities and Investments Commission Act 2001*, as amended (ASIC Act). Under section 227B of the ASIC Act, the AUASB may formulate Auditing Standards for other purposes.

Under the Strategic Direction given to the AUASB by the Financial Reporting Council (FRC), the AUASB is required to have regard to any programme initiated by the International Auditing and Assurance Standards Board (IAASB) for the revision and enhancement of the International Standards on Auditing (ISAs) and to make appropriate consequential amendments to the Australian Auditing Standards. Accordingly, the AUASB has decided to revise and redraft the Australian Auditing Standards using the equivalent redrafted ISAs.

ASA

Main Features

This Auditing Standard establishes requirements and provides application and other explanatory material regarding the auditor's responsibilities relating to undertaking an engagement to report on summary financial statements derived from a financial report audited in accordance with Australian Auditing Standards by that same auditor.

This Auditing Standard:

(a) establishes the engagement acceptance terms for the auditor;

(b) sets out the nature of audit procedures in respect of summary financial statements;

(c) deals with the timing of the auditor's work, and events subsequent to the auditor's report on the audited financial report; and

(d) sets out the form of the auditor's opinion.

Authority Statement

The Auditing and Assurance Standards Board (AUASB) formulates this Auditing Standard ASA 810 *Engagements to Report on Summary Financial Statements* pursuant to section 227B of the *Australian Securities and Investments Commission Act 2001.*

This Auditing Standard is to be read in conjunction with ASA 101 *Preamble to Australian Auditing Standards*, which sets out the intentions of the AUASB on how the Australian Auditing Standards, operative for financial reporting periods commencing on or after 1 January 2010, are to be understood, interpreted and applied. This Auditing Standard is to be read also in conjunction with ASA 200 *Overall Objectives of the Independent Auditor and the Conduct of the Audit in Accordance with Australian Accounting Standards.*

Dated: 27 October 2009

M H Kelsall
Chairman - AUASB

Auditing Standard ASA 810

Engagements to Report on Summary Financial Statements

Application

Aus 0.1 This Auditing Standard applies to an auditor's responsibilities to report on summary financial statements that are derived from a financial report, or a complete set of financial statements, audited in accordance with Australian Auditing Standards, by that same auditor.

Operative Date

Aus 0.2 This Auditing Standard is operative for financial reporting periods commencing on or after 1 January 2010.

Introduction

Scope of this Auditing Standard

1. This Auditing Standard deals with the auditor's responsibilities relating to undertaking an engagement to report on summary financial statements derived from a financial report audited in accordance with Australian Auditing Standards by that same auditor.

Aus 1.1 Auditors that are required to issue an auditor's report on a concise financial report prepared under the *Corporations Act 2001* and Accounting Standard AASB 1039 *Concise Financial Reports* should refer to guidance contained in GS 001 *Concise Financial Reports*.*

Effective Date

2. [Deleted by the AUASB. Refer Aus 0.2]

Objectives

3. The objectives of the auditor are:
   (a) To determine whether it is appropriate to accept the engagement to report on summary financial statements;
   (b) If engaged to report on summary financial statements:
      (i) To form an opinion on the summary financial statements based on an evaluation of the conclusions drawn from the evidence obtained; and
      (ii) To express clearly that opinion through a written report that also describes the basis for that opinion.

Definitions

4. For purposes of this Auditing Standard, the following terms have the meanings attributed below:
   (a) Applied criteria means the criteria applied by management in the preparation of the summary financial statements.
   (b) Audited financial report means a financial report[1] audited by the auditor in accordance with Australian Auditing Standards, and from which the summary financial statements are derived.
   (c) [Deleted by the AUASB. Refer Aus 4.1]

* Issued by the Auditing and Assurance Standards Board (December 2008).

1 See ASA 200 *Overall Objectives of the Independent Auditor and the Conduct of an Audit in Accordance with Australian Auditing Standards*, paragraphs Aus 13.1, Aus 13.2, Aus 13.3, and Aus 13.4.

Aus 4.1 Summary financial statements means historical financial information that is derived from a financial report, but that contains less detail than the financial report, while still providing a structured representation consistent with that provided by the financial report, of the entity's economic resources or obligations at a point in time or the changes therein for a period of time.[2] Summary financial statements may include an assertion by those responsible for the summary financial statements. Different jurisdictions may use different terminology to describe such historical financial information.

Requirements

Engagement Acceptance

5. The auditor shall accept an engagement to report on summary financial statements in accordance with this Auditing Standard only when the auditor has been engaged to conduct an audit in accordance with Australian Auditing Standards of the financial report from which the summary financial statements are derived. (Ref: Para. A1)

6. Before accepting an engagement to report on summary financial statements, the auditor shall: (Ref: Para. A2)
   (a) Determine whether the applied criteria are acceptable; (Ref: Para. A3-A7)
   (b) Obtain the agreement of management that it acknowledges and understands its responsibility:
      (i) For the preparation of the summary financial statements in accordance with the applied criteria;
      (ii) To make the audited financial report available to the intended users of the summary financial statements without undue difficulty (or, if law or regulation provides that the audited financial report need not be made available to the intended users of the summary financial statements and establishes the criteria for the preparation of the summary financial statements, to describe that law or regulation in the summary financial statements); and
      (iii) To include the auditor's report on the summary financial statements in any document that contains the summary financial statements and that indicates that the auditor has reported on them.
   (c) Agree with management the form of opinion to be expressed on the summary financial statements (see paragraphs 9-11 of this Auditing Standard).

7. If the auditor concludes that the applied criteria are unacceptable or is unable to obtain the agreement of management set out in paragraph 6(b) of this Auditing Standard, the auditor shall not accept the engagement to report on the summary financial statements, unless required by law or regulation to do so. An engagement conducted in accordance with such law or regulation does not comply with this Auditing Standard. Accordingly, the auditor's report on the summary financial statements shall not indicate that the engagement was conducted in accordance with this Auditing Standard. The auditor shall include appropriate reference to this fact in the terms of the engagement. The auditor shall also determine the effect that this may have on the engagement to audit the financial report from which the summary financial statements are derived.

Nature of Procedures

8. The auditor shall perform the following procedures, and any other procedures that the auditor may consider necessary, as the basis for the auditor's opinion on the summary financial statements:
   (a) Evaluate whether the summary financial statements adequately disclose their summarised nature and identify the audited financial report.

2 See ASA 200, paragraph Aus 13.2.

(b) When summary financial statements are not accompanied by the audited financial report, evaluate whether they describe clearly:
   (i) From whom or where the audited financial report is available; or
   (ii) The law or regulation that specifies that the audited financial report need not be made available to the intended users of the summary financial statements and establishes the criteria for the preparation of the summary financial statements.

(c) Evaluate whether the summary financial statements adequately disclose the applied criteria.

(d) Compare the summary financial statements with the related information in the audited financial report to determine whether the summary financial statements agree with, or can be recalculated from, the related information in the audited financial report.

(e) Evaluate whether the summary financial statements are prepared in accordance with the applied criteria.

(f) Evaluate, in view of the purpose of the summary financial statements, whether the summary financial statements contain the information necessary, and are at an appropriate level of aggregation, so as not to be misleading in the circumstances.

(g) Evaluate whether the audited financial report is available to the intended users of the summary financial statements without undue difficulty, unless law or regulation provides that they need not be made available and establishes the criteria for the preparation of the summary financial statements. (Ref: Para. A8)

Form of Opinion

9. When the auditor has concluded that an unmodified opinion on the summary financial statements is appropriate, the auditor's opinion shall, unless otherwise required by law or regulation, use one of the following phrases: (Ref: Para. A9)
   (a) The summary financial statements are consistent, in all material respects, with the audited financial report, in accordance with [the applied criteria]; or
   (b) The summary financial statements are a fair summary of the audited financial report, in accordance with [the applied criteria].

10. If law or regulation prescribes the wording of the opinion on summary financial statements in terms that are different from those described in paragraph 9 of this Auditing Standard, the auditor shall:
   (a) Apply the procedures described in paragraph 8 of this Auditing Standard and any further procedures necessary to enable the auditor to express the prescribed opinion; and
   (b) Evaluate whether users of the summary financial statements might misunderstand the auditor's opinion on the summary financial statements and, if so, whether additional explanation in the auditor's report on the summary financial statements can mitigate possible misunderstanding.

11. If, in the case of paragraph 10(b) of this Auditing Standard, the auditor concludes that additional explanation in the auditor's report on the summary financial statements cannot mitigate possible misunderstanding, the auditor shall not accept the engagement, unless required by law or regulation to do so. An engagement conducted in accordance with such law or regulation does not comply with this Auditing Standard. Accordingly, the auditor's report on the summary financial statements shall not indicate that the engagement was conducted in accordance with this Auditing Standard.

Timing of Work and Events Subsequent to the Date of the Auditor's Report on the Audited Financial Report

12. The auditor's report on the summary financial statements may be dated later than the date of the auditor's report on the audited financial report. In such cases, the auditor's report on the summary financial statements shall state that the summary financial statements and audited financial report do not reflect the effects of events that occurred subsequent to the

date of the auditor's report on the audited financial report that may require adjustment of, or disclosure in, the audited financial report. (Ref: Para. A10)

13. The auditor may become aware of facts that existed at the date of the auditor's report on the audited financial report, but of which the auditor previously was unaware. In such cases, the auditor shall not issue the auditor's report on the summary financial statements until the auditor's consideration of such facts in relation to the audited financial report in accordance with ASA 560[3] has been completed.

Auditor's Report on Summary Financial Statements

Elements of the Auditor's Report

14. The auditor's report on summary financial statements shall include the following elements:[4] (Ref: Para. A15)
   (a) A title clearly indicating it as the report of an independent auditor. (Ref: Para. A11)
   (b) An addressee. (Ref: Para. A12)
   (c) An introductory paragraph that:
      (i) Identifies the summary financial statements on which the auditor is reporting, including the title of each statement included in the summary financial statements; (Ref: Para. A13)
      (ii) Identifies the audited financial report;
      (iii) Refers to the auditor's report on the audited financial report, the date of that report, and, subject to paragraphs Aus 14.1 and 17-18 of this Auditing Standard, the fact that an unmodified opinion is expressed on the audited financial report;
      (iv) If the date of the auditor's report on the summary financial statements is later than the date of the auditor's report on the audited financial report, states that the summary financial statements and the audited financial report do not reflect the effects of events that occurred subsequent to the date of the auditor's report on the audited financial report; and
      (v) A statement indicating that the summary financial statements do not contain all the disclosures required by the financial reporting framework applied in the preparation of the audited financial report, and that reading the summary financial statements is not a substitute for reading the audited financial report.
   (d) A description of management's[5] responsibility for the financial statements, explaining that management[6] is responsible for the preparation of the summary financial statements in accordance with the applied criteria.
   (e) A statement that the auditor is responsible for expressing an opinion on the summary financial statements based on procedures required by this Auditing Standard.
   (f) A paragraph clearly expressing an opinion (see paragraphs 9-11 of this Auditing Standard).
   (g) The auditor's signature.
   (h) The date of the auditor's report. (Ref: Para. A14)
   (i) The auditor's address.

Aus 14.1 In circumstances where the auditor's report on the audited financial report has been modified, paragraphs 17-18 of this Auditing Standard require additional elements to be included in the auditor's report on the summary financial statements.

15. If the addressee of the summary financial statements is not the same as the addressee of the auditor's report on the audited financial report, the auditor shall evaluate the appropriateness of using a different addressee. (Ref: Para. A12)

---

3 See ASA 560 *Subsequent Events*.

4 [Footnote deleted by the AUASB. Refer Aus 14.1]

5 Or other term that is appropriate in the context of the legal framework in the jurisdiction.

6 Or other term that is appropriate in the context of the legal framework in the jurisdiction.

16. The auditor shall date the auditor's report on the summary financial statements no earlier than: (Ref: Para. A14)

    (a) The date on which the auditor has obtained sufficient appropriate evidence on which to base the opinion, including evidence that the summary financial statements have been prepared and those with the recognised authority have asserted that they have taken responsibility for them; and

    (b) The date of the auditor's report on the audited financial report.

Modifications to the Opinion, Emphasis of Matter Paragraph or Other Matter Paragraph in the Auditor's Report on the Audited Financial Report (Ref: Para. A15)

17. When the auditor's report on the audited financial report contains a qualified opinion, an Emphasis of Matter paragraph, or an Other Matter paragraph, but the auditor is satisfied that the summary financial statements are consistent, in all material respects, with or are a fair summary of the audited financial report, in accordance with the applied criteria, the auditor's report on the summary financial statements shall, in addition to the elements in paragraph 14 of this Auditing Standard:

    (a) State that the auditor's report on the audited financial report contains a qualified opinion, an Emphasis of Matter paragraph, or an Other Matter paragraph; and

    (b) Describe:

        (i) The basis for the qualified opinion on the audited financial report, and that qualified opinion; or the Emphasis of Matter or the Other Matter paragraph in the auditor's report on the audited financial report; and

        (ii) The effect thereof on the summary financial statements, if any.

18. When the auditor's report on the audited financial report contains an adverse opinion or a disclaimer of opinion, the auditor's report on the summary financial statements shall, in addition to the elements in paragraphs 14 and Aus 14.1 of this Auditing Standard:

    (a) State that the auditor's report on the audited financial report contains an adverse opinion or disclaimer of opinion;

    (b) Describe the basis for that adverse opinion or disclaimer of opinion; and

    (c) State that, as a result of the adverse opinion or disclaimer of opinion, it is inappropriate to express an opinion on the summary financial statements.

Modified Opinion on the Summary Financial Statements

19. If the summary financial statements are not consistent, in all material respects with, or are not a fair summary of, the audited financial report, in accordance with the applied criteria, and management does not agree to make the necessary changes, the auditor shall express an adverse opinion on the summary financial statements. (Ref: Para. A15)

Restriction on Distribution or Use or Alerting Readers to the Basis of Accounting

20. When distribution or use of the auditor's report on the audited financial report is restricted, or the auditor's report on the audited financial report alerts readers that the audited financial report is prepared in accordance with a special purpose framework, the auditor shall include a similar restriction or alert in the auditor's report on the summary financial statements.

Comparatives

21. If the audited financial report contains comparatives, but the summary financial statements do not, the auditor shall determine whether such omission is reasonable in the circumstances of the engagement. The auditor shall determine the effect of an unreasonable omission on the auditor's report on the summary financial statements. (Ref: Para. A16)

22. If the summary financial statements contain comparatives that were reported on by another auditor, the auditor's report on the summary financial statements shall also contain the

matters that ASA 710 requires the auditor to include in the auditor's report on the audited financial report.[7] (Ref: Para. A17)

Unaudited Supplementary Information Presented with Summary Financial Statements

23. The auditor shall evaluate whether any unaudited supplementary information presented with the summary financial statements is clearly differentiated from the summary financial statements. If the auditor concludes that the entity's presentation of the unaudited supplementary information is not clearly differentiated from the summary financial statements, the auditor shall ask management to change the presentation of the unaudited supplementary information. If management refuses to do so, the auditor shall explain in the auditor's report on the summary financial statements that such information is not covered by that report. (Ref: Para. A18-Aus A18.1)

Other Information in Documents Containing Summary Financial Statements

24. The auditor shall read other information included in a document containing the summary financial statements and related auditor's report to identify material inconsistencies, if any, with the summary financial statements. If, on reading the other information, the auditor identifies a material inconsistency, the auditor shall determine whether the summary financial statements or the other information needs to be revised. If, on reading the other information, the auditor becomes aware of an apparent material misstatement of fact, the auditor shall discuss the matter with management. (Ref: Para. 19-Aus A19.1)

Auditor Association

25. If the auditor becomes aware that the entity plans to state that the auditor has reported on summary financial statements in a document containing the summary financial statements, but does not plan to include the related auditor's report, the auditor shall request management to include the auditor's report in the document. If management does not do so, the auditor shall determine and carry out other appropriate actions designed to prevent management from inappropriately associating the auditor with the summary financial statements in that document. (Ref: Para. A20)

26. The auditor may be engaged to report on the financial report of an entity, while not engaged to report on the summary financial statements. If, in this case, the auditor becomes aware that the entity plans to make a statement in a document that refers to the auditor and the fact that summary financial statements are derived from the financial report audited by the auditor, the auditor shall be satisfied that:

    (a) The reference to the auditor is made in the context of the auditor's report on the audited financial report; and

    (b) The statement does not give the impression that the auditor has reported on the summary financial statements.

    If (a) or (b) are not met, the auditor shall request management to change the statement to meet them, or not to refer to the auditor in the document. Alternatively, the entity may engage the auditor to report on the summary financial statements and include the related auditor's report in the document. If management, and where appropriate those charged with governance, does not change the statement, delete the reference to the auditor, or include an auditor's report on the summary financial statements in the document containing the summary financial statements, the auditor shall advise management, and where appropriate those charged with governance, that the auditor disagrees with the reference to the auditor, and the auditor shall determine and carry out other appropriate actions designed to prevent management from inappropriately referring to the auditor. (Ref: Para. A20)

❖ ❖ ❖

7 See ASA 710 *Comparative Information—Corresponding Figures and Comparative Financial Reports.*

Application and Other Explanatory Material

Engagement Acceptance (Ref: Para. 5-6)

A1. The audit of the financial report from which the summary financial statements are derived provides the auditor with the necessary knowledge to discharge the auditor's responsibilities in relation to the summary financial statements in accordance with this Auditing Standard. Application of this Auditing Standard will not provide sufficient appropriate evidence on which to base the opinion on the summary financial statements if the auditor has not also audited the financial report from which the summary financial statements are derived.

A2. Management's agreement with the matters described in paragraph 6 may be evidenced by its written acceptance of the terms of the engagement.

Criteria (Ref: Para. 6(a))

A3. The preparation of summary financial statements requires management to determine the information that needs to be reflected in the summary financial statements so that they are consistent, in all material respects, with or represent a fair summary of the audited financial report. Because summary financial statements by their nature contain aggregated information and limited disclosure, there is an increased risk that they may not contain the information necessary so as not to be misleading in the circumstances. This risk increases when established criteria for the preparation of summary financial statements do not exist.

A4. Factors that may affect the auditor's determination of the acceptability of the applied criteria include:

- The nature of the entity;
- The purpose of the summary financial statements;
- The information needs of the intended users of the summary financial statements; and
- Whether the applied criteria will result in summary financial statements that are not misleading in the circumstances.

A5. The criteria for the preparation of summary financial statements may be established by an authorised or recognised standards-setting organisation or by law or regulation. Similar to the case of a financial report, as explained in ASA 210,[8] in many such cases, the auditor may presume that such criteria are acceptable.

A6. Where established criteria for the preparation of summary financial statements do not exist, criteria may be developed by management, for example, based on practice in a particular industry. Criteria that are acceptable in the circumstances will result in summary financial statements that:

(a) Adequately disclose their summarised nature and identify the audited financial report;

(b) Clearly describe from whom or where the audited financial report is available or, if law or regulation provides that the audited financial report need not be made available to the intended users of the summary financial statements and establishes the criteria for the preparation of the summary financial statements, that law or regulation;

(c) Adequately disclose the applied criteria;

(d) Agree with or can be recalculated from the related information in the audited financial report; and

(e) In view of the purpose of the summary financial statements, contain the information necessary, and are at an appropriate level of aggregation, so as not to be misleading in the circumstances.

A7. Adequate disclosure of the summarised nature of the summary financial statements and the identity of the audited financial report, as referred to in paragraph A6(a), may, for example, be provided by a title such as "Summary Financial Statements Prepared from the Audited Financial Report for the Year Ended 30 June 20X1."

8 See ASA 210 *Agreeing the Terms of Audit Engagements,* paragraphs A3 and A8-A9.

Evaluating the Availability of the Audited Financial Report (Ref: Para. 8(g))

A8. The auditor's evaluation whether the audited financial report is available to the intended users of the summary financial statements without undue difficulty is affected by factors such as whether:

- The summary financial statements describe clearly from whom or where the audited financial report is available;
- The audited financial report is on public record; or
- Management has established a process by which the intended users of the summary financial statements can obtain ready access to the audited financial report.

Form of Opinion (Ref: Para. 9)

A9. A conclusion, based on an evaluation of the evidence obtained by performing the procedures in paragraph 8, that an unmodified opinion on the summary financial statements is appropriate enables the auditor to express an opinion containing one of the phrases in paragraph 9. The auditor's decision as to which of the phrases to use may be affected by generally accepted practice in the particular jurisdiction.

Timing of Work and Events Subsequent to the Date of the Auditor's Report on the Audited Financial Report (Ref: Para. 12)

A10. The procedures described in paragraph 8 are often performed during or immediately after the audit of the financial report. When the auditor reports on the summary financial statements after the completion of the audit of the financial report, the auditor is not required to obtain additional audit evidence on the audited financial report, or report on the effects of events that occurred subsequent to the date of the auditor's report on the audited financial report since the summary financial statements are derived from the audited financial report and does not update them.

Auditor's Report on Summary Financial Statements

Elements of the Auditor's Report

Title (Ref: Para. 14(a))

A11. A title indicating the report is the report of an independent auditor, for example, "Report of the Independent Auditor", affirms that the auditor has met all of the relevant ethical requirements regarding independence. This distinguishes the report of the independent auditor from reports issued by others.

Addressee (Ref: Para. 14(b), 15)

A12. Factors that may affect the auditor's evaluation of the appropriateness of the addressee of the summary financial statements include the terms of the engagement, the nature of the entity, and the purpose of the summary financial statements.

Introductory Paragraph (Ref: Para. 14(c)(i))

A13. When the auditor is aware that the summary financial statements will be included in a document that contains other information, the auditor may consider, if the form of presentation allows, identifying the page numbers on which the summary financial statements are presented. This helps readers to identify the summary financial statements to which the auditor's report relates.

Date of the Auditor's Report (Ref: Para. 14(h), 16)

A14. The person or persons with recognised authority to conclude that the summary financial statements have been prepared and take responsibility for them depends on the terms of the engagement, the nature of the entity, and the purpose of the summary financial statements.

***Illustrations** (Ref: Para. 14, 17-19)*

A15. Appendix 1 to this Auditing Standard contains illustrations of auditors' reports on summary financial statements that:

(a) Contain unmodified opinions;

(b) Are derived from audited financial reports on which the auditor issued modified opinions; and

(c) Contain a modified opinion.

Comparatives (Ref: Para. 21-22)

A16. If the audited financial report contains comparatives, there is a presumption that the summary financial statements also would contain comparatives. Comparatives in the audited financial report may be regarded as corresponding figures or as comparative financial information. ASA 710 describes how this difference affects the auditor's report on the financial report, including, in particular, reference to other auditors who audited the financial report for the prior period.

A17. Circumstances that may affect the auditor's determination whether an omission of comparatives is reasonable include the nature and objective of the summary financial statements, the applied criteria, and the information needs of the intended users of the summary financial statements.

Unaudited Supplementary Information Presented with Summary Financial Statements (Ref: Para. 23)

A18. [Deleted by the AUASB. Refer Aus A18.1]

Aus A18.1 ASA 700[9] contains requirements and guidance to be applied when unaudited supplementary information is presented with an audited financial report, which may be helpful in applying the requirement in paragraph 23.

Other Information in Documents Containing Summary Financial Statements (Ref: Para. 24)

A19. [Deleted by the AUASB. Refer Aus A19.1]

Aus A19.1 ASA 720[10] contains requirements and guidance relating to reading other information included in a document containing the audited financial report and related auditor's report, and responding to material inconsistencies and material misstatements of fact. They may be helpful in applying the requirement in paragraph 24.

Auditor Association (Ref: Para. 25-26)

A20. Other appropriate actions the auditor may take when management, and where appropriate those charged with governance, do not take the requested action may include informing the intended users and other known third-party users of the inappropriate reference to the auditor. The auditor's course of action depends on the auditor's legal rights and obligations. Consequently, the auditor may consider it appropriate to seek legal advice.

❖ ❖ ❖

9 See ASA 700 *Forming an Opinion and Reporting on the Financial Report*, paragraphs 46-47.

10 See ASA 720 *The Auditor's Responsibility Relating to Other Information in Documents Containing an Audited Financial Report.*

Conformity with International Standards on Auditing

This Auditing Standard conforms with International Standard on Auditing ISA 810 *Engagements to Report on Summary Financial Statements*, issued by the International Auditing and Assurance Standards Board (IAASB), an independent standard-setting board of the International Federation of Accountants (IFAC).

Paragraphs that have been added to this Auditing Standard (and do not appear in the text of the equivalent ISA) are identified with the prefix "Aus".

The following requirement is additional to ISA 810:

- In circumstances where the auditor's report on the audited financial report has been modified, paragraphs 17-18 of this Auditing Standard require additional elements to be included in the auditor's report on the summary financial statements. (Ref: Para. Aus 14.1)

Compliance with this Auditing Standard enables compliance with ISA 810.

Appendix 1

(Ref: Para. A15)

Illustrations of Auditors' Reports on Summary Financial Statements

- Illustration 1: An auditor's report containing an unmodified opinion on the summary financial statements prepared in accordance with established criteria. The auditor's report on the summary financial statements is dated later than the date of the auditor's report on the financial report from which summary financial statements are derived. An unmodified opinion is expressed on the audited financial report.
- Illustration 2: An auditor's report containing an unmodified opinion on the summary financial statements prepared in accordance with criteria developed by management and adequately disclosed in the summary financial statements. The auditor has determined that the applied criteria are acceptable in the circumstances. An unmodified opinion is expressed on the audited financial report.
- Illustration 3: An auditor's report containing a qualified opinion on the summary financial statements prepared in accordance with criteria developed by management and adequately disclosed in the summary financial statements. The auditor has determined that the applied criteria are acceptable in the circumstances. A qualified opinion is expressed on the audited financial report.
- Illustration 4: An auditor's report containing a disclaimer of opinion on the summary financial statements prepared in accordance with criteria developed by management and adequately disclosed in the summary financial statements. The auditor has determined that the applied criteria are acceptable in the circumstances. An adverse opinion is expressed on the audited financial report.
- Illustration 5: An auditor's report containing an adverse opinion on the summary financial statements prepared in accordance with established criteria. The auditor concludes that it is not possible to express an unmodified opinion on the summary financial statements. An unmodified opinion is expressed on the audited financial report.

Example Auditor's Report
Auditor's opinion on the financial report is unmodified Auditor's opinion on the summary financial statements is unmodified and dated later than the financial report opinion (Compliance Framework)

Illustration 1:

Circumstances include the following:

- **An unmodified opinion is expressed on the audited financial report.**
- **Established criteria exist for the preparation of summary financial statements.**
- **The auditor's report on the summary financial statements is dated later than the date of the auditor's report on the financial report from which the summary financial statements are derived.**
- **The summary financial statements are *not* prepared under the *Corporations Act 2001.***

REPORT OF THE INDEPENDENT AUDITOR ON THE SUMMARY FINANCIAL STATEMENTS

[Appropriate Addressee]

The accompanying summary financial statements, which comprises the summary statement of financial position as at 30 June 20X1, the summary statement of comprehensive income, summary statement of changes in equity and summary cash flow statement for the year then ended, related notes and management's assertion statement*, are derived from the audited financial report of ABC Entity for the year ended 30 June 20X1. We expressed an unmodified audit opinion on that financial report in our report dated 15 September 20X1. That financial report, and the summary financial statements, do not reflect the effects of events that occurred subsequent to the date of our report on that financial report.

The summary financial statements do not contain all the disclosures required by [describe financial reporting framework applied in the preparation of the audited financial report of ABC Entity]. Reading the summary financial statements, therefore, is not a substitute for reading the audited financial report of ABC Entity.

Management's[11] Responsibility for the Summary Financial Statements

Management is responsible for the preparation of a summary of the audited financial report in accordance with [describe established criteria].

Auditor's Responsibility

Our responsibility is to express an opinion on the summary financial statements based on our procedures, which were conducted in accordance with Auditing Standard ASA 810 *Engagements to Report on Summary Financial Statements*.

Opinion

In our opinion, the summary financial statements derived from the audited financial report of ABC Entity for the year ended 30 June 20X1 are consistent, in all material respects, with (or *a fair summary of*) that audited financial report, in accordance with [describe established criteria].

[Auditor's signature]**

[Date of the auditor's report]#

[Auditor's address]

---

* Or other appropriate term.

11 Or other term that is appropriate in the context of the legal framework in the particular jurisdiction.

** The auditor's report needs to be signed in one or more of the following ways: name of the audit firm, the name of the audit company or the personal name of the auditor as appropriate.

The date of the auditor's report is the date the auditor signs the report.

Example Auditor's Report
Auditor's opinion on the financial report is unmodified
Auditor's opinion on the summary financial statements is unmodified
(Compliance Framework)

Illustration 2:

Circumstances include the following:

- **An unmodified opinion is expressed on the audited financial report.**
- **Criteria are developed by management and adequately disclosed in Note X. The auditor has determined that the criteria are acceptable in the circumstances.**
- **The summary financial statements are *not* prepared under the *Corporations Act 2001*.**

ASA

REPORT OF THE INDEPENDENT AUDITOR ON THE SUMMARY FINANCIAL STATEMENTS

[Appropriate Addressee]

The accompanying summary financial statements, which comprises the summary statement of financial position as at 30 June 20X1, the summary statement of comprehensive income, summary statement of changes in equity and summary cash flow statement for the year then ended, related notes and management's assertion statement*, are derived from the audited financial report of ABC Entity for the year ended 30 June 20X1. We expressed an unmodified audit opinion on that financial report in our report dated 15 September 20X1.[12]

The summary financial statements do not contain all the disclosures required by [describe financial reporting framework applied in the preparation of the audited financial report of ABC Entity]. Reading the summary financial statements, therefore, is not a substitute for reading the audited financial report of ABC Entity.

Management's[13] Responsibility for the Summary Financial Statements

Management is responsible for the preparation of a summary of the audited financial report on the basis described in Note X.

Auditor's Responsibility

Our responsibility is to express an opinion on the summary financial statements based on our procedures, which were conducted in accordance with Auditing Standard ASA 810 *Engagements to Report on Summary Financial Statements*.

Opinion

In our opinion, the summary financial statements derived from the audited financial report of ABC Entity for the year ended 30 June 20X1 are consistent, in all material respects, with (or *a fair summary of*) that audited financial report, on the basis described in Note X.

[Auditor's signature]**

[Date of the auditor's report]#

[Auditor's address]

---

* Or other appropriate term.

12 When the auditor's report on the summary financial statements is dated later than the date of the auditor's report on the audited financial report from which they are derived, the following sentence is added to this paragraph: "That audited financial report, and the summary financial statements, do not reflect the effects of events that occurred subsequent to the date of our report on that audited financial report."

13 Or other term that is appropriate in the context of the legal framework in the particular jurisdiction.

** The auditor's report needs to be signed in one or more of the following ways: name of the audit firm, the name of the audit company or the personal name of the auditor as appropriate.

The date of the auditor's report is the date the auditor signs the report.

Example Auditor's Report
Auditor's opinion on the financial report is qualified
Auditor's opinion on the summary financial statements is qualified
(Compliance Framework)

Illustration 3:

Circumstances include the following:

- **A qualified opinion is expressed on the audited financial report.**
- **Criteria are developed by management and adequately disclosed in Note X. The auditor has determined that the criteria are acceptable in the circumstances.**
- **The summary financial statements are *not* prepared under the *Corporations Act 2001*.**

Note: The layout of the 'Qualified opinion' paragraph is different from that in ASA 705 due to the nature of the inter-relationship between the auditor's opinion on the audited financial report and the auditor's reporting on the derived summary financial statements.**

REPORT OF THE INDEPENDENT AUDITOR ON THE SUMMARY FINANCIAL STATEMENTS

[Appropriate Addressee]

The accompanying summary financial statements, which comprises the summary statement of financial position as at 30 June 20X1, the summary statement of comprehensive income, summary statement of changes in equity and summary cash flow statement for the year then ended, related notes and management's assertion statement[##], are derived from the audited financial report of ABC Entity for the year ended 30 June 20X1.[14] We expressed a qualified audit opinion on that financial report in our report dated 15 September 20X1 (see below).

The summary financial statements do not contain all the disclosures required by [describe financial reporting framework applied in the preparation of the audited financial report of ABC Entity]. Reading the summary financial statements, therefore, is not a substitute for reading the audited financial report of ABC Entity.

Management's[15] Responsibility for the Summary Financial Statements

Management is responsible for the preparation of a summary of the audited financial report on the basis described in Note X.

Auditor's Responsibility

Our responsibility is to express an opinion on the summary financial statements based on our procedures, which were conducted in accordance with Auditing Standard ASA 810 *Engagements to Report on Summary Financial Statements*.

Qualified Opinion

In our opinion, the summary financial statements derived from the audited financial report of ABC Entity for the year ended 30 June 20X1 are consistent, in all material respects, with (or *a fair summary of*) that audited financial report, on the basis described in Note X. However, the summary financial statements are misstated to the equivalent extent as the audited financial report of ABC Entity for the year ended 30 June 20X1.

** See ASA 705 *Modifications to the Opinion in the Independent Auditor's Report*.

Or other appropriate term

14 When the auditor's report on the summary financial statements is dated later than the date of the auditor's report on the audited financial report from which they are derived, the following sentence is added to this paragraph: "The audited financial report, and the summary financial statements, do not reflect the effects of events that occurred subsequent to the date of our report on that audited financial report."

15 Or other term that is appropriate in the context of the legal framework in the particular jurisdiction.

The misstatement of the audited financial report is described in our qualified audit opinion in our report dated 15 September 20X1. Our qualified audit opinion is based on the fact that the entity's inventories are carried in the balance sheet in that financial report at xxx. Management has not stated the inventories at the lower of cost and net realisable value but has stated them solely at cost, which constitutes a departure from Australian Accounting Standards. The entity's records indicate that had management stated the inventories at the lower of cost and net realisable value, an amount of xxx would have been required to write the inventories down to their net realisable value. Accordingly, cost of sales would have been increased by xxx, and income tax, net income and shareholders' equity would have been reduced by xxx, xxx and xxx, respectively. Our qualified audit opinion states that, except for the effects of the described matter, the financial report presents fairly, in all material respects, (or *gives a true and fair view of*) the financial position of ABC Entity as at 30 June 20X1, and (*of*) its financial performance and its cash flows for the year then ended in accordance with Australian Accounting Standards.

[Auditor's signature]*

[Date of the auditor's report]#

[Auditor's address]

* The auditor's report needs to be signed in one or more of the following ways: name of the audit firm, the name of the audit company or the personal name of the auditor as appropriate.

\# The date of the auditor's report is the date the auditor signs the report.

Example Auditor's Report
Auditor's opinion on the financial report is adverse Auditor's opinion on the summary financial statements is a disclaimer of opinion (Compliance Framework)

Illustration 4:

Circumstances include the following:

- **An adverse opinion is expressed on the audited financial report.**
- **Criteria are developed by management and adequately disclosed in Note X. The auditor has determined that the criteria are acceptable in the circumstances.**
- **The summary financial statements are *not* prepared under the *Corporations Act 2001*.**

REPORT OF THE INDEPENDENT AUDITOR ON THE SUMMARY FINANCIAL STATEMENTS

[Appropriate Addressee]

The accompanying summary financial statements, which comprises the summary statement of financial position as at 30 June 20X1, the summary statement of comprehensive income, summary statement of changes in equity and summary cash flow statement for the year then ended, related notes and management's assertion statement*, are derived from the audited financial report of ABC Entity for the year ended 30 June 20X1.[16]

The summary financial statements do not contain all the disclosures required by [describe financial reporting framework applied in the preparation of the audited financial report of ABC Entity]. Reading the summary financial statements, therefore, is not a substitute for reading the audited financial report of ABC Entity.

Management's[17] Responsibility for the Summary Financial Statements

Management is responsible for the preparation of a summary of the audited financial report on the basis described in Note X.

Auditor's Responsibility

Our responsibility is to express an opinion on the summary financial statements based on our procedures, which were conducted in accordance with Auditing Standard ASA 810 *Engagements to Report on Summary Financial Statements*.

Disclaimer of Opinion

In our report dated 15 September 20X1, we expressed an adverse audit opinion on the financial report of ABC Entity for the year ended 30 June 20X1. The basis for our adverse audit opinion was [describe basis for adverse audit opinion]. Our adverse audit opinion stated that [describe adverse audit opinion].

* Or other appropriate term.

16 When the auditor's report on the summary financial statements is dated later than the date of the auditor's report on the audited financial report from which they are derived, the following sentence is added to this paragraph: "The audited financial report, and the summary financial statements, do not reflect the effects of events that occurred subsequent to the date of our report on that audited financial report."

17 Or other term that is appropriate in the context of the legal framework in the particular jurisdiction.

Because of the significance of the matter discussed above, it is inappropriate to express an opinion on the summary financial statements of ABC Entity for the year ended 30 June 20X1.

[Auditor's signature]*

[Date of the auditor's report]#

[Auditor's address]

Example Auditor's Report
Auditor's report on the financial report is unmodified
Auditor's report on the summary financial statements is adverse
(Compliance Framework)

Illustration 5:

Circumstances include the following:

- **An unmodified opinion is expressed on the audited financial report.**
- **Established criteria exist for the preparation of summary financial statements.**
- **The auditor concludes that it is not possible to express an unmodified opinion on the summary financial statements.**
- **The summary financial statements are *not* prepared under the *Corporations Act 2001*.**

REPORT OF THE INDEPENDENT AUDITOR ON THE SUMMARY FINANCIAL STATEMENTS

[Appropriate Addressee]

The accompanying summary financial statements, which comprises the summary statement of financial position as at 30 June 20X1, the summary statement of comprehensive income, summary statement of changes in equity and summary cash flow statement for the year then ended, related notes and management's assertion statement**, are derived from the audited financial report of ABC Entity for the year ended 30 June 20X1. We expressed an unmodified audit opinion on that financial report in our report dated September 15 20X1.[18]

The summary financial statements do not contain all the disclosures required by [describe financial reporting framework applied in the preparation of the audited financial report of ABC Entity]. Reading the summary financial statements, therefore, is not a substitute for reading the audited financial report of ABC Entity.

Management's[19] Responsibility for the Summary Audited Financial Statements

Management is responsible for the preparation of a summary of the audited financial report in accordance with [describe established criteria].

---

* The auditor's report needs to be signed in one or more of the following ways: name of the audit firm, the name of the audit company or the personal name of the auditor as appropriate.

The date of the auditor's report is the date the auditor signs the report.

** Or other appropriate term.

18 When the auditor's report on the summary financial statements is dated later than the date of the auditor's report on the audited financial report from which they are derived, the following sentence is added to this paragraph: "The audited financial report, and the summary financial statements, do not reflect the effects of events that occurred subsequent to the date of our report on that audited financial report."

19 Or other term that is appropriate in the context of the legal framework in the particular jurisdiction.

Auditor's Responsibility

Our responsibility is to express an opinion on the summary financial statements based on our procedures, which were conducted in accordance with Auditing Standard ASA 810 *Engagements to Report on Summary Financial Statements*.

Basis for Adverse Opinion

[Describe matter that caused the summary financial statements not to be consistent, in all material respects, with (or *a fair summary of*) the audited financial report, in accordance with the applied criteria.]

Adverse Opinion

In our opinion, because of the significance of the matter discussed in the Basis for Adverse Opinion paragraph, the summary financial statements referred to above are not consistent with (or *a fair summary of*) the audited financial report of ABC Entity for the year ended 30 June 20X1, in accordance with [describe established criteria].

[Auditor's signature]*

[Date of the auditor's report]#

[Auditor's address]

* The auditor's report needs to be signed in one or more of the following ways: name of the audit firm, the name of the audit company or the personal name of the auditor as appropriate.

\# The date of the auditor's report is the date the auditor signs the report.

Explanatory Guide to AUASB Standards Applicable to Review Engagements

(Issued August 2008)

Issued by the Auditing and Assurance Standards Board.

Note from the Institute of Chartered Accountants Australia

This note, prepared by the technical editor, is not part of ASRE 2410.

Historical development

August 2008: The Explanatory Guide was issued following the issue of the series of Standards on Review Engagements, ASREs 2400, 2405 and 2410, to provide information on the use of Auditing and Assurance Standards Board (AUASB) Standards by auditors and assurance practitioners undertaking a review engagement, particularly in the context of a review of non-financial information, now that the ASRE Standards on review engagements are directed towards the review of financial information.

The AUASB formulates *Explanatory Guide to AUASB Standards Applicable to Review Engagements* pursuant to section 227B of the *Australian Securities and Investments Commission Act 2001*. This explanatory guidance does not itself establish or extend mandatory requirements or the assurance practitioner's obligations for the performance of audit, review, assurance or related service engagements under the AUASB Standards. Accordingly, the AUASB has not issued this Explanatory Guide for the purposes of the *Corporations Act 2001*.

This Explanatory Guide should be read in conjunction with ASA 100 *Preamble to AUASB Standards*, which sets out the intentions of the AUASB on how the Standards on Review Engagements are to be understood, interpreted and applied.

This Explanatory Guide is not an AUASB Guidance Statement (GS) that provides guidance to assist auditors and assurance practitioners to fulfil the objectives of the audit or assurance engagement.

Explanatory Guide to AUASB Standards Applicable to Review Engagements

Purpose

The purpose of this explanatory guide is to provide information on the use of Auditing and Assurance Standards Board (AUASB) Standards to auditors and assurance practitioners undertaking review engagements.

Introduction

With the issuance of ASRE 2400 *Review of a Financial Report Performed by an Assurance Practitioner Who is not the Auditor of the Entity* and ASRE 2405 *Review of Historical Financial Information Other than a Financial Report*, the AUASB has completed its revision of the suite of Standards relating to review engagements of historical financial information.

In October 1991, the former Auditing & Assurance Standards Board of the Australian Accounting Research Foundation issued AUS 902 *Review of Financial Reports*. This Standard had very broad application covering reviews of

(i) financial information, both historical and prospective; and

(ii) non-financial information.

With the normal development of standards, a number of new Standards that apply to review engagements have been, or are in the process of being, issued overseas and in Australia. Consequently, AUS 902 has become superseded, and the AUASB has replaced it with a series of Standards that apply to specific types of review engagements.

Background

AUS 902

AUS 902 was released in October 1995 and was operative for reporting periods commencing on or after 1 July 1996. The Standard was directed towards the review of financial reports. However, it could also be applied, to the extent practicable, to engagements to review financial or other information (such as reports on internal control). Furthermore, AUS 902 was to be read in conjunction with AUS 106 *Explanatory Framework for Standards on Audit and Audit Related Services*.

An important feature of AUS 902 was that mandatory Requirement paragraph .05 stated "***The auditor should conduct a review in accordance with Australian Auditing Standards applicable to review engagements***". The accompanying guidance described the AUSs as being mostly written in the context of audits, however, they are "to be applied and adapted as necessary to review engagements".

Other Pronouncements

- In April 2006, the AUASB issued ASRE 2410 *Review of an Interim Financial Report Performed by the Independent Auditor of the Entity*. This Standard is part of the suite of Auditing Standards made under section 336 of the Corporations Act 2001 (the Act).
- In June 2007, the AUASB issued the non-mandatory Pronouncement, *Framework for Assurance Engagements*, which provides the assurance practitioner with an explanation of the overall context for how to apply Standards on Review Engagements (ASREs) and Standards on Assurance Engagements (ASAEs). *The Framework for Assurance Engagements* also defines and describes the elements and objectives of an assurance engagement, including the concepts of reasonable assurance and limited assurance. "Reasonable assurance" is defined as high, but not absolute, level of assurance, and is the basis for a positive form of the assurance practitioner's expression. "Limited assurance" engagements provide a lower level of assurance and are the basis for a negative form of the assurance practitioner's expression. Review engagements, by nature, are limited assurance engagements.
- In July 2007, the AUASB issued ASAE 3000 *Assurance Engagements Other than Audits or Reviews of Historical Financial Information*. This Standard is not part of the Auditing Standards made under the Act. Inter alia, it is to be applied in the review of prospective financial information. AUS 804 *The Audit of Prospective Financial Information* establishes requirements and guidance in relation to audits of prospective financial information. For review engagements, AUS 804 refers to AUS 902.
- In June 2008, the AUASB issued Standard on Assurance Engagements ASAE 3100 *Compliance Engagements*. The Standard has been developed as an adjunct Standard to ASAE 3000. The Standard applies to review engagements as well as to audit engagements.
- In July 2008, the AUASB issued Standard on Assurance Engagements ASAE 3500 *Performance Engagements*. The Standard is a composite revision of both AUS 806 *Performance Auditing* and AUS 808 *Planning Performance Audits*. The Standard applies to performance reviews and performance audits.

ASRE

International Auditing And Assurance Standards Board (IAASB)

In December 2007, the IAASB approved changes to the application of ISRE 2400 *Engagements to Review Financial Statements* and ISRE 2410 *Review of Interim Financial Information Performed by the Independent Auditor of the Entity*. The changes were made effective for financial reporting periods commencing on or after 1 January 2008.

When the IAASB originally issued ISRE 2410, the intention was for that Standard to be used only by the auditor of the entity. This was in recognition that the auditor's knowledge of the entity's business differs from that of an assurance practitioner, who does not initially have the same level of knowledge of the business as the auditor of the entity. The amendments made by the IAASB in December 2007 were to enable ISRE 2410 to be used, by the auditor of the entity, for reviews of historical financial information for periods other than interim periods. ISRE 2400 is to be used by assurance practitioners who are *not* the auditor of the entity.

Situation

With the issuance of ASRE 2410, ASAE 3000, ASAE 3100 and ASAE 3500, and the recent changes to ISRE 2400 and ISRE 2410, AUS 902 has become outdated. Accordingly, it has become necessary to:

- develop Standards to address review engagements not covered by ASRE 2410, ASAE 3000, ASAE 3100 and ASAE 3500;
- make appropriate amendments to ASRE 2410 in response to the IAASB changes; and
- withdraw AUS 902.

The Approach

ASRE 2410

To align with the ISREs, the AUASB has amended ASRE 2410 so that the Standard is to be applied by the auditor of the entity in the review of a financial report for *any* period. Previously, the Standard was applicable only to the review of a financial report for an interim period.

Furthermore, the AUASB has amended the Standard to include guidance on the composition of a "financial report" and on the intended financial reporting framework. The AUASB considers these changes to ASRE 2410 as necessary because the AUASB supports the IAASB's intention for ISRE 2410 to be used for financial report reviews conducted only by the auditor of the entity. The IAASB's changes acknowledge that the auditor's knowledge of the business, gained through conducting an audit in compliance with Auditing Standards, differs from an assurance practitioner who does not initially have the same level of knowledge of the business as the auditor of the entity. The changes also mean that an auditor conducting a review of a financial report for a period equal to or greater than 12 months will in future, use ASRE 2410 instead of AUS 902.

ASRE 2400

The AUASB has developed a new Standard for use by an assurance practitioner who is *not* the auditor of the entity. In this regard, the Standard conforms with ISRE 2400. The Requirements and Explanatory Guidance are designed to ensure that the same objective and level of assurance as ASRE 2410 are achieved by the assurance practitioner who does not initially have the same level of knowledge of the business as the auditor.

ASRE 2400 is directed towards the review of a financial report comprising historical financial information.

Reviews of financial reports by assurance practitioners, who are not the auditor of the entity, are reviews that are not required by the Act. Accordingly, it is necessary to address these types of review in a Standard other than ASRE 2410 (which is the Standard applicable under the Act).

The AUASB is of the view that Standards applicable to the review of a financial report should consist of similar mandatory Requirements regardless of whether the review is performed by the auditor of the entity, or an assurance practitioner who is not the auditor of the entity. As the objectives, procedures and level of assurance are the same, so too should be the form and content of the Standards. Accordingly, ASRE 2400 has been developed using ASRE 2410 as the base Standard.

To mirror the changes to ASRE 2410, ASRE 2400 covers the review of a financial report for *any* period and includes guidance on the composition of a financial report and the intended financial reporting framework.

ASRE 2405

To complete the suite of Standards applicable to review engagements of historical financial information, the remaining area to be addressed is the review of historical financial information that is not in the form of a financial report prepared in accordance with a financial reporting framework designed for fair presentation (covered by ASRE 2400 and ASRE 2410). Examples of such financial information include a single financial statement, such as a Balance Sheet; a listing of accounts receivable; other information derived from financial records; and financial statements prepared in accordance with a reporting framework that is not designed for fair presentation (e.g. condensed financial statements and internal management accounts). The AUASB is of the view that due to the nature of these engagements, the Requirements applicable to them differ from those necessary for the review of a financial report. Accordingly, the AUASB has decided a separate Standard is more appropriate than ASRE 2410 being adapted by the auditor for this purpose. Furthermore, the AUASB acknowledges these types of review engagements are unlikely, if ever, to be required by legislation or regulation. ASRE 2405 has been developed by the AUASB using AUS 902 as the base Standard.

Reporting Format Types

The terms of the review engagement will stipulate the nature and reporting requirements of the review. Accordingly, the auditor or assurance practitioner will plan and perform the engagement so as to provide a report that concludes using either of the following format types:

a. "Based on our review, which is not an audit, nothing has come to our attention that causes us to believe that the [name of report or historical financial information] of [name of entity] [as at date or for the period ended] is not prepared, in all material respects, in accordance with [applicable criteria] used.

or

b. "Based on our review, which is not an audit, nothing has come to our attention that causes us to believe that the [name of report or historical financial information] of [name of entity] [as at date or for the period ended] does not present fairly, in all material respects, in accordance with [applicable criteria] used.

Obligations

An auditor's obligations under ASRE 2410 or ASRE 2405, and an assurance practitioner's obligations under ASRE 2400 or ASRE 2405 are not less than their obligations were under AUS 902.

Tables and Diagrams

To provide a summarised view of the Standards described above, the Tables and Diagrams on the following pages present key application information for each Standard. The information is arranged so as to clearly identify the two categories of AUASB Standards that apply to review engagements, namely:

- tables A, B, C: Standards on Review Engagements (ASREs).

  These Standards apply **only** to engagements to review historical financial information—ASRE 2400, ASRE 2405 and ASRE 2410; and

- tables D, E, F: Standards on Assurance Engagements (ASAEs).

  These Standards apply to audit or review engagements not covered by the Auditing Standards (ASAs) or ASREs and include reviews of information other than historical financial information—ASAE 3000, ASAE 3100 and ASAE 3500.

Standards on Review Engagements (ASREs): applicable only to reviews of historical financial information.

Table A

ASRE 2400 *Review of a Financial Report Performed by an Assurance Practitioner Who is not the Auditor of the Entity*	
Application	*Criteria*
• Review of a financial report comprising historical financial information, performed by an assurance practitioner who is not the auditor of the entity.	• The assurance practitioner must *not* be the auditor of the entity; • Must be a financial report comprising historical financial information; *and* • The financial report may be for any period.

Table B

ASRE 2405 *Review of Historical Financial Information Other than a Financial Report*	
Application	*Criteria*
• Review of historical financial information, other than a financial report.	• Used by an auditor of the entity or assurance practitioner who is not the auditor of the entity; • Financial information is not in the form of a financial report; *and* • Financial information must be historical.

Table C

ASRE 2410 *Review of Interim and Other Financial Reports Performed by the Independant Auditor of the Entity*	
Application	*Criteria*
• Review, by the independent auditor of the entity, of a financial report for a half-year in accordance with Part 2M.3 of the *Corporations Act 2001*; or • Review, by the independent auditor of the entity, of a financial report, comprising historical financial information, for any other purpose.	• Used only by the auditor of the entity; • Must be a financial report, comprising historical financial information, *and* • The financial report may be for any period.

Australian Standards on Assurance Engagements (ASAEs): applicable to engagements other than engagements covered by the ASAs or ASREs.

Table D

ASAE 3000 *Assurance Engagements Other than Audits or Reviews of Historical Financial Information*	
Application	*Criteria*
• Assurance engagements other than audits or reviews of historical financial information.	• Used by an auditor of the entity or an assurance practitioner who is not the auditor of the entity. • General application to assurance engagements other than audits or reviews of historical financial information covered by ASAs or ASREs. • If the subject of the engagement is financial information, the financial information must not be historical. • Applies to reviews of prospective financial information.

Table E

ASAE 3100 *Compliance Engagements Application Criteria*	
Application	*Criteria*
• Compliance Engagements.	• Used by the auditor of the entity or an assurance practitioner who is not the auditor of the entity; and • Provide assurance on an entity's compliance with internally or externally imposed requirements as measured by the suitable criteria.

Table F

ASAE 3500 *Performance Engagements Application Criteria*	
Application	*Criteria*
• Performance Engagements.	• Used by the auditor of the entity or an assurance practitioner who is not the auditor of the entity; and • Reasonable and acceptable standards of performance against which the extent of economy, efficiency or effectiveness of an activity may be assessed.

Diagram 1

Review Standards applicable to Reviews of Financial Reports (comprising historical financial information), and other Historical Financial Information.

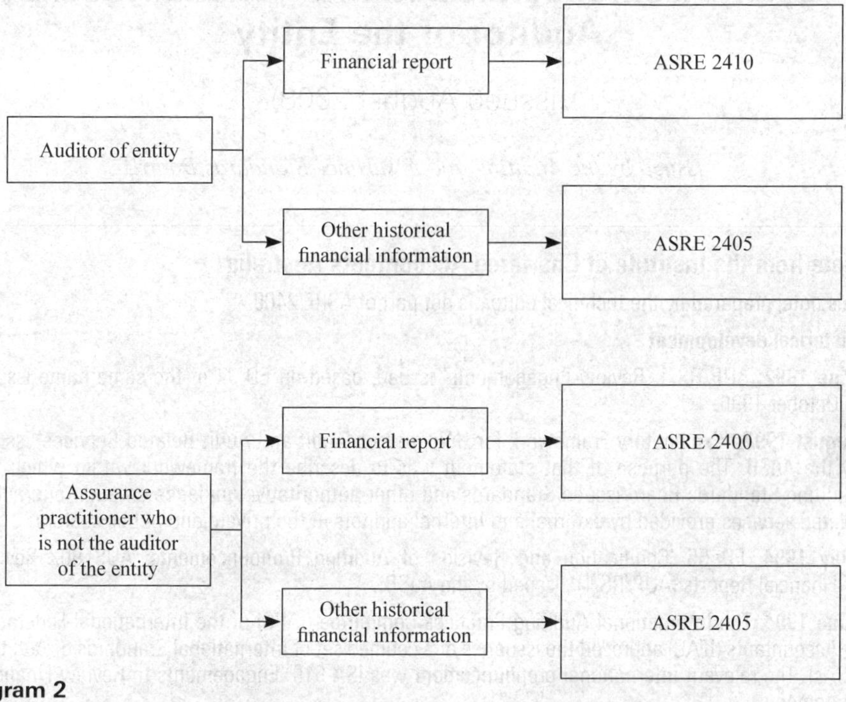

Diagram 2

Standards applicable to Review Engagements, not covered by ASREs.

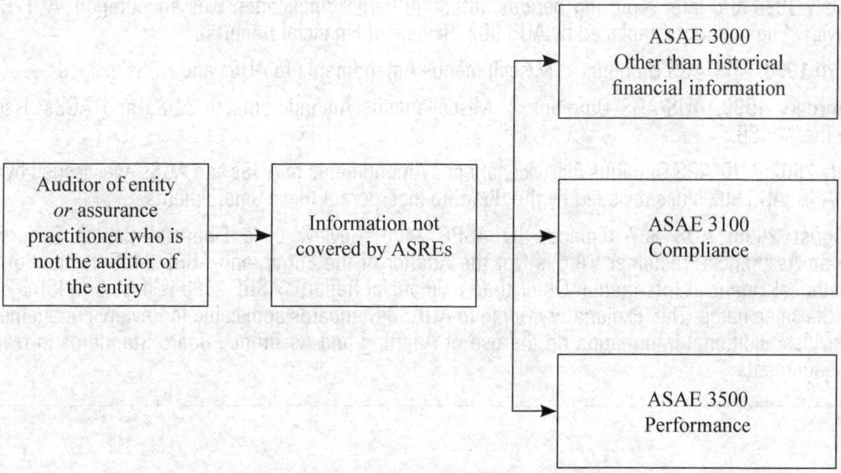

This explanatory guide should be read in conjunction with:

- the AUASB pronouncements outlined in this explanatory guide; and
- ASA 100 *Preamble to AUASB Standards.*

ASRE 2400

Review of a Financial Report Performed by an Assurance Practitioner Who is Not the Auditor of the Entity

(Issued August 2008)

Issued by the Auditing and Assurance Standards Board.

Note from the Institute of Chartered Accountants Australia

This note, prepared by the technical editor, is not part of ASRE 2400.

Historical development

June 1992: AUP/RS 1 'Review Engagements' issued, based on ED 34 of the same name issued in October 1990.

August 1992: 'Explanatory Framework for Guidance on Audit and Audit Related Services' issued by the AuSB. The purpose of that statement was to describe the framework within which the Auditing Standards Board issued Standards and other authoritative guidance on audit and audit-related services provided by external and internal auditors in the private and public sectors.

May 1994: ED 55 'Codification and Revision of Auditing Pronouncements: AUS 902 Review of Financial Reports (AUP/RS 1)', issued by the AuSB.

June 1994: The International Auditing Practices Committee (IAPC) of the International Federation of Accountants (IFAC) approved the issuance of a codified set of International Standards of Auditing (ISAs). The relevant international pronouncement was ISA 910 'Engagements to Review Financial Statements'.

October 1995: The Codified Australian Auditing Standards and Auditing Guidance Statements released. These Standards became operative for the first reporting period commencing on or after 1 July 1996 and later reporting periods, although earlier application was encouraged. AUP/RS 1 'Review Engagements' replaced by AUS 902 'Review of Financial Reports'.

April 1998: AUS/AGS Omnibus 1 'Miscellaneous Amendments to AUSs and AGSs' issued.

February 1999: AUS/AGS Omnibus 2 'Miscellaneous Amendments to AUSs and AGSs' issued by the AuASB.

July 2002: AUS/AGS Omnibus 3 'Miscellaneous Amendments to AUSs and AGSs' was issued by the AuASB. AUS 902 since reissued by the Board to incorporate these amendments.

August 2008: AUS 902 replaced by ASRE 2400 'Review of a Financial Report Performed by an Assurance Practioner Who is Not the Auditor of the Entity' and ASRE 2405 'Review of the Historical Financial Information Other than a Financial Report'. ASRE 2400 is based on ISRE 2400 of the same name. The 'Explanatory Guide to AUASB Standards applicable to Review Engagements' provides additional information on the use of Auditing and Assurance Board Standards in review engagements.

Contents

Preface

Reasons for Issuing Standard on Review Engagements ASRE 2400 *Review of a Financial Report Performed by an Assurance Practitioner Who is Not the Auditor of the Entity*

The Auditing and Assurance Standards Board (AUASB) makes Auditing Standards under section 336 of the *Corporations Act 2001* for the purposes of the corporations legislation and formulates auditing and assurance standards for other purposes.

The AUASB issues Standard on Review Engagements ASRE 2400 *Review of a Financial Report Performed by an Assurance Practitioner Who is Not the Auditor of the Entity* pursuant to the requirements of the legislative provisions explained below.

The *Corporate Law Economic Reform Program (Audit Reform and Corporate Disclosure) Act 2004* (the CLERP 9 Act) established the AUASB as an independent statutory body under section 227A of the *Australian Securities and Investments Commission Act 2001*(ASIC Act), as from 1 July 2004. Under section 227B of the ASIC Act, the AUASB may formulate Assurance Standards for purposes other than the corporations legislation.

Revision of AUS 902

In October 1995, the former Auditing & Assurance Standards Board (AuASB) of the Australian Accounting Research Foundation (AARF) issued the Standard AUS 902 *Review of Financial Reports*. The Standard was based on the International Standard on Review Engagements ISRE 2400. AUS 902 had very broad application covering reviews of (i) financial information, both historical and prospective; and (ii) non-financial information.

With the subsequent progression of standard-setting, a number of new Standards that apply to review engagements have been issued by the AUASB. As a consequence, AUS 902 has become outdated by these new standards that are designed to be applied in specific circumstances and which therefore differ markedly in scope from the broad application of AUS 902. The AUASB takes the view that standards applicable to specific circumstances are more useful to assurance practitioners than are broad-based standards that may require significant interpretation in the context of specific circumstances.

Accordingly, the various review engagement types, previously conducted in accordance with AUS 902, are to be conducted in accordance with the relevant AUASB Standard.

Details of the background and current application of the suite of AUASB Standards that apply to review engagements, are contained in the *Explanatory Guide to Review Engagements*, a copy of which may be obtained from the AUASB website: www.auasb.gov.au

Appendix 6 of this Standard contains a table and diagrams that illustrate the application of AUASB Standards by review engagement type.

Main Features

This Standard on Review Engagements (ASRE) establishes mandatory requirements and provides explanatory guidance on the responsibilities of an assurance practitioner who is not the auditor of an entity, when engaged to undertake a review of a financial report, and on the form and content of the assurance practitioner's review report.

Operative Date

This Standard on Review Engagements is operative for engagements commencing on or after 1 October 2008.

Main changes from AUS 902 (July 2002)

The main differences between this Standard on Review Engagements (ASRE) and the Auditing Standard issued by the Auditing and Assurance Standards Board of the Australian Accounting Research Foundation that it supersedes, AUS 902 *Review of Financial Reports* (July 2002), are that in this ASRE:

1. The word 'shall', in the **bold-type** paragraphs, is the terminology used to describe an assurance practitioner's mandatory requirements, whereas an assurance practitioner's degree of responsibility was described in AUS 902 by the word 'should'.
2. The Explanatory Guidance paragraphs provide guidance and illustrative examples to assist the assurance practitioner in fulfilling the mandatory requirements, whereas in AUS 902 some obligations were implied within certain explanatory paragraphs. Accordingly, such paragraphs have been redrafted to clarify that the matter forms part of the explanatory guidance.
3. Application is restricted to reviews of financial reports comprising historical financial information, by assurance practitioners who are not the auditor of the entity. The application of AUS 902 was not restricted in this way.
4. ASRE 2400 has been based on Auditing Standard on Review Engagements ASRE 2410 *Review of Interim and Other Financial Reports Performed by the Independent Auditor of the Entity* so as to recognise the common basis for reviews of financial reports. Accordingly, ASRE 2400 includes a number of additional mandatory requirements to those in AUS 902 (see listing in paragraph 5 below).

   It is not practical here to compare the wording of each Requirement in ASRE 2400 to the equivalent Requirement in AUS 902. However, an assurance practitioner's obligations under ASRE 2400 are not less than those under AUS 902.
5. The following additional mandatory Requirements have been included:

   5.1 This Standard on Review Engagements (ASRE) applies to a review of a financial report comprising historical financial information, performed by an assurance practitioner who is not the auditor of the entity (paragraph 1).

   5.2 Where in rare and exceptional circumstances, factors outside the assurance practitioner's control prevent the assurance practitioner from complying with a relevant mandatory requirement of this ASRE, the assurance practitioner shall:

   (a) if possible, perform appropriate alternative procedures; and

   (b) document in the working papers:

   (i) the circumstances surrounding the inability to comply;

   (ii) the reasons for the inability to comply; and

   (iii) justification of how alternative procedures achieve the objectives of the mandatory requirement.

   When the assurance practitioner is unable to perform appropriate alternative procedures, the assurance practitioner shall consider the implications for the assurance practitioner's review report (paragraph 6).

   5.3 The assurance practitioner shall implement quality control procedures to address the following elements of a quality control system that apply to the individual engagement:

   (a) leadership responsibilities for quality on the assurance engagement;

   (b) ethical requirements;

   (c) acceptance and continuance of client relationships and specific engagements;

   (d) assignment of engagement teams;

   (e) engagement performance; and

   (f) monitoring (paragraph 10).

   5.4 The assurance practitioner shall obtain evidence that the financial report agrees or reconciles with the underlying accounting records (paragraph 37).

5.5 The assurance practitioner shall enquire whether those charged with governance have changed their assessment of the entity's ability to continue as a going concern. When, as the result of this enquiry or other review procedures, the assurance practitioner becomes aware of events or conditions that may cast significant doubt on the entity's ability to continue as a going concern, the assurance practitioner shall:

(a) enquire of those charged with governance as to their plans for future actions based on their going concern assessment, the feasibility of these plans, and whether they believe that the outcome of these plans will improve the situation; and

(b) consider the adequacy of the disclosure about such matters in the financial report (paragraph 41).

5.6 When comparative information is included for the first time in a financial report, the assurance practitioner shall perform similar procedures on the comparative information as applied to the current period financial report (paragraph 45).

5.7 The assurance practitioner shall evaluate, individually and in the aggregate, whether uncorrected misstatements that have come to the assurance practitioner's attention are material to the financial report (paragraph 50).

5.8 The assurance practitioner shall endeavour to obtain written representations from management that:

(a) it acknowledges its responsibility for the design and implementation of internal control to prevent and detect fraud and error;

(b) the financial report is prepared and presented in accordance with the applicable financial reporting framework;

(c) it believes the effect of those uncorrected misstatements aggregated by the assurance practitioner during the review are immaterial, both individually and in the aggregate, to the financial report taken as a whole. A summary of such items is included in, or attached to, the written representations;

(d) it has disclosed to the assurance practitioner all significant facts relating to any fraud(s) or suspected fraud(s) known to it that may have affected the entity;

(e) it has disclosed to the assurance practitioner the results of its assessment of the risk that the financial report may be materially misstated as a result of fraud;

(f) it has disclosed to the assurance practitioner all known actual or possible non-compliance with laws and regulations the effects of which are to be considered when preparing the financial report; and

(g) it has disclosed to the assurance practitioner all significant events that have occurred subsequent to the balance sheet date and through to the date of the review report that may require adjustment to, or disclosure in, the financial report (paragraph 54).

5.9 If those charged with governance refuse to provide a written representation that the assurance practitioner considers necessary, this constitutes a limitation on the scope of the assurance practitioner's work and the assurance practitioner shall express a qualified conclusion or a disclaimer of conclusion (paragraph 56).

5.10 The assurance practitioner shall read the other information that accompanies the financial report to consider whether any such information is materially inconsistent with the financial report (paragraph 57).

5.11 If a matter comes to the assurance practitioner's attention that causes the assurance practitioner to believe that the other information appears to include a material misstatement of fact, the assurance practitioner shall discuss the matter with the entity's management (paragraph 60).

5.12 When, as a result of performing the review of a financial report, a matter comes to the assurance practitioner's attention that causes the assurance practitioner to believe that it is necessary to make a material adjustment to the financial report for it to be prepared, in all material respects, in accordance with the applicable financial reporting framework, the assurance practitioner shall communicate this matter as soon as practicable to the appropriate level of management (paragraph 62).

5.13 When, in the assurance practitioner's judgement, management does not respond appropriately within a reasonable period of time, the assurance practitioner shall inform those charged with governance (paragraph 63).

5.14 When, in the assurance practitioner's judgement, those charged with governance do not respond appropriately within a reasonable period of time, the assurance practitioner shall consider:

(a) whether to modify the report; or

(b) the possibility of withdrawing from the engagement (paragraph 65).

5.15 When, as a result of performing the review of a financial report, a matter comes to the assurance practitioner's attention that causes the assurance practitioner to believe in the existence of fraud or non-compliance by the entity with laws and regulations, the assurance practitioner shall communicate the matter as soon as practicable to those charged with governance and shall consider the implications for the review (paragraph 66).

5.16 The assurance practitioner shall communicate relevant matters of governance interest arising from the review of the financial report to those charged with governance (paragraph 68).

6. The "Objective of a Review Engagement" is included in AUS 902 as a mandatory paragraph (**bold-type**). However, the equivalent "Objective of an Engagement to Review a Financial Report" paragraph has been included in ASRE 2400 as explanatory guidance. This change has been adopted to acknowledge the contextual nature of the matter and to be consistent with ASRE 2405 *Review of Historical Financial Information Other than a Financial Report* and ASRE 2410 *Review of Interim and Other Financial Reports Performed by the Independent Auditor of the Entity*. The amendment does not diminish the quality of the standard or the obligations of an assurance practitioner (paragraphs 14-16).

7. AUS 902 included a separate mandatory paragraph relating to the direction, supervision and review of work performed by assistants. In ASRE 2400, this Requirement is addressed by the mandatory requirements to comply with Professional Standards (paragraph 7) and quality control procedures (paragraph 10).

8. AUS 902 includes a mandatory paragraph requiring the auditor, when using the work of another auditor, to determine how the work of the other auditor will affect the review engagement. In addition, AUS 902 includes a mandatory paragraph requiring the auditor, when using the work of an expert, to obtain sufficient appropriate evidence that such work is adequate for the purposes of the review engagement. These requirements have not been included as specific requirements in ASRE 2400 so as to keep ASRE 2400 consistent with ASRE 2410 and ISRE 2410. ASRE 2400 paragraph 32 requires the assurance practitioner to perform review procedures to enable the assurance practitioner to reach a conclusion. Furthermore, the explanatory guidance at paragraph 34 explicitly refers to considering the adequacy of the work of another assurance practitioner or expert (Requirement paragraph 32 and Explanatory Guidance paragraph 34).

9. AUS 902 includes five explanatory guidance paragraphs under the heading "Moderate Assurance". This guidance has not been included in this ASRE as it would duplicate the equivalent information contained within the AUASB pronouncement, *Framework for Assurance Engagements*, which comprehensively explains "limited assurance".

Authority Statement

The Auditing and Assurance Standards Board (AUASB) formulates this Standard on Review Engagements ASRE 2400 *Review of a Financial Report Performed by an Assurance Practitioner Who is Not the Auditor of the Entity* as set out in paragraphs 1 to 97 and Appendices 1 to 6, pursuant to section 227B of the *Australian Securities and Investments Commission Act 2001*.

This Standard on Review Engagements is to be read in conjunction with the *Preamble to AUASB Standards*, which sets out the intentions of the AUASB on how the Standards on Review Engagements are to be understood, interpreted and applied.

The mandatory Requirements of this Standard on Review Engagements are set out in **bold-type** paragraphs.

Dated 21 August 2008

M H Kelsall
Chairman - AUASB

Standard On Review Engagements ASRE 2400

Review of a Financial Report Performed by an Assurance Practitioner Who is Not the Auditor of the Entity

Application

1 **This Standard on Review Engagements (ASRE) applies to a review of a financial report comprising historical financial information, performed by an assurance practitioner who is not the auditor of the entity.**

Operative Date

2 **This ASRE is operative for engagements commencing on or after 1 October 2008.**

Introduction

3 The purpose of this ASRE is to establish mandatory Requirements and to provide Explanatory Guidance on the assurance practitioner's professional responsibilities when undertaking an engagement to review a financial report, and on the form and content of the assurance practitioner's review report.

4 For purposes of this ASRE:

(a) a financial report is a complete financial report which ordinarily includes accompanying notes and an assertion by those responsible for the financial report. The requirements of the applicable financial reporting framework determine the form and content of the financial report and what constitutes a complete financial report;

(b) a financial report is prepared in accordance with a financial reporting framework that is designed to achieve fair presentation;

(c) an assurance practitioner is a person or an organisation, whether in public practice, industry, commerce or the public sector, involved in the provision of assurance services; and

(d) the assurance practitioner is not the auditor of the entity.

5 **The assurance practitioner who is engaged to perform a review of a financial report shall perform the review in accordance with this ASRE.**

6 **Where in rare and exceptional circumstances, factors outside the assurance practitioner's control prevent the assurance practitioner from complying with a relevant mandatory Requirement of this ASRE, the assurance practitioner shall:**

(a) if possible, perform appropriate alternative procedures; and

(b) document in the working papers:

(i) the circumstances surrounding the inability to comply;

(ii) the reasons for the inability to comply; and

(iii) justification of how alternative procedures achieve the objectives of the mandatory requirement.

When the assurance practitioner is unable to perform appropriate alternative procedures, the assurance practitioner shall consider the implications for the assurance practitioner's review report.

General Principles of a Review of a Financial Report

7 **The assurance practitioner shall comply with the fundamental ethical principles of integrity, objectivity, professional competence and due care, confidentiality and professional behaviour.**

8 The applicable code of conduct of a professional accounting body[1] provides appropriate guidance on the application of fundamental ethical principles.

9 The applicable code of conduct of a professional accounting body provides a framework of principles that members of assurance teams, firms and network firms use to identify threats to independence, evaluate the significance of those threats and, if the threats are other than clearly insignificant:

(a) identify and apply safeguards to eliminate the threats; or

(b) reduce them to an acceptable level,

such that independence of mind and independence in appearance are not compromised.

10 The assurance practitioner shall implement quality control procedures to address the following elements of a quality control system that apply to the individual engagement:

(a) leadership responsibilities for quality on the assurance engagement;

(b) ethical requirements;

(c) acceptance and continuance of client relationships and specific engagements;

(d) assignment of engagement teams;

(e) engagement performance; and

(f) monitoring.

11 The quality control procedures relevant to an audit engagement are contained in Auditing Standard ASA 220 *Quality Control for an Audit of Historical Financial Information*, and may be helpful in determining quality control procedures relevant to a review engagement.

12 The assurance practitioner shall plan and perform the review by exercising professional judgement and with an attitude of professional scepticism, recognising that circumstances may exist that cause the financial report to require a material adjustment for it to be prepared, in all material respects, in accordance with the applicable financial reporting framework.

13 An attitude of professional scepticism means that the assurance practitioner makes a critical assessment, with a questioning mind, of the validity of evidence obtained and is alert to evidence that contradicts or brings into question the reliability of documents or representations by management of the entity.

Objective of an Engagement to Review a Financial Report

14 The objective of an engagement to review a financial report is to enable the assurance practitioner to express a conclusion whether, on the basis of the review, anything has come to the assurance practitioner's attention that causes the assurance practitioner to believe that the financial report is not prepared, in all material respects, in accordance with the applicable financial reporting framework. Under paragraph 21 of this ASRE, the assurance practitioner needs to make enquiries and perform analytical and other review procedures in order to reduce, to a limited level, the risk of expressing an inappropriate conclusion when the financial report is materially misstated.

15 The objective of a review of a financial report differs significantly from that of an audit conducted in accordance with Auditing Standards. A review of a financial report does not provide a basis for expressing an opinion whether the financial report gives a true and fair view, or is presented fairly, in all material respects, in accordance with the applicable financial reporting framework.

16 A review, in contrast to an audit, is not designed to obtain reasonable assurance that the financial report is free from material misstatement. A review consists of making enquiries, primarily of persons responsible for financial and accounting matters, and applying analytical and other review procedures. A review may bring significant matters affecting the financial

1 The applicable code of conduct of the professional accounting bodies is *APES 110 Code of Ethics for Professional Accountants*, as issued from time to time by the Accounting Professional and Ethical Standards Board (APESB). This code of conduct has been adopted by CPA Australia, National Institute of Accountants and the Institute of Chartered Accountants in Australia. In addition, codes of conduct issued by other professional bodies may apply.

ASRE

report to the assurance practitioner's attention, but it does not provide all of the evidence that would be required in an audit.

Agreeing the Terms of the Engagement

17 **The assurance practitioner shall agree the terms of the engagement with the entity, which shall be recorded in writing by the assurance practitioner and forwarded to the entity. When the review engagement is undertaken pursuant to legislation, the minimum applicable terms are those contained in the legislation.**

18 Such a communication helps to avoid misunderstandings regarding the nature of the engagement and, in particular, the objective and scope of the review, the responsibilities of those charged with governance, the extent of the assurance practitioner's responsibilities, the assurance obtained, and the nature and form of the report. The communication ordinarily covers the following matters:

- The objective of a review of a financial report.
- The scope of the review.
- The responsibilities of those charged with governance for:
  - ♦ the financial report;
  - ♦ establishing and maintaining effective internal control relevant to the preparation of the financial report; and
  - ♦ making all financial records and related information available to the assurance practitioner.
- Agreement from those charged with governance:
  - ♦ to provide written representations to the assurance practitioner to confirm representations made orally during the review, as well as representations that are implicit in the entity's records.
  - ♦ that where any document containing the financial report indicates that the financial report has been reviewed by the entity's assurance practitioner, the review report will also be included in the document; and
  - ♦ the anticipated form and content of the report to be issued, including the identity of the addressee of the report and provision that the report may be modified.

Appendix 1 to this ASRE contains an illustrative engagement letter.

19 **Unless required by law or regulation, an assurance practitioner shall not accept an engagement to review a financial report when management has imposed a limitation on the scope of the assurance practitioner's review.**

20 Under paragraph 19 of this ASRE, the assurance practitioner needs to refuse to accept an engagement to review a financial report if the assurance practitioner's preliminary knowledge of the engagement circumstances indicates that the assurance practitioner would be unable to complete the review because there will be a limitation on the scope of the assurance practitioner's review imposed by management of the entity.

Procedures for a Review of a Financial Report

Understanding the Entity and its Environment

21 **The assurance practitioner shall obtain an understanding of the entity and its environment, including its internal control, as it relates to the preparation of the financial report, sufficient to plan and conduct the engagement so as to be able to:**

(a) identify the types of potential material misstatements and consider the likelihood of their occurrence; and

(b) select the enquiries, analytical and other review procedures that will provide the assurance practitioner with a basis for reporting whether anything has come to the assurance practitioner's attention that causes the assurance practitioner to believe that the financial report is not prepared, in all material respects, in accordance with the applicable financial reporting framework.

22 Under paragraph 21 of this ASRE, the assurance practitioner needs to use the understanding of the entity and its environment, including its internal control, to determine the enquiries to be made and the analytical and other review procedures to be applied, and to identify the particular events, transactions or assertions to which enquiries may be directed or analytical or other review procedures applied.

23 The procedures performed by the assurance practitioner to obtain or update the understanding of the entity and its environment, including its internal control, may include, for example, the following:

- reading the documentation of the preceding year's audit, and review(s) of prior period(s) of the current year, and corresponding period(s) of the prior year, to enable the assurance practitioner to identify matters that may affect the current-period financial report;
- considering any significant risks, including the risk of management override of controls, that were identified in the audit of the prior year's financial report;
- reading the most recent annual and comparable prior period financial report;
- considering materiality with reference to the applicable financial reporting framework, as it relates to the financial report, to assist in determining the nature and extent of the procedures to be performed and evaluating the effect of misstatements;
- considering the nature of any corrected material misstatements and any identified uncorrected immaterial misstatements in the prior year's financial report;
- considering significant financial accounting and reporting matters that may be of continuing significance, such as material weaknesses in internal control;
- considering the results of any internal audit performed and the subsequent actions taken by management;
- enquiring of management about the results of management's assessment of the risk that the financial report may be materially misstated as a result of fraud;
- enquiring of management about the effect of changes in the entity's business activities;
- enquiring of management about any significant changes in internal control and the potential effect of any such changes on the preparation of the financial report; and
- enquiring of management of the process by which the financial report has been prepared and the reliability of the underlying accounting records to which the financial report is agreed or reconciled.

24 Under paragraph 21, the assurance practitioner needs to determine the nature of the review procedures, if any, to be performed for components and, where applicable, communicate these matters to other assurance practitioners involved in the review. Factors considered ordinarily include the materiality of, and risk of misstatement in, the financial report components, and the assurance practitioner's understanding of the extent to which internal control over the preparation of such reports is centralised or decentralised.

25 The understanding required under paragraph 21, enables the assurance practitioner to focus the enquiries made, and the analytical and other review procedures applied in performing a review of the financial report in accordance with this ASRE. As part of obtaining this understanding, ordinarily the assurance practitioner makes enquiries, where relevant, of the entity's auditor and, where practicable, reviews the auditor's documentation for the preceding annual audit and for any prior periods in the current year that have been reviewed by the auditor. In doing so, ordinarily the assurance practitioner considers the nature of any corrected misstatements, and any uncorrected misstatements aggregated by the auditor, any significant risks, including the risk of management override of controls, and significant accounting and any reporting matters that may be of continuing significance, such as material weaknesses in internal control. See also paragraph 23 above.

ASRE

Materiality

26 **The assurance practitioner shall consider materiality, using professional judgement, when:**

(a) determining the nature, timing and extent of review procedures; and

(b) evaluating the effect of misstatements.

27 Under paragraph 26 of this ASRE, the assurance practitioner needs to use professional judgement and consider qualitative and quantitative factors in determining materiality.

28 Ordinarily, the assurance practitioner's consideration of materiality for a review of an interim financial report is based on the interim period financial data and accordingly materiality based on interim period financial data may be less than materiality for annual financial data. If the entity's business is subject to cyclical variations, or if the financial results for the current period show an exceptional decrease or increase compared to prior periods and expected results for the current period, the assurance practitioner may, for example, conclude that materiality is more appropriately determined using a normalised amount for the period.

29 The assurance practitioner's consideration of materiality, in evaluating the effects of misstatements, is a matter of professional judgement and is affected by the assurance practitioner's perception of the financial information needs of users of the financial report.

30 If the applicable financial reporting framework contains a definition of materiality, it will ordinarily provide a reference to the assurance practitioner when determining materiality for planning and performing the review.

31 Under paragraph 26 of this ASRE, the assurance practitioner needs, when relevant, to consider materiality from the perspective of both the entity and the consolidated entity.

Enquiries, Analytical and Other Review Procedures

32 **The assurance practitioner shall make enquiries, primarily of persons responsible for financial and accounting matters, and perform analytical and other review procedures to enable the assurance practitioner to conclude whether, on the basis of the procedures performed, anything has come to the assurance practitioner's attention that causes the assurance practitioner to believe that the financial report is not prepared, in all material respects, in accordance with the applicable financial reporting framework.**

33 A review ordinarily does not require tests of the accounting records through inspection, observation or confirmation. Procedures for performing a review of a financial report ordinarily are limited to making enquiries, primarily of persons responsible for financial and accounting matters and applying analytical and other review procedures, rather than corroborating information obtained concerning matters relating to the financial report. The assurance practitioner's understanding of the entity and its environment, including its internal control, the results of risk assessments and the assurance practitioner's consideration of materiality as it relates to the financial report, affect the nature and extent of the enquiries made, and analytical and other review procedures applied.

34 The assurance practitioner ordinarily performs the following review procedures:

- Reading the minutes of the meetings of shareholders, those charged with governance, and other appropriate committees, to identify matters that may affect the financial report, and enquiring about matters dealt with at meetings for which minutes are not available that may affect the financial report.
- Considering the effect, if any, of matters giving rise to a modification of the audit or review report, accounting adjustments or unadjusted misstatements, at the time of the previous audit or reviews.
- Communicating, where appropriate, with other assurance practitioners who are performing a review of the financial report of the entity's significant components.

- When using the work performed by another assurance practitioner or an expert, considering the adequacy of such work for the purposes of the review.[2]
- Enquiring of members of management responsible for financial and accounting matters, and others as appropriate, about the following:
  - ♦ whether the financial report has been prepared and presented in accordance with the applicable financial reporting framework;
  - ♦ whether there have been any changes in accounting principles or in the methods of applying them;
  - ♦ whether any new transactions have necessitated the application of a new accounting principle;
  - ♦ whether the financial report contains any known uncorrected misstatements;
  - ♦ unusual or complex situations that may have affected the financial report, such as a business combination or disposal of a segment of the business;
  - ♦ significant assumptions that are relevant to the fair value measurement or disclosures and management's intention and ability to carry out specific courses of action on behalf of the entity;
  - ♦ whether related party transactions have been appropriately accounted for and disclosed in the financial report;
  - ♦ significant changes in commitments and contractual obligations;
  - ♦ significant changes in contingent assets and contingent liabilities including litigation or claims;
  - ♦ compliance with debt covenants;
  - ♦ matters about which questions have arisen in the course of applying the review procedures;
  - ♦ significant transactions occurring in the last several days of the period or the first several days of the next period;
  - ♦ knowledge of any fraud or suspected fraud affecting the entity involving:
    - ◦ management;
    - ◦ employees who have significant roles in internal control; or
    - ◦ others where the fraud could have a material effect on the financial report;
  - ♦ knowledge of any allegations of fraud, or suspected fraud, affecting the entity's financial information, communicated by employees, former employees, analysts, regulators or others; and
  - ♦ knowledge of any actual or possible non-compliance with laws and regulations that could have a material effect on the financial report;
- Applying analytical procedures to the financial report designed to identify relationships and individual items that appear to be unusual and that may reflect a material misstatement in the financial report. Analytical procedures may include ratio analysis and statistical techniques such as trend analysis or regression analysis and may be performed manually or with the use of computer assisted techniques. Appendix 3 to this ASRE contains examples of analytical procedures the assurance practitioner may consider when performing a review of a financial report.
- Reading the financial report and considering whether anything has come to the assurance practitioner's attention that causes the assurance practitioner to believe that the financial report is not prepared in accordance with the applicable financial reporting framework.

Appendix 4 to this ASRE contains illustrative detailed procedures that the assurance practitioner may consider when performing a review of a financial report. The list is not exhaustive, nor is it intended that all procedures suggested apply to every review engagement.

---

2 Auditing Standard ASA 600 *Using the Work of Another Auditor* and Auditing Standard ASA 620 *Using the Work of an Expert* contain information that the assurance practitioner may find helpful in this context.

35 The assurance practitioner may perform many of the review procedures before, or simultaneously with, the entity's preparation of the financial report. For example, it may be practical to obtain or update the understanding of the entity and its environment, including its internal control, and begin reading applicable minutes before the end of the period. Performing some of the review procedures earlier in the period also permits early identification and consideration of significant accounting matters affecting the financial report.

36 A review of a financial report ordinarily does not require corroborating the enquiries about litigation or claims. It is, therefore, ordinarily not necessary to send an enquiry letter to the entity's lawyer. Direct communication with the entity's lawyer with respect to litigation or claims, or alternative procedures, may, however, be appropriate if a matter comes to the assurance practitioner's attention that causes the assurance practitioner to question whether the financial report is in accordance with the applicable financial reporting framework.

37 The assurance practitioner shall obtain evidence that the financial report agrees or reconciles with the underlying accounting records.

38 The assurance practitioner may obtain evidence that the financial report agrees or reconciles with the underlying accounting records by tracing the financial report to:

(a) the accounting records, such as the general ledger, or a consolidating schedule that agrees or reconciles with the accounting records; and

(b) other supporting data in the entity's records as necessary.

39 The assurance practitioner shall enquire whether management has identified all events up to the date of the review report that may require adjustment to, or disclosure in, the financial report.

40 Under paragraph 39 of this ASRE, the assurance practitioner need not perform procedures to identify events occurring after the date of the review report.

41 The assurance practitioner shall enquire whether those charged with governance have changed their assessment of the entity's ability to continue as a going concern. When, as the result of this enquiry or other review procedures, the assurance practitioner becomes aware of events or conditions that may cast significant doubt on the entity's ability to continue as a going concern, the assurance practitioner shall:

(a) enquire of those charged with governance as to their plans for future actions based on their going concern assessment, the feasibility of these plans, and whether they believe that the outcome of these plans will improve the situation; and

(b) consider the adequacy of the disclosure about such matters in the financial report.

42 Events or conditions which may cast significant doubt on the entity's ability to continue as a going concern may have existed at the date of the annual financial report or may be identified as a result of enquiries of management or in the course of performing other review procedures. When such events or conditions come to the assurance practitioner's attention, under paragraph 41 of this ASRE, the assurance practitioner needs to enquire of those charged with governance as to their plans for future action, such as their plans to liquidate assets, borrow money or restructure debt, reduce or delay expenditures, or increase capital. Under paragraph 41 of this ASRE, the assurance practitioner needs to enquire also as to the feasibility of the plans of those charged with governance and whether they believe that the outcome of these plans will improve the situation. Ordinarily, the assurance practitioner considers, based on procedures performed, whether it is necessary to corroborate the feasibility of the plans of those charged with governance and whether the outcome of these plans will improve the situation.

43 When a matter comes to the assurance practitioner's attention that leads the assurance practitioner to question whether a material adjustment should be made for the financial report to be prepared, in all material respects, in accordance with the applicable financial reporting framework, the assurance practitioner shall make additional enquiries or perform other procedures to enable the assurance practitioner to express a conclusion in the review report.

44 For example, if the assurance practitioner's review procedures lead the assurance practitioner to question whether a significant sales transaction is recorded in accordance with the

applicable financial reporting framework, the assurance practitioner performs additional procedures sufficient to resolve the assurance practitioner's questions, such as discussing the terms of the transaction with senior marketing and accounting personnel, or reading the sales contract.

Comparatives

45 **When comparative information is included for the first time in the financial report, the assurance practitioner shall perform similar procedures on the comparative information as applied to the current period financial report.**

46 When comparative information is included for the first time in the financial report, and the assurance practitioner is unable to obtain sufficient appropriate review evidence to achieve the review objective, a limitation on the scope of the review exists. Under paragraph 82 of this ASRE, the assurance practitioner needs to modify[3] the review report. In such cases, ordinarily an assurance practitioner encourages clear disclosure in the financial report, that the assurance practitioner has been unable to review the comparatives. Appendix 5 to this ASRE contains an example of a modified review report.

47 When comparative information is included in the first financial report and the assurance practitioner believes a material adjustment should be made to the financial report, under paragraph 72 of this ASRE, the assurance practitioner needs to modify the review report.

48 When an entity has come into existence within the first period, comparative information will not be provided in the first financial report and no modified review report is required.

49 Accounting Standard AASB 101 *Presentation of Financial Statements*, provides Requirements and Explanatory Guidance relating to comparative information included in a financial report prepared in accordance with Australian Accounting Standards. Accounting Standard AASB 1 *First-time Adoption of Australian Equivalents to International Financial Reporting Standards*, provides Requirements and guidance relating to comparative information when an entity adopts Australian Equivalents to International Financial Reporting Standards (AIFRS) for the first time.

Evaluation of Misstatements

50 **The assurance practitioner shall evaluate, individually and in the aggregate, whether uncorrected misstatements that have come to the assurance practitioner's attention are material to the financial report.**

51 A review of a financial report, in contrast to an audit engagement, is not designed to obtain reasonable assurance that the financial report is free from material misstatement. However, under paragraph 50 of this ASRE, misstatements which come to the assurance practitioner's attention, including inadequate disclosures, need to be evaluated individually and in the aggregate, to determine whether a material adjustment is required to be made to the financial report, for it to be prepared, in all material respects, in accordance with the applicable financial reporting framework.

52 Under paragraph 50 of this ASRE, the assurance practitioner needs to exercise professional judgement in evaluating the materiality of any misstatements that the entity has not corrected. Ordinarily, the assurance practitioner considers matters such as the nature, cause and amount of the misstatements, whether the misstatements originated in the preceding year or period of the current year, and the potential effect of the misstatements on future periods.

53 The assurance practitioner may designate an amount below which misstatements need not be aggregated, because the assurance practitioner expects that the aggregation of such amounts clearly would not have a material effect on the financial report. In so doing, under paragraph 26 of this ASRE, the assurance practitioner needs to consider the fact that the determination of materiality involves quantitative as well as qualitative considerations and that misstatements of a relatively small amount could nevertheless have a material effect on the financial report.

3 Ordinarily, a limitation on the scope of the assurance practitioner's work will result in a qualified ("except for") conclusion.

ASRE

Management Representations

54 **The assurance practitioner shall endeavour to obtain written representations from management that:**

(a) it acknowledges its responsibility for the design and implementation of internal control to prevent and detect fraud and error;

(b) the financial report is prepared and presented in accordance with the applicable financial reporting framework;

(c) it believes the effect of those uncorrected misstatements aggregated by the assurance practitioner during the review are immaterial, both individually and in the aggregate, to the financial report taken as a whole. A summary of such items is included, in or attached to, the written representations;

(d) it has disclosed to the assurance practitioner all significant facts relating to any fraud(s) or suspected fraud(s) known to it that may have affected the entity;

(e) it has disclosed to the assurance practitioner the results of its assessment of the risk that the financial report may be materially misstated as a result of fraud;

(f) it has disclosed to the assurance practitioner all known actual or possible non-compliance with laws and regulations the effects of which are to be considered when preparing the financial report; and

(g) it has disclosed to the assurance practitioner all significant events that have occurred subsequent to the balance sheet date and through to the date of the review report that may require adjustment to, or disclosure in, the financial report.

55 Under paragraph 54 of this ASRE, the assurance practitioner needs to endeavour to obtain additional representations, as are appropriate, to matters specific to the entity's business or industry. Appendix 2 to this ASRE contains an illustrative management representation letter.

56 **If those charged with governance refuse to provide a written representation that the assurance practitioner considers necessary, this constitutes a limitation on the scope of the assurance practitioner's work and the assurance practitioner shall express a qualified conclusion or a disclaimer of conclusion.**

Assurance Practitioner's Responsibility for Accompanying Information

57 **The assurance practitioner shall read the other information that accompanies the financial report to consider whether any such information is materially inconsistent with the financial report.**

58 Ordinarily, the assurance practitioner makes appropriate arrangements with the entity to obtain the other information on a timely basis.

59 If the assurance practitioner identifies a material inconsistency, under paragraph 57 of this ASRE, the assurance practitioner needs to consider whether the financial report or the other information needs to be amended. If an amendment is necessary in the financial report, and those charged with governance refuse to make the amendment, under paragraph 65 of this ASRE, the assurance practitioner needs to consider the implications for the review report. If an amendment is necessary in the other information and those charged with governance refuse to make the amendment, the assurance practitioner may, for example, consider including in the review report an additional paragraph (emphasis of matter) describing the material inconsistency, or may take other actions, such as withholding the issuance of the review report or withdrawing from the engagement. For example, those charged with governance may present alternative measures of earnings that more positively portray financial performance than the financial report, and such alternative measures are given excessive prominence, are not clearly defined, or not clearly reconciled to the financial report such that they are confusing and potentially misleading.

60 **If a matter comes to the assurance practitioner's attention that causes the assurance practitioner to believe that the other information appears to include a material misstatement of fact, the assurance practitioner shall discuss the matter with the entity's management.**

61 While reading the other information for the purpose of identifying material inconsistencies, an apparent material misstatement of fact may come to the assurance practitioner's attention (i.e. information, not related to matters appearing in the financial report, that is incorrectly stated or presented). When discussing the matter with the entity's management, ordinarily the assurance practitioner considers the validity of the other information and management's responses to the assurance practitioner's enquiries, whether valid differences of judgement or opinion exist and whether to request management to consult with a qualified third party to resolve the apparent misstatement of fact. If an amendment is necessary to correct a material misstatement of fact and management refuses to make the amendment, ordinarily the assurance practitioner considers taking further action as appropriate, such as notifying those charged with governance and, if necessary, obtaining legal advice.

Communication

62 When, as a result of performing the review of a financial report, a matter comes to the assurance practitioner's attention that causes the assurance practitioner to believe that it is necessary to make a material adjustment to the financial report for it to be prepared, in all material respects, in accordance with the applicable financial reporting framework, the assurance practitioner shall communicate this matter as soon as practicable to the appropriate level of management.

63 When, in the assurance practitioner's judgement, management does not respond appropriately within a reasonable period of time, the assurance practitioner shall inform those charged with governance.

ASRE

64 Such communications are made as soon as practicable, either orally or in writing. The assurance practitioner's decision whether to communicate orally or in writing ordinarily is affected by factors such as the nature, sensitivity and significance of the matter to be communicated and the timing of the communications. If the information is communicated orally, under paragraph 95 of this ASRE, the assurance practitioner needs to document the communication.

65 When, in the assurance practitioner's judgement, those charged with governance do not respond appropriately within a reasonable period of time, the assurance practitioner shall consider:

(a) whether to modify the report; or

(b) the possibility of withdrawing from the engagement.

66 When, as a result of performing the review of a financial report, a matter comes to the assurance practitioner's attention that causes the assurance practitioner to believe in the existence of fraud or non-compliance by the entity with laws and regulations, the assurance practitioner shall communicate the matter as soon as practicable to those charged with governance and shall consider the implications for the review.

67 The determination of which level of management may also be informed is affected by the likelihood of collusion or the involvement of a member(s) of management. Under paragraph 66 of this ASRE, the assurance practitioner needs to report such matters to those charged with governance.

68 The assurance practitioner shall communicate relevant matters of governance interest arising from the review of the financial report to those charged with governance.

69 As a result of performing the review of the financial report, the assurance practitioner may become aware of matters that in the opinion of the assurance practitioner are both important and relevant to those charged with governance in overseeing the financial reporting and disclosure process. Under paragraph 68 of this ASRE, the assurance practitioner needs to communicate such matters to those charged with governance.

Reporting the Nature, Extent and Results of the Review of a Financial Report

70 **The assurance practitioner shall issue a written report that contains the following:**

(a) An appropriate title clearly identifying it as a review report of the independent assurance practitioner.

(b) An addressee, as required by the circumstances of the engagement.

(c) Identification of the financial report reviewed including identification of the title of each of the statements contained in the financial report and the date and period covered by the financial report.

(d) A statement that those charged with governance are responsible for the preparation and fair presentation of the financial report in accordance with the applicable financial reporting framework.

(e) A statement that the assurance practitioner is responsible for expressing a conclusion on the financial report based on the review.

(f) A statement that the review of the financial report was conducted in accordance with Standard on Review Engagements ASRE 2400 *Review of Financial Reports Performed by an Assurance Practitioner Who is Not the Auditor of the Entity*, and that the Standard on Review Engagements requires the assurance practitioner to comply with ethical requirements.

(g) A statement that a review consists of making enquiries, primarily of persons responsible for financial and accounting matters, and applying analytical and other review procedures.

(h) A statement that a review is substantially less in scope than an audit conducted in accordance with Auditing Standards and consequently does not enable the assurance practitioner to obtain assurance that the assurance practitioner would become aware of all significant matters that might be identified in an audit and that accordingly no audit opinion is expressed.

(i) A conclusion as to whether anything has come to the assurance practitioner's attention that causes the assurance practitioner to believe that the financial report does not present fairly, or if applicable, is not true and fair, in all material respects, in accordance with the applicable financial reporting framework (including a reference to the jurisdiction or country of origin of the financial reporting framework when Australia is not the origin of the financial reporting framework used).

(j) The date of the assurance practitioner's review report.

(k) The location in the country or jurisdiction where the assurance practitioner practices.

(l) The assurance practitioner's signature.

71 In some cases, laws or regulations governing the review of a financial report may prescribe wording for the assurance practitioner's conclusion that is different from the wording described in paragraph 70(i). Although the assurance practitioner may be obliged to use the prescribed wording, the assurance practitioner's responsibilities as described in this ASRE for coming to the conclusion remain the same[4]. Appendix 5 to this ASRE contains illustrative review reports.

Departure from the Applicable Financial Reporting Framework

72 **The assurance practitioner shall express a qualified or adverse conclusion when a matter has come to the assurance practitioner's attention that causes the assurance practitioner to believe that a material adjustment should be made to the financial report, for it to be prepared, in all material respects, in accordance with the applicable financial**

4 Auditing Standard ASA 700 *The Auditor's Report on a General Purpose Financial Report*, contains information on the wording of reports that may be helpful.

reporting framework. The assurance practitioner shall include a basis for modification paragraph in the report, that describes the nature of the departure and, if practicable, state the effects on the financial report. If the effects or possible effects are incapable of being measured reliably, a statement to that effect and the reasons therefore shall be included in the basis for modification paragraph. The conclusion paragraph shall be headed "Qualified Conclusion" or "Adverse Conclusion" whichever is relevant.

73 If matters have come to the assurance practitioner's attention that cause the assurance practitioner to believe that the financial report is or may be materially affected by a departure from the applicable financial reporting framework, and those charged with governance do not correct the financial report, under paragraph 72 of this ASRE, the assurance practitioner needs to modify the review report. If the information that the assurance practitioner believes is necessary for adequate disclosure is not included in the financial report, under paragraph 72 of this ASRE, the assurance practitioner needs to modify the review report and, if practicable, include the necessary information in the review report. Appendix 5 to this ASRE contains illustrative review reports with a qualified conclusion.

74 When the effect of the departure is so material and pervasive to the financial report that the assurance practitioner concludes a qualified conclusion is not adequate to disclose the misleading or incomplete nature of the financial report, the assurance practitioner shall express an adverse conclusion.

75 Appendix 5 to this ASRE contains an illustrative review report with an adverse conclusion.

Limitation on Scope

76 Ordinarily, a limitation on scope prevents the assurance practitioner from completing the review.

77 When the assurance practitioner is unable to complete the review, the assurance practitioner shall communicate, in writing, to the appropriate level of management and to those charged with governance the reason why the review cannot be completed, and consider whether it is appropriate to issue a review report.

Limitation on Scope Imposed by Management

78 If, after accepting the engagement, management imposes a limitation on the scope of the review, the assurance practitioner shall request management to remove the limitation. If management refuses the assurance practitioner's request to remove the limitation, the assurance practitioner shall communicate, in writing, to the appropriate level of management and those charged with governance, the reason(s) why the review cannot be completed.

79 If, after accepting the engagement, management imposes a limitation on the scope of the review, under paragraph 78 of this ASRE, the assurance practitioner needs to request the removal of that limitation. If management refuses to do so, the assurance practitioner is unable to complete the review and express a conclusion. In such cases, under paragraph 78 of this ASRE, the assurance practitioner needs to communicate, in writing, to the appropriate level of management and those charged with governance, the reason(s) why the review cannot be completed. Nevertheless, if a matter comes to the assurance practitioner's attention that causes the assurance practitioner to believe that a material adjustment to the financial report is necessary for it to be prepared, in all material respects, in accordance with the applicable financial reporting framework, under paragraphs 62, 63 and 66 of this ASRE, the assurance practitioner needs to communicate such matters to the appropriate level of management and those charged with governance.

80 If management refuses the assurance practitioner's request to remove a limitation that has been imposed on the scope of the review, but there is a legal or regulatory requirement for the assurance practitioner to issue a report, the assurance practitioner shall issue a disclaimer of conclusion or qualified conclusion report containing the reason(s) why the review cannot be completed.

81 Under paragraph 80 of this ASRE, the assurance practitioner needs to consider the legal and regulatory responsibilities, including whether there is a legal or regulatory requirement for the assurance practitioner to issue a report. If there is such a requirement, under paragraph 80

of this ASRE, the assurance practitioner needs to disclaim a conclusion, and provide in the review report the reason why the review cannot be completed. However, if a matter comes to the assurance practitioner's attention that causes the assurance practitioner to believe that a material adjustment to the financial report is necessary for it to be prepared, in all material respects, in accordance with the applicable financial reporting framework, the assurance practitioner, ordinarily under the terms of the engagement, needs to communicate such a matter in the report.

Other Limitations on Scope Not Imposed by Management

82 **When the assurance practitioner concludes that an unqualified conclusion cannot be expressed, the assurance practitioner shall express a qualified conclusion when in rare circumstances there is a limitation on the scope of an assurance practitioner's work, that is confined to one or more specific matters that, while material, are not in the assurance practitioner's judgement pervasive to the financial report. A qualified conclusion shall be expressed as being "except for" the effects of the matter to which the qualification relates. The conclusion paragraph shall be headed "Qualified Conclusion".**

83 A limitation on scope may occur due to circumstances other than a limitation on scope imposed by management or those charged with governance. In such circumstances, the assurance practitioner is ordinarily unable to complete the review and express a conclusion and is guided by paragraphs 80 and 82. There may be, however, some rare circumstances where the limitation on the scope of the assurance practitioner's work is clearly confined to one or more specific matters that, while material, are not in the assurance practitioner's judgement pervasive to the financial report. In such circumstances, under paragraph 82 of this ASRE, the assurance practitioner needs to modify the review report by indicating that, except for the matter which is described in the basis for qualification paragraph to the review report, the review was conducted in accordance with this ASRE, and by qualifying the conclusion. Appendix 5 to this ASRE contains illustrative review reports with a qualified conclusion.

84 The auditor may have expressed a qualified opinion on the audit of the latest annual financial report because of a limitation on the scope of that audit. Under paragraph 82 of this ASRE, the assurance practitioner needs to consider whether that limitation on scope still exists and, if so, the implications for the review report.

Going Concern and Significant Uncertainties

85 In certain circumstances, an emphasis of matter paragraph may be added to a review report, without affecting the assurance practitioner's conclusion, to highlight a matter that is included in a note to the financial report that more extensively discusses the matter. The paragraph would preferably be included after the conclusion paragraph and ordinarily refers to the fact that the conclusion is not qualified in this respect.

86 **If adequate disclosure is made in the financial report, the assurance practitioner shall add an emphasis of matter paragraph to the review report to highlight a material uncertainty relating to an event or condition that may cast significant doubt on the entity's ability to continue as a going concern.**

87 An assurance practitioner, or the auditor of the entity, may have modified a prior audit or review report by adding an emphasis of matter paragraph to highlight a material uncertainty relating to an event or condition that may cast significant doubt on the entity's ability to continue as a going concern. If the material uncertainty still exists and adequate disclosure is made in the financial report, under paragraph 86 of this ASRE, the assurance practitioner needs to modify the review report on the current financial report by adding a paragraph to highlight the continued material uncertainty.

88 If, as a result of enquiries or other review procedures, a material uncertainty relating to an event or condition comes to the assurance practitioner's attention that may cast significant doubt on the entity's ability to continue as a going concern, and adequate disclosure is made in the financial report, under paragraph 86 of this ASRE, the assurance practitioner needs to modify the review report by adding an emphasis of matter paragraph.

89 If a material uncertainty that casts significant doubt about the entity's ability to continue as a going concern is not adequately disclosed in the financial report, the assurance practitioner shall express a qualified or adverse conclusion, as appropriate. The report shall include specific reference to the fact that there is such a material uncertainty.

90 The assurance practitioner shall modify the review report by adding a paragraph to highlight a significant uncertainty (other than a going concern problem) that is adequately disclosed in the financial report, that came to the assurance practitioner's attention, the resolution of which is dependent upon future events and which may materially affect the financial report.

91 If a significant uncertainty (other than a going concern problem) is not adequately disclosed in the financial report, the assurance practitioner shall express a qualified or adverse conclusion, as appropriate. The report shall include specific reference to the fact that there is such a significant uncertainty.

Other Considerations

92 The terms of the engagement include agreement by those charged with governance that where any document containing the financial report indicates that the financial report has been reviewed by the assurance practitioner, the review report will be also included in the document. If those charged with governance have not included the review report in the document, ordinarily the assurance practitioner considers seeking legal advice to assist in determining the appropriate course of action in the circumstances.

93 If the assurance practitioner has issued a modified review report and those charged with governance issue the financial report without including the modified review report in the document containing the financial report, ordinarily the assurance practitioner considers seeking legal advice to assist in determining the appropriate course of action in the circumstances, and the possibility of resigning from the appointment.

94 A summarised financial report does not include all of the information that would be included in a general purpose financial report, but may rather present an explanation of the events and changes that are significant to an understanding of the changes in the financial position and performance of the entity since the annual reporting date. This is because it is presumed that the users of the financial report will have access to the latest audited financial report, such as is the case with listed entities. In other circumstances, ordinarily the assurance practitioner discusses with management the need for the financial report to include a statement that it is to be read in conjunction with the latest audited financial report. In the absence of such a statement, ordinarily the assurance practitioner considers whether, without a reference to the latest audited financial report, the financial report is misleading in the circumstances as well as the implications for the review report.

Documentation

95 The assurance practitioner shall prepare review documentation that is sufficient and appropriate to provide a basis for the assurance practitioner's conclusion and to provide evidence that the review was performed in accordance with this ASRE and applicable legal and regulatory requirements.

96 Under paragraph 95 of this ASRE, the assurance practitioner needs to prepare documentation that enables an experienced assurance practitioner, having no previous connection with the engagement, to understand the nature, timing and extent of the enquiries made and analytical and other review procedures applied, information obtained, and any significant matters considered during the performance of the review, including the disposition of such matters.

Conformity with International Standards on Review Engagements

97 ISRE 2400 *Engagements to Review Financial Statements*, establishes standards and provides guidance to practitioners who are not the auditor of the entity, when engaged to review financial statements. ISRE 2400 is to be applied, adapted as necessary in the circumstances, to engagements to review other historical financial information.

The AUASB has decided that:

- due to the existence of ASRE 2410 *Review of Interim and Other Financial Reports Performed by the Independent Auditor of the Entity* in Australia, ASRE 2400 is to apply only to the review of a financial report and accordingly, is to be consistent with ASRE 2410;
- due to the nature of reviews of other historical financial information, a separate Standard is more appropriate than ASRE 2400 and ASRE 2410 being adapted by the auditor or assurance practitioner for this purpose; and
- ASRE 2405 *Review of Historical Financial Information Other than a Financial Report*, as developed by the AUASB, will more comprehensively deal with reviews of other historical financial information and is based on AUS 902 *Review of Financial Reports* (equivalent ISRE 2400).

Accordingly, ASRE 2400 is not designed to be equivalent to ISRE 2400, however, is intended to conform, with the exceptions listed below, to ISRE 2400 to the extent that ISRE 2400 deals with the review of a financial report by a practitioner who is not the auditor of the entity.

Except as noted below, this ASRE conforms, to the extent described above, with International Standard on Review Engagements ISRE 2400 *Engagements to Review Financial Statements* issued by the International Auditing and Assurance Standards Board (IAASB), an independent standard-setting board of the International Federation of Accountants (IFAC). The main differences between this ASRE and ISRE 2400 are:

- ASRE 2400 includes the following mandatory requirements that are not in ISRE 2400:
  - ♦ This ASRE applies to a review of a financial report comprising historical financial information, performed by an assurance practitioner who is not the auditor of the entity (paragraph 1).
  - ♦ Where in rare and exceptional circumstances, factors outside the assurance practitioner's control prevent the assurance practitioner from complying with a relevant mandatory Requirement in this ASRE, the assurance practitioner shall:
    - (a) if possible, perform appropriate alternative procedures; and
    - (b) document in the working papers:
      - (i) the circumstances surrounding the inability to comply;
      - (ii) the reasons for the inability to comply; and
      - (iii) justification of how alternative procedures achieve the objectives of the mandatory Requirement.

    When the assurance practitioner is unable to perform appropriate alternative procedures, the assurance practitioner shall consider the implications for the assurance practitioner's review report (paragraph 6).
  - ♦ The assurance practitioner shall implement quality control procedures to address the following elements of a quality control system that apply to the individual engagement:
    - (a) leadership responsibilities for quality on the assurance engagement;
    - (b) ethical requirements;
    - (c) acceptance and continuance of client relationships and specific engagements;
    - (d) assignment of engagement teams;
    - (e) engagement performance; and
    - (f) monitoring (paragraph 10).
  - ♦ The assurance practitioner shall obtain evidence that the financial report agrees or reconciles with the underlying accounting records (paragraph 37).
  - ♦ The assurance practitioner shall enquire whether those charged with governance have changed their assessment of the entity's ability to continue as a going concern.

When, as the result of this enquiry or other review procedures, the assurance practitioner becomes aware of events or conditions that may cast significant doubt on the entity's ability to continue as a going concern, the assurance practitioner shall:

(a) enquire of those charged with governance as to their plans for future actions based on their going concern assessment, the feasibility of these plans, and whether they believe that the outcome of these plans will improve the situation; and

(b) consider the adequacy of the disclosure about such matters in the financial report (paragraph 41).

- When comparative information is included for the first time in a financial report, the assurance practitioner shall perform similar procedures on the comparative information as applied to the current period financial report (paragraph 45).
- The assurance practitioner shall evaluate, individually and in the aggregate, whether uncorrected misstatements that have come to the assurance practitioner's attention are material to the financial report (paragraph 50).
- The assurance practitioner shall endeavour to obtain written representations from management that:
  (a) it acknowledges their responsibility for the design and implementation of internal control to prevent and detect fraud and error;
  (b) the financial report is prepared and presented in accordance with the applicable financial reporting framework;
  (c) it believes the effect of those uncorrected misstatements aggregated by the assurance practitioner during the review are immaterial, both individually and in the aggregate, to the financial report taken as a whole. A summary of such items is included in, or attached to, the written representations;
  (d) it has have disclosed to the assurance practitioner all significant facts relating to any fraud(s) or suspected fraud(s) known to it that may have affected the entity;
  (e) it has disclosed to the assurance practitioner the results of its assessment of the risk that the financial report may be materially misstated as a result of fraud;
  (f) it has disclosed to the assurance practitioner all known actual or possible non-compliance with laws and regulations the effects of which are to be considered when preparing the financial report; and
  (g) it has disclosed to the assurance practitioner all significant events that have occurred subsequent to the balance sheet date and through to the date of the review report that may require adjustment to or disclosure in the financial report (paragraph 54).
- If those charged with governance refuse to provide a written representation that the assurance practitioner considers necessary, this constitutes a limitation on the scope of the assurance practitioner's work and the assurance practitioner shall express a qualified conclusion or a disclaimer of conclusion (paragraph 56).
- The assurance practitioner shall read the other information that accompanies the financial report to consider whether any such information is materially inconsistent with the financial report (paragraph 57).
- If a matter comes to the assurance practitioner's attention that causes the assurance practitioner to believe that the other information appears to include a material misstatement of fact, the assurance practitioner shall discuss the matter with the entity's management (paragraph 60).
- When, as a result of performing the review of a financial report, a matter comes to the assurance practitioner's attention that causes the assurance practitioner to believe that it is necessary to make a material adjustment to the financial report for it to be prepared, in all material respects, in accordance with the applicable financial

ASRE

reporting framework, the assurance practitioner shall communicate this matter as soon as practicable to the appropriate level of management (paragraph 62).

- When, in the assurance practitioner's judgement, management does not respond appropriately within a reasonable period of time, the assurance practitioner shall inform those charged with governance (paragraph 63).
- When, in the assurance practitioner's judgement, those charged with governance do not respond appropriately within a reasonable period of time, the assurance practitioner shall consider:
  (a) whether to modify the report; or
  (b) the possibility of withdrawing from the engagement (paragraph 65).
- When, as a result of performing the review of a financial report, a matter comes to the assurance practitioner's attention that causes the assurance practitioner to believe in the existence of fraud or non-compliance by the entity with laws and regulations, the assurance practitioner shall communicate the matter as soon as practicable to those charged with governance and shall consider the implications for the review (paragraph 66).
- The assurance practitioner shall communicate relevant matters of governance interest arising from the review of the financial report to those charged with governance (paragraph 68).

- The "Objective of a Review Engagement" is included in ISRE 2400 as a mandatory paragraph (**bold-type** lettering). However, the equivalent "Objective of an Engagement to Review a Financial Report" paragraph has been included in this proposed ASRE 2400 as explanatory guidance (paragraphs 14-16).
- ISRE 2400 includes a mandatory paragraph requiring the assurance practitioner, when using the work of another assurance practitioner or an expert, to be satisfied that such work is adequate for the purposes of the review. This requirement has not been included as a specific requirement in ASRE 2400 so as to keep ASRE 2400 consistent with ASRE 2410 and ISRE 2410. ASRE 2400 paragraph 32 requires the assurance practitioner to perform review procedures to enable the assurance practitioner to reach a conclusion. Furthermore, the explanatory guidance at paragraph 34 explicitly refers to considering the adequacy of the work of another assurance practitioner or expert (Requirement paragraph 32 and Explanatory Guidance paragraph 34).

Compliance with this Standard on Review Engagements enables compliance with ISRE 2400 to the extent described above.

Appendix 1
Example of an Engagement Letter for a Review Engagement

The following letter is not intended to be a standardised letter. It is to be used as a guide only and will need to be adapted according to the engagement requirements and circumstances.

To [title of those charged with governance:[5]]

Scope

You have requested that we review the financial report of [name of entity], which comprises the balance sheet as at 31 December 20XX, and the related statements of income, changes in equity and cash flows for the [period] ended on that date, and a summary of significant accounting policies and other explanatory notes. We are pleased to confirm our acceptance and our understanding of the terms and objectives of our engagement by means of this letter.

Our review will be conducted in accordance with Standard on Review Engagements ASRE 2400 *Reviews of Financial Reports Performed by an Assurance Practitioner Who is Not the Auditor of the Entity* issued by the Auditing and Assurance Standards Board, with the objective of providing us with a basis for reporting whether anything has come to our attention that causes us to believe that the financial report of [name of entity] is not prepared, in all material respects, in accordance with [applicable financial reporting framework]. Such a review consists of making enquiries, primarily of persons responsible for financial and accounting matters, and applying analytical and other review procedures and does not, ordinarily, require corroboration of the information obtained. The scope of a review of a financial report is substantially less than the scope of an audit conducted in accordance with Auditing Standards whose objective is the expression of an opinion regarding the financial report and accordingly, we shall express no such opinion. ASRE 2400 requires us to also comply with ethical requirements.

We expect to report on the financial report as follows, however, our report may be modified:

[Include text of sample review report - see Appendix 5]

Responsibility for the financial report, including adequate disclosure, is that of [those charged with governance.[6]] This includes establishing and maintaining internal control relevant to the preparation and fair presentation of the financial report that is free from material misstatement, whether due to fraud or error, selecting and applying appropriate accounting policies, and making accounting estimates that are reasonable in the circumstances. As part of our review, we shall request written representations from management concerning assertions made in connection with the review. We shall also request that where any document containing the financial report indicates that the financial report has been reviewed, our report will also be included in the document.

A review of the financial report does not provide assurance that we shall become aware of all significant matters that might be identified in an audit. Further, our engagement cannot be relied upon to identify whether fraud or errors, or illegal acts exist. However, we shall inform you of any material matters that come to our attention.

Presentation of the reviewed financial report on the Internet [Insert if applicable]

It is our understanding that [the entity] intends to publish a hard copy of the reviewed financial report and the assurance practitioner's review report, and to electronically present the reviewed financial report and our review report on its internet web site. When information is presented electronically on a web site, the security and controls over information on the web site should be addressed by [the entity] to maintain the integrity of the data presented. The examination of the controls over the electronic presentation of reviewed financial information on the entity's web site is beyond the scope of the review of the financial report. Responsibility for the electronic presentation of the financial report on the entity's web site is that of the [governing body of the entity].

5 Insert the appropriate term, such as "Directors" or "Board of Management".

6 Insert the appropriate term, such as "Directors" or "Board of Management".

Fees

[Insert additional information here regarding fee arrangements and billings, as appropriate.]

We look forward to full co-operation with your staff and we trust that they will make available to us whatever records, documentation and other information are requested in connection with our review.

[This letter will be effective for future years unless it is terminated, amended or superseded.][7]

Please sign and return the attached copy of this letter to indicate that it is in accordance with your understanding of the arrangements for our review of the financial report.

Yours faithfully,

(signed)

....

Name and Title Date

Acknowledged on behalf of [entity] by

(signed)

....

Name and Title Date

Appendix 2

Example of a Management Representation Letter for a Review Engagement

The following letter is not intended to be a standardised letter. It is to be used as a guide only and will need to be adapted according to the engagement requirements and circumstances.

Representations by management will vary from one entity to another and from one period to the next. Representation letters are ordinarily useful where evidence, other than that obtained by enquiry, may not be reasonably expected to be available or when management have made oral representations which the assurance practitioner wishes to confirm in writing.

[Entity Letterhead]

[Addressee – Assurance Practitioner]

[Date]

This representation letter is provided in connection with your review of the financial report of [name of entity] for the [period] ended [date], for the purpose of you expressing a conclusion as to whether anything has come to your attention that causes you to believe that the financial report of [name of entity] is not prepared, in all material respect, in accordance with [applicable financial reporting framework].

We acknowledge our responsibility for ensuring that the financial report is prepared and presented [fairly] in accordance with [indicate applicable financial reporting framework] and confirm that the financial report is free of material misstatement including omissions.

We confirm, to the best of our knowledge and belief, the following representations made to you during your review.

7 Use if applicable.

[Include representations required by this ASRE (paragraph 54) and those relevant to the entity. Such representations may include the following examples.]

1. We have made available to you:
   (a) all financial records and related data, other information, explanations and assistance necessary for the conduct of the review; and
   (b) minutes of all meetings of [shareholders, directors, committees of directors, Boards of Management].
2. We have disclosed to you the results of our assessment of the risk that the [financial report] may be materially misstated as a result of fraud.
3. There:
   (a) has been no fraud or suspected fraud, error or non-compliance with laws and regulations involving management or employees who have a significant role in the internal control structure;
   (b) has been no fraud or suspected fraud, error or non-compliance with laws and regulations that could have a material effect on the financial report; and
   (c) have been no communications from regulatory agencies concerning non-compliance with, or deficiencies in, financial reporting practices that could have a material effect on the financial report.
4. We are responsible for, and have established and maintained, an adequate internal control structure to prevent and detect fraud and error and to facilitate the preparation of a reliable financial report, and adequate financial records have been maintained. There are no material transactions that have not been recorded properly in the accounting records underlying the financial report.
5. We have no plans or intentions that may affect materially the carrying values, or classification, of assets and liabilities.
6. We have considered the requirements of Accounting Standard AASB 136 *Impairment of Assets*, when assessing the impairment of assets and in ensuring that no assets are stated in excess of their recoverable amount.
7. We believe the effects of uncorrected misstatements summarised in the accompanying schedule are immaterial, both individually and in the aggregate, to the financial report taken as a whole.
8. The following have been recorded and/or disclosed properly in the financial report:
   (a) related party transactions and related amounts receivable or payable, including sales, purchases, loans, transfers, leasing arrangements and guarantees (written or oral);
   (b) share options, warrants, conversions or other requirements;
   (c) arrangements involving restrictions on cash balances, compensating balances and line-of-credit or similar arrangements;
   (d) agreements to repurchase assets previously sold;
   (e) material liabilities or assets (including contingent liabilities / assets and those arising under derivative financial instruments);
   (f) unasserted claims or assessments that our lawyer(s) has advised us are probable of assertion; and
   (g) losses arising from the fulfilment of, or an inability to fulfil, any sale commitments or as a result of purchase commitments for inventory quantities in excess of normal requirements or at prices in excess of prevailing market prices.
9. There are no violations or possible violations of laws or regulations the effects of which should be considered for disclosure in the financial report or as a basis for recording an expense.
10. The entity has satisfactory title to all assets, and there are no liens or encumbrances on such assets that have not been disclosed nor has any asset been pledged as collateral. Allowances for depreciation have been adjusted for all significant items of property, plant and equipment that have been abandoned or are otherwise unusable.

11. The entity has complied with all aspects of contractual agreements that would have a material effect on the financial report in the event of non-compliance.
12. There were no material commitments for construction or acquisition of property, plant and equipment or to acquire other non-current assets, such as investments or intangible assets, other than those disclosed in the financial report.
13. We have no plans to abandon any significant lines of product, or other plans or intentions that will result in any excess or obsolete inventory, and no inventory is stated at an amount in excess of its net realisable value.
14. No events have occurred subsequent to the balance sheet date through to the date of this letter that would require adjustment to, or disclosure in, the financial report.

We understand that your review was made in accordance with Standard on Review Engagements ASRE 2400 *Reviews of Financial Reports Performed by an Assurance Practitioner Who is Not the Auditor of the Entity* and was, therefore, designed primarily for the purpose of expressing a conclusion on the financial report of [the entity], and that your procedures were limited to those which you considered necessary for that purpose.

Yours faithfully

[Name of signing officer and title]

Notes:

[*The above example representation letter may need to be amended in certain circumstances. The following illustrate some of those situations.*]

(a) **Exceptions**

Where matters are disclosed in the financial report, the associated representation needs to be amended, for example:

- If a subsequent event has been disclosed, Item 14 (above) could be modified to read: "Except as discussed in Note X to the financial report, no events have occurred"
- If the entity has plans that impact the carrying values of assets and liabilities, Item 13 (above) could be modified to read:

  "The entity has no plans or intentions that may materially affect the carrying amount or classification of assets and liabilities, except for our plan to dispose of segment X, as disclosed in note Y in the in the financial report, and which is discussed in the minutes of the meeting of the governing body[8] held on [date]".

(b) **Other Required Information**

Certain entities may be required to include other information in the financial report, for example, performance indicators for government entities. In addition to identifying this information and the applicable financial reporting framework in paragraphs 1 and 2 of the example Management Representation Letter, an additional paragraph similar to the following may be appropriate:

"The disclosures of key performance indicators have been prepared and presented in conformity with [relevant statutory requirements] and we consider the indicators reported to be relevant to the stated objectives of the [entity]".

(c) **Management's Opinions and Representations in the Notes to the Financial Statements**

Where the notes to the financial statements include opinions and representations by management, such matters may be addressed in the representation letter. This may include, for example, notes relating to the anticipated outcome of litigation, the intention and ability of the entity regarding held-to-maturity investments and plans necessary to support the going concern basis.

8 Insert the appropriate term, such as "Directors" or "Board of Management".

(d) **Environmental Matters**

In situations where there are environmental matters that may, but probably will not, require an outflow of resources, this may be reflected in an addition to Item 9 (above), for example:

> "However, the [entity] has received a notice from the Environmental Protection Agency that it may be required to share in the cost of cleanup of the [name] waste disposal site. This matter has been disclosed in Note A in the financial report and we believe that the disclosure and estimated contingent loss is reasonable based on available information."

(e) **Compliance**

If, as part of the review, the assurance practitioner is required also to report on the entity's compliance with laws and regulations, a representation may be appropriate acknowledging that management is responsible for the entity's compliance with applicable laws and regulations and that the requirements have been met.

(f) **Other Matters**

Additional representations that may be appropriate in specific situations may include the following:

- Justification for a change in accounting policy.
- The work of an expert has been used.
- Arrangements for controlling the dissemination of the financial report and assurance practitioner's review report on the Internet.

Appendix 3

Analytical Procedures the Assurance Practitioner May Consider when Performing a Review of a Financial Report

The analytical procedures carried out in a review of a financial report are determined by the assurance practitioner exercising professional judgement. The procedures listed below are for illustrative purposes only. It is not intended that all the procedures suggested apply to every review engagement, nor is the Appendix intended to serve as a program or checklist in the conduct of a review.

Examples of analytical procedures the assurance practitioner may consider when performing a review of a financial report include the following:

- Comparing the financial report with the financial report of the immediately preceding period, with the financial report of the corresponding period of the preceding financial year, with the financial report that was expected by management for the current period, and with the most recent audited annual financial report.
- Comparing the current financial report with anticipated results, such as budgets or forecasts. For example, comparing tax balances and the relationship between the provision for income taxes to pre-tax income in the current financial report with corresponding information in:
  - ♦ budgets, using expected rates; and
  - ♦ financial information for prior periods.
- Comparing the current financial report with relevant non-financial information.
- Comparing the recorded amounts, or ratios developed from recorded amounts, to expectations developed by the assurance practitioner. The assurance practitioner develops such expectations by identifying and applying relationships that reasonably are expected to exist based on the assurance practitioner's understanding of the entity and of the industry in which the entity operates.
- Comparing ratios and indicators for the current period with those of entities in the same industry.

- Comparing relationships among elements in the current financial report with corresponding relationships in the financial report of prior periods, for example, expense by type as a percentage of revenue, assets by type as a percentage of total assets, and percentage of change in revenue to percentage of change in receivables.
- Comparing disaggregated data. The following are examples of how data may be disaggregated:
  - ♦ by period, for example, revenue or expense items disaggregated into quarterly, monthly, or weekly amounts;
  - ♦ by product line or source of revenue;
  - ♦ by location, for example by component;
  - ♦ by attributes of the transaction, for example, revenue generated by designers, architects, or craftsmen; and
  - ♦ by several attributes of the transaction, for example, revenue by product and month.

Appendix 4

Illustrative Detailed Procedures that the Assurance Practitioner may Consider when Performing a Review Engagement

1. The enquiry and analytical procedures carried out in a review engagement are determined by the assurance practitioner exercising professional judgement. The procedures listed below are for illustrative purposes only and are considered by the assurance practitioner, who is presumed to have obtained an understanding of the entity and its environment, including internal control relative to the preparation of the financial report. It is not intended that all the procedures suggested apply to every review engagement. This Appendix is not intended to serve as a program or checklist in the conduct of a review.

General

2. Discuss terms and scope of the engagement with the engagement team.
3. Enquire whether all financial information is recorded:

   (a) completely;

   (b) promptly; and

   (c) after the necessary authorisation.
4. Enquire about the accounting policies and consider whether:

   (a) they comply with the applicable financial reporting framework;

   (b) they have been applied appropriately; and

   (c) they have been applied consistently and, if not, consider whether disclosure has been made of any changes in the accounting policies.
5. Enquire about the policies and procedures to assess impairment of assets and any consequential estimation of recoverable amount.
6. Enquire about the policies and procedures to determine the fair value of assets and liabilities.
7. Enquire if actions taken at meetings of shareholders or those charged with governance which affect the financial report have been appropriately reflected therein.
8. Enquire about plans to dispose of major assets or business/geographical segments.
9. Obtain the financial report and discuss it with management and those charged with governance.
10. Consider the adequacy, classification and presentation of disclosures in the financial report.

11. Compare the outcomes shown in the current period financial report with those shown in financial reports for comparable prior periods and, if available, with the relevant budgets and forecasts.
12. Obtain explanations from management for any unusual fluctuations or inconsistencies in the financial report.

Cash

13. Obtain the bank reconciliations. Enquire about any old or unusual reconciling items.
14. Enquire about transfers between cash accounts for the period immediately before and after the review date.
15. Enquire whether there are any restrictions on cash accounts.

Receivables

16. Enquire about the accounting policies for initially recording trade receivables and determine whether any allowances for doubtful debts are made on such transactions.
17. Obtain a schedule of receivables and determine whether the total agrees with the trial balance.
18. Obtain and consider explanations of significant variations in account balances from previous periods or from those anticipated.
19. Obtain an aged analysis of the trade receivables. Enquire about the reason for unusually large accounts, credit balances on accounts or any other unusual balances and enquire about the collectibility of aged receivables.
20. Discuss with management the classification of receivables, including non-current balances, net credit balances and amounts due from shareholders, those charged with governance, and other related parties in the financial report.
21. Enquire about the methods for identifying and calculating the impairment of assets and consider them for reasonableness.
22. Enquire whether receivables have been pledged, factored or discounted.
23. Enquire about procedures applied to ensure that a proper cut-off of revenue transactions and sales returns has been achieved.
24. Enquire whether receivables balances represent goods shipped on consignment and, if so, whether adjustments have been made to reverse these transactions and include the goods in inventory.
25. Enquire whether any large credits relating to recorded income have been issued after the balance sheet reporting period and whether provision has been made for such amounts.

Inventories

26. Obtain the inventory list and determine whether:
    (a) the total agrees with the balance in the trial balance; and
    (b) the list is based on a physical count of inventory.
27. Enquire about the method for counting inventory.
28. Where a physical count was not carried out on the date of the reporting period, enquire whether:
    (a) a perpetual inventory system is used and whether periodic comparisons are made with actual quantities on hand; and
    (b) an integrated cost system is used and whether it has produced reliable information in the past.
29. Discuss adjustments made resulting from the last physical inventory count.
30. Enquire about procedures applied to control cut-off and any inventory movements at period end.

ASRE

31. Enquire about the basis used in valuing each inventory classification and, in particular, regarding the elimination of intra-group income. Enquire whether inventory is valued at the lower of cost and net realisable value (or lower of cost and current replacement cost for not-for-profit organisations).
32. Consider the consistency with which inventory valuation methods have been applied, including factors such as material, labour and overhead.
33. Compare amounts of major inventory categories with those of prior periods and with those anticipated for the current period. Enquire about major fluctuations and differences.
34. Compare inventory turnover with that in previous periods.
35. Enquire about the method used for identifying slow moving and obsolete inventory and whether such inventory has been accounted for at the lower of cost and net realisable value.
36. Enquire whether any inventory has been consigned to the entity and, if so, whether adjustments have been made to exclude such goods from inventory.
37. Enquire whether any inventory is pledged, stored at other locations or on consignment to others and consider whether such transactions have been accounted for appropriately.

Investments (Including Investments in Associates and Financial Instruments)

38. Obtain a schedule of investments at the date of the reporting period and determine whether it agrees with the trial balance.
39. Enquire about the accounting policies applied to investments.
40. Enquire from management about the carrying amounts of investments. Consider whether there are any realisation or other impairment problems.
41. Consider whether there has been proper accounting for gains and losses and investment income.
42. Enquire about the classification of long-term and short-term investments.

Property, Plant and Equipment and Depreciation

43. Obtain a schedule of the property, plant and equipment indicating the cost and accumulated depreciation and determine whether it agrees with the trial balance.
44. Enquire about the accounting policy applied regarding residual values, provisions to allocate the cost of property, plant and equipment over their estimated useful lives using the expected pattern of consumption of the future economic benefits and distinguishing between capital and maintenance items. Consider whether the property, plant and equipment have suffered an impairment in value.
45. Discuss with management significant additions and disposals to property, plant and equipment accounts and accounting for gains and losses on disposals or de-recognition. Enquire whether all such transactions have been accounted for.
46. Enquire about the consistency with which the depreciation method and rates have been applied and compare depreciation accumulations with prior years.
47. Enquire whether there are any restrictions on the property, plant and equipment.
48. Discuss whether lease agreements have been properly reflected in the financial report in conformity with current accounting pronouncements.

Prepaid Expenses, Intangibles and Other Assets

49. Obtain schedules identifying the nature of these accounts and discuss with management the recoverability thereof.
50. Enquire about the basis for recording these accounts and the amortisation methods used.
51. Compare balances of related expense accounts with those of prior periods and discuss significant variations with management.
52. Discuss the classification basis between current and non-current accounts with management.

Loans Payable

53. Obtain from management a schedule of loans payable and determine whether the total agrees with the trial balance.
54. Enquire whether there are any loans where management has not complied with the provisions of the loan agreement and, if so, enquire as to management's actions and whether appropriate adjustments have been made in the financial report.
55. Consider the reasonableness of interest expense in relation to loan balances.
56. Enquire whether loans payable are secured.
57. Enquire whether loans payable have been appropriately classified between current and non-current.

Trade Payables

58. Enquire about the accounting policies for initially recording trade payables and whether the entity is entitled to any allowances given on such transactions.
59. Obtain and consider explanations of significant variations in account balances from previous periods or from those anticipated.
60. Obtain a schedule of trade payables and determine whether the total agrees with the trial balance.
61. Enquire whether balances are reconciled with the creditors' statements and compare with prior period balances. Compare turnover with prior periods.
62. Consider whether there could be material unrecorded liabilities.
63. Enquire whether payables to shareholders, those charged with governance and other related parties are disclosed separately.

Other Liabilities and Contingent Liabilities

64. Obtain a schedule of the other liabilities and determine whether the total agrees with the trial balance.
65. Compare major balances of related expense accounts with similar accounts for prior periods.
66. Enquire about approvals for such other liabilities, terms of payment, compliance with terms, collateral and classification.
67. Enquire about the method for determining other liabilities.
68. Enquire as to the nature of amounts disclosed in contingent liabilities and commitments.
69. Enquire whether any actual or contingent liabilities exist which have not been recognised/disclosed in the financial report. If so, discuss with management and/or those charged with governance whether provisions need to be made in the accounts or whether disclosure should be made in the notes to the financial report.

Income and Other Taxes

70. Discuss with management if there were any events, including disputes with taxation authorities, which could have a significant effect on the taxes payable by the entity.
71. Consider the tax expense in relation to the entity's income for the period.
72. Discuss with management the adequacy of the recognised deferred tax assets and/or liabilities and amounts in respect of prior periods.

Subsequent Events

73. Obtain from management the latest financial report and compare it with the financial report being reviewed or with those for comparable periods from the preceding year.
74. Enquire about events after the balance sheet date that would have a material effect on the financial report under review and, in particular, enquire whether:
    (a) any substantial commitments or uncertainties have arisen subsequent to the balance sheet date;
    (b) any significant changes in the share capital, long-term debt or working capital have occurred up to the date of enquiry; and

(c) any unusual adjustments have been made during the period between the balance sheet date and the date of enquiry.

Consider the need for adjustments or disclosure in the financial report.

75. Obtain and read the minutes of meetings of shareholders, those charged with governance and appropriate committees subsequent to the review date.

Litigation

76. Discuss with management whether the entity is the subject of any legal actions - threatened, pending or in process. Consider the effect on the financial report.

Equity

77. Obtain and consider a schedule of the transactions in the equity accounts, including equity contributions, buy-backs of the entity's own equity instruments and dividends.

78. Enquire whether there are any restrictions on retained earnings or other equity accounts.

Operations

79. Compare results with those of prior periods and those expected for the current period. Discuss significant movements/variations with management.

80. Discuss whether the recognition of major revenue and expense items have taken place in the appropriate periods.

81. Enquire about the policies and procedures related to accrued revenue and/or expenses.

82. Consider and discuss with management the relationship between related items in the revenue accounts and assess the reasonableness thereof in the context of similar relationships for prior periods and other available information.

Appendix 5

Example Review Engagement Reports

The following example review reports are to be used as a guide only and will need to be adapted according to the engagement requirements and circumstances.

Example 1: Financial report prepared in accordance with a financial reporting framework designed to achieve fair presentation.

EXAMPLE OF AN UNMODIFIED ASSURANCE PRACTITIONER'S REVIEW REPORT ON A FINANCIAL REPORT

INDEPENDENT ASSURANCE PRACTIONER'S REVIEW REPORT

To [appropriate addressee]

Report on the [appropriate title for the financial report] Financial Report

We have reviewed the accompanying [period] financial report of [name of entity], which comprises the balance sheet as at [date], and the income statement, statement of changes in equity and cash flow statement for the [period] ended on that date, a [statement or description of accounting policies[9]], other selected explanatory notes [and the declaration of those charged with governance[10]].[11] [12]

---

9 Insert relevant statement or description of accounting policies.

10 Amend this term to reflect the appropriate title for those charged with governance.

11 When the assurance practitioner is aware that the financial report will be included in a document that contains other information, the assurance practitioner may consider, if the form of presentation allows, identifying the page numbers on which the reviewed financial report is presented.

12 The assurance practitioner may wish to specify the regulatory authority or equivalent with whom the financial report is filed.

[Title of those charged with governance]' Responsibility for the [period] Financial Report

The [title of those charged with governance] of the [type of entity] are responsible for the preparation and fair presentation of the [period] financial report in accordance with the [applicable financial reporting framework]. This responsibility includes establishing and maintaining internal control relevant to the preparation and fair presentation of the [period] financial report that is free from material misstatement, whether due to fraud or error; selecting and applying appropriate accounting policies; and making accounting estimates that are reasonable in the circumstances.

Assurance Practitioner's Responsibility

Our responsibility is to express a conclusion on the [period] financial report based on our review. We conducted our review in accordance with Standard on Review Engagements ASRE 2400 *Review of a Financial Report Performed by an Assurance Practitioner Who is Not the Auditor of the Entity*, in order to state whether, on the basis of the procedures described, anything has come to our attention that causes us to believe that the financial report is not presented fairly, in all material respects, in accordance with the [applicable financial reporting framework]. ASRE 2400 requires us to comply with the requirements of the applicable code of professional conduct of a professional accounting body.

A review of a [period] financial report consists of making enquiries, primarily of persons responsible for financial and accounting matters, and applying analytical and other review procedures. A review is substantially less in scope than an audit conducted in accordance with Australian Auditing Standards and consequently does not enable us to obtain assurance that we would become aware of all significant matters that might be identified in an audit. Accordingly, we do not express an audit opinion.

[*Independence*

In conducting our review, we have complied with the independence requirements of the Australian professional accounting bodies[13]].

Conclusion

Based on our review, which is not an audit, nothing has come to our attention that causes us to believe that the [period] financial report of [name of entity] does not present fairly, in all material respects, [or "give a true and fair view of[14]"] the financial position of the [type of entity] as at [date], and of its financial performance and its cash flows for the [period] ended on that date, in accordance with [applicable financial reporting framework].

Report on Other Legal and Regulatory Requirements

[Form and content of this section of the assurance practitioner's review report will vary depending on the nature of the assurance practitioner's other reporting responsibilities.]

[Assurance Practitioner's signature[15]]

[Date of the Assurance Practitioner's review report]

[Assurance Practitioner's address]

13 Use when appropriate.

14 Auditing Standard ASA 700 *The Auditor's Report on a General Purpose Financial Report*, contains information on the wording of reports that may be helpful.

15 The assurance practitioner's review report is required to be signed in one or more of the name of the assurance practitioner's firm, the name of the assurance practitioner's company or the personal name of the assurance practitioner as appropriate.

Example 2: Financial report prepared in accordance with a financial reporting framework designed to achieve fair presentation.

EXAMPLE OF AN ASSURANCE PRACTITIONER'S REVIEW REPORT WITH A QUALIFIED CONCLUSION FOR A DEPARTURE FROM THE APPLICABLE FINANCIAL REPORTING FRAMEWORK

INDEPENDENT ASSURANCE PRACTITIONER'S REVIEW REPORT

To [appropriate addressee]

Report on the [appropriate title for the financial report] Financial Report

We have reviewed the accompanying [period] financial report of [name of entity], which comprises the balance sheet as at [date], and the income statement, statement of changes in equity and cash flow statement for the [period] ended on that date, a [statement or description of accounting policies,[16]] other selected explanatory notes [and the declaration of those charged with governance[17]] [18] [19]

[*Title of those charged with governance*]*' Responsibility for the* [*period*] *Financial Report*

The [title of those charged with governance] of the [type of entity] are responsible for the preparation and fair presentation of the [period] financial report in accordance with the [applicable financial reporting framework]. This responsibility includes establishing and maintaining internal control relevant to the preparation and fair presentation of the [period] financial report that is free from material misstatement, whether due to fraud or error; selecting and applying appropriate accounting policies; and making accounting estimates that are reasonable in the circumstances.

Assurance Practitioner's Responsibility

Our responsibility is to express a conclusion on the [period] financial report based on our review. We conducted our review in accordance with Standard on Review Engagements ASRE 2400 *Review of a Financial Report Performed by an Assurance Practitioner Who is Not the Auditor of the Entity*, in order to state whether, on the basis of the procedures described, anything has come to our attention that causes us to believe that the financial report is not presented fairly, in all material respects, in accordance with the [applicable financial reporting framework]. ASRE 2400 requires us to comply with the requirements of the applicable code of professional conduct of a professional accounting body.

A review of a [period] financial report consists of making enquiries, primarily of persons responsible for financial and accounting matters, and applying analytical and other review procedures. A review is substantially less in scope than an audit conducted in accordance with Australian Auditing Standards and consequently does not enable us to obtain assurance that we would become aware of all significant matters that might be identified in an audit. Accordingly, we do not express an audit opinion.

[*Independence*

In conducting our review, we have complied with the independence requirements of the Australian professional accounting bodies[20]].

Basis for Qualified Conclusion

Based on information provided to us by management, [name of entity] has excluded from property, plant and equipment and long-term debt certain lease obligations that we believe should be capitalised to conform with [indicate applicable financial reporting framework]. This information indicates that if these lease obligations were capitalised at 31 December 20XX, property, plant and

16 Insert relevant statement or description of accounting policies.

17 Amend this term to reflect the appropriate title for those charged with governance.

18 When the assurance practitioner is aware that the financial report will be included in a document that contains other information, the assurance practitioner may consider, if the form of presentation allows, identifying the page numbers on which the reviewed financial report is presented.

19 The assurance practitioner may wish to specify the regulatory authority or equivalent with whom the financial report is filed.

20 Use when appropriate.

equipment would be increased by $_______, long-term debt by $_______, and net income and earnings per share would be increased (decreased) by $_________ and $_________ respectively for the [period] ended on that date.

Qualified Conclusion

Based on our review, which is not an audit, with the exception of the matter described in the preceding paragraph, nothing has come to our attention that causes us to believe that the [period] financial report of [name of entity] does not present fairly, in all material respects, [or "give a true and fair view of"[21]] the financial position of the [type of entity] as at [date], and of its financial performance and its cash flows for the [period] period ended on that date, in accordance with [applicable financial reporting framework].

Report on Other Legal and Regulatory Requirements

[Form and content of this section of the assurance practitioner's review report will vary depending on the nature of the assurance practitioner's other reporting responsibilities].

[Assurance Practitioner's signature[22]]

[Date of the Assurance Practitioner's review report]

[Assurance Practitioner's address]

Example 3: Financial report prepared in accordance with a financial reporting framework designed to achieve fair presentation.

EXAMPLE OF AN ASSURANCE PRACTITIONER'S REVIEW REPORT WITH A QUALIFIED CONCLUSION FOR A LIMITATION ON SCOPE NOT IMPOSED BY MANAGEMENT

INDEPENDENT ASSURANCE PRACTITIONER'S REVIEW REPORT

To [appropriate addressee]

Report on the [appropriate title for the financial report] Financial Report

We have reviewed the accompanying [period] financial report of [name of entity], which comprises the balance sheet as at [date], and the income statement, statement of changes in equity and cash flow statement for the [period] ended on that date, a [statement or description of accounting policies[23]], other selected explanatory notes [and the declaration of those charged with governance[24]] [25] [26]

[Title of those charged with governance]' Responsibility for the [period] Financial Report

The [title of those charged with governance] of the [type of entity] are responsible for the preparation and fair presentation of the [period] financial report in accordance with the [applicable financial reporting framework]. This responsibility includes: establishing and maintaining internal control relevant to the preparation and fair presentation of the [period] financial report that is free from material misstatement, whether due to fraud or error; selecting and applying appropriate accounting policies; and making accounting estimates that are reasonable in the circumstances.

---

21 Auditing Standard ASA 700 *The Auditor's Report on a General Purpose Financial Report*, contains information on the wording of reports that may be helpful.

22 The assurance practitioner's review report is required to be signed in one or more of the name of the audit firm, the name of the audit company or the personal name of the assurance practitioner as appropriate.

23 Insert relevant statement or description of accounting policies.

24 Amend this term to reflect the appropriate title for those charged with governance.

25 When the assurance practitioner is aware that the financial report will be included in a document that contains other information, the assurance practitioner may consider, if the form of presentation allows, identifying the page numbers on which the reviewed financial report is presented.

26 The assurance practitioner may wish to specify the regulatory authority or equivalent with whom the financial report is filed.

Assurance Practitioner's Responsibility

Our responsibility is to express a conclusion on the [period] financial report based on our review. We conducted our review in accordance with Standard on Review Engagements ASRE 2400 *Review of a Financial Report Performed by an Assurance Practitioner Who is Not the Auditor of the Entity*, in order to state whether, on the basis of the procedures described, anything has come to our attention that causes us to believe that the financial report is not presented fairly, in all material respects, in accordance with the [applicable financial reporting framework]. ASRE 2400 requires us to comply with the requirements of the applicable code of professional conduct of a professional accounting body.

A review of a [period] financial report consists of making enquiries, primarily of persons responsible for financial and accounting matters, and applying analytical and other review procedures. A review is substantially less in scope than an audit conducted in accordance with Australian Auditing Standards and consequently does not enable us to obtain assurance that we would become aware of all significant matters that might be identified in an audit. Accordingly, we do not express an audit opinion.

[*Independence*

In conducting our review, we have complied with the independence requirements of the Australian professional accounting bodies[27]].

Basis for Qualified Conclusion

As a result of a fire in a branch office on [date] that destroyed its accounts receivable records, we were unable to complete our review of accounts receivable totalling $XXX included in the [period] financial report. The [type of entity] is in the process of reconstructing these records and is uncertain as to whether these records will support the amount shown above and the related allowance for uncollectible accounts. Had we been able to complete our review of accounts receivable, matters might have come to our attention indicating that adjustments might be necessary to the [period] financial report.

Qualified Conclusion

Except for the adjustments to the [period] financial report that we might have become aware of had it not been for the situation described above, based on our review, which is not an audit, nothing has come to our attention that causes us to believe that the [period] financial report of [name of entity] does not present fairly, in all material respects, [or "give a true and fair view of[28]]" the financial position of the [type of entity] as at [date], and of its financial performance and its cash flows for the [period] period ended on that date, in accordance with [applicable financial reporting framework].

Report on Other Legal and Regulatory Requirements

[Form and content of this section of the assurance practitioner's review report will vary depending on the nature of the assurance practitioner's other reporting responsibilities.]

[Assurance Practitioner's signature[29]]

[Date of the Assurance Practitioner's review report]

[Assurance Practitioner's address]

27 Use when appropriate.

28 Auditing Standard ASA 700 *The Auditor's Report on a General Purpose Financial Report*, contains information on the wording of reports that may be helpful.

29 The assurance practitioner's review report is required to be signed in one or more of the name of the audit firm, the name of the audit company or the personal name of the assurance practitioner as appropriate.

Example 4: Financial report prepared in accordance with a financial reporting framework designed to achieve fair presentation.

EXAMPLE OF AN ASSURANCE PRACTITIONER'S REVIEW REPORT WITH AN ADVERSE CONCLUSION FOR A DEPARTURE FROM THE APPLICABLE FINANCIAL REPORTING FRAMEWORK

INDEPENDENT ASSURANCE PRACTITIONER'S REVIEW REPORT

To [appropriate addressee]

Report on the [appropriate title for the financial report] Financial Report

We have reviewed the accompanying [period] financial report of [name of entity], which comprises the balance sheet as at [date], and the income statement, statement of changes in equity and cash flow statement for the [period] ended on that date, a [statement or description of accounting policies[30]], other selected explanatory notes [and the declaration of those charged with governance.[31]] [32] [33]

[Title of those charged with governance]' Responsibility for the [period] Financial Report

The [title of those charged with governance] of the [type of entity] are responsible for the preparation and fair presentation of the [period] financial report in accordance with the [applicable financial reporting framework]. This responsibility includes: establishing and maintaining internal control relevant to the preparation and fair presentation of the [period] financial report that is free from material misstatement, whether due to fraud or error; selecting and applying appropriate accounting policies; and making accounting estimates that are reasonable in the circumstances.

ASRE

Assurance Practitioner's Responsibility

Our responsibility is to express a conclusion on the [period] financial report based on our review. We conducted our review in accordance with Standard on Review Engagements ASRE 2400 *Review of a Financial Report Performed by an Assurance Practitioner Who is Not the Auditor of the Entity*, in order to state whether, on the basis of the procedures described, anything has come to our attention that causes us to believe that the financial report is not presented fairly, in all material respects, in accordance with the [applicable financial reporting framework]. ASRE 2400 requires us to comply with the requirements of the applicable code of professional conduct of a professional accounting body.

A review of a [period] financial report consists of making enquiries, primarily of persons responsible for financial and accounting matters, and applying analytical and other review procedures. A review is substantially less in scope than an audit conducted in accordance with Australian Auditing Standards and consequently does not enable us to obtain assurance that we would become aware of all significant matters that might be identified in an audit. Accordingly, we do not express an audit opinion.

[Independence

In conducting our review, we have complied with the independence requirements of the Australian professional accounting bodies[34]].

Basis for Adverse Conclusion

Commencing this period, the [title of those charged with governance] of the [type of entity] ceased to consolidate the financial reports of its subsidiary companies since the [title of those charged with governance] considers consolidation to be inappropriate because of the existence of new substantial non-controlling interests. This is not in accordance with [applicable financial

30 Insert relevant statement or description of accounting policies.

31 Amend this term to reflect the appropriate title for those charged with governance.

32 When the assurance practitioner is aware that the financial report will be included in a document that contains other information, the assurance practitioner may consider, if the form of presentation allows, identifying the page numbers on which the reviewed financial report is presented.

33 The assurance practitioner may wish to specify the regulatory authority or equivalent with whom the financial report is filed.

34 Use when appropriate.

reporting framework]. Had a consolidated financial report been prepared, virtually every account in the financial report would have been materially different.

Adverse Conclusion

Our review indicates, because the [type of entity's] investment in subsidiary companies is not accounted for on a consolidation basis, as described in the preceding paragraph, this [period] financial report of [name of entity] does not present fairly, in all material respects, [or "give a true and fair view of[35]]" the financial position of the [type of entity] as at [date], and of its financial performance and its cash flows for the [period] period ended on that date, in accordance with [applicable financial reporting framework].

Report on Other Legal and Regulatory Requirements

[Form and content of this section of the assurance practitioner's review report will vary depending on the nature of the assurance practitioner's other reporting responsibilities.]

[Assurance Practitioner's signature[36]]

[Date of the Assurance Practitioner's review report]

[Assurance Practitioner's address]

Example 5: Financial report prepared in accordance with a financial reporting framework designed to achieve fair presentation

EXAMPLE OF AN ASSURANCE PRACTITIONER'S REVIEW REPORT WITH A QUALIFIED CONCLUSION ON THE BASIS THAT COMPARATIVES HAVE NOT BEEN REVIEWED OR AUDITED

INDEPENDENT ASSURANCE PRACTITIONER'S REVIEW REPORT

To [appropriate addressee]

Report on the [appropriate title for the financial report] Financial Report

We have reviewed the accompanying [period] financial report of [name of entity], which comprises the balance sheet as at [date], and the income statement, statement of changes in equity and cash flow statement for the [period] ended on that date, a [statement or description of accounting policies[37]], other selected explanatory notes [and the declaration of those charged with governance.[38]] [39] [40]

[Title of those charged with governance]' Responsibility for the [period] Financial Report

The [title of those charged with governance] of the [type of entity] are responsible for the preparation and fair presentation of the [period] financial report in accordance with the [applicable financial reporting framework]. This responsibility includes: establishing and maintaining internal control relevant to the preparation and fair presentation of the [period] financial report that is free from material misstatement, whether due to fraud or error; selecting and applying appropriate accounting policies; and making accounting estimates that are reasonable in the circumstances.

35 Auditing Standard ASA 700 *The Auditor's Report on a General Purpose Financial Report*, contains information on the wording of reports that may be helpful.

36 The assurance practitioner's review report is required to be signed in one or more of the name of the audit firm, the name of the audit company or the personal name of the assurance practitioner as appropriate.

37 Insert relevant statement or description of accounting policies.

38 Amend this term to reflect the appropriate title for those charged with governance.

39 When the assurance practitioner is aware that the financial report will be included in a document that contains other information, the assurance practitioner may consider, if the form of presentation allows, identifying the page numbers on which the reviewed financial report is presented.

40 The assurance practitioner may wish to specify the regulatory authority or equivalent with whom the financial report is filed.

Assurance Practitioner's Responsibility

Our responsibility is to express a conclusion on the [period] financial report based on our review. We conducted our review in accordance with Standard on Review Engagements ASRE 2400 *Review of a Financial Report Performed by an Assurance Practitioner Who is Not the Auditor of the Entity*, in order to state whether, on the basis of the procedures described, anything has come to our attention that causes us to believe that the financial report is not presented fairly, in all material respects, in accordance with the [applicable financial reporting framework. ASRE 2400 requires us to comply with the requirements of the applicable code of professional conduct of a professional accounting body.

A review of a [period] financial report consists of making enquiries, primarily of persons responsible for financial and accounting matters, and applying analytical and other review procedures. A review is substantially less in scope than an audit conducted in accordance with Australian Auditing Standards and consequently does not enable us to obtain assurance that we would become aware of all significant matters that might be identified in an audit. Accordingly, we do not express an audit opinion.

[*Independence*]

In conducting our review, we have complied with the independence requirements of the Australian professional accounting bodies[41]].

Basis for Qualified Conclusion

As this is the first year that [name of entity] has prepared a [period] financial report and had it reviewed, the income statement, the balance sheet, statement of changes in equity, cash flow statement, summary of significant accounting policies and other explanatory notes[42] for the preceding corresponding [period] have not been reviewed or audited. Accordingly, we are not in a position to, and do not, express any assurance in respect of the comparative information for the [period] ended [date of preceding corresponding period]. The financial report for the preceding financial year ended [date of preceding financial year] has been audited and therefore our review conclusion is not qualified in respect of the comparative information for the year ended [date of preceding financial year] included in the balance sheet.

Qualified Conclusion

Except for the effect, if any, on the comparatives for the preceding corresponding [period] that may result from the qualification in the preceding paragraph, based on our review, which is not an audit, nothing has come to our attention that causes us to believe that the [period] financial report of [name of entity] does not present fairly, in all material respects, [or "give a true and fair view of [43]]" the financial position of the [type of entity] as at [date], and of its financial performance and its cash flows for the [period] period ended on that date, in accordance with [applicable financial reporting framework].

Report on Other Legal and Regulatory Requirements

[Form and content of this section of the assurance practitioner's review report will vary depending on the nature of the assurance practitioner's other reporting responsibilities.]

[Assurance Practitioner's signature[44]]

[Date of the Assurance Practitioner's review report]

[Assurance Practitioner's address]

---

41 Use when appropriate.

42 Insert relevant description of the summary of significant accounting policies and other explanatory notes.

43 Auditing Standard ASA 700 *The Auditor's Report on a General Purpose Financial Report*, contains information on the wording of reports that may be helpful.

44 The assurance practitioner's review report is required to be signed in one or more of the name of the audit firm, the name of the audit company or the personal name of the assurance practitioner as appropriate.

Appendix 6

Standards Applicable to Review Engagements

The pre-existing Standard AUS 902 *Review of Financial Reports* had broad application covering reviews of (i) financial information, both historical and prospective; and (ii) non-financial information. The following table and diagrams identify the applicable AUASB Standard in each of the various review engagement types that were previously conducted under AUS 902.

Review Engagement Type [Previously Conducted Under Aus 902]	**Applicable AUASB Standards**
Review of a financial report comprising historical financial information. (**assurance practitioner who is *not* the auditor**)	**ASRE 2400** *Review of a Financial Report Performed by an Assurance Practitioner Who is Not the Auditor of the Entity*
Review of historical financial information other than a financial report.	**ASRE 2405** *Review of Historical Financial Information Other than a Financial Report*
Review of a financial report comprising historical financial information (**auditor**).	**ASRE 2410** *Review of Interim and Other Financial Reports Performed by the Independent Auditor of the Entity*
Review other than a review of historical financial information covered by the ASREs.	**ASAE 3000** *Assurance Engagements Other than Audits or Reviews of Historical Financial Information*
Review of an entity s compliance with internally or externally imposed requirements as measured by the suitable criteria.	**ASAE 3100** *Compliance Engagements*
Reviews of performance against which the extent of economy, efficiency or effectiveness of an activity may be assessed	**ASAE 3500** *Performance Engagements*

Diagram 1

Review Standards applicable to Reviews of Financial Reports (comprising historical financial information), and other Historical Financial Information. [To be read in conjunction with the Table above.]

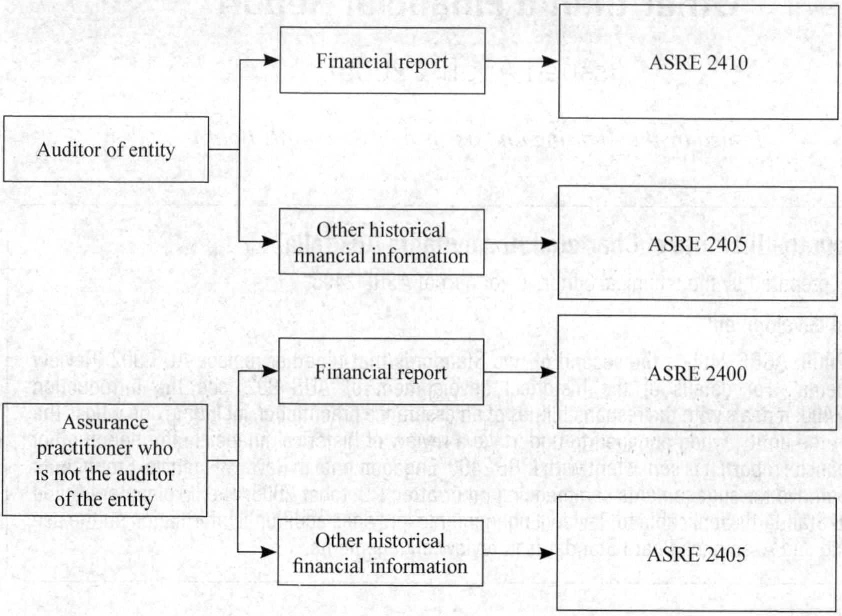

Diagram 2

Standards applicable to Review Engagements, not covered by ASREs. [To be read in conjunction with the Table above.]

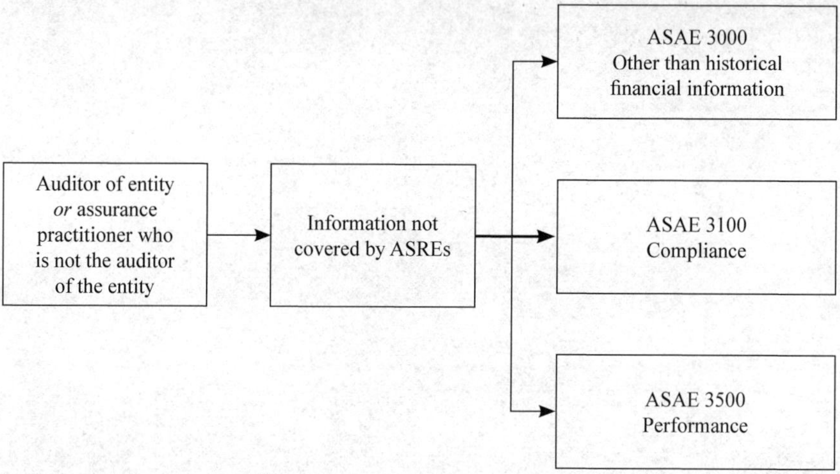

ASRE

ASRE 2405
Review of Historical Financial Information Other than a Financial Report

(Issued August 2008)

Issued by the Auditing and Assurance Standards Board.

Note from the Institute of Chartered Accountants Australia

This note, prepared by the technical editor, is not part of ASRE 2405.

Historical development

August 2008: ASRE 2405 is the second of two Standards that together replace AUS 902 'Review Engagements'. For details of the historical development of AUS 902, see the introduction to ASRE 2400. It deals with the responsibilities of an assurance practitioner, including one who is the auditor of the entity, when engaged to undertake a review of historical financial information other than a financial report. It is consistent with ISRE 2400 'Engagements to Review Financial Statements' and is operative for engagements commencing on or after 1 October 2008. The 'Explanatory Guide to AUASB Standards applicable to Review Engagements' provides additional information on the use of Auditing and Assurance Board Standards in review engagements.

Contents

ASRE

Preface

Reasons for Issuing Standard on Review Engagements ASRE 2405 *Review of Historical Financial Information Other than a Financial Report*

The Auditing and Assurance Standards Board (AUASB) makes Auditing Standards under section 336 of the *Corporations Act 2001* for the purposes of the corporations legislation and formulates auditing and assurance standards for other purposes.

The AUASB issues Standard on Review Engagements ASRE 2405 *Review of Historical Financial Information Other than a Financial Report* pursuant to the requirements of the legislative provisions explained below.

The *Corporate Law Economic Reform Program (Audit Reform and Corporate Disclosure) Act 2004* (the CLERP 9 Act) established the AUASB as an independent statutory body under section 227A of the *Australian Securities and Investments Commission Act 2001* (ASIC Act), as from

1 July 2004. Under section 227B of the ASIC Act, the AUASB may formulate Assurance Standards for purposes other than the corporations legislation.

Revision of AUS 902

In October 1995, the former Auditing & Assurance Standards Board (AuASB) of the Australian Accounting Research Foundation (AARF) issued the Standard AUS 902 *Review of Financial Reports*. The Standard was based on the International Standard on Review Engagements ISRE 2400. AUS 902 had very broad application covering reviews of (i) financial information, both historical and prospective; and (ii) non-financial information.

With the subsequent progression of standard-setting, a number of new Standards that apply to review engagements have been issued by the AUASB. As a consequence, AUS 902 has become outdated by these new standards that are designed to be applied in specific circumstances and which therefore differ markedly in scope from the broad application of AUS 902. The AUASB takes the view that standards applicable to specific circumstances are more useful to assurance practitioners than are broad-based standards that may require significant interpretation in the context of specific circumstances.

Accordingly, the various review engagement types, previously conducted in accordance with AUS 902, are to be conducted in accordance with the relevant AUASB Standard.

Details of the background and current application of the suite of AUASB Standards that apply to review engagements, are contained in the *Explanatory Guide to Review Engagements*, a copy of which may be obtained from the AUASB website: www.auasb.gov.au

Appendix 6 of this Standard contains a table and diagrams that illustrate the application of AUASB Standards by review engagement type.

Main Features

This Standard on Review Engagements (ASRE) establishes mandatory Requirements and provides Explanatory Guidance on the responsibilities of an assurance practitioner, including those who are the auditor of the entity, when engaged to undertake a review of historical financial information other than a financial report, and on the form and content of the assurance practitioner's review report.

The term "assurance practitioner", used throughout this ASRE, includes the auditor of the entity.

Operative Date

This Standard on Review Engagements is operative for engagements commencing on or after 1 October 2008.

Main changes from AUS 902 (July 2002)

The main differences between this Standard on Review Engagements (ASRE) and the Auditing Standard issued by the Auditing and Assurance Standards Board of the Australian Accounting Research Foundation that it supersedes, AUS 902 *Review of Financial Reports* (July 2002) are that in this ASRE:

1. The word 'shall', in the **bold-type** paragraphs, is the terminology used to describe an assurance practitioner's mandatory requirements, whereas an assurance practitioner's degree of responsibility was described in AUS 902 by the word 'should'.
2. The Explanatory Guidance paragraphs provide guidance and illustrative examples to assist the assurance practitioner in fulfilling the mandatory requirements, whereas in AUS 902 some obligations were implied within certain explanatory paragraphs. Accordingly, such paragraphs have been redrafted to clarify that the matter forms part of the explanatory guidance.
3. Application is restricted to reviews of historical financial information other than a financial report. The application of AUS 902 was not restricted in this way.
4. It is not practical here to compare the wording of each Requirement in ASRE 2405 to the equivalent Requirement in AUS 902. However, an assurance practitioner's obligations under ASRE 2405 are not less than those under AUS 902

5. The following additional mandatory requirements have been included:

5.1 This Standard on Review Engagements (ASRE) applies to a review of historical financial information, other than a financial report (paragraph 1).

5.2 Where in rare and exceptional circumstances, factors outside the assurance practitioner's control prevent the assurance practitioner from complying with a relevant mandatory requirement of this ASRE, the assurance practitioner shall:

(a) if possible, perform appropriate alternative procedures; and

(b) document in the working papers:

(i) the circumstances surrounding the inability to comply;

(ii) the reasons for the inability to comply; and

(iii) justification of how alternative procedures achieve the objectives of the mandatory Requirement.

When the assurance practitioner is unable to perform appropriate alternative review procedures, the assurance practitioner shall consider the implications for the review report (paragraph 7).

[Note: Although a similar paragraph is included in AUS 902, paragraph 7 is included in this listing to highlight the conditions and specific requirements in this ASRE].

5.3 The assurance practitioner shall implement quality control procedures that are relevant to the individual engagement (paragraph 11).

5.4 The assurance practitioner shall evaluate, individually and in the aggregate, whether uncorrected misstatements that have come to the assurance practitioner's attention are material to the historical financial information (paragraph 38).

5.5 The assurance practitioner shall endeavour to obtain written representations from management that:

(a) it acknowledges its responsibility for the design and implementation of internal control to prevent and detect fraud and error;

(b) the historical financial information is prepared and presented in accordance with the applicable criteria;

(c) it believes the effect of those uncorrected misstatements aggregated by the assurance practitioner during the review are immaterial, both individually and in the aggregate, to the historical financial information taken as a whole. A summary of such items is included in, or attached to, the written representations;

(d) it has disclosed to the assurance practitioner all significant facts relating to any fraud(s) or suspected fraud(s) known to it that may have affected the entity;

(e) it has disclosed to the assurance practitioner the results of its assessment of the risk that the historical financial information may be materially misstated as a result of fraud;

(f) it has disclosed to the assurance practitioner all known actual or possible non-compliance with laws and regulations the effects of which are to be considered when preparing the historical financial information; and

(g) it has disclosed to the assurance practitioner all significant events that have occurred subsequent to the date of the historical financial information and through to the date of the review report, that may require adjustment to or disclosure in the historical financial information (paragraph 42).

5.6 If those charged with governance refuse to provide a written representation that the assurance practitioner considers necessary, this constitutes a limitation on the scope of the assurance practitioner's work and the assurance practitioner shall express a qualified conclusion or a disclaimer of conclusion (paragraph 44).

5.7 The assurance practitioner shall read the other information that accompanies the historical financial information to consider whether any such information is materially inconsistent with the historical financial information (paragraph 45).

ASRE

5.8 If a matter comes to the assurance practitioner's attention that causes the assurance practitioner to believe that the other information appears to include a material misstatement of fact, the assurance practitioner shall discuss the matter with the entity's management (paragraph 48).

5.9 When, as a result of performing the review of historical financial information, a matter comes to the assurance practitioner's attention that causes the assurance practitioner to believe that it is necessary to make a material adjustment to the historical financial information for it to be prepared, or presented fairly, in all material respects, in accordance with the applicable criteria, the assurance practitioner shall communicate this matter as soon as practicable to the appropriate level of management (paragraph 50).

5.10 When, in the assurance practitioner's judgement, management does not respond appropriately within a reasonable period of time, the assurance practitioner shall inform those charged with governance (paragraph 51).

5.11 When, in the assurance practitioner's judgement, those charged with governance do not respond appropriately within a reasonable period of time, the assurance practitioner shall consider:

(a) whether to modify the report; or

(b) the possibility of withdrawing from the engagement; and

(c) when also the auditor, the possibility of resigning from the appointment to audit the annual financial report (paragraph 53).

5.12 When, as a result of performing the review of historical financial information, a matter comes to the assurance practitioner's attention that causes the assurance practitioner to believe in the existence of fraud or non-compliance by the entity with laws and regulations, the assurance practitioner shall communicate the matter as soon as practicable to those charged with governance and shall consider the implications for the review (paragraph 54).

5.13 The assurance practitioner shall communicate relevant matters of governance interest arising from the review of the historical financial information to those charged with governance (paragraph 54).

6. The "Objective of a Review Engagement" is included in AUS 902 as a mandatory paragraph (**bold-type** lettering). However, the equivalent "Objective of a Review of Historical Financial Information, Other than a Financial Report" paragraph has been included in ASRE 2405 as Explanatory Guidance. This change has been adopted to acknowledge the contextual nature of the subject matter and to be consistent with ASRE 2400 *Review of a Financial Report Performed by an Assurance Practitioner Who is Not the Auditor of the Entity* and ASRE 2410 *Review of Interim and Other Financial Reports Performed by the Independent Auditor of the Entity*. The amendment does not diminish the quality of the standard or the obligations of an assurance practitioner (paragraphs 16-18).

7. AUS 902 includes a separate mandatory paragraph relating to the direction, supervision and review of work performed by assistants. In this ASRE, this requirement is addressed by the mandatory Requirements to comply with professional standards (paragraph 8) and with quality control procedures (paragraph 11).

8. AUS 902 includes a mandatory paragraph relating to the use of the work of another auditor and a mandatory paragraph relating to the use of the work of an expert. In this ASRE, these Requirements have been combined and are addressed by a single mandatory Requirement paragraph (paragraph 28).

9. Where appropriate, the wording of mandatory Requirements in this ASRE that originate from AUS 902, has been updated to conform with ASRE 2400 and other applicable AUASB pronouncements.

10. AUS 902 includes five explanatory guidance paragraphs under the heading "Moderate Assurance". This guidance has not been included in ASRE 2405 as it would duplicate the equivalent information contained within the AUASB pronouncement *Framework for Assurance Engagements* which comprehensively explains "limited assurance".

Authority Statement

The Auditing and Assurance Standards Board (AUASB) formulates this Standard on Review Engagements ASRE 2405 *Review of Historical Financial Information Other than a Financial Report* as set out in paragraphs 1 to 67, and Appendices 1 to 6 pursuant to section 227B of the *Australian Securities and Investments Commission Act 2001*.

This Standard on Review Engagements is to be read in conjunction with the *Preamble to AUASB Standards*, which sets out the intentions of the AUASB on how the Standards on Review Engagements are to be understood, interpreted and applied.

The mandatory Requirements of this Standard on Review Engagements are set out in **bold-type** paragraphs.

Dated 21 August 2008

M H Kelsall
Chairman - AUASB

Standard on Review Engagements ASRE 2405

Review of Historical Financial Information Other than a Financial Report

ASRE

Application

1 **This Standard on Review Engagements (ASRE) applies to a review of historical financial information, other than a financial report.**

Operative Date

2 **This ASRE is operative for engagements commencing on or after 1 October 2008.**

Introduction

3 The purpose of this ASRE is to establish mandatory Requirements and to provide Explanatory Guidance on the assurance practitioner's professional responsibilities when undertaking an engagement to review historical financial information, other than a financial report, and on the form and content of the assurance practitioner's review report.

4 For purposes of this ASRE, an assurance practitioner is a person or an organisation, whether in public practice, industry, commerce or the public sector, involved in the provision of assurance services.

5 For purposes of this ASRE, historical financial information, other than a financial report includes:

- Specific components, elements, accounts or items of a financial report, such as:
  - ♦ A single financial statement, for example, an income statement or balance sheet.
  - ♦ Accounts receivable.
  - ♦ Impairment of asset accounts.
  - ♦ Inventory.
  - ♦ The liability for accrued benefits of a defined benefits plan.
  - ♦ The recorded value of identified intangible assets.
  - ♦ Pro-forma historical financial information and adjustments.
  - ♦ The liability for "incurred but not reported" claims in an insurance portfolio, including related explanatory notes.
- Other information derived from financial records, such as:
  - ♦ A schedule of externally managed assets and income of a private pension plan, including related explanatory notes.
  - ♦ A schedule of net tangible assets, including related explanatory notes.

- ♦ A schedule of disbursements in relation to a leased property, including related explanatory notes
- ♦ A schedule of profit participation or employee bonuses, including related explanatory notes.

- Financial statements prepared in accordance with a financial reporting framework that is not designed to achieve fair presentation, such as condensed financial statements and an entity's internal management accounts.

6 **The assurance practitioner shall conduct a review of historical financial information, other than a financial report, in accordance with this ASRE.**

7 **Where in rare and exceptional circumstances, factors outside the assurance practitioner's control prevent the assurance practitioner from complying with a relevant mandatory requirement of this ASRE, the assurance practitioner shall:**

(a) if possible, perform appropriate alternative procedures; and

(b) document in the working papers:

(i) the circumstances surrounding the inability to comply;

(ii) the reasons for the inability to comply; and

(iii) justification of how alternative procedures achieve the objectives of the mandatory Requirement.

When the assurance practitioner is unable to perform appropriate alternative review procedures, the assurance practitioner shall consider the implications for the review report.

General Principles of a Review of Historical Financial Information, Other than a Financial Report

8 **The assurance practitioner shall comply with the fundamental ethical principles of integrity, objectivity, professional competence and due care, confidentiality and professional behaviour.**

9 The applicable code of conduct of a professional accounting body[1] provides appropriate guidance on the application of fundamental ethical principles.

10 The applicable code of conduct of a professional accounting body provides a framework of principles that members of assurance teams, firms and network firms use to identify threats to independence, evaluate the significance of those threats and, if the threats are other than clearly insignificant:

(a) identify and apply safeguards to eliminate the threats; or

(b) reduce them to an acceptable level,

such that independence of mind and independence in appearance are not compromised.

11 **The assurance practitioner shall implement quality control procedures to address the following elements of a quality control system that apply to the individual engagement:**

(a) leadership responsibilities for quality on the assurance engagement;

(b) ethical requirements;

(c) acceptance and continuance of client relationships and specific engagements;

(d) assignment of engagement teams;

(e) engagement performance; and

(f) monitoring.

1 The applicable code of conduct of the professional accounting bodies is APES 110 *Code of Ethics for Professional Accountants*, as issued from time to time by the Accounting Professional and Ethical Standards Board. This code of conduct has been adopted by CPA Australia, National Institute of Accountants and The Institute of Chartered Accountants in Australia. In addition, codes of conduct issued by other professional bodies may apply.

12 The quality control procedures relevant to an audit engagement are contained in Auditing Standard ASA 220 *Quality Control for an Audit of Historical Financial Information*, and may be helpful in determining quality control procedures relevant to a review engagement.

13 The assurance practitioner shall plan and perform the review by exercising professional judgement and with an attitude of professional scepticism, recognising that circumstances may exist that cause the historical financial information to be materially misstated.

14 An attitude of professional scepticism means that the assurance practitioner makes a critical assessment, with a questioning mind, of the validity of evidence obtained and is alert to evidence that contradicts or brings into question the reliability of documents or representations by management of the entity.

15 For the purpose of expressing limited assurance in the review report, the assurance practitioner shall obtain sufficient appropriate evidence primarily through enquiry and analytical procedures to be able to draw conclusions.

Objective of a Review of Historical Financial Information Other than a Financial Report

16 The objective of a review of historical financial information, other than a financial report, is to enable the assurance practitioner to express a conclusion whether, on the basis of the review, anything has come to the assurance practitioner's attention that causes the assurance practitioner to believe that the historical financial information, other than a financial report, is not prepared, or presented fairly, in all material respects, in accordance with the applicable criteria (limited assurance). Under paragraph 15 of this ASRE, the assurance practitioner needs to make enquiries and perform analytical and other review procedures in order to reduce to a limited level the risk of expressing an inappropriate conclusion when the historical financial information, other than a financial report, is materially misstated.

17 The objective of a review of historical financial information, other than a financial report, differs significantly from that of an audit conducted in accordance with Auditing Standards. A review of historical financial information, other than a financial report, does not provide a basis for expressing an opinion whether the historical financial information, other than a financial report, gives a true and fair view, or is presented fairly, in all material respects, in accordance with the applicable criteria or financial reporting framework.

18 A review, in contrast to an audit, is not designed to obtain reasonable assurance that the historical financial information, other than a financial report, is free from material misstatement. A review consists of making enquiries, primarily of persons responsible for financial and accounting matters, and applying analytical and other review procedures. A review may bring significant matters affecting the historical financial information, other than a financial report to the assurance practitioner's attention, but it does not provide all of the evidence that would be required in an audit.

Scope of a Review of Historical Financial Information Other than a Financial Report

19 The procedures required to conduct a review of historical financial information, other than a financial report, shall be determined by the assurance practitioner having regard to the requirements of this ASRE, relevant professional bodies, legislation, regulation, the terms of the review engagement and, where appropriate, prescribed reporting requirements.

20 The term "scope of an engagement to review historical financial information, other than a financial report," refers to the review procedures deemed necessary in the circumstances to achieve the objective of the review.

Agreeing the Terms of the Engagement

21 The assurance practitioner shall agree the terms of the engagement with the entity, which shall be recorded in writing by the assurance practitioner and forwarded to the entity. When the review engagement is undertaken pursuant to legislation, the minimum applicable terms are those contained in the legislation.

22 An engagement letter, or other suitable form, will be of assistance in planning the review work. It is in the interests of both the assurance practitioner and the entity that the assurance practitioner sends an engagement letter, preferably before the commencement of the engagement, documenting the key terms of the appointment.

23 An engagement letter confirms the assurance practitioner's acceptance of the appointment and helps avoid misunderstanding regarding such matters as the objective(s) and scope of the engagement, the extent of the assurance practitioner's responsibilities and the form of report to be issued.

24 Ordinarily, matters that are contained in the engagement letter include the following:

- The objective(s) of the review being performed.
- The scope of the review, including reference to this ASRE.
- The criteria being applied as the basis of reporting.
- The responsibilities of management, and where appropriate, those charged with governance, for the financial information and criteria used.
- Agreement from management to provide unrestricted access to whatever records, documentation and other information requested in connection with the review.
- Agreement from management and, where appropriate, those charged with governance, to provide written representations.
- A sample of the review report expected to be rendered, with provision that the review report may be modified.
- The fact that the engagement cannot be relied upon to identify fraud(s), errors, illegal acts or other irregularities that may exist.
- A statement that an audit is not being performed and that an audit opinion will not be expressed. To emphasise this point and to avoid confusion, the assurance practitioner may also consider pointing out that a review engagement will not satisfy any statutory or third party requirements for an audit.

Appendix 1 to this ASRE contains an illustrative engagement letter.

Planning

25 The assurance practitioner shall plan the review so that an effective engagement will be performed.

26 In planning a review of historical financial information, the assurance practitioner shall obtain or update their knowledge of the business including consideration of the entity's organisation, accounting systems, operating characteristics and the nature of its assets, liabilities, revenues and expenses, to the extent required to achieve the objective of the engagement.

27 Under paragraph 26 of this ASRE, the assurance practitioner needs to obtain an understanding of such matters and other matters relevant to the historical financial information, for example, a knowledge of the entity's production and distribution methods, product lines, operating locations and related parties. Under paragraphs 25 and 26 of this ASRE, the assurance practitioner needs this understanding to be able to make relevant enquiries and to design appropriate procedures, as well as to assess the responses and other information obtained.

Work Performed by Others

28 When using work performed by another assurance practitioner or an expert, the assurance practitioner shall be satisfied that such work is adequate for the purposes of the review.

Procedures and Evidence

29 The assurance practitioner shall apply judgement in determining the specific nature, timing and extent of review procedures.

30 The assurance practitioner may be guided by such matters as the following:

- Any knowledge acquired by carrying out audits or reviews of financial statements or reports for prior periods.
- The assurance practitioner's knowledge of the business including knowledge of the accounting principles and practices of the industry in which the entity operates.
- The entity's accounting systems.
- The extent to which a particular item is affected by management judgement.
- The materiality of transactions and account balances in the context of the historical financial information.
- Any first-time inclusion of comparative historical financial information.

31 The assurance practitioner shall consider materiality, using professional judgement, when:

(a) determining the nature, timing and extent of review procedures; and

(b) evaluating the effect of misstatements.

32 Under paragraph 31 of this ASRE, the assurance practitioner needs to use professional judgement and consider qualitative and quantitative factors in determining materiality.

33 Although there is a greater risk that misstatements will not be detected in a review than in an audit, the judgement as to what is material is made by reference to the historical financial information on which the assurance practitioner is reporting and the needs of those relying on that information, not to the level of assurance provided.

34 Procedures for the review of historical financial information, other than a financial report may ordinarily include the following:

- Obtaining an understanding of the industry in which the entity operates.
- Enquiries concerning the entity's accounting principles and practices.
- Enquiries concerning the entity's procedures for recording, classifying and summarising transactions, accumulating information for disclosure and preparing the historical financial information.
- Enquiries concerning all material assertions in the financial information.
- Analytical procedures designed to identify relationships and individual items that appear unusual. Such procedures may include:
  - ♦ Comparison of the historical financial information with information from prior periods.
  - ♦ Comparison of the historical financial information with expectations.
  - ♦ Study of the relationships of the elements of the historical financial information that would be expected to conform to a predictable pattern based on the entity's experience or industry norm.

  In applying these procedures, the assurance practitioner ordinarily considers the nature of matters that required accounting adjustments in prior periods.
- Enquiries concerning actions taken at meetings of shareholders, those charged with governance and other meetings that may affect the historical financial information.
- Reading the historical financial information to consider, on the basis of any matter that comes to the assurance practitioner's attention, whether the historical financial information appears to conform with the basis of accounting indicated.
- Obtaining reports from other assurance practitioners, if any, and if considered necessary, who have been engaged to audit or review the financial statements of the entity or components of the entity.

ASRE

- Enquiries of persons having responsibility for financial, accounting and other matters concerning, for example:
  - ♦ Whether all transactions have been recorded.
  - ♦ Whether the financial information has been prepared and presented in accordance with the applicable criteria e.g., basis of accounting.
  - ♦ Whether there have been significant changes in the entity's business activities and/or accounting principles and practices.
  - ♦ Matters as to which questions have arisen in the course of applying the review procedures.
- Obtaining written representations from management.

Appendix 4 to this ASRE provides an illustrative list of procedures that the assurance practitioner may consider when performing a review engagement. The list is not exhaustive, nor is it intended that all the procedures suggested apply to every review engagement.

35 **The assurance practitioner shall enquire about events subsequent to the date of the historical financial information that may require adjustment of, or disclosure in, the historical financial information.**

36 Under paragraph 35 of this ASRE, the assurance practitioner need not perform procedures to identify events occurring after the date of the review report.

37 **If the assurance practitioner has reason to believe that the historical financial information subject to review may be materially misstated, the assurance practitioner shall carry out additional or more extensive procedures as are considered necessary to be able to express a limited assurance conclusion or to confirm that a modified report is required.**

Evaluation of Misstatements

38 **The assurance practitioner shall evaluate, individually and in the aggregate, whether uncorrected misstatements that have come to the assurance practitioner's attention are material to the historical financial information.**

39 A review of historical financial information, in contrast to an audit engagement, is not designed to obtain reasonable assurance that the financial information is free from material misstatement. However, under paragraph 38 of this ASRE, misstatements which come to the assurance practitioner's attention, including inadequate disclosures, need to be evaluated individually and in the aggregate to determine whether a material adjustment is required to be made to the historical financial information for it to be prepared, or presented fairly, in all material respects, in accordance with the applicable criteria.

40 Under paragraph 38 of this ASRE, the assurance practitioner needs to exercise professional judgement in evaluating the materiality of any misstatements that the entity has not corrected. Ordinarily, the assurance practitioner considers matters such as the nature, cause and amount of the misstatements, whether the misstatements originated in the preceding year or period of the current year, and the potential effect of the misstatements on future periods.

41 The assurance practitioner may designate an amount below which misstatements need not be aggregated, because the assurance practitioner expects that the aggregation of such amounts clearly would not have a material effect on the financial information. In so doing, under paragraph 31 of this ASRE, the assurance practitioner needs to consider the fact that the determination of materiality involves quantitative as well as qualitative considerations and that misstatements of a relatively small amount could nevertheless have a material effect on the historical financial information.

Management Representations

42 **The assurance practitioner shall endeavour to obtain written representations from management that:**

(a) it acknowledges its responsibility for the design and implementation of internal control to prevent and detect fraud and error;

(b) the historical financial information is prepared and presented in accordance with the applicable criteria;

(c) it believes the effect of those uncorrected misstatements aggregated by the assurance practitioner during the review are immaterial, both individually and in the aggregate, to the historical financial information taken as a whole. A summary of such items is included in, or attached to, the written representations;

(d) it has disclosed to the assurance practitioner all significant facts relating to any fraud(s) or suspected fraud(s) known to it that may have affected the entity;

(e) it has disclosed to the assurance practitioner the results of its assessment of the risk that the historical financial information may be materially misstated as a result of fraud;

(f) it has disclosed to the assurance practitioner all known actual or possible non-compliance with laws and regulations the effects of which are to be considered when preparing the historical financial information; and

(g) it has disclosed to the assurance practitioner all significant events that have occurred subsequent to the date of the historical financial information and through to the date of the review report, that may require adjustment to or disclosure in the historical financial information.

43 Under paragraph 42 of this ASRE, the assurance practitioner needs to endeavour to obtain additional representations as are considered appropriate to matters specific to the entity's business or industry. Appendix 2 to this ASRE contains an illustrative management representation letter.

44 If those charged with governance refuse to provide a written representation that the assurance practitioner considers necessary, this constitutes a limitation on the scope of the assurance practitioner's work and the assurance practitioner shall express a qualified conclusion or a disclaimer of conclusion.

Assurance Practitioner's Responsibility for Accompanying Information

45 The assurance practitioner shall read the other information that accompanies the historical financial information to consider whether any such information is materially inconsistent with the historical financial information.

46 Ordinarily, the practitioner makes appropriate arrangements with the entity to obtain the other information on a timely basis.

47 If the assurance practitioner identifies a material inconsistency, under paragraph 45 of this ASRE, the assurance practitioner needs to consider whether the historical financial information or the other accompanying information needs to be amended. If an amendment is necessary in the historical financial information and those charged with governance refuse to make the amendment, under paragraph 53 of this ASRE, the assurance practitioner needs to consider the implications for the review report. If an amendment is necessary in the accompanying other information and those charged with governance refuse to make the amendment, the assurance practitioner may, for example, consider including in the review report, an additional paragraph (emphasis of matter) describing the material inconsistency or may take other actions, such as withholding the issuance of the review report, or withdrawing from the engagement.

48 If a matter comes to the assurance practitioner's attention that causes the assurance practitioner to believe that the other information appears to include a material misstatement of fact, the assurance practitioner shall discuss the matter with the entity's management.

49 While reading the other information for the purpose of identifying material inconsistencies, an apparent material misstatement of fact may come to the assurance practitioner's attention (i.e. information, not related to matters appearing in the historical financial information, that is incorrectly stated or presented). When discussing the matter with the entity's management, ordinarily the assurance practitioner considers the validity of the other information and management's responses to the assurance practitioner's enquiries, whether valid differences of judgement or opinion exist, and whether to request management to consult with a qualified third party to resolve the apparent misstatement of fact. If an amendment is necessary to

correct a material misstatement of fact and management refuses to make the amendment, ordinarily the assurance practitioner considers taking further action as appropriate, such as notifying those charged with governance and, if necessary, obtaining legal advice.

Communication

50 **When, as a result of performing the review of historical financial information, a matter comes to the assurance practitioner's attention that causes the assurance practitioner to believe that it is necessary to make a material adjustment to the historical financial information for it to be prepared, or presented fairly, in all material respects, in accordance with the applicable criteria, the assurance practitioner shall communicate this matter as soon as practicable to the appropriate level of management.**

51 **When, in the assurance practitioner's judgement, management does not respond appropriately within a reasonable period of time, the assurance practitioner shall inform those charged with governance.**

52 Such communications are made as soon as practicable, either orally or in writing. The assurance practitioner's decision whether to communicate orally or in writing ordinarily is affected by factors such as the nature, sensitivity and significance of the matter to be communicated and the timing of the communications. If the information is communicated orally, under paragraph 65 of this ASRE, the assurance practitioner needs to document the communication.

53 **When, in the assurance practitioner's judgement, those charged with governance do not respond appropriately within a reasonable period of time, the assurance practitioner shall consider:**

(a) whether to modify the report; or

(b) the possibility of withdrawing from the engagement; and

(c) when also the auditor, the possibility of resigning from the appointment to audit the annual financial report.

54 **When, as a result of performing the review of historical financial information, a matter comes to the assurance practitioner's attention that causes the assurance practitioner to believe in the existence of fraud or non-compliance by the entity with laws and regulations, the assurance practitioner shall communicate the matter as soon as practicable to those charged with governance and shall consider the implications for the review.**

55 The determination of which level of management may also be informed is affected by the likelihood of collusion or the involvement of a member(s) of management. Under paragraph 54 of this ASRE, the assurance practitioner needs to report such matters to those charged with governance.

56 **The assurance practitioner shall communicate relevant matters of governance interest arising from the review of the historical financial information to those charged with governance.**

57 As a result of performing a review of historical financial information, the assurance practitioner may become aware of matters that, in the opinion of the assurance practitioner, are both important and relevant to those charged with governance. Under paragraph 56 of this ASRE, the assurance practitioner needs to communicate such matters to those charged with governance.

Conclusions and Reporting

58 **An unmodified review report shall contain a clear written expression of limited assurance. The assurance practitioner shall review and assess the conclusions drawn from the evidence obtained as the basis for the expression of limited assurance.**

59 **Based on the work performed, the assurance practitioner shall assess whether any information obtained during the review indicates that the historical financial information is not prepared, or presented fairly, in all material respects, in accordance with the applicable criteria.**

60 Under paragraph 61, the report on a review of financial information needs to describe the scope of the engagement to enable the reader to understand the nature of the work performed and make it clear that an audit was not performed and, therefore, that an audit opinion is not expressed.

61 The report on a review of historical financial information shall contain the following basic elements:

(a) Title[2];

(b) Addressee;

(c) Opening or introductory paragraph including:

(i) Identification of the historical financial information on which the review has been performed;

(ii) A statement of the responsibility of those charged with governance of the entity, including the identification of the applicable criteria, and the responsibilities of the assurance practitioner; and

(iii) A statement, where appropriate, that the historical financial information has been prepared for a particular purpose and user(s), and any express restriction on the distribution of the review report or on those entitled to rely on it;

(d) A paragraph describing the nature of a review, including:

(i) A statement that the review is conducted in accordance with this ASRE;

(ii) A statement that a review is limited primarily to enquiries and analytical procedures; and

(iii) A statement that an audit has not been performed, that the procedures undertaken provide less assurance than an audit and that an audit opinion is not expressed;

(e) A conclusion of limited assurance;

(f) Date of the review report;

(g) Assurance practitioner's address; and

(h) Assurance practitioner's signature.

Appendix 5 to this ASRE contains an illustrative review report.

62 The review report shall:

(a) State a conclusion that, on the basis of the review, nothing has come to the assurance practitioner's attention that causes the assurance practitioner to believe that the historical financial information is not prepared, or presented fairly, in all material respects, in accordance with the applicable criteria; or

(b) If matters have come to the assurance practitioner's attention, describe those matters that cause the assurance practitioner to believe that the historical financial information is not prepared, or presented fairly, in all material respects, in accordance with the applicable criteria, including, unless impracticable, a quantification of the possible effect(s) on the historical financial information, and either:

(i) Express a qualification of the limited assurance provided; or

(ii) When the effect of the matter is so material and pervasive to the historical financial information that the assurance practitioner concludes that a qualification is not adequate to disclose the misleading or incomplete nature of the historical financial information, express an adverse conclusion that

2 It may be appropriate to use the term "independent" in the review report title to distinguish the assurance practitioner's report from reports that might be issued by others, such as officers of the entity, or from the reports of other practitioners who may not have to abide by the same ethical requirements as an independent assurance practitioner.

ASRE

the financial information is not prepared, or presented fairly, in all material respects, in accordance with the applicable criteria; or

(c) If there has been a material scope limitation, describe the limitation and either:

(i) Express a qualification of the limited assurance provided regarding the possible adjustments to the historical financial information that might have been determined to be necessary had the limitation not existed; or

(ii) When the possible effect of the limitation is so significant and pervasive that the assurance practitioner concludes that no level of assurance can be provided, not provide any assurance; and

(d) When considered necessary by the assurance practitioner, include an emphasis of matter section, suitably headed and placed immediately after the review conclusion.

63 The circumstances under which an auditor is required to include an emphasis of matter paragraph in the auditor's report, and the form of such reporting, are described in ASA 701 *Modifications to the Auditor's Report*. ASA 701 may be helpful in determining the need for an emphasis of matter paragraph, and the form of such reporting, in an assurance practitioner's review report.

64 The assurance practitioner shall date the review report as of the date the review is completed, which includes performing procedures relating to events occurring up to the date of the report. However, since the assurance practitioner's responsibility is to report on the historical financial information as prepared and presented by management, or where applicable, those charged with governance, the assurance practitioner shall not date the review report earlier than the date on which the historical financial information was approved by management, or where applicable, those charged with governance.

Documentation

65 The assurance practitioner shall prepare review documentation that is sufficient and appropriate to provide a basis for the assurance practitioner's conclusion and to provide evidence that the review was performed in accordance with this ASRE.

66 Under paragraph 65 of this ASRE, the assurance practitioner needs to prepare documentation that enables an experienced assurance practitioner, having no previous connection with the review engagement, to understand the nature, timing and extent of the enquiries made and analytical and other review procedures applied, information obtained, and any significant matters considered during the performance of the review, including the disposition of such matters.

Conformity with International Standards on Review Engagements

67 ISRE 2400 *Engagements to Review Financial Statements*, establishes standards and provides guidance to practitioners who are not the auditor of the entity, when engaged to review financial statements. ISRE 2400 is to be applied, adapted as necessary in the circumstances, to engagements to review other historical financial information.

The AUASB has decided that:

- due to the nature of reviews of other historical financial information, a separate Standard is more appropriate than ASRE 2400 and ASRE 2410 being adapted by the auditor or assurance practitioner for this purpose; and
- ASRE 2405 *Review of Historical Financial Information Other than a Financial Report*, as developed by the AUASB, will more comprehensively deal with reviews of other historical financial information and is based on AUS 902 *Review of Financial Reports* (equivalent ISRE 2400).

Accordingly, ASRE 2405 is not designed to be equivalent to ISRE 2400, however, is intended to conform, with the exceptions listed below, to ISRE 2400 to the extent that

ISRE 2400 deals with the review of historical financial information other than a financial report.

Except as noted below, this ASRE conforms, to the extent described above, with International Standard on Review Engagements ISRE 2400 *Engagements to Review Financial Statements* issued by the International Auditing and Assurance Standards Board (IAASB), an independent standard-setting board of the International Federation of Accountants (IFAC). The main differences between this ASRE and ISRE 2400 are:

- ASRE 2405 includes the following mandatory Requirements and related Explanatory Guidance paragraphs that are not in ISRE 2400:
  - This ASRE applies to a review of historical financial information, other than a financial report (paragraph 1).
  - Where in rare and exceptional circumstances, factors outside the assurance practitioner's control prevent the assurance practitioner from complying with a relevant mandatory requirement of this ASRE, the assurance practitioner shall:
    (a) if possible, perform appropriate alternative procedures; and
    (b) document in the working papers:
      (i) the circumstances surrounding the inability to comply;
      (ii) the reasons for the inability to comply; and
      (iii) justification of how alternative procedures achieve the objectives of the mandatory requirement.

    When the assurance practitioner is unable to perform appropriate alternative procedures, the assurance practitioner shall consider the implications for the assurance practitioner's review report (paragraph 7).
  - The assurance practitioner shall implement quality control procedures that are relevant to the individual engagement (paragraph 11).
  - The assurance practitioner shall evaluate, individually and in the aggregate, whether uncorrected misstatements that have come to the assurance practitioner's attention are material to the historical financial information (paragraph 38).
  - The assurance practitioner shall endeavour to obtain written representations from management that:
    (a) it acknowledges its responsibility for the design and implementation of internal control to prevent and detect fraud and error;
    (b) the historical financial information is prepared and presented in accordance with the applicable criteria;
    (c) it believes the effect of those uncorrected misstatements aggregated by the assurance practitioner during the review are immaterial, both individually and in the aggregate, to the historical financial information taken as a whole. A summary of such items is included in, or attached to, the written representations;
    (d) it has disclosed to the assurance practitioner all significant facts relating to any fraud(s) or suspected frauds known to it that may have affected the entity;
    (e) it has disclosed to the assurance practitioner the results of its assessment of the risk that the historical financial information may be materially misstated as a result of fraud;
    (f) it has disclosed to the assurance practitioner all known actual or possible non-compliance with laws and regulations the effects of which are to be considered when preparing the historical financial information; and
    (g) it has have disclosed to the assurance practitioner all significant events that have occurred subsequent to the date of the historical financial information and through to the date of the review report, that may require adjustment to or disclosure in the historical financial information (paragraph 42).

ASRE

- ♦ If those charged with governance refuse to provide a written representation that the assurance practitioner considers necessary, this constitutes a limitation on the scope of the assurance practitioner's work and the assurance practitioner shall express a qualified conclusion or a disclaimer of conclusion (paragraph 44).
- ♦ The assurance practitioner shall read the other information that accompanies the historical financial information to consider whether any such information is materially inconsistent with the historical financial information (paragraph 45).
- ♦ If a matter comes to the assurance practitioner's attention that causes the assurance practitioner to believe that the other information appears to include a material misstatement of fact, the assurance practitioner shall discuss the matter with the entity's management (paragraph 48).
- ♦ When, as a result of performing the review of historical financial information, a matter comes to the assurance practitioner's attention that causes the assurance practitioner to believe that it is necessary to make a material adjustment to the historical financial information for it to be prepared, or presented fairly, in all material respects, in accordance with the applicable criteria, the assurance practitioner shall communicate this matter as soon as practicable to the appropriate level of management (paragraph 50).
- ♦ When, in the assurance practitioner's judgement, management does not respond appropriately within a reasonable period of time, the assurance practitioner shall inform those charged with governance (paragraph 51).
- ♦ When, in the assurance practitioner's judgement, those charged with governance do not respond appropriately within a reasonable period of time, the assurance practitioner shall consider:
  (a) whether to modify the report; or
  (b) the possibility of withdrawing from the engagement; and
  (c) when also the auditor, the possibility of resigning from the appointment to audit the annual financial report (paragraph 53).
- ♦ When, as a result of performing the review of historical financial information, a matter comes to the assurance practitioner's attention that causes the assurance practitioner to believe in the existence of fraud or non-compliance by the entity with laws and regulations, the assurance practitioner shall communicate the matter as soon as practicable to those charged with governance and shall consider the implications for the review (paragraph 54).
- ♦ The assurance practitioner shall communicate relevant matters of governance interest arising from the review of the historical financial information to those charged with governance (paragraph 56).

- The "Objective of a Review Engagement" is included in ISRE 2400 as a mandatory paragraph (**bold-type** lettering). However, the equivalent "Objective of a Review of Historical Financial Information, Other than a Financial Report," paragraph is included in this ASRE as Explanatory Guidance (paragraph 16-18).

Compliance with this Standard on Review Engagements enables compliance with ISRE 2400 to the extent described above.

Appendix 1
Example of an Engagement Letter for a Review Engagement

The following letter is not intended to be a standardised letter. It is to be used as a guide only and will need to be adapted according to the engagement requirements and circumstances.

To [title of those charged with governance:[3]]

Scope

You have requested that we review the Accounts Receivable Aged Trial Balance [name of document] of [name of entity], which comprises [insert relevant information] as at 31 December 20XX [or for the period ended] [and other explanatory notes (if applicable)]. We are pleased to confirm our acceptance and our understanding of the terms and objectives of our engagement by means of this letter.

Our review will be conducted in accordance with Standard on Review Engagements ASRE 2405 *Review of Historical Financial Information Other than a Financial Report*, issued by the Auditing and Assurance Standards Board, with the objective of providing us with a basis for reporting whether anything has come to our attention that causes us to believe that the Accounts Receivable Aged Trial Balance [name of document] of [name of entity] is not prepared, in all material respects, in accordance with Accounting Standard AASB 139 *Financial Instruments: Recognition and Measurement* and the accompanying explanatory notes [the applicable criteria]. Such a review consists of making enquiries, primarily of persons responsible for financial and accounting matters, and applying analytical and other review procedures and does not, ordinarily, require corroboration of the information obtained. The scope of a review is substantially less than the scope of an audit conducted in accordance with Auditing Standards whose objective is the expression of an opinion regarding a financial report and accordingly, we shall express no such opinion. ASRE 2405 requires us to also comply with ethical requirements.

We expect to report on the Accounts Receivable Aged Trial Balance [name of document] as follows, however, our report may be modified:

[Include text of sample review report - see Appendix 5]

Responsibility for the Accounts Receivable Aged Trial Balance [name of document] is that of [those charged with governance.[4]] This includes establishing and maintaining internal control relevant to the preparation and fair presentation of the Accounts Receivable Aged Trial Balance [name of document] that is free from material misstatement, whether due to fraud or error, selecting and applying appropriate accounting policies, and making accounting estimates that are reasonable in the circumstances. As part of our review, we shall request written representations from management concerning assertions made in connection with the review. We shall also request that where any document containing the Accounts Receivable Aged Trial Balance [name of document] indicates that the Accounts Receivable Aged Trial Balance [name of document] has been reviewed, our report will also be included in the document.

A review of the Accounts Receivable Aged Trial Balance [name of document] does not provide assurance that we shall become aware of all significant matters that might be identified in an audit. Further, our engagement cannot be relied upon to disclose whether fraud or errors, or illegal acts exist. However, we shall inform you of any material matters that come to our attention.

Fees

[Insert additional information here regarding fee arrangements and billings, as appropriate.]

We look forward to full co-operation with your staff and we trust that they will make available to us whatever records, documentation and other information are requested in connection with our review.

3 Insert the appropriate term, such as "Directors" or "Board of Management".

4 Insert the appropriate term, such as "Directors" or "Board of Management".

[This letter will be effective for future years unless it is terminated, amended or superseded.][5]

Please sign and return the attached copy of this letter to indicate that it is in accordance with your understanding of the arrangements for our review of the Accounts Receivable Aged Trial Balance [name of document].

Yours faithfully,

(signed)

....

Name and Title

Date

Acknowledged on behalf of [entity] by

(signed)

....

Name and Title

Date

Appendix 2
Example of a Management Representation Letter for a Review Engagement

The following letter is not intended to be a standardised letter. It is to be used as a guide only and will need to be adapted according to the engagement requirements and circumstances.

Representations by management will vary from one entity to another and from one period to the next. Representation letters are ordinarily useful where evidence, other than that obtained by enquiry, may not be reasonably expected to be available or when management have made oral representations which the assurance practitioner wishes to confirm in writing.

[Entity Letterhead]

[Addressee – Assurance Practitioner]

[Date]

This representation letter is provided in connection with your review of the Accounts Receivable Aged Trial Balance [name of document] of [name of entity] as at 31 December 20XX [period/date], for the purpose of you expressing a conclusion as to whether anything has come to your attention that causes you to believe that the Accounts Receivable Aged Trial Balance is not prepared, in all material respect, in accordance with Accounting Standard AASB 139 *Financial Instruments: Recognition and Measurement* ("AASB 139") and the accompanying explanatory notes [the applicable criteria].

We acknowledge our responsibility for ensuring that the Accounts Receivable Aged Trial Balance as at 31 December 20XX is prepared and presented in all material respects in accordance with AASB 139 and the accompanying explanatory notes, and confirm that the Accounts Receivable Aged Trial Balance is free of material misstatements including omissions.

We confirm, to the best of our knowledge and belief, the following representations made to you during your review.

5 Use if applicable.

[Include representations required by this ASRE (paragraph 42) and those relevant to the entity. Such representations may include the following examples.]

1. We have made available to you all financial records and related data, other information, explanations and assistance necessary for the conduct of the review.
2. We have disclosed to you the results of our risk assessment that the Accounts Receivable Aged Trial Balance may be materially misstated as result of fraud.
3. There:
   (a) has been no fraud or suspected fraud, error or non-compliance with laws and regulations involving management or employees who have a significant role in the internal control structure;
   (b) has been no fraud or suspected fraud, error or non-compliance with laws and regulations that could have a material effect on the Accounts Receivable Aged Trial; and
   (c) have been no communications from regulatory agencies concerning non-compliance with, or deficiencies in, financial reporting practices that could have a material effect on the Accounts Receivable Aged Trial Balance.
4. We are responsible for, and have established and maintained, an adequate internal control structure to prevent and detect fraud and error and to facilitate the preparation of the Accounts Receivable Aged Trial Balance, and adequate financial records have been maintained. There are no material transactions that have not been recorded properly in the accounting records underlying the Accounts Receivable Aged Trial Balance.
5. We have no plans or intentions that may affect materially the carrying values, or classification, of accounts receivable balances included in the Accounts Receivable Aged Trial Balance.
6. We have considered the requirements of Accounting Standard AASB 139 *Financial Instruments: Recognition and Measurement*, when assessing the impairment of accounts receivable balances recorded in the Accounts Receivable Aged Trial Balance and in ensuring that the balances are not stated in excess of their recoverable amount.
7. We believe the effects of uncorrected misstatements summarised in the accompanying schedule are immaterial, both individually and in the aggregate, to the Accounts Receivable Aged Trial Balance.
8. The entity has satisfactory title to all balances recorded in the Accounts Receivable Aged Trial Balance, and there are no liens or encumbrances over such balances that have not been disclosed, nor has any asset(s) been pledged as collateral.
9. The entity has complied with all aspects of contractual agreements that would have a material effect on the Accounts Receivable Aged Trial Balance in the event of non-compliance.
10. No events have occurred subsequent to the date of the Accounts Receivable Aged Trial Balance and through to the date of this letter that would require adjustment to, or disclosure in, the Accounts Receivable Aged Trial Balance as at 31 December 20XX.

We understand that your examination was made in accordance with Standard on Review Engagements ASRE 2405 *Review of Historical Financial Information Other than a Financial Report*, and was, therefore, designed primarily for the purpose of expressing a conclusion on the Accounts Receivable Aged Trial Balance as at 31 December 20XX of [the entity], and that your procedures were limited to those which you considered necessary for that purpose.

Yours faithfully

[Name of signing officer and title]

Appendix 3

Analytical Procedures the Assurance Practitioner May Consider When Performing a Review of Historical Financial Information

The analytical procedures carried out in a review are determined by the assurance practitioner exercising professional judgement. The procedures listed below are for illustrative purposes only. It is not intended that all the procedures suggested apply to every review engagement nor is the Appendix intended to serve as a program or checklist in the conduct of a review.

Examples of analytical procedures the assurance practitioner may consider when performing a review of historical financial information include the following:

- Comparing the historical financial information with the historical financial information of the immediately preceding period, with the historical financial information of the corresponding period of the preceding financial year, with the historical financial information that was expected by management for the current period, and with the most recent audited annual financial report.
- Comparing the current historical financial information with anticipated results, such as budgets or forecasts
- Comparing the current historical financial information with relevant non-financial information.
- Comparing the recorded amounts, or ratios developed from recorded amounts, to expectations developed by the assurance practitioner. The assurance practitioner develops such expectations by identifying and applying relationships that reasonably are expected to exist based on the assurance practitioner's understanding of the entity and of the industry in which the entity operates.
- Comparing ratios and indicators for the current period with those of entities in the same industry.
- Comparing relationships among elements in the current historical financial information with corresponding relationships in the financial information of prior periods.
- Comparing disaggregated data. The following are examples of how data may be disaggregated:
  - ♦ by period, for example, revenue or expense items disaggregated into quarterly, monthly, or weekly amounts;
  - ♦ by product line or source of revenue;
  - ♦ by location, for example by component;
  - ♦ by attributes of the transaction, for example, revenue generated by designers, architects, or craftsmen; and
  - ♦ by several attributes of the transaction, for example, revenue by product and month.

Appendix 4

Illustrative Detailed Procedures That the Assurance Practitioner May Consider When Performing a Review Engagement

1. The enquiry and analytical procedures carried out in a review engagement are determined by the assurance practitioner exercising professional judgement. The procedures listed below are for illustrative purposes only and are considered by the assurance practitioner who is presumed to have obtained an understanding of the entity and its environment, including internal controls relative to the preparation of the historical financial information. It is not intended that all the procedures listed apply to every review engagement. This Appendix is intended as helpful guidance and not to serve as a program or checklist in the conduct of a review.

General

2. Discuss terms and scope of the engagement with the engagement team.
3. Enquire whether all historical financial information is recorded:
   (a) completely;
   (b) promptly; and
   (c) after the necessary authorisation.
4. Enquire about the accounting policies and consider whether:
   (a) they comply with the applicable criteria;
   (b) they have been applied appropriately; and
   (c) they have been applied consistently and, if not, consider whether disclosure has been made of any changes in the accounting policies.
5. Enquire about the policies and procedures to assess impairment of assets and any consequential estimation of recoverable amount.
6. Enquire about the policies and procedures to determine the fair value of assets and liabilities.
7. Enquire if actions taken at meetings of shareholders or those charged with governance which affect the historical financial information have been appropriately reflected therein.
8. Enquire about plans to dispose of major assets or business/geographical segments.
9. Obtain the historical financial information and discuss it with management and those charged with governance.
10. Consider the adequacy, classification and presentation of disclosures in the historical financial information.
11. Compare the outcomes shown in the current period historical financial information with those shown in historical financial information for comparable prior periods and, if available, with the relevant budgets and forecasts.
12. Obtain explanations from management for any unusual fluctuations or inconsistencies in the historical financial information.

Cash

13. Obtain the bank reconciliations. Enquire about any old or unusual reconciling items.
14. Enquire about transfers between cash accounts for the period immediately before and after the review date.
15. Enquire whether there are any restrictions on cash accounts.

Receivables

16. Enquire about the accounting policies for initially recording trade receivables and determine whether any allowances for doubtful debts are made on such transactions.

17. Obtain a schedule of receivables and determine whether the total agrees with the trial balance.
18. Obtain and consider explanations of significant variations in account balances from previous periods or from those anticipated.
19. Obtain an aged analysis of the trade receivables. Enquire about the reason for unusually large accounts, credit balances on accounts or any other unusual balances and enquire about the collectibility of aged receivables.
20. Discuss with management the classification of receivables, including non-current balances, net credit balances and amounts due from shareholders, those charged with governance, and other related parties.
21. Enquire about the methods for identifying and calculating the impairment of assets and consider them for reasonableness.
22. Enquire whether receivables have been pledged, factored or discounted.
23. Enquire about procedures applied to ensure that a proper cut-off of revenue transactions and sales returns has been achieved.
24. Enquire whether receivables balances represent goods shipped on consignment and, if so, whether adjustments have been made to reverse these transactions and include the goods in inventory.
25. Enquire whether any large credits relating to recorded income have been issued after the reporting period and whether provision has been made for such amounts.

Inventories

26. Obtain the inventory list and determine whether:
    (a) the total agrees with the balance in the trial balance; and
    (b) the list is based on a physical count of inventory.
27. Enquire about the method for counting inventory.
28. Where a physical count was not carried out on the date of the reporting period, enquire whether:
    (a) a perpetual inventory system is used and whether periodic comparisons are made with actual quantities on hand; and
    (b) an integrated cost system is used and whether it has produced reliable information in the past.
29. Discuss adjustments made resulting from the last physical inventory count.
30. Enquire about procedures applied to control cut-off and any inventory movements at period end.
31. Enquire about the basis used in valuing each inventory classification and, in particular, regarding the elimination of intra-group income. Enquire whether inventory is valued at the lower of cost and net realisable value (or lower of cost and current replacement cost for not-for-profit organisations).
32. Consider the consistency with which inventory valuation methods have been applied, including factors such as material, labour and overhead.
33. Compare amounts of major inventory categories with those of prior periods and with those anticipated for the current period. Enquire about major fluctuations and differences.
34. Compare inventory turnover with that in previous periods.
35. Enquire about the method used for identifying slow moving and obsolete inventory and whether such inventory has been accounted for at the lower of cost and net realisable value.
36. Enquire whether any inventory has been consigned to the entity and, if so, whether adjustments have been made to exclude such goods from inventory.
37. Enquire whether any inventory is pledged, stored at other locations or on consignment to others and consider whether such transactions have been accounted for appropriately.

Investments (Including Investments in Associates and Financial Instruments)

38. Obtain a schedule of investments at the date of the reporting period and determine whether it agrees with the trial balance.
39. Enquire about the accounting policies applied to investments.
40. Enquire from management about the carrying amounts of investments. Consider whether there are any realisation or other impairment problems.
41. Consider whether there has been proper accounting for gains and losses and investment income.
42. Enquire about the classification of long-term and short-term investments.

Property, Plant and Equipment and Depreciation

43. Obtain a schedule of the property, plant and equipment indicating the cost and accumulated depreciation and determine whether it agrees with the trial balance.
44. Enquire about the accounting policy applied regarding residual values, provisions to allocate the cost of property, plant and equipment over their estimated useful lives using the expected pattern of consumption of the future economic benefits and distinguishing between capital and maintenance items. Consider whether the property, plant and equipment have suffered an impairment in value.
45. Discuss with management significant additions and disposals to property, plant and equipment accounts and accounting for gains and losses on disposals or de-recognition. Enquire whether all such transactions have been accounted for.
46. Enquire about the consistency with which the depreciation method and rates have been applied and compare depreciation accumulations with prior years.
47. Enquire whether there are any restrictions on the property, plant and equipment.
48. Discuss whether lease agreements have been properly reflected in the historical financial information in conformity with current accounting pronouncements.

Prepaid Expenses, Intangibles and Other Assets

49. Obtain schedules identifying the nature of these accounts and discuss with management the recoverability thereof.
50. Enquire about the basis for recording these accounts and the amortisation methods used.
51. Compare balances of related expense accounts with those of prior periods and discuss significant variations with management.
52. Discuss the classification basis between current and non-current accounts with management.

Loans Payable

53. Obtain from management a schedule of loans payable and determine whether the total agrees with the trial balance.
54. Enquire whether there are any loans where management has not complied with the provisions of the loan agreement and, if so, enquire as to management's actions and whether appropriate adjustments have been made in the financial information.
55. Consider the reasonableness of interest expense in relation to loan balances.
56. Enquire whether loans payable are secured.
57. Enquire whether loans payable have been appropriately classified between current and non-current.

Trade Payables

58. Enquire about the accounting policies for initially recording trade payables and whether the entity is entitled to any allowances given on such transactions.
59. Obtain and consider explanations of significant variations in account balances from previous periods or from those anticipated.
60. Obtain a schedule of trade payables and determine whether the total agrees with the trial balance.

61. Enquire whether balances are reconciled with the creditors' statements and compare with prior period balances. Compare turnover with prior periods.

62. Consider whether there could be material unrecorded liabilities.

63. Enquire whether payables to shareholders, those charged with governance and other related parties are disclosed separately.

Other Liabilities and Contingent Liabilities

64. Obtain a schedule of the other liabilities and determine whether the total agrees with the trial balance.

65. Compare major balances of related expense accounts with similar accounts for prior periods.

66. Enquire about approvals for such other liabilities, terms of payment, compliance with terms, collateral and classification.

67. Enquire about the method for determining other liabilities.

68. Enquire as to the nature of amounts disclosed in contingent liabilities and commitments.

69. Enquire whether any relevant actual or contingent liabilities exist which have not been recognised/disclosed in the financial information. If so, discuss with management and/or those charged with governance whether provisions need to be recognised/disclosed in the financial information.

Income and Other Taxes

70. Discuss with management if there were any events, including disputes with taxation authorities, which could have a significant effect on the taxes payable by the entity.

71. Consider the tax expense in relation to the entity's income for the period.

72. Discuss with management the adequacy of the recognised deferred tax assets and/or liabilities and amounts in respect of prior periods.

Subsequent Events

73. Obtain from management the latest financial report and compare it, where appropriate, with the historical financial information being reviewed or with that for comparable periods from the preceding year.

74. Enquire about events after the reporting date that would have a material effect on the historical financial information under review and, in particular, enquire whether:
    (a) any substantial commitments or uncertainties have arisen subsequent to the reporting date;
    (b) any significant changes in the share capital, long-term debt or working capital have occurred up to the date of enquiry; and
    (c) any unusual adjustments have been made during the period between the reporting date and the date of enquiry.

    Consider the need for adjustments or disclosure in the financial information.

75. Obtain and read the minutes of meetings of shareholders, those charged with governance and appropriate committees subsequent to the review date.

Litigation

76. Discuss with management whether the entity is the subject of any legal actions - threatened, pending or in process. Consider the effect on the historical financial information.

Equity

77. Obtain and consider a schedule of the transactions in the equity accounts, including equity contributions, buy-backs of the entity's own equity instruments and dividends.

78. Enquire whether there are any restrictions on retained earnings or other equity accounts.

Operations

79. Compare results with those of prior periods and those expected for the current period. Discuss significant movements/variations with management.
80. Discuss whether the recognition of major revenue and expense items have taken place in the appropriate periods.
81. Enquire about the policies and procedures related to accrued revenue and/or expenses.
82. Consider and discuss with management the relationship between related items in the revenue accounts and assess the reasonableness thereof in the context of similar relationships for prior periods and other available information.

Appendix 5

Example Review Engagement Reports

The following example reports are to be used as a guide only and will need to be adapted according to the engagement requirements and circumstances.

Example 1: Example of an unmodified assurance practitioner's review report on a Schedule of Accounts Receivable.

INDEPENDENT ASSURANCE PRACTIONER'S [AUDITOR'S] REVIEW REPORT

To [appropriate addressee]

Report on the Schedule of Accounts Receivable

We have reviewed the attached Schedule of Accounts Receivable of [name of entity] as at 30 June 20X1(the Schedule).

The Schedule has been prepared for the [appropriate party[6]] to assess the value of the [type of entity's] receivables portfolio.

Management's [Appropriate Title] Responsibility for the Schedule

Management [Appropriate Title] is responsible for the preparation of the Schedule and has determined that the accounting policies [applicable criteria] used are appropriate to the needs of the[appropriate party]. This responsibility includes establishing and maintaining internal control relevant to the preparation of the Schedule that is free from material misstatement, whether due to fraud or error.

Assurance Practitioner's [Auditor's] Responsibility

Our responsibility is to express a conclusion on the Schedule based on our review. We have conducted our review in accordance with Standard on Review Engagements ASRE 2405 *Review of Historical Financial Information Other than a Financial Report* in order to state whether, on the basis of the procedures described, anything has come to our attention that causes us to believe that the Schedule is not prepared, in all material respects, in accordance with the accounting policies [applicable criteria] used. No opinion is expressed as to whether the accounting policies [applicable criteria] used are appropriate to the needs of the [appropriate party].

ASRE 2405 requires us to comply with the requirements of the applicable code of professional conduct of a professional accounting body.

A review consists of making enquiries, primarily of persons responsible for financial and accounting matters, and applying analytical and other review procedures. A review is substantially less in scope than an audit conducted in accordance with Australian Auditing Standards and consequently does not enable us to obtain assurance that we would become aware of all significant matters that might be identified in an audit. Accordingly, we do not express an audit opinion.

6 Insert the appropriate party such as "Directors" or "Board of Management".

Conclusion

Based on our review, which is not an audit, nothing has come to our attention that causes us to believe that the Schedule of Accounts Receivable of [name of entity] as at 30 June 20X1 is not prepared, in all material respects, in accordance with the accounting policies [applicable criteria] used.

[Assurance Practitioner's signature[7]]

[Date of the Assurance Practitioner's review report]

[Assurance Practitioner's address]

Example 2: Example of an assurance practitioner's review report on a Schedule of Accounts Receivable with a qualified conclusion for a limitation on scope not imposed by management.

INDEPENDENT ASSURANCE PRACTIONER'S [AUDITOR'S] REVIEW REPORT

To [appropriate addressee]

Report on the Schedule of Accounts Receivable

We have reviewed the attached Schedule of Accounts Receivable of [name of entity] as at 30 June 20X1 (the Schedule).

The Schedule has been prepared for the [appropriate party[8]] to assess the value of the [type of entity's] receivables portfolio.

Management's [Appropriate Title] Responsibility for the Schedule

Management [Appropriate Title] is responsible for the preparation of the Schedule and has determined that the accounting policies [applicable criteria] used are appropriate to the needs of the [appropriate party]. This responsibility includes establishing and maintaining internal control relevant to the preparation of the Schedule that is free from material misstatement, whether due to fraud or error.

Assurance Practitioner's [Auditor's] Responsibility

Our responsibility is to express a conclusion on the Schedule based on our review. We have conducted our review in accordance with Standard on Review Engagements ASRE 2405 *Review of Historical Financial Information Other than a Financial Report* in order to state whether, on the basis of the procedures described, anything has come to our attention that causes us to believe that the Schedule is not prepared, in all material respects, in accordance with the accounting policies [applicable criteria] used. No opinion is expressed as to whether the accounting policies [applicable criteria] used are appropriate to the needs of the [appropriate party]. ASRE 2405 requires us to comply with the requirements of the applicable code of professional conduct of a professional accounting body.

A review consists of making enquiries, primarily of persons responsible for financial and accounting matters, and applying analytical and other review procedures. A review is substantially less in scope than an audit conducted in accordance with Australian Auditing Standards and consequently does not enable us to obtain assurance that we would become aware of all significant matters that might be identified in an audit. Accordingly, we do not express an audit opinion.

Basis for Qualified Conclusion

The Schedule includes four separate balances receivable from individual debtors in the Republic of XXX, a country suffering from civil unrest. These balances amount in total to AUS$ XXX and represent 15% of the total receivable balances listed in the Schedule. We have been unable to obtain the evidence we consider necessary to review and ascertain the collectibility of these four balances. Had we been able to obtain the information we require, matters might have come to our attention indicating that adjustments might be necessary to the Schedule.

7 The assurance practitioner's review report is required to be signed in one or more of the name of the audit firm, the name of the audit company or the personal name of the assurance practitioner as appropriate.

8 Insert the appropriate party such as "Directors" or "Board of Management".

Qualified Conclusion

Except for the adjustments to the Schedule that we might have become aware of had it not been for the situation described in the preceding paragraph, based on our review, which is not an audit, nothing has come to our attention that causes us to believe that the Schedule of Accounts Receivable of [name of entity] as at 30 June 20X1 is not prepared, in all material respects, in accordance with the accounting policies [applicable criteria] used.

[Assurance Practitioner's signature[9]]

[Date of the Assurance Practitioner's review report]

[Assurance Practitioner's address]

Appendix 6

Standards Applicable to Review Engagements

The pre-existing Standard AUS 902 *Review of Financial Reports* had broad application covering reviews of (i) financial information, both historical and prospective; and (ii) non-financial information. The following table and diagrams identify the applicable AUASB Standard in each of the various review engagement types that were previously conducted under AUS 902.

Review Engagement Type [Previously conducted under AUS 902]	**Applicable AUASB Standards**
Review of a financial report comprising historical financial information. (**assurance practitioner who is *not* the auditor**)	**ASRE 2400** *Review of a Financial Report Performed by an Assurance Practitioner Who is Not the Auditor of the Entity*
Review of historical financial information other than a financial report.	**ASRE 2405** *Review of Historical Financial Information Other than a Financial Report*
Review of a financial report comprising historical financial information (**auditor**).	**ASRE 2410** *Review of Interim and Other Financial Reports Performed by the Independent Auditor of the Entity*
Review other than a review of historical financial information covered by the ASREs.	**ASAE 3000** *Assurance Engagements Other than Audits or Reviews of Historical Financial Information*
Review of an entity's compliance with internally or externally imposed requirements as measured by the suitable criteria.	**ASAE 3100** *Compliance Engagements*
Reviews of performance against which the extent of economy, efficiency or effectiveness of an activity may be assessed.	**ASAE 3500** *Performance Engagements*

Diagram 1

Review Standards applicable to Reviews of Financial Reports (comprising historical financial information), and other Historical Financial Information. [To be read in conjunction with the Table above.]

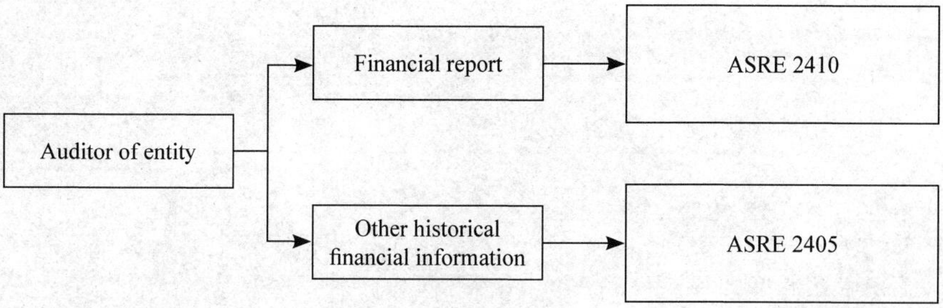

9 The assurance practitioner's review report is required to be signed in one or more of the name of the audit firm, the name of the audit company or the personal name of the assurance practitioner as appropriate

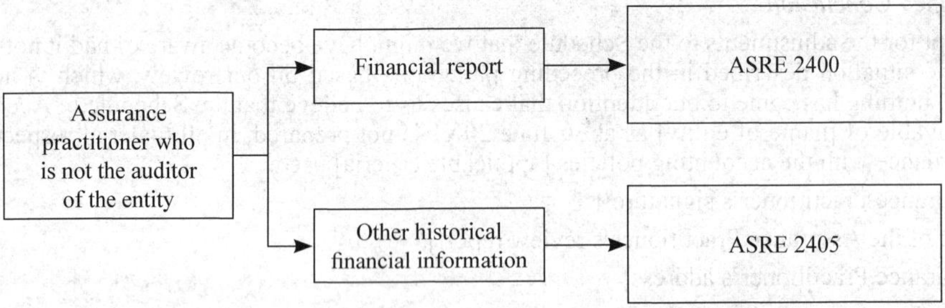

Diagram 2

Standards applicable to Review Engagements not covered by ASREs.

[To be read in conjunction with the Table above.]

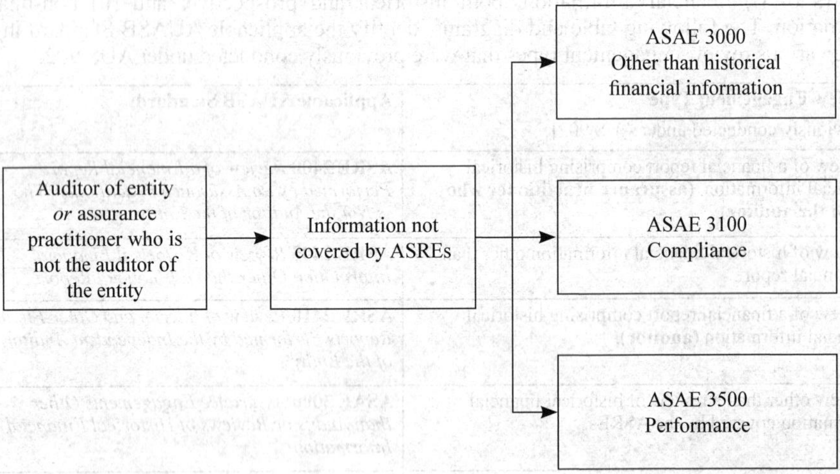

ASRE 2410

Review of a Financial Report Performed by the Independent Auditor of the Entity

(Reissued October 2009: amended and compiled June 2011)

Issued by the Auditing and Assurance Standards Board.

Note from the Institute of Chartered Accountants Australia

This note, prepared by the technical editor, is not part of ASRE 2410.

Historical development

April 2006: Standard on Review Engagements ASRE 2410 'Review of Interim and Other Financial Reports Performed by the Independent Auditor of the Entity' was issued as a legally binding Standard. It is based on ISRE 2410 of the same name.

August 2008: ASRE 2410 reissued to be consistent with the new ASRE 2400 and ASRE 2405. The 'Explanatory Guide to AUASB Standards applicable to Review Engagements' was issued to provide information on the use of AUASB Standards in review engagements.

October 2009: ASRE 2410 reissued as 'Review of a Financial Report Performed by the Independent Auditor of the Entity' as part of the AUASB's Clarity Project to make it consistent with changes made to other auditing Standards under the project. It is based on ISRE 2410 'Review of Interim Financial Information Performed by the Independent Auditor of the Entity' which has not been redrafted in 'clarity' format by the IAASB. It has been modified to take into account *Corporations Act 2001* requirements, but conforms to ISRE 2410 to the extent that that Standard deals with the review of financial statements by the auditor of the entity.

June 2011: ASRE 2410 updated for editorial amendments contained in ASA 2011-1 'Amendments to Australian Auditing Standards'.

Contents

Compilation Details

Auditing Standard ASRE 2410 *Review of a Financial Report Performed by the Independent Auditor of the Entity* as Amended

This compilation takes into account amendments made up to and including 27 June 2011 and was prepared on 27 June 2011 by the Auditing and Assurance Standards Board (AUASB).

This compilation is not a separate Auditing Standard made by the AUASB. Instead, it is a representation of ASRE 2410 (October 2009) as amended by another Auditing Standard which is listed in the Table below.

Table of Standards

Standard	Date made	Operative date
ASRE 2410	27 October 2009	1 January 2010
ASA 2011-1	27 June 2011	1 July 2011

Table of Amendments

Paragraph affected	How affected	By … [paragraph]
39	Amended	ASA 2011-1 [87]
Appendix 1: Example Engagement Letter	Amended	ASA 2011-1 [88]
Appendix 1: Example Engagement Letter	Amended	ASA 2011-1 [89]
Appendix 1: Example Representation Letter	Amended	ASA 2011-1 [90]
Appendix 3: Example Auditor's Report	Amended	ASA 2011-1 [91]
Appendix 3: Example Auditor's Report	Amended	ASA 2011-1 [92]
Appendix 3: Example Auditor's Report	Amended	ASA 2011-1 [93]
Appendix 4: Example Auditor's Report	Amended	ASA 2011-1 [94]
Appendix 4: Example Auditor's Report	Amended	ASA 2011-1 [95]
Appendix 4: Example Auditor's Report	Amended	ASA 2011-1 [96]
Appendix 4: Example Auditor's Report	Amended	ASA 2011-1 [97]
Appendix 4: Example Auditor's Report	Amended	ASA 2011-1 [98]
Appendix 4: Example Auditor's Report	Amended	ASA 2011-1 [99]

Preface

[Preface extracted from the original Auditing Standard issued 27 October 2009]

Reasons for Issuing Auditing Standard on Review Engagements ASRE 2410 *Review of a Financial Report Performed by the Independent Auditor of the Entity*

The Auditing and Assurance Standards Board (AUASB) issues Auditing Standard on Review Engagements ASRE 2410 *Review of a Financial Report Performed by the Independent Auditor of the Entity* pursuant to the requirements of the legislative provisions and the Strategic Direction explained below.

The AUASB is an independent statutory board of the Australian Government established under section 227A of the *Australian Securities and Investments Commission Act 2001*, as amended (ASIC Act). Under section 336 of the *Corporations Act 2001*, the AUASB may make Australian Auditing Standards for the purposes of the corporations legislation. These Auditing Standards are legislative instruments under the *Legislative Instruments Act 2003*.

Under the Strategic Direction given to the AUASB by the Financial Reporting Council (FRC), the AUASB is required to have regard to any programme initiated by the International Auditing and Assurance Standards Board (IAASB) for the revision and enhancement of the International Standards on Auditing (ISAs) and to make appropriate consequential amendments to the Australian Auditing Standards. Accordingly, the AUASB has decided to revise and redraft the Australian Auditing Standards using the equivalent redrafted ISAs.

ASRE 2410 is an Auditing Standard made under the *Corporations Act 2001*. Consequently, the AUASB has redrafted the extant Auditing Standard, ASRE 2410 *Review of Interim and Other Financial Reports Performed by the Independent Auditor of the Entity* in a format that is consistent with the other revised and redrafted Australian Auditing Standards operative for financial reporting periods commencing on or after 1 January 2010. A further revision of this Auditing Standard will occur at a later date, once the IAASB undertakes a revision of its equivalent International Standard.

Main Features

This Auditing Standard on Review Engagements establishes requirements and provides application and other explanatory material regarding the responsibilities of an auditor of an entity when engaged to undertake a review of a financial report and on the form and content of the auditor's review report.

This Auditing Standard:

(a) describes the general principles of a review of a financial report;

(b) sets out the requirements on agreeing the terms of engagement;

(c) details the procedures for a review of a financial report;

(d) lists the matters to be included in written representations that an auditor seeks to obtain from management, and where appropriate, those charged with governance;

(e) stipulates the matters that an auditor communicates to management and those charged with governance;

(f) details the form and content of the auditor's review report;

(g) describes the circumstances under which the auditor's review report is to be modified and the type of modification applicable;

(h) sets out requirements regarding going concern and significant uncertainty; and

(i) describes the auditor's documentation requirements.

Authority Statement

Auditing Standard on Review Engagements ASRE 2410 *Review of a Financial Report Performed by the Independent Auditor of the Entity* (as amended at 27 June 2011) is set out in paragraphs 1 to A60 and Appendices 1 to 4.

This Auditing Standard on Review Engagements is to be read in conjunction with ASA 101 *Preamble to Australian Auditing Standards*, which sets out the intentions of the AUASB on how the Australian Auditing Standards, operative for financial reporting periods commencing on or after 1 January 2010, are to be understood, interpreted and applied.

Dated: 27 June 2011

M H Kelsall
Chairman - AUASB

Auditing Standard ASRE 2410

The Auditing and Assurance Standards Board (AUASB) made Auditing Standard ASRE 2410 *Review of a Financial Report Performed by the Independent Auditor of the Entity*, pursuant to section 227B of the *Australian Securities and Investments Commission Act 2001* and section 336 of the *Corporations Act 2001*, on 27 October 2009.

This compiled version of ASRE 2410 incorporates subsequent amendments contained in another Auditing Standard made by the AUASB up to and including 27 June 2011 (see Compilation Details).

Auditing Standard on Review Engagements ASRE 2410

Review of a Financial Report Performed by the Independent Auditor of the Entity

Application

1. This Auditing Standard on Review Engagements applies to:
   (a) a review by the independent auditor of the entity, of a financial report for a half-year, in accordance with the *Corporations Act 2001*; and
   (b) a review, by the independent auditor of the entity, of a financial report, or a complete set of financial statements, comprising historical financial information, for any other purpose.

Operative Date

2. This Auditing Standard on Review Engagements is operative for financial reporting periods commencing on or after 1 January 2010.
   [Note: For operative dates of paragraphs changed or added by an amending Standard, see Compilation Details.]

Introduction

Scope of this Auditing Standard on Review Engagements

3. This Auditing Standard on Review Engagements (Auditing Standard) deals with the auditor's responsibilities when an auditor undertakes an engagement to review a financial report of an audit client, and on the form and content of the auditor's review report. The term "auditor" is used throughout this Auditing Standard, not because the auditor is performing an audit function but because the scope of this Auditing Standard is limited to a review of a financial report performed by the independent auditor of the financial report of the entity.

Objective

4. The objective of the auditor is to plan and perform the review to enable the auditor to express a conclusion whether, on the basis of the review, anything has come to the auditor's attention that causes the auditor to believe that the financial report, or complete set of financial statements, is (are) not prepared, in all material respects, in accordance with the applicable financial reporting framework. (Ref: Para. A1-A3)

Definitions

5. For the purposes of this Auditing Standard, the following terms have the meanings attributed below:
   (a) An interim financial report means a financial report that is prepared in accordance with an applicable financial reporting framework[1] for a period that is shorter than the entity's financial year.
   (b) A financial report means a complete set of financial statements including the related notes and an assertion statement by those responsible for the financial report. The related notes ordinarily comprise a summary of significant accounting policies and other explanatory information. The requirements of the applicable financial reporting framework determine the form and content of the financial report. For example, a financial report, as defined under section 303 of the *Corporations Act 2001* consists of financial statements for the half-year, notes to the financial statements and the directors' declaration about the statements and notes.

1 See, for example, Accounting Standard AASB 134 *Interim Financial Reporting* and the *Corporations Act 2001.*

(c) An applicable financial reporting framework means a financial reporting framework that is designed to achieve fair presentation.

Requirements

Performing a Review

6. The auditor who is engaged to perform a review of a financial report shall perform the review in accordance with this Auditing Standard. (Ref: Para. A4)

7. Where in rare and exceptional circumstances, factors outside the auditor's control prevent the auditor from complying with an essential procedure contained within a relevant requirement in this Auditing Standard, the auditor shall:
   (a) if possible, perform appropriate alternative procedures; and
   (b) document in the working papers:
      (i) the circumstances surrounding the inability to comply;
      (ii) the reasons for the inability to comply; and
      (iii) justification of how alternative procedures achieve the objectives of the requirement.

   When the auditor is unable to perform appropriate alternative procedures, the auditor shall consider the implications for the auditor's review report.

General Principles of a Review of a Financial Report

8. The auditor shall comply with relevant ethical requirements relating to the audit of the annual financial report of the entity. (Ref: Para. A5)

9. The auditor shall implement quality control procedures that are applicable to the individual engagement. (Ref: Para. A6)

10. The auditor shall plan and perform the review by exercising professional judgement and with an attitude of professional scepticism, recognising that circumstances may exist that cause the financial report to require a material adjustment for it to be prepared, in all material respects, in accordance with the applicable financial reporting framework. (Ref: Para. A7)

Agreeing the Terms of the Engagement (Ref: Para. A8, A55 and A57)

Preconditions for a Review

11. The auditor shall, prior to agreeing the terms of the engagement, determine whether the financial reporting framework is acceptable and obtain agreement from management and, where appropriate, those charged with governance, that it acknowledges and understands its responsibility:
   (a) for the preparation and fair presentation of the financial report;
   (b) for such internal controls as management and, where appropriate, those charged with governance, deems necessary to enable the preparation of the financial report that is free from material misstatement; and
   (c) to provide the auditor with:
      - access to information relevant to the preparation of the financial report;
      - additional information that the auditor may request for the purposes of the review engagement; and
      - unrestricted access to persons from whom the auditor determines it necessary to obtain evidence.

Agreement on Review Engagement Terms

12. The auditor shall agree the terms of the engagement with the entity, which shall be recorded in writing by the auditor and forwarded to the entity. When the review engagement is undertaken pursuant to legislation, the minimum applicable terms are those contained in the legislation.

Procedures for a Review of a Financial Report

Understanding the Entity and its Environment, Including its Internal Control

13. The auditor shall obtain an understanding of the entity and its environment, including its internal control, as it relates to the preparation of both the annual and interim or other financial reports, sufficient to plan and conduct the engagement so as to be able to:

    (a) identify the types of potential material misstatements and consider the likelihood of their occurrence; and

    (b) select the enquiries, analytical and other review procedures that will provide the auditor with a basis for reporting whether anything has come to the auditor's attention that causes the auditor to believe that the financial report is not prepared, in all material respects, in accordance with the applicable financial reporting framework. (Ref: Para. A9-A12)

14. In order to plan and conduct a review of a financial report, a recently appointed auditor, who has not yet performed an audit of the annual financial report in accordance with Australian Auditing Standards, shall obtain an understanding of the entity and its environment, including its internal control, as it relates to the preparation of both the annual and interim or other financial reports. (Ref: Para. A13)

Materiality (Ref: Para. A14-A18)

15. The auditor shall consider materiality, using professional judgement, when:

    (a) determining the nature, timing and extent of review procedures; and

    (b) evaluating the effect of misstatements.

Enquiries, Analytical and Other Review Procedures

16. The auditor shall make enquiries, primarily of persons responsible for financial and accounting matters, and perform analytical and other review procedures to enable the auditor to conclude whether, on the basis of the procedures performed, anything has come to the auditor's attention that causes the auditor to believe that the financial report is not prepared, in all material respects, in accordance with the applicable financial reporting framework. (Ref: Para. A19-A23)

17. The auditor shall obtain evidence that the financial report agrees or reconciles with the underlying accounting records. (Ref: Para. A24)

18. The auditor shall enquire whether management has identified all events up to the date of the review report that may require adjustment to or disclosure in the financial report. (Ref: Para. A25)

19. The auditor shall enquire whether those charged with governance have changed their assessment of the entity's ability to continue as a going concern. When, as the result of this enquiry or other review procedures, the auditor becomes aware of events or conditions that may cast significant doubt on the entity's ability to continue as a going concern, the auditor shall:

    (a) enquire of those charged with governance as to their plans for future actions based on their going concern assessment, the feasibility of these plans, and whether they believe that the outcome of these plans will improve the situation; and

    (b) consider the adequacy of the disclosure about such matters in the financial report. (Ref: Para. A26)

20. When a matter comes to the auditor's attention that leads the auditor to question whether a material adjustment should be made for the financial report to be prepared, in all material respects, in accordance with the applicable financial reporting framework, the auditor shall make additional enquiries or perform other procedures to enable the auditor to express a conclusion in the review report. (Ref: Para. A27)

Comparatives – First Financial Report (Ref: Para. A28-A31)

21. When comparative information is included for the first time in a financial report, an auditor shall perform similar procedures on the comparative information as applied to the current period financial report.

Evaluation of Misstatements (Ref: Para. A32-A34)

22. The auditor shall evaluate, individually and in the aggregate, whether uncorrected misstatements that have come to the auditor's attention are material to the financial report.

Written Representations

23. The auditor shall endeavour to obtain written representations from management and, where appropriate, those charged with governance, that:
    (a) they acknowledge their responsibility for the design and implementation of internal control to prevent and detect fraud and error;
    (b) the financial report is prepared and presented in accordance with the applicable financial reporting framework;
    (c) they believe the effect of those uncorrected misstatements aggregated by the auditor during the review are immaterial, both individually and in the aggregate, to the financial report taken as a whole. A summary of such items is included in or attached to the written representations;
    (d) they have disclosed to the auditor all significant facts relating to any frauds or suspected frauds known to them that may have affected the entity;
    (e) they have disclosed to the auditor the results of their assessment of the risk that the financial report may be materially misstated as a result of fraud;
    (f) they have disclosed to the auditor all known actual or possible non-compliance with laws and regulations, the effects of which are to be considered when preparing the financial report; and
    (g) they have disclosed to the auditor all significant events that have occurred subsequent to the balance sheet date and through to the date of the review report that may require adjustment to or disclosure in the financial report. (Ref: Para. A35)
24. If management and, where appropriate, those charged with governance refuse to provide a written representation that the auditor considers necessary, this constitutes a limitation on the scope of the auditor's work and the auditor shall express a qualified conclusion or a disclaimer of conclusion, as appropriate.

Auditor's Responsibility for Accompanying Information

25. The auditor shall read the other information that accompanies the financial report to consider whether any such information is materially inconsistent with the financial report. (Ref: Para. A36)
26. If a matter comes to the auditor's attention that causes the auditor to believe that the other information appears to include a material misstatement of fact, the auditor shall discuss the matter with the entity's management, and where appropriate, those charged with governance. (Ref: Para. A37)

Communication

27. When, as a result of performing a review of a financial report, a matter comes to the auditor's attention that causes the auditor to believe that it is necessary to make a material adjustment to the financial report for it to be prepared, in all material respects, in accordance with the applicable financial reporting framework, the auditor shall communicate this matter as soon as practicable to the appropriate level of management.
28. When, in the auditor's judgement, management does not respond appropriately within a reasonable period of time, the auditor shall inform those charged with governance. (Ref: Para. A38)

29. When, in the auditor's judgement, those charged with governance do not respond appropriately within a reasonable period of time, the auditor shall consider:

(a) whether to modify the review report; or

(b) the possibility of withdrawing from the engagement; and

(c) the possibility of resigning from the appointment to audit the annual financial report. (Ref: Para. Aus A36.1 and A58)

30. When, as a result of performing the review of a financial report, a matter comes to the auditor's attention that causes the auditor to believe in the existence of fraud or non-compliance by the entity with laws and regulations, the auditor shall communicate the matter as soon as practicable to those charged with governance and shall consider the implications for the review. (Ref: Para. A39)

31. The auditor shall communicate relevant matters of governance interest arising from the review of the financial report to those charged with governance. (Ref: Para. A40 and A59)

Reporting the Nature, Extent and Results of the Review of a Financial Report

32. The auditor shall issue a written report that contains the following:

(a) An appropriate title clearly identifying it as a review report of the independent auditor of the entity.

(b) An addressee, as required by the circumstances of the engagement.

(c) Identification of the financial report reviewed, including identification of the title of each of the statements contained in the financial report and the date and period covered by the financial report.

(d) A statement that those charged with governance are responsible for the preparation and fair presentation of the financial report in accordance with the applicable financial reporting framework.

(e) A statement that the auditor is responsible for expressing a conclusion on the financial report based on the review.

(f) A statement that the review of the financial report was conducted in accordance with Auditing Standard on Review Engagements ASRE 2410 *Review of a Financial Report Performed by the Independent Auditor of the Entity*, and that that Auditing Standard requires the auditor to comply with ethical requirements relevant to the audit of the annual financial report.

(g) A statement that a review consists of making enquiries, primarily of persons responsible for financial and accounting matters, and applying analytical and other review procedures.

(h) A statement that a review is substantially less in scope than an audit conducted in accordance with Australian Auditing Standards and consequently does not enable the auditor to obtain assurance that the auditor would become aware of all significant matters that might be identified in an audit, and that accordingly no audit opinion is expressed.

(i) A conclusion as to whether anything has come to the auditor's attention that causes the auditor to believe that the financial report does not present fairly, or if applicable, is not true and fair, in all material respects, in accordance with the applicable financial reporting framework (including a reference to the jurisdiction or country of origin of the financial reporting framework when Australia is not the origin of the financial reporting framework used).

(j) The date of the auditor's review report.

(k) The location in the country or jurisdiction where the auditor practices.

(l) The auditor's signature. (Ref: Para. A41)

Departure from the Applicable Financial Reporting Framework

33. The auditor shall express a qualified or adverse conclusion when a matter has come to the auditor's attention that causes the auditor to believe that a material adjustment should be made to the financial report for it to be prepared, in all material respects, in accordance with the applicable financial reporting framework. The auditor shall include a basis for modification paragraph in the report, that describes the nature of the departure and, if practicable, states the effects on the financial report. If the effects or possible effects are incapable of being measured reliably, a statement to that effect and the reasons therefor shall be included in the basis for modification paragraph. The conclusion paragraph shall be headed "Qualified Conclusion" or "Adverse Conclusion", whichever is relevant. (Ref: Para. A42)

34. When the effect of the departure is so material and pervasive to the financial report that the auditor concludes a qualified conclusion is not adequate to disclose the misleading or incomplete nature of the financial report, the auditor shall express an adverse conclusion. (Ref: Para. A43)

Limitation on Scope (Ref: Para. A44)

35. When the auditor is unable to complete the review, the auditor shall communicate, in writing, to the appropriate level of management and to those charged with governance the reason why the review cannot be completed, and consider whether it is appropriate to issue a review report.

Limitation on Scope Imposed by Management

36. Unless required by law or regulation, an auditor shall not accept an engagement to review a financial report when management has imposed a limitation on the scope of the auditor's review. (Ref: Para. A45 and A58)

37. If, after accepting the engagement, management imposes a limitation on the scope of the review, the auditor shall request management to remove the limitation. If management refuses the auditor's request to remove the limitation, the auditor shall communicate, in writing, to the appropriate level of management and those charged with governance, the reason(s) why the review cannot be completed. (Ref: Para. A46)

38. If management and, where appropriate, those charged with governance, refuses the auditor's request to remove a limitation that has been imposed on the scope of the review, but there is a legal or regulatory requirement for the auditor to issue a report, the auditor shall issue a disclaimer of conclusion or qualified conclusion report, as appropriate, containing the reason(s) why the review cannot be completed. (Ref: Para. A47)

Other Limitations on Scope Not Imposed by Management (Ref: Para. A48-A49)

39. The auditor shall express a qualified conclusion when, in rare circumstances, there is a limitation on the scope of the auditor's work that is confined to one or more specific matters, which while material, is not in the auditor's judgement pervasive to the financial report, and when the auditor concludes that an unqualified opinion cannot be expressed. A qualified conclusion shall be expressed as being "except for" the effects of the matter to which the qualification relates. The conclusion paragraph shall be headed "Qualified Conclusion".

Going Concern and Significant Uncertainties (Ref: Para. A50-A54)

40. If adequate disclosure is made in the financial report, the auditor shall add an emphasis of matter paragraph to the review report to highlight a material uncertainty relating to an event or condition that casts significant doubt on the entity's ability to continue as a going concern.

41. If a material uncertainty that casts significant doubt on the entity's ability to continue as a going concern is not adequately disclosed in the financial report, the auditor shall express a qualified or adverse conclusion, as appropriate. The report shall include specific reference to the fact that there is such a material uncertainty.

42. In circumstances other than a going concern problem, the auditor shall consider adding an emphasis of matter paragraph to highlight a significant uncertainty that is adequately disclosed in the financial report, that came to the auditor's attention, the resolution of which is dependent upon future events and which may materially affect the financial report.

43. If a significant uncertainty (other than a going concern problem) is not adequately disclosed in the financial report, the auditor shall express a qualified or adverse conclusion, as appropriate. The report shall include specific reference to the fact that there is such a significant uncertainty.

Documentation (Ref: Para. A60)

44. The auditor shall prepare review documentation that is sufficient and appropriate to provide a basis for the auditor's conclusion, and to provide evidence that the review was performed in accordance with this Auditing Standard and applicable legal and regulatory requirements.

❖ ❖ ❖

Application and Other Explanatory Material

Objective (Ref: Para. 4)

A1. Under paragraph 13, the auditor needs to make enquiries, and perform analytical and other review procedures in order to reduce to a limited level the risk of expressing an inappropriate conclusion when the financial report is materially misstated.

A2. The objective of a review of a financial report differs significantly from that of an audit conducted in accordance with Australian Auditing Standards. A review of a financial report does not provide a basis for expressing an opinion whether the financial report gives a true and fair view, or is presented fairly, in all material respects, in accordance with the applicable financial reporting framework.

A3. A review, in contrast to an audit, is not designed to obtain reasonable assurance that the financial report is free from material misstatement. A review consists of making enquiries, primarily of persons responsible for financial and accounting matters, and applying analytical and other review procedures. A review may bring significant matters affecting the financial report to the auditor's attention, but it does not provide all of the evidence that would be required in an audit.

Performing a Review (Ref: Para 6)

A4. Through performing the audit of the annual financial report, the auditor obtains an understanding of the entity and its environment, including its internal control. When the auditor is engaged to review the financial report, under paragraph 13, the auditor needs to update this understanding through enquiries made in the course of the review, to assist the auditor in focusing the enquiries to be made and the analytical and other review procedures to be applied. A practitioner who is engaged to perform a review of a financial report, and who is not the auditor of the entity, does not perform the review in accordance with ASRE 2410*, as the practitioner ordinarily does not have the same understanding of the entity and its environment, including its internal control, as the auditor of the entity.

Although other Auditing Standards do not apply to review engagements, they include guidance which may be helpful to auditors performing reviews covered by this Auditing Standard.

General Principles of a Review of a Financial Report

A5. Relevant ethical requirements[2] govern the auditor's professional responsibilities in the following areas: independence, integrity, objectivity, professional competence and due care, confidentiality, professional behaviour, and technical standards. (Ref: Para. 8)

A6. The elements of quality control that are relevant to an individual engagement include leadership responsibilities for quality on the engagement, ethical requirements, acceptance and continuance of client relationships and specific engagements, assignment

---

* See ASRE 2400 *Review of a Financial Report Performed by an Assurance Practitioner Who is Not the Auditor of the Entity.*

2 See ASA 102 *Compliance with Ethical Requirements when Performing Audits, Reviews and Other Assurance Engagements.*

of engagement teams, engagement performance, and monitoring. ASQC 1 and ASA 220[3] include guidance that may be helpful. (Ref: Para. 9)

A7. An attitude of professional scepticism denotes that the auditor makes a critical assessment, with a questioning mind, of the validity of evidence obtained and is alert to evidence that contradicts or brings into question the reliability of documents or representations by management of the entity. ASA 200 includes guidance which may be helpful.[*] (Ref: Para. 10)

Agreeing the Terms of the Engagement

A8. Written agreement of the terms of the engagement helps to avoid misunderstandings regarding the nature of the engagement and, in particular, the objective and scope of the review, the responsibilities of management and, where appropriate, those charged with governance, the extent of the auditor's responsibilities, the assurance obtained, and the nature and form of the report. The communication ordinarily covers the following matters:

(a) the objective of a review of a financial report;

(b) the scope of the review;

(c) the responsibilities of management and, where appropriate, those charged with governance for:

  (i) the financial report;

  (ii) establishing and maintaining effective internal control relevant to the preparation of the financial report; and

  (iii) making all financial records and related information available to the auditor;

(d) agreement from management and, where appropriate, those charged with governance:

  (i) to provide written representations to the auditor to confirm representations made orally during the review, as well as representations that are implicit in the entity's records; and

  (ii) that where any document containing the financial report indicates that the financial report has been reviewed by the entity's auditor, the review report also will be included in the document; and

(e) the anticipated form and content of the report to be issued, including the identity of the addressee of the report.

An illustrative engagement letter is set out in Appendix 1. The terms of engagement to review a financial report can also be combined with the terms of engagement to audit the annual financial report. ASA 210 includes guidance which may be helpful.[**] (Ref: Para. 12)

Procedures for a Review of a Financial Report

Understanding the Entity and its Environment, Including its Internal Control

A9. Under ASA 315 *Identifying and Assessing the Risks of Material Misstatement through Understanding the Entity and Its Environment*, the auditor who has audited the entity's financial report for one or more annual periods has obtained an understanding of the entity and its environment, including its internal control, as it relates to the preparation of the annual financial report, that was sufficient to conduct the audit. In planning a review of a financial report, the auditor needs to update this understanding. The auditor also needs to obtain a sufficient understanding of internal control as it relates to the preparation of the financial report subject to review, as it may differ from internal control as it relates to the preparation of the annual financial report. (Ref: Para. 13)

---

3 See ASQC 1 *Quality Control for Firms that Perform Audits and Reviews of Financial Reports and Other Financial Information, and Other Assurance Engagements* and ASA 220 *Quality Control for an Audit of a Financial Report and Other Historical Financial Information.*

* See ASA 200 *Overall Objectives of the Independent Auditor and the Conduct of an Audit in Accordance with Australian Auditing Standards.*

** See ASA 210 *Agreeing the Terms of Audit Engagements.*

ASRE

A10. The auditor needs to use the understanding of the entity and its environment, including its internal control, to determine the enquiries to be made and the analytical and other review procedures to be applied, and to identify the particular events, transactions or assertions to which enquiries may be directed or analytical or other review procedures applied. (Ref: Para. 13)

A11. The procedures performed by the auditor to update the understanding of the entity and its environment, including its internal control, ordinarily include the following:

(a) reading the documentation, to the extent necessary, of the preceding year's audit, reviews of prior period(s) of the current year, and corresponding period(s) of the prior year, to enable the auditor to identify matters that may affect the current-period financial report;

(b) considering any significant risks, including the risk of management override of controls, that were identified in the audit of the prior year's financial report;

(c) reading the most recent annual and comparable prior period financial report;

(d) considering materiality with reference to the applicable financial reporting framework as it relates to the financial report, to assist in determining the nature and extent of the procedures to be performed and evaluating the effect of misstatements;

(e) considering the nature of any corrected material misstatements and any identified uncorrected immaterial misstatements in the prior year's financial report;

(f) considering significant financial accounting and reporting matters that may be of continuing significance, such as material weaknesses in internal control;

(g) considering the results of any audit procedures performed with respect to the current year's financial report;

(h) considering the results of any internal audit performed and the subsequent actions taken by management;

(i) enquiring of management about the results of management's assessment of the risk that the financial report may be materially misstated as a result of fraud;

(j) enquiring of management about the effect of changes in the entity's business activities;

(k) enquiring of management about any significant changes in internal control and the potential effect of any such changes on the preparation of the financial report; and

(l) enquiring of management of the process by which the financial report has been prepared and the reliability of the underlying accounting records to which the financial report is agreed or reconciled. (Ref: Para. 13)

A12. The auditor needs to determine the nature of the review procedures, if any, to be performed for components and, where applicable, communicate these matters to other auditors involved in the review. Factors considered ordinarily include the materiality of, and risk of misstatement in, the financial report components, and the auditor's understanding of the extent to which internal control over the preparation of such reports is centralised or decentralised. (Ref: Para. 13)

A13. Obtaining an understanding of the entity and its environment enables the auditor to focus the enquiries made, and the analytical and other review procedures applied in performing a review of the financial report in accordance with this Auditing Standard. As part of obtaining this understanding, ordinarily the auditor makes enquiries of the predecessor auditor and, where practicable, reviews the predecessor auditor's documentation for the preceding annual audit and for any prior periods in the current year that have been reviewed by the predecessor auditor. In doing so, ordinarily the auditor considers the nature of any corrected misstatements, and any uncorrected misstatements aggregated by the auditor, any significant risks, including the risk of management override of controls, and significant accounting and any reporting matters that may be of continuing significance, such as material weaknesses in internal control. (Ref: Para. 14)

Materiality (Ref: Para. 15)

A14. The auditor needs to use professional judgement and consider qualitative and quantitative factors in determining materiality.

A15. Ordinarily, the auditor's consideration of materiality for a review of a financial report is based on the period financial data and accordingly, materiality based on interim period financial data may be less than materiality for annual financial data. If the entity's business is subject to cyclical variations or if the financial results for the current period show an exceptional decrease or increase compared to prior periods and expected results for the current year, the auditor may, for example, conclude that materiality is more appropriately determined using a normalised figure for the period.

A16. The auditor's consideration of materiality, in evaluating the effects of misstatements, is a matter of professional judgement and is affected by the auditor's perception of the financial information needs of users of the financial report.

A17. If the applicable financial reporting framework contains a definition of materiality, it will ordinarily provide a frame of reference to the auditor when determining materiality for planning and performing the review.

A18. The auditor needs, when relevant, to consider materiality from the perspective of both the entity and the consolidated entity.

Enquiries, Analytical and Other Review Procedures

A19. A review ordinarily does not require tests of the accounting records through inspection, observation or confirmation. Procedures for performing a review of a financial report ordinarily are limited to making enquiries, primarily of persons responsible for financial and accounting matters and applying analytical and other review procedures, rather than corroborating information obtained concerning matters relating to the financial report. The auditor's understanding of the entity and its environment, including its internal control, the results of the risk assessments relating to the preceding audit and the auditor's consideration of materiality as it relates to the financial report, affects the nature and extent of the enquiries made, and analytical and other review procedures applied. (Ref: Para. 16)

A20. The auditor ordinarily performs the following procedures:

(a) Reading the minutes of the meetings of shareholders, those charged with governance and other appropriate committees to identify matters that may affect the financial report, and enquiring about matters dealt with at meetings for which minutes are not available that may affect the financial report.

(b) Considering the effect, if any, of matters giving rise to a modification of the audit or review report, accounting adjustments or unadjusted misstatements, at the time of the previous audit or reviews.

(c) Communicating, where appropriate, with other auditors who are performing a review of the financial report of the entity's significant components.

(d) Enquiring of members of management responsible for financial and accounting matters, and others as appropriate, about the following:

(i) whether the financial report has been prepared and presented in accordance with the applicable financial reporting framework;

(ii) whether there have been any changes in accounting principles or in the methods of applying them;

(iii) whether any new transactions have necessitated the application of a new accounting principle;

(iv) whether the financial report contains any known uncorrected misstatements;

(v) unusual or complex situations that may have affected the financial report, such as a business combination or disposal of a segment of the business;

(vi) significant assumptions that are relevant to the fair value measurement or disclosures and management's intention and ability to carry out specific courses of action on behalf of the entity;

(vii) whether related party transactions have been appropriately accounted for and disclosed in the financial report;

(viii) significant changes in commitments and contractual obligations;

(ix) significant changes in contingent assets and contingent liabilities including litigation or claims;

(x) compliance with debt covenants;

(xi) matters about which questions have arisen in the course of applying the review procedures;

(xii) significant transactions occurring in the last several days of the period or the first several days of the next period;

(xiii) knowledge of any fraud or suspected fraud affecting the entity involving:

- management;
- employees who have significant roles in internal control; or
- others where the fraud could have a material effect on the financial report; and

(xiv) knowledge of any allegations of fraud, or suspected fraud, affecting the entity's financial information communicated by employees, former employees, analysts, regulators or others; and

(xv) knowledge of any actual or possible non-compliance with laws and regulations that could have a material effect on the financial report.

(e) Applying analytical procedures to the financial report designed to identify relationships and individual items that appear to be unusual and that may reflect a material misstatement in the financial report. Analytical procedures may include ratio analysis and statistical techniques such as trend analysis or regression analysis and may be performed manually or with the use of computer-assisted auditing techniques. Appendix 2 to this Auditing Standard contains examples of analytical procedures the auditor may consider when performing a review of a financial report.

(f) Reading the financial report and considering whether anything has come to the auditor's attention that causes the auditor to believe that the financial report is not in accordance with the applicable financial reporting framework. (Ref: Para. 16)

A21. The auditor may perform many of the review procedures before or simultaneously with the entity's preparation of the financial report. For example, it may be practicable to update the understanding of the entity and its environment, including its internal control, and begin reading applicable minutes before the end of the period. Performing some of the review procedures earlier in the period also permits early identification and consideration of significant accounting matters affecting the financial report. (Ref: Para. 16)

A22. The auditor performing a review of the financial report is also the auditor of the annual financial report of the entity. For convenience and efficiency, the auditor may decide to perform certain audit procedures concurrently with the review of the financial report. For example, information gained from reading the minutes of meetings of the board of directors in connection with the review of the financial report may also be used for the annual audit. The auditor may decide also to perform, at the time of the review, auditing procedures that would need to be performed for the purpose of the audit of the annual financial report, for example, performing auditing procedures on:

(a) significant or unusual transactions that occurred during the period, such as business combinations, restructurings, or significant revenue transactions, or

(b) opening balances (when applicable). (Ref: Para. 16)

A23. A review of a financial report ordinarily does not require corroborating the enquiries about litigation or claims. It is, therefore, ordinarily not necessary to send an enquiry letter to the entity's lawyer. Direct communication with the entity's lawyer with respect to litigation or claims, or alternative procedures, may, however, be appropriate if a matter comes to the auditor's attention that causes the auditor to question whether the financial report is in accordance with the applicable financial reporting framework. (Ref: Para. 16)

A24. The auditor may obtain evidence that the financial report agrees or reconciles with the underlying accounting records by tracing the financial report to:

(a) the accounting records, such as the general ledger, or a consolidating schedule that agrees or reconciles with the accounting records; and

(b) other supporting data in the entity's records as necessary. (Ref: Para. 17)

A25. The auditor need not perform procedures to identify events occurring after the date of the review report. (Ref: Para. 18)

A26. Events or conditions which may cast significant doubt on the entity's ability to continue as a going concern may have existed at the date of the annual financial report, or may be identified as a result of enquiries of management or in the course of performing other review procedures. When such events or conditions come to the auditor's attention, the auditor needs to enquire of those charged with governance as to their plans for future action, such as their plans to liquidate assets, borrow money or restructure debt, reduce or delay expenditures, or increase capital. The auditor needs to enquire also as to the feasibility of the plans of those charged with governance and whether they believe that the outcome of these plans will improve the situation. Ordinarily, the auditor considers, based on procedures performed, whether it is necessary to corroborate the feasibility of the plans of those charged with governance and whether the outcome of these plans will improve the situation. (Ref: Para. 19)

A27. For example, if the auditor's review procedures lead the auditor to question whether a significant sales transaction is recorded in accordance with the applicable financial reporting framework, the auditor performs additional procedures sufficient to resolve the auditor's questions, such as discussing the terms of the transaction with senior marketing and accounting personnel or reading the sales contract. (Ref: Para. 20)

Comparatives – First Financial Report (Ref: Para. 21)

A28. When comparative information is included in the first financial report and the auditor is unable to obtain sufficient appropriate review evidence to achieve the review objective, a limitation on the scope of the review exists and the auditor needs to modify the review report. Ordinarily, a restriction on the scope of the auditor's work will result in a qualified ("except for") conclusion. In such cases, ordinarily an auditor encourages clear disclosure in the financial report, that the auditor has been unable to review the comparatives. An example of a modified review report is included in Appendix 4.

A29. When comparative information is included in the first financial report and the auditor believes a material adjustment should be made to the financial report, under paragraph 33, the auditor needs to modify the review report.

A30. When an entity has come into existence only within the first financial reporting period, comparative information will not be provided in the first financial report and no modified review report is required.

A31. Accounting Standard AASB 101 *Presentation of Financial Statements* provides requirements and explanatory guidance relating to comparative information included in a financial report prepared in accordance with Australian Accounting Standards. Accounting Standard AASB 1 *First-time Adoption of Australian Accounting Standards* provides requirements and guidance relating to comparative information when an entity adopts Australian Accounting Standards for the first time.

Evaluation of Misstatements (Ref: Para. 22)

A32. A review of a financial report, in contrast to an audit engagement, is not designed to obtain reasonable assurance that the financial report is free from material misstatement. However, misstatements which come to the auditor's attention, including inadequate disclosures, need to be evaluated individually and in the aggregate to determine whether a material adjustment is required to be made to the financial report for it to be prepared, in all material respects, in accordance with the applicable financial reporting framework.

A33. The auditor needs to exercise professional judgement in evaluating the materiality of any misstatements that the entity has not corrected. Ordinarily, the auditor considers matters such as the nature, cause and amount of the misstatements, whether the misstatements originated in the preceding year or current year, and the potential effect of the misstatements on future interim or annual periods.

A34. The auditor may designate an amount below which misstatements need not be aggregated, because the auditor expects that the aggregation of such amounts clearly would not have a material effect on the financial report. In so doing, under paragraph 15, the auditor needs to consider the fact that the determination of materiality involves quantitative as well as qualitative considerations and that misstatements of a relatively small amount could nevertheless have a material effect on the financial report.

Written Representations

A35. The auditor needs to endeavour to obtain additional representations as are appropriate to matters specific to the entity's business or industry. An illustrative representation letter is set out in Appendix 1. (Ref: Para. 23)

Auditor's Responsibility for Accompanying Information

A36. If the auditor identifies a material inconsistency, the auditor needs to consider whether the financial report or the other information needs to be amended. If an amendment is necessary in the financial report and those charged with governance refuse to make the amendment, under paragraph 29, the auditor needs to consider the implications for the review report. If an amendment is necessary in the other information and those charged with governance refuse to make the amendment, the auditor may, for example, consider including in the review report an Other Matter Paragraph describing the material inconsistency (ASA 720 and ASA 706 include guidance which may be helpful[4]) or taking other actions, such as withholding the issuance of the review report or withdrawing from the engagement. For example, those charged with governance may present alternative measures of earnings that more positively portray financial performance than the financial report, and such alternative measures are given excessive prominence, or are not clearly defined, or not clearly reconciled to the financial report such that they are confusing and potentially misleading. (Ref: Para. 25)

Aus A36.1 For a review of a half-year financial report under the *Corporations Act 2001* (Act), withholding the issuance of the review report and/or withdrawing from the review engagement are not options available under the Act. (Ref: Para. 29)

A37. While reading the other information for the purpose of identifying material inconsistencies, an apparent material misstatement of fact may come to the auditor's attention (that is, information, not related to matters appearing in the financial report, that is incorrectly stated or presented). When discussing the matter with the entity's management, ordinarily the auditor considers the validity of the other information and management's responses to the auditor's enquiries, whether valid differences of judgement or opinion exist and whether to request management to consult with a qualified third party to resolve the apparent misstatement of fact. If an amendment is necessary to correct a material misstatement of fact and management refuses to make the amendment, ordinarily the auditor considers taking further action as appropriate, such as notifying those charged with governance and, if necessary, obtaining legal advice. (Ref: Para. 26)

Communication

A38. Communications with management and/or those charged with governance are made as soon as practicable, either orally or in writing. The auditor's decision whether to communicate orally or in writing ordinarily is affected by factors such as the nature, sensitivity and significance of the matter to be communicated and the timing of the communications. If the information is communicated orally, under paragraph 44, the auditor needs to document the communication. (Ref: Para. 28)

4 See ASA 720 *The Auditor's Responsibilities Relating to Other Information in Documents Containing an Audited Financial Report*; and ASA 706 *Emphasis of Matter Paragraphs or Other Matter Paragraphs in the Independent Auditor's Report.*

A39. The determination of which level of management may also be informed is affected by the likelihood of collusion or the involvement of a member of management. (Ref: Para. 30)

A40. As a result of performing a review of a financial report, the auditor may become aware of matters that in the opinion of the auditor are both important and relevant to those charged with governance in overseeing the financial reporting and disclosure process. (Ref: Para. 31)

Reporting the Nature, Extent and Results of the Review of a Financial Report (Ref: Para. 32)

A41. In some cases, law or regulation governing the review of a financial report may prescribe wording for the auditor's conclusion that is different from the wording described in paragraph 32(i). Although the auditor may be obliged to use the prescribed wording, the auditor's responsibilities as described in this Auditing Standard for coming to the conclusion remain the same. ASA 700 includes guidance which may be helpful.[5] Illustrative review reports are set out in Appendices 3 and 4.

Departure from the Applicable Financial Reporting Framework (Ref: Para. 33–34)

A42. If matters have come to the auditor's attention that cause the auditor to believe that the financial report is or may be materially affected by a departure from the applicable financial reporting framework, and those charged with governance do not correct the financial report, the auditor needs to modify the review report. If the information that the auditor believes is necessary for adequate disclosure is not included in the financial report, the auditor needs to modify the review report and, if practicable, include the necessary information in the review report. Illustrative review reports with a qualified conclusion are set out in Appendix 4.

A43. Departures from the applicable financial reporting framework, may result in an adverse conclusion. An illustrative review report with an adverse conclusion is set out in Appendix 4.

Limitation on Scope (Ref: Para. 35)

A44. Ordinarily, a limitation on scope prevents the auditor from completing the review.

Limitation on Scope Imposed by Management

A45. The auditor needs to refuse to accept an engagement to review a financial report if the auditor's preliminary knowledge of the engagement circumstances indicates that the auditor would be unable to complete the review because there will be a limitation on the scope of the auditor's review imposed by management of the entity. (Ref: Para. 36)

A46. If, after accepting the engagement, management imposes a limitation on the scope of the review, the auditor needs to request the removal of that limitation. If management refuses to do so, the auditor is unable to complete the review and express a conclusion. In such cases, the auditor needs to communicate, in writing, to the appropriate level of management and those charged with governance, the reason(s) why the review cannot be completed. Nevertheless, if a matter comes to the auditor's attention that causes the auditor to believe that a material adjustment to the financial report is necessary for it to be prepared, in all material respects, in accordance with the applicable financial reporting framework, under paragraphs 27, 28 and 30, the auditor needs to communicate such matters to the appropriate level of management and, where appropriate, those charged with governance. (Ref: Para. 37)

A47. The auditor needs to consider the legal and regulatory requirements, including whether there is a legal requirement for the auditor to issue a report. If there is such a requirement, the auditor needs to disclaim a conclusion and provide in the review report the reason why the review cannot be completed. However, if a matter comes to the auditor's attention that causes the auditor to believe that a material adjustment to the financial report is necessary for it to be prepared, in all material respects, in accordance with the applicable financial reporting framework the auditor needs to communicate such a matter in the report. (Ref: Para. 38)

5 See ASA 700 *Forming an Opinion and Reporting on a Financial Report.*

Other Limitations on Scope Not Imposed by Management (Ref: Para. 39)

A48. A limitation on scope may occur due to circumstances other than a limitation on scope imposed by management or those charged with governance. In such circumstances, the auditor is ordinarily unable to complete the review and express a conclusion, and is guided by paragraphs 38 and 39. There may be, however, some rare circumstances where the limitation on the scope of the auditor's work is clearly confined to one or more specific matters that, while material, are not in the auditor's judgement pervasive to the financial report. In such circumstances, the auditor needs to modify the review report by indicating that, except for the matter which is described in an explanatory paragraph to the review report, the review was conducted in accordance with this Auditing Standard, and by qualifying the conclusion. Illustrative review reports with a qualified conclusion are set out in Appendix 4.

A49. The auditor may have expressed a qualified opinion on the audit of the latest annual financial report because of a limitation on the scope of that audit. The auditor needs to consider whether that limitation on scope still exists and, if so, the implications for the review report.

Going Concern and Significant Uncertainties (Ref: Para. 40-43)

A50. In certain circumstances, an emphasis of matter paragraph may be added to a review report, without affecting the auditor's conclusion, to highlight a matter that is included in a note to the financial report that more extensively discusses the matter. The paragraph would preferably be included after the conclusion paragraph and ordinarily refers to the fact that the conclusion is not qualified in this respect.

A51. The auditor may have modified a prior audit or review report by adding an emphasis of matter paragraph to highlight a material uncertainty relating to an event or condition that casts significant doubt on the entity's ability to continue as a going concern. If the material uncertainty still exists and adequate disclosure is made in the financial report, the auditor needs to modify the review report on the current financial report by adding a paragraph to highlight the continued material uncertainty.

A52. If, as a result of enquiries or other review procedures, a material uncertainty relating to an event or condition comes to the auditor's attention that casts significant doubt on the entity's ability to continue as a going concern, and adequate disclosure is made in the financial report, the auditor needs to modify the review report by adding an emphasis of matter paragraph.

A53. ASA 570 *Going Concern* provides information that the auditor may find helpful in considering going concern in the context of the review engagement.

A54. Ordinarily, a significant uncertainty in relation to any other matter, the resolution of which may materially affect the financial report, would warrant an emphasis of matter paragraph in the auditor's review report.

Other Considerations

A55. The terms of the engagement include agreement by those charged with governance that, where any document containing a financial report indicates that the report has been reviewed by the entity's auditor, the review report will be also included in the document. If those charged with governance have not included the review report in the document, ordinarily the auditor considers seeking legal advice to assist in determining the appropriate course of action in the circumstances. (Ref: Para. 12)

A56. If the auditor has issued a modified review report and those charged with governance issue the financial report without including the modified review report in the document containing the financial report, ordinarily the auditor considers seeking legal advice to assist in determining the appropriate course of action in the circumstances, and the possibility of resigning from the appointment to audit the annual financial report.

Considerations Specific to Public Sector Entities

A57. The auditor needs to agree with the client the terms of engagement. When agreeing the terms of engagement, an engagement letter helps to avoid misunderstandings regarding the nature of the engagement and, in particular, the objective and scope of the review, management's responsibilities, the extent of the auditor's responsibilities, the assurance obtained, and the nature and form of the report. Law or regulation governing review engagements in the public sector ordinarily mandates the appointment of the auditor. Nevertheless, an engagement letter setting out the matters referred to in paragraph A8 may be useful to both the public sector auditor and the client. Public sector auditors, therefore, consider agreeing with the client the terms of a review engagement by way of an engagement letter. (Ref: Para. 12)

A58. In the public sector, the auditor's statutory audit obligation may extend to other work, such as a review of interim financial information. Where this is the case, the public sector auditor cannot avoid such an obligation and, consequently, may not be in a position not to accept, or to withdraw from a review engagement. The public sector auditor also may not be in the position to resign from the appointment to audit the annual financial report. (Ref: Para. 29(b)-29(c) and 36)

A59. The auditor needs to communicate to those charged with governance and consider the implications for the review when a matter comes to the auditor's attention that causes the auditor to believe in the existence of fraud or non-compliance by the entity with laws and regulations. In the public sector, the auditor may be subject to statutory or other regulatory requirements to report such a matter to regulatory or other public authorities. (Ref: Para. 31)

Documentation (Ref: Para. 44)

A60. The auditor needs to prepare documentation that enables an experienced auditor having no previous connection with the engagement to understand the nature, timing and extent of the enquiries made and analytical and other review procedures applied, information obtained, and any significant matters considered during the performance of the review, including the disposition of such matters.

❖ ❖ ❖

Conformity with International Standards on Auditing

This Auditing Standard on Review Engagements conforms with International Standard on Review Engagements ISRE 2410 *Review of Interim Financial Information Performed by the Independent Auditor of the Entity*, issued by the International Auditing and Assurance Standards Board (IAASB), an independent standard-setting board of the International Federation of Accountants (IFAC).

The underlying standard is extant ASRE 2410 *Review of Interim and Other Financial Reports Performed by the Independent Auditor of the Entity*. The underlying standard to extant ASRE 2410 is ISRE 2410 which has not been drafted in "clarity" format by the IAASB.

Following consultation with constituents in Australia in accordance with normal exposure draft processes, the AUASB has decided that:

- due to the nature of reviews of other historical financial information, a separate Standard is more appropriate than ASRE 2410 being adapted by the auditor for this purpose; and
- ASRE 2405 *Review of Historical Financial Information Other than a Financial Report*, developed by the AUASB, deals with reviews of other historical financial information.

Accordingly, ASRE 2410 is intended to conform, with the exceptions listed below, to ISRE 2410 to the extent that ISRE 2410 deals with the review of financial statements by the auditor of the entity.

Except as noted below, this Auditing Standard conforms, to the extent described above, with International Standard ISRE 2410 *Review of Interim Financial Information Performed by the Independent Auditor of the Entity* issued by the IAASB. The main differences between this Auditing Standard and ISRE 2410 are:

1. This Auditing Standard contains the following requirements that are not contained in ISRE 2410:
   - This Auditing Standard applies to:
     (a) a review, by the independent auditor of the entity, of a financial report for a half-year in accordance with the *Corporations Act 2001*; and

(b) a review, by the independent auditor of the entity, of a financial report, or a complete set of financial statements, comprising historical financial information, for any other purpose (Ref: Para. 1(a) and (b)).

- Where in rare and exceptional circumstances, factors outside the auditor's control prevent the auditor from complying with an essential procedure contained within a relevant requirement, the auditor shall:
  - ♦ if possible, perform appropriate alternative procedures; and
  - ♦ document in the working papers:
    - the circumstances surrounding the inability to comply;
    - the reasons for the inability to comply; and
    - justification of how alternative procedures achieve the objectives of the requirement.

  When the auditor is unable to perform appropriate alternative procedures, the auditor shall consider the implications for the auditor's review report (Ref: Para. 7).
- The auditor shall, prior to agreeing the terms of the engagement, determine whether the financial reporting framework is acceptable and obtain agreement from management and, where appropriate, those charged with governance, that it acknowledges and understands its responsibility:
  - ♦ for the preparation and fair presentation of the financial report;
  - ♦ for such internal controls as management and, where appropriate, those charged with governance, deems necessary to enable the preparation of the financial report that is free from material misstatement; and
  - ♦ to provide the auditor with:
    - access to information relevant to the preparation of the financial report;
    - additional information that the auditor may request for the purposes of the review engagement; and
    - unrestricted access to persons from whom the auditor determines it necessary to obtain evidence (Ref: Para. 11).
- The auditor shall agree the terms of the engagement with the entity, which shall be recorded in writing by the auditor and forwarded to the entity. When the review engagement is undertaken pursuant to legislation, the minimum applicable terms are those contained in the legislation (Ref: Para. 12).
- The auditor shall consider materiality, using professional judgement, when:
  - ♦ determining the nature, timing and extent of review procedures; and
  - ♦ evaluating the effect of misstatements (Ref: Para. 15).
- When comparative information is included for the first time in a financial report, an auditor shall perform similar procedures on the comparative information as applied to the current period financial report (Ref: Para. 21).
- If management and, where appropriate, those charged with governance refuse to provide a written representation that the auditor considers necessary, this constitutes a limitation of the scope of the auditor's work and the auditor shall express a qualified conclusion or a disclaimer of conclusion, as appropriate (Ref: Para. 24).
- When, as a result of performing the review of a financial report, a matter comes to the auditor's attention that causes the auditor to believe in the existence of fraud or non-compliance by the entity with laws and regulations, the auditor shall communicate the matter as soon as practicable to those charged with governance and shall consider the implications for the review (Ref: Para. 30).
- The auditor shall express a qualified or adverse conclusion when a matter has come to the auditor's attention that causes the auditor to believe a material adjustment should be made to the financial report for it to be prepared, in all material respects,

in accordance with the applicable financial reporting framework. The auditor shall include a basis for modification paragraph in the report, that describes the nature of the departure and, if practicable, states the effects on the financial report. If the effects or possible effects are incapable of being measured reliably, a statement to that effect and the reasons therefor shall be included in the basis for modification paragraph. The conclusion paragraph shall be headed "Qualified Conclusion" or "Adverse Conclusion", whichever is relevant (Ref: Para 33).

- When the effect of the departure is so material and pervasive to the financial report that the auditor concludes a qualified conclusion is not adequate to disclose the misleading or incomplete nature of the financial report, the auditor shall express an adverse conclusion (Ref: Para. 34).
- Unless required by law or regulation, an auditor shall not accept an engagement to review a financial report when management has imposed a limitation on the scope of the auditor's review (Ref: Para. 36).
- If, after accepting the engagement, management imposes a limitation on the scope of the review, the auditor shall request management to remove the limitation. If management refuses the auditor's request to remove the limitation, the auditor shall communicate, in writing, to the appropriate level of management and those charged with governance, the reasons why the review cannot be completed (Ref: Para. 37).
- If management and, where appropriate, those charged with governance, refuses the auditor's request to remove a limitation that has been imposed on the scope of the review, but there is a legal or regulatory requirement for the auditor to issue a report, the auditor shall issue a disclaimer of conclusion or qualified conclusion report, as appropriate, containing the reason(s) why the review cannot be completed (Ref: Para. 38).
- The auditor shall express a qualified opinion when, in rare circumstances, there is a limitation on the scope of the auditor's work that is confined to one or more specific matters, which while material, is not in the auditor's judgement pervasive to the financial report, and when the auditor concludes that an unqualified opinion cannot be expressed. A qualified conclusion shall be expressed as being "except for" the effects of the matter to which the qualification relates. The conclusion paragraph shall be headed "Qualified Conclusion" (Ref: Para. 39).

2. The following requirements in ISRE 2410, paragraph 43(e) and paragraph 43(j), are not contained in this Auditing Standard:

   Paragraph 43(e)

   "In other circumstances, a statement that management is responsible for the preparation and presentation of the interim financial information in accordance with the applicable financial reporting framework".

   Paragraph 43(j)

   "In other circumstances, a conclusion as to whether anything has come to the auditor's attention that causes the auditor to believe that the interim financial information is not prepared, in all material respects, in accordance with the applicable financial reporting framework (including a reference to the jurisdiction or country of origin of the financial reporting framework when the financial reporting framework used is not International Financial Reporting Standards)."

   Requirements and guidance on the review of financial statements that are prepared in accordance with a financial reporting framework that is not designed to achieve fair presentation are included in ASRE 2405 *Review of Historical Financial Information Other than a Financial Report.*

3. This Auditing Standard includes explanatory guidance not contained within ISRE 2410 on:

   - Materiality (Ref: Para.A14 to A18); and
   - Comparatives (Ref: Para.A28 to A31).

4. This Auditing Standard provides illustrative examples that differ in form and content from those contained in ISRE 2410, namely:
   - An engagement letter (Appendix 1).
   - A written representation letter (Appendix 1).
   - The auditor's unmodified review reports (Appendices 3 and 4).
   - The auditor's modified review reports (Appendix 4).
5. This Auditing Standard provides illustrative detailed procedures that may be performed in an engagement to review a financial report that are not contained in ISRE 2410 (Appendix 2).

Compliance with this Auditing Standard on Review Engagements enables compliance with ISRE 2410 to the extent described above.

Appendix 1

(Ref: Para. A8)

Example of an Engagement Letter for a Review of a Financial Report

The following letter is not intended to be a standard letter. It is to be used as a guide only and will need to be adapted according to individual requirements and circumstances. This illustrative letter is written in the context of a half-year financial report under the *Corporations Act 2001.*

To [those charged with governance:[6]]

Scope

You have requested that we review the half-year financial report[7] of [name of entity], which comprises the statement of financial position as at 31 December 20XX, and the statement of comprehensive income, statement of changes in equity and statement of cash flows for the six-month[8] period ended on that date, and notes comprising a summary of significant accounting policies and other explanatory information and the directors' declaration. We are pleased to confirm our acceptance and our understanding of the terms and objectives of our engagement by means of this letter.

Our review will be conducted in accordance with Auditing Standard on Review Engagements ASRE 2410 *Review of a Financial Report Performed by the Independent Auditor of the Entity*, issued by the Auditing and Assurance Standards Board, with the objective of providing us with a basis for reporting whether we have become aware of any matter [anything has come to our attention[9]] that makes [causes[9]] us [to[9]] believe that the half-year financial report is not prepared, in all material respects, in accordance with Accounting Standard AASB 134 *Interim Financial Reporting* and the *Corporations Act 2001* [indicate applicable financial reporting framework]. Such a review consists of making enquiries, primarily of persons responsible for financial and accounting matters, and applying analytical and other review procedures and does not, ordinarily, require corroboration of the information obtained. The scope of a review of a financial report is substantially less than the scope of an audit conducted in accordance with Auditing Standards whose objective is the expression of an opinion regarding the financial report and accordingly, we shall express no such opinion. ASRE 2410 requires us to also comply with the ethical requirements relevant to the audit of the annual financial report of the entity.

---

6 Insert the appropriate term, such as "Directors' or 'Board of Management".

7 If the term "half-year financial report" is not appropriate, then this term should be changed to reflect the report being reviewed.

8 If the period being reviewed is other than six months, then this should be amended as appropriate.

9 Use in a review of a half-year financial report prepared other than in accordance with the *Corporations Act 2001.*

Appendix 1 (continued)

We expect to report on the half-year financial report[10] as follows:

[Include text of sample review report - see Appendix 3 or 4 as appropriate.]

The directors [those charged with governance[11]] of the [company/registered scheme/disclosing entity] are responsible for the preparation of the half-year financial report that gives a true and fair view in accordance with Australian Accounting Standards and the *Corporations Act 2001* and for such internal control as the directors [those charged with governance] determine is necessary to enable the preparation of the half-year financial report that is free from material misstatement, whether due to fraud or error. As part of our review, we shall request written representations from management concerning assertions made in connection with the review. We shall also request that where any document containing the half-year financial report indicates that the half-year financial report has been reviewed, our review report will also be included in the document.

The directors [those charged with governance] of the [company/registered scheme/disclosing entity] acknowledge and understand they have responsibility to provide us with:

(i) access to information relevant to the preparation of the financial report;

(ii) additional information that we may request for the purposes of the review engagement; and

(iii) unrestricted access to persons from whom we determine it is necessary to obtain evidence.

A review of the half-year financial report does not provide assurance that we shall become aware of all significant matters that might be identified in an audit. Further, our engagement cannot be relied upon to disclose whether fraud or errors, or illegal acts exist. However, we shall inform you of any material matters that come to our attention.

Independence

We confirm that, to the best of our knowledge and belief, we currently meet the independence requirements of the *Corporations Act 2001* in relation to the review of the half-year financial report. In conducting our review of the half-year financial report, should we become aware that we have contravened the independence requirements of the *Corporations Act 2001*, we shall notify you on a timely basis. As part of our review process, we shall also provide you with a written independence declaration as required by the *Corporations Act 2001*.

The *Corporations Act 2001* includes specific restrictions on the employment relationships that can exist between the reviewed entity and its auditors. To assist us in meeting the independence requirements of the *Corporations Act 2001*, and to the extent permitted by law and regulation, we request you discuss with us:

- The provision of services offered to you by [insert firm name] prior to engaging or accepting the service; and
- The prospective employment opportunities of any current or former partner or professional employee of [insert firm name] prior to the commencement of formal employment discussions with the current or former partner or professional employee.

Presentation of the reviewed half-year financial report in electronic format

It is our understanding that [the entity] intends to publish a hard copy of the reviewed half-year financial report and the auditor's review report for members, and to electronically present the reviewed half-year financial report and the auditor's review report on its internet web site. When information is presented electronically on a web site, the security and controls over information on the web site should be addressed by [the entity] to maintain the integrity of the data presented. The examination of the controls over the electronic presentation of reviewed financial information on the entity's web site is beyond the scope of the review of the half-year financial report. Responsibility for the electronic presentation of the half-year financial report on the entity's web site is that of the [governing body of the entity].

10 If the term "half-year financial report" is not appropriate, then this term should be changed to reflect the report being reviewed.

11 Insert the appropriate term, such as "Directors or Board of Management".

Appendix 1 (continued)

Fees

[Insert additional information here regarding fee arrangements and billings, as appropriate.]

We look forward to full co-operation with your staff and we trust that they will make available to us whatever records, documentation and other information are requested in connection with our review.

[This letter will be effective for future years unless it is terminated, amended or superseded.[12]]
Please sign and return the attached copy of this letter to indicate that it is in accordance with your understanding of the arrangements for our review of the half-year financial report.

Yours faithfully,

(signed)

....

Name and Title

Date

Acknowledged on behalf of [entity] by

(signed)

....

Name and Title

Date

Example of a Representation Letter

The following letter is not intended to be a standard letter. It is to be used as a guide only and will need to be adapted according to individual requirements and circumstances. This illustrative letter is written in the context of a half-year financial report under the *Corporations Act 2001*.

Representations by management will vary from one entity to another and from one period to the next. Representation letters are ordinarily useful where evidence, other than that obtained by enquiry, may not be reasonably expected to be available or when management have made oral representations which the auditor wishes to confirm in writing.

[Entity Letterhead]

[Addressee – Auditor]

[Date]

This representation letter is provided in connection with your review of the half-year[13] financial report[14] of [name of entity] for the [period] ended [date], for the purpose of you expressing a conclusion as to whether you became aware of any matter in the course of the review that makes you believe that the half-year financial report is not in accordance with the *Corporations Act 2001*.

We acknowledge our responsibility for ensuring that the half-year financial report is in accordance with the *Corporations Act 2001*, including:

(i) giving a true and fair view of the [company/entity]'s financial position as at [date] and of its performance for the half-year ended on that date; and

(ii) complying with Australian Accounting Standards (including the Australian Accounting Interpretations) and the *Corporations Regulations 2001*.

---

12 Use if applicable.

13 If the period being reviewed is other than six months, then this should be amended as appropriate.

14 If the term "half-year financial report" is not appropriate, then this term should be changed to reflect the type of report being reviewed.

Appendix 1 (continued)

We confirm that the half-year financial report is prepared and presented in accordance with the *Corporations Act 2001* and is free of material misstatements, including omissions.

OR

[This representation letter is provided in connection with your review of the financial report[15] of [name of entity] for the [period] ended [date], for the purpose of you expressing a conclusion as to whether anything has come to your attention that causes you to believe that the financial report is not, in all material respects, presented fairly in accordance with [applicable financial reporting framework[16]].

We acknowledge our responsibility for ensuring that the financial report is in accordance with [applicable financial reporting framework].

We confirm that the financial report is prepared and presented fairly in accordance with [applicable financial reporting framework] and is free of material misstatements, including omissions].

We confirm, to the best of our knowledge and belief, the following representations made to you during your review.

[Include representations required by this Auditing Standard (paragraph 23) and those relevant to the entity. Such representations may include the following examples.]

1. We have made available to you:
   (a) all financial records and related data, other information, explanations and assistance necessary for the conduct of the review; and
   (b) minutes of all meetings of [shareholders, directors, committees of directors, Boards of Management].
2. We have disclosed to you the results of our assessment of the risk that the [financial report] may be materially misstated as a result of fraud.
3. There:
   (a) has been no fraud or suspected fraud, error or non-compliance with laws and regulations involving management or employees who have a significant role in the internal control structure;
   (b) has been no fraud or suspected fraud, error or non-compliance with laws and regulations that could have a material effect on the financial report; and
   (c) have been no communications from regulatory agencies concerning non-compliance with, or deficiencies in, financial reporting practices that could have a material effect on the financial report.
4. We are responsible for an adequate internal control structure to prevent and detect fraud and error and to facilitate the preparation of a reliable financial report, and adequate financial records have been maintained. There are no material transactions that have not been recorded properly in the accounting records underlying the financial report.
5. We have no plans or intentions that may affect materially the carrying values, or classification, of assets and liabilities.
6. We have considered the requirements of Accounting Standard AASB 136 *Impairment of Assets*, when assessing the impairment of assets and in ensuring that no assets are stated in excess of their recoverable amount.
7. We believe the effects of uncorrected misstatements summarised in the accompanying schedule are immaterial, both individually and in the aggregate, to the [half-year] financial report taken as a whole.

15 The term "financial report" should be changed to reflect the type of report being reviewed, as appropriate.

16 Specify the applicable financial reporting framework/requirements.

Appendix 1 (continued)

8. The following have been recorded and/or disclosed properly in the [half-year] financial report:
   (a) related party transactions and related amounts receivable or payable, including sales, purchases, loans, transfers, leasing arrangements and guarantees (written or oral);
   (b) share options, warrants, conversions or other requirements;
   (c) arrangements involving restrictions on cash balances, compensating balances and line-of-credit or similar arrangements;
   (d) agreements to repurchase assets previously sold;
   (e) material liabilities or contingent liabilities or assets including those arising under derivative financial instruments;
   (f) unasserted claims or assessments that our lawyer(s) has advised us are probable of assertion; and
   (g) losses arising from the fulfilment of, or an inability to fulfil, any sale commitments or as a result of purchase commitments for inventory quantities in excess of normal requirements or at prices in excess of prevailing market prices.
9. There are no violations or possible violations of laws or regulations the effects of which should be considered for disclosure in the financial report or as a basis for recording an expense.
10. The entity has satisfactory title to all assets, and there are no liens or encumbrances on such assets that have not been disclosed nor has any asset been pledged as collateral. Allowances for depreciation have been adjusted for all important items of property, plant and equipment that have been abandoned or are otherwise unusable.
11. The entity has complied with all aspects of contractual agreements that would have a material effect on the financial report in the event of non-compliance.
12. There were no material commitments for construction or acquisition of property, plant and equipment or to acquire other non-current assets, such as investments or intangibles, other than those disclosed in the financial report.
13. We have no plans to abandon lines of product or other plans or intentions that will result in any excess or obsolete inventory, and no inventory is stated at an amount in excess of net realisable value.
14. No events have occurred subsequent to the balance sheet date through to the date of this letter that would require adjustment to, or disclosure in, the [financial report].

We understand that your examination was made in accordance with Auditing Standard on Review Engagements ASRE 2410 and was, therefore, designed primarily for the purpose of expressing a conclusion on the financial report of [the entity], and that your procedures were limited to those which you considered necessary for that purpose.

Yours faithfully

[Name of signing officer and title]

Notes:

[The above example representation letter may need to be amended in certain circumstances. The following illustrate some of those situations.]

(a) Exceptions

Where matters are disclosed in the financial report, the associated representation needs to be amended, for example:

- If a subsequent event has been disclosed, Item 14 (above) could be modified to read:

  "Except as discussed in Note X to the financial report, no events have occurred ….."

Appendix 1 (continued)

- If the entity has plans that impact the carrying values of assets and liabilities, Item 5 (above) could be modified to read:

  "The entity has no plans or intentions that may materially affect the carrying value or classification of assets and liabilities, except for our plan to dispose of segment X, as disclosed in note Y in the financial report, which is discussed in the minutes of the meeting of the governing body[17] held on [date]".

(b) Other Required Information

Certain entities may be required to include other information in the financial report, for example, performance indicators for government entities. In addition to identifying this information and the applicable financial reporting framework in paragraphs 1 and 2 of the example management representation letter, an additional paragraph similar to the following may be appropriate:

"The disclosures of key performance indicators have been prepared and presented in conformity with [relevant statutory requirements] and we consider the indicators reported to be relevant to the stated objectives of the [entity]".

(c) Management's Opinions and Representation in the Notes to the Financial Statements

Where the notes to the financial statements include opinions and representations by management, such matters may be addressed in the representation letter. For example, notes relating to the anticipated outcome of litigation, the intent and ability to hold long-term securities to maturity and plans necessary to support the going concern basis.

(d) Environmental Matters

In situations where there are environmental matters that may, but probably will not, require an outflow of resources, this may be reflected in an addition to Item 9 (above), for example:

"However, the [entity] has received a notice from the Environmental Protection Agency that it may be required to share in the cost of cleanup of the [name] waste disposal site. This matter has been disclosed in Note A in the financial report and we believe that the disclosure and estimated contingent loss is reasonable based on available information."

(e) Compliance

If, as part of the review, the auditor is required also to report on the entity's compliance with laws and regulations, a representation may be appropriate acknowledging that management is responsible for the entity's compliance with applicable laws and regulations and that the requirements have been met. For example, for reviews under the *Corporations Act 2001*, the following paragraph may be added:

"The financial records of the [company, registered scheme or disclosing entity] have been kept so as to be sufficient to enable a financial report to be prepared and reviewed, and other records and registers required by the *Corporations Act 2001* have been kept properly and are up-to-date."

(f) Other Matters

Additional representations that may be appropriate in specific situations may include the following:

- Justification for a change in accounting policy.
- The work of a management expert has been used.
- Arrangements for controlling the dissemination of the financial report and auditor's review report on the Internet.

17 Insert the appropriate term, such as "Directors or Board of Management".

Appendix 2

(Ref: Para. A20)

Analytical Procedures the Auditor May Consider When Performing a Review of a Financial Report

The analytical procedures carried out in a review of a financial report are determined by the auditor's judgement. The procedures listed below are for illustrative purposes only. It is not intended that all the procedures suggested apply to every review engagement. This Appendix is not intended to serve as a program or checklist in the conduct of a review.

Examples of analytical procedures the auditor may consider when performing a review of a financial report include the following:

- Comparing the financial report with the financial report of the immediately preceding period, with the financial report of the corresponding period of the preceding financial year, with the financial report that was expected by management for the current period, and with the most recent audited annual financial report.
- Comparing the current financial report with anticipated results, such as budgets or forecasts. For example, comparing sources of revenue and the and the cost of sales in the current financial report with corresponding information in:
  - budgets, including expected gross margin(s); and
  - financial information for prior periods.
- Comparing the current financial report with relevant non-financial information.
- Comparing the recorded amounts, or ratios developed from recorded amounts, to expectations developed by the auditor. The auditor develops such expectations by identifying and applying relationships that reasonably are expected to exist based on the auditor's understanding of the entity and of the industry in which the entity operates.
- Comparing ratios and indicators for the current period with those of entities in the same industry.
- Comparing relationships among elements in the current financial report with corresponding relationships in the financial report of prior periods, for example, expense by type as a percentage of sales, assets by type as a percentage of total assets, and percentage of change in sales to percentage of change in receivables.
- Comparing disaggregated data. The following are examples of how data may be disaggregated:
  - by period, for example, revenue or expense items disaggregated into quarterly, monthly, or weekly amounts;
  - by product line or source of revenue;
  - by location, for example by component;
  - by attributes of the transaction, for example, revenue generated by designers, architects, or craftsmen; and
  - by several attributes of the transaction, for example, sales by product and month.

Appendix 2 (continued)

Illustrative Detailed Procedures that may be Performed in an Engagement to Review a Financial Report

The enquiry, analytical and other procedures carried out in a review of a financial report are determined by the auditor exercising professional judgement in light of the auditor's assessment of the risk of material misstatement. The procedures listed below are for illustrative purposes only. It is not intended that all the procedures suggested apply to every review engagement. This Appendix is not intended to serve as a program or checklist in the conduct of a review.

General

1. Confirm that the engagement team complies with relevant independence and ethical requirements.
2. Prepare and send an engagement letter to the entity.
3. Discuss the terms and scope of the engagement with the engagement team.
4. Obtain or update knowledge and understanding of the business, the key internal and external changes (including laws and regulations), and their effect on the scope of the review, materiality and risk assessment. This can be performed through the following:
   (a) Ascertaining whether there have been any significant changes to the nature and scope of operations.
   (b) Considering the results and effects of previous audits and review engagements.
   (c) Enquiring of persons responsible for financial reporting in respect of matters that impact on the reliability of the underlying accounting records. For example, considering fraud risk, material weaknesses in internal controls and any significant changes to internal control policies and procedures
   (d) Considering the results of any internal audits performed and the subsequent actions taken by management.
   (e) Considering whether additional procedures will be required on any significant accounts where internal controls relating to significant processes have been historically unreliable in detecting and preventing errors in the financial report.

   Assess the relevance and impact of the results of the above procedures on the current period.
5. Determine materiality, exercising professional judgement, considering both qualitative and quantitative factors.
6. Enquire of persons responsible for financial reporting about the following:
   (a) Accounting policies adopted and consider whether:
      (i) they comply with the applicable financial reporting framework;
      (ii) they have been applied appropriately; and
      (iii) they have been applied consistently and, if not, consider whether disclosure has been made of any changes in the accounting policies.
   (b) Policies and procedures used to assess asset impairment and any consequential estimation of recoverable amount.
   (c) The policies and procedures to determine the fair value of financial assets and financial liabilities.
   (d) New, unusual or complex situations that may have affected the financial report such as a business combination or disposal of a segment of the business. Consider adequacy of additional note disclosures in the financial report.
   (e) Plans to dispose of major assets or business segments.

ASRE

Appendix 2 (continued)

(f) Material off-balance sheet transactions, special purpose entities and other equity investments and related accounting treatment and disclosure.

(g) Knowledge of any allegations of fraud, or suspected fraud.

(h) Knowledge of any actual or possible significant non-compliance with laws and regulations.

(i) Compliance with debt covenants.

(j) Material or unusual related party transactions.

(k) New or significant changes in commitments, contractual obligations.

7. Obtain and read the minutes of meetings of shareholders, those charged with governance and other appropriate committees to identify matters that may affect the financial report, and enquire about matters dealt with at meetings for which minutes are not yet available that may affect the financial report.

8. Enquire if actions taken at meetings of shareholders or those charged with governance that affect the financial report have been appropriately reflected therein.

9. Ensure the financial report is agreed to the trial balance and is fairly presented including additional disclosure notes. If applicable, enquire as to whether all intercompany balances have been eliminated.

10. Review other information included in the financial report and document findings. Discuss any material misstatements of fact with the entity's management.

Cash

11. Obtain the bank reconciliations. Enquire about any old or unusual reconciling items with client personnel to assess reasonableness.

12. Enquire about transfers between cash accounts for the period before and after the review date.

13. Enquire whether there are any restrictions on cash accounts.

Revenue and Receivables

14. Enquire about the accounting policies for recognising sales revenue and trade receivables and determine whether they have been consistently and appropriately applied.

15. Obtain a schedule of receivables and determine whether the total agrees with the trial balance.

16. Obtain and consider explanations of significant variations in account balances from previous periods or from those anticipated.

17. Obtain an aged analysis of the trade receivables. Enquire about the reason for unusually large accounts, credit balances on accounts or any other unusual balances and enquire about the collectibility of receivables.

18. Consider, with management, the classification of receivables, including non-current balances, net credit balances and amounts due from shareholders, those charged with governance and other related parties in the financial report.

19. Enquire about the method for identifying "slow payment" accounts and setting allowances for doubtful accounts and consider it for reasonableness.

20. Enquire whether receivables have been pledged, factored or discounted and determine whether they have been properly accounted for.

21. Enquire about procedures applied to ensure that a proper cut-off of sales transactions and sales returns has been achieved.

22. Enquire whether accounts represent goods shipped on consignment and, if so, whether adjustments have been made to reverse these transactions and include the goods in inventory.

23. Enquire whether any large credits relating to recorded income have been issued after the balance sheet reporting date and whether provision has been made for such amounts. Consider the reasonableness of any provisions.

Appendix 2 (continued)

Inventories

24. Obtain the inventory list and determine whether:
    (a) the total agrees with the balance in the trial balance; and
    (b) the list is based on a physical count of inventory.
25. Enquire about the method for counting inventory.
26. Where a physical count was not carried out on the balance sheet date, enquire whether:
    (a) a perpetual inventory system is used and whether periodic comparisons are made with actual quantities on hand; and
    (b) an integrated cost system is used and whether it has produced reliable information in the past.
27. Consider adjustments made resulting from the last physical inventory count.
28. Enquire about procedures applied to control cut-off and any inventory movements.
29. Enquire about the basis used in valuing each inventory classification and, in particular, regarding the elimination of inter-branch profits. Enquire whether inventory is valued at the lower of cost and net realisable value (or lower of cost and replacement cost for not-for-profit organisations).
30. Consider the consistency with which inventory valuation methods have been applied, including factors such as material, labour and overhead.
31. Compare amounts of major inventory categories with those of prior periods and with those anticipated for the current period. Enquire about major fluctuations and differences.
32. Compare inventory turnover with that in previous periods.
33. Enquire about the method used for identifying slow moving and obsolete inventory and whether such inventory has been accounted for at net realisable value.
34. Enquire whether any inventory has been consigned to the entity and, if so, whether adjustments have been made to exclude such goods from inventory.
35. Enquire whether any inventory is pledged, stored at other locations or on consignment to others and consider whether such transactions have been accounted for appropriately.

Investments (Including Associated Entities and Financial Instruments)

36. Obtain a schedule of the investments at the balance sheet reporting date and determine whether it agrees with the trial balance.
37. Enquire whether the accounting policy applied to investments is consistent with prior periods.
38. Enquire from management about the carrying values of investments. Consider whether there are any realisation problems.
39. Enquire whether there are any new investments, including business combinations. Consider classification, measurement and disclosure in respect of material or significant acquisitions.
40. Consider whether gains and losses and investment income have been properly accounted for.
41. Enquire about the classification of long-term and short-term investments.

Property Plant and Equipment and Depreciation

42. Obtain a schedule of the property, plant and equipment indicating the cost and accumulated depreciation and determine whether it agrees with the trial balance.
43. Enquire about the accounting policy applied regarding residual values, provisions to allocate the cost of property, plant and equipment over their estimated useful lives using the expected pattern of consumption of the future economic benefits and distinguishing between capital and maintenance items. Consider whether there are any indicators of impairment and whether the property, plant and equipment have suffered a material, permanent impairment in value.

Appendix 2 (continued)

44. Discuss with management the additions and deletions to property, plant and equipment accounts and accounting for gains and losses on disposals or de-recognition. Enquire whether all such transactions have been properly accounted for.

45. Enquire about the consistency with which the depreciation method and rates have been applied and compare depreciation provisions with prior years.

46. Enquire whether there are any restrictions on the property, plant and equipment.

47. Enquire whether lease agreements have been properly reflected in the financial report in conformity with current accounting pronouncements.

Prepaid Expenses, Intangibles and Other Assets

48. Obtain schedules identifying the nature of these accounts and determine whether they agree with the trial balance. Discuss recoverability thereof with management.

49. Enquire whether management have updated their impairment calculations in respect of goodwill or other intangibles. Consider whether there have been any indicators of impairment for intangibles and enquire whether management have appropriately considered discount rates, growth rates, etc.

50. Enquire about the basis for recording these accounts and the amortisation methods used.

51. Compare balances of related expense accounts with those of prior periods and obtain explanations for significant variations with management.

52. Discuss the classification between current and non-current accounts with management.

Investment Property

53. Obtain a schedule of investment property and determine whether it agrees with the trial balance.

54. Enquire whether the accounting policy applied to investment property is consistent with prior periods.

55. Update with management the acquisitions and disposals to investment property and accounting for gains and losses on disposals or de-recognition. Determine whether all significant transactions have been accounted for appropriately.

56. Consider whether there are any indicators of impairment and whether any investment property was subject to recent valuations.

Loans Payable

57. Obtain from management a schedule of loans payable and determine whether the total agrees with the trial balance.

58. Enquire whether there are any loans where there has been a change to the terms and conditions or management has not complied with the provisions of the loan agreement, including any debt covenants. Assess whether loans have been appropriately classified as current or non-current in the financial report.

59. Where material, consider the reasonableness of interest expense in relation to loan balances.

60. Enquire whether loans payable are secured. Review loan and working capital facilities. Enquire if options to extend terms have been exercised or if any debt requires refinancing.

Trade Payables

61. Enquire about the accounting policies for initially recording trade payables and whether the entity is entitled to any allowances given on such transactions.

62. Obtain and consider explanations of significant variations in account balances from previous periods or from those anticipated.

63. Obtain a schedule of trade payables and determine whether the total agrees with the trial balance.

64. Enquire whether balances are reconciled with the creditors' statements and compare with prior period balances. Compare turnover with prior periods.

Appendix 2 (continued)

65. Consider whether there could be material unrecorded liabilities.

66. Enquire whether payables to shareholders, those charged with governance and other related parties are separately disclosed.

Other Liabilities and Contingent Liabilities

67. Obtain a schedule of other liabilities and determine whether the total agrees with the trial balance.

68. Compare major balances of related expense accounts with similar accounts for prior periods.

69. Enquire about approvals for such other liabilities, terms of payment, compliance with terms, collateral and classification.

70. Enquire about other liabilities to assess whether the methodology and assumptions adopted are consistent with prior periods. Enquire whether there are any unusual trends and developments affecting accounting estimates.

71. Enquire as to the nature of amounts included in contingent liabilities and commitments.

72. Enquire whether any actual or contingent liabilities exist which have not been recognised in the accounts. If so, enquire with management and/or those charged with governance whether provisions need to be made in the accounts or whether disclosure should be made in the notes to the financial report.

Income and Other Taxes

73. Enquire from management if there were any events, including disputes with taxation authorities, which could have a significant effect on the taxes payable by the entity. Examine correspondence in relation to any significant matters arising and assess whether events have been reflected appropriately in the financial report.

74. Consider the tax expense in relation to the entity's income for the period.

75. Enquire from management as to the adequacy of the recognised deferred and current tax assets and/or liabilities including provisions in respect of prior periods.

Financial Instruments

76. Enquire or update knowledge and understanding with persons responsible for financial reporting (including any treasury specialist), of what derivatives are in place, what accounting policies are applied to these derivatives and whether they have been consistently applied.

77. Enquire whether any hedges have been entered into for speculative purposes.

78. Enquire whether there are adequate policies and procedures to determine the fair value of financial assets and financial liabilities.

79. Enquire whether there are any sales and transfers that may call into question the classification of investments in securities, including management's intent and ability with respect to the remaining securities classified as held to maturity.

Employee Share Plans

80. Enquire about any new employee share plans or changes to existing plans, and where employee share plans are material, assess whether the accounting methodology has been consistently applied.

Subsequent Events

81. Obtain from management the latest financial report and compare it with the financial report being reviewed or with those for comparable periods from the preceding year.

82. Enquire about events after the balance sheet reporting date that would have a material effect on the financial report under review and, in particular, enquire whether:

    (a) any substantial commitments or uncertainties have arisen subsequent to the balance sheet date;

    (b) any significant changes in the share capital, long-term debt or working capital have occurred up to the date of enquiry; and

ASRE

Appendix 2 (continued)

(c) any unusual adjustments have been made during the period between the balance sheet reporting date and the date of enquiry.

Consider the need for adjustments or disclosure in the financial report.

83. Obtain and read the minutes of meetings of shareholders, those charged with governance and appropriate committees subsequent to the balance sheet date and consider any impact of the financial report and disclosures.

Litigation

84. Enquire from persons responsible for financial reporting, and where appropriate in-house litigation specialists, whether the entity is the subject of any legal actions - threatened, pending or in process. Consider the effect thereof on the financial report and any provision for loss.

Equity

85. Obtain and consider a schedule of the transactions in the equity accounts, including new issues, retirements and dividends. Consider whether there are any unusual terms for new issues of debt or equity which could affect classification.

86. Enquire whether there are any restrictions on retained earnings or other equity accounts.

Operations

87. Compare results with those of prior periods and those expected for the current period. Obtain explanations of significant variations with management.

88. Enquire whether the recognition of major revenue and expenses have taken place in the appropriate periods.

89. Enquire whether the policies and procedures related to revenue recognition, including accrued income, have been consistently applied and whether there are any new or complex changes, including any changes in major contracts with customers or suppliers.

90. Consider and update with management the relationship between related items in the revenue account and assess the reasonableness thereof in the context of similar relationships for prior periods and other information available to the auditor.

91. Discuss the policy in respect of capitalisation of interest and whether it is in accordance with Australian Accounting Standards.

Going Concern Assessment

92. Consider the going concern assumption. When events or conditions come to attention which cast significant doubt on the entity's ability to continue as a going concern, perform additional procedures to assess the impact on the financial report and review report. Additional procedures may include:

- Discussion with those charged with governance to understand the events and circumstances that have contributed to the current situation to determine whether the risk arising can be mitigated.
- Plans for future actions, such as plans or intentions to liquidate assets, borrow money or restructure debt, reduce or delay expenditures, or increase capital.
- Feasibility of the plans and whether those charged with governance believe that the outcome of these plans will improve the situation.

93. Consider the adequacy of disclosure about such matters in the financial report.

Evaluation of Misstatements

94. Ensure significant review differences have been summarised and their effect evaluated.

95. Ensure material adjustments identified are notified to management/those charged with governance (as appropriate).

Written Representations

96. Obtain written representation from the directors/management/those charged with governance (as appropriate) to confirm matters arising during the course of the review engagement.

Documentation

97. Ensure that review documentation is sufficient and appropriate to provide a basis for the conclusion and to provide evidence of compliance with ASRE 2410.

Appendix 3
(Ref: Para. A41)

An Auditor's Review Report Under the *Corporations Act 2001*

Financial Report For A Half-Year

Introduction

1. This Appendix has been prepared to assist an auditor, engaged to undertake a review engagement, by providing an example of an auditor's review report on a review of a financial report for a half- year prepared in accordance with Part 2M.3 of the *Corporations Act 2001* ("The Act"). The example reflects both requirements of this Auditing Standard and the Act, but is not intended to require standard wording for the circumstances of particular modifications.
2. This Appendix contains limited extracts from the Act and the Australian Accounting Standards in order to provide a context for the example report included in this Appendix. These selected extracts are included in this Appendix only for the purpose stated and accordingly are not intended to be an exhaustive list of an auditor's obligations and requirements which are found elsewhere in this Auditing Standard, the Act, the Australian Accounting Standards and other relevant mandates.
3. This Appendix:
   - Includes selected extracts from the Act and Australian Accounting Standards, and references to other relevant information, to provide a contextual framework; and
   - Provides an example of a review report.

Contextual Framework

Corporations Act 2001

The following selected extracts from the Act are included in this Appendix only to point to some of the important requirements of the Act that affect auditors engaged to undertake a review engagement in accordance with the Act.

4. Section 302 states:

   "A disclosing entity[18] must:

   (a) prepare a financial report and directors' report for each half-year; and

   (b) have the financial report audited or reviewed in accordance with Division 3 and obtain an auditor's report; and

   (c) lodge the financial report, the director's report and the auditor's report on the financial report with ASIC;

   unless the entity is not a disclosing entity when lodgement is due".

18 The definition of a "disclosing entity" is found in Part 1.2A, Division 2, section 111AC of the *Corporations Act 2001.*

ASRE

Appendix 3 (continued)

5. Section 303(1) states:

"The financial report for a half-year consists of:

(a) the financial statements for the half-year;

(b) the notes to the financial statements; and

(c) the directors' declaration about the statements and notes".

6. Section 304 states:

"The financial report for a half-year must comply with the accounting standards and any further requirements in the regulations".

7. Section 305 states:

"The financial statements and notes for a half-year must give a true and fair view of:

(a) the financial position and performance of the disclosing entity; or

(b) if consolidated financial statements are required the financial position and performance of the consolidated entity.

This section does not affect the obligation under section 304 for financial reports to comply with accounting standards.

Note: If the financial statements prepared in compliance with the accounting standards would not give a true and fair view, additional information must be included in the notes to the financial statements under paragraph 303(3)(c)".

8. Section 309(4) states:

"An auditor who reviews the financial report for a half-year must report to members on whether the auditor became aware of any matter in the course of the review that makes the auditor believe the financial report does not comply with Division 2".

9. Section 309(5) states:

"A report under subsection (4) must:

(a) Describe any matter referred to in subsection (4); and

(b) Say why that matter makes the auditor believe that the financial report does not comply with Division 2".

10. Section 309(5A) states:

"The auditor's report must include any statements or disclosures required by the auditing standards".

11. Section 320 states:

"A disclosing entity that has to prepare or obtain a report for a half- year under Division 2 must lodge the report with ASIC within 75 days after the end of the half-year".

Other Information – ASIC and ASX

12. An auditor, in the role of auditor, is required by section 311 of the Act to notify ASIC if the auditor is aware of certain circumstances. ASIC Regulatory Guide 34 *Auditors' obligations: reporting to ASIC* (December 2007), provides guidance to help auditors comply with their obligations under section 311 of the Act.

13. ASIC and the ASX have agreed that listed entities can satisfy the requirements of the Act by lodging the half-year financial report, the directors' report, and the review report on the financial report with the ASX. Details are provided in ASIC Regulatory Guide 28 *Relief from dual lodgement of financial reports* (July 2003) and *Class Order* 98/104 (as amended by Class Orders 99/90 and 99/837).

Australian Accounting Standards

14. Minimum Components of an Interim Financial Report - AASB 134 *Interim Financial Reporting*, paragraph 8:

Appendix 3 (continued)

An interim financial report shall include, at a minimum, the following components:

(a) a condensed statement of financial position;

(b) a condensed statement of comprehensive income;

(c) a condensed statement of changes in equity showing either:

(i) all changes in equity; or

(ii) changes in equity other than those arising from capital transactions with owners and distributions to owners;

(d) a condensed statement of cash flows; and

(e) selected explanatory notes.

15. Form and Content of Interim Financial Reports - AASB 134 paragraph 9 states:

"If an entity publishes a complete financial report as its interim financial report, the form and content of that report shall conform to the requirements of AASB 101 for a financial report".

16. Form and Content of Interim Financial Reports - AASB 134 paragraph 10 states:

"If an entity publishes a condensed financial report as its interim financial report, that condensed report shall include, at a minimum, each of the headings and subtotals that were included in its most recent annual financial report and the selected explanatory notes as required by this Standard. Additional line items or notes shall be included if their omission would make the condensed interim financial report misleading".

17. Materiality - AASB 134 paragraph 23 states:

"In deciding how to recognise, measure, classify, or disclose an item for interim financial reporting purposes, materiality shall be assessed in relation to the interim period financial data. In making assessments of materiality, it shall be recognised that interim measurements may rely on estimates to a greater extent than measurements of annual financial data".

Example of an Unmodified Auditor's Review Report on a Half-Year Financial Report – Single Disclosing Entity

INDEPENDENT AUDITOR'S REVIEW REPORT

To the members of [name of entity]

Report on the Half-Year Financial Report

We have reviewed the accompanying half-year financial report of [name of entity], which comprises the condensed statement of financial position as at 31 December 20XX, the condensed statement of comprehensive income, condensed statement of changes in equity and condensed statement of cash flows for the half-year ended on that date, notes comprising a summary of significant accounting policies [statement or description of accounting policies[19]] and other explanatory information, and the directors' declaration.[20]

Directors' Responsibility for the Half-Year Financial Report

The directors of the [company/registered scheme/disclosing entity] are responsible for the preparation of the half-year financial report that gives a true and fair view in accordance with Australian Accounting Standards and the *Corporations Act 2001* and for such internal control as the directors [those charged with governance] determine is necessary to enable the preparation

19 Insert relevant statement or description of accounting policies as required by AASB 134.

20 When the auditor is aware that the half-year financial report will be included in a document that contains other information, the auditor may consider, if the form of presentation allows, identifying the page numbers on which the audited half-year financial report is presented.

Appendix 3 (continued)

of the half-year financial report that is free from material misstatement, whether due to fraud or error.

Auditor's Responsibility

Our responsibility is to express a conclusion on the half-year financial report based on our review. We conducted our review in accordance with Auditing Standard on Review Engagements ASRE 2410 *Review of a Financial Report Performed by the Independent Auditor of the Entity*, in order to state whether, on the basis of the procedures described, we have become aware of any matter that makes us believe that the half-year financial report is not in accordance with the *Corporations Act 2001* including: giving a true and fair view of the [company's/registered scheme's/disclosing entity's] financial position as at 31 December 20XX and its performance for the half-year ended on that date; and complying with Accounting Standard AASB 134 *Interim Financial Reporting* and the *Corporations Regulations 2001*. As the auditor of [name of entity], ASRE 2410 requires that we comply with the ethical requirements relevant to the audit of the annual financial report.

A review of a half-year financial report consists of making enquiries, primarily of persons responsible for financial and accounting matters, and applying analytical and other review procedures. A review is substantially less in scope than an audit conducted in accordance with Australian Auditing Standards and consequently does not enable us to obtain assurance that we would become aware of all significant matters that might be identified in an audit. Accordingly, we do not express an audit opinion.

Independence

In conducting our review, we have complied with the independence requirements of the *Corporations Act 2001*. We confirm that the independence declaration required by the *Corporations Act 2001*, which has been given to the directors of [name of entity], would be in the same terms if given to the directors as at the time of this auditor's report.[21]

Conclusion

Based on our review, which is not an audit, we have not become aware of any matter that makes us believe that the half-year financial report of [name of company/registered scheme/disclosing entity] is not in accordance with the *Corporations Act 2001* including:

(a) giving a true and fair view of the [company's/registered scheme's/disclosing entity's] financial position as at 31 December 20XX and of its performance for the half-year ended on that date; and

(b) complying with Accounting Standard AASB 134 *Interim Financial Reporting* and *Corporations Regulations 2001*.

Report on Other Legal and Regulatory Requirements

[Form and content of this section of the auditor's review report will vary depending on the nature of the auditor's other reporting responsibilities].

[Auditor's signature][22]

[Date of the auditor's review report][23]

[Auditor's address]

21 Or, alternatively, include statements (a) to the effect that circumstances have changed since the declaration was given to the relevant directors; and (b) setting out how the declaration would differ if it had been given to the relevant directors at the time the auditor's report was made.

22 The auditor's review report is required to be signed in one or more of the name of the audit firm, the name of the audit company or the personal name of the auditor as appropriate.

23 The date of the auditor's report is the date the auditor signs the report.

Appendix 4
(Ref: Para. A41)

Illustrations of Auditors' Review Reports—Unmodified and Modified Conclusions

Example of an Unmodified Auditor's Review Report on a Financial Report
Financial Report Prepared in Accordance with a Financial Reporting Framework Designed to Achieve Fair Presentation

Example of an Auditor's Review Report with a Qualified Conclusion (Except For) for a Departure from the Applicable Financial Reporting Framework
Financial Report Prepared in Accordance with a Financial Reporting Framework Designed to Achieve Fair Presentation

Example of an Auditor's Review Report with a Qualified Conclusion for a Limitation On Scope Not Imposed by Management
Financial Report Prepared in Accordance with a Financial Reporting Framework Designed to Achieve Fair Presentation

Example of An Auditor's Review Report with an Adverse Conclusion for a Departure from the Applicable Financial Reporting Framework
Financial Report Prepared in Accordance with a Financial Reporting Framework Designed to Achieve Fair Presentation

Example of an Auditor's Review Report with a Qualified Conclusion (Except for) on the Basis that Comparatives have not been Reviewed or Audited
Financial Report Prepared in Accordance with a Financial Reporting Framework Designed to Achieve Fair Presentation

Example of an Unmodified Auditor's Review Report on a Financial Report

Financial Report Prepared in Accordance with a Financial Reporting Framework Designed to Achieve Fair Presentation

INDEPENDENT AUDITOR'S REVIEW REPORT

To [appropriate addressee]

Report on the [appropriate title for the financial report] Financial Report

We have reviewed the accompanying [period] financial report of [name of entity], which comprises the balance sheet as at [date], and the income statement, statement of changes in equity and cash flow statement for the [period] ended on that date, a [statement or description of accounting policies[24]], other selected explanatory notes, and [the declaration of those charged with governance[25]].[26, 27]

[Title of those charged with governance] Responsibility for the [period] Financial Report

The [title of those charged with governance] of the [type of entity] are responsible for the preparation and fair presentation of the [period] financial report in accordance with the [applicable

24 Insert relevant statement or description of accounting policies.

25 Amend these terms to reflect the appropriate assertion statement and title for those charged with governance.

26 When the auditor is aware that the financial report will be included in a document that contains other information, the auditor may consider, if the form of presentation allows, identifying the page numbers on which the reviewed financial report is presented.

27 The auditor may wish to specify the regulatory authority or equivalent with whom the financial report is filed.

Appendix 4 (continued)

financial reporting framework] and for such internal control as the directors [those charged with governance] determine is necessary to enable the preparation and fair presentation of the [period] financial report that is free from material misstatement, whether due to fraud or error.

Auditor's Responsibility

Our responsibility is to express a conclusion on the [period] financial report based on our review. We conducted our review in accordance with Auditing Standard on Review Engagements ASRE 2410 *Review of a Financial Report Performed by the Independent Auditor of the Entity*, in order to state whether, on the basis of the procedures described, anything has come to our attention that causes us to believe that the financial report is not presented fairly, in all material respects, in accordance with the [applicable financial reporting framework]. As the auditor of [name of entity], ASRE 2410 requires that we comply with the ethical requirements relevant to the audit of the annual financial report.

A review of a [period] financial report consists of making enquiries, primarily of persons responsible for financial and accounting matters, and applying analytical and other review procedures. A review is substantially less in scope than an audit conducted in accordance with Australian Auditing Standards and consequently does not enable us to obtain assurance that we would become aware of all significant matters that might be identified in an audit. Accordingly, we do not express an audit opinion.

[*Independence*

In conducting our review, we have complied with the independence requirements of the Australian professional accounting bodies[28]].

Conclusion

Based on our review, which is not an audit, nothing has come to our attention that causes us to believe that the [period] financial report of [name of entity] does not present fairly, in all material respects, [or "give a true and fair view of[29]"] the financial position of the [entity] as at [date], and of its financial performance and its cash flows for the [period] ended on that date, in accordance with [applicable financial reporting framework].

Report on Other Legal and Regulatory Requirements

[Form and content of this section of the auditor's review report will vary depending on the nature of the auditor's other reporting responsibilities.]

[Auditor's signature][30]

[Date of the auditor's review report][31]

[Auditor's address]

28 Use when appropriate.

29 ASA 700 *Forming an Opinion and Reporting on a Financial Report*, contains information on the wording of reports that may be helpful.

30 The auditor's review report is required to be signed in one or more of the name of the audit firm, the name of the audit company or the personal name of the auditor, as appropriate.

31 The date of the auditor's report is the date the auditor signs the report.

Appendix 4 (continued)

Example of an Auditor's Review Report with a Qualified Conclusion (Except for) for a Departure from the Applicable Financial Reporting Framework

Financial Report Prepared in Accordance with a Financial Reporting Framework Designed to Achieve Fair Presentation

INDEPENDENT AUDITOR'S REVIEW REPORT

To [appropriate addressee]

Report on the [appropriate title for the financial report] Financial Report

We have reviewed the accompanying [period] financial report of [name of entity], which comprises the balance sheet as at [date], and the income statement, statement of changes in equity and cash flow statement for the [period] ended on that date, a [statement or description of accounting policies,[32]] other selected explanatory notes, and [the declaration of those charged with governance[33]].[34, 35]

[Title of those charged with governance] Responsibility for the [period] Financial Report

The [title of those charged with governance] of the [type of entity] are responsible for the preparation and fair presentation of the [period] financial report in accordance with the [applicable financial reporting framework]and for such internal control as the directors [those charged with governance] determine is necessary to enable the preparation and fair presentation of the [period] financial report that is free from material misstatement, whether due to fraud or error.

Auditor's Responsibility

Our responsibility is to express a conclusion on the [period] financial report based on our review. We conducted our review in accordance with Auditing Standard on Review Engagements ASRE 2410 *Review of a Financial Report Performed by the Independent Auditor of the Entity*, in order to state whether, on the basis of the procedures described, anything has come to our attention that causes us to believe that the financial report is not presented fairly, in all material respects, in accordance with the [applicable financial reporting framework]. As the auditor of [name of entity], ASRE 2410 requires that we comply with the ethical requirements relevant to the audit of the annual financial report.

A review of a [period] financial report consists of making enquiries, primarily of persons responsible for financial and accounting matters, and applying analytical and other review procedures. A review is substantially less in scope than an audit conducted in accordance with Australian Auditing Standards and consequently does not enable us to obtain assurance that we would become aware of all significant matters that might be identified in an audit. Accordingly, we do not express an audit opinion.

[Independence

In conducting our review, we have complied with the independence requirements of the Australian professional accounting bodies[36]].

Basis for Qualified Conclusion

Based on information provided to us by management, [name of entity] has excluded from property and long-term debt certain lease obligations that we believe should be capitalised to conform with [indicate applicable financial reporting framework]. This information indicates that

---

32 Insert relevant statement or description of accounting policies.

33 Amend these terms to reflect the appropriate assertion statement and title for those charged with governance.

34 When the auditor is aware that the financial report will be included in a document that contains other information, the auditor may consider, if the form of presentation allows, identifying the page numbers on which the reviewed financial report is presented.

35 The auditor may wish to specify the regulatory authority or equivalent with whom the financial report is filed.

36 Use when appropriate.

Appendix 4 (continued)

if these lease obligations were capitalised at 31 December 20XX, property would be increased by $_______, long-term debt by $_______ , and net income and earnings per share would be increased (decreased) by $_______ and $_______ respectively for the [period] ended on that date.

Qualified Conclusion

Based on our review, which is not an audit, with the exception of the matter described in the preceding paragraph, nothing has come to our attention that causes us to believe that the [period] financial report of [name of entity] does not present fairly, in all material respects, [or "give a true and fair view of"[37]] the financial position of the [entity] as at [date], and of its financial performance and its cash flows for the [period] period ended on that date, in accordance with [applicable financial reporting framework].

Report on Other Legal and Regulatory Requirements

[Form and content of this section of the auditor's review report will vary depending on the nature of the auditor's other reporting responsibilities].

[Auditor's signature][38]

[Date of the auditor's review report][39]

[Auditor's address]

Example of an Auditor's Review Report with a Qualified Conclusion for a Limitation on Scope Not Imposed by Management

Financial Report Prepared In Accordance with a Financial Reporting Framework Designed to Achieve Fair Presentation

INDEPENDENT AUDITOR'S REVIEW REPORT

To [appropriate addressee]

Report on the [appropriate title for the financial report] Financial Report

We have reviewed the accompanying [period] financial report of [name of entity], which comprises the balance sheet as at [date], and the income statement, statement of changes in equity and cash flow statement for the [period] ended on that date, a [statement or description of accounting policies[40]], other selected explanatory notes, and [the declaration of those charged with governance [41]].[42, 43]

[Title of those charged with governance] Responsibility for the [period] Financial Report

The [title of those charged with governance] of the [type of entity] are responsible for the preparation and fair presentation of the [period] financial report in accordance with the [applicable financial reporting framework] and for such internal control as the directors [those charged with governance] determine is necessary to enable the preparation and fair presentation of the [period] financial report that is free from material misstatement, whether due to fraud or error.

---

37 ASA 700 *Forming an Opinion and Reporting on a Financial Report*, contains information on the wording of reports that may be helpful.

38 The auditor's review report is required to be signed in one or more of the name of the audit firm, the name of the audit company or the personal name of the auditor, as appropriate.

39 The date of the auditor's report is the date the auditor signs the report.

40 Insert relevant statement or description of accounting policies.

41 Amend these terms to reflect the appropriate assertion statement and title for those charged with governance.

42 When the auditor is aware that the financial report will be included in a document that contains other information, the auditor may consider, if the form of presentation allows, identifying the page numbers on which the reviewed financial report is presented.

43 The auditor may wish to specify the regulatory authority or equivalent with whom the financial report is filed.

Appendix 4 (continued)

Auditor's Responsibility

Our responsibility is to express a conclusion on the [period] financial report based on our review. We conducted our review in accordance with Auditing Standard on Review Engagements ASRE 2410 *Review of a Financial Report Performed by the Independent Auditor of the Entity*, in order to state whether, on the basis of the procedures described, anything has come to our attention that causes us to believe that the financial report is not presented fairly, in all material respects, in accordance with the [applicable financial reporting framework]. As the auditor of [name of entity], ASRE 2410 requires that we comply with the ethical requirements relevant to the audit of the annual financial report.

A review of a [period] financial report consists of making enquiries, primarily of persons responsible for financial and accounting matters, and applying analytical and other review procedures. A review is substantially less in scope than an audit conducted in accordance with Australian Auditing Standards and consequently does not enable us to obtain assurance that we would become aware of all significant matters that might be identified in an audit. Accordingly, we do not express an audit opinion.

[*Independence*

In conducting our review, we have complied with the independence requirements of the Australian professional accounting bodies[44]].

Basis for Qualified Conclusion

As a result of a fire in a branch office on [date] that destroyed its accounts receivable records, we were unable to complete our review of accounts receivable totalling $______ included in the [period] financial report. The [entity] is in the process of reconstructing these records and is uncertain as to whether these records will support the amount shown above and the related allowance for uncollectible accounts. Had we been able to complete our review of accounts receivable, matters might have come to our attention indicating that adjustments might be necessary to the [period] financial report.

Qualified Conclusion

Except for the adjustments to the [period] financial report that we might have become aware of had it not been for the situation described above, based on our review, which is not an audit, nothing has come to our attention that causes us to believe that the [period] financial report of [name of entity] does not present fairly, in all material respects, [or "give a true and fair view of[45]]" the financial position of the [entity] as at [date], and of its financial performance and its cash flows for the [period] period ended on that date, in accordance with [applicable financial reporting framework].

Report on Other Legal and Regulatory Requirements

[Form and content of this section of the auditor's review report will vary depending on the nature of the auditor's other reporting responsibilities.]

[Auditor's signature[46]]

[Date of the auditor's review report][47]

[Auditor's address]

44 Use when appropriate.

45 ASA 700 *Forming an Opinion and Reporting on a Financial Report*, contains information on the wording of reports that may be helpful.

46 The auditor's review report is required to be signed in one or more of the name of the audit firm, the name of the audit company or the personal name of the auditor, as appropriate.

47 The date of the auditor's report is the date the auditor signs the report.

Appendix 4 (continued)

Example of an Auditor's Review Report with an Adverse Conclusion for a Departure from the Applicable Financial Reporting Framework

Financial Report Prepared in Accordance with a Financial Reporting Framework Designed to Achieve Fair Presentation

INDEPENDENT AUDITOR'S REVIEW REPORT

To [appropriate addressee]

Report on the [appropriate title for the financial report] Financial Report

We have reviewed the accompanying [period] financial report of [name of entity], which comprises the balance sheet as at [date], and the income statement, statement of changes in equity and cash flow statement for the [period] ended on that date, a [statement or description of accounting policies[48]], other selected explanatory notes, and [the declaration of those charged with governance[49]].[50, 51]

[Title of those charged with governance] Responsibility for the [period] Financial Report

The [title of those charged with governance] of the [type of entity] are responsible for the preparation and fair presentation of the [period] financial report in accordance with the [applicable financial reporting framework] and for such internal control as the directors [those charged with governance] determine is necessary to enable the preparation and fair presentation of the [period] financial report that is free from material misstatement, whether due to fraud or error.

Auditor's Responsibility

Our responsibility is to express a conclusion on the [period] financial report based on our review. We conducted our review in accordance with Auditing Standard on Review Engagements ASRE 2410 *Review of a Financial Report Performed by the Independent Auditor of the Entity*, in order to state whether, on the basis of the procedures described, anything has come to our attention that causes us to believe that the financial report is not presented fairly, in all material respects, in accordance with the [applicable financial reporting framework]. As the auditor of [name of entity], ASRE 2410 requires that we comply with the ethical requirements relevant to the audit of the annual financial report.

A review of a [period] financial report consists of making enquiries, primarily of persons responsible for financial and accounting matters, and applying analytical and other review procedures. A review is substantially less in scope than an audit conducted in accordance with Australian Auditing Standards and consequently does not enable us to obtain assurance that we would become aware of all significant matters that might be identified in an audit. Accordingly, we do not express an audit opinion.

[*Independence*

In conducting our review, we have complied with the independence requirements of the Australian professional accounting bodies[52]].

Basis for Adverse Conclusion

Commencing this period, [title of those charged with governance] of the [entity] ceased to consolidate the financial reports of its subsidiary companies since [title of those charged with governance] considers consolidation to be inappropriate because of the existence of new

48 Insert relevant statement or description of accounting policies.

49 Amend these terms to reflect the appropriate assertion statement and title for those charged with governance.

50 When the auditor is aware that the financial report will be included in a document that contains other information, the auditor may consider, if the form of presentation allows, identifying the page numbers on which the reviewed financial report is presented.

51 The auditor may wish to specify the regulatory authority or equivalent with whom the financial report is filed.

52 Use when appropriate.

Appendix 4 (continued)

substantial non-controlling interests. This is not in accordance with [applicable financial reporting framework]. Had a consolidated financial report been prepared, virtually every account in the financial report would have been materially different.

Adverse Conclusion

Our review indicates, because the [entity's] investment in subsidiary companies is not accounted for on a consolidation basis, as described in the previous paragraph, this [period] financial report of [name of entity] does not present fairly, in all material respects, [or "give a true and fair view of[53]]" the financial position of the [entity] as at [date], and of its financial performance and its cash flows for the [period] period ended on that date, in accordance with [applicable financial reporting framework].

Report on Other Legal and Regulatory Requirements

[Form and content of this section of the auditor's review report will vary depending on the nature of the auditor's other reporting responsibilities.]

[Auditor's signature[54]]

[Date of the auditor's review report][55]

[Auditor's address]

ASRE

Example of an Auditor's Review Report with a Qualified Conclusion (Except For) on the Basis that Comparatives have not been Reviewed or Audited

Financial Report Prepared in Accordance with a Financial Reporting Framework Designed to Achieve Fair Presentation

INDEPENDENT AUDITOR'S REVIEW REPORT

To [appropriate addressee]

Report on the [appropriate title for the financial report] Financial Report

We have reviewed the accompanying [period] financial report of [name of entity], which comprises the balance sheet as at [date], and the income statement, statement of changes in equity and cash flow statement for the [period] ended on that date, a [statement or description of accounting policies[56]], other selected explanatory notes, and [the declaration of those charged with governance[57]].[58, 59]

[Title of those charged with governance] Responsibility for the [period] Financial Report

The [title of those charged with governance] of the [type of entity] are responsible for the preparation and fair presentation of the [period] financial report in accordance with the [applicable financial reporting framework] and for such internal control as the directors [those charged with governance] determine is necessary to enable the preparation and fair presentation of the [period] financial report that is free from material misstatement, whether due to fraud or error.

53 ASA 700 *Forming an Opinion and Reporting on a Financial Report*, contains information on the wording of reports that may be helpful.

54 The auditor's review report is required to be signed in one or more of the name of the audit firm, the name of the audit company or the personal name of the auditor, as appropriate.

55 The date of the auditor's report is the date the auditor signs the report.

56 Insert relevant statement or description of accounting policies.

57 Amend these terms to reflect the appropriate assertion and title for those charged with governance.

58 When the auditor is aware that the interim financial report will be included in a document that contains other information, the auditor may consider, if the form of presentation allows, identifying the page numbers on which the reviewed interim financial report is presented.

59 The auditor may wish to specify the regulatory authority or equivalent with whom the financial report is filed.

Appendix 4 (continued)

Auditor's Responsibility

Our responsibility is to express a conclusion on the [period] financial report based on our review. We conducted our review in accordance with Auditing Standard on Review Engagements ASRE 2410 *Review of a Financial Report Performed by the Independent Auditor of the Entity*, in order to state whether, on the basis of the procedures described, anything has come to our attention that causes us to believe that the financial report is not presented fairly, in all material respects, in accordance with the [applicable financial reporting framework]. As the auditor of [name of entity], ASRE 2410 requires that we comply with the ethical requirements relevant to the audit of the annual financial report.

A review of a [period] financial report consists of making enquiries, primarily of persons responsible for financial and accounting matters, and applying analytical and other review procedures. A review is substantially less in scope than an audit conducted in accordance with Australian Auditing Standards and consequently does not enable us to obtain assurance that we would become aware of all significant matters that might be identified in an audit. Accordingly, we do not express an audit opinion.

[*Independence*

In conducting our review, we have complied with the independence requirements of the Australian professional accounting bodies[60]].

Basis for Qualified Conclusion

As this is the first year that [name of entity] is required to prepare a [period] financial report and have it reviewed, the balance sheet, income statement, statement of changes in equity, cash flow statement, [statement or description of accounting policies[61]] and other selected explanatory notes for the preceding corresponding [period] have not been reviewed or audited. Accordingly, we are not in a position to and do not express any assurance in respect of the comparative information for the [period] ended [date of preceding corresponding period]. We have, however, audited the financial report for the preceding financial year ended [date of preceding financial year] and therefore our review statement is not qualified in respect of the comparative information for the year ended [date of preceding financial year] included in the balance sheet.

Qualified Conclusion

Except for the effect, if any, on the comparatives for the preceding corresponding [period] that may result from the qualification in the preceding paragraph, based on our review, which is not an audit, nothing has come to our attention that causes us to believe that the [period] financial report of [name of entity] does not present fairly, in all material respects, [or "give a true and fair view of[62]]" the financial position of the [entity] as at [date], and of its financial performance and its cash flows for the [period] period ended on that date, in accordance with [applicable financial reporting framework].

Report on Other Legal and Regulatory Requirements

[Form and content of this section of the auditor's review report will vary depending on the nature of the auditor's other reporting responsibilities.]

[Auditor's signature[63]]

[Date of the auditor's review report][64]

[Auditor's address]

60 Use when appropriate.

61 Insert relevant statement or description of accounting policies.

62 ASA 700 *Forming an Opinion and Reporting on a Financial Report*, contains information on the wording of reports that may be helpful.

63 The auditor's review report is required to be signed in one or more of the name of the audit firm, the name of the audit company or the personal name of the auditor, as appropriate.

64 The date of the auditor's report is the date the auditor signs the report.

ASRE 2415
Review of a Financial Report – Company Limited by Guarantee

(Issued June 2010)

Issued by the Auditing and Assurance Standards Board.

Note from the Institute of Chartered Accountants Australia

This note, prepared by the technical editor, is not part of ASRE 2415.

Historical development

June 2010: ASRE 2415 was issued in response to changes to the *Corporations Act 2001* that permit certain companies limited by guarantee to have a review rather than an audit. It contains an example review report and is operative for periods ending on or after 30 June 2010. It has no international equivalent.

An Explanatory Guide to ASRE 2415 was also published by the AUASB in June 2010 and is available at auasb.gov.au. It explains the legislative context for the issue of ASRE 2415.

Contents

Preface

Reasons for Issuing Auditing Standard on Review Engagements ASRE 2415 *Review of a Financial Report – Company Limited by Guarantee*

The Auditing and Assurance Standards Board (AUASB) issues Auditing Standard on Review Engagements ASRE 2415 *Review of a Financial Report – Company Limited by Guarantee* pursuant to the requirements of the legislative provisions explained below.

The AUASB is an independent statutory board of the Australian Government established under section 227A of the *Australian Securities and Investments Commission Act 2001*, as amended (ASIC Act). Under section 336 of the *Corporations Act 2001* (the Act), the AUASB may make Australian Auditing Standards for the purposes of the corporations legislation. These Auditing Standards are legislative instruments under the *Legislative Instruments Act 2003*.

Under the *Corporations Amendment (Corporate Reporting Reform) Act 2010*, the Act and related Regulations have been amended to enable certain companies limited by guarantee to elect for their financial report for a financial year to be reviewed instead of audited. Accordingly, the AUASB issues ASRE 2415 as an Auditing Standard under section 336 of the Act, to address the changes to the Act and related Regulations.

Main Features

This transitional Auditing Standard on Review Engagements establishes requirements and provides application and other explanatory material regarding a review of a financial report for a financial year of certain companies limited by guarantee and on the form and content of the auditor's review report.

This Auditing Standard:

(a) Directs an auditor who has conducted an audit of the company's previous financial report, to conduct a review in the first reporting period under the revised legislation, in accordance with:

(i) ASRE 2410 *Review of Interim and Other Financial Reports Performed by the Independent Auditor of the Entity*; or

(ii) ASRE 2410 *Review of a Financial Report Performed by the Independent Auditor of the Entity* for financial reporting periods commencing on or after 1 January 2010, as applicable.

(b) Directs an auditor who has not conducted an audit of the company's previous financial report, to conduct a review in accordance with ASRE 2400 *Review of a Financial Report Performed by an Assurance Practitioner Who is not the Auditor of the Entity*.

(c) Requires the auditor to comply with relevant ethical requirements; and to implement quality control relevant to the individual engagement.

Operative Date

This Auditing Standard on Review Engagements is operative for financial reporting periods ending on or after 30 June 2010.

Authority Statement

The Auditing and Assurance Standards Board (AUASB) makes this Auditing Standard on Review Engagements ASRE 2415 *Review of a Financial Report – Company Limited by Guarantee* pursuant to section 227B of the *Australian Securities and Investments Commission Act 2001* and section 336 of the *Corporations Act 2001*.

Dated: 30 June 2010

M H Kelsall
Chairman - AUASB

ASRE

Auditing Standard on Review Engagements ASRE 2415

Review of a Financial Report – Company Limited by Guarantee

Application

1 This Auditing Standard on Review Engagements applies to a review of a financial report for a financial year for a company limited by guarantee in accordance with the *Corporations Act 2001* (the Act).

Operative Date

2 This Auditing Standard on Review Engagements (Auditing Standard) is operative for financial reporting periods ending on or after 30 June 2010.

Introduction

Scope of this Auditing Standard on Review Engagements

3 This transitional Auditing Standard deals with the responsibilities of the auditor to review the financial report of a company limited by guarantee that has elected, under section 301(3) of the Act, to have its financial report reviewed instead of audited. It also deals with the form and content of the review report, which is based on the example review reports contained within existing review standards.[1]

4 This Auditing Standard does not apply to the review of a half-year financial report under the Act. Refer ASRE 2410 *Review of Interim and Other Financial Reports Performed by the Independent Auditor of the Entity* or ASRE 2410 *Review of a Financial Report Performed by the Independent Auditor of the Entity*, as applicable.

Objective

5 The objective of the auditor, is to plan and perform the review of a financial report prepared by a company limited by guarantee, to enable the auditor to express a conclusion whether, on the basis of the review, anything has come to the auditor's attention that causes the auditor to believe that the financial report is not prepared, in all material respects, in accordance with the applicable financial reporting framework.

1 See Appendix 1 for an illustrative example review report.

Definitions

6 For purposes of this Auditing Standard, the following terms have the meanings attributed below:

(a) A company limited by guarantee means a company limited by guarantee whose obligations are set out in section 285A of the Act.

(b) A registered company auditor includes an individual who meets the requirements of section 324BE of the Act.

(c) Revised Legislation means *Corporations Amendment* (*Corporate Reporting Reform*) *Act 2010*.

7 The term "auditor" as used in this Auditing Standard, refers to a registered company auditor or an individual taken to be a registered company auditor under section 324BE of the Act.

8 The term "financial report", as used in this Auditing Standard, refers to a financial report for a financial year. A financial report for a financial year may be for a period that is greater than or less than 12 months.

Requirements

Applicable Standards

Company Previously Audited

9 When a company limited by guarantee elects to have its financial report reviewed instead of audited, an auditor who has conducted an audit of the previous financial report of the company in accordance with the Act and the Australian Auditing Standards, shall, in the first financial reporting period under the revised legislation, conduct the review in accordance with:[2]

(a) ASRE 2410 *Review of Interim and Other Financial Reports Performed by the Independent Auditor of the Entity*; or

(b) ASRE 2410 *Review of a Financial Report Performed by the Independent Auditor of the Entity* as applicable (Ref: Para. A1)

Company Not Previously Audited by the Auditor

10 When a company limited by guarantee elects to have its financial report reviewed instead of audited, an auditor who has not conducted an audit of the previous financial report of the company in accordance with the Act and the Australian Auditing Standards, shall conduct the review in accordance with ASRE 2400 *Review of a Financial Report Performed by an Assurance Practitioner Who is Not the Auditor of the Entity*.[3] (Ref: Para. A2)

11 For purposes of this Auditing Standard, requirements under ASRE 2400 are identified in **bold-type** in that standard.[4]

General Principles

12 The auditor shall comply with relevant ethical requirements relating to the review of the financial report.[5] (Ref: Para. A3)

13 The auditor shall implement quality control procedures that are applicable to the individual engagement.[6]

2 See ASRE 2410 *Review of Interim and Other Financial Reports Performed by the Independent Auditor of the Entity* (Compiled), issued August 2008. For financial reporting periods commencing on or after 1 January 2010, see ASRE 2410 *Review of a Financial Report Performed by the Independent Auditor of the Entity*, issued October 2009.

3 See ASRE 2400 *Review of a Financial Report Performed by an Assurance Practitioner Who is Not the Auditor of the Entity*, issued August 2008.

4 See ASA 100 *Preamble to AUASB Standards*, paragraph 9(a).

5 See ASA 102 *Compliance with Ethical Requirements when Performing Audits, Reviews and Other Assurance Engagements*.

6 See ASA 220 *Quality Control for an Audit of a Financial Report and Other Historical Financial Information* which may be helpful in determining quality control procedures applicable to a review engagement.

❖❖❖

Application and Other Explanatory Material

Applicable Standards

Company Previously Audited

A1 At the time of the amendments to the Act there will be companies limited by guarantee that have been in existence for some time and will have appointed an auditor. Where that auditor has conducted an audit of the company's previous financial report, that auditor will have obtained an understanding of the company and its environment, including the company's internal control, in accordance with the Australian Auditing Standards. Accordingly, the auditor conducting a review, does so in accordance with ASRE 2410.[7] ASRE 2410 is to be read in conjunction with ASA 100 *Preamble to AUASB Standards* or ASA 101 *Preamble to Australian Auditing Standards*, as applicable. (Ref: Para. 9)

Company Not Previously Audited by the Auditor

A2 A company limited by guarantee may engage an auditor, who has not conducted an audit of the company's previous financial report, to conduct a review of its financial report. In such cases, that auditor will not have recently obtained an understanding of the company and its environment, including the company's internal control, through compliance with Australian Auditing Standards. Accordingly, that auditor conducts the review in accordance with ASRE 2400.[8] ASRE 2400 is to be read in conjunction with ASA 100 *Preamble to AUASB Standards*. (Para. 10)

General Principles

A3 When complying with the fundamental ethical principles in accordance with ASRE 2400, an auditor with no previous engagement experience with the company, pays particular attention to the principle of professional competence and due care. (Ref: Para. 12)

❖❖❖

Conformity with International Standards on Review Engagements

This Auditing Standard on Review Engagements has been made for Australian legislative purposes and accordingly there is no equivalent International Standard on Review Engagements (ISRE) issued by the International Auditing and Assurance Standards Board (IAASB).

7 See ASRE 2410 *Review of Interim and Other Financial Reports Performed by the Independent Auditor of the Entity (Compiled)*, issued August 2008. For financial reporting periods commencing on or after 1 January 2010, refer ASRE 2410 *Review of a Financial Report Performed by the Independent Auditor of the Entity*, issued October 2009.

8 See ASRE 2400 *Review of a Financial Report Performed by an Assurance Practitioner Who is Not the Auditor of the Entity*, issued August 2008.

Appendix 1

(Ref: Para. 3)

Example Auditor's Review Report

The following example auditor's review report is to be used as a guide only and will need to be adapted according to the review engagement requirements and circumstances. It is based on the example review reports contained in the Appendices of ASRE 2400 and ASRE 2410.

Example 1: Financial report of a company limited by guarantee prepared under the *Corporations Act 2001*. The financial reporting framework is designed to achieve fair presentation.

EXAMPLE OF AN UNMODIFIED REVIEW REPORT

INDEPENDENT AUDITOR'S REVIEW REPORT

To the members of [name of company]

Report on the Financial Report

We [I][9] have reviewed the accompanying financial report of [name of company], which comprises the statement of financial position as at 30 June 20XX, the statement of comprehensive income, statement of changes in equity and statement of cash flows for the year ended on that date, notes comprising a summary of significant accounting policies and other explanatory information, and the directors' declaration.[10]

Directors' Responsibility for the Financial Report

The directors of the company are responsible for the preparation of the financial report that gives a true and fair view in accordance with Australian Accounting Standards and the *Corporations Act 2001* and for such internal control as the directors determine is necessary to enable the preparation of the financial report that is free from material misstatement, whether due to fraud or error.

Auditor's Responsibility

Our [My] responsibility is to express a conclusion on the financial report based on our [my] review. We [I] conducted our [my] review in accordance with Auditing Standard on Review Engagements ASRE 2415 *Review of a Financial Report - Company Limited by Guarantee*, in order to state whether, on the basis of the procedures described, we [I] have become aware of any matter that makes us [me] believe that the financial report is not in accordance with the *Corporations Act 2001* including: giving a true and fair view of the company's financial position as at 30 June 20XX and its performance for the year ended on that date; and complying with the Australian Accounting Standards and *Corporations Regulations 2001*. ASRE 2415 requires that we [I] comply with the ethical requirements relevant to the review of the financial report.

A review of a financial report consists of making enquiries, primarily of persons responsible for financial and accounting matters, and applying analytical and other review procedures. A review is substantially less in scope than an audit conducted in accordance with Australian Auditing Standards and consequently does not enable us [me] to obtain assurance that we [I] would become aware of all significant matters that might be identified in an audit. Accordingly, we [I] do not express an audit opinion.

9 When an individual is taken to be a registered company auditor under section 324BE of the Act, the auditor's report is to be written in singular form.

10 When the auditor is aware that the financial report will be included in a document that contains other information, the auditor may consider, if the form of presentation allows, identifying the page numbers on which the reviewed financial report is presented.

Independence

In conducting our [my] review, we [I] have complied with the independence requirements of the *Corporations Act 2001*. We [I] confirm that the independence declaration required by the *Corporations Act 2001*, which has been given to the directors of [name of company], would be in the same terms if given to the directors as at the time of this auditor's report.*

Conclusion

Based on our [my] review, which is not an audit, we [I] have not become aware of any matter that makes us [me] believe that the financial report of [name of company] is not in accordance with the *Corporations Act 2001* including:

(a) giving a true and fair view of the company's financial position as at 30 June 20XX and of its performance for the year ended on that date; and

(b) complying with Australian Accounting Standards and *Corporations Regulations 2001*.

Report on Other Legal and Regulatory Requirements

[Form and content of this section of the review report will vary depending on the nature of the auditor's other reporting responsibilities].

[Auditor's signature][11]

[Date of the auditor's review report][12]

[Auditor's address]

---

* Or, alternatively, include statements (a) to the effect that circumstances have changed since the declaration was given to the relevant directors; and (b) setting out how the declaration would differ if it had been given to the relevant directors at the time the auditor's report was made.

11 The auditor's review report is required to be signed in one or more of the following ways: the name of the audit firm, the name of the audit company or the personal name of the individual auditor as appropriate.

12 The date of the auditor's report is the date the auditor signs the report.

ASAE 3000
Assurance Engagements other than Audits or Reviews of Historical Financial Information

(July 2007)

Issued by the Auditing and Assurance Standards Board.

Note from the Institute of Chartered Accountants Australia

This note, prepared by the technical editor, is not part of ASAE 3000.

Historical development

June 2006: AUS 110 issued. Based on the International Standard on Assurance Engagements (ISAE) 3000, of the same name, it established basic principles and essential procedures for all assurance engagements other than audits or reviews of historical information covered by other AUSs.

July 2007: ASAE 3000 issued, again based on ISAE 3000. It was redrafted in the style of the ASA legally binding Standards. It is operative for periods beginning on or after 1 July 2007.

Contents

ASAE

Preface

Reasons for Issuing Standard on Assurance Engagements ASAE 3000 *Assurance Engagements Other than Audits or Reviews of Historical Financial Information*

The Auditing and Assurance Board (AUASB) makes Auditing Standards under section 336 of the *Corporations Act 2001* for the purposes of the corporation's legislation and formulates auditing and assurance standards for other purposes.

The AUASB issues Standard on Assurance Engagements ASAE 3000 *Assurance Engagements Other than Audits or Reviews of Historical Financial Information* pursuant to the requirements of the legislative provisions explained below.

The *Corporate Law Economic Reform Program (Audit Reform and Corporate Disclosure) Act 2004* (the CLERP 9 Act) established the AUASB as an independent statutory body under section 227A of the *Australian Securities and Investments Commission Act 2001* (ASIC Act), as from 1 July 2004. Under section 227B of the ASIC Act the AUASB may formulate Assurance Standards for other purposes.

Main Features

This Standard on Assurance Engagements establishes mandatory requirements and provides explanatory guidance for undertaking and reporting on assurance engagements other than audits or reviews of historical financial information covered by Auditing Standards (ASAs) or Auditing Standards on Review Engagements (ASREs).

Operative Date

This Standard on Assurance Engagements is operative for reporting periods commencing on or after 1 July 2007.

Main changes from AUS 110 (June 2004) *Assurance Engagements Other than Audits or Reviews of Historical Financial Information*

The main differences between this Standard on Assurance Engagements (ASAE) and the Auditing Standard issued by the Auditing & Assurance Standards Board of the Australian Accounting Research Foundation, AUS 110 (June 2004) *Assurance Engagements Other than Audits or Reviews of Historical Financial Information,* are that in this ASAE:

1. The word 'shall', in the **bold-type** paragraphs, is the terminology used to describe an assurance practitioner's mandatory requirements, whereas an assurance practitioner's degree of responsibility was described in AUS 110 by the word 'should'.
2. The explanatory paragraphs provide guidance and illustrative examples to assist the assurance practitioner in fulfilling the mandatory requirements, whereas in AUS 110 some obligations were implied within certain explanatory paragraphs.
3. The term 'practitioner' has been replaced with 'assurance practitioner' to extend the application of the ASAE to other professionals. Assurance practitioner has been defined as follows:
   (a) for the purpose of this ASAE, an "assurance practitioner" means a person or an organisation, whether in public practice, industry, commerce or the public sector, involved in the provision of assurance services (paragraph 4).
4. The definition of reasonable assurance has been expanded as follows:
   (a) reasonable assurance means a high, but not absolute, level of assurance (paragraph 5(a)).
5. The following implied obligation in AUS 110 has been elevated and re-stated as a specific mandatory requirement:
   (a) the assurance practitioner shall comply with this ASAE and other relevant ASAEs when performing an assurance engagement other than an audit or review of historical financial information covered by ASAs or ASREs (paragraph 6).
6. The following additional and/or extended mandatory requirements, not in AUS 110, have been included:
   (a) this Standard on Assurance Engagements (ASAE) applies to assurance engagements other than audits or reviews of historical financial information (paragraph 1);
   (b) where in rare and exceptional circumstances, factors outside the assurance practitioner's control prevent the assurance practitioner from complying with a relevant mandatory requirement in this ASAE, the assurance practitioner shall:
      (i) if possible, perform appropriate alternative evidence-gathering procedures; and
      (ii) document in the working papers:
         - the circumstances surrounding the inability to comply;
         - the reasons for the inability to comply; and
         - justification of how alternative evidence-gathering procedures achieve the objectives of the mandatory requirement.

When the assurance practitioner is unable to perform appropriate alternative evidence-gathering procedures, the assurance practitioner shall consider the implications for the assurance practitioner's report (paragraph 8);

(c) the assurance practitioner shall comply with the fundamental ethical principles of integrity, objectivity, professional competence and due care, confidentiality and professional behaviour (paragraph 9);

(d) the assurance practitioner shall implement procedures to address the following elements of a quality control system that apply to the individual assurance engagement:

(i) leadership responsibilities for quality on the assurance engagement;

(ii) ethical requirements;

(iii) acceptance and continuance of client relationships and specific assurance engagements;

(iv) assignment of assurance engagement teams;

(v) assurance engagement performance; and

(vi) monitoring (paragraph 12);

(e) the assurance practitioner shall accept (or continue where applicable) an assurance engagement only if, on the basis of a preliminary knowledge of the assurance engagement circumstances, nothing comes to the attention of the assurance practitioner to indicate that the requirements of the fundamental ethical principles or of the ASAEs will not be satisfied (paragraph 16);

(f) the assurance practitioner shall agree on the terms of the assurance engagement with the engaging party, which shall be recorded in writing by the assurance practitioner and forwarded to the engaging party. When the assurance engagement is undertaken pursuant to legislation, the minimum applicable assurance engagement terms shall be those contained in the legislation (paragraph 20);

(g) when the terms of an assurance engagement are changed, the assurance practitioner shall agree on the new terms with the engaging party and confirm them in writing (paragraph 23);

(h) the assurance practitioner shall prepare, on a timely basis, documentation that is sufficient and appropriate to provide:

(i) a basis for the assurance practitioner's conclusion; and

(ii) evidence that the assurance engagement was performed in accordance with ASAEs (paragraph 70);

(i) an assurance practitioner shall modify the assurance report by adding an emphasis of matter paragraph to highlight a matter that is fundamental to the users' understanding of the subject matter information. The addition of an emphasis of matter paragraph does not affect the assurance practitioner's conclusion (paragraph 82); and

(j) in some cases the assurance practitioner shall consider withdrawing from the assurance engagement (paragraph 83(c)).

7. Explanatory guidance on the level of documentation has been enhanced at paragraph 72 and explanatory guidance on modifications has been included at paragraph 81.

8. Footnote references have been made to ASAs that provide helpful guidance to assurance practitioners (paragraphs 13, 21, 26, 48, 57, 65, 66, 71, 79, 81 and 85).

9. References to paragraphs in the *Framework for Assurance Engagements* have been replaced with the following explanatory guidance paragraphs:

(a) preliminary knowledge of the assurance engagement circumstances prior to acceptance of an assurance engagement (paragraph 17);

(b) characteristics of an appropriate subject matter (paragraph 34); and

(c) characteristics of suitable criteria (paragraph 36).

10. The Public Sector Perspective section is not included as this ASAE is sector neutral.

ASAE

Authority Statement

The Auditing and Assurance Standards Board (AUASB) formulates this Standard on Assurance Engagements ASAE 3000 *Assurance Engagements Other than Audits or Reviews of Historical Financial Information* as set out in paragraphs 1 to 89, pursuant to section 227B of the *Australian Securities and Investments Commission Act 2001*.

This Standard on Assurance Engagements is to be read in conjunction with the *Preamble to AUASB Standards*, which sets out the intentions of the AUASB on how the Standards on Assurance Engagements are to be understood, interpreted and applied.

The mandatory requirements of this Standard on Assurance Engagements are set out in **bold-type** paragraphs.

Dated 9 July 2007

M H Kelsall
Chairman - AUASB

Standard On Assurance Engagements ASAE 3000

Assurance Engagements Other than Audits or Reviews of Historical Financial Information

Application

1 **This Standard on Assurance Engagements (ASAE) applies to assurance engagements other than audits or reviews of historical financial information.**

Operative Date

2 **This ASAE is operative for reporting periods commencing on or after 1 July 2007.**

Introduction

3 The purpose of this ASAE is to establish mandatory requirements and to provide explanatory guidance for undertaking and reporting on assurance engagements other than audits or reviews of historical financial information covered by Auditing Standards (ASAs) or Standards on Review Engagements (ASREs). This ASAE applies to assurance practitioners and others involved in performing assurance engagements.

4 For the purpose of this ASAE, an "assurance practitioner" means a person or an organisation, whether in public practice, industry, commerce or the public sector, involved in the provision of assurance services.

5 This ASAE uses the terms "reasonable assurance engagement" and "limited assurance engagement" to distinguish between the two types of assurance engagements that an assurance practitioner may perform:

(a) A reasonable assurance engagement. The objective of a reasonable assurance engagement is a reduction in assurance engagement risk to an acceptably low level in the circumstances of the assurance engagement[1] as the basis for a positive form of expression of the assurance practitioner's conclusion. Reasonable assurance means a high, but not absolute, level of assurance.

(b) A limited assurance engagement. The objective of a limited assurance engagement is a reduction in assurance engagement risk to a level that is acceptable in the circumstances of the assurance engagement, but where that risk is greater than for a reasonable assurance engagement, as the basis for a negative form of expression of the assurance practitioner's conclusion.

1 Engagement circumstances include the terms of the engagement, including whether it is a reasonable assurance engagement or a limited assurance engagement, the characteristics of the subject matter, the criteria to be used, the needs of the intended users, relevant characteristics of the responsible party and its environment, and other matters, for example events, transactions, conditions and practices, that may have a significant effect on the engagement.

Relationship with Other ASAEs, ASAs and ASREs

6 **The assurance practitioner shall comply with this ASAE and other relevant ASAEs when performing an assurance engagement other than an audit or review of historical financial information covered by ASAs or ASREs.**

7 This ASAE has been written for general application to assurance engagements other than audits or reviews of historical financial information covered by ASAs or ASREs. Other ASAEs may relate to topics that apply to all subject matters or be subject matter specific. Although ASAs and ASREs do not apply to assurance engagements covered by ASAEs, they may nevertheless provide helpful guidance to assurance practitioners.

Inability to Comply with Mandatory Requirements

8 **Where in rare and exceptional circumstances, factors outside the assurance practitioner's control prevent the assurance practitioner from complying with a relevant mandatory requirement in this ASAE, the assurance practitioner shall:**

(a) if possible, perform appropriate alternative evidence-gathering procedures; and

(b) document in the working papers:

(i) the circumstances surrounding the inability to comply;

(ii) the reasons for the inability to comply; and

(iii) justification of how alternative evidence-gathering procedures achieve the objectives of the mandatory requirement.

When the assurance practitioner is unable to perform appropriate alternative evidence-gathering procedures, the assurance practitioner shall consider the implications for the assurance practitioner's report.

Ethical Requirements

9 **The assurance practitioner shall comply with the fundamental ethical principles of integrity, objectivity, professional competence and due care, confidentiality and professional behaviour.**

10 The applicable code of conduct of a professional accounting body[2] provides appropriate guidance on the application of fundamental ethical principles to assurance engagements.

11 The applicable code of conduct of a professional accounting body provides a framework of principles that members of assurance teams, firms and network firms use to identify threats to independence, evaluate the significance of those threats and, if the threats are other than clearly insignificant:

(a) identify and apply safeguards to eliminate the threats; or

(b) reduce them to an acceptable level,

such that independence of mind and independence in appearance are not compromised.

Quality Control

12 **The assurance practitioner shall implement procedures to address the following elements of a quality control system that apply to the individual assurance engagement:**

(a) leadership responsibilities for quality on the assurance engagement;

(b) ethical requirements;

(c) acceptance and continuance of client relationships and specific assurance engagements;

(d) assignment of assurance engagement teams;

(e) assurance engagement performance; and

(f) monitoring.

2 The applicable code of conduct of the professional accounting bodies is APES 110 *Code of Ethics for Professional Accountants,* as issued from time to time by the Accounting Professional and Ethical Standards Board. This code of conduct has been adopted by CPA Australia, National Institute of Accountants and The Institute of Chartered Accountants in Australia. In addition, codes of conduct issued by other professional bodies may apply.

13 The quality control requirements for firms[3], specify the obligations of a firm of professional accountants to establish a system of quality control[4] designed to provide it with reasonable assurance that the firm and its personnel comply with ASAs, ASAEs and ASREs, the applicable code of conduct of a professional accounting body, and regulatory and legal requirements, and that the assurance reports issued by the assurance firm or engagement partners are appropriate in the circumstances.

Assurance Engagement Acceptance and Continuance

14 The assurance practitioner shall accept (or continue where applicable) an assurance engagement only if the subject matter is the responsibility of a party other than the intended users or the assurance practitioner.

15 The responsible party can be one of the intended users, but not the only one. Acknowledgement by the responsible party provides evidence that the appropriate relationship exists, and also establishes a basis for a common understanding of the responsibility of each party. A written acknowledgement is the most appropriate form of documenting the responsible party's understanding. In the absence of an acknowledgement of responsibility, the practitioner ordinarily considers:

(a) whether it is appropriate to accept the assurance engagement. Accepting it may be appropriate when, for example, other sources, such as legislation or a contract, indicate responsibility; and

(b) if the assurance engagement is accepted, whether to disclose these circumstances in the assurance report.

16 The assurance practitioner shall accept (or continue where applicable) an assurance engagement only if, on the basis of a preliminary knowledge of the assurance engagement circumstances, nothing comes to the attention of the assurance practitioner to indicate that the requirements of the fundamental ethical principles or of the ASAEs will not be satisfied.

17 Under paragraph 16 of this ASAE, the assurance practitioner does not accept the assurance engagement unless the preliminary knowledge of the assurance engagement circumstances indicates that:

(a) relevant ethical requirements, such as independence and professional competence will be satisfied; and

(b) the assurance engagement exhibits the following characteristics:

(i) the subject matter is appropriate;

(ii) the criteria to be used are suitable and are available to the intended users;

(iii) the assurance practitioner has access to sufficient appropriate evidence to support the assurance practitioner's conclusion;

(iv) the assurance practitioner's conclusion, in the form appropriate to either a reasonable assurance engagement or a limited assurance engagement, is to be contained in a written report; and

(v) the assurance practitioner is satisfied that there is a rational purpose for the assurance engagement. If there is a significant limitation on the scope of the assurance practitioner's work, it may be unlikely that the assurance engagement has a rational purpose. Also, an assurance practitioner may believe the engaging party intends to associate the assurance practitioner's name with the subject matter in an inappropriate manner.

---

3 The quality control requirements for firms are set out in APES 320 *Quality Control for Firms*, as issued from time to time by the Accounting Professional and Ethical Standards Board. These quality control requirements for firms have been adopted by CPA Australia, National Institute of Accountants and The Institute of Chartered Accountants in Australia.

4 The quality control procedures relevant to an audit engagement are contained in Auditing Standard ASA 220 *Quality Control for Audits of Historical Financial Information,* and may be helpful in determining quality control procedures applicable to an assurance engagement.

Also, if the party engaging the assurance practitioner (the "engaging party") is not the responsible party, the assurance practitioner ordinarily considers the effect of this on access to records, documentation and other information the assurance practitioner may need to complete the assurance engagement.

18 **The assurance practitioner shall accept (or continue where applicable) an assurance engagement only if the assurance practitioner is satisfied that those persons who are to perform the assurance engagement collectively possess the necessary professional competencies.**

19 An assurance practitioner may be requested to perform assurance engagements on a wide range of subject matters. Some subject matters may need specialised skills and knowledge beyond those ordinarily possessed by an individual assurance practitioner (see paragraphs 47-55).

Agreeing on the Terms of the Assurance Engagement

20 **The assurance practitioner shall agree on the terms of the assurance engagement with the engaging party, which shall be recorded in writing by the assurance practitioner and forwarded to the engaging party. When the assurance engagement is undertaken pursuant to legislation, the minimum applicable assurance engagement terms shall be those contained in the legislation.**

21 To avoid misunderstandings, under paragraph 20 of this ASAE, the agreed terms of the assurance engagement need to be recorded in an assurance engagement letter or other suitable form of contract. If the engaging party is not the responsible party, the nature and content of an assurance engagement letter or contract may vary. The existence of a legislative mandate may satisfy the requirement to agree on the terms of the assurance engagement. Even in those situations an assurance engagement letter may be useful for both the assurance practitioner and engaging party.[5]

22 **An assurance practitioner shall consider the appropriateness of a request, made before the completion of an assurance engagement, to change the assurance engagement to a non-assurance engagement or from a reasonable assurance engagement to a limited assurance engagement, and shall not agree to a change without reasonable justification.**

23 **When the terms of an assurance engagement are changed, the assurance practitioner shall agree on the new terms with the engaging party and confirm them in writing.**

24 A change in circumstances that affects the intended users' needs, or a misunderstanding concerning the nature of the assurance engagement, ordinarily will justify a request for a change in the assurance engagement. If such a change is made, the assurance practitioner does not disregard evidence that was obtained prior to the change.

Planning and Performing the Assurance Engagement

25 **The assurance practitioner shall plan an assurance engagement so that it will be performed effectively.**

26 Planning involves developing an overall strategy for the scope, emphasis, timing and conduct of the assurance engagement, and an assurance engagement plan, consisting of a detailed approach for the nature, timing and extent of evidence-gathering procedures to be performed and the reasons for selecting them.[6] Ordinarily, adequate planning:

- Helps to devote appropriate attention to important areas of the assurance engagement, identify potential problems on a timely basis and properly organise and manage the assurance engagement in order for it to be performed in an effective and efficient manner.

5 An illustrative example of an engagement letter relevant to an audit engagement is contained in Auditing Standard ASA 210 *Terms of Audit Engagements,* and may be helpful in determining terms of engagement applicable to an assurance engagement.

6 The planning procedures relevant to an audit engagement are contained in Auditing Standard ASA 300 *Planning an Audit of a Financial Report,* and may be helpful in determining planning procedures applicable to an assurance engagement.

- Assists the assurance practitioner to properly assign work to assurance engagement team members, and facilitates their direction and supervision and the review of their work.
- Assists, where applicable, the coordination of work done by other assurance practitioners and experts.

The nature and extent of planning activities will vary with the assurance engagement circumstances, for example the size and complexity of the entity and the assurance practitioner's previous experience with it. Examples of the main matters to be considered include:

- The terms of the assurance engagement.
- The characteristics of the subject matter and the identified criteria.
- The assurance engagement process and possible sources of evidence.
- The assurance practitioner's understanding of the entity and its environment, including the risks that the subject matter information may be materially misstated.
- Identification of intended users and their needs, and consideration of materiality and the components of assurance engagement risk.
- Personnel and expertise requirements, including the nature and extent of experts' involvement.

27 Planning is not a discrete phase, but rather a continual and iterative process throughout the assurance engagement. As a result of unexpected events, changes in conditions, or the evidence obtained from the results of evidence-gathering procedures, the assurance practitioner may need to revise the overall strategy and assurance engagement plan, and thereby the resulting planned nature, timing and extent of further evidence-gathering procedures.

28 The assurance practitioner shall plan and perform an assurance engagement with an attitude of professional scepticism recognising that circumstances may exist that cause the subject matter information to be materially misstated.

29 An attitude of professional scepticism means the assurance practitioner makes a critical assessment, with a questioning mind, of the validity of evidence obtained and is alert to evidence that contradicts or brings into question the reliability of documents and responses to enquiries and other information obtained from management and those charged with governance.

30 The assurance practitioner shall obtain an understanding of the subject matter and other assurance engagement circumstances, sufficient to identify and assess the risks of the subject matter information being materially misstated, and sufficient to design and perform further evidence-gathering procedures.

31 Obtaining an understanding of the subject matter and other assurance engagement circumstances is an essential part of planning and performing an assurance engagement. That understanding ordinarily provides the assurance practitioner with a frame of reference for exercising professional judgement throughout the assurance engagement, for example when:

- Considering the characteristics of the subject matter.
- Assessing the suitability of criteria.
- Identifying where special consideration may be necessary, for example factors indicative of fraud, and the need for specialised skills or the work of an expert.
- Establishing and evaluating the continued appropriateness of quantitative materiality levels (where appropriate), and considering qualitative materiality factors.
- Developing expectations for use when performing analytical procedures.
- Designing and performing further evidence-gathering procedures to reduce assurance engagement risk to an appropriate level.
- Evaluating evidence, including the reasonableness of the responsible party's oral and written representations.

32 The assurance practitioner uses professional judgement to determine the extent of the understanding that is needed of the subject matter and other assurance engagement circumstances. The assurance practitioner ordinarily considers whether the understanding is sufficient to assess the risks that the subject matter information may be materially misstated. The assurance practitioner ordinarily has a lesser depth of understanding than the responsible party.

Assessing the Appropriateness of the Subject Matter

33 **The assurance practitioner shall assess the appropriateness of the subject matter.**

34 An appropriate subject matter has the following characteristics:

(a) identifiable, and capable of consistent evaluation or measurement against the identified criteria; and

(b) such that the information about it can be subjected to procedures for gathering sufficient appropriate evidence to support a reasonable assurance or limited assurance conclusion, as appropriate.

The assurance practitioner also ordinarily identifies those characteristics of the subject matter that are particularly relevant to the intended users, which are to be described in the assurance report. An assurance practitioner does not accept an assurance engagement unless the assurance practitioner's preliminary knowledge of the assurance engagement circumstances indicates that the subject matter is appropriate. After accepting the assurance engagement, however, if the assurance practitioner concludes that the subject matter is not appropriate, under paragraph 83(c) of this ASAE, the assurance practitioner needs to express a qualified or adverse conclusion or a disclaimer of conclusion. In some cases the assurance practitioner considers withdrawing from the assurance engagement.

Assessing the Suitability of the Criteria

35 **The assurance practitioner shall assess the suitability of the criteria to evaluate or measure the subject matter.**

36 Suitable criteria have the following characteristics:

- Relevance: relevant criteria contribute to conclusions that assist decision-making by the intended users.
- Completeness: criteria are sufficiently complete when relevant factors that could affect the conclusions in the context of the assurance engagement circumstances are not omitted. Complete criteria include, where relevant, benchmarks for presentation and disclosure.
- Reliability: reliable criteria allow reasonably consistent evaluation or measurement of the subject matter including, where relevant, presentation and disclosure, when used in similar circumstances by similarly qualified assurance practitioners.
- Neutrality: neutral criteria contribute to conclusions that are free from bias.
- Understandability: understandable criteria contribute to conclusions that are clear, comprehensive, and not subject to significantly different interpretations.

37 As indicated in paragraph 16 of this ASAE, an assurance practitioner does not accept an assurance engagement unless the assurance practitioner's preliminary knowledge of the assurance engagement circumstances indicates that the criteria to be used are suitable. After accepting the assurance engagement, however, if the assurance practitioner concludes that the criteria are not suitable, under paragraph 83(c) of this ASAE, the assurance practitioner needs to express a qualified or adverse conclusion or a disclaimer of conclusion. Under paragraph 83(c) of this ASAE, in some cases the assurance practitioner needs to consider withdrawing from the assurance engagement.

38 Criteria can either be established or specifically developed. Ordinarily, established criteria are suitable when they are relevant to the needs of the intended users. When established criteria exist for a subject matter, specific users may agree to other criteria for their specific purposes. For example, various frameworks can be used as established criteria for evaluating the effectiveness of internal control. Specific users may, however, develop a more detailed

set of criteria that meet their specific needs in relation to, for example, prudential supervision. In such cases, the assurance report:

(a) notes, when it is relevant to the circumstances of the assurance engagement, that the criteria are not embodied in laws or regulations, or issued by authorised or recognised bodies of experts that follow a transparent due process; and

(b) states that it is only for the use of the specific users and for their purposes.

39 For some subject matters, it is likely that no established criteria exist. In those cases, criteria are specifically developed. Ordinarily, the assurance practitioner:

- Considers whether specifically developed criteria result in an assurance report that is misleading to the intended users.
- Attempts to have the intended users or the engaging party acknowledge that specifically developed criteria are suitable for the intended users' purposes.
- Considers how the absence of such an acknowledgement affects what is to be done to assess the suitability of the identified criteria, and the information provided about the criteria in the assurance report.

Materiality and Assurance Engagement Risk

40 The assurance practitioner shall consider materiality and assurance engagement risk when planning and performing an assurance engagement.

41 Under paragraph 40 of this ASAE, the assurance practitioner needs to consider materiality when determining the nature, timing and extent of evidence-gathering procedures, and when evaluating whether the subject matter information is free of misstatement. In considering materiality the assurance practitioner needs to understand and assess what factors might influence the decisions of the intended users. For example, when the identified criteria allow for variations in the presentation of the subject matter information, the assurance practitioner ordinarily considers how the adopted presentation might influence the decisions of the intended users.

42 Materiality is considered in the context of quantitative and qualitative factors, such as relative magnitude, the nature and extent of the effect of these factors on the evaluation or measurement of the subject matter, and the interests of the intended users. The assessment of materiality and the relative importance of quantitative and qualitative factors in a particular assurance engagement are matters for the assurance practitioner's judgement.

43 The assurance practitioner shall reduce assurance engagement risk to an acceptable level in the circumstances of the assurance engagement.

44 In a reasonable assurance engagement, under paragraph 43 of this ASAE, the assurance practitioner needs to reduce assurance engagement risk to an acceptably low level in the circumstances of the assurance engagement to obtain reasonable assurance as the basis for a positive form of expression of the assurance practitioner's conclusion. The level of assurance engagement risk is higher in a limited assurance engagement than in a reasonable assurance engagement because of the different nature, timing or extent of evidence-gathering procedures.

45 In a limited assurance engagement, the combination of the nature, timing, and extent of evidence-gathering procedures is at least sufficient for the assurance practitioner to obtain a meaningful level of assurance as the basis for a negative form of expression of the assurance practitioner's conclusion. To be meaningful, the level of assurance obtained is likely to enhance the intended users' confidence about the subject matter information to a degree that is clearly more than inconsequential.

46 In general, assurance engagement risk comprises inherent risk, control risk and detection risk. The degree to which the assurance practitioner's consideration of these components is reflected in the assurance engagement evidence gathering process is affected by the assurance engagement circumstances, in particular the nature of the subject matter and whether a reasonable assurance or a limited assurance engagement is being performed.

Using the Work of an Expert

47 **When the work of an expert is used in the collection and evaluation of evidence, the assurance practitioner and the expert shall, on a combined basis, possess adequate skill and knowledge regarding the subject matter and the criteria for the assurance practitioner to determine that sufficient appropriate evidence has been obtained.**

48 The subject matter and related criteria of some assurance engagements may include aspects requiring specialised knowledge and skills in the collection and evaluation of evidence.[7] In these situations, the assurance practitioner may decide to use the work of persons from other professional disciplines, referred to as experts, who have the required knowledge and skills. This ASAE does not provide explanatory guidance with respect to using the work of an expert for assurance engagements where there is joint responsibility and reporting by an assurance practitioner and one or more experts.

49 Due care is a required professional quality for all assurance practitioners and experts, involved in an assurance engagement. Persons involved in assurance engagements will have different responsibilities assigned to them. The extent of proficiency needed for performing those assurance engagements will vary with the nature of their responsibilities. While experts do not need to have the same proficiency as the assurance practitioner in performing all aspects of an assurance engagement, under paragraph 47 of this ASAE, the assurance practitioner needs to determine that the experts have a sufficient understanding of the ASAEs to enable them to relate the work assigned to them to the assurance engagement objective.

50 Under paragraph 12 of this ASAE, the assurance practitioner needs to adopt quality control procedures that address the responsibility of each person performing the assurance engagement, including the work of any experts who are not assurance practitioners, to ensure compliance with this ASAE and other relevant ASAEs in the context of their responsibilities.

ASAE

51 **The assurance practitioner shall be involved in the assurance engagement and understand the work for which an expert is used, to an extent that is sufficient to enable the assurance practitioner to accept responsibility for the conclusion on the subject matter information.**

52 Under paragraph 51 of this ASAE, the assurance practitioner needs to consider the extent to which it is reasonable to use the work of an expert in forming the assurance practitioner's conclusion.

53 The assurance practitioner is not expected to possess the same specialised knowledge and skills as the expert. The assurance practitioner has however, sufficient skill and knowledge to:

(a) define the objectives of the assigned work and how this work relates to the objective of the assurance engagement;

(b) consider the reasonableness of the assumptions, methods and source data used by the expert; and

(c) consider the reasonableness of the expert's findings in relation to the assurance engagement circumstances and the assurance practitioner's conclusion.

54 **The assurance practitioner shall obtain sufficient appropriate evidence that the expert's work is adequate for the purposes of the assurance engagement.**

55 In assessing the sufficiency and appropriateness of the evidence provided by the expert, ordinarily the assurance practitioner evaluates:

- The professional competence, including experience, and objectivity of the expert.
- The reasonableness of the assumptions, methods and source data used by the expert.
- The reasonableness and significance of the expert's findings in relation to the circumstances of the assurance engagement and the assurance practitioner's conclusion.

7 Using the work of experts as evidence in the context of an audit engagement is contained in Auditing Standard ASA 620 *Using the Work of an Expert,* and may be helpful in using the work of experts as evidence in an assurance engagement.

Obtaining Evidence

56 The assurance practitioner shall obtain sufficient appropriate evidence on which to base the conclusion.

57 Sufficiency is the measure of the quantity of evidence. Appropriateness is the measure of the quality of evidence; that is, its relevance and its reliability.[8] The assurance practitioner ordinarily considers the relationship between the cost of obtaining evidence and the usefulness of the information obtained. However, the matter of difficulty or expense involved is not in itself a valid basis for omitting an evidence-gathering procedure for which there is no alternative. The assurance practitioner uses professional judgement and exercises professional scepticism in evaluating the quantity and quality of evidence, and thus its sufficiency and appropriateness, to support the assurance report.

58 An assurance engagement rarely involves the authentication of documentation, nor is the assurance practitioner trained as or expected to be an expert in such authentication. However, under paragraph 56 of this ASAE, the assurance practitioner needs to consider the reliability of the information to be used as evidence, for example photocopies, facsimiles, filmed, digitised or other electronic documents, including consideration of controls over their preparation and maintenance where relevant.

59 Sufficient appropriate evidence in a reasonable assurance engagement is obtained as part of an iterative, systematic assurance engagement process involving:

(a) obtaining an understanding of the subject matter and other assurance engagement circumstances which, depending on the subject matter, includes obtaining an understanding of internal control;

(b) based on that understanding, assessing the risks that the subject matter information may be materially misstated;

(c) responding to assessed risks, including developing overall responses, and determining the nature, timing and extent of further evidence-gathering procedures;

(d) performing further evidence-gathering procedures clearly linked to the identified risks, using a combination of inspection, observation, confirmation, recalculation, re-performance, analytical procedures and enquiry. Such further evidence-gathering procedures involve substantive procedures, including obtaining corroborating information from sources independent of the entity, and depending on the nature of the subject matter, tests of the operating effectiveness of controls; and

(e) evaluating the sufficiency and appropriateness of evidence.

60 Reasonable assurance is less than absolute assurance. Reducing assurance engagement risk to zero is very rarely attainable or cost beneficial as a result of factors such as the following:

- The use of selective testing.
- The inherent limitations of internal control.
- The fact that much of the evidence available to the assurance practitioner is persuasive rather than conclusive.
- The use of judgement in gathering and evaluating evidence and forming conclusions based on that evidence.
- In some cases, the characteristics of the subject matter.

61 Both reasonable assurance and limited assurance engagements require the application of assurance skills and techniques and the gathering of sufficient appropriate evidence as part of an iterative, systematic assurance engagement process that includes obtaining an understanding of the subject matter and other assurance engagement circumstances.

62 The nature, timing and extent of evidence-gathering procedures for gathering sufficient appropriate evidence in a limited assurance engagement are, however, deliberately limited relative to a reasonable assurance engagement. For some subject matters, there may be

8 The concepts and discussions on evidence relevant to an audit engagement are contained in Auditing Standard ASA 500 *Audit Evidence,* and may be helpful in determining the evidence applicable to an assurance engagement.

specific ASAEs to provide guidance on procedures for gathering sufficient appropriate evidence for a limited assurance engagement. In the absence of a specific ASAE, the procedures for gathering sufficient appropriate evidence will vary with the circumstances of the assurance engagement, in particular the subject matter, and the needs of the intended users and the engaging party, including relevant time and cost constraints.

63 For both reasonable assurance and limited assurance engagements, if the assurance practitioner becomes aware of a matter that leads the assurance practitioner to question whether a material revision needs to be made to the subject matter information, the assurance practitioner pursues the matter by performing other evidence-gathering procedures sufficient to enable the assurance practitioner to report.

Representations by the Responsible Party

64 The assurance practitioner shall endeavour to obtain written representations from the responsible party, as appropriate.

65 Written confirmation of oral representations reduces the possibility of misunderstandings between the assurance practitioner and the responsible party.[9] In particular, the assurance practitioner ordinarily requests from the responsible party a written representation that evaluates or measures the subject matter against the identified criteria, whether or not it is to be made available as an assertion to the intended users. Having no written representation may result in a qualified conclusion or a disclaimer of conclusion on the basis of a limitation on the scope of the assurance engagement. The assurance practitioner may also include a restriction on the use of the assurance report.

66 During an assurance engagement, the responsible party may make representations to the assurance practitioner, either unsolicited or in response to specific enquiries. When such representations relate to matters that are material to the subject matter's evaluation or measurement, the assurance practitioner ordinarily:

- Evaluates their reasonableness and consistency with other evidence obtained, including other representations.
- Considers whether those making the representations can be expected to be well informed on the particular matters.
- Obtains appropriate corroborative evidence.[10]

67 Representations by the responsible party cannot replace other evidence the assurance practitioner could reasonably expect to be available. An inability to obtain sufficient appropriate evidence regarding a matter that has, or may have, a material effect on the evaluation or measurement of the subject matter, when such evidence would ordinarily be available, constitutes a limitation on the scope of the assurance engagement, even if a representation from the responsible party has been received on the matter.

Considering Subsequent Events

68 The assurance practitioner shall consider the effect on the subject matter information and on the assurance report of events up to the date of the assurance report.

69 The extent of consideration of subsequent events depends on the potential for such events to affect the subject matter information and to affect the appropriateness of the assurance practitioner's conclusion. Consideration of subsequent events in some assurance engagements may not be relevant because of the nature of the subject matter. For example, when the assurance engagement requires a conclusion about the accuracy of a statistical return at a point in time, events occurring between that point in time and the date of the assurance report may not affect the conclusion, or require disclosure in the statistical return or the assurance report.

---

9 Matters for consideration and an illustrative example of a representation letter relevant to an audit engagement are contained in Auditing Standard ASA 580 *Management Representations*, and may be helpful in determining representations applicable to an assurance engagement.

10 Guidance on corroborative evidence relevant in investigating unusual fluctuations in an audit engagement is contained in Auditing Standard ASA 520 *Analytical Procedures*, and may be helpful in determining appropriate corroborative evidence in an assurance engagement.

ASAE

Documentation

70 The assurance practitioner shall prepare, on a timely basis, documentation that is sufficient and appropriate to provide:

(a) a basis for the assurance practitioner's conclusion; and

(b) evidence that the assurance engagement was performed in accordance with ASAEs.

71 Documentation includes a record of the assurance practitioner's reasoning on all significant matters that require the exercise of judgement, and related conclusions.[11] The existence of difficult questions of principle or judgement, calls for the documentation to include the relevant facts that were known by the assurance practitioner at the time the conclusion was reached.

72 In applying professional judgement to assessing the extent of documentation to be prepared and retained, the assurance practitioner ordinarily considers what is necessary to provide an understanding of the work performed and the basis of the principal decisions taken to another experienced assurance practitioner who has no previous experience with the assurance engagement. It is, however, neither necessary nor practicable to document every matter the assurance practitioner considers during the assurance engagement.

Preparing the Assurance Report

73 The assurance practitioner shall conclude whether sufficient appropriate evidence has been obtained to support the conclusion expressed in the assurance report.

74 In developing the conclusion, the assurance practitioner ordinarily considers all relevant evidence obtained, regardless of whether it appears to corroborate or to contradict the subject matter information.

75 The assurance report shall be in writing and shall contain a clear expression of the assurance practitioner's conclusion about the subject matter information.

76 Oral and other forms of expressing conclusions can be misunderstood without the support of a written report. For this reason, the assurance practitioner does not report orally or by use of symbols without also providing a definitive written assurance report that is readily available whenever the oral report is provided or the symbol is used. For example, a symbol could be hyperlinked to a written assurance report on the Internet.

77 This ASAE does not require a standardised format for reporting on all assurance engagements. Instead it identifies in paragraph 78 the basic elements the assurance report is to include. Assurance reports are tailored to the specific assurance engagement circumstances. The assurance practitioner chooses a short form or long form style of reporting to facilitate effective communication to the intended users. Short-form reports ordinarily include only the basic elements. Long form reports often describe in detail the terms of the assurance engagement, the criteria being used, findings relating to particular aspects of the assurance engagement and, in some cases, recommendations, as well as the basic elements. Any findings and recommendations are clearly separated from the assurance practitioner's conclusion on the subject matter information, and the wording used in presenting them makes it clear they are not intended to affect the assurance practitioner's conclusion. The assurance practitioner may use headings, paragraph numbers, typographical devices, for example the bolding of text, and other mechanisms to enhance the clarity and readability of the assurance report.

Assurance Report Content

78 The assurance report shall include the following basic elements:

(a) a title that clearly indicates the report is an independent assurance report;

(b) an addressee;

(c) an identification and description of the subject matter information and, when appropriate, the subject matter;

11 The nature, form content and extent of documentation relevant to an audit engagement are contained in Auditing Standard ASA 230 *Audit Documentation*, and may be helpful in determining the nature, form content and extent of documentation applicable to an assurance engagement.

(d) identification of the criteria;

(e) where appropriate, a description of any significant, inherent limitation associated with the evaluation or measurement of the subject matter against the criteria;

(f) when the criteria used to evaluate or measure the subject matter are available only to specific intended users, or are relevant only to a specific purpose, a statement restricting the use of the assurance report to those intended users or that purpose;

(g) a statement to identify the responsible party and to describe the responsible party's and the assurance practitioner's responsibilities;

(h) a statement that the assurance engagement was performed in accordance with ASAEs and the level of assurance provided;

(i) a summary of the work performed;

(j) the assurance practitioner's conclusion:

(i) where appropriate, the conclusion shall inform the intended users of the context in which the assurance practitioner's conclusion is to be read;

(ii) in a reasonable assurance engagement, the conclusion shall be expressed in the positive form;

(iii) in a limited assurance engagement, the conclusion shall be expressed in the negative form; and

(iv) where the assurance practitioner expresses a conclusion that is other than unqualified, the assurance report shall contain a clear description of all the reasons;

(k) the assurance report date; and

(l) the name of the firm or the assurance practitioner, and a specific location, which ordinarily is the city where the assurance practitioner maintains the office that has responsibility for the assurance engagement.

ASAE

79 The basic elements of an assurance report under paragraph 78 of this ASAE may assist the assurance practitioner as follows:

(a) the title described at paragraph 78(a) of this ASAE, indicates whether the report is an independent assurance report.[12] An appropriate title helps to identify the nature of the assurance report, and to distinguish it from reports issued by others, such as those who do not have to comply with the same ethical requirements as the assurance practitioner;

(b) an addressee identifies the party or parties to whom the assurance report is directed. Whenever practical, the assurance report is addressed to all the intended users, but in some cases there may be other intended users;

(c) identification and description of the subject matter information and, when appropriate, the subject matter may for example include:

(i) the point in time or period of time to which the evaluation or measurement of the subject matter relates;

(ii) where applicable, the name of the entity or component of the entity to which the subject matter relates; and

(iii) an explanation of those characteristics of the subject matter or the subject matter information of which the intended users ought to be aware, and how such characteristics may influence the precision of the evaluation or measurement of

12 If the assurance practitioner is not in public practice, for example an internal auditor, and if the assurance practitioner or other members of the assurance team and, when applicable, the assurance practitioner's employer, are not independent of the entity in respect of which the assurance engagement is being performed, the lack of independence and the nature of the relationship(s) with the assurance client are prominently disclosed in the assurance report. Also, that report does not include the word "independent" in its title, and the purpose and users of the report are restricted.

the subject matter against the identified criteria, or the persuasiveness of available evidence. For example:

- the degree to which the subject matter information is qualitative versus quantitative, objective versus subjective, or historical versus prospective; and
- changes in the subject matter or other assurance engagement circumstances that affect the comparability of the subject matter information from one period to the next. When the assurance practitioner's conclusion is worded in terms of the responsible party's assertion, that assertion is appended to the assurance report, reproduced in the assurance report or referenced therein to a source that is available to the intended users;

(d) the assurance report identifies the criteria against which the subject matter was evaluated or measured so the intended users can understand the basis for the assurance practitioner's conclusion. The assurance report may include the criteria, or refer to them if they are contained in an assertion prepared by the responsible party that is available to the intended users or if they are otherwise available from a readily accessible source. The assurance practitioner considers whether it is relevant to the circumstances, to disclose:

(i) the source of the criteria, and whether or not the criteria are embodied in laws or regulations, or issued by authorised or recognised bodies of experts that follow a transparent due process, that is, whether they are established criteria in the context of the subject matter (and if they are not, a description of why they are considered suitable);

(ii) measurement methods used when the criteria allow for choice between a number of methods;

(iii) any significant interpretations made in applying the criteria in the assurance engagement circumstances; and

(iv) whether there have been any changes in the measurement methods used;

(e) in terms of the appropriateness of a description of any significant, inherent limitation, in some cases inherent limitations can be expected to be well understood by readers of an assurance report, while in other cases it may be appropriate to make explicit reference in the assurance report. For example, in an assurance report related to the effectiveness of internal control, it may be appropriate to note that the historic evaluation of effectiveness is not relevant to future periods due to the risk that internal control may become inadequate because of changes in conditions, or that the degree of compliance with policies or procedures may deteriorate;

(f) whenever the assurance report is intended only for specific intended users or a specific purpose, under paragraph 78(f) of this ASAE, the assurance practitioner needs to consider stating this fact in the assurance report.[13] This provides a caution to readers that the assurance report is restricted to specific users or for specific purposes;

(g) the statement described at paragraph 78(g) of this ASAE informs the intended users that the responsible party is responsible for the subject matter in the case of a direct reporting assurance engagement, or the subject matter information in the case of an assertion-based assurance engagement, and that the assurance practitioner's role is to independently express a conclusion about the subject matter information;

(h) where there is a subject matter specific ASAE, that ASAE may require that the assurance report refer specifically to it;

13 While an assurance report may be restricted whenever it is intended only for specified intended users or for a specific purpose, the absence of a restriction regarding a particular reader or purpose does not itself indicate that a legal responsibility is owed by the assurance practitioner in relation to that reader or for that purpose. Whether a legal responsibility is owed will depend on the legal circumstances of each case and the relevant jurisdiction.

(i) a summary of the work performed will help the intended users understand the nature of the assurance conveyed by the assurance report.[14] Where no specific ASAE provides guidance on evidence-gathering procedures for a particular subject matter, the summary might include a more detailed description of the work performed. Because in a limited assurance engagement an appreciation of the nature, timing, and extent of evidence-gathering procedures performed is essential to understanding the assurance conveyed by a conclusion expressed in the negative form, the summary of the work performed:

(i) is ordinarily more detailed than for a reasonable assurance engagement and identifies the limitations on the nature, timing, and extent of evidence-gathering procedures. It may be appropriate to indicate evidence-gathering procedures that were not performed that would ordinarily be performed in a reasonable assurance engagement; and

(ii) states that the evidence-gathering procedures are more limited than for a reasonable assurance engagement, and that therefore less assurance is obtained than in a reasonable assurance engagement;

(j) separate conclusions may be provided on each aspect, where the subject matter information is made up of a number of aspects. While not all such conclusions need to relate to the same level of evidence-gathering procedures, each conclusion is expressed in the form that is appropriate to either a reasonable assurance or a limited assurance engagement:

(i) the assurance practitioner's conclusion may, for example, include wording such as: "This conclusion has been formed on the basis of, and is subject to the inherent limitations outlined elsewhere in this independent assurance report." This would be appropriate, for example, when the report includes an explanation of particular characteristics of the subject matter of which the intended users ought to be aware;

(ii) an example of a positive conclusion is: "In our opinion internal control is effective, in all material respects, based on *XYZ criteria*" or "In our opinion *the responsible party's* assertion that internal control is effective, in all material respects, based on *XYZ criteria,* is fairly stated"; and

(iii) an example of a negative conclusion is: "Based on our work described in this report, nothing has come to our attention that causes us to believe that internal control is not effective, in all material respects, based on *XYZ criteria*" or "Based on our work described in this report, nothing has come to our attention that causes us to believe that *the responsible party's* assertion that internal control is effective, in all material respects, based on *XYZ criteria,* is not fairly stated";

(k) the assurance report date informs the intended users that the assurance practitioner has considered the effect on the subject matter information and on the assurance report of events that occurred up to that date; and

(l) the name and location of the assurance practitioner informs the intended users of the individual or firm assuming responsibility for the assurance engagement.

80 The assurance practitioner may expand the assurance report to include other information and explanations that are not intended to affect the assurance practitioner's conclusion. Examples include:

- details of the qualifications and experience of the assurance practitioner and others involved with the assurance engagement;
- disclosure of materiality levels;
- findings relating to particular aspects of the assurance engagement; and
- recommendations.

Whether to include any such information depends on its significance to the needs of the intended users. Additional information is clearly separated from the assurance practitioner's conclusion and worded in such a manner so as not to affect that conclusion.

14 Auditing Standards ASA 700 *The Auditor's Report on a General Purpose Financial Report* and ASRE 2410 *Review of an Interim Financial Report Performed by the Independent Auditor of the Entity,* may provide helpful guidance in relation to the appropriate type of summary.

Modifications to the Assurance Report

81 Modifications[15] to the assurance report relate to circumstances:

(a) that require an emphasis of matter paragraph; or

(b) when the assurance practitioner is unable to express an unqualified conclusion and an assurance report is issued with either:

(i) a qualified conclusion; or

(ii) an adverse conclusion; or

(iii) a disclaimer of conclusion.

Emphasis of Matter Paragraphs, Qualified Conclusions, Adverse Conclusions and Disclaimers of Conclusion

82 An assurance practitioner shall modify the assurance report by adding an emphasis of matter paragraph to highlight a matter that is fundamental to the users' understanding of the subject matter information. The addition of an emphasis of matter paragraph does not affect the assurance practitioner's conclusion.

83 The assurance practitioner shall not express an unqualified conclusion when the following circumstances exist and, in the assurance practitioner's judgement, the effect of the matter is or may be material:

(a) there is a limitation on the scope of the assurance practitioner's work, that is, circumstances prevent, or the responsible party or the engaging party imposes a restriction that prevents, the assurance practitioner from obtaining evidence required to reduce assurance engagement risk to the appropriate level. The assurance practitioner shall express a qualified conclusion or a disclaimer of conclusion;

(b) in those cases where:

(i) the assurance practitioner's conclusion is worded in terms of the responsible party's assertion, and that assertion is not fairly stated, in all material respects; or

(ii) the assurance practitioner's conclusion is worded directly in terms of the subject matter and the criteria, and the subject matter information is materially misstated, the assurance practitioner shall express a qualified conclusion or adverse conclusion; or

(c) when it is discovered, after the assurance engagement has been accepted, that the criteria are unsuitable or the subject matter is not appropriate for an assurance engagement. The assurance practitioner shall express:

(i) a qualified conclusion or adverse conclusion when the unsuitable criteria or inappropriate subject matter is likely to mislead the intended users; or

(ii) a qualified conclusion or a disclaimer of conclusion in other cases.

In some cases the assurance practitioner shall consider withdrawing from the assurance engagement.

84 The assurance practitioner shall express a qualified conclusion when the effect of a matter is not so material or pervasive as to require an adverse conclusion or a disclaimer of conclusion. A qualified conclusion is expressed as being "except for" the effects of the matter to which the qualification relates.

85 In those cases where the assurance practitioner's unqualified conclusion would be worded in terms of the responsible party's assertion, and that assertion has identified and properly

15 Auditing Standard ASA 701 *Modifications to the Auditor's Report* may be helpful in considering modifications to the assurance report.

described that the subject matter information is materially misstated, under paragraph 84 of this ASAE, the assurance practitioner needs to either:

(a) express a qualified or adverse conclusion[16] worded directly in terms of the subject matter and the criteria; or

(b) if specifically required by the terms of the assurance engagement to word the conclusion in terms of the responsible party's assertion, express an unqualified conclusion but use an emphasis of matter[17] paragraph to specifically refer to it in the assurance report.

Other Reporting Responsibilities

86 **The assurance practitioner shall consider other reporting responsibilities, including the appropriateness of communicating relevant matters of governance interest arising from the assurance engagement with those charged with governance.**

87 In this ASAE, "governance" describes the role of persons entrusted with the supervision, control and direction of a responsible party.[18] Those charged with governance ordinarily are accountable for ensuring that an entity achieves its objectives and for reporting to interested parties. If the engaging party is different from the responsible party it may not be appropriate to communicate directly with the responsible party or those charged with governance over the responsible party.

88 In this ASAE, "relevant matters of governance interest" are those that arise from the assurance engagement and, in the assurance practitioner's opinion, are both important and relevant to those charged with governance. Relevant matters of governance interest include only those matters that have come to the attention of the assurance practitioner while performing the assurance engagement. If the terms of the assurance engagement do not specifically require it, the assurance practitioner is not required to design procedures for the specific purpose of identifying matters of governance interest.

Conformity with International Standards on Assurance Engagements

89 Except as noted below, this ASAE conforms with International Standard on Assurance Engagements ISAE 3000, *Assurance Engagements Other than Audits or Reviews of Historical Financial Information* issued by the International Auditing and Assurance Standards Board of the International Federation of Accountants. The main differences between this ASAE and ISAE 3000 are:

- This ASAE contains the following application paragraph that is not contained in ISAE 3000:
  - this Standard on Assurance Engagements (ASAE) applies to assurance engagements other than audits or reviews of historical financial information (paragraph 1).

16 In those direct reporting assurance engagements where the subject matter information is presented only in the assurance practitioner's conclusion, and the assurance practitioner concludes that the subject matter does not, in all material respects, conform with the criteria, for example: "In our opinion, except for […], internal control is effective, in all material respects, based on XYZ criteria," such a conclusion would also be considered to be qualified (or adverse as appropriate).

17 Example emphasis of matter paragraphs relevant to an audit engagement are contained in ASA 701 and may be helpful guidance in developing emphasis of matter paragraphs applicable to an assurance engagement.

18 Principles of corporate governance have generally been developed by various countries as a point of reference for the establishment of good corporate behaviour. Such principles generally focus on publicly listed companies; however, they may also serve to improve governance in other forms of entities. As board and governance structures and practices vary from country to country, there is no single model of good corporate governance. A common principle is that the entity has in place a governance structure which enables the board to exercise objective oversight over the business and management of the entity including financial reporting. Internationally, it may be appropriate to refer to the Principles of Corporate Governance, as issued from time to time, by the Organisation for Economic Co-operation and Development (OECD). In Australia, it may be appropriate to refer to the Principles of Good Corporate Governance and Best Practice Recommendations, as issued from time to time, by the Corporate Governance Council of the Australian Securities Exchange Ltd.

- In this ASAE, the term 'practitioner' has been replaced with 'assurance practitioner' to expand the application of the ASAE by other professionals. Assurance practitioner has been defined as follows:
    - for the purpose of this ASAE, an "assurance practitioner" means a person or an organisation, whether in public practice, industry, commerce or the public sector, involved in the provision of assurance services (paragraph 4).
- In this ASAE, the definition of reasonable assurance has been expanded as follows:
    - reasonable assurance means a high, but not absolute, level of assurance (paragraph 5(a)).
- This ASAE contains the following mandatory requirements that are not contained in ISAE 3000:
    - where in rare and exceptional circumstances, factors outside the assurance practitioner's control prevent the assurance practitioner from complying with a relevant mandatory requirement in this ASAE, the assurance practitioner shall:
        - if possible, perform appropriate alternative evidence-gathering procedures; and
        - document in the working papers:
            - the circumstances surrounding the inability to comply;
            - the reasons for the inability to comply; and
            - justification of how alternative evidence-gathering procedures achieve the objectives of the mandatory requirement.

      When the assurance practitioner is unable to perform appropriate alternative evidence-gathering procedures, the assurance practitioner shall consider the implications for the assurance practitioner's report (paragraph 8);
    - the assurance practitioner shall comply with the fundamental ethical principles of integrity, objectivity, professional competence and due care, confidentiality and professional behaviour (paragraph 9);
    - the assurance practitioner shall implement procedures to address the following elements of a quality control system that apply to the individual assurance engagement:
        - leadership responsibilities for quality on the assurance engagement;
        - ethical requirements;
        - acceptance and continuance of client relationships and specific assurance engagements;
        - assignment of assurance engagement teams;
        - assurance engagement performance; and
        - monitoring (paragraph 12);
    - the assurance practitioner shall accept (or continue where applicable) an assurance engagement only if, on the basis of a preliminary knowledge of the assurance engagement circumstances, nothing comes to the attention of the assurance practitioner to indicate that the requirements of the fundamental ethical principles or of the ASAEs will not be satisfied (paragraph 16);
    - the assurance practitioner shall agree on the terms of the assurance engagement with the engaging party, which shall be recorded in writing by the assurance practitioner and forwarded to the engaging party. When the assurance engagement is undertaken pursuant to legislation, the minimum applicable assurance engagement terms shall be those contained in the legislation (paragraph 20);
    - when the terms of an assurance engagement are changed, the assurance practitioner shall agree on the new terms with the engaging party and confirm them in writing (paragraph 23);

- the assurance practitioner shall prepare, on a timely basis, documentation that is sufficient and appropriate to provide:
  - a basis for the assurance practitioner's conclusion; and
  - evidence that the assurance engagement was performed in accordance with ASAEs (paragraph 70);
- an assurance practitioner shall modify the assurance report by adding an emphasis of matter paragraph to highlight a matter that is fundamental to the users' understanding of the subject matter information. The addition of an emphasis of matter paragraph does not affect the assurance practitioner's conclusion (paragraph 82); and
- in some cases the assurance practitioner shall consider withdrawing from the assurance engagement (paragraph 83 (c)).

- References to paragraphs in the *Framework for Assurance Engagements* have been replaced with the following explanatory guidance paragraphs:
  - preliminary knowledge of the assurance engagement circumstances prior to acceptance of an assurance engagement (paragraph 17);
  - characteristics of an appropriate subject matter has the following characteristics (paragraph 34); and
  - characteristics of suitable criteria (paragraph 36).
- This ASAE contains enhanced explanatory guidance on the level of documentation at paragraph 72 and explanatory guidance on modifications at paragraph 81.
- This ASAE contains footnote references to Auditing Standards (ASAs) that provide helpful guidance to assurance practitioners (paragraphs 13, 21, 26, 48, 57, 65, 66, 71, 79, 81 and 85).
- ISAE 3000 includes a Public Sector Perspective section. This ASAE does not include a separate section on the public sector as it is sector neutral.

Compliance with this Standard on Assurance Engagements enables compliance with ISAE 3000.

ASAE 3100

Compliance Engagements

(Issued June 2008: revised and reissued September 2008)

Issued by the Auditing and Assurance Standards Board.

Note from the Institute of Chartered Accountants Australia

This note, prepared by the technical editor, is not part of ASAE 3100.

Historical development

June 2008: ASAE 3100 establishes mandatory requirements and provides explanatory guidance for performing and reporting on compliance engagements other than audits or reviews of historical financial reports. There is no corresponding international statement. It is operative for engagements commencing on or after 1 October 2008.

September 2008: ASAE 3100 reissued because of subsequent technical and editorial amendments made by the AUASB.

Contents

ASAE

Preface

Reasons for Issuing Standard on Assurance Engagements ASAE 3100 *Compliance Engagements*

The AUASB makes Auditing Standards under section 336 of the *Corporations Act 2001* for the purposes of the corporations legislation and formulates auditing and assurance standards for other purposes.

The AUASB has reissued Standard on Assurance Engagements ASAE 3100 *Compliance Engagements* pursuant to the requirements of the legislative provisions explained below. This Standard was issued on 24 June 2008 and has been reissued as a result of various subsequent technical and editorial amendments made by the AUASB.

The *Corporate Law Economic Reform Program (Audit Reform and Corporate Disclosure) Act 2004* (the CLERP 9 Act) established the AUASB as an independent statutory body under section 227A of the *Australian Securities and Investments Commission Act 2001* (ASIC Act), as from 1 July 2004. Under section 227B of the ASIC Act, the AUASB may formulate Assurance Standards for purposes other than the corporations legislation.

Main Features

This Standard on Assurance Engagements (ASAE) establishes mandatory requirements and provides explanatory guidance for performing and reporting on compliance engagements other than audits or reviews of historical financial reports.

This ASAE establishes standards for compliance engagements conducted by assurance practitioners to meet emerging needs of key stakeholders as regulators and others place greater emphasis on assurance of specific reporting obligations under contracts, legislation or regulatory frameworks.

ASAE 3100 has been developed as an adjunct standard to ASAE 3000 *Assurance Engagements Other than Audits or Reviews of Historical Financial Information*. Consistent with ASAE 3000, ASAE 3100 is directed towards the conduct of both compliance audit and compliance review engagements by assurance practitioners in accordance with ASAEs.

For explanatory guidance on compliance with subject matter specific reporting obligations, under pronouncements issued by regulators, legislators or statutory bodies, the AUASB has issued subject matter specific Guidance Statements. The AUASB will continue to issue this type of guidance, from time to time as appropriate, which may supplement this Standard.

Operative Date

This Standard on Assurance Engagements is operative for reporting periods or engagements commencing on or after 1 October 2008. Early adoption of this ASAE is permitted prior to this date.

Authority Statement

The Auditing and Assurance Standards Board (AUASB) formulates this Standard on Assurance Engagements ASAE 3100 *Compliance Engagements* as set out in paragraphs 1 to 90 and Appendix 1, pursuant to section 227B of the *Australian Securities and Investments Commission Act 2001*.

This Standard on Assurance Engagements is to be read in conjunction with the *Preamble to AUASB Standards*, which sets out the intentions of the AUASB on how the Standards on Assurance Engagements are to be understood, interpreted and applied.

The mandatory requirements of this Standard on Assurance Engagements are set out in **bold-type** paragraphs.

Dated 9 September 2008

M H Kelsall
Chairman - AUASB

Standard on Assurance Engagements ASAE 3100 Compliance Engagements

Application

1 **This Standard on Assurance Engagements (ASAE) applies to compliance engagements, including both reasonable assurance and limited assurance engagements, on an entity's compliance with requirements as measured by the suitable criteria.**

Operative Date

2 **This ASAE is operative for reporting periods or engagements commencing on or after 1 October 2008. Early adoption of this ASAE is permitted prior to this date.**

Introduction

3 The purpose of this ASAE is to establish mandatory requirements and to provide explanatory guidance for performing and reporting on compliance engagements other than audits or reviews of historical financial reports.

4 An entity may have an obligation to comply with externally and/or internally imposed requirements. These requirements may be established through law and regulation, contractual arrangements or internally imposed requirements, for example company policies. This ASAE establishes mandatory requirements and explanatory guidance for practitioners engaged to provide assurance on an entity's compliance with such requirements as measured by the suitable criteria.

5 This ASAE uses the terms "reasonable assurance engagement" and "limited assurance engagement" to distinguish between the two types of compliance engagements that an assurance practitioner may perform.

Relationship with Other ASAEs, ASAs and ASREs

6 **The assurance practitioner shall comply with this ASAE, ASAE 3000 *Assurance Engagements Other than Audit or Reviews of Historical Financial Information*, and other applicable ASAEs, when performing a compliance engagement.**

7 ASAE 3000 has been written for general application to assurance engagements other than audits or reviews of historical financial information covered by ASAs or ASREs. This ASAE has been written for specific application to compliance engagements. Other ASAEs may relate to topics that apply to all subject matters or be subject matter specific. When an assurance engagement includes a number of subject matters on which there are topic specific ASAEs, e.g. performance engagements and compliance engagements, in accordance with paragraph 6 of this ASAE, the assurance practitioner needs to apply the relevant topic specific ASAEs, as well as ASAE 3000, in performing the assurance engagement.

Inability to Comply with Mandatory Requirements

8 **Where in rare and exceptional circumstances, factors outside the assurance practitioner's control prevent the assurance practitioner from complying with a relevant mandatory requirement in this ASAE, ASAE 3000 and/or any other applicable ASAE, the assurance practitioner shall:**

(a) if possible, perform appropriate alternative assurance procedures; and

(b) document in the working papers:

(i) the circumstances surrounding the inability to comply;

(ii) the reasons for the inability to comply; and

(iii) justification of how alternative assurance procedures achieve the objectives of the mandatory requirement.

When the assurance practitioner is unable to perform appropriate alternative assurance procedures, the assurance practitioner shall consider the implications for the assurance practitioner's report.

ASAE

Objective of a Compliance Engagement

9 **The objective of a compliance engagement is to enable the assurance practitioner to express a conclusion on whether an entity has complied in all material respects, with requirements as measured by the suitable criteria.**

10 The responsibility for an entity's compliance with requirements as measured by the suitable criteria rests with the responsible party. A compliance engagement performed by an assurance practitioner does not relieve the responsible party of its obligations to ensure compliance with requirements as measured by the suitable criteria.

Definitions

11 In this ASAE the following terms have the meanings attributed below:

(a) "An attitude of professional scepticism" means the assurance practitioner makes a critical assessment, with a questioning mind, of the validity of evidence obtained and is alert to evidence that contradicts or brings into question the reliability of documents and responses to enquiries and other information obtained from management and the responsible party.

(b) "Assurance Practitioner" means a person or an organisation, whether in public practice, industry, commerce or the public sector, involved in the provision of assurance services.

(c) "Assertion-based Engagement" means a compliance engagement where an entity asserts compliance with requirements as measured by the suitable criteria, and the assurance practitioner evaluates and expresses a conclusion to enhance the intended user's confidence in the entity's assertion.

(d) (i) "Compliance" means, in the context of the compliance engagement, adherence by the entity to the requirements as measured by the suitable criteria.

(ii) "Compliance Framework", for the purposes of this ASAE, means a framework used by the entity, which is designed to ensure that the entity achieves compliance, and includes governance structures, programs, processes, systems, controls and procedures.

(e) "Compliance Engagement" means an assurance engagement in which an assurance practitioner expresses a conclusion, after evaluating an entity's compliance with the requirements as measured by the suitable criteria.

(f) "Compliance Engagement Risk" means the risk that the assurance practitioner expresses an inappropriate conclusion when the entity is materially non compliant with the requirements as measured by the suitable criteria.

(g) "Direct Reporting Engagement" means a compliance engagement where the assurance practitioner directly evaluates an entity's compliance with requirements as measured by the suitable criteria and expresses a conclusion to the intended users in a compliance report.

(h) "Intended users" means the person, persons or class of persons for whom the assurance practitioner prepares the compliance report. The responsible party may be one of the intended users, but not the sole user.

(i) "Limited Assurance Engagement" means an assurance engagement where the assurance practitioner's objective is a reduction in compliance engagement risk to a level that is acceptable in the circumstances of the assurance engagement but where that risk is greater than that for a reasonable assurance engagement, as the basis for a negative form of expression of the assurance practitioner's conclusion. A limited assurance engagement is commonly referred to as a review.

(j) "Material" in the context of a compliance engagement means:

(i) in relation to potential (for risk assessment purposes) or detected (for evaluation purposes) breaches - instance(s) of non compliance that are significant, individually or collectively, in the context of the entity's compliance with the requirements as measured by the suitable criteria, and that affect the assurance practitioner's conclusion; and/or

(ii) in relation to the compliance framework and controls - instance(s) of deficiency that are significant in the context of the entity's control environment and that may raise the compliance engagement risk sufficiently to affect the assurance practitioner's conclusion.

(k) "Reasonable Assurance Engagement" means an assurance engagement where the assurance practitioner's objective is a reduction in compliance engagement risk to an acceptably low level in the circumstances of the compliance engagement as the basis for a positive form of expression of the assurance practitioner's conclusion. Reasonable assurance means a high, but not absolute, level of assurance. A reasonable assurance engagement is commonly referred to as an audit.

(l) "Responsible Party" means the person (or persons) who:

(i) In a direct reporting engagement, is responsible for the subject matter.

(ii) In an assertion-based engagement, is responsible for the subject matter information (the assertion).

(m) "Suitable criteria" means the reasonable and acceptable standards of compliance which are subject to the compliance engagement. Suitable criteria have the following characteristics:

(i) reliability: reliable criteria allow reasonably consistent evaluation or measurement of the subject matter, when used in similar circumstances by similarly qualified assurance practitioners;

(ii) neutrality: neutral criteria contribute to conclusions that are free from bias;

(iii) understandability: understandable criteria contribute to conclusions that are clear, comprehensive, and not subject to significantly different interpretations;

(iv) relevance: relevant criteria contribute to conclusions that assist decision-making by the intended users; and

(v) completeness: criteria are sufficiently complete when relevant factors that could affect the conclusions in the context of the assurance engagement circumstances are not omitted.

ASAE

General Principles of a Compliance Engagement

Ethical Requirements

12 **The assurance practitioner shall comply with the fundamental ethical principles of integrity, objectivity, professional competence and due care, confidentiality and professional behaviour.**

13 The concept of independence is fundamental to the assurance practitioner's compliance with the principles of integrity and objectivity under paragraph 12 of this ASAE.

14 The applicable code of ethics of a professional accounting body[1] provides a framework of principles that members of assurance teams, firms and network firms use to identify threats to independence, evaluate the significance of those threats and, if the threats are other than clearly insignificant:

(a) identify and apply safeguards to eliminate the threats; or

(b) reduce them to an acceptable level,

such that independence of mind and independence in appearance are not compromised.

Where the practitioner is not able to comply with the fundamental ethical principles, including those relating to independence, the practitioner cannot claim compliance with this ASAE. In such circumstances, ASAE 3100 may still provide useful guidance.

1 The applicable code of ethics of the professional accounting bodies in Australia is *APES 110 Code of Ethics for Professional Accountants,* as issued from time to time by the Accounting Professional and Ethical Standards Board. This code of ethics has been adopted by CPA Australia, National Institute of Accountants, and The Institute of Chartered Accountants in Australia. In addition, codes of ethics issued by other professional bodies may apply.

Quality Control

15 **The assurance practitioner shall implement procedures to address the following elements of a quality control system that apply to an individual compliance engagement:**

(a) **leadership responsibilities for quality on the compliance engagement;**

(b) **ethical requirements;**

(c) **acceptance and continuance of client relationships and specific compliance engagements;**

(d) **assignment of compliance engagement teams;**

(e) **conduct of the compliance engagement; and**

(f) **monitoring.**

16 For further guidance on quality control refer to ASAE 3000[2].

Compliance Engagement Acceptance and Continuance

17 **The assurance practitioner shall accept (or continue where applicable) a compliance engagement in accordance with the requirements of ASAE 3000.**

18 For further guidance on engagement acceptance and continuance refer to ASAE 3000[3].

Agreeing on the Terms of the Compliance Engagement

19 **The assurance practitioner shall communicate or agree on the terms of the compliance engagement with the responsible party, which shall be recorded in writing by the assurance practitioner and forwarded to the responsible party. Where the compliance engagement is undertaken pursuant to legislation, the minimum applicable compliance engagement terms shall be those contained in the legislation.**

20 Under paragraph 19 of this ASAE the assurance practitioner needs to consider:

(a) the objectives of the compliance engagement;

(b) the scope of the compliance engagement; and

(c) the suitable criteria against which compliance is to be assessed.

21 For further guidance on agreeing on the terms of the compliance engagement refer to ASAE 3000[4].

Planning and Performing the Compliance Engagement

22 **The assurance practitioner shall plan a compliance engagement so that it will be performed effectively.**

23 Planning involves developing an overall strategy for the scope, emphasis, timing and conduct of the compliance engagement, and a compliance engagement plan, consisting of a detailed approach outlining the nature, timing and extent of evidence gathering procedures to be performed and the reasons for selecting them.[5] Ordinarily, adequate planning:

- Helps to ensure that appropriate attention is devoted to important areas of the engagement based on an assessment of compliance engagement risk, identify potential problems on a timely basis and properly organise and manage the compliance engagement in order for it to be performed in an effective manner.
- Assists the assurance practitioner to properly assign work to compliance engagement team members, and facilitates their direction and supervision and the review of their work.
- Assists, where applicable, in the coordination of work done by other assurance practitioners and experts.

2 See ASAE 3000, paragraph 13.

3 See ASAE 3000, paragraphs 15, 17 and 19.

4 See ASAE 3000, paragraphs 21 and 24.

5 The planning procedures relevant to an audit engagement are contained in Auditing Standard ASA 300 *Planning an Audit of a Financial Report*, and may be helpful in determining planning procedures applicable to a compliance engagement.

24 Ordinarily, the matters the assurance practitioner considers as part of the planning activities include:

- The terms of the engagement.
- The characteristics of the requirements and the suitable criteria.
- The engagement process and possible sources of evidence.
- Understanding of the entity, its environment and the compliance framework, including the risks that the entity may not be compliant with the requirements as measured by the suitable criteria.
- Identification of intended users and their needs, and consideration of materiality and the components of compliance engagement risk.
- Personnel and expertise requirements, including the nature and extent of experts' involvement if required.

25 Planning is not a discrete phase, but rather a continual and iterative process throughout the compliance engagement. As a result of unexpected events, changes in conditions, or the evidence obtained from the results of evidence-gathering procedures, the assurance practitioner may need to revise the overall strategy and compliance engagement plan, and the nature, timing and extent of further evidence-gathering procedures.

26 As part of the planning phase of the compliance engagement the assurance practitioner ordinarily performs a combination of evidence-gathering procedures. The types of procedures that may be undertaken include:

- Risk assessment on the overall compliance framework.
- Compliance framework process review.
- Compliance framework controls review.
- Review of work performed by the internal compliance function and assessment of the reliance that may be placed on this work by the assurance practitioner.

27 The assurance practitioner shall plan and perform a compliance engagement with an attitude of professional scepticism recognising that circumstances may exist that cause the entity to be non compliant with the requirements as measured by the suitable criteria.

Understanding the Entity

28 The assurance practitioner shall obtain an understanding of the entity, the requirements, suitable criteria and other compliance engagement circumstances, sufficient to identify and assess the risks of the entity's non compliance with the requirements as measured by the suitable criteria, and sufficient to design and perform further evidence-gathering procedures.

29 Obtaining an understanding of the entity, requirements, suitable criteria and other engagement circumstances is an essential part of planning and performing a compliance engagement. That understanding ordinarily provides the assurance practitioner with a frame of reference for exercising professional judgement throughout the compliance engagement, for example when:

- Considering the elements of the compliance framework.
- Identifying where special consideration may be necessary, for example factors indicative of fraud, and the need for specialised skills or the work of an expert.
- Establishing and evaluating the continued appropriateness of quantitative materiality levels (where appropriate), and/or considering qualitative materiality factors.
- Designing and performing further evidence-gathering procedures to reduce compliance engagement risk to an acceptable level.
- Evaluating evidence, including the reasonableness of the responsible party's oral and written representations.

30 The assurance practitioner considers whether the understanding is sufficient to assess the risks that the entity is materially noncompliant with the requirements as measured by the suitable criteria.

Elements of a Compliance Framework

31 **In planning a compliance engagement to facilitate the design of appropriate evidence-gathering procedures, the assurance practitioner shall obtain an understanding of the entity's compliance environment, and shall document the key elements of the entity's compliance framework.**

32 The nature and extent of planning and subsequent evidence-gathering procedures will vary with the engagement circumstances, and the maturity of the entity's compliance framework.

Elements of an entity's compliance framework ordinarily include the following:

- Procedures for identifying and updating compliance obligations.
- Staff training and awareness programs.
- Procedures for assessing the impact of compliance obligations on the entity's key business activities.
- Controls embedded within key business processes designed to ensure compliance with obligations.
- Processes to identify and monitor the implementation of further mitigating actions required to ensure that compliance obligations are met.
- A monitoring plan to test key compliance controls on a periodic basis and report exceptions.
- Procedures for identifying, assessing, rectifying and reporting compliance incidents and breaches.
- Periodic sign off by management and/or external third party outsourced service providers as to compliance with obligations.
- A compliance governance structure that establishes responsibility for the oversight of compliance control activities with those charged with governance, typically a Board Audit, Risk Management or Compliance Committee.

Assessing the Appropriateness of the Subject Matter

33 **The assurance practitioner shall assess the appropriateness of the subject matter.**

34 An appropriate subject matter is:

(a) identifiable, and capable of consistent evaluation or measurement against the identified criteria; and

(b) such that the information about it can be subjected to procedures for gathering sufficient appropriate evidence to support a reasonable assurance or limited assurance conclusion, as appropriate.

Examples of subject matters that may be appropriate for a compliance engagement include compliance with the following:

- Risk Management Strategy & Plan (RMS/RMP).
- Treasurer's Instructions.
- Managed Investment Schemes – Compliance Plan.

35 For further guidance on assessing the appropriateness of the subject matter refer to ASAE 3000[6].

Assessing the Suitability of the Criteria

36 **The assurance practitioner shall assess the suitability of the criteria to evaluate or measure the subject matter.**

37 Where the criteria are prescribed by legislation or regulation, paragraph 36 of this ASAE may be deemed to be complied with by the assurance practitioner. In circumstances where this is not the case, the assurance practitioner needs to assess the suitability of the criteria to measure the requirement.

6 See ASAE 3000, paragraph 34.

38 In the context of a compliance engagement, examples of suitable criteria include:

- Externally imposed criteria under law or directives, including:
  - Legislation.
  - Regulation.
  - Other statutory requirements (e.g. ASIC Regulatory Guides and Practice Notes or APRA Prudential Standards).
  - Ministerial directives.
  - Industry or professional obligations (professional standards or guidance, codes of practice or conduct).
  - Enforceable contractual obligations.
  - Enforceable undertakings.
- Internally imposed criteria, as determined by management, including:
  - Organisational policies and procedures.
  - Frameworks, for example, compliance framework based on AS 3806 – Australian Standard Compliance Programs

39 For further guidance on assessing the suitability of the criteria refer to ASAE 3000[7].

Materiality and Compliance Engagement Risk

40 The assurance practitioner shall consider materiality and compliance engagement risk when planning and performing a compliance engagement.

Materiality

41 Under paragraph 40 of this ASAE, the assurance practitioner needs to consider materiality when determining the nature, timing and extent of evidence-gathering procedures, and when evaluating whether a compliance breach is material. In considering materiality, the assurance practitioner ordinarily understands and assesses what factors might influence the decisions of the intended users.

42 Ordinarily, the assurance practitioner considers materiality in the context of quantitative and qualitative factors, such as relative magnitude of instances of detected or suspected non compliance, the nature and extent of the effect of these factors on the evaluation of compliance with the requirements as measured by the suitable criteria, and the interests of the intended users. The assessment of materiality and the relative importance of quantitative and qualitative factors in a particular engagement are matters for the assurance practitioner's professional judgement.

Compliance Engagement Risk

43 The assurance practitioner shall reduce compliance engagement risk to an acceptable level in the circumstances of the compliance engagement.

44 In a reasonable assurance engagement, under paragraph 43 of this ASAE, the assurance practitioner needs to reduce compliance engagement risk to an acceptably low level in the circumstances of the engagement to obtain reasonable assurance as the basis for a positive form of expression of the assurance practitioner's conclusion.

45 In a limited assurance engagement, the combination of the nature, timing, and extent of evidence-gathering procedures is at least sufficient for the assurance practitioner to obtain a meaningful level of assurance as the basis for a negative form of expression of the assurance practitioner's conclusion. The level of accepted compliance engagement risk is higher in a limited assurance engagement than in a reasonable assurance engagement because of the different nature, timing and extent of evidence gathering procedures.

46 In general, compliance engagement risk comprises inherent risk, control risk and detection risk. The degree to which the assurance practitioner's consideration of these components is reflected in the engagement evidence gathering process is affected by the engagement

7 See ASAE 3000, paragraphs 36 to 39.

circumstances, in particular the nature of the requirements and whether a reasonable assurance or a limited assurance engagement is being performed. The components of risk that may require further consideration include those pertaining to compliance policies, resources, monitoring, detection and documentation as outlined in paragraph 31 and 32 of this ASAE.

47 **Where there are material deficiencies in the entity's compliance framework the assurance practitioner shall assess the impact on the risk of non-compliance with the requirements as measured by the suitable criteria, and the implication for planning and performing the engagement.**

48 Under paragraph 31 of this ASAE, if the assurance practitioner becomes aware of material deficiencies in the compliance framework for example:

- a limited or inadequate monitoring plan for key compliance controls over the period; and/or
- a lack of staff training and awareness of the need to identify, assess and report compliance breaches

the assurance practitioner needs to consider the following implications:

(a) risk of non compliance being increased;

(b) amount and type of evidence gathering procedures to obtain sufficient appropriate evidence; and

(c) reporting of material deficiencies to the responsible party and the intended users.

49 **The assurance practitioner shall evaluate any compliance breach with the requirements as measured by the suitable criteria to determine if the breach is material, and how this may impact on the assurance practitioner's planned engagement approach under paragraph 22 of this ASAE.**

50 The assurance practitioner ordinarily considers the following factors in evaluating if a compliance breach by the entity with the requirements, is material:

(a) size, complexity and nature of the entity's activities;

(b) nature of the breach – one off or systemic;

(c) evidence of a robust compliance framework in place to detect, rectify and report compliance breaches;

(d) commonly accepted practice within the relevant industry;

(e) regulatory, legislative or contractual requirements;

(f) impact on the decisions of the intended users and stakeholders of the entity; and

(g) specific terms of the compliance engagement.

Obtaining Evidence

51 **The assurance practitioner shall obtain sufficient appropriate evidence on which to base the conclusion.**

52 Sufficiency is the measure of the quantity of evidence. Appropriateness is the measure of the quality of evidence; that is, its relevance and its reliability. The assurance practitioner ordinarily considers the relationship between the cost of obtaining evidence and the usefulness of the information obtained. However, the matter of difficulty or expense involved is not in itself a valid basis for omitting an evidence-gathering procedure for which there is no alternative. The assurance practitioner uses professional judgement and exercises professional scepticism in evaluating the quantity and quality of evidence, and thus its sufficiency and appropriateness, to support the conclusion in the compliance report.

53 In a compliance engagement evidence may be gathered through enquiry and observation, tests of controls, substantive testing, and representations received from management.[8]

8 The concepts and discussions on evidence relevant to an audit engagement are contained in Auditing Standard ASA 500 *Audit Evidence*, and may be helpful in determining the evidence applicable to a compliance engagement.

54 The amount of evidence from each source which is deemed by the assurance practitioner to constitute sufficient, reliable evidence to reduce compliance engagement risk to an acceptable level is a matter for the assurance practitioner's professional judgement.

55 A compliance engagement rarely involves the authentication of documentation, nor is the assurance practitioner trained as or expected to be an expert in such authentication. Under paragraph 51of this ASAE, the assurance practitioner needs to consider the reliability of the information to be used as evidence, for example photocopies, facsimiles, filmed, digitised or other electronic documents, including consideration of controls over their preparation and maintenance where relevant.

56 In a compliance engagement sufficient appropriate evidence is obtained as part of an iterative, systematic engagement process involving:

(a) obtaining an understanding of the entity's business and its compliance environment which includes the key elements of the entity's compliance framework;

(b) obtaining an understanding of the requirements, the suitable criteria and other engagement circumstances which, depending on the subject matter, may include obtaining an understanding of internal controls and testing the effectiveness of these controls;

(c) obtaining an understanding of the internal compliance function where appropriate and any relevant testing of compliance controls performed as part of that function during the period. Evaluating the results of this testing and the level of reliance that can be placed on this work and the impact on further control and substantive procedures;

(d) based on the understanding acquired under (a), (b) and (c), assessing the risks that the entity may be non compliant with requirements as measured by the suitable criteria;

(e) responding to assessed risks, including developing overall responses, and determining the nature, timing and extent of further procedures; and

(f) performing further evidence-gathering procedures clearly linked to the identified compliance engagement risks, using a combination of inspection, observation, confirmation, recalculation, re-performance and enquiry. Such further evidence-gathering procedures may involve substantive procedures, including obtaining corroborating information from sources independent of the entity, and depending on the nature of the activity or subject matter, tests of the operating effectiveness of controls.

57 In a compliance engagement the assurance practitioner ordinarily performs a combination of evidence gathering procedures that reflect a strategy to obtain planned levels of assurance from testing of the compliance framework, controls and substantive testing. It is unlikely that sufficient assurance may be obtained from only performing one type of testing. The type and extent of these procedures will be based on the complexity of the entity, nature of the business and initial risk assessment. The types of procedures that may be undertaken are:

(a) controls testing and walk throughs in key risk areas;

(b) substantive testing; and

(c) enquiries of management and representations.

The results of the above testing are ordinarily evaluated by the assurance practitioner to ensure the evidence gathered is sufficient and appropriate for the purposes of the engagement.

Representations by the Responsible Party

58 The assurance practitioner shall endeavour to obtain written representations from the responsible party, as appropriate.

59 Written confirmation of oral representations reduces the possibility of misunderstandings between the assurance practitioner and the responsible party.[9] In particular, the assurance practitioner ordinarily requests from the responsible party a written representation that measures the requirements against the suitable criteria, whether or not it is to be made available as an assertion to the intended users. Having no written representation may result

9 Matters for consideration and an illustrative example of an representation letter relevant to an audit engagement are contained in Auditing Standard ASA 580 *Management Representations*, and may be helpful in determining representations applicable to a compliance engagement.

ASAE

in a qualified conclusion or a disclaimer of conclusion on the basis of a limitation on the scope of the engagement. The assurance practitioner may also include a restriction on the use of the compliance report.

60 During a compliance engagement, the responsible party may make representations to the assurance practitioner, either unsolicited or in response to specific enquiries. When such representations relate to matters that are material to the requirements' evaluation or measurement, the assurance practitioner ordinarily:

- Evaluates their reasonableness and consistency with other evidence obtained, including other representations.
- Considers whether those making the representations can be expected to be well informed on the particular matters.
- Obtains appropriate corroborative evidence.

61 Representations by the responsible party cannot replace other evidence the assurance practitioner may reasonably expect to be available. An inability to obtain sufficient appropriate evidence regarding a matter that has, or may have, a material effect on the evaluation or measurement of the requirement, when such evidence would ordinarily be available, constitutes a limitation on the scope of the engagement, even if a representation from the responsible party has been received on the matter.

Using the Work of an Expert

62 When using the work of an expert in a compliance engagement, the assurance practitioner shall collect and evaluate evidence, in accordance with ASAE 3000.

63 For further guidance on using the work of an expert refer to ASAE 3000[10].

Evaluation and Communication of Deficiencies and Breaches

64 The assurance practitioner shall evaluate, individually and in aggregate, whether deficiencies and/or compliance breaches that have come to the attention of the assurance practitioner are material.

65 Under paragraph 64 of this ASAE, the assurance practitioner needs to exercise professional judgement in evaluating the materiality of deficiencies and compliance breaches.

66 In evaluating any deficiencies and compliance breaches the assurance practitioner ordinarily considers materiality as specified in the terms of engagement, any relevant legislative, regulatory or other (e.g. contractual) requirements which may apply and the effect on the decisions of the intended users of the compliance report and the assurance practitioner's conclusion.

67 For both reasonable assurance and limited assurance engagements, if the assurance practitioner becomes aware of a matter that leads the assurance practitioner to question whether a material compliance breach or deficiency exists, the assurance practitioner would ordinarily pursue the matter by performing other evidence-gathering procedures sufficient to enable the assurance practitioner to form a conclusion.

68 The assurance practitioner shall make the responsible party aware as soon as practicable, of material deficiencies and/or compliance breaches which have come to the assurance practitioner's attention.

69 The assurance practitioner's communications with the responsible party may be made orally or in writing. Ordinarily, the assurance practitioner's decision whether to communicate orally or in writing is affected by factors including the following:

- The size, operating structure, legal structure, and communications processes of the entity.
- The nature, sensitivity and significance of the matters to be communicated.

10 See ASAE 3000, paragraphs 48, 49, 50, 52, 53 and 55.

- The arrangements made with respect to periodic meetings or reporting of findings from the engagement.
- The extent of on-going contact and dialogue the assurance practitioner has with the responsible party.

Considering Subsequent Events

70 **The assurance practitioner shall consider the effect on the entity's compliance with requirements and the compliance report of events up to the date of the compliance report.**

71 The extent of consideration of subsequent events depends on the potential for such events to affect compliance with the requirements as measured by the suitable criteria, and to affect the appropriateness of the assurance practitioner's conclusion. Consideration of subsequent events in some compliance engagements may not be relevant because of the nature of the subject matter and the period which is being reported on. For example, if a one off material breach occurs in the period subsequent to the period that is being reported, this may not impact on the assurance practitioner's conclusion, however, it would ordinarily be reported to the responsible party. If the material breach was indicative of a systemic issue that has potential to impact the period on which the assurance practitioner is reporting, then, under paragraph 71 of this ASAE, those events need further consideration in assessing the assurance practitioner's conclusion.

Documentation

72 **The assurance practitioner shall prepare, on a timely basis, documentation that is sufficient and appropriate to provide:**

(a) a basis for the assurance practitioner's conclusion; and

(b) evidence that the compliance engagement was performed in accordance with this ASAE, ASAE 3000 and other applicable ASAEs.

73 Documentation required under paragraph 72 of this ASAE, includes a record of the assurance practitioner's reasoning on all significant matters that require the exercise of judgement, and related conclusions.[11] The existence of difficult questions of principle or judgement calls for the documentation to include the relevant facts that were known by the assurance practitioner at the time the conclusion was reached.

74 It is neither necessary nor practical to document every matter the assurance practitioner considers. In applying professional judgement in assessing the extent of documentation to be prepared and retained, the assurance practitioner may consider what is necessary to provide an understanding of the work performed and the basis of the principal decisions taken (but not the detailed aspects of the engagement) to another experienced assurance practitioner who has no previous experience with the engagement. That other assurance practitioner may only be able to obtain an understanding of detailed aspects of the engagement by discussing them with the assurance practitioner who prepared the documentation.

Preparing the Compliance Report

75 **The assurance practitioner shall determine whether sufficient appropriate evidence has been obtained to support the conclusion expressed in the compliance report.**

76 In circumstances when a compliance engagement incorporates both reasonable assurance and limited assurance conclusions, under paragraph 75 of this ASAE, the assurance practitioner needs to clearly separate the two types of conclusions expressed.

77 In developing the conclusion, the assurance practitioner ordinarily considers all relevant evidence obtained, regardless of whether it appears to corroborate or to contradict the subject matter information.

11 The nature, form content and extent of documentation relevant to an audit engagement are contained in Auditing Standard ASA 230 *Audit Documentation*, and may be helpful in determining the nature, form content and extent of documentation applicable to a compliance engagement.

78 **The compliance report shall be in writing and shall contain a clear expression of the assurance practitioner's conclusion about the entity's compliance with the requirements as measured by the suitable criteria.**

79 ASAE 3000 and this ASAE do not require a standardised format for reporting on all compliance engagements. Instead, this ASAE identifies in paragraph 80 the basic elements the compliance report is to include. Compliance reports are tailored to the specific compliance engagement circumstances. The assurance practitioner may choose a short form or long form style of reporting to facilitate effective communication to the intended users. Short form reports ordinarily include only the basic elements. Long form reports often describe in detail the terms of the compliance engagement, the suitable criteria being used, findings relating to particular aspects of the compliance engagement and, in some cases, recommendations, as well as the basic elements. The assurance practitioner may use headings, paragraph numbers, typographical devices, for example the bolding of text, and other mechanisms, to enhance the clarity and readability of the compliance report.

Compliance Report Content

80 **The compliance report shall include the following basic elements:**

(a) a title that clearly indicates the report is an independent assurance report;

(b) an addressee;

(c) identification and description of the requirements;

(d) the period of compliance being reported on by the assurance practitioner;

(e) identification of the suitable criteria;

(f) where appropriate, a description of any significant, inherent limitation associated with the evaluation of compliance with the requirements as measured by the suitable criteria;

(g) when the suitable criteria used to evaluate the requirements are available only to specific intended users, or are relevant only for a specific purpose, a statement restricting the use of the compliance report to those intended users or that purpose;

(h) a statement to identify the responsible party and to describe the responsible party's and the assurance practitioner's responsibilities;

(i) a statement that the engagement was performed in accordance with applicable ASAEs (ASAE 3100 *Compliance Engagements*) and the level of assurance provided;

(j) a summary of the work performed;

(k) the assurance practitioner's conclusion:

(i) in a reasonable assurance engagement, the conclusion shall be expressed in the positive form;

(ii) in a limited assurance engagement, the conclusion shall be expressed in the negative form; and

(iii) where the assurance practitioner expresses a conclusion that is other than unqualified, the compliance report shall contain a clear description of all the reasons;

(l) the compliance report date; and

(m) the name of the firm or the assurance practitioner, and a specific location, which is ordinarily the city where the assurance practitioner maintains the office that has responsibility for the engagement.

other than to the extent that these elements are inconsistent with legislation or regulation.

81 A compliance report ordinarily describes relevant facts and findings sufficient to allow readers to understand the basis upon which the assurance practitioner's conclusion has been formed. Findings arise from an examination of the underlying facts, comparisons with suitable criteria and the assurance practitioner's analysis of differences between what is

observed and the suitable criteria, including, where applicable, the causes and effects of the differences.

82 For further guidance on compliance report content refer to ASAE 3000[12].

Reporting Additional Information - Findings and Recommendations

83 The assurance practitioner may expand the compliance report to include other information and explanations that do not directly affect the assurance practitioner's conclusion, but provide additional useful information to the users. Examples include:

- Disclosure of materiality considerations applied.
- Findings relating to particular aspects of the compliance engagement.
- Recommendations.

The inclusion of this information depends on its significance to the needs of the intended users. Additional information is clearly separated from the assurance practitioner's conclusion and worded in a manner that does not affect that conclusion.

Modifications to the Compliance Report

84 The assurance practitioner shall not express an unqualified conclusion when the following circumstances exist and, in the assurance practitioner's judgement, the effect of the matter is that material non compliance with the requirements as measured by the suitable criteria may exist:

(a) there is a limitation on the scope of the assurance practitioner's work, that is, circumstances prevent, or the responsible party or the engaging party imposes a restriction that prevents the assurance practitioner from obtaining evidence required to reduce compliance engagement risk to the appropriate level. The assurance practitioner shall express a qualified conclusion or a disclaimer of conclusion;

(b) in those cases where:

(i) the assurance practitioner's conclusion is worded in terms of the responsible party's assertion, and that assertion is not fairly stated, in all material respects; or

(ii) the assurance practitioner's conclusion is worded directly in terms of the requirements and the suitable criteria, and the entity is non compliant with the requirements as measured by the suitable criteria in all material respects,[13] the assurance practitioner shall express a qualified or adverse conclusion; or

(c) when it is discovered, after the engagement has been accepted, that the criteria are unsuitable or the subject matter is not appropriate for a compliance engagement, the assurance practitioner shall express:

(i) a qualified or adverse conclusion when the unsuitable criteria or inappropriate subject matter is likely to mislead the intended users; or

(ii) a qualified conclusion or a disclaimer of conclusion in other cases.

Where appropriate, the assurance practitioner shall consider withdrawing from the engagement.

85 The assurance practitioner shall express a qualified conclusion when the effect of a matter is not so material or pervasive as to require an adverse conclusion or a disclaimer of conclusion. A qualified conclusion is expressed as being "except for" or otherwise discloses the effects of the matter to which the qualification relates.

---

12 See ASAE 3000, paragraph 79.

13 In those direct reporting engagements where the requirement information is presented only in the practitioner's conclusion, and the practitioner concludes that the requirement does not, in all material respects, conform with the criteria, for example: "In our opinion, except for […], the compliance plan of XYZ meets the requirements under s601HG(3) of the *Corporations Act 2001*, in all material respects, based on XYZ criteria," such a conclusion would be considered also to be qualified (or adverse as appropriate).

86 In those cases where the assurance practitioner's unqualified conclusion would be worded in terms of the responsible party's assertion, and that assertion has identified and properly described that the entity is non compliant with the requirements as measured by the suitable criteria, under paragraph 85 of this ASAE, the assurance practitioner needs to either:

(a) express a qualified or adverse conclusion worded directly in terms of the requirements and the suitable criteria; or

(b) if specifically required by the terms of the engagement to word the conclusion in terms of the responsible party's assertion, express an unqualified conclusion but emphasise the matter by specifically referring to it in the compliance report.

87 Where an assurance practitioner identifies a matter that gives rise to a qualified, adverse or a disclaimer of conclusion under paragraphs 84 and 85 of this ASAE, the assurance practitioner needs to consider any obligations under the terms of the engagement to separately report these matters to the responsible party and/or the intended users of the compliance report.

Other Reporting Responsibilities

88 In addition to communicating material deficiencies and compliance breaches, as required by paragraphs 68 and 87 of this ASAE, the assurance practitioner shall consider other reporting responsibilities as specified in the terms of the engagement, including the appropriateness of communicating relevant matters of governance interest arising from the compliance engagement with the responsible party.

89 The assurance practitioner shall consider any other reporting obligations set by regulators, legislators and statutory bodies.

Conformity with International Standards on Assurance Engagements

90 There is no corresponding International Standard on Assurance Engagements.

Appendix 1

Example Assurance Practitioner Reports

The following example reports are to be used as a guide only and will need to be adapted according to individual engagement requirements and circumstances.

Note: Each example report provides two illustrative conclusions:

(A) Unqualified and (B) Qualified.

Example 1

EXAMPLE OF A COMPLIANCE REPORT - REASONABLE ASSURANCE {AUDIT} REPORT

INDEPENDENT ASSURANCE PRACTIONER'S COMPLIANCE AUDIT REPORT

To [Intended Users]

Report on the [appropriate title for the compliance report]

We have audited the compliance of [name of entity] with the [requirements] as measured by the [suitable criteria] for the [period from …./…/….. to…./…./…..].

Respective Responsibilities

The [Responsible Party] is responsible for compliance with the [requirements] as measured by the [suitable criteria].

Our responsibility is to express a conclusion on compliance with the [requirements] as measured by the [suitable criteria], in all material respects. Our audit has been conducted in accordance with applicable Standards on Assurance Engagements (ASAE 3100 *Compliance Engagements*) to provide reasonable assurance that the [name of entity] has complied with the [requirements] as measured by the [suitable criteria]. Our procedures included [level of detail included to be determined by the assurance practitioner]. These procedures have been undertaken to form a conclusionas to whether the [name of entity] has complied in all material respects, withthe [requirements], as measured by the [suitable criteria] for the [period from…./…/….. to…./…./…..].

Use of Report

This compliance audit report has been prepared for the [Intended Users] of [name of entity] in accordance with [suitable criteria which may be prescribed by legislation or regulation]. We disclaim any assumption ofresponsibility for any reliance on this report to any persons or users other than the [Intended Users] of [name of entity], or for any purpose other than that for which it was prepared.

Inherent Limitations (include where appropriate under paragraph 80(f) of ASAE 3100)

Because of the inherent limitations of any [details provided as appropriate by the assurance practitioner, refer to limitations in evidence gathering procedures and limitations in the responsible party's internal control framework], it is possible that fraud, error or non compliance may occur and not be detected. An audit is not designed to detect all instances of non compliance with the [requirements] as measured by the [suitable criteria], as an audit is not performed continuously throughout the [period] and the audit procedures performed in respect of compliance with [requirements] as measured by the [suitable criteria] are undertaken on a test basis. The audit conclusion expressed in this report has been formed on the above basis.

Conclusion

(A) Unqualified

In our opinion, [name of entity] has complied, in all material respects, with the [requirements] as measured by the [suitable criteria] for the [period from…./…/….. to…./…./…..].

Or

(B) Qualified (under paragraph 84(b)(ii) of ASAE 3100 *Compliance Engagements*)

In our opinion, except for [detail the exception(s) or provide details under a separate section of the report], [name of entity] has complied, in all material respects, with the [requirements] as measured by the [suitable criteria] for the [period from …./…/….. to…../…./…..].

Findings and Recommendations (include as determined by the assurance practitioner under paragraph 83 of ASAE 3100)

[This section of the report would provide relevant and sufficient information to allow readers to understand the basis upon which the assurance practitioner's conclusion has been formed. The inclusion of this information depends on its significance to the needs of the intended users].

[Assurance Practitioner's signature]

[Date of the Assurance Practitioner's review report]

[Assurance Practitioner's address]

Example 2

EXAMPLE OF A COMPLIANCE REPORT - LIMITED ASSURANCE {REVIEW} REPORT

INDEPENDENT ASSURANCE PRACTIONER'S COMPLIANCE REVIEW REPORT

To [Intended Users]

Report on the [appropriate title for the compliance report]

We have reviewed the compliance of [name of entity] with the [requirements] as measured by the [suitable criteria] for the [period from …./…/….. to…./…./…..].

Respective Responsibilities

The [Responsible Party] is responsible for compliance with the [requirements] as measured by the [suitable criteria].

Our responsibility is to express a conclusion on compliance with the [requirements] as measured by the [suitable criteria], in all material respects. Our review has been conducted in accordance with applicable Standards on Assurance Engagements (ASAE 3100 *Compliance Engagements*)

to provide limited assurance that the [name of entity] has complied with the [requirements] as measured by the [suitable criteria]. Our procedures included [level of detail included to be determined by the assurance practitioner]. These procedures have been undertaken to form a conclusion, that nothing has come to our attention that causes us to believe that [name of entity] does not comply in all material respects, with the [requirements], as measured by the [suitable criteria] for the [period from …./…/….. to…./…./…..].

Use of Report

The compliance review report was prepared for the [Intended Users] of [name of entity] in accordance with [suitable criteria which may be prescribed by legislation or regulation]. We disclaim any assumption of responsibility for any reliance on this report to any persons or users other than the [Intended Users] of [name of entity], or for any purpose other than that for which it was prepared.

Inherent Limitations (include where appropriate under paragraph 80(f) of ASAE 3100)

Because of the inherent limitations of any [details provided as appropriate by the assurance practitioner, refer to limitations in evidence gathering procedures and limitations in the responsible party's internal control framework], it is possible that fraud, error or non compliance may occur and not be detected. A review is not designed to detect all instances of non compliance with the [requirements] as measured by the [suitable criteria], as it generally comprises making enquiries, primarily of the responsible party, and applying analytical and other review procedures. The review conclusion expressed in this report has been formed on the above basis.

Conclusion

(A) Unqualified

Based on our review, which is not an audit, nothing has come to our attention that causes us to believe that [name of entity] does not comply, in all material respects, with the [requirements] as measured by the [suitable criteria] for the [period from …./…/….. to…./…./…..].

Or

(B) Qualified (under paragraph 84(b)(ii) of ASAE 3100)

Based on our review, which is not an audit, except for the matter noted [detail the exception(s) or provide details under a separate section of the report], nothing has come to our attention that causes us to believe that [name of entity] does not comply, in all material respects, with the [requirements] as measured by the [suitable criteria] for the [period from …./…/….. to…./…./…..].

Findings and Recommendations (include as determined by the assurance practitioner under paragraph 83 of ASAE 3100)

[This section of the report would provide relevant and sufficient information to allow readers to understand the basis upon which the assurance practitioner's conclusion has been formed. The inclusion of this information depends on its significance to the needs of the intended users].

[Assurance Practitioner's signature]

[Date of the Assurance Practitioner's review report]

[Assurance Practitioner's address]

ASAE 3402
Assurance Reports on Controls at a Service Organisation

(Issued June 2010)

Issued by the Auditing and Assurance Standards Board.

Note from the Institute of Chartered Accountants Australia

This note, prepared by the technical editor, is not part of ASAE 3402.

Historical development

June 2010: ASAE 3402 was issued to complement ASA 402 'Audit Considerations Relating to an Entity Using a Service Organisation'. It covers assurance reports for periods beginning on or after 1 July 2010. It assists assurance practitioners who are preparing reports on controls at service organisations. Service organisations provide reports for use by user entities and their auditors on the operation of controls at the service organisation. ASAE 3402 provides guidance and example reports for use on such engagements. It is based on the International ISAE 3402 'Assurance Reports on Controls at a Service Organisation'.

To assist auditors in understanding the various pronouncements applicable to service organisations and when they apply, the AUASB has also issued 'Explanation of the Applicability of AUASB Pronouncements where a User Entity uses a Service Organisation'.

October 2011: 'Explanation of the Applicability of AUASB Pronouncements where a User Entity Uses a Service Organisation' updated to reflect the issue of the revised GS 007. It is attached at the end of ASAE 3402.

Contents

Preface

Reasons for Issuing Standard on Assurance Engagements ASAE 3402 *Assurance Reports on Controls at a Service Organisation*

The AUASB is an independent statutory board of the Australian Government established under section 227A of the *Australian Securities and Investments Commission Act 2001*, as amended (ASIC Act). Under section 227B of the ASIC Act the AUASB may formulate Assurance Standards for purposes other than the corporations legislation.

Under the Strategic Direction given to the AUASB by the Financial Reporting Council (FRC), the AUASB is required to have regard to any programme initiated by the International Auditing and Assurance Standards Board (IAASB) for the development, revision and enhancement of its standards and to make appropriate consequential amendments to the Australian Auditing and Assurance Standards. Accordingly, the AUASB has decided to issue ASAE 3402 using the equivalent International Standard on Assurance Engagements ISAE 3402 *Assurance Reports on Controls at a Service Organization*.

Main Features

This Standard on Assurance Engagements (ASAE) establishes requirements and provides application and other explanatory material regarding the assurance practitioner's responsibilities when providing a report for use by user entities and their auditors, on the controls at a service organisation that provides a service to user entities that is likely to be relevant to user entities' internal control as it relates to financial reporting.

Authority Statement

The Auditing and Assurance Standards Board (AUASB) formulates this Standard on Assurance Engagements ASAE 3402 *Assurance Reports on Controls at a Service Organisation* pursuant to section 227B of the *Australian Securities and Investments Commission Act 2001*.

This Standard on Assurance Engagements is to be read in conjunction with ASA 100 *Preamble to AUASB Standards*, which sets out the intentions of the AUASB on how the AUASB Standards are to be understood, interpreted and applied.

Dated: 29 June 2010

M H Kelsall
Chairman - AUASB

Standard on Assurance Engagements ASAE 3402

Assurance Reports on Controls at a Service Organisation

Application

Aus 0.1 This Standard on Assurance Engagements applies to an assurance engagement to provide an assurance report for use by user entities and their auditors on the controls at a service organisation.

Operative Date

Aus 0.2 This Standard on Assurance Engagements is operative for service auditors' assurance reports covering periods commencing on or after 1 July 2010.

Introduction

Scope of this Standard on Assurance Engagements

1. This Standard on Assurance Engagements deals with assurance engagements undertaken by an assurance practitioner[1*] to provide a report for use by user entities and their auditors, on the controls at a service organisation that provides a service to user entities that is likely to be relevant to user entities' internal control as it relates to financial reporting. It complements ASA 402,[2] in that reports prepared in accordance with this standard are capable of providing appropriate evidence under ASA 402. (Ref: Para. A1)

2. The *Framework for Assurance Engagements* (the Assurance Framework) states that an assurance engagement may be a "reasonable assurance" engagement or a "limited assurance" engagement; that an assurance engagement may be either an "assertion-based" engagement or a "direct reporting" engagement; and, that the assurance conclusion for an assertion-based engagement can be worded either in terms of the responsible party's assertion or directly in terms of the subject matter and the criteria.[3] This standard only deals with assertion-based engagements that convey reasonable assurance, with the assurance conclusion worded directly in terms of the subject matter and the criteria.[4]

3. [Deleted by the AUASB. Refer Aus 3.1][5].

Aus 3.1 This standard applies only when the service organisation is responsible for, or otherwise able to make an assertion about, the suitable design of controls as they relate to financial reporting. Therefore, this standard only deals with assurance engagements which include reporting on:

(a) the suitability of design of controls,[**] and

(b) controls which are likely to be relevant to user entities' internal control as it relates to financial reporting (for example, reports only on controls that affect user entities' production or quality control are not dealt with in this standard).[***]

---

1 [Footnote deleted by the AUASB. Refer following footnote "*"]

* See ASQC 1 *Quality Control for Firms that Perform Audits and Reviews of Financial Reports and Other Financial Information, and Other Assurance Engagements*, Para. Aus 12.2 and ASA 220 *Quality Control for an Audit of a Financial Report and Other Historical Financial Information*, Para. Aus 7.1.

2 See ASA 402 *Audit Considerations Relating to an Entity Using a Service Organisation.*

3 See Assurance Framework.

4 See paragraphs 13 and 53(k) of this standard.

5 [Footnote deleted by the AUASB.]

** This standard, however, provides some guidance for engagements which do not include reporting on the suitability of design, carried out under ASAE 3000. (Ref: Para. A2)

*** This standard, however, provides some guidance for engagements which do not include reporting on controls which are likely to be relevant to user entities' internal control as it relates to financial reporting, carried out under ASAE 3000. (Ref: Para. A2)

4. In addition to issuing an assurance report on controls, a service auditor may also be engaged to provide reports such as the following, which are not dealt with in this standard:
   (a) A report on a user entity's transactions or balances maintained by a service organisation; or
   (b) An agreed-upon procedures report on controls at a service organisation.

Relationship with Other Professional Pronouncements

5. The performance of assurance engagements other than audits or reviews of historical financial information requires the service auditor to comply with ASAE 3000. ASAE 3000 includes requirements in relation to such topics as engagement acceptance, planning, evidence, and documentation that apply to all assurance engagements, including engagements in accordance with this standard. This standard expands on how ASAE 3000 is to be applied in a reasonable assurance engagement to report on controls at a service organisation. The Assurance Framework, which defines and describes the elements and objectives of an assurance engagement, provides the context for understanding this standard and ASAE 3000.

6. [Deleted by the AUASB. Refer Aus 6.1].[6]

Aus 6.1 Compliance with ASAE 3000 requires, among other things, that the service auditor comply with the fundamental ethical principles of integrity, objectivity, professional competence and due care, confidentiality and professional behaviour, and implement quality control procedures that are applicable to the individual engagement.[#]

Effective Date

7. [Deleted by the AUASB. Refer Aus 0.2]

Objectives

8. The objectives of the service auditor are:
   (a) To obtain reasonable assurance about whether, in all material respects, based on suitable criteria:
      (i) The service organisation's description of its system fairly presents the system as designed and implemented throughout the specified period (or in the case of a type 1 report, as at a specified date);
      (ii) The controls related to the control objectives stated in the service organisation's description of its system were suitably designed throughout the specified period (or in the case of a type 1 report, as at a specified date); and
      (iii) Where included in the scope of the engagement, the controls operated effectively to provide reasonable assurance that the control objectives stated in the service organisation's description of its system were achieved throughout the specified period.
   (b) To report on the matters in (a) above in accordance with the service auditor's findings.

Definitions

9. For purposes of this Standard on Assurance Engagements, the following terms have the meanings attributed below:
   (a) Carve-out method means method of dealing with the services provided by a subservice organisation, whereby the service organisation's description of its system includes the nature of the services provided by a subservice organisation, but that subservice organisation's relevant control objectives and related controls are excluded from the service organisation's description of its system and from the scope of the service auditor's engagement. The service organisation's description of its system and the

6 [Footnote deleted by the AUASB.]

\# See ASAE 3000, paragraphs 9 and 12 and ASA 102 *Compliance with Ethical Requirements when Performing Audits, Reviews and Other Assurance Engagements.*

scope of the service auditor's engagement include controls at the service organisation to monitor the effectiveness of controls at the subservice organisation, which may include the service organisation's review of an assurance report on controls at the subservice organisation.

(b) Complementary user entity controls means controls that the service organisation assumes, in the design of its service, will be implemented by user entities, and which, if necessary to achieve control objectives stated in the service organisation's description of its system, are identified in that description.

(c) Control objective means the aim or purpose of a particular aspect of controls. Control objectives relate to risks that controls seek to mitigate.

(d) Controls at the service organisation means controls over the achievement of a control objective that is covered by the service auditor's assurance report. (Ref: Para. A3)

(e) Controls at a subservice organisation means controls at a subservice organisation to provide reasonable assurance about the achievement of a control objective.

(f) Criteria means benchmarks used to evaluate or measure a subject matter including, where relevant, benchmarks for presentation and disclosure.

(g) Inclusive method means method of dealing with the services provided by a subservice organisation, whereby the service organisation's description of its system includes the nature of the services provided by a subservice organisation, and that subservice organisation's relevant control objectives and related controls are included in the service organisation's description of its system and in the scope of the service auditor's engagement. (Ref: Para. A4)

(h) Internal audit function means an appraisal activity established or provided as a service to the service organisation. Its functions include, amongst other things, examining, evaluating and monitoring the adequacy and effectiveness of internal control.

(i) Internal auditors means those individuals who perform the activities of the internal audit function. Internal auditors may belong to an internal audit department or equivalent function.

(j) Report on the description and design of controls at a service organisation (referred to in this standard as a "type 1 report") means a report that comprises:

  (i) The service organisation's description of its system;

  (ii) A written assertion by the service organisation that, in all material respects, and based on suitable criteria:

    a. The description fairly presents the service organisation's system as designed and implemented as at the specified date; and

    b. The controls related to the control objectives stated in the service organisation's description of its system were suitably designed as at the specified date; and

  (iii) A service auditor's assurance report that conveys reasonable assurance about the matters in (ii)a.-b. above.

(k) Report on the description, design and operating effectiveness of controls at a service organisation (referred to in this standard as a "type 2 report") means a report that comprises:

  (i) The service organisation's description of its system;

  (ii) A written assertion by the service organisation that, in all material respects, and based on suitable criteria:

    a. The description fairly presents the service organisation's system as designed and implemented throughout the specified period;

    b. The controls related to the control objectives stated in the service organisation's description of its system were suitably designed throughout the specified period; and

    c. The controls related to the control objectives stated in the service organisation's description of its system operated effectively throughout the specified period; and

(iii) A service auditor's assurance report that:

a. Conveys reasonable assurance about the matters in (ii)a.-c. above; and

b. Includes a description of the tests of controls and the results thereof.

(l) Service auditor means an assurance practitioner who, at the request of the service organisation, provides an assurance report on controls at a service organisation.

(m) Service organisation means a third-party organisation (or segment of a third-party organisation) that provides services to user entities that are likely to be relevant to user entities' internal control as it relates to financial reporting.

(n) Service organisation's system (or the system) means the policies and procedures designed and implemented by the service organisation to provide user entities with the services covered by the service auditor's assurance report. The service organisation's description of its system includes identification of: the services covered; the period, or in the case of a type 1 report, the date, to which the description relates; control objectives; and related controls.

(o) Service organisation's assertion means the written assertion about the matters referred to in paragraph 9(k)(ii) (or paragraph 9(j)(ii) in the case of a type 1 report).

(p) Subservice organisation means a service organisation used by another service organisation to perform some of the services provided to user entities that are likely to be relevant to user entities' internal control as it relates to financial reporting.

(q) Test of controls means a procedure designed to evaluate the operating effectiveness of controls in achieving the control objectives stated in the service organisation's description of its system.

(r) User auditor means an auditor who audits and reports on the financial report/statements of a user entity.[7]

Aus 9.1 In the case of a subservice organisation, the service auditor of a service organisation that uses the services of the subservice organisation is also a user auditor.

(s) User entity means an entity that uses a service organisation.

Requirements

ASAE 3000

10. The service auditor shall not represent compliance with this standard unless the service auditor has complied with the requirements of this standard and ASAE 3000.

Ethical Requirements

11. The service auditor shall comply with relevant ethical requirements, including those pertaining to independence, relating to assurance engagements.* (Ref: Para. Aus A5.1)

Management and Those Charged with Governance

12. Where this standard requires the service auditor to enquire of, request representations from, communicate with, or otherwise interact with the service organisation, the service auditor shall determine the appropriate person(s) within the service organisation's management or governance structure with whom to interact. This shall include consideration of which person(s) have the appropriate responsibilities for and knowledge of the matters concerned. (Ref: Para. A6)

---

7 [Footnote deleted by the AUASB. See Aus 9.1]

* See ASA 102 *Compliance with Ethical Requirements when Performing Audits, Reviews and Other Assurance Engagements.*

Acceptance and Continuance

13. Before agreeing to accept, or continue, an engagement, the service auditor shall:
    (a) Determine whether:
        (i) The service auditor has the capabilities and competence to perform the engagement; (Ref: Para. A7)
        (ii) The criteria to be applied by the service organisation to prepare the description of its system will be suitable and available to user entities and their auditors; and
        (iii) The scope of the engagement and the service organisation's description of its system will not be so limited that they are unlikely to be useful to user entities and their auditors.
    (b) Obtain the agreement of the service organisation that it acknowledges and understands its responsibility:
        (i) For the preparation of the description of its system, and accompanying service organisation's assertion, including the completeness, accuracy and method of presentation of that description and assertion; (Ref: Para. A8)
        (ii) To have a reasonable basis for the service organisation's assertion accompanying the description of its system; (Ref: Para. A9)
        (iii) For stating in the service organisation's assertion the criteria it used to prepare the description of its system;
        (iv) For stating in the description of its system:
            a. The control objectives; and,
            b. Where they are specified by law or regulation, or another party (for example, a user group or a professional body), the party who specified them;
        (v) For identifying the risks that threaten achievement of the control objectives stated in the description of its system, and designing and implementing controls to provide reasonable assurance that those risks will not prevent achievement of the control objectives stated in the description of its system, and therefore that the stated control objectives will be achieved; and (Ref: Para. A10)
        (vi) To provide the service auditor with:
            a. Access to all information, such as records, documentation and other matters, including service level agreements, of which the service organisation is aware that is relevant to the description of the service organisation's system and the accompanying service organisation's assertion;
            b. Additional information that the service auditor may request from the service organisation for the purpose of the assurance engagement; and
            c. Unrestricted access to persons within the service organisation from whom the service auditor determines it necessary to obtain evidence.

Acceptance of a Change in the Terms of the Engagement

14. If the service organisation requests a change in the scope of the engagement before the completion of the engagement, the service auditor shall be satisfied that there is a reasonable justification for the change. (Ref: Para. A11-Aus A12.1)

Assessing the Suitability of the Criteria

15. As required by ASAE 3000, the service auditor shall assess whether the service organisation has used suitable criteria in preparing the description of its system, in evaluating whether controls are suitably designed, and, in the case of a type 2 report, in evaluating whether controls are operating effectively.[8]

8 See ASAE 3000, paragraph 35.

16. In assessing the suitability of the criteria to evaluate the service organisation's description of its system, the service auditor shall determine if the criteria encompass, at a minimum:
   (a) Whether the description presents how the service organisation's system was designed and implemented, including, as appropriate:
      (i) The types of services provided, including, as appropriate, classes of transactions processed;
      (ii) The procedures, within both information technology and manual systems, by which services are provided, including, as appropriate, procedures by which transactions are initiated, recorded, processed, corrected as necessary, and transferred to the reports and other information prepared for user entities;
      (iii) The related records and supporting information, including, as appropriate, accounting records, supporting information and specific accounts that are used to initiate, record, process and report transactions; this includes the correction of incorrect information and how information is transferred to the reports and other information prepared for user entities;
      (iv) How the service organisation's system deals with significant events and conditions, other than transactions;
      (v) The process used to prepare reports and other information for user entities;
      (vi) The specified control objectives and controls designed to achieve those objectives;
      (vii) Complementary user entity controls contemplated in the design of the controls; and
      (viii) Other aspects of the service organisation's control environment, risk assessment process, information system (including the related business processes) and communication, control activities and monitoring controls that are relevant to the services provided. (Ref: Para. A15)
   (b) In the case of a type 2 report, whether the description includes relevant details of changes to the service organisation's system during the period covered by the description.
   (c) Whether the description omits or distorts information relevant to the scope of the service organisation's system being described, while acknowledging that the description is prepared to meet the common needs of a broad range of user entities and their auditors and may not, therefore, include every aspect of the service organisation's system that each individual user entity and its auditor may consider important in its particular environment.
17. In assessing the suitability of the criteria to evaluate the design of controls, the service auditor shall determine if the criteria encompass, at a minimum, whether:
   (a) The service organisation has identified the risks that threaten achievement of the control objectives stated in the description of its system; and
   (b) The controls identified in that description would, if operated as described, provide reasonable assurance that those risks do not prevent the stated control objectives from being achieved.
18. In assessing the suitability of the criteria to evaluate the operating effectiveness of controls in providing reasonable assurance that the stated control objectives identified in the description will be achieved, the service auditor shall determine if the criteria encompass, at a minimum, whether the controls were consistently applied as designed throughout the specified period. This includes whether manual controls were applied by individuals who have the appropriate competence and authority. (Ref: Para. A13-A14)

Materiality

19. When planning and performing the engagement, the service auditor shall consider materiality with respect to the fair presentation of the description, the suitability of the design of controls and, in the case of a type 2 report, the operating effectiveness of controls. (Ref: Para. A16-A18)

ASAE

Obtaining an Understanding of the Service Organisation's System

20. The service auditor shall obtain an understanding of the service organisation's system, including controls that are included in the scope of the engagement. (Ref: Para. A19-A20)

Obtaining Evidence Regarding the Description

21. The service auditor shall obtain and read the service organisation's description of its system, and shall evaluate whether those aspects of the description included in the scope of the engagement are fairly presented, including whether: (Ref: Para. A21-A22)
    - (a) Control objectives stated in the service organisation's description of its system are reasonable in the circumstances; (Ref: Para. A23)
    - (b) Controls identified in that description were implemented;
    - (c) Complementary user entity controls, if any, are adequately described; and
    - (d) Services performed by a subservice organisation, if any, are adequately described, including whether the inclusive method or the carve-out method has been used in relation to them.
22. The service auditor shall determine, through other procedures in combination with enquiries, whether the service organisation's system has been implemented. Those other procedures shall include observation, and inspection of records and other documentation, of the manner in which the service organisation's system operates and controls are applied. (Ref: Para. A24)

Obtaining Evidence Regarding Design of Controls

23. The service auditor shall determine which of the controls at the service organisation are necessary to achieve the control objectives stated in the service organisation's description of its system, and shall assess whether those controls were suitably designed. This determination shall include: (Ref: Para. A25-A27)
    - (a) Identifying the risks that threaten the achievement of the control objectives stated in the service organisation's description of its system; and
    - (b) Evaluating the linkage of controls identified in the service organisation's description of its system with those risks.

Obtaining Evidence Regarding Operating Effectiveness of Controls

24. When providing a type 2 report, the service auditor shall test those controls that the service auditor has determined are necessary to achieve the control objectives stated in the service organisation's description of its system, and assess their operating effectiveness throughout the period. Evidence obtained in prior engagements about the satisfactory operation of controls in prior periods does not provide a basis for a reduction in testing, even if it is supplemented with evidence obtained during the current period. (Ref: Para. A28-A32)
25. When designing and performing tests of controls, the service auditor shall:
    - (a) Perform other procedures in combination with enquiry to obtain evidence about:
        - (i) How the control was applied;
        - (ii) The consistency with which the control was applied; and
        - (iii) By whom or by what means the control was applied;
    - (b) Determine whether controls to be tested depend upon other controls (indirect controls) and, if so, whether it is necessary to obtain evidence supporting the operating effectiveness of those indirect controls; and (Ref: Para. A33-A34)
    - (c) Determine means of selecting items for testing that are effective in meeting the objectives of the procedure. (Ref: Para. A35-A36)
26. When determining the extent of tests of controls, the service auditor shall consider matters including the characteristics of the population to be tested, which includes the nature of controls, the frequency of their application (for example, monthly, daily, a number of times per day), and the expected rate of deviation.

Sampling

27. When the service auditor uses sampling, the service auditor shall: (Ref: Para. A35-A36)
    (a) Consider the purpose of the procedure and the characteristics of the population from which the sample will be drawn when designing the sample;
    (b) Determine a sample size sufficient to reduce sampling risk to an appropriately low level;
    (c) Select items for the sample in such a way that each sampling unit in the population has a chance of selection;
    (d) If a designed procedure is not applicable to a selected item, perform the procedure on a replacement item; and
    (e) If unable to apply the designed procedures, or suitable alternative procedures, to a selected item, treat that item as a deviation.

Nature and Cause of Deviations

28. The service auditor shall investigate the nature and cause of any deviations identified and shall determine whether:
    (a) Identified deviations are within the expected rate of deviation and are acceptable; therefore, the testing that has been performed provides an appropriate basis for concluding that the control is operating effectively throughout the specified period;
    (b) Additional testing of the control or of other controls is necessary to reach a conclusion on whether the controls relative to a particular control objective are operating effectively throughout the specified period; or (Ref: Para. A25)
    (c) The testing that has been performed provides an appropriate basis for concluding that the control did not operate effectively throughout the specified period.

29. In the extremely rare circumstances when the service auditor considers a deviation discovered in a sample to be an anomaly and no other controls have been identified that allow the service auditor to conclude that the relevant control objective is operating effectively throughout the specified period, the service auditor shall obtain a high degree of certainty that such deviation is not representative of the population. The service auditor shall obtain this degree of certainty by performing additional procedures to obtain sufficient appropriate evidence that the deviation does not affect the remainder of the population.

The Work of an Internal Audit Function[9]

Obtaining an Understanding of the Internal Audit Function

30. If the service organisation has an internal audit function, the service auditor shall obtain an understanding of the nature of the responsibilities of the internal audit function and of the activities performed in order to determine whether the internal audit function is likely to be relevant to the engagement. (Ref: Para. A37)

Aus 30.1 This standard does not deal with instances when individual internal auditors provide direct assistance to the service auditor in carrying out assurance procedures.

Determining Whether and to What Extent to Use the Work of the Internal Auditors

31. The service auditor shall determine:
    (a) Whether the work of the internal auditors is likely to be adequate for purposes of the engagement; and
    (b) If so, the planned effect of the work of the internal auditors on the nature, timing or extent of the service auditor's procedures.

32. In determining whether the work of the internal auditors is likely to be adequate for purposes of the engagement, the service auditor shall evaluate:
    (a) The objectivity of the internal audit function;
    (b) The technical competence of the internal auditors;

9 [Footnote deleted by the AUASB. Refer Aus 30.1]

(c) Whether the work of the internal auditors is likely to be carried out with due professional care; and

(d) Whether there is likely to be effective communication between the internal auditors and the service auditor.

33. In determining the planned effect of the work of the internal auditors on the nature, timing or extent of the service auditor's procedures, the service auditor shall consider: (Ref: Para. A38)

(a) The nature and scope of specific work performed, or to be performed, by the internal auditors;

(b) The significance of that work to the service auditor's conclusions; and

(c) The degree of subjectivity involved in the evaluation of the evidence gathered in support of those conclusions.

Using the Work of the Internal Audit Function

34. In order for the service auditor to use specific work of the internal auditors, the service auditor shall evaluate and perform procedures on that work to determine its adequacy for the service auditor's purposes. (Ref: Para. A39)

35. To determine the adequacy of specific work performed by the internal auditors for the service auditor's purposes, the service auditor shall evaluate whether:

(a) The work was performed by internal auditors having adequate technical training and proficiency;

(b) The work was properly supervised, reviewed and documented;

(c) Adequate evidence has been obtained to enable the internal auditors to draw reasonable conclusions;

(d) Conclusions reached are appropriate in the circumstances and any reports prepared by the internal auditors are consistent with the results of the work performed; and

(e) Exceptions relevant to the engagement or unusual matters disclosed by the internal auditors are properly resolved.

Effect on the Service Auditor's Assurance Report

36. If the work of the internal audit function has been used, the service auditor shall make no reference to that work in the section of the service auditor's assurance report that contains the service auditor's opinion. (Ref: Para. A40)

37. In the case of a type 2 report, if the work of the internal audit function has been used in performing tests of controls, that part of the service auditor's assurance report that describes the service auditor's tests of controls and the results thereof shall include a description of the internal auditor's work and of the service auditor's procedures with respect to that work. (Ref: Para. A41)

Written Representations

38. The service auditor shall request the service organisation to provide written representations: (Ref: Para. A42)

(a) That reaffirm the assertion accompanying the description of the system;

(b) That it has provided the service auditor with all relevant information and access agreed to;[10] and

(c) That it has disclosed to the service auditor any of the following of which it is aware:

(i) Non-compliance with laws and regulations, fraud, or uncorrected deviations attributable to the service organisation that may affect one or more user entities;

(ii) Design deficiencies in controls;

(iii) Instances where controls have not operated as described; and

(iv) Any events subsequent to the period covered by the service organisation's description of its system up to the date of the service auditor's assurance report that could have a significant effect on the service auditor's assurance report.

10 See paragraph 13(b)(vi) of this standard.

39. The written representations shall be in the form of a representation letter addressed to the service auditor.* The date of the written representations shall be as near as practicable to, but not after, the date of the service auditor's assurance report.

40. If, having discussed the matter with the service auditor, the service organisation does not provide one or more of the written representations requested in accordance with paragraph 38(a) and (b) of this standard, the service auditor shall disclaim an opinion. (Ref: Para. A43)

Other Information

41. The service auditor shall read the other information, if any, included in a document containing the service organisation's description of its system and the service auditor's assurance report, to identify material inconsistencies, if any, with that description. While reading the other information for the purpose of identifying material inconsistencies, the service auditor may become aware of an apparent misstatement of fact in that other information.

42. If the service auditor becomes aware of a material inconsistency or an apparent misstatement of fact in the other information, the service auditor shall discuss the matter with the service organisation. If the service auditor concludes that there is a material inconsistency or a misstatement of fact in the other information that the service organisation refuses to correct, the service auditor shall take further appropriate action. (Ref: Para. A44-A45)

Subsequent Events

43. The service auditor shall enquire whether the service organisation is aware of any events subsequent to the period covered by the service organisation's description of its system up to the date of the service auditor's assurance report that could have a significant effect on the service auditor's assurance report. If the service auditor is aware of such an event, and information about that event is not disclosed by the service organisation, the service auditor shall disclose it in the service auditor's assurance report.

44. The service auditor has no obligation to perform any procedures regarding the description of the service organisation's system, or the suitability of design or operating effectiveness of controls, after the date of the service auditor's assurance report.

ASAE

Documentation

45. The service auditor shall prepare documentation that is sufficient to enable an experienced service auditor, having no previous connection with the engagement, to understand:
   (a) The nature, timing, and extent of the procedures performed to comply with this standard and applicable legal and regulatory requirements;
   (b) The results of the procedures performed, and the evidence obtained; and
   (c) Significant matters arising during the engagement, and the conclusions reached thereon and significant professional judgements made in reaching those conclusions.

46. In documenting the nature, timing and extent of procedures performed, the service auditor shall record:
   (a) The identifying characteristics of the specific items or matters being tested;
   (b) Who performed the work and the date such work was completed; and
   (c) Who reviewed the work performed and the date and extent of such review.

47. If the service auditor uses specific work of the internal auditors, the service auditor shall document the conclusions reached regarding the evaluation of the adequacy of the work of the internal auditors, and the procedures performed by the service auditor on that work.

48. The service auditor shall document discussions of significant matters with the service organisation and others including the nature of the significant matters discussed and when and with whom the discussions took place.

49. If the service auditor has identified information that is inconsistent with the service auditor's final conclusion regarding a significant matter, the service auditor shall document how the service auditor addressed the inconsistency.

* An example representation letter is included in [Aus] Appendix 0B.

50. The service auditor shall assemble the documentation in an engagement file and complete the administrative process of assembling the final engagement file on a timely basis after the date of the service auditor's assurance report.[11]

51. After the assembly of the final engagement file has been completed, the service auditor shall not delete or discard documentation before the end of its retention period. (Ref: Para. A46)

52. If the service auditor finds it necessary to modify existing engagement documentation or add new documentation after the assembly of the final engagement file has been completed and that documentation does not affect the service auditor's report, the service auditor shall, regardless of the nature of the modifications or additions, document:

(a) The specific reasons for making them; and

(b) When and by whom they were made and reviewed.

Preparing the Service Auditor's Assurance Report

Content of the Service Auditor's Assurance Report

53. The service auditor's assurance report shall include the following basic elements: (Ref: Para. A47)

(a) A title that clearly indicates the report is an independent service auditor's assurance report.

(b) An addressee.

(c) Identification of:

(i) The service organisation's description of its system, and the service organisation's assertion, which includes the matters described in paragraph 9(k)(ii) of this standard for a type 2 report, or paragraph 9(j)(ii) of this standard for a type 1 report.

(ii) Those parts of the service organisation's description of its system, if any, that are not covered by the service auditor's opinion.

(iii) If the description refers to the need for complementary user entity controls, a statement that the service auditor has not evaluated the suitability of design or operating effectiveness of complementary user entity controls, and that the control objectives stated in the service organisation's description of its system can be achieved only if complementary user entity controls are suitably designed or operating effectively, along with the controls at the service organisation.

(iv) If services are performed by a subservice organisation, the nature of activities performed by the subservice organisation as described in the service organisation's description of its system and whether the inclusive method or the carve-out method has been used in relation to them. Where the carve-out method has been used, a statement that the service organisation's description of its system excludes the control objectives and related controls at relevant subservice organisations, and that the service auditor's procedures do not extend to controls at the subservice organisation. Where the inclusive method has been used, a statement that the service organisation's description of its system includes control objectives and related controls at the subservice organisation, and that the service auditor's procedures extended to controls at the subservice organisation.

(d) Identification of the criteria, and the party specifying the control objectives.

(e) A statement that the report and, in the case of a type 2 report, the description of tests of controls are intended only for user entities and their auditors, who have a sufficient understanding to consider it, along with other information including information about controls operated by user entities themselves, when assessing the risks of material misstatements of user entities' financial reports/statements. (Ref: Para. A48)

11 See Auditing Standard ASQC 1, paragraphs 45 and A54-A55.

(f) A statement that the service organisation is responsible for:

(i) Preparing the description of its system, and the accompanying assertion, including the completeness, accuracy and method of presentation of that description and that assertion;

(ii) Providing the services covered by the service organisation's description of its system;

(iii) Stating the control objectives (where not identified by law or regulation, or another party, for example, a user group or a professional body); and

(iv) Designing and implementing controls to achieve the control objectives stated in the service organisation's description of its system.

(g) A statement that the service auditor's responsibility is to express an opinion on the service organisation's description, on the design of controls related to the control objectives stated in that description and, in the case of a type 2 report, on the operating effectiveness of those controls, based on the service auditor's procedures.

(h) A statement that the engagement was performed in accordance with ASAE 3402 *Assurance Reports on Controls at a Service Organisation*, which requires that the service auditor comply with ethical requirements and plan and perform procedures to obtain reasonable assurance about whether, in all material respects, the service organisation's description of its system is fairly presented and the controls are suitably designed and, in the case of a type 2 report, are operating effectively.

(i) A summary of the service auditor's procedures to obtain reasonable assurance and a statement of the service auditor's belief that the evidence obtained is sufficient and appropriate to provide a basis for the service auditor's opinion, and, in the case of a type 1 report, a statement that the service auditor has not performed any procedures regarding the operating effectiveness of controls and therefore no opinion is expressed thereon.

(j) A statement of the limitations of controls and, in the case of a type 2 report, of the risk of projecting to future periods any evaluation of the operating effectiveness of controls.

(k) The service auditor's opinion, expressed in the positive form, on whether, in all material respects, based on suitable criteria:

(i) In the case of a type 2 report:

a. The description fairly presents the service organisation's system that had been designed and implemented throughout the specified period;

b. The controls related to the control objectives stated in the service organisation's description of its system were suitably designed throughout the specified period; and

c. The controls tested, which were those necessary to provide reasonable assurance that the control objectives stated in the description were achieved, operated effectively throughout the specified period.

(ii) In the case of a type 1 report:

a. The description fairly presents the service organisation's system that had been designed and implemented as at the specified date; and

b. The controls related to the control objectives stated in the service organisation's description of its system were suitably designed as at the specified date.

(l) The date of the service auditor's assurance report, which shall be no earlier than the date on which the service auditor has obtained sufficient appropriate evidence on which to base the opinion.

(m) The name of the service auditor, and the location in the jurisdiction where the service auditor practices.

54. In the case of a type 2 report, the service auditor's assurance report shall include a separate section after the opinion, or an attachment, that describes the tests of controls that were performed and the results of those tests. In describing the tests of controls, the service

auditor shall clearly state which controls were tested, identify whether the items tested represent all or a selection of the items in the population, and indicate the nature of the tests in sufficient detail to enable user auditors to determine the effect of such tests on their risk assessments. If deviations have been identified, the service auditor shall include the extent of testing performed that led to identification of the deviations (including the sample size where sampling has been used), and the number and nature of the deviations noted. The service auditor shall report deviations even if, on the basis of tests performed, the service auditor has concluded that the related control objective was achieved. (Ref: Para. A18 and A49)

Modified Opinions

55. If the service auditor concludes that: (Ref: Para. A50-A52)
    (a) The service organisation's description does not fairly present, in all material respects, the system as designed and implemented;
    (b) The controls related to the control objectives stated in the description were not suitably designed, in all material respects;
    (c) In the case of a type 2 report, the controls tested, which were those necessary to provide reasonable assurance that the control objectives stated in the service organisation's description of its system were achieved, did not operate effectively, in all material respects; or
    (d) The service auditor is unable to obtain sufficient appropriate evidence,

    the service auditor's opinion shall be modified, and the service auditor's assurance report shall contain a clear description of all the reasons for the modification.

Other Communication Responsibilities

56. If the service auditor becomes aware of non-compliance with laws and regulations, fraud, or uncorrected errors attributable to the service organisation that are not clearly trivial and may affect one or more user entities, the service auditor shall determine whether the matter has been communicated appropriately to affected user entities. If the matter has not been so communicated and the service organisation is unwilling to do so, the service auditor shall take appropriate action. (Ref: Para. A53)

❖ ❖ ❖

Application and Other Explanatory Material

Scope of this Standard on Assurance Engagements (Ref: Para. 1 and 3)

A1. Internal control is a process designed to provide reasonable assurance regarding the achievement of objectives related to the reliability of financial reporting, effectiveness and efficiency of operations and compliance with applicable laws and regulations. Controls related to a service organisation's operations and compliance objectives may be relevant to a user entities' internal control as it relates to financial reporting. Such controls may pertain to assertions about presentation and disclosure relating to account balances, classes of transactions or disclosures, or may pertain to evidence that the user auditor evaluates or uses in applying auditing procedures. For example, a payroll processing service organisation's controls related to the timely remittance of payroll deductions to government authorities may be relevant to a user entity as late remittances could incur interest and penalties that would result in a liability for the user entity. Similarly, a service organisation's controls over the acceptability of investment transactions from a regulatory perspective may be considered relevant to a user entity's presentation and disclosure of transactions and account balances in its financial report/statements. The determination of whether controls at a service organisation related to operations and compliance are likely to be relevant to user entities' internal control as it relates to financial reporting is a matter of professional judgement, having regard to the control objectives set by the service organisation and the suitability of the criteria.

A2. The service organisation may not be able to assert that the system is suitably designed when, for example, the service organisation is operating a system that has been designed by a user entity or is stipulated in a contract between a user entity and the service organisation. Because of the inextricable link between the suitable design of controls and their operating effectiveness, the absence of an assertion with respect to the suitability of design will likely preclude the service auditor from concluding that the controls provide reasonable assurance that the control objectives have been met and thus from opining on the operating effectiveness of controls. As an alternative, the practitioner may choose to accept an agreed-upon procedures engagement to perform tests of controls, or an assurance engagement under ASAE 3000 to conclude on whether, based on tests of controls, the controls have operated as described.

Definitions (Ref: Para. 9(d) and 9(g))

A3. The definition of "controls at the service organisation" includes aspects of user entities' information systems maintained by the service organisation, and may also include aspects of one or more of the other components of internal control at a service organisation. For example, it may include aspects of a service organisation's control environment, monitoring, and control activities when they relate to the services provided. It does not, however, include controls at a service organisation that are not related to the achievement of the control objectives stated in the service organisation's description of its system, for example, controls related to the preparation of the service organisation's own financial report/statements.

A4. When the inclusive method is used, the requirements in this standard also apply to the services provided by the subservice organisation, including obtaining agreement regarding the matters in paragraph 13(b)(i)-(vi) as applied to the subservice organisation rather than the service organisation. Performing procedures at the subservice organisation entails coordination and communication between the service organisation, the subservice organisation, and the service auditor. The inclusive method generally is feasible only if the service organisation and the subservice organisation are related, or if the contract between the service organisation and the subservice organisation provides for its use.

Ethical Requirements (Ref: Para. 11)

A5. [Deleted by the AUASB. Refer Aus A5.1].

Aus A5.1 The service auditor is subject to relevant independence requirements, which comprise the requirements referenced in ASA 102 *Compliance with Ethical Requirements when Performing Audits, Reviews and Other Assurance Engagements*. In performing an engagement in accordance with this standard, relevant independence requirements do not require the service auditor to be independent from each user entity.

Management and Those Charged with Governance (Ref: Para. 12)

A6. Management and governance structures vary by jurisdiction and by entity, reflecting influences such as different cultural and legal backgrounds, and size and ownership characteristics. Such diversity means that it is not possible for this standard to specify for all engagements the person(s) with whom the service auditor is to interact regarding particular matters. For example, the service organisation may be a segment of a third-party organisation and not a separate legal entity. In such cases, identifying the appropriate management personnel or those charged with governance from whom to request written representations may require the exercise of professional judgement.

Acceptance and Continuance

Capabilities and Competence to Perform the Engagement (Ref: Para. 13(a)(i))

A7. Relevant capabilities and competence to perform the engagement include matters such as the following:

- Knowledge of the relevant industry;
- An understanding of information technology and systems;
- Experience in evaluating risks as they relate to the suitable design of controls; and
- Experience in the design and execution of tests of controls and the evaluation of the results.

Service Organisation's Assertion (Ref: Para. 13(b)(i))

A8. Refusal, by a service organisation, to provide a written assertion, subsequent to an agreement by the service auditor to accept, or continue, an engagement, represents a scope limitation that causes the service auditor to withdraw from the engagement. If law or regulation does not allow the service auditor to withdraw from the engagement, the service auditor disclaims an opinion.

Reasonable Basis for Service Organisation's Assertion (Ref: Para. 13(b)(ii))

A9. In the case of a type 2 report, the service organisation's assertion includes a statement that the controls related to the control objectives stated in the service organisation's description of its system operated effectively throughout the specified period. This assertion may be based on the service organisation's monitoring activities. Monitoring of controls is a process to assess the effectiveness of controls over time. It involves assessing the effectiveness of controls on a timely basis, identifying and reporting deficiencies to appropriate individuals within the service organisation, and taking necessary corrective actions. The service organisation accomplishes monitoring of controls through ongoing activities, separate evaluations, or a combination of both. The greater the degree and effectiveness of ongoing monitoring activities, the less need for separate evaluations. Ongoing monitoring activities are often built into the normal recurring activities of a service organisation and include regular management and supervisory activities. Internal auditors or personnel performing similar functions may contribute to the monitoring of a service organisation's activities. Monitoring activities may also include using information communicated by external parties, such as customer complaints and regulator comments, which may indicate problems or highlight areas in need of improvement. The fact that the service auditor will report on the operating effectiveness of controls is not a substitute for the service organisation's own processes to provide a reasonable basis for its assertion.

Identification of Risks (Ref: Para. 13(b)(v))

A10. As noted in paragraph 9(c), control objectives relate to risks that controls seek to mitigate. For example, the risk that a transaction is recorded at the wrong amount or in the wrong period can be expressed as a control objective that transactions are recorded at the correct amount and in the correct period. The service organisation is responsible for identifying the risks that threaten achievement of the control objectives stated in the description of its system. The service organisation may have a formal or informal process for identifying relevant risks. A formal process may include estimating the significance of identified risks, assessing the likelihood of their occurrence, and deciding about actions to address them. However, since control objectives relate to risks that controls seek to mitigate, thoughtful identification of control objectives when designing and implementing the service organisation's system may itself comprise an informal process for identifying relevant risks.

Acceptance of a Change in the Terms of the Engagement (Ref: Para. 14)

A11. A request to change the scope of the engagement may not have a reasonable justification when, for example, the request is made to exclude certain control objectives from the scope of the engagement because of the likelihood that the service auditor's opinion would be modified; or the service organisation will not provide the service auditor with a written assertion and the request is made to perform the engagement under ASAE 3000.

A12. A request to change the scope of the engagement may have a reasonable justification when, for example, the request is made to exclude from the engagement a subservice organisation when the service organisation cannot arrange for access by the service auditor, and the method used for dealing with the services provided by that subservice organisation is changed from the inclusive method to the carve-out method.

Aus A12.1 An example engagement letter is contained in [Aus] Appendix 0A.

Assessing the Suitability of the Criteria (Ref: Para. 15-18)

A13. Criteria need to be available to the intended users to allow them to understand the basis for the service organisation's assertion about the fair presentation of its description of the system, the suitability of the design of controls and, in the case of a type 2 report, the operating effectiveness of the controls related to the control objectives.

A14. ASAE 3000 requires the service auditor, among other things, to assess the suitability of criteria, and the appropriateness of the subject matter.[12] The subject matter is the underlying condition of interest to intended users of an assurance report. The following table identifies the subject matter and minimum criteria for each of the opinions in type 2 and type 1 reports.

	Subject matter	Criteria	Comment
Opinion about the fair presentation of the description of the service organisation's system (type 1 and type 2 reports)	The service organisation's system that is likely to be relevant to user entities' internal control as it relates to financial reporting and is covered by the service auditor's assurance report.	The description is fairly presented if it: (a) presents how the service organisation's system was designed and implemented including, as appropriate, the matters identified in paragraph 16(a)(i)-(viii); (b) in the case of a type 2 report, includes relevant details of changes to the service organisation's system during the period covered by the description; and (c) does not omit or distort information relevant to the scope of the service organisation's system being described, while acknowledging that the description is prepared to meet the common needs of a broad range of user entities and may not, therefore, include every aspect of the service organisation's system that each individual user entity may consider important in its own particular environment.	The specific wording of the criteria for this opinion may need to be tailored to be consistent with criteria established by, for example, law or regulation, user groups, or a professional body. Examples of criteria for this opinion are provided in the illustrative service organisation's assertion in Appendix 1. Paragraphs A21-A24 offer further guidance on determining whether these criteria are met. (In terms of the requirements of ASAE 3000, the subject matter information[13] for this opinion is the service organisation's description of its system and the service organisation's assertion that the description is fairly presented.)

12 See ASAE 3000, paragraphs 33-39.

13 The "subject matter information" is the outcome of the evaluation or measurement of the subject matter that results from applying the criteria to the subject matter.

	Subject matter	Criteria	Comment	
Opinion about suitability of design, and operating effectiveness (type 2 reports)	The suitability of the design and operating effectiveness of those controls that are necessary to achieve the control objectives stated in the service organisation's description of its system.	The controls are suitably designed and operating effectively if: (a) the service organisation has identified the risks that threaten achievement of the control objectives stated in the description of its system; (b) the controls identified in that description would, if operated as described, provide reasonable assurance that those risks do not prevent the stated control objectives from being achieved; and (c) the controls were consistently applied as designed throughout the specified period. This includes whether manual controls were applied by individuals who have the appropriate competence and authority.	When the criteria for this opinion are met, controls will have provided reasonable assurance that the related control objectives were achieved throughout the specified period. (In terms of the requirements of ASAE 3000, the subject matter information for this opinion is the service organisation's assertion that controls are suitably designed and that they are operating effectively.)	The control objectives, which are stated in the service organisation's description of its system, are part of the criteria for these opinions. The stated control objectives will differ from engagement to engagement. If, as part of forming the opinion on the description, the service auditor concludes the stated control objectives are not fairly presented then those control objectives would not be suitable as part of the criteria for forming an opinion on either the design or operating effectiveness of controls.
Opinion about suitability of design (type 1 reports)	The suitability of the design of those controls that are necessary to achieve the control objectives stated in the service organisation's description of its system.	The controls are suitably designed if: (a) the service organisation has identified the risks that threaten achievement of the control objectives stated in the description of its system; and (b) the controls identified in that description would, if operated as described, provide reasonable assurance that those risks do not prevent the stated control objectives from being achieved.	Meeting these criteria does not, of itself, provide any assurance that the related control objectives were achieved because no assurance has been obtained about the operation of controls. (In terms of the requirements of ASAE 3000, the subject matter information for this opinion is the service organisation's assertion that controls are suitably designed.)	The control objectives, which are stated in the service organisation's description of its system, are part of the criteria for these opinions. The stated control objectives will differ from engagement to engagement. If, as part of forming the opinion on the description, the service auditor concludes the stated control objectives are not fairly presented then those control objectives would not be suitable as part of the criteria for forming an opinion on the design.

A15. Paragraph 16(a) identifies a number of elements that are included in the service organisation's description of its system as appropriate. These elements may not be appropriate if the system being described is not a system that processes transactions, for example, if the system relates to general controls over the hosting of an IT application but not the controls embedded in the application itself.

Materiality (Ref: Para. 19 and 54)

A16. In an engagement to report on controls at a service organisation, the concept of materiality relates to the system being reported on, not the financial reports/statements of user entities. The service auditor plans and performs procedures to determine whether the service organisation's description of its system is fairly presented in all material respects, whether controls at the service organisation are suitably designed in all material respects and, in the case of a type 2 report, whether controls at the service organisation are operating effectively in all material respects. The concept of materiality takes into account that the service auditor's assurance report provides information about the service organisation's system to meet the common information needs of a broad range of user entities and their auditors who have an understanding of the manner in which that system has been used.

A17. Materiality with respect to the fair presentation of the service organisation's description of its system, and with respect to the design of controls, includes primarily the consideration of qualitative factors, for example: whether the description includes the significant aspects of processing significant transactions; whether the description omits or distorts relevant information; and the ability of controls, as designed, to provide reasonable assurance that control objectives would be achieved. Materiality with respect to the service auditor's opinion on the operating effectiveness of controls includes the consideration of both quantitative and qualitative factors, for example, the tolerable rate and observed rate of deviation (a quantitative matter), and the nature and cause of any observed deviation (a qualitative matter).

ASAE

A18. The concept of materiality is not applied when disclosing, in the description of the tests of controls, the results of those tests where deviations have been identified. This is because, in the particular circumstances of a specific user entity or user auditor, a deviation may have significance beyond whether or not, in the opinion of the service auditor, it prevents a control from operating effectively. For example, the control to which the deviation relates may be particularly significant in preventing a certain type of error that may be material in the particular circumstances of a user entity's financial report/statements.

Obtaining an Understanding of the Service Organisation's System (Ref: Para. 20)

A19. Obtaining an understanding of the service organisation's system, including controls, included in the scope of the engagement, assists the service auditor in:

- Identifying the boundaries of that system, and how it interfaces with other systems.
- Assessing whether the service organisation's description fairly presents the system that has been designed and implemented.
- Determining which controls are necessary to achieve the control objectives stated in the service organisation's description of its system.
- Assessing whether controls were suitably designed.
- Assessing, in the case of a type 2 report, whether controls were operating effectively.

A20. The service auditor's procedures to obtain this understanding may include:

- Enquiring of those within the service organisation who, in the service auditor's judgement, may have relevant information.
- Observing operations and inspecting documents, reports, printed and electronic records of transaction processing.

- Inspecting a selection of agreements between the service organisation and user entities to identify their common terms.
- Reperforming control procedures.

Obtaining Evidence Regarding the Description (Ref: Para. 21-22)

A21. Considering the following questions may assist the service auditor in determining whether those aspects of the description included in the scope of the engagement are fairly presented in all material respects:

- Does the description address the major aspects of the service provided (within the scope of the engagement) that could reasonably be expected to be relevant to the common needs of a broad range of user auditors in planning their audits of user entities' financial reports/statements?
- Is the description prepared at a level of detail that could reasonably be expected to provide a broad range of user auditors with sufficient information to obtain an understanding of internal control in accordance with ASA 315?[14] The description need not address every aspect of the service organisation's processing or the services provided to user entities, and need not be so detailed as to potentially allow a reader to compromise security or other controls at the service organisation.
- Is the description prepared in a manner that does not omit or distort information that may affect the common needs of a broad range of user auditors' decisions, for example, does the description contain any significant omissions or inaccuracies in processing of which the service auditor is aware?
- Where some of the control objectives stated in the service organisation's description of its system have been excluded from the scope of the engagement, does the description clearly identify the excluded objectives?
- Have the controls identified in the description been implemented?
- Are complementary user entity controls, if any, described adequately? In most cases, the description of control objectives is worded such that the control objectives are capable of being achieved through effective operation of controls implemented by the service organisation alone. In some cases, however, the control objectives stated in the service organisation's description of its system cannot be achieved by the service organisation alone because their achievement requires particular controls to be implemented by user entities. This may be the case where, for example, the control objectives are specified by a regulatory authority. When the description does include complementary user entity controls, the description separately identifies those controls along with the specific control objectives that cannot be achieved by the service organisation alone.
- If the inclusive method has been used, does the description separately identify controls at the service organisation and controls at the subservice organisation? If the carve-out method is used, does the description identify the functions that are performed by the subservice organisation? When the carve-out method is used, the description need not describe the detailed processing or controls at the subservice organisation.

A22. The service auditor's procedures to evaluate the fair presentation of the description may include:

- Considering the nature of user entities and how the services provided by the service organisation are likely to affect them, for example, whether user entities are from a particular industry and whether they are regulated by government agencies.
- Reading standard contracts, or standard terms of contracts, (if applicable) with user entities to gain an understanding of the service organisation's contractual obligations.

14 See ASA 315 *Identifying and Assessing Risks of Material Misstatement through Understanding the Entity and Its Environment.*

- Observing procedures performed by service organisation personnel.
- Reviewing the service organisation's policy and procedure manuals and other systems documentation, for example, flowcharts and narratives.

A23. Paragraph 21(a) requires the service auditor to evaluate whether the control objectives stated in the service organisation's description of its system are reasonable in the circumstances. Considering the following questions may assist the service auditor in this evaluation:

- Have the stated control objectives been designated by the service organisation or by outside parties such as a regulatory authority, a user group, or a professional body that follows a transparent due process?
- Where the stated control objectives have been specified by the service organisation, do they relate to the types of assertions commonly embodied in the broad range of user entities' financial reports/statements to which controls at the service organisation could reasonably be expected to relate? Although the service auditor ordinarily will not be able to determine how controls at a service organisation specifically relate to the assertions embodied in individual user entities' financial reports/statements, the service auditor's understanding of the nature of the service organisation's system, including controls, and services being provided is used to identify the types of assertions to which those controls are likely to relate.
- Where the stated control objectives have been specified by the service organisation, are they complete? A complete set of control objectives can provide a broad range of user auditors with a framework to assess the effect of controls at the service organisation on the assertions commonly embodied in user entities' financial reports/statements.

A24. The service auditor's procedures to determine whether the service organisation's system has been implemented may be similar to, and performed in conjunction with, procedures to obtain an understanding of that system. They may also include tracing items through the service organisation's system and, in the case of a type 2 report, specific enquiries about changes in controls that were implemented during the period. Changes that are significant to user entities or their auditors are included in the description of the service organisation's system.

ASAE

Obtaining Evidence Regarding Design of Controls (Ref: Para. 23 and 28(b))

A25. From the viewpoint of a user entity or a user auditor, a control is suitably designed if, individually or in combination with other controls, it would, when complied with satisfactorily, provide reasonable assurance that material misstatements are prevented, or detected and corrected. A service organisation or a service auditor, however, is not aware of the circumstances at individual user entities that would determine whether or not a misstatement resulting from a control deviation is material to those user entities. Therefore, from the viewpoint of a service auditor, a control is suitably designed if, individually or in combination with other controls, it would, when complied with satisfactorily, provide reasonable assurance that control objectives stated in the service organisation's description of its system are achieved.

A26. A service auditor may consider using flowcharts, questionnaires, or decision tables to facilitate understanding the design of the controls.

A27. Controls may consist of a number of activities directed at the achievement of a control objective. Consequently, if the service auditor evaluates certain activities as being ineffective in achieving a particular control objective, the existence of other activities may allow the service auditor to conclude that controls related to the control objective are suitably designed.

Obtaining Evidence Regarding Operating Effectiveness of Controls

Assessing Operating Effectiveness (Ref: Para. 24)

A28. From the viewpoint of a user entity or a user auditor, a control is operating effectively if, individually or in combination with other controls, it provides reasonable assurance that material misstatements, whether due to fraud or error, are prevented, or detected and corrected. A service organisation or a service auditor, however, is not aware of the circumstances at individual user entities that would determine whether a misstatement resulting from a control deviation had occurred and, if so, whether it is material. Therefore, from the viewpoint of a service auditor, a control is operating effectively if, individually or in combination with other controls, it provides reasonable assurance that control objectives stated in the service organisation's description of its system are achieved. Similarly, a service organisation or a service auditor is not in a position to determine whether any observed control deviation would result in a material misstatement from the viewpoint of an individual user entity.

A29. Obtaining an understanding of controls sufficient to opine on the suitability of their design is not sufficient evidence regarding their operating effectiveness, unless there is some automation that provides for the consistent operation of the controls as they were designed and implemented. For example, obtaining information about the implementation of a manual control at a point in time does not provide evidence about operation of the control at other times. However, because of the inherent consistency of IT processing, performing procedures to determine the design of an automated control, and whether it has been implemented, may serve as evidence of that control's operating effectiveness, depending on the service auditor's assessment and testing of other controls, such as those over program changes.

A30. To be useful to user auditors, a type 2 report ordinarily covers a minimum period of six months. If the period is less than six months, the service auditor may consider it appropriate to describe the reasons for the shorter period in the service auditor's assurance report. Circumstances that may result in a report covering a period of less than six months include when (a) the service auditor is engaged close to the date by which the report on controls is to be issued; (b) the service organisation (or a particular system or application) has been in operation for less than six months; or (c) significant changes have been made to the controls and it is not practicable either to wait six months before issuing a report or to issue a report covering the system both before and after the changes.

A31. Certain control procedures may not leave evidence of their operation that can be tested at a later date and, accordingly, the service auditor may find it necessary to test the operating effectiveness of such control procedures at various times throughout the reporting period.

A32. The service auditor provides an opinion on the operating effectiveness of controls throughout each period, therefore, sufficient appropriate evidence about the operation of controls during the current period is required for the service auditor to express that opinion. Knowledge of deviations observed in prior engagements may, however, lead the service auditor to increase the extent of testing during the current period.

Testing of Indirect Controls (Ref: Para. 25(b))

A33. In some circumstances, it may be necessary to obtain evidence supporting the effective operation of indirect controls. For example, when the service auditor decides to test the effectiveness of a review of exception reports detailing sales in excess of authorised credit limits, the review and related follow up is the control that is directly of relevance to the service auditor. Controls over the accuracy of the information in the reports (for example, the general IT controls) are described as "indirect" controls.

A34. Because of the inherent consistency of IT processing, evidence about the implementation of an automated application control, when considered in combination with evidence about the operating effectiveness of the service organisation's general controls (in particular, change controls), may also provide substantial evidence about its operating effectiveness.

Means of Selecting Items for Testing (Ref: Para. 25(c) and 27)

A35. The means of selecting items for testing available to the service auditor are:

(a) Selecting all items (100% examination). This may be appropriate for testing controls that are applied infrequently, for example, quarterly, or when evidence regarding application of the control makes 100% examination efficient;

(b) Selecting specific items. This may be appropriate where 100% examination would not be efficient and sampling would not be effective, such as testing controls that are not applied sufficiently frequently to render a large population for sampling, for example, controls that are applied monthly or weekly; and

(c) Sampling. This may be appropriate for testing controls that are applied frequently in a uniform manner and which leave documentary evidence of their application.

A36. While selective examination of specific items will often be an efficient means of obtaining evidence, it does not constitute sampling. The results of procedures applied to items selected in this way cannot be projected to the entire population; accordingly, selective examination of specific items does not provide evidence concerning the remainder of the population. Sampling, on the other hand, is designed to enable conclusions to be drawn about an entire population on the basis of testing a sample drawn from it.

The Work of an Internal Audit Function

Obtaining an Understanding of the Internal Audit Function (Ref: Para. 30)

A37. An internal audit function may be responsible for providing analyses, evaluations, assurances, recommendations, and other information to management and those charged with governance. An internal audit function at a service organisation may perform activities related to the service organisation's own system of internal control, or activities related to the services and systems, including controls, that the service organisation is providing to user entities.

Determining Whether and to What Extent to Use the Work of the Internal Auditors (Ref: Para. 33)

A38. In determining the planned effect of the work of the internal auditors on the nature, timing or extent of the service auditor's procedures, the following factors may suggest the need for different or less extensive procedures than would otherwise be the case:

- The nature and scope of specific work performed, or to be performed, by the internal auditors is quite limited.
- The work of the internal auditors relates to controls that are less significant to the service auditor's conclusions.
- The work performed, or to be performed, by the internal auditors does not require subjective or complex judgements.

Using the Work of the Internal Audit Function (Ref: Para. 34)

A39. The nature, timing and extent of the service auditor's procedures on specific work of the internal auditors will depend on the service auditor's assessment of the significance of that work to the service auditor's conclusions (for example, the significance of the risks that the controls tested seek to mitigate), the evaluation of the internal audit function and the evaluation of the specific work of the internal auditors. Such procedures may include:

- Examination of items already examined by the internal auditors;
- Examination of other similar items; and
- Observation of procedures performed by the internal auditors.

Effect on the Service Auditor's Assurance Report (Ref: Para. 36-37)

A40. Irrespective of the degree of autonomy and objectivity of the internal audit function, such function is not independent of the service organisation as is required of the service auditor when performing the engagement. The service auditor has sole responsibility for the opinion expressed in the service auditor's assurance report, and that responsibility is not reduced by the service auditor's use of the work of the internal auditors.

A41. The service auditor's description of work performed by the internal audit function may be presented in a number of ways, for example:

- By including introductory material to the description of tests of controls indicating that certain work of the internal audit function was used in performing tests of controls.
- Attribution of individual tests to internal audit.

Written Representations (Ref: Para. 38 and 40)

A42. The written representations required by paragraph 38 are separate from, and in addition to, the service organisation's assertion, as defined at paragraph 9(o).

A43. If the service organisation does not provide the written representations requested in accordance with paragraph 38(c) of this standard, it may be appropriate for the service auditor's opinion to be modified in accordance with paragraph 55(d) of this standard.

Other Information (Ref: Para. 42)

A44. Relevant ethical requirements require that a service auditor not be associated with information where the service auditor believes that the information:

(a) Contains a materially false or misleading statement;

(b) Contains statements or information furnished recklessly; or

(c) Omits or obscures information required to be included where such omission or obscurity would be misleading.[15]

If other information included in a document containing the service organisation's description of its system and the service auditor's assurance report contains future-oriented information such as recovery or contingency plans, or plans for modifications to the system that will address deviations identified in the service auditor's assurance report, or claims of a promotional nature that cannot be reasonably substantiated, the service auditor may request that information be removed or restated.

A45. If the service organisation refuses to remove or restate the other information, further actions that may be appropriate include, for example:

- Requesting the service organisation to consult with its legal counsel as to the appropriate course of action.
- Describing the material inconsistency or material misstatement of fact in the assurance report.
- Withholding the assurance report until the matter is resolved.
- Withdrawing from the engagement.

Documentation (Ref: Para. 51)

A46. ASQC 1 requires firms to establish policies and procedures for the timely completion of the assembly of engagement files.[16] An appropriate time limit within which to complete the assembly of the final engagement file is ordinarily not more than 60 days after the date of the service auditor's report.[17]

Preparing the Service Auditor's Assurance Report

Content of the Service Auditor's Assurance Report (Ref: Para. 53)

A47. Illustrative examples of service auditors' assurance reports, related service organisations' assertions and a description of the system are contained in Appendices 1, [Aus] 1A and 2.

15 See ASA 102.

16 See ASQC 1, paragraph 45.

17 See ASQC 1, paragraph A54.

Intended Users and Purposes of the Service Auditor's Assurance Report (Ref: Para. 53(e))

A48. The criteria used for engagements to report on controls at a service organisation are relevant only for the purposes of providing information about the service organisation's system, including controls, to those who have an understanding of how the system has been used for financial reporting by user entities. Accordingly this is stated in the service auditor's assurance report. In addition, the service auditor may consider it appropriate to include wording that specifically restricts distribution of the assurance report other than to intended users, its use by others, or its use for other purposes.

Description of the Tests of Controls (Ref: Para. 54)

A49. In describing the nature of the tests of controls for a type 2 report, it assists readers of the service auditor's assurance report if the service auditor includes:

- The results of all tests where deviations have been identified, even if other controls have been identified that allow the service auditor to conclude that the relevant control objective has been achieved or the control tested has subsequently been removed from the service organisation's description of its system.
- Information about causative factors for identified deviations, to the extent the service auditor has identified such factors.

Modified Opinions (Ref: Para. 55)

A50. Illustrative examples of elements of modified service auditor's assurance reports are contained in Appendix 3.

A51. Even if the service auditor has expressed an adverse opinion or disclaimed an opinion, it may be appropriate to describe in the basis for modification paragraph the reasons for any other matters of which the service auditor is aware that would have required a modification to the opinion, and the effects thereof.

A52. When expressing a disclaimer of opinion because of a scope limitation, it is not ordinarily appropriate to identify the procedures that were performed nor include statements describing the characteristics of a service auditor's engagement; to do so might overshadow the disclaimer of opinion.

Other Communication Responsibilities (Ref: Para. 56)

A53. Appropriate actions to respond to the circumstances identified in paragraph 56 may include:

- Obtaining legal advice about the consequences of different courses of action.
- Communicating with those charged with governance of the service organisation.
- Communicating with third parties (for example, a regulator) when required to do so.
- Modifying the service auditor's opinion, or adding an Other Matter paragraph.
- Withdrawing from the engagement.

❖ ❖ ❖

Conformity with International Standards on Assurance Engagements

This Standard on Assurance Engagements conforms with International Standard on Assurance Engagements ISAE 3402 *Assurance Reports on Controls at a Service Organization*, issued by the International Auditing and Assurance Standards Board (IAASB), an independent standard-setting board of the International Federation of Accountants (IFAC).

Paragraphs that have been added to this Standard on Assurance Engagements (and do not appear in the text of the equivalent ISAE) are identified with the prefix "Aus".

The following requirement is additional to ISAE 3402:

- The standard does not deal with instances when individual internal auditors provide direct assistance to the service auditor in carrying out assurance procedures. (Ref: Para. Aus 30.1)

ASAE

Appendices containing guidance which have been added to this Standard on Assurance Engagements (and do not appear in the appendices of the equivalent ISAE) are identified with the prefix "Aus".

The following appendices are additional to ISAE 3402:

- [Aus] Appendix 0A *Example Engagement Letter*
- [Aus] Appendix 0B *Example Representation Letter*
- [Aus] Appendix 1A: *Illustrative Example of a Service Organisation's Description of the System Accompanying XYZ Service Organisation Management's Assertion*

Compliance with this Standard enables compliance with ISAE 3402.

[Aus] Appendix 0A

(Ref: Para. Aus A12.1)

Example Engagement Letter

The following example of a service auditor's engagement letter is for guidance only and is not intended to be exhaustive or applicable to all situations.

Service Auditor's Engagement Letter for a Type 2 Report

To [the appropriate representative of management or those charged with governance] of XYZ Service Organisation:

[The objective and scope of the engagement]

You have requested that we report on the description of XYZ Service Organisation's [the type or name of] system and management's assertion with respect to that description, which you will provide and which will accompany our report. The description of XYZ Service Organisation's [the type or name of] system comprises control objectives and related controls designed to achieve those objectives for the [period] ended [date]. The control objectives included are those which are likely to be relevant to internal control as it relates to financial reporting of customers who have used [the type and name of system].

We are pleased to confirm our acceptance and our understanding of this assurance engagement by means of this letter. Our assurance engagement will be conducted with the objective of our expressing an opinion on the fair presentation of the [the type or name of] system, suitability of the design of the controls to achieve the control objectives throughout the period and the operating effectiveness of the controls necessary to provide reasonable assurance that the control objectives were achieved throughout the period.

[Responsibilities of the assurance practitioner]

We will conduct our assurance engagement in accordance with Standard on Assurance Engagements ASAE 3402 *Assurance Reports on Controls at a Service Organisation*. That standard requires that we comply with ethical requirements and plan and perform procedures to obtain reasonable assurance about whether, in all material respects, XYZ Service Organisation's description of the [the type or name of] system is fairly presented, the controls are suitably designed and operating effectively. An assurance engagement involves performing procedures to obtain evidence about the description, design and operating effectiveness of controls. The procedures selected depend on the assurance practitioner's judgement, including the assessment of the risks of significant deficiencies in the [the type or name of] system.

Because of the inherent limitations of an assurance engagement, together with the inherent limitations of any internal control system there is an unavoidable risk that some significant deficiencies may not be detected, even though the engagement is properly planned and performed in accordance with Standards on Assurance Engagements.

The system, within which the controls that we will test operate, will not be examined except to the extent the system is likely to be relevant to customers, as it relates to financial reporting. Hence no opinion will be expressed as to the effectiveness of the internal control system as a whole.

The work undertaken by us to form an opinion is permeated by judgement, in particular regarding the nature, timing and extent of assurance procedures for gathering evidence and the drawing of conclusions based on the evidence gathered. In addition to the inherent limitations in any assurance engagement, which include the use of testing, inherent limitations of any internal control structure, and the possibility of collusion, most evidence is persuasive rather than conclusive. As a result, an assurance engagement can only provide reasonable – not absolute – assurance that the description is fairly presented, controls are suitably designed and controls have operated effectively throughout the period.

[The responsibilities of management and identification of the applicable control framework]

Our assurance engagement will be conducted on the basis that [management or, where appropriate, those charged with governance] acknowledge and understand that they have responsibility:

(a) For the preparation of a written assertion that, in all material respects, and based on suitable criteria:

  (i) the description fairly presents the XYZ Service Organisation's [the type or name of] system designed and implemented throughout the period;

  (ii) The controls related to the control objectives stated in XYZ Service Organisation's description of its system were suitably designed throughout the specified period;

  (iii) The controls related to the control objectives stated in XYZ Service Organisation's description of its system operated effectively throughout the specified period.

(b) For design of the system, comprising controls which will achieve control objectives which are likely to be relevant to customers', who have used [the type or name of] system, internal control as it relates to financial reporting;

(c) To provide us with:

  (i) Access to all information of which those charged with governance and management are aware that is relevant to the design, implementation and operation of the [the type or name of] system;

  (ii) Additional information that we may request from those charged with governance and management for the purposes of this assurance engagement; and

  (iii) Unrestricted access to persons within the entity from whom we determine it necessary to obtain evidence.

As part of our assurance process, we will request from [management and, where appropriate, those charged with governance], written confirmation concerning representations made to us in connection with the engagement.

[Assurance Approach]

We will examine and evaluate the control objectives and controls for [the type or name of] system described above. The "Description of [the type or name of] System" will include details of controls with which customers should comply. While our evaluation will include assessment of the appropriateness of the complementary customer controls, our testing will not encompass evaluation of the suitability of design or operating effectiveness of controls carried out by users of XYZ Service Organisation's [the type or name of] system. The control objectives stated in XYZ Service Organisation's description of its system can be achieved only if complementary user entity controls are suitably designed or operating effectively, along with the controls at the service organisation.

Our procedures will extend to the control objectives and related controls at relevant subservice organisations only to the extent that those controls are included in XYZ Service Organisation's description of [the type or name of] system and are necessary to achieve the relevant control objectives.

Due to the complex nature of internal control, our assurance procedures will not encompass all individual controls at XYZ Service Organisation, but will be restricted to an examination of those controls reported which achieve the control objectives identified by XYZ Service Organisation's management in the "Description of the [the type or name of] System" provided to us.

[Assurance Procedures]

Our assurance procedures are likely to include:

1. Performing a preliminary review of the control environment of XYZ Service Organisation relevant to the [the type or name of] system;
2. Evaluating the reasonableness of the control objectives;
3. Evaluating the completeness, accuracy and presentation of the Description of the [the type or name of] System against the controls implemented.
4. Evaluating the design of specific controls by:
   - Assessing the risks that threaten the achievement of the control objectives.
   - Evaluating whether the controls described are capable of addressing those risks and achieving the related objectives.
5. Performing tests of controls to ascertain whether the degree of compliance with controls is sufficient to provide reasonable assurance that the controls have achieved their objectives throughout the period.

In undertaking this engagement, we shall work closely with XYZ Service Organisation's internal audit function and place reliance on their work in accordance with ASA 610 *Using the Work of Internal Auditors* [this paragraph is applicable where the work of internal audit is an integral part of the assurance engagement].

[Assurance Report]

The format of the report will be in accordance with ASAE 3402 and will consist of an opinion on the "Description of the [the type or name of] system" by XYZ Service Organisation management and an accompanying description of the tests of controls that we performed and the results of those tests. An example of the proposed report is contained in the appendix to this letter.

Our report will be issued [frequency] and will cover [period reported on] (paragraph is appropriate for recurring engagements).

The assurance report will be incorporated in a report issued by the XYZ Service Organisation containing information prepared by XYZ Service Organisation management to provide customers and their auditors with an overall understanding of [subject matter]. We will review the contents of the report issued by XYZ Service Organisation to identify any material inconsistencies with the Description of the [the type or name of] System.

[Distribution of the Assurance Report]

Our report and the accompanying description of tests of controls are intended only for customers of XYZ Service Organisation which use the [the type or name of] system and their auditors, who have a sufficient understanding to consider it, along with other information including information about controls operated by customers themselves, when assessing the risks of material misstatements of customers' financial reports.

The assurance report will be prepared for this purpose only and we disclaim any assumption of responsibility for any reliance on our report to any person other than to XYZ Service Organisation's customers and their auditors, or for any purpose other than that for which it was prepared.

[Significant Deficiencies in Controls]

We will issue an assurance report without modification, to provide assurance on the [the type or name of] system where our procedures do not disclose a significant deficiency in the controls necessary to achieve the control objectives contained in the Description of the [the type or name of] System by XYZ Service Organisation management. For this purpose, a significant deficiency exists when prescribed control procedures, or the degree of compliance with them:

(a) does not provide XYZ Service Organisation management with reasonable assurance that the control objectives will be met or that fraud, error, or non-compliance with laws and regulations would be prevented or detected by employees in the normal course of their assigned functions; and

(b) knowledge of that deficiency would be material to users of the assurance report.

If our assurance engagement discloses that there are significant deficiencies in the system of controls in operation during the period covered by the report, such deficiencies will be disclosed in our report even if they were corrected prior to the end of the reporting period. However, our report will indicate that such deficiencies were corrected if that is the case. If any significant deficiencies disclosed in our report have been corrected subsequent to this period (or are in the process of being corrected), we will refer to this in our report.

Although the primary purpose of our assurance engagement will be to enable us to issue the above described report, we will also periodically provide you with letters containing recommendations for strengthening controls if such matters are observed during the process of the assurance engagement. Although issues raised may not represent significant deficiencies in the system of controls, recommendations will address areas where we believe controls could be improved.

We look forward to full cooperation from your staff during our assurance engagement.

[Other relevant information]

[Insert other information, such as fee arrangements, billings and other specific terms, as appropriate.]

Please sign and return the attached copy of this letter to indicate your acknowledgement of, and agreement with, the arrangements for our assurance engagement to report on the control procedures over your services to customers, including our respective responsibilities.

Yours faithfully,

(signed)

....

Name and Title

Date

Acknowledged on behalf of XYZ Service Organisation

(signed)

....

Name and Title

Date

ASAE

[Aus] Appendix 0B

(Ref: Para. 39)

Example Representation Letter

The following example of a representation letter is for guidance only and is not intended to be exhaustive or applicable to all situations.

Representation Letter for a Type 2 Engagement

[To auditor]

This representation letter is provided in connection with your assurance engagement to report on XYZ Service Organisation's [the type or name of] system (the system) for the period [date] to [date], set forth in XYZ Service Organisation's (XYZ) description of the system pages [bb-cc], for the purpose of expressing an opinion on the fair presentation of the description of the system, suitability of the design to achieve the control objectives and the operating effectiveness of controls throughout the period.

We confirm that, to the best of our knowledge and belief, having made such enquiries as we considered necessary for the purpose of appropriately informing ourselves:

Description of the System

1. We have fulfilled our responsibilities, as set out in the terms of the engagement dated [insert date], for the preparation of the description of the system pages [bb-cc] and the accompanying XYZ's assertion page [aa], including the completeness, accuracy and method of presentation of that description and assertion and we have a reasonable basis for making that assertion.
2. We have identified the risks that threaten achievement of the control objectives stated in the description of the system, and designed and implemented controls to provide reasonable assurance that those risks will not prevent achievement of the control objectives stated in the description of the system, and therefore the stated control objectives will be achieved.
3. The description of the system set out in our report fairly presents the system for processing customers' transactions throughout the period [date] to [date].
4. The controls related to the control objectives stated in the accompanying description were suitably designed and operated effectively throughout the period [date] to [date].

Information Provided

1. We have provided you with:
   (a) access to all information of which we are aware that is relevant to the purposes of your engagement such as records, documentation and other matters;
   (b) additional information that you have requested from us for the purpose of the assurance engagement; and
   (c) unrestricted access to persons within XYZ from whom you determined it necessary to obtain evidence.
2. We have disclosed to you:
   (a) all known instances of non-compliance or suspected non-compliance with laws and regulations, fraud or suspected fraud and uncorrected deviations attributable to ABC that may effect one or more customers of [type of services];
   (b) all control design deficiencies of which we are aware;
   (c) all instances, of which we are aware, where controls have not operated as described; and
   (d) any events subsequent to the period [date] to[date] up to [date of the assurance report] that could have a significant effect on your report.

Yours faithfully,

XYZ Service Organisation

....

Management Management

Appendix 1

(Ref: Para. A47)

Example Service Organisation's Assertions

The following examples of service organisations' assertions are for guidance only and are not intended to be exhaustive or applicable to all situations.

Example 1: Type 2 Service Organisation's Assertion

Assertion by the Service Organisation

The accompanying description has been prepared for customers who have used [the type or name of] system and their auditors who have a sufficient understanding to consider the description, along with other information including information about controls operated by customers themselves, when assessing the risks of material misstatements of customers' financial reports/statements. [Entity's name] confirms that:

(a) The accompanying description at pages [bb-cc] fairly presents [the type or name of] system for processing customers' transactions throughout the period [date] to [date]. The criteria used in making this assertion were that the accompanying description:

(i) Presents how the system was designed and implemented, including:

- The types of services provided, including, as appropriate, classes of transactions processed.
- The procedures, within both information technology and manual systems, by which those transactions were initiated, recorded, processed, corrected as necessary, and transferred to the reports prepared for customers.
- The related accounting records, supporting information and specific accounts that were used to initiate, record, process and report transactions; this includes the correction of incorrect information and how information was transferred to the reports prepared for customers.
- How the system dealt with significant events and conditions, other than transactions.
- The process used to prepare reports for customers.
- Relevant control objectives and controls designed to achieve those objectives.
- Controls that we assumed, in the design of the system, would be implemented by customers, and which, if necessary to achieve control objectives stated in the accompanying description, are identified in the description along with the specific control objectives that cannot be achieved by ourselves alone.
- Other aspects of our control environment, risk assessment process, information system (including the related business processes) and communication, control activities and monitoring controls that were relevant to processing and reporting customers' transactions.

(ii) Includes relevant details of changes to the service organisation's system during the period [date] to [date].

(iii) Does not omit or distort information relevant to the scope of the system being described, while acknowledging that the description is prepared to meet the common needs of a broad range of customers and their auditors and may not, therefore, include every aspect of the system that each individual customer may consider important in its own particular environment.

(b) The controls related to the control objectives stated in the accompanying description were suitably designed and operated effectively throughout the period [date] to [date]. The criteria used in making this assertion were that:

(i) The risks that threatened achievement of the control objectives stated in the description were identified;

(ii) The identified controls would, if operated as described, provide reasonable assurance that those risks did not prevent the stated control objectives from being achieved; and

(iii) The controls were consistently applied as designed, including that manual controls were applied by individuals who have the appropriate competence and authority, throughout the period [date] to [date].

Example 2: Type 1 Service Organisation's Assertion

The accompanying description has been prepared for customers who have used [the type or name of] system and their auditors who have a sufficient understanding to consider the description, along with other information including information about controls operated by customers themselves, when obtaining an understanding of customers' information systems relevant to financial reporting. [Entity's name] confirms that:

(a) The accompanying description at pages [bb-cc] fairly presents [the type or name of] system for processing customers' transactions as at [date]. The criteria used in making this assertion were that the accompanying description:

(i) Presents how the system was designed and implemented, including:

- The types of services provided, including, as appropriate, classes of transactions processed.
- The procedures, within both information technology and manual systems, by which those transactions were initiated, recorded, processed, corrected as necessary, and transferred to the reports prepared for customers.
- The related accounting records, supporting information and specific accounts that were used to initiate, record, process and report transactions; this includes the correction of incorrect information and how information is transferred to the reports prepared for customers.
- How the system dealt with significant events and conditions, other than transactions.
- The process used to prepare reports for customers.
- Relevant control objectives and controls designed to achieve those objectives.
- Controls that we assumed, in the design of the system, would be implemented by customers, and which, if necessary to achieve control objectives stated in the accompanying description, are identified in the description along with the specific control objectives that cannot be achieved by ourselves alone.
- Other aspects of our control environment, risk assessment process, information system (including the related business processes) and communication, control activities and monitoring controls that were relevant to processing and reporting customers' transactions.

(ii) Does not omit or distort information relevant to the scope of the system being described, while acknowledging that the description is prepared to meet the common needs of a broad range of customers and their auditors and may not, therefore, include every aspect of the system that each individual customer may consider important in its own particular environment.

(b) The controls related to the control objectives stated in the accompanying description were suitably designed as at [date]. The criteria used in making this assertion were that:

(i) The risks that threatened achievement of the control objectives stated in the description were identified; and

(ii) The identified controls would, if operated as described, provide reasonable assurance that those risks did not prevent the stated control objectives from being achieved.

[Aus] Appendix 1A

(Ref: Para. A47)

Illustrative Example of a Service Organisation's Description of the System Accompanying XYZ Service Organisation Management's Assertion

The following example of the service organisation's description of the system is illustrative only and is not intended to be exhaustive or applicable to all situations. The preparation and presentation of the description of the service organisation's system is the responsibility of management of the service organisation and the format is not prescribed by this standard, including this appendix. Management's description of the service organisation's system should be developed as appropriate to suit the individual circumstances of the assurance engagement.

XYZ Service Organisation's Computer Timeshare System

Services Provided

XYZ Service Organisation (XYZ) operates a data centre that provides its customers timeshare for on-line computer based systems. Batch generation of reports extracted from on-line data is also available upon request.

The data centre houses computer hardware and system software and accommodates operators responsible for day-to-day operations of the network, computer systems and production scheduling, the hardware, and an operations support function responsible for disk support, maintenance and back-up of data and software.

ASAE

The System

The stated internal control objectives and related controls included in this report apply to XYZ operations as they relate only to computer timesharing services. Specifically excluded from this report are controls within individual systems, controls executed at customer premises and other services provided by XYZ, including data conversion services, custom application development and facilities management.

The effectiveness of controls performed by customers of XYZ should also be considered as part of the overall system of control relating to processing performed at the XYZ data centre.

*[Describe, as appropriate:**

- *The procedures, within both information technology and manual systems, by which those transactions were initiated, recorded, processed, corrected as necessary, and transferred to the reports prepared for customers.*
- *The related accounting records, supporting information and specific accounts that were used to initiate, record, process and report transactions; this includes the correction of incorrect information and how information is transferred to the reports prepared for customers.*
- *How the system dealt with significant events and conditions, other than transactions.*
- *The process used to prepare reports for customers.*

This may include a description of the flow of transactions or a flowchart].

* Aspects of the system to be described here relate to the manner in which the system operates to provide services to customers but do not include specific controls which are designed to achieve the control objectives.

[Controls at Subservice Organisations]**

[XYZ Service Organisation uses [name of subservice organisation] to provide [type or name of] services, which form part of the [type or name of] system used by XYZ Service Organisation's customers. The [type or name of] services provided by [subservice organisation] are [describe the nature of the services provided]. XYZ Service Organisation's description of the system includes XYZ Service Organisation's monitoring controls over the operating effectiveness of the controls at [subservice organisation] and [includes/excludes]*** the relevant control objectives and related controls of [subservice organisation].]

We set out in this report the control objectives [specified by [identify law, regulation or another party]]**** and related controls implemented for the XYZ data centre of XYZ Service Organisation. The specific controls set out in the remainder of the report have been designed to achieve each of the control objectives. The controls have been in place throughout the period from [date] to [date] unless otherwise indicated.

Internal Control Objective

1. Effective segregation of duties exists at the XYZ data centre.

Related Controls#

1.1 There is a formal organisation structure for all functions at the XYZ data centre. Each functional group reports to a separate manager, who in turn reports to the Senior Manager - Data Processing Services.

*[**Period of operation:** If the control has not been in operation the entire period or has changed, state the period during which the control was operating and the period during which the change was effective.]*†

*[**Complementary customer controls:** Describe any complementary user entity controls contemplated in the design of the controls.]*‡

1.2 Segregation of functions exists for computer operations, systems support, hardware support, applications development and administrative functions.

Internal Control Objective

2. Physical security is restricted to prevent inadvertent or unauthorised access to computer facilities, software and documentation.

Related Controls

2.1 Security guards are in attendance 24 hours per day, 7 days per week. Entrances are either manned or locked and alarmed.

2.2 All exterior doors are locked, alarmed and subject to visual surveillance.

2.3 Access to and within the data centre is restricted by a cardkey security system that provides on-line monitoring of physical access and intrusion. Procedures exist for security guards to monitor accesses and intrusions.

** Insert this section if XYZ Service Organisation uses a subservice organisation which performs some of the services provided to customers which use the system.

*** Use "includes" if the inclusive method is used and "excludes" if the carve-out method is used with respect to the subservice organisation's services.

**** Insert if control objectives are specified by law, regulation or another party.

Controls may include other aspects of the service organisation's control environment, risk assessment process, information system (including the related business processes) and communication, control activities and monitoring controls which are designed to achieve the control objective and that are relevant to the services provided.

† This section should be inserted for each control which has not been in operation for the whole period or has changed during the period.

‡ This section should be inserted for each control for which there are complementary user entity controls contemplated in the design of the control.

2.4 All authorised personnel are required to wear colour-coded badges that identify the individual and specify the areas to which access is allowed within the data centre.

2.5 Visitors must be signed in/out by an authorised individual and escorted whilst on the premises.

Internal Control Objective

3. Logical access is restricted to prevent inadvertent or unauthorised access to systems software, application programs and data.

Related Controls

3.1 Procedures exist to ensure all accesses are authorised.

3.2 All authorised personnel are issued unique user identification codes and are responsible for maintaining the corresponding passwords.

3.3 Access control software is implemented to restrict access and report violations of logical security.

3.4 Access violation reports are reviewed on a timely basis and followed-up.

3.5 Network transmissions originate from pre-determined terminal locations. Remote access is restricted.

3.6 Utilities identified as having special capabilities are restricted in their use and usage is monitored and justified.

Internal Control Objective

4. Systems software changes and enhancements are subject to authorisation and testing to maintain the integrity of the system software environment.

Related Controls

4.1 Responsibilities for the support and maintenance of system software are documented.

4.2 Changes and enhancements to system software components are scheduled.

4.3 All changes and enhancements to system software are authorised by the manager responsible for system software.

4.4 Testing of system software changes and enhancements are subject to pre-determined test criteria. Achievement of the criteria is required prior to implementation in the production environment.

4.5 Documentation for system software, including all changes and enhancements, exists in libraries organised by the software support function.

Internal Control Objective

5. An environmentally controlled facility exists to ensure continuity of data processing operations.

Related Controls

5.1 The data centre building is constructed of non-combustible materials.

5.2 The data centre is protected with fire, water and heat detection systems that are tested periodically. Fire suppression systems exist and are tested on a regular basis.

5.3 The data centre has an uninterruptible power supply (UPS) to prevent deviations in power supply to computer equipment and support facilities.

5.4 Preventive maintenance is carried out on a regular basis on the detection, air conditioning and fire suppression systems.

Internal Control Objective

6. Back-up procedures are adequate to ensure the continuity of processing in the event of a disaster.

Related Controls

6.1 A disaster recovery plan, designed to provide reasonable assurance that processing can be maintained, exists, is documented and maintained.

6.2 An off-site facility has been contracted in order to execute the disaster recovery plan.

6.3 System software is backed up on a weekly basis and stored off-site. Application programs and data are backed up daily and stored off-site. Documentation is backed up monthly and stored off-site.

6.4 On-site back-ups exist to facilitate the resumption of processing operations in the event of minor interruptions in processing.

6.5 The disaster recovery plan is tested at least once on an annual basis.

Internal Control Objective

7. Problems relating to data centre operations, including the communications network, are identified and resolved on a timely basis.

Related Controls

7.1 Schedules establishing the operations of the data centre are pre-determined and authorised.

7.2 All special requests of the operations support function must be documented and authorised.

7.3 Performance of the data centre operations, including the communications network, is monitored on a regular basis.

7.4 Problems identified with computer operations are logged and the status is monitored to resolution.

7.5 Operations support prepares a weekly report describing major incidents and summarising system performance as compared to established performance criteria. The report is reviewed by data centre management.

Appendix 2

(Ref: Para. A47)

Example Service Auditor's Assurance Reports

The following examples of reports are for guidance only and are not intended to be exhaustive or applicable to all situations.

Example 1: Type 2 Service Auditor's Assurance Report

Independent Service Auditor's Assurance Report on the Description of Controls, their Design and Operating Effectiveness

To: XYZ Service Organisation

Scope

We have been engaged to report on XYZ Service Organisation's description at pages [bb-cc] of its [type or name of] system for processing customers' transactions throughout the period [date] to [date] (the description), and on the design and operation of controls related to the control objectives stated in the description.[18]

XYZ Service Organisation's Responsibilities

XYZ Service Organisation is responsible for: preparing the description and accompanying assertion at page [aa], including the completeness, accuracy and method of presentation of the description and assertion; providing the services covered by the description; stating the control objectives; and designing, implementing and effectively operating controls to achieve the stated control objectives.

Service Auditor's Responsibilities

Our responsibility is to express an opinion on XYZ Service Organisation's description and on the design and operation of controls related to the control objectives stated in that description, based on our procedures. We conducted our engagement in accordance with Standard on Assurance Engagements ASAE 3402 *Assurance Reports on Controls at a Service Organisation*, issued by the Auditing and Assurance Standards Board. That standard requires that we comply with relevant ethical requirements and plan and perform our procedures to obtain reasonable assurance about whether, in all material respects, the description is fairly presented and the controls are suitably designed and operating effectively.

An assurance engagement to report on the description, design and operating effectiveness of controls at a service organisation involves performing procedures to obtain evidence about the disclosures in the service organisation's description of its system, and the design and operating effectiveness of controls. The procedures selected depend on our judgement, including the assessment of the risks that the description is not fairly presented, and that controls are not suitably designed or operating effectively. Our procedures included testing the operating effectiveness of those controls that we consider necessary to provide reasonable assurance that the control objectives stated in the description were achieved. An assurance engagement of this type also includes evaluating the overall presentation of the description, the suitability of the objectives stated therein, and the suitability of the criteria specified by the service organisation and described at page [aa].

We believe that the evidence we have obtained is sufficient and appropriate to provide a basis for our opinion.

Limitations of Controls at a Service Organisation

XYZ Service Organisation's description is prepared to meet the common needs of a broad range of customers and their auditors and may not, therefore, include every aspect of the system that each individual customer may consider important in its own particular environment. Also, because of their nature, controls at a service organisation may not prevent or detect all errors

18 If some elements of the description are not included in the scope of the engagement, this is made clear in the assurance report.

ASAE

or omissions in processing or reporting transactions. Also, the projection of any evaluation of effectiveness to future periods is subject to the risk that controls at a service organisation may become inadequate or fail.

Opinion

Our opinion has been formed on the basis of the matters outlined in this report. The criteria we used in forming our opinion are those described at page [aa]. In our opinion, in all material respects:

(a) The description fairly presents the [the type or name of] system as designed and implemented throughout the period from [date] to [date];

(b) The controls related to the control objectives stated in the description were suitably designed throughout the period from [date] to [date]; and

(c) The controls tested, which were those necessary to provide reasonable assurance that the control objectives stated in the description were achieved, operated effectively throughout the period from [date] to [date].

Description of Tests of Controls

The specific controls tested and the nature, timing and results of those tests are listed on pages [yy-zz].

Intended Users and Purpose

This report and the description of tests of controls on pages [yy-zz] are intended only for customers who have used XYZ Service Organisation's [type or name of] system, and their auditors, who have a sufficient understanding to consider it, along with other information including information about controls operated by customers themselves, when assessing the risks of material misstatements of customers' financial reports/statements.

[Service auditor's signature]

[Date of the service auditor's assurance report]

[Service auditor's address]

Example 2: Type 1 Service Auditor's Assurance Report

Independent Service Auditor's Assurance Report on the Description of Controls and their Design

To: XYZ Service Organisation

Scope

We have been engaged to report on XYZ Service Organisation's description at pages [bb-cc] of its [type or name of] system for processing customers' transactions as at [date] (the description), and on the design of controls related to the control objectives stated in the description.[19]

We did not perform any procedures regarding the operating effectiveness of controls included in the description and, accordingly, do not express an opinion thereon.

XYZ Service Organisation's Responsibilities

XYZ Service Organisation is responsible for: preparing the description and accompanying assertion at page [aa], including the completeness, accuracy and method of presentation of the description and the assertion; providing the services covered by the description; stating the control objectives; and designing, implementing and effectively operating controls to achieve the stated control objectives.

19 If some elements of the description are not included in the scope of the engagement, this is made clear in the assurance report.

Service Auditor's Responsibilities

Our responsibility is to express an opinion on XYZ Service Organisation's description and on the design of controls related to the control objectives stated in that description, based on our procedures. We conducted our engagement in accordance with Standard on Assurance Engagements ASAE 3402 *Assurance Reports on Controls at a Service Organisation*, issued by the Auditing and Assurance Standards Board. That standard requires that we comply with ethical requirements and plan and perform our procedures to obtain reasonable assurance about whether, in all material respects, the description is fairly presented and the controls are suitably designed in all material respects.

An assurance engagement to report on the description and design of controls at a service organisation involves performing procedures to obtain evidence about the disclosures in the service organisation's description of its system, and the design of controls. The procedures selected depend on our judgement, including the assessment that the description is not fairly presented, and that controls are not suitably designed. An assurance engagement of this type also includes evaluating the overall presentation of the description, the suitability of the control objectives stated therein, and the suitability of the criteria specified by the service organisation and described at page [aa].

As noted above, we did not perform any procedures regarding the operating effectiveness of controls included in the description and, accordingly, do not express an opinion thereon.

We believe that the evidence we have obtained is sufficient and appropriate to provide a basis for our opinion.

Limitations of Controls at a Service Organisation

XYZ Service Organisation's description is prepared to meet the common needs of a broad range of customers and their auditors and may not, therefore, include every aspect of the system that each individual customer may consider important in its own particular environment. Also, because of their nature, controls at a service organisation may not prevent or detect all errors or omissions in processing or reporting transactions.

Opinion

Our opinion has been formed on the basis of the matters outlined in this report. The criteria we used in forming our opinion are those described at page [aa]. In our opinion, in all material respects:

(a) The description fairly presents the [the type or name of] system as designed and implemented as at [date]; and

(b) The controls related to the control objectives stated in the description were suitably designed as at [date].

Intended Users and Purpose

This report is intended only for customers who have used XYZ Service Organisation's [type or name of] system, and their auditors, who have a sufficient understanding to consider it, along with other information including information about controls operated by customers themselves, when obtaining an understanding of customers' information systems relevant to financial reporting.

[Service auditor's signature]

[Date of the service auditor's assurance report]

[Service auditor's address]

Appendix 3

(Ref: Para. A50)

Example Modified Service Auditor's Assurance Reports

The following examples of modified reports are for guidance only and are not intended to be exhaustive or applicable to all situations. They are based on the examples of reports in Appendix 2.

Example 1: Qualified opinion – the service organisation's description of the system is not fairly presented in all material respects

…

Service Auditor's Responsibilities

…

We believe that the evidence we have obtained is sufficient and appropriate to provide a basis for our qualified opinion.

Basis for Qualified Opinion

The accompanying description states at page [mn] that XYZ Service Organisation uses operator identification numbers and passwords to prevent unauthorised access to the system. Based on our procedures, which included enquiries of staff personnel and observation of activities, we have determined that operator identification numbers and passwords are employed in Applications A and B but not in Applications C and D.

Qualified Opinion

Our opinion has been formed on the basis of the matters outlined in this report. The criteria we used in forming our opinion were those described in XYZ Service Organisation's assertion at page [aa]. In our opinion, except for the matter described in the Basis for Qualified Opinion paragraph:

(a) …

Example 2: Qualified opinion – the controls are not suitably designed to provide reasonable assurance that the control objectives stated in the service organisation's description of its system will be achieved if the controls operate effectively

…

Service Auditor's Responsibilities

…

We believe that the evidence we have obtained is sufficient and appropriate to provide a basis for our qualified opinion.

Basis for Qualified Opinion

As discussed at page [mn] of the accompanying description, from time to time XYZ Service Organisation makes changes in application programs to correct deficiencies or to enhance capabilities. The procedures followed in determining whether to make changes, in designing the changes and in implementing them, do not include review and approval by authorised individuals who are independent from those involved in making the changes. There are also no specified requirements to test such changes or provide test results to an authorised reviewer prior to implementing the changes.

Qualified Opinion

Our opinion has been formed on the basis of the matters outlined in this report. The criteria we used in forming our opinion were those described in XYZ Service Organisation's assertion at page [aa]. In our opinion, except for the matter described in the Basis for Qualified Opinion paragraph:

(a) …

Example 3: Qualified opinion – the controls did not operate effectively throughout the specified period (type 2 report only)

…

Service Auditor's Responsibilities

…

We believe that the evidence we have obtained is sufficient and appropriate to provide a basis for our qualified opinion.

Basis for Qualified Opinion

XYZ Service Organisation states in its description that it has automated controls in place to reconcile loan payments received with the output generated. However, as noted at page [mn] of the description, this control was not operating effectively during the period from [date] to [date] due to a programming error. This resulted in the non-achievement of the control objective "Controls provide reasonable assurance that loan payments received are properly recorded" during the period from [date] to [date]. XYZ implemented a change to the program performing the calculation as of [date], and our tests indicate that it was operating effectively during the period from [date] to [date].

ASAE

Qualified Opinion

Our opinion has been formed on the basis of the matters outlined in this report. The criteria we used in forming our opinion were those described in XYZ Service Organisation's assertion at page [aa]. In our opinion, except for the matter described in the Basis for Qualified Opinion paragraph:

…

Example 4: Qualified opinion – the service auditor is unable to obtain sufficient appropriate evidence

…

Service Auditor's Responsibilities

…

We believe that the evidence we have obtained is sufficient and appropriate to provide a basis for our qualified opinion.

Basis for Qualified Opinion

XYZ Service Organisation states in its description that it has automated controls in place to reconcile loan payments received with the output generated. However, electronic records of the performance of this reconciliation for the period from [date] to [date] were deleted as a result of a computer processing error, and we were therefore unable to test the operation of this control for that period. Consequently, we were unable to determine whether the control objective "Controls provide reasonable assurance that loan payments received are properly recorded" operated effectively during the period from [date] to [date].

Qualified Opinion

Our opinion has been formed on the basis of the matters outlined in this report. The criteria we used in forming our opinion were those described in XYZ Service Organisation's assertion at page [aa]. In our opinion, except for the matter described in the Basis for Qualified Opinion paragraph:

(a) …

Explanation of the Applicability of AUASB pronouncements when conducting Internal Control Engagements

(Issued 26 October 2011)

Assurance engagements to report on controls at an entity may be conducted and reported on by the assurance practitioner under a number of different pronouncements depending on the subject matter and the whether or not assurance is being provided. The objective of this explanation is to assist the assurance practitioner in determining the appropriate pronouncement to apply in any given circumstance.

The following pronouncements may be applicable when conducting an engagement on controls:

- ASAE 3000 *Assurance Engagements other than Audits or Reviews of Historical Financial Information*
- AUS 810 *Special Purpose Reports on the Effectiveness of Control Procedures*
- ASAE 3402 *Assurance Reports on Controls at a Service Organisation*
- GS 007 *Audit Implications of the Use of Service Organisations for Investment Management Services*
- ASRS 4400 *Agreed-Upon Procedures Engagements to Report Factual Findings*

The overarching standard for engagements to report on controls when assurance is to be provided is ASAE 3000, which provides the broad requirements for all assurance engagements, other than audits or reviews of historical financial information. Consequently, ASAE 3000 will need to be applied in all assurance engagements on controls.

ASAE

In addition, AUS 810, which was issued under a previous framework by the former AuASB in 2002 and predates ASAE 3000, is applicable to certain assurance and agreed-upon procedures engagements to report on controls and provides additional requirements relating specifically to controls. AUS 810 requires updating and is expected to be replaced with a new Assurance Standard in the 2011-12 financial year. Consequently, AUS 810 may be applied only to the extent that the requirements of ASAE 3000 are also met. Where inconsistencies are identified, the requirements of ASAE 3000 take precedence over AUS 810.

For engagements to conduct agreed-upon procedures on controls and report factual findings, AUS 810 is applied alongside ASRS 4400.

Where a controls engagement relates to reporting on a service organisation for use by user entities and their auditors, ASAE 3402 specifically applies. AUS 810 does not need to be applied in these circumstances as ASAE 3402 provides all of the necessary requirements. Further guidance is provided by GS 007 where the services provided by the service organisation are investment management services.

The following table summarises the applicability of the AUASB's pronouncements when conducting internal controls engagements:

AUASB Standard or Guidance	ASAE 3000	AUS 810	ASAE 3402	GS 007 (2011)	ASRS 4400
Title	*Assurance Engagements other than Audits or Reviews of Historical Financial Information*	*Special Purpose Reports on the Effectiveness of Control Procedures*	*Assurance Reports on Controls at a Service Organisation*	*Audit Implications of the Use of Service Organisations for Investment Management Services*	*Agreed-Upon Procedures Engagements to Report Factual Findings*

Disclaimer: The above information is provided by the AUASB Technical Group to assist auditors and assurance practitioners when conducting internal control engagements. No responsibility is taken by the AUASB for the results of actions or omissions to act on the basis of any information contained in this document or for any errors or omissions in it.

AUASB Standard or Guidance	ASAE 3000	AUS 810	ASAE 3402	GS 007 (2011)	ASRS 4400
Applicable to reporting periods commencing ON or AFTER	I July 2007	July 2002	1 July 2010	1 January 2012[1]	1 July 2011
Applicable practitioners	Assurance practitioners	Auditors (generally)	Assurance practitioners engaged to report on service organisation controls (service auditor)	Service auditors for investment management services organisations	Assurance practitioners
Subject matter of assurance engagement	Other than Historical Financial Information (including controls)	Design and operating effectiveness of control procedures	Description, design and/ or operating effectiveness of controls at a service organisation	Description, design and/ or operating effectiveness of controls at an investment management service organisation	Any subject matter subject to agreed-upon procedures
Nature of Report	Reasonable or limited assurance	Reasonable or limited assurance or factual findings	Reasonable assurance	Reasonable assurance	Factual findings
Issue date	9 July 2007	July 2002	29 June 2010	25 October 2011	June 2011

1 The superseded GS 007 (2008) was operative for reporting periods commencing on or after 1 July 2008.

Disclaimer: The above information is provided by the AUASB Technical Group to assist auditors and assurance practitioners when conducting internal control engagements. No responsibility is taken by the AUASB for the results of actions or omissions to act on the basis of any information contained in this document or for any errors or omissions in it.

ASAE 3410

Assurance Engagements on Greenhouse Gas Statements

(Issued June 2012)

Issued by the Auditing and Assurance Standards Board.

Note from the Institute of Chartered Accountants Australia

This note, prepared by the technical editor, is not part of ASAE 3410.

Historical development

June 2012: ASAE 3410 issued to provide requirements and application material for practitioners providing assurance on statements of greenhouse gas emissions. It conforms with ISAE 3410 of the same name and is operative for periods beginning on or after 1 July 2012.

November 2012: The AUASB approved for issue GS 021 'Engagements under the National Greenhouse and Energy Reporting, Clean Energy and Related Schemes'. It is due to be issued during December 2012 and is operative from 1 July 2012. It will be available from auasb.gov.au. It relates the Standard in ASAE 3410 to the Australian legislative context.

Contents

Preface

Reasons for Issuing ASAE 3410

The AUASB issues Standard on Assurance Engagements ASAE 3410 *Assurance Engagements on Greenhouse Gas Statements,* pursuant to the requirements of the legislative provisions explained below.

The AUASB is an independent statutory committee of the Australian Government established under section 227A of the *Australian Securities and Investments Commission Act 2001*, as amended (ASIC Act). Under section 227B of the ASIC Act, the AUASB may formulate assurance standards for other purposes.

New Standard on Assurance Engagements

This Standard on Assurance Engagements is a new pronouncement of the AUASB and accordingly does not supersede a pre-existing Standard on Assurance Engagements. It conforms with ISAE 3410 Assurance Engagements on Greenhouse Gas Statements to be issued by the International Auditing and Assurance Standards Board (IAASB) in 2012.

Main Features

This Standard on Assurance Engagements establishes requirements and provides application and other explanatory material regarding the assurance practitioner's responsibilities when accepting, conducting and reporting on an engagement to provide reasonable or limited assurance on a greenhouse gas statement.

The AUASB intends for this new standard to mirror ISAE 3410 to ensure conformity with IAASB standards. In Australia, greenhouse gas statements include reports on emissions, energy consumption and energy production under the *National Greenhouse and Energy Reporting* (NGER) *Act 2007* and legislative requirements for assurance on those reports are also provided under the NGER Act and related regulations. These reporting and assurance requirements underpin the NGER and Clean Energy Schemes, which provide for emissions reporting and a carbon pricing mechanism respectively. The AUASB intends to develop and issue a Guidance Statement to provide guidance for the assurance practitioner on how to meet these legislative and regulatory requirements when conducting an engagement under ASAE 3410. These legislative requirements are not addressed in detail in this proposed standard.

Authority Statement

The Auditing and Assurance Standards Board (AUASB) formulates this Standard on Assurance Engagements ASAE 3410 *Assurance Engagements on Greenhouse Gas Statements,* pursuant to section 227B of the *Australian Securities and Investments Commission Act 2001.*

This Standard on Assurance Engagements is to be read in conjunction with ASA 100 *Preamble to AUASB Standards*, which sets out the intentions of the AUASB on how the AUASB Standards are to be understood, interpreted and applied.

Dated: 28 June 2012

M H Kelsall
Chairman - AUASB

Standard on Assurance Engagements ASAE 3410

Assurance Engagements on Greenhouse Gas Statements

Application

Aus 0.1 This Standard on Assurance Engagements applies to an assurance engagement to provide either a reasonable assurance or limited assurance report on a greenhouse gas statement.

Operative Date

Aus 0.2 This Standard on Assurance Engagements is operative for reporting periods commencing on or after 1 July 2012.

Introduction

1. Given the link between greenhouse gas (GHG) emissions and climate change, many entities are quantifying their GHG emissions for internal management purposes, and many are also preparing a GHG statement:
   (a) As part of a regulatory disclosure regime;*
   (b) As part of an emissions trading scheme;# or
   (c) To inform investors and others on a voluntary basis. Voluntary disclosures may be, for example, published as a stand-alone document; included as part of a broader sustainability report or in an entity's annual report; or made to support inclusion in a "carbon register."

Scope of this Standard on Assurance Engagements

2. This Standard on Assurance Engagements (ASAE) deals with assurance engagements to report on an entity's GHG statement.
3. The assurance practitioner's conclusion in an assurance engagement may cover information in addition to a GHG statement, for example, when the assurance practitioner is engaged to report on a sustainability report of which a GHG statement is only one part. In such cases: (Ref: Para. A1–A2)
   (a) This ASAE applies to assurance procedures performed with respect to the GHG statement other than when the GHG statement is a relatively minor part of the overall information subject to assurance; and
   (b) ASAE 3000[1] (or another ASAE dealing with a specific subject matter) applies to assurance procedures performed with respect to the remainder of the information covered by the assurance practitioner's conclusion.
4. This ASAE does not deal with, or provide specific guidance for, assurance engagements to report on the following:
   (a) Statements of emissions other than GHG emissions, for example, nitrogen oxides (NOx) and sulphur dioxide (SO_2). This ASAE may nonetheless provide guidance for such engagements;[2]

* In Australia this includes the National Greenhouse and Energy Reporting Scheme (NGERS), which establishes emission, energy consumption and energy production reporting.

\# In Australia this includes the Clean Energy Scheme, which establishes a carbon pricing mechanism.

1 ASAE 3000 *Assurance Engagements Other than Audits or Reviews of Historical Financial Information.* ISAE 3000 is currently being revised by the IAASB. There may be conforming amendments to ASAE 3000 and in turn to this ASAE as a result of changes to ISAE 3000.

2 NOx (i.e., NO and NO_2, which differ from the GHG nitrous oxide, N_2O) and SO_2 are associated with "acid rain" rather than climate change.

(b) Other GHG-related information, such as product lifecycle "footprints," hypothetical "baseline" information, and key performance indicators based on emissions data; or (Ref: Para. A3)

(c) Instruments, processes or mechanisms, such as offset projects, used by other entities as emissions deductions. However, where an entity's GHG statement includes emissions deductions that are subject to assurance, the requirements of this ASAE apply in relation to those emissions deductions as appropriate (see paragraph 76(f)).

Assertion-Based and Direct Reporting Engagements

5. The *Framework for Assurance Engagements* (the Assurance Framework) notes that an assurance engagement may be either an assertion-based engagement or a direct reporting engagement. This ASAE deals only with assertion-based engagements.[3]

Procedures for Reasonable Assurance and Limited Assurance Engagements

6. The Assurance Framework notes that an assurance engagement may be either a reasonable assurance engagement or a limited assurance engagement.[4] This ASAE deals with both reasonable and limited assurance engagements.

7. In both reasonable assurance and limited assurance engagements on a GHG statement, the assurance practitioner chooses a combination of assurance procedures, which can include: inspection; observation; confirmation; recalculation; reperformance; analytical procedures; and enquiry. Determining the assurance procedures to be performed on a particular engagement is a matter of professional judgement. Because GHG statements cover a wide range of circumstances, the nature, timing and extent of procedures are likely to vary considerably from engagement to engagement.

8. Unless otherwise stated, each requirement of this ASAE applies to both reasonable and limited assurance engagements. Because the level of assurance obtained in a limited assurance engagement is lower than in a reasonable assurance engagement, the procedures the assurance practitioner will perform in a limited assurance engagement will vary in nature from, and are less in extent than for, a reasonable assurance engagement.[5] Requirements that apply to only one or the other type of engagement have been presented in a columnar format with the letter "L" (limited assurance) or "R" (reasonable assurance) after the paragraph number. Although some procedures are required only for reasonable assurance engagements, they may nonetheless be appropriate in some limited assurance engagements (see also paragraph A90, which outlines the primary differences between the assurance practitioner's further procedures for a reasonable assurance engagement and a limited assurance engagement on a GHG statement). (Ref: Para. A4, A90)

Relationship with ASAE 3000, Other Pronouncements, and Other Requirements

9. The performance of assurance engagements other than audits or reviews of historical financial information requires the assurance practitioner to comply with ASAE 3000. ASAE 3000 includes requirements in relation to such topics as engagement acceptance, planning, evidence, and documentation that apply to all assurance engagements, including engagements in accordance with this ASAE. This ASAE expands on how ASAE 3000 is to be applied in an assurance engagement to report on an entity's GHG statement. The Assurance Framework, which defines and describes the elements and objectives of an assurance engagement, provides context for understanding this ASAE and ASAE 3000. (Ref: Para. A17)

10. [Deleted by the AUASB. Ref: Para. Aus 10.1]

Aus 10.1 ASA 102[†] requires that the assurance practitioner comply with relevant ethical requirements relating to assurance engagements, including those pertaining to

---

3 Assurance Framework, paragraph 10.

4 Assurance Framework, paragraph 11.

5 Assurance Framework, paragraph 53, and ASAE 3000 paragraphs 61-63.

† See ASA 102 *Compliance with Ethical Requirements when Performing Audits, Reviews and Other Assurance Engagements,* para.5

ASAE

independence and implement quality control procedures that are applicable to the individual engagement.[6] (Ref: Para. A5–A6)

11. Where the engagement is subject to laws or regulations or the provisions of an emissions trading scheme, this ASAE does not override those laws, regulations or provisions. In the event that laws or regulations or the provisions of an emissions trading scheme differ from this ASAE, an engagement conducted in accordance with laws or regulations or the provisions of a particular scheme will not automatically comply with this ASAE. The assurance practitioner is entitled to represent compliance with this ASAE in addition to compliance with laws or regulations or the provisions of the emissions trading scheme only when all applicable requirements of this ASAE have been met. (Ref: Para. A7)

Effective Date

12. [Deleted by the AUASB. Refer AUS 0.2]

Objectives

13. The objectives of the assurance practitioner are:

    (a) To obtain reasonable or limited assurance, as appropriate, about whether the GHG statement is free from material misstatement, whether due to fraud or error, thereby enabling the assurance practitioner to express a conclusion conveying that level of assurance;

    (b) To report, in accordance with the assurance practitioner's findings, about whether:

        (i) In the case of a reasonable assurance engagement, the GHG statement is prepared, in all material respects, in accordance with the applicable criteria; or

        (ii) In the case of a limited assurance engagement, anything has come to the assurance practitioner's attention that causes the assurance practitioner to believe, on the basis of the procedures performed and evidence obtained, that the GHG statement is not prepared, in all material respects, in accordance with the applicable criteria; and

    (c) To communicate as otherwise required by this ASAE, in accordance with the assurance practitioner's findings.

Definitions

14. For the purposes of this Standard on Assurance Engagements, the following terms have the meanings attributed below:

    (a) Applicable criteria – The criteria used by the entity to quantify and report its emissions in the GHG statement.

    (b) Assertions – Representations by the entity, explicit or otherwise, that are embodied in the GHG statement, as used by the assurance practitioner to consider the different types of potential misstatements that may occur.

    (c) Base year – A specific year or an average over multiple years against which an entity's emissions are compared over time.

    (d) Cap and trade – A system that sets overall emissions limits, allocates emissions allowances to participants, and allows them to trade allowances and emission credits with each other.

    (e) Comparative information – The amounts and disclosures included in the GHG statement in respect of one or more prior periods.

    (f) Emissions – The GHGs that, during the relevant period, have been emitted into the atmosphere or would have been emitted into the atmosphere had they not been captured and channelled into a sink. Emissions can be categorised as:

        - Direct emissions (also known as Scope 1 emissions), which are emissions from sources that are owned or controlled by the entity. (Ref: Para. A8)

6 ASAE 3000, paragraphs 9 and 12.

- Indirect emissions, which are emissions that are a consequence of the activities of the entity, but which occur at sources that are owned or controlled by another entity. Indirect emissions can be further categorised as:
    - Scope 2 emissions, which are emissions associated with energy that is transferred to and consumed by the entity. (Ref: Para. A9)
    - Scope 3 emissions, which are all other indirect emissions. (Ref: Para. A10)

(g) Emissions deduction – Any item included in the entity's GHG statement that is deducted from the total reported emissions, but which is not a removal; it commonly includes purchased offsets, but can also include a variety of other instruments or mechanisms such as performance credits and allowances that are recognised by a regulatory or other scheme of which the entity is a part. (Ref: Para. A11–A12)

(h) Emissions factor – A mathematical factor or ratio for converting the measure of an activity (for example, litres of fuel consumed, kilometres travelled, the number of animals in husbandry, or tonnes of product produced) into an estimate of the quantity of GHGs associated with that activity.

(i) Emissions trading scheme – A market-based approach used to control greenhouse gases by providing economic incentives for achieving reductions in the emissions of such gases.

(j) Entity – The legal entity, economic entity, or the identifiable portion of a legal or economic entity (for example, a single factory or other form of facility, such as a land fill site), or combination of legal or other entities or portions of those entities (for example, a joint venture) to which the emissions in the GHG statement relate.

(k) Fraud – An intentional act by one or more individuals among management, those charged with governance, employees, or third parties, involving the use of deception to obtain an unjust or illegal advantage.

(l) Further procedures – Procedures performed in response to assessed risks of material misstatement, including tests of controls (if any), tests of details and analytical procedures.

(m) GHG statement – A statement setting out constituent elements and quantifying an entity's GHG emissions for a period (sometimes known as an emissions inventory) and, where applicable, comparative information and explanatory notes including a summary of significant quantification and reporting policies. An entity's GHG statement may also include a categorised listing of removals or emissions deductions. Where the engagement does not cover the entire GHG statement, the term "GHG statement" is to be read as that portion that is covered by the engagement. The GHG statement is the "subject matter information" of the engagement.[7]

(n) Greenhouse gases (GHGs) – Carbon dioxide (CO_2) and any other gases required by the applicable criteria to be included in the GHG statement, such as: methane; nitrous oxide; sulphur hexafluoride; hydro fluorocarbons; perfluorocarbons; and chlorofluorocarbons. Gases other than carbon dioxide are often expressed in terms of carbon dioxide equivalents (CO_2-e).

(o) Organisational boundary – The boundary that determines which operations to include in the entity's GHG statement.

(p) Performance materiality – The amount or amounts set by the assurance practitioner at less than materiality for the GHG statement to reduce to an appropriately low level the probability that the aggregate of uncorrected and undetected misstatements exceeds materiality for the GHG statement. If applicable, performance materiality also refers to the amount or amounts set by the assurance practitioner at less than the materiality level or levels for particular types of emissions or disclosures.

(q) Purchased offset – An emissions deduction in which the entity pays for the lowering of another entity's emissions (emissions reductions) or the increasing of another

7 Assurance Framework, paragraph 8.

entity's removals (removal enhancements), compared to a hypothetical baseline. (Ref: Para. A13)

(r) Quantification – The process of determining the quantity of GHGs that relate to the entity, either directly or indirectly, as emitted (or removed) by particular sources (or sinks).

(s) Removal – The GHGs that the entity has, during the period, removed from the atmosphere, or that would have been emitted to the atmosphere had they not been captured and channelled to a sink. (Ref: Para. A14)

(t) Significant facility – A facility that is of individual significance due to the size of its emissions relative to the aggregate emissions included in the GHG statement or its specific nature or circumstances which give rise to particular risks of material misstatement. (Ref: Para. A15–A16)

(u) Sink – A physical unit or process that removes GHGs from the atmosphere.

(v) Source – A physical unit or process that releases GHGs into the atmosphere.

(w) Type of emission – A grouping of emissions based on, for example, source of emission, type of gas, region, or facility.

Requirements

ASAE 3000

15. The assurance practitioner shall not represent compliance with this ASAE unless the assurance practitioner has complied with the requirements of both this ASAE and ASAE 3000. (Ref: Para. A5–A6, A17, A21–A22, A37, A127)

Acceptance and Continuance of the Engagement

Skills, Knowledge and Experience

16. The engagement partner shall:

(a) Have sufficient assurance skills, knowledge and experience, and sufficient competence in the quantification and reporting of emissions, to accept responsibility for the assurance conclusion; and

(b) Be satisfied that the engagement team and any assurance practitioner's external experts collectively possess the necessary professional competencies, including in the quantification and reporting of emissions and in assurance, to perform the assurance engagement in accordance with this ASAE. (Ref: Para. A18–A19)

Preconditions for the Engagement

17. In order to establish whether the preconditions for the engagement are present:

(a) The engagement partner shall determine that both the GHG statement and the engagement have sufficient scope to be useful to intended users, considering, in particular: (Ref: Para. A20)

(i) If the GHG statement is to exclude significant emissions that have been, or could readily be, quantified, whether such exclusions are reasonable in the circumstances;

(ii) If the engagement is to exclude assurance with respect to significant emissions that are reported by the entity, whether such exclusions are reasonable in the circumstances; and

(iii) If the engagement is to include assurance with respect to emissions deductions, whether the nature of the assurance the assurance practitioner will obtain with respect to the deductions and the intended content of the assurance report with respect to them are clear, reasonable in the circumstances, and understood by the engaging party. (Ref: Para. A11-A12)

(b) When assessing the suitability of the applicable criteria, as required by ASAE 3000,[8] the assurance practitioner shall determine whether the criteria encompass at a minimum: (Ref: Para. A23–A26)

  (i) The method for determining the entity's organisational boundary; (Ref: Para. A27–A28)

  (ii) The GHGs to be accounted for;

  (iii) Acceptable quantification methods, including methods for making adjustments to the base year (if applicable); and

  (iv) Adequate disclosures such that intended users can understand the significant judgements made in preparing the GHG statement. (Ref: Para. A29–A34)

(c) The assurance practitioner shall obtain the agreement of the entity that it acknowledges and understands its responsibility:

  (i) For designing, implementing and maintaining such internal control as the entity determines is necessary to enable the preparation of a GHG statement that is free from material misstatement, whether due to fraud or error;

  (ii) For the preparation of its GHG statement in accordance with the applicable criteria; and (Ref: Para. A35)

  (iii) For referring to or describing in its GHG statement the applicable criteria it has used and, when it is not readily apparent from the engagement circumstances, who developed them. (Ref: Para. A36)

Agreement on Engagement Terms

18. The agreed terms of the engagement required by ASAE 3000[9] shall include: (Ref: Para. A37)

  (a) The objective and scope of the engagement;

  (b) The responsibilities of the assurance practitioner;

  (c) The responsibilities of the entity, including those described in paragraph 17(c);

  (d) Identification of the applicable criteria for the preparation of the GHG statement;

  (e) Reference to the expected form and content of any reports to be issued by the assurance practitioner and a statement that there may be circumstances in which a report may differ from its expected form and content; and

  (f) An acknowledgement that the entity agrees to provide written representations at the conclusion of the engagement.

Planning

19. When planning the engagement as required by ASAE 3000,[10] the assurance practitioner shall: (Ref: Para. A38–A41)

  (a) Identify the characteristics of the engagement that define its scope;

  (b) Ascertain the reporting objectives of the engagement to plan the timing of the engagement and the nature of the communications required;

  (c) Consider the factors that, in the assurance practitioner's professional judgement, are significant in directing the engagement team's efforts;

  (d) Consider the results of engagement acceptance or continuance procedures and, where applicable, whether knowledge gained on other engagements performed by the engagement partner for the entity is relevant;

  (e) Ascertain the nature, timing and extent of resources necessary to perform the engagement, including the involvement of experts and of other assurance practitioners; and (Ref: Para. A42–A43)

  (f) Determine the impact of the entity's internal audit function, if any, on the engagement.

8 ASAE 3000, paragraphs 35-37.

9 ASAE 3000, paragraphs 20-21.

10 ASAE 3000, paragraphs 25-26.

ASAE

Materiality in Planning and Performing the Engagement

Determining Materiality and Performance Materiality When Planning the Engagement

20. When establishing the overall engagement strategy, the assurance practitioner shall determine materiality for the GHG statement. (Ref: Para. A44–A50)

21. The assurance practitioner shall determine performance materiality for purposes of assessing the risks of material misstatement and determining the nature, timing and extent of further procedures.

Revision as the Engagement Progresses

22. The assurance practitioner shall revise materiality for the GHG statement in the event of becoming aware of information during the engagement that would have caused the assurance practitioner to have determined a different amount initially. (Ref: Para. A51)

Understanding the Entity and Its Environment, Including the Entity's Internal Control, and Identifying and Assessing Risks of Material Misstatement

Obtaining an Understanding of the Entity and Its Environment

23. The assurance practitioner shall obtain an understanding of the following: (Ref: Para. A52-A53)

    (a) Relevant industry, regulatory, and other external factors including the applicable criteria.

    (b) The nature of the entity, including:

    (i) The nature of the operations included in the entity's organisational boundary, including: (Ref: Para. A27–A28)

    a. The sources and completeness of emissions and, if any, sinks and emissions deductions;

    b. The contribution of each to the entity's overall emissions; and

    c. The uncertainties associated with the quantities reported in the GHG statement. (Ref: Para. A54–A59)

    (ii) Changes from the prior period in the nature or extent of operations, including whether there have been any mergers, acquisitions, or sales of emissions sources, or outsourcing of functions with significant emissions; and

    (iii) The frequency and nature of interruptions to operations. (Ref: Para. A60)

    (c) The entity's selection and application of quantification methods and reporting policies, including the reasons for changes thereto and the potential for double-counting of emissions in the GHG statement.

    (d) The requirements of the applicable criteria relevant to estimates, including related disclosures.

    (e) The entity's climate change objective and strategy, if any, and associated economic, regulatory, physical and reputational risks. (Ref: Para. A61)

    (f) The oversight of, and responsibility for, emissions information within the entity.

    (g) Whether the entity has an internal audit function and, if so, its activities and main findings with respect to emissions.

Procedures to Obtain an Understanding and to Identify and Assess Risks of Material Misstatement

24. The procedures to obtain an understanding of the entity and its environment and to identify and assess risks of material misstatement shall include the following: (Ref: Para. A52–A53, A62)

    (a) Enquiries of those within the entity who, in the assurance practitioner's judgement, have information that is likely to assist in identifying and assessing risks of material misstatement due to fraud or error.

    (b) Analytical procedures. (Ref: Para. A63–A65)

    (c) Observation and inspection. (Ref: Para. A66–A68)

Obtaining an Understanding of the Entity's Internal Control

Limited Assurance	Reasonable Assurance
25L. For internal control relevant to emissions quantification and reporting, as the basis for identifying and assessing the risks of material misstatement, the assurance practitioner shall obtain an understanding, through enquiries, about: (Ref: Para. A52–A53, A69–A70) (a) The control environment; (b) The information system, including the related business processes, and communication of emissions reporting roles and responsibilities and significant matters relating to emissions reporting; and (c) The results of the entity's risk assessment process.	25R. The assurance practitioner shall obtain an understanding of the following components of the entity's internal control relevant to emissions quantification and reporting as the basis for identifying and assessing risks of material misstatement: (Ref: Para. A52–A53, A70) (a) The control environment; (b) The information system, including the related business processes, and communication of emissions reporting roles and responsibilities and significant matters relating to emissions reporting; (c) The entity's risk assessment process; (d) Control activities relevant to the engagement, being those the assurance practitioner judges it necessary to understand in order to assess the risks of material misstatement at the assertion level and design further procedures responsive to assessed risks. An assurance engagement does not require an understanding of all the control activities related to each significant type of emission and disclosure in the GHG statement or to every assertion relevant to them; and (Ref: Para. A71–A72) (e) Monitoring of controls.
	26R. When obtaining the understanding required by paragraph 25R, the assurance practitioner shall evaluate the design of controls and determine whether they have been implemented by performing procedures in addition to enquiry of the entity's personnel. (Ref: Para. A52–A53)

Other Procedures to Obtain an Understanding and to Identify and Assess Risks of Material Misstatement

27. If the engagement partner has performed other engagements for the entity, the engagement partner shall consider whether information obtained is relevant to identifying and assessing risks of material misstatement. (Ref: Para. A73)

28. The assurance practitioner shall make enquiries of management, and others within the entity as appropriate, to determine whether they have knowledge of any actual, suspected or alleged fraud or non-compliance with laws and regulations affecting the GHG statement. (Ref: Para. A84–A86)

29. The engagement partner and other key members of the engagement team, and any key assurance practitioner's external experts, shall discuss the susceptibility of the entity's GHG statement to material misstatement whether due to fraud or error, and the application of the applicable criteria to the entity's facts and circumstances. The engagement partner shall determine which matters are to be communicated to members of the engagement team, and to any assurance practitioner's external experts not involved in the discussion.

30. The assurance practitioner shall evaluate whether the entity's quantification methods and reporting policies, including the determination of the entity's organisational boundary, are appropriate for its operations, and are consistent with the applicable criteria and quantification and reporting policies used in the relevant industry and in prior periods.

Performing Procedures on Location at the Entity's Facilities

31. The assurance practitioner shall determine whether it is necessary in the circumstances of the engagement to perform procedures on location at significant facilities. (Ref: Para. A15–A16, A74–A77)

Internal Audit

32. Where the entity has an internal audit function that is relevant to the engagement, the assurance practitioner shall: (Ref: Para. A78)

(a) Determine whether, and to what extent, to use specific work of the internal audit function; and

(b) If using the specific work of the internal audit function, determine whether that work is adequate for the purposes of the engagement.

Identifying and Assessing Risks of Material Misstatement

Limited Assurance	Reasonable Assurance
33L. The assurance practitioner shall identify and assess risks of material misstatement: (a) At the GHG statement level; and (Ref: Para. A79–A80) (b) For material types of emissions and disclosures, (Ref: Para. A81) as the basis for designing and performing procedures whose nature, timing and extent: (c) Are responsive to assessed risks of material misstatement; and (d) Allow the assurance practitioner to obtain limited assurance about whether the GHG statement is prepared, in all material respects, in accordance with the applicable criteria.	33R. The assurance practitioner shall identify and assess risks of material misstatement: (a) At the GHG statement level; and (Ref: Para. A79–A80) (b) At the assertion level for material types of emissions and disclosures, (Ref: Para. A81–A82) as the basis for designing and performing procedures whose nature, timing and extent: (Ref: Para. A83) (c) Are responsive to assessed risks of material misstatement; and (d) Allow the assurance practitioner to obtain reasonable assurance about whether the GHG statement is prepared, in all material respects, in accordance with the applicable criteria.

Causes of Risks of Material Misstatement

34. When performing the procedures required by paragraphs 33L or 33R, the assurance practitioner shall consider at least the following factors: (Ref: Para. A84–A89)

(a) The likelihood of intentional misstatement in the GHG statement; (Ref: Para. A84– A86)

(b) The likelihood of non-compliance with the provisions of those laws and regulations generally recognised to have a direct effect on the content of the GHG statement; (Ref: Para. A87)

(c) The likelihood of omission of a potentially significant emission; (Ref: Para. A88(a))

(d) Significant economic or regulatory changes; (Ref: Para. A88(b))

(e) The nature of operations; (Ref: Para. A88(c))

(f) The nature of quantification methods; (Ref: Para. A88(d))

(g) The degree of complexity in determining the organisational boundary and whether related parties are involved; (Ref: Para. A27–A28)

(h) Whether there are significant emissions that are outside the normal course of business for the entity, or that otherwise appear to be unusual; (Ref: Para. A88(e))

(i) The degree of subjectivity in the quantification of emissions; (Ref: Para. A88(e))

(j) Whether Scope 3 emissions are included in the GHG statement; and (Ref: Para. A88(f))

(k) How the entity makes significant estimates and the data on which they are based. (Ref: Para. A88(g))

Overall Responses to Assessed Risks of Material Misstatement and Further Procedures

35. The assurance practitioner shall design and implement overall responses to address the assessed risks of material misstatement at the GHG statement level. (Ref: Para. A90–A93)

36. The assurance practitioner shall design and perform further procedures whose nature, timing and extent are responsive to the assessed risks of material misstatement, having regard to the level of assurance, reasonable or limited, as appropriate. (Ref: Para. A90)

Limited Assurance	Reasonable Assurance
37L. In designing and performing the further procedures in accordance with paragraph 36, the assurance practitioner shall: (Ref: Para. A90, A94) (a) Consider the reasons for the assessment given to the risks of material misstatement for material types of emissions and disclosures; and (Ref: Para. A95) (b) Obtain more persuasive evidence the higher the assurance practitioner's assessment of risk. (Ref: Para. A97)	37R. In designing and performing the further procedures in accordance with paragraph 36, the assurance practitioner shall: (Ref: Para. A90, A94) (a) Consider the reasons for the assessment given to the risks of material misstatement at the assertion level for material types of emissions and disclosures, including: (Ref: Para. A95) (i) The likelihood of material misstatement due to the particular characteristics of the relevant type of emission or disclosure (that is, the inherent risk); and (ii) Whether the assurance practitioner intends to rely on the operating effectiveness of controls in determining the nature, timing and extent of other procedures; and (Ref: Para. A96) (b) Obtain more persuasive evidence the higher the assurance practitioner's assessment of risk. (Ref: Para. A97)

Limited Assurance	Reasonable Assurance
	Tests of Controls 38R. The assurance practitioner shall design and perform tests of controls to obtain sufficient appropriate evidence as to the operating effectiveness of relevant controls if: (a) The assurance practitioner intends to rely on the operating effectiveness of controls in determining the nature, timing and extent of other procedures; or (Ref: Para. A96) (b) Procedures other than tests of controls cannot alone provide sufficient appropriate evidence at the assertion level. (Ref: Para. A98)
	39R. If deviations from controls upon which the assurance practitioner intends to rely are detected, the assurance practitioner shall make specific enquiries to understand these matters and their potential consequences, and shall determine whether: (a) The tests of controls that have been performed provide an appropriate basis for reliance on the controls; (b) Additional tests of controls are necessary; or (c) The potential risks of material misstatement need to be addressed using other procedures.
	Procedures Other than Tests of Controls 40R. Irrespective of the assessed risks of material misstatement, the assurance practitioner shall design and perform tests of details or analytical procedures in addition to tests of controls, if any, for each material type of emission and disclosure. (Ref: Para. A94)
	41R. The assurance practitioner shall consider whether external confirmation procedures are to be performed. (Ref: Para. A99)

Limited Assurance	Reasonable Assurance
Analytical Procedures Performed in Response to Assessed Risks of Material Misstatement	**Analytical Procedures Performed in Response to Assessed Risks of Material Misstatement**
42L. If designing and performing analytical procedures, the assurance practitioner shall: (Ref: Para. A90(c), A100–A102) (a) Determine the suitability of particular analytical procedures, taking account of the assessed risks of material misstatement and tests of details, if any; (b) Evaluate the reliability of data from which the assurance practitioner's expectation of recorded quantities or ratios is developed, taking account of the source, comparability, and nature and relevance of information available, and controls over preparation; and (c) Develop an expectation with respect to recorded quantities or ratios.	42R. If designing and performing analytical procedures, the assurance practitioner shall: (Ref: Para. A90(c), A100–A102) (a) Determine the suitability of particular analytical procedures for given assertions, taking account of the assessed risks of material misstatement and tests of details, if any, for these assertions; (b) Evaluate the reliability of data from which the assurance practitioner's expectation of recorded quantities or ratios is developed, taking account of the source, comparability, and nature and relevance of information available, and controls over preparation; and (c) Develop an expectation of recorded quantities or ratios which is sufficiently precise to identify possible material misstatements.
43L. If analytical procedures identify fluctuations or relationships that are inconsistent with other relevant information or that differ significantly from expected quantities or ratios, the assurance practitioner shall make enquiries of the entity about such differences. The assurance practitioner shall consider the responses to these enquiries to determine whether other procedures are necessary in the circumstances. (Ref: Para. A90(c))	43R. If analytical procedures identify fluctuations or relationships that are inconsistent with other relevant information or that differ significantly from expected quantities or ratios, the assurance practitioner shall investigate such differences by: (Ref: Para. A90(c)) (a) Enquiring of the entity and obtaining additional evidence relevant to the entity's responses; and (b) Performing other procedures as necessary in the circumstances.

ASAE

Limited Assurance	Reasonable Assurance
Procedures Reqarding Estimates 44L. Based on the assessed risks of material misstatement, the assurance practitioner shall: (Ref: Para. A103–A104) (a) Evaluate whether: (i) The entity has appropriately applied the requirements of the applicable criteria relevant to estimates; and (ii) The methods for making estimates are appropriate and have been applied consistently, and whether changes, if any, in reported estimates or in the method for making them from the prior period are appropriate in the circumstances; and (b) Consider whether other procedures are necessary in the circumstances.	**Procedures Reqarding Estimates** 44R. Based on the assessed risks of material misstatement, the assurance practitioner shall evaluate whether: (Ref: Para. A103) (a) The entity has appropriately applied the requirements of the applicable criteria relevant to estimates; and (b) The methods for making estimates are appropriate and have been applied consistently, and whether changes, if any, in reported estimates or in the method for making them from the prior period are appropriate in the circumstances.

Limited Assurance	Reasonable Assurance
	45R. In responding to an assessed risk of material misstatement, the assurance practitioner shall undertake one or more of the following, taking account of the nature of estimates: (Ref: Para. A103) (a) Test how the entity made the estimate and the data on which it is based. In doing so, the assurance practitioner shall evaluate whether: (i) The method of quantification used is appropriate in the circumstances; and (ii) The assumptions used by the entity are reasonable. (b) Test the operating effectiveness of the controls over how the entity made the estimate, together with other appropriate procedures. (c) Develop a point estimate or a range to evaluate the entity's estimate. For this purpose: (i) If the assurance practitioner uses assumptions or methods that differ from the entity's, the assurance practitioner shall obtain an understanding of the entity's assumptions or methods sufficient to establish that the assurance practitioner's point estimate or range takes into account relevant variables and to evaluate any significant differences from the entity's point estimate. (iii) If the assurance practitioner concludes that it is appropriate to use a range, the assurance practitioner shall narrow the range, based on evidence available, until all outcomes within the range are considered reasonable.

ASAE

Sampling

46. If sampling is used, the assurance practitioner shall, when designing the sample, consider the purpose of the procedure and the characteristics of the population from which the sample will be drawn. (Ref: Para. A90(b), A105)

Fraud, Laws and Regulations

47. The assurance practitioner shall respond appropriately to fraud or suspected fraud and non-compliance or suspected non-compliance with laws and regulations identified during the engagement. (Ref: Para. A106–A107)

Limited Assurance	Reasonable Assurance
Procedures Regarding the GHG Statement Aggregation Process 48L. The assurance practitioner's procedures shall include the following procedures related to the GHG statement aggregation process: (Ref: Para. A108) (a) Agreeing or reconciling the GHG statement with the underlying records; and (b) Obtaining, through enquiry of the entity, an understanding of material adjustments made during the course of preparing the GHG statement and considering whether other procedures are necessary in the circumstances.	**Procedures Regarding the GHG Statement Aggregation Process** 48R. The assurance practitioner's procedures shall include the following procedures related to the GHG statement aggregation process: (Ref: Para. A108) (a) Agreeing or reconciling the GHG statement with the underlying records; and (b) Examining material adjustments made during the course of preparing the GHG statement.
Determining Whether Additional Procedures Are Necessary in a Limited Assurance Engagement 49L. If the assurance practitioner becomes aware of a matter(s) that causes the assurance practitioner to believe the GHG statement may be materially misstated, the assurance practitioner shall design and perform additional procedures sufficient to enable the assurance practitioner to: (Ref: Para. A109-A110) (a) Conclude that the matter(s) is not likely to cause the GHG statement to be materially misstated; or (b) Determine that the matter(s) causes the GHG statement to be materially misstated. (Ref: Para. A111)	**Revision of Risk Assessment in a Reasonable Assurance Engagement** 49R. The assurance practitioner's assessment of the risks of material misstatement at the assertion level may change during the course of the engagement as additional evidence is obtained. In circumstances where the assurance practitioner obtains evidence from performing further procedures, or if new information is obtained, either of which is inconsistent with the evidence on which the assurance practitioner originally based the assessment, the assurance practitioner shall revise the assessment and modify the planned procedures accordingly. (Ref: Para. A109)

Accumulation of Identified Misstatements

50. The assurance practitioner shall accumulate misstatements identified during the engagement, other than those that are clearly trivial. (Ref: Para. A112)

Consideration of Identified Misstatements as the Engagement Progresses

51. The assurance practitioner shall determine whether the overall engagement strategy and engagement plan need to be revised if:
    (a) The nature of identified misstatements and the circumstances of their occurrence indicate that other misstatements may exist that, when aggregated with misstatements accumulated during the engagement, could be material; or
    (b) The aggregate of misstatements accumulated during the engagement approaches materiality determined in accordance with paragraphs 20–22 of this ASAE.

52. If, at the assurance practitioner's request, the entity has examined a type of emission or disclosure and corrected misstatements that were detected, the assurance practitioner shall perform procedures with respect to the work performed by the entity to determine whether material misstatements remain.

Communication and Correction of Misstatements

53. The assurance practitioner shall communicate on a timely basis all misstatements accumulated during the engagement with the appropriate level within the entity and shall request the entity to correct those misstatements.

54. If the entity refuses to correct some or all of the misstatements communicated by the assurance practitioner, the assurance practitioner shall obtain an understanding of the entity's reasons for not making the corrections and shall take that understanding into account when forming the assurance practitioner's conclusion.

Evaluating the Effect of Uncorrected Misstatements

55. Prior to evaluating the effect of uncorrected misstatements, the assurance practitioner shall reassess materiality determined in accordance with paragraphs 20–22 of this ASAE to confirm whether it remains appropriate in the context of the entity's actual emissions.

56. The assurance practitioner shall determine whether uncorrected misstatements are material, individually or in the aggregate. In making this determination, the assurance practitioner shall consider the size and nature of the misstatements, and the particular circumstances of their occurrence, in relation to particular types of emissions or disclosures and the GHG statement. (See paragraph 72)

ASAE

Using the Work of Other Assurance Practitioners

57. When the assurance practitioner intends using the work of other assurance practitioners, the assurance practitioner shall:
    (a) Communicate clearly with those other assurance practitioners about the scope and timing of their work and their findings; and (Ref: Para. A113–A114)
    (b) Evaluate the sufficiency and appropriateness of evidence obtained and the process for including related information in the GHG statement. (Ref: Para. A115)

Written Representations

58. The assurance practitioner shall request written representations from a person(s) within the entity with appropriate responsibilities for, and knowledge of, the matters concerned: (Ref: Para. A116)
    (a) That they have fulfilled their responsibility for the preparation of the GHG statement, including comparative information where appropriate, in accordance with the applicable criteria, as set out in the terms of the engagement;
    (b) That they have provided the assurance practitioner with all relevant information and access as agreed in the terms of the engagement and reflected all relevant matters in the GHG statement;
    (c) Whether they believe the effects of uncorrected misstatements are immaterial, individually and in the aggregate, to the GHG statement. A summary of such items shall be included in, or attached to, the written representation;
    (d) Whether they believe that significant assumptions used in making estimates are reasonable;

(e) That they have communicated to the assurance practitioner all deficiencies in internal control relevant to the engagement that are not clearly trivial of which they are aware; and

(f) Whether they have disclosed to the assurance practitioner their knowledge of actual, suspected or alleged fraud or non-compliance with laws and regulations where the fraud or non-compliance could have a material effect on the GHG statement.

59. The date of the written representations shall be as near as practicable to, but not after, the date of the assurance report.

60. The assurance practitioner shall disclaim a conclusion on the GHG statement or withdraw from the engagement, where withdrawal is possible under applicable laws or regulations, if:

(a) The assurance practitioner concludes that there is sufficient doubt about the integrity of the person(s) providing the written representations required by paragraphs 58(a) and (b) that written representations in these regards are not reliable; or

(b) The entity does not provide the written representations required by paragraphs 58(a) and (b).

Subsequent Events

61. The assurance practitioner shall: (Ref: Para. A117)

(a) Consider whether events occurring between the date of the GHG statement and the date of the assurance report require adjustment of, or disclosure in, the GHG statement, and evaluate the sufficiency and appropriateness of evidence obtained about whether such events are appropriately reflected in that GHG statement in accordance with the applicable criteria; and

(b) Respond appropriately to facts that become known to the assurance practitioner after the date of the assurance report, that, had they been known to the assurance practitioner at that date, may have caused the assurance practitioner to amend the assurance report.

Comparative Information

62. When comparative information is presented with the current emissions information and some or all of that comparative information is covered by the assurance practitioner's conclusion, the assurance practitioner's procedures with respect to the comparative information shall include evaluating whether: (Ref: Para. A118–A121)

(a) The comparative information agrees with the amounts and other disclosures presented in the prior period or, when appropriate, has been properly restated and that restatement has been adequately disclosed; and (Ref Para. A121)

(b) The quantification policies reflected in the comparative information are consistent with those applied in the current period or, if there have been changes, whether they have been properly applied and adequately disclosed.

63. Irrespective of whether the assurance practitioner's conclusion covers the comparative information, if the assurance practitioner becomes aware that there may be a material misstatement in the comparative information presented the assurance practitioner shall:

(a) Discuss the matter with those person(s) within the entity with appropriate responsibilities for, and knowledge of, the matters concerned and perform procedures appropriate in the circumstances; and (Ref: Para. A122–A123)

(b) Consider the effect on the assurance report. If the comparative information presented contains a material misstatement, and the comparative information has not been restated:

(i) Where the assurance practitioner's conclusion covers the comparative information, the assurance practitioner shall express a qualified conclusion or an adverse conclusion in the assurance report; or

(ii) Where the assurance practitioner's conclusion does not cover the comparative information, the assurance practitioner shall include an Other Matter paragraph in the assurance report describing the circumstances affecting the comparative information.

Other Information

64. The assurance practitioner shall read other information included in documents containing the GHG statement and the assurance report thereon and, if, in the assurance practitioner's judgement, that other information could undermine the credibility of the GHG statement and the assurance report, shall discuss the matter with the entity and take further action as appropriate. (Ref: Para. A124–A126)

Documentation

65. In documenting the nature, timing and extent of procedures performed, the assurance practitioner shall record: (Ref: Para. A127)
    (a) The identifying characteristics of the specific items or matters tested;
    (b) Who performed the engagement work and the date such work was completed; and
    (c) Who reviewed the engagement work performed and the date and extent of such review.

66. The assurance practitioner shall document discussions of significant matters with the entity and others, including the nature of the significant matters discussed, and when and with whom the discussions took place. (Ref: Para. A127)

Quality Control

67. The assurance practitioner shall include in the engagement documentation:
    (a) Issues identified with respect to compliance with relevant ethical requirements and how they were resolved;
    (b) Conclusions on compliance with independence requirements that apply to the engagement, and any relevant discussions with the firm that support these conclusions;
    (c) Conclusions reached regarding the acceptance and continuance of client relationships and assurance engagements; and
    (d) The nature and scope of, and conclusions resulting from, consultations undertaken during the course of the engagement.

Matters Arising after the Date of the Assurance Report

68. If, in exceptional circumstances, the assurance practitioner performs new or additional procedures or draws new conclusions after the date of the assurance report, the assurance practitioner shall document: (Ref: Para. A128)
    (a) The circumstances encountered;
    (b) The new or additional procedures performed, evidence obtained, and conclusions reached, and their effect on the assurance report; and
    (c) When and by whom the resulting changes to engagement documentation were made and reviewed.

Assembly of the Final Engagement File

69. The assurance practitioner shall assemble the engagement documentation in an engagement file and complete the administrative process of assembling the final engagement file on a timely basis after the date of the assurance report. After the assembly of the final engagement file has been completed, the assurance practitioner shall not delete or discard engagement documentation of any nature before the end of its retention period. (Ref: Para. A129)

70. In circumstances other than those envisaged in paragraph 68 where the assurance practitioner finds it necessary to modify existing engagement documentation or add new engagement documentation after the assembly of the final engagement file has been completed, the assurance practitioner shall, regardless of the nature of the modifications or additions, document:
    (a) The specific reasons for making them; and
    (b) When and by whom they were made and reviewed.

Engagement Quality Control Review

71. For those engagements, if any, for which a quality control review is required by laws or regulations or for which the firm has determined that an engagement quality control review is required, the engagement quality control reviewer shall perform an objective evaluation of the significant judgements made by the engagement team, and the conclusions reached in formulating the assurance report. This evaluation shall involve: (Ref: Para. A130)
   (a) Discussion of significant matters with the engagement partner, including the engagement team's professional competencies with respect to the quantification and reporting of emissions and assurance;
   (b) Review of the GHG statement and the proposed assurance report;
   (c) Review of selected engagement documentation relating to the significant judgements the engagement team made and the conclusions it reached; and
   (d) Evaluation of the conclusions reached in formulating the assurance report and consideration of whether the proposed assurance report is appropriate.

Forming the Assurance Conclusion

72. The assurance practitioner shall conclude as to whether the assurance practitioner has obtained reasonable or limited assurance, as appropriate, about the GHG statement. That conclusion shall take into account the requirements of paragraphs 56 and 73–75 of this ASAE.

Limited Assurance	Reasonable Assurance
73L. The assurance practitioner shall evaluate whether anything has come to the assurance practitioner's attention that causes the assurance practitioner to believe that the GHG statement is not prepared, in all material respects, in accordance with the applicable criteria.	73R. The assurance practitioner shall evaluate whether the GHG statement is prepared, in all material respects, in accordance with the applicable criteria.

74. This evaluation shall include consideration of the qualitative aspects of the entity's quantification methods and reporting practices, including indicators of possible bias in judgements and decisions in the making of estimates and in preparing the GHG statement,[11] and whether, in view of the applicable criteria:
   (a) The quantification methods and reporting policies selected and applied are consistent with the applicable criteria and are appropriate;
   (b) Estimates made in preparing the GHG statement are reasonable;
   (c) The information presented in the GHG statement is relevant, reliable, complete, comparable and understandable;
   (d) The GHG statement provides adequate disclosure of the applicable criteria, and other matters, including uncertainties, such that intended users can understand the significant judgements made in its preparation; and (Ref: Para. A29, A131–A133)
   (e) The terminology used in the GHG statement is appropriate.
75. The evaluation required by paragraph 73 shall also include consideration of:
   (a) The overall presentation, structure and content of the GHG statement; and
   (b) When appropriate in the context of the criteria, the wording of the assurance conclusion, or other engagement circumstances, whether the GHG statement represents the underlying emissions in a manner that achieves fair presentation.

11 Indicators of possible bias do not themselves constitute misstatements for the purposes of drawing conclusions on the reasonableness of individual estimates.

Assurance Report Content

76. The assurance report shall include the following basic elements: (Ref: Para. A134)

(a) A title that clearly indicates the report is an independent limited assurance or reasonable assurance report.

(b) The addressee of the assurance report.

(c) Identification of the GHG statement, including the period(s) it covers, and, if any information in that statement is not covered by the assurance practitioner's conclusion, clear identification of the information subject to assurance as well as the excluded information, together with a statement that the assurance practitioner has not performed any procedures with respect to the excluded information and, therefore, that no conclusion on it is expressed. (Ref: Para. A120, A135)

(d) A description of the entity's responsibilities. (Ref: Para. A35)

(e) A statement that GHG quantification is subject to inherent uncertainty. (Ref: Para. A54–A59)

(f) If the GHG statement includes emissions deductions that are covered by the assurance practitioner's conclusion, identification of those emissions deductions, and a statement of the assurance practitioner's responsibility with respect to them. (Ref: Para. A136–A139)

(g) (i) Identification of the applicable criteria;

(ii) Identification of how those criteria can be accessed;

(iii) If those criteria are available only to specific intended users, or are relevant only to a specific purpose, a statement restricting the use of the assurance report to those intended users or that purpose; and (Ref: Para. A140–A141)

(iii) If established criteria need to be supplemented by disclosures in the explanatory notes to the GHG statement for those criteria to be suitable, identification of the relevant note(s). (Ref: Para. A131)

(h) A description of the assurance practitioner's responsibility, including:

(i) A statement that the engagement was performed in accordance with ASAE 3410 *Assurance Engagements on Greenhouse Gas Statements*; and

(ii) A summary of the assurance practitioner's procedures. In the case of a limited assurance engagement, this shall include a statement that the procedures performed in a limited assurance engagement vary in nature from, and are less in extent than for, a reasonable assurance engagement. As a result, the level of assurance obtained in a limited assurance engagement is substantially lower than the assurance that would have been obtained had a reasonable assurance engagement been performed. (Ref: Para. A142–A144)

(i) The assurance practitioner's conclusion, expressed in the positive form in the case of a reasonable assurance engagement or in the negative form in the case of a limited assurance engagement, about whether the GHG statement is prepared, in all material respects, in accordance with the applicable criteria.

(j) If the assurance practitioner expresses a conclusion that is modified, a clear description of all the reasons therefore.§

(k) The assurance practitioner's signature. (Ref: Para. A145)

(l) The date of the assurance report.

(m) The location in the jurisdiction where the assurance practitioner practices.

§ ASAE 3000, paragraphs 81-84, explain the modifications which can be included in the assurance practitioner's report and when each modification may be applied.

ASAE

Emphasis of Matter Paragraphs and Other Matter Paragraphs

77. If the assurance practitioner considers it necessary to: (Ref: Para. A146–A152)

 (a) Draw intended users' attention to a matter presented or disclosed in the GHG statement that, in the assurance practitioner's judgement, is of such importance that it is fundamental to intended users' understanding of the GHG statement (an Emphasis of Matter paragraph); or

 (b) Communicate a matter other than those that are presented or disclosed in the GHG statement that, in the assurance practitioner's judgement, is relevant to intended users' understanding of the engagement, the assurance practitioner's responsibilities or the assurance report (an Other Matter paragraph),

 and this is not prohibited by laws or regulations, the assurance practitioner shall do so in a paragraph in the assurance report, with an appropriate heading, that clearly indicates the assurance practitioner's conclusion is not modified in respect of the matter.

Other Communication Requirements

78. The assurance practitioner shall communicate to those person(s) with oversight responsibilities for the GHG statement the following matters that come to the assurance practitioner's attention during the course of the engagement, and shall determine whether there is a responsibility to report them to another party within or outside the entity:

 (a) Deficiencies in internal control that, in the assurance practitioner's professional judgement, are of sufficient importance to merit attention;

 (b) Identified or suspected fraud; and

 (c) Matters involving non-compliance with laws and regulations, other than when the matters are clearly trivial. (Ref: Para. A87)

❖❖❖

Application and Other Explanatory Material

Introduction

Assurance Engagements Covering Information in Addition to the GHG Statement (Ref: Para. 3)

A1. In some cases, the assurance practitioner may perform an assurance engagement on a report that includes GHG information, but that GHG information does not comprise a GHG statement as defined in paragraph 14(m). In such cases, this ASAE may provide guidance for such an engagement.

A2. Where a GHG statement is a relatively minor part of the overall information that is covered by the assurance practitioner's conclusion, the extent to which this ASAE is relevant is a matter for the assurance practitioner's professional judgement in the circumstances of the engagement.

Key Performance Indicators Based on GHG Data (Ref: Para. 4(b))

A3. An example of a key performance indicator based on GHG data is the weighted average of emissions per kilometre of vehicles manufactured by an entity during a period, which is required to be calculated and disclosed by laws or regulations in some jurisdictions.

Procedures for Reasonable Assurance and Limited Assurance Engagements (Ref: Para. 8)

A4. Some procedures that are required only for reasonable assurance engagements may nonetheless be appropriate in some limited assurance engagements. For example, although obtaining an understanding of control activities is not required for limited assurance engagements, in some cases, such as when information is recorded, processed, or reported only in electronic form, the assurance practitioner may nonetheless decide that testing controls, and therefore obtaining an understanding of relevant control activities, is necessary for a limited assurance engagement (see also paragraph A90).

Independence (Ref: Para. Aus 10.1 and 15)

A5. Relevant ethical requirements relating to assurance engagements‡ may require a threats and safeguards approach to independence. Compliance with relevant ethical requirements may potentially be threatened by a broad range of circumstances. Many threats fall into the following categories:

- Self-interest, for example, undue dependence on total fees from the entity.
- Self-review, for example, performing another service for the entity that directly affects the GHG statement, such as involvement in the quantification of the entity's emissions.
- Advocacy, for example, acting as an advocate on behalf of the entity with respect to the interpretation of the applicable criteria.
- Familiarity, for example, a member of the engagement team having a long association, or close or immediate family relationship, with an employee of the entity who is in a position to exert direct and significant influence over the preparation of the GHG statement.
- Intimidation, for example, being pressured to reduce inappropriately the extent of work performed in order to lower fees, or being threatened with withdrawal of the assurance practitioner's registration by a registering authority that is associated with the entity's industry group.

A6. Safeguards created by relevant ethical requirements, laws or regulations, or safeguards in the work environment, may eliminate or reduce such threats to an acceptable level.

Laws and Regulations and the Provisions of an Emissions Trading Scheme (Ref: Para. 11)

A7. Laws or regulations or the provisions of an emissions trading scheme may: include requirements in addition to the requirements of this ASAE; require that specific procedures be undertaken on all engagements; or require that procedures be undertaken in a particular way. For example, laws or regulations or the provisions of an emissions trading scheme may require the assurance practitioner to report in a format that is not in compliance with this ASAE. When the law or regulation prescribes the layout or wording of the assurance report in a form or in terms that are significantly different from this ASAE, and the assurance practitioner concludes that additional explanation in the assurance report cannot mitigate possible misunderstanding, the assurance practitioner may consider including a statement in the report that the engagement is not conducted in accordance with this ASAE.

Definitions

Emissions (Ref: Para. 14(f), Appendix 1)

A8. Scope 1 emissions may include stationary combustion (from fuel burned in the entity's stationary equipment, such as boilers, incinerators, engines, and flares), mobile combustion (from fuel burned in the entity's transport devices, such as trucks, trains, airplanes and boats), process emissions (from physical or chemical processes, such as cement manufacturing, petrochemical processing, and aluminium smelting), and fugitive emissions (intentional and unintentional releases, such as equipment leaks from joints and seals and emissions from wastewater treatment, pits, and cooling towers).

A9. Almost all entities purchase energy in a form such as electricity, heat or steam; therefore, almost all entities have Scope 2 emissions. Scope 2 emissions are indirect because the emissions associated with, for example, electricity that the entity purchases occur at the power station, which is outside the entity's organisational boundary.

A10. Scope 3 emissions may include emissions associated with, for example: employee business travel; outsourced activities; consumption of fossil fuel or electricity required to use the entity's products; extraction and production of materials purchased as inputs to the entity's processes; and transportation of purchased fuels. Scope 3 emissions are further discussed in paragraphs A31–A34.

‡ Relevant ethical requirements are defined in ASA 102 *Compliance with Ethical Requirements when Performing Audits, Reviews and Other Assurance Engagements.*

ASAE

Emissions Deductions (Ref: Para. 14(g), 17(a)(iii), Appendix 1)

A11. In some cases, emissions deductions include jurisdiction-specific credits and allowances for which there is no established link between the quantity of emissions allowed by the criteria to be deducted, and any lowering of emissions that may occur as a result of money paid or other action taken by the entity in order for it to claim the emissions deduction.

A12. Where an entity's GHG statement includes emissions deductions that are within the scope of the engagement, the requirements of this ASAE apply in relation to emissions deductions as appropriate (see also paragraphs A136-A139).

Purchased Offset (Ref: Para. 14(q), Appendix 1)

A13. When the entity purchases an offset from another entity, that other entity may spend the money it receives from the sale on emissions reduction projects (such as replacing energy generation using fossil fuels with renewable energy sources, or implementing energy efficiency measures), or on removing emissions from the atmosphere (for example, by planting and maintaining trees that would otherwise not have been planted or maintained), or the money may be compensation for not undertaking an action that would otherwise be undertaken (such as deforestation or forest degradation). In some jurisdictions, offsets can only be purchased if the emissions reduction or removal enhancement has already occurred.

Removal (Ref: Para. 14(s), Appendix 1)

A14. Removal may be achieved by storing GHGs in geological sinks (for example, underground) or biological sinks (for example, trees). Where the GHG statement includes the removal of GHGs that the entity would have otherwise emitted to the atmosphere, they are commonly reported in the GHG statement on a gross basis, that is, both the source and the sink are quantified in the GHG statement. Where removals are covered by the assurance practitioner's conclusion, the requirements of this ASAE apply in relation to those removals as appropriate.

Significant Facility (Ref: Para. 14(t) and 31)

A15. As the individual contribution of a facility to the aggregate emissions reported in the GHG statement increases, the risks of material misstatement to the GHG statement ordinarily increase. The assurance practitioner may apply a percentage to a chosen benchmark as an aid to identify facilities that are of individual significance due to the size of their emissions relative to the aggregate emissions included in the GHG statement. Identifying a benchmark and determining a percentage to be applied to it involve the exercise of professional judgement. For example, the assurance practitioner may consider that facilities exceeding 15% of total production volume are significant facilities. A higher or lower percentage may, however, be determined to be appropriate in the circumstances in the assurance practitioner's professional judgement. This may be the case when, for example: there is a small number of facilities, none of which is less than 15% of total production volume, but in the assurance practitioner's professional judgement not all the facilities are significant; or when there are a number of facilities that are marginally below 15% of total production volume which in the assurance practitioner's professional judgement are significant.

A16. The assurance practitioner may also identify a facility as significant due to its specific nature or circumstances which give rise to particular risks of material misstatement. For example, a facility could be using different data gathering processes or quantification techniques from other facilities, require the use of particularly complex or specialised calculations, or involve particularly complex or specialised chemical or physical processes.

ASAE 3000 (Ref: Para. 9, 15)

A17. ASAE 3000 includes a number of requirements that apply to all assurance engagements, including engagements in accordance with this ASAE. In some cases, this ASAE may include additional requirements or application material in relation to those topics.

Acceptance and Continuance of the Engagement

Competency (Ref: Para 16(b))

A18. GHG competencies may include:

- General understanding of climate science, including the scientific processes that relate GHGs to climate change.
- Understanding who the intended users of the information in the entity's GHG statement are, and how they are likely to use that information (see paragraph A47).
- Understanding emissions trading schemes and related market mechanisms, when relevant.
- Knowledge of applicable laws and regulations, if any, that affect how the entity should report its emissions, and may also, for example, impose a limit on the entity's emissions.
- GHG quantification and measurement methodologies, including the associated scientific and estimation uncertainties, and alternative methodologies available.
- Knowledge of the applicable criteria, including, for example:
    - Identifying appropriate emissions factors.
    - Identifying those aspects of the criteria that call for significant or sensitive estimates to be made, or for the application of considerable judgement.
    - Methods used for determining organisational boundaries, i.e., the entities whose emissions are to be included in the GHG statement.
    - Which emissions deductions are permitted to be included in the entity's GHG statement.

A19. The complexity of assurance engagements with respect to a GHG statement varies. In some cases, the engagement may be relatively straightforward, for instance, when an entity has no Scope 1 emissions and is reporting only Scope 2 emissions using an emissions factor specified in regulation, applied to electricity consumption at a single location. In this case, the engagement may focus largely on the system used to record and process electricity consumption figures identified on invoices, and arithmetical application of the specified emissions factor. When, however, the engagement is relatively complex, it is likely to require specialist competence in the quantification and reporting of emissions. Particular areas of expertise that may be relevant in such cases include:

Information systems expertise

- Understanding how emissions information is generated, including how data is initiated, recorded, processed, corrected as necessary, collated and reported in a GHG statement.

Scientific and engineering expertise

- Mapping the flow of materials through a production process, and the accompanying processes that create emissions, including identifying the relevant points at which source data is gathered. This may be particularly important in considering whether the entity's identification of emissions sources is complete.
- Analysing chemical and physical relationships between inputs, processes and outputs, and relationships between emissions and other variables. The capacity to understand and analyse these relationships will often be important in designing analytical procedures.
- Identifying the effect of uncertainty on the GHG statement.
- Knowledge of the quality control policies and procedures implemented at testing laboratories, whether internal or external.
- Experience with specific industries and related emissions creation and removal processes. Procedures for Scope 1 emissions quantification vary greatly depending on the industries and processes involved, for example, the nature of electrolytic processes in aluminium production; combustion processes in the production of

electricity using fossil fuels; and chemical processes in cement production are all different.

- The operation of physical sensors and other quantification methods, and the selection of appropriate emissions factors.

Scope of the GHG Statement and the Engagement (Ref: Para. 17(a))

A20. Examples of circumstances where the reasons for excluding known emissions sources from the GHG statement, or excluding disclosed emissions sources from the engagement, may not be reasonable in the circumstances include where:

- The entity has significant Scope 1 emissions but only includes Scope 2 emissions in the GHG statement.
- The entity is a part of a larger legal entity that has significant emissions that are not being reported on because of the way the organisational boundary has been determined when this is likely to mislead intended users.
- The emissions that the assurance practitioner is reporting on are only a small proportion of the total emissions included in the GHG statement.

Assessing the Appropriateness of the Subject Matter (Ref: Para. 15)

A21. ASAE 3000 requires the assurance practitioner to assess the appropriateness of the subject matter.[12] In the case of a GHG statement, the entity's emissions (and removals and emissions deductions if applicable) are the subject matter of the engagement. That subject matter will be appropriate if, among other things, the entity's emissions are capable of consistent quantification using suitable criteria.[13]

A22. GHG sources may be quantified by:

(a) Direct measurement (or direct monitoring) of GHG concentration and flow rates using continuous emissions monitoring or periodic sampling; or

(d) Measuring a surrogate activity, such as fuel consumption, and calculating emissions using, for example, mass balance equations,[14] entity-specific emissions factors, or average emissions factors for a region, source, industry or process.

Assessing the Suitability of the Criteria

Specifically Developed and Established Criteria *(Ref: Para. 17(b))*

A23. Suitable criteria exhibit the following characteristics: relevance, completeness, reliability, neutrality, and understandability. Criteria may be "specifically developed" or they may be "established," that is, embodied in laws or regulations, or issued by authorised or recognised bodies of experts that follow a transparent due process.[15] Although criteria established by a regulator can be presumed to be relevant when that regulator is the intended user, some established criteria may be developed for a special purpose and be unsuitable for application in other circumstances. For example, criteria developed by a regulator that include emissions factors for a particular region may render misleading information if used for emissions in another region; or criteria that are designed to report only on particular regulatory aspects of emissions may be unsuitable for reporting to intended users other than the regulator that established the criteria.

A24. Specifically developed criteria may be appropriate when, for example, the entity has very specialised machinery or is aggregating emissions information from different jurisdictions where the established criteria used in those jurisdictions differ. Special care may be necessary when assessing the neutrality and other characteristics of specifically developed criteria, particularly if they are not substantially based on established criteria generally used in the entity's industry or region, or are inconsistent with such criteria.

12 ASAE 3000, paragraphs 33-34.

13 Assurance Framework, paragraphs 34-Aus 38.1, and ASAE 3000, paragraphs 35-39.

14 That is, equating the amount of a substance entering and exiting a defined boundary, for example, the amount of carbon in a hydrocarbon-based fuel entering a combustion device equals the amount of carbon exiting the device in the form of carbon dioxide.

15 Assurance Framework, paragraphs 36–37.

A25. The applicable criteria may comprise established criteria supplemented by disclosures, in the explanatory notes to the GHG statement, of specific boundaries, methods, assumptions, emissions factors, etc. In some cases, established criteria may not be suitable, even when supplemented by disclosures in the explanatory notes to the GHG statement, for example, when they do not encompass the matters noted in paragraph 17(b).

A26. It should be noted that the suitability of the applicable criteria is not affected by the level of assurance, that is, if they are not suitable for a reasonable assurance engagement, they are also not suitable for a limited assurance engagement, and vice versa.

Operations Included in the Entity's Organisational Boundary
(Ref: Para. 17(b)(i), 23(b)(i), 34(g))

A27. Determining which operations owned or controlled by the entity to include in the entity's GHG statement is known as determining the entity's organisational boundary. In some cases, laws and regulations define the boundaries of the entity for reporting GHG emissions for regulatory purposes. In other cases, the applicable criteria may allow a choice between different methods for determining the entity's organisational boundary, for example, the criteria may allow a choice between an approach that aligns the entity's GHG statement with its financial statements and another approach that treats, for example, joint ventures or associates differently. Determining the entity's organisational boundary may require the analysis of complex organisational structures such as joint ventures, partnerships, and trusts, and complex or unusual contractual relationships. For example, a facility may be owned by one party, operated by another, and process materials solely for another party.

A28. Determining the entity's organisational boundary is different from what some criteria describe as determining the entity's "operational boundary." The operational boundary relates to which categories of Scope 1, 2 and 3 emissions will be included in the GHG statement, and is determined after setting the organisational boundary.

Adequate Disclosures (Ref: Para. 17(b)(iv), 74(d))

A29. In regulatory disclosure regimes, disclosures specified in the relevant laws or regulations are adequate for reporting to the regulator. Disclosure in the GHG statement of such matters as the following may be necessary in voluntary reporting situations for intended users to understand the significant judgements made in preparing the GHG statement:

(a) Which operations are included in the entity's organisational boundary, and the method used for determining that boundary if the applicable criteria allow a choice between different methods (see paragraphs A27–A28);

(b) Significant quantification methods and reporting policies selected, including:

(i) The method used to determine which Scope 1 and Scope 2 emissions have been included in the GHG statement (see paragraph A30);

(ii) Any significant interpretations made in applying the applicable criteria in the entity's circumstances, including data sources and, when choices between different methods are allowed, or entity-specific methods are used, disclosure of the method used and the rationale for doing so; and

(iii) How the entity determines whether previously reported emissions should be restated.

(c) The categorisation of emissions in the GHG statement. As noted in paragraph A14, where the GHG statement includes the removal of GHGs that the entity would have otherwise emitted to the atmosphere, both emissions and removals are commonly reported in the GHG statement on a gross basis, that is, both the source and the sink are quantified in the GHG statement;

(d) A statement regarding the uncertainties relevant to the entity's quantification of its emissions, including: their causes; how they have been addressed; their effects on the GHG statement; and, where the GHG statement includes Scope 3 emissions, an explanation of: (see paragraphs A31–A34)

(i) The nature of Scope 3 emissions, including that it is not practicable for an entity to include all Scope 3 emissions in its GHG statement; and

(ii) The basis for selecting those Scope 3 emissions sources that have been included; and

(e) Changes, if any, in the matters mentioned in this paragraph or in other matters that materially affect the comparability of the GHG statement with a prior period(s) or base year.

Scope 1 and Scope 2 Emissions

A30. Criteria commonly call for all material Scope 1, Scope 2, or both Scope 1 and Scope 2 emissions to be included in the GHG statement. Where some Scope 1 or Scope 2 emissions have been excluded, it is important that the explanatory notes to the GHG statement disclose the basis for determining which emissions are included and which are excluded, particularly if those that are included are not likely to be the largest for which the entity is responsible.

Scope 3 Emissions

A31. While some criteria require the reporting of specific Scope 3 emissions, more commonly the inclusion of Scope 3 emissions is optional because it would be impracticable for nearly any entity to attempt to quantify the full extent of its indirect emissions as this includes all sources both up and down the entity's supply chain. For some entities, reporting particular categories of Scope 3 emissions provides important information for intended users, for example, where an entity's Scope 3 emissions are considerably larger than its Scope 1 and Scope 2 emissions, as may be the case with many service sector entities. In these cases, the assurance practitioner may consider it inappropriate to undertake an assurance engagement if significant Scope 3 emissions are not included in the GHG statement.

A32. Where some Scope 3 emissions sources have been included in the GHG statement, it is important that the basis for selecting which sources to include is reasonable, particularly if those included are not likely to be the largest sources for which the entity is responsible.

A33. In some cases, the source data used to quantify Scope 3 emissions may be maintained by the entity. For example, the entity may keep detailed records as the basis for quantifying emissions associated with employee air travel. In some other cases, the source data used to quantify Scope 3 emissions may be maintained in a well-controlled and accessible source outside the entity. Where this is not the case, however, it may be unlikely that the assurance practitioner will be able to obtain sufficient appropriate evidence with respect to such Scope 3 emissions. In such cases, it may be appropriate to exclude those Scope 3 emissions sources from the engagement.

A34. It may also be appropriate to exclude Scope 3 emissions from the engagement where the quantification methods in use are heavily dependent on estimation and lead to a high degree of uncertainty in reported emissions. For example, various quantification methods for estimating the emissions associated with air travel can give widely varying quantifications even when identical source data is used. If such Scope 3 emissions sources are included in the engagement, it is important that the quantification methods used are selected objectively and that they are fully described along with the uncertainties associated with their use.

The Entity's Responsibility for the Preparation of the GHG Statement
(Ref: Para. 17(c)(ii), 76(d))

A35. As noted in paragraph A70, for some engagements concerns about the condition and reliability of an entity's records may cause the assurance practitioner to conclude that it is unlikely that sufficient appropriate evidence will be available to support an unmodified conclusion on the GHG statement. This may occur when the entity has little experience with the preparation of GHG statements. In such circumstances, it may be more appropriate for the quantification and reporting of emissions to be subject to an agreed-upon procedures engagement or a consulting engagement in preparation for an assurance engagement in a later period.

Who Developed the Criteria (Ref: Para. 17(c)(iii))

A36. When the GHG statement has been prepared for a regulatory disclosure regime or emissions trading scheme where the applicable criteria and form of reporting are prescribed, it is likely to be apparent from the engagement circumstances that it is the regulator or body in charge of the scheme that developed the criteria. In voluntary reporting situations, however, it may not be clear who developed the criteria unless it is stated in the explanatory notes to the GHG statement.

Changing the Terms of the Engagement (Ref: Para. 15, 18)

A37. ASAE 3000 requires that the assurance practitioner not agree to a change in the terms of the engagement where there is no reasonable justification for doing so.[16] A request to change the scope of the engagement may not have a reasonable justification when, for example, the request is made to exclude certain emissions sources from the scope of the engagement because of the likelihood that the assurance practitioner's conclusion would be modified.

Planning (Ref: Para. 19)

A38. When establishing the overall engagement strategy, it may be relevant to consider the emphasis given to different aspects of the design and implementation of the GHG information system. For example, in some cases the entity may have been particularly conscious of the need for adequate internal control to ensure the reliability of reported information, while in other cases the entity may have focused more on accurately determining the scientific, operational or technical characteristics of the information to be gathered.

A39. Smaller engagements or more straightforward engagements (see paragraph A19) may be conducted by a very small engagement team. With a smaller team, co-ordination of, and communication between, team members is easier. Establishing the overall engagement strategy for a smaller engagement, or for a more straightforward engagement, need not be a complex or time-consuming exercise. For example, a brief memorandum, based on discussions with the entity, may serve as the documented engagement strategy if it covers the matters noted in paragraph 19.

A40. The assurance practitioner may decide to discuss elements of planning with the entity when determining the scope of the engagement or to facilitate the conduct and management of the engagement (for example, to co-ordinate some of the planned procedures with the work of the entity's personnel). Although these discussions often occur, the overall engagement strategy and the engagement plan remain the assurance practitioner's responsibility. When discussing matters included in the overall engagement strategy or engagement plan, care is required in order not to compromise the effectiveness of the engagement. For example, discussing the nature and timing of detailed procedures with the entity may compromise the effectiveness of the engagement by making the procedures too predictable.

A41. The performance of an assurance engagement is an iterative process. As the assurance practitioner performs planned procedures, the evidence obtained may cause the assurance practitioner to modify the nature, timing or extent of other planned procedures. In some cases, information may come to the assurance practitioner's attention that differs significantly from that expected at an earlier stage of the engagement. For example, systematic errors discovered when performing procedures on location at selected facilities may indicate that it is necessary to visit additional facilities.

Planning to Use the Work of Experts or of Other Assurance Practitioners (Ref: Para. 19(e))

A42. The engagement may be performed by a multi-disciplinary team that includes one or more experts, particularly on relatively complex engagements when specialist competence in the quantification and reporting of emissions is likely to be required (see paragraph A19). ASAE 3000 contains a number of requirements with respect to using the work of an expert that may need to be considered at the planning stage when ascertaining the nature, timing and extent of resources necessary to perform the engagement.[17]

16 ASAE 3000, paragraph 22-24.

17 ASAE 3000, paragraphs 47-55.

A43. The work of another assurance practitioner may be used in relation to, for example, a factory or other form of facility at a remote location; a subsidiary, division or branch in a foreign jurisdiction; or a joint venture or associate. Relevant considerations when the engagement team plans to request another assurance practitioner to perform work on information to be included in the GHG statement may include:

- Whether the other assurance practitioner understands and complies with the ethical requirements that are relevant to the engagement and, in particular, is independent.
- The other assurance practitioner's professional competence.
- The extent of the engagement team's involvement in the work of the other assurance practitioner.
- Whether the other assurance practitioner operates in a regulatory environment that actively oversees that assurance practitioner.

Materiality in Planning and Performing the Engagement

Determining Materiality When Planning the Engagement (Ref: Para. 20–21)

A44. The criteria may discuss the concept of materiality in the context of the preparation and presentation of the GHG statement. Although criteria may discuss materiality in different terms, the concept of materiality generally includes that:

- Misstatements, including omissions, are considered to be material if they, individually or in the aggregate, could reasonably be expected to influence relevant decisions of users taken on the basis of the GHG statement;
- Judgements about materiality are made in light of surrounding circumstances, and are affected by the size or nature of a misstatement, or a combination of both; and
- Judgements about matters that are material to intended users of the GHG statement are based on a consideration of the common information needs of intended users as a group. The possible effect of misstatements on specific individual users, whose needs may vary widely, is not considered.

A45. Such a discussion, if present in the applicable criteria, provides a frame of reference to the assurance practitioner in determining materiality for the engagement. If the applicable criteria do not include a discussion of the concept of materiality, the characteristics referred to above provide the assurance practitioner with such a frame of reference.

A46. The assurance practitioner's determination of materiality is a matter of professional judgement, and is affected by the assurance practitioner's perception of the common information needs of intended users as a group. In this context, it is reasonable for the assurance practitioner to assume that intended users:

(a) Have a reasonable knowledge of GHG related activities, and a willingness to study the information in the GHG statement with reasonable diligence;

(b) Understand that the GHG statement is prepared and assured to levels of materiality, and have an understanding of any materiality concepts included in the applicable criteria;

(c) Understand that the quantification of emissions involves uncertainties (see paragraphs A54–A59); and

(d) Make reasonable decisions on the basis of the information in the GHG statement.

A47. Intended users and their information needs may include, for example:

- Investors and other stakeholders such as suppliers, customers, employees, and the broader community in the case of voluntary disclosures. Their information needs may relate to decisions to buy or sell equity in the entity; lend to, trade with, or be employed by the entity; or make representations to the entity or others, for example, politicians.
- Market participants in the case of an emissions trading scheme, whose information needs may relate to decisions to trade negotiable instruments (such as permits, credits or allowances) created by the scheme, or impose fines or other penalties on the basis of excess emissions.

- Regulators and policy makers in the case of a regulatory disclosure regime. Their information needs may relate to monitoring compliance with the disclosure regime, and a broad range of government policy decisions related to climate change mitigation and adaptation, usually based on aggregated information.
- Management and those charged with governance of the entity who use information about emissions for strategic and operational decisions, such as choosing between alternative technologies and investment and divestment decisions, perhaps in anticipation of a regulatory disclosure regime or entering an emissions trading scheme.

The assurance practitioner may not be able to identify all those who will read the assurance report, particularly where there are a large number of people who have access to it. In such cases, particularly where possible readers are likely to have a broad range of interests with respect to emissions, intended users may be limited to major stakeholders with significant and common interests. Intended users may be identified in different ways, for example, by agreement between the assurance practitioner and the engaging party, or by laws or regulations.

A48. Judgements about materiality are made in light of surrounding circumstances, and are affected by both quantitative and qualitative factors. It should be noted, however, that decisions regarding materiality are not affected by the level of assurance, that is, materiality for a reasonable assurance engagement is the same as for a limited assurance engagement.

A49. A percentage is often applied to a chosen benchmark as a starting point in determining materiality. Factors that may affect the identification of an appropriate benchmark and percentage include:

- The elements included in the GHG statement (for example, Scope 1, Scope 2 and Scope 3 emissions, emissions deductions, and removals). A benchmark that may be appropriate, depending on the circumstances, is gross reported emissions, that is, the aggregate of reported Scope 1, Scope 2 and Scope 3 emissions before subtracting any emissions deductions or removals. Materiality relates to the emissions covered by the assurance practitioner's conclusion. Therefore, when the assurance practitioner's conclusion does not cover the entire GHG statement, materiality is set in relation to only that portion of the GHG statement that is covered by the assurance practitioner's conclusion as if it were the GHG statement.
- The quantity of a particular type of emission or the nature of a particular disclosure. In some cases, there are particular types of emissions or disclosures for which misstatements of lesser or greater amounts than materiality for the GHG statement in its entirety are acceptable. For example, the assurance practitioner may consider it appropriate to set a lower or greater materiality for emissions from a particular jurisdiction, or for a particular gas, scope or facility.
- How the GHG statement presents relevant information, for example, whether it includes a comparison of emissions with a prior period(s), a base year, or a "cap," in which case determining materiality in relation to the comparative information may be a relevant consideration. Where a "cap" is relevant, materiality may be set in relation to the entity's allocation of the cap if it is lower than reported emissions.
- The relative volatility of emissions. For example, if emissions vary significantly from period to period, it may be appropriate to set materiality relative to the lower end of the fluctuation range even if the current period is higher.
- The requirements of the applicable criteria. In some cases, the applicable criteria may set a threshold for accuracy and may refer to this as materiality. For example, the criteria may state an expectation that emissions are measured using a stipulated percentage as the "materiality threshold." Where this is the case, the threshold set by the criteria provides a frame of reference to the assurance practitioner in determining materiality for the engagement.

ASAE

A50. Qualitative factors may include:

- The sources of emissions.
- The types of gases involved.
- The context in which the information in the GHG statement will be used (for example, whether the information is for use in an emissions trading scheme, is for submission to a regulator, or is for inclusion in a widely distributed sustainability report); and the types of decisions that intended users are likely to make.
- Whether there are one or more types of emissions or disclosures on which the attention of the intended users tends to be focused, for example, gases that, as well as contributing to climate change, are ozone depleting.
- The nature of the entity, its climate change strategies and progress toward related objectives.
- The industry and the economic and regulatory environment in which the entity operates.

Revision as the Engagement Progresses (Ref: Para. 22)

A51. Materiality may need to be revised as a result of a change in circumstances during the engagement (for example, the disposal of a major part of the entity's business), new information, or a change in the assurance practitioner's understanding of the entity and its operations as a result of performing procedures. For example, it may become apparent during the engagement that actual emissions are likely to be substantially different from those used initially to determine materiality. If during the engagement the assurance practitioner concludes that a lower materiality for the GHG statement (and, if applicable, materiality level or levels for particular types of emissions or disclosures) than that initially determined is appropriate, it may be necessary to revise performance materiality, and the nature, timing and extent of the further procedures.

Understanding the Entity and Its Environment, Including the Entity's Internal Control, and Identifying and Assessing Risks of Material Misstatement (Ref: Para. 23–26)

A52. The assurance practitioner uses professional judgement to determine the extent of the understanding and the nature, timing and extent of procedures to identify and assess risks of material misstatement that are required to obtain reasonable or limited assurance, as appropriate. The assurance practitioner's primary consideration is whether the understanding that has been obtained and the identification and assessment of risks are sufficient to meet the objective stated in this ASAE. The depth of the understanding that is required by the assurance practitioner is less than that possessed by management in managing the entity, and both the depth of the understanding and the nature, timing and extent of procedures to identify and assess risks of material misstatement are less for a limited assurance engagement than for a reasonable assurance engagement.

A53. Obtaining an understanding and identifying and assessing risks of material misstatement is an iterative process. Procedures to obtain an understanding of the entity and its environment and to identify and assess risks of material misstatement by themselves do not provide sufficient appropriate evidence on which to base the assurance conclusion.

Uncertainty (Ref: Para: 23(b)(i)c, 76(e))

A54. The GHG quantification process can rarely be 100% accurate due to:

(a) *Scientific uncertainty:* This arises because of incomplete scientific knowledge about the measurement of GHGs. For example, the rate of GHG sequestration in biological sinks, and the "global warming potential" values used to combine emissions of different gases and report them as carbon dioxide equivalents, are subject to incomplete scientific knowledge. The degree to which scientific uncertainty affects the quantification of reported emissions is beyond the control of the entity. However, the potential for scientific uncertainty to result in unreasonable variations in reported emissions can be negated by the use of criteria that stipulate particular scientific assumptions to be used in preparing the GHG statement, or particular factors that embody those assumptions; and

(b) *Estimation (or measurement) uncertainty:* This results from the measurement and calculation processes used to quantify emissions within the bounds of existing scientific knowledge. Estimation uncertainty may relate to the data on which an estimate is based (for example, it may relate to uncertainty inherent in measurement instruments used), or the method, including where applicable the model, used in making the estimate (sometimes known as parameter and model uncertainty, respectively). The degree of estimation uncertainty is often controllable by the entity. Reducing the degree of estimation uncertainty may involve greater cost.

A55. The fact that quantifying an entity's emissions is subject to uncertainty does not mean that an entity's emissions are inappropriate as a subject matter. For example, the applicable criteria may require Scope 2 emissions from electricity to be calculated by applying a prescribed emissions factor to the number of kilowatt hours consumed. The prescribed emissions factor will be based on assumptions and models that may not hold true in all circumstances. However, as long as the assumptions and models are reasonable in the circumstances and adequately disclosed, information in the GHG statement will ordinarily be capable of being assured.

A56. The situation in paragraph A55 can be contrasted with quantification in accordance with criteria that use models and assumptions based on an entity's individual circumstances. Using entity-specific models and assumptions will likely result in more accurate quantification than using, for example, average emissions factors for an industry; it will also likely introduce additional risks of material misstatement with respect to how the entity-specific models and assumptions were arrived at. As noted in paragraph A55, as long as the assumptions and models are reasonable in the circumstances and adequately disclosed, information in the GHG statement will ordinarily be capable of being assured.

A57. In some cases, however, the assurance practitioner may decide that it is inappropriate to undertake an assurance engagement if the impact of uncertainty on information in the GHG statement is very high. This may be the case when, for example, a significant proportion of the entity's reported emissions are from fugitive sources (see paragraph A8) that are not monitored and estimation methods are not sufficiently sophisticated, or when a significant proportion of the entity's reported removals are attributable to biological sinks. It should be noted that decisions whether to undertake an assurance engagement in such circumstances are not affected by the level of assurance, that is, if it is not appropriate for a reasonable assurance engagement, it is also not appropriate for a limited assurance engagement, and vice versa.

A58. A discussion in the explanatory notes to the GHG statement of the nature, causes, and effects of the uncertainties that affect the entity's GHG statement alerts intended users to the uncertainties associated with the quantification of emissions. This may be particularly important where the intended users did not determine the criteria to be used. For example, a GHG statement may be available to a broad range of intended users even though the criteria used were developed for a particular regulatory purpose.

A59. Because uncertainty is a significant characteristic of all GHG statements, paragraph 76(e) requires it to be mentioned in the assurance report regardless of what, if any, disclosures are included in the explanatory notes to the GHG statement.[18]

The Entity and Its Environment

Interruptions to Operations (Ref: Para. 23(b)(iii))

A60. Interruptions may include incidents such as shut downs, which may occur unexpectedly, or may be planned, for example, as part of a maintenance schedule. In some cases, the nature of operations may be intermittent, for example, when a facility is only used at peak periods.

Climate Change Objectives and Strategies (Ref: Para. 23(e))

A61. Consideration of the entity's climate change strategy, if any, and associated economic, regulatory, physical and reputational risks, may assist the assurance practitioner to identify risks of material misstatement. For example, if the entity has made commitments to become carbon neutral, this may provide an incentive to understate emissions so the

18 See also ASAE 3000, paragraphs 78(e) and 79(e).

target will appear to be achieved within a declared timeframe. Conversely, if the entity is expecting to be subject to a regulated emissions trading scheme in the future, this may provide an incentive to overstate emissions in the meantime to increase the opportunity for it to receive a larger allowance at the outset of the scheme.

Procedures to Obtain an Understanding and to Identify and Assess Risks of Material Misstatement (Ref: Para. 24)

A62. Although the assurance practitioner is required to perform all the procedures in paragraph 24 in the course of obtaining the required understanding of the entity, the assurance practitioner is not required to perform all of them for each aspect of that understanding.

Analytical Procedures for Obtaining an Understanding of the Entity and Its Environment and Identifying and Assessing Risks of Material Misstatement (Ref: Para. 24(b))

A63. Analytical procedures performed to obtain an understanding of the entity and its environment and to identify and assess risks of material misstatement may identify aspects of the entity of which the assurance practitioner was unaware and may assist in assessing the risks of material misstatement in order to provide a basis for designing and implementing responses to the assessed risks. Analytical procedures may include, for example, comparing GHG emissions from various facilities with production figures for those facilities.

A64. Analytical procedures may help identify the existence of unusual events, and amounts, ratios, and trends that might indicate matters that have implications for the engagement. Unusual or unexpected relationships that are identified may assist the assurance practitioner in identifying risks of material misstatement.

A65. However, when such analytical procedures use data aggregated at a high level (which may be the situation with analytical procedures performed to obtain an understanding of the entity and its environment and to identify and assess risks of material misstatement), the results of those analytical procedures only provide a broad initial indication about whether a material misstatement may exist. Accordingly, in such cases, consideration of other evidence that has been gathered when identifying the risks of material misstatement together with the results of such analytical procedures may assist the assurance practitioner in understanding and evaluating the results of the analytical procedures.

Observation and Inspection (Ref: Para. 24(c))

A66. Observation consists of looking at a process or procedure being performed by others, for example, the assurance practitioner's observation of monitoring devices being calibrated by the entity's personnel, or of the performance of control activities. Observation provides evidence about the performance of a process or procedure, but is limited to the point in time at which the observation takes place, and by the fact that the act of being observed may affect how the process or procedure is performed.

A67. Inspection involves:

(a) Examining records or documents, whether internal or external, in paper form, electronic form, or other media, for example, calibration records of a monitoring device. Inspection of records and documents provides evidence of varying degrees of reliability, depending on their nature and source and, in the case of internal records and documents, on the effectiveness of the controls over their production; or

(e) A physical examination of, for example, a calibrating device.

A68. Observation and inspection may support enquiries of management and others, and may also provide information about the entity and its environment. Examples of such procedures include observation or inspection of the following:

- The entity's operations. Observing processes and equipment, including monitoring equipment, at facilities may be particularly relevant where significant Scope 1 emissions are included in the GHG statement.
- Documents (such as emissions mitigation plans and strategies), records (such as calibration records and results from testing laboratories), and manuals detailing information collection procedures and internal controls.

- Reports prepared for management or those charged with governance, such as internal or external reports with respect to the entity's environmental management systems.
- Reports prepared by management (such as quarterly management reports) and those charged with governance (such as minutes of board of directors' meetings).

Obtaining an Understanding of the Entity's Internal Control (Ref: Para. 25L–26R)

A69. In a limited assurance engagement, the assurance practitioner is not required to obtain an understanding of all of the components of the entity's internal control relevant to emissions quantification and reporting as is required in a reasonable assurance engagement. In addition, the assurance practitioner is not required to evaluate the design of controls and determine whether they have been implemented. Therefore, in a limited assurance engagement, while it may often be appropriate to enquire of the entity about control activities and monitoring of controls relevant to the quantification and reporting of emissions, it will often not be necessary to obtain a detailed understanding of these components of the entity's internal control.

A70. The assurance practitioner's understanding of relevant components of internal control may raise doubts about whether sufficient appropriate evidence is available for the assurance practitioner to complete the engagement. For example (see also paragraphs A71–A72, A92–A93, and A96):

- Concerns about the integrity of those preparing the GHG statement may be so serious as to cause the assurance practitioner to conclude that the risk of management misrepresentation in the GHG statement is such that an engagement cannot be conducted.
- Concerns about the condition and reliability of an entity's records may cause the assurance practitioner to conclude that it is unlikely that sufficient appropriate evidence will be available to support an unmodified conclusion on the GHG statement.

ASAE

Control Activities Relevant to the Engagement (Ref: Para. 25R(d))

A71. The assurance practitioner's judgement about whether particular control activities are relevant to the engagement may be affected by the level of sophistication, documentation and formality of the entity's information system, including the related business processes, relevant to reporting emissions. As reporting of emissions evolves, it can be expected that so too will the level of sophistication, documentation and formality of information systems and related control activities relevant to the quantification and reporting of emissions.

A72. In the case of very small entities or immature information systems, particular control activities are likely to be more rudimentary, less well-documented, and may only exist informally. When this is the case, it is less likely the assurance practitioner will judge it necessary to understand particular control activities in order to assess the risks of material misstatement and design further procedures responsive to assessed risks. In some regulated schemes, on the other hand, the information system and control activities may be required to be formally documented and their design approved by the regulator. Even in some of these cases, however, not all relevant data flows and associated controls may be documented. For example, it may be more likely that control activities with respect to source data collection from continuous monitoring are sophisticated, well-documented, and more formal than control activities with respect to subsequent data processing and reporting (see also paragraphs A70, A92–A93, and A96).

Other Engagements Performed for the Entity (Ref: Para. 27)

A73. Information obtained from other engagements performed for the entity may relate to, for example, aspects of the entity's control environment.

Performing Procedures on Location at the Entity's Facilities (Ref: Para. 31)

A74. Performing observation and inspection, as well as other procedures, on location at a facility (often referred to as a "site visit") may be important in building on the understanding of the entity that the assurance practitioner develops by performing procedures at head office.

Because the assurance practitioner's understanding of the entity and identification and assessment of risks of material misstatement can be expected to be more comprehensive for a reasonable assurance engagement than for a limited assurance engagement, the number of facilities at which procedures are performed on location in the case of a reasonable assurance engagement will ordinarily be greater than in the case of a limited assurance engagement.

A75. Performing procedures on location at a facility (or having another assurance practitioner perform such procedures on behalf of the assurance practitioner) may be done as part of planning, when performing procedures to identify and assess risks of material misstatement, or when responding to assessed risks of material misstatement. Performing procedures at significant facilities is often particularly important for an engagement being undertaken for the first time when considering the completeness of Scope 1 sources and of sinks included in the GHG statement, and when establishing whether the entity's data collection and processing systems, and its estimation techniques, are appropriate relative to the underlying physical processes and related uncertainties.

A76. As noted in paragraph A74, performing procedures on location at a facility may be important in building on the understanding of the entity that the assurance practitioner develops by performing procedures at head office. For many reasonable assurance engagements, the assurance practitioner will also judge it necessary to perform procedures on location at each significant facility to respond to assessed risks of material misstatement, particularly when the entity has significant facilities with Scope 1 emissions. For a limited assurance engagement where the entity has a number of significant facilities with Scope 1 emissions, a meaningful level of assurance may not be able to be obtained without the assurance practitioner having performed procedures at a selection of significant facilities. Where the entity has significant facilities with Scope 1 emissions and the assurance practitioner determines that effective and efficient procedures cannot be performed on location at the facility by the assurance practitioner (or another assurance practitioner on their behalf), alternative procedures may include one or more of the following:

- Reviewing source documents, energy flow diagrams, and material flow diagrams.
- Analysing questionnaire responses from facility management.
- Inspecting satellite imagery of the facility.

A77. To obtain adequate coverage of total emissions, particularly in a reasonable assurance engagement, the assurance practitioner may decide that it is appropriate to perform procedures on location at a selection of facilities that are not significant facilities. Factors that may be relevant to such a decision include:

- The nature of emissions at different facilities. For example, it is more likely that an assurance practitioner may choose to visit a facility with Scope 1 emissions than a facility with only Scope 2 emissions. In the latter case, the examination of energy invoices at head office is more likely to be a primary source of evidence.
- The number and size of facilities, and their contribution to overall emissions.
- Whether facilities use different processes, or processes using different technologies. Where this is the case, it may be appropriate to perform procedures on location at a selection of facilities using different processes or technologies.
- The methods used at different facilities to gather emissions information.
- The experience of relevant staff at different facilities.
- Varying the selection of facilities over time.

Internal Audit (Ref: Para. 32)

A78. The entity's internal audit function is likely to be relevant to the engagement if the nature of the internal audit function's responsibilities and activities are related to the quantification and reporting of emissions and the assurance practitioner expects to use the work of the internal audit function to modify the nature or timing, or reduce the extent, of procedures to be performed.

Risks of Material Misstatement at the GHG Statement Level (Ref: Para. 33L(a)–33R(a))

A79. Risks of material misstatement at the GHG statement level refer to risks that relate pervasively to the GHG statement as a whole. Risks of this nature are not necessarily risks identifiable with a specific type of emission or disclosure level. Rather, they represent circumstances that may increase the risks of material misstatement more generally, for example, through management override of internal control. Risks of material misstatement at the GHG statement level may be especially relevant to the assurance practitioner's consideration of the risks of material misstatement arising from fraud.

A80. Risks at the GHG statement level may derive in particular from a deficient control environment. For example, deficiencies such as management's lack of competence may have a pervasive effect on the GHG statement and may require an overall response by the assurance practitioner. Other risks of material misstatement at the GHG statement level may include, for example:

- Inadequate, poorly controlled or poorly documented mechanisms for collecting data, quantifying emissions and preparing GHG statements.
- Lack of staff competence in collecting data, quantifying emissions and preparing GHG statements.
- Lack of management involvement in quantifying emissions and preparing GHG statements.
- Failure to identify accurately all sources of GHGs.
- Risk of fraud, for example, in connection with emissions trading markets.
- Presenting information covering prior periods that is not prepared on a consistent basis, for example, because of changed boundaries or changes in measurement methodologies.
- Misleading presentation of information in the GHG statement, for example, unduly highlighting particularly favourable data or trends.
- Inconsistent quantification methods and reporting policies, including different methods for determining the organisational boundary, at different facilities.
- Errors in unit conversion when consolidating information from facilities.
- Inadequate disclosure of scientific uncertainties and key assumptions in relation to estimates.

ASAE

The Use of Assertions (Ref: Para. 33L(b)–33R(b))

A81. Assertions are used by the assurance practitioner in a reasonable assurance engagement, and may be used in a limited assurance engagement, to consider the different types of potential misstatements that may occur.

A82. In representing that the GHG statement is in accordance with the applicable criteria, the entity implicitly or explicitly makes assertions regarding the quantification, presentation and disclosure of emissions. Assertions fall into the following categories and may take the following forms:

(a) Assertions about the quantification of emissions for the period subject to assurance:

(i) Occurrence—emissions that have been recorded have occurred and pertain to the entity.

(ii) Completeness—all emissions that should have been recorded, have been recorded (see paragraphs A30–A34 for a discussion of completeness with respect to various Scopes).

(iii) Accuracy—the quantification of emissions has been recorded appropriately.

(iv) Cut-off—emissions have been recorded in the correct reporting period.

(v) Classification—emissions have been recorded as the proper type.

(b) Assertions about presentation and disclosure:

(i) Occurrence and responsibility—disclosed emissions and other matters have occurred and pertain to the entity.

(ii) Completeness—all disclosures that should have been included in the GHG statement have been included.

(iii) Classification and understandability—emissions information is appropriately presented and described, and disclosures are clearly expressed.

(iv) Accuracy and quantification—emissions quantification and related information included in the GHG statement are appropriately disclosed.

(v) Consistency—quantification policies are consistent with those applied in the prior period, or changes are justified and have been properly applied and adequately disclosed; and comparative information, if any, is as reported in the prior period or has been appropriately restated.

Reliance on Internal Control (Ref: Para. 33R)

A83. If the assurance practitioner's assessment of risks of material misstatement at the assertion level includes an expectation that the controls are operating effectively (that is, the assurance practitioner intends to rely on the operating effectiveness of controls in determining the nature, timing and extent of other procedures), the assurance practitioner is required by paragraph 38R to design and perform tests of the operating effectiveness of those controls.

Causes of Risks of Material Misstatement (Ref: Para. 34)

Fraud (Ref: Para. 28, 34(a))

A84. Misstatements in the GHG statement can arise from either fraud or error. The distinguishing factor between fraud and error is whether the underlying action that results in the misstatement of the GHG statement is intentional or unintentional.

A85. Incentives for intentional misstatement of the GHG statement may arise if, for example, those who are directly involved with, or have the opportunity to influence, the emissions reporting process have a significant portion of their compensation contingent upon achieving aggressive GHG targets. As noted in paragraph A61, other incentives to either under or overstate emissions may result from the entity's climate change strategy, if any, and associated economic, regulatory, physical and reputational risks.

A86. Although fraud is a broad legal concept, for the purposes of this ASAE, the assurance practitioner is concerned with fraud that causes a material misstatement in the GHG statement. Although the assurance practitioner may suspect or, in rare cases, identify the occurrence of fraud, the assurance practitioner does not make legal determinations of whether fraud has actually occurred.

Non-Compliance with Laws and Regulations (Ref: Para. 34(b), 78(c))

A87. This ASAE distinguishes the assurance practitioner's responsibilities in relation to compliance with two different categories of laws and regulations as follows:

(a) The provisions of those laws and regulations generally recognised to have a direct effect on the determination of material amounts and disclosures in the GHG statement in that they determine the reported quantities and disclosures in an entity's GHG statement. Paragraph 34(b) requires the assurance practitioner to consider the likelihood of material misstatement due to non-compliance with the provisions of such laws and regulations when performing the procedures required by paragraphs 33L or 33R; and

(b) Other laws and regulations that do not have a direct effect on the determination of the quantities and disclosures in the GHG statement, but compliance with which may be fundamental to the operating aspects of the business, to an entity's ability to continue its business, or to avoid material penalties (for example, compliance with the terms of an operating license, or compliance with environmental regulations). Maintaining professional scepticism throughout the engagement, as required by ASAE 3000,[19] is important in the context of remaining alert to the possibility that procedures applied for the purpose of forming a conclusion on the GHG statement may bring instances of identified or suspected non-compliance with such laws and regulations to the assurance practitioner's attention.

19 ASAE 3000, paragraph 28-29.

Other Causes of Risks of Material Misstatement *(Ref: Para. 34)*

A88. Examples of factors referred to in paragraph 34(c)–(k) include:

(a) Omission of one or more emissions sources is more likely for sources that are less obvious and may be overlooked, such as fugitive emissions.

(b) Significant economic or regulatory changes may include, for example, increases in renewable energy targets or significant price changes for allowances under an emissions trading scheme, which may lead to, for example, increased risk of misclassification of sources at an electricity generator.

(c) The nature of the entity's operations may be complex (for example, it may involve multiple and disparate facilities and processes), discontinuous (for example, peak load electricity generation), or result in few or weak relationships between the entity's emissions and other measurable activity levels (for example, a cobalt nickel plant). In such cases, the opportunity for meaningful analytical procedures may be significantly reduced.

Changes in operations or boundaries (for example, introduction of new processes, or the sale, acquisition or outsourcing of emissions sources or removal sinks) may also introduce risks of material misstatement (for example, through unfamiliarity with quantification or reporting procedures). Also, double counting of an emissions source or removals sink may occur due to inadequate co-ordination in the identification of sources and sinks at a complex installation.

(d) Selection of an inappropriate quantification method (for example, calculating Scope 1 emissions using an emissions factor when using a more accurate direct measurement method is available and would be more appropriate). Selecting an appropriate quantification method is particularly important when the method has been changed. This is because intended users are often interested in emissions trends over time, or relative to a base year. Some criteria may require that quantification methods are only changed when a more accurate method is to be used. Other factors related to the nature of quantification methods include:

- Incorrect application of a quantification method, such as not calibrating meters or not reading them sufficiently frequently, or use of an emissions factor that is inappropriate in the circumstances. For example, an emissions factor may be predicated on an assumption of continuous use and may not be appropriate to use after a shut down.
- Complexity in quantification methods, which will likely involve higher risk of material misstatement, for example: extensive or complex mathematical manipulation of source data (such as the use of complex mathematical models); extensive use of state conversion factors (such as those to convert measures of liquid to measures of gas); or extensive use of unit conversion factors (such as those to convert imperial measures to metric measures).
- Changes in quantification methods or input variables (for example, if the quantification method used is based on the carbon content of biomass, and the composition of the biomass used changes during the period).

(e) Significant non-routine emissions or judgemental matters are a source of greater risk of material misstatement relative to routine, non-complex emissions that are subject to systematic quantification and reporting. Non-routine emissions are those that are unusual, in size or nature, and that therefore occur infrequently (for example, one-off events such as a plant malfunction or major leak). Judgemental matters may include the development of subjective estimates. Risks of material misstatement may be greater because of matters such as:

- Greater management intervention to specify the quantification methods or reporting treatment.
- Greater manual intervention for data collection and processing.
- Complex calculations or quantification methods and reporting principles.

- The nature of non-routine emissions, which may make it difficult for the entity to implement effective controls over the risks.
- Quantification methods and reporting principles for estimates may be subject to differing interpretation.
- Required judgements may be subjective or complex.

(f) The inclusion of Scope 3 emissions where the source data used in quantification are not maintained by the entity, or where quantification methods commonly in use are imprecise or lead to large variations in reported emissions (see paragraphs A31–A34).

(g) Matters that the assurance practitioner may consider in obtaining an understanding of how the entity makes significant estimates and the data on which they are based include, for example:

- An understanding of the data on which estimates are based;
- The method, including where applicable the model, used in making estimates;
- Relevant aspects of the control environment and information system;
- Whether the entity has used an expert;
- The assumptions underlying estimates;
- Whether there has been or ought to have been a change from the prior period in the methods for making estimates and, if so, why; and
- Whether and, if so, how the entity has assessed the effect of estimation uncertainty on the GHG statement, including:
    - Whether and, if so, how the entity has considered alternative assumptions or outcomes by, for example, performing a sensitivity analysis to determine the effect of changes in the assumptions on an estimate;
    - How the entity determines the estimate when analysis indicates a number of outcome scenarios; and
    - Whether the entity monitors the outcome of estimates made in the prior period, and whether it has appropriately responded to the outcome of that monitoring procedure.

A89. Examples of other factors that may lead to risks of material misstatement include:

- Human error in the quantification of emissions, which may be more likely to occur if personnel are unfamiliar with, or not well-trained regarding, emissions processes or data recording.
- Undue reliance on a poorly designed information system, which may have few effective controls, for example, the use of spreadsheets without adequate controls.
- Manual adjustment of otherwise automatically recorded activity levels, for example, manual input may be required if a flare meter becomes overloaded.
- Significant external developments such as heightened public scrutiny of a particular facility.

Overall Responses to Assessed Risks of Material Misstatement and Further Procedures

Limited and Reasonable Assurance Engagements (Ref: Para. 8, 35–41R,42L–43R, 46)

A90. Because the level of assurance obtained in a limited assurance engagement is lower than in a reasonable assurance engagement, the procedures the assurance practitioner will perform in a limited assurance engagement will vary in nature from, and are less in extent than for, a reasonable assurance engagement. The primary differences between the assurance practitioner's overall responses to address the assessed risks of material misstatement and further procedures for a reasonable assurance engagement and a limited assurance engagement on a GHG statement are as follows:

(a) *The emphasis placed on the nature of various procedures:* The emphasis placed on the nature of various procedures as a source of evidence will likely differ, depending on the engagement circumstances. For example:

- The assurance practitioner may judge it to be appropriate in the circumstances of a particular limited assurance engagement to place relatively greater emphasis on enquiries of the entity's personnel and analytical procedures, and relatively less emphasis, if any, on tests of controls and obtaining evidence from external sources than would be the case for a reasonable assurance engagement.
- Where the entity uses continuous measuring equipment to quantify emissions flows, the assurance practitioner may decide in a limited assurance engagement to respond to an assessed risk of material misstatement by enquiring about the frequency with which the equipment is calibrated. In the same circumstances for a reasonable assurance engagement, the assurance practitioner may decide to examine the entity's records of the equipment's calibration or independently test its calibration.
- Where the entity burns coal, the assurance practitioner may decide in a reasonable assurance engagement to independently analyse the characteristics of the coal, but in a limited assurance engagement the assurance practitioner may decide that reviewing the entity's records of laboratory test results is an adequate response to an assessed risk of material misstatement.

(b) *The extent of further procedures:* The extent of further procedures performed in a limited assurance engagement is less than in a reasonable assurance engagement. This may involve:

- Reducing the number of items to be examined, for example, reducing sample sizes for tests of details;
- Performing fewer procedures (for example, performing only analytical procedures in circumstances when, in a reasonable assurance engagement, both analytical procedures and tests of detail would be performed); or
- Performing procedures on location at fewer facilities.

(c) *The nature of analytical procedures:* In a reasonable assurance engagement, analytical procedures performed in response to assessed risks of material misstatement involve developing expectations of quantities or ratios that are sufficiently precise to identify material misstatements. In a limited assurance engagement, on the other hand, analytical procedures are often designed to support expectations regarding the direction of trends, relationships and ratios rather than to identify misstatements with the level of precision expected in a reasonable assurance engagement.[20]

Further, when significant fluctuations, relationships or differences are identified, appropriate evidence in a limited assurance engagement may often be obtained by making enquiries of the entity and considering responses received in the light of known engagement circumstances, without obtaining additional evidence as is required by paragraph 43R(a) in the case of a reasonable assurance engagement.

In addition, when undertaking analytical procedures in a limited assurance engagement the assurance practitioner may, for example:

- Use data that is more highly aggregated, for example, data at a regional level rather than at a facility level, or monthly data rather than weekly data.
- Use data that has not been subjected to separate procedures to test its reliability to the same extent as it would be for a reasonable assurance engagement.

20 This may not always be the case; for example, in some circumstances the practitioner may develop a precise expectation based on fixed physical or chemical relationships even in a limited assurance engagement.

ASAE

Overall Responses to Assessed Risks of Material Misstatement (Ref: Para. 35)

A91. Overall responses to address the assessed risks of material misstatement at the GHG statement level may include:

- Emphasising to the assurance personnel the need to maintain professional scepticism.
- Assigning more experienced staff or those with special skills or using experts.
- Providing more supervision.
- Incorporating additional elements of unpredictability in the selection of further procedures to be performed.
- Making general changes to the nature, timing, or extent of procedures, for example: performing procedures at the period end instead of at an interim date; or modifying the nature of procedures to obtain more persuasive evidence.

A92. The assessment of the risks of material misstatement at the GHG statement level, and thereby the practitioner's overall responses, is affected by the assurance practitioner's understanding of the control environment. An effective control environment may allow the assurance practitioner to have more confidence in internal control and the reliability of evidence generated internally within the entity and thus, for example, allow the assurance practitioner to conduct some procedures at an interim date rather than at the period end. Deficiencies in the control environment, however, have the opposite effect. For example, the assurance practitioner may respond to an ineffective control environment by:

- Conducting more procedures as of the period end rather than at an interim date.
- Obtaining more extensive evidence from procedures other than tests of controls.
- Increasing sample sizes and the extent of procedures, such as the number of facilities at which procedures are performed.

A93. Such considerations, therefore, have a significant bearing on the assurance practitioner's general approach, for example, the relative emphasis on tests of controls versus other procedures (see also paragraphs A70–A72, and A96).

Examples of Further Procedures (Ref: Para. 37L–37R, 40R)

A94. Further procedures may include, for example:

- Testing the operating effectiveness of controls over the collection and recording of activity data, such as kilowatt hours of electricity purchased.
- Agreeing emissions factors to appropriate sources (for example, government publications), and considering their applicability in the circumstances.
- Reviewing joint venture agreements and other contracts relevant to determining the entity's organisational boundary.
- Reconciling recorded data to, for example, odometers on vehicles owned by the entity.
- Reperforming calculations (for example, mass balance and energy balance calculations), and reconciling differences noted.
- Taking readings from continuous monitoring equipment.
- Observing or re-performing physical measurements, such as dipping oil tanks.
- Analysing the soundness and appropriateness of unique measurement or quantification techniques, particularly complex methods that may involve, for example, recycle or feedback loops.
- Sampling and independently analysing the characteristics of materials such as coal, or observing the entity's sampling techniques and reviewing records of laboratory test results.
- Checking the accuracy of calculations and the suitability of calculation methods used (for example, the conversion and aggregation of input measurements).
- Agreeing recorded data back to source documents, such as production records, fuel usage records, and invoices for purchased energy.

Factors that May Influence Assessed Risks of Material Misstatement (Ref: Para. 37L(a)–37R(a))

A95. Factors that may influence the assessed risks of material misstatement include:

- Inherent limitations on the capabilities of measurement instruments and the frequency of their calibration.
- The number, nature, geographical spread, and ownership characteristics of facilities from which data is collected.
- The number and nature of the various gases and emissions sources included in the GHG statement.
- Whether processes to which emissions relate are continuous or intermittent, and the risk of disruption to such processes.
- The complexity of methods for activity measurement and for calculating emissions, for example, some processes require unique measurement and calculation methods.
- The risk of unidentified fugitive emissions.
- The extent to which the quantity of emissions correlates with readily available input data.
- Whether personnel who perform data collection are trained in relevant methods, and the frequency of turnover of such personnel.
- The nature and level of automation used in data capture and manipulation.
- The quality control policies and procedures implemented at testing laboratories, whether internal or external.
- The complexity of criteria and of quantification and reporting policies, including how the organisational boundary is determined.

Operating Effectiveness of Controls (Ref: Para. 37R(a)(ii), 38R(a))

A96. In the case of very small entities or immature information systems, there may not be many control activities that could be identified by the assurance practitioner, or the extent to which their existence or operation have been documented by the entity may be limited. In such cases, it may be more efficient for the assurance practitioner to perform further procedures that are primarily other than tests of controls. In some rare cases, however, the absence of control activities or of other components of control may make it impossible to obtain sufficient appropriate evidence (see also paragraphs A70–A72, and A92–A93).

Persuasiveness of Evidence (Ref: Para. 37L(b)–37R(b))

A97. To obtain more persuasive evidence because of a higher assessment of risk of material misstatement, the assurance practitioner may increase the quantity of the evidence, or obtain evidence that is more relevant or reliable, for example, by obtaining corroborating evidence from a number of independent sources.

Risks for Which Tests of Controls Are Necessary to Provide Sufficient Appropriate Evidence (Ref: 38R(b))

A98. The quantification of emissions may include processes that are highly automated with little or no manual intervention, for example, where relevant information is recorded, processed, or reported only in electronic form such as in a continuous monitoring system, or when the processing of activity data is integrated with an information technology-based operational or financial reporting system. In such cases:

- Evidence may be available only in electronic form, and its sufficiency and appropriateness dependent on the effectiveness of controls over its accuracy and completeness.
- The potential for improper initiation or alteration of information to occur and not be detected may be greater if appropriate controls are not operating effectively.

Confirmation Procedures (Ref: Para. 41R)

A99. External confirmation procedures may provide relevant evidence about such information as:

- Activity data collected by a third party, such as data about: employee air travel collated by a travel agent; the inflow of energy to a facility metered by a supplier; or kilometres travelled by entity-owned vehicles recorded by an external fleet manager.
- Industry benchmark data used in calculating emissions factors.
- The terms of agreements, contracts, or transactions between the entity and other parties, or information about whether other parties are, or are not, including particular emissions in their GHG statement, when considering the entity's organisational boundary.
- The results of laboratory analysis of samples (for example, the calorific value of input samples).

Analytical Procedures Performed in Response to Assessed Risks of Material Misstatement (Ref: Para. 42L–42R)

A100. In many cases, the fixed nature of physical or chemical relationships between particular emissions and other measurable phenomena allows for the design of powerful analytical procedures (for example, the relationship between fuel consumption and carbon dioxide and nitrous oxide emissions).

A101. Similarly, a reasonably predictable relationship may exist between emissions and financial or operational information (for example, the relationship between Scope 2 emissions from electricity and the general ledger balance for electricity purchases or hours of operation). Other analytical procedures may involve comparisons of information about the entity's emissions with external data such as industry averages; or the analysis of trends during the period to identify anomalies for further investigation and trends across periods for consistency with other circumstances such as the acquisition or disposal of facilities.

A102. Analytical procedures may be particularly effective when disaggregated data is readily available, or when the assurance practitioner has reason to consider the data to be used is reliable, such as when it is extracted from a well-controlled source. In some cases, data to be used may be captured by the financial reporting information system, or may be entered in another information system in parallel with the entry of related financial data and some common input controls applied. For example, the quantity of fuel purchased as recorded on suppliers' invoices may be input under the same conditions that relevant invoices are entered into an accounts payable system. In some cases, data to be used may be an integral input to operational decisions and therefore subject to increased scrutiny by operational personnel, or subject to separate external audit procedures (for example, as part of a joint venture agreement or oversight by a regulator).

Procedures Regarding Estimates (Ref: Para. 44L–45R)

A103. In some cases, it may be appropriate for the assurance practitioner to evaluate how the entity has considered alternative assumptions or outcomes, and why it has rejected them.

A104. In some limited assurance engagements, it may be appropriate for the assurance practitioner to undertake one or more of the procedures identified in paragraph 45R.

Sampling (Ref: Para. 46)

A105. Sampling involves:

(a) Determining a sample size sufficient to reduce sampling risk to an acceptably low level. Because the acceptable level of assurance engagement risk is lower for a reasonable assurance engagement than for a limited assurance engagement, so too may be the level of sampling risk that is acceptable in the case of tests of details. Therefore, when sampling is used for tests of details in a reasonable assurance engagement, the sample size may be larger than when used in similar circumstances in a limited assurance engagement.

(b) Selecting items for the sample in such a way that each sampling unit in the population has a chance of selection, and performing procedures, appropriate to the purpose, on each item selected. If the assurance practitioner is unable to apply the designed procedures, or suitable alternative procedures, to a selected item, that item is treated as a deviation from the prescribed control, in the case of tests of controls, or a misstatement, in the case of tests of details.

(c) Investigating the nature and cause of deviations or misstatements identified, and evaluating their possible effect on the purpose of the procedure and on other areas of the engagement.

(d) Evaluating:

(i) The results of the sample, including, for tests of details, projecting misstatements found in the sample to the population; and

(ii) Whether the use of sampling has provided an appropriate basis for conclusions about the population that has been tested.

Fraud, Laws and Regulations (Ref: Para. 47)

A106. In responding to fraud or suspected fraud identified during the engagement, it may be appropriate for the assurance practitioner to, for example:

- Discuss the matter with the entity.
- Request the entity to consult with an appropriately qualified third party, such as the entity's legal counsel or a regulator.
- Consider the implications of the matter in relation to other aspects of the engagement, including the assurance practitioner's risk assessment and the reliability of written representations from the entity.
- Obtain legal advice about the consequences of different courses of action.
- Communicate with third parties (for example, a regulator).
- Withhold the assurance report.
- Withdraw from the engagement.

A107. The actions noted in the paragraph A106 may be appropriate in responding to non-compliance or suspected non-compliance with laws and regulations identified during the engagement. It may also be appropriate to describe the matter in an Other Matter paragraph in the assurance report in accordance with paragraph 77 of this ASAE, unless the assurance practitioner:

(a) Concludes that the non-compliance has a material effect on the GHG statement and has not been adequately reflected in the GHG statement; or

(b) Is precluded by the entity from obtaining sufficient appropriate evidence to evaluate whether non-compliance that may be material to the GHG statement has, or is likely to have, occurred, in which case paragraph 51 of ASAE 3000 applies.

Procedures Regarding the GHG Statement Aggregation Process (Ref: Para. 48L–48R)

A108. As noted in paragraph A71, as reporting of emissions evolves, it can be expected that so too will the level of sophistication, documentation and formality of information systems relevant to the quantification and reporting of emissions. In immature information systems, the aggregation process may be very informal. In more sophisticated systems, the aggregation process may be more systematic and formally documented. The nature, and also the extent, of the assurance practitioner's procedures with respect to adjustments and the manner in which the assurance practitioner agrees or reconciles the GHG statement with the underlying records depends on the nature and complexity of the entity's quantifications and reporting process and the related risks of material misstatement.

ASAE

Additional Procedures (Ref: Para. 49L–49R)

A109. An assurance engagement is an iterative process and information may come to the assurance practitioner's attention that differs significantly from that on which the determination of planned procedures was based. As the assurance practitioner performs planned procedures, the evidence obtained may cause the assurance practitioner to perform additional procedures. Such procedures may include asking the entity to examine the matter(s) identified by the practitioner and to make adjustments to the GHG statement if appropriate.

Determining Whether Additional Procedures Are Necessary in a Limited Assurance Engagement (Ref: Para. 49L)

A110. The assurance practitioner may become aware of a matter(s) that causes the assurance practitioner to believe the GHG statement may be materially misstated. For example, when performing site visits, the assurance practitioner may identify a potential source of emissions which does not appear to be included in the GHG statement. In such cases, the assurance practitioner makes further enquiries as to whether the potential source has been incorporated into the GHG statement. The extent of additional procedures performed, in accordance with paragraph 49L, will be a matter of professional judgement. The greater the likelihood of material misstatement the more persuasive the evidence the assurance practitioner obtains.

A111. If, in the case of a limited assurance engagement, a matter(s) comes to the assurance practitioner's attention that causes the assurance practitioner to believe the GHG statement may be materially misstated, the assurance practitioner is required by paragraph 49L to design and perform additional procedures. If having done so, however, the assurance practitioner is not able to obtain sufficient appropriate evidence to either conclude that the matter(s) is not likely to cause the GHG statement to be materially misstated or determine that it does cause the GHG statement to be materially misstated, a scope limitation exists.

Accumulation of Identified Misstatements (Ref: Para. 50)

A112. The assurance practitioner may designate an amount below which misstatements would be clearly trivial and would not need to be accumulated because the assurance practitioner expects that the accumulation of such amounts clearly would not have a material effect on the GHG statement. "Clearly trivial" is not another expression for "not material." Matters that are clearly trivial will be of a wholly different (smaller) order of magnitude than materiality determined in accordance with this ASAE, and will be matters that are clearly inconsequential, whether taken individually or in the aggregate and whether judged by any criteria of size, nature or circumstances. When there is any uncertainty about whether one or more items are clearly trivial, the matter is considered not to be clearly trivial.

Using the Work of Other Assurance Practitioners

Communication to Other Assurance Practitioners (Ref: Para. 57(a))

A113. Relevant matters that the engagement team may communicate to other assurance practitioners in respect of the work to be performed, the use to be made of that work, and the form and content of the other assurance practitioner's communication with the engagement team may include:

- A request that the other assurance practitioner, knowing the context in which the engagement team will use the work of the other assurance practitioner, confirms that the other practitioner will cooperate with the engagement team.
- Performance materiality for the work of the other assurance practitioner, which may be lower than performance materiality for the GHG statement (and, if applicable, the materiality level or levels for particular types of emissions or disclosures) and the threshold above which misstatements cannot be regarded as clearly trivial to the GHG statement.
- Identified risks of material misstatement of the GHG statement that are relevant to the work of the other assurance practitioner; and a request that the other assurance practitioner communicate on a timely basis any other risks identified during the

engagement that may be material to the GHG statement, and the other assurance practitioner's responses to such risks.

Communication from Other Assurance practitioners (Ref: Para. 57(a))

A114. Relevant matters that the engagement team may request the other assurance practitioner to communicate include:

- Whether the other assurance practitioner has complied with ethical requirements that are relevant to the group engagement, including independence and professional competence.
- Whether the other assurance practitioner has complied with the group engagement team's requirements.
- Information on instances of non-compliance with laws or regulations that could give rise to a material misstatement of the GHG statement.
- A list of uncorrected misstatements identified by the other assurance practitioner during the engagement that are not clearly trivial.
- Indicators of possible bias in the preparation of relevant information.
- Description of any identified significant deficiencies in internal control identified by the other assurance practitioner during the engagement.
- Other significant matters that the other assurance practitioner has communicated or expects to communicate to the entity, including fraud or suspected fraud.
- Any other matters that may be relevant to the GHG statement, or that the other assurance practitioner wishes to draw to the attention of the engagement team, including exceptions noted in any written representations that the other assurance practitioner requested from the entity.
- The other assurance practitioner's overall findings, conclusion or opinion.

Evidence (Ref: Para. 57(b))

A115. Relevant considerations when obtaining evidence regarding the work of the other assurance practitioner may include:

- Discussions with the other assurance practitioner regarding business activities relevant to that other assurance practitioner's work that are significant to the GHG statement.
- Discussions with the other assurance practitioner regarding the susceptibility of relevant information to material misstatement.
- Reviewing the other assurance practitioner's documentation of identified risks of material misstatement, responses to those risks, and conclusions. Such documentation may take the form of a memorandum that reflects the other assurance practitioner's conclusion with regard to the identified risks.

Written Representations (Ref: Para. 58)

A116. In addition to the written representations required by paragraph 58, the assurance practitioner may consider it necessary to request other written representations. The person(s) from whom the assurance practitioner requests written representations will ordinarily be a member of senior management or those charged with governance. However, because management and governance structures vary by jurisdiction and by entity, reflecting influences such as different cultural and legal backgrounds, and size and ownership characteristics, it is not possible for this ASAE to specify for all engagements the appropriate person(s) from whom to request written representations. For example, the entity may be a facility that is not a separate legal entity in its own right. In such cases, identifying the appropriate management personnel or those charged with governance from whom to request written representations may require the exercise of professional judgement.

Subsequent Events (Ref: Para. 61)

A117. Subsequent events may include, for example, the publication of revised emissions factors by a body such as a government agency, changes to relevant legislation or regulations, improved scientific knowledge, significant structural changes in the entity, the availability of more accurate quantification methods, or the discovery of a significant error.

Comparative Information (Ref: Para. 62–63, 76(c))

A118. Law or regulation, or the terms of the engagement, may specify the requirements in respect of presentation, reporting and assurance of the comparative information in a GHG statement. A key difference between financial statements and a GHG statement is that the amounts presented in a GHG statement measures emissions for a discrete period and are not based on cumulative amounts over time. As a result, the comparative information presented does not affect current year information unless emissions have been recorded in the wrong period and therefore the amounts may be based on the incorrect starting period for measurement.

A119. Where a GHG statement includes references to percentage reductions in emissions, or a similar comparison of period on period information, it is important that the assurance practitioner consider the appropriateness of the comparisons. These may be inappropriate due to:

(a) Significant changes in operations from the prior period;

(b) Significant changes in conversion factors; or

(c) Inconsistency of sources or methods of measurement.

A120. When comparative information is presented with the current emissions information but some or all of that comparative information is not covered by the assurance practitioner's conclusion, it is important that the status of such information is clearly identified in both the GHG statement and the assurance report.

Restatements (Ref: Para. 62(a))

A121. The GHG quantities reported in a prior period may need to be restated in accordance with laws or regulations or the applicable criteria because of, for example, improved scientific knowledge, significant structural changes in the entity, the availability of more accurate quantification methods, or the discovery of a significant error.

Performing Procedures on Comparative Information (Ref: Para 63(a))

A122. In a limited assurance engagement that includes assurance on comparative information, if the assurance practitioner becomes aware that there may be a material misstatement in the comparative information presented, the procedures to be performed are to be in accordance with the requirements of paragraph 49L. In the case of a reasonable assurance engagement, the procedures to be performed are to be sufficient to form an opinion on the comparative information.

A123. If the engagement does not include assurance on comparative information, the requirement to perform procedures in the circumstances addressed by paragraph 63(a) is to satisfy the assurance practitioner's ethical obligation to not knowingly be associated with materially false or misleading information.

Other Information (Ref: Para. 64)

A124. A GHG statement may be published with other information that is not covered by the assurance practitioner's conclusion, for example, a GHG statement may be included as part of an entity's annual report or sustainability report, or included with other climate change-specific information such as:

- A strategic analysis, including a statement about the impact climate change has on the entity's strategic objectives.
- An explanation and qualitative assessment of current and anticipated significant risks and opportunities associated with climate change.
- Disclosures about the entity's actions, including its long-term and short-term plan to address climate change-related risks, opportunities and impacts.

- Disclosures about future outlook, including trends and factors related to climate change that are likely to affect the entity's strategy or the timescale over which achievement of the strategy is planned.
- A description of governance processes and the entity's resources that have been assigned to the identification, management and oversight of climate change-related issues.

A125. In some cases, the entity may publish emissions information that is calculated on a different basis from that used in preparing the GHG statement, for example, the other information may be prepared on a "like-for-like" basis whereby emissions are recalculated to omit the effect of non-recurring events, such as the commissioning of a new plant or the closing down of a facility. The assurance practitioner may seek to have such information removed if the methods used to prepare it would be disallowed by the criteria used to prepare the GHG statement. The assurance practitioner may also seek to have removed any narrative information that is inconsistent with the quantitative data included in the GHG statement or cannot be substantiated (for example, speculative projections or claims about future action).

A126. Further actions that may be appropriate when other information could undermine the credibility of the GHG statement and the assurance report include, for example:

- Requesting the entity to consult with a qualified third party, such as the entity's legal counsel.
- Obtaining legal advice about the consequences of different courses of action.
- Communicating with third parties, for example, a regulator.
- Withholding the assurance report.
- Withdrawing from the engagement, where withdrawal is possible under applicable laws or regulations.
- Describing the matter in the assurance report.

ASAE

Documentation

Documentation of the Procedures Performed and Evidence Obtained (Ref: Para. 15, 65–66)

A127. ASAE 3000 requires the assurance practitioner to document matters that are significant in providing evidence that supports the assurance report and that the engagement was performed in accordance with ASAEs.[21] The following are examples of matters that may be appropriate to include in the engagement documentation:

- Fraud: The risks of material misstatement and the nature, timing and extent of procedures with respect to fraud; and communications about fraud made to the entity, regulators and others.
- Laws and Regulations: Identified or suspected non-compliance with laws and regulations and the results of discussion with the entity and other parties outside the entity.
- Planning: The overall engagement strategy, the engagement plan, and any significant changes made during the engagement, and the reasons for such changes.
- Materiality: The following amounts and the factors considered in their determination: materiality for the GHG statement; if applicable, the materiality level or levels for particular types of emissions or disclosures; performance materiality; and any revision of materiality as the engagement progresses.
- Risks of Material Misstatement: the discussion required by paragraph 29, and the significant decisions reached, key elements of the understanding obtained regarding each of the aspects of the entity and its environment specified in paragraph 23, and the risks of material misstatement for which in the assurance practitioner's professional judgement further procedures were required.

21 ASAE 3000, paragraph 70.

- Further Procedures: the nature, timing and extent of the further procedures performed, the linkage of those further procedures with the risks of material misstatement, and the results of the procedures.
- Evaluation of Misstatements: The amount below which misstatements would be regarded as clearly trivial, misstatements accumulated during the engagement and whether they have been corrected, and the assurance practitioner's conclusion as to whether uncorrected misstatements are material, individually or in the aggregate, and the basis for that conclusion.

Matters Arising after the Date of the Assurance Report (Ref: Para. 68)

A128. Examples of exceptional circumstances include facts which become known to the assurance practitioner after the date of the assurance report but which existed at that date and which, if known at that date, might have caused the GHG statement to be amended or the assurance practitioner to modify the conclusion in the assurance report, for example, the discovery of a significant uncorrected error. The resulting changes to the engagement documentation are reviewed in accordance with the firm's policies and procedures with respect to review responsibilities as required by ASQC 1, with the engagement partner taking final responsibility for the changes.[22]

Assembly of the Final Engagement File (Ref: Para. 69)

A129. ASQC 1 requires firms to establish policies and procedures for the timely completion of the assembly of engagement files.[23] An appropriate time limit within which to complete the assembly of the final engagement file is ordinarily not more than 60 days after the date of the assurance report.[24]

Engagement Quality Control Review (Ref: Para. 71)

A130. Other matters that may be considered in an engagement quality control review include:

- The engagement team's evaluation of the firm's independence in relation to the engagement.
- Whether appropriate consultation has taken place on matters involving differences of opinion or other difficult or contentious matters, and the conclusions arising from those consultations.
- Whether engagement documentation selected for review reflects the work performed in relation to the significant judgements and supports the conclusions reached.

Forming the Assurance Conclusion

Description of the Applicable Criteria (Ref: Para. 74(d), 76(g)(iv))

A131. The preparation of the GHG statement by the entity requires the inclusion of an adequate description of the applicable criteria in the explanatory notes to the GHG statement. That description advises intended users of the framework on which the GHG statement is based, and is particularly important when there are significant differences between various criteria regarding how particular matters are treated in a GHG statement, for example: which emissions deductions are included, if any; how they have been quantified and what they represent; and the basis for selecting which Scope 3 emissions are included, and how they have been quantified.

A132. A description that the GHG statement is prepared in accordance with particular criteria is appropriate only if the GHG statement complies with all the requirements of those criteria that are effective during the period covered by the GHG statement.

---

22 ASQC 1 *Quality Control for Firms that Perform Audits and Reviews of Financial Reports and Other Financial Information, and Other Assurance Engagements*, paragraphs 32–33.

23 ASQC 1, paragraph 45.

24 ASQC 1, paragraph A54.

A133. A description of the applicable criteria that contains imprecise qualifying or limiting language (for example, "the GHG statement is in substantial compliance with the requirements of XYZ") is not an adequate description as it may mislead users of the GHG statement.

Assurance Report Content

Illustrative Assurance Reports (Ref: Para. 76)

A134. Appendix 2 contains illustrations of assurance reports on GHG statements incorporating the elements set forth in paragraph 76.

Information Not Covered by the Assurance practitioner's Conclusion (Ref: Para. 76(c))

A135. To avoid misunderstanding and undue reliance on information that has not been subject to assurance, where the GHG statement includes information, such as comparatives, that is not covered by the assurance practitioner's conclusion, that information is ordinarily identified as such in the GHG statement and in the assurance practitioner's assurance report.

Emissions Deductions (Ref: Para. 76(f))

A136. The wording of the statement to be included in the assurance report when the GHG statement includes emissions deductions may vary considerably depending on the circumstances.

A137. The availability of relevant and reliable information in relation to offsets and other emissions deductions varies greatly and, therefore, so does the evidence available to assurance practitioners to support entities' claimed emissions deductions.

A138. Because of the varied nature of emissions deductions and the often reduced number and nature of procedures that can be applied to emissions deductions by the assurance practitioner, this ASAE requires identification in the assurance report of those emissions deductions, if any, that are covered by the assurance practitioner's conclusion, and a statement of the assurance practitioner's responsibility with respect to them.

A139. A statement of the assurance practitioner's responsibility with respect to emissions deductions may be worded as follows when the emissions deductions are comprised of offsets: "The GHG statement includes a deduction from ABC's emissions for the year of yyy tonnes of CO2-e relating to offsets. We have performed procedures as to whether these offsets were acquired during the year, and whether the description of them in the GHG statement is a reasonable summary of the relevant contracts and related documentation. We have not, however, performed any procedures regarding the external providers of these offsets, and express no opinion about whether the offsets have resulted, or will result, in a reduction of yyy tonnes of CO2-e."

Use of the Assurance Report (Ref: Para. 76(g)(iii))

A140. As well as identifying the addressee of the assurance report, the assurance practitioner may consider it appropriate to include wording in the body of the assurance report that specifies the purpose for which, or the intended users for whom, the report was prepared. For example, when the GHG statement will be lodged on the public record, it may be appropriate for the explanatory notes to the GHG statement and the assurance report to include a statement that the report is intended for users who have a reasonable knowledge of GHG related activities, and who have studied the information in the GHG statement with reasonable diligence and understand that the GHG statement is prepared and assured to appropriate levels of materiality.

A141. In addition, the assurance practitioner may consider it appropriate to include wording that specifically restricts distribution of the assurance report other than to intended users, its use by others, or its use for other purposes.

Summary of the Assurance practitioner's Procedures (Ref: Para. 76(h)(ii))

A142. The assurance report in a reasonable assurance engagement normally follows a standard wording and only briefly describes procedures performed. This is because, in a reasonable assurance engagement, describing in any level of detail the specific procedures performed would not assist users to understand that, in all cases where an unmodified report is issued, sufficient appropriate evidence has been obtained to enable the assurance practitioner to express an opinion.

A143. In a limited assurance engagement, an appreciation of the nature, timing and extent of procedures performed is essential for the intended users to understand the conclusion expressed in a limited assurance report. The description of the assurance practitioner's procedures in a limited assurance engagement is therefore ordinarily more detailed than in a reasonable assurance engagement. It also may be appropriate to include a description of procedures that were not performed that would ordinarily be performed in a reasonable assurance engagement. However, a complete identification of all such procedures may not be possible because the assurance practitioner's required understanding and assessment of risks of material misstatement are less than in a reasonable assurance engagement.

Factors to consider in making that determination and the level of detail to be provided include:

- Circumstances specific to the entity (e.g., the differing nature of the entity's activities compared to those typical in the sector).
- Specific engagement circumstances affecting the nature and extent of the procedures performed.
- The intended users' expectations of the level of detail to be provided in the report, based on market practice, or applicable laws or regulations.

A144. In describing the procedures performed in the limited assurance report, it is important that they are written in an objective way but are not summarised to the extent that they are ambiguous, nor written in a way that is overstated or embellished or that implies that reasonable assurance has been obtained. It is also important that the description of the procedures not give the impression that an agreed-upon procedures engagement has been undertaken, and in most cases will not detail the entire work plan.

The Assurance practitioner's Signature (Ref: Para. 76(k))

A145. The assurance practitioner's signature is either in the name of the assurance practitioner's firm, the personal name of the assurance practitioner, or both, as appropriate for the particular jurisdiction. In addition to the assurance practitioner's signature, in certain jurisdictions, the assurance practitioner may be required to declare in the assurance report the assurance practitioner's professional designation or the fact that the assurance practitioner or firm, as appropriate, has been recognised by the appropriate licensing authority in that jurisdiction.

Emphasis of Matter Paragraphs and Other Matter Paragraphs (Ref: Para. 77)

A146. A widespread use of Emphasis of Matter or Other Matter paragraphs diminishes the effectiveness of the practitioner's communication of such matters.

A147. An Emphasis of Matter paragraph may be appropriate when, for example, different criteria have been used or the criteria have been revised, updated or interpreted differently than in prior periods and this has had a fundamental effect on reported emissions, or a system breakdown for part of the period being accounted for means that extrapolation was used to estimate emissions for that time and this has been stated in the GHG statement.

A148. An Other Matter paragraph may be appropriate when, for example, the scope of the engagement has changed significantly from the prior period and this has not been stated in the GHG statement.

A149. The content of an Emphasis of Matter paragraph includes a clear reference to the matter being emphasised and to where relevant disclosures that fully describe the matter can be found in the GHG statement. It also indicates that the assurance practitioner's conclusion is not modified in respect of the matter emphasised. (See also paragraph A125)

A150. The content of an Other Matter paragraph reflects clearly that such other matter is not required to be presented and disclosed in the GHG statement. Paragraph 77 limits the use of an Other Matter paragraph to matters relevant to users' understanding of the engagement, the assurance practitioner's responsibilities or the assurance report, that the assurance practitioner considers it necessary to communicate in the assurance report. (See also paragraph A124)

A151. Including the assurance practitioner's recommendations on matters such as improvements to the entity's information system in the assurance report may imply that those matters have not been appropriately dealt with in preparing the GHG statement. Such recommendations may be communicated, for example, in a management letter or in discussion with those charged with governance. Considerations relevant to deciding whether to include recommendations in the assurance report include whether their nature is relevant to the information needs of intended users, and whether they are worded appropriately to ensure they will not be misunderstood as a qualification of the assurance practitioner's conclusion on the GHG statement.

A152. An Other Matter paragraph does not include information that the assurance practitioner is prohibited from providing by laws, regulations or other professional standards, for example, ethical standards relating to confidentiality of information. An Other Matter paragraph also does not include information that is required to be provided by management.

❖ ❖ ❖

Conformity with International Standards on Assurance Engagements

This Standard on Assurance Engagements conforms with International Standard on Assurance Engagements ISAE 3410 *Assurance Engagements on Greenhouse Gas Statements* issued by the International Auditing and Assurance Standards Board (AUASB), an independent standard-setting board of the International Federation of Accountants (IFAC).

Paragraphs that have been added to this Standard on Assurance Engagements (and do not appear in the text of the equivalent ISAE) are identified with the prefix "Aus".

This Standard on Assurance Engagements incorporates terminology and definitions used in Australia.

The equivalent requirements and related application and other explanatory material included in ISAE 3410 in respect of "relevant ethical requirements", are included in another Auditing Standard, ASA 102 *Compliance with Ethical Requirements when Performing Audits, Reviews and Other Assurance Engagements,* rather than this standard. There is no international equivalent to ASA 102.

Compliance with this Standard on Assurance Engagements enables compliance with ISAE 3410.

Appendix 1

(Ref: Para.A8–A14)

Emissions, Removals and Emissions Deductions

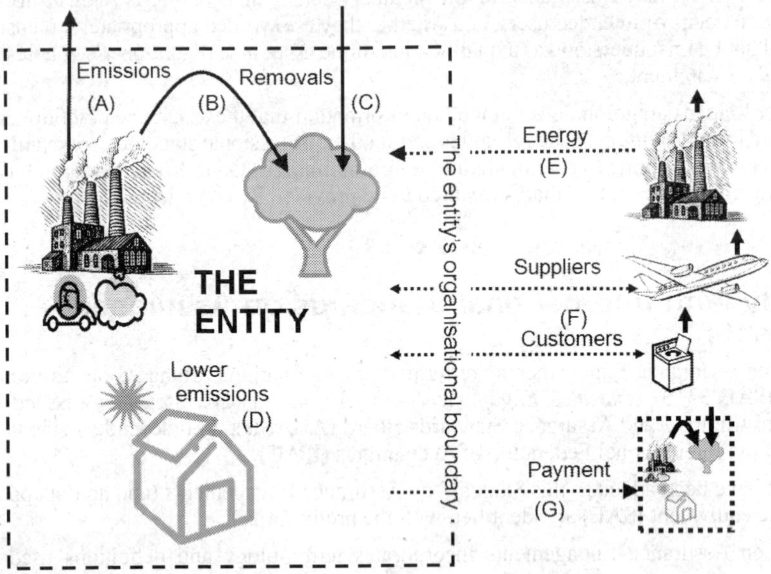

A = Direct, or Scope 1, emissions (see paragraph A8).

B = Removals (emissions that are generated within the entity's boundary but captured and stored within that boundary rather than released into the atmosphere. They are commonly accounted for on a gross basis, that is, as a Scope 1 emission and a removal) (see paragraph A14).

C = Removals (GHGs the entity has removed from the atmosphere) (see paragraph A14).

D = Actions the entity takes to lower its emissions. Such actions might reduce Scope 1 emissions (for example, using more fuel efficient vehicles), Scope 2 emissions (for example, installing solar panels to reduce the quantity of purchased electricity), or Scope 3 emissions (for example, reducing business travel or selling products that require less energy to use). The entity might discuss such actions in the explanatory notes to the GHG statement, but they only affect the quantification of emissions on the face of the entity's GHG statement to the extent that reported emissions are lower than they would otherwise be or they constitute an emissions deduction in accordance with the applicable criteria (see paragraph A11).

E = Scope 2 emissions (see paragraph A9).

F = Scope 3 emissions (see paragraph A10).

G = Emissions deductions, including purchased offsets (see paragraphs A11–A13).

Appendix 2

(Ref: Para. A134)

Illustrations of Assurance Reports on GHG Statements

Illustration 1:*

Circumstances include the following:

- **Reasonable assurance engagement.**
- **The entity's GHG statement contains no Scope 3 emissions.**
- **The entity's GHG statement contains no emissions deductions.**
- **The GHG statement contains no comparative information.**

The following illustrative report is for guidance only and is not intended to be exhaustive or applicable to all situations.

INDEPENDENT ASSURANCE PRACTITIONER'S REASONABLE ASSURANCE REPORT ON ABC'S GREENHOUSE GAS (GHG) STATEMENT

[Appropriate Addressee]

Report on GHG Statement *(this heading is not needed if this is the only section)*

We have undertaken a reasonable assurance engagement of the accompanying GHG statement of ABC for the year ended 30 June 20X1, comprising the Emissions Inventory and the Explanatory Notes on pages xx–yy. [This engagement was conducted by a multidisciplinary team including assurance practitioners, engineers and environmental scientists.] [25]

ABC's Responsibility for the GHG Statement

ABC is responsible for the preparation of the GHG statement in accordance with [*applicable criteria*], applied as explained in Note 1 to the GHG statement. This responsibility includes the design, implementation and maintenance of internal control relevant to the preparation of a GHG statement that is free from material misstatement, whether due to fraud or error.

[As discussed in Note 1 to the GHG statement,][26] GHG quantification is subject to inherent uncertainty because of incomplete scientific knowledge used to determine emissions factors and the values needed to combine emissions of different gases.

Our Independence and Quality Control

We have complied with the relevant ethical requirements relating to assurance engagements, which include independence and other requirements founded on fundamental principles of integrity, objectivity, professional competence and due care, confidentiality and professional behaviour.

In accordance with Auditing Standard ASQC 1,[27] [*name of firm*] maintains a comprehensive system of quality control including documented policies and procedures regarding compliance with ethical requirements, professional standards and applicable legal and regulatory requirements.

* When reporting under NGERS, the assurance practitioner needs to comply with the requirements of the NGER (Audit) Determination 2009 and use the reporting templates in the NGER Audit Determination Handbook issued by the Department of Climate Change and Energy Efficiency. A Guidance Statement will be developed by the AUASB which will apply ASAE 3410 to the conduct of assurance engagements under NGERS.

25 The sentence should be deleted if it is not applicable to the engagement (for example, if the engagement was to report only on Scope 2 emissions and no other experts were used).

26 Where there is no discussion of the inherent uncertainty in Note 1 to the GHG statement, this should be deleted.

27 ASQC 1 *Quality Control for Firms that Perform Audits and Reviews of Financial Reports and Other Financial Information, and Other Assurance Engagements.*

Our Responsibility

Our responsibility is to express an opinion on the GHG statement based on the evidence we have obtained. We conducted our reasonable assurance engagement in accordance with Standard on Assurance Engagements ASAE 3410 *Assurance Engagements on Greenhouse Gas Statements* ("ASAE 3410"), issued by the Auditing and Assurance Standards Board. That standard requires that we plan and perform this engagement to obtain reasonable assurance about whether the GHG statement is free from material misstatement.

A reasonable assurance engagement in accordance with ASAE 3410 involves performing procedures to obtain evidence about the quantification of emissions and related information in the GHG statement. The nature, timing and extent of procedures selected depend on the assurance practitioner's judgement, including the assessment of the risks of material misstatement, whether due to fraud or error, in the GHG statement. In making those risk assessments, we considered internal control relevant to ABC's preparation of the GHG statement. A reasonable assurance engagement also includes:

- Assessing the suitability in the circumstances of ABC's use of [applicable criteria], applied as explained in Note 1 to the GHG statement, as the basis for preparing the GHG statement;
- Evaluating the appropriateness of quantification methods and reporting policies used, and the reasonableness of estimates made by ABC; and
- Evaluating the overall presentation of the GHG statement.

We believe that the evidence we have obtained is sufficient and appropriate to provide a basis for our opinion.

Opinion

In our opinion, the GHG statement for the year ended 30 June 20X1 is prepared, in all material respects, in accordance with the [*applicable criteria*] applied as explained in Note 1 to the GHG statement.

Report on Other Legal and Regulatory Requirements *(applicable for some engagements only)*

[Form and content of this section of the assurance report will vary depending on the nature of the assurance practitioner's other reporting responsibilities.]

[Assurance practitioner's signature]

[Date of the assurance report]

[Assurance practitioner's address]

Illustration 2#

Circumstances include the following:

- **Limited assurance engagement.**
- **The entity's GHG statement contains no Scope 3 emissions.**
- **The entity's GHG statement contains no emissions deductions.**
- **The GHG statement contains no comparative information.**

The following illustrative report is for guidance only and is not intended to be exhaustive or applicable to all situations.

INDEPENDENT ASSURANCE PRACTITIONER'S LIMITED ASSURANCE REPORT ON ABC'S GREENHOUSE GAS (GHG) STATEMENT

[Appropriate Addressee]

Report on GHG Statement *(this heading is not needed if this is the only section)*

We have undertaken a limited assurance engagement of the accompanying GHG statement of ABC for the year ended 30 June 20X1, comprising the Emissions Inventory [and the Explanatory Notes on pages xx–yy]. [This engagement was conducted by a multidisciplinary team including assurance practitioners, engineers and environmental scientists.][28]

ABC's Responsibility for the GHG Statement

ABC is responsible for the preparation of the GHG statement in accordance with [*applicable criteria*], applied as explained in Note 1 to the GHG statement. This responsibility includes the design, implementation and maintenance of internal control relevant to the preparation of a GHG statement that is free from material misstatement, whether due to fraud or error.

[As discussed in Note 1 to the GHG statement,][29] GHG quantification is subject to inherent uncertainty because of incomplete scientific knowledge used to determine emissions factors and the values needed to combine emissions of different gases.

Our Independence and Quality Control

We have complied with the relevant ethical requirements relating to assurance engagements, which include independence and other requirements founded on fundamental principles of integrity, objectivity, professional competence and due care, confidentiality and professional behaviour.

In accordance with Australian Standard on Quality Control 1,[30] [*name of firm*] maintains a comprehensive system of quality control including documented policies and procedures regarding compliance with ethical requirements, professional standards and applicable legal and regulatory requirements.

Our Responsibility

Our responsibility is to express a limited assurance conclusion on the GHG statement based on the procedures we have performed and the evidence we have obtained. We conducted our limited assurance engagement in accordance with Standard on Assurance Engagements ASAE 3410, *Assurance Engagements on Greenhouse Gas Statements* ("ASAE 3410"), issued by the Auditing and Assurance Standards Board. That standard requires that we plan and perform this engagement to obtain limited assurance about whether the GHG statement is free from material misstatement.

\# When reporting under NGERS the assurance practitioner needs to comply with the form of reporting required by the NGER (Audit) Determination 2009 and use the reporting templates in the NGER Audit Determination Handbook issued by the Department of Climate Change and Energy Efficiency. A Guidance Statement will be developed by the AUASB which will apply ASAE 3410 to the conduct of assurance engagements under NGERS.

28 The sentence should be deleted if it is not applicable to the engagement (for example, if the engagement was to report only on Scope 2 emissions and no other experts were used).

29 Where there is no discussion of the inherent uncertainty in Note 1 to the GHG statement, this should be deleted.

30 ASQC 1 *Quality Control for Firms that Perform Audits and Reviews of Financial Reports and Other Financial Information, and Other Assurance Engagements.*

A limited assurance engagement undertaken in accordance with ASAE 3410 involves assessing the suitability in the circumstances of ABC's use of [applicable criteria] as the basis for the preparation of the GHG statement, assessing the risks of material misstatement of the GHG statement whether due to fraud or error, responding to the assessed risks as necessary in the circumstances, and evaluating the overall presentation of the GHG statement. A limited assurance engagement is substantially less in scope than a reasonable assurance engagement in relation to both the risk assessment procedures, including an understanding of internal control, and the procedures performed in response to the assessed risks.

The procedures we performed were based on our professional judgement and included enquiries, observation of processes performed, inspection of documents, analytical procedures, evaluating the appropriateness of quantification methods and reporting policies, and agreeing or reconciling with underlying records.

[The assurance practitioner may insert a summary of the nature and extent of procedures performed that, in the assurance practitioner's judgement, provides additional information that may be relevant to the users' understanding of the basis for the assurance practitioner's conclusion.[31] *The following section has been provided as guidance, and the example procedures are not an exhaustive list of either the type, or extent, of the procedures which may be important for the users' understanding of the work done.]*[32]

Given the circumstances of the engagement, in performing the procedures listed above we:

- Through enquiries, obtained an understanding of ABC's control environment and information systems relevant to emissions quantification and reporting, but did not evaluate the design of particular control activities, obtain evidence about their implementation or test their operating effectiveness.
- Evaluated whether ABC's methods for developing estimates are appropriate and had been consistently applied. However, our procedures did not include testing the data on which the estimates are based or separately developing our own estimates against which to evaluate ABC's estimates.
- Undertook site visits [at three sites] to assess the completeness of the emissions sources, data collection methods, source data and relevant assumptions applicable to the sites. The sites selected for testing were chosen taking into consideration their emissions in relation to total emissions, emissions sources, and sites selected in prior periods. Our procedures [did/did not] include testing information systems to collect and aggregate facility data, or the controls at these sites.][33]

The procedures performed in a limited assurance engagement vary in nature from, and are less in extent than for, a reasonable assurance engagement. As a result, the level of assurance obtained in a limited assurance engagement is substantially lower than the assurance that would have been obtained had we performed a reasonable assurance engagement. Accordingly, we do not express a reasonable assurance opinion about whether ABC's GHG statement has been prepared, in all material respects, in accordance with the [*applicable criteria*] applied as explained in Note 1 to the GHG statement.

Limited Assurance Conclusion

Based on the procedures we have performed and the evidence we have obtained, nothing has come to our attention that causes us to believe that ABC's GHG statement for the year ended 30 June 20X1 is not prepared, in all material respects, in accordance with the [*applicable criteria*] applied as explained in Note 1 to the GHG statement.

31 The procedures are to be summarised but not to the extent that they are ambiguous, nor described in a way that is overstated or embellished or that implies that reasonable assurance has been obtained. It is important that the description of the procedures does not give the impression that an agreed-upon procedures engagement has been undertaken, and in most cases will not detail the entire work plan.

32 In the final report, this explanatory paragraph will be deleted.

33 This section should be deleted if the practitioner concludes that the expanded information on the procedures performed is not needed in the circumstances of the engagement.

Report on Other Legal and Regulatory Requirements (*applicable for some engagements only*)

[Form and content of this section of the assurance report will vary depending on the nature of the assurance practitioner's other reporting responsibilities.]

[Assurance practitioner's signature]

[Date of the assurance report]

[Assurance practitioner's address]

ASAE

ASAE 3420
Assurance Engagements to Report on the Compilation of Pro Forma Historical Financial Information included in a Prospectus or other Document

(Issued November 2012)

Issued by the Auditing and Assurance Standards Board

Note from the Institute of Chartered Accountants Australia

This note, prepared by the technical editor, is not part of ASAE 3420

Historical development

November 2012: ASAE 3420 issued. It provides detailed requirements and related guidance for auditors when determining whether to accept an engagement to report on the compilation of pro forma historical financial information, the appropriate level of assurance, how the engagement is to be performed and what to include in the assurance report. It is operative for engagements commencing on or after 1 July 2013 and conforms with the International Standard ISAE 3420.

Contents

PREFACE

AUTHORITY STATEMENT

Paragraphs

ASAE

Preface

Reasons for Issuing ASAE 3420

The AUASB issues Standard on Assurance Engagements ASAE 3420 *Assurance Engagements To Report on the Compilation of Pro Forma Historical Financial Information included in a Prospectus or other Document,* pursuant to the requirements of the legislative provisions explained below.

The AUASB is an independent statutory board of the Australian Government established under section 227A of the *Australian Securities and Investments Commission Act 2001*, as amended (ASIC Act). Under section 227B of the ASIC Act, the AUASB may formulate assurance standards for other purposes.

Main Features

This Standard on Assurance Engagements establishes requirements and provides application and other explanatory material regarding reporting on the compilation of pro forma historical financial information related to a prospectus, other public document, or prepared for other purposes.

Authority Statement

The Auditing and Assurance Standards Board (AUASB) formulates this Standard on Assurance Engagements ASAE 3420 *Assurance Engagements To Report on the Compilation of Pro Forma Historical Financial Information included in a Prospectus or other Document,* pursuant to section 227B of the *Australian Securities and Investments Commission Act 2001.*

This Standard on Assurance Engagements is to be read in conjunction with ASA 100 *Preamble to AUASB Pronouncements*, which sets out the intentions of the AUASB on how the AUASB Standards are to be understood, interpreted and applied.

Dated: 26 November 2012

M H Kelsall
Chairman - AUASB

Standard on Assurance Engagements ASAE 3420

Assurance Engagements To Report on the Compilation of Pro Forma Historical Financial Information included in a Prospectus or other Document

Application

Aus 0.1 This Standard on Assurance Engagements applies to assurance engagements to provide reasonable assurance on the compilation of pro forma historical financial information included in a prospectus, other public document, or prepared for any other purpose.

Aus 0.2 This Standard on Assurance Engagements also applies, as appropriate, to assurance engagements to provide limited assurance on the compilation of pro forma historical financial information included in a prospectus, other public document, or prepared for any other purpose.

Operative Date

Aus 0.3 This Standard on Assurance Engagements is operative for engagements commencing on or after 1 July 2013.

Introduction

Scope of this Standard on Assurance Engagements

1. [Deleted by the AUASB. Refer Aus 1.1]

Aus 1.1 This Australian Standard on Assurance Engagements (ASAE) deals with limited or reasonable assurance engagements undertaken by an assurance practitioner[1] to report on the responsible party's[2] compilation of pro forma historical financial information included in a prospectus, other public document, or prepared for any other purpose. For ease of reference, in this ASAE the term 'prospectus' is taken to include an other public document or nonpublic document prepared for any other purpose, unless otherwise noted. (Ref: Para. A1)

Aus 1.2 When the assurance practitioner is requested to provide assurance on the pro forma financial information itself, refer to ASAE 3450 *Assurance Engagements involving Corporate Fundraisings and/or Prospective Financial Information.*

Nature of the Assurance Practitioner's Responsibility

2. In an engagement performed under this ASAE, the assurance practitioner has no responsibility to compile the pro forma financial information for the entity; such responsibility rests with the responsible party. The assurance practitioner's sole responsibility is to report on whether the pro forma financial information has been compiled, in all material respects, by the responsible party on the basis of the applicable criteria.

3. This ASAE does not deal with nonassurance engagements in which the assurance practitioner is engaged by the entity to compile its historical financial statements.

Purpose of Pro Forma Financial Information Included in a Prospectus

4. The purpose of pro forma financial information included in a prospectus is solely to illustrate the impact of a significant event(s) or transaction(s) on unadjusted financial information of the entity as if the event had occurred or the transaction had been undertaken at an earlier date selected for purposes of the illustration. This is achieved by applying pro forma adjustments to the unadjusted financial information. Pro forma financial information does not represent the entity's actual financial position, financial performance, or cash flows. (Ref: Para. A2-A3)

Aus 4.1 In this ASAE 'pro forma financial information' is taken to mean pro forma historical financial information. Reporting on the compilation of pro forma financial information in the form of a pro forma forecast is not included within the scope of this ASAE.

Compilation of Pro Forma Financial Information

5. The compilation of pro forma financial information involves the responsible party gathering, classifying, summarising and presenting financial information that illustrates the impact of a significant event(s) or transaction(s) on unadjusted financial information of the entity as if the event had occurred or the transaction had been undertaken at the selected date. Steps involved in this process include:

- Identifying the source of the unadjusted financial information to be used in compiling the pro forma financial information, and extracting the unadjusted financial information from that source; (Ref: Para. A4-A5)
- Making pro forma adjustments to the unadjusted financial information for the purpose for which the pro forma financial information is presented; and
- Presenting the resulting pro forma financial information with accompanying disclosures.

1 The term "assurance practitioner" is described in ASAE 3000, *Assurance Engagements Other than Audits or Reviews of Historical Financial Information*, paragraph 4.

2 See the *Framework for Assurance Engagements* (the Assurance Framework), paragraphs 25-26, which describes the meaning of the term "responsible party."

ASAE

Nature of Reasonable Assurance Engagement

6. A reasonable assurance engagement to report on the compilation of pro forma financial information involves performing the procedures set out in this ASAE to assess whether the applicable criteria used by the responsible party in the compilation of the pro forma financial information provide a reasonable basis for presenting the significant effects directly attributable to the event(s) or transaction(s), and to obtain sufficient appropriate evidence about whether: (Ref: Para. A6)

 - The related pro forma adjustments give appropriate effect to those criteria; and
 - The resultant pro forma column (see paragraph 11(c) of this ASAE) reflects the proper application of those adjustments to the unadjusted financial information.

 It also involves evaluating the overall presentation of the pro forma financial information. The engagement, however, does not involve the assurance practitioner updating or reissuing any reports or opinions on any historical financial information used in compiling the pro forma financial information, or performing an audit or review of the financial information used in compiling the pro forma financial information.

Nature of Limited Assurance Engagement

Aus 6.1 A limited assurance engagement to report on the compilation of pro forma financial information involves performing the procedures set out in this ASAE to assess whether anything comes to the assurance practitioner's attention that causes the assurance practitioner to believe that the applicable criteria used by the responsible party in the compilation of the pro forma financial information does not provide a reasonable basis for presenting the significant effects directly attributable to the event(s) or transaction(s), or that: (Ref: Para. Aus A6.1-A6.4)

 - The related pro forma adjustments do not give appropriate effect to those criteria; and
 - The resultant pro forma column (see paragraph 11(c) of this ASAE) does not reflect the proper application of those adjustments to the unadjusted financial information.

 It also involves evaluating the overall presentation of the pro forma financial information. The engagement, however, does not involve the assurance practitioner updating or reissuing any previously issued reports or opinions on any historical financial information used in compiling the pro forma financial information, or performing an audit or review of the financial information used in compiling the pro forma financial information.

Relationship with Other Professional Pronouncements

7. The performance of assurance engagements other than audits or reviews of historical financial information requires the assurance practitioner to comply with ASAE 3000.[3] ASAE 3000 includes requirements in relation to such topics as engagement acceptance, planning, evidence, and documentation that apply to all assurance engagements, including engagements in accordance with this ASAE. This ASAE expands on how ASAE 3000 is to be applied in a reasonable or limited assurance engagement to report on the compilation of pro forma financial information included in a prospectus. The *Framework for Assurance Engagements* which defines and describes the elements and objectives of an assurance engagement, provides context for understanding this ASAE and ASAE 3000.

8. [Deleted by the AUASB. Refer Aus 8.1]

3 See ASAE 3000.

Aus 8.1 Compliance with ASAE 3000 requires, among other things, that the assurance practitioner:

(a) complies with the fundamental ethical principles of integrity, objectivity, professional competence and due care, confidentiality and professional behaviour; and

(b) implements quality control procedures that are applicable to the individual assurance engagement.[4,*]

Aus 8.2 In addition to compliance with ASAE 3000 described in paragraph Aus 8.1 of this ASAE, the assurance practitioner is also required to comply with the relevant ethical requirements relating to assurance engagements contained in ASA 102.[#]

Effective Date

9. [Deleted by the AUASB. Refer Aus 0.3]

Objectives

10. The objectives of the assurance practitioner are:

(a) [Deleted by the AUASB. Refer Aus 10.1(a)]

(b) [Deleted by the AUASB. Refer Aus 10.1(b)]

Aus 10.1 (a) To obtain reasonable or limited assurance, as appropriate, about whether the pro forma financial information has been compiled by the responsible party on the basis of the applicable criteria, thereby enabling the assurance practitioner to express a conclusion conveying that level of assurance; and

(b) To report in accordance with the assurance practitioner's findings.

Definitions

11. For the purposes of this Standard on Assurance Engagements, the following terms have the meanings attributed below:

(a) Applicable criteria – The criteria used by the responsible party when compiling the pro forma financial information. Criteria may be established by applicable law or regulation or in the absence of established criteria, be developed by the responsible party. (Ref: Para. A7-A9)

(b) Pro forma adjustments – In relation to unadjusted financial information, these include:

(i) Adjustments to unadjusted financial information that illustrate the impact of a significant event(s) or transaction(s) ("events" or "transactions") as if the event had occurred or the transaction had been undertaken at an earlier date selected for purposes of the illustration; and

(ii) Adjustments to unadjusted financial information that are necessary for the pro forma financial information to be compiled on a basis consistent with the applicable financial reporting framework of the reporting entity ("entity") and its accounting policies under that framework. (Ref: Para. A15-A16)

Pro forma adjustments include the relevant financial information of a business that has been, or is to be, acquired ("acquiree"), or a business that has been, or is to be, divested ("divestee"), to the extent that such information is used in compiling the pro forma financial information ("acquiree or divestee financial information").

(c) [Deleted by the AUASB. Refer Aus 11.1]

4 See ASAE 3000, paragraphs 12 and 13.

* See ASQC 1 Quality Control for Firms that Perform Audits and Reviews of Financial Reports and Other Financial Information, and Other Assurance Engagements.

\# See ASA 102 *Compliance with Ethical Requirements when Performing Audits, Reviews and Other Assurance Engagements.*

ASAE

Aus 11.1 Pro forma financial information – Historical financial information shown together with adjustments to illustrate the impact of an event(s) or transaction(s) on unadjusted financial information as if the event had occurred or the transaction had been undertaken at an earlier date selected for purposes of the illustration. In this ASAE, it is assumed that pro forma financial information is presented in columnar format consisting of (a) the unadjusted historical financial information; (b) the pro forma adjustments; and (c) the resulting pro forma column. (Ref: Para. A2)

(d) Prospectus – A document issued pursuant to applicable law or regulation relating to the entity's securities on which it is intended that a third party should make an investment decision.

Aus 11.2 Public document – a disclosure document, product disclosure statement or other documentation provided to shareholders, unit holders, or holders of a relevant interest in an entity (or which is provided to management of any entity) in relation to a scheme of arrangement under the Part 5.1 of the *Corporations Act 2001*, or a takeover or compulsory acquisition under Chapter 6 of the *Corporations Act 2001*.

(e) Published financial information – Financial information of the entity or of an acquiree or a divestee that is made available publicly.

(f) [Deleted by the AUASB. Refer Aus 11.3]

Aus 11.3 Unadjusted financial information – Historical financial information of the entity to which pro forma adjustments are applied by the responsible party. (Ref: Para. A4A5)

Requirements

ASAE 3000

12. The assurance practitioner shall not represent compliance with this ASAE unless the assurance practitioner has complied with the requirements of both this ASAE and ASAE 3000.

Engagement Acceptance

Preconditions for Acceptance

13. Before agreeing to accept an engagement to report on whether pro forma financial information included in a prospectus has been compiled, in all material respects, on the basis of the applicable criteria, the assurance practitioner shall:

(a) Determine that the assurance practitioner has the capabilities and competence to perform the engagement; (Ref: Para. A10-Aus A10.2)

(b) On the basis of a preliminary knowledge of the engagement circumstances and discussion with the responsible party, determine that the applicable criteria are suitable and that it is unlikely that the compilation of the pro forma financial information will be misleading for the purpose for which it is intended;

(c) If applicable, evaluate the wording of the assurance practitioner's conclusion prescribed by applicable law or regulation to determine that it will be possible for the assurance practitioner to express the conclusion so prescribed based on performing the procedures specified in this ASAE; (Ref: Para. A54-A56)

(d) Where the sources from which the unadjusted financial information and any acquiree or divestee financial information have been extracted have been audited or reviewed and a modified audit opinion or review conclusion has been expressed, or the report contains an Emphasis of Matter paragraph, consider whether or not applicable law or regulation permits the use of, or reference in the assurance practitioner's report to, the modified audit opinion or review conclusion or the report containing the Emphasis of Matter paragraph with respect to such sources;

(e) If the entity's historical financial information has never been audited or reviewed, consider whether the assurance practitioner can obtain a sufficient understanding of the entity and its accounting and financial reporting practices to perform the engagement; (Ref: Para. A31)

(f) If the event(s) or transaction(s) include(s) an acquisition and the acquiree's historical financial information has never been audited or reviewed, consider whether the assurance practitioner can obtain a sufficient understanding of the acquiree and its accounting and financial reporting practices to perform the engagement;

(g) Obtain the agreement of the responsible party that it acknowledges and understands its responsibility for: (Ref: Para. A11-A12)

(i) Adequately disclosing and describing the applicable criteria to the intended users if these are not publicly available;

(ii) Compiling the pro forma financial information on the basis of the applicable criteria; and

(iii) Providing the assurance practitioner with:

- Access to all information (including, if applicable for the purposes of the engagement, information the responsible party has in respect of any acquiree(s) in a business combination transaction), such as records, documentation, and other material, relevant to evaluating whether the pro forma financial information has been compiled, in all material respects, on the basis of the applicable criteria;
- Additional information that the assurance practitioner may request from the responsible party for the purpose of the engagement;
- Access to those within the entity and the entity's advisors from whom the assurance practitioner determines it necessary to obtain evidence relating to evaluating whether the pro forma financial information has been compiled, in all material respects, on the basis of the applicable criteria; and
- When needed for purposes of the engagement, access to appropriate individuals within the acquiree(s) in a business combination;

(iv) Aus 13.1 The preparation of the unadjusted financial information used in preparing the pro forma financial information;

(v) Aus 13.2 The preparation of the pro forma financial information itself;

(vi) Aus 13.3 The selection of the applicable criteria; and

(h) Aus 13.4 Determine whether the type of assurance requested is acceptable (Ref: Para. Aus A10.2)

Agreeing the Terms of the Assurance Engagement

Aus 13.5 As required by ASAE 3000* the assurance practitioner shall agree the terms of the assurance engagement with the responsible party in writing. (Ref: Para. Aus A10.3)

Aus 13.6 The agreed terms of the assurance engagement, as required by ASAE 3000, shall at a minimum, include:

(a) the objective(s) and scope of the engagement, including:

(i) the assurance practitioner's understanding of the purpose of the engagement and the intended users of the assurance report;

(ii) confirmation that the assurance practitioner will conduct the engagement in accordance with this ASAE;

(iii) the nature, source, time period covered and purpose of the pro forma financial information;

(iv) a statement that the assurance practitioner is not responsible for the preparation of the pro forma financial information or for applicable criteria;

(v) if applicable, a statement that an audit is not being performed and that consequently, an audit opinion will be not be expressed;

* See ASAE 3000, paragraphs 20-21.

ASAE

(b) a reference to the expected form and content of any reports to be issued by the assurance practitioner and a statement that there may be circumstances in which a report may differ from its expected form and content; and

(i) an acknowledgement that the entity agrees to provide written representations at the conclusion of the engagement; and;

(ii) a statement that the engagement cannot be relied upon to identify fraud, error(s), illegal action(s) or other irregularities that may exist within the entity;

(c) the responsibilities of the assurance practitioner, including:

(i) compliance with relevant ethical requirements, including independence;

(ii) providing limited or reasonable assurance, as applicable, on whether the pro forma financial information has been compiled, in all material respects, on the basis of the applicable criteria;

(iii) determining whether the applicable criteria, selected by the responsible party for illustrating the significant effects directly attributable to the event(s) or transaction(s), are suitable;

(iv) performing assurance procedures on the responsible party's compilation of the pro forma financial information on the basis of the responsible party's specified applicable criteria to obtain sufficient appropriate evidence for the type of assurance required; (Ref: Para. Aus A10.4)

(v) issuing a written assurance report and any other reporting agreed with the responsible party;*

(vi) where applicable, and once satisfied it is appropriate to, providing consent in the required form to the responsible party to the inclusion of the assurance practitioner's name and assurance report in the prospectus;

(vii) for the purposes of the engagement, the assurance practitioner is not responsible for:

- updating or reissuing any previously issued audit report or review conclusion on any financial information used in compiling the pro forma financial information; and

- performing an audit or review of any financial information used in compiling the pro forma financial information or the pro forma financial information itself;

(d) the responsibilities of the responsible party including those set out in paragraph 13(g) of this ASAE; and

(e) such other terms and conditions that the assurance practitioner determines are appropriate in the engagement circumstances.

* See ASA 260 *Communication with Those Charged with Governance* for guidance on specific matters that may be communicated in an audit engagement that may be helpful in an assurance engagement involving reasonable assurance on historical financial information. Additionally, ASRE 2405 *Review of Historical Financial Information Other than a Financial Report* provides guidance on specific matters that may be communicated in a review engagement that may also be helpful in an assurance engagement involving a review of historical financial information.

Changes in the Terms of the Assurance Engagement

Aus 13.7 If the assurance practitioner is unable to agree to a change in the terms of the engagement, and is not permitted by the responsible party to continue the original engagement, the assurance practitioner shall: (Ref: Para. Aus A12.1)

(a) withdraw from the engagement where possible under applicable law or regulation; and

(b) determine whether there is any obligation, either contractual or otherwise, to report the circumstances to parties other than the responsible party.

Planning and Performing the Engagement

Aus 13.8 The assurance practitioner shall use professional judgement** to design and perform procedures whose nature, timing and extent are appropriate to the type of assurance required. (Ref: Para. Aus A12.2)

Assessing the Suitability of the Applicable Criteria

14 The assurance practitioner shall assess whether the applicable criteria are suitable, as required by ASAE 3000[5], and in particular shall determine that they include, at a minimum, that:

(a) The unadjusted financial information be extracted from an appropriate source; (Ref: Para. A4-A5, A27)

(b) The pro forma adjustments be:

(i) directly attributable to the event(s) or transaction(s); (Ref: Para. A13-Aus A13.1)

(ii) factually supportable; and (Ref: Para. A14)

(iii) consistent with the entity's applicable financial reporting framework and its accounting policies under that framework; and (Ref: Para. A15-A16)

(c) Appropriate presentation be made and disclosures be provided to enable the intended users to understand the information conveyed. (Ref: Para. A2-A3, A42)

15. In addition, the assurance practitioner shall assess whether the applicable criteria are:

(a) Consistent, and do not conflict, with applicable law or regulation; and

(b) Unlikely to result in pro forma financial information that is misleading.

Materiality

16. When planning and performing the engagement, the assurance practitioner shall consider materiality# with respect to evaluating whether the pro forma financial information has been compiled, in all material respects, on the basis of the applicable criteria. (Ref: Para. A17-Aus A18.1)

Obtaining an Understanding of How the Responsible Party Has Compiled the Pro Forma Financial Information and Other Engagement Circumstances

17. The assurance practitioner shall obtain an understanding of: (Ref: Para. A19)

(a) The event(s) or transaction(s) in respect of which the pro forma financial information is being compiled;

(b) How the responsible party has compiled the pro forma financial information; (Ref: Para. A20-A21)

** The concepts and discussions on professional judgement relevant to audit engagements are contained in ASA 200 *Overall Objectives of the Independent Auditor and the Conduct of an Audit in Accordance with Australian Auditing Standards* and may be helpful in applying professional judgement in an assurance engagement.

5 See ASAE 3000, paragraph 35.

See ASA 320 *Materiality in Planning and Performing an Audit* for guidance on planning materiality.

ASAE

(c) The nature of the entity and any acquiree or divestee, including: (Ref: Para. A22-A23)

(i) Their operations;

(ii) Their assets and liabilities; and

(iii) The way they are structured and how they are financed; and

(d) Relevant industry, legal and regulatory, and other external factors pertaining to the entity and any acquiree or divestee; and (Ref: Para. A24-A26)

(e) The applicable financial reporting framework and the accounting and financial reporting practices of the entity and of any acquiree or divestee, including their selection and application of accounting policies.

Aus 17.1 The understanding shall be sufficient to enable the assurance practitioner to plan and design assurance procedures appropriate to the type of assurance required.

Obtaining Evidence about the Appropriateness of the Source from Which the Unadjusted Financial Information Has Been Extracted

18. The assurance practitioner shall determine whether the responsible party has extracted the unadjusted financial information from an appropriate source. (Ref: Para. A27-Aus A28.2)

19. If there is no audit or review report on the source from which the unadjusted financial information has been extracted, the assurance practitioner shall perform procedures to be satisfied that the source is appropriate. (Ref: Para. A29-A31)

Aus 19.1 If the assurance practitioner is not able to perform the procedures stated in paragraph 19 of this ASAE in order to obtain sufficient appropriate evidence*** on which to assess whether the source from which the unadjusted financial information has been extracted is appropriate, this constitutes a limitation of scope on the assurance practitioner's work, and the assurance practitioner shall modify the conclusion in the assurance report in accordance with ASAE 3000.#

20. The assurance practitioner shall determine whether the responsible party has appropriately extracted the unadjusted financial information from the source.

Obtaining Evidence about the Appropriateness of the Pro Forma Adjustments

21. In evaluating whether the pro forma adjustments are appropriate, the assurance practitioner shall determine whether the responsible party has identified the pro forma adjustments necessary to illustrate the impact of the event(s) or transaction(s) at the date or for the period of the illustration. (Ref: Para. A32)

22. In determining whether the pro forma adjustments are in accordance with the applicable criteria, the assurance practitioner shall determine whether they are:

(a) Directly attributable to the event(s) or transaction(s); (Ref: Para. A13-Aus A13.1)

(b) Factually supportable. If acquiree or divestee financial information is included in the pro forma adjustments and there is no audit or review report on the source from which such financial information has been extracted, the assurance practitioner shall perform procedures to be satisfied that the financial information is factually supportable; and (Ref: Para. A14, A33-A38)

(c) Consistent with the entity's applicable financial reporting framework and its accounting policies under that framework. (Ref: Para. A15-A16)

Modified Audit Opinion or Review Conclusion, or Emphasis of Matter Paragraph, with Respect to the Source from Which the Unadjusted Financial Information Has Been Extracted or the Source from Which the Acquiree or Divestee Financial Information Has Been Extracted

23. A modified audit opinion or review conclusion may have been expressed with respect to either the source from which the unadjusted financial information has been extracted or the source from which the acquiree or divestee financial information has been extracted,

*** See ASAE 3000, paragraphs 56-63 for further information on obtaining evidence.

See ASAE 3000, paragraphs 82-84 for further information.

or a report containing an Emphasis of Matter paragraph may have been issued with respect to such source. In such circumstances, if the applicable law or regulation does not prohibit the use of such a source, the assurance practitioner shall evaluate:

(a) The potential consequence on whether the pro forma financial information has been compiled, in all material respects, on the basis of the applicable criteria; (Ref: Para. A39)

(b) What further appropriate action to take; and (Ref: Para. A40)

(c) Whether there is any effect on the assurance practitioner's ability to report in accordance with the terms of the engagement, including any effect on the assurance report.

Source from Which the Unadjusted Financial Information Has Been Extracted or Pro Forma Adjustments Not Appropriate

24. If, on the basis of the procedures performed, the assurance practitioner identifies that the responsible party has:

(a) Used an inappropriate source from which to extract the unadjusted financial information; or

(b) Omitted a pro forma adjustment that should be included, applied a pro forma adjustment that is not in accordance with the applicable criteria or otherwise inappropriately applied a pro forma adjustment,

the assurance practitioner shall discuss the matter with the responsible party. If the assurance practitioner is unable to agree with the responsible party as to how the matter can be resolved, the assurance practitioner shall evaluate what further action to take. (Ref: Para. A40)

Obtaining Evidence about the Calculations within the Pro Forma Financial Information

25. The assurance practitioner shall determine whether the calculations within the pro forma financial information are arithmetically accurate.

Evaluating the Presentation of the Pro Forma Financial Information

26. The assurance practitioner shall evaluate the presentation of the pro forma financial information. This shall include consideration of:

(a) The overall presentation and structure of the pro forma financial information, including whether it is clearly labelled to distinguish it from historical or other financial information; (Ref: Para. A2-A3)

(b) Whether the pro forma financial information and related explanatory notes illustrate the impact of the event(s) or transaction(s) in a manner that is not misleading; (Ref: Para. A41-Aus A41.1)

(c) Whether appropriate disclosures are provided with the pro forma financial information to enable the intended users to understand the information conveyed; and (Ref: Para. A42)

(d) [Deleted by the AUASB. Refer Aus 26.1]

Aus 26.1 Whether the assurance practitioner has become aware of any significant events, related to the unadjusted financial information that have occurred subsequent to the date of the source from which the unadjusted financial information has been extracted, that may require reference to, or disclosure in, the pro forma financial information. (Ref: Para. Aus A43.1)

27. The assurance practitioner shall read the other information included in the prospectus containing the pro forma financial information to identify material inconsistencies, if any, with the pro forma financial information. If, on reading the other information, the assurance practitioner identifies a material inconsistency or becomes aware of a material misstatement of fact in relation to the pro forma financial information in that other information, the assurance practitioner shall discuss the matter with the responsible party. If correction of the matter is necessary and the responsible party refuses to do so, the assurance practitioner shall take further appropriate action. (Ref: Para. A44)

Written Representations

28. The assurance practitioner shall request written representations* from the responsible party that:

(a) In compiling the pro forma financial information, the responsible party has identified all appropriate pro forma adjustments necessary to illustrate the impact of the event(s) or transaction(s) at the date or for the period of the illustration in accordance with the applicable criteria; (Ref: Para. A45)

(b) The pro forma financial information has been compiled, in all material respects, on the basis of the applicable criteria;

Aus 28.1 (c) They accept, acknowledge, and understand their responsibility for those matters described in paragraphs 13(g) to Aus 13.4 inclusive of this ASAE;

(d) They acknowledge the intended use of the pro forma financial information;

(e) There are no currently anticipated material changes to be made to the pro forma financial information between the date of the assurance report and the relevant date;

(f) There has been no matter, event, transaction, or issue that has arisen or been discovered subsequent to the preparation of the pro forma financial information that may impact, or require adjustment to, the pro forma financial information;

(g) They have provided the assurance practitioner with a listing of all known uncorrected immaterial misstatements in the pro forma financial information, together with an acknowledgement that the responsible party is responsible for confirming that such misstatements are immaterial; and

(h) Cover such other written representations as that the assurance practitioner determines are appropriate in the engagement circumstances.

Aus 28.2 The date of the representation letter shall be as near as practicable to, but not after, the date of the assurance report.

Aus 28.3 If the assurance practitioner has sufficient doubt about the competence, integrity, ethical values, or diligence of those providing the written representations or if the representations received are inconsistent with other evidence, the assurance practitioner shall:

(a) discuss the matter with the responsible party;

(b) perform other procedures to attempt to resolve any inconsistencies;

(c) re-evaluate the integrity of the responsible party and evaluate the effect this may have on the reliability of representations (oral or written) and evidence in general; and

(d) take appropriate action, including determining the possible effect on the assurance conclusion in the assurance report.

Aus 28.4 If the representations remain inconsistent with other evidence, the assurance practitioner shall reconsider the assessment of the competence, integrity, ethical values, or diligence of the responsible party or of its commitment to an enforcement of these, and shall determine the effect that this may have on the reliability of representations (oral or written) and evidence in general.

Forming the Conclusion

29. [Deleted by the AUASB. Refer Aus 29.1]

Aus 29.1 The assurance practitioner shall conclude as to whether the assurance practitioner has obtained reasonable or limited assurance, as appropriate, on the compilation of the pro forma financial information. (Ref: Para. A46-A48)

---

* The concepts and discussions on obtaining written representations relevant to audit engagement are contained in ASA 580 *Written Representations* and may be helpful in determining the form and content of written representations applicable to an assurance engagement.

30. In order to form that conclusion, the assurance practitioner shall conclude whether the assurance practitioner has obtained sufficient appropriate evidence about whether the compilation of the pro forma financial information is free from material omission, or inappropriate use or application of, a pro forma adjustment(s). That conclusion shall include an evaluation of whether the responsible party has adequately disclosed and described the applicable criteria in the prospectus to the extent that these are not publicly available. (Ref: Para. A49-A50)

Form of Conclusion

Unmodified Conclusion

31. The assurance practitioner shall express an unmodified conclusion when the assurance practitioner concludes with reasonable assurance that the pro forma financial information has been compiled, in all material respects, by the responsible party on the basis of the applicable criteria.

Aus 31.1 In a limited assurance engagement, the assurance practitioner shall express an unmodified conclusion when the assurance practitioner concludes that nothing has come to the assurance practitioner's attention that causes the assurance practitioner to believe that the pro forma financial information has not been compiled, in all material respects, by the responsible party on the basis of the applicable criteria.

Modified Conclusion

32. [Deleted by the AUASB. Refer Aus 32.1]

Aus 32.1 If the assurance practitioner concludes that a modified conclusion is appropriate in accordance with ASAE 3000, the assurance practitioner shall discuss the matter with the responsible party. If the responsible party does not agree to make the necessary changes, the assurance practitioner shall either:

(a) withhold the assurance report;

(b) consider seeking legal advice;

(c) withdraw from the engagement, where practical and possible under applicable law or regulation; or

(d) modify the conclusion in accordance with the requirements in ASAE 3000[6] regarding modified conclusions.

33. [Deleted by the AUASB. Refer Aus 32.1(d)]

Emphasis of Matter Paragraph

34. In some circumstances, the assurance practitioner may consider it necessary to draw users' attention to a matter presented or disclosed in the pro forma financial information or the accompanying explanatory notes. This would be the case when, in the assurance practitioner's opinion, the matter is of such importance that it is fundamental to users' understanding of whether the pro forma financial information has been compiled, in all material respects, on the basis of the applicable criteria. In such circumstances, the assurance practitioner shall include an Emphasis of Matter paragraph[*] in the assurance practitioner's report provided that the assurance practitioner has obtained sufficient appropriate evidence that the matter does not affect whether the pro forma financial information has been compiled, in all material respects, on the basis of the applicable criteria. Such a paragraph shall refer only to information presented or disclosed in the pro forma financial information or the accompanying explanatory notes.

6 See ASAE 3000, paragraphs 83 and 84.

* The concepts and discussions on the circumstances under which an emphasis of matter paragraph is included in an auditor's report are contained in ASA 706 *Emphasis of Matter Paragraphs and Other Matter Paragraphs in the Independent Auditor's Report* and may be helpful in an assurance engagement.

Preparing the Assurance Report

Aus 34.1 If applicable, the assurance practitioner's conclusion on the compilation of the pro forma financial information shall be clearly separated from assurance on any other type of financial information within the assurance report.

35. The assurance practitioner's report shall include the following basic elements: (Ref: Para. A57–Aus A57.1)

(a) A title that clearly indicates that the report is an independent assurance report; (Ref: Para. A51)

(b) An addressee(s), as agreed in the terms of engagement; (Ref: Para. A52)

(c) Introductory paragraphs that identify: (Ref: Para. A53)

(i) The pro forma financial information;

(ii) The source from which the unadjusted financial information has been extracted, and whether or not an audit or review report on such a source has been published;

(iii) The period covered by, or the date of, the pro forma financial information; and

(iv) The applicable criteria on the basis of which the responsible party has performed the compilation of the pro forma financial information, and the source of the criteria;

(d) A statement that the responsible party is responsible for compiling the pro forma financial information on the basis of the applicable criteria;

(e) A description of the assurance practitioner's responsibilities, including statements that:

(i) The assurance practitioner's responsibility is to conclude about whether the pro forma financial information has been compiled, in all material respects, by the responsible party on the basis of the applicable criteria;

(ii) For purposes of this engagement, the assurance practitioner is not responsible for updating or reissuing any reports or opinions on any historical financial information used in compiling the pro forma financial information, nor has the assurance practitioner, in the course of this engagement, performed an audit or review of the financial information used in compiling the pro forma financial information;

(iii) The purpose of pro forma financial information included in a prospectus is solely to illustrate the impact of a significant event(s) or transaction(s) on unadjusted financial information of the entity as if the event had occurred or the transaction had been undertaken at an earlier date selected for purposes of the illustration. Accordingly, the assurance practitioner does not provide any assurance that the actual outcome of the event(s) or transaction(s) at that date would have been as presented; and

(f) A statement that the engagement was performed in accordance with ASAE 3420, *Assurance Engagements to Report on the Compilation of Pro Forma Historical Financial Information Included in a Prospectus or other Document*, which requires that the assurance practitioner comply with relevant ethical requirements and plan and perform procedures to obtain the required type of assurance about whether the responsible party has compiled, in all material respects, the pro forma financial information on the basis of the applicable criteria;

(g) Statements that:

(i) In a reasonable assurance engagement to report on whether the pro forma financial information has been compiled, in all material respects, on the basis of the applicable criteria, the engagement has involved performing procedures to assess whether the applicable criteria used by the responsible party in the compilation of the pro forma financial information provide a reasonable basis for presenting the significant effects directly attributable to the event(s) or transaction(s), and to obtain sufficient appropriate evidence about whether:

- ♦ The related pro forma adjustments give appropriate effect to those criteria; and
- ♦ The pro forma financial information reflects the proper application of those adjustments to the unadjusted financial information; or

(ii) Aus 35.1 In a limited assurance engagement to report on whether anything comes to the assurance practitioner's attention that causes the assurance practitioner to believe that the pro forma financial information has not been compiled, in all material respects, on the basis of the applicable criteria, the engagement has involved performing limited procedures to assess whether the applicable criteria used by the responsible party in the compilation of the pro forma financial information provide a reasonable basis for presenting the significant effects directly attributable to the event(s) or transaction(s), and to obtain sufficient appropriate evidence about whether:

- ♦ The related pro forma adjustments give appropriate effect to those criteria; and
- ♦ The pro forma financial information reflects the proper application of those adjustments to the unadjusted financial information; and

(iii) The procedures selected depend on the assurance practitioner's professional judgement, having regard to the assurance practitioner's understanding of the nature of the entity, the event(s) or transaction(s) in respect of which the pro forma financial information has been compiled, the type of assurance to be expressed on the compilation, and other relevant engagement circumstances; and

(iv) The engagement also involves evaluating the overall presentation of the pro forma financial information;

(h) Unless otherwise required by applicable law or regulation:

(i) The assurance practitioner's reasonable assurance unmodified conclusion uses one of the following phrases, which are regarded as being equivalent: (Ref: Para. A54-A56)

- ◊ The pro forma financial information has been compiled, in all material respects, on the basis of the applicable criteria; or
- ◊ The pro forma financial information has been properly compiled on the basis stated; or

(ii) Aus 35.2 The assurance practitioner's limited assurance unmodified conclusion uses one of the following phrases, which are regarded as being equivalent: (Ref: Para. A54-A56)

- ◊ nothing has come to the assurance practitioner's attention that causes the assurance practitioner to believe that the pro forma financial information has not been compiled, in all material respects, on the basis of the applicable criteria; or
- ◊ nothing has come to the assurance practitioner's attention that causes the assurance practitioner to believe that the pro forma financial information has not been properly compiled on the basis stated; or

(iii) If the assurance practitioner's conclusion is modified, include a clear description of the reasons for the modification, with the effects appropriately quantified, to the extent reasonably practicable and disclosed in the report;

Aus 35.3 An independence, or disclosure of interest, statement;

(i) The assurance practitioner's signature;

(j) [Deleted by the AUASB. Refer Aus 35.4]

Aus 35.4 The date of the assurance practitioner's report shall be the date the assurance practitioner signs the report; and

(k) The assurance practitioner's address.

❖❖❖

Application and Other Explanatory Material

Scope of this ASAE (Ref: Para. Aus 1.1)

A1. This ASAE does not deal with circumstances where pro forma financial information is provided as part of the entity's financial statements pursuant to the requirements of an applicable financial reporting framework.

Purpose of Pro Forma Financial Information Included in a Prospectus (Ref: Para. 4, Aus 11.1, 14(c), 26(a))

A2. Pro forma financial information is accompanied by related explanatory notes that often disclose the matters set out in paragraph A42.

A3. Different presentations of pro forma financial information may be included in the prospectus depending on the nature of the event(s) or transaction(s) and how the responsible party intends to illustrate the impact of such event(s) or transaction(s) on the unadjusted financial information of the entity. For example, the entity may acquire a number of businesses prior to an initial public offering. In such circumstances, the responsible party may choose to present a pro forma net asset statement to illustrate the impact of the acquisitions on the entity's financial position and key ratios such as debt to equity as if the acquired businesses had been combined with the entity at an earlier date. The responsible party may also choose to present a pro forma income statement to illustrate what the results of operations might have been for the period ended on that date. In such cases, the nature of the pro forma financial information may be described by titles such as "Statement of Pro Forma Net Assets as at 30 June 20X1" and "Pro Forma Income Statement for the Year Ended 30 June 20X1."

Compilation of Pro Forma Financial Information

Unadjusted Financial Information (Ref: Para. 5, Aus 11.2-Aus 11.3, 14(a))

A4. In many cases, the source from which the unadjusted financial information has been extracted will be published financial information such as annual or interim financial statements.

A5. Depending on how the responsible party chooses to illustrate the impact of the event(s) or transaction(s), the unadjusted financial information may comprise either:

- One or more single financial statements, such as a statement of financial position and a statement of comprehensive income; or
- Financial information that is appropriately condensed from a complete set of financial statements, for example, a statement of net assets.

Nature of the Assurance Engagement

A6. In this ASAE, describing the pro forma financial information as being "properly compiled" means that the pro forma financial information has been compiled, in all material respects, by the responsible party, on the basis of the applicable criteria. (Ref: Para. 6)

Aus A6.1 The determination of the type of assurance to be provided on the responsible party's compilation of pro forma financial information is a matter for discussion and agreement between the responsible party and the assurance practitioner, having regard to the information requirements of intended users of the compiled pro forma financial information, the availability of sufficient appropriate evidence to support the compilation, time considerations and cost constraints.# (Ref: Para. Aus 6.1)

Aus A6.2 In Australia, it is often the case that the responsible party will request an assurance practitioner to conduct an assurance engagement to report on the compilation of pro forma financial information in engagement circumstances where it is known that the assurance practitioner will not be able to access, on a timely basis, or at all, certain documentation (for example, detailed financial information and supporting records) or financial information from those entities whose financial information is included in the compilation (for example, in an acquisition). In such circumstances, the assurance practitioner may be able to plan and perform other procedures on the available documentation (for example, through being able to access the auditor's working paper file) in order to obtain sufficient appropriate evidence on the compilation of the pro forma financial information for that entity. The level of assurance obtained may however be lower than that required for a reasonable assurance engagement, but commensurate with limited assurance. If the assurance practitioner is not able to perform such other procedures, this represents a limitation of scope on the assurance practitioner's work which would at the minimum result in a modified assurance conclusion. If the assurance practitioner knows at the time of the responsible party's engagement request that the assurance practitioner will not be able to obtain sufficient appropriate evidence through performing other procedures, the assurance practitioner ordinarily would not accept the engagement, as these engagement circumstances represent a limitation of scope on the assurance practitioner's work which would at the minimum result in a modified assurance conclusion. (Ref: Para. Aus 6.1, Aus A10.2)

Aus A6.3 In circumstances where the assurance practitioner will be able to access, on a timely basis, all required documentation of all entities whose financial information is included in the compilation, it would ordinarily be the case that the assurance practitioner would be able to provide reasonable assurance on the compilation of the pro forma financial information and hence conduct the engagement as a reasonable assurance engagement. (Ref: Para. Aus 6.1, Aus A10.2)

Aus A6.4 The differences between the procedures performed in a reasonable assurance engagement as compared to a limited assurance engagement are explained at paragraph Aus A12.2. (Ref: Para. Aus 6.1)

Definitions

Applicable Criteria (Ref: Para. 11(a))

A7. Where established criteria for compiling the pro forma financial information do not exist, the responsible party will have developed the criteria based on, for example, practice in a particular industry or the criteria of a jurisdiction that has developed established criteria, and disclosed that fact.

A8. The applicable criteria for compiling the pro forma financial information will be suitable in the circumstances if they meet the benchmarks set out in paragraph 14.

A9. Accompanying explanatory notes may include some additional detail about the criteria to describe how they illustrate the effects of the particular event(s) or transaction(s). This may include, for example:

- The date at which the event(s) is assumed to have occurred or the transaction(s) been undertaken; or
- The approach used for allocating income, overheads, assets and liabilities between relevant businesses in a divestment.

See ASAE 3000, paragraph 62 for further guidance.

ASAE

Engagement Acceptance

Capabilities and Competence to Perform the Engagement (Ref: Para. 13(a))

A10. [Deleted by the AUASB. Refer Aus A10.1[7]]

Aus A10.1 ASA 102[*] issued by the AUASB requires the assurance practitioner to comply with relevant ethical requirements.

Preconditions for Acceptance (Ref: Para. Aus 13.4, 13(a))

Aus A10.2 Refer paragraphs Aus A6.2 and Aus A6.3 for guidance on determining the type of assurance to be provided.

Agreeing on the Terms of the Assurance Engagement

Aus A10.3 If the responsible party does not agree to sign the engagement letter, the assurance practitioner needs to consider whether it is appropriate to accept the engagement, taking into account that applicable law, regulation, or a preexisting contract, may acknowledge or indicate such responsibility in sufficient detail the engagement terms. For example, under the *Corporations Act 2001*,[†] the directors of an entity are deemed responsible for financial information included in a public document used in offering securities. In such circumstances, the assurance practitioner may, using professional judgement, agree to accept the engagement terms. (Ref: Para. Aus 13.5)

Aus A10.4 The assurance practitioner exercises professional judgement as to what assurance procedures may be summarised in the engagement letter, taking into account the nature of the pro forma financial information, and the type of assurance required in the engagement circumstances. The assurance practitioner may include such terms and conditions as in the assurance practitioner's professional judgement are appropriate to the engagement. They may include: (Ref: Para. Aus 13.6(c)(iv))

(a) important deadlines/timelines for the completion of the engagement. This may include deadlines such as the expected date of publication of the document and when the assurance practitioner's consent is required;

(b) arrangements regarding the planning and performance of the engagement, including the composition of the engagement team (including any experts);

(c) arrangements for the assurance practitioner to:

(i) attend meetings such as the due diligence committee meetings (if appropriate under the terms of the engagement)[§];

(ii) receive draft and final versions of the prospectus in a timely manner when requested;

(iii) use the service(s) of the responsible party's experts and/or the assurance practitioner's experts; and

(iv) communicate directly with the entity's external auditor and/or other professional advisers regarding matters relevant to the pro forma financial information; and

(v) provide consent to the inclusion of the assurance practitioner's report in the prospectus. If the prospectus is prepared in accordance with the *Corporations Act 2001*,[**] the form of the consent must be consistent with how the prospectus is intended to be distributed. For example, entities intending to distribute the prospectus in both electronic and

7 [Footnote deleted by the AUASB. Refer Aus A10.1[*]]

* See ASA 102 *Compliance with Ethical Requirements when Performing Audits, Reviews and Other Assurance Engagements.*

† See Section 717 of the *Corporations Act 2001* for an overview of the procedures for offering securities.

§ See APES 350 *Participation by Members in Public Practice in Due Diligence Committees in Connection with a Public Document*, as issued by the Accounting Professional & Ethical Standards Board, for further guidance.

** See Section 716 of the *Corporations Act 2001.*

paper forms must also obtain the assurance practitioner's consent to the inclusion of the assurance report in both forms.[#]

The Responsible Party's Responsibilities (Ref: Para. 13(g))

A11. An engagement in accordance with this ASAE is conducted on the premise that the responsible party has acknowledged and understands that it has the responsibilities set out in paragraph 13(g). An engagement to report on whether pro forma financial information has been compiled, in all material respects, on the basis of the applicable criteria is based on the assumption that:

(a) The assurance practitioner's role does not involve taking responsibility for compiling such information;

(b) The assurance practitioner has a reasonable expectation of obtaining the information necessary for the engagement; and

Aus A11.1 (c) The assurance practitioner's role does not include expressing a conclusion on the pro forma financial information itself, or for updating or reissuing any previously issued audit reports or review conclusions related to the unadjusted financial information.

Accordingly, this premise is fundamental to the conduct of the engagement. To avoid misunderstanding, agreement is reached with the responsible party that it acknowledges and understands that it has such responsibilities as part of agreeing and recording the terms of the engagement as required by ASAE 3000.[8]

A12. If applicable law or regulation prescribes in sufficient detail the terms of the engagement, the assurance practitioner needs only record the fact that such law or regulation applies and that the responsible party acknowledges and understands its responsibilities as set out in paragraph 13(g).

Changes in the Terms of the Assurance Engagement

Aus A12.1 Examples of when requests from the responsible party to change the terms of the engagement may be received include where there has been a change in circumstances affecting the need for the service or a misunderstanding of the nature of the assurance services to be provided. The assurance practitioner considers the justification for the proposed change and any implications for the conduct and reporting of the engagement, as well as any evidence that was obtained prior to the assurance practitioner agreeing to the change. Changes requested by the responsible party that may be unacceptable to the assurance practitioner include: (Ref: Para. Aus 13.7)

(a) a change that relates to historical financial information that is incorrect, incomplete or otherwise unsatisfactory;

(b) limiting the time available for the assurance practitioner to perform the engagement;

(c) preventing access to all relevant documents or persons requested; and/or

(d) not providing documents when requested, leading to time constraints that make the satisfactory completion of the engagement by the date required unachievable.

ASAE

See ASIC RG 107 *Electronic Prospectuses.*

8 See ASAE 3000, paragraph 25.

Planning and Performing the Engagement

Limited and Reasonable Assurance Engagements (Ref: Para. Aus 13.8)

Aus A12.2 Because the level of assurance obtained in a limited assurance engagement is lower than in a reasonable assurance engagement, the procedures the assurance practitioner will perform in a limited assurance engagement will vary in nature from, and are less in extent than for, a reasonable assurance engagement. Procedures performed in a reasonable assurance engagement are not incremental to those performed in a limited assurance engagement. Depending on the engagement circumstances, reasonable assurance procedures may include none, some, or all, of the limited assurance procedures specified, as well as other procedures, in order to obtain the higher level of reasonable assurance. The primary differences between the assurance practitioner's overall responses to address the assessed risks of material misstatement and further procedures for a reasonable assurance engagement and a limited assurance engagement on financial information are as follows:

(a) *The emphasis placed on the nature of various procedures*: The emphasis placed on the nature of various procedures as a source of evidence will likely differ, depending on the engagement circumstances.

(b) *The extent of further procedures*: The extent of further procedures performed in a limited assurance engagement is less than in a reasonable assurance engagement. This may involve:

- reducing the number of items to be examined, for example, reducing sample sizes for tests of details; or
- performing fewer procedures (for example, performing only analytical procedures in circumstances when, in a reasonable assurance engagement, both analytical procedures and tests of details would be performed).

(c) *The nature of analytical procedures*: In a reasonable assurance engagement, analytical procedures performed in response to assessed risks of material misstatement involve developing expectations of quantities or ratios that are sufficiently precise to identify material misstatements. In a limited assurance engagement, on the other hand, analytical procedures are often designed to support expectations regarding the direction of trends, relationships and ratios rather than to identify misstatements with the level of precision expected in a reasonable assurance engagement.

Further, when significant fluctuations, relationships or differences are identified, appropriate evidence in a limited assurance engagement may often be obtained by making enquiries of the entity and considering responses received in the light of known engagement circumstances, without obtaining the additional evidence that would be required in the case of a reasonable assurance engagement.

In addition, when undertaking analytical procedures in a limited assurance engagement the assurance practitioner may, for example:

- Use data that is more highly aggregated.
- Use data that has not been subjected to separate procedures to test its reliability to the same extent as it would be for a reasonable assurance engagement.

Assessing the Suitability of the Applicable Criteria

Directly Attributable Adjustments (Ref: Para. 14(b)(i), 22(a))

A13. It is necessary that the pro forma adjustments be directly attributable to the event(s) or transaction(s) to avoid the pro forma financial information reflecting matters that do not arise solely as a result of the event or that are not an integral part of the transaction.

Directly attributable adjustments exclude those that relate to future events or are dependent on actions to be taken once the transaction(s) has been completed, even if such actions are key to the entity entering into the transaction (for example, closing of redundant production sites after an acquisition).

Aus A13.1 The assurance practitioner uses professional judgement in determining the extent of sufficient appropriate evidence required to support the pro forma adjustments being directly attributable to the event(s) or transaction(s), taking into consideration:

- the nature of the event(s) or transaction(s);
- the nature, type and materiality of the pro forma adjustments; and
- the type of assurance required.

Factually Supportable Adjustments (Ref: Para. 14(b)(ii), 22(b))

A14. It is also necessary that the pro forma adjustments be factually supportable in order to provide a reliable basis for the pro forma financial information. Factually supportable adjustments are capable of objective determination. Sources of factual support for the pro forma adjustments include, for example:

- Purchase and sale agreements.
- Financing documents for the event(s) or transaction(s), such as debt agreements.
- Independent valuation reports.
- Other documents relating to the event(s) or transaction(s).
- Published financial statements.
- Other financial information disclosed in the prospectus.
- Applicable legal or regulatory actions, such as in the area of taxation.
- Employment agreements.
- Actions of those charged with governance.

Adjustments Consistent with the Entity's Applicable Financial Reporting Framework and Its Accounting Policies under that Framework (Ref: Para. 11(b)(ii), 14(b)(iii), 22(c))

A15. For the pro forma financial information to be meaningful, it is necessary that the pro forma adjustments be consistent with the entity's applicable financial reporting framework and the accounting policies under that framework. In the context of a business combination, for example, compiling the pro forma financial information on the basis of the applicable criteria involves consideration of such matters as:

- Whether differences exist between the acquiree's accounting policies and those of the entity; and
- Whether accounting policies for transactions undertaken by the acquiree that the entity has not previously entered into, are policies that the entity would have adopted for such transactions under its applicable financial reporting framework, taking into account the entity's particular circumstances.

A16. Consideration of the appropriateness of the entity's accounting policies may also be necessary in some circumstances. For example, as part of the event(s) or transaction(s), the entity may propose to issue complex financial instruments for the first time. If this is the case, it may be necessary to consider:

- Whether the responsible party has selected appropriate accounting policies to be used in accounting for such financial instruments under its applicable financial reporting framework; and
- Whether it has appropriately applied such policies in compiling the pro forma financial information.

ASAE

Materiality (Ref: Para. 16)

A17. Materiality with regard to whether the pro forma financial information has been compiled, in all material respects, on the basis of the applicable criteria, does not depend on a single quantitative measure. Instead, it depends on the size and nature of the omission or inappropriate application of an element of the compilation as described in paragraphs A18 and Aus A18.1, whether or not intentional. Professional judgement about these aspects of size and nature will, in turn, depend on such matters as:

- The context of the event(s) or transaction(s);
- The purpose for which the pro forma financial information is being compiled; and
- The related engagement circumstances.

The determining factor could be the size or the nature of the matter, or a combination of both.

A18. The risk of the pro forma financial information not being considered compiled, in all material respects, on the basis of the applicable criteria may arise when there is evidence of, for example:

- Use of an inappropriate source from which to extract the unadjusted financial information.
- Incorrect extraction of the unadjusted financial information from an appropriate source.
- In relation to adjustments, the misapplication of accounting policies or the failure of the adjustments to be consistent with the entity's accounting policies.
- Failure to make an adjustment required by the applicable criteria.
- Making an adjustment that is not in accordance with the applicable criteria.
- A mathematical or clerical mistake in the calculations within the pro forma financial information.
- Inadequate, incorrect or omitted disclosures.

Aus A18.1 Judgements about materiality are made in light of surrounding circumstances, and are affected by both quantitative and qualitative factors. It should be noted, however, that decisions regarding materiality are not affected by the level of assurance, that is, materiality for a reasonable assurance engagement is the same as for a limited assurance engagement.

Obtaining an Understanding of How the Responsible Party Has Compiled the Pro Forma Financial Information and Other Engagement Circumstances (Ref: Para. 17-Aus 17.1)

A19. The assurance practitioner may obtain this understanding through a combination of procedures such as:

- Enquiring of the responsible party and other entity personnel involved in compiling the pro forma financial information.
- Enquiring of other appropriate parties such as those charged with governance and the entity's advisors.
- Reading relevant supporting documentation such as contracts or agreements.
- Reading minutes of meetings of those charged with governance.

How the Responsible Party Has Compiled the Pro Forma Financial Information *(Ref: Para. 17(b))*

A20. The assurance practitioner may obtain an understanding of how the responsible party has compiled the pro forma financial information by considering, for example:

- The source from which the unadjusted financial information has been extracted.

- The steps taken by the responsible party to:
  - Extract the unadjusted financial information from the source.
  - Identify the appropriate pro forma adjustments, for example, how the responsible party has obtained acquiree financial information in compiling the pro forma financial information.
- The responsible party's competence in compiling pro forma financial information.
- The nature and extent of oversight by the responsible party of other entity personnel involved in compiling the pro forma financial information.
- The responsible party's approach to identifying appropriate disclosures to support the pro forma financial information.

A21. In a business combination or divestment, areas that may give rise to complexity in the compilation of the pro forma financial information include allocations of income, overheads, and assets and liabilities among or between the relevant businesses. Accordingly, it is important that the assurance practitioner understand the responsible party's approach and criteria for such allocations and that the explanatory notes accompanying the pro forma financial information disclose these matters.

Nature of the Entity and Any Acquiree or Divestee *(Ref: Para. 17(c))*

A22. An acquiree may be an incorporated entity or a separately identifiable unincorporated operation within another entity such as a division, branch or line of business. A divestee may be an incorporated entity such as a subsidiary or joint venture, or a separately identifiable unincorporated operation within the entity such as a division, branch or line of business.

A23. The assurance practitioner may have all or part of the required understanding of the entity and any acquiree or divestee, and their respective environments, if the assurance practitioner has audited or reviewed their financial information.

Relevant Industry, Legal and Regulatory, and Other External Factors *(Ref: Para. 17(d))*

A24. Relevant industry factors include industry conditions such as the competitive environment, supplier and customer relationships, and technological developments. Examples of matters the assurance practitioner may consider include:

- The market and competition, including demand, capacity, and price competition.
- Common business practices within the industry.
- Cyclical or seasonal activity.
- Product technology relating to the entity's products.

A25. Relevant legal and regulatory factors include the legal and regulatory environment. This encompasses, among other matters, the applicable financial reporting framework in accordance with which the entity or, if applicable, the acquiree prepares its periodic financial information, and the legal and political environment. Examples of matters the assurance practitioner may consider include:

- Industry-specific accounting practices.
- Legal and regulatory framework for a regulated industry.
- Legislation and regulation that significantly affect the entity's or, if applicable, the acquiree's or divestee's operations, including direct supervisory activities.
- Taxation.
- Government policies currently affecting the conduct of the entity's or, if applicable, the acquiree's or divestee's business, such as monetary policies (including foreign exchange controls), fiscal policies, financial incentives (for example, government aid programs), and tariffs or trade restrictions policies.
- Environmental requirements affecting the entity's or acquiree's or divestee's industry and business.

A26. Examples of other external factors affecting the entity and, if applicable, the acquiree or divestee that the assurance practitioner may consider include the general economic conditions, interest rates and availability of financing, and inflation or currency revaluation.

Obtaining Evidence about the Appropriateness of the Source from Which the Unadjusted Financial Information Has Been Extracted

Relevant Factors to Consider *(Ref: Para. 14(a), 18)*

A27. Factors that affect the appropriateness of the source from which the unadjusted financial information has been extracted include whether there is an audit or review report on the source and whether the source:

- Is permitted or specifically prescribed by the applicable law or regulation, is permitted by the relevant securities exchange with which the prospectus is to be filed, or is used as such under normal market custom and practice.
- Is clearly identifiable.
- Represents a reasonable starting point for compiling the pro forma financial information in the context of the event(s) or transaction(s), including whether it is consistent with the entity's accounting policies and is at an appropriate date or covers an appropriate period.

A28. An audit or review report on the source from which the unadjusted financial information has been extracted may have been issued by another assurance practitioner. In this situation, the need by the assurance practitioner reporting under this ASAE for an understanding of the entity and its accounting and financial reporting practices pursuant to the requirements of paragraphs 17(c) and (e), and to be satisfied that the source from which the unadjusted financial information has been extracted is appropriate, is not diminished.

Aus A28.1 The assurance practitioner's understanding of the entity and its accounting and financial reporting practices referred to in paragraph A28 may be obtained by:

(a) Requesting a copy of the audit or review report accompanying the unadjusted financial information and, if obtained, reading it to understand if the report was modified or unmodified. If the report was modified, understanding the reasons for the modification;

(b) Contacting the other assurance practitioner to request access to the audit working papers supporting the audit or review report and, if provided, reading the work papers to assess the appropriateness of the audit approach taken for the purposes of placing reliance on that audit or review report in assessing the appropriateness of the source of the unadjusted financial information;

(c) Reading the unadjusted financial information to which the audit or review report relates to establish if its basis of preparation (that is, its accounting policies) and time frame covered are acceptable; and/or

(d) Planning to perform further procedures as is considered necessary in the engagement circumstances.

Aus A28.2 If the assurance practitioner requests access to the audit working papers of another assurance practitioner and is unable to obtain such access, this constitutes a limitation of scope on the assurance practitioner being able to assess the appropriateness of the source of the unadjusted financial information. If the assurance practitioner is unable to perform alternative procedures to obtain sufficient appropriate evidence on its appropriateness, the assurance practitioner modifies the conclusion in the assurance report in accordance with ASAE 3000*.

* See ASAE 3000, paragraphs 82-84 for further information.

No Audit or Review Report on the Source from Which the Unadjusted Financial Information Has Been Extracted (Ref: Para. 19)

A29. When there is no audit or review report on the source from which the unadjusted financial information has been extracted, it is necessary for the assurance practitioner to perform procedures in relation to the appropriateness of that source. Factors that may affect the nature and extent of these procedures include, for example:

- Whether the assurance practitioner has previously audited or reviewed the entity's historical financial information, and the assurance practitioner's knowledge of the entity from such engagement.
- How recently the entity's historical financial information was audited or reviewed.
- Whether the entity's financial information is subject to periodic review by the assurance practitioner, for example, for purposes of meeting regulatory filing requirements.
- Aus A29.1 Whether the assurance practitioner is able to access documentation describing, and supporting, the source of the unadjusted financial information.
- Aus A29.2 The type of assurance to be provided.

Aus A29.3 This ASAE does not require the assurance practitioner to perform an audit or review of the source from which the unadjusted financial information has been extracted as part of the engagement, if such an audit or review has not already been performed.

A30. The entity's financial statements for the period immediately preceding that of the source from which the unadjusted financial information has been extracted are likely to have been audited or reviewed, even if the source from which the unadjusted financial information has been extracted itself is not. For example, the source from which the unadjusted financial information has been extracted may be interim financial statements that have not been audited or reviewed whereas the entity's financial statements for the immediately preceding financial year may have been audited. In such a case, procedures that the assurance practitioner may perform, having regard to the factors in paragraphs A29-Aus A29.3, in relation to the appropriateness of the source from which the unadjusted financial information has been extracted, may, depending on the type of assurance required, include:

- Enquiring of the responsible party about:
  - The process by which the source has been prepared and the reliability of the underlying accounting records to which the source is agreed or reconciled.
  - Whether all transactions for the time period have been recorded.
  - Whether the source has been prepared in accordance with the entity's accounting policies.
  - Whether there have been any changes in accounting policies from the most recent audited or reviewed period, and if so, how such changes have been dealt with.
  - Its assessment of the risk that the source may be materially misstated as a result of error or fraud.
  - The effect of changes in the entity's business activities and operations.
- If the assurance practitioner has audited or reviewed the immediately preceding annual or interim financial information, considering the findings of such audit or review and whether these might indicate any issues with the preparation of the source from which the unadjusted financial information has been extracted.
- Corroborating the information provided by the responsible party in response to the assurance practitioner's enquiries when the responses appear inconsistent with the assurance practitioner's understanding of the entity or the engagement circumstances.

- Comparing the source with the corresponding prior period financial information and, as applicable, the immediately preceding annual or interim financial information, and discussing significant changes with the responsible party.
- Aus A30.1 Agreeing or reconciling the source of the unadjusted financial information with underlying records.
- Aus A30.2 Performing audit tests of certain material balances within the unadjusted financial information.

***Historical financial information of the entity never audited or reviewed** (Ref: Para. 13(e))*

A31. Other than in the case of an entity formed for purposes of the transaction and which has never had any trading activity, applicable law or regulation may not permit an entity to issue a prospectus if its historical financial information has never been audited or reviewed.

Obtaining Evidence about the Appropriateness of the Pro Forma Adjustments

***Identification of Appropriate Pro Forma Adjustments** (Ref: Para. 21)*

A32. Informed by the assurance practitioner's understanding of how the responsible party has compiled the pro forma financial information and other engagement circumstances, the assurance practitioner may obtain evidence regarding whether the responsible party has appropriately identified the necessary pro forma adjustments through a combination of procedures (depending on the type of assurance required), such as:

- Enquiring of relevant parties within an acquiree regarding the approach to extracting the acquiree financial information.
- Evaluating the reasonableness of the responsible party's approach to identifying and quantifying the appropriate pro forma adjustments, for example, the method used in identifying appropriate allocations of income, overheads, assets and liabilities among the relevant business.
- Evaluating specific aspects of the relevant contracts, agreements or other documents.
- Enquiring of the entity's advisors regarding specific aspects of the event or transaction and related contracts and agreements that are relevant to the identification of appropriate adjustment.
- Evaluating relevant analyses and worksheets prepared by the responsible party and other entity personnel involved in compiling the pro forma financial information.
- Obtaining evidence of the responsible party's oversight of other entity personnel involved in compiling the pro forma financial information.
- Performing analytical procedures.

***Factual Support for Any Acquiree or Divestee Financial Information Included in the Pro Forma Adjustments** (Ref: Para. 22(b))*

Divestee financial information

A33. In the case of a divestment, the divestee's financial information will be derived from the source from which the unadjusted financial information has been extracted, which will often be audited or reviewed. The source from which the unadjusted financial information has been extracted will therefore provide the basis for the assurance practitioner to determine whether there is factual support for the divestee financial information. In such a case, matters to consider include, for example, whether income and expenses attributable to the divestee that are recorded at the consolidated level have been appropriately reflected in the pro forma adjustments.

A34. Where the source from which the unadjusted financial information has been extracted has not been audited or reviewed, the assurance practitioner may refer to the guidance in paragraphs A29–Aus A29.3 in determining whether the divestee financial information is factually supportable.

Acquiree financial information

A35. The source from which the acquiree financial information has been extracted may have been audited or reviewed. Where the source from which the acquiree financial information has been extracted has been audited or reviewed by the assurance practitioner, the acquiree financial information will, subject to any implications arising from the circumstances addressed in paragraph 23, be factually supportable.

A36. The source from which the acquiree financial information has been extracted may have been audited or reviewed by another assurance practitioner. In this situation, the need by the assurance practitioner reporting under this ASAE for an understanding of the acquiree and its accounting and financial reporting practices pursuant to the requirements of paragraphs 17(c) and (e), and to be satisfied that the acquiree financial information is factually supportable, is not diminished.

Aus A36.1 The assurance practitioner uses professional judgement to determine, based on the type of assurance, how to obtain such an understanding of the acquiree and its accounting and financial reporting practices such that the assurance practitioner can be satisfied that the acquiree's source from which the unadjusted financial information has been extracted is appropriate. See paragraphs A28–Aus A28.2 for procedures that may be helpful in obtaining such an understanding.

A37. When the source from which the acquiree financial information has been extracted has not been audited or reviewed, it is necessary for the assurance practitioner to perform procedures in relation to the appropriateness of that source. Factors that may affect the nature and extent of these procedures include, for example:

- Whether the assurance practitioner has previously audited or reviewed the acquiree's historical financial information, and the assurance practitioner's knowledge of the acquiree from such engagement.
- How recently the acquiree's historical financial information was audited or reviewed.
- Whether the acquiree's financial information is subject to periodic review by the assurance practitioner, for example, for purposes of meeting applicable law or regulatory reporting requirements.
- Aus A37.1 Whether the assurance practitioner is able to access documentation describing the source of the acquiree's unadjusted financial information.
- Aus A37.2 The type of assurance to be provided.

Aus A37.3 This ASAE does not require the assurance practitioner to perform an audit or review of the acquiree's unadjusted financial information as part of the engagement, if such an audit or review has not already been performed.

A38. The acquiree's financial statements for the period immediately preceding that of the source from which the acquiree financial information has been extracted often will have been audited or reviewed, even if the source from which the acquiree financial information has been extracted itself is not. In such a case, procedures that the assurance practitioner may perform, having regard to the factors in paragraphs A37–Aus A37.3, in relation to whether the acquiree financial information is factually supportable include:

- Enquiring of the acquiree's management about:
  - The process by which the source from which the acquiree's financial information has been extracted has been prepared and the reliability of the underlying accounting records to which the source is agreed or reconciled.
  - Whether all transactions have been recorded.
  - Whether the source from which the acquiree's financial information has been extracted has been prepared in accordance with the acquiree's accounting policies.
  - Whether there have been any changes in accounting policies from the most recently audited or reviewed financial statements and, if so, how such changes have been dealt with.

 - Its assessment of the risk that the source from which the acquiree's financial information has been extracted may be materially misstated as a result of error or fraud.
 - The effect of changes in the acquiree's business activities and operations.

- If the assurance practitioner has audited or reviewed the immediately preceding annual or interim financial information, considering the findings of such audit or review and whether these might indicate any issues with the preparation of the source from which the acquiree financial information has been extracted.
- Corroborating the information provided by the acquiree's management in response to the assurance practitioner's enquiries when the responses appear inconsistent with the assurance practitioner's understanding of the acquiree or the engagement circumstances.
- Comparing the source from which the acquiree's financial information has been extracted with the corresponding prior period financial information and, as applicable, the immediately preceding annual or interim financial information, and discussing significant changes with the acquiree's management.

Modified Audit Opinion or Review Conclusion, or Emphasis of Matter Paragraph, with Respect to the Source from Which the Unadjusted Financial Information Has Been Extracted or the Source from Which the Acquiree or Divestee Financial Information Has Been Extracted

***Potential Consequence** (Ref: Para. 23(a))*

A39. Not all modified audit opinions, review conclusions or Emphasis of Matter paragraphs with respect to either the source from which the unadjusted financial information has been extracted or the source from which the acquiree or divestee financial information has been extracted may necessarily affect whether the pro forma financial information can be compiled, in all material respects, on the basis of the applicable criteria. For example, a qualified audit opinion may have been expressed on the entity's financial statements because of the nondisclosure of remuneration for those charged with governance as required by the applicable financial reporting framework. If this is the case and these financial statements are used as the source from which the unadjusted financial information has been extracted, such qualification may have no consequence on whether pro forma net asset and income statements can be compiled, in all material respects, on the basis of the applicable criteria.

***Further Appropriate Action** (Ref: Para. 23(b), 24)*

A40. Further appropriate action that the assurance practitioner may take includes, for example:

- In relation to the requirement in paragraph 23(b):
 - Discussing the matter with the responsible party.
 - Where possible under applicable law or regulation, making a reference in the assurance practitioner's report to the modified audit opinion, review conclusion, or the Emphasis of Matter paragraph, if, in the assurance practitioner's professional judgement, the matter is of sufficient relevance and importance to users' understanding of the pro forma financial information.
- In relation to the requirement in paragraph 24, where possible under applicable law or regulation, modifying the assurance practitioner's conclusion.
- Seeking legal advice.
- Where possible under applicable law or regulation, withholding the assurance report or withdrawing from the engagement.

Evaluating the Presentation of the Pro Forma Financial Information

Avoiding Association with Misleading Financial Information (Ref: Para. 26(b))

A41. [Deleted by the AUASB. Refer Aus A41.1[9]]

Aus A41.1 Applicable law or regulation ordinarily requires that the assurance practitioner not knowingly be associated with reports, returns, communications or other information that the assurance practitioner believes contain misleading or deceptive statements[*] Additionally relevant ethical requirement[#] also contain requirements for the assurance practitioner to comply with.

Disclosures Accompanying the Pro Forma Financial Information (Ref: Para. 14(c), 26(c))

A42. Appropriate disclosures may include matters such as:

- The nature and purpose of the pro forma financial information, including the nature of the event(s) or transaction(s), and the date at which such event is assumed to have occurred or transaction been undertaken;
- The source from which the unadjusted financial information has been extracted, and whether or not an audit or review report on such a source has been published;
- The pro forma adjustments, including a description and explanation of each adjustment. This includes, in the case of acquiree or divestee financial information, the source from which such information has been extracted and whether or not an audit or review report on such a source has been published;
- If not publicly available, a description of the applicable criteria on the basis of which the pro forma financial information has been compiled; and
- A statement to the effect that the pro forma financial information has been compiled for illustrative purposes only and that, because of its nature, it does not represent the entity's actual financial position, financial performance, or cash flows.

Applicable law or regulation may require these or other specific disclosures.

Consideration of Significant Subsequent Events (Ref: Para. Aus 26.1)

A43. [Deleted by the AUASB. Refer Aus A43.1]

Aus A43.1 As the assurance practitioner is not reporting on the source from which the unadjusted financial information has been extracted, there is no requirement for the assurance practitioner to perform procedures to identify events related to the unadjusted financial information after the date of the source that require adjustment of, or disclosure in, such a source. Nevertheless, it is necessary for the assurance practitioner to consider whether any significant events relating to the unadjusted financial information subsequent to the date of the source from which the unadjusted financial information has been extracted have come to the assurance practitioner's attention that may require reference to, or disclosure in, the explanatory notes to the pro forma financial information to avoid the latter being misleading. Such consideration is based on performing the procedures under this ASAE or the assurance practitioner's knowledge of the entity and the engagement circumstances.

Material Inconsistency with Other Information (Ref: Para. 27)

A44. Further appropriate action that the assurance practitioner may take if the responsible party refuses to revise the pro forma financial information or the other information as appropriate includes, for example:

- Where possible under applicable law or regulation:
  - Describing the material inconsistency in the assurance practitioner's report.
  - Modifying the assurance practitioner's conclusion.
  - Withholding the assurance report or withdrawing from the engagement.
- Seeking legal advice.

---

9 [Footnote deleted by the AUASB. Refer Aus A41.1[#]]

* See the *Corporations Act 2001* for further information.

\# See ASA 102.

ASAE

Written Representations (Ref: Para. 28(a))

A45. In some circumstances, the types of transactions involved may require the responsible party to select accounting policies for the pro forma adjustments that the entity has not previously had to articulate because it had no relevant transactions. In such a case, the assurance practitioner may request the responsible party to expand the written representations to include confirmation that the selected accounting policies constitute the entity's adopted policies for such types of transactions.

Forming the Conclusion

Assurance on Further Matters Required by Applicable Law or Regulation (Ref: Para. Aus 29.1)

A46. Applicable law or regulation may require the assurance practitioner to express a conclusion on matters other than whether the pro forma financial information has been compiled, in all material respects, on the basis of the applicable criteria. In some of these circumstances, it may not be necessary for the assurance practitioner to perform additional procedures. For example applicable law or regulation may require the assurance practitioner to express an opinion about whether the basis on which the responsible party has compiled the pro forma financial information is consistent with the entity's accounting policies. Compliance with the requirements in paragraphs 18 and 22(c) of this ASAE provides a basis for expressing such an opinion.

A47. In other circumstances, the assurance practitioner may need to perform additional procedures. The nature and extent of such additional procedures will vary with the nature of the other matters on which the applicable law or regulation requires the assurance practitioner to express a conclusion.

Statement of the Assurance Practitioner's Responsibility for the Report

A48. Applicable law or regulation may require the assurance practitioner to include in the assurance practitioner's report an explicit statement asserting or confirming the assurance practitioner's responsibility for the report. The inclusion of such an additional legal or regulatory statement in the assurance practitioner's report is not incompatible with the requirements of this ASAE.

Disclosure of the Applicable Criteria (Ref: Para. 30)

A49. The responsible party need not repeat in the explanatory notes accompanying the pro forma financial information any criteria that are prescribed by the applicable law or regulation, or promulgated by an authorised or recognised standardsetting organisation. Such criteria will be publicly available as part of the reporting regime and are therefore implicit in the responsible party's compilation of the pro forma financial information.

A50. Where the responsible party has developed any specific criteria, it is necessary that those criteria be disclosed so that users may obtain a proper understanding of how the pro forma financial information has been compiled by the responsible party.

Preparing the Assurance Report

Title (Ref: Para. 35(a))

A51. A title indicating that the report is the report of an independent assurance practitioner, for example, "Independent Assurance Practitioner's Assurance Report on the Compilation of Pro Forma Financial Information Included [in a Prospectus or other Document]," affirms that the assurance practitioner has met all of the relevant ethical requirements regarding independence as required by ASAE 3000.[10] This distinguishes the report of the independent assurance practitioner from reports issued by others.

Addressee(s) (Ref: Para. 35(b))

A52. The relevant law or regulation may specify the addressee(s) of the report. Alternatively, the assurance practitioner may agree with the entity who the addressee(s) will be, as part of the terms of the engagement.

10 See ASAE 3000, paragraph 9.

Introductory Paragraphs (Ref: Para. 35(c))

A53. As the pro forma financial information will be included in a prospectus that contains other information, the assurance practitioner may consider, if the form of presentation allows, including a reference that identifies the section where the pro forma financial information is presented. This helps readers identify the pro forma financial information to which the assurance practitioner's report relates.

Conclusion (Ref: Para. 13(c), 35(h))

A54. Whether the phrase "pro forma financial information has been compiled, in all material respects, on the basis of the [*applicable criteria*]," or the phrase "pro forma financial information has been properly compiled on the basis stated" is used to express the reasonable assurance conclusion is determined by applicable law or regulation or by generally accepted practice.

Aus A54.1 In a limited assurance engagement, whether the phrase "nothing has come to the assurance practitioner's attention that causes the assurance practitioner to believe that the pro forma financial information has not been compiled, in all material respects, on the basis of the [*applicable criteria*]," or the phrase "nothing has come to the assurance practitioner's attention that causes the assurance practitioner to believe that the pro forma financial information has not been properly compiled on the basis stated" is used to express the limited assurance conclusion is determined by applicable law or regulation or by generally accepted practice.

A55. Applicable law or regulation may prescribe the wording of the assurance practitioner's conclusion in terms other than those specified above. Where this is the case, it may be necessary for the assurance practitioner to exercise professional judgement to determine whether performing the procedures set out in this ASAE would enable the assurance practitioner to express the conclusion in the wording prescribed by that applicable law or regulation, or whether further procedures would be necessary.

A56. When the assurance practitioner concludes that performing the procedures set out in this ASAE would be sufficient to enable the assurance practitioner to express the conclusion in the wording prescribed by applicable law or regulation, it may be appropriate to regard that wording as being equivalent to the two alternative wordings of the conclusion specified in this ASAE.

Illustrative Reports (Ref: Para. 35)

A57. An assurance practitioner's report in a reasonable assurance engagement with an unmodified conclusion is set out in Appendix 1.

Aus A57.1 An assurance practitioner's report in a limited assurance engagement with an unmodified conclusion is set out in Appendix 2.

❖ ❖ ❖

Conformity with International Standards on Assurance Engagements

This Standard on Assurance Engagements conforms with International Standard on Assurance Engagements ISAE 3420 *Assurance Engagements To Report on the Compilation of Pro Forma Financial Information included in a Prospectus or other Document,* issued by the International Auditing and Assurance Standards Board (IAASB), an independent standardsetting board of the International Federation of Accountants (IFAC).

Paragraphs that have been added to this Standard on Assurance Engagements (and do not appear in the text of the equivalent ISAE) are identified with the prefix "Aus".

The following requirements are additional to ISAE 3420:

- Extending the application of the Standard to include assurance engagements to report on the compilation of pro forma financial information included in public documents (other than a prospectus) or prepared for any other purpose. (Ref: Para. Aus 0.1)
- Requirements related to the assurance practitioner being able to perform the engagement to report on the compilation of pro forma financial information as a limited assurance engagement. (Ref: Para. Aus 6.1, and Aus 35.2-Aus 35.4)
- Requirements related to the terms of the engagement. (Ref: Para. Aus 13.5-Aus 13.7)
- Requirements related to planning and performing the engagement. (Ref: Para. Aus 13.8, Aus 17.1, Aus 19.1, and Aus 26.1)
- Requirements related to the responsible party's written representations. (Ref: Para. Aus 28.1, Aus 28.4)
- Requirements related to Forming the Conclusion. (Ref: Para. Aus 29.1, Aus 31.1, Aus 32.1, Aus 34.1, Aus 35.1-Aus 35.4)

The following application and other explanatory material is additional to ISAE 3420:

- Related application and other explanatory material related to the engagement being a limited assurance engagement.
- The inclusion of [Aus] Appendix 2 containing an illustrative assurance practitioner's report in a limited assurance engagement.

This Standard on Assurance Engagements incorporates terminology and definitions used in Australia.

The equivalent requirements and related application and other explanatory material included in ISAE 3420 in respect of "relevant ethical requirements", have been included in another Auditing Standard, ASA 102 *Compliance with Ethical Requirements when Performing Audits, Reviews and Other Assurance Engagements*. There is no international equivalent to ASA 102.

Compliance with this Standard on Assurance Engagements enables compliance with ISAE 3420 to the extent the assurance practitioner conducts the engagement to report on the compilation of pro forma financial information included in a prospectus as a reasonable assurance engagement.

Appendix 1

(Ref: Para. A57)

Illustrative Assurance Practitioner's Report in a Reasonable Assurance Engagement with an Unmodified Conclusion

[Date]*

[Addressee]

[Name of Entity]

[Address]

Independent Reasonable Assurance Report on ABC Company's Compilation of Pro Forma Historical Financial Information Included in a Prospectus

Dear [Addressee]#

We have completed our reasonable assurance engagement to report on ABC Company's compilation of pro forma financial information by [the responsible party]. The pro forma financial information consists of [the pro forma net asset statement as at [date]], [the pro forma Statement of Financial Performance for the period ended [date]], [the pro forma cash flow statement for the period ended [date],] and related notes [as set out on pages XX of the prospectus issued by the company]. The applicable criteria is the basis of which [the responsible party] has compiled the pro forma financial information and are [specified in [insert details] and described in [Note X]/[described in [Note X]].

Expressions and terms defined in the prospectus have the same meaning in this report.

[Insert any background information relating to ABC Company and/or the proposed fundraising deemed relevant; if any.]

The pro forma financial information has been compiled by [the responsible party] to illustrate the impact of the [event(s) or transaction(s)] [described in Note X] on the [company's financial position as at insert date] [and] [the company's/its financial performance [and cash flows] for the period ended specify date] as if the [event(s) or transaction(s)] had taken place at [specify date] [and specify date respectively]. As part of this process, information about the company's [financial position], [financial performance] [and cash flows] has been extracted by [the responsible party] from the company's financial statements [for the period ended [date]], on which [[an audit]/[a review] report]/[no audit or review report] has been published.[11]

[The Responsible Party's] Responsibility for the Pro Forma Financial Information

[The responsible party] is responsible for compiling the pro forma financial information on the basis of the applicable criteria.

Our Responsibilities

Our responsibility is to express an opinion about whether the pro forma financial information has been properly compiled, in all material respects, by [the responsible party] of ABC Company on the basis of the applicable criteria, as described in section [X] of the prospectus.

* The date of both the hard copy and electronic version of the report should be the same. See ASIC's RG 107 *Electronic Prospectuses.*

11 Where the audit or review report has been modified, reference may be made to where the modification has been described in the prospectus.

\# For example, the directors or other title as appropriate in the circumstances of the assurance engagement.

We conducted our engagement in accordance with Standard on Assurance Engagements ASAE 3420, *Assurance Engagements To Report on the Compilation of Pro Forma Historical Financial Information included in a Prospectus or other Document* (ASAE 3420), issued by the Auditing and Assurance Standards Board.

For purposes of this engagement, we are not responsible for updating or reissuing any reports or opinions on any historical financial information used in compiling the pro forma financial information, nor have we, in the course of this engagement, performed an audit or review of the historical financial information used in compiling the pro forma financial information, or of the pro forma financial information itself.

The purpose of the pro forma financial information being included in a prospectus is solely to illustrate the impact of a significant event(s) or transaction(s) on unadjusted financial information of the company as if the event(s) had occurred or the transaction(s) had been undertaken at an earlier date selected for purposes of the illustration. Accordingly, we do not provide any assurance that the actual outcome of the event(s) or transaction(s) at [insert date] would have been as presented.

A reasonable assurance engagement to report on whether the pro forma financial information has been compiled, in all material respects, on the basis of the applicable criteria involves performing procedures to assess whether the applicable criteria used by [the responsible party] in the compilation of the pro forma financial information provide a reasonable basis for presenting the significant effects directly attributable to the event(s) or transaction(s), and to obtain sufficient appropriate evidence about whether:

- The related pro forma adjustments give appropriate effect to those criteria; and
- The pro forma financial information reflects the proper application of those adjustments to the unadjusted financial information.

The procedures selected depend on the assurance practitioner's professional judgement, having regard to the assurance practitioner's understanding of the nature of the company, the event(s) or transaction(s) in respect of which the pro forma financial information has been compiled, and other relevant engagement circumstances.

The engagement also involves evaluating the overall presentation of the pro forma financial information.

We believe that the evidence we have obtained is sufficient and appropriate to provide a basis for our opinion.

Opinion

In our opinion, [the pro forma financial information has been compiled, in all material respects, on the basis of the applicable criteria as described in section [X] of the prospectus]/[the pro forma financial information has been properly compiled on the basis stated].

Consent

[Firm name] has consented to the inclusion of this report in the prospectus in the form and context in which it is included.

Liability

[*Liability wording to be inserted for individual Firm practice.*]

Declaration of Independence [or Disclosure of Interest Statement]

[Firm Name] does not have any interest in the outcome of this [transaction] other than in [state interest] for which normal professional fees will be received.

Yours faithfully

[Assurance practitioner's signature]

[Date of the assurance practitioner's report]

[Assurance practitioner's address]

[Aus] Appendix 2

(Ref: Para. Aus A57.1)

Illustrative Assurance Practitioner's Report in a Limited Assurance Engagement with an Unmodified Conclusion

[Date]*

[Addressee]

[Name of Entity]

[Address]

Independent Limited Assurance Report on ABC Company's Compilation of Pro Forma Historical Financial Information for a Document

Dear [Addressee]#

We have completed our limited assurance engagement to report on ABC Company's compilation of pro forma financial information. The pro forma financial information consists of [the pro forma net asset statement as at [date]], [the pro forma Statement of Financial Performance for the period ended [date]], [the pro forma cash flow statement for the period ended [date],] and related notes as set out on pages XX of the [insert details] issued by the company (collectively "the pro forma financial information"). The applicable criteria on which the [responsible party] have compiled the pro forma financial information are specified in [insert details] and described in [note X]/described in Note X] for inclusion in [insert details], dated on or about [insert date], and relating to the issue of [X shares/units] in ABC Company.

Expressions and terms defined in the [insert title] have the same meaning in this report.

[*Insert any background information relating to ABC Company and/or the proposed fundraising deemed relevant; if any.*]

The pro forma financial information has been compiled by the [responsible party] to illustrate the impact of the [event(s) or transaction(s)] [described in Note X] on the [company's financial position as at [insert date] [and] [the company's/its financial performance [and cash flows] for the period ended [insert date],] as if the [event(s) or transaction(s)] had taken place at [insert details] [and insert date respectively]. As part of this process, information about the company's [financial position], [financial performance] [and cash flows] has been extracted by the [responsible party] from the company's financial statements [for the period ended [date]], on which [[an audit]/[a review] report]/[no audit or review report] has been published.†

[The Responsible Party's] Responsibilities for the Pro Forma Financial Information

The [responsible party] of ABC Company are responsible for properly compiling the pro forma financial information on the basis of the applicable criteria.

Our Responsibilities

Our responsibility is to express a conclusion on whether anything has come to our attention that the pro forma financial information has not been properly compiled, in all material respects, by the [responsible party] on the basis of the applicable criteria, as described in section [X] of the [insert details.]

We have conducted our limited assurance engagement in accordance with the Standard on Assurance Engagements ASAE 3420 *Assurance Engagements To Report on the Compilation of Pro Forma Historical Financial Information included in a Prospectus or other Document* (ASAE 3420), issued by the Auditing and Assurance Standards Board (AUASB).

* The date of both the hard copy and electronic version of the report should be the same. See ASIC's RG 107 *Electronic Prospectuses.*

† Where the audit or review report has been modified, reference may be made to where the modification has been described in the prospectus.

For purposes of this engagement, we are not responsible for updating or reissuing any reports or opinions on any historical financial information used in compiling the pro forma financial information, nor have we, in the course of this engagement, performed an audit or review of the financial information used in compiling the pro forma financial information, or of the pro forma financial information itself.

The purpose of the compilation of the pro forma financial information being included in a [insert details] is solely to illustrate the impact of a significant event(s) or transaction(s) on unadjusted financial information of the company as if the event(s) had occurred or the transaction(s) had been undertaken at an earlier date selected for purposes of the illustration. Accordingly, we do not provide any assurance that the actual outcome of the event(s) or transaction(s) at [insert date] would have been as presented.

A limited assurance engagement to report on whether anything comes to our attention that the pro forma financial information has not been properly compiled, in all material respects, on the basis of the applicable criteria involves performing procedures to assess whether the applicable criteria used by [the responsible party] in the compilation of the pro forma financial information does not provide a reasonable basis for presenting the significant effects directly attributable to the event(s) or transaction(s), and that the:

- related pro forma adjustments do not give appropriate effect to those criteria; and
- resultant pro forma financial information does not reflect the proper application of those adjustments to the unadjusted financial information.

The procedures we performed were based on our professional judgement and included making enquiries, primarily of persons responsible for financial and accounting matters, observation of processes performed, inspection of documents, analytical procedures, evaluating the appropriateness of supporting documentation and agreeing or reconciling with underlying records, and other procedures. The procedures performed in a limited assurance engagement vary in nature from, and are less in extent than for, a reasonable assurance engagement. As a result, the level of assurance obtained in a limited assurance engagement is substantially lower than the assurance that would have been obtained had we performed a reasonable assurance engagement. Accordingly, we do not express a reasonable assurance opinion about whether the compilation of the pro forma financial information has been prepared, in all material respects, in accordance with the applicable criteria.

The engagement also involves evaluating the overall presentation of the pro forma financial information.

We believe that the evidence we have obtained is sufficient and appropriate to provide a basis for our conclusion.

Limited Assurance Conclusion

Based on the procedures we have performed and the evidence we have obtained, nothing has come to our attention that causes us to believe that the pro forma financial information is not compiled, in all material respects, by the [responsible party] of ABC Company on the basis of the applicable criteria as described in section [X] of the [insert details.]

Consent

[Firm name] has consented to the inclusion of this report in the [insert details] in the form and context in which it is included.

Liability

[*Liability wording to be inserted for individual Firm practice.*]

Declaration of Interest [or Disclosure of Interest Statement]

[Firm Name] does not have any interest in the outcome of this [transaction] other than in [state interest] for which normal professional fees will be received.

Yours faithfully

[Assurance practitioner's signature]

[Date of the assurance practitioner's report]

[Assurance practitioner's address]

ASAE 3450

Assurance Engagements involving Corporate Fundraisings and/or Prospective Financial Information

(Issued November 2012)

Issued by the Auditing and Assurance Standards Board

Note from the Institute of Chartered Accountants Australia

This note, prepared by the technical editor, is not part of ASAE 3450

Historical development

November 2012: ASAE 3450 issued. It applies where an assurance practitioner is asked to report on historical, prospective or pro forma financial information that has been prepared for inclusion in a document such as a prospectus, and also to any assurance report on prospective financial information. It provides detailed requirements and related guidance for auditors when determining whether to accept such an engagement, the appropriate level of assurance, how the engagement is to be performed and what to include in the assurance report. It replaces AUS 804 'The Audit of Prospective Financial Information' and AGS 1062 'Reporting in Connection with Proposed Fundraisings' and is operative for engagements commencing on or after 1 July 2013 and has no international equivalent.

Summary Contents

Detailed Contents

Preface

Reasons for Issuing ASAE 3450

The AUASB issues Standard on Assurance Engagements ASAE 3450 *Assurance Engagements involving Corporate Fundraisings and/or Prospective Financial Information,* pursuant to the requirements of the legislative provisions explained below.

The AUASB is an independent statutory board of the Australian Government established under section 227A of the *Australian Securities and Investments Commission Act 2001*, as amended (ASIC Act). Under section 227B of the ASIC Act, the AUASB may formulate assurance standards for other purposes.

Main Features

This Standard on Assurance Engagements establishes requirements and provides application and other explanatory material regarding the reporting on financial information included in, or to be included in, a public or nonpublic document and the reporting on prospective financial information prepared for other purposes.

Authority Statement

The Auditing and Assurance Standards Board (AUASB) formulates this Standard on Assurance Engagements ASAE 3450 *Assurance Engagements involving Corporate Fundraisings and/or Prospective Financial Information,* pursuant to section 227B of the *Australian Securities and Investments Commission Act 2001.*

This Standard on Assurance Engagements is to be read in conjunction with ASA 100 *Preamble to AUASB Standards*, which sets out the intentions of the AUASB on how the AUASB Standards are to be understood, interpreted and applied.

Dated: 26 November 2012

M H Kelsall
Chairman - AUASB

ASAE

Standard on Assurance Engagements ASAE 3450

Assurance Engagements involving Corporate Fundraisings and/or Prospective Financial Information

Application

1. This Standard on Assurance Engagements applies to reporting on:

   (a) historical financial information, pro forma historical financial information, prospective financial information and/or pro forma forecast prepared in connection with a corporate fundraising, and included in, or to be included in, a public or non-public document; and

   (b) prospective financial information, including a pro forma forecast or a projection, prepared for any other purpose.

Operative Date

2. This Standard on Assurance Engagements is operative for engagements commencing on or after 1 July 2013.

Introduction

Scope of this Standard on Assurance Engagements

3. This ASAE deals with the responsibilities of the assurance practitioner when undertaking an engagement to report on the responsible party's preparation of financial information related to a corporate fundraising, or if the financial information is prospective, if it is prepared for another purpose. It applies to an assurance engagement to provide either a reasonable assurance or limited assurance report, or a combination report, on that financial information.

4. In some circumstances, the assurance practitioner may also have separately agreed to provide other assurance or non-assurance services related to the corporate fundraising. Such services are outside the scope of this ASAE. (Ref: Para A1-A2)

Types of Financial Information Covered

5. The types of financial information covered by this ASAE are historical financial information, pro forma historical financial information and prospective financial information (including a forecast, projection, or a pro forma forecast) prepared in respect of a corporate fundraising, or additionally if the financial information is prospective, if it is prepared for another purpose. The financial information may be in respect of one entity or multiple entities (for example, in the case of a merger or acquisition).

6. It is acknowledged that assurance engagements covered by this ASAE often involve the assurance practitioner providing assurance, and reporting, on more than one type of financial information. In such circumstances, the assurance practitioner conducts the engagement in accordance with the applicable requirements and related application and other explanatory material in the appropriate section of the ASAE, and reports the assurance conclusion for each type of financial information either in individual assurance reports (by type), or a composite assurance report (all types). Appendix 3 contains illustrative examples of composite assurance reports.

Using this ASAE

7. Paragraphs 16 to 92 inclusive of this ASAE set out core requirements, and paragraphs A4 to A71 inclusive set out the core related application and other explanatory material applicable to assurance engagements to report on the responsible party's preparation of financial information in respect of a corporate fundraising, or prospective financial information prepared for another purpose. Requirements and related application and other explanatory material setting out the additional special considerations applicable to each of the different types of financial information covered by this ASAE are to be read in

conjunction with the core requirements and related applications and other explanatory material, and are as follows:

(a) Historical financial information - refer requirements contained in paragraphs 93 to 95 inclusive and related application and other explanatory material contained in paragraphs A72 to A74 inclusive.

(b) Pro forma historical financial information - refer requirements contained in paragraphs 96 to 104 inclusive and related application and other explanatory material contained in paragraphs A75 to A84 inclusive.

(c) Prospective financial information - refer requirements contained in paragraphs 105 to 118 inclusive and related application and other explanatory material contained in paragraphs A85 to A95 inclusive.

(d) Projection – refer requirements contained in paragraphs 120 to 127 inclusive and related application and other explanatory material contained in paragraphs A96 to A98 inclusive.

(e) Pro forma forecast - refer requirements contained in paragraphs 128 to 136 inclusive and related application and other explanatory material contained in paragraphs A99 to A106 inclusive.

Types of Assurance provided in the Engagement

8. In this ASAE, the following types of assurance are permitted on the different types of financial information:

(a) Historical financial information – limited or reasonable assurance.

(b) Pro forma historical financial information – limited or reasonable assurance.

(c) Prospective financial information (element 1 – assumptions) – limited assurance.

(d) Prospective financial information (element 2 – basis of preparation) – limited or reasonable assurance.

(e) Prospective financial information (element 1 – overall) – limited assurance.

ASAE

9. The assurance practitioner may be requested to provide assurance on a single type of financial information (for example, a forecast), or multiple types of financial information (for example, a pro forma forecast and historical financial information). The assurance practitioner may be requested to provide limited or reasonable assurance on the financial information, or if the financial information is prospective, a mixture of limited and reasonable assurance on its different elements.

(a) An example of a limited assurance engagement involving a single type of financial information is a review of historical financial information.

(b) An example of a limited assurance engagement that involves providing assurance on multiple types of financial information is a review of historical financial information and pro forma historical financial information.

(c) An example of an assurance engagement involving a single type of financial information in which there are elements of the assurance conclusion which will be on a reasonable assurance basis and other elements will be on a limited assurance basis involves a forecast.

(d) An example of an assurance engagement that involves providing assurance on multiple types of financial information involves a review of historical financial information (limited assurance) and a pro forma forecast where there are elements of the assurance conclusion which will be on a reasonable assurance basis and other elements which will be on a limited assurance basis.

The assurance practitioner exercises professional judgement[1] in determining the type of assurance that is appropriate to the type of financial information and possible in the individual engagement circumstances. (Ref: Para. A3)

1 See ASA 200 *Overall Objectives of the Independent Auditor and the Conduct of an Audit in Accordance with Australian Auditing Standards*, paragraph 13(k) for further guidance on the principle of "professional judgement".

10. In both reasonable and limited assurance engagements on financial information the assurance practitioner chooses a combination of assurance procedures which can include: inspection; observation; confirmation; recalculation; re-performance; analytical procedures; and enquiry. Determining the nature, timing and extent of assurance procedures to be performed on a particular engagement is a matter of professional judgement, taking into account the engagement circumstances (including the type of assurance to be provided), and consequently is likely to vary considerably from engagement to engagement.

Applying Requirements in this ASAE

11. In this ASAE, unless otherwise stated, the requirements are based on the engagement being to express limited assurance on the financial information. Because the level of assurance obtained in a limited assurance engagement is lower than in a reasonable assurance engagement, the procedures the assurance practitioner performs in a limited assurance engagement will vary in nature from, and are less in extent than for, a reasonable assurance engagement.[2] A reference in the requirements to "if applicable, in a reasonable assurance engagement" is taken to mean that these requirements are to be performed in a reasonable assurance engagement either:

(a) in addition to the limited assurance requirements within the same paragraph reference; or

(b) performed on a standalone basis, as a minimum requirement,

depending on the engagement circumstances.

Relationship with Other AUASB Standards

12. Assurance engagements other than audits or reviews of historical financial information are conducted in accordance with ASAE 3000 *Assurance Engagements Other than Audits or Reviews of Historical Financial Information*. Assurance engagements that are reviews of historical financial information are conducted in accordance with ASRE 2405 *Review of Historical Financial Information Other than a Financial Report*. Both ASRE 2405 and ASAE 3000 include requirements in relation to such topics as engagement acceptance, planning, performance, evidence, and documentation that apply to all assurance engagements, including those conducted in accordance with this ASAE. This ASAE deals with specific considerations in the application of ASRE 2405 and/or ASAE 3000 to assurance engagements relating to reporting on financial information related to corporate fundraisings and/or reporting on prospective financial information for other purposes. *The Framework for Assurance Engagements*, which defines and describes the elements and objectives of an assurance engagement, provides context for understanding this ASAE, ASRE 2405 and ASAE 3000.

13. This ASAE does not override the requirements of ASRE 2405 or ASAE 3000 which may apply in the engagement circumstances. It does not purport to deal with all engagement circumstances.

Objectives

14. The objectives of the assurance practitioner are:

(a) to obtain the required level(s) of assurance on elements of the financial information thereby enabling the assurance practitioner to express a conclusion conveying that level(s) of assurance;

(b) to report in accordance with the assurance practitioner's findings; and

(c) to communicate, as required by this ASAE, in accordance with the assurance practitioner's findings.

2 See *Framework for Assurance Engagements*, paragraph 53, and ASAE 3000 *Assurance Engagements other than Audits or Reviews of Historical Financial Information*, paragraphs 61-63 for further information.

Definitions

15. For the purposes of this Standard on Assurance Engagements, the following terms have the meanings attributed below:

(a) Assumptions mean expectations made by the responsible party as to future events and actions expected to take place as at the date the prospective financial information is prepared and exclude hypothetical assumptions, unless otherwise stated[3].

(b) Assurance report means a written report prepared by an independent assurance practitioner that provides assurance on a single type of financial information (individual assurance report) or on multiple types of financial information (either a composite assurance report or separate assurance reports for each type of financial information). When prepared in connection with a fundraising it is often referred to as an "Independent Assurance Report" or "Investigating Accountant's Report".

(c) AUASB Standards means standards issued by the Auditing and Assurance Standards Board (AUASB) comprising:

(i) Australian Auditing Standards;

(ii) Standards on Review Engagements;

(iii) Standards on Assurance Engagements; and

(iv) Standards on Related Services.

(d) Base financial information means financial information that is used as the starting point for the application of pro forma adjustments[4] by the responsible party. Base financial information is ordinarily historical in nature, however, it can also be prospective (for example a profit forecast). It may or may not have been previously audited or reviewed. Base financial information may also be referred to as unadjusted or source financial information.

(e) Corporate fundraising ("fundraising") means any transaction involving shares, debentures, units or interests in a management investment scheme undertaken to raise debt or equity funds, or issue equity, and/or offer and/or respond to an offer of, cash and/or scrip consideration to effect a transaction through the issuance of a public or non-public document. It includes initial public offerings, fundraisings[5], takeovers, schemes of arrangement or other corporate restructures.

(f) Different elements of prospective financial information means:

(i) the assumptions used in the preparation of the prospective financial information; (element 1)

(ii) the stated basis of preparation and the assumptions referred to in (i) above; (element 2) and

(iii) its reasonableness (element 3).

(g) Document means a public document or non-public document related to a corporate fundraising or other document containing prospective financial information.

(h) Engaging party means the body or person(s) that requested the services of the assurance practitioner for the assurance engagement. The engaging party is ordinarily the responsible party, as defined in paragraph (cc) below of this ASAE. References in this ASAE to "responsible party" are taken to include the engaging party unless otherwise stated.

(i) Entity means the entity responsible for the preparation and issuance of the public document or other document.

3 See paragraph 15(m) for a definition of "hypothetical assumptions".

4 See paragraph 15(v) for a definition of "pro forma adjustments".

5 See Section 700 of the *Corporations Act 2001*.

(j) Event(s) or transaction(s) means underlying event(s) or transaction(s) that is (are):

 (i) primarily the subject of the document; or

 (ii) not the subject of the document but the effect(s) of which have been reflected in the financial information.

(k) Financial information means information of a financial nature prepared by the responsible party in the form of:

 (i) base financial information;

 (ii) historical financial information;

 (iii) pro forma historical financial information;

 (iv) prospective financial information; or

 (v) a pro forma forecast.

(l) Historical financial information means information expressed in financial terms in relation to a particular entity, which is derived primarily from that entity's accounting system and relates to events occurring in past time periods or about conditions or circumstances at points in time in the past.[6]

(m) Hypothetical assumptions[7] means assumptions made by the responsible party in preparing prospective financial information in the form of a projection about future events and management actions which may not necessarily be expected to take place or that may be expected to take place, and may not be based on reasonable grounds.[8]

(n) Limited assurance engagement means an assurance engagement in which the assurance practitioner reduces the assurance engagement risk to a level that is acceptable in the circumstances of the assurance engagement, but where the risk is greater than for a reasonable assurance engagement. The set of procedures performed in a limited assurance engagement is limited compared with that necessary in a reasonable assurance engagement, but is planned to obtain a level of assurance that is, in the assurance practitioner's professional judgement acceptable in the circumstances of the assurance engagement. An example of a limited assurance engagement is a review.

(o) Management means the person(s) with executive responsibility for the conduct of the operations or individual business units of the entity. For some entities, in some circumstances, management includes some or all of those charged with governance, for example, executive members of a governance board, or an owner-manager.

(p) Materiality means in relation to information, that if certain information is omitted, misstated, or not disclosed, that information has the potential to affect the economic decisions of users of the document, or the discharge of accountability by management or those charged with governance of the entity (the responsible party).[9]

(q) Material inconsistency means information within the document that materially contradicts the financial information that is the subject of the assurance report.[10]

---

6 See ASA 200, paragraph Aus 13.1, for guidance on determining the nature of historical financial information for an assurance engagement.

7 See RG 170 *Prospective Financial Information,* issued by the Australian Securities and Investments commission (ASIC) (April 2011) for further guidance on hypothetical assumptions.

8 See paragraph 15(a) for a definition of "assumptions".

9 See AASB 101 *Presentation of Financial Statements*, paragraph 7, issued by the Australian Accounting Standards Board for a definition of materiality, and ASA 320 *Materiality in Planning and Performing an Audit* for further guidance on the concept of materiality in the preparation of a financial report, and may also be helpful in considering materiality in assurance engagements.

10 See ASA 720 *The Auditor's Responsibilities Relating to Other Information in Documents Containing an Audited Financial Report* for guidance on material inconsistencies in an audit engagement, which may be helpful in assurance engagements.

(r) Misstatement of fact means information that is incorrectly stated or presented in the document. A material misstatement of fact may undermine the credibility of financial information that is the subject of the assurance report.[11]

(s) Multiple types of financial information mean financial information that involves more than one type.[12]

(t) Non-IFRS financial information[13] is financial information that is presented other than in accordance with all relevant accounting standards.[14]

(u) Non-public document means a document in relation to a fundraising or a document containing prospective financial information, which is not a public document. It is not prepared in accordance with the *Corporations Act 2001*.

(v) Pro forma adjustments means adjustments selected by the responsible party in accordance with the stated basis of preparation to make to base financial information[15] (historical or prospective) to:

(i) illustrate the impact of a significant event or transaction ("event" or "transaction") as if the event had occurred or the transaction had been undertaken at an earlier date than actually occurred, or as if it had not occurred at all; and/or

(ii) eliminate the effects of unusual or non-recurring event(s) or transaction(s) that are not part of the normal operations of the entity; and/or

(iii) exclude certain event(s) or transaction(s), or present transactions or balances on a different recognition and measurement basis from that required or permitted by Australian Accounting Standards; and/or

(iv) correct errors or uncertainties.

(w) Pro forma financial information means base financial information adjusted for pro forma adjustments in accordance with the stated basis of preparation, resulting in non-IFRS financial information that is not prepared in accordance with Australian Accounting Standards. It is subject to the assumptions inherent in the responsible party's stated basis of preparation.

(x) Prospective financial information means financial information of a predictive character prepared based on assumptions made by the responsible party, in accordance with the stated basis of preparation. Prospective financial information may be either:

(i) a forecast which is prepared based on the responsible party's assumptions as to future events expected to take place on the dates, or in the period, described and the actions expected to be taken at the date the financial information is prepared. It is commonly referred to as a "directors' forecast"; or

(ii) a projection[16] which is prepared based on the responsible party's material hypothetical assumptions, or a mixture of assumptions and material hypothetical assumptions as to future events which are not necessarily expected to take place on the dates, or in the period, described and the actions not necessarily expected to be taken at the date the financial information is prepared (a "what-if" scenario).

---

11 See ASA 720 for guidance on the concept of misstatement of fact which may be helpful in assurance engagements.

12 See paragraph 15(k) for the different types covered by this ASAE.

13 See RG 230 *Disclosing non-IFRS financial Information* (December 2011), issued by ASIC for a definition of, and discussion on, non-IFRS financial information (see RG 230.14), as well as further guidance on pro forma financial information included in transaction documents.

14 Accounting Standards are ordinarily those issued by the Australian Accounting Standards Board.

15 See paragraph 14(d) for a definition of "base financial information."

16 See RG 170, which contains guidance that prospective financial information that includes a projection (that is, supported by material hypothetical assumptions) rather than reasonable grounds is likely to be misleading and therefore is not permitted to be included in a public document.

(y) Public document means a disclosure document, product disclosure statement or other documentation provided to shareholders, unit holders, or holders of a relevant interest in an entity (or which is provided to management of an entity) in relation to a scheme of arrangement under Part 5.1 of the *Corporations Act 2001*, or a takeover or compulsory acquisition under Chapter 6 of the *Corporations Act 2001*. Examples include:

   (i) A prospectus prepared by an entity that is a corporation in accordance with relevant sections of the *Corporations Act 2001*.[17]

   (ii) A Short-Form Prospectus; lodged with the Australian Securities and Investments Commission (ASIC), instead of including in the body of the prospectus the relevant information discussed in such materials.[18]

   (iii) Scheme Booklets.

   (iv) Target Statements.

   (v) Bidder Statements.

   (vi) Profile Statements; this is a brief statement that may be sent out with offers, with ASIC's approval, instead of a prospectus.[19]

   (vii) Offer Information Statements; this is a document that may be used instead of a prospectus under certain criteria set by the *Corporations Act 2001*.[20]

   (viii) Product Disclosure Statements (PDS) used where the entity is a trust or other type of managed investment scheme.

(z) Reasonable assurance engagement means an assurance engagement where the assurance practitioner reduces the assurance engagement risk to an acceptably low level in the circumstances of the assurance engagement as the basis for the assurance practitioner's conclusion.

(aa) Reasonable grounds means, in relation to a statement made, that there must be a sufficient objective foundation for that statement.[21]

(bb) Relevant Date means as applicable:

   (i) the allotment date;

   (ii) the effective date of the relevant proposed fundraising;

   (iii) the implementation date of the relevant proposed merger transaction; or

   (iv) in the case of a scheme of arrangement, the date of the shareholders or unit-holders meeting to vote on the scheme.

(cc) Responsible party means those charged with governance of the entity (ordinarily the Board of Directors), who are also responsible for the preparation and issuance of the financial information included in the document. It may also mean the management of the entity in circumstances where the assurance practitioner has been requested to provide assurance to those charged with governance in relation to financial information prepared by management. Alternatively it may also mean the party responsible for the preparation of the financial information. The responsible party may be different from the party that is the engaging party.

(dd) Stated basis of preparation means the basis on which the responsible party has chosen to prepare the financial information that is acceptable in view of the nature

17 See Sections 710, 711, and 713 of the *Corporations Act 2001*.

18 See Section 712 of the *Corporations Act 2001*.

19 See Sections 705 and 721 of the *Corporations Act 2001*.

20 See Section 709 of the *Corporations Act 2001* for the criteria as to when an Offer Information Statement may be used instead of a prospectus.

21 See RG 170 for further guidance on the concept of reasonable grounds in relation to public documents.

and objective of the document, or as required by applicable law or regulation. A stated basis of preparation may include:

(i) the recognition and measurement principles contained in the Australian Accounting Standards (but not all the presentation and disclosure requirements), and the entity's adopted accounting policies;

(ii) recognition and measurement principles contained in the Australian Accounting Standards adjusted by pro forma adjustments, selected for the purpose for which the pro forma financial information (i.e. non-IFRS financial information) is presented;

(iii) recognition and measurement principles other than those contained in Australian Accounting Standards; or

(iv) a basis selected by the responsible party, in order to present the financial information for its intended purpose.

(ee) Subsequent events mean events or facts that become known to the assurance practitioner after the date of the assurance report and prior to the relevant date.

(ff) Takeover means the acquisition of control of listed or unlisted entities conducted in accordance with Chapter 6 of the *Corporations Act 2001*.

Requirements

Complying with Standards that are Relevant to the Engagement

16. In respect of assurance engagements involving: (Ref: Para. A4)

(a) reasonable or limited assurance on non-historical financial information, the assurance practitioner shall not represent compliance with this ASAE unless the assurance practitioner has complied with the requirements of both this ASAE and ASAE 3000; and/or

(b) limited assurance on historical financial information, the assurance practitioner shall not represent compliance with this ASAE unless the assurance practitioner has complied with the requirements of both this ASAE and ASRE 2405.

17. The assurance practitioner shall have an understanding of the entire section(s) of this ASAE that is applicable in the engagement circumstances, including the application and other explanatory material, to understand its objectives and to apply its requirements properly.

Ethical Requirements

18. The assurance practitioner shall comply with relevant ethical requirements relating to assurance engagements, including those pertaining to independence, and implement quality control procedures that are applicable to the individual engagement in accordance with ASA 102.[22]

Quality Control

19. The assurance practitioner shall establish and maintain a system of quality control in accordance with ASQC 1.[23]

Professional Scepticism

20. The assurance practitioner shall plan and perform the engagement with professional scepticism, recognising that circumstances may exist that causes the financial information to be materially misstated.

22 See ASA 102 *Compliance with Ethical Requirements when Performing Audits, Reviews and Other Assurance Engagements*, paragraph 5.

23 See ASQC 1 *Quality Control for Firms that Perform Audits and Reviews of Financial Reports and Other Financial Information, and Other Assurance Engagements.*

Professional Judgement

21. The assurance practitioner shall exercise professional judgement in planning and performing assurance engagements involving reporting on financial information.

Inability to Comply with the Requirements of this ASAE or Other AUASB Standards

22. Where in rare and exceptional circumstances, factors outside the assurance practitioner's control prevent the assurance practitioner from complying with an essential procedure contained within a relevant requirement[24] in this ASAE, the assurance practitioner shall:
    (a) if possible, perform appropriate alternative procedures; and
    (b) document in the working papers:
        (i) the circumstances surrounding the inability to comply;
        (ii) the reasons for the inability to comply; and
        (iii) the justification of how the alternative procedures achieve the objective(s) of the requirement.

23. When the assurance practitioner is unable to perform the appropriate alternative procedures, the assurance practitioner shall consider the implications for the engagement. (Ref: Para. A5)

Assurance Engagement Acceptance

Preconditions for Acceptance (Ref: Para. A6-A7)

24. In order to establish whether the preconditions for the engagement are present, the assurance practitioner shall obtain agreement from the responsible party that they:
    (a) understand and accept the terms of the assurance engagement, including the assurance practitioner's reporting responsibilities and the type(s) of assurance to be expressed;
    (b) acknowledge and understand their responsibility for:
        (i) the selection of the financial information, including whether it contains comparatives;
        (ii) the preparation of the financial information in accordance with the stated basis of preparation;[25,26]
        (iii) determining the applicable time period to be covered by the financial information;
        (iv) the determination, selection, development, adequate disclosure and consistent application, of the stated basis of preparation in the document; the

24 The concepts and discussion on which requirements are relevant in the circumstances of the audit engagement are contained in ASA 200 (paragraphs 22 and Aus 23.1), and may be helpful in determining how to ensure compliance with relevant requirements for assurance engagements related to a corporate fundraising.

25 The concepts and discussions on the audit of historical financial information in the form of a complete set of financial statements that is prepared in accordance with a special purpose framework (that is, other than a general purpose framework) are contained in ASA 800 *Special Considerations–Audits of Financial Reports Prepared in Accordance with Special Purpose Frameworks*. It may be helpful in assisting the assurance practitioner's special considerations in planning, performing and providing reasonable assurance on this type of historical financial information related to fundraisings. Alternatively, ASRE 2400 *Review of a Financial Report Performed by an Assurance Practitioner Who is Not the Auditor of the Entity* contains the concepts and discussions on the review of historical financial information in the form of a complete set of financial statements. It may be helpful in assisting the assurance practitioner to plan, design, perform and provide limited assurance on historical financial information related to fundraisings.

26 If the historical financial information is in the form of a single financial statement (s), or specific elements, accounts or items of a financial statement, then in addition to ASA 800, ASA 805 *Special Consideration–Audits of Single Financial Statements and Specific Elements, Accounts or Items of Financial Statements* may be helpful in assisting the assurance practitioner's special considerations in planning, performing and providing reasonable assurance on this type of historical financial information related to fundraisings.

contents, preparation and issuance of the document[27] in which the financial information is contained;

(v) complying with the requirements of all applicable laws and regulations in the preparation of the financial information and the document;[28] and

(vi) such internal control as is determined to be necessary to enable the preparation of financial information that is free from material misstatement; and

(c) will provide the assurance practitioner with:

(i) unrestricted access to all requested information relevant to the financial information, where possible;

(ii) unrestricted access to those persons within the entity or the responsible party's experts, from whom the assurance practitioner determines it is necessary to obtain evidence, where possible;

(iii) a listing of all known uncorrected misstatements in the financial information, together with an acknowledgement that the responsible party is responsible for confirming that such misstatements are immaterial; and

(iv) written representations covering all matters requested by the assurance practitioner in relation to the engagement, within the timeframe required.

Other Factors Affecting Engagement Acceptance

25. The assurance practitioner shall accept the engagement only when:

(a) on the basis of preliminary knowledge of the assurance engagement circumstances, nothing has come to the assurance practitioner's attention to indicate that:

(i) the requirements of the relevant ethical principles described in ASA 102 will not be satisfied;

(ii) the stated basis of preparation chosen by the responsible party, and used in the preparation of the financial information, is likely to be misleading or deceptive;

(iii) there will be significant limitations on the scope of the assurance practitioner's work, including limited access to information or persons;

(iv) the responsible party intends to associate the assurance practitioner's name with the financial information in an inappropriate manner;

(v) the time period covered by the financial information is not acceptable;[29] or

(vi) the assurance engagement does not have a rational purpose;[30]

(b) the preconditions for the engagement, as stated in paragraph 24 of this ASAE are present;

(c) the type(s) of assurance requested by the responsible party is/(are) acceptable to the assurance practitioner;

(d) the assurance practitioner has the capabilities, competence and necessary qualifications to perform the engagement; and

(e) the assurance practitioner believes that the assurance report will be used for its intended purpose.

26. If the preconditions for the assurance engagement or other factors affecting engagement acceptance as set out in paragraphs 24 and 25 of this ASAE are not present, the assurance

27 The *Corporations Act 2001* places specific requirements on directors in relation to the preparation of public documents, including presentation of financial information included therein.

28 For example, See RG 228 *Prospectus: Effective Disclosure for retail investors* (November 2011), issued by ASIC for further guidance in respect of public documents.

29 See RG 170, for further guidance on what is an acceptable time period. It is ordinarily the case that the longer the period, the less likely it is that there are reasonable grounds for disclosed.

30 See ASAE 3000, paragraph 17(b)(v), for further guidance.

practitioner shall discuss the matter with the responsible party. If changes cannot be made to meet the preconditions, the assurance practitioner shall not accept the engagement as an assurance engagement, unless required by applicable law or regulation.

Agreeing on the Terms of the Assurance Engagement

27. The agreed terms of the assurance engagement shall include, at a minimum: (Ref: Para. A8, A10)
    (a) the objective(s) and scope of the assurance engagement, including:
        (i) the assurance practitioner's understanding of the purpose of the assurance engagement, the nature of, and time period covered by, the financial information, and the intended users of the assurance report;
        (ii) confirmation that the assurance practitioner will conduct the engagement in accordance with this ASAE;
        (iii) a statement that the assurance practitioner is not responsible for the preparation of the financial information;
        (iv) a statement that the assurance practitioner has no responsibility to perform an assessment of the appropriateness, or otherwise, of the selected stated basis of preparation of the financial information;
        (v) a statement that the assurance practitioner will assess whether the financial information has been prepared in accordance with the stated basis of preparation;
        (vi) in connection with a non-public document, a statement that the assurance practitioner will disclaim responsibility for any reliance on the assurance report by any party other than intended users, and for any use of the assurance report for any purpose other than that for which the assurance report was prepared;
        (vii) if applicable, a statement that an audit is not being performed and that consequently, an audit opinion will be not be expressed;
        (viii) the type(s) and proposed wording of the assurance conclusion; and
        (ix) a statement that the engagement cannot be relied upon to identify fraud, error(s), illegal act(s) or other irregularities that may exist within the entity;
    (b) the responsibilities of the assurance practitioner, including:
        (i) compliance with relevant ethical requirements, including independence;
        (ii) performing assurance procedures on the financial information to obtain sufficient appropriate evidence for the type(s) of assurance required;
        (iii) issuing a written assurance report and any other report agreed with the responsible party;[31] and
        (iv) if applicable, and once satisfied it is appropriate to, providing consent in the required form to the responsible party for the inclusion of the assurance practitioner's name and assurance report in the document;
    (c) the responsibilities of the responsible party including those set out in paragraphs 24(b) and 24(c) of this ASAE; and
    (d) such other terms and conditions that the assurance practitioner determines are appropriate in the engagement circumstances. (Ref: Para. A9)

31 See ASA 260 *Communication with Those Charged with Governance* for guidance on specific matters that may be communicated in an audit engagement that may be helpful in an assurance engagement involving reasonable assurance on historical financial information. Additionally, ASRE 2405 provides guidance on specific matters that may be communicated in a review engagement on historical financial information that may also be helpful in an assurance engagement that involves a review of financial information that is historical.

Changes in the Terms of the Engagement

28. The assurance practitioner shall not agree to a change in the terms of the assurance engagement where there is no reasonable justification for doing so. If such a change is made, the assurance practitioner shall not disregard evidence that was obtained prior to the change. (Ref: Para. A11)

29. If the terms of the assurance engagement are to change, the assurance practitioner and the responsible party shall agree on, and record, the new terms of the assurance engagement in an engagement letter or other suitable form of written agreement. (Ref: Para. A12)

30. If the assurance practitioner is unable to agree to a change in the terms of the engagement, and is not permitted by the responsible party to continue the original engagement, the assurance practitioner shall:
    (a) withdraw from the engagement, where possible under applicable law or regulation; and
    (b) determine whether there is any obligation, either contractual or otherwise, to report the circumstances to parties other than the responsible party.

Planning the Engagement

31. The assurance practitioner shall plan the engagement so that it will be performed effectively.[32] (Ref: Para. A13)

Planning Activities

32. The assurance practitioner's planning procedures shall include, at a minimum: (Ref: Para. A14-A15)
    (a) establishing an overall engagement strategy that sets the scope, timing and direction of the engagement and that guides the development of the plan;
    (b) ascertaining the responsible party's reporting objectives and key milestones of the engagement, to plan the timing of the engagement and the nature of the communications required;
    (c) considering the factors that in the assurance practitioner's professional judgement are significant in directing the engagement team's efforts;
    (d) considering the results of preliminary engagement activities, including engagement acceptance;
    (e) if applicable, whether knowledge gained from other engagements performed by the engagement partner for the entity is relevant;
    (f) considering the nature, timing and extent of planned risk assessment procedures;[33]
    (g) assessing assurance engagement risk;[34] (Ref: Para. A16)
    (h) determining if the entity's auditor will need to be contacted in respect of the audit opinion or review conclusion expressed on the latest financial report; and
    (i) ascertaining the nature, timing and extent of resources necessary to perform the engagement, including considering the involvement of experts.

Materiality in Planning and Performing the Engagement

Determining Materiality when Planning the Engagement (Ref: Para. A17-A18)

33. When establishing the overall engagement strategy, the assurance practitioner shall determine materiality for the financial information.[35]

32 See ASAE 3000, paragraphs 25-26 or ASRE 2405, paragraphs 25-27, as appropriate.

33 See ASA 315 *Identifying and Assessing the Risks of Material Misstatement through Understanding the Entity and Its Environment*, for guidance on planned risks assessment procedures which may be helpful.

34 See ASA 200, paragraphs A32-A44 for guidance on the different elements of assurance engagement risk.

35 See ASA 320 *Materiality in Planning and Performing an Audit* for guidance on planning materiality.

34. The assurance practitioner shall determine performance materiality for purposes of assessing the risks of material misstatement and determining the nature, timing and extent of further procedures.

Revision as the Engagement Progresses

35. The assurance practitioner shall revise materiality in the event of becoming aware of information during the engagement that would have caused the assurance practitioner to have determined a different amount initially. (Ref: Para. A19)

Understanding the Entity and Its Environment and Identifying and Assessing Risks of Material Misstatement

Obtaining an Understanding of the Entity and Its Environment

36. The procedures to obtain an understanding of the entity and its environment, and to identify and assess risks of material misstatement in the financial information shall include the following:
   (a) Enquiries of those persons within the entity who, in the assurance practitioner's judgement, have information that is likely to assist in identifying and assessing risks of material misstatement.
   (b) Analytical procedures. (Ref: Para. A20-A22)
   (c) Observation and inspection. (Ref: Para. A23-A25)

Overall Considerations

37. If the assurance practitioner does not have a prior knowledge of the entity, the assurance practitioner shall obtain an understanding of: (Ref: Para. A26)
   (a) the type of document that the financial information will be included in;
   (b) any applicable legal and regulatory requirements related to the financial information being included in that type of document;
   (c) the nature of the entity, and any acquiree or divestee whose financial information is included in the financial information that is the subject of the assurance report including:
      (i) its size, complexity, industry or industries in which it operates, its ownership, financial and regulatory structures, key strategies and products/services, competitors, regulatory environment, management structure, and available financial resources;
      (ii) its operating history;
      (iii) if applicable, any changes from prior financial reporting periods in the nature or extent of its operations, including whether there have been any mergers and/or acquisitions; and
      (iv) its assets and liabilities;
   (d) relevant industry, legal and regulatory and other external factors pertaining to the entity and any acquiree or divestee; and (Ref: Para. A27-A29)
   (e) the stated basis of preparation of the financial information of the entity and of any acquiree or divestee and how these differ, if at all, from the accounting policies contained in the most recent financial report. (Ref: Para. A30)

38. Notwithstanding any prior knowledge, the assurance practitioner shall obtain an understanding of:
   (a) the stated basis of preparation chosen by the responsible party for the financial information, if it is different from prior audited or reviewed historical financial information also included in the document, and if so, why;

(b) the financial information including:
   (i) its type,[36] source, and nature;[37]
   (ii) the time period covered and reasons for its selection;
   (iii) its intended use;
   (iv) the extent to which it may be affected by the responsible party's judgements;
   (v) obtaining an understanding of whether it contains comparative financial information, whether such financial information will be restated, and if so, why;
   (vi) identifying relevant financial information available in the public domain;
   (vii) identifying expected and plausible relationships within the financial information for use when performing analytical procedures;
   (viii) whether the entity's financial report has already been audited or reviewed, and, if so, whether the audit or review was conducted in accordance with Australian Auditing Standards; and what type of audit opinion or review conclusion was expressed in the auditor's report;
   (ix) if any part of the financial information has been audited or reviewed;
   (x) whether it has been prepared on a consistent basis with that of any prior period audited or reviewed historical financial information included in the document. For example, the audited or reviewed comparatives may have been restated by the responsible party to ensure consistency of basis of preparation;[38] and
   (xi) whether adjustments have been made that were previously considered immaterial in the prior period audit or review of the financial report;

(c) the event(s) and transaction(s) that may have a significant impact on the preparation of the financial information;

(d) the nature and type of other information to be included in the document, if available, sufficient to enable the assessment of whether it is consistent with the financial information;

(e) the requirements of any applicable law or regulation that may impact the financial information;[39]

(f) an understanding of any recent key changes in the entity's business activities, and how they affect the financial information;

(g) an understanding of whether experts are required, or whether reliance will be required to be placed on their work;

(h) the expertise of the preparers of the financial information; and

(i) internal control over the process used to prepare the financial information.

ASAE

36 For example, historical financial information, pro forma historical financial information, prospective financial information, or pro forma forecast.

37 For example, its relevance, completeness, reliability and understandability.

38 See RG 230 and RG 228, for further guidance on the nature and type of comparatives that should be included in a public document.

39 Prospective financial information included in a public document under the *Corporations Act 2001* is required to be based on reasonable grounds to be considered not misleading. See section 728(2) and section 769C of the *Corporations Act 2001*. See ASIC's RG 170 *Prospective Financial Information,* for further guidance on what constitutes "reasonable grounds", as well as some non-exhaustive examples of indicative factors that may suggest or demonstrate reasonable grounds.

39. The understanding required in paragraph 38 of this ASAE shall be: (Ref: Para. A31-A32)

    (a) sufficient to enable the assurance practitioner to identify and assess any risks that the financial information may not be prepared in accordance with the stated basis of preparation; and

    (b) enable the assurance practitioner to plan and design assurance procedures whose nature, timing and extent are responsive to assessed risks of material misstatement and allow the assurance practitioner to obtain the required level of assurance.

Other Procedures to Obtain an Understanding and to Identify and Assess Risks of Material Misstatement

40. If the assurance practitioner has performed other engagements for the entity, the assurance practitioner shall consider whether information obtained from other engagements is relevant to identifying and assessing risks of material misstatement. (Ref: Para. A33)

41. The assurance practitioner shall make enquiries of the responsible party, and others within the entity as appropriate, to determine whether they have knowledge of any actual, suspected or alleged fraud or non-compliance with laws and regulations affecting the financial information.

42. The engagement partner and other key members of the engagement team, and any key assurance practitioner's external experts, shall discuss the susceptibility of the entity's financial information to material misstatement whether due to fraud or error, and the application of the stated basis of preparation to the entity's facts and circumstances. The engagement partner shall determine which matters are to be communicated to members of the engagement team, and to any assurance practitioner's external experts not involved in the discussion.

Reliance on the work performed by others

43. The assurance practitioner shall consider whether to use the work of any expert,[40] including the responsible party's expert[41] or other assurance practitioner, in respect of obtaining sufficient appropriate evidence in respect of a material area or item within the financial information, including:

    (a) evaluating whether any material adjustments made to, or assumptions included within, the financial information are in accordance with the stated basis of preparation;

    (b) evaluating the suitability of the stated basis of preparation; and/or

    (c) assessing the impact of any contractual requirements on the financial information.

44. In considering whether to use the work of an expert, the assurance practitioner shall take into account:

    (a) the purpose for which the expert's work is to be, or, was, performed;

    (b) the risks of material misstatement in the material area or item within the financial information to which the expert's work relates;

    (c) the significance of the expert's work to the engagement;

    (d) the assurance practitioner's assessment of the competence, capabilities and objectivity of the expert for the assurance practitioner's purposes;

    (e) whether the assurance practitioner will be able to obtain access to the relevant working papers supporting the expert's report; and

    (f) any prior knowledge of the expert's work.

---

40 The concepts and discussions on auditors using the work of other experts are contained in ASA 620 *Using the Work of an Auditor's Expert* and may be helpful in determining the extent of reliance by an assurance practitioner in an assurance engagement.

41 The concepts and discussions on auditors assessing and placing reliance on the work performed by the entity's expert are contained in ASA 500 *Audit Evidence* and may be helpful in determining the extent of reliance by an assurance practitioner in an assurance engagement.

45. If the assurance practitioner does intend to use the work of an expert, and consequently place reliance on the expert's work, for the purposes of the engagement, the assurance practitioner shall consider if a written acknowledgement by the expert or other assurance practitioner is required in order for the assurance practitioner to place such reliance, and if so, shall request such an acknowledgement.

46. If the expert does not provide a required written acknowledgement, the assurance practitioner shall consider what additional procedures, if any, are necessary, in order for the assurance practitioner to place reliance on the expert's work and conclude on the material area or item. (Ref: Para. A34(a))

47. If the expert does permit reliance to be placed on the work performed, the assurance practitioner shall evaluate the adequacy of the expert's work for the assurance practitioner's purposes by requesting access to the expert's working papers in order to:

(a) evaluate the competence, capabilities, objectivity and independence of that expert;

(b) understand the scope, timing and type of work performed and outcomes;

(c) evaluate the appropriateness of the work performed as evidence for the purpose of the engagement;

(d) if applicable, understand the materiality levels set by the expert;

(e) if applicable, evaluate the expert's work methodology;

(f) if applicable, evaluate any audit or review differences identified by that expert;

(g) understand the type of audit opinion, review conclusion or report issued by that expert, and if applicable, the reasons for any modification;

(h) if applicable, ascertain whether the financial information has been prepared in accordance with the stated basis of preparation of the entity;

(i) determine, based on the results of the expert's work, whether additional assurance procedures will be required to be performed on the financial information in order to obtain sufficient appropriate evidence on which to base the required assurance conclusion; and

(j) if applicable, evaluate whether the other assurance practitioner's audit opinion or review conclusion was modified, and determine the implications for the engagement, including considering:

(i) the assurance practitioner's ability to undertake the engagement in accordance with the agreed terms; and

(ii) the potential impact, if any, on the assurance procedures to be performed.

Causes of Risks of Material Misstatement

48. When designing the procedures to obtain an understanding of the entity and its environment, and to identify and assess risks of material misstatement in the financial information, required in paragraph 36 of this ASAE, the assurance practitioner shall consider the following factors:

(a) the likelihood of intentional misstatement in the financial information;

(b) applicable law or regulatory requirements with respect to the preparation or presentation of the financial information;

(c) the complexity and degree of subjectivity underlying calculations of information which are included in the financial information; and

(d) how the responsible party makes all significant accounting estimates included in the financial information. (Ref: Para A35)

ASAE

Overall Responses to Assessed Risks of Material Misstatement and Further Procedures

Assurance Procedures

49. The assurance practitioner shall design and implement procedures to respond to, and address the assessed risks of material misstatement of the financial information. (Ref: Para. A36-A37)

50. The assurance practitioner shall use professional judgement to design and perform assurance procedures whose nature, timing and extent are responsive to the assessed risks of material misstatement, after:

    (a) considering the likelihood of material misstatement in the financial information due to the particular characteristics of the financial information (that is, the inherent risk); (Ref: Para. A38-A39)

    (b) assessing the need to obtain more persuasive evidence the higher the assurance practitioner's assessment of risk, such as external confirmation procedures; and/or (Ref: Para. A40-A41)

    (c) if applicable, in a reasonable assurance engagement, and irrespective of the assessed risks of material misstatement, designing and performing tests of details or analytical procedures for each material account balance within the financial information.

51. In designing analytical procedures, the assurance practitioner shall determine the suitability of particular analytical procedures in relation to the financial information, taking into consideration the assessed risks of material misstatement of the financial information.

52. The assurance procedures shall include:

    (a) if applicable, in respect of comparative information:

        (i) comparing, for consistency, its stated basis of preparation against the entity's previously audited or reviewed historical financial information and if applicable, the most unaudited or unreviewed recent annual or interim financial report, and

            ♦ evaluating the reasons for any differences; and

            ♦ ensuring any restatements or adjustments made are appropriate;

        (ii) reading the most recent audited or reviewed financial report in order to identify any matters that may affect the financial information;

    (b) evaluating the reasonableness and appropriateness of the time period covered;

    (c) enquiring of the responsible party in respect of the financial information:

        (i) that it agrees to, and has been reconciled to underlying, supporting accounting records and documentation;

        (ii) that it reflects any changes made to the stated basis of preparation from the most recent audited or reviewed financial statements;

        (iii) that it reflects the results of any identified misstatements from the prior year's financial statements;

        (iv) if any part of the financial information has been previously audited or reviewed, that it agrees to those audited or reviewed records; and/or

    (d) if applicable, performing external confirmation procedures in respect of material balances within the financial information;

    (e) assessing the appropriateness and suitability of any adjustments made by the responsible party as compared to the stated basis of preparation; performing the analytical procedures referred to in paragraph 51 of this ASAE on the financial information that the assurance practitioner considers are responsive to the assessed risks of material misstatement in the financial information: (Ref: Para. A42)

(i) evaluating the reliability of data from which the assurance practitioner's expectation of recorded amounts or ratios is developed, taking account of the source, comparability, and nature and relevance of information available;

(ii) developing an expectation with respect to recorded amounts or ratios in the financial information; and

(iii) if applicable, in a reasonable assurance engagement, the expectation developed in (ii) above must be sufficiently precise to identify possible material misstatements in the financial information; and/or

(f) if applicable, in a reasonable assurance engagement, performing tests of details of material classes of transactions or account balances within the financial information;

(g) if applicable, in respect of material accounting estimates included in the financial information: (Ref: Para. A43)

(i) confirming that the responsible party has appropriately applied the requirements of the stated basis of preparation relevant to material accounting estimates;

(ii) verifying the methodology chosen for making material accounting estimates:

- has been applied consistently;
- is appropriate when compared with the most recent audited/reviewed financial statements;
- reflects any changes in methodology from prior periods; and
- any changes in methodology are consistent with the stated basis of preparation;

(iii) considering whether other procedures are necessary in the circumstances including testing how the responsible party made the accounting estimate and the data on which it is based, including evaluating whether the method of quantification used is appropriate in the circumstances, and the assumptions used by the responsible party are reasonable;

(h) in respect of the stated basis of preparation:

(i) understanding the process for its selection and approval;

(ii) understanding what accounting policies have been adopted;

(iii) assessing its reasonableness and suitability for presenting the significant effects attributable to the event(s) or transaction(s) that is the subject of the document by understanding the nature, effect of, and reasons for any changes made to the stated basis of preparation as compared to that used in the most recent audited or reviewed financial statements;

(iv) performing consistency checks in the application of the stated basis of preparation to the financial information;

(v) assessing, based on the assurance practitioner's understanding, whether the stated basis of preparation is adequately described in the document; and

(i) assessing whether the financial information is prepared in accordance with the stated basis of preparation;

ASAE

(j) enquiring of the responsible party and/or other parties[42] relating to whether there were:

   (i) any changes in accounting policies, financial reporting practices and other reporting requirements that occurred during the time period under examination;

   (ii) any corrections made to convert the financial information from an overseas jurisdiction's generally accepted accounting principles to the stated basis of preparation;

   (iii) any unadjusted audit differences from the most recently audited or reviewed financial report that may be material for the purposes of the document;

   (iv) any other provisions and other accounting estimates (such as asset revaluations) in the financial information; and

   (v) any significant transactions with related parties (for example, assets purchased from an associated entity); and

(k) considering the use of sampling. (Ref: Para. A44)

53. If the analytical procedures described in paragraph 52(e) of this ASAE identify fluctuations or relationships that are inconsistent with other relevant information, or differ significantly from expected amounts or ratios in the financial information, the assurance practitioner shall investigate such differences by:

(a) enquiring of the responsible party;

(b) evaluating the responses received; and/or

(c) if applicable:

   (i) determining whether other procedures are necessary in the circumstances; and (Ref: Para. A45)

   (ii) obtaining additional evidence supporting the responsible party's responses to the enquiries made.

Oral Representations

54. If the assurance practitioner obtains oral representations from the responsible party in respect of matters supporting the financial information, the assurance practitioner shall:

(a) evaluate their reasonableness and consistency with other evidence obtained, including other representations;

(b) consider whether those making the representations can be expected to be well informed on the particular matters;

(c) obtain appropriate corroborative evidence;[43] and

(d) document the key aspects of the oral representation.

Additional Procedures

55. The assurance practitioner shall remain alert throughout the engagement for any event(s), condition(s), transaction(s), or error(s) that may:

(a) cast doubt over the reliability, accuracy, or completeness of the information used by the assurance practitioner as evidence for the financial information; and/or

(b) require a reassessment, or revision, of the assurance practitioner's risk assessment; and/or

42 The concepts and discussions on using the work of another auditor or internal auditor relevant to an audit engagement are contained in Auditing Standard ASA 600 *Special Considerations—Audits of a Group Financial Report (including the Work of Component Auditors)* and Auditing Standard ASA 610 *Using the Work of Internal Auditors,* which may be helpful in considering the work of other auditors for the purposes of an assurance engagement.

43 The concepts and discussions on corroborative evidence relevant in investigating unusual fluctuations relevant to an audit engagement are contained in Auditing ASA 520 *Analytical Procedures,* and may be helpful in determining appropriate corroborative evidence in an assurance engagement.

(c) require changes, or additions, to the planned assurance procedures in order to obtain sufficient appropriate evidence on which to base the assurance conclusion on the financial information. (Ref: Para. A46)

56. If the assurance practitioner becomes aware of an event(s), condition(s), transaction(s) or error(s) that causes the assurance practitioner to believe the financial information may be materially misstated, the assurance practitioner shall use professional judgement to design and perform additional procedures sufficient to enable the assurance practitioner to: (Ref: Para. A46)

(a) conclude that the event(s), condition(s), transaction(s) or error(s) is (are) not likely to cause the financial information to be materially misstated; or

(b) determine that the event(s), condition(s), transaction(s) or error(s) cause(s) the financial information to be materially misstated.

Communication and Correction of Misstatements

57. Prior to evaluating the effect of any identified uncorrected misstatements the assurance practitioner shall reassess materiality determined in accordance with paragraphs 33 and 34 of this ASAE to confirm whether it remains appropriate in the context of the financial information.

58. The assurance practitioner shall determine whether the uncorrected misstatements are material, individually or in aggregate to the financial information, taking into consideration the size and nature of the misstatements, and the particular circumstances of their occurrence.

59. If the assurance practitioner believes that it is necessary to correct an identified misstatement for the financial information to be prepared in accordance with the stated basis of preparation, the assurance practitioner shall communicate this as soon as practicable to the responsible party to enable them to make the correction.

60. If, at the assurance practitioner's request, the responsible party has corrected an identified misstatement(s), the assurance practitioner shall perform additional procedures on the corrected misstatements to ensure they have been appropriately made and determine whether any material misstatements remain in the financial information.

61. If the responsible party refuses to correct some or all of the identified material misstatements in the financial information communicated by the assurance practitioner, the assurance practitioner:

(a) shall obtain an understanding of the responsible party's reasons for not making the adjustments, and take this into account when forming the assurance practitioner's conclusion; and

(b) if the misstatement is material, the assurance practitioner shall express an adverse conclusion in accordance with paragraph 84(b) of this ASAE.

Identified Misstatements

62. The assurance practitioner shall accumulate misstatements identified during the engagement, other than those that are clearly trivial. (Ref: Para. A47-A48)

63. The assurance practitioner shall determine whether the overall engagement strategy and engagement plan needs to be revised if:

(a) the nature of identified misstatements and the circumstances of their occurrence indicate that other misstatements may exist that, when aggregated with misstatements already identified, could be material; or

(b) the aggregate of identified misstatements approaches materiality levels set in accordance with paragraphs 33 and 34 of this ASAE.

Evidence

64. The assurance practitioner considers the adequacy, relevance and reliability of the information obtained as evidence and shall evaluate whether the assurance practitioner has

obtained sufficient appropriate evidence[44] on which to express an assurance conclusion on the financial information. (Ref: Para. A49)

Other Information Included in the Document

65. When the document containing the financial information includes, or will include, other information, the assurance practitioner shall request from the responsible party a copy of that document and read its entire contents for the sole purpose of identifying any material inconsistencies with, or material misstatements of fact in relation to, the financial information. (Ref: Para. A50-A51)

66. If the assurance practitioner:

    (a) identifies a material inconsistency between the other information and the financial information; and/or

    (b) becomes aware of a material misstatement of fact in that other information that is related to the financial information; and/or

    (c) identifies a potentially misleading or deceptive statement in relation to the financial information;

    the assurance practitioner shall discuss this with the responsible party and:

    (d) if the responsible party agrees to a revision of the document the assurance practitioner shall request an updated copy of the document to ensure the revision has been made; or

    (e) if the responsible party refuses to make the revision, the assurance practitioner shall consider whether to:

        (i) obtain expert advice on the appropriate course of action for the assurance practitioner; and/or

        (ii) include in the assurance report an Other Matter paragraph[45] that describes the material inconsistency and/or misstatement of fact; and/or

        (iii) withdraw consent for the responsible party to include the assurance report in the document; and/or

        (iv) withdraw from the engagement, where withdrawal is possible under applicable law or regulation.

Going Concern Considerations

67. The assurance practitioner shall determine if an assessment of the entity's ability to continue as a going concern is relevant to the engagement.[46] (Ref: Para. A52)

68. If the assurance practitioner determines that an assessment of the entity's ability to continue as a going concern is relevant, the assurance practitioner shall perform such an assessment in order to obtain sufficient appropriate evidence regarding the appropriateness of the responsible party's use of the going concern assumption in the preparation of the financial information. (Ref: Para. A53)

69. If the assurance practitioner concludes the entity is not a going concern, or if there is a material uncertainty related to event(s) or condition(s) that individually, or collectively, may cast significant doubt on the entity's ability to continue as a going concern, the assurance practitioner shall consider the implications for the engagement and the assurance report. (Ref: Para. A54)

---

44 The concepts and discussions on the sufficiency and appropriates of evidence related to an audit engagement are contained in ASA 500 and may be helpful in evaluating the evidence for an assurance engagement.

45 The concepts and discussion on the use of an Other Matter paragraph relevant to an audit engagement are contained in ASA 706 *Emphasis of Matter Paragraphs and Other Matter Paragraphs in the Independent Auditor's Report*, paragraphs 8-Aus 8.1, and may be helpful in determining its form, content and location in the assurance report applicable to an assurance engagement.

46 The concepts and discussions on the going concern assessment relevant to an audit engagement are contained in ASA 570 *Going Concern*, and may be helpful in performing a going concern assessment in an assurance engagement. Australian Accounting Standard AASB 101 *Presentation of Financial Statements*, paragraphs 25-26 contains relevant guidance on the going concern assessment.

Consideration of Events Up to the Date of the Assurance Report

(Ref: Para. A55)

70. The assurance practitioner shall consider the impact of any event(s), transaction(s), correction(s), or error(s) of which the assurance practitioner becomes aware, that may materially affect the financial information, for the time period up to and including the date of the assurance report.[47]

71. The assurance practitioner shall discuss with the responsible party any such event(s), transaction(s), correction(s), or error(s) identified during the engagement in order to establish whether the effect on the financial information is material. If the effect is material, the assurance practitioner must perform additional procedures to confirm if the event(s), transaction(s), correction(s), or error(s) has (have) been corrected in the financial information and/or elsewhere in the document, if applicable. If the required correction(s) is(are) not made, the assurance practitioner shall consider what further action is appropriate in the engagement circumstances, including the implications for the assurance report.

72. The assurance practitioner shall revoke any consent to include the assurance report in the document that may have been previously provided, if the event(s), transaction(s), correction(s), or error(s) referred to in paragraph 70 of this ASAE is (are) not, in the assurance practitioner's professional judgement, appropriately addressed by the responsible party.

Consideration of Events Identified After the Date of the Assurance Report (Ref: Para. A56-A57)

73. If the assurance practitioner becomes aware of event(s), transaction(s) or error(s) after the date of the issuance of the assurance report and before the relevant date that may have caused the assurance practitioner to amend the assurance report, had the assurance practitioner known of such matters at the date of that assurance report, the assurance practitioner shall:

(a) discuss such event(s), correction(s), transaction(s) or error(s) with the responsible party; and

(b) consider what further action is appropriate in the engagement circumstances, including the implications for the assurance report.

74. The assurance practitioner shall revoke any consent to include the assurance report in the document that may have been previously provided, if the event(s), transaction(s), correction(s), or error(s) referred to in paragraph 73 of this ASAE are not, in the assurance practitioner's professional judgement, appropriately addressed by the responsible party.

Written Representations

75. The assurance practitioner shall request the responsible party to provide written representations at the completion of the engagement containing the following: (Ref: Para. A58-A61)

(a) the preconditions described in paragraphs 24(b) and 24(c) of this ASAE;

(b) confirmation of the intended use of the financial information;

(c) confirmation that the going concern basis of preparation of the financial information is appropriate in the document;

(d) confirmation that there are no currently anticipated material changes to be made to the financial information between the date of the assurance report and the relevant date;

(e) confirmation that there has been no event(s), transactions, correction(s), error(s) or other matter(s) that has(have) arisen or been discovered subsequent to the preparation of the financial information that may impact, or require adjustment to, the financial information;

47 The concepts and discussions on the subsequent events relevant to a financial report audit engagement are contained in ASA 560 *Subsequent Events,* and may be helpful in assessing subsequent events in an assurance engagement.

(f) confirmation that the assurance practitioner has been provided with a listing of all known uncorrected immaterial misstatements in the financial information, together with an acknowledgement that the responsible party is responsible for confirming that such misstatements are immaterial; and

(g) such other written representations that the assurance practitioner determines are appropriate in the engagement circumstances.

76. The date of the written representations shall be as near as practicable to, but not after, the date of the assurance report.

77. If the assurance practitioner has sufficient doubt about the competence, integrity, ethical values, or diligence of those providing the written representations, or if the representations received are inconsistent with other evidence, the assurance practitioner shall:

(a) if practical, discuss the matter(s) with the responsible party;

(b) perform other procedures to attempt to resolve any inconsistencies;

(c) re-evaluate the integrity of the responsible party and evaluate the effect this may have on the reliability of representations (oral or written) and evidence in general; and

(d) take appropriate action, including determining the possible effect on the assurance conclusion in the assurance report.

78. If the representations remain inconsistent with other evidence, the assurance practitioner shall reconsider the assessment of the competence, integrity, ethical values, or diligence of the responsible party or of its commitment to an enforcement of these, and shall determine the effect that this may have on the reliability of representations (oral or written) and evidence in general.

79. If the responsible party does not provide such written representations, or refuses to provide them, the assurance practitioner shall qualify or disclaim the conclusion in the assurance report, based on a limitation on the scope of the engagement.

Forming the Assurance Conclusion

80. The assurance practitioner shall conclude as to whether the assurance practitioner has obtained the required level of assurance on the financial information, or elements of the financial information. That conclusion shall take into consideration the requirement in paragraph 64 of this ASAE.

81. In forming the conclusion the assurance practitioner shall consider:

(a) the assurance practitioner's conclusion regarding the sufficiency and appropriateness of evidence obtained; and

(b) an evaluation of whether any uncorrected misstatements are material, either individually or in aggregate, to the financial information.

Unmodified Conclusion

82. The assurance practitioner shall express an unmodified conclusion in the assurance report when the assurance practitioner, having obtained sufficient appropriate evidence, concludes that the financial information, or elements of the financial information, do not require material modification.

Emphasis of Matter Paragraph

83. The assurance practitioner shall include an Emphasis of Matter paragraph in the assurance report when the assurance practitioner concludes it is necessary to draw users' attention to a matter disclosed in the financial information or accompanying explanatory notes on the basis that the matter is of such importance that it is fundamental to users' understanding of the financial information.[48] (Ref: Para. A62)

48 The concepts and discussions on the circumstances under which an emphasis of matter is included in an auditor's report are contained in ASA 706 and may be helpful in assisting the assurance practitioner decide if an Emphasis of Matter paragraph is appropriate for an assurance engagement.

Modified Conclusion

84. The assurance practitioner shall, subject to paragraph 85 of this ASAE, express a modified conclusion[49] in the assurance report if:

(a) having obtained sufficient appropriate evidence, the assurance practitioner concludes that the effects, or possible effects, of a matter are material but not pervasive as to require an adverse conclusion or a disclaimer of conclusion, (qualified conclusion);

(b) having obtained sufficient appropriate evidence, the assurance practitioner concludes that misstatements, individually or in the aggregate, are both material and pervasive to the financial information (adverse conclusion); (Ref: Para. 61(b))

(c) the assurance practitioner is unable to obtain sufficient appropriate evidence on which to base an assurance conclusion, and concludes that the possible effects on the financial information of undetected misstatements, if any, could be both material and pervasive (disclaimer of conclusion); or (Ref: Para. A63, A79)

(d) the responsible party has not made the required disclosures, relating to material uncertainties in respect of going concern[50], in the document (a qualified or adverse conclusion, as appropriate).

85. The assurance practitioner shall discuss with the responsible party any conclusion that is intended to be modified prior to preparing the assurance report. If the responsible party does not agree to make the necessary changes to appropriately resolve the matter, the assurance practitioner shall include the modified conclusion in the assurance report and consider any other implications for the engagement. (Ref: Para. A64)

Preparing the Assurance Report

86. The assurance practitioner shall provide a written assurance report to the responsible party containing a clear expression of the assurance practitioner's conclusion on each type of financial information that is the subject of the engagement. (Ref: Para. A65, A67)

87. The assurance practitioner's conclusion shall clearly distinguish and separate each type of financial information from any other types of financial information within the assurance report. (Ref: Para. A66)

88. If the assurance practitioner is required by law or regulation to use a specific layout or wording in the assurance report, the assurance practitioner shall evaluate whether the assurance report is acceptable in the circumstances of the engagement, and if not, whether additional explanation in the assurance practitioner's report can mitigate possible misunderstanding. (Ref: Para. A67)

Consent to the Inclusion of the Assurance Report in a Public Document

(Ref: Para. A69)

89. The assurance practitioner shall consider applicable law or regulation when the assurance practitioner has been requested to provide consent in writing to the responsible party for the inclusion of the assurance report in the document.

90. Where the assurance practitioner considers it inappropriate for the assurance report to be included in the document, consent shall either not be provided, or be revoked prior to the relevant date of the document's release.

Documentation

91. The assurance practitioner shall prepare documentation on a timely basis that is sufficient to enable an experienced assurance practitioner, having no previous connection with the engagement, to understand: (Ref: Para. A70-A71)

(a) the nature, timing and extent of the assurance procedures performed to comply with this ASAE and applicable legal and regulatory requirements;

(b) the results of the procedures performed, and the evidence obtained; and

---

49 See ASA 705 *Modifications to the Opinion in the Independent Auditor's Report*, for further guidance.

50 See ASA 570 for further guidance.

ASAE

(c) significant matters arising during the engagement, the conclusions reached thereon, and significant professional judgements made in reaching those conclusions.

Quality Control

92. The assurance practitioner shall include in the engagement documentation:
   (a) issues identified with respect to compliance with relevant ethical requirements and how they were resolved;
   (b) conclusions on compliance with independence requirements that apply to the engagement, and any relevant discussions within the assurance practitioner's firm that support these conclusions;
   (c) conclusions reached regarding the acceptance and continuance of client relationships and engagements;
   (d) evidence of compliance with applicable systems of quality control requirements within the firm;[51] and
   (e) the nature and scope of, and conclusions resulting from, consultations undertaken during the course of the engagement.

Historical Financial Information

93. This section deals with the additional special consideration in the application of requirements in paragraphs 16 to 92 inclusive of this ASAE when the assurance practitioner is requested to provide assurance on historical financial information prepared by the responsible party in connection with a corporate fundraising. Paragraphs 96 to 104 inclusive of this ASAE deal with additional special considerations when the historical financial information includes pro forma adjustments, resulting in pro forma historical financial information.

Preparing the Assurance Report

94. The assurance practitioner shall not report compliance with this ASAE in the assurance report unless it includes, at a minimum, each of the elements identified in paragraph 95 of this ASAE.

Basic Elements of the Assurance Report

95. The assurance report shall include, at a minimum, the following elements:
   (a) a title that clearly indicates the report is an independent limited or reasonable assurance report;
   (b) an addressee;
   (c) a background section that identifies the purpose of the assurance report, and if applicable, the fact that it will be included in the document;
   (d) a scope section that:
      (i) identifies the entity (entities) whose historical financial information is the subject of the assurance report, and if applicable, the responsible party of the entity;
      (ii) identifies the financial information being reported on, the time period covered; and if applicable;
      (iii) cross reference to, or describes, the source of the financial information and the stated basis of preparation selected by the responsible party in the preparation of the historical financial information; and
      (iv) whether the historical financial information has been previously audited or reviewed and by whom, and the type of conclusion expressed;
   (e) a description of the responsible party's responsibilities, including those set out in paragraph 27(c) of this ASAE;

51 See ASQC 1 *Quality Control for Firms that Perform Audits and Reviews of Financial Reports and Other Financial Information, and Other Assurance Engagements*, for further guidance.

(f) a description of the assurance practitioner's responsibilities, including:

(i) a statement that the engagement was performed in accordance with this ASAE;

(ii) if applicable, a summary of the assurance practitioner's procedures. In the case of a limited assurance engagement, this shall include a statement that the procedures performed in a limited assurance engagement vary in nature from, and are less in extent than for, a reasonable assurance engagement. As a result, the level of assurance obtained in a limited assurance engagement is substantially lower than the assurance that would have been obtained had a reasonable assurance engagement been performed; (Ref: Para. A72-A74)

(iii) if applicable, a statement that the engagement did not include updating or re-issuing any previous audit or review report on financial information used as a source of the historical financial information;

(g) the assurance practitioner's conclusion on the historical financial information:

(i) in a limited assurance engagement:

- if the conclusion is unmodified, that nothing has come to the assurance practitioner's attention that causes the assurance practitioner to believe that the historical financial information [as described in section [X] of the document] is not presented fairly, in all material respects, in accordance with the stated basis of preparation [as described in section [X] of the document or the scope section of this report]; or
- if the conclusion is modified, a clear description of the reasons for the modification in a Basis for Modification qualification paragraph, with the effects appropriately quantified, to the extent reasonably practical, and disclosed in the assurance report; and/or
- where the assurance practitioner has identified material event(s), transaction(s), correction(s), or error(s) outside the entity's ordinary business that in the assurance practitioner's professional judgement require comment, or adjustment to, the historical financial information, but are not adequately addressed in the historical financial information, and/or the document, the assurance practitioner shall include a section covering such material event(s) or transaction(s) and if applicable, their potential impact to the extent it can be reasonably estimated; or

(ii) in a reasonable assurance engagement:

- if the conclusion is unmodified, that the historical financial information is presented fairly, in all material respects, in accordance with the stated basis of preparation, [as described in section [X] of the document or the scope section of this report]; or
- if the conclusion is modified, a clear description of the reasons for the modification in a Basis for Modification qualification paragraph, with the effects appropriately quantified, to the extent reasonably practical, and disclosed in the assurance report; and/or
- where the assurance practitioner has identified material event(s), transaction(s), correction(s), or error(s) outside the entity's ordinary business that in the assurance practitioner's professional judgement require comment, or adjustment to, the historical financial information, but are not adequately addressed in the historical financial information, and/or the document, the assurance practitioner shall include a section covering such material event(s) or transaction(s) and if applicable, their potential impact to the extent it can be reasonably estimated; and

(h) if applicable, an Emphasis of Matter paragraph[52] when the assurance practitioner concludes it is necessary to draw users' attention to a matter disclosed in the historical financial information or accompanying explanatory notes on the basis that the matter is of such importance that it is fundamental to users' understanding of the historical financial information;

(i) a statement that the historical financial information has been prepared for inclusion in the document, and that as a result, the historical financial information may not be suitable for use for another purpose;

(j) a declaration of interest, or disclosure of interest, statement;

(k) if applicable, a consent statement;

(l) if applicable, a liability statement;

(m) the assurance practitioner's signature;

(n) the date of the assurance practitioner's report that shall be the date the assurance practitioner signs the report; and

(o) the assurance practitioner's address.

Pro Forma Historical Financial Information

96. This section deals with additional special considerations in the application of requirements in paragraphs 16 to 92 inclusive of this ASAE, when the assurance practitioner is required to provide assurance on pro forma financial information that is historical. When the assurance practitioner is requested to provide assurance on whether the pro forma financial information has been properly compiled, refer to ASAE 3420 *Assurance Engagements to Report on the Compilation of Pro Forma Historical Financial Information Included in a Prospectus or other Document.* (Ref: Para. A75-A76)

Engagement Acceptance

Preconditions for Acceptance

97. In addition to the requirements in paragraph 24 of this ASAE, the assurance practitioner shall, prior to agreeing the terms of the engagement, obtain agreement from the responsible party that it accepts its responsibility for:

(a) selecting the basis of preparation of the pro forma historical financial information;

(b) selecting the unadjusted historical financial information used as the source for the pro forma historical financial information;

(c) selecting and determining the pro forma adjustments;

(d) complying with the requirements of all applicable laws and regulation;[53] and

(e) preparing pro forma historical financial information in accordance with the stated basis of preparation.

Other Factors Affecting Engagement Acceptance

98. In addition to the requirements in paragraph 25 of this ASAE, the assurance practitioner shall only accept the engagement if the level of assurance to be provided on the pro forma historical financial information is not higher than the level of assurance expressed on the source of the unadjusted historical financial information, if it has been previously audited or reviewed. (Ref: Para. A77)

52 The concepts and discussions on the inclusion of an emphasis of matter paragraph relating to a financial report being prepared in accordance with a special purpose framework are contained in ASA 800 *Special Considerations–Audits of Financial Reports Prepared in Accordance with Special Purpose Frameworks.* It may be helpful in assisting the assurance practitioner preparing an assurance report for an assurance engagement.

53 For example, see RG 228 and RG 230, issued by ASIC, for further guidance.

Understanding the Entity and Its Environment and Identifying and Assessing Risks of Material Misstatement

Obtaining an Understanding of the Entity and Its Environment

99. In addition to the requirements in paragraphs 37 and 38 of this ASAE, the assurance practitioner shall obtain:
   (a) an understanding of the source of the unadjusted historical financial information used in the preparation of the pro forma historical financial information including:
      (i) whether it has been previously audited or reviewed, and
      (ii) if so, if the audit opinion/review conclusion was modified, considering the implications, if any, for the pro forma historical financial information including: (Ref: Para. A78-A79)
         ♦ what appropriate action to take; and
         ♦ whether there is any effect on the assurance practitioner's ability to report in accordance with the terms of the engagement, including any effect on the assurance report; or
      (iii) planning the additional procedures required if the source of the unadjusted historical financial information has not been previously audited or reviewed; and
   (b) in respect of the pro forma adjustments:
      (i) identifying all the pro forma adjustments;
      (ii) understanding the event(s) or transaction(s) that the pro forma adjustments are intending to record; and
      (iii) understanding the methodology used by the responsible party in formulating the pro forma adjustments, including the basis for, and calculations underlying, them.[54]

Overall Responses to Assessed Risks of Material Misstatement and Further Procedures

Assurance Procedures

100. In addition to the requirements in paragraph 52 of this ASAE, the assurance procedures performed on the pro forma historical financial information shall include:
   (a) if the source of the unadjusted historical financial information has not been previously audited or reviewed, such procedures as are necessary, in the assurance practitioner's professional judgement, to obtain sufficient appropriate evidence in relation to that financial information on which to rely for engagement purposes; (Ref: Para. A80)
   (b) if the source of the unadjusted historical financial information has been previously audited or reviewed, such procedures as are necessary, in the assurance practitioner's professional judgement, to obtain sufficient appropriate evidence on which to rely for engagement purposes; (Ref: Para. A81)
   (c) understanding the stated basis of preparation for the pro forma historical financial information;
   (d) understanding the basis for, and calculations underlying, the pro forma adjustments;

54 See RG 230 for further guidance.

(e) determining whether the pro forma adjustments: (Ref: Para. A82-A83)

(i) have been selected and applied to the unadjusted historical financial information by the responsible party in accordance with the stated basis of preparation;

(ii) are supported by sufficient appropriate evidence, and are arithmetically correct;[55] and

(f) determining whether the resultant pro forma historical financial information reflects the results of applying the pro forma adjustments to the unadjusted financial information.

101. If the assurance practitioner is not satisfied that the pro forma adjustments:

(a) have been made in accordance with the stated basis of preparation; and/or

(b) lack sufficient appropriate evidence;

the assurance practitioner shall discuss this with the responsible party, and:

(c) if the responsible party agrees to make a revision of the pro forma adjustments, the assurance practitioner shall request an updated copy of the document in order to ensure the revision has been made; or

(d) if the responsible party refuses to make a required revision to the pro forma adjustments, the assurance practitioner shall consider whether to:

(i) obtain expert advice on the appropriate course of action of the assurance practitioner;

(ii) withdraw consent for the responsible party to include the assurance report in the document; and/or

(iii) withdraw from the engagement, where withdrawal is possible under applicable law or regulation.

Written Representations

102. In addition to the requirements in paragraph 75 of this ASAE, the assurance practitioner shall request the responsible party to include in the written representations an acknowledgement of their responsibility for the matters described in paragraph 97 of this ASAE.

Preparing the Assurance Report

103. The assurance practitioner shall not report compliance with this ASAE in the assurance report unless it includes, at a minimum, each of the elements identified in paragraph 104 of this ASAE.

Basic Elements of the Assurance Report

104. In addition to the requirements in paragraph 95 of this ASAE, the assurance report shall include, at a minimum, the following elements:

(a) statements in the scope section that:

(i) identify the pro forma historical financial information being reported on, including the time period it covers;

(ii) identify whether there has been an audit or review conducted on the source from which the unadjusted historical financial information was prepared; and

(iii) cross reference to, or describe, the stated basis of preparation selected by the responsible party for the pro forma historical financial information; (Ref: Para. A84)

(b) if applicable, a statement that the firm of which the assurance practitioner is a member holds all applicable license(s) and/or other designation(s) required under the *Corporations Act 2001*;

55 See RG 170 and RG 228, for further guidance on the nature of pro forma adjustments.

(c) if applicable, a statement that the engagement did not include updating or re-issuing any previous audit or review report on the unadjusted historical financial information used in the preparation of the pro forma historical financial information;

(d) the assurance practitioner's conclusion on the pro forma historical financial information:

(i) in a limited assurance engagement:

- with an unmodified conclusion, a statement that nothing has come to the assurance practitioner's attention that causes the assurance practitioner to believe that the pro forma historical financial information is not presented fairly, in all material respects, in accordance with the stated basis of preparation being [insert details/cross reference]; or
- with a modified conclusion, a clear description of the reasons for the modification, with the effects appropriately quantified, to the extent reasonably practical, and disclosed in the assurance report; or

(ii) in a reasonable assurance engagement:

- with an unmodified conclusion, a statement that the assurance practitioner believes that the pro forma historical financial information is presented fairly, in all material respects, in accordance with the stated basis of preparation being [insert details/cross reference]; or
- with a modified conclusion, a clear description of the reasons for the modification, with the effects appropriately quantified, to the extent reasonably practical, and disclosed in the assurance report; and

(e) if applicable, a reference to the assurance practitioner's financial services guide.

Prospective Financial Information

105. This section deals with additional special considerations in the application of requirements in paragraphs 16 to 92 inclusive of this ASAE, when the assurance practitioner is requested to provide assurance on prospective financial information prepared by the responsible party based on their assumptions (excluding material hypothetical assumptions). Paragraphs 119 to 127 inclusive of this ASAE deal with the additional special considerations when the prospective financial information includes only hypothetical assumptions, or a mixture of assumptions and material hypothetical assumptions, resulting in a projection that is for inclusion in a non-public document. Paragraphs 128 to 136 inclusive of this ASAE deal with the additional special considerations when the prospective financial information includes pro forma adjustments, resulting in a pro forma forecast.

Assurance Engagement Acceptance

Preconditions for Acceptance

106. In addition to the requirements in paragraph 24 of this ASAE, the assurance practitioner shall, prior to agreeing the terms of the engagement, obtain agreement from the responsible party that they:

(a) understand and accept the type of assurance to be expressed on each of the three different elements of the prospective financial information; and (Ref: Para. A85-A86)

(b) acknowledge and understand their responsibility for the preparation of the prospective financial information:

(i) in accordance with the stated basis of preparation; and

(ii) based on assumptions selected by the responsible party that:[56]

- provide reasonable grounds[57] for the preparation of the prospective financial information, if it is to be included in a public document; or
- are clearly realistic for the preparation of the prospective financial information, if it is to be included in a non-public document;
- are not misleading or deceptive, having regard to applicable law and regulation.[58]

Other Factors Affecting Engagement Acceptance

107. In addition to the requirements in paragraph 25 of this ASAE, the assurance practitioner shall accept the engagement only when:

(a) on the basis of preliminary knowledge of the assurance engagement circumstances, nothing has come to the assurance practitioner's attention to indicate that:

(i) if the prospective financial information is to be included in a public document, it has been prepared based on:

- assumptions that do not have reasonable grounds; (Ref: Para. A87) and/or
- material hypothetical assumptions; or

(ii) if the prospective financial information is to be included in a non-public document, it has been prepared based on assumptions that are clearly unrealistic;

(iii) any historical financial information used as a source for the prospective financial information and that is material to such prospective financial information:

- has not been previously audited or reviewed, and
- is not planned to be reviewed as part of the engagement; (Ref: Para. A88)

(b) the prospective financial information will be inappropriate for its intended use;

(c) the preconditions for the engagement, as stated in paragraph 106 of this ASAE, are present; and (Ref: Para. A89)

(d) the type(s) of assurance required on different elements of the prospective financial information by the responsible party is acceptable to the assurance practitioner.

Understanding the Entity and Its Environment and Identifying and Assessing Risks of Material Misstatement

Obtaining an Understanding of the Entity and its Environment

108. In addition to the requirements in paragraphs 37 and 38 of this ASAE, the assurance practitioner shall, at the minimum, obtain an understanding of:

(a) whether the prospective financial information is a forecast, a projection, or a pro forma forecast;

(b) the stated basis of preparation chosen by the responsible party including:

(i) its relevance, completeness, reliability, and understandability; and

(ii) any differences between the basis and that used in the most recent audited or reviewed historical financial information;

56 See ASA 540 *Auditing Accounting Estimates, Including Fair Value Accounting Estimates, and Related Disclosures,* for further guidance on assessing the reasonableness of assumptions.

57 See paragraph 14(aa) of this ASAE for the definition. What constitutes "reasonable grounds" for preparation depends on the specific circumstances of the assurance engagement, but ordinarily does not include material hypothetical assumptions. Where the prospective financial information is intended to be included in a public document, see RG 170 for further guidance.

58 In relation to public documents, see section 728 or section 769C of the *Corporations Act 2001,* and RG 170.

(c) the accuracy of any forecast(s) prepared in prior time periods, and the reasons for any material variances;

(d) whether comparative information is to be included in the document, and whether it will be restated;

(e) relevant financial information available in the public domain; and

(f) key expectations and relationships in the prospective financial information for use when designing and performing analytical procedures.

Overall Responses to Assessed Risks of Material Misstatement and Further Procedures

Assurance Procedures

Source of the Prospective Financial Information

109. In addition to the requirements in paragraph 52 of this ASAE, the assurance practitioner's procedures to determine whether the responsible party has extracted the source of the prospective financial information from an appropriate source shall include:

(a) making relevant enquiries of the responsible party, other experts and relevant parties on the nature of the source of the prospective financial information;

(b) if the source of the prospective financial information includes material historical financial information which has been previously audited or reviewed:

(i) reading the historical financial information to which the audit or review report relates to establish if its stated basis of preparation and time frame covered are acceptable; and

(ii) requesting, and obtaining, a copy of the audit or review report accompanying the historical financial information and, if obtained, reading it to assess whether:

- the audit or review report was modified, and if so, why, and the impact, if any, on the engagement; and
- there are any matters that may affect the prospective financial information; and/or

(iii) if applicable, in a reasonable assurance engagement:

- contacting the other assurance practitioner to obtain access to the audit working papers supporting the audit or review on the historical financial information and evaluating the extent of evidence, if any, provided by the results of that prior audit or review;
- designing and performing further procedures on the historical financial information in order to obtain further evidence of the adequacy, relevance and reliability of the historical financial information to be used as evidence, including:
  - ◊ agreeing or reconciling some or all the historical financial information with supporting records;
  - ◊ re-performing audit tests of material account balances;
  - ◊ evaluating the adequacy and reliability of the historical financial information as a source of the prospective financial information; and
- comparing the source with the corresponding prior period financial information and, as applicable, the immediately preceding annual or interim historical financial information, and discussing any significant changes with the responsible party;

(c) if the source of the prospective financial information includes material historical financial information which has not been previously audited or reviewed, or is a forecast, the assurance practitioner shall perform assurance procedures to be satisfied that the source is appropriate, including: (Ref: Para. A90)

ASAE

(i) ascertaining whether the assurance practitioner is able to access all required documentation describing and supporting the source;

(ii) enquiring of the responsible party about:

- the process by which the source has been prepared and the reliability of its underlying accounting records;
- whether all transactions for the time period have been recorded;
- identifying the stated basis of preparation of the source;
- whether the source has been prepared in accordance with the entity's accounting policies and stated basis of preparation;
- whether there have been any changes in accounting policies from that adopted in the most recent audited or reviewed financial statements and, if so, how such changes have been dealt with;
- their assessment of the risk that the source may be materially misstated as a result of error or fraud;
- how recently the entity's historical financial information was audited or reviewed;
- whether there has been any changes in the entity's business activities and operations, and if so, their effect on the source; and
- the extent to which statistical and mathematical modelling, computer-assisted techniques and other techniques have been used in the preparation of the prospective financial information, and the reliability of those techniques; and

(iii) if the assurance practitioner has audited or reviewed the immediately preceding annual or interim historical financial information, considering the findings and whether these might indicate any issues with the preparation of the source from which the historical financial information has been extracted; and/or

(iv) if applicable, in a reasonable assurance engagement:

- corroborating the information provided by the responsible party in response to the assurance practitioner's enquiries when the responses appear inconsistent with the assurance practitioner's understanding of the entity, the prospective financial information, or engagement circumstances:
- agreeing or reconciling some or all the financial information with supporting records;
- performing selected audit tests of material account balances within the financial information; and
- comparing the source with the corresponding prior period financial information and, as applicable, the immediately preceding annual or interim financial information, and discussing significant changes with the responsible party;

(d) evaluating the adequacy and reliability of the financial information as a source of the prospective financial information;

(e) evaluating the accuracy of any prospective financial information prepared in prior time periods as compared to actual financial results, and the reasons provided for significant variances; and

(f) ensuring the source of the prospective financial information reflects any changes made to the stated basis of preparation from the prior audited or reviewed period, and if so:

(i) determining the nature of, and reasons for, the changes and their effect on the prospective financial information;

(ii) evaluating whether there have been any reclassifications or adjustments made by the responsible party to reflect unusual or non-recurring items, or to correct known errors and uncertainties; and

(iii) evaluating any differences between the basis of preparation of the prospective financial information and that of other financial information included in the document.

110. If the assurance practitioner is not able to perform the procedures in paragraph 109 of this ASAE in order to assess whether the source of the prospective financial information is appropriate, the assurance practitioner shall consider the implications for the engagement and the assurance report.

Assumptions

111. The assurance practitioner's assurance procedures on the assumptions shall include:

(a) reading the most recent audited or reviewed financial report, and, if appropriate, the most recently prepared annual or interim financial information, to enable the assessment of the assumptions used in the preparation of the prospective financial information;

(b) enquiry of the responsible party of:

(i) the source, degree of reliability, uncertainty, verifiability, and validity of the assumptions, including whether the assumptions are objectively reasonable;

(ii) the time period the assumptions cover;

(iii) the methodology used in their development and quantification, including the extent to which they are affected by the responsible party's judgement;

(iv) the likelihood of the assumptions actually occurring; (Ref: Para. A91)

(v) whether the assumptions have a wide range of possibilities, or their outcomes are particularly sensitive to fluctuations, and if so, the effect on the prospective financial information of such sensitivities; and/or

(vi) whether any hypothetical assumptions are included, and if so, their materiality to the prospective financial information;

(c) evaluating whether all material assumptions required for the preparation of the prospective financial information have been identified;

(d) determining whether the assumptions used in the preparation of the prospective financial information are consistent with the stated basis of preparation;

(e) determining whether the assumptions are arithmetically correct;

(f) obtaining appropriate evidence to support all material assumptions;

(g) evaluating whether the assumptions are within the entity's capacity to achieve in light of the assurance practitioner's understanding of the prospective financial information;

(h) performing, or reviewing the responsible party's sensitivity analysis to test the responsiveness, or otherwise, of the prospective financial information to material changes in key assumptions underlying that prospective financial information; and

(i) considering the responsible party's reliance on the work of experts in relation to the assumptions.

112. If the responsible party's assumptions on which the prospective financial information has been prepared lack supporting evidence, and are determined by the assurance practitioner not to have reasonable grounds, the assurance practitioner shall consider such assumptions to be hypothetical and shall determine the implications for the engagement and the assurance report, taking into account any applicable law or regulation.[59]

59 See RG 170, for further guidance.

Prospective Financial Information prepared in accordance with the Stated Basis of Preparation and Assumptions

113. The assurance practitioner's assurance procedures to ascertain if the prospective financial information has been prepared in accordance with the stated basis of preparation and the assumptions shall include:

(a) evaluating the chosen stated basis of preparation; (Ref: Para. A92)

(b) assessing whether the stated basis of preparation described in the financial information section of the document is consistent with the assurance practitioner's understanding;

(c) making clerical checks such as re-computations and reviewing internal consistency of assumptions including those with common variables (that is, the actions the responsible party intends to take are compatible with each other and there are no inconsistences in the determination of the amounts that are based on common variables, such as interest rates);

(d) ensuring the prospective financial information reflects any changes made to the stated basis of preparation from the previously audited or reviewed financial report included in the document;

(e) considering the interrelationships of elements within the prospective financial information;

(f) agreeing or reconciling the assumptions included to the stated basis of preparation;

(g) obtaining through enquiry of the responsible party, an understanding of all material assumptions and considering whether any other procedures are necessary in the circumstances; and/or

(h) if applicable, in a reasonable assurance engagement:

(i) performing consistency checks in the application of the stated basis of preparation to the prospective financial information;

(ii) performing test checks of items within the prospective financial information to ensure they have been prepared in accordance with the assumptions; and

(iii) obtaining evidence to support an assessment of whether any uncorrected misstatements or adjustments are material, individually or in aggregate, to the prospective financial information.

Prospective Financial Information Itself

114. The assurance practitioner's assurance procedures on the prospective financial information itself shall include:

(a) evaluating the length of time covered by the prospective financial information, taking into account that information ordinarily becomes more speculative and less verifiable as the length of the period covered increases,[60] and by:

(i) enquiring of the responsible party the reasons for the choice of time period;

(ii) considering whether the time period is consistent with the entity's normal reporting period and operating cycle so as to make it comparable to any previously issued historical financial information; and

(iii) considering whether any elapsed portion of the current time period is included in the prospective financial information;

(b) evaluating the type of business conducted by the entity, the assumptions included in the prospective financial information, and consequently the assessed volatility of the overall prospective financial information;

60 For example, see ASIC's RG 170 for guidance regarding what timeframe ASIC considers is reasonable for the inclusion of prospective financial information.

(c) assessing the accuracy of any prospective financial information prepared in prior time periods as compared to actual financial results and obtaining and assessing the responsible party's reasons for any significant variances; and

(d) assessing whether the prospective financial information is prepared on a reasonable basis, based on evidence obtained throughout the engagement.

Written Representations

115. In addition to the requirements in paragraph 75 of this ASAE, the assurance practitioner shall request the responsible party to include in written representations confirmation:

(a) of the completeness of all material assumptions used in the preparation of the prospective financial information; and

(b) that the material assumptions remain appropriate, even if the underlying information has been accumulated over a period of time.

Forming the Assurance Conclusion

Unmodified Conclusion

116. The assurance practitioner shall express an unmodified conclusion in the assurance report on each element of the prospective financial information when the assurance practitioner concludes:

(a) with limited assurance on each of the different elements of the prospective financial information, that based on the procedures performed, nothing has come to the assurance practitioner's attention that causes the assurance practitioner to believe that:

(i) the assumptions used in the preparation of the prospective financial information, as described in section [X] of the document, do not provide reasonable grounds for the preparation of the prospective financial information;

(ii) in all material respects, the prospective financial information:

- is not prepared on the basis of the assumptions as described in section [X] of the document; and
- is not presented fairly in accordance with the stated basis of preparation as described in section [X] of the document; and

(iii) the prospective financial information itself is unreasonable; or

(b) with a combination of limited or reasonable assurance on each of the different elements of the prospective financial information, that based on the procedures performed:

(i) nothing has come to the assurance practitioner's attention that causes the assurance practitioner to believe that the assumptions used in the preparation of the prospective financial information do not provide reasonable grounds for the prospective financial information;

(ii) in all material respects, the prospective financial information:

- is not prepared on the basis of the assumptions as described in section [X] of the document; and
- is not presented fairly in accordance with the stated basis of preparation as described in section [X] of the document; and

(iii) nothing has come to the assurance practitioner's attention that causes the assurance practitioner to believe that the prospective financial information is itself unreasonable.

Preparing the Assurance Report

117. The assurance practitioner shall not report compliance with this ASAE in the assurance report unless it includes, at a minimum, each of the elements identified in paragraph 118 of this ASAE.

Basic Elements of the Assurance Report

118. The assurance report shall include, at a minimum, the following elements:

(a) a title that clearly indicates the report is an independent assurance report;

(b) an addressee;

(c) a background section that identifies the purpose of the assurance report, and if applicable, the fact that it will be included in the document;

(d) statements in the scope section that:

(i) identify the entity (entities) whose prospective financial information is the subject of the assurance report and if applicable, the responsible party;

(ii) identify the source of the prospective financial information being reported on, its purpose, the time period covered, and if applicable, a statement that the prospective financial information has been prepared for inclusion in the document, and that as a result, the prospective financial information may not be suitable for another purpose;

(iii) cross reference to, or describe the stated basis of preparation selected by the responsible party in the preparation of the prospective financial information; and

(iv) if applicable, states that the firm which the assurance practitioner is a member of holds all applicable license(s) and/or other designation(s) required under the *Corporations Act 2001*;

(e) a description of the responsible party's responsibilities, including those set out in paragraph 27(c) of this ASAE;

(f) a description of the assurance practitioner's responsibilities, including:

(i) a statement that the engagement was performed in accordance with this ASAE;

(ii) if applicable, a summary of the assurance practitioner's procedures. In a limited assurance engagement, this shall include a statement "that the procedures performed in a limited assurance engagement vary in nature from, and are less in extent than for, a reasonable assurance engagement. As a result, the level of assurance obtained in a limited assurance engagement is substantially lower than the assurance that would have been obtained had a reasonable assurance engagement been performed"; (Ref: Para. A93-A95)

(iii) if applicable, a statement that the engagement did not include updating or re-issuing any previous audit or review report on the financial information used as the source of the prospective financial information;

(g) statements that:

(i) actual results are likely to be different from the prospective financial information since anticipated event(s) or transaction(s) frequently do not occur as expected and the variation could be material;

(ii) disclaim the assurance practitioner's responsibility for the achievability of the results indicated by the prospective financial information; and

(iii) if applicable, clearly identify any hypothetical assumptions[61] in the prospective financial information and confirm that they have no significant impact upon the forecast outcome;

61 See RG 170.

(h) the assurance practitioner's assurance conclusion on the different elements of the prospective financial information:

 (i) with limited assurance and an unmodified conclusion, that nothing has come to the assurance practitioner's attention that causes the assurance practitioner to believe:

  - that the assumptions used in the preparation of the prospective financial information do not provide reasonable grounds for the preparation of the prospective financial information;
  - in all material respects, that the prospective financial information is not properly prepared on the basis of the assumptions as described in section [X] of the document, and is not presented fairly in accordance with the stated basis of preparation as described in section [X] of the document]; and
  - the prospective financial information itself is unreasonable; or

 (ii) with limited assurance and a modified conclusion, a clear description of the reasons for the modification, with the effects appropriately quantified, to the extent reasonably practical, and disclosed in the assurance report; or

 (iii) with a combination of limited and reasonable assurance on each of the different elements of the prospective financial information:

  - limited assurance that nothing has come to the assurance practitioner's attention that causes the assurance practitioner to believe that the assumptions do not provide reasonable grounds for the preparation of the prospective financial information;
  - reasonable assurance that in all material respects, the prospective financial information is prepared on the basis of the assumptions as described in section [X] of the document; and is presented fairly in accordance with the stated basis of preparation as described in section [X] of the document; and
  - limited assurance that nothing has come to the assurance practitioner's attention that causes the assurance practitioner to believe the prospective financial information itself is unreasonable; or

 (iv) with both reasonable or limited assurance on each of the different elements of the prospective financial information, and part of the conclusion is modified, a clear description of the reasons for the modification, with the effects appropriately quantified, to the extent reasonably practical, and disclosed in the assurance report;

(i) if applicable, an Emphasis of Matter paragraph[62] when the assurance practitioner concludes it is necessary to draw users' attention to a matter disclosed in the prospective financial information or accompanying explanatory notes on the basis that the matter is of such importance that it is fundamental to users' understanding of the prospective financial information;

(j) a statement that the prospective financial information has been prepared for inclusion in the document and that as a result, the prospective financial information may not be suitable for use for another purpose;

(k) where the assurance practitioner has become aware of material event(s), transaction(s), correction(s), or error(s) that in the assurance practitioner's professional judgement require comment, or adjustment to, the prospective financial information, but that are not adequately addressed in the prospective financial information and/or offering document, the assurance practitioner shall

---

62 The concepts and discussions on the inclusion of an emphasis of matter paragraph relating to a financial report being prepared in accordance with a special purpose framework are contained in ASA 800 *Special Considerations–Audits of Financial Reports Prepared in Accordance with Special Purpose Frameworks*. It may be helpful in assisting the assurance practitioner preparing an assurance report for an assurance engagement.

ASAE

include a section covering such material event(s), transaction(s), correction(s), or error(s) and if applicable, their potential impact to the extent it can be reasonably estimated;

(l) a declaration of interest, or disclosure of interest, statement;

(m) if applicable, a consent statement;

(n) if applicable, a liability statement;

(o) if applicable, a reference to the assurance practitioner's financial services guide;

(p) the assurance practitioner's signature;

(q) the date of the assurance practitioner's report that shall be the date the assurance practitioner signs the report; and

(r) the assurance practitioner's address.

Projection

119. This section deals with the additional special considerations in the application of requirements in paragraphs 16 to 92 inclusive of this ASAE, when the assurance practitioner is required to provide assurance on prospective financial information that includes only hypothetical assumptions, or a mixture of assumptions and material hypothetical assumptions, resulting in a projection. Such a projection is only for inclusion in a non-public document.[63]

Assurance Engagement Acceptance

Preconditions for Acceptance

120. In addition to the requirements in paragraph 106 of this ASAE, the assurance practitioner shall, prior to agreeing the terms of the engagement, obtain agreement from the responsible party that they:

(a) understand and accept that the assurance practitioner will not express any assurance on any hypothetical assumptions included in the projection; (Ref: Para. A96)

(b) acknowledge and understand their responsibility for the preparation of the projection:

(i) for an intended use that is not for inclusion in a public document;

(ii) in selecting, determining and disclosing the assumptions and hypothetical assumptions underlying the projection and their stated basis of preparation;

(iii) based on hypothetical assumptions selected by the responsible party that are clearly realistic for the preparation of the projection;

(iv) that takes into consideration all material implications for the assumptions and hypothetical assumptions used; and

(v) that clearly identifies and differentiates any hypothetical assumptions from other assumptions used.

Other Factors Affecting Engagement Acceptance

121. In addition to the requirements in paragraph 107 of this ASAE, the assurance practitioner shall accept the engagement only when:

(a) on the basis of preliminary knowledge of the engagement circumstances:

(i) nothing has come to the assurance practitioner's attention to indicate that the projection is prepared based on material hypothetical assumptions that are clearly unrealistic and/or inconsistent with the stated purpose of the projection; and

(ii) the assurance practitioner considers that the intended users are able to understand that the stated basis of preparation for the projection includes hypothetical assumptions, and that these assumptions relate to future events

63 See RG 170 for further information.

and management actions that may not necessarily be expected to take place, or that may be expected to take place and may not be based on reasonable grounds; and

(b) the preconditions for the engagement, as stated in paragraph 120 of this ASAE, are present.

Understanding the Entity and Its Environment and Identifying and Assessing Risks of Material Misstatement

Obtaining an Understanding of the Entity and Its Environment

122. In addition to the requirements in paragraph 36 and 37 of this ASAE, the assurance practitioner shall obtain an understanding of:

(a) the assumptions used including:

(i) the use of, and materiality of, hypothetical assumptions within the projection;

(ii) understanding the basis for, and calculations underlying, all material assumptions and hypothetical assumptions used in preparing the projection;

(b) the stated basis of preparation chosen by the responsible party including:

(i) its relevance, completeness, reliability, and understandability; and

(ii) any differences between the basis and that used in the most recent audited or reviewed historical financial information;

(c) the accuracy of any projection(s) prepared in prior time periods, and the reasons for any material variances;

(d) whether comparative information is to be included in the document, and whether it will be restated;

(e) relevant financial information available in the public domain; and

(f) key expectations and relationships in the projection for use when designing and performing analytical procedures.

Overall Responses to Assessed Risks of Material Misstatement and Further Procedures

Assurance Procedures

Hypothetical Assumptions

123. In addition to the requirements in paragraphs 109 to 114 inclusive of this ASAE, the assurance procedures performed on assumptions that are hypothetical shall include: (Ref: Para. A97)

(a) enquiry of the responsible party of:

(i) the source, degree of reliability, uncertainty, and validity of the assumptions including whether the assumptions are objectively reasonable;

(ii) the time period the hypothetical assumptions cover;

(iii) the methodology used in their development and quantification, including the extent to which they are affected by the responsible party's judgement;

(iv) the likelihood of the hypothetical assumptions actually occurring;

(v) whether the hypothetical assumptions have a wide range of possibilities, or their outcomes are particularly sensitive to fluctuations, and if so, the effect on the projection of such sensitivities; and

(vi) of the materiality of hypothetical assumptions to the projection;

(b) determining whether material hypothetical assumptions are:

(i) arithmetically correct;

(ii) consistent with the stated basis of preparation of the projection;

(iii) consistent with the purpose of the projection;

(c) evaluating whether all material hypothetical assumptions are within the entity's capacity to achieve in light of the assurance practitioner's understanding of the projection;

(d) evaluating whether all significant implications of the hypothetical assumptions have been taken into consideration by the responsible party;

(e) if applicable, considering the responsible party's reliance on the work of experts in relation to the projection, or the hypothetical assumptions underlying it; and

(f) evaluating whether anything has come to the assurance practitioner's attention during the engagement that causes the assurance practitioner to believe that any of the material hypothetical assumptions are clearly unrealistic;

(g) performing, or reviewing the responsible party's sensitivity analysis to test the responsiveness, or otherwise, of the projection to material changes in key hypothetical assumptions underlying that projection; and

(h) considering whether anything has come to the assurance practitioner's attention that may result in the intended users of the projection being misled by the inclusion of hypothetical assumptions.

Projection Itself

124. The assurance practitioner's assurance procedures on the projection itself shall include evaluating whether the projection reflects all assumptions and hypothetical assumptions, consistent with the stated basis of preparation.

Written Representations

125. In addition to the requirements in paragraph 115 of this ASAE, the assurance practitioner shall request the responsible party to include in the written representations an acknowledgement of their responsibilities for the matters described in paragraph 120 of this ASAE.

Preparing the Assurance Report

126. The assurance practitioner shall not report compliance with this ASAE in the assurance report unless it includes, at a minimum, each of the elements identified in paragraph 127 of this ASAE.

Basic Elements of the Assurance Report

127. In addition to the requirements in paragraph 118 of this ASAE, the assurance report shall include, at a minimum, the following elements:

(a) statements in the scope section that:

(i) identify the projection being reported on, its purpose, the time period covered, and if applicable, a statement that the projection has been prepared for inclusion in the document, and that as a result, the projection may not be suitable for another purpose;

(ii) cross reference to, or describe the stated basis of preparation selected by the responsible party for the projection; (Ref: Para. A98)

(b) the assurance practitioner's assurance conclusion on the different elements of a projection that includes both assumptions and hypothetical assumptions:

(i) with limited assurance and an unmodified conclusion, that nothing has come to the assurance practitioner's attention that causes the assurance practitioner to believe:

- that the assumptions do not provide reasonable grounds for the preparation of the projection, giving the occurrence of hypothetical assumptions;
- in all material respects, that the projection is not properly prepared on the basis of the assumptions and the hypothetical assumptions as described in section [X] of the document; and is not presented

fairly in accordance with the stated basis of preparation as described in section [X] of the document; and

- the projection itself is unreasonable; or

(ii) with limited assurance and a modified conclusion, a clear description of the reasons for the modification, with the effects appropriately quantified, to the extent reasonably practical, and disclosed in the assurance report; or

(iii) with a combination of limited and reasonable assurance on each of the different elements of the projection:

- limited assurance that nothing has come to the assurance practitioner's attention that causes the assurance practitioner to believe the assumptions do not provide reasonable grounds for the preparation of the projection giving the occurrence of hypothetical assumptions;
- reasonable assurance that in all material respects, the projection is prepared on the basis of the assumptions as described in section [X] of the document; and is presented fairly in accordance with the stated basis of preparation as described in section [X] of the document; and
- limited assurance that nothing has come to the assurance practitioner's attention that causes the assurance practitioner to believe the projection itself is unreasonable; or
- with both reasonable and limited assurance on each of the different elements of the projection, and part of the conclusion is modified, a clear description of the reasons for the modification, with the effects appropriately quantified, to the extent reasonably practical, and disclosed in the assurance report; or

(c) the assurance practitioner's assurance conclusion on the different elements of a projection that includes only hypothetical assumptions:

(i) with limited assurance and an unmodified conclusion, that nothing has come to the assurance practitioner's attention that causes the assurance practitioner to believe:

- in all material respects, that the projection is not properly prepared on the basis of the hypothetical assumptions as described in section [X] of the document; and is not presented fairly in accordance with the stated basis of preparation as described in section [X] of the document; and
- the projection itself is unreasonable; or

(ii) with limited assurance and a modified conclusion, a clear description of the reasons for the modification, with the effects appropriately quantified, to the extent reasonably practical, and disclosed in the assurance report; or

(iii) with a combination of limited and reasonable assurance on each of the different elements of the projection:

- reasonable assurance that in all material respects, the projection is prepared on the basis of the hypothetical assumptions as described in section [X] of the document; and is presented fairly in accordance with the stated basis of preparation as described in section [X] of the document; and
- limited assurance that nothing has come to the assurance practitioner's attention that causes the assurance practitioner to believe the projection itself is unreasonable; or
- with both reasonable and limited assurance on each of the different elements of the projection, and part of the conclusion is modified, a clear description of the reasons for the modification, with the effects appropriately quantified, to the extent reasonably practical, and disclosed in the assurance report.

Pro Forma Forecast

128. This section deals with the additional special considerations in the application of requirements in paragraphs 16 to 92 inclusive of this ASAE, when the assurance practitioner is required to provide assurance on prospective financial information in the form of a pro forma forecast.

Assurance Engagement Acceptance

Preconditions for Acceptance

129. In addition to the requirements in paragraph 106 of this ASAE, the assurance practitioner shall obtain agreement from the responsible party that they acknowledge and understand their responsibility for:
   (a) selecting the basis of preparation of the pro forma forecast;
   (b) selecting the unadjusted forecast financial information used as the source of the pro forma forecast;
   (c) selecting and determining the pro forma adjustments; preparing the pro forma forecast in accordance with the stated basis of preparation.

Other Factors Affecting Engagement Acceptance

130. In addition to the requirements in paragraph 107 of this ASAE, the assurance practitioner shall only accept the engagement if the level of assurance to be provided on the pro forma forecast is not higher than the level of assurance expressed on the source of the unadjusted financial information, in circumstances where it has been previously audited or reviewed. (Ref: Para. A99)

Understanding the Entity and Its Environment and Identifying and Assessing Risks of Material Misstatement

Obtaining an Understanding of the Entity and Its Environment

131. In addition to the requirements in paragraphs 37 and 38 of this ASAE, the assurance practitioner shall obtain:
   (a) an understanding of the source of the unadjusted financial information used in the preparation of the pro forma forecast including:
      (i) whether it has been previously audited or reviewed; and
      (ii) if the audit opinion/review conclusion was modified, considering the implications, if any for the pro forma forecast; including:
         - what appropriate action to take; (Ref: Para. A100-A101) and
         - whether there is any effect on the assurance practitioner's ability to report in accordance with the terms of the engagement, including any effect on the assurance report; or
      (iii) planning the additional procedures required if the source of the unadjusted financial information has not been previously audited or reviewed;
   (b) an understanding of the stated basis of preparation for the pro forma forecast;
   (c) an understanding of the pro forma adjustments:
      (i) identifying all the adjustments made that have been made and the event(s) or transaction(s) the effects of which they intend to record;
      (ii) an understanding of the event(s) or transaction(s) that the pro forma adjustments are intending to record; and
      (iii) understanding the methodology used by the responsible party in formulating the pro forma adjustments, including the basis for, and calculations underlying them;[64]
   (d) an understanding of any recent key changes in the entity's business activities, and how they affect the pro forma forecast;

64 See RG 230 for further guidance.

(e) an understanding of whether experts[65] are required to be used for the assurance engagement for:
  (i) evaluating pro forma adjustments, including whether they were prepared in accordance with the stated basis of preparation;
  (ii) evaluating the suitability of the stated basis of preparation; and
  (iii) assessing the impact of any contractual requirements on the pro forma forecast.

Overall Responses to Assessed Risks of Material Misstatement and Further Procedures

Assurance Procedures

132. In addition to the requirements in paragraphs 109 to 114 inclusive of this ASAE, the assurance procedures performed on the pro forma forecast shall include:
  (a) if the source of the unadjusted financial information has not been previously audited or reviewed, such procedures as are necessary, in the assurance practitioner's professional judgement, to obtain sufficient appropriate evidence in relation to that financial information on which to rely for engagement purposes; (Ref: Para. A102)
  (b) if the source of the unadjusted historical financial information has been previously audited or reviewed, such procedures as are necessary, in the assurance practitioner's professional judgement, to obtain sufficient appropriate evidence on which to rely for engagement purposes; (Ref: Para. A103)
  (c) determining whether the pro forma adjustments: (Ref: Para. A104-A105)
    (i) are directly attributable to the event(s) or transaction(s) requiring the preparation of the pro forma forecast;
    (ii) have been selected and applied by the responsible party on a basis consistent with the stated basis of preparation;
    (iii) are supported by sufficient appropriate evidence, and are arithmetically correct;[66]
    (iv) reflect the planned event(s) or transaction(s) in the time period in which they are expected to occur; and
  (d) determining whether the resultant pro forma forecast reflects the results of applying the pro forma adjustments to the unadjusted financial information.

133. If the assurance practitioner is not satisfied that the pro forma adjustments:
  (a) have been made in accordance with the stated basis of preparation, and/or
  (b) lack sufficient appropriate evidence;

  the assurance practitioner shall discuss this with the responsible party, and:
  (c) if the responsible party agrees to make a revision of the pro forma adjustments, the assurance practitioner shall request an updated copy of the document in order to ensure the revision has been made; or
  (d) if the responsible party refuses to make the required revision to the pro forma adjustments, the assurance practitioner shall consider whether to:
    (i) obtain expert advice on the appropriate course of action of the assurance practitioner;
    (ii) withdraw consent for the responsible party to include the assurance report in the document; and/or
    (iii) withdraw from the engagement, where withdrawal is possible under applicable law or regulation.

---

65 The concepts and discussions on placing reliance on the work of another auditor relevant to an audit engagement are contained in ASA 620 which may be useful to assurance practitioners when determining the extent, if any, of such reliance in the conduct of an assurance engagement.

66 See RG 170 and RG 228 for further guidance on the nature of pro forma adjustments.

Written Representations

134. In addition to the requirements in paragraph 115 of this ASAE, the assurance practitioner shall request the responsible party to include in the written representations an acknowledgement of their responsibilities for the matters described in paragraph 129 of this ASAE.

Preparing the Assurance Report

135. The assurance practitioner shall not report compliance with this ASAE in the assurance report unless it includes, at a minimum, each of the elements identified in paragraph 136 of this ASAE.

Basic Elements of the Assurance Report

136. In addition to the requirements in paragraph 118 of this ASAE, the assurance report shall include, at a minimum, the following elements:

(a) statements in the scope section that:

(i) identify the pro forma forecast being reported on, including the time period covered, and if applicable, a statement that the pro forma forecast has been prepared for inclusion in the document, and that as a result, the pro forma forecast may not be suitable for another purposes;

(ii) if applicable, identify whether there has been an audit or review conducted on the source from which the unadjusted financial information was prepared;

(iii) cross reference to, or describe the stated basis of preparation selected by the responsible party for the pro forma forecast; (Ref: Para. A106)

(b) the assurance practitioner's assurance conclusion on the different elements of the pro forma forecast:

(i) with limited assurance and an unmodified conclusion, that nothing has come to the assurance practitioner's attention that causes the assurance practitioner to believe:

- that the assumptions do not provide reasonable grounds for the pro forma forecast;
- in all material respects, that the pro forma forecast is not properly prepared on the basis of the assumptions as described in section [X] of the document; and is not presented fairly in accordance with the stated basis of preparation as described in section [X] of the document; and
- the pro forma forecast itself is unreasonable; or

(ii) with limited assurance and a modified conclusion, a clear description of the reasons for the modification, with the effects appropriately quantified, to the extent reasonably practical, and disclosed in the assurance report; or

(iii) with a combination of limited and reasonable assurance on each of the different elements of the pro forma forecast:

- limited assurance that nothing has come to the assurance practitioner's attention that causes the assurance practitioner to believe the assumptions do not provide reasonable grounds for the preparation of the pro forma forecast;
- reasonable assurance that in all material respects, the pro forma forecast is prepared on the basis of the assumptions as described in section [X] of the document; and is presented fairly in accordance with the stated basis of preparation as described in section [X] of the document; and
- limited assurance that nothing has come to the assurance practitioner's attention that causes the assurance practitioner to believe the pro forma forecast itself is unreasonable; or

(iv) with both reasonable and limited assurance on each of the different elements of the pro forma forecast, and part of the conclusion is modified, a clear description of the reasons for the modification, with the effects appropriately quantified, to the extent reasonably practical, and disclosed in the assurance report.

❖ ❖ ❖

Application and Other Explanatory Material

Scope of this Standard on Assurance Engagements (Ref: Para. 4)

A1. The assurance practitioner may agree to provide non-assurance services in accordance with the agreed terms of an engagement[67] or may be a member of a firm that is to provide such non-assurance services. Non-assurance services are not within the scope of this ASAE. The assurance practitioner should consider relevant ethical requirements (including independence), and the requirements of applicable law, regulation and professional standards[68] when considering whether they are able to agree to provide such non-assurance services. If non-assurance services are able to be provided, they may be included in a separate engagement letter from the assurance services, or combined into a single engagement letter.

A2. Examples of non-assurance services include:

(a) the preparation and issuance of a Materiality Advice Letter or similar document to an entity's due diligence committee related to the fundraising;

(b) participation in the entity's due diligence committee;[69]

(c) the preparation of taxation information which is to be disclosed in the document and is unrelated to the financial information that is the subject of the assurance engagement;

(d) agreed upon procedures engagements, where no assurance conclusion is expressed (for example, a report of factual findings in respect of subsets of financial information included in the public document or the document; or earnings per share calculations);[70]

(e) comfort letter engagements performed by an assurance practitioner who is also the appointed auditor of the entity;[71] and

(f) accounting services in respect of financial information that is not the subject of the assurance engagement.

Types of Assurance provided in the Engagement (Ref: Para. 9)

A3. Factors to consider include:

(a) the actual type of information, including its source and extent;

(b) the nature and extent of documentation that is known to be available to support the financial information;

(c) whether all, or part, of the financial information has been previously audited or reviewed;

---

67 See *Framework for Assurance Engagements* for further guidance on the elements of an assurance engagement (paragraph 20) and consulting engagements (paragraphs 12-Aus 16.1).

68 See for example APES 110 *Code of Ethics for Professional Accountants* (Reissued December 2010, as amended) issued by the Accounting Professional and Ethical Standards Board for the assurance practitioners professional responsibilities in these circumstances.

69 See APES 350 *Participation by Members in Public Practice in Due Diligence Committees in connection with a Public Document* (March 2011, as amended), issued by the Accounting Professional and Ethical Standards Board for assurance practitioner's professional responsibilities in these circumstances.

70 See ASRS 4400 *Agreed-Upon Procedures Engagements to Report Factual Findings*.

71 See ASRS 4450 *Comfort Letter Engagements*.

ASAE

(d) the nature, purpose and intended users of the financial information; and

(e) the engagement circumstances.

Complying with Standards that are Relevant to the Engagement (Ref: Para. 16)

A4. ASAE 3000 and ASRE 2405 include requirements that apply to relevant assurance engagements. This ASAE includes additional requirements or application and other explanatory material in relation to those topics, as applicable to assurance engagements related to corporate fundraisings or prospective financial information prepared for other purposes.

Inability to Comply with the Requirements of this ASAE or Other AUASB Standards (Ref: Para. 23)

A5. Implications for the engagement may include:

(a) whether to continue to perform the engagement;

(b) issuing a modified conclusion in the assurance report;

(c) refusing to issue the assurance report; or

(d) withdrawing from the engagement, where it is possible under any applicable law or regulation.

The assurance practitioner should discuss the above implications with the responsible party.

Assurance Engagement Acceptance

Preconditions for Acceptance (Ref: Para. 24)

A6. The responsible party is ultimately responsible for the preparation and presentation of all information in the document. The responsible party may engage other experts (for example, tax advisors, business advisors, or legal counsel) who may prepare, assist with the preparation of, or provide independent advice on, the information included in the document, however the responsible party retains responsibility for such information. The only exception to this is in respect of the content of reports prepared by other parties/experts, which are included, by consent, in the document.

A7. If the responsible party is not also the engaging party, the assurance practitioner ordinarily considers the effect this may have on their ability to access records, documentation and other information that may be needed by the assurance practitioner to complete the engagement.

Agreeing on the Terms of the Assurance Engagement

A8. If the responsible party does not agree to sign the engagement letter, the assurance practitioner needs to consider whether it is appropriate to accept the engagement. Such considerations should take into account that applicable law, regulation, or a pre-existing contract may already acknowledge the terms included in the engagement letter, or set out the responsible party's responsibility in sufficient detail, such that the engagement letter is not required. For example, under the *Corporations Act 2001*,[72] the directors of an entity are deemed responsible for the financial information included in a public document used in offering securities. In such circumstances, the assurance practitioner may, using professional judgement, agree to accept the engagement, without requiring the engagement letter be signed. (Ref: Para. 27)

A9. Other terms and conditions that may be included in the agreed terms are: (Ref: Para. 27(d))

(a) a description of assurance procedures to be performed, for example:

(i) analytical review procedures;

(ii) review and consideration of key working papers, accounting records and other documents prepared by the responsible party and other experts;

72 See Section 717 of the *Corporations Act 2001*, for an overview of the procedures for offering securities.

(iii) enquiry of, and discussion with, the responsible party and other experts related to the source and stated basis of preparation used for the historical financial information;

(iv) the examination of, on a test basis, evidence supporting the financial information;

(v) consideration of events up to, and including the date of the assurance report;

(vi) consistency checks of the stated basis of preparation compared to the accounting policies disclosed in the most recent historical financial information also disclosed in the document;

(b) important deadlines/timelines for the completion of the engagement. This may include deadlines such as the expected date of publication of the document and when the assurance practitioner's consent is required;

(c) arrangements regarding the planning and performance of the engagement, including the composition of the engagement team (including any experts); and

(d) arrangements for the assurance practitioner to:

(i) attend meetings such as the due diligence committee meetings (if applicable under the terms of the engagement);[73]

(ii) receive draft and final versions of the document in a timely manner, when requested;

(iii) use the service(s) of the responsible party's experts and/or the assurance practitioner's experts;

(iv) communicate directly with the entity's external auditor and/or other professional advisers regarding matters relevant to the financial information; and

(v) provide consent to the inclusion of the assurance practitioner's assurance report in the document. If the document is a prospectus, prepared in accordance with the *Corporations Act 2001*,[74] the form of the consent must be consistent with how the prospectus is intended to be distributed. For example, entities intending to distribute the prospectus in both electronic and paper forms must also obtain the assurance practitioner's consent to the inclusion of the assurance report in both forms.[75]

A10. Appendix 1 provides an illustrative example engagement letter for an engagement. (Ref: Para. 27)

Changes in the Terms of the Engagement

A11. Examples of when requests from the responsible party to change the terms of the engagement may be received include where there has been a change in circumstances affecting the need for the service, or a misunderstanding of the type or nature of the assurance services to be provided. The assurance practitioner considers the justification for the proposed change, implications for the conduct and reporting of the engagement, as well as any evidence that was obtained prior to the assurance practitioner agreeing to the change. Changes that may be unacceptable to the assurance practitioner include: (Ref: Para. 28)

(a) a change that relates to historical financial information that is incorrect, incomplete or otherwise unsatisfactory;

(b) limiting time available to perform the engagement;

(c) preventing access to all relevant documents or persons requested; and/or

(d) not providing documents when requested, leading to time constraints that make the satisfactory completion of the engagement by the date required unachievable.

---

73 See for example, APES 350, for further guidance.

74 See Section 716 of the *Corporations Act 2001*.

75 See ASIC RG 107 *Electronic Prospectuses*.

A12. It is important that all changes agreed to by the responsible party and the assurance practitioner be documented in writing to ensure no misunderstanding occurs between the parties of what has been agreed. (Ref: Para. 29)

Planning the Engagement

A13. The assurance practitioner uses professional judgement to determine the extent of understanding that it is necessary to obtain of the financial information and other relevant engagement circumstances.[76] (Ref: Para. 31)

Planning Activities

A14. The type of planning activities the assurance practitioner performs depends on the level of understanding of the entity the assurance practitioner has. Such an understanding may have been obtained from prior audit or review engagements performed. This understanding would ordinarily include knowledge of the entity's management skills and resources, and information technology systems (including financial systems). This understanding would need to be updated to ensure it had not changed in the current time period. Note that in certain engagement circumstances, the assurance practitioner may not be able to obtain such an understanding. For example, in a takeover or merger fundraising transaction, the assurance practitioner may not be able to access an entity's financial information, other than that available in the public domain. Hence, the level of understanding will be necessarily more limited, as will the nature of the assurance conclusion. The entity's document is also unlikely to be drafted at the time of engagement planning, so the assurance practitioner's opportunity to gain an understanding of the other information to be included in the document at this stage is ordinarily very limited. (Ref: Para. 32)

A15. The assurance practitioner may decide to discuss elements of planning with the responsible party when determining the scope of the engagement or to facilitate the conduct and management of the engagement (for example, to coordinate some of the planned procedures with the work of the entity's personnel). Although these discussions often occur, the overall engagement strategy and the engagement plan remain the assurance practitioner's responsibility. When discussing matters included in the overall engagement plan, care is needed in order to not compromise the effectiveness of the engagement. For example, discussing the nature, timing and extent of all planned detailed procedures with the entity may compromise the effectiveness of the engagement by making the procedures too predictable. (Ref: Para. 32)

A16. Assurance engagement risk comprises inherent risk, control risk and detection risk and the assurance practitioner considers these risk components in terms of the assurance engagement circumstances; in particular the nature of the financial information and whether a reasonable or limited assurance conclusion is sought. These considerations are then reflected in the extent of the planned procedures to be performed and the evidence-gathering process. (Ref: Para. 32(g))

Materiality in Planning and Performing the Engagement

Determining Materiality when Planning the Engagement (Ref: Para. 33-34)

A17. The concept of materiality ordinarily includes the principles that:

(a) misstatements, including omissions, are considered to be material if they, individually or in the aggregate, could reasonably be expected to influence relevant decisions of users taken on the basis of the financial information;

(b) judgements about materiality are made in light of surrounding circumstances, and are affected by the size or nature of a misstatement, or a combination of both; and

(c) judgements about matters that are material to intended users of the financial information are based on a consideration of the common information needs of intended users as a group. The possible effect of misstatements on specific individual users, whose needs may vary widely, is not considered.

76 The concepts and discussions on complete set of financial statements relevant to an audit engagement are contained in ASA 200, paragraph Aus 13.1, and may be helpful in determining the components of a complete set of financial statements applicable to an assurance engagement.

A18. The assurance practitioner's determination of materiality[77] is a matter of professional judgement, and is affected by:

(a) the assurance practitioner's perception of the common information needs of intended users as a group. In this context, it is reasonable for the assurance practitioner to assume that intended users:

(i) understand that the financial information is prepared and assured to levels of materiality, and have an understanding of any materiality concepts included in the stated basis of preparation;

(ii) understand that the quantification of any prospective financial information involves uncertainties; and

(iii) make reasonable decisions on the basis of the information in the financial information;

(b) whether the stated basis of preparation includes references to materiality. This provides a frame of reference to the assurance practitioner in determining materiality for the engagement. If the stated basis of preparation does not include a discussion of the concept of materiality, the characteristics referred to above provide the assurance practitioner with such a frame of reference;

(c) the engagement circumstances; and

(d) both quantitative and qualitative factors.

It should be noted, however, that decisions regarding materiality are not affected by the level of assurance, that is, materiality for a reasonable assurance engagement is the same as for a limited assurance engagement.

Revision as the Engagement Progresses (Ref: Para. 35)

A19. Materiality may need to be revised as a result of a change in circumstances during the engagement (for example, the disposal of a major part of the entity's business), new information, or a change in the assurance practitioner's understanding of the entity and its operations as a result of performing procedures. For example, it may become apparent during the engagement that accounting estimates used are likely to be substantially different from those included in the financial information used initially to determine materiality. If, during the engagement, the assurance practitioner concludes that a lower materiality for the financial information (and, if applicable, materiality level or levels for particular types of accounts or disclosures within it) is appropriate than that initially determined, it may be necessary to revise performance materiality, and consequently the nature, timing and extent of the further planned procedures.

Understanding the Entity and Its Environment and Identifying and Assessing Risks of Material Misstatement

Obtaining an Understanding of the Entity and Its Environment

Analytical Procedures (Ref: Para. 36(b))

A20. Analytical procedures performed to obtain an understanding of the entity and its environment and to identify and assess risks of material misstatement may identify aspects of the entity of which the assurance practitioner was unaware and may assist in assessing the risks of material misstatement in order to provide a basis for designing and implementing responses to the assessed risks.

A21. Analytical procedures may help identify the existence of unusual events, and amounts, ratios, and trends that might indicate matters that have implications for the engagement. Unusual or unexpected relationships that are identified may assist the assurance practitioner in identifying risks of material misstatement.

A22. However, when such analytical procedures use data aggregated at a high level (which may be the situation with analytical procedures performed to obtain an understanding of the entity and its environment and to identify and assess risks of material misstatement),

77 See ASA 320 for helpful guidance on the concept of materiality. Additionally APES 350 provides further helpful guidance in respect of materiality with respect to capital raisings.

the results of those analytical procedures only provide a broad initial indication about whether a material misstatement may exist. Accordingly, in such cases, consideration of other evidence that has been gathered when identifying the risks of material misstatement together with the results of such analytical procedures may assist the assurance practitioner in understanding and evaluating the results of the analytical procedures.

Observation and Inspection **(Ref: Para. 36(c))**

A23. Observation consists of looking at a process or procedure being performed by others, for example, the assurance practitioner's observation of monitoring devices being calibrated by the entity's personnel, or of the performance of control activities. Observation provides evidence about the performance of a process or procedure, but is limited to the point in time at which the observation takes place, and by the fact that the act of being observed may affect how the process or procedure is performed.

A24. Inspection involves examining records, documents or reports, whether internal or external, in paper form, electronic form, or other media. Inspection of records, documents and reports provides evidence of varying degrees of reliability, depending on their nature and source and, in the case of internal records and documents, on the effectiveness of the controls over their production.

A25. Observation and inspection may support enquiries of management and others, and may also provide information about the entity and its environment. Examples of such procedures include observation or inspection of the following:

(a) The entity's operations.

(b) Relevant documents supporting the financial information.

(c) Reports prepared for management or those charged with governance.

(d) If the entity is relying on the fundraising to ensure its continued going concern in future time periods, the assurance practitioner may request from the entity a copy of the signed underwriting agreement to assist in the assurance practitioner's going concern assessment considerations. Such an agreement may be used as a potential mitigating factor.

Overall Considerations

A26. The assurance practitioner uses professional judgement to determine the extent of the understanding required and of the nature, timing and extent of procedures required to identify and assess risks of material misstatement appropriate to the level of assurance required. The assurance practitioner's primary consideration is whether the understanding that has been obtained and the identification and assessment of risks are sufficient to meet the objective stated in this ASAE. The depth of the understanding that is required by the assurance practitioner is less than that possessed by management in managing the entity, and both the depth of the understanding and the nature, timing and extent of procedures to identify and assess risks of material misstatement are less for a limited assurance engagement than for a reasonable assurance engagement. (Ref: Para. 37)

A27. Relevant industry factors include industry conditions such as the competitive environment, supplier and customer relationships, and technological developments. Examples of matters the assurance practitioner may consider include: (Ref: Para. 37(d))

(a) The market and competition, including demand, capacity, and price competition.

(b) Common business practices within the industry.

(c) Cyclical or seasonal activity.

(d) Product technology relating to the entity's products.

A28. Relevant legal and regulatory factors encompass, among other matters, the applicable financial reporting framework in accordance with which the entity or, if applicable, the acquiree prepares its periodic financial information, and the legal and political environment. Examples of matters the assurance practitioner may consider include: (Ref: Para. 37(d))

(a) Industry-specific accounting practices.

(b) Legal and regulatory framework for a regulated industry.

(c) Legislation and regulation that significantly affect the entity's or, if applicable, the acquiree's or divestee's operations, including direct supervisory activities.

(d) Taxation.

(e) Government policies currently affecting the conduct of the entity's or, if applicable, the acquiree's or divestee's business, such as monetary policies (including foreign exchange controls), fiscal policies, financial incentives (for example, government aid programs), and tariffs or trade restrictions policies.

(f) Environmental requirements affecting the entity's or acquiree's or divestee's industry and business.

A29. Examples of other external factors affecting the entity and, if applicable, the acquiree or divestee that the assurance practitioner may consider include the general economic conditions, interest rates and availability of financing. (Ref: Para. 37(d))

A30. The assurance practitioner ordinarily has no responsibility to perform an assessment of the appropriateness, or otherwise, of the chosen stated basis of preparation. The stated basis of preparation chosen by the responsible party is ordinarily represented by the recognition and measurement accounting principles contained in Australian Accounting Standards and the accounting policies adopted by the entity. The stated basis of preparation described in the document should include the extent to which the entity has been consistent with that basis selected by the responsible party. (Ref: Para. 37(e))

The Use of Assertions (Ref: Para. 39(a))

A31. Assertions are ordinarily used by the assurance practitioner in a reasonable assurance engagement, and may be used in a limited assurance engagement, to consider the different types of potential misstatements within the financial information that may occur.[78]

A32. In representing that the financial information is in accordance with the stated basis of preparation, the responsible party implicitly or explicitly makes assertions regarding the quantification and presentation and disclosure of the financial information. Assertions made by the responsible party fall into the following categories and may take the following forms:

(a) Assertions about the quantification of the financial information for the period subject to assurance:

(i) Occurrence—events or transactions that have been recorded have occurred and pertain to the entity.

(ii) Completeness—all events or transactions that should have been recorded (in accordance with the stated basis of preparation) have been recorded.

(iii) Accuracy—the amounts and other data related to the recorded event(s) or transaction(s) has (have) been recorded appropriately.

(iv) Cut-off—event(s) and transaction(s) has (have) been recorded in the correct reporting period.

(v) Classification—financial information classes (for example, assets, liabilities) have been recorded in the proper accounts.

(b) Assertions about presentation and disclosure of the financial information in the document:

(i) Occurrence and rights and obligations—disclosed financial information and other matters have occurred and pertain to the entity.

(ii) Completeness—all disclosures that should have been included in the financial information have been included.

(iii) Classification and understandability—financial information is appropriately presented and described, and disclosures are clearly expressed.

78 See ASA 315, paragraphs A110-A112, for helpful guidance on the use of the assertions.

(iv) Accuracy and valuation—all event(s) or transaction(s) included in the financial information are in accordance with the stated basis of preparation and disclosed fairly and at appropriate amounts.

(v) Consistency—accounting policies are consistent with those applied in the prior period, or changes made are justified and have been properly applied and adequately disclosed; and comparative information, if any, is as reported in the prior period or has been appropriately restated.

Notwithstanding the presentation and disclosure assertions made by the responsible party, the assurance practitioner only designs assurance procedures related to the quantification of the financial information, as this ASAE does not require the assurance practitioner to provide assurance on the presentation and disclosure of the financial information in the document.

Other Procedures to Obtain an Understanding and to Identify and Assess Risks of Material Misstatement (Ref: Para. 40)

A33. Obtaining an understanding, and identifying and assessing risks of material misstatement, is an iterative process. Procedures to obtain an understanding of the entity and its environment and to identify and assess risks of material misstatement by themselves do not provide sufficient appropriate evidence on which to base the assurance conclusion.

Reliance on the work performed by others (Ref: Para. 43-47)

A34. The other assurance practitioner may not permit reliance on a previously issued audit or review report, due to the fact that the report was prepared and issued for a purpose other than the subject of the current engagement. In the absence of the assurance practitioner being able to place reliance, additional procedures are ordinarily performed with respect to the financial information, in order to obtain sufficient and appropriate evidence necessary for the engagement, including:[79]

(a) Requesting to review the other assurance practitioner's working paper file supporting the issued audit or review report, and reading it, in order to ascertain the appropriateness of the audit approach taken. (Ref: Para. 46)

(b) Re-performing some, or all, audit procedures with respect to the financial information, including enquiry, observation, analytical procedures, and tests of details.

(c) Performing audit test checks of certain balances within the financial information.

Causes of Risks of Material Misstatement

A35. Matters that the assurance practitioner may consider in obtaining an understanding of how the entity makes significant accounting estimates included in the financial information, and the data on which they are based include, for example: (Ref: Para. 48(d))

(a) an understanding of the data on which the accounting estimates are based including its source, reliability, and whether it has been previously audited or reviewed;

(b) the method, including if applicable the model, used in making accounting estimates;

(c) relevant aspects of the control environment and information system;

(d) whether the responsible party has used an expert;

(e) the assumptions underlying accounting estimates;

(f) whether there has been, or ought to have been, a change from the prior period in the methods for making accounting estimates and, if so, why; and

(g) whether and, if so, how the entity's responsible party has assessed the effect of any uncertainty in their estimation on the financial information, including:

79 The concepts and discussions on placing reliance on the work of another auditor relevant to an audit engagement are contained in ASA 620 and ASA 600 which may be useful to assurance practitioners when determining the extent, if any, of such reliance in the conduct of an assurance engagement.

(i) whether and, if so, how the entity has considered alternative assumptions or outcomes by, for example, performing a sensitivity analysis to determine the effect of changes in the assumptions on an estimate;

(ii) scenarios; and

(iii) whether the entity monitors the outcome of accounting estimates made in the prior period, and whether it has appropriately responded to the outcome of that monitoring procedure.

Overall Responses to the Assessed Risks of Material Misstatement and Further Procedures

Assurance Procedures (Ref: Para. 49)

A36. When designing and performing assurance procedures, the assurance practitioner considers the adequacy, relevance and reliability of the information obtained to be used as evidence.[80]

A37. Because the level of assurance obtained in a limited assurance engagement is lower than in a reasonable assurance engagement, the procedures the assurance practitioner will perform in a limited assurance engagement will vary in nature from, and are less in extent than for, a reasonable assurance engagement. The primary differences between the assurance practitioner's overall responses to address the assessed risks of material misstatement in the financial information and the further procedures performed in a reasonable assurance engagement as compared to a limited assurance engagement are as follows:

(a) *The emphasis placed on the nature of various procedures*: The emphasis placed on the nature of various procedures as a source of evidence will likely differ, depending on the engagement circumstances.

(b) *The extent of further procedures*: The extent of further procedures performed in a limited assurance engagement is less than in a reasonable assurance engagement. This may involve:

(i) reducing the number of items to be examined, for example, reducing sample sizes for tests of details; or

(ii) performing fewer procedures (for example, performing only analytical procedures in circumstances when, in a reasonable assurance engagement, both analytical procedures and tests of detail would be performed).

(c) *The nature of analytical procedures*: In a reasonable assurance engagement, analytical procedures performed in response to assessed risks of material misstatement involve developing expectations of quantities or ratios related to the financial information that are sufficiently precise to identify material misstatements. In a limited assurance engagement, on the other hand, analytical procedures are often designed to support expectations regarding the direction of trends, relationships and ratios, rather than to identify misstatements with the level of precision expected in a reasonable assurance engagement. Further, when significant fluctuations, relationships or differences are identified, appropriate evidence in a limited assurance engagement may often be obtained by making enquiries of the entity and considering responses received in the light of known engagement circumstances, without obtaining additional evidence as is required by paragraph 53 in the case of a reasonable assurance engagement.

In addition, when undertaking analytical procedures in a limited assurance engagement the assurance practitioner may, for example:

(i) Use data that is more highly aggregated.

(ii) Use data that has not been subjected to separate procedures to test its reliability to the same extent as it would be for a reasonable assurance engagement.

80 The concepts and discussions on obtaining evidence relevant to an audit engagement are contained in ASA 500, which may be useful to assurance practitioners when determining the extent, if any, of evidence required in the conduct of an assurance engagement.

***Overall Responses to the Assessed Risks** (Ref: Para. 50(a))*

A38. Overall responses to address the assessed risks of material misstatement in the financial information level may include:

(a) emphasising to the assurance team the need to maintain professional scepticism;

(b) assigning more experienced staff or those with special skills or using experts;

(c) providing more supervision of engagement staff;

(d) incorporating additional elements of unpredictability in the selection of further procedures to be performed; and

(e) making general changes to the nature, timing, or extent of procedures, and modifying the nature of procedures to obtain more persuasive evidence.

A39. The nature, timing, and extent of assurance procedures to be carried out are influenced by various factors, including, but not limited to:

(a) the assurance practitioner's assessment of risk and its impact on the sufficiency and appropriateness of evidence;

(b) the stated basis of preparation chosen by the responsible party;

(c) whether some of the financial information has already been audited or reviewed, and if so whether the audit or review was conducted in accordance with Australian Auditing Standards; and what type of audit opinion or review conclusion was expressed in the auditor's report;

(d) whether the financial information included in the document is prepared on the same basis as that of the prior period audited or reviewed historical financial information, and if not, the reasons for the differences;

(e) whether the source and time period covered by the financial information are appropriate, and consistent with the stated basis of preparation; and

(f) whether there is a need to make corrections in the financial information previously considered immaterial in the prior period audit or review of the financial report.

***Persuasiveness of Evidence** (Ref: Para. 50(b))*

A40. To obtain more persuasive evidence because of a higher assessment of risk of material misstatement, the assurance practitioner may increase the quantity of the evidence, or obtain evidence that is more relevant or reliable, for example, by obtaining corroborating evidence from a number of independent sources.

***Confirmation Procedures** (Ref: Para. 50(b))*

A41. External confirmation procedures may provide relevant evidence about such information as terms of agreements, contracts, or transactions between the entity and other parties, related to the financial information that is the subject of the engagement.

***Analytical Procedures Performed in Response to Assessed Risks of Material Misstatement.** (Ref: Para. 52(e))*

A42. Analytical procedures may be particularly effective when disaggregated data is readily available, or when the assurance practitioner has reason to consider the data to be used is reliable, such as when it is extracted from a well-controlled source. In some cases, data to be used may be captured by the financial reporting information system, or may be entered in another information system in parallel with the entry of related financial data and some common input controls applied.

A43. In some cases, it may be appropriate for the assurance practitioner to evaluate how the responsible party has considered alternative assumptions or outcomes in determining the accounting estimates, and why it has rejected them. (Ref: Para. 52(g))

Sampling (Ref: Para. 52(k))

A44. Sampling[81] involves:

(a) Determining a sample size sufficient to reduce sampling risk to an acceptably low level. Because the acceptable level of assurance engagement risk is lower for a reasonable assurance engagement than for a limited assurance engagement, so too may be the level of sampling risk that is acceptable in the case of tests of details. Therefore, when sampling is used for tests of details in a reasonable assurance engagement, the sample size may be larger than when used in similar circumstances in a limited assurance engagement.

(b) Selecting items for the sample in such a way that each sampling unit in the population has a chance of selection, and performing procedures, appropriate to the purpose, on each item selected. If the assurance practitioner is unable to apply the designed procedures, or suitable alternative procedures, to a selected item, that item is treated as a deviation from the prescribed control, in the case of tests of controls, or a misstatement, in the case of tests of details.

(c) Investigating the nature and cause of deviations or misstatements identified, and evaluating their possible effect on the purpose of the procedure and on other areas of the engagement.

(d) Evaluating:

(i) the results of the sample, including, for tests of details, projecting misstatements found in the sample to the population; and

(ii) whether the use of sampling has provided an appropriate basis for conclusions about the population that has been tested.

Examples of Other Procedures (Ref: Para. 53(c)(i))

A45. Other procedures may include, for example:

(a) reviewing key contracts relevant to the financial information;

(b) reconciling key recorded accounts and balances to supporting documentation; and

(c) re-performing key calculations such as accounting estimates and reconciling any differences noted.

Additional Procedures *(Ref: Para. 55-56)*

A46. Examples of additional procedures are making further enquiries of the responsible party, or requesting further supporting documentation to ascertain whether the financial information is materially misstated. If however, having performed additional procedures, the assurance practitioner is not able to obtain sufficient appropriate evidence to either conclude that the event(s), condition(s), transaction(s) or error(s) is (are) not likely to cause the financial information to be materially misstated or determine that it does cause the financial information to be materially misstated, a scope limitation exists and the assurance practitioner should consider the implications for the assurance engagement.

Identified Misstatements *(Ref: Para. 62)*

A47. The assurance practitioner may designate an amount below which misstatements[82] would be clearly trivial and would not need to be accumulated because the assurance practitioner expects that the accumulation of such amounts clearly would not have a material effect on the financial information. "Clearly trivial" is not another expression for "not material." Event(s), condition(s), transaction(s) or error(s) that are clearly trivial will be of a wholly different (smaller) order of magnitude than materiality determined in accordance with this ASAE, and will be matters that are clearly inconsequential, whether taken individually or in the aggregate and whether judged by any criteria of size, nature or circumstances.

81 See ASA 530 *Audit Sampling*, which describes audit sampling techniques, and may be useful to assurance practitioners when performing an assurance engagement involving sampling.

82 The concepts and discussions on evaluating misstatements in an audit engagement are contained in ASA 450 *Evaluation of Misstatements Identified during the Audit*; paragraph A2, which may be useful to assurance practitioners when evaluating misstatements in an assurance engagement.

When there is any uncertainty about whether one or more items are clearly trivial, the matter is considered not to be clearly trivial.

A48. The assurance practitioner may communicate such matters verbally or in writing, as soon as the event(s), condition(s), transaction(s) or error(s) is (are) identified, to enable the responsible party to investigate the matter(s). The responsible party is then able to advise the assurance practitioner of their findings, provide supporting evidence and their decision on whether the adjustment(s) will be made to the financial information. The assurance practitioner is then able to evaluate the evidence provided to consider if the responsible party's decision on the adjustment(s) is acceptable to the assurance practitioner.

Evidence (Ref: Para. 64)

A49. The quantity of evidence obtained by the assurance practitioner is a measure of the sufficiency of the evidence, whilst the quality of the evidence obtained is a measure of its appropriateness; that is, its relevance and its reliability.[83] The extent of evidence required depends on the type of assurance required in respect of the financial information.

Other Information Included in the Document (Ref: Para. 65)

A50. The assurance practitioner's reading of the other information does not infer any assurance on that information, as the assurance practitioner reads it only to establish if there are any material inconsistencies or misstatements which may impact the financial information. Further, the assurance practitioner performs the assessment as if the event(s) or transaction(s) giving rise to the fundraising or report on prospective financial information had occurred. Material inconsistencies in other information that come to the assurance practitioner's attention may raise doubt about the conclusions drawn from evidence already obtained, and possibly, about the basis for the assurance practitioner's conclusion in the assurance report.

A51. The assurance practitioner ordinarily pays particular attention to the following disclosure areas within the document:

(a) other financial information not subject to the assurance engagement including:

(i) summarised financial information, for example in tabular or graphical forms;

(ii) any disclosures related to other financial information that has been previously audited or reviewed; and

(iii) management discussion and analysis section discussing the other financial information;

(b) disclosures about the nature of the event(s) or transaction(s) giving rise to the preparation of the document, including:

(i) the purpose of the document;

(ii) if applicable, the nature and amount of the securities, their value and rights, as well as any minimum subscription and how the proceeds will be applied; and

(iii) if applicable, the risks associated with the fundraising;

(c) qualitative and quantitative disclosures about the entity's plans and future outlooks, including:

(i) its long-term and short-term plans to address key challenges; and

(ii) change-related risks, opportunities and impacts;

(d) key trends and factors related to the entity's industry or nature of operations that are likely to affect the entity's strategy or the timescale over which achievement of the strategy is planned; and

83 The concepts and discussions on evidence relevant to an audit engagement are contained in Auditing Standard ASA 500, and may be helpful in determining the evidence applicable to an assurance engagement.

(e) other relevant disclosures, including:

(i) explanations of how revenue would be generated, including summaries of relevant contracts;

(ii) nature and extent of related party disclosures; and

(iii) valuation of material assets.

Going Concern Considerations

Assessment

A52. The assurance practitioner considers the appropriateness of the going concern assumption of the entity when the nature of the assurance engagement means that such an assessment could have implications for the assurance report. Ordinarily the assessment of going concern is appropriate for assurance engagements relating to historical financial information. Ordinarily in an engagement to report on prospective financial information, the going concern assumption is not relevant to the assurance practitioner's conclusion as the nature of the information is subjective, prospective (based on anticipated event(s) or transaction(s) that have not occurred) and its preparation requires the exercise of considerable judgement by the responsible party. (Ref: Para. 67)

A53. If the assurance practitioner considers that performing a going concern assessment[84] is relevant, the assurance practitioner ordinarily performs the assessment as if the event(s) or transaction(s) giving rise to the corporate fundraising or reporting on prospective financial information had occurred, and considers the entity's prepared future forecasts, future cash flow statements, the directors' working capital statements, and financial position and any other event(s) or condition(s) that are relevant to the assessment. For example, if the prospects for profitability are not supported by adequate positive future cash flows, then both the forecast financial performance statement and the ongoing viability of the entity are at risk. There may also be mitigating factors that in the assurance practitioner's professional judgement eliminate the going concern uncertainty. These mitigating factors may include: (Ref: Para. 68)

(a) a review of recently prepared forecasts, cash flow statements, working capital statements or statements of financial performance;

(b) unequivocal financial support provided from another entity which has the capacity to provide support;

(c) a signed underwriting agreement being in place; and/or

(d) the underlying event(s) or transaction(s) giving rise to the document (for example, a capital raising) which will, if completed successfully, raise sufficient funds to result in the entity becoming a going concern.

Mitigating factors should be supported by appropriate written evidence. In such circumstances, the assurance practitioner needs to evaluate and document how the unequivocal financial support or proceeds from the fundraising issue will provide funding for future operations of the entity that will result in the entity becoming a going concern. Consideration should be given to any proposed underwriting of any capital raising, and the circumstances in which the proposed underwriting may not occur. The assurance practitioner should also consider requesting a written representation from the responsible party regarding the appropriateness of the going concern assumption.

84 The concepts and discussions on performing a going concern assessment of an entity, relevant to an audit engagement are contained in Auditing Standard ASA 570, and may be helpful in performing a going concern assessment in an assurance engagement.

ASAE

Going Concern Assumption Inappropriate (Ref: Para. 69)

A54. If the assurance practitioner does not consider the going concern assumption to be appropriate to the entity, the implications for the assurance report depend on whether the responsible party has modified the basis of preparation of the financial information from that of a going concern basis:

(a) if the basis has not been modified, then the conclusion in the assurance report should be modified (adverse conclusion) on the basis of the going concern assumption being inappropriate to the historical financial information; or

(b) if the basis has been modified, and the assurance practitioner considers the basis to be appropriate, then the assurance practitioner may still include an Emphasis of Matter paragraph in the assurance report to draw attention to the disclosure of this alternate basis.

Consideration of Events up to the Date of the Assurance Report (Ref: Para. 70-72)

A55. In considering the impact of an identified event(s), transaction(s), correction(s) or error(s), the assurance practitioner takes into account issues such as:

(a) the potential for such event(s), condition(s), transaction(s) or error(s) to materially affect the financial information in the document in terms of requiring comment on, or correction to, the financial information;

(b) whether such event(s), condition(s), transaction(s) or error(s) are within the ordinary business of the entity; and

(c) whether such event(s), condition(s), transaction(s) or error(s) cause the financial information to be potentially misleading or deceptive.

Consideration of Events Identified after the date of the Assurance Report (Ref: Para. 73-74)

A56. If there are event(s), condition(s), transaction(s) or error(s) omitted from the document, which come to the assurance practitioner's attention after:

(a) the document has been lodged with the appropriate regulatory body, if it is a public document; or

(b) the document has been finalised and issued to its intended user(s) and before the relevant date, if it is not a public document;

the assurance practitioner considers the implications for the assurance report, as well as any reporting obligations the assurance practitioner may have to inform the entity issuing the document.

A57. If event(s), condition(s), transaction(s) or error(s) with a potentially material impact on the financial information come to the assurance practitioner's attention prior to the relevant date, the assurance practitioner discusses the omissions with the responsible party. If the responsible party refuses to correct such omissions, the assurance practitioner ordinarily withdraws consent for the entity to include the assurance report in the document, and evaluates if there are any applicable laws, regulations, agreements or other professional responsibilities that impose particular reporting obligations on the assurance practitioner (for example, reporting such matters to the entity's due diligence committee).

Written Representations (Ref: Para. 75-79)

A58. The assurance practitioner requests and obtains written representations from the responsible party at the completion of the assurance engagement.[85] If the responsible party is those charged with governance in the entity, the representation letter should be provided by them and not management. The assurance practitioner ordinarily provides the responsible party with a specific list of representations required. Such matters may already be contained in documentation reviewed by the assurance practitioner, including

85 The concepts and discussions on obtaining written representations relevant to an audit engagement are contained in Auditing Standard ASA 580 *Written Representations*, and may be helpful in determining the form and content of written representations applicable to an assurance engagement.

minutes of meetings, written acceptance of the assurance engagement terms, and due diligence committee reports. Therefore the assurance practitioner only needs to request the inclusion of such matters in the written representations if the assurance practitioner considers it appropriate in the assurance engagement circumstances.

A59. Appendix 2 provides an illustrative representation letter.

A60. Oral or written representations made by the responsible party cannot replace other evidence the assurance practitioner could reasonably expect to be available. For example, relevant minutes of meetings of the Board of Directors, or a published statement by the Board of Directors acknowledging responsibility for the preparation and presentation of the financial information, may be considered sufficient appropriate evidence under the circumstances. To the extent the other evidence obtained is inconsistent with the responsible party's oral or written representations, the assurance practitioner investigates and evaluates such inconsistencies in terms of their impact on the assurance report and whether additional procedures are required in order to resolve the inconsistencies and obtain sufficient appropriate evidence.

A61. An inability to obtain sufficient appropriate evidence regarding a matter that has, or may have, a material effect on the evaluation of the financial information in the document, when such evidence would ordinarily be available, constitutes a limitation on the scope of the assurance engagement, even if a written representation from the responsible party has been received by the assurance practitioner on the matter.

Forming the Assurance Conclusion

Emphasis of Matter Paragraph (Ref: Para. 83)

A62. An example of a matter that may give rise to an emphasis of matter paragraph is when the assurance practitioner believes the going concern assumption is appropriate, but a material uncertainty exists. In such circumstances, the assurance practitioner ordinarily considers the adequacy of the going concern related disclosures within the financial information and the other parts of the document. If the assurance practitioner considers the responsible party has adequately disclosed:

(a) a description of the principal event(s) or condition(s) that cast significant doubt on the entity's going concern ability; and

(b) the fact that a material uncertainty exists related to the event(s) or condition(s); and

(c) therefore the entity may be unable to realise its assets and discharge its liabilities in the normal course of business;

then the assurance practitioner is able to express an unmodified conclusion on the financial information, with an Emphasis of Matter paragraph to highlight the existence of the material uncertainty and to draw attention to the responsible party's disclosures. If there is not adequate disclosure, then the assurance practitioner expresses a qualified conclusion or adverse conclusion, as appropriate.

Modified Conclusion

A63. An inability to obtain sufficient appropriate evidence regarding a matter that has, or may have, a material effect on the evaluation of the financial information, when such evidence would ordinarily be available, constitutes a limitation on the scope of the assurance engagement, even if a written representation from the responsible party has been received by the assurance practitioner on the matter. (Ref: Para. 84(c))

A64. Applicable law or regulation may preclude the assurance practitioner from expressing a modified conclusion in an assurance report that is to be included in a public document. Where this is the case, and the assurance practitioner concludes that a modified conclusion is nevertheless appropriate, the assurance practitioner discusses the matter with the responsible party. If the responsible party does not agree to make the changes required to enable the assurance practitioner to issue an unmodified conclusion, the assurance practitioner considers whether to withhold the assurance report, withdraw from the assurance engagement, or obtain legal advice. If the responsible party decides to omit the modified assurance report from the document, the assurance practitioner considers any other professional reporting obligations such as, for example, to the entity's due diligence committee. (Ref: Para. 85)

Preparing the Assurance Report

A65. The assurance report may be prepared solely in respect of one type of financial information or be a composite report where two or more types of financial information are the subject of the assurance report (for example historical and prospective financial information). (Ref: Para. 86)

A66. If the assurance practitioner is preparing a composite assurance report, the assurance practitioner needs to ensure that: (Ref: Para. 87)

(a) the different types of financial information are clearly identified in the document, and separately referred to in the assurance report; and

(b) the assurance report clearly identifies and segregates the work carried out, and type of assurance expressed, on the different types of financial information.

A67. In respect of an assurance report that is being included in a public document prepared in accordance with the *Corporations Act 2001*, the assurance practitioner also needs to ensure that the assurance report is appropriately: (Ref: Para. 88)

(a) cross referenced, and consistent with, other information disclosed in the public document; and

(b) positioned in the public document.

A68. Appendix 3 contains illustrative examples of assurance reports. (Ref: Para. 86)

Consent to the Inclusion of the Assurance Report in a Public Document (Ref: Para. 89-90)

A69. For assurance reports in connection with a public document prepared in accordance with the *Corporations Act 2001*, the assurance practitioner is required to consent to the form and context in which the assurance report is included in that public document.[86] Such consent is ordinarily provided by way of a separate consent letter issued to the entity prior to the assurance report. Consequently, the assurance practitioner ordinarily reads all other information included in the public document for consistency. If there are material inconsistencies, or material misstatements of fact, related to the financial information which remain uncorrected by the responsible party, or the assurance practitioner does not consider the assurance report will be used for the intended purpose, the assurance practitioner ordinarily does not provide consent.

Documentation (Ref: Para. 91)

A70. Sufficient appropriate documentation[87] should include a record of the assurance practitioner's reasoning on all significant matters that required the exercise of professional judgement, together with the assurance practitioner's conclusions on the matters. In areas involving difficult questions of estimate, principle or judgement, the documentation should include the relevant facts that were known by the assurance practitioner at the time the conclusion was reached.

A71. In applying professional judgement to assessing the extent of documentation to be prepared and retained, the assurance practitioner ordinarily considers what would be necessary for another experienced assurance practitioner who has no previous experience with the assurance engagement to obtain an understanding of the work performed and the basis of the significant decisions taken. It is, however, neither necessary nor practicable to document every matter the assurance practitioner considers during the assurance engagement.

86 See Section 716 of the *Corporations Act 2001*.

87 The concepts and discussions on documentation relevant to an audit engagement are contained in Auditing Standard ASA 230 *Audit Documentation*, and may be helpful in determining appropriate documentation to be obtained in an assurance engagement.

Historical Financial Information

Preparing the Assurance Report (Ref: Para. 95)

Basic Elements of the Assurance Report

Reasonable Assurance

A72. The assurance report in a reasonable assurance engagement ordinarily follows a standard wording and only in summary form describes the procedures performed. This is because, in a reasonable assurance engagement, describing in any level of detail the specific procedures performed would not assist users to understand that, in all cases where an unmodified report is issued, sufficient appropriate evidence has been obtained to enable the assurance practitioner to express an opinion.

Limited Assurance

A73. In a limited assurance engagement, an appreciation of the nature, timing and extent of procedures performed is essential for the intended users to understand the conclusion expressed in a limited assurance report. A description of the assurance practitioner's procedures in a limited assurance engagement is ordinarily therefore more detailed than in a reasonable assurance engagement. It also may be appropriate to include a description of the procedures that were not performed that would ordinarily be performed in a reasonable assurance engagement. However, a complete identification of all such procedures may not be possible because the assurance practitioner's understanding and assessment of the risks of material misstatement are less than in a reasonable assurance engagement. The assurance practitioner does not ordinarily detail all procedures in the assurance report.

Factors to consider in making that determination and the level of detail to be provided include:

(a) circumstances specific to the entity (for example, the differing nature of the entity's activities compared to those typical in the sector);

(b) specific engagement circumstances affecting the nature and extent of the procedures performed; and

(c) the intended users' expectations of the level of detail to be provided in the assurance report based on market practice, or applicable laws or regulations.

A74. In describing the procedures performed in a limited assurance report, it is important that they are written in an objective way but are not summarised to the extent that they are ambiguous, nor written in a way that is overstated or embellished or that implies that reasonable assurance has been obtained. It is also important that the description of the procedures does not give the impression that an agreed-upon procedures engagement has been undertaken.

Pro Forma Historical Financial Information

A75. In Australia, assurance practitioners are ordinarily requested by the responsible party to provide assurance on the pro forma historical financial information. In circumstances where the assurance practitioner: (Ref: Para. 96)

(a) cannot access, or obtain sufficient access to, documentation supporting the source of the unadjusted historical financial information or the pro forma adjustments; or

(b) does not audit one of the entities whose financial information is included in the pro forma historical financial information;

the assurance practitioner and responsible party may alternatively agree for an assurance engagement to be conducted to report on the compilation of the pro forma historical financial information. In such circumstances, refer ASAE 3420 *Assurance Engagements to Report on the Compilation of Pro Forma Historical Financial Information Included in a Prospectus or other Document.*

A76. Circumstances such as those outlined in paragraph A75 may occur, for example: (Ref: Para. 96)

(a) when the fundraising involves a takeover transaction in which neither the assurance practitioner nor the responsible party of the entity are able to access the other entity's financial information;

(b) when the fundraising involves a takeover transaction where the other entity has not been subject to an audit or review; or

(c) when there is insufficient time in which to conduct the engagement to enable the expression of assurance on the pro forma historical financial information itself.

Engagement Acceptance

Other Factors Affecting Engagement Acceptance (Ref: Para. 98)

A77. Ordinarily, the assurance practitioner only provides limited assurance on pro forma historical financial information, as the pro forma adjustments made to the unadjusted financial information (which is historical) are based on the responsible party's stated basis of preparation. The assurance practitioner has no responsibility under the terms of the assurance engagement to perform an assessment of the appropriateness, or otherwise, of the selected stated basis of preparation.

Understanding the Entity and Its Environment and Identifying and Assessing Risks of Material Misstatement

Obtaining an Understanding of the Entity and Its Environment

Unadjusted Financial Information has been Audited or Reviewed (Ref: Para. 99(a)(ii))

A78. The assurance practitioner may:

(a) Request a copy of the audit or review report accompanying the unadjusted financial information and, if obtained, read it to understand if the report was modified or unmodified. If the report was modified, understand the reasons for the modification;

(b) Contact the other assurance practitioner to request access to the audit working papers supporting the audit or review report and, if provided, read the work papers to assess the appropriateness of the audit approach taken for the purposes of placing reliance on that audit or review report in assessing the appropriateness of the source of the unadjusted financial information;

(c) Read the unadjusted financial information to which the audit or review report relates to establish if its stated basis of preparation (that is, its accounting policies) and time frame covered are acceptable; and/or

(d) Plan to perform further procedures as is considered necessary in the engagement circumstances.

A79. If the assurance practitioner requests access to the audit working papers of another assurance practitioner and is unable to obtain such access, this constitutes a limitation of scope on the assurance practitioner being able to assess the appropriateness of the source of the unadjusted financial information. If the assurance practitioner is unable to perform alternative procedures to obtain sufficient appropriate evidence on its appropriateness, the assurance practitioner modifies the conclusion in the assurance report in accordance with paragraph 84(c).*

Overall Responses to Assessed Risks of Material Misstatement and Further Procedures

Assurance Procedures

A80. The assurance procedures may include: (Ref: Para. 100(a))

(a) enquiring of the responsible party about:

(i) the process by which the source has been prepared and the reliability of the underlying accounting records to which the source is agreed or reconciled;

* See ASAE 3000, paragraphs 82-84 for further information.

(ii) whether all transactions for the time period have been recorded;

(iii) whether the source has been prepared in accordance with the entity's accounting policies;

(iv) whether there have been any changes in accounting policies from the most recent audited or reviewed period, and, if so, how such changes have been dealt with;

(v) its assessment of the risk that the source may be materially misstated as a result of error or fraud; and

(vi) the effect of changes in the entity's business activities and operations;

(b) if the assurance practitioner has audited or reviewed the immediately preceding annual or interim financial information, considering the findings of such audit or review and whether these might indicate any issues with the preparation of the source from which the unadjusted financial information has been extracted;

(c) corroborating the information provided by the responsible party in response to the assurance practitioner's enquiries, when the responses appear inconsistent with the assurance practitioner's understanding of the entity, or the engagement circumstances; and

(d) comparing the source with the corresponding prior period financial information and, as applicable, the immediately preceding annual or interim financial information, and discussing significant changes with the responsible party.

***No Audit or Review of the Unadjusted Financial Information** (Ref: Para. 100(b))*

A81. When there is no audit or review report on the source from which the unadjusted financial information has been extracted, it is necessary for the assurance practitioner to perform procedures in relation to the appropriateness of that source. Factors that may affect the nature and extent of these procedures include, for example:

(a) Whether the assurance practitioner has previously audited or reviewed the entity's historical financial information, and the assurance practitioner's knowledge of the entity from such engagement.

(b) How recently the entity's historical financial information was audited or reviewed.

(c) Whether the entity's financial information is subject to periodic review by the assurance practitioner, for example, for purposes of meeting regulatory filing requirements.

(d) Whether the assurance practitioner is able to access documentation describing, and supporting, the source of the unadjusted historical financial information.

(e) The type of assurance to be provided.

***Pro Forma Adjustments** (Ref: Para. 100(e))*

A82. For the pro forma financial information to be meaningful, it is necessary that the pro forma adjustments be consistent with the stated basis of preparation. In the context of a business combination, for example, this may involve consideration of such matters as:

(a) whether differences exist between the acquiree's accounting policies and those of the entity; and

(b) whether accounting policies for transactions undertaken by the acquiree that the entity has not previously entered into, are policies that the entity would have adopted for such transactions under its applicable financial reporting framework, taking into account the entity's particular circumstances.

ASAE

A83. Consideration of the appropriateness of the entity's accounting policies may also be necessary in some circumstances. For example, as part of the event(s) or transaction(s), the entity may propose to issue complex financial instruments for the first time. If this is the case, it may be necessary to consider:

(a) whether the responsible party has selected appropriate accounting policies to be used in accounting for such financial instruments under its applicable financial reporting framework; and

(b) whether it has appropriately applied such policies in preparing the pro forma historical financial information.

Preparing the Assurance Report

Basic Elements of the Assurance Report (Ref: Para. 104(a)(iii))

A84. The stated basis of preparation for the pro forma historical financial information, as chosen by the responsible party, is ordinarily represented by the application to its base historical financial information of the recognition and measurement principles contained in Australian Accounting Standards and the adopted accounting policies, as well as the pro forma adjustments made.

Prospective Financial Information

Assurance Engagement Acceptance

Preconditions for Acceptance

Type of assurance (Ref: Para. 106(a))

A85. The nature of prospective financial information, being information prepared based on events and actions that have not yet occurred, and may not occur, means that the engagement is conducted either as a limited assurance engagement, or in certain circumstances, a combined limited assurance and reasonable assurance engagement on different elements of the prospective financial information:

(a) Assumptions - evidence may be available to support the responsible party's underlying assumptions, however such evidence is itself generally future orientated and, therefore, speculative in nature, as distinct from being factually supportable. Due to this, the assurance practitioner is not able to provide any assurance on the reasonableness of the assumptions but may be able to provide limited assurance on whether they provide reasonable grounds for the preparation of the prospective financial information.

(b) Basis of the prospective financial information - the assurance practitioner is ordinarily able to provide limited or reasonable assurance (depending on the terms of the engagement and the sufficiency and availability of evidence) that the prospective financial information has been prepared on the basis of those assumptions, and presented fairly in accordance with the entity's stated basis of preparation.

(c) Prospective financial information itself - given the nature of the evidence available to support the underlying source of the prospective financial information is inherently uncertain, the assurance practitioner is not able to conclude as to whether the results shown in the prospective financial information overall will be achieved, however the assurance practitioner may be in a position to provide limited assurance on whether the prospective financial information itself is unreasonable, based on the results of (a) and (b) above.

A86. The type of assurance that the assurance practitioner agrees to provide on different elements of the prospective financial information may depend on the assurance practitioner's assessment of the following:

(a) the engagement circumstances, including the nature (for example, complexity or simplicity) and type of the entity (for example, start up or ongoing), timeframe covered and overall purpose of including the prospective financial information in the document;

(b) the assurance practitioner's professional judgement in whether there is, or will be, sufficient appropriate evidence available to support the level of assurance requested; and

(c) any prior experience the assurance practitioner may have with the entity in terms of the accuracy, completeness and timeliness of financial information prepared by the responsible party.

Other Factors Affecting Engagement Acceptance

A87. In obtaining a preliminary understanding of whether the assumptions have reasonable grounds, the assurance practitioner considers matters such as: (Ref: Para. 107(a)(i))

(a) whether the time available to complete the engagement is adequate;

(b) the nature of the assumptions (best-estimate or hypothetical), and whether their impact is material to the prospective financial information;

(c) the economic viability, stability and financial strength of the entity;

(d) the economic viability and substance of the fundraising and the assumptions related to it;

(e) the source, availability, and quality of the data supporting the assumptions (for example, the data is sourced from third parties/experts or by using statistical, mathematical or computer-assisted techniques); and

(f) if applicable, the assurance practitioner's past experience with the accuracy of the entity's previous prospective financial information, as against actual results.

A88. If the source of the base financial information is historical and has not been previously audited or reviewed, the assurance practitioner, in order to obtain sufficient appropriate evidence on which to conclude and express limited assurance on the different elements of the prospective financial information, needs to be able to conduct a review of such historical financial information as part of the assurance engagement terms. (Ref: Para. 107(a)(iii))

ASAE

A89. The assurance practitioner should be satisfied based on preliminary knowledge that the assurance engagement has a rational purpose. Examples where this may not be the case include: (Ref: Para. 107(b))

(a) the reason for the preparation of the prospective financial information is unclear;

(b) the prospective financial information does not have a reasonable basis for inclusion in a public document (for example it is a projection);[88]

(c) the prospective financial information is materially affected by hypothetical assumptions;

(d) there will be significant limitations on the scope of the assurance practitioner's work; or

(e) the engagement circumstances lead the assurance practitioner to believe that the responsible party intends to associate the assurance practitioner's name with the prospective financial information in an inappropriate manner.

No Audit or Review Report on the Source of the Prospective Financial Information (Ref: Para. 109(c))

A90. This ASAE does not require the assurance practitioner to perform an audit or review of the source from which the unadjusted financial information has been extracted as part of the engagement, if such an audit or review has not already been performed.

Assumptions (Ref: Para. 111(b)(iv))

A91. A high risk that there may be a significant difference between the prospective financial information and actual results may call into question the suitability and reasonableness of the assumptions used as the basis for the preparation of the prospective financial information and their characterisation as reasonable.

88 For prospective financial information included in a public document, see the *Corporations Act 2001* and Corporations Regulations for requirements. See RG 170, for guidance on what constitutes reasonable grounds for inclusion.

Prospective Financial Information prepared in accordance with the Stated Basis of Preparation and Assumptions

A92. The assurance practitioner's evaluation of the stated basis of preparation used by the responsible party ordinarily includes: (Ref: Para. 113(a))

(a) the process for its selection and approval;

(b) the differences, if any to the basis of preparation, adopted in the most recent financial report; and

(c) its suitability for the preparation of the prospective financial information, based on the stated purpose of the prospective financial information.

Preparing the Assurance Report

Basic Elements of the Assurance Report (Ref: Para. 118(f)(ii))

Reasonable Assurance

A93. The assurance report in a reasonable assurance engagement ordinarily follows a standard wording and only in summary form describes the procedures performed. This is because, in a reasonable assurance engagement, describing in any level of detail the specific procedures performed would not assist users to understand that, in all cases where an unmodified report is issued, sufficient appropriate evidence has been obtained to enable the assurance practitioner to express an opinion.

Limited Assurance

A94. In a limited assurance engagement, an appreciation of the nature, timing and extent of procedures performed is essential for the intended users to understand the conclusion expressed in a limited assurance report. A description of the assurance practitioner's procedures in a limited assurance engagement is ordinarily therefore more detailed than in a reasonable assurance engagement. It also may be appropriate to include a description of the procedures that were not performed that would ordinarily be performed in a reasonable assurance engagement. However, a complete identification of all such procedures may not be possible because the assurance practitioner's understanding and assessment of the risks of material misstatement are less than in a reasonable assurance engagement. The assurance practitioner does not ordinarily detail all procedures in the assurance report.

Factors to consider in making that determination and the level of detail to be provided include:

(a) circumstances specific to the entity (for example, the differing nature of the entity's activities compared to those typical in the sector);

(b) specific engagement circumstances affecting the nature and extent of the procedures performed; and

(c) the intended users' expectations of the level of detail to be provided in the report, based on market practice, or applicable laws or regulations.

A95. In describing the procedures performed in a limited assurance report, it is important that they are written in an objective way but are not summarised to the extent that they are ambiguous, nor written in a way that is overstated or embellished or that implies that reasonable assurance has been obtained. It is also important that the description of the procedures does not give the impression that an agreed-upon procedures engagement has been undertaken.

Projection

Assurance Engagement Acceptance

Preconditions for Acceptance (Ref: Para. 120(a))

A96. The assurance practitioner does not express any assurance on the hypothetical assumptions as by their nature, sufficient appropriate evidence is not available to support such assumptions.

Overall Responses to the Assessed Risks of Material Misstatement and Further Procedures

Assurance Procedures

Hypothetical Assumptions (Ref: Para. 123)

A97. The assurance practitioner ordinarily considers, when hypothetical assumptions are used, all significant implications of the assumptions have been taken into consideration. For example, if sales are assumed to grow beyond the entity's current plant capacity, the prospective financial information will need to include the necessary investment in the additional plant capacity or the costs of alternative means of meeting the anticipated sales, such as by sub-contracting production.

Preparing the Assurance Report

Basic Elements of the Assurance Report (Ref: Para. 127(a)(ii))

A98. The stated basis of preparation for the projection, as chosen by the responsible party is ordinarily represented by the recognition and measurement principles contained in Australian Accounting Standards and the accounting policies adopted, as applied to the financial information, as if the future events or actions included in the projection will occur within the time frame covered by the projection (a "what-if" scenario).

Pro Forma Forecast

Assurance Engagement Acceptance

Other Factors Affecting Engagement Acceptance (Ref: Para. 130)

A99. Ordinarily, the assurance practitioner only provides limited assurance on a pro forma forecast, as the pro forma adjustments made to the unadjusted financial information are based on the responsible party's stated basis of preparation. The assurance practitioner has no responsibility under the terms of the assurance engagement to perform an assessment of the appropriateness, or otherwise, of the selected stated basis of preparation.

Understanding the Entity and Its Environment and Identifying and Assessing Risks of Material Misstatement

Obtaining an Understanding of the Entity and Its Environment

Audited or Reviewed Unadjusted Financial Information (Ref: Para. 131(a))

A100. The assurance practitioner may:

(a) request a copy of the audit or review report accompanying the unadjusted financial information and, if obtained, read it to understand if the report was modified or unmodified. If the report was modified, understand the reasons for the modification;

(b) contact the other assurance practitioner to request access to the audit working papers supporting the audit or review report and, if provided, read the work papers to assess the appropriateness of the audit approach taken for the purposes of placing reliance on that audit or review report in assessing the appropriateness of the source of the unadjusted financial information;

(c) read the unadjusted financial information to which the audit or review report relates to establish if its stated basis of preparation (that is, its accounting policies) and time frame covered are acceptable; and/or

(d) plan to perform further procedures as is considered necessary in the engagement circumstances.

A101. If the assurance practitioner requests access to the audit working papers of another assurance practitioner and is unable to obtain such access, this constitutes a limitation of scope on the assurance practitioner being able to assess the appropriateness of the source of the unadjusted financial information. If the assurance practitioner is unable to perform alternative procedures to obtain sufficient appropriate evidence on its appropriateness, the assurance practitioner modifies the conclusion in the assurance report in accordance with paragraph 84(c).*

Overall Responses to Assessed Risks of Material Misstatement and Further Procedures

Assurance Procedures

A102. The assurance procedures may include: (Ref: Para. 132(a))

(a) enquiring of the responsible party about:

(i) the process by which the source has been prepared and the reliability of the underlying accounting records to which the source is agreed or reconciled;

(ii) whether all transactions for the time period have been recorded;

(iii) whether the source has been prepared in accordance with the entity's accounting policies;

(iv) whether there have been any changes in accounting policies from the most recent audited or reviewed period, and, if so, how such changes have been dealt with;

(v) its assessment of the risk that the source may be materially misstated as a result of error or fraud; and

(vi) the effect of changes in the entity's business activities and operations;

(b) if the assurance practitioner has audited or reviewed the immediately preceding annual or interim financial information, considering the findings of such audit or review and whether these might indicate any issues with the preparation of the source from which the unadjusted financial information has been extracted;

(c) corroborating the information provided by the responsible party in response to the assurance practitioner's enquiries, when the responses appear inconsistent with the assurance practitioner's understanding of the entity, or the engagement circumstances; and

(d) comparing the source with the corresponding prior period financial information and, as applicable, the immediately preceding annual or interim financial information, and discussing significant changes with the responsible party.

No Audit or Review of the Unadjusted Financial Information (Ref: Para. 132(b))

A103. When there is no audit or review report on the source from which the unadjusted financial information has been extracted, it is necessary for the assurance practitioner to perform procedures in relation to the appropriateness of that source. Factors that may affect the nature and extent of these procedures include, for example:

(a) Whether the assurance practitioner has previously audited or reviewed the entity's historical financial information, and the assurance practitioner's knowledge of the entity from such engagement.

(b) How recently the entity's historical financial information was audited or reviewed.

(c) Whether the entity's financial information is subject to periodic review by the assurance practitioner, for example, for purposes of meeting regulatory filing requirements.

(d) Whether the assurance practitioner is able to access documentation describing, and supporting, the source of the unadjusted historical financial information.

(e) The type of assurance to be provided.

* See ASAE 3000, paragraphs 82-84 for further information.

***Pro Forma Adjustments** (Ref: Para. 132(c))*

A104. For the pro forma financial information to be meaningful, it is necessary that the pro forma adjustments be consistent with the stated basis of preparation. In the context of a business combination, for example, this may involve consideration of such matters as:

(a) Whether differences exist between the acquiree's accounting policies and those of the entity; and

(b) Whether accounting policies for transactions undertaken by the acquiree that the entity has not previously entered into, are policies that the entity would have adopted for such transactions under its applicable financial reporting framework, taking into account the entity's particular circumstances.

A105. Consideration of the appropriateness of the entity's accounting policies may also be necessary in some circumstances. For example, as part of the event(s) or transaction(s), the entity may propose to issue complex financial instruments for the first time. If this is the case, it may be necessary to consider:

(a) whether the responsible party has selected appropriate accounting policies to be used in accounting for such financial instruments under its applicable financial reporting framework; and

(b) whether it has appropriately applied such policies in preparing the pro forma forecast.

Preparing the Assurance Report

Basic Elements of the Assurance Report (Ref: Para. 136(a)(iii))

A106. The stated basis of preparation for the pro forma forecast, as chosen by the responsible party, is ordinarily represented by the application to its base financial information of the recognition and measurement principles contained in Australian Accounting Standards and the adopted accounting policies, as well as pro forma adjustments made.

❖ ❖ ❖

Conformity with International Standards on Assurance Engagements

This Standard on Assurance Engagements has been made for Australian public interest purposes, and accordingly there is no equivalent International Standard on Assurance Engagements, issued by the International Auditing and Assurance Standards Board (IAASB), an independent standard-setting board of the International Federation of Accountants (IFAC).

Compliance with this Standard on Assurance Engagements does not affect compliance with the ISAEs.

ASAE

Appendix 1

(Ref: Para. A10)

Illustrative Engagement Letter

The following illustrative engagement letter is not authoritative but is intended only to be a guide that may be used in conjunction with the considerations outlined in this ASAE. It will need to be varied according to individual requirements and circumstances.

Engagement Circumstances are:
ABC Company proposes a takeover of XYZ Target company.
Limited assurance engagement on historical financial information, pro forma historical financial information and a forecast.

Introduction

This letter confirms our understanding of the terms of engagement requiring our services as investigating accountant in respect of financial information to be included in the proposed public document of ABC Company Limited ("ABC Company") to be issued in connection with the proposed acquisition of XYZ Target Limited ("Target"). The purpose of this letter is to outline the role and approach of [firm name] and the assurance report we will deliver.

Scope of our work

Our firm will:

- perform procedures, described below, to enable us to report on the ABC Company's historical Statement of Financial Position as at 30 June 20X1, Statements of Financial Performance for the years ended 30 June 20XX and 20X1 and Statements of Cash Flows for the years ended 30 June 20XX and 20X1 (the "historical financial information");
- perform procedures, described below, to enable us to report on ABC Company's pro forma historical Statement of Financial Position, shown with pro forma adjustments to show the effect of events and transactions related to the takeover as if they had occurred at 30 June 20XX, pro forma historical Statements of Financial Performance for the years ended 30 June 20XX and 20X1 and pro forma historical Statements of Cash Flows for the years ended 30 June 20XX and 20X1 (the "pro forma historical financial information");
- perform procedures, described below, to enable us to report on ABC Company's forecast Statements of Financial Performance for the year ending 30 June 20XX ("the forecast"); and
- perform procedures, described below, to enable us to report on ABC Company's forecast Statement of Financial Performance for the year ending 30 June 20XX ("the forecast");

collectively referred to as the "financial information".

We will conduct our engagement in accordance with ASAE 3450 *Assurance Engagements involving Corporate Fundraisings and/or Prospective Financial Information*.

Review of ABC Company's historical financial information

We will review the historical financial information of ABC Company, comprising the Statement of Financial Position as at 30 June 20X1, Statements of Financial Performance and Statements of Cash Flows for the years ended 30 June 20XX and 20X1, in order to state whether on the basis of the procedures described, anything has come to our attention that would cause us to believe that the historical financial information is not prepared, in all material respects, in accordance with the recognition and measurement principles contained in Australian Accounting Standards and the entity's adopted accounting policies, as described in the proposed public document (the "stated basis of preparation").

The review procedures will include, but are not limited to:

- analytical procedures on the unaudited Statement of Financial Position of ABC Company as at 30 June 20X1, Statements of Financial Performance and Statements of Cash Flows of ABC Company for the years ended 30 June 20XX and 20X1;

- a consistency check of the application of the stated basis of preparation, as described in the proposed public document, to the historical financial information;
- a review of ABC Company's work papers, accounting records and other documents; and
- enquiry of directors, management and others in relation to the historical financial information.

Our review procedures will not provide all the evidence that would be required in an audit, thus the level of assurance (limited assurance) provided will be less than given in an audit. Our review is not an audit and, accordingly, we will not express an audit opinion.

Review of ABC Company's pro forma historical financial information

We will review the director's pro forma historical financial information in order to state whether, on the basis of the procedures described, anything comes to our attention that would cause us to believe that the pro forma historical financial information is not prepared, in all material respects, by the directors on the basis of the stated basis of preparation. The stated basis of preparation is:

- the historical financial information of ABC Company extracted from the audited financial statements of ABC Company for the years ended 30 June 20XX and 20X1; and
- the pro forma adjustments applied to the historical financial information from ABC Company to illustrate the effects of the takeover on ABC Company described in section [X] of the proposed public document.

The review procedures will include, but are not limited to:

- consideration of work papers, accounting records and other documents, including those dealing with the extraction of historical financial information of ABC Company from its audited financial statements for the years ended 30 June 20XX and 20X1;
- consideration of the pro forma adjustments described in section [X] of the proposed public document;
- enquiry of directors, management, personnel and advisors;
- the performance of analytical procedures applied to the pro forma historical financial information;
- a review of work papers, accounting records and other documents of ABC Company and its auditors; and
- a review of accounting policies for consistency of application.

The procedures will not provide all the evidence that would be required in an audit, thus, the level of assurance provided (limited assurance) will be less than given in an audit. Our review is not an audit and, accordingly, we will not express an audit opinion.

Review of ABC Company forecast

We will review the ABC Company forecast and the directors' best-estimate assumptions underlying it in order to state whether, on the basis of the procedures described, anything has come to our attention that causes us to believe that:

- the directors' best-estimate assumptions do not provide reasonable grounds for the ABC Company forecast;
- in all material respects the forecast is not:
  - prepared on the basis of the directors' best-estimate assumptions as described in section [X] of the proposed public document; and
  - presented fairly in accordance with the stated basis of preparation, being the recognition and measurement principles contained in Australian Accounting Standards, applied to the forecast and the company's adopted accounting policies;
- the forecast itself is unreasonable.

The review procedures will include, but are not limited to enquiry, comparison, and other such analytical review procedures we consider necessary.

ASAE

Our review of the ABC Company forecast will be limited primarily to:

- comparison and analytical review procedures;
- discussions with management and directors of ABC Company of the factors considered in determining their assumptions; and
- examination, on a test basis, of evidence supporting:
  - the assumptions and amounts in the forecast; and
  - the evaluation of accounting policies used in the forecast.

We will require written representations and confirmations from the directors and management to be provided to ensure the assumptions applied in the preparation of the ABC Company forecast are consistent with the directors' knowledge and expectation.

Our review of the ABC Company forecast will be substantially less in scope than an audit examination conducted in accordance with Australian Auditing Standards. A review of this nature provides less assurance than an audit. Our review is not an audit and we will not express an audit opinion on the ABC Company forecast or the directors' best-estimate assumptions underlying the ABC Company forecast. Our Firm will not express any opinion as to whether the ABC Company forecast will be achieved, or warrant or guarantee any statements as to the future prospects of ABC Company.

Review of the ABC company pro forma forecast

We will review the directors' pro forma forecast in order to state whether based on the procedures performed anything has come to our attention that causes us to believe that the pro forma forecast is prepared, in all material respects by the directors, in accordance with the stated basis of preparation. The stated basis of preparation is:

- the ABC Company forecast; and
- the directors' best-estimate assumptions underlying the pro forma forecast.

Our review procedures will include, but are not limited to enquiry, comparison, and other such analytical review procedures we consider necessary.

Our review of the ABC Company pro forma forecast will be substantially less in scope than an audit examination conducted in accordance with Australian Auditing Standards. A review of this nature provides less assurance than an audit. Our review is not an audit and we will not express an audit opinion on the pro forma forecast or the directors' best-estimate assumptions underlying the pro forma forecast. Our Firm will not express any opinion as to whether the pro forma forecast will be achieved, or warrant or guarantee any statements as to the future prospects of ABC Company.

Reporting

As a result of the above work procedures, we intend to issue an Independent Assurance Report to the directors of ABC Company for inclusion in the proposed public document.

Reliance on information

The directors of ABC Company are responsible for:

- the content of the proposed public document, other than the content of our Independent Assurance Report, and any other experts' reports;
- issuing the proposed public document;
- the preparation and presentation of the financial information included in the proposed public document;
- the directors' best-estimate assumptions on which the ABC Company forecast is based;
- the directors' best-estimate assumptions on which the pro forma forecast is based; and
- the inclusion in the proposed public document of information regarding the sensitivity of the ABC Company forecast and the pro forma forecast to changes in key assumptions.

We do not assume any liability for information or statements included in the public document other than our Independent Assurance Report.

We will require written representations from ABC Company that all material information relevant to the financial information within the company's possession has been provided prior to the finalisation of our reports, and that no material changes have occurred between the date of our report and the date of lodgement of the proposed public document with the Australian Securities and Investments Commission ("ASIC") which could affect our findings.

Consent

Prior to the issue of the proposed public document, we will review the document in its entirety, to consider whether we consent to the form and context in which we are named as Investigating Accountant, and to consider whether we consent to the inclusion of our Independent Assurance Report in the form and context in which it is included. Our consent will be issued on the letterhead of [firm name] and should then be quoted in the proposed public document.

The consent relates to the use of our name and report in the context of the whole proposed public document. Our name or report, or any extract, may not be included in any analysts' briefings, in any display on an internet site or in any other media without our prior consent. [Firm name] will be giving the consent pursuant to section 636(3) of the *Corporations Act 2001* but will not otherwise be authorising or causing the issue of the public document.

In the event of any misuse of our name or our reports, [firm name] reserves the right to withdraw its consent by written notification to ABC Company at its registered office and to ASIC.

[*Insert other information such as fee arrangements, billings and other specific terms and conditions, as appropriate.*]

Acceptance of Engagement Terms

We look forward to working closely with the directors of ABC Company in relation to this engagement.

Please sign and return the attached copy of this engagement letter to indicate your acknowledgement of, and agreement with, the terms and conditions detailed in this engagement letter, including our respective responsibilities. If you wish to discuss any aspect of this letter, please do not hesitate to contact me.

Yours Faithfully

[Firm name]

[Name of partner]

Partner

Client Acceptance

I have read and understood the terms and conditions of this letter, and the attached Appendix 1, and I agree to and accept them for and on behalf of ABC Company, by whom I am duly authorised:

Signature ....

Name ....

Position ....

ASAE

Appendix 2

(Ref: Para. A59)

Illustrative Representation Letter

The following illustrative representation letter is not authoritative but is intended only to be a guide that may be used in conjunction with the considerations outlined in this ASAE. It will need to be varied according to individual engagement requirements and circumstances.

Engagement Circumstances include the following:
ABC Company proposes to issue a public document.
Limited assurance engagement reporting on historical financial information, pro forma historical financial information and a directors' forecast.

Entity Letterhead

Firm Name

Address

[Date]

Dear Sirs,

This letter is provided in connection with your engagement to provide an independent assurance report on the financial information (comprising historical financial information, pro forma historical financial information and the Directors' forecast included in the public document of ABC Company Limited ("ABC Company") to be dated on or around [31 October 20XX], in accordance with the terms and conditions contained in your engagement letter dated [insert date].

Expressions and terms defined in the public document have the same meaning in this letter.

General Representations

We acknowledge that your engagement has been conducted in accordance with Standard on Assurance engagement ASAE 3450 *Assurance Engagements involving Corporate Fundraisings and/or Prospective Financial Information.* We understand that your engagement involved a review of the financial information in order to provide limited assurance, and consequently the procedures performed were limited primarily to enquiries of ABC Company personnel and analytical review procedures applied to the financial information, and thus provide less assurance than in an audit. You have not performed an audit and accordingly you do not express an audit opinion. [*Note that this paragraph will need to be amended if the assurance engagement involves providing reasonable assurance in relation to any of the financial information.*]

We acknowledge our responsibility for the preparation of the public document, including the preparation and presentation of all financial information contained therein, in accordance with the *Corporations Act 2001* (the Act).

We confirm that, to the best of our knowledge and belief (having made such enquiries as we considered necessary for the purposes of appropriately informing ourselves):

- ABC Company's financial information has been prepared on a going concern basis. Having considered the circumstances likely to affect ABC Company during the next 12 months, and the circumstances that we know will arise thereafter, we are satisfied that the going concern basis of preparing the financial information is appropriate.
- All material financial information, financial records, related data and other information relevant to the historical financial information and pro forma historical financial information within the possession of ABC Company have been provided to [Firm Name] prior to the finalisation of the assurance report. [Firm Name] is entitled to rely on the information provided by ABC Company and to assume that the information provided is, to the best knowledge and belief of management and the directors, accurate and, except where otherwise indicated, complete.

- In the performance of the assurance engagement, [Firm Name] has been entitled to rely on the information provided by ABC Company and to assume that the information provided is, to the best knowledge and belief of management and the directors of ABC Company, accurate and, except where otherwise indicated, complete.
- Any material changes that may have occurred between the date of the assurance report and the lodgement date of the public document with the Australian Securities and Investments Commission ("ASIC") have been advised to [Firm Name].
- All material events and transactions have been properly recorded in the accounting records underlying the financial information.
- We are responsible for, and have established and maintained, an adequate internal control structure to facilitate the preparation of reliable financial information. We acknowledge our responsibility for the implementation and operation of accounting and internal controls systems that are designed to prevent and detect fraud and error.
- There has been no fraud or suspected fraud involving any member of management or employee with a significant role in monitoring or implementing ABC Company's system of internal controls, or any other employee, that could have had a material effect on the financial information.
- [Other than detailed in the public document], there have been no violations, or possible violations, of laws, regulations or contractual agreements, the effects of which should be considered as the basis for recording a liability or for disclosure in the public document.
- [Other than detailed in the public document], there have been no communications from governmental or other regulatory authorities concerning non-compliance with, or deficiencies in, the group's adherence to relevant legislation. ABC Company has put in place appropriate procedures to ensure compliance with such legislation and the procedures have been applied throughout the financial periods under review.
- [Other than detailed in the public document], there have been no changes in accounting policies, or the application of the accounting policies, that have a material effect on the financial information. The accounting policies have been consistently applied in the preparation of the financial information.
- We believe there have been no uncorrected misstatements that are material, both individually and in aggregate, to any of the financial information under review. The uncorrected misstatements contained in [Appendix 1] are, we believe, immaterial, both individually and in aggregate to the financial information to which it relates.
- All material risks that may impact on the business have been adequately disclosed in the public document and considered in relation to their impact on the financial information.
- Other than those already adjusted for, and/or disclosed, there have been no matters or events that have arisen, or been discovered, subsequent to the preparation of the financial information that would require adjustment to that financial information or disclosure in the public document.
- There will not be any deficiencies or encumbrances attaching to the title of ABC Company's assets during the period covered by the financial information, other than those already reflected in the public document.
- ABC Company has no plans or intentions that could materially affect the book value or classification of assets or liabilities during the period of the financial information that are not already reflected therein.
- The ABC Company's board of directors is not aware of any breach or non-compliance with the terms of any contractual arrangements, however caused, that could initiate claims against ABC Company, and which would have a material effect on the financial information.
- [*Include any other matters that the assurance practitioner considers appropriate*.]

Historical financial information and pro forma historical financial information

With respect to the historical financial information and pro forma historical financial information of ABC Company for the year's ended 30 June 20XX and 20X1, we acknowledge our responsibility for the preparation and presentation of that financial information to which the independent assurance report relates. These financial statements include the Statement of Financial Position, Statements of Financial Performance, Statement of Cash flows and related notes. We confirm that, to the best of our knowledge and belief (having made such enquiries as we considered necessary for the purposes of appropriately informing ourselves):

- ABC Company's historical financial information included in the public document has been prepared in accordance with the stated basis of preparation, being the recognition and measurement principles contained in Australian Accounting Standards and the adopted accounting policies of ABC Company as described in section [X] of the public document.
- ABC Company's pro forma historical financial information included in the public document has been prepared in accordance with the stated basis of preparation, being the recognition and measurement principles contained in Australian Accounting Standards and the adopted accounting policies applied to:
    - ABC Company's historical financial information, as described in section [X] of the public document; and
    - pro forma adjustments as described in section [X] of the public document as if those adjustments had occurred as at the date of ABC Company's historical financial information.
- Disclosures not included in the public document with respect to the financial information have been determined by us to be not material to users of the public document.

Directors' forecast

With respect to the directors' forecast prepared in respect of the financial period 30 June 20XX to 30 June 20X2, we acknowledge our responsibility for the preparation and presentation of that information, the best-estimate assumptions used therein and its compliance with the stated basis of preparation.

We confirm that, to the best of our knowledge and belief (having made such enquiries as we considered necessary for the purposes of appropriately informing ourselves):

- The best-estimate assumptions described in section [X] of the public document have been agreed by ABC Company's board of directors, and provide a reasonable basis for the directors' forecast.
- The best-estimate assumptions underlying the directors' forecast have reasonable grounds, are supportable and consistent between themselves and with ABC Company's strategic plans, and have been consistently applied.
- The Directors' forecast has been prepared using the best-estimate assumptions, based on present circumstances, as to both the most likely set of economic, operating, developmental, and trading conditions and the course of action ABC Company is most likely to take. Accordingly, the Directors' forecast is appropriately called a forecast.
- All liabilities which will arise out of the activities of ABC Company have been included in the directors' forecast.
- During your review we have made available to you all records and information available to us at the time and on which we have based our financial model.
- The accounting policies adopted in preparing the directors' forecast for the year ending 30 June 20XX are those that are expected to be used for reporting historical financial information for the corresponding period.
- No transactions(s) or event(s) have occurred to the time of signing this letter that would necessitate adjustment to the directors' forecast, or disclosure in the public document, which we have not brought to your attention.
- [*Include any other matters that the assurance practitioner considers appropriate*].

Conclusion

This representation is provided to [Firm Name], [its Directors and employees], in connection with the public document dated 30 June 20XX to be issued by ABC Company.

Yours faithfully

ABC Company Limited

Name

Director

Appendix 3

(Ref: Para. A68)

Illustrative Assurance Reports

The following illustrative assurance reports can be tailored for specific engagement circumstances.

- Illustration 1: Independent Assurance Report on historical financial information and pro forma historical financial information included in a public document, with unmodified limited assurance conclusions
- Illustration 2: Independent Assurance Report on a forecast and pro forma forecast included in a public document, with unmodified limited assurance conclusions
- Illustration 3: Independent Assurance Report on prospective financial information in the form of a forecast, not included in a public document, with an unmodified limited assurance conclusion
- Illustration 4: Independent Assurance Report on prospective financial information in the form of a forecast, not included in a public document, with a mixture of unmodified limited assurance and reasonable assurance on different elements of the prospective financial information

Illustration 1: Engagement Circumstances include the following:

- **ABC Company proposes to issue a public document which includes historical financial information and pro forma historical financial information.**
- **Limited assurance engagement on historical financial information and pro forma historical financial information, with unmodified conclusions.**

[Date][89]

[The Addressees]

ABC Company Limited

[Address]

Dear [Addressees][90]

Independent Limited Assurance Report on ABC Company historical and pro forma historical financial information

We have been engaged by ABC Company Limited ("ABC Company") to report on the historical financial information and pro forma historical financial information of ABC Company [as at/for the period [date]] for inclusion in the public document dated on or about [insert date] and relating to the issue of [X] shares in ABC Company ("the document").

Expressions and terms defined in the document have the same meaning in this report.

The nature of this report is such that it can only be issued by an entity which holds an [please specify][91] under the *Corporations Act 2001*. [Firm name] holds the appropriate [please specify] under the *Corporations Act 2001*.

[Insert any background information relating to ABC Company and/or the proposed fundraising deemed relevant; if any.]

Scope

Historical Financial Information

You have requested [Firm Name] to review the following historical financial information of ABC Company (the responsible party) included in the public document:

89 The date of both the hard copy and electronic version of the report should be the same. See ASIC's RG 107 *Electronic Prospectuses*.

90 For example, the Directors or other title, as appropriate, in the circumstances of the assurance engagement.

91 An example is an Australian Financial Services License (AFSL)

- the Statement of Financial Performance for the [year(s)/period(s)] ended [insert date];
- the Statement of Financial Position as at [insert date];
- the Statement of Cash Flows for the [(year(s)/period(s)] ended [insert date];

The historical financial information has been prepared in accordance with the stated basis of preparation, being the recognition and measurement principles contained in Australian Accounting Standards and the company's adopted accounting policies. The historical financial information has been extracted from the financial report of ABC Company for the year(s) ended [insert date], which was audited by [Firm Name] in accordance with the Australian Auditing Standards. [Firm Name] issued a [modified/unmodified] audit opinion on the financial report. The historical financial information is presented in the public document in an abbreviated form, insofar as it does not include all of the presentation and disclosures required by Australian Accounting Standards and other mandatory professional reporting requirements applicable to general purpose financial reports prepared in accordance with the *Corporations Act 2001*.

Pro Forma historical financial information

You have requested [Firm Name] to review the pro forma historical Statement of Financial Position as at [insert date] referred to as "the pro forma historical financial information".

The pro forma historical financial information has been derived from the historical financial information of ABC Company, after adjusting for the effects of pro forma adjustments described in section [X] of the public document. The stated basis of preparation is the recognition and measurement principles contained in Australian Accounting Standards applied to the historical financial information and the event(s) or transaction(s) to which the pro forma adjustments relate, as described in section [X] of the public document, as if those event(s) or transaction(s) had occurred as at the date of the historical financial information. Due to its nature, the pro forma historical financial information does not represent the company's actual or prospective [financial position], [financial performance], and/or [cash flows].

[*Insert any other information relating to the underlying event(s) or transaction(s), which is deemed appropriate.*]

Directors' responsibility

The directors of ABC Company are responsible for the preparation of the historical financial information and pro forma historical financial information, including the selection and determination of pro forma adjustments made to the historical financial information and included in the pro forma historical financial information. This includes responsibility for such internal controls as the directors determine are necessary to enable the preparation of historical financial information and pro forma historical financial information that are free from material misstatement, whether due to fraud or error.

Our responsibility

Our responsibility is to express a limited assurance conclusion on the financial information based on the procedures performed and the evidence we have obtained. We have conducted our engagement in accordance with the Standard on Assurance Engagement ASAE 3450 *Assurance Engagements involving Corporate Fundraisings and/or Prospective Financial Information*.

A review consists of making enquiries, primarily of persons responsible for financial and accounting matters, and applying analytical and other review procedures. A review is substantially less in scope than an audit conducted in accordance with Australian Auditing Standards and consequently does not enable us to obtain reasonable assurance that we would become aware of all significant matters that might be identified in an audit. Accordingly, we do not express an audit opinion.

Our engagement did not involve updating or re-issuing any previously issued audit or review report on any financial information used as a source of the financial information.

Conclusions

Historical financial information

Based on our review, which is not an audit, nothing has come to our attention that causes us to believe that the historical financial information, as described in section [X] of the public document, and comprising:

- the Statement of Financial Performance of ABC Company for the [year(s)/period(s)] ended [insert date];
- the Statement of Financial Position as at [insert date]; and
- the Statement of Cash flows for the [year(s)/period(s)] ended [insert date];

are not presented fairly, in all material respects, in accordance with the stated basis of preparation, as described in section [X] of the document.[92]

Pro Forma historical financial information

Based on our review, which is not an audit, nothing has come to our attention that causes us to believe that the pro forma historical financial information being the Statement of Financial Position as at [insert date] is not presented fairly in all material respects, in accordance with the stated basis of preparation as described in section [X] of the document.

Restriction on Use

Without modifying our conclusions, we draw attention to section [X] of the public document, which describes the purpose of the financial information, being for inclusion in the public document. As a result, the financial information may not be suitable for use for another purpose.

Consent [Firm name] has consented[93] to the inclusion of this assurance report in the public document in the form and context in which it is included.

Liability

[*Liability wording to be inserted for individual Firm practice.*]

Declaration of Interest [or Disclosure of Interest]

[Firm Name] does not have any interest in the outcome of this [transaction][94] other than in [state interest] for which normal professional fees will be received.

Financial Services Guide

[*If applicable, insert wording.*]

Yours faithfully

[Firm Name][95] Date

92 Identify any departures from the recognition and measurement principles contained in the Australian Accounting Standards.

93 Consent is ordinarily provided in a separate consent letter, which can be referenced here.

94 Identify the nature of the event(s) or transaction(s), for example, the issue of shares or scheme of arrangement.

95 Where applicable, this may be replaced with "representative of the licensee".

Illustration 2: Engagement Circumstances include the following:

- **ABC Company proposes to issue a public document in accordance with the *Corporations Act 2001* which includes prospective financial information.**
- **Limited assurance engagement on prospective financial information in the form of a forecast and a pro forma forecast, with unmodified conclusions.**

[Date][96]

The [Addressees]

ABC Company Limited

[Address]

Dear [Addressees][97]

Independent Limited Assurance Report on ABC Company forecast and pro forma forecast

We have been engaged by ABC Company Limited ["ABC Company"] to report on the forecast Statement of Financial Performance ("forecast") and pro forma forecast Statement of Financial Performance ("pro forma forecast") [for the period ending] 30 June 20X0 of ABC Company for inclusion in the [public document][98] dated on or about [insert date] and relating to the issue of [X shares/units] in ABC Company.

Expressions and terms defined in the public document have the same meaning in this report.

The nature of this report is such that it can only be issued by an entity which holds an [please specify][99] under the *Corporations Act 2001*. [Firm name] holds the appropriate [please specify] under the *Corporations Act 2001*.

[*Insert any background information relating to ABC Company and/or the proposed fundraising deemed appropriate; if any.*]

Scope

You have requested [Firm Name] to review the following financial information of ABC Company (the responsible party) included in the public document:

- the forecast Statement of Financial Performance of ABC Company for the period(s) ending [insert date], as described in section [X] of the public document. The directors' best-estimate assumptions underlying the forecast are described in section [X] of the public document. The stated basis of preparation used in the preparation of the forecast is [include a reference to, or a description of the stated basis of preparation, for example, the recognition and measurement principles contained in Australian Accounting Standards and the entity's adopted accounting policies]; and
- the pro forma forecast Statement of Financial Performance of ABC Company for the period(s) ending [insert date], described in section [X] of the public document. The pro forma forecast has been derived from ABC Company's forecast, after adjusting for the effects of the pro forma adjustments described in section [X] of the public document. The stated basis of preparation used in the preparation of the pro forma forecast is [include a reference to, or a description of the stated basis of preparation, for example, the recognition and measurement principles contained in Australian Accounting Standards applied to the forecast and the event(s) or transaction(s) to which the pro forma adjustments relate, as described in section [X] of the public document, as if those event(s) or transaction(s) had occurred as at 1 July 20XX]. Due to its nature, the pro forma forecast does not represent the company's actual prospective [financial position], [financial performance], and/or [cash flows] [for the period(s) ending/as at] [insert date].

---

96 The date of both the hard copy and electronic version of the report should be the same. See ASIC's RG 107 *Electronic Prospectuses*.

97 For example, the Directors or other title, as appropriate, in the circumstances of the assurance engagement.

98 Specify the type of the public document.

99 An example is an Australian Financial Services License (AFSL).

Directors' Responsibility

The directors of ABC Company are responsible for the preparation of the forecast [for the period(s) ending/as at] [insert date], including the best-estimate assumptions underlying the forecast. They are also responsible for the preparation of the pro forma forecast for the period ending [insert date], including the selection and determination of the pro forma adjustments made to the forecast and included in the pro forma forecast. This includes responsibility for such internal control as the directors determine are necessary to enable the preparation of a forecast and a pro forma forecast that are free from material misstatement, whether due to fraud or error.

Our Responsibility

Our responsibility is to express limited assurance conclusions on the forecast and pro forma forecast, the best-estimate assumptions underlying the forecast and pro forma forecast, and the reasonableness of the forecast and pro forma forecast themselves, based on our review. We have conducted our engagement in accordance with the Standard on Assurance Engagements ASAE 3450 *Assurance Engagements involving Corporate Fundraisings and/or Prospective Financial Information.*

Our limited assurance procedures consisted of making enquiries, primarily of persons responsible for financial and accounting matters, and applying analytical and other review procedures. A limited assurance engagement is substantially less in scope than an audit conducted in accordance with Australian Auditing Standards and consequently does not enable us to obtain reasonable assurance that we would become aware of all significant matters that might be identified in a reasonable assurance engagement. Accordingly, we do not express an audit opinion.

Our engagement did not involve updating or re-issuing any previously issued audit or review report on any financial information used as a source of the financial information.

Conclusions

Forecast

Based on our limited assurance engagement, which is not a reasonable assurance engagement, nothing has come to our attention which causes us to believe that:

- the directors' best-estimate assumptions used in the preparation of the forecast Statement of Financial Performance of ABC Company [for the year(s)/period(s) ending] [insert date] do not provide reasonable grounds for the forecast; and
- in all material respects, the forecast:
  - is not prepared on the basis of the directors' best-estimate assumptions as described in section [X] of the public document; and
  - is not presented fairly in accordance with the stated basis of preparation, being [insert a reference to, or a description of the stated basis of preparation, for example, the recognition and measurement principles contained in Australian Accounting Standards and the entity's adopted accounting policies]; and
- the forecast itself is unreasonable.

Pro Forma Forecast

Based on our review, which is not an audit, nothing has come to our attention that causes us to believe that:

- the directors' best-estimate assumptions used in the preparation of the pro forma forecast Statement of Financial Performance of ABC Company [for the year(s) ended/period(s) ending] [insert date] do not provide reasonable grounds for the pro forma forecast; and
- in all material respects, the pro forma forecast:
  - is not prepared on the basis of the directors' best-estimate assumptions, as described in section [X] of the public document; and
  - is not presented fairly in accordance with the stated basis of preparation, being [insert reference to, or a description of the stated basis of preparation, for example, the recognition and measurement principles contained in Australian Accounting Standards and the company's adopted accounting policies, applied to the forecast

and the pro forma adjustments as if those adjustments had occurred as at the date of the forecast]; and

- the pro forma forecast itself is unreasonable.

Forecast and Pro Forma Forecast

The forecast and pro forma forecast have been prepared by management and adopted by the directors in order to provide prospective investors with a guide to the potential financial performance of ABC Company [for the period(s)/year(s) ending] [insert date]. There is a considerable degree of subjective judgement involved in preparing forecasts since they relate to event(s) and transaction(s) that have not yet occurred and may not occur. Actual results are likely to be different from the forecast and pro forma forecast since anticipated event(s) or transaction(s) frequently do not occur as expected and the variation may be material. The directors' best-estimate assumptions on which the forecast and pro forma forecast are based relate to future event(s) and/or transaction(s) that management expect to occur and actions that management expect to take and are also subject to uncertainties and contingencies, which are often outside the control of the ABC Company. Evidence may be available to support the directors' best-estimate assumptions on which the forecast and pro forma are based however such evidence is generally future-oriented and therefore speculative in nature. We are therefore not in a position to express a reasonable assurance conclusion on those best-estimate assumptions, and accordingly, provide a lesser level of assurance on the reasonableness of the directors' best-estimate assumptions. The limited assurance conclusion expressed in this report has been formed on the above basis.

Prospective investors should be aware of the material risks and uncertainties in relation to an investment in ABC Company, which are detailed in the public document, and the inherent uncertainty relating to the forecast and pro forma forecast. Accordingly, prospective investors should have regard to the investment risks and sensitivities as described in section [X] of the public document. The sensitivity analysis described in section [X] of the public document demonstrates the impact on the forecast and pro forma forecast of changes in key best-estimate assumptions. We express no opinion as to whether the forecast or pro forma forecast will be achieved.

The forecast and pro forma forecast have been prepared by the directors for the purpose of [insert description].[100] We disclaim any assumption of responsibility for any reliance on this report, or on the forecast or pro forma forecast to which it relates, for any purpose other than that for which it was prepared. We have assumed, and relied on representations from certain members of management of ABC Company, that all material information concerning the prospects and proposed operations of ABC Company has been disclosed to use and that the information provided to use for the purpose of our work is true, complete and accurate in all respects. We have no reason to believe that those representations are false.

Restriction on Use

Without modifying our conclusions, we draw attention to section [X] of the public document, which describes the purpose of the forecast and pro forma forecast, being for inclusion in the public document. As a result, the forecast and pro forma forecast may not be suitable for use for another purpose.

Consent

[Firm name] has consented[101] to the inclusion of this assurance report in the public document in the form and context in which it is included.

Liability

[*Liability wording to be inserted for individual Firm practice.*]

100 Indicate the Directors' purpose for preparing the forecast, for example: "*to provide prospective investors with a guide to the potential financial performance of ABC Company for the year(s) ending [insert date].*"

101 Consent is ordinarily provided in a separate consent letter, which can be referenced here.

Declaration of Interest [or Disclosure of Interest]

[Firm Name] does not have any interest in the outcome of this [transaction][102] other than in [state interest] for which normal professional fees will be received.

Financial Services Guide

[*If applicable, insert wording*.]

Yours faithfully

[Firm Name][103] Date

Illustration 3: Engagement Circumstances include the following:

- **ABC Company has prepared a non-public document, and includes prospective financial information.**
- **Limited assurance engagement on prospective financial information in the form of a forecast, with an unmodified limited assurance conclusion.**

[Date][104]

The [Addressees]

[Name of Entity]

[Address]

Dear [Addressees][105]

Independent Assurance Report on ABC Company forecast

We have been engaged by ACB Company Limited ("ABC Company") to report on the forecast Statement of Financial Performance for the period ending 30 June 20X0 of ABC Company for inclusion in section [X] of the [describe document], dated on or about [insert date], and relating to [please specify] ("the document"). As agreed in our engagement letter dated [insert date], this report is prepared solely for distribution to users specified in section [X] of the document.

Expressions and terms defined in the document have the same meaning in this report.

[*Insert any background information relating to ABC Company and/or the proposed fundraising deemed appropriate; if any*.]

Scope

You have requested [Firm Name] to review the ABC Company forecast included in the document. The stated basis of preparation used in the preparation of the forecast by ABC Company (the responsible party) is [include a reference to, or a description of the stated basis of preparation, for example, the recognition and measurement principles contained in Australian Accounting Standards and the company's adopted accounting policies.]

Management's Responsibility

The management of ABC Company is responsible for the preparation of the forecast for the period(s) ending [insert date], including the best-estimate assumptions underlying the forecast. This includes responsibility for such internal controls as management determines are necessary to enable the preparation of a forecast that is free from material misstatement, whether due to fraud or error.

Our Responsibility

Our responsibility is to express limited assurance conclusions on the forecast, the best-estimate assumptions underlying the forecast, and the reasonableness of the forecast itself, based on our work. We have conducted our engagement in accordance with the Standard on Assurance

102 Identify the nature of the event(s) or transaction(s), for example, the issue of shares or scheme of arrangement.

103 Where applicable, this may be replaced with "representative of the licensee".

104 The date of both the hard copy and electronic version of the report should be the same. See ASIC's RG 107 *Electronic Prospectuses*.

105 For example, the Directors or other title, as appropriate, in the circumstances of the assurance engagement.

Engagements ASAE 3450 *Assurance Engagements involving Corporate Fundraisings and/or Prospective Financial Information.*

Our limited assurance engagement consisted of making enquiries, primarily of persons responsible for financial and accounting matters, and applying analytical and other review procedures. It is substantially less in scope than an reasonable assurance engagement conducted in accordance with Australian Auditing Standards and consequently does not enable us to obtain reasonable assurance that we would become aware of all significant matters that might be identified in an reasonable assurance engagement. Accordingly, we do not express a reasonable assurance conclusion.

Conclusion

Based on our limited assurance engagement, which is not a reasonable assurance engagement, nothing has come to our attention which causes us to believe that:

- management's best-estimate assumptions do not provide reasonable grounds for the preparation of the forecast Statement of Financial Performance of ABC Company [for the year(s)/period(s) ending] [insert date]; and
- in all material respects, the forecast:
  - is not prepared on the basis of management's best-estimate assumptions as described in section [X] of the document; and
  - is not presented fairly in accordance with the stated basis of preparation, being [insert a reference to, or a description of the stated basis of preparation, for example, the recognition and measurement principles contained in Australian Accounting Standards and the entity's adopted accounting policies]; and
- the forecast itself is unreasonable.

The forecast has been prepared by management and adopted by the directors in order to provide [please specify] with a guide to the potential financial performance of the ABC Company [for the period(s)/year(s) ending] [date]. There is a considerable degree of subjective judgement involved in preparing a forecast since it relates to event(s) and transaction(s) that have not yet occurred and may not occur. Actual results are likely to be different from the forecast since anticipated event(s) or transaction(s) frequently do not occur as expected and the variation may be material.

Management's best-estimate assumptions on which the forecast is based relate to future event(s) and/or transaction(s) that management expect to occur and actions that management expect to take and are also subject to uncertainties and contingencies, which are often outside the control of the ABC Company. Evidence may be available to support management's best-estimate assumptions on which the forecast is based; however such evidence is generally future-oriented and therefore speculative in nature. We are therefore not in a position to obtain the level of assurance necessary to express a reasonable assurance conclusion on those best-estimate assumptions, and accordingly provide a lesser level of assurance on the reasonableness of management's best-estimate assumptions. The limited assurance conclusion expressed in this assurance report has been formed on the above basis.

Readers of the document should be aware of the material risks and uncertainties in relation to [please insert details], which are detailed in the [public document], and the inherent uncertainty relating to the forecast. Accordingly, readers should have regard to the risks and sensitivities as described in section [X] of the document. The sensitivity analysis as described in section [X] of the document demonstrates the impact on the forecast of changes in key best-estimate assumptions. We express no opinion as to whether the forecast will be achieved.

The forecast has been prepared by management for [the purpose of]. We disclaim any assumption of responsibility for any reliance on this report, or on the forecast to which it relates, for any purpose other than that for which it was prepared. We have assumed, and relied on representations from certain members of management of ABC Company that all material information concerning the prospects and proposed operations of ABC Company has been disclosed to us and that the information provided to us for the purpose of our work is true, complete and accurate in all respects. We have no reason to believe that those representations are false.

Reliance on this report

This report is addressed to the directors of ABC Company (as responsible party for ABC Company) and [specify]. [*Include any other matters that the assurance practitioner considers appropriate*].

Restriction on Use

Without modifying our conclusions, we draw attention to section [X] of the public document, which describes the purpose of the financial information, being for inclusion in the public document. As a result, the forecast may not be suitable for use for another purpose.

Consent

[Firm name] has consented[106] to the inclusion of this assurance report in the public document in the form and context in which it is included.

Liability

[*Liability wording to be inserted for individual Firm practice.*]

Declaration of Interest [or Disclosure of Interest]

[Firm Name] does not have any interest in the outcome of this [transaction] other than in [state interest] for which normal professional fees will be received.

Financial Services Guide

[*If applicable, insert wording.*]

Yours faithfully

[Firm Name] Date

Illustration 4: Engagement Circumstances include the following:

- **ABC Company has prepared a non-public document, which includes prospective financial information.**
- **The engagement is a mixture of unmodified limited assurance and unmodified reasonable assurance on different elements of the prospective financial information in the form of a forecast.**

[Date][107]

The [Addressees]

[Name of Entity]

[Address]

Dear [Addressees][108]

Independent Assurance Report on ABC Company forecast

We have been engaged to report on the forecast Statement of Financial Performance for the period ending 30 June 20X0 of ABC Company Limited ("ABC Company") for inclusion in section [X] of the [describe document], dated on or about [insert date], and relating to [insert what document relates to] ("the document"). As agreed in our engagement letter dated [insert date], this report is prepared solely for distribution to users specified in section [X] of the document.

Expressions and terms defined in the document have the same meaning in this report.

[*Insert any background information relating to ABC Company and/or the proposed fundraising deemed appropriate; if any.*]

Scope

You have requested [Firm Name] to review the forecast prepared by ABC Company (the responsible party) included in the document. The stated basis of preparation used in the preparation of the forecast is [include a reference to, or a description of the stated basis

106 Consent is ordinarily provided in a separate consent letter, which can be referenced here.

107 The date of both the hard copy and electronic version of the report should be the same. See ASIC's RG 107.

108 For example, the Directors or other title, as appropriate, in the circumstances of the assurance engagement.

of preparation, for example, the recognition and measurement principles contained in Australian Accounting Standards and the company's adopted accounting policies.]

Management's Responsibility

The management of ABC Company is responsible for the preparation of the forecast for the period(s) ending [insert date], including the best-estimate assumptions underlying the forecast. This includes responsibility for such internal controls as management determines are necessary to enable the preparation of a forecast that is free from material misstatement, whether due to fraud or error.

Our Responsibility

Our responsibility, based on our work performed is to express limited assurance on the best-estimate assumptions underlying the forecast and on the reasonableness of the forecast itself, and reasonable assurance on whether the forecast is prepared based on those assumptions and the stated basis of preparation. We have conducted our engagement in accordance with the Standard on Assurance Engagements ASAE 3450 *Assurance Engagements involving Corporate Fundraisings and/or Prospective Financial Information.*

The forecast has been prepared by management and adopted by the directors in order to provide [please specify] with a guide to the potential financial performance of the ABC Company [for the period(s)/year(s) ending] [date]. There is a considerable degree of subjective judgement involved in preparing a forecast since it relates to event(s) and transaction(s) that have not yet occurred and may not occur. Actual results are likely to be different from the forecast since anticipated event(s) or transaction(s) frequently do not occur as expected and the variation may be material.

Management's best-estimate assumptions on which the forecast is based relate to future event(s) and/or transaction(s) that management expect to occur and actions that management expect to take and are also subject to uncertainties and contingencies, which are often outside the control of the ABC Company. Evidence may be available to support management's best-estimate assumptions on which the forecast is based; however such evidence is generally future-oriented and therefore speculative in nature. We are therefore not in a position to obtain the level of assurance necessary to express a reasonable assurance conclusion on those best-estimate assumptions, and accordingly provide a lesser level of assurance on the reasonableness of management's best-estimate assumptions. The limited assurance conclusion expressed in this assurance report has been formed on the above basis.

Readers of the document should be aware of the material risks and uncertainties in relation to an investment in the ABC Company, which are detailed in the [public document], and the inherent uncertainty relating to the forecast. Accordingly, readers should have regard to the risks and sensitivities as described in section [X] of the document. The sensitivity analysis as described in section [X] of the document demonstrates the impact on the forecast of changes in key best-estimate assumptions. We express no opinion as to whether the forecast will be achieved.

The forecast has been prepared by management for [the purpose of]. We disclaim any assumption of responsibility for any reliance on this report, or on the forecast to which it relates, for any purpose other than that for which it was prepared. We have assumed, and relied on representations from certain members of management of ABC Company that all material information concerning the prospects and proposed operations of ABC Company has been disclosed to us and that the information provided to us for the purpose of our work is true, complete and accurate in all respects. We have no reason to believe that those representations are false.

Conclusion

- based on our limited assurance procedures, nothing has come to our attention which causes us to believe that management's best-estimate assumptions do not provide reasonable grounds for the preparation of the forecast Statement of Financial Performance of ABC Company [for the year(s)/period(s) ending] [insert date];
- based on our reasonable assurance procedures, the forecast is, in all material respects, prepared on the basis of management's best-estimate assumptions as described in section [X] of the document; and is presented fairly in accordance with the stated basis of preparation, being [insert a reference to, or a description of the stated basis of preparation, for example,

the recognition and measurement principles contained in Australian Accounting Standards and the entity's adopted accounting policies]; and

- based on our limited assurance procedures, nothing has come to our attention which causes us to believe that the forecast itself is unreasonable.

Reliance on this report

This report is addressed to the directors of ABC Company (as responsible party for ABC Company) and [specify]. [*Include any other matters that the assurance practitioner considers appropriate*].

Consent

[Firm name] has consented[109] to the inclusion of this assurance report in the public document in the form and context in which it is included.

Liability

[*Liability wording to be inserted for individual Firm practice.*]

Declaration of Interest [or Disclosure of Interest]

[Firm Name] does not have any interest in the outcome of this [transaction] other than in [state interest] for which normal professional fees will be received.

Yours faithfully

[Firm Name] Date

ASAE

109 Consent is ordinarily provided in a separate consent letter, which can be referenced here.

ASAE 3500

Performance Engagements

(Issued July 2008: amended October 2008)

Issued by the Auditing and Assurance Standards Board.

Note from the Institute of Chartered Accountants Australia

This note, prepared by the technical editor, is not part of ASAE 3500.

Historical development

July 2008: ASAE 3500 establishes mandatory requirements and provides explanatory guidance for conducting and reporting on performance engagements. This ASAE is operative for performance engagements commencing on or after 1 January 2009. There is no corresponding international statement. The AUASB had reviewed AUS 806 'Performance Auditing' (July 2002) and AUS 808 'Planning Performance Audits' (October 1995), prepared by its predecessor Board and identified the need to update these Standards.

October 2008: ASAE 3500 reissued with editorial amendments.

Contents

ASAE

Preface

Reasons for Issuing Standard on Assurance Engagements ASAE 3500 *Performance Engagements*

The AUASB makes Auditing Standards under section 336 of the *Corporations Act 2001* for the purposes of the corporations legislation and formulates auditing and assurance standards for other purposes.

The AUASB issues Standard on Assurance Engagements ASAE 3500 *Performance Engagements* pursuant to the requirements of the legislative provisions explained below.

The *Corporate Law Economic Reform Program (Audit Reform and Corporate Disclosure) Act 2004* (the CLERP 9 Act) established the AUASB as an independent statutory body under section 227A of the *Australian Securities and Investments Commission Act 2001* (ASIC Act), as from 1 July 2004. Under section 227B of the ASIC Act, the AUASB may formulate Assurance Standards for purposes other than the corporations legislation.

Following the issuance of the *Framework for Assurance Engagements* (Framework) and ASAE 3000 *Assurance Engagements Other than Audits or Reviews of Historical Financial Information*, the AUASB reviewed existing assurance standards issued by the former Auditing & Assurance Standards Board of the Australian Accounting Research Foundation, including AUS 806 *Performance Auditing* (July 2002) and AUS 808 *Planning Performance Audits* (October 1995), and identified the need to update these standards.

Main Features

This Standard on Assurance Engagements (ASAE) establishes mandatory requirements and provides explanatory guidance for conducting and reporting on performance engagements.

Operative Date

This ASAE is operative for performance engagements commencing on or after 1 January 2009.

Authority Statement

The Auditing and Assurance Standards Board (AUASB) formulates this Standard on Assurance Engagements ASAE 3500 *Performance Engagements* as set out in paragraphs 1 to 94, pursuant to section 227B of the *Australian Securities and Investments Commission Act 2001*.

This Standard on Assurance Engagements is to be read in conjunction with the *Preamble to AUASB Standards*, which sets out the intentions of the AUASB on how the Standards on Assurance Engagements are to be understood, interpreted and applied.

The mandatory requirements of this Standard on Assurance Engagements are set out in **bold-type** paragraphs.

Dated 31 July 2008

M H Kelsall
Chairman - AUASB

Standard on Assurance Engagements ASAE 3500 Performance Engagements

Application

1 **This Standard on Assurance Engagements (ASAE) applies to performance engagements which may be a performance audit or a performance review engagement.**

Operative Date

2 **This ASAE is operative for performance engagements commencing on or after 1 January 2009.**

Introduction

3 The purpose of this ASAE, in addition to the mandatory requirements and explanatory guidance for assurance engagements provided by ASAE 3000 *Assurance Engagements Other than Audits or Reviews of Historical Financial Information*, is to establish mandatory requirements and to provide explanatory guidance for undertaking and reporting on performance engagements. This ASAE applies to assurance practitioners conducting performance engagements.

4 The terms "performance audit engagement" and "performance review engagement" distinguish between the two types of performance engagements that an assurance practitioner may conduct under this ASAE. A performance audit engagement provides reasonable assurance, whereas a performance review engagement provides limited assurance.

5 A performance engagement with multiple objectives and sub-objectives, which incorporates either or both levels of assurance in the same engagement, may also be conducted under this ASAE. In these circumstances, the activity on which a performance audit is conducted needs to be clearly distinguished from the activity on which a performance review is conducted.

6 The essential elements of performance engagements are:

(a) a three party relationship involving an assurance practitioner, a responsible party or a number of responsible parties, and intended users, where either the responsible party or the intended user may also be the engaging party;

(b) an appropriate activity;

(c) suitable criteria;

(d) sufficient appropriate evidence; and

(e) a written assurance report in a form appropriate to a performance audit engagement or a performance review engagement or a report addressing both levels of assurance.

7 The responsible party and the intended users may be from different entities or the same entity. The relationship between the responsible party and the intended users needs to be viewed within the context of a specific performance engagement and may differ from more traditionally defined lines of responsibility. For example, an entity's senior management (the intended user) may engage an assurance practitioner to conduct a performance engagement of a particular aspect of the entity's activities that is the immediate responsibility of a lower level of management (the responsible party), but for which senior management is ultimately responsible. In the public sector, performance engagements may be conducted by an Auditor-General (the assurance practitioner) pursuant to a legislative mandate on a government agency or agencies (the responsible party or parties) for the purpose of reporting to the Parliament (the intended user).

Relationship with Other ASAEs, ASAs and ASREs

8 **The assurance practitioner shall comply with this ASAE, ASAE 3000 and other applicable ASAEs when conducting a performance engagement of an entity or selected activity of an entity, or a selected activity across a number of entities.**

ASAE

9 ASAE 3000 has been written for general application to assurance engagements other than audits or reviews of historical financial information covered by ASAs or ASREs. Other ASAEs may relate to topics that apply to all subject matters or be subject matter specific. This ASAE has been written for specific application to performance engagements as an adjunct standard to ASAE 3000.

10 In circumstances when a performance engagement includes a compliance component, in accordance with paragraph 8 of this ASAE, the assurance practitioner needs to apply both ASAE 3100 and ASAE 3500 as applicable, as well as ASAE 3000, in conducting the assurance engagement. However, if there is any inconsistency, ASAE 3500 applies.

Inability to Comply with Mandatory Requirements

11 Where in rare and exceptional circumstances, factors outside the assurance practitioner's control prevent the assurance practitioner from complying with a relevant mandatory requirement in this ASAE and/or ASAE 3000, the assurance practitioner shall:

(a) if possible, undertake appropriate alternative evidence-gathering procedures; and

(b) document in the working papers:

(i) the circumstances surrounding the inability to comply;

(ii) the reasons for the inability to comply; and

(iii) justification of how alternative evidence-gathering procedures achieve the objectives of the mandatory requirement.

When the assurance practitioner is unable to undertake appropriate alternative evidence-gathering procedures, the assurance practitioner shall assess the implications for the assurance report.

Objective of a Performance Engagement

12 The objective of a performance engagement is to enable the assurance practitioner to express a conclusion designed to enhance the degree of confidence of the intended users other than the responsible party by reporting on assertions, or information obtained directly, concerning the economy, efficiency or effectiveness of an activity against identified criteria.

13 In expressing a conclusion, under paragraph 12 of this ASAE, the assurance practitioner uses professional judgement to assess the performance of an activity against the identified criteria and whether:

(a) performance is within the tolerances of materiality (that is, the activity has been carried out economically, efficiently or effectively); or

(b) performance is outside the tolerances of materiality (that is, the activity has not been carried out economically, efficiently or effectively).

14 While legislation, regulations, predetermined policies or custom may establish the responsible party's responsibility, it may not necessarily be described using the terms economy, efficiency and effectiveness. In these circumstances, the assurance practitioner exercises professional judgement in determining the use of the most appropriate terminology throughout the performance engagement and especially in the assurance report. In conducting a performance engagement, the assurance practitioner is not limited to only using the terms economy, efficiency and effectiveness.

15 Ordinarily, performance engagements address a range of activities including:

- Systems for planning, budgeting, authorisation, control and evaluation of resource allocation.
- Systems established and maintained to ensure compliance with an entity's mandate as expressed in policies or legislation.
- Appropriateness of resource management.
- Measures aimed at deriving economies of scale, such as centralised resource acquisition, sharing common resources across a number of business units.

- Measures aimed at improving economy, efficiency or effectiveness.
- Appropriateness of the assignment of responsibilities, and accountability.
- Measures to monitor outcomes against predetermined objectives and performance benchmarks.

16 In the public sector, the conduct of performance engagements by Auditors-General is legislated in the respective jurisdictions. While the legislative requirements may have either a narrow or broad scope, ordinarily performance engagements include examination of:

- Economy, efficiency or effectiveness:
  - in terms of management systems or an entity's management in order to contribute to improvements;
  - of the operations of an entity or an activity of an entity;
  - of the internal controls applied by an entity in relation to an activity;
  - in the implementation of government policies or programs and the application of government grants;
  - in terms of financial prudence in the application of public resources; and
  - of administrative arrangements.
- The validity and reliability of performance measurement systems and/or statements published by the responsible party in annual reports.
- Compliance with legislation and accompanying instruments and identification of breaches.
- Intended and unintended impacts of the implementation of government policies or programs and the extent to which community needs and stated objectives of an activity or entity have been met.
- Probity processes and identification of weaknesses.

Definitions

17 In this ASAE, the following terms have the meanings attributed below:

(a) "Activity" means an action or actions associated with a function or program, including administrative and internal control functions, that are integral to the operations of a business unit or an entity. In the context of this ASAE the economy, efficiency or effectiveness of the activity is the subject matter of a performance engagement.

(b) "Assertion-based Engagement" in the context of a performance engagement means a performance engagement where the assurance practitioner reports on assertions prepared by the responsible party regarding the economy, efficiency or effectiveness of the activity.

(c) "Assurance practitioner" means a person or an organisation, whether in public practice, industry, commerce or the public sector, involved in the provision of assurance services.

(d) "Criteria" in the context of a performance engagement means reasonable and acceptable standards of performance against which the extent of economy, efficiency or effectiveness of an activity may be assessed.

Suitable criteria have the following characteristics:

(i) *relevance*: relevant criteria contribute to conclusions that assist decision-making by the intended users;

(ii) *completeness*: criteria are sufficiently complete when relevant factors that could affect the conclusions in the context of the performance engagement circumstances are not omitted. Complete criteria include, where relevant, benchmarks for presentation and disclosure;

(iii) *reliability*: reliable criteria allow reasonably consistent evaluation or measurement of the activity, including when used in similar circumstances by similarly qualified assurance practitioners;

(iv) *neutrality*: neutral criteria contribute to conclusions that are free from bias; and

(v) *understandability*: understandable criteria contribute to conclusions that are clear, comprehensive, and not subject to significantly different interpretations.

(e) "Direct Reporting Engagement" means performance engagements where the assurance practitioner directly undertakes the evaluation or measurement of the activity to report on the economy, efficiency or effectiveness of the activity.

(f) "Intended users" means the person, persons or class of persons for whom the assurance practitioner prepares the assurance report. The responsible party can be one of the intended users, but not the sole user.

(g) "Materiality" in the context of a performance engagement means variations of the measure or assertions from identified criteria for the evaluation or measurement of performance of the activity which, if omitted, misstated or not disclosed has the potential to adversely affect decisions about the economy, efficiency or effectiveness made by users or the discharge of accountability by the responsible party or the governing body of the entity.

(h) "Performance engagement" means a performance audit or a performance review of all or a part of the activities of an entity (or entities) to assess economy, efficiency or effectiveness. It includes a "performance audit engagement" or a "performance review engagement" directed to assess:

(i) the adequacy of an internal control structure or specific internal controls, in particular those intended to safeguard assets and to ensure due regard for economy, efficiency or effectiveness;

(ii) the extent to which resources have been managed economically or efficiently; and

(iii) the extent to which activities have been effective.

Using identified criteria to evaluate or measure the economy, efficiency or effectiveness of an activity results in assertions or information concerning the performance of that activity. The assurance practitioner gathers sufficient appropriate evidence about these assertions or information to provide a basis for expressing a conclusion in an assurance report. For example, a performance engagement may be directed at management's assertions or information concerning the effectiveness of an entity's road maintenance program (activity) in reducing traffic accidents as measured against identified criteria.

The terms "performance audit" and "performance review" are predominantly applied in the public sector. In the private sector these audits and reviews are commonly referred to as "operational audits" and "operational reviews".

(i) "Performance audit engagement" means a performance engagement where the assurance practitioner provides reasonable assurance. This is where the assurance practitioner's objective is a reduction in performance engagement risk to an acceptably low level in the circumstances of the performance engagement as the basis for a positive form of expression of the assurance practitioner's conclusion. Reasonable assurance means a high, but not absolute, level of assurance.

(j) "Performance review engagement" means a performance engagement where the assurance practitioner provides limited assurance. In a limited assurance engagement the assurance practitioner's objective is a reduction in performance engagement risk to a level that is acceptable in the circumstances of the assurance engagement, as the basis for a negative form of expression of the assurance practitioner's conclusion. The acceptable performance engagement risk in a limited assurance engagement is greater than for a reasonable assurance engagement.

(k) "Performance engagement risk" means the risk that the assurance practitioner expresses an inappropriate conclusion when the performance of an activity is not materially economic, efficient or effective. This would arise where the assurance practitioner draws conclusions based on evidence that is not soundly based or that is improper or incomplete as a result of inadequacies in the evidence gathering process, misrepresentation or fraud.

(l) "Professional scepticism" means where the assurance practitioner makes a critical assessment, with a questioning mind, of the validity of evidence obtained and is alert to evidence that contradicts or brings into question the reliability of documents and responses to enquiries and other information obtained from management and the responsible party.

(m) "Responsible Party" means the person (or persons) who:

(i) in a direct reporting engagement, is responsible for the activity; and

(ii) in an assertion-based engagement, is responsible for the assertions or information concerning the performance of the activity and may also be responsible for the activity itself. An example of when the responsible party is responsible for the assertions or information concerning the performance of an activity but not responsible for the activity itself is when a central government agency, such as a Treasury or Department of Finance, prepares assertions or information concerning the performance of activities conducted by other government departments.

18 In addition to the definitions included at paragraph 17 of this ASAE, the following definitions have the meanings attributed below. These definitions may have broader application in the public sector and should not be seen as limiting existing legislative arrangements or custom.

(a) "Economy" means the acquisition of the appropriate quality and quantity of resources at the appropriate times and at the lowest cost.

(b) "Efficiency" means the use of resources such that output is optimised for any given set of resource inputs, or input is minimised for any given quantity and quality of output.

(c) "Effectiveness" means the achievement of the objectives or other intended effects of activities at a program or entity level.

ASAE

General Principles of a Performance Engagement

Ethical Requirements

19 The assurance practitioner shall comply with the fundamental ethical principles of integrity, objectivity, professional competence and due care, confidentiality and professional behaviour.

20 The concept of independence is fundamental to the assurance practitioner's compliance with the principles of integrity and objectivity under paragraph 19 of this ASAE.

21 The applicable code of ethics of a professional accounting body[1] provides a framework of principles that members of assurance teams, firms and network firms use to identify threats to independence, evaluate the significance of those threats and, if the threats are other than clearly insignificant:

(a) identify and apply safeguards to eliminate the threats; or

(b) reduce them to an acceptable level,

such that independence of mind and independence in appearance are not compromised.

1 The applicable code of ethics of the professional accounting bodies in Australia is *APES 110 Code of Ethics for Professional Accountants*, as issued from time to time by the Accounting Professional and Ethical Standards Board. This code of ethics has been adopted by CPA Australia, National Institute of Accountants, and The Institute of Chartered Accountants in Australia. In addition, codes of ethics issued by other professional bodies may apply.

22 Where the practitioner is not able to comply with the fundamental ethical principles, including those relating to independence, the practitioner can not claim compliance with this ASAE. In such circumstances, ASAE 3500 may still provide useful guidance.

Quality Control

23 **The assurance practitioner shall implement procedures to address the following elements of a quality control system that apply to the individual performance engagement:**

(a) leadership responsibilities for quality on the performance engagement;

(b) ethical requirements;

(c) acceptance of client relationships and specific performance engagements;

(d) assignment of performance engagement teams;

(e) conduct of the performance engagement; and

(f) monitoring.

24 For further guidance on quality control refer to ASAE 3000.

25 Depending on the nature of the performance engagement, the assurance practitioner may need to either assemble a multi-disciplinary team or be a specialist in the relevant discipline. A multi-disciplinary team may include expertise in, for example, accounting, economics, legal, organisational psychology, political science and sociology.

26 When multi-disciplinary teams are used in a performance engagement, adequate direction, supervision and review are particularly important so that the team members' different perspectives, experience and specialties are appropriately used. It is important that all team members understand the objectives of the particular performance engagement and the terms of reference of work assigned to them. Adequate direction, supervision and review are important so that the work of all team members is executed properly and is in compliance with this ASAE and ASAE 3000.

Performance Engagement Initiation or Acceptance

27 **The assurance practitioner shall initiate or accept a performance engagement only if:**

(a) the activity is the responsibility of a party who is not the sole intended user or the assurance practitioner;

(b) on the basis of a preliminary knowledge of the performance engagement circumstances, the assurance practitioner forms the view that:

(i) the requirements of the fundamental ethical principles will be satisfied;

(ii) the activity is appropriate as a subject matter for the performance engagement in that it is identifiable, its performance is capable of consistent measurement against identified criteria or assertions, and[2] information about it is capable of being subjected to procedures for gathering sufficient appropriate evidence;

(iii) the identified criteria are suitable; and

(iv) the requirements of this ASAE or ASAE 3000 will be satisfied; and

(c) the assurance practitioner is satisfied that those persons who are to conduct the performance engagement collectively possess the necessary professional and technical competencies.

Communicating or Agreeing on the Terms of the Performance Engagement

28 **The assurance practitioner shall communicate or agree on the terms of the performance engagement with the engaging party, which shall be recorded in writing by the assurance practitioner and forwarded to the engaging party. When the**

2 Amended October 2008.

terms of a performance engagement are changed, the assurance practitioner shall communicate or agree the new terms with the engaging party in writing. When the performance engagement is undertaken or changed pursuant to legislation, the applicable performance engagement terms shall be those contained in the legislation.

29 To avoid misunderstandings, under paragraph 28 of this ASAE, the agreed terms of the performance engagement need to be recorded in a performance engagement letter or other suitable form of contract. If the engaging party is not the responsible party, the nature and content of a performance engagement letter or contract may be different from when the engaging party is the responsible party. The existence of a legislative mandate may satisfy the requirement to agree on the terms of the performance engagement. Even in those situations an assurance engagement letter may be useful for both the assurance practitioner and engaging party.

30 Where there is a legislated mandate that gives an assurance practitioner the discretion to determine or change the terms of the performance engagement, the assurance practitioner's notification of the legislative mandate and focus of the proposed performance engagement to the responsible party satisfies the requirements under paragraph 28 of this ASAE.

31 A change in circumstances that affects the intended users' needs, or a misunderstanding concerning the nature of the performance engagement, ordinarily may justify a change in the terms of the performance engagement. If such a change is made, the assurance practitioner does not disregard evidence that was obtained prior to the change.

Planning and Conducting the Performance Engagement

32 The assurance practitioner shall plan a performance engagement so that it will be conducted effectively and achieves the objectives communicated or agreed in the terms of the performance engagement.

33 Planning involves developing an overall strategy for the scope, emphasis, timing and conduct of the performance engagement, and a performance engagement plan, consisting of a detailed approach for the nature, timing and extent of evidence-gathering procedures to be undertaken and the reasons for selecting them. Ordinarily, adequate planning:

- Helps to devote appropriate attention to important areas of the performance engagement, identify potential problems on a timely basis and properly organise and manage the performance engagement in order for it to be conducted in an effective and efficient manner.
- Assists the assurance practitioner to properly assign work to performance engagement team members, and facilitates their direction and supervision and the review of their work.
- Assists, where applicable, the coordination of work done by other assurance practitioners and experts.

34 The nature and extent of planning activities will vary with the performance engagement circumstances, for example the size and complexity of the activity and the assurance practitioner's previous experience with it. Examples of the main matters to be considered include:

- The terms of the performance engagement.
- The characteristics of the activity and the identified criteria.
- The performance engagement process and possible sources of evidence.
- The assurance practitioner's understanding of the activity and other performance engagement circumstances.
- Identification of intended users and their needs, and consideration of materiality and the components of performance engagement risk.
- Personnel and expertise requirements, including the nature and extent of involvement by experts.

35 Planning is not a discrete phase, but rather a continual and iterative process throughout the performance engagement. As a result of unexpected events, changes in conditions, or

the evidence obtained from the results of evidence-gathering procedures, the assurance practitioner may need to revise the overall strategy and performance engagement plan, and thereby the resulting planned nature, timing and extent of further evidence-gathering procedures.

36 **The assurance practitioner shall plan and conduct a performance engagement with an attitude of professional scepticism recognising that circumstances may exist that cause the:**

(a) activity not to be economic, efficient or effective; and/or

(b) assertions or information concerning the activity to be materially misstated.

Understanding the Activity

37 **The assurance practitioner shall obtain an understanding of the activity and other performance engagement circumstances sufficient to identify and assess the performance engagement risks of the activity not being economic, efficient or effective, and sufficient to design and undertake further evidence-gathering procedures.**

38 Obtaining an understanding of the activity and other performance engagement circumstances is an essential part of planning and conducting a performance engagement. That understanding ordinarily provides the assurance practitioner with a frame of reference for exercising professional judgement throughout the performance engagement, for example, when:

- Considering the characteristics of the activity.
- Assessing the suitability of criteria.
- Assessing systems established and maintained for ensuring compliance with an entity's mandate or internal controls as expressed in policies and legislation.
- Identifying where special consideration may be necessary, for example factors indicative of wastage or fraud, and the need for specialised skills or the work of an expert.
- Establishing and evaluating the continued appropriateness of quantitative levels of performance (where appropriate), and considering qualitative materiality factors or benchmarks.
- Developing expectations for use when undertaking analytical procedures.
- Designing and undertaking further evidence-gathering procedures to reduce performance engagement risk to an appropriate level.
- Evaluating evidence, including the reasonableness of the responsible party's oral and written representations.

39 The assurance practitioner uses professional judgement to determine the extent of the understanding that is needed of the activity and other performance engagement circumstances. Under paragraph 37 of this ASAE, the assurance practitioner needs to consider whether the understanding is sufficient to assess the performance engagement risk that the activity may not be materially economic, efficient or effective or information asserted about the activity is materially misstated. The assurance practitioner ordinarily has a lesser depth of understanding than the responsible party.

Assessing the Appropriateness of the Activity as the Subject Matter

40 **The assurance practitioner shall assess the appropriateness of the activity as the subject matter, in terms of:**

(a) being identifiable, and its performance capable of consistent assessment against identified criteria; and

(b) ensuring the information about it is capable of being subjected to procedures for gathering sufficient appropriate evidence to support a reasonable assurance or limited assurance conclusion, as appropriate.

41 The assurance practitioner also ordinarily identifies those characteristics of the activity that are particularly relevant to the intended users, which are to be described in the assurance report. As indicated in paragraph 27(b) of this ASAE, an assurance practitioner does not initiate or accept a performance engagement unless the assurance practitioner's preliminary knowledge of the performance engagement circumstances indicates the appropriateness of the activity as the subject matter prior to commencing the engagement.

42 If after initiating or accepting the performance engagement, the assurance practitioner concludes that the activity is not a subject matter appropriate to being subjected to audit or review, the assurance practitioner shall assess whether to:

(a) change the terms of the performance engagement as described in paragraph 28 of this ASAE; or

(b) withdraw from or discontinue the performance engagement.

43 In the event that the assurance practitioner is unable to change the terms of, or withdraw from or discontinue, the performance engagement, under paragraph 89(c) of this ASAE, the assurance practitioner needs to consider the implications for the assurance report.

Assessing the Suitability of the Criteria

44 The assurance practitioner shall assess the suitability of the criteria to evaluate or measure the performance of the activity.

45 Criteria may range from general to specific. General criteria are broad statements of acceptable and reasonable performance. Specific criteria are derived from general criteria and are more closely related to an entity's governing legislation or mandate, objectives, programs, systems and controls. The level of detail of the assurance practitioner's conclusions is affected by the level of detail at which the criteria are specified.

46 Suitable criteria may be derived from sources such as:

- Regulatory bodies, legislation or policy statements.
- Standards of good practice developed by professions, associations or other recognised authorities.
- Statistics or practices developed within the entity or among similar entities.
- Criteria identified in similar circumstances.

47 As indicated in paragraph 27(b) of this ASAE, an assurance practitioner does not initiate or accept a performance engagement unless the assurance practitioner's preliminary knowledge of the performance engagement circumstances indicates that the identified criteria are suitable.

48 If after initiating or accepting the performance engagement, the assurance practitioner concludes that the identified criteria are not suitable, the assurance practitioner shall assess whether to:

(a) change the terms of the performance engagement as described in paragraph 28 of this ASAE; or

(b) withdraw from or discontinue the performance engagement.

49 In the event that the assurance practitioner is unable to change the terms of, or withdraw from or discontinue, the performance engagement, under paragraph 89(c) of this ASAE, the assurance practitioner needs to consider the implications for the assurance report.

50 Criteria are either established or specifically developed. Ordinarily, established criteria are suitable when they are relevant to the needs of the intended users. When established criteria exist for an activity, specific users may agree to other criteria for their specific purposes. For example, various frameworks can be used as established criteria for evaluating the effectiveness of internal control. Specific users may, however, develop

ASAE

a more detailed set of criteria that meet their specific needs in relation to, for example, program administration where the assurance report may state:

(a) when it is relevant to the circumstances of the performance engagement, that the criteria are not embodied in laws or regulations, or issued by authorised or recognised bodies of experts that follow a transparent due process; and

(b) that it is only for the use of the specific users and for their purposes.

51 For some activities it is likely that no established criteria exist. In those cases, criteria are specifically developed. Ordinarily, the assurance practitioner:

- Considers whether specifically developed criteria result in an assurance report that is misleading to the intended users.
- Attempts to have the intended users or the responsible party acknowledge that specifically developed criteria are suitable for the intended users' purposes.
- Considers how the absence of such an acknowledgement affects what is to be done to assess the suitability of the identified criteria, and the information provided about the criteria in the assurance report.

52 The assurance practitioner may use criteria developed by the responsible party for evaluating or measuring an activity if, in the assurance practitioner's opinion, they are suitable. The responsible party may have developed a system of performance assessment and monitoring incorporating the use of internally developed criteria. In assertion-based engagements, this system of performance assessment may form the basis of the responsible party's written assertions regarding economy, efficiency or effectiveness of an activity.

Materiality and Performance Engagement Risk

53 The assurance practitioner shall consider materiality and performance engagement risk when planning and conducting a performance engagement.

54 Under paragraph 53 of this ASAE, the assurance practitioner needs to consider materiality and performance engagement risk together when:

(a) determining the nature, timing and extent of evidence-gathering procedures; and

(b) evaluating whether the assertion or information concerning the economy, efficiency or effectiveness of the activity is free of misstatement.

In considering materiality the assurance practitioner needs to understand and assess what deficiencies in systems and controls or variations from the identified criteria might influence the decisions of the intended users. For example, in an assertion-based engagement, when the identified criteria allow for variations in the presentation of the information about the economy, efficiency or effectiveness of the activity, the assurance practitioner ordinarily considers how the adopted presentation might influence the decisions of the intended users.

55 Ordinarily, the assurance practitioner plans to examine material areas where the performance engagement risk is assessed to be high as well as material areas where the performance engagement risk is assessed as low but where any significant variation from or deficiency, when evaluated or measured against identified criteria in that area, could have a material effect on decisions about the economy, efficiency or effectiveness of the activity.

56 Materiality is considered in the context of quantitative and qualitative factors, such as relative magnitude, the nature and extent of the effect of these factors on the evaluation or measurement of the activity and the interests of the intended users. The assessment of materiality and the relative importance of quantitative and qualitative factors in a particular performance engagement are matters for the assurance practitioner's judgement.

57 Ordinarily, the assurance practitioner considers quantitative and qualitative factors when assessing materiality and performance engagement risk. These factors include:

- The importance of the activity to achieving the entity's objectives.
- The financial impact the activity has on the entity as a whole.

- The nature of transactions, for example, high volumes, large dollar values and complex transactions.
- The extent of interest shown in particular aspects of the activity by, for example, the legislature or other governing body, regulatory authorities or the public.
- The economic, social, political and environmental impact of the activity.
- The extent of management's actions regarding issues raised in previous performance engagements.
- The diversity, consistency and clarity of the entity's objectives and goals.
- The nature, size and complexity of the activity.
- The complexity and quality of management information and external reporting.
- The effectiveness of internal control, including the level of coverage by the internal auditors.
- The nature and degree of change in the environment or within the entity that impact on the activity.
- Management's effectiveness in a particular area.

58 **The assurance practitioner shall reduce performance engagement risk to an acceptable level in the circumstances of the performance engagement.**

59 In a performance audit engagement, under paragraph 58 of this ASAE, the assurance practitioner needs to reduce performance engagement risk to an acceptably low level in the circumstances of the performance engagement to obtain reasonable assurance as the basis for a positive form of expression of the assurance practitioner's conclusion.

60 In a performance review engagement, the combination of the nature, timing, and extent of evidence-gathering procedures is at least sufficient to reduce performance engagement risk to a level that is acceptable in the circumstances of the assurance engagement, but where that risk is greater than that for a reasonable assurance engagement, as the basis for a negative form of expression of the assurance practitioner's conclusion.

Using the Work of an Expert

61 **When using the work of an expert in the performance engagement, the assurance practitioner shall collect and evaluate evidence in accordance with ASAE 3000.**

Obtaining Evidence

62 **The assurance practitioner shall obtain sufficient appropriate evidence on which to base the assurance practitioner's conclusions.**

63 Sufficiency is the measure of the quantity of evidence. Appropriateness is the measure of the quality of evidence; that is, its relevance and its reliability. The assurance practitioner ordinarily considers the relationship between the cost of obtaining evidence and the usefulness of the information obtained. However, the matter of difficulty or expense involved is not in itself a valid basis for omitting an evidence-gathering procedure for which there is no alternative. The assurance practitioner uses professional judgement and exercises professional scepticism in evaluating the quantity and quality of evidence, and thus its sufficiency and appropriateness, to support the conclusions in the assurance report.

64 Performance audit and performance review engagements both require the application of assurance skills and techniques and the gathering of sufficient appropriate evidence as part of an iterative, systematic assurance engagement process. For further guidance on the nature, timing and extent of evidence-gathering procedures for performance audit and performance review engagements, refer to ASAE 3000.

65 For both performance audit and performance review engagements, if the assurance practitioner becomes aware of a matter that leads the assurance practitioner to question whether sufficient appropriate evidence has been obtained, the assurance practitioner ordinarily pursues the matter by undertaking other evidence-gathering procedures sufficient to enable the assurance practitioner to report.

Evaluation and Communication of Deficiencies and Variations

66 **The assurance practitioner shall evaluate, individually and in aggregate, whether:**

(a) **deficiencies in systems or controls; and/or**

(b) **variations of the measures or assertions from the identified criteria**

that have come to the attention of the assurance practitioner are material to the conclusions in the assurance report.

67 Under paragraph 66 of this ASAE, the assurance practitioner needs to exercise professional judgement in evaluating the materiality of deficiencies in systems and controls and variations in economy, efficiency or effectiveness of the activity.

68 **The assurance practitioner shall make the responsible party aware of:**

(a) **deficiencies in systems and controls; and**

(b) **variations of the measures or assertions from the identified criteria,**

that have come to the attention of the assurance practitioner and are material to the conclusions in the assurance report.

69 Under paragraph 66 of this ASAE, the assurance practitioner needs to consider the impact of material system or control deficiencies and material variations in the performance of the activity when evaluated or measured against the identified criteria, on the conclusions in the assurance report. A variation or deficiency is material when, in the assurance practitioner's judgement, it has the potential to adversely affect[3]:

(a) decisions made by intended users about the economy, efficiency or effectiveness of an activity; or

(b) the discharge of accountability by the responsible party or the governing party of the entity.

Representations by the Responsible Party

70 **The assurance practitioner shall endeavour to obtain written representations from the responsible party, as appropriate for the engagement.**

71 When the responsible party's responsibilities are prescribed by law or regulation, the written representations required under paragraph 70 of this ASAE are ordinarily described in the same manner as that prescribed by law or regulation. Ordinarily, in a direct reporting performance engagement, the responsible party may not be in a position to provide representations to the assurance practitioner.

72 In the public sector, written representations may involve the responsible party's comments on the factual accuracy of the assurance practitioner's findings, which form the basis of the assurance practitioner's conclusions and which may be included in the assurance report.

73 Representations by the responsible party cannot replace other evidence the assurance practitioner could reasonably expect to be available. An inability to obtain sufficient appropriate evidence regarding a matter that has, or may have, a material effect on the evaluation or measurement of the activity, when such evidence would ordinarily be available, constitutes a limitation on the scope of the performance engagement, even if a representation from the responsible party has been received on the activity.

Considering Subsequent Events

74 **The assurance practitioner shall consider the effect on the activity and on the assurance report of events up to the date of the assurance report.**

75 The extent of consideration of subsequent events, that come to the attention of the assurance practitioner, depends on the potential for such events to affect the activity and to affect the appropriateness of the assurance practitioner's conclusions. Consideration of subsequent events in some performance engagements may not be relevant because of the nature of the activity.

3 Amended October 2008.

Documentation

76 **The assurance practitioner shall prepare, on a timely basis, documentation that is sufficient and appropriate to provide:**

(a) a basis for the assurance practitioner's conclusion and recommendations; and

(b) evidence that the performance engagement was conducted in accordance with this ASAE and ASAE 3000.

77 Documentation includes a record of the assurance practitioner's reasoning on all significant matters that require the exercise of judgement, and related conclusions. The existence of difficult questions of principle or judgement, calls for the documentation to include the relevant facts that were known by the assurance practitioner at the time the conclusion was reached.

78 In applying professional judgement to assessing the extent of documentation to be prepared and retained, the assurance practitioner ordinarily considers what is necessary to provide an understanding of the work undertaken and the basis of the principal decisions taken to another experienced assurance practitioner who has no previous experience with the performance engagement. It is, however, neither necessary nor practicable to document every matter the assurance practitioner considers during the performance engagement.

Preparing the Assurance Report

79 **The assurance practitioner shall determine whether sufficient appropriate evidence has been obtained to support the conclusions expressed in the assurance report.**

80 In circumstances when a performance engagement incorporates both performance audit of an activity and performance review on another activity, under paragraph 79 of this ASAE, the assurance practitioner needs to clearly distinguish the two types of conclusions expressed.

81 In developing the conclusion, the assurance practitioner ordinarily considers all relevant evidence obtained, regardless of whether it appears to corroborate or to contradict information about the economy, efficiency or effectiveness of the activity. The assurance practitioner's conclusion in a direct reporting engagement may consist of a series of conclusions about different aspects of a number of activities where this is appropriate in the context of the particular performance engagement.

82 **The assurance report shall be in writing and shall contain a clear expression of the assurance practitioner's conclusion against the objectives communicated or agreed in the terms of the performance engagement.**

Assurance Report Content

83 **Other than to the extent that it is inconsistent with relevant legislation or regulation, the assurance report shall include the following basic elements:**

(a) a title that clearly indicates the report is an independent assurance report;

(b) an addressee;

(c) an identification and description of the activity;

(d) identification of the criteria;

(e) where appropriate, a description of any significant, inherent limitation associated with the evaluation or measurement of the activity against the criteria;

(f) when the criteria used to evaluate or measure the activity are available only to specific intended users, or are relevant only to a specific purpose, a statement restricting the use of the assurance report to those intended users or that purpose;

(g) a statement to identify the responsible party and to describe the responsible party's and the assurance practitioner's responsibilities;

ASAE

(h) a statement that the performance engagement was conducted in accordance with applicable ASAEs (ASAE 3500 *Performance Engagements*) and the level of assurance provided;

(i) a summary of the work undertaken;

(j) the assurance practitioner's conclusions:

(i) where appropriate, shall inform the intended users of the context in which the assurance practitioner's conclusions are to be read;

(ii) shall be expressed in the positive form where reasonable assurance is provided;

(iii) shall be expressed in the negative form where limited assurance is provided;

(iv) where both positive and negative forms are expressed, shall clearly separate the two types of conclusions; and

(v) where the assurance practitioner expresses a conclusion that is other than unqualified, the assurance report shall contain a clear description of the reasons;

(k) the assurance report date; and

(l) the name of the firm or the assurance practitioner, and a specific location, which ordinarily is the city where the assurance practitioner maintains the office that has responsibility for the performance engagement.

84 This ASAE does not require a standardised format for reporting on all performance engagements even though at paragraph 83 it identifies the basic elements of the assurance report. For instance, under:

- Paragraph 83(a), the title of the assurance report may differ depending on whether the assurance practitioner is an Auditor-General or a practitioner in the private sector. However, in both instances the title would convey that it is an independent report.
- Paragraph 83(j), the assurance practitioner's conclusions on an activity may include a combination of positive and negative forms which may be inseparable but essential to be reported as such for the purposes of effectively communicating the assurance practitioner's conclusions to the intended users.
- Paragraph 83(j)(i), the assurance practitioner's conclusions may be drafted as appropriate to recognise local legislation or custom.

85 Therefore, assurance reports are tailored to the specific performance engagement circumstances with the assurance practitioner using professional judgement in deciding how best to meet the reporting requirements detailed in paragraph 83 in conveying the conclusion(s). The assurance practitioner may choose a short form or long form style of reporting to facilitate effective communication to the intended users. Short-form reports ordinarily include only the basic elements. Long form reports often describe in detail the terms of the performance engagement, the criteria being used, findings relating to particular aspects of the performance engagement and, in some cases, recommendations, as well as the basic elements. Ordinarily, any findings and recommendations are clearly separated from the assurance practitioner's conclusion on the economy, efficiency or effectiveness of the activity, and the wording used in presenting them makes it clear they are not intended to affect the assurance practitioner's conclusion.

Reporting Findings, Recommendations and Responsible Party Comments

86 The assurance practitioner may expand the assurance report to include other information and explanations that are not intended to affect the assurance practitioner's conclusion. Examples include:

- Disclosure of materiality levels.
- Findings relating to particular aspects of the performance engagement.

- Recommendations.
- Comments received from the responsible party.

The decision to include any such information depends on its significance to the needs of the intended users. Additional information is clearly separated from the assurance practitioner's conclusion and worded in such a manner so as not to affect that conclusion.

87 Under a direct reporting engagement, the assurance report ordinarily describes relevant facts and findings to allow intended users to understand the basis upon which the assurance practitioner's conclusions and recommendations have been formed. Findings arise from an examination of the underlying facts, comparison with identified criteria and the assurance practitioner's analysis of the variations in the performance of the activity against criteria, including, where applicable, the causes and effects of the variations.

Modifications to the Assurance Report

88 Modifications to the assurance report relate to circumstances when the assurance practitioner is unable to express an unqualified conclusion and an assurance report is issued with either:

(a) a qualified conclusion;

(b) an adverse conclusion; or

(c) a disclaimer of conclusion.

Qualified Conclusions, Adverse Conclusions and Disclaimers of Conclusion

89 The assurance practitioner shall not express an unqualified conclusion when the following circumstances exist and, in the assurance practitioner's judgement, the effect of the matter is or may be material:

(a) there is a limitation on the scope of the assurance practitioner's work, that is, circumstances prevent, or the responsible party or the engaging party imposes a restriction that prevents the assurance practitioner from obtaining evidence required to reduce performance engagement risk to the appropriate level. The assurance practitioner shall express a qualified conclusion or a disclaimer of conclusion; or

(b) in those cases where:

(i) the assurance practitioner's conclusion is worded in terms of the responsible party's assertion, and that assertion is not fairly stated in all material respects; or

(ii) the assurance practitioner's conclusion is worded directly in terms of the activity and the performance against identified criteria is not materially economic, efficient or effective,

the assurance practitioner shall express a qualified conclusion or adverse conclusion.

(c) in the case of an assertion-based engagement when it is discovered, after the engagement has been initiated or accepted, that the activity is not a subject matter appropriate to being subjected to audit or review, or the identified criteria are not suitable, the assurance practitioner shall express:

(i) a qualified or adverse conclusion when the unsuitable criteria or inappropriate subject matter is likely to mislead the intended users; or

(ii) a qualified conclusion or a disclaimer of conclusion in other cases.

90 The assurance practitioner shall express a qualified conclusion when the effect of a matter is not so material or pervasive as to require an adverse conclusion or a disclaimer of conclusion. A qualified conclusion is expressed as being "except for" or otherwise discloses the effects of the matter to which the qualification relates.

Other Reporting Responsibilities

91 **In addition to communicating material deficiencies and variations, as required by paragraph 68 of this ASAE, the assurance practitioner shall consider other reporting responsibilities, including the appropriateness of communicating relevant matters of governance interest arising from the performance engagement with the responsible party.**

92 Relevant matters of governance interest include only those matters that have come to the attention of the assurance practitioner while conducting the performance engagement. If the terms of the performance engagement do not specifically require it, the assurance practitioner is not required to design procedures for the specific purpose of identifying matters of governance interest.

93 **The assurance practitioner shall consider any other reporting responsibilities set by legislation.**

Conformity with International Standards on Assurance Engagements

94 There is no corresponding International Standard on Assurance Engagements.

ASRS 4400

Agreed-Upon Procedures Engagements to Report Factual Findings

(Issued June 2011)

Issued by the Auditing and Assurance Standards Board.

Note from the Institute of Chartered Accountants Australia

This note, prepared by the technical editor, is not part of ASRS 4400.

Historical development

June 1992: AUP/RS 2 'Engagements to Perform Agreed-upon Procedures' issued, based on ED 38 of the same name issued in January 1991.

May 1994: ED 55 'Codification and Revision of Auditing Pronouncements: AUS 904 Engagements to Perform Agreed-upon Procedures (AUP/RS 2)' issued by the AuSB.

June 1994: The International Auditing Practices Committee (IAPC) of the International Federation of Accountants (IFAC) approved the issuance of a codified set of International Standards of Auditing (ISAs). The relevant international pronouncement was ISA 920 'Engagements to Perform Agreed-upon Procedures Regarding Financial Information'.

October 1995: Australian Auditing Standards and Auditing Guidance Statements released. The status of these was explained in APS 1.1 'Conformity With Auditing Standards'. These Standards became operative for the first reporting period commencing on or after 1 July 1996 and later reporting periods, although earlier application was encouraged. AUP/RS 2 'Engagements to Perform Agreed-upon Procedures' replaced by AUS 904 'Engagements to Perform Agreed-upon Procedures'.

April 1998: AUS/AGS Omnibus 1 'Miscellaneous Amendments to AUSs and AGSs' issued.

July 2002: AUS/AGS Omnibus 3 'Miscellaneous Amendments to AUSs and AGSs' issued by the AuASB. AUS 904 since reissued by the Board to incorporate these amendments.

June 2011: Standard on Related Services ASRS 4400 was issued to replace AUS 904 'Engagements to Perform Agreed-upon Procedures' issued by the predecessor board, the AuASB. It is based on the International Standard on Related Services ISRS 4400 'Engagements to Perform Agreed-Upon Procedures Regarding Financial Information'.

Contents

Preface

Reasons for Issuing Standard on Related Services ASRS 4400

The Auditing and Assurance Standards Board (AUASB) issues Standard on Related Services ASRS 4400 *Agreed-Upon Procedures Engagements to Report Factual Findings*, pursuant to the requirements of the legislative provisions and the Strategic Direction explained below.

The AUASB is an independent statutory board of the Australian Government established under section 227A of the *Australian Securities and Investments Commission Act 2001*, as amended (ASIC Act). Under section 227B of the ASIC Act, the AUASB may formulate assurance standards for other purposes.

Under the Strategic Direction given to the AUASB by the Financial Reporting Council (FRC), the AUASB develops auditing and assurance standards other than for historical financial information. The AUASB uses the standards of the International Auditing and Assurance Standards Board as a base on which to develop standards and incorporates additional requirements considered to be in the public interest. Accordingly, the AUASB has decided to issue ASRS 4400 using the equivalent International Standard on Related Services ISRS 4400 *Engagements to Perform Agreed-Upon Procedures Regarding Financial Information.*

Main Features

This Standard on Related Services establishes mandatory requirements and provides application and other explanatory material for assurance practitioners when accepting, undertaking and reporting on engagements to perform agreed-upon procedures.

This Standard on Related Services:

(a) details ethical requirements, including independence, applicable to agreed-upon procedures engagements;

(b) describes acceptance requirements for agreed-upon procedures engagements;

(c) requires terms of the engagement to be agreed;

(d) requires the assurance practitioner to plan the work;

(e) specifies that the assurance practitioner does not perform a risk assessment and does not apply materiality;

(f) describes quality control requirements;

(g) describes requirements for using the work of others;

(h) describes the documentation requirements;

(i) requires the procedures to be performed when conducting the engagement to be limited to those agreed; and

(j) describes the form and content of the report of factual findings.

Authority Statement

The Auditing and Assurance Standards Board (AUASB) formulates this Standard on Related Services ASRS 4400 *Agreed-Upon Procedures Engagements to Report Factual Findings*, pursuant to section 227B of the *Australian Securities and Investments Commission Act 2001*.

This Standard on Related Services ASRS 4400 is to be read in conjunction with the *Preamble to AUASB Standards*, which sets out the intentions of the AUASB on how its standards are to be understood, interpreted and applied.

Dated: 8 June 2011

M H Kelsall
Chairman - AUASB

Standard on Related Services ASRS 4400

Agreed-Upon Procedures Engagements to Report Factual Findings

Application

1. This Standard on Related Services applies to agreed-upon procedures engagements to be performed by an assurance practitioner, where factual findings are reported but no conclusion or opinion is expressed and no assurance is provided by the assurance practitioner. The intended users draw their own conclusions based on the factual findings reported combined with any other information they have obtained.

2. This standard may also be applied, as appropriate, to agreed-upon procedures engagements to be performed by a practitioner other than an assurance practitioner.

Operative Date

3. This standard is operative for agreed-upon procedures engagements commencing on or after 1 October 2011.

Introduction

4. An agreed-upon procedures engagement involves the performance of procedures of an assurance nature from which no conclusion or opinion is expressed by the assurance practitioner and no assurance is provided to intended users. Instead only factual findings obtained as a result of the procedures performed are reported.

5. An assurance practitioner may be asked to perform other types of engagements for which assurance is also not provided but in contrast to agreed-upon procedures engagements, the procedures conducted are not primarily of an assurance nature. These engagements are not dealt with in this standard and include:

   (a) consulting (or advisory) services;

   (b) compilation engagements; and

   (c) business services, such as accounting and taxation services.

   The objective of consulting services is the provision of professional advice and recommendations with respect to the subject matter. The objective of compilation engagements is the presentation of financial information in a specified form. The objective of business services is the conduct of accounting procedures, computations or the provision of business or taxation advice. These engagements are not subject to the requirements of this standard.

6. An agreed-upon procedures engagement is not an assurance engagement,[1] even though similar procedures are performed, as the purpose of the procedures performed is not to obtain sufficient appropriate evidence on which to base a conclusion. In contrast, the sufficiency and appropriateness of the evidence obtained in an assurance engagement is based on the assurance practitioner's assessment of materiality and risk of material misstatement or non-compliance. As the assurance practitioner does not assess materiality or engagement risk to determine the evidence gathering procedures to be performed in an agreed-upon procedures engagement, the assurance practitioner is unable to determine whether the evidence is sufficient and appropriate to reduce risk to an acceptable level as a basis for a conclusion.

1 See *Framework for Assurance Engagements*, paragraph Aus 7.1. "Assurance engagement" is defined as an engagement in which an assurance practitioner expresses a conclusion designed to enhance the degree of confidence of the intended users, other than the responsible party, about the outcome of the evaluation or measurement of a subject matter against criteria.

7. ASRS 4400 addresses the assurance practitioner's professional responsibilities to accept agreed-upon procedures engagements to report factual findings only if:

(a) the assurance practitioner has the capabilities and competence to perform the procedures;

(b) assurance is not deemed to be necessary to meet the needs of intended users of the assurance practitioner's report;

(c) the assurance practitioner is not required to determine the sufficiency of the procedures to be performed;

(d) neither an assurance conclusion nor assurance opinion will be provided on the findings but the intended users may draw their own conclusions with respect to the subject matter; and

(e) each of the procedures to be performed is to be clearly specified in the engagement letter.

8. ASRS 4400 deals with the conduct of agreed-upon procedures engagements and identifies that risk assessment, responding to assessed risks, evaluation of evidence gathered and expressing a conclusion or opinion are aspects of an assurance engagement which are not performed when no assurance is to be provided.

9. An agreed-upon procedures engagement may be misunderstood as providing assurance, as the engagement is performed by an assurance practitioner and involves the conduct of the same or similar procedures to an assurance engagement. The *Framework for Assurance Engagements*[2] states that the assurance practitioner should clearly distinguish a report on an engagement that is not an assurance engagement from an assurance report. This standard deals with the content of a report of factual findings in order to differentiate it from an assurance report.

10. This standard deals with how the form, content and restrictions on distribution of an assurance practitioner's report of factual findings helps to minimise misinterpretation and promote the intended users' understanding of that report.

Objective

11. The objective of the assurance practitioner in an agreed-upon procedures engagement is to apply their professional capabilities and competence in carrying out procedures of an assurance nature, to which the assurance practitioner, the engaging party and any third party (as applicable) have agreed, and to report factual findings, without providing assurance or implying that assurance has been provided.

Definitions

12. Assurance practitioner means a person or an organisation, whether in public practice, industry, commerce or the public sector, involved in the provision of assurance services.[3]

13. Engaging party means the party(ies) that engages the assurance practitioner to perform the agreed-upon procedures engagement.

14. Intended users means the individual(s) or organisation(s), or class(es) thereof for whom the assurance practitioner prepares the report of factual findings.

15. Procedures of an assurance nature means procedures performed by an assurance practitioner which are the same or similar to procedures performed in an assurance engagement.

---

2 See *Framework for Assurance Engagements*, paragraph 15.

3 The term "assurance practitioner" is used throughout this ASRS as defined in ASAE 3000 *Assurance Engagements Other than Audits or Reviews of Historical Financial Information*. Such reference is not intended to imply that assurance is being provided. The term is used to indicate that the work is required to be performed and the report prepared by persons who have adequate training, experience and competence in conducting assurance engagements.

Requirements

Conduct of an Agreed-Upon Procedures Engagement

16. The assurance practitioner shall comply with this standard and with the terms of the engagement agreed with the engaging party.

Ethical Requirements Relating to an Agreed-Upon Procedures Engagement

17. When conducting an agreed-upon procedures engagement, the assurance practitioner shall comply with ethical requirements equivalent to the ethical requirements applicable to Other Assurance Engagements,[4] including those pertaining to independence, unless the engaging party has explicitly agreed to modified independence requirements in the terms of the engagement.[5] If modified independence requirements have been agreed in the terms of the engagement, the level of independence applied shall be described in the report of factual findings.[6] (Ref: Para. A1)

Acceptance of an Agreed-Upon Procedures Engagement

18. The assurance practitioner shall obtain an understanding of the needs and objectives of the intended users, including a class of intended users, of the assurance practitioner's report of factual findings and the purpose for which that report will be used. (Ref: Para. A2-A3)

19. A regulator or representative of a class of users, industry or the accounting profession may specify the agreed-upon procedures to be performed to meet the needs of a class of intended users. In these circumstances, the assurance practitioner shall be satisfied that the needs of the class of users for whom the engagement is intended have been appropriately considered and addressed.

20. Before accepting an agreed-upon procedures engagement, the assurance practitioner shall determine that the persons who are to perform the engagement collectively have the appropriate competence and capabilities to perform the procedures.

21. The assurance practitioner shall not accept an agreed-upon procedures engagement if, in the professional judgement of the assurance practitioner:
    (a) the provision of factual findings alone which provide no assurance is unlikely to meet the needs of the intended users; or (Ref: Para. A3)
    (b) the circumstances of the engagement indicate that the intended users are likely to construe the outcome of the engagement as providing an assurance conclusion about the subject matter; or
    (c) distribution of the report of factual findings cannot be restricted to the engaging party and any intended users identified, due to legal requirements or other circumstances; or
    (d) all of the elements of an assurance engagement[7] are met; or (Ref: Para. A4-A6)
    (e) the engagement has no rational purpose; or
    (f) the circumstances of the engagement indicate that it will be necessary for the assurance practitioner to do any of the following:
        (i) determine the sufficiency of the procedures to be performed; (Ref: Para. A7)
        (ii) perform a risk assessment in order to determine the procedures to be undertaken; (Ref: Para. A8)

4 The ethical requirements, including independence, applicable to Other Assurance Engagements are defined in ASA 102 *Compliance with Ethical Requirements when Performing Audits, Reviews and Other Assurance Engagements*. For ethical requirements specifically relating to Other Assurance Engagements, refer to APES 110 *Code of Ethics for Professional Accountants*, section 291 *Independence - Other Assurance Engagements* (December 2010), issued by the Accounting Professional & Ethical Standards Board Ltd (APESB), subsequent to ASA 102 (October 2009).

5 See sub-paragraph 24(f) of this standard.

6 See sub-paragraph 43(f) of this standard.

7 See *Framework for Assurance Engagements*, paragraph 20.

(iii) evaluate the findings in order to determine the sufficiency and appropriateness of the evidence gathered; (Ref: Para. A8) or

(iv) reach a conclusion or form an opinion based on the evidence gathered. (Ref: Para. A8)

22. In order to establish whether the preconditions of an agreed-upon procedures engagement are present, the assurance practitioner shall obtain agreement from management [and, where appropriate, those charged with governance and intended users] that it acknowledges and understands its responsibility:

(a) for determining the adequacy or otherwise of the procedures agreed to be performed;

(b) for determining whether the factual findings reported, in combination with any other information obtained, provide an appropriate basis for any conclusions which management or the intended users wish to draw on the subject matter;

(c) to provide the assurance practitioner with:

(i) access to all information of which management is aware that is necessary for the performance of the procedures agreed;

(ii) additional information that the auditor may request from management for the purpose of the engagement; and

(iii) unrestricted access to persons within the entity from whom the assurance practitioner requires co-operation in order to perform the procedures agreed.

Agreeing the Terms of the Agreed-Upon Procedures Engagement

23. The assurance practitioner shall agree the terms of the agreed-upon procedures engagement with the engaging party, and other specified parties who will receive copies of the report.[8] If additional parties are intended users of the report of factual findings but are not signatories to the terms of the engagement, those parties shall be identified in the terms of the engagement and all other parties shall be excluded from using the report. (Ref: Para. A9-A10)

24. The agreed terms of the engagement shall be recorded in an engagement letter or other suitable form of written agreement and shall include: (Ref: Para. A11-A13)

(a) the objective and scope of the engagement;

(b) confirmation of the assurance practitioner's acceptance of the appointment;

(c) the nature of the engagement, including a statement that the procedures performed will not constitute a reasonable or limited assurance engagement and that accordingly no assurance will be provided;

(d) a statement that intended users are expected to conduct their own assessment of the findings, combined with other information available to them and, if necessary, perform further procedures in order to obtain sufficient appropriate evidence on which to base any conclusion on the subject matter;

(e) the assurance practitioner's responsibilities to the engaging party and other specified parties;

(f) confirmation that the assurance practitioner will apply ethical requirements equivalent to those applicable to Other Assurance Engagements or, if modified independence requirements have been agreed, the level of independence agreed;

(g) identification of the subject matter to which the procedures will be applied;

(h) the nature, timing and extent of the specific procedures to be performed;

(i) management's responsibilities;

(j) identification of the intended users of the report including those users who may not be party to the terms of the engagement, such as a class of user, regulator or bank;

8 See Appendix 3 of this standard for an example of an engagement letter for an agreed-upon procedures engagement.

ASRS

(k) a statement that the distribution of the report of factual findings would be restricted to the engaging party, who has agreed to the procedures to be performed, and the intended users identified; and

(l) reference to the expected form of any reports to be issued by the assurance practitioner, which may be illustrated by attaching to the engagement letter a draft of the report of factual findings that will be issued, omitting the factual findings.

25. The nature, timing and extent of procedures shall be specified in the terms of the engagement in sufficient detail such that the assurance practitioner will not be required, during the course of the engagement, to exercise professional judgement in determining or modifying the procedures to be performed. (Ref: Para. A11)

26. When conducting an agreed-upon procedures engagement, if the assurance practitioner is unable to perform the exact nature, timing or extent of procedures agreed, but alternative procedures can be performed and the engaging party requires those procedures to be performed, then new terms of the engagement shall be agreed with the engaging party in writing.

Planning

27. The assurance practitioner shall plan the work so that the engagement will be performed in an effective manner, in accordance with the terms of the engagement and this standard.

28. The engagement plan for an agreed-upon procedures engagement shall be restricted to the nature, timing and extent of procedures agreed in the terms of the engagement. The plan does not include alternative or further procedures unless agreed with the engaging party in amended terms of the engagement. (Ref: Para. A14)

Risk Assessment

29. The assurance practitioner does not perform a risk assessment for an agreed-upon procedures engagement, as the nature, timing and extent of procedures to be performed are agreed with the engaging party rather than determined by the assurance practitioner in response to assessed risks.

Materiality

30. The assurance practitioner does not apply materiality to designing the procedures to be performed nor to assessing the factual findings to determine whether the subject matter information is free from material misstatement or non-compliance, as this is the responsibility of the intended users.

Quality Control

31. The assurance practitioner shall take responsibility for the overall quality of the agreed-upon procedures engagement and shall apply the firm's quality control procedures equivalent to those applicable to Other Assurance Engagements.[9]

32. Throughout the engagement, the assurance practitioner shall remain alert, through observation and making enquiries as necessary, for evidence of non-compliance with relevant ethical requirements, including independence, by members of the engagement team. If matters come to the assurance practitioner's attention that indicate that members of the engagement team have not complied with relevant ethical requirements, the assurance practitioner shall determine the appropriate action.

33. The assurance practitioner shall be satisfied that the engagement team,[10] and any experts engaged who are not part of the engagement team, collectively have the appropriate competence, capabilities and resources to perform the agreed-upon procedures in accordance with this standard.

---

9 See ASQC 1 *Quality Control for Firms that Perform Audits and Reviews of Financial Reports and Other Financial Information and Other Assurance Engagements.*

10 Engagement team, as defined in ASQC 1, paragraph 12(f), means all partners and staff performing the engagement, and any individuals engaged by the firm or a network firm who perform procedures on the engagement. This excludes external experts engaged by the firm or a network firm.

Using the Work of Others

34. The assurance practitioner shall take responsibility for the direction, supervision and performance of the engagement and the accurate reporting of factual findings.

35. When the assurance practitioner uses the work of another assurance practitioner, internal auditor or an expert, the assurance practitioner shall evaluate the adequacy of their work, including their objectivity and technical competence in conducting the procedures, whether the nature, timing and extent of procedures conducted agrees with procedures in the terms of the engagement and whether the factual findings communicated detail adequately the result of the procedures conducted.

Documentation

36. The assurance practitioner shall document:
    (a) issues identified with respect to compliance with relevant ethical requirements and how they were resolved;
    (b) conclusions on compliance with independence requirements equivalent to 'Other Assurance Engagements' or modified independence agreed;
    (c) conclusions reached regarding the acceptance and continuance of client relationships and acceptance of the agreed-upon procedures engagement;
    (d) the nature, timing and extent of procedures performed and the factual findings obtained, as identified in the agreed-upon procedures report; and
    (e) evidence that the engagement was carried out in accordance with this standard and the terms of the engagement.

Performing the engagement

37. As no assurance is to be provided, the assurance practitioner shall carry out only the procedures agreed in the terms of the engagement and use the results of the procedures to provide a report of factual findings. (Ref: Para. A15-16)

38. If the engaging party's requirements alter during the course of the engagement which require the assurance practitioner to draw conclusions from the findings, the terms of the agreed-upon procedures engagement cannot be extended to the provision of assurance. However, a new engagement may be agreed for the provision of assurance, if appropriate, to be conducted in accordance with applicable AUASB standards.

ASRS

Reporting

39. The assurance practitioner shall provide a report of factual findings for the agreed-upon procedures engagement. In contrast to an assurance report, a report of factual findings does not include an evaluation of those findings in order to draw a conclusion or form an opinion. (Ref: Para. A17)

40. The assurance practitioner shall not express a conclusion or opinion in an agreed-upon procedures engagement as the assurance practitioner has not performed a risk assessment, responded to assessed risks by determining the procedures to be performed or assessed whether sufficient appropriate evidence has been obtained as a reasonable basis for expressing a conclusion.

41. If the assurance practitioner is undertaking an agreed-upon procedures engagement in parallel with an assurance engagement, the factual findings from the agreed-upon procedures engagement shall be presented separately from the report on the assurance engagement.

42. Use of the report shall be restricted to those parties that have either agreed to the procedures to be performed or have been specifically included as intended users in the engagement letter since others, unaware of the reasons for the procedures, may misinterpret the results.

43. The report of factual findings for an agreed-upon procedures engagement shall contain: (Ref: Para. A18-A19)
    (a) a title;
    (b) an addressee (ordinarily the engaging party);

(c) identification of the specific information to which the procedures have been applied;

(d) a statement that the procedures performed were those agreed with the engaging party;

(e) a statement that the engagement was performed in accordance with ASRS 4400;

(f) a statement that either ethical requirements equivalent to those applicable to Other Assurance Engagements have been complied with, including independence, or, if modified independence requirements have been agreed in the terms of the engagement, a description of the level of independence applied;

(g) identification of the purpose for which the agreed-upon procedures engagement was performed;

(h) a statement that the responsibility for determining the adequacy or otherwise of the procedures agreed to be performed by the assurance practitioner is that of the engaging party;

(i) a listing of the specific procedures performed, detailing the nature, timing and extent of each procedure;

(j) a description of the assurance practitioner's factual findings in relation to each procedure performed, including sufficient details of errors and exceptions found;

(k) identification of any of the procedures agreed in the terms of the engagement which could not be performed and why that has arisen;

(l) a statement that the procedures performed do not constitute either a reasonable or limited assurance engagement and, as such, no assurance is provided;

(m) a statement that had the assurance practitioner performed additional procedures, a reasonable assurance engagement or a limited assurance engagement, other matters might have come to the assurance practitioner's attention which would have been reported;

(n) a statement that use and distribution of the report is restricted to those parties identified in the report, who have agreed to the procedures to be performed or were identified in the terms of the engagement;

(o) a statement (when applicable) that the report relates only to the elements, accounts, items or financial and non-financial information specified and that it does not extend to the entity's financial report, or other specified report, taken as a whole;

(p) the date of the report;

(q) the assurance practitioner's address; and

(r) the assurance practitioner's signature.

44. If the assurance practitioner is required by law or regulation to use a specific layout or wording for the report of factual findings, the report of factual findings shall refer to ASRS 4400 only if the assurance practitioner's report includes, at a minimum, each of the elements in paragraph 43.

45. Law or regulation of the relevant jurisdiction may prescribe the layout or wording of the report of factual findings in a form or in terms which are significantly different from the requirements of this standard. In these circumstances, the assurance practitioner shall evaluate:

(a) whether intended users might misunderstand the factual findings reported and the fact that no assurance is provided; and, if so;

(b) whether additional explanation in the report of factual findings can mitigate possible misunderstanding.

If the assurance practitioner considers that additional explanation in the report of factual findings cannot mitigate possible misunderstanding, the auditor shall not accept the engagement unless required by law or regulation to do so. As an agreed-upon procedures engagement conducted in accordance with such law or regulation does not comply with this standard, the assurance practitioner shall not include any reference in the report of factual findings to the engagement having been conducted in accordance with ASRS 4400. (Ref: Para. A20)

46. The assurance practitioner shall not issue modifications or an emphasis of matter in a report of factual findings, as no conclusion or opinion is expressed. Nevertheless, the following matters, if applicable, are reported as part of the factual findings:

(a) errors or exceptions identified as a result of the procedures performed, regardless of whether they were subsequently rectified by the entity; and (Ref: Para. A21)

(b) the inability of the assurance practitioner to perform any of the agreed-upon procedures. (Ref: Para. A22)

47. The report of factual findings for an agreed-upon procedures engagement shall be clearly distinguished from an assurance report in that it shall not contain:

(a) a statement of compliance with AUASB standards, except for reference to ASRS 4400;

(b) inappropriate use of the terms "assurance", "audit", "review", "opinion" or "conclusion"; or

(c) any statement that could reasonably be mistaken for a conclusion designed to enhance the degree of confidence of intended users about the outcome of the evaluation or measurement of a subject matter against criteria.[11]

❖ ❖ ❖

Application and Other Explanatory Material

Ethical Requirements Relating to an Agreed-Upon Procedures Engagement (Ref: Para. 17)

A1. Ethical requirements, applicable to Other Assurance Engagements, permit the independence requirements to be modified, if the intended users of the assurance practitioner's report are knowledgeable as to the purpose, subject matter information and limitations of the report and explicitly agree to the application of the modified independence requirements. In these circumstances, the report is to include a restriction on use and distribution to the intended users only, which is already included in the report of factual findings. If modified independence requirements are adopted in the terms of the engagement, but the intended users include a class of users who are not party to the terms of the engagement, they are required to be made aware of the modified independence requirements, such as by reference to them in the report of factual findings. In any case, the independence of the assurance practitioner and the engagement team will need to be assessed.

Acceptance of an Agreed-Upon Procedures Engagement (Ref: Para. 18-22)

A2. The assurance practitioner needs to understand the engaging party's objectives in engaging the assurance practitioner to ensure that an engagement is agreed which is appropriate to those objectives and to avoid any misunderstandings with respect to the scope of the engagement.

A3. In determining whether a report of factual findings is likely to meet the needs of intended users, or class of intended users, of the report, the assurance practitioner considers the purpose for which users intend to use the report. In doing so, the assurance practitioner, does not take responsibility for the sufficiency of the agreed-upon procedures to be performed to meet the needs of intended users. If intended users are likely to be able to interpret the factual findings resulting from procedures performed, whether alone or in combination with other available evidence, to reach appropriate conclusions, then an engagement to report factual findings may be acceptable. If intended users are unlikely to be able to interpret the factual findings to reach appropriate conclusions, then the

11 See *Framework for Assurance Engagements*, paragraph 16.

assurance practitioner does not accept an agreed-upon procedures engagement, but may accept an assurance engagement if appropriate.

A4. An agreed-upon procedures engagement may be accepted if it satisfies some but not all of the elements of an assurance engagement,[12] with the exception of a written assurance report, as that requires the provision of assurance.

A5. If all of the elements of an assurance engagement are met,[13] the assurance practitioner declines an agreed-upon procedures engagement, however an assurance engagement may be accepted if appropriate and applicable AUASB standards are applied. Appendix 1 provides a table of *Differentiating Factors between Agreed-Upon Procedures Engagements and Assurance Engagements* to assist the assurance practitioner in determining whether the engagement is an agreed-upon procedures engagement or an assurance engagement.

A6. The extent of the subject matter does not affect whether an engagement is an assurance engagement or not. Even if the subject matter of an engagement is very specific, when the engagement contains the elements of an assurance engagement, the assurance practitioner complies with the requirements of either:

(a) ASA 805 *Special Considerations - Audits of Single Financial Statements and Specific Elements, Accounts or Items of a Financial Statement* when providing reasonable assurance on historical financial information other than a financial report;

(b) ASA 2405 *Review of Historical Financial Information Other than a Financial Report* when providing limited assurance on historical financial information other than a financial report; or

(c) ASAE 3000 *Assurance Engagements Other than Audits or Reviews of Historical Financial Information* when providing reasonable or limited assurance on matters other than historical financial information.[14]

Example engagements are described in Appendix 2 illustrating how an engagement could be scoped as an agreed-upon procedures engagement or an assurance engagement for the same subject matter.

A7. The assurance practitioner may assist the engaging party and intended users in determining the procedures to be performed to ensure that the procedures are able to be performed and are likely to meet the needs of the intended users. Nevertheless, the assurance practitioner is not responsible for the adequacy of the agreed-upon procedures nor for assessing whether the findings will be sufficient either alone or in combination with other evidence to support any conclusions which the users intend to draw. The assurance practitioner's role in an agreed-upon procedures engagement is to use their professional competence and capabilities in the performance of the agreed-upon procedures and to report the findings accurately.

A8. If it is necessary for the assurance practitioner to perform a risk assessment, respond to assessed risks or evaluate the evidence gathered, then this indicates that the assurance practitioner is using their professional judgement to gather sufficient appropriate evidence to support a conclusion. In these circumstances, the engagement may be an assurance engagement and, if so, the relevant requirements in the AUASB standards need to be applied.

Agreeing the Terms of the Agreed-Upon Procedures Engagement (Ref: Para. 23-26)

A9. The agreed terms would ordinarily be recorded in an engagement letter or other suitable form of written agreement. It is in the interests of both the engaging party and the assurance practitioner that the assurance practitioner sends an engagement letter, preferably before the commencement of the engagement, to help in avoiding misunderstandings with respect to the engagement.

---

12 See *Framework for Assurance Engagements*, paragraph 20 for the elements of an assurance engagement.

13 See *Framework for Assurance Engagements*, paragraph 20 for the elements of an assurance engagement.

14 See ASAE 3100 *Compliance Engagements* and ASAE 3500 *Performance Engagements*, as appropriate.

A10. In certain circumstances, for example when the procedures have been agreed to between the regulator, industry representatives and representatives of the accounting profession, the assurance practitioner may not be able to discuss the procedures with all the parties who will receive the report of factual findings. In such cases, the assurance practitioner may consider, for example, discussing the procedures to be applied with appropriate representatives of the parties involved, reviewing relevant correspondence from such parties or sending them a draft of the report of factual findings that will be issued.

A11. In an agreed-upon procedures engagement, as the assurance practitioner does not express a conclusion, it is the engaging party's responsibility to determine the procedures which will provide sufficient appropriate evidence to support their own or intended users' conclusions. It is only appropriate for the assurance practitioner to select the procedures if they will be assessing the evidence to support a conclusion provided in an assurance engagement.

A12. Not all intended users may be available to agree to the terms of the engagement or the agreed-upon procedures to be performed. These intended users may still be specified in the letter of engagement where the assurance practitioner is satisfied that those users will understand the purpose for which the report of factual findings is intended to be used. These intended users may include:

(a) regulators or industry bodies which issue requirements for procedures to be performed and factual findings to be reported; and

(b) an identifiable class of users which are intended to receive the report of factual findings for a specified purpose.

A13. An example of an engagement letter for an agreed-upon procedures engagement is set out in Appendix 3.

Planning (Ref: Para. 27-28)

A14. Planning in an agreed-upon procedures engagement is restricted by the nature, timing and extent of procedures as agreed in the terms of the engagement. Therefore, the assurance practitioner does not have the discretion to perform alternative or additional procedures without obtaining the engaging party's agreement. Nevertheless, the assurance practitioner will still need to plan the nature, timing and extent of the resources necessary to perform the engagement.

Performing the Engagement (Ref: Para. 37-38)

A15. The procedures applied in an engagement to perform agreed-upon procedures may include:

(a) inspection;

(b) observation;

(c) external confirmation;

(d) re-calculation;

(e) re-performance;

(f) analytical review procedures, where those procedures are based solely on comparison against expectations defined in the terms of the engagement; and

(g) enquiry.

A16. Analytical procedures are not performed in an agreed-upon procedures engagement unless the engaging party provides an expectation of recorded amounts or ratios on which the assurance practitioner may base the analytical procedures. The engaging party's expectations are defined in the procedures described in the terms of the engagement. It is necessary for the engaging party to provide the expectations as a basis for the analytical procedures so that the assurance practitioner does not use their professional judgement to develop expectations, which is only appropriate when conducting an assurance engagement. The assurance practitioner does not interpret the findings from the analytical procedures but simply presents the findings against the expectations provided by the engaging party.

Reporting (Ref: Para. 39-47)

A17. Even though assurance is not provided by the assurance practitioner, the intended users are entitled to rely on the accuracy of the reported findings by virtue of the assurance practitioner's capabilities and competence in conducting the agreed-upon procedures.

A18. The report of factual findings needs to describe the procedures performed and findings in sufficient detail to enable the intended users to understand the nature, timing and extent of the work performed as well as the nature of the errors and exceptions identified in order to assess the findings reported and draw their own conclusions on the subject matter. In order to draw conclusions, intended users may need to assess the factual findings along with information from other sources. Intended users will need to satisfy themselves that the evidence, which the report of factual findings and other sources provide, is sufficient and appropriate to provide a basis for any conclusion which they may reach.

A19. An illustrative report of factual findings, incorporating the elements set forth in paragraph 43, is set out in Appendix 4.

A20. If the law or regulation prescribes the layout or wording of the assurance practitioner's report in a form or in terms that are significantly different from the requirements of this standard and an additional explanation cannot mitigate possible misunderstanding, in addition to excluding any reference to this standard in the report, the assurance practitioner may consider including a statement that the agreed-upon procedures engagement is not conducted in accordance with this standard.

A21. If the assurance practitioner is aware that an error or exception identified has been substantially rectified, the fact that it has been rectified may be included in the report.

A22. The assurance practitioner's inability to perform the agreed-upon procedures may arise from:

(a) circumstances beyond the control of the engaging party;

(b) circumstances relating to the nature or timing of the assurance practitioner's work; or

(c) limitations imposed by management of the engaging party.

❖ ❖ ❖

Conformity with International Standards on Related Services

Except as noted below, this Standard on Related Services conforms with International Standard on Related Services ISRS 4400, issued by the International Auditing and Assurance Standards Board, an independent standard-setting board of the International Federation of Accountants (IFAC). The main differences between ASRS 4400 and ISRS 4400 are:

- ASRS 4400 is not limited to procedures regarding "financial information", whereas ISRS 4400 is limited to financial information. (Ref: Para. 4)
- ASRS 4400 applies to "procedures of an assurance nature" whereas ISRS 4400 applies to "procedures of an audit nature". Whilst the terms differ, they can be taken to have the same meaning as indicated by the procedures listed in ISRS 4400, paragraph 16, which are equivalent to those listed in ASRS 4400, paragraph A15. (Ref: Para. 4 & 11)
- ASRS 4400 applies to the "assurance practitioner", whereas ISRS 4400 applies to the "auditor". Whilst the terms differ, they can be taken to have the same meaning. (Ref: Para. 1)
- The AUASB is of the view that the assurance practitioner, when carrying out procedures of an assurance nature and reporting factual findings, needs to either be independent or to have agreed modified independence requirements with the engaging party and agreed or disclosed those modified independence with intended users. Therefore, ASRS 4400 requires the assurance practitioner to maintain independence equivalent to the independence requirements applicable to Other Assurance Engagements and to disclose in their report if modified independence requirements are agreed. ISRS 4400 does not

require the auditor to be independent, but requires the auditor to state in the report of factual findings if they are not independent. (Ref: Para. 17)

- ASRS 4400 includes requirements, which are additional to those contained in ISRS 4400, for the assurance practitioner to:
  - understand the needs and objectives of the intended users; (Ref: Para. 18)
  - satisfy themselves that a regulator or representative of a class of users, industry or the accounting profession does represent the class of users for whom the engagement is intended; (Ref: Para. 19)
  - only accept the engagement if those persons who are to perform the engagement collectively have the capabilities and competence to perform the procedures; (Ref: Para. 20)
  - not accept an agreed-upon procedures engagement if: (Ref: Para. 21)
    - it is unlikely to meet the needs of intended users;
    - users are likely to construe the outcome as providing assurance;
    - all of the elements of an assurance engagement are met;
    - the engagement has no rational purpose; or
    - the assurance practitioner needs to determine the sufficiency of procedures to be performed, perform a risk assessment, evaluate the sufficiency and appropriateness of the evidence or reach a conclusion;
  - state in the terms of the engagement that intended users are responsible for reaching any conclusions on the subject matter; (Ref: Para. 22)
  - not exercise professional judgement to determine or modify the procedures to be performed during the course of the engagement; (Ref: Para. 25)
  - request amended terms of the engagement if alternative or further procedures are to be performed; (Ref: Para. 26)
  - limit planning to the procedures agreed in the terms of the engagement; (Ref: Para. 28)
  - not perform a risk assessment; (Ref: Para. 29)
  - not apply materiality to design procedures nor to assess factual findings; (Ref: Para. 30)
  - establish and maintain a system of quality control within the firm, although this requirement is imposed indirectly on engagements under ISRS 4400 by virtue of ISQC1[15] which, unlike ASQC 1, applies to related services engagements; (Ref: Para. 31)
  - take responsibility for overall quality control and apply quality control procedures on the engagement, including the engagement team's compliance with ethical requirements; (Ref: Para. 31-32)
  - satisfy themselves that the engagement team and any experts collectively have competence, capabilities and resources to perform the agreed-upon procedures; (Ref: Para. 33)
  - take responsibility for the direction, supervision and performance of the engagement and the accurate reporting of factual findings and, when using the work of others, evaluate the adequacy of their work and the findings communicated; (Ref: Para. 34-35)
  - document matters with respect to compliance with ethical requirements, including independence, acceptance and continuance of client relationships and acceptance of the engagement; (Ref: Para. 36)
  - not extend the terms of engagement to the provision of assurance; (Ref: Para. 38)
  - not evaluate the findings or provide a conclusion or opinion; (Ref: Para. 39)

15 See ISQC1 *Quality Control for Firms the Perform Audits and Reviews of Financial Reports and Other Financial Information, and Other Assurance Engagements.*

- state in the report of factual findings that the responsibility for determining the adequacy of the agreed-upon procedures is that of the engaging party; (Ref: Para. 43(h))
- not issue a modified report or emphasis of matter, but instead report all errors or exceptions in the factual findings, even if they are subsequently rectified, or the inability to perform any of the agreed-upon procedures; and (Ref: Para. 46)
- exclude wording from the report of factual findings which may indicate that assurance is being provided. (Ref: Para. 47)

Compliance with this standard enables compliance with ISRS 4400.

Appendix 1

(Ref: Para. A5)

Differentiating Factors between Agreed-Upon Procedures Engagements and Assurance Engagements

Differentiating Factor	Agreed-Upon Procedures Engagement	Assurance Engagement
Nature, timing and extent of procedures responsibility of:	Engaging party	Assurance practitioner
Nature, timing and extent of procedures determined in:	Terms of the engagement	Engagement plan
Changes to the nature, timing and extent of procedures are documented in:	Terms of the engagement	Engagement plan
Extent of assurance practitioner's professional judgement exercised in selecting procedures:	Professional judgement may be exercised in assisting the engaging party to identify procedures when agreeing the terms of the engagement, but only professional competence is exercised when conducting the agreed-upon procedures.	Professional judgement exercised in selecting procedures
Sufficiency and appropriateness of evidence assessed by:	Intended user	Assurance practitioner
Form and content of report:	Factual findings, no conclusion or assurance provided	Conclusion providing assurance
Reporting of procedures performed:	Detail of the exact nature, timing and extent of all procedures performed are reported	Summary of work performed
Reporting of findings:	Detail of exact findings resulting from each procedure performed, including errors and exceptions identified, even if rectified.	No detail of findings, unless a modified report is to be issued when the basis for modification is provided or if a management letter is provided in addition to the assurance report.

Appendix 2

(Ref: Para. A6)

Examples of Differences in Scope between an Agreed-Upon Procedures Engagement and an Assurance Engagement

The following brief descriptions of engagements are intended to illustrate that engagements relating to the same subject matter may be scoped in the terms of the engagement as an agreed-upon procedures engagement providing no assurance or an assurance engagement depending on the needs of the engaging party and intended users. The scope provided in each of the following examples, which would be reflected in the terms of the engagement, is to be used as a guide only and will need to be adapted to the individual engagement requirements and circumstances.

Nature of Engagement	Purpose of Engagement	Scope of an Agreed-Upon Procedures Engagement	Scope of an Assurance Engagement
1. Turnover lease agreement	To assist parties to a lease agreement based on turnover in assessing compliance with the agreement.	• Agree gross turnover to underlying data; • Recalculate adjusted turnover based on agreed formula; and • Recalculate the turnover rent payable under the lease agreement.	• Audit/review compliance with the turnover lease agreement to provide a reasonable/limited assurance conclusion as to whether the entity has complied, in all material respects, with the lease agreement over the period.
2. Management agreement	To assist the directors of each entity to fulfil their reporting requirements under management agreements with the managing entity.	• Agree specified data from entities' income statements to the entities' trial balances, parent entity consolidation schedule and audited consolidated financial report.	• Audit/review compliance with the reporting requirements of the management agreement to provide a reasonable/limited assurance conclusion as to whether each entity has complied, in all material respects, with the management agreement over the period.
3. Leave provisions	To assist management assessment of whether leave provisions were calculated in accordance with corporate policy as a basis for negotiating the consideration for transferring staff.	• Agree start date and employment terms for a random sample of X staff to employment contracts. • Agree leave taken to employee records. • Recalculate long service leave and annual leave provisions for X staff to be transferred as part of a novation agreement.	• Audit/review employee leave provisions to provide a reasonable/limited assurance conclusion as to whether leave balances are calculated, in all material respects, in accordance with corporate policy.
4. Loan securitisation	To assist the engaging party and potential investors in determining the data on which to base the securitisation of a pool of loans.	• Select X loans based on criteria provided by the engaging party. • Agree specified loan data to supporting documentation and check loan data against given criteria. • Recalculate total loan pool data.	• Audit/review the loan pool to provide a reasonable/limited assurance conclusion as to whether the loan pool is reported, in all material respects, in accordance with the agreed basis.

ASRS

Nature of Engagement	Purpose of Engagement	Scope of an Agreed-Upon Procedures Engagement	Scope of an Assurance Engagement
5. Stocktake procedures	To assist management in determining the value of stock on hand.	• Attend X sites randomly selected, test count X randomly selected stock items to stock count sheets. • Trace those stock count sheets to summary stock data. • Agree X randomly selected stock items to inventory account and agree cost to supplier invoices.	• Audit/review stock at period end to provide a reasonable/limited assurance conclusion as to whether stock is valued fairly, in all material respects, in accordance with corporate policy.
6. Debtors' balances	To assist management in identifying issues in debtors' collection.	• Agree aged debtors to the trial balance at period end. • Agree the largest (at period end) X debtors to sales invoices. • Trace X randomly selected debtor balances to subsequent receipts. • Itemise bad debt written off for the period with explanations provided by management. • Itemise customers on stop supply or COD. • Determine value and number of credit notes for the period. • Calculate debtors ageing percentages at period end.	• Audit/review debtors and provision for doubtful debts to provide a reasonable/limited assurance conclusion as to whether debtors and provision for doubtful debts are presented fairly, in all material respects, in accordance with the agreed basis of accounting.
7. Controls to meet contractual obligations	To assist client in completing their certificate of compliance with respect to confidentiality and privacy agreements, in circumstances where data supplied by providers under confidentiality and privacy agreements requiring controls to protect data.	• Agree list of users with access to restricted data for any part of the reporting period to signed confidentiality statements. • Agree individual confidentiality statements to confidentiality agreement. • Identify confidentiality training held over reporting period, percentage of users attended and average hours training attended per user. • Trace data access log for X days, spread throughout the period, to list of approved users.	• Audit/review controls in place to comply with confidentiality and privacy agreements in order to provide a reasonable/limited assurance conclusion as to whether the description fairly presents the controls, the controls are suitably designed and operating effectively throughout the reporting period.

Appendix 3

(Ref: Para. A13)

Example of an Engagement Letter for an Agreed-Upon Procedures Engagement

The following is an example of an engagement letter for an agreed-upon procedures engagement prepared in accordance with ASRS 4400. This letter is not authoritative but is intended only to be a guide that may be used in conjunction with the considerations outlined in this standard. It will need to be varied according to individual requirements and circumstances of each engagement. It may be appropriate to seek legal advice that any proposed letter is suitable.

❖❖❖

To the appropriate representative of management or those charged with governance[16] of name of Entity [and name of other intended users or class of users as appropriate]:

[The objective and scope of the engagement]

You have requested that we perform the agreed-upon procedures specified below [as required by [name of representative of class of intended users or regulator] to meet the needs of [class of intended users]]. We are pleased to confirm our acceptance and understanding of this agreed-upon procedures engagement and the nature and limitations of the procedures we will conduct. Our engagement will be conducted with the objective of reporting factual findings resulting from each procedure for the purpose of [specify purpose]. The procedures performed will not constitute a reasonable or limited assurance engagement, accordingly, no assurance will be provided.

[The responsibilities of the assurance practitioner]

We will conduct our engagement in accordance with Standard on Related Services ASRS 4400 *Agreed-Upon Procedures Engagements to Report Factual Findings*. That standard requires that we comply with ethical requirements equivalent to Other Assurance Engagements,[17] [including independence/except with respect to independence for which modified independence requirements will be applied], and plan and perform the agreed procedures to obtain factual findings. [If applicable:[18] We will apply modified independence requirements agreed with you, which will consist of (describe level of independence to be applied).] The procedures which we will perform will be restricted to those procedures agreed with you [which include procedures required by [name of representative of class of intended users or regulator]] and listed below. Information acquired by us in the course of our engagement is subject to strict confidentiality requirements and will not be disclosed by us to other parties except as required or allowed for by law or professional standards, or with your express consent.

We have agreed to perform the following procedures and report to you the factual findings resulting from our work:

> [describe the nature, timing and extent of each procedure to be performed, including specific reference, where applicable, to the identity of documents and records to be read, individuals to be contacted and parties from whom confirmations will be obtained.]

---

16 *Those charged with governance* means the person(s) or organisation(s) (for example a corporate trustee) with responsibility for overseeing the strategic direction of the entity. This includes overseeing the financial reporting process. For some entities in some jurisdictions, those charged with governance may include management personnel, for example, executive members of a governance board of a private or public sector entity, or an owner-manager.

17 See APES 110 *Code of Ethics for Professional Accountants*, (Dec 2010), Section 291 *Independence - Other Assurance Engagements*.

18 See APES 110, Section 291. Modified independence requirements are only permitted under the ethical requirements applicable to Other Assurance Engagements if the intended users of the report (a) are knowledgeable as to the purpose, subject matter information and limitations of the report and (b) explicitly agree to the application of the modified independence requirements.

ASRS

If we are unable to perform the exact nature, timing or extent of procedures agreed above but alternative procedures are available, we will only perform these alternative procedures if modified terms of the engagement are agreed with [name of entity and other intended users].

[The responsibilities of management or those charged with governance and intended users (if appropriate)]

Our agreed-upon procedures will be performed on the basis that [management and, where appropriate, those charged with governance and intended users] acknowledge and understand that:

(a) they have responsibility for determining the adequacy or otherwise of the procedures agreed to be performed by us;

(b) they have responsibility for determining whether the factual findings provided by us, in combination with any other information obtained, provide a reasonable basis for any conclusions which you or the intended users wish to draw on the subject matter;

(c) they have responsibility to provide us with:

  (i) access to all information of which management is aware that is necessary for the performance of the procedures agreed;

  (ii) additional information that we may request from you for the purpose of the engagement; and

  (iii) unrestricted access to persons within the entity from whom we require co-operation in order to perform the procedures agreed.

(d) the procedures we will perform are solely to assist you [and name of intended users] in [state purpose]. Our report of factual findings is not to be used for any other purpose and is solely for your [and name of intended users'] information.

(e) the procedures that we will perform will not constitute a reasonable or limited assurance engagement in accordance with AUASB standards and, consequently, no assurance will be provided.

We look forward to full co-operation with your staff during our engagement.

[Other relevant information]

[Insert other information, such as fee arrangements, billings and other specific terms as appropriate]

[Reporting]

Our report of factual findings will consist of a detailed listing of the procedures performed and our findings in relation to each procedure, including any errors or exceptions identified regardless of whether those errors or exceptions have since been rectified. Use of our report will be restricted to you [and [name of other intended users or class of users]] and all other parties will be excluded from using the report.

Please sign and return the attached copy of this letter to indicate your acknowledgement of, and agreement with, the arrangements for our agreed-upon procedures engagement including the specific procedures which we have agreed will be performed and our respective responsibilities.

Yours faithfully,

....

Partner

XYZ & Co

Acknowledged on behalf of [name of Entity] by

(signed)

....

Name and Title

Date

[Acknowledged on behalf of [name of Intended User] by

(signed)

....

Name and Title

Date

Appendix 4

(Ref: Para. A19)

Example of a Report of Factual Findings in Connection with Accounts Payable

REPORT OF FACTUAL FINDINGS

To [appropriate addressee]

Report of Factual Findings

We have performed the procedures agreed with you and [name of any intended users party to the terms of the engagement] to report factual findings for the purpose of assisting you [and [name of other intended users or class of intended users]] in assessing, in combination with other information obtained by you, the accuracy of accounts payable as at [date]. The procedures performed are detailed in the terms of the engagement of [date] and described below [(or if appropriate) set forth in the attached schedules][19] with respect to the accounts payable of [entity] as of [date].

[Management/Those Charged with Governance]'s Responsibility for the Procedures Agreed

[Management/Those Charged with Governance and any intended users party to the terms of the engagement] are responsible for the adequacy or otherwise of the procedures agreed to be performed by us. You and [name of other intended users or class of intended users] are responsible for determining whether the factual findings provided by us, in combination with any other information obtained, provide a reasonable basis for any conclusions which you or other intended users wish to draw on the subject matter.

Assurance Practitioner's Responsibility

Our responsibility is to report factual findings obtained from conducting the procedures agreed. We conducted the engagement in accordance with Standard on Related Services ASRS 4400 *Agreed-Upon Procedures Engagements to Report Factual Findings*. We have complied with ethical requirements equivalent to those applicable to Other Assurance Engagements,[20] [including independence/except that we applied modified independence requirements as agreed with you in the terms of the engagement consisting of (describe level of independence applied)].

Because the agreed-upon procedures do not constitute either a reasonable or limited assurance engagement in accordance with AUASB standards, we do not express any conclusion and provide no assurance on the accounts payable of [entity] as of [date]. Had we performed additional procedures or had we performed an audit or a review of the accounts payable in accordance with AUASB standards, other matters might have come to our attention that would have been reported to you.

19 If schedules are attached, describe and reference the schedules (not shown in this example).

20 See APES 110 (Dec 2010), Section 291.

Factual Findings[21]

The procedures were performed solely to assist you in evaluating the accuracy of the accounts payable. The procedures performed and the factual findings obtained are as follows:

Procedures Performed	Factual Findings	Errors or Exceptions Identified
1. We obtained and checked the addition of the trial balance of accounts payable as at [date] prepared by [entity], and we compared the total to the balance in the related general ledger account.	We found the addition to be correct and the total amount to be in agreement.	None
2 We compared the attached schedule (not shown in this example) provided by [entity] of major suppliers and the amounts owing at [date] to each of the related names and amounts in the trial balance.	We found the amounts compared to be in agreement, except for the exceptions noted.	*[Detail the exceptions]*
3. For X suppliers randomly selected from the attached schedule we obtained suppliers' statements or requested suppliers to confirm balances owing at [date].	We found there were suppliers' statements for all such suppliers.	None
4. We compared such statements or confirmations to the amounts referred to in 2. For amounts which did not agree, we obtained reconciliations from [entity]. For reconciliations obtained, we identified and listed outstanding invoices, credit notes and payments, each of which was greater than $XXX. We agreed outstanding invoices over $XXX for suppliers selected to accounts payable for the subsequent period, invoices subsequently received and either credit notes or payment made.	We found the amounts agreed, or with respect to amounts which did not agree, we found [entity] had prepared reconciliations and that the credit notes, invoices and payments over $XXX as agreed to reconciling items unless exceptions noted.	*[Detail exceptions]*

[The following procedures included in the terms of the engagement could not be performed for the reasons set out below:][22]

[Procedure Unable to be Performed]	[Reasons Procedure was Unable to be Performed]
[Detail procedure in terms of the engagement]	*[Detail reasons]*

Restriction on Distribution and Use of Report

This report is intended solely for the use of [entity] and [intended users identified in the terms of the engagement] for the purpose set out above. As the intended user of our report, it is for you and other intended users to assess both the procedures and our factual findings to determine whether they provide, in combination with any other information you have obtained, a reasonable basis for any conclusions which you wish to draw on the subject matter. As required by ASRS 4400, distribution of this report is restricted to those parties that have agreed the procedures to be performed with us and other intended users identified in the terms of the engagement (since others, unaware of the reasons for the procedures, may misinterpret the results). Accordingly, we expressly disclaim and do not accept any responsibility or liability to any party other than [company full name, name of intended users and name of class of users] for any consequences of reliance on this report for any purpose.

[Assurance practitioner's signature]

[Date of the report of factual findings]

[Assurance practitioner's address]

21 The assurance practitioner may choose instead to present the table of factual findings as an attachment to the report, particularly if it is lengthy.

22 Insert this table where there has been a limitation of scope such that certain procedures could not be performed.

ASRS 4450

Comfort Letter Engagements

(Issued May 2012)

Issued by the Auditing and Assurance Standards Board.

Note from the Institute of Chartered Accountants Australia

This note, prepared by the technical editor, is not part of ASRS 4450.

Historical development

May 2012: ASRS 4450 issued. It provides detailed requirements and related guidance for auditors when determining whether to accept a comfort letter engagement, how it is to be performed and how and what to report. It is operative for engagements commencing on or after 1 July 2013 and there is no international equivalent, but it is based on the US Standard SAS 72 'Letters for Underwriters and Certain Other Requesting Parties'. ASRS 4450 is supported by the 'Explanatory Guide to applying ASRS 4450 Comfort Letter Engagements', which provides additional information on when to apply the Standard. The Explanatory Guide can be found at auasb.gov.au.

ASRS

Contents

Preface

Reasons for Issuing ASRS 4450

The AUASB issues a Standard on Related Services ASRS 4450 *Comfort Letter Engagements,* pursuant to the requirements of the legislative provisions explained below.

The AUASB is an independent statutory board of the Australian Government established under section 227A of the *Australian Securities and Investments Commission Act 2001*, as amended (ASIC Act). Under section 227B of the ASIC Act, the AUASB may formulate standards for other purposes.

Under the Strategic Direction given to the AUASB by the Financial Reporting Council (FRC), the AUASB develops auditing and assurance standards for historical and non-historical financial information. The AUASB issues standards considered to be in the public interest. Accordingly, the AUASB has decided to issue ASRS 4450 *Comfort Letter Engagements*.

Main Features

This Standard on Related Services establishes requirements and provides application and other explanatory material for auditors undertaking and reporting in comfort letter engagements.

Authority Statement

The Auditing and Assurance Standards Board (AUASB) formulates this Standard on Related Services ASRS 4450 *Comfort Letter Engagements,* pursuant to section 227B of the *Australian Securities and Investments Commission Act 2001.*

This Standard on Related Services is to be read in conjunction with ASA 100 *Preamble to AUASB Standards,* which sets out the intentions of the AUASB on how the AUASB Standards are to be understood, interpreted and applied.

Dated: 30 May 2012

Merran Kelsall
Chairman - AUASB

ASRS

Standard on Related Services ASRS 4450 Comfort Letter Engagements

Application

1. This Standard on Related Services applies to engagements relating to the auditor of an entity providing a comfort letter to certain requesting parties in respect of particular financial information related to, and/or included in, an offering document.

Operative Date

2. This Standard on Related Services is operative for comfort letter engagements commencing on or after 1 July 2013.

Introduction

Scope of this Standard on Related Services

3. This Standard on Related Services (ASRS) addresses the auditor's responsibilities when requested by the responsible party of the entity making an offering of securities to provide a comfort letter to certain requesting parties relating to particular financial information included in the entity's offering document. The auditor is ordinarily the appointed auditor of the entity for the period covered by the comfort letter and the entity ordinarily receives a copy of the comfort letter. The requesting parties may be underwriters, buyers, sellers, brokers, selling agents, or other auditors appointed by the entity in connection with an offering being undertaken by the entity. The entity may or may not be the issuer of the securities included in the offering document. References in this ASRS to 'entity' are taken to mean the issuer unless otherwise stated. The comfort letter is prepared based on the

auditor having performed the requesting parties' specified procedures and consequently no assurance is expressed in the comfort letter. The auditor is not required by any AUASB Standard to accept the engagement, and ordinarily does so only if certain preconditions are met by both the responsible party of the entity and requesting parties. (Ref: Para. A1)

4. Any request by the entity to the auditor to perform an audit or review of the entity's interim financial information included in the offering document is covered by a separate engagement to the comfort letter engagement and performed in accordance with applicable AUASB Standards.

5. The subject matter that may be covered in a comfort letter includes:

   (a) the independence of the auditor;

   (b) unaudited financial statements, interim financial information, pro forma historical financial information and changes in selected financial statement items during a period subsequent to the date and period of the latest audited and /or reviewed financial statements of the entity; and

   (c) tables, statistics, and other financial information included in the offering document.

Types of Offerings Covered by this ASRS

6. The following types of offerings are included within the scope of this ASRS: (Ref: Para. A2)

   (a) initial public offerings;

   (b) overseas private placements of equity or debt securities;

   (c) offerings of debt securities that are issued or backed by public sector entities in overseas jurisdictions; and

   (d) acquisition of, or merger with, another entity domiciled in an overseas jurisdiction, where there is an exchange of equity shares between the two entities.

Comfort Letters Provided to Requesting Parties outside Australia

7. In certain jurisdictions, requesting parties who are underwriters may be held liable under applicable law or regulation for any material omissions or misstatements in an offering document. Requesting the entity's auditor to issue a comfort letter in respect of particular financial information included in the offering document is one of a number of procedures that may be used by the requesting parties to establish a due diligence defence against exposure to any liability.

Relationship with applicable Standards of other jurisdictions

8. The auditor may undertake a comfort letter engagement in accordance with:

   (a) this ASRS, when issuing a comfort letter to requesting parties in a jurisdiction where there is no existing standard issued by a national auditing standards setting body; or

   (b) the requirements of another standard, when issuing a comfort letter to requesting parties in jurisdictions where the other standard has been issued by a national auditing standards setting body.[1]

Objective

9. The objectives of the auditor when requested to provide a comfort letter are to ensure:

   (a) that the preconditions for accepting the engagement are met; and

   (b) the appropriate form and content of the comfort letter are used to report the results of performing the procedures specified by the requesting parties on particular financial information related to, and/or included in, an offering document.

1 For example, SAS 72 *Letters for Underwriters and Certain Other Requesting Parties*, issued by the American Institute of Certified Public Accountants and Hong Kong Standard on Investment Circular Reporting Engagements 400 *Comfort Letters and Due Diligence Meetings on Financial and Non-Financial Information*, issued by the Hong Kong Institute of Certified Public Accountants.

Definitions

10. For purposes of this ASRS, the following terms have the meanings attributed below:

(a) Applicable financial reporting framework means the financial reporting framework adopted by the entity in the preparation of general or special purpose financial information of the entity that is acceptable based on the nature of the entity or as required by applicable law or regulation. In Australia, an applicable financial reporting framework that may be used in preparing such financial information is represented by the Australian Accounting Standards which are International Financial Reporting Standards (IFRS) compliant (as issued by the International Accounting Standards Board), or applicable law, such as the *Corporations Act 2001*. Other frameworks that may be used are the International Financial Reporting Standards, issued by the International Accounting Standards Board and the Generally Accepted Accounting Principles of the United States.

(b) Addressees mean the parties to whom the auditor addresses the comfort letter, and includes the requesting parties and the responsible party of the entity.

(c) Auditor means the person or firm appointed to audit an entity's financial report.

(d) Auditor's statement means a statement made by the auditor that based on the procedures performed, nothing has come to the auditor's attention that caused the auditor to believe that specified matters do not meet specified criteria.

(e) Bring down comfort letter means a letter prepared and issued by the auditor subsequent to the issuance of the initial comfort letter, that updates and reaffirms the results of the specified procedures described in that comfort letter as at a certain date.

(f) Change period means the period specified by the requesting parties ending on the cut-off date and begins for balance sheet items, immediately after the date of the latest balance sheet, and for profit and loss items, immediately after the latest period for which such items are included in, or incorporated by reference, in the offering document and does not extend beyond the day before the date of the end of the entity's next financial reporting period.

(g) Closing date means the date on which the issuer of the securities or selling security holder delivers the securities to the underwriter in exchange for the proceeds of the offering.

(h) Comfort letter means a letter issued by an auditor in accordance with this ASRS under the terms of the engagement letter to requesting parties in relation to an entity's financial information related to, and/or included in an offering document.

(i) Comparison date and comparison period mean the dates as of which, and periods for which, data at the cut-off date and data for the change period are to be compared.

(j) Cross-border offering means an offering or listing that occurs in a jurisdiction other than the entity's domicile, and which may or may not occur concurrently in the entity's domicile.

(k) Cut-off date means the date to which certain procedures performed on change period financial information, as described in the comfort letter, are to relate.

(l) Domestic offering means a securities offering that occurs in Australia.

(m) Entity means the party whose financial statements or financial information is the subject of the comfort letter engagement. The entity may or may not be the Issuer.

(n) Financial forecast means financial information of a predictive character prepared based on assumptions made by the entity as to future events, expected to take place on the dates described, and the actions expected to be taken at the date the financial information is prepared.

(o) Financial information means information of a historical or pro forma financial nature that is the subject matter of the comfort letter.

(p) Offering means the making available of an entity's equity or debt securities to parties (who may be in overseas jurisdictions) ordinarily through:

(i) the sale of securities to the public under a prospectus;

(ii) foreign offerings;

(iii) an exempt transaction or offering (for example, a private placement of equity or debt securities to a limited number of investors, or an offering of debt securities issued or backed by public sector entities);

(iv) certain securities transactions covered by specific laws or regulations (for example, exchange of shares in merger transactions); or

(v) acquisition transactions in which there is an exchange of equity.

(q) Private placement means securities offered for sale or issue in a prospectus to a limited number of investors, which are exempt, by law or regulation from certain content, distribution or registration requests in certain jurisdictions ("exempt offering").

(r) Procedures mean procedures performed by the auditor which are specified by the requesting parties. The auditor does not determine whether the extent of such procedures is sufficient for the purposes of the requesting parties. Procedures may also be referred to as agreed-upon procedures.

(s) Pro forma financial information means non-IFRS financial information that is intended to show the effects of proposed or completed transactions for illustrative purposes.[2] The non-IFRS financial information is adjusted by pro forma adjustments to illustrate the impact of an event(s) or transaction(s) in the financial information as if the event had occurred, or the transaction had been undertaken at an earlier date selected for the purposes of the illustration, ordinarily the beginning of the reporting period.

(t) Representation letter means a letter prepared by the entity at the request of the auditor that confirms to the auditor specific matters relating to the comfort letter engagement.

(u) Requesting parties means third party underwriter(s) and/or other parties involved with the entity's securities offering (such as financial intermediaries, buyers, sellers, brokers or selling agents or group or component auditors) that have agreed to be bound by the auditor's engagement letter (including by authorising the lead manager to sign on their behalf) in order to request the auditor's comfort letter, and may receive the comfort letter if they sign the auditor's engagement letter.

(v) Responsible party of the entity means those charged with governance of the entity (ordinarily the Board of Directors) who are responsible for the preparation of the offering document, and who engage the auditor to issue a comfort letter to the requesting parties and provide a copy to the responsible party.

(w) Underwriter means any person or their agent who has purchased, or intends to purchase securities from an issuer with a view to, or offers or sells for an issuer in connection with, the distribution of any security, or participates or has a direct or indirect participation in any such undertaking. This ASRS also uses the term underwriter to refer to the managing or lead underwriter who ordinarily negotiates the underwriting agreement on behalf of a group of underwriters whose exact composition is not determined until shortly before an offering document becomes effective. The underwriters may or may not be named in the offering document, and are commonly the requesting parties.

(x) Underwriting agreement means a formal agreement between the underwriter(s) and the responsible party of the entity with respect to the entity's offering document. It may specify the form and content of the comfort letter to be requested of the

2 See RG 230 *Disclosing non-IFRS financial information (December 2011)* issued by Australian Securities and Investments Commission for further guidance on pro forma financial information included in transaction documents such as those referred to in this ASRS.

auditor, or that the form and content is to be specified by the requesting parties at a later time. The auditor is not a party to the underwriting agreement.

Requirements

Ethical Requirements

11. When conducting a comfort letter engagement, the auditor shall comply with relevant ethical requirements.[3]

Engagement Acceptance

12. Nothing in this ASRS requires the auditor of an entity to accept a request to prepare a comfort letter, and the auditor shall evaluate all such requests in terms of individual engagement circumstances.

13. When a comfort letter is requested from more than one auditor, the requirements of this ASRS apply to each auditor.

Preconditions for Providing a Comfort Letter

14. The auditor shall, prior to agreeing the terms of providing the comfort letter:

(a) discuss with the responsible party of the entity who the requesting parties are that the comfort letter will be provided to;

(b) obtain an understanding of the applicable financial reporting framework used in the preparation of each type of financial information and the internal control environment for any change period financial information;

(c) discuss with the requesting parties and the responsible party of the entity to: (Ref: Para. A3)

(i) understand the specific matters to be addressed in the comfort letter;

(ii) understand whether a bring down comfort letter will be required covering change period financial information;

(iii) understand the nature of the transaction giving rise to the preparation of the offering document, the jurisdiction(s) into which the offering document will be issued and applicable law or regulation that may affect the comfort letter;

(iv) confirm that the financial information that is the subject of the comfort letter does not include a financial forecast; (Ref: Para. A4)

(v) understand the procedures that the requesting parties have specified to be performed for each type of financial information, and explain in any discussion of procedures that the auditor cannot and will not provide any assurance regarding the sufficiency of the procedures for the requesting parties' purposes;

(d) confirm whether the responsible party of the entity[4] acknowledges and accepts their responsibility for:

(i) the preparation of the offering document;

(ii) the preparation and presentation of the financial information included in the offering document in accordance with the entity's selected applicable financial reporting framework;

(iii) the inclusion of financial and other information in the offering document that is complete and does not include any information that is unacceptable or misleading for its intended purpose;

(iv) the maintenance of proper financial records and systems which facilitate the preparation of the financial information;

3 The auditor's ethical requirements in respect of the responsible party of the entity, including independence applicable to other assurance engagements which include comfort letter engagements, are set out in ASA 102 *Compliance with Ethical Requirements when Performing Audits, Reviews and Other Assurance Engagements.*

4 Where the entity is not the Issuer (e.g. a target in an acquisition or a guarantor), they may not have primary responsibility for (i), (ii) or (iii). Their responsibility would primarily be the financial statements.

(v) such internal control related to financial reporting as the entity determines is necessary to enable the preparation of financial information that is free from material misstatement and fraud;

(vi) providing the auditor in a timely manner with:

- access to all information (including a copy of the final offering document) and persons within the entity;
- written representations covering all matters requested by the auditor; and
- an update on any information the responsible party becomes aware of during the engagement that may impact the comfort letter;

(e) confirm whether the requesting parties acknowledge and accept their responsibility for:

(i) providing a signed final underwriting agreement to the auditor before the comfort letter is issued;

(ii) selecting and determining the nature, timing and extent of the procedures to be performed by the auditor, as well as determining the sufficiency of such procedures for the requesting parties purposes;

(iii) communicating to the auditor the procedures to be performed in sufficient detail that the auditor will not be required to exercise any professional judgement in determining or modifying the procedures, or be held responsible for the sufficiency of such procedures for the requesting parties' purposes;

(iv) conducting a due diligence investigation; and

(v) providing signed representations to the auditor prior to the commencement of the engagement that confirms: (Ref: Para. A4-A5)

- that the requesting parties have a due diligence defence available to them under applicable law or regulation (Ref. Para. A6); or
- that the requesting parties have conducted, or are in the process of conducting, a review process on the offering document substantially consistent with the due diligence process that would be performed if the offering were being undertaken pursuant to applicable law or regulation. (Ref. Para. A7)

15. If the preconditions for providing the comfort letter set out in paragraph 14 of this ASRS are not present, the auditor either:

(a) does not agree to prepare the comfort letter in accordance with this ASRS; or

(b) chooses not to accept the engagement.

Agreeing on the Terms of Engagement

16. The auditor shall document the agreed terms of engagement in an engagement letter, addressed to the responsible party of the entity and requesting parties, which shall include, at a minimum:

(a) an introduction that summarises the auditor's understanding of the nature of the transaction giving rise to the preparation of an offering document;

(b) a statement identifying the addressees of the comfort letter; (Ref: Para. A8)

(c) statements that the engagement will be conducted in accordance with this ASRS, in compliance with relevant ethical requirements, including independence,[5] and the applicable law and regulation of Australia; (Ref: Para. A9)

(d) a statement that the agreed purpose of the engagement is to provide a comfort letter to the addressees solely for use by the responsible party of the entity and requesting parties in seeking to establish a due diligence defence, and accordingly the comfort

5 See ASA 102.

letter is restricted in its distribution to only the addressees, or otherwise by prior written consent;

(e) statements in respect of the work to be performed:

(i) that the auditor will perform the procedures specified by the requesting parties up to a certain date in respect of particular financial information related to, and/or included in the offering document and will report results or the auditor's statement in the comfort letter within the agreed timeframe; (Ref: Para. A9)

(ii) if applicable, that the auditor will provide a draft copy of the comfort letter, containing the expected form and content of the comfort letter, together with a statement that there may be circumstances where the final comfort letter may differ from the draft; (Ref: Para. A10)

(iii) that the sufficiency of the comfort letter procedures for the requesting parties' purposes is for the requesting parties to decide, and not the auditor; (Ref: Para. A11)

(iv) if applicable, that the auditor will provide a draft copy of the bring down comfort letter in respect of certain change period financial information selected by the requesting parties;

(f) the responsibilities of the responsible party of the entity, including those set out in paragraph 14(d) of this ASRS;

(g) the responsibilities of the requesting parties, including those set out in paragraph 14(e) of this ASRS; and

(h) other such terms or conditions that the auditor considers appropriate in the circumstances. (Ref: Para A12-A13)

17. The auditor shall endeavour to obtain a signed engagement letter from the responsible party of the entity and requesting parties. If the requesting parties do not agree to sign the engagement letter, the auditor shall perform such procedures as in the auditor's professional judgement are appropriate to ensure the auditor is satisfied the requesting parties understand the terms of the engagement. If the responsible party of the entity does not agree to sign the engagement letter, the auditor shall not accept the engagement. (Ref: Para. A14)

Draft Comfort Letter

18. If agreed to in the terms of engagement as set out in paragraph 16 of this ASRS, the auditor shall provide a draft of the expected form and content of the comfort letter to the requesting parties in a timely manner. (Ref: Para. A15)

19. The draft comfort letter shall be clearly identified as a draft to avoid giving the impression that the procedures described in the draft have been performed. To the extent possible, the draft comfort letter shall deal with all matters to be covered in the final comfort letter and use exactly the same terms as those to be used in the final comfort letter, subject to the understanding that the comments in the final comfort letter cannot be determined until the procedures underlying it have been performed. It shall clearly describe that the procedures to be performed by the auditor are those specified by the requesting parties, and that the requesting parties above are responsible for the sufficiency of the procedures for their purposes. (Ref: Para. A16-A17)

20. If the auditor is unable to have a discussion with the requesting parties about the requesting parties' required procedures for the auditor to perform at the time of preparing the draft comfort letter, the auditor shall either:

(a) describe in the draft comfort letter those procedures specified in the draft underwriting agreement that the auditor is willing to perform; or

(b) if the draft underwriting agreement is not available at the time of being requested to prepare the draft, the auditor is unable to agree to provide a draft comfort letter. (Ref: Para. A18)

21. In competitive bidding situations in which legal counsel for the requesting parties acts as the requesting parties' representative prior to opening and acceptance of the bid, the

auditor shall carry out the discussions and other communications required by this ASRS with the legal counsel until the requesting parties are selected. In such circumstances, the auditor shall not agree to provide a comfort letter addressed to the entity, legal counsel, or a non-specific addressee such as any or all underwriters to be selected. If the auditor agrees to provide a draft comfort letter, the draft comfort letter shall include a legend describing the comfort letter's purpose and limitations. (Ref: Para. A19)

Changes in the Terms of Providing the Comfort Letter

22. The auditor shall not agree to a change in the scope of services agreed to in the engagement letter if there is no reasonable justification for doing so. (Ref: Para. A20)

23. If the terms of providing the comfort letter are agreed to be changed, the terms shall be documented in writing and co-signed by the auditor, the responsible party of the entity and the requesting parties. (Ref: Para. A21)

24. If the terms of providing the comfort letter are unable to be agreed by the auditor, the auditor shall withdraw from the engagement and not agree to issue the comfort letter.

Performing the Engagement (Ref: Para. A22)

25. The auditor shall perform the requesting parties' specified procedures as agreed in the engagement letter.

Commenting in a Comfort Letter on Financial Information Other Than Audited or Reviewed Financial Statements

General

26. If the auditor is required to comment in a comfort letter on financial information other than audited financial statements, the auditor shall: (Ref: Para. A23)

    (a) describe the procedures specified by the requesting parties to be performed by the auditor;

    (b) describe the applicable criteria specified by the requesting parties; and

    (c) state that the procedures performed with respect to interim financial reporting periods may not disclose matters of significance regarding the particular financial information about which the auditor's statement is requested.

27. The auditor shall not in the comfort letter:

    (a) make any statements that the auditor has applied procedures that the auditor determined to be necessary or sufficient for the requesting parties' purposes;

    (b) use terms of uncertain meaning (such as general review, limited review, reconcile, check, or test) in describing the work performed unless the procedures encompassed by these terms are described in the comfort letter; or

    (c) make a statement that nothing else has come to the auditor's attention that would be of interest to the requesting parties as a result of carrying out the specified procedures. (Ref: Para. A24-A25)

28. When an auditor's report on audited financial statements or a review report on reviewed financial statements in the offering document includes a modified opinion or conclusion, the auditor shall consider the effect on the comfort letter regarding subsequent interim financial information included in the offering document or regarding an absence of specified subsequent changes. (Ref: Para. A26)

Knowledge of Internal Control (Ref: Para. A27)

29. The auditor shall obtain an understanding of the entity's internal control over financial reporting of both year-end and interim periods when commenting in a comfort letter on:

    (a) unaudited interim financial information; and/or

    (b) subsequent changes in selected financial statement items.

Unaudited Interim Financial Information

30. The auditor may only provide limited assurance on interim financial information included in the offering document if the auditor has, as agreed to under a separate engagement,

conducted a review in accordance with the applicable Australian Standard on Review Engagements. If included in the agreed terms of the comfort letter engagement, the auditor may attach a copy of the review report to the comfort letter unless it is already included in the offering document, or is otherwise publicly available. (Ref: Para. A28)

31. When unaudited interim financial information has been included in the offering document with respect to a period that has not been audited or reviewed, the auditor is not able to provide an auditor's statement on the interim financial information. The auditor may alternatively agree to perform procedures on the interim financial information, provided it:

(a) has been prepared using an applicable financial reporting framework that is consistent with that used in the most recent audited or reviewed financial statements; and

(b) is disclosed as being unaudited or unreviewed by the auditor; and report results in the comfort letter based on the procedures specified by the requesting parties.

Pro Forma Historical Financial Information

32. If the auditor is required to comment on pro forma historical financial information, the auditor shall not provide such a comment unless the auditor has an appropriate level of knowledge of the accounting and financial reporting practices of the entity. (Ref: Para. A29)

33. The auditor shall not provide an auditor's statement in a comfort letter with respect to: (Ref: Para. A30)

(a) the application of pro forma adjustments to historical financial information amounts;

(b) the compilation of any pro forma historical financial information; or

(c) whether the pro forma historical financial information has been prepared in all material respects in accordance with the applicable financial reporting framework chosen by the responsible party of the entity;

unless the auditor has obtained the required knowledge described in paragraph 29 of this ASRS and has performed, in respect of the historical financial statements to which the pro forma adjustments are applied, either an audit in accordance with applicable Australian Auditing Standards, or a review in accordance with the applicable Standard on Review Engagements. If the auditor has not performed such an audit or review, the auditor shall only report results in the comfort letter based on the procedures specified by the requesting parties.

34. If the auditor is requested by the requesting parties to provide limited assurance on pro forma historical financial information included in the offering document, the auditor shall only agree to such a request if:

(a) this is conducted as a separate engagement to the comfort letter engagement; and

(b) it is performed in accordance with the applicable AUASB Standard.

Financial Forecasts (Ref: Para. A31)

35. The auditor shall not agree, as part of a comfort letter engagement, to perform procedures specified by the requesting parties in relation to a financial forecast.

Tables, Statistics, and Other Financial Information

36. The auditor may be requested to perform procedures specified by the requesting parties and report results on tables, statistics and other financial information. If the auditor is requested to comment in a comfort letter on tables, statistics and other financial information appearing in the offering document, the auditor shall comment only on information that: (Ref: Para. A32)

(a) is expressed in dollars (or percentages or ratios derived from such dollar amounts) and that has been obtained from accounting records that are subject to internal control over financial reporting; or

(b) has been derived directly from such accounting records by analysis or computation.

ASRS

37. The auditor shall not comment in a comfort letter:
    (a) on quantitative information that has been obtained from accounting records unless the information is subject to the same controls over financial reporting as the dollar amounts; or
    (b) on tables, statistics, and other financial information relating to an unaudited period unless the auditor has:
        (i) performed an audit of the entity's financial statements for a period including, or immediately prior to, the unaudited period, or completed an audit for a later period, or
        (ii) otherwise obtained knowledge of the entity's internal control over financial reporting for that period.

38. The auditor shall not use the terms "presents fairly" or "true and fair" in comments concerning tables, statistics, and other financial information and shall not comment on: (Ref: Para. A33)
    (a) information subject to legal interpretation, such as beneficial share ownership; or
    (b) matter(s) merely because the auditor is capable of reading, counting, measuring or performing other functions that might be applicable.

39. The auditor's reporting of results from the performance of the procedures in the comfort letter concerning tables, statistics, and other financial information included in the offering document shall include: (Ref: Para. A34)
    (a) a clear identification of the specific information commented on;
    (b) a description of the procedures performed; and
    (c) the results, expressed in terms of agreement between items compared.

40. With respect to the acceptability of methods of allocation used in deriving the figures commented on, the auditor shall comment only to the extent to which such allocation is made in, or can be derived directly by, analysis or computation from the entity's accounting records. Such comments, if made, shall make clear that:
    (a) such allocations may be, to a substantial extent, arbitrary;
    (b) the method of allocation used is not the only acceptable method; and
    (c) other acceptable methods of allocation might produce significantly different results.

41. The comfort letter shall state that the auditor makes no representations regarding:
    (a) any matter of legal interpretation;
    (b) the completeness or adequacy of disclosure; and
    (c) the adequacy of the procedures followed, and that such procedures would not necessarily identify material misstatements or omissions in the financial information to which the comments relate.

Change Period Financial Information

42. If agreed to under the terms of the engagement, the auditor shall perform the procedures specified by the requesting parties on financial information during the change period, in order to provide an auditor's statement on such financial information in the comfort letter. (Ref: Para. A35)

43. The auditor shall base the auditor's statement regarding any subsequent changes in the change period financial information solely on the procedures performed with respect to the change period. (Ref: Para. A36)

44. The auditor shall provide an auditor's statement in the comfort letter regarding subsequent changes in the change period financial information only as of a date less than the date specified in paragraph 10(f) of this ASRS. (Ref: Para. A37)

45. When the requesting parties request an auditor's statement regarding subsequent changes in specified financial information as of a date after the date specified in paragraph 10(f) of this ASRS, the auditor is not permitted to include an auditor's statement in the comfort

letter and is restricted to reporting on the results based on the procedures specified by the requesting parties.

46. In commenting on subsequent changes, the auditor shall not characterise subsequent changes using ambiguous terms, such as referring to a change as adverse. (Ref: Para. A38)

47. The auditor shall comment only on the occurrence of subsequent changes in the change period financial information that are not disclosed in the offering document. Accordingly, the auditor shall include the statement "except for changes, increases, or decreases that the offering document discloses have occurred or may occur" in the comfort letter when it has come to the auditor's attention that a change, increase, or decrease has occurred during the change period, and the amount of such change, increase, or decrease is disclosed in the offering document. This statement need not be included in the comfort letter when there are no changes, increases, or decreases in the change period financial information or if they are already disclosed in the offering document. (Ref: Para. A38)

48. The auditor shall comment in the comfort letter if as a result of the procedures performed, the auditor identifies there has been a change in the application of the applicable financial reporting framework to the change period financial information such that the financial information is not prepared on a basis consistent with the latest audited or reviewed financial statements. (Ref: Para. A39)

49. The auditor shall identify in the comfort letter the dates as of which, and periods for which, data at the cut-off date and data for the change period are to be compared. (Ref: Para. A40-A42)

50. If the requesting parties request the use of an earlier change period or change periods other than that defined in paragraph 10(f) of this ASRS, the auditor shall explain to the requesting parties the implications of using an earlier date. If the requesting parties, nonetheless, request the use of a change period or periods other than that defined in paragraph 10(f) of this ASRS, the auditor is permitted to use the change period or periods requested. (Ref: Para. A43)

51. If the auditor is unable to perform the exact nature, timing or extent of the requesting parties' specified procedures, the auditor shall discuss this as soon as possible with the requesting parties. If alternative procedures are requested by the requesting parties, then these new procedures shall be agreed between the auditor and the requesting parties, and documented in writing and co-signed by the auditor and the requesting parties.

52. If the terms of engagement include the auditor preparing a bring down comfort letter, to be dated at or shortly before the closing date of the offering, the auditor shall carry out the specified procedures set out in the engagement letter and make enquiries of the entity as of the cut-off date for the bring down comfort letter. The subsequent bring down comfort letter shall relate only to financial information in the offering document as most recently amended.

Entity Written Representations (Ref: Para. A44-A45)

53. The auditor shall request a written representation letter from the entity's Chief Executive Officer and Chief Financial Officer[6] that includes the following representations, at a minimum:
    (a) a reaffirmation of the representations previously provided in the most recent audit or review of the entity's financial statements;
    (b) that all information requested by the auditor has been provided, including the final version of the offering document;
    (c) that all matters relevant to the comfort letter have been advised to the auditor;
    (d) an acceptance of responsibility for the offering document, including that it complies with the applicable legal requirements of all jurisdiction(s) in which it will be, or is, issued;
    (e) that all financial information that is the subject of the comfort letter has:
        (i) been derived from the same accounting records and subject to the same internal control as the most recent audited or reviewed financial statements;

6 Or equivalent roles, responsibilities, or positions within the entity.

(ii) a reasonable basis of preparation, and is prepared in accordance with the applicable financial reporting framework chosen by the responsible party of the entity; and

(iii) been prepared on a basis consistent with that of the most recent audited or reviewed financial statements; or if not, that appropriate disclosure of any changes has been made to the financial information in the offering document; and

(f) such other representations that the auditor determines are appropriate in the engagement circumstances.

54. The date of the representation letter shall be either the cut-off date of the offering document, or as near as practicable to, but not after, the date of the comfort letter.

55. If the required representations set out in paragraph 53 of this ASRS are not received, the auditor shall not issue the comfort letter.

Completing the Engagement

56. The auditor shall determine if all the requesting parties' specified procedures have been completed in order to prepare the comfort letter.

57. The auditor shall request a copy of the signed underwriting agreement from the requesting parties.

58. The auditor shall agree to provide a comfort letter to the requesting parties only if the auditor has received a signed copy of the underwriting agreement.

Subsequently Discovered Matters (Ref: Para. A46)

59. The auditor shall inform the requesting parties as soon as possible when the auditor has discovered matters, as a result of the procedures performed by the auditor, not included in the offering document, that require inclusion in the final comfort letter and that were not previously included in the draft comfort letter provided to the requesting parties. If the responsible party of the entity decides not to amend the offering document, the auditor shall inform the responsible party of the entity that the matters will be included in the final comfort letter.

Format and Contents of the Comfort Letter

60. The auditor's comfort letter shall include, at a minimum, each of the following elements: (Ref: Para. A50)

(a) addressees, being only the responsible party of the entity and the requesting parties;

(b) the date of issue, being the date the auditor signs the comfort letter; (Ref: Para. A47-A49)

(c) identification of the offering document to which the comfort letter relates;

(d) the purpose of the comfort letter and that it has been prepared in accordance with this ASRS and the engagement letter;

(e) the specified procedures requested by the requesting parties which have been performed by the auditor on each type of financial information in order to report factual findings, and that no assurance is expressed on that financial information;

(f) a statement that the auditor is not responsible for the sufficiency of the procedures performed;

(g) the results of the procedures;

(h) if applicable, for the change period financial information:

(i) the change period financial information;

(ii) the applicable cut-off period, as well as the dates and periods of comparison for the cut-off period financial information; (Ref: Para. A47)

(iii) the procedures performed and that they did not cover the period from the cut-off date to the date of the comfort letter; (Ref: Para. A47)

(iv) the auditor's statement as to whether, based on the procedures described, nothing has come to the auditor's attention that there are any changes, increases or decreases in the change period financial information, as compared to the corresponding period:

- ♦ if there are such changes, increases or decreases, that are actual or contemplated, disclosed in the offering document, the auditor's statement states that "except for changes, increases or decreases disclosed in the offering document as having occurred or which may occur"; or
- ♦ if the changes are not disclosed in the offering document, the auditor's statement shall include the amount of the changes, increases or decreases in the selected financial information during the change period;

(v) the auditor's statement that no audit or review was performed on the change period financial information, and accordingly no assurance is expressed on that financial information; and

(vi) a statement that the auditor is not responsible for updating the comfort letter for events and circumstances occurring after the cut-off date.

(i) confirmation that the use of the comfort letter is restricted to its addressees and is prepared for the sole purpose of assisting the requesting parties in their due diligence defence of the offering document, and consequently is to be used only in connection with the stated purpose of the comfort letter. Consequently the auditor is not responsible for any reliance that may be placed on the comfort letter for any other purpose;

(j) the auditor's firm name; and

(k) the auditor's address.

61. If the auditor is required by law or regulation to use a specific layout and/or wording in the comfort letter, the auditor shall refer to compliance with this ASRS only if the comfort letter includes, at a minimum, each of the elements identified in paragraph 60 of this ASRS.

62. When issuing a comfort letter in accordance with this ASRS, the auditor shall not circumvent the intent of this ASRS by issuing any additional letters or reports to requesting parties in connection with the offering document in which the auditor comments on items for which commenting is otherwise precluded by this ASRS.

63. The auditor shall not refer to in, or attach to, the comfort letter any restricted use reports.

64. If the auditor does not receive the requested signed representation letter containing a confirmation that the requesting parties have a due diligence defence as required in paragraph 14(e)(v) of this ASRS, the auditor shall not agree to issue the comfort letter to the requesting parties.

Preparing a Bring Down Comfort Letter

65. If the agreed terms of engagement require the auditor to issue a letter subsequent to the comfort letter in order to report procedures performed on financial information for a new change period, the auditor shall perform the new change period procedures specified by the requesting parties. (Ref: Para. A51)

66. The auditor shall request an updated written representation letter from the entity's Chief Executive Officer and Chief Financial Officer, containing such representations that the auditor determines are appropriate in the engagement circumstances.

67. The date of the updated representation letter shall be either the cut-off date of the offering document or as near as practical to, but not after, the date of the bring down comfort letter.

68. If the required representations set out in paragraph 66 of this ASRS are not received, the auditor shall not issue the comfort letter.

69. The auditor shall provide a written bring down comfort letter to the requesting parties including a clear expression of the results of the auditor's procedures on the change period financial information. (Ref: Para A51)

***Basic Elements of the Bring Down Comfort Letter** (Ref: Para. A52)*

70. The bring down comfort letter shall include, at a minimum, each of the following elements:

(a) date issued;

(b) addressees;

(c) a reference to the previously issued comfort letter and the purpose of the bring down comfort letter;

(d) a statement as to whether the auditor reaffirms the statements previously included in the comfort letter;

(e) details of the updated procedures specified by the requesting parties and performed by the auditor, including when the procedures were performed, and the change period subsequent to the date of the comfort letter to which the procedures relate; and

(f) a statement that the bring down comfort letter is restricted to the addressees and is to be used only in connection with the stated purpose of the letter.

Documentation

71. The auditor shall document on a timely basis:

(a) the nature, timing and extent of the procedures performed by the auditor as specified by the requesting parties and the results obtained, as identified in the comfort letter; and

(b) evidence that the procedures were carried out in accordance with this ASRS and the agreed terms of engagement.

❖ ❖ ❖

Application and Other Explanatory Material

Scope of this Standard on Related Services (Ref: Para. 3)

A1. The requesting parties ordinarily request the auditor of the entity to perform certain procedures as a part of their due diligence investigation on selected financial information disclosed in the entity's offering document and report results by way of issuing a comfort letter. The request is ordinarily made through the responsible party of the entity, and the auditor's agreement to undertake the engagement is both with the requesting parties and the responsible party of the entity. Comfort letters are not included in the offering document. It is ordinarily a condition of the underwriting agreement between the entity and its underwriters (as requesting parties) that an auditor's comfort letter is provided in respect of the financial information. The issuance of the comfort letter is restricted to those parties that have agreed to the procedures to be performed by the auditor since others, unaware of the reasons for the procedures, may misinterpret the results. The comfort letter is ordinarily issued upon pricing of the offering or when a debt program is established provided the engagement letter has been signed. The comfort letter is ordinarily updated on closing, settlement date or when the requesting parties request multiple updates through the issue of a bring down comfort letter.

Types of Offerings Covered by this ASRS (Ref: Para. 6)

A2. While the types of offerings covered by this ASRS are specifically aimed at international offerings, this ASRS also applies if the auditor is requested to issue a comfort letter in relation to domestic debt or equity offerings, notwithstanding that in Australia, auditors ordinarily are not requested to issue comfort letters for such domestic offerings.

Engagement Acceptance

Preconditions for Providing a Comfort Letter

A3. If the requesting parties refuse to meet the auditor, the auditor considers whether to accept the engagement. (Ref: Para. 14(c))

A4. In Australia, auditors do not ordinarily provide review conclusions or audit opinions on non-historical financial information such as a financial forecast and consequently do not agree to perform any other procedures on such financial information. If the auditor is requested to provide a comfort letter on financial information that includes a financial forecast, the auditor shall not agree to such a request and shall consider the implications for the engagement. (Ref: Para 14(c)(iv))

A5. The signed representations may be provided by way of a specific letter or agreed to be included by the auditor in the engagement letter terms which are then co-signed by the requesting parties with the responsible party of the entity. (Ref: Para. 14(e)(v))

A6. A legal counsel's letter indicating that a requesting party may be deemed to be an underwriter or has a liability substantially equivalent to that of an underwriter under the applicable law would ordinarily not meet this requirement. (Ref: Para.14(e)(v))

A7. What is substantially consistent may vary from situation to situation and may not be the same as that done in a registered offering of the same securities for the same issuer. Whether the procedures being, or to be, followed will be substantially consistent is determined by the requesting parties on a case-by-case basis. (Ref: Para.14(e)(v))

Agreeing on the Terms of Engagement

A8. The responsible party of the entity who signs the engagement letter ordinarily is the ultimate responsible party of the entity, or an authorised representative/officer thereof, recognising that, in certain circumstances, the directors of the entity (being those charged with governance) may not be appointed by the time of agreeing the terms of the engagement or the entity may not be in existence when the engagement commences (for example, a new company structure). If there is a change of responsible party of the entity, the auditor considers whether to update and re-issue the engagement letter for their signature as approval of the terms. (Ref: Para. 16(b))

A9. A factor in considering whether to accept the engagement is whether the period between the cut-off date and the date of the comfort letter provides sufficient time to allow the auditor to perform the procedures and prepare the comfort letter. (Ref: Para.16(e)(i))

A10. The underwriting agreement ordinarily outlines either the expected form or content of the comfort letter (including the specific matters to be addressed in the comfort letter), or that such form and content are to be determined by the requesting parties separately. At the time of engagement acceptance, the agreement may be in draft form, as it is not ordinarily finalised and signed by the entity and the requesting parties until closer to the offering document's date of issue. The auditor ordinarily receives a copy of the underwriting agreement. As the auditor is not a party to the underwriting agreement, the procedures the auditor will perform need to be agreed between the responsible party of the entity, requesting parties and auditor, and documented in the engagement letter. (Ref: Para 16(e)(ii))

A11. When financial information in an offering document has not been audited in accordance with Australian Auditing Standards and, accordingly, is not covered by an auditor's opinion, the nature of the comments that the auditor can make in the comfort letter with respect to that financial information is limited. What constitutes a reasonable investigation of unaudited financial information sufficient to satisfy the requesting parties' purposes for the comfort letter can vary from jurisdiction to jurisdiction. Consequently, only the requesting party can determine what is sufficient for the requesting party's purposes. (Ref: Para.16(e)(iii))

A12. The assistance that the auditor can provide by way of a comfort letter is subject to limitations. One limitation is that auditors can properly comment in their professional capacity only on matters to which their professional expertise is relevant. Another limitation is that procedures contemplated in a comfort letter, which do not constitute an audit of financial statements, do not provide the auditor with a basis for expressing an opinion. Such procedures may bring to the auditor's attention significant matters affecting the financial information, but they do not provide any assurance that the auditor will become aware of any or all significant matters that would be disclosed in an audit. Accordingly, a risk exists that the auditor may have provided assurance on the absence of conditions or matters that may prove to have existed. (Ref: Para. 16(h))

A13. Appendix 1 contains an illustrative auditor's engagement letter. (Ref: Para. 16(h))

A14. Acknowledgement by the responsible party of the entity and the requesting parties in writing of their acceptance of the engagement letter provides evidence that the entity and the requesting parties accept their engagement responsibilities and establishes a basis of common understanding of the responsibility of each party. It also avoids misunderstandings of the agreed terms. If the requesting parties do not agree to sign, or do not sign the engagement letter, the auditor may: (Ref. Para: 17)

(a) be satisfied that the requesting parties' responsibilities in the engagement are already contained in applicable law or regulation thereby not requiring the requesting parties' written acknowledgement as a signatory to the engagement letter;

(b) if the requesting parties' responsibilities are not already contained in applicable law or regulation, not agree to issue the comfort letter; or

(c) agree to report only factual findings on the financial information in accordance with ASRS 4400 *Agreed-Upon Procedures Engagements to Report Factual Findings*.

Draft Comfort Letter

A15. By providing a draft comfort letter early in the process, the auditor has the opportunity to clearly show the requesting parties what they may expect to receive from the auditor. The requesting parties therefore also have the opportunity to discuss further with the auditor the procedures and to request any additional procedures. If the additional procedures relate to matters within the auditor's professional competence, and the auditor agrees to perform them, a revised draft may be prepared. (Ref: Para. 18)

A16. Acceptance by the requesting parties of the draft comfort letter (and subsequently by acceptance of the comfort letter in final form) is an indication to the auditor that the requesting parties consider the procedures described to be sufficient for the requesting parties' purposes. Clearly describing the procedures to be followed by the auditor in the comfort letter avoids misunderstanding about the basis on which the auditor's comments have been made and assists the requesting parties in deciding whether the procedures performed are sufficient for the requesting parties' purposes. (Ref: Para.19)

A17. The following is an example of a paragraph that may be placed in the draft letter for identification and explanation of its purposes and limitations: (Ref: Para. 19)

"This draft is provided solely for the purpose of indicating the form of letter that we would expect to be able to furnish [*names of the requesting party*] in response to their request, the matters expected to be covered in the letter, and the nature of the procedures that we would expect to carry out with respect to such matters. Based on our discussions with [*name of requesting party*], it is our understanding that the procedures outlined in this draft letter are those they wish us to follow. Unless [*names of the requesting party*] informs us otherwise, we shall assume that there are no additional procedures they wish us to follow. The text of the letter itself will depend, of course, on the results of the procedures, which we would not expect to complete until shortly before the letter is given and in no event before the cut-off date indicated therein."

A18. If the auditor has not had any discussions with the requesting parties about the procedures required to be performed by the requesting parties, the second sentence in this paragraph would be revised as follows: "In the absence of any discussions with [*names of the requesting party*], we have set out in this draft letter those procedures referred to in the draft underwriting agreement (of which we have been furnished a copy) that we are willing to follow." (Ref: Para. 20)

A19. Situations may exist in which more than one auditor is involved in the audit of the financial statements of an entity and in which the reports of more than one auditor appear in the offering document. This is ordinarily the case when the entity is involved in a business combination. Other examples may include the audit of significant divisions, branches, or subsidiaries by component auditors. Comfort letters are requested occasionally from more than one auditor, for example, in connection with an offering document to be used in the subsequent sale of shares issued in recently effected mergers, and from predecessor auditors. In such circumstances, it is the responsible party of the entity's responsibility, at the earliest practicable date, to inform any other auditors who may be involved about any comfort letter that may be requested of them and arrange for those other auditors to receive a draft of the underwriting agreement so that those other auditors may make arrangements at an early date for the preparation of a draft comfort letter and for the performance of specified procedures. The responsible party of the entity or requesting parties are also responsible for arranging for a copy of the comfort letters of component auditors in draft and final form to be provided to the auditor of the group financial statements provided that the group auditor has signed the component auditor's engagement letter as one of the requesting parties. (Ref: Para. 21)

Changes in the Terms of Providing the Comfort Letter

A20. Any change in agreed terms proposed by the responsible party of the entity during the engagement needs to be appropriately justified to the auditor's satisfaction before the auditor agrees to such a change. Examples of when requests from the entity may be received include a change to reflect a change in circumstances or a misunderstanding of the nature of the services to be provided. The auditor considers the implications of the proposed change on the conduct and reporting of the engagement, as well as any evidence that was obtained prior to the change. A change in circumstances that affects the entity's requirements, or a misunderstanding concerning the nature of the auditor's Comfort letter originally agreed, may be considered a reasonable basis for requesting a change in the engagement terms. (Ref: Para. 22)

A21. It is important that all changes agreed to by the entity, the requesting parties and the auditor be documented and approved in writing to ensure there is no misunderstanding of what has been agreed. (Ref: Para. 23)

Performing the Engagement

A22. Comfort letter engagements ordinarily require the following procedures be performed by the auditor: (Ref: Para. 25)

(a) procedures specified by the requesting parties on unaudited interim financial information; and

(b) procedures specified by the requesting parties in respect of selected financial information during the change period.

Commenting in a Comfort Letter on Financial Information Other than Audited or Reviewed Financial Statements

General

A23. Comments included in the letter will often be related to: (Ref: Para. 26)

(a) Unaudited interim financial information.

(b) Pro forma financial information.

(c) Tables, statistics and other financial information.

(d) Subsequent changes in other specified financial statement items.

A24. The procedures performed with respect to interim periods may not disclose subsequent changes in the specified financial statement items, inconsistencies in the application of the applicable financial reporting framework, instances of non-compliance as to form with applicable legal or regulatory requirements, or other matters about which an auditor's statement is requested.

A25. The auditor is not allowed to make a general statement in the comfort letter to the effect that "nothing else has come to the auditor's attention that would be of interest to the requesting parties" because there is no way for the auditor to anticipate other matters that would be of interest to the requesting parties. (Ref: Para. 27(c))

A26. The effect of any modification needs to be assessed by the auditor based on the nature of the modification and whether and how it relates to any of the financial information that is the subject of the comfort letter. The auditor uses professional judgement in making such an assessment. (Ref: Para. 28)

Knowledge of Internal Control (Ref: Para. 29)

A27. The auditor should have obtained a sufficient understanding of an entity's internal control over financial reporting for both year-end and interim periods through performing an audit of the entity's financial statements for one or more financial reporting periods.

Unaudited Interim Financial Information (Ref: Para. 30)

A28. The applicable financial reporting framework used for the review of interim financial information is ordinarily represented by Australian Accounting Standard AASB 134 *Interim Financial Reporting*, issued by the Australian Accounting Standards Board.

Pro Forma Financial Information

A29. An appropriate level of knowledge of the accounting and financial reporting practices of the entity may be obtained by the auditor auditing, or reviewing, in accordance with Australian Auditing Standards, historical financial statements of the entity (or, in the case of a business combination, a significant constituent part of the combined entity) for the most recent year end or interim period for which the pro forma financial information is presented. (Ref: Para. 32)

A30. Pro forma financial information is ordinarily included in the offering document when the entity is involved in a business combination. (Ref: Para. 33)

Financial Forecast (Ref: Para. 35)

A31. A financial forecast prepared by the entity may or may not be included in the offering document.

Tables, Statistics, and Other Financial Information

A32. Other financial information appearing in the offering document does not include financial information that is covered by the auditor's report on the financial statements. (Ref: Para. 36)

A33. As the audit terms "presents fairly" or "true and fair" ordinarily relates to presentations of financial statements, the use of the terms by auditors in commenting on other types of information may be misleading and should not be used in the comfort letter. (Ref: Para. 38)

A34. Options for describing the procedures performed and the findings obtained include: (Ref: Para. 39)

(a) describing them individually for each item of specific information on which comment is made;

(b) grouping or summarising some or all of the descriptions, provided:

  (i) the procedures and factual findings are adequately described;

  (ii) the applicability of the descriptions to items in the offering document is clear; and

  (iii) the descriptions do not imply that the auditor assumes responsibility for the adequacy of the procedures;

(c) presenting a matrix listing the financial information and common procedures employed and indicating the procedures applied to the specific items; and

(d) identifying procedures performed with specified symbols and identifying items to which those procedures have been applied directly on a copy of the offering document, which is attached to the comfort letter.

Change Period Financial Information

A35. Comments regarding subsequent changes typically relate to whether, during the change period, there have been any: (Ref: Para. 42)

(a) changes in share capital;

(b) increases in long-term debt;

(c) decreases in other specified financial statement items;

(c) decreases in net current assets or equity and equity attributable to the company;

(d) decreases in net sales or the total per-share amounts of income from continuing operations and of net income or net income attributable to the company; or

(e) changes in the basis of preparation of the financial information (e.g. different accounting policies adopted).

A36. Procedures may include: (Ref: Para. 43)

(a) reading minutes during the change period and discussing with those charged with governance those meetings for which minutes have not been approved;

(b) reading the unaudited or unreviewed financial information for the change period; or

(c) making enquiries of entity relating to the whole of the change period and obtaining appropriate written representations from the entity to support the answers to the enquiries;

to enable the auditor to state whether anything has come to the auditor's attention that a change, increase, or decrease has occurred during the change period.

A37. In determining whether to accept the comfort letter engagement, the auditor ordinarily considers whether the length of the cut-off period proposed by the requesting parties for the change period financial information is appropriate, having regard to factors such as: (Ref: Para. 44)

(a) the timeframe proposed to be covered;

(b) the time that has elapsed since the issue date of the latest audit or review report on the entity's financial statements;

(c) when the next audit or review report is expected to be issued; and

(d) whether the basis of preparation is consistent with that of the most recent audited or reviewed financial statements.

Publicly listed entities ordinarily have a change period up to six months from the date of the latest audited or reviewed financial statements whilst privately incorporated entities ordinarily have a change period up to twelve months. If the auditor is not comfortable with the proposed change period, it should be discussed with the requesting parties. If the auditor does not accept the proposed change period, the auditor does not agree to provide an auditor's statement in respect of the change period financial information and consequently only reports the results of the procedures performed as specified by the requesting parties in the comfort letter.

ASRS

A38. In commenting on subsequent changes, the auditor may use terms such as 'change', 'increase', or 'decrease'. Terms such as 'adverse' are not clearly understood and may cause the comments on subsequent changes to be ambiguous and hence are not used. (Ref: Para. 46-47)

A39. An example of a change in the financial reporting framework may be as a result of the entity changing the selection or application of accounting policies applied to the change period financial information. (Ref: Para. 48)

A40. The comparison for the change period relates to the entire period and not to portions of that period. A decrease during one part of the period may be offset by an equal or larger increase in another part of the period; however, because no decrease for the period as a whole existed, the comfort letter would not report the decrease occurring during one part of the period. (Ref: Para. 49)

A41. Dates as of which, and periods for which, data at the cut-off date and data for the change period are to be compared are to be agreed in the engagement letter. For balance sheet items, the comparison date is normally that of the latest balance sheet included in the offering document (that is, immediately prior to the beginning of the change period). For income statement items, the comparison period or periods might be one or more of the following: (Ref: Para. 49)

(a) the corresponding period of the preceding year;

(b) a period of corresponding length immediately preceding the change period;

(c) a proportionate part of the preceding fiscal year; or

(d) any other period of corresponding length chosen by the requesting parties.

A42. The purpose of identifying the date and period used for comparison is to avoid misunderstandings about the matters being compared, and so that the requesting parties can determine whether the comparison period is suitable for the requesting parties' purposes. (Ref: Para. 49)

A43. Requesting parties occasionally request that the change period begins immediately after the date of the latest audited balance sheet (which is, ordinarily also the closing date of the latest audited statement of comprehensive income) in the offering document, even though the offering document includes a more recent unaudited balance sheet and statement of income. The use of the earlier date may defeat the requesting parties' purpose because it is possible that an increase in one of the items referred to in paragraph A35 occurring between the dates of the latest audited and unaudited balance sheets included in the offering document might more than offset a decrease occurring after the later date. A similar situation might arise in the comparison of income statement items. In these circumstances, the decrease occurring after the date of the latest unaudited interim financial statements included in the offering document would not be reported in the comfort letter. (Ref: Para. 50)

Entity Written Representations (Ref: Para. 53-55)

A44. The auditor ordinarily requests to receive a written representation letter from the responsible party of the entity at the completion of the engagement.[7] The auditor ordinarily provides the responsible party of the entity with a specific list of matters requiring the entity's representations. Such matters may already be contained in documentation reviewed by the auditor, including minutes of meetings, and written acceptance of the engagement letter, and therefore the auditor only needs to request the inclusion of such matters in the written representation letter if the auditor considers it appropriate in the engagement circumstances. If the responsible party of the entity does not provide a written representation letter, or refuses to provide it, the auditor informs them that the auditor is unable to provide a comfort letter.

A45. Appendix 2 contains an illustrative representation letter.

Subsequently Discovered Matters (Ref: Para. 59)

A46. The auditor ordinarily requests a copy of the final offering document (and any document incorporated by reference in it) for the sole purpose of reading it to identify any possible matters that may impact providing the comfort letter, or its final form and content to the entity. Subsequently discovered matters may include matters identified from reading the final offering document and changes in specified items that are the subject of the comfort letter and have been identified as a result of the procedures performed, but which are not already disclosed in the offering document. If the matters are already disclosed in the offering document, there is ordinarily no need to include such matters in the comfort letter, except by way of reference to where they are disclosed in the offering document. If matters are not already disclosed in the offering document, the auditor ordinarily discusses them with the entity and advises that the auditor will include details of the matters in the final comfort letter. The auditor may also advise the requesting parties of the matters and/or suggest to the entity that the requesting parties be advised.

Format and Contents of the Comfort Letter

Date of the Comfort Letter (Ref: Para. 60(b))

A47. The comfort letter is dated when issued which is ordinarily on, or shortly after:

(a) the entity's representation letter is received;

(b) when the underwriting agreement(s) is/are signed;

(c) when the signed engagement letter is received; and

(d) before finalisation of the offering document.

---

7 The concepts and discussions on obtaining written representations relevant to an audit engagement are contained in Auditing Standard ASA 580 *Written Representations*, and may be helpful in determining the form and content of written representations applicable to a comfort letter engagement.

A48. The engagement letter ordinarily specifies the date, often referred to as the cut-off date, to which the procedures specified by the requesting parties in the letter are to relate, ordinarily between three and five working days before the date of the comfort letter. A factor in considering whether to accept the engagement is whether the period between the cut-off date and the date of the letter provides sufficient time to allow the auditor to perform the procedures and prepare the comfort letter.

A49. Comments included in an earlier comfort letter that relate to information in the offering document may be incorporated by reference in a subsequent bring down comfort letter.

A50. Appendix 3 contains an illustrative comfort letter. (Ref: Para. 60)

Preparing a Bring Down Comfort Letter

A51. The requesting parties may request the auditor to issue an updated comfort letter, ordinarily referred to as a bring down comfort letter, at the offering pricing, closing of the offering document and/or subsequent dates depending on the offering circumstances. (Ref: Para. 65-66)

A52. Appendix 4 contains an illustrative bring down comfort letter. (Ref: Para. 70)

❖ ❖ ❖

Conformity with International Standards on Related Services

This Standard on Related Services has been made for Australian public interest purposes and accordingly there is no equivalent International Standard on Related Services (ISRS) issued by the International Auditing and Assurance Standards Board (IAASB), an independent standard-setting board of the International Federation of Accountants (IFAC).

Compliance with this Standard on Related Services does not affect compliance with the ISRSs.

Appendix 1

(Ref: Para. A13)

Example Engagement Letter

The following illustrative letter includes example terms of engagement that can be tailored for specific engagement circumstances.

[The Directors]

[Entity Limited]

[Address]

The Lead Manager and Dealers

[Addressee]

[Date]

Dear Sirs/Mesdames

PROPOSED [insert type of offering] ISSUE BY [Issuer Name] ("the Issuer")

Introduction

1. This Engagement Letter sets out the scope and limitations of the work to be performed by [Firm name] ("we" or "us") as auditor of [entity] in connection with the proposed issue of [insert details] ("the Issue") which will involve the preparation by the Issuer of, and for which the Issuer will be solely responsible, an Offering Document [in accordance with the [Listing Rules of the [relevant] Stock Exchange or other listing authority].

This letter is written in the context of the respective roles of the directors of the Issuer, [the Lead Manager] ("the Lead Manager"), the other Managers (as defined in Paragraph 2 below) and ourselves. Any work contemplated by this arrangement which is performed before the date of this letter will also be governed by the terms and conditions of this letter.

Addressees

2. This Engagement Letter is addressed to the directors of the Issuer, the Lead Manager and to each of the managers who have agreed, or prior to the issue of our Comfort Letter will agree, to participate in the proposed Issue and who have, or prior to the issue of our Comfort Letter will have, validly authorised the Lead Manager to sign this engagement letter on their behalf (together being the "Addressees"). All managers' legal names are set out in Appendix 1 to this Engagement Letter.

3. By signing and accepting the terms of this Engagement Letter, the Lead Manager confirms that it will ensure that it receives prima facie authority from each Manager identified in Appendix 1 authorising it to enter into this engagement letter on the relevant Manager's behalf.[8]

4. Up to the date of the relevant Comfort Letter, a Manager may be added to Appendix 1 by the Issuer or by the Lead Manager by written notice to us and the Issuer or the Lead Manager. A Manager may also be deleted from Appendix 1 where the Manager withdraws from the Issue and/or advises the Lead Manager that it does not wish to receive the benefit of the Comfort Letter or for this Engagement Letter to be signed on its behalf or where the Lead Manager does not receive authority to sign this engagement letter on behalf of the relevant Manager. The revised managers shall then, together with the Lead Manager, be referred to in this engagement letter as "the Managers".

Comfort Letter

5. The Lead Manager confirms that, in connection with the proposed Issue, it is aware of [state applicable law, regulation, standard or industry guidance] relating to due diligence issued by the [state name of body] from time to time, which will be followed by it in connection with the proposed issue.

6. Our Comfort Letter will be provided to the addressees of this letter solely in the context of the due diligence procedures that you undertake pursuant to the guidance referred to in Paragraph 5 above for the purpose of seeking to establish any due diligence defence the Addressees are entitled to advance in any claim or proceeding in connection with the contents of the Offering Document. Accordingly our Comfort Letter will be addressed to you solely for that purpose and may not be relied on by you for any other purpose. Our engagement will be conducted with the objective of reporting results resulting from each procedure requested by the Addressees. The procedures performed will not constitute an audit or review engagement, and accordingly no assurance will be provided.

7. Any Comfort Letter issued pursuant to this Engagement Letter will not have been provided in accordance with the professional standards of [insert jurisdiction] and accordingly should not be relied upon in connection with any obligations or responsibilities that you may have under any legislation, regulations and/or rule of law in [insert jurisdiction] and, in the event of any such use in [insert jurisdiction], we accept no responsibility in this regard.

8. Our work and findings shall not in any way constitute advice or recommendations (and we accept no liability in relation to any advice or recommendations) regarding any commercial decisions associated with the Issue, including, in particular, but without limitation, any which may be taken by the Managers (or any person connected to the Managers or any one of them) in the capacity of investor or in providing investment advice to their clients.

9. Our Comfort Letter will be provided solely for your private information and should not be used for any purpose other than as set out in Paragraph 6 above. Our Comfort Letter may not be referred to in any other document (except that reference may be made to its existence

8 The auditor should not accept any limitations on the level of scope of the Lead Manager's authority.

in any contract or other communication between the Issuer and/or the Managers, and/or ourselves), nor made available to any other party (except that a copy may be included in the [describe the documents] prepared for the Issuer and the Managers).

10. Nothing in paragraphs 7 and 9 above shall prevent you from disclosing our Comfort Letter to your professional advisers or as may be required by law or regulation, and/or referring to and/or producing our Comfort Letter in court proceedings relating to the Issue or the Offering Document. Provided that you first obtain our prior written consent, you may disclose our Comfort Letter to third parties where to do so would reasonably be necessary in the interest of a resolution of a dispute with that third party relating to the Issue or the Offering Document.

11. Other than to those who have validly accepted this Engagement Letter, we will not accept any responsibility to any party to whom our Comfort Letter is shown or into whose hands it may come, and for those who have validly accepted, only then on the terms set out in this letter.

12. You may only rely on information and comments set out in our Comfort Letter on the basis of this Engagement Letter.

Work and procedures

13. Our work will be conducted in accordance with ASRS 4450 *Comfort Letter Engagements*, issued by the Australian Auditing and Assurance Standards Board and we will indicate so in the Comfort Letter. In other jurisdictions, standards and practice relevant to reporting accountants may be different and may not provide for reporting in the manner contemplated herein. Accordingly, the Comfort Letter should not be relied on as if it had been provided in accordance with the standards and practice of any professional body in any other jurisdiction.

14. The procedures that we will perform in accordance with this Engagement Letter have been requested by the Lead Manager and will be recorded in the Comfort Letter itself. [If applicable, describe the nature of the procedures]. Accordingly, we have not carried out an audit or review performed in accordance with Australian Auditing Standards or the Standards on Review Engagements respectively ("AUASB Standards") of any financial information relating to the Issuer for any period subsequent to [date of last audited balance sheet] and consequently no audit opinion or review conclusion will be expressed. The Addressees draw their own conclusions from the procedures and the Comfort Letter. We will make no representation as to the adequacy of any disclosure or information in the Offering Document. Furthermore, the procedures we will perform are not designed, and are not likely to reveal fraud or matters of significance with respect to any material misstatement of the information referred to below.

15. Our work will be carried out on the basis that information provided to us by the Addressees for the purposes of the procedures is reliable, accurate and complete. In no circumstances will we be responsible for any loss or damage, of whatsoever nature, arising from information material to our work being withheld or concealed from us or misrepresented to us.

16. The procedures that we have been requested by the Addressees to conduct have been discussed between the Issuer, the Lead Manager and us and will be recorded in the Comfort Letter itself. We will undertake those procedures agreed with the Addressees as set out in the final draft of the Comfort Letter, and in doing so, we will address ourselves solely to the data provided to us by the Addressees for the purpose of performing those procedures. The Addressees have sole responsibility for determining the adequacy or otherwise of the procedures that we agree to perform. We will only carry out those procedures expressly provided for in the Comfort Letter. Accordingly, we make no representations as to the sufficiency for your purposes of such procedures and, therefore, our responsibility shall be limited to performing the work agreed upon in this engagement letter and/or recorded in the Comfort Letter with due skill, care and attention. If we were to perform additional procedures or if we were to conduct an audit or review of the financial statements of the Issuer in accordance with applicable AUASB Standards, other matters might come to our attention which we would report to you. The procedures to be performed by us should not

be taken to supplant any additional enquiries or procedures that may be appropriate in the performance of your role in connection with the proposed offering.

17. In relation to the contents of the Offering Document, we will address ourselves solely to such financial information in the Offering Document as is identified in the Comfort Letter and we will make no representations as to the adequacy of disclosure in the Offering Document or as to whether any material facts have been omitted by the Issuer.

18. Any opinions expressed on financial information outside the context of this Engagement Letter were, or are, expressed solely in the context of the specific terms and conditions governing their preparation. In particular, the terms of this Engagement Letter and any action pursuant to it shall be additional to and shall not detract from or change in any way any legal rights which any party to this letter may otherwise have acquired, whether in contract or in tort, in connection with our audits of the financial statements of the Issuer.

19. Except as may be expressly included in the Comfort Letter, we do not accept any responsibility for any other reports or letters beyond any responsibility that we owed to those to whom our reports or letters were addressed at the date of their issue. Our procedures will be performed on the basis that:

(a) the Lead Manager acknowledges and understands:

(i) their responsibility for determining the adequacy or otherwise of the procedures agreed to be performed by us;

(ii) their responsibility for determining whether the results provided by us, in combination with other information obtained, provide a reasonable basis for any conclusions which the Addressees wish to draw on the subject matter;

(iii) their responsibility to provide us with:

- access to all information of which the Addressees are aware is necessary for the performance of the agreed-upon procedures; and
- such additional information that we may request for the purpose of the engagement;

(b) the responsible party of the entity acknowledges and understands its responsibility to provide unrestricted access to persons within the entity from whom we require co-operation in order to perform the agreed-upon procedures; and

(c) the Addressees acknowledge and understand that:

(i) the procedures we will perform are solely to assist the Addressees in their due diligence defence. Our Comfort Letter is not to be used for any other purposes and is solely for the Addressees information; and

(ii) the procedures that we will perform will not constitute an audit or review performed in accordance with applicable AUASB Standards, and consequently, no assurance will be provided.

Contents of the Comfort Letter

20. We would be grateful if you would review the draft Comfort Letter at [Appendix 3] [that we expect to be able to provide you with] and advise us of any amendments you propose to the procedures as soon as possible, so that we can consider the proposed amendments and, if agreed, provide you with a revised draft for your further consideration and approval.

21. Once an advanced draft of the Offering Document is available and you have identified, and we have agreed, the procedures to be performed, we will provide you with a further revised draft of the Comfort Letter for your approval of its scope prior to finalisation. In so far as any such draft or oral discussions are inconsistent with the subsequent final Comfort Letter, it will be deemed to be superseded by such final Comfort Letter.

22. For the avoidance of doubt, we will not comment on, or otherwise give comfort in relation to, the prospects or trading position or, save as expressly stated in the Comfort Letter, comment on or provide any opinion or other conclusion as to the current overall financial position of the Issuer.

Meetings

23. It [will be] [has been] necessary for us to receive copies of the draft Offering Document as it [is] [was] produced and it [may be] [has been] necessary for us to attend meetings (including, but not limited to, meetings with the Issuer, and its directors and/or employees, and the Lead Manager and its employees or agents) at which the Offering Document [is] [has been] discussed and drafted or at which other related matters [are] [have been] discussed. We [shall answer] [have answered] queries raised at such meetings on an informal basis but you should neither act nor refrain from acting on the basis of such informal answers unless and until they are confirmed in writing by us, whether in the final Comfort Letter or otherwise. In the absence of such written confirmation we shall have no liability to you in contract or in tort (including negligence or otherwise) for our answers.

24. Unless otherwise specifically agreed between the parties, we are authorised by the Issuer to speak to the Managers and other professional advisers advising on the proposed Issue. In connection with our work pursuant to this Engagement Letter, we may release to the Managers and such other professional advisers any information relating to the Issuer, whether confidential or not and obtained during the course of our work or otherwise and shall not be liable to the Issuer for any use subsequently made of that information.

Timetable

25. [We will endeavour to carry out our work in accordance with a timetable to be agreed between all parties that will satisfy the requirements of the Issue]. We [intend to provide] [are providing] you with our Comfort Letter on the date of the final Offering Document relating to the Issue and to provide you with an updated Comfort Letter or to reissue our Comfort Letter on the date of closing of the Offering Document.

Fees

26. Our fees will primarily reflect such factors as complexity, specialist input, urgency, inherent risks, and the use of techniques, expertise and the time spent on performing the specified procedures. Our out of pocket expenses plus GST (if applicable) will be advised under separate cover and will be the sole responsibility of, and will be paid by, the Issuer.

Issues

27. We will discuss with you any difficulties we encounter during the conduct of this engagement, or with meeting the required timetable, as soon as any problems arise.

Applicable law and jurisdiction

28. Each Addressee and we covenant with the other not to bring any claim or proceeding of any nature in relation to this Engagement Letter in any jurisdiction other than [insert applicable State, Australia].

Other Terms and Conditions

29. The terms and conditions, which are attached as Appendix 2, also form part of this Engagement Letter. Terms and conditions shall apply, as indicated, to the Addressees [except that Paragraphs [X] and [X] shall not apply to all the Managers of this Engagement Letter.] In the event of any inconsistency between this Engagement Letter and such terms and conditions, the terms of this letter shall prevail as being the relevant terms and conditions.

30. [Insert any other terms and conditions that are applicable in the engagement circumstances].

Prohibition on Assignment

31. No party may assign any of its rights in relation to this Engagement Letter without the prior written consent of the other parties.

Counterparts

32. This Engagement Letter may be executed in any number of counterparts, all of which taken together shall constitute one and the same instrument and as if the signatures on the counterparts were on a single copy of this Engagement Letter.

Entire Agreement

33. This Engagement Letter and the Appendices to it constitute the entire agreement between us and, except as provided in this Engagement.Letter, no change in the terms of our agreement will be effective unless agreed in writing and signed by all parties to this Engagement Letter or their respective legal counsel.

Please sign and return the attached copy of this letter to indicate your acknowledgement of, and agreement with, the arrangement for our Comfort Letter engagement including the specific procedures which we have agreed will be performed and our respective responsibilities.

Yours faithfully

Firm name

Acknowledgement and Acceptance

We acknowledge receipt of this letter and agree with the terms of your engagement set out therein:

.... Director Date ....

.... Name

for and on behalf of Issuer

.... Title Date ....

.... Name

for and on behalf of Lead Manager

.... Title Date ....

.... Name

Encl.

Appendix 1: Names of all Managers involved in the Offering Document

Appendix 2: [Firm name] Terms and Conditions of Engagement

Appendix 3: Draft Comfort Letter

Appendix 2

(Ref: Para. A45)

Example Entity Representation Letter

The following illustrative letter is an example representation letter provided by the responsible party of the entity in respect of an auditor's comfort letter, when the representations are not otherwise included within the engagement letter. The Issuer of the offering document is assumed to be the same entity as that which appointed the auditor. It can be tailored for specific engagement circumstances.

[Date]

[Name of Firm Name]

[Address]

Dear Sirs/Mesdames

Issue of [X] ("the Issue") by [type of issue by Issuer] ("Issuer")

In connection with the above mentioned issue, you have been asked to provide to us and to the [Managers/Dealers] under the terms of your engagement letter dated [Date], an auditor's Comfort Letter concerning certain financial information of the Issuer included in the Offering Document dated [Date] and changes in the financial position of the Issuer since [Date].

We reaffirm to you all the statements made to you in the letter dated [date of last management representation letter obtained for the audited financial statements] and issued to you in connection with your audit of our financial statements for the years ended [Date] and [Date]. Nothing has come to our attention which causes us to believe that the audited financial statements of the entity for the years ended [Date] and [Date] did not give a true and fair view, in all material respects, of the Issuer's state of affairs at the respective balance dates and of the Issuer's profits for the years ended on those dates. Nothing has come to our attention that would cause us to believe that there is a need to restate the audited consolidated financial statements for the years ended [Date] and [Date] due to material misstatements.

We are responsible for the information contained in the Offering Document and the information contained in the ["Schedule of Changes Prepared by Management" (the "Schedule")] attached at Appendix 1 to this letter.

We confirm that to the best of our knowledge and belief, and having made appropriate enquiries of [relevant persons] of the Issuer, the following representations:

1. The facts as stated in your Comfort Letter are accurate in all material respects, any opinions attributable to us are fair and reasonable, we have made available to you all significant information relevant to your Comfort Letter of which we have knowledge and we are not aware of any matters relevant to your engagement letter dated [Date] which have been excluded.
2. The Issuer has with reasonable care and due diligence performed appropriate procedures to ensure that the information contained in the Offering Document is in accordance with the facts and does not omit anything likely to affect the importance of the information provided.
3. The Issuer has taken appropriate legal and other advice in order to ensure that the Offering Document complies with the relevant requirements of the [insert applicable law].
4. The Issuer has, for the period since [Date], had in place a system to ensure compliance with the continuous disclosure requirements of Australian law, and we are not aware of any instances of non-compliance with those requirements during that period.
5. Any events or decisions of the Board of Directors up to the Cut-off Date [Date] that could impact the figures included in the Schedule were accounted for in the management accounts. These include the items within paragraph [98(b) to (e) of AASB 101 *Presentation of Financial Statements* issued by the [Australian Accounting Standards Board] being: [insert details of items].
6. All decisions of the executive management or directors of the Issuer which might materially affect the carrying value or classification of the entity's assets and liabilities has been advised to you. No events have occurred up to [Date] (the "Cut-off date") other than already disclosed in the Offering Document or as set out in the Issuer's [Date] audited financial statements that would require additional disclosure to you.
7. All approved minutes of meetings of the shareholders, Board of Directors and [identify any other bodies], containing all substantive actions taken at such meetings, agenda items and board papers for all board meetings held since [Date] to the Cut-off date have been made available for inspection by you.
8. The unaudited monthly management accounts for [Date] (the "[Month, this year] Management Accounts") of the Issuer have been prepared and presented in conformity with [Australian Accounting Standards] applied on a basis which is substantially consistent[9] with that of the published audited financial statements for the year ended [Date], [except that it is incomplete in that it omits [insert details].] No management accounts or financial statements exist for the period subsequent to [Date].
9. The management accounts properly deal with all of the following matters identified by you from the minutes referred to in Paragraph 7 above [insert details].
10. [If applicable, the Board has considered the matters identified by [Firm name] in the course of their procedures on changes since [last audited balance sheet date] and confirmed that

9 In circumstances when management accounts are not prepared on a substantially consistent basis, additional representations should be included to state what differences exist, such as year-end adjustments for impairment, fair value of certain financial instruments, or equity accounting adjustments for investments.

ASRS

they had been properly reflected in the management accounts for the [insert number] months ended [Date]].

11. Provisions which are believed to be adequate have been made in the entity's accounting records as reflected in the [Month, this year] Management Accounts for significant litigation and claims against the entity other than where the likelihood of loss is considered less than likely. The Issuer is not aware of any material litigation that is both probable and capable of reliable estimation which is not currently recorded as a liability in the [Date] audited financial statements or the [Month, this year] Management Accounts.

12. The information in the Schedule attached to this letter (other than information as of the Cut-off date, which agrees to the accounting records of the Issuer) agrees to the [Month, this year] Management Accounts, [Month, prior year] Management Accounts, or the [Date] audited financial statements.

    (a) [If applicable, that, having advised you that no financial statements or management accounts as of any date subsequent or for any period subsequent to [Date] are available, other than as disclosed in the Schedule, there was no:

        (i) decrease in [revenue from continuing operations, consolidated net profit] for the [X] month(s) period ended [Date], compared with the [corresponding period in the preceding year];

        (ii) change in the [number of issued ordinary shares, decrease in net current assets, consolidated total assets or shareholders' equity], at [Date], compared with the corresponding figures in the [Date] audited financial statements; or

        (iii) increase in [total borrowings or total liabilities] at [Date], compared with the corresponding figures in the [Date] audited financial statements], or

    (b) [If applicable, there has been no change in the [number of issued ordinary shares] or increase in [total borrowings] at the Cut-off date as compared with the respective amounts shown in the [Date] audited financial statements, except in all instances for changes, increases or decreases that the Offering Document (including the financial statements incorporated by reference in it) discloses have occurred or may occur, and except as are disclosed in the Schedule.]

13. We confirm that, to the best of our knowledge and belief, in the period between [Date] and the date of this letter, there has been no event reported in the minutes or decisions of the Board documented in the minutes that could be given accounting recognition in accordance with [paragraph 98(b) to (e) of AASB 101 *Presentation of Financial Statements*] in the next published audited financial statements of the Issuer following the date of this letter.

14. The Board is not aware of any matters to which attention should be drawn in the statement on page [X] of [[proof [] of] the Offering Document that there has been no material adverse change in the financial position or prospects of the Issuer since the date of its last published financial statements.

15. The [describe document] which has been used as a basis for the [describe information in the document] has been [prepared/derived] from the Group's accounting records.

16. [The statement of capitalisation for the Issuer as at [Date] contained on page [X] of [proof [] of] the Offering Document dated [Date] related to the Issue ("the Offering Document") has been properly prepared by our management after due and careful consideration and the Directors further confirm that they are not aware of any relevant factor which has not been taken into account therein.]

17. During the course of your work you have been provided with all of the information and explanations which we believe may be relevant to your work and there are no other matters of which you should be aware.

Yours faithfully

For and on behalf of the directors of [Issuer]

.... Title Date ……………..

.... Name

Encl.

Appendix 1: Schedule of Changes prepared by Management

$'000 unless otherwise stated	Unaudited As at [Date]	Audited /Unaudited (if from reviewed financial statements) As at [Date]	Increase/Decrease
Units on issue (number in thousands)			
Net current assets			
Consolidated total assets			
Shareholders' equity			
Total borrowings			
Total liabilities			
	Unaudited **for the [X] months ended [Date]**	**Unaudited** **for the [X]months ended [Date]**	**Increase/Decrease**
Revenue from continuing operations			
Consolidated net profit			

Appendix 3

(Ref: Para. A50)

Example Comfort Letter

The following illustrative letter represents an example comfort letter that can be tailored for specific engagement circumstances. The Issuer of the offering document is assumed to be the same entity as that which appointed the auditor.

Private and Confidential

The Lead Manager and Dealers

[Addressee]

[Date]

Dear Sirs/Mesdames

PROPOSED [insert type of offering] ISSUE BY [insert issuer name] ("the Issuer")

We attach as Appendix 1, a copy of the Offering Document [insert name] and dated [Date] which we have initialled for identification purposes. We attach as Appendix 2, a copy of the Engagement Letter dated [*insert date*] (the "Engagement Letter"), the terms of which have been agreed between us, are deemed to have been incorporated in this Comfort Letter and govern the matters addressed by this Comfort Letter and its use.

This letter is addressed to the Directors of the Issuer, to the Lead Manager ("the Lead Manager") and to each of the [other managers whose names are set out above] [the Managers identified in Appendix 2 of the Engagement Letter] who have agreed to participate in the proposed issue of [the Securities] ("the Issue") provided they have validly authorised the Lead Manager to accept the Engagement Letter on their behalf. Together with the Lead Manager, they are referred to as "the Managers".

This letter is provided solely for the private information of its addressees in the context of the due diligence procedures that you are undertaking, or intend to undertake, in connection with the contents of the Offering Document solely for the purpose of seeking to establish a due diligence defence in such context that you may wish to advance in any claim or proceeding in connection with the contents of the Offering Document on the basis set out in the Engagement Letter.

Accordingly, this letter is addressed to you solely for that purpose and may not be relied on by you or used for any other purpose, nor be referred to in any other document (except that reference may be made to its existence in any contract or other communication between the Issuer and/or the Managers and/or ourselves), nor made available to any other party (except that a copy may be included in [specify document] prepared for the Issuer and the Managers).

We will not accept any responsibility to any other party to whom our letter is shown, or into whose hands it may come (including any Manager who has not validly authorised the Lead Manager to accept the Engagement Letter).

We have performed the engagement in accordance with Australian Standard on Related Services ASRS 4450 *Comfort Letter Engagements*, issued by the Australian Auditing and Assurance Standards Board.

In accordance with the terms of the Engagement Letter referred to above, we set out below the procedures we have carried out and our results from the performance of those procedures.

Pro forma Financial Information

At your request, we have:

1. Read the unaudited pro forma condensed consolidated balance sheets as of [Date] and the unaudited pro forma condensed consolidated statements of income for the year ended [date], and the [insert number] month period ended [Date] included in the Offering Document.
2. Enquired of [give names and positions of directors, managers and other staff of the Issuer with responsibility for financial and accounting matters to whom enquiries were addressed] about:
   (a) the basis of their determination of the pro forma adjustments; and
   (b) whether the unaudited pro forma condensed consolidated financial information referred to in (a) above has been prepared and presented on a basis consistent with the accounting policies adopted by the Issuer in preparing the latest audited or reviewed financial statements.

The foregoing procedures are substantially less in scope than an examination, the objective of which is the expression of an opinion on management's assumptions, the pro forma adjustments, and the application of those adjustments to historical financial information and accordingly, we do not express such an opinion. The foregoing procedures would not necessarily reveal matters of significance with respect to the comments in the following paragraph. Accordingly, we make no representation about the sufficiency of such procedures for your purpose.

Nothing came to our attention as a result of the procedures described above that caused us to believe that the unaudited pro forma condensed consolidated financial statements referred to in 1 above have not been properly compiled on the pro forma basis described in the notes. Had we performed additional procedures, or had we made an examination of the pro forma condensed consolidated financial statements, other matters might have come to our attention that would have been reported to you.

Financial Information

On pages [insert pages], the Offering Document sets out certain financial information for the [insert number] years [and insert period] ended [Date] of the Issuer. We have read this information and have compared it with that shown in the audited financial statements [and the unaudited published interim financial statements for the [insert number] months ended [Date]] of the Issuer. We confirm that this financial information has been accurately extracted from the audited financial statements for the relevant years [or, as the case may be, the published reviewed interim financial statements for such period]. [If applicable, we did not conduct a review of such interim financial statements in accordance with the applicable Standard on Review Engagements issued by the Auditing and Assurance Standards Board].

Other Financial Information

For the purposes of this letter, we have also read the items that you have identified as indicated on the attached copy of the Offering Document and have performed the following procedures, which were applied as indicated [by the symbols explained below]:[10]

- [Symbol] [Compared the specific dollar amount or percentage to a dollar amount or percentage included in or derived from the audited financial statements of the Issuer at [Date] and found them to be in agreement [after giving effect to aggregation or rounding, if applicable].
- [Symbol] [Compared the [specific dollar amount or percentage to a dollar amount or percentage] included in or derived from the [unaudited financial statements] which the Issuer has represented was [prepared/derived] from the accounting records and found the [dollar amount or percentage] to be in agreement, after giving effect to aggregation or rounding, if applicable. We have not traced the information to the accounting records themselves. [We make no comment as to the appropriateness of the Issuer's method of derivation used in the unaudited schedules.] [We make no comment with respect to reasons given for changes between periods or any other matter.]
- [Symbol] [Recomputed the [percentages/ratios etc.] and found them to be correctly calculated.][11] [We make no comment as to the appropriateness of the Issuer's method of derivation used in the calculation the [percentages/ratios etc.] [We make no comment with respect to reasons given for changes between periods or any other matter.]

[If applicable - Capitalisation and Indebtedness Table

1. On page [X] of the Offering Document there is a statement of the capitalisation and indebtedness of the Issuer. We have read the capitalisation and indebtedness statement and we confirm that the shareholders' funds, borrowings and [contingent liabilities] at [insert date of last previously published financial statements] included in that statement have been accurately extracted from the [audited financial statements/reviewed interim results] of the Issuer as at [insert date of last audited financial statements/reviewed interim results], [if applicable, in relation to which we did not conduct a review in accordance with the applicable Standard on Review Engagements issued by the Auditing and Assurance Standards Board].]

Changes in Financial Position

Agreed-Upon Procedures

2. For the purpose of this letter, we have performed the following procedures. We have:
   (a) [read the minutes of meetings of [the Board or Directors, the Board Audit Committee, other board committees where relevant] of the Issuer held since [insert the date of its last published year-end financial statements] as set out in minute books at [insert date] (the "cut-off date") ([together with/excluding] the papers provided to the board for that meeting), which the directors have advised us are complete; and
   (b) read the [insert date of latest] unaudited management accounts for the [insert number of months] months ended [insert date] (the "[Month, this year] management accounts") (which the directors have advised us are the most recent management accounts available) and the corresponding unaudited management accounts from the previous year (the "[Month, last year] management accounts").
3. Our objective in reading the documents referred to in Paragraph (2) (a) and (b) above was to identify those matters which, in our view, might, prima facie, be expected to impact the figures and ratios set out in Paragraph (6) below.
4. In the case of the minutes referred to in Paragraph (2) (a) above, our objective was also to identify such matters in those minutes, which would on their face, without further enquiry, require accounting recognition in accordance with [items (b) to (e) inclusive

10 The method of identification of the procedures should be agreed between the parties.

11 These procedures are illustrative only, and should be amended to reflect the specified procedures requested by the Lead Manager and agreed by the auditor as set out in the Engagement Letter.

ASRS

of paragraph 98 of AASB 101 *Presentation of Financial Statements*][12] [issued by the Australian Accounting Standards Board] in the next published financial statements of the Issuer following the date of this letter (being matters that will be disclosed under Paragraph (8) (a) below).

5. We have made enquiries of [give name and positions of directors, managers and other staff of the Issuer with responsibility for financial and accounting matters to whom enquiries were addressed] (the "Persons Responsible for Financial and Accounting Matters") as to whether:

   (a) those matters identified by us in the course of the work undertaken pursuant to Paragraph (8) below have been reflected in the [month, this year] management accounts upon which the figures and ratios referred to in Paragraph (6) below are based; and

   (b) the [Month, this year] management accounts have been prepared and presented on a basis consistent with the accounting policies normally adopted by the Issuer and applied in preparing the [insert date of latest] audited financial statements.

6. We have compared the amounts shown in Appendix 3 prepared by management of the Issuer, (the "Schedule"), relating to [specify items e.g. revenue, profits before tax, net interest expense, depreciation of fixed assets, share capital, long-term debt, net current assets, total current assets and total current liabilities] to the [month, this year] management accounts, [month, last year] management accounts or [insert date of latest] audited financial statements as appropriate and found them to be in agreement. [We have recomputed the ratios set out in the schedule on the bases set out therein and found them to be correctly calculated.]

7. The procedures described above do not constitute an audit or review performed in accordance with AUASB Standards. Nor do they provide any assurance that the [month, this year] management accounts have been prepared on a basis consistent with the [month, last year] management accounts, that such management accounts have been prepared in a reliable manner nor that either have been prepared on a basis consistent with the [insert date of latest] audited financial statements. Consequently, our procedures would not necessarily reveal matters of significance with respect to the comments made in the following paragraphs and we make no representations as to the sufficiency for your purposes of any such procedures.

8. Solely on the basis of the foregoing procedures, we note and draw to your attention:

   (a) [Insert findings in relation to the matters referred to in Paragraph (5) above which are relevant to the findings in Paragraph (6) above;]

   (b) [Insert changes, if any, identified in the basis of preparing or presenting the accounts reviewed or, if there are none, state this; and]

   (c) [Insert matters revealed by the minutes of the Issuer from which it is evident without further enquiry that the events reported or decisions of the Board will be given accounting recognition in accordance with [items (b) to (e) inclusive of paragraph 98 of AASB 101 *Presentation of Financial Statements*], issued by the [Australian Accounting Standards Board] in the next published financial statements of the Issuer following the date of this letter or, if there are none, state this.]

Auditor's Statement

9. [Except for the matter(s) detailed in Paragraph (8) above and except in all circumstances for increases or decreases that the Offering Document discloses have occurred or may occur], nothing came to our attention as a result of the foregoing procedures that caused us to believe that:

   (a) at [insert date of latest management accounts] there were any decreases in the [specify items e.g. share capital, net current assets, total current assets] or increase in [specify items e.g. long-term debt, current liabilities] of the Issuer compared with the corresponding figures in the [insert date of latest] audited financial statements; and

12 Or other applicable professional standards if those financial statements are not prepared in accordance with Australian Accounting Standards.

(b) in the period from [insert date of first day after end of last audited financial statements] to [date of latest management accounts] there was any decrease in [specify items e.g. revenue, profit before tax] or increase in [specify items e.g. interest expense, costs of goods sold], compared to the corresponding period in the preceding year as shown in the [month, last year] management accounts.

Agreed-Upon Procedures

10. Since the Directors have advised us that no financial statements have been prepared up to any date subsequent to [insert date of latest management accounts], the procedures carried out by us with respect to changes in financial statement items after [insert date of latest management accounts] have of necessity been even more limited than those carried out for the period up to that date. Up to the cut-off date, we have made enquiries of the persons responsible for financial and accounting matters identified in Paragraph (5) above as to:

(a) whether there has been any decrease in [specify items e.g. share capital, net current assets, net assets [same items as in Paragraph (5) above]] or increase in [specify items e.g. long term debt [same items as in Paragraph (5) above]] at the cut-off date as compared with the amounts shown in the [insert date of latest] audited financial statements of the Issuer; and

(b) whether for the period from [insert date of first day after end of last audited financial statements] up to the cut-off date there have been any decreases in [specify items e.g. revenue, profit before tax [same items as in Paragraph (5) above]] as compared with the corresponding period in the preceding year.

Auditor's Statement

11. The persons responsible for financial and accounting matters identified in Paragraph (5) above confirmed that [except for the matters set out in Paragraph (9) above and except for [insert changes communicated by persons responsible for financial and accounting matters]] they were not aware of any such increase in [specify items] or decreases in any of the other items in Paragraph (10) (a) or (b) above. On the basis of the responses to these enquiries and our reading of the minutes as described in Paragraph (4) above, nothing has come to our attention which causes us to believe that [except for the matters set out in Paragraph (10) (a) above,] there has been any such increase or decrease.

General

12. The procedures described above do not constitute an audit or review performed in accordance with AUASB Standards and, as such, no assurance is expressed. Had we performed additional procedures, or conducted an audit or a review in accordance with AUASB Standards, other matters may have come to our attention that would have been reported to you.

13. The Addressees had sole responsibility for determining the adequacy or otherwise of the procedures we agreed to perform for the purpose of issuing this letter and we make no representations as to the sufficiency of these procedures for your purposes.

14. Our work did not extend to the period from the cut-off date to the date of this letter.

15. This letter should not be relied on as if it had been provided in accordance with the standards and practice of any professional body in any jurisdiction other than Australia.

16. We make no representation regarding any matters of legal interpretation or the completeness or adequacy of disclosures in the offering document.

17. This Comfort Letter may only be relied upon in respect of the matters to which it refers and as of its date. In relying upon this Comfort Letter, you agree that we have no responsibility to and we will not perform any work subsequent to the date of this Comfort Letter nor to consider, monitor, communicate or report any events or circumstances which may occur or may come to light subsequent to the date of this letter [except if we are required to issue a updated Comfort Letter, which will be issued in the form and on the basis set out in the Engagement Letter].

18. This letter is prepared in accordance with ASRS 4450 *Comfort Letter Engagements*. This letter is not issued in accordance with [SAS 72 *Letters for Underwriters and Certain*

Other Requesting Parties] issued by [American Institute of Certified Public Accountants]. Furthermore, this letter is not intended to be relied on in the jurisdiction of the [United States of America] and we accept no responsibility for any use that you may make of it in the [United States of America]. Subject always to the previous sentence, it may be disclosed, referred to and/or produced as provided for in paragraph [X] of the Engagement Letter.

Yours faithfully

Firm Name

cc The Directors, Issuer Ltd

.... Title Date ....

.... Name

Encl.

Appendix 1: Offering Document of [Issuer Name]

Appendix 2: Engagement Letter

Appendix 3: Schedule prepared by management of the Issuer

Appendix 4

(Ref: Para. A52)

Example Bring Down Comfort Letter

The following illustrative Bring Down Comfort Letter is issued subsequently to the original Comfort Letter. It can be tailored for specific engagement circumstances. The Issuer of the offering document is assumed to be the same entity as that which appointed the auditor.

[The Directors]

[ABC Company Limited]

[Address]

The Lead Manager and Dealers

[Addressee]

[Date]

Dear Sirs/Mesdames

[Insert type of offering] ISSUE BY [insert issuer name] ("the Issuer")

1. We attach as Appendix 1 a copy of the Engagement Letter dated [*insert date*] (the "Engagement Letter"), the terms of which have been agreed between us, are deemed to have been incorporated into this bring down letter and govern the matters addressed by this bring down letter and its use.

2. We refer to our letter of [Date] relating to the [Offering Document] dated [Date] of ABC Company Limited (the "Company"), attached as Appendix 2. We reaffirm as of the date hereof, and as though made on the date hereof, all statements made in that letter, except that for the purposes of this letter:

   (a) The Offering Document to which this letter relates is as amended on [Effective Date].[13]

   (b) The reading of minutes described in [paragraph number] of that letter has been carried out through [the New Cut-Off date].

13 Effective date means the date on which the securities offering becomes effective.

(c) The procedures and enquiries covered in [paragraph number] of that letter were carried out to [the new cut-off date] (our work did not extend to the period from [day after the new cut-off date] to [date of letter], inclusive).

(d) The period covered in [paragraph number] of that letter is changed to the period from [Date] officials of the Issuer having advised us that no such financial statements as of any date or for any period subsequent to [Date], were available.

(e) The references to [Date], in [paragraph number] of that letter are changed to [Date].

3. This letter is intended solely for the information of the directors of the Issuer ("the Directors"), the Lead Manager and to each of the Dealers who at the date of issue of the Comfort Letter had agreed to participate in the Issue and agreed in writing to be bound by the terms of the Engagement Letter ("the managers") (the Issuer, the Lead manager, the Directors and the managers collectively being the "Addressees").

4. This letter is provided solely for the purpose of any due diligence defence the Addressees are entitled to advance in any claim or proceedings in connection with the contents of the Offering Document referred to in the Engagement Letter, on the basis set out in the Engagement Letter. Accordingly, this letter is addressed to you for that purpose and may not be relied on by you or be used, circulated, quoted or otherwise referred to for any purpose, including but not limited to the purchase or sale of securities, nor is it to be filed with or referred to in whole or in part in the [Offering Document] or any other document, except that reference may be made to its existence in any contract or other communication between any of the Addressees or ourselves) nor made available to any other party except as permitted by the Engagement Letter.

5. Other than those who have signed the Engagement Letter, or have validly accepted or otherwise agreed with the terms of the Engagement Letter in accordance with paragraph [X] of the Engagement Letter, we will not accept any responsibility to any other party to whom our letter is shown or into whose hands it may come.

General

6. The Addressees had sole responsibility for determining the adequacy or otherwise of the procedures we agreed to perform for the purpose of issuing this letter and we make no representations as to the sufficiency of these procedures for your purposes.

7. Our work did not extend to the period from the New Cut-off Date to the date of this letter.

8. This letter should not be relied on as if it had been provided in accordance with the standards and practice of any professional body in any jurisdiction other than Australia.

9. This letter may only be relied on in respect of the matters to which it refers and as of its date. In relying on this letter, you agree we have no responsibility to and we will not perform any work subsequent to the date of this bring down letter nor to consider, monitor, communicate or report any events or circumstances which may occur or may come to light subsequent to the date of this letter.

Yours faithfully

Firm Name

cc The Directors, Issuer Ltd

.... Title Date ....

.... Name

Encl.

Appendix 1: Engagement Letter

Appendix 2: Comfort Letter

ASRS

AUS 804
The Audit of Prospective Financial Information

(As amended July 2002)

Prepared by the Auditing and Assurance Standards Board of the Australian Accounting Research Foundation.

Issued by the Australian Accounting Research Foundation on behalf of CPA Australia and The Institute of Chartered Accountants in Australia.

Note from the Institute of Chartered Accountants Australia

This note, prepared by the technical editor, is not part of AUS 804.

Historical development

March 1993: AUP 36 'The Audit of Prospective Financial Information' issued following a period of exposure as ED 49. The purpose of AUP 36 was to provide guidance to auditors on the general procedures to be performed in an audit of prospective financial information. The statement required the auditor, in normal circumstances, to provide a negative expression of opinion on the reasonableness of management's best-estimate assumptions. No opinion should be expressed on hypothetical assumptions.

June 1994: The International Auditing Practices Committee (IAPC) of the International Federation of Accountants (IFAC) approved the issuance of a codified set of International Standards of Auditing (ISAs). The relevant international pronouncement was ISA 810 'The Examination of Prospective Financial Information'.

September 1994: ED 62 'Codification and Revision of Auditing Pronouncements: AUS 810 The Audit of Prospective Financial Information' issued by the AuSB.

October 1995: Australian Auditing Standards and Auditing Guidance Statements released. The status of these is explained in APS 1.1 'Conformity With Auditing Standards'. These Standards became operative for the first reporting period commencing on or after 1 July 1996 and later reporting periods, although earlier application was encouraged. AUP 36 'The Audit of Prospective Financial Information' replaced by AUS 804 'The Audit of Prospective Financial Information'.

April 1998: AUS/AGS Omnibus 1 'Miscellaneous Amendments to AUSs and AGSs' issued. The changes to AUS 804 embodied in Omnibus 1 were incorporated in this version of AUS 804.

July 2002: AUS/AGS Omnibus 3 'Miscellaneous Amendments to AUSs and AGSs' issued by the AuASB, operative from the date of issue. AUS 804 since reissued by the Board to incorporate these amendments.

November 2012: The AUASB issued ASAE 3450 'Assurance Engagements involving Corporate Fundraisings and/or Prospective Financial Information', which will supersede AUS 802 for engagements commencing after July 2013.

Contents

Auditing Standards contain the basic principles and essential procedures identified in **bold-type (black lettering)** which are mandatory, together with related guidance. For further information about the responsibility of members for compliance with AUSs refer Miscellaneous Professional Statement APS 1.1 "Conformity with Auditing Standards".

Auditing Standard AUS 804

The Audit of Prospective Financial Information

Introduction

.01 The purpose of this Auditing Standard (AUS) is to establish standards and provide guidance on engagements to audit and report on prospective financial information prepared using best-estimate and/or hypothetical assumptions. For engagements to review prospective financial information, refer to AUS 902 "Review of Financial Reports".

.02 ***In an engagement to audit prospective financial information, the auditor should obtain sufficient appropriate audit evidence as to whether:***

(a) management's best-estimate assumptions on which the prospective financial information is based are reasonable for the preparation of the prospective financial information;

(b) the prospective financial information is properly prepared on the basis of the assumptions;

(c) the prospective financial information is properly presented and all material assumptions are adequately disclosed, including a clear indication as to whether they are best-estimate assumptions or hypothetical assumptions; and

(d) the prospective financial information is prepared on a consistent basis with historical financial reports, using appropriate accounting principles.

.03 This AUS does not apply to the audit of prospective financial information expressed in general or narrative terms, such as that found in management's discussion and analysis in an entity's annual report, though many of the procedures outlined herein may be suitable for such an audit.

AUS

.04 "Prospective financial information" means financial information based on assumptions about events that may occur in the future and possible actions by an entity. It is highly subjective in nature and its preparation requires the exercise of considerable judgement. Prospective financial information can be in the form of a forecast, or projection or a combination of both, for example a one year forecast plus a five year projection.

.05 A "forecast" means prospective financial information prepared on the basis of assumptions as to future events which management expects to take place, and the actions management expects to take as of the date the information is prepared (best- estimate assumptions).

.06 A "projection" means prospective financial information prepared on the basis of:

(a) hypothetical assumptions about future events and management actions which are not necessarily expected to take place, such as when some entities are in a start- up phase or are considering a major change in the nature of operations; or

(b) a mixture of best-estimate and hypothetical assumptions.

Such information illustrates the possible consequences, as of the date the information is prepared, if the events and actions were to occur (a "what-if" scenario).

.07 Prospective financial information can include financial reports or one or more elements of financial reports and may be prepared:

(a) as an internal management tool, for example to assist in evaluating a possible capital investment; or

(b) for the distribution to third parties in, for example:

  (i) a prospectus to provide potential investors with information about future expectations;

  (ii) an annual report to provide information to shareholders, regulatory bodies and other interested parties; and

  (iii) a document for the information of lenders which may include, for example cash flow forecasts.

.08 Management is responsible for the preparation and presentation of the prospective financial information, including the identification and disclosure of the underlying assumptions. The auditor may be asked to audit and report on the prospective financial information to enhance its credibility, whether it is intended for use by third parties or for internal purposes.

The Auditor's Assurance regarding Prospective Financial Information

.09 Prospective financial information relates to events and actions that have not yet occurred and may not occur. While evidence may be available to support the underlying assumptions, such evidence is itself generally future oriented and, therefore, speculative in nature, as distinct from the evidence ordinarily available in the audit of historical financial information. The auditor is therefore not in a position to express an opinion as to whether the results shown in the prospective financial information will be achieved.

.10 Further, given the nature of the evidence available in assessing the reasonableness of the assumptions on which the prospective financial information is based, it may be difficult for the auditor to obtain a level of satisfaction sufficient to express a positive opinion that the assumptions are free of material misstatement. Consequently, in this AUS, when reporting on the reasonableness of management's assumptions, the auditor:

(a) ordinarily provides only a moderate level of assurance by issuing a statement of negative assurance on best-estimate assumptions. This does not imply that the auditor can limit the procedures performed to that of a review engagement. The auditor is required to perform audit procedures to obtain sufficient appropriate audit evidence to issue a statement of negative assurance on the reasonableness of management's assumptions; and

(b) does not express an opinion on hypothetical assumptions.

Acceptance of Engagement

.11 Before accepting an engagement to audit prospective financial information, the auditor would consider, amongst other things:

(a) the intended use of the information;

(b) whether the information will be used by persons with whom the preparer is or is not negotiating directly;

(c) the nature of the assumptions, that is whether they are best-estimate or hypothetical assumptions;

(d) the elements to be included in the information;

(e) the period covered by the information; and

(f) whether any prior period financial information was subject to a modified audit opinion and the nature of the modification.

.12 ***The auditor should not accept an engagement when the assumptions are clearly unrealistic or the auditor believes that the prospective financial information will be inappropriate for its intended use.***

.13 In deciding whether to accept an engagement, the auditor would consider matters such as:

(a) whether the time available to complete the engagement is adequate;

(b) the economic substance and viability of the entity and/or transaction or project of the entity;

(c) the economic environment and the industry in which the entity operates;

(d) the stability of the entity's business;

(e) the financial strength of the entity;

(f) the reputation of management responsible for the assumptions underlying the prospective financial information;

(g) the past record of management in the preparation of prospective financial information;

(h) the engagement team's experience with the business and the industry in which the entity operates and with reporting on prospective financial information;

(i) the governing body's understanding of its responsibility in respect of the underlying assumptions; and

(j) the availability of data derived from third parties to support the assumptions, such as industry statistics.

If the auditor concludes that one or more of these factors is unsatisfactory, consideration needs to be given to the significance of the matters.

.14 In some circumstances an engagement would not be accepted because of an unsatisfactory response to one of the matters in AUS 804.13 (for example if there is insufficient time to adequately complete the engagement), in other cases a combination of matters may indicate that the engagement is impracticable. In other circumstances, the auditor may accept the engagement, but use the knowledge of an unsatisfactory matter in determining the nature, timing and extent of procedures to be applied to obtain sufficient appropriate audit evidence to form an opinion on the prospective financial information (for example, if the entity's business is unstable or management has a poor record in preparing prospective financial information).

.15 In accordance with AUS 204 "Terms of Audit Engagements", it is necessary for the auditor and the client to agree on the terms of the engagement. It is in the interest of both the entity and the auditor that the auditor sends an engagement letter, preferably before the commencement of the engagement, to help in avoiding misunderstandings with respect to the engagement. An engagement letter would address the matters in AUS 804.11, and set out management's responsibilities for the assumptions and for providing the auditor with all relevant information and source data in developing the assumptions.

Knowledge of the Business

.16 ***The auditor should obtain a sufficient level of knowledge of the business to be able to evaluate whether all significant assumptions required for the preparation of the prospective financial information have been identified.*** The auditor would also need to become familiar with the entity's process for preparing prospective financial information, for example, by considering:

(a) the internal controls over the system used to prepare prospective financial information and the expertise and experience of those persons preparing the prospective financial information;

(b) the nature of the documentation prepared by the entity supporting management's assumptions;

(c) the extent to which statistical, mathematical and computer-assisted techniques are used and the reliability thereof;

(d) the methods used to develop and apply assumptions; and

(e) the accuracy of prospective financial information prepared in prior periods and the reasons for significant variances.

.17 The knowledge and understanding of the entity required by the auditor would have been acquired by an auditor who has carried out an audit or review of the entity's financial reports in recent previous periods. Where this form of engagement is undertaken by an auditor who does not have the knowledge acquired from recent previous audits, that auditor needs to be satisfied that sufficient knowledge and understanding can be obtained to meet the requirements of this AUS.

.18 ***The auditor should consider the extent to which reliance on the entity's historical financial information is justified.*** The auditor requires a knowledge of the entity's historical financial information to assess whether the prospective financial information has been prepared on a basis consistent with the historical financial information and to provide a historical yardstick for considering management's assumptions. The auditor will need to establish, for example, whether relevant historical information was audited or reviewed and whether acceptable accounting principles were used in its preparation.

.19 If the audit or review report on the prior period historical financial information was qualified, or if the entity is in a start-up phase, the auditor would consider the surrounding facts and the impact on the approach to the audit of the prospective financial information.

Period Covered

.20 ***The auditor should consider the period of time covered by the prospective financial information.*** Since assumptions become more speculative as the length of the period covered increases, as that period lengthens, the ability of management to make best-estimate assumptions decreases. The period would not extend beyond the time for which management has a reasonable basis for the assumptions. The following are some of the factors that are relevant to the auditor's consideration of the period of time covered by the prospective financial information:

(a) the operating cycle, for example in the case of a major construction project the time required to complete the project may dictate the period covered;

(b) the degree of reliability of assumptions, for example if the entity is introducing a new product, the prospective period covered could be short and broken into small segments, such as weeks or months. Alternatively, if the entity's sole business is owning property under long-term lease, a relatively long prospective period might be reasonable; and

(c) the needs of users, for example prospective financial information may be prepared in connection with an application for a loan, for the period of time required to generate sufficient funds for repayment. Alternatively, the information may be prepared for investors in connection with the sale of debentures to illustrate the intended use of the proceeds in the subsequent period.

Audit Procedures

.21 ***When determining the nature, timing and extent of audit procedures, the auditor's considerations should include:***

(a) ***the likelihood of material misstatement;***

(b) ***knowledge obtained during any previous engagements;***

(c) ***management's competence regarding the preparation of prospective financial information;***

(d) ***the extent to which the prospective financial information is affected by management's judgement; and***

(e) ***the adequacy and reliability of the underlying data.***

.22 The auditor would assess the source and reliability of the evidence supporting management's best-estimate assumptions. Sufficient appropriate audit evidence supporting such assumptions would be obtained from internal and external sources, including consideration of the assumptions in the light of historical information and an evaluation of whether they are based on plans that are within the entity's capacity.

.23 The auditor would consider whether, when hypothetical assumptions are used, all significant implications of the assumptions have been taken into consideration. For example if sales are assumed to grow beyond the entity's current plant capacity, the prospective financial information will need to include the necessary investment in the additional plant capacity or the costs of alternative means of meeting the anticipated sales, such as by sub-contracting production.

.24 Although evidence supporting hypothetical assumptions need not be obtained, the auditor would need to be satisfied that they are consistent with the purpose of the prospective financial information and that there is no reason to believe they are clearly unrealistic.

.25 The auditor will need to be satisfied that the prospective financial information is properly prepared from management's assumptions by, for example, making clerical checks such as recomputations and reviewing internal consistency, that is, the actions management intends to take are compatible with each other and there are no inconsistencies in the determination of the amounts that are based on common variables, such as interest rates.

.26 The auditor would focus on the extent to which those areas that are particularly sensitive to variation will have a material effect on the results shown in the prospective financial information. This will influence the extent to which the auditor will seek appropriate audit evidence. It will also influence the auditor's evaluation of the appropriateness and adequacy of disclosure.

.27 When engaged to audit one or more elements of prospective financial information, such as an individual financial statement, it is important that the auditor consider the interrelationship of other elements in the financial report.

.28 When any elapsed portion of the current period is included in the prospective financial information, the auditor would consider the extent to which procedures need be applied to the historical information. Procedures will vary depending on the circumstances, for example, how much of the prospective period has elapsed.

.29 ***The auditor should obtain written representations from management regarding the intended use of the prospective financial information, the completeness of significant management assumptions and management's acceptance of its responsibility for the prospective financial information.*** These representations may be in the form of relevant minutes of meetings of the governing body, a written representation from management or a published statement by the management acknowledging such responsibility.

AUS

Presentation and Disclosure

.30 ***The auditor should assess the appropriateness of the presentation and disclosure of the prospective financial information and the underlying assumptions.*** In addition to any relevant statutory requirements, regulations, Accounting Standards or UIG Consensus Views, the auditor would consider whether:

(a) the presentation of prospective financial information is informative and not misleading;

(b) the accounting policies are clearly disclosed in the notes to the prospective financial information;

(c) the assumptions are adequately disclosed in the notes to the prospective financial information. It needs to be clear whether assumptions represent management's best-estimates or are hypothetical. When assumptions are made in areas that are material and are subject to a high degree of uncertainty, this uncertainty and the resulting sensitivity of results needs to be adequately disclosed;

(d) the date at which the prospective financial information was prepared is disclosed. The governing body needs to confirm that the assumptions are appropriate as of this date, even though the underlying information may have been accumulated over a period of time;

(e) the basis of establishing points in a range is clearly indicated, and the range is not selected in a biased or misleading manner when results shown in the prospective financial information are expressed in terms of a range; and

(f) any change in accounting policy since the most recent historical financial report is disclosed along with the reason for the change and its effect on the prospective financial information.

Audit Reporting

.31 ***The report by an auditor on an audit of prospective financial information should contain the following, ordinarily in the following order:***

(a) the title;

(b) the addressee;

(c) a section describing the audit scope which includes the following:

(i) identification of the prospective financial information;

(ii) a statement that the governing body is responsible for the prospective financial information, including the assumptions on which it is based;

(iii) a statement that the auditor has conducted an independent audit of the prospective financial information in order to express an opinion thereon to the addressee;

(iv) a statement that the audit has been conducted in accordance with Australian Auditing Standards;

(v) in rare and exceptional circumstances, when a departure from a basic principle or essential procedure may be necessary, as indicated in Miscellaneous Professional Statement APS 1.1 "Conformity with Auditing Standards", the statement required under paragraph (iv) should provide details of the particular basic principle(s) or essential procedure(s) that has been departed from together with the justification for the departure. As indicated in APS 1.1, this statement is not required where the basic principle or essential procedure relates to a matter that is not material or where the Auditing Standard contains an exceptional circumstance departure provision in the black-lettering. (For example, refer AUS 504.02 "Confirmation of Receivables".);

(vi) a statement that the auditor's procedures included examination, on a test basis, of evidence supporting the assumptions, amounts and other disclosures in the forecast or projection and the evaluation of accounting policies;

(vii) ***a statement indicating that these procedures have been undertaken to form an opinion as to whether:***

- ***anything has come to the auditor's attention which causes the auditor to believe that management's assumptions do not provide a reasonable basis for the preparation of the forecast or projection; and***
- ***in all material respects, the forecast or projection is properly prepared on the basis of the assumptions and is presented fairly in accordance with the identified reporting framework, and on a basis consistent with the accounting policies adopted and disclosed by the entity in its previous financial report so as to present a view of the entity which is consistent with the auditor's understanding of the entity's past, current and future operations; and***

(viii) ***a statement that the audit opinion has been formed on the basis identified in the scope section above;***

(d) ***a section expressing the auditor's opinion in respect of whether:***

(i) ***management's best-estimate assumptions are reasonable for the preparation of the prospective financial information;***

(ii) ***the prospective financial information is properly prepared on the basis of the assumptions; and***

(iii) ***the prospective financial information is presented fairly in accordance with an identified reporting framework and, where appropriate, on a basis consistent with the accounting policies adopted and disclosed by the entity in its audited financial report;***

(e) ***appropriate caveats concerning the achievability of the results indicated by the prospective financial information;***

(f) ***the auditor's signature;***

(g) ***the auditor's address; and***

(h) ***the date of the audit report.***

The attached Appendix contains examples of audit reports on prospective financial information.

AUS

.32 Such a report would state that:

(a) the actual results are likely to be different from the prospective financial information since anticipated events frequently do not occur as expected and the variation could be material. Likewise, when the prospective financial information is expressed as a range, it would be stated that there can be no assurance that actual results will fall within the range; and

(b) in the case of a projection, the prospective financial information has been prepared for (state purpose), using a set of assumptions that include hypothetical assumptions about future events and management's actions that are not necessarily expected to occur. Consequently, readers are cautioned that the prospective financial information ought not be used for purposes other than that described.

.33 The audit report would be dated as of the date the auditor signs that report. The auditor has no responsibility to update the audit report except when the auditor becomes aware of facts which were not known at that date and which may require adjustment of, or disclosure in, the prospective financial information. In these circumstances, the auditor would refer to AUS 706 "Subsequent Events".

.34 When reporting on the reasonableness of best-estimate assumptions, the auditor would ordinarily issue a statement of negative assurance due to the nature of the evidence available. However, when in the auditor's judgement, sufficient appropriate audit evidence has been obtained, the auditor is not precluded from expressing a positive opinion on the assumptions.

.35 The auditor does not express an opinion on hypothetical assumptions because, by their nature, sufficient appropriate audit evidence is not available to support those assumptions.

.36 Where the prospective financial information is prepared on the basis of best-estimate and hypothetical assumptions, the auditor reports on the best-estimate assumptions and the prospective financial information on the presumption that the hypothetical assumptions will occur.

.37 ***When the auditor believes that the presentation and disclosure of the prospective financial information is not adequate, the auditor should express an "except for" or an adverse opinion on the prospective financial information, as appropriate, setting out the reasons in a separate qualification section in the audit report.*** An example would be where the financial information fails to disclose the consequences of any assumptions which are highly sensitive.

.38 ***When the auditor believes that one or more significant assumptions do not provide a reasonable basis for the prospective financial information prepared on the basis of best-estimate assumptions, or that one or more significant assumptions do not provide a reasonable basis for the prospective financial information given the hypothetical assumptions, the auditor should express an adverse opinion, setting out the reasons in a separate qualification section in the audit report.***

.39 ***When the audit is affected by conditions that preclude application of one or more procedures considered necessary in the circumstances, the auditor should express an "except for" or an inability to form an opinion on the basis of a limitation on the scope of the audit.***

.40 The duty of the auditor is to convey information, not merely arouse enquiry. ***Whenever the auditor expresses a qualified opinion, the audit report should, in accordance with AUS 702 "The Audit Report on a General Purpose Financial Report", contain:***

(a) a clear description of all the substantive reasons therefor;

(b) a quantification of the effects or possible effects on the amounts and other disclosures contained in, or omitted from, the financial report; or

(c) if the effects or possible effects are incapable of being measured reliably, a statement to that effect and the reasons therefor.

Operative Date

.41 This AUS, which incorporates amendments made by AUS/AGS Omnibus 3 "Miscellaneous Amendments to AUSs and AGSs", is operative from July 2002. This version of AUS 804 supersedes AUS 804 "The Audit of Prospective Financial Information", as revised in April 1998.

Compatibility with International Standards on Auditing

.42 Except for the matters noted below, the basic principles and essential procedures of this AUS and International Standard on Auditing ISA 810, The Examination of Prospective Financial Information, are consistent in all material respects:

(a) ISA 810 remains silent as to whether the auditor should report that the prospective financial information has, or has not been prepared on a basis consistent with the accounting policies adopted and disclosed by the entity in its audited financial report. When relevant, the Auditing & Assurance Standards Board considers it appropriate to report on this matter as this provides useful information to the addressee of the audit report;

(b) AUS 804 requires the auditor to include a scope section in the audit report to explain the nature and extent of the auditor's work and the degree of assurance provided. ISA 810 does not contain an equivalent requirement. The Auditing & Assurance Standards Board is of the view that as many members of the community do not have an adequate appreciation of the role and responsibilities of the auditor, the inclusion of a scope section will help clarify the audit function;

(c) AUS 804 paragraph 30 contains a basic principle/essential procedure which requires the auditor to assess the appropriateness of the presentation and disclosure of the prospective financial information and the underlying assumptions. ISA 810 only provides guidance on the matters to consider when assessing the presentation and disclosure. The Auditing & Assurance Standards Board is of the view that given the nature of prospective information, and the fact that such information is often prepared without a formal reporting framework in place, the auditor should assess the appropriateness of the presentation and disclosure; and

(d) ISA 810 allows the auditor to withdraw from an engagement if the auditor believes:
   (i) the presentation and disclosure of the prospective financial information is not adequate;
   (ii) one or more significant assumptions do not provide a reasonable basis for the best-estimate assumptions, or that one or more significant assumptions do not provide a reasonable basis given the hypothetical assumptions;
   (iii) the audit is affected by conditions that preclude one or more procedures considered necessary; or
   (iv) the assumptions are clearly unrealistic or that the prospective financial information will be inappropriate for its intended use.

   AUS 804 does not follow that approach. Rather this AUS requires the auditor to qualify the audit report in these circumstances. The Auditing & Assurance Standards Board is of the view that once the auditor accepts an engagement, the auditor has a responsibility to fulfil the contract by reporting to the client.

Appendix

Examples of Audit Reports on Prospective Financial Information

Example 1: Best-estimate Assumptions – a Forecast, where a Statement of Negative Assurance is Issued on the Reasonableness of Management's Assumptions

Independent Audit Report

To [addressee]

Scope

We have audited the forecast of [entity] for the [period] as set out on pages ... to ... . The [members of the governing body] are responsible for the preparation and presentation of the forecast and the information contained therein, including the assumptions as set out in note ... on which the forecast is based. We have conducted an independent audit of the forecast in order to express an opinion on it to [addressee].

The forecast has been prepared for distribution to [addressee] for the purpose ... . We disclaim any assumption of responsibility for any reliance on this report or on the forecast to which it relates to any person other than to [addressee] or for any purpose other than that for which it was prepared.[1]

Our audit has been conducted in accordance with Australian Auditing Standards. Our procedures included examination, on a test basis, of evidence supporting the assumptions, amounts and other disclosures in the forecast and the evaluation of accounting policies. These procedures have been undertaken to form an opinion whether anything has come to our attention which causes us to believe that management's assumptions as set out in note ... do not provide a reasonable basis for the preparation of the forecast, and whether, in all material respects, the forecast is properly prepared on the basis of the assumptions as set out in note ... and is presented fairly in accordance

1 When the audit report has been prepared for users beyond the addressee, this paragraph should be amended to state:

"The forecast has been prepared for the purpose... . We disclaim any assumption of responsibility for any reliance on this report or on the forecast to which it relates for any purposes other than that for which it was prepared."

with ...[2] (and on a basis consistent with the accounting policies adopted and disclosed by the entity in its audited financial report for the [period] ended [date])[3] so as to present a view of the [entity] which is consistent with our understanding of the [entity's] past, current and future operations.

Prospective financial information relates to events and actions that have not yet occurred and may not occur. While evidence may be available to support the assumptions on which prospective financial information is based, such evidence is generally future oriented and therefore speculative in nature. Given the nature of the evidence available in assessing the reasonableness of management's assumptions, we are not in a position to obtain the level of assurance necessary to express a positive opinion on those assumptions. Accordingly, we provide a lesser level of assurance on the reasonableness of management's assumptions[4].

The audit opinion expressed in this report has been formed on the above basis.

Audit Opinion

Based on our examination of the evidence supporting the assumptions, nothing has come to our attention which causes us to believe that the assumptions as set out in note ... do not provide a reasonable basis for the preparation of the forecast.

In our opinion,

(a) the forecast is properly prepared on the basis of the assumptions as set out in note ... ; and

(b) the forecast is presented fairly in accordance with:

  (i) ...[5]; and

  (ii) on a basis consistent with the accounting policies adopted and disclosed by the entity in its audited financial report for the [period] ended [date][6] (except for the changes in accounting policies as disclosed in note ...)[7].

Actual results are likely to be different from the forecast since anticipated events frequently do not occur as expected and the variation may be material. Accordingly, we express no opinion as to whether the forecast will be achieved.

Date Firm

Address Partner

Example 2: Hypothetical Assumptions – a Projection

Independent Audit Report

To [addressee]

Scope

We have audited the projection of [entity] for the [period] as set out on pages ... to ... . The [members of the governing body] are responsible for the preparation and presentation of the projection and the information contained therein, including the assumptions as set out in note ... on which the projection is based. We have conducted an independent audit of the projection in order to express an opinion on it to [addressee].

The projection has been prepared for distribution to [addressee] for the purpose ... . We disclaim any assumption of responsibility for any reliance on this report or on the projection to which

2 Indicate the reporting framework.

3 Where appropriate.

4 Where appropriate.

5 Indicate the reporting framework.

6 Where appropriate.

7 Where appropriate.

it relates to any person other than to [addressee] or for any purpose other than that for which it was prepared[8]. In addition, (as [the entity] is in a start-up phase)[9] the projection has been prepared using a set of assumptions that include hypothetical assumptions about future events and management's actions that are not necessarily expected to occur. Consequently, readers are cautioned that this projection may not be appropriate for purposes other than that described above.

Our audit has been conducted in accordance with Australian Auditing Standards. Our procedures included examination, on a test basis, of evidence supporting the assumptions, amounts and other disclosures in the projection and the evaluation of accounting policies. Because hypothetical assumptions relate to future events and management actions which are not necessarily expected to take place, we are not in a position to, and do not express an opinion on the hypothetical assumptions. The procedures have been undertaken to form an opinion whether (anything has come to our attention which causes us to believe that management's best-estimate assumptions as set out in note ... do not provide a reasonable basis for the preparation of the projection given the occurrence of the hypothetical assumptions, and whether)[10], in all material respects, the projection is properly prepared on the basis of the assumptions as set out in note ... and is presented fairly in accordance with ...[11] (and on a basis consistent with the accounting policies adopted and disclosed by the entity in its audited financial report for the [period] ended [date])[12] so as to present a view of the [entity] which is consistent with our understanding of the [entity's] current and future operations.

(Prospective financial information relates to events and actions that have not yet occurred and may not occur. While evidence may be available to support the best-estimate assumptions on which prospective financial information is based, such evidence is generally future oriented and therefore speculative in nature. Given the nature of the evidence available in assessing the reasonableness of management's best-estimate assumptions, we are not in a position to obtain the level of assurance necessary to express a positive opinion on those assumptions. Accordingly, we provide a lesser level of assurance on the reasonableness of management's assumptions)[13].

The audit opinion expressed in this report has been formed on the above basis.

Audit Opinion

(Based on our examination of the evidence supporting the assumptions, nothing has come to our attention which causes us to believe that the best-estimate assumptions as set out in note ... do not provide a reasonable basis for the preparation of the projection, given the occurrence of the hypothetical assumptions)[14].

In our opinion,

(a) the projection is properly prepared on the basis of the assumptions as set out in note ...; and

(b) the projection is presented fairly in accordance with:

  (i) ...[15]; and

8 When the projection has been prepared for users beyond the addressee, this paragraph should be amended to state:

"The projection has been prepared for the purpose.... We disclaim any assumption of responsibility for any reliance on this report or on the projection to which it relates for any purpose other than that for which it was prepared. In addition, (as [the entity] is in a start-up phase)[9] the projection has been prepared using a set of assumptions that include hypothetical assumptions about future events and management's actions that are not necessarily expected to occur. Consequently, readers are cautioned that this projection may not be appropriate for purposes other than that described above."

9 where appropriate.

10 include only in circumstances where best-estimate assumptions are presented with hypothetical assumptions.

11 indicate the reporting framework.

12 where appropriate.

13 include only in circumstances where best-estimate assumptions are presented with hypothetical assumptions.

14 include only in circumstances where best-estimate assumptions are presented with hypothetical assumptions.

15 indicate the reporting framework.

(ii) a basis consistent with the accounting policies adopted and disclosed by the entity in its audited financial report for the [period] ended [date][16] (except for the changes in accounting policies as disclosed in note ...)[17].

Even if the events anticipated under the hypothetical assumptions described above occur, actual results are still likely to be different from the projection since other anticipated events frequently do not occur as expected and the variation may be material. Accordingly, we express no opinion as to whether the projection will be achieved.

Date	Firm
Address	Partner

16 where appropriate.

17 where appropriate.

AUS 810

Special Purpose Reports on the Effectiveness of Control Procedures

(As amended July 2002)

Prepared by the Auditing and Assurance Standards Board of the Australian Accounting Research Foundation.

Issued by the Australian Accounting Research Foundation on behalf of CPA Australia and The Institute of Chartered Accountants in Australia.

Note from the Institute of Chartered Accountants Australia

This note, prepared by the technical editor, is not part of AUS 810.

Historical development

May 1999: AUS 810 'Special Purpose Reports on the Effectiveness of Control Procedures' issued by the AuASB, based on ED 68 with the same title issued in April 1998, and operative for reporting periods ending on or after 1 July 1999.

July 2002: AUS/AGS Omnibus 3 'Miscellaneous Amendments to AUSs and AGSs' issued by the AuASB, operative from the date of issue. AUS 810 since reissued by the Board to incorporate these amendments.

March 2011: The AUASB published an explanation of the applicability of AUASB pronouncements when conducting Internal Control Engagements. It can be downloaded from auasb.gov.au under the AUS 810 'Extra', and is reproduced in this book after ASAE 3402 'Assurance Reports at a Service Organisation'.

Contents

Auditing Standards contain the basic principles and essential procedures identified in **bold-type (black lettering)** which are mandatory, together with related guidance. For further information about the responsibility of members for compliance with AUSs refer Miscellaneous Professional Statement APS 1.1 "Conformity with Auditing Standards".

Auditing Standard AUS 810

Special Purpose Reports on the Effectiveness of Control Procedures

Main Features of the Standard

The Standard:

(a) establishes standards and provides guidance on engagements to report in relation to special purpose reports about the effectiveness of control procedures;

(b) differentiates the different types of engagements that an auditor can be engaged to undertake;

(c) provides guidance on the audit process and procedures to be applied to engagements to report on control procedures;

(d) provides guidance on the process for identifying suitable criteria against which to report; and

(e) identifies the basic elements for reporting on control procedures and the circumstances that result in a modified opinion.

Introduction

.01 The purpose of this Auditing Standard is to establish standards and provide guidance to auditors engaged to report to either:

(a) an entity's management either at the governing body or operational level; or

(b) a specified third party, for example a regulator or another auditor,

on whether control procedures for a specified area of activity are effective. It is recognised that an auditor may be engaged to report on design effectiveness, for example if evaluating a proposed system, or operating effectiveness, and not necessarily both. However, unless otherwise stated this Standard applies to engagements to report on both the design and operation of control procedures. This Standard does not deal with engagements to:

(i) report publicly (ie. where the report is intended to meet the information needs common to users who are unable to command the preparation of reports tailored so as to satisfy specifically all of their information needs regarding control procedures for the area of activity); or

(ii) report on an entity's entire internal control structure, control environment and/or information system.

.02 ***The objective of an engagement to report on control procedures for a specific area of activity is for the auditor to provide:***

(a) a level of assurance (in the case of an audit or review); or

(b) a report of factual findings (in the case of agreed-upon procedures);

about the design and operating effectiveness of those procedures based on identified suitable criteria.

.03 This Standard is to be read in conjunction with Australian Auditing Standards applicable to performance audits, and other AUSs as indicated.

AUS

Definitions

.04 "Area of activity" is the specific aspect(s) of the subject matter (internal control) relating to the entity's activities that is being reported upon by the auditor, for example, compliance with specified laws, the preparation of annual financial reports, the management of risks in trading in financial derivatives or the effectiveness of motor vehicle fleet management.

.05 "Attest reporting engagement" means an engagement where management makes a written assertion about the effectiveness of their control procedures, and the auditor provides an opinion to enhance the credibility of management's assertion. The auditor's report can either be in the form of an opinion:

(a) about the effectiveness of the control procedures themselves. In this case, by expressing an opinion on the same subject matter as the written assertion by management, the auditor enhances the credibility of that assertion; or

(b) about management's assertion about the effectiveness of the control procedures.

The standards and guidance in this Standard are directed towards the former type of opinion. If the terms of the engagement require the latter type of opinion, the reporting requirements may need to be adapted.

.06 "Control procedures" means those policies and procedures in addition to the control environment that management has established to ensure, as far as possible, that specific entity objectives will be achieved.

.07 "Control weakness" means a deficiency in the design of control procedures or a deficiency in operation of a control procedure that could potentially result in risks relevant to the area of activity not being reduced to an acceptable level. Relevant risks are those that threaten achievement of the objectives relevant to the area of activity being examined.

.08 "Criteria" means reasonable and attainable standards against which the effectiveness of the control procedures in relation to the area of activity can be assessed.

.09 "Direct reporting engagement" means an engagement where management does not make a written assertion about the effectiveness of their control procedures, and the auditor:

(a) provides an opinion about the effectiveness of the control procedures; and

(b) when appropriate, provides relevant and reliable information about the procedures in the form of facts and findings.

.10 "Internal control structure" (internal control) means the dynamic, integrated processes, effected by the governing body, management and all other staff, that are designed to provide reasonable assurance regarding the achievement of the following general objectives:

(a) effectiveness, efficiency and economy of operations;

(b) reliability of management and financial reporting; and

(c) compliance with applicable laws and regulations and internal policies.

Management's strategies for achieving these general objectives are affected by the design and operation of the following components:

(i) the control environment;

(ii) the information system; and

(iii) control procedures.

Each of these components is discussed further in AUS 402 "Risk Assessments and Internal Controls". The relationship between the general objectives and the components of internal control can be depicted as shown below[1]:

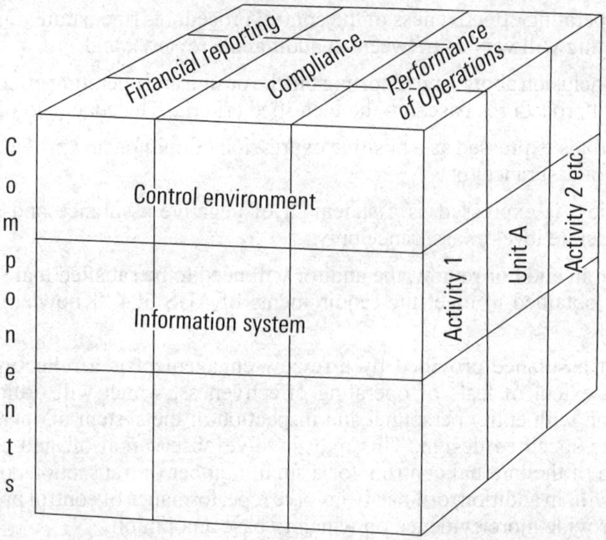

.11 "Materiality" refers to the potential for knowledge of a control weakness to affect the decisions of the addressee of the auditor's report.

Assurance

Types of Engagement

.12 An auditor may be engaged to perform any of the following types of engagement:

(a) audit (direct or attest);

(b) review (direct or attest); or

(c) agreed-upon procedures.

Audit and Review

.13 An audit provides a high but not absolute level of assurance about the effectiveness of control procedures. This is expressed as reasonable assurance in recognition of the fact that absolute assurance is rarely attainable due to such factors as the need for judgement, the use of testing, the inherent limitations of internal control and because much of the evidence available to the auditor is persuasive rather than conclusive in nature.

.14 A review provides a moderate level of assurance about the effectiveness of control procedures. The level of assurance provided is less than that provided in an audit because the scope of the auditor's work is less extensive than that of an audit, and the nature, timing and extent of the procedures performed do not provide sufficient appropriate audit evidence to enable the auditor to express a positive opinion. The objective of a review is to enable the auditor to state whether, on the basis of procedures which do not provide all the evidence that would be required in an audit, anything has come to the auditor's attention that causes the auditor to believe that the control procedures were not effective based on identified criteria (expression of negative assurance). AUS 902 "Review of Financial Reports" is to be applied to the extent practicable in an engagement to review the effectiveness of control procedures.

1 This diagram has been adapted from "Internal Control – Integrated Framework" the Committee of Sponsoring Organizations of the Treadway Commission (COSO), 1992.

AUS

.15 Both audits and reviews of control procedures involve:

(a) planning the engagement;

(b) evaluating the design effectiveness of control procedures;

(c) testing the operating effectiveness of the control procedures (the nature, timing and extent of testing will vary as between an audit and a review); and

(d) forming a conclusion about, and reporting on, the design and operating effectiveness of the control procedures based on the identified criteria. The conclusion for:

(i) an audit is expressed as a positive expression of opinion and provides a high level of assurance; or

(ii) a review is expressed as a statement of negative assurance and provides a moderate level of assurance only.

.16 To undertake either an audit or review, the auditor will need to be satisfied that sufficient knowledge can be obtained to meet the requirements of AUS 304 "Knowledge of the Business".

.17 The lower level of assurance provided by a review engagement is a reflection of the nature, timing and extent of tests of operating effectiveness, which will ordinarily be limited to discussion with entity personnel and inspection of the system in operation for deviations from the specified design. This may involve observation of, and enquiring about the operation of the internal controls for a small number of transactions or events. An audit however will, in addition, ordinarily involve reperformance of control procedures on a test basis to provide more evidence on which to base an opinion.

.18 The auditor applies professional judgement in determining the specific nature, timing and extent of procedures to be conducted in either an audit or review. This will depend on the individual circumstances faced by the auditor. For example in a review engagement, the auditor may decide that additional examination procedures are required to dispel or confirm a suspicion that a significant control weakness exists. The performance of such additional examination procedures does not convert the engagement to an audit. These procedures relate to the resolution of a specific matter and do not necessarily provide all the evidence needed to raise the overall assurance capable of being provided from moderate to high.

.19 Audits and reviews can result in either a direct report or an attest report, depending on whether management have made a written assertion about the effectiveness of their control procedures.

Agreed-Upon Procedures

.20 An agreed-upon procedures engagement does not result in the expression of any assurance by the auditor. The auditor is engaged to carry out specific procedures to meet the information needs of those parties who have agreed to the procedures to be performed. The auditor issues a report of factual findings to those parties that have agreed to the procedures. The recipients must form their own conclusions from this report because the auditor has not determined the nature, timing and extent of procedures to be able to express any assurance. The report is restricted to those parties (for example, a regulatory body) that have agreed to the procedures to be performed, since others are not aware of the reasons for the procedures and may misinterpret the results.

Engagement Mandate

.21 Where an engagement is to be undertaken to meet a regulatory or similarly imposed requirement, it is important that the auditor be satisfied that the type of engagement is clear from the relevant legislation or other source of the engagement mandate. If there is any uncertainty, it is recommended that the auditor and/or appointing party communicate with the relevant regulator or other party responsible for establishing or regulating the requirement and agree the engagement type and the assurance to be provided.

.22 An auditor, who before the completion of an engagement, is requested to change the engagement from an audit to a review or agreed-upon procedures engagement, needs to consider the appropriateness of doing so, and cannot agree to a change where there is no reasonable justification for the change. For example, a change is not appropriate in order to avoid a modified report.

Scope of Standard

.23 Except as otherwise stated, the remainder of this AUS is directed towards audit engagements. For review engagements the auditor would apply this AUS in the context of AUS 902. For agreed-upon procedures engagements the auditor would apply this AUS in the context of AUS 904 "Engagements to Perform Agreed-upon Procedures".

Limitations

.24 The auditor's opinion is based on the procedures determined to be necessary for the collection of sufficient appropriate evidence, that evidence being persuasive rather than conclusive in nature. The assurance provided by an auditor on the effectiveness of internal controls is however restricted because of the nature of internal controls and the inherent limitations of any set of internal controls and their operations. These limitations include:

(a) management's usual requirement that the cost of an internal control does not exceed the expected benefits to be derived;

(b) most internal controls tend to be directed at routine rather than non-routine transactions/events;

(c) the potential for human error due to carelessness, distraction or fatigue, misunderstanding of instructions and mistakes in judgement;

(d) the possibility of circumvention of internal controls through the collusion of employees with one another or with parties outside the entity;

(e) the possibility that a person responsible for exercising an internal control could abuse that responsibility, for example, a member of management overriding a control procedure;

(f) the possibility that management may not be subject to the same internal controls applicable to other personnel; and

(g) the possibility that internal controls may become inadequate due to changes in conditions, and compliance with procedures may deteriorate.

.25 Custom, culture, and the corporate governance system may inhibit fraud, error, or non-compliance with laws and regulations by management, but they are not infallible deterrents. An effective control environment, may help mitigate the probability of such fraud, error, or non-compliance with laws and regulations. Control environment factors such as an effective governing body, audit committee, and internal audit function may constrain improper conduct by management. Alternatively, an ineffective control environment may negate the effectiveness of control procedures within the internal control structure. For example, although an entity has good control procedures relating to compliance with environmental regulations, management may have a strong bias to suppress information about any detected breaches that would reflect adversely on the entity's public image. The effectiveness of internal controls might also be affected by factors such as a change in ownership or control, changes in management or other personnel, or developments in the entity's market or industry.

Terms of Engagement

.26 ***The auditor and the appointing party should agree on the terms of the engagement.*** Particular attention needs to be paid to defining the area of activity to be examined and the criteria against which the effectiveness of control procedures are to be assessed. The agreed terms would ordinarily be included in legislation or a contract, or recorded in an engagement letter or other suitable form. It is important that the terms are clear as to whether the engagement is an audit, review or agreed-upon procedures engagement, and whether it is an attest or direct reporting engagement. The auditor would include in the engagement letter a reference to management's responsibility for establishing and maintaining an effective internal control structure, including control procedures in relation to the area of activity.

AUS

Planning

.27 ***The auditor should plan the work so that the engagement will be performed in an effective manner.*** This will affect the auditor's judgement about what comprises sufficient appropriate audit evidence, and will also assist in determining the nature, timing and extent of audit procedures, to achieve the engagement objective.

.28 ***In planning the engagement, the auditor should obtain a general understanding of the internal control structure and a more detailed understanding of the control procedures in relation to the area of activity to be examined.*** This may be done by making inquiries of appropriate personnel, inspecting documents, and observing activities and operations. The nature and extent of these procedures will vary from engagement to engagement, due to factors such as:

(a) the entity's size and complexity;

(b) the nature of the area of activity to be examined, including the objective(s) to which the control procedures are directed and the risk that those objectives will not be achieved;

(c) the extent to which information technology is used; and

(d) the documentation available.

.29 The extent to which an understanding of the information technology controls is required, and the level of specialist skills necessary, will be affected by the complexity of the computer system, extent of computer use and importance to the entity, and the extent to which significant control procedures are incorporated into computer programs.

.30 Where specialist skills are required the auditor would apply the guidance in AUS 206 "Quality Control for Audit Work" for experts employed by the auditor and AUS 606 "Using the Work of an Expert" for experts engaged by the entity or auditor.

.31 ***The auditor should develop and document an engagement plan describing the expected scope and conduct of the engagement. The auditor should develop and document an audit program setting out the nature, timing and extent of procedures required to implement the plan. The plan and program should be revised as necessary during the course of the audit.*** When developing the audit plan and program, the auditor would consider factors such as:

(a) matters affecting the industry in which the entity operates, for example economic conditions, laws and regulations, and technology;

(b) risks to which the business is exposed that are relevant to the area of activity being examined;

(c) the quality of the control environment within the entity and the role of the governing body, audit committee and internal auditing;

(d) knowledge of the entity's internal control structure obtained during other engagements;

(e) the extent of recent changes if any, in the entity, its operations or its internal control structure;

(f) methods adopted by management to evaluate the effectiveness of the internal control structure;

(g) preliminary judgements about significant risk;

(h) the nature and extent of evidence likely to be available;

(i) the nature of control procedures relevant to the subject matter and their relationship to the internal control structure taken as a whole; and

(j) the auditor's preliminary judgement about the effectiveness of the internal control structure taken as a whole and of the control procedures for the area of activity.

Materiality

.32 ***The auditor should consider materiality when:***

(a) determining the nature, timing and extent of audit procedures; and

(b) evaluating the effect of identified control weaknesses on the auditor's conclusion.

The auditor applies the same considerations in a review as in an audit to judgements as to what is material, since such judgements are not affected by the level of assurance being provided.

.33 Materiality is addressed in the context of the entity's objectives relevant to the area of activity being examined, and whether the internal controls will reduce to an acceptably low level the risks that threaten achievement of those objectives.

.34 When assessing materiality, the auditor would consider qualitative factors as well as quantitative factors. The following are examples of qualitative factors that may be relevant:

(a) the purpose of the engagement and any specific requirements of the terms of the engagement;

(b) the economic, social, political and environmental impact of a control weakness;

(c) the importance of an identified control weakness in relation to the area of activity and the entity's overall objectives;

(d) the impact of a centralised function (for example computer security, central budgeting or human resource management) on other parts of the entity;

(e) public perceptions and/or interest in the area of activity;

(f) the cost of alternative controls relative to their likely benefit; and

(g) the length of time an identified control weakness was in existence.

The auditor would also consider those factors affecting materiality and risk that are identified in AUS 808 "Planning Performance Audits", paragraph .17.

The Link between Objectives, Risks, Control Procedures and Criteria

.35 Internal controls exist to reduce to an acceptably low level the risks that threaten achievement of the entity's objectives. To implement effective internal controls, the entity needs to:

(a) establish objectives;

(b) identify the significant risks that threaten achievement of those objectives; and

(c) have in place control procedures that reduce those risks to an acceptable level.

Examples of each of these are attached as Appendix 2.

.36 Objectives are set at various levels. At the highest level they may be represented by the entity's mission or vision statement. These would be complemented at lower levels by specific objectives for each activity, for example the reliability of financial reporting and the efficient use of motor vehicles. Objectives need to be consistent throughout the entity because an internal control structure cannot provide reasonable assurance about the achievement of conflicting objectives, and therefore suitable criteria could not be established to assess the effectiveness of control procedures.

.37 It is recognised that there are, legitimately, different approaches to establishing criteria. The basis for determining the criteria needs to be relevant to the engagement circumstances, and the level of detail at which criteria are set will also vary with the circumstances of each engagement. Criteria can be established by reference to the specific objectives for an area of activity, and expressed as the outcomes of the control process. For example, if the objective is to comply with applicable laws and regulations, the criteria expressed in terms of outcomes may be that all applicable laws and regulations are identified, communicated to all relevant staff and any instances of non-compliance detected are notified to the governing body on a timely basis. They can also be expressed in terms of relevant risks, or some combination of objectives and risks. Alternatively, criteria may be expressed in terms of the control policy or methodology establishing what should be in place to reduce the risks that threaten the achievement of the objective(s) to an acceptable level. When the criteria are related to residual risk, that is the risk left after the operation of control procedures, they will need to be expressed in such a way that it is clear the auditor is not responsible for forming an opinion about what level of risk is, or should be, acceptable to users.

.38 Control procedures, for example segregation of duties, custodial controls, logic checks etc., are the mechanism by which entities seek to reduce the risks that threaten achievement of objectives. The internal control procedures are not therefore the criteria in their own right, but are assessed as to their effectiveness to determine whether the criteria have been achieved, for example that the objective(s) has been met and/or the risks that threaten the achievement of those objectives reduced to an acceptable level.

Suitable Criteria

.39 Suitable criteria need to be identified by the parties to the engagement and agreed by the appointing party and the auditor. The auditor may need to discuss the criteria to be used with management and the intended user of the report. Criteria can be either established or specifically developed. The auditor normally concludes that established criteria embodied in laws or regulations or issued by professions, associations or other recognised authorities that follow due process are suitable when the criteria are consistent with the objective. Other criteria may be agreed to by the addressee of the auditor's report, or a party entitled to act on their behalf, and may also be specifically developed for the engagement.

.40 In situations where the criteria have been specifically developed for the engagement, including where the auditor assists in developing suitable criteria, the auditor would obtain from the addressee or a party entitled to act on their behalf, acknowledgment that the specifically developed criteria are sufficient for the addressee's purpose.

Assessing the Suitability of Criteria

.41 ***The auditor should determine that there are suitable criteria to enable the assessment of the effectiveness of the control procedures.*** Suitable criteria are those that are relevant to the matters being examined, are appropriate to the circumstances and are in a form that will allow for the expression of a meaningful opinion. At the initial planning stage, criteria may be identified at a relatively general level, however, more specific criteria will need to be identified for use during the engagement process. The auditor needs to be satisfied that specifically developed criteria do not result in a report that would be misleading to intended users.

.42 Characteristics of suitable criteria include:

(a) *Relevance:* Relevant criteria contribute to a conclusion to meet the engagement objective and assist decision-making by the intended user.

(b) *Reliability:* Reliable criteria result in consistent conclusions when used by other auditors in the same circumstances;

(c) *Neutrality:* Neutral criteria are free from any bias of the auditor or management and do not cause the auditor's opinion to mislead the intended users;

(d) *Understandability:* Understandable criteria are clearly stated and are not subject to significantly different interpretations;

(e) *Completeness:* Complete criteria include all significant criteria necessary to assess internal controls in the circumstances.

These characteristics would be considered together in identifying and assessing the suitability of criteria. The relative importance of the characteristics in different circumstances is a matter of professional judgement and would, depending on the engagement mandate, be discussed with the user of the auditor's report.

.43 Criteria may need to be amended as the engagement proceeds. For example, more information may become available or the circumstances of the entity may change. This would ordinarily be discussed with the user of the auditor's report.

.44 AUS 808 deals further with criteria and factors to consider in assessing the suitability of criteria.

The Consequence of Unsuitable Criteria

.45 The auditor needs to consider whether the identified criteria are in a suitable form to allow for the expression of a meaningful opinion. ***If the auditor believes the identified criteria are unsuitable, the auditor should either:***

(a) ***agree on suitable criteria with the addressee of the auditor's report, or a party entitled to act on their behalf, prior to continuing with the engagement. If unable to agree on suitable criteria, the auditor would not continue with the engagement; or***

(b) ***issue a qualified report where the auditor is required to perform the engagement under a legislative mandate.***

Internal Auditing

.46 ***During the planning phase, the auditor should determine whether the entity has an internal auditing function and its effect on the internal control structure.*** Internal auditing is an appraisal activity established within an entity as a service to the entity. Its functions include, among other things, examining, evaluating and monitoring the adequacy and effectiveness of other components of the internal control structure.

.47 An effective internal auditing function will often allow a modification in the nature and/or timing, and/or a reduction in the extent, of procedures performed by the external auditor, but cannot eliminate them entirely. Where the entity has an internal auditing function, the external auditor would obtain an understanding and perform a preliminary assessment of internal auditing regarding:

(a) its impact on the effectiveness of the control structure and, in particular, control procedures in relation to the subject matter; and

(b) its effect on procedures to be performed by the external auditor.

Evaluating Design Effectiveness

.48 ***The auditor should obtain a general understanding of the control environment and information system to identify matters that are likely to have a significant impact on the effectiveness of particular control procedures.*** Evaluating design effectiveness is done in the context of the auditor's general understanding of the control environment and information system as gained for the purpose of planning the engagement. A weakness in the control environment could undermine the effectiveness of control procedures, and this would be taken into account in determining the nature, timing and extent of procedures to test operating effectiveness. However, unless specifically required by the terms of the engagement, the auditor is not expressing an opinion on the control environment and information system. This is recognised in the auditor's report.

.49 ***The auditor should evaluate the design effectiveness of the control procedures based on the identified criteria.*** This evaluation would be based on whether the control procedures have been suitably designed to reduce to an acceptably low level, the risks that threaten achievement of the objectives relevant to the area of activity. Where the auditor is unable to identify control procedures designed to provide reasonable assurance about the reduction of risk, this would constitute a weakness in relation to design effectiveness.

.50 Where, in the auditor's opinion, a material weakness exists which has extreme implications in relation to design effectiveness, the auditor would consider issuing a modified report without performing any tests of operating effectiveness. In such situations, an adverse opinion would ordinarily be appropriate.

.51 Control consists of a number of integrated processes directed at the achievement of objectives. Some controls may have a pervasive effect on achieving many overall objectives, whereas others are designed with a particular objective in mind. Because of the pervasive nature of some controls, the auditor may often find several control procedures that affect the risks relevant to a particular objective. Consequently, where the auditor evaluates a control procedure as being ineffective for a particular objective the auditor would not, on this basis alone, conclude that a material weakness exists. Where a control procedure has been evaluated as ineffective however, the auditor will need to consider the effect of this evaluation on other control procedures.

Testing Operating Effectiveness

.52 ***The auditor should perform tests to obtain sufficient appropriate evidence about whether the control procedures are operating as contemplated in the evaluation of design effectiveness.*** Tests of operating effectiveness are concerned with how the control procedures were applied, the consistency with which they were applied, and by whom they were applied. The auditor would also need to consider the period of time over which the control procedures were applied. These tests ordinarily include procedures such as inquiry of appropriate personnel, inspection of relevant documentation, observation of the entity's operations, and:

(a) for an audit, detailed procedures to substantiate the effective operation of control procedures. Detailed procedures will include reperformance or other examination and follow-up of the application of significant control procedures; or

(b) for a review, inspection of the control procedures in operation for deviations from the specified design. This may involve observation of, and enquiring about the operation of the control procedures for a small number of transactions or events.

.53 The auditor's evaluation of the design effectiveness of control procedures often influences the nature, timing and extent of tests of operating effectiveness.

.54 The nature of a control procedure often influences the nature of tests of operating effectiveness that can be performed. For example, the auditor may examine evidence regarding control where such evidence exists, however documentary evidence regarding some control procedures often does not exist. In these circumstances, the tests of operating effectiveness may consist of inquiry and observation only. As such controls may operate only because of inquiry and observation and may not operate at other times during the period, the auditor would, in conjunction with those procedures, seek to obtain other supporting evidence by looking to the outcomes from the system, for example substantive testing of the accuracy of the information over which the controls operate.

.55 The decision about what comprises sufficient appropriate audit evidence is a matter of professional judgement. The auditor would consider for example:

(a) the nature of the area of activity;

(b) the significance of the control procedure in achieving the relevant objective(s);

(c) the nature and extent of any tests of operating effectiveness performed by the entity (management, internal auditing or other personnel); and

(d) the likelihood that the control procedure will not reduce to an acceptably low level the risks relevant to the objective(s). This may involve consideration of:

(i) the design effectiveness of the internal control;

(ii) changes in the volume or nature of transactions that might affect design or operating effectiveness (for example, an increase in the volume of transactions may make it tedious to identify and correct errors thus creating a disincentive to perform the control among entity personnel);

(iii) whether there have been any changes in the control procedure (personnel may not be aware of the change or may not understand the way it operates thus inhibiting effective implementation);

(iv) the interdependence of the control procedure upon other controls (for example the design of control procedures associated with the cash receipts function may be assessed as effective however their operating effectiveness may be poor due to a lack of segregation of duties);

(v) changes in key personnel who perform the control procedure or monitor its performance (this may result in insufficient knowledge about how the control should operate);

(vi) whether the control procedure is manual or computerised and the significance of the information system's general controls (manual controls may allow a greater degree of override in a weak control environment, whereas adequately tested computer controls will consistently perform a function based on agreed specifications);

(vii) the complexity of the control procedure (a complex procedure may promote non compliance if personnel are not adequately trained in the operation of the procedure);

(viii) whether more than one control procedure achieves the same objective (the assessment of a procedure as ineffective would not necessarily preclude its objective from being achieved as other procedures that are pervasive in nature may address this objective); and

(ix) whether there have been any changes in the processes adopted by an entity (for example, a change in a process may render a particular control procedure ineffective).

.56 Management, internal auditing or other entity personnel may provide the auditor with the results of their tests of the operating effectiveness of certain aspects of internal control. Although the auditor would consider the results of such tests when evaluating operating effectiveness, it is the auditor's responsibility to obtain sufficient appropriate evidence to support the auditor's opinion and, if appropriate, corroborate the results of such tests. When evaluating whether sufficient appropriate evidence has been obtained, the auditor would consider that evidence obtained through direct personal knowledge, observation, reperformance, and inspection is more persuasive than information obtained indirectly, such as from management, internal auditing or other entity personnel. Further, judgements about the sufficiency and appropriateness of evidence obtained and other factors affecting the auditor's opinion, such as the significance of identified control weaknesses, should be those of the auditor.

Period of Testing

Current System

.57 Where the terms of the engagement require an opinion on the current control procedures only, that is the system in place at reporting date, the period of time over which the auditor would perform tests of operating effectiveness is a matter of judgement. This may vary with the nature of the control being tested and also with the frequency with which the procedures operate. Some procedures operate continuously, for example, in relation to sales, while others operate only at particular times, for example, procedure in relation to physical inventory counts. ***The tests of operating effectiveness should be performed over a period of time that is adequate to determine that the control procedures are operating effectively.***

.58 Where control procedures have changed during the period subject to examination, the auditor would need to consider whether the new control procedures have been in place for a sufficient period to assess their effectiveness.

Extended Period

.59 When the auditor is reporting in relation to an extended period of time, for example a full year, the auditor will need to consider whether the control procedures currently in use were in use throughout the period. If substantially different control procedures were used at different times during the period, the auditor would consider each separately.

Management's Representations

.60 ***The auditor should obtain evidence that management acknowledges its responsibility for establishing and maintaining the entity's internal control structure.*** This may be in the form of a published assertion or obtained from relevant minutes of meetings or by obtaining a written representation from management.

Subsequent Events

.61 ***The auditor should perform procedures designed to provide sufficient appropriate evidence that all matters up to the date of the auditor's report that may impact upon the conclusion about the effectiveness of the internal control procedures have been***

AUS

identified. This does not require an extension of the detailed audit procedures on which the initial conclusion was based at the specified date or period end. The procedures are limited to review of relevant reports, for example reports on control procedures, minutes of relevant committees and inquiry of management or other personnel as to significant non-compliance with control procedures.

.62 The matters identified may:

(a) provide additional evidence or reveal for the first time conditions that existed during the period on which the auditor is reporting; or

(b) provide evidence about conditions that existed subsequent to the period on which the auditor is reporting that may significantly affect the operation of the control procedures.

.63 In the circumstances described in paragraph .62(a), the auditor would reassess any conclusions previously formed that are likely to be affected by the additional evidence obtained.

.64 In the circumstances described in paragraph .62(b) when the auditor's report has not already been issued:

(a) in an attest engagement, the auditor would:

(i) include an emphasis of matter where the report by management adequately discloses the subsequent event; or

(ii) issue a qualified opinion if the report by management does not adequately disclose the subsequent event; and

(b) in a direct reporting engagement, the auditor would include as part of the description of facts and findings a section headed "Subsequent Events" describing the events and indicating they may affect the future effectiveness of the control procedures.

.65 The auditor does not have any responsibility to perform procedures or make any inquiry after the date of the report. If however, after the date of the report, the auditor becomes aware of a matter identified in paragraph .62(a), the auditor would consider re-issuing the report. In an attest engagement where the report has already been issued, the new report would include an emphasis of matter discussing the reason for the new report. In a direct reporting engagement, the new report would discuss the reason for the new report in the description of facts and findings section under a heading "Subsequent Events".

Conclusions and Reporting

.66 ***The auditor should review and assess the conclusions drawn from the evidence obtained as the basis for forming an opinion on the effectiveness of the control procedures based on the identified criteria.***

.67 ***An auditor's report about the effectiveness of control procedures should include the following:***

(a) the title;

(b) the addressee;

(c) a description of the scope of the audit, including:

(i) an identification or description of the area of activity;

(ii) the criteria used as a basis for the auditor's conclusion; and

(iii) a statement that the maintenance of an effective internal control structure, including control procedures for the area of activity, is the responsibility of management;

(d) where the engagement is an attest engagement, a statement identifying the source of managements representation about the effectiveness of control procedures;

(e) a statement that the auditor has conducted the engagement in order to express an opinion on the effectiveness of control procedures;

(f) an identification of the purpose for which the auditor's report has been prepared and of those entitled to rely on it, and a disclaimer of liability for its use for any other purpose or by any other person;

- (g) *a description of the criteria or disclosure of the source of the criteria;*
- (h) *a statement that the audit has been conducted in accordance with Australian Auditing Standards;*
- (i) *in rare and exceptional circumstances, when a departure from a basic principle or essential procedure may be necessary, as indicated in Miscellaneous Professional Statements APS 1.1 "Conformity with Auditing Standards", the statement required under paragraph (h) should provide details of the particular basic principle(s) or essential procedure(s) that has been departed from together with the justification for the departure;*
- (j) *further explanatory details about the variables that affect the assurance provided and other information as appropriate;*
- (k) *a paragraph section headed "Inherent Limitations" stating that:*
  - (i) *because of inherent limitations in any internal control structure, it is possible that fraud, error, or non-compliance with laws and regulations may occur and not be detected. Further, the internal control structure, within which the control procedures that have been audited operate, has not been audited and no opinion is expressed as to its effectiveness;*
  - (ii) *an audit is not designed to detect all weaknesses in control procedures as it is not performed continuously throughout the period and the tests performed on the control procedures are on a sample basis; and*
  - (iii) *any projection of the evaluation of the control procedures to future periods is subject to the risk that the procedures may become inadequate because of changes in conditions, or that the degree of compliance with them may deteriorate;*
- (l) *when the auditor's opinion is qualified, a section headed "Qualification" which clearly describes the qualification;*
- (m) *an expression of opinion about whether, in all material respects and based on the identified criteria, the design and operation of control procedures in relation to the area of activity were effective;*
- (n) *the auditor's signature;*
- (o) *the auditor's address; and*
- (p) *the date of the auditor's report.*

.68 Where the auditor undertakes a review engagement, the reporting principles in AUS 902.33 are to be adopted and applied. The report indicates that the auditor's conclusion relates to design and operating effectiveness, and that the auditor's work in relation to operating effectiveness was limited primarily to inquiries, inspection and minimal testing of the operation of the internal controls. The report includes a statement that an audit has not been performed, that the procedures undertaken provide less assurance than an audit and that an audit opinion is not expressed. The expression of negative assurance states that nothing has come to the auditor's attention that cause the auditor to believe the entity's control procedures were, in any material respect, ineffective in relation to the area of activity, based on the identified criteria.

.69 In addition, the auditor may expand the report to include other information not intended as a qualification of the auditor's opinion or statement. For example, a description of the facts and findings relating to particular aspects of the engagement recommendations about identified control weaknesses and control weaknesses not considered significant because the cost of control exceeds the benefit. When considering whether to include any such information the auditor assesses the materiality of that information in the context of the objectives of the engagement. Additional information is not to be worded in such a manner that it may be regarded as a qualification of the auditor's opinion or statement.

.70 If the criteria are adequately described in a source that is readily accessible to the addressee of the auditor's report, the auditor may identify those criteria by reference, rather than by repetition of the description in the auditor's report or an appendix to the report.

AUS

For example, if the criteria are published and generally available, or if they are detailed in an engagement letter.

Modifications to the Auditor's Report

.71 ***The auditor's report should be modified as indicated in the following table.*** This table lists the circumstances in which a modified report would be issued and the type of opinion appropriate in the circumstances:

	Material but not extreme	Extreme
Scope limitation	"except for"	inability to form an opinion
Control weakness	"except for"[2]	adverse
Unsuitable criteria		
• Contractual mandate	No report (withdraw from engagement)	No report (withdraw from engagement)
• Legislative mandate	"except for"	adverse
Subsequent Events Attest Report		
• Inadequate Disclosure	"except for"	"adverse"

[An emphasis of matter would be used in the circumstances described in paragraph .64(a)(i).]

.72 In a modified auditor's report, reference would be made to all relevant matters. For example, a qualification on one matter would not be regarded as a reason for omitting other, perhaps unrelated, qualifications which otherwise would have been reported.

Scope Limitation

.73 A limitation on the scope of the auditor's work may be imposed by the terms of the engagement or by the circumstances of the particular engagement. ***When the limitation is imposed by the terms of the engagement, and the auditor believes that an inability to form an opinion would need to be expressed, the engagement should not be accepted or continued past the current period.***

.74 ***When a scope limitation is imposed by the circumstances of the particular engagement, the auditor should attempt to perform reasonable alternative procedures to overcome the limitation. When a scope limitation exists, the wording of the auditor's opinion should indicate that it is qualified as to the effects of any significant weakness that might have been identified had the limitation not existed.***

.75 Where a material weakness exists, the auditor will not be able to conclude that control procedures are effective. The type of report to be issued by the auditor will be determined by the significance of the weakness.

.76 The duty of the auditor is to convey information, not merely arouse inquiry. ***Whenever the auditor expresses a qualified opinion, the auditor's report should include a clear description of all the substantive reasons therefor, and:***

(a) a description of the effect of all identified matters on the residual risk of not achieving relevant objectives; or

(b) if the auditor is unable to reliably determine the effect of a matter, a statement to that effect and the reasons therefor.

Unsuitable Criteria – Legislative Mandate

.77 ***When the auditor's report is qualified as required by paragraph .45(b), it should:***

(a) state that in the auditor's opinion the criteria are unsuitable;

(b) explain the reasons why the auditor believes the criteria are unsuitable.

---

2 In an attest reporting engagement where the auditor's opinion is to be expressed in terms of an opinion about management's assertion, and management adequately identify the weakness in their assertion, an unqualified opinion with an emphasis of matter would be appropriate.

Reporting to Management

.78 During the course of the engagement the auditor may become aware of control weaknesses. ***The auditor should report to an appropriate level of management on a timely basis any identified control weaknesses.*** The engagement procedures are designed to gather sufficient appropriate evidence to form a conclusion in accordance with the terms of the engagement. In the absence of a specific requirement in the terms of engagement the auditor does not have a responsibility to design procedures to identify matters that may be appropriate to report to management.

.79 Certain matters may be of such importance that they would be reported to the audit committee or the governing body of the entity. Unless stated otherwise in the terms of engagement, less important matters would be reported to a level of management that has the authority to take appropriate action.

Operative Date

.80 This AUS, which incorporates amendments made by AUS/AGS Omnibus 3 "Miscellaneous Amendments to AUSs and AGSs", is operative from July 2002. This version of AUS 810 supersedes AUS 810 "Special Purpose Reports on the Effectiveness of Control Procedures", as revised in May 1999.

Compatibility with International Standards on Auditing

.81 There is no corresponding International Auditing Standard.

Appendix 1

Examples of Audit Reports

Example 1: Unqualified Attest Report [In the form of an opinion about the effectiveness of the control procedures themselves – refer paragraph .05]

Independent Audit Report

To *addressee*

Scope

We have audited [name of entity] control procedures in relation to [area of activity] [as at/for the period] ended [date] in order to express an opinion about their effectiveness based on [describe or identify criteria].

[The area of activity and the criteria would be identified either:

(a) by cross-reference to an accessible source, for example an engagement letter; or

(b) described in full here or in another place in the report. If a detailed description is appropriate to the circumstances of the engagement, it may be appropriate to include details under separate headings or as attachments.]

The [members of the governing body] are responsible for maintaining an effective internal control structure including control procedures in relation to [area of activity]. Management's assertion about the effectiveness of these control procedures is included in the accompanying report [title of report]. We have conducted an independent audit of the control procedures in order to express an opinion on them to [addressee].

Our audit has been conducted in accordance with Australian Auditing Standard AUS 810 "Special Purpose Reports on the Effectiveness of Control Procedures" and accordingly included such tests and procedures as we considered necessary in the circumstances. These procedures have been undertaken to form an opinion whether in all material respects, the control procedures in relation to [area of activity] were adequately designed and operated effectively based on the criteria referred to above.

This report has been prepared for distribution to [addressee] for the purpose of [explain purpose]. We disclaim any assumption of responsibility for any reliance on this report to any person other than [addressee], or for any purpose other than that for which it was prepared.

Inherent Limitations

Because of the inherent limitations of any internal control structure it is possible that fraud, error, or non-compliance with laws and regulations may occur and not be detected. Further, the internal control structure, within which the control procedures that we have audited operate, has not been audited and no opinion is expressed as to its effectiveness.

An audit is not designed to detect all weaknesses in control procedures as it is not performed continuously throughout the period and the tests performed are on a sample basis.

Any projection of the evaluation of control procedures to future periods is subject to the risk that the procedures may become inadequate because of changes in conditions, or that the degree of compliance with them may deteriorate.

The audit opinion expressed in this report has been formed on the above basis.

Findings [or other appropriate heading or headings]

[Additional details per paragraphs .67(j) and .69 as appropriate]

Audit Opinion

In our opinion, [name of entity] maintained, in all material respects, effective control procedures in relation to [area of activity] [as at/for the period] ended [date] based on the criteria referred to above.

Date	Firm
Address	Partner

Example 2: Unqualified Attest Report [In the form of an opinion on managements assertion about the effectiveness of the control procedures – refer paragraph .05]

Independent Audit Report

To *addressee*

Scope

We have audited the assertions made by [governing body of other appropriate party] which are contained in [identify report and report date] that the [name of entity] control procedures in relation to [area of activity] [as at/for the period] ended [date] are effective based on [describe or identify criteria].

[The area of activity and the criteria would be identified either:

(a) by cross-reference to an accessible source, for example an engagement letter; or

(b) described in full here or in another place in the report. If a detailed description is appropriate to include details under separate headings or as attachments.]

The [members of the governing body] are responsible for maintaining an effective internal control structure including control procedures in relation to [area of activity]. We have conducted an independent audit in order to express an opinion on the assertions by [governing body or other appropriate party] to [addressee].

Our audit has been conducted in accordance with Australian Auditing Standard AUS 810 "Special Purpose Reports on the Effectiveness of Control Procedures" and accordingly included such tests and procedures as we considered necessary in the circumstances. These procedures have been undertaken to form an opinion whether in all material respects, the control procedures in relation to [area of activity] were adequately designed and operated effectively based on the criteria referred to above in order to support our opinion on the assertions contained in the [report of the governing body or other appropriate party] [date].

This report has been prepared for distribution to [addressee] for the purpose of [explain purpose]. We disclaim any assumption of responsibility for any reliance on this report to any person other than [addressee], or for any purpose other than that for which it was prepared.

Inherent Limitations

Because of the inherent limitations of any internal control structure it is possible that fraud, error, or non-compliance with laws and regulations may occur and not be detected. Further, the internal control structure, within which the control procedures that we have audited operate, has not been audited and no opinion is expressed as to its effectiveness.

An audit is not designed to detect all weaknesses in control procedures as it is not performed continuously throughout the period and the tests performed are on a sample basis.

Any projection of the evaluation of control procedures to future periods is subject to the risk that the procedures may become inadequate because of changes in conditions, or that the degree of compliance with them may deteriorate.

The audit opinion expressed in this report has been formed on the above basis.

Findings [or other appropriate heading or headings]

[Additional details per paragraphs .67(j) and .69 as appropriate]

Audit Opinion

In our opinion, the assertion by the [governing body] that [name of entity] [has/has not] maintained, in all material respects, effective control procedures in relation to the [area of activity] [as at/for the period] ended [date] based on the criteria referred to above, is fairly stated.

Date Firm

Address Partner

Example 3: Unqualified Direct Report

A direct report would be the same as the attest report except that the following sentence would be deleted from the first paragraph of the "Scope" section in Example 1:

> "Management's assertion about the effectiveness of the internal controls in relation to [area of activity] is included in the accompanying report [title of report]".

Example 4: Modified Audit Report – Material, but not extreme, control weakness identified

The following qualification section and opinion section would be used in Example 1:

Qualification

Our evaluation of the design of the internal controls identified a material weakness in relation to control procedures in the [area of activity]. [Give details.] The effect of this design weakness is that the entity did not have reasonable assurance that the [specific objective] was being consistently achieved.

Further, our tests of operating effectiveness identified that the control procedures designed to ensure achievement of [specific objective] were not operating effectively. [Give details.] The entity could not therefore have had reasonable assurance that the [specific objective] was consistently achieved. (While management has taken steps to overcome this weakness [give details], the revised procedures have not been in place for a sufficient period for us to evaluate their effectiveness.)

Qualified Audit Opinion

In our opinion, except for the matters referred to in the qualification section, [name of entity] maintained, in all material respects, effective control procedures in relation to [area of activity] [as at/for the period] ended [date] based on the criteria referred to above.

Example 5: Modified Audit Report – Material, but not extreme, control weakness identified that was corrected during the period (extended period reporting only)

The following qualification section and opinion section would be used in Example 1:

Qualification

Our tests of operating effectiveness identified that the control procedures designed to ensure achievement of [specific objective] were not operating effectively during the period [... to ...].

[Give details]. The entity could not therefore have had reasonable assurance that this objective was consistently achieved. Action taken by management rectified this situation as of [date].

Qualified Audit Opinion

In our opinion, except for the matter referred to in the qualification section, [name of entity] maintained, in all material respects, effective control procedures in relation to [area of activity] for the [period] ended [date] based on the criteria referred to above.

Example 6: Unqualified Direct Review Report

Independent Review Report

To *addressee*

Scope

We have reviewed [name of entity] control procedures in relation to [area of activity] [as at/for the period] ended [date]. The [members of the governing body] are responsible for maintaining an effective internal control structure including control procedures in relation to [area of activity]. We have conducted an independent review of the control procedures in order to state whether, on the basis of our examination as described, anything has come to our attention that would indicate that they are not adequately designed and effectively operated, in order to, based on [identify criteria].

[The area of activity and the criteria would be identified either:

(a) by cross-reference to an accessible source, for example an engagement letter; or

(b) described in full here or in another place in the report. If a detailed description is appropriate to the circumstances to the engagement, it may be appropriate to include details under separate headings or as attachments.]

Our review has been conducted in accordance with Australian Auditing Standards AUS 902 "Review of Financial Reports" and AUS 810 "Special Purpose Reports on the Effectiveness of Control Procedures. A review is limited primarily to inquiries of entity personnel, inspection of evidence and observation of, and enquiry about, the operation of the control procedures for a small number of transactions or events.

Inherent Limitations

Because of the inherent limitations of any internal control structure it is possible that fraud, error, or non-compliance with laws and regulations may occur and not be detected. Further, the internal control structure, within which the control procedures that we have reviewed operate, has not been reviewed and no view is expressed as to its effectiveness.

A review is not designed to detect all weaknesses in control procedures as it is not performed continuously throughout the period and the tests performed are on a sample basis. Also, a review does not provide all the evidence that would be required in an audit, thus the level of assurance provided is less than given in an audit. We have not performed an audit and, accordingly, we do not express an audit opinion.

Any projection of the evaluation of control procedures to future periods is subject to the risk that the procedures may become inadequate because of changes in conditions, or that the degree of compliance with them may deteriorate.

Findings (or other appropriate heading or headings)

[Additional details per paragraphs .67(j) and .69 as appropriate.]

Statement

Based on our review, which is not an audit, nothing has come to our attention that causes us to believe that [name of entity] did not maintain, in all significant respects, effective control procedures in relation to [area of activity] [as at/for the period] ended [date] based on the criteria referred to above.

Date	Firm
Address	Partner

Appendix 2

Examples of Significant Objectives, Risks Control Elements and Levels of Remaining Risks[1]

Objective 1	Objective 2	Objective 3
To comply with applicable laws and regulations	**To secure ongoing funding for program delivery**	**To provide services to all eligible citizens**
Significant risks related to these objectives		
• failure to identify applicable laws and regulations • failure to communicate applicable laws and regulations to staff • failure to promptly act on any instances of non-compliance of applicable laws and regulations	• failure to identify and cultivate new sources and means of funding • failure to manage the relations (communications, recognition, participation) with existing funders • increased competition for funding dollars	• the consequences of incorrectly refusing services to eligible citizens such as erosion of staff morale, loss of reputation with the community and funders, legal liability • the consequences of incorrectly providing services to ineligible citizens such as inefficient and ineffective use of limited resources, loss of reputation of the organisation with the community and funders, erosion of staff morale, loss of not-for-profit status

1 Example based on material relating to a not-for-profit organisation adapted from the Canadian Institute of Chartered Accountants Criteria of Control Board "Guidance on Assessing Control – The CoCo Principles", June 1997.

AUS

Objective 1 To comply with applicable laws and regulations	Objective 2 To secure ongoing funding for program delivery	Objective 3 To provide services to all eligible citizens
Key elements of control to manage these risks		
• ongoing monthly review of industry publications to identify applicable laws and regulations • yearly discussion with the organisation's legal counsel • weekly staff meetings which provide an opportunity to discuss applicable laws and regulations, compliance with laws and regulations and to deal with the consequences of non-compliance • requirements in code of conduct to comply with applicable laws and regulations and to report any instances of non-compliance to the chief executive officers • organisational culture that encourages and rewards timely communication about "bad news"	• employment of a fundraising professional • development and approval by the board of directors of a three year fundraising plan • monthly reviews of fundraising results to date and projections for the next twelve months • semi-annual meetings with major funders • diversification of fundraising sources • a funders recognition program	• development of eligibility criteria for providing services which were approved by the board of directors • shared values within the organisation about mission of the organisation and the need to serve the community • training for staff to learn how to apply the criteria and approve eligibility • weekly reporting and analysis of the number of citizens receiving service and refused service • monitoring of a "complaints" program for people who were refused service

1 Example based on material relating to a not-for-profit organisation adapted from the Canadian Institute of Chartered Accountants Criteria of Control Board "Guidance on Assessing Control – The CoCo Principles", June 1997.

AGS 1014

Privity Letter Requests

(As amended July 2002)

Prepared by the Auditing and Assurance Standards Board of the Australian Accounting Research Foundation.

Issued by the Australian Accounting Research Foundation on behalf of CPA Australia and The Institute of Chartered Accountants in Australia.

Note from the Institute of Chartered Accountants Australia

This note, prepared by the technical editor, is not part of AGS 1014.

Historical development

July 1991: Auditing Guidance Release AUG 9 'Privity Letter Requests' issued by the AuASB.

October 1995: Australian Auditing Standards and Auditing Guidance Statements released. The status of the guidance is explained in APS 1.1 'Conformity with Auditing Standards'. These Standards became operative for the first reporting period commencing on or after 1 July 1996 and later reporting periods, although earlier application was encouraged. AUG 9 'Privity Letter Requests' replaced by AGS 1014 'Privity Letter Requests'.

February 1998: AGS 1014 'Privity Letter Requests' issued by the AuASB.

February 1999: AUS/AGS Omnibus 2 'Miscellaneous Amendments to AUSs and AGSs' issued by the AuASB, operative from date of issue.

July 2002: AUS/AGS Omnibus 3 'Miscellaneous Amendments to AUSs and AGSs' issued by the AuASB. AGS 1014 since reissued by the Board to incorporate these amendments, operative from the date of issue.

AGS

Contents

Paragraph

Auditing Guidance Statement AGS 1014

Privity Letter Requests

Introduction

.01 This auditing guidance statement relates to circumstances where third parties such as investors, lenders or providers of goods or services seek reliance on a general purpose financial report.

.02 The English decision in *Caparo Industries PLC v Dickman & Others* [1990] established that an auditor's statutory duty to audit and report an opinion on a company's financial report is owed to the body of shareholders as a whole and not to shareholders or potential shareholders acting as individuals or as groups of individuals. Furthermore, no duty of care is owed to a third party unless, at the time the audit report is prepared, the auditor had knowledge of the third party and knew, or should reasonably have known, that the audited financial report would be shown to and relied upon by the third party and the particular purpose for which the third party intended to place reliance on the audited financial report. The Australian High Court judgment in *Esanda Finance Corporation Limited v Peat Marwick Hungerford* [1997] 142 ALR 750 is consistent with the *Caparo* decision in its approach to the circumstances in which an auditor may be found liable to a third party.

.03 In Australia the common law concerning the nature and extent of an auditor's duty of care to third parties remains complex as judgments contain differences of judicial opinion and interpretation. However, the judgment in *Esanda* was a positive development for auditors because the court rejected the contention that liability could be based on foreseeability of reliance alone. The High Court found that there had to be circumstances establishing a relationship of proximity between the auditor and the third party before a duty of care could be said to exist. This indicates that the auditor has to come into a real relationship with the third party for liability to arise rather than just knowledge of the third party's existence as a theoretical possibility.

.04 However, even after *Esanda*, it remains difficult to predict exactly what conduct or circumstance will expose auditors to this risk of undue reliance. The High Court did not establish a single definitive test since the individual judgments described various possibilities. The position is also complicated because third party liability is part of the law of negligence, which is still evolving. The applicability of the Esanda judgment may also be affected by the legislation under which the audit is performed, the terms of the audit engagement and the audit report itself.

.05 Situations may arise where a third party seeks a letter from the auditor in which the auditor is requested to acknowledge that the third party intends to rely on an audited financial report. In this way the third party is seeking to establish a relationship with the auditor, with the required foreseeability and proximity, which would give rise to a duty of care by the auditor to the third party. These letters are commonly referred to as "privity", "reliance" or "comfort" letters. The term "privity letters" is used in this Guidance Statement.

.06 The purpose of this Guidance Statement is to alert auditors to the risks associated with a privity letter request and to provide guidance to reduce the risk of undue reliance on the auditor's report in specific circumstances. The Auditing and Assurance Standards Board is not advising on the application of the *Esanda* judgment, and any decision by an auditor as to how to respond to a privity letter request is to be made by that auditor after consideration of the risks involved in giving such acknowledgment. An auditor will exercise judgment whether an acknowledgment of facts giving rise to a duty of care is appropriate in the circumstances or whether a separate engagement would be necessary to meet the needs of the third party making the request.

Request from Third Party

.07 Requests for a privity letter may arise in various circumstances seeking comfort for different purposes. For example:

(a) the auditor is requested to acknowledge and accept in writing the third party's intention to rely on a general purpose financial report and the auditor's report thereon;

(b) the request relates to a transaction(s) planned either prior to or subsequent to the issue of the general purpose financial report and auditor's report thereon, about which the auditor has not had any knowledge in planning and performing the audit;

(c) in respect of debt transactions, the period of intended reliance may extend to the period over which the debt is repaid, and reference may be made to the lender's concern regarding compliance with the terms and conditions of the planned agreement.

.08 Requests from a third party are of concern to the auditor because:

(a) there are inherent limitations in any financial report. A financial report presents an entity's state of affairs only at balance sheet date. A financial report presents an historical view of the entity's results for the period and must be interpreted having careful regard to the underlying accounting policies. Furthermore, a financial report may not reflect items considered to be immaterial and certain revenues, expenses, assets and liabilities, for which no precise means of measurement exist, may be included on the basis of the directors'/managements' best estimates. The only events occurring after balance date taken into account are those which impact on the financial report in accordance with AAS 8 and AASB 1002 "Events Occurring After Reporting Date". While a financial report is normally prepared on a going concern basis, it does not give any indication of the level of future profitability or cash flows of the business;

(b) there are inherent limitations in the audit of a financial report. An audit provides reasonable, but not absolute assurance that the financial report is free of material misstatement. The auditor exercises a significant level of professional judgment on such issues as materiality and audit risk, the application of procedures on a test basis, the evaluation of management's accounting estimates and the ability to rely on management's internal control structure. The auditor's consideration of subsequent events and going concern assumptions are in accordance with AUS 706 "Subsequent Events" and AUS 708 "Going Concern". The audit of a general purpose financial report does not extend to confirmation of future profitability or cash flows – matters which may be significant to a third party seeking to place reliance on the financial report;

(c) the auditor may lack knowledge of the third party's specific needs. The audit of a financial report may not be planned or performed for the benefit of, or to take into account the special needs of the third party who may wish to rely on the audited financial report for a specific decision(s). At the time of the audit, the auditor is often not aware of a third party's decision to enter into a transaction or their specific needs. The auditor may not, therefore, give consideration to procedures which might otherwise be considered necessary and appropriate;

(d) a third party may be substituting reliance on the audited financial report for assurance which should be obtained from the third party carrying out its own due diligence and monitoring procedures. It would be a reasonable expectation to assume that an experienced third party would have a degree of business experience and sophistication to properly assess the risks of entering into a particular transaction using information from various sources. Furthermore, once that transaction has occurred, the third party should carry out procedures to monitor the position of the investee/borrower; and

(e) in certain circumstances, the period of intended reliance by a lender, for example, may extend to the entire period during which the debt is outstanding. While the auditor may be aware of this transaction during subsequent audits, special procedures over and above those necessary for the audit of the borrower's financial reports may be necessary to address all the lender's concerns, for example in relation to debt covenants. This may require a separate engagement to address the lender's specific requirements.

The Auditor's Position

.09 Before responding to a request, the auditor makes appropriate inquiries of management, for example, to ascertain whether the third party is seeking to rely on the audited financial report in relation to an unspecified or specified transaction(s), and considers carefully all the circumstances relating to the request, for example, whether the request is received before or after signing the audit report. The auditor also considers taking legal advice before responding to the request.

.10 The effectiveness of any form of response containing a disclaimer in restricting responsibility or liability with respect to a statutory duty is uncertain. It is likely that disclaimers of responsibility to third parties will only be upheld by a court where they are reasonable in all circumstances. Therefore, the auditor's response to the third party clearly states the reasons why the auditor is not assuming responsibility to the third party. The auditor continues to behave consistently with that disclaimer. If a third party has evidence to support an allegation that an auditor's conduct was misleading and deceptive, in breach of Section 52 of the Trade Practices Act or its equivalent section in the various State Fair Trading Acts, then the existence of a disclaimer will not of itself, protect the auditor.

The Auditor's Response

.11 In view of the circumstances associated with a request for a privity letter and the audit concerns noted, unless an auditor intends to accept responsibility to a third party, an auditor responds unequivocally to a request for a privity letter stating that the body of shareholders is the only group entitled to rely on the audit report. Additional reasons are given to state why it is unreasonable for the third party to rely on the audit report as appropriate. Failure to decline responsibility to a third party presents a risk of responsibility being established if silence is taken as agreement. A copy of the response is sent to the auditee to ensure that the auditor, third party and auditee have a common understanding of the context in which the auditor's report on the financial statements is issued.

.12 The form of the auditor's response should reflect the circumstances of the request. The following guidance indicates the form of response possible for the circumstances indicated:

(a) where the proposed reliance by the third party is not for a specific purpose, the auditor responds by declining to accept responsibility to the third party (refer Appendix 1);

(b) where the proposed reliance by the third party is in relation to a specific transaction, the auditor responds by declining to accept responsibility (refer Appendix 2), unless the auditor intends to extend the duty of care to the third party, or the relationship between the auditor and the third party is such that a duty of care may already exist. If the auditor intends to extend the duty of care, or where the duty of care may already exist in the particular circumstances, the auditor responds by acknowledging a responsibility to the third party, but emphasising that such acknowledgment is confined to the context and scope of the financial report audit (refer Appendix 3).

.13 Irrespective of the effectiveness of any disclaimer of responsibility that an auditor may issue, a duty of care may result from the auditor's knowledge of the specific purpose for which the financial report is to be used. For example, the auditor would be expected to be aware a lender is placing reliance on the audited financial report where an unqualified audit report and a new loan facility agreement are signed contemporaneously, and the auditor has been informed that the former is a condition precedent of the latter.

.14 Where the auditor acknowledges a responsibility to a specific third party, the nature and scope of the duty of care will depend on the circumstances of the particular case, and may impose on the auditor a continuing obligation to advise the third party of events occurring after the date of the audit report. For example, having assumed a duty of care to a lender, the auditor may be under an obligation to advise the lender of a change in circumstances arising after the audit report is signed where the auditor is aware the lender intends taking further action, such as extending the loan facility, in reliance on the audit report.

.15 If a specific third party requires assurance from the auditor on matters outside the normal audit scope, for example, on the adequacy of the entity's internal control structure, the efficiency of management, or on other matters in which the third party may be primarily interested for its own specific needs, this should be the subject of a separate engagement between the auditee and the auditor.

.16 Before entering into a separate engagement to meet the specific needs of a third party, an auditor carefully considers the position in light of any potential conflict of interest with respect to the auditor's duties and responsibilities under the original audit engagement. The auditor obtains the consent of the management of the auditee to undertake the engagement. Such an engagement is separate from, for example, the audit of a financial report under the *Corporations Act 2001*, and is the subject of a separate engagement letter and separate fee arrangements with the parties for which the engagement is carried out.

Representations from the Third Party

.17 In situations where the auditor intends to acknowledge a responsibility, the auditor obtains a written representation from the third party stating that:

(a) the third party is aware of the nature and scope of the audit as explained in the audit engagement letter;

(b) the third party acknowledges that the audit will not be specifically planned for the specific benefit of the third party and will not necessarily address the third party's needs;

(c) the third party is a sophisticated investor/lender/provider of goods/services and will diligently perform their own inquiries, with due care, in connection with the transaction; and

(d) if the third party enters into the transaction, it will subsequently perform its own on-going monitoring activities.

This representation is obtained prior to issuing a privity letter and, once obtained, a copy should be forwarded to the auditee. Appendix 4 provides an example third party representation letter.

.18 If the third party refuses to provide the required representation, the auditor refuses to issue a privity letter and declines responsibility (refer Appendix 2).

Operative Date

.19 This AGS, which incorporates amendments made by AUS/AGS Omnibus 3 "Miscellaneous Amendments to AUSs and AGSs", is operative from July 2002. This version of AGS 1014 supersedes AGS 1014 "Privity Letter Requests", as revised in February 1999.

Compatibility with International Standards and Statements on Auditing

.20 There is no corresponding International Standard or Statement on Auditing.

Appendix 1

Example Letter for Declining Responsibility to a Third Party Seeking General Reliance on an Audited General Purpose Financial Report and Auditor's Report Thereon

The letter contained in this appendix is for an auditor engaged to report on a company financial report and is for the purpose of illustration only. It should be amended as appropriate to suit individual circumstances.

ABC Limited

(Third Party)

Dear ...

XYZ Limited (Auditee)

We acknowledge receipt of your letter of [date].

As the statutory auditor of [Company], we were appointed by the shareholders to perform an audit and report to them. The objective of our audit is to form an opinion whether the financial report, the preparation and presentation of which is the responsibility of the directors of the company, is in accordance with the *Corporations Act 2001*, including: giving a true and fair view of the company's [and consolidated entity's] financial position as at [date] and of its [their] performance for the period ended on that date; and complying with Accounting Standards and the Corporations Regulations; and other mandatory professional reporting requirements. Our audit was planned and performed for this purpose only and should not be relied upon for any other purpose.

Your proposed reliance on the financial report of [Company] is for the purpose of unspecified transactions and for an indefinite period of time. We do not know what factors you regard as being significant in relation to the transaction(s) which you envisage undertaking [and any future monitoring thereof]. Therefore our audit of the financial report prepared in accordance with statutory requirements has not necessarily addressed (will not necessarily address) such factors. We therefore cannot issue any letter which assumes responsibility to you in respect of our audit opinion on which you could reasonably rely, and disclaim any assumption of responsibility for any reliance by you on the report or the financial report to which the report relates.

If [the third party] require us to investigate the affairs of [Company] for their particular purposes, we could do so, but only with the express consent of the directors of [Company] and within the relevant regulatory parameters. We would naturally charge a fee for any such services provided. We would also have to be satisfied that conducting a special engagement for the purpose of [the third party] will not create a conflict between our resulting duty to [the third party] and our duty to [Company] and its shareholders.

We also note that any report issued to [the third party] as a result of additional services provided would be issued solely for use by [the specific third party] and would not be suitable for distribution to or use by any other party.

Yours faithfully,

(Auditor)

NOTE: Items in brackets are for completion as required.

Appendix 2

Example Letter for Declining Responsibility to a Third Party Seeking Reliance on the General Purpose Financial Report and Auditor's Report Thereon in Relation to a Specific Transaction

The letter contained in this appendix is for an auditor engaged to report on a company financial report and is for the purpose of illustration only. It should be amended as appropriate to suit individual circumstances.

ABC Limited

(Third Party)

Dear ...

XYZ Limited (Auditee)

We acknowledge receipt of your letter of [date] in which you state your intention to rely on the audited financial report of [Company] for the [period] ended [date] and our report thereon [date] in connection with [describe transaction].

As the statutory auditor of [Company], we were appointed by the shareholders to perform an audit and report to them. The objective of our audit is to form an opinion whether the financial report, the preparation and presentation of which is the responsibility of the directors of the company, is in accordance with the *Corporations Act 2001*, including: giving a true and fair view of the company's [and consolidated entity's] financial position as at [date] and of its [their] performance for the period ended on that date; and complying with Accounting Standards and the Corporations Regulations; and other mandatory professional reporting requirements. Our audit was planned and performed for this purpose only and should not be relied upon for any other purpose.

We do not know what factors you regard as being significant in the transaction(s) which you envisage undertaking [and any future monitoring thereof]. Therefore our audit of the financial report prepared in accordance with statutory requirements has not necessarily addressed such factors. We therefore cannot issue any letter which assumes responsibility to you in respect of our audit opinion on which you could reasonably rely, and disclaim any assumption of responsibility for any reliance by you on the report or the financial report to which the report relates.

If [the third party] require us to investigate the affairs of [Company] for their particular purposes, we could do so, but only with the express consent of the directors of [Company] and within the relevant regulatory parameters. We would naturally charge a fee for any such services provided. We would also have to be satisfied that conducting a special engagement for the purpose of [the third party] will not create a conflict between our resulting duty to [the third party] and our duty to [Company] and its shareholders.

We also note that any report issued to [the third party] as a result of additional services provided would be issued solely for use by [the specific third party] and would not be suitable for distribution to or use by any other party.

Yours faithfully,

(Auditor)

NOTE: Items in brackets are for completion as required.

Appendix 3

Example Letter for Acknowledging Responsibility to a Third Party in Relation to a Specific Transaction within the Context of the Scope of a General Purpose Financial Report Audit

The letter contained in this appendix is for an auditor engaged to report on a company financial report and is for the purpose of illustration only. It should be amended as appropriate to suit individual circumstances.

ABC Limited

(Third Party)

Dear ...

XYZ Limited (Auditee)

We acknowledge receipt of your letter of [date].

We understand that you intend to use the audited financial report of [Company] for the year ended [date] and our report thereon in connection with a proposed [transaction/event] with the company. We also understand that [third party] is a sophisticated [investor/lender/provider of goods/services] in [identify business/industry].

As the statutory auditor of [Company], we were appointed by the shareholders to perform an audit and report to them. The objective of our audit is to form an opinion whether the financial report, the preparation and presentation of which is the responsibility of the directors of the company, is in accordance with the *Corporations Act 2001*, including: giving a true and fair view of the company's [and consolidated entity's] financial position as at [date] and of its [their] performance for the period ended on that date; and complying with Accounting Standards and the Corporations Regulations; and other mandatory professional reporting requirements. Our audit was planned and performed for this purpose only and should not be relied upon for any other purpose.

The financial report is not designed for the specific purpose for which [third party] wish to rely on it, nor do we have such a purpose in mind when carrying out our audit. Accordingly this firm, its partners and employees do not assume any additional responsibility to [the third party] or any other third party for our audit report and, without affecting the generality, we deny that by writing your above-mentioned letter you have imposed any obligation to take any special steps in the interest of [the third party] or any other third party.

Our audits are planned and performed in accordance with Australian Auditing Standards to provide reasonable assurance whether the financial report are free of material misstatement. The application of these professional standards requires judgment in the design, completion and evaluation of the results of our procedures. Those procedures include:

(i) examining, on a test basis, evidence supporting the amounts and other disclosures in the financial report;

(ii) the evaluation of the accounting policies and significant accounting estimates; and

(iii) forming an opinion whether, in all material respects, the financial report presents a view of the company which is consistent with our understanding of its operations.

Our audit is not designed to provide absolute assurance that there are no misstatements in the financial report resulting from fraud, irregularities or error, and the audit report does not represent any form of guarantee or warranty in that regard, nor is it a guarantee or prediction of the present or future performance or sagacity of management.

If [the third party] requires us to investigate the affairs of [Company] for their particular purposes, we could do so, but only with the express consent of the directors of [Company] and within the relevant regulatory parameters. We would naturally charge a fee for any such services provided. We would also have to be satisfied that conducting a special engagement for the purpose of [the third party] will not create a conflict between our resulting duty to [the third party] and our duty to the company and its shareholders.

We also note that any report issued to [the third party] as a result of additional services provided would be issued solely for use by [the specific third party] and would not be suitable for distribution to or use by any other party.

We also understand that [third party] will exercise due care to diligently obtain whatever information it feels is necessary to determine whether to undertake the proposed [specify transaction/event], and will monitor the future activities of [Company] on an on-going basis to the extent it deems necessary.

Information obtained by us during our audit cannot be disclosed by us to third parties such as [the third party] except pursuant to our statutory obligations or with the express consent of the company. That being so, may we suggest that any questions that [the third party] may have regarding the affairs of the company be referred to the company which will, if it sees fit, request us to respond.

This letter applies only to the financial report of [Company] for the year ended [date] and to [specify transaction/event]. Reliance relates only to the financial report as indicated as at the date of the audit report and cannot extend to events occurring after the date of that report.

Yours faithfully,

(Auditor)

NOTE: Items in brackets are for completion as required.

Appendix 4

Example Representation Letter from Third Party – Obtained Prior to Issue of a Privity Letter

The letter contained in this appendix is for an auditor engaged to report on a company financial report and is for the purpose of illustration only. It should be amended as appropriate to suit individual circumstances.

DEF

(Auditor)

Dear ...

XYZ Limited (Auditee)

In connection with [specify transaction/event] that we propose to enter into with [Company] you have agreed to provide us with a copy of the company's financial report for the year ended [date] together with the audit report thereon as well as a privity letter and a copy of a letter from the company indicating that they are aware of, and consent to, this action.

In making this request, we acknowledge:

(a) that we have read and understand the terms of the audit as explained in your engagement letter dated [date]; and

(b) in view of the terms of the audit engagement letter, that the audit was neither planned for the specific benefit of [third party] nor does it necessarily address our needs.

We also confirm that:

(a) [third party] is a sophisticated [investor/lender/provider of goods/services] and we will exercise due care to diligently obtain whatever information we believe is necessary to determine whether to undertake [specify transaction/event] and will not rely solely on your report on the financial report of [Company] for the year ended [date], and

(b) [third party] will monitor future activities of [Company] on an ongoing basis to the extent we deem necessary.

We also acknowledge that the letter which you will provide will apply only to the company's financial report for the year ended [date] and to [specify transaction/event].

Yours faithfully,

(Third Party)

NOTE: Items in brackets are for completion as required.

AGS

AGS 1062

Reporting in Connection with Proposed Fundraisings

(August 2002)

Prepared by the Auditing and Assurance Standards Board of the Australian Accounting Research Foundation.

Issued by the Australian Accounting Research Foundation on behalf of CPA Australia and The Institute of Chartered Accountants in Australia.

Note from the Institute of Chartered Accountants Australia

This note, prepared by the technical editor, is not part of AGS 1062.

Historical development

August 2002: AGS 1062 'Reporting in Connection with Proposed Fundraisings' issued by the AuASB. It has no international equivalents and was operative from the date of issue.

November 2012: The AUASB issued ASAE 3450 'Assurance Engagements involving Corporate Fundraisings and/or Prospective Financial Information', which will supersede AGS 1062 for engagements commencing on or after 1 July 2013.

Contents

Auditing Guidance Statement AGS 1062

Reporting in Connection with Proposed Fundraisings

Main Features

This Auditing and Assurance Guidance Statement (AGS):

(a) provides general guidance to auditors and other professional accountants on engagements in relation to fundraising, particularly those engagements regulated by *Chapter 6D* of the *Corporations Act 2001*;

(b) identifies the types of disclosure documents required under *Chapter 6D* of the *Corporations Act 2001*;

(c) outlines the responsibilities of management and the professional accountant in connection with *Chapter 6D* fundraising engagements; and

(d) provides guidance to the professional accountant when reporting on the engagement.

Introduction

.01 This Auditing and Assurance Guidance Statement (AGS) has been prepared by the Auditing & Assurance Standards Board (AuASB) to provide general guidance to auditors and other professional accountants (hereafter the professional accountant) on engagements in relation to fundraising that are regulated by the Australian Securities and Investments Commission (ASIC) and are subject to Chapter 6D provisions of the *Corporations Act 2001* (Cth) (the "Act"), and the provisions of the *Financial Services Reform Act 2001* (Cth) ("FSR Act")[1] that may be applicable. Fundraising involves offering securities for issue or for sale including inviting applications for the issue of the securities and inviting offers to purchase the securities. Fundraising offer documents may be required, for instance, when entities make initial and secondary public offerings, or when there are offers of interests in managed investment schemes.

.02 Audit and other assurance engagements relating to fundraising are required to adhere to the basic principles and essential procedures contained in Auditing and Assurance Standards (AUSs). This AGS has been developed to clarify the responsibilities of professional accountants in respect of such engagements, and to provide guidance to the professional accountant on additional considerations which may be taken into account when undertaking engagements agreed with the "client entity"[2] involved in fundraising. This AGS applies to assurance engagements relating to historical data including pro forma historical financial information, forecasts and projections in disclosure documents for potential investors. The guidance in this AGS should be read in conjunction with that contained in AUS 804 "The Audit of Prospective Financial Information" and AUS 902 "Review of Financial Reports". This AGS is not intended to apply to taxation opinions provided on fundraising documents, or when reporting in connection with a Bidder Statement, Target Statement, or Scheme of Arrangement for the purposes of raising or restructuring debt or equity.

.03 It is important to note that this AGS does not impose any responsibilities on the professional accountant beyond those which are imposed by AUSs and the requirements of the Act. The provisions of the Act are augmented by ASIC Policy Statement 170 "Prospective financial information", and other regulatory pronouncements. Access to this and other ASIC policy statements (PS), practice notes (PN), and information releases (IR) that also

1 See the ASIC website http://www.asic.gov.au for an update of the latest developments and transitional issues that may be applicable in relation to proposed fundraisings.

2 The term "client entity" is synonymous with "commissioning party" in ASIC's Practice Note 43 "Valuation reports and profit forecasts". The client entity may be the responsible party, the intended user, or both, in an assurance engagement. It also includes a body, scheme or person defined under the fundraising provisions of the Act. See paragraph .04 of this AGS for this and other definitions.

could be relevant to specific types of fundraising activities is available through the ASIC website (http://www.asic.gov.au).

Definitions

.04 For the purposes of this AGS:

(a) "Securities" are shares in a body, debentures in a body, or interests in a registered managed investment scheme. Securities also include legal or equitable interests or options to acquire shares, debentures, or interests in a registered managed investment scheme that are subject to the transitional provisions of the FSR Act. Interests in a managed investment scheme may also be securities pending the transition under the provisions of the FSR Act. Securities do not cover a futures contract or an option approved by a prescribed financial market as an exchange traded option[3].

(b) "Management" means the governing body, audit committee, individual member of the governing body, officer(s) and/or other person(s) having responsibility for planning and directing the activities of an entity. The Act places specific requirements on Directors as members of the governing body in relation to disclosure documents.

(c) "Client entity" is synonymous with "commissioning party" in ASIC's PN 43 "Valuation reports and profit forecasts". The client entity may be the responsible party, the intended user, or both, in an assurance engagement. It also includes a body, scheme or person defined under the fundraising provisions of the Act.

(d) "Fundraising" involves offering securities for issue or for sale including inviting applications for the issue of the securities and inviting offers to purchase the securities[4].

(e) "Financial information" in relation to fundraising may include:

(i) "historical financial information" that may be audited or unaudited financial information with or without adjustment(s). Adjustments to historical information may relate to the financial statements, such as the statement of financial position, statement of cash flows, and/or the statement of financial performance, and accompanying notes if applicable. The adjustments comprise "historical adjustments" which are adjustments made to correct for errors and uncertainties, and adjustments made for consistency with current Accounting Standards and/or accounting policies. The adjustments could include, for instance, restatement of provision accounts for consistency, or restatement of depreciation charges based upon current depreciation rates.

(ii) "pro forma historical information" comprises historical information, adjusted for significant subsequent events and other matters relating to transactions associated with the fundraising. Pro forma historical information also includes adjustments for presentation and/or disclosure. Specific adjustments involved in preparing pro forma historical information include adjustments to the financial statements, including the statement of financial position, which may have formed part of the historical financial report, to show the impact of transactions associated with fundraising. The adjustments may also include, for example, adjustments for a discontinued part of operations, or sale of a business segment.

(iii) "prospective financial information" is financial information based on assumptions about events that may occur in the future and on possible actions by the client entity. It is highly subjective in nature and its preparation requires the exercise of considerable judgement. Prospective financial information can be in the form of a forecast, or a projection, or a

AGS

3 The definition of "securities" is consistent with Section 92(3) of the Act. Securities may also include financial instruments classified as equity in AASB 1040 "Statement of Financial Position".

4 The definition of "fundraising" is consistent with the offers and invitations covered under Section 700 (2) (a) & (b) of the Act.

combination of both. For example, a one-year forecast plus a projection for several years.

(f) prospective financial information must have "reasonable grounds" for its inclusion in a disclosure document. The disclosure obligations in the Act do not allow disclosure of information that is misleading. ASIC takes the view that what constitutes reasonable grounds under Section 728(2) of the Act is an objective test in that it requires a reasonable person to view the grounds for the statement as reasonable. The view of management alone in relation to assumptions about events that may occur in the future and on possible actions by the client entity as the basis for prospective financial information may be considered as being subjective, and may not meet the "reasonable grounds" requirement under the Act. Under PS 170 and the Act, prospective financial information should not be included in a disclosure document if there are no reasonable grounds for it. Prospective financial information without reasonable grounds would be misleading to potential investors. Furthermore, potential investors and their professional advisers should not reasonably require such financial information or reasonably expect to find it in a disclosure document. A decision whether or not to include prospective financial information in a disclosure document requires a balance between the information value of what is disclosed against the likelihood that the information is misleading. The two elements are interrelated. So the less reliable information is, the less relevant it becomes to investors, and the less likely it should be included in the disclosure document. PS 170 also provides indicative factors that may suggest reasonable grounds for the inclusion of prospective financial information.

(g) A "forecast" means prospective financial information prepared on the basis of assumptions as to future events which management expects to take place, and the actions management expects to take as of the date the information is prepared (best-estimate assumptions). The period for a forecast is generally consistent with the reporting period of the issuer, and may cover several periods[5]. Forecasts are generally prepared by management on a comparable basis to the historical information in an offer document, to assist potential investors in making an informed assessment of the prospects of the client entity. Forecasts may also be "estimated actual forecasts" that combine historical information over part of a reporting period, with forecast information over the remainder of the period.

(h) A "projection" means prospective financial information prepared on the basis of:

(i) hypothetical assumptions about future events and management actions which are not necessarily expected to take place. This may include circumstances when entities are in a start-up phase or are considering a major change in the nature of operations; or

(ii) a mixture of best-estimate and hypothetical assumptions.

Such information illustrates the possible consequences, as of the date the information is prepared, if the events and actions were to occur (a "what-if" scenario). A projection will not usually have reasonable grounds. If a projection does not have reasonable grounds it will be misleading under Section 728(2) of the Act, and should not be disclosed.

(i) "Listing Rules" are the rules governing the listing of securities on a prescribed financial market[6] such as the Australian Stock Exchange (ASX)[7]. The Listing Rules include specific conditions and tests for securities to be admitted and listed[8] on an ongoing basis on a prescribed financial market such as the ASX. A selection of ASX Listing Rules, that may be relevant in relation to fundraising includes for example:

5 PS 170 notes that longer range forecasts (greater than one or two years) may be subject to greater uncertainty.

6 The definition of prescribed financial market is consistent with Section 9 of the Act.

7 A complete set of the Listing Rules and guidance notes is available from the Australian Stock Exchange website (http://www.asx.com.au).

8 The ASX List is known as the "official list" and is defined in Chapter 19 "Interpretation and definitions" as the list of entities that ASIC has admitted and not removed.

(i) A client entity's securities need to be substantiated by a disclosure document that is issued and lodged with ASIC (except for ASX Foreign Exempt Listing or an ASX Debt Listing) [ASX 1.1, Condition 3].

(ii) There are specific requirements, known as "spread requirements" that are required for security holders of client entities seeking admission and listing on the ASX [ASX 1.1, Condition 7]. The spread requirements specify the minimum number of holders and value of securities, and the class of securities, for ASX admission. The determination of the appropriate disclosure document (i.e. information memorandum, or prospectus) that the ASX is willing to accept for client entities that have already issued an Offer Information Statement and are seeking to be admitted and listed are contingent upon the spread requirements. Under the ASX Listing Rules an Offer Information Statement is not a Prospectus.

(iii) In addition, client entities seeking admission need to satisfy the "profit" or "assets" test [ASX 1.1, Condition 8].

- The profit test [ASX 1.2] places specific consolidated and aggregated profit requirements on the client entity, and also requires the client entity to be a going concern and have undertaken the same main business activity over the last three years. The test also identifies the specific accounts[9] and Directors Statements that need to be lodged with the ASX.
- The assets test [ASX 1.3] places specific requirements on the client entity in terms of net tangible assets and working capital. The test also identifies the specific accounts, independent expert reports and statements that may or may not be included as part of the disclosure document, and that need to be lodged with the ASX.

(j) A "disclosure document" also known as an "offer document", is a document prepared for the benefit of potential investors under the Act for fundraising. A disclosure document includes: prospectuses, short form prospectuses, profile statements and offer information statements. Disclosure documents also include an information memorandum prepared under the Listing Rules for client entities seeking admission to a prescribed financial market such as the ASX for fundraising from potential investors. Information memorandum requirements are outlined, for example, in Appendix 1A "ASX Listing application and agreement".

(k) "Professional accountant" means those persons, whether they be in public practice (including a sole practitioner, partnership or corporate body), industry, commerce, the public sector or education, who are members of CPA Australia or The Institute of Chartered Accountants in Australia, and includes affiliates, practice entity participants and registered graduates of the Institute. It should be noted however, that graduates of the Institute or associates from CPA Australia may not be sufficiently qualified or have sufficient experience to act as a professional accountant for the purposes of authorising an Independent Accountant's Report.

(l) "An Independent Accountant's Report" is a report prepared by a qualified professional accountant on financial information provided in disclosure documents. This report is included in a separate section of the disclosure document in close proximity to the financial information section to enable the investors and professional advisors to make an informed assessment of the prospects of the client entity. The report may also be called a "Professional Accountant'sReport" or an "Investigating Accountant's Report".

9 The usage of the term "accounts" is consistent with the ASX Listing Rules [ASX 19.12]. The term "accounts" is defined in Chapter 19 "Interpretation and definitions". "Accounts" includes the balance sheet, profit and loss statement, statement of cash flows, notes or disclosures in relation to the balance sheet, profit and loss statement, and statement of cash flows required by any law, regulation, rule or Accounting Standards. Accounts also includes any other information necessary to give a true and fair view of the financial position and performance of the entity required by any law, regulation, rule or Accounting Standards.

Regulatory Framework

.05 The regulatory framework for fundraising consists principally of:

(a) a requirement for the person or client entity offering securities to comply with the Chapter 6D fundraising provisions of the Act and the requirements of the FSR Act that may be applicable;

(b) relevant ASIC policy statements (PS), practice notes (PN) and information releases (IR) applicable to specific activities in relation to fundraising[10]; and

(c) for entities seeking admission to a prescribed financial market such as the ASX, the relevant ASX Listing Rules that may be applicable to the entity[11].

.06 Section 706 of the Act states that an offer of securities needs disclosure to investors. Under Section 707 of the Act offers are[12]:

(a) *An off market sale by the controller (sale by a person controlling the body).* Circumstances when the person making the offer controls the body[13] and either the securities are not quoted, or if quoted, are not offered for sale in the ordinary course of trading on a stock market or prescribed financial market.

(b) *A sale amounting to indirect issue (sale of securities).* Circumstances when an offer of a body's previously undisclosed securities are available for sale within twelve months after the issue, and the securities were issued to a person with the purpose of:

(i) selling or transferring the securities; or

(ii) granting, issuing or transferring interests, in, or options or warrants over, the securities.

(c) *A sale amounting to an indirect off market sale by a controller (sale of securities by a person controlling the body).* Covers circumstances when a person who controlled the body at the time of sale has either offered a body's securities for sale, or grants, issues or transfers, options warrants or interests over the securities within a twelve month period. The securities were previously undisclosed securities, and either the securities were not quoted or, if quoted, were not offered for sale in the ordinary course of trading on a stock market or prescribed financial market.

.07 Subject to the exemptions that are outlined in the FSR Act, the Act also identifies offers that do not need disclosure including:

(a) *Small scale offerings.* These are offers to investors or sales of securities to no more than twenty persons within twelve months [Section 708(1)-(7)];

(b) *Offers to sophisticated investors* [Section 708(8)] and professional investors[14] [Section 708(11)];

(c) *Offers to people associated with the body* [Section 708(12)];

(d) *Certain offers to present holders of securities* [Section 708(13) – (14)];

(e) *Issues to investors or sales for no consideration* [Section 708(15) – (16)];

(f) *Compromise or arrangement under Part 5.1 of the Act* when a body is being wound up [Section 708(17)];

(g) *Takeovers* under a takeover bid regulated under Chapter 6 of the Act and accompanied by a bidder's statement [Section 708(18)];

---

10 Policy Statements (PS), Practice Notes (PN) and Information Releases (IR) are available at the ASIC website (http://www.asic.gov.au).

11 See the Australian Stock Exchange website (http://www.asx.com.au) for a complete set of Listing Rules and ASX guidelines.

12 Sections 707 and 708 of the Act have been amended by the FSR Act which commenced operation on the 11 March 2002.

13 Section 9 of the Act defines body as "body corporate or an unincorporated body and includes, for example, a society or association".

14 See Audit & Assurance Alert (AAA) 9: "Sophisticated Investor Reports under the Corporations Law" (now the *Corporations Act 2001*) available at (http://www.aarf.asn.au).

(h) *Offers of debentures* of an Australian Authorised Deposittaking Institution or a body registered under the Life Insurance Act 1995 [Section 708(19)]; and

(i) *Offers by an exempt body or exempt public authority* of a state or territory [Section 708(20) – (21)].

.08 When a disclosure document under the fundraising provisions is required, the disclosure documents are required to comply with the provisions of the Act, and to be lodged with ASIC unless relief has been given. ASIC may grant relief from lodgement either by class order or on a case by case basis. Examples where class order relief applies include short term money market deposits, horse breeding schemes and film investment schemes. Examples where case by case lodgement relief applies include share purchase plans and business introduction services. However, ASIC will not give relief from the requirement to lodge a disclosure document for friendly societies or regular savings plans[15].

Types of Disclosure Documents

.09 When an offer of securities needs disclosure, the following disclosure documents may be used under the Act:

(a) *Prospectus*. The full disclosure document prepared in accordance with Sections 710, 711 and 713 of the Act;

(b) *Short-Form Prospectus*. A prospectus that refers to material previously lodged with ASIC. The material is not included in the body of the prospectus. A short-form prospectus may be used for any offer[16]. Investors are entitled to receive a copy of the material that is lodged with ASIC if they request it;

(c) *Profile Statement*. With ASIC's approval, a brief disclosure document may be sent out with offers instead of a prospectus[17]. In such a circumstance, the prospectus is still required to be prepared and lodged with ASIC. Investors are entitled to receive a copy of the prospectus if they request it; and

(d) *Offer Information Statement*. This is a document that has a lower level of disclosure than that of a prospectus. It may be used instead of a prospectus if the amount raised over the entity's lifetime through Offer Information Statements, including the current Offer Information Statement, is five million dollars or less[18].

Electronic Prospectuses

.10 Subject to the requirements of the FSR Act, prospectuses may be in paper or electronic form. ASIC PS 107 "Electronic prospectuses" allows electronic documents for fundraising when the disclosure requirements under the Act are satisfied. PS107.29 requires the electronic prospectus to be a "copy", that is, a reproduction, transcript or imitation that is faithful to the original paper form. An electronic version is a copy of the lodged original paper version if the electronic prospectus contains the same information, and no more information, in the same sequence as the lodged prospectus with no material differences[19].

AGS

Prospectus Content

.11 Sections 710, 711 and 713 of the Act outline the content requirements of a prospectus. There are general and specific content disclosure requirements in relation to managed investment schemes, offers and sales of securities.

General Disclosure Requirements

.12 A prospectus for a body's securities must contain all the information that investors and their professional advisers would reasonably require to make an informed assessment. The specific matters that need to be considered are outlined in Section 710 of the Act.

15 See the ASIC website or contact ASIC for further information in relation to relief from lodgement.

16 See Section 712 of the Act.

17 See Section 721 of the Act.

18 See Section 709 of the Act.

19 See PS 107.45 (p.13) for a summary of ASIC's electronic prospectuses policy.

There are also special prospectus content rules that may be applicable under Section 713 of the Act for continuously quoted securities[20]. The following needs to be included for offers in relation to offers and sale of securities and managed investment schemes that remain subject to the requirements of Chapter 6D (for example by virtue of the transitional provisions of the FSR Act):

(a) *offers and sale of securities*:

  (i) the rights and liabilities attaching to the interest or option, or the underlying securities;

  (ii) the assets and liabilities, financial position and performance, profits and losses and prospects of the body whose securities are offered; and

  (iii) for an option - the capacity of the person making the offer to issue or deliver the underlying securities.

(b) *managed investment schemes that are subject to Chapter 6D*:

  (i) the rights and liabilities attaching to the securities offered; and

  (ii) the assets and liabilities, financial position and performance, profits and losses and prospects of the body that has issued or is to issue the shares, debentures or interests[21].

Continuously Quoted Securities

.13 The Listing Rules that may be considered when preparing a prospectus, include, for instance, admission rules for Client Entities [ASX 1.1-1.7], and Debt Listing Rules [ASX 1.8–1.10][22]. There are also additional disclosure requirements in the Act for a prospectus of continuously quoted securities listed on a stock exchange. These include:[23]

(a) information that investors and their professional advisers would reasonably require to make an informed assessment of the effects of the offer on the body or managed investment scheme;

(b) the prospectus is also required to state that:

  (i) as a disclosing entity, the body or managed investment scheme is subject to regular reporting and disclosure obligations; and

  (ii) copies of documents lodged with ASIC in relation to the body may be obtained from, or inspected at, an ASIC office; and

(c) the prospectus should also:

  (i) inform people of their right to obtain a copy of the most recent annual report, half-year, or interim financial report or continuous disclosure notices issued by the body or managed investment scheme that are made available free of charge to anyone who asks for a copy of the document during the application period of a prospectus[24]; or

  (ii) be accompanied by, or include, a copy of the document.

---

20 The reduced disclosure obligations for offers of continuously quoted securities in Section 713 operate in place of the requirements in Section 710 of the Act.

21 For managed investment schemes that are regulated by the FSR Act, a different regulatory regime applies. Managed investment schemes regulated under the FSR Act require a Product Disclosure Statement defined in section 761A of the Act. Also see PS 168 "Disclosure: product disclosure statements (and other disclosure obligations)", PN 64 "Accounting and disclosure issues for property trust prospectuses", PN 70 "Prospectuses for cash box and investment companies", PS 148 "Investor directed portfolio services" and other regulatory policy pronouncements, that may be applicable to the fundraising activity of the client entity, located on the ASIC website.

22 Chapter 1 of the ASX Listing Rules summarises the conditions and tests for admission to the ASX.

23 The interpretation of continuously quoted securities is consistent with Section 9 of the Act.

24 Under Section 713(5) of the Act, information about the offer that is excluded from the continuous disclosure notice of a prescribed financial market in accordance with the Listing Rules must also be included in the prospectus if it is reasonable for investors and their professional advisers to expect to find the information in the prospectus.

Specific Disclosure Requirements

.14 Under Section 711 of the Act, a prospectus is required to disclose all necessary information prescribed by the Act including the following:

(a) the terms and conditions of the offer;

(b) fees and interests of people involved in the offer. These people may include:

(i) a director or proposed director of the body or responsible entity of a managed investment scheme;

(ii) a person named in the prospectus who performs a function in a professional, advisory, or other capacity;

(iii) a promoter of the body; and

(iv) a stockbroker or underwriter (but not subunderwriter) to the issue or sale;

(c) for securities quoted on a stock market of a prescribed financial market, a prospectus is also required to state that the securities have been admitted for quotation on the exchange, or, an admission for quotation has been made, or an application for admission of the securities to quotation on that stock market will be made to the prescribed financial market within 7 days after the date of the prospectus;

(d) its expiry date, and a statement that no securities will be issued after the expiry date specified in the prospectus. The expiry date must not be later than 13 months after the date of the prospectus. The expiry date of a replacement prospectus must be the same as that of the original prospectus it replaces; and

(e) that a copy of the prospectus has been lodged with ASIC, and ASIC takes no responsibility for the content of the prospectus.

Short-Form Prospectus Content

.15 A short-form prospectus is required to meet the general and specific disclosure requirements of a prospectus. The Act, under Section 712, allows a prospectus to refer to a document lodged with ASIC instead of setting out the information. The reference is required to identify the document, or part of the document, that contains the information and inform people of the right to obtain a copy of the document. While a short-form prospectus is primarily of interest to users with specialist information needs, such as professional analysts, advisers or investors, the reference is required to include:

(a) a description of the contents of the document or its part; and

(b) a statement to the effect that the information in the document or part is primarily of interest to those users.

In any other case, there should be sufficient information about the contents of the document to allow a person to whom the offer is made to decide whether to obtain a copy of the document or part of the document.

Profile Statement Content

.16 Under Section 714 of the Act, a profile statement is required to disclose all necessary information prescribed by the regulations including the following:

(a) identification of the body and the nature of the securities;

(b) the nature of the risks involved in investing in the securities;

(c) details of all amounts payable in respect of the securities. These include any amounts by way of fee, commission or charge;

(d) a disclosure that the person given the profile statement is entitled to a copy of the prospectus free of charge; and

(e) a disclosure that a copy of the profile statement has been lodged with ASIC and that ASIC takes no responsibility for the content of the statement.

The profile statement is also required to disclose that no securities will be issued on the basis of the statement after the expiry date specified in the statement[25].

25 Under Section 714 of the Act, the expiry date must not be later than 13 months after the date of the prospectus. The expiry date of a replacement statement must be the same as that of the original statement it replaces.

Offer Information Statement Content

.17 Under Section 715 of the Act, an offer information statement is required to include all necessary information including the following:

(a) identification of the body and the nature of the securities;

(b) description of the body's business;

(c) description of what the funds raised by the offer(s) are to be used for;

(d) description of the nature of the risks involved in investing in the securities;

(e) details of all amounts payable in respect of the securities;

(f) a disclosure that a copy of the offer information statement has been lodged with ASIC, and that ASIC takes no responsibility for the content of the statement;

(g) a disclosure that the statement is not a prospectus and that it has a lower level of disclosure requirements than that of a prospectus;

(h) a statement that investors should obtain professional investment advice before accepting the offer; and

(i) a copy of a financial report for the body that complies with PS 157 "Financial reports for offer information statements". The financial report is required to:

(i) be a report for a 12 month period and have a reporting date that occurs within the last 6 months before the securities are first offered under the statement;

(ii) be prepared in accordance with Australian Accounting Standards; and

(iii) be audited.

In addition, the Statement is required to disclose that no securities will be issued on the basis of the Statement after the expiry date specified in the Statement[26].

.18 For a client entity seeking admission to a prescribed financial market such as the ASX, the Listing Rules require the issue and lodgement of a prospectus as a condition for admission [Rule 1.1 Condition 3]. Under the Listing Rules of a prescribed financial market such as the ASX, an offer information statement prepared by management is not a prospectus. However, if the client entity establishes that it has not raised capital in the past three months, and does not expect to raise capital in the next three months, the ASX may agree with the client entity's management to the issue of an information memorandum, that is generally sent to all security holders provided the spread requirements are met. Information memorandum requirements are outlined in Appendix 1A "ASX Listing application and agreement" of the Listing Rules.

.19 The information memorandum is generally a document that is prepared by the client entity's management and may refer to the financial or other information in the offer information statement or other disclosure documents required under the Act. Unless the professional accountant is specifically engaged to prepare an Independent Accountant's Report on the financial information included in an information memorandum, it is expected that management would need to obtain consent from the professional accountant to include the Independent Accountant's Report in an information memorandum. This is because the Independent Accountant's Report may have been prepared for another disclosure document such as an offer information statement.

Responsibilities of Management

.20 When a client entity produces a disclosure document for fundraising, the Directors have primary responsibility for the information provided to investors about the body, or managed investment scheme. In particular the Act requires that the disclosure document[27]:

(a) sets out all the information, including financial information that is required;

26 Under Section 715 of the Act, the expiry date must not be later than 13 months after the date of the Statement. The expiry date of a replacement statement must be the same as that of the original statement it replaces.

27 See Section 717 of the Act which provides an overview of the procedures for offering securities.

(b) does not contain any misleading or deceptive statements[28]. A disclosure document may also be considered to be misleading if significant information is presented in a way that investors are likely to overlook[29]. PS 170 also requires that the information needed to assess the reliability of a forecast be presented in a way that enables a connection between the information and the forecast;

(c) is dated; and

(d) evidences that the Directors consent to the disclosure document.

.21 For client entities seeking admission to and listing on a prescribed financial market such as the ASX, it is the responsibility of the Directors to comply with the terms and conditions of the listing application rules[30]. Listing Rules of prescribed financial markets such as the ASX also require Directors to provide a statement on the adequacy of working capital[31] following the proposed fundraising, for the entity to carry out its stated objectives. This ordinarily would require the Directors of the client entity to provide a statement on the adequacy of working capital, which is supported by work undertaken by the Directors or a specialist, and reviewed by a professional accountant. After the client entity is admitted to a securities exchange such as the ASX, the Directors also have the responsibility for compliance with the Listing Rules on an ongoing basis.

.22 Disclosure documents under the Act are prepared by Directors to assist investors in making an informed assessment in relation to the prospects of the body or managed investment scheme. The documents may therefore include historical financial information, pro forma historical financial information and prospective financial information. Under PS 170, the Directors need to assess, on a case by case basis, whether there are reasonable grounds for the preparation and inclusion of prospective financial information in disclosure documents[32]. Directors should generally refrain from including prospective financial information in disclosure documents in the following non-exhaustive circumstances[33]:

(a) the client entity is in the start-up phase[34];

(b) the client entity will substantially change its operations following the capital raising;

(c) the client entity's present activities in relation to its products constitute research and development, and the product development is not significantly advanced to warrant a reasonable expectation of commercialisation; and

(d) the client entity's future operations are difficult to predict.

In the absence of prospective financial information, the Directors are required to disclose information on the prospects of the client entity. This could include information, for example, on expected expenditures, and the point in time when the client entity will exhaust cash if sufficient revenue is not derived.

AGS

28 Due to the interaction of Section 769 C and Section 1041 H in the Act, management also has a responsibility not to make misleading and deceptive statements in advertisements in relation to disclosure documents.

29 See *Fraser v NRMA Holdings Ltd* (1995) 13 ACLC 132; *Pancontinental Mining Ltd v Goldfields Limited* (1995) 16 ACSR 463.

30 See Appendix 1A "ASX Listing application and agreement" of the ASX Listing Rules for a checklist of the information that needs to be completed as part of the application for admission to the ASX.

31 The statement is provided in a prospectus or information memorandum. See for example, the working capital requirement under "The assets test" of Chapter 1 "Admission" under the ASX Listing Rules [ASX Listing Rules 1.3.3 (a)].

32 PS 170 suggests in determining the disclosure of prospects in a disclosure document, the entity should also consider its business plan that includes budgets and other forward looking information.

33 The view of management alone that there are reasonable grounds for a particular statement in relation to prospective financial information may not be sufficient to meet the requirements under Section 728(2) of the Act. There needs to be other indicators to meet the reasonable grounds requirement under Section 728(2) of the Act. See PS 170 for indicative factors of reasonable grounds.

34 For bodies in the start-up phase, management may disclose other information on the prospects of the client entity. This may include information in relation to "cash burn" that encompasses, for example, the likely rate of expenditure, the source of further funding if and when it is required, and the method of further fundraising.

.23 If it is found that the disclosure document lodged by the Directors of the body or scheme is deficient, or a significant new matter has arisen, then management needs to consider the following under Section 717 of the Act:

(a) lodging a supplementary or replacement document; or

(b) returning application money that is held in trust to the applicants.

Considerations for the Professional Accountant

.24 The responsibilities of the professional accountant in relation to fundraising vary from engagement to engagement. However, in all such engagements, the professional accountant needs to adopt quality control policies and procedures in accordance with AUS 206 "Quality Control for Audit Work". Quality control policies and procedures apply at two levels. Quality control policy and procedures relate to the overall policies and procedures for all engagements, such as procedures in relation to client acceptance, and also to the direction, supervision and review of work delegated to personnel involved in a specific assurance engagement. For example, in evaluating a prospective client or reviewing an existing client, the professional accountant ordinarily carries out a preliminary review of the client entity's operations and financial information to consider whether there may be factors which might restrict the scope of work to be carried out, or give rise to a qualification of the report.

.25 The professional accountant is also required to hold the appropriate licences, which may be, for example, the Australian Financial Services Licence required by the licensing provisions of the Act and other regulations that may be applicable[35].

.26 The professional accountant also needs to comply with the requirements of the Joint Code of Professional Conduct (The Code). A professional accountant who performs such an engagement needs to be independent. Professional Statements, Sections F.1 and F.2, in The Code indicate some of the situations which, because of the actual or apparent lack of independence, may give a reasonable observer grounds for doubting the independence of a professional accountant. Furthermore, Professional Statements, Sections F.3 and F.4, in The Code require the professional accountant to communicate with the existing accountant and client entity prior to acceptance of the engagement.

Agreeing on the Terms of the Engagement

.27 Professional accountants may be engaged in a variety of engagements in relation to fundraising. These include for example:

(a) reporting on historical and/or pro forma historical financial information;

(b) reporting on prospective financial information;

(c) compilation engagements in relation to historical and prospective financial information; and

(d) due diligence engagements such as managing or participating in the due diligence process in relation to the fundraising.

The conduct by the professional accountant of an audit or review engagement in accordance with Australian Auditing and Assurance Standards may not, of itself, provide a sufficient basis for the professional accountant to meet the obligations placed by the Act on experts named in the disclosure document. In circumstances when this occurs, the professional accountant extends the procedures to meet the objectives of the Act that may be applicable.

.28 The professional accountant and the client entity agree on the terms of engagement in writing in accordance with AUS 204 "Terms of Audit Engagements" and/or Professional Statement Section F in the Joint Code of Professional Conduct[36]. The engagement letter:

(a) clarifies Directors' responsibilities in relation to disclosure documents and financial information;

35 The professional accountant is required to meet the legislative requirements of the Act and ASIC's Policy Statements, Practice Notes and other guidance that may be applicable. See (http://www.asic.gov.au).

36 For engagements such as compilation engagements.

(b) clarifies the considerations for the professional accountant in relation to:

(i) the preparation of a professional report for inclusion in the disclosure document and the level of assurance obtained for supporting the conclusion in the report[37]. The engagement letter also clarifies the scope of the Professional Accountant's Report, the responsibility for the information in the report and the format in which the report will be presented; and

(ii) the nature of the published consent given by the professional accountant in relation to the form and context of statements made in the disclosure document for securities under Section 716 of the Act[38]. For example, when the client entity wishes to distribute a disclosure document in electronic and paper form, PS 107.72 requires that consent from the professional accountant is obtained for both forms. The professional accountant may also consider limiting the consent and involvement to the reports issued, or the segments of the disclosure document for which the professional accountant is directly responsible; and

(c) outlines other matters in relation to the engagement such as:

(i) audit or review of interim financial reports;

(ii) review of any profit forecasts and preparation of any report by the professional accountant to be included in the prospectus with the forecast;

(iii) the nature of any comfort letters required in relation to the Directors' Statement(s) concerning borrowings, the adequacy of working capital, or other financial information;

(iv) arrangements for the professional accountant to:

- attend meetings in relation to the engagement such as the due diligence and risk committee meetings; and
- use the work of experts;

(v) the timescale for the preparation and publication of the disclosure document(s) and deadlines to be met;

(vi) the need to communicate with the client entity's external auditor if applicable, and/or other professional advisers; and

(vii) arrangements to ensure an opportunity for the professional accountant to receive draft and final versions of the disclosure document in order to be satisfied with their form and content before consenting to the issue of the disclosure document. The professional accountant also may request management of the client entity to acknowledge and confirm in writing the report of the professional accountant, in order to confirm management's understanding of the form that the report is to take and its broad content.

.29 If the engagement is a joint reporting engagement, the terms of the engagement also may include procedures to enable professional accountants from separate accounting practices to liaise on a regular basis with regard to any problems identified.

Planning

.30 In accordance with AUS 304 "Knowledge of the Business"[39], the professional accountant obtains knowledge of the business sufficient to enable the identification and understanding of the events, transactions and practices that may have a significant effect on the financial information or on the Professional Accountant's Report. Knowledge of the business includes a general knowledge of the economy and the industry within which the client entity operates (AUS 304.03).

37 PN 43.7 requires the commissioning party to provide the expert with written instructions that clearly set out the scope and purpose of the report.

38 For managed investment schemes the FSR Act specifies separate consent obligations.

39 AUS 304 may be adapted for review engagements as necessary. For Compilation engagements also see APS 9 "Statement on Compilation of Financial Reports".

.31 The professional accountant uses knowledge of the business to:

(a) assess risks and identify problems;

(b) plan the engagement; and

(c) perform efficient and effective procedures during the engagement.

.32 The professional accountant also uses knowledge of the business to consider the appropriateness of accounting policies and financial information disclosures such as:

(a) the appropriateness of any adjustments made to historical financial information presented in the disclosure document; and

(b) the suitability of the assumptions used as the basis for the preparation of prospective financial information.

.33 The professional accountant plans the engagement in accordance with AUS 302 "Planning"[40]. In planning the engagement the professional accountant considers:

(a) review of the financial report(s) and interim financial reports of current and prior reporting periods;

(b) review of the audit working papers, where available; and

(c) comparison of actual amounts to budgets, for example, sales, profit and loss, and capital expenditures that may provide indications of the prospects of the client entity; and,

(d) the implications for the engagement arising from the Listing Rules of a prescribed financial market such as the ASX and other regulations such as the FSR Act. For example, the professional accountant reviews the forecast statement of financial performance, statement of cash flows and statement of financial position in order to gain comfort with respect to the director's working capital statement [see for example ASX 1.3.3 (a)] where appropriate.

.34 The professional accountant also considers materiality and engagement risk when planning and conducting an assurance engagement in relation to disclosure documents. Consideration of materiality and engagement risk reduces the risk of expressing an inappropriate conclusion.

.35 When the professional accountant is not the appointed external auditor of the client entity and uses the work of another auditor in relation to the disclosure document, the professional accountant needs to consider how the work of the other auditor affects the engagement[41]. Furthermore, Professional Statements F3 (paragraph .13) and F4 provide guidance on communicating with the other auditor and the client entity when professional work is performed.

Financial Information Included in a Disclosure Document

.36 Financial information included in a disclosure document that is prepared by management forms part of the content requirements prepared for the benefit of potential investors and their professional advisers, to assist them to make an informed assessment of the prospects of the client entity. The conduct by the professional accountant of an audit or review engagement in accordance with Australian Auditing and Assurance Standards may not provide a sufficient basis for the professional accountant to meet the obligations placed by the Act on experts named in the disclosure document. The professional accountant also has a responsibility to consider whether the financial information in a disclosure document is sufficient to enable investors and their professional advisors to make an informed assessment of the prospects of the client entity[42].

.37 The financial information prepared by management in disclosure documents may comprise historical, pro forma historical and prospective financial information. Generally, the financial information needs to comply with the recognition and measurement principles in the Australian Accounting Standards, Urgent Issues Group (UIG) Consensus

40 AUS 302 may be adapted for review engagements as necessary. For Compilation engagements also see APS 9.

41 See AUS 602 "Using the Work of Another Auditor" which may be modified for fundraising engagements.

42 See Section 710 Prospectus content - general disclosure test.

Views, and other Australian accounting pronouncements. The presentation and disclosure requirements of Accounting Standards may also be relevant. In particular, information is generally classified in a manner that is not inconsistent with the requirements of Accounting Standards. However, the presentation and disclosure requirements from the ASX Listing Rules, AUS 804, and PS 170 need to be followed to the extent that compliance with these requirements would generally assist investors and their professional advisors with their investment decisions. When compliance with the presentation and disclosure requirements of the applicable accounting framework is misleading for investors and their professional advisors, and a departure from the applicable accounting framework is necessary, PS 170 requires that as a general principle management disclose the following in the disclosure document:

(a) the reason for departure from any current Accounting Standard or UIG Consensus View;

(b) the reason for applying an Accounting Standard in a particular way when discretion is involved;

(c) the reason for adopting a particular accounting or disclosure treatment. For example, there may be circumstances where the past may not be relevant to the client entity's financial position or future prospects; and

(d) whenever comparative information is included in a disclosure document to meet the needs of investors and their professional advisors, it should generally be provided with appropriate restatements that management considers necessary. Omission of comparatives may be appropriate, with historical information however, when a major restructuring has occurred since the comparative period.

Historical Information

.38 The professional accountant has regard to the terms of the engagement concerning historical information included in the disclosure document. Ordinarily the professional accountant ensures that the financial information provided is, where appropriate, consistent with prior period audited financial information.

.39 The nature and extent of work to be carried out by the professional accountant varies significantly from engagement to engagement and will be influenced by:

(a) whether all the financial reports have previously been subject to audit or review;

(b) whether a modified or qualified report has been issued previously;

(c) whether the professional accountant audited or reviewed the financial report on which the report is to be based;

(d) whether there is a need to reclassify or adjust historical amounts such as unusual and/or non-recurring and extraordinary items and prior restructuring costs, and correct for errors and uncertainties such as provisions;

(e) whether there is consistency with current Australian Accounting Standards, UIG Consensus Views and other Australian accounting pronouncements;

(f) whether there are transaction specific effects that clearly necessitate adjustments, such as the sale of a subsidiary or division; and

(g) responses to enquiries of management, the external auditor (if applicable) and internal auditors where they exist[43]. The enquires may be directed towards matters such as:

  (i) changes in accounting policies which occurred during the period under review;

  (ii) changes in Accounting Standards, and practices and other mandatory reporting requirements subsequent to the latest period;

  (iii) adjustments needed to convert from overseas Generally Accepted Accounting Principles (GAAP) to Australian Accounting Standards, UIG

43 Also see AUS 602 "Using the Work of Another Auditor" and AUS 604 "Considering the Work of Internal Auditing".

Consensus Views, and other Australian accounting pronouncements and other mandatory reporting requirements (if applicable);

(iv) unadjusted audit differences that may now become material;

(v) the treatment of provisions and other significant estimation areas such as revaluations; and

(vi) whether assets have been purchased from an associated entity or revalued prior to or after the sale.

.40 There is no stipulation in the Act as to how many years of historical financial information should be prepared and presented by management in a disclosure document. However prescribed financial markets such as the ASX place the following requirements generally on client entities seeking admission under the profit [ASX 1.2.3] or assets test [ASX 1.3.5]:

(a) client entities are required to prepare and lodge financial statements together with any audit or review report for the last three full financial years (or shorter period if ASX agrees) under the profit test. Under the assets test, historical financial information does not need to be audited or reviewed; and

(b) under the profit test, if the last full financial year ended more than eight months before the entity applied for admission, interim financial statements for the last halfyear (or longer period if available) from the end of the last financial year, together with an audit or review report[44], must be provided.

Therefore, depending on the date of the last audit, listing requirements might not be satisfied, and an audit or review of a General Purpose Financial Report drawn up to an interim reporting date may be required[45].

Pro Forma Historical Information

.41 The professional accountant considers the need for management to make adjustments, by altering the figures previously reported in the audited financial report, or altering the presentation, to promote consistency and comparability with prospective financial information. The professional accountant also considers management's response to:

(a) the effects of proposed operating changes that may result in adjustments being made to the financial information in the disclosure document; and

(b) whether the changes to the presentation of financial information ensure that matters of particular importance in the context of the client entity are given due prominence.

.42 Material adjustments should generally be adequately disclosed, quantified and the reasons for adjustment explained[46]. Adjustments that can be reliably estimated may be made by management to the historical financial information to:

(a) reclassify historical amounts. Reclassification may include for example, opening adjustments on adoption of new standards or accounting policies. Reclassification also includes consistency and hindsight adjustments between different years and may also include a re-assessment of the unusual and/or non-recurring nature of items in the light of current circumstances and Accounting Standards, and from a potential investor's perspective. The professional accountant needs to consider the effects of items that constitute the profit history of the client entity such as unusual and/or non-recurring items, extraordinary items or prior restructuring costs; and

(b) account for transaction-specific effects which clearly necessitate adjustment. These may include, for example:

(i) significant changes to the financing structure rendering historic interest and taxation charges irrelevant. The presentation of earnings before interest and

44 Also see AGS 1016 "Audit and Review Reports on Half-Year Financial Reports of Disclosing Entities under the *Corporations Act 2001*".

45 Furthermore, it is the responsibility of management of the client entity to inform the ASX if the financial statements have not been audited or reviewed [see for example the asset test 1.3.5 (a)]. Also see Section 715 and PS 157 in relation to financial reports in offer information statements.

46 See Section 728 of the Act which addresses misstatements in, or omissions from, disclosure documents.

tax rather than net profit after tax and extraordinary items may be more appropriate;

(ii) significant changes to the asset structure resulting in the reporting of earnings before depreciation, interest and taxes;

(iii) notional consolidation for multiple entities, or exclusion of the consolidated results of parts of a group when only parts of a group are floated; and

(iv) sale of a former subsidiary or division with any gain or loss on disposal being separately identified for the purposes of the offer.

.43 The professional accountant considers management's adjustments in accordance with AUS 306 "Materiality and Audit Adjustments". Adjustments are made to the historical information only if they are material. Materiality should also be considered under Section 728 of the Act from the perspective of investors which determines that an offence has occurred if the misleading or deceptive statement, omission or new circumstance is materially adverse from the point of view of investors[47]. Generally:

(a) older information will be of less relevance;

(b) information that indicates trends may become more significant than other information that does not capture trends; and

(c) items of a recurring nature may also become more significant than non-recurring items, particularly if the items affect the prospects of the client entity. The professional accountant considers making potential adjustments for non-recurring items only where appropriate.

In obtaining assurance for drawing conclusions, the professional accountant avoids making misleading statements in a disclosure document by stating in the report or elsewhere in the contents of the disclosure document that all adjustments considered necessary have been made, or alternatively that no adjustments are necessary.

Prospective Financial Information

.44 AUS 804 provides guidance regarding the appropriate procedures to be applied to prospective financial information. Furthermore, PS 170 provides guidance with respect to the expected disclosures in relation to forecasts and projections. PS 170 states that a disclosure document must disclose the basis of any forecast so that investors can properly assess the forecast or projection. A supplementary disclosure document may be required if a forecast or projection changes significantly.

.45 Where the professional accountant as an expert engages a specialist(s) to assist with the engagement, the principles in AUS 606 "Using the Work of an Expert" may be modified as necessary to suit the engagement. Furthermore, PN 43.27 places a responsibility on the professional accountant to:

(a) assess whether the specialist(s) is competent in the field;

(b) assess whether the assumptions and methodologies that have been used seem reasonable, and draw on source data that appears to be appropriate;

(c) ensure that the specialist(s) is independent of, and is perceived to be independent of, interested parties[48];

(d) have a clear agreement with the specialist(s) concerning the purpose and scope of the work performed by the specialist(s); and

(e) require the specialist(s) to sign his or her report and consent to the use of it in the form and context in which it will be published[49].

AGS

47 The provisions of the Act would override the requirements of AUS 306 should the application of the Act and AUS 306 yield a different result.

48 PN 43.27 requires that any lack of independence by the specialist should be clearly and prominently disclosed. The Professional Accountant's Report should not be described as an independent report if the expert is not independent.

49 PN 43.27 also requires that if the professional accountant as expert does not ensure that the specialist take responsibility for the report, and does not consent to the use of the report in an appropriate form and context, the professional accountant must accept the entire responsibility for the statements in the report as his or her own, and must have reasonable grounds for believing that the statements are not misleading.

Forecasts

.46 The professional accountant(s) may have separate engagements in relation to the historical and prospective financial information contained in a disclosure document. However, when the professional accountant is engaged to obtain assurance in relation to prospective financial information that is prepared by the client entity, the professional accountant considers also the historical financial information to ensure that both prospective and historical information are developed on a consistent basis and presented in a consistent manner. The professional accountant obtains assurance in relation to the prospective financial information in forecasts in accordance with the requirements of AUS 804 and the guidance in this AGS. Furthermore, PS 170 requires also that an investor must be able to make an informed assessment of the reliability of a forecast and therefore must be able to assess:

(a) the validity of the assumptions on which the forecast is based;

(b) the likelihood of the assumptions actually occurring; and

(c) the effect on the forecast if the assumptions vary.

.47 Therefore, a disclosure document containing a forecast prepared by management is required to clearly disclose information for investors concerning:

(a) the specific assumptions used by management to compile a forecast that materially affect the significant variables, such as net profit or net assets in a forecast, and the overall forecast outcome [PS 170][50];

(b) explanations of the material details about the enquiries and research undertaken and the process followed by management in preparing the forecast [PS 170];

(c) the specific period of the forecast and an explanation of the choice of period[51]. For forecasts beyond 2 years, ASIC generally will require supporting material to ensure that there is reasonable grounds for the forecast(s). Moreover, forecasts should generally be consistent with the reporting period of the issuer [PS 170];

(d) the risks or factors that may or may not be within management's control that could result in the forecast not being achieved, and that there may be a significant difference between forecast and actual results. PS 170 suggests that presenting a forecast in terms of a range may make the uncertainty in a forecast clearer for significant variables such as net profits or net assets in a disclosure document. The disclosure document should state which variables will have a significant effect on the outcome within the range. Moreover, the linkage between the assumptions, the significant variables, and the upper and lower ends of the range should be clear. A range in a forecast needs to be small enough to provide meaningful information about future prospects. Furthermore, it may be misleading to include a range when the expectation is for results at the lower end of the range [PS 170]. A more favourable figure or fact in a management forecast should not be given undue prominence; and

(e) the sensitivity of the forecast to changes in key assumptions, and its impact on significant variables such as net profits or net assets included in the forecast. Furthermore, when a range is used by management in a sensitivity analysis, it should be realistic.

.48 The professional accountant considers the reasonableness of the client entity's best-estimate assumptions used to prepare profit forecasts, and the adequacy of the disclosures given in the disclosure document regarding those assumptions, and gathers sufficient appropriate evidence to obtain assurance for the conclusion in the report.

Projections

.49 The professional accountant considers evidence in relation to the client entity's projections, and collects evidence to gain an understanding whether the projection has been prepared on a basis consistent with the purpose of the prospective financial information provided by management in the disclosure document. Under Section 728(2) of the Act, Director's

50 See *GIO Australia Holdings Ltd v AMP Insurance Investment Holdings Pty Ltd* (1998) 29 ACSR 584, which requires the specific impact of the assumption to be set out.

51 See PN 43.49.

Projections need to meet the reasonable grounds test for inclusion in a disclosure document[52]. It may be useful to note that in general ASIC is of the view that projections will not have reasonable grounds (because they are based on hypothetical assumptions or a combination of best-estimate and hypothetical assumptions).

.50 The professional accountant also considers:

(a) the significant implications arising from the hypothetical assumptions in accordance with AUS 804.23; and

(b) management responses to enquiries made by the professional accountant in relation to the material details in the projection. The professional accountant seeks explanations of the material details, such as the research undertaken, and the process followed by management to establish the hypothetical assumptions in preparing the projection. PS 170 also requires the professional accountant to document the procedures conducted on the hypothetical assumptions established by management.

.51 When prospective information that comprises both forecasts and projections is significantly affected by hypothetical assumptions, the prospective information should be treated as a projection rather than a forecast. Also, if any of the hypothetical assumptions underlying the projection are material, then in accordance with PS 170 the projection is very unlikely to have reasonable grounds. As a result, such a projection should not be included in any disclosure document. The professional accountant also has particular regard to the nature of the disclosures made. For example, the professional accountant considers whether:

(a) forecasts based on best-estimate assumptions have been clearly differentiated from projections based on hypothetical assumptions; and

(b) best-estimate assumptions and hypothetical assumptions have been clearly differentiated in the disclosures given.

Other Considerations

.52 The professional accountant adapts AUS 502 "Audit Evidence" as necessary to suit the engagement. The professional accountant obtains sufficient appropriate evidence on which to base the conclusion. Sufficiency is the measure of the quantity of evidence obtained and appropriateness is the measure of its quality, including its relevance to the subject matter. The decision as to whether a sufficient quantity of evidence has been obtained will be influenced by its quality. The quality of evidence available to the professional accountant will be affected by the nature of the subject matter and the quality of the criteria, and also by the nature and extent of the procedures applied by the professional accountant. A determination as to the sufficiency and appropriateness of evidence is a matter of professional judgement. The professional accountant collects and evaluates evidence to evaluate whether the subject matter is in conformity with the identified criteria. The conclusions expressed and the level of assurance obtained is determined by the nature and extent of the procedures and the nature of the subject matter, which reflect on the quality of evidence obtained.

.53 The professional accountant adapts AUS 208 "Documentation" to document matters that are important in providing evidence to support the conclusion expressed in the Professional Accountant's Report, and in providing evidence that the engagement was performed in accordance with applicable Auditing and Assurance Standards. Documentation includes a record of the professional accountant's reasoning on all significant matters, that require the exercise of judgement, together with the professional accountant's conclusion thereon. In areas involving difficult questions of principle or judgement, the documentation will include the relevant facts that were known by the professional accountant at the time the conclusion was reached[53].

52 Also see paragraph .04(e)(iii) in the "Definitions" section and paragraph .22 "Responsibilities of Management" section of this AGS in relation to section 728(2).

53 The professional accountant may also use the evidence and if necessary documentation for defending a potential liability that may arise under Sections 728 and 729 of the Act. For example, evidence and documentation may be used for due diligence defences for disclosure documents (Section 731); lack of knowledge defence for offer information statements and profile statements (Section 732); and as a general defence for all disclosure documents (Section 733).

AGS

.54 The professional accountant considers if the client entity is a going concern in accordance with AUS 708 "Going Concern". Expressing a going concern uncertainty would preclude the client entity from being listed on a prescribed financial market such as the ASX[54], and also results in the professional accountant withdrawing from the engagement. The professional accountant also considers the forecasts and/or projections, cash flows, and the statement of financial position in conjunction with the Directors' working capital statement when establishing whether the client entity is a going concern. The professional accountant also considers the cash flow information that supports the prospective financial information because if the prospects for profitability are not also supported by adequate cash flows, then both the forecast of the statement of financial performance and the ongoing viability of the entity are at risk. There may, however, be mitigating factors that may eliminate the going concern uncertainty with fundraising for the client entity. These factors include unequivocal financial support from another entity which has the capacity to provide support, or when the proceeds from the issue will result in the client entity becoming a going concern. In such circumstances, the professional accountant documents how unequivocal financial support and the proceeds from the issue will provide the funding for future operations of the client entity, and will result in the client entity becoming a going concern.

.55 The professional accountant also has regard to events occurring after the reporting date to ensure that events between the date of the latest audited financial report and the publication of the disclosure document are identified and reflected in the financial information presented in the disclosure document, including the Independent Accountant's Report. The basic principles and essential procedures in AUS 706 "Subsequent Events" may be adapted as necessary to suit fundraising engagements.

.56 Section 716 of the Act requires the professional accountant to consent to the form and content of the report included in a disclosure document. Therefore, the professional accountant considers the information in the entire disclosure document to ensure that there are no material omissions or misleading or deceptive statements or inconsistent statements in the disclosure document, that may be related to the Independent Accountant's Report. The professional accountant pays specific attention to areas such as:

(a) summarised financial information and its cross referencing and consistency with the report issued for the engagement;
(b) other financial information such as asset values in other expert reports;
(c) the clarity in the specification of assumptions in relation to prospective financial information, the level of assurance obtained[55];
(d) management discussion and analysis of historical and forecast results;
(e) the terms of the issue such as the nature and amount of the securities, their value and rights as well as any minimum subscription;
(f) the purpose of the offer as well as how the proceeds will be applied;
(g) the risks associated with the offer; and
(h) other relevant and material information such as:
    (i) explanations of how revenue would be generated, including relevant contracts;
    (ii) other forward looking statements on the prospects of the client entity in the disclosure document that may be of a qualitative nature[56];
    (iii) nature and extent of related party disclosures;
    (iv) valuation of assets including intangible assets; and
    (v) subsequent losses.

If there are material deficiencies, misleading or deceptive statements, or significant new matters omitted from the disclosure document, which come to the professional accountant's attention, even after the disclosure document is lodged with ASIC, Section 730 of the Act

54 See the profit test in ASX 1.2 "Admission".

55 See PS 170.

56 Forward looking statements may require additional disclosure such as material assumptions.

requires the professional accountant to inform the person making the offer[57]. When the client entity is notified about material deficiencies, misleading or deceptive statements, or significant new matters that are omitted from the disclosure document and these are not corrected in the disclosure document, the professional accountant withdraws consent from the disclosure document and advises the client entity and ASIC accordingly.

Reporting on the Engagement

.57 The Professional Accountant's Report, known as the "Independent Accountant's Report" is prepared in accordance with the scope and nature of the engagement. The Independent Accountant's Report may be a report that is specifically directed towards historical, pro forma historical, or prospective financial information. The Independent Accountant's Report may also be a composite report that addresses historical (and pro forma historical information) and prospective financial information. When preparing a composite report covering both historical and prospective financial information, the professional accountant ensures:

(a) the historical and prospective financial information is clearly and separately identified in the disclosure document; and

(b) the Independent Accountant's Report clearly identifies and segregates the work carried out on the different components of financial information.

.58 The Independent Accountant's Report adapts the basic principles and essential procedures in existing Auditing and Assurance Standards and Guidance to provide the client entity with the agreed level of assurance in relation to the information prepared for the potential investor. For example :

(a) *Historical (and pro forma historical) information.* The professional accountant may adopt the basic principles and essential procedures in AUS 702 "The Audit Report on a General Purpose Financial Report" for positive assurance on historical and pro forma historical information respectively. AUS 902 may also be adapted for negative assurance engagements. On pro forma historical information, PS 170 requires the professional accountant provide at least negative assurance in relation to whether the pro forma historical information has been properly prepared on the basis of pro forma transactions. When an audit is conducted, the professional accountant expresses the conclusion in the form of positive (audit level) assurance rather than negative assurance.

(b) *Prospective financial information.* The professional accountant applies the basic principles and essential procedures in AUS 804 or in AUS 902 adapted as necessary for negative assurance. In relation to the assumptions in prospective financial information, the professional accountant in accordance with PS 170 generally provides negative assurance in relation to best-estimate assumptions[58], and does not provide any assurance in relation to hypothetical assumptions[59]. PS 170 requires that the report of the professional accountant, as an expert, clearly identifies which assumptions made by the Directors may be subject to negative

AGS

57 Section 728 of the Act makes the person making the statement liable for material deficiencies, misleading or deceptive statements, or significant new matters omitted from the disclosure document.

58 Although the conclusion may be a statement of negative assurance, AUS 804.10(a) requires the auditor to perform sufficient appropriate audit level procedures to obtain sufficient appropriate evidence to issue a statement of negative assurance on the reasonableness of management's best-estimate assumptions.

59 AUS 804.10(b) requires the professional accountant not to express a conclusion on the hypothetical assumptions. However, when there are best-estimate and hypothetical assumptions and the hypothetical assumptions are not material to the projection, then it may be possible to express negative assurance on the projection in accordance with PS 170. PS 170 requests the professional accountant to consider whether a particular assumption is "significant". In the context of assessing whether assumptions are "significant" in accordance with PS 170, the professional accountant applies the basic principles and essential procedures in AUS 306 "Materiality and Audit Adjustments". In applying the basic principles and essential procedures in accordance with AUS 306, the professional accountant gives consideration to both the quantitative and qualitative nature of the assumption(s), the potential for the assumption(s) to be material in the context of the investment decision of a prospective investor, and the impact of the assumption(s) on the reasonable grounds test for the prospective financial information to which the assumption(s) pertains. PS 170 specifies only the minimum assurance that is required for hypothetical assumptions (no assurance) and best-estimate assumptions (review assurance).

assurance (bestestimate assumptions) and which are not subject to any assurance (hypothetical assumptions). The professional accountant is required to check whether the assumptions are appropriately disclosed. If the disclosure document does not include this disclosure, the professional accountant considers issuing a qualified report or withdrawing from the engagement.

(c) *Other assurance engagements*:

(i) *Compilation engagements*. The professional accountant may report in accordance with AUS 904 "Engagements to Perform Agreedupon Procedures" and APS 9 "Statement on Compilation of Financial Reports". The professional accountant clarifies management's acceptance of responsibility in relation to the compilation; and

(ii) *Other engagements*. In due diligence engagements in relation to fundraising, the professional accountant communicates with management by adapting the basic principles and essential procedures in AUS 710 "Communicating with Management on Matters Arising from an Audit".

.59 The responsibility for the preparation of the financial information including historical information, pro forma historical information, projections and forecasts rests with management. PS 170 requires that where the professional accountant, as expert, is also engaged to compile the financial report, the professional accountant needs to disclose the extent of responsibility for the preparation of the financial information in the report.

.60 The "Independent Accountant's Report" includes the following basic elements, ordinarily laid out as:

(a) a title;

(b) the addressee;

(c) a background section that:

(i) identifies the purpose of the report;

(ii) identifies the information being reported on;

(iii) states that the Independent Accountant's Report has been prepared for inclusion in the disclosure document; and

(iv) defines the responsibilities of each of the professional accountant and management in relation to the disclosure document;

(d) section(s) describing the scope of the engagement. The scope section(s) generally:

(i) includes similar content to that normally included for audit and review engagements;

(ii) separates audit and review procedures; and

(iii) refers to the financial information section that outlines the basis of accounting, and any adjustments that have been made to the financial information for the disclosure document[60].

The scope section(s) may also refer to the source(s) of the financial information in instances where the professional accountant was the prior year external auditor. When the professional accountant was not the prior year auditor, the professional accountant refers to the prior year auditor. The prior year auditor would also be named in the disclosure document and a formal consent needs to be obtained for that disclosure from the external auditor. The scope section may also indicate how a previous financial report qualification(s) is addressed in the disclosure document[61].

(e) in circumstances, when there are matters that come to the professional accountant's attention that require the assurance provided to be qualified, the Independent

60 The adjustments may be detailed in a separate section of the disclosure document and the section may only be referred to in the report.

61 In instances where there may be a limitation of scope on the work performed, the scope section may include a disclaimer with respect to future events for prospective information, and a statement that the work was less in scope than an audit.

Accountant's Report draws attention to these matters in a separate section describing the qualification[62];

(f) a section expressing the professional accountant's conclusions on the financial information. Separate conclusions may be required for historical information, pro forma historical information, and prospective financial information and also to distinguish assurance provided in different reports;

(g) a section on the potential impact of subsequent events, if applicable;

(h) an independence or disclosure of interest statement[63];

(i) the professional accountant's signature;

(j) the professional accountant's address; and

(k) the date of the report (generally on or after the date of the disclosure document)[64].

.61 The professional accountant obtains assurance to support the conclusion in the Independent Accountant's Report in accordance with the requirements of the Act and the terms of engagement. The professional accountant considers the nature of the financial information (i.e. historical or prospective financial information) in the disclosure document when obtaining assurance. Appendix 1 to this AGS clarifies the reporting guidance for the professional accountant in AUS 804 and this AGS in relation to financial information in disclosure documents. Appendix 2 includes sample Independent Accountant's Reports on historical and prospective financial information.

.62 As the professional accountant consents to the report being issued as part of the disclosure document under the Act, the professional accountant needs to ensure that the Independent Accountant's Report is:

(a) issued by the professional accountant, and included in the disclosure document. The professional accountant takes responsibility only for the specific section(s) in the disclosure document that the professional accountant has agreed to in the terms of engagement with management;

(b) appropriately cross referenced and consistent with other information disclosed in the disclosure document; and

(c) appropriately positioned in the disclosure document in relation to the information on which the professional accountant gives assurance[65].

Operative Date

.63 This AGS is operative from date of issue.

Compatibility with International Standards and Statements on Auditing

.64 There is no corresponding International Standard or Statement on Auditing.

AGS

62 See PS 170.

63 See PN 42.

64 The offer information date is the date the Directors date the prospectus, and the date to which subsequent events are considered. The date is generally as close to the disclosure document issue date as practicable.

65 See PS 170.

Appendix 1

Reporting on Financial Information in a Disclosure Document#

<table>
<tr><td colspan="2"></td><td colspan="3">Financial Information in a Disclosure Document</td></tr>
<tr><td colspan="2" rowspan="2">The Independent Accountant's Report</td><td rowspan="2">Historical Information*</td><td colspan="2">Prospectives (Note 3)</td></tr>
<tr><td>Forecasts (Best Estimate Assumptions Only)</td><td>Projections (Best Estimate and/ or Hypothetical Assumptions)</td></tr>
<tr><td></td><td>Conclusion</td><td></td><td></td><td></td></tr>
<tr><td rowspan="2">Reporting Guidance</td><td>Audit
(positive statement of expression)</td><td>Appendix 2 (Example 1)</td><td>Note 2</td><td>Note 1</td></tr>
<tr><td>Review
(negative statement of expression)</td><td>Appendix 2 (Example 2)</td><td>Appendix 2 (Example 3)</td><td>Appendix 2 (Example 3 Modified as necessary - also see Note 4)</td></tr>
</table>

\# In a number of circumstances a composite report may be issued that combines a forecast with pro forma historical information.

* Historical information includes pro forma historical financial information.

Notes:

(1) Shading of the "Audit Conclusion" under "Projections" above indicates that the audit conclusion does not apply to projections.

(2) An audit report on forecasts may be issued only in rare and exceptional circumstances. For guidance on audits of forecasts see AUS 804.

(3) Prospective financial information in a disclosure document must have reasonable grounds for its inclusion. Where hypothetical assumptions are used, the report should state whether or not those assumptions may have a significant impact upon the prospective financial information presented. The larger the impact of hypothetical assumptions on a projected outcome, the more likely it is the projection will not be based on reasonable grounds. Where the prospective financial information is a forecast, the best-estimate assumptions must be objectively reasonable. See PS 170.

(4) Directors include projections as part of the disclosure document only when there are reasonable grounds under Section 728(2) of the Act. Also, in accordance with paragraph .51 of this AGS, if any of the hypothetical assumptions underlying the Director's Projections are material, then in accordance with PS 170 it is very unlikely that the projection has reasonable grounds. Therefore projections with material hypothetical assumptions should generally not be included in any disclosure document. The professional accountant issues a report on projected financial information only in rare and exceptional circumstances to avoid making misleading or deceptive statements under Section 728(1) of the Act.

Appendix 2

Examples of Independent Accountants' Reports

This example report incorporates the requirements of this AGS. However, it is not intended to suggest standard wording for circumstances relating to all engagements.

Example 1: Independent Accountant's Report on Audited Historical Financial Information

The Directors

[Name of Company / Trust]

[Address]

[Date][1]

Subject: Independent Accountant's Report on Audited Historical Financial Information

Dear [Addressee],

We have prepared this Independent Accountant's Report (report) on historical financial information of ______ [and controlled entities] (the Company / Trust) for inclusion in a {disclosure document} dated on or about ______, the {disclosure document[2]} relating to the issue of __________ [ordinary shares / units] in the [Company / Trust].

Expressions defined in the {disclosure document} have the same meaning in this report.

Background

[insert any background information relating to the Company / Trust which is deemed relevant]

Scope

You have requested [Firm Name] to prepare a report covering the following information:

(a) the historical financial performance of the [Company / Trust] for the [year(s) / period(s)] ended __________;

(b) the historical statement of financial position as at ________ and the pro forma statement of financial position as at ________ which assumes completion of the contemplated transactions disclosed in Section [ ] of the {disclosure document} (the pro forma transactions);

(c) the statement of cash flows (if applicable).

[insert any other information relating to the Company / Trust which is deemed relevant[3]] (referred to collectively as the historical financial information)

Audit of Historical Financial Information

The historical financial information set out in Section [ ] of the {disclosure document} has been extracted from the [audited] financial statements of the [Company / Trust] which was previously audited by [Firm Name] that issued a [qualified/unqualified] audit opinion in respect of the historical financial information. The [Directors / Directors of the client entity] are responsible for the preparation of the historical financial information, including determination of the adjustments.

We have audited the historical financial information of the [Company / Trust] for the period(s) ended [insert end(s) of the period(s)]. Our audit has been conducted in accordance with Australian Auditing and Assurance Standards to provide reasonable assurance whether the historical financial information is free of material misstatement. Our procedures included examination,

---

1 The date of both the hard copy and electronic versions of the report should be the same. The professional accountant may provide the electronic report in Adobe Acrobat© PDF format where possible to ensure the electronic report is an identical copy of the hard copy report. See PS 107.

2 Specify the type of disclosure document.

3 Include, for example, any departure from the disclosure requirements of an Accounting Standard or UIG Consensus View and the reasons for the departure, in relation to the financial information prepared for the benefit of the potential investor (see paragraph .37 of this AGS).

on a test basis, of evidence supporting the amounts and other disclosures in the historical financial information, and the evaluation of accounting policies and significant accounting estimates. Our procedures also included:

- consideration of the assumptions used to compile the pro forma statement of financial position and/or statement of financial performance;
- audit of the pro forma historical financial information; and
- comparison of consistency in application of the recognition and measurement principles in Accounting Standards and other mandatory professional reporting requirements in Australia, and the accounting policies adopted by the [Company / Trust] disclosed in Section [ ] of the {disclosure document} [and the requirements of the constitution].

These procedures have been undertaken to form an opinion whether, in all material respects, the historical financial information is presented fairly in accordance with the recognition and measurement principles prescribed in Accounting Standards and other mandatory professional reporting requirements [and relevant statutory and other requirements] in Australia so as to present a view which is consistent with our understanding of the [Company / Trust] financial position, the results of its operations and its cash flows. The audit opinion expressed in this report has been formed on the above basis.

Conclusion:

Audit Opinion on Historical Financial Information

In our opinion:

- the pro forma statement of financial position has been properly prepared on the basis of the transactions described in Section [ ] Notes to the Financial Information in the {disclosure document}; and
- the other historical financial information, as set out in Section [ ] of the {disclosure document} presents fairly:

  (a) the historical financial performance of the [Company / Trust] for the [year(s) / period(s)] ended ________; and

  (b) the historical statement of financial position of the [Company / Trust] as at ________,

  in accordance with the recognition and measurement principles prescribed in Accounting Standards and other mandatory professional reporting requirements, and accounting policies adopted by the [Company / Trust] disclosed in Section [ ] of the {disclosure document} [and the requirements of the constitution][4].

Subsequent events

Apart from the matters dealt with in this report, and having regard to the scope of our report, to the best of our knowledge and belief, no material transactions or events outside of the ordinary business of the [Company / Trust] have come to our attention that would require comment on, or adjustment to, the information referred to in our report or that would cause such information to be misleading or deceptive.

Independence or Disclosure of Interest[5]

[Firm Name] does not have any interest in the outcome of this issue other than in [state interest] for which normal professional fees will be received.

Yours faithfully

[Partner]

[Firm Name]

---

4 Identify departures from the disclosure requirements of Accounting Standards and UIG Consensus Views if applicable (see paragraph .37 of this AGS).

5 See PN 42.

Example 2: Independent Accountant's Report on Reviewed Historical Financial Information

The Directors

[Name of Company / Trust]

[Address]

[Date][6]

Subject: Independent Accountant's Report on Reviewed Historical Financial Information

Dear [Addressee],

We have prepared this Independent Accountant's Report (report) on historical financial information of _______ [and controlled entities] (the Company / Trust) for inclusion in a {disclosure document} dated on or about _______ the {disclosure document[7]}relating to the issue of [ordinary shares / units] in the [Company / Trust].

Expressions defined in the {disclosure document} have the same meaning in this report.

Background

[insert any background information relating to the Company / Trust which is deemed relevant]

Scope

You have requested [Firm Name] to prepare a report covering the following information:

(a) the historical financial performance of the [Company / Trust] for the [year(s) / period(s)] ended _________;

(b) the historical statement of financial position as at _______ and the pro forma statement of financial position as at _______, which assumes completion of the contemplated transactions disclosed in Section [ ] of the {disclosure document} (the pro forma transactions);

(c) the statement of cash flows (if applicable).

[insert any other information relating to the Company / Trust which is deemed relevant[8]]
(referred to collectively as the historical financial information)

Review of Pro Forma Historical Financial Information

The historical financial information set out in Section [ ] of the {disclosure document} has been extracted from the [audited] financial statements of the [Company / Trust] which was previously audited by [Firm Name] that issued a [qualified/unqualified] audit opinion in respect of the historical financial information. The [Directors / Directors of the client entity] are responsible for the preparation of the historical financial information, including determination of the adjustments.

We have conducted our review of the historical financial information in accordance with the Australian Auditing and Assurance Standard AUS 902 "Review of Financial Reports". We made such inquiries and performed such procedures as we, in our professional judgement, considered reasonable in the circumstances including:

- analytical procedures on the [audited] financial performance of the [Company / Trust] for the relevant historical period;
- a review of work papers, accounting records and other documents;
- a review of the assumptions used to compile the pro forma statement of financial position and/or statement of financial performance;
- a review of the adjustments made to the pro forma historical financial information;

6 The date of both the hard copy and electronic versions of the report should be the same. The professional accountant may provide the electronic report in Adobe Acrobat© PDF format where possible to ensure the electronic report is an identical copy of the hard copy report. See PS 107.

7 Specify the type of disclosure document.

8 Include for example, any departure from the disclosure requirements of an Accounting Standard or UIG Consensus View and the reasons for the departure, in relation to the financial information prepared for the benefit of the potential investor (see paragraph .37 of this AGS).

- a comparison of consistency in application of the recognition and measurement principles in Accounting Standards and other mandatory professional reporting requirements in Australia, and the accounting policies adopted by the [Company / Trust] disclosed in Section [ ] of the {disclosure document} [and the requirements of the constitution], and
- enquiry of Directors, management and others.

These procedures do not provide all the evidence that would be required in an audit, thus the level of assurance provided is less than given in an audit. We have not performed an audit and, accordingly, we do not express an audit opinion.

Conclusion:

Review Statement on Historical Financial Information

Based on our review, which is not an audit, nothing has come to our attention which causes us to believe that:

- the pro forma statement of financial position has not been properly prepared on the basis of the pro forma transactions;
- the historical financial information, as set out in Section [ ] of the {disclosure document} does not present fairly:
  - (a) the historical financial performance of the [Company / Trust] for the [year(s) / period(s)] ended ____________; and
  - (b) the historical statement of financial position of the [Company / Trust] as at ________,

  in accordance with the recognition and measurement principles prescribed in Accounting Standards and other mandatory professional reporting requirements, and accounting policies adopted by the [Company / Trust] disclosed in Section [ ] of the {disclosure document} [and the requirements of the constitution][9].

Subsequent events

Apart from the matters dealt with in this report, and having regard to the scope of our report, to the best of our knowledge and belief no material transactions or events outside of the ordinary business of the [Company / Trust] have come to our attention that would require comment on, or adjustment to, the information referred to in our report or that would cause such information to be misleading or deceptive.

Independence or Disclosure of Interest[10]

[Firm Name] does not have any interest in the outcome of this issue other than in [state interest] for which normal professional fees will be received.

Yours faithfully

[Partner]

[Firm Name]

9 Identify departures from the disclosure requirements of Accounting Standards and UIG Consensus Views if applicable (see paragraph .37 of this AGS).

10 See PN 42.

Example 3: Independent Accountant's Report on Forecast Financial Information[11,12]

The Directors

[Name of Company / Trust]

[Address]

[Date][13]

Subject: Independent Accountant's Report on Forecast Financial Information

Dear [Addressee],

We have prepared this Independent Accountant's Report (report) on the forecast financial information of ______[and controlled entities] (of the [Company / Trust]) for the financial year(s) / period(s)ending ____________ for inclusion in a {disclosure document}[14] dated on or about __________ (the {disclosure document}) relating to the issue of __________ [ordinary shares / units] in the [Company / Trust]. This report is prepared in accordance with AUS 804 "The Audit of Prospective Financial Information" and PS 170 "Prospective financial information".

Expressions defined in the {disclosure document} have the same meaning in this report.

The nature of this report is such that it can be given only by an entity which holds a [specific[15]] licence. [Firm Name] holds the appropriate [specify] licence under the *Corporations Act 2001*.

Background

[insert any background information relating to the Company / Trust which is deemed relevant]

Scope

You have requested [Firm Name] to prepare a report covering the following information:

(a) forecast financial performance of the [Company / Trust] for the [year(s) / period(s)] ending ____________; and

(b) the statement of financial position of the [Company / Trust] as at __________, which assumes completion of the contemplated transactions disclosed in Section [ ] of the {disclosure document} (the pro forma transactions).

AGS

11 In rare and exceptional circumstances, when the Directors' hypothetical assumptions have no material impact on the projected outcome, the professional accountant modifies the report for the Directors' Projection(s) in accordance with the requirements of PS 170. When issuing a report on Directors' Projection(s) the professional accountant considers whether the Directors' Projection(s) included in the disclosure document clearly identify and differentiate hypothetical assumptions from best-estimate assumptions. In addition, in accordance with requirements of PS 170 the professional accountant provides a statement as part of the conclusion in the Independent Accountant's Report that the Directors' hypothetical assumptions have no material impact on the projected outcome in the Directors' Projections. When the hypothetical assumptions have a material impact on the projected outcome, the professional accountant avoids issuing an Independent Accountant's Report on the projection as it is unlikely that the Directors' Projection, as a forward looking statement, has reasonable grounds under Section 728(2) of the Act.

12 The Independent Accountant's Report on Forecast Financial Information may be modified for Directors' Projections. The modifications include, for example, replacement of the word "forecast(s)" with "projection(s)" and referring to "hypothetical assumptions" in conjunction with "best-estimate assumptions" where appropriate (see for example, footnote 18).

13 The date of both the hard copy and electronic versions of the report should be the same. The professional accountant may provide the electronic report in Adobe Acrobat© PDF format where possible to ensure the electronic report is a copy of the hard copy report. See PS 107.

14 Specify the type of disclosure document.

15 The specific licence may be, for example, the Australian Financial Services Licence required by the Act.

[insert any other information relating to the Company / Trust which is deemed relevant[16,17]]

(referred to collectively as the forecasts)

The [Directors / Directors of the client entity] are responsible for the preparation and presentation of the forecasts, including the best-estimate assumptions[18], which include the pro forma transactions, on which they are based. The forecasts have been prepared for inclusion in the {disclosure document}. We disclaim any assumption of responsibility for any reliance on this report or on the forecasts to which it relates for any purposes other than for which it was prepared.

Review of Directors' Best-Estimate Assumptions[19]

Our review of the best-estimate assumptions underlying the Directors' forecasts was conducted in accordance with the Australian Auditing and Assurance Standard AUS 902 "Review of Financial Reports". Our procedures consisted primarily of enquiry and comparison and other such analytical review procedures we considered necessary. These procedures included discussion with the Directors and management of the [Company / Trust] and have been undertaken to form an opinion whether anything has come to our attention which causes us to believe that the best-estimate assumptions do not provide a reasonable basis for the preparation of the forecasts and whether, in all material respects, the forecasts are properly prepared on the basis of the best-estimate assumptions and are presented fairly in accordance with the recognition and measurement principles prescribed in Accounting Standards and other mandatory professional reporting requirements in Australia, and the accounting policies of the [Company / Trust] disclosed in Section [ ] of the {disclosure document} [and the Trust Deed of the Trust dated ______ (the constitution)] so as to present a view of the [Company / Trust] which is consistent with our understanding of the [Company's / Trust's] past, current and future operations.

The forecasts have been prepared by the Directors to provide investors with a guide to the [Company's / Trust's] potential future financial performance based upon the achievement of certain economic, operating, developmental and trading assumptions about future events and actions that have not yet occurred and may not necessarily occur. There is a considerable degree of subjective judgement involved in the preparation of forecasts. Actual results may vary materially from those forecasts and the variation may be materially positive or negative. Accordingly, investors should have regard to the investment risks and sensitivities set out in Section [ ] of the {disclosure document}.

---

16 For Directors' Projections, the Independent Accountant's Report needs to identify and differentiate the hypothetical assumptions and best-estimate assumptions in the disclosure document. The following wording may be used for a projection:

"The Directors' Projections have been prepared by the Directors using a set of assumptions which include:

- best-estimate assumptions relating to future events and management actions that the Directors expect to occur. The Directors' best-estimate assumptions are set out in Section [ ] on pages [ ] and [] of the {disclosure document}; and
- hypothetical assumptions about future events and management actions that may not necessarily occur. The Directors' hypothetical assumptions are set out in Section [ ] on pages [ ] and [ ] of the {disclosure document}."

17 Include for example, any departure from the disclosure requirements of an Accounting Standard or UIG Consensus View and the reasons for the departure, in relation to the financial information prepared for the benefit of the potential investor (see paragraph .37 of this AGS).

18 Include "and hypothetical assumptions" for Directors' Projections.

19 For Directors' Projections modify title to *Review of Directors' Assumptions*. Create a subheading *Best-Estimate Assumptions* under *Review of Directors' Assumptions*.v

Our review of the forecast information that is based on best-estimate assumptions, is substantially less in scope than an audit examination conducted in accordance with Australian Auditing and Assurance Standards. A review of this nature provides less assurance than an audit. We have not performed an audit and we do not express an audit opinion on the forecasts included in the {disclosure document}[20].

Conclusion:

Review Statement on the Forecasts[21]

Based on our review of the forecasts, which is not an audit, and based on an investigation of the reasonableness of the Directors' best-estimate assumptions giving rise to the prospective financial information, nothing has come to our attention which causes us to believe that:

(a) the Directors' best-estimate assumptions set out in Section [ ] of the {disclosure document} do not provide reasonable grounds for the preparation of the forecasts;

(b) the forecasts are not properly compiled on the basis of the Directors' best-estimate assumptions and are presented fairly in accordance with the recognition and measurement principles prescribed in Accounting Standards and other mandatory professional reporting requirements in Australia, and the accounting policies adopted by the [Company / Trust] disclosed in Section [ ] of the {disclosure document} [and the requirements of the constitution];

(c) that the forecast itself is unreasonable; and

(d) the statement of financial position has not been properly prepared on the basis of the pro forma transactions[22].

The underlying assumptions are subject to significant uncertainties and contingencies often outside the control of the [Company / Trust]. If events do not occur as assumed, actual results and distributions achieved by the [Company / Trust] may vary significantly from the forecasts. Accordingly, we do not confirm or guarantee the achievement of the forecasts, as future events, by their very nature, are not capable of independent substantiation.

Subsequent events

Apart from the matters dealt with in this report, and having regard to the scope of our report, to the best of our knowledge and belief no material transactions or events outside of the ordinary business of the [Company / Trust] have come to our attention that would require comment on, or adjustment to, the information referred to in our report or that would cause such information to be misleading or deceptive.

Independence or Disclosure of Interest[23]

[Firm Name] does not have any interest in the outcome of this issue other than in [state interest] for which normal professional fees will be received.

Yours faithfully

[Partner]

[Firm Name]

20 For Directors' Projections, create a subheading Hypothetical Assumptions and introduce the following text below:

"We have also reviewed the Directors' Projections for the years ending [insert date] and [insert date] to assess whether the Directors' have prepared the projections, in all material respects, in accordance with:

- the stated hypothetical assumptions; and
- the accounting policies disclosed in Note 1 set out in Section [ ] of the [disclosure document]."

21 For a projection, modify subheading to *Review Statement on the Projections* and replace "forecast(s)" with "projection(s)" where appropriate.

22 In accordance with PS 170 the following additional statement is required for a projection:
"(e) the hypothetical assumptions identified in Section [ ] on pages [ ] and [ ] of the {disclosure document} have no significant impact on the projected outcome in the Directors' Projections."

23 See PN 42.

GS 001

Concise Financial Reports Under the *Corporations Act 2001*

(Revised March 2010)

Prepared and issued by the Auditing and Assurance Standards Board.

Note from the Institute of Chartered Accountants Australia

This note, prepared by the technical editor, is not part of GS 001.

Historical development

July 2007: GS 001 issued to provide guidance to auditors on reporting on a concise financial report under the *Corporations Act 2001*. The guidance used to form part of AUS 702 and has now been moved to this separate statement. There is no international equivalent.

December 2008: GS 001 revised and reissued following changes to the Accounting Standard AASB 1039 'Concise Financial Reports' in August 2008.

March 2010: GS 001 revised and reissued to reflect the amendments to AASB 1039 'Concise Financial Reports' in June 2009 and the new ASA 810 'Engagements to Report on Summary Financial Statements' issued in October 2009. It is operative for periods beginning on or after 1 January 2010 and there is no equivalent international pronouncement.

Contents

Authority Statement

The Auditing and Assurance Standards Board (AUASB) formulates Guidance Statement GS 001 *Concise Financial Reports Under the Corporations Act 2001* pursuant to section 227B of the *Australian Securities and Investments Commission Act 2001*, for the purposes of providing guidance on auditing and assurance matters.

This Guidance Statement provides guidance to assist the auditor to fulfil the objectives of the audit or assurance engagement. It includes explanatory details on specific matters for the purposes of understanding and complying with AUASB Standards. The auditor exercises professional judgement when using this Guidance Statement.

The Guidance Statement does not prescribe or create new Requirements.

Dated 12 March 2010

M H Kelsall
Chairman - AUASB

Guidance Statement GS 001

Concise Financial Reports Under the *Corporations Act 2001*

Application

1 This Guidance Statement has been formulated by the Auditing and Assurance Standards Board (AUASB) to provide guidance to auditors reporting on a concise financial report prepared under the *Corporations Act 2001* ("the Act") and in accordance with Accounting Standard AASB 1039 *Concise Financial Reports* (as amended June 2009) (AASB 1039).

2 For audits of other concise financial reports, the auditor complies with Auditing Standard ASA 810 *Engagements to Report on Summary Financial Statements*.

3 This Guidance Statement should be used when an auditor conducts an audit under the Australian Auditing Standards.

Issuance Date

4 This Guidance Statement is issued on 1 March 2010 by the AUASB.

Introduction

5 The auditor's objective in respect of a concise financial report prepared under the Act, is to express an opinion:

(a) whether the concise financial report complies with AASB 1039; and

GS

(b) when included, whether the discussion and analysis complies with the requirements of AASB 1039.

Regulatory Requirements

6 The annual financial reporting requirements of a company, registered scheme and disclosing entity are found in section 314(1) of the Act.

7 Section 314(2) of the Act states:

A concise report for a financial year consists of:

(a) a concise financial report for the year drawn up in accordance with accounting standards made for the purpose of this paragraph; and

(b) the directors' report for the year (see sections 298-300A); and

(c) a statement by the auditor:

(i) that the financial report has been audited; and

(ii) whether, in the auditor's opinion, the concise financial report complies with the accounting standards made for the purpose of paragraph (a); and

(d) a copy of any qualification in, and of any statements included in the emphasis of matter section of, the auditor's report on the financial report; and

(e) a statement that the report is a concise report and that the full financial report and auditor's report will be sent to the member free of charge if the member asks for them.

8 Section 314 of the Act does not require a concise report to include the directors' declaration made under section 295(4) of the Act in respect of the (full) financial report for the year. Consequently, where the directors of an entity decide to include the directors' declaration as part of the concise report, the auditor, under ASA 720 *The Auditor's Responsibilities Relating to Other Information in Documents Containing an Audited Financial Report*, needs to read the declaration, along with other documents comprising the concise report, to identify material inconsistencies with the concise financial report and material misstatements of fact.

9 Section 314(3) of the Act requires the auditor to report on whether the discussion and analysis, if required by the Accounting Standard to be included in the concise financial report[1], complies with the requirements laid down by the Accounting Standard. Furthermore, section 314(3)(b) specifies that the auditor need not otherwise audit the statements made in the discussion and analysis.

10 The requirements of the Act relating to concise financial reports are based on the view that a concise financial report can provide members with information relevant to evaluating the business, without giving them fully detailed accounting disclosures. The concise report will, in many cases, be the only report that is sent to members[2]. The provision, to some members, of less detailed information is expected to be sufficient to meet their needs for an understanding of the financial performance, financial position and financing and investing activities of the company, registered scheme or disclosing entity.

Accounting Standard AASB 1039

11 The Australian Accounting Standards Board issued Accounting Standard AASB 1039 *Concise Financial Reports*, the latest revision of which, dated June 2009, is operative for financial reporting periods beginning on or after 1 January 2009.

Discussion and Analysis

12 The Accounting Standard, inter alia, specifies the minimum content of a concise financial report, including a requirement that the financial statements forming part of the concise financial report, other than those of a listed company, be accompanied by discussion and analysis to assist the understanding of members.

---

1 *Discussion and analysis* are not required for listed companies – see AASB 1039 paragraph 24. This is because, unlike other entities, listed companies are required by section 299A of the Act to provide an operational and financial report in the directors' report (which is included in the concise report).

2 Unless members request a copy of the full financial report (annual financial report) – see section 314(2(e) of the Act.

13 AASB 1039 adopts the view that the information reported in the financial statements forming part of the concise financial report will be enhanced by discussion and analysis of the principal factors which affect the financial performance, financial position and financing and investing activities of an entity. According to AASB 1039, the extent of discussion and analysis which is required to be provided in concise financial reports will vary from entity to entity, and from year to year, as is necessary in the circumstances to compensate for the brevity of the concise financial report, compared with the (full) financial report for the year.

14 AASB 1039 does not require the financial statements, forming part of the concise financial report of listed companies, to be accompanied by discussion and analysis. This is so as to avoid repetition of information required to be included in the directors' report by section 299A of the Act.

15 Whilst AASB 1039 does not mandate specific discussion and analysis disclosures, paragraph 27 of the Standard provides examples of the types of disclosures that may, at least, be expected to accompany the financial statements.

Materiality

16 AASB 1039 paragraph 5 specifies that the requirements in AASB 1039 are subject to the requirements of AASB 1031 *Materiality*.

Audit Activities

Engagement Acceptance

17 Given that the concise financial report is an alternative form of reporting to members under the Act, and that the Act prescribes the auditor's reporting requirements, the AUASB takes the view that the audit of the concise financial report is treated, by auditors, as a separate engagement from the audit of the (full) financial report for the year. This view has been taken also because procedures, additional to those performed on the (full) financial report for the year, will be necessary when undertaking the audit of the concise financial report, particularly given that AASB 1039 requires, in certain circumstances, the inclusion of other information not found in the (full) financial report for the year, such as discussion and analysis.

18 In order to avoid any misunderstandings in relation to the audit of the concise financial report, the auditor complies with the engagement acceptance requirements in ASA 810 *Engagements to Report on Summary Financial Statements*. The auditor agrees the terms of the audit engagement with the appropriate person(s) within the entity's governance structure. The prudent auditor records the terms of engagement in writing and obtains written acceptance from the appropriate person representing the entity. These terms may be included in the written terms of the audit engagement for the (full) financial report. On recurring audits, the terms of the engagement are revised and re-confirmed as appropriate.

19 In addition to the specific requirements in ASA 810, the terms of engagement ordinarily include the objective and scope of the audit of the concise financial report (including the audit of discussion and analysis disclosures in that report). Such inclusions differentiate the engagement to audit the concise report from the engagement to audit the (full) financial report.

Audit Procedures

Auditing Standards

20 AASB 1039 requires the concise financial report to be derived from the (full) financial report for the year and each financial statement to be presented as it is in the (full) financial report for the year. Consequently, the audit procedures performed under the Auditing Standards by the auditor when auditing the (full) financial report for the year are effectively performed on that information in the concise financial report that has been derived from the (full) financial report for the year. Accordingly, there is no expectation that such audit procedures need be repeated on the relevant information in the concise financial report.

21 Reference to "audit" and "audit procedures" in the illustrative examples of an auditor's report on the concise financial report (see Appendix 1) relate to all procedures that have

GS

been performed by the auditor (i.e. regarding both the (full) financial report and the concise financial report).

22 When selecting and applying procedures in addition to those performed in relation to the (full) financial report for the year, the auditor complies with ASA 810.

23 Under ASA 810, paragraph 8, the auditor is required to perform specified procedures. Furthermore, the auditor is required to perform additional procedures that the auditor considers necessary as the basis for the auditor's opinion (on the concise financial report), for example, procedures addressing discussion and analysis.

Discussion and Analysis

24 As the inclusion of discussion and analysis is not required in the (full) financial report for the year of some entities reporting under the Act, the audit of a concise financial report will include procedures to enable the auditor to reach a conclusion on the discussion and analysis, as part of forming an opinion on the concise financial report.

25 These procedures may include, a recalculation of ratios and/or trend analyses which have been included in the discussion and analysis; and ensuring that these disclosures are consistent with the information in the (full) financial report for the year.

26 Whilst AASB 1039 requires that the financial statements and the specific disclosures in a concise financial report be consistent with the (full) financial report for the year of the entity, it is recognised that because of the nature of discussion and analysis, such information (for example, a discussion and analysis of the main influences on the costs of the operations of the entity) goes beyond the type of disclosure which is included normally in the audited (full) financial report for the year.

27 In such circumstances, the auditor selects and applies appropriate procedures to be able to reach a conclusion on the discussion and analysis and evaluates the results of such procedures when forming an opinion on whether the discussion and analysis complies with the requirements of AASB 1039. In selecting and applying procedures and evaluating results, the auditor exercises professional judgement in accordance with ASA 200 *Overall Objectives of the Independent Auditor and the Conduct of an Audit in Accordance with Australian Auditing Standards*.

28 Where information of a subjective and/or prospective nature is included in the discussion and analysis, either to comment on, or to augment the entity's financial statements forming part of the concise financial report (for example, a discussion of the impact of significant economic or other events on the operations of the entity), the auditor assesses whether the inclusion of such information in the audited concise financial report has the potential to mislead users.

29 Under ASA 200, the auditor exercises professional judgement in assessing the inclusion of such information in the discussion and analysis. If the auditor considers that this information is overly subjective and/or prospective in nature, and/or that it is information which cannot be quantified or verified, then the auditor refers to Auditing Standard ASA 705 *Modifications to the Opinion in the Independent Auditor's Report*, for requirements and guidance on modifying the auditor's report. Depending on the circumstances, the modification to the auditor's report may be as a result of a disagreement with the directors (those charged with governance) on the adequacy or appropriateness of disclosures in the concise financial report or may be as a result of a limitation in scope.

30 In view of the matters discussed above, it is generally important that the auditor ascertains from the directors (those charged with governance), at an early stage in the audit, the extent and nature of the discussion and analysis that they intend to include in the concise financial report.

31 In ascertaining the extent and nature of the discussion and analysis at an early stage the auditor seeks to avert any difficulties which might otherwise arise with regard to the inclusion of such information. The directors (those charged with governance) are thus informed at that stage if, in the auditor's opinion, there is any possibility that users of the concise financial report might be misled by the inclusion of overly subjective and/or prospective terminology and information in the discussion and analysis which forms part of the concise financial report.

Representations

32 Given that the Act does not require a directors' declaration to be included in the concise report, prior to issuing the auditor's report, it would be prudent for the auditor, under ASA 580 *Written Representations*, to obtain a written representation from the entity's directors which attests that the concise financial report (including, when applicable, discussion and analysis disclosures) complies with the requirements of AASB 1039 and the Act.

The Auditor's Report

33 When reporting on a concise financial report, the auditor complies with the Act and ASA 810. As section 314 of the Act prescribes the auditor's reporting obligations, the auditor adheres to the requirements in ASA 810, paragraph 10 in respect of the prescribed reporting obligations.

34 Under ASA 810, paragraph 10(b), the auditor evaluates whether the users of a concise financial report might misunderstand the auditor's opinion. Due to the precision of wording recommended in this Guidance Statement; and the requirements of the Act, an auditor ordinarily concludes that users will not misunderstand the auditor's opinion.

35 ASA 810, paragraph 14 lists the elements required to be included in an auditor's report.

Modifications to the Opinion, Emphasis of Matter Paragraph and Other Matter Paragraph

36 Under ASA 810, paragraph 17, all modifications to the auditor's report on the (full) financial report are to be included in the auditor's report on the concise financial report. The form of inclusion is dependent on whether the modification to the opinion, emphasis of matter paragraph or other matter paragraph contained in the auditor's report on the (full) financial report is applicable, or not applicable, to the concise financial report.

37 Examples:

(a) AASB 1039 requires the concise financial report to be derived from, and consistent with, the (full) financial report for the year. Accordingly, modifications to the auditor's opinion on the (full) financial report for the year will commonly be applicable to the auditor's opinion on the concise financial report. Certain modifications to the auditor's opinion on the (full) financial report for the year, however, may not be applicable to the auditor's opinion on the concise financial report, such as those relating solely to disclosures in the notes to the (full) financial report for the year.

(b) The auditor may modify the auditor's report relating to the concise financial report only. An example is when an auditor is of the opinion that the discussion and analysis does not comply with the requirements of AASB 1039.

38 Where the auditor's report on the (full) financial report contains an adverse or disclaimer of opinion, the auditor's report on the concise financial report must, under ASA 810, paragraph 18:

(a) state that the auditor's report on the audited financial report contains an adverse opinion or disclaimer of opinion;

(b) describe the basis for that adverse opinion or disclaimer of opinion; and

(c) state that, as a result of the adverse opinion or disclaimer of opinion, it is inappropriate to express an opinion on the concise financial report.

Remuneration Report[3]

39 Where a company includes a Remuneration Report in the annual directors' report, the auditor reports thereon to members. Whilst there is no legal requirement to do so, it is in the public interest that a copy of the auditor's report on the Remuneration Report is included with the auditor's report on the concise financial report.

GS

3 See Guidance Statement GS 008 *The Auditor's Report on a Remuneration Report Pursuant to Section 300A of the Corporations Act 2001.*

Illustrative Examples

40 The illustrative reports in Appendix 1 provide examples of an auditor's report on a concise financial report covering:

- an unmodified opinion;
- modified opinions; and
- an Emphasis of Matter paragraph.

Conformity with International Pronouncements

41 As this Guidance Statement relates to Australian legislative requirements under the Act, there is no equivalent International Standard on Auditing or International Auditing Practice Statement to this Guidance Statement.

Appendix 1

(Ref: Para. 40)

Illustrative Examples of the Auditor's Report on a Concise Financial Report

Introduction

A. *Examples Provided in this Appendix*

Consideration of the examples in this Appendix is as follows:

(i) Unmodified report—consider Example 1.

(ii) Modified report—qualification on (full) financial report that does not affect the opinion on the concise financial report—consider Example 2.

(iii) Modified report—qualification on either:

(a) the concise financial report only; or

(b) both the (full) financial report and the concise financial report—i.e. qualification on (full) financial report that <u>does</u> affect the opinion on the concise financial report—consider Example 3.

(iv) Modified report—Emphasis of Matter Paragraph relating to either:

(a) the concise financial report only; or

(b) both the (full) financial report for the year and the concise financial report—consider Example 4.

Note: Wording used in an auditor's report to describe an auditor's responsibilities will differ according to the circumstances described above.

A schematic of these illustrative examples is provided at paragraph E. below.

B. *Form of Reporting*

AASB 1039 does not specify whether a concise financial report prepared under section 314 of the Act is a "general purpose financial report" within the meaning described in Accounting Standard AASB 101 *Presentation of Financial Statements*. The auditor's reporting obligations, under section 314 , require an opinion on compliance (with AASB 1039), not an expression of opinion on the fair presentation of the financial information. Accordingly, the illustrative example auditor's reports, contained within this Appendix, are not developed from a classification (general purpose or special purpose) of the concise financial report and are not based on the expression of an opinion on fair presentation.

Instead, the illustrative example auditor's reports contained within this Appendix are discrete and have been developed from:

(i) the auditor's reporting obligations specified in the Act;

(ii) the reporting requirements under ASA 810;

(iii) the principles of auditor's reporting found in Auditing Standard ASA 700 *Forming an Opinion and Reporting on a Financial Report* in relation to a compliance financial reporting framework;

(iv) consideration of the nature of concise reports, including concise financial reports, prepared under the Act and AASB 1039; and

(v) recognition of the relationship, prescribed in AASB 1039, of a concise financial report to the audited (full) financial report for the year.

It should be noted that as AASB 1039 does not require parent entity information to be separately disclosed when consolidated financial information is presented in concise financial reports, separate references to the parent entity and consolidated entity are therefore not required in the auditor's report on a concise financial report.

C. *Qualifications*

Section 314(2)(d) of the Act specifies that — "a copy of any qualification in, and of any statements included in the emphasis of matter section of, the auditor's report on the financial report"—is to be included in a concise report.

At the time section 314 was introduced into the Act, the word "qualification" was a generic term and had the same meaning and expression as used in the then Auditing Standards (AUSs) issued by the former Auditing and Assurance Standards Board (AuASB) of the Australian Accounting Research Foundation. Specifically, AUS 702.25(b) stated that a "qualified" opinion should be expressed as:

(i) an "except for" opinion;

(ii) an adverse opinion; or

(iii) an inability to form an opinion.

However, under the current Auditing Standard (ASA 705), the term "qualified" has a specific and different meaning—it refers only to an "except for" type modification to the auditor's opinion. The terminology used in this Guidance Statement is consistent with ASA 705.

The meaning of the term Emphasis of Matter Paragraph does not differ between the Act, the AUSs, the ASAs and this Guidance Statement.

The term "Other Matter Paragraph" has been introduced to the Australian Auditing Standards applicable for financial reporting periods commencing on or after 1 January 2010. Accordingly, the term is not used in the Act but its use has no consequence under the Act.

The use of differing terminology between the Act and this Guidance Statement, as described above, does not mean that the requirements of section 314 of the Act have changed in so far that only "except for" type modifications are included in a concise report. The requirements of the Act remain unchanged and the term "qualification" in the Act covers all three types of modification to the auditor's opinion listed above, regardless of how they may be described in this Guidance Statement (or the Auditing Standards).

D. *Directors' Obligations under the Act*

This Guidance Statement, including the illustrative auditor's reports, is prepared to provide guidance to the auditor reporting on a concise financial report prepared under the *Corporations Act 2001*. It is not prepared to provide guidance to directors on their obligations under the Act, especially regarding section 314(2)(d) that requires a copy of any qualification and/or emphasis of matter [from the auditor's report on the (full) financial report] to be included in the "concise report".

See "Important Notes" at Example 3 with respect to "appropriately restating" a qualification.

E. *Schematic of Illustrative Examples*

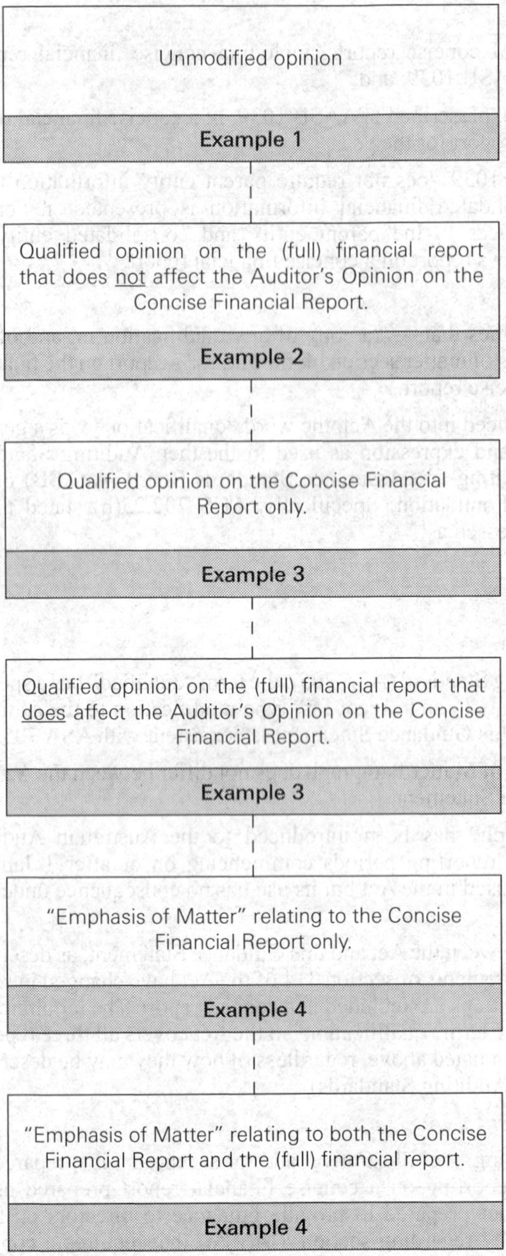

Example 1: Unmodified Report

Unmodified Auditor's Report on a Concise Financial Report prepared under section 314 of the *Corporations Act 2001*.

INDEPENDENT AUDITOR'S REPORT

To the members of [name of entity]:

Report on the Concise Financial Report[4]

We have audited the accompanying concise financial report of [name of entity] which comprises the statement of financial position as at 30 June 20X1, the statement of comprehensive income, statement of changes in equity, statement of cash flows[5] for the year then ended, and related notes, derived from the audited financial report of [name of entity] for the year ended 30 June 20X1 [and the discussion and analysis[6]][7]. The concise financial report does not contain all the disclosures required by the Australian Accounting Standards and accordingly, reading the concise financial report is not a substitute for reading the audited financial report.

Directors'[8] Responsibility for the Concise Financial Report

The Directors are responsible for the preparation of the concise financial report in accordance with Accounting Standard AASB 1039 *Concise Financial Reports*, and the *Corporations Act 2001*, and for such internal control as the directors determine are necessary to enable the preparation of the concise financial report.

Auditor's Responsibility

Our responsibility is to express an opinion on the concise financial report based on our procedures which were conducted in accordance with Auditing Standard ASA 810 *Engagements to Report on Summary Financial Statements*. We have conducted an independent audit, in accordance with Australian Auditing Standards, of the financial report of [name of entity] for the year ended 30 June 20X1. We expressed an unmodified audit opinion on that financial report in our report dated [date]. The Australian Auditing Standards require that we comply with relevant ethical requirements relating to audit engagements and plan and perform the audit to obtain reasonable assurance whether the financial report for the year is free from material misstatement.

An audit involves performing procedures to obtain audit evidence about the amounts and disclosures in the concise financial report. The procedures selected depend on the auditor's judgement, including the assessment of the risks of material misstatement of the concise financial report, whether due to fraud or error. In making those risk assessments, the auditor considers internal control relevant to the entity's preparation of the concise financial report in order to design audit procedures that are appropriate in the circumstances, but not for the purpose of expressing an opinion on the effectiveness of the entity's internal control. Our procedures included testing that the information in the concise financial report is derived from, and is consistent with, the financial report for the year, and examination on a test basis, of audit evidence supporting the amounts [, discussion and analysis,] and other disclosures which were not directly derived from the financial report for the year. These procedures have been undertaken to form an opinion whether, in all material respects, the concise financial report complies with AASB 1039 *Concise*

4 The subheading "Report on the Concise Financial Report" is unnecessary in circumstances when the subheadings "Report on Other Legal and Regulatory Requirements" and "Report on the Remuneration Report" are not applicable.

5 The titles used for financial statements in this example are consistent with those used in AASB 101 *Presentation of Financial* Statements and AASB 1039 *Concise Financial Reports* applicable for annual reporting periods beginning on or after 1 January 2009. AASB 101 permits the use of other appropriate titles, and consequently, auditors should ensure consistency of terms used in the auditor's report with those used in the concise financial report.

6 A discussion and analysis is not required for listed companies due to their section 299A reporting requirement (AASB 1039 paragraph 24-25).

7 As the concise financial report will be included in a document that contains other information (the concise report), the auditor may consider, if the form of presentation allows, identifying the page numbers on which the audited concise financial report is presented.

8 Alternatively, insert the title of those charged with governance.

Financial Reports [and whether the discussion and analysis complies with the requirements laid down in AASB 1039 *Concise Financial Reports*][9].

[The concise financial report and the audited financial report do not reflect the effects of events that occurred subsequent to the date of the auditor's report on the audited financial report.]*

We believe that the audit evidence we have obtained is sufficient and appropriate to provide a basis for our audit opinion.

Independence

In conducting our audit, we have complied with the independence requirements of the *Corporations Act 2001*. We confirm that the independence declaration required by the *Corporations Act 2001*, which has been given to the directors of [name of entity] would be in the same terms if given to the directors as at the time of this auditor's report.#

Opinion

In our opinion, the concise financial report [, including the discussion and analysis[10]] of [name of entity] for the year ended 30 June 20X1 complies with Accounting Standard AASB 1039 *Concise Financial Reports*.

Report on Other Legal and Regulatory Requirements[11]

[Form and content of this section of the auditor's report will vary depending on the nature of the auditor's other reporting responsibilities.]

Report on the Remuneration Report[12]

The following paragraphs are copied from our Report on the Remuneration Report for the [period] ended 30 June 20X1.

[Insert the exact wording, including headings, of the Report on the Remuneration Report for the [period] ended 30 June 20X1.]

[Auditor's signature][13]

[Date of the auditor's report]

[Auditor's address]

---

9 Include when a discussion and analysis is required (i.e. other than listed companies) – AASB 1039 paragraph 24.

* Include if the date of the auditor's report on the concise financial report is later than the date of the auditor's report on the audited financial report.

\# Or, alternatively, include statements: (a) to the effect that circumstances have changed since the declaration was given to the relevant directors; and (b) setting out how the declaration would differ if it had been given to the relevant directors at the time the auditor's report was made.

10 Include when a discussion and analysis has been included in the concise financial report.

11 Include when applicable, such as when a matter has been reported under this heading in the auditor's report on the (full) financial report for the year.

12 Include only when an auditor's Report on the Remuneration Report has been included with the auditor's report on the (full) financial report.

13 The auditor's report needs to be signed in one or more of the following ways: the name of the audit firm, the name of the audit company or the personal name of the auditor as appropriate.

Example 2: Modified Report

Unmodified Auditor's Opinion on a Concise Financial Report prepared under section 314 of the *Corporations Act 2001* – Qualified Auditor's Opinion on the (full) financial report for the year that does not affect the Auditor's Opinion on the Concise Financial Report.

INDEPENDENT AUDITOR'S REPORT

To the members of [name of entity]:

Report on the Concise Financial Report[14]

We have audited the accompanying concise financial report of [name of entity] which comprises the statement of financial position as at 30 June 20X1, the statement of comprehensive income, statement of changes in equity, statement of cash flows[15] for the year then ended, and related notes, derived from the audited financial report of [name of entity] for the year ended 30 June 20X1 [and the discussion and analysis[16]][17]. The concise financial report does not contain all the disclosures required by the Australian Accounting Standards and accordingly, reading the concise financial report is not a substitute for reading the audited financial report.

Directors'[18] Responsibility for the Concise Financial Report

The Directors are responsible for the preparation of the concise financial report in accordance with Accounting Standard AASB 1039 *Concise Financial Reports*, and the *Corporations Act 2001* and for such internal control as the directors determine are necessary to enable the preparation of the concise financial report.

Auditor's Responsibility

Our responsibility is to express an opinion on the concise financial report based on our procedures which were conducted in accordance with Auditing Standard ASA 810 *Engagements to Report on Summary Financial Statements*. We have conducted an independent audit, in accordance with Australian Auditing Standards, of the financial report of [name of entity] for the year ended 30 June 20X1. We expressed a modified audit opinion on that financial report in our report dated [date]. The modification, stated below does not qualify our opinion on the concise financial report[19] because [insert reason(s)]. The Australian Auditing Standards require that we comply with relevant ethical requirements relating to audit engagements and plan and perform the audit to obtain reasonable assurance whether the financial report for the year is free from material misstatement.

An audit involves performing procedures to obtain audit evidence about the amounts and disclosures in the concise financial report. The procedures selected depend on the auditor's judgement, including the assessment of the risks of material misstatement of the concise financial report, whether due to fraud or error. In making those risk assessments, the auditor considers

14 The subheading "Report on the Concise Financial Report" is unnecessary in circumstances when the subheadings "Report on Other Legal and Regulatory Requirements", "Modification to the Auditor's Report on the Financial Report for the Year" and "Report on the Remuneration Report" are not applicable.

15 The titles used for financial statements in this example are consistent with those used in AASB 101 *Presentation of Financial* Statements and AASB 1039 *Concise Financial Reports* applicable for annual reporting periods beginning on or after 1 January 2009. AASB 101 permits the use of other appropriate titles, and consequently, auditors should ensure consistency of terms used in the auditor's report with those used in the concise financial report.

16 A discussion and analysis is not required for listed companies due to their section 299A reporting requirement (see AASB 1039, paragraph 24-25).

17 As the concise financial report will be included in a document that contains other information (the concise report), the auditor may consider, if the form of presentation allows, identifying the page numbers on which the audited concise financial report is presented.

18 Alternatively, insert the title of those charged with governance.

19 An example of a modification to the (full) financial report for the year that does *not* affect the concise financial report is a qualification ("except for") on disclosures in the notes to the financial statements where no such notes are included in the concise financial report. A copy of the modification paragraphs are included in a section of this auditor's report that follows the opinion and is clearly identified as *not* affecting the auditor's opinion on the concise financial report.

internal control relevant to the entity's preparation of the concise financial report in order to design audit procedures that are appropriate in the circumstances, but not for the purpose of expressing an opinion on the effectiveness of the entity's internal control. Our procedures included testing that the information in the concise financial report is derived from, and is consistent with, the financial report for the year, and examination on a test basis, of audit evidence supporting the amounts [, discussion and analysis,] and other disclosures which were not directly derived from the financial report for the year. These procedures have been undertaken to form an opinion whether, in all material respects, the concise financial report complies with Accounting Standard AASB 1039 *Concise Financial Reports* [and whether the discussion and analysis complies with the requirements laid down in AASB 1039 *Concise Financial Reports*][20].

[The concise financial report and the audited financial report do not reflect the effects of events that occurred subsequent to the date of the auditor's report on the audited financial report.]*

We believe that the audit evidence we have obtained is sufficient and appropriate to provide a basis for our audit opinion.

Independence

In conducting our audit, we have complied with the independence requirements of the *Corporations Act 2001*. We confirm that the independence declaration required by the *Corporations Act 2001*, which has been given to the directors of [name of entity] would be in the same terms if given to the directors as at the time of this auditor's report.#

Opinion

In our opinion, the concise financial report [, including the discussion and analysis[21]] of [name of entity] for the year ended 30 June 20X1 complies with Accounting Standard AASB 1039 *Concise Financial Reports*.

Report on Other Legal and Regulatory Requirements[22]

[Form and content of this section of the auditor's report will vary depending on the nature of the auditor's other reporting responsibilities.]

Modification to the Auditor's Report on the Financial Report for the Year

The following paragraphs are copied from our report on the financial report for the year. The modification to the opinion in that report does not apply to our opinion on the Concise Financial Report for the reason(s) stated above.

[Insert the exact wording, including headings, of the basis of modification paragraph(s) and the modified opinion paragraph from the auditor's report on the financial report for the year.]

Report on the Remuneration Report[23]

The following paragraphs are copied from our Report on the Remuneration Report for the [period] ended 30 June 20X1.

[Insert the exact wording, including headings, of the Report on the Remuneration Report for the [period] ended 30 June 20X1.]

---

20 Include when a discussion and analysis is required (i.e. other than listed companies) – see AASB 1039, paragraph 24.

* Include if the date of the auditor's report on the concise financial report is later than the date of the auditor's report on the audited financial report.

\# Or, alternatively, include statements: (a) to the effect that circumstances have changed since the declaration was given to the relevant directors; and (b) setting out how the declaration would differ if it had been given to the relevant directors at the time the auditor's report was made.

21 Include when a discussion and analysis has been included in the concise financial report.

22 Include when applicable, such as when a matter has been reported under this heading in the auditor's report on the (full) financial report for the year.

23 Include only when an auditor's report on the Remuneration Report has been included with the auditor's report on the (full) financial report.

[Auditor's signature][24]

[Date of the auditor's report]

[Auditor's address]

Example 3: Modified Report

Modified Auditor's Opinion on a Concise Financial Report prepared under section 314 of the *Corporations Act 2001* – Qualified Auditor's Opinion ("Except for") relating to either:

a. the Concise Financial Report only; or

b. the (full) financial report and the Concise Financial Report – i.e. Qualified Auditor's Opinion on the (full) financial report for the year that does affect the Auditor's Opinion on the Concise Financial Report.

IMPORTANT NOTES:

1. This example auditor's report (Example 3) illustrates a qualification affecting the opinion on the concise financial report only and a qualification on the (full) financial report for the year that affects the auditor's opinion on the concise financial report.
2. Where a qualification on the (full) financial report for the year affects the auditor's opinion on the concise financial report, the following point is important:

   The primary obligation is for the auditor to opine on the concise financial report and accordingly it may not be appropriate to copy the exact wording of the basis for qualification paragraph from the auditor's report on the (full) financial report. For example, the basis for qualification paragraph on the (full) financial report may include reference to a note to the financial statements which note is not present in the concise financial report. In such circumstances, it will be necessary to "appropriately restate" the wording [from the basis for qualification paragraph on the (full) financial report] in the auditor's report on the concise financial report. Any such "restatement" must reflect the meaning of the basis for qualification on the (full) financial report.

   It is important to remember the qualification on the (full) financial report is the basis for qualifying the concise financial report; however, the wording of the qualification(s) may differ.

GS

24 The auditor's report needs to be signed in one or more of the following ways: the name of the audit firm, the name of the audit company or the personal name of the auditor as appropriate.

INDEPENDENT AUDITOR'S REPORT

To the members of [name of entity]:

Report on the Concise Financial Report[25]

We have audited the accompanying concise financial report of [name of entity], which comprises the statement of financial position as at 30 June 20X1, the statement of comprehensive income, statement of changes in equity, statement of cash flows[26] for the year then ended and related notes, derived from the audited financial report of [name of entity] for the year ended 30 June 20X1 [and the discussion and analysis[27]][28]. The concise financial report does not contain all the disclosures required by the Australian Accounting Standards and accordingly, reading the concise financial report is not a substitute for reading the audited financial report.

Directors'[29] *Responsibility for the Concise Financial Report*

The Directors are responsible for the preparation of the concise financial report in accordance with Accounting Standard AASB 1039 *Concise Financial Reports*, and the *Corporations Act 2001* and for such internal control as the directors determine are necessary to enable the preparation of the concise financial report.

Auditor's Responsibility

Our responsibility is to express an opinion on the concise financial report based on our procedures which were conducted in accordance with Auditing Standard ASA 810 *Engagements to Report on Summary Financial Statements*. We have conducted an independent audit, in accordance with Australian Auditing Standards, of the financial report of [name of entity] for the year ended 30 June 20X1. We expressed a modified audit opinion on that financial report in our report dated [date]. The modification affects our report on the concise financial report and is a modification to our opinion[30] on the concise financial report. The Australian Auditing Standards require that we comply with relevant ethical requirements relating to audit engagements and plan and perform the audit to obtain reasonable assurance whether the financial report for the year is free from material misstatement.

An audit involves performing procedures to obtain audit evidence about the amounts and disclosures in the concise financial report. The procedures selected depend on the auditor's judgement, including the assessment of the risks of material misstatement of the concise financial report, whether due to fraud or error. In making those risk assessments, the auditor considers internal control relevant to the entity's preparation of the concise financial report in order to design audit procedures that are appropriate in the circumstances, but not for the purpose of expressing an opinion on the effectiveness of the entity's internal control. Our procedures included testing that the information in the concise financial report is derived from and consistent with the financial report for the year, and examination on a test basis, of audit evidence supporting the amounts [, discussion and analysis,] and other disclosures which were not directly derived from the financial report for the year. These procedures have been undertaken to form an opinion whether, in all material respects, the concise financial report complies with Accounting Standard

25 The subheading "Report on the Concise Financial Report" is unnecessary in circumstances when the subheadings "Report on Other Legal and Regulatory Requirements" and "Report on the Remuneration Report" are not applicable.

26 The titles used for financial statements in this example are consistent with those used in AASB 101 *Presentation of Financial* Statements and AASB 1039 *Concise Financial Reports* applicable for annual reporting periods beginning on or after 1 January 2009. AASB 101 permits the use of other appropriate titles, and consequently, auditors should ensure consistency of terms used in the auditor's report with those used in the concise financial report.

27 A discussion and analysis is not required for listed companies due to their section 299A reporting requirement (AASB 1039, paragraph 24-25).

28 As the concise financial report will be included in a document that contains other information (the concise report), the auditor may consider, if the form of presentation allows, identifying the page numbers on which the audited concise financial report is presented.

29 Alternatively, insert the title of those charged with governance.

30 An emphasis of matter is not a modification to the auditor's opinion - it is a modification to the auditor's report (see Example 4).

AASB 1039 *Concise Financial Reports* [and whether the discussion and analysis complies with the requirements laid down in AASB 1039 *Concise Financial Reports*][31].

[The concise financial report and the audited financial report do not reflect the effects of events that occurred subsequent to the date of the auditor's report on the audited financial report.]*

We believe that the audit evidence we have obtained is sufficient and appropriate to provide a basis for our audit opinion.

Independence

In conducting our audit, we have complied with the independence requirements of the *Corporations Act 2001*. We confirm that the independence declaration required by the *Corporations Act 2001*, which has been given to the directors of [name of entity] would be in the same terms if given to the directors as at the time of this auditor's report.#

Basis for Qualified Opinion

[Include a clear description of all the substantive reasons for the qualification and quantification of the effects.][32]

[Copy exactly, or appropriately restate, the Basis for Qualified Opinion paragraph(s) from the auditor's report on the financial report for the year.] This basis for qualification to our opinion on the concise financial report is also a basis for qualification to our opinion on the financial report of (name of entity) for the year[33].

Qualified Opinion

In our opinion, except for the effect on the concise financial report of the matter(s) referred to in the preceding paragraph(s), the concise financial report [, including the discussion and analysis[34]] of [name of entity] for the year ended 30 June 20X1 complies with Accounting Standard AASB 1039 *Concise Financial Reports*.

Report on Other Legal and Regulatory Requirements[35]

[Form and content of this section of the auditor's report will vary depending on the nature of the auditor's other reporting responsibilities.]

Report on the Remuneration Report[36]

The following paragraphs are copied from our Report on the Remuneration Report for the [period] ended 30 June 20X1.

[Insert the exact wording, including headings, of the Report on the Remuneration Report for the [period] ended 30 June 20X1.]

[Auditor's signature][37]

31 Include when a discussion and analysis is required (i.e. other than listed companies) – AASB 1039, paragraph 24.

* Include if the date of the auditor's report on the concise financial report is later than the date of the auditor's report on the audited financial report.

\# Or, alternatively, include statements: (a) to the effect that circumstances have changed since the declaration was given to the relevant directors; and (b) setting out how the declaration would differ if it had been given to the relevant directors at the time the auditor's report was made.

32 The qualification affects the opinion on the concise financial report ONLY – for example, a qualification on the *discussion and analysis.*

33 Copy exactly or appropriately restate the wording from the basis for modification paragraph(s) from the auditor's report on the (full) financial report for the year that affects the opinion on the concise financial report. Ensure the modification is described as a copy or restatement of a qualification to the opinion on the financial report for the year.

34 Include when a discussion and analysis has been included in the concise financial report.

35 Include when applicable, such as when a matter has been reported under this heading in the auditor's report on the financial report for the year.

36 Include only when an auditor's Report on the Remuneration Report has been included with the auditor's report on the (full) financial report.

37 The auditor's report needs to be signed in one or more of the following ways: the name of the audit firm, the name of the audit company or the personal name of the auditor as appropriate.

[Date of the auditor's report]

[Auditor's address]

Example 4: Modified Report

Modified Auditor's Report on a Concise Financial Report prepared under section 314 of the *Corporations Act 2001* – Emphasis of Matter Paragraph relating to either:

a. the Concise Financial Report only; or

b. both the (full) financial report for the year and the Concise Financial Report.

INDEPENDENT AUDITOR'S REPORT

To the members of [name of entity]:

Report on the Concise Financial Report[38]

We have audited the accompanying concise financial report of [name of entity] which comprises the statement of financial position as at 30 June 20X1, the statement of comprehensive income, statement of changes in equity (or statement of recognised income and expenses), statement of cash flows[39] for the year then ended, and related notes, derived from the audited financial report of [name of entity] for the year ended 30 June 20X1 [and the discussion and analysis[40]][41]. The concise financial report does not contain all the disclosures required by the Australian Accounting Standards and accordingly, reading the concise financial report is not a substitute for reading the audited financial report.

Directors'[42] Responsibility for the Concise Financial Report

The Directors are responsible for the preparation of the concise financial report in accordance with Accounting Standard AASB 1039 *Concise Financial Reports*, and the *Corporations Act 001* and for such internal control as the directors determine are necessary to enable the preparation of the concise financial report.

Auditor's Responsibility

Our responsibility is to express an opinion on the concise financial report based on our procedures which were conducted in accordance with Auditing Standard ASA 810 *Engagements to Report on Summary Financial Statements*. We have conducted an independent audit, in accordance with Australian Auditing Standards, of the financial report of [name of entity] for the year ended 30 June 20X1. We expressed a modified [unmodified[43]] audit opinion on that financial report in our report dated [date]. The modification, an emphasis of matter, affects [does not affect] the concise financial report [because (state reasons)][44]. The Australian Auditing Standards require that we comply with relevant ethical requirements relating to audit engagements and plan and perform the audit to obtain reasonable assurance whether the financial report for the year is free from material misstatement.

38 The subheading "Report on the Concise Financial Report" is unnecessary in circumstances when the subheadings "Emphasis of Matter in the Auditor's Report on the Financial Report for the Year", "Report on Other Legal and Regulatory Requirements" and "Report on the Remuneration Report" are not applicable.

39 The titles used for financial statements in this example are consistent with those used in AASB 101 *Presentation of Financial* Statements and AASB 1039 *Concise Financial Reports* applicable for annual reporting periods beginning on or after 1 January 2009. AASB 101 permits the use of other appropriate titles, and consequently, auditors should ensure consistency of terms used in the auditor's report with those used in the concise financial report.

40 A discussion and analysis is not required for listed companies due to their section 299A reporting requirement (AASB 1039, paragraph 24-25).

41 As the concise financial report will be included in a document that contains other information (the concise report), the auditor may consider, if the form of presentation allows, identifying the page numbers on which the audited concise financial report is presented.

42 Alternatively, insert the title of those charged with governance.

43 Use only when the auditor's report on the (full) financial report is unmodified (i.e. contains no emphasis of matter paragraph and/or no modification to the opinion.

44 Use this sentence only when the auditor's report on the (full) financial report for the year is modified.

An audit involves performing procedures to obtain audit evidence about the amounts and disclosures in the concise financial report. The procedures selected depend on the auditor's judgement, including the assessment of the risks of material misstatement of the concise financial report, whether due to fraud or error. In making those risk assessments, the auditor considers internal control relevant to the entity's preparation of the concise financial report in order to design audit procedures that are appropriate in the circumstances, but not for the purpose of expressing an opinion on the effectiveness of the entity's internal control. Our included testing that the information in the concise financial report is derived from, and is consistent with, the financial report for the year, and examination on a test basis, of audit evidence supporting the amounts [, discussion and analysis,] and other disclosures which were not directly derived from the financial report for the year. These procedures have been undertaken to form an opinion whether, in all material respects, the concise financial report complies with Accounting Standard AASB 1039 *Concise Financial Reports* [and whether the discussion and analysis complies with the requirements laid down in AASB 1039 *Concise Financial Reports*][45].

[The concise financial report and the audited financial report do not reflect the effects of events that occurred subsequent to the date of the auditor's report on the audited financial report.][*]

We believe that the audit evidence we have obtained is sufficient and appropriate to provide a basis for our audit opinion.

Independence

In conducting our audit, we have complied with the independence requirements of the *Corporations Act 2001*. We confirm that the independence declaration required by the *Corporations Act 2001*, which has been given to the directors of [name of entity] would be in the same terms if given to the directors as at the time of this auditor's report.[#]

Opinion(s)

In our opinion, the concise financial report [, including the discussion and analysis[46]] of [name of entity] for the year ended 30 June 20X1 complies with Accounting Standard AASB 1039 *Concise Financial Reports*.

Description of Emphasis of Matter

Without qualification (or without further qualification) to the opinion expressed above, attention is drawn to… (include details)[47]. [This emphasis of matter paragraph is included in our auditor's report on the financial report of (name of entity) for the year.][48]

Emphasis of Matter in the Auditor's Report on the Financial Report for the Year[49]

The following paragraph(s) are copied from our report on the financial report for the year. The emphasis of matter paragraph in that report does not apply to the Concise Financial Report for the reason(s) stated above.

[Insert the exact wording of the Emphasis of Matter paragraph included in the auditor's report on the financial report for the year.]

45 Include when a discussion and analysis is required (i.e. other than listed companies) – AASB 1039, paragraph 24.

* Include if the date of the auditor's report on the concise financial report is later than the date of the auditor's report on the audited financial report.

\# Or, alternatively, include statements: (a) to the effect that circumstances have changed since the declaration was given to the relevant directors; and (b) setting out how the declaration would differ if it had been given to the relevant directors at the time the auditor's report was made.

46 Include when a discussion and analysis has been included in the concise financial report.

47 Include when the Emphasis of Matter paragraph relates to either: (a) the concise financial report; or (b) both the concise financial report and the (full) financial report for the year.

48 Include only when the Emphasis of Matter paragraph relates to both the concise financial report and the (full) financial report for the year.

49 Include only when the Emphasis of Matter paragraph in the auditor's report on the (full) financial report for the year does not relate to the concise financial report.

Report on Other Legal and Regulatory Requirements[50]

[Form and content of this section of the auditor's report will vary depending on the nature of the auditor's other reporting responsibilities.]

Report on the Remuneration Report[51]

The following paragraphs are copied from our Report on the Remuneration Report for the [period] ended 30 June 20X1.

[Insert the exact wording, including headings, of the Report on the Remuneration Report for the [period] ended 30 June 20X1.]

[Auditor's signature][52]

[Date of the auditor's report]

[Auditor's address]

50 Include when applicable, such as when a matter has been reported under this heading in the auditor's report on the (full) financial report for the year.

51 Include only when an auditor's Report on the Remuneration Report has been included with the auditor's report on the (full) financial report.

52 The auditor's report needs to be signed in one or more of the following ways: the name of the audit firm, the name of the audit company or the personal name of the auditor as appropriate.

GS 002

Special Considerations in the Audit of Risk Management Requirements for Registrable Superannuation Entities and Licensees

(Revised September 2010)

Issued by the Auditing and Assurance Standards Board.

Note from the Institute of Chartered Accountants Australia

This note, prepared by the technical editor, is not part of GS 002.

Historical development

July 2006: AGS 1070 issued in response to a need for guidance in auditing the risk management requirements imposed on registrable superannuation entities and licensees under the *Superannuation Industry Supervision Act 1993* and Regulations. It only relates to entities regulated by the Australian Prudential Regulation Authority and not to self-managed superannuation funds regulated by the Australian Taxation Office.

July 2007: Revised and reissued as GS 002 to reflect the issue of ASAE 3000 'Assurance Engagements other than Audits or Reviews of Historical Financial Information'.

September 2010: Revised and reissued to reflect changes in the format of the auditor's report and the issue of the Clarity Auditing Standards in October 2009. It has no international equivalent.

GS

Contents

AUTHORITY STATEMENT

Authority Statement

The Auditing and Assurance Standards Board (AUASB) formulates Guidance Statement GS 002 *Special Considerations in the Audit of Risk Management Requirements for Registrable Superannuation Entities and Licensees* pursuant to section 227B of the *Australian Securities and Investments Commission Act 2001*, for the purposes of providing guidance on auditing and assurance matters.

This Guidance Statement provides guidance to assist the auditor to fulfil the objectives of the audit or assurance engagement. It includes explanatory material on specific matters for the purposes of understanding and complying with AUASB Standards. The auditor exercises professional judgement when using this Guidance Statement.

The Guidance Statement does not prescribe or create new requirements.

Dated 20 September 2010

M H Kelsall
Chairman - AUASB

Guidance Statement GS 002

Special Considerations in the Audit of Risk Management Requirements for Registrable Superannuation Entities and Licensees

Application

1 This Guidance Statement has been formulated by the Auditing and Assurance Standards Board (AUASB) to provide guidance to auditors on matters relating to:

(a) the audit of compliance with Risk Management Strategies (RMS) for Trustees of the Registrable Superannuation Entity (RSE) Licensee;

(b) the audit of compliance with Risk Management Plans (RMP) of RSEs; and

(c) the review of risk management systems (being the relevant processes and procedures) to maintain future compliance with the RMS and RMP.

Issuance Date

2 This Guidance Statement is issued on 20 September 2010 by the AUASB and replaces GS 002 *Special Considerations in the Audit of Risk Management Requirements for Registrable Superannuation Entities and Licensees* issued in July 2007.

Introduction

3 The audit of compliance with the RMS or the RMP and the review of risk management systems may give rise to a number of special audit considerations. Accordingly, this Guidance Statement clarifies certain responsibilities of the auditor on such engagements, and to provide guidance to the auditor on additional factors which the auditor may consider when planning, conducting and reporting on the audit of compliance with the RMS and RMP and review of the risk management systems of the RSE and the RSE Licensee.

4 This Guidance Statement provides guidance on the existing responsibilities of the auditor of the RSE Licensee and RSE imposed by Australian Auditing Standards (ASA)[1], Standards on Assurance Engagements (ASAE), Standards on Review Engagements (ASRE) and the requirements of the *Superannuation Industry (Supervision) Act 1993* (SIS Act) and the *Superannuation Industry (Supervision) Regulations 1994* (SIS Regulations) but does not add to the auditor's responsibilities contained therein.

5 This Guidance Statement is to be read in conjunction with ASAE 3000 *Assurance Engagements Other than Audits or Reviews of Historical Financial Information* and relevant Australian Prudential Regulation Authority (APRA) guidance in this area. This Guidance Statement only applies to APRA regulated superannuation entities and does not apply to self-managed superannuation funds (Australian Taxation Office (ATO) regulated funds).

Background

6 On 1 July 2004, the *Superannuation Safety Amendment Act 2004* (the SSA Act) introduced requirements for all superannuation trustees to be licensed and for all superannuation entities to become registered by 30 June 2006. As part of obtaining and retaining a licence, the SIS Act requires a Trustee (the RSE Licensee) to maintain the RMS for its operations and a RMP for each superannuation entity (RSE) managed by the RSE Licensee. Where the RSE Licensee manages several similar funds, it may have very similar or identical RMPs for each RSE, if the risks are similar for each fund.

7 The SSA Act introduced sections 29E and 29L in the SIS Act, which require the RSE licensee to maintain the RMS and the RMP for each RSE. The SSA Act also introduced section 113(3)(c) of the SIS Act which requires an opinion by the auditor confirming compliance with the RMS and each RMP for the RSEs, and that the RSE Licensee's risk management systems (being the relevant processes and procedures) are adequate to maintain future compliance with the RMS and each RMP for the RSEs.

8 The prescribed format of the auditor's audit reports and review reports are specified in APRA's Approved Form titled *Superannuation Industry (Supervision) Act 1993 Act 1993 (SIS Act) Section 35C – Approved* issued June 2010 for reporting periods commencing on or after 1 July 2009, and subsequent versions.

Regulatory Requirements for the RMS and the RMP

Contents of the RMS

9 Before APRA will grant a Trustee the RSE Licence, the Trustee is required to have the RMS in place that satisfies the requirements of section 29H of the SIS Act. Once a licence has been granted, the RSE Licensee is required to maintain compliance with the RMS under the SIS Act.

1 The Australian Auditing Standards (ASAs) referred to in this guidance statement are those ASAs issued by the AUASB in October 2009, which apply to audits of financial reports with reporting periods commencing on or after 1 January 2010.

10 In August 2010, APRA issued Prudential Practice Guide SPG 200 – Risk Management[2] which provides guidance on areas the RMS should include.

SPG 200 paragraph 32, states that a non-exhaustive list of the areas of inherent risk that should be considered in developing the *RSE Licensee's RMS* includes:

- Governance risks;
- Investment risks;
- Solvency Risk;
- Liquidity risk;
- Operational risks;
- Outsourcing risk;
- Agency risk;
- Fraud risk;
- External risks; and
- Any other risks - relevant to the operations of the trustee and its compliance with relevant legislation.

Maintaining and reviewing the RMS

11 Section 29HA(1) of the SIS Act requires the RSE Licensee to:

(a) ensure that at all times the RMS is up to date;

(b) ensure that the RMS is reviewed at least once each year to ensure that it complies with section 29H of the SIS Act; and

(c) modify, or replace, the RMS in accordance with section 29HB of the SIS Act if at any time the RSE Licensee becomes aware that the RMS no longer complies with section 29H of the SIS Act.

12 Section 29HA(2) of the SIS Act requires the RSE Licensee to review its risk management strategy within 60 days after the RSE Licensee becomes the RSE Licensee of an additional fund or becomes an acting trustee appointed under Part 17 of the SIS Act. Section 29HC of the SIS Act requires the Trustee to provide a copy of any modified RMS to APRA within 14 days of making the modification.

Contents of the RMP

13 The RSE Licensee is required under the RSE licence to register all superannuation entities for which it is responsible. For each superannuation entity that is registered, the RSE Licensee is required to provide the RMP that meets the requirements of section 29P of the SIS Act. Once the RSE has been registered, the RSE Licensee is required to remain in compliance with the RMP under the SIS Act.

14 SPG 200 provides guidance on areas the RMP may contain. SPG 200 paragraph 53, states that a non-exhaustive list of inherent risks that could be included in the RMP are:

- Specific fund or trust governance risks;
- Risks associated with benefit design;
- Investment risks;
- Operational risks;
- Liquidity risk;
- Valuation risk;
- Outsourcing risk;
- Agency risk;
- Fraud;
- Insurance risk; and
- Any other risk particular to the fund.

2 SPG 200 – Risk Management supersedes Superannuation Guidance Note SGN 120.1 Risk Management July 2004

Maintaining and reviewing the RMP

15 Section 29PA(1) of the SIS Act requires the RSE Licensee of the RSE that has been registered to:

(a) ensure that at all times the RMP for the RSE is up to date; and

(b) ensure that the RMP for the RSE is reviewed at least once each year to ensure that it complies with section 29P of the SIS Act; and

(c) modify or replace, the RMP for the RSE in accordance with section 29PB of the SIS Act if at any time the RSE Licensee becomes aware that the RMP no longer complies with section 29P of the SIS Act.

16 Section 29PA(2) of the SIS Act requires the RSE Licensee to review the RMP within 60 days after the RSE licensee becomes the (new) RSE Licensee or becomes the acting trustee appointed under Part 17 of the SIS Act. Section 29PC of the SIS Act further requires the Trustee to provide a copy of any modified RMP to APRA within 14 days of making the modification.

Risk Management Systems

17 In order to develop the RMS and the RMP for each RSE, the RSE Licensee is required by SPG 200 to establish a risk management system. SPG 200 sets out the main elements of an effective risk management system. These include:

- A continuous process of identification and assessment of all material risks that could adversely affect current and future operations.
- Risk tolerance objectives/thresholds to be determined regarding the overall risk posed to the trustee's business.
- A process to determine and rank residual risks and in the context of the Trustee's risk appetite, develop a risk management plan to accept, mitigate, transfer or avoid the identified risk.
- Control mechanisms in place to mitigate identified risks and to ensure compliance with the risk management framework.
- A process to be implemented and documented to regularly monitor risk profiles and material exposures to losses according to the nature, scale and complexity of the operations.
- Effective management information systems to be established, maintained and documented commensurate with the size and complexity of the operations.

Audit and Review Procedures

Those Who May Conduct the Audit and Review

18 Section 113(1) of the SIS Act, states that "For each year of income, each trustee of a superannuation entity must ensure that an approved auditor is appointed to give the trustee, or the trustees, a report, in the approved form, of the operations of the entity, and the RSE licensee (if any) of the entity, for that year." SIS Regulation 1.04(2) defines an "approved auditor" as follows:

"For the purposes of the definition of "approved auditor" in section 10 of the Act, the following class of persons is specified, namely, individuals each of whom:

(b) in the case of an auditor of a superannuation entity other than a self managed superannuation fund:

(i) is, under Division 2 of Part 9.2 of the Corporations Law, registered, or taken to be registered, as an auditor and is either:

(A) associated with a professional organisation specified in Schedule 1AAA in the manner specified, in respect of that organisation, in that Schedule; or

(B) approved by the Regulator under subregulation (2A); or

(ii) is the Auditor-General of the Commonwealth, a State or Territory."

Schedule 1AAA includes the following professional organisations:

1. CPA Australia (Member);
2. The Institute of Chartered Accountants in Australia (Member);
3. National Institute of Accountants (Member);
4. Association of Taxation and Management Accountants (Member or Fellow); and
5. National Tax and Accountants Association Ltd (Fellow).

The approved auditor may conduct both the financial report audit and the audit and review required under section 113(3)(c) of the SIS Act.

Agreeing on the Terms of the Engagement with the RSE Licensee

19 The approved auditor and the RSE Licensee agree on the terms of the engagement. Such terms may be detailed in a terms of engagement letter[3]. The auditor has regard to Auditing Standard ASA 210 *Agreeing the Terms of Audit Engagements* when agreeing on the terms of the engagement.

20 The terms of engagement may also detail arrangements for liaison with the RSE Licensee's audit and/or compliance committee (if applicable), other compliance advisors, and other auditors, including the internal auditor of the RSE Licensee and the auditor of the RSE Licensee's outsourced service provider(s) (if applicable).

21 The approved auditor may also use the terms of engagement to clarify the respective roles of the RSE Licensee's directors or individual trustee members, by contrasting the respective statutory responsibilities of the RSE Licensee and the approved auditor under Part 13 of the SIS Act. In particular, it is important to highlight in the terms of engagement the RSE Licensee's obligation to establish and maintain an adequate risk management system and have in place adequate measures and structures to ensure compliance with the RMS, RMP and the SIS Act. The auditor obtains acknowledgment of this obligation from the RSE Licensee's directors or individual trustee members when obtaining agreement on the terms of the engagement. An example engagement letter illustrating such agreement is provided in Appendix 1 to this Guidance Statement.

Clarifying the Approved Auditor's Role

Role of the RSE Licensee

22 The RSE Licensee is required under the SIS Act to develop the RMS for its own operations and the RMP for each RSE it manages, together with descriptions of the measures in place to monitor and control material risks identified in the RMS and RMP. These measures are to be in place and fully operational once the RSE licence is granted. Section 29HA of the SIS Act requires the RSE Licensee to ensure that at all times the RMS is up-to-date and to review the RMS at least once a year to ensure that it complies with section 29H of the SIS Act. The RMS is required, under the SIS Act, to be modified once the RSE Licensee becomes aware that the RMS no longer complies with section 29H of the SIS Act. Section 29PA of the SIS Act imposes similar requirements on the RSE Licensee to maintain the RMPs for the RSEs that it manages.

23 The RSE Licensee's directors or individual trustee members are responsible, under the SIS Act, for establishing and maintaining an appropriate risk management system. The RSE Licensee's directors or individual trustee members are responsible, under the SIS Act, for identifying risks, setting risk tolerances and designing and implementing processes to manage and monitor those risks. The RSE Licensee's directors or individual trustee members are responsible, under the SIS Act, for determining the adequacy of the RSE Licensee's response to the identified risks.

3 Or other suitable form of audit contract.

Role of the Approved Auditor

24 Section 113(3)(c) of the SIS Act states that an approved form "must if it is approved for a registrable superannuation entity that is registered under Part 2B, include a statement by the auditor as to whether, in the opinion of the auditor, the RSE licensee of the entity:

(i) has complied with each risk management plan for the entity that applied during that year; and

(ii) has adequate systems to ensure future compliance with any risk management plan for the entity; and

(iii) has complied with each risk management strategy that applied to the RSE licensee during that year in relation to risks arising from any activities, and proposed activities, as RSE licensee of the entity, and all other activities, or proposed activities, relevant to those activities; and

(iv) has adequate systems to ensure future compliance with the risk management strategy for the RSE licensee in relation to future risks arising from any proposed future activities as RSE licensee of the entity, and all other proposed future activities relevant to those activities."

APRA has specified that reports (i) and (iii) above will contain auditor's audit opinions providing reasonable assurance and reports (ii) and (iv) will contain auditor's review conclusions providing limited assurance. The prescribed format of the reports is set out in APRA's Approved Form titled *Superannuation Industry (Supervision) Act 1993 (SIS Act) Section 35C – Approved Form* issued June 2010 for reporting periods commencing on or after 1 July 2009, and subsequent versions.

25 The approved auditor's responsibility, under the SIS Act, is to assess whether the RSE Licensee has complied with the requirements contained within the RMS and RMP. This may include whether key controls identified in the RMS or RMP are in place and/or whether any residual risk treatment strategies have been implemented.

26 During the course of the audit and review the approved auditor may become aware of material deficiencies in the RMS and RMP and/or material control weaknesses in the RSE Licensee's risk management systems. Section 129 of the SIS Act requires the approved auditor to report these instances to the Trustee and APRA, if the matter affects the interests of members or beneficiaries. SPG 200 paragraph 77 further notes that '*matters identified with respect to the RMS and RMP by the approved auditor would be reported to the Trustee and not excluded by a financial materiality threshold*'. The auditor may also find Auditing Standard ASA 260 *Communication with Those Charged With Governance* useful for this purpose.

Inherent Limitations of Auditing Compliance with the RMS and RMP

27 Due to the nature of audit testing and other inherent limitations of an audit, together with the inherent limitations of the RMS and the RMP and their related control measures, there is a possibility that a properly planned and executed audit will not detect all deficiencies in the RSE Licensee's compliance with its RMS and RMP. Accordingly, the auditor's audit reports under section 113(3)(c) are expressed in terms of reasonable assurance and cannot constitute a guarantee that the RSE Licensee's compliance with the RMS and RMP is completely free from any deficiency, or that all breaches have been detected.

28 There are also practical limitations in requiring an auditor to perform a continuous examination of compliance with the RMS and RMP and in forming an opinion that the entity has complied at all times with the RMS and RMP during the reporting period. The approved auditor performs tests periodically throughout the financial year to obtain evidence and have reasonable assurance that the Licensee has complied with the written descriptions within the RMS and RMP throughout the period under examination.

Inherent Limitations of Reviewing Systems to Ensure Future Compliance with the RMS and RMP

29 Due to the nature of review procedures and other inherent limitations of a review, together with the inherent limitations of the RMS and the RMP and their related control measures,

there is a possibility that a properly planned and executed review will not detect all deficiencies in the RSE Licensee's risk management systems (being the relevant processes and procedures) to manage and monitor future compliance with the RMS and the RMP, ie., the twelve month period following the date of the auditor's review report. Accordingly, the auditor's review reports under section 113(3)(c) provide limited assurance and cannot constitute a guarantee that the risk management systems are completely free from any deficiency, or that they will always ensure future compliance with the RMS and RMP.

30 There are also practical limitations in requiring an auditor to provide limited assurance that the RSE Licensee's risk management systems are adequate to ensure future compliance with the RMS and RMP. The approved auditor performs procedures appropriate to provide limited assurance on the risk management systems to confirm that they exist at the review date and whether those systems have operated as documented throughout the period and considered risks that may arise from the RSE Licensee's business operations and business planning. APRA's Approved Form titled *Superannuation Industry (Supervision) Act 1993 (SIS Act) Section 35C – Approved Form* defines the future to be the 12 month period following the date the review report is signed. Another inherent limitation is that after the auditor's review reports are signed, the RSE Licensee's risk management processes may change and/or its business operations and business plans may change such that deficiencies may emerge that result in non-compliance with the current RMS and RMP.

Planning the Audit and Review

Materiality

31 The auditor considers materiality when:

(a) determining the nature, timing and extent of audit and review procedures;

(b) evaluating the effect of identified breaches of the RMS and/or RMP when forming an auditor's audit opinion on compliance with the RMS and RMP; and

(c) considering whether identified weaknesses in risk management systems (being the relevant processes and procedures) may affect the Licensee's future compliance with the RMS and RMP for the purposes of providing an auditor's review report on the adequacy of systems to ensure future compliance with the RMS and the RMP.

32 Materiality is addressed in the context of the RSE Licensee's risk management objectives, which are developed having regard to the protection of the interests of the RSE members as a whole. Materiality considerations are therefore viewed within the context of setting out adequate measures that the RSE Licensee is to apply in managing its business operations to ensure compliance with the RMS and RMP.

33 The explanatory guidance on the meaning and application of the concept of materiality contained in Auditing Standard ASA 320 *Materiality in Planning and Performing an Audit* is adapted by the approved auditor, as appropriate, to the task of judging adherence to the RMS and RMP and considering other qualitative factors such as conformity with the relevant provisions of the SIS Act. However, it is not possible to give a definitive view on what may constitute a significant or material breach of the RMS or the RMP. The auditor exercises appropriate professional judgement having regard to the RSE Licensee's obligations, together with the size, complexity and nature of the RSE Licensee's activities when determining whether a breach is to be considered significant or material. Section 29JA(1)(b) of the SIS Act requires the RSE Licensee to report all significant breaches of the RMS or the RMP to APRA. Section 129 of the SIS Act requires the auditor to report all detected instances of non-compliance with the SIS Act to APRA if the breach is of such a nature that it may materially affect the interests of members or beneficiaries of the entity. Breaches can be reported to APRA via the breach reporting portal, D2A and/or the auditor's report.

34 As identified in ASA 320, when assessing materiality, the auditor considers qualitative factors. The following are examples of qualitative factors that may be relevant:

- The specific requirements of the terms of the engagement.
- The significance of identified RMS/RMP breaches or weaknesses in existing risk management measures.

- The nature of any incidents which indicate a weakness in the governance structures.
- The length of time for which an identified breach or weakness was in existence, both before it was identified and before it was rectified.
- Indications of systemic and pervasive weaknesses in the existing risk management systems.

Other Planning Considerations

35 The approved auditor considers:

(a) the date the RMS and RMP were last reviewed by the RSE Licensee and updated, and whether the modified version was provided to APRA in the required timeframe;

(b) key responsibilities and risks identified in the RMS and RMP;

(c) processes established by the RSE Licensee to identify and manage risks;

(d) processes established by the RSE Licensee to identify risks emerging from current or proposed business activities;

(e) processes established by the RSE Licensee to monitor adherence to the RMS and RMP; and

(f) processes established to ensure that the RMS and RMP comply with the relevant requirements of the SIS Act.

36 When evaluating the RSE Licensee's adherence to the RMS and RMP, the approved auditor obtains from the RSE Licensee a copy of each RMS and RMP that applied during the period covered by the audit, together with a written description of the procedures and structures which the RSE Licensee has established to ensure compliance with the relevant RMS and RMP. As the RMS and RMP are high level summaries of the risk management systems the RSE Licensee has in place, the approved auditor obtains sufficient information to enable an understanding of the risk management systems and supporting processes and procedures.

37 To further assist in the audit and review, the approved auditor considers various matters when planning the work, including:

- The structure of the RSE Licensee and the nature of its operations.
- The most recent business plan of the RSE Licensee.
- The nature and extent of any changes to the RMS and RMP in the reporting period.
- The nature and extent of any changes to the RSE Licensee's operations.
- Correspondence with APRA and other regulators including, the results of any recent field visits.
- Reports and other documents submitted to the compliance committee and/or the board of the RSE Licensee regarding the operation of the Trustee and the RSEs and its risk management functions.
- Previous auditor's reports, including the auditor's report on financial statements of the RSE Licensee, the RSE and related management letters.

Matters to be Considered During the Audit and Review

Reasonable Assurance on Compliance with the RMS and RMP

38 As part of the audit of compliance with the RMS and RMP and review of the risk management systems for compliance with the RMS and RMP, the approved auditor considers the measures in place which relate to the RSE Licensee's monitoring of, and reporting on, specific matters incorporated into the RMS and RMP. Such a consideration may include the following matters:

- Whether breaches of the RMS and RMP have been detected and reported by the monitoring systems implemented by the RSE Licensee. Where breaches of the RMS and or RMP have been detected, the approved auditor considers whether such breaches are material either in themselves, or where they are of a recurring nature and have

GS

not been rectified, whether their cumulative effect renders them to be a material non-compliance.

- Identifying systems which the RSE Licensee uses to ensure that business units and staff comply with the measures in the RMS and RMP on a day to day basis.
- Whether the RSE Licensee has a process in place to identify and review the risks arising from its business processes and operations on a periodic basis so as to ensure that its RMS and RMP remain up-to-date at all times.
- Testing of selected controls identified in the RMS and RMP.

39 As part of the audit of compliance with the RMS and RMP the approved auditor may seek the following types of information and documentation to the extent relevant:

- Documentation that identifies the policies and procedures that are in place to manage identified risks and representations that policies and procedures have been complied with.
- Details of changes to the RMS and RMP and related policies and procedures and the reasons for the revisions.
- Minutes of the meetings of Board and sub-committees that are responsible for monitoring compliance with aspects of the RMS and RMP and the RSE Licensee's risk management framework.
- Reasons for changes to outsourced service providers and documentation of the tender process to the extent that this impacts upon the material risks identified in the RMS and/or RMP.
- Results of monitoring of outsource service providers.
- Reports from outsourced service providers confirming compliance with the service level agreements.
- Breach registers and complaints registers and follow up actions taken to the extent that recorded items may indicate a failure to comply with the RMS or RMP.
- Training registers and new responsible officer induction processes.
- Internal audit reports.
- Results of disaster recovery and business continuity planning and testing.
- Conflicts register.
- Business plan of the licensee.
- Certifications made by the licensee and relevant supporting documentation to substantiate compliance with the RMS and RMP during the reporting period.
- Internal and external incident and breach reports.
- Other supporting evidence to confirm that the controls identified in the RMS and RMP have been in place during the reporting period.
- Unit pricing systems, procedures and controls.

The above is not meant to represent a complete list and there may be other evidence that is relevant to the specific circumstances of each RSE Licensee and the RSEs it manages.

40 Some RSE Licensees may have a number of RSEs with very similar RMPs, or a master RMP covering more than one RSE under the control of a single RSE Licensee. In such situations, the approved auditor may choose to design and apply common audit tests and review procedures across more than one RSE, as considered necessary in the circumstances. However, the approved auditor ensures that the tests and procedures which are applied are representative across all RSEs under the master RMP, and that they provide sufficient and appropriate evidence to enable the expression of the auditor's audit opinion on each RMP as required by section 113(3)(c) of the SIS Act.

41 In addition, the RSE Licensee may choose to outsource various functions (e.g. administration and custody services) and engage external service providers. The RSE Licensee includes measures in the RMS and RMP to supervise these service providers, given that the RSE

Licensee is considered to be accountable under the SIS Act both for the compliance of those activities which are performed within the RSE Licensee itself, as well as those functions which may be outsourced to external service providers, which where material will be subject to a 'complying' service agreement.

42 In such circumstances, the approved auditor reviews compliance with the measures in the RMP and RMS relating to the supervision by the RSE Licensee of its service provider(s). However, the approved auditor is not expected to conduct an audit of the service provider(s), as it is the obligation of the RSE Licensee and not the approved auditor, to ensure that the service provider(s) adhere to the RSE Licensee's RMS and RMP for each RSE under its control. The auditor may also be mindful of the 'access to premises' clause contained in any material service agreement. In this context, the auditor has particular regard to matters raised in Auditing Standard ASA 402 *Audit Considerations Relating to an Entity Using a Service Organisation.*

Limited Assurance on Adequacy of Systems to Ensure Future Compliance with the RMS and RMP

43 As part of the review of the risk management systems (being the relevant processes and procedures) to assess the ability of the RSE Licensee to maintain compliance with the RMS and RMP the approved auditor may seek the following types of information and documentation to the extent relevant:

- The most recent business plan of the RSE Licensee and confirmation of the activities it proposes to undertake in the 12 months following the review.
- Details of proposed changes to the RMS and RMP which reflect initiatives identified in the business plan.
- Minutes of meetings of the Board and sub-committees that are responsible for monitoring compliance with aspects of the RMS and RMP (since the end of the reporting period).
- Confirmation of the use of experts by the RSE Licensee where appropriate.
- Progress reports on major business or operational initiatives.
- Proposed future activities, changes to its business plan or any other significant changes to its current activities or operations identified from enquiries of the RSE Licensee and/or management.
- Whether the RSE Licensee has a process in place to identify emerging risks arising from its current or proposed activities.

The above is not meant to represent a complete list and there may be other evidence that is relevant to the specific circumstances of each RSE Licensee and the RSEs it manages.

The Auditor's Audit Report and Auditor's Review Report

44 Prior to issuing the auditor's audit reports on compliance with the RMS and RMP and the auditor's review reports on the risk management systems, the auditor may seek a written representation from the RSE Licensee's directors or individual trustee members which contain their assertions that the RSE Licensee has complied with the RMS and RMP during the financial year, and that the RSE Licensee has adequate systems to ensure future compliance with the RMS and RMP. This representation will include a statement to the effect that the RMS and RMP have been updated to reflect identified risks arising from proposed future business activities after the assessment of possible risks emerging from those activities by the RSE Licensee and the assistance of outside experts if required. An example representation letter is provided in Appendix 2 to this Guidance Statement.

45 Reports required to be issued under section 113(3) of the SIS Act are required to be issued no later than 4 months after the financial year end of the RSE. The auditor's audit reports and review reports are required to be addressed to the RSE Licensee. The auditor's audit reports and review reports on the RMP are available to RSE members on request via the RSE Licensee.

46 The auditor's audit reports on the RMS and RMP will be for the year of income of the fund. The auditor's review reports will be expressed as being for "the twelve month period

following the date of this review report". Where the licence is granted during the financial year, the auditor's audit report will be for the period commencing on the date the licence was granted to the end of the financial year.

47 Where the financial year of the RSE Licensee and the RSE differ, it may be appropriate to align the RMS and the RMP audit reporting periods.

48 When reporting on the matters required by section 35C, the auditor adheres to APRA's Approved Form titled *Superannuation Industry (Supervision) Act 1993 (SIS Act) Section 35C – Approved Form* issued June 2010 for reporting periods commencing on or after 1 July 2009, and subsequent versions. If the auditor is required to modify the audit report because of a material breach of the RMS or RMP or because of some ongoing material weakness in the adequacy of systems to manage and monitor future compliance, the auditor refers to Auditing Standard ASA 705 *Modifications to the Opinion in the Independent Auditor's Report*, which may be helpful when drafting the modified audit reports or review reports.

49 Evidence gathered to support the auditor's audit opinions and review conclusions is documented in accordance with Auditing Standard ASA 230 *Audit Documentation*. APRA may seek to review the approved auditor's working papers to obtain an understanding on how the approved auditor's views were formed and APRA has stated that it expects the documentation to be consistent with the requirements of the Australian Auditing Standards.

50 Where the RSE licensee has trusteeship of Small APRA Funds (SAFs) and has used the same RMP for each SAF (where specific requirements have been met), it is acceptable to APRA, as noted in the instructions to APRA's Approved Form titled *Superannuation Industry (Supervision) Act 1993 (SIS Act) Section 35C – Approved Form* issued June 2010 for reporting periods commencing on or after 1 July 2009, and subsequent versions, to issue one auditor's audit report on the RMP provided that all SAFs to which the RMP applies are identified by the auditor.

Conformity with International Pronouncements

51 There is no equivalent International Auditing Practice Statement (IAPS) or Auditing Standard to this Guidance Statement.

Appendix 1

Example Engagement Letter

The following example audit and review engagement letter is for use as a guide only, in conjunction with the considerations described in this Guidance Statement, and will need to be varied according to individual requirements and circumstances.

To [the governing body of the Trustee (e.g. the directors or individual trustee members)]:

Engagement Letter for Risk Management Strategy and Risk Management Plans

Australian Auditing Standards require that there is a common understanding in writing, between the auditor and the client as to the terms of the audit engagement. Accordingly, following our recent discussions with you, we set out below brief details of our responsibilities as auditors and our understanding of the services you require us to perform. This letter relates to the audit of compliance with the Risk Management Strategy for [name of Trustee] ("Trustee") and to the following superannuation entities' Risk Management Plans:

- [Name of Superannuation Fund]
- [Name of Superannuation Fund]

We will also conduct a review of the Trustee's systems which are designed to manage and maintain future compliance with the RMS and RMP.

Audit and Review

Our function as auditor under section 113(3)(c) of the *Superannuation Industry (Supervision) Act 1993* is to examine and report on the Trustee's Risk Management Strategy ("RMS") and each superannuation entity's Risk Management Plan ("RMP") which has been supplied to us by the Trustee. We are required to report whether:

- The Trustee has complied with the RMS in all material respects for the year ended [date].
- The Trustee has complied with the RMP for each superannuation entity in all material respects for the year ended [date].
- Based on our review, which is not an audit, nothing has come to our attention that causes us to believe that the Trustee does not have adequate systems, to manage and monitor future compliance with the risk management plan of each superannuation entity.
- Based on our review, which is not an audit, nothing has come to our attention that causes us to believe that the Trustee does not have adequate systems, to identify future risks arising from proposed future activities and to manage and monitor future compliance with the risk management strategy.

As auditors we are not responsible for the identification of risks, design, documentation, operation and monitoring of the RMS and RMP, nor for the adequacy of controls, risk assessments contained in the RMS and RMP, including the relevant internal control systems, policies and procedures and compliance, including future compliance therewith. These duties are imposed on the Trustee by the *Superannuation Industry (Supervision) Act 1993*.

The work undertaken by us to form an opinion is permeated by judgement, in particular, regarding the nature, timing and extent of the audit and review procedures for gathering of audit and review evidence and the drawing of conclusions based on the audit and review evidence gathered. In addition, there are inherent limitations in any audit and review, and these include the use of testing, the inherent limitations of any internal control and compliance structure, the possibility of collusion to commit fraud, and the fact that most audit evidence is persuasive rather than conclusive. As a result, our audit can only provide reasonable, not absolute assurance, that in all material respects the Trustee, as the registered entity, has complied with the RMS and RMP presented to us by the Trustee and our review can only provide limited assurance that the Trustee has adequate systems to manage and maintain future compliance with the RMS and RMP.

In accordance with normal practice, our audit and review will be planned primarily to enable us to express our professional opinion and reach conclusions. It should not be relied on to disclose fraud or error, but their disclosure, if they exist, may possibly result from the audit and review tests we undertake.

Procedures

The work we do to enable us to form our opinion on the auditor's audit reports and conclusion on the review reports will include the following:

- Auditing compliance with the relevant RMS and RMP to ensure that they are up-to-date and approved by the Trustee.
- Reviewing the processes (including monitoring and reporting procedures) the Trustee has in place to ensure ongoing compliance with the RMS and RMP and the law and other licence conditions.
- Reviewing the evidence supporting the Trustee's attestation in the APRA annual return in relation to compliance with the RMS and RMP.
- Testing the controls in place used by the Trustee to manage the risks identified in the RMS and RMP.

The auditor's review report on future compliance defines "future" as the twelve month period following the date of the review report.

In considering the systems which the Trustee has to identify future risks arising from its proposed future activities, we will assess the reasonableness of the processes and procedures used by the Trustee to identify risks which arise from current business operations. In this regard we will review the current business plan and confirm the activities which the Trustee proposes to undertake in the 12 months following the date of the review.

After the completion of our auditor's audit report and review report, it is our normal practice to report any matters of significance together with suggestions for their rectification and any other recommendations we may have on the systems and processes in general.

However, we should point out that the examination will be limited to the audit and review implications of the systems and processes and will not constitute a comprehensive study of the identified risks. You cannot assume that any matters reported to you indicate that there are no additional matters, or matters that you should be aware of in meeting your responsibilities.

Our Reporting Responsibilities Under s. 129 of the SIS Act

Section 129 of the SIS Act requires us to report to you in writing if we believe a contravention of the legislation has occurred, is occurring or may occur. We need to also advise APRA at the same time as advising the Trustee if we believe the contravention may affect the interest of members or beneficiaries.

Presentation of RMP on the Internet

It is our understanding that the [entity/Trustee] intends to publish a hard copy of the RMP and related auditor's audit and review reports for members, and to present electronically the RMP and related auditor's audit and review reports on its internet web site. When information is presented electronically on a web site, the security and controls over information on the web site should be addressed by the Trustee to maintain the integrity of the data presented. The examination of the controls over the electronic presentation of the RMP on the entity's web site is beyond the scope of the audit of compliance with the RMP. Responsibility for the electronic presentation of the RMP on the entity's web site is that of the governing body of the entity/directors of the Trustee.

Fees

We look forward to full cooperation from your staff and we trust that they will make available to us whatever records, documentation and other information we request in connection with our audits and reviews.

[*Insert additional information here regarding fee arrangements and billings, as appropriate.*]

Other

This letter will be effective for future years unless we advise you of its amendment or replacement, or the engagement is terminated.

Please sign and return the attached copy of this letter to indicate that it is in accordance with your understanding of the arrangements for our audit and review of the RMS and RMP(s).

Yours faithfully,

(signed)

....

Name and Title

Date

Acknowledged on behalf of [entity] by (signed)

....

Name and Title

Date

Appendix 2

Example RSE Licensee Representation Letter

[Trustee Letterhead]

[Addressee – Auditor]

[Date]

This representation letter is provided in connection with your audit of compliance with the Risk Management Strategy (RMS) for [name of Trustee] ("Trustee") and to the following superannuation entities' Risk Management Plans (RMP):

- [Name of Superannuation Fund];
- [Name of Superannuation Fund];

and including your review of the Trustee's systems to manage and maintain future compliance.

We acknowledge our responsibility for the identification of risks, design, documentation, operation and monitoring of the RMS and RMP, the adequacy of controls, risk assessments contained in the RMS and RMP, including the relevant internal control systems, policies and procedures and compliance, including future compliance therewith. These duties are imposed on the Trustee by the *Superannuation Industry (Supervision) Act 1993*.

We confirm that to the best of our knowledge and belief, the following representations made to you during your audit and review.

[Include representations relevant to the entity. Such representations may include the following examples.]

1 We have provided you with:

(a) copies of the RMS and RMP in force during the year ended [date], relevant business plans, policy and procedure documents, breach registers, other information, explanations and assistance necessary for the conduct of the audit and review; and

(b) minutes of all meetings of the [audit and compliance committee and/or other relevant committees].

2 There:

(a) has been no fraud, error, or non-compliance with laws and regulations involving management or employees who have a significant role in the internal control structure;

(b) has been no fraud, error, or non-compliance with laws and regulations that could result in non-compliance with the RMS and/or RMP; and

(c) have been no communications from regulatory agencies concerning non-compliance with, or deficiencies in, risk management systems that could have a material effect on future compliance with the RMS and RMP.

3 We have established and maintained an adequate internal control structure to facilitate compliance with the RMS and RMP, and adequate records have been maintained evidencing on-going compliance. There are no known breaches of compliance with the RMS and RMP that have not been properly recorded in the breach registers provided to you.

4 The business plan(s) provided to you adequately reflect the Trustee's proposed activities over the next 12 months. We have no plans or intentions that may materially impact future compliance with the RMS and RMP. [or] Material risks that arise from activities proposed in the business plan(s) have been factored into proposed changes to the RMS and/or RMP.

5 There are no violations or possible violations of laws or regulations the effects of which should be considered for disclosure to any regulator or which would impact compliance with the RMS and RMP.

6 No events have occurred subsequent to [reporting period date] that would impact the Trustee's ability to manage and maintain future compliance with the RMS and RMP.

We understand that your examination was made in accordance with Australian Auditing Standards, as applicable, and was, therefore, designed primarily for the purpose of expressing an opinion on compliance with the RMS and RMP and our ability to manage and maintain future compliance, and that your tests of our records and controls and other auditing procedures were limited to those which you considered necessary for that purpose.

Yours faithfully

[Name of signing officer and title]

GS 003

Audit and Review Requirements for Australian Financial Services Licensees under the *Corporations Act 2001*

(Issued October 2007)

Issued by the Auditing and Assurance Standards Board.

Note from the Institute of Chartered Accountants Australia

This note, prepared by the technical editor, is not part of GS 003.

Historical development

October 2004: Auditing Guidance Statement 1068 'Audit Requirements for Australian Financial Services Licensees under the Corporations Act 2001' issued in response to requests from auditors for guidance in performing audits of Australian financial services licensees under the *Corporations Act 2001*. The statement has no international equivalent and was operative from the date of issue.

October 2007: This statement was revised and reissued as GS 003 'Audit and Review Requirements to Australian Financial Services Licencees under the *Corporations Act 2001*'.

GS

Contents

Authority Statement

The Auditing and Assurance Standards Board (AUASB) formulates Guidance Statement GS 003 *Audit and Review Requirements for Australian Financial Services Licensees under the Corporations Act 2001* as set out in paragraphs 1 to 81 and Appendices 1 to 4, pursuant to section 227B of the *Australian Securities and Investments Commission Act 2001,* for the purposes of providing guidance on procedural auditing and assurance matters.

This Guidance Statement provides guidance to assist the auditor to fulfil the objectives of the audit or assurance engagement. It includes explanatory details and suggested procedures on specific matters for the purposes of understanding and complying with AUASB Standards. The auditor exercises professional judgement when using this Guidance Statement.

This Guidance Statement does not prescribe or create mandatory requirements.

Dated 31 October 2007

M H Kelsall
Chairman - AUASB

Guidance Statement GS 003

Audit and Review Requirements for Australian Financial Services Licensees under the *Corporations Act 2001*

Application

1 This Guidance Statement has been formulated by the Auditing and Assurance Standards Board (AUASB) to provide guidance to the auditor of an Australian financial services (AFS) licensee reporting in accordance with the requirements of the *Corporations Act 2001* (the Corporations Act).

Issuance Date

2 This Guidance Statement is issued on 31 October 2007 by the AUASB and replaces AGS 1068 *Audit Requirements for Australian Financial Services Licensees under the Corporations Act 2001*(issued in October 2004).

Introduction

3 The audit of AFS licensees may give rise to a number of special audit considerations. Accordingly, this Guidance Statement has been developed to identify the auditor's responsibilities on such engagements, and to provide guidance to the auditor on additional factors which the auditor may consider when planning, conducting and reporting on the audit of an AFS licensee.

4 This Guidance Statement provides guidance on the existing responsibilities of the auditor of an AFS licensee imposed by Auditing Standards (ASAs), Standards on Assurance Engagements (ASAEs), Standards on Review Engagements (ASREs) and the requirements of the Corporations Act and the *Corporations Regulations 2001* (Corporations Regulations) but does not add to the auditor's responsibilities contained therein.

5 This Guidance Statement is to be read in conjunction with Standard on Assurance Engagements ASAE 3000 *Assurance Engagements Other than Audits or Reviews of Historical Financial Information,* ASA 800 *The Auditor's Report on Special Purpose Audit Engagements* and relevant Australian Securities and Investments Commission (ASIC) regulatory documents in this area issued from time to time, such as Regulatory Guide 166 *Licensing: Financial requirements* (RG 166) reissued on 25 June 2007 and Pro Forma 209 *Australian financial services licence conditions* (PF 209) reissued on 25 June 2007.

6 It is not intended that this Guidance Statement replace the need for the auditor of an AFS licensee to refer to the Corporations Act, Corporations Regulations or other relevant ASIC regulatory documents. This Guidance Statement should not be used as a checklist of issues to be considered by the auditor. Furthermore it is not intended that this Guidance Statement limits or replaces the auditor's professional judgement and initiative or limits the application of AUASB Standards on such engagements. AUASB Standards contain the basic principles

GS

and essential procedures to be applied to audit and review engagements. Audit and review programs for each engagement are to be designed to meet the requirements of the particular situation, giving careful consideration to the size and type of AFS licensee and the adequacy of its internal control structure.

Legislative Background

7 The *Financial Services Reform Act 2001* (FSR Act) and the overall AFS licensing regulatory regime which is administered by ASIC, formally commenced on 11 March 2002. The full provisions of the FSR Act are operative for all AFS licensees under Chapter 7 of the Corporations Act.

8 The FSR Act amendments to the Corporations Act introduced a single licensing regime for financial advice and dealings in relation to financial products. The Corporations Act requires an entity that operates a financial services business to hold an AFS licence or be authorised by a licensee.

Regulatory Requirements for AFS Licensees

Corporations Act Requirements

9 Section 989B of Part 7.8 of the Corporations Act requires an AFS licensee to lodge a profit and loss statement, balance sheet and auditor's report with ASIC for each financial year. Regulation 7.8.13(1) of the Corporations Regulations requires that for subsection 989B(3), the auditor's report on the profit and loss statement and balance sheet in respect of a financial year be lodged with ASIC in the prescribed form. ASIC requires the profit and loss statement (Statement of Financial Performance) and balance sheet (Statement of Financial Position) and notes to the Statement of Financial Performance and Statement of Financial Position (the "financial statements") to accompany Australian financial services licensees: profit and loss statement and balance sheet (FS 70) and Australian financial services licensees: audit report (FS 71). FS 70 and FS 71 can be found on the ASIC website www.asic.gov.au under Download Forms.

10 Section 989D(1) of the Corporations Act and regulation 7.8.14A of the Corporations Regulations requires an AFS licensee to lodge FS 70 and FS 71 with ASIC within the following periods:

(a) if not a body corporate – the day that is 2 months after the end of that financial year;

(b) if a body corporate that is a disclosing entity or a registered scheme – the day that is 3 months after the end of that financial year; or

(c) if a body corporate that is not a disclosing entity or registered scheme – the day that is 4 months after the end of that financial year.

11 Many AFS licensees already lodge annual financial reports and the auditor's report under Chapter 2M of the Corporations Act (usually within 4 months of the financial year, but within 3 months of the financial year for a disclosing entity or registered scheme) with ASIC. The lodgement requirements under Chapter 2M of the Corporations Act apply to companies in general and are not affected by the FSR Act amendments. The FSR Act requires AFS licensees to lodge FS 70 (which includes the annual financial reports) and FS 71 (auditor's report) under Part 7.8 of the Corporations Act. The lodgement requirements under Chapter 2M and Part 7.8 of the Corporations Act are independent obligations so it is necessary to lodge financial reports separately under both provisions. Only the financial reports lodged under Chapter 2M are on public record while FS 70 and FS 71 contain information that is not required under Chapter 2M. If an AFS licensee is not required to lodge annual financial reports under Chapter 2M, they are still required to lodge FS 70 and FS 71 with ASIC under Part 7.8 of the Corporations Act.

12 An AFS licensee can apply to ASIC for an extension of time to lodge FS 70 and FS 71 under Section 989D(3) of the Corporations Act.

Financial Requirements for APRA Regulated Entities, Market and Clearing Participants

13 The base level financial requirements and other financial requirement conditions, as set out in ASIC Pro Forma 209 (PF 209), do not apply but FS 70 and FS 71 are still required to be lodged with ASIC if the licensee is either:

(a) a body regulated by the Australian Prudential Regulation Authority (APRA) as defined in Section 3(2) of the *Australian Prudential Regulation Authority Act 1998*; or

(b) a market participant, as defined in the operating rules of ASX Limited (ASX) (other than a principal trader, unless the principal trader is registered as a market maker) who complies with the ASX's operating rules for financial requirements, taking into account any waiver by ASX; or a participant in the licensed market operated by the Sydney Futures Exchange Limited (SFE) that restricts its financial services business to participation in the licensed market and incidental business supervised by SFE and complies with the SFE operating rules for financial requirements, taking into account any waiver by SFE; or

(c) a clearing participant in the licensed clearing and settlement facility, as defined in the operating rules of the Licensed Clearing and Settlement Facility (CS Facility), operated by Australian Clearing House Pty Ltd (ACH), that complies with the operating rules of the CS Facility operated by ACH relating to financial requirements, taking into account any waiver by ACH.

14 Where a licensee is a body regulated by APRA, PF209 condition 27 requires the audit opinion in FS 71 to state whether for the relevant period, on a reasonable assurance basis, the licensee was a body regulated by APRA at the end of the financial year or for any period of time that ASIC requests. Example 1 in Appendix 1 shows an example FS 71 paragraph 3 for a licensee regulated by APRA.

15 Where a licensee is a market participant or clearing participant, ASIC requires the audit opinion in FS 71 to state whether, during any part of the period for which the licensee relied on being a market participant or clearing participant, on a reasonable assurance basis, the licensee was a participant in the market conducted by:

(a) ASX; or

(b) ACH; or

(c) SFE, that restricted its financial services business to participating in the market and incidental business supervised by SFE.

Example 2 in Appendix 1 shows an example FS 71 paragraph 3 for a market participant or clearing participant.

Financial Requirements for all other AFS Licensees

16 All other licensees that are not exempted from the base level financial requirements are required to comply with these requirements under the Corporations Act. The base level financial requirements are that the licensee must:

(a) be able to pay all its debts as and when they become due and payable; and

(b) either:

(i) have total assets that exceed total liabilities as shown in the licensee's most recent balance sheet lodged with ASIC and have no reason to suspect that the licensee's total assets would not currently exceed its total liabilities; or

(ii) have adjusted assets that exceed adjusted liabilities calculated at the balance date shown in the licensee's most recent balance sheet lodged with ASIC and have no reason to suspect that the licensee's adjusted assets would currently not exceed its adjusted liabilities; and

(c) meet the cash needs requirement by complying with one of the following five options:

(i) Option 1 (reasonable estimate projection plus cash buffer) - refer to definition of Option 1 in Appendix 4; or

(ii) Option 2 (contingency based projection) - refer to definition of Option 2 in Appendix 4; or

GS

(iii) Option 3 (financial commitment by an Australian ADI or comparable foreign institution) – refer to Base Level Financial Requirements in Appendix 4; or

(iv) Option 4 (expectation of support from an Australian ADI or comparable foreign institution) – refer to Base Level Financial Requirements in Appendix 4; or

(v) Option 5 (parent entity prepares cash flow projections on a consolidated basis) – refer to Base Level Financial Requirements in Appendix 4.

17 There are also additional financial requirements specified in PF 209 and RG 166 for:

(a) managed investments and custody services (net tangible assets requirement, refer to PF 209 conditions 14-19 and RG 166 Section C);

(b) foreign exchange dealers (tier one capital requirement, refer to PF 209 condition 20 and RG 166 Section G);

(c) holding client money or property (tiered surplus liquid funds requirement, refer to PF 209, condition 21 and RG 166 Section E);

(d) transacting with clients as principal (adjusted surplus liquid funds requirement, refer to PF 209, condition 22 and RG 166 Section F); and

(e) reporting triggers (refer to PF 209, conditions 23-26).

The auditor has an obligation to consider whether these financial requirements are applicable depending upon the licensee's licence and business activities. If any of the additional financial requirements are applicable to the licensee, then the FS 71 audit report requires reasonable assurance on those financial requirements.

18 If the licensee is authorised to operate an Investor Directed Portfolio Services ("IDPS"), the licensee will need to comply with Class Order 02/294 *Investor directed portfolio services* (CO 02/294). CO 02/294 as amended:

- on 1 June 2004, by Class Order 04/606 *Investor directed portfolio services - amendment* (CO 04/606);
- on 28 June 2004 by CO 04/734 Investor directed portfolio services - amendment (CO 04/734); and
- on 27 June 2007 by CO 07/480 Investor directed portfolio se*rvices, investor directed portfolio-like services and managed discretionary accounts - amendments* (CO 07/480).

This class order as amended provides an exemption from certain fundraising, financial product disclosure and managed investments provisions of the Corporations Act for persons who are operating, or are involved in the operation or promotion of, an investor directed portfolio service subject to some conditions and disclosure requirements.

19 If the licensee is authorised to operate a Managed Discretionary Account (MDA) Service or act as an external MDA custodian that will directly contract with retail clients, the licensee will need to comply with Class Order 04/194 *Managed Discretionary Accounts.* CO 04/194 was amended on 27 June 2007 by CO 07/480 *Investor directed portfolio services, investor directed portfolio-like services and managed discretionary accounts - amendments* (CO 07/480).

FS 71 Auditor Reporting Requirements

20 The FS 71 audit report requires:

(a) Reasonable assurance on the financial statements.

(b) Limited assurance on certain statements made in FS 70 relating to dealing with clients' money and other property of clients.

(c) Reasonable assurance that the licensee:

(i) is a body regulated by APRA; or

(ii) is a market or clearing participant; or

(iii) complies with all the financial requirements under the licence other than the cash needs requirement, except for paragraph (e) of the definition of Option 1 if the licensee purports to comply with Option 1.

(d) If the licensee is not a body regulated by APRA or a market or clearing participant then the licensee will need to meet the cash needs requirements by complying with one of the following options:

(i) If the licensee is relying on satisfying the cash needs requirement by Option 1 or Option 2 then ASIC requires the following:

- Reasonable assurance that the licensee had at all times a projection (covering at least the following 3 months) that purports to, and appears on its face to comply with, paragraph (a) of the definition of Option 1 or paragraph (a) of the definition of Option 2 (depending on which option the licensee purports to be complying with); and
- Reasonable assurance that the licensee has correctly calculated the projections on the basis of the assumptions the licensee adopted for the projections described) above; and
- Limited assurance that the licensee is managing the risk of having insufficient financial resources to comply with the conditions of the licence; and
- Limited assurance over the cash needs requirement using either Option 1 or Option 2 except for paragraphs (a), (c) and (e) of the definition of Option 1 or paragraphs (a) and (c) of the definition of Option 2; and
- If the licensee relied on Option 1, limited assurance that the assumptions the licensee adopted for its projection were not unreasonable; or
- If the licensee relied on Option 2, limited assurance that the basis for the selection of assumptions to meet the requirements for the projection adopted was not unreasonable; or

(ii) If the licensee is relying on satisfying the cash needs requirement with a financial commitment by an Australian ADI or comparable foreign institution (Option 3) then ASIC requires:

- Reasonable assurance that the licensee has obtained from an Australian ADI or a foreign deposit-taking institution approved in writing by ASIC as an eligible provider an enforceable and unqualified commitment to pay on demand from time to time an unlimited amount to the licensee, or the amount for which the licensee is liable to its creditors at the time of demand to the licensee's creditors or a trustee for the licensee's creditors; and
- Limited assurance that the licensee is managing the risk of having insufficient financial resources to comply with the conditions of the licence; and
- Limited assurance that the basis for the selection of the assumptions adopted was not unreasonable; or

(iii) If the licensee is relying on satisfying the cash needs requirement by relying on licence condition 13(c)(iv) (Option 4) then ASIC requires:

- Reasonable assurance that the licensee is a subsidiary of an Australian ADI or a corporation approved by ASIC in writing; and
- Reasonable assurance that a responsible officer of the licensee has documented that the officer has the reasonable expectation for at least the following three month period together with the reasons for forming the expectation, the contingencies for which the licensee considers it is reasonable to plan, the assumptions made concerning the contingencies and the basis for selecting those assumptions; and
- Limited assurance that the licensee is managing the risk of having insufficient financial resources to comply with the conditions of the licence; and
- Limited assurance that the basis for the selection of the assumptions adopted was not unreasonable; or

(iv) If the licensee is relying on satisfying the cash needs requirement by relying on licence condition 13(c)(v) (Option 5), then ASIC requires:

- Reasonable assurance that the cash flows of the licensee and each of its related bodies corporate, other than any body regulated by APRA ("licensee group"), are managed on a consolidated basis and there is a body corporate within the licensee group of which all members of the licensee group are subsidiaries that is not a body regulated by APRA ("parent entity"); and
- If the licensee is relying on Alternative A, reasonable assurance that the parent entity has provided an enforceable and unqualified commitment to pay on demand from time to time an unlimited amount to the licensee or to meet the licensee's liabilities; or
- If the licensee is relying on Alternative B:
  - ◊ Limited assurance that the licensee is managing the risk of having insufficient financial resources to comply with the conditions of the licence; and
  - ◊ Limited assurance that the basis for the selection of the assumptions adopted was not unreasonable.

(e) Reasonable assurance on the following matters as stated in Regulation 7.8.13(2) of the Corporations Regulations:

(i) the effectiveness of internal controls used by an AFS licensee to comply with:

- Divisions 2, 3, 4, 5 and 6 of Part 7.8 of the Corporations Act; and
- Division 7 of Part 7.8 of the Corporations Act other than section 991A; and

(ii) whether each account required by sections 981B and 982B of the Corporations Act to be maintained by the AFS licensee has been operated and controlled in accordance with those sections; and

(iii) whether all necessary records, information and explanations were received from the AFS licensee.

(f) A statement that there are no matters that should have been reported to ASIC in accordance with section 990K of the Corporations Act during or since the financial year that have not previously been reported to ASIC, other than the matters detailed in FS 71.

21 FS 71 is a prescribed form, however, paragraph 3 of FS 71 has been left blank for the auditor to insert their opinions and/or statements required under the licensee's licence. Appendix 1 contains examples of paragraph 3 to be included in different circumstances.

22 The AFS financial requirements are complex and ASIC reissued *Regulatory Guide 166 Licensing: Financial requirements* (RG 166) on 25 June 2007. This regulatory guide sets out the financial requirements for holders of an AFS licence.

23 In addition, ASIC *Pro Forma 209 Australian Financial Services Licence Conditions* (PF 209), reissued on 25 June 2007, sets out the standard licence conditions which subject to individual circumstances, will usually be applied to licences authorising a person to provide financial services under an AFS licence. It is important that the individual AFS licence conditions are examined carefully so that the appropriate reporting and auditing obligations are met.

Exemptions From Lodging Form FS 71

24 A foreign Authorised Deposit-taking Institution ("ADI") which holds an AFS licence that has relief under Class Order 03/823 *Relief from licensing, accounting and audit requirements for foreign authorised deposit-taking institutions,* is not required to lodge FS 71 with ASIC. It is exempt from the requirements of section 989B of the Corporations Act, where equivalent reports prepared for the overseas regulator of the foreign ADI are lodged with ASIC at least once in every calendar year and at intervals of not more than 15 months.

25 Where the foreign ADI is also regulated by APRA and the AFS licence contains condition 27 in PF 209, then it is necessary for the foreign ADI to lodge an audit report (even if the foreign

ADI is exempt under Class Order 03/823), that states whether for the relevant period, on a reasonable assurance basis, the licensee was a body regulated by APRA at the end of the financial year or for any period of time that ASIC requests. This is because the APRA regulation confirmation requirement is in addition to Section 989B or Class Order 03/823. The format of this audit report does not need to be in accordance with FS 71. To avoid any processing problems, ASIC requires the audit report to be lodged and accompanied by a letter identifying the licensee, licence number and financial year, and clearly stating the reasons why FS 71 has not been lodged. ASIC requires this letter to include reference to the class order and to the requirement for a report pursuant to the relevant licence condition.

26 Class Order 06/68 *Conditional relief for foreign licensees from financial reporting and record keeping obligations,* issued 3 February 2006 provides that a foreign company AFS Licence holder (other than a foreign ADI) can lodge accounts prepared for their home regulator with ASIC to meet their AFS Licence requirements. As a result the foreign company does not have to comply with regulations made for the purposes of sections 989B and 989C and hence is not required to lodge FS 70 or FS 71.

27 RG 166.8 also states that if the licensee is prudentially regulated overseas, they can apply to ASIC for relief from the financial requirements. ASIC will give this relief on a case-by-case basis if they are satisfied that the applicant is regulated in a way that is comparable to regulation by APRA for entities of that kind. If applicable, ASIC will consider the extent to which the relevant foreign prudential regulation is consistent with the Basel Committee guidelines for regulating deposit-taking institutions.

Considerations for the Auditor

Those Who May Audit the AFS Licensee

28 Section 990B(1) of the Corporations Act, requires the AFS licensee to ensure that at all times a registered company auditor is engaged to audit the licensee's financial statements.

Agreeing on the Terms of the Engagement

29 The auditor and the AFS licensee agree on the terms of the AFS licensee engagement in writing. Such terms may be outlined in an engagement letter[1], an example of which is provided in Appendix 2 to this Guidance Statement. The auditor has regard to the requirements of ASA 210 Terms of Audit Engagements when agreeing on the terms of the engagement.

30 The auditor may also use the engagement letter to clarify the respective roles of the AFS licensee and the auditor. In particular, it is important to highlight in the engagement letter the AFS licensee's obligation to establish and maintain effective internal controls in relation to compliance with the requirements of the Corporations Act. It is the responsibility of the AFS licensee to comply with all the conditions under its licence, including all the financial requirements. The auditor obtains acknowledgment of this obligation from the directors of the AFS licensee when obtaining agreement on the terms of the engagement.

Planning

31 ASA 315 *Understanding the Entity and Its Environment and Assessing the Risks of Material Misstatement* requires that, the auditor obtains an understanding of the entity and its environment, including its internal control, sufficient to identify and asses the risks of material misstatement of the financial report whether due to fraud or error, and sufficient to design and perform further audit procedures which may also impact on the FS 71 audit report.

32 The auditor plans the engagement in accordance with ASA 300 *Planning an Audit of a Financial Report.* In planning the engagement the auditor considers comparison of actual amounts to budgets, for example, when considering the projection of the licensee's cash flows over the next 3 months to the actual cash flows.

GS

1 Or other suitable form of audit contract.

33 The auditor of the AFS licensee considers:

(a) key responsibilities and risks identified;

(b) processes established by the AFS licensee to implement the licence conditions; and

(c) processes established by the licensee to monitor adherence to the licence conditions and the Corporations Act requirements.

34 When evaluating the licensee's adherence to the licence conditions and the ongoing adequacy of its processes, the auditor will need to obtain from management a copy of the licence conditions, together with a written description of the procedures and structures which the licensee has established to ensure compliance with those licence conditions.

35 In planning the audit or review, the auditor considers various matters including:

- The licence conditions.
- The nature and extent of any recent changes to the licence conditions and whether any detected breaches are deemed to be material in light of the revised licence conditions.
- The nature of and extent of any changes to, the operations of the licensee itself.
- Changes to the Corporations Act and Corporations Regulations.
- Reports and other documents submitted to the board of the licensee regarding the operation of the licence and its compliance functions.
- Previous auditor's reports, including the auditor's report on financial statements of the licensee, and related management letters.

Materiality

36 The auditor considers materiality when determining the nature, timing and extent of audit and review procedures.

37 Materiality is addressed in the context of the AFS licensee's objectives, which are developed having regard to the protection of the interests of clients as a whole. Materiality considerations are therefore viewed within the context of setting out adequate measures that the licensee is to apply in operating to ensure compliance with the Corporations Act and the licence conditions.

38 The meaning and application of the concept of materiality contained in ASA 320 *Materiality and Audit Adjustments* is adapted by the AFS licensee auditor, as appropriate, to the task of judging adherence to the AFS licence and conformity with the relevant provisions in Part 7.8 of the Corporations Act. However, it is not possible to give a definitive view on what may constitute material, other than to suggest that the auditor exercises appropriate professional judgement having regard to the AFS licensee's obligations to clients, together with the size, complexity and nature of an AFS licensee's activities.

39 As identified in ASA 320, when assessing materiality, the auditor considers qualitative factors as well as quantitative factors. The following are examples of qualitative factors that may be relevant:

- The specific requirements of the terms of the engagement.
- The significance of identified weaknesses or breaches in compliance measures.
- The cost of alternative compliance measures relative to their likely benefit.
- Public perceptions and/or interest.

Quality Control

40 The auditor needs to adopt quality control policies and procedures in accordance with ASA 220 *Quality Control for Audits of Historical Financial Information.* Quality control policies and procedures apply at two levels. Quality control policy and procedures relate to the overall policies and procedures for all engagements, such as procedures in relation to client acceptance, and also to the direction, supervision and review of work delegated to personnel involved in a specific engagement.

Reporting Entity Concept

41 AFS licensees are required to lodge annual financial statements attached to FS 70 and FS 71. Where licensees have not previously prepared financial statements or, in very rare situations, have previously prepared special purpose financial statements, then the auditor considers whether the licensee is a reporting entity. Guidance as to what constitutes a reporting entity is contained in Statement of Accounting Concepts SAC 1 'Definition of the Reporting Entity' and Miscellaneous Professional Statement APS 1 'Conformity with Accounting Standards and UIG Consensus Views'. The decision as to whether an entity is a reporting entity needs to be made on a case by case basis in accordance with SAC 1 and APS 1. A requirement to prepare and/or lodge a financial report with ASIC pursuant to the Corporations Act does not, of itself, deem that entity to be a reporting entity.

42 Whilst the current legislation allows for a non-reporting entity to prepare "special purpose" financial statements, in most circumstances an AFS licensee will be a reporting entity and hence lodge "general purpose" financial statements (i.e. adopt all of the Australian Accounting Standards). FS 71 requires a statement as to whether the licensee is a reporting entity or not.

Natural Persons

43 ASIC has issued class order CO 03/748 on reporting requirements for AFS licensees who are natural persons. A natural person is defined as an individual, as opposed to a company, partnership or trustee. CO 03/748 states that where the licensee is a natural person, the licensee may exclude from the profit and loss statement, the revenue and expense that do not relate to any business of the licensee or all the revenue and expenses that do not relate to a financial services business of the licensee.

44 Alternatively, a natural person licensee can choose not to rely on CO 03/748 and instead include in a profit and loss statement all of their revenues and expenses, whether personal or business. The relief under CO 03/748 is confined to the preparation of the profit and loss statement. ASIC requires a natural person licensee to still prepare a balance sheet that discloses all of his or her assets and liabilities, including his or her personal assets and liabilities and the assets and liabilities of any other business.

Reporting Requirements

Limited Assurance on Certain Statements Made in FS 70 relating to Dealing with Clients' Money and Dealing with Other Property of Clients

45 The FS 71 audit report requires limited assurance on certain statements at paragraphs 6 (has the licensee received client monies), 7 (has the licensee received client property) and 8 (has the licensee received a loan from a client) of FS 70. The auditor considers the licensee's statements on FS 70 and through performing other evidence gathering procedures including, knowledge of the client and corroborative enquiry, concludes as to the reasonableness of the statements.

Statement on Section 990K(2) Matters

46 FS 71 requires a statement about any matter referred to in subsection 990K(2) of the Corporations Act and covers the year under audit and up until the date the FS 71 auditor's report is signed . This 990K(2) statement only deals with those matters that have not already been reported by the auditor as required under 990K(1). The section 990K(2) statement is no longer part of the opinion section on FS 71. Section 990K(2) requires a report to be given in relation to any matter that, in the opinion of the auditor:

(a) has adversely affected, is adversely affecting or may adversely affect the ability of the licensee to meet the licensee's obligations as a licensee; or

(b) constitutes or may constitute a contravention of:

(i) a provision of Subdivision A or B of Division 2 (or a provision of regulations made for the purposes of such a provision); or

(ii) a provision of Division 3 (or a provision of regulations made for the purposes of such a provision); or

GS

(iii) a provision of Subdivision B or C of this Division (or a provision of regulations made for the purposes of such a provision); or

(iv) a condition of the licensee's licence; or

(c) constitutes an attempt to unduly influence, coerce, manipulate or mislead the auditor in the conduct of the audit.

47 The auditor's obligation is to report on the above relevant matters (a) - (c), if they have become aware of them during the course of the audit of the financial statements, performing work on FS 71 or undertaking other audit work (e.g. Managed investments compliance plan audits). However, if the auditor becomes aware of a 990K(2) matter that is outside the Corporations Act sections under audit, then the auditor would report on these section 990K(2) matters but has no obligation to look for matters outside the sections under audit.

48 As this statement specifically covers both the financial year and the period between the end of the financial year and the date of signing the FS71 auditor's report (unlike the other reporting requirements in FS71), the auditor is obliged to formally consider the existence of relevant matters up to the date of signing the report. To determine the existence of such matters, the auditor considers matters including:

- Reading minutes of the meetings of those charged with governance, and compliance, audit and executive committees, held after the reporting date, and enquiring about matters discussed at meetings for which minutes are not yet available.
- Examining the licensee's breach registers up to the date of signing.
- Obtaining copies of all correspondence with ASIC up to the date of signing.
- Enquiring of management as to whether any subsequent events have occurred which might represent matters referred to under section 990K(2).

49 To determine whether the licensee is meeting its obligations as a licensee, the auditor considers matters including:

- A compliance manual exists and whether it has been distributed.
- The licensee monitors the conduct of its representatives.
- Procedures exist to ensure all staff are appropriately qualified and receive ongoing training.
- Recruitment procedures assess the competence of candidates.
- The licensee has a documented complaints and dispute resolution policy.
- The licensee is a member of an approved external dispute resolution scheme.
- The licensee has written approval from ASIC of its compensation arrangements for retail clients.
- Any non-compliance with ASIC directions or ASIC requests for information exists.
- There has been any business changes that may impact on the licence conditions eg: has the licensee either become or ceased to be a participant in a licensed market or a licensed clearing settlement facility.
- Due diligence procedures exist for client documents such as financial services guides, product disclosure statements and other public documents.
- Copies of all correspondence with ASIC during the period have been received.
- The licensee's breach registers have been obtained to determine whether any breaches identified by the licensee are required to be reported in FS 71.

50 Apart from the requirement to report section 990K(2) breaches in FS 71, section 990K(1) requires auditors to report such breaches to ASIC (and any relevant market or clearing authority e.g. ASX for stockbrokers) within 7 days of becoming aware of the matter. Auditors consider this obligation at all times of the year, but particularly during the planning, interim and final stages of their audits. The licensee will have already reported any such breaches within 5 business days of them becoming aware of the matter as required by section 912D(1). However, there is potential conflict between the auditor's obligation to report <u>any</u> breaches and the licensee's obligation to only report <u>significant</u> breaches to ASIC.

Limited Assurance on Risk Management Systems

51 FS 71 requires limited assurance on risk management systems in relation to compliance with financial requirements. Section 912A(1)(h) requires an AFS licensee to have adequate risk management systems. To satisfy this obligation, ASIC expects that the risk management systems will specifically deal with the risk that the licensee's financial resources will not be adequate to ensure that they are able to carry on their business in compliance with their licence obligations.

52 The auditor considers enquiry of management as to the processes by which they manage these risks. The auditor considers whether a formal documented risk management system exists, although the formality and extent of the processes required will depend on the size, nature and complexity of the business. Aside from periodic calculations of compliance with financial requirements, the auditor considers processes that also exist to identify and address matters that may arise between these periodic calculations that have the potential to cause non-compliance with the financial requirements, although the extent of these processes will depend on how much of a buffer the licensee has above the requirements and the sensitivity of these buffers to fluctuations in the performance and financial position of the licensee.

Reasonable Assurance on Certain Provisions in Part 7.8 of the Corporations Act

53 The FS 71 audit report requires reasonable assurance on compliance with the requirements of Divisions 2, 3, 4, 5 and 6 of Part 7.8 of the Corporations Act and Division 7 of Part 7.8 other than section 991A. These provisions include:

- Dealing with clients' money.
- Dealing with other property of clients.
- Special provisions relating to insurance.
- Obligations to report.
- Financial records, statements and audit.
- Other rules about conduct (i.e.: giving priority to client orders, transmission of instructions through licensed markets, maintaining records of instruction, dealing with non-licensees and employees).

54 Division 2 of Part 7.8 subdivision A and Corporations Regulations 7.8.01 – 7.8.05 relates to handling of client money including:

- What constitutes client money?
- Establishing an approved trust account.
- Payment of client money into the trust account within one business day.
- Circumstances where money can be withdrawn from the trust account.
- Treatment of interest on client money.

55 The auditor establishes whether the licensee holds client money, and then the auditor performs procedures including:

- Determining whether a trust account has been appropriately established for the financial period.
- Sample testing to establish whether client money received has been appropriately paid into the trust account.
- Sample testing to establish whether withdrawals from the trust account are in accordance with Corporations Regulation 7.8.02. If a licensee does hold client money, the auditor considers whether they also have to comply with the Surplus Liquid Funds requirement.

56 Division 2 of Part 7.8 subdivision B and Corporations Regulations 7.8.06 relates to monies paid to a licensee by way of a loan from a client, including:

- What constitutes a loan from a client (excludes deposit and debenture payments)?
- Establishing an approved trust account.

- Payment of money lent into the trust account within 1 business day.
- Statement required to be given to the client setting out terms and conditions of use of the loan and purpose for which funds will be used.
- Requirement to only use funds for specified purpose outlined in the terms and conditions or subsequently agreed to in writing.

57 The auditor establishes whether the licensee has received a loan from a client, and then the auditor performs procedures including:

- Determining whether a trust account has been appropriately established for the financial period;
- Sample testing to establish whether money received has been appropriately paid into the trust account;
- Testing to establish whether clients have been given the appropriate statements;
- Sample testing to establish whether money lent has been used for an agreed purpose.

58 Division 3 of Part 7.8 and Corporations Regulation 7.8.07 relates to the handing of property other than money given to the licensee, including:

- What constitutes client property?
- How the licensee deposits or register that client property.
- Circumstances in which a licensee can hold property as security.
- The requirement to return secured property to the client within one business day of the client settling their obligation to the licensee.
- The requirement to provide clients with statements of property held as security every 3 months.

59 The auditor establishes whether the licensee handles client property, and then the auditor performs procedures including:

- Sample testing to establish whether property received has been appropriately deposited or registered;
- Establishing whether property is received as security;
- Sample testing to establish whether the licensee has complied with the requirements relating to property received as security.

60 Division 4 of Part 7.8 and Corporations Regulations 7.8.08 relates to the receipt of monies by licensees who are insurance brokers and agents of general and life insurance contracts but not the actual insurer. Auditors consider the applicable legislation and design appropriate tests to determine whether the licensee has designed and is operating effective internal controls in order to comply with the relevant requirements.

61 Division 5 of Part 7.8 makes provision for the regulations to impose reporting requirements in relation to money to which Division 2 or 3 applies, or to a licensee dealing in derivatives. Currently, there are no regulations relating to this Division.

62 Division 6 of Part 7.8 relates to financial records, statements and audit. Auditors consider the applicable legislation and design appropriate tests to determine whether the licensee has complied with the relevant requirements.

63 Division 7 of Part 7.8 (other than section 991A) relates to other rules about conduct in licensed markets. The auditor considers firstly whether the legislation is applicable to the licensee. If the legislation is applicable, the auditor then designs appropriate tests to determine whether the licensee has designed and is operating effectively internal controls in order to comply with the relevant requirements.

Financial Requirements

64 When auditing compliance with the AFS Licensee requirements throughout the period, it is important for the auditor to:

(a) understand how the licensee derives their calculations, so the auditor can conclude as to whether this method is in accordance with the requirements

(b) ascertain whether all the calculations prepared during the period demonstrate a compliant position; and

(c) sample test a number of calculations for accuracy based on underlying financial information.

65 The auditor considers the relevant financial requirements by referring to the licence conditions and the client's documented procedures for monitoring compliance with the financial requirements.

Cash Needs Requirement

66 ASIC requires a reasonable assurance opinion on the entity's compliance with the financial licensee requirements for the entire year, not just year end. Hence, evidence-gathering procedures will need to include an understanding of the processes adopted by the licensee to ensure compliance throughout the year, such as formal policies, monthly calculations, use of standard calculation templates and monitoring by the licensee's board or appropriate delegate. The auditor considers testing to be performed on a sample basis depending on the assessment of effectiveness of controls.

67 If the licensee has adopted Option 1 for the cash needs requirement, the auditor considers compliance throughout the period with the cash holding requirement in Part (e) of the Option 1 definition.

68 The auditor considers obtaining the cash flow projections throughout the relevant period and determining whether the cash flow projections are either:

(a) a projection of the licensee's cash flows over at least the next 3 months based on the licensee's reasonable estimate of what is likely to happen over this term (Option 1); or

(b) a projection of the licensee's cash flows over at least the next 3 months based on the licensee's estimate of what would happen if the licensee's ability to meet its liabilities over the projected term (including any liabilities the licensee might incur during the term of the projection) is adversely affected by commercial contingencies taking into account all contingencies that are sufficiently likely for a reasonable licensee to plan how they might manage them (Option 2).

The auditor considers establishing how often and when the cash flow projection is updated to ensure it continuously covers at least the next 3 months.

69 The auditor considers obtaining the licensee's documented assumptions used to prepare the cash flow projections and checking whether the assumptions have been correctly applied in preparing the projections. This may include ensuring that the documented assumptions on the timing of cash flows have been correctly applied to budgeted revenues, expenses and capital expenditure.

70 Based on the cash flow projections already obtained, the auditor considers whether there is evidence that the cash flow assumptions are not appropriately documented or that the projections do not demonstrate that the licensee had access as needed to sufficient financial resources at all times in compliance with paragraphs (b) and (d) of either the Option 1 or Option 2 definitions throughout the period. The auditor considers whether the documentation is sufficient to enable the auditor to ascertain whether the assumptions have been correctly applied in preparing the projections. This may involve reviewing the documentation of budget assumptions if the cash flow documentation does not stand alone.

71 If the licensee relied on Option 1, then based on reviewing the assumptions in line with the auditor's knowledge of the business and on enquiries of management, the auditor considers whether there is evidence that the assumptions used are unreasonable. This may involve obtaining an understanding of the licensee's budgeting process if budgets are used to prepare the cash flow projections, or considering the historical accuracy of the assumptions in predicting actual cash flows.

72 If the licensee relies on Option 2, then based on reviewing the basis of selecting the assumptions in line with the auditor's knowledge of the business and on enquiries of management, the auditor considers determining whether there is evidence that the basis for selecting the assumptions is unreasonable. For Option 2, there is no requirement to consider whether the assumptions themselves are reasonable, unlike for Option 1.

73 Where the licensee uses group cash flow projections to meet the cash needs requirement, on the basis of alternative A (under licence condition 13(c)(v)), the auditor is required to include an audit opinion on whether there is an enforceable and unqualified commitment to pay on demand an unlimited amount to the licensee, or to meet the licensee's liabilities (including any additional liabilities that the licensee might incur while the commitment applies). In addition, the report is required to contain a statement on whether the auditor has any reason to believe that the documented basis for selecting the assumptions, on which the licensee's expectation concerning the period during which the commitment will apply, is unreasonable.

74 Where the licensee relies on alternative B (under licence condition 13(d)(v)), the audit report is required contain a statement about whether the auditor has any reason to believe that the documented basis for selecting the assumptions, on which the licensee's expectation concerning the adequacy of the resources required under alternative B, is unreasonable.

75 Where the licensee is a subsidiary of an Australian ADI or ASIC-approved prudentially regulated body that does not prepare cash flow projections, on the basis of its expectation concerning the adequacy of resources (under licence condition 13(c)(iv)), the audit report is required to contain a statement about whether the auditor has any reason to believe that the basis for selecting the assumptions documented by the licensee in forming the expectation is unreasonable.

Inherent Limitations

76 Due to the nature of audit testing and other inherent limitations of an audit, together with the inherent limitations of an AFS licensee and its related licence conditions, there is a possibility that a properly planned and executed audit will not detect all deficiencies in a licensee's licence conditions. Accordingly, the audit opinion under section 989B(3) is expressed in terms of reasonable assurance and cannot constitute a guarantee that the AFS licensee is completely free from any deficiency, or that all compliance breaches have been detected.

77 There are also practical limitations in requiring an auditor to perform a continuous examination of the AFS licensee, and form an opinion that the entity has complied at all times with the Corporations Act during the period covered by the AFS licensee audit report. However, the auditor performs tests periodically throughout the financial year to obtain evidence and have reasonable assurance that the measures complied with the written descriptions and were adequate throughout the period under examination.

The FS 71 Audit Report

78 Prior to issuing the FS 71 audit report, the auditor considers obtaining a written representation from the directors of the AFS licensee which contains their assertions that the AFS licensee has complied with the licence conditions during the financial year and up to the date the FS71audit report is signed, and that the AFS licensee continues to meet the requirements of Part 7.8 of the Corporations Act.

79 The FS 71 audit report is an ASIC prescribed form and can be found on the ASIC web site www.asic.gov.au under Download Forms. ASIC requires form FS 71 to be lodged in the prescribed form and that no modifications or deletions be made, unless consented to by ASIC.

80 It is important to check the ASIC website to ensure that the latest version of FS71 is adopted.

Conformity with International Pronouncements

81 There is no equivalent International Standard on Auditing or International Auditing Practice Statement to this Guidance Statement.

Appendix 1

Example FS 71 Paragraph 3 Insertions

Example 1: Paragraph 3 for a Licensee regulated by APRA

This suggested example paragraph 3 is to be included on ASIC's Form FS 71 and applies where the licensee is a body regulated by APRA for the entire financial year. This example also applies if the licensee is both a body regulated by APRA and a market participant or clearing participant.

3. Except as stated at paragraph 7, the licensee relied on being a body regulated by the Australian Prudential Regulation Authority ("APRA") for the financial year and in my/our opinion the licensee was a body regulated by APRA at the end of the financial year.

Example 2: Paragraph 3 for a Market or Clearing Participant

This suggested example paragraph 3 is to be included on ASIC's Form FS 71 and applies where the licensee was a market participant or clearing participant for the entire financial year and is not a body regulated by APRA.

3. Except as stated at paragraph 7, based on the definitions under the licensee's licence, the licensee relied on being a market participant or a clearing participant for the financial year, and in my/our opinion, the licensee was a participant in the market conducted by [ASX Limited (ASX)], [the Australian Clearing House Pty Ltd (ACH)] *or* [Sydney Futures Exchange Limited (SFE) that restricted its financial services business to participating in the market and incidental business supervised by SFE] for the financial year.

Example 3: Paragraph 3 relying on Option 1 or Option 2

This suggested example paragraph 3 is to be included on ASIC's Form FS 71 and is for licensees not regulated by APRA or market participants or clearing participants and where the licensee is relying on satisfying the cash needs requirement by Option 1 or Option 2. The licence conditions specified have been taken from PF 209 reissued on 25 June 2007, however the auditor is expected to use the actual licence conditions of the licensee.

3. Except as stated at paragraph 7,

   (i) in my/our opinion, for the financial year, the licensee:

   (A) complied with all the financial requirements under conditions 13 to 26 (inclusive) of this licence, other than paragraph 13(c) of this licence, [except for paragraph (e) of the definition of Option 1 under this licence if the licensee purports to comply with Option 1]; and

   (B) had at all times a projection (covering at least the following 3 months) that purported to, and appears on its face to comply with, [paragraph (a) of the definition of Option 1] *or* [paragraph (a) of the definition of Option 2]; and

   (C) correctly calculated the projections on the basis of the assumptions the licensee adopted for the projections described in subparagraph 4(i)(B) above; and

   (ii) based on my/our review, following an examination of the documents the licensee relied on in complying with Option 1 or Option 2, we have no reason to believe that:

   (A) the licensee did not satisfy the requirements of subsection 912A(1)(h) of the Act for managing the risk of having insufficient financial resources to comply with the conditions of this licence; or

   (B) the licensee failed to comply with the cash needs requirement using either Option 1 or Option 2 (as applicable) except for paragraphs (a), (c) and (e) of the definition of Option 1 or paragraphs (a) and (c) of the definition of Option 2; or

   (C) if the licensee relied on Option 1, the assumptions the licensee adopted for its projections were unreasonable; or

   (D) if the licensee relied on Option 2, the basis for the selection of assumptions to meet the requirements for the projections adopted was unreasonable.

GS

Example 4: Paragraph 3 relying on licence condition 13(c)(iii) (Option 3)

This suggested example paragraph 3 is to be included on ASIC's Form FS 71 and is for licensees not regulated by APRA or market participants or clearing participants and where the licensee is relying on satisfying the cash needs requirement with PF 209 licence condition 13(d)(iii). The licence conditions specified have been taken from PF 209 reissued on 25 June 2007, however the auditor is expected to use the actual licence conditions of the licensee.

3. Except as stated at paragraph 7,

   (i) in my opinion the licensee has complied with all the financial requirements under conditions 13 to 26 (inclusive) of this licence, other than paragraph 13(c) of this licence for the financial year; and

   (ii) in my/our opinion, for the financial year when the licensee relied on subparagraph 13(c)(iii), the licensee has obtained from [an Australian ADI] *or* [a foreign deposit-taking institution] approved in writing by ASIC as an eligible provider an enforceable and unqualified commitment to pay on demand from time to time an unlimited amount to the licensee, or the amount for which the licensee is liable to its creditors at the time of demand to the licensee's creditors or a trustee for the licensee's creditors; and

   (iii) based on my/our review, for the financial year, following an examination of the documented assumptions that the licensee relied on in forming the reasonable expectation referred to in licence condition 13(c)(iii), we have no reason to believe that:

      (A) the licensee did not satisfy the requirements of subsection 912A(1)(h) of the Act for managing the risk of having insufficient financial resources to comply with the conditions of this licence; or

      (B) the basis for the selection of the assumptions adopted was unreasonable.

Example 5: Paragraph 3 relying on licence condition 13(c)(iv) (Option 4)

This suggested example paragraph 3 is to be included on ASIC's Form FS 71 and is for licensees not regulated by APRA or market participants or clearing participants and where the licensee is relying on satisfying the cash needs requirement with PF 209 licence condition 13(c)(iv). The licence conditions specified have been taken from PF 209 reissued on 25 June 2007, however the auditor is expected to use the actual licence conditions of the licensee.

3. Except as stated at paragraph 7:

   (i) in my opinion the licensee has complied with all the financial requirements under conditions 13 to 26 (inclusive) of this licence, other than paragraph 13(c) of this licence for the financial year; and

   (ii) in my opinion, for the financial year when the licensee relied on subparagraph 13(c)(iv), following an examination of the documents prepared for subparagraphs 13(c)(iv)(C), the licensee complied with subparagraphs 13(c)(iv)(A) and subparagraph 13(c)(iv)(C) for the period to which the report relates; and

   (iii) based on my/our review, for the financial year when the licensee relied on subparagraph 13(c)(iv), following an examination of the documents prepared for subparagraph 13(c)(iv)(C), we have no reason to believe that:

      (A) the licensee did not satisfy the requirements of subsection 912A(1)(h) of the Act for managing the risk of having insufficient financial resources to comply with the conditions of this licence; and

      (B) the basis for the selection of the assumptions adopted was unreasonable.

Example 6: Paragraph 3 relying on licence condition 13(c)(v) (Option 5)

This suggested example paragraph 3 is to be included on ASIC's Form FS 71 and is for licensees not regulated by APRA or market participants or clearing participants and where the licensee is relying on satisfying the cash needs requirement with PF 209 licence condition 13(c)(v). The licence conditions specified have been taken from PF 209 reissued on 25 June 2007, however the auditor is expected to use the actual licence conditions of the licensee.

3. Except as stated at paragraph 7,:
   (i) in my opinion the licensee has complied with all the financial requirements under conditions 13 to 26 (inclusive) of this licence, other than paragraph 13(c) of this licence for the financial year; and
   (ii) in my opinion, for the financial year when the licensee relied on subparagraph 13(c) (v), the licensee complied with licence condition 13(c)(v)(A) and (B); and
   (iii) in my opinion, when the licensee relied on Alternative A in subparagraph 13(c) (v) (E), the parent entity has provided an enforceable and unqualified commitment to pay on demand from time to time an unlimited amount to the licensee or to meet the licensee's liabilities;

   or

   (iii) based on my/our review, for the financial year when the licensee relied on subparagraph 13(c)(v) under Alternative B, following an examination of the documents prepared for Alternative B, we have no reason to believe that:
      (A) the licensee did not satisfy the requirements of subsection 912A(1)(h) of the Act for managing the risk of having insufficient financial resources to comply with the conditions of this licence; or
      (B) the basis for the selection of the assumptions adopted was unreasonable.

Appendix 2

Example Audit Engagement Letter

The following example audit engagement letter is for use as a guide only, in conjunction with the considerations described in GS 003, and will need to be varied according to individual requirements and circumstances.

To [Board of Directors]

Engagement Letter for Australian Financial Services Licensee

Australian Auditing Standards require that there be a clear understanding in writing, between the auditor and the client as to the extent of audit duties. Accordingly, we set out below details of our responsibilities as auditor and our understanding of the services you require us to perform.

Our Role

Section 989B of the *Corporations Act 2001* (the "Corporations Act") requires an Australian Financial Services Licence ("AFSL") holder ("Licensee") to lodge the auditor's report on the Licensee together with a profit and loss statement and balance sheet (being the audited financial statements). This letter outlines the scope for the auditor's report for the year ending *[year-end]*.

The Corporations Act and Corporations Regulations determine the scope of the auditor's report. Reference to the auditor's report is also made in the conditions of the AFSL. Currently the required format of the auditor's report is set out in ASIC Form 71.

Audit Scope and Approach

The audit scope is summarised as follows:

- Audit of the financial statements (covered by a separate engagement letter);
- Audit of compliance with specified provisions of Part 7.8 of the Corporations Act (being Divisions 2 to 7, except for section 991A);

GS

- Audit of compliance with sections 981B and 982B of the Corporations Act (relating to the control and operation of trust accounts);
- Audit of compliance with specific AFSL conditions relating to financial requirements, including internal procedures used by the Licensee to comply with the financial requirements under the Licence;
- Review of projections required under the cash needs requirements conditions of the AFSL; and
- Consideration of Guidance Statement GS 003 *Audit Requirements for Australian Financial Services Licensees under the Corporations Act 2001* and section 990K of the Corporations Act. These procedures will be limited primarily to inquiries of Licensee management, review of minutes and related documents, review of correspondence with regulatory bodies and observation of the operation of the internal compliance controls. These procedures will not constitute an audit of the overall internal compliance structure and framework.

Audit procedures will be conducted in accordance with Australian Auditing Standards, and accordingly will include such tests and procedures as we consider necessary in the circumstances. This will involve an examination of the internal control procedures used by the Licensee to comply with the financial requirements of the AFSL, the specified provisions of Part 7.8 and the control and operation of each account maintained for section 981B or section 982B of the Corporations Act.

Our review of the projections required under the cash needs requirements conditions of the AFSL will be conducted in accordance with Australian Auditing Standards applicable to review engagements in order to state whether anything has come to our attention, which causes us to believe that the Licensee did not satisfy the cash needs requirements. A review is substantially less in scope than an audit examination conducted in accordance with Australian Auditing Standards. A review of this nature provides less assurance than an audit.

Inherent Limitations

Because of the inherent limitations of any internal control structure it is possible that errors or irregularities may occur and not be detected. We will not audit the overall internal control structure (including procedures that do not relate to the financial requirements) and no opinion will be expressed as to its effectiveness.

The projections prepared by the Directors in accordance with the cash needs requirements conditions of the AFSL are based upon the achievement of certain economic, operating and developmental assumptions about future events and actions that have not yet occurred and may not necessarily occur. There is a considerable degree of subjective judgement involved in the preparation of projections. Actual results may vary materially from those projections and the variation may be materially positive or negative.

Directors' Responsibilities

The Licensee is responsible for maintaining effective internal control procedures, including control procedures in relation to compliance with the requirements of Part 7.8 of the Corporations Act, the conditions of the AFSL and the provisions of the financial services laws. These duties are imposed on the Licensee by the Corporations Act and the AFSL.

Fees

We look forward to full cooperation from your staff and we trust that they will make available to us whatever records, documentation and other information we request in connection with our audit.

[Insert additional information here regarding fee arrangements and billings, as appropriate]

Other

This letter will be effective for future years unless we advise you of its amendment or replacement, or the engagement is terminated.

Please sign and return the attached copy of this letter to indicate that it is in accordance with your understanding of the arrangements for our audit of [Name of the AFS Licensee] as required by Section 989(B) of the Corporations Act.

Yours faithfully,

(signed)

....

Name and Title

Date

Acknowledged on behalf of [entity] by (signed)

....

Name and Title

Date

Appendix 3

Example Management Representation Letter

[Client Letterhead]
[Addressee – Auditor]
[Date]

This representation letter is provided in connection with your audit of the Australian Financial Services Licence ("AFSL") of [Name of the AFS Licensee] (Licence No: [xx] as required by Section 989(B) of the Corporations Act 2001 for the financial year ended [balance date].

We confirm, to the best of our knowledge and belief, the following representations:

1. We have made available to you, and your representatives:
   (a) all financial records and related data, other information, explanations and assistance necessary for the conduct of the audit; and
   (b) minutes of all meetings of *(shareholders, directors, and committees of directors)*.
2. There:
   (a) has been no knowledge of any fraud, error or non-compliance with laws and regulations involving management or employees who have a significant role in the internal control structure;
   (b) has been no knowledge of any fraud, error or non-compliance with laws and regulations that could have a material effect on the either the financial reports for [Name of the AFS Licensee], or ongoing compliance with the AFSL; and
   (c) has been no communications from regulatory agencies concerning non-compliance with, or deficiencies in, financial reporting or compliance practices that that could have a material effect on the financial report of [Name of the AFS Licensee] or our ongoing ability to comply with financial services laws or conditions of the AFSL.
3. We have disclosed to you:
   (a) all significant facts relating to any frauds or suspected frauds which are known to us that may have affected the respective entities; and
   (b) the results of our assessment of the risk that the financial report may be materially misstated as a result of fraud.
4. There has been no matter during or since the end of the year/period ended **[selected date]** which has adversely affected, is adversely affecting or may adversely affect our ability to meet our obligations as a licensee or constitutes a contravention of :
   (a) a provision of Subdivision A or B of Division 2 of Part 7.8 of the Act (or a provision of regulations made for the purposes of such a provision); or
   (b) a provision of Division 3 of Part 7.8 of the Act (or a provision of regulations made for the purposes of such a provision); or

GS

(c) a provision of Subdivision B or C of Division 6 of the Part 7.8 of the Act (or a provision of regulations made for the purposes of such a provision); or

(d) a condition of the licence.

5. We have reported any significant breaches to ASIC as required under:

   (a) section 912D of the Act; and

   (b) section 601FC(1)(l) of the Act ***[delete if licensee is not a responsible entity of a managed investment scheme]***

   and have provided you with details of all breaches, reported and unreported, of the Licence or the Act that occurred during or since the end of the year/period.

6. We have complied with all the financial requirements under the Licence throughout the year/period.

7. We acknowledge our responsibility for the preparation of cash flow projections and the assumptions underpinning those projections, and confirm that the assumptions adopted for the projections were reasonable/the basis for the selection of assumptions to meet the requirements for the projections adopted was reasonable. ***[delete as applicable depending on whether the licensee is complying with Option 1 or Option 2]***

8. We confirm that we have access as needed to enough financial resources to meet our liabilities over the next 3 months, including any additional liabilities that we project we will incur during that term/we might incur during that term. ***[delete as applicable depending on whether the licensee is complying with Option 1 or Option 2]***

9. We have maintained adequate risk management systems throughout the year/period to manage the risk of having insufficient financial resources to comply with the conditions of the Licence. ***[delete if APRA-regulated]***

10. We have maintained effective controls to ensure that we comply with Divisions 2, 3, 4, 5, 6 and 7 of Part 7.8 of the Act (other than section 991A);

11. We have operated and controlled each account required by sections 981B and 982B in accordance with those sections;

12. In relation to forecast financial information provided to you for the purpose of your report (in particular the cash needs requirements prescribed by Option 1 or Option 2 as referred to in your AFSL and ASIC Form FS 71), it is confirmed, to the best of our knowledge and belief, that:

    (a) the financial position and operating results for the forecast period reflect the best judgement of our directors and management based on expected future market conditions and the likely course of action to be taken;

    (b) the accounting principles used in the preparation of the forecast data are consistent with those used in our historical financial statements and are the same as those expected to be used in the eventual preparation of the historical financial statements come the end of the forecast period;

    (c) there are no contingent liabilities, unusual contractual obligations or substantial commitments which would materially affect the financial forecast except as otherwise specifically disclosed to you;

    (d) the key assumptions have been consistently applied during the forecast period; and

    (e) no factors that may be relevant have been omitted.

13. We understand that your examination was made in accordance with Australian Auditing Standards and was, therefore, designed primarily for the purpose of expressing an opinion to the Australian Securities and Investments Commission for the financial year ended [balance date] and that your tests of the financial records and other auditing procedures were limited to those which you considered necessary for that purpose.

14. We have established and maintained an adequate compliance structure to ensure compliance with the conditions applicable to in the AFSL.

Yours faithfully

Name of signing officer and title]

Appendix 4

Extract from ASIC Pro Forma 209

Base Level Financial Requirements

13. The licensee must:

(a) be able to pay all its debts as and when they become due and payable; and

(b) either:

(i) have total assets that exceed total liabilities as shown in the licensee's most recent balance sheet lodged with ASIC and have no reason to suspect that the licensee's total assets would not currently exceed its total liabilities; or

(ii) have adjusted assets that exceed adjusted liabilities calculated at the balance date shown in the licensee's most recent balance sheet lodged with ASIC and have no reason to suspect that the licensee's adjusted assets would currently not exceed its adjusted liabilities; and

(c) meet the cash needs requirement by complying with one of the following five options:

(i) Option 1 (reasonable estimate projection plus cash buffer) - refer to definition of "Option 1" under this licence; or

(ii) Option 2 (contingency based projection) – refer to definition of "Option 2" under this licence; or

(iii) Option 3 (financial commitment by an Australian ADI or comparable foreign institution) – a requirement that an Australian ADI or a foreign deposit-taking institution approved in writing by ASIC as an eligible provider gives the licensee an enforceable and unqualified commitment to pay on demand from time to time an unlimited amount to the licensee, or the amount for which the licensee is liable to its creditors at the time of the demand to the licensee's creditors or a trustee for the licensee's creditors, that the licensee reasonably expects will apply for at least three months, taking into account all commercial contingencies for which the licensee should reasonably plan; or

(iv) Option 4 (expectation of support from an Australian ADI or comparable foreign institution) – a requirement that the licensee:

(A) is a subsidiary of an Australian ADI or a corporation approved by ASIC in writing for the purpose of this condition; and

(B) reasonably expects that (based on access to cash from its related bodies corporate) it will have adequate resources (when needed) to meet its liabilities for at least the next three months (including any additional liabilities that the licensee might incur during that period), taking into account all adverse commercial contingencies for which the licensee should reasonably plan; and

(C) ensures that a responsible officer of the licensee has documented that the officer has the reasonable expectation for at least the following three month period together with the reasons for forming the expectation, the contingencies for which the licensee considers it is reasonable to plan, the assumptions made concerning the contingencies and the basis for selecting those assumptions; or

(v) Option 5 (parent entity prepares cash flow projections on a consolidated basis) – a requirement that the licensee ensures that:

(A) the cash flows of the licensee and each of its related bodies corporate, other than any body regulated by APRA ("licensee group"), are managed on a consolidated basis; and

(B) there is a body corporate within the licensee group of which all members of the licensee group are subsidiaries that is not a body regulated by APRA ("parent entity"); and

(C) the parent entity complies with Option 1 or Option 2 as if it were the licensee, cash flows of any member of the licensee group were cash flows of the licensee and any cash held by a member of the licensee group, other than as trustee or as trustee of a relevant trust, were so held by the licensee; and

(D) a report by the parent entity's auditor that is a registered company auditor is given to ASIC with the licensee's annual audit report under condition 28 of this licence, in relation to each financial year of the licensee and for any other period that ASIC requests, by a date that ASIC requests, with respect to compliance by the parent entity with Option 1 or Option 2 as they would apply in accordance with subparagraph (C), reflecting the report that would be required from the auditor of a licensee, for that period purporting to comply with Option 1 or Option 2; and

(E) either of the following applies:

Alternative A – the parent entity has provided an enforceable and unqualified commitment to pay on demand from time to time an unlimited amount to the licensee or to meet the licensee's liabilities which the licensee reasonably expects will apply for at least the next three months taking into account all adverse commercial contingencies for which the licensee should reasonably plan; or

Alternative B – the licensee reasonably expects that (based on access to cash from members of the licensee group), it will have adequate resources to meet its liabilities (including any additional liabilities that the licensee might incur while the commitment applies) for at least the next three months taking into account all adverse commercial contingencies for which the licensee should reasonably plan and a responsible officer of the licensee has documented that the officer has the reasonable expectation in respect of at least the following three months together with the reasons for forming the expectation, the contingencies for which the licensee considers it is reasonable to plan, the assumptions made concerning the contingencies and the basis for selecting those assumptions; and

(F) the licensee has no reason to believe that the parent entity has not complied with the requirement at subparagraph (C) or has failed to comply in a material respect with its obligations under Chapter 2M of the Corporations Act or, if the parent entity is not a company, under any other laws (whether law in Australia or not) relating to financial reporting that apply to it.

For 5 years after the end of the last financial year that includes a part of the period to which any document prepared for subparagraph (c)(iv)(C) or Alternative B in subparagraph (c)(v)(E) relates, the licensee must keep the document and give it to ASIC if ASIC requests.

Option 1 means the reasonable estimate projection plus cash buffer basis where the licensee is required to:

(a) prepare a projection of the licensee's cash flows over at least the next 3 months based on the licensee's reasonable estimate of what is likely to happen over this term; and

(b) document the licensee's calculations and assumptions, and describe in writing why the assumptions relied upon are the appropriate assumptions; and

(c) update the projection of the licensee's cash flows when those cash flows cease to cover the next 3 months or if the licensee has reason to suspect that an updated projection would show that the licensee was not meeting paragraph (d) of this definition; and

(d) demonstrate, based on the projection of the licensee's cash flows, that the licensee will have access when needed to enough financial resources to meet its liabilities over the projected term of at least 3 months, including any additional liabilities the licensee projects will be incurred during that term; and

(e) hold (other than as trustee) or be the trustee of a relevant trusts that holds, in cash an amount equal to 20% of the greater of:

(i) the cash outflow for the projected period of at least 3 months (if the projection covers a period longer than 3 months, the cash outflow may be adjusted to product a 3-month average, or

(ii) the licensee's actual cash outflow for the most recent financial year for which the licensee has prepared a profit and loss statement, adjusted to produce a 3-month average.

For the purposes of this definition, references to the licensee's cash flow include the licensee's own cash flow and any cash flow of a relevant trust but do not include cash flows of any other trust.

For the purposes of paragraph (e) of this definition, "cash" means:

(A) current assets valued at the amount of cash for which they can be expected to be exchanged within 5 business days; or

(B) a commitment to provide cash from an eligible provider that can be drawn down within 5 business days and has a maturity of at least a month;

but does not include any cash in a relevant trust if the licensee has reason to believe that the cash will not be available to meet all of the projected cash flows of the licensee.

(This definition is imposed where the licensee is not a body regulated by APRA.)

Option 2 means the cash needs requirement on the contingency-based projection basis where the licensee is required to:

(a) prepare a projection of the licensee's cash flows over at least the next 3 months based on the licensee's estimate of what would happen if the licensee's ability to meet its liabilities over the projected term (including any liabilities the licensee might incur during the term of the projection) was adversely affected by commercial contingencies taking into account all contingencies that are sufficiently likely for a reasonable licensee to plan how they might manage them; and

(b) document the licensee's calculations and assumptions, and describe in writing why the assumptions relied upon are the appropriate assumptions; and

(c) update the projection of the licensee's cash flows when those cash flows cease to cover the next 3 months or if the licensee has reason to suspect that an updated projection would show that the licensee was not meeting paragraph (d) of this definition; and

(d) demonstrate, based on the projection of the licensee's cash flow, that the licensee will have access when needed to enough financial resources to meet its liabilities over the projected term of at least 3 months, including any additional liabilities the licensee might incur during that term.

For the purposes of this definition references to the licensee's cash flow include any cash flow of a relevant trust.

(This definition is imposed where the licensee is authorised to provide financial services in the capacity of a Principal Trader only).

GS 004

Audit Implications of Prudential Reporting Requirements for General Insurers

(Issued October 2007)

Issued by the Auditing and Assurance Standards Board.

Note from the Institute of Chartered Accountants Australia

This note, prepared by the technial editor, is not part of GS 004.

Historical development

March 2003: AGS 1064 issued to provide guidance for auditors undertaking a reporting engagement under GPS 220 'Risk Management' and related guidance notes issued by the Australian Prudential Regulation Authority. It also provides example report formats and engagement letters. The AGS was operative from the date of issue and there is no corresponding International Standard or statement on auditing.

October 2006: Addendum added to provide guidance to auditors on changes to the reporting requirements of general insurers following the release of new and revised Prudential Standards by APRA. It includes an example Independent Review Report in accordance with APRA Prudential Standard GPS 310 'Audit and Actuarial Reporting and Valuation' and related transitional rules for insurers that are required to report on or after 1 October 2006.

October 2007: AGS 1064 and its Addendum replaced by GS 004 of the same name updated to reflect the Insurance Act, effective 1 January 2008.

Contents

AUTHORITY STATEMENT

Authority Statement

The Auditing and Assurance Standards Board (AUASB) formulates Guidance Statement GS 004 *Audit Implications of Prudential Reporting Requirements for General Insurers,* as set out in paragraphs 1 to 121 and Appendices 1 to 4, pursuant to section 227B of the *Australian Securities and Investments Commission Act 2001,* for the purposes of providing guidance on procedural auditing and assurance matters.

This Guidance Statement provides guidance to assist the auditor to fulfil the objectives of the audit or assurance engagement. It includes explanatory details and suggested procedures on specific matters for the purposes of understanding and complying with AUASB Standards. The auditor exercises professional judgement when using this Guidance Statement.

The Guidance Statement does not prescribe or create mandatory requirements.

Dated 31 October 2007

M H Kelsall
Chairman - AUASB

Guidance Statement GS 004

Audit Implications of Prudential Reporting Requirements for General Insurers

Application

1 This Guidance Statement has been formulated by the Auditing and Assurance Standards Board (AUASB) in consultation with the Australian Prudential Regulation Authority (APRA) to provide guidance to the auditor of a general insurer in reporting pursuant to the prudential reporting requirements specified by APRA for general insurers reporting on a stand-alone basis (Level 1 reporting).

GS

A 'general insurer' is defined, under section 11 of the *Insurance Act 1973* (Act) as amended, as a body corporate that is authorised in writing by APRA, under section 12 of the Act, to carry on general insurance business in Australia. The term 'general insurer' (insurer) includes a foreign general insurer (foreign insurer) as defined in subsection 3(1) of the Act[1].

2 This Guidance Statement incorporates amendments to the Act, made under the *Financial Sector Legislation Amendment (Simplifying Regulation and Review) Act 2007,* which take effect on 1 January 2008.

Issuance Date

3 This Guidance Statement is issued on 31 October 2007 by the AUASB and replaces AGS 1064 *Audit Implications of Prudential Reporting Requirements for General Insurers* (issued March 2003) and the Addendum to AGS 1064 *Audit Implications of Prudential Reporting Requirements for General Insurers* (issued October 2006).

This Guidance Statement is effective from the date of issue, with the exception of amended requirements of the Act relating to the appointment and removal of the auditor of an insurer (refer paragraphs 27 and 29) and the auditor's non-routine reporting requirements under the Act (refer paragraphs 67 and 112), which take effect on 1 January 2008.

Introduction

4 The primary objective of general insurance Prudential Requirements (refer paragraph 16) is the protection of the interests of policyholders and prospective policyholders. This Guidance Statement acknowledges that the auditor of an insurer has an important role to play in the prudential supervision process.

5 Reporting requirements imposed on the auditor of an insurer by APRA are in addition to the audit and review of financial reports required under the *Corporations Act 2001.* Section 49 of the Act, in conjunction with APRA Prudential Standard GPS 310 *Audit and Actuarial Reporting and Valuation* (GPS 310), extend the responsibilities of the auditor as follows:

(a) an audit (reasonable assurance) of the insurer's yearly statutory accounts[2];

(b) a review (limited assurance), on an annual basis, of the insurer's systems, procedures and controls designed to address compliance with all applicable Prudential Requirements and to enable the insurer to report reliable financial and statistical information to APRA;

(c) a review (limited assurance), on an annual basis, of the insurer's compliance, in all significant respects, with its Risk Management Strategy (RMS) and Reinsurance Management Strategy (REMS);

(d) a special purpose engagement (which may be an audit, review or agreed-upon procedures), where requested by APRA in writing, of specific matters relating to the insurer's operations, risk management or financial affairs; and

(e) non-routine reporting under sections 49, 49A and 49B of the Act, where APRA requests specific information, or where the auditor possesses reportable information specified in that Act or where the auditor considers that the provision of information would assist APRA in performing its functions under the Act.

6 This Guidance Statement has been developed to assist the auditor of an insurer in reporting pursuant to the prudential reporting requirements specified by APRA and not in relation to reporting on the audit of the financial report of an insurer, for which mandatory requirements and explanatory guidance are provided in Auditing Standard ASA 700 *The Auditor's Report on a General Purpose Financial Report.*

7 This Guidance Statement is to be read in conjunction with Standard on Assurance Engagements ASAE 3000 *Assurance Engagements Other than Audits or Reviews of Historical Financial Information,* Auditing Standard ASA 800 *The Auditor's Report on*

1 Reference to insurer hereafter includes also a foreign insurer, unless specified otherwise.

2 Yearly statutory accounts, in relation to a body corporate, means the reporting documents that the body corporate is required to lodge with APRA in respect of a financial year, under section 13 of the *Financial Sector (Collection of Data) Act 2001.*

Special Purpose Audit Engagements, and relevant APRA Prudential Requirements and best practice guidance in this area.

8 It is not intended that this Guidance Statement replace the need for the auditor of an insurer to refer to APRA Prudential Requirements and guidance. This Guidance Statement is not be used as a checklist of issues to be considered by the auditor. Furthermore it is not intended that this Guidance Statement limits or replaces the auditor's professional judgement and initiative or limits the application of AUASB Standards on engagements detailed in paragraph 5. AUASB Standards contain the basic principles and essential procedures to be applied to audit and review engagements. Audit and review programs for each engagement are to be designed to meet the requirements of the particular situation, giving careful consideration to the size and type of general insurer and the adequacy of its internal control structure.

9 Auditing Standard ASA 315 *Understanding the Entity and its Environment and Assessing the Risks of Material Misstatement* requires that the auditor obtain an understanding of the entity and its environment, including its internal control, sufficient to identify and assess the risks of material misstatement, whether due to fraud or error, and to design and perform further audit procedures. Due to the extended scope imposed by APRA Prudential Requirements, the auditor gives further consideration as to whether the auditor has, or will be able to obtain, adequate knowledge and the required skills to undertake the engagement.

Trilateral Relationship

10 Periodic APRA liaison with the auditor will be conducted normally under trilateral arrangements involving APRA, the insurer and the insurer's auditor. Under GPS 310, any one of APRA, the insurer or the auditor may initiate meetings or discussions at any time, when considered necessary.

11 Under normal circumstances, APRA does not consult directly with the auditor on matters concerning an individual insurer. However, notwithstanding the trilateral relationship, in exceptional circumstances, such as that required under the statutory obligations imposed by sections 49, 49A and 49B of the Act, an insurer's auditor and APRA may engage with each other on a bilateral basis where either party considers this to be necessary (refer paragraphs 110-118). APRA may communicate with the auditor of an insurer on a bilateral basis to obtain or discuss information for whatever reason(s) it considers appropriate.

12 The continual development of the trilateral arrangements assists in achieving:

(a) greater clarity of expectations by APRA of the auditor;

(b) more meaningful contribution to the prudential supervisory process through special purpose engagements (refer paragraphs 97-109) undertaken by the auditor in accordance with instructions from the insurer to meet the requirements of APRA; and

(c) improved value-added feedback to insurer management in areas such as the RMS and the REMS and systems to implement insurer strategies.

APRA Prudential Requirements

13 The Act provides for the prudential supervision of insurers by APRA, the national prudential regulator created on 1 July 1998[3].

14 APRA formulates, promulgates and enforces prudential policy and practice applicable to insurers. It does this through General Insurance Prudential Standards (GPSs), which have the force of law. Non-enforceable best practice guidance in relation to prudential matters is contained in Prudential Practice Guides (GPGs).

15 Without limiting the role of the Prudential Standards in their entirety, the Prudential Standard of most relevance to the auditor of an insurer is GPS 310 *Audit and Actuarial Reporting and Valuation.*

16 Under GPS 310, the term 'Prudential Requirements'[4] includes requirements imposed by:

3 *Australian Prudential Regulation Authority Act 1998.*

4 These requirements may differ between locally incorporated and foreign insurers.

GS

(a) the Act;

(b) *Insurance Regulations 2002;*

(c) APRA Prudential Standards;

(d) *Financial Sector (Collection of Data) Act 2001* (the Collection of Data Act);

(e) APRA Reporting Standards (made under the Collection of Data Act);

(f) APRA conditions on the insurer's authorisation;

(g) Directions issued by APRA pursuant to the Act; and

(h) Any other requirements imposed by APRA in writing[5].

Access to the Prudential Standards, Practice Guides and legislation relevant to insurers is available through APRA's website (http://www.apra.gov.au).

Obligations of the Insurer

Lodgement of Auditor's Reports

17 Under section 49L of the Act, an insurer is required to submit to APRA all certificates and reports required to be prepared by its auditor in accordance with the Prudential Requirements and within the time specified in GPS 310.

Responsibility to Keep Auditor Informed

18 Under section 49J of the Act, an insurer is required to make arrangements necessary to enable its auditor to undertake the audit function as required by the Act and Prudential Standards made under the Act. Under GPS 310, these arrangements include ensuring that the auditor is kept fully informed of all APRA Prudential Requirements applicable to the insurer.

19 Under GPS 310, the insurer is furthermore required to ensure that the auditor has access to all relevant data, information, reports and staff of the insurer that the auditor reasonably believes is necessary to fulfil their responsibilities. This includes access to those charged with governance[6] of the insurer and to the Board Audit Committee.

20 In particular, the insurer is required to provide the auditor with access to the insurer's RMS and REMS documents, as discussed below, approved by those charged with governance and forwarded to APRA by the insurer, including information relating to the timing of their supply to APRA and any changes in the documents.

21 In relation to the insurer's responsibility to keep the auditor informed, the auditor requests management of the insurer to sign an appropriate management representation letter[7].

RMS and REMS Documents

22 Prudential Standard GPS 220 *Risk Management* (GPS 220) requires an insurer to have in place a Risk Management Framework (RMF) to manage the risks arising from its business. Prudential Standard GPS 230 *Reinsurance Management* (GPS 230) requires an insurer to have in place, as part of its overall RMF, a Reinsurance Management Framework (REMF) to manage the risks arising from its reinsurance arrangements. There must be a clear link between the insurer's REMF (including its REMS) and the insurer's RMF.

23 The RMS is a high level, strategic document intended to describe the key elements of an insurer's RMF, including the insurer's risk appetite, policies, procedures, managerial responsibilities and controls to identify, assess, monitor, report on and mitigate all material risks, financial and non-financial, having regard to such factors as the size, business mix and

---

5 In relation to the Prudential Review Report, the auditor will report on the Prudential Requirements specified in writing by APRA of which the auditor is aware. Also refer to paragraphs 18 and 78.

6 The term "those charged with governance" refers to either the board (for a locally incorporated Insurer) or the senior officer outside Australia to whom authority has been delegated in accordance with Prudential Standard GPS 510 *Governance* (for a foreign insurer).

7 The auditor has regard to the requirements and guidance provided in Auditing Standard ASA 580 *Management Representations* when requesting this letter.

complexity of the insurer's operations. Appendix 4 of this Guidance Statement includes a list of some of the key aspects to be included in an insurer's RMS.

24 The REMS is a high level, strategic document intended to describe the key elements of the insurer's REMF, including policies, procedures, management responsibilities and controls to manage the selection, implementation, monitoring, review, amendment and documentation of reinsurance arrangements of the insurer. Appendix 4 of this Guidance Statement includes a list of some of the key aspects to be included in an insurer's REMS.

Risk Management and Financial Information Declarations

25 Under GPS 220, an insurer is required to submit to APRA, at the same time as lodgement of the yearly statutory accounts, a declaration on risk management and on financial information. These Declarations include statements by the insurer on: the reliability of financial information lodged with APRA by the insurer; the adequacy of the insurer's systems in place to ensure compliance with APRA Prudential Requirements; the efficacy of the insurer's processes and systems surrounding the production of financial information; and compliance with the insurer's RMS and REMS. Refer to GPS 220 for information in relation to an insurer's Risk Management and Financial Information Declarations.

26 The auditor is not required to form an opinion on these Declarations other than in the context of the auditor's responsibility to express a conclusion on the insurer's compliance with the responsibilities and reporting requirements of GPS 310.

Role and Responsibilities of the Auditor

Those Who May Conduct the Audit and Review

27 Section 39 of the Act outlines the mechanism for the appointment of an auditor by an insurer. Under this section, an insurer must not appoint a person as the auditor unless:

(a) the insurer is reasonably satisfied that the person meets the eligibility criteria for such an appointment set out in the Prudential Standards; and

(b) no determination is in force under section 44 which disqualifies the person from holding such an appointment[8].

Prudential Standard GPS 520 *Fit and Proper* (GPS 520) sets out the eligibility criteria for appointment as auditor of an insurer.

28 Prudential Standard GPS 510 *Governance* (GPS 510) includes provisions relating to the independence of an auditor engaged to perform work of a prudential nature in relation to the Act, APRA Prudential Standards and APRA Reporting Standards.

29 Section 44 of the Act sets out the circumstances under which APRA may disqualify a person from holding an appointment as an auditor of an insurer.[9] APRA may, if satisfied that grounds exist under section 49R[10], direct an insurer to remove an auditor.

Role and Responsibilities of the Auditor

30 Under section 41 of the Act, an auditor appointed by an insurer must comply with the Prudential Standards in performing their duties and exercising their powers.

31 Broadly, section 49J of the Act, together with GPS 310, require the auditor to:

(a) conduct an audit of the yearly statutory accounts of the insurer and provide a certificate (auditor's report) to the insurer which contains the auditor's opinion in relation to the audit (refer paragraphs 39-44 and Appendix 1);

(b) undertake a review and prepare a report, on an annual basis, which contains the auditor's review conclusions providing limited assurance in relation to the matters specified in paragraph 45 (refer paragraphs 45-96 and Appendix 2);

GS

8 With effect from 1 January 2008, APRA will no longer be required to approve the appointment of a person as the auditor of an insurer.

9 Individuals disqualified in this manner may request that APRA review that decision. An appeal process is set out in Part VI of the Act.

10 With effect from 1 January 2008.

(c) undertake a special purpose engagement, when requested by APRA in writing, of specific matters relating to the insurer's operations, risk management or financial affairs, and to prepare a report in respect of that engagement (refer paragraphs 97-109); and

(d) perform such other work considered necessary to fulfil the auditor's responsibilities under the Prudential Standards.

32 Sections 49, 49A and 49B of the Act, together with GPS 310, specify certain circumstances where the auditor is required to report to APRA on a non-routine basis, where APRA requests specific information, or where an auditor possesses reportable information specified in the Act or where the auditor considers that the provision of information would assist APRA in performing its functions under the Act (refer paragraphs 110-118).

Agreeing the Terms of Engagement

33 The auditor and the insurer agree on the terms of the engagement. Such terms may be detailed in an engagement letter or other suitable form of written contract.

34 The requirement to audit the yearly statutory accounts of the insurer is in addition to the audit or review of financial reports required under the *Corporations Act 2001* and is to be treated by the auditor as a separate audit engagement. In addition to the requirements of ASA 800, the auditor has regard to ASA 210 *Terms of Audit Engagements* when agreeing on the terms of the engagement with the insurer.

35 The audit or review of financial reports required under the *Corporations Act 2001* and the audit of the yearly statutory accounts required under the Act are directed towards obtaining sufficient evidence to form an opinion or conclusion under the appropriate legislation. These audit and review procedures are not designed to enable the auditor to conclude on matters specified in paragraph 45 of this Guidance Statement. The requirement for an auditor to provide a review report under GPS 310 therefore constitutes a separate engagement with separate reporting requirements. The auditor has regard to ASAE 3000[11] when agreeing on the terms of this review engagement.

36 It is important that those charged with governance of the insurer are aware of the auditor's obligations referred to in GPS 310 and of the implications for confidentiality. It is important also that the engagement letter includes a reference to the responsibility of those charged with governance of the Insurer for establishing and maintaining effective internal control.

37 The engagement letter explains that any special purpose engagement of specific matters relating to the insurer's operations, risk management or financial affairs, will constitute a separate engagement(s) and that the details of such engagement(s) will be the subject of a separate engagement letter(s).

38 An example engagement letter to accommodate APRA reporting requirements as per GPS 310 is set out in Appendix 3 of this Guidance Statement.

Report on Audit of Yearly Statutory Accounts

Reporting Requirements

39 Section 49J of the Act, together with GPS 310, include a requirement for the auditor to audit the yearly statutory accounts of the insurer and to provide a certificate (auditor's report) to the insurer in relation to those accounts. GPS 310 requires the auditor's report to include the auditor's opinion on whether the yearly statutory accounts of the insurer present a true and fair view of the results of the insurer's operations for the year and financial position at year end, in accordance with:

(a) the provisions of the Act and APRA Prudential Standards, the Collection of Data Act and APRA Reporting Standards; and

(b) to the extent that they do not contain any requirements that conflict with the aforementioned, Australian Accounting Standards and other mandatory professional reporting requirements in Australia.

11 Reference to Auditing Standard ASA 210 *Terms of Audit Engagements*, may provide useful guidance when agreeing the terms of the review engagement.

In accordance with GPS 310, where the auditor is unable to provide an auditor's opinion as above, the opinion must be modified and include details of the relevant matters[12].

40 Under GPS 310, the auditor's report, addressed to those charged with governance of the insurer, must be prepared on an annual basis. Furthermore, it must be submitted to the insurer within such time as to enable the insurer to provide the report to APRA on or before the day that the insurer's yearly statutory accounts are required to be submitted to APRA in accordance with APRA Reporting Standards[13].

41 In preparing this auditor's report, APRA requires the auditor to have regard to relevant AUASB Standards and Guidance Statements, to the extent that these pronouncements are not inconsistent with the requirements of GPS 310.

42 ASA 800 establishes the mandatory requirements and provides explanatory guidance in relation to the audit of special purpose financial reports.

43 The auditor considers materiality in providing auditor's reports and in reporting exceptions. In considering materiality, the auditor exercises professional judgement, having regard to the requirements and guidance provided in ASA 320 *Materiality and Audit Adjustments*. Australian Accounting Standard AASB 1031 *Materiality* may provide further useful guidance. In the context of APRA's reporting requirements, the insurer's Minimum Capital Requirement (MCR) is an important consideration with respect to materiality. However, the auditor may need to consider whether an alternative base (such as profit, assets or revenue) is more appropriate.

Format of Reporting Requirements

44 An illustrative example of an auditor's report on the yearly statutory accounts of an insurer can be found in Appendix 1.

Annual Prudential Review Report

Reporting Requirements

45 In accordance with GPS 310, the auditor is required to perform a review and provide the insurer with a report specifying the auditor's review conclusions, namely whether:

(a) there exist systems, procedures and controls, that are kept up to date, which address the insurer's compliance with all applicable Prudential Requirements;

(b) the insurer's systems, procedures and controls relating to actuarial data integrity and financial reporting risks[14] are adequate and effective;

(c) the insurer has complied, in all significant respects, with its RMS and REMS;

(d) the insurer has systems, procedures and controls in place to ensure that reliable statistical and financial data are provided to APRA in the Quarterly Returns required by APRA Reporting Standards; and

(e) there are matters which have come to the auditor's attention which will, or are likely to, affect adversely the interests of policyholders of the insurer.

46 Where the auditor identifies instances of non-compliance with Prudential Requirements during the course of reviewing the insurer's systems, procedures and controls, GPS 310 requires the review report to include details of these matters[15]. Refer to *Part E* of the Prudential Review Report in Appendix 2.

---

12 Modifying an auditor's opinion is a matter for auditor judgement. However, GPS 310 lists the following examples of matters to be included: accounting records that have not been kept appropriately, transactions that appear irregular or that have not been recorded accurately or properly, requests for information and explanations that have not been met, or aspects of the accounts that do not represent a true and fair view of the transactions and financial position.

13 Generally, this will be within four months after reporting date.

14 The risks that incorrect source data will be used in completing returns to APRA in accordance with the *Collection of Data Act*.

15 Whether or not the insurer has reported the non-compliance to APRA.

GS

47 In accordance with GPS 310, the review report is to be on an annual basis and to cover the same period as the yearly statutory accounts, unless other arrangements between APRA and either the insurer and/or the auditor apply. The review report is to be issued on a timely basis so as to enable the insurer to submit the report to APRA on or before the day that the insurer's yearly statutory accounts are required to be submitted to APRA in accordance with APRA Reporting Standards[16].

48 The prudential review report is required to be addressed to those charged with governance of the insurer and must be based on a limited assurance engagement. The report is to indicate that it is limited to the use of the insurer and APRA. In preparing the report, APRA requires the auditor to have regard to AUASB Standards and Guidance Statements, to the extent that these pronouncements are not inconsistent with the requirements of GPS 310.

49 The auditor undertakes the review engagement in accordance with ASAE 3000[17].

50 The auditor considers materiality in providing reports as per GPS 310 and in the reporting of exceptions (refer paragraphs 62 to 67).

51 Where the auditor determines it necessary to issue a modified review conclusion because of, for example, a significant breach of the RMS and the REMS or because of the existence of a material weakness in systems, procedures and controls reviewed, the auditor has regard to the requirements of, and guidance provided in, AUASB Standards on Review Engagements (ASREs) and Standards on Assurance Engagements (ASAEs), as appropriate.

52 Where the auditor becomes aware of material weaknesses in internal controls, compliance errors or irregularities highlighted during the review, the auditor reports these instances to an appropriate level of management of the insurer on a timely basis[18].

53 Prior to issuing the auditor's review report, the auditor obtains a written representation from the insurer's management[19] which contains its assertions, for example, that the insurer has complied with its RMS and REMS during the period under review and that the auditor has been kept informed fully of all APRA's Prudential Requirements applicable to the insurer. However, representations by management cannot be a substitute for other audit evidence that the auditor could reasonably expect to be available.

Format of Reporting Requirements

54 An illustrative example of an annual Prudential Review Report, prepared by the auditor in compliance with APRA annual reporting requirements, is set out in Appendix 2. This format has been agreed to by APRA.

Matters to Consider in Planning and Conducting the Review

55 To assist in the effective and efficient operation of the reporting process, there is a need to avoid misunderstanding and to clarify what is required or can be achieved in providing the reports as per GPS 310. There is furthermore a need to avoid excessive or unwarranted work that is not cost beneficial to the regulatory process.

56 In a limited assurance engagement, the combination of the nature, timing, and extent of evidence-gathering procedures is at least sufficient for the assurance practitioner to obtain a meaningful level of assurance as the basis for a negative form of expression of the auditor's conclusion. To be meaningful, the level of assurance obtained is likely to enhance the intended users' confidence about the subject matter information to a degree that is clearly more than inconsequential.

57 For the purpose of expressing a conclusion in the review report, the auditor, through limited procedures, obtains sufficient appropriate evidence to support the conclusion. These limited

16 Refer to footnote 13.

17 AUASB Standards on Review Engagements (ASREs), Standards on Assurance Engagements (ASAEs) and this Guidance Statement may provide helpful information to assist the auditor in conducting the review.

18 Reference to Auditing Standard ASA 260 *Communication of Audit Matters with Those Charged With Governance* may provide useful guidance in this regard.

19 Matters for consideration and an illustrative example of a representation letter relevant to an audit engagement are contained in Auditing Standard ASA 580 *Management Representations*, which may be helpful in determining representations applicable to the review engagement.

procedures comprise primarily of enquiries of the insurer's staff and analytical procedures. The nature, timing and extent of procedures deemed necessary by the auditor to reduce assurance engagement risk to an acceptable level, are a matter for the auditor's professional judgement, taking into consideration the specific engagement circumstances.

58 The auditor is not required by GPS 310 to extend the scope of the review engagement in order to report to APRA matters which will, or are likely to, affect adversely the interests of policyholders of the insurer, or instances in which the insurer has not complied with all aspects of relevant Prudential Requirements, or in relation to the auditor's obligations as regards non-routine reporting requirements under sections 49A and 49B of the Act. Although there is no requirement for the auditor to perform any specific procedures to identify such matters required to be reported to APRA, during the course of the review engagement the auditor exercises professional judgement and considers whether additional procedures are necessary in relation to these matters.

Inherent Limitations of the Review

59 While reviews involve the application of audit related skills and techniques, usually they do not involve many of the procedures performed during an audit. In an audit, as the auditor's objective is to provide a high, but not absolute, level of assurance on the truth and fairness of financial information, the auditor uses more extensive audit procedures than in a review. Review procedures do not provide all the evidence required in an audit and, consequently, the level of assurance provided is less than that given in an audit.

60 There are inherent limitations in any internal control structure. Furthermore, fraud, error or non-compliance with laws and regulations may occur and not be detected. As the systems, procedures and controls to ensure compliance with APRA Prudential Requirements are part of the insurer's operations, it is possible that either the inherent limitations of the internal control structure, or weaknesses in it, impact on the effective operation of the insurer's specific control procedures.

61 Projections of any evaluation of internal control procedures to future periods are subject to the risk that control procedures may become inadequate because of changes in conditions after the review reports are signed, or that the degree of compliance may deteriorate.

Materiality

62 In accordance with ASAE 3000, the auditor considers materiality when:

(a) determining the nature, timing and extent of review procedures;

(b) considering the effect of identified weaknesses in systems, procedures and controls designed to address compliance with Prudential Requirements and to enable the insurer to report reliable financial and statistical information to APRA;

(c) evaluating the significance of identified breaches of the RMS and the REMS;

(d) reporting instances of non-compliance with Prudential Requirements identified during the course of the review of the insurer's systems, procedures and controls; and

(e) reporting matters that will, or are likely to, affect adversely the interests of the policyholders of the insurer.

63 Materiality is to be addressed in the context of the insurer's objectives relevant to the particular area of activity being examined (see paragraph 45) and whether the internal controls will reduce to an acceptable level the risks that threaten achievement of those objectives. These objectives are developed having regard to the protection of the interests of the policyholders and prospective policyholders of the insurer.

64 In addition to the guidance provided in ASAE 3000 and other relevant ASAEs, the auditor may find ASA 320 helpful when assessing materiality. However, it is not possible to give a definitive view on what may constitute, for example, a material breach of Prudential Requirements or a material control weakness. The auditor exercises professional judgement in considering materiality appropriate to the insurer's circumstances, having regard to the insurer's obligations, the purpose and terms of the specific engagement, together with the size, complexity and nature of the insurer's activities.

65 AASB 1031 may provide useful guidance to the auditor also. Matters likely to affect adversely the interests of policyholders are related generally to solvency issues and going concern assumptions. In the context of APRA's reporting requirements, the insurer's MCR is therefore an important consideration with respect to materiality. However, the auditor needs to consider whether alternative bases such as profit, assets or revenue may be more appropriate.

66 For the purpose of paragraphs 82-89, the significance of a matter is to be judged by the auditor in the context in which it is being considered, taking into account both quantitative and qualitative factors. This may, for example, include consideration of the significance in terms of the potential impact of the non-compliance with the RMS and the REMS rather than the actual impact. Where the auditor considers that non-compliance potentially could be significant to the insurer as a whole and/or to policyholder interests, or where the matter may be considered as important by APRA in performing its functions under the Act, then that is a matter to be reported to APRA.

67 Reference to section 49A(7)[20] of the Act, which defines the term 'significant' in the context of matters to be notified to APRA by the auditor (as part of the auditor's non-routine reporting requirements – refer paragraph 112), provides helpful guidance when considering the significance of matters in relation to the insurer's RMS and REMS.

Internal Audit

68 GPS 510 requires an insurer[21] to have in place an independent and adequately resourced internal audit function[22]. GPS 510 and APRA Prudential Practice Guide GPG 200 *Risk Management,* set out the requirements and provide guidance to insurers in relation to internal audit.

69 GPS 220 requires an insurer's RMF to be reviewed by operationally independent, appropriately trained and competent staff. Commonly, this evaluation of the adequacy and effectiveness of the RMF, which includes a review of the insurer's risk management function (or role), RMS and internal control system, will be undertaken by the internal audit function.

70 Auditing Standard ASA 610 *Considering the Work of Internal Audit* sets out the requirements and provides guidance to the auditor in considering the activities of the internal audit function and evaluating the effect, if any, on audit procedures.

Existence of Controls Addressing Compliance with Prudential Requirements

71 The auditor is required to express a conclusion as to whether anything has come to the auditor's attention that causes the auditor to believe that the insurer does not have systems, procedures and controls in place, that are kept up-to-date, to address the insurer's compliance with all applicable Prudential Requirements (refer *Part A* of the Prudential Review Report as per Appendix 2). Items included under 'Prudential Requirements' are listed in paragraph 16 of this Guidance Statement.

72 The auditor reviews whether the high level controls over systems and procedures pertinent to the Prudential Requirements, as documented in the RMS and the REMS, exist and whether the insurer has in place a periodic review process to ensure that relevant systems, procedures and controls remain up-to-date at all times. Existence is addressed normally when evaluating the design of controls during the planning phase of the review.

73 As part of the review, the auditor obtains an understanding of the insurer's compliance framework, which may include the following key elements:

- Procedures for identifying and updating compliance obligations.
- Staff training and awareness programs.

20 Section 49A(7) of the Act is effective from 1 January 2008.

21 This will include a foreign insurer in relation to its Australian business.

22 Under GPS 510, APRA may approve alternative arrangements where APRA is satisfied that they will achieve the same objectives.

- Procedures for assessing the impact of compliance obligations on the insurer's key business activities.
- Controls embedded within key business processes to ensure compliance with obligations.
- Processes to identify and monitor the implementation of further mitigating actions required to ensure that compliance obligations are met.
- A monitoring plan to test key compliance controls on a periodic basis and to report exceptions.
- Procedures for identifying, assessing and reporting compliance incidents and breaches.
- Periodic sign off by management as to compliance with obligations.
- A compliance governance structure that establishes responsibility for the oversight of compliance control activities with those charged with governance, typically a Board Audit, Risk Management or Compliance Committee.

74 Insurers have different systems and procedures in place to monitor compliance with specific Prudential Standards. Projections and estimates are likely to be part of the monitoring process, as the preparation of a full financial report is unlikely to be practical on a day-by-day or week-by-week basis. Varying degrees of precision may exist therefore in applying the monitoring process. Notwithstanding these differences, such systems seek to ensure that insurers comply with all Prudential Standards on a continuous basis.

75 As part of the auditor's review of whether systems, procedures and controls exist to address compliance with the relevant statutory and regulatory requirements and conditions on the insurer's authority to carry on insurance business, or other conditions imposed by APRA in relation to the insurer's operations, including bilateral APRA-insurer requirements and conditions, the auditor makes enquiries of insurer management as to (but not limited to):

- The nature of authorisation to carry on general insurance business under section 12 of the Act.
- Conditions or change in conditions imposed by APRA on the section 12 authorisation.
- Exemption granted by APRA to the insurer in relation to specific sections of the Act.
- Directions by APRA to the insurer under section 36 of the Act in relation to compliance with a Prudential Standard where there has been a breach of the Standard or is likely to be a breach.
- Directions issued by APRA to the insurer under section 62 of the Act in the context of an investigation.
- Formal correspondence issued to an insurer in relation to an APRA prudential visit/ review.

76 An auditor's review of an insurer's compliance with relevant statutory or regulatory requirements includes a review of compliance with the following sections of the Act:

- Authorisation under section 12 of the Act[23].
- Conditions imposed under section 13 of the Act.
- Directions issued by APRA pursuant to sections 7, 36, 49M, 49Q, 51, and 62 of the Act.
- Other specified matter(s).

77 Conditions on the insurer's authority to carry on insurance business may vary from one insurer to another and the auditor makes enquiries with respect to conditions imposed on the insurer by APRA.

78 In relation to Prudential Requirements specified in writing by APRA, the auditor of an insurer limits the review to the Prudential Requirements specified in writing by APRA of which the auditor is aware.

79 While the auditor is not expected to review the design or operating effectiveness of control procedures, during the course of the review, the auditor may become aware of material

23 Or in the case of an authorised non-operating holding company (NOHC), section 18 of the Act.

control weaknesses in this regard which are reported to an appropriate level of management of the insurer.

Adequacy and Effectiveness of Controls Relating to Actuarial Data Integrity and Financial Reporting Risks

80 The auditor is required to express a conclusion as to whether anything has come to the auditor's attention that causes the auditor to believe that the insurer's systems, procedures and controls relating to actuarial data integrity and financial reporting risks[24] are not adequate and effective to address the risk of material error in the APRA returns. Refer *Part B* of the Prudential Review Report as per Appendix 2.

81 The auditor reviews whether systems, procedures and controls in place are adequate and operating effectively to ensure that source data used for actuarial valuations and completion of returns to APRA in accordance with the requirements of the Collection of Data Act, are accurate and complete, consistent with the accounting records of the insurer, and a true representation of the transactions for the year and the financial position of the insurer. The auditor performs review procedures covering the period to obtain evidence regarding the continuity of systems, procedures and controls in place for the period under review.

Compliance with RMS and REMS

82 The auditor is required to express a conclusion as to whether anything has come to the auditor's attention that causes the auditor to believe that the insurer has not complied, in all significant respects (refer paragraphs 66-67), with its RMS and REMS[25]. Refer *Part C* of the Prudential Review Report as per Appendix 2.

83 The objective of the auditor's review of the insurer's compliance with its RMS and REMS is whether the insurer has complied substantially with key systems, policies, procedures, structures and controls documented in the RMS and the REMS for the period under review. There is no expectation that the auditor expresses assurance on the adequacy of the RMS and the REMS.

84 The auditor's review of compliance with the RMS and the REMS may include the following procedures:

- Obtaining an understanding of the insurer's RMF and the process to identify material risks.
- Reviewing the relevant RMS and the REMS to confirm that they are up-to-date and approved by the insurer.
- Reviewing the processes (including monitoring and reporting procedures) the insurer has in place to ensure ongoing compliance with the RMS and the REMS. The auditor may find reference to paragraph 73 useful in this regard. It identifies some of the key elements that may form part of an insurer's compliance framework.
- Reviewing the evidence supporting the insurer's attestation in the APRA Annual Return in relation to compliance with the RMS and the REMS.

85 As part of the auditor's review, the auditor may consider the measures in place which relate to the insurer's monitoring of, and reporting on, specific matters incorporated into the RMS and the REMS. Such a review may include the following matters:

- Whether breaches of the RMS and the REMS have been detected and reported by the monitoring systems. When breaches have been detected, whether such breaches are significant either in themselves or, when they are of a recurring nature and have not been rectified, whether their cumulative effect renders them to be a significant non-compliance.
- Identifying systems which the insurer uses to ensure that business units and staff comply with the measures in the RMS and the REMS on a day-to-day basis.

24 That is, the risks that incorrect source data will be used in completing returns to APRA in accordance with the requirements of the *Collection of Data Act*.

25 Refer to paragraphs 22-24 and Appendix 4 for a description of, and Prudential Requirements in relation to, the RMS and REMS documents.

86 As part of the review of compliance with the RMS and the REMS the auditor may seek the following types of information and documentation:

- Copies of the RMS and the REMS that applied during the period covered by the review.
- Details of changes to the RMS and the REMS and related policies and procedures and the reasons for the revisions.
- Documentation that identifies and describes the policies, procedures and structures that are in place to manage identified risks and representations that such policies, procedures and structures have been complied with.
- Minutes of the meetings of those charged with governance and sub-committees responsible for monitoring compliance with aspects of the RMS and the REMS.
- Internal and external incident and breach reports, breach and complaints registers and follow up action taken to the extent that recorded items may indicate a failure to comply with the RMS and the REMS.
- Internal audit reports.
- Certifications made by the insurer and relevant supporting documentation to substantiate compliance with the RMS and the REMS during the reporting period.
- Other supporting evidence to confirm that the controls identified in the RMS and the REMS have been in place during the reporting period.

The above is not meant to represent an exhaustive list and there may be other evidence that is relevant to the specific circumstances of each insurer.

87 There are practical limitations in requiring the auditor to express a conclusion as to the insurer's compliance at all times with the RMS and the REMS during the review period. However, the auditor performs review procedures to the extent that the auditor considers to be appropriate in order to obtain sufficient appropriate evidence as to the insurer's compliance with the written descriptions within the RMS and the REMS throughout the period under review.

88 While the auditor is not expected to review the adequacy of the RMS and the REMS, during the course of the review the auditor may become aware of significant deficiencies in the RMS and the REMS which are reported to an appropriate level of the insurer's management.

89 The auditor lists any key strategies included in the RMS and the REMS provided to APRA by the insurer, but not reviewed by the auditor as a consequence of a circumstance that makes the review impractical (for example, any period for which the strategy has not been in place).

Controls in place to ensure Reliability of Statistical and Financial Data

90 The auditor of an insurer is required to express a conclusion as to whether anything has come to the auditor's attention that causes the auditor to believe that the insurer does not have systems, procedures and controls in place to ensure that reliable statistical and financial data are provided by the insurer in its Quarterly Returns to APRA, as required by APRA Reporting Standards. Refer *Part D* of the Prudential Review Report as per Appendix 2.

91 Interpretation of the word 'reliable' in the context of paragraph 90 requires mutual understanding in that it has practical limitations in the present circumstances. For many insurers it is at reporting period-end only that the insurer's accounts, including all the appropriate adjustments for accruals, prepayments, provisioning and valuations, are prepared. Some insurers report their results half-yearly also, and therefore would incorporate the necessary adjustments, but generally an audit is not carried out on these balances unless the insurer requires an audit rather than a review of the half-year financial report.

92 APRA expects review procedures to include limited tests of control in relation to the compilation of the required statistical and financial information included in the APRA Quarterly Returns, to the extent the auditor considers appropriate. This involves, at a minimum, test checking from the Quarterly Returns to the insurer's general ledger or appropriate sub-ledger or sub-system but does not extend to auditing the financial or statistical information presented in the Quarterly Returns.

GS

Policyholders' Interests

93 The auditor is required to express a conclusion as to whether anything has come to the auditor's attention that causes the auditor to believe that there are matters which, in the auditor's opinion, will, or are likely to, affect adversely the interests of the policyholders[26] of the insurer. Matters likely to affect adversely the interests of the policyholders are related generally to solvency issues and going concern assumptions, for example, the insurer's compliance with MCR as per Prudential Standard GPS 110. Refer *Part E* of the Prudential Review Report as per Appendix 2.

94 The auditor will report to APRA on the basis of information obtained during the course of the auditor's financial report audit under the *Corporations Act 2001*, the audit of the yearly statutory accounts prepared in accordance with the Act, additional review procedures undertaken for APRA reporting purposes, and current knowledge of the insurer's affairs at the time of issuing the report.

95 The auditor of a foreign insurer is unlikely to have complete knowledge of the overseas operations of the parent or related entities of the foreign insurer. The auditor may not have had responsibility for the financial report audit of the foreign insurer. As a result, the auditor is limited in the level of assurance that can be provided with respect to foreign insurer policyholders' interests.

96 Where a situation described at paragraph 95 exists, the auditor of a foreign insurer is not expected to expand the scope of the review engagement in order to meet the reporting requirements of GPS 310, or to be aware of all material issues or events that are outside the Australian operations of the foreign insurer. Rather, in meeting APRA's reporting requirements, the auditor reports the scope of any financial report audit work performed with respect to the foreign insurer and, where no financial report audit has been conducted, reports only on matters that come to the auditor's attention during the course of the auditor's work in relation to APRA's additional reporting requirements.

Special Purpose Engagements

Reporting Requirements

97 In addition to APRA's annual prudential reporting requirements, the auditor may be requested by the insurer, under GPS 310, to undertake a special purpose engagement in relation to matters specified by APRA in writing, relating to the insurer's operations, risk management or financial affairs, and to prepare a report in respect of that engagement[27].

98 APRA requires such special purpose engagements to be completed in accordance with relevant AUASB Standards and Guidance Statements, to the extent that these pronouncements are not inconsistent with the requirements of GPS 310.

99 Under GPS 310, the auditor's special purpose engagement report is required to be submitted to APRA and the insurer simultaneously, within 3 months of the engagement being commissioned, unless APRA grants an extension of time in writing.

100 APRA may meet with the insurer and its auditor periodically to discuss the auditor's report and to agree on the area(s) to be examined. Timing of these trilateral meetings is negotiated with the insurer and the auditor at the initiative of APRA. The area(s) to be examined may vary among insurers.

101 APRA has indicated that the auditor may be requested to perform any of the following types of engagement:

(a) audit (reasonable assurance);

(b) review (limited assurance); and

(c) agreed-upon procedures (no assurance).

26 Reference to policyholders relates to a class of policyholders rather than to individual policyholders.

27 Furthermore, in accordance with Prudential Standard GPS 231 *Outsourcing*, APRA may request the auditor of the insurer to provide an assessment of the risk management processes in place with respect to an arrangement to outsource a material business activity.

102 It must be appreciated that the auditor of an insurer does not evaluate all aspects of the internal control structure and systems of controls when performing an audit or review of financial reports required under the *Corporations Act 2001* and is therefore not in a position to express an opinion on the adequacy of the systems of accounting and internal control taken as a whole.

103 The APRA requirement for an auditor to undertake a special purpose engagement in a selected area of the insurer's operations, constitutes a separate engagement and reporting. The auditor undertakes the engagement in accordance with ASAE 3000 and having due regard to relevant Auditing Standards (ASAs), ASREs, ASAEs and Standards on Related Services (ASRSs).

104 Due to the nature of audit testing and review procedures, and other inherent limitations of audits and reviews, together with the inherent limitations of all control systems, there is a possibility that a properly planned and executed audit or review will not detect all deficiencies in relation to the insurer's operations, risk management or financial affairs.

105 The extent of reporting matters that could be improved depends on the auditor's judgement. Materiality is to be addressed in the context of the insurer's objectives relevant to the particular area of activity being examined and whether the internal controls will reduce to an acceptable level the risks that threaten achievement of those objectives. Minor omissions, weaknesses and failures are not required to be reported upon. Matters that are commented on are those which, in the view of the auditor, indicate individually or collectively that the objectives of the system may not be achieved. Materiality is addressed in paragraphs 62-67.

106 The report is to be restricted to the parties that have agreed to the terms of the special purpose engagement, namely those charged with governance and management of the insurer, and APRA.

Format of Reporting Requirements

107 The format of the special purpose engagement report will vary depending on the type of engagement; that is, an audit (reasonable assurance), a review (limited assurance) or agreed-upon procedures (no assurance), as well as the topic and the findings. The auditor has regard to the requirements, guidance and illustrative examples of reports provided in ASAs, ASREs, ASAEs and ASRSs, as applicable, when preparing the special purpose engagement report.

Terms of Engagement

108 Following the determination by APRA of the specific area to be examined, the auditor, APRA and the insurer agree on the terms of the engagement. It is in the interests of both the insurer and the auditor that an engagement letter is compiled to help avoid misunderstandings with respect to the engagement. When agreeing on the terms of the engagement, the auditor has regard to the requirements of ASAs, ASREs, ASAEs and ASRSs, as applicable.

109 To ensure that there is a clear understanding regarding the terms of the engagement, the following are examples of matters to be agreed:

- APRA is to identify the scope of the insurer's operations, risk management or financial affairs to be the subject of the engagement.
- APRA is to identify clearly whether the engagement is an audit, review or agreed-upon procedures engagement.
- The auditor, APRA and the insurer are to agree on the objectives of the engagement, key features and criteria of the area to be examined, and the period to be covered by the engagement.
- For an agreed-upon procedures engagement, the auditor, APRA and the insurer are to agree on the nature and extent of procedures to be performed.

Non-routine Reporting Requirements

110 It is important that the auditor of an insurer, an authorised non-operating holding company (NOHC), or a subsidiary of an insurer or authorised NOHC, understands the additional responsibilities in relation to non-routine reporting to APRA, imposed under sections 49, 49A and 49B of the Act.

111 Under section 49 of the Act, APRA may give written notice to a person who is, or who has been, the auditor of either an insurer, an authorised NOHC, or a subsidiary of an insurer or authorised NOHC, to provide information about such entities to APRA if APRA considers that the provision of such information will assist APRA in performing its functions under the Act.[28]

112 Section 49A of the Act identifies matters of which APRA needs to be notified of:

(a) immediately (for example, where an existing or proposed state of affairs may prejudice materially the interests of policyholders); and

(b) as soon as is practicable[29] (for example, where an insurer's failure to comply with the Prudential Standards or a condition of its authorisation is or will be significant).[30]

These matters are to be reported to APRA in writing. When an auditor contravenes this section of the Act, the auditor will be guilty of an offence under the Act.

113 Section 49B of the Act provides that a person who is, or who has been, the auditor of either an insurer, an authorised NOHC or a subsidiary of an insurer or authorised NOHC, may provide information about such entities to APRA if the person considers that the provision of that information to APRA will assist APRA in performing its functions under the Act or the Collection of Data Act.

114 GPS 310 requires the auditor, in assessing whether the interests of policyholders may be prejudiced materially[31], to consider not only a single activity or a single deficiency in isolation, as policyholders' interests may be prejudiced materially by a number of activities or deficiencies which, although not individually material, do amount to a material threat when considered in totality.

115 In circumstances where the auditor has reasonable grounds to believe that the interests of policyholders are, or are likely to be compromised, the auditor may need to consider the whistle blowing provisions in both the Act and GPS 520.

116 GPS 310 requires matters reported to APRA by an auditor also to be reported to the insurer to which the matter relates, unless the auditor considers that by doing so the interests of policyholders would be jeopardised, or where a situation of mistrust between an auditor and those charged with governance or senior management of the insurer exists.

117 In relation to reporting under sections 49A and 49B of the Act, there is no requirement for the auditor of an insurer to carry out additional work to satisfy the auditor with respect to the above matters. Thus, subject to the reporting requirements as per GPS 310, the auditor is not required to extend the scope of the work to ascertain that the insurer is complying with all aspects of all applicable Prudential Requirements for insurers. If the auditor becomes aware of any of the matters identified under sections 49A and 49B of the Act, the auditor brings the matter(s) to the attention of an appropriate level of management and those charged with governance of the insurer. If the response provided by the insurer is unsatisfactory, the auditor is obliged to report the matter(s) to APRA in a timely manner, having regard to materiality as described in paragraphs 62-67.

118 Section 49C of the Act and GPS 310 include provisions to protect an auditor providing information to APRA, in good faith and without negligence, from any action, claim or demand by, or any liability to, any other person in respect of the information.

---

28 To ensure that the auditor is able to comply with any such request from APRA, GPS 310 requires that all working papers and other documentation of the auditor in relation to the insurer be maintained for a period of seven years after the date of the report or certificate to which the working papers or documentation relate, as required under the *Corporations Act 2001*.

29 No longer than 10 business days.

30 Section 49A of the Act has been amended with effect from 1 January 2008.

31 Prejudice materially is taken to be the same as affect adversely. In cases where there is doubt, the auditor may need to obtain a legal opinion. Circumstances that may affect adversely the interests of policyholders are discussed in paragraphs 93-96.

Other Reporting Responsibilities

119 GPS 510 requires all locally incorporated insurers and authorised NOHCs to have a Board Audit Committee. GPS 510 sets out the specific requirements with respect to the size, composition, responsibilities and powers of the Board Audit Committee.

120 Although the type of engagement to which this Guidance Statement relates is not that in relation to the audit of a financial report under the *Corporations Act 2001,* guidance on matters of governance interest that the auditor considers communicating to the Audit Committee can be found in ASA 260 *Communication of Audit Matters with Those Charged With Governance*[32].

Conformity with International Pronouncements

121 There is no equivalent International Standard on Auditing or International Auditing Practice Statement to this Guidance Statement.

Appendix 1

Example of an Unmodified Auditor's Report on the Yearly Statutory Accounts

INDEPENDENT AUDITOR'S REPORT

To [Title of those charged with governance[33]] of [Insurer]

REPORT ON THE YEARLY STATUTORY ACCOUNTS

We have audited the accompanying yearly statutory accounts, being a special purpose financial report, of [Insurer] for the financial year ended [date]. The yearly statutory accounts comprise [specify form numbers] with the authentication code of [……].

The Responsibility of [Those Charged with Governance] for the Yearly Statutory Accounts

[Title of those charged with governance] of [Insurer] are responsible for the preparation and fair presentation of the yearly statutory accounts and the information they contain, in accordance with the requirements of the *Insurance Act 1973* and Australian Prudential Regulation Authority (APRA) Prudential Standards, the *Financial Sector (Collection of Data) Act 2001* and APRA Reporting Standards, and, to the extent that they do not contain any requirements to the contrary, Australian Accounting Standards (including Australian Accounting Interpretations). This responsibility includes establishing and maintaining internal control relevant to the preparation and fair presentation of the yearly statutory accounts that are free from material misstatement, whether due to fraud or error; selecting and applying appropriate accounting policies; and making accounting estimates that are reasonable in the circumstances.

Auditor's Responsibility

Our responsibility is to express an opinion on the yearly statutory accounts based on our audit. We conducted our audit in accordance with Australian Auditing Standards. These Auditing Standards require that we comply with relevant ethical requirements relating to audit engagements and plan and perform the audit to obtain reasonable assurance whether, in all material respects, the yearly statutory accounts present a true and fair view of the results of [Insurer]'s operations for the year and financial position at reporting end, in accordance with the provisions of the *Insurance Act 1973* and APRA Prudential Standards, the *Financial Sector (Collection of Data) Act 2001* and APRA Reporting Standards, and, to the extent that they do not contain any requirements to the contrary, Australian Accounting Standards (including Australian Accounting Interpretations). The *Insurance Act 1973* and Prudential Standards do not require the application of all Australian Accounting Standards.

GS

32 In the absence of a Board Audit Committee (for a foreign insurer), the auditor will normally communicate with the senior officer outside Australia.

33 Amend this term to reflect the appropriate title for those charged with governance, for example, Board of Directors for a locally incorporated insurer or senior officer outside Australia for a foreign insurer. Insert appropriate title, when prompted, throughout the report.

Our audit involves performing procedures to obtain audit evidence about the amounts and disclosures in the yearly statutory accounts. The procedures selected depend on our judgement, including assessment of the risks of material misstatement of the yearly statutory accounts, whether due to fraud or error. In making those risk assessments, we consider internal control relevant to [Insurer]'s preparation and fair presentation of the yearly statutory accounts in order to design audit procedures that are appropriate in the circumstances, but not for the purpose of expressing an opinion on the effectiveness of [Insurer]'s internal control. An audit includes evaluating the appropriateness of accounting policies used and the reasonableness of accounting estimates made by [Title of those charged with governance], as well as evaluating the overall presentation of the financial report.

The yearly statutory accounts have been prepared for the purpose of fulfilling the reporting requirements of [Insurer] under the *Insurance Act 1973*, Section 13 of the *Financial Sector (Collection of Data) Act 2001* and the Prudential Standards. We disclaim any assumption of responsibility for any reliance on this report or on the yearly statutory accounts to which it relates to any party other than the [Insurer] and APRA, or for any purpose other than that for which it was prepared.

We believe that the audit evidence we have obtained is sufficient and appropriate to provide a basis for our audit opinion.

Independence

In conducting our audit we have, to the best of our knowledge and belief, complied with the independence requirements specified by APRA in Prudential Standard GPS 510 *Governance.*

Auditor's Opinion[34]

In our opinion, the yearly statutory accounts of [Insurer], in respect of the year ended [date], present a true and fair view of the results of [Insurer]'s operations for the year and financial position at year end, in accordance with:

(a) the provisions of the *Insurance Act 1973* and APRA Prudential Standards, the *Financial Sector (Collection of Data) Act 2001* and APRA Reporting Standards; and

(b) to the extent that they do not contain any requirements that conflict with the aforementioned, Australian Accounting Standards (including the Australian Accounting Interpretations).

[Auditor's signature]

[Date of the Auditor's report]

[Auditor's address]

34 Where the auditor determines it necessary to issue a modified auditor's report on the yearly statutory accounts of an insurer, the principles contained in ASA 701 *Modifications to the Auditor's Report* may provide useful guidance.

Appendix 2

Example of an Unmodified Prudential Review Report

Prepared by the Auditor of a General Insurer Pursuant to the Reporting Requirements Specified in Australian Prudential Regulation Authority Prudential Standard GPS 310 *Audit and Actuarial Reporting and Valuation*

INDEPENDENT AUDITOR'S REVIEW REPORT

To [Title of Those Charged with Governance[35]] of [Insurer]

Prudential Review Report as required by Australian Prudential Regulation Authority – Prudential Standard GPS 310 *Audit and Actuarial Reporting and Valuation*

We have performed a review pursuant to the reporting requirements specified in Australian Prudential Regulation Authority (APRA) Prudential Standard GPS 310 *Audit and Actuarial Reporting and Valuation* (GPS 310), described in the *Scope* section, paragraphs *Part A* to *Part E*, of this report.

[Title of Those Charged with Governance]' Responsibility

The [Title of those charged with governance] of [Insurer] are responsible for establishing and maintaining systems to ensure compliance with all applicable APRA Prudential Requirements, which includes providing APRA with:

(a) a Risk Management Declaration, as set out in Attachment A to APRA Prudential Standard GPS 220 *Risk Management* (GPS 220); and

(b) a Financial Information Declaration (signed by the Chief Executive Officer and the Chief Financial Officer) as set out in Attachment B to APRA Prudential Standard GPS 220.

Auditor's Responsibility

Our responsibility is to perform a review as required by GPS 310, described in *Scope* paragraphs *Part A* to *Part E* of this report, and to express a conclusion based on our review.

We conducted our review in accordance with Standard on Assurance Engagements ASAE 3000 *Assurance Engagements Other than Audits or Reviews of Historical Financial Information,* in order to state whether, on the basis of the procedures described, anything has come to our attention that causes us to believe that [Insurer] has not complied, in all material respects, with its responsibilities and reporting requirements. ASAE 3000 requires us to comply with fundamental ethical requirements.

Our audit [and review] of the financial report(s) required under the *Corporations Act 2001* and our audit of the yearly statutory accounts required under the *Insurance Act 1973* are directed towards obtaining sufficient evidence to form an opinion [and conclusion] under the appropriate legislation. These procedures were not designed to enable us to conclude on other matters required by APRA's Prudential Standards. We have therefore performed additional procedures beyond those undertaken in order to meet our responsibilities in relation to our audit [and review] of the financial report(s) required under the *Corporations Act 2001*, and our audit of the yearly statutory accounts required under the *Insurance Act 1973.*

Our review consists primarily of making enquiries of [Insurer's] personnel and applying analytical and other review procedures. We have performed our review procedures having regard to relevant standards and guidance issued by the Auditing and Assurance Standards Board.

Inherent Limitations

A review is substantially less in scope than an audit conducted in accordance with Australian Auditing Standards and consequently does not enable us to obtain assurance that we would become aware of all significant matters that might be identified in an audit. Accordingly, we do not express an audit opinion.

---

35 Amend this term to reflect the appropriate title for those charged with governance, for example, Board of Directors for a locally incorporated insurer or senior officer outside Australia for a foreign insurer. Insert appropriate title, when prompted, throughout the report.

There are inherent limitations in any internal control structure, and fraud, error or non-compliance with laws and regulations may occur and not be detected. As the systems, procedures and controls to ensure compliance with APRA Prudential Requirements are part of the operations of [Insurer], it is possible that either the inherent limitations of the general internal control structure, or weaknesses in it, can impact on the effective operation of the specific control procedures of [Insurer].

Furthermore, projections of any evaluation of internal control procedures to future periods are subject to the risk that control procedures may become inadequate because of changes in conditions, or that the degree of compliance may deteriorate. Consequently, there are inherent limitations on the level of assurance that can be provided.

Accounting records and data relied on for prudential reporting and compliance are not continuously audited and do not necessarily reflect accounting adjustments necessary for end of reporting period financial report preparation, or events occurring after the end of the reporting period.

This report has been prepared solely for the [Title of those charged with governance] in order to meet the APRA reporting requirements of [Insurer]. This report is not to be used for any other purpose or distributed to any other party. We disclaim any assumption of responsibility for any reliance on this report to any party other than [Insurer] and APRA, or for any purpose other than that for which it was prepared.

The conclusions in this report expressed below are to be read in the context of the foregoing comments.

Scope

Part A – Existence of Controls Addressing Compliance with Prudential Requirements

During [insert month and year] we performed review procedures that we consider necessary in relation to [Insurer]'s systems, procedures and controls that address compliance with all applicable Prudential Requirements. Prudential Requirements include requirements imposed by the:

(a) *Insurance Act 1973;*

(b) *Insurance Regulations 2002;*

(c) APRA Prudential Standards;

(d) *Financial Sector (Collection of Data) Act 2001;*

(e) APRA Reporting Standards;

(f) APRA conditions on the Insurer's authorisation;

(g) Directions issued by APRA pursuant to the *Insurance Act 1973;* and

(h) Other requirements imposed by APRA in writing (if applicable).

We have performed these procedures to enable us to state, on the basis of our review as described, whether anything has come to our attention that causes us to believe that, at the date of our review, there did not exist systems, procedures and controls that address compliance, in all material respects, with applicable Prudential Requirements, specified above, and that these systems, procedures and controls were not kept up-to-date.

We have not tested whether these systems, procedures and controls operated effectively throughout the full period, and express no opinion on their operating effectiveness.

Part B – Adequacy and Effectiveness of Controls Relating to Actuarial Data Integrity and Financial Reporting Risks

We have performed review procedures that we consider necessary in relation to [Insurer]'s systems, procedures and controls relating to actuarial data integrity and financial reporting risks (the risks that incorrect source data will be used in completing the quarterly and annual returns provided to APRA in accordance with the requirements of the *Financial Sector (Collection of Data) Act 2001),* that address the risk of material error in the APRA returns.

We have performed these procedures to enable us to state, on the basis of our review as described, whether anything has come to our attention that causes us to believe that for the [insert period]

[Insurer] did not have systems, procedures and controls relating to actuarial data integrity and financial reporting risks, that are adequate and operating effectively to address the risk of material error in the APRA returns.

Part C – Compliance with RMS and REMS

We have performed review procedures that we consider necessary in relation to [Insurer]'s compliance, in all significant respects, with its Risk Management Strategy (RMS) and Reinsurance Management Strategy (REMS) for the [insert period].

We have performed these procedures to enable us to state, on the basis of our review as described, whether anything has come to our attention that causes us to believe that for the [insert period] [Insurer] did not comply, in all significant respects, with its RMS and REMS.

Part D – Controls in Place to ensure reliable Statistical and Financial Data

We have performed review procedures that we consider necessary in relation to [Insurer]'s systems, procedures and controls in place to ensure that reliable statistical and financial data are provided to APRA in the Quarterly APRA Returns, required by APRA Reporting Standards made under the *Financial Sector (Collection of Data) Act 2001,* for the [insert period].

We have performed the review of systems, procedures and controls in order to state whether, on the basis of the review procedures described, anything has come to our attention that causes us to believe that [Insurer] does not have in place systems, procedures and controls to ensure that, in all material respects, reliable statistical and financial data are provided to APRA in the Quarterly APRA Returns.

Our review procedures include test checking to the general ledger or appropriate sub ledger or sub system but do not extend to auditing the financial or statistical information presented in the Quarterly Returns.

Part E – Issues Identified in the Conduct of our Review Procedures

We have evaluated the results of our procedures conducted during (i) this review, (ii) our audit of the yearly statutory accounts prepared in accordance with the *Insurance Act 1973* and (iii) our audit [and review] performed under the *Corporations Act 2001,* in order to report to [Title of those charged with governance] of [Insurer] and APRA:

(a) matters which will, or are likely to, affect adversely the interests of policyholders of the Insurer; and

(b) instances in which the Insurer has not complied with all applicable Prudential Requirements (refer *Part A* of this report).

We have not performed any review procedures that were designed specifically to identify such circumstances or breaches and therefore provide no assurance that all such circumstances and breaches have been identified and reported.

[The overseas operations of a foreign insurer are excluded from the scope of this review.]

Independence

In conducting our review we have, to the best of our knowledge and belief, complied with the independence requirements specified by APRA in Prudential Standard GPS 510 *Governance.*

Conclusions[36]

Part A – Existence of Controls addressing Compliance with Prudential Requirements

Based on our review, which is not an audit, nothing has come to our attention that causes us to believe that, at the date of our review [insert date], [Insurer] did not have in place systems, procedures and controls to address compliance, in all material respects, with the specified Prudential Requirements, and that these systems, procedures and controls were not kept up-to-date.

36 Where the auditor determines it necessary to issue a modified review conclusion, the principles contained in ASAs, ASREs and ASAEs (as appropriate) may provide useful guidance.

GS

Part B – Adequacy and Effectiveness of Controls Relating to Actuarial Data Integrity and Financial Reporting Risks

Based on our review, which is not an audit, nothing has come to our attention that causes us to believe that, for the [insert period], [Insurer] did not have systems, procedures and controls relating to actuarial data integrity and financial reporting risks (the risks that incorrect source data will be used in completing the returns to APRA in accordance with the requirements of the *Financial Sector (Collection of Data Act) 2001)* that are adequate and effective to address the risk of material error in the APRA returns.

Part C – Compliance with RMS and REMS

Based on our review, which is not an audit, nothing has come to our attention that causes us to believe that, for the [insert period], [Insurer] did not comply, in all significant respects, with its RMS and REMS.

Part D – Controls in place to ensure Reliable Statistical and Financial Data

Based on our review, which is not an audit, nothing has come to our attention that causes us to believe that, for the [insert period], [Insurer] did not have in place systems, procedures and controls to ensure that, in all material respects, reliable statistical and financial data were provided to APRA in the Quarterly APRA Returns required by APRA Reporting Standards made under the *Financial Sector (Collection of Data) Act 2001.*

Part E – Issues Identified in the Conduct of our Review Procedures

Based on our review, which is not an audit, nothing has come to our attention that causes us to believe that during the [insert period]:

(a) there are matters which will, or are likely to, affect adversely the interests of policyholders of [Insurer]; and

(b) [Insurer] did not comply with all applicable Prudential Requirements.

Appendix 3

Example of an Engagement Letter

For Reporting Engagements Undertaken Pursuant To Australian Prudential Regulation Authority - Prudential Standard GPS 310 *Audit and Actuarial Reporting and Valuation*

The following example engagement letter is for use as a guide only, in conjunction with the considerations described in GS 004 *Audit Implications of Prudential Reporting Requirements for General Insurers,* and may need to be varied according to individual requirements and circumstances.

To [Title of Those Charged with Governance[37]] of [Insurer]

The *Insurance Act 1973*, Section 13 of the *Financial Sector (Collection of Data) Act 2001* and the Australian Prudential Regulation Authority (APRA) Prudential Standard GPS 310 *Audit and Actuarial Reporting and Valuation* (GPS 310) identify APRA's reporting requirements for general insurers and their auditors.

We set out below, in general terms, our understanding of the terms and objectives of this engagement. This engagement is a separate engagement from our audit [and half-year review] appointment(s) under the *Corporations Act 2001.*

37 Amend this term to reflect the appropriate title for those charged with governance, for example, Board of Directors for a locally incorporated insurer or senior officer outside Australia for a foreign insurer. Insert appropriate title, when prompted, throughout the letter.

Scope

APRA has requested you to obtain from us:

(a) an auditor's report on the yearly statutory accounts; and

(b) a review report, on an annual basis, which contains our review conclusions providing limited assurance in relation to the following matters insofar as they relate to [Insurer], namely whether:

  (i) there exist systems, procedures and controls, that are kept up-to-date, which address compliance with all applicable Prudential Requirements;

  (ii) systems, procedures and controls relating to actuarial data integrity and financial reporting risks (the risks that incorrect source data will be used in completing returns to APRA in accordance with the *Financial Sector (Collection of Data) Act 2001*) are adequate and effective;

  (iii) [Insurer] has complied, in all significant respects, with its Risk Management Strategy (RMS) and Reinsurance Management Strategy (REMS);

  (iv) [Insurer] has systems, procedures and controls in place to ensure that reliable statistical and financial data are provided to APRA in the Quarterly Returns required by APRA Reporting Standards made under the *Financial Sector (Collection of Data) Act 2001*; and

  (v) there are matters which have come to the auditor's attention which will, or are likely to, affect adversely the interests of policyholders of [Insurer].

The auditor's report and review report will cover the same period as the annual financial report required under the *Corporations Act 2001* and are to be issued within four months of the reporting date.

Responsibility of [Those charged with Governance]

The [Title of those charged with governance] of [Insurer] are responsible for:

(a) The preparation and fair presentation of the yearly statutory accounts and the information they contain, in accordance with the requirements of the *Insurance Act 1973* and APRA Prudential Standards, the *Financial Sector (Collection of Data) Act 2001* and APRA Reporting Standards and, to the extent that they do not contain any requirements to the contrary, Australian Accounting Standards (including Australian Accounting Interpretations). This responsibility includes establishing and maintaining internal control relevant to the preparation and fair presentation of the yearly statutory accounts that are free from material misstatement, whether due to fraud or error; selecting and applying appropriate accounting policies; and making accounting estimates that are reasonable in the circumstances.

(b) Establishing and maintaining systems to ensure compliance with all applicable APRA Prudential Requirements, which includes providing APRA with:

  (i) a Risk Management Declaration, as set out in Attachment A to APRA Prudential Standard GPS 220 *Risk Management* (GPS 220); and

  (ii) a Financial Information Declaration (signed by the Chief Executive Officer and the Chief Financial Officer) as set out in Attachment B to APRA Prudential Standard GPS 220.

Auditor's Responsibilities

As the auditor of [Insurer], we carry out sufficient procedures to enable us to form an opinion on the state of [Insurer]'s affairs and its results and to report thereon to the members of [Insurer] in accordance with the requirements of the *Corporations Act 2001* [or other appropriate local or overseas requirements]. Although our audit [and review] under the *Corporations Act 2001* will include such review of [Insurer]'s systems of accounting and internal control and performing such tests and inquiries as we consider necessary, these audit [and review] procedures are not designed to form an opinion or conclude on the systems of accounting and internal control taken as a whole.

Our audit [and review] procedures under the *Corporations Act 2001* are therefore not designed to enable us to express an opinion on the adequacy of systems and procedures operating within [Insurer] to generate [Insurer]'s yearly statutory accounts pursuant to APRA reporting requirements applicable to the Insurer; nor are they designed to enable us to conclude on the existence or adequacy and operating effectiveness of systems, procedures and controls operating within [Insurer] to generate reliable financial and statistical information and to ensure compliance with all Prudential Requirements; nor are our procedures designed to enable us to conclude as to [Insurer]'s compliance with its RMS and its REMS.

> [The auditor of a foreign insurer amends the above paragraphs to reflect the applicable circumstances. The overseas operations of a foreign insurer are excluded from the scope of this review.]

Therefore, in order to satisfy the requirements of APRA, we shall have to carry out additional procedures over and above those which are performed in our capacity as the auditor under the *Corporations Act 2001* [other legislation]. These additional procedures will include a review of [Insurer]'s management systems and performing such tests and enquiries as we consider necessary in the circumstances.

Despite our involvement in examining the [Insurer]'s systems of control, it must be appreciated that it is the responsibility of those charged with governance of [Insurer] to establish and maintain all of [Insurer]'s internal control systems (refer to *Responsibility of [Those charged with Governance]* above). All such systems have their limitations and, this being so, errors or irregularities may occur and which may not be detected. Our work is not to be relied upon for the purposes of discovering fraud, error, or non-compliance with laws and regulations, although we shall report to the appropriate level of management any fraud, error, or non-compliance that may be identified as a result of our review.

As part of our procedures, we shall request representations from management and, where appropriate, those charged with governance, concerning assertions made in connection with the engagement.

After the completion of our auditor's report and review report, it is our normal practice to report any matters of significance, together with suggestions for their rectification and any recommendations we may have on the systems, procedures and controls in general. However, as our examination will be limited to the audit and review in relation to matters set out in the Scope section above, you cannot assume that any matters reported to you indicate that there are no additional matters or matters that you should be aware of in meeting your responsibilities.

We recognise that there may be some overlap between our audit [and review] under the *Corporations Act 2001* and work that is necessary to fulfil APRA's requirements. In order to help ensure the most efficient use of resources, wherever possible, reliance will be placed on work that is carried out for statutory financial report audit [and review] purposes.

(a) Audit of Yearly Statutory Accounts

Our responsibility is to express an opinion on the yearly statutory accounts based on our audit. The yearly statutory accounts are prepared for the purpose of fulfilling the reporting requirements of [Insurer] under the *Insurance Act 1973,* APRA Prudential Standards, Section 13 of the *Financial Sector (Collection of Data) Act 2001* and APRA Reporting Standards. We shall conduct our audit in accordance with Australian Auditing Standards. These Auditing Standards require that we comply with relevant ethical requirements relating to audit engagements and plan and perform the audit to obtain reasonable assurance whether, in all material respects, the yearly statutory accounts present a true and fair view of the results of [Insurer]'s operations for the year and financial position at reporting date, in accordance with the provisions of the *Insurance Act 1973,* APRA Prudential Standards, the *Financial Sector (Collection of Data) Act 2001* and APRA Reporting Standards, and, to the extent that they do not contain any requirements to the contrary, Australian Accounting Standards (including Australian Accounting Interpretations). The *Insurance Act 1973* and APRA Prudential Standards do not require the application of all Australian Accounting Standards.

Our audit involves performing procedures to obtain audit evidence about the amounts and disclosures in the yearly statutory accounts. The procedures selected depend on our judgement, including the assessment of the risks of material misstatement of the yearly statutory accounts, whether due to fraud or error. In making those risk assessments, we consider internal control relevant to [Insurer]'s preparation and fair presentation of the yearly statutory accounts in order to design audit procedures that are appropriate in the circumstances, but not for the purpose of expressing an opinion on the effectiveness of [Insurer]'s internal control. An audit includes evaluating the appropriateness of accounting policies used and the reasonableness of accounting estimates made by [Title of those charged with governance], as well as evaluating the overall presentation of the financial report.

(b) Annual Prudential Review Report

Our responsibility is to perform a review as required by GPS 310, in relation to the matters set out under *paragraph (b)* of the *Scope* section of this letter, and to express a conclusion based on our review.

We shall conduct our review in accordance with Standard on Assurance Engagements ASAE 3000 *Assurance Engagements Other than Audits or Reviews of Historical Financial Information,* in order to state whether, on the basis of the procedures described, anything has come to our attention that causes us to believe that [Insurer] has not complied, in all material respects, with its responsibilities and reporting requirements. ASAE 3000 requires us to comply with fundamental ethical requirements.

Our review consists primarily of making enquiries of [Insurer]'s personnel and applying analytical and other review procedures. We shall perform our review procedures having regard to relevant standards and guidance issued by the Auditing and Assurance Standards Board.

A review is substantially less in scope than an audit conducted in accordance with Australian Auditing Standards and consequently will not enable us to obtain assurance that we would become aware of all significant matters that might be identified in an audit. According, we shall not express an audit opinion.

Independence

We confirm that, to the best of our knowledge and belief, we currently meet the independence requirements specified by APRA in Prudential Standard GPS 510 *Governance*.

Internal Audit (where applicable)

[Insurer]'s internal audit function is considered well placed to review and test properly documented systems, procedures and controls operating within [Insurer]. Consequently, it is our intention to liaise closely with the Internal Audit Function throughout the year.

Where work is carried out by Internal Audit as part of [Insurer]'s internal control procedures, we intend to review the work performed and carry out such reperformance tests and other procedures as we consider necessary. Where we are satisfied with the work carried out by Internal Audit, it is our intention to place reliance on such work in accordance with Auditing Standard ASA 610 *Considering the Work of Internal Audit* and accordingly reduce the extent of our own procedures relating to internal controls.

Special Purpose Engagements

As a separate engagement, we shall undertake an [audit/review/agreed-upon procedures (insert as appropriate)] and issue a report on a specific area identified by APRA. The details of this engagement will be the subject of a specific request from APRA and result in a separate engagement letter based on that request.

Confidentiality

Our annual APRA reports and special purpose engagement report will be issued to [Title of those charged with governance] of [Insurer] with a copy of the special purpose engagement report sent to APRA at the same time. Any further requests or enquiries from APRA will be communicated to us through [Insurer]. In this way our confidential relationship with [Insurer] will be maintained. However, the *Insurance Act 1973* sections 49, 49A and 49B provide that an Insurer's auditor and APRA may communicate with each other on a bilateral basis in certain circumstances.

The Auditor's Report on the yearly statutory accounts and the auditor's Prudential Review Report are prepared for [Title of those charged with governance] in order to meet [Insurer]'s APRA reporting requirements. These reports are not to be used for any other purpose or distributed to any other party. We disclaim any assumption of responsibility for any reliance on these reports to any party other than [Insurer] and APRA, or for any purpose other than that for which they were prepared.

Fees

APRA requirements will result in additional audit and review procedures being carried out. Fees relating to this work will be based on the degree of responsibility and skill involved and the time necessarily occupied by the work undertaken.

As the fees will not relate to our audit [and review] carried out in our capacity as the statutory auditor under the *Corporations Act 2001*, our invoices will be rendered separately so as to clearly identify the additional costs of APRA's requirements in relation to the audit of the yearly statutory accounts and the prudential review report.

[Insert additional information here regarding fee arrangements and billings, as appropriate.]

We look forward to full co-operation with you and your staff and we trust that you will make available to us whatever records, documentation and other information are requested in connection with our audit and review.

This letter will be effective for future years unless we advise you of its amendment or replacement, or the engagement is terminated.

Please sign and return the attached copy of this letter to indicate that it is in accordance with your understanding of the arrangements for our audit of the yearly statutory accounts and our review pursuant to APRA Prudential Standard GPS 310.

Yours faithfully,

(signed)

....

Name and Title

Date

Acknowledged on behalf of [Insurer] by

(signed)

....

Name and Title

Date

Appendix 4

Risk Management Strategy (RMS) and Reinsurance Management Strategy (REMS) Documents

Risk Management Strategy (RMS)

1 The RMS is a high level, strategic document intended to describe the key elements of an insurer's Risk Management Framework (RMF), including the insurer's risk appetite, policies, procedures, managerial responsibilities and controls to identify, assess, monitor, report on and mitigate all material risks[38], financial and non-financial, having regard to such factors as the size, business mix and complexity of the insurer's operations.

2 Prudential Standard GPS 220 *Risk Management* sets out the key requirements for an insurer's RMF and RMS document. Where specifically indicated in GPS 220, certain requirements (including the requirement for a RMS) may be complied with on an insurance group basis, provided APRA has agreed.

38 Under GPS 220, material risks must, at a minimum, include: balance sheet and market risk; credit risk; operational risk; insurance risk; risks arising out of reinsurance arrangements; concentration risk; and strategic and tactical risks that arise out of the insurer's business plan.

3 The following is a list of some of the key aspects which are to be included in an insurer's RMS[39]:

- Outline of the risk governance relationship between the Board, Board committees and senior management.
- Description of the processes for identifying and assessing risks.
- Description of the process for establishing mitigation and control mechanisms for individual risks.
- Description of the process for monitoring and reporting risk issues.
- Description of the approach to ensuring relevant staff have an awareness of risk issues and instilling an appropriate risk culture, including the level of accessibility of the RMS.
- Identification of those persons or groups of persons with managerial responsibility for the RMF, including their roles and responsibilities.
- Description of the process by which the RMF (including the RMS, the Reinsurance Management Framework (REMF) and REMS, the risk management function (or role), and the internal control system) is to be reviewed to ensure that the framework remains effective.
- Overview of the mechanisms in place for monitoring and ensuring continual compliance with the Minimum Capital Requirement (MCR).
- Overview of the processes and controls in place for ensuring compliance with all other Prudential Requirements.
- Identification of local risks and the risks arising from the overseas operations of the insurer that could impact on the Australian operations of the insurer.

Reinsurance Management Strategy (REMS)

4 The REMS is a high level, strategic document intended to describe the key elements of the insurer's REMF, including all policies, procedures, management responsibilities and controls to manage the selection, implementation, monitoring, review, amendment and documentation of reinsurance arrangements of the insurer.

5 Prudential Standard GPS 230 *Reinsurance Management* sets out the key requirements for the REMF, REMS document, as well as the Reinsurance Arrangements Statement and the annual Reinsurance Declaration. Where specifically indicated in GPS 230, certain requirements (including the requirement for a REMS) may be complied with on an insurance group basis, provided the relevant Insurer has notified APRA of this prior to doing so, and APRA has agreed.

6 The following is a list of some of the key aspects which must be included in an insurer's REMS[40]:

- Definition and documentation of the insurer's objectives and strategy for reinsurance management and control, reflecting the insurer's appetite for risk.
- Identification of the key elements of the insurer's policies and procedures, processes and controls that comprise the insurer's REMF.
- Summary of the processes for selecting, implementing, monitoring and reviewing reinsurance arrangements.
- Summary of the process for ensuring accurate and complete reinsurance documentation is put in place.
- Summary of the insurer's process for setting and monitoring its Maximum Event Retention (MER), including the process for setting and monitoring retentions so that the insurer's MER is not exceeded.

GS

39 Refer to GPS 220 for a complete list of requirements. It should be noted that, where the insurer is part of an Australian or global corporate group, or is a foreign insurer, GPS 220 and GPS 230 identify additional requirements for the RMS and the REMS.

40 Refer to GPS 230 for a complete list of requirements.

- Identification of those persons or groups of persons with managerial responsibility for the REMF and setting out their roles and responsibilities in relation to that framework.
- Identification of local risks and the risks arising from the overseas operations of the insurer that could impact on the Australian operations of the insurer.

7 The RMS and REMS documents, prepared in accordance with the requirements of GPS 220 and GPS 230, respectively, must be submitted to APRA after being approved by those charged with governance of the insurer. The insurer is required to review its RMS and REMS at least annually (or as close to annually as is practicable) to ensure that its RMF and REMF are documented accurately. Material changes to the RMS and REMS must be submitted to APRA within 10 business days of being approved by those charged with governance of the insurer.

GS 005
Using the Work of an Actuary

(Issued October 2007)

Issued by the Auditing and Assurance Standards Board.

Note from the Institute of Chartered Accountants Australia

This note, prepared by the technical editor, is not part of GS 005.

Historical development

September 1994: ED 60 'Codification and Revision of Auditing Pronouncements: AUS 526 The Auditor's Use of the Work of an Actuary and the Actuary's Use of the Work of the Auditor in Connection with the Preparation and Presentation and the Audit of a Financial Report' issued for comment.

June 1996: Auditing Standard AUS 524 'The Auditor's Use of the Work of an Actuary and the Actuary's Use of the Work of the Auditor in Connection with the Preparation and Presentation of the Audit of a Financial Report' issued by the AuSB, based on ED 60 of the same title. This Standard was prepared jointly by the AuSB and The Institute of Actuaries of Australia. AUS 524 became operative for the first financial reporting period commencing on or after 1 July 1996 and later reporting periods, although earlier application was encouraged. There is no equivalent IAPC Statement. AUS 524 replaced the appendix 'An Auditor's Relationship with an Actuary Concerning Actuarial Valuation of Policy Liabilities of Life Insurance Company', issued in June 1985, in Statement of Auditing Practice AUP 22 'Using the Work of an Expert'.

October 2007: GS 005 issued to give guidance to audit on using the work of actuaries. It is to be read in conjunction with ASA 620, 'Using the Work of an Expert', and has no international equivalent.

GS

Contents

AUTHORITY STATEMENT

Authority Statement

The Auditing and Assurance Standards Board (AUASB) formulates Guidance Statement GS 005 *Using the Work of an Actuary* as set out in paragraphs 1 to 32, pursuant to section 227B of the *Australian Securities and Investments Commission Act 2001*, for the purposes of providing guidance on procedural auditing and assurance matters.

This Guidance Statement provides guidance to assist the auditor to fulfil the objectives of the audit or assurance engagement. It includes explanatory details and suggested procedures on specific matters for the purposes of understanding and complying with AUASB Standards. The auditor exercises professional judgement when using this Guidance Statement.

The Guidance Statement does not prescribe or create mandatory requirements.

Dated 31 October 2007

M H Kelsall
Chairman - AUASB

Guidance Statement GS 005

Using the Work of an Actuary

Application

1 This Guidance Statement has been formulated by the Auditing and Assurance Standards Board (AUASB) to provide guidance to the auditor when using the work of an actuary as audit evidence in relation to:

(a) the audit or review of a financial report for a financial year or a half-year, in accordance with the *Corporations Act 2001*;

(b) the audit or review of a financial report for any other purpose; and

(c) the audit or review of other financial information[1].

Issuance Date

2 This Guidance Statement is issued on 31 October 2007 by the AUASB and supersedes AUS 524 *The Auditor's Use of the Work of the Actuary and the Actuary's Use of the Work of the Auditor in connection with the preparation and audit of a Financial Report* issued in July 2002.

1 Other financial information may include the annual Australian Prudential Regulation Authority (APRA) return and Regulatory financial statements for life insurers (PR 35).

Introduction

3 This Guidance Statement has been developed to provide guidance on:

(a) the circumstances under which the auditor uses the work of the actuary in carrying out the responsibilities of the auditor with respect to an entity's financial report or other financial information;

(b) how the auditor assesses the competency and objectivity of the actuary and determines the scope of the actuary's work; and

(c) how the auditor evaluates the work of an actuary and any impact of this work on the responsibilities of the auditor with respect to an entity's financial report or other financial information.

4 This guidance applies equally to the use of the work of actuaries whether they are internal or external to an entity and an actuary fulfilling the role of an External Peer Reviewer ("EPR").

5 The auditor ordinarily considers the general principles of materiality and audit risk[2] in determining the application of this Guidance Statement in gathering sufficient and appropriate audit evidence.

6 ASA 620 *Using the Work of an Expert,* which establishes mandatory requirements and provides explanatory guidance on using the work of an expert as audit evidence, needs to be considered by the auditor in conjunction with this Guidance Statement.

7 Although the auditor may use the work of an actuary as audit evidence, under ASA 700 *The Auditor's Report on a General Purpose Financial Report* the auditor retains full responsibility for the audit opinion on the financial report or other financial information.

Roles and Responsibilities of the Auditor when Expressing Opinions in Respect of a Financial Report or Other Financial Information

8 The preparation and presentation of a financial report and other financial information of an entity are the responsibility of those charged with governance. The representations contained in the financial report or other financial information may include amounts determined by the actuary or may be based upon actuarial valuations.

9 The auditor is responsible for forming and expressing an opinion on a financial report or other financial information. When a financial report or other financial information includes amounts determined by, or based upon the work of, the actuary the auditor considers using the work of the actuary as audit evidence.

10 In preparing reports and analyses, ordinarily the actuary relies on data provided by the entity, however an actuary has a professional obligation to take reasonable steps to verify the appropriateness of the data provided (i.e. its consistency, completeness and accuracy). An actuary's specific responsibilities in relation to data are set out in the *Actuarial Code of Professional Conduct, Actuarial Professional Standards*[3] and where relevant other regulatory and legislative requirements, APRA Prudential Standards and the *Life Insurance Act 1995*.

11 An auditor in using the work of an actuary assesses whether the actuary has performed sufficient procedures to determine if the data is reliable and appropriate for the purposes of the report. In assessing this work, the auditor considers the steps taken by the actuary in relation to the appropriateness of data used. If, as part of the audit procedures, the auditor becomes aware of matters material to the accuracy or completeness of data, ordinarily the auditor (having obtained client permission, where appropriate) communicates those findings to the actuary.

GS

2 Procedures involving Materiality and Audit Risk relevant to an audit are contained in Auditing Standard ASA 320 *Materiality and Audit Adjustments,* and may be helpful in determining procedures in relation to the use of the work of an actuary.

3 "Actuarial Professional Standards" means those standards issued by The Institute of Actuaries of Australia and/or the APRA Prudential Standards and/or equivalent International professional standards.

Determining the Need to Use the Work of an Actuary

12 In obtaining an understanding of the entity and performing further procedures in response to assessed risks, the auditor may need to obtain audit evidence in the form of reports, opinions, valuations and statements by an actuary.

13 When determining the need to use the work of an actuary, ordinarily the auditor considers:

(a) the engagement team's knowledge and previous experience of the matter being considered;

(b) the risk of material misstatement based on the nature, complexity and materiality of the matter being considered; and

(c) the quantity and quality of other audit evidence expected to be obtained.

Communication between the Auditor and the Actuary

14 The auditor communicates any information that may be relevant to the actuary's work. The level of communication may differ in detail depending on whether the actuary is internal or external to the entity and this is a matter for the auditor's professional judgement. Such communication is established during the planning stage and further communication would take place as necessary throughout the engagement. If the right to communicate with the actuary was not obtained from management the auditor would need to consider any impact on the engagement.

15 Ordinarily, the auditor:

- Informs the actuary of the intended use of the actuary's work including the possible communication to third parties of the actuary's identity and extent of involvement in accordance with this Guidance Statement.
- Makes the actuary aware of the auditor's needs. This includes a discussion of:
  - ♦ materiality, to establish that the actuary considers using a materiality level that is appropriate in the circumstances;
  - ♦ subsequent events, to establish that the actuary understands how subsequent events are to be treated and that the actuary will consider the effect of matters which come to the actuary's attention up to the date of the actuary's report;
  - ♦ verification of data, so that reasonable assurance will be obtained with respect to the accuracy, completeness and consistency of the required data;
  - ♦ the timing of the work to be carried out by the actuary and the date of the actuary's report; and
  - ♦ any questions relating to the actuary's work.

Competence and Objectivity of an Actuary

16 When planning to use the work of the actuary, the auditor evaluates the professional competence and objectivity of the actuary.

17 The auditor ordinarily considers the actuary's:

(a) professional qualification, for example a Fellowship or Accredited Membership of The Institute of Actuaries of Australia and/or other recognised equivalent qualifications; and

(b) experience and reputation in the field of expertise[4].

18 ASA 500 *Audit Evidence* indicates that evidence from external sources is generally more reliable than that generated internally. The existence of a relationship between the actuary and the entity being audited may impair the actuary's ability to be objective. ASA 620 indicates that where an expert is employed or related to the entity, the auditor needs to consider whether there are any mitigating factors such as professional and/or statutory obligations governing the work of an expert that would impact on the objectivity of the expert. If the auditor is

4 The auditor may consider the Fit and Proper Requirements that need to be met in order for the Actuary to be appointed, to an entity regulated by the APRA Prudential Standards.

concerned regarding the competence or objectivity of the actuary, the auditor discusses any reservations with management and considers whether sufficient appropriate audit evidence can be obtained concerning the work of the actuary. The auditor may undertake additional procedures or seek audit evidence from another expert.

19 Mitigating factors which enhance the ability of the actuary, when the actuary is an employee of the entity, to be objective, and therefore may compensate for the lack of independence, include:

- Adherence to the professional standards issued by The Institute of Actuaries of Australia and/or the APRA Prudential Standards and/or equivalent International professional standards where appropriate.
- The requirement to provide an opinion and a detailed report on the appropriateness of the actuarial liabilities to regulatory authorities, and to provide an opinion on the appropriateness of the actuarial liabilities to, for example policy holders and/or members.
- Formal appointment of the actuary by those charged with governance and access to those charged with governance by the actuary.
- Legislation requiring that regulatory authorities are informed of the actuary's appointment and any change to the appointment by those charged with governance.
- Consideration of the results of any EPR or similar review.

Ordinarily, the basis on which the actuary is remunerated and or incentives offered as part of that remuneration are considered also by the auditor when assessing the actuary's objectivity.

Consideration of the above may be relevant also in evaluating the objectivity of an actuary external to the entity.

20 The decision as to whether to perform more extensive procedures or engage an independent actuary to review some or all of the work of the actuary is a matter of professional judgement. In making this judgement, the auditor considers:

(a) economic and competitive conditions;

(b) significant concern by management about operating results; and

(c) evidence of undue management pressure on the actuary.

21 The auditor may consider performing more extensive procedures or engaging an independent actuary to review some or all of the work of the actuary when inherent audit risk has been assessed as high for a particular audit engagement.

Scope of the Actuary's Work

22 The auditor considers the scope of the actuary's work to ensure it is adequate for the purposes of the audit and provides sufficient appropriate audit evidence.

23 In assessing the appropriateness and adequacy of the actuary's terms of reference, consideration is given to the scope disclosed in the actuary's report.

24 The appropriateness and reasonableness of assumptions and methods used and their application are the responsibility of the actuary. Although not having the same expertise as the actuary, the auditor will need to obtain an understanding of the assumptions and methods used and to consider whether they are reasonable, based on the auditor's knowledge of the business and the results of other procedures performed. In situations where the amounts to be included in the financial report or other financial information are based on the work of the actuary, but have been finalised with further input from the those charged with governance, the auditor determines the reasonableness of that input.

Evaluating the Work of an Actuary

25 In accordance with ASA 620, the auditor evaluates the appropriateness of the actuary's work as audit evidence and whether the substance of the actuary's findings is properly reflected in the financial report or other financial information, and supports the assertions with, consideration of:

(a) source data used;

(b) assumptions and methods used and their consistency with prior periods; and

(c) results of the actuary's work in the light of the auditor's overall knowledge of the business and the results of other audit procedures.

26 ASA 620 requires that if the results of the actuary's work do not provide sufficient appropriate audit evidence, or if the results are not consistent with other audit evidence, the auditor needs to resolve the matter. This may involve discussions with the entity and the actuary, applying additional audit procedures, including possibly engaging another expert, or modifying the auditor's report.

27 Ordinarily, the actuary's work is documented in a report which complies with the Institute of Actuaries of Australia, *Code of Professional Conduct* and any relevant regulatory requirements or equivalent International professional standards or relevant regulatory requirements.

28 During the course of the engagement, the auditor uses the report of the actuary. If the auditor has a question about an aspect of the actuary's work, the auditor discusses this aspect with the actuary to obtain an explanation about that aspect of the work performed. This does not, however, limit the right of the auditor to any information or explanation that may be required in the performance of their duties in accordance with the auditor's professional standards.

Reference to the Work of an Actuary in the Auditor's Report

29 ASA 620 requires that, when issuing an unmodified auditor's report, the auditor does not refer to the work of an expert.

30 If as a result of the work of the actuary the auditor decides to issue a modified auditor's report, in some circumstances it may be appropriate in explaining the nature of the modification, to refer to or describe the work of the actuary (including the identity of the actuary and the extent of the actuary's involvement). In these circumstances, ordinarily the auditor obtains the permission of the actuary before making such a reference. If permission is refused and the auditor considers that a reference is necessary, the auditor may need to seek legal advice.

31 ASA 701 *Modifications to the Auditor's Report* provides further mandatory requirements and explanatory guidance regarding modifications in the auditor's report.

Conformity with International Pronouncements

32 There is no equivalent International Standard on Auditing or International Auditing Practice Statement to this Guidance Statement.

GS 006

Electronic Publication of the Auditor's Report

(Issued December 2007: revised March 2010)

Issued by the Auditing and Assurance Standards Board.

Note from the Institute of Chartered Accountants Australia

This note, prepared by the technical editor, is not part of GS 006.

Historical development

December 1999: AGS 1050 'Audit Issues Relating to the Electronic Presentation of Financial Reports' issued by the AUASB, operative from the date of issue.

December 2007: GS 006 issued to replace AGS 1050 in response to changes in the *Corporations Act 2001* that permit companies to distribute their annual reports electronically.

March 2010: GS 006 reissued, applicable to reporting periods commencing on or after 1 January 2010. The guidance in the new version is more specific and refers to the Clarity Auditing Standards issued in October 2009. There is no equivalent International Auditing Practice Statement.

Contents

AUTHORITY STATEMENT

Authority Statement

The Auditing and Assurance Standards Board (AUASB) formulates Guidance Statement GS 006 *Electronic Publication of the Auditor's Report* pursuant to section 227B of the *Australian Securities and Investments Commission Act 2001*, for the purposes of providing guidance on auditing and assurance matters.

This Guidance Statement provides guidance to assist the auditor to fulfil the objectives of the audit or assurance engagement. It includes explanatory details on specific matters for the purposes of understanding and complying with AUASB Standards. The auditor exercises professional judgement when using this Guidance Statement.

The Guidance Statement does not prescribe or create new Requirements.

Dated: 12 March 2010

M H Kelsall
Chairman - AUASB

Guidance Statement GS 006

Electronic Publication of the Auditor's Report

Application

1 This Guidance Statement has been formulated by the Auditing and Assurance Standards Board (AUASB) to provide guidance to auditors on matters relating to the electronic publication of the auditor's report.

2 This Guidance Statement should be used when an auditor conducts an audit under the Australian Auditing Standards applicable to financial reporting periods commencing on or after 1 January 2010.

Issuance Date

3 This Guidance Statement is issued on 1 March 2010.

Introduction

4 Various types of financial and non-financial information can be distributed electronically or published on websites, including:

(a) information that has been audited (for example the annual financial report);

(b) information which the auditor has reviewed (for example an interim financial report);

(c) the auditor's report(s);

(d) information with which the auditor has had no direct involvement, such as financial highlights in an entity's annual report or other information the auditor may never have seen, such as presentations for analysts; and

(e) a considerable amount of non-financial information.

5 Under the *Corporations Act 2001* (the Act) companies, registered schemes and disclosing entities may choose to meet their statutory reporting obligations to members by distributing annual financial reports, including the concise report, electronically. Alternatively, the Act provides for entities wishing to publish their financial reports, including the concise report, on their website. See section 314 (1AA) of the Act for details and requirements.

Definitions

6 For the purposes of this Guidance Statement, the term electronic publication includes the electronic distribution of documents.[1]

7 For purposes of this Guidance Statement, the term management should be read hereafter as management, or where appropriate, those charged with governance.

The Auditor's Considerations when the Auditor's Report is Electronically Published

8 The requirements of the Australian Auditing Standards do not differ according to whether the audited financial report and the auditor's report are distributed to members in hard copy format or electronic copy format. However, in the latter case, the auditor considers performing additional procedures in response to the nature of electronic publication. For example:

- where applicable, determining that the requirements of the Act have been adhered to when the financial report is distributed electronically; and
- evaluating whether unaudited supplementary information is clearly differentiated from the audited financial report when such documentation is presented on a web site.

The following paragraphs provide application guidance on relevant requirements of the Auditing Standards.

Terms of Engagement

9 Under ASA 210 *Agreeing the Terms of Audit Engagements*, the auditor is required to obtain the agreement of management, and where appropriate, those charged with governance, that it acknowledges and understands its responsibility for the preparation of the financial report. This responsibility includes the distribution and publication, regardless of method, of the audited financial report and the auditor's report.

10 In order to clarify responsibilities, the auditor may include in the engagement letter details regarding responsibilities and internal control in relation to the electronic distribution and publication of the audited financial reports and the auditor's report. The engagement letter may include, for example, acknowledgements that:

(a) the electronic presentation of the audited financial report and auditor's report is the responsibility of those charged with governance;

(b) security and controls over information on the entity's website are the responsibility of the entity; and

(c) the examination of controls over the electronic presentation of audited financial information on the entity's website is beyond the scope of the audit of the financial report.

Appendix 1 contains an example of an additional paragraph that may be included in an engagement letter.

GS

1 The term electronic publication includes all formats of electronic publication, for example 'pdf' documents or documents published in the format used under Australia's Standard Business Reporting regime (refer www.sbr.gov.au).

Communications

11 ASA 260 *Communications with Those Charged with Governance*, provides an overarching framework for the auditor's effective two-way communication with those charged with governance; and identifies some specific matters to be communicated with them.

12 The auditor discusses with those charged with governance how the audited financial report and the auditor's report will be published or distributed in electronic form. Particular attention must be paid to compliance with the Act (where applicable) and minimising the risk that the auditor's report is inappropriately associated with other information.

Representations

13 Under ASA 580 *Written Representations*, the auditor is required to obtain written representations from management that it has fulfilled its responsibility for the preparation of the financial report. This responsibility covers distribution and publication of the audited financial report and the auditor's report regardless of whether it is in hard copy or electronic copy form.

14 When financial reporting is under the Act, management is required to comply with the reporting requirements of the Act. See, for example, section 314 (1AA) which relates to the electronic distribution and publication of financial reports.

15 Accordingly and in the case of electronic publication of the audited financial report and the auditor's report, the auditor obtains written representations that management acknowledges its responsibility for the electronic presentation of the audited financial report and the auditor's report.

16 Under ASA 580, paragraph 13, the auditor may determine that written representations are necessary to support other audit evidence relevant to the financial report. Accordingly, the auditor may request written representations that:

(a) the electronic version of the audited financial report and auditor's report published on the website are identical to the final signed version of the audited financial report and auditor's report;

(b) management has in place a process to clearly differentiate between audited and unaudited information on the entity's website and understands the risk of potential misrepresentation;

(c) management has assessed the controls over audited financial information and the auditor's report and is satisfied that procedures in place are adequate to ensure the integrity of the information provided;

(d) where the auditor's report on the full financial report is provided on the website, the financial report is also provided in full; and

(e) where applicable, management has complied with the requirements of the Act with respect to the electronic presentation of the audited financial reports.

Appendix 2 contains an example of an additional paragraph that may be included in a written representation letter.

Auditor's Report

17 The auditor is not required to provide a separate auditor's report for the electronic presentation of an audited financial report on an entity's website.

18 The auditor may consider including an "Other Matter Paragraph" in the auditor's report which advises readers that the report refers only to the statements named in the auditor's report and does not provide an opinion on any other information which may have been hyperlinked to/from the audited financial report. See ASA 706 *Emphasis of Matter Paragraphs and Other Matter Paragraphs in the Independent Auditor's Report*.

Appendix 3 contains an example of an "Other Matter Paragraph" that may be included in an auditor's report.

19 If the auditor's report is used without the auditor's consent, and the auditor has concerns about the electronic presentation of the audited financial report or the auditor's report and appropriate action is not taken by management, the auditor seeks legal advice as necessary. The auditor also considers whether it would be appropriate to resign, where possible under applicable law or regulation.

Other Information

20 The Auditing Standards require particular attention when the audited financial report and auditor's report are published with other information - which is common practice on internet websites.

21 Under ASA 700 *Forming an Opinion and Reporting on a Financial Report*, when unaudited supplementary information that is not required by the applicable financial reporting framework is presented with the audited financial report, the auditor is required to evaluate whether such supplementary information is clearly differentiated from the audited financial report

(a) If such supplementary information is not clearly differentiated from the audited financial report, the auditor asks management to change how the unaudited supplementary information is presented.

(b) If management refuses to do so, the auditor explains in the auditor's report that such supplementary information has not been audited. Such explanation is contained in an "Other Matter Paragraph" under ASA 706.

(c) Techniques that may be used to differentiate material within a website include:

- Icons or watermarks.
- Colour borders.
- Labels/banners such as "annual report" or "audited financial statements".

22 The appropriate mode of differentiation between audited and unaudited information will be dependent on the electronic format selected, and the nature of other information published on the website.

23 The auditor remains alert to unaudited supplementary information that is not required by the applicable financial reporting framework, but is nevertheless an integral part of the financial report because it cannot be clearly differentiated from the audited financial report due to its nature and how it is presented. Such information is covered by the auditor's opinion. See ASA 700, paragraph 47.

24 Under ASA 720 *The Auditor's Responsibilities Relating to Other Information in Documents Containing an Audited Financial Report*, the auditor establishes that the auditor's report is not inappropriately associated with other information. The auditor's objective is to respond appropriately when documents containing an audited financial report and the auditor's report thereon include other information that could undermine the credibility of that financial report and the auditor's report.

25 An important requirement of ASA 720 is for the auditor to make arrangements with management to obtain the other information prior to the date of the auditor's report.

26 Where a material inconsistency is identified in the other information and management refuse to revise that information, the auditor is required to include in the auditor's report an "Other Matter Paragraph" describing the material inconsistency in accordance with ASA 706. See ASA 720, paragraph 10(a).

GS

Conformity with International Pronouncements

27 There is no equivalent International Auditing Practice Statement (IAPS) to this Guidance Statement.

Appendix 1

(Ref: Para. 10)

Example of an Additional Paragraph that may be Included in an Engagement Letter when the Audited Financial Report is Electronically Published on an Entity's Website

Electronic Publication of Audited Financial Report

It is our understanding that the [type of entity] intends to electronically present the audited financial report and auditor's report on its internet website. Responsibility for the electronic presentation of the financial report on the [type of entity's] website is that of management [or appropriate term] of the [type of entity]. The security and controls over information on the website should be addressed by the [type of entity] to maintain the integrity of the data presented. The examination of the controls over the electronic presentation of audited financial report(s) on the [type of entity's] website is beyond the scope of the audit of the financial report.

Appendix 2

(Ref: Para. 16)

Example of an Additional Paragraph that may be Included in a Management Representation Letter when the Audited Financial Report is Electronically Published on an Entity's Website

Publication on a Website

With respect to publication of the audited financial report on our website, we acknowledge that:

(a) we are responsible for the electronic presentation of the audited financial report;

(b) we will ensure that the electronic version of the audited financial report and the auditor's report on the website will be identical to the final signed hard copy version;

(c) we will clearly differentiate between audited and unaudited information in the construction of the entity's website as we understand the risk of potential misrepresentation;

(d) we have assessed the controls over the security and integrity of the data on the website and that adequate procedures are in place to ensure the integrity of the information published;

(e) we will not present the auditor's report on the full financial report with extracts only of the full financial report; and

(f) where applicable, we have complied with the requirements of the *Corporations Act 2001* with respect to the electronic presentation of the audited financial reports.

Appendix 3

(Ref: Para. 18)

Example of an Other Matter Paragraph that may be Included in an Auditor's Report when the Audited Financial Report is Electronically Published on an Entity's Website

Matters Relating to the Electronic Publication of the Audited Financial Report

This auditor's report relates to the financial report of [name of entity] for the year ended 30 June 20X1 included on [name of entity's] website. The [type of entity's] directors [or appropriate term] are responsible for the integrity of [name of entity's] website. We have not been engaged to report on the integrity of the [name of entity's] website. The auditor's report refers only to the subject matter described above. It does not provide an opinion on any other information which may have been hyperlinked to/from these statements. If users of the financial report are concerned with the inherent risks arising from publication on a website, they are advised to refer to the hard copy of the audited financial report to confirm the information contained in this website version of the financial report.

GS

GS 007

Audit Implications of the Use of Service Organisations for Investment Management Services

(Reissued October 2011)

Issued by the Auditing and Assurance Standards Board.

Note from the Institute of Chartered Accountants Australia

This note, prepared by the technical editor, is not part of GS 007.

Historical development

September 2008: GS 007 applies to both auditors of entities that use service organisations to provide investment management services, and that auditors of those service organisations who provide audit and assurance reports that may be used as audit evidence in the audit of the user entity's financial report.

It replaced AGS 1026 'Superannuation Funds – Auditor Reports on Externally Managed Assets' and superseded AUS 522 'Audit Evidence Implications of Externally Managed Assets of Superannuation, Provident or Similar Funds'. It was operative for reporting periods commencing on or after 1 July 2008.

October 2011: GS 007 updated for the requirements and terminology of the new Clarity Auditing Standards as well as the changes made to related pronouncements dealing with the audit of service organisations including ASA 402 and ASAE 3402. The reissued Guidance is operative for periods commencing 1 January 2012. It has no international equivalent. The AUASB also published 'Explanation of the Applicability of AUASB pronouncements when conducting Internal Control Engagements' in October 2011. This can be found in this book after ASAE3402.

Contents

AUTHORITY STATEMENT

GS

Authority Statement

The Auditing and Assurance Standards Board (AUASB) formulates Guidance Statement GS 007 *Audit Implications of the Use of Service Organisations for Investment Management Services*, pursuant to section 227B of the *Australian Securities and Investments Commission Act 2001* for the purposes of providing guidance on auditing and assurance matters.

This Guidance Statement provides guidance to assist the auditor to fulfil the objectives of the audit or assurance engagement. It includes explanatory material on specific matters for the purposes of understanding and complying with AUASB Standards. The auditor exercises professional judgement when using this Guidance Statement.

The Guidance Statement does not prescribe or create new requirements.

Dated: 25 October 2011

M H Kelsall
Chairman - AUASB

Guidance Statement GS 007

Audit Implications of the Use of Service Organisations for Investment Management Services

Application

1. This Guidance Statement has been formulated by the Auditing and Assurance Standards Board (AUASB) to provide guidance to:
   (a) auditors (user auditors) of a financial report of an entity (user entity) which uses a third party service organisation to provide investment management services; and
   (b) auditors (service auditors) of those service organisations, who provide reports on controls or financial information which may be used as audit evidence in the audit of the user entity's financial report.

Issuance Date

2. This Guidance Statement is issued on 25 October 2011 by the AUASB and replaces Guidance Statement GS 007 *Audit Implications of the Use of Service Organisations for Investment Management Services*, issued in March 2008. It is operative for reporting periods commencing on or after 1 January 2012.

Introduction

3. This Guidance Statement provides guidance to:
   (a) user auditors in applying Auditing Standard ASA 402 *Audit Considerations Relating to an Entity Using a Service Organisation*, when using reports on controls at a service organisation, and other Australian Auditing Standards, when using service auditor's reports on financial information as audit evidence relating to investment management services provided by the service organisation; and
   (b) service auditors in applying Standard on Assurance Engagements ASAE 3402 *Assurance Reports on Controls at a Service Organisation*, when engaged to report on controls, and other Australian Auditing Standards, when engaged to report on financial information, relating to components of user entities for which investment management services are provided by the service organisation.

4. Part A of this Guidance Statement (paragraphs 20-50) provides guidance to user auditors but is to be read in conjunction with, and is not a substitute for referring to the requirements and application material contained in, ASA 402, when using a service auditor's report on controls, or Australian Auditing Standards, when using a service auditor's report on financial information. This Guidance Statement is applicable to user auditors when:
   (a) the services provided are part of the user entity's information system, including related business processes, relevant to financial reporting;[1]
   (b) audit evidence required by the user auditor regarding internal controls and/or assertions is located at the service organisation; and

1 See ASA 402, paragraph 3.

(c) reports on controls at the service organisation and/or a service auditor's report on specified assertions or a financial statement of the user entity's balances or transactions relating to the services provided by the service organisation are available.

5. Part B of this Guidance Statement (paragraphs 51-90) provides guidance to the service auditor but is to be read in conjunction with, and is not a substitute for referring to the requirements and application material contained in ASAE 3402, when reporting on controls, and Auditing Standard ASA 805,[2] when reporting on financial information.

6. ASA 402 does not apply to services provided by financial institutions which are limited to processing of transactions that are specifically authorised by the user entity.[3] Therefore reports prepared under ASAE 3402 are not usually necessary for banks processing clients' account transactions or brokers processing clients' securities transactions. Nor does ASA 402 apply to transactions relating to financial interests in other entities when those interests are accounted for and reported to interest holders. Therefore, reports under ASAE 3402 are not generally necessary for unitised funds or other investments of an entity for which prices are publicly available. However, unitised funds or other investments may use service organisations to provide investment management services, in which case it is appropriate for the service organisation to provide a type 1 or 2 report. Unitised funds and unit pricing of those funds are addressed in the control objectives within this Guidance Statement only in the context of service organisations which provide investment management services to unitised funds.

Types of Reports

7. This Guidance Statement provides guidance for the preparation and use as audit evidence of the following reports:

(a) Reports on the description and design of controls at a service organisation (type 1 report) or description, design and operating effectiveness of controls at a service organisation (type 2 report), relating to the service organisation's system over the investment management services provided to user entities, prepared in accordance with ASAE 3402.

(b) Service auditor's reports on financial information, prepared in accordance with ASA 805,[4] comprising either:

(i) a service auditor's report on specified assertions regarding balances or transactions of the user entity reported in a financial statement by the service organisation, which provides investment management services, ("service auditor's report on specified assertions"); or

(ii) a service auditor's report on a financial statement of the user entity's balances or transactions ("statement") reported by the service organisation which provides investment management services ("service auditor's report on a statement").

8. Type 1 and 2 reports on controls comprise:[5]

(a) A service organisation's description of its investment management services system, including identification of:

(i) the services covered;

(ii) the date or period to which the description relates;

GS

2 See ASA 805 *Special Considerations—Audits of Single Financial Statements and Specific Elements, Accounts or Items of a Financial Statement.*

3 See ASA 402, paragraph 5.

4 ASA 800 *Special Considerations—Audits of Financial Reports Prepared in Accordance with Special Purpose Frameworks* is also applicable if the financial information is a financial report or complete set of financial statements prepared in accordance with a special purpose framework.

5 See ASAE 3402, paragraph 9.

(iii) control objectives, including the control objectives listed in Appendix 3 of this Guidance Statement, for the relevant investment management services provided; and

(iv) related controls.

(b) A written assertion by the service organisation that, in all material respects, and based on suitable criteria:

(i) the description fairly presents the service organisation's system as designed and implemented;

(ii) the controls related to the control objectives stated in the service organisation's description of its system were suitably designed as at the specified date, for a type 1 report, or throughout the period, for a type 2 report; and

(iii) for a type 2 report, the controls operated effectively throughout the specified period.

(c) A service auditor's assurance report that conveys reasonable assurance about the service organisation's assertions, including for type 2 reports, a description of the tests of controls and the results thereof.

9. The use of a type 1 report by a user auditor is limited to understanding the entity in accordance with Auditing Standard ASA 315,[6] whereas a type 2 report may also be used by a user auditor in responding to assessed risks in accordance with Auditing Standard ASA 330.[7]

10. Other reports may be required by the user entity as set out in the contract and/or service level agreement for purposes such as monitoring the performance of the service organisation, however the reports covered by this Guidance Statement are limited to those that may be used by user auditors as audit evidence for the audit of the user entity's financial report.

11. The following table, entitled *Table 1: Service Auditor's Reports*, outlines the context in which each of these reports is prepared and used as audit evidence. Table 1 lists the reports included in this Guidance Statement, the subject matter covered by each report, the circumstances for which each report may be useful to user auditors, standards relevant to the preparation and use of each report and references to appendices containing examples of each report and related engagement letters.

12. The guidance in this Guidance Statement is based on engagements to provide an opinion based on reasonable assurance, with respect to controls or financial information. It does not apply to an engagement to provide a review conclusion on controls based on limited assurance, however, it may be adapted, as necessary in the circumstances, to an engagement to provide limited assurance on specified assertions or a Statement. A review conclusion from the service auditor may be appropriate where the user auditor is engaged to perform a review of the user entity's financial report. The service auditor exercises professional judgement in applying this Guidance Statement to a review and, when reporting on specified assertions or a Statement, complies with the requirements of relevant standards on review engagements.

---

6 See ASA 315 *Identifying and Assessing the Risks of Material Misstatement through Understanding the Entity and Its Environment.*

7 See ASA 330 *The Auditor's Responses to Assessed Risks.*

Table 1: Service Auditor's Reports

Title of Report	Subject Matter Covered by Report	Circumstances for Which Report is Used by User Auditors	Relevant Standards	Appendix Reference for Examples
Reports on controls				
1. Type 1 report[8]	Description and design of controls at the service organisation.	Planning: Obtaining an understanding of the user entity and its environment, including controls over services provided by the service organisation, in order to assess the risk of material misstatement and design further audit procedures. This report cannot be relied on to reduce substantive procedures.	User Auditor: ASA 402 and ASA 315 Service Auditor: ASAE 3402	Engagement letter and service auditor's type 1 report: No example provided as this report is not likely to meet the needs of all user auditors.
2. Type 2 report[9]	Description, design, and operating effectiveness of controls at the service organisation.	Planning: Obtaining an understanding of the user entity and its environment: as for type 1 reports. Responding to the assessed risks of material misstatement when evidence is required of the operating effectiveness of controls over the services provided at the service organisation	User Auditor: ASA 402 and ASA 330 Service Auditor: ASAE 3402	Engagement letter: Appendix 1 Example 1. Service Organisation's assertion and description of its system: Appendix 2. Minimum Control Objectives: Appendix 3. Service auditor's type 2 report: Appendices 4 and 5.
Reports on financial information				
3. Service auditor's report on specified assertions[10]	Specified assertions regarding balances or transactions of the user entity reported in a Statement.	Require evidence from procedures conducted at the service organisation regarding certain assertions with respect to balances or transactions of the user entity, reported in a Statement.	Service Auditor: ASA 805	Engagement letter: Appendix 1 Example 2 Service auditor's report: Appendix 6 Example 1
4. Service auditor's report on a Statement[11]	Balances or transactions of the user entity reported in a Statement.	Require evidence from procedures conducted at the service organisation regarding the balances or transactions of the user entity, reported in a Statement.	Service Auditor: ASA 805	Engagement letter: Appendix 1 Example 3 Service auditor's report: Appendix 6 Example 2

13. The user auditor may request the user entity to obtain from the service auditor, or directly engage the service auditor to provide, a report on agreed-upon procedures. Agreed-upon procedures engagements may be appropriate in certain circumstances to provide evidence that the user auditor requires, for example when:

- A type 2 report is provided, however the user auditor requires more evidence with respect to controls over a specified area, such as unit pricing.
- Provision of a service auditor report on controls is not agreed in the service level agreement or contract, but the user auditor nevertheless requires selected controls to be tested at the service organisation.
- A service auditor's report on specified assertions is provided for assets under the custody of a custodian, but does not address assets outside the custody of the

8 See paragraph 8 of this Guidance Statement.

9 See paragraph 8 of this Guidance Statement.

10 See paragraph 7(b)(i) of this Guidance Statement.

11 See paragraph 7(b)(ii) of this Guidance Statement.

custodian for which the custodian provides investment administration services. Additional agreed-upon procedures are performed to assist the user auditor to obtain evidence on the existence or valuation of the assets outside the custody of the custodian.

- A service auditor's report on specified assertions is provided as described in this Guidance Statement, however further audit procedures are required by the user auditor in obtaining sufficient appropriate audit evidence with respect to particular assertions. For example, with respect to the assertion of valuation, agreement of valuation input variables to source data may be required by the user auditor.

Such engagements are conducted under Standards on Related Services[12] and no further guidance on agreed-upon procedures engagements is provided in this Guidance Statement.

Services Relevant to this Guidance Statement

14. This Guidance Statement has been developed specifically for circumstances where service organisations provide investment management services to user entities, where those services and the controls over them, are part of the user entity's information system, including business processes, relevant to financial reporting,[13] and as a result are relevant to the audit of a user entity's financial report. The Investment Management Services addressed in this Guidance Statement are:
    - Custody.
    - Asset Management.
    - Property Management.
    - Superannuation Member Administration.
    - Investment Administration.
    - Registry.

    Each of these services is defined in Appendix 3.

15. Controls over the calculation of unit pricing are not included as part of the services addressed in this Guidance Statement as reliance can generally be placed on the publicly available unit price, where appropriate, with additional procedures to assess the bona fides of the fund such as sighting audited financial statements of the fund, for the assertion of valuation for investments in unitised funds. If user auditors require assurance over unit pricing, for governance or compliance purposes, they may request that control objectives and controls for unit pricing are included in the service organisation's description of the system and audited by the service auditor.

16. Operators of investor directed portfolio services (IDPS)[14] and investor directed portfolio-like services are required by ASIC Class Order 02/294[15] and Class Order 02/296[16] to obtain an auditor's report providing:

    (a) an opinion on the internal controls and other relevant accounting procedures as they relate to the specific annual investor statements; and

    (b) a review conclusion on the annual investor statements, quarterly reports in certain circumstances and information accessible to clients electronically.

---

12 See ASRS 4400 *Agreed-upon Procedures Engagements to Report Factual Findings.*

13 The circumstances under which a service organisation's services are part of a user entity's information system, including business processes, relevant to financial reporting, are provided in ASA 402, paragraph 3.

14 "IDPS" means an investor directed portfolio service, consisting of a number of functions including a custody, settlement and reporting system and service. The clients of the service have the sole discretion to decide what assets will be acquired or disposed of. The service is provided in such a way that clients are led to expect, and are likely to receive, benefits in the form of access to investments that the client could not otherwise access directly or cost reductions by using assets contributed by the client or derived directly or indirectly from assets contributed by the client with assets contributed by other clients or derived directly or indirectly from assets contributed by other clients.

15 See ASIC Class Order 02/294 *Investor Directed Portfolio Services.*

16 See ASIC Class Order 02/296 *Investor Directed Portfolio-like Services Provided Through a Registered Managed Investment Scheme.*

These class orders provide requirements for the form and content of the report in these circumstances. Reports provided under these class orders may provide sufficient appropriate audit evidence for a user auditor. If additional evidence is required by the user auditor, a service auditor's report on controls or on financial information may be requested. IDPS or IDPS-like services generally include custody and investment administration, consequently, if a type 1 or 2 report is provided, the user auditor can reasonably expect the operator (service organisation) and service auditor to report on the control objectives for the relevant services provided in this Guidance Statement.

17. Types of service organisations which provide some or all of the investment management services addressed in this Guidance Statement include:
- Custodians.
- Third Party Administrators.
- Investment Managers.
- Registrars.
- Trust Departments of Financial Institutions.
- Prime Brokers.

18. The responsible parties which typically engage the services of these service organisations on behalf of user entities, include but are not limited to:
- Trustees of Superannuation Funds.
- Responsible Entities for Registered Managed Investment Schemes.
- Trustees of Unregistered Unit Trusts.
- Boards of Insurance Companies.

19. The responsibilities of the responsible party of a user entity are set out in the relevant laws and regulations governing their role and the particular services they oversee.

A: Guidance for the User Auditor

20. The use of a service organisation for the provision of investment management services by a user entity does not alter the overall objective of the audit of the user entity's financial report, therefore it remains the responsibility of the user auditor to obtain sufficient appropriate audit evidence to support the auditor's opinion. The requirements of the Auditing Standards relating to obtaining sufficient appropriate evidence on which to form an opinion are the same as would apply if the records and supporting documentation were maintained by the user entity.

Using a Type 1 or Type 2 Report on Controls

21. ASA 402 provides requirements for the user auditor in obtaining an understanding of the user entity and its environment when the user entity uses the services of a service organisation and states that a type 1 or 2 report may be used to obtain that understanding, if the user auditor is unable to obtain a sufficient understanding from the user entity. The user auditor is required to determine whether the type 1 or 2 report provides sufficient appropriate audit evidence to support the user auditor's understanding of the design and implementation of controls at the service organisation.[17]

22. A type 1 report cannot be relied upon to reduce the level of substantive procedures conducted by the user auditor, as it does not provide any evidence of the operating effectiveness of the controls reported upon. Consequently, the usefulness of a type 1 report to a user auditor is limited to planning the audit, assessing the risk of material misstatement and designing further audit procedures.

23. When the user auditor's risk assessment includes an expectation that controls at the service organisation are operating effectively, ASA 402 requires the user auditor to obtain evidence about the operating effectiveness of those controls, which may be obtained from

17 See ASA 402, paragraphs 9-14.

a type 2 report.[18] Type 2 reports are prepared for the purposes of multiple user entities, not specifically for the purposes of any individual user auditor, so the user auditor is required to determine the sufficiency and appropriateness of the audit evidence provided by that report in accordance with ASA 402.[19]

24. Whilst the user auditor makes their own assessment of the relevance of the service auditor's tests of controls to the assertions in the user entity's financial report, when investment management services are provided, the user auditor can reasonably expect:

(a) each of the control objectives specified in this Guidance Statement[20] for the relevant investment management service/s to be addressed in the service organisation's description of its system and assertion;

(b) the related controls identified to be reported on by the service auditor; and

(c) adequate justification to be provided by the service organisation for any control objectives for which no related controls are identified.

25. When the service organisation reports against the minimum control objectives provided in this Guidance Statement it assists the user auditor to:

- Compare directly the controls in place at different service organisations providing the same investment management services.
- Collate the results of the controls tested where multiple service organisations are used to provide the same service.
- Identify omissions in the user entity's description of the system or gaps in the system of control over the relevant investment management services.

26. If the controls report is prepared by a service auditor practicing in another jurisdiction, the report may not address the minimum control objectives in this Guidance Statement for the investment management services provided. Nevertheless, the report may still provide useful audit evidence. In assessing the sufficiency and appropriateness of the evidence that the controls report provides, in addition to consideration of the matters required in ASA 402,[21] the user auditor may use the minimum control objectives as a means of assessing the suitability of the control objectives used as criteria in the controls report provided.

27. When assessing the sufficiency and appropriateness of the evidence provided by a type 2 report, ASA 402[22] requires the user auditor to evaluate the adequacy of the time period covered and the time elapsed since performance of the tests of controls. Whilst the longer the time elapsed since the performance of the tests, the less evidence the test may provide, it is necessary for the type 2 report to be available with sufficient time for the user auditor to use the evidence it contains prior to completion of the user entity's audit. It may be necessary for the user auditor to conduct further procedures in response to a modified opinion or deviations reported in the results of the tests performed. Consequently, a type 2 report issued for a time period ending prior to the user entity's period end may be more useful for the user auditor, even if the user auditor needs to obtain additional evidence about the operation of controls in the intervening period.

28. When the service organisation has used a subservice organisation in providing investment management services to the user entity and those services are excluded from the type 1 or 2 report, ASA 402 requires, if those services are relevant to the audit of the user entity, the user auditor to apply the requirements of ASA 402 with respect to the services of the subservice organisation.[23]

29. If a type 2 report provides the user auditor with sufficient appropriate audit evidence as to the reliability of controls over the investment management services provided by the service organisation to the user entity, it will enable the user auditor to reduce the

18 See ASA 402, paragraph 16.

19 See ASA 402, paragraph 17.

20 See Appendix 3 of this Guidance Statement.

21 See ASA 402, paragraphs 13 and A21.

22 See ASA 402, paragraphs 17(c) and A32.

23 See ASA 402, paragraph 18.

extent of substantive testing that might otherwise have been necessary with respect to the balances or transactions subject to those services.

30. A type 2 report is not necessary, if the user auditor concludes that the risk of material misstatement will not be affected by the controls at the service organisation or that it is more appropriate to gather the evidence required by alternative procedures. These alternative procedures may include obtaining a service auditor's report on financial information.

Using a Service Auditor's Report on Financial Information

31. In responding to the assessed risks of material misstatement, if sufficient appropriate audit evidence is not available from records held at the user entity, ASA 402 requires the user auditor to perform further audit procedures or use another auditor to perform those procedures at the service organisation.[24] Whilst the user auditor may be able to rely on a type 2 report as audit evidence of the operating effectiveness of controls to mitigate identified risks of material misstatement, a type 2 report alone cannot provide sufficient appropriate audit evidence with respect to material balances or classes of transactions of the user entity. ASA 330 requires the user auditor to design and perform substantive procedures for each material class of transactions, account balance and disclosure.

32. Service organisations which provide investment management services may provide the user entity with a single financial statement regarding financial information of the user entity ("Statement") periodically in accordance with either a general purpose framework or special purpose framework.[25] Examples of a Statement include: a portfolio valuation report, a financial report or a component of a financial report. The requirements of the applicable financial reporting framework determine the form and content of the Statement. An unaudited Statement is an unverified source of evidence, which is a representation not independent from the user entity. If the financial report of the user entity has been prepared using unaudited financial information obtained from the service organisation, such information may not constitute sufficient appropriate audit evidence on which the user auditor could form an opinion.

33. The user auditor's procedures at the user entity with respect to the balances and transactions relating to the services provided by the service organisation are usually limited to:

- A review of the contract or service level agreement between the user entity and the service organisation so as to understand the rights and obligations of each party.
- A review and evaluation of the monitoring controls exercised by the user entity over the service organisation.
- A review of representations given by the service organisation concerning the user entity's balances or transactions.
- Verification of the receipt of income from the service organisation (if not re-invested).
- Analytical procedures on the financial information supplied by the service organisation.
- A review of the most recent audited financial report of the service organisation.

These procedures alone, or even in combination with a type 1 or 2 report on controls over the relevant investment management services, may not generate sufficient appropriate audit evidence.

34. The user auditor exercises professional judgement to determine whether the results of procedures conducted at the user entity as described in paragraph 33 of this Guidance Statement, considered alone or in combination with a type 1 or 2 report, provide sufficient appropriate evidence on which to form an audit opinion. If the user auditor requires further audit evidence, which the user auditor believes to be held at the service organisation, the user auditor either:

(a) obtains a service auditor's report on financial information; or

(b) gains access to the records and other information relating to the user entity in the possession of the service organisation.

24 See ASA 402, paragraph 15.

25 See ASA 700 *Forming an Opinion and Reporting on a Financial Report* for the definition of general purpose framework and ASA 800 for the definition of special purpose framework.

35. Individual circumstances determine whether a service auditor's report on financial information is the more effective or efficient method of obtaining the audit evidence required by the user auditor. If the user auditor is able to specify whether the service auditor prepares a service auditor's report on specified assertions or on a Statement, the user auditor must exercise professional judgement to make this determination in the particular circumstances of the engagement.

36. A service auditor's report on a Statement, as defined in paragraph 7(b)(ii) of this Guidance Statement, may be the most effective way to obtain sufficient appropriate audit evidence for all assertions regarding the user entity's balances or transactions contained in the Statement provided by the service organisation. This type of report may also be required by the user auditor if there is a potential or identified significant deficiency in the service organisation's controls, or there are material errors identified in the service organisation's reports.

37. The user auditor may be able to obtain sufficient appropriate audit evidence only for certain assertions relating to the user entity's balances or transactions contained in the Statement from information available from the user entity's records and from audit procedures performed thereon by the user auditor. For the remaining assertions, a service auditor's report on specified assertions, as defined in paragraph 7(b)(i) of this Guidance Statement, could provide the audit evidence required. This may include any of the assertions identified in ASA 315, which are:

(a) for classes of transactions and events for the period under audit: occurrence, completeness, accuracy, cut-off and classification;

(b) for account balances at the period end: existence, rights and obligations, completeness, valuation and allocation; and

(c) for presentation and disclosure: occurrence and rights and obligations, completeness, classification and understandability, and accuracy and valuation.

In many circumstances, the use of a service auditor's report on specified assertions in conjunction with a type 2 report provide the user auditor with sufficient appropriate audit evidence concerning the balances or transactions reported in the Statement.

38. In evaluating the audit evidence provided by a service auditor's report on financial information, the user auditor considers:

(a) the professional competence of the service auditor in the context of the assignment conducted;

(b) the sufficiency and appropriateness of the evidence, whether on its own or in conjunction with a type 1 or 2 report, provided by the service auditor's report on financial information regarding the assertions on which evidence is required;

(c) the impact of any modification to the service auditor's report on financial information on the sufficiency and appropriateness of the evidence provided by the report;

(d) the effect of any uncorrected misstatements reported by the service auditor in an attachment to their report, as described in paragraph 89 of this Guidance Statement; and

(e) the effect of any other matters, including significant deficiencies in internal control, significant findings from the audit, or fraud identified during the audit or reported by the service organisation to the user entity.

Materiality for Service Auditor's Reports on Financial Information

39. Paragraphs 84 to 85 of this Guidance Statement provide an appropriate basis for the service auditor to determine materiality for auditing specified assertions or a Statement. The user auditor, in determining performance materiality under Auditing Standard ASA 320[26] for the classes of transactions, account balances or disclosures affected by the services of the service organisation, may determine that the performance materiality level which would

26 See ASA 320 *Materiality in Planning and Performing an Audit.*

be determined by the service auditor in applying this Guidance Statement is not suitable for the purposes of the audit of the user entity's financial report. In these circumstances, the user auditor may request that an alternative benchmark and/or percentage is used by the service auditor to determine performance materiality. The manner in which such a request is ordinarily communicated is discussed in paragraphs 42 and 44 of this Guidance Statement.

40. The user auditor makes the user auditor's own assessment of the materiality of any uncorrected misstatements communicated by the service auditor in the attachment, if any, to the service auditor's report on financial information, as described in paragraph 89 of this Guidance Statement.

Communicating with the Service Auditor

41. ASA 402 requires the user auditor to obtain an understanding of the nature of the relationship between the user entity and the service organisation, including the relevant contractual terms for the activities undertaken by the service organisation. The contract or service level agreement may specify whether:[27]

(a) a type 1 or 2 report on controls will be provided;

(b) the user auditor will have access to the accounting records of the user entity maintained by the service organisation and other information relevant to the audit; and

(c) the agreement allows for direct communication between the user auditor and service auditor.

42. If there is no direct relationship between the user auditor and the service auditor, communication is conducted through the user entity and service organisation. This is often the case when using a report on controls as there may be multiple user entities for which the report is provided. In considering the reliability of the information to be used as audit evidence,[28] if a report on controls is provided indirectly through the user entity and service organisation, the user auditor remains alert to fraud risk factors in the context of establishing the report's authenticity.

43. The user auditor may engage the service auditor directly, subject to relevant ethical and confidentiality considerations, to provide a report on financial information of the user entity maintained by the service organisation.[29]

44. The user auditor's engagement letter may provide for the user entity to obtain from the service organisation, where possible, a type 1 or 2 report, a service auditor's report on financial information or agreement to direct communication between the user auditor and the service auditor.

Communicating With Those Charged With Governance of the User Entity

45. The user auditor is required under the Australian Auditing Standards to communicate any of the following matters identified to those charged with governance of the user entity on a timely basis:

(a) significant deficiencies in internal control identified during the audit;[30]

(b) significant findings from the audit;[31]

(c) uncorrected misstatements and the effect they, individually or in aggregate, may have on the opinion in the auditor's report;[32] and

GS

27 See ASA 402, paragraphs 9(d) and A8.

28 See ASA 500 *Audit Evidence*.

29 See ASA 402, paragraph A9.

30 See ASA 265 *Communicating Deficiencies in Internal Control to Those Charged with Governance and Management*.

31 See ASA 260 *Communication with Those Charged with Governance*.

32 See ASA 450 *Evaluation of Misstatements Identified during the Audit*.

(d) fraud, identified or suspected, involving management, employees who have significant roles in internal control or others where the fraud results in a material misstatement, as well as any other matters related to fraud that are relevant to their responsibilities.[33]

46. In determining whether there are any matters which the user auditor needs to report to those charged with governance of the user entity, as outlined in paragraph 45 of this Guidance Statement, with respect to the investment management services provided by the service organisation, the user auditor's procedures may include:

- A review of documentation and correspondence at the user entity regarding oversight and monitoring of the performance of the contract and/or service level agreement by the service organisation.
- Enquiries of those charged with governance, management or others within the user entity regarding whether any matters reported to those charged with governance of the service organisation, which may affect one or more user entities, have been reported by the service organisation to the user entity.
- Identification of any deviations reported by the service auditor in the type 1 or 2 report and evaluation of whether those deviations represent significant deficiencies in the user entity's internal control.
- Enquiries regarding the reasons for any modification to the service auditor's type 1 or 2 report or report on financial information.
- Identification of any uncorrected misstatements reported by the service auditor, in an attachment to the service auditor's report on financial information as described in paragraph 89 of this Guidance Statement.

47. If a type 1 or 2 controls report is available, ASA 402 requires the user auditor to enquire of management of the user entity whether the service organisation has reported to the user entity, or the user entity is aware of, any fraud, non-compliance with laws and regulations or uncorrected misstatements affecting the financial report of the user entity. These matters of governance interest may be communicated to the user entity by the service organisation, otherwise the service auditor is required to take appropriate action, which may include communication of such matters directly to the user entity. The service auditor may become aware of such matters as a result of the written representations which it is required to obtain from the service organisation. In addition, a service organisation may be required under the contract or service level agreement with the user entity to disclose matters, including those listed in paragraph 45 of this Guidance Statement, that may affect the user entity. The user auditor evaluates the effect of any matters reported on the nature, timing and extent of further audit procedures.[34]

48. Where the user auditor does not have sufficient information regarding the matters of governance interest to fulfil the user auditor's responsibility, as outlined in paragraph 45 of this Guidance Statement, the user auditor may request further information to be provided. Whilst this information may be provided by the service auditor, the request is ordinarily made through the user entity.

Reporting by the User Auditor

49. If the user auditor concludes that the user entity's financial report contains material misstatements with respect to the services provided by the service organisation or that the user auditor is unable to obtain sufficient appropriate audit evidence regarding the services provided by the service organisation relevant to the audit to form an opinion, Auditing Standard ASA 705 requires the user auditor to modify their opinion on the user entity's financial report.[35]

33 See ASA 240 *The Auditor's Responsibilities Relating to Fraud in an Audit of a Financial Report.*

34 See ASA 402, paragraphs 19 and A41, and ASAE 3402, paragraphs 38 and 56.

35 See ASA 705 *Modifications to the Opinion in the Independent Auditor's Report* and ASA 402, paragraph 20.

50. In accordance with ASA 402,[36] when using a type 1 or 2 report on controls, and Auditing Standards ASA 600 and ASA 620,[37] when using a service auditor's report on financial information, the user auditor does not refer to the work of a service auditor in the user auditor's report, unless required to do so by law or regulation or if it is relevant to understanding a modification to the user auditor's opinion.

B: Guidance for the Service Auditor

Types of Engagements

51. Under a contract, offer document or service level agreement, the service organisation may agree to provide the user entity periodically with a type 1 or 2 report on controls, prepared in accordance with ASAE 3402, with respect to the services provided to the user entity and/or a Statement, with respect to the user entity's assets, liabilities or transactions recorded by the service organisation for the period, accompanied by a service auditor's report on the Statement or specified assertions, issued in accordance with ASA 805.

Engagements to Report on Controls

Nature of Engagement

52. Service auditor's engagements to report on controls are assurance engagements, which are defined under the *Framework for Assurance Engagements* as engagements in which the auditor expresses a conclusion or opinion about the outcome of the evaluation of a subject matter against criteria. The criteria for an engagement to report on a service organisation's controls, include control objectives.[38] The control objectives collectively reflect the level of control over user entities' balances or transactions that the user entity could reasonably expect from the service organisation for the purpose of the user entity's financial reporting. The service organisation's controls are designed to meet those control objectives. Appendix 3 of this Guidance Statement sets out the control objectives which the user entity can expect to be included in type 1 or 2 reports for each of the relevant investment management services. The service organisation may choose to include additional control objectives in the type 1 or 2 report. Additional control objectives may be included where those objectives are relevant to user entities' financial reporting or to meet compliance reporting requirements or the terms of the service level agreement, offer document or contract.

Acceptance and Continuance of Engagements to Report on Controls

53. When agreeing to accept, or continue, an engagement to report on controls at a service organisation, ASAE 3402[39] requires the service auditor to assess whether the criteria will be suitable and available to user entities and their auditors. In doing so, the service auditor determines whether the criteria include the control objectives provided in this Guidance Statement for the relevant investment management services and, if any objectives are omitted or amended, whether the service organisation has adequately disclosed and justified that omission or amendment.

54. An example of an engagement letter for engagements to report on controls is provided in Appendix 1 Example 1.

GS

36 See ASA 402, paragraphs 21 and 22.

37 See ASA 600 *Special Considerations—Audits of a Group Financial report (Including the Work of Component Auditors)* and ASA 620 *Using the Work of an Auditor's Expert*.

38 See ASAE 3402, paragraph 16.

39 See ASAE 3402, paragraphs 13-14 for requirements in accepting and continuing an engagement to report on controls at a service organisation.

Ethical Requirements

55. ASAE 3402 requires the service auditor to comply with relevant ethical requirements including those pertaining to independence, relating to assurance engagements, which does not necessitate the service auditor being independent from each user entity.[40]

56. However, threats to independence may arise with respect to user entities where there are only one or few user entities for the services subject to audit. Threats to independence may also arise with respect to subservice organisations where the controls of the subservice organisation are included in the service organisation's description of its system, under the inclusive method.[41]

57. Service auditors may also need to consider the manner in which their type 1 or 2 report is used and distributed by the service organisation. Examples of how this matter may be addressed in the engagement letter and in the service auditor's type 2 report are contained in Appendix 1 Example 1 and Appendix 4 respectively.

Responsibilities of the Service Organisation

58. It is for management, or, where appropriate, those charged with governance, of the service organisation to decide whether to prepare a report on controls and whether to have this report audited by a service auditor. In certain circumstances, the service organisation may, for example, consider it more appropriate to allow access for user entities and user auditors to the service organisation's records or provide a report on a specific aspect of its operations as it impacts an individual user entity. However, the following guidance is only applicable if the service organisation provides a controls assertion and a description of the system on which the service auditor is engaged to provide an assurance report.

59. The service organisation typically prepares a description of its system to meet the needs of all user entities of a particular investment management service or services. A type 1 or 2 report on the controls at a service organisation covers investment management services provided to user entities which are likely to form part of those user entities' information systems relevant to financial reporting. Circumstances in which the user auditor may require a type 1 report on design and implementation of controls only are set out in paragraph 22 of this Guidance Statement. The value of a type 1 report to the audit of the user entity is limited, so it is appropriate for the service auditor to prepare a type 1 report only in the first year of reporting on controls, to provide a starting point for future reports, or if none of the user entities require a report on the operating effectiveness of controls. Due to its limited value, an example of this report is not provided in this Guidance Statement.

60. The frequency with which the service organisation provides a report on controls and the time period to be covered may be agreed in the contract and/or service level agreement between the user entity and the service organisation or may be set out in an offer document.

61. An example of a service organisation's assertion and description of its system is shown in Appendix 2 of this Guidance Statement.

Assessing the Suitability of the Criteria

62. In assessing whether the service organisation has used suitable criteria in preparing the description of the system, evaluating whether controls are suitably designed and, in the case of type 2 reports, in evaluating whether controls are operating effectively, in accordance with ASAE 3402,[42] the service auditor determines whether the minimum control objectives provided in this Guidance Statement[43] for the relevant investment management service or services are included in the description of the system.

63. It is the responsibility of the service organisation to ensure that the control objectives are sufficient to meet the expectations of user entities and that any omissions or amendments to the minimum control objectives are appropriate. A service organisation may therefore

40 See ASAE 3402, paragraph 11.

41 See ASAE 3402, paragraph 9(g).

42 See ASAE 3402, paragraphs 15-18 for further requirements in assessing the suitability of the criteria.

43 See Appendix 3 of this Guidance Statement.

consider the need to add further objectives and supporting controls where appropriate. The service auditor evaluates the suitability of any additional control objectives specified by the service organisation, by determining if they meet the characteristics of relevance, completeness, reliability, neutrality and understandability.[44]

64. If the service organisation omits or amends a control objective from GS 007 or adds further control objectives, the service auditor can expect those omissions, amendments or additional objectives to be clearly identified in the service organisation's description of the system. If a control objective is omitted, the service organisation may list that objective and note briefly the reasons for its omission. If a control objective is amended to clarify the intended meaning, such as use of terms appropriate to the service organisation's circumstances, or the control objective is expanded, the relevant GS 007 control objective may be treated as included. However, if the meaning of the control objective is changed or the scope of the objective reduced by the modifications, then it is appropriate for the service organisation to report the relevant GS 007 objective as omitted and report the modified objective as an additional objective in the description of the system.

Obtaining an Understanding of the Service Organisation's System

65. ASAE 3402[45] requires the service auditor to obtain an understanding of the service organisation's system, including controls that are included in the scope of the engagement. In doing so, the service auditor identifies the boundaries of that system and ensures that the boundary of the investment management services included in the description of the system does not omit aspects of the services provided which are part of user entities' information system relevant to financial reporting. The description of each investment management service provided in this Guidance Statement is indicative and not definitive. The service organisation may provide multiple investment management services, in which case the service auditor identifies how the services interface.

Conducting the Assurance Engagement to Report on Controls

66. The service auditor complies with the requirements of ASAE 3402 when conducting an assurance engagement to report on controls at the service organisation when:[46]

(a) obtaining evidence regarding the description, design and operating effectiveness of controls;

(b) considering the work of an internal audit function;

(c) obtaining written representations from the service organisation;

(d) considering other information;

(e) enquiring and, if necessary, disclosing subsequent events; and

(f) preparing and assembling documentation.

67. In obtaining evidence regarding the fair presentation of the description, the service auditor evaluates whether the control objectives are reasonable in the circumstances. In doing so, the service auditor determines whether the control objectives from Appendix 3 of this Guidance Statement for the relevant investment management service/s have been included or, for any objectives which have been omitted or amended, the adequacy of the reasons for their omission or amendment. If there are any unjustified omissions or misstatements with regard to the control objectives, the service auditor asks management, or those charged with governance, to amend the description. If it is not amended, the service auditor considers the reasons, if known, for the omission or misstatement and the effect on the service auditor's type 1 or 2 report.

GS

44 See ASAE 3000 *Assurance Engagements other than Audits or Reviews of Historical Financial Information*, on assessing the suitability of criteria.

45 See ASAE 3402, paragraph 20.

46 See ASAE 3402, paragraphs 21-52.

The Service Auditor's Assurance Report[47]

68. The service auditor's opinion is expressed in a written assurance report on controls attached to the service organisation's description of its system and assertion.

69. The service auditor's type 1 or 2 report, includes the basic elements required by ASAE 3402 with specific consideration of matters relevant to investment management services, including:

    (a) A statement that the criteria include the minimum control objectives provided in this Guidance Statement for the relevant investment management services; and

    (b) A statement that the service organisation is responsible for:

        (i) Providing the investment management services covered by the service organisation's description of its system; and

        (ii) Stating the control objectives, including those for the relevant investment management services from this Guidance Statement, and if any minimum control objectives are omitted or amended, providing an explanation of that omission or amendment.

An example of a service auditor's type 2 assurance report is shown at Appendix 4.

Describing Tests of Operating Effectiveness

70. The service auditor's type 2 report includes a separate attachment that describes the service auditor's tests of controls and the results thereof. An explanation of the service auditor's description of the nature, timing and extent of tests applied to controls is in Appendix 5 of this Guidance Statement.

Modified Opinions

71. When preparing the assurance report, the service auditor is required to modify their opinion in the circumstances set out in ASAE 3402. If the service auditor concludes that the control objectives for the investment management services are incomplete and the service organisation refuses to amend their report to address those control objectives, the service auditor may modify their opinion if it has a material impact on the fair presentation of the description.

Other Communication Responsibilities

72. ASAE 3402 requires the service auditor to determine whether non-compliance with laws and regulations, fraud, or uncorrected errors which are not clearly trivial, have been communicated to affected user entities and, if not, to take appropriate action.

Engagements to Report on Financial Information

Nature of Engagements

73. If the service auditor is engaged to provide a report on financial information, the service auditor issues a separate auditor's report in respect of each user entity concerning only that user entity's balances and/or transactions.

74. In performing an engagement to report on specified assertions or on a Statement the service auditor applies the Australian Auditing Standards and reports on the engagement under ASA 805.

75. If the service auditor has provided assurance on controls in a type 2 report, it provides assurance as to the reliability of controls over the investment management services which relate to the user entity's balances and/or transactions. Accordingly, the service auditor may be able to reduce the extent of substantive testing that might otherwise be necessary in preparing a service auditor's report on financial information.

47 See ASAE 3402, paragraphs 53-56.

Acceptance and Continuance of Audit Engagements to Report on Financial Information

76. Before accepting the engagement, the service auditor is required under Auditing Standard ASA 210[48] to determine the acceptability of the financial reporting framework, which in the case of a single financial statement or element, includes determining whether application of the financial reporting framework will result in a presentation that provides adequate disclosures to enable the intended users to understand the information conveyed and the effect of material transactions and events on the information conveyed.[49]

77. The service auditor also complies with ASA 210 in agreeing the terms of engagement. In addition to the matters specified in ASA 210, the engagement letter or other written agreement between the service auditor and the engaging party may include:

- The service auditor's responsibility to conduct the engagement with reference to this Guidance Statement.
- The service auditor's responsibility to report, in an attachment to the service auditor's report, uncorrected misstatements which have been aggregated during the audit, other than amounts which are clearly trivial.
- Reference to the performance materiality level provided by the user auditor, if applicable.

Example engagement letters for engagements to report on specified assertions and on a Statement are included in Appendix 1, Examples 2 and 3 respectively.

78. The service auditor may be engaged by the service organisation or directly by the user entity or user auditor. If the user entity or user auditor engages the service auditor directly, access to the service organisation's records will need to be agreed with the service organisation. Access to the service organisation's records may be allowed for in the service level agreement with the user entity or by separate agreement. The agreement may provide for the service organisation to receive a copy of the auditor's report and notification of any matters of governance interest communicated as described in paragraph 88 of this Guidance Statement.

Ethical Requirements

79. In accordance with Auditing Standard ASA 200,[50] the service auditor is required to comply with relevant ethical requirements, including those pertaining to independence, when performing an audit of a Statement or specified assertions.

80. Relevant ethical requirements, defined in Auditing Standard ASA 102, include the fundamental principles of professional ethics, relating to the engagement to be undertaken, which are:

(a) integrity;

(b) objectivity;

(c) professional competence and due care;

(d) confidentiality; and

(e) professional behaviour.

81. Where the service auditor is undertaking an audit of a Statement or specified assertion particular consideration needs to be given to any threats to independence with respect to the user entity since the service auditor is reporting on financial information of the user entity. Threats to independence with respect to the user entity may be present, such as self-interest or familiarity threats, notwithstanding that the user entity may not be an assurance client of the service auditor.

82. In evaluating threats to independence and considering applicable safeguards, the service auditor considers the nature of the engagement. It may be sufficient, for example in the

---

48 See ASA 210 *Agreeing the Terms of Audit Engagements.*

49 See ASA 805.

50 See ASA 200 *Overall Objectives of the Independent Auditor and the Conduct of an Audit in Accordance with Australian Auditing Standards.*

GS

case of a restricted use report, to apply independence requirements in evaluating the independence of the engagement team members and their immediate and close family with respect to the user entity, along with limited consideration of the firm's interests and relationships with the user entity.

83. Examples of safeguards that may be considered appropriate by service auditors to manage identified threats to independence include:

- Prohibiting the holding of direct, or material indirect, financial interests in the user entity or its affiliates by members of the service auditor's engagement team and their immediate and close family.
- Removal from the service auditor's engagement team of any personnel with a close relationship with directors, officers or employees of the user entity or its affiliates.

Materiality to be Applied by the Service Auditor

84. When conducting an audit of specified assertions or a Statement, the service auditor considers materiality under ASA 320 in determining the nature, timing and extent of audit procedures and evaluating the effect of misstatements. The relevant benchmark, for investment management services, on which the service auditor bases materiality, under ASA 320, in most cases is either:

(a) the assets of the user entity for which specific assertions are being audited;

(b) total assets of the user entity reported in the Statement; or

(c) net assets, where assets and liabilities are reported, of the user entity reported in the Statement.

85. The service auditor often applies a percentage to the benchmark as a starting point in determining materiality under ASA 320. The user auditor may request that a particular benchmark or percentage be used by the service auditor as a basis for determining performance materiality. In the absence of a basis for materiality specified by the user auditor, the service auditor may apply a percentage of 0.5% to any of the benchmarks listed in paragraph 84 of this Guidance Statement as a reasonable basis for determining performance materiality for auditing specified assertions or a Statement, where investment management services are provided. Where an alternative benchmark is used, this percentage may not be appropriate for determining materiality.

The Service Auditor's Report on Financial Information

86. Service auditor's reports on specified assertions or on a Statement, need to comply with the requirements in ASA 805 and as such include the basic elements of an auditor's report as set out in that standard. In addition to these elements, the service auditor includes in their report:

(a) identification of the specific assertions audited (if the report is limited to specific assertions);

(b) identification of the investment management services provided by the service organisation to the user entity;

(c) a description of the responsible party's (management, or those charged with governance, of the service organisation) responsibilities for the investment management services provided to the user entity; and

(d) reference to the use of the report by the user entity and the user auditor.

Examples of a service auditor's report on specified assertions is provided in Appendix 6 Example 1 and a service auditor's report on a Statement is provided in Appendix 6 Example 2 of this Guidance Statement.

Information Excluded from the Service Auditor's Report

87. When performing an audit engagement at a service organisation, the service auditor may restrict the audit procedures to information that is held by the service organisation on behalf of the user entity. The Statement, however, may include information which is provided by the user entity or by another party to the service organisation for inclusion

in the Statement. Documentation or other audit evidence may not be available at the service organisation to substantiate that information. Where certain information within the Statement has not been audited, the service auditor identifies that information and specifically excludes it from the scope of the audit opinion.

Reporting of Matters of Governance Interest Arising in an Audit Engagement on Financial Information

88. In the course of performing procedures for an audit engagement at a service organisation on financial information of the user entity, the service auditor is required to communicate any of the following matters identified to those charged with governance of the engaging party on a timely basis:

(a) significant deficiencies in internal control;[51]

(b) significant findings from the audit;[52]

(c) uncorrected misstatements and the effect they, individually or in aggregate, may have on the opinion in the auditor's report;[53] and

(d) fraud, identified or suspected involving management, employees who have significant roles in internal control or others where the fraud results in a material misstatement, as well as any other matters related to fraud that are relevant to their responsibilities.[54]

89. In addition, the service auditor states in their report whether they have identified any uncorrected misstatements in the course of the audit, other than amounts which are clearly trivial, and, if so, details the uncorrected misstatements in an attachment to their report. An outline for an attachment on uncorrected misstatements is shown in Appendix 6, Examples 1 and 2.

90. When the service auditor is engaged by the service organisation and considers that any of the matters reported to those charged with governance of the service organisation may affect one or more user entities, the service auditor determines from the appropriate level of management whether this information has been communicated to the affected user entities. If the matter is not communicated satisfactorily, the service auditor may consider whether it affects the service auditor's ability to conduct the engagement or necessitates a modification to the service auditor's report.

Conformity with International Pronouncements

91. There is no pronouncement issued by the International Auditing and Assurance Standards Board equivalent to this Guidance Statement.

GS

51 See ASA 265.

52 See ASA 260.

53 See ASA 450.

54 See ASA 240.

Appendix 1

(Ref: Para. 54 and 77)

Example Engagement Letters

The following example engagement letters are not authoritative and are intended only to be a guide that may be used in conjunction with the considerations outlined in GS 007. The engagement letters will need to be varied according to individual requirements and circumstances. They are drafted to refer to an engagement for a single reporting period and would require adaptation if intended or expected to apply to recurring engagements.[55] It may be appropriate to seek legal advice that any proposed engagement letter is suitable.

Example 1: A service auditor's engagement letter to a service organisation for provision of assurance over a type 2 report on the description, design and operating effectiveness of a service organisation's controls.

Example 2: A service auditor's engagement letter to the engaging party for audit of specified assertions of the user entity's assets, liabilities or transactions in a financial statement prepared by a service organisation.

Example 3: A service auditor's engagement letter to the engaging party for an audit of a financial statement of a user entity's assets, liabilities or transactions prepared by a service organisation.

Example 1: Engagement Letter for a Type 2 Report on a Service Organisation's Controls

To [the appropriate representative of management or those charged with governance] of XYZ Service Organisation (XYZ):

[*The objective and scope of the engagement*]

You have requested that we report on the description of XYZ's [investment management service/s provided: custody, asset management, property management, superannuation member administration, investment administration or registry] system and management's assertion with respect to that description, which you will provide and which will accompany our report. The description of XYZ's [investment management service] system comprises control objectives and related controls designed to achieve those objectives for the [period] ended [date]. The control objectives included are the objectives for [investment management service] specified in Guidance Statement GS 007[56] and any additional objectives which are likely to be relevant to internal control as it relates to financial reporting of clients who have used the [investment management service] system.

We are pleased to confirm our acceptance and understanding of this assurance engagement by means of this letter. Our assurance engagement will be conducted with the objective of our expressing an opinion on the fair presentation of the [investment management service] system, suitability of the design of the controls to achieve the control objectives throughout the period and the operating effectiveness of the controls necessary to provide reasonable assurance that the control objectives were achieved throughout the period.

[The responsibilities of the assurance practitioner]

We will conduct our assurance engagement in accordance with Standard on Assurance Engagements ASAE 3402 *Assurance Reports on Controls at a Service Organisation* and with reference to Guidance Statement GS 007 *Audit Implications of the Use of Service Organisations for Investment Management Services*. ASAE 3402 requires that we comply with ethical requirements and plan and perform procedures to obtain reasonable assurance about whether, in all material respects, XYZ's description of the [investment management service] system is fairly presented, the controls are suitably designed, and operating effectively throughout the reporting period. An assurance engagement involves performing procedures to obtain evidence about the description, design and operating effectiveness of controls. The procedures selected depend

55 See ASA 210.

56 See Appendix 3 of this Guidance Statement.

Appendix 1 (continued)

on the assurance practitioner's judgement, including the assessment of the risks of significant deficiencies in the [investment management service] system.

Because of the inherent limitations of an assurance engagement, together with the inherent limitations of any internal control system there is an unavoidable risk that some significant deficiencies may not be detected, even though the engagement is properly planned and performed in accordance with Standards on Assurance Engagements.

The system, within which the controls that we will test operate, will not be examined except to the extent the system is likely to be relevant to clients, as it relates to financial reporting. Hence no opinion will be expressed as to the effectiveness of the internal control system as a whole.

The work undertaken by us to form an opinion, is permeated by judgement, in particular regarding the nature, timing and extent of assurance procedures for gathering evidence and the drawing of conclusions based on the evidence gathered. In addition to the inherent limitations in any assurance engagement, which include the use of testing, inherent limitations of any internal control structure, and the possibility of collusion, most evidence is persuasive rather than conclusive. As a result, an assurance engagement can only provide reasonable – not absolute – assurance that the description is fairly presented, controls are suitably designed and controls have operated effectively throughout the period.

[The responsibilities of management and identification of the applicable control framework]

Our assurance engagement will be conducted on the basis that [management or, where appropriate, those charged with governance] acknowledge and understand that they have responsibility:

(a) for the preparation of a written assertion that, in all material respects, and based on suitable criteria:

  (i) the description fairly presents XYZ's [investment management service] system designed and implemented throughout the period;

  (ii) the controls related to the control objectives stated in XYZ's description of its system were suitably designed throughout the specified period; and

  (iii) the controls related to the control objectives stated in XYZ's description of its system operated effectively throughout the specified period.

(b) for design of the system, comprising controls which will achieve control objectives which are likely to be relevant to clients', who have used the [investment management service] system, internal control as it relates to financial reporting;

(c) to provide us with:

  (i) Access to all information of which those charged with governance and management are aware that is relevant to the design, implementation and operation of the [investment management service] system;

  (ii) Additional information that we may request from those charged with governance and management for the purposes of this assurance engagement; and

  (iii) Unrestricted access to persons within the entity from whom we determine it necessary to obtain evidence.

As part of our assurance process, we will request from [management and, where appropriate, those charged with governance], written confirmation concerning representations made to us in connection with the engagement.

XYZ's description of the system will include the minimum control objectives for [investment management service] set out in GS 007, but they may add to or amend these to the extent necessary such that the control objectives are likely to be relevant to internal control as it relates to financial reporting of clients, who have used the [investment management service] system. If [management/those charged with governance] consider any of the control objectives from GS 007 for [investment management service] are not applicable to XYZ or require amendment, then they will include an explanation of the omission of or amendment to that objective in XYZ's description of the system.

GS

Appendix 1 (continued)

[Assurance Approach]

We will examine and evaluate the control objectives and controls for the [investment management service] system described above. The "Description of the [investment management service] System" will include details of controls with which clients should comply. While our evaluation will include assessment of the appropriateness of the complementary client controls, our testing will not encompass evaluation of the suitability of design or operating effectiveness of controls carried out by users of XYZ's [investment management service] system. The control objectives stated in XYZ's description of its system can be achieved only if complementary user entity controls are suitably designed or operating effectively, along with the controls at the service organisation.

Our procedures will extend to the control objectives and related controls at relevant subservice organisations only to the extent that those controls are included in XYZ's description of the [investment management service] system and are necessary to achieve the relevant control objectives.

Due to the complex nature of internal control, our assurance procedures will not encompass all individual controls at XYZ, but will be restricted to an examination of those controls reported which achieve the control objectives identified by XYZ's management in the "Description of the [investment management service] System" provided to us.

[Assurance Procedures]

Our assurance procedures are likely to include:

1. Performing a preliminary review of the control environment of XYZ relevant to the [investment management service] system.
2. Evaluating the reasonableness of the control objectives, including assessing how they address the minimum control objectives for [investment management service] provided in GS 007.
3. Evaluating the completeness, accuracy and presentation of the "Description of the [investment management service] System" against the controls implemented.
4. Evaluating the design of specific controls by:
   - Assessing the risks that threaten the achievement of the control objectives.
   - Evaluating whether the controls described are capable of addressing those risks and achieving the related objectives.
5. Performing tests of controls to ascertain whether the degree of compliance with controls is sufficient to provide reasonable assurance that the controls have achieved their objectives throughout the period.

In undertaking this engagement, we shall work closely with XYZ's internal audit function and place reliance on their work in accordance with Auditing Standard ASA 610 *Using the Work of Internal Auditors* [this paragraph is applicable where the work of internal audit is an integral part of the assurance engagement].

[Assurance Report]

The format of the report will be in accordance with ASAE 3402 and will include an opinion on the "Description of the [investment management service] System" by XYZ management and an accompanying description of the tests of controls that we performed and the results of those tests. An example of the proposed report is contained in the appendix to this letter.

Our report will be issued [frequency] and will cover [period reported on] (paragraph is appropriate for recurring engagements).

The assurance report will be incorporated in a report issued by XYZ containing information prepared by XYZ management to provide clients and their auditors with an overall understanding of [subject matter]. We will review the contents of the report issued by XYZ to identify any material inconsistencies with the "Description of the [investment management service] System".

[Distribution of the Assurance Report]

Our report and the accompanying description of tests of controls are intended only for clients of XYZ that use the [investment management service] system and their auditors, who have a

Appendix 1 (continued)

sufficient understanding to consider it, along with other information including information about controls operated by clients themselves, when assessing the risks of material misstatements of clients' financial reports.

Our assurance report will be prepared for this purpose only and we disclaim any assumption of responsibility for any reliance on our report to any person other than to XYZ's clients and their auditors or for any purpose other than that for which it was prepared.[57]

[Significant Deficiencies in Controls]

We will issue an assurance report without modification, to provide reasonable assurance on the [investment management service] system where our procedures do not disclose a significant deficiency in the controls necessary to achieve the control objectives contained in the "Description of the [investment management service] System" by XYZ management. For this purpose, a significant deficiency exists when prescribed control procedures, or the degree of compliance with them:

(a) does not provide XYZ management with reasonable assurance that the control objectives will be met or that fraud, error, or non-compliance with laws and regulations would be prevented or detected by employees in the normal course of their assigned functions; and

(b) knowledge of that deficiency would be material to users of the assurance report.

If our assurance engagement discloses that there are significant deficiencies in the system of controls in operation during the period covered by the report, such deficiencies will be disclosed in our report even if they were corrected prior to the end of the reporting period. However, our report will indicate that such deficiencies were corrected if that is the case. If any significant deficiencies disclosed in our report have been corrected subsequent to this period (or are in the process of being corrected), we will refer to this in our report.

Although the primary purpose of our assurance engagement will be to enable us to issue the above described report, we will also periodically provide you with letters containing recommendations for strengthening controls if such matters are observed during the process of the assurance engagement. Although issues raised may not represent significant deficiencies in the system of controls, recommendations will address areas where we believe controls could be improved.

We look forward to full co-operation from your staff during our assurance engagement.

[Other relevant information]

[Insert additional information such as fee arrangements, billings and other specific terms, as appropriate.]

Please sign and return the attached copy of this letter to indicate your acknowledgement of, and agreement with, the arrangements for our assurance engagement to report on the controls over XYZ's [investment management service] services to clients, including our respective responsibilities.

Yours faithfully

(signed)

....

Name and Title

Date

Acknowledged on behalf of XYZ

(signed)

....

Name and Title

Date

57 Use of the report and liability limitation: insert additional wording, if any, required to reflect any liability arrangements agreed between the service auditor, the service organisation and other users, including confirmation of the purpose for which the service auditor's report has been prepared and the basis on which other parties may use the report.

Appendix 1 (continued)

Example 2: Engagement Letter for an Audit of Specified Assertions

To [the engaging party]:[58]

[The objective and scope of the audit]

You[59] have requested that we audit the [specified assertions][60] of the assets [and liabilities or transactions] in the [title of the financial statement] of [user entity/entities] ("the Statement"), which comprises the [statement of assets and liabilities] as at [date], and the [statement of transactions] for the [period] then ended, concerning the assets and liabilities of [user entity/entities][61] [nature of investment management service: managed by or in the custody] of the XYZ Service Organisation (XYZ) as at [date].

We are pleased to confirm our acceptance and our understanding of this engagement by means of this letter. Our audit will be conducted with the objective of our expressing an opinion on the [specified assertions] of the assets [and liabilities or transactions] in the Statement.

[The responsibilities of the auditor]

We will conduct our audit in accordance with the Australian Auditing Standards, in particular ASA 805 *Special Considerations—Audit of Single Financial Statements and Specific Elements, Accounts or Items of a Financial Statement*, and with reference to AUASB Guidance Statement GS 007 *Audit Implications of the Use of Service Organisations for Investment Management Services*. Australian Auditing Standards require that we comply with ethical requirements and plan and perform the audit to obtain reasonable assurance whether the Statement is free from material misstatement with respect to the assertions specified. This audit involves performing procedures to obtain audit evidence about the [specified assertions] of the assets [and liabilities or transactions] in the Statement. The procedures selected depend on the auditor's judgement, including the assessment of the risks of material misstatement with respect to the [specified assertions] of the assets [and liabilities or transactions] in the Statement, whether due to fraud or error. An audit also includes evaluating the appropriateness of accounting policies used and the reasonableness of accounting estimates made by management, as well as evaluating the presentation of the Statement with respect to the [specified assertions] of the assets [and liabilities or transactions].

Because of the inherent limitations of an audit, together with the inherent limitations of internal control, there is an unavoidable risk that some material misstatements may not be detected, even though the audit is properly planned and performed in accordance with Australian Auditing Standards.

In making our risk assessments, we consider internal control relevant to XYZ's [specified assertions] of the assets [and liabilities or transactions] in the Statement in order to design audit procedures that are appropriate in the circumstances, but not for the purpose of expressing an opinion on the effectiveness of XYZ's controls.[62] However, we will communicate to you in writing concerning any significant deficiencies in internal controls over financial reporting on

58 The addressees and references in the letter would be those that are appropriate in the circumstances of the engagement, including the relevant jurisdiction. It is important to refer to the appropriate persons – see ASA 210.

59 Throughout this letter, references to "you," "we," "us," "management," "those charged with governance" and "auditor" would be used or amended as appropriate in the circumstances.

60 Insert specified assertions to be audited:

- for transactions or events: occurrence, completeness, accuracy, cut-off and classification;
- for balances: existence, rights and obligations, completeness or valuation and allocation; or
- for presentation and disclosure: occurrence, rights and obligations, completeness, classification and understandability and accuracy and valuation.

61 Where the assets are held in the name of a nominee holding company insert "held in the name of [nominee holding company]".

62 In circumstances when the auditor also has responsibility to express an opinion on the effectiveness of internal control in conjunction with the audit of the specified assertions of the assets [and liabilities or transactions] in the Statement, this sentence would be worded as follows: "In making those risk assessments, the auditor considers internal control relevant to [name of service organisation]'s preparation and fair presentation of [specified assertions] of the assets [and liabilities or transactions] in the Statement in order to design audit procedures that are appropriate in the circumstances."

Appendix 1 (continued)

behalf of [user entity/entities], that we have identified during the audit of the [specified assertions] of the assets [and liabilities or transactions] in the Statement.

We will report any uncorrected misstatements which we have aggregated during the audit but that were determined by management to be immaterial, both individually and in aggregate, to [specified assertions] of the assets [and liabilities or transactions] in the Statement, other than amounts which are clearly trivial, in an attachment to our report.

[The responsibilities of management]

Our audit will be conducted on the basis that [[the engaging party] confirm that][63] management and, where appropriate, those charged with governance,[64] of XYZ acknowledge and understand that they have responsibility:

(a) for the [specified assertions] of the assets [and liabilities or transactions] in the Statement fairly in accordance with the basis of preparation;[65]

(b) for such internal control as XYZ [management] determines is necessary to enable [specified assertions] of the assets [and liabilities or transactions] in the Statement that is free from misstatement, whether due to fraud or error;

(c) to provide us with:

  (i) Access to all information of which those charged with governance and management of XYZ are aware that is relevant to the [specified assertions] of the assets [and liabilities or transactions] in the Statement such as records, documentation and other matters;

  (ii) Additional information that we may request from those charged with governance and management of XYZ for the purpose of the audit; and

  (iii) Unrestricted access to persons within XYZ from whom we determine it necessary to obtain audit evidence.

As part of our audit process, we will request from [management and, where appropriate, those charged with governance of XYZ] written confirmation concerning representations made to us in connection with the audit.

We look forward to full cooperation from [XYZ and][66] your staff during our audit.

[Distribution of the Auditor's Report]

We understand that our report may be incorporated in a report prepared by XYZ for distribution to [the engaging party and] the [Trustee/those charged with governance] of [user entity] for the purpose of fulfilling the [those charged with governance] of XYZ's reporting obligations under the [title of contract or service level agreement]. Our report will be prepared for this purpose only and we disclaim any assumption of responsibility for any reliance on our report, or on the Statement to which it relates, to any person other than [the engaging party], [those charged with governance] of XYZ, [the Trustee/those charged with governance] of [user entity/entities] and their auditor, or for any other purpose other than that for which it was prepared.[67]

[Other relevant information]

[Insert other information, such as fee arrangements, billings and other specific terms, as appropriate.]

[Reporting]

63 Insert where the engaging party is not XYZ Service Organisation, so the engaging party needs to obtain XYZ's acknowledgement of their responsibilities.

64 Use terminology as appropriate in the circumstances, such as "the Directors".

65 Insert "applicable Australian Accounting Standards" where multiple Australian Accounting Standards were applied; insert reference to a specific Australian Accounting Standard where appropriate (for example: "the measurement standards of AAS 25 Financial Reporting by Superannuation Plans."); or "the accounting policies described in Note X to the Statement".

66 Insert where the engaging party is not XYZ Service Organisation.

67 Use of the report and liability limitation: insert additional wording, if any, required to reflect any liability arrangements agreed between the service auditor, the service organisation and other users, including confirmation of the purpose for which the service auditor's report has been prepared and the basis on which other parties may use the report.

Appendix 1 (continued)

[Insert appropriate reference to the expected form and content of the auditor's report.]

The form and content of our report may need to be amended in the light of our audit findings.

[Independence]

We confirm that, to the best of our knowledge and belief, the engagement team are independent of [user entity/entities] in accordance with [specify relevant ethical requirements] in relation to the audit of the [specified assertions] of the assets [and liabilities or transactions] in the Statement. In conducting our audit of the [specified assertions] of the assets [and liabilities or transactions] in the Statement, should we become aware that we are not in compliance with the independence requirements of [specify relevant ethical requirements] we shall notify you on a timely basis.

Please sign and return the attached copy of this letter to indicate your acknowledgement of, and agreement with, the arrangements for our audit of [specified assertions] of the assets [and liabilities or transactions] in the Statement including our respective responsibilities.

Yours faithfully

(signed)

....

Partner

Firm

Acknowledged and agreed on behalf of [engaging party] by

(signed)

....

Name and Title

Date

Example 3: Engagement Letter for an Audit of a Statement

To [the engaging party]:[68]

[The objective and scope of the audit]

You[69] have requested that we audit the [title of financial statement] of [user entity/entities][70] ("the Statement"), which comprises the [statement of assets and liabilities] as at [date], and the [statement of transactions] for the year then ended, concerning the assets [and liabilities or transactions] of [user entity/entities][71] [insert nature of investment management service: managed by or in the custody of] XYZ Service Organisation (XYZ) as at [date].

We are pleased to confirm our acceptance and our understanding of this engagement by means of this letter. Our audit will be conducted with the objective of our expressing an opinion on the Statement.

[The responsibilities of the auditor]

We will conduct our audit in accordance with the Australian Auditing Standards, in particular ASA 805 *Special Considerations—Audits of Single Financial Statements and Specific Elements, Accounts or Items of a Financial Statement*, and with reference to AUASB Guidance Statement GS 007 *Audit Implications of the Use of Service Organisations for Investment Management Services*. Australian Auditing Standards require that we comply with ethical requirements and plan and perform the audit to obtain reasonable assurance whether the Statement is free from material misstatement. [If the user auditor has provided a materiality level to apply in the audit insert: The performance materiality level, which we will apply in determining the nature,

68 The addressees and references in the letter would be those that are appropriate in the circumstances of the engagement, including the relevant jurisdiction. It is important to refer to the appropriate persons – see ASA 210.

69 Throughout this letter, references to "you," "we," "us," "management," "those charged with governance" and "auditor" would be used or amended as appropriate in the circumstances.

70 If certain assertions are specifically excluded from the audit then insert: "except for [specify assertions excluded, e.g. presentation and disclosure] of the Statement".

71 Where the assets are held in the name of a nominee holding company insert "held in the name of [nominee holding company]".

Appendix 1 (continued)

timing and extent of audit procedures and in evaluating the effect of misstatements identified, has been provided by the auditor of [user entity/entities] and is [x] percent of [total assets/net assets]. This audit involves performing procedures to obtain audit evidence about the amounts and disclosures in the Statement. The procedures selected depend on the auditor's judgement, including the assessment of the risks of material misstatement of the Statement, whether due to fraud or error. An audit also includes evaluating the appropriateness of accounting policies used and the reasonableness of accounting estimates made by management, as well as evaluating the overall presentation of the Statement.

Because of the other inherent limitations of an audit, together with the inherent limitations of internal control, there is an unavoidable risk that some material misstatements may not be detected, even though the audit is properly planned and performed in accordance with Australian Auditing Standards.

In making our risk assessments, we consider internal control relevant to XYZ's preparation of the Statement in order to design audit procedures that are appropriate in the circumstances, but not for the purpose of expressing an opinion on the effectiveness of XYZ's controls.[72] However, we will communicate to you in writing concerning any significant deficiencies in internal controls over financial reporting on behalf of [user entity/entities], that we have identified during the audit of the Statement.

We will report any uncorrected misstatements which we have aggregated during the audit but that were determined by management to be immaterial, both individually and in aggregate, to the Statement taken as a whole, other than amounts which are clearly trivial, in an attachment to our report.

[The responsibilities of management and identification of the applicable financial reporting framework]

Our audit will be conducted on the basis that [[the engaging party] confirm that][73] management and, where appropriate, those charged with governance[74] of XYZ acknowledge and understand that they have responsibility:

(a) For the preparation of the Statement that gives a true and fair view in accordance with [specify framework].[75]

(b) For such internal control as XYZ [management] determines is necessary to enable the preparation of a Statement that is free from misstatement, whether due to fraud or error.

(c) To provide us with:

  (i) Access to all information of which those charged with governance and management of XYZ are aware that is relevant to the preparation of the Statement such as records, documentation and other matters;

  (ii) Additional information that we may request from those charged with governance and management of XYZ for the purpose of the audit; and

  (iii) Unrestricted access to persons within XYZ from whom we determine it necessary to obtain audit evidence.

As part of our audit process, we will request from [management and, where appropriate, from those charged with governance of XYZ], written confirmation concerning representations made to us in connection with the audit.

GS

---

72 In circumstances when the auditor also has responsibility to express an opinion on the effectiveness of internal control in conjunction with the audit of the Statement, this sentence would be worded as follows: "In making those risk assessments, the auditor considers internal control relevant to [name of service organisation]'s preparation and fair presentation of the Statement in order to design audit procedures that are appropriate in the circumstances."

73 Insert where the engaging party is not XYZ Service Organisation, so the engaging party needs to obtain XYZ's acknowledgement of their responsibilities.

74 Use terminology as appropriate in the circumstances, such as "the Directors".

75 Insert "applicable Australian Accounting Standards" where multiple Australian Accounting Standards were applied; insert reference to a specific Australian Accounting Standard where appropriate (for example: "the measurement standards of AAS 25 Financial Reporting by Superannuation Plans."); or "the accounting policies described in Note X to the Statement".

Appendix 1 (continued)

We look forward to full cooperation from [XYZ and][76] your staff during our audit.

[Distribution of the Auditor's Report]

We understand that our report may be incorporated in a report prepared by XYZ for distribution to [the engaging party and] the [Trustee/those charged with governance] of [user entity] for the purpose of fulfilling the [those charged with governance] of XYZ's reporting obligations under the [title of contract or service level agreement]. Our report will be prepared for this purpose only and we disclaim any assumption of responsibility for any reliance on our report, or on the Statement to which it relates, to any person other than [the engaging party], [those charged with governance] of XYZ, [the Trustee/those charged with governance] of [user entity/entities] and their auditor, or for any other purpose other than that for which it was prepared.[77]

[Other relevant information]

[Insert other information, such as fee arrangements, billings and other specific terms, as appropriate.]

[Reporting]

[Insert appropriate reference to the expected form and content of the auditor's report.]

The form and content of our report may need to be amended in the light of our audit findings.

[Independence]

We confirm that, to the best of our knowledge and belief, the engagement team is independent of [user entity/entities] in accordance with [specify relevant ethical requirements] in relation to the audit of the Statement. In conducting our audit of the Statement, should we become aware that we have contravened the independence requirements of [specify relevant ethical requirements] we shall notify you on a timely basis.

Please sign and return the attached copy of this letter to indicate your acknowledgement of, and agreement with, the arrangements for our audit of the Statement including our respective responsibilities.

Yours faithfully

(signed)

....

Partner

Firm

Acknowledged and agreed on behalf of [the engaging party] by

(signed)

....

Name and Title

Date

76 Insert where the engaging party is not XYZ Service Organisation.

77 Use of the report and liability limitation: insert additional wording, if any, required to reflect any liability arrangements agreed between the service auditor, the service organisation and other users, including confirmation of the purpose for which the service auditor's report has been prepared and the basis on which other parties may use the report.

Appendix 2

(Ref: Para. 61)

Service Organisation's Type 2 Controls Assertion and Description of the System

The following example is for use as a guide only, in conjunction with the considerations described in this Guidance Statement, and is not intended to be exhaustive or applicable to all situations.

Service Organisation's Type 2 Assertion on the [Investment Management Service] System

Assertion by XYZ Service Organisation (XYZ)

The accompanying description has been prepared for clients who have used the [investment management service] system and their auditors who have a sufficient understanding to consider the description, along with other information including information about controls operated by clients themselves, when assessing the risks of material misstatements of clients' financial reports/statements. XYZ confirms that:

(a) The accompanying description at pages [bb-cc] fairly presents the [investment management service] system for processing clients' transactions throughout the period [date] to [date]. The criteria used in making this assertion were that the accompanying description:

(i) Presents how the system was designed and implemented, including:

- The types of services provided, including, as appropriate, classes of transactions processed.
- The procedures, within both information technology and manual systems, by which those transactions were initiated, recorded, processed, corrected as necessary, and transferred to the reports prepared for clients.
- The related accounting records, supporting information and specific accounts that were used to initiate, record, process and report transactions; this includes the correction of incorrect information and how information was transferred to the reports prepared for clients.
- How the system dealt with significant events and conditions, other than transactions.
- The process used to prepare reports for clients.
- Relevant control objectives and controls designed to achieve those objectives, including the control objectives for [investment management service] provided in Guidance Statement 007 *Audit Implications of the Use of Service Organisations for Investment Management Services* except for [number excluded] control objectives which have been amended or omitted for the reasons set out in the attached Description of Controls in Operation.[78]
- Controls that we assumed, in the design of the system, would be implemented by clients, and which, if necessary to achieve control objectives stated in the accompanying description, are identified in the description along with the specific control objectives that cannot be achieved by ourselves alone.
- Other aspects of our control environment, risk assessment process, information system (including the related business processes) and communication, control activities and monitoring controls that were relevant to processing and reporting clients' transactions.

(ii) Includes relevant details of changes to the system during the period [date] to [date].

(iii) Does not omit or distort information relevant to the scope of the system being described, while acknowledging that the description is prepared to meet the common

78 Insert if certain control objectives specified in this Guidance Statement are not met by relevant controls.

GS

Appendix 2 (continued)

needs of a broad range of clients and their auditors and may not, therefore, include every aspect of the system that each individual client may consider important in its own particular environment.

(b) The controls related to the control objectives stated in the accompanying description were suitably designed and operated effectively throughout the period [date] to [date]. The criteria used in making this assertion were that:

(i) The risks that threatened achievement of the control objectives stated in the description were identified;

(ii) The identified controls would, if operated as described, provide reasonable assurance that those risks did not prevent the stated control objectives from being achieved; and

(iii) The controls were consistently applied as designed, including that manual controls were applied by individuals who have the appropriate competence and authority, throughout the period [date] to [date].

....

Signed on behalf of [management or those charged with governance] of XYZ

Date

Attachment 1: Description of the [Investment Management Service] System Accompanying XYZ Service Organisation Management's Assertion

XYZ Service Organisation's [Investment Management Service] System

Services Provided

XYZ Service Organisation (XYZ) provides its clients with [investment management service/s: custody; asset management, property management, superannuation member administration, investment administration or registry] services, which involves [describe services provided].

The System

The stated internal control objectives and related controls included in this report apply to XYZ operations as they relate only to [investment management service] services. Specifically excluded from this report are controls within individual systems, controls executed at client premises and other services provided by XYZ, including [other related services provided to clients].

The effectiveness of controls performed by clients of XYZ should also be considered as part of the overall system of control relating to XYZ's [investment management service] services.

[Describe, as appropriate:[79]

- *The procedures, within both information technology and manual systems, by which those transactions were initiated, recorded, processed, corrected as necessary, and transferred to the reports prepared for clients.*
- *The related accounting records, supporting information and specific accounts that were used to initiate, record, process and report transactions; this includes the correction of incorrect information and how information is transferred to the reports prepared for clients.*
- *How the system dealt with significant events and conditions, other than transactions.*
- *The process used to prepare reports for clients.*

This may include a description of the flow of transactions or a flowchart].[80]

79 Aspects of the system to be described here relate to the manner in which the system operates to provide services to clients but do not include specific controls which are designed to achieve the control objectives.

80 The description may be presented in various formats such as narratives, flowcharts, tables or graphics, with an indication of the extent of manual and computer processing used.

Appendix 2 (continued)

[Controls at Subservice Organisations][81]

[XYZ uses [name of subservice organisation] to provide [type or name of] services, which form part of the [investment management service] system used by XYZ clients. The [type or name of] services provided by [subservice organisation] are [describe the nature of the services provided]. XYZ's description of the system includes XYZ's monitoring controls over the operating effectiveness of the controls at [subservice organisation] and [includes/excludes][82] the relevant control objectives and related controls of [subservice organisation].

Internal Control Objectives and Related Controls

We set out in this report the control objectives and related controls implemented for XYZ. The specific controls set out in the remainder of the report have been designed to achieve each of the control objectives. The controls have been in place throughout the period from [date] to [date] unless otherwise indicated.

The controls which were in operation at XYZ throughout the period from [date] to [date], or during a lesser period where specified, to ensure that the identified control objectives over [investment management service] are achieved were:

Internal Control Objective

[Control objectives, including the minimum control objectives for the relevant investment management service/s from GS 007 Appendix 3 and, for any minimum control objectives omitted, the reason for that omission.][83]

Related Controls

[List controls in operation during the specified period relating to each control objective.]

*[**Period of operation:** If the control has not been in operation the entire period or has changed, state the period during which the control was operating and the period during which the change was effective.]*[84]

*[**Complementary client controls:** Describe any complementary user entity controls contemplated in the design of the controls.]* [85]

81 Insert this section if XYZ uses a subservice organisation which performs some of the services provided to clients which use the system.

82 Use "includes" if the inclusive method is used and "excludes" if the carve-out method is used with respect to the subservice organisation's services. See ASAE 3402, paragraph 9(a) for definition of carve-out method and paragraph 9(g) for definition of inclusive method.

83 Where the control objective is excluded from the system description, insert: "This control objective is not relevant to the operation of [service organisation]'s [investment management service] services because [specify reasons] and so has not been addressed by related controls."

84 This section should be inserted for each control which has not been in operation for the whole period or has changed during the period.

85 This section should be inserted for each control for which there are complementary user entity controls contemplated in the design of the control. See ASAE 3402 paragraph 9(b) for definition of complementary user entity controls.

Appendix 3

(Ref: Para. 14, 62)

Minimum Control Objectives for Each Investment Management Service

This Appendix sets out detailed control objectives for the investment management services referred to in paragraph 14 of this Guidance Statement and further defined below. The control objectives listed are the minimum objectives which the service auditor and users of a type 1 or 2 report may reasonably expect to be addressed in the service organisation's description of its investment management service system for each service, but are not intended to be exhaustive. Where a combination of multiple investment management services are provided the service organisation ensures that the combined control objectives adequately address the service offering and that additional objectives are added where there are gaps between the set of objectives for each service.

The control objectives included are those which are likely to be relevant to user entities' controls as they relate to financial reporting and not for other purposes, such as to meet compliance requirements or to assess performance with respect to service level agreements. It remains the responsibility of management, or those charged with governance, of the service organisation to ensure that the described control objectives are likely to be relevant to client's controls as they relate to financial reporting. Unitised funds themselves will not usually prepare controls reports, unless specifically requested to do so, as investors in unitised funds usually rely on publicly available unit prices, where appropriate, with additional procedures to assess the bona fides of the fund such as sighting audited financial statements of the fund, for valuation of their investments, so investors' auditors will not usually need to rely on the unitised fund's controls.

Control objectives for transition of specific user entities to a new investment management service organisation are also not addressed in these minimum control objectives, as they are not relevant to the general financial reporting needs of all user entities, rather they relate to each individual transitioning user entity. A separate engagement may be agreed with the service organisation and service auditor where assurance over the transition is required by the affected user entity.

Control objectives for services provided by unitised funds, unit pricing, transitions or other purposes may be included if the service organisation requires those objectives to be addressed in the engagement.

A. Custody

Definition:

"Custody" is the performance of the following functions on behalf of user entities:

- Maintaining custody of assets and records of the assets held for user entities (such assets may exist in physical or electronic form).
- Collecting income and distributing such income to user entities.
- Receiving notification of corporate events and reflecting such events in the records of user entities.
- Receiving notification of asset purchase and sale transactions on behalf of user entities for which the custodian is holding assets, and reflecting such transactions in the records of user entities.
- Receiving payments from purchasers and disbursing proceeds to sellers for asset purchase and sale transactions.

Control Objectives:

Accepting clients

A1. New accounts[86] are set up completely and accurately in accordance with client agreements and any applicable regulations.

86 Controls over the transition of specific user entities' funds to the custody of the service organisation are not addressed in this objective.

Appendix 3 (continued)

A2. Complete and authorised client agreements are established prior to initiating custody activity.

Authorising and processing transactions

A3. Investment and related cash and foreign exchange transactions are authorised and recorded completely, accurately and on a timely basis in accordance with client instructions.

A4. Investment and related cash and foreign exchange transactions are settled completely, accurately and on a timely basis and failures are resolved in a timely manner.

A5. Corporate actions are identified, actioned, processed and recorded on a timely basis.

A6. Cash receipts and payments are authorised, processed and recorded completely, accurately and on a timely basis.

A7. Securities lending programs are authorised and loan initiation, maintenance and termination are recorded on an accurate and timely basis.

A8. Loans are collateralised in accordance with the lender's agreement and the collateral together with its related income is recorded completely, accurately and on a timely basis.

A9. Collateral is completely and accurately invested in accordance with the lender's agreement.

Maintaining financial and other records

A10. Accounts are administered in accordance with client agreements and any applicable regulations.

A11. Changes to non-monetary static data (for example, address changes and changes in allocation instructions) are authorised and correctly recorded on a timely basis.

A12. Investment income and related tax reclaims are collected and recorded accurately and on a timely basis.

A13. Asset positions for securities held by third parties such as sub custodians and depositories are accurately recorded and regularly reconciled.

Safeguarding assets

A14. Assets held (including investments held with depositories, cash and physically held assets) are safeguarded from loss, misappropriation and unauthorised use.

A15. Assets held are appropriately registered and client money is segregated.

Monitoring compliance

A16. Transaction errors are rectified promptly.

Monitoring subservice organisations[87]

A17. Appointments of subservice organisations, including sub-custodians, are approved, subservice organisations are managed in accordance with the requirements of the client agreement and their activities are adequately monitored.

Reporting

A18. Client reporting in respect of client asset holdings is complete and accurate and provided within required timescales.

A19. Asset positions and details of securities lent (including collateral) are reported to interested parties accurately and within the required timescale.

Information technology

See control objectives: **G.1 – G.13**

87 Control objective for monitoring subservice organisations applies when the carve-out method is used to deal with subservice organisations. See ASAE 3402, paragraph 9(a) for definition of carve-out method.

GS

Appendix 3 (continued)

B. Asset Management

Definition:

"Asset management" is the investment of money on behalf of clients and involves the performance of the following functions:

- Initiating and executing purchase and sale transactions, either by specific direction from the client or under discretionary authority granted by the client.
- Determining whether transactions comply with guidelines and restrictions.
- Reconciling records of security transactions and portfolio holdings, for each client, to statements received from the custodian.
- Reporting to the client on portfolio performance and activities.

Assets may be managed in accordance with specific client directions, under a discretionary mandate agreed by the client or through a unitised fund, with the investment strategy mandated in an offer document or client agreement. These control objectives are relevant to service organisations providing mandate business, where the investors (user entities) are required to prepare audited financial reports. The objectives are also relevant to service organisations providing asset management services to unitised funds (user entities) but do not include objectives for controls within unitised funds themselves.

Control Objectives:

Accepting clients

B.1 New accounts[88] are set up completely and accurately in accordance with client agreements and/or offer documents and any applicable regulations.

B.2 Complete and authorised client agreements, including investment guidelines and restrictions, are established prior to initiating investment activity.

Authorising and processing transactions

B.3 Asset investment transactions are properly authorised, executed and allocated in a timely and accurate manner.

B.4 Transactions are undertaken only with approved brokers.

B.5 Asset investment and related cash transactions are completely and accurately recorded and settled in a timely manner.

B.6 Corporate events are identified and generated, respectively, and then actioned, processed and recorded accurately and in a timely manner.

B.7 Client new monies and withdrawals are processed and recorded completely and accurately, on a timely basis, and withdrawals are authorised.[89]

Maintaining financial and other records

B.8 Accounts are administered in accordance with client agreements and/or offer documents.

B.9 Changes to non-monetary client data (for example, address changes and changes in allocation instructions) are authorised and correctly recorded on a timely basis.[90]

B.10 Investment income and related tax are accurately recorded in the proper period.

B.11 Investments are valued using current prices obtained from independent external pricing sources or an alternative basis in accordance with client agreements.[91]

B.12 Cash and securities positions are completely and accurately recorded and reconciled to third party data.

88 Controls over the transition of specific user entities' assets to the management of the service organisation are not addressed in this objective.

89 Where user entities are unitised funds this objective is not usually applicable but is instead covered by the control objectives for Registry (Section F).

90 Where user entities are unitised funds, this objective is not applicable but is instead covered by the control objectives for Registry (Section F).

91 This objective is not intended to extend to the detailed controls over unit pricing.

Appendix 3 (continued)

B.13 Investment management fees and other account expenses are accurately calculated and recorded in accordance with client agreements and/or offer documents.

Safeguarding of assets

B.14 Investments are properly registered and client money is segregated.

B.15 Appropriate segregation exists between the service organisation's asset management and custody services, which may give rise to a conflict of interest.[92]

Monitoring compliance

B.16 Client portfolios are managed in accordance with investment objectives, monitored for compliance with investment guidelines and restrictions and performance is measured.

B.17 Transaction errors are rectified promptly in accordance with the service level agreement and/or offer document or client instructions.

B.18 Broker exposures are monitored in accordance with client agreements and/or offer document.

Monitoring subservice organisations[93]

B.19 Appointments of subservice organisations, including those providing asset management services, are approved, subservice organisations are properly managed and their activities are adequately monitored on a timely basis.

Reporting to clients

B.20 Client reporting in respect of portfolio transactions and holdings (including collateral) is complete and accurate and provided within required timescales.

Information technology

See control objectives: **G.1 – G.13**

C. Property Management

Definition:

"Property management" is the performance of the following functions:

- Initiating and executing property purchase and sale transactions either by specific direction from the client or under discretionary authority granted by the client.
- Determining whether transactions comply with guidelines and restrictions.
- Reconciling records of transactions for each client, to statements received from the custodian.
- Reporting to the client on performance and activities.

Control Objectives:

Accepting clients

C.1 New accounts[94] are set up completely and accurately in accordance with client agreements and any applicable regulations.

C.2 Complete and authorised client agreements are established prior to initiating investment activity.

C.3 Investment guidelines and restrictions are established and agreed prior to investment management activity.

---

92 Control objective applies if the investment administrator also provides custody services which may give rise to a conflict of interest.

93 Control objective for monitoring subservice organisations applies when the carve-out method is used to deal with subservice organisations. See ASAE 3402, paragraph 9(a) for definition of carve-out method.

94 Controls over the transition of specific user entities' property to the management of the service organisation are not addressed in this objective.

Appendix 3 (continued)

Authorising and processing transactions

C.4 Investment decisions are properly formulated in accordance with investment guidelines, authorised, implemented and reviewed on a timely basis.

C.5 Property developments are only undertaken in accordance with acceptable risk criteria.

C.6 Costs associated with buying and selling properties are authorised and recorded accurately.

C.7 Tenants' covenants and lease conditions are assessed and authorised on a timely basis.

C.8 Property and related cash transactions are completely and accurately recorded and settled in a timely manner.

C.9 Rental income and service charges are accurately calculated and recorded on a timely basis.

C.10 Client new monies and withdrawals are processed and recorded completely and accurately, withdrawals are appropriately authorised.

Maintaining financial and other records

C.11 Accounts are administered in accordance with client agreements and any applicable regulations.

C.12 Changes to non-monetary client data (for example, address changes and changes in allocation instructions) are authorised and correctly recorded on a timely basis.

C.13 Complete and accurate records of each property are maintained.

C.14 Properties are valued in accordance with regulatory requirements, client agreements or industry standard.

C.15 Income entitlements are received in full, wherever possible, and expenses, both recoverable and irrecoverable, are controlled.

C.16 Property management fees and other account expenses are accurately calculated and recorded.

C.17 Rents are monitored and rent reviews are recorded promptly and accurately.

C.18 Unitholders' funds are priced and administered accurately and in a timely manner.

Safeguarding assets

C.19 Properties purchased are of good and marketable title.

C.20 Title deeds are safeguarded from loss, misappropriation and unauthorised use.

C.21 Uninvested cash is appropriately registered and client money is segregated.

C.22 Risks arising from investing in property are insured in accordance with client instructions.

Monitoring compliance

C.23 Client portfolios are managed in accordance with investment objectives, monitored for compliance with investment guidelines and restrictions and performance is measured.

C.24 Transaction errors (including guideline breaches) are rectified promptly.

Monitoring subservice organisations[95]

C.25 Appointments of subservice organisations, including those providing property management services, are approved, subservice organisations are properly managed and their activities are adequately monitored on a timely basis.

Reporting to clients

C.26 Client reporting in respect of property transactions, holdings and performance is complete and accurate and provided within required timescales.

Information technology

See control objectives: **G.1 – G.13**

95 Control objective for monitoring subservice organisations applies when the carve-out method is used to deal with subservice organisations. See ASAE 3402, paragraph 9(a) for definition of carve-out method.

Appendix 3 (continued)

D. Superannuation Member Administration

Definition:

"Superannuation member administration" is the performance of the following functions:

- Maintaining membership data, including the addition of new members and updating existing members' data.
- Receiving contributions and transfers in from employers, members or government and allocating to members' accounts.
- Calculation and payment of benefits to members, beneficiaries, other superannuation funds and/or other third parties where applicable (e.g. financial hardship).
- Receiving instructions from members and trustees regarding investment elections and investment switch requests, and executing these instructions.
- Processing deductions from member accounts, including insurance premiums, administration fees and contribution tax, and remittance of expenses and tax to appropriate parties.
- Liaison with insurers regarding insurance claims, receipt of insurance proceeds and payment of death, TPD and income protection benefits.
- Allocation of fund earnings to members' accounts, through application of crediting rate or adjustment of unit prices.
- Annual review of fund, including roll up of members' accounts and calculation of vested benefits/accrued benefits and annual reporting to members and trustees.

Where the service organisation maintains financial records in addition to member records, the control objectives in Appendix 3 Section E Investment Administration will also be applicable.

Control Objectives:

Accepting clients

D.1 New accounts[96] for superannuation funds and sub-plans are set up completely and accurately in accordance with client agreements and any applicable regulations.

D.2 Member accounts are set up completely and accurately in accordance with fund rules and individual investment and insurance elections.

Authorising and processing transactions

D.3 Contributions and transfers in are correctly classified and allocated to members' accounts, processed accurately and on a timely basis.

D.4 Superannuation benefits payable and transfer values are calculated and recorded accurately and payments are authorised and made on a timely basis.

D.5 Instructions from members and trustees regarding investment elections and investment switch requests are actioned and accurately processed.

D.6 Deductions from member accounts, including insurance premiums, administration fees and contribution tax, are calculated in accordance with member elections, fund rules, relevant legislation and regulations and accurately recorded.

D.7 Expenses and tax deducted are remitted to the appropriate parties on a timely basis.

Maintaining member records

D.8 Changes to members' standing data (for example, address changes and changes in allocation instructions) are authorised and correctly recorded on a timely basis.

D.9 Investment earnings are accurately allocated (using authorised crediting rates or unit prices) to member accounts, in accordance with trustee directions and fund rules.

96 Controls over the transition of individual existing superannuation funds to the superannuation member administrator are not addressed in this objective.

GS

Appendix 3 (continued)

Safeguarding assets

D.10 Superannuation fund, sub-plan and member data is appropriately stored to ensure security and protection from unauthorised use.

Monitoring compliance

D.11 Contributions are received in accordance with fund rules and relevant legislation.

D.12 Transaction errors are identified, notified to members or trustees in accordance with client agreements and rectified promptly if required.

D.13 Benefits payable and transfer values are calculated and paid in accordance with superannuation fund rules, relevant legislation and regulations.

Monitoring subservice organisations[97]

D.14 Appointments of subservice organisations, including those providing superannuation member administration, are approved, subservice organisations are properly managed and their activities are adequately monitored on a timely basis.

Reporting to clients

D.15 Periodic member statements issued to members are accurate and complete and distributed on a timely basis.

Information technology

See control objectives: **G.1 – G.13**

E: Investment Administration

Definition:

"Investment Administration" is the performance of the following functions:

- Maintaining records of securities, cash, and other portfolio assets and liabilities based on information received from the Trustee/Responsible Entity, investment manager, registrar, custodian and others (as applicable).
- Valuations of portfolio assets and liabilities, determining net asset values and reporting thereof.
- Periodic reporting of performance and investment compliance to the Trustee/Responsible Entity, investment manager, and others (as applicable).
- Periodic financial reporting.

Unit pricing and crediting rate calculations are also a function performed in investment administration, for which the control objectives include the accurate calculation of daily or other periodic unit prices or crediting rates with detailed controls allied to that objective. Control objectives relevant to unit pricing, distributions and credit rate calculations have not been listed below, because it would not ordinarily be necessary to meet these objectives in obtaining assurance over the operating effectiveness of controls for investment administration services provided by a service organisation for the purpose of the audit of user entities' financial reports.

Control Objectives:

Accepting clients

E.1 New accounts[98] are set up completely and accurately in accordance with client agreements and any applicable regulations.

E.2 Complete and authorised client agreements are established prior to initiating accounting activity.

Authorising and processing transactions

E.3 Portfolio transactions are recorded completely, accurately and on a timely basis.

97 Include control objectives for monitoring subservice organisations when the carve-out method is used to deal with subservice organisations. See ASAE 3402, paragraph 9(a) for definition of carve-out method.

98 Controls over the transition of specific user entities' administration to the management of the service organisation are not addressed in this objective.

Appendix 3 (continued)

E.4 Corporate actions are actioned, processed and recorded accurately and on a timely basis.

E.5 Expenses are appropriately authorised and recorded in accordance with the service level agreement and/or client instructions, on a timely basis.

Maintaining financial and other records

E.6 Accounts are administered in accordance with client agreements.

E.7 Changes to non-monetary static data (for example, address changes and changes in allocation instructions) are authorised and correctly recorded on a timely basis.

E.8 Investment income and related tax are accurately calculated and recorded on a timely basis.

E.9 Investments are valued using current prices obtained from independent external pricing sources, or an alternative basis in accordance with client agreements.

E.10 Issue and cancellations of shares/units are recorded completely and accurately in the financial records and units on issue are regularly reconciled to data provided by registry.

E.11 Cash and securities positions are completely and accurately recorded and reconciled to third party data on a timely basis.

E.12 Reconciliations between different systems, including the investment ledger, general ledger and administration system, are performed on a timely basis.

Monitoring compliance

E.13 Errors are identified, notified to clients and rectified promptly in accordance with client agreements.

Monitoring subservice organisations[99]

E.14 Appointments of subservice organisations, including those providing investment administration, are approved, subservice organisations are properly managed and their activities are adequately monitored on a timely basis.

Reporting to clients

E.15 Periodic reports to clients, including calculation of net asset value if required, are accurate and complete and distributed on a timely basis.

E.16 Annual reports and accounts are prepared in accordance with applicable laws and regulations.

Taxation

E.17 Tax policy is updated and reviewed on a timely basis.

E.18 Tax information components and attributes used in the preparation of the income tax computation (current and deferred) are complete and calculated accurately in accordance with tax policy or as agreed with clients.

E.19 Differences between tax and accounting treatments are identified and calculated in accordance with tax policy or as agreed with clients and reported in a timely manner to clients.

E.20 Current and deferred tax balances in the general ledger are accurately recorded in accordance with the tax computation, and processed in a timely manner in accordance with tax policy or as agreed with clients.

Information technology

See control objectives: **G.1 – G.13**

99 Include control objectives for monitoring subservice organisations when the carve-out method is used to deal with subservice organisations. See ASAE 3402, paragraph 9(a) for definition of carve-out method.

Appendix 3 (continued)

F. Registry

Definition:

"Registry" is the performance of the following functions:

- Maintaining records of the name and address of each shareholder or unitholder investing in the client/issuer, the amount of shares or units in the client owned by each share/unitholder, any reference corresponding to a share/unit holder's positions, the issue date of the share/unit, and the cancellation date of the share/unit (if applicable).
- Recording the amount of shares/units purchased, redeemed, switched, transferred or reinvested by a shareholder or unitholder on the issuer's books upon receipt of a validated request.
- Recording changes to share/unit holdings as a consequence of a corporate action upon receipt of a validated instruction.
- Monitoring the issuance of shares/units in an issue to prevent the unauthorised issuance of shares/units.
- Ensuring that any issuance of shares/units will not cause the authorised number of shares/units in an issue to be exceeded and that the number of new shares/units represented corresponds to the number of cancelled shares/units.
- Performing stakeholder meeting and voting processes such as document design and print procurement, postage, other distribution of documentation and reporting.

Control Objectives:

Accepting clients

F.1 New accounts[100] are set up completely and accurately in accordance with client/issuers agreements.

F.2 Complete and authorised client agreements are established prior to initiating accounting activity.

Authorising and processing transactions

F.3 New share/unitholder activity is clearly established and recorded completely, accurately and in a timely manner.

F.4 Share/unitholder applications, redemptions and switches received are checked, sorted and distributed for processing in a timely manner.

F.5 Share/unitholder transactions and adjustments are authorised, processed accurately, completely and in a timely manner.

F.6 Cash receipts are processed accurately and banked promptly.

F.7 Cheques and confirmation letters issued are accurately generated, matched and authorised prior to despatch.

F.8 Where issued capital is fixed, the number of shares in the registry records match the number of shares on issue.

F.9 Distribution payments and reinvestments are complete, calculated in accordance with the authorised distribution and processed in a timely manner.

Maintaining financial and other records

F.10 Accounts are administered in accordance with client agreements.

F.11 Changes to non-monetary share/unitholder data (for example, address changes and changes in allocation instructions) are authorised and correctly recorded on a timely basis.

F.12 Registrar records accurately reflect shares, units and cash held by third parties.

F.13 Share/unit activity is recorded completely, accurately and positions are regularly reconciled.

100 Controls over the transition of specific user entities' registry to the management of the service organisation are not addressed in this objective.

Appendix 3 (continued)

Safeguarding assets

F.14 Lost and stolen certificates are recorded in a timely manner.

Monitoring compliance

F.15 Transaction errors are identified, notified to clients and share/unit holders in accordance with client agreements and rectified if necessary.

Monitoring subservice organisations[101]

F.16 Appointments of subservice organisations, including those providing registry services, are approved, subservice organisations are properly managed and their activities are adequately monitored on a timely basis.

Reporting to clients

F.17 Client reporting is complete, accurate and processed within required timescales.

Taxation

F.18 Withholding tax for non-residents, or where no TFN/ABN has been provided, is calculated completely, accurately and on a timely basis.

Information technology

See control objectives: **G.1 – G.13**

G. Information Technology

Scope:

Information technology (IT) control objectives are applicable to all investment management services as IT is integral to providing those services. The IT control objectives are addressed for each investment management service reported on, in addition to the specific control objectives that are provided for each investment management service in this Appendix. The IT systems which are addressed in the controls identified to meet these objectives are those which are relevant to the investment management services provided to user entities, specifically the financial reporting of user entities with respect to those services.

Control Objectives:

Restricting access to systems and data

G.1 Physical access to computer networks, equipment, storage media and program documentation is restricted to authorised individuals.

G.2 Logical access to computer systems, programs, master data, client data, transaction data and parameters, including access by administrators to applications, databases, systems and networks, is restricted to authorised individuals via information security tools and techniques.

G.3 Segregation of incompatible duties is defined, implemented and enforced by logical security controls in accordance with job roles.

Authorising and processing transactions

G.4 IT processing is authorised and scheduled appropriately and deviations are identified and resolved in a timely manner.

Safeguarding assets

G.5 Appropriate measures, including firewalls and anti-virus software, are implemented to counter the threat from malicious electronic attack.

G.6 The physical IT equipment is maintained in a controlled environment.

Maintaining and developing systems hardware and software

G.7 Development and implementation of new systems, applications and software, and changes to existing systems, applications and software, are authorised, tested, approved, implemented and documented.

101 Include control objectives for monitoring subservice organisations when the carve-out method is used to deal with subservice organisations. See ASAE 3402, paragraph 9(a) for definition of carve-out method.

Appendix 3 (continued)

G.8 Data migration or modification is authorised, tested and, once performed, reconciled back to the source data.

Recovering from processing interruptions

G.9 Data and systems are backed up regularly offsite and tested for recoverability on a periodic basis.

G.10 IT hardware and software issues are monitored and resolved in a timely manner.

G.11 Business and information systems recovery plans are documented, approved, tested and maintained.

Monitoring compliance

G.12 Information technology services provided to clients are approved, managed and performance thresholds met in accordance with the requirements of the client agreement.

Monitoring subservice organisations[102]

G.13 Appointment of subservice organisations, including those providing IT services, are approved, subservice organisations are managed in accordance with the requirements of the client agreement and their activities are adequately monitored.

Appendix 4

(Ref: Para. 69)

Service Auditor's Type 2 Assurance Report

Independent Service Auditor's Assurance Report on the Description of Controls over [Investment Management Service], their Design and Operating Effectiveness

To: XYZ Service Organisation

Scope

We have been engaged to report on XYZ Service Organisation's (XYZ) description at pages [bb-cc] of its [specify investment management service: custody, asset management, property management, superannuation member administration, investment administration or registry] system provided to XYZ's clients throughout the period [date] to [date] (the description), and on the design and operations of those controls related to the control objectives stated in the description.[103]

XYZ's Responsibilities

XYZ is responsible for: preparing the description and accompanying assertion at page [aa], including the completeness, accuracy and method of presentation of the description and assertion; providing the [investment management service/s] covered by the description; stating the control objectives, including relevant controls objectives for [investment management service/s] as outlined in AUASB Guidance Statement GS 007 *Audit Implications of the Use of Service Organisations for Investment Management Services,* and designing, implementing and effectively operating controls to achieve the stated control objectives.

Service Auditor's Responsibilities

Our responsibility is to express an opinion on XYZ 's description and on the design and operation of controls related to the control objectives stated in that description based on our procedures. We conducted our engagement in accordance with Standard on Assurance Engagements ASAE 3402 *Assurance Reports on Controls at a Service Organisation* and with reference to Guidance Statement GS 007 *Audit Implications of the Use of Service Organisations*

102 Include control objectives for monitoring subservice organisations when the carve-out method is used to deal with subservice organisations. See ASAE 3402, paragraph 9(a) for definition of carve-out method.

103 If some elements of the description are not included in the scope of the engagement, this is made clear in the assurance report.

Appendix 4 (continued)

for Investment Management Services. ASAE 3402 requires that we comply with relevant ethical requirements and plan and perform our procedures to obtain reasonable assurance about whether, in all material respects, the description is fairly presented and the controls are suitably designed and operating effectively.

An assurance engagement to report on the description, design and operating effectiveness of controls at a service organisation involves performing procedures to obtain evidence about the disclosures in the service organisation's description of its system, and the design and operating effectiveness of controls. The procedures selected depend on our judgement, including the assessment of the risks that the description is not fairly presented, and that controls are not suitably designed or operating effectively. Our procedures included testing the operating effectiveness of those controls that we consider necessary to provide reasonable assurance that the control objectives stated in the description were achieved. An assurance engagement of this type also includes evaluating the overall presentation of the description, the suitability of the objectives stated therein, and the suitability of the criteria specified by the service organisation and described at page [aa]. In evaluating the suitability of the objectives stated in the description, we have determined whether each of the minimum control objectives provided in GS 007 for [investment management service/s] is included, or, if any of the minimum objectives are omitted or amended, that the reason for the omission or amendment is adequately disclosed in the description.

We believe that the evidence we have obtained is sufficient and appropriate to provide a basis for our opinion.

Limitations of Controls at a Service Organisation

XYZ's description is prepared to meet the common needs of a broad range of clients and their auditors and may not, therefore, include every aspect of the system that each individual client may consider important in its own particular environment. Also, because of their nature, controls at a service organisation may not prevent or detect all errors or omissions in processing or reporting transactions. Also, the projection of any evaluation of effectiveness to future periods is subject to the risk that controls at a service organisation may become inadequate or fail.

Opinion

Our opinion has been formed on the basis of the matters outlined in this report. The criteria we used in forming our opinion are those described at page [aa]. In our opinion, in all material respects:

(a) the description fairly presents the [investment management service] system as designed and implemented throughout the period from [date] to [date];

(b) the controls related to the control objectives stated in the description were suitably designed throughout the period from [date] to [date]; and

(c) the controls tested, which were those necessary to provide reasonable assurance that the control objectives stated in the description were achieved, operated effectively throughout the period from date] to [date].

Description of Tests of Controls

The specific controls tested and the nature, timing and results of those tests are listed on pages [yy-zz].

Intended Users and Purpose

This report and the description of tests of controls on pages [yy-zz] are intended only for clients who have used XYZ's [investment management service] system, and their auditors, who have a sufficient understanding to consider it, along with other information including information about controls operated by clients themselves, when assessing the risks of material misstatements of clients' financial reports/statements.

[*Service auditor's signature*]

[*Date of the service auditor's assurance report*]

[*Service auditor's address*]

GS

Appendix 5

(Ref: Para. 70))

Service Auditor's Description of the Nature, Timing and Extent of Tests Applied to Controls

The description does not duplicate the service auditor's detailed assurance programme, since that would provide more than the appropriate level of detail. There is no standardised format for presenting a description of tests applied to controls, however the following elements are ordinarily included in the description:

1. Cross reference to the control objectives and allied controls[104] intended to achieve those objectives described in the service organisation's description of its system.
2. Assessment of the fair presentation of the description, including:
   (a) identification of any inadequacies, omissions or inaccuracies in the description of control objectives;
   (b) identification of any inaccuracies in the description of controls, as designed and implemented.
3. Assessment of the suitability of the design, including identification of any inadequacies in the design of the controls to achieve their stated objectives.
4. Tests of operating effectiveness, including:
   (a) nature, timing and extent of tests conducted including whether the whole population was tested or a sample, in this case the size of the sample;
   (b) number and nature of deviations noted;
   (c) remedial action taken by management, if any; and
   (d) results of the tests in sufficient detail to enable user auditors to assess the effect of those tests on their assessment of control risk.

Description of nature of tests

The nature of tests carried out by the service auditor may include such procedures as enquiry, inspection, observation and re-performance. Examples of descriptions of these procedures, which may assist the service auditor in describing tests of controls are set out below.

1. Enquiry:
   - Enquired of appropriate XYZ personnel.
   - Conducted enquiries seeking relevant information or representation from personnel to obtain, among other things:
     - Knowledge, additional information and affirmation regarding the control of procedures.
     - Corroborating evidence of the controls.
2. Inspection:
   - Inspected documents and records indicating performance of the controls. This included, among other things:
     - Inspection of reconciliations and management reports that age and/or quantify reconciling items to assess whether balances and reconciling items appear to be properly monitored, controlled and resolved on a timely basis, as required by the related control.
     - Examination of source documentation and authorisations related to selected transactions processed.

104 If applicable, complementary user entity controls would also be described. See ASAE 3402, paragraph 9(b) for definition of complementary user entity controls.

Appendix 5 (continued)

- Examination of documents or records for evidence of performance, such as the existence of initials or signatures.
- Inspection of XYZ's systems documentation, such as operations, manuals, flow charts and job descriptions.

3. Observation:
   - Observed the application or existence of specific controls as represented.
4. Re-performance:
   - Re-performed the control or processing application of the controls to check the accuracy of their operation. This included, among other things:
     - Obtaining evidence of the arithmetical accuracy and correct processing of transactions by performing independent calculations.
     - Re-performing the matching of various system records by independently matching the same records and comparing reconciling items to reconciliations prepared by XYZ.

Appendix 6

(Ref: Para. 86 and 89)

Examples of Service Auditor's Reports on Financial Information

The following example service auditor's reports are for use as a guide only, in conjunction with the considerations described in this Guidance Statement, and will need to be varied according to individual requirements and circumstances.

Example 1: A service auditor's report to the engaging party on the audit of specified assertions of the user entity's assets, liabilities or transactions in a financial statement prepared by a service organisation.

Example 2: A service auditor's report to the engaging party on the audit of a financial statement of the user entity's assets, liabilities or transactions prepared by a service organisation.

Example 1: Service Auditor's Report on Specified Assertions

INDEPENDENT AUDITOR'S REPORT

To [the engaging party][105]

Report on Specified Assertions of Assets [and liabilities or transactions] in the Statement[106]

We have audited the [specify assertions audited][107] of the assets [and liabilities or transactions] of the accompanying [title of financial statement] ("the Statement"), which comprises the [statement of assets and liabilities] as at [date], and the [statement of transactions] for the year then ended, concerning the assets [and liabilities or transactions] of [user entity][108] for which XYZ Service Organisation (XYZ) provides [specify investment management service provided:

105 Insert name of user entity or the name of the engaging party, if other than the user entity.

106 The subheading "Report on the Statement" is unnecessary in circumstances when the second subheading "Report on Other Legal and Regulatory Requirements" is not applicable.

107 Insert specified assertions audited:

- for transactions or events: occurrence, completeness, accuracy, cut-off and classification;
- for balances: existence, rights and obligations, completeness or valuation and allocation; or
- for presentation and disclosure: occurrence, rights and obligations, completeness, classification and understandability and accuracy and valuation.

108 Where the assets are held in the name of a nominee holding company insert "held in the name of [nominee holding company]".

GS

Appendix 6 (continued)

custody, asset management, property management, superannuation member administration, investment administration or registry] services, set out on pages [bb] to [cc].[109] The Statement has been prepared by management of XYZ using the basis of preparation described in Note X.

XYZ Management's Responsibility for the Statement

XYZ is responsible for [investment management service] on behalf of [user entity]. Management of XYZ is responsible for the preparation and fair presentation of the Statement in accordance with [specify framework applied][110] and has determined that the accounting policies described in Note X to the Statement are appropriate to meet the financial reporting requirements of the [title of contract or service level agreement] and are appropriate to meet the needs of [user entity]. Management is also responsible for such internal control as management determines is necessary to enable the preparation of the Statement that is free from material misstatement, whether due to fraud or error.

Auditor's Responsibility

Our responsibility is to express an opinion on the [specify assertions audited] in respect of the assets [and liabilities or transactions] in the accompanying Statement, based on our audit. We conducted our audit in accordance with Australian Auditing Standards. Those Standards require that we comply with relevant ethical requirements and plan and perform the audit to obtain reasonable assurance about whether the assets [and liabilities or transactions] set out in the Statement are free of material misstatement in respect of the specified audit assertions.

An audit of the [specify assertions audited] of the assets [and liabilities or transactions] in the Statement involves performing procedures to obtain audit evidence that the assets [and liabilities or transactions] set out in the Statement [insert relevant assertion: for example for existence insert "exist as at [date]" or for valuation insert: "have been appropriately valued in accordance with [specify framework]"]. The procedures selected depend on the auditor's judgement, including the assessment of the risks of material misstatement of the Statement in relation to the specified assertions, whether due to fraud or error. In making those risk assessments, the auditor considers internal control relevant to the [specify assertions audited] of the assets [and liabilities or transactions] in the Statement in order to design audit procedures that are appropriate in the circumstances, but not for the purpose of expressing an opinion on the effectiveness of XYZ's internal control.[111] An audit also includes evaluating the appropriateness of accounting policies used and the reasonableness of accounting estimates, if any, made by management of XYZ with respect to the [specified assertions] of the assets [and liabilities or transactions].

We believe that the audit evidence we obtained is sufficient and appropriate to provide a basis for our audit opinion.

[Insert either:

No uncorrected misstatements, other than amounts which are clearly trivial, have been identified during the course of our audit; or

Uncorrected misstatements, other than amounts which are clearly trivial, which, have come to our attention during the course of our audit and are not material individually or in aggregate in relation to the [specify assertions audited] in respect of the assets [and liabilities or transactions] in the accompanying Statement but may be material when aggregated with any uncorrected misstatements identified by [user entity]'s auditor, are listed in an attachment to this report. These uncorrected misstatements do not affect our audit opinion.]

---

109 When the auditor is aware that the Statement will be included in a document that contains other information, the auditor may consider, if the form of the presentation allows, identifying the page numbers on which the Statement is presented.

110 Insert "applicable Australian Accounting Standards" where multiple Australian Accounting Standards were applied; insert reference to specific Australian Accounting Standard where appropriate (for example: "in accordance with the measurement standards of AAS 25 *Financial Reporting by Superannuation Plans.*"); or "the accounting policies described in Note X to the Statement".

111 In circumstances when the auditor also has responsibility to express an opinion on the effectiveness of internal control in conjunction with the audit of the specified assertions of the assets [and liabilities or transactions] in the Statement, this sentence would be worded as follows: "In making those risk assessments, the auditor considers internal control relevant to the [specify assertions audited] of the assets [and liabilities or transactions] in the Statement in order to design audit procedures that are appropriate in the circumstances."

Appendix 6 (continued)

Opinion

In our opinion, the Statement presents fairly, in all material respects, the [specify assertions audited] of the assets [and liabilities or transactions] of [user entity], for which XYZ provides [investment management service] services, as of [date] in accordance with [specify framework].

Basis of Accounting and Restriction on Distribution

Without modifying our opinion, we draw attention to Note X to the Statement, which describes the basis of accounting. The Statement has been prepared by XYZ for distribution to the [the Trustee/those charged with governance] of [user entity]. As a result, the Statement may not be suitable for another purpose. Our report is intended solely for XYZ, [user entity] and their auditor and should not be distributed to any other parties or used for any other purpose other than that for which they are prepared.[112]

Report on Other Legal and Regulatory Requirements

[Form and content of this section of the auditor's report will vary depending on the nature of the auditor's other reporting responsibilities].

[Auditor's signature]

[Date of the auditor's report]

[Auditor's address]

[Attachment: Uncorrected Misstatements][113]

In the course of conducting our audit procedures at XYZ for the purpose of reporting on [specific assertions] we have identified the following uncorrected misstatements, other than amounts which are clearly trivial, which were determined by [management/those charged with governance] to be immaterial, both individually and in aggregate, to the [specific assets and liabilities or transactions] taken as a whole. These misstatements are reported solely for the purpose of providing information to clients of XYZ and their auditors and they do not affect our audit opinion:

[Insert: List of uncorrected misstatements]

Example 2: Service Auditor's Report on a Statement

INDEPENDENT AUDITOR'S REPORT

To [the engaging party] [114]

Report on the Statement[115]

We have audited the accompanying [title of financial statement] ("the Statement"),[116] which comprises the [statement of assets and liabilities] as at [date], and the [statement of transactions] for the year then ended, concerning the assets [and liabilities or transactions] of [user entity][117] for which XYZ Service Organisation (XYZ) provides [specify investment management services provided: custody, asset management, property management, superannuation member administration, investment administration or registry] services set out on pages [bb] to [cc].[118]

112 Use of the report and liability limitation: insert additional/alternative wording, if any, required to reflect any liability arrangements agreed between the service auditor, the service organisation and other users, including confirmation of the purpose for which the service auditor's report has been prepared and the basis on which other parties may use the report.

113 Include attachment where uncorrected misstatements were identified.

114 Insert name of user entity or the name of the engaging party, if it is not the user entity.

115 The subheading "Report on the Statement" is unnecessary in circumstances when the second subheading "Report on Other Legal and Regulatory Requirements" is not applicable.

116 If certain assertions are specifically excluded from the audit then insert: "except for [specify assertions excluded, e.g. presentation and disclosure] of the Statement."

117 Where the assets are held in the name of a nominee holding company insert "held in the name of [nominee holding company]."

118 When the auditor is aware that the Statement will be included in a document that contains other information, the auditor may consider, if the form of the presentation allows, identifying the page numbers on which the Statement is presented.

GS

Appendix 6 (continued)

The Statement has been prepared by management of XYZ on the basis of preparation described in Note X.

Management's[119] Responsibility for the Statement

XYZ is responsible for [investment management service] on behalf of [user entity]. Management of XYZ is responsible for the preparation and fair presentation of the Statement in accordance with [specify framework][120] and has determined that the accounting policies described in Note X to the Statement are appropriate to meet the financial reporting requirements of the [title of contract or service level agreement] and are appropriate to meet the needs of [user entity]. Management is also responsible for such internal control as management determines is necessary to enable the preparation of the Statement that is free from material misstatement, whether due to fraud or error.

Auditor's Responsibility

Our responsibility is to express an opinion on the Statement based on our audit. We conducted our audit in accordance with Australian Auditing Standards. Those Standards require that we comply with relevant ethical requirements and plan and perform the audit to obtain reasonable assurance about whether the Statement is free from material misstatement.

An audit of the Statement involves performing procedures to obtain audit evidence about the amounts and disclosures in the Statement. The procedures selected depend on the auditor's judgement, including the assessment of the risks of material misstatement of the Statement, whether due to fraud or error. In making those risk assessments, the auditor considers internal controls relevant to XYZ's preparation and fair presentation of the Statement in order to design audit procedures that are appropriate in the circumstances, but not for the purpose of expressing an opinion on the effectiveness of XYZ's internal control[121]. An audit also includes evaluating the appropriateness of accounting policies used and the reasonableness of accounting estimates, if any, made by management, as well as evaluating the overall presentation of the Statement.

We believe that the audit evidence we obtained is sufficient and appropriate to provide a basis for our audit opinion.

[Insert either:

No uncorrected misstatements, other than amounts which are clearly trivial, have been identified during the course of our audit; or

Uncorrected misstatements, other than amounts which are clearly trivial, which have come to our attention during the course of our audit and are not material individually or in aggregate in relation to the Statement, but may be material when aggregated with any uncorrected misstatements identified by [user entity]'s Auditor, are listed in an attachment to this report. These uncorrected misstatements do not affect our audit opinion.]

Opinion

In our opinion, the attached Statement presents fairly, in all material respects, the assets [and liabilities] of [user entity] as of [date] and transactions for the [period] then ended, for which XYZ provides [investment management service] services, in accordance with in accordance with the basis of accounting described in Note X.

Basis of Accounting and Restriction on Distribution

Without modifying our opinion, we draw attention to Note X to the Statement, which describes the basis of accounting. The Statement has been prepared by XYZ for distribution to the [the Trustee/those charged with governance] of [user entity]. As a result, the Statement may not

119 Insert the title of those charged with governance, e.g. directors/trustees/committees. For example, "Director's Responsibility for the Statement". Insert appropriate title, when prompted, throughout the report.

120 Insert "applicable Australian Accounting Standards" where multiple Australian Accounting Standards were applied; insert reference to specific Australian Accounting Standard where appropriate (for example: "in accordance with the measurement standards of AAS 25 *Financial Reporting by Superannuation Plans.*") or "the accounting policies described in Note X to the Statement".

121 In circumstances when the auditor also has responsibility to express an opinion on the effectiveness of internal control in conjunction with the audit of the Statement, this sentence would be worded as follows: "In making those risk assessments, the auditor considers internal control relevant to XYZ's preparation and fair presentation of the Statement in order to design audit procedures that are appropriate in the circumstances."

Appendix 6 (continued)

be suitable for another purpose. Our report is intended solely for XYZ, [user entity] and their auditor and should not be distributed to any other parties or used for any other purpose other than that for which they are prepared.[122]

Report on Other Legal and Regulatory Requirements

[Form and content of this section of the auditor's report will vary depending on the nature of the auditor's other reporting responsibilities].

[Auditor's signature]

[Date of the auditor's report]

[Auditor's address]

[Attachment: Uncorrected Misstatements][123]

In the course of conducting our audit procedures at XYZ Service Organisation for the purpose of reporting on [the Statement] we have identified the following uncorrected misstatements, other than amounts which are clearly trivial, which were determined by [management/those charged with governance] to be immaterial, both individually and in aggregate, to the [specific assets and liabilities or transactions/Statement] taken as a whole. These misstatements are reported solely for the purpose of providing information to clients of XYZ and their auditors and they do not affect our audit opinion:

[Insert: List of uncorrected misstatements]

122 Use of the report and liability limitation: insert additional/alternative wording, if any, required to reflect any liability arrangements agreed between the service auditor, the service organisation and other users, including confirmation of the purpose for which the service auditor's report has been prepared and the basis on which other parties may use the report.

123 Include attachment where uncorrected misstatements were identified.

GS 008

The Auditor's Report on a Remuneration Report under Section 300A of the *Corporations Act 2001*

(Revised March 2010)

(Issued by the Auditing and Assurance Standards Board.

Note from the Institute of Chartered Accountants Australia

This note, prepared by the technical editor, is not part of GS 008.

Historical development

August 2006: This guidance was first issued as a Guidance Note to replace the previous guidance on disclosures required by AASB 1046 'Director and Executive Disclosures by Disclosing Entities' after AASB 1046 was replaced by additional requirements in AASB 124 'Related Party Disclosures'.

June 2008: Following changes to the *Corporations Act 2001*, the Guidance was revised and reissued as GS 008.

March 2010: GS 008 was updated to reflect the Clarity changes to the audit reporting standards issued in October 2009. It has no international equivalent.

Contents

AUTHORITY STATEMENT

Authority Statement

The Auditing and Assurance Standards Board (AUASB) formulates Guidance Statement GS 008 *The Auditor's Report on a Remuneration Report Under Section 300A of the Corporations Act 2001* pursuant to section 227B of the *Australian Securities and Investments Commission Act 2001*, for the purposes of providing guidance on auditing and assurance matters.

This Guidance Statement provides guidance to assist the auditor to fulfil the objectives of the audit or assurance engagement. It includes explanatory details on specific matters for the purposes of understanding and complying with AUASB Standards. The auditor exercises professional judgement when using this Guidance Statement.

The Guidance Statement does not prescribe or create new Requirements.

Dated 12 March 2010

M H Kelsall
Chairman - AUASB

Guidance Statement GS 008

The Auditor's Report on a Remuneration Report Under Section 300A of the *Corporations Act 2001*

GS

Application

1 This Guidance Statement has been formulated by the Auditing and Assurance Standards Board (AUASB) to provide guidance to auditors reporting pursuant to section 308(3C) of the *Corporations Act 2001* ("the Act") regarding the Remuneration Report required to be included in the annual directors' report pursuant to section 300A of the Act ("the Remuneration Report").

2 This Guidance Statement should be used when an auditor conducts an audit under the Australian Auditing Standards applicable to financial reporting periods commencing on or after 1 January 2010.

Issuance Date

3 This Guidance Statement is operative on 1 March 2010.

Introduction

4 The auditor's objective is to express an opinion on whether the Remuneration Report complies with section 300A of the Act.

5 Section 300A applies to any disclosing entity[1] that is a company. In recognition of the section 300A requirements and so as to avoid unnecessary duplication, Accounting Standard AASB 124 *Related Party Disclosures* lists certain disclosure requirements that do not apply to disclosing entities that are companies.

Auditor's Reporting Requirements

Responsibility to Express an Opinion on the Remuneration Report

6 Section 308(3C) of the Act requires that, if the directors' report for the financial year includes a Remuneration Report, the auditor must report also to members on whether the auditor is of the opinion that the Remuneration Report complies with section 300A of the Act. If not of that opinion, the auditor's report must state why.

7 The requirement to express a distinct opinion on the Remuneration Report in the directors' report is additional to the auditor's responsibility to express an opinion on the financial report. In accordance with Auditing Standard ASA 700 *Forming an Opinion and Reporting on a Financial Report*, the auditor is required to address other reporting responsibilities in a separate section of the auditor's report that follows the opinion paragraph on the financial report, in order to clearly distinguish them from the auditor's primary responsibility to express an opinion on the financial report.[2]

8 Where a company has included a Remuneration Report in the annual directors' report pursuant to section 300A of the Act, the auditor's report should identify clearly the paragraph numbers or pages of the directors' report that have been audited pursuant to section 308(3C) of the Act. This is necessary to avoid any misunderstanding by users as to which part of the directors' report has been subjected to audit.

9 Furthermore, the auditor's report describes the respective responsibilities of the directors and the auditor in relation to the Remuneration Report. See Appendix 1 for an illustrative example of an unmodified report.

Materiality

10 The suggested form of opinion on the Remuneration Report, included in the Appendices to this Guidance Statement, does not make reference to materiality. An auditor exercises professional judgement in considering reporting responsibilities under the Act, including considering additional regulatory reporting obligations, such as under section 311 of the Act, for significant breaches of the Act.

Modifications

11 Modifications to the auditor's report in relation to the Remuneration Report are made in accordance with ASA 705 *Modifications to the Opinion in the Independent Auditor's Report*. See Appendix 2 for an illustrative example of a modified report.

The Auditor's Report

12 The example of an unmodified auditor's report, that is included as Illustration 1A in Appendix 1 of ASA 700 incorporates the audit reporting requirements of the Act and the Auditing Standards. This auditor's report format has been used in the Appendices to this Guidance Statement to illustrate example wording regarding the auditor's reporting responsibilities regarding the Remuneration Report, pursuant to section 308(3C) of the Act.

---

1 Disclosing Entity is defined in the *Corporations Act 2001*.

2 See ASA 700, paragraph 38.

Conformity with International Pronouncements

13 As this Guidance Statement relates to Australian legislative requirements under the Act, there is no equivalent International Standard on Auditing or Auditing Practice Statement to this Guidance Statement.

Appendix 1

(Ref: Para. 9)

Illustrative Example of an Unmodified Auditor's Report Addressing the Auditor's Additional Reporting Responsibilities Pursuant to Section 308(3C) of the *Corporations Act 2001*

The illustrative example auditor's report in this Appendix to Guidance Statement GS 008 incorporates the reporting requirements of the Act, including:

(a) section 308(3C); and

(b) the Auditing Standards.

The auditor's reporting requirements regarding the Remuneration Report are additional to the auditor's reporting requirements regarding the financial report and, accordingly, are contained in a separate section of the auditor's report following the opinion paragraph on the financial report—see ASA 700, paragraph 38.

[See: **Report on the Remuneration Report** in the example below.]

INDEPENDENT AUDITOR'S REPORT

[Appropriate Addressee]

Report on the Financial Report[3]

We have audited the accompanying financial report of ABC Company Ltd., which comprises the statement of financial position as at 30 June 20X1, the statement of comprehensive income, statement of changes in equity, statement of cash flows for the year then ended, notes comprising a summary of significant accounting policies and other explanatory information, and the directors' declaration.[4]

Directors' Responsibility for the Financial Report

The directors of the company are responsible for the preparation of the financial report that gives a true and fair view in accordance with Australian Accounting Standards and the *Corporations Act 2001* and for such internal control as the directors determine is necessary to enable the preparation of the financial report that is free from material misstatement, whether due to fraud or error. [In Note XX, the directors also state, in accordance with Accounting Standard AASB 101 *Presentation of Financial Statements*, that the financial statements comply with *International Financial Reporting Standards*.[5]]

Auditor's Responsibility

Our responsibility is to express an opinion on the financial report based on our audit. We conducted our audit in accordance with Australian Auditing Standards. Those standards require that we comply with relevant ethical requirements relating to audit engagements and plan and perform

3 The subheading "Report on the Financial Report" is only necessary in circumstances when the auditor addresses "other reporting responsibilities" in accordance with ASA 700, paragraph 38—see also footnote 7 below.

4 When the auditor is aware that the financial report will be included in a document that contains other information, the auditor may consider, if the form of presentation allows, identifying the page numbers on which the audited financial report is presented.

5 Insert only where the entity has included in the notes to the financial statements, an explicit and unreserved statement of compliance with International Financial Reporting Standards in accordance with AASB 101.

the audit to obtain reasonable assurance about whether the financial report is free from material misstatement.

An audit involves performing procedures to obtain audit evidence about the amounts and disclosures in the financial report. The procedures selected depend on the auditor's judgement, including the assessment of the risks of material misstatement of the financial report, whether due to fraud or error. In making those risk assessments, the auditor considers internal control relevant to the entity's preparation and fair presentation of the financial report in order to design audit procedures that are appropriate in the circumstances, but not for the purpose of expressing an opinion on the effectiveness of the entity's internal control. An audit also includes evaluating the appropriateness of accounting policies used and the reasonableness of accounting estimates made by the directors, as well as evaluating the overall presentation of the financial report.

We believe that the audit evidence we have obtained is sufficient and appropriate to provide a basis for our audit opinion.

Independence

In conducting our audit, we have complied with the independence requirements of the *Corporations Act 2001*. We confirm that the independence declaration required by the *Corporations Act 2001*, which has been given to the directors of ABC Company Ltd., would be in the same terms if given to the directors as at the time of this auditor's report.*

Opinion

In our opinion the financial report of ABC Company Ltd., is in accordance with the *Corporations Act 2001*, including:

(a) giving a true and fair view of the company's financial position as at 30 June 20X1 and of its performance for the year ended on that date; and

(b) complying with Australian Accounting Standards and the *Corporations Regulations 2001*.

OR

[In our opinion:

(a) the financial report of ABC Company Ltd., is in accordance with the *Corporations Act 2001*, including:

  (i) giving a true and fair view of the company's financial position as at 30 June 20X1 and of its performance for the year ended on that date; and

  (ii) complying with Australian Accounting Standards and the *Corporations Regulations 2001*; and

(b) the financial report also complies with *International Financial Reporting Standards* as disclosed in Note XX.[6]]

Report on the Remuneration Report[7]

We have audited the Remuneration Report included in [paragraphs a to b or pages x to y] of the directors' report for the [period] ended 30 June 20X1. The directors of the company are responsible for the preparation and presentation of the Remuneration Report in accordance with section 300A of the *Corporations Act 2001*. Our responsibility is to express an opinion on the Remuneration Report, based on our audit conducted in accordance with Australian Auditing Standards.

---

* Or, alternatively, include statements: (a) to the effect that circumstances have changed since the declaration was given to the relevant directors; and (b) setting out how the declaration would differ if it had been given to the relevant directors at the time the auditor's report was made.

6 Insert only where the entity has included in the notes to the financial statements, an explicit and unreserved statement of compliance with *International Financial Reporting Standards* in accordance with AASB 101 and the auditor agrees with the entity's statement. If the auditor does not agree with the statement, the auditor refers to ASA 705.

7 The "Report on the Remuneration Report" is an example of "other reporting responsibilities"—refer ASA 700, paragraph 38. Any additional "other reporting responsibilities" that the auditor needs to address will also be included in a separate section of the auditor's report following the opinion paragraph on the financial report.

Opinion

In our opinion the Remuneration Report of ABC Company Ltd., for the [period] ended 30 June 20X1, complies with section 300A of the *Corporations Act 2001*.

[Auditor's signature][8]

[Date of the auditor's report]

[Auditor's address]

Appendix 2

(Ref: Para. 11)

Illustrative Example of a Modified Auditor's Report Addressing the Auditor's Additional Reporting Responsibilities Pursuant to Section 308(3c) of the *Corporations Act 2001* – Qualified Opinion

The illustrative example auditor's report in this Appendix to Guidance Statement GS 008 incorporates the reporting requirements of the Act, including:

(a) section 308(3C); and

(b) the Auditing Standards.

The auditor's reporting requirements regarding the Remuneration Report are additional to the auditor's reporting requirements regarding the financial report and accordingly are contained in a separate section of the auditor's report following the opinion paragraph on the financial report—see ASA 700, paragraph 38.

[See: **Report on the Remuneration Report** in the example below.]

Note: As the example below relates to a qualified opinion, the report on the Remuneration Report will need to be amended accordingly where an adverse or disclaimer of opinion is required.

INDEPENDENT AUDITOR'S REPORT

[Appropriate Addressee]

Report on the Financial Report[9]

We have audited the accompanying financial report of ABC Company Ltd., which comprises the statement of financial position as at 30 June 20X1, the statement of comprehensive income, statement of changes in equity, statement of cash flows for the year then ended, notes comprising a summary of significant accounting policies and other explanatory information and the directors' declaration.[10]

Directors' Responsibility for the Financial Report

The directors of the company are responsible for the preparation of the financial report that gives a true and fair view in accordance with Australian Accounting Standards and the *Corporations*

GS

8 ASA 700 requires the auditor's report to be signed in one or more of the following ways: the name of the audit firm, the name of the audit company or the personal name of the auditor as appropriate.

9 The subheading "Report on the Financial Report" is only necessary in circumstances when the auditor addresses "other reporting responsibilities" in accordance with ASA 700, paragraph 38—see also footnote 13 below.

10 When the auditor is aware that the financial report will be included in a document that contains other information, the auditor may consider, if the form of presentation allows, identifying the page numbers on which the audited financial report is presented.

Act 2001 and for such internal control as the directors determine is necessary to enable the preparation of the financial report that is free from material misstatement, whether due to fraud or error. [In Note XX, the directors also state, in accordance with Accounting Standard AASB 101 *Presentation of Financial Statements*, that the financial statements comply with *International Financial Reporting Standards*.[11]]

Auditor's Responsibility

Our responsibility is to express an opinion on the financial report based on our audit. We conducted our audit in accordance with Australian Auditing Standards. Those Auditing Standards require that we comply with relevant ethical requirements relating to audit engagements and plan and perform the audit to obtain reasonable assurance about whether the financial report is free from material misstatement.

An audit involves performing procedures to obtain audit evidence about the amounts and disclosures in the financial report. The procedures selected depend on the auditor's judgement, including the assessment of the risks of material misstatement of the financial report, whether due to fraud or error. In making those risk assessments, the auditor considers internal control relevant to the entity's preparation and fair presentation of the financial report in order to design audit procedures that are appropriate in the circumstances, but not for the purpose of expressing an opinion on the effectiveness of the entity's internal control. An audit also includes evaluating the appropriateness of accounting policies used and the reasonableness of accounting estimates made by the directors, as well as evaluating the overall presentation of the financial report.

We believe that the audit evidence we have obtained is sufficient and appropriate to provide a basis for our audit opinion.

Independence

In conducting our audit, we have complied with the independence requirements of the *Corporations Act 2001*. We confirm that the independence declaration required by the *Corporations Act 2001*, which has been given to the directors of ABC Company Ltd., would be in the same terms if given to the directors as at the time of this auditor's report.*

Opinion

In our opinion the financial report of ABC Company Ltd., is in accordance with the *Corporations Act 2001*, including:

(a) giving a true and fair view of the company's financial position as at 30 June 20X1 and of its performance for the year ended on that date; and

(b) complying with Australian Accounting Standards and the *Corporations Regulations 2001*.

OR

[In our opinion:

(a) the financial report of ABC Company Ltd., is in accordance with the *Corporations Act 2001*, including:

   (i) giving a true and fair view of the company's financial position as at 30 June 20X1 and of its performance for the year ended on that date; and

   (ii) complying with Australian Accounting Standards and the *Corporations Regulations 2001*; and

(b) the financial report also complies with *International Financial Reporting Standards* as disclosed in Note XX.[12]]

11 Insert only where the entity has included in the notes to the financial statements, an explicit and unreserved statement of compliance with *International Financial Reporting Standards* in accordance with AASB 101.

* Or, alternatively, include statements: (a) to the effect that circumstances have changed since the declaration was given to the relevant directors; and (b) setting out how the declaration would differ if it had been given to the relevant directors at the time the auditor's report was made.

12 Insert only where the entity has included in the notes to the financial statements, an explicit and unreserved statement of compliance with *International Financial Reporting Standards* in accordance with AASB 101 and the auditor agrees with the entity's statement. If the auditor does not agree with the statement, the auditor refers to ASA 705.

Report on the Remuneration Report[13]

We have audited the Remuneration Report included in [paragraphs a to b or pages x to y] of the directors' report for the [period] ended 30 June 20X1. The directors of the company are responsible for the preparation and presentation of the Remuneration Report in accordance with section 300A of the *Corporations Act 2001*. Our responsibility is to express an opinion on the Remuneration Report, based on our audit conducted in accordance with Australian Auditing Standards.

Basis for Qualified Opinion on the Remuneration Report

[Include a clear description of all the substantive reasons for the modification].

Qualified Opinion on the Remuneration Report

In our opinion, except for the effect(s) on the Remuneration Report of the matter(s) referred to in the preceding paragraph, the Remuneration Report of ABC Company Ltd., for the [period] ended 30 June 20X1, complies with section 300A of the *Corporations Act 2001*.

[Auditor's signature][14]

[Date of the auditor's report]

[Auditor's address]

GS

13 The "Report on the Remuneration Report" is an example of "other reporting responsibilities"—refer ASA 700, paragraph 38. Any additional "other reporting responsibilities" that the auditor needs to address, will also be included in a separate section of the auditor's report following the opinion paragraph on the financial report.

14 ASA 700 requires the auditor's report to be signed in one or more of the following ways: the name of the audit firm, the name of the audit company or the personal name of the auditor as appropriate.

GS 009

Auditing Self-Managed Superannuation Funds

(Revised August 2011)

Issued by the Auditing and Assurance Standards Board.

Note from the Institute of Chartered Accountants Australia

This note, prepared by the technical editor, is not part of GS 009.

Historical development

October 2008: GS 009 issued. The GS guides auditors through the application of AUASB Standards and the requirements of the legislation and regulations governing the audits of self-managed superannuation funds (SMSFs). It replaces the old Audit Guide 4 'The Audit of Superannuation Funds' and is operative immediately. It has no international equivalent.

August 2011: GS 009 revised to reflect changes introduced by the Clarity Auditing Standards operative for periods beginning on or after 1 January 2010, current requirements of the ATO for the 2010/11 year, updates to superannuation legislation and practical issues that may be encountered on SMSF audits.

Contents

AUTHORITY STATEMENT

GS

Authority Statement

The Auditing and Assurance Standards Board (AUASB) formulates Guidance Statement GS 009 *Auditing Self-Managed Superannuation Funds*, pursuant to section 227B of the *Australian Securities and Investments Commission Act 2001*, for the purposes of providing guidance on auditing and assurance matters.

This Guidance Statement provides guidance to assist the auditor to fulfil the objectives of the audit or assurance engagement. It includes explanatory material on specific matters for the purposes of understanding and complying with AUASB Standards. The auditor exercises professional judgement when using this Guidance Statement.

The Guidance Statement does not prescribe or create new requirements.

Dated: 31 August 2011

M H Kelsall
Chairman - AUASB

Guidance Statement GS 009

Auditing Self-Managed Superannuation Funds

Application

1. This Guidance Statement has been formulated by the Auditing and Assurance Standards Board (AUASB) to provide guidance to auditors conducting:

   (a) the audit of a self-managed superannuation fund's (SMSF's) special purpose financial report[1], [2](financial audit); and

   (b) the audit of a SMSF's compliance with the *Superannuation Industry (Supervision) Act 1993* (SISA) and the *Superannuation Industry (Supervision) Regulations 1994* (SISR) (compliance engagement).

2. This Guidance Statement does not apply to Australian Prudential Regulation Authority (APRA) regulated superannuation entities.[3]

Issuance Date

3. This Guidance statement is issued in August 2011 by the AUASB and replaces GS 009 *Auditing Self Managed Superannuation Funds*, issued in October 2008.

Introduction

4. SMSFs are a specific type of superannuation fund which have fewer than five members and are regulated by the Australian Taxation Office (ATO). SMSFs are primarily governed by the requirements of the SISA, SISR, the *Income Taxation Assessment Acts 1936* and *1997* (ITAA) and the fund's governing rules, which include the trust deed and applicable case law. Complying SMSFs are eligible for tax concessions, and may also receive Superannuation Guarantee (SG) contributions. Complying SMSFs are Australian superannuation funds which meet the requirements of the SISA and SISR and are "regulated"[4] under the SISA.

5. The SISA, subsection 35C(1), requires SMSFs to be audited each financial year by an approved auditor[5], who must complete both the financial audit and the compliance engagement and sign the auditor's report before a SMSF may submit its Annual Return.[6] The auditor reports to the trustees in the "approved form", as issued and updated from time to time, by the ATO,[7] which includes opinions under two sections:

   (a) Part A: Financial report; and

   (b) Part B: Compliance.

---

1 SMSFs prepare different special purpose financial reports depending on whether the fund is an accumulation fund (defined contribution), a defined benefit fund or the benefit is wholly determined by reference to a life assurance policy. The specific reports are defined in paragraph 137.

2 If the SMSF is a reporting entity then it will be required to prepare a general purpose financial report in accordance with the Australian Accounting Standards and the guidance in this Guidance Statement will have to be adapted accordingly. To determine whether a SMSF is a reporting entity, refer to Statement of Accounting Concepts SAC1: *Definition of the Reporting Entity* issued by the Australian Accounting Standards Board.

3 Auditors of APRA regulated superannuation entities, particularly auditors of small APRA funds, may find this Guidance Statement useful in designing, planning and conducting their audits, but it does not relate specifically to APRA funds.

4 Regulated funds, under section 19 of the SISA, are funds which have a trustee, either a corporate trustee or governing rules which contain a pension fund and have made an irrevocable election to become regulated in the approved form within the specified time.

5 Approved auditor is defined in paragraph 14.

6 The SMSF Annual Return (NAT 71226-6.2011) is required to be submitted, which combines the information previously contained in the Income Tax and Regulatory Return and Member Contribution Statement.

7 The approved form auditor's report is contained within the *Instructions and form for approved auditors of SMSFs - Self-managed superannuation fund independent auditor's report* (NAT11466.07.2011). The auditor's report has been reproduced in Appendix 3 of this Guidance Statement and is available from the ATO's website www.ato.gov.au/Superfunds.

6. This Guidance Statement has been developed to identify, clarify and summarise the existing responsibilities which auditors have with respect to conducting SMSF audit engagements, and to provide guidance to auditors on matters which auditors consider when planning, conducting and reporting on the financial audit and compliance engagement of a SMSF.

7. This Guidance Statement does not extend the responsibilities of the auditor beyond those which are imposed by the SISA, SISR, Auditing Standards (ASAs), Standards on Assurance Engagements (ASAEs) or other applicable legislation.

8. This Guidance Statement comprises:
   - (a) an introductory section, which provides guidance on matters common to both the financial audit and compliance engagement;
   - (b) Part A, which provides guidance on the financial audit; and
   - (c) Part B, which provides guidance on the compliance engagement.

9. This Guidance Statement is to be read in conjunction with, and is not a substitute for referring to the requirements and guidance contained in:
   - (a) the *Australian Auditing Standards* (ASAs), in which references to the "auditor" includes an auditor conducting the financial audit of a SMSF;
   - (b) applicable *Standards on Assurance Engagements* (ASAEs), specifically ASAE 3100 *Compliance Engagements*, in which references to the "assurance practitioner" include an auditor conducting a compliance engagement of a SMSF;
   - (c) the SISA and SISR; and
   - (d) ATO Rulings, Interpretive Decisions and Guides and the Income Tax Assessment Acts.

Definitions

10. A SMSF meets the definition of a SMSF of the SISA[8] if:
    - (a) it has fewer than five members;
    - (b) each individual trustee or director of the corporate trustee is a member of the fund, unless it is a single member fund, in which case the sole member is either:
      - (i) a director of the corporate trustee or one of two directors who are related; or
      - (ii) one of two individual trustees of whom the additional trustee may be anyone apart from an employee of the member, unless the employee is related;
    - (c) each member of the fund is a trustee or a director of the corporate trustee;
    - (d) no member is an employee of another member, unless they are relatives; and
    - (e) no trustee, or director of a corporate trustee, receives remuneration for any duties or services performed by the trustee or director in relation to the fund.

11. A SMSF does not fail to satisfy the definition of a SMSF of the SISA[9] if:
    - (a) a member of the fund has died and the legal personal representative of the member is a trustee of the fund or a director of a body corporate that is the trustee of the fund, in place of the member, during the period:
      - (i) beginning when the member of the fund died; and
      - (ii) ending when death benefits commence to be payable in respect of the member of the fund; or

8 Subsections 17A(1) & (2) of the SISA.

9 Subsections 17A(3) & (4) of the SISA.

(b) the legal personal representative of a member of the fund is a trustee of the fund or a director of a body corporate that is the trustee of the fund, in place of the member, during any period when:

(i) the member of the fund is under a legal disability; or

(ii) the legal personal representative has an enduring power of attorney[10] in respect of the member of the fund; or

(c) if a member of the fund is under a legal disability because of age and does not have a legal personal representative—the parent or guardian of the member is a trustee of the fund in place of the member; or

(d) an appointment under section 134 of an acting trustee of the fund is in force.

Trustees' Responsibilities

12. The responsibilities of the SMSF's trustees are contained in the SISA, SISR, the trust deed and any other governing rules of the fund. The trustees have ultimate responsibility for the compliance of the SMSF with the SISA and SISR and any other legislation, such as the taxation legislation affecting SMSFs. Certain covenants affecting the behaviour of the trustees of a SMSF are deemed to be contained in the SMSF's governing rules under section 52 of the SISA, which are in summary:

(a) to act honestly;

(b) to exercise care, skill and diligence;

(c) to act in the best interests of beneficiaries;

(d) to keep the money and assets of the SMSF separate from the money and assets held personally by the trustees and from those of any employer-sponsor of the SMSF;

(e) not to enter into a contract or agreement that would hinder the trustees in properly performing their duties; and

(f) to formulate and give effect to a reserves strategy;[11]

The trustees' compliance responsibilities are summarised in the ATO's Guide for SMSF trustees *Running a self-managed super fund – Your role and responsibilities as a trustee.*[12]

13. The trustees of a SMSF are required, under the SISA, to ensure that financial reports of the SMSF are prepared and signed for each year of income and that an approved auditor is appointed no later than 30 days before the due date of the auditor's report.

Auditor's Responsibilities

14. An approved auditor[13] of a SMSF under the SISR[14] is required to be an individual who is currently either:

(a) a registered company auditor;

(b) a member of CPA Australia Ltd (CPA Australia), The Institute of Chartered Accountants in Australia (ICAA) or the Institute of Public Accountants (IPA);

(c) a member or fellow of the Association of Taxation and Management Accountants (ATMA);

GS

10 The applicability of enduring powers of attorney in this circumstance will vary depending on the relevant state legislation. Guidance is also provided in Self-Managed Superannuation Funds Ruling SMSFR 2010/2.

11 A reserves strategy is only required if reserves are held within the SMSF.

12 The ATO's Guide for SMSF trustees *Running a self-managed super fund - Your role and responsibilities as a trustee* (NAT 11032-06.2010) is available at www.ato.gov.au/Superfunds.

13 Approved auditor is defined under subsection 10(1) of the SISA.

14 Regulation 1.04(2) (a) and Schedule 1AAA of the SISR detail who may be an approved auditor of a SMSF. This differs from approved auditors of other superannuation entities under regulation 1.04(2)(b) of the SISR who must be either a registered company auditor or the Auditor-General of the Commonwealth, a State or a Territory.

(d) a fellow of the National Tax and Accountants Association Ltd (NTAA);[15]

(e) an SMSF Specialist Auditor for the SMSF professionals' Association of Australia Limited; or

(f) the Auditor-General of the Commonwealth, a State or a Territory;

and is not a person in respect of whom a disqualification order is in force under section 131 of the SISA.[16]

15. In addition, SMSF auditors may be subject to competency requirements, for the audit of SMSFs, by virtue of their membership of a professional body.[17] For example, members of CPA Australia, ICAA and IPA are required to comply with competency requirements[18] when accepting and conducting SMSF audits. These include requirements to hold a practising certificate, maintain appropriate professional indemnity insurance, complete minimum continuing professional development in the audit of SMSFs and ensure staff have appropriate knowledge and experience and are properly supervised. Auditors ensure that they are up-to-date and compliant with any applicable competency requirements imposed by their professional bodies in accepting and conducting SMSF audits.

16. The auditor is required under the SISA to:

(a) provide an auditor's report on the SMSF's operations for the year to the trustees in the approved form;[19]

(b) report in writing to a trustee, if the auditor forms the opinion in the course of or in connection with the performance of the audit of the SMSF, that:

(i) any contraventions of the SISA or SISR, may have occurred, may be occurring or may occur in relation to the SMSF (section 129 of the SISA); or

(ii) the financial position of the SMSF may be, or may be about to become, unsatisfactory (section 130 of the SISA); and

(c) report in writing to the ATO using the approved form Auditor/actuary contravention report (ACR) and instructions (ACR instructions),[20] if the auditor forms the opinion in the course of or in connection with the performance of the audit of a SMSF, that:

(i) it is likely that a contravention, may have occurred, may be occurring or may occur, of the requirements of the SISA or SISR, specified by the ATO in the ACR, which meet the tests specified in the ACR instructions (section 129 of the SISA); or

(ii) the financial position of the SMSF may be, or may be about to become, unsatisfactory (section 130 of the SISA).

17. The auditor may also provide information in the ACR to the ATO about the SMSF or a trustee of the SMSF, if the auditor considers it will assist the ATO in performing its functions under the SISA and SISR (section 130A of the SISA).

---

15 Fellows of the NTAA must have a practising certificate from one of the professional accounting bodies, or at least three years full time experience as a practitioner and hold a recognised degree with an accounting major.

16 At the time of publication, the Government is considering *Stronger Super* reforms which will change eligibility requirements for SMSF auditors, including new competency standards and an SMSF auditor registration requirement.

17 *Competency standards for Fellows of the NTAA auditing SMSFs* (December 2008) issued by NTAA.

18 *Competency Requirements for Auditors of Self-Managed Superannuation Funds* (February 2008) issued by Representatives of the Australian Accounting Profession, CPA Australia, ICAA and IPA (http://www.charteredaccountants.com.au/Industry-Topics/Superannuation/SMSF/~/media/Files/Industry%20topics/Superannuation/CompReqSMSF.ashx).

19 Section 35C of the SISA.

20 *Instructions for SMSF auditors and actuaries – Completing the Auditor/actuary contravention report containing the Auditor/actuary contravention report* (NAT 11299-07.2011) together comprise the approved form for the purposes of sections 129 and 130 of the SISA. See: www.ato.gov.au/Superfunds.

18. The approved form of the auditor's report, issued by the ATO, is divided into two parts:

(a) *Part A: Financial report*, which requires the auditor to express an opinion on the financial report, based on the audit, conducted "in accordance with Australian Auditing Standards" (ASAs).

(b) *Part B: Compliance*, which requires the auditor to express an opinion on compliance with sections and regulations of the SISA and SISR specified in the approved form auditor's report based on the compliance engagement, conducted "in accordance with applicable Standards on Assurance Engagements" (ASAEs).

Conduct the Financial Audit and Compliance Engagement in Accordance with ASQC 1

19. ASQC 1 *Quality Control for Firms that Perform Audits and Reviews of Financial Reports and Other Financial Information, and Other Assurance Engagements* establishes requirements and provides application and other explanatory material regarding the firm's responsibilities for its system of quality control for audits and reviews of financial reports and other financial information, and other assurance engagements.[21]

Conduct the Financial Audit in Accordance with ASAs

20. The auditor complies with all of the requirements in each of the ASAs relevant to the financial audit in determining the audit procedures to be performed in conducting an audit in accordance with the ASAs. The key ASAs which are relevant to the conduct of the financial audit of a SMSF include, but are not limited to:

(a) ASA 102 *Compliance with Ethical Requirements when Performing Audits, Reviews and Other Assurance Engagements* requires the auditor to comply with relevant ethical requirements, including those pertaining to independence.

(b) ASA 200 *Overall Objectives of the Independent Auditor and the Conduct of an Audit in Accordance with Australian Auditing Standards* requires the auditor to:

(i) comply with the relevant ethical requirements, including those pertaining to independence, relating to financial report audit engagements;

(ii) comply with all Australian Auditing Standards relevant to the audit;

(iii) plan and perform an audit of a financial report by exercising professional judgement;

(iv) plan and perform an audit with professional scepticism recognising that circumstances may exist that cause the financial report to be materially misstated; and

(v) To obtain reasonable assurance about whether the financial report as a whole is free from material misstatement, whether due to fraud or error, thereby enabling the auditor to express an opinion on whether the financial report is prepared, in all material respects, in accordance with an applicable financial reporting framework.

(c) ASA 210 *Agreeing the Terms of Audit Engagements* requires the terms of the audit engagement to be agreed with management or those charged with governance, in an audit engagement letter or other suitable form of written agreement. On recurring audits, the auditor assesses whether circumstances require the terms of the audit engagement to be revised and whether there is a need to remind the entity of the existing terms of the audit engagement. The auditor obtains the trustees' acknowledgement that their responsibilities under SIS include the preparation of financial statements and records, establishing and maintaining internal controls, particularly those preventing and detecting fraud and error, and providing the auditors with any information, explanations and assistance required for the audit.

21 Also refer to APES110: *Code of Ethics for Professional Accountants.*

GS

(d) ASA 220 *Quality Control for an Audit of a Financial Report and Other Financial Information* requires the engagement partner to:

(i) remain alert, through observation and making enquiries as necessary, for evidence of non-compliance with relevant ethical requirements by members of the engagement team, throughout the audit engagement;

(ii) form a conclusion on compliance with the independence requirements that apply to the audit engagement;

(iii) be satisfied that appropriate procedures regarding the acceptance and continuance of client relationships and audit engagements have been followed, and determine that conclusions reached in this regard are appropriate;

(iv) be satisfied that the engagement team, and any auditor's experts who are not part of the engagement team, collectively have the appropriate competence and capability to perform the audit engagement;

(v) take responsibility for the direction, supervision and performance of the audit engagement; and

(vi) take responsibility for the auditor's report being appropriate in the circumstances.

(e) ASA 230 *Audit Documentation* requires preparation of documentation:

(i) that is sufficient to enable an experienced auditor, having no previous connection with the audit, to understand the nature, timing and extent of the audit procedures performed to comply with the Australian Auditing Standards and applicable legal and regulatory requirements;

(ii) that is sufficient to enable an experienced auditor, having no previous connection with the audit, to understand the results of the audit procedures performed, the audit evidence obtained, significant matters arising during the audit, the audit conclusion reached thereon and significant professional judgements made in reaching those conclusions; and

(iii) which is assembled in an audit file on a timely basis (ordinarily not more than 60 days) after the date of the auditor's report.

(f) ASA 240 *The Auditor's Responsibilities Relating to Fraud in an Audit of a Financial Report* requires the auditor to consider the risks of material misstatements in the financial report due to fraud.[22]

(g) ASA 250 *Consideration of Laws and Regulations in an Audit of a Financial Report* requires the auditor to obtain a general understanding of the legal and regulatory framework applicable to the entity, how the entity is complying with that framework, perform further audit procedures to help identify instances of non-compliance with those laws and regulations that may have a material effect on the financial report and obtain sufficient appropriate audit evidence regarding compliance with those laws and regulations generally recognised to have a direct effect on the determination of material amounts and disclosures in the financial report. For example, non-compliance with requirements of the SISA, SISR or taxation legislation by an SMSF, such as the failure to meet the definition of a SMSF, may expose the SMSF to additional tax liabilities which may impact materially on the SMSF's financial report.

(h) ASA 260 *Communication with Those Charged with Governance* requires the auditor to determine the appropriate person(s) within the entity's governance structure with whom to communicate, usually the trustees in the audit of an SMSF, and communicate with them the responsibilities of the auditor in relation to the

22 Due to the few persons involved in the operation of an SMSF, there is ordinarily limited segregation of duties, which may impact on the auditor's assessment of fraud risk, as trustees, administrators or advisers may have an ability to override controls. SMSFs are not afforded the same level of protection as APRA regulated funds, for which provision is made, in certain circumstances, for members to be compensated for losses incurred in the event of fraud.

financial report audit, an overview of the planned scope and timing of the audit, significant findings from the audit, and auditor independence on a timely basis.

(i) ASA 265 *Communication Deficiencies in Internal Control to Those Charged with Governance and Management* requires the auditor to communicate appropriately to those charged with governance and management, deficiencies in internal control that the auditor has identified during the audit and that, in the auditor's professional judgement, are of sufficient importance to merit their respective attentions. This ASA may not be applicable for smaller audits.

(j) ASA 300 *Planning an Audit of a Financial Report* requires the auditor to perform preliminary engagement activities, including evaluation of their own compliance with relevant ethical requirements including independence, to establish and document an overall audit strategy that sets the scope, timing and direction of the audit, that guides the development of the audit plan and plan the nature, timing and extent of direction and supervision of the engagement team members and review of their work.

(k) ASA 315 *Identifying and Assessing the Risks of Material Misstatement through Understanding the Entity and Its Environment* requires the auditor to obtain an understanding of the entity (the SMSF) and its environment, including its internal controls to provide a basis for the identification and assessment of risks of material misstatement at the financial report and assertion level.

(l) ASA 320 *Materiality in Planning and Performing an Audit* requires the auditor to determine materiality for the financial report as a whole when determining the overall audit strategy, and to determine performance materiality for purposes of assessing the risks of material misstatement and determining the nature, timing and extent of further audit procedures.

(m) ASA 330 *The Auditor's Responses to Assessed Risks* requires the auditor to design and implement overall responses to address the assessed risks of material misstatement at the financial report level and design and perform further audit procedures whose nature, timing and extent are based on and are responsive to the assessed risks of material misstatement at the assertion level. Further audit procedures may comprise only substantive procedures or, when reliance is placed on the operating effectiveness of controls to reduce substantive testing, include tests of controls.

(n) ASA 402 *Audit Considerations Relating to an Entity Using a Service Organisation* requires the auditor to determine whether the service organisation's activities are of significance to the entity and relevant to the audit and, if so, the auditor is required to obtain a sufficient understanding of the entity and its environment to identify and assess the risks of material misstatement and design further audit procedures in response to the assessed risk. The auditor may need to obtain evidence of the operating effectiveness of the service organisation's controls and may use a report of a service organisation auditor to provide that evidence. In using the service auditor's report, the auditor considers the professional competence of the service auditor, the nature and content of the report, the scope of the work performed and whether the nature, timing and extent of the tests of controls and results that are relevant, provide sufficient appropriate audit evidence about the operating effectiveness of those controls to support the assessed risks of material misstatement. Guidance Statement GS 007 *Audit Implications of the Use of Service Organisations for Investment Management Services* provides further guidance to an auditor in obtaining sufficient appropriate audit evidence when the SMSF uses a third party service organisation for investment management services, including custody, asset management, property management, superannuation member administration, investment administration or registry.

(o) ASA 450 *Evaluation of Misstatements Identified during the Audit* requires the auditor to determine whether the overall audit strategy and audit plan needs to be revised if the nature of identified misstatements and the circumstances of their occurrence indicate that other misstatements may exist that, when aggregated

GS

with misstatements accumulated during the audit, could be material or approaches materiality determined in accordance with ASA 320.

(p) ASA 500 *Audit Evidence* requires the auditor to design and perform audit procedures that are appropriate in the circumstances for the purpose of obtaining sufficient appropriate audit evidence to be able to draw reasonable conclusions on which to base the audit opinion. It requires the auditor to consider the relevance and reliability of the information to be used as audit evidence.

(q) ASA 502 *Audit Evidence – Specific Considerations for Litigation and Claims* requires the auditor to design and perform audit procedures to identify litigation and claims which may give rise to a risk of material misstatement, and accounted for and disclosed in accordance with the applicable financial reporting framework. For an SMSF, material legal matters may include: the divorce of a member which may threaten the liquidity of the SMSF, an ATO investigation into the trustee or legal action commenced by the SMSF against the SMSF's administrators or investment managers, each of which may have a material effect on the financial report.

(r) ASA 505 *External Confirmations* requires the auditor to request external confirmations where they are necessary to obtain sufficient appropriate audit evidence.

(s) ASA 510 *Initial Audit Engagements – Opening Balances* requires the auditor to obtain sufficient appropriate audit evidence about whether the opening balances contain misstatements that materially affect the current period's financial report, whether the prior period closing balances have been correctly brought forward and that appropriate accounting policies are applied consistently.

(t) ASA 520 *Analytical Procedures* requires the auditor to design and perform analytical procedures to address the assessed risks of material misstatement near the end of the audit that assist the auditor when forming an overall conclusion as to whether the financial report is consistent with the auditor's understanding of the entity.

(u) ASA 540 *Auditing Accounting Estimates, Including Fair Value Accounting Estimates and Related Disclosures* requires the auditor to obtain sufficient appropriate audit evidence that accounting estimates, including fair value accounting estimates and disclosures are reasonable and are in accordance with the applicable financial reporting framework, which is chosen by the trustee in the case of an SMSF. The requirements and guidance in ASA 540 are particularly relevant to the audit of trustees' valuations, which are common in SMSF's.

(v) ASA 560 *Subsequent Events* requires the auditor to perform audit procedures designed to obtain sufficient appropriate audit evidence that all events up to the date of the auditor's report have been identified, and if material, are properly disclosed and accounted for.

(w) ASA 570 *Going Concern* requires the auditor to consider the appropriateness of use of the going concern assumption in the preparation of the financial report.

(x) ASA 580 *Written Representations* requires the auditor to request written representations from management that they are responsible for the preparation of the financial report in accordance with the applicable reporting framework, they have provided the auditor with all relevant information and access, and that all transactions have been recorded and reflected in the financial report. In the case of a SMSF these representations are obtained from the trustees.

(y) ASA 620 *Using the Work of an Auditor's Expert* requires the auditor, when using the work of an auditor's expert, to obtain sufficient appropriate audit evidence that such work is adequate for the purposes of the audit and to evaluate the competence, capabilities and objectives of the auditor's expert.

(z) ASA 700 *Forming an Opinion and Reporting on a Financial Report* requires the auditor to form an opinion on whether the financial report is prepared, in all material respects, in accordance with the applicable financial framework, and to express the auditor's report in writing.

(aa) ASA 705 *Modifications to the Opinion in the Independent Auditor's Report* requires the auditor to modify the auditor's report when it is not possible to issue an unmodified audit opinion. The circumstances may dictate that, due to a conflict, a significant uncertainty, a limitation of scope or a lack of sufficient appropriate audit evidence, that it is not possible to issue an unqualified audit opinion. In these circumstances, ASA 705 requires the auditor to issue either a qualified audit opinion, a disclaimer of opinion or an adverse opinion.

(bb) ASA 706 *Emphasis of Matter Paragraphs and Other Matter Paragraphs in the Independent Auditor's Report* contains the requirements of how the emphasis matter of paragraph is to be shown in the auditor's report.

(cc) ASA 710 *Comparative Information – Corresponding Figures and Comparative Financial Reports* requires the auditor to determine whether the financial report includes the comparative information required by the applicable financial reporting framework and whether such information is appropriately classified.

(dd) ASA 800 *Special Considerations – Audits of Financial Reports Prepared in Accordance with Special Purpose Frameworks* specifies the form of the auditor's report on special purpose financial reports, which for SMSFs is reflected in the approved form auditor's report issued by the ATO.[23] Auditor's reports for SMSF's are to include an Emphasis of Matter paragraph for periods commencing on or after 1 January 2010. This paragraph draws attention to the note of the financial report which describes the basis of accounting.

Conduct the Compliance Engagement in Accordance with Applicable ASAEs

21. ASAE 3100, which is to be read in conjunction with ASAE 3000 *Assurance Engagements Other Than Audits or Reviews of Historical Financial Information*, is applicable to the conduct of the compliance engagement of SMSFs. ASAE 3100 requires the auditor to:

- Comply with applicable ASAEs.
- Comply with the fundamental ethical principles of integrity, objectivity, professional competence and due care, confidentiality and professional behaviour.
- Implement quality control procedures.
- Meet acceptance and continuance procedures.
- Agree the terms of the engagement in writing.
- Plan the compliance engagement so that it will be performed effectively.
- Consider materiality and compliance engagement risk[24] when planning and performing the compliance engagement.
- Reduce compliance engagement risk to an acceptable level in the circumstances of the compliance engagement.
- Obtain sufficient appropriate evidence on which to base the conclusion and evaluate the impact on the conclusion of any compliance breaches noted.
- Consider the effect of events up to the date of the compliance report.
- Prepare, on a timely basis, documentation that is sufficient and appropriate to provide a basis for the auditor's conclusion and evidence that the engagement was performed in accordance with ASAE 3000 and ASAE 3100.
- Express a conclusion about the subject matter information, which for an SMSF is compliance in all material respects with the SISA and SISR requirements specified in the approved form auditor's report.

23 If the SMSF is a reporting entity, the SMSF is required to prepare a general purpose financial report and the auditor refers to the requirements in ASA 700 *The Auditor's Report on a General Purpose Financial Report*.

24 Compliance engagement risk is defined in ASAE 3100 paragraph 11 as: the risk that the assurance practitioner expresses an inappropriate conclusion when the entity (SMSF) is materially non-compliant with the requirements as measured by the suitable criteria (SISA sections and SISR regulations as specified in the ATO approved form auditor's report).

GS

22. Since ASAE 3100 is read in conjunction with ASAE 3000, where specific guidance is contained in ASAE 3000 and only referenced in ASAE 3100, this guidance statement makes direct reference to ASAE 3000. Although ASAs do not apply to compliance engagements, they may nevertheless provide helpful guidance in the conduct of a compliance engagement.

23. ASAE 3402, *Assurance Reports on Controls at a Service Organisation*, is applicable to the conduct of the compliance engagement of SMSFs. ASAE 3402 deals with assurance engagements undertaken by an auditor to provide a report for use by user entities and their auditors, on the controls at a service organisation that provides a service to user entities that is likely to be relevant to user entities' internal controls as they relate to financial reporting. It complements ASA 402, in that reports prepared in accordance with this standard are capable of providing appropriate evidence under ASA 402.

Preliminary Engagement Activities

24. Prior to commencing the audit, the auditor performs a number of preliminary tasks to gain confidence that undertaking the audit is appropriate from a client and ethical point of view. ASA 300 requires the auditor, prior to beginning an audit engagement, to:

    (a) perform procedures regarding the acceptance and continuance of the client relationship and the specific audit engagement;

    (b) evaluate compliance with relevant ethical requirements relating to the audit engagement, including independence; and

    (c) establish an understanding of the terms of engagement.

    These procedures are outlined below.

Acceptance and Continuance Procedures

25. Under the ASAs and ASAE 3000, the auditor only accepts or continues an engagement if nothing comes to the auditor's attention to indicate that the requirements of the fundamental ethical principles, the Auditing Standards and ASAE 3000 will not be satisfied.

26. For an initial audit, where there has been a change of auditor, the auditor communicates with the previous auditor in accordance with the relevant ethical requirements to ensure that there is no impediment or restriction in accepting and conducting the audit. The new auditor may need to seek permission from the trustees to communicate with the previous auditor.

Ethical Requirements

27. In accordance with ASA 102, ASA 200 and ASAE 3000, the auditor is required to comply with relevant ethical requirements relating to audit engagements, which include the applicable code of ethics of a professional accounting body (the Code of Ethics).[25] The fundamental principles of professional ethics comprise:

    (a) integrity;

    (b) objectivity;

    (c) professional competence and due care;

    (d) confidentiality; and

    (e) professional behaviour.

    The concept of independence is fundamental to compliance with the principles of integrity and objectivity.

---

25 In Australia, the applicable code of ethics of the professional accounting bodies is APES 110 *Code of Ethics for Professional Accountants*, as issued from time to time by the Accounting Professional and Ethical Standards Board. This Code of Ethics has been adopted by CPA Australia, IPA and ICAA and is applicable to their members. Members of the ATMA are also required to conform with this code under the ATMA by-laws. Fellows of the NTAA who obtained fellowship by virtue of holding a practising certificate from one of the professional accounting bodies, will be members of one of those bodies and consequently are also required to comply with the Code of Ethics.

28. Under ASA 220 and ASAE 3100, the auditor accepts an engagement only when the auditor is satisfied that they, and the engagement team if applicable, have met the relevant ethical requirements.

29. The auditor ensures that they possess, or if applicable the engagement team conducting the audit collectively possess, the appropriate capabilities, competence and time to conduct the audit in accordance with the ASAs, applicable ASAEs and legislative requirements. Capabilities and competence are developed through a variety of means, including professional education, training, practical experience, coaching and mentoring by more experienced staff. Meeting the applicable competency requirements of their professional bodies will assist SMSF auditors to maintain the competence, knowledge, skills and capabilities necessary to perform SMSF audits satisfactorily.

30. Under ASA 250, the auditor obtains a general understanding of the legal and regulatory environment applicable to the SMSF. A sound and current knowledge of superannuation legislation, including the SISA and SISR, relevant taxation legislation and ATO Rulings and Determinations, is necessary for the auditor to meet this requirement.

Independence

31. ASA 220 requires the engagement partner to form a conclusion on compliance with the independence requirements applying to the audit engagement which are contained in the Code of Ethics. ASAE 3100 requires compliance with the fundamental ethical principles on compliance engagements, for which the concept of independence is integral.

32. Overall, independence requires both:
    (a) independence of mind - the state of mind that permits the expression of a conclusion without being affected by influences that compromise professional judgment, allowing an individual to act with integrity, and exercise objectivity and professional scepticism; and
    (b) independence in appearance - the avoidance of facts and circumstances that are so significant that a reasonable and informed third party, having knowledge of all relevant information, including safeguards applied, would reasonably conclude a firm's, or a member of the engagement team's, integrity, objectivity or professional scepticism had been compromised.

33. The Code of Ethics provides a framework of principles that auditors and members of audit teams use to ensure that independence of mind and independence in appearance are not compromised.

34. When assessing independence the auditor:
    (a) identifies any threats to independence;
    (b) evaluates the significance of the threats; and
    (c) if the threats are other than clearly insignificant, identifies and applies safeguards to eliminate or reduce the threats to an acceptable level.

35. The threats to independence in a SMSF audit engagement may include:
    - *Self-interest threat*, which occurs when a firm or a member of the audit team *could benefit from a financial interest in, or other self-interest conflict with*, an audit client. For example, this could arise if the auditor, member of the audit team or their immediate family member is a trustee or member of the SMSF or the SMSF is the sole client or a significant client of the firm.
    - *Self-review threat*, which occurs when any product such as a set of financial accounts, or a judgement of a previous engagement needs to be re-evaluated in reaching conclusions on the audit engagement so that the auditor is reviewing their own work. For example, where a member of the audit team prepared the SMSF's financial report or accounting records.
    - *Advocacy threat*, which occurs when a firm, or member of the audit team, promotes, or may be perceived to promote an audit client's position to the point that objectivity may be, or be perceived to be, compromised. For example, when an audit team member acts as an advocate for the SMSF in litigation or a dispute.

GS

- *Familiarity threat*, which is when, by virtue of a close relationship with an audit client, its directors, officers or employees, the firm or a member of the audit team becomes too sympathetic to the client's interests. For example, when a close family member of the auditor is a trustee or member of the SMSF or an employee of the SMSF's administrator or where the auditor has a long association with a trustee.
- *Intimidation threat*, which is when a member of the audit team is deterred from acting objectively by threats, actual or perceived, from the trustees of the SMSF or the directors, officers or employees of a related entity of a trustee. For example, a threat of replacement over a disagreement with the application of an accounting principle or the loss of other general accounting or tax work if the auditor's opinion is modified or an ACR is submitted to the ATO. An intimidation threat may also arise where a SMSF administrator pressures the auditor to reduce inappropriately the extent of work performed in order to reduce fees in circumstances where the administrator refers a significant number of SMSF audit clients.

36. Safeguards to independence may be:
    (a) created by the profession, legislation or regulation;
    (b) within the SMSF; or
    (c) within the firm's own systems and procedures.

37. Safeguards created by the profession, legislation or regulation, generally include the following:
    - Educational, training and experience requirements for entry into the profession.
    - Continuing education requirements.
    - Professional standards, monitoring and disciplinary processes.
    - External review of a firm's quality control system.
    - Legislation covering the independence requirements of the firm.
    - Recommendations on independence from relevant regulators.

38. Safeguards within the SMSF may be limited, as by its very nature, a SMSF is a small entity with limited scope for segregation of duties. Hence reliance on internal safeguards may not be possible and the auditor ordinarily relies on the safeguards created by the profession, legislation and regulation and those safeguards created by internal systems within the auditor's firm to enhance independence.

39. In evaluating threats to independence and considering applicable safeguards, the auditor considers the nature of the SMSF, the range of services provided to the audit client and the relationships the auditor and the audit team have with the SMSF's trustees, financial adviser, accountants, administrator, actuary and any other person or organisation involved with the management or operation of the SMSF.

40. Assisting an audit client in the preparation of accounting records or financial reports may create a self-review threat when those records and reports are subsequently audited by the same firm. If the firm's staff also make management decisions for the SMSF, which may occur if the firm is providing administrative services to the SMSF, there are no safeguards available to reduce the self-review threat to an acceptably low level, other than withdrawal from either the administration or the audit engagement.

41. If, however, the accounting services provided are of a routine or mechanical nature, such as posting transactions and entries approved by the SMSF or preparing the financial report based on a trial balance provided by the SMSF, the self-review threat may be reduced to an acceptably low level by applying safeguards, including:
    - Making arrangements so accounting services are not performed by a member of the audit team.
    - Implementing policies and procedures to prohibit the individual providing such services from making any managerial decisions on behalf of the SMSF.
    - Requiring the source data for the accounting entries to be originated by the SMSF.
    - Requiring the underlying assumptions to be originated and approved by the SMSF.

- Obtaining the SMSF's approval for any proposed journal entries or other changes affecting the financial report.
- Obtaining the SMSF's acknowledgement of their responsibility for the accounting work performed by the firm.
- Disclosing to the trustees the firm's involvement in both engagements.

42. Provision of taxation services to a SMSF which is also an audit client would not generally create a threat to independence.

43. Provision of financial advice to a SMSF which is also an audit client may create advocacy and self-review threats. These threats may be reduced to an acceptably low level by safeguards such as:
    - Implementing policies and procedures to prohibit individuals providing advice from making managerial decisions on behalf of the SMSF.
    - Using staff and partners who are not members of the audit team to provide the financial advice.
    - Ensuring that the individual providing the advice does not commit the SMSF to the terms of any transaction or consummate a transaction on behalf of the SMSF.

44. Where the audit firm or individual partner is unduly reliant on the audit fees from a particular SMSF or group of SMSFs, such as those SMSFs referred by a certain advisor or administrator, the concern about the possibility of losing the referrals may create a self-interest or intimidation threat. Safeguards may include diversifying the client base to spread the source of revenue so that the potential for undue influence is removed or obtaining an external quality review.

45. Safeguards that the auditor may apply to manage other identified self-interest, advocacy, familiarity or intimidation threats to independence may include:
    - Prohibiting the holding of direct, or material indirect, financial interests by the auditor in closely held investments of the SMSF, such as a joint venture or property syndicate.
    - Removal from the SMSF audit team of any personnel with a close relationship with the trustees of the SMSF, including relatives of the trustees.

46. In situations in which no safeguards are available to reduce the threat to an acceptable level, the only possible actions are to eliminate the activities or interest creating the threat, or to refuse to accept or continue the audit engagement.[26]

47. Appendix 6 of this Guidance Statement provides a number of practical examples of SMSF audit engagements and the threats to independence posed by those engagements, as well as some appropriate safeguards which may address those threats.

Professional Judgement and Scepticism

48. ASA 200 requires the auditor to plan and perform an audit exercising professional judgement, and with an attitude of professional scepticism.
    - *Professional judgement* emanates typically from the auditor's expertise, experience, knowledge and training. When exercising professional judgement, the auditor maintains independence and objectivity and adopts an attitude of professional scepticism in order to achieve the audit objectives.
    - *Professional scepticism* requires the auditor to maintain a questioning mind as to the validity of audit evidence presented and representations of the trustees. The auditor remains alert to contradictory information or information that brings into question the validity of the evidence presented.

GS

26 The ATO has stated that they consider there is a significant breach of professional requirements where an auditor has accepted an audit engagement for a fund where the auditor is:
- a trustee / director of the corporate trustee or a member of the fund
- a relative or close associate of the trustee / director of the corporate trustee or member of the fund, or has personally prepared the accounts and statements for the fund.

Quality Control

49. Under ASA 220 and ASAE 3100, the engagement partner implements procedures to ensure quality control systems are applied to both the financial audit and compliance engagement including:
    - Taking responsibility for overall quality on the financial audit and compliance engagement.
    - Considering whether members of the engagement team have complied with relevant ethical requirements.
    - Forming a conclusion on compliance with relevant independence requirements.
    - Ensuring that requirements in relation to acceptance and continuance of client relationships and specific audit engagements have been followed and that conclusions reached are appropriate and have been adequately documented.
    - Assigning audit engagement teams which possess collectively the appropriate capabilities, competence and time to perform the engagements in accordance with AUASB Standards and regulatory and legal requirements.
    - Directing, supervising and performing the audit engagement in accordance with AUASB Standards and regulatory and legal requirements.
    - Issuing an auditor's report that is appropriate in the circumstances and supported by sufficient appropriate audit evidence.
    - Consulting appropriately on difficult or contentious matters both within the engagement team and with others within or outside the firm, and documenting and implementing agreed conclusions.
    - Monitoring quality adequately against firm and professional standards, including the ASAs and ASAEs.

Agree the Terms of Engagement

50. Under ASA 210, the auditor is required to agree the terms of the audit engagement in writing with the SMSF prior to conducting the audit. This is usually in the form of an engagement letter to the trustees. ASA 210 provides guidance on the principal contents of an engagement letter.

51. The trustees are required to appoint the auditor at least 30 days prior to the date that the auditor's report is due.[27] Either the trustees may be involved in the selection and appointment of the auditor or the SMSF's accountants, administrators or financial planners may assist with the sourcing and recruitment of an auditor for the SMSF. In either case, the trustees approve the appointment in writing before the audit commences, usually by signing the engagement letter and indicating their approval in a trustee minute.

52. For a SMSF audit engagement, the engagement letter ordinarily:
    - Describes the objective and scope of the financial audit and compliance engagement, including the sections and regulations of SISA and SISR against which the auditor will be reporting.
    - Identifies the responsibilities of the auditor.
    - Identifies the responsibilities of the trustees, including:
        - Establishing and maintaining an adequate internal control structure.
        - Preparing the SMSF's financial report.
        - Keeping the records of the SMSF secure and for the statutory time periods.
        - Conducting the affairs of the SMSF in compliance with all relevant provisions of SISA, SISR and the trust deed throughout the year.

27 Requirement under regulation 8.02A of the SISR. If the auditor is appointed less than 30 days before the audit report is due, then the auditor may report the contravention to the trustee under section 129 or decline the engagement.

- Sets out the reporting requirements of the auditor, including those imposed by sections 129 and 130 of the SISA.
- Includes a notice to the trustees that the audit records and auditor's work may be subject to review by the professional body of which the auditor is a member or by the ATO.

53. ASA 210 does not require engagement letters to be issued every year. However, on recurring audits, the auditor considers whether it is appropriate to confirm the terms of the engagement in writing due to the circumstances of the engagement, including when there is:
    - A revision of the terms of the engagement.
    - An indication that the trustees misunderstand the objective and scope of the audit.
    - A change in trustees.
    - A significant change in the nature or size of the SMSF.
    - Significant changes in the SISA, SISR or other regulatory requirements, such as changes to the requirements to be reported on in the approved form auditor's report or ACR.
54. An example engagement letter is attached as Appendix 1 of this Guidance Statement.

Planning

55. Planning an audit involves a number of closely related procedures which include:
    - Establishing the overall audit strategy for the audit.
    - Developing and documenting an audit plan in order to reduce audit risk and compliance engagement risk to an acceptably low level.
    - Updating the audit strategy and the audit plan during the course of the audit.
    - Planning the nature, timing and extent of direction and supervision of engagement team members and review of their work.
56. The auditor plans the financial audit and compliance engagement so that they may be conducted in an effective manner in order to reduce audit risk and compliance engagement risk to an acceptably low level.
57. Adequate planning may:
    - Ensure appropriate attention to important areas of the audit engagement.
    - Identify potential problems on a timely basis.
    - Assist in the proper organisation and management of the audit engagement in order for it to be performed in an effective manner.
    - Assist the auditor in assigning work properly to audit team members, and facilitates the direction, supervision and review of the team's work.
    - Assist, where applicable, in the coordination of work performed by other auditors, actuaries and experts.
58. The nature, timing and extent of planning activities will vary according to:
    - The size and complexity of the SMSF.
    - Whether the SMSF was a complying fund in prior years.
    - Whether the SMSF is a defined benefit or accumulation fund.
    - The level of trustee involvement and knowledge of the operations of the SMSF.
    - Whether the SMSF is self-administered or administered by a third party service organisation.
    - The nature and range of investments held and whether they are internally or externally managed.
    - The availability of service auditor's reports for services provided by service organisations.

GS

- Whether the employer-sponsor is also a client of the firm preparing the accounts or the auditor.
- The potential and any known previous compliance issues.
- The auditor's previous experience, if any, with the SMSF.
- The due date for lodgement of the SMSF's Annual Return to the ATO.

59. Annual review of the audit plan is necessary to ensure that it is updated to reflect the current circumstances of the SMSF and any changes in legislation that may affect the SMSF.

Overall Audit Strategy

60. Under ASA 300, the auditor is required to establish the overall audit strategy for the financial audit and this is mirrored in the guidance in ASAE 3100 for the compliance engagement. The overall audit strategy sets the scope, emphasis, timing, direction and conduct of the audit, including the resources required for the audit and supervision of the audit team. The audit strategy is based on the results of the preliminary work performed and the auditor's experience gained on any previous audit engagements with the SMSF.

61. The complexity of the audit strategy will vary with the size and complexity of the SMSF.[28] The strategy guides the development of the more detailed audit plan for the nature, timing and extent of evidence gathering procedures to be performed and the reasons for selecting them.

62. In conducting a SMSF audit, the auditor obtains a preliminary understanding of the SMSF, including the SMSF's trust structure, nature of its investments and administration, the parties involved in the management and trusteeship of the SMSF and related parties of the trustees and members.

63. In gaining this preliminary understanding of the SMSF, the auditor reviews the current trust deed to verify whether:

    (a) The trust deed was properly executed.

    (b) The SMSF has current and appropriately empowered trustees.

    (c) The SMSF was established with either a corporate trustee, individual trustees or to pay a pension.

    (d) The trust deed complies with or has a mechanism to comply with the SISA and SISR and changes thereto.

    (e) The powers to accept contributions and pay benefits, in the form permitted by the SISA and SISR, are included.

    The covenants in subsection 52(2) of the SISA are deemed to be included in the governing rules, even if they are not specifically included. A comprehensive list of considerations in examining the SMSF's trust deed is included in Appendix 4 *Self-Managed Superannuation Fund Trust Deed Audit Planning Checklist*.

64. It is possible for the trust deed to be more restrictive than the SISA and SISR and prohibit or limit the trustees' actions or powers. However, if the Deed is more expansive than the SISA and SISR, then the SISA and SISR will prevail.

The Audit Plan

65. ASA 300 requires the auditor to develop and document the audit plan to record the key decisions and the nature, timing and extent of risk assessment procedures to be undertaken. The form and extent of the audit plan depends on the complexity of the SMSF and the circumstances of the specific audit engagement. The audit plan documents the procedures proposed to be undertaken at the assertion level and evidences work performed to facilitate proper review, supervision of the audit team and any external quality review.

28 ASA 300 provides guidance on establishing the audit strategy for smaller entities.

66. The audit plan is dynamic and is required to be updated if necessary during the course of the audit. Audit evidence obtained may trigger a revision of the initial risk assessment and a need for further audit procedures, which is documented accordingly.

67. Often, the audit plan for a SMSF takes the form of a checklist which assists in maintaining quality control for the engagement as required by ASA 220. However, standardised checklists need to be tailored specifically to reflect the particular circumstances and nature of the SMSF and the audit evidence available.

68. The audit plan encompasses financial audit procedures, such as the illustrative financial audit procedures listed in Appendix 5 of this Guidance Statement, as well as compliance procedures.[29]

Risk Assessment Procedures

69. The auditor obtains a sufficient understanding of the SMSF and its environment, including its internal control, to identify and assess the risks of material misstatement of the financial report, whether due to fraud or error, and the risk of non-compliance with the specified requirements of the SISA and SISR, in order to design and perform further audit procedures. The risk assessment for the financial audit includes identifying and assessing risks at the financial report level and at the assertion level for classes of transactions, account balances and disclosures, as required by ASA 330.

70. Under ASA 315, the auditor is required to examine the internal controls of the SMSF and document the auditor's understanding of the control environment. ASAE 3100 requires the auditor to document the key elements of the compliance framework, such as procedures for identifying, assessing and reporting compliance incidents and breaches.

71. Under ASA 250, the auditor is required to consider whether the SMSF has breached the SISA or SISR previously and whether there is any outstanding correspondence or unresolved issues with the ATO. Any such matters identified will impact on the risk assessment and the auditor's assessment of the compliance framework.

72. SMSFs are often small entities, with a close and related membership where control is vested in a few individuals. There may be little or no opportunity for implementing proper segregation of duties in these circumstances. Consequently, the auditor may assess the SMSF's control environment and compliance framework as ineffective, in which case the auditor will be unable to rely on the effectiveness of the internal controls to reduce substantive testing. As a result, the auditor may design and perform further audit procedures which are primarily or entirely substantive procedures. If the administration of the SMSF is outsourced, the auditor looks at the controls prevailing at the administrator.

Materiality

73. ASA 320 requires the auditor to consider performance materiality[30] when determining the nature, timing and extent of financial audit procedures and ASA 450 requires the auditor to consider materiality when evaluating the effect of misstatements identified during the audit. Similarly, under ASAE 3100, the auditor considers materiality when planning and performing the compliance engagement and in assessing any compliance breaches identified. Information is material if its omission, misstatement or non-disclosure has the potential to adversely affect decisions made by users of the report. An auditor's consideration of materiality is a matter of professional judgement, and is affected by the auditor's perception of the information needs of users and the level of audit risk.

GS

29 Illustrative compliance procedures or compliance checklists are available as guidance for the SMSF auditor, such as *Instructions for Auditors of SMSFs - Auditing a Self-Managed Super Fund –Questions and statements to consider when auditing a self-managed super fund* (NAT 16308-08.2008) issued by the ATO, which is available at www.ato.gov.au/Superfunds. In addition, the ATO's electronic SMSF audit tool (eSAT), for use in conducting the compliance engagement, is available on the ATO website.

30 Performance materiality refers to the amount or amounts set by the auditor at less than materiality for the financial report as a whole to reduce to an appropriate low level the probability that the aggregate of uncorrected and undetected misstatements exceeds materiality for the financial report as a whole. If applicable, performance materiality also refers to the amount or amounts set by the auditor at less than the materiality level or levels for particular classes of transactions, account balances or disclosures.

74. The auditor's preliminary assessment of materiality is based largely on quantitative factors, whereas when assessing the outcome of audit procedures, including the materiality of misstatements identified in the financial audit or contraventions identified in the compliance engagement, the auditor considers both their amount (quantitative) and nature (qualitative).

75. Materiality differs in nature between a financial audit and a compliance engagement and is discussed separately within both Part A (paragraphs 146 to 149) and Part B (paragraph 285) respectively of this Guidance Statement.

Audit Evidence

76. The results of the risk assessment procedures enable the auditor to design and perform further audit procedures to respond to the assessed risks for the compliance engagement and financial audit. The auditor determines the nature, timing and extent of audit procedures to be performed, which may be either tests of controls or substantive procedures.

77. ASA 500 and ASAE 3100 require the auditor in the conduct of the financial audit and compliance engagement to obtain sufficient appropriate audit evidence on which to base the auditor's opinion. Sufficiency is the measure of the quantity of evidence, which is affected by the risk of misstatement, the higher the risk the more evidence is likely to be required. Appropriateness is the measure of the quality of evidence, that is, its relevance and its reliability, the higher the quality the less evidence may be required. The auditor considers the relationship between the cost of obtaining evidence and the usefulness of the information obtained. However, the matter of difficulty or expense involved is not in itself a valid basis for omitting an evidence gathering procedure for which there is no alternative. The auditor uses professional judgement and exercises professional scepticism in evaluating the quantity and quality of evidence, and thus its sufficiency and appropriateness, to support the audit opinion.

78. Audit evidence means all the information used by the auditor in arriving at the conclusions on which the auditor's opinion is based, and includes the information contained in the accounting records underlying the financial report and other information. For a SMSF this includes financial reports, trustees' minutes, investment holding certificates, contracts of sale, bank statements, invoices, receipts, titles, legal advice, correspondence, emails, Annual Returns, deposit books and cheque butts, which may be in paper or electronic form. Audit evidence, which is cumulative in nature, includes evidence obtained from audit procedures performed during the course of the audit and may include evidence obtained from previous audits and other sources.

79. Audit evidence is generally more reliable when:

- Obtained from an independent source.
- Controls are operating effectively.
- Obtained directly by the auditor.
- In documentary form.
- It comprises of original documents.

Evidence received directly by the auditor is substantially more reliable than evidence that has passed through other parties.

80. A SMSF audit rarely involves the authentication of documentation, nor is the auditor trained as, or expected to be, an expert in such authentication. However, ASA 500 and ASAE 3000 require the auditor to consider the reliability of the information to be used as evidence, for example photocopies, facsimiles, filmed, digitised or other electronic documents which are easily altered, including consideration of controls over their preparation and maintenance where relevant. The auditor remains aware of the potential for fraud in the presentation of audit evidence. If an auditor is aware that any documentation has been altered or differs from expected results, then further audit procedures should be applied.

81. ASA 500 provides guidance on the substantive audit procedures which the auditor may conduct to collect appropriate evidence, which include:
- Inspection of records or documents.
- Inspection of tangible assets.
- Observation.
- Enquiry.
- Confirmation.
- Recalculation.
- Reperformance.
- Analytical review.

82. ASA 530 *Audit Sampling and Other Means of Testing* requires the auditor to determine the appropriate means for selecting items for testing. Due to the specific nature of SMSFs and limited internal control environment, the auditor may decide on a highly substantive method of testing. This may involve examining the entire population of items that make up a class of transactions or account balance, when the population constitutes a small number of large value items or when there is a significant level of risk and other means do not provide sufficient appropriate audit evidence.

Inspection of Records or Documents

83. Inspection of records or documents consists of examining records or documents, whether internal or external, in paper form, electronic form, or other media. Inspection of records and documents provides audit evidence of varying degrees of reliability, depending on their nature and source and, in the case of internal records and documents, on the effectiveness of the controls over their production.

84. Some documents represent direct audit evidence of the existence of an asset, for example, a document constituting a financial instrument such as a share or bond. Inspection of such documents may not necessarily provide audit evidence about ownership or value. In addition, inspecting an executed contract may provide audit evidence relevant to the SMSF's application of accounting policies, such as revenue recognition.

Inspection of Tangible Assets

85. Inspection of tangible assets consists of physical examination of the assets. Inspection of tangible assets may provide reliable audit evidence with respect to their existence, but not necessarily about the SMSF's rights and obligations or the valuation of the assets.

Observation

86. Observation consists of watching a process or procedure being performed by others. Observation provides audit evidence about the performance of a process or procedure, but is limited to the point in time at which the observation takes place and by the fact that the act of being observed may affect how the process or procedure is performed.

Enquiry

87. Enquiry consists of seeking financial or non-financial information from knowledgeable persons, either within the SMSF or outside the SMSF. Enquiry is an audit procedure that is used extensively throughout the audit and often is complementary to performing other audit procedures. Enquiries may range from formal written enquiries to informal oral enquiries. Evaluating responses to enquiries is an integral part of the enquiry process.

88. Responses received to enquiries may provide the auditor with information not previously possessed or with corroborative audit evidence supporting the audit opinion. Alternatively, responses to enquiries may provide information that differs significantly from other information that the auditor has obtained. In all cases, the auditor evaluates the responses received to enquiries to assess whether there is a need to modify or perform additional audit procedures to support the audit opinion.

89. Enquiry alone ordinarily does not provide sufficient audit evidence to detect a material misstatement at the assertion level, nor sufficient evidence of the operating effectiveness

GS

of controls, therefore the auditor performs further audit procedures to obtain sufficient appropriate audit evidence.

90. The auditor obtains written representations from the trustees or management to confirm responses to oral enquiries on material matters when other sufficient appropriate audit evidence cannot reasonably be expected to exist or when the other audit evidence obtained is of a lower quality.[31]

Confirmation

91. Confirmation, which is a specific type of enquiry, is the process of obtaining a representation of an existing condition or information directly from a third party. For example, the auditor may seek direct confirmation of cash balances with the SMSF's bank. Confirmations are frequently used in relation to account balances and their components.[32]

Recalculation

92. Recalculation consists of checking the mathematical accuracy of documents, records or account balances. Recalculation may be performed electronically, for example through the use of through the use of computer assisted audit techniques (CAATs) to check the accuracy of the summarisation of the electronic accounts, or manually, for example to recalculate account balances from primary documentation to validate the balance.

Reperformance

93. Reperformance is the auditor's independent execution of procedures and controls that were originally performed as part of the SMSF's operations, for example reperforming the calculation of net market movement for a range of listed securities. Reperformance may be conducted either manually or through the use of CAATs.

Analytical Procedures

94. Under ASA 520, the auditor is required to apply analytical procedures as risk assessment procedures to obtain an understanding of the SMSF and its environment and in the overall review at the end of the audit.

95. Analytical review procedures may be utilised to compare and contrast how the SMSF has performed over two or more consecutive reporting periods. Common analytical procedures include comparing balances, calculating ratios and trend analysis. Major variations, inconsistencies or other deviations may warrant further investigation particularly where the difference is not easily understood, not explained sufficiently by the trustees or deviates from predicted amounts.

96. Ordinarily, an auditor reviews the movement in the member balances from one period to another in the preliminary planning phase of the audit. This process identifies the movement in the balance from contributions and investment earnings as well as any reduction in balances due to benefit payments or expenses such as fees, charges or insurance premiums deducted. The auditor uses analytical review to assess whether the member balances are reasonable given the overall circumstances of the SMSF.

Audit Documentation

97. ASA 230 and ASAE 3100 require the auditor to prepare, on a timely basis, audit documentation that is sufficient and appropriate to provide:

    (a) a basis for the auditor's report; and

    (b) evidence that the audit was performed in accordance with ASAs, applicable ASAEs and applicable legal and regulatory requirements.

98. Preparing sufficient appropriate audit documentation on a timely basis helps to enhance the quality of the audit and facilitates the effective review and evaluation of the audit evidence obtained and conclusions reached before the auditor's report is finalised.

31 See ASA 580 for further requirements and explanatory guidance on written representations.

32 See ASA 505 for further requirements and explanatory guidance on confirmations.

Documentation prepared at the time the work is performed is likely to be more accurate than documentation prepared subsequently.

99. In assessing the extent of documentation, the auditor considers what audit documentation is necessary to enable an experienced auditor, having no previous connection with the audit, to understand:

(a) the nature, timing, and extent of the audit procedures performed to comply with ASAs, applicable ASAEs and applicable legal and regulatory requirements;

(b) the results of the audit procedures and the audit evidence obtained; and

(c) significant matters arising during the audit and the conclusions reached thereon.

100. The form, content and extent of audit documentation depend on factors such as:

- The nature of the audit procedures to be performed.
- The identified risks of material misstatement.
- The extent of judgement required in performing the work and evaluating the results.
- The significance of the audit evidence obtained.
- The nature and extent of exceptions identified.
- The need to document a conclusion or the basis for a conclusion not readily determinable from the documentation of the work performed or audit evidence obtained.
- The audit methodology and tools used.

It is, however, neither necessary nor practicable to document every matter the auditor considers during the audit.

Nature of Documentation

101. Audit documentation may be recorded on paper, electronically or on other media. It includes, for example, audit programs, analyses, records of audit testing and results of that testing, issues memoranda, summaries of significant matters, letters of confirmation and representation, checklists, and correspondence (including email) concerning significant matters. Abstracts or copies of the SMSF's records, for example, significant and specific contracts and agreements, may be included as part of audit documentation if considered appropriate. Audit documentation, however, is not a substitute for the SMSF's accounting records.

102. Oral explanations by the auditor, on their own, do not represent adequate support for the work the auditor performed or conclusions the auditor reached, but may be used to explain or clarify information contained in the audit documentation.

103. ASA 230 requires the auditor in documenting the nature, timing and extent of audit procedures to record by whom and when the audit work was performed and, if applicable, who reviewed the audit work and the extent of the review.

104. The auditor completes the assembly of the final audit file on a timely basis after the date of the auditor's report. This facilitates justification and verification that appropriate audit procedures were performed in the audit. Quality reviews, internal and external, are able to be performed more quickly and efficiently if a file is constructed in an orderly and logical manner.

105. Under ASA 230, the auditor is required to adopt appropriate procedures for maintaining the confidentiality, safe custody, integrity, accessibility and retrievability of audit documentation.

Significant Matters

106. The auditor may consider it helpful to prepare and retain as part of the audit documentation a summary (sometimes known as a completion memorandum) that describes the significant matters identified during the audit and how they were addressed, or that includes cross-references to other relevant supporting audit documentation that provides such information.

Such a summary may facilitate effective and efficient reviews and inspections of the audit documentation. The preparation of such a summary may assist the auditor's consideration of the significant matters.

107. Judging the significance of a matter requires an objective analysis of the facts and circumstances of the situation. Significant matters include:

- Matters that give rise to significant risks (as defined in ASA 315).
- Results of audit procedures indicating that the financial information could be materially misstated; or a need to revise the auditor's previous assessment of the risks of material misstatement and the auditor's responses to those risks.
- Circumstances that cause the auditor significant difficulty in applying necessary audit procedures.
- Findings that could result in a modification to the auditor's report.

108. If the auditor identifies information that contradicts or is inconsistent with the auditor's final conclusion regarding a significant matter, the auditor documents how the contradiction or inconsistency has been addressed in forming the auditor's final opinion.

Representations

109. Under ASA 580 and ASAE 3100, the auditor seeks written representations from the trustees regarding financial and compliance matters. These written representations are generally in the form of a representation letter which may confirm both verbal representations made during the course of the audit as well as other matters requiring written confirmation.

110. With respect to the financial audit of a SMSF, under ASA 580 the auditor obtains written representations from the trustees, including that they:

- Acknowledge responsibility for the fair presentation of the financial report in accordance with the adopted applicable financial reporting framework.
- Have approved the financial report.
- Confirm specified matters material to the financial report, when other sufficient appropriate audit evidence cannot reasonably be expected to exist.
- Acknowledge their responsibility for the design and implementation of internal control to prevent and detect error.
- Believe the effect of uncorrected misstatements aggregated by the auditor are immaterial, both individually and in aggregate, to the financial report.

111. The auditor may also seek representations under ASAE 3100, with respect to the compliance engagement, that the trustees:

- Confirm specified matters material to the compliance engagement.
- Have conducted the affairs of the SMSF in compliance with the SISA and SISR throughout the period.

112. Upon receipt of a written representation, the auditor evaluates the representation for reasonableness against other audit evidence collected and the knowledge of the individual making the representation and, where possible, obtains corroborative evidence.

113. Representations by the trustees cannot replace other evidence the auditor could reasonably expect to be available. An inability to obtain sufficient appropriate evidence regarding a matter that has, or may have, a material effect on the financial report or evaluation or measurement of the subject matter, when such evidence would ordinarily be available, constitutes a limitation on the scope of the audit, even if a representation from the responsible party has been received on the matter. In such circumstances, ASA 705 and ASAE 3100 require the auditor to express a qualified opinion or a disclaimer of opinion.

114. An example Trustee Representation Letter which covers both the financial audit and compliance engagement is included as Appendix 2 of this Guidance Statement.

Service Organisations

115. SMSFs may use service organisations to provide services such as investment management services including:
    - Custody.
    - Asset management (including Hedge fund management and Private Equity).
    - Property management.
    - Superannuation member administration.
    - Investment administration, including fund accounting and/or fund administration.
    - Registry.

    These management services may take various forms including WRAP[33] accounts, individually managed portfolio services, individual mandates or platform investments. Further guidance is provided in GS 007[34].

116. The use of a service organisation by a SMSF may render the audit evidence required less readily accessible to the auditor if the service organisation provides some of the record keeping or compliance functions of the SMSF.

117. Nevertheless, location of audit evidence at the service organisation does not alter the overall scope and objective of the financial audit and compliance engagement of the SMSF. Therefore, it remains the responsibility of the auditor to obtain sufficient appropriate audit evidence to support the auditor's financial audit and compliance assurance opinions. The requirements of the AUASB Standards relating to obtaining sufficient appropriate evidence on which to form an opinion are the same as would apply if the records and supporting documentation were maintained by the SMSF.

118. The use of a service organisation may provide the auditor with the opportunity to reduce substantive testing for balances and transactions maintained by the service organisation, if reliance can be placed on the service organisation's controls. ASA 402 establishes requirements and provides guidance regarding the use of controls reports from service organisations as evidence for a financial audit. In addition, GS 007 provides further guidance where the services provided to the SMSF are investment management services. Controls reports prepared under ASA 402, ASAE 3402 and GS 007 are not intended to provide any assurance with respect to controls over compliance with SISA or SISR and consequently those reports may not contain any evidence of the operating effectiveness of controls over compliance. Nevertheless, where controls over compliance with the requirements of SISA and SISR relevant to the SMSF are included in the controls report prepared by a service organisation, then it may provide the auditor with the opportunity to reduce substantive testing over compliance matters maintained by the service organisation.

119. In obtaining an understanding of the SMSF and its environment for the financial audit, under ASA 402 the auditor determines the significance of the service organisation's activities to the SMSF and the relevance to the audit. In doing so, the user auditor determines:
    - The nature and materiality of the transactions processed or accounts affected by the service organisation.
    - The nature of the relationship between the SMSF and the service organisation, including the contractual terms applying to the services provided by the service organisation.

GS

33 A "WRAP" or "Wrap Service" is an administrative and reporting service that combines and reports on an investor's total investment portfolio in a single report. WRAPS combine reporting on such investments including bank accounts, listed securities, corporate actions and managed funds which are held within the portfolio. Some Wrap Services also provide a service where other assets, such as property and exotic assets, can be added to the report independently to provide a more comprehensive report for the investor.

34 The revised GS 007 is applicable for periods commencing 1 January 2012.

120. Where the auditor concludes that the services provided by the service organisation are significant to the SMSF and relevant to the audit, under ASA 402 there are four options for obtaining evidence for the financial audit relating to the controls at the service organisation over the services provided to the SMSF. These are:

(a) contacting the service organisation through the user entity, to obtain specific information;

(b) visiting the service organisation and performing procedures that will provide necessary information about the relevant controls at the service organisation;

(c) obtaining a "type 1" or "type 2" report, if available; or

(d) using another auditor to perform procedures that will provide the necessary information about the relevant controls at the service organisation.

These sources of evidence may also be utilised in obtaining evidence relating to controls for the compliance engagement.

121. In certain circumstances, an auditor may have access to the service organisation's records, such as when the auditor is engaged to audit a number of SMSFs administered by the same service organisation or the auditor also audits the service organisation. In these circumstances, it may be possible to conduct testing of the service organisation's controls in order to rely on the operating effectiveness of those controls for the financial audit and compliance engagement of all of the SMSFs administered to reduce substantive testing.

122. Unless the SMSF is a significant client of the service organisation, it is unlikely that the SMSF's auditor can obtain access to the service organisation's records. Furthermore, reliance on an SMSF's monitoring controls over the service organisation may not be appropriate, as controls at the SMSF may be limited. A type 1 report is useful for obtaining an understanding of the SMSF and its environment as part of the planning work only, as it does not provide any assurance on the operating effectiveness of the service organisation's controls. The auditor may, however, seek to place reliance on the controls at the service organisation by obtaining and assessing the evidence contained in a type 2 report.

123. A type 2 report comprises:

(a) a description, prepared by management of the service organisation, of the service organisation's systems, control objectives and related controls, their design and implementation as at a specified date or throughout a specified period and, in some cases, their operating effectiveness throughout a specified period; and

(b) a report by the service auditor with the objective of conveying reasonable assurance that includes:

(i) the service auditor's opinion on the description of the service organisation's system, control objectives and related controls, the suitability of the design of the controls to achieve the specified control objectives, and the operating effectiveness of the controls; and

(ii) a description of the service auditor's tests of the controls and the results thereof.

124. Even if the auditor obtains sufficient appropriate audit evidence of the operating effectiveness of controls over the services outsourced, substantive procedures must still be conducted for all material balances, transactions and compliance requirements. Further guidance on substantive procedures, where the services provided by a service organisation are significant to the SMSF and relevant to the audit, are contained in paragraphs 180 to 185 of this Guidance Statement for the financial audit and paragraphs 373 to 374 for the compliance engagement.

125. Operators of investor directed portfolio services (IDPS)[35] and investor directed portfolio-like services are required by ASIC Class Order 02/294[36] and Class Order 02/296[37] to obtain an auditor's report providing an opinion on the internal controls and other relevant accounting procedures as they relate to the specific annual investor statements, and a review conclusion on the annual investor statements, quarterly reports in certain circumstances and information accessible to clients electronically. These class orders provide requirements for the form and content of the report in these circumstances. Reports provided under these class orders may provide sufficient appropriate audit evidence for a user auditor. If additional evidence is required by the user auditor, a service auditor's report on controls or on financial information may be requested. IDPS or IDPS-like services generally include custody and investment administration, consequently, if a type 1 or 2 report is provided the user auditor can reasonably expect the operator (service organisation) and service auditor of an IDPS to report on the control objectives for the relevant services provided in this guidance statement.

Using the Work of a Service Auditor

126. In relying on the work of a service organisation's auditor under ASA 402, the auditor considers the professional competence of the service auditor in the context of the specific assignment and assesses whether the work of the service auditor is adequate for the SMSF auditor's purposes.

127. In assessing professional competence of the service auditor, the auditor may gain some comfort from the other auditor having membership of a professional accounting body or affiliation with a reputable accounting firm.

128. With respect to the appropriateness of the service auditor's work, the auditor needs to consider whether:

(a) controls, balances, transactions or compliance with requirements relevant to the SMSF have been audited;

(b) the materiality level applied is appropriate to the SMSF's audit;

(c) an audit opinion, providing reasonable assurance, or a review conclusion, providing limited assurance, has been provided; and

(d) the service auditor's report contains any modifications which may impact the audit of the SMSF.

Using the Work of an Expert

129. Some SMSF audit engagements may include aspects requiring specialised knowledge and skills in the collection and evaluation of sufficient appropriate audit evidence. In these situations, the auditor may decide to use the work of an expert who has the required knowledge and skills to assist the auditor, such as property valuers, actuaries, legal professionals or other professionals. Either the auditor or the trustee may engage the required expert. ASA 620 applies for an auditor's expert.

130. When using the work of a management's expert, ASA 500 paragraph 8 and ASAE 3100 require the auditor to obtain sufficient appropriate evidence that the expert's work is adequate for the purposes of the audit. In doing so, the auditor evaluates:

(a) the competence, capabilities and objectivity of the expert;

(b) whether the scope of the expert's work is adequate for the purposes of the audit, including the reasonableness of the assumptions, method and source data used by the expert; and

GS

35 "IDPS" means an investor directed portfolio service, consisting of a number of functions including a custody, settlement and reporting system and service. The clients of the service have the sole discretion to decide what assets will be acquired or disposed of. The service is provided in such a way that clients are led to expect, and are likely to receive, benefits in the form of access to investments that the client could not otherwise access directly or cost reductions by using assets contributed by the client or derived directly or indirectly from assets contributed by the client with assets contributed by other clients or derived directly or indirectly from assets contributed by other clients.

36 See ASIC Class Order 02/294 *Investor Directed Portfolio Services.*

37 See ASIC Class Order 02/296 *Investor Directed Portfolio-like Services provided through a registered managed investment Scheme.*

(c) the appropriateness of the expert's work as audit evidence, including the reasonableness and significance of the expert's findings in relation to the audit of the SMSF.

Using the Work of an Actuary

131. Actuaries are experts generally appointed by the trustees to provide actuarial valuations and certificates required by the SISA, SISR or the ITAA. The auditor applies the requirements of ASA 500 paragraph 8 and ASAE 3100 and refers to Guidance Statement GS 005 for guidance on using the actuary's work as audit evidence, in particular the auditor:

(a) evaluates the competence, capabilities and objectivity of the actuary;

(b) evaluates the adequacy of the scope of the actuary's work for the purposes of the audit;

(c) evaluates the appropriateness of the actuarial certificates as audit evidence; and

(d) assesses whether the actuary's findings are properly reflected in the financial report.

132. In assessing the actuary's competence, capabilities and objectivity, the auditor ordinarily relies on the actuary's membership of The Institute of Actuaries of Australia or equivalent body, including adherence to their code of professional conduct and professional standards, and the actuary's experience and reputation in the field.

133. The trustees are required to obtain the following actuarial reports and certificates:

(a) Actuarial report for defined benefits funds, covering the value of assets, adequacy of assets to meet accrued benefit liabilities, recommended contribution rates and the SMSF's financial position, prepared:

(i) on establishment or conversion to the defined benefit fund;[38],[39]

(ii) triennially when in the accumulation phase;[40] and

(iii) annually when in pension mode.[41]

(b) Funding and solvency certificate for defined benefit funds, covering solvency and the minimum contributions required to secure the SMSF's solvency, for provision to employer-sponsors,[42] prepared:

(i) on establishment of the defined benefit fund;[43]

(ii) within 3 months of the expiry of the existing certificate;[44]

(iii) on occurrence of a notifiable event;[45] and

(iv) under a number of other circumstances.

(c) Actuarial certificate for accumulation funds with members in both pension and accumulation phases, where the assets are un-segregated, covering the proportion of income which is tax exempt, obtained annually.[46]

Actuarial certificates are not required for accumulation funds paying pensions with segregated assets.

134. Actuarial reports are a means of reviewing a SMSF's progress in achieving its objectives of providing the member's future benefits. The results of an actuarial valuation for a defined benefit fund are used to determine the appropriate contribution levels and to indicate any surplus or deficiency in the funding of the SMSF. Employer–sponsors need to pay contributions which are not less than the certified minimum contributions in order to maintain the defined benefit fund's solvency.

38 Regulation 9.29 of the SISR.

39 Since May 2004, establishment of or conversion to defined benefits funds is no longer permitted.

40 Regulation 9.29 of the SISR.

41 Regulation 9.29A of the SISR.

42 Regulation 9.09 of the SISR.

43 Regulation 9.11 of the SISR.

44 Regulation 9.14 of the SISR.

45 Regulation 9.13 of the SISR.

46 Section 295-390 of the ITAA 1997.

Part A - Financial Audit

135. The ATO's approved form auditor's report Part A: *Financial report* requires the auditor to conduct the audit in accordance with Australian Auditing Standards to form an opinion regarding the fair presentation of the financial report of the SMSF for the reporting period, in accordance with stated accounting policies, which are consistent with the financial reporting requirements of the SMSF's governing rules, compliant with the SISA and SISR and are appropriate to meet the needs of members.

136. ASA 200 requires the auditor to express an opinion on whether the financial report is prepared, in all material respects, in accordance with an applicable financial reporting framework. As SMSFs generally prepare special purpose financial reports they are not required to formally adopt Australian Accounting Standards and the trustees determine the applicable financial reporting framework which they will apply to the SMSF's financial report.[47] The basis for preparation of the report is disclosed in the accounting policy notes in the financial report.

Financial Reports

137. The type of financial report which a SMSF prepares depends on whether it is an accumulation or a defined benefit fund.

138. An accumulation fund, or defined contribution fund,[48] is a fund which is not a defined benefits fund.[49] The benefits payable to members on satisfying a condition of release in an accumulation fund are determined by the accumulated contributions made to the fund and the investment income thereon, as well as any insurance benefit available, less any expenses or other deductions.

139. A defined benefit fund is a fund with at least one defined benefit member and some or all of the contributions to which are not paid into the fund, or accumulated, in respect of any individual member but are paid into the fund, or accumulated, in the form of an aggregate amount.[50] A defined benefit member is a member entitled to benefits determined by reference to a formula specified in the trust deed or governing rules, which is generally based on the member's salary at a particular date or the member's salary averaged over a period before retirement.

140. The financial report of a SMSF comprises, either:

 (a) for a SMSF that is an accumulation fund, or a defined benefit fund with an actuarial review at the reporting date[51]:
  (i) a statement of financial position; and
  (ii) an operating statement; or

 (b) for a SMSF that is a defined benefit fund[52]:
  (i) a statement of net assets; and
  (ii) a statement of changes in net assets.

These are special purpose financial reports for the purposes of the Australian Auditing Standards. Funds, where the benefits are wholly determined by reference to life assurance policies, prepare significantly different financial reports to other SMSFs. Guidance on these reports is provided in the SISR.[53] This Guidance Statement does not deal with the audit of these funds.

GS

47 If a SMSF is a reporting entity, the SMSF prepares general purpose financial reports and adheres to the Australian Accounting Standards in the preparation of that report.

48 Term used in Australian Accounting Standard AAS 25 *Financial Reporting of Superannuation Plans.*

49 Definition from regulation 1.03(1) of the SISR.

50 Definition from regulation 1.03(1) of the SISR.

51 Section 35B of the SISA.

52 Regulation 8.01 of the SISR.

53 Regulations 8.02 and 8.03 of the SISR.

141. The key differences in the two types of financial reports are that:

(a) A statement of financial position includes the liability for accrued benefits whereas a statement of net assets refers to the liability for accrued benefits only in a note to the financial statements. A statement of net assets is prepared where the defined benefit fund does not have an actuarial valuation of the liability for accrued benefits at the reporting date and so it cannot be included on the face of the statement.

(b) A statement of changes in net assets, in addition to including all of the items in an operating statement, shows the opening and closing balances of net assets available to pay benefits and includes benefits paid in order to reconcile those balances.

142. Although the presentation differs between the two types of reports that a SMSF may prepare, the same account categories will require auditing, including:

- Assets:
  - Cash and cash equivalents.
  - Investments.
  - Receivables.
  - Prepayments.
- Liabilities:
  - Tax liabilities (current and deferred).
  - Accounts payable.
  - Borrowings.
  - Accrued benefits (disclosed in the notes to the financial statements for defined benefit funds).
  - Vested benefits (disclosed in the notes to the financial statements).
- Reserves.
- Revenue:
  - Investment revenue, including changes in net market values.
  - Proceeds from term insurance policies.
  - Contributions and transfers in.
- Expenses:
  - General administration expenses.
  - Tax expenses.
  - Benefits paid.

Guidance on auditing each of these balances and transactions is provided in paragraphs 156 to 249, and illustrative financial audit procedures are also provided in Appendix 5 of this Guidance Statement.

Assertions and Audit Evidence

143. In representing that the financial report gives a fair presentation of the SMSF's position, results and disclosure during the reporting period and is prepared in accordance with the applicable financial reporting framework, the trustees make assertions implicitly or explicitly (positive confirmations) regarding the recognition, measurement, presentation and disclosure of the various elements of a financial report and related disclosures.

144. In accordance with ASA 315, the auditor uses assertions for classes of transactions, account balances, and presentation and disclosures in sufficient detail to form a basis for the assessment of risks of material misstatement and the design and performance of further audit procedures.

145. Assertions used by the auditor fall into the following categories:

(a) Assertions about classes of transactions and events reflected in the SMSF's operating statement or statement of changes in net assets for the period under audit:

(i) *Occurrence* - transactions and events that have been recorded have occurred and pertain to the SMSF.

(ii) *Completeness* - all transactions and events that should have been recorded have been recorded.

(iii) *Accuracy* - amounts and other data relating to recorded transactions and events have been recorded appropriately.

(iv) *Cut-off* - transactions and events have been recorded in the correct accounting period.

(v) *Classification* - transactions and events have been recorded in the proper accounts.

(b) Assertions about SMSF account balances reflected in the SMSF's statement of financial position or statement of net assets at the period end:

(i) *Existence* - assets, liabilities, and member entitlements exist.

(ii) *Rights and obligations (ownership)* - the SMSF holds or controls the rights to assets, either directly or beneficially, and liabilities are the obligations of the SMSF.

(iii) *Completeness* - all assets, liabilities and member entitlements that should have been recorded have been recorded.

(iv) *Valuation and allocation* - assets, liabilities and member entitlements are included in the financial report at appropriate amounts and any resulting valuation or allocation adjustments are appropriately recorded.

(c) Assertions about presentation and disclosure within the SMSFs special purpose financial reports:

(i) *Occurrence and rights and obligations* - disclosed events, transactions, and other matters have occurred and pertain to the SMSF.

(ii) *Completeness* - all disclosures that should have been included in the financial report have been included.

(iii) *Classification and understandability* - financial information is presented and described appropriately, and disclosures are expressed clearly.

(iv) *Accuracy and valuation* - financial and other information is disclosed fairly and at appropriate amounts.

Materiality

146. ASA 320 requires the auditor to make a preliminary assessment of materiality to establish an appropriate quantitative materiality level to plan risk assessment procedures, further audit procedures, selection strategies and other audit procedures for the financial audit. Ordinarily, a quantitative materiality level is calculated by applying a percentage, based on the auditor's professional judgement, to the selected benchmark or benchmarks, which may include:

- Total gross assets.
- Net assets.
- Total member entitlements.
- Total gross income.

147. The auditor uses the preliminary quantitative materiality level and the assessed risk of material misstatement at both the financial report level and at the assertion level, for classes of transactions and account balances, to determine the nature, timing and extent of audit procedures for the financial audit.

GS

148. In assessing the materiality of any misstatements identified during the audit and their impact on the auditor's report, the auditor considers both quantitative and qualitative factors. Qualitative factors which the auditor considers include:

- The significance of a misstatement to the SMSF.
- The pervasiveness of a misstatement.
- The effect of misstatement on the financial report as a whole.

149. ASA 450 requires the auditor to consider the possibility that the cumulative result of uncorrected misstatements below the materiality level could have a material effect on the financial report.

Opening Balances

150. Upon appointment to a new engagement, ASA 510 requires the auditor to obtain sufficient appropriate audit evidence that:

(a) the opening balances (account balances which exist at the beginning of the period) do not contain misstatements that materially affect the current period's financial report;

(b) the prior period's closing balances have been correctly brought forward to the current period or, when appropriate, have been restated; and

(c) appropriate accounting policies reflected in the opening balances have been consistently applied in the current period's financial report or changes thereto are appropriately accounted for and adequately presented and disclosed in accordance with the applicable financial reporting framework.

151. When the prior period's financial report was audited by another auditor, the current auditor may be able to obtain sufficient audit evidence by reviewing the predecessor auditor's working papers. In these circumstances, the current auditor considers the professional competence and independence of the predecessor auditor. If the prior period's auditor's opinion was modified, under ASA 705, the auditor pays particular attention in the current period to the matter which resulted in the prior period modification.

152. Prior to communicating with the predecessor auditor, under ASA 220, the current auditor is required to consider the relevant ethical requirements.

153. If the prior period's financial report was not audited or when the auditor is not able to obtain sufficient appropriate audit evidence by examining the work of the previous auditor, the auditor undertakes further audit procedures to obtain sufficient appropriate audit evidence to ascertain whether the opening balances are stated fairly.

154. Ordinarily, some audit evidence may be obtained as part of the current period's audit procedures for the opening balances of current assets and liabilities. Performing audit procedures on the valuation of the opening bank account and other smaller items may provide sufficient appropriate audit evidence. For investments and material balances, the auditor examines the accounting records and other information underlying the investments which may contain the opening balances of such investments. In certain cases, the auditor may be able to obtain confirmation of opening balances with third parties such as share registries or fund managers. When the auditor cannot obtain this information, the auditor may need to carry out additional audit procedures to verify the opening balances.

155. If audit procedures do not result in sufficient appropriate audit evidence concerning opening balances, ASA 510 requires that the auditor's report is modified. Further guidance on modifications to the auditor's report is provided in paragraphs 269 to 276.

Cash and Cash Equivalents

156. Cash and cash equivalents include bank accounts, cash management trusts and other cash transactional facilities held with banks, fund managers, credit unions and other approved financial or deposit taking institutions. These accounts provide either a paper based record or electronic record of transactions and may have cheque, direct debit or internet banking facilities.

157. The audit assertions for auditing a SMSF's cash and cash equivalents are:

- *Existence* – obtaining evidence that the cash exists.
- *Rights and obligations (ownership)* – obtaining evidence that the cash is owned directly or beneficially by the SMSF.
- *Completeness* – obtaining evidence that all cash owned by the SMSF is recorded.
- *Valuation and allocation* – obtaining evidence that the cash is valued at face value in accordance with the accounting policies.

158. Cash and cash equivalents are a SMSF's most liquid assets and so may carry a high fraud risk. The auditor remains alert to fraud and the risk of fraud with respect to the SMSF's bank accounts. The auditor makes enquires regarding who has access to the account via internet or phone banking and access to cheque books. The auditor assesses the internal controls surrounding the authorisation of payments and receipts to ascertain whether the cash of the SMSF are safeguarded adequately. The auditor remains sceptical of transactions in the bank accounts that may relate to early access or fraud perpetrated not by the members or trustees but by those related parties that may have access to fund bank accounts.

159. If the banking operations are significant to the audit, the auditor sends bank confirmation requests[54] to the SMSF's banks. A bank confirmation is a request to a bank to provide independent confirmation for audit purposes of such information as the SMSF's account balances, securities, treasury management instruments, documents and other related information held by the bank on behalf of the SMSF. The confirmation will also seek to identify any deliberate or inadvertent borrowings with the bank.

160. Some SMSFs may utilise a cash account established with their broker, investment account or other investment platform (for example, IDPS) as part of their securities trading activity. This account may facilitate trading, settlement and receipt of dividends and interest. The auditor establishes who has access to this account and who may authorise transactions to ensure that only authorised investment trading takes place. The auditor also needs to obtain sufficient audit evidence that the controls at the broker, investment account or other investment platform are effective.

Investments

161. The investments of a SMSF may include:

- Listed securities.
- Fixed rate securities such as government, semi-government or corporate bonds, loans (secured or unsecured) and mortgages.
- Variable rate and discount securities such as bank bills, promissory notes or floating rate notes.
- Hybrid securities which have both interest and equity components, such as convertible notes or converting preference shares.
- Managed products such as units in managed funds, managed investment schemes, PSTs and insurance policies.
- Unlisted investments including shares and units in widely held entities.
- Unlisted investments including shares and units in closely held or related entities.
- Derivatives such as futures and options.
- Instalment warrants.
- Real property.
- Other assets such as artwork, antiques, wine, vehicles, boats, equipment, fishing licences, timber plantations and other agricultural investments.

162. Investments may be domestic, international or a combination of both and may be held by a custodian, the individual trustees or a corporate trustee.

54 For an example of a Bank Audit Confirmation, refer to GS 016.

163. The audit assertions for auditing a SMSF's investments are:

- *Existence* – obtaining evidence that the investment exists.
- *Rights and obligations (ownership)* – obtaining evidence that the investments are owned directly or beneficially by the SMSF.
- *Completeness* – obtaining evidence that all investments owned by the SMSF are recorded in the accounts.
- *Valuation and allocation* – obtaining evidence that investments are valued in accordance with the accounting policies adopted, allocated to the correct account and disclosed fairly in accordance with the stated policies.

164. Audit risks to be considered in relation to auditing investments may include, but are not limited to:

- Overstatement of investment values, including investment values not being adjusted for dividends or distributions which are included as income.
- Investments not beneficially owned by the SMSF.

165. The audit procedures relating to investments will vary depending on the administration and management arrangements adopted by the trustees, the type of investments held and the trustee structure that holds the assets. The auditor exercises professional judgement in determining the appropriate auditing procedures.

Existence and Ownership

166. In auditing existence of the SMSF's assets, the auditor may either physically inspect the assets or examine documentation supporting their existence. The documentation may also verify ownership. If assets are registered in the name of the trustees, corporate trustee or custodian, the auditor also obtains audit evidence that the SMSF is the beneficial owner and that the assets are being held on behalf of the SMSF. Evidence of beneficial ownership may include an acknowledgement of trust or equivalent document.

Completeness

167. The auditor ensures that all investments of the SMSF have been recorded at the correct amounts and in the correct period. The auditor reviews supporting documentation to ensure that no asset of the SMSF has been excluded. This may extend to obtaining investment schedules from previous years and examining them for changes and movements and reconciling the schedules with purchase and sale transactions for the current period to ensure that all movements in investments have been recorded. The auditor may also obtain representations from the trustees that they have provided a full disclosure of all assets of the SMSF and made available all records relating to those assets.

Valuation and Allocation of Assets

168. As the SMSF's financial report is generally a special purpose financial report, the trustees choose the financial reporting framework under which the SMSF reports and exercise their discretion when determining the most appropriate valuation methods to be applied to each investment of the SMSF.[55] Under ASA 800, the auditor's responsibility is to form an opinion regarding fair presentation in accordance with the identified financial reporting framework or identified basis of accounting. Under ASA 540, the auditor is required to obtain sufficient appropriate audit evidence that fair value measurements and disclosures are in accordance with the SMSF's applicable financial reporting framework. The auditor evaluates whether the valuation method employed is consistent with the financial reporting framework adopted and the policies described in the accounting policy notes, whether the method of measurement is appropriate in the circumstances and that the method adopted has been applied consistently.

---

55 If the SMSF is a reporting entity it is required to prepare general purpose financial reports, in which case the auditor assesses that the accounting policies applied are consistent with the Australian Accounting Standards, in particular AAS 25 *Financial Reporting by Superannuation Plans*, which requires that assets be measured at *net market value*, derived after deducting the costs of disposal from market value. AAS 25 is under review at the time of publication of this Guidance Statement. Any subsequent changes made to AAS 25 or its replacement should be considered, if relevant, in planning the auditor's procedures with respect to auditing the valuation of assets in general purpose financial reports.

169. Multiple valuation methods exist, including:
- Market value.
- Fair market value.
- Independent valuation by an expert.
- Net tangible asset backing.
- Latest sale prices.
- Cost.
- Present value method.
- Using valuations from similar investments.
- Sworn valuations.
- Application of indices or benchmarks.

170. The auditor obtains an understanding of the trustees' rationale for selecting the valuation method and exercises professional judgement in assessing whether the method employed is appropriate given the nature of the asset and the financial and investment markets in which the SMSF operates.

171. The ATO's preferred valuation method, as outlined in its Superannuation Circular 2003/1, is that SMSFs' assets are carried at market value[56] and valued annually at the SMSF's reporting date. Market value is defined in the SISA.[57]

172. It is not the role of the auditor to value the assets. The auditor assesses the valuation method and evaluates the valuation for accuracy and reasonableness. The auditor assesses the risks of material misstatement of the asset values and designs and performs audit procedures in response to the assessed risks.

173. SMSFs may invest directly in unit trusts, listed securities, PSTs or other investment products for which market prices are published and readily available. If market value is employed, the auditor verifies that the unit price used is consistent with reference to cum-distribution or ex-distribution price and any accrual of income. For these investments, the product or unit is recorded as an asset in the records of the SMSF rather than the underlying investments.

174. Non-monetary items, such as property and collectibles, require alternative methods to arrive at an estimate that approximates market value. Property valuations may be based on sworn valuations by appropriately qualified valuers, market appraisals by real estate agents or the trustees' assessment of market value. Collectibles may be valued by the trustee or an expert valuer.

175. The accounting treatment which may be applied to investments in instalment warrants may be either net asset value or separate balances for the gross asset and the liability.

176. Foreign assets are stated in Australian dollars and valued in a manner consistent with Australian assets.

177. Where the auditor is unable to form an opinion in assessing whether the valuation is in accordance with the financial reporting framework adopted, due to uncertainty, and no expert valuation can be obtained, the auditor considers modification of the auditor's report, taking into account materiality and the risk of material misstatement.

178. To protect the value of their assets, SMSFs may obtain insurance cover over the assets. In auditing ownership and valuation of assets, the auditor obtains evidence that:

(a) the insurance exists;

(b) the SMSF is both the owner and beneficiary of the policy;

(c) the premium is paid by the SMSF; and

(d) the cover is effected and current.

---

56 ATO Superannuation Circular 2003/1 *Self-Managed Superannuation Funds* states that SMSFs should use market values for all valuation purposes. This includes valuations for determining the purchase price of a pension and the use of market value accounting for all financial reports.

57 Subsection 10(1) of the SISA.

GS

179. With respect to investment properties, residential or commercial, circumstances may exist where the SMSF's tenancy lease agreement stipulates that the tenant is required to pay for the insurance. In these cases, the auditor checks to see if the policy is up to date and the beneficiary of the insurance benefit is the SMSF and not the tenant.

Service Organisations

180. Whilst the auditor of a SMSF may be able to rely on a type 2 report[58] from the service organisation as audit evidence of the operating effectiveness of controls over the services outsourced, the auditor must still conduct substantive procedures for all material balances and transactions under ASA 330 to support their financial audit opinion. It may be impractical or impossible to gain access to the service organisation's records to conduct substantive testing, in which case, the auditor may rely on the type 2 report in conjunction with:

- Analytical review of the balances and transactions of the SMSF reported by the service organisation, such as comparison of investment returns with market indices or comparison of expected contribution rates and benefit payments with changes in assets managed by the service organisation.
- Reconciliation of balances and transactions reported by the service provider with records maintained by the SMSF.
- Confirmation of balances or transactions recorded on behalf of the SMSF from the service organisation.
- A special purpose auditor's report on a statement of the SMSF's balances and transactions or on specified assertions in relation to such balances and transactions provided by the service organisation under GS 007.

181. The nature of the audit procedures required to obtain sufficient appropriate audit evidence regarding a SMSF's investments which are managed by or in the custody of a service organisation will depend on the extent to which the records of the SMSF are maintained by the service organisation.

182. By comparison, for investments in listed securities, units or products for which prices are readily or publicly available, such as managed funds, Pooled Superannuation Trusts (PSTs) and listed property trusts, registered in the name of the trustee on behalf of the SMSF, for which the SMSF maintains its own accounting records, the auditor is ordinarily able to confirm the number of units held in the end of period statements and taxation summaries or directly with the registry, coupled with substantive testing of the SMSF's records for investments and redemptions. Valuation may be tested against published unit prices using the number of units held.

183. For investments for which recording of material balances or transactions is controlled by the service organisation but accounting records are still maintained by the SMSF and the SMSF has access to the source documentation, such as when assets are held in custody, the end of period statements and taxation summaries may be insufficient evidence alone but may be coupled with evidence of the operating effectiveness of controls within the service organisation as evidenced in a type 2 report, confirmation of balances with the service organisation and analytical review of the SMSF's investment activity.

184. For a standalone investment mandate where the service organisation maintains the SMSF's accounting records, including source documentation, makes investment decisions based on the mandate and holds the investments on behalf of the SMSF, the SMSF may maintain only limited independent accounting records, source documentation or banking records, in which case the SMSF relies on the service organisation's reports as a basis for preparation of their financial report. Audit evidence in these circumstances may include a type 2 report from the service organisation and substantive testing of balances and transactions by either visiting the service organisation, obtaining a special purpose auditor's report from the service organisation on the balances and transactions of the SMSF or conducting testing at the SMSF. Testing at the SMSF may include: valuation using independent sources, confirmation of contributions with employers, verification of benefit payments against

58 See paragraph 123 of this Guidance Statement for a description of a type 2 report.

members' records, if available, and verification of dividend and trust distributions against independent sources.

185. It may be impossible or impractical to obtain sufficient appropriate audit evidence with respect to material balances or transactions of the SMSF controlled by the service organisation, in which case either the auditor qualifies their opinion on the basis of a limitation of scope or issues a disclaimer of opinion, if the effects or possible effects are material and pervasive.

Receivables and Prepayments

186. Where the SMSF accounts on an accruals basis, receivables may include contributions, interest or trust distributions receivable and current tax assets. Receivables are tested primarily for existence, valuation and allocation by confirming the receipt in the subsequent period.

187. If the SMSF accounts on an accruals basis and invests in managed funds that pay distributions post balance date, the auditor verifies that the SMSF has accrued these distributions of income correctly and consistently and that the investment value of the underlying asset has been adjusted accordingly.

188. Prepayments are tested against cash payments and particular attention paid to transactions with related parties to ensure they relate to a genuine expense.

Liabilities

189. Liabilities of a SMSF, other than accrued benefits which are discussed separately, may include:

- Benefits payable, including benefits arising from insurance claims.
- Bank overdrafts, other borrowings and related interest payable.
- Goods and Services Tax (GST) payable, if the SMSF is registered for GST.
- Income tax liabilities, current and deferred.
- Accruals for accounting and audit fees.
- Liabilities relating to instalment warrants, where the accounting treatment is on a gross basis.
- Any other accrued expense the trustees have provided for or incurred.

Many of these liabilities will only be recorded if the SMSF accounts on an accruals basis.

190. The audit assertions with respect to a SMSF's liabilities are:

- *Existence* – the liabilities exist.
- *Rights and obligations (ownership)* – the liabilities are obligations of the SMSF.
- *Completeness* – all liabilities of the SMSF have been recorded.
- *Valuation and allocation* – liabilities are recorded at appropriate amounts and allocated to the appropriate account.

191. Generally, SMSFs are not allowed to borrow under SISA. Permitted exceptions are temporary borrowings which are required for the payment of member benefits, payment of the superannuation contributions surcharge,[59] settlement of securities transactions or borrowings under instalment warrant arrangements.

192. Audit risks to be considered in relation to auditing liabilities may include but are not limited to:

- Liability values being understated.
- Liabilities being omitted.
- Excessive accruals for expenses that will not be paid or which are not legitimate expenses of the SMSF.

59 The superannuation contributions surcharge was abolished from 1 July 2005; however there may be circumstances where the surcharge may still be levied on contributions relating to periods prior to this date.

GS

193. Normally, the auditor performs a search for unrecorded liabilities by examining brokers' statements for outstanding balances, bank confirmation letters for borrowings or evidence of security provided, banking records for payments after period end and by reviewing the financial records for expenses that were paid in previous years, but billed infrequently or annually such as insurance or accountancy fees, which may not have been included in the current period's accruals. The auditor may seek representations from the trustee that all liabilities of the SMSF have been disclosed and recorded.

194. Many SMSFs record expenses on a cash basis with little or no adjustments for prepayments or accruals. Where expenses are accrued, the auditor reviews the basis for accrual and determines whether the expense was paid subsequent to year end.

Accrued Benefits

195. The liability for accrued benefits, or member entitlements, is the present obligation to pay benefits to members or beneficiaries in the future.

196. Accrued benefits of a SMSF may arise from:

- Accumulation entitlements where the member bears the investment risk.
- Defined benefit entitlements where a party, other than the member, bears the investment risk. The other party is generally an employer before the beneficiary ceases employment or the SMSF post cessation of the member's employment.
- Insurance claims paid or payable to the SMSF owing to members.

197. The audit assertions with respect to a SMSF's accrued benefits are:

- *Existence* – the accrued benefits are entitlements of members.
- *Rights and obligations (ownership)* – the accrued benefits are obligations of the SMSF.
- *Completeness* – all accrued benefits of each member of the SMSF have been recorded.
- *Valuation and allocation* – accrued benefits are recorded at appropriate amounts and allocated to the appropriate account/member.

198. Audit risks for accrued benefits include, but are not limited to:

- Contributions not being allocated correctly to members.
- Income not being allocated correctly or appropriately to individual members.
- Benefit payments or expenses being allocated incorrectly to member's balances.
- Member balances and components not being carried forward correctly from one period to another.

199. Accrued benefits are calculated differently for accumulation and defined benefit funds. For accumulation funds, benefits are based on the performance of the SMSF's investments and do not exceed the assets available in the SMSF. Accrued benefits in an accumulation fund are calculated as the difference between the carrying value of the assets and the carrying value of tax and sundry liabilities as at the reporting period. Any liability for accrued benefits is included in the statement of financial position for an accumulation fund.

200. The defined benefits component of a defined benefit fund is payable by reference to a formula based on some combination of each member's salary, years of service, contribution rate and/or some other measure such as life expectancy or other actuarial derived amount. Accrued benefits in a defined benefit fund are based on actuarial valuations which must be conducted:

(a) triennially when in accumulation mode;[60] or

(b) annually when in pension mode.[61]

60 Regulation 9.29 of the SISR.

61 Regulation 9.29A of the SISR.

201. Actuarial valuations are based on the application of a market-based risk-adjusted discount rate and relevant actuarial assumptions to expected future pension payments. For defined benefit funds with an actuarial valuation at period end, a liability for accrued benefits is shown on the face of the statement of financial position. For a defined benefit fund which does not have an actuarial valuation at period end, a statement of net assets is prepared and the liability for accrued benefits is disclosed as a note to the financial statements as at the last actuarial valuation date.

Vested Benefits

202. Vested benefits are those benefits to which the member is currently entitled irrespective of the member's continued membership of the SMSF, on-going employment with a particular employer or maintenance of other conditions. Although vested benefits are an unconditional benefit of the member within the SMSF, those benefits can be accessed only upon satisfying an appropriate condition of release, such as retirement, death, rollover, reaching age 65 or reaching at least preservation age[62] and accessing a transition to retirement income stream. Usually vested benefits are disclosed in the notes to the financial statements.

203. Vested benefits equate to the minimum benefits of the SMSF's members. Minimum benefits include member concessional and non-concessional contributions, mandated contributions (compulsory employer contributions) such as Superannuation Guarantee (SG) contributions or superannuation payments made pursuant to an Award or other employment agreement, amounts rolled over or transferred in as minimum benefits and the earnings thereon. Some older SMSFs may have a vesting scale which provides for certain contributions and earnings to progressively vest. Minimum benefits must be maintained in the SMSF until they are cashed, rolled over or transferred in accordance with the SISA and SISR benefit payment rules.[63]

204. Audit procedures to test for vesting of minimum benefits include examining the trust deed to ensure that the trust deed fully vests the contributions in the member and testing member and employer contributions for the period to inclusion in members' accounts. In addition, the auditor reviews any transfers to reserves to ensure that the minimum benefits are not being reduced.

205. In circumstances where the SMSF is converting from a defined benefit fund to an accumulation fund, the auditor examines whether the conversion will adversely affect members' rights to minimum benefits. Ordinarily, the auditor reviews the actuarial advice issued in relation to the conversion and the resultant figures derived.

Reserves

206. A reserve is an amount held within a SMSF that is not allocated specifically to members. Generally, reserves are permitted unless specifically prohibited under a SMSF's trust deed. Typically, reserves are created from excess investment returns or in accordance with actuarial requirements.

207. Types of reserves permitted for SMSFs may include, but are not limited to:
- Investment.
- Solvency.
- Miscellaneous.

208. Investment reserves are used to smooth returns and assist with meeting payment obligations for some defined benefit pensions.

209. Solvency reserves provide an asset/income buffer to assist in guaranteeing payments of defined benefit pensions and are determined actuarially.

62 Preservation age is the age at which super benefits can be accessed. Preservation age will rise from 55 to 60 between 2015 and 2024. This will mean that for someone born before 1 July 1960, their preservation age is 55 years, while for someone born after 30 June 1964, their preservation age will be 60.

63 Refer regulation 5.08 SISR.

210. Generally, miscellaneous reserves are created by the death of the last defined benefit pensioner within the SMSF with the residual sums being transferred to the miscellaneous reserve. They can also be created intentionally for other purposes.

211. Contribution reserves could be established prior to mid-2004, but the establishment of new contributions reserves is no longer permissible as contributions received by a SMSF must be allocated within 28 days of receipt. Some long established SMSFs may still have contribution reserves which can be retained but cannot be increased.

212. Anti-detriment payment reserves may be established to pay an additional benefit upon death, equivalent to the tax already paid on contributions for the member. Various methods may be used to calculate the exact amount of the anti-detriment payment and auditors should refer to the relevant sections of the ITAA 1997. The reserve may be funded from excess investment returns or allocated from miscellaneous reserves and needs to be established prior to death.

213. Audit considerations for reserves include whether:

- The trust deed permits the making of reserves.
- The assets of the particular reserve are segregated appropriately from the rest of the SMSF's assets.
- Amounts transferred in or out of the reserves are appropriate.
- Actuarial recommendations are met.

Investment and Other Revenue

214. Revenue of a SMSF, other than contributions, may include:

- Dividends.
- Interest.
- Rental income.
- Unit trust distributions.
- Insurance policy proceeds, rebates and bonuses.
- Changes in net market value – both realised and unrealised.

215. The audit assertions for revenue received by a SMSF are:

- *Occurrence* – revenue received by the SMSF is real and has occurred.
- *Completeness* – all revenue received by the SMSF has been recorded.
- *Accuracy* – all the revenue received by the SMSF has been recorded appropriately. Changes in net market value are based on appropriate and accurate asset valuations.
- *Cut-off* – all the revenue received by the SMSF has been recorded in the correct period.
- *Classification* – all the revenue received by the SMSF has been allocated correctly, either to the correct members' accounts or to the asset pool and the tax status of that income is appropriate.

216. Audit risks to be considered in relation to auditing revenue may include:

- Revenue is recognised before it is earned.
- Revenue is not being accounted for in accordance with the SMSF's accounting policies.
- Misstatement of changes in net market value due to under or overstatement of market valuation.

Contributions and Transfers In

217. Typically, contributions into SMSFs are sourced from either the members or the members' employers. Transfers in are benefits transferred from other superannuation entities. Contributions are classified as either concessional, for which a tax deduction has been claimed by the contributor, or non-concessional, for which no tax deduction has been claimed by the member. Contributions and transfers in to a SMSF may include[64]:

- Employer contributions, including SG, award and salary sacrifice contributions.
- Member contributions, both concessional and non-concessional.
- Spouse contributions.
- Child contributions.
- Rollovers from other complying funds.
- Small business rollovers (CGT small business retirement exemption and CGT small business 15 year exemption amount).
- Amounts transferred from a foreign fund.
- Government co-contributions.
- Transfers from the Superannuation Holding Accounts Reserve (SHAR) held by the ATO.
- Personal injury election.
- Other family and friend contributions.
- Directed termination (taxable component) payments.

Contributions may be made in cash or *in specie* (by transferring an asset) or a combination of both. However, the trust deed must permit the SMSF to accept contributions that are made *in specie*.

218. The objectives for auditing contributions received by a SMSF are:

- *Occurrence* – contributions and transfers in recorded by the SMSF are real and have occurred.
- *Completeness* – all contributions and transfers in receivable from or on behalf of members have been received and recorded.
- *Accuracy* – all contributions and transfers in have been recorded appropriately.
- *Cut-off* – all contributions and transfers in have been recorded in the correct period.
- *Classification* – all contributions and transfers in have been allocated to the correct member and correctly classified as concessional or non-concessional.

219. Audit risks to be considered in relation to contributions and transfers in may include, but are not limited to:

- Incorrect classification and allocation of concessional and non-concessional contributions.
- Incorrect tax treatment of contributions.
- Incorrect cut-off for contributions resulting in failure to recognise that contribution caps have been exceeded.
- Incorrect allocation of the components of transfers in.
- Acceptance of contributions in excess of the fund contributions cap.[65]
- Understatement of market values for in specie contributions to avoid exceeding the contributions caps.
- Overstatement of market values for *in specie* contributions either to provide early access to benefits or to disguise loans to members.

---

64 Refer to the Self-Managed Superannuation Fund annual return 2011 (NAT 71226- 6.2011).

65 Contributions caps are discussed in paragraph 231 of this Guidance Statement.

GS

220. Where the auditor also audits the employer-sponsor, the auditor may be able to use evidence from testing of payments and payroll deductions at the employer to verify contributions received by the SMSF. Alternatively, confirmation may be sought from the employers.

Expenses

221. The typical expenses of a SMSF may include:
- Administration fees.
- Audit fees.
- Actuarial advice.
- Legal advice.
- Valuation fees.
- Accounting and tax agent fees.
- Superannuation supervisory levy.
- Investment management fees and financial planning advice.
- Bank fees.
- Property fees – if the SMSF invests in property.
- Insurance premiums paid.
- Taxation.

222. The audit objectives with respect to a SMSF's expenses are:
- *Occurrence* – all expenses recorded by the SMSF were incurred.
- *Completeness* – all expenses incurred by the SMSF have been recorded.
- *Accuracy* – all expenses have been recorded appropriately.
- *Cut-off* – all expenses have been recorded in the correct period.
- *Classification* – all expenses have been allocated to the proper accounts or members to which they relate.

223. Audit risks to be considered in relation to auditing expenses may include:
- Personal expenses of the members or trustees are recorded as expenses of the SMSF.
- Expenses of the SMSF paid by a member or an employer are not recorded as concessional or non-concessional contributions.
- Incorrect tax treatment of an expense.

224. Ordinarily, the auditor reviews any payments made to individual trustees or corporate trustees to validate that the payment was *bona fide* and not an early benefit or a payment for services to the SMSF, which are prohibited.

Tax Expenses and Benefits

225. The main areas of focus for an auditor with respect to tax are the tax calculation and allocation of any tax expense or benefit to the members' accounts. The taxation legislation is amended periodically and interpretation of that legislation by the ATO and the courts may change from time to time, consequently, the guidance in this section may become outdated over time and it is the responsibility of the auditor to ensure that they remain up-to-date with the taxation requirements affecting SMSFs. The audit objectives with respect to a SMSF's tax expenses and benefits include:
- *Occurrence* – Deductions were incurred and imputation credits, carried forward losses and any other offsets are attributable to the SMSF.
- *Completeness* – All assessable income, including capital gains, received by the SMSF has been declared.
- *Accuracy* – Assessable income, including capital gains, allowable deductions, rebates, offsets and eligible credits attributable to the SMSF are calculated and recorded appropriately.

- *Cut-off* – Assessable income, including capital gains, allowable deductions, rebates, offsets and eligible credits attributable to the SMSF are declared or claimed in the correct period.
- *Classification* – The tax status of contributions is correctly determined. Timing differences have been correctly identified and accounted for.

226. Income tax is payable on investment earnings (net of expenses) and capital gains, with full imputation credits for dividends received from Australian companies and credits for dividend and withholding tax on foreign income to the extent of Australian tax payable on the foreign sourced income. Income tax is also payable on employer contributions and on member contributions where the member has notified the trustees of an intention to claim a personal tax deduction (concessional contributions). Deductions are available for certain payments and expenses.

227. Some SMSFs account for deferred income taxes in accordance with Australian Accounting Standard AASB 112 *Income Taxes*, in which case the auditor assesses the impact of this accounting standard upon the SMSF. Ordinarily, the auditor considers whether the recognition of any current or deferred tax liabilities or tax assets is appropriate given likelihood of payment of the liabilities or recovery of the assets based on the age of the members and the circumstances of the SMSF. However, most SMSFs operate under the special purpose framework and do not need to comply with AASB 112.

Ordinary Income

228. The ordinary income of the SMSF for tax purposes includes:
    - Investment earnings, such as interest, dividends, rent, trust distributions, and realised capital gains.
    - Concessional contributions received during the year.
    - Insurance premium rebates or refunds.

229. Ordinary income does not include:
    - Non-concessional contributions.
    - Income not derived.
    - Dividend income derived but not yet received.
    - Non-reversionary bonuses on life policies.
    - Income from assets used to fund pensions.

230. Income from assets used to fund pensions is still included for the purpose of accounting and auditing. It is, however, exempt from tax. The auditor, in reviewing the tax calculation, ordinarily establishes that exempt income has been identified and that the income is correctly treated.

Contributions

231. SMSFs are prohibited from accepting fund-capped contributions,[66] in a financial year in excess of the caps specified in the SISR,[67] and must return any amount which is inconsistent with these caps within 30 days of receipt.[68] The auditor makes enquiries to satisfy themselves that excess contributions are returned and excluded from the tax calculations.

GS

66 Fund-capped contributions are defined in regulation 7.04(7) of the SISR.

67 Regulation 7.04(3) of the SISR. Legislation surrounding contributions and contribution caps can and does change. It is the auditors' responsibility to ensure that they are auditing according to the relevant and applicable legislation and regulation.

68 The ATO's Interpretative Decision, ATO ID 2007/225, states that the trustee is only expected to consider whether contributions individually exceed the contribution caps and the trustee does not need to aggregate contributions by a member for the year in determining whether excess contributions should be returned. Also refer to ATO ID 2009/29 Superannuation Contributions: return of contribution by SMSF – after 30 day time limit and ATO ID 2008/90 Superannuation Contributions: return of fund capped contributions by SMSF.

232. The auditor verifies contributions against the documentation from the member or member's employer (for example, remittance advices), for correct allocation to members' accounts and appropriate classification as concessional or non-concessional, so that the correct tax treatment is applied.

233. Upon the sale of certain small business assets, members may be able to contribute some or all of the sale proceeds to the SMSF and may be able to exclude all or part of the contribution from the non-concessional contributions cap. In these circumstances, the auditor examines the documentation surrounding the contribution and verifies that any small business capital gains tax (CGT) concessional contributions have been calculated appropriately and classified correctly.

Non-arm's Length Income

234. Non-arm's length[69] income of a SMSF, which includes private company dividends (unless arm's length), income from non-arm's length transactions and certain trust distributions, is not taxed concessionally. The auditor checks that any non-arm's length income has been classified correctly.

Franked Dividends

235. The auditor checks that any imputation credits attached to a franked dividend to which the SMSF is entitled have been recorded and that the respective franking credit of each dividend is accounted for correctly and that these have been included in the tax calculation appropriately. This extends to checking that the SMSF has held the security for the requisite period to qualify for the franking credit.

Capital Gains Tax

236. Growth in the value of most SMSF assets, excluding cash, are subject to CGT on their disposal, with assets purchased prior to 30 June 1988 deemed to be purchased on that date. The auditor examines any asset disposal that may trigger a CGT event to verify that any CGT loss or gain is taken into account in determining the current tax liability. The auditor also verifies that capital losses and discounts appropriate to capital gains have been correctly calculated and applied.

Goods and Service Tax

237. If the SMSF is registered for GST, generally due to owning business real property, and has taxed supplies (income) and input taxed supplies (expenses) the auditor , where material, reviews the GST calculation and business activity statements (BAS) to ensure that the correct amounts are being disclosed and the SMSF is meeting its reporting and payment obligations with respect to GST. Input tax credits are claimable on supplies relating to commercial property, on other supplies at the reduced rate of 75% and not claimable on certain expenses, such as tax and audit fees.

Deductions

238. Expenses incurred by a SMSF may be deductible by the SMSF under the ITAA subject to the normal principles governing the tax deductibility of expenditure incurred by superannuation funds.[70] The auditor tests the deductions claimed to verify their occurrence, deductibility and that they were incurred by the SMSF and were not personal in nature, or if they were shared, the correct proportion of the expense has been claimed by the SMSF. In general, the following expenses are deductible – administration fees, actuarial costs, accountancy and audit fees, investment management fees and custody fees. Other expenses such as capital allowances (depreciation) may be deductible depending on the circumstances of the SMSF. Depending on the type of insurance policy, the insurance premium may also

69 Prior to 1 July 2007, non-arm's length income was special income under the ITAA. Section 273 of the ITAA (1936) was repealed on 1 July 2007 and replaced by section 295-550 of the ITAA (1997). Refer to Public Tax Ruling TR2006/7 for further information.

70 The ATO has issued a number of publications which provide further guidance on the deductibility of expenses incurred by the SMSF. They include Taxation Ruling TR 93/17 *Income tax: income tax deductions available to superannuation funds*, and its addendum TR 93/17A, which provides general guidance, Miscellaneous Tax Ruling MT 2005/1, which provides specific guidance on expenses paid by members or employers, and Tax Ruling IT 2672, which discusses the deductibility of amending a deed.

be deductible, in part or in full. The auditor may also check that capital items have been correctly treated, as items of a strictly capital nature may not be tax deductible.

239. The auditor verifies that expenses are not claimed if they relate to exempt pension income.[71]

Actuarial Reports for Un-segregated Assets

240. Where a fund has un-segregated assets and at least one member in accumulation mode and another in pension mode during the year, it is necessary to obtain an actuarial certificate to certify the portion of exempt pension income. In these circumstances, the auditor sights and evaluates the actuarial tax certificate that is used in the calculation of taxable income and reviews the accuracy of the information provided to the actuary to prepare the actuarial tax certificate. The auditor confirms that the correct percentage figure certified by the actuary has been applied to derive the exempt pension income for the SMSF.

Benefits Paid

241. Generally, benefits paid by a SMSF are triggered by the member's retirement, death, ill-health,[72] termination of employment, request to rollover their benefit to another complying superannuation fund, commencement of a transition to retirement income stream (upon turning 55) or commencement of an income stream upon the member retiring or turning 65.[73] In the event of divorce, benefits may be split pursuant to a superannuation agreement, consent order or an arbitrated court order.[74]

242. SMSFs may pay benefits by way of a lump sum (in cash or *in specie*), pension or insurance benefit.[75] An accumulation fund may pay the following types of pensions:

(a) account based income streams, including transition to retirement income streams; and

(b) existing allocated pensions and market linked income streams (formerly known as market linked pensions).

243. New defined benefit pensions have been prohibited since 2004. However, existing defined benefit funds may continue to pay the following types of pensions:

(a) flexi pensions (also known as commutable life-time pensions);

(b) life-time income streams; or

(c) complying fixed term income streams.

Benefits may be paid to the member, the member's spouse, the member's financial dependant, the member's estate or another superannuation fund depending on the circumstances.

244. The relevant assertions with respect to benefits paid are:

- *Occurrence* – all benefits recorded by the SMSF as paid have been incurred and paid.
- *Completeness* – all benefits paid or payable, if appropriate, by the SMSF have been recorded.
- *Accuracy* – benefits paid by the SMSF have been calculated appropriately and the correct amount of Pay-As-You-Go (PAYG) withholding tax, if applicable, has been deducted.
- *Cut-off* – all benefits paid by the SMSF have been recorded in the correct period.

71 Guidance and information on how exempt current pension income and relevant deductions should be applied for funds with segregated or unsegregated assets is available on the ATO website www.ato.gov.au (search under ECPI).

72 Ill-health may include total and permanent disability, total and temporary disability or trauma, depending on the insurance policies held on behalf of members.

73 Other circumstances may also trigger a condition of release, such as financial hardship.

74 In circumstances where a benefit payment has been split, the auditor reviews the documentation surrounding the split and mechanism by which the superannuation entitlement was dealt with in the property settlement arrangements. See paragraphs 247 to 249 for further guidance on benefit splitting.

75 A total and temporary disability benefit (salary continuance/income protection benefit) is generally paid as a regular income payment without reference to an account balance.

- *Classification* – all benefits paid by the SMSF have been recorded in the proper accounts and are allocated to the appropriate member's account.

245. Audit risks to be considered in relation to auditing benefits may include, but are not limited to:
    - Payment of a benefit to which the member or beneficiary are not entitled, providing early access to benefits.
    - Incorrect calculation of a benefit payment, including any PAYG withholding tax.
    - Payment of a benefit to an incorrect member or beneficiary.

246. Upon the death of a pensioner, many SMSF pensions are reversionary and continue to pay the pension to the surviving spouse or reversionary beneficiary. The reversionary feature is generally established at commencement of the pension, but some trust deeds may permit establishment under a discretionary power in the deed. The auditor, in the case of death of a pensioner with a reversionary benefit, checks that the pension is being paid to the nominated reversionary beneficiary and that the benefit has not been transferred to reserves or paid out as a lump sum.

Divorce and Splitting of Benefits

247. In circumstances where a member's benefit within a SMSF is subject to a property settlement upon divorce or a "splitting arrangement", the auditor reviews the documentation supporting the splitting of the benefit. A settlement is evidenced by one or more of the following documents:
    (a) Superannuation agreement – negotiated between the divorcing parties and certified by two legal practitioners who represent the respective divorcing parties.
    (b) Consent order – an order of the court frequently negotiated between two legal practitioners who represent the respective divorcing parties and submitted to the court for approval.
    (c) Arbitrated court order – where the divorcing parties are unable to agree on the settlement terms and the court decides the settlement amount and terms.
    (d) Notice by a non-member.[76]
    (e) Notice by a trustee of information regarding an interest subject to a payment split.[77]
    (f) Payment split notice by a trustee to both member and non-member.[78]
    (g) One of the following notices by the non-member spouse to the trustees to:
        (i) create a new interest;[79]
        (ii) rollover or transfer benefits;[80]
        (iii) pay a lump sum where non-member has met a condition for release.[81]

248. Once an order or agreement has been executed properly, the trustees are required to implement the order or agreement. In general, this may mean one of the parties exits the SMSF. Where there is a two member SMSF, the exiting member may take part of the other party's interest as well as their own. The auditor then treats the exit as per a normal member rollover or cashing out of a benefit. The auditor is careful to ensure that the capital gains issues are addressed, and that the tax components and preservation status of the superannuation payments are maintained. If a member exits the SMSF, the remaining trustee needs to ensure compliance with section 17A by:
    (a) appointing a new individual member; or
    (b) appointing a corporate trust of which the member is the sole director.

---

76 Notice under regulation 72 of the Family Law (Superannuation) Regulations 2001.

77 Notice under regulation 2.36C of the SISR.

78 Notice under regulation 7A.03 of the SISR.

79 Notice under regulation 7A.03C or 7A.05 of the SISR.

80 Notice under regulation 7A.03D or 7A.06 of the SISR.

81 Notice under regulations 7A.03E or 7A.07 of the SISR.

249. Due to the potential complexities and subtleties of the court orders, the possibility of court orders inadvertently conflicting with the SISA or SISR, and the trustees' obligations to perform the order irrespective of the implications for compliance with the SISA and SISR, the auditor may seek legal advice where benefits payments under a court order may be in contravention of the SISA or SISR.

Other Audit Considerations

Going Concern

250. The SMSF's financial report is prepared on the basis that the SMSF is a going concern. Under ASA 570, the auditor is required to consider and remain alert to whether there are any events, conditions and related business risks which may cast significant doubt on the SMSF's ability to continue as a going concern.[82] In assessing going concern, the auditor considers the period of approximately 12 months following the date of the current auditor's report, being the period up until the expected date of the auditor's report for the next annual reporting period.

251. To view a SMSF as a going concern, the SMSF is expected to be able to pay its debts as and when they fall due and continue in operation without any intention or necessity to liquidate or otherwise wind up its operations. For a SMSF, the primary concern is whether the SMSF will be able to pay benefits and entitlements to members, in addition to tax and other expenses, payable over the coming year. If the SMSF is in an unsatisfactory financial position for the purposes of reporting under SISA section 130,[83] the auditor still makes a separate assessment as to whether the SMSF is a going concern in forming their opinion on the financial report.

252. For an accumulation fund, the auditor is concerned with whether the net assets of the SMSF exceed the vested benefits, which are payable to members irrespective of whether they continue as a member. If there is a deficiency in net assets with respect to vested benefits the SMSF may not be a going concern, so the auditor undertakes further audit procedures to investigate the deficiency. These procedures include identifying whether an actuarially determined technical insolvency program is in place and assessing whether it enables the SMSF to continue as a going concern. The trustee is required to initiate a technical insolvency program, designed by an actuary to return the SMSF to a solvent position within five years, if the SMSF is technically insolvent under the SISR.[84] An accumulation fund is technically insolvent under the SISR if the net realisable value of the assets of the SMSF is less than the minimum guaranteed benefits to members.[85]

253. For a defined benefit fund, the value of accrued benefits may be an indicator of future funding deficiencies and inadequacies in the current contribution arrangements in funding future benefits that may arise. Therefore, the auditor determines whether the value of accrued benefits exceeds the value of the SMSF's net assets. If this is the case, the SMSF may not be a going concern, so the auditor undertakes further audit procedures to investigate the deficiency, including determining whether:

(a) The net assets exceed the value of vested benefits;

(b) the SMSF has a current actuarial funding and solvency certificate;[86] or

(c) the SMSF is technically insolvent under the SISR, due to the minimum benefit index[87] being less than 1[88] and if so, whether an actuarially determined technical insolvency program has been initiated by the trustees and a special funding and solvency certificate has been obtained.

GS

82 ASA 570 provides requirements and guidance to the auditor where going concern issues exist.

83 Reporting an unsatisfactory financial position is addressed in the compliance engagement, paragraphs 370 to 371 of this Guidance Statement.

84 Regulation 9.38(1) of the SISR.

85 Regulation 9.35 of the SISR.

86 Regulation 9.90 of the SISR.

87 The minimum benefits index is calculated in accordance with regulation 9.15 of the SISR.

88 Regulation 9.21 of the SISR.

254. A deficiency in net assets with respect to the value of vested benefits of a defined benefits fund indicates that the SMSF may be experiencing going concern problems and the auditor assesses the actuarial certificates and any technical insolvency program in place to determine if this deficiency can be overcome. The auditor considers:
   (a) whether the employer has been making contributions in accordance with the actuarially determined recommendations in the funding and solvency certificate;
   (b) the employers' or members' ability to remediate the funding deficiency in the long term, including any material uncertainties regarding their ability to do so; and
   (c) whether the pension or income streams have been commuted to a lower pension after period end, such that the SMSF's assets will be sufficient to fund the reduced pension or income stream.

255. The trustee of a defined benefits fund is required to obtain an actuarial funding and solvency certificate.[89] The actuary certifies the solvency of the SMSF as at the effective date of the certificate and the minimum contributions expected to be required to secure the solvency of the SMSF on the expiry date,[90] which may be between one to five years after the effective date of the certificate. The auditor checks whether the certificate has ceased to have effect due to any of the reasons set out in the SISR,[91] including expiry of the certificate or occurrence of a notifiable event.

256. If the SMSF is technically insolvent, the auditor ascertains whether a special funding and solvency certificate has been obtained by the trustee and a technical insolvency program initiated, to ensure that the SMSF is in a solvent position within five years, or alternatively winding-up proceedings have been initiated, as required under the SISR.[92] The auditor assesses whether any technical insolvency program enables the SMSF to continue as a going concern. If winding-up proceedings have commenced the SMSF is not a going concern.

257. Having considered the matters above, under ASA 570, the auditor may conclude that either:
   (a) an unmodified auditor's opinion may be issued due to the fact that:
      (i) the auditor is satisfied that it is appropriate, based on all reasonably foreseeable circumstances facing the SMSF, for the financial report to be prepared on a going concern basis; or
      (ii) there is adequate disclosure of the principal conditions which caused the auditor to question the going concern basis, including, as appropriate, the trustees' evaluation of their significance and possible effects and any funding plans and other mitigating factors; or
   (b) a modified auditor's opinion is necessary due to the existence of a material uncertainty which may cast significant doubt on the SMSF's ability to continue as a going concern, expressed as either:
      (i) an emphasis of matter section in the auditor's report regarding a going concern uncertainty, where there is adequate disclosure of the uncertainty; or
      (ii) a qualified or adverse opinion in the auditor's report, where there is inadequate disclosure of the uncertainty; or
   (c) a modified auditor's opinion is necessary, due to the fact that the SMSF will not be able to continue as a going concern where the financial report had been prepared on a going concern basis, expressed as an adverse opinion.

89 Regulation 9.09 of the SISR.

90 Regulation 9.10 of the SISR.

91 Regulation 9.12(2) of the SISR.

92 Regulation 9.17 of the SISR.

258. Under ASA 570, the auditor communicates to the trustees if a modified opinion is to be issued on the basis of going concern. This communication may be done in conjunction with communication of other matters of governance interest arising from the audit, discussed further in paragraphs 277 to 281.

Subsequent Events

259. ASA 560 requires the auditor to apply audit procedures designed to obtain sufficient appropriate audit evidence that all events up to the date of the auditor's report that may require adjustment of, or disclosure in, the financial report have been identified. Under ASA 560, audit procedures to identify such events, are performed as near as practicable to the date of the auditor's report and may include reading the trustees' minutes, making enquiries of the SMSF's lawyers concerning litigation or a marital split and making enquiries of the trustees as to whether any subsequent events have occurred which might affect the financial report, such as sales of investments or significant adjustments to investment values.

260. The auditor's response to the subsequent events depends on the potential for such events to affect the financial report and the appropriateness of the auditor's opinion. For example, if the trustees decide to wind up the SMSF, this would be a material event requiring appropriate disclosure and amendments to the financial report. Whereas, if an immaterial investment of the SMSF became worthless, this may not warrant any amendment.

Winding-Up

261. If the trustees decide to wind up the SMSF, the SMSF still needs to be audited for the relevant financial year, except in situations where an approval has been given by the ATO for a return not necessary to be required.

262. Upon winding-up, an audit is performed with increased testing in the areas of:

- Liquidated investments – to determine whether they were realised for cash or transferred in specie and what value was received.
- Benefit payments – to test that they are bona fide, calculated correctly and paid to the correct individual with the correct amount of tax deducted and remitted.
- Cash – to ensure there are no transactions post balance date and that the balance is nil at balance date.
- Rollovers – to test whether they were paid to complying superannuation funds, where applicable.

Change of Auditor

263. When SMSFs transfer from one administrator to another, the auditor needs to follow ASA 510 to determine whether the opening balances contain misstatements that materially affect the current period's financial report, whether the prior year closing balances have been correctly brought forward and that appropriate accounting policies are applied consistently. The auditor obtains the prior year signed audit report and undertakes further investigation if the report was modified. Any contributions and benefit payments made prior to the transfer date are tested substantively.

Anti-Money Laundering

264. *The Anti-Money Laundering and Counter-Terrorism Financing Act 2006* (AML/CTF Act) is legislation designed to deter money laundering and terrorism financing. The AML/CTF Act sets out which entities are reporting entities and then imposes obligations on them when they provide one or more of the 'designated services' as set out in the AML/CTF Act. Currently, SMSFs do not provide a designated service and accordingly are not required to report under the AML/CTF Act. Auditors of SMSFs also have no formal AML/CTF reporting obligations, but they remain alert to potential money laundering or terrorist activities and report suspicions voluntarily, if appropriate. For newly established SMSFs, auditors of SMSFs would typically check for the 100 point identification as part of the application process.

Reporting

265. With respect to the financial audit, the SISA, section 35C, requires the auditor to:

(a) report on the audit of the SMSF's financial report for the year of income; and

(b) give the trustees the report in the approved form,[93] as issued by the ATO, within the prescribed time as set out in the SISR, being a day before the latest date stipulated by the ATO for lodgement of the Annual Return.[94]

266. ASA 700 requires the auditor to form an opinion as to whether the financial report is prepared, in all material respects, in accordance with the applicable financial reporting framework. In order to form that opinion the auditor shall conclude as to whether the auditor has obtained reasonable assurance about whether the financial report as a whole is free from material misstatement, whether due to fraud or error.

267. ASA 220 requires that before the auditor's report is issued, the auditor performs a review of the audit documentation and conducts a discussion with the engagement team, in order to be satisfied that sufficient appropriate audit evidence has been obtained to support the conclusions reached.

268. In forming an opinion, the auditor considers all relevant evidence obtained, regardless of whether it appears to corroborate, or to contradict, information contained in the financial report.

Modifications to the Auditor's Opinion

269. Modifications to the auditor's opinion may be either:

(a) a qualified opinion;

(b) a disclaimer of opinion; or

(c) an adverse opinion.

ASA 705 contains requirements and guidance regarding when a modification to the auditor's opinion on the financial audit is necessary.

270. ASA 800 requires an auditor's report for a SMSF to include an emphasis of matter paragraph to highlight the financial report is prepared in accordance with a special purpose framework and as a result, the financial report may not be suitable for another purpose. The inclusion of an emphasis of matter paragraph does not affect the auditor's opinion, but draws the user's attention to the matter raised. ASA 706 contains the requirements and guidance regarding an emphasis of matter paragraph.

271. An auditor's report may also include an emphasis of matter paragraph to highlight:

(a) that a material uncertainty exists regarding a going concern matter that is adequately disclosed in the financial report;

(b) that additional disclosure is required to highlight that the financial report may be potentially misleading; or

(c) that the financial report has been revised due to the discovery of a subsequent fact, and replaces a previously issued financial report for which an auditor's report was issued.

The addition of such an emphasis of matter paragraph does not affect the auditor's opinion, but draws the user's attention to the matter raised.

272. An auditor's report may include another matter paragraph to highlight:

(a) that the financial report has been revised due to the discovery of a subsequent fact, and replaces a previously issued financial report for which an auditor's report was issued.

(b) that the financial report of the prior period was audited by the predecessor auditor, the type of opinion expressed, the reasons if the opinion was modified and the date of the report;

93 The approved form auditor's report is contained in Appendix 3 of this Guidance Statement and is also available at www.ato.gov.au/Superfunds.

94 Regulation 8.03 of the SISR.

(c) that the auditor's opinion on a prior period financial report differs from the opinion the auditor previously expressed;

(d) that the prior period financial report was not audited and the corresponding figures are unaudited; or

(e) a material inconsistency in a document containing the financial report.

ASA 706 contains the requirements and guidance regarding when another matter paragraph is necessary in the auditor's report.

273. A qualified opinion may be issued for a SMSF where the financial report is materially misstated or there is an inability to obtain sufficient appropriate evidence which is not as material and pervasive as to require an adverse opinion or a disclaimer of opinion. The auditor's inability to obtain sufficient appropriate audit evidence may arise from circumstances beyond the control of the entity, circumstances relating to the nature or timing of the auditor's work or limitations imposed by management. Examples of circumstances beyond the control of the entity include when the entity's accounting records have been destroyed or the accounting records of a significant component have been seized indefinitely by governmental authorities. A qualified opinion is expressed as being "except for" the effects of the matter to which the qualification relates. The opinion paragraph is headed "Qualified Opinion".

274. A disclaimer of opinion is expressed when the possible effect of an inability to obtain sufficient appropriate evidence is so material and pervasive that the auditor has not been able to obtain sufficient appropriate audit evidence and, accordingly, is unable to express an opinion on the financial report. In these circumstances, the opinion paragraph is headed "Disclaimer of Opinion".

275. An adverse opinion is expressed when the effect of the misstatement is so material and pervasive to the financial report that the auditor concludes that a qualification of the auditor's report is not adequate to disclose the misleading or incomplete nature of the financial report. The opinion paragraph is headed "Adverse Opinion".

276. Whenever the auditor expresses an opinion that is other than unmodified, a clear description of all the substantive reasons is included in the auditor's report and, unless impracticable, a quantification of the possible effect on the financial report. If the effects or possible effects are incapable of being measured reliably, a statement to that effect and the reasons therefore are included in the basis for modification paragraph of the auditor's report.

Communication of Audit Matters

277. Under ASA 260, the auditor communicates matters of governance interest arising from the audit to the trustees on a timely basis, to enable the trustees to take appropriate action. Ordinarily, the auditor initially discusses with the trustees and/or management those matters arising from an audit that are causing concern, including expected modifications, if any, to the auditor's report. This provides the trustees with an opportunity to clarify facts and issues and to provide further information.

278. The auditor is also required under ASA 260 to inform the trustees of those uncorrected misstatements, other than clearly trivial amounts, aggregated by the auditor during the audit that were determined to be immaterial, both individually and in the aggregate, to the financial report taken as a whole.

279. Under ASA 260, the communication may be made orally or in writing, however, to meet the documentation requirements of ASA 230, the matters communicated and any responses need to be documented in the working papers. Oral communications may need to be confirmed in writing depending on the nature, sensitivity and significance of the discussions.

280. Under ASA 265, the auditor communicates deficiencies in internal control that the auditor has identified during the audit and that, in the auditor's professional judgement, are of sufficient importance to merit their respective attentions.

281. Under ASA 250, any non-compliance which the auditor considers to be intentional and material, is communicated to the trustees without delay. The auditor's statutory reporting responsibilities in relation to non-compliance also necessitate reporting of such matters to the trustees under section 129 of the SISA.[95]

Part B – Compliance engagement

282. The compliance engagement of a SMSF is driven by the provisions of the SISA and SISR specified in the approved form auditor's report and in the ACR, which comprise the compliance criteria for the engagement. These criteria can be grouped within the following categories:
   (a) establishment and operation of the SMSF;
   (b) sole purpose;
   (c) investment restrictions;
   (d) benefits restrictions;
   (e) contributions restrictions;
   (f) solvency; and
   (g) other regulatory information.

283. The specific criteria and corresponding provisions of the SISA and SISR which are required to be reported on in the auditor's report and the ACR under each of these categories are listed in Table 1 below. From time to time, the SISA, SISR and the approved form auditor's report may be amended and new Tax Rulings and Interpretive Decisions may be issued by the ATO. In these circumstances, the auditor will need to adapt the approach in this Guidance Statement to address changes to the compliance criteria.

284. The auditor may use a checklist as an aide in conducting and documenting the compliance engagement. Standardised checklists are available from a number of professional organisations and from the ATO, which is contained in Instructions for Auditors of SMSFs *Auditing a Self-Managed Super Fund – Questions and statements to consider when auditing a self-managed super fund.*[96]

95 Reporting under section 129 of the SISA is discussed in paragraphs 376 to 378.

96 The ATO's compliance checklist is included in appendix A of the ATO publication Approved auditors and self-managed super funds: Your roles and responsibilities as an approved auditor (NAT 11375) which can be found at www.ato.gov.au/Superfunds. In addition, the ATO's electronic SMSF audit tool (eSAT), for use in conducting compliance engagements, is available on the ATO website (www.ato.gov.au/eSAT).

Table 1: Summary of Criteria for Compliance Engagement

This table provides a summary of the sections of the SISA and SISR which are the criteria reported on in Part B: *Compliance* of the approved form auditor's report and/or in the ACR.

Category	Specific Criteria	Auditor's Report Part B SISA/SISR	ACR SISA/SISR
Establishment and operation of the SMSF	Meets the definition of a SMSF.	S.17A[97]	S.17A
	Trustees are not disqualified persons.	S.126K[98]	S.126K
	Maintains minutes and records for specified time periods.	S.103	S.103
	Maintains trustees' declarations regarding duties for those who become trustees for the first time after 30 June 2007.	S.104A[99]	S.104A
	Proper accounting records kept and retained for 5 years.	S.35A	–
	Annual financial report prepared, signed and retained for 5 years.	S.35B	–
	Trustee provides auditor documents within 14 days of request (14 day letter).	S.35C(2)	S.35C(2)
	Prohibition on entering contracts restricting trustees' functions and powers.	S.52(2)(e)	–
	Trustees formulate and give effect to an investment strategy.	R.4.09	R.4.09
Sole purpose	Established for the sole purpose of funding a member's benefits for retirement, attainment of a certain age, death, ill-health or termination.	S.62	S.62

97 Section 17A of the SISA is a requirement which is included in the approved form auditor's report for periods ending on or after 30 June 2008, but was not included in the approved form auditor's report for the previous period.

98 Section 121 was repealed and replaced with section 126K of the SISA, on 26 May 2008.

99 Section 104A of the SISA is a requirement which is included in the approved form auditor's report for periods ending on or after 30 June 2008, but was not previously opined upon.

GS

Category	Specific Criteria	Auditor's Report Part B SISA/SISR	ACR SISA/SISR
Investment restrictions	Restrictions on acquiring or holding "in-house" assets.	Ss.69-71E; Ss.73-75; Ss.80-85	S.82, S.83, S.84 & S.85
	Restrictions on acquisitions of assets from related parties.	S.66	S.66
	Maintains arm's length investments.	S.109	S.109
	Maintains SMSF money and other assets separate from those of the trustees and employer-sponsors and other related parties.	S.52(2)(d)	S.52(2)(d)
	Prohibition on lending or providing financial assistance to member or relative.	S.65	S.65
	Restrictions on borrowings.	S.67	S.67
	Prohibition on charges over SMSF assets.	R.13.14	R.13.14
Benefits Restrictions	Trustees maintain members' minimum benefits.	R.5.08	R.5.08
	Minimum pension amount to be paid annually.	R.1.06(9A)	–
	Restrictions on payment of benefits.	R.6.17	R.6.17
	Prohibition on assignment of members' superannuation interest.	R.13.12	–
	Prohibition on creating charges over members' benefits.	R.13.13	–
Contributions restrictions	Accepts contributions within specified restrictions.	R.7.04	R.7.04
Reserves/Investment Return Allocation	Reserves to be used appropriately and investment returns must be allocated to members' accounts in a manner that is fair and reasonable.	R. 5.03	–
Solvency	Unsatisfactory financial position.	–	S.130[100]
Other regulatory information	Information regarding the SMSF or trustees which may assist the ATO, including compliance with other relevant SISA sections and SISR regulations.	–	S.130A[101]

100 Unsatisfactory financial position is reported separately from other contraventions in Section F of the ACR and the seven tests set out in the ACR instructions are not applicable. Also see Reg 9.04 of the SISR for the narrow definition of "unsatisfactory financial position."

101 Other regulatory information is reported separately from other contraventions in Section G of the ACR and the seven tests set out in the ACR instructions are not applicable.

Materiality

285. In planning and performing the compliance engagement, ASAE 3100 requires the auditor to consider materiality and compliance engagement risk. In assessing materiality, the auditor considers qualitative and quantitative factors including

- Potential damage to members of a breach of the SISA or SISR occurring.
- Whether disclosure of a breach would influence members', trustees' or the ATO's perceptions or decisions, including whether the breach would be reportable in an ACR.
- Potential monetary value of increased tax resulting from a breach.
- Potential monetary value or severity of any penalties.
- Whether there are any arm's length members, such as members who are subject to a legal disability.

Establishment and Operation of the SMSF

286. In auditing the SMSF's compliance with the requirements regarding establishment and operation of the SMSF, the auditor conducts testing to determine that:

(a) the SMSF meets the definition of SMSF;

(b) the trustees are not disqualified persons;

(c) the SMSF's minutes and records are retained for the prescribed periods;

(d) the SMSF has and retains trustee declarations of duties signed by any new trustees after 30 June 2007;

(e) the SMSF's accounting records are kept and retained for five years;

(f) annual financial reports have been prepared for the SMSF, either signed by two individual trustees, two directors of the corporate trustee or the sole director of the corporate trustee, and retained for five years along with the SMSF's accounts;

(g) the SMSF has not entered into any contract or act that may prevent or hinder the trustees from properly performing or exercising their powers and functions; and

(h) an investment strategy which takes into account the risk, diversification, cash flows and liquidity of the SMSF has been formulated and given effect.

In addition, the auditor can expect the trustees to provide documents within 14 days that are requested in writing and are relevant to the preparation of the auditor's report, as required under the SISA.[102]

Definition of SMSF

287. To determine if the SMSF meets the definition of SMSF,[103] the auditor may conduct procedures including:

- Examination of the trust deed, member applications and minutes of trustees' meetings to identify the members and trustees and that they comply with the relevant legislation.
- Enquiry of management to identify members, employers and trustees and their relationships with one another.
- Testing SMSF payments to ensure no payments have been made to the trustees for duties or services to the SMSF.
- Obtaining trustee representations.

GS

102 Subsection 35C(2) of the SISA.

103 The definition of a SMSF is in section 17A of the SISA. Also refer to SMSFR 2010/2. The scope and operation of subparagraph 17(A)(3)(b)(ii) of the SISA and ATO ID 2010/139 Subparagraph 17(A)(3)(b)(i) of the SISA – tribunal appointed administrator of the plenary estate of a person with a mental disability.

Disqualified Persons

288. An individual SMSF trustee is disqualified under the SISA[104] if they are:
   (a) convicted of an offence in respect of dishonest conduct;
   (b) the subject of a civil penalty order;
   (c) an insolvent under administration (includes an undischarged bankrupt under the *Bankruptcy Act 1966*); or
   (d) disqualified by the ATO.

289. A corporate trustee is disqualified if:
   (a) the responsible officer is a disqualified person; or
   (b) the company is in receivership, administration, provisional liquidation or has begun winding-up proceedings.

290. Ordinarily, the auditor verifies that the trustees are not disqualified by obtaining trustee representations to that effect. During the course of the audit the auditor remains alert to circumstances which may indicate that a trustee may be technically disqualified, such as personal financial difficulties or a trustee's involvement in legal proceedings. In this case, the auditor may make enquiries such as checking the trustee's details against APRA's disqualification register,[105] the National Personal Insolvency Index listing bankrupts, ASIC Company Register for Company Status or other commercial databases providing record search facilities.

Maintenance and Provision of SMSF Records

291. The auditor obtains representations from the trustees that the minutes and records of meetings have been held for 10 years (or from SMSF inception for funds under 10 years old), accounting records and financial reports have been retained for 5 years (or from SMSF inception for funds under 5 years old) and trustees appointed after 30 June 2007 have signed a "Trustee Declaration".[106]

292. The auditor examines the company secretarial records (for a corporate trustee) or SMSF records provided by the trustee or administrator to corroborate the trustees' representations regarding retention of records.

293. The SISA requires that the records be kept in the English language or a form that is readily convertible to English.[107] Generally, investment documentation in a foreign language, required as audit evidence, is translated at the SMSF's expense into English. This facilitates more efficient and effective auditing and quality control.

294. The auditor may request documents from the trustees required to conduct the audit. If the trustees fails to provide the documents required within the specified time period, this is a compliance breach which, if material, the auditor reports in the compliance report provided a written request was made under section 35C (2) of SISA and the documents were not supplied within 14 days.

Contracts Restricting Trustees' Functions and Powers

295. The auditor considers contracts entered into on behalf of the SMSF, the trust deed and any other arrangements in the light of the SISA's prohibition on entering a contract or doing anything which prevents the trustees from, or hinders the trustees in, properly performing or exercising their functions and powers.[108] The auditor may obtain representations from the trustees that no such arrangement has been entered into.

---

104 Subsection 120(1) of the SISA. Also refer to ATO ID 2011/24 *Waiver of disqualified person status – meaning of 'serious dishonest conduct'.*

105 The ATO does not publish a trustee disqualification register, however as APRA was the regulator of SMSFs prior to the ATO, APRA's register reflects disqualifications imposed when APRA regulated SMSFs.

106 The *Trustee Declaration* is an approved form issued by the ATO (NAT 71089), available from the ATO's website at www.ato.gov.au.

107 Section 35A of the SISA.

108 Section 52(2)(e) of the SISA.

Investment Strategy

296. In the approved form auditor's report the auditor states that their procedures "included testing that the fund trustee has an investment strategy, that the trustee has given consideration to risk, return, liquidity and diversification and that the fund's investments are made in line with that investment strategy". The SISR[109] requires the trustees of a SMSF to formulate and give effect to an investment strategy that has regard to all the circumstances of the SMSF, including:

- The risk involved in making, holding and realising, and the likely return from, the SMSF's investments, having regard to its objectives and expected cash flow requirements.
- The composition of the SMSF's investments as a whole, including the extent to which they are diverse or involve exposure of the SMSF to risks from inadequate diversification.
- The liquidity of the SMSF's investments, having regard to its expected cash flow requirements.
- The ability of the SMSF to discharge its existing and prospective liabilities.

297. Ordinarily the investment strategy is documented in writing and the auditor assesses that the trustees have properly considered all the circumstances of the SMSF, however the auditor is not required to assess whether the investment strategy is adequate to meet the long term investment needs of the SMSF and the auditor states in their report that "no opinion is made on the investment strategy or its appropriateness to the fund members".

298. For defined benefit funds, liquidity is of particular concern as members' benefits are not based on the SMSF's return on investments, so the auditor conducts additional procedures to test whether the trustee has properly considered liquidity, having regard to expected cash flow requirements necessary to fund liabilities, particularly benefit payments.[110]

299. In order to determine whether the trustees have given effect to the investment strategy, the auditor assesses whether the investments made during the period are invested according to the documented investment strategy as approved by the trustees. The auditor enquires as to whether the trustees have reviewed or modified their investment strategy during the period to accommodate the SMSF's changing needs and changes in the investment environment.

Sole Purpose

300. The SISA[111] requires the trustees to ensure that the SMSF is maintained solely for one or more of the allowable core purposes and, in addition, may also be maintained for one or more of the allowable ancillary purposes. The allowable core purposes are the provision of benefits for each member on their retirement, attainment of a prescribed age or death prior to retirement or attaining the prescribed age. The allowable ancillary purposes are the provision of benefits for each member on termination of employment, cessation of work due to ill-health, death after retirement or attainment of a prescribed age, or a benefit approved by the ATO. The "sole purpose test" is a conceptual test that when satisfied demonstrates that the SMSF has in fact been maintained solely for the allowable purposes and requires a higher standard than maintenance of the SMSF for a dominant or principal purpose. The approved form auditor's report, in Appendix 3 of this Guidance Statement, requires the auditor to separately state that their procedures "included testing that the fund trust deed establishes the fund solely for the provision of retirement benefits for fund members or their dependents in the case of a member's death before retirement".

GS

109 Regulation 4.09 of the SISR.

110 Going concern, including liquidity issues, for defined benefit funds are discussed in paragraphs 250 to 258 of this Guidance Statement.

111 Section 62 of the SISA.

301. The trustees of a SMSF are required to maintain a SMSF in a manner that complies with the sole purpose test at all times while the SMSF is in existence. This extends to all activities of the SMSF including:
- Accepting contributions.
- Acquiring and investing the SMSF's assets.
- Administering the funds (including maintaining the SMSF's structure).
- Employing and using the SMSF's assets.
- Paying benefits, including those benefits on or after retirement.

302. In assessing whether a SMSF has complied with the sole purpose test, the auditor may refer to the ATO's Ruling SMSFR 2008/2 on the application of the sole purpose test to circumstances where the SMSF is maintained for the purposes prescribed while providing benefits, particularly to members or related parties, other than those specified in section 62 of the SISA. SMSFR 2008/2 states that a SMSF may still satisfy the sole purpose test despite the provision of benefits not specified in section 62, if the benefits are "incidental, remote or insignificant". In order to determine whether the benefits are incidental, remote or insignificant, the circumstances surrounding the SMSF's maintenance need to be viewed "holistically and objectively".

303. In assuring compliance with the sole purpose test, the auditor looks for the provision of current day benefits, being benefits to a member or related party before the member's retirement, employment termination or death, and assesses whether those benefits fail the sole purpose test. An asset of a SMSF which provides current day benefits to a related party is generally an "in-house" asset and, even if it does not breach the sole purpose test, it still cannot exceed, in combination with other in-house assets, the restriction on the value of in-house assets which may be held by the SMSF. In-house assets are discussed further in paragraphs 319 to 322.

304. Current day benefits are likely to fail the sole purpose test if the benefit:
- Was negotiated or sought out by the trustees.
- Has influenced the decision making of the trustees.
- Has been provided at a cost or financial detriment to the SMSF.
- Is part of a pattern or preponderance of events which, when viewed in their entirety, amount to a material benefit being provided that is not specified under section 62(1).

305. Current day benefits are more likely to comply with the sole purpose test if:
- The benefit is an inherent and unavoidable part of activities for allowable purposes.
- The benefit is remote, isolated or insignificant.
- The benefit is provided on arm's length commercial terms, at no cost or financial detriment to the SMSF.[112]
- The trustees comply with the covenants in section 52 of the SISA.
- The benefit relates to activities which are part of a properly considered and formulated investment strategy.

306. The sole purpose test is complemented by other restrictions in SISA relating to dealings with members and related parties, such as prohibitions on:
- Transactions not at arm's length.[113]
- Borrowings.[114]
- Loans or financial assistance to members or relatives.[115]

---

112 SMSFD 2010/1 provides guidance where a fund purchases trauma insurance for a member and considerations for compliance with s62 of SISA.

113 Section 109 of the SISA.

114 Section 67 of the SISA.

115 Section 65 of the SISA.

- Acquisitions from related parties.[116]
- Charges over assets.[117]
- Assignment of, or charges over, member's benefits.[118]
- SMSF assets not held separately from the members' personal assets.[119]
- Acquisition of "in-house" assets in excess of 5% of the total market value of the SMSF assets.[120]

Breaches of one or more of these restrictions may be indicative of circumstances establishing a breach of the sole purpose test.

Running a Business

307. The auditor remains alert to circumstances which indicate that the SMSF is running a business or conducting operations which may be akin to running a business, as this activity may breach the sole purpose test. Indications that a business is being conducted by the SMSF may include revenues from trading activities, employing staff and paying operating expenses. A business is not usually administered for the sole purpose of providing the allowable benefits to members or beneficiaries of the SMSF, as there is an inherent risk that running a business may jeopardise the member's benefits.[121]

308. In addition, running a business may breach other restrictions. Running the business may not be consistent with the SMSF's investment strategy. Many businesses routinely borrow to provide working capital and purchase goods on credit, which prima facie breach the borrowing restrictions[122], discussed further below. If a trustee is also an employee of the business, payment of salary or wages to the trustee may be construed as remuneration to the trustee for the duties or services performed by the trustee in relation to the SMSF, which is a breach of the definition of SMSF under the SISA.[123] The auditor assesses all circumstances of a SMSF running a business to determine whether it is in breach of the SISA or SISR.

309. SMSFs that engage in high volume trading of derivatives, listed securities, real property or other investments or a series of property developments may be running a business for purposes other than solely for providing specified benefits to members and beneficiaries. For SMSFs conducting activities of this kind, the auditor considers whether the activities are justified in giving effect to the investment strategy.

Collectables[124]

310. Collectables may be permitted investments for SMSF, however they lend themselves to personal enjoyment and, therefore, may involve significant current day benefits if members or related parties use or access the collectibles. Audit procedures, to establish whether members or related parties are deriving personal enjoyment or benefit from the collectable, may include:
    - Verifying registration and insurance in the SMSF's name.
    - Identifying where the collectable is located or stored.
    - Establishing whether it was used during the period and, if so, whether commercial rates of hire or lease were paid for that use.

116 Section 66 of the SISA.

117 Regulation 13.14 of the SISR.

118 Regulations 13.12 and 13.13, SISR.

119 Section 52(2)(d) of the SISA.

120 Part 8 of the SISA.

121 Also refer to SMSFR 2008/2: The application of the sole purpose test in section 62 of the SISA to the provision of benefits other than retirement, employment termination or death benefits.

122 Section 67 of the SISA.

123 Section 17A of the SISA.

124 At the time of publication, legislation has been passed which includes additional requirements for SMSF trustees investing in artwork and collectables. These changes will be a consideration for the fund audit for the reporting period commencing 1 July 2011.

GS

311. The treatment and classification of collectables is an area where the auditor exercises professional judgment to determine whether the investment is compliant with the sole purpose test and other requirements of the SISA and SISR. The auditor satisfies themselves that the underlying reason or rationale for investment in collectables is reasonable, including whether the risks involved in making, holding and realising the investment, and the likely return, are consistent with the SMSF's investment strategy and cash flow requirements, given potential difficulties in realising the investment in some collectibles.

Table 2: Examples of Assurance Procedures for Collectables

Table 2 provides examples of the threats in meeting the sole purpose test and related SISA and SISR compliance posed by investments in collectables, and suggested assurance procedures to determine whether the sole purpose test is satisfied. Detailed examples are provided in SMSFR 2008/2. The list is not exhaustive.

Collectable	Sole purpose test threats	Suggested assurance procedures
Artworks	• On display/view at member's or related party's home/office. • On display without an arm's length lease at commercial rates. • Investments in artworks are not consistent with the investment strategy and purchased to provide current day benefits to members or related parties.	• If on display with a third party, verify arm's length lease in place at commercial rates. • If on display with a member or related party it is unlikely to pass the sole purpose test, nevertheless it may be possible if the auditor can verify that benefit from displaying the art work is remote, isolated or insignificant, the benefit is an inherent part of other activities and the SMSF did not suffer any financial detriment. • Verify if the artwork is insured in the SMSF's name. • Validate that artwork is stored in a safe and secure manner. • Check whether holding artwork is consistent with the investment strategy. • Consider sighting artwork to test above.
Jewellery	• Worn or displayed by member or related party for little or no consideration. • Investments in jewellery are not consistent with the investment strategy and purchased to provide current day benefits to members or related parties.	• Verify storage in a bank safe deposit or similar off site repository or, if held at a member's private address, verify an arm's length lease is in place at commercial rates and current day benefits are not enjoyed. • Verify if the jewellery is insured in the SMSF's name. • Check whether holding jewellery is consistent with the investment strategy. • Sight bank safe deposit arrangement to test above. Consider inclusion in bank audit confirmation letter request.

Collectable	Sole purpose test threats	Suggested assurance procedures
Classic cars	• Driven by member or related party for pleasure, competition or rallying for little or no consideration. • Displayed by member or related party for little or no consideration. • Investments in cars are not consistent with the investment strategy and purchased to provide current day benefits to members or related parties.	• Verify where the car is garaged. If kept at a member's home or office, verify if an arm's length lease is in place at commercial rates and current day benefits are not enjoyed. • Compare odometer readings at beginning of year and at year end to see mileage during the year which may indicate provision of current day benefits. • Some very limited driving for maintenance may be permissible. Sight invoices for description of any work. • Ensure any expenditure on restoration is appropriate. • Verify that the car is registered and insured in the SMSF's name. • Check whether holding cars is consistent with the investment strategy.
Coins/stamps	• Enjoyed or displayed in the member's home or related party's home. • Displayed by member as trading stock or lent to a related party as stock or display stock for little or no return. • Investments in coins or stamps are not consistent with the investment strategy and purchased to provide current day benefits to members or related parties.	• Verify storage in a bank safe deposit or similar off site repository and not with a member's personal effects unless a lease is in place at commercial rates and current day benefits are not enjoyed. • Check that coins/stamps are insured by SMSF, not by a member or trustee. • Check whether holding coins or stamps is consistent with the investment strategy.
Antiques	• Used, enjoyed or displayed in the member's or related party's home, office or other building owned by the member or related party. • Investments in antiques are not consistent with the investment strategy and purchased to provide current day benefits to members or related parties.	• If on display, verify that an arm's length lease is in place at commercial rates and current day benefits are not enjoyed. • Verify that the antiques are insured in the SMSF's name. • Verify stored in a safe and secure manner. • Check whether holding antiques is consistent with the investment strategy.
Sporting memorabilia	• Displayed in the member's or related party's home, office or other building owned by the member or related party. • Investments in memorabilia are not consistent with the investment strategy and purchased to provide current day benefits to members or related parties.	• If on display, verify arm's length lease in place at commercial rates and current day benefits are not enjoyed. • Verify that the memorabilia is insured in the SMSF's name. • Verify that memorabilia is stored in a safe and secure manner. • Check whether holding memorabilia is consistent with the investment strategy.
Wine	• Wine stored at member's or related parties' home, office or other building owned by the member or related party on display or accessible for consumption. • Investments in wine are not consistent with the investment strategy and purchased to provide current day benefits to members or related parties.	• Check that wine is stored correctly in a temperature / humidity controlled environment. • Identify a strategy in place to dispose of non-investment quality wine or vintages. • Check that when wine is no longer required it is not consumed by a member or trustee unless sold to them at arm's length.[125] • Check whether holding wine is consistent with the investment strategy.

GS

312. Other collectables, such as precious metals or fine china, may be allowable investments. However, the general principle, that the investment in a collectable should not provide a current day benefit, remains. Ordinarily, the auditor considers the full circumstances of the investment before forming an opinion as to whether it is in compliance with the SISA and SISR.

Lifestyle Assets

313. Membership investments, such as ski lodge, country club or golf club memberships, providing a right to use a facility or service, will usually fail the sole purpose test if the trustees or members derive a current day benefit from the investment. The auditor may refer to the examples in ATO Ruling SMSFR 2008/02 to assist them in assessing whether or not an investment in a lifestyle asset is a breach of the SISA and SISR.

314. Investments in broadly held schemes or arrangements to develop and sell recreational property may be permitted, if there is no residual entitlement to utilise the facilities, or otherwise enjoy the benefits of the development and where the scheme does not involve running a business.

315. Investments in holiday houses or apartments need to be justifiable as a legitimate part of the SMSF's investment strategy, and the accommodation is required to be rented out, or be made available for rent at commercial rates. Use or enjoyment of the property by the trustees, members or a related party is a strong indication that the sole purpose test may have been breached and may also render the investment an "in-house" asset,[126] in which case the in-house asset limits will apply. However, if use of the property by the trustees, members or a related party is at arm's length, for short periods only, and in circumstances where there is an independent third party real estate agent/manager that is in charge of the rental arrangements, the SMSF may still satisfy the sole purpose test.

316. Generally, investments that provide an ancillary benefit as part of the investment need to be examined to determine whether the investment as a whole meets the sole purpose test. Ancillary benefits include, but are not limited to, such things as a discount on a product or service, priority access to a facility, upgrades or free products or services.

Units in a Related Unit Trust

317. Investments in related unit trusts, where trustees or members of the SMSF are also trustees of the related unit trust, are common SMSF investments. The auditor considers the sole purpose test in light of the investments held in, and by, the related unit trust to ensure that the investments held are for the long-term provision of allowable benefits to members and not to provide other benefits to the trustees, members or their relatives. The auditor will also need to consider whether the investment breaches the prohibition on acquisitions from related parties, the prohibition on borrowings or exceeds the "in-house" asset limits.

Investment Restrictions

318. The SISA contains a number of investment restrictions with which the trustees are required to comply. In assessing whether these prohibitions have been complied with, the auditor examines the nature of each material investment to ensure that the investment is permitted under the SISA. In particular, the auditor:

(a) Examines the documentation supporting the investment to determine whether it was undertaken and maintained on a commercial and arm's length basis.

(b) Evaluates whether the investment has been held separately from the personal assets of the trustees.

(c) Evaluates whether other entities may be benefiting inappropriately from the transaction.

125 Purchasing wine from a SMSF is only permitted if the purchase complies with the requirement to make and maintain investments of the SMSF at arm's length in accordance with section 109 of the SISA.

126 Guidance on "in-house" assets is provided in paragraphs 319 to 322 of this Guidance Statement.

"In-house Assets"

319. An "in-house" asset of a SMSF is an asset that is loaned to a related party, an investment in a related party, an investment in a related trust or an asset of the SMSF subject to a lease between the trustees and a related party of the SMSF.[127] A related trust is a trust that a member or employer-sponsor controls.[128] There are a number of exceptions to the definition of in-house assets and transitional provisions included in Part 8 of the SISA.[129] The auditor needs to be familiar with these exceptions when considering in-house asset requirements.

320. The SISA has strict limits on the level of "in-house assets" permitted to be held by the SMSF. The market value of the in-house asset must not exceed 5% of the total market value of the SMSF's assets at the time of acquisition[130] and at year end.[131] Also the trustees are prohibited from acquiring an in-house asset that would cause the total of all in-house assets to exceed this 5% ratio. The auditor examines the investments of the SMSF to identify potential in-house assets to ensure that the legislative limits are not exceeded either when they were acquired or at year end.

321. If a SMSF invests in in-house assets but does not account for its investments at market value, the auditor obtains market values in order to ascertain whether a breach has occurred.

322. The auditor remains alert to schemes intentionally entered into or carried out by the trustees which have the effect of artificially reducing the market value ratio of the SMSF's in-house assets. Such actions are prohibited under the SISA.[132]

Acquisition of Assets from Related Parties

323. Trustees and investment managers are prohibited, under the SISA,[133] from acquiring assets from a related party unless the assets are acquired at market value and are either:
   (a) listed securities;
   (b) business real property; or
   (c) in-house assets within the 5% ratio limit.

324. Business real property[134] is land and buildings used wholly and exclusively for business purposes.[135] It does not extend to:
   (a) vacant land, unless used in primary production;
   (b) land used for property development or shares held in an unlisted property owning company; or
   (c) residential properties except where the residence forms part of a primary production business and does not exceed two hectares in area or the provision of accommodation is in the nature of a business (e.g. for a motel).

325. Ordinarily, the auditor examines the documentation surrounding the purchase of material investments, other than those which fall into one of the exceptions above, to ascertain whether the vendor was a related party. This may involve checking the contract or sale document to confirm who the parties to the transaction were and, to the extent possible, their relationship with the trustees and members. The auditor makes enquiries in the

GS

---

127 Defined in subsection 10(1) of the SISA. Also refer to SMSFR 2009/4 the meaning of 'asset', 'loan', 'investment in', 'lease' and 'lease arrangement' in the definition of an 'in-house asset' in the SISA.

128 Defined in subsection 10(1) of the SISA.

129 See also regulations 13.22B, 13.22C and 13.22D of the SISR. SMSFR 2009/I is also relevant to the definition of business real property and the exceptions under S71(1) of SISA.

130 Section 83 of the SISA.

131 Section 82 of the SISA.

132 Section 85 of the SISA.

133 Section 66 of the SISA.

134 Defined in subsection 66(5) of the SISA. Refer to SMSFR 2010/1 *The application of subsection 66(1) of the SISA to the acquisition of an asset by a SMSF from a related party.*

135 Refer to SMSFR 2009/1 *Business real property for the purposes of the SISA.*

planning phase of the audit in order to identify related parties, whether individuals or entities related to the trustees or members.

Arm's Length Investments

326. The SISA[136] requires the trustees and investment managers to invest and maintain the SMSF's assets at arm's length. Indicators of non-arm's length investments may include:

- Investments in a related party.
- Investments being managed by a related party.
- Details of parties to a contract indicate related parties.
- Uncommercial or disadvantageous terms of a lease or loan.
- No formal contracts established for loan, lease or other arrangement.
- Assets, such as rental properties, deriving little or no income, or income well below commercial rates.
- Investments which are inconsistent with the investment strategy or entered into without a sound rationale.

327. The auditor assesses all aspects of the transaction, including that the settlement terms, interest rates, rents, lease refurbishment term, warranties, security and repayment terms are commercial in nature.

Assets Held Separately

328. The trustees are required[137] to keep the money and the assets of the SMSF separate from their personal or business assets of the trustees and from the assets of employer-sponsors. The auditor examines the affairs of the SMSF to identify possible situations where the assets of the SMSF may have become intermingled with assets of the trustees or employer-sponsors. The auditor checks that the assets of the SMSF are registered in the SMSF's name or, where assets cannot be held directly by the SMSF, there is evidence that those assets are held beneficially on behalf of the SMSF, such as a declaration of trust.

329. The auditor examines payments and receipts to ascertain that dividends, interest and other income of the SMSF are not banked into personal or business accounts, particularly where a corporate trustee operates a number of bank accounts as well as conducting the affairs of the SMSF. The auditor may test that dividends declared for listed securities held are received and banked by the SMSF.

Loans and Financial Assistance to Members or their Relatives

330. SMSFs are not permitted to lend money or provide financial assistance to members or their relatives[138] and the approved form auditor's report states that the auditor procedures included "a review of investments to ensure the fund is not providing financial assistance to members, unless allowed under the legislation". The auditor examines the bank account and obtains explanations for material withdrawals and deposits in order to ascertain whether any loan or financial assistance benefit has been provided to a trustee, member or relative of a member or trustee. In certain circumstances, access by members or their relatives to SMSF funds may be considered to be an early access to benefits without meeting a condition of release.[139]

331. In cases where funds are accessed in error by the trustees for non-SMSF use, the breach may affect the audit opinion, unless the amount is immaterial, the event is infrequent and repayment is made in full. Interest at commercial rates may also be appropriate.

---

136 Section 109 of the SISA.

137 Subsection 52(2)(d) of the SISA.

138 Section 65 of the SISA. Also refer to SMSFR 2008/1 *Giving financial assistance using the resources of a SMSF to a member or relative of a member that is prohibited for the purposes of section 65(1)(b) of the SISA*.

139 Determining whether benefits have been accessed prior to meeting a condition of release is a question of fact and any penalty is at the discretion of the ATO.

332. The auditor reviews the ownership of the SMSF's assets to ensure that a charge or other form of security has not been taken over any of the SMSF's assets to secure a member's or relative's borrowings, which would be a form of financial assistance. This may require performing a title search for the SMSF's real property to identify any encumbrances.

Borrowings

333. SMSFs are not permitted to borrow money,[140] with the exceptions of borrowings:

(a) to pay a benefit, pension or superannuation contribution surcharge liability (no longer levied), for a maximum of 90 days for up to 10% of the value of the SMSF's assets;

(b) to cover settlement on a security transaction for a maximum period of 7 days, for up to 10% of the value of the SMSF's assets provided that, at the time the relevant investment decision was made, it was likely that the borrowing would not be needed; or

(c) that are part of an instalment warrant arrangement.

334. Ordinarily, the auditor reviews the bank statements to ascertain whether any non-compliant borrowings were made during the period, whether by way of an overdraft or a loan account.

335. Margin lending, in general, involves a borrowing arrangement where a loan is taken out using the listed securities purchased as security for that loan. Margin loan facilities breach the SISA and SISR by virtue of the fact that the borrowing is not an approved exception to the borrowing prohibition and SMSFs are not permitted to give a charge over some or all of the fund assets as required by a margin lending arrangement. If the SMSF is involved in trading of securities or derivatives, the auditor examines related documentation for indications of the existence of margin lending arrangements, such as interest payments on broker's statements, margin call payments or significant listed securities purchases without corresponding payments.

336. The auditor reviews any investments in derivatives, including options, futures, or swaps, to ascertain that the investments are in accordance with the investment strategy, any current legislative requirement and that the investment is not putting the assets of the SMSF at risk. Derivatives, due to their inherent nature, may be high risk and involve borrowings that may have recourse to the SMSF. Where the auditor is unsure of the legality of the investment, the auditor may need to seek legal advice as to whether the investment meets the investment restrictions. Active trading of derivatives may be construed as running a business and, consequently, may be a breach of the sole purpose test.

337. Investments in limited recourse borrowing arrangements are an exception to the prohibition on borrowings. Limited recourse borrowing arrangements, sometimes referred to as instalment warrants, are complex financial arrangements whereby the SMSF buys an asset via a limited recourse agreement where there is some debt funding or borrowing to purchase the asset. The transaction is characterised by an asset held in trust for the SMSF, where the SMSF holds an interest in the income and the rights to acquire the asset. The SMSF may be required to make regular instalments or repayments. Recourse by the lender, in the case of failure to settle the loan, is required to be solely over, and limited to, the asset held in the trust arrangement. After commencing the borrowing, the SMSF is required to make at least one payment before purchasing the asset. Whilst there is no formal requirement for regular repayments/instalments, the lack of repayments may bring into question the commercial rationale of the underlying investment and whether the sole purpose test is being breached.

338. From 24 September 2007, superannuation funds were allowed to invest in certain limited recourse borrowing arrangements involving borrowing money to acquire a permitted asset. Those arrangements need to meet the conditions stipulated by the law in the former subsection 67(4A) of the SISA. Those rules continue to apply to limited recourse borrowing arrangements that were entered into before 7 July 2010.

140 Section 67 of the SISA. Also refer to SMSFR 2009/2 *The meaning of "borrow money" or "maintain an existing borrowing of money" for the purposes of section 67 of the SISA*.

339. For limited recourse borrowing arrangements entered into by superannuation funds on or after 7 July 2010, the superannuation laws have been amended so that:

(a) the asset within the arrangement can only be replaced by a different asset in very limited circumstances specified in the law;

(b) superannuation fund trustees cannot borrow to improve an asset (for example, real property);

(c) the borrowing is permitted only over a single asset or a collection of identical assets that have the same market value;

(d) the asset within the arrangement is not subject to a charge other than to the lender in respect of the borrowing by the superannuation fund trustee.[141]

340. Procedures which the auditor may conduct in auditing compliance of instalment warrants with the SISA and SISR may include:

- Examination of the trust deed to determine if the SMSF is permitted to borrow.
- Examination of the investment strategy, or discussions with the trustees if there is no written investment strategy, to determine if instalment warrant arrangements and the percentage of funds devoted to them are allowed within that strategy.
- Identification of the nature of the asset purchased and whether the vendor is a related party so as to ensure that the transaction is permitted under the SISA, SISR and trust deed.
- Determination of whether the debt arrangement or loan agreement is a non-recourse agreement as required by the SISA,[142] whereby the other assets of the SMSF are not used as security for the loan.
- Determination of whether the finance is provided by a related party, such as a family trust, in order to identify any potential non arm's length dealings.
- Determination of whether the funds borrowed were used to purchase an asset held in the instalment warrant arrangement.
- Identification of whether the terms of the loan are commercial. Less than commercial interest rates may be a means of making additional contributions to the SMSF, whereas an excessively high interest rate may fail the sole purpose test, or potentially be a scheme to access benefits.
- Identification of any arrangements outside the SMSF, such as a personal guarantee, which may have recourse to the assets of the SMSF, other than the asset acquired (or any replacement), as this may be a breach of the borrowing restriction exception granted to instalment warrant arrangements.
- Determination of whether the original asset has been added to in any way, either by additional shares or further purchases, since if the instalment warrant asset has increased, this would indicate a further borrowing and therefore a potential breach of the prohibition on borrowing.
- For limited recourse borrowing arrangements entered into from 1 July 2010, determination of whether:
    - a replacement to the asset has been made contrary to the law;
    - the fund has not borrowed to improve an asset in the arrangement;
    - the trust asset is a single asset or identical assets that have the same value, for e.g. ordinary shares; and
    - there is no charge over the asset except per the limited recourse arrangement.[143]

141 Refer to ATO Interpretative Decisions 2010/162, 184 and 185 for further guidance.

142 Subsection 67(4A)(d) of the SISA.

143 At the time of publication, it is anticipated the ATO will issue a ruling to provide further guidance on the new requirements for limited recourse borrowing arrangements. Also refer to ATO ID 2010/162, 2010/184 and 2010/185.

Charges Over Assets

341. SMSFs are not permitted to use the assets of the SMSF to secure a debt facility[144] and, hence, charges and liens over assets are not permitted. Also, charges and liens over any member benefits are prohibited. Accordingly, the auditor reviews the minutes, correspondence and records of the trustees to identify whether any charges or debt facilities have been applied for or established. Additional audit procedures include review of any bank confirmations for charges, dividend reinvestment options, title searches on properties of the SMSF to identify any charges or liens and examination of the accounting records or bank statements to identify any interest payments made by the SMSF, which may indicate a loan facility.

342. Similarly, the auditor ordinarily reviews the ownership of the SMSF's assets to ensure that a charge, or other form of security, has not been taken over any of the SMSF's assets. This may extend to reviewing any product disclosure statement relating to assets acquired to determine whether the product has any recourse to the SMSF. Even if the marketing or summary material claims there is no recourse to the SMSF, the auditor still checks the actual provisions of the arrangement.

343. Where the SMSF has investments in related or unlisted unit trusts, the auditor is alert to any borrowings the unit trust may have and whether there is any recourse to the SMSF. Any borrowings by the unit trust must be in accordance with the SISA and SISR. Certain unit trusts established pre-July 1999 may be subject to transitional legislation that permits borrowings. The auditor assesses the legislative requirements that apply to the trust and whether the borrowing is permitted on an ongoing basis or needs to be repaid. Additional audit procedures may need to be conducted to assess this. Specialist legal advice may be sought if the auditor is unsure whether the investment exposes the SMSF to borrowings.

344. Ordinarily, the auditor requests a financial report, the tax return and distribution statements, for investments in unit trusts, to identify income, net asset value and any debts owing by the unit trust. In certain cases, the unit trust deed may be required to assist the auditor in assessing compliance.

Benefit Restrictions

345. The member's ability to receive a benefit normally depends on:
   (a) the type of benefit the member has accumulated in the SMSF;
   (b) the member's age and whether any preservation restrictions apply to the benefit; and
   (c) whether the rules of the SMSF permit the benefit to be paid at the time.

Minimum Benefits

346. The trustees are required[145] to maintain the members' minimum benefits until the benefits are paid out, rolled over or transferred. For defined benefit funds, the auditor ensures that the minimum benefits have been calculated correctly by reference to the formula provided in the trust deed, the SMSF's records and the actuarial valuation, if appropriate. The SISR require annual or triennial actuarial reports to be obtained by the trustees for defined benefit funds, depending on the circumstances. The actuarial report states whether, in the actuary's opinion, the value of the SMSF's assets is adequate to meet the accrued benefits of members at the valuation date. For accumulation funds, the minimum benefit which needs to be maintained is the value of vested benefits.

Payment of Benefits

347. Generally, benefits are triggered due to a condition of release being met and the approved form auditor's report states that the auditor's procedures include testing "that no preserved benefits have been paid before a condition of release has been met". Conditions of release are specified in the SISR[146] and may be further restricted by the SMSF's trust deed.

144 Regulation 13.14 of the SISR. Also refer to ATO ID 2010/162, 2010/184 and 2010/185.

145 Regulation 5.08 of the SISR.

146 Conditions of release are listed in Schedule 1 and detailed in Part 6 of the SISR.

Conditions of release may include retirement, death, temporary incapacity, terminal medical condition, permanent incapacity, attaining the prescribed preservation age for a transition to retirement benefit,[147] severe financial hardship, compassionate grounds approved by APRA,[148] attaining age 65 or a request to rollover. A condition of release triggers either a lump sum payment or a pension.

348. For pension payments, the auditor ensures that any payments meet the minimum or maximum[149] payment conditions as stipulated in the SISA and SISR and an appropriate condition of release has been met. In particular, funds paying account based pensions must pay an annual minimum pension which is calculated by applying a percentage rate, dependent on the member's age, at the 1st July of the reporting year being audited, to the member's account balance. Where a minimum pension has not been paid, the income stream from the assets providing pension will no longer be tax exempt.[150]

349. For lump sum payments, the auditor ensures that the trust deed permits such payments and that an appropriate condition of release has been satisfied.

350. In relation to testing the compliance of both lump sum or pension-type benefits, the auditor considers whether:

(a) the circumstances of the individual in triggering the payment of the benefit are consistent with a condition of release;

(b) the member has satisfied the payment criteria; and

(c) the benefit has been calculated correctly in accordance with the method provided in the trust deed and the governing rules.

351. Ordinarily, the auditor tests the validity of the payment by checking to source documents that the benefit payment is *bona fide*, such as sighting a signed letter to the trustees requesting the benefit be paid and that retirement is evidenced by a statutory declaration or similar document stating that the individual has retired and will not be seeking paid employment in the future.

352. Total and permanent disability generally requires at least two appropriately qualified medical practitioners to certify that the individual is unlikely to work in paid employment or meets such similar definition as may be contained in the trust deed or governing rules of the SMSF. The SMSF may or may not have insurance for total and permanent disability.

353. With respect to death benefits, the auditor confirms that the member is deceased by sighting a funeral notice or death certificate and verifies that the correct death benefit has been paid. The auditor enquires as to whether any additional insurance benefit is payable and whether the trustees have claimed any available tax deductions for anti-detriment payments.

354. If an appropriately witnessed and executed binding death benefit nomination has been made, ordinarily, the auditor enquires to ensure that the benefit was paid appropriately according to the nomination's intent.

355. If the SMSF has an insurance policy covering total and permanent disability, total and temporary disability or death or a combination of these benefits, ordinarily the auditor enquires to see if a claim has been made or paid to support the benefit. If the proceeds of any such claim have been paid, ordinarily, the auditor checks to see that the benefit has been applied either to the member's account or paid to the legal personal representative or beneficiaries.

147 Members need to reach their preservation age before commencing a transition to retirement benefit. This is age 55 for those born prior to 1 July 1960 and increasing up to age 60 for those born after 1 July 1964.

148 The Commissioner of Taxation delegated the authority as regulator with respect to approval of compassionate reasons to APRA.

149 Maximum payments exist for transition to retirement income streams.

150 Refer to sub-regulation 1.06(9A) and Schedule 7 of SISR.

Assignment of Members' Interests and Charges over Members' Benefits

356. The trustees are not permitted to recognise, or in any way encourage or sanction, an assignment of a superannuation interest, of a member or beneficiary,[151] or a charge over, or in relation to, a member's benefits.[152]

357. The auditor reviews the trustees' minutes, contracts and correspondence to identify any arrangements which may amount to an encumbrance over members' interests or benefits. Similarly, the auditor reviews the same documentation to ensure that the benefit or member's interest has not been assigned to another individual or corporation. The auditor may obtain representations from the trustees that no such arrangements have been entered into as far as they are aware.

Contribution Restrictions

358. A contribution is defined as anything of value that increases the capital of a superannuation fund provided by a person whose purpose is to benefit one or more particular members of the fund or all of the members in general.[153] Ordinarily, the auditor examines all contributions made to the SMSF to assess whether they have been made in accordance with the trust deed, SISA and SISR and, that in accepting the contribution, the SMSF is not contravening the SISA and SISR. In making this assessment, the auditor identifies the type of contribution made, the age of the member and the source of the contribution.

359. The auditor tests that the SMSF has accepted contributions only in accordance with the SISR,[154] which are either:

(a) mandated employer contributions received irrespective of the member's age, such as SG contributions, superannuation guarantee shortfall, award related and certain payments from superannuation holding accounts;

(b) member contributions or employer contributions (except mandated contributions) when:

(i) the member is under 65 years old;

(ii) the member is not under 65 but is under 70 and has been gainfully employed at least on a part-time basis during the financial year in which the contribution is made;[155] or

(iii) the member is not under 70 but is under 75 and has been gainfully employed at least on a part-time basis during the financial year in which the contribution is made and the contribution is received no later than 28 days after the month end when the member turned 75 and, in the case of a member contribution, it is made by the member.

(c) other contributions for a member who is under 65 years of age; or

(d) contributions received at a later date in respect of a period in which the member met the age restrictions.

360. The auditor also tests that contributions are:

(a) within contribution caps specified in the SISR, being:

(i) if the member is 64 or less on 1 July of the financial year – three times the amount of the non-concessional contributions cap; or

(ii) if the member is 65 but less than 75 on 1 July of the financial year – the non-concessional contributions cap; and

(b) for a member for whom a tax file number (TFN) has been supplied.

GS

---

151 Regulation 13.12 of the SISR.

152 Regulation 13.13 of the SISR.

153 TR 2010/1 *Income tax: Superannuation contributions.*

154 Regulation 7.04 of the SISR.

155 The basic work test for accepting contributions is to work for remuneration for at least 40 hours in a continual 30 day period within the year the contribution was made.

361. In verifying the appropriateness of contributions received the auditor considers factors including:
- The type and source of the contribution.
- The age of the member.
- Whether a tax file number has been provided.
- The amount contributed.
- The timing of when the contribution was made.

362. Ordinarily, the auditor checks to see that the classification of any taxable contributions is appropriate and allocated to the correct member account. If a single inappropriate contribution or contribution in excess of the contributions caps is accepted, the SMSF is not in breach of the SISA or SISR if the SMSF returns the amount within 30 days of becoming aware that the amount was received in a manner that was inconsistent with the regulations.[156] The contribution is not required to be returned unless all or part of the contribution itself will cause the member to have excess non-concessional contributions for the income year.[157]

363. With respect to the Government co-contribution, the auditor ordinarily checks that the co-contribution has been allocated correctly where material.

In specie Contributions

364. *In specie* contributions are contributions to a SMSF where a physical asset (e.g. a commercial property) or an intangible asset (e.g. a share, or an option) are contributed to the SMSF on behalf a member without any cash being exchanged.

365. Where contributions are accepted *in specie*, the auditor assesses whether:
(a) the trust deed permits in specie contributions; and
(b) the SISA prohibitions on acquiring assets from related parties (including members) have been satisfied.

366. Once it is established that the *in specie* contribution may be accepted, the auditor assesses whether the *in specie* contribution is:
(a) within the contributions cap;
(b) valued fairly, generally at market value or independent valuation; and
(c) not in breach of any other SISA prohibition.

Use of Reserves

367. Where reserves are present in an SMSF, an auditor ordinarily checks to ensure the use of the reserves by the trustees is appropriate and within the requirements of the SISA and SISR. In particular, the allocation from an investment reserve to members' accounts should take into consideration the return on the investments, any costs attributable to the members' accounts and the level of the reserves held by the fund.[158] For contributions held in any reserves, the auditor checks to ensure the amounts have been allocated to members' accounts within 28 days of receipt by the fund.

Investment Returns

368. An auditor ordinarily checks to ensure that any fund investment returns or losses are accurately credited or debited to relevant members' benefits in a way that is fair and reasonable.[159] The allocation should take into consideration all the members of the fund and the various kinds of benefits of each member of the fund.

156 Regulation 7.04 of the SISR.
157 ATO Interpretative Decision 2008/17, 2008/18, 2008/90, 2009/29, 2010/104.
158 Sub-regulation 5.03(1) of the SISR.
159 Sub-regulation 5.03(2) of the SISR.

Solvency

369. If the auditor, in the course of, or in connection with, performance of the audit of a SMSF, forms the opinion that the financial position of the SMSF may be, or may be about to become, unsatisfactory, the auditor is required to report to the ATO (in an ACR) and to the trustees in writing under section 130 of the SISA.

370. Under the SISR,[160] the financial position of a SMSF is treated as unsatisfactory if, in the auditor's opinion:

(a) for a defined benefit fund: the value of vested benefits exceed the value of the assets; or

(b) for an accumulation fund: either the aggregate members' benefits accounts exceed the value of the assets or the accrued members' benefits exceed the value of the assets.

Other Regulatory Information

371. In the course of conducting the audit, the auditor may obtain information regarding the SMSF or a trustee which the auditor considers may assist the ATO in performing its functions under the SISA or SISR. This information may relate to compliance with requirements of the SISA or SISR which are not specified in the approved form auditor's report or the ACR. Under section 130A of the SISA, the auditor is required to report any such information to the ATO in the ACR.

372. The auditor considers whether any regulatory information reported in the ACR under section 130A needs to be included in the auditor's report on compliance, as the approved form auditor's report allows for reporting on additional sections of the SISA and SISR, and whether the information affects the compliance assurance opinion.

Other Compliance Engagement Considerations

Service Organisations

373. If a service organisation is used by the SMSF, the auditor cannot merely rely on the type 2 report as evidence of the SMSF's compliance with the SISA and SISR. The auditor should perform additional procedures necessary to ensure the SMSF's compliance with the SISA and SISR. If insufficient evidence of compliance is obtained by assurance procedures at the SMSF and further evidence of compliance is located at the service organisation, the auditor may either visit the service organisation to conduct compliance testing or request the SMSF to engage another auditor to conduct the testing required. This may consist of an agreed upon procedures engagement, which may comprise completion of a compliance checklist with respect to the services provided.

374. It may be impossible or impractical to obtain sufficient appropriate audit evidence of compliance with respect to the services provided, in which case either the auditor qualifies their opinion on the basis of a limitation of scope or issues a disclaimer of opinion.

Subsequent Events

375. The auditor considers the effect of subsequent events on the auditor's compliance report occurring up to the date the report is signed. If a material compliance breach has occurred after year end and the breach indicates a systemic issue with potential to impact the reporting period, it may result in modifications to the compliance report.

160 Regulation 9.04 of the SISR.

Reporting Compliance Breaches

376. In determining whether to report potential or actual contraventions (breaches) identified during the compliance engagement, the auditor applies different criteria in relation to their reporting obligations to:

(a) a trustee under SISA sections 129 or 130[161] (management letter);

(b) the ATO, in an ACR, under SISA sections 129 or 130; and

(c) the trustees in the auditor's compliance report.

377. The auditor reports to a trustee in writing under SISA section 129 any contraventions of the SISA or SISR, which it is likely may have occurred, may be occurring or may occur, regardless of the materiality of those contraventions. The auditor also reports to a trustee under section 130 if the financial position of the SMSF may be, or may be about to become, unsatisfactory.

378. The auditor reports events which may lead, or have led, to one or more contraventions of the SISA or SISR to the ATO in an ACR where they are contraventions of sections or regulations specified in the ACR and, either:

(a) those contraventions meet the reporting criteria, which comprise seven mandatory tests specified in the ACR instructions;[162] or

(b) those contraventions do not meet the specified tests, but the auditor wishes to report them as a result of the exercise of professional judgement.

In addition, the auditor reports to the ATO in an ACR under section 130 if the financial position of the SMSF may be or may be about to become unsatisfactory.[163]

379. ASAE 3100 requires the auditor's report on compliance to be modified if, in the auditor's judgement, material non-compliance with a requirement being reported on may exist. Consequently, the auditor determines whether any potential or actual contraventions of the SISA or SISR identified during the audit are:

(a) contraventions of sections of the SISA or SISR specified in the approved form auditor's report; and

(b) material to the SMSF.

380. In determining whether a contravention identified is material to the SMSF, and therefore whether a modification to the auditor's report is warranted, the auditor considers the factors in paragraph 282 as well as factors such as:

- The value of the breach.
- The time taken to rectify the breach, or if not yet rectified, the trustees' proposed actions and timeline for rectification.
- Whether the auditor has previously reported the breach in a section 129 report to a trustee or in an ACR.
- The extent to which a limit has been exceeded or a statutory deadline missed.
- Whether the breach was intentional.

381. Even if a contravention is reported in an ACR, it does not necessarily result in a modification to the auditor's compliance report. The auditor, nevertheless, considers the contraventions which meet the reporting criteria specified in the ACR instructions, and uses professional judgement in determining the impact, if any, on the auditor's compliance report.

---

161 Where an auditor forms an opinion that it is likely that a contravention may have occurred, may be occurring or may occur, the reporting criteria and the list of reportable sections and regulations that an auditor applies to determine whether a report to the ATO is required, are listed in the ACR instructions (NAT 11299-07.2011) www.ato.gov.au/Superfunds.

162 The ACR instructions (NAT 11299-07.2011) is an approved form and can be obtained through the ATO's website at www.ato.gov.au/Superfunds. Additionally, eSAT software is available free of charge from the tax office to assist in completing the compliance assurance engagement and reporting any ACRs appropriately to the ATO. See www. Ato.gov.au/eSAT for further details.

163 See "Solvency" at paras 369-370.

382. The circumstances which may result in a modification to the auditor's compliance report are where:

(a) a limitation of scope of the auditor's work exists, due either to circumstances or a trustee imposing a restriction, which prevents the auditor from obtaining the evidence required, in which case the auditor expresses a qualified opinion or a disclaimer of opinion; or

(b) the SMSF did not comply in all material respects with the requirements included in the approved form, in which case the auditor expresses a qualified or adverse opinion.

383. A qualified opinion is expressed as being "except for" the matter to which the qualification relates when that matter is not as material or pervasive as to require an adverse or disclaimer of opinion.

Conformity with International Pronouncements

384. As this Guidance Statement relates to Australian legislative requirements, there is no equivalent International Practice Statement (IAPS) to this Guidance Statement.

Appendix 1

Example of an Engagement Letter for the Audit of a Self-Managed Superannuation Fund

The following example audit engagement letter is for use as a guide only, in conjunction with the considerations described in GS 009, and may need to be modified according to the individual requirements and circumstances of each engagement.

To [the Trustees/Directors of the Corporate Trustee] of [name of SMSF]

The Objective and Scope of the Audit

You have requested that we audit the [name of SMSF]'s (the Fund):

1. financial report, which comprises the [statement of financial position/statement of net assets] as at [date] and the [operating statement/statement of changes in net assets] for the [period] then ended and the notes to the financial statements; and
2. compliance during the same period with the requirements of the Superannuation Industry (Supervision) Act 1993 (SISA) and SIS Regulations (SISR) specified in the approved form auditor's report as issued by the ATO, which are sections 17A, 35A, 35B, 35C(2), 52(2)(d), 52(2)(e), 62, 65, 66, 67, 69-71E, 73-75, 80-85, 103, 104A, 109 and 126K of the SISA and regulations 1.06(9A), 4.09, 5.03, 5.08, 6.17, 7.04, 13.12, 13.13, and 13.14 of the SISR.[164]

We are pleased to confirm our acceptance and our understanding of this engagement by means of this letter. Our audit will be conducted pursuant to the SISA with the objective of our expressing an opinion on the financial report and the fund's compliance with the specified requirements of the SISA and SISR.

The Responsibilities of the Auditor

We will conduct our financial audit in accordance with Australian Auditing Standards and our compliance engagement in accordance with applicable Standards on Assurance Engagements, issued by the Auditing and Assurance Standards Board (AUASB). These standards require that we comply with relevant ethical requirements relating to audit and assurance engagements and plan and perform the audit to obtain reasonable assurance whether the financial report is free from material misstatement and that you have complied, in all material respects, with the specified requirements of the SISA and SISR.

164 These sections and regulations need to be amended if there are any changes to the sections and regulations in the approved form auditor's report.

The annual audit of the financial reports and records of the Fund must be carried out during and after the end of each year of income. In accordance with section 35 of the SISA, we are required to provide to the trustees of the Fund an auditor's report in the approved form within the prescribed time as set out in the SISR, being a day before the latest date stipulated by the ATO for lodgement of the fund's Annual Return.

Financial Audit

A financial audit involves performing audit procedures to obtain audit evidence about the amounts and disclosures in the financial report. The procedures selected depend on the auditor's judgement, including the assessment of the risks of material misstatement of the financial report, whether due to fraud or error. A financial audit also includes evaluating the appropriateness of the financial reporting framework, accounting policies used and the reasonableness of accounting estimates made by the trustees, as well as evaluating the overall presentation of the financial report. Due to the test nature and other inherent limitations of an audit, together with the inherent limitations of any accounting and internal control system, there is an unavoidable risk that even some material misstatements may remain undiscovered.

In making our risk assessments, we consider internal controls relevant to the fund's preparation of the financial report in order to design audit procedures that are appropriate in the circumstances, but not for the purpose of expressing an opinion on the effectiveness of the fund's internal controls. However, we expect to provide you with a separate letter concerning any significant deficiencies in the fund's system of accounting and internal controls that come to our attention during the audit of the financial report. This will be in the form of a trustee letter.

Compliance Engagement

A compliance engagement involves performing audit procedures to obtain audit evidence about the fund's compliance with the provisions of the SISA and SISR specified in the ATO's approved form auditor's report.

Our compliance engagement with respect to investments includes determining whether the investments are made for the sole purpose of funding members' retirement, death or disability benefits and whether you have an investment strategy for the fund, which gives due consideration to risk, return, liquidity and diversification. Our procedures will include testing whether the investments are made for the allowable purposes in accordance with the investment strategy, but not for the purpose of assessing the appropriateness of those investments to the members.

The Responsibilities of the Trustees

We take this opportunity to remind you that it is the responsibility of the trustees to ensure that the fund, at all times, complies with the SISA and SISR as well as any other legislation relevant to the fund. The trustees are also responsible for the preparation and fair presentation of the financial report.

Our auditor's report will explain that the trustees are responsible for the preparation and the fair presentation of the financial report and for determining that the accounting policies used are consistent with the financial reporting requirements of the SMSF's governing rules, comply with the requirements of SISA and SISR and are appropriate to meet the needs of the members.[165] This responsibility includes:

- Establishing and maintaining controls relevant to the preparation of a financial report that is free from misstatement, whether due to fraud or error. The system of accounting and internal control should be adequate in ensuring that all transactions are recorded and that the recorded transactions are valid, accurate, authorised, properly classified and promptly recorded, so as to facilitate the preparation of reliable financial information. This responsibility to maintain adequate internal controls also extends to the Fund's compliance with SIS including any Circulars and Guidelines issued by a relevant regulator to the extent applicable. The internal controls should be sufficient to prevent and/or detect material non-compliance with such legislative requirements.
- Selecting and applying appropriate accounting policies.

165 If the SMSF is a reporting entity this sentence requires amendment to read: "Our auditor's report will explain that the trustees are responsible for the preparation and the fair presentation of the financial report in accordance with Australian Accounting Standards (including the Australian Accounting Interpretations)."

- Making accounting estimates that are reasonable in the circumstances.
- Making available to us all the books of the Funds, including any registers and general documents, minutes and other relevant papers of all Trustee meetings and giving us any information, explanations and assistance we require for the purposes of our audit. Section 35C(2) of SIS requires that Trustees must give to the auditor any document that the auditor requests in writing within 14 days of the request.

As part of our audit process, we will request from the trustees written confirmation concerning representations made to us in connection with the audit.

Our audit report is prepared for the members of the Fund and we disclaim any assumption of responsibility for any reliance on our report, or on the financial report to which it relates, to any person other than the members of the fund, or for any purpose other than that for which it was prepared.

Independence

We confirm that, to the best of our knowledge and belief, the engagement team meets the current independence requirements of [specify relevant ethical requirements such as *the Code of Ethics for Professional Accountants*, as issued by the Accounting Professional & Ethical Standards Board] in relation to the audit of the fund. In conducting our financial audit and compliance engagement, should we become aware that we have contravened the independence requirements, we shall notify you on a timely basis.

Report on Matters Identified

Under section 129 of the SISA, we are required to report to you in writing, if during the course of, or in connection with, our audit, we become aware of any contravention of the SISA or SISR which we believe has occurred, is occurring or may occur. Furthermore, you should be aware that we are also required to notify the Australian Taxation Office (ATO) of certain contraventions of the SISA and SISR that we become aware of during the audit, which meet the tests stipulated by the ATO, irrespective of the materiality of the contravention or action taken by the trustees to rectify the matter. Finally, under section 130 we are required to report to you and the ATO if we believe the financial position of the Fund may be, or may be about to become unsatisfactory.

You should not assume that any matters reported to you, or that a report that there are no matters to be communicated, indicates that there are no additional matters, or matters that you should be aware of in meeting your responsibilities. The completed audit report may be provided to you as a signed hard copy or a signed electronic version.[166]

Compliance Program

The conduct of our engagement in accordance with Australian Auditing Standards and applicable Standards on Assurance Engagements means that information acquired by us in the course of our engagement is subject to strict confidentiality requirements. Information will not be disclosed by us to other parties except as required or allowed for by law or professional standards, or with your express consent. Our audit files may, however, be subject to review as part of the compliance program of a professional accounting body or the ATO. We advise you that by signing this letter you acknowledge that, if requested, our audit files relating to this audit will be made available under these programs. Should this occur, we will advise you. The same strict confidentiality requirements apply under these programs as apply to us as your auditor.

[Limitation of liability[167]

As a practitioner/firm participating in a scheme approved under Professional Services Legislation, our liability may be limited under the scheme.]

GS

166 The auditor should retain an original hard copy in the working papers.

167 Applicable to participants in a limitation of liability scheme. Accounting Professional and Ethical Standard APES 305 *Terms of Engagement*, issued by the Accounting Professional & Ethical Standards Board in December 2007, which is applicable to members of the professional accounting bodies in Australia in public practice, requires participants in a limitation of liability scheme under Professional Services Legislation to advise the client that the member's liability may be limited under the scheme.

Fees

We look forward to full co-operation with [you/your administrator] and we trust that you will make available to us whatever records, documentation and other information are requested in connection with our audit.

[Insert additional information here regarding fee arrangements and billings, as appropriate.]

Other

This letter will be effective for future years unless we advise you of its amendment or replacement, or the engagement is terminated.

Please sign and return the attached copy of this letter to indicate that it is in accordance with your understanding of the arrangements for our financial audit and compliance engagement of the [name of SMSF].

[*Insert here or attach any additional matters specific to the engagement, such as business terms and conditions, as appropriate.*]

Yours faithfully,

....

Name and Title

Date

Acknowledged on behalf of the trustees of [name of SMSF] by (signed).

....

Name and Title

Date

Appendix 2

Example of a Self-Managed Superannuation Fund Trustee Representation Letter

This illustrative letter is provided as an example only and may need to be modified according to the individual requirements and circumstances of each engagement. Representations by the trustees will vary between SMSFs and from one period to the next.

[SMSF letterhead]

Date

[Addressee - Auditor]

Dear [Sir/Madam],

Trustee Representation Letter

This representation letter is provided in connection with your audit of the financial report of the [SMSF Name] (the Fund) and the Fund's compliance with the Superannuation Industry (Supervision) Act 1993 (SISA) and SIS Regulations (SISR), for the [period] ended [date], for the purpose of you expressing an opinion as to whether the financial report is, in all material respects, presented fairly in accordance with the accounting policies adopted by the Fund and the Fund complied, in all material respects, with the relevant requirements of SISA and SISR.

The trustees have determined that the Fund is not a reporting entity for the [period] ended [date] and that the requirement to apply Australian Accounting Standards and other mandatory reporting requirements do not apply to the Fund.[168] Accordingly, the financial report prepared is a special purpose financial report which is for distribution to members of the Fund and to satisfy the requirements of the SISA and SISR. We acknowledge our responsibility for ensuring that the financial report is in accordance with the accounting policies as selected by ourselves and requirements of SISA and SISR, and confirm that the financial report is free of material misstatements, including omissions.

We confirm, to the best of our knowledge and belief, the following representations made to you during your audit.

[*Include representations relevant to the Fund. Such representations may include the following examples.*]

1. Sole purpose test

   The Fund is maintained for the sole purpose of providing benefits for each member on their retirement, death, termination of employment or ill-health.

2. Trustees are not disqualified

   No disqualified person acts as a director of the trustee company or as an individual trustee.

3. Trust deed, trustees' responsibilities and fund conduct

   The Fund meets the definition of a self-managed superannuation fund under SISA, including that no member is an employee of another member, unless they are relatives and no trustee [or director of the corporate trustee] receives any remuneration for any duties or services performed by the trustee [or director] in relation to the fund.

   The Fund has been conducted in accordance with its constituent trust deed at all times during the year and there were no amendments to the trust deed during the year, except as notified to you.

   The trustees have complied with all aspects of the trustee requirements of the SISA and SISR.

   The trustees are not subject to any contract or obligation which would prevent or hinder the trustees in properly executing their functions and powers.

   The Fund has been conducted in accordance with SISA, SISR and the governing rules of the Fund.

   The Fund has complied with the requirements of the SISA and SISR specified in the approved form auditor's report as issued by the ATO, which are sections 17A, 35A, 35B, 35C(2), 52(2)(d), 52(2)(e), 62, 65, 66, 67, 69-71E, 73-75, 80-85, 103, 104A, 109 and 126K of the SISA and regulations 1.06(9A), 4.09, 5.03, 5.08, 6.17, 7.04, 13.12, 13.13, and 13.14 of the SISR.

   All contributions accepted and benefits paid have been in accordance with the governing rules of the Fund and relevant provisions of the SISA and SISR.

   There have been no communications from regulatory agencies concerning non-compliance with, or deficiencies in, financial reporting practices that could have a material effect on the financial report.

4. Investment strategy

   The investment strategy has been determined with due regard to risk, return, liquidity and diversity, and the assets of the Fund are in line with this strategy.

168 If the SMSF is a reporting entity then it will be required to prepare a general purpose financial report in accordance with the Australian Accounting Standards and this paragraph will need to be adapted accordingly.

GS

5. Accounting policies

All the significant accounting policies of the Fund are adequately described in the financial report and the notes attached thereto. These policies are consistent with the policies adopted last year.

6. Fund books and records

We have made available to you all financial records and related data, other information, explanations and assistance necessary for the conduct of the audit; and minutes of all meetings of the trustees.

We acknowledge our responsibility for the design and implementation of internal control to prevent and detect error. We have established and maintained an adequate internal control structure to facilitate the preparation of reliable financial reports, and adequate financial records have been maintained. There are no material transactions that have not been properly recorded in the accounting records underlying the financial report.

All accounting records and financial reports have been kept for 5 years, minutes and records of trustees' [or directors of the corporate trustee] meetings [or for sole trustee: decisions] have been kept for 10 years and trustee declarations in the approved form have been signed and kept for each trustee appointed after 30 June 2007.

7. Asset form and valuation

The assets of the Fund are being held in a form suitable for the benefit of the members of the Fund, and are in accordance with our investment strategy.

Investments are carried in the books at [insert valuation method: e.g. market value]. Such amounts are considered reasonable in light of present circumstances.

We have no plans or intentions that may materially affect the carrying values, or classification, of assets and liabilities.

There are no commitments, fixed or contingent, for the purchase or sale of long term investments.

8. Uncorrected misstatements

We believe the effects of those uncorrected financial report misstatements aggregated by the auditor during the audit are immaterial, both individually and in aggregate, to the financial report taken as a whole. A summary of such items is attached.

9. Ownership and pledging of assets

The Fund has satisfactory title to all assets appearing in the statement of [financial position/net assets]. All investments are registered in the name of the Fund, where possible, and are in the custody of the respective manager/trustee.

There are no liens or encumbrances on any assets or benefits and no assets, benefits or interests in the Fund have been pledged or assigned to secure liabilities of others.

All assets of the Fund are held separately from the assets of the members, employers and the trustees. All assets are acquired, maintained and disposed of on an arm's length basis and appropriate action is taken to protect the assets of the Fund.

10. Related parties

Related party transactions and related amounts receivable have been properly recorded or disclosed in the financial report. Acquisitions from, loans to, leasing of assets to and investments in related parties have not exceeded the in-house asset restrictions in the SISA at the time of the investment, acquisition or at year end.

The Fund has not made any loans or provided financial assistance to members of the Fund or their relatives.

11. Borrowings

The Fund has not borrowed money or maintained any borrowings during the period, with the exception of borrowings which were allowable under SISA.

12. Subsequent events

No events or transactions have occurred since the date of the financial report, or are pending, which would have a significant adverse effect on the Fund's financial position at that date, or which are of such significance in relation to the Fund as to require mention in the notes to the financial statements in order to ensure they are not misleading as to the financial position of the Fund or its operations.

13. Outstanding legal action

The trustees confirm that there is no outstanding legal action or claims against the Fund.

There have been no communications from the ATO concerning a contravention of SISA or SISR which has occurred, is occurring, or is about to occur.

14. Additional matters

[*Include any additional matters relevant to the particular circumstances of the audit, for example:*

- the work of an expert has been used; or
- *justification for a change in accounting policy.*]

We understand that your examination was made in accordance with Australian Auditing Standards and applicable Standards on Assurance Engagements and was, therefore, designed primarily for the purpose of expressing an opinion on the financial report of the Fund taken as a whole, and on the compliance of the Fund with specified requirements of SISA and SISR, and that your tests of the financial and compliance records and other auditing procedures were limited to those which you considered necessary for that purpose.

Yours faithfully

(signed)

………………………..

[Director/Trustee]

[Date]

………………………..

[Director/Trustee]

[Date]

GS

Appendix 3

(Ref. Para.)

ATO's Approved Form Auditor's Report for a Self-Managed Superannuation Fund

The approved form auditor's report in this Appendix has been extracted from the ATO's *Instructions and form for approved auditors of SMSFs, Self-managed superannuation fund independent auditor's report* (NAT11466.07.2011)[169] and should be read in conjunction with those instructions. Since this approved form is updated from time to time, the applicable version may be checked on the ATO's website.

SELF-MANAGED SUPERANNUATION FUND INDEPENDENT AUDITOR'S REPORT

Auditor details

Name ....

Postal address ....

Business name ....

Business postal address ....

Professional organisation ....

Professional membership or registration number ....

Self-managed superannuation fund details

Self-managed superannuation fund (SMSF) name ....

Australian business number (ABN) or tax file number (TFN) ....

Address...

Year of income being audited...

To the trustees

To the trustees of [SMSF name]

Part A: Financial report

I have audited the special purpose financial report comprising [Insert the title of statements audited including reference to the summary of significant accounting policies and other explanatory notes. For example: 'the statement of financial position as at 30 June [year], and the operating statement, statement of changes in equity for the year then ended, a summary of significant accounting policies and other explanatory notes.'] of the [SMSF name] for the year ended 30 June [year].

Trustee's responsibility for the financial report

The trustee is responsible for the preparation of the financial report in accordance with the financial reporting requirements of the *Superannuation Industry (Supervision) Act 1993* (SISA) and the Superannuation Industry (Supervision) Regulations 1994 (SISR), and for such internal control as the trustee determines is necessary to enable the preparation of a financial report that is free from material misstatement, whether due to fraud or error.

Auditor's responsibility

My responsibility is to express an opinion on the financial report based on the audit. I have conducted an independent audit of the financial report in order to express an opinion on it to the trustee.

169 The ATO's *Instructions and form for approved auditors of SMSFs, Self-managed superannuation fund independent auditor's report* (NAT11466.07.2011) is available at: www.ato.gov.au/Superfunds.

My audit has been conducted in accordance with Australian Auditing Standards. These standards require that I comply with relevant ethical requirements relating to audit engagements and plan and perform the audit to obtain reasonable assurance as to whether the financial report is free from material misstatement.

An audit involves performing procedures to obtain audit evidence about the amounts and disclosures in the financial report. The procedures selected depend on the auditor's judgement, including the assessment of the risks of material misstatement of the financial report, whether due to fraud or error. In making those risk assessments, the auditor considers internal control relevant to the trustee's preparation and fair presentation of the financial report in order to design audit procedures that are appropriate in the circumstances, but not for the purpose of expressing an opinion or the effectiveness of the trustee's internal control. An audit also includes evaluating the appropriateness of accounting policies used and the reasonableness of accounting estimates made by the trustees, as well as evaluating the overall presentation of the financial report.

I believe that the audit evidence I have obtained is sufficient and appropriate to provide a basis for my audit opinion.

[*Additional material may be inserted here at the discretion of the auditor.*]

[Basis for Qualified / Disclaimer of / Adverse Auditor's Opinion

[*This section should be modified if the financial report is not a true and fair presentation of the financial position of the fund, or if in the opinion of the auditor the financial position of the fund may be, or may be about to become unsatisfactory or there are other conditions that warrant a qualification.*]

[Qualified / Disclaimer of / Adverse] Auditor's Opinion

In my opinion, [except for the effects on the financial statements of the matter/s referred to in the preceding paragraph,] the financial report

[*Select one option*]

(a) presents fairly, in all material respects, in accordance with the accounting policies described in the notes to the financial statements, the financial position of the fund at 30 June [year] and the results of its operations for the year then ended.

OR

(b) presents fairly, in all material respects, in accordance with the accounting policies described in the notes to the financial statements, the net assets of the fund as at 30 June [year] and the changes in net assets for the year then ended.

OR

(c) presents fairly, in all material respects, in accordance with the accounting policies described in the notes to the financial statements (and the Trust Deed), the operations of the fund for the year ended 30 June [year].

[The following "Basis of Accounting" section is required if the audit report is for a reporting period commencing on and from 1 January 2010, otherwise delete it.]

Basis of Accounting

Without modifying our opinion, we draw attention to Note [X] of the financial report, which describes the basis of accounting. The financial report has been prepared to assist [SMSF Name] to meet the requirements of the Superannuation Industry (Supervision) Act 1993 (SISA) and the Superannuation Industry (Supervision) Regulations 1994 (SISR). As a result, the financial report may not be suitable for another purpose.

Part B: Compliance Report

Trustee's responsibility for compliance

The trustee is responsible for complying with the requirements of the SISA and the SISR.

Auditor's responsibility

My responsibility is to express an opinion on the trustee's compliance, based on the compliance engagement. My audit has been conducted in accordance with applicable Standards on Assurance Engagements, to provide reasonable assurance that the trustee of the fund has complied, in all material respects, with the relevant requirements of the following provisions (to the extent applicable) of the SISA and the SISR.

Sections: 17A, 35A, 35B, 35C(2), 52(2)(d), 52 (2)(e), 62, 65, 66, 67, 69-71E, 73-75, 80-85, 103, 104A, 109, 126K

Regulations: 1.06(9A), 4.09, 5.03, 5.08, 6.17, 7.04, 13.12, 13.13, 13.14[170]

[*Additional sections and regulations may be inserted here at the discretion of the auditor.*]

My procedures included examination, on a test basis, of evidence supporting compliance with those requirements of the SISA and the SISR.

These tests have not been performed continuously throughout the period, were not designed to detect all instances of non-compliance, and have not covered any other provisions of the SISA and the SISR apart from those specified. My procedures with respect to section 62 included testing that the fund trust deed establishes the fund solely for the provision of retirement benefits for fund members or their dependants in the case of the member's death before retirement; a review of investments to ensure the fund is not providing financial assistance to members, unless allowed under the legislation; and testing that no preserved benefits have been paid before a condition of release has been met.

My procedures with respect to regulation 4.09 included testing that the fund trustee has an investment strategy, that the trustee has given consideration to risk, return, liquidity and diversification and that the fund's investments are made in line with that investment strategy. No opinion is made on the investment strategy or its appropriateness to the fund members.

I believe that the audit evidence I have obtained is sufficient and appropriate to provide a basis for my audit opinion.

[Basis for Qualified / Disclaimer of / Adverse Auditor's Conclusion]

[*This section should be modified if, in the opinion of the auditor, a contravention of one of the provisions listed is material.*]

[Qualified / Disclaimer of / Adverse] Auditor's Conclusion

In my opinion, [except for the matter/s referred to above] the trustee of [SMSF name] has complied, in all material respects, with the requirements of the SISA or the SISR specified above, for the year ended 30 June [year].

Signature

Signature of approved auditor ______________________

Date ______________

170 An explanation of each of these sections and regulations is attached as an appendix to assist trustees. Please ensure that it is attached to the fund's audit report.

Appendix 4

Self-Managed Superannuation Fund Trust Deed Audit Planning Checklist

In obtaining a preliminary understanding of the SMSF, as part of the planning process, the auditor examines the trust deed to obtain a sound understanding of the trustee structure, requirements of the deed and the powers vested in the trustees. The following suggested procedures are examples only and should be reviewed and adapted for the specific circumstances and audit risks associated with each SMSF audit engagement.

The auditor exercises professional judgement and due care in interpreting the provisions of the trust deed. If the auditor is unsure of the meaning or interpretation of a clause, provision or section of the deed, then the auditor may seek the advice of an experienced superannuation lawyer.

Ref	Questions to be addressed in examining the trust deed
A	**ESTABLISHMENT AND EXECUTION**
A.1	Is the date of establishment of the SMSF recorded?
A.2	Has the trust deed been: • Properly executed? • Signed by all the members who are individual trustees? • Witnessed? • Dated? • Stamped (if required)?
A.3	Do the rules incorporate the SISA, SISR and applicable taxation rules?
A.4	Does the deed outline the core and ancillary purposes of the SMSF?
A.5	Does the deed require an irrevocable election to be made to be a regulated superannuation fund or a fund subject to the SISA and SISR?
A.6	Does the deed have a clause which deems the appropriate legislation into or out of the deed to allow the SMSF to remain complying?
B	**AMENDMENTS TO THE DEED**
B.1	Does the deed allow amendments?
B.2	Has the trust deed been amended since the last audit? If so: • Has the deed amendment been properly executed? • Is confirmation of the deed's compliance with SISA and SISR required from the solicitor or other party involved in the amendment? • Is the amendment signed off by the current trustees? • Could the amendments impact the audit?
C	**TRUSTEE AND MEMBERSHIP**
C.1	Does the trust deed specify who may be a trustee? Either: • Two or more individual trustees; or • A trustee company.
C.2	Does the deed specifically identify the trustee as either an individual or a corporate entity?
C.3	Are all individual trustees or directors of the trustee company required to be members?
C.4	Does the deed permit members to be • A non-working spouse? • A retired person? • A child?

GS

Ref	Questions to be addressed in examining the trust deed
C.5	Does the deed limit the maximum number of members to 4 members?
C.6	Is membership open to anyone else?
C.7	Do the members of the SMSF meet the definitions? • No member of the SMSF is an employee of another member, unless related. • No trustee receives remuneration for their services to the SMSF.
C.8	Does the trust deed contain the trustee covenants in s. 52 of the SISA?
D	**AUDIT AND FINANCIAL REPORTS**
D.1	Does the trust deed require the appointment of an approved auditor?
D.2	Does the trust deed require the trustees to prepare a financial report annually and for it to be audited?
D.3	Does the trust deed require the trustees to keep the minutes and records of trustee decisions for at least 10 years and accounting records and signed financial reports for at least 5 years?
E	**CONTRIBUTIONS**
E.1	Does the deed allow: • Concessional contributions, including • Employer contributions, including contributions made pursuant to a salary sacrifice agreement? • Member contributions for which a tax deduction is claimed? • Non-concessional contributions, including • Member contributions for which no tax deduction is claimed? • Eligible spouse contributions? • Contributions in respect of minors? • Rollovers and transfers in? • Government co-contributions? • Contribution splitting to a spouse? • Contributions by members who are under 65 and not working? • Contributions by members who are working part-time and are over 65 and under 75? • Mandated contributions to be accepted at any age? • Contribution splitting arrangements pursuant to family law matters?
E.2	Does the deed allow for *in specie* contributions of assets to be made by members or related parties?
E.3	Does the deed permit spouse accounts and may employers make contributions to spouse accounts?
E.4	Does the deed provide a basis for rejecting excess contributions?
E.5	May excess contributions tax levied on the member be paid by the SMSF, irrespective of preservations rules and conditions of release?
F	**BENEFIT PAYMENTS**
F.1	Does the SMSF require compulsory cashing of the members balance at a specific age?
F.2	Does the SMSF require a lump sum benefit to be paid in lieu of a pension?
G	**PENSIONS**
G.1	Does the deed expressly allow for payment of pensions by the SMSF, including*: • Account based pensions? • Transition to retirement income stream? • Allocated pensions? • Term allocated or market linked or growth pensions? • Complying lifetime or fixed term pensions • Non-complying lifetime or fixed term pensions? * This list includes a number of pensions which may no longer be permitted but if already established may continue being paid.
G.2	Does the deed allow for commutation of a pension?
G.3	Does the deed allow for the segregation of assets to meet pension requirements?

Ref	Questions to be addressed in examining the trust deed
G.4	Does the deed make reference to nominated beneficiaries?
H	**RESERVES (If applicable)**
H.1	Does the deed provide rules in relation to the establishment, maintenance and operation of SMSF Reserves?
H.2	Does the deed require different or parallel investment strategies for each reserve account?
I.	**INVESTMENTS**
I.1	Does the deed provide powers to the trustees to invest the assets of the SMSF?
I.2	Does the deed specify specific assets/asset classes that the SMSF may invest in?
I.3	Does the deed prevent investments in, or loans to, related parties?
I.4	Does the deed require an investment strategy to be formulated and given effect?
J	**BORROWINGS**
J.1	Does the deed prohibit borrowings?
J.2	Does the deed permit borrowing in specific circumstances, including: • Temporary borrowings which are required for the payment of member benefits, short term settlement of securities or superannuation contributions surcharges (no longer levied)? • Borrowings for instalment warrant arrangements?
K	**WINDING-UP**
K.1	Does the deed provide for the winding-up of the SMSF?

Appendix 5

Illustrative Financial Audit Procedures for a Self-Managed Superannuation Fund

The following suggested procedures are for illustrative purposes only and should be reviewed and adapted for the specific circumstances and audit risks associated with each SMSF audit engagement. The auditor exercises professional judgement to ensure that the procedures adopted are appropriate to the audit engagement. No allowance has been made for materiality or extent of testing and changes may be necessary when reliance is placed on internal controls. This appendix is not intended to serve as an audit program or checklist in the conduct of a SMSF's financial audit and not all of the procedures suggested will apply to every SMSF's financial audit.

The procedures detailed are designed to address the financial audit of a SMSF, however, in some instances, where compliance matters are integral to the financial audit, these may also be included. For procedures in conducting a compliance engagement, a compliance checklist may be used. Standardised checklists are available from a number of professional organisations and from the ATO, which is contained in *Instructions for auditors of SMSFs Auditing a self-managed super fund – Questions and statements to consider when auditing a self-managed super fund.*[171]

GS

171 The ATO's compliance checklist (NAT 16308-08.2008) is available on the ATO's website at www.ato.gov.au/Superfunds.

Ref	Audit Procedure
A	ENGAGEMENT ACCEPTANCE
A.1	Confirm that the appropriate procedures relating to new and ongoing engagements have been completed prior to commencing the audit, including: • Clearance from previous auditor on new engagements. • Confirmation of independence of the engagement partner and each audit team member.
A.2	Confirm that an engagement letter, that it is relevant to the scope of this audit, has been issued and signed by a trustee.
B	AUDIT PLANNING
B.1	Obtain a copy of the following documents before commencing the audit: • Trust deed and amendments. • Signed financial report, audit opinion and annual return for the prior year. • Minutes of trustee meetings.
B.2	Prepare an audit strategy and audit plan for this engagement addressing, as a minimum, the following matters: • Client profile, audit and reporting arrangements. • Audit approach - Nature: o Controls testing, including use of service organisations' controls reports. o Substantive testing – inspection, observation, enquiry, confirmation, recalculation, reperformance and analytical review. - Timing. - Extent – fully substantive, sampling, analytical review or representations. - Resources, including extent of direction and supervision. Consider interviewing the trustees and/or their advisors, reviewing the draft financial report and the minutes prior to and during the development of the audit plan.
B.3	Complete a risk assessment and determine preliminary materiality levels, covering: • Risk assessment - Current period events. - Fraud risks. - Control environment. - Computer/IT environment. - Compliance environment. • Materiality - Financial audit. - Compliance engagement.
B.4	<u>Regulatory matters</u> • Confirm that the SMSF is a regulated superannuation fund and listed as an ATO regulated fund on the Australian Business Register www.abn.business.gov.au • Enquire of the trustee if there has been any correspondence or requests from the ATO and if so, the current status of such matters.

Ref	Audit Procedure	
C	**FINANCIAL REPORT AND DISCLOSURE**	
C.1	Clerical accuracy and cross references Check that: • The financial report for an accumulation fund (or a defined benefits fund with an actuarial review at period end) includes an operating statement and statement of financial position. The financial report for a defined benefit fund (usually a fund paying a complying pension) includes a statement of changes in net assets and a statement of net assets. • The table of contents or index agrees to the financial report, including the page numbers and content. • The footnotes refer to the notes to the financial statements and do not mention compilation reports or "unaudited" information. • The audit report is situated appropriately in the financial report so as not to suggest that the member's statements or other information have been audited. • Prior period comparatives agree to those from the prior year signed financial report. • Additions in the financial report are correct. • The notes to the financial statements cross-reference correctly to and from the financial report.	
C.2	Opening Balances - new engagements • Review the opening balances for reasonableness. • Check that the bank account balance from the prior year financial report agrees with the bank statement at the beginning of the audit period. • To verify the liabilities for accrued benefits in the prior year, confirm the member's balances have increased by the expected amounts for the current period.	
C.3	Accounting policies • If the SMSF is not a reporting entity, check that the accounting policy notes reflect this, obtain an understanding of the relevant accounting policies the trustee has used to prepare the financial report and check that the accounting policy notes adequately explain the policies adopted. • If the SMSF is a reporting entity, check that the financial report complies with AAS 25 and other Australian Accounting Standards. • Determine if there are any changes in the accounting policies applied in prior periods, and if so, check that these been appropriately disclosed in the accounting policy notes.	
D	**UNDERLYING ACCOUNTING RECORDS**	
D.1	Obtain a copy of the SMSF's trial balance and general ledger and agree the trial balance to the financial report and note any discrepancies.	
D.2	Review the general ledger and identify material journal entries and other adjustments and review these to ensure that they are reasonable and consistent with the financial report.	
E	**CASH AND CASH EQUIVALENTS**	**ASSERTION MET OR SATISFIED**
E.1	Confirm ownership of the bank accounts from the bank statement to the SMSF for each bank account held.	
E.2	Sight original bank statements and review statements for the year, examining accounts for large or unusual transactions and seek explanation for those transactions.	
E.3	Test large and unusual payments and receipts to ensure these are *bona fide* and correctly recorded and authorised.	
E.4	Trace payments and receipts to bank statements and agree to the source documents.	
E.5	Review bank reconciliation at year end: • Following up and investigating large, unusual or recurring reconciling items. • Follow up uncleared deposits and unpresented cheques ensuring correct cut off. • Trace unpresented cheques to bank statement subsequent to year end.	

GS

Ref	Audit Procedure	
E.6	Where banking activities are significant to the audit and you are unable to gain sufficient appropriate audit evidence (in the case of certain term deposits, passbooks or other accounts where regular statements are not issued): • Confirm the bank balance by way of a bank confirmation letter. • Seek explanations for any material differences. • Check for any debit balances, undisclosed liabilities and security for borrowings.	
E.7	Ensure that cash investments are correctly classified as investments.	
E.8	Agree undeposited cheques or cash to bank statements after period end. Obtain documentary evidence or confirmation from the trustee that the cash was received by the SMSF prior to period end.	
F	**INVESTMENTS**	**ASSERTION MET OR SATISFIED**
F.1	General An auditor should use professional judgement to determine what evidence is appropriate and the size of the sample to be verified for each investment.	
F.2	Foreign Currency Transactions Check to ensure that all investments are recorded in Australian dollars and that if foreign currency transactions occur they are converted at the appropriate currency rates and accounted for correctly.	
F.3	Managed Portfolios and Custodial Investments • If the SMSF uses an investment manager or managers that have the authority to transact on behalf of the SMSF, obtain directly from each manager and/or custodian confirmation of the assets held at period end. • Check that the confirmation refers to the correct trustee and SMSF. • Obtain appropriate auditor's reports on the investment manager and/or custodian's controls over the services provided. Assess any modifications to the auditor's report and the evidence of operating effectiveness of relevant controls contained therein. • Verify the carrying value at period end with an independent source. • Confirm that the method used to value the investments is consistent with that disclosed in the accounting policy notes.	
F.4	Pooled Superannuation Trusts (PSTs) • Sight original statement issued by the PST, or obtain a confirmation directly from the PST at period end. • Confirm that the investment is in the correct name. • Confirm the number of units and carrying value at period end, for investments at market value ensure that the unit price is the redemption price. • Confirm that the method used to value the investments is consistent with that disclosed in the accounting policy notes.	
F.5	Life Insurance Policies • Sight the original life insurance policy and statement from the Life Office at period end. • Obtain direct third party confirmation of the market value of the product or an actuarial valuation at period end. Assess the reasonableness of the valuation based on the assumptions applied. • Confirm policy or product is in the correct name. • Agree transactions on the statement to premiums paid, bonuses or benefits received in the SMSF's records.	

Ref	Audit Procedure	
F.6	<u>Interest Bearing Investments</u> • Obtain bank confirmation letter, reconcile to cash balances and check classification. • Confirm that the investments are in the name of the trustee and that the documentation clearly identifies that the investment is an asset of the SMSF.	
F.7	<u>Fixed and Deferred Interest Securities</u> • Complete the following for each fixed or deferred interest security including debentures and bonds held by the SMSF at the end of the period: - Sight original certificates and confirm correct ownership, date of issue of the certificates and date of maturity of the investment. - Agree the value of securities held at period end with quoted market prices. - For bonds, either confirm the net market value at period end with the originator of the security or with published market prices. - For unlisted non-transferable debentures, agree the net market value with the face value. • Confirm that the investments are in the name of the trustee and that the documentation clearly identifies that the investment is an asset of the Fund. • Confirm that the method used to value the investments is consistent with that disclosed in the accounting policy notes.	
F.8	<u>Property</u> • Complete independent property searches annually for all real estate investments owned by the SMSF. • Check that each property is owned by the trustee and is correctly and appropriately recorded as an investment of the SMSF. This may involve viewing a declaration of trust or similar documentation. • Check that there are no registered encumbrances, or if so, the related liabilities are correctly reflected in the financial report. • Review the accounting policies to determine how the trustee has valued each property. Generally, property investments will be carried at market value determined in line with ATO Superannuation Circular 2003/1. • If the trustees have relied on an independent market appraisal or valuation, obtain a copy of this and confirm that: - The value is correctly reflected in the financial report. - The valuation/appraisal refers to the correct property. - The valuation was based on reasonable assumptions and is current. - The valuation takes into account redemption costs. - The value takes into account GST (if applicable). - If the property has been subsequently sold, that the sale price does not differ significantly from the valuation/appraisal. - That the method used to value the property is consistent with that disclosed in the accounting policy notes. • Where the property includes "buildings and other fixtures" verify existence of adequate insurance and, where these are being depreciated, ensure that the depreciation adjustments are correctly and appropriately reflected in the market value and accounting policies.	

GS

Ref	Audit Procedure	
F.9	Listed Securities Review the number of listed securities including shares, units, instalment receipts, options, warrants and futures held by the SMSF at the end of the period. If the SMSF has units in unit trusts, obtain a listing of these and identify any unit trusts that are listed on the Australian Stock Exchange, those that are widely held trusts and those that are closely held trusts. • Agree the number of securities held at period end to the CHESS statement issued at period year, the share or unit registry or other appropriate sources. • Check that each listed security is owned by the trustee and is correctly and appropriately recorded as an investment of the SMSF. • Confirm the closing market price of the securities at the period end against an independent source. • Confirm that the method used to value the investments is consistent with that disclosed in the accounting policy notes. • If the SMSF invested or redeemed listed securities during the period, trace transactions to and/or from the SMSF to confirm that they have been dealt with in an appropriate and timely manner.	
F.10	Unlisted Unit Trusts	
F.10.1	Widely Held Trusts These are usually arm's length and professionally managed trusts that provide regular reports on unit holdings, distributions and unit prices. • Sight the original unit certificates, a confirmation from the unit trust or similar documentation and agree: - The number of securities held at period end. - That each investment is owned by the trustee and is correctly and appropriately recorded as an investment of the SMSF. - The closing price of the units at the period end. - The method used to value the investments is consistent with that disclosed in the accounting policy notes. - Check if the units are valued cum or ex-distribution and that this is correctly and consistently calculated and reported. • If the SMSF invested or redeemed units during the period, trace transactions to and/or from the SMSF to confirm that they have been dealt with in an appropriate and timely manner. • If acquired during the year, ensure not acquired from related parties to avoid breach of section 66.	

Ref	Audit Procedure	
F.10.2	Closely Held Trusts These are usually related trusts that require additional audit procedures to confirm ownership and value. • Sight the original unit certificates, a confirmation from the unit trust or similar documentation and agree the following: - The number of units held at period end. - That each investment is owned by the trustee and is correctly and appropriately recorded as an investment of the SMSF. • Identify the valuation method used and test the value by: - Assessing whether the method and valuation process were reasonable and the valuation is current. - Obtaining documentary evidence to support the valuation. - Verifying that the method used to value the investments is consistent with that disclosed in the accounting policy notes. • Review the assets and liabilities of the unit trust and test for existence and valuation and allocation: - in the case of listed shares, by obtaining a current share certificate and a third party valuation). - in the case of a property, by obtaining a current title search and a third party valuation. • If the SMSF invested or redeemed units during the period, trace transactions to and/or from the SMSF to confirm that they have been dealt with in an appropriate and timely manner.	
F.11	Assets subject to Limited Recourse Debt/Instalment Warrant Arrangements • If the asset is subject to an instalment warrant arrangement, determine how the investment has been valued, either net asset value or gross assets and liabilities, and confirm that this is consistent with that disclosed in the accounting policy notes. • Audit procedures should be undertaken (as outlined above) based on the type of arrangement.	
F.12	Other Investments (collectables etc.) • Verify adequate and valid insurance in place in name of the SMSF. • If the asset is a type that does not have any form of title obtain evidence to confirm existence and ownership including: - Minutes or resolution relating to the acquisition of the asset, and its use/storage in the relevant financial year. - Invoice and evidence of payment from the SMSF for the purchase of the asset. - Sighting asset. - Insurance policy or premium payment for insurance of the asset. - Lease documents, if leased to another party. • If the trustee has relied on an independent valuation, obtain a copy of this and confirm that: - The valuation or appraisal refers to the correct SMSF. - The valuation refers to the correct period. - If the asset has been subsequently sold, that the sale price does not differ significantly from the valuation or appraisal. - If sold to a related party, that it was sold at market value. - That the method used to value the property is reasonable and consistent with that disclosed in the accounting policy notes. - The assumptions on which the valuation is based are reasonable and the valuation is current.	

GS

Ref	Audit Procedure	
	• If the trustee has not obtained an independent valuation, obtain documentary evidence (trustee declaration) of the valuation method used, including that: - All relevant factors and considerations likely to affect the value of the asset have been taken into account. - The valuation was undertaken in good faith. - The valuation was based on a rational process and reasonable assumptions and the valuation is current. - The basis of the valuation is capable of explanation to a third party. - If the property has been subsequently sold, the sale price does not differ significantly from the valuation. - The method used to value the property is consistent with that disclosed in the accounting policy notes.	
G	**RECEIVABLES**	
G.1	If the SMSF uses accrual accounting, review each investment class and determine if the SMSF was entitled to receive income for the year and if this had been received or accrued at balance date.	
G.2	Obtain details of other receivables and ensure that they are correctly accounted for.	
G.3	Verify that the receivable is current and has been received by the SMSF subsequent to period end or that it will be received by the SMSF.	
G.4	If the amount is receivable from a related party, check that the disclosures are appropriate.	
H	**LIABILITIES**	
H.1	Review the value at which liabilities have been disclosed in the financial report and vouch to supporting documentation. Review the documentation and assess whether the amount and nature of the liabilities appears reasonable.	
H.2	Vouch payment of liabilities, accruals and benefits payable to payments subsequent to year end.	
H.3	Review ageing of liabilities/payables and comment on any delay in payment.	
H.4	Vouch prior year payables and accruals to payments during the year, or re-accrue or adjust against expense items.	
H.5	Test for unrecorded liabilities by reviewing client documentation and subsequent payments.	
H.6	Review prior year accounts to identify expenses that have been paid for in previous years but not paid/accrued for this year.	
I	**ACCRUED AND VESTED BENEFITS**	
	Note, that in most cases the vested benefits in a SMSF will equal the accrued benefits. However, these will differ if the SMSF is a defined benefit fund, in which case the actuary will need to value the liabilities in order to determine the accrued and vested benefits. If an accumulation fund is holding reserves, the accrued benefits will also differ from the vested benefits by the value of that those reserves.	

Ref	Audit Procedure	
I.1	<u>Accumulation Funds</u> • Determine if the net assets of the SMSF have been allocated between the members, if so, the vested benefits will generally agree to the accrued benefits. • Obtain listing of all members account balances and check that the total agrees with accrued benefits in the financial report. • Review the allocation of revenue, expenses, income tax, superannuation contribution surcharge and other items to members to ensure that they have been correctly apportioned. • Ensure that the disclosures in the financial report are appropriate and consistent with the member's entitlements. • Check that vested benefits do not exceed net assets.	
I.2	<u>Defined Benefit Funds</u> • Obtain and review a copy of the most recent actuarial valuation for consistency with your understanding of the SMSF, member details and pension terms. • Ensure that the actuarial valuation is within the past three years and if for a year other than the current financial year, this has been disclosed correctly and the appropriate financial report prepared. • Check the values in the valuation with accrued and vested benefits in the financial report. • Check that accrued benefits do not exceed net assets.	
J	**RESERVES**	
J.1	Review the SMSF's documentation including the trust deed and trustee minutes to ensure that the reserve is permitted and recorded in accordance with trustee policy.	
J.2	Review the movements in the reserve during the period to ensure that they are clerically accurate and in accordance with the trustee's policy.	
J.3	Ensure that the disclosures in the financial report are appropriate and consistent with the members' entitlements.	
K	**INVESTMENT AND OTHER REVENUE**	
K.1	<u>Analytical Review</u> • Calculate the SMSF's investment return as a percentage based on the net income as a proportion of average assets held by the SMSF over the period. • Compare this to the prior year as well as average market performance (for example, superratings) for the period of the audit and confirm that the return is reasonable and not under or overstated.	
K.2	<u>Interest Income</u> • Obtain a listing of interest income (if material) and ensure that this is consistent with the investments and what should have been received. • For bank interest, analytical review against ROI on the bank audit confirmations.	
K.3	<u>Changes in Net Market Value</u> • Test the changes in net market value calculations including realised changes in net market value to ensure that they are correct. • Analytical review. • Tying into investments , for substantive audits.	

Ref	Audit Procedure	
K.4	Dividends • Vouch dividends received to dividend slips, published dividend rates or registry details. • Confirm the accounting treatment of franking credits (either on a net or gross basis) and ascertain accounting treatment is consistent with the details disclosed in the accounting policy notes.	
K.5	Trust Distributions • Vouch distributions received to distribution advice, ensuring that the discounted capital gains and other income have been correctly classified.	
K.6	Rental Income • Vouch rental income against agent's statements or other records and cash receipts, as appropriate. • If the SMSF is complying with accounting standards, rental expenses should be deducted from rental income to provide net investment revenue. • Analytical review against rental agreement.	
K.7	Other Income • If the SMSF receives other forms of income ensure that these are correctly calculated and disclosed. • Ensure income is classified correctly between investment and other income.	
L	CONTRIBUTIONS AND TRANSFERS IN	
L.1	Concessional contributions • Obtain confirmation of employer contributions (or, for related employers, obtain the employer's trial balance and general ledger to verify contributions). • Test that contributions have been allocated to the member for whom they were remitted. • For concessional contributions made by the member, obtain a copy of the section 290-170 Notice of Intention to Deduct and confirm the details are consistent with the accounting treatment. • For members > 65, ensure that the work test has been met. • Ensure no-TFN contributions were received. • If transfers in, ensure transfer in fund is a complying superannuation fund. • Ensure SG contributions are not over 9%.	
L.2	Non-concessional contributions • Obtain confirmation from the members as to the personal non-concessional contributions made by them and test that they have been allocated to the member for whom they were received.	
L.3	• Where co-contributions have been received test that they have been allocated to the member for whom they were remitted.	
L.4	• Vouch transfers in to supporting documentation ensuring that the transfers in are from a complying source and correctly recorded as taxed or untaxed. • For members > 75, ensure that the work test has been met and that contributions are employer mandated contributions. • Ensure that all contributions not complying with Regulation 7.04 are refunded within 30 days.	
L.5	Verify and trace contributions to the bank statements with additional testing at year end for correct cut-off.	

Ref	Audit Procedure	
M	**EXPENSES**	
M.1	Perform an analytical review of expenses and assess for reasonableness against your knowledge of the SMSF and in comparison to the prior year's expenditure.	
M.2	Vouch material items to invoices, ensuring the expenses are attributable to the SMSF or are apportioned correctly.	
M.3	Agree administration fees to the agreement with the administrator.	
M.4	Agree management fees to the agreement with the investment manager.	
N	**BENEFITS PAID**	
N.1	Lump Sums • Obtain a listing of all benefits paid and reconcile benefits paid between general ledger and bank statement. • For each benefit paid, review documentation including correspondence to the members and rollover institutions and ensure that the benefit was duly authorised. • Confirm that each benefit was paid in accordance with the terms of the trust deed. • Where resignation or other benefits are based on an accumulation of contributions and earnings, test reasonableness of the benefit based on the number of years of membership, contribution amounts for the member, any earnings-related contributions by the associated employer, concessional and non-concessional contributions and your knowledge of the SMSF's earning rates and reasonableness of interim earning rate calculations. Agree member information to trust minutes and records. • For retirement or other defined benefits check calculation is in accordance with the trust deed and agree member's age, final average or highest average salary and years of service to payroll, personnel records or trust records. • Ensure payment is made to authorised beneficiaries. • Obtain minutes supporting the final payment decision. • For death benefits, sight death certificate and confirm if the benefit was paid in accordance with the trust deed and, if applicable, a binding death benefit nomination. • For a total and permanent disability benefit, sight the medical certification regarding the inability of the member to work again. • For a total and temporary permanent disability benefit, sight the medical certification regarding the temporary inability of the member to work. • For each benefit paid ensure that the PAYG obligations have been correctly calculated and remitted by the SMSF.	
N.2	Pension Payments • Sight documentation (member request and trustee minutes confirming member's request for pension) and trustee acknowledgement and agreement to pay pension. • Ensure that pensions paid are within the minimum and maximum thresholds and that pensions are paid at least once annually. • Investigate liabilities at year end to ensure that pensions have been paid, and not just accrued. • Review the terms of the pensions to ensure that the pensions have been calculated and paid in accordance with these terms. • Trace pension payments to bank statements.	

GS

Ref	Audit Procedure	
O	TAX	Assertion
O.1	Review tax work papers to ensure that the income tax is correctly calculated and disclosed in accordance with the accounting policies, including: • Member contributions have been treated correctly as non-assessable unless the SMSF received a notice in accordance with section 290-170 of the ITAA 1997 stating that the member contribution is assessable. • Capital gains from the disposal of PSTs and insurance policies have been excluded from taxable income. • Fee rebates and other income from PSTs have been excluded from taxable income. • Income from assets used to pay current pensions is identified as not assessable and an actuarial certificate has been obtained to apportion the income, if required. • The non-assessable pension income proportion has been correctly applied to income but not contributions. • Cash bonuses (not rebates) received on life insurance policies are not included as taxable income. • If the SMSF derives exempt income, check that expenses have been apportioned between deductible and non-deductible expenses in accordance with section 8-1 of the ITAA 1997. • If the SMSF pays a complying pension and assets are segregated, ensure that income is allocated correctly between assessable and non-assessable components. • Franking credits from dividends are correctly adjusted. • Trust distributions have been correctly apportioned to different classes of income and adjusted accordingly. • Foreign tax credits are correctly adjusted, note that foreign tax credits may only be claimed to the extent of tax payable on foreign income. • CGT calculations are correct, including, discounted gains, indexed gains and capital losses. Note that capital losses must be applied before any discount. • Ensure CGT cost base adjustments required by section 104-70 of the ITAA 1997 (relating to differences between accounting and tax distributions from trusts) have been recorded and adjusted correctly. • Non arm's length income has been correctly identified and tax applied at the appropriate rate.	
O.2	If the SMSF applies AASB 112, check the deferred tax assets and liabilities are correctly calculated and reflected in the financial report, including: • Deferred tax assets arising from unrealised losses are after discounting. • Deferred tax assets arising from tax losses have only been brought to account where the trustee is confident that these will be recoverable in the future. • Proving the deferred tax assets and liabilities represent the tax effect of timing differences.	
O.3	If the SMSF is accounting for income tax in accordance with AASB 112, ensure that this is appropriate for the SMSF, especially if the SMSF is paying pensions.	
O.4	If the SMSF does not adopt AASB 112 check that this departure from Accounting Standards is disclosed in the accounting policies notes.	
O.5	Confirm that tax has been calculated for ordinary income at 15%, unless the SMSF has received a notice advising it is non-complying for taxation purposes.	

Ref	Audit Procedure
O.6	Confirm that PAYG instalments and TFN credits paid by the SMSF during the period have been correctly identified and applied against the current tax liability.
P	**GOING CONCERN**
P.1	Review all circumstances, investments, transactions and other matters from the audit to assess if the SMSF is a going concern.
P.2	<u>Accumulation Funds</u> • Determine if the vested benefits exceed the net assets of the SMSF. • If vested benefits exceed net assets, review any measures by the employer-sponsor or trustee to remediate the deficiency and consider whether a modification to the auditor's report is necessary.
P.3	<u>Defined Benefit Funds</u> • If the actuarial review discloses that the accrued benefits exceed the net assets of the SMSF: - Review the actuarial funding recommendations for reasonableness. - Ensure that the employer-sponsor and the trustees are taking remedial action. • If the actuarial review discloses that the vested benefits exceed the net assets of the SMSF: - Assess the adequacy of any immediate measures taken by the employer-sponsor or the trustees to cover the deficiency. - Consider a modification to the auditor's report.
Q	**SUBSEQUENT EVENTS**
Q.1	Identify any subsequent events which would affect the financial report of the current or future periods.
Q.2	Test receipts and payments after balance date to ensure correct cut off of contributions, benefits, income and expenses.
Q.3	Check for significant fluctuations in investment valuations after period end.
R	**OTHER AUDIT CONSIDERATIONS**
R.1	If there have been any transactions with related parties, ensure that these matters have been appropriately addressed and reported in accordance with the accounting policies adopted by the SMSF.
R.2	Check whether material commitments and contingencies are properly disclosed by reviewing or obtaining: • Trustee minutes. • Solicitors' representations. • Trustees' representations. • Contracts with investment managers.
S	**TRUSTEE REPRESENTATIONS**
S.1	Obtain written representations from the trustee.
S.2	Evaluate that the representations appear reasonable and consistent with the other audit evidence and conclusions.
S.3	If necessary, seek corroborative evidence on trustee representations.
T	**COMMUNICATIONS WITH TRUSTEES**
	Check that all matters of governance interest, if any, arising from the audit are communicated to the trustees on a timely basis, including: • Uncorrected misstatements aggregated by the auditor during the audit that were determined by the trustees to be immaterial, both individually and in the aggregate, to the financial report taken as a whole.

GS

Appendix 6

Illustrative Examples of Threats to Independence in a Self-Managed Superannuation Fund

The following table provides examples of some of the scenarios which practitioners may face when auditing SMSFs, the type of threats to independence the scenarios present and appropriate safeguards which may address those threats.[172]

	Type of threat					
Scenario	**Self interest**	**Self-review**	**Advocacy**	**Familiarity**	**Intimidation**	**Appropriate safeguards**
1. An auditor is a trustee or director of a corporate trustee and/or a member of the fund	X	X		X		No safeguards are available which would enable the practitioner to perform audit work, as this involves clear self-interest threats. An auditor who undertakes such an engagement is in clear breach of their professional and ethical obligations.
2. A sole practitioner prepares a SMSF's accounts and performs the financial audit and compliance engagement.	X	X				No safeguards are available which would enable the practitioner to perform both the accounting and audit work, as this involves the auditor reviewing their own work. The auditor withdraws from either the accounting or audit engagement. The resultant loss of work by withdrawing may be overcome by entering a reciprocal arrangement with an independent practitioner or firm for referral of SMSF audit engagements.
3. A sole practitioner signs the auditor's report for a SMSF and uses staff to perform the financial audit and compliance engagement work and to prepare the SMSF's accounts.	X	X			X	No safeguards are available which would enable the practitioner to sign the auditor's report as well as supervising the accounting work, as the practitioner is ultimately responsible for the accounting work and this amounts to reviewing their own work. The auditor withdraws from either the accounting or audit engagement.
4. A sole practitioner provides financial advice and audits the SMSF.	X	X	X			No safeguards are available which would enable the practitioner to perform both the financial advisory and audit work, as this involves the auditor in assessing the compliance implications of their own advice. The auditor withdraws from either the financial advisory or the audit engagement. The resultant loss of work by withdrawing may be overcome by entering a reciprocal arrangement with an independent practitioner or firm for referral of SMSF audit engagements.

172 These examples are based on principles stated in APES 110 *Code of Ethics for Professional Accountants*.

Scenario	Type of threat: Self interest	Self-review	Advocacy	Familiarity	Intimidation	Appropriate safeguards
5. A two partner practice in which one partner prepares the SMSF's accounts and the other partner conducts the audit. Common staff work on both engagements.	X	X			X	Threats may be overcome by safeguards including removal of staff who prepare the accounts from the audit team, implementing policies and procedures prohibiting those in the firm who provide accounting services from making decisions on behalf of the SMSF, requiring source data and underlying assumptions to be generated by the SMSF, obtaining SMSF approval for any journal entries, obtaining the SMSF's acknowledgement of their responsibility for the accounting work performed by the firm and disclosing to the trustees the firm's involvement in both engagements.
6. A two partner practice where one partner provides financial advice to the SMSF and the other partner audits the SMSF and prepares the SMSF's accounts.	X	X	X			Threats may be overcome by applying safeguards which include each of the two partners performing one of the engagements, with appropriate segregation of the engagement teams, and the firm withdrawing from the third engagement. For example, if one partner conducts the financial advisory work, the second partner prepares the accounts and then the firm withdraws from the audit and segregates the staff working on the engagements which are retained. Additional safeguards may include: implementing policies and procedures to prohibit individuals providing advice from making managerial decisions on behalf of the SMSF and ensuring that the individual providing the advice does not commit the SMSF to the terms of any transaction or consummate a transaction on behalf of the SMSF.
7. A firm prepares the SMSF's annual return and also undertakes the audit of the SMSF.						Provision of taxation services to audit clients will not generally create threats to independence.
8. A sole practitioner audits numerous SMSFs but they are all administered by the same service provider who engages the auditor on behalf of the trustees. The sole practitioner is very reliant on fees generated by referrals from the service provider.	X				X	Safeguards include expanding the client base so that reliance on the administrator is reduced, declining to accept any further audits from the administrator, obtaining external quality reviews and ensuring that the practitioner has direct access to the trustees of each SMSF, so that matters arising during the audit may be communicated without fear of intimidation.
9. A member of the audit engagement team has a close or immediate relationship with the trustees of the SMSF. The auditor signing the audit opinion supervises the team member's work.				X		Safeguards include removing the audit member from the audit engagement team.

GS

Scenario	Type of threat					Appropriate safeguards
	Self interest	Self-review	Advocacy	Familiarity	Intimidation	
10. The auditor has provided accounting advice in relation to a material transaction of the SMSF which was then entered into on the basis of that advice.		X				Technical assistance on accounting principles and advice an accounting issues often form part of the normal audit process and may promote fair presentation of the financial report and may not create a threat to independence. However, in certain instances, the advice may have influenced the decision making of the SMSF and safeguards may include segregation of the partners and staff providing accounting advice from the audit team or withdrawal from the audit engagement.
11. A partner in a multi-partner practice has had the SMSF as an audit client for "years" and regularly socialises with the SMSF's trustee.				X		The long and personal association with the trustee may compromise the partner's objectivity. Safeguards include transferring the engagement to another partner within the firm or quality control review of the audit findings, including conclusions on significant matters arising in the audit by another partner prior to sign-off of the audit opinion.
12. A practitioner or firm providing administrative services to numerous SMSFs, outsources all of the SMSF audits to one approved auditor.						The practitioner has implemented appropriate safeguards to avoid a self-review threat by referring the audit work to another auditor and it is the responsibility of that auditor to ensure that they are not as reliant on the referrals from the practitioner as to create a self-interest or intimidation threat.

GS 010

Responding to Questions at an Annual General Meeting

(Issued March 2009)

Issued by the Auditing and Assurance Standards Board.

Note from the Institute of Chartered Accountants Australia

This note, prepared by the technical editor, is not part of GS 010.

Historical development

March 2009: GS 010 issued. This GS provides guidance to auditors on responding to both written questions submitted prior to an Annual General Meeting and questions raised at the Annual General Meeting of a listed company. It replaces AGS 1046 'Responding to Questions at an AGM', which was first issued in June 1999 and, following changes to the Corporations Act, was revised and reissued in Oct 2005.

Contents

Authority Statement

The Auditing and Assurance Standards Board (AUASB) formulates Guidance Statement GS 010 *Responding to Questions at an Annual General Meeting* as set out in paragraphs 1 to 44, pursuant to section 227B of the *Australian Securities and Investments Commission Act 2001*, for the purposes of providing guidance on procedural auditing and assurance matters.

This Guidance Statement provides guidance to assist the auditor to fulfil the objectives of the audit or assurance engagement. It includes explanatory details and suggested procedures on specific matters for the purposes of understanding and complying with AUASB Standards. The auditor exercises professional judgement when using this Guidance Statement.

The Guidance Statement does not prescribe or create new mandatory requirements.

Dated: 12 March 2009

M H Kelsall
Chairman - AUASB

Guidance Statement GS 010

Responding to Questions at an Annual General Meeting

Application

1 This Guidance Statement has been formulated by the Auditing and Assurance Standards Board (AUASB) to provide guidance to auditors on responding to questions at an Annual General Meeting (AGM) of a listed public company.

Issuance Date

2 This Guidance Statement is issued in March 2009 by the AUASB and replaces AGS 1046 *Responding to Questions at an Annual General Meeting* issued in October 2005.

Introduction

3 The *Corporations Act 2001* (the Act) includes provisions for members to obtain information from the auditor relevant to their investment by submitting written questions before the AGM or by raising questions at the AGM.

Definition

4 "Those charged with governance" include those persons accountable for ensuring that the entity achieves its objectives with regard to reliability of financial reporting, effectiveness and efficiency of operations, compliance with applicable laws, and reporting to interested parties. Those charged with governance include management only when it performs such functions. In the context of this Guidance Statement, those charged with governance include those persons accountable for the preparation for, and conduct of, an AGM. For some entities, in addition to the directors, this may include management, for example, the company secretary.

Written Questions to the Auditor before the AGM

5 Section 250PA of the Act states:

"(1) A member of a listed company who is entitled to cast a vote at the AGM may submit a written question to the auditor under this section if the question is relevant to:

(a) the content of the auditor's report to be considered at the AGM; or

(b) the conduct of the audit of the annual financial report to be considered at the AGM.

The member submits the question to the auditor under this subsection by giving the question to the listed company no later than the fifth business day before the day on which the AGM is held."

6 In accordance with section 250PA(3) of the Act, the listed company must pass the question on to the auditor as soon as practicable after the question is received by the company, even if the company believes the question is not relevant to the matters specified in section 250PA(1)(a) and (b).

7 In accordance with sections 250PA(4) and (5) of the Act, the auditor must prepare, and give to the listed company, a list of the questions that the listed company has passed on to the auditor which the auditor considers to be relevant to the matters specified in section 250PA(1)(a) and (b). This must be done as soon as practicable after the end of the time for submitting questions under section 250PA(1) and a reasonable time before the AGM.

8 The listed company must, at or before the start of the AGM, make copies of the question list reasonably available to the members attending the AGM.

9 In accordance with section 250T(1)(b) of the Act, if the auditor or their representative is at the AGM[1], the chair must allow a reasonable opportunity for the auditor or their representative to answer written questions submitted to the auditor under section 250PA.

10 In accordance with sections 250T(3) and (4) of the Act, the auditor may be permitted to table a written answer to a written question submitted to the auditor under section 250PA and the listed company must make that written answer reasonably available to members as soon as practicable after the AGM.

Questions to the Auditor at the AGM

11 In addition to submitting written questions to the auditor prior to the AGM[2], members are able to direct questions to the auditor at the AGM. Section 250T of the Act states:

"(1) If the company's auditor or their representative is at the meeting[3], the chair of an AGM must:

(a) allow a reasonable opportunity for the members as a whole at the meeting to ask the auditor or the auditor's representative questions relevant to:

(i) the conduct of the audit; and

---

1 See section 250RA of the Act relating to the requirement for a listed company's auditor to attend the company's AGM at which the audit report is considered.

2 See paragraphs 5-10 of this guidance statement.

3 See section 250RA of the Act relating to the requirement for a listed company's auditor to attend the company's AGM at which the audit report is considered.

GS

(ii) the preparation and content of the auditor's report; and

(iii) the accounting policies adopted by the company in relation to the preparation of the financial statements; and

(iv) the independence of the auditor in relation to the conduct of the audit; and

(b) allow a reasonable opportunity for the auditor or their representative to answer written questions submitted to the auditor under section 250PA."

Auditor's Responsibilities in Responding to Questions

12 In contrast to the responsibilities of those charged with governance for all aspects of the business, the auditor has specific responsibilities which are established by the Act[4], but which may be extended when agreed with the entity as part of the terms of the engagement. Members may not be generally familiar with the scope of an audit. Therefore, without due consideration of the role of the auditor, there is the risk that questions from members may be directed to the auditor on matters that should be addressed by those charged with governance.

13 The auditor does not respond to questions dealing with issues beyond the scope of the audit mandate and/or questions relating to matters that are the responsibility of those charged with governance. Therefore it is important that the auditor, together with the chair of the AGM and others charged with governance, adequately prepare for participation at an AGM. If auditors are asked to respond to inappropriate questions or if responses are not understood in an appropriate context, there is the risk that any information provided could be misleading.

AGM Planning

14 Adequate planning and preparation for the AGM enable authoritative responses to be provided to questions raised. The auditor prepares for questions that may be received whether in writing before the AGM or verbally at the AGM.

15 The chair should be familiar with the responsibility and authority of both those charged with governance and the auditor, and with matters arising from the financial report, to ensure that inappropriate questions do not delay proceedings. A question is inappropriate if the person to whom it has been directed is not able to respond with an appropriate level of authority.

16 Auditors assist the AGM planning process by meeting with the chair and directors in an AGM planning meeting, and/or by having discussions with directors, management, and/or audit committee members, to ascertain whether there are particular issues which are likely to be of interest.

17 The auditor ascertains the protocol for questions at the AGM from the chair of the AGM prior to the meeting. Usually, the chair will communicate to the meeting the protocol for presenting questions and, as a rule, questions are to be addressed to the chair who can direct them to the appropriate respondent.

18 Questions directed to the auditor may not be within the scope of the audit or the auditor's responsibilities. The auditor refers such questions to the chair of the AGM. If the question is about an area where the responsibility is divided between the auditor and those charged with governance, the auditor endeavours to respond and invites the chair to consider the question as well. For example, a question on accounting policies might be put to the auditor. The auditor can state that the policy complies with Australian Accounting Standards. The chair and/or others charged with governance may explain the choice of that policy within the allowable choices available under Australian Accounting Standards. Where the auditor plans to ask those charged with governance to respond to a written question directed to the auditor, the auditor informs the chair of the intention. This enables those charged with governance to provide an appropriate response at the AGM.

4 See Part 2M.3 Division 3 of the Act.

19 Written questions are to be encouraged to ensure that an informed, authoritative response can be provided by the relevant party. If written questions are received before the AGM, the company will pass these questions to the auditor. The auditor ensures that responses to such questions are prepared prior to the meeting. Where written questions have been received, the auditor considers whether a written response to the meeting is appropriate.

20 Prior notification of issues enables the auditor to seek professional consultation and/or legal advice if appropriate. However, some members may prefer to reserve questions for the meeting. Adequate planning is imperative to identify areas of potential interest to ensure that questions directed to the auditor at the AGM can be properly addressed.

Context

21 In response to any question at the AGM, the auditor first conveys to the meeting the context within which the auditor's response is provided by explaining key aspects of an audit which include:

(a) The auditor conducts an audit in accordance with Australian Auditing Standards, as required by the Act.

(b) The auditor is not responsible for the preparation and fair presentation of the financial report. This is the responsibility of those charged with governance.

(c) The auditor provides reasonable, not absolute, assurance that the financial report taken as a whole is free from material misstatement.

(d) The objective of an audit of a financial report is to enable the auditor to express an opinion as to whether the financial report is prepared, in all material respects, in accordance with the applicable financial reporting framework, such as the Act and Australian Accounting Standards.

(e) The audit involves performing procedures to obtain audit evidence about amounts and disclosures in the financial report.

(f) The auditor determines the procedures required to conduct an audit in accordance with Australian Auditing Standards, having regard to the requirements of these Standards, as well as the Act, other legislation and, when appropriate, the terms of the audit engagement.

(g) The auditor exercises professional judgement in selecting audit procedures to be performed. Audit procedures include the assessment of the risks of material misstatement of the financial report whether due to fraud or error. In making such risk assessments, the auditor considers internal controls relevant to the entity's preparation and fair presentation of the financial report in order to design audit procedures that are appropriate in the circumstances, but not for the purpose of expressing an opinion on the effectiveness of the entity's internal control.

(h) The audit involves a systematic examination for which audit-based skills, which include skills such as analysis of financial information, knowledge of internal control structures, risk assessment, sample selection, knowledge of accounting standards and other aspects of reporting, are required.

(i) The auditor's report does not provide assurance in relation to individual elements of the financial report, or other aspects of operations such as the adequacy of the entity's systems of internal control or the selection of accounting policies.

Responses to Questions

22 The auditor responds to questions relevant to the conduct of the audit, the preparation and content of the auditor's report, the accounting policies adopted by the company in relation to the preparation of the financial report and the independence of the auditor. The auditor is not able to provide an authoritative response to questions dealing with issues that go beyond the scope of the audit mandate and/or questions which should have been addressed to those charged with governance, and therefore such questions are declined by the auditor. Paragraphs 23–38 below discuss a number of factors which the auditor takes into account when considering questions.

Auditor Independence

23 The auditor responds to question about auditor independence with reference to the Act[5], Australian Auditing Standards and relevant ethical requirements[6]. Where an individual auditor or an audit firm or audit company has prepared a written auditor independence declaration in accordance with section 307C of the Act, the auditor may choose to refer to the declaration in responding to questions at the AGM.

Audit Approach and Audit Plan

24 Auditing Standard ASA 200 *Objective and General Principles Governing an Audit of a Financial Report* requires the auditor to plan and perform an audit by exercising professional judgement and with an attitude of professional scepticism recognising that circumstances may exist that cause the financial report to be materially misstated.

25 In accordance with ASA 300 *Planning an Audit of a Financial Report*, the auditor exercises professional judgement to assess audit risk and to design audit procedures to ensure audit risk is reduced to an acceptable level. The auditor's assessment of risk requires as prerequisites both a "knowledge of the business" (economy, industry, entity operations, management, legislation and regulation) and an assessment of materiality. When members raise questions relating to the audit approach or audit plan it is possible that they will not have an understanding of these prerequisites, nor of their significance to the audit process. Similarly members' perceptions of risk may vary considerably. Therefore the auditor informs the meeting about the auditor's approach to risk with reference to ASA 315 *Understanding the Entity and Its Environment and Assessing the Risks of Material Misstatement* and ASA 330 *The Auditor's Procedures in Response to Assessed Risks*.

26 It is possible that members may not be familiar with the relevant statutory requirements governing an audit of a financial report. Responses to questions at an AGM provide an opportunity to inform members of the requirements mandated by Australian Auditing Standards, relevant requirements of the Act and the professional and ethical standards[6] governing auditors. It provides further opportunity to explain that adherence to Australian Auditing Standards and professional ethics promote quality in the audit process and commitment to due care.

Audit Procedures

27 Questions which relate to specific audit procedures and/or in relation to specific parts of the financial report are addressed by reference to the fact that the auditor's report relates to the financial report taken as a whole. In this context, it is not appropriate for the auditor to address individual audit procedures or financial report components. The auditor indicates that the nature of audit procedures result in many types of audit evidence being obtained and drawn upon to provide sufficient appropriate audit evidence with which to form an opinion on a financial report. Discussion of particular procedures in isolation could be misleading.

28 Auditors may find it useful to refer also to ASA 100 *Preamble to AUASB Standards*, which sets out how the AUASB Standards are to be understood, interpreted and applied, to explain that Australian Auditing Standards contain mandatory requirements relating to the planning, conduct and reporting of an audit. Each Auditing Standard describes the procedures to be performed for various aspects of the audit, and is relevant only as an integral component of the whole audit process.

Accounting Policies

29 Members may request the auditor to comment on accounting policies adopted by the entity. Selection of accounting policies is the responsibility of those charged with governance, therefore the auditor responds to the question by stating that the policies comply, or do not comply, with Australian Accounting Standards. Those charged with governance may

5 See Part 2M.4 Division 3 of the Act relating to the requirements for auditor independence.

6 See APES 110 *Code of Ethics for Professional Accountants* issued by the Accounting Professional and Ethical Standards Board.

wish to comment on the appropriateness of the choice of accounting policies within those choices permitted by Australian Accounting Standards.

Internal Control

30 The auditor ensures that responses given in respect of questions on internal control are provided within the context of the financial report audit. An audit of a financial report conducted in accordance with Australian Auditing Standards is not designed to, and therefore does not, provide sufficient appropriate evidence on which to base an opinion on the adequacy of the internal control structure. Evidence on which to base an opinion on internal control would require the application of audit procedures beyond the scope of an audit of a financial report.

31 In particular, the auditor communicates clearly that assurance is not provided on internal control, but rather that control procedures are examined only to the extent that reliance thereon might reduce other audit work. An auditor engaged to report on the financial report has no responsibility under Australian Auditing Standards to understand and evaluate the internal control structure beyond that level sufficient to plan and develop an effective audit approach unless there is a specific statutory, regulatory or additional contractual requirement to the contrary. Questions regarding internal control should be addressed to those charged with governance who are responsible for ensuring that an adequate internal control structure exists. (See also paragraph 21(g) above.)

The Auditor's Report

Report on the Financial Report

32 The auditor responds to questions about the auditor's report by referring to the auditor's report included with the financial report. Where necessary, the auditor explains the meaning of the terms used in the auditor's report.

33 The auditor provides assurance on the financial report taken as a whole. Hence individual items are audited within the framework of materiality appropriate to the financial report as a whole, rather than a materiality level appropriate to a specific individual item. Since audit procedures are not directed towards providing assurance on specific items, the auditor explains why providing such information might be misleading, and ordinarily explains, in general terms, the requirements of Australian Auditing Standards. The auditor may conclude by referring the question to the chair.

34 Members may be interested in errors detected by the auditor and/or disagreements with management. The auditor explains the significance of an unmodified report to indicate that any errors or disagreements have been resolved satisfactorily and that such items are considered in the context of materiality appropriate to the financial report as a whole.

Report on Other Legal and Regulatory Requirements

35 In some cases, the auditor may have additional responsibilities to report on other matters that are supplementary to the auditor's responsibility to express an opinion on the financial report.

36 For example, the auditor may be asked to report certain matters if they come to the auditor's attention during the course of the audit of the financial report. Alternatively, the auditor may be asked to perform and report on additional specified procedures, or to express an opinion on specific matters. When the audit is conducted pursuant to the Act, section 308(3)(b) also requires the auditor to report on any deficiency, failure or shortcoming in respect of certain matters relating to the completeness of information, explanation and assistance given to the auditor and the maintenance of financial and other records by the entity[7]. These items are referred to in the auditor's report if there is cause for concern; alternatively, silence in the auditor's report indicates satisfaction.

7 See sections 307(b), (c) and (d) of the Act.

37 When the auditor addresses other reporting responsibilities within the auditor's report on the financial report, these other reporting responsibilities are included in a separate section of the auditor's report that follows the opinion on the financial report.

38 The auditor responds to questions relating to these other matters by reference to the auditor's report.

Modification to the Independent Auditor's Report

39 If the auditor has issued a modified auditor's report, the auditor may expect to be asked questions about issues leading to that modification. The auditor addresses any such questions by reference to the auditor's report. Auditors are reminded that ASA 701 *Modifications to the Auditor's Report* requires that the auditor's report includes all relevant information to explain matters that result in a modified auditor's report

40 In certain circumstances the auditor may seek legal advice or professional consultation in preparing responses to issues raised in respect of a modified auditor's report. If further information regarding such issues is required, it may be more appropriate for the auditor to request that those charged with governance provide the response.

Audit Files

41 While responses given by the auditor will be supported by sufficient appropriate audit evidence, audit files are not taken into the AGM. The level of detail relating to specific issues, as contained in audit files, is not appropriate in responses to questions at AGMs.

Auditor's Representative at the AGM

42 On those occasions when the auditor is not able to attend an AGM and questions for the auditor have been notified, the auditor arranges for a representative to attend the meeting on the auditor's behalf. In this situation, the auditor ensures that the representative has sufficient knowledge of the engagement and is provided with sufficient information to provide an adequate response to the matters raised.

Inability to Provide a Response to a Question

43 A question may arise at the AGM in relation to the audit to which the auditor is not able to provide an immediate response. For example, the auditor may wish to seek legal advice prior to providing the response. In these circumstances, the auditor, in conjunction with the entity's management, makes alternative arrangements, as appropriate, to communicate the information to the members. This may include posting the response on the entity's website.

Conformity with International Pronouncements

44 There is no equivalent International Standard on Auditing or International Auditing Practice Statement to this Guidance Statement.

GS 011

Third Party Access to Audit Working Papers

(Issued April 2009)

Issued by the Auditing and Assurance Standards Board.

Note from the Institute of Chartered Accountants Australia

This note, prepared by the technical editor, is not part of GS 011.

Historical development

April 2009: GS 011 issued. This GS provides guidance to auditors on how to deal with third-party requests for access to audit or review working papers. It replaces AGS 1038 'Access to Audit Working Papers', which was first issued in February 1999 and revised and reissued in February 2006.

GS

Contents

Authority Statement

The Auditing and Assurance Standards Board (AUASB) formulates Guidance Statement GS 011 *Third Party Access to Audit Working Papers* pursuant to section 227B of the *Australian Securities and Investments Commission Act 2001*, for the purposes of providing guidance on auditing and assurance matters.

This Guidance Statement provides guidance to assist the auditor to fulfil the objectives of the audit or assurance engagement. It includes explanatory details and suggested procedures on specific matters for the purposes of understanding and complying with AUASB Auditing Standards. The auditor exercises professional judgement when using this Guidance Statement.

The Guidance Statement does not prescribe or create new mandatory Requirements.

Dated 7 April 2009

M H Kelsall
Chairman - AUASB

Guidance Statement GS 011

Third Party Access to Audit Working Papers

Application

1 This Guidance Statement has been formulated by the Auditing and Assurance Standards Board (AUASB) to provide guidance to auditors regarding third party requests for access to audit or review working papers relating to:

(a) audits or reviews of a financial report in accordance with the *Corporations Act 2001* ("the Act");

(b) audits or reviews of a financial report for any other purpose; and

(c) audits or reviews of other financial information.

2 This Guidance Statement also applies, as appropriate, to external auditor's requests for access to internal auditor's audit working papers.

Issuance Date

3 This Guidance Statement is issued in April 2009 by the AUASB and replaces AGS 1038 *Access to Audit Working Papers* issued in February 2006.

Introduction

4 This Guidance Statement provides guidance to auditors when establishing and agreeing the conditions under which third parties are voluntarily granted access to their audit working papers and related documentation. Such documentation is required to be prepared in accordance with applicable Auditing Standards.[1] The protocols outlined in this Guidance Statement have resulted from consultation with practitioners, on the basis of a willingness by practitioners to co-operate in providing access to their audit working papers to third parties in certain circumstances.

5 The protocols in this Guidance Statement endeavour to promote cooperation when access to an auditor's audit working papers is requested. Audit working papers are the auditor's property, and they may, at their discretion, grant, decline or restrict access (subject to regulatory, legislative or other legal requirements). Each request to access audit working papers is decided on its merits. An auditor might, for example, exercise their discretion to restrict or decline access to their audit working papers when their audit fees are outstanding, or if litigation has commenced or is threatened (unless the auditor becomes compelled to produce audit working papers in connection with that litigation).

6 Regulators may also, pursuant to legislative requirements, request access to audit working papers. When access to audit working papers is required by a regulator, the auditor provides access in accordance with the requirements of the relevant legislation.

Definitions

7 For the purposes of this Guidance Statement, the following terms have the meanings attributed below:

(a) "Auditor" means an individual auditor, audit firm or audit company.[2] Unless specified, auditor refers to an external auditor conducting an audit or review of an entity's financial report or other financial information.

(b) "Audit (or review) working papers" (herein referred to as audit working papers in this Guidance Statement) contained within an audit file may include:

(i) documents or any other records of information, produced or acquired by an auditor (whether from the client or third parties) during an engagement that

GS

1 Auditing Standard ASA 230 *Audit Documentation* (paragraph 11) requires an auditor to prepare audit documentation that will enable an experienced auditor, having no previous connection with the audit, to understand: (a) the nature, timing and extent of the audit procedures performed, (b) results of the audit and evidence obtained and (c) significant matters arising during the audit and the conclusions reached thereon.

2 This is consistent with Section 324AA of the *Corporations Act 2001*.

are used, or developed, to undertake the engagement and fulfil the auditor's responsibilities under that engagement.

(ii) copies of documents, records or schedules produced by the client and utilised by the auditor to undertake an engagement;

(iii) internal documents and records created or developed by the auditor to perform or support any audit or audit-based procedures undertaken or conclusion derived from these documents, such as memorandums, external correspondence with the client or third parties, and final reports;

(iv) audit work programs (other than those considered proprietary by the audit firm); and

(v) for an internal audit engagement—the internal audit working papers.

(c) An "audit file" is a file that contains the audit working papers as defined in (b) above, and those other documents that are excluded for the purposes of allowing third party access, as enumerated in paragraph 8 below.

(d) "Internal audit function" means an appraisal activity, established within, or provided as a service to the entity. Its functions include, amongst other things, examining, evaluating and monitoring the adequacy and effectiveness of internal control.

(e) "Internal auditors" means those individuals who perform the activities of the internal audit function. Internal auditors may belong to an internal audit department of an entity or equivalent function or an internal audit provider.

(f) "Internal audit provider" means a third party contracted to provide internal audit services to an entity.

(g) "Third parties", in addition to internal audit providers defined in (f) above, may also include regulators, auditors of controlling entities or joint ventures, advisers to prospective purchasers, investors or lenders, and successor auditors.

(h) "Regulators" may include the Australian Securities and Investments Commission (ASIC), the Australian Prudential Regulation Authority (APRA) or the Australian Taxation Office (ATO).

8 For the purposes of this Guidance Statement, the following documents and information which are ordinarily contained in an audit file, do not form part of the auditor's audit working papers defined in paragraph 7 (b) that are normally provided to third parties when access is requested:

(a) the auditor's internal budgeting documents concerning costing or billing records for the audit client;

(b) internal staffing-related documents for the engagement and any incidental personnel records or information about the engagement team;

(c) documents or information that are subject to legal professional privilege; and

(d) proprietary work programs (e.g. client acceptance checklists and internal firm independence review checklists).

The information contained in audit working papers can be in any form, including handwritten data, text, image or audio, and may be stored electronically or in hard copy.

9 When a regulator seeks access to audit working papers, the relevant legislative provisions may permit the regulator to access documents or information that do not form part of the auditor's audit working papers as outlined in paragraph 8 above.

10 For the purposes of this Guidance Statement, documents or information included in the audit file may be subject to "legal professional privilege" because an audit client, or relevant laws or regulations, at the time it was originally provided, required that such information or audit working paper be legally privileged. An example is legal advice regarding litigation against the audit client, as provided by its legal counsel. Paragraphs 28–31 of this Guidance Statement contain further discussion related to legal professional privilege.

Circumstances When Requests for Access Are Made

11 The table below outlines:

(a) common circumstances when requests for access to an external auditor's audit working papers may arise;

(b) specific paragraphs in this Guidance Statement that could be considered in deciding whether access will be granted; and

(c) the example letter(s) auditors may use for each specific circumstance listed.

Circumstances	Relevant Guidance Statement Paragraph	Example Letters in Appendix 1
1. Audit of a Group Financial Report When a controlling entity's auditor wishes to review the audit working papers of the auditor of a controlled entity, in connection with the audit or review of the consolidated financial reports (including consolidated financial statements) of the controlling entity.[3]	32-40	Letter A Letter C
2. Prospective Purchaser, Investor or Lender When a third party adviser to a prospective purchaser, investor or lender of the auditor's client wishes to review the audit working papers to obtain information to assist them advise their client about a transaction.	42	Letter B1 Letter B2 Letter C
3. Predecessor/Successor Auditor When an entity's newly appointed auditor (successor auditor) wants to consider the predecessor auditor's audit working papers in connection with the next audit or review of the entity.	49-50	Letter E Letter C
4. Internal Audit Where the internal audit function is outsourced to an internal audit provider and the entity's external auditor wants to review the entity's internal audit working papers belonging to the internal audit provider to gain an understanding of the entity's internal auditing activities relevant to the audit of the financial report.	43	Letter C Letter D
5. Joint Venture When an auditor of a joint venture participant may want to review the audit working papers of the auditor of the joint venture audit.	41	Letter A Letter C

General Considerations Applicable to all Requests for Access to Audit Working Papers

12 Certain matters need to be considered when an auditor receives a request for access to audit working papers. They include:

(a) client confidentiality requirements concerning access to audit working papers;

(b) risk of legal claims resulting from allowing access and appropriate legal protection to mitigate that risk, such as indemnities that may be required (depending on the circumstances governing the request including the form of the release, waiver or indemnity);

(c) the appropriate sequence of indemnities between the auditor, auditor's client and any third parties;

(d) how and when the auditor grants access to their audit working papers, including having regard to whether the audit is complete; and

(e) whether the audit working papers contain documents or information that are subject to legal professional privilege, which should not form part of the audit working papers to be accessed by third parties.

3 In these circumstances, Section 323B of the *Corporations Act 2001* requires the controlled entity's auditor to give the controlling entity's auditor any information, explanation or assistance required under Section 323A of the Act.

GS

13 The guidance provided in this Guidance Statement needs to be adapted to the specific client or other circumstances faced by the auditor. For example, when an auditor is responding to a request to access their audit working papers by a regulator, some of the above considerations may not be applicable, as access is granted in accordance with the requirements of the relevant legislation.

Client Confidentiality

14 Before the auditor grants third party access to audit working papers, the client's consent is necessary to ensure the auditor complies with their common law duty of confidentiality to the client, as well as applicable professional ethical standards on confidentiality[4] and any contractual undertakings that the auditor may have given to the client. Unless consent is given, preferably in writing, the auditor cannot voluntarily grant access to third parties unless required by law to do so.

15 When access to audit working papers is required by a regulator, the auditor (unless prohibited by the terms of the regulator) needs to consider informing their client that access is being sought and will be granted in accordance with legislative requirements.

16 The letter of consent required from the client needs to be signed by a person(s) appropriately authorised to legally bind the client. If the client wishes to give consent under a power of attorney, the auditor considers whether it is necessary to sight the power of attorney document.

Client Indemnity

External Auditor

17 Whenever the auditor's client, or any third party, seeks access to audit working papers, the auditor ought to obtain from the client and any third party (as the case may be) an indemnity against any liability which arises as a result of that access.

18 A company cannot under the Act[5] indemnify its auditor from a liability to the company or a related body corporate incurred in the capacity of being the company's auditor. However, the company can indemnify its auditor against liabilities to third parties (i.e. parties other than the company and its related bodies corporate), and third parties themselves can indemnify the auditor against liability to those or other parties. Moreover, the company can indemnify its auditor from a liability to the company or a related body corporate incurred in a capacity other than as auditor.

Internal Auditor

19 The internal audit function of an external auditor's client may be undertaken by employees of the entity, or, might be outsourced to an internal audit provider. Where the internal audit services are outsourced to an internal audit provider, the opportunity for the external auditor to access the internal audit working papers of the internal audit provider will depend on who "owns" such working papers. Normally, the letter of engagement between the client and the internal audit provider specifies who "owns" internal audit working papers.

20 When the internal audit working papers are "owned" by the client, a consent letter to access the internal audit working papers is not required. Nonetheless, prior to allowing access, the internal audit provider or the client may request the external auditor to acknowledge that their access is subject to their obligations to comply with the requirements of Auditing Standard ASA 610 *Considering the Work of Internal Audit*. When the internal audit working papers are "owned" by the internal audit provider:

(a) The internal audit provider would ordinarily first require consent from its client before granting access to its working papers to the external auditor. Refer Example Letter C in Appendix 1 for an example client consent letter.

(b) Once the internal audit provider has obtained the signed client consent letter, it would then request the external auditor to provide a signed request letter to access

4 See Compiled APES 110 *Code of Ethics for Professional Accountants*, issued by the Accounting Professional and Ethical Standards Board.

5 See Section 199A, *Corporations Act 2001*.

the internal audit working papers. Refer Example Letter D in Appendix 1 for an example of this letter.

See paragraph 43 for additional considerations related to granting access to internal audit working papers.

Indemnities from Third Parties

21 The audit working papers which form part of an audit file are ordinarily prepared for the sole purpose of an internal or external audit or review. Their preparation for an external financial report audit or review is for the sole purpose of documenting and supporting the auditor's conclusions included in the auditor's report on the financial report. Consequently, audit working papers may not be suitable for any intended use by a third party, as the scope and nature of the third party's needs are not known by the auditor, and thus, did not form part of the scope of the audit.

22 Access to the audit working papers by third parties, without receipt of appropriate releases, indemnities and waivers of reliance, could place the auditor at risk of a legal claim by the third party based on the results of their access to the audit working papers. Accordingly, it would not be prudent for the auditor to grant such access to their audit working papers, unless the auditor has:

(a) obtained the client's consent letter; and

(b) agreed terms of access with the third party in writing, including appropriate releases and/or indemnities.

23 If access is provided to audit working papers, in most cases the letter of consent includes an express disclaimer of reliance and exclusion of liability.

24 The Example Letters in Appendix 1 incorporate a suggested form of release, indemnity and waiver of reliance that an auditor ordinarily seeks when responding to a request to access their audit working papers.

25 The Example Letters in Appendix 1 are designed to facilitate access to the auditor's audit working papers when access is sought by a third party. The Example Letters record the agreed basis on which an auditor may be prepared to provide access to their audit working papers to a third party agent. Access may be denied to the third party agent if a letter is not executed and obtained from the third party and the agent.

Auditor's Control Over Access to Audit Working Papers

26 An auditor may decide to allow limited access to some of their audit working papers and inform the third party that certain audit working papers have been omitted.

27 When access to audit working papers is granted, the auditor controls how access is to be administered. Ordinarily, the auditor will:

(a) agree on the format (electronic or hard copy) with the third party in which access to the audit working papers will be provided. The auditor is entitled to determine the format so as not to place at risk the confidentiality of any of their proprietary audit software and methodologies, as well as other clients' confidential information.

(b) agree on and control the extent of access to original audit working papers granted to a third party.

(c) oversee the physical inspection of audit working papers;

(d) request that any questions arising from the examination of the audit working papers be put in writing. The auditor's response will be restricted to matters in the audit working papers, rather than for example, answering questions of a general nature or matters concerning events subsequent to the reporting period covered by the audit engagement; and

(e) not permit making copies of audit working papers without specific consent. When permission to make copies of audit working papers is granted, the auditor ordinarily:

(i) maintains control over which audit working papers can be copied;

GS

(ii) reviews all audit working papers that are to be copied, prior to making them available to the third party;

(iii) retains a record of which audit working papers have been copied; and

(iv) considers what (if any) charge is to be made for the cost of making copies of the requested audit working papers.

Legal Professional Privilege

28 In undertaking an engagement, the auditor might access or incorporate within their audit file confidential communications made between, or confidential documents prepared by, the audit client and their legal counsel(s). When the dominant purpose of these communications is for the client's legal counsel to provide legal advice to the client or where the documents have been created in contemplation of existing or anticipated legal proceedings, the communications may be subject to legal professional privilege.

29 Documents or information included in the audit file that are subject to legal professional privilege are owned by the client and not the auditor. When granting access to audit working papers is being contemplated, the auditor needs to consider obtaining legal advice from its own legal counsel as to how to deal with documents or information that may be subject to legal professional privilege. A client also ought to have an opportunity to review all documents and information that are to be produced so that the client can assess whether a claim for legal professional privilege will be made in relation to specified documents.

30 The following are example communications, documents and information that may attract legal professional privilege:

(a) Correspondence between the client and their legal advisers for the dominant purpose of giving or receiving legal advice, or for use in existing or anticipated litigation, that has been provided to the auditor for the engagement;

(b) Opinions from the legal counsel, and associated billing costs (including details of legal costs), where such information would disclose the nature of the advice sought or given;

(c) Correspondence between the auditor and the client's legal counsel; or

(d) Documents that incorporate the types of documents listed (a) to (c) above.

31 If any of the documents or information listed in paragraph 30 above are contained in the audit working papers, or if the auditor is in any doubt about whether any client communications, documents or information are subject to legal professional privilege, the auditor notifies their client in accordance with paragraph 29 above. In these circumstances, the auditor might also need to consult with their own legal counsel in order to correctly identify the status of communications and documents that could potentially be the subject of legal professional privilege.

Granting Access to the Auditor of a Controlling Entity

Basis for Granting Access

32 The auditor of a controlling entity has a duty to form an opinion on various matters as may be required by laws or regulations, such as the *Corporations Act 2001* (or other relevant statutory requirements) regarding the consolidated financial report of the entity. There may also be circumstances when the auditor of a controlling entity may be engaged to perform a non-statutory audit of the consolidated financial report of the entity. The auditor of the controlling entity may wish to access the audit working papers of the auditor of a controlled entity in order to assist them in the audit of the controlling entity. Under Auditing Standard ASA 600 *Using the Work of Another Auditor*, the auditor of the controlling entity is required to perform procedures to obtain sufficient appropriate audit evidence, that the work of the auditor of the controlled entity is adequate for the purposes of the auditor of the controlling entity, in the context of the specific engagement.[6]

6 See Auditing Standard ASA 600 *Using the Work of Another Auditor*.

Relevant Factors to Consider

33 For an audit or review conducted under the *Corporations Act 2001* of a financial report that includes consolidated financial statements, the auditor of a controlled entity must allow the auditor of the controlling entity access to the controlled entity's books and must give the auditor of the controlling entity any information, explanation or assistance required, for the purposes of the audit or review.[7] The meaning attaching to these statutory requirements is not precise, as there is no judicial or statutory authority about what is meant by the words "information, explanation or assistance". The Act does not specify that the external auditor of the controlling entity has a statutory right to inspect the audit working papers of the external auditor of the controlled entity. Nonetheless, the auditor of a controlled entity ordinarily endeavours to be open and frank with the auditor of the controlling entity and seeks to ensure compliance with any reasonable request by the auditor of the controlling entity to discharge their responsibilities under the *Corporations Act 2001*. In determining the extent of obligations when the auditor of the controlled entity gives the controlling entity's auditor access to their audit working papers, the requirements of Auditing Standard ASA 600 are to be complied with.

34 The auditor of a controlled entity may grant the auditor of the controlling entity access to its audit working papers. For example, access is normally given for audit or review engagements (under the Act or otherwise), but only if:

(a) the controlled entity agrees to the terms of access as set out in Example Letter C in Appendix 1, including a release and indemnity in favour of the auditor of the controlled entity from liability which might arise through access being given to the auditor of the controlling entity; and

(b) the auditor of the controlling entity agrees to the terms of access as set out in Example Letter A in Appendix 1.

35 When access to audit working papers is granted, for audit or review engagements under the Act, the controlling entity cannot release or indemnify the auditor of the controlled entity under the Act's relevant provisions.[8] The auditor of the controlling entity will also often not agree to release or indemnify the auditor of the controlled entity by virtue of reliance by the controlling entity's auditor on the auditor of the controlled entity's performance of its obligations required by the Act.[9] Where the auditor of the controlled entity gives assistance or information to the auditor of the controlling entity more than is required by the Act[8], the auditor of the controlled entity could seek a release and an indemnity from the auditor of the controlling entity (and arguably from the controlling entity itself). Any release or indemnity referred to in this paragraph must extend to liability that arises through access to audit working papers, other files maintained by the auditor and their audit staff.

36 Notwithstanding some uncertainty about the working paper access obligations of an auditor of a controlled entity under the Act[10], Example Letter A in Appendix 1 identifies the basis upon which the auditor of a controlled entity may make audit working papers available to the auditor of the controlling entity. Example Letter A is completed and exchanged between both auditors, before access is granted by the auditor of a controlled entity to their audit working papers.

Circumstances in Which an Auditor of a Controlled Entity can Provide Access to their Audit Working Papers

37 Ordinarily, the auditor of the controlled entity will not allow the auditor of the controlling entity access to its audit working papers until the auditor of the controlled entity has completed its audit or review.

GS

7 See Sections 323A and 323B of the *Corporations Act 2001*.

8 Under the relevant provisions of Section 199A, *Corporations Act 2001*.

9 Refers to legal obligations of the auditor of the controlled entity required by Section 323B, *Corporations Act 2001*.

10 See Section 323B, *Corporations Act 2001*.

38 For the purposes of this Guidance Statement, the audit of a controlled entity is complete when:

(a) the directors' declaration about the financial statements[11] or similar representation by the entity's governing body, attached to the financial report, is signed; and

(b) the auditor's report on the financial report is signed and dated.

39 Some practical issues that may be encountered by an auditor of a controlled entity regarding access to their audit working papers by the auditor of the controlling entity include:

(a) Where the controlled entity is a subsidiary of an overseas controlling entity and the management of the controlling entity has forwarded a group consolidation package, access may not be granted to the controlling entity's auditor until the controlled entity's audit has been completed in accordance with paragraph 38 (a) and (b) above. Prior to this, the controlled entity's auditor may consider if it is prepared to provide a written response on the stage of completion of the audit, the basis of the review of the consolidation package and the opinion on the appropriateness of the package for group consolidation purposes.

(b) If the controlled entity's financial report has been finalised, and submitted for group consolidation purposes, but the requirements in paragraph 38 (a) and (b) above are not yet complete, then access to the auditor's audit working papers is inappropriate, and is unlikely to be granted. Until the directors have provided the auditor the signed directors' declaration, the auditor of the controlled entity will not be able to confirm that the directors have agreed with, and adopted the representations of management. Once this occurs, the auditor of the controlled entity may be requested to advise the auditor of the controlling entity, in writing, of any differences between the previously reported upon group consolidation package and the statutory financial report.

40 The following guidance is also relevant with regard to access to audit working papers by the auditor of the controlling entity:

(a) At the completion of the audit of a controlled entity, the auditor of the controlled entity may grant the auditor of the controlling entity access to their audit working papers, when the auditor of the controlling entity has provided to the auditor of the controlled entity a letter of understanding in the form of Example Letter A in Appendix 1.

(b) Access to the controlled entity's auditor's audit working papers and audit staff is likely to be denied to all parties and, similarly, access ought not be requested until the completion of the audit of the controlled entity or until adoption of the controlled entity's financial report. Nonetheless, the respective auditors may negotiate access to audit working papers at an earlier time. When access to incomplete audit working papers is permitted, it is prudent to acknowledge that the audit work or accompanying audit working papers may not reflect significant events or matters which are material to the audit or review at the date when access is agreed. The acknowledgement ought to also contain the extent to which the controlled entity's auditor has any obligation or responsibility to update the audit working papers or inform the reviewing auditor of information obtained subsequent to the date access is provided to the incomplete audit working papers.

(c) Until completion of the audit of the controlled entity, or until completion of a group's consolidation reporting package, requests by the auditor of the controlling entity to the auditor of the controlled entity for progress reports, advice on or information on the audit of the controlled entity are best made in writing, detailing specific matters on which a response is sought, and allowing the auditor of the controlled entity to respond in writing.

11 As required by Section 295, *Corporations Act 2001*.

Access to Audit Working Papers of the Joint Venture Auditor

41 When an audit client is one of the parties in a joint venture, the audit client's auditor may seek access to the audit working papers belonging to the auditor of the joint venture. In this context, issues similar to those related to access to audit working papers of the auditor of a controlled entity by the controlling entity's auditor (discussed above) will need to be considered. Normally, audit arrangements are outlined in the joint venture agreement, wherein one auditor is appointed to audit the joint venture. However, as the investment in the joint venture may be material to one or more of the joint venturers (whose financial report may be audited by another auditor), it may be necessary for that auditor to gain access to the audit working papers of the joint venture's auditor. Unless specifically provided for in the auditor's contract of appointment with the joint venture, the auditors of the joint venture parties may not be legally entitled to such access. However, to assist the auditor of a joint venture party, access may be granted at the discretion of all the relevant parties to the joint venture and the joint venture's auditor by completing and exchanging Example Letter A in Appendix 1.

Granting Access to Prospective Purchasers, Investors or Lenders

Basis for Granting Access

42 Owners of an entity seeking to sell their investment, or entities seeking further equity or loan funding from third parties, often believe their objectives might be facilitated by requesting the entity's auditor to make available their audit working papers to third parties. As such a request potentially exposes an auditor to significant legal risk, access to audit working papers for this purpose necessitates the following matters be considered by the auditor before access is given:

(a) whether to obtain legal advice; and

(b) ensure the auditor's client and third parties, to whom access is to be given, confirm and acknowledge, in favour of the auditor:

  (i) that no representation is made about the accuracy or completeness of the audit working papers or any additional information provided in connection with that access, or of any individual amounts, accounts, balances, transactions or disclosures, or the accuracy or completeness of other information included in the audit working papers or any additional information;

  (ii) that the auditor is not responsible to the audit client and/or other third parties for any loss suffered in connection with access, to or use of, the audit working papers; and

  (iii) that the auditor will receive an indemnity against any loss, action, liability, claim, suit, demand, claim for costs or expenses or any other proceeding that the auditor may suffer arising out of, or in connection with, granting access to the audit working papers and the additional information given in connection with that access.

Granting Access to Internal Audit Working Papers in an Outsourced Internal Audit Arrangement

43 When the internal audit function of an entity is outsourced to an internal audit provider, or where personnel from the internal audit provider are seconded to an internal audit client, and the audit working papers belong to the internal audit provider, the external auditor may seek access to the entity's internal audit working papers to gain an understanding of relevant internal auditing activities that are relevant to the audit or review of the financial report. In such circumstances, the following matters may be considered:

(a) the external auditor seeking access to the internal auditor's audit working papers needs to comply with the requirements and guidance in Auditing Standard ASA 610 *Considering the Work of Internal Audit*. This includes acknowledging that an understanding of the audit client's internal control structure and subsequent assessment of audit risk, gained from the review of the internal auditor's audit working papers, are based solely on the external auditor's professional judgement; and

(b) generally, internal audit working papers prepared by an internal audit provider will not be released for review by the external auditor until after the related internal audit report is finalised and/or has been tabled with the Audit Committee (or equivalent governing body), subject to the terms of the outsourcing arrangement.

Granting Access to Audit Working Papers by Regulators

44 An auditor is required to produce, or give access to their audit working papers when:

(a) legally requested to do so pursuant to the issue of a subpoena, search warrant or court order or pursuant to discovery obligations during court proceedings; or

(b) required by a regulator such as ASIC, APRA and the ATO, under relevant legislative provisions.

45 Regulators may seek to access an auditor's audit working papers when, for example, they are undertaking:

(a) an investigation of an alleged or suspected contravention of the relevant legislation by the auditor's client; or

(b) compliance-related surveillance activities concerning legislative obligations or monitoring of industry-wide issues that affect the auditor's client.

46 If under the relevant legislation regulatory authorities seek access to audit working papers, the auditor's statutory obligations under normal circumstances will override common law or professional responsibilities to respect the confidentiality of the client. The level of access granted by the external auditor will need to be in accordance with the requirements of the relevant legislation.

47 When a regulator requests an auditor to provide access to their audit working papers, the request is normally made on a formal basis, by issuing a written notice under the legislation. The notice typically sets out for example, the nature of the matter to be investigated, to whom and when audit working papers are required to be made available and a description of the specific audit working papers to be provided.

48 When regulators, pursuant to their legal/regulatory powers, require access to audit working papers, auditors would normally, subject to legal advice and internal firm requirements, undertake the following procedures:

(a) inform the client, or former client that a request for audit working papers concerning the audit client's engagement has been made and the purpose for which access is required, except where such disclosure is prohibited by law;

(b) consult their legal counsel;

(c) where appropriate, and in consultation with the client, inform the regulator seeking access to their audit working papers that certain audit working papers may not be accessed, because they are the subject of client legal professional privilege (see paragraph 28); and

(d) maintain a written record of action taken to comply with the regulator's request, as well as a list of the audit working papers provided pursuant to such request; and

(e) ensure the regulator provides a written receipt for all audit working papers accessed.

Reviewing the Audit Working Papers of a Predecessor Auditor

49 A recently appointed auditor (successor auditor) of an entity which requires an audit in accordance with the Act has a statutory responsibility to report on the financial report of the entity in the year of appointment pursuant to the provisions of the Act (or other relevant legislation). The financial report on which the successor auditor reports is affected by the account balances carried forward from the previous reporting period on which the predecessor auditor issued an audit report. Consequently, the successor auditor will need to form a view about whether the opening balances for the year are fairly stated in accordance with Auditing Standard ASA 510 *Initial Engagements–Opening Balances*.

It is for this purpose access to the predecessor auditor's audit working papers may be obtained. The auditor's client consent prior to granting access is considered essential in these circumstances and Example Letter C in Appendix 1 sets out the matters that are ordinarily addressed.

Appropriate Procedures

50 Where the predecessor auditor agrees to provide the successor auditor access to the auditor's audit working papers, such access ordinarily involves an exchange of letters between the two auditors. Example Letter E in Appendix 1 sets out the matters ordinarily addressed, though amendments may be required to reflect circumstances specific to the engagement.

Conformity with International Pronouncements

51 There is no equivalent International Auditing Practice Statement (IAPS) to this Guidance Statement.

Appendix 1

Example Letter A: Terms and Consent of a Controlled Entity's Auditor for Access to the Audit Working Papers by the Controlling Entity's Auditor

The following example letter can be tailored to specific circumstances where the external auditor of a controlling entity is seeking to review the audit working papers of the external auditor of the controlled entity for an audit or review of a financial report prepared under the Corporations Act 2001. It can also be tailored for entities subject to other statutory requirements. A client consent letter (Example Letter C) is required to be obtained before this letter can be provided.

Auditor's Letterhead

[Date]

(Reviewing Auditor)

[Address]

Dear [**Insert controlling entity's auditor's name**]

You have asked for access to our audit working papers of the statutory audit of [**name of controlled entity**] for the year ended [**date**] (the "Audit Working Papers") under section 323B of the *Corporations Act 2001* in connection with your statutory audit of [**name of controlling entity**] for the year ended [**financial year end for controlling entity**]. You have also asked us to answer any questions you may have in relation to the Audit Working Papers ("Additional Information").

This letter sets out the terms on which we are prepared to grant you access to the Audit Working Papers and to provide you with the Additional Information. You acknowledge and agree that:

1. You may only use the Audit Working Papers and Additional Information in connection with your audit of **[name of controlling entity]** for the year ended **[financial year end for controlling entity]**.
2. You will make a request for any Additional Information in writing.
3. Our work was performed and the Audit Working Papers were prepared in connection with our role as the statutory auditor of **[insert name of controlled entity]** for the year ended **[insert year end]** and for no other purpose.
4. Our Audit Working Papers or any Additional Information may not be sufficient or appropriate for your purpose. In performing our statutory audit of **[insert name of**

GS

controlled entity] we may not have addressed matters in which you **[or the controlling entity]** may be interested or which may be material to you or **[controlling entity]**.

5. The Audit Working Papers and any Additional Information relate to the period ended **[insert date]**. Events may have occurred since that date which may impact on the information contained in the Audit Working Papers or your statutory audit of **[name of controlling entity]**. To the extent permitted by law, access to our audit working papers will not be made available until the audit of **[name of controlled entity]** is completed.
6. To the maximum extent permitted by law (including subject to the *Corporations Act 2001* and Australian Auditing Standards), we are not responsible to you or any other party for any loss you or any other party may suffer in connection with your access to or use of the Audit Working Papers or any Additional Information.
7. The Audit Working Papers and any Additional Information are confidential information and must be treated as such by you. They must not be copied or used for any other purpose or disclosed or distributed to anyone (other than disclosure as required by law), without our prior written consent, which may be granted at our absolute discretion and may be subject to conditions.
8. We reserve the right to withhold any information from the Audit Working Papers which is confidential to us. Accordingly, unless we have a legal obligation not to do so, we reserve the right to remove files from our Audit Working Papers relating to practice management issues such as budgets, time/cost records, proprietary software, staffing records and any other information that is confidential to us, or is the subject of legal professional privilege.
9. In accordance with Auditing Standard ASA 600 *Using the Work of Another Auditor*, you have sole responsibility for the opinion expressed on the consolidated financial report of [**controlling entity**] for the year ended [**insert date**].
10. You must not name us in any report or document which will be publicly available or lodged or filed with any regulator without our prior written consent, such consent will be granted at our absolute discretion and may be subject to conditions.
11. In accordance with Auditing Standard ASA 600 *Using the Work of Another Auditor*, you will, subject to legal and professional considerations, bring to our attention any matters of which you are aware that might have an important bearing on our audit of [**name of controlled entity**].

Please acknowledge that you accept these terms by signing dating and returning this letter to us at **[insert address].**

Yours faithfully

[Signature of Partner]

[Auditor of Controlled Entity]

We accept the terms on which access to the Audit Working Papers and Additional Information is to be provided.

[Signature of Partner]

[Auditor of Controlling Entity]

[Date]

Example Letter B1: Auditor's Terms and Consent for Access to Audit Working Papers by an Adviser/Firm in Connection with a Transaction

The following example letter may be tailored to the specific client circumstances as well as for access to audit working papers for a review engagement. A client consent letter (Example Letter C) is required before this letter can be provided.

Auditor's Letterhead

[Date]

[Reviewing firm/adviser]

[Address]

Dear **[Insert addressee(s)]**

You, **[name of reviewing firm/adviser]**, have asked for access to our audit working papers of the statutory audit of **[name of entity]** for the year ended **[date]** (the "Audit Working Papers") in connection with **[describe transaction]** (the "Transaction"). You have also asked us to answer any questions you may have in relation to the Audit Working Papers ("Additional Information"). **[name of entity]** has authorised us at our discretion to give you access to the Audit Working Papers and provide you with Additional Information. This letter sets out the terms on which we are prepared to grant you access to the Audit Working Papers and to provide you with any Additional Information. You acknowledge and agree that:

1. You may only use the Audit Working Papers and Additional Information in connection with the Transaction.
2. You will make a request for any Additional Information in writing.
3. Our work was performed and the Audit Working Papers were prepared in connection with our role as the statutory auditor of **[insert name of entity]** for the year ended **[insert year end]** and for no other purpose.
4. Events may have occurred since we prepared the Audit Working Papers, which may impact on the information contained in the Audit Working Papers and on the Transaction, however, we are not obliged to update our Audit Working Papers after the financial report has been issued.
5. In accordance with Australian Auditing Standards, there are inherent limitations in an audit of a financial report, accordingly our audit report is not a guarantee that the financial report is free of material misstatement. In undertaking the audit, we exercised our professional judgement regarding for example:
   (a) our assessment of materiality, and
   (b) our selective testing of the data being audited, which involves judgement about both the number of transactions to be audited and the areas to be tested.

   This means our Audit Working Papers and any Additional Information may include information and conclusions that may be assessed differently by you in the context of the Transaction.

   In addition, the scope of an audit is normally narrower than an investigation that a **[reviewing firm/adviser]** might undertake. Therefore, our Audit Working Papers or any Additional Information are subject to these limitations and may not be sufficient or appropriate for the purposes of the Transaction. You should not rely on them or treat them as such. Furthermore, the **[name of entity]**'s financial report, our audit of the financial report and accompanying Audit Working Papers, were not planned, conducted or prepared in either contemplation or for the purposes of the Transaction.
6. We make no representation about the accuracy or completeness of the Audit Working Papers or any Additional Information or of any individual amounts, accounts, balances,

GS

transactions or disclosures, or the accuracy or completeness of other information included in our Audit Working Papers or any Additional Information. Accordingly, any notations, comments and individual conclusions appearing on the Audit Working Papers or in any Additional Information do not stand alone, and should not be read or relied upon by you as an opinion or conclusion regarding any individual amounts, accounts, balances, transactions or disclosures. While we will provide the Audit Working Papers and any Additional Information in good faith, you are responsible for verifying the accuracy and completeness of anything we provide to you.

7. We reserve the right to withhold any information from the Audit Working Papers which is confidential to us. Accordingly, unless we have a legal obligation not to do so, we reserve the right to remove files from our Audit Working Papers relating to practice management issues such as budgets, time/cost records, proprietary software, staffing records and any other information that is confidential to us, or is subject to legal professional privilege.

8. The Audit Working Papers and any Additional Information are confidential information and must be treated as such by you. They must not be copied or used for any other purpose or disclosed or distributed to anyone (other than disclosure as required by law), without our prior written consent, which may be granted at our absolute discretion and may be subject to conditions.

9. To the maximum extent permitted by law, we are not responsible to you or any other party for any loss you or any other party may suffer in connection with your access to or use of the Audit Working Papers or any Additional Information.

10. You must not name us in any report or document which will be publicly available or lodged or filed with any regulator without our prior written consent, such consent will be granted at our absolute discretion and may be subject to conditions.

11. You, **[reviewing firm/advisers]**, will indemnify **[name of audit firm]**, its partners, officers and employees against any loss, action, liability, claim, suit, demand, claim for costs or expenses or any other proceeding we may suffer arising out of, or in connection with a breach of clauses 1, 8 and 10 of this letter.[12]

12. You agree to release and forever discharge **[name of audit firm]**, its partners, officers and employees from, and not assert against us, any action, liability, claim, suit, demand, claims for costs or expenses or any other proceedings arising out of, or in connection with, your access to the Audit Working Papers and the Additional Information.

13. We reserve the right to withdraw our consent to you having access to the Audit Working Papers or to providing any further Additional Information at any time including if you breach any of the terms of this letter.

Please acknowledge that you accept these terms by signing, dating and returning this letter to us at **[insert address]**.

Yours faithfully

[Signature of partner]

[Audit Firm]

We confirm our acceptance of the terms on which access to the Audit Working Papers and Additional Information is to be provided.

____

[Signature]

[Name of Reviewing Firm/Advisers]

____

[Date]

12 When agreeing to provide the indemnity contained in Clause 11 of this letter, you should also consider, unless prohibited by law or regulation, obtaining a similar indemnity from the client.

Example Letter B2: Auditor's Terms and Consent for Access to Audit Working Papers by a Prospective Purchaser, Investor or Lender in Connection with a Transaction

The following example letter can be used to inform the prospective purchase/lender/investor of the terms on which access to audit working papers and Additional Information are made available to a reviewing firm/adviser in relation to a transaction. The letter may be tailored to the specific client circumstances. The letter is from the perspective that the usual practice is to allow access to the audit working papers and any additional information only to the reviewing firm/adviser, rather than the prospective purchaser/lender/investor.[13] *A client consent letter (Example Letter C) is required before this can be provided.*

Auditor's Letterhead

[Date]

[Prospective purchaser/investor/lender]

[Address]

[Adviser]

[Address]

Dear **[Insert addressee(s)]**

You, **[Prospective Purchaser/Investor/Lender]**, have asked **[name of reviewing firm/advisers]** to seek access to our audit working papers of the statutory audit of **[name of entity]** for the year ended **[date]** (the "Audit Working Papers") in connection with **[describe transaction]** (the "Transaction"). You have also asked us to answer any questions they may have in relation to the Audit Working Papers ("Additional Information").

[Name of entity] has authorised us at our discretion to give **[name of reviewing firm/advisers]** access to the Audit Working Papers and provide them with Additional Information. Accordingly, this letter sets out the terms on which we are prepared to grant access to the Audit Working Papers and to provide any Additional Information to **[name of reviewing firm/advisers]**.

You **[Prospective Purchaser/Investor/Lender]** acknowledge and agree that

1. **[Name of reviewing firm/advisers]** may only use the Audit Working Papers and Additional Information in connection with the Transaction.
2. **[Name of reviewing firm/advisers]** will make a request for any Additional Information in writing.
3. Our work was performed and the Audit Working Papers were prepared in connection with our role as the statutory auditor of **[insert name of entity]** for the year ended **[insert year end]** and for no other purpose.
4. Events may have occurred since we prepared the Audit Working Papers, which may impact on the information contained in the Audit Working Papers and on the Transaction, however, we are not obliged to update our Audit Working Papers after the financial report has been issued.
5. In accordance with Australian Auditing Standards, there are inherent limitations in an audit of a financial report, accordingly our audit report is not a guarantee that the financial

GS

13 When it is contemplated that access to the auditor's Audit Working Papers will be given to an individual, firm or organisation, other than a professional assurance services (audit) firm, there is risk the party seeking access to the Audit Working Papers may not clearly understand the content, purpose and limitations inherent in the Audit Working Papers. In such circumstances, this Letter may need to be adapted to mitigate this risk.

report is free of material misstatement. In undertaking the audit, we exercised our professional judgement regarding for example:

(a) our assessment of materiality, and

(b) our selective testing of the data being audited, which involves judgement about both the number of transactions to be audited and the areas to be tested.

This means our Audit Working Papers and any Additional Information may include information and conclusions that may be assessed differently by you in the context of the Transaction.

In addition, the scope of an audit is normally narrower than an investigation that you or a **[reviewing firm/advisers]** might undertake. Therefore, our Audit Working Papers or any Additional Information are subject to these limitations and may not be sufficient or appropriate for the purposes of the Transaction. You should not rely on them or treat them as such. The **[name of entity]**'s financial report, our audit of the financial report and accompanying Audit Working Papers, were not planned, conducted or prepared in either contemplation or for the purposes of the Transaction.

6. We make no representation about the accuracy or completeness of the Audit Working Papers or any Additional Information or of any individual amounts, accounts, balances, transactions or disclosures, or the accuracy or completeness of other information included in our Audit Working Papers or any Additional Information. Accordingly, any notations, comments and individual conclusions appearing on the Audit Working Papers or in any Additional Information do not stand alone, and should not be read or relied upon by you as an opinion or conclusion regarding any individual amounts, accounts, balances, transactions or disclosures. While we will provide the Audit Working Papers and any Additional Information in good faith, you are responsible for verifying the accuracy and completeness of anything we provide to **[name of reviewing firm/advisers]**.

7. We reserve the right to withhold any information from the Audit Working Papers which is confidential to us. Accordingly, unless we have a legal obligation not to do so, we reserve the right to remove files from our Audit Working Papers relating to practice management issues such as budgets, time/cost records, proprietary software, staffing records and any other information that is confidential to us, or is subject to legal professional privilege.

8. The Audit Working Papers and any Additional Information are confidential information and must be treated as such by you. They must not be copied or used for any other purpose or disclosed or distributed to anyone (other than disclosure as required by law), without our prior written consent, which may be granted at our absolute discretion and may be subject to conditions.

9. To the maximum extent permitted by law, we are not responsible to you or any other party for any loss you or any other party may suffer in connection with **[name of reviewing firm's/adviser's]** access to or use of the Audit Working Papers or any Additional Information.

10. You must not name us in any report or document which will be publicly available or lodged or filed with any regulator without our prior written consent, such consent will be granted at our absolute discretion and may be subject to conditions.

11. You, **[purchaser/investor/lender]**, will indemnify **[name of audit firm]**, its partners, officers and employees against any loss, action, liability, claim, suit, demand, claim for costs or expenses or any other proceeding we may suffer arising out of or in connection with **[reviewing firm's/adviser's]** access to our Audit Working Papers and the Additional Information or arising out of, or in connection with, a breach of clauses 8 and/or 10 of this letter.

12. You agree to release and forever discharge **[name of audit firm]**, its partners, officers and employees from, and not assert against us, any action, liability, claim, suit, demand, claims for costs or expenses or any other proceedings arising out of, or in connection with, your access to the Audit Working Papers and the Additional Information.

13. We reserve the right to withdraw our consent to **[name of reviewing firm/advisers]** having access to the Audit Working Papers or to providing any further Additional Information at

any time including if you or **[name of reviewing firm/advisers]** breach any of the terms of this letter.

Please acknowledge that you accept these terms by signing, dating and returning this letter to us at **[insert address].**

Yours faithfully

[Signature of Partner]

[Audit Firm]

We confirm our acceptance of the terms on which access to the Audit Working Papers and Additional Information relating to the statutory audit of **[name of entity]** for the year ended **[date]** is to be provided to **[name of reviewing firm/advisers]**.

____

[Signature]

[Name of Purchaser/Investor/Lender]

____

[Date]

GS

Example Letter C: Auditor's Client Consent Letter to Allow Third Party Access to Audit Working Papers

The following example letter is forwarded to the auditor's client in connection with a request by a third party to access the auditor's audit working papers by:

(a) *the external auditor of the controlling entity, when seeking to access the audit working papers of the external auditor of the controlled entity for the audit of a financial report prepared under the Corporations Act 2001;*

(b) *a purchaser/investor, lending institution, company and/or the reviewing firm/advisers, when seeking to access the audit working papers of the external auditor in connection with a proposed transaction;*

(c) *the external auditor of the entity, when seeking to access the internal audit working papers of the internal auditor where the internal audit function has been outsourced; or*

(d) *a successor auditor, when seeking to access the audit working papers of the predecessor auditor.*

Auditor's Letterhead

[Date]

[Client]

[Address]

Dear **[Insert client contact person]**

You have asked us to provide access to our audit working papers for **[See Insert 1]**[14] for the year ended **[date]** (the "Audit Working Papers") to **[See Insert 2]**[15] in connection with **[Insert description of purpose e.g. external audit/ transaction]**. You have also requested that we answer any questions they may have in relation to the Audit Working Papers ("Additional Information"). This letter sets out the basis on which we are prepared to grant access to our Audit Working Papers and any Additional Information to **[Insert 2]**.

You acknowledge that the Audit Working Papers and any Additional Information relate to the work that was undertaken by **[name of firm]** under the terms and conditions contained in our engagement letter dated **[insert date]**. Accordingly, the Audit Working Papers (including Additional Information) and the scope of our work may not be sufficient or appropriate for the purposes for which **[Insert 2]** has requested access.

---

14 **Insert 1** – Insert here either:
1. 'the statutory audit of [name of controlled entity]'
2. 'the internal audit of [name of entity]', or
3. 'name of entity / target company'—when in relation to a specific transaction.

15 **Insert 2** – Insert here either:
1. **'name of external auditor of controlling entity'**—when the request is in relation to accessing the audit working papers of the controlled entity
2. **'reviewing firm/advisers'**—when the request is in relation to accessing the audit working papers of the entity for a proposed transaction
3. **'name of external auditor'**—when the request is for access to the audit working papers relating to the internal audit pursuant to Auditing Standard ASA 610 *Considering the Work of Internal Audit*, or
4. **'name of successor auditor'**—when the request is for access to the audit working papers of the predecessor auditor by the successor auditor.
5. **'prospective purchaser, investor or lender'**—when the request is in relation to accessing the audit working papers of the entity for a proposed transaction.

We agree to make the Audit Working Papers and any Additional Information available to **[Insert 3 – Refer to Table below regarding the relevant text to be inserted]**:

Insert the following text in the letter	Attach accompanying letter
'**[name of external auditor]** if they sign a letter in the form attached, confirming the terms on which we are willing to provide access.'	If for the release of audit working papers to the: (a) external auditor of the controlling entity, attach Letter A. (b) external auditor in relation to the internal audit working papers for the internal audit, attach Letter D. (c) newly appointed external auditor of the client entity, attach Letter E.
'**[reviewing firm/advisers]** if they sign a letter in the form attached, confirming the terms on which we are willing to provide access. In particular, please note clauses 5, 7 and 13 of the attached letter.'	If for the release of audit working papers in relation to a Transaction attach Letter B1.
'**[prospective purchaser, investor or lender]** if they sign a letter in the form attached, confirming the terms on which we are willing to provide access. In particular, please note clauses 5, 7 and 13 of the attached letter.'	If for the release of audit working papers in relation to a Transaction attach Letter B2.

To the maximum extent permitted by law:

(a) we are not responsible to you or any other party for any loss you or any other party may suffer in connection with the access to or use of the Audit Working Papers or any Additional Information by **[Insert 2]**.

(b) you agree to release and forever discharge **[name of audit firm]** its partners, officers and employees from, and not assert against us, any action, liability, claim, suit, demand, claims for costs or other expenses or any other proceedings arising out of, or in connection with, the release of our Audit Working Papers and the Additional Information to **[Insert 2]**.

(c) you will indemnify **[name of audit firm]**, its partners, officers and employees against any loss, action, liability, claim, suit, demand, claim for costs or expenses or any other proceeding we may suffer arising out of, or in connection with, access to the Audit Working Papers and any Additional Information by **[Insert 2]**.

Please acknowledge that you agree to these terms and to the release of the Audit Working Papers and any Additional Information to **[Insert 2]** by signing, dating and returning this letter to us at **[insert address]**.[16]

Yours sincerely

[Signature of Partner]

[Audit Firm]

____

We consent to the Audit Working Papers and any Additional Information being made available to **[Insert 2]** and to provide any Additional Information and accept the terms set out above on which such access will be provided.

You have our consent to bill any time and other costs to us at your standard rate. I warrant that I have the necessary authority of the company to commit the company to these terms.

____

[Signature of Client's Authorised Officer(s)]

____

[Date]

16 If vendor is not also the target company then include the following: Please also arrange for this letter to be signed on behalf of [insert target].

GS

Example Letter D: Internal Auditor's Terms and Consent to Grant the Entity's External Auditor Access to Internal Audit Working Papers

The following example letter can be used where the internal auditor has received a request from the entity's external auditor to access their internal audit working papers which belong to the internal auditor, in connection with the external auditor's audit of the financial report of the entity. The internal audit working papers could relate to an assurance engagement conducted by the internal auditor or a non-assurance engagement conducted by the internal auditor (such as an agreed upon procedures engagement). This letter can be tailored to the specific client circumstances. A client consent letter (Example Letter C) is required before this letter can be provided.

Internal Auditor's Letterhead

[Date]

[Reviewing Auditor]

[Address]

Dear **[Insert addressee(s)]**

You have asked for access to our audit working papers of the internal audit of **[name of entity]**[17] for the year ended **[date]** (the "Internal Audit Working Papers"), under Auditing Standard ASA 610 *Considering the Work of Internal Audit* in connection with your audit of the financial report of **[name of entity]** for the year ended **[financial year end for entity]**. You have also asked us to answer any questions you may have in relation to the Internal Audit Working Papers ("Additional Information").

This letter sets out the terms on which we are prepared to grant you access to the Internal Audit Working Papers and to provide you with the Additional Information. You acknowledge and agree that:

1. You may only use the Internal Audit Working Papers and Additional Information in connection with your audit of **[name of entity]** for the year ended **[date]**.
2. You will make a request for any Additional Information in writing.
3. Our work was performed, and the Internal Audit Working Papers were prepared, in connection with our internal audit engagement with **[name of entity]** for the year ended **[date]** and for no other purpose.
4. Our Internal Audit Working Papers or any Additional Information may not be sufficient or appropriate for your purposes and in performing our work for the internal audit of **[insert name of entity]** we may not have addressed matters which you may be interested or which may be material to you.
5. The Internal Audit Working Papers and any Additional Information relate to the periods specified within the Internal Audit Working Papers. Events may have occurred since we prepared the Internal Audit Working Papers, which may impact on the information contained in the Internal Audit Working Papers and on your statutory audit of **[name of entity]**.
6. We reserve the right to withhold any information from the Internal Audit Working Papers that is confidential to us. Accordingly, unless we have a legal obligation not to do so, we reserve the right to remove files from our Internal Audit Working Papers relating to practice management issues such as budgets, time/cost records, proprietary software, staffing records, and any other information that is confidential to us, or is subject to legal professional privilege.

17 Where not an internal audit, refer to other type of engagement, as the case may be.

7. To the maximum extent permitted by law, we are not responsible to you or any other party for any loss you or any other party may suffer in connection with your access to or use of the Internal Audit Working Papers or any Additional Information.

8. The Audit Working Papers and any Additional Information are confidential information and must be treated as such by you. They must not be copied or used for any other purpose or disclosed or distributed to anyone (other than disclosure as required by law), without our prior written consent, which may be granted at our absolute discretion and may be subject to conditions.

   In accordance with Auditing Standard ASA 610 *Considering the Work of Internal Audit*, you have sole responsibility for the opinion expressed on the financial report of **[name of entity]** for the year ended **[insert date]**.

9. You must not name us in any report or document which will be publicly available or lodged or filed with any regulator without our prior written consent, such consent will be granted at our absolute discretion and may be subject to conditions.

10. You agree that, in accordance with Auditing Standard ASA 610, you will bring to our attention any matters of which you are aware which might have an important bearing on our internal audit of **[name of entity]**.

11. You agree to indemnify [name of audit firm], its partners, officers and employees against any loss, action, liability, claim, suit, demand, claim for costs or expenses or any other proceeding arising out of or in connection with a breach of clauses 8 or 10 of this letter.

Please acknowledge that you accept these terms by signing, dating and returning this letter to us at **[insert address]**.

Yours faithfully

[Signature of Partner]

[Internal auditor]

We accept the terms on which access to the Internal Audit Working Papers and Additional Information is to be provided.

____

[Signature of Partner]

____

[Date]

[Reviewing external auditor]

GS

Example Letter E: Predecessor Auditor's Terms and Consent to Allow Access to Audit Working Papers by the Successor Auditor

The following example letter can be tailored to the specific client circumstances. A client consent letter (Example Letter C) is required before this letter can be provided.

Auditor's Letterhead

[Date]

[Reviewing Auditor]

[Address]

Dear **[Name of newly appointed auditor]**

You have asked for access to our audit working papers for the statutory audit of **[name of entity]** for the year ended **[date]** (the "Audit Working Papers") in connection with your appointment as the statutory auditor of **[name of entity]** for the year ended **[date].** You have also asked us to answer any questions you may have in relation to the Audit Working Papers ("Additional Information").

This letter sets out the terms on which we are prepared to grant you access to the Audit Working Papers and to provide you with the Additional Information. You acknowledge and agree that:

1. You may only use the Audit Working Papers and Additional Information in connection with your audit of **[name of entity]** for the year ended **[date]**.
2. You will make a request for any Additional Information in writing.
3. Our work was performed and the Audit Working Papers were prepared in connection with our role as the statutory auditor of **[insert name of entity]** for the year ended **[insert year end]** and for no other purpose.
4. The Audit Working Papers or any Additional Information may not be sufficient or appropriate for your purposes. This is because in performing our statutory audit of **[insert name of entity]** for the year ended **[date]** we may not have addressed matters in which you **[or entity]** may be interested or are material to you regarding **[name of entity]**. You therefore agree it is your responsibility to ensure compliance with applicable Australian Auditing Standards, including the requirements in Auditing Standard ASA 510 *Initial Engagement–Opening balances*, Auditing Standard ASA 710 *Comparatives* and Auditing Standard ASA 600 *Using the Work of Another Auditor*, particularly with regard to your sole responsibility for the opinion expressed on the financial report of **[insert name of entity]** for the year ended **[insert date]**.
5. The Audit Working Papers and any Additional Information relate to the period(s) ended **[insert date]**. Events may have occurred since that date which may impact on the information contained in the Audit Working Papers or your statutory audit of **[name of entity]**.
6. To the maximum extent permitted by law, we are not responsible to you or any other party for any loss you or any other party may suffer in connection with your access to or use of the Audit Working Papers or any Additional Information.
7. The Audit Working Papers and any Additional Information are confidential information and must be treated as such by you. They must not be copied or used for any other purpose or disclosed or distributed to anyone (other than disclosure as required by law), without our prior written consent, which may be granted at our absolute discretion and may be subject to conditions.
8. We reserve the right to withhold any information from the Audit Working Papers which is confidential to us. Accordingly, unless we have a legal obligation not to do so, we reserve

the right to remove files from our Audit Working Papers relating to practice management issues such as budgets, time/cost records, proprietary software, staffing records, and any other information that is confidential to us, or is subject to legal professional privilege.

9. You have sole responsibility for any opinion expressed, or any advice you give **[name of entity]** on the financial report of **[entity]** for the year ended **[insert date]** or any other period.

10. You must not name us in any report or document which will be publicly available or lodged or filed with any regulator without our prior written consent, such consent will be granted at our absolute discretion and may be subject to conditions.

11. Please acknowledge that you accept these terms by signing, dating and returning this letter to us at **[insert address]**.

Yours faithfully

[Signature of Partner]

[Predecessor auditor]

We accept the terms on which access to the Audit Working Papers and Additional Information is to be provided.

____

Signature of Partner]

[Successor auditor of entity]

____

[Date]

GS

GS 012

Prudential Reporting Requirements for Auditors of Authorised Deposit-taking Institutions

(Issued June 2009)

Issued by the Auditing and Assurance Standards Board.

Note from the Institute of Chartered Accountants Australia

This note, prepared by the technical editor, is not part of GS 012.

Historical development

July 2009: GS 012 issued. The new GS is a response to the revision by the Australian Prudential Regulation Authority (APRA) in late 2008 of its prudential statement APS 310 'Audit and Related Matters' which is effective from 1 January 2009. The APS 310 revisions sought to ensure that APRA is provided with independent advice from an ADI's auditor in relation to its operations and risk control environment, as well as to provide assurance that the data provided to APRA is reliable. GS 012 replaces AGS 1008 'Audit Implications of Prudential Reporting Requirements for Authorised Deposit-taking Institutions' and applies to prudential reporting engagements undertaken in relation to reporting periods commencing on or after 1 January 2009.

AGS 1008 was initially issued in December 1987 and subsequently revised in October 1995, July 1997, September 2001 and July 2002.

Contents

Preface

How this Guidance Statement is to be used

This Guidance Statement has been formulated by the Auditing and Assurance Standards Board (AUASB), in consultation with the Australian Prudential Regulation Authority (APRA), to provide guidance to the appointed auditor of an Authorised Deposit-taking Institution (ADI), reporting in accordance with the prudential reporting requirements specified by APRA in its ADI Prudential Standard APS 310 *Audit and Related Matters* (APS 310).

This Guidance Statement is to be read in conjunction with, and is not a substitute for referring to, the requirements contained in:

(a) APS 310 and other applicable APRA Prudential Requirements, including the *Banking Act 1959* (Banking Act), the *Financial Sector (Collection of Data) Act 2001* (FSCODA), and APRA Prudential and Reporting Standards;

(b) applicable AUASB Standards; and

(c) relevant ethical and professional standards.

This Guidance Statement does not extend the responsibilities of an appointed auditor of an ADI beyond those which are imposed by the Banking Act, the FSCODA, APRA Prudential and Reporting Standards, AUASB Standards and other applicable legislation.

GS

It is not the intention of this Guidance Statement to provide step-by-step guidance in relation to the conduct of a prudential reporting engagement and it is not to be used as a checklist of all issues to be considered by the appointed auditor.

It is not intended that this Guidance Statement limits or replaces the appointed auditor's professional judgement and initiative, or limits the application of relevant AUASB Standards. AUASB Standards contain the basic principles and essential procedures to be applied by the auditor when performing reasonable assurance (audit) and limited assurance (review) engagements. Audit and review programs for each engagement are to be designed to meet the requirements of the particular situation, giving careful consideration to the size and type of ADI and the adequacy of its internal controls.

Authority Statement

The Auditing and Assurance Standards Board (AUASB) formulates Guidance Statement GS 012 *Prudential Reporting Requirements for Auditors of Authorised Deposit-taking Institutions* pursuant to section 227B of the *Australian Securities and Investments Commission Act 2001*, for the purposes of providing guidance on procedural auditing and assurance matters.

This Guidance Statement provides guidance to assist the auditor to fulfil the objectives of the audit or assurance engagement. It includes explanatory details and suggested procedures on specific matters for the purposes of understanding and complying with *AUASB Standards*. The auditor exercises professional judgement when using this Guidance Statement.

The Guidance Statement does not prescribe or create new mandatory requirements.

Dated 24 June 2009

M H Kelsall
Chairman - AUASB

Guidance Statement GS 012

Prudential Reporting Requirements for Auditors of Authorised Deposit-taking Institutions

Application

1 This Guidance Statement has been formulated by the Auditing and Assurance Standards Board (AUASB), in consultation with the Australian Prudential Regulation Authority (APRA), to provide guidance to the appointed auditor[1] of an Authorised Deposit-taking Institution (ADI)[1], reporting in accordance with the prudential reporting requirements specified by APRA in its ADI Prudential Standard APS 310 *Audit and Related Matters* (January 2009) (APS 310).

2 The table in Appendix 1 to this Guidance Statement, entitled *Reporting Requirements for Appointed Auditors*, outlines relevant reporting requirements applicable to the appointed auditor of an ADI reporting pursuant to APS 310.

3 Reference, in this Guidance Statement, to an ADI will be taken, in the case of a:

(a) 'locally incorporated ADI', as a reference to:

(i) an ADI on a Level 1 basis; and

(ii) a group of which an ADI is a member on a Level 2 basis; or

(b) 'foreign ADI'[1], as a reference to the foreign ADI's Australian operations as if they were a stand-alone ADI.

Level 1 and Level 2, as applied in this Guidance Statement, have the meaning given in ADI Prudential Standard APS 110 *Capital Adequacy* (APS 110) and APS 310.

1 The terms 'appointed auditor', 'ADI', 'foreign ADI' and authorised NOHC are defined in paragraph 34 of this Guidance Statement.

Issuance Date

4 This Guidance Statement is issued in June 2009 by the AUASB and replaces AGS 1008 *Audit Implications of Prudential Reporting Requirements for Authorised Deposit-taking Institutions* (ADIs), issued in July 2002.

5 This Guidance Statement is effective for assurance engagements undertaken in relation to reporting periods commencing on or after 1 January 2009.

Introduction

Prudential Supervision of ADIs

6 Under the *Banking Act 1959* (Banking Act), APRA is responsible for the prudential supervision and monitoring of prudential matters relating to ADIs, authorised non-operating holding companies (authorised NOHCs),[1] and groups of bodies corporate which are their subsidiaries, in order to protect the interests of depositors of the ADIs and to promote financial system stability in Australia.

7 APRA formulates, promulgates and enforces prudential policy and practice through ADI Prudential Standards (APSs). In addition, APRA may also issue non-enforceable ADI Prudential Practice Guides (APGs) and other guidelines, to assist ADIs in complying with the requirements in its Prudential Standards and, more generally, to outline prudent practices in relation to certain elements of an ADI's operations.[2]

8 An ADI is required to appoint an auditor (the appointed auditor) for the purposes of APS 310. The appointed auditor of an ADI has an important role to play in the prudential supervision process. Requirements for appointed auditors of ADIs to provide reports on prudential matters to APRA are intended to assist APRA in assessing the reliability of information supplied to it by an ADI.

9 The use by ADIs and APRA of assurance reports prepared by appointed auditors needs to be evaluated in the context of the inherent limitations of an audit or review and the subject matter of the audit or review (refer paragraphs 183-188 of this Guidance Statement).

10 APS 310 warns that all persons involved in the provision of information (which includes the appointed auditor) are to note that it is an offence under subsection 137.1 and 137.2 of the *Criminal Code 1995* to provide, whether directly or indirectly, false and misleading information to a Commonwealth entity (such as APRA).

Responsibilities of the Appointed Auditor

11 The responsibilities and reporting requirements of the appointed auditor of an ADI are contained in:

(a) applicable AUASB Standards;

(b) APS 310;

(c) other applicable APRA Prudential Requirements[3], including the Banking Act, the *Financial Sector (Collection of Data) Act 2001* (FSCODA), and APRA Prudential and Reporting Standards; and

(d) relevant ethical and professional standards.

12 APRA places reliance on accounting and auditing standards to the extent that they do not conflict with Prudential Requirements applicable to the ADI. APS 310 requires the appointed auditor, in meeting their role and responsibilities, to comply with the Auditing Standards and Guidance Statements issued by the AUASB, except where:

(a) they are inconsistent with the requirements of APS 310, in which case APS 310 prevails; or

(b) APRA otherwise specifies, in writing, to the ADI that alternative standards and guidance are to be used by the appointed auditor.

GS

1 The terms 'appointed auditor', 'ADI', 'foreign ADI' and authorised NOHC are defined in paragraph 34 of this Guidance Statement.

2 Access to APRA Prudential Standards, Prudential Practice Guides and legislation relevant to ADIs is available on APRA's website (www.apra.gov.au).

3 See paragraph 34(i) of this Guidance Statement.

13 The following AUASB Standards are applicable to the engagement:

(a) Auditing Standards (ASAs) - where reasonable assurance on financial information is required; and

(b) Standard on Assurance Engagements ASAE 3000 *Assurance Engagements Other than Audits or Reviews of Historical Financial Information* – where limited assurance is required in relation to information other than historical financial information and in relation to internal controls.

ASAE 3000 has been written for general application to assurance engagements other than audits or reviews of historical financial information covered by ASAs or Standards on Review Engagements (ASREs). Where topic specific ASAEs exist, for example ASAE 3100 *Compliance Engagements*, the appointed auditor applies the relevant topic-specific ASAEs, as well as ASAE 3000.

(For an outline of the relevant AUASB Standards applicable to each part of the prudential assurance engagement, refer to Appendix 1 to this Guidance Statement.)

14 The appointed auditor accepts the prudential reporting engagement only when the auditor is satisfied that they, and the engagement team if applicable, have met the relevant ethical requirements relating to the assurance engagement.

15 The concept of independence is important to the appointed auditor's compliance with the fundamental ethical principles of integrity and objectivity. The appointed auditor is required to meet the independence requirements set out in:

(a) APRA's ADI Prudential Standard APS 510 *Governance* (APS 510); and

(b) the Accounting Professional and Ethical Standards Board's (APESB's) APES 110 *Code of Ethics for Professional Accountants* (APES 110).

16 It is important that the appointed auditor of an ADI recognises the additional responsibilities under sections 16B, 16BA and 16C of the Banking Act, imposed on any auditor of an ADI, an authorised NOHC, or their subsidiaries, to provide information to APRA upon request, or where the auditor possesses reportable information specified in that Act, or where the auditor considers that the provision of information would assist APRA in performing its functions under the Banking Act or the FSCODA (see paragraphs 206-219 of this Guidance Statement).

17 Under section 70B of the Banking Act, where any conflict between provisions applied to ADIs pursuant to the Banking Act *vis a vis* provisions applied to ADIs pursuant to the *Corporations Act 2001* (Corporations Act) exist, the Banking Act provisions take precedence over the Corporations Act provisions. Therefore, any provisions made under the Banking Act governing auditor reporting to APRA (refer paragraphs 206-219 of this Guidance Statement) will override any conflicting Corporations Act provisions which may apply to such reporting.

Tripartite Relationship

18 Under normal circumstances, APRA does not consult directly with an appointed auditor of an ADI on matters concerning an individual ADI. APRA liaison with an appointed auditor of an ADI is conducted normally under tripartite arrangements involving APRA, the ADI and its appointed auditor(s) (see APS 310).

19 Any one of the parties involved in the tripartite relationship may initiate meetings or discussions at any time, when considered necessary. In the normal course, regular tripartite meetings are held to discuss the appointed auditor's annual prudential assurance report, prepared pursuant to APS 310.

20 Where an ADI is part of a Level 2 group, APRA may meet with the ADI, the head ADI of the Level 2 group and the appointed auditor at the same time, or separately, on a Level 1 and Level 2 basis, as APRA deems appropriate (see APS 310).

21 Notwithstanding the tripartite relationship, APRA and the appointed auditor may meet, at any time, on a bilateral basis at the request of either party. APRA may communicate with an auditor of an ADI on a bilateral basis to obtain or discuss information for whatever reason(s) it considers appropriate.

22 Under APS 510 an ADI is required to ensure that its internal policy and contractual arrangements do not explicitly or implicitly restrict or discourage auditors (or other parties) from communicating with APRA.

Implementation of the Basel II Framework[4] in Australia

23 APRA's new suite of Prudential Standards became effective on 1 January 2008 and implemented the Basel II Framework in Australia.

24 The Basel II Framework is applicable to all ADIs in Australia. The Framework provides for two broad approaches to the measurement of an ADI's regulatory capital, namely:

(a) relatively simple methodologies ('standardised approaches'); and

(b) more complex approaches that rely on an ADI's own quantitative estimates ('advanced approaches').

25 The majority of ADIs in Australia have adopted the standardised approaches under Basel II to determine their regulatory capital (Standardised ADIs). For these ADIs, changes to risk management and reporting systems were minimal upon transitioning to Basel II.

26 ADIs choosing to adopt the advanced approaches under Basel II (Advanced ADIs), require prior approval from APRA (APRA accreditation). Under the advanced approaches for measuring capital adequacy, an ADI is permitted to use its own quantitative risk estimates in calculating regulatory capital. This involves a greater use of internal modelling and other forms of statistical analysis, as well as qualitative assessment.

27 Due to the changes arising from the introduction of Basel II in Australia, APRA introduced new reporting requirements for ADIs on a Level 1 and Level 2 basis from 1 January 2008.

28 For Standardised ADIs, the reporting requirements are similar to the previous capital reporting requirements, with new additional reporting requirements in areas such as operational risk, securitisation and amendments to risk weighted assets for investment ratings and loan quality. For Advanced ADIs, the majority of the reporting requirements relating to capital are new.

29 The reissued APS 310 takes into account the introduction of Basel II as well as other changes to the Banking Act, the FSCODA and other Prudential Requirements which have occurred since APS 310 was last updated in 2000.

Scope of APS 310 Prudential Reporting Engagements

30 APS 310 provides for two types of engagements to be conducted by the appointed auditor of an ADI, namely:

(a) annual prudential reporting engagements (routine reporting) (see paragraphs 38-205); and

(b) special purpose engagements (see paragraphs 220-230)

31 APRA Prudential Standards[5] may include further requirements for 'independent'[6] audit or review engagements to be undertaken in relation to specific aspects of an ADI's risk management framework and risk data inputs used by an ADI in the calculation of its regulatory capital (refer paragraph 150). The appointed auditor of an ADI may be engaged to undertake engagements of this type.

These requirements for 'independent' audit or review engagements are additional, and separate, to the APS 310 prudential reporting requirements, and fall outside the scope of this Guidance Statement.

GS

4 The Basel II Framework is the commonly used description for a document entitled *International Convergence of Capital Measurement and Capital Standards, a Revised Framework*. Background information on the Basel II Framework, and its implementation in Australia, is available on APRA's website at www.apra.gov.au.

5 For example: APS 112 *Capital Adequacy: Standardised Approach to Credit Risk*; APS 113 *Capital Adequacy: Internal Ratings-based Approach to Credit Risk*; APS 115 *Capital Adequacy: Advanced Measurement Approaches to Operational Risk*; and APS 116 *Capital Adequacy: Market Risk*.

6 To be undertaken by a party or parties who are independent within the meaning of the relevant APRA Prudential Standards.

32 The audit [and review] of financial reports required under the Corporations Act (where required) is directed towards obtaining sufficient appropriate evidence to form an opinion or conclusion on whether the financial report is presented fairly in accordance with the required financial reporting framework. The financial report audit [and review] is not designed to enable the appointed auditor to conclude in relation to the matters specified in APS 310.

33 The APS 310 prudential reporting requirements, imposed on the appointed auditor via the terms of engagement with an ADI, are in addition to the audit [and review] of financial reports required under the Corporations Act.

Definitions

34 For the purpose of this Guidance Statement, the following terms have the meanings attributed below:

(a) 'ADI Reporting Form' (or Data Collection Form), means a form used for the collection and reporting of information in relation to an ADI, as required to be provided to APRA by an ADI in accordance with APRA Reporting Standards made under the FSCODA.

'Specified ADI Reporting Forms', means ADI Reporting Forms listed in APRA Prudential Standard APS 310 *Attachment A – Data Collections subject to reasonable and/or limited assurance*. Also refer to paragraphs 109-113 of this Guidance Statement.

(b) 'Accounting records' is defined in the AUASB Glossary as including "the records of initial entries and supporting records, such as cheques and records of electronic fund transfers, invoices, contracts, the general and subsidiary ledgers, journal entries and other adjustments to the financial report that are not reflected in formal journal entries, and records such as work sheets and spreadsheets supporting cost allocations, computations, reconciliations and disclosures."

For guidance on the application of the definition of 'accounting records' to the audit and/or review of ADI Reporting Forms, refer to paragraphs 99-108.

(c) 'Advanced ADI', means an ADI that has APRA's approval to use the advanced measurement approaches, available under APRA Prudential Standards, for capital adequacy purposes.

(d) 'Appointed auditor', means an independent auditor(s) appointed by an ADI to meet the prudential reporting requirements under APS 310. APS 310 allows for separate auditors to be appointed to meet the APS 310 reporting requirements on a Level 1 and Level 2 basis, and to undertake the different types of engagements provided for in APS 310. APRA may also require, by notice in writing, that an ADI appoint another auditor, in addition to any auditor already appointed by the ADI, for the purposes of APS 310.

Therefore, under APS 310, it is possible for an ADI to have more than one appointed auditor at any time, and for an APS 310 appointed auditor to be different from the auditor responsible for undertaking the financial report audit [and review] under the Corporations Act.

Where the Banking Act refers to 'the auditor' of an ADI, this can be an 'appointed auditor' (under APS 310) or another auditor, such as the auditor responsible for the audit [and review] of financial reports required under the Corporations Act (see paragraphs 206-219).

(e) 'Authorised Deposit-taking Institution (ADI)' is defined, under the Banking Act, as a body corporate in relation to which an authority to carry on banking business in Australia under subsection 9(3) of the Banking Act is in force.

ADIs include, but are not limited to: Australian owned banks, foreign subsidiary banks, branches of foreign banks, building societies, credit unions, providers of purchased payment facilities, and specialist credit card institutions.

(f) 'Authorised non-operating holding company (authorised NOHC)' is defined under section 5 of the Banking Act.

(g) 'Foreign ADI' is defined under section 5 of the Banking Act (also refer to paragraph 177 of this Guidance Statement).

(h) 'Limited assurance', means a level of assurance that is less than that provided in an audit. The objective of a limited assurance engagement is a reduction in assurance engagement risk to a level that is acceptable in the circumstances of the assurance engagement, but where that risk is greater than for a reasonable assurance engagement, as the basis for a negative form of expression of the appointed auditor's conclusion. A limited assurance engagement is commonly referred to as a review.

(i) 'Prudential Requirements[7], is defined in APS 310 and includes requirements imposed by:

- (i) the Banking Act;
- (ii) Regulations (made under the Banking Act);
- (iii) APRA Prudential Standards (made under the Banking Act);
- (iv) the FSCODA;
- (v) APRA Reporting Standards (made under the FSCODA);
- (vi) APRA conditions on the ADI's authorisation; and
- (vii) any other requirements imposed by APRA, in writing, in relation to an ADI.

(j) 'Reasonable assurance', means a high, but not absolute, level of assurance. The objective of a reasonable assurance engagement is a reduction in assurance engagement risk to an acceptably low level in the circumstances of the assurance engagement as the basis for a positive form of expression of the appointed auditor's conclusion. A reasonable assurance engagement is commonly referred to as an audit.

(k) 'Routine reporting', refers to the appointed auditor's responsibility under APS 310 to report to APRA and the ADI, on an annual basis, in relation to the matters identified in paragraph 38 of this Guidance Statement.

(l) 'Standardised ADI', means an ADI that uses the standardised measurement approaches, available under APRA Prudential Standards, for capital adequacy purposes in respect of the whole of its operations.

Responsibilities of the ADI

35 It is the responsibility of an ADI's Board and management to ensure that the ADI meets prudential and statutory requirements and has management practices to limit risks to prudent levels (refer to APS 310 and APS 510).

36 APS 310 requires an ADI to appoint an auditor(s) to meet the prudential reporting requirements under APS 310. APS 310 sets out the eligibility criteria for the appointment of an auditor as well as the permitted use of group auditors under APS 310.[8]

37 The ADI is required to ensure that its appointed auditor(s):

- has access to all data, information, reports and staff of the ADI, which the appointed auditor reasonably believes is necessary to fulfil its role and responsibilities under APS 310. This includes, access to the ADI's Board, Board Audit Committee and internal auditors, as required;
- is kept fully informed of all APRA Prudential Requirements applicable to the ADI; and
- is provided with any other information that APRA has provided to the ADI that may assist the appointed auditor in fulfilling its role and responsibilities under APS 310.

GS

7 These requirements may differ between locally incorporated and foreign ADIs.

8 See APS 310, paragraphs 15-16.

Role and Responsibilities of the Appointed Auditor (Routine Reporting)

38 APS 310 requires the appointed auditor of an ADI to report simultaneously to APRA and the ADI's Board (or Board Audit Committee)[9] , within three[10] months of the end of the financial year of the ADI, in relation to the following matters[11]:

(a) *Assurance on Specified[12] ADI Reporting Forms at the financial year-end:*

(i) Reporting Forms with Data Sourced from Accounting Records

The appointed auditor is required to provide reasonable assurance that the information included in the specified ADI Reporting Forms at the financial year-end, sourced from the ADI's accounting records, is, in all material respects, reliable and in accordance with the relevant APRA Prudential and Reporting Standards;

(ii) Reporting Forms with Data Sourced from Non-Accounting Records

Unless otherwise indicated, in writing, by APRA, the appointed auditor is required to provide limited assurance that the information, included in the specified ADI Reporting Forms at the financial year-end, sourced from non-accounting records, is, in all material respects, reliable and in accordance with the relevant APRA Prudential and Reporting Standards;

(iii) Reporting Forms with Data Sourced from a Combination of Accounting and Non-Accounting Records

Unless otherwise indicated, in writing, by APRA, the appointed auditor is required to provide reasonable assurance on information sourced from accounting records, and limited assurance that information sourced from non-accounting records, at the financial year-end, is, in all material respects, reliable and in accordance with the relevant APRA Prudential and Reporting Standards (also refer to paragraphs 108 and 112).

(b) *Limited Assurance on Internal Controls addressing Compliance with Prudential Requirements and the Reliability of Data included in ADI Reporting Forms*

APS 310 requires the appointed auditor to provide limited assurance that, in all material respects:

(i) the ADI has implemented internal controls that are designed to ensure the ADI has:

a. complied with all applicable Prudential Requirements; and

b. provided reliable data to APRA in the ADI Reporting Forms prepared under the FSCODA; and

(ii) the controls in paragraph 38(b)(i) have operated effectively throughout the financial year.

(c) *Limited Assurance on Compliance with Prudential Requirements*

APS 310 requires the appointed auditor to provide limited assurance, based on the appointed auditor's work under (a) and (b) above, that the ADI has complied, in all material respects, with all relevant Prudential Requirements under the Banking Act and the FSCODA, including compliance with APRA Prudential and Reporting Standards, during the financial year.

9 Or, for a foreign ADI, a senior officer outside Australia to whom authority has been delegated in accordance with APS 510, for overseeing the Australian operations.

10 For a non-disclosing ADI the relevant period is four months.

11 Subject to paragraph 40 of this Guidance Statement.

12 For a listing of ADI Reporting Forms to be subjected to audit and/or review, refer to APRA Prudential Standard APS 310 *Attachment A – Data Collections subject to reasonable and/or limited assurance.* The requirements are different for Standardised, Advanced and Foreign ADIs.

39 Under APS 310, it is the responsibility of the appointed auditor, as provided for in the required terms of engagement by an ADI, to submit directly to APRA:

(a) all reports required to be prepared in accordance with the terms of engagement with the ADI under APS 310; and

(b) all assessments and other material associated with these reports, if requested by APRA.

40 Ordinarily, matters reported to APRA under paragraph 39 are also reported to the ADI to which the matter relates. However, APS 310 specifically prohibits the appointed auditor from notifying the ADI of, or from providing the ADI with, the documents referred to in paragraph 39, where:

(a) the appointed auditor considers that by doing so the interests of depositors of the ADI would be jeopardised; or

(b) there is a situation of mistrust between the appointed auditor and the Board or senior management of the ADI.

41 In accordance with APS 310, an appointed auditor, whether as part of routine or special purpose engagements, must not place sole reliance on the work performed by APRA.

42 The appointed auditor of an ADI is required to attend all meetings with APRA related to APS 310, whether on a bilateral, tripartite or other basis, unless APRA indicates otherwise in writing.

Agreeing the Terms of the Annual Prudential Reporting Engagement (Routine Reporting)

43 The requirement to report pursuant to APRA's annual prudential reporting requirements, is in addition to the audit [and review] of financial reports required under the Corporations Act, and is to be treated by the appointed auditor as a separate audit engagement.

44 The appointed auditor and the ADI agree on the terms of the engagement in accordance with the requirements of Auditing Standard ASA 210 *Terms of Audit Engagements* and ASAE 3000. These arrangements have to be legally binding and include the required terms of engagement specified in APS 310.

45 An engagement letter (or other suitable form) confirms both the client's and the appointed auditor's understanding of the terms of the engagement, helping to avoid misunderstanding, and the appointed auditor's acceptance of the appointment. Both parties sign the engagement letter to acknowledge that it is a legally binding contract.

46 For recurring engagements, the appointed auditor considers whether circumstances require the terms of the engagement to be revised and whether there is a need to re-confirm in writing the existing terms of the engagement. While the appointed auditor may decide not to re-confirm the terms of engagement each year, factors that may make it appropriate to do so include a recent change of senior management or those charged with governance, or any indication that the ADI misunderstands the objectives and scope of the APS 310 prudential reporting engagements.

47 Ordinarily, matters that are contained in the engagement letter include the following:

- The objectives and scope of the annual prudential reporting engagement pursuant to APS 310.
- The responsibilities of management and, where appropriate, those charged with governance, for the subject matter reported on.
- The role and responsibilities of the appointed auditor in accordance with the requirements of APS 310.
- Acknowledgement that the appointed auditor, in meeting its role and responsibilities, will comply with the requirements of applicable AUASB Standards and will consider relevant Guidance Statements issued by the AUASB, except where inconsistent with the requirements of APS 310 or where APRA specifies alternative standards and guidance to be used.

GS

- Identification of the relevant AUASB Standards under which the engagement will be conducted and inclusion of a statement that, although it does not prescribe or create new mandatory requirements, the auditor will consider the guidance contained in this Guidance Statement.
- Agreement by the ADI to provide unrestricted access to whatever records, documentation and other information requested in connection with the prudential reporting engagement.
- Agreement from management and, where appropriate, those charged with governance, to provide written representations.
- Any limitations of the engagement (see paragraphs 183-188).
- The agreed use of the assurance report(s) issued by the appointed auditor, and the extent to which, and the basis on which, the assurance reports may be made available to others (refer paragraphs 72-73).
- The auditor's additional responsibilities to report to APRA under sections 16B, 16BA and 16C of the Banking Act, including reference to Part VIA of the Banking Act which provides for protection in relation to the disclosure of such information (refer paragraphs 206-219).
- Confirmation that the appointed auditor will meet the independence requirements under APS 510 and APES 110.
- The form of reporting and communication in relation to the engagement.

48 The engagement letter explains that any special purpose engagement of any aspect of the ADI's operations, prudential reporting, risk management systems or financial position, will constitute a separate engagement(s) and that the details of such engagement(s) will be the subject of a separate engagement letter(s).

49 The engagement letter furthermore clarifies that, in accordance with APS 310 and APS 510, the appointed auditor is not to be a party to any contractual arrangements, or any understandings with an ADI, that seeks in any way to limit the auditor's ability or willingness to communicate to APRA. APRA may liaise bilaterally with an appointed auditor and may, although not usually, request information directly from the appointed auditor (see paragraph 21 above). The appointed auditor notifies APRA of any attempts by an ADI to achieve such arrangements or understandings.

50 Refer to Appendix 2 of this Guidance Statement for an illustrative example engagement letter to accommodate APRA reporting requirements as per APS 310.

Planning the Annual Prudential Reporting Engagement (Routine Reporting)

51 The nature and extent of planning activities will vary with the engagement circumstances. Specific matters to be considered by the appointed auditor as part of the planning process include:

- The appointed auditor's understanding of the ADI and its environment, including its internal control and compliance framework (see paragraphs 52-58).
- The appointed auditor's previous experience with the ADI.
- The characteristics of the subject matter and the identified assessment criteria (see paragraphs 59-71).
- The intended users of the appointed auditor's assurance report and their needs (see paragraphs 72-73).
- Materiality (see paragraphs 74-90).
- Assurance engagement risk.
- The appropriate assurance strategy to adopt for each part of the engagement and possible sources of evidence.
- Personnel and expertise requirements, including the nature and extent of experts' involvement (see paragraphs 91-94).

- Work performed by another auditor (see paragraph 95).
- The activities of the internal audit function and the effect on audit and review procedures (see paragraphs 96-98).
- The auditor's additional reporting responsibilities under the Banking Act (see paragraphs 206-219).

The Appointed Auditor's Understanding of the ADI and its Environment, including its Internal Control and Compliance Framework

52 The appointed auditor obtains an understanding of the ADI and its environment, including its internal control and compliance framework, and other assurance engagement circumstances, sufficient to:

(a) identify and assess the risks of the subject matter information being materially misstated, that significant deficiencies in internal controls may exist (in relation to the area of activity to be examined), and/or that the ADI may not be complying with applicable Prudential Requirements; and

(b) design and perform further evidence-gathering procedures.

53 The appointed auditor exercises professional judgement to determine the nature and extent of the understanding that is needed. When performing procedures to obtain an understanding of the ADI and its environment, consideration of the following matters may be helpful:

- The size, nature and complexity of the ADI and its activities.
- Any changes in the market environment.
- Whether the ADI is an Advanced or Standardised ADI (see definitions under paragraph 34(c) and (l)).
- Whether the ADI is a foreign ADI (see definition under paragraph 34(g)).
- Governance and management functions within the ADI, including the attitude and awareness of those charged with governance and of management concerning the ADI's compliance with Prudential Requirements, and the respective roles and responsibilities attributed to the finance, risk management, compliance and internal audit functions.
- Relevant aspects of the ADI's risk management framework and systems applicable to the engagement, including the ADI's risk assessment process for identifying risks relevant to prudential reporting objectives and deciding on actions to address those risks through its risk management systems.
- The ADI's internal control relevant to the assurance engagement.
- The ADI's compliance framework, processes and controls (refer to ASAE 3100).
- The significance and complexity of the ADI's information technology environment and systems.
- Any (formal) communications between APRA and the ADI, and the results of any supervisory visits conducted by APRA in relation to the engagement. Refer also to paragraph 92 of this Guidance Statement.
- Recent reports prepared by other auditors appointed to report on any aspect of the ADI.
- Work performed by the internal audit and compliance functions, and any reliance that may be placed on this work.
- Discussions with ADI staff responsible for monitoring regulatory compliance, such as the ADI's Compliance Officer.

The ADI's Internal Control Relevant to the Assurance Engagement

54 The appointed auditor obtains an understanding of internal control relevant to the assurance engagement.

GS

55 Internal control is the process designed and effected by those charged with governance, management, and other personnel of an ADI, to provide reasonable assurance about the achievement of the ADI's objectives. Prudential Requirements generally require ADIs to have in place internal controls corresponding to their size and complexity aimed at ensuring that:

(a) risks are managed within prudent limits set by senior management and those charged with governance;

(b) information provided to management and those charged with governance is adequate and timely; and

(c) the ADI complies with applicable prudential and statutory requirements.

56 The term 'internal control', as used in this Guidance Statement, encompasses the following components:

(a) the control environment;
(b) the ADI's risk assessment process;
(c) the information system, including the related business processes, relevant to financial and prudential reporting, and communication;
(d) control activities; and
(e) monitoring of controls.

57 The way in which internal control is designed and implemented varies with an ADI's size and complexity. Specifically, smaller Standardised ADIs may use less formal means and simpler processes and procedures to achieve the objectives in paragraph 55.

58 In addition to the general planning considerations, the appointed auditor takes into consideration the following factors when planning the review of the ADI's internal controls relevant to the assurance engagement:

- The size, nature and complexity of the ADI under review, and specifically whether or not it is an Advanced ADI, as this will influence the degree of complexity impacting the ADI's control environment, compliance framework and control policies and processes.
- The overall compliance framework adopted by the ADI to ensure compliance with all applicable Prudential Requirements, including its controls, policies and processes, and consideration of whether or not these are appropriate given the size, nature and complexity of the ADI.
- The sufficiency and appropriateness of the ADI's Risk Management Systems descriptions and similar policy documents issued in accordance with specific Prudential Standards, and consideration of whether these are up to date and in sufficient detail to facilitate compliance with the relevant Prudential Standards.
- Matters relating to the ADI's organisational structure and operating characteristics, and recent significant changes thereof, which could impact on the ADI's internal controls.
- Knowledge of the ADIs internal controls obtained during other assurance engagements conducted in relation to the ADI.
- The method adopted, and the process used, by the ADI to develop risk information to be disclosed in ADI Reporting Forms.
- Previously communicated instances of material non-compliance with Prudential Requirements and/or material deficiencies in internal controls designed to ensure compliance with all applicable Prudential Requirements and the provision of reliable data to APRA in Reporting Forms, that have not been resolved by the ADI.

The above is not meant to represent an exhaustive list and there may be other factors relevant to the specific circumstances of an ADI.

The Characteristics of the Subject Matter and the Identified Assessment Criteria

59 The table in Appendix 1 of this Guidance Statement outlines the relevant APS 310 reporting requirements applicable to each part of the assurance engagement.

60 The level of assurance required to be provided by the appointed auditor for Parts A and B of the engagement (see Appendix 1), is determined by the source of the data included in each specified ADI Reporting Form. A reasonable level of assurance (audit) is required for data sourced from 'accounting records'. A limited level of assurance (review) is required for all other data. The AUASB's definition of 'accounting records' (refer paragraph 34(b) of this Guidance Statement) therefore needs to be applied with care. Paragraphs 99-108 below, provide guidance on the application of this definition.

61 The appointed auditor identifies the most recent year-end ADI Reporting Forms submitted to APRA for audit and/or review. Further guidance is provided in paragraphs 109-113 below.

62 The appointed auditor is to note that, in relation to ADI Reporting Forms prepared under the FSCODA, there are additional Reporting Forms, beyond the specific Reporting Forms listed in Attachment A to APS 310 (which is the subject matter for Parts A and B). These additional Reporting Forms are to be included in the scope of Part C of the assurance engagement (see Appendix 1), together with the Reporting Forms identified in Attachment A to APS 310.

63 The appointed auditor identifies, and obtains an understanding of, all the Prudential Requirements (refer to definition under paragraph 34(i)) applicable to the specific ADI (including any additional guidance provided by APRA to the ADI), with particular attention to changes in these requirements during the reporting period. The auditor makes enquiries with respect to any requirements that are imposed in writing by APRA on a bilateral APRA-ADI basis, or in relation to conditions on the ADI's authorisation, as these requirements may vary from one ADI to another.

64 Compliance with Prudential Requirements (see paragraphs 38(b) and 38(c) of this Guidance Statement) is broader than compliance with only the quantitative limits in APRA Prudential Standards (for example, capital requirements). The appointed auditor is required to provide assurance in relation to compliance with *all* relevant/applicable Prudential Requirements under the Banking Act and the FSCODA, including compliance with APRA Prudential and Reporting Standards.

The scope of the prudential assurance engagement therefore includes compliance with APRA Prudential Standards dealing with, for example, governance, risk management systems, business continuity management and outsourcing and the APS 310 requirements relating to the appointment of the auditor and the use of group auditors.

65 In relation to an ADI's responsibility to keep the appointed auditor informed of all APRA Prudential Requirements applicable to the ADI, the appointed auditor obtains written representations from those responsible (see paragraphs 174-176).

Concept of "Reliability"

66 Under the Australian Accounting Standards Board's *Framework for the Preparation and Presentation of Financial Statements*, information has the quality of reliability *"... when it is free from material error and bias and can be depended upon by users to represent faithfully that which it either purports to represent or could reasonably be expected to represent"*.

67 In applying this concept of reliability to the prudential reporting engagement, information in ADI Reporting Forms is not to lead users to conclusions that serve the particular needs of an ADI. Furthermore, such information needs to be capable of reliable measurement.

68 The concept of reliability is to be viewed in the context of the reliability of the data for the intended use by the identified users (see paragraphs 72-73 below). Materiality is to be applied as outlined in paragraphs 74-90 below.

69 APRA Prudential and Reporting Standards provide the frame of reference (benchmarks) for reasonably consistent evaluation or measurement, within the context of the appointed

GS

auditor's professional judgement, of the reliability of the information included in ADI Reporting Forms.

70 The appointed auditor identifies and obtains an understanding of the applicable Prudential Requirements that govern the preparation of data within ADI Reporting Forms, with particular attention to changes in these requirements during the reporting period under review. In addition to the Prudential and Reporting Standards issued by APRA, other Prudential Requirements, including the specific ADI Reporting Form Instruction Guides, will also have an impact on the provision of reliable data to APRA under the FSCODA and, therefore, the appointed auditor has regard to all relevant Prudential Requirements when planning and conducting the engagement.

71 It is important that the appointed auditor obtains an understanding of how APRA Prudential Standards and APRA Reporting Standards differ from the financial reporting framework (Australian Accounting Standards) which are used to record data in the ADI's accounting records.

The Intended Users of the Appointed Auditor's Assurance Report and Their Needs

72 Data collected in ADI Reporting Forms are primarily used by APRA and the Reserve Bank of Australia for the purpose of prudential regulation and supervision of individual ADIs, overall supervision of the stability of the financial system and for setting monetary policy. It may also be used by the Australian Bureau of Statistics to construct a range of important statistical macro-economic indicia. Requirements for appointed auditors of ADIs to provide assurance reports on prudential matters to APRA are intended to assist APRA in assessing the reliability of information supplied to it by an ADI.

73 APRA has the power under subsection 56(5) of the *Australian Prudential Regulation Authority Act 1998* to make 'protected information' (which may include auditors' reports or information extracted from such reports) available to another financial sector supervisory agency (for example, the Reserve Bank of Australia and Treasury), or any other 'specified' agency (including foreign agencies), when APRA is satisfied such information will assist those agencies in performing its functions or exercising its powers.

Materiality

74 The appointed auditor considers materiality when:

(a) determining the nature, timing and extent of audit and review procedures;

(b) evaluating the effect of uncorrected misstatements identified in ADI Reporting Forms;

(c) evaluating the effect of identified deficiencies in internal controls designed to ensure:

(i) compliance with Prudential Requirements; and

(ii) reliable data is provided in the ADI Reporting Forms; and

(d) assessing the significance of identified instances of non-compliance with relevant Prudential Requirements.

75 Determining materiality involves the exercise of professional judgement. Judgements about materiality are made in light of relevant circumstances, and are affected by quantitative and qualitative factors as well as consideration of the potential of misstatements, control deficiencies and/or instances of non compliance that are individually immaterial but in the aggregate may be of concern.

76 Since the concept of materiality applies differently in the context of an audit or review of financial and other information, a review of internal controls, and for the purpose of reporting on an ADI's compliance with Prudential Requirements, it is considered separately below.

77 Although there is a greater risk that misstatements, control deficiencies or instances of non-compliance may not be detected in a review than in an audit, the judgement as to what is material is made by reference to the subject matter on which the appointed auditor is

reporting and the needs of those relying on that information, not to the level of assurance provided.

Audit and/or Review of Specified[13] ADI Reporting Forms

78 The principles of assessing materiality for the purpose of an audit and/or review of ADI Reporting Forms will generally be similar to that applying to the audit or review of a financial report.

79 For the purposes of the audit and/or review of specified ADI Reporting Forms, the appointed auditor considers materiality, as appropriate, under Auditing Standard ASA 320 *Materiality and Audit Adjustments* (for financial information) and/or ASAE 3000 (for information other than historical financial information). In the absence of specific requirements issued by APRA, the Australian Accounting Standards Board's Accounting Standard AASB 1031 *Materiality* may provide a useful frame of reference to the appointed auditor in determining materiality for the engagement.

80 A misstatement in the specified ADI Reporting Forms, either individually or in aggregate with other misstatements, is considered material if the appointed auditor believes the intended users (refer paragraphs 72-73) may be influenced by the misstatement of the information.

81 ASA 320 and AASB 1031 deal with materiality in the context of the financial statements taken as a whole. For the purpose of reporting on the reliability of information included in specified ADI Reporting Forms, the appointed auditor considers and applies materiality at the level of individual Reporting forms, or data items, as appropriate.

82 In applying ASA 320 and ASAE 3000, as appropriate, to individual Reporting Forms, the appointed auditor has regard to the nature, purpose and use of the information included in each Reporting Form. The collection and analysis of data in specified Reporting Forms is a critical component of APRA's supervisory function. Information provided to APRA in ADI Reporting Forms are used to construct institutional risk profiles that are used in conjunction with other information to monitor individual ADIs, identify industry trends, and establish benchmarks and trigger points for prudential and financial ratios. This analysis assists APRA in prioritising its supervisory activities. APRA data collections are also used by the Reserve Bank of Australia and the Bureau of Statistics. The appointed auditor refers to ADI Reporting Forms and Instructions, and associated Prudential and Reporting Standards, for information regarding the nature and purpose of each individual ADI Reporting Form.

83 The appointed auditor's preliminary assessment of materiality is based largely on quantitative factors. A percentage is often applied to a chosen benchmark as a starting point in determining materiality. The base and percentage may vary depending upon the ADI Reporting Form in question.

84 A key concern with any misstatement within ADI Reporting Forms is its potential impact on the ADIs 'capital base' and 'capital adequacy ratio', that are determined in accordance with APRA's prudential standards[14]. This is taken into consideration by the appointed auditor when evaluating whether a misstatement in the ADI Reporting Forms, especially within the *Capital Adequacy* ADI Reporting Forms, is material.

85 APRA has advised the AUASB that a materiality threshold of 25 basis points of *Risk Weighted Assets* (determined in accordance with APS 110) may be applied in aggregate by the appointed auditor as a reasonable basis for determining quantitative materiality for the purpose of the audit and/or review of *Capital Adequacy* ADI Reporting Forms. This threshold may be used as indicative guidance only, in conjunction with the considerations described within this Guidance Statement, which includes consideration of qualitative factors. The appointed auditor exercises professional judgement when applying the threshold in specific circumstances. A lower level of materiality may be appropriate as the level of surplus capital reduces.

13 For a listing of ADI Reporting Forms to be subjected to audit and/or review, refer to APS 310 *Attachment A – Data Collections subject to reasonable and/or limited assurance*. The requirements are different for Standardised, Advanced and Foreign ADIs.

14 Refer to APS 110.

86 The appointed auditor also needs to have regard to alternative bases such as profit, revenue or assets when considering whether a misstatement within ADI Reporting Forms such as the *Statement of Financial Performance, Statement of Financial Position, Provisions and Impaired Assets*, is material.

Review of Internal Controls

87 In accordance with ASAE 3000, when reviewing internal controls, the appointed auditor assesses materiality in the context of the ADI's objectives relevant to the particular area of activity being examined, and whether the internal controls will reduce to an acceptably low level, the risks that threaten achievement of those objectives.

88 In assessing materiality, the appointed auditor has regard to the measures the ADI has adopted to ensure:

(a) reliable data is provided to APRA in all ADI Reporting Forms prepared under the FSCODA; and

(b) compliance with all applicable Prudential Requirements.

89 ASAE 3100 sets out the requirements and provides guidance to the appointed auditor in applying materiality in the context of a compliance engagement.

Reporting on Compliance with Prudential Requirements

90 APS 310 requires the appointed auditor to provide limited assurance that the ADI has complied, in all material respects, with all relevant Prudential Requirements (see paragraph 38(c) of this Guidance Statement). This conclusion is to be based on the appointed auditor's audit and reviews undertaken to provide assurance in relation to specified ADI Reporting Forms (see paragraph 38(a)) and internal controls (see paragraph 38(b)).

The appointed auditor considers materiality when evaluating the significance of identified instances of non-compliance with relevant Prudential Requirements (refer to paragraphs 166-170).

Personnel and Expertise Requirements, Including the Nature and Extent of Experts' Involvement

91 An appointed auditor gives further consideration as to whether the auditor has, or will be able to obtain, adequate knowledge and the required skills to undertake the engagement.

92 APS 310 prohibits an appointed auditor from placing sole reliance on the work performed by APRA (for example, refer to paragraphs 135 and 150 of this Guidance Statement). APRA expects appointed auditors to exercise their professional judgement and reach their own conclusions.

93 The nature and complexity of the ADI increases the likelihood that the appointed auditor may need to involve experts in the engagement. For example, obtaining an understanding of the process and assumptions used by an Advanced ADI to develop risk information, may require technical knowledge of risk measurement methodologies which can be complex.

94 When planning to use an expert, the appointed auditor complies with the requirements of, as appropriate, Auditing Standard ASA 620 *Using the Work of an Expert* and ASAE 3000.

Work Performed by Another Auditor

95 Where the appointed auditor plans to use the work of another independent auditor, the appointed auditor:

- for the audit of financial information, complies with the requirements of Auditing Standard ASA 600 Using the Work of Another Auditor; and
- for other assurance, has regard to the principles of ASA 600.

The Activities of the Internal Audit Function and the Effect on Audit and Review Procedures

96 APS 510 requires all ADIs (including a foreign ADI in relation to its Australian business) and authorised NOHCs, to have in place an independent and adequately resourced internal audit function.[15]

97 APS 310 requires an ADI to ensure that the scope of internal audit includes a review of the policies, processes and controls put in place by management to ensure compliance with Prudential Requirements. Furthermore, APS 510 requires that the objectives of the internal audit function include an evaluation of the adequacy and effectiveness of the financial and risk management framework of the ADI.

98 In considering the activities of the internal audit function and evaluating the effect, if any, on audit and review procedures, the appointed auditor:

- for the audit of financial information, complies with the requirements of Auditing Standard ASA 610 *Considering the Work of Internal Audit*; and
- for other assurance, has regard to the principles of ASA 610.

Matters to Consider in Conducting the Annual Prudential Reporting Engagement (Routine Reporting)

Special Considerations Relating to the Audit and/or Review of Specified[16] ADI Reporting Forms

Application of the AUASB Definition of 'Accounting Records'

99 APS 310 requires the appointed auditor to provide two different levels of assurance over the reliability of a specific set of ADI Reporting Forms at the ADI's financial year-end (refer paragraph 38(a) of this Guidance Statement). The level of assurance required to be provided by the appointed auditor is determined by the source of the data included in the Reporting Forms. Data sourced from 'accounting records', requires a reasonable level of assurance (audit). All other data requires a limited level of assurance (review).

100 'Accounting records', is defined in paragraph 34(b) of this Guidance Statement and, ordinarily, includes all the data used by an ADI to manage its financial affairs and to report the results of its operations and its financial position in its financial report on an annual or half-yearly basis (that is, the underlying evidence in support of the financial report). The expectation is, generally, that such data would be subject to rigorous internal controls.

101 However, the initial books of entry may also comprise other data which is stored alongside accounting data. Such data may not be used for financial management and financial reporting, and may not be subject to rigorous controls, and therefore fall outside the scope of the reasonable assurance opinion.

102 Data in ADI Reporting Forms may be sourced from systems that are not used to produce financial report information and are not readily reconcilable to financial report information (see paragraph 106 below). The initial entries to these systems may be the same as for the accounting records, but both the level of control over the systems and the amount of manipulation/aggregation of the data within such systems may result in the output being significantly different from the accounting records and not readily reconcilable back to these records.

103 The appointed auditor makes an assessment of whether or not a data item has been sourced from accounting records, by exercising professional judgement and referring to the definition of accounting records (see paragraph 34(b)). The appointed auditor carefully considers the source and the use of the data, and whether it is appropriately controlled and, therefore, capable of being subjected to audit.

15 Under APS 510, APRA may approve alternative arrangements where APRA is satisfied that it will achieve the same objectives.

16 For a listing of ADI Reporting Forms to be subjected to audit and/or review, refer to APS 310 *Attachment A – Data Collections subject to reasonable and/or limited assurance*. The requirements are different for Standardised, Advanced and Foreign ADIs.

GS

104 APRA's expectation is that most of the information reported in the ADI Reporting Forms specified in Attachment A to APS 310, fall within the scope of the reasonable assurance opinion (*Part A of the Auditor's Prudential Assurance Report*).

105 Ordinarily, most of the Reporting Forms for Standardised ADIs, and most of the 'non-capital' Reporting Forms for Advanced ADIs, are sourced from an ADI's accounting records and fall within the scope of the reasonable assurance opinion.

106 For Advanced ADIs, where the ADI's risk management systems provide internal estimates for some or all of the risk components in determining capital, the 'capital' Reporting Forms will include data items sourced from non-accounting records. Examples include measures for 'probability of default' and 'loss given default'.

107 Certain data items may have been sourced indirectly from the accounting records, for example, data sourced from accounting records that involve additional examination, computation, re-classification or segmentation. APRA has indicated that these data items are deemed to have been sourced from the accounting records and will fall within the scope of the reasonable assurance opinion.

108 Where ADI Reporting Forms combine elements that are derived from accounting records and non-accounting records (see paragraph 38(a)(iii)), the appointed auditor provides reasonable assurance on information derived from the accounting records (for example, totals derived from the balance sheet such as values for assets, liabilities and derivatives, in the ADI Reporting Forms listed below) and limited assurance on the information derived from non-accounting records, for example:

- *ADI Reporting Form ARF 117.0* - the repricing period allocations to time periods set out in the interest rate sensitivity tables (which are subjective).
- *ADI Reporting Form ARF 112.1A* - the risk rating for loans based on the loan-to-valuation ratio (LVR) where the security values are subject to variation over time.

Also refer to paragraph 112 below.

Identification of Financial Year-end ADI Reporting Forms

109 Identification of the year-end ADI Reporting Forms to be subjected to audit and/or review, requires careful consideration by the appointed auditor.

110 The initial submission of ADI Reporting Forms, to meet APRA's reporting timetable, may be too soon in the ADI's year-end process for the ADI to have processed all relevant year-end journals and adjustments. As a result, the ADI may have submitted revised Reporting Form(s) after the due reporting date. As the audit requirement is to report on the "reliability" of the year-end Reporting Forms, the appointed auditor selects the most up to date (recent) Reporting Forms submitted to APRA for audit or review, rather than the Reporting Forms initially submitted in accordance with APRA's reporting timetable. The appointed auditor conducts further procedures to ensure that the selected Reporting Forms include all relevant year-end journals and adjustments.

111 The ADI Reporting Forms which are the subject of the assurance report, are clearly identified in the assurance report. This may be achieved, for example, by:

(a) attaching the Reporting Forms to the assurance report; or

(b) noting the time and date of submission of the Reporting Forms to APRA in the assurance report.

112 Certain ADI Reporting Forms may include data sourced from a combination of accounting and non-accounting records, as provided for in APS 310, paragraph 38(c) (see paragraphs 38(a)(iii) and 108 of this Guidance Statement). The appointed auditor needs to clearly identify such data so that the intended user of the assurance report understands the level of assurance attached to each data item. This could be achieved in a number of ways, for example:

- Attaching the Reporting Forms to the assurance report and clearly identifying the level of assurance attached to each individual section (or data item) within each Reporting Form.

- Listing the Reporting Form and the individual sections (or data items) for which reasonable and limited assurance have been provided within the body of the assurance report under the sections "Appointed Auditor's Responsibilities" and "Auditor's Opinion and Conclusions".
- Providing a detailed list in an attachment to the assurance report which clearly identifies the Reporting Form and the individual sections (or data items) for which reasonable and limited assurance have been provided.

113 Where the ADI Reporting Form subject to audit and/or review at the financial year-end, is not the ADI Reporting Form submitted on the due date in accordance with APRA's reporting timetable, the appointed auditor needs to consider this issue when providing assurance on the design and operational effectiveness of controls over the reliability of Reporting Forms (refer paragraph 136 below).

Audit of Specified ADI Reporting Forms - Data Sourced from Accounting Records

Audit Objective

114 The appointed auditor is required to provide reasonable assurance that information included in ADI Reporting Forms, as specified in Attachment A of APS 310, at the financial year-end, sourced from the ADI's accounting records, is, in all material respects, reliable and in accordance with the relevant APRA Prudential and Reporting Standards.

Refer *Part A* of the illustrative *Auditor's Annual Prudential Assurance Report in Appendix 4* of this Guidance Statement.

AUASB Standards

115 In order to form an opinion on the reliability of financial information included in specified ADI Reporting Forms at the financial year-end, sourced from the ADI's accounting records, the appointed auditor conducts an audit in accordance with the Australian Auditing Standards.

Gathering Audit Evidence

116 To identify the Reporting Forms, or data items in a Reporting Form, that are to be subjected to audit (the subject matter), the appointed auditor applies the definition of accounting records (refer paragraph 34(b)) to each item of data within each Reporting Form as specified in Attachment A of APS 310.

117 Having identified the ADI Reporting Forms, or data items within a Reporting Form, that are to be subjected to audit, the appointed auditor obtains sufficient appropriate audit evidence as part of a systematic process, that includes:

- Obtaining an understanding of the specified ADI Reporting Forms and individual data items included in these Reporting Forms (subject matter), the intended use of the information included in the Reporting Forms by the intended users, and the Prudential Requirements applicable to the preparation and submission of Reporting Forms.
- Obtaining an understanding of the ADI's system of internal control and the compliance function.
- Evaluating the controls over ADI Reporting Forms.
- Assessing the risk that information in Reporting Forms may be materially misstated.
- Responding to assessed risks and determining the nature, timing and extent of further evidence-gathering procedures.
- Performing further evidence-gathering procedures clearly linked to the identified risks.
- Evaluating the sufficiency and appropriateness of evidence.

118 The appointed auditor exercises professional judgement in determining the nature, timing and extent of audit procedures to gather sufficient appropriate evidence on which to base the audit opinion.

GS

119 A controls based assurance approach is often the most appropriate approach to adopt in these circumstances. However, where the appointed auditor judges that a material weakness exists in the ADI's internal controls designed to ensure reliable data is provided to APRA in the ADI Reporting Forms, and/or where the appointed auditor makes a determination based on effectiveness and/or efficiency, a substantive approach may be more appropriate (for example, for smaller Standardised ADIs).

120 Audit procedures for obtaining audit evidence include, but are not limited to, testing of specific controls aimed at ensuring Reporting Forms are reliable and are prepared in accordance with APRA Prudential Standards and Reporting Standards. Audit procedures may include observation, inspection, confirmation, recalculation, re-performance, analytical procedures, enquiry, obtaining independent corroborating information, testing of controls over the compilation of Reporting Forms, testing of controls over the extraction of data from the underlying accounting records (including all relevant year-end adjustments) and obtaining management representations.

121 The appointed auditor may decide to place reliance on work undertaken by the auditor appointed for the purpose of the audit of the general purpose financial report, required under the Corporations Act (the statutory audit), as the basis for opining on the reliability of the specified ADI Reporting Forms, or data items included in these forms. However, the appointed auditor is still required to obtain additional audit evidence to ensure that the Reporting Forms, or data items in a Reporting Form:

(a) have been appropriately extracted from the underlying accounting records (which were the subject of the statutory audit); and

(b) are in accordance with APRA's Prudential Standards and Reporting Standards (which may be different from the Australian Accounting Standards Framework used to record items in the ADI's underlying accounting and statutory records).

122 Where reliance is being placed on work performed for the statutory audit, the appointed auditor ensures that events occurring subsequent to the date of signing the accounts, but before the date of issuing the Auditor's Annual Prudential Assurance Report, are taken into consideration in forming the opinion issued in the Report.

123 Materiality is to be applied as outlined in paragraphs 74-90 of this Guidance Statement.

Review of Specified ADI Reporting Forms - Data Sourced from Non-Accounting Records

Review Objective

124 The appointed auditor is required to express a conclusion, based on a review, on whether anything has come to the appointed auditor's attention that causes the auditor to believe that information included in ADI Reporting Forms, as specified in Attachment A to APS 310, at the financial year-end, sourced from non-accounting records of the ADI, is not, in all material respects reliable and in accordance with the relevant APRA Prudential and Reporting Standards.

Refer *Part B* of the illustrative *Auditor's Annual Prudential Assurance Report in Appendix 4* of this Guidance Statement.

AUASB Standards

125 In order to form a conclusion on the reliability of information included in specified ADI Reporting Forms at the financial year-end, sourced from non-accounting records, the appointed auditor conducts a review in accordance with ASAE 3000.

Gathering Assurance Evidence

126 All ADI Reporting Forms, or data items within Reporting Forms, as specified in Attachment A of APS 310, that have been excluded under paragraphs 114-123 above as not having been sourced from accounting records, are included in this section as the subject matter for review.

127 Having identified the ADI Reporting Forms, or data items within Reporting Forms, that are to be subjected to review, the appointed auditor obtains evidence, as part of a systematic

process directed by the risk assessment carried out during the planning phase of the engagement.

128 The review is substantially less in scope than the audit undertaken in paragraphs 114-123 in order to provide reasonable assurance under Part A of the Auditor's Annual Prudential Assurance Report. The review procedures do not provide all the evidence required in an audit and, consequently, the level of assurance provided is less than that given in an audit.

129 The appointed auditor exercises professional judgement in determining the specific nature, timing and extent of review procedures to gather evidence on which to base the conclusion.

130 Ordinarily, review procedures include a review of specific controls aimed at ensuring Reporting Forms are reliable and are prepared in accordance with APRA Prudential Standards and Reporting Standards. Review procedures may include analytical procedures, enquiry, limited testing of controls over the compilation of Reporting Forms, limited testing of controls over the extraction of data from the underlying source systems and obtaining management representations.

131 Materiality is to be applied as outlined in paragraphs 74-90 of this Guidance Statement.

Advanced ADIs

132 Under the advanced approaches for measuring capital adequacy, an Advanced ADI is permitted to use its own quantitative risk estimates in calculating regulatory capital. This involves a greater use of internal risk measurement models that generate the credit risk, operational risk, market risk and interest rate risk in the banking book (instead of the standardised risk assessments used by Standardised ADIs). As a result, a smaller proportion of information contained in APRA's capital adequacy Reporting Forms, under the advanced approaches, is derived from accounting records.

133 At the planning stage of the engagement, the appointed auditor decides on the appropriate assurance approach to adopt in order to gather evidence to reduce the assurance engagement risk to an acceptable low level to provide limited assurance in relation to the reliability of Reporting Forms, or data items in a Reporting Form, which are sourced from the internal risk measurement models.

134 A controls based assurance approach is often the most appropriate approach to adopt in these circumstances. The appointed auditor gathers evidence regarding the internal control structure, and that key controls around the risk measurement models, as identified during the planning phase of the audit, are operating effectively to support the assurance conclusion.

135 In concluding on any data produced from the internal risk measurement models, the appointed auditor cannot place sole reliance on the work performed by APRA, as part of the initial accreditation process for becoming an Advanced ADI or in any subsequent reviews undertaken by APRA.

Review of Internal Controls over Compliance with Prudential Requirements and Reliability of ADI Reporting Forms

Review Objective

136 The appointed auditor is required to express a conclusion, based on a review, as to whether anything has come to the attention of the auditor to cause the auditor to believe that, in all material respects:

(a) the ADI has not implemented internal controls that are designed to ensure the ADI has:

(i) complied with all applicable Prudential Requirements; and

(ii) provided reliable data to APRA in the ADI Reporting Forms prepared under the FSCODA; and

(b) the controls in paragraph 136(a) have not operated effectively throughout the financial year.

Refer *Part C* of the illustrative *Auditor's Annual Prudential Assurance Report* in Appendix 4 of this Guidance Statement.

GS

AUASB Standards

137 The appointed auditor conducts the review of internal controls in accordance with ASAE 3000 and other relevant topic specific ASAEs, for example, ASAE 3100.

Gathering Assurance Evidence

138 The evaluation of whether the ADI has implemented internal controls that are designed to achieve the relevant control objectives as set out in paragraph 136 above, is performed in the context of the appointed auditor's general understanding of the ADI and its environment, the ADI's risk management practices, and its internal control and compliance framework, as obtained for the purpose of planning the engagement. This evaluation is based on whether the ADI has implemented internal controls that have been suitably designed to reduce to an acceptably low level, the risks that threaten achievement of the relevant control objectives.

139 The appointed auditor generally adopts a 'top down' approach in gathering evidence, by making enquiries of key personnel, observing the ADI's operations, performing 'walk-through' tests of controls, and inspecting relevant documentation, in order to achieve the following:

- obtaining an understanding of the ADI's overall control environment and compliance framework;
- identifying the internal compliance function(s) designed to ensure compliance with all applicable Prudential Requirements;
- identifying policies, procedures and controls designed to ensure compliance with all applicable Prudential Requirements, by reviewing documents such as the ADI's Risk Management Systems descriptions and similar policy documents issued by the ADI in accordance with applicable Prudential Standards;
- identifying the processes used by the ADI to support the Chief Executive Officer's attestation to APRA over its Risk Management Systems descriptions;
- identifying the internal compliance functions designed to oversee the provision of data to APRA in ADI Reporting Forms;
- identifying significant processes for the preparation of ADI Reporting Forms; and
- identifying the key controls over these significant processes that are designed to ensure that reliable data is provided to APRA in ADI Reporting Forms.

The above is not an exhaustive list, nor is it intended to direct the auditor as to the conclusion over the ADI's internal controls.

140 The way in which internal control is designed and implemented varies with an ADI's size and complexity. Smaller ADIs may use less formal means and simpler processes to achieve their objectives.

141 The appointed auditor gathers evidence in response to assessed risks with a focus on identifying key controls within the control systems design. The appointed auditor exercises professional judgement in determining the specific nature, timing and extent of review procedures to achieve the review objective.

142 Following the evaluation of whether the ADI has internal controls designed to achieve the relevant control objectives, the appointed auditor performs review procedures to obtain evidence about whether these controls have operated as designed throughout the financial year. The auditor may consider how the controls were applied, the consistency with which they were applied, by whom they were applied and the period of time over which the controls were applied.

143 The review of operating effectiveness may include procedures such as:

- enquiry of appropriate ADI personnel (and obtaining written representations);
- observation of the control process;
- ascertaining whether the person(s) performing the control(s) possesses the necessary authority and competence to perform the control(s) effectively;
- review of relevant documentation;

- 'walk-through' tests; and
- limited re-performance of the controls.

144 Interpretation of the word 'reliable' in the context of the review of controls over ADI Reporting Forms has practical limitations in some circumstances. For many ADIs, it is only at the financial year-end (or for ADIs that are disclosing entities, also at the half year-end) that all the necessary accounting adjustments, such as accruals, prepayments, provisioning and valuations, are prepared and subjected to audit or review. APRA is aware of this position and has indicated it accepts ADI Reporting Forms prepared throughout the year based on the ADI's normal accounting process.

145 The appointed auditor enquires whether there were any changes in internal control, or other matters, subsequent to the financial year-end date and up to the date of the appointed auditor's assurance report, that may have an impact on the appointed auditor's conclusion about the effectiveness of internal controls, and obtains written representations from management relating to such matters.

146 Materiality is to be applied as outlined in paragraphs 74-90 of this Guidance Statement.

Advanced ADIs

147 For an Advanced ADI, the appointed auditor furthermore considers the ADI's internal controls over the risk measurement models used to meet the requirements of specific Prudential Standards and to generate certain risk data provided to APRA in Reporting Forms prepared under the FSCODA.

148 The appointed auditor undertakes an appropriate risk assessment of the controls over these models within the context of the stated review objective, and plans the assurance engagement accordingly.

149 The appointed auditor obtains an understanding of any deficiencies in the models, identified either by APRA, the ADI, or through any independent review, and how such deficiencies have been addressed by the ADI.

150 In concluding on the controls over internal risk models, the appointed auditor cannot place sole reliance on the work performed by APRA during the accreditation process to become an Advanced ADI, or on reports issued as a result of any "independent review"[17] required under specific APRA Prudential Standards dealing with credit risk, operational risk, market risk and interest rate risk in the banking book[18]. Under these Standards, APRA may require Advanced ADIs to obtain an independent review of the use of any internal models, statistical techniques, other methods relevant to estimating or assessing risks, and risk data inputs used.[19]

151 The appointed auditor reviews any reports issued as a result of independent reviews. In drawing a conclusion on whether or not to use these reports, the appointed auditor has regard to the level of independence of the reviewer, and their qualifications and competency to carry out such a review. In making this assessment, the appointed auditor complies with the requirements of ASAE 3000.

---

17 To be undertaken by a party or parties who are independent within the meaning of the relevant APRA Prudential Standards.

18 For example, APS 115 includes a requirement for an independent review of the ADI's operational risk management framework, both initially at the time that approval is sought from APRA to use the advanced approach and thereafter, on an ongoing basis (at least once every three years or when a material change is made to the framework).

19 The scope of an independent review of an Advanced ADI's risk management framework, may cover the following:

- the accuracy of the analytics underlying the calculation of the risk adjusted regulatory capital, the outputs of the risk measurement model and the consistency of this methodology;
- assessment of the reasonableness of any assumptions made in the risk measurement model; and
- the continuing appropriateness and adequacy of the risk modelling approach given industry developments in the modelling of risk.

The scope of an independent review of the risk data inputs to the internal risk models (to ensure the continued quality of the data and the effectiveness of internal controls) ordinarily includes an assessment of the controls surrounding the data collection and maintenance processes, as well as data inspection.

152 The appointed auditor makes enquiries about the overall system controls over such models, including controls that ensure the consistency and integrity of the models.

153 Review procedures over the models would ordinarily include a review of:

- the control environment and general controls, including the IT function; and
- change controls (including limited testing).

154 Review procedures of data produced from the risk measurement models would ordinarily include a review of:

- the key controls over inputs to the models; and
- how management review and use the data outputs from the models in the Reporting Forms.

Such review procedures may include making enquiries of management and persons operating the control(s), assessing whether such persons have the appropriate degree of skill and authority to effectively operate the control(s), observation, 'walk through' tests, limited re-performance and analytical review of the resulting Reporting Forms, or data items in a Reporting Form.

Evaluation of Findings

Audit and/or Review of Specified ADI Reporting Forms

155 The appointed auditor evaluates, individually and in the aggregate, whether uncorrected misstatements that have come to the auditor's attention, are material to the reported information. Materiality is to be applied in the context of paragraphs 74-90 of this Guidance Statement.

156 In evaluating whether or not the specified ADI Reporting Forms, or data in Reporting Forms, are, in all material respects, reliable and in accordance with the relevant APRA Prudential and Reporting Standards, the appointed auditor exercises professional judgement, having regard to both the user and intended uses of the information in the Reporting Forms.

157 The magnitude of a misstatement alone is only one factor used to assess the misstatement. The appointed auditor evaluates each identified misstatement in the context of information relevant to users of the Reporting Form, by considering qualitative factors and the circumstances in which each misstatement has been made. For example, in evaluating identified misstatements, the appointed auditor has regard to factors such as the level of the ADI's buffer above the particular minimum prudential requirements (determined under periodic quantitative calculations) and the sensitivity of these buffers to fluctuations in the ADI's financial performance and position.

158 The appointed auditor may designate an amount below which misstatements need not be aggregated, because the auditor expects that the aggregation of such amounts clearly would not have a material effect on the reported information. In doing so, the appointed auditor needs to consider the fact that the materiality of misstatements involves qualitative as well as quantitative considerations and that misstatements of a relatively small amount could nevertheless have a material effect on the reported information.

159 In extremely rare circumstances, the appointed auditor may conclude that information reported in ADI Reporting Forms in accordance with the relevant APRA Prudential and Reporting Standards, are misleading. The appointed auditor discusses the matter with management and, depending how it is resolved, determines whether, and how, to communicate the matter in the auditor's assurance report.

Review of Internal Controls

160 The appointed auditor evaluates, individually and in aggregate, whether internal control deficiencies that have come to the auditor's attention are material. Materiality is to be applied in the context of paragraphs 74-90.

161 The appointed auditor exercises professional judgement in evaluating the materiality of internal control deficiencies, having regard to the intended users of the auditor's assurance report.

162 In evaluating the severity of identified internal control deficiencies, the appointed auditor considers, based on materiality:

(a) the likelihood that the relevant internal controls may fail to prevent or detect:

(i) non-compliance with a Prudential Requirement; or

(ii) a misstatement in the data being provided to APRA in ADI Reporting Forms; and

(b) the magnitude of the potential resulting non-compliance with a Prudential Requirement on the ADI's overall compliance with applicable Prudential Requirements; and

(c) the magnitude of the potential misstatement resulting from the internal control deficiency on the information reported in the ADI Reporting Forms.

163 The evaluation of the severity of a deficiency in internal control does not depend on whether a misstatement or non-compliance with a Prudential Requirement has actually occurred, but rather the likelihood that the ADI's controls may fail to prevent or detect a material misstatement or material non-compliance with a Prudential Requirement.

Reporting on Compliance with Prudential Requirements

164 The appointed auditor is required to express a conclusion, based on the appointed auditor's audit and reviews conducted under paragraphs 114, 124 and 136 above, as to whether anything has come to the attention of the appointed auditor to cause the auditor to believe that, during the financial year, the ADI has not complied, in all material respects, with all relevant Prudential Requirements under the Banking Act and the FSCODA, including compliance with APRA Prudential and Reporting Standards.

Refer *Part D* of the illustrative *Auditor's Annual Prudential Assurance Report in Appendix 4* of this Guidance Statement.

165 The APS 310 requirement to report matters of non-compliance to APRA on an annual basis, is in addition to the reporting obligations under section 16BA of the Banking Act, which requires certain matters to be reported to APRA immediately and certain other matters to be reported to APRA as soon as is practicable. See paragraphs 206-219 of this Guidance Statement.

166 The appointed auditor considers materiality when assessing the significance of identified instances of non-compliance with relevant Prudential Requirements.

167 Section 16BA(7) of the Banking Act defines the term 'significant' in the context of matters that are required to be notified to APRA by the appointed auditor as part of the auditor's additional statutory reporting responsibilities under the Banking Act (refer paragraph 218 of this Guidance Statement).

168 The significance of a matter is to be judged by the appointed auditor in the context in which it is being considered, taking into account both quantitative and qualitative factors. This may, for example, include consideration of the significance of the potential impact of the non-compliance rather than the actual impact.

169 Furthermore, it is possible that an instance of non-compliance, which is not significant in isolation, may become so when considered in totality with other identified instances of non-compliance.

170 Where the appointed auditor considers identified instances of non-compliance as being potentially significant to the ADI as a whole and/or to its depositors' interests, or where the matter may be considered important by APRA in performing its functions under the Act, then the identified instance of non-compliance is a matter to be reported to APRA.

171 In order to conclude on an ADI's compliance with all relevant Prudential Requirements, the appointed auditor considers the existence of relevant matters, that may indicate instances of non-compliance, throughout the reporting period and up to the date of signing the auditor's assurance report.

172 The appointed auditor's review of subsequent events may include the following procedures:

- reading minutes of the ADI's Board, as well as minutes of any sub committees responsible, for example, for compliance and audit, held after balance date and enquiring about matters discussed at these meetings for which minutes are not yet available;
- examining the ADI's breach registers up to the date of the auditor's assurance report; and
- enquiring of the ADI's management as to whether any subsequent events have occurred which might represent non-compliance with relevant Prudential Requirements.

173 The appointed auditor reports instances of significant non-compliance which have not previously been reported to APRA by the appointed auditor. This will include matters the ADI indicated it was notifying, and which an auditor relied upon as a reason for the auditor not notifying APRA.[20]

Written Representations

174 Prior to issuing the Auditor's Annual Prudential Assurance Report, the appointed auditor obtains written representations, as are considered appropriate to matters specific to the ADI, from the party responsible[21] for the ADI.

175 These written representations are generally in the form of a representation letter. In obtaining and using these written representations, the appointed auditor complies with the requirements of, as appropriate, Auditing Standard ASA 580 *Management Representations* and ASAE 3000.

176 Refer to Appendix 3 of this Guidance Statement for an illustrative example of the format of a representation letter, as well as examples of representations that may be considered appropriate in the specific engagement circumstances.

Foreign ADIs

177 By definition (refer paragraph 34(g)), a foreign ADI is a foreign bank authorised to operate in Australia, effectively as a branch operation. Reference to a foreign ADI does not capture locally incorporated ADI subsidiaries of foreign banks.

The terms 'branch of a foreign bank' and 'branch of a foreign ADI' are also used in APRA Reporting Standards and ADI Reporting Forms when referring to a 'foreign ADI'.

178 Prudential Requirements for foreign ADIs (branches) may differ from those of locally incorporated ADIs[22] and, consequently, these are considered by the appointed auditor. For example, foreign ADIs are not required to report in Australia with respect to branch capital adequacy. However, the Banking Act authority restricts the source and quantum of deposits that foreign ADIs may accept. In addition, APRA has set guidelines relating to the manner in which foreign ADIs inform depositors of the requirements of the Banking Act that do not apply to those ADIs. The appointed auditor reports to APRA on the foreign ADI's compliance with all relevant Prudential Requirements.

179 APRA requires the appointed auditor of a foreign ADI (branch) to conform to APS 310[23] and other relevant Prudential Requirements as they apply to foreign ADIs (branches). The appointed auditor of a foreign ADI considers the individual engagement requirements and circumstances at the foreign ADI (branch) when interpreting the guidance contained in this Guidance Statement.

---

20 Under subsections 16BA(5) and 16BA(10) of the Banking Act, an auditor is not required to notify APRA of matters that have been brought to the auditor's attention by the ADI, where the auditor is informed that APRA has been notified of the matter in writing by the ADI and the auditor has no reason to disbelieve the ADI.

21 Management and, where appropriate, those charged with governance of the ADI.

22 Which includes a locally incorporated subsidiary of a foreign ADI.

23 For example, under paragraph 38 of APS 310 (refer paragraph 38 of this Guidance Statement), appointed auditors are required to provide a consistent level of assurance for foreign ADIs and locally incorporated 'stand-alone' ADIs.

180 As part of the requirements under APS 310, the appointed auditor of a foreign ADI (branch) is required to provide reasonable assurance over data sourced from accounting records, included in ADI Reporting Forms such as the 'Statement of Financial Performance' and 'Statement of Financial Position'[24].

181 As a foreign ADI (branch) is not required to prepare a financial report under the Corporations Act, there is no requirement for a statutory financial report audit to be undertaken. Therefore, the accounting records of a foreign ADI (branch) would not generally be subjected to a full scope audit, unless the branch is included in the scope of the foreign ADI group audit, where the audit arrangements will be driven by head office audit requirements and applying materiality relevant to the entire group.

182 Since generally the appointed auditor of a foreign ADI (branch) has incomplete knowledge of the overseas operations of the foreign ADI, and has not undertaken the statutory financial report audit of the foreign ADI, the appointed auditor of a foreign ADI considers the following additional matters (this is not a complete list):

- The reliance to be placed on work performed by overseas auditors (such as comfort over systems and processes hosted offshore which impact the foreign ADI's (branch's) prudential reporting) and the requirements of ASA 600.
- The financial reporting framework applied by the foreign ADI for head office (group) reporting and whether adjustments are required to comply with APRA Prudential Requirements.
- Assessing materiality for APRA prudential reporting purposes, which may differ from materiality considerations for the purpose of head office (group) reporting.
- The requirements of Auditing Standard ASA 701 *Modifications to the Auditor's Report*, in particular, where sufficient appropriate evidence cannot be obtained.
- In the first year of reporting, the requirements of Auditing Standard ASA 510 *Initial Engagements – Opening Balances*, in particular, with respect to the level of assurance which can be provided over opening balances.

Inherent Limitations of the Engagement

183 As the systems, procedures and controls to ensure compliance with Prudential Requirements are part of the ADI's operations, it is possible that either the inherent limitations of the internal control structure, or weaknesses in it, may impact on the effective operation of the ADI's specific control procedures. Furthermore, fraud, error or non-compliance with laws and regulations may occur and not be detected.

184 Due to the nature of audit and review procedures and other inherent limitations of an audit and review, there is a possibility that a properly planned and executed audit or review may not detect all errors or omissions in ADI Reporting Forms, deficiencies in controls, or instances of non-compliance with Prudential Requirements.

185 An audit provides reasonable assurance and cannot constitute a guarantee that the information included in ADI Reporting Forms specified in Attachment A to APS 310, sourced from accounting records, are reliable, or that all instances of non-compliance with relevant APRA Prudential and Reporting Standards have been detected.

186 While reviews involve the application of audit related skills and techniques, usually they do not involve many of the procedures performed during an audit. In an audit, as the auditor's objective is to provide a high, but not absolute, level of assurance on the reliability of information included in ADI Reporting Forms, the auditor uses more extensive audit procedures than in a review. Review procedures therefore do not provide all the evidence required in an audit and, consequently, the level of assurance provided is less than that given in an audit.

24 Refer to Attachment A of APS 310 for a complete list of foreign ADI Reporting Forms to be subjected to audit and/or review.

187 Accordingly, review procedures undertaken by the appointed auditor provides only limited assurance that:

(a) information in ADI Reporting Forms, specified in Attachment A to APS 310, sourced from non-accounting records, are reliable and in accordance with the relevant APRA Prudential and Reporting Standards;

(b) the ADI has implemented internal controls that are designed to ensure:

(i) compliance with all applicable Prudential Requirements; and

(ii) reliable data is provided to APRA in ADI Reporting Forms;

(c) the controls in paragraph 187(b) have operated effectively throughout the financial year; and

(d) the ADI has complied with all relevant Prudential Requirements.

188 The appointed auditor performs procedures appropriate to provide limited assurance in relation to internal controls existing at the review date, and whether those controls have operated as documented throughout the financial year. Projections of any evaluation of control procedures to future periods are subject to the risk that control procedures may become inadequate because of changes in conditions after the auditor's annual prudential assurance report is signed, or that the degree of compliance may deteriorate.

Communication

189 It is the responsibility of the appointed auditor to make the ADI aware, as soon as practicable, of any identified material misstatements in ADI Reporting Forms, material deficiencies in internal controls and instances of material non-compliance arising from the prudential reporting engagement.

190 Such communications are made as soon as practicable, either orally or in writing. The appointed auditor's decision whether to communicate orally or in writing ordinarily is affected by factors such as the nature, sensitivity and significance of the matter to be communicated and the timing of the communications. If the information is communicated orally, the appointed auditor needs to document the communication.

191 When, in the appointed auditor's judgement, those charged with governance do not respond appropriately within a reasonable period of time, the appointed auditor considers whether to modify the auditor's annual prudential assurance report.

192 It is important that the appointed auditor understands their additional statutory responsibilities to report certain matters to APRA under the Banking Act. Failure to notify APRA as required represent criminal offences, which attracts criminal penalties. Refer also to paragraphs 206-219 below.

193 Material findings (misstatements, control deficiencies and non-compliance) are reported to APRA and the ADI's Board (or Board Audit Committee) as modifications to the appointed auditor's assurance report (Refer paragraph 198).

194 Under Auditing Standard ASA 260 *Communication of Audit Matters with Those Charged With Governance* and ASAE 3000, the appointed auditor communicates relevant matters of governance interest arising from the engagement to those charged with governance on a timely basis. Examples of such matters may include:

- The general approach and overall scope of the engagement, or any additional requirements.
- Fraud or information that indicates that fraud may exist.
- Significant deficiencies in internal controls identified during the engagement. A significant deficiency is a deficiency or combination of deficiencies in internal control relevant to the engagement that, although not material, in the appointed auditor's professional judgement is of sufficient importance to merit the attention of those charged with governance.
- Disagreements with management about matters that, individually or in aggregate, could be significant to the engagement.
- Expected modifications to the auditor's prudential assurance report.

195 The appointed auditor informs those charged with governance of the ADI of those uncorrected misstatements, other than clearly trivial amounts, aggregated by the appointed auditor during and pertaining to the engagement that were considered to be immaterial, both individually and in the aggregate, to the assurance engagement.

196 Under APS 310, if requested by APRA, the appointed auditor submits directly to APRA all assessments and other material associated with the auditor's report, such as management letters issued by the appointed auditor to the ADI which contain material findings relating to the auditor's prudential assurance report.

The Appointed Auditor's Annual Prudential Assurance Report (Routine Reporting)

197 The appointed auditor evaluates the conclusions drawn from the evidence obtained in conducting the assurance engagement as the basis for the auditor's opinion/conclusions as required under APS 310.

198 If the appointed auditor:

(a) concludes that a material misstatement, internal control deficiency and/or non-compliance exists; or

(b) is unable to obtain sufficient appropriate assurance evidence to conclude whether a material misstatement, internal control deficiency and/or non-compliance may exist,

the appointed auditor modifies their opinion/conclusion, and includes a clear description of the reasons in their assurance report, in accordance with the requirements of, as appropriate, ASA 701 and applicable ASAEs.

199 As required under APS 310, the appointed auditor of an ADI reports simultaneously to APRA and the ADI's Board (or Board Audit Committee)[25], within three[26] months of the end of the financial year of the ADI. [27]

200 The appointed auditor's report may, unless otherwise instructed in writing by APRA, be prepared to cover, as appropriate:

(a) both the ADI on a Level 1 basis and the Level 2 group, provided it is clear when the appointed auditor is referring to matters relating to the ADI or the Level 2 group; or

(b) the ADI on a Level 1 basis and Level 2 group separately.

201 To avoid the possibility of the assurance report being used for purposes for which it was not intended, the appointed auditor ordinarily indicates in the auditor's report the purpose for which the report is prepared and any restrictions on its distribution and use (refer paragraphs 72-73).

Format of Auditor's Annual Prudential Assurance Report

202 AUASB Standards do not prescribe a standardised format for reporting on all assurance engagements. Instead, both Auditing Standard ASA 800 *The Auditor's Report on Special Purpose Audit Engagements* and ASAE 3000 identify the basic elements required to be included in the assurance report. The 'short form' auditor's report ordinarily includes only the basic elements.

203 Assurance reports are tailored to the specific assurance engagement circumstances. Although not specifically required under APS 310, the appointed auditor may consider it appropriate to include other information and explanations that do not directly affect the appointed auditor's opinion or conclusions, but provide additional useful information to the users (that is, a 'long form' style of reporting). The inclusion of this information

GS

25 Or, for a foreign ADI, a senior officer outside Australia to whom authority has been delegated in accordance with APS 510, for overseeing the Australian operations.

26 For a non-disclosing ADI, the relevant period is four months.

27 Subject to paragraph 40.

depends on its significance to the needs of the intended users. The following are examples of additional information that may be considered for inclusion:

- Disclosure of materiality considerations (materiality levels) applied.
- Significant findings or exceptions relating to particular aspects of the assurance engagement.
- Recommendations.

204 The appointed auditor needs to ensure that this additional information is clearly separated from the auditor's opinion and conclusions, and worded in a manner to ensure that it does not affect the opinion and conclusions. This can be achieved, for example, by including any additional information in a:

(a) separate appendix to the auditor's short form assurance report; or

(b) separate section of the auditor's short form assurance report, following the 'opinion and conclusions'[28] section.

This will enable users to clearly distinguish this additional information from the appointed auditor's responsibility to report on the matters identified in APS 310.

205 Refer to Appendix 4 of this Guidance Statement for an illustrative example of the appointed auditor's annual prudential assurance report (short form report), prepared pursuant to APRA's APS 310 annual reporting requirements.

Additional Reporting Requirements under the Banking Act

206 It is important that the auditor[29] of:

(a) an ADI; or

(b) an authorised NOHC; or

(c) a subsidiary of an ADI or authorised NOHC; or

(d) if the ADI[30] is a subsidiary of a foreign corporation:

(i) another subsidiary (a relevant Australian-incorporated subsidiary) of the foreign corporation (other than an ADI listed in paragraphs (a), (b) or (c) above), being a subsidiary that is incorporated in Australia; or

(ii) another subsidiary (a relevant foreign-incorporated subsidiary) of the foreign corporation (other than an ADI listed in paragraphs (a), (b) or (c) above), being a subsidiary that is not incorporated in Australia and carries on business in Australia;

understands the additional responsibilities to report to APRA under sections 16B, 16BA and 16C of the Banking Act.

207 An auditor risks committing an offence under the Banking Act for any contravention of sections 16B and 16BA of that Act. Under section 6B of the Banking Act, the *Criminal Code 1995* applies to all offences against the Banking Act[31].

208 Part VIA of the Banking Act include provisions to protect an auditor providing information to APRA, in good faith and without negligence, from any action, claim or demand by, or any liability to, any other person in respect of the information.

Auditors to Give Information to APRA on Request

209 Under section 16B of the Banking Act, APRA may give written notice to a person who is, or who has been, the auditor of an ADI listed in paragraph 206 above, to provide information, or to produce books, accounts or documents, about such entities to APRA, if APRA considers that the provision of such information will assist APRA in performing its functions under the Act.

28 See examples of assurance practitioner reports included in *Attachment 1* to ASAE 3100.

29 Including the appointed auditor - refer definitions at paragraph 34(d).

30 Whether or not the ADI is itself a foreign ADI.

31 Criminal penalties include provisions for terms of imprisonment.

Requirement for Auditors to Give Information about ADIs

210 Section 16BA of the Banking Act identifies matters of which APRA needs to be notified of:

(a) *immediately*, if the auditor has reasonable grounds for believing that, for example:

(i) the ADI is insolvent, or there is a significant risk that the ADI will become insolvent; or

(ii) an existing or proposed state of affairs may prejudice materially the interests of depositors of the ADI; and

(b) *as soon as is practicable*[32], if the auditor has reasonable grounds for believing that an ADI has failed to comply with a provision of:

(i) the Banking Act, the Regulations, or the FSCODA; or

(ii) a Prudential Standard; or

(iii) a Direction under Division 1BA of Part II of the Banking Act; or

(iv) a condition of its authority;

and the failure to comply is or will be *significant*[33].

211 Under the Banking Act, these matters are to be reported to APRA in writing.

Auditor may Provide Information to APRA

212 Section 16C of the Banking Act provides that a person who is, or who has been, the auditor of an ADI listed in paragraph 206 above, may provide information, or produce books, accounts or documents, about such entities to APRA, if the person considers that the provision of that information to APRA will assist APRA in performing its functions under the Banking Act or the FSCODA.

Discussion of Additional Reporting Requirements under the Banking Act

213 Sections 16B, 16BA and 16C of the Banking Act is applicable to *all* and *any* auditor of an ADI, authorised NOHCs, or their subsidiaries, not only to auditors appointed by an ADI to meet the prudential requirements under APS 310.

214 In relation to reporting under sections 16B and 16BA of the Banking Act, there is no requirement for the appointed auditor of an ADI to carry out additional work to satisfy the auditor with respect to the above matters. The appointed auditor reports to APRA on the basis of, for example:

(a) information obtained during the course of the auditor's financial report audit [and review] under the Corporations Act;

(b) additional audit and review procedures undertaken for APRA prudential reporting purposes (pursuant to APS 310 or in accordance with the requirements of another specific ADI Prudential Standard);

(c) other audit work undertaken at the ADI (for example, Australian Financial Services Licence audits); and

(d) the appointed auditor's current knowledge of the ADI's affairs at the time of issuing the auditor's assurance report.

215 In circumstances where the appointed auditor identifies that a reportable matter may exist, the auditor carries out such additional work as considered appropriate, to determine whether the facts and circumstances provide reasonable grounds for believing that the matter does in fact exist. In reaching this conclusion, the appointed auditor exercises professional judgement and seeks appropriate legal advice if necessary.

216 The ADI may also notify APRA of the matter(s) identified by the appointed auditor, and provide details of any action(s) taken, or to be taken, in response. However, such notification by the ADI does not relieve the appointed auditor of the statutory obligation to report directly to APRA.

32 No longer than 10 business days.

33 For the purpose of this paragraph, the term 'significant' is defined in subsection 16BA(7) of the Banking Act. See paragraph 218 of this Guidance Statement.

217 Matters likely to prejudice materially the interests of depositors are related generally to capital adequacy, solvency and going concern matters, for example, the ADI's compliance with minimum capital levels as per APRA Prudential Standard APS 110. Materiality is addressed in paragraphs 74-90 of this Guidance Statement.

218 In determining whether a failure to comply with Prudential Requirements is or will be significant, the appointed auditor considers the factors listed in subsection 16BA(7) of the Banking Act, namely:

(a) the number or frequency of similar failures;

(b) the impact the failure has or will have on the ADI's ability to conduct its business;

(c) the extent to which the failure indicates that the ADI's arrangements to ensure compliance with the Banking Act, the Prudential Standards or the Regulations might be inadequate;

(d) the actual or potential financial loss arising, or that will arise from the failure, to the depositors of the ADI or to the ADI; and

(e) any matters prescribed by the Regulations for the purposes of this subsection of the Banking Act.

219 In assessing whether the interests of depositors may be prejudiced materially, the appointed auditor considers not only a single activity or a single deficiency in isolation, as depositors' interests may be prejudiced materially by a number of activities or deficiencies which, although not individually material, do amount to a material threat when considered in totality. Similarly, it is possible that a breach in compliance, although not significant in isolation, may become so when considered in the context of other possible breaches.

Special Purpose Engagements

APRA Prudential Reporting Requirements (APS 310)

220 Under APS 310, in addition to the annual prudential reporting requirements (routine reporting), APRA may require an ADI, by notice in writing, to appoint an auditor (who may be the existing appointed auditor or another auditor), to provide a report on a particular aspect of the ADI's operations, prudential reporting, risk management systems or financial position. Although a special purpose engagement report will normally only be requested following consultation with an ADI, APRA may commission such a report without prior consultation with an ADI.

221 Unless otherwise determined by APRA, an auditor appointed to undertake a special purpose engagement will be required to provide limited assurance on the matters required to be reported on.

222 Under APS 310, the appointed auditor's special purpose engagement assurance report is to be submitted simultaneously[34] to APRA and the ADI's Board (or Board Audit Committee)[35], within three months of the date of the notice commissioning the report, unless otherwise determined by APRA, and advised to the ADI by notice in writing.

223 The APRA requirement for an auditor to undertake a special purpose engagement in a selected area of the ADI's operations, prudential reporting, risk management systems or financial position constitutes a separate reporting engagement. The details of the engagement will normally be the subject of a specific request from APRA to the ADI and a separate engagement letter from the ADI to the appointed auditor based on that request.

Terms of the Engagement

224 Following the determination by APRA of the specific area to be examined, the appointed auditor, APRA and the ADI agree on the terms of the engagement in accordance with the requirements of applicable AUASB Standards. These arrangements are legally binding and include the required terms of engagement specified in APS 310.

34 Subject to paragraph 40.

35 Or, for a foreign ADI, a senior officer outside Australia to whom authority has been delegated in accordance with APS 510 for overseeing the Australian operations.

225 The appointed auditor accepts the engagement only when the auditor is satisfied that they, and the engagement team, if applicable, have met the relevant ethical requirements relating to the assurance engagement. The concept of independence is important to the appointed auditor's compliance with the fundamental ethical principles of integrity and objectivity and the appointed auditor must be able to meet the independence requirements stipulated under both APS 510 and APES 110.

226 An engagement letter (or other suitable form) helps to avoid misunderstandings with respect to the engagement and confirms both the client ADI's and the appointed auditor's understanding of the terms of the engagement, and the appointed auditor's acceptance of the appointment. Both parties sign the engagement letter to acknowledge that it is a legally binding contract.

227 To ensure that there is a clear understanding regarding the terms of the engagement, the following are examples of matters to be agreed:

- APRA is to identify the scope of the ADI's operations, prudential reporting, risk management or financial position to be the subject of the engagement.
- The appointed auditor, APRA and the ADI are to agree on the objectives of the engagement, key features and criteria of the area(s) to be examined, and the period to be covered by the engagement.
- APRA is to identify clearly the level of assurance required, that is, limited or reasonable assurance.
- The format of reports required (for example, long and/or short form reports) or other communication of results of the engagement.
- Responsibility of those charged with governance for the subject matter of the engagement.
- Understanding of the inherent limitations of an assurance engagement.

Format of Reporting Requirements

228 The format of the special purpose assurance report may vary depending on the type of engagement; that is, an audit (reasonable assurance) or a review (limited assurance), as well as the subject matter and the findings. The appointed auditor has regard to the requirements, guidance and illustrative examples of reports provided in relevant AUASB Standards — ASAs, ASREs and ASAEs, as applicable, when preparing the special purpose assurance report.

229 AUASB Standards do not require a standardised format for special purpose reporting under APS 310. Instead, these Standards identify the basic elements to be included in the auditor's report. Ordinarily, the appointed auditor adopts a long form style of reporting and the report may include a description of the terms of the engagement, materiality considerations applied, the assurance approach, findings relating to particular aspects of the engagement and, in some cases, recommendations.

230 The appointed auditor's assurance report is to be restricted to the parties that have agreed to the terms of the special purpose engagement, namely the ADI and APRA, as well as other parties that APRA is lawfully entitled to share information with (refer paragraphs 72-73).

Conformity with International Pronouncements

231 As this Guidance Statement relates to Australian legislative requirements, there is no equivalent International Standard on Auditing or International Auditing Practice Statement to this Guidance Statement.

232 International Auditing Practice Statement IAPS 1004 *The Relationship Between Bank Supervisors and External Auditors* provides general guidance on managing the relationship between bank auditors and bank supervisors. The primary purpose of this Guidance Statement is to provide guidance to the appointed auditor of an ADI reporting in accordance with the prudential reporting requirements for appointed auditors of ADIs, specified by APRA in APS 310. As a consequence, this Guidance Statement differs in its purpose, form and content from IAPS 1004.

Appendix 1

Reporting Requirements for Appointed Auditors

The following table outlines the relevant reporting requirements applicable to the appointed auditor of an ADI reporting pursuant to APRA's ADI Prudential Standard APS 310 *Audit and Related Matters* (APS 310). This table contains only limited extracts from APS 310 and sections 16B, 16BA and 16C of the *Banking Act 1959* (Banking Act) and, accordingly, is not intended to be an exhaustive summary of an appointed auditor's obligations and requirements which are found in the *Banking Act 1959*, the *Financial Sector (Collection of Data) Act 2001*, APRA Prudential and Reporting Standards, other relevant APRA Prudential Requirements, applicable AUASB Standards, and other relevant mandates.

APS 310 PRUDENTIAL REPORTING REQUIREMENTS				
A. ANNUAL PRUDENTIAL REPORTING ENGAGEMENTS (ROUTINE REPORTING)				
Part of Assurance Engagement	*Level of Assurance*	*Subject Matter*	*Assessment Criteria*	*Applicable AUASB Standards*
Part A - Audit of Specified[36] ADI Reporting Forms	Reasonable assurance	Information included in specified[36] ADI Reporting Forms at the financial year-end of the ADI, sourced from *accounting records*.	Concept of reliability. APRA Prudential and Reporting Standards.	Applicable Australian Auditing Standards.
Part B – Review of Specified[36] ADI Reporting Forms	Limited assurance	Information included in specified[36] ADI Reporting Forms at the financial year-end of the ADI, sourced from *non-accounting records*.	Concept of reliability. APRA Prudential and Reporting Standards.	ASAE 3000.
Part C (i) – Review of Internal Controls over Compliance with Prudential Requirements	Limited assurance	Internal Controls implemented to ensure compliance with all applicable Prudential Requirements.	Applicable Prudential Requirements.	ASAE 3000 and other relevant topic specific ASAEs, for example ASAE 3100.
Part C (ii) – Review of Internal Controls over the Reliability of ADI Reporting Forms	Limited assurance	Internal Controls implemented to ensure *all* ADI Reporting Forms, that the ADI is required to provide to APRA throughout the financial year, are reliable and in accordance with relevant APRA Prudential and Reporting Standards.	Concept of reliability. APRA Prudential and Reporting Standards.	ASAE 3000 and other relevant topic specific ASAEs.

36 For a listing of ADI Reporting Forms to be subjected to audit and/or review, refer to APRA Prudential Standard APS 310 *Attachment A – Data Collections subject to reasonable and/or limited assurance*.

APS 310 PRUDENTIAL REPORTING REQUIREMENTS				
Part D – Reporting on Compliance with Prudential Requirements	Limited assurance	All of the above.	All relevant Prudential Requirements.	No requirement for an appointed auditor to carry out additional audit or review procedures.

B. SPECIAL PURPOSE ENGAGEMENTS UNDER APS 310				
Part of Assurance Engagement	*Level of Assurance*	*Subject Matter*	*Assessment Criteria*	*Applicable AUASB Standards*
-	Limited assurance[37] (review)	A particular aspect of the ADI's operations, prudential reporting, risk management systems or financial position, as determined by APRA and agreed to by the appointed auditor, APRA and the ADI.	In normal circumstances, as agreed to by the appointed auditor, APRA and the ADI.	ASAE 3000 and other relevant topic specific ASAEs, for example ASAE 3100.

ADDITIONAL REPORTING REQUIREMENTS UNDER THE BANKING ACT[38]		
Section of Banking Act	*Statutory Reporting Requirement*	*Applicable AUASB Standards*
Section 16B	Duty to provide information to APRA on request.	No requirement for an auditor to carry out additional audit or review procedures.
Section 16BA	Requirement to provide information to APRA where the auditor possesses specified reportable information. Section 16BA identifies matters of which APRA needs to be notified of: (a) immediately; and (b) as soon as is practicable (no longer than 10 business days).	
Section 16C	Auditor may provide information to APRA where the auditor considers that the provision of such information would assist APRA in performing its functions under the Banking Act or FSCODA.	

37 Unless otherwise determined by APRA.

38 Sections 16B, 16BA and 16C of the Banking Act is applicable to *all* auditors of ADIs, authorised NOHCs, or their subsidiaries, not only to auditors appointed by an ADI to meet the prudential reporting requirements under APS 310.

Appendix 2

Example Engagement Letter

For an Annual Prudential Reporting Engagement Undertaken Pursuant to APRA Prudential Standard APS 310 *Audit and Related Matters* (Routine Reporting)

The following example engagement letter is to be used as a guide only and will need to be adapted according to individual engagement requirements and circumstances of the ADI.

[Note: If this report covers both the 'Level 1 ADI' and 'Level 2 group', this fact must be indicated by using the appropriate terminology, that is, 'the ADI' and 'the ADI and its controlled entities' (the Group).]

To [Chairman of Board or Board Audit Committee[39]] of [name of ADI]

The Australian Prudential Regulation Authority's (APRA's) Prudential Standard APS 310 *Audit and Related Matters* (APS 310) identifies APRA's reporting requirements for appointed auditors of ADIs.

We set out below, in general terms, our understanding of the terms, objectives and scope of this engagement, as well as a description of the responsibilities of both those charged with governance of the ADI and the appointed auditor. This engagement is a separate engagement from our audit [and half-year review] appointment(s) under the *Corporations Act 2001* (Corporations Act).

Objective and Scope of Engagement

APS 310 requires us to report simultaneously, on an annual basis, to APRA and your Board (or Board Audit Committee)[39], on the matters set out below, insofar as they relate to [name of ADI].

We are required to provide:

(a) reasonable assurance that the information, sourced from the [type of ADI]'s accounting records, included in the ADI Reporting Forms at the financial year-end as specified in Attachment A of APS 310, is, in all material respects, reliable and in accordance with the relevant APRA Prudential and Reporting Standards;

(b) limited assurance, unless otherwise indicated by APRA in writing, that the information, sourced from non-accounting records, included in the ADI Reporting Forms at the financial year-end as specified in Attachment A of APS 310, is, in all material respects, reliable and in accordance with the relevant APRA Prudential and Reporting Standards;

(c) limited assurance that, in all material respects:

  (i) the [type of ADI] has implemented internal controls that are designed to ensure:

    a. compliance with all applicable Prudential Requirements; and

    b. reliable data is provided to APRA in the ADI Reporting Forms prepared under the *Financial Sector (Collection of Data) Act 2001* (FSCODA); and

  (ii) the controls in (c)(i) have operated effectively throughout the financial year; and

(d) limited assurance, based on our work under (a) to (c) above, that the [type of ADI] has complied, in all material respects, with all relevant Prudential Requirements under the *Banking Act 1959* (Banking Act) and the FSCODA, including compliance with APRA Prudential and Reporting Standards during the financial year.

Our annual prudential report will cover the same period as the annual financial report required under the Corporations Act and is to be issued within three [four] months of the financial year-end of the [type of ADI].

We are pleased to confirm our acceptance and our understanding of the terms, objectives and scope of our engagement by means of this letter.

39 Or, for a foreign ADI, a senior officer outside Australia to whom authority has been delegated in accordance with APRA's ADI Prudential Standard APS 510 *Governance*, for overseeing the Australian operations.

Responsibilities of the [Title of Those Charged with Governance[40]]

In accordance with APS 310, it is the responsibility of [name of ADI]'s [Title of those charged with governance] and management to ensure that the [type of ADI] meets prudential and statutory requirements and has management practices to limit risks to prudent levels. This responsibility includes:

(a) ensuring that the information included in ADI Reporting Forms at the financial year-end is reliable and in accordance with the relevant APRA Prudential and Reporting Standards;

(b) establishing and maintaining internal controls that are designed to ensure:

   (i) the [type of ADI] complies with all applicable Prudential Requirements; and

   (ii) reliable data is provided to APRA in the ADI Reporting Forms prepared under the FSCODA; and

(c) ensuring that the controls under (b) operate effectively throughout the financial year; and

(d) ensuring that the [type of ADI] complies with all relevant Prudential Requirements under the Banking Act and the FSCODA, including compliance with APRA Prudential and Reporting Standards during the financial year.

Responsibilities of the Appointed Auditor

[If applicable: As the statutory auditor of [name of ADI], we carry out sufficient procedures to enable us to form an opinion on the state of the [type of ADI]'s affairs and its results, and to report thereon to the members of the [type of ADI] in accordance with the requirements of the Corporations Act [or other appropriate local or overseas requirements]. Although our audit [and review] under the Corporations Act will include such review of the [type of ADI]'s systems of accounting and internal control and performing such tests and enquiries as we consider necessary, these audit [and review] procedures are not designed to form an opinion on the systems of accounting and internal control taken as a whole.

In order to satisfy the requirements of APRA, we will carry out additional procedures over and above those which are performed in our capacity as the auditor under the Corporations Act [other legislation].

Despite our involvement in examining the [type of ADI]'s systems of control, it must be appreciated that it is the responsibility of the [Title of those charged with governance] of the [type of ADI] to establish and maintain all of the [type of ADI]'s internal control systems. All such systems have their limitations and, this being so, errors or irregularities may occur and which may not be detected. Our work is not to be relied upon for the purposes of discovering fraud, error, deficiencies, or non-compliance with laws and regulations, although we will report to the appropriate level of management any fraud, error, deficiencies, or non-compliance that may be identified as a result of our review.

We recognise that there may be some overlap between our audit [and review] under the Corporations Act and work that is necessary to fulfil APRA's APS 310 prudential reporting requirements. In order to help ensure the most efficient use of resources, wherever possible, reliance will be placed on work that is carried out for the statutory financial report audit [and review] purposes.

In order to report on the matters set out in the *Objective and Scope of Engagement* section of this letter, we are required to conduct an audit and review, described in PARTS A to D below, and to report our opinions and conclusions based on our audit and review.

We will conduct our engagement in accordance with applicable Australian Auditing Standards and Standards on Assurance Engagements, and with reference to Guidance Statement GS 012 *Prudential Reporting Requirements for Auditors of Authorised Deposit-taking Institutions (ADIs)*, issued by the Australian Auditing and Assurance Standards Board (AUASB).

40 Amend this term to reflect the appropriate title for those charged with governance of the ADI, for example, "Board of Directors" for a locally incorporated ADI or "senior country manager" (a senior officer outside Australia to whom authority has been delegated in accordance with APS 510, for overseeing the Australian operations) for a foreign ADI. Insert appropriate title, when prompted, throughout the letter.

As part of our procedures, we will request representations from management and, where appropriate, those charged with governance, concerning assertions made in connection with the engagement.

After the completion of our prudential engagement report, it is our normal practice to report any matters of significance, together with suggestions for their correction and any recommendations we may have on the systems, procedures and controls in general. However, as our examination will be limited to the audit and review in relation to matters set out in the *Objective and Scope of Engagement* section above, you cannot assume that any matters reported to you indicate that there are no additional matters or matters that you need to be aware of in meeting your responsibilities.

PART A: Audit of Information Included in Specified ADI Reporting Forms at the Financial Year-end, Sourced from Accounting Records

Our responsibility is to express an opinion, based on our audit, on whether the information sourced from [name of ADI]'s accounting records, included in the ADI Reporting Forms at the financial year-end as specified in Attachment A to APS 310 is, in all material respects, reliable and in accordance with the relevant APRA Prudential and Reporting Standards.

We will conduct our audit in accordance with applicable Australian Auditing Standards. These Auditing Standards require that we comply with relevant ethical requirements relating to audit engagements and plan and perform the audit to obtain reasonable assurance whether the relevant data included in the specified ADI Reporting Forms are free from material misstatement.

An audit involves performing procedures to obtain audit evidence on whether the information sourced from the accounting records included in the specified ADI Reporting Forms are, in all material respects, reliable and in accordance with the relevant APRA Prudential and Reporting Standards. The procedures selected depend on our judgement, including our assessment of the risks of material misstatement of the data in the ADI Reporting Forms, whether due to fraud or error. In making those risk assessments, we consider internal control systems and compliance functions relevant to the preparation of the ADI Reporting Forms, in order to design audit procedures that are appropriate in the circumstances.

PART B: Review of Information Included in Specified ADI Reporting Forms at the Financial Year-end, Sourced from Non-Accounting Records

Our responsibility is to perform a review of the information sourced from [name of ADI]'s non-accounting records, included in ADI Reporting Forms at the financial year-end as specified in Attachment A to APS 310, and to express a conclusion on whether anything has come to our attention that causes us to believe that this information is not, in all material respects, reliable and in accordance with the relevant APRA Prudential and Reporting Standards.

We will conduct our review in accordance with Standard on Assurance Engagements ASAE 3000 *Assurance Engagements other than Audits or Reviews of Historical Financial Information*, issued by the AUASB.

Under ASAE 3000 we are required to comply with relevant ethical requirements relating to assurance engagements.

The objective of our review is to provide us with a basis for reporting whether anything has come to our attention that causes us to believe that the relevant data in the specified ADI Reporting Forms, are not, in all material respects, reliable and in accordance with the relevant APRA Prudential and Reporting Standards.

Such a review consists of making enquiries of responsible [name of ADI] personnel and applying analytical and other review procedures considered necessary and does not, ordinarily, require corroboration of the information obtained. The scope of a review is substantially less than the scope of an audit conducted in accordance with Australian Auditing Standards and, consequently, does not enable us to obtain assurance that we would become aware of all significant matters that might be identified in an audit. Accordingly, we do not express an audit opinion.

Our review procedures depend on our judgement, including our assessment of the risks of material misstatement of the ADI Reporting Forms, whether due to fraud or error. In making those risk assessments, we consider internal control systems and compliance functions relevant to the preparation of ADI Reporting Forms in order to design review procedures that are appropriate in the circumstances.

PART C: Review of Internal Controls Addressing Compliance with Prudential Requirements and Reliability of Data Included in APRA Reporting Forms

Our responsibility is to perform a review and express a conclusion, based on our review as described below, on whether anything has come to our attention that causes us to believe that, for the financial year ended [date], in all material respects:

(a) [name of ADI] has not implemented internal controls, that are designed to ensure:

 (i) compliance with all applicable Prudential Requirements; and

 (ii) reliable data is provided to APRA in the ADI Reporting Forms prepared under the FSCODA; and

(b) the controls in paragraph (a) have not operated effectively.

We have conducted our review in accordance with Standards on Assurance Engagements ASAE 3000 and ASAE 3100 *Compliance Engagements*. These ASAEs require us to comply with relevant ethical requirements relating to assurance engagements.

A review consists of making enquiries of responsible personnel and applying analytical and other review procedures considered necessary, and does not, ordinarily, require corroboration of the information obtained. The scope of a review is substantially less than the scope of an audit conducted in accordance with Australian Auditing Standards and consequently does not enable us to obtain assurance that we would become aware of all significant matters that might be identified in an audit. Accordingly, we do not express an audit opinion.

Review procedures selected depend on our judgement, including our assessment of the risks of a material breakdown in controls. In making those risk assessments, we consider internal control systems and compliance functions relevant to ensuring compliance with all applicable Prudential Requirements and provision of reliable data to APRA in ADI Reporting Forms prepared under the FSCODA, in order to design assurance procedures that are appropriate in the circumstances.

PART D: Reporting on Compliance with Prudential Requirements

Our responsibility is to express a conclusion, based on our work performed under Parts A to C above, on whether anything has come to our attention that causes us to believe that, for the financial year ended [date], [name of ADI] has not, in all material respects, complied with all relevant Prudential Requirements under the Banking Act and the FSCODA, including compliance with APRA Prudential and Reporting Standards.

Inherent Limitations

There are inherent limitations in any internal control and compliance framework, and fraud, error or non-compliance with Prudential Requirements may occur and not be detected. As the systems, procedures and controls to ensure compliance with applicable Prudential Requirements are part of the operations of the [type of ADI], it is possible that either the inherent limitations of the general internal control structure, or weaknesses in it, can impact on the effective operation of the specific controls of the [type of ADI].

Projection of any evaluation of internal controls to future periods is subject to the risk that controls may become inadequate because of changes in conditions, or that the degree of compliance may deteriorate.

An audit or review is not designed to detect all misstatements in ADI Reporting Forms, or deficiencies in internal controls, or instances of non-compliance with applicable Prudential Requirements, as audit and review procedures are not performed continuously throughout the [period], and audit and review procedures performed are undertaken on a test basis.

Consequently, there are inherent limitations on the level of assurance that can be provided.

Internal Audit

[Name of ADI]'s internal audit function is considered well placed to review and test properly documented systems, procedures and controls operating within the [type of ADI]. Consequently, it is our intention to liaise closely with internal auditors throughout the year.

Where work is carried out by internal auditors as part of the [type of ADI]'s internal control procedures, we intend to [may] review the work performed and carry out such re-performance tests and other procedures as we consider necessary. Where we are satisfied with the work carried out by internal auditors, it is our intention to place reliance on such work in accordance with Auditing Standard ASA 610 *Considering the Work of Internal Audit*, and, where appropriate, reduce the extent of our own procedures relating to internal controls.

Independence

We confirm that, to the best of our knowledge and belief, we currently meet the independence requirements specified by APRA in ADI Prudential Standard APS 510 *Governance*.

Special Purpose Engagements

Under APS 310, APRA may require you, by notice in writing, to appoint an auditor to provide a report on a particular aspect of the [type of ADI]'s operations, prudential reporting, risk management systems or financial position. The details of such an engagement will be the subject of a specific request from APRA and will constitute a separate engagement and reporting. In these circumstances, a separate engagement letter will be issued.

Liaison with APRA

Under normal circumstances, liaison with APRA will take place under tripartite arrangements involving APRA, the [type of ADI] and its appointed auditor(s). Notwithstanding the tripartite relationship, APS 310 allows for communication between an appointed auditor and APRA on a bilateral basis, at the request of either party. APRA can, although not commonly, request information directly from an appointed auditor. Under APS 510, an ADI is required to ensure that its internal policy and contractual arrangements do not explicitly or implicitly restrict or discourage auditors from communication with APRA.

Additional Reporting Responsibilities under the Banking Act

Under sections 16B, 16BA and 16C of the Banking Act, we are required to provide information to APRA upon request, or where we possess reportable information specified in Banking Act, or where we consider that the provision of information would assist APRA in performing its functions under the Banking Act or the FSCODA.

Part VIA of the Banking Act includes provisions to protect an auditor providing information to APRA, in good faith and without negligence, from any action, claim or demand by, or any liability to, any other person in respect of the information.

Use of Report(s)

Our annual APS 310 prudential assurance report and any special purpose engagement report will be prepared for distribution to the [Board, or Board Audit Committee], of [name of ADI] and APRA. These assurance reports will be prepared in accordance with the terms of our engagement letter dated [date], in order to satisfy APRA's prudential reporting requirements for appointed auditor's of ADIs, as specified in APS 310.

In accordance with the Australian *Prudential Regulation Authority Act 1998*, APRA may make our assurance reports available to other specified agencies when APRA is satisfied that such information may assist these agencies in performing their functions or exercising their powers.

These reports are not to be distributed to any party other than [name of ADI], APRA, and other parties that APRA is lawfully entitled to provide relevant information.

We disclaim any assumption of responsibility for any reliance on these reports or the subject matter to which it relates to any party other than the Board, or Board Audit Committee, of [name of ADI], APRA, and other parties that APRA is lawfully entitled to provide relevant information.

Fees

The requirement to report pursuant to APS 310 is in addition to, and separate from, the audit [and review] of financial reports required under the Corporations Act and will result in additional audit and review procedures being carried out. Fees relating to this work will be based on the degree of responsibility and skill involved and the time necessarily occupied by the work undertaken.

As the fees will not relate to our audit [and review] carried out in our capacity as the statutory auditor under the Corporations Act, our invoices will be rendered separately, so as to clearly identify the additional cost of APRA's prudential reporting requirements.

[Insert additional information here regarding fee arrangements and billings, as appropriate.]

We look forward to full co-operation with you and your staff and we trust that you will make available to us whatever records, documentation and other information are requested in connection with our audit and reviews.

This letter will be effective for future years unless we advise you of its amendment or replacement, or the engagement is terminated.

Please sign and return the attached copy of this letter to indicate that it is in accordance with your understanding of the arrangements for our prudential engagement pursuant to APS 310.

Yours faithfully,

(signed)

....

Name and Title

Date

Acknowledged on behalf of [name of ADI] by

(signed)

....

Name and Title

Date

Appendix 3

Example Management Representation Letter

For an Annual Prudential Reporting Engagement Undertaken Pursuant to APRA Prudential Standard APS 310 *Audit and Related Matters* (Routine Reporting)

The following example management representation letter is to be used as a guide only and will need to be adapted according to individual engagement requirements and circumstances of the ADI.

[Note: If the report covers both the 'Level 1 ADI' and 'Level 2 group', this fact must be indicated by using the appropriate terminology, that is, 'the ADI' and 'the ADI and its controlled entities' (the Group).]

[[name of ADI] Letterhead]

[Addressee – Appointed Auditor]

[Date]

Dear Sir/Madam

LETTER OF REPRESENTATION

This representation letter is provided in connection with your audit and review, as required by APRA's Prudential Standard APS 310 *Audit and Related Matters* (APS 310), of [name of ADI] for the [period] ended [date], for the purpose of you providing:

(a) reasonable assurance that the information, sourced from the [type of ADI]'s accounting records, included in the ADI Reporting Forms at the financial year-end as specified in Attachment A of APS 310, is, in all material respects, reliable and in accordance with the relevant APRA Prudential and Reporting Standards;

GS

(b) limited assurance, unless otherwise indicated in writing by APRA, that the information, sourced from the [type of ADI]'s non-accounting records, included in the ADI Reporting Forms at the financial year-end as specified in Attachment A of APS 310, is, in all material respects, reliable and in accordance with the relevant APRA Prudential and Reporting Standards;

(c) limited assurance that, in all material respects:

(i) the [type of ADI] has implemented internal controls that are designed to ensure:

a. compliance with all applicable Prudential Requirements; and

b. reliable data is provided to APRA in the ADI Reporting Forms prepared under the *Financial Sector (Collections of Data) Act 2001* (FSCODA); and

(ii) the controls in (c)(i) have operated effectively throughout the financial year; and

(d) limited assurance, based on your work under (a) to (c) above, that the [type of ADI] has complied, in all material respects, with all relevant Prudential Requirements under the *Banking Act 1959* (Banking Act) and the FSCODA, including compliance with APRA Prudential and Reporting Standards during the financial year.

We acknowledge our responsibility for ensuring that:

- the [type of ADI] complies with prudential and statutory requirements and has management practices to limit risks to prudent levels.
- risk management practices are detailed in descriptions of risk management systems and are regularly reviewed and updated, at least annually, to take account of changing circumstances;
- APRA is provided with high-level descriptions of our key risk management systems covering all major areas of risk, and APRA is informed of all material changes to the [type of ADI]'s risk management systems descriptions when they are made;
- adequate internal controls have been established and maintained to ensure:
  (i) compliance with all applicable Prudential Requirements; and
  (ii) reliable data is provided to APRA in the ADI Reporting Forms prepared under the FSCODA; and
- the information included in ADI Reporting Forms at the financial year-end is reliable, and in accordance with the relevant APRA Prudential Standards and Reporting Standards;
- you are informed of all Prudential Requirements applicable to the [type of ADI];
- we provide you with access to all data, information, reports and staff of the [type of ADI] that you reasonably believe are necessary to fulfil your role and responsibilities under APS 310. This includes access to the [type of ADI]'s Board, Board Audit Committee and internal auditors as required.

We confirm, to the best of our knowledge and belief, the following representations made to you during your assurance engagement:

[*Include representations relevant to the ADI. Such representations may include the following examples.*]

1. We have made available to you for the purpose of your assurance engagement:

(a) all data, information, reports and staff of the [type of ADI] that you have required to fulfil your role and responsibilities under APS 310;

(b) access to the [type of ADI]'s Board, Board Audit Committee and internal auditors as required, and related data, minutes of meetings, reports, other information, explanations and assistance necessary for the conduct of the assurance engagement;

(c) all correspondence with APRA concerning all Prudential Requirements applicable to the [type of ADI];

(d) all policies and procedures (including all changes in the reporting period) that are designed to ensure the [type of ADI] has:

(i) complied with all applicable Prudential Requirements; and

(ii) provided reliable data to APRA in the ADI Reporting Forms prepared under the FSCODA;

(e) all high level descriptions of our key risk management systems covering all major areas of risk, approved by the Board and management, and including all material changes to the risk management systems descriptions issued to APRA during the year; and

(f) all other information APRA has provided to the [type of ADI] that may assist you in fulfilling your role and responsibilities under APS 310.

2. There has been:

(a) no fraud, error or non-compliance with APRA Prudential Requirements that could have a material effect on the reporting of data to APRA under the FSCODA, or compliance with applicable Prudential Requirements;

(b) no fraud, error or non-compliance with APRA Prudential Requirements involving management or employees who have a significant role in the internal control structure; and

(c) no communications from APRA concerning non-compliance with, or deficiencies in, prudential reporting practices that could have a material effect on your report,

other than instances that have been provided to you in the course of your engagement

3. We have established and maintained adequate internal control to prevent and detect fraud and error, to ensure the [type of ADI] has:

(a) complied with all applicable Prudential Requirements; and

(b) provided reliable data to APRA in the ADI Reporting Forms prepared under the FSCODA;

4. There has been no breakdown in internal control or non compliance with the policies and procedures which are designed to ensure the [type of ADI] has:

(a) complied with all applicable Prudential Requirements; and

(b) provided reliable data to APRA in the ADI Reporting Forms prepared under the FSCODA,

other than instances that have been provided to you in the course of your engagement;

5. We have issued to APRA:

(a) all high level descriptions of our key risk management systems covering all major areas of risk, approved by the Board and management, and including all material changes to the risk management systems descriptions made during the year; and

(b) all information as prescribed by the Prudential Standards for disclosure to APRA within the prescribed period.

6. We have consulted with APRA on all matters such as new business ventures and other initiatives, where prescribed by the Prudential Standards, and provided you with the responses from APRA.

7. We have complied with all prudential and statutory requirements applicable to the [type of ADI] throughout the [period].

8. We have signed [or intend to sign] an unqualified declaration to APRA, from our CEO endorsed by the Board, in accordance with APS 310, attesting that for the financial year ended [date]:

(a) the key risks of the [type of ADI] have been identified;

(b) systems to monitor and manage those risks have been established including, where appropriate, by setting and requiring adherence to a series of prudent limits, and by adequate and timely reporting processes;

(c) the risk management systems are operating effectively and are adequate having regard to the risks they are designed to control; and

(d) the descriptions of risk management systems provided to APRA are accurate and current.

GS

9. With respect to ADI Reporting Forms prepared under the FSCODA:
   (a) the data has been compiled in accordance with the relevant APRA Prudential and Reporting Standards, and related guidance applicable to each form;
   (b) the Reporting Forms have been resubmitted where assurance engagement adjustments of a material nature were identified;
   (c) we believe the effects of the uncorrected misstatements identified by you during the assurance engagement, summarised in the accompanying schedule, are immaterial, both individually and in the aggregate, to the ADI Reporting Forms prepared under the FSCODA taken as a whole;
   (d) there are no material transactions that have not been recorded properly in the records supporting the ADI Reporting Forms; and
   (e) information in the ADI Reporting Forms, sourced from records other than the [type of ADI]'s accounting records, are prepared from reliable records applicable to the matters to be provided to APRA, in accordance with the applicable guidance provided by APRA.

10. No events have occurred subsequent to the financial year-end date and through to the date of this letter that would require adjustment to, or disclosure in, ADI Reporting Forms.

11. Additional Matters

    [*Include any additional matters relevant to the particular circumstances of the engagement.*]

We understand that your examination was made in accordance with Australian Auditing Standards and applicable Standards on Assurance Engagements, and was, therefore, designed primarily for the purpose of reporting pursuant to the requirements of APS 310, and that your procedures were limited to those which you considered necessary for that purpose.

Yours faithfully

[Name of signing officer and title]

Appendix 4

Example Auditor's Report

For an Annual Prudential Reporting Engagement Undertaken Pursuant to APRA Prudential Standard APS 310 *Audit and Related Matters* (Routine Reporting)

The following example auditor's report is to be used as a guide only and will need to be adapted according to individual engagement requirements and circumstances of the ADI.

[Note: If the report covers both the 'Level 1 ADI' and 'Level 2 group', this fact must be indicated by using the appropriate terminology, that is, 'the ADI' and 'the ADI and its controlled entities' (the Group).]

To [Chairman of Board or Board Audit Committee[41]] of [name of ADI]

Auditor's Annual Prudential Assurance Report for the Financial Year Ended [date]

We have performed an audit and reviews, as applicable, pursuant to the reporting requirements specified in Australian Prudential Regulation Authority (APRA) Prudential Standard APS 310 *Audit and Related Matters* (APS 310) for [name of ADI].

APS 310 requires an ADI to appoint an auditor to undertake an annual assurance engagement, as set out in that Prudential Standard. The responsibilities and reporting requirements arising from this appointment, have been outlined in our letter of engagement dated [date].

41 Or, for a foreign ADI, a senior officer outside Australia to whom authority has been delegated, in accordance with Prudential Standard APS 510 *Governance* (APS 510), for overseeing the Australian operations.

[Include only if applicable: "Our audit [and review] of the financial report(s) required under the *Corporations Act 2001* (Corporations Act) [or other appropriate local or overseas legislation] is directed towards obtaining sufficient evidence to form an opinion under the appropriate legislation. Our procedures were not designed to enable us to conclude on other matters required under APRA's Prudential Requirements. We have therefore performed additional procedures beyond those undertaken in order to meet our responsibilities in relation to our audit [and review] of the financial report(s) required under the [appropriate legislation]."

Use of Report(s)

This report has been prepared for distribution to the [Board (or Board Audit Committee)[42]], of [name of ADI] and APRA. This report is prepared in accordance with the terms of our engagement letter dated [date], in order to satisfy APRA's prudential reporting requirements for appointed auditors of ADIs, as specified in APS 310.

In accordance with the *Australian Prudential Regulation Authority Act 1998*, APRA may make this report available to other specified agencies when APRA is satisfied that such information may assist those agencies in performing their functions or exercising their powers.

This report is not to be distributed to any party other than [name of ADI], APRA, and other parties that APRA is lawfully entitled to provide relevant information. We disclaim any assumption of responsibility for any reliance on this report or the subject matter to which it relates to any party other than the Board, or Board Audit Committee, of [name of ADI], APRA, and other parties that APRA is lawfully entitled to provide relevant information.

Responsibilities of the [Title of Those Charged with Governance[43]]

In accordance with APS 310, it is the responsibility of [name of ADI]'s [Title of those charged with governance] and management to ensure that the [type of ADI] meets prudential and statutory requirements and has management practices to limit risks to prudent levels. This responsibility includes:

(a) ensuring that the information included in ADI Reporting Forms at the financial year-end is reliable and in accordance with the relevant APRA Prudential and Reporting Standards;

(b) establishing and maintaining internal controls that are designed to ensure:

- (i) the [type of ADI] complies with all applicable Prudential Requirements; and
- (ii) reliable data is provided to APRA in the ADI Reporting Forms prepared under the *Financial Sector (Collection of Data) Act 2001* (FSCODA);

(c) ensuring that the controls in (b) operate effectively throughout the financial year; and

(d) ensuring that the [type of ADI] complies with all relevant Prudential Requirements under the Banking Act and the FSCODA, including compliance with APRA Prudential Standards and Reporting Standards, during the financial year.

Appointed Auditor's Responsibility

Our responsibility is to conduct an audit and review as required under APS 310, described in PARTS A to D below, and to report our opinions and conclusions based on our audit and review.

PART A – Audit of Information Included in Specified ADI Reporting Forms at the Financial Year-end, Sourced from Accounting Records

Our responsibility is to express an opinion, based on our audit, on whether information sourced from [name of ADI]'s accounting records, included in the following ADI Reporting Forms of the [type of ADI] as at [financial year-end] is, in all material respects, reliable and in accordance with the relevant APRA Prudential and Reporting Standards:

[Attach all the ADI Reporting Forms, which are the subject matter of this assurance report, to the report, and identify on each ADI Reporting Form the date it was submitted

42 Or, for a foreign ADI, a senior officer outside Australia to whom authority has been delegated in accordance with APS 510 for overseeing the Australian operations.

43 Amend this term to reflect the appropriate title for those charged with governance of the ADI, for example, "Board of Directors" for a locally incorporated ADI or "senior country manager" (a senior officer outside Australia to whom authority has been delegated in accordance with APS 510, for overseeing the Australian operations) for a foreign ADI. Insert appropriate title, when prompted, throughout the report.

and whether or not the data items have been subjected to audit or review. Include in the assurance report by reference to "the data identified on the ADI Reporting Forms attached under Attachment 1 – XX"]

[Alternatively, list here, or include a reference to an appendix which lists the specific title, number and date submitted of each relevant ADI Reporting Form, based on those specified in Attachment A of APS 310, where such forms contain information sourced from accounting records, which have been subjected to audit.

Note: Clearly identify data items within each ADI Reporting Form that have been sourced from accounting records and are therefore the subject matter of this opinion.]

We have conducted our audit in accordance with applicable Australian Auditing Standards. These Auditing Standards require that we comply with relevant ethical requirements relating to audit engagements and plan and perform the audit to obtain reasonable assurance as to whether the relevant data, as listed above, is free from material misstatement.

An audit involves performing procedures to obtain audit evidence on whether the information sourced from the accounting records included in the specified ADI Reporting Forms is, in all material respects, reliable and in accordance with the relevant APRA Prudential and Reporting Standards. The procedures selected depend on our judgement, including our assessment of the risks of material misstatement of the data in the ADI Reporting Forms, whether due to fraud or error. In making those risk assessments, we considered internal control systems and compliance functions relevant to the preparation of the ADI Reporting Forms, in order to design audit procedures that are appropriate in the circumstances.

[If applicable: We have performed an independent audit [and review] of the financial report of [name of ADI] for the year [half-year] ended [date]. Our auditor's report on the financial report was signed on [date], and [was/was not] subject to modification.]

We believe that the audit evidence we have obtained is sufficient and appropriate to provide a basis for our audit opinion

PART B – Review of Information Included in Specified ADI Reporting Forms at the Financial Year-end, Sourced from Non-accounting Records

Our responsibility is to perform a review of the information sourced from non-accounting records, included in the following ADI Reporting Forms of [name of ADI] as at [financial year-end], and to express a conclusion based on our review.

[Attach all the ADI Reporting Forms, which are the subject matter of this assurance report, to the report, and identify on each ADI Reporting Form the date it was submitted and whether or not the data items have been subjected to audit or review. Include in the assurance report by reference to "the data identified on the ADI Reporting Forms attached under Attachment 1 – XX"]

[Alternatively, list here, or include a reference to an appendix which lists the specific title, number and date submitted of each relevant ADI Reporting Form, based on those specified in Attachment A of APS 310, where such forms contain information sourced from non-accounting records, which have been subjected to review.

Note: Clearly identify data items within each ADI Reporting Form that have been sourced from non-accounting records and therefore the subject matter of this conclusion.]

We have conducted our review in accordance with the AUASB's Standard on Assurance Engagements ASAE 3000 *Assurance Engagements Other than Audits or Reviews of Historical Financial Information*, in order to state whether, on the basis of the procedures described, anything has come to our attention that causes us to believe that the information in the relevant Reporting Forms as listed above, sourced from non-accounting records, is not, in all material respects, reliable and in accordance with the relevant APRA Prudential and Reporting Standards.

A review consists of making enquiries of responsible [name of ADI] personnel and applying analytical and other review procedures. A review is substantially less in scope than an audit conducted in accordance with Australian Auditing Standards, and consequently, does not enable us to obtain assurance that we would become aware of all significant matters that might be identified in an audit. Accordingly, we do not express an audit opinion.

Review procedures selected depend on our judgement, including our assessment of the risks of material misstatement of the ADI Reporting Forms, whether due to fraud or error. In making those risk assessments, we considered internal control systems and compliance functions relevant to the preparation of ADI Reporting Forms in order to design review procedures that are appropriate in the circumstances.

PART C – Review of Internal Controls Addressing Compliance with Prudential Requirements and Reliability of Data Included in APRA Reporting Forms

Our responsibility is to perform a review and express a conclusion, based on our review as described, on whether anything has come to our attention that causes us to believe that, for the financial year ended [date], in all material respects:

(a) [name of ADI] has not implemented internal controls that are designed to ensure:

   (i) compliance with all applicable Prudential Requirements; and

   (ii) reliable data is provided to APRA in the ADI Reporting Forms prepared under the FSCODA; and

(b) the controls in (a) have not operated effectively.

We have conducted our review in accordance with the AUASB's Standards on Assurance Engagements ASAE 3000 and ASAE 3100 *Compliance Engagements*. These ASAEs require us to comply with relevant ethical requirements relating to assurance engagements.

A review consists of making enquiries of responsible personnel and applying analytical and other review procedures. A review is substantially less in scope than an audit conducted in accordance with Australian Auditing Standards and consequently does not enable us to obtain assurance that we would become aware of all significant matters that might be identified in an audit. Accordingly, we do not express an audit opinion.

Review procedures selected depend on our judgement, including our assessment of the risks of a material breakdown in controls. In making those risk assessments, we considered internal control systems and compliance functions relevant to ensuring compliance with all Prudential Requirements and provision of reliable data to APRA in ADI Reporting Forms prepared under the FSCODA, in order to design assurance procedures that are appropriate in the circumstances.

PART D – Reporting on Compliance with Prudential Requirements

Our responsibility is to express a conclusion, based on our work performed under Parts A to C above, on whether anything has come to our attention that causes us to believe that, for the financial year ended [date], [name of ADI] has not, in all material respects, complied with all relevant Prudential Requirements under the Banking Act and the FSCODA, including compliance with APRA Prudential and Reporting Standards.

Inherent Limitations

There are inherent limitations in any internal control and compliance framework, and fraud, error or non-compliance with Prudential Requirements may occur and not be detected. As the systems, procedures and controls to ensure compliance with applicable APRA Prudential Requirements are part of the operations of the [type of ADI], it is possible that either the inherent limitations of the general internal control structure, or weaknesses in it, can impact on the effective operation of the specific controls of the [type of ADI].

Projection of any evaluation of internal controls to future periods is subject to the risk that controls may become inadequate because of changes in conditions, or that the degree of compliance may deteriorate.

An audit or review is not designed to detect all misstatements in ADI Reporting Forms, or deficiencies in internal controls, or instances of non-compliance with applicable Prudential Requirements, as procedures are not performed continuously throughout the [period] and procedures performed are undertaken on a test basis.

Consequently, there are inherent limitations on the level of assurance that can be provided.

Independence

In conducting our audit and review we have, to the best of our knowledge and belief, complied with the independence requirements specified by APRA in ADI Prudential Standard APS 510 *Governance*.

The opinion and conclusions in this report, expressed below, are to be read in the context of the foregoing comments.

[Basis for Qualified/Disclaimer of/Adverse Auditor's Opinion/Conclusion]

[Provide details or refer to attachment. Appendix 5 of this Guidance Statement provides an example format for reporting these findings.]

[Qualified/Disclaimer of/Adverse] Auditor's Opinion and Conclusions

PART A – Audit of Information Included in Specified ADI Reporting Forms at the Financial Year-end, Sourced from Accounting Records

In our opinion, the information in the following ADI Reporting Forms of [name of ADI] as at [financial year-end], sourced from the [type of ADI]'s accounting records, is, in all material respects, reliable and in accordance with the relevant APRA Prudential and Reporting Standards.

> [Attach all the ADI Reporting Forms, which are the subject matter of this assurance report, to the report, and identify on each ADI Reporting Form the date it was submitted and whether or not the data items have been subjected to audit or review. Include in the assurance report by reference to "the data identified on the ADI Reporting Forms attached under Attachment 1 – XX".]
>
> [Alternatively, list here, or include a reference to an appendix which lists the specific title, number and date submitted of each relevant ADI Reporting Form, based on those specified in Attachment A of APS 310, where such forms contain information sourced from accounting records, which have been subjected to reasonable assurance.
>
> Note: Clearly identify data items within each ADI Reporting Form that have been sourced from accounting records and therefore the subject matter of this opinion.]

PART B – Review of Information Included in Specified ADI Reporting Forms at the Financial Year-end, Sourced from Non-accounting Records

Based on our review, which is not an audit, nothing has come to our attention that causes us to believe that the information in the following ADI Reporting Forms of [name of ADI] as at [financial year-end], sourced from the [type of ADI]'s non-accounting records, is not, in all material respects, reliable and in accordance with the relevant APRA Prudential and Reporting Standards.

> [Attach all the ADI Reporting Forms, which are the subject matter of this assurance report, to the report, and identify on each ADI Reporting Form the date it was submitted and whether or not the data items have been subjected to audit or review. Include in the assurance report by reference to "the data identified on the ADI Reporting Forms attached under Attachment 1 – XX"]
>
> [Alternatively, list here, or include a reference to an appendix which lists the specific title, number and date submitted of each relevant ADI Reporting Form, based on those specified in Attachment A of APS 310, where such forms contain information sourced from non-accounting records, which have been subjected to limited assurance.
>
> Note: Clearly identify data items within each ADI Reporting Form that have been sourced from non-accounting records and therefore the subject matter of this conclusion.]

PART C – Review of Internal Controls Addressing Compliance with Prudential Requirements and Reliability of Data Included in ADI Reporting Forms

Based on our review, which is not an audit, nothing has come to our attention that causes us to believe that, for the financial year ended [date], in all material respects:

(a) [name of ADI] has not implemented internal controls that are designed to ensure:
   (i) compliance with all applicable Prudential Requirements; and
   (ii) reliable data is provided to APRA in the ADI Reporting Forms prepared under the FSCODA; and

(b) the controls in (a) have not operated effectively.

PART D – Reporting on Compliance with Prudential Requirements

Based on our audit and reviews in Parts A to C above, nothing has come to our attention that causes us to believe that, for the financial year ended [date], [name of ADI] has not complied, in all material respects, with all relevant Prudential Requirements under the Banking Act and the FSCODA, including compliance with APRA Prudential and Reporting Standards.

[Auditor's signature]

[Date of the Auditor's report]

[Auditor's address]

Appendix 5

Example Attachment to the Auditor's Report - Material Findings or Exceptions

The following example attachment to the appointed auditor's Annual Prudential Assurance Report is to be used as a guide only, and will need to be adapted according to the engagement requirements and circumstances of the ADI.

This attachment accompanies, and forms part of, the example Auditor's Report provided in Appendix 4.

ATTACHMENT 1: MATERIAL FINDINGS OR EXCEPTIONS

This attachment has been prepared for distribution to the [Board (or Board Audit Committee)][44] of [name of ADI] and APRA. It accompanies, and forms part of, the Auditor's Annual Prudential Assurance Report dated [date], for the financial year ended [date], prepared pursuant to the reporting requirements specified in APRA's Prudential Standard APS 310 - *Audit and Related Matters*.

(a) Material Misstatements in ADI Reporting Form(s) not previously advised by the [type of ADI] to APRA

During our audit and/or review of ADI Reporting Forms, we noted the following:

(i) Errors in Reporting Form XXX

Error: Line [ ]

This error was due to ……………………………………..

We recommend that ……………………………………

[The appropriate correct disclosure accompanies the reporting of any error(s)]

(b) Significant non-compliance with relevant Prudential Requirements under the *Banking Act 1959* and the *Financial Sector (Collection of Data) Act 2001*, including APRA Prudential and Reporting Standards, identified during the financial year and up to the date of signing the auditor's assurance report.

(i) Matters previously reported to APRA by the appointed auditor:

……………

(ii) Matters previously reported to APRA by the [type of ADI]:

……………

(iii) Matters not previously reported to APRA:

……………

[Auditor's signature]

[Date of the Auditor's report]

[Auditor's address]

44 Or, for a foreign ADI, a senior officer outside Australia to whom authority has been delegated in accordance with Prudential Standard APS 510 *Governance*, for overseeing the Australian operations.

GS

GS 013

Special Considerations in the Audit of Compliance Plans of Managed Investment Schemes

(Issued August 2009)

Issued by the Auditing and Assurance Standards Board.

Note from the Institute of Chartered Accountants Australia

This note, prepared by the technical editor, is not part of GS 013.

Historical development

August 2009: GS 013 issued. The new GS replaces AGS 1052 'Special Considerations in the Audit of Compliance Plans of Managed Investment Schemes', initially issued in December 1999 and revised in July 2002, which has now been withdrawn. It contains updated references to the *Corporations Act 2001* and relevant ASIC Regulatory Guides to reflect regulatory changes since AGS 1052 was last revised in 2002.

Contents

AUTHORITY STATEMENT

Authority Statement

The Auditing and Assurance Standards Board (AUASB) issues Guidance Statement GS 013 *Special Considerations in the Audit of Compliance Plans of Managed Investment Schemes* pursuant to section 227B of the *Australian Securities and Investments Commission Act 2001*, for the purposes of providing guidance on auditing and assurance matters.

This Guidance Statement is the reissuance of AGS 1052 *Special Considerations in the Audit of Compliance Plans of Managed Investment Schemes* (June 2002), with updated references to the *Corporations Act 2001* and relevant *ASIC Regulatory Guides* to reflect subsequent regulatory changes affecting managed investment schemes. Further consideration of these changes will be undertaken by the AUASB as part of the future revision of this Guidance Statement.

This Guidance Statement provides guidance to assist the auditor to fulfil the objectives of the audit or assurance engagement. It includes explanatory material on specific matters for the purposes of understanding and complying with AUASB Standards. The auditor exercises professional judgement when using this Guidance Statement and needs to refer to the *ASIC Regulatory Guides* where relevant.

The Guidance Statement does not prescribe or create new mandatory Requirements.

Dated: 12 August 2009

M H Kelsall
Chairman - AUASB

GS

Guidance Statement GS 013

Special Considerations in the Audit of Compliance Plans of Managed Investment Schemes

Application

1 This Guidance Statement has been formulated by the Auditing and Assurance Standards Board (AUASB) to provide guidance to auditors on various matters relating to the audit of compliance plans of registered managed investment schemes established in accordance with the requirements of the *Corporations Act 2001* ("the Act").

Issuance Date

2 This Guidance Statement is issued on 12 August 2009 by the AUASB and replaces AGS 1052 *Special Considerations in the Audit of Compliance Plans of Managed Investment Schemes* which was issued in July 2002.

Introduction

3 The auditor of a managed investment scheme compliance plan is required to adhere to the requirements contained in the Standards on Assurance Engagements, including ASAE 3100 *Compliance Engagements*. The AUASB recognises that the audit of compliance plans may give rise to a number of special audit considerations. Accordingly, this Guidance Statement has been developed to clarify the auditor's responsibilities on such engagements, and to provide guidance to the auditor on additional factors which the auditor may consider when planning, conducting and reporting on the audit of a scheme's compliance plan.

4 It is important to note that this Guidance Statement does not impose any responsibilities on the auditor of a managed investment scheme compliance plan beyond those which are imposed by Standards on Assurance Engagements and the requirements of the Act. Nonetheless, the provisions of the Act in this area may be augmented by Regulatory Guides (RGs) and any modifications to the Act effected by individual orders or class orders issued by the Australian Securities and Investments Commission (ASIC).

Legislative Background

5 The managed investments regulatory regime which is administered by ASIC, is contained in Chapter 5C of the Act. Part 5C.4 of Chapter 5C specifically deals with scheme compliance plans, and *inter alia* requires that each registered scheme have in place a compliance plan to ensure compliance with the scheme's constitution and the Act.

Regulatory Requirements for Compliance Plans

Significance of Compliance Plans to the Registration of Schemes

6 Under section 601EB(1) of the Act, ASIC must register a managed investment scheme within the prescribed timeframe, unless it appears to ASIC that certain requirements of the Act as specified in that provision have not been met, including whether the scheme's compliance plan meets the requirements of Part 5C.4 of the Act. Consequently, ASIC will review a scheme's compliance plan before approving a scheme's application for registration. ASIC Regulatory Guide RG 132 *Managed investments: Compliance plans* identifies the following approach which ASIC has stated it will adopt when reviewing the compliance plans of schemes prior to registration:

> **RG 132.14:** *We will actively assess compliance plans when we are deciding whether or not to register a scheme under s 601EB(1). We will consider, in the context of the type of scheme, whether the responsible entity has designed measures which adequately address the risks of not complying with its obligations. For example, a responsible entity must continuously monitor, review and audit the outcomes of its compliance activities. We will therefore assess whether the responsible entity's arrangements for doing this are adequate.*

7 RG 132 provides guidance to responsible entities on how to prepare a compliance plan and in particular, on the structured and systematic process which needs to be undertaken when developing such plans. Consequently, when reviewing a compliance plan for registration purposes, it is likely that ASIC considers matters outlined in RG 132 such as:

(a) the responsible entity's obligations under the Act and the scheme's constitution;

(b) the risks to ongoing compliance, given such matters as the nature of the scheme, its operating environment, its size, and the nature of its assets;

(c) the likelihood and potential impact of failing to achieve the outcomes intended by the Act and the scheme's constitution;

(d) the appropriateness of the focus adopted in the compliance plan and the compliance measures in terms of stated outcomes; and

(e) the specific requirements of Part 5C.4 of the Act.

8 ASIC has the authority to withhold the scheme's registration, until such time as any deficiencies in the compliance plan which it may have identified during the registration process are rectified by the responsible entity.

9 Section 601HE(1) of the Act enables the responsible entity to make changes to the compliance plan, to facilitate the updating of the compliance plan as circumstances change, or in the case that particular measures are found to be ineffective. Under section 601HE(2), ASIC may also require that the responsible entity make changes to the compliance plan in certain circumstances. Where modifications to the compliance plan are made or a compliance plan is repealed and replaced, the auditor ascertains that it is lodged with ASIC in accordance with the requirements of section 601HE(3).

Contents of the Compliance Plan

10 Section 601HA of the Act requires each registered scheme to have in place a compliance plan which sets out "adequate measures" that the responsible entity is to apply in operating the scheme to ensure compliance with the Act and the scheme's constitution.

11 Specific matters which are identified in section 601HA that are to be included in compliance plans include arrangements for:

(a) the identification and custody of scheme property;

(b) the operation and functions of the scheme's compliance committee, where required;

(c) the valuation of scheme property;

(d) ensuring the compliance plan is audited as required by section 601HG;

(e) ensuring adequate records are kept of the scheme's operations; and

(f) compliance with other matters prescribed in the regulations.

12 RG 132 outlines considerations which a responsible entity is to take into account when preparing compliance plans in order to satisfy the requirements of section 601HA. RG 132 also emphasises that compliance plans for each scheme are to include compliance measures which provide clear links with the requirements of the Act and the scheme's constitution. Such measures are to be set out in the compliance plan with sufficient clarity and detail to enable the responsible entity's directors and where required, the compliance committee, as well as the compliance plan auditor to assess whether the responsible entity has complied with the compliance plan and the requirements of section 601HA.

13 RG 45 *Mortgage schemes—improving disclosure for retail investors* (September 2008) and RG 46 *Unlisted property schemes—improving disclosure for retail investors* (September 2008) expects compliance plans of the relevant schemes to contain adequate procedures to ensure disclosure against the benchmarks specified in the regulatory guides. The Act imposes various obligations on the responsible entity and its officers to ensure that the requirements of section 601HA are met. These obligations include:

(a) Section 601FC(1)(g) – which specifically requires the responsible entity of a registered scheme to ensure that the scheme's compliance plan meets the requirements of section 601HA.

(b) Section 601FC(1)(h) – which requires the responsible entity to comply with the scheme's compliance plan.

(c) Section 601JA(1) – which obliges the responsible entity to establish a compliance committee, if less than half of the directors of the responsible entity are external directors. Such a committee is *inter alia* required to monitor compliance with the compliance plan and assess the adequacy of the compliance plan in accordance with section 601JC(1).

(d) Notwithstanding the above, section 601FD(1)(f) places the onus on the officers of the responsible entity to take all steps that a reasonable person would take to ensure that the responsible entity complies with the compliance plan.

14 RG 132 expects the responsible entity, when preparing a compliance plan for the first time and continuously thereafter, to undertake a due diligence process to consider its responsibilities under the Act and the scheme's constitution, identify risks of non-compliance and establish measures to address those risks. ASIC has benchmarked compliance plans for schemes within various industries and provided examples of better compliance plans for those schemes in the following regulatory guides:

- RG 116 Commentary on compliance plans: Agricultural industry schemes (April 2004).
- RG 117 Commentary on compliance plans: Financial asset schemes (April 2004)
- RG 118 Commentary on compliance plans: Contributory mortgage schemes (April 2004)
- RG 119 Commentary on compliance plans: Pooled mortgage schemes (April 2004).
- RG 120 Commentary on compliance plans: Property schemes (April 2004).

Compliance Structure

15 RG 132 sets out ASIC's expectations of responsible entities when preparing compliance plans for registered schemes to meet the requirements of the Act. As identified in RG 132, the responsible entity is expected to continuously monitor the outcomes of its compliance activities in order to satisfy the requirements of section 601HA. To enable such monitoring and assessment to occur, the responsible entity is expected to establish and maintain compliance reporting structures to prevent, and where necessary to identify and respond to breaches of its compliance plan, and to promote what ASIC has described as a "culture of compliance".

16 With regard to the above, ASIC has indicated that it expects such compliance structures to include clear procedures for recording and reporting on compliance, a complaints handling system[1], systems to identify, investigate and rectify recurring and systemic problems, and appropriately trained staff. The responsible entity is also expected to have adequate compliance measures in place for monitoring and maintaining an adequate level of control over any activities which it may outsource to external service providers.

Auditing the Compliance Plan

Who May Audit the Compliance Plan?

17 In accordance with section 601HG(1) of the Act, the responsible entity of a registered scheme is required to ensure that at all times a registered company auditor, an audit firm or an authorised audit company is engaged to audit compliance with the scheme's compliance plan. Section 601HG(2) *inter alia* prohibits the auditor of the responsible entity's financial report from also acting as the auditor of the compliance plan. However, section 601HG(2A) allows another auditor from the same firm or company to undertake the compliance plan audit of a scheme managed by the responsible entity. Furthermore, there is no prohibition on the compliance plan auditor from also performing the statutory audit of the scheme's financial report.

1 See RG 139 *Approval and oversight of external dispute resolution schemes.*

Agreeing on the Terms of the Audit Engagement with the Responsible Entity

18 ASAE 3100 requires the auditor of the compliance plan to agree on the terms of the compliance plan audit engagement with the responsible entity, which are required to be recorded in writing by the auditor and forwarded to the responsible entity. Such terms may be outlined in an audit engagement letter.[2] The auditor has regard to the requirements of ASAE 3100 relevant on agreeing the terms of the assurance engagement and applies those requirements when agreeing on the terms of a compliance plan audit engagement.[3]

19 Other than matters covered by ASAE 3100, the engagement letter may also outline arrangements for liaison with the responsible entity's compliance committee (if applicable), other compliance advisors, and other auditors, including the auditor of the responsible entity's financial report and the auditor of the scheme's financial report.

20 The compliance plan auditor may also use the engagement letter to clarify the respective roles of the responsible entity's directors and the auditor, by contrasting the respective statutory responsibilities of the responsible entity and the compliance plan auditor under Part 5C.4 of the Act. In particular, it is important to highlight in the engagement letter the responsible entity's obligation to establish and maintain an adequate compliance plan and have in place adequate measures and structures to ensure compliance with the Act and the scheme's constitution. The auditor obtains acknowledgment of this obligation from the directors of the responsible entity when obtaining agreement on the terms of the compliance plan audit engagement. An example engagement letter illustrating such agreement is provided in Appendix 1 to this Guidance Statement.

Clarifying the Compliance Plan Auditor's Role

Role of the Responsible Entity

21 Under the Act, the responsible entity is required to ensure that the scheme has a compliance plan which meets the requirements of section 601HA. This includes that the compliance plan must set out adequate measures that the responsible entity is to apply in operating the scheme to ensure compliance with the Act and the scheme's constitution. The compliance plan, which is lodged with ASIC with the application to register as a managed investment scheme under section 601EA, must be signed by all the directors of the responsible entity under section 601HC and arrangements must be in place for the audit of the compliance plan under section 601HG. Section 601FD(1)(f) requires the directors of the responsible entity to take all steps that a reasonable person would take to ensure that the responsible entity complies with the Act, the scheme's constitution and the scheme's compliance plan.

Role of the Compliance Plan Auditor

22 The role of the compliance plan auditor under section 601HG(3) of the Act is to examine the scheme's compliance plan and carry out an audit of the responsible entity's compliance with the compliance plan for the financial year. Furthermore, the auditor of the compliance plan must give the responsible entity an audit report which states whether in the auditor's opinion:

(a) the responsible entity has complied with the scheme's compliance plan during the financial year; and

(b) the compliance plan continues to meet the requirements of Part 5C.4 of the Act.

The second part of the auditor's opinion as stated in (b) above, is to be expressed "as at" the date of the end of the financial year.[4]

GS

2 Or other suitable form of audit contract.

3 The procedures for agreeing the terms of an engagement relevant to a financial report audit engagement are contained in ASA 210 *Terms of Audit Engagements*, and may be helpful in determining procedures for agreeing the terms of an engagement applicable to a compliance plan audit engagement

4 As the wording in section 601HG(3)(c)(ii) is ambiguous, the AUASB believes that the expression "continues to meet" may be interpreted to mean "as at" the end of the scheme's financial year.

Inherent Limitations of Auditing Compliance with the Compliance Plan

23 Due to the nature of audit testing and other inherent limitations of an audit, together with the inherent limitations of a compliance plan and its related compliance measures, there is a possibility that a properly planned and executed audit will not detect all deficiencies in a scheme's compliance plan. Accordingly, the audit opinion under section 601HG(3) is expressed in terms of reasonable assurance and cannot constitute a guarantee that the compliance plan is completely free from any deficiency, or that all compliance breaches have been detected.

24 There are also practical limitations in requiring an auditor to perform a continuous examination of the compliance plan, and form an opinion that the entity has complied at all times with the Act during the period covered by the compliance plan audit report. However, the auditor performs tests periodically throughout the financial year to obtain evidence and have reasonable assurance that the measures complied with the written descriptions and were adequate throughout the period under examination.

Reporting on Whether the Compliance Plan "Continues to Meet" the Requirements of Part 5C.4 of the Corporations Act

25 The requirements of the Act relating to reporting on whether the compliance plan "continues to meet" the requirements of Part 5C.4, including matters under section 601HA(1), are stated in broad terms. Such requirements are augmented by the examples and guidance in the Annexure to RG 132 and the additional expectation that compliance plan auditors consider whether the compliance plan is adequate to ensure compliance with the disclosure and advertising obligations of RG 45 for mortgage schemes and RG 46 for unlisted property schemes. The auditor uses such criteria to assess the appropriateness of the design of the compliance measures contained in a scheme's compliance plan.

26 The compliance plan auditor considers how the responsible entity has satisfied itself that the scheme's compliance plan and the measures within it continue to be appropriate throughout the financial year. The Annexure to RG 132 provides general guidance about various matters which may be considered by responsible entities when developing the scheme's compliance plan. In addition, ASIC has benchmarked compliance plans for various industry schemes and provided examples of better compliance plans for those types of schemes in RG 116, RG 117, RG 118, RG 119 and RG 120. The compliance plan auditor may also consider these matters when planning and undertaking a compliance plan audit. However, as compliance plans will vary between different responsible entities and their respective managed investment schemes, it will be necessary for the auditor to apply professional judgement when applying audit procedures and evaluating compliance plans and the design of compliance measures, having regard to the size and complexity of the particular managed investment scheme under examination.

Planning the Compliance Plan Audit

Materiality

27 The auditor considers materiality when:

(a) determining the nature, timing and extent of audit procedures; and

(b) evaluating the effect of identified compliance plan breaches or weaknesses in compliance measures.

28 Materiality is addressed in the context of the responsible entity's compliance objectives, which are developed having regard to the protection of the interests of scheme members as a whole. Materiality considerations are therefore viewed within the context of setting out adequate measures that the responsible entity is to apply in operating the scheme to ensure compliance with the Act and the scheme's constitution. In this respect, materiality is assessed for the compliance plan of each managed investment scheme being audited, relevant to the area of activity being examined, and whether the compliance measures in the compliance plan will reduce to an acceptably low level the risks that threaten achievement of those objectives and which otherwise could adversely affect the interests of scheme members.

29 The auditor is expected to report significant detected breaches, which either individually or collectively, the auditor judges to be material. The guidance on the meaning and application of the concept of materiality contained in ASAE 3100 is adapted by the compliance plan auditor, as appropriate, to the task of judging adherence to the compliance plan and conformity with the relevant provisions in Part 5C.4 of the Act. However, it is not possible to give a definitive view on what may constitute a material breach of a scheme's compliance plan, other than to suggest that the auditor exercises appropriate professional judgement having regard to the responsible entity's obligations to scheme members, together with the size, complexity and nature of a scheme's activities when determining whether a breach is to be considered material.

30 As identified in ASAE 3100, when assessing materiality, the auditor considers qualitative factors as well as quantitative factors. The following are examples of qualitative factors that may be relevant:

(a) the specific requirements of the terms of the engagement;

(b) the significance of identified compliance plan breaches or weaknesses in compliance measures;

(c) the cost of alternative compliance measures relative to their likely benefit; and

(d) the length of time which an identified compliance breach was in existence.

Other Audit Planning Considerations

31 The auditor of the compliance plan considers:

(a) the adequacy of the measures set out in the compliance plan;

(b) key responsibilities and risks identified in the compliance plan;

(c) processes established by the responsible entity to implement the measures outlined in the compliance plan; and

(d) processes established by the responsible entity to monitor adherence to the compliance plan.

32 When evaluating the responsible entity's adherence to the compliance plan and the ongoing adequacy of its measures, the auditor will need to obtain from management a copy of the plan and the detailed measures which it provides, together with a written description of the procedures and structures which the responsible entity has established to ensure compliance. RG 132 indicates that a scheme's compliance plan needs to describe compliance activities in sufficient detail and certainty to enable the auditor to assess whether or not the plan has been complied with. Such information will be required by the auditor when designing audit procedures to assess whether the compliance measures and systems are operating effectively and are adequately managing compliance risks.

33 To further assist in the audit of the compliance plan, the auditor considers various matters when planning the audit, including:

(a) the scheme's constitution;

(b) the Australian financial services licence held by the responsible entity and, in particular, any conditions imposed thereon. In this regard, the auditor may choose to examine details of the responsible entity's licence application, in particular those sections relating to the nature of the scheme's business and the compliance structure put in place by the responsible entity.

(c) the nature and extent of any recent changes to the scheme's compliance plan and whether any detected breaches are deemed to be material in light of the revised compliance plan;

(d) the nature and extent of any changes to the operation of the scheme itself;

(e) changes to the Act and related regulations;

(f) reports and other documents submitted to the compliance committee and/or the board of the responsible entity regarding the operation of the scheme and its compliance functions; and

(g) previous auditor's reports, including the auditor's report on financial reports of the responsible entity, the scheme and other schemes operated by the responsible entity, and related management letters.

Other Matters to be Considered During the Audit of the Compliance Plan

34 As part of the audit of the compliance plan, the auditor considers the measures in the compliance plan which relate to the responsible entity's monitoring of, and reporting on specific matters incorporated into the plan. Such a consideration may include, but is not limited to, the following matters:

(a) whether reporting to the board of directors or compliance committee by management on compliance matters is adequate in terms of the extent and frequency of reporting, having regard to the size and complexity of the scheme;

(b) whether compliance plan breaches are likely to be detected and reported by the monitoring systems that have been implemented by the responsible entity. Where breaches of compliance procedures have been detected, the auditor considers whether such breaches are material either in themselves, or where they are of a recurring nature and have not been rectified, whether their cumulative effect renders them to be a material non-compliance;

(c) identifying systems which the responsible entity uses to ensure that business units and staff comply with the measures in the compliance plan on a day to day basis. It is also important for the auditor to determine whether the systems and procedures which the responsible entity has in place under its compliance plan are able to correct the effects of significant compliance breaches of which management becomes aware; and

(d) whether the responsible entity has a process in place to identify and review the scheme's compliance risks on a periodic basis so as to ensure that its compliance plan contains "adequate" measures and that it complies with the scheme's constitution and the requirements in Part 5C.4 of the Act.

35 Some responsible entities may have a number of schemes with very similar compliance plans, electing (in some instances) to incorporate, into a compliance plan, the provisions of an existing compliance plan by reference. In such situations, the compliance plan auditor may choose to design and apply common audit tests and procedures across more than one scheme, as considered necessary in the circumstances. However, the compliance plan auditor ensures that the tests and procedures which are applied are representative across all schemes that incorporate the provisions of the incorporated (original) compliance plan, and that they provide sufficient and appropriate audit evidence to enable the expression of the auditor's opinion on each scheme's compliance plan as required by section 601HG(3) of the Act.

36 In addition, a responsible entity may choose to outsource various functions (e.g. information technology services or registry services) and engage external service providers. The responsible entity is expected to include measures in the compliance plan to supervise these service providers, given that the responsible entity is considered to be responsible under the Act both for the compliance of those activities which are performed by the responsible entity itself, as well as those functions which may be outsourced to external service providers.

37 In such circumstances, the compliance plan auditor audits compliance with the measures in the compliance plan relating to the supervision by the responsible entity of its service providers. However, the compliance plan auditor is not expected to conduct an audit of these service providers, as it is the obligation of the responsible entity and not the compliance plan auditor, to ensure that the service providers adhere to the responsible entity's compliance plan for each scheme under its control. In this context, the auditor has particular regard to matters raised in ASA 402 *Audit Considerations Relating to Entities Using Service Organisations* and GS 007 *Audit Implications of the Use of Service Organisations for Investment Management Services*.

The Auditor's Report on the Compliance Plan Audit

38 Prior to issuing the auditor's report on the compliance plan audit, the auditor seeks a written representation from the directors of the responsible entity which contains their assertions that the responsible entity has complied with the scheme's compliance plan during the financial year, and that the plan continues to meet the requirements of Part 5C.4 of the Act.

39 Section 601HG(3) requires the auditor to give their auditor's report to the current responsible entity, therefore the auditor's report is addressed to the scheme's responsible entity. In addition, section 601HG(7) requires the responsible entity to lodge the auditor's report with ASIC at the same time as the financial statements and reports of the scheme are lodged with ASIC.

40 When reporting on the matters required by section 601HG(3), the auditor follows the requirements contained in ASAE 3100. If the auditor is required to modify the auditor's report because of a material breach of the compliance plan or because of some ongoing material weakness in compliance measures, the auditor applies the requirements in ASAE 3100 when drafting the modified auditor's report. Examples of auditor's reports that may be appropriate for this type of engagement are included in Appendix 2 to this Guidance Statement.

Conformity with International Pronouncements

41 There is no equivalent International Auditing Practice Statement (IAPS) to this Guidance Statement.

Appendix 1

Example Engagement Letter for the Audit of a Managed Investment Scheme Compliance Plan

To the Board of Directors[5] of [name of responsible entity]:

Scope

You have requested that we audit the compliance plan of the [name of managed investment scheme] ("the scheme")[6], for which [name of responsible entity] acts as its responsible entity in accordance with the requirements of Chapter 5C of the *Corporations Act 2001*. We are pleased to confirm our acceptance and our understanding of this engagement by means of this letter. Our audit will be conducted pursuant to section 601HG of the *Corporations Act 2001* with the objective of our expressing an opinion on:

(a) compliance by the responsible entity with the scheme's compliance plan during the financial year ended 30 June 20XX; and

(b) whether the compliance plan of the scheme continues to meet the requirements of Part 5C.4 of the *Corporations Act 2001* as at 30 June 20XX.

We will conduct our audit in accordance with Standards on Assurance Engagements. Those Standards require that we comply with relevant ethical requirements relating to assurance engagements and plan and perform the audit to obtain reasonable assurance whether the responsible entity has complied with the compliance plan and the compliance plan meets the requirements of the Act in all material respects. The audit will involve performing audit procedures to obtain an understanding of the compliance plan and the compliance measures which have been operated by the responsible entity under that plan. The procedures selected depend on the auditor's judgement and the auditor's assessment of the risks of non-compliance with the plan.

Because of the test nature and other inherent limitations of an audit, together with the inherent limitations of a compliance plan and the measures contained within it, there is an unavoidable

5 Or Chairman/Managing Director.

6 Or other suitable description e.g. "the fund".

GS

risk that even some material breaches of the compliance plan or inadequacies in the plan's measures may remain undiscovered. However, we expect to provide you with a separate letter concerning any material weaknesses in the scheme's compliance plan or breaches thereof, that come to our attention during the audit of the scheme's compliance plan.

We take this opportunity to remind you that the responsibility for ensuring compliance with the scheme's compliance plan and that the scheme's plan meets the requirements of section 601HA of the *Corporations Act 2001* is that of [the directors] of [name of responsible entity]. Our auditor's report will explain that [the directors] are responsible for the adequacy of the measures in the scheme's compliance plan to ensure compliance with the *Corporations Act 2001* and the scheme's constitution and for compliance with the measures and structures described in the compliance plan.

As part of our audit process, we will request from management written confirmation concerning representations made to us in connection with the audit.

Liaison with Compliance Committee[7]

We understand that the responsible entity has established a compliance committee to monitor compliance with the scheme's compliance plan. We will accordingly, unless requested otherwise by you, liaise directly with the scheme's compliance committee in respect of matters pertaining to our audit of the scheme's compliance plan. In the first instance however, we will address all reports and correspondence to the Board of Directors[8] of the [name of responsible entity].

Internal Audit Function[9]

As a component of the compliance measures established by the responsible entity, the internal audit function may be relevant in determining the nature, timing and extent of our audit procedures. In view of this, it is our intention to evaluate the internal audit function in so far as we believe it may be relevant to our audit of the compliance plan, and liaise closely with the internal auditor and to agree certain areas where we may use the internal auditor's work.

Where we intend to use the work carried out by the internal audit function, we will evaluate and review the work performed and carry out such tests and other procedures as we consider necessary.

Liaison with Other Auditors[10]

It is our understanding that [name of firm] has been appointed under the *Corporations Act 2001* as the external auditor of the responsible entity's financial report. We also understand that [name of firm] has been appointed to perform the statutory audit of the scheme's financial report. It may be necessary from time to time, for us to communicate with [name(s) of firm(s)] on matters relevant to our audit of the compliance plan, and similarly, for [name(s) of firm(s)] to make enquiries of us in the context of their audits. Unless otherwise stated, the return of a signed copy of this engagement letter will be acknowledged as your approval for us to communicate with [name(s) of firm(s)] in respect of such matters involving the scheme and the responsible entity.

Changes to the Compliance Plan

As you may be aware, section 601HE(1) of the Act enables a responsible entity to make modifications to a compliance plan, or repeal it and replace it with a new compliance plan. Accordingly, as directors of the responsible entity, we would ask that you note your responsibilities in this regard, and ensure that where any modifications are made to the compliance plan or a compliance plan is repealed and replaced, that the modifications or the new compliance plan are lodged with ASIC within the prescribed period. Furthermore, in order to facilitate the planning of the audit, we request that you ensure that we are advised of any changes to the compliance plan on a timely basis.

7 Omit if not applicable.

8 Or Chairman/Managing Director.

9 Omit if not applicable.

10 Omit if not applicable.

Other Matters

We confirm that, to the best of our knowledge and belief, we currently are eligible under Section 601HG of the *Corporations Act 2001* to audit the scheme's compliance plan. In conducting our audit of the compliance plan, should we become aware that we are not eligible to act as auditor of the compliance plan under the *Corporations Act 2001*, we shall notify you on a timely basis.

The *Corporations Act 2001* includes specific restrictions on the relationships that can exist between the responsible entity and the auditors of the scheme's compliance plan. To assist us in meeting the eligibility requirements of the *Corporations Act 2001*, and to the extent permitted by law and regulation, we request you discuss with us the provision of services offered to you by [insert auditor's firm name] prior to engaging or accepting the service.

Fees

We look forward to full co-operation with your staff and we trust that they will make available to us whatever records, documentation and other information we request in connection with our audit.

[*Insert additional information here regarding fee arrangements and billings, as appropriate.*]

Please sign and return the attached copy of this letter to indicate that it is in accordance with your understanding of our agreement.

Yours faithfully,

(signed)

....

[Auditor's name] [Date]

Acknowledged on behalf of [name of responsible entity] by:

....

[Name and Title] [Date]

Appendix 2

Example Audit Reports on Managed Investment Scheme Compliance Plans Pursuant to Section 601HG of the *Corporations Act 2001*

Example 1: Unmodified Auditor's Report

INDEPENDENT AUDITOR'S REPORT

To the Directors of [name of responsible entity]:

We have audited the compliance plan of [name of managed investment scheme] which was established by [name of responsible entity] as the responsible entity for the scheme[11] for the financial year ended [date]. The compliance plan was approved by the directors of the responsible entity on [date] and lodged with the Australian Securities and Investment Commission on [date].

Directors' Responsibility for the Compliance Plan

The directors of the responsible entity are responsible for ensuring that the scheme's compliance plan meets the requirements of Section 601HA of the *Corporations Act 2001*, including that it sets out adequate measures that the responsible entity is to apply in operating the scheme to ensure compliance with the *Corporations Act 2001* and the scheme's constitution, and for

11 Or other suitable description e.g. "the fund".

GS

complying with the compliance plan. These responsibilities are set out in Part 5C.2 of the *Corporations Act 2001*.[12]

Auditor's Responsibility

Our responsibility is to express an opinion on whether the responsible entity complied with the compliance plan during the financial year ended 30 June 20XX and the compliance plan continues to meet the requirements of Part 5C.4 of the *Corporations Act 2001* as at that date, in all material respects. We conducted our audit in accordance with Standards on Assurance Engagements. These Standards on Assurance Engagements require that we comply with relevant ethical requirements relating to assurance engagements and plan and perform the engagement to obtain reasonable assurance that the responsible entity complied with the compliance plan and the plan met the requirements of the *Corporations Act 2001.* Our procedures included obtaining an understanding of the compliance plan and the measures which it contains and examining, on a test basis, evidence supporting the operation of these measures. These procedures have been undertaken to form an opinion whether, in all material respects, the responsible entity has complied with the compliance plan during the financial year ended 30 June 20XX, and the compliance plan continues to meet the requirements of Part 5C.4 of the *Corporations Act 2001* as at that date.

Use of Report

This audit report has been prepared for [name of responsible entity] as the responsible entity of [name of scheme] in accordance with section 601HG of the *Corporations Act 2001.* We disclaim any assumption of responsibility for any reliance on this report to any persons or users other than the [intended users] of the responsible entity, or for any purpose other than that for which it was prepared.

Inherent Limitations

Because of the inherent limitations of any compliance measures, as documented in the compliance plan, it is possible that fraud, error, or non-compliance with laws and regulations may occur and not be detected. An audit is not designed to detect all weaknesses in a compliance plan and the measures in the plan, as an audit is not performed continuously throughout the financial year and the audit procedures performed on the compliance plan and measures are undertaken on a test basis.

Any projection of the evaluation of the compliance plan to future periods is subject to the risk that the compliance measures in the plan may become inadequate because of changes in conditions or circumstances, or that the degree of compliance with them may deteriorate.

The audit opinion expressed in this report has been formed on the above basis.

Audit Opinion

In my opinion, in all material respects:

(a) [name of responsible entity] has complied with the compliance plan of [name of scheme] for the financial year ended 30 June 20XX; and

(b) the compliance plan continues to meet the requirements of Part 5C.4 of the *Corporations Act 2001* as at that date.

[Auditor's signature]

[Date of the auditor's report]

[Auditor's address]

12 The auditor is encouraged to obtain a statement (or letter of representation) signed by the directors of the responsible entity which affirms these responsibilities.

Example 2: Modified Auditor's Report – Qualified Audit Opinion

The following example is to be used as a guide only and is not intended to suggest standard wording for the circumstances of particular modifications giving rise to a qualified opinion.

INDEPENDENT AUDITOR'S REPORT

To the Directors of [name of responsible entity]:

We have audited the compliance plan of [name of managed investment scheme] which was established by [name of responsible entity] as the responsible entity for the scheme[13] for the financial year ended [date]. The compliance plan was approved by the directors of the responsible entity on [date] and lodged with the Australian Securities and Investment Commission on [date].

Directors' Responsibility for the Compliance Plan

The directors of the responsible entity are responsible for ensuring that the scheme's compliance plan meets the requirements of Section 601HA of the *Corporations Act 2001*, including that it sets out adequate measures that the responsible entity is to apply in operating the scheme to ensure compliance with the *Corporations Act 2001* and the scheme's constitution, and for complying with the compliance plan. These responsibilities are set out in Part 5C.2 of the *Corporations Act 2001*.[14]

Auditor's Responsibility

Our responsibility is to express an opinion on whether the responsible entity complied with the compliance plan during the financial year ended 30 June 20XX and the compliance plan continues to meet the requirements of Part 5C.4 of the *Corporations Act 2001* as at that date, in all material respects. We conducted our audit in accordance with Standards on Assurance Engagements. These Standards on Assurance Engagements require that we comply with relevant ethical requirements relating to assurance engagements and plan and perform the engagement to obtain reasonable assurance that the responsible entity complied with the compliance plan and the plan met the requirements of the *Corporations Act 2001*. Our procedures included obtaining an understanding of the compliance plan and the measures which it contains and examining, on a test basis, evidence supporting the operation of these measures. These procedures have been undertaken to form an opinion whether, in all material respects, the responsible entity has complied with the compliance plan during the financial year ended 30 June 20XX, and the compliance plan continues to meet the requirements of Part 5C.4 of the *Corporations Act 2001* as at that date.

Use of Report

This audit report has been prepared for [name of responsible entity] as the responsible entity of [name of scheme] in accordance with section 601HG of the *Corporations Act 2001*. We disclaim any assumption of responsibility for any reliance on this report to any persons or users other than the [intended users] of the responsible entity, or for any purpose other than that for which it was prepared.

Inherent Limitations

Because of the inherent limitations of any compliance measures, as documented in the compliance plan, it is possible that fraud, error, or non-compliance with laws and regulations may occur and not be detected. An audit is not designed to detect all weaknesses in a compliance plan and the measures in the plan, as an audit is not performed continuously throughout the financial year and the audit procedures performed on the compliance plan and measures are undertaken on a test basis.

Any projection of the evaluation of the compliance plan to future periods is subject to the risk that the compliance measures in the plan may become inadequate because of changes in conditions or circumstances, or that the degree of compliance with them may deteriorate.

13 Or other suitable description e.g. "the fund".

14 The auditor is encouraged to obtain a statement (or letter of representation) signed by the directors of the responsible entity which affirms these responsibilities.

The audit opinion expressed in this report has been formed on the above basis.

Basis for Qualified Auditor's Opinion

Our audit of the compliance plan has identified instances of material non-compliance with measures in the compliance plan relating to [describe area of scheme operations]. The effect of this breach is that [describe effect].

Furthermore, our audit has identified that the measures in the compliance plan designed to meet the requirement to [describe and identify requirement in the *Corporations Act 2001*] were not effective because of [give reasons]. We are therefore unable to provide reasonable assurance in relation to the appropriateness of the design of these compliance plan measures throughout the financial year. While steps have been taken to overcome this matter by [give details], the revised compliance plan measures have not been in place for a sufficient period of time for us to be able to fully assess their effectiveness.

Qualified Auditor's Opinion

In our opinion, except for the matters referred to in the basis for qualified auditor's opinion section, in all material respects:

(a) [name of responsible entity] has complied with the compliance plan of [name of scheme] for the financial year ended 30 June 20XX; and

(b) the compliance plan continues to meet the requirements of Part 5C.4 of the *Corporations Act 2001* as at that date.

[Auditor's signature]

[Date of the auditor's report]

[Auditor's address]

GS 014

Auditing Mortgage Schemes

(Issued August 2009)

Issued by the Auditing and Assurance Standards Board.

Note from the Institute of Chartered Accountants Australia

This note, prepared by the technical editor, is not part of GS 014.

Historical development

August 2009: GS 014 issued. The new GS replaces AGS 1058 'Auditing Mortgage Investment Schemes', first issued in August 2001 and revised in July 2002, which has been withdrawn. It contains updated references to the *Corporation Act 2001* and relevant ASIC Regulatory Guides to reflect regulatory changes since AGS 1058 was last revised in 2002.

GS

Contents

AUTHORITY STATEMENT

Authority Statement

The Auditing and Assurance Standards Board (AUASB) issues Guidance Statement GS 014 *Auditing Mortgage Schemes* pursuant to section 227B of the *Australian Securities and Investments Commission Act 2001*, for the purposes of providing guidance on auditing and assurance matters.

This Guidance Statement is the re-issuance of AGS 1058 *Auditing Mortgage Investment Schemes* (July 2002), with updated references to the *Corporations Act 2001* and relevant *ASIC Regulatory Guides* to reflect subsequent regulatory changes affecting mortgage schemes. Further consideration of these changes will be undertaken by the AUASB as part of the future revision of this Guidance Statement.

This Guidance Statement provides guidance to assist the auditor to fulfil the objectives of the audit or assurance engagement. It includes explanatory material on specific matters for the purposes of understanding and complying with AUASB Standards. The auditor exercises professional judgement when using this Guidance Statement and needs to refer to the *ASIC Regulatory Guides* where relevant.

The Guidance Statement does not prescribe or create new mandatory Requirements.

Dated 12 August 2009

M H Kelsall
Chairman - AUASB

Guidance Statement GS 014

Auditing Mortgage Schemes

Application

1 This Guidance Statement has been formulated by the Auditing and Assurance Standards Board (AUASB) to provide guidance to auditors of mortgage schemes which are regulated by the Australian Securities and Investments Commission (ASIC) and are subject to Chapter 5C of the *Corporations Act 2001* (the "Act").

Issuance Date

2 This Guidance Statement is issued on 12 August 2009 by the AUASB and replaces AGS 1058 *Auditing Mortgage Investment Schemes* which was issued in July 2002.

Introduction

3 The guidance in this Guidance Statement is to be read in conjunction with that contained in GS 013 *Special Considerations in the Audit of Compliance Plans of Managed Investment Schemes* for audits of mortgage schemes' compliance plans undertaken pursuant to section 601HG of the Act.

4 Auditors of mortgage schemes are required to adhere to the mandatory requirements contained in Auditing Standards (ASAs) when undertaking financial report audits and the requirements contained in Standards on Assurance Engagements (ASAEs) when undertaking audits of compliance plans. This Guidance Statement has been developed to clarify auditors' responsibilities in respect of such engagements, and to provide guidance to the auditors on additional considerations which may be taken into account when undertaking financial report and compliance plan audits of mortgage schemes.

5 It is important to note that this Guidance Statement does not impose any responsibilities on the auditor beyond those which are imposed by ASAs, ASAEs and the requirements of the Act. The provisions of the Act in this area are supported by ASIC Regulatory Guide 144 *Mortgage investment schemes* (RG 144), Regulatory Guide 45 *Mortgage schemes – improving disclosure for retail investors* (RG 45) and other ASIC regulatory guides, including those applicable to managed investment schemes, as well as modifications to the Act made by individual orders or class orders issued by ASIC.

Regulatory Background

6 ASIC's regulatory framework for mortgage schemes principally consists of:

(a) a requirement for operators of mortgage schemes, that meet the criteria for registration as a managed investment scheme, to comply with Chapter 5C of the Act;

(b) application of RG 144 and RG 45, as well as other relevant ASIC regulatory guides applicable to managed investment schemes generally; and

(c) relief to mortgage scheme operators in certain cases, such as operators of small, low risk schemes e.g. solicitors' mortgage practices, may be permitted to comply with an approved industry body's rules (for example, those of the relevant State or Territory professional law bodies) rather than all of Chapter 5C, if the body can demonstrate effective supervision over such participants.[1]

7 RG 144 indicates that a mortgage scheme is likely to be regarded as being a managed investment scheme if:

(a) the legal or commercial character of the investment is determined by the nature of the business operations of the promoter e.g. where money contributed by different investors is lent under one mortgage; and

(b) commercial decisions are taken by the operator or the promoter of the scheme and not by investors.

8 RG 144 recognises that subsection 601ED(1) must also be satisfied for a mortgage scheme to be required to be registered as a managed investment scheme under Chapter 5C. In particular registration may be required under subsection 601ED(1) if:

(a) the scheme has more than 20 members (investors); or

(b) the scheme was promoted by a person, or an associate of a person, who was, when the scheme was promoted, in the business of promoting managed investment schemes; or

(c) ASIC has determined that the scheme is one of a number of schemes that are closely related and the total number of members is greater than 20.[2]

GS

1 For schemes of this kind with no more than 20 investors and no more than $7.5 million in total loan capital, ASIC allows such operators to participate in an industry-based compliance structure approved by ASIC. However, ASIC has indicated that it will impose various conditions on such schemes, including the application of the disclosure and anti-hawking provisions of the Act.

2 Auditors of smaller schemes not directly regulated by ASIC but administered as part of an industry-based compliance structure may also be required to report on various compliance matters as part of the auditing arrangements which are agreed to with the individual State or Territory industry supervisory bodies.

Responsibilities of Management and Auditors

Management's Responsibilities

9 Section 285 of the Act imposes a responsibility on registered schemes, which includes mortgage schemes, to comply with the requirements of Chapter 2M of the Act dealing with financial reports and audit requirements. Furthermore, section 285(3) deems a scheme's responsible entity responsible for the performance of the financial reporting obligations in that Chapter in respect of the scheme.

10 In addition to the above obligations, the responsible entity of a scheme is required to comply with Part 5C.4 of the Act and expected to apply ASIC Regulatory Guide 132 *Managed investments: Compliance plans*. The requirements of the Act impose obligations on the responsible entity to ensure that compliance plans are in place which set out adequate measures that the responsible entity is to apply in operating the scheme to ensure compliance with the Act and the scheme's constitution.

11 As with managed investment schemes generally, the responsible entity of a mortgage scheme which is registered under section 601ED, operates the scheme on behalf of the members of the scheme. To this end, the responsible entity and the directors of that entity, are responsible to the members of the scheme for the operation of the scheme, including for meeting it's statutory and other legal obligations. The responsible entity will need to establish and maintain an adequate system of internal control to protect the interests of members who have invested in the scheme.

12 A scheme's internal control structure is to provide its management, i.e. the responsible entity, with reasonable, but not absolute assurance, that the operations of the scheme are orderly and efficient, and that irregularities are prevented as far as possible and detected should they occur. An adequate internal control system will also provide management with reasonable assurance that assets are safeguarded from unauthorised use or disposal, and that the financial and other records of the scheme reflect the entire operational activities of the scheme and permit the timely preparation of financial reports required by the Act.

Auditors' Responsibilities

13 The auditor of a scheme's financial report ordinarily obtains a preliminary understanding of the scheme and its environment, including its internal control, sufficient to identify and assess the risks of material misstatement of the financial report whether due to fraud or error, and sufficient to design and perform further audit procedures, which may include, where appropriate, tests of the operating effectiveness of controls and other compliance measures in the context of the scope of the scheme's financial report audit, in order to be able to form an opinion on it as required by Chapter 2M.[3]

14 Similarly, the compliance plan auditor[4] who conducts the audit of a scheme's compliance plan under section 601HG, is required under ASAE 3100 *Compliance Audits* to obtain an understanding of the scheme's compliance plan (the subject matter) and other engagement circumstances sufficient to identify and assess the risks of non-compliance, either of the responsible entity with the compliance plan or of the compliance plan with the Act, and be mindful of the compliance related expectations set out in RG 144, RG 45 and the other relevant ASIC regulatory guides, including those regulatory guides applicable to managed investment schemes generally.

Agreeing on the Terms of the Audit Engagements

15 Under section 331AAA, the scheme's responsible entity is responsible for the appointment of the scheme's financial report auditor. This is also the case for the scheme's compliance plan auditor who is appointed by the responsible entity under section 601HG. It is therefore essential that the auditors and the scheme's responsible entity separately agree on the terms of the respective audit engagements, which are to be recorded in writing. Such

3 See ASA 315 *Understanding the Entity and its Environment and Assessing the Risk of Material Misstatements*.

4 Under section 601HG(2) the compliance plan auditor and the financial report auditor of the responsible entity must be different persons, notwithstanding that they may be from the same firm. See also GS 013 *Special Considerations in the Audit of Managed Investment Schemes*.

terms are normally outlined in separate audit engagement letters[5] which are forwarded to the responsible entity.

16 The auditors may use the engagement letters to clarify the respective roles of the responsible entity's directors, the financial report auditor and the compliance plan auditor, by contrasting the respective statutory responsibilities of the responsible entity and the auditors under the Act. Both the financial report auditor and compliance plan auditor obtain acknowledgment of management's responsibilities from the directors of the scheme's responsible entity when obtaining agreement on the terms of the audit engagements.

Issues for Auditors to Consider

17 In addition to the issues normally considered when undertaking financial report audits and compliance plan audits, auditors of mortgage schemes will need to consider several matters that are particularly important to the operation of such schemes. These matters include whether:

(a) appropriate documentation is available in respect of all deposits or receipts to the scheme and its bank accounts, and in relation to payments and withdrawals from the scheme and its bank accounts;

(b) appropriate documentation is available in respect of all loans made by the scheme, including detailed loan agreements, securities held, guarantees, terms of repayments and external independent valuations;

(c) the mortgage scheme's circumstances are consistent with the basis of reporting, that is whether it is a going concern for the relevant period; and

(d) the compliance plan adequately addresses the expectations about disclosure and advertising specified by ASIC in RG 45 and the relevant measures are complied with to ensure disclosure against the benchmarks provided in RG 45.

18 The auditors of mortgage schemes may also take into account other specific compliance related considerations relevant to such schemes. These considerations include whether:

(a) investor funds have been placed in the mortgage scheme on the basis of the written approval of the investor;

(b) specific disbursements of investor funds are supported by written authorities from investors;

(c) investor funds are capable of being remitted back to the investor within the time period agreed by the investor and that the net monies loaned (after agent's commission or loan establishment fees) are sufficient to enable payment of the amount that has been agreed to be paid to the investor;

(d) investor funds have been appropriately secured e.g. first mortgage or other charges or liens are taken out over the assets and undertakings of the investee or borrower;

(e) commissions or loan establishment fees paid to agents are in accordance with legally binding agreements between the parties;

(f) interest and principal payments from the investee or borrower are being received in accordance with loan agreements;

(g) interest paid to the investors is financed from receipt of investee or borrowers funds and not from the commissions or other monies due to solicitors or agents;

(h) periodic statements are provided to investors in respect of the disbursement of their funds until the funds are fully utilised in the mortgage scheme; and

(i) that monthly bank reconciliations have been prepared in respect of each "trust" account.

19 It is important that auditors take the above considerations into account when planning and undertaking both financial report audits and compliance plan audits of mortgage schemes. While not purporting to be an exhaustive list of compliance matters to be considered by auditors, they represent areas in which there should be appropriate controls in place, so as

GS

5 Or other suitable form of audit contract. See ASA 210 *Terms of Audit Engagements* and ASAE 3100.

to adequately mitigate the risk of a material misstatement in a scheme's financial report and/or material non-compliance with a scheme's compliance plan.

Conformity with International Pronouncements

20 There is no equivalent International Auditing Practice Statement (IAPS) to this Guidance Statement.

GS 015

Audit Implications of Accounting for Investments in Associates

(Issued November 2009)

Issued by the Auditing and Assurance Standards Board.

Note from the Institute of Chartered Accountants Australia

This note, prepared by the technical editor, is not part of GS 015.

Historical development

November 2009: GS 015 issued. The new GS replaces AGS 1032 'The Audit Implications of Accounting for Investments in Associates', first issued in November 1997 and revised in July 2002, which has been withdrawn. It provides guidance for auditors on the implications of Accounting Standard AASB 123 'Investments in Associates'.

GS

Contents

AUTHORITY STATEMENT

Authority Statement

The Auditing and Assurance Standards Board (AUASB) issues Guidance Statement GS 015 *Audit Implications of Accounting for Investments in Associates* pursuant to section 227B of the *Australian Securities and Investments Commission Act 2001*, for the purposes of providing guidance on auditing and assurance matters.

This Guidance Statement provides guidance to assist the auditor to fulfil the objectives of the audit or assurance engagement. It includes explanatory material on specific matters for the purposes of understanding and complying with AUASB Standards. The auditor exercises professional judgement when using this Guidance Statement.

The Guidance Statement does not prescribe or create new mandatory requirements.

Dated: 24 November 2009

M H Kelsall
Chairman - AUASB

Guidance Statement GS 015

Audit Implications of Accounting for Investments in Associates

Application

1 This Guidance Statement has been formulated by the Auditing and Assurance Standards Board (AUASB) to provide guidance to auditors on audit implications arising from the application of Accounting Standard AASB 128 *Investments in Associates*.

Issuance Date

2 This Guidance Statement is issued on 24 November 2009 and replaces AGS 1032 *The Audit Implications of Accounting for Investments in Associates* which was issued in July 2002.

Introduction

3 AASB 128 requires an investor to recognise an investment in an associate by applying the equity method in its consolidated financial statements and at cost or in accordance with Accounting Standard AASB 139 *Financial Instruments: Recognition and Measurement* in its own separate financial statements.

If the investor is not required to prepare consolidated financial statements, AASB 128 requires recognition of an investment in an associate by applying the equity method in its own separate financial statements.

4 This Guidance Statement does not apply to the audit of investments in associates held by venture capital organisations, mutual funds, unit trusts and similar entities including investment-linked insurance funds when they are measured at fair value through profit and loss or are classified as held for trading and accounted for in accordance with AASB 39 or are an investment classified as held for sale in accordance with AASB 5 *Non-current Assets Held for Sale and Discontinued Operations*.

5 This Guidance Statement discusses audit implications for auditors who do not have direct access to information from an associate of an investor and which may restrict the auditor's ability to gather sufficient appropriate audit evidence.

6 The audit implications and audit responses included in this Guidance Statement may apply to obtaining audit evidence for Joint Ventures that may be equity accounted for under Accounting Standard AASB 131 *Interests in Joint Ventures*.

Definitions

7 For the purpose of this Guidance Statement, the following term has the meaning attributed below:

Associate means an entity, including an unincorporated entity such as a partnership, over which the investor has significant influence and that is neither a subsidiary nor an interest in a joint venture. [See also AASB 128].

Objectives of the Audit

8 The overall objective of the auditor as described in ASA 200 *Overall Objectives of the Independent Auditor and the Conduct of an Audit in Accordance with Australian Auditing Standards*, is to obtain reasonable assurance about whether the financial report as a whole is free from material misstatement, whether due to fraud or error, thereby enabling the auditor to express an opinion on whether the financial report is prepared, in all material respects, in accordance with an applicable financial reporting framework.

9 To obtain reasonable assurance, the auditor obtains sufficient appropriate audit evidence to reduce audit risk to an acceptably low level and thereby enables the auditor to draw reasonable conclusions on which to base the auditor's opinion.

10 The investor's auditor gathers sufficient appropriate audit evidence to evaluate:

(a) representations made by those charged with governance of the investor as to the existence and ownership of the investment, and the existence or otherwise of significant influence;

(b) the appropriateness of the carrying amounts of an investment, the investor's share of the associate's profits and losses, including the required adjustments and dividends received or receivable from an associate;

(c) the appropriateness of adjustments to the carrying amounts of an investment due to post-acquisition changes in an associate's reserves;

(d) the adequacy of financial report disclosure; and

(e) the appropriateness of other equity accounting adjustments such as adjustments for dissimilar accounting policies and elimination of unrealised profits and losses.

Planning

Understanding the Entity and its Environment and Assessing the Risks of Material Misstatement

11 The auditor needs to obtain an understanding of the entity and its environment and assess the risks of material misstatement in a financial report audit in accordance with ASA 315 *Understanding the Entity and Its Environment and Assessing the Risks of Material Misstatement*. The auditor needs to perform risk assessment procedures to obtain an understanding of the entity and its environment, including its internal control.

12 If the auditor assesses significant risks in the area of investments in associates, this will impact all areas of the audit including planning, audit testing and gathering of appropriate audit evidence to mitigate these risks.

Planning an Audit of Investments in Associates

13 The audit of equity accounting balances and adjustments requires adequate attention during the planning of the audit. The auditor develops the audit plan in accordance with ASA 300 *Planning an Audit of a Financial Report* and ASA 330 *The Auditor's Responses to Assessed Risks* to ensure that sufficient appropriate audit evidence concerning the investment in associates is made available to the auditor of the investor. The auditor considers materiality and its relationship with audit risk in accordance with ASA 320 *Materiality and Audit Adjustments* and in conjunction with the auditor's risk assessments, in the planning and conduct of the audit.

14 The investor's auditor may meet with the management of the investor and plan in relation to such matters as:

(a) the provision of evidence to support identification of associates;

(b) the nature and the adequacy of policies and adjustments between the investor and the associate for dissimilar accounting policies, transactions, balances, and reciprocal shareholdings;

(c) the accounting timetable and the availability of the associate's financial reports (especially in relation to the provision of information required for the application of equity accounting), and any other information considered necessary;

(d) the procedures to identify events subsequent to balance date for the associate; and

(e) contact with the associate's auditor where necessary, when the associate is not audited by the investor's auditor.

15 The investor's auditor also considers whether there are any legal restrictions that may affect the availability of information from an associate. There may be legal restrictions applicable to the communication of confidential information by those charged with governance, to third parties. However, representatives of the investor on the investee's governing body may make available information to the investor they represent. This is normally subject to the condition that it is done with the knowledge of the investee governance body, and is in the best interests of the investee. If the investor is not able to obtain necessary information from the investee, the presumption of significant influence requires further clarification. The refusal by the investee may demonstrate a lack of significant influence by the investor or may be the result of a legal restriction on the investee as to the information it can make available. Legal restrictions may also apply to the investor publishing information about the associate which has not been made available to the other equity holders of the associate.

Identification of Associates

16 The responsibility for establishing whether or not significant influence exists rests with those charged with governance of the investor. The evidence used to determine significant influence is obtained by the auditor and documented in the audit working papers.

17 Generally, where an investor holds directly or indirectly, 20 per cent or more of the voting power in an investee, in the absence of evidence to the contrary, there could be the presumption of significant influence. However, this percentage is not an absolute cut-

off point. In certain cases, an investee will qualify as an associate, notwithstanding that the investor's voting power in the investee is less than, or has fallen below, 20 per cent. The converse also applies. Hence, voting power in an investee comprises only part of the audit evidence to support significant influence.

18 AASB 128 provides examples of factors which individually, or in combination, may indicate the existence of significant influence. In cases where those charged with governance of the investor are asserting that the provisions of AASB 128 apply, the auditor would expect to be provided with evidence to support the assertion. The auditor examines and evaluates that evidence in accordance with ASA 500 *Audit Evidence*.

19 Examples of the evidence that the auditor examines, depending on the assertions being made, are:

(a) the investee's constituent document. This may indicate that the remainder of the voting power of the investee is concentrated with a limited number of equity holders, which precludes the investor from exercising significant influence, or alternatively, that the remainder of the voting power is so widely dispersed that the investor is able to exercise significant influence;

(b) the composition of the investee governance body, and if available, extracts of documents indicating that policy decisions made by the investor concerning the investee have been implemented by the investee, with particular reference to control over the distribution or retention of the investee's profits;

(c) the agreements and actual level of technical and/or physical facility dependence by the investee on the investor, and an evaluation of that dependence in terms of the investee's overall technical and physical facilities;

(d) the type and volume of transactions between the investor and the investee and the terms of trading between the entities, the status and details of loans and current accounts with the investee, and details of any guarantees to third parties provided by or on behalf of the investee, with an evaluation, in terms of the investee's overall position, of the level of financial dependence by the investee on the investor; and

(e) the agreements and actual level and type of staff interchange or staff services between the investor and investee.

20 The auditor evaluates the information presented by the management or governing body of the investee, and applies a combination of procedures appropriate to the circumstances, to form an opinion on the assertion of significant influence, or otherwise, made by those charged with governance. Such procedures could include:

(a) an examination and evaluation of the investor's system of internal control over transactions between the investor and investee as a basis for understanding the type and volume of transactions between the investor and investee;

(b) inspection of relevant contracts and agreements between the investor and investee;

(c) inspection of the investor's minutes of meetings for details of decisions made concerning the relationship between the investor and the investee, and the activities of both parties;

(d) discussions with relevant investor personnel, and where possible, relevant investee personnel, and/or examination of a statement from the investee stating that it accepts the investor is in a position to exercise significant influence over it;

(e) confirmation of transactions and balances with the investee;

(f) confirmation and enquiry with external parties, for example: solicitors as to the existence and interpretation of agreements; banks as to the existence and details of guarantees; and credit agencies as to enquiries that cannot be dealt with directly by the auditor;

(g) computation and checking of details with supporting accounting records; and

(h) analysis of the financial reports of the associate.

Information from Associates

21 To audit equity accounting adjustments, relevant information about an associate is required for the auditor to obtain sufficient appropriate audit evidence to be able to draw reasonable conclusions. AASB 128 requires the investor to use the most recent financial information available to the equity holders of the associate and if the reporting dates of the associate and that of the investor are different; the difference shall be no more than three months. The auditor ascertains whether this information is adequate, and in form and content appropriate for the purpose of accounting for the equity interests of an investor. This aspect of the audit emphasises the need for adequate planning as detailed in paragraphs 13 and 14.

Adjustments are required to:

(a) address differences in the accounting policies adopted by an associate to achieve consistency with the accounting policies of the investor;

(b) eliminate intra group balances, transactions, income and expenses in full between the associate and:

(i) the investor and its controlled entities (the economic entity);

(ii) another associate of the investor.

22 Using materiality and knowledge of internal controls, the auditor assesses the risk attached to these adjustments.

23 In some cases unaudited financial information is provided by the associate for equity accounting purposes. Unaudited financial reports or other information and data provide evidential matter which is not of itself sufficient appropriate audit evidence for the investor's auditor to evaluate the accounting for investments in associates. In this respect, the auditor needs to consider the impact of matters noted in the following paragraphs to assess whether there is a limitation of scope.

Audit Evidence

The Reliability of Financial Reports and Other Information Provided about an Associate

24 Evidence pertaining to the application of the equity method may be available in the following forms:

(a) Audited Financial Reports

Financial reports of an associate available to the equity holders of that associate generally constitute sufficient appropriate audit evidence as to the equity in the underlying net assets and results of operations of an associate when such statements have been audited by the investor's auditor, or by another independent auditor. Where an associate is audited by another auditor, the investor's auditor considers the principles in ASA 600 *Special Considerations—Audits of a Group Financial Report (Including the Work of Component Auditors)*, in particular those in relation to understanding the work of component auditors.

(b) Unaudited Financial Reports

When the information provided about the investee is unaudited, the investor's auditor uses professional judgment to assess audit risk and to design appropriate audit procedures to evaluate the equity accounting adjustments and disclosures. Sufficient appropriate audit evidence may be obtained for example:

(i) by having the associate's auditor perform appropriate audit procedures, in which case the principles of ASA 600 apply; or

(ii) by gaining access to the associate to apply audit procedures; or

(iii) by supplementing a review or agreed-upon procedures report provided by another auditor on the financial information, with additional procedures as appropriate.

In those cases where the auditor of the investor is unable to obtain the access required to enable audit procedures to be carried out, or is unable to obtain evidence of sufficient quality from another auditor, there may be a limitation on the scope of the audit. In such cases, the auditor complies with the requirements in ASA 705 *Modifications to the Opinion in the Independent Auditor's Report*.

Subsequent Events

25 Where a time lag exists between the balance date of an associate and that of the investor, the auditor ascertains the procedures by which those charged with governance of the investor have attempted to make themselves aware of any significant events or transactions of the associate, that have arisen subsequent to the date of the associate's financial statements, to the date on which the auditor signs the auditor's report on the investor's financial report. Audit procedures could include:

(a) enquiry of the appropriate levels of the investor's management, and review of actions taken;

(b) comparison to any interim financial statements and/or management reports of the associate, where possible;

(c) examination of any correspondence between the investor and associate;

(d) where possible, discussion with those charged with governance and/or auditors of the associate; and

(e) comparison to other appropriate evidence, including industry literature, financial press disclosures, external credit organisations.

26 In the event of the investor auditor being informed of, or becoming aware of, any significant events or transactions of an associate occurring during the period between balance dates and the date on which the auditor signs the auditor's report on the investor's financial report, the auditor makes additional enquiries to evaluate the impact of these events or transactions on the carrying amount of the investment in the financial report. The auditor obtains evidence that management has accounted for or adequately disclosed such events in the financial report.

27 The investor auditor considers whether there are any significant events or transactions involving the investor which impact on the equity interest in an associate disclosed in the financial report. The provisions of Accounting Standard AASB 110 *Events After Balance Sheet Date*, and ASA 560 *Subsequent Events* apply.

Audit Reporting

The Auditor's Report

28 The auditor's opinion is on the investor's financial report which includes the equity accounting adjustments. The auditor's report is prepared in accordance with ASA 700 *Forming an Opinion and Reporting on a Financial Report* and where appropriate, ASA 800 *Special Considerations—Audits of Financial Reports Prepared in Accordance with Special Purpose Frameworks*.

29 In those cases where the auditor of the investor is unable to obtain sufficient appropriate audit evidence, there may be a limitation on the scope of the audit. In such cases, the auditor complies with the requirements in ASA 705 *Modifications to the Opinion in the Independent Auditor's Report*.

30 Where a significant uncertainty about the associate exists, the resolution of which may materially affect the financial report, the auditor complies with the requirements in ASA 706 *Emphasis of Matter Paragraphs and Other Matter Paragraphs in the Independent Auditor's Report*.

Review Engagements

31 In a review of a financial report the auditor or the assurance practitioner makes enquiries and performs analytical and other review procedures to enable the auditor to conclude whether, on the basis of the procedures performed, anything has come to the auditor's attention that causes the auditor to believe that the financial report is not prepared (or presents fairly), in all material respects, in accordance with the applicable financial reporting framework.

32 The guidance in this Guidance Statement for planning an audit and audit evidence issues regarding an investment in an associate, applies, as appropriate, to the review of an investor's financial report.

33 Where a review is conducted by the auditor of the entity, ASRE 2410 *Review of a Financial Report Performed by the Independent Auditor of the Entity* applies. Where reviews are undertaken by assurance practitioners who are not the auditor of the entity, ASRE 2400 *Review of a Financial Report Performed by an Assurance Practitioner Who is Not the Auditor of the Entity* applies. Both ASRE 2400 and ASRE 2410 contain illustrative procedures in the Appendices that may be helpful when completing review engagements.

Conformity with International Pronouncements

34 There is no equivalent International Auditing Practice Statement (IAPS) to this Guidance Statement.

GS 016

Bank Confirmation Requests

(Issued June 2010)

Prepared and issued by the Auditing and Assurance Standards Board.

Note from the Institute of Chartered Accountants Australia

This note, prepared by the technical editor, is not part of GS 016.

Historical development

March 1976: Statement CP1 'Bank Confirmation Requests', prepared by the Audit Standards Committee of the Australian Accounting Research Foundation, and issued by The Institute of Chartered Accountants in Australia and the Australian Society of Accountants. No effective date was indicated in the statement. It was reissued, without amendment, as AUP 1 in August 1979.

May 1990: ED 32 'Bank Confirmation Requests' issued by the AuSB, with comments being sought by 31 August 1990.

May 1991: AUP 1 'Bank Confirmation Requests' revised and issued, operative for the first financial reporting period ending on or after 1 January 1992, although earlier application was encouraged. The major revisions to AUP 1 (5/91) were the introduction of guidance on Bank Confirmation requests as audit evidence and revision of the confirmation request to take into account new financial instruments, this being accomplished by two separate Bank Confirmations — General and Treasury.

There was no corresponding IFAC statement, although 'Inter-Bank Confirmation Procedures', which was published in February 1984 by the International Auditing Practice Committee of IFAC and The Committee on Banking Regulations and Supervisory Practices of the Group of Ten Major Industrialised Countries and Switzerland, was relevant. This statement did not include the pro-formas included in the exposure draft.

December 1993: ED 53 'Codification and Revision of Auditing Pronouncements: AUS 506 Bank Confirmation Requests (AUP 1)' issued by the AuSB.

October 1995: Australian Auditing Standards and Auditing Guidance Statements released. The status of these is explained in APS 1.1 'Conformity With Auditing Standards'. These Standards became operative for the first reporting period commencing on or after 1 July 1996 and later reporting periods, although earlier application was encouraged. AUP 1 'Bank Confirmation Requests' replaced by AGS 1002 'Bank Confirmation Requests'.

June 2010: GS 016 issued, applicable for reporting periods ending on or after 30 September 2010. It has been developed with the Australian Bankers Association to ensure that audit requests are better designed and banks are better able to respond in a timely manner. There is no equivalent international statement.

GS

Contents

AUTHORITY STATEMENT

Authority Statement

The Auditing and Assurance Standards Board (AUASB) formulates Guidance Statement GS 016 *Bank Confirmation Requests* pursuant to section 227B of the *Australian Securities and Investments Commission Act 2001*, for the purposes of providing guidance on auditing and assurance matters.

This Guidance Statement provides guidance to assist the auditor to fulfil the objectives of the audit or assurance engagement. It includes explanatory material on specific matters for the purposes of understanding and complying with AUASB Standards. The auditor exercises professional judgement when using this Guidance Statement.

The Guidance Statement does not prescribe or create new mandatory requirements.

Dated: 10 June 2010

M H Kelsall
Chairman - AUASB

Guidance Statement GS 016

Bank Confirmation Requests

Application

1 This Guidance Statement has been formulated by the Auditing and Assurance Standards Board (AUASB) to provide guidance to auditors on the enquiry and confirmation methods for obtaining audit evidence regarding an entity's bank accounts and transactions, in accordance with the Australian Auditing Standards.[1]

2 This Guidance Statement is applicable to audit engagements with financial reporting periods ending on or after 30 September 2010.

Issuance Date

3 This Guidance Statement is issued on 10 June 2010 by the AUASB.

Introduction

4 This Guidance Statement has been developed by the AUASB in consultation with the Australian Bankers' Association (ABA), and with the co-operation of its members.[2]

5 While this Guidance Statement deals specifically with communications with banks that are members of the ABA, the guidance may be applied to confirmation requests directed to other authorised deposit-taking institutions, for example, building societies and credit unions.

Definitions

6 For the purposes of this Guidance Statement, the following terms have the meanings attributed below:

(a) Bank means banks and other authorised deposit-taking institutions.

(b) External confirmation means audit evidence obtained by the auditor as a direct written response to the auditor from a third party (the confirming party), in paper form, or by electronic or other medium.[3]

(c) Bank confirmation is a particular type of external confirmation used by an auditor to obtain independent confirmation from a bank or other authorised deposit-taking institution for audit purposes of information such as an entity's bank account balances, securities, treasury management instruments, documents and other related information held by the bank, or authorised deposit-taking institution, on behalf of the entity.

Bank Confirmations

7 Information obtained from a bank confirmation assists the auditor in discharging the auditor's responsibility to obtain reasonable assurance about whether the financial report as a whole is free from material misstatement, thereby enabling the auditor to express an opinion on the financial report.[4]

8 Under Australian Auditing Standards, the auditor is required to obtain sufficient appropriate audit evidence to reduce risk to an acceptably low level, thereby enabling the auditor to draw reasonable conclusions on which to base the auditor's opinion.[5] Information obtained from a bank confirmation may assist the auditor in obtaining sufficient appropriate audit

1 For the purposes of this Guidance Statement, Australian Auditing Standards are those standards issued by the AUASB in October 2009 that apply to audits and reviews of financial reports for reporting periods commencing on or after 1 January 2010.

2 See www.bankers.asn.au for a list of the banks that are members of the ABA.

3 See ASA 505 *External Confirmations*, paragraph 6(a).

4 See ASA 200 *Overall Objectives of the Independent Auditor and the Conduct of an Audit in Accordance with Australian Auditing Standards*, paragraph 11.

5 See ASA 200, paragraph 17.

evidence regarding bank-related transactions and account balances, and their presentation and disclosure in the financial report.

The Audit Process and Bank Confirmations

9 ASA 300 *Planning an Audit of a Financial Report* requires the auditor to plan the audit through establishing an overall audit strategy and developing an audit plan, so that the engagement will be performed in an effective manner. The audit plan is more detailed than the overall audit strategy in that it includes the nature, timing and extent of audit procedures to be performed by engagement team members.

10 ASA 315 *Identifying and Assessing the Risks of Material Misstatement through Understanding the Entity and Its Environment* requires the auditor to identify and assess the risks of material misstatement, whether due to fraud or error, at the financial report and assertion levels.

11 Risks of material misstatement:

(a) at the financial report level—may derive from a deficient control environment (or relate to other factors, such as declining economic conditions);[6] and

(b) at the assertion level[7]— may relate to assertions made, implicitly or explicitly, by management or where appropriate those charged with governance regarding the recognition, measurement, presentation and disclosure of bank-related elements of the financial report and related disclosures. This may include assertions regarding:

(i) bank-related classes of transactions and events for the period under audit, including:
- occurrence;
- completeness;
- accuracy;
- cut-off; and
- classification; and

(ii) account balances at the period end, including:
- existence;
- rights and obligations;
- completeness; and
- valuation; and

(iii) presentation and disclosure, including:
- occurrence and rights and obligations;
- completeness;
- classification and understandability; and
- accuracy and valuation.

Deciding Whether to Request a Bank Confirmation

12 ASA 330 *The Auditor's Responses to Assessed Risks* requires the auditor to design and implement responses to the assessed risks of material misstatement in the financial report. For each material class of transactions, account balance, and disclosure, irrespective of the assessed risks of material misstatement, the auditor is required to design and perform substantive procedures.[8] In particular, in respect of bank-related transactions, account balances and disclosures, the auditor shall consider whether external confirmation procedures are to be performed.[9]

6 See ASA 315, paragraphs A105-A107.

7 See ASA 315, paragraphs A109-A112.

8 See ASA 330, paragraph 18.

9 See ASA 330, paragraphs 19 and A48-A51.

13 When the entity's banking activities, including treasury operations, are significant, complex, or unusual, or there are deficiencies in the entity's control environment that may impact the assertions and disclosures regarding the entity's banking activities, the auditor would ordinarily send a bank confirmation request(s).

14 In other instances, when:

(a) an entity's banking activities are simple and straightforward; and

(b) the auditor has considered the entity's control environment and assessed the risk of material misstatement of bank-related account balances and disclosures as low; and

(c) there are other means to obtain sufficient appropriate audit evidence in respect of banking activities;

the auditor may decide not to request a bank confirmation.

15 Alternative sources of audit evidence may include, for example, bank statements for the relevant period provided on bank letterhead; together with:

(a) the bank facilities letter, on bank letterhead, documenting the banking facilities used by, or made available to, the entity; and

(b) bank reconciliations that agree to the bank statements.

Nature of the Evidence Obtained from a Bank Confirmation

16 ASA 500 *Audit Evidence* requires the auditor to design and perform audit procedures that are appropriate in the circumstances to obtain sufficient appropriate audit evidence[10] and discusses the relevance and reliability of audit evidence in an audit of a financial report.[11]

17 Relevance deals with the logical connections with, or bearing upon, the purpose of the audit procedure and, where appropriate, the assertion under consideration. A given set of audit procedures may provide audit evidence that is relevant to certain assertions, but not others. Thus, for example, for certain investments a bank confirmation may provide information that addresses the existence assertion, but not the valuation assertion. In such circumstances, it may be necessary to consider performing alternative or additional audit procedures to address the valuation assertion.

18 The reliability of audit evidence is influenced by its source and by its nature and is dependent on the individual circumstances under which it is obtained. The reliability of the evidence obtained from information contained in a response to a bank confirmation request, is influenced by the circumstances in which the request is made and the response is received.

19 ASA 500 states that audit evidence is generally more reliable when it is obtained from independent sources outside the entity.[12] However, even when audit evidence, such as a bank confirmation, is obtained from sources external to the entity, circumstances may exist that could affect the reliability of the information obtained. For example, all confirmation responses carry some risk of interception, alteration or fraud. Such risk exists regardless of whether a response is obtained in paper form, or through electronic or other medium.

20 ASA 500 further states that audit evidence obtained by original documents is generally more reliable than audit evidence provided by photocopies or facsimiles, or documents that have been filmed, digitised or otherwise transformed into electronic form. Where an auditor chooses to send or receive bank confirmations electronically, it is important to consider the controls built into this process to determine the reliability of the information obtained. (See *Electronic Bank Confirmation Processes* below)

21 The auditor is required to exercise professional scepticism in accordance with ASA 200.[13] ASA 200 explains that an attitude of professional scepticism means the auditor makes a critical assessment, with a questioning mind, of the validity of audit evidence obtained and is alert to audit evidence that contradicts or brings into question the reliability of

GS

10 See ASA 500, paragraph 6.

11 See ASA 500, paragraphs 7 and A26-A33.

12 See ASA 500, paragraph A31 and ASA 505, paragraph 2.

13 See ASA 200, paragraph 15.

documents and responses to enquiries.[14] However, unless the auditor has reason to believe the contrary, the auditor may accept records and documents as genuine.[15] If there is any indication that a confirmation response may not be reliable, ASA 505 *External Confirmations* emphasises the need for the auditor to consider the response's reliability and to perform audit procedures to dispel any concern (for example, the auditor may choose to verify the source and contents of the response in a telephone call to the purported sender).[16]

Remaining Alert to the Possibility of Fraud

22 While the primary responsibility for the prevention and detection of fraud rests with both those charged with governance of the entity and management,[17] the auditor, in exercising professional scepticism, remains alert to the possibility of fraud in the bank confirmation process.

23 When determining whether to use bank confirmation requests, it may be important to be alert to the entity's circumstances and its environment, the circumstances surrounding the confirmation process, and the information obtained from the confirmation process that may indicate a risk of material misstatement.

24 Being alert to the possibility of fraud may be particularly important when an external confirmation is the primary audit evidence for a material financial report item, particularly if the item itself is susceptible to fraud. This risk may arise, for example, when requesting confirmation of the existence of liquid funds and investments held by the entity in an offshore bank.

25 Heightened professional scepticism may also be called for when dealing with unusual or unexpected responses to confirmation requests, such as a significant change in the number or timeliness of responses to bank confirmation requests relative to prior audits, or a non-response when a response would be expected.

Bank Confirmation Procedures

26 ASA 505 emphasises the importance of the auditor maintaining control over the external confirmation process to enhance the reliability of the audit evidence obtained through the process.

27 When using bank confirmations, the auditor maintains control over the process through:[18]

(a) determining the bank information to be requested;

(b) selecting the appropriate confirming party(parties);

(c) designing the bank confirmation request, ensuring that it:

(i) is properly addressed;

(ii) is clear, accurate and sufficiently detailed; and

(iii) contains an accurate return address, for responses to be sent directly to the auditor.

(d) considering the timing of the lodgement of the request and the date by which a response is required; and

(e) taking follow-up action when a response is overdue.

14 See ASA 200, paragraphs A18-A22.

15 See ASA 200, paragraph A21.

16 See ASA 505, paragraph 10.

17 See ASA 240 *The Auditor's Responsibilities Relating to Fraud in an Audit of a Financial Report*, paragraph 4.

18 See ASA 505, paragraph 7.

Determining the Bank Information to be Confirmed and Selecting the Appropriate Confirming Party (Parties)

28 The auditor may determine the bank information to be confirmed and select the appropriate confirming party (parties) through:

(a) discussions with management or where appropriate those charged with governance;

(b) analysing the assertions made by the entity in the financial report being audited;

(c) checking the annual banking facilities letter, if any;

(d) inspecting bank statements;

(e) inspecting the minutes of meetings of the Board, audit committee, finance committee, management team or other internal committee;

(f) evaluating the work of internal audit; or

(g) knowledge of the entity's banking relationships from prior periods.

29 The information to be confirmed may relate to:

(a) normal banking activities, such as:

(i) account balances at the period end for current accounts, interest bearing deposit accounts, foreign currency accounts, money market deposits, overdraft accounts, bank loans and term loans;

(ii) interest rates and terms of other liabilities to the bank, such as bills of exchange, forward exchange contracts, letters of credit, guarantees and indemnities undertaken by the bank;

(iii) items held as security for the entity's liabilities to the bank;

(iv) accounts opened or closed by the entity during the period; and

(v) unused limits and facilities; and/or

(b) treasury operations, such as:

(i) forward rate agreements;

(ii) foreign currency contracts;

(iii) interest rate swaps;

(iv) options; and

(v) treasury futures contracts; and

(c) other contractual arrangements.

Designing the Bank Confirmation Request

30 Standard bank confirmation request forms provide for the confirmation or provision of information which is customarily held by banks. Accordingly, two standard bank confirmation request forms have been developed through consultation with auditors and the ABA. The two forms are:

(a) *Bank Confirmation—Audit Request (General)* (Appendix 1) – the information to be confirmed or requested relates to normal banking activities and is substantially the same for a range of entities; and

(b) *Bank Confirmation—Audit Request (Treasury and Other Operations)* (Appendix 2) – the information to be confirmed or requested relates to the entity's treasury operations and use of treasury management instruments.

These forms are also available as separate documents on the AUASB website[19], to facilitate their use in the confirmation process, if required.

31 While the standard bank confirmation request forms will generally provide the information required by the auditor in a range of audit engagements, there may be instances where the standard forms are not appropriate. For example, the auditor may require confirmation

GS

19 See www.auasb.gov.au.

of matters not covered by the standard bank confirmation request forms and may write a separate letter requesting confirmation of specific matters.

32 Where a letter is used by the auditor to request bank confirmation, the letter would clearly identify the details of the information for which confirmation is required and would carry the entity's authorisation for the bank to provide the confirmation to the auditor.

33 To avoid unnecessary delays in the confirmation process, the auditor ensures that a bank confirmation request is properly addressed. It is not sufficient, for example, to address a request to "The Manager, ABC Bank". Similarly, a request needs to contain sufficient, accurate information to enable the request to be clearly understood. For example, where the auditor is seeking bank information relating to a parent entity and its subsidiaries, that should be made clear in the bank confirmation request. A valid return address, direct to the auditor, is also important to minimise delays in the process.

Pre-completing the Standard Bank Confirmation Request Form

34 Where the auditor uses the standard bank confirmation request forms provided in this Guidance Statement, the auditor, in consultation with the entity, is responsible for pre-completing all known details in the shaded areas of the forms prior to forwarding the forms to the bank. It is important to complete known account names and the corresponding BSB and account numbers, as this will assist the bank in locating the relevant information.

35 The bank is responsible for checking the information supplied by the auditor and completing the information requested in the unshaded areas of the forms.

Submitting the Bank Confirmation Request

36 Having decided to obtain a bank confirmation, and selected and completed the appropriate bank confirmation request form, the auditor plans the submission of the request to the bank.

37 The auditor determines where to submit the bank confirmation request. In some instances, banks process bank confirmation requests at the branch level; therefore the auditor should address the bank confirmation request to the relevant branch. In other instances, banks have a single, centralised point of contact for the lodgement of all bank confirmation requests. Some banks may have different addresses for the lodgement of requests depending on the customer type. For example, the address for general requests may be different to the address for requests regarding treasury and other operations.

38 It is the auditor's responsibility to determine the appropriate address for the bank confirmation request. To assist the auditor, the ABA has agreed to publish on its website[20] the addresses of its members for the lodgement of bank confirmation requests.

Authority to Disclose

39 Banks require the explicit authority of the entity to disclose information to the auditor in response to a bank confirmation request. For this reason, the auditor would ordinarily request the entity to complete and sign a letter of authorisation to be forwarded to the bank together with the bank confirmation request. An example authorisation letter is provided in Appendix 3 of this Guidance Statement.

40 When a third party is involved, the auditor, with the assistance of the entity, may seek authorisation from the third party allowing disclosure or confirmation of relevant information by the bank. (See *Guarantees and Other Third Party Securities* below.)

41 One authorisation letter may be used to cover several bank confirmation requests, for example, requests relating to a parent and its subsidiaries, provided all entities and the relevant authorising officers are listed in the authorisation letter.

42 It is the auditor's responsibility to confirm with the entity that the names and titles of the authorising officers provided in the authorisation letter are up to date. Incorrect or invalid information regarding authorising officers may result in delays in the bank's response to a bank confirmation request.

20 See www.bankers.asn.au.

Guarantees and Other Third Party Securities

43 The provision of information about guarantees and other third party securities has, on occasion, resulted in significant delays in the completion of bank confirmation requests because the bank does not have sufficient authority to provide full disclosure of the information requested, due to data protection regulations concerning the counter-parties. When the bank does not have sufficient authority to provide full disclosure, the bank advises the auditor that further authority is required to provide full disclosure of such guarantees or third party securities. The auditor can then obtain details of the arrangements from the entity, for example, by requesting a copy of the relevant facility letter, loan agreement or contract. In some cases, these procedures may provide sufficient appropriate audit evidence. In other cases, the auditor may require further independent evidence and may seek further authority from the guarantor or third party for the bank to provide information to the auditor.

Timing of Bank Confirmation Requests

44 Where practicable, the auditor sends the bank confirmation request to the bank at least 15 working days in advance of the period end date. It is advisable to allow more time for requests covering the June and December period ends, as the banks receive large numbers of bank confirmation requests at this time.

45 Late lodgement of bank confirmation requests may result in delays in the bank's response.

Acknowledgement of Receipt by the Bank

46 The ABA has agreed to publish on its website a list of its members and whether or not they acknowledge receipt of audit requests for bank confirmations.

47 If acknowledgement is required, the auditor should include a Request for Acknowledgement of Receipt with the request for a bank confirmation. An example Request for Acknowledgement of Receipt letter is provided in Appendix 4 of this Guidance Statement.

48 Those banks that provide acknowledgements of receipt of audit requests if asked, will endeavour to do so within 5 working days of receipt. As part of the acknowledgement process, banks may indicate either a date by which they expect to respond to the auditor regarding the bank confirmation request, or provide an indication of the time allowed in their standard service level agreement for this process.

Following-Up Bank Confirmation Requests

49 The auditor should allow an appropriate time for the bank to process a bank confirmation request before following-up for a response.

50 The bank may have a service level agreement with an entity or a standard service level agreement applicable to all entities regarding response times for bank confirmation requests. In general, the ABA has agreed that its members will endeavour, *once a request is received and the confirmation date has passed*, to process bank confirmation requests within the following timeframes:

(a) Simple requests (for example, account balances only) – within 5-10 working days; and

(b) Complex requests (for example, multiple facilities, guarantees, third party securities, group comprising a parent entity and subsidiaries) – within 10-15 working days.

51 The auditor should not follow-up before the expected response time has passed, as these types of pre-production enquiries lead to significant delays and unnecessary costs in the bank confirmation process.

52 Where the bank confirmation request is not received by the bank on a timely basis, or contains incomplete, unclear or incorrect information, or the bank does not have the necessary authority to disclose information, a response may take longer than the times indicated above.

GS

53 Where the customer has banking arrangements across a number of jurisdictions or a bank maintains its records for certain bank transactions or accounts in different jurisdictions, a response may take longer than the times indicated above.

54 The ABA has agreed to publish on its website bank contact details for follow-up of audit requests for bank confirmation requests. It is important that auditors use these contact details, where provided, as telephone calls and electronic mail to other areas of the bank lead to unnecessary work and cost for the banks involved. The auditor should note that banks may have different addresses for the follow up of general requests compared to requests regarding treasury and other operations.

Results of the Bank Confirmation Process

55 The auditor evaluates the bank's response to a bank confirmation request and determines whether the response provides relevant and reliable audit evidence about the entity's bank accounts and transactions, or whether further audit evidence is required.[21]

56 The auditor may need to carry out additional audit procedures. For example, it is generally unwarranted for the auditor to place sole reliance on the information obtained through a bank confirmation request to satisfy the completeness assertion. This may be due to various factors such as:

(a) other audit procedures indicate doubt as to the completeness of the information provided by the bank;

(b) a question on the bank confirmation request remains unanswered by the bank;

(c) the auditor believes there is a risk that material accounts, agreements or transactions exist, that have not been disclosed in the bank confirmation;

(d) the bank's disclaimer regarding the information provided (see paragraphs 67-70 of this Guidance Statement); or

(e) limitations arising from the bank's ability to gather all information in respect of an entity's banking activities (see paragraph 74 of this Guidance Statement).

57 The auditor therefore considers performing additional audit procedures to obtain evidence over the completeness of information about bank accounts and transactions. The appropriateness of performing such procedures is dependent on the entity's circumstances and the assessed level of risk, and may include:

(a) requesting separate confirmation of the completeness of the information directly from the entity's relationship manager at the bank;

(b) contacting the bank separately about specific issues of concern;

(c) performing additional journal entry test work around cash and disbursements and reviewing cash transactions for unusual flows of funds;

(d) asking the entity to include a paragraph in the management representation letter confirming that the bank information is complete;

(e) reviewing minutes of meetings where new bank accounts or arrangements may have been agreed; or

(f) enquiring of the entity's treasury department, or other appropriate personnel in the entity, whether they are aware of any additional banking arrangements.

58 On its own, an oral response to a bank confirmation request does not meet the definition of an external confirmation because it is not a direct written response to the auditor. However, upon obtaining an oral response to a bank confirmation request, the auditor may, depending on the circumstances, request the bank to respond in writing directly to the auditor. If no such response is received, in accordance with ASA 505,[22] the auditor seeks other audit evidence to support the information in the oral response.

---

21 See ASA 505, paragraphs 10-11 and 16.

22 See ASA 505, paragraph 12.

Electronic Bank Confirmation Processes

59 Largely in an effort to make the external confirmation process more efficient and effective, auditors and banks have been increasingly relying on new technologies to facilitate the bank confirmation process. Electronic mail, facsimiles, and other electronic communications have become accepted methods of communication in addition to traditional mail. In some jurisdictions, certain confirmation processes also now involve the use of third party service providers serving as intermediaries between the auditor and the bank through an electronic medium. For example, some banks and authorised deposit-taking institutions will no longer accept and respond to paper confirmation requests received by mail and will only respond to confirmation requests sent electronically through designated third party service providers. Confirmations obtained through these various technological means may broadly be described as electronic confirmations.

60 ASA 505 does not preclude the use of an electronic confirmation process or the acceptance of electronic confirmations as audit evidence. While electronic confirmations may improve response times and claim to increase the reliability of responses, they may also give rise to new risks that the responses might not be reliable. For example, with electronic responses, proof of origin and authority of the respondents to respond may be difficult to establish, and alterations may be difficult to detect.

61 An electronic bank confirmation process used by the auditor and the bank that creates a secure environment for executing the confirmation request and receiving the response may mitigate the risk of inappropriate human intervention and manipulation. An important factor may therefore be the mechanism that is established between the auditor and the bank to minimise the risk that the electronic bank confirmation will be compromised because of interception, alteration, or fraud.

62 The auditor may need to design and perform tests of controls[23] to obtain sufficient appropriate audit evidence as to the operating effectiveness of controls over the electronic confirmation process before relying on the information obtained. If the auditor is satisfied that such a process is secure and properly controlled, the reliability of the related responses is enhanced.

63 If the auditor has doubts about the reliability of an electronic bank confirmation arising from the risks that:

(a) the response may not be from the proper source;

(b) a respondent may not be authorised to respond; and

(c) the integrity of the transmission may have been compromised,

it may be possible to verify the source and contents of the response by contacting the bank.

64 For example, when a confirmation response is transmitted by electronic mail or facsimile, it may be appropriate to telephone the bank to determine whether the bank did, in fact, send the response. It may also be possible to ask the bank to mail the original confirmation directly to the auditor. If a response is received indirectly (for example, because the bank incorrectly addressed it to the entity rather than to the auditor), it may be appropriate to ask the bank to respond again in writing directly to the auditor.

65 If a bank will only respond to a confirmation request through a third party service provider and the auditor plans to rely on the service provider's process, it may be important that the auditor be satisfied with the controls over the information sent by the entity to the service provider to initiate the process, and the controls applied during processing of the data and preparation and sending of the confirmation response to the auditor. A service auditor's report on the service provider's process may assist the auditor in evaluating the design and operating effectiveness of the electronic and manual controls with respect to that process. In the absence of a service auditor's report on the service provider, it may be important that the auditor designs other procedures to evaluate the design and operating effectiveness of the electronic and manual controls with respect to that process, and/or check the accuracy and completeness of the electronic confirmations received.

23 See ASA 330, paragraphs 8-11 regarding the requirements for the auditor to design and perform tests of controls.

66 An electronic confirmation process might incorporate various techniques for validating the identity of the sender of electronic information and that person's authority to confirm the requested information, for example, the use of data encryption,[24] electronic digital signatures[25] and procedures to verify web site authenticity.[26]

Disclaimers or Restrictive Language

67 The auditor considers the nature of any disclaimer or restrictive language used in a response to a bank confirmation request[27] to determine whether or not the disclaimer or restrictive language affects the reliability of the response as audit evidence. In general, the auditor can reasonably rely upon information given by the bank provided it corroborates the assertions made by management and is not clearly wrong, suspicious, inconsistent in itself, ambiguous, or in conflict with other evidence gathered during the course of the audit, even where the response includes a standard disclaimer of liability.

68 However, certain restrictive language may cast doubt on the completeness or accuracy of the information contained in the response, or the auditor's ability to rely on that information. Examples of such restrictive language include statements such as:

(a) Information is obtained from electronic data sources, which may not contain all information in the bank's possession.

(b) Information is not guaranteed to be accurate nor current and may be a matter of opinion.

(c) The recipient may not rely upon the information in the bank confirmation.

69 Whether the auditor may rely on the information confirmed and the degree of such reliance depends on the nature and substance of the restrictive language. Where the practical effect of the restrictive language is difficult to ascertain in the particular circumstances, the auditor may consider it appropriate to seek clarification from the bank or seek legal advice.

70 If restrictive language limits the extent to which the auditor can rely on the bank confirmation response as audit evidence, additional or alternative audit procedures may need to be performed. The nature and extent of such procedures depends on factors such as the nature of the item being confirmed, the assertion being tested, the nature and substance of the restrictive language, and relevant information obtained through other audit procedures. If the auditor is unable to obtain sufficient appropriate audit evidence through alternative or additional audit procedures, the auditor is required to consider the implications for the auditor's report in accordance with ASA 705.[28]

Co-operation with the Banking Industry

71 To facilitate effective and efficient processes for bank confirmation requests, the ABA, on behalf of banks in Australia, has:

(a) requested that the auditor forward the bank confirmation request to the bank at least 15 working days prior to the period end date for which confirmation is required. This will allow sufficient time for the bank to process the request and respond to the auditor within the agreed timeframes; (see paragraph 44 above)

---

24 Encryption is the process of encoding electronic data in such a way that it cannot be read without the second party using a matching encryption "key." Use of encryption reduces the risk of unintended intervention in a communication.

25 Digital signatures may use the encryption of codes or text or other means to ensure that only the claimed signer of the document could have affixed the symbol. The signature and its characteristics are uniquely linked to the signer. Digital signature routines allow for the creation of the signature and the checking of the signature at a later date for authenticity.

26 Website authenticity routines may use various means including mathematical algorithms to monitor data or a website to ensure that its content has not been altered without authorisation. For example, Webtrust or Verisign certifications may be earned and affixed to a website, indicating an active program of protecting the underlying content of the information.

27 The standard bank confirmation request forms (Bank Confirmation—Audit Request (General) and Bank Confirmation—Audit Request (Treasury and Other Operations)) include a disclaimer in favour of the bank and its staff.

28 See ASA 705 *Modifications to the Opinion in the Independent Auditor's Report*.

(b) undertaken to remind its members of the need for the timely completion of bank confirmation requests in order to facilitate the timely completion of audits;

(c) agreed with members preferred turnaround times for responding to audit requests for bank confirmation; (see paragraph 50 above)

(d) agreed to publish on its website:

(i) the addresses of members for the lodgement of bank confirmation requests; (see paragraph 38 above)

(ii) a list of those members who acknowledge the receipt of audit requests for bank confirmation on request; and (see paragraph 46 above)

(iii) contact details for its members for the follow up of overdue responses to audit requests for bank confirmation; and (see paragraph 54 above)

The auditor should note that banks may have different addresses for lodgement and follow up depending on the customer type. For example, addresses for general requests may be different from addresses for requests regarding treasury and other operations.

72 The ABA has separately issued guidance to banks in Australia regarding audit requests for bank confirmation, including the matters outlined in paragraph 71 above.

73 The ABA has advised that a charge may be made for completing a bank confirmation request form and the auditor is asked to advise the entity of this fact.

74 The ABA has also advised that the record-keeping systems of Australian banks ordinarily do not maintain together information for all entities within a reporting entity, or all accounts of a customer. For example, many Australian entities have current accounts based in other countries. In addition, many banks based in Australia are global and certain transactions and accounts for an entity, such as foreign exchange contracts, may be recorded by the bank in another country. Requests for bank confirmation in such circumstances would be considered non-standard, or complex, and would take longer to process.

Conformity with International Pronouncements

75 There is no equivalent International Auditing Practice Statement (IAPS) to this Guidance Statement.

Appendix 1

Bank Confirmation—Audit Request (General)

Instructions

Auditor

(a) Complete all known details in the shaded areas of this form before forwarding to the bank, including all known account names and the corresponding BSB and account numbers.

(b) If the space provided on the form is inadequate, attach a separate request giving full details of the information required.

Bank

(a) Confirm that the details provided in the shaded areas are correct as at the confirmation date shown below, and highlight any variation/s. Also add any relevant information that may have been omitted by the customer/auditor.

(b) Complete the unshaded areas in sections 1-10.

(c) Sign the completed form and return the original direct to the auditor, and a duplicate to the customer, in the stamped addressed envelopes provided. A copy may be retained by the bank.

GS

Bank (Name & Address)	Customer/Entity (Name & Address) "Entity" includes companies, companies in a parent-subsidiary relationship, joint ventures, partnerships, trusts, and unincorporated associations.

Auditor (Name & Address)	Confirmation Date (DD/MM/YYYY)
Contact Name: Telephone Number:	Authority to Disclose Information attached Yes/No
Fax Number: Email Address:	Third Party Authority attached Yes/No/ Not applicable
Date of Audit Request (DD/MM/YYYY)	Request for Acknowledgement attached Yes/No

1. CREDIT ACCOUNT BALANCES

Provide details of all account balances in favour of the bank customer as at the confirmation date, in respect of current accounts, interest bearing deposits, foreign currency accounts, convertible certificates of deposit, money market deposits, cash management trusts and any other credit balances. Provide details for the accounts listed below and for any other accounts not listed.

Provide details of any account or balance that is subject to any restriction(s) whatsoever and indicate the nature and extent of the restriction, e.g. garnishee order.

Account Name	BSB Number	Account Number	Currency	Balance
Auditor/customer to complete known details in shaded areas			Bank to complete unshaded areas	
Bank to provide information on other accounts not identified by auditor/customer				

2. DEBIT ACCOUNT BALANCES

Provide details of all account balances owed to the bank by the bank customer as at the confirmation date, in respect of overdraft accounts, bank loans, term loans, credit cards and any other debit balances.

Provide details of any account or balance that is subject to any restriction(s) whatsoever and indicate the nature and extent of the restriction, e.g. garnishee order.

Account Name	BSB Number	Account Number	Currency	Balance
Auditor/customer to complete known details in shaded areas			Bank to complete unshaded areas	
Bank to provide information on other accounts not identified by auditor/customer				

3. PROMISSORY NOTES/BILLS OF EXCHANGE HELD FOR COLLECTION ON BEHALF OF THE CUSTOMER

(Bank to complete)

Maker/Acceptor	Due Date	Balance

4. CUSTOMER'S OTHER LIABILITIES TO THE BANK (Bank to complete)

Provide details of the following as at the confirmation date:

(a) Acceptances, bills discounted with recourse to the customer or any subsidiary or related party of the customer, endorsed drafts/notes, forward exchange contracts, letters of credit, liability in respect of shipping documents where customer's account not yet debited.

(b) Bonds, guarantees, indemnities or other undertakings given to the bank by the customer in favour of third parties (including separately any such items in favour of any subsidiary or related party of the customer). Give details of the parties in favour of whom guarantees or undertakings have been given, whether such guarantees or undertakings are written or oral and their nature.

(c) Bonds guarantees, indemnities or other undertakings given by you, on your customer's behalf, stating whether there is recourse to your customer and/or any other related entity.

(d) Other liabilities—give details.

Nature of Liability	Terms of Liability	Currency	Name of Beneficiary	Balance

5. ITEMS HELD AS SECURITY FOR CUSTOMER'S LIABILITIES TO THE BANK (Bank to complete)

With respect to items held as security for customer's liabilities to the bank indicate whether the security:

(a) relates to particular borrowings or liabilities to the bank and whether it is lodged in the customer's name or by a third party. (If lodged by a third party, that party's authority to disclose details must be attached).

(b) is formally charged (provide details of date, ownership and type of charge);

(c) supports facilities granted by the bank to the customer or to another party.

(d) is limited in amount or to a specific borrowing or, if to your knowledge, there is a prior, equal or subordinate charge;

Provide details of any arrangements for set-off of balances or compensating balances e.g., back to back loans. Include details of date, type of document and account covered, any acknowledgement of set-off, whether given by specific letter of set-off or incorporated in some other document;

Provide details of any negative pledge arrangements that exist.

Provide details here

GS

6. LEASES (Bank to complete)

Provide details of all known finance leasing commitments

Leased Item	Restrictions/Special Arrangements	Lease Term	Currency	Implicit Interest Rate	Repayment Terms	Balance

7. ACCOUNTS OPENED/CLOSED (Bank to complete)

List details of any accounts opened or closed during the twelve months prior to confirmation date.

Account Name	BSB Number	Account Number	Open or Closed?	Date opened/closed

8. UNUSED LIMITS/FACILITIES (Bank to complete)

Please confirm details of all available unused limits/facilities at confirmation date.

Types of Facility	Facility Limit	Unused Limit	Terms of Facility Use

9. DEFAULTS AND BREACHES (Bank to complete)

With reference to the customer's accounts with the bank, provide details of any defaults or breaches during the period and full details of such defaults and breaches. Include details, for example, of:

(a) loans payable in default at the confirmation date and whether they have since been re-negotiated, and

(b) bank covenants breached during the twelve months up to the confirmation date and whether the breach was remedied.

Provide details here

10. OTHER INFORMATION

Please confirm (see shaded area below) and/or provide any other details (unshaded area below) relating to any financial relationships not dealt with under sections to 1-9 above.

Auditor/customer to complete known details in shaded area
Bank to provide other information not identified by customer

11. BANK AUTHORISATION (Bank to complete)

This certificate has been completed from our records at .... (bank details).

The Bank and its staff are unable to warrant the correctness of that information and accordingly hereby disclaim all liability in respect of the same. The information contained herein is confidential and provided for private use in confirmation of our customer accounts for audit purposes only. It may not be used for any other purpose or by any other persons. In particular this is not a credit reference.

AUTHORISED BY:	Other authorisation details (where applicable)
Signature: ________	
Name (print name) ________	
Title ________	
Telephone Number ________	
Email Address ________	
Date Completed ________	

Appendix 2

Bank Confirmation—Audit Request (Treasury and Other Operations)

Instructions

Auditor

(a) Complete all known details in the shaded areas of this form before forwarding to the bank, including all known account names and the corresponding account numbers.

(b) If the space provided on the form is inadequate, attach a separate request giving the full details of the information required.

Bank

(a) Confirm that the details provided in the shaded areas are correct as at the confirmation date shown below, and highlight any variation/s. Also add any relevant information that may have been omitted by the customer/auditor.

(b) Complete the unshaded areas in sections 1-9.

(d) Sign the completed form and return the original direct to the auditor, and a duplicate to the customer, in the stamped addressed envelopes provided. A copy may be retained by the bank.

Bank (Name & Address)	Customer/Entity (Name & Address)
	"Entity" includes companies, companies in a parent-subsidiary relationship, joint ventures, partnerships, trusts, and unincorporated associations.

GS

Auditor (Name & Address)	Confirmation Date (DD/MM/YYYY)
Contact Name: Telephone Number: Fax Number: Email Address:	Authority to Disclose Information attached Yes/No Third Party Authority attached Yes/No/ Not applicable
Date of Audit Request (DD/MM/YYYY)	Request for Acknowledgement attached Yes/No

1. BALANCES OF ACCOUNTS (DEPOSIT & ADVANCES), SECURITIES HELD

(a) Please confirm details of all account balances as at the confirmation date.

(b) Include details of: nostro accounts, vostro accounts, current accounts, interest bearing deposits, foreign currency accounts, convertible certificates of deposit, money market deposits, etc. Confirm details of any securities held for payment, e.g., Promissory Notes.

(c) Confirm details of direct liabilities (bank & term loans etc), indicating the collateral lodged by the customer in respect to each outstanding loan. Details of repayment terms should also be confirmed.

Account Name	Account Number	Balance DR/CR	Currency	Interest Rate	Interest Accrued	Date Paid	Other Charges	Maturity Date	Collateral Lodged
Auditor/customer to complete		Bank to complete unshaded areas							
Bank to provide information on other accounts not identified by auditor/customer									

2. FORWARD RATE AGREEMENTS (FRAs) (Bank to complete)

Please confirm details of all outstanding forward rate agreement contracts at the confirmation date.

Name and Number of contract	Period of Contract Start Date	Maturity Date	Notional Principal Amount	Currency	Contract/ Hedge Rate	Fixed/ Floating	Contract Borrower/ Contract Lender

3. FOREIGN EXCHANGE CONTRACTS (Bank to complete)

Please confirm details of all outstanding foreign exchange contracts at the confirmation date. Obligations to purchase/sell currency should be confirmed in terms of the bank's indebtedness.

Purchase Currency	Amount	Sell Currency	Amount	Exchange Rate	Deal Date	Maturity Date

4. SINGLE CURRENCY INTEREST RATE SWAPS (Bank to complete)

Please confirm details of outstanding single currency interest rate swaps.

			Receive					Pay			
Start Date	Maturity Date	Notional Principal Amount	Currency	Fixed/ Floating	Payment Frequency	Interest Rate	Last Received	Fixed/ Floating	Payment Frequency	Interest Rate	Last Paid

5. CROSS CURRENCY INTEREST RATE SWAPS (Bank to complete)

Please confirm details of outstanding cross-currency interest rate swaps.

		Received/Purchase Currency					Pay/Sell Currency				
Start Date	Maturity Date	Notional Principal Amount	Currency	Payment Frequency	Interest Rate	Last Received	Notional Principal Amount	Currency	Payment Frequency	Interest Rate	Last Paid

6. OPTIONS CONTRACTS (e.g., INTEREST, CURRENCY AND COMMODITIES) (Bank to complete)

Please confirm details listed of outstanding options contracts as at the confirmation date. Indicate the nature of each option contract e.g., Interest Rate Options (cap, collar etc).

Nature of Option Contract	Option Type American/European	Premium	Strike Price	Currency	Expiry Date	Put/Call Option	Buy/Sell	Contracts Outstanding (No.)

7. TREASURY FUTURES CONTRACTS (Bank to complete)

Please confirm details listed of outstanding Treasury Futures Contracts e.g., BABs, Bonds.

Type of Futures Contract	Value Month	Number of Contracts	Funds on Deposit & Margin Calls	Long/Short	Contracted Sales Price

8. NETTING (OFFSET) ARRANGEMENTS (Bank to complete)

Please confirm the details of any arrangements for offset of compensating balances e.g., back to back loans. Give particulars of any acknowledgement of offset, whether given by specific letter of offset or incorporated in some other document (i.e., date, type of document and accounts covered).

Item Subject to Netting Arrangements	Conditions of Netting

GS

9. OTHER CONTRACTUAL ARRANGEMENTS (Bank to complete)

Provide details of any other contractual arrangement(s) between the customer and the bank e.g., forward bank bills/bonds, repurchase agreements, transactions packaged as a unique product for the customer, bullion contracts, commodity contracts, swap arrangements (near and far dates), credit derivatives including collateralised debt obligations (CDOs), and others (indicate their nature).

Nature of Contract	Deal Date	Maturity Date	Value Date	Face Value	Consideration	Coupon

10. BANK AUTHORISATION (Bank to complete)

This certificate has been completed from our records at .... (bank details).

The Bank and its staff are unable to warrant the correctness of that information and accordingly hereby disclaim all liability in respect of the same. The information contained herein is confidential and provided for private use in confirmation of our customer accounts for audit purposes only. It may not be used for any other purpose or by any other persons. In particular this is not a credit reference.

AUTHORISED BY:		Other authorisation details (where applicable)
Signature:	______	
Name (print name)	______	
Title	______	
Telephone Number	______	
Email Address	______	
Date Completed	______	

Appendix 3

Example Letter: Customer Request and Authority to Disclose

Addressee

Name of Bank

Address of Bank

Date

Dear ....

[Entity's (ies') Name(s)][29]—Bank Confirmation Request and Authority to Disclose Information

29 The entity's (ies') name(s) on the Authority to Disclose letter should match the name(s) shown in the bank confirmation request.

I/We[30] authorise you, [Name of Bank], including all branches and subsidiaries of the bank, to provide to our auditor [Name of Auditor] any information that the auditor may request from you regarding all and any of our accounts and dealings with you.

More specifically, it would be appreciated if you would complete and return, for audit purposes, the information requested in the attached form(s) by (insert date):

- Bank Confirmation—Audit Request (General)
- Bank Confirmation—Audit Request (Treasury and Other Operations)

Please mail the original of the completed form(s) direct to our auditor as named in the form(s) and the duplicate(s) to us in the stamped, addressed envelopes enclosed for this purpose.

Any charge for providing this information is to be debited to the following account: [insert account details]

Yours faithfully

(Authorising Officer's Signature)[30]	(Authorising Officer' Signature)
(Authorising Officer's Name)	(Authorising Officer's Name)
(Authorising Officer's Title)	(Authorising Officer's Title)

Appendix 4

Example Form: Request for Acknowledgement of Receipt of Bank Confirmation Request

Part A - to completed by the Auditor

Please acknowledge receipt of the:

- Bank Confirmation—Audit Request (General)
- Bank Confirmation—Audit Request (Treasury and Other Operations) [Delete if not applicable]

for the following entity (ies):

Entity (Name & address)[31]	

This acknowledgement should be returned to:

Auditor (Name & address)	

Please contact the following person if you have any queries about this request:

Contact name:

Telephone Number:

Fax Number:

Email Address:

30 The person(s) signing this Authority to Disclose letter should be duly authorised to do so as the entity's representative.

31 The entity name should match the relevant information contained in the Bank Confirmation Request.

GS

Part B - to be completed by the Bank

Thank you for your:

- Bank Confirmation—Audit Request (General)
- Bank Confirmation—Audit Request (Treasury and Other Operations)
  [Delete if not applicable]

in respect of:

Entity (Name & address)	
The request was received on (DD/MM/YYYY)	

Your request is being processed and we expect to respond to you by ________ (DD/MM/YYYY), in accordance with our general service level agreement for processing bank confirmation requests.

In the event that you need to contact us, please address any enquiries to:

Bank (Name & address)	

Contact name:

Telephone Number:

Fax Number:

Email Address:

GS 017

Prudential Reporting Requirements for Auditors of a Life Company

(Issued June 2010)

Prepared and issued by the Auditing and Assurance Standards Board.

Note from the Institute of Chartered Accountants Australia

This note, prepared by the technical editor, is not part of GS 017.

Historical development

December 1995: AGS 1024 'Life Insurance Act 1995 – Audit Obligations' released by the AuASB to assist the auditor of a life insurance company, operating under the *Life Insurance Act 1995* (the Act), to discharge the audit obligations under the Act.

December 2002: A revised AGS 1024 issued in response to legislative and regulatory changes. This AGS has been endorsed by the Australian Prudential Regulation Authority (APRA).

June 2010: GS 017 issued to replace AGS 1024, in response to prudential Standards issued by APRA in March 2010. It is effective for reporting periods beginning on or after 1 July 2010. There is no equivalent international statement.

GS

Contents

Preface

How this Guidance Statement is to be used

This Guidance Statement has been formulated by the Auditing and Assurance Standards Board (AUASB), in consultation with the Australian Prudential Regulation Authority (APRA), to provide guidance to the auditor of a life company, reporting in accordance with the prudential reporting requirements specified by APRA in its life company Prudential Standard LPS 310 *Audit and Related Matters* (LPS 310).

This Guidance Statement is to be read in conjunction with, and is not a substitute for referring to:

(a) LPS 310 and other applicable APRA Prudential Requirements and Reporting Standards, including the *Life Insurance Act 1995* (Life Act), the *Financial Sector (Collection of Data) Act 2001* (FSCODA);

(b) applicable AUASB Standards; and

(c) relevant ethical and professional standards.

This Guidance Statement does not extend the responsibilities of an auditor of a life company beyond those which are imposed by the Life Act, the FSCODA, APRA Prudential and Reporting Standards, AUASB Standards and other applicable legislation.

It is not the intention of this Guidance Statement to provide step-by-step guidance in relation to the conduct of a prudential reporting engagement and it is not to be used as a checklist of all issues to be considered by the auditor.

It is not intended that this Guidance Statement limits or replaces the auditor's professional judgement and initiative, or limits the application of relevant AUASB Standards. AUASB Standards contain the basic principles and essential procedures to be applied by the auditor when performing reasonable assurance (audit) and limited assurance (review) engagements. Audit and review programs for each engagement are to be designed to meet the circumstances of the particular engagement, giving careful consideration to the size and type of life company and the adequacy of its internal controls.

Authority Statement

The Auditing and Assurance Standards Board (AUASB) formulates Guidance Statement GS 017 *Prudential Reporting Requirements for Auditors of a Life Company* pursuant to section 227B of the *Australian Securities and Investments Commission Act 2001*, for the purposes of providing guidance on auditing and assurance matters.

This Guidance Statement provides guidance to assist the auditor to fulfil the objectives of the audit or assurance engagement. It includes explanatory material on specific matters for the purposes of understanding and complying with AUASB Standards. The auditor exercises professional judgement when using this Guidance Statement.

The Guidance Statement does not prescribe or create new requirements.

Dated: 24 June 2010

M H Kelsall
Chairman - AUASB

Guidance Statement GS 017

Prudential Reporting Requirements for Auditors of a Life Company

Application

1 This Guidance Statement has been formulated by the Auditing and Assurance Standards Board (AUASB), in consultation with the Australian Prudential Regulation Authority (APRA), to provide guidance to the auditor of a life company[1], reporting in accordance with the prudential reporting requirements specified by APRA in its life company Prudential Standard LPS 310 *Audit and Related Matters* (March 2010) (LPS 310).

Issuance Date

2 This Guidance Statement is issued on 24 June 2010 by the AUASB and replaces AGS 1024 *Life Insurance Act 1995 – Audit Obligations,* issued in December 2002.

3 This Guidance Statement is effective for assurance engagements undertaken in relation to reporting periods commencing on or after 1 July 2010.

Introduction

Prudential Supervision of a Life company

4 Under the *Life Insurance Act 1995* (Life Act), APRA is responsible for the prudential supervision and monitoring of prudential matters relating to all life companies, a specified class of life companies or one or more specified life companies in order to protect the interests of policy holders or prospective policy holders of the life companies concerned.

5 APRA formulates, promulgates and enforces prudential policy and practice through life company Prudential Standards (LPSs). In addition, APRA may also issue non-enforceable life company Prudential Practice Guides (LPGs) and other guidelines, to assist life companies in complying with the requirements in its Prudential Standards and, more

GS

1 The terms auditor and life company are defined in paragraph 21 of this Guidance Statement.

generally, to outline prudent practices in relation to certain elements of a life company's operations.[2]

6 Under the Life Act a life company is required to appoint an auditor. LPS 310 provides eligibility criteria for auditors. The auditor of a life company has an important role to play in the prudential supervision process. Requirements for auditors of life companies to provide reports on prudential matters to APRA are intended to assist APRA in assessing the reliability of information supplied to it by a life company.

7 The use by life companies and APRA of assurance reports prepared by auditors needs to be evaluated in the context of the inherent limitations of an audit or review (refer paragraphs 107 – 111) and the subject matter of the audit or review (refer paragraphs 41 – 47 of this Guidance Statement).

8 LPS 310 warns that all persons involved in the provision of information (which includes the auditor) are to note that it is an offence under subsection 137.1 and 137.2 of the Criminal Code 1995 to provide, whether directly or indirectly, false or misleading documents or information to a Commonwealth entity (such as APRA).

Responsibilities of the Auditor

9 The responsibilities and reporting requirements of the auditor of a life company are contained in:

(a) applicable AUASB Standards;

(b) LPS 310;

(c) other applicable APRA Prudential Requirements[3], including the *Life Insurance Act*, the *Financial Sector (Collection of Data) Act 2001* (FSCODA), and APRA Prudential and Reporting Standards; and

(d) relevant ethical and professional standards.

10 APRA places reliance on accounting and auditing standards to the extent that they do not conflict with Prudential Requirements applicable to life companies. LPS 310 requires auditors in meeting their role and responsibilities, to comply with the Australian Auditing Standards and consider Guidance Statements issued by the AUASB, except where:

(a) they are inconsistent with the requirements of LPS 310, in which case LPS 310 prevails; or

(b) APRA otherwise specifies, in writing, to the life company that alternative standards and guidance are to be used by the auditor.

In the case of an eligible foreign life insurance company (EFLIC), APRA requires compliance with Australian Accounting Standards in the completion of APRA annual returns under LPS 310.

11 The following AUASB Standards are applicable to the engagement:

(a) Auditing Standards - where reasonable assurance on financial information is required; and

(b) Standard on Assurance Engagements ASAE 3000 *Assurance Engagements Other than Audits or Reviews of Historical Financial Information* (ASAE 3000) – where limited assurance is required in relation to information other than historical financial information and in relation to internal controls.

ASAE 3000 has been written for general application to assurance engagements other than audits or reviews of historical financial information covered by Auditing Standards or Standards on Review Engagements. Where topic-specific ASAEs exist, for example ASAE 3100 *Compliance Engagements*, the auditor applies the relevant topic-specific ASAEs, as well as ASAE 3000.

2 Access to APRA Prudential Standards, Prudential Practice Guides and legislation relevant to Life company's is available on APRA's website (www.apra.gov.au).

3 See paragraph 21 of this Guidance Statement.

12 The auditor accepts the prudential reporting engagement only when the auditor is satisfied that the auditor and the engagement team if applicable, have met the relevant ethical requirements relating to the assurance engagement.

13 The concept of independence is important to the auditor's compliance with the fundamental ethical principles of integrity and objectivity. The auditor is required to meet the independence requirements set out in:

(a) APRA's life company Prudential Standard LPS 510 *Governance* (LPS 510); and

(b) ASA 102 *Compliance with Ethical Requirements when Performing Audits, Reviews and Other Assurance Engagements* (ASA 102).

Tripartite Relationship

14 Under normal circumstances, APRA does not consult directly with an auditor of a life company on matters concerning an individual life company. APRA's liaison with an auditor of a life company is normally conducted under tripartite arrangements involving APRA, the life company and its auditor(s) (see LPS 310).

15 Any one of the parties involved in the tripartite relationship may initiate meetings or discussions at any time, when considered necessary.

16 Notwithstanding the tripartite relationship, APRA and the auditor may meet, at any time, on a bilateral basis at the request of either party. APRA may communicate with an auditor of a life company on a bilateral basis to obtain or discuss information for whatever reason(s) it considers appropriate.

17 Under LPS 510, a life company is required to ensure that its internal policy and contractual arrangements do not explicitly or implicitly restrict or discourage auditors (or other parties) from communicating with APRA.

Scope of LPS 310 Prudential Reporting Engagements

18 LPS 310 provides for two types of engagements to be conducted by the auditor of a life company, namely:

(a) annual prudential reporting engagements (see paragraphs 30-127); and

(b) special purpose engagements (see paragraphs 133-143).

19 The audit [and review] of financial reports required under the *Corporations Act 2001* (the Act) (where required) is directed towards obtaining sufficient appropriate evidence to form an opinion [or conclusion] on whether the financial report is presented fairly in accordance with the required financial reporting framework. The financial report audit [and review] is not designed to enable the auditor to conclude in relation to the matters specified in LPS 310.

20 The LPS 310 prudential reporting requirements, imposed on the auditor via the terms of engagement with a life company, are in addition to the audit [and review] of financial reports required under the Act.

Definitions

21 For the purpose of this Guidance Statement, the following terms have the meanings attributed below:

(a) Assurance engagement means an engagement in which an assurance practitioner expresses a conclusion designed to enhance the degree of confidence of the intended users other than the responsible party about the outcome of the evaluation or measurement of a subject matter against criteria.

(b) Assurance engagement risk means the risk that the practitioner expresses an inappropriate conclusion when the subject matter information is materially misstated.

(c) Auditor means an independent auditor(s) appointed by a life company to meet the prudential reporting requirements under LPS 310.

Under LPS 310 it is possible for a life company to have more than one auditor at any time, and for an auditor appointed under LPS 310 to be different from the auditor

GS

responsible for undertaking the financial report audit [and review] under the Act if agreed to by APRA and the auditor satisfies the criteria under LPS 310.

Where the Life Act refers to 'the auditor' of a life company, this may be an 'auditor' (under LPS 310) or another auditor, such as the auditor responsible for the audit [and review] of financial reports required under the Act.

(d) Internal control encompasses the following components:

(i) the control environment;

(ii) the life company's risk assessment process;

(iii) information systems, including the related business processes, relevant to financial and prudential reporting, and communication;

(iv) control activities; and

(v) monitoring of controls.

The way in which internal control is designed and implemented varies depending on the life company's size and complexity.

(e) Life company means all life companies (including friendly societies) registered under section 21 of the *Life Insurance Act 1995*.

(f) Life company auditable annual return(s), means a form used for the collection and reporting of information in relation to a life company, as required to be provided to APRA by a life company in accordance with APRA Reporting Standards made under the FSCODA.

(g) Limited assurance engagement means an assurance engagement where the assurance practitioner's objective is a reduction in assurance engagement risk to a level that is acceptable in the circumstances of the assurance engagement, but where that risk is greater than for a reasonable assurance engagement, as the basis for a negative form of expression of the assurance practitioner's conclusion. A limited assurance engagement is commonly referred to as a review.

(h) Prudential Requirements[4], are outlined in LPS 310 and include requirements imposed by:

(i) the *Life Insurance Act 1995*;

(ii) Regulations (made under the *Life Insurance Act 1995*);

(iii) APRA Prudential Standards (made under the *Life Insurance Act 1995*);

(iv) APRA Prudential Rules (made under the *Life Insurance Act 1995*);

(v) the FSCODA;

(vi) APRA Reporting Standards (made under the FSCODA);

(vii) APRA conditions on the registration of a life company; and

(viii) any other requirements imposed by APRA, in writing, in relation to the life company.

(i) Reasonable assurance engagement means an assurance engagement where the assurance practitioner's objective is a reduction in assurance engagement risk to an acceptably low level in the circumstances of the assurance engagement as the basis for a positive form of expression of the assurance practitioner's conclusion. A reasonable assurance engagement is commonly referred to as an audit.

(j) Reliability under the Australian Accounting Standards Board's *Framework for the Preparation and Presentation of Financial Statements* means information has the quality of reliability "... *when it is free from material error and bias and can be depended upon by users to represent faithfully that which it either purports to represent or could reasonably expected to represent*".

4 These requirements may differ between locally incorporated and foreign life companies.

Responsibilities of the Life Company

22 It is the responsibility of a life company's Board and management to ensure that the life company meets prudential and statutory requirements and has management practices in place to limit risks to prudent levels (refer LPS 510).

23 Under the Life Act a life company is required to appoint an auditor(s) to meet the prudential reporting requirements under LPS 310. LPS 310 sets out the eligibility criteria for the appointment of an auditor.[5]

24 The life company is required to ensure that its auditor(s):

(i) has access to all relevant data, information, reports and staff of the life company, which the auditor reasonably believes is necessary to fulfil their role and responsibilities under LPS 310. This includes, access to the life company's Board[6], Board Audit Committee and internal auditors as required;

(ii) is kept fully informed of all APRA prudential requirements applicable to the life company; and

(iii) is provided with any other information that APRA has provided to the life company that may assist the auditor in fulfilling their role and responsibilities under LPS 310.

25 A life company must ensure that the following are provided to its Board or Board Audit Committee (if not already sighted by one of them):

(i) reports, provided by the auditor in accordance with LPS 310, and any associated assessments and other material prepared in connection with fulfilling the requirements of LPS 310;

(ii) commentary or responses provided by APRA to the life company on reports provided by the auditor, and any associated assessments and other material; and

(iii) any commentary or response on the reports, associated assessments and other material provided by the auditor that is given by the life company to APRA.

26 A life company, if requested by APRA, must within a reasonable time provide APRA with the terms of engagement and other instructions or correspondence, including management letters, that may have a bearing on the:

(i) scope or conduct of the work undertaken by the auditor in accordance with LPS 310; and

(ii) form, content (including findings made or opinions expressed by the auditor) or coverage of the reports provided in accordance with LPS 310.

Role and Responsibilities of the Auditor

27 LPS 310 requires the auditor of a life company to report to the Board within four months of the end of the financial year of the life company, in relation to the following matters:

(a) *Reasonable Assurance on Life company annual returns*[7]*:*

LPS 310 requires the auditor to prepare a report that provides reasonable assurance that, in all material respects the:

(i) annual returns are reliable and in accordance with the relevant prudential requirements, and

(ii) prudential requirements in relation to the accounting for statutory funds have been met.

The requirements in (i) above are largely met by work performed by the auditor and the engagement team as part of the financial report audit required under the Act.

(b) *Limited Assurance on Systems, Procedures and Internal Controls that are designed to ensure Compliance with Prudential Requirements and the Reliability of Data included in the Life company annual returns*

5 See LPS 310, paragraph 5.

6 In the case of an eligible foreign life insurance company (EFLIC), the Compliance Committee.

7 For a listing of life company annual returns to be subjected to audit refer to APRA Prudential Standard LPS 310 *Attachment A – Auditable annual returns.*

GS

LPS 310 requires the auditor to prepare a report that provides limited assurance that, based on the review which is not an audit, in all material respects, nothing has come to the attention of the auditor that:

(i) the life company has not implemented systems, procedures and internal controls that are designed to ensure the life company has:
   a. complied with all applicable prudential requirements; and
   b. provided reliable data to APRA in the life company auditable annual returns prepared under the FSCODA; and

(ii) the controls in paragraph 27(b)(i) have not operated effectively throughout the financial year; and

(iii) the life company's systems, procedures and internal controls relating to actuarial data integrity and financial reporting risks (the risks that incorrect source data will be used in completing the annual returns under FSCODA) are not adequate and effective.

Refer to paragraphs 120-123 for further guidance on the auditor's opinion/conclusions.

28 The Life Act specifies in section 88 the circumstances where the auditor is required to report to APRA in the instance where a life company or its directors may have contravened the Life Act or any other law and the contravention may significantly prejudice the interests of the holders of policies issued by the life company.

When a report is made to APRA, the auditor should not disclose this to the life company if the auditor:

(a) has lost confidence in or mistrusts the Board or senior management of the life company; or

(b) the auditor considers that by doing so the interests of policy holders may be jeopardised.

29 In accordance with LPS 310, an auditor, whether as part of the annual prudential reporting or special purpose engagements, must not place sole reliance on work performed by APRA.

Agreeing the Terms of the Annual Prudential Reporting Engagement

30 The requirement to report in accordance with APRA's annual prudential reporting requirements, is in addition to the audit [and review] of financial reports required under the Act, and is to be treated by the auditor as a separate audit engagement.

31 The auditor and the life company agree on the terms of the engagement in accordance with the requirements of Auditing Standard ASA 210 *Agreeing the Terms of Audit Engagements* (ASA 210) and ASAE 3000. These arrangements have to be legally binding and include the required terms of engagement specified in LPS 310.

32 An engagement letter (or other suitable form) confirms both the client's and the auditor's understanding of the terms of the engagement and the auditor's acceptance of the appointment. Both parties sign the engagement letter to acknowledge that it is a legally binding contract.

33 For recurring engagements, the auditor considers whether circumstances require the terms of the engagement to be revised and whether there is a need to re-confirm in writing the existing terms of the engagement. While the auditor may decide not to re-confirm the terms of engagement each year, factors that may make it appropriate to do so include a recent change of senior management or those charged with governance, or any indication that the life company misunderstands the objectives and scope of LPS 310 prudential reporting engagements.

34 Ordinarily, matters that are contained in the engagement letter include the following:

- The objectives and scope of the annual prudential reporting engagement pursuant to LPS 310.
- The responsibilities of management and, where appropriate, those charged with governance, for the subject matter of the report.
- The role and responsibilities of the auditor in accordance with the requirements of LPS 310.

- Acknowledgement that the auditor, in meeting their role and responsibilities, will comply with the requirements of applicable AUASB Standards and will consider relevant Guidance Statements issued by the AUASB, except where inconsistent with the requirements of LPS 310 or where APRA specifies alternative standards and guidance to be used.
- Identification of the relevant AUASB Standards under which the engagement will be conducted and inclusion of a statement that, although it does not prescribe or create new mandatory requirements, the auditor will consider the guidance contained in this Guidance Statement.
- Agreement from management and, where appropriate, those charged with governance, to provide unrestricted access to whatever records, documentation and other information requested in connection with the prudential reporting engagement.
- Agreement from management and, where appropriate, those charged with governance, to provide written representations requested by the auditor.
- Any limitations on the engagement (see paragraphs 107-111).
- The agreed use of the assurance report(s) issued by the auditor, and the extent to which, and the basis on which, the assurance reports may be made available to others (refer paragraphs 120-123).
- The auditor's additional responsibilities to report to APRA under sections 80(3), 88 and 88A of the Life Act and section 89 which provides for protection in relation to the disclosure of such information.
- Confirmation that the auditor will meet the independence requirements under LPS 510 and ASA 102.
- The form of reporting and communication in relation to the engagement.

35 The engagement letter explains that any special purpose engagement of any aspect of the life company's operations, risk management or financial affairs, will constitute a separate engagement(s) and that the details of such engagement(s) will be the subject of a separate engagement letter(s).

36 The engagement letter furthermore clarifies that, in accordance with LPS 310 and LPS 510, the auditor is not to be a party to any contractual arrangements, or any understandings with a life company, that seek in any way to limit the auditor's ability or willingness to communicate to APRA. The auditor notifies APRA of any attempts by a life company to achieve such arrangements or understandings. APRA may liaise bilaterally with an auditor and may although not usually, request information directly from the auditor.

Planning the Annual Prudential Reporting Engagement

37 The nature and extent of planning activities will vary with the engagement circumstances. Specific matters that may be considered by the auditor as part of the planning process include:

- The auditor's understanding of the life company and its environment, including its internal control and compliance framework (see paragraphs 38-40).
- The auditor's previous experience with the life company.
- The characteristics of the subject matter and the identified assessment criteria (see paragraphs 41-47).
- The internal controls relating to actuarial data integrity and financial reporting risks and the reliability and accuracy of the underlying source data.
- The intended users of the auditor's assurance report and their needs (see paragraphs 48-49).
- Materiality (see paragraphs 50-64).
- Assurance engagement risk.
- The appropriate assurance strategy to adopt for each part of the engagement and possible sources of evidence.

GS

- Personnel and expertise requirements, including the nature and extent of experts' involvement (see paragraphs 65-69).
- Work to be performed by another auditor (see paragraph 70).
- The activities of the internal audit function and the effect on audit and review procedures (see paragraphs 71-73).
- The auditor's additional reporting responsibilities under the Life Act (see paragraphs 130-134).

Further guidance on planning an audit may be found in ASAE 3000 and ASA 300 *Planning an Audit of a Financial report* (ASA 300).

The Auditor's Understanding of the Life Company and its Environment, including its Internal Control and Compliance Framework

38 The auditor obtains an understanding of the life company and its environment, including its internal control and compliance framework, and other assurance engagement circumstances, sufficient to:

(a) identify and assess the risks of the subject matter information being materially misstated, that significant deficiencies in internal controls may exist (in relation to the area of activity to be examined), and/or that the life company may not be complying with applicable prudential requirements; and

(b) design and perform further evidence-gathering procedures.

39 The auditor exercises professional judgement to determine the nature and extent of the understanding that is needed. When performing procedures to obtain an understanding of the life company and its environment, consideration of the following matters may be helpful:

- The size, nature and complexity of the life company and its activities.
- Any changes in the market environment.
- Governance and management functions within the life company, including the attitude, awareness and actions of those charged with governance and of management concerning the life company's compliance with Prudential Requirements, and the respective roles and responsibilities attributed to the finance, risk management, compliance and internal audit functions.
- Relevant aspects of the life company's risk management framework and systems applicable to the engagement, including the life company's risk assessment process for identifying risks relevant to prudential reporting objectives and deciding on actions to address those risks through its risk management systems.
- The life company's internal control relevant to the assurance engagement.
- The life company's compliance framework, processes and controls (refer to ASAE 3100).
- The significance and complexity of the life company's information technology environment and systems.
- Any formal communications between APRA and the life company, and the results of any supervisory visits conducted by APRA in relation to the engagement.
- Recent reports prepared by other assurance practitioners appointed to report on any aspect of the life company.
- Work performed by the internal audit, risk management and compliance functions, for example key findings, control deficiencies, compliance register or incident reporting, and any reliance that may be placed on this work.
- Discussions with life company staff responsible for monitoring regulatory compliance, such as the life company's compliance officer or chief risk officer.

40 In addition to the general planning considerations, the auditor takes the following factors into account when planning the review of the life company's internal controls relevant to the assurance engagement:

- The overall compliance framework adopted by the life company to ensure compliance with all applicable prudential requirements, including its controls, policies and processes, and consideration of whether or not these are appropriate given the size, nature and complexity of the life company.
- The sufficiency and appropriateness of the life company's risk management strategy, including systems, policies and controls adopted in accordance with specific prudential standards, and consideration of whether these are up to date and in sufficient detail to facilitate compliance with the relevant prudential standards.
- Matters relating to the life company's organisational structure and operating characteristics, and recent significant changes thereto, which could impact on the life company's internal controls.
- Knowledge of the life company's internal controls obtained during other assurance engagements conducted in relation to the life company.
- Previously communicated instances of material non-compliance with prudential requirements and/or material deficiencies in internal controls designed to ensure compliance with all applicable prudential requirements and the provision of reliable data to APRA in annual returns that have and have not been resolved by the life company.
- In relation to actuarial data integrity and financial reporting risks the auditor may consider some of the following:
    - Sufficiency of expert resources within the life company e.g. actuarial or financial analysis and modelling;
    - Level/frequency of internal/external review of actuarial forecasting systems, models and associated controls;
    - Complexity of the underlying IT systems and general IT controls including:
        - storage and protection of data;
        - number of source systems;
        - system interfaces;
        - data transfer processes;
        - updating of actuarial data/key fields in the source systems; and
        - end user computing controls in relation to spreadsheets or other business owned applications e.g. version control, integrity, password control and logic tests.

The above is not meant to represent an exhaustive list and there may be other factors relevant to the specific circumstances of a life company.

The Characteristics of the Subject Matter and the Identified Assessment Criteria

41 The auditor identifies the most recent year-end life company annual returns submitted to APRA for audit and/or review.

42 The auditor identifies, and obtains an understanding of, all the prudential requirements (refer to definition under paragraph 21) applicable to the specific life company (including any additional guidance provided by APRA to the life company), with particular attention to changes in these requirements during the reporting period. The auditor makes enquiries with respect to any requirements that are imposed in writing by APRA on a bilateral APRA - life company basis, or in relation to conditions on the life company's authorisation, as these requirements may vary from one life company to another.

43 Compliance with prudential requirements (see paragraphs 27(a) and 27(b) of this Guidance Statement) is broader than compliance with only the quantitative limits in APRA Prudential Standards (for example, capital adequacy requirements). The auditor is required to provide reasonable assurance in relation to the preparation of the annual return(s) in accordance

GS

with the Life Act, the *FSCODA Act 2001* and the applicable APRA reporting standards (Refer Auditor's Opinion in Appendix 1 Part A).

44 In relation to a life company's responsibility to keep the auditor informed of all APRA prudential requirements applicable to the life company, the auditor obtains written representations from those responsible (see paragraphs 106-107).

45 APRA Prudential and Reporting Standards provide the frame of reference (criteria) for reasonably consistent evaluation or measurement, within the context of the auditor's professional judgement, of the reliability of the information included in life company annual returns.

46 The auditor identifies and obtains an understanding of the applicable prudential requirements that govern the preparation of data within life company annual returns, with particular attention to changes in these requirements during the reporting period under review. In addition to the Prudential and Reporting Standards issued by APRA, other Prudential Requirements, including the life company *Reporting Form Instruction Guides*, will also have an impact on the provision of reliable data to APRA under the FSCODA and, therefore, the auditor has regard to all relevant Prudential Requirements when planning and conducting the engagement.

47 It is important that the auditor obtains an understanding of how APRA Prudential Standards and APRA Reporting Standards differ from the financial reporting framework (Australian Accounting Standards) which determines data recorded in the life company's accounting records.

The Intended Users of the Auditor's Assurance Report and Their Needs

48 Data collected in a life company annual return(s) is primarily used by APRA to ensure that:

(a) the regulated entity has met requirements of all prudential standards;

(b) statutory and regulatory requirements are met;

(c) statistical and financial data provided to APRA is reliable; and

(d) other matters that could materially prejudice/adversely affect the interests of policyholders are concluded upon.

49 APRA has the power under subsection 56(5) of the *Australian Prudential Regulation Authority Act 1998* to make 'protected information' (which may include auditors' reports or information extracted from such reports) available to another financial sector supervisory agency (for example, the Reserve Bank of Australia (RBA), the Australian Bureau of Statistics (ABS) and the Australian Securities and Investments Commission (ASIC)), or any other 'specified' agency (including foreign agencies), when APRA is satisfied such information will assist those agencies in performing their functions or exercising their powers.

Materiality

50 The auditor considers materiality when:

(a) determining the nature, timing and extent of audit and review procedures;

(b) evaluating the effect of uncorrected misstatements identified in life company annual returns;

(c) evaluating the effect of identified deficiencies in internal controls designed to ensure:

(i) compliance with Prudential Requirements; and

(ii) reliable data is provided in the life company annual returns; and

(iii) integrity of actuarial data;

(d) assessing the significance of identified instances of non-compliance with relevant Prudential Requirements.

51 Determining materiality involves the exercise of professional judgement. Judgements about materiality are made in light of relevant circumstances, and are affected by quantitative and qualitative factors as well as consideration of the potential impact of misstatements, control

deficiencies and/or instances of non compliance that are individually immaterial but in the aggregate may be of concern.

52 Since the concept of materiality is applied differently in the context of an audit or review of financial and other information, a review of internal controls, and for the purpose of reporting on a life company's compliance with Prudential Requirements, it is considered separately below in paragraphs 61 to 63.

53 Although there is a greater risk that misstatements, control deficiencies or instances of non-compliance may not be detected in a review than in an audit, the judgement as to what is material is made by reference to the subject matter on which the auditor is reporting and the needs of those relying on that information, as opposed to the level of assurance provided.

Audit of Life Company Annual Returns

54 The principles of assessing materiality for the purpose of expressing a positive assurance opinion on a life company's annual returns (an audit), will generally be similar to that applying to the audit of a financial report.

55 For the purposes of the audit of life company annual returns the auditor considers materiality, as appropriate, under Auditing Standard ASA 320 *Materiality in Planning and Performing an Audit* (ASA 320). In the absence of specific requirements issued by APRA, the Australian Accounting Standards Board's Accounting Standard AASB 1031 *Materiality* may provide a useful frame of reference to the auditor in determining materiality for the engagement.

56 Misstatements in the life company annual returns, either individually or in aggregate with other misstatements, are considered material if the auditor believes the intended users (refer paragraphs 48-49) may be influenced by the misstatement(s) of the information.

57 ASA 320 and AASB 1031 deal with materiality in the context of the financial statements taken as a whole. For the purpose of reporting on the reliability of information included in specified life company annual returns, the auditor considers and applies materiality at the level of individual annual returns, or data items, as appropriate.

58 In applying ASA 320 and ASAE 3000, as appropriate, to individual annual returns, the auditor has regard to the nature, purpose and use of the information included in each annual return. The collection and analysis of data in specified annual returns is a critical component of APRA's supervisory function. APRA collects data from life companies and friendly societies (and other APRA-regulated entities) in order to:

(a) verify compliance with prudential requirements (e.g. solvency and capital requirements);

(b) understand the operations of the company and the industry;

(c) identify emerging issues in both the company and the industry;

(d) pass on data to other government agencies; and

(e) provide information on the finance sector to research organisations and the general public.

59 The auditor's preliminary assessment of materiality is based largely on quantitative factors. A percentage is often applied to a chosen benchmark as a starting point in determining materiality. The base and percentage may vary depending upon the life company annual return in question.

60 The auditor also needs to have regard to alternative bases such as profit, revenue or assets when considering whether a misstatement within a life company's annual returns such as the *Statement of Financial Performance*, *Statement of Financial Position*, *Summary of Revenue and Expenses and Retained Profits*, is material.

Review of Internal Controls

61 In accordance with ASAE 3000, when reviewing internal controls, the auditor assesses materiality in the context of the life company's objectives relevant to the particular area of activity being examined, and whether the internal controls will reduce to an acceptably low level, the risks that may jeopardise the achievement of control objectives – in this case compliance with prudential requirements and integrity of actuarial data.

62 In assessing materiality, the auditor has regard to the measures the life company has adopted to ensure:

(a) reliable data is provided to APRA in all of the life company's annual returns prepared under the FSCODA;

(b) compliance with all applicable Prudential Requirements; and

(c) integrity of actuarial data.

63 ASAE 3100 sets out the requirements and provides guidance to the auditor in applying materiality in the context of a compliance engagement.

Reporting on Compliance with Prudential Requirements and Actuarial Data Integrity

64 LPS 310 requires the auditor to provide limited assurance that the life company has complied, in all material respects, with all applicable Prudential Requirements (see paragraph 27(b) of this Guidance Statement). This conclusion is to be based on the auditor's audit and reviews undertaken to provide assurance in relation to the life company's annual returns (see paragraph 27(a)) and internal controls (see paragraph 27(b)).

The auditor considers materiality when evaluating the significance of identified instances of non-compliance with relevant Prudential Requirements (refer to paragraphs 89-95).

For further guidance in relation to the controls relating to actuarial data integrity and appropriate audit evidence (refer to paragraphs 87 –88) and the evaluation of findings by the auditor (refer to paragraphs 96-99).

Personnel and Expertise Requirements, Including the Nature and Extent of Experts' Involvement

65 An auditor gives further consideration as to whether the auditor has, or will be able to obtain, adequate knowledge and the required skills to undertake the engagement.

66 LPS 310 prohibits an auditor from placing sole reliance on the work performed by APRA. As required by professional ethical requirements, auditors exercise their professional judgement and reach their own conclusions when undertaking any assurance engagement.

67 The nature and complexity of the life company determines whether the auditor may need to involve experts in the engagement. When conducting this type of engagement there are a number of considerations that need to be addressed by the auditor in relation to the use of, for example, an actuarial expert:

- whether there is an expert appointed by management or those charged with governance (internal expert) under the requirements outlined in LPS 320 *Actuarial and Related Matters* (LPS 320);
- whether there is a requirement for an auditor's expert (external expert) in which case ASA 620 *Using the Work of an Auditor's Expert*(ASA 620) and ASAE 3000[8] will need to be considered; and
- where the engagement team includes actuarial experts.

Under the Life Act, a life company must appoint an appointed actuary. One of the key requirements to be met by the appointed actuary is to complete a financial condition report on the company or in the case of a friendly society investigate the financial condition of the society. As outlined in LPS 320, this is the minimum requirement for a life company or a friendly society.

68 The complexity and nature of the life company may warrant the use of both a management's expert and an auditor's expert on the same engagement. Generally this is the case for the larger more complex life companies, however, in the case of a friendly society the management expert may be able to provide the auditor with sufficient appropriate audit/review evidence.

69 The life company auditor will also need to liaise with the life company appointed actuary with regard to the requirements of s80(2) of the Life Act in order for the auditor to obtain assurance that the income and outgoings apportionments have been made equitably and in accordance with generally accepted accounting principles (refer to paragraph 129).

8 Further guidance on this area is available in GS 005 *Using the Work of an Actuary*.

Work Performed by Another Auditor

70 Where the auditor plans to use the work of another independent auditor, the auditor:

- for the audit of financial information, complies with the requirements of Auditing Standard ASA 600 *Special Considerations-Audits of a group Financial Report (Including the Work of Component Auditors)* (ASA 600); and
- for other assurance, has regard to the principles of ASA 600 and ASAE 3000.

The Activities of the Internal Audit Function and the Effect on Audit and Review Procedures

71 LPS 510 requires all life companies (including an eligible foreign life insurance companies (EFLICs)), to have in place independent and adequately resourced internal audit function.[9]

72 LPS 510 requires that the objectives of the internal audit function include an evaluation of the adequacy and effectiveness of the financial and risk management framework of the life company.

73 In considering the activities of the internal audit function and evaluating the effect, if any, on audit and review procedures, the auditor:

- for the audit of financial information, complies with the requirements of Auditing Standard ASA 610 *Using the Work of Internal Auditors* (ASA 610); and
- for other assurance, has regard to the principles of ASA 610 and ASAE 3000.

Matters to Consider in Conducting the Annual Prudential Reporting Engagement

Audit of Annual returns to APRA

Audit Objective

74 The auditor is required to prepare a report that provides reasonable assurance on the life company's annual returns to APRA, as specified in attachment A to LPS 310. In particular, the report must specify whether in all material respects, the auditor concludes the:

(a) annual returns are reliable in accordance with relevant prudential requirements; and

(b) prudential requirements in relation to the accounting for statutory funds have been met.

The report to the life company is addressed to the board of the life company.

Review of Internal Controls over Compliance with Prudential Requirements and Reliability of Life company's Annual returns

Review Objective

75 Under LPS 310 the auditor is required to express a conclusion, based on a review, as to whether anything has come to the attention of the auditor to cause the auditor to believe that, in all material respects:

(a) The life company has not implemented internal controls that are designed to ensure the life company has:

(i) complied with all applicable Prudential Requirements; and

(ii) provided reliable data to APRA in the life company's annual returns prepared under the FSCODA.

(b) The controls in paragraph 75(a) have not operated effectively throughout the financial year.

(c) The life company's systems, procedures and internal controls relating to actuarial data integrity and financial reporting risks (the risks that incorrect source data will be used in completing the Annual returns under FSCODA) are not adequate and effective.

9 Under LPS 510, APRA may approve alternative arrangements where APRA is satisfied that it will achieve the same objectives.

GS

AUASB Standards

76 The auditor conducts the review of internal controls in accordance with ASAE 3000 and other relevant topic specific ASAEs, for example, ASAE 3100 *Compliance Engagements*.

Gathering Assurance Evidence

77 The evaluation of whether the life company has implemented internal controls that are designed to achieve the relevant control objectives as set out in paragraph 75 above, is performed in the context of the auditor's general understanding of the life company and its environment, the life company's risk management practices, and its internal control and compliance framework, as obtained for the purpose of planning the engagement. This review is based on whether the life company has implemented internal controls that have been suitably designed to reduce to an acceptably low level, the risks that threaten achievement of the relevant control objectives.

78 The auditor generally adopts a 'top down' approach in gathering evidence, by making enquiries of key personnel, observing the life company's operations, performing 'walk-through' tests of controls, and inspecting relevant documentation, as appropriate, in order to achieve the following:

- Obtaining an understanding of the life company's overall control environment and compliance framework.
- Identifying the internal compliance function(s) designed to ensure compliance with all applicable Prudential Requirements.
- Identifying policies, procedures and controls designed to ensure compliance with all applicable Prudential Requirements, by reviewing documents such as the life company's Risk Management Framework, Risk Management Strategy and similar risk management policy documents issued by the life company in accordance with applicable prudential standards.
- Identifying the processes used by the Board of the life company to support its Risk Management Declaration to APRA as outlined in LPS 220 *Risk Management* (LPS 220).
- Identifying key Board and operational matters by reviewing the minutes of the life company's Board, as well as minutes of any sub committees responsible, for example, for oversight of compliance and audit, held during the year and enquiring about matters discussed and outcomes from Board decisions.
- Identifying the internal compliance functions designed to oversee the provision of data to APRA in life company annual returns.
- Identifying significant processes for the preparation of life company annual returns.
- Identifying the key controls over these significant processes that are designed to ensure that reliable data is provided to APRA in life company annual returns.

The above is not an exhaustive list, nor is it intended to direct the auditor as to the conclusion over the life company's internal controls.

79 Life companies have different systems and procedures in place to monitor compliance with specific Prudential Standards. Projections and estimates are likely to be part of the monitoring process, as the preparation of a full financial report is unlikely to be practical on a day-by-day or week-by-week basis. Varying degrees of precision may exist therefore in applying the monitoring process. Notwithstanding these differences, such systems seek to ensure that life companies comply with all Prudential Standards on a continuous basis.

80 The way in which internal control is designed and implemented varies with a life company's size and complexity. Smaller life companies may use less formal means and simpler processes to achieve their control objectives.

81 The auditor gathers evidence in response to assessed risks with a focus on identifying key controls within the control systems design. The auditor exercises professional judgement in determining the specific nature, timing and extent of review procedures to achieve the review objective.

82 Following the evaluation of whether the life company has internal controls designed to achieve the relevant control objectives, the auditor performs review procedures to obtain evidence about whether these controls have operated as designed throughout the financial year. The auditor may consider how the controls were applied, the consistency with which they were applied, by whom they were applied and the period of time over which the controls were applied.

83 The review of operating effectiveness may include procedures such as:

- Enquiry of appropriate life company personnel (and obtaining written representations).
- Observation of the control process.
- Ascertaining whether the person(s) performing the control(s) possesses the necessary authority and competence to perform the control(s) effectively.
- Review of relevant documentation.
- 'Walk-through' tests; and
- Limited re-performance of the controls.

84 Interpretation of the word 'reliable' in the context of the review of controls over life company annual returns has practical limitations in some circumstances. For many life companies, it is only at the financial year-end (or for life companies that are disclosing entities, also at the half year-end) that all the necessary accounting adjustments, such as accruals, prepayments, provisioning and valuations, are prepared and subjected to audit or review. APRA accepts this position that annual returns prepared throughout the year are based on the life company's normal accounting process.

85 The auditor enquires whether there were any changes in internal control, or other matters, subsequent to the financial year-end date and up to the date of the auditor's assurance report, that may have an impact on the auditor's conclusion about the effectiveness of internal controls, and obtains written representations from management relating to such matters.

86 Materiality is to be considered as outlined in paragraphs 50-63 of this Guidance Statement.

Adequacy and Effectiveness of Controls Relating to Actuarial Data Integrity and Financial Reporting Risks

87 The auditor under LPS 310 is required to express a conclusion as to whether anything has come to the auditor's attention that causes the auditor to believe that the company's systems, procedures and controls relating to actuarial data integrity and financial reporting risks[10] are not adequate and effective to address the risk of material error in the APRA returns. Refer *Part B* of the Special Purpose Report as per Appendix 1.

88 The auditor reviews whether systems, procedures and controls in place are adequate and operating effectively to ensure that source data used for actuarial valuations and completion of returns to APRA in accordance with the requirements of the *Collection of Data Act*, is accurate and complete, consistent with the accounting records of the life company, and a true representation of the transactions for the year and the financial position of the life company. The auditor performs review procedures covering the period to obtain evidence regarding the continuity of systems, procedures and controls in place for the period under review.

Evaluation of Misstatements

Audit of Life Company Annual Returns

89 The auditor evaluates, individually and in the aggregate, whether uncorrected misstatements that have come to the auditor's attention, are material to the reported information. Materiality is to be applied in the context of paragraphs 50-63 of this Guidance Statement.

90 In evaluating whether or not the specified life company annual returns, or data in annual returns, are, in all material respects, reliable and in accordance with the relevant APRA Prudential and Reporting Standards, the auditor exercises professional judgement, having regard to both the users and intended uses of the information in the annual returns.

10 That is, the risks that incorrect source data will be used in completing returns to APRA in accordance with the requirements of the *Collection of Data Act*.

GS

91 The magnitude of a misstatement alone is only one factor used to assess the misstatement. The auditor evaluates each identified misstatement in the context of information relevant to users of the annual return, by considering qualitative factors and the circumstances in which each misstatement has been made. For example, in evaluating identified misstatements, the auditor has regard to factors such as the level of the life company's buffer above the particular minimum prudential capital requirements (determined under periodic quantitative calculations) and the sensitivity of these buffers to fluctuations in the life company's financial performance and position.

92 The auditor may designate an amount below which misstatements need not be aggregated, because the auditor expects that the aggregation of such amounts clearly would not have a material effect on the reported information. In doing so, the auditor needs to consider the fact that the materiality of misstatements involves qualitative as well as quantitative considerations and those misstatements of a relatively small amount could nevertheless have a material effect on the reported information.

93 A key concern with any misstatement within a life company's annual returns is its potential impact on the life company's 'solvency requirement', 'capital adequacy requirement' and 'management capital requirement' that are determined in accordance with APRA's prudential standards[11]. This is taken into consideration by the auditor when evaluating whether a misstatement in the life company's annual returns, has a material impact on *Solvency, Capital Adequacy and Management Capital.*

94 The assurance practitioners should be aware of LPS 3.04 *Capital Adequacy Standard*, where materiality in relation to solvency, capital adequacy and management capital must be considered/evaluated and applied at the statutory fund level. The materiality of the statutory fund relative to the size of the company overall may be taken into account for the purposes of assessing the impact on Capital Adequacy.

95 In extremely rare circumstances, the auditor may conclude that information reported in life company annual return(s) in accordance with the relevant APRA Prudential and Reporting Standards is misleading. The auditor discusses the matter with management and, depending how it is resolved, determines whether, and how, to communicate the matter in the auditor's assurance report.

Review of Internal Controls

96 The auditor evaluates, individually and in aggregate, whether internal control deficiencies that have come to the auditor's attention are material. Materiality is to be applied in the context of paragraphs 63-65.

97 The auditor exercises professional judgement in evaluating the materiality of internal control deficiencies, having regard to the intended users of the auditor's assurance report.

98 In evaluating the severity of identified internal control deficiencies, the auditor having regard to materiality, considers:

(a) the likelihood that the relevant internal controls may fail to prevent or detect:

(i) non-compliance with a Prudential Requirement;

(ii) a misstatement in the data being provided to APRA in life company annual returns;

(iii) misstatements in actuarial data used in financial reporting;

(b) the significance of the potential resulting non-compliance with a Prudential Requirement in the context of the life company's overall compliance with applicable Prudential Requirements;

(c) the magnitude of the potential misstatement that could result from the internal control deficiency in the information reported in the life company annual returns; and

(d) the magnitude of the potential misstatement that could result from a deficiency in internal control over the adequacy and effectiveness of actuarial data integrity and financial reporting risks.

99 The evaluation of the severity of a deficiency in internal control does not depend on whether a misstatement or non-compliance with a Prudential Requirement has actually occurred, but

11 Refer to LPS 100 *Solvency*, LPS 110 *Capital Adequacy* and LPS 120 *Management Capital*.

rather the likelihood that the life company's controls may fail to prevent or detect a material misstatement or material non-compliance with a Prudential Requirement.

Reporting on Compliance with Prudential Requirements

100 The auditor is required to express a conclusion, based on the audit or review(s) conducted under paragraphs 76-99 above, as to whether anything has come to the attention of the auditor to cause the auditor to believe that, during the financial year, the life company has not complied, in all material respects, with all applicable Prudential Requirements in the Life Act and the FSCODA, including compliance with APRA Prudential and Reporting Standards.

101 Under sections 88 and 88A of the Life Act, auditors are required to report to APRA when the auditor believes the life company or its directors may have contravened the Life Act or to assist APRA to perform its functions under the Life Act (refer to paragraphs 28, 128-132 of this Guidance Statement for further detail).

102 The auditor considers materiality when assessing the significance of identified instances of non-compliance with relevant Prudential Requirements.

103 In order to conclude on a life company's compliance with all applicable Prudential Requirements, the auditor considers the existence of relevant matters that may indicate instances of non-compliance, throughout the reporting period and up to the date of signing the auditor's assurance report.

104 The auditor complies with the requirements of Auditing Standard ASA 560 *Subsequent Events* (ASA 560), as appropriate, which may include the following audit procedures:

- Reading minutes of the life company's Board, as well as minutes of any sub committees responsible, for example, for oversight of compliance and audit, held after balance date and enquiring about matters discussed at these meetings for which minutes are not yet available.
- Examining the life company's breach registers up to the date of the auditor's assurance report.
- Enquiring of the life company's management as to whether any subsequent events have occurred which might represent non-compliance with applicable Prudential Requirements.

Written Representations

105 Prior to issuing the Auditor's Annual Prudential Assurance Report, the auditor obtains written representations, as are considered appropriate to matters specific to the life company, from the party responsible[12] for the life company.

106 These written representations are generally in the form of a representation letter. In obtaining and using these written representations, the auditor complies with the requirements of, as appropriate, Auditing Standard ASA 580 *Written Representations* (ASA 580) and ASAE 3000.

Inherent Limitations of the Engagement

107 As the systems, procedures and controls to ensure compliance with Prudential Requirements are part of the life company's operations, it is possible that either the inherent limitations of the internal control structure, or weaknesses in it, may impact on the effective operation of the life company's specific control procedures. Furthermore, fraud, error or non-compliance with laws and regulations may occur and not be detected.

108 Due to the nature of audit and review procedures and other inherent limitations of an audit and review, there is a possibility that a properly planned and executed audit or review may not detect all errors or omissions in life company annual returns, deficiencies in controls, or instances of non-compliance with Prudential Requirements.

109 An audit provides reasonable assurance and cannot constitute a guarantee that the information included in life company annual returns specified in Attachment A to LPS 310,

12 Management and, where appropriate, those charged with governance of the life company.

GS

sourced from accounting records, is reliable, or that all instances of non-compliance with relevant APRA Prudential and Reporting Standards have been detected.

110 While reviews involve the application of audit related skills and techniques, usually they do not involve many of the procedures performed during an audit. In an audit, as the auditor's objective is to provide a high, but not absolute, level of assurance on the reliability of information included in life company annual returns, the auditor uses more extensive audit procedures than in a review. Review procedures, therefore, do not provide all the evidence required in an audit and, consequently, the level of assurance provided is less than that given in an audit.

111 The auditor performs procedures appropriate to provide limited assurance in relation to internal controls existing at the review date, and whether those controls have operated as documented throughout the financial year.

Communication

112 It is the responsibility of the auditor to make the life company aware, as soon as practicable, of any identified material misstatements in life company annual returns, material deficiencies in internal controls and instances of material non-compliance arising from the prudential reporting engagement.

113 Such communications are made as soon as practicable, either orally or in writing. The auditor's decision whether to communicate orally or in writing ordinarily is affected by factors such as the nature, sensitivity and significance of the matter to be communicated and the timing of the communications. If the information is communicated orally, the auditor needs to document the communication.

114 When, in the auditor's judgement, those charged with governance do not respond appropriately within a reasonable period of time, the auditor considers whether to modify the auditor's annual prudential assurance report.

115 It is important that the auditor understands the additional statutory responsibilities to report certain matters to APRA under the Life Act. Failure to notify APRA as required represents a criminal offence, which attracts criminal penalties. Refer also to paragraphs 128-132 below.

116 Material findings (misstatements, control deficiencies and non-compliance) are reported to APRA and the life company's Board (or Board Audit Committee) as modifications to the auditor's assurance report (Refer paragraph 121).

117 Under Auditing Standard ASA 260 *Communication with Those Charged With Governance* (ASA 260), ASA 265 *Communicating Deficiencies in Internal Control to Those Charged with Governance and Management* (ASA 265) and ASAE 3000, the auditor communicates relevant matters of governance interest arising from the engagement to those charged with governance on a timely basis. Examples of such matters may include:

- The general approach and overall scope of the engagement, or any additional requirements.
- Fraud or information that indicates that fraud may exist.
- Significant deficiencies in internal controls identified during the engagement. A significant deficiency in internal control means a deficiency or combination of deficiencies in internal control that, in the auditor's professional judgement is of sufficient importance to merit the attention of those charged with governance.
- Disagreements with management about matters that, individually or in aggregate, could be significant to the engagement.
- Expected modifications to the auditor's prudential assurance report.

118 The auditor informs those charged with governance of the life company of those uncorrected misstatements, other than clearly trivial amounts, aggregated by the auditor during and pertaining to the engagement that were considered to be immaterial, both individually and in the aggregate, to the assurance engagement.

119 Under LPS 310, if requested by APRA, the auditor submits directly to APRA all assessments and other material associated with the auditor's report, such as management letters issued by the auditor to the life company which contain material findings relating to the auditor's prudential assurance report.

The Auditor's Annual Prudential Assurance Report

120 The auditor evaluates the conclusions drawn from the evidence obtained in conducting the assurance engagement as the basis for the auditor's opinion/conclusions as required under LPS 310.

121 If the auditor:

(a) concludes that a material misstatement, internal control deficiency and/or non-compliance exists; or

(b) is unable to obtain sufficient appropriate assurance evidence to conclude whether a material misstatement, internal control deficiency and/or non-compliance may exist,

the auditor modifies their opinion/conclusion, and includes a clear description of the reasons in their assurance report, in accordance with the requirements of, as appropriate, ASA 705 *Modifications to the Opinion in the Independent Auditor's Report* (ASA 705) or ASA 706 *Emphasis of Matter Paragraphs and Other Matter Paragraphs in the Independent Auditor's Report* (ASA 706) and applicable ASAEs. (Refer Appendix 2 of this Guidance Statement).

122 As required under LPS 310, the auditor of a life company reports simultaneously to APRA and the life company's Board (or Board Audit Committee)[13], within four months of the end of the financial year of the life company.

123 To avoid the possibility of the assurance report being used for purposes for which it was not intended, the auditor indicates in the auditor's report the purpose for which the report is prepared and any restrictions on its distribution and use in an emphasis of matter paragraph as required by ASA 800 *Special Considerations-Audits of Financial Reports Prepared in Accordance with Special Purpose Frameworks* (ASA 800) (refer paragraphs 30-36).

Format of Auditor's Annual Prudential Assurance Report

124 AUASB Standards do not prescribe a standardised format for reporting on all assurance engagements. Instead, both Auditing Standard ASA 800 and ASAE 3000 identify the basic elements required to be included in the assurance report. The short form auditor's report ordinarily includes only the basic elements.

125 Assurance reports are tailored to the specific assurance engagement circumstances. Although not specifically required under LPS 310, the auditor may consider it appropriate to include other information and explanations that do not directly affect the auditor's opinion or conclusions, but provide additional useful information to the users (that is, a 'long form' style of reporting). The inclusion of this information depends on its significance to the needs of the intended users. The following are examples of additional information that may be considered for inclusion:

- Disclosure of materiality considerations (materiality levels) applied.
- Significant findings or exceptions relating to particular aspects of the assurance engagement.
- Recommendations.

126 The auditor needs to ensure that this additional information is clearly separated from the auditor's opinion and conclusions, and worded in a manner to ensure that it does not affect the opinion and conclusions. This can be achieved, for example, by including any additional information in:

(a) a separate appendix to the auditor's short form assurance report; or

(b) a separate section of the auditor's short form assurance report, following the 'opinion and conclusions'[14] in an other matter paragraph as required by ASA 706 *Emphasis of Matter Paragraphs and Other Matter Paragraphs in the Independent Auditor's Report* (ASA 706).

This will enable users to clearly distinguish this additional information from the auditor's responsibility to report on the matters identified in LPS 310.

GS

13 Or for a foreign Life company, a senior officer outside Australia to whom authority has been delegated in accordance with LPS 510, for overseeing the Australian operations.

14 See examples of assurance practitioner reports included in Appendix 1 to ASAE 3100.

127 Refer to Appendix 1 of this Guidance Statement for an illustrative example of the auditor's annual prudential assurance report (short form report), prepared pursuant to APRA's LPS 310 annual reporting requirements.

Additional Reporting Requirements under the Life Insurance Act

128 It is important that management, those charged with governance and the auditor of a life company[15] understand the additional responsibilities to report to APRA under sections 80, 88 and 88A of the Life Act (refer paragraph 28).

129 The Life Act specifies under section 80(3) that the apportionment of income and outgoings for a life company carrying on other business as well as its Life Insurance business is not effective unless a report given by the auditor of the life company for the purposes of FSCODA states that the apportionment has been made equitably and in accordance with generally accepted accounting principles. Section 80(2) of the Life Act states that before an apportionment is made, those charged with governance of the company concerned must obtain the appointed actuary's written advice whether the basis of the proposed apportionment is appropriate.

This report is provided by the auditor as part of the annual return(s) audit opinion. An example is given in Appendix 1 Part A.

130 Under section 88 of the Life Act the auditor has certain obligations to report to the company or those charged with governance any matters that come to the attention of the auditor that the auditor thinks requires action to be taken by the company or its directors. If the auditor of a Life company thinks that there are reasonable grounds for believing that the company or those charged with governance have contravened the Life Act or any other law and it may significantly affect the interests of the policy holders the auditor must immediately inform APRA in writing. Persons involved in the provision of information should note that it is a serious offence under sub section 137.1 and 137.2 of the *Criminal Code 1995* to provide, whether directly or indirectly, false or misleading documents or information to a Commonwealth entity such as APRA.

131 Section 89 of the Life Act applies the concept of qualified privilege to auditors of a life company and is in addition to any privilege conferred on a person by the *Corporations Act 2001*.

Auditor may provide information to APRA

132 Section 88A of the Life Act states:

(a) a person who is or was the auditor of a life company may give information, or produce books, accounts or documents, about the life company to APRA if the person considers that doing so will assist APRA in performing its functions under this Act or under the FSCODA.

(b) a person who, in good faith and without negligence, gives information to APRA in accordance with this section is not subject to any action, claim or demand by, or any liability to, any other person in respect of the information.

Special Purpose Engagements

APRA Prudential Reporting Requirements (LPS 310)

133 Under LPS 310, in addition to the annual prudential reporting requirements, APRA may require a life company, by notice in writing, to arrange for its auditor (who may be the existing auditor or another auditor agreed to by APRA and satisfies the criteria in LPS 310), to provide a report on a particular aspect of the life company's operations, risk management or financial affairs. Although a special purpose engagement report will normally only be requested following consultation with a life company, APRA may commission such a report without prior consultation with a life company.

15 See definitions at paragraph 21(e).

134 Unless otherwise determined by APRA, an auditor appointed to undertake a special purpose engagement will be required to provide limited assurance [review] on the matters required to be reported on.

135 Under LPS 310, the auditor's special purpose engagement assurance report is to be submitted simultaneously to APRA and the life company's Board (or Board Audit Committee)[16], within three months of the date of the notice commissioning the report, unless otherwise determined by APRA, and advised to the life company by notice in writing.

136 The APRA requirement for an auditor to undertake a special purpose engagement in a selected area of the life company's operations, risk management or financial affairs constitutes a separate reporting engagement. The details of the engagement will normally be the subject of a specific request from APRA to the life company and a separate engagement letter from the life company to the auditor based on that request.

Terms of the Engagement

137 Following the determination by APRA of the specific area to be examined, the auditor, APRA and the life company agree on the terms of the engagement in accordance with the requirements of applicable AUASB Standards. These arrangements are legally binding and include the required terms of engagement specified in LPS 310.

138 The auditor accepts the engagement only when the auditor is satisfied that the auditor and the engagement team, if applicable, have met the relevant ethical requirements relating to the assurance engagement. The concept of independence is important to the auditor's compliance with the fundamental ethical principles of integrity and objectivity and the auditor must be able to meet the independence requirements stipulated under both LPS 510 and ASA 102.

139 An engagement letter (or other suitable form) helps to avoid misunderstandings with respect to the engagement and confirms both the life company's and the auditor's understanding of the terms of the engagement, and the auditor's acceptance of the appointment. Both parties sign the engagement letter to acknowledge that it is a legally binding contract.

140 To ensure that there is a clear understanding regarding the terms of the engagement, the following are examples of matters to be agreed:

- APRA is to identify the scope of the life company's operations, risk management or financial affairs to be the subject of the engagement.
- The auditor, APRA and the life company are to agree on the objectives of the engagement, key features and criteria of the area(s) to be examined, and the period to be covered by the engagement.
- APRA is to identify clearly the level of assurance required, that is, limited or reasonable assurance.
- The format of reports required (for example, long and/or short form reports) and other communication of results of the engagement.
- Responsibility of those charged with governance for the subject matter of the engagement.
- Understanding of the inherent limitations of an assurance engagement.

Format of Reporting Requirements

141 The format of the special purpose assurance report may vary depending on the type of engagement: that is, an audit (reasonable assurance) or a review (limited assurance), as well as the subject matter and the findings. The auditor has regard to the requirements, guidance and illustrative examples of reports provided in relevant AUASB Standards - ASAs, ASREs and ASAEs, as applicable, when preparing the special purpose assurance report.

142 AUASB Standards do not require a standardised format for special purpose reporting under LPS 310. Instead, these Standards identify the basic elements to be included in the auditor's report. Ordinarily, the auditor adopts a long form style of reporting and the report may

16 Or, for a foreign life company, a senior officer outside Australia to whom authority has been delegated in accordance with LPS 510 for overseeing the Australian operations.

include a description of the terms of the engagement, materiality considerations applied, the assurance approach and an other matter paragraph which may include - findings relating to particular aspects of the engagement and, in some cases, recommendations.

143 The auditor's assurance report is to be restricted to the parties that have agreed to the terms of the special purpose engagement, namely the life company and APRA, as well as other parties with whom APRA is lawfully entitled to share the information, by means of an emphasis of matter paragraph required by ASA 706 (refer example at Appendix 1).

Conformity with International Pronouncements

144 As this Guidance Statement relates to Australian legislative requirements, there is no equivalent International Standard on Auditing or International Auditing Practice Statement to this Guidance Statement.

Appendix 1

(Ref: Para.126)

Example Special Purpose Auditor's Report

For an Annual Prudential Reporting Engagement Undertaken Pursuant to APRA Prudential Standard LPS 310 *Audit and Related Matters*

The following example auditor's report is to be used as a guide only and will need to be adapted according to individual engagement requirements and circumstances of the life company. The auditor's opinion and conclusions given in the examples are based on the requirements set by APRA in LPS 310.

[Note: Generally the reports illustrated in *Section A* and *Section B* below are formulated as separate special purpose reports. This however, does not preclude the auditor from issuing one special purpose report that covers both the reasonable and limited assurance opinions if it were appropriate under the engagement requirements and circumstances]

Section A [Reasonable Assurance on APRA Annual Returns]

To [Title of Those Charged with Governance[17]] of [name of life company]

We have audited the attached Annual APRA Return, being a special purpose financial report of [name of Life company] for the year ended [date]. The Annual APRA Return comprises forms:

LRF 100.0 - ....

LRF 120.0 - ....

[include a full list of Annual APRA Forms as appropriate]

Responsibilities of Management and [Title of Those Charged with Governance]

Management and [Title of Those charged with Governance] of [name of life company] are responsible for the preparation and fair presentation of the Annual APRA return and the information it contains, in accordance with the requirements of the *Life Insurance Act 1995*, the *Financial Sector (Collection of Data) Act 2001* and Australian Prudential Regulation Authority (APRA) Reporting Standards, insofar as they do not conflict with the above Australian Accounting Standards; and for such internal control as management determines is necessary to enable the preparation and fair presentation of the Annual APRA return that is free from material misstatement, whether due to fraud or error.

17 Or, for a foreign life company, a senior officer outside Australia to whom authority has been delegated, in accordance with Prudential Standard LPS 510 *Governance* (LPS 510), for overseeing the Australian operations.

Auditor's Responsibility

Our responsibility is to express an opinion on the Annual APRA Return based on our audit. We conducted our audit in accordance with Australian Auditing Standards. Those Auditing Standards require that we comply with relevant ethical requirements and plan and perform the audit to obtain reasonable assurance whether, in all material respects, the Annual APRA Return:

(a) has been prepared in accordance with the *Life Insurance Act 1995*, the *Financial Sector (Collection of Data) Act 2001* and APRA Reporting Standards LRS 100.0 to LRS 340.0;

(b) is reliable;

(c) meets prudential requirements in relation to the accounting for statutory funds;

(d) presents fairly, the financial position of the company at year end in accordance with APRA Reporting Standards LRS 100.0 to LRS 340.0; and

(e) the apportionments made under Division 2 of Part 6 of the *Life Insurance Act 1995* have been made in accordance with generally acceptable accounting principles.

Our audit did not involve an analysis of the prudence of business decisions made by those charged with governance. Our audit involves performing procedures to obtain audit evidence about the amounts and disclosures in the Annual APRA Return. The procedures selected depend on our judgement, including assessment of the risks of material misstatement of the Annual APRA Return, whether due to fraud or error. In making those risk assessments, we consider internal control relevant to the company's preparation and fair presentation of the Annual APRA Return in order to design audit procedures that are appropriate in the circumstances, but not for the purpose of expressing an opinion on the effectiveness of the company's internal control. An audit also includes evaluating the appropriateness of accounting policies used and the reasonableness of accounting estimates made by those charged with governance (management), as well as evaluating the overall presentation of the financial report.

We believe that the audit evidence we have obtained is sufficient and appropriate to provide a basis for our audit opinion.

Independence

In conducting our audit we have met the independence requirements of the Australian professional accounting bodies and those specified by APRA in Prudential Standard LPS 510 *Governance*.

[Basis for Qualified / Adverse / Disclaimer of Opinion]

[Provide details or refer to attachment. Appendix 2 of this Guidance Statement provides an example format for reporting these findings.]

Opinion[18]

In our opinion, in all material respects:

(a) the Annual APRA return of [name of entity], in respect of the year ended [date], comprising forms LRF 100.0 to LRF 340.0:

  (i) has been prepared in accordance with the *Life Insurance Act 1995*, the *Financial Sector (Collection of Data) Act 2001* and APRA Reporting Standards LRS 100.0 to LRS 340.0;

  (ii) is reliable;

  (iii) meets prudential requirements in relation to the accounting for statutory funds; and

  (iv) presents fairly, the financial position of the company at [year end] in accordance with APRA Reporting Standards LRS 100.0 to LRS 340.0.

(b) the apportionments made under Division 2 of Part 6 of the *Life Insurance Act 1995* have been made in accordance with generally acceptable accounting principles.

Basis of Restriction on Distribution

The Annual APRA Return has been prepared for the purpose of fulfilling the reporting requirements of the company under the *Life Insurance Act 1995*, Section 13 of the *Financial*

18 If the auditor's opinion includes a qualification / adverse or disclaimer opinion the words in the opinion paragraph will need to change accordingly.

GS

Sector (Collection of Data) Act 2001 and the APRA Reporting Standards. We disclaim any assumption of responsibility for any reliance on this report or on the Annual APRA Return to which it relates to any party other than the company and APRA, or for any purpose other than that for which it was prepared.

[Auditor's signature]

[Date of the Auditor's report]

[Auditor's address]

Section B [Limited Assurance on Controls to Ensure Compliance with APRA Prudential Requirements]

To [Title of Those Charged with Governance] of [name of life company]

We have performed a review pursuant to the reporting requirements specified in Australian Prudential Regulation Authority (APRA) Prudential Standard LPS 310 *Audit and Related Matters* (LPS 310), described in the *Scope* section, paragraphs *Part A* to *Part D*, of this report.

Responsibilities of Management and [Title of Those Charged with Governance]

Management and [Title of Those Charged with Governance] of, [name of life company] are responsible for ensuring that there are adequate systems, procedures and internal controls to ensure compliance with all applicable prudential standards, the *Life Insurance Act 1995*, the Regulations, the *Financial Sector (Collection of Data) Act 2001*, reporting standards, authorisation conditions, directions and any other requirements imposed by APRA in writing.

Auditor's Responsibility

Our responsibility is to perform a review as required by LPS 310, described in *Scope* paragraphs *Part A* to *Part D* of this report, and to express a conclusion based on our review.

We conducted our review in accordance with Standard on Assurance Engagements ASAE 3000 *Assurance Engagements Other than Audits or Reviews of Historical Financial Information*, in order to state whether, on the basis of the procedures described, anything has come to our attention that causes us to believe that [name of life company] has not complied, in all material respects, with its responsibilities and reporting requirements. ASAE 3000 requires us to comply with fundamental ethical requirements.

Our audit of the financial report required under the *Corporations Act 2001* and our audit of the yearly statutory accounts (Annual APRA Return) required under the *Life Insurance Act 1995*, the *Financial Sector (Collection of Data) Act 2001* and Australian Prudential Regulation Authority (APRA) Reporting Standards is directed towards obtaining sufficient evidence to form an opinion under the appropriate legislation. Our audit was not designed to enable us to conclude on other matters required by the APRA Reporting Standards. We have therefore performed review procedures in order to meet our responsibilities in relation to controls designed to ensure compliance with APRA Prudential Requirements.

Our review procedures include test checking to the general ledger or appropriate sub ledger or sub system but do not extend to auditing the financial or statistical information presented in the Quarterly APRA Returns nor forms LRF 400.0 to 430.0 in the Annual APRA Return. Our review consists primarily of making enquiries of the life company's personnel and applying analytical and other review procedures. A review is substantially less in scope than an audit conducted in accordance with Australian Auditing Standards and consequently does not enable us to obtain assurance that we would become aware of all significant matters that might be identified in an audit. Accordingly, we do not express an audit opinion.

Inherent limitations

There are inherent limitations in any internal control structure, and fraud, error or non-compliance with laws and regulations may occur and not be detected. As the systems, procedures and controls to ensure compliance with APRA Prudential Requirements are part of the operations of [name of life company], it is possible that either the inherent limitations of the general internal control structure, or weaknesses in it, can impact on the effective operation of the specific control procedures of [name of life company].

Furthermore, projections of any evaluation of internal control to future periods are subject to the risk that control procedures may become inadequate because of changes in conditions, or that the degree of compliance may deteriorate. Consequently, there are inherent limitations on the level of assurance that can be provided.

Accounting records and data relied on for prudential reporting and compliance are not continuously audited and do not necessarily reflect accounting adjustments necessary for end of reporting period financial report preparations, or events occurring after the end of the reporting period.

The conclusions in this report expressed below are to be read in the context of the foregoing comments.

Scope

Part A – Existence of Controls Addressing Compliance with Prudential Requirements

We performed review procedures that we considered necessary in relation to [name of life company] systems, procedures and controls that address compliance with all applicable Prudential Requirements. Prudential Requirements are imposed by the:

(a) *Life Insurance Act 1995*;

(b) Insurance Regulations 2002;

(c) APRA Prudential Standards and Rules;

(d) *Financial Sector (Collection of Data) Act 2001*;

(e) APRA Reporting Standards;

(f) APRA conditions on the company's registration;

(g) Directions issued by APRA pursuant to the *Life Insurance Act 1995*; and

(h) Other requirements imposed by APRA in writing (if applicable).

[*Note :- If the company does not comply with any prudential standards, a list of all the prudential standards complied with by the company should be listed under section (e) above*]

We have preformed these procedures to enable us to state, on the basis of our review as described, whether anything has come to our attention that causes us to believe that, at the date of our review, there did not exist systems, procedures and internal controls that are designed to ensure that the life company has complied, in all material respects, with all applicable Prudential Requirements, specified above, and that these systems, procedures and internal controls have operated effectively throughout the financial year of the company.

Part B – Controls in Place to Ensure Reliable Statistical and Financial Data

We have performed review procedures that we considered necessary in relation to [name of life company] systems, procedures and internal controls in place for the [insert period], to ensure that reliable statistical and financial data are provided to APRA in the APRA Returns, required by APRA Reporting Standards made under the *Financial Sector (Collection of Data) Act 2001*:

LRF 100.0 *Solvency;*

LRF 110.0 *Capital Adequacy;* and

LRF 340.2 *Retained Profits*

We have performed a review of systems, procedures and controls in order to state whether, on the basis of the review procedures described, anything has come to our attention that causes us to believe that [name of life company] does not have in place systems, procedures and controls to ensure that, in all material respects, reliable statistical and financial data are provided to APRA in the APRA Returns.

Our review procedures included test checking to the general ledger or appropriate sub ledger or sub system but did not extend to auditing the financial or statistical information presented in all APRA Returns.

Part C – Adequacy and Effectiveness of Controls Relating to Actuarial Data Integrity and Financial Reporting Risks.

We have performed review procedures that we considered necessary in relation to [name of life company] systems, procedures and controls relating to actuarial data integrity and financial reporting risks (risks that incorrect source data will be used in completing the reporting forms under the *Financial Sector (Collection of Data) Act 2001,* that address the risk of material error in the APRA returns for the [insert period].

We have performed these procedures to enable us to state, on the basis of our review as described, whether anything has come to our attention that causes us to believe that for the [insert period] [name of life company]did not have systems, procedures and internal controls relating to actuarial data integrity and financial reporting risks [risks that incorrect source data will be used in completing the reporting forms under FSCODA], that are in all material respects, adequate and operating effectively to address the risk of material error in the APRA returns.

Part D – Issues Identified in the Conduct of our Review Procedures

We have evaluated the results of our procedures conducted during:

(a) this review;

(b) our audit of the relevant APRA Returns prepared in accordance with the *Life Insurance Act 1995*; and

(c) our audit [and review] performed under the *Corporations Act 2001*,

in order to report to [Title of Those Charged with Governance] of [name of life company] and APRA, instances in which the company has not complied with all applicable Prudential Requirements (refer *Part A* of this report).

We have not performed any review procedures that were designed specifically to identify such circumstances or instances of non compliance and therefore provide no assurance that all such circumstances or instances of non compliance have been identified and reported.

Independence

In conducting our review we have met the independence requirements of the Australian professional accounting bodies and those specified by APRA in Prudential Standard LPS 510 *Governance*.

[Basis for Qualified / Adverse / Disclaimer of Opinion]

Part A – Existence of Controls Addressing Compliance with Prudential Requirements

[Provide details where a qualification is included]

Part B – Controls in place to ensure reliable Statistical and Financial Data.

[Provide details where a qualification is included]

Part C – Adequacy and Effectiveness of Controls Relating to Actuarial Data Integrity and Financial Reporting Risks.

[Provide details where a qualification is included]

Part D – Issues Identified in the Conduct of our Review Procedures

[Provide details where a qualification is included]

[Qualified] Conclusion[19]

Part A – Existence of Controls Addressing Compliance with Prudential Requirements

Based on our review, which is not an audit, [except for the matters referred to in the basis for qualified opinion paragraph above], nothing has come to our attention that causes us to believe

19 If the auditor's opinion includes an adverse or disclaimer opinion the words in the opinion paragraph(s) will need to change accordingly.

that, at the date of our review [insert date], [name of life company] did not have in place systems, procedures and controls to address compliance, in all material respects, with the specified Prudential Requirements, and that these systems, procedures and controls did not operate effectively throughout the financial year [date].

Part B – Controls in place to ensure reliable Statistical and Financial Data

Based on our review, which is not an audit, [except for the matters referred to in the basis for qualified opinion paragraph above], nothing has come to our attention that causes us to believe that, for the [insert period], [name of life company] did not have in place systems, procedures and controls to ensure that, in all material respects, reliable statistical and financial data were provided to APRA in the APRA Returns required by APRA Reporting Standards made under the FSCODA, [insert period].

Part C – Adequacy and Effectiveness of Controls Relating to Actuarial Data Integrity and Financial Reporting Risks

Based on our review, which is not an audit, [except for the matters referred to in the basis for qualified opinion paragraph above,], nothing has come to our attention that causes us to believe that, for the [insert period], [life company] did not have systems, procedures and controls relating to actuarial data integrity and financial reporting risks (the risks that incorrect source data will be used in completing the returns to APRA in accordance with the requirements of FSCODA that are adequate and effective to address the risk of material error in the APRA returns.

Part D – Issues Identified in the Conduct of our Review Procedures

Based on our review, which is not an audit, [except for the matters referred to in the basis for qualified opinion paragraph above], nothing has come to our attention that causes us to believe that during the [insert period] the [name of life company] did not comply with, in all material respects:

(a) all applicable Prudential Requirements as listed in the scope section Part A

(b) has provided reliable data to APRA in the reporting forms prepared under FSCODA (including those provided quarterly); and

(c) the internal controls over (a) and (b) have operated effectively throughout the financial period; and

(d) systems, procedures and internal controls relating to actuarial data integrity and financial reporting risks (the risks that incorrect source data will be used in completing the reporting forms under FSCODA) are adequate and effective.

Basis of Restriction on Distribution

This report has been prepared solely for [Title of Those Charged with Governance] in order to meet the APRA reporting requirements of [name of life company]. This report is not to be used for any other purpose or be distributed to any other party. We disclaim any assumption of responsibility for any reliance on this report to any party other than [name of life company] and APRA, or for any purpose other than that for which it was prepared.

Firm

[Name of Partner]

Partner

[Date]

GS

Appendix 2

(Ref: Para.123)

Example Attachment to the Auditor's Special Purpose Report - Material Findings or Exceptions

The following example attachment to the auditor's Special Purpose Report (reasonable or limited assurance) is to be used as a guide only, and will need to be adapted according to the engagement requirements and circumstances of the life company.

This attachment accompanies, and forms part of, the example Auditor's Report provided in Appendix 1.

Attachment 1: Material Findings or Exceptions

This attachment has been prepared for distribution to [Title of Those Charged with Governance][20] of [name of life company] and APRA. It accompanies, and forms part of, the Auditor's Special Purpose Report dated [date], for the financial year ended [date], prepared pursuant to the reporting requirements specified in APRA's Prudential Standard LPS 310 *Audit and Related Matters*.

(a) Material Misstatements in Life Company Annual Return(s) not previously advised by the [type of life company] to APRA

During our audit and/or review of the life company Annual return(s), we noted the following:

a. Errors in Annual Return XXX

Error: Line [ ]

This error was due to ....

We recommend that ....

[The appropriate correct disclosure accompanies the reporting of any error(s)]

(b) Significant non-compliance with relevant Prudential Requirements under the *Life Insurance Act 1995* and the *Financial Sector (Collection of Data) Act 2001*, including APRA Prudential and Reporting Standards, identified during the financial year and up to the date of signing the auditor's assurance report.

a. Matters previously reported to APRA by the auditor:

....

b. Matters previously reported to APRA by the [type of Life company]:

....

c. Matters not previously reported to APRA:

....

[Auditor's signature]

[Date of the Auditor's report]

[Auditor's address]

20 Or, for a EFLIC, a senior officer outside Australia to whom authority has been delegated in accordance with Prudential Standard LPS 510 *Governance*, for overseeing the Australian operations.

GS 018

Franchising Code of Conduct – Auditor's Reports

(Issued October 2010)

Issued by the Auditing and Assurance Standards Board.

Note from the Institute of Chartered Accountants Australia

This note, prepared by the technical editor, is not part of GS 018.

Historical development

March 1999: AGS 1040 'Franchising Code of Conduct – Auditor's Reports' issued by the AuASB.

November 2002: AGS 1040 reissued in response to amendments to the 'Franchising Code of Conduct'. The AGS assists auditors in preparing an audit report to support a statement by the directors of a franchisor that there are reasonable grounds to believe that the franchisor will be able to pay its debts as and when they fall due. AGS 1040 has no international equivalent and was operative from the date of issue.

October 2010: GS 018 issued to reflect changes to the 'Franchising Code of Conduct' released in June 2010. It is operative from the date of issue and has no international equivalent.

Contents

Authority Statement

The Auditing and Assurance Standards Board (AUASB) formulates Guidance Statement GS 018 *Franchising Code of Conduct – Auditor's Reports,* pursuant to section 227B of the *Australian Securities and Investments Commission Act 2001*, for the purposes of providing guidance on auditing and assurance matters.

This Guidance Statement provides guidance to assist the auditor to fulfil the objectives of the audit or assurance engagement. It includes explanatory material on specific matters for the purposes of understanding and complying with AUASB Standards. The auditor exercises professional judgement when using this Guidance Statement.

The Guidance Statement does not prescribe or create new requirements.

Dated: 28 October 2010

M H Kelsall
Chairman - AUASB

Guidance Statement GS 018

Franchising Code of Conduct – Auditor's Reports

Application

1 This Guidance Statement has been formulated by the Auditing and Assurance Standards Board (AUASB) to assist auditors to interpret, discharge and report under Item 20 of Annexure 1 to the Franchising Code of Conduct[1] (the "Franchising Code").

Issuance Date

2 This Guidance Statement is issued on 28 October 2010 by the AUASB and replaces AGS 1040 *Franchising Code of Conduct – Auditor's Reports* issued in November 2002.

1 The *Franchising Code of Conduct* came into operation on 1 July 1998 and was last amended on 3 June 2010. A copy of the Code is available from the Australian Competition and Consumer Commission (ACCC) website (http://www.accc.gov.au).

Introduction

3 Item 20 of Annexure 1[2] to the *Franchising Code* imposes mandatory disclosure requirements in relation to financial details, which must be provided by franchisors to franchisees when entering into a new franchise agreement on or after 1 October 1998, as follows:

20. Financial details

20.1 A statement as at the end of the last financial year, signed by at least one director of the franchisor, whether in its directors' opinion there are reasonable grounds to believe that the franchisor will be able to pay its debts as and when they fall due.

20.2 Financial reports for each of the last two completed financial years in accordance with sections 295 to 297 of the *Corporations Act 2001*, or a foreign equivalent of that Act applicable to the franchisor, prepared by the franchisor.

20.2A If:

(a) the franchisor is part of a consolidated entity that is required to provide audited financial reports under the *Corporations Act 2001*, or a foreign equivalent of that Act applicable to the consolidated entity; and

(b) a franchisee requests those financial reports;

financial reports for each of the last two completed financial years, prepared by the consolidated entity.

20.3 Item 20.2 and 20.2A do not apply if:

(a) the statement under item 20.1 is supported by an independent audit [report specifically relating to that statement] provided by:

(i) a registered company auditor; or

(ii) if the franchisor is a foreign franchisor – a foreign equivalent for that franchisor;

within 12 months after the end of the financial year to which the statement relates; and

(b) a copy of the independent audit [report] is provided with the statement under item 20.1.

4 Generally, the financial report of the franchisor needs to be accompanied by an independent audit report addressed to the directors of the franchisor entity for the specific purpose of being provided to franchisees as part of the disclosure document. However, as indicated in Item 20.3, a franchisor will not be required to provide a financial report where the directors' statement relating to solvency which is provided pursuant to Item 20.1 is supported by an independent audit report provided by a registered company auditor.

Nature and Extent of the Audit Engagement

5 The directors' statement required by Item 20.1 of Annexure 1 to the *Franchising Code* contains their opinion on "solvency" as at the end of the last financial year in respect of recorded liabilities as at the end of that year, and which relates to the ability to meet those liabilities over the 12 month period from the end of the last financial year. The auditor's direct responsibility is to form and express an opinion on the directors' statement made pursuant to Item 20.1 of Annexure 1 to the *Franchising Code*. The substance of this responsibility is similar to that assumed by a company auditor in relation to the "solvency" statement by directors which forms part of the directors' declaration under Section 295(4) of the *Corporations Act 2001* (the "Act"), and on which the auditor forms an opinion and reports, as a component of the financial report, under the *Corporations Act*. For audits under the *Act*, the auditor's opinion on the directors' solvency statement is derived from, and is

2 Annexure 1 to the *Franchising Code* sets out the content requirements of the franchising disclosure document when the expected annual turnover of a franchised business is $50,000 or more. Annexure 2 to the *Franchising Code* sets out the content requirements of the franchising disclosure document when the expected annual turnover of a franchised business is less than $50,000. For the purpose of this Guidance Statement, the guidance applicable to the auditing requirements of the solvency statements under Annexure 1 and Annexure 2 is the same.

GS

integral to, the audit process related to forming an opinion on the financial report and the appropriateness of the going concern basis in accordance with ASA 570 *Going Concern.*[3]

6 In the case of an audit under the *Act*, the auditor's responsibility is to consider the appropriateness of the going concern basis (defined for financial reporting purposes) in the context of the audit of a financial report. The auditor therefore considers the going concern assumption (including solvency) for the "relevant period", being the period from the date of the auditor's current report to the expected date of the next auditor's report on the financial report for the next period. Due to the specific nature of the engagement under the *Franchising Code* which generally occurs outside the annual financial reporting process, the *Franchising Code* specifies that the directors' statement must be provided within a 12 month period from the end of the financial year to which it relates.

7 Whilst recognising that for entities subject to audit under the *Act*, there is an interrelationship between the opinion under the *Act* and that required under Item 20.3 of Annexure 1 to the *Franchising Code*, the audit report issued under Item 20.3 is undertaken as a separate audit engagement. It is acknowledged, however, that in situations where the reports are to be provided by the same auditor, much of the evidence to support the opinion under Item 20.3 will be derived from the financial report audit under the *Act*.

8 For engagements under Item 20.3 of Annexure 1 to the *Franchising Code*, the auditor considers the risks inherent in issuing an audit report without the support of an accompanying financial report. For example, unlike the auditor's opinion on solvency under the *Act*, which is one element of the information reported on by the auditor, the Item 20.3 opinion is a specific report on solvency and stands in its own right.

9 In situations where no audit has been conducted as at the end of the last financial year, the nature and extent of the audit procedures to be undertaken by an auditor on an entity's financial information, may be similar to those required to express an opinion under the *Act*, before being able to report under Item 20.3. Whilst the audit process need not be directed to supporting an opinion on a complete financial report, but rather on the directors' assertion in their statement, the auditor may, for example need to have obtained sufficient appropriate audit evidence under ASA 500 *Audit Evidence* about the assets, liabilities, revenues, expenses, cash flows, budgets and projections etc. of the entity in order to assess the basis for the directors' "solvency" statement.

10 The audit procedures performed are likely to include analysis and assessment of prospective information in relation to cash flows, revenue and payment streams and reflects assumptions that are dependent upon future events which may be subject to risks inherent in the business and future economic conditions. The auditor applies professional judgement in auditing any assumptions to determine their reasonableness as such evidence is future oriented and speculative in nature.

Audit Approach

11 The nature, timing and extent of the audit procedures appropriate to achieve reasonable assurance are a function of the circumstances of each engagement, and will depend on:

(a) whether the auditor is a new or continuing auditor;

(b) the proximity of the most recent audited financial report;

(c) the extent and nature of changes in the entity's activities and/or industry/industries in which it operates since the issue of the most recent audited financial report; and

(d) the nature, timing and extent of the audit procedures conducted since the issue of the most recent audited financial report.

Continuity in Auditor

12 For the continuing auditor where an audited financial report has recently been issued under the *Act,* the audit process may be limited to a consideration of any changes in the entity's

3 The Australian Auditing Standards (ASAs) referred to in this Guidance Statement are those ASAs issued by the AUASB in October 2009, which apply to audits of financial reports with reporting periods commencing on or after 1 January 2010.

circumstances since the audit of the directors' opinion on solvency included in the directors' declaration is already required under the *Act*. This may involve the auditor:

(a) enquiring of management/directors as to the basis on which they have formed their opinion on solvency under Item 20.1, and evaluating the appropriateness of any new assumptions underlying their opinion;

(b) updating knowledge of the entity's business and industry, to evaluate whether there have been any significant changes to the appropriateness of significant assumptions underlying the previous solvency opinion. Procedures to be applied in this regard could include, for example, those identified in Appendix 1 of ASA 315 *Identifying and Assessing the Risks of Material Misstatement through Understanding the Entity and Its Environment*. Particular emphasis may need to be given to any changes in expectations concerning cash flow, trading conditions, financial commitments, financing arrangements etc;

(c) enquiring as to any changes to the entity's internal control structure in relation to cash flow and management of debt; and

(d) applying appropriate analytical review procedures, for example comparing the latest management accounts with budgets and cash flow forecasts.

In the absence of evidence contrary to the representations made by the directors in their Item 20.1 solvency statement, and for the auditor to report under Item 20.3, ASA 700 *Forming an Opinion and Reporting on a Financial Report* states that the auditor shall form an unmodified opinion.

13 Significant changes in fundamental assumptions and/or conditions, for example changes in the nature of the entity's business, plans for significant acquisitions and disposals may require application of more extensive procedures.

Initial Engagement – New Auditor

14 For a new auditor, and/or a situation where there has been a significant time lag since the issue of the latest audited financial report, and limited audit procedures applied in relation to forming an audit opinion on the financial report in the current financial period, the nature, timing and extent of the audit procedures may need to be more extensive. This may involve the auditor placing further emphasis on certain areas of the audit, but is not limited to, the following:

(a) Understanding the entity and its environment and assessing the risks of material misstatement under ASA 315.

(b) Obtaining sufficient appropriate audit evidence under ASA 500 to support the solvency statement by Directors:

(i) enquiring of management as to the basis on which they have formed their opinion on solvency and evaluating the appropriateness of the assumptions on which this is based;

(ii) reviewing procedures and controls over cash flows, trading conditions, financial commitments etc that may affect cash flow and budgetary forecasts and the ability of the entity to pay its debts as and when they fall due;

(iii) appropriateness of management's use of the going concern assumption in the preparation of the solvency statement under ASA 570 *Going Concern*; and

(iv) obtaining written representations under ASA 580 *Written Representations* from management based on the assertions made throughout the engagement.

(c) Consideration of subsequent events under ASA 560 *Subsequent Events* that may have the potential to affect the solvency statement by Directors.

15 In any of the situations described above where the audit procedures create doubts as to the directors' representations concerning solvency, additional audit procedures may need to be undertaken to enable an opinion to be expressed.

Auditor's Report

16 The auditor is concerned with obtaining sufficient appropriate audit evidence that the opinion stated in the directors' solvency statement is reasonable, based on the foreseeable commercial circumstances facing the entity and which the auditor can reasonably perceive to exist.

17 If, as a result of applying the appropriate level of audit procedures, the auditor forms the opinion that there is sufficient and appropriate audit evidence obtained to support the representation made by the directors in their solvency statement, the auditor issues an unmodified auditor's report under ASA 700. An example report is provided in Appendix 1 to this Guidance Statement.

18 If the auditor is of the opinion that the audit evidence is inconsistent with the representation made by the directors, the auditor issues a modified report under ASA 705 *Modifications to the Opinion in the Independent Auditor's Report*.

19 If the auditor is of the opinion that there is sufficient and appropriate audit evidence to support the representation made by the directors that events exist that put into doubt the ability of the entity to pay its debts as and when they fall due, the auditor expresses an unqualified opinion but adds an emphasis of matter section. ASA 706 *Emphasis of Matter Paragraphs and Other Matter Paragraphs in the Independent Auditor's Report* may provide the auditor with some further guidance in this area.

20 Item 20.3(b) of Annexure 1, requires the copy of the independent audit [report] to be provided with the directors' statement before distribution of that report to any franchisee or prospective franchisee.

Conformity with International Pronouncements

21 There is no equivalent International Auditing Practice Statement (IAPS) or Auditing Standard to this Guidance Statement.

Appendix 1

Example of An Unmodified Auditor's Report

INDEPENDENT AUDITOR'S REPORT

[Appropriate Addressee]

Report on Solvency

We have audited the statement by directors ("the statement") of [name of entity] dated [insert date] made for the purposes of fulfilling the requirements of Item 20 of Annexure 1[4] to the *Franchising Code of Conduct*.

Directors' Responsibility for the Statement

The [name of entity] directors are responsible for the preparation and fair presentation of the statement which has been prepared as at [date of financial year end] to reflect the debts of the entity at that date, and the ability of [name of entity] to meet these debts as and when they fall due over the 12 month period from that date. This responsibility includes establishing, designing, implementing and maintaining internal controls relevant to the preparation and fair presentation of the statement that is free from material misstatement, whether due to fraud or errors; selecting and applying appropriate accounting policies; and making accounting estimates that are reasonable in the circumstances.

4 The requirements of Item 20 of Annexure 1 are the same as those of Item 10 of Annexure 2 to the *Franchising Code*. Therefore the phrase 'Item 20 of Annexure 1' in the auditor's report may be replaced with "Item 10 of Annexure 2", as applicable to the relevant franchised business.

Auditor's Responsibility

Our responsibility is to express an opinion on the statement based on our audit. We conducted our audit in accordance with Australian Auditing and Assurance Standards. These standards require that we comply with relevant ethical requirements relating to audit engagements and plan and perform the audit to obtain reasonable assurance whether the statement is free from material misstatement.

Our audit, in accordance with Australian Auditing and Assurance Standards, involved such tests and procedures as we considered necessary in the circumstances. Our procedures included examination, on a test basis, of evidence supporting the reasonableness of assumptions and procedures used by the directors in forming their opinion as at [date of financial year end] whether there are reasonable grounds to believe [name of entity] will be able to pay its debts as and when they fall due over the 12 month period from [date of financial year end].

Because of the subjective nature of prospective information required to fulfil the requirements of Item 20 of Annexure 1[4] to the *Franchising Code*, the persuasiveness of the evidence available is limited. Prospective information relates to events and actions that have not yet occurred and may not occur, and reflect assumptions that are dependent upon future events and subject to the risks inherent in the business and future economic conditions. Whilst evidence is available to support the assumptions on which the directors' opinion is based, such evidence is future orientated and speculative in nature. As a consequence, actual results are likely to be different from the information on which the opinion is based, since anticipated events frequently do not occur as expected or assumed and the variations between the prospective opinion and the actual outcome may be significant.

The statement has been prepared pursuant to Item 20 of Annexure 1[4] to the *Franchising Code of Conduct* for distribution to the franchisees and prospective franchisees of [name of entity]. We disclaim any assumption of responsibility for any reliance on this audit report or on the statement to which it relates to any other party, or for any purpose other than that for which it was prepared.

We believe that the audit evidence we have obtained is sufficient and appropriate to provide a basis for our audit opinion.

Opinion

In our opinion, the statement by directors dated [insert date], presents fairly, in all material respects, the directors' opinion pursuant to Item 20 of Annexure 1[4] to the *Franchising Code of Conduct*, that there are reasonable grounds to believe that [name of entity] will be able to pay its debts as and when they fall due.

[Auditor's signature]

[Date of the auditor's report]

[Auditor's address]

GS

4 The requirements of Item 20 of Annexure 1 are the same as those of Item 10 of Annexure 2 to the *Franchising Code*. Therefore the phrase 'Item 20 of Annexure 1' in the auditor's report may be replaced with "Item 10 of Annexure 2", as applicable to the relevant franchised business.

GS 019
Auditing Fundraising Revenue of Not-for-Profit Entities

(Issued April 2011)

Issued by the Auditing and Assurance Standards Board.

Note from the Institute of Chartered Accountants Australia

This note, prepared by the technical editor, is not part of GS 019.

Historical development

April 2011: GS 019 issued to replace AGS 1054 'Auditing Revenue of Charitable Entities' issued by the predecessor board, the AuASB. AGS 1054 was first issued in February 2000 and reissued to incorporate minor amendments in July 2002. There is no equivalent international pronouncement.

Contents

AUTHORITY STATEMENT

Authority Statement

The Auditing and Assurance Standards Board (AUASB) formulates Guidance Statement GS 019 *Auditing Fundraising Revenue of Not-for-Profit Entities* pursuant to section 227B of the *Australian Securities and Investments Commission Act 2001*, for the purposes of providing guidance on auditing and assurance matters.

This Guidance Statement provides guidance to assist the auditor to fulfil the objectives of the audit or assurance engagement. It includes explanatory material on specific matters for the purposes of understanding and complying with AUASB Standards. The auditor exercises professional judgement when using this Guidance Statement.

The Guidance Statement does not prescribe or create new requirements.

Dated: 21 April 2011

M H Kelsall
Chairman - AUASB

GS

Guidance Statement GS 019

Auditing Fundraising Revenue of Not-for-Profit Entities

Application

1. This Guidance Statement has been formulated by the Auditing and Assurance Standards Board (AUASB) to provide guidance to auditors on the factors to consider when planning, performing and reporting on the completeness of fundraising revenue for not-for-profit entities.

Issuance Date

2. This Guidance statement is issued on 21 April 2011 by the AUASB and replaces 1054 *Auditing Revenue of Charitable Entities*, issued in July 2002.

Introduction

3. Australian Auditing Standards contain requirements, application and other explanatory material that apply to the audit of the financial report of any entity, including not-for-profit entities, irrespective of their size, legal form, or the nature of their activities. However, the AUASB recognises that the audit of not-for-profit entities gives rise to a number of specific audit issues, a significant one of which is forming a conclusion and reporting on the completeness assertion in relation to fundraising revenue from sources such as cash donations, appeals, raffles and other fundraising activities.

4. From an audit perspective, there can often be uncertainty as to whether a not-for-profit entity has received all cash donations to which it has a right from its respective fundraising or other revenue generating activities as adequate controls may not be in place over all sources of revenue. Consequently, an auditor may find it difficult to perform tests of controls and substantive procedures that are necessary to reduce assurance engagement risk, particularly in respect of the completeness of cash donations, to an acceptable level. When such a scope limitation exists, the auditor considers expressing a qualified opinion. However, the expression of a qualified opinion in respect of the completeness of cash donations as a portion of fundraising revenue ought not occur as a matter of course for all not-for-profit entities that receive cash donations. Consideration needs to be given to materiality and mitigation of risks through internal control structures or other factors affecting the environment in which the not-for-profit entity operates.

5. The guidance provided is applicable to all audits of not-for-profit entities as typically these entities are more reliant on cash donations from fundraising activities as a significant source of their revenue base as compared to a for-profit entity. The guidance is designed to assist the auditor in exercising professional judgement in the application of the Auditing Standards. This guidance statement also contains Appendix 1 which outlines various audit risks associated with different sources of fundraising revenue and indicative audit procedures that may be adopted for each source of fundraising revenue.

Characteristics of a Not-for-Profit Entity

6. Significant diversity can exist in the activities, operations, size, and legal structures of not-for-profit entities. There is also significant public interest in the accountability of not-for-profit entities, because they are generally supported by voluntary contributions of both physical and financial resources and their purpose is largely to serve some public need, as opposed to being in business for profit. To varying degrees, such characteristics impact on the audit of not-for-profit entities, including the audit of fundraising revenue.

Regulatory Framework Affecting a Not-for-Profit Entity

7. The regulatory framework for not-for-profit entities can be complex. not-for-profit entities may operate under a variety of legal structures, such as a company limited by guarantee, a trust, an incorporated or unincorporated association, Royal Charter or pursuant to

legislation enacted specifically to establish the entity (e.g. *Charitable Fundraising Act 1991*). Each of these legal structures may impose specific financial reporting and auditing requirements. A not-for-profit entity's governing documents may prescribe specific disclosure requirements to be made in its financial report or other responsibilities which impact on the scope of the audit. The legal structure may also affect the financial reporting framework, for example, the extent to which compliance with Australian Accounting Standards is required.

8. For a not-for-profit entity that is a company limited by guarantee, further consideration needs to be given to the recent changes to the *Corporations Act 2000*. Refer to *Corporations Amendment (Corporate Reporting Reform) Act 2010* which establishes a three tier system for these entities based on annual revenue and the status of the entity, as to whether they are required to prepare a financial report and have the report audited or reviewed. If the company limited by guarantee meets the criteria and the auditor is able to conduct a review instead of an audit this guidance statement provides an illustration of a Qualified Review Report (Limitation of Scope) as set out in Appendix 4. For further information, refer to ASRE 2415 *Review of a Financial Report - Company Limited by Guarantee*.

9. The conduct of some activities undertaken by not-for-profit entities, for example, major fundraising events or other activities associated therewith may be governed by specific regulations. Such regulations may prescribe compliance and reporting obligations by the entity's governing body and the auditor in connection with the particular event. Any material non-compliance with these regulations could have a significant financial impact should any limitation be placed on the not-for-profit entity undertaking similar activities in the future.

Nature of Fundraising Revenue

10. The revenue of not-for-profit entities may be derived from a variety of sources including: cash donations from members of the public, donated materials, restricted and unrestricted grants from government. Fundraising revenue may be obtained from street, door-to-door or postal collections, special events or other methods of fundraising. Revenue from fundraising activities can be geographically dispersed, and may be directed to a not-for-profit entity from professional third parties or voluntary fundraisers. However, unlike revenue of a for-profit business entity, the collection of such revenue may not be supported by invoices or equivalent documentation, or subject to internal controls commonly found in a for-profit business entity. Consequently, from an audit perspective the control systems usually found in a for-profit business environment may not be present for some sources of fundraising revenue.

11. It can sometimes be difficult to accurately estimate the level of fundraising revenue from cash donations, contributions or grants. This is generally because:

    (a) donors' patterns of giving may change, due for example, to economic hardship or competing demands on limited resources; and

    (b) some contributions, such as grants to undertake particular activities, being dependent on a tendering process. Such funding decisions are usually based on considerations by third parties over whom the not-for-profit entity has little influence. Receipt of these funds can be for a specific purpose, with their use and recognition subject to compliance with specific conditions.

12. It may be difficult to establish a relationship between cash donations and other amounts in the financial report, as expenditure levels may not have any direct relationship with such fundraising revenue.

Internal Control

13. It is important that the governing body of a not-for-profit entity maintains an effective internal control structure over its activities. The governing body has responsibility for ensuring that all fundraising and other revenues to which the not-for-profit entity gains control are accounted for properly. This involves establishing controls to ensure that cash donations are recorded correctly in the financial records of the entity, and that the revenue

recognised in the financial report is calculated in accordance with Australian Accounting Standards and the entity's accounting policies adopted for revenue recognition[1]. Many aspects of a not-for-profit's control environment and individual control procedures will be the same as those of a for-profit business entity. However, the internal control structure for a not-for-profit entity is likely to be affected, to varying degrees, by the following factors:

(a) limited resources being available to achieve internal control objectives, as generally a not-for-profit entity keeps administrative staff and management tools to a minimum so that resources are allocated to activities that will help achieve its mission;

(b) the likelihood that volunteers will be involved in the not-for-profit entity. The involvement of volunteers can range from serving in a voluntary capacity on the not-for-profit entity's governing board to daily involvement in the entity's operations or management, including performing accounting and fundraising functions;

(c) the culture that underlies various facets of the control environment, including attitudes towards the importance of accountability, how authority and responsibility are assigned, and personnel management policies and practices;

(d) the existence of any externally imposed requirements by governments, contributors, or national or international bodies affiliated with the not-for-profit entity that may require certain control procedures be implemented, such as ensuring that government grants are only expended / recognised in accordance with a grant agreement or certain expenses are approved by the governing body;

(e) the regulatory requirements relating to its fundraising activities;

(f) the existence of accountability requirements over operations in the form of key performance indicators, for example the ratio of organisational and fundraising expenditure to fundraising revenue, or cost of fundraising to funds raised; and

(g) where third party specialist fundraisers or other non-controlled entities e.g. branches or associates, undertake fundraising on behalf of a not-for-profit entity (under a documented agreement).

Communicating Deficiencies in Internal Control

14. The auditor may also need to consider any obligations under ASA 265 *Communicating Deficiencies in Internal Control to Those Charged with Governance and Management* to communicate significant or other deficiencies in internal control while performing the audit.

Audit of Fundraising Revenue

Audit Planning

15. In forming an opinion on management's assertions about whether fundraising revenue is presented fairly in all material respects, the auditor develops an audit plan based on an assessment of:

(a) inherent and control risk in accordance with ASA 315 *Identifying and Assessing the Risks of Material Misstatement through Understanding the Entity and Its Environment*. For the audit of fundraising revenue, as well as other material account balances or classes of transactions, the auditor assesses inherent risk and obtains an understanding of the internal control structure to assess control risk, and to determine whether the evaluation and testing of controls and the application of substantive tests will reduce assurance engagement risk to an acceptably low level with respect to the assertions about the completeness and recording of fundraising revenue;

1 See paragraphs 77 – 80, AASB ED 180 *Income from Non-exchange Transactions (Taxes and Transfers)*, to be issued as an AASB Standard in June 2011.

(b) fraud risk – in accordance with ASA 240 *The Auditor's Responsibilities Relating to Fraud in an Audit of a Financial Report* when the auditor performs risk assessment procedures and related activities under ASA 315, the auditor needs to perform certain procedures[2] to obtain information for use in identifying, assessing and responding to risks of material misstatement due to fraud. ASA 240 paragraphs 26 and 47 deem that there are risks of fraud in revenue recognition and the auditor needs to document their conclusion on the risks associated with revenue recognition even if they are of the opinion that it is not applicable in the engagement circumstances; and

(c) materiality of fundraising revenue – in accordance with ASA 320 *Materiality in Planning and Performing an Audit*, and the discussion of materiality in Accounting Standards AASB 1031 *Materiality*. In determining the materiality of fundraising revenue, qualitative materiality considerations may be significant, given the characteristics of a not-for-profit entity, and the nature of and sources from which fundraising revenue is derived. Qualitative factors that the auditor may consider include:

(i) governing documents or reporting frameworks prescribing specific recognition and/or disclosure requirements in the financial report;

(ii) whether law, regulation or the applicable financial reporting framework affect users' expectations regarding the measurement or disclosure of certain items;

(iii) key disclosures in relation to the industry in which the entity operates;

(iv) whether attention is focused on a particular aspect of the entity's business that is separately disclosed in the financial report; and

(v) indicators of deviations from normal activities such as the reversal of a trend, turning a loss into a profit or creating or eliminating the net asset position in the balance sheet.

Completeness of Fundraising Revenue

16. ASA 315 states that the auditor needs to perform risk assessment procedures to provide a basis for the identification and assessment of risks of material misstatement at the financial report and assertion levels. Sufficient appropriate audit evidence needs to be obtained to provide a basis on which to conclude whether the cash donations portion of fundraising revenue included in a not-for-profit entity's financial report is, in all material respects, complete. In some cases there may be assurance engagement risk that cash donations may not be recorded from all sources, and consequently, materially understated.

17. In accordance with ASA 330 *The Auditor's Responses to Assessed Risks*, "the auditor shall design and perform further audit procedures whose nature, timing and extent are based on and are responsive to the assessed risks of material misstatement at the assertion level". ASA 330 states that in designing these further audit procedures consideration should be given to the likelihood of material misstatement due to the particular characteristics of the relevant class of transactions and whether the risk assessment takes account of relevant controls, their operating effectiveness and the overall responsibility by management/ governing body for effectively monitoring these activities/controls, in determining the extent of substantive procedures to be undertaken[3].

18. ASA 330 also requires the auditor to evaluate before the conclusion of the audit whether the assessments of the risks of material misstatement at the assertion level remain appropriate and whether sufficient appropriate audit evidence has been obtained[4].

19. As the revenue of each not-for-profit entity may be derived from, and obtained by, different sources and methods, each source has its own distinct inherent and control risk.

GS

2 See ASA 240, paragraphs 17-29.

3 See ASA 330 *The Auditor's Responses to Assessed Risks*, paragraphs 8-23.

4 ASA 330 *The Auditor's Responses to Assessed Risks*, paragraphs 25-27.

In assessing whether cash donations as a portion of fundraising revenue are properly stated the auditor's considerations may include an assessment of the following:

(a) nature of the various sources of fundraising revenue received by the not-for-profit entity, the risks associated with their method of receipt, including any specific risks in the context of the entity's activities;

(b) loss of incoming resources through fraud: the possibility that the not-for-profit's records of incoming resources to which it is legally entitled may be incomplete as a result of fraud. A common type of fraud against not-for-profit entities is the diversion of donations to bank or building society accounts which the not-for-profit governing body does not control;

(c) effectiveness of the controls that are applied, given that some controls can usually be established for each source of fundraising revenue; and

(d) materiality of each source of fundraising revenue in relation to all of the not-for-profit entity's revenue.

Appendix 1 to this guidance statement sets out, for illustrative purposes only, the risks associated with various sources of fundraising revenue, the controls which a not-for-profit entity may implement in respect of those fundraising revenues, and some indicative substantive procedures which the auditor may consider in relation to the audit of each source of fundraising revenue.

Forming an Opinion and Reporting on a Financial Report

Forming an Opinion

20. In order to form an opinion under ASA 700[5] *Forming an Opinion and Reporting on a Financial Report* "the auditor shall conclude as to whether the auditor has obtained reasonable assurance about whether the financial report as a whole is free from material misstatement, whether due to fraud or error". In relation to the above the auditor needs to consider:

(a) whether sufficient appropriate evidence has been obtained and under ASA 330[6] in particular, the auditor needs to consider the controls and the effectiveness of controls over each source of fundraising revenue;

(b) whether uncorrected misstatements are material, individually or in aggregate[7], under ASA 450 *Evaluation of Misstatements Identified during the Audit*; and

(c) whether the financial report, in all material respects, is in accordance with the requirements of the applicable financial reporting framework[8]. This evaluation shall include consideration of the qualitative aspects of the entity's accounting practices, including indicators of possible bias in management's judgements, In particular consideration may be given to whether:

  (i) adequate disclosure of significant accounting policies for fundraising revenue has been made, their selection appropriate and that they have been consistently applied within the reporting framework;

  (ii) accounting estimates made by management are reasonable;

  (iii) information presented in the financial report is relevant, reliable, comparable and understandable; and

  (iv) the financial report provides adequate disclosures to enable intended users to understand material transactions and events in the information conveyed in the financial report.

5 See ASA 700 *Forming an Opinion and Reporting on a Financial Report*, paragraphs 10-15.

6 See paragraphs 17 and 18 of this guidance statement.

7 See ASA 450 *Evaluation of Misstatements Identified during the Audit*, paragraph 11.

8 See ASA 700 *Forming an Opinion and Reporting on a Financial Report*, paragraphs 13-15.

Communication with Those Charged with Governance

21. The auditor may also need to consider any obligations under ASA 260 *Communication with Those Charged with Governance* to communicate significant findings from the audit.

Reporting

22. Where the auditor obtains sufficient appropriate audit evidence to conclude that fundraising revenue reported in a not-for-profit entity's financial report is, in all material respects, presented fairly in accordance with Australian Accounting Standards and other relevant professional reporting requirements, the auditor issues an unmodified audit opinion. This may be the case where for example, a not-for-profit entity receives most of its fundraising revenue in the form of grants, contributions or fees and adequate and effective controls are in place over these sources of revenue and there is only an immaterial amount from cash donations and other fundraising sources.

23. Where considered fundamental to the users' understanding of the financial report, the auditor may deem it necessary to draw to the attention of users, the inherent risk of the not-for-profit entity's operating environment as it relates to revenue recognition from fundraising sources. This may be achieved by the inclusion of an Emphasis of Matter paragraph, in accordance with ASA 706 *Emphasis of Matter Paragraphs and Other Matter Paragraphs in the Independent Auditor's Report*[9]. Appendix 2 provides an illustration of an auditor's report with the inclusion of an example Emphasis of Matter paragraph.

24. A not-for-profit entity may derive a material proportion of its fundraising revenue from sources for which there are limited controls e.g. street collections. It may be impracticable to maintain effective controls due to resource constraints, prior to the recording of fundraising revenue in the financial records. Accordingly, it may not be possible to obtain reasonable assurance about the completeness of fundraising revenue from these sources. In the absence of other evidence and qualitative factors, and where cash donations as a portion of total fundraising revenue is material, the scope of the auditor's work may be limited in so far as being able to obtain sufficient appropriate audit evidence to conclude whether the financial records reflect fundraising revenue from the point at which the not-for-profit entity should have gained control of the cash donations.

25. ASA 705 *Modifications to the Opinion in the Independent Auditor's Report* describes the circumstances when a modification to the auditor's opinion is required including when the auditor is unable to obtain sufficient appropriate audit evidence to conclude that the financial report as a whole is free from material misstatement. In these circumstances the auditor would issue a qualified audit opinion as illustrated in Appendix 3.

Conformity with International Pronouncements

26. There is no equivalent International Auditing Practice Statement (IAPS) or Auditing Standard to this Guidance Statement.

GS

9 See ASA 706 *Emphasis of Matter Paragraphs and Other Matter Paragraphs in the Independent Auditor's Report*, paragraphs 6-7.

Appendix 1

(Ref: Para. 5)

Example Controls and Audit Procedures Relating to Fundraising Revenue

While this Appendix contains certain example internal controls and indicative audit procedures, it does not describe all of the internal controls or procedures necessary to establish control over fundraising revenue or to perform an audit of a not-for-profit entity's fundraising revenue in accordance with Australian Auditing Standards. The guidance in this Appendix is neither intended to be comprehensive, nor is it intended to limit or supplant individual professional judgement. Audit programs and audit procedures for each audit need to be designed to meet the requirements of the particular engagement, which is a matter that can be determined only by the exercise of professional judgement in the light of the circumstances present in a particular case.

The example controls listed below for fundraising revenue assist in improving control over the collection of these sources of fundraising revenue. However, overall control of fundraising revenue is enhanced if the governing body implements policies governing the undertaking of fundraising activities, establishes operational and financial internal controls for fundraising and has in place procedures to ensure compliance therewith.

Fundraising Revenue & Risks	Methods of Collection	Example Controls	Indicative Audit Procedures
Cash donations			
• Inherent risk high, as cash donations are highly susceptible to inadvertent misplacement, or loss through fraud or theft • Control risk associated with the completeness of cash donations usually assessed as high	• Direct cash donations (e.g. door-to-door or street collection, or small special events e.g. raffle)	• Establish numerical control over collection boxes • Ensure appropriate sealing of collection boxes so that any opening prior to recording cash is apparent • Maintain regular collection and recording of proceeds from collection boxes • Establish dual control over counting and recording of proceeds independent of collectors • Reconcile receipts issued with cash received • Issue receipts, where appropriate • Require collectors to operate in pairs so that one collector is able to observe the actions of the other • Where collections are solicited from a designated geographical area, require a report on the response of each collection unit (e.g. each household)	• Review and test procedures implemented to collect cash donations and their systems of control • Review and test policies and procedures followed by staff or volunteers when collecting cash donations • Reconcile total of tax receipts issued with cash recorded and banked • Design analytical procedures for each different source or geographical area from which cash donations are obtained, e.g. compare cash donations from a particular activity or geographical area with previous years or budgeted cash donations

Fundraising Revenue & Risks	Methods of Collection	Example Controls	Indicative Audit Procedures
	• Postal cash donations e.g. received from a fundraising appeal	• Segregate mail opening and bank deposit functions • Ensure immediate recording of donations on opening of mail or receipt • Agree bank paying-in slips with a record of receipts by an independent person	• Observe control procedures • Analyse donations received to donations requested, and compare with previous years or industry statistics (if available)
Monthly Subscriptions/ Mailing List Donations • Inherent risk medium, as monthly credit card payments and standing orders are less susceptible to misplacement or theft • Control risk associated with the completeness of credit card or online subscriptions usually assessed as med/low	• Standing Order, Credit card, Direct debit and online EFT	• Monthly bank reconciliations that are reviewed and signed off • Issue receipts, where appropriate • Enquire about procedures over establishing new subscription accounts and reviewing controls on an ongoing basis	• Review of monthly bank reconciliations with specific consideration for any unusual reconciling items • Estimate revenue based on # of subscribers x average donation to determine reasonableness of revenue recorded
Fundraising campaigns and other special events • Given the range and size of specific fundraising events that a not-for-profit entity may undertake, each event will have its own inherent and control risk, though like cash donations, assurance engagement risk in respect of the completeness of fundraising revenue from these sources is usually high	• Telemarketing campaigns • Bingos, raffles and lotteries • Social events • Large appeals	• Establish procedures to ensure compliance with any regulatory requirements that pertain specifically to the fundraising event • Ensure persons responsible for handling collections from ticket sales account for each pre numbered ticket sold, and provide a reconciliation to tickets issued for sale • Independent person to reconcile tickets issued against tickets sold or returned unsold, with the person being segregated from the person responsible for counting and depositing monies received	• Review compliance with any regulations that are applicable to the fundraising event • Comparison of cash donations actually received to past results for similar special events and statistics for response rates for NFPs in general • To determine completeness of revenue recorded from social events, assess the reasonableness of related expenditure, compare amounts recorded with past revenue and expenditure for the event • For each material fundraising event, review procedures adopted by the charitable entity for capturing and recording fundraising revenue which it controls

Fundraising Revenue & Risks	Methods of Collection	Example Controls	Indicative Audit Procedures
Donated materials • Inherent risk in estimating the fair value of donated materials		• Develop policies to ensure immediate recording of donated materials, with periodic review of policies by the appropriate level of management • Segregate incompatible tasks, for example, responsibility for receipt and recording of donated materials • Supervise collections to prevent collusion or theft	• Enquire about the accounting policies adopted for recording donated materials, test the extent and effectiveness of the accounting procedures and internal controls • Compare data collected on current year donated materials with budgeted material contributions or previous years' receipts • Consider confirming contributions from significant donors
Bequests and Legacies • Potential for breach of restrictions (if any) regarding the use of a bequest or legacy through inadequate implementation of accounting controls		• Maintain comprehensive correspondence files for each bequest or legacy received or receivable • Implement systematic procedures to detect if any restrictions are imposed on the expenditure of funds, and ensure details about restrictions are communicated to those responsible for expenditure of funds • Separately record legacies with restrictions imposed and deposit in trust or separate bank account	• Review correspondence relating to bequests and legacies, noting the imposition of any restrictions and the consequences of non-compliance therewith • Test controls over expenditure and approval • Review procedures for recording bequests and legacies

Fundraising Revenue & Risks	Methods of Collection	Example Controls	Indicative Audit Procedures
Pledges			
• Inherent risk associated with estimation of the realisable value of pledges receivable is particularly significant	• Solicited from regular or special fundraising campaigns and can be made by telephone, other electronic methods or in writing	• Establish a method of recording and maintaining control over pledges when obtained, including procedures to ensure detection of, and compliance with, restrictions or conditions (if any) • Establish a collections policy for pledges, for the purposes of providing for uncollectible pledges	• Review and test the process used by management to estimate pledges receivable • Review the ageing of pledges • Consider obtaining confirmation of unusual or significant pledges • Compare pledges receivable with subsequent receipt of donations • Determine whether the materialisation ratios used to estimate pledges receivable are reasonable
Contributions from grants or restricted income			
• Potential for breach of the conditions or restrictions on the use of the grant	• Contributions from government possibly following from tendering process • Receipt from major donors or supporters	• Maintain comprehensive records of applications made and implement follow-up procedures for grant applications not discharged	• For evidence on the completeness assertion, examine grant applications and correspondence • Confirm grants received or receivable with grantor bodies

Appendix 2

(Ref: Para. 23)

Example Auditor's Report General Purpose Financial Report - Unmodified Opinion, Emphasis of Matter

Financial report is prepared for a general purpose by the governing body of the entity and is in accordance with Australian Accounting Standards. The financial report is *not* prepared under the *Corporations Act 2001*.

INDEPENDENT AUDITOR'S REPORT

[Appropriate Addressee]

Report on the Financial Report

We have audited the accompanying financial report of [name of not-for-profit entity] [which comprises…….][10], for the year ended [insert date].

Governing Body's Responsibility for the Financial Report

The [members of the governing body] are responsible for the preparation and fair presentation of the financial report in accordance with Australian Accounting Standards and [relevant reporting

10 or identify the individual components when appropriate.

framework], and for such internal control as the governing body determines is necessary to enable the preparation of the financial report that is free from material misstatement, whether due to fraud or error.

Auditor's Responsibility

Our responsibility is to express an opinion on the financial report based on our audit. We conducted our audit in accordance with Australian Auditing Standards. Those standards require that we comply with relevant ethical requirements relating to audit engagements and plan and perform the audit to obtain reasonable assurance about whether the financial report is free from material misstatement.

An audit involves performing procedures to obtain audit evidence about the amounts and disclosures in the financial report. The procedures selected depend on the auditor's judgement, including the assessment of the risks of material misstatement of the financial report, whether due to fraud or error. In making those risk assessments, the auditor considers internal control relevant to the entity's preparation and fair presentation of the financial report in order to design audit procedures that are appropriate in the circumstances, but not for the purpose of expressing an opinion on the effectiveness of the entity's internal control. An audit also includes evaluating the appropriateness of accounting policies used and the reasonableness of accounting estimates made by [governing body], as well as evaluating the overall presentation of the financial report.

We believe that the audit evidence we have obtained is sufficient and appropriate to provide a basis for our audit opinion.

Opinion

In our opinion, the financial report of [name of not-for-profit entity], presents fairly, in all material respects (or gives a true and fair view of) the financial position as at [year end], and (of) its financial performance and its cash flows for the year then ended in accordance with Australian Accounting Standards and [relevant reporting framework].

Emphasis of Matter

We draw attention to Note X to the financial report which describes the revenue recognition policy of [name of not-for-profit entity], including the limitations that exist in relation to the recording of cash receipts from [name of source of fundraising revenue]. Revenue from this source represents a significant proportion of [name of not-for-profit entity's] revenue. Our opinion is unmodified in respect of this matter.

Report on Other Legal and Regulatory Requirements

[Form and content of this section of the auditor's report will vary depending on the nature of the auditor's other reporting responsibilities.]

[Auditor's signature]

[Date of the auditor's report]

[Auditor's address]

Appendix 3

(Ref: Para. 25)

Example Auditor's Report General Purpose Financial Report - Qualified Opinion (Limitation of Scope)

Financial report is prepared for a general purpose by the governing body of the entity and is in accordance with Australian Accounting Standards. The financial report is *not* prepared under the *Corporations Act 2001*.

INDEPENDENT AUDITOR'S REPORT

[Appropriate Addressee]

Report on the Financial Report

We have audited the accompanying financial report of [name of not-for-profit entity] [which comprises…….][11], for the year ended [insert date].

Governing Body's Responsibility for the Financial Report

The [members of the governing body] are responsible for the preparation and fair presentation of the financial report in accordance with Australian Accounting Standards and [relevant reporting framework], and for such internal control as the governing body determines is necessary to enable the preparation of the financial report that is free from material misstatement, whether due to fraud or error.

Auditor's Responsibility

Our responsibility is to express an opinion on the financial report based on our audit. We conducted our audit in accordance with Australian Auditing Standards. Those standards require that we comply with relevant ethical requirements relating to audit engagements and plan and perform the audit to obtain reasonable assurance about whether the financial report is free from material misstatement.

An audit involves performing procedures to obtain audit evidence about the amounts and disclosures in the financial report. The procedures selected depend on the auditor's judgement, including the assessment of the risks of material misstatement of the financial report, whether due to fraud or error. In making those risk assessments, the auditor considers internal control relevant to the entity's preparation and fair presentation of the financial report in order to design audit procedures that are appropriate in the circumstances, but not for the purpose of expressing an opinion on the effectiveness of the entity's internal control. An audit also includes evaluating the appropriateness of accounting policies used and the reasonableness of accounting estimates made by [governing body], as well as evaluating the overall presentation of the financial report.

We believe that the audit evidence we have obtained is sufficient and appropriate to provide a basis for our qualified audit opinion.

Basis for Qualified Opinion

[Identify type(s) of fundraising revenue] are a significant source of fundraising revenue for the [name of not-for-profit entity]. The [name of not-for-profit entity] has determined that it is impracticable to establish control over the collection of [identify type(s) of fundraising revenue] prior to entry into its financial records. Accordingly, as the evidence available to us regarding fundraising revenue from this source was limited, our audit procedures with respect to [identify type(s) of fundraising revenue] had to be restricted to the amounts recorded in the financial records. We therefore are unable to express an opinion whether [identify type(s) of fundraising revenue] of [name of not-for-profit entity] recorded is complete.

GS

11 or identify the individual components when appropriate.

Example Basis for Qualified Opinion

Cash donations are a significant source of fundraising revenue for the XYZ Society. The XYZ Society has determined that it is impracticable to establish control over the collection of cash donations prior to entry into its financial records. Accordingly, as the evidence available to us regarding fundraising revenue from this source was limited, our audit procedures with respect to cash donations had to be restricted to the amounts recorded in the financial records. We therefore are unable to express an opinion whether cash donations the XYZ Society recorded are complete.

Qualified Opinion

In our opinion, except for the possible effects of the matter described in the Basis for Qualified Opinion paragraph, the financial report of [name of not-for-profit entity], presents fairly, in all material respects (or gives a true and fair view of) the financial position as at [year end], and (of) its financial performance and its cash flows for the year then ended in accordance with Australian Accounting Standards and [relevant reporting framework].

Report on Other Legal and Regulatory Requirements

[Form and content of this section of the auditor's report will vary depending on the nature of the auditor's other reporting responsibilities.]

[Auditor's signature]

[Date of the auditor's report]

[Auditor's address]

Appendix 4

(Ref: Para. 8)

Example Auditor's Review Report with a Qualified Conclusion for a Limitation on Scope

The following example auditor's review report is to be used only for those entities that meet the revenue and status requirements as described in ASRE 2415 *Review of a Financial Report - Company Limited by Guarantee.*

Financial report of a company limited by guarantee prepared under the *Corporations Act 2001*. The financial reporting framework is designed to achieve fair presentation.

INDEPENDENT AUDITOR'S REVIEW REPORT

[Appropriate Addressee]

Report on the Financial Report

We [I][12] have reviewed the accompanying financial report of [name of not-for-profit entity], which comprises the statement of financial position as at [insert date], the statement of comprehensive income, statement of changes in equity and statement of cash flows for the year ended on that date, notes comprising a summary of significant accounting policies and other explanatory information, and the directors' declaration.[13]

Governing Body's Responsibility for the Financial Report

The [members of the governing body] are responsible for the preparation of the financial report that gives a true and fair view in accordance with Australian Accounting Standards and the *Corporations Act 2001* and for such internal control as the directors determine is necessary to enable the preparation of the financial report that is free from material misstatement, whether due to fraud or error.

---

12 When an individual is taken to be a registered company auditor under section 324BE of the *Corporations Act 2001*, the auditor's report is to be written in singular form.

13 When the auditor is aware that the financial report will be included in a document that contains other information, the auditor may consider, if the form of presentation allows, identifying the page numbers on which the reviewed financial report is presented.

Auditor's Responsibility

Our [My] responsibility is to express a conclusion on the financial report based on our [my] review. We [I] conducted our [my] review in accordance with Auditing Standard on Review Engagements ASRE 2415 *Review of a Financial Report - Company Limited by Guarantee*, in order to state whether, on the basis of the procedures described, we [I] have become aware of any matter that makes us [me] believe that the financial report is not in accordance with the *Corporations Act 2001* including: giving a true and fair view of the not-for-profit entity's financial position as at [insert date] and its performance for the year ended on that date; and complying with the Australian Accounting Standards and *Corporations Regulations 2001*. ASRE 2415 requires that we [I] comply with the ethical requirements relevant to the review of the financial report.

A review of a financial report consists of making enquiries, primarily of persons responsible for financial and accounting matters, and applying analytical and other review procedures. A review is substantially less in scope than an audit conducted in accordance with Australian Auditing Standards and consequently does not enable us [me] to obtain assurance that we [I] would become aware of all significant matters that might be identified in an audit. Accordingly, we [I] do not express an audit opinion.

Independence

In conducting our [my] review, we [I] have complied with the independence requirements of the *Corporations Act 2001*. We [I] confirm that the independence declaration required by the *Corporations Act 2001*, which has been given to the governing body of [name of not-for-profit entity], would be in the same terms if given to the governing body as at the time of this auditor's report.*

Basis for Qualified Conclusion

[Identify type(s) of fundraising revenue] are a significant source of fundraising revenue for the [name of not-for-profit entity]. The [name of not-for-profit entity] has determined that it is impracticable to establish control over the collection of [identify type(s) of fundraising revenue] prior to entry into its financial records. Accordingly, as the evidence available to us regarding fundraising revenue from this source was limited, our audit procedures with respect to [identify type(s) of fundraising revenue] had to be restricted to the amounts recorded in the financial records. We therefore are unable to express an opinion whether [identify type(s) of fundraising revenue] of [name of not-for-profit entity] recorded is complete.

Example Basis for Qualified Conclusion

Cash donations are a significant source of fundraising revenue for the XYZ Society. The XYZ Society has determined that it is impracticable to establish control over the collection of cash donations prior to entry into its financial records. Accordingly, as the evidence available to us regarding fundraising revenue from this source was limited, our audit procedures with respect to cash donations had to be restricted to the amounts recorded in the financial records. We therefore are unable to express an opinion whether cash donations the XYZ Society recorded is complete.

Qualified Conclusion

Except for the possible effects of the matter described in the Basis for Qualified Conclusion paragraph, based on our [my] review, which is not an audit, we [I] have not become aware of any matter that makes us [me] believe that the financial report of [name of not-for-profit entity] is not in accordance with the *Corporations Act 2001* including:

(a) giving a true and fair view of the not-for-profit entity's financial position as at [insert date] and of its performance for the year ended on that date; and

(b) complying with Australian Accounting Standards and *Corporations Regulations 2001*.

* Or, alternatively, include statements (a) to the effect that circumstances have changed since the declaration was given to the relevant directors; and (b) setting out how the declaration would differ if it had been given to the relevant directors at the time the auditor's report was made.

GS

Report on Other Legal and Regulatory Requirements

[Form and content of this section of the review report will vary depending on the nature of the auditor's other reporting responsibilities].

[Auditor's signature][14]

[Date of the auditor's review report][15]

[Auditor's address]

14 The auditor's review report is required to be signed in one or more of the following ways: the name of the audit firm, the name of the audit company or the personal name of the individual auditor as appropriate. Under ASRE 2415 the review report can be signed by a registered company auditor which includes an individual who meets the requirements of section 324BE of the *Corporations Act 2001*.

15 The date of the auditor's report is the date the auditor signs the report.

GS 020

Special Considerations in Auditing Financial Instruments

(Issued March 2012)

Issued by the Auditing and Assurance Standards Board.

Note from the Institute of Chartered Accountants Australia

This note, prepared by the technical editor, is not part of GS 020.

Historical development

May 2012: GS 20 issued. It provides extensive explanatory background on financial instruments and then goes on to give guidance to auditors on the special considerations relating to their audit, such as when financial instruments are held at valuation.

It is applicable from the date of issue and replaces AGS 1030 'Auditing Derivative Financial Instruments'. It conforms with IAPN 1000 'Special Considerations in Auditing Financial Instruments'.

GS

Contents

AUTHORITY STATEMENT

Authority Statement

The Auditing and Assurance Standards Board (AUASB) formulates Guidance Statement GS 020 *Special Considerations in Auditing Financial Instruments* pursuant to section 227B of the *Australian Securities and Investments Commission Act 2001*, for the purposes of providing guidance on auditing and assurance matters.

This Guidance Statement provides guidance to assist the auditor to fulfil the objectives of the audit or assurance engagement. It includes explanatory material on specific matters for the purposes of understanding and complying with AUASB Standards. The auditor exercises professional judgement when using this Guidance Statement.

The Guidance Statement does not prescribe or create new requirements.

Dated: 8 March 2012

M H Kelsall
Chairman - AUASB

Guidance Statement GS 020

Special Considerations in Auditing Financial Instruments

Application

Aus 0.1 This Guidance Statement has been formulated by the Auditing and Assurance Standards Board (AUASB) to provide background information about financial instruments (Section 1) and guidance to auditors on audit considerations relating to financial instruments (Section II).

GS

Issuance Date

Aus 0.2 This Guidance Statement is issued on 8 March 2012 by the AUASB and replaces AGS 1030 *Auditing Derivative Financial Instruments*.

Introduction

1. Financial instruments may be used by financial and non-financial entities of all sizes for a variety of purposes. Some entities have large holdings and transaction volumes while other entities may only engage in a few financial instrument transactions. Some entities may take positions in financial instruments to assume and benefit from risk while other

entities may use financial instruments to reduce certain risks by hedging or managing exposures. This Guidance Statement is relevant to all of these situations.

2. The following Australian Auditing Standards are particularly relevant to audits of financial instruments:

(a) ASA 540[1] deals with the auditor's responsibilities relating to auditing accounting estimates, including accounting estimates related to financial instruments measured at fair value;

(b) ASA 315[2] and ASA 330[3] deal with identifying and assessing risks of material misstatement and responding to those risks; and

(c) ASA 500[4] explains what constitutes audit evidence and deals with the auditor's responsibility to design and perform audit procedures to obtain sufficient appropriate audit evidence to be able to draw reasonable conclusions on which to base the auditor's opinion.

3. [Deleted by the AUASB. Refer Aus 0.1].

4. This Guidance Statement is relevant to entities of all sizes, as all entities may be subject to risks of material misstatement when using financial instruments.

5. The guidance on valuation[5] in this Guidance Statement is likely to be more relevant for financial instruments measured or disclosed at fair value, while the guidance on areas other than valuation applies equally to financial instruments either measured at fair value or amortised cost. This Guidance Statement is also applicable to both financial assets and financial liabilities. This Guidance Statement does not deal with instruments such as:

(a) The simplest financial instruments such as cash, simple loans, trade accounts receivable and trade accounts payable;

(b) Investments in unlisted equity instruments; or

(c) Insurance contracts.

6. Also, this Guidance Statement does not deal with specific accounting issues relevant to financial instruments, such as hedge accounting, profit or loss on inception (often known as "Day 1" profit or loss), offsetting, risk transfers or impairment, including loan loss provisioning. Although these subject matters can relate to an entity's accounting for financial instruments, a discussion of the auditor's consideration regarding how to address specific accounting requirements is beyond the scope of this Guidance Statement.

7. An audit in accordance with Australian Auditing Standards is conducted on the premise that management and, where appropriate, those charged with governance have acknowledged certain responsibilities. Such responsibilities subsume making fair value measurements. This Guidance Statement does not impose responsibilities on management or those charged with governance nor override laws and regulation that govern their responsibilities.

8. This Guidance Statement has been written in the context of general purpose fair presentation financial reporting frameworks, but may also be useful, as appropriate in the circumstance, in other financial reporting frameworks such as special purpose financial reporting frameworks.

Aus 8.1 Australian Accounting Standards on financial instruments include AASB 7 *Financial Instruments: Disclosures*, AASB 132 *Financial Instruments: Presentation*, AASB 139 *Financial Instruments: Recognition and Measurement*, AASB 9 *Financial Instruments* and AASB 13 *Fair Value Measurement*.

---

1 See ASA 540 *Auditing Accounting Estimates, Including Fair Value Accounting Estimates, and Related Disclosures.*

2 See ASA 315 *Identifying and Assessing the Risks of Material Misstatement through Understanding the Entity and Its Environment.*

3 See ASA 330 *The Auditor's Responses to Assessed Risks.*

4 See ASA 500 *Audit Evidence.*

5 In this Guidance Statement, the terms "valuation" and "measurement" are used interchangeably.

9. This Guidance Statement focuses on the assertions of valuation, and presentation and disclosure, but also covers, in less detail, completeness, accuracy, existence, and rights and obligations.

10. Financial instruments are susceptible to estimation uncertainty, which is defined in ASA 540 as "the susceptibility of an accounting estimate and related disclosures to an inherent lack of precision in its measurement."[6] Estimation uncertainty is affected by the complexity of financial instruments, among other factors. The nature and reliability of information available to support the measurement of financial instruments varies widely, which affects the estimation uncertainty associated with their measurement. This Guidance Statement uses the term "measurement uncertainty" to refer to the estimation uncertainty associated with fair value measurements.

Section I—Background Information about Financial Instruments

11. Different definitions of financial instruments may exist among financial reporting frameworks. For example, Australian Accounting Standards define a financial instrument as any contract that gives rise to a financial asset of one entity and a financial liability or equity instrument of another entity.[7] Financial instruments may be cash, the equity of another entity, the contractual right or obligation to receive or deliver cash or exchange financial assets or liabilities, certain contracts settled in an entity's own equity instruments, certain contracts on non-financial items, or certain contracts issued by insurers that do not meet the definition of an insurance contract. This definition encompasses a wide range of financial instruments from simple loans and deposits to complex derivatives, structured products, and some commodity contracts.

12. Financial instruments vary in complexity, though the complexity of the financial instrument can come from difference sources, such as:
    - A very high volume of individual cash flows, where a lack of homogeneity requires analysis of each one or a large number of grouped cash flows to evaluate, for example, credit risk (for example, collateralised debt obligations (CDOs)).
    - Complex formulae for determining the cash flows.
    - Uncertainty or variability of future cash flows, such as that arising from credit risk, option contracts or financial instruments with lengthy contractual terms.

    The higher the variability of cash flows to changes in market conditions, the more complex and uncertain the fair value measurement of the financial instrument is likely to be. In addition, sometimes financial instruments that, ordinarily, are relatively easy to value become complex to value because of particular circumstances, for example, instruments for which the market has become inactive or which have lengthy contractual terms. Derivatives and structured products become more complex when they are a combination of individual financial instruments. In addition, the accounting for financial instruments under certain financial reporting frameworks or certain market conditions may be complex.

13. Another source of complexity is the volume of financial instruments held or traded. While a "plain vanilla" interest rate swap may not be complex, an entity holding a large number of them may use a sophisticated information system to identify, value and transact these instruments.

Purpose and Risks of Using Financial Instruments

14. Financial instruments are used for:
    - Hedging purposes (that is, to change an existing risk profile to which an entity is exposed). This includes:
        - The forward purchase or sale of currency to fix a future exchange rate;
        - Converting future interest rates to fixed rates or floating rates through the use of swaps; and

6 See ASA 540, paragraph 7(c).

7 See Australian Accounting Standard 132 (AASB 132) *Financial Instruments: Presentation*, paragraph 11.

  - The purchase of option contracts to provide an entity with protection against a particular price movement, including contracts which may contain embedded derivatives;
- Trading purposes (for example, to enable an entity to take a risk position to benefit from short term market movements); and
- Investment purposes (for example, to enable an entity to benefit from long term investment returns).

15. The use of financial instruments can reduce exposures to certain business risks, for example changes in exchange rates, interest rates and commodity prices, or a combination of those risks. On the other hand, the inherent complexities of some financial instruments also may result in increased risk.

16. Business risk and the risk of material misstatement increase when management and those charged with governance:
    - Do not fully understand the risks of using financial instruments and have insufficient skills and experience to manage those risks;
    - Do not have the expertise to value them appropriately in accordance with the applicable financial reporting framework;
    - Do not have sufficient controls in place over financial instrument activities; or
    - Inappropriately hedge risks or speculate.

17. Management's failure to fully understand the risks inherent in a financial instrument can have a direct effect on management's ability to manage these risks appropriately, and may ultimately threaten the viability of the entity.

18. The principal types of risk applicable to financial instruments are listed below. This list is not meant to be exhaustive and different terminology may be used to describe these risks or classify the components of individual risks.

    (a) Credit (or counterparty) risk is the risk that one party to a financial instrument will cause a financial loss to another party by failing to discharge an obligation and is often associated with default. Credit risk includes settlement risk, which is the risk that one side of a transaction will be settled without consideration being received from the customer or counterparty.

    (b) Market risk is the risk that the fair value or future cash flows of a financial instrument will fluctuate because of changes in market prices. Examples of market risk include currency risk, interest rate risk, and commodity and equity price risk.

    (c) Liquidity risk includes the risk of not being able to buy or sell a financial instrument at an appropriate price in a timely manner due to a lack of marketability for that financial instrument.

    (d) Operational risk relates to the specific processing required for financial instruments. Operational risk may increase as the complexity of a financial instrument increases, and poor management of operational risk may increase other types of risk. Operational risk includes:

        (i) The risk that confirmation and reconciliation controls are inadequate resulting in incomplete or inaccurate recording of financial instruments;

        (ii) The risks that there is inappropriate documentation of transactions and insufficient monitoring of these transactions;

        (iii) The risk that transactions are incorrectly recorded, processed or risk managed and, therefore, do not reflect the economics of the overall trade;

        (iv) The risk that undue reliance is placed by staff on the accuracy of valuation techniques, without adequate review, and transactions are therefore incorrectly valued or their risk is improperly measured;

        (v) The risk that the use of financial instruments is not adequately incorporated into the entity's risk management policies and procedures;

(vi) The risk of loss resulting from inadequate or failed internal processes and systems, or from external events, including the risk of fraud from both internal and external sources;

(vii) The risk that there is inadequate or non-timely maintenance of valuation techniques used to measure financial instruments; and

(viii) Legal risk, which is a component of operational risk, and relates to losses resulting from a legal or regulatory action that invalidates or otherwise precludes performance by the end user or its counterparty under the terms of the contract or related netting arrangements. For example, legal risk could arise from insufficient or incorrect documentation for the contract, an inability to enforce a netting arrangement in bankruptcy, adverse changes in tax laws, or statutes that prohibit entities from investing in certain types of financial instruments.

19. Other considerations relevant to risks of using financial instruments include:

- The risk of fraud that may be increased if, for example, an employee in a position to perpetrate a financial fraud understands both the financial instruments and the processes for accounting for them, but management and those charged with governance have a lesser degree of understanding.
- The risk that master netting arrangements[8] may not be properly reflected in the financial report.
- The risk that some financial instruments may change between being assets or liabilities during their term and that such change may occur rapidly.

Controls Relating to Financial Instruments

20. The extent of an entity's use of financial instruments and the degree of complexity of the instruments are important determinants of the necessary level of sophistication of the entity's internal control. For example, smaller entities may use less structured products and simple processes and procedures to achieve their objectives.

21. Often, it is the role of those charged with governance to set the tone regarding, and approve and oversee the extent of use of, financial instruments while it is management's role to manage and monitor the entity's exposures to those risks. Management and, where appropriate, those charged with governance are also responsible for designing and implementing a system of internal control to enable the preparation of financial report in accordance with the applicable financial reporting framework. An entity's internal control over financial instruments is more likely to be effective when management and those charged with governance have:

(a) Established an appropriate control environment, including active participation by those charged with governance in controlling the use of financial instruments, a logical organisational structure with clear assignment of authority and responsibility, and appropriate human resource policies and procedures. In particular, clear rules are needed on the extent to which those responsible for financial instrument activities are permitted to act. Such rules have regard to any legal or regulatory restrictions on using financial instruments. For example, certain public sector entities may not have the power to conduct business using derivatives;

(b) Established a risk management process relative to the size of the entity and the complexity of its financial instruments (for example, in some entities a formal risk management function may exist);

(c) Established information systems that provide those charged with governance with an understanding of the nature of the financial instrument activities and the associated risks, including adequate documentation of transactions;

8 An entity that undertakes a number of financial instrument transactions with a single counterparty may enter into a master netting arrangement with that counterparty. Such an agreement provides for a single net settlement of all financial instruments covered by the agreement in the event of default of any one contract.

(d) Designed, implemented and documented a system of internal control to:

- ◦ Provide reasonable assurance that the entity's use of financial instruments is within its risk management policies;
- ◦ Properly present financial instruments in the financial report;
- ◦ Ensure that the entity is in compliance with applicable laws and regulations; and
- ◦ Monitor risk.

The Appendix provides examples of controls that may exist in an entity that deals in a high volume of financial instrument transactions; and

(e) Established appropriate accounting policies, including valuation policies, in accordance with the applicable financial reporting framework.

22. Key elements of risk management processes and internal control relating to an entity's financial instruments include:

- Setting an approach to define the amount of risk exposure that the entity is willing to accept when engaging in financial instrument transactions (this may be referred to as its "risk appetite"), including policies for investing in financial instruments, and the control framework in which the financial instrument activities are conducted;
- Establishing processes for the documentation and authorisation of new types of financial instrument transactions which consider the accounting, regulatory, legal, financial and operational risks that are associated with such instruments;
- Processing financial instrument transactions, including confirmation and reconciliation of cash and asset holdings to external statements, and the payments process;
- Segregation of duties between those investing or trading in the financial instruments and those responsible for processing, valuing and confirming such instruments. For example, a model development function that is involved in assisting in pricing deals is less objective than one that is functionally and organisationally separate from the front office;
- Valuation processes and controls, including controls over data obtained from third-party pricing sources; and
- Monitoring of controls.

23. The nature of risks often differs between entities with a high volume and variety of financial instruments and those with only a few financial instrument transactions. This results in different approaches to internal control. For example:

- Typically, an institution with high volumes of financial instruments will have a dealing room type environment in which there are specialist traders and segregation of duties between those traders and the back office (which refers to the operations function that data-checks trades that have been conducted, ensuring that they are not erroneous, and transacting the required transfers). In such environments, the traders will typically initiate contracts verbally over the phone or via an electronic trading platform. Capturing relevant transactions and accurately recording financial instruments in such an environment is significantly more challenging than for an entity with only a few financial instruments, whose existence and completeness often can be confirmed with a bank confirmation to a few banks.
- On the other hand, entities with only a small number of financial instruments often do not have segregation of duties, and access to the market is limited. In such cases, although it may be easier to identify financial instrument transactions, there is a risk that management may rely on a limited number of personnel, which may increase the risk that unauthorised transactions may be initiated or transactions may not be recorded.

Completeness, Accuracy, and Existence

24. Paragraphs 25–33 of this Guidance Statement describe controls and processes which may be in place in entities with a high volume of financial instrument transactions, including those with trading rooms. By contrast, an entity that does not have a high volume of financial instrument transactions may not have these controls and processes but may instead confirm their transactions with the counterparty or clearing house. Doing so may be relatively straightforward in that the entity may only transact with one or two counterparties.

Trade Confirmations and Clearing Houses

25. Generally, for transactions undertaken by financial institutions, the terms of financial instruments are documented in confirmations exchanged between counterparties and legal agreements. Clearing houses serve to monitor the exchange of confirmations by matching trades and settling them. A central clearing house is associated with an exchange and entities that clear through clearing houses typically have processes to manage the information delivered to the clearing house.

26. Not all transactions are settled through such an exchange. In many other markets there is an established practice of agreeing the terms of transactions before settlement begins. To be effective, this process needs to be run separately from those who trade the financial instruments to minimise the risk of fraud. In other markets, transactions are confirmed after settlement has begun and sometimes confirmation backlogs result in settlement beginning before all terms have been fully agreed. This presents additional risk because the transacting entities need to rely on alternative means of agreeing trades. These may include:

- Enforcing rigorous reconciliations between the records of those trading the financial instruments and those settling them (strong segregation of duties between the two are important), combined with strong supervisory controls over those trading the financial instruments to ensure the integrity of the transactions;
- Reviewing summary documentation from counterparties that highlights the key terms even if the full terms have not been agreed; and
- Thorough review of traders' profits and losses to ensure that they reconcile to what the back office has calculated.

Reconciliations with Banks and Custodians

27. Some components of financial instruments, such as bonds and shares, may be held in separate depositories. In addition, most financial instruments result in payments of cash at some point and often these cash flows begin early in the contract's life. These cash payments and receipts will pass through an entity's bank account. Regular reconciliation of the entity's records to external banks' and custodians' records enables the entity to ensure transactions are properly recorded.

28. It should be noted that not all financial instruments result in a cash flow in the early stages of the contract's life or are capable of being recorded with an exchange or custodian. Where this is the case, reconciliation processes will not identify an omitted or inaccurately recorded trade and confirmation controls are more important. Even where such a cash flow is accurately recorded in the early stages of an instrument's life, this does not ensure that all characteristics or terms of the instrument (for example, the maturity or an early termination option) have been recorded accurately.

29. In addition, cash movements may be quite small in the context of the overall size of the trade or the entity's own balance sheet and may therefore be difficult to identify. The value of reconciliations is enhanced when finance, or other back office staff, review entries in all general ledger accounts to ensure that they are valid and supportable. This process will help identify if the other side to cash entries relating to financial instruments has not been properly recorded. Reviewing suspense and clearing accounts is important regardless of the account balance, as there may be offsetting reconciling items in the account.

30. In entities with a high volume of financial instrument transactions, reconciliation and confirmation controls may be automated and, if so, adequate IT controls need to be in place

to support them. In particular, controls are needed to ensure that data is completely and accurately picked up from external sources (such as banks and custodians) and from the entity's records and is not tampered with before or during reconciliation. Controls are also needed to ensure that the criteria on which entries are matched are sufficiently restrictive to prevent inaccurate clearance of reconciling items.

Other Controls over Completeness, Accuracy, and Existence

31. The complexity inherent in some financial instruments means that it will not always be obvious how they should be recorded in the entity's systems. In such cases, management may set up control processes to monitor policies that prescribe how particular types of transactions are measured, recorded and accounted for. These policies are typically established and reviewed in advance by suitably qualified personnel who are capable of understanding the full effects of the financial instruments being booked.

32. Some transactions may be cancelled or amended after initial execution. Application of appropriate controls relating to cancellation or amendment can mitigate the risks of material misstatement due to fraud or error. In addition, an entity may have a process in place to reconfirm trades that are cancelled or amended.

33. In financial institutions with a high volume of trading, a senior employee typically reviews daily profits and losses on individual traders' books to evaluate whether they are reasonable based on the employee's knowledge of the market. Doing so may enable management to determine that particular trades were not completely or accurately recorded, or may identify fraud by a particular trader. It is important that there are transaction authorisation procedures that support the more senior review.

Valuation of Financial Instruments

Financial Reporting Requirements

34. In many financial reporting frameworks, including Australian Accounting Standards, financial instruments, including embedded derivatives, are often measured at fair value for the purpose of balance sheet presentation, calculating profit or loss, and/or disclosure. In general, the objective of fair value measurement is to arrive at the price at which an orderly transaction would take place between market participants at the measurement date under current market conditions; that is, it is not the transaction price for a forced liquidation or distressed sale. In meeting this objective, all relevant available market information is taken into account.

35. Fair value measurements of financial assets and financial liabilities may arise both at the initial recording of transactions and later when there are changes in value. Changes in fair value measurements that occur over time may be treated in different ways under different financial reporting frameworks. For example, such changes may be recorded as profit or loss, or may be recorded in the other comprehensive income. Also, depending on the applicable financial reporting framework, the whole financial instrument or only a component of it (for example, an embedded derivative when it is separately accounted for) may be required to be measured at fair value.

36. Some financial reporting frameworks, for example, Australian Accounting Standards, establish a fair value hierarchy to develop increased consistency and comparability in fair value measurements and related disclosures. The inputs may be classified into different levels such as:

- Level 1 inputs—Quoted prices (unadjusted) in active markets for identical financial assets or financial liabilities that the entity can access at the measurement date.
- Level 2 inputs—Inputs other than quoted prices included within level 1 that are observable for the financial asset or financial liability, either directly or indirectly. If the financial asset or financial liability has a specified (contractual) term, a level 2 input must be observable for substantially the full term of the financial asset or financial liability. Level 2 inputs include the following:
    - Quoted prices for similar financial assets or financial liabilities in active markets.

- ◦ Quoted prices for identical or similar financial assets or financial liabilities in markets that are not active.
- ◦ Inputs other than quoted prices that are observable for the financial asset or financial liability (for example, interest rates and yield curves observable at commonly quoted intervals, implied volatilities and credit spreads).
- ◦ Inputs that are derived principally from, or corroborated by, observable market data by correlation or other means (market-corroborated inputs).

- Level 3 inputs—Unobservable inputs for the financial asset or financial liability. Unobservable inputs are used to measure fair value to the extent that relevant observable inputs are not available, thereby allowing for situations in which there is little, if any, market activity for the financial asset or financial liability at the measurement date.

In general, measurement uncertainty increases as a financial instrument moves from level 1 to level 2, or level 2 to level 3. Also, within level 2 there may be a wide range of measurement uncertainty depending on the observability of inputs, the complexity of the financial instrument, its valuation, and other factors.

37. Australian Accounting Standards may require or permit the entity to adjust for measurement uncertainties, in order to adjust for risks that a market participant would make in the pricing to take account of the uncertainties of the risks associated with the pricing or cash flows of the financial instrument. For example:

- Model adjustments. Some models may have a known deficiency or the result of calibration may highlight the deficiency for the fair value measurement in accordance with the financial reporting framework.
- Credit-risk adjustments. Some models do not take into account credit risk, including counterparty risk or own credit risk.
- Liquidity adjustments. Some models calculate a mid-market price, even though the financial reporting framework may require use of a liquidity adjusted amount such as a bid/offer spread. Another, more judgemental, liquidity adjustment recognises that some financial instruments are illiquid which affects the valuation.
- Other risk adjustments. A value measured using a model that does not take into account all other factors that market participants would consider in pricing the financial instrument may not represent fair value on the measurement date, and therefore may need to be adjusted separately to comply with the applicable financial reporting framework.

Adjustments are not appropriate if they adjust the measurement and valuation of the financial instrument away from fair value as defined by the applicable financial reporting framework, for example for conservatism.

Observable and Unobservable Inputs

38. As mentioned above, financial reporting frameworks often categorise inputs according to the degree of observability. As activity in a market for financial instruments declines and the observability of inputs declines, measurement uncertainty increases. The nature and reliability of information available to support valuation of financial instruments varies depending on the observability of inputs to its measurement, which is influenced by the nature of the market (for example, the level of market activity and whether it is through an exchange or over-the-counter (OTC)). Accordingly, there is a continuum of the nature and reliability of evidence used to support valuation, and it becomes more difficult for management to obtain information to support a valuation when markets become inactive and inputs become less observable.

39. When observable inputs are not available, an entity uses unobservable inputs (level 3 inputs) that reflect the assumption that market participants would use when pricing the financial asset or the financial liability, including assumptions about risk. Unobservable inputs are developed using the best information available in the circumstances. In developing unobservable inputs, an entity may begin with its own data, which is adjusted if reasonably available information indicates that (a) other market participants would use different

GS

data or (b) there is something particular to the entity that is not available to other market participants (for example, an entity-specific synergy).

Effects of Inactive Markets

40. Measurement uncertainty increases and valuation is more complicated when the markets in which financial instruments or their component parts are traded become inactive. There is no clear point at which an active market becomes inactive, though financial reporting frameworks, including Australian Accounting Standards, may provide guidance on this issue. Characteristics of an inactive market include a significant decline in the volume and level of trading activity, available prices vary significantly over time or among market participants or the prices are not current. However, assessing whether a market is inactive requires judgement.

41. When markets are inactive, prices quoted may be stale (that is, out of date), may not represent prices at which market participants may trade or may represent forced transactions (such as when a seller is required to sell an asset to meet regulatory or legal requirements, needs to dispose of an asset immediately to create liquidity or the existence of a single potential buyer as a result of the legal or time restrictions imposed). Accordingly, valuations are developed based on level 2 and level 3 inputs. Under such circumstances, entities may have:

- A valuation policy that includes a process for determining whether level 1 inputs are available;
- An understanding of how particular prices or inputs from external sources used as inputs to valuation techniques were calculated in order to assess their reliability. For example, in an active market, a broker quote on a financial instrument that has not traded is likely to reflect actual transactions on a similar financial instrument, but, as the market becomes less active, the broker quote may rely more on proprietary valuation techniques to determine prices;
- An understanding of how deteriorating business conditions affect the counterparty, as well as whether deteriorating business conditions in entities similar to the counterparty may indicate that the counterparty may not fulfil its obligations (that is, non-performance risk);
- Policies for adjusting for measurement uncertainties. Such adjustments can include model adjustments, lack of liquidity adjustments, credit risk adjustments, and other risk adjustments;
- The capability to calculate the range of realistic outcomes given the uncertainties involved, for example by performing a sensitivity analysis; and
- Policies for identifying when a fair value measurement input moves to a different level of the fair value hierarchy.

42. Particular difficulties may develop where there is severe curtailment or even cessation of trading in particular financial instruments. In these circumstances, financial instruments that have previously been valued using market prices may need to be valued using a model.

Management's Valuation Process

43. Techniques that management may use to value their financial instruments include observable prices, recent transactions, and models that use observable or unobservable inputs. Management may also make use of:

(a) A third-party pricing source, such as a pricing service or broker quote; or

(b) A valuation expert.

Third-party pricing sources and valuation experts may use one or more of these valuation techniques.

44. In many financial reporting frameworks, including Australian Accounting Standards, the best evidence of a financial instrument's fair value is found in contemporaneous transactions in an active market (that is, level 1 inputs). In such cases, the valuation of a financial instrument may be relatively simple. Quoted prices for financial instruments

that are listed on exchanges or traded in liquid over-the-counter markets may be available from sources such as financial publications, the exchanges themselves or third-party pricing sources. When using quoted prices, it is important that management understand the basis on which the quote is given to ensure that the price reflects market conditions at the measurement date. Quoted prices obtained from publications or exchanges may provide sufficient evidence of fair value when, for example:

(a) The prices are not out of date or "stale" (for example, if the quote is based on the last traded price and the trade occurred some time ago); and

(b) The quotes are prices at which dealers would actually trade the financial instrument with sufficient frequency and volume.

45. Where there is no current observable market price for the financial instrument (that is, a level 1 input), it will be necessary for the entity to gather other price indicators to use in a valuation technique to value the financial instrument. Price indicators may include:

- Recent transactions, including transactions after the date of the financial statements in the same instrument. Consideration is given to whether an adjustment needs to be made for changes in market conditions between the measurement date and the date the transaction was made, as these transactions are not necessarily indicative of the market conditions that existed at the date of the financial statements. In addition it is possible that the transaction represents a forced transaction and is therefore not indicative of a price in an orderly trade.
- Current or recent transactions in similar instruments, often known as "proxy pricing." Adjustments will need to be made to the price of the proxy to reflect the differences between them and the instrument being priced, for example, to take account of differences in liquidity or credit risk between the two instruments.
- Indices for similar instruments. As with transactions in similar instruments, adjustments will need to be made to reflect the difference between the instrument being priced and the instrument(s) from which the index used is derived.

46. It is expected that management will document its valuation policies and model used to value a particular financial instrument, including the rationale for the model(s) used, the selection of assumptions in the valuation methodology, and the entity's consideration of whether adjustments for measurement uncertainty are necessary.

Models

47. Models may be used to value financial instruments when the price cannot be directly observed in the market. Models can be as simple as a commonly used bond pricing formula or involve complex, specifically developed software tools to value financial instruments with level 3 inputs. Many models are based on discounted cash flow calculations.

48. Models comprise a methodology, assumptions and data. The methodology describes rules or principles governing the relationship between the variables in the valuation. Assumptions include estimates of uncertain variables which are used in the model. Data may comprise actual or hypothetical information about the financial instrument, or other inputs to the financial instrument.

49. Depending on the circumstances, matters that the entity may address when establishing or validating a model for a financial instrument include whether:

- The model is validated prior to usage, with periodic reviews to ensure it is still suitable for its intended use. The entity's validation process may include evaluation of:
  - The methodology's theoretical soundness and mathematical integrity, including the appropriateness of parameters and sensitivities.
  - The consistency and completeness of the model's inputs with market practices, and whether the appropriate inputs are available for use in the model.
- There are appropriate change control policies, procedures and security controls over the model.

GS

- The model is appropriately changed or adjusted on a timely basis for changes in market conditions.
- The model is periodically calibrated, reviewed and tested for validity by a separate and objective function. Doing so is a means of ensuring that the model's output is a fair representation of the value that marketplace participants would ascribe to a financial instrument.
- The model maximises the use of relevant observable inputs and minimises the use of unobservable inputs.
- Adjustments are made to the output of the model to reflect the assumptions marketplace participants would use in similar circumstances.
- The model is adequately documented, including the model's intended applications and limitations and its key parameters, required data, results of any validation analysis performed and any adjustments made to the output of the model.

An Example of a Common Financial Instrument

50. The following describes how models may be applied to value a common financial instrument, known as an asset backed security.[9] Because asset backed securities are often valued based on level 2 or 3 inputs, they are frequently valued using models and involve:
    - Understanding the type of security—considering (a) the underlying collateral; and (b) the terms of the security. The underlying collateral is used to estimate the timing and amounts of cash flows such as mortgage or credit card interest and principal payments.
    - Understanding the terms of the security—this includes evaluating contractual cash flow rights, such as the order of repayment, and any default events. The order of repayment, often known as seniority, refers to terms which require that some classes of security holders (senior debt) are repaid before others (subordinated debt). The rights of each class of security holder to the cash flows, frequently referred to as the cash flow "waterfall," together with assumptions of the timing and amount of cash flows are used to derive a set of estimated cash flows for each class of security holder. The expected cash flows are then discounted to derive an estimated fair value.

51. The cash flows of an asset backed security may be affected by prepayments of the underlying collateral and by potential default risk and resulting estimated loss severities. Prepayment assumptions, if applicable, are generally based on evaluating market interest rates for similar collateral to the rates on the collateral underlying the security. For example, if market interest rates for mortgages have declined then the underlying mortgages in a security may experience higher prepayment rates than originally expected. Estimating potential default and loss severity involves close evaluation of the underlying collateral and borrowers to estimate default rates. For example, when the underlying collateral comprises residential mortgages, loss severities may be affected by estimates of residential housing prices over the term of the security.

Third-Party Pricing Sources

52. Entities may use third-party pricing sources in order to obtain fair value information. The preparation of an entity's financial statements, including the valuation of financial instruments and the preparation of financial statement disclosures relating to these instruments, may require expertise that management does not possess. Entities may not be able to develop appropriate valuation techniques, including models that may be used in a valuation, and may use a third-party pricing source to arrive at a valuation or to provide disclosures for the financial statements. This may particularly be the case in smaller entities or in entities that do not engage in a high volume of financial instruments transactions (for example, non-financial institutions with treasury departments). Even though management has used a third-party pricing source, management is ultimately responsible for the valuation.

9 An asset backed security is a financial instrument which is backed by a pool of underlying assets (known as the collateral, such as credit card receivables or vehicle loans) and derives value and income from those underlying assets.

53. Third-party pricing sources may also be used because the volume of securities to price over a short timeframe may not be possible by the entity. This is often the case for traded investment funds that must determine a net asset value each day. In other cases, management may have their own pricing process but use third-party pricing sources to corroborate their own valuations.

54. For one or more of these reasons most entities use third-party pricing sources when valuing securities either as a primary source or as a source of corroboration for their own valuations. Third-party pricing sources generally fall into the following categories:

- Pricing services, including consensus pricing services; and
- Brokers proving broker quotes.

Pricing services

55. Pricing services provide entities with prices and price-related data for a variety of financial instruments, often performing daily valuations of large numbers of financial instruments. These valuations may be made by collecting market data and prices from a wide variety of sources, including market makers, and, in certain instances, using internal valuations techniques to derive estimated fair values. Pricing services may combine a number of approaches to arrive at a price. Pricing services are often used as a source of prices based on level 2 inputs. Pricing services may have strong controls around how prices are developed and their customers often include a wide variety of parties, including buy and sell side investors, back and middle office functions, auditors and others.

56. Pricing services often have a formalised process for customers to challenge the prices received from the pricing services. These challenge processes usually require the customer to provide evidence to support an alternative price, with challenges categorised based on the quality of evidence provided. For example, a challenge based on a recent sale of that instrument that the pricing service was not aware of may be upheld, whereas a challenge based on a customer's own valuation technique may be more heavily scrutinised. In this way, a pricing service with a large number of leading participants, both buy and sell side, may be able to constantly correct prices to more fully reflect the information available to market participants.

Consensus pricing services

57. Some entities may use pricing data from consensus pricing services which differ from other pricing services. Consensus pricing services obtain pricing information about an instrument from several participating entities (subscribers). Each subscriber submits prices to the pricing service. The pricing service treats this information confidentially and returns to each subscriber the consensus price, which is usually an arithmetical average of the data after a data cleansing routine has been employed to eliminate outliers. For some markets, such as for exotic derivatives, consensus prices might constitute the best available data. However, many factors are considered when assessing the representational faithfulness of the consensus prices including, for example:

- Whether the prices submitted by the subscribers reflect actual transactions or just indicative prices based on their own valuation techniques.
- The number of sources from which prices have been obtained.
- The quality of the sources used by the consensus pricing service.
- Whether participants include leading market participants.

58. Typically consensus prices are only available to subscribers who have submitted their own prices to the service. Accordingly not all entities will have direct access to consensus prices. Because a subscriber generally cannot know how the prices submitted were estimated, other sources of evidence in addition to information from consensus pricing services may be needed for management to support their valuation. In particular, this may be the case if the sources are providing indicative prices based on their own valuation techniques and management is unable to obtain an understanding of how these sources calculated their prices.

Brokers providing broker quotes

59. As brokers provide quotes only as an incidental service for their clients, quotes they provide differ in many respects from prices obtained in pricing services. Brokers may be unwilling to provide information about the process used to develop their quote, but may have access to information on transactions about which a pricing service may not be aware. Broker quotes may be executable or indicative. Indicative quotes are a broker's best estimate of fair value, whereas an executable quote shows that the broker is willing to transact at this price. Executable quotes are strong evidence of fair value. Indicative quotes are less so because of the lack of transparency into the methods used by the broker to establish the quote. In addition the rigour of controls over the brokers' quote often will differ depending on whether the broker also holds the same security in its own portfolio. Broker quotes are often used for securities with level 3 inputs and sometimes may be the only external information available.

Further considerations relating to third-party pricing sources

60. Understanding how the pricing sources calculated a price enables management to determine whether such information is suitable for use in its valuation, including as an input to a valuation technique and in what level of inputs the security should be categorised for disclosure purposes. For example, third-party pricing sources may value financial instruments using proprietary models, and it is important that management understands the methodology, assumptions and data used.

61. If fair value measurements obtained from third-party pricing sources are not based on the current prices of an active market, it will be necessary for management to evaluate whether the fair value measurements were derived in a manner that is consistent with the applicable financial reporting framework. Management's understanding of the fair value measurement includes:

- How the fair value measurement was determined—for example, whether the fair value measurement was determined by a valuation technique, in order to assess whether it is consistent with the fair value measurement objective;
- Whether the quotes are indicative prices, indicative spread, or binding offers; and
- How frequently the fair value measurement is estimated by the third-party pricing sources—in order to assess whether it reflects market conditions at the measurement date.

Understanding the bases on which third-party pricing sources have determined their quotes in the context of the particular financial instruments held by the entity assists management in evaluating the relevance and reliability of this evidence to support its valuations.

62. It is possible that there will be disparities between price indicators from different sources. Understanding how the price indicators were derived, and investigating these disparities, assists management in corroborating the evidence used in developing its valuation of financial instruments in order to evaluate whether the valuation is reasonable. Simply taking the average of the quotes provided, without doing further research, may not be appropriate, because one price in the range may be the most representative of fair value and this may not be the average. To evaluate whether its valuations of financial instruments are reasonable, management may:

- Consider whether actual transactions represent forced transactions rather than transactions between willing buyers and willing sellers. This may invalidate the price as a comparison;
- Analyse the expected future cash flows of the instrument. This could be performed as an indicator of the most relevant pricing data;
- Depending on the nature of what is unobservable, extrapolate from observed prices to unobserved ones (for example, there may be observed prices for maturities up to ten years but not longer, but the ten year price curve may be capable of being extrapolated beyond ten years as an indicator). Care is needed to ensure that extrapolation is not carried so far beyond the observable curve that its link to observable prices becomes too tenuous to be reliable;

- Compare prices within a portfolio of financial instruments to each other to make sure that they are consistent among similar financial instruments;
- Use more than one model to corroborate the results from each one, having regard to the data and assumptions used in each; or
- Evaluate movements in the prices for related hedging instruments and collateral.

In coming to its judgement as to its valuation, an entity may also consider other factors that may be specific to the entity's circumstances.

Use of Valuation Experts

63. Management may engage a valuation expert from an investment bank, broker, or other valuation firm to value some or all of its securities. Unlike pricing services and broker quotes, generally the methodology and data used are more readily available to management when they have engaged an expert to perform a valuation on their behalf. Even though management has engaged an expert, management is ultimately responsible for the valuation used.

Issues Related to Financial Liabilities

64. Understanding the effect of credit risk is an important aspect of valuing both financial assets and financial liabilities. This valuation reflects the credit quality and financial strength of both the issuer and any credit support providers. In some financial reporting frameworks, including Australian Accounting Standards, the measurement of a financial liability assumes that it is transferred to a market participant at the measurement date. Where there is not an observable market price for a financial liability, its value is typically measured using the same method as a counterparty would use to measure the value of the corresponding asset, unless there are factors specific to the liability (such as third-party credit enhancement). In particular, the entity's own credit risk[10] can often be difficult to measure.

Presentation and Disclosure about Financial Instruments

65. Most financial reporting frameworks, including Australian Accounting Standards, require disclosures in the financial report to enable users of the financial report to make meaningful assessments of the effects of the entity's financial instrument activities, including the risks and uncertainties associated with financial instruments.

66. Most frameworks require the disclosure of quantitative and qualitative information (including accounting policies) relating to financial instruments. The accounting requirements for fair value measurements in financial statement presentation and disclosures are extensive in most financial reporting frameworks and encompass more than just valuation of the financial instruments. For example, qualitative disclosures about financial instruments provide important contextual information about the characteristics of the financial instruments and their future cash flows that may help inform investors about the risks to which entities are exposed.

Categories of Disclosures

67. Disclosure requirements include:

    (a) Quantitative disclosures that are derived from the amounts included in the financial report—for example, categories of financial assets and liabilities;

    (b) Quantitative disclosures that require significant judgement—for example, sensitivity analysis for each type of market risk to which the entity is exposed; and

    (c) Qualitative disclosures—for example, those that describe the entity's governance over financial instruments; objectives; controls, policies and processes for managing each type of risk arising from financial instruments; and the methods used to measure the risks.

68. The more sensitive the valuation is to movements in a particular variable, the more likely it is that disclosure will be necessary to indicate the uncertainties surrounding the valuation. Certain financial reporting frameworks, including Australian Accounting Standards, may

10 Own credit risk is the amount of change in fair value that is not attributable to changes in market conditions.

also require disclosure of sensitivity analyses, including the effects of changes in assumptions used in the entity's valuation techniques. For example, the additional disclosures required for financial instruments with fair value measurements that are categorised within level 3 inputs of the fair value hierarchy are aimed at informing users of financial report about the effects of those fair value measurements that use the most subjective inputs.

69. Some financial reporting frameworks, for example, Australian Accounting Standards, require disclosure of information that enables users of the financial report to evaluate the nature and extent of the risks arising from financial instruments to which the entity is exposed at the reporting date. This disclosure may be contained in the notes to the financial statements, or in management's discussion and analysis within its annual report cross-referenced from the audited financial report. The extent of disclosure depends on the extent of the entity's exposure to risks arising from financial instruments. This includes qualitative disclosures about:

- The exposures to risk and how they arise, including the possible effects on an entity's future liquidity and collateral requirements;
- The entity's objectives, policies and processes for managing the risk and the methods used to measure the risk; and
- Any changes in exposures to risk or objectives, policies or processes for managing risk from the previous period.

Section II Audit Considerations Relating to Financial Instruments

70. Certain factors may make auditing financial instruments particularly challenging. For example:

- It may be difficult for both management and the auditor to understand the nature of financial instruments and what they are used for, and the risks to which the entity is exposed.
- Market sentiment and liquidity can change quickly, placing pressure on management to manage their exposures effectively.
- Evidence supporting valuation may be difficult to obtain.
- Individual payments associated with certain financial instruments may be significant, which may increase the risk of misappropriation of assets.
- The amounts recorded in the financial report relating to financial instruments may not be significant, but there may be significant risks and exposures associated with these financial instruments.
- A few employees may exert significant influence on the entity's financial instruments transactions, in particular where their compensation arrangements are tied to revenue from financial instruments, and there may be possible undue reliance on these individuals by others within the entity.

These factors may cause risks and relevant facts to be obscured, which may affect the auditor's assessment of the risks of material misstatement, and latent risks can emerge rapidly, especially in adverse market conditions.

Professional Scepticism[11]

71. Professional scepticism is necessary to the critical assessment of audit evidence and assists the auditor in remaining alert for possible indications of management bias. This includes questioning contradictory audit evidence and the reliability of documents, responses to inquiries and other information obtained from management and those charged with governance. It also includes being alert to conditions that may indicate possible misstatement due to error or fraud and considering the sufficiency and appropriateness of audit evidence obtained in light of the circumstances.

11 See ASA 200 *Overall Objectives of the Independent Auditor and the Conduct of an Audit in Accordance with Australian Accounting Standards*, paragraph 15.

72. Application of professional scepticism is required in all circumstances, and the need for professional scepticism increases with the complexity of financial instruments, for example with regard to:

- Evaluating whether sufficient appropriate audit evidence has been obtained, which can be particularly challenging when models are used or in determining if markets are inactive.
- Evaluating management's judgements, and the potential for management bias, in applying the entity's applicable financial reporting framework, in particular management's choice of valuation techniques, use of assumptions in valuation techniques, and addressing circumstances in which the auditor's judgements and management's judgements differ.
- Drawing conclusions based on the audit evidence obtained, for example assessing the reasonableness of valuations prepared by management's experts and evaluating whether disclosures in the financial report achieve fair presentation.

Planning Considerations[12]

73. The auditor's focus in planning the audit is particularly on:

- Understanding the accounting and disclosure requirements;
- Understanding the financial instruments to which the entity is exposed, and their purpose and risks;
- Determining whether specialised skills and knowledge are needed in the audit;
- Understanding and evaluating the system of internal control in light of the entity's financial instrument transactions and the information systems that fall within the scope of the audit;
- Understanding the nature, role and activities of the internal audit function;
- Understanding management's process for valuing financial instruments, including whether management has used an expert or a service organisation; and
- Assessing and responding to the risk of material misstatement.

Understanding the Accounting and Disclosure Requirements

74. ASA 540 requires the auditor to obtain an understanding of the requirements of the applicable financial reporting framework relevant to accounting estimates, including related disclosures and any regulatory requirements.[13] The requirements of the applicable financial reporting framework regarding financial instruments may themselves be complex and require extensive disclosures. Reading this Guidance Statement is not a substitute for a full understanding of all the requirements of the applicable financial reporting framework. For example, Australian Accounting Standards require consideration of areas such as:

- Hedge accounting;
- Accounting for "Day 1" profits or losses;
- Recognition and derecognition of financial instrument transactions;
- Own credit risk; and
- Risk transfer and derecognition, in particular where the entity has been involved in the origination and structuring of complex financial instruments.

Understanding the Financial Instruments

75. The characteristics of financial instruments may obscure certain elements of risk and exposure. Obtaining an understanding of the instruments in which the entity has invested or to which it is exposed, including the characteristics of the instruments, helps the auditor to identify whether:

12 ASA 300 *Planning an Audit of a Financial Report* deals with the auditor's responsibility to plan an audit of a financial report.

13 See ASA 540, paragraph 8(a).

- Important aspects of a transaction are missing or inaccurately recorded;
- A valuation appears appropriate;
- The risks inherent in them are fully understood and managed by the entity; and
- The financial instruments are appropriately classified into current and non-current assets and liabilities.

76. Examples of matters that the auditor may consider when obtaining an understanding of the entity's financial instruments include:
    - To which types of financial instruments the entity is exposed.
    - The use to which they are put.
    - Management's and, where appropriate, those charged with governance's understanding of the financial instruments, their use and the accounting requirements.
    - Their exact terms and characteristics so that their implications can be fully understood and, in particular where transactions are linked, the overall impact of the financial instrument transactions.
    - How they fit into the entity's overall risk management strategy.

    Inquiries of the internal audit function and the risk management function, if such functions exist, and discussions with those charged with governance may inform the auditor's understanding.

77. In some cases, a contract, including a contract for a non-financial instrument may contain a derivative. Some financial reporting frameworks, including Australian Accounting Standards, permit or require such "embedded" derivatives to be separated from the host contract in some circumstances. Understanding management's process for identifying, and accounting for, embedded derivatives will assist the auditor in understanding the risks to which the entity is exposed.

Using Those with Specialised Skills and Knowledge in the Audit[14]

78. A key consideration in audits involving financial instruments, particularly complex financial instruments, is the competence of the auditor. ASA 220[15] requires the engagement partner to be satisfied that the engagement team, and any auditor's experts who are not part of the engagement team, collectively have the appropriate competence and capabilities to perform the audit engagement in accordance with professional standards and applicable legal and regulatory requirements and to enable an auditor's report that is appropriate in the circumstances to be issued. Further, relevant ethical requirements[16] require the auditor to determine whether acceptance of the engagement would create any threats to compliance with the fundamental principles, including the professional competence and due care. Paragraph 79 below provides examples of the types of matters that may be relevant to the auditor's considerations in the context of financial instruments.

79. Accordingly, auditing financial instruments may require the involvement of one or more experts or specialists, for example, in the areas of:
    - Understanding the financial instruments used by the entity and their characteristics, including their level of complexity. Using specialised skills and knowledge may be needed in checking whether all aspects of the financial instrument and related considerations have been captured in the financial statements, and evaluating whether

14 When such a person's expertise is in auditing and accounting, regardless of whether the person is from within or external to the firm, this person is considered to be part of the engagement team and is subject to the requirements of ASA 220 *Quality Control for an Audit of a Financial Report and Other Historical Financial Information.* When such a person's expertise is in a field other than accounting or auditing, such person is considered to be an auditor's expert and the provisions of ASA 620 *Using the Work of an Auditor's Expert* apply. ASA 620 explains that distinguishing between specialised areas of accounting or auditing, and expertise in another field, will be a matter of professional judgement, but notes the distinction may be made between expertise in methods of accounting for financial instruments (accounting and auditing expertise) and expertise in complex valuation techniques for financial instruments (expertise in a field other than accounting or auditing).

15 See ASA 220, paragraph 14.

16 See ASA 102 *Compliance with Ethical Requirements when Performing Audits, Reviews and Other Assurance Engagements.*

adequate disclosure in accordance with the applicable financial reporting framework has been made where disclosure of risks is required.

- Understanding the applicable financial reporting framework, especially when there are areas known to be subject to differing interpretations, or practice is inconsistent or developing.
- Understanding the legal, regulatory, and tax implications resulting from the financial instruments, including whether the contracts are enforceable by the entity (for example, reviewing the underlying contracts), may require specialised skills and knowledge.
- Assessing the risks inherent in a financial instrument.
- Assisting the engagement team gather evidence to support management's valuations or to develop a point estimate or range, especially when fair value is determined by a complex model; when markets are inactive and data and assumptions are difficult to obtain; when unobservable inputs are used; or when management has used an expert.
- Evaluating information technology controls, especially in entities with a high volume of financial instruments. In such entities information technology may be highly complex, for example when significant information about those financial instruments is transmitted, processed, maintained or accessed electronically. In addition, it may include relevant services provided by a service organisation.

80. The nature and use of particular types of financial instruments, the complexities associated with accounting requirements, and market conditions may lead to a need for the engagement team to consult[17] with other accounting and audit professionals, from within or outside the firm, with relevant technical accounting or auditing expertise and experience, taking into account factors such as:

- The capabilities and competence of the engagement team, including the experience of the members of the engagement team.
- The attributes of the financial instruments used by the entity.
- The identification of unusual circumstances or risks in the engagement, as well as the need for professional judgement, particularly with respect to materiality and significant risks.
- Market conditions.

Understanding Internal Control

81. ASA 315 establishes requirements for the auditor to understand the entity and its environment, including its internal control. Obtaining an understanding of the entity and its environment, including the entity's internal control, is a continuous, dynamic process of gathering, updating and analysing information throughout the audit. The understanding obtained enables the auditor to identify and assess the risks of material misstatement at the financial statement and assertion levels, thereby providing a basis for designing and implementing responses to the assessed risks of material misstatement. The volume and variety of the financial instrument transactions of an entity typically determines the nature and extent of controls that may exist at an entity. An understanding of how financial instruments are monitored and controlled assists the auditor in determining the nature, timing and extent of audit procedures. The Appendix describes controls that may exist in an entity that deals in a high volume of financial instrument transactions.

Understanding the Nature, Role and Activities of the Internal Audit Function

82. In many large entities, the internal audit function may perform work that enables senior management and those charged with governance to review and evaluate the entity's controls relating to the use of financial instruments. The internal audit function may assist in

---

17 ASA 220, paragraph 18(b), requires the engagement partner to be satisfied that members of the engagement team have undertaken appropriate consultation during the course of the engagement, both within the engagement team and between the engagement team and others at the appropriate level within or outside the firm.

identifying the risks of material misstatement due to fraud or error. However, the knowledge and skills required of an internal audit function to understand and perform procedures to provide assurance to management or those charged with governance on the entity's use of financial instruments are generally quite different from those needed for other parts of the business. The extent to which the internal audit function has the knowledge and skill to cover, and has in fact covered, the entity's financial instrument activities, as well as the competence and objectivity of the internal audit function, is a relevant consideration in the external auditor's determination of whether the internal audit function is likely to be relevant to the overall audit strategy and audit plan.

83. Areas where the work of the internal audit function may be particularly relevant are:[18]

- Developing a general overview of the extent of use of financial instruments;
- Evaluating the appropriateness of policies and procedures and management's compliance with them;
- Evaluating the operating effectiveness of financial instrument control activities;
- Evaluating systems relevant to financial instrument activities; and
- Assessing whether new risks relating to financial instruments are identified, assessed and managed.

Understanding Management's Methodology for Valuing Financial Instruments

84. Management's responsibility for the preparation of the financial report includes applying the requirements of the applicable financial reporting framework to the valuation of financial instruments. ASA 540 requires the auditor to obtain an understanding of how management makes accounting estimates and the data on which accounting estimates are based.[19] Management's approach to valuation also takes into account the selection of an appropriate valuation methodology and the level of the evidence expected to be available. To meet the objective of a fair value measurement, an entity develops a valuation methodology to measure the fair value of financial instruments that considers all relevant market information that is available. A thorough understanding of the financial instrument being valued allows an entity to identify and evaluate the relevant market information available about identical or similar instruments that should be incorporated into the valuation methodology.

Assessing and Responding to the Risks of Material Misstatement

Overall Considerations Relating to Financial Instruments

85. ASA 540[20] explains that the degree of estimation uncertainty affects the risk of material misstatement of accounting estimates. The use of more complex financial instruments, such as those that have a high level of uncertainty and variability of future cash flows, may lead to an increased risk of material misstatement, particularly regarding valuation. Other matters affecting the risk of material misstatement include:

- The volume of financial instruments to which the entity is exposed.
- The terms of the financial instrument, including whether the financial instrument itself includes other financial instruments.
- The nature of the financial instruments.

18 Work performed by functions such as the risk management function, model review functions, and product control, may also be relevant.

19 See ASA 540, paragraph 8(c).

20 See ASA 540, paragraph 2.

Fraud Risk Factors[21]

86. Incentives for fraudulent financial reporting by employees may exist where compensation schemes are dependent on returns made from the use of financial instruments. Understanding how an entity's compensation policies interact with its risk appetite, and the incentives that this may create for its management and traders, may be important in assessing the risk of fraud.

87. Difficult financial market conditions may give rise to increased incentives for management or employees to engage in fraudulent financial reporting: to protect personal bonuses, to hide employee or management fraud or error, to avoid breaching regulatory, liquidity or borrowing limits or to avoid reporting losses. For example, at times of market instability, unexpected losses may arise from extreme fluctuations in market prices, from unanticipated weakness in asset prices, through trading misjudgements, or for other reasons. In addition, financing difficulties create pressures on management concerned about the solvency of the business.

88. Misappropriation of assets and fraudulent financial reporting may often involve override of controls that otherwise may appear to be operating effectively. This may include override of controls over data, assumptions and detailed process controls that allow losses and theft to be hidden. For example, difficult market conditions may increase pressure to conceal or offset trades as they attempt to recover losses.

Assessing the Risk of Material Misstatement

89. The auditor's assessment of the identified risks at the assertion level in accordance with ASA 315 includes evaluating the design and implementation of internal control. It provides a basis for considering the appropriate audit approach for designing and performing further audit procedures in accordance with ASA 330, including both substantive procedures and tests of controls. The approach taken is influenced by the auditor's understanding of internal control relevant to the audit, including the strength of the control environment and any risk management function, the size and complexity of the entity's operations and whether the auditor's assessment of the risks of material misstatement include an expectation that controls are operating effectively.

90. The auditor's assessment of the risk of material misstatement at the assertion level may change during the course of the audit as additional information is obtained. Remaining alert during the audit, for example, when inspecting records or documents may assist the auditor in identifying arrangements or other information that may indicate the existence of financial instruments that management has not previously identified or disclosed to the auditor. Such records and documents may include, for example:

- Minutes of meetings of those charged with governance; and
- Specific invoices from, and correspondence with, the entity's professional advisors.

Factors to Consider in Determining Whether, and to What Extent, to Test the Operating Effectiveness of Controls

91. An expectation that controls are operating effectively may be more common when dealing with a financial institution with well-established controls, and therefore controls testing may be an effective means of obtaining audit evidence. When an entity has a trading function, substantive tests alone may not provide sufficient appropriate audit evidence due to the volume of contracts and the different systems used. Tests of controls, however, will not be sufficient on their own as the auditor is required by ASA 330 to design and perform substantive procedures for each material class of transactions, account balance and disclosure.[22]

GS

21 See ASA 240 *The Auditor's Responsibilities Relating to Fraud in an Audit of a Financial Report* for requirements and guidance dealing with fraud risk factors.

22 See ASA 330, paragraph 18.

92. Entities with a high volume of trading and use of financial instruments may have more sophisticated controls, and an effective risk management function, and therefore the auditor may be more likely to test controls in obtaining evidence about:

- The occurrence, completeness, accuracy, and cut-off of the transactions; and
- The existence, rights and obligations, and completeness of account balances.

93. In those entities with relatively few financial instrument transactions:

- Management and those charged with governance may have only a limited understanding of financial instruments and how they affect the business;
- The entity may only have a few different types of instruments with little or no interaction between them;
- There is unlikely to be a complex control environment (for example, the controls described in the Appendix may not be in place at the entity);
- Management may use pricing information from third-party pricing sources to value their instruments; and
- Controls over the use of pricing information from third-party pricing sources may be less sophisticated.

94. When an entity has relatively few transactions involving financial instruments, it may be relatively easy for the auditor to obtain an understanding of the entity's objectives for using the financial instruments and the characteristics of the instruments. In such circumstances, much of the audit evidence is likely to be substantive in nature, the auditor may perform the majority of the audit work at year-end, and third-party confirmations are likely to provide evidence in relation to the completeness, accuracy, and existence of the transactions.

95. In reaching a decision on the nature, timing and extent of testing of controls, the auditor may consider factors such as:

- The nature, frequency and volume of financial instrument transactions;
- The strength of controls, including whether controls are appropriately designed to respond to the risks associated with an entity's volume of financial instrument transactions and whether there is a governance framework over the entity's financial instrument activities;
- The importance of particular controls to the overall control objectives and processes in place at the entity, including the sophistication of the information systems to support financial instrument transactions;
- The monitoring of controls and identified deficiencies in control procedures;
- The issues the controls are intended to address, for example, controls related to the exercise of judgements compared with controls over supporting data. Substantive tests are more likely to be effective than relying on controls related to the exercise of judgement;
- The competency of those involved in the control activities, for example whether the entity has adequate capacity, including during periods of stress, and ability to establish and verify valuations for the financial instruments to which it is exposed;
- The frequency of performance of these control activities;
- The level of precision the controls are intended to achieve;
- The evidence of performance of control activities; and
- The timing of key financial instrument transactions, for example, whether they are close to the period end.

Substantive Procedures

96. Designing substantive procedures includes consideration of:
- The use of analytical procedures[23]—While analytical procedures undertaken by the auditor can be effective as risk assessment procedures to provide the auditor with information about an entity's business, they may be less effective as substantive procedures when performed alone. This is because the complex interplay of the drivers of the valuation often masks any unusual trends that might arise.
- Non-routine transactions—Many financial transactions are negotiated contracts between an entity and its counterparty (often known as "over the counter" or OTC.) To the extent that financial instrument transactions are not routine and outside an entity's normal activities, a substantive audit approach may be the most effective means of achieving the planned audit objectives. In instances where financial instrument transactions are not undertaken routinely, the auditor's responses to assessed risk, including designing and performing audit procedures, have regard to the entity's possible lack of experience in this area.
- Availability of evidence—For example, when the entity uses a third-party pricing source, evidence concerning the relevant financial statement assertions may not be available from the entity.
- Procedures performed in other audit areas—Procedures performed in other financial statement areas may provide evidence about the completeness of financial instrument transactions. These procedures may include tests of subsequent cash receipts and payments, and the search for unrecorded liabilities.
- Selection of items for testing—In some cases, the financial instrument portfolio will comprise instruments with varying complexity and risk. In such cases, judgemental sampling may be useful.

97. For example, in the case of an asset-backed security, in responding to the risks of material misstatement for such a security, the auditor may consider performing some of the following audit procedures:
- Examining contractual documentation to understand the terms of the security, the underlying collateral and the rights of each class of security holder.
- Enquiring about management's process of estimating cash flows.
- Evaluating the reasonableness of assumptions, such as prepayment rates, default rates and loss severities.
- Obtaining an understanding of the method used to determine the cash flow waterfall.
- Comparing the results of the fair value measurement with the valuations of other securities with similar underlying collateral and terms.
- Reperforming calculations.

Dual-Purpose Tests

98. Although the purpose of a test of controls is different from the purpose of a test of details, it may be efficient to perform both at the same time by, for example:
- Performing a test of controls and a test of details on the same transaction (for example, testing whether a signed contract has been maintained and whether the details of the financial instrument have been appropriately captured in a summary sheet; or
- Testing controls when testing management's process of making valuation estimates.

GS

23 ASA 315, paragraph 6(b), requires the auditor to apply analytical procedures as risk assessment procedures to assist in assessing the risks of material misstatement in order to provide a basis for designing and implementing responses to the assessed risks. ASA 520 *Analytical Procedures*, paragraph 6, requires the auditor to use analytical procedures in forming an overall conclusion on the financial report. Analytical procedures may also be applied at other stages of the audit.

Timing of the Auditor's Procedures[24]

99. After assessing the risks associated with financial instruments, the engagement team determines the timing of planned tests of controls and substantive audit procedures. The timing of planned audit procedures varies depending on a number of factors, including the frequency of the control operation, the significance of the activity being controlled, and the related risk of material misstatement.

100. While it is necessary to undertake most of the audit procedures in relation to valuation and presentation at the period end, audit procedures in relation to other assertions such as completeness and existence can usefully be tested at an interim period. For example tests of controls may be performed at an interim period for more routine controls, such as IT controls and authorisations for new products. Also, it may be effective to test the operating effectiveness of controls over new product approval by gathering evidence of the appropriate level of management sign-off on a new financial instrument for an interim period.

101. Auditors may perform some tests on models as of an interim date, for example, by comparing the output of the model to market transactions. Another possible interim procedure for instruments with observable inputs is to test the reasonableness of the pricing information provided by a third-party pricing source.

102. Areas of more significant judgement are often tested close to, or at, the period end as:

- Valuations can change significantly in a short period of time, making it difficult to compare and reconcile interim balances with comparable information at the balance sheet date;
- An entity may engage in an increased volume of financial instrument transactions between an interim period and year-end;
- Manual journal entries may only be made after the end of the accounting period; and
- Non-routine or significant transactions may take place late in the accounting period.

Procedures Relating to Completeness, Accuracy, Existence, Occurrence and Rights and Obligations

103. Many of the auditor's procedures can be used to address a number of assertions. For example, procedures to address the existence of an account balance at period end will also address the occurrence of a class of transactions, and may also assist in establishing proper cut-off. This is because financial instruments arise from legal contracts and, by verifying the accuracy of the recording of the transaction, the auditor can also verify its existence, and obtain evidence to support the occurrence and rights and obligations assertions at the same time, and confirm that transactions are recorded in the correct accounting period.

104. Procedures that may provide audit evidence to support the completeness, accuracy, and existence assertions include:

- External confirmation[25] of bank accounts, trades, and custodian statements. This can be done by direct confirmation with the counterparty (including the use of bank confirmations), where a reply is sent to the auditor directly. Alternatively this information may be obtained from the counterparty's systems through a data feed. Where this is done, controls to prevent tampering with the computer systems through which the information is transmitted may be considered by the auditor in evaluating the reliability of the evidence from the confirmation. If confirmations are not received, the auditor may be able to obtain evidence by reviewing contracts and testing relevant controls. External confirmations, however, often do not provide

---

24 Paragraphs 11–12 and 22–23 of ASA 330 establish requirements when the auditor performs procedures at an interim period and explains how such audit evidence can be used.

25 ASA 505 *External Confirmations* deals with the auditor's use of external confirmation procedures to obtain audit evidence in accordance with the requirements of ASA 330 and ASA 500. See also Guidance Statement GS 016 *Bank Confirmation Requests* and the Staff Audit Practice Alert *Emerging Practice Issues Regarding the Use of External Confirmations in an Audit of Financial Statements* issued by the staff of the International Auditing and Assurance Standards Board in November 2009.

adequate audit evidence with respect to the valuation assertion though they may assist in identifying any side agreements.

- Reviewing reconciliations of statements or data feeds from custodians with the entity's own records. This may necessitate evaluating IT controls around and within automated reconciliation processes and to evaluate whether reconciling items are properly understood and resolved.
- Reviewing journal entries and the controls over the recording of such entries. This may assist in, for example:
  - Determining if entries have been made by employees other than those authorised to do so.
  - Identifying unusual or inappropriate end-of-period journal entries, which may be relevant to fraud risk.
- Reading individual contracts and reviewing supporting documentation of the entity's financial instrument transactions, including accounting records, thereby verifying existence and rights and obligations. For example, an auditor may read individual contracts associated with financial instruments and review supporting documentation, including the accounting entries made when the contract was initially recorded, and may also subsequently review accounting entries made for valuation purposes. Doing so allows the auditor to evaluate whether the complexities inherent in a transaction have been fully identified and reflected in the accounts. Legal arrangements and their associated risks need to be considered by those with suitable expertise to ensure that rights exist.
- Testing controls, for example by reperforming controls.
- Reviewing the entity's complaints management systems. Unrecorded transactions may result in the entity's failure to make a cash payment to a counterparty, and may be detected by reviewing complaints received.
- Reviewing master netting arrangements to identify unrecorded instruments.

105. These procedures are particularly important for some financial instruments, such as derivatives or guarantees. This is because they may not have a large initial investment, meaning it may be hard to identify their existence. For example, embedded derivatives are often contained in contracts for non-financial instruments which may not be included in confirmation procedures.

Valuation of Financial Instruments

Financial Reporting Requirements

106. Fair presentation financial reporting frameworks often use fair value hierarchies, for example those used in Australian Accounting Standards. This usually means that the volume and detail of the required disclosures increases as the level of measurement uncertainty increases. The distinction between the levels in the hierarchy may require judgement.

107. The auditor may find it useful to obtain an understanding of how the financial instruments relate to the fair value hierarchy. Ordinarily, the risk of material misstatement, and the level of audit procedures to be applied, increases as the level of measurement uncertainty increases. The use of level 3, and some level 2, inputs from the fair value hierarchy may be a useful guide to the level of measurement uncertainty. Level 2 inputs vary from those which are easily obtained to those which are closer to level 3 inputs. The auditor evaluates available evidence and understands both the fair value hierarchy and the risk of management bias in management's categorisation of financial instruments in the fair value hierarchy.

108. In accordance with ASA 540,[26] the auditor considers the entity's valuation policies and methodology for data and assumptions used in the valuation methodology. In many cases, the applicable financial reporting framework does not prescribe the valuation methodology.

26 See ASA 540, paragraph 8(c).

GS

When this is the case, matters that may be relevant to the auditor's understanding of how management values financial instruments include, for example:

- Whether management has a formal valuation policy and, if so, whether the valuation technique used for a financial instrument is appropriately documented in accordance with that policy;
- Which models may give rise to the greatest risk of material misstatement;
- How management considered the complexity of the valuation of the financial instrument when selecting a particular valuation technique;
- Whether there is a greater risk of material misstatement because management has internally developed a model to be used to value financial instruments or is departing from a valuation technique commonly used to value the particular financial instrument;
- Whether management made use of a third-party pricing source;
- Whether those involved in developing and applying the valuation technique have the appropriate skills and expertise to do so, including whether a management's expert has been used; and
- Whether there are indicators of management bias in selecting the valuation technique to be used.

Assessing the Risk of Material Misstatement Related to Valuation

109. When evaluating whether the valuation techniques used by an entity are appropriate in the circumstances, and whether controls over valuation techniques are in place, the factors considered by the auditor may include:

- Whether the valuation techniques are commonly used by other market participants and have been previously demonstrated to provide a reliable estimate of prices obtained from market transactions;
- Whether the valuation techniques operate as intended and there are no flaws in their design, particularly under extreme conditions, and whether they have been objectively validated. Indicators of flaws include inconsistent movements relative to benchmarks;
- Whether the valuation techniques take account of the risks inherent in the financial instrument being valued, including counterparty creditworthiness, and own credit risk in the case of valuation techniques used to measure financial liabilities;
- How the valuation techniques are calibrated to the market, including the sensitivity of the valuation techniques to changes in variables;
- Whether market variables and assumptions are used consistently and whether new conditions justify a change in the valuation techniques, market variables or assumptions used;
- Whether sensitivity analyses indicate that valuations would change significantly with only small or moderate changes in assumptions;
- The organisational structure, such as the existence of an internal department responsible for developing models to value certain instruments, particularly where level 3 inputs are involved. For example, a model development function that is involved in assisting in pricing deals is less objective than one which is functionally and organisationally segregated from the front office; and
- The competence and objectivity of those responsible for the development and application of the valuation techniques, including management's relative experience with particular models that may be newly developed.

The auditor (or auditor's expert) may also independently develop one or more valuation techniques to compare its output with that of the valuation techniques used by management.

Significant Risks

110. The auditor's risk assessment process may lead the auditor to identify one or more significant risks relating to the valuation of financial instruments, when any of the following circumstances exist:

- High measurement uncertainty related to the valuation of financial instruments (for example, those with unobservable inputs).[27]
- Lack of sufficient evidence to support management's valuation of its financial instruments.
- Lack of management understanding of its financial instruments or expertise necessary to value such instruments properly, including the ability to determine whether valuation adjustments are needed.
- Lack of management understanding of complex requirements in the applicable financial reporting framework relating to measurement and disclosure of financial instruments, and inability of management to make the judgements required to properly apply those requirements.
- The significance of valuation adjustments made to valuation technique outputs when the applicable financial reporting framework requires or permits such adjustments.

111. For accounting estimates that give rise to significant risks, in addition to other substantive procedures performed to meet the requirements of ASA 330, ASA 540[28] requires the auditor to evaluate the following:

(a) How management has considered alternative assumptions or outcomes, and why it has rejected them, or how management has otherwise addressed measurement uncertainty in making the accounting estimate;

(b) Whether the significant assumptions used by management are reasonable; and

(c) Where relevant to the reasonableness of the significant assumptions used by management, or the appropriate application of the applicable financial reporting framework, management's intent to carry out specific courses of action and its ability to do so.

112. As markets become inactive, the change in circumstances may lead to a move from valuation by market price to valuation by model, or may result in a change from one particular model to another. Reacting to changes in market conditions may be difficult if management does not have policies in place prior to their occurrence. Management may also not possess the expertise necessary to develop a model on an urgent basis, or select the valuation technique that may be appropriate in the circumstances. Even where valuation techniques have been consistently used, there is a need for management to examine the continuing appropriateness of the valuation techniques and assumptions used for determining valuation of financial instruments. Further, valuation techniques may have been selected in times where reasonable market information was available, but may not provide reasonable valuations in times of unanticipated stress.

113. The susceptibility to management bias, whether intentional or unintentional, increases with the subjectivity of the valuation and the degree of measurement uncertainty. For example, management may tend to ignore observable marketplace assumptions or data and instead use their own internally-developed model if the model yields more favourable results. Even without fraudulent intent, there may be a natural temptation to bias judgements towards the most favourable end of what may be a wide spectrum, rather than the point in the spectrum that might be considered to be most consistent with the applicable financial reporting framework. Changing the valuation technique from period to period without a clear and appropriate reason for doing so may also be an indicator of management bias. Although some form of management bias is inherent in subjective decisions relating to

GS

27 Where the auditor determines that the high estimation uncertainty related to the valuation of complex financial instruments gives rise to a significant risk, ASA 540 requires the auditor to perform substantive procedures and evaluate the adequacy of the disclosure of their estimation uncertainty. See ASA 540, paragraphs 11, 15 and 20.

28 See ASA 540, paragraph 15(a)-(b).

the valuation of financial instruments, when there is intention to mislead, management bias is fraudulent in nature.

Developing an Audit Approach

114. In testing how management values the financial instrument and in responding to the assessed risks of material misstatement in accordance with ASA 540,[29] the auditor undertakes one or more of the following procedures, taking account of the nature of the accounting estimates:

(a) Test how management made the accounting estimate and the data on which it is based (including valuation techniques used by the entity in its valuations).

(b) Test the operating effectiveness of the controls over how management made the accounting estimate, together with appropriate substantive procedures.

(c) Develop a point estimate or a range to evaluate management's point estimate.

(d) Determine whether events occurring up to the date of the auditor's report provide audit evidence regarding the accounting estimate.

Many auditors find that a combination of testing how management valued the financial instrument, and the data on which it is based, and testing the operating effectiveness of controls, will be an effective and efficient audit approach. While subsequent events may provide some evidence about the valuation of financial instruments, other factors may need to be taken into account to address any changes in market conditions subsequent to the balance sheet date.[30] If the auditor is unable to test how management made the estimate, the auditor may choose to develop a point estimate or range.

115. As described in Section I, to estimate the fair value of financial instruments management may:

- Utilise information from third-party pricing sources;
- Gather data to develop their own estimate using various techniques including models; and
- Engage an expert to develop an estimate.

Management often may use a combination of these approaches. For example, management may have their own pricing process but use third-party pricing sources to corroborate their own values.

Audit Considerations When Management Uses a Third-Party Pricing Source

116. Management may make use of a third-party pricing source, such as a pricing service or broker, in valuing the entity's financial instruments. Understanding how management uses the information and how the pricing service operates assists the auditor in determining the nature and extent of audit procedures needed.

117. The following matters may be relevant where management uses a third-party pricing source:

- *The type of third-party pricing source* – Some third-party pricing sources make more information available about their process. For example, a pricing service often provides information about their methodology, assumptions and data in valuing financial instruments at the asset class level. By contrast, brokers often provide no, or only limited, information about the inputs and assumptions used in developing the quote.
- *The nature of inputs used and the complexity of the valuation technique* – The reliability of prices from third-party pricing sources varies depending on the observability of inputs (and accordingly, the level of inputs in the fair value hierarchy), and the complexity of the methodology for valuing a specific security or asset class. For example, the reliability of a price for an equity investment actively

29 See ASA 540, paragraphs 12–14.

30 Paragraphs A63-A66 of ASA 540 provide examples of some of the factors that may be relevant.

traded in a liquid market is higher than that of a corporate bond traded in a liquid market that has not traded on the measurement date, which, in turn, is more reliable than that of an asset-backed security that is valued using a discounted cash flow model.

- *The reputation and experience of the third-party pricing source* – For example, a third-party pricing source may be experienced in a certain type of financial instrument, and be recognised as such, but may not be similarly experienced in other types of financial instruments. The auditor's past experience with the third-party pricing source may also be relevant in this regard.
- *The objectivity of the third-party pricing source* – For example, if a price obtained by management comes from a counterparty such as the broker who sold the financial instrument to the entity, or an entity with a close relationship with the entity being audited, the price may not be reliable.
- *The entity's controls over the use of third-party pricing sources* – The degree to which management has controls in place to assess the reliability of information from third-party pricing sources affects the reliability of the fair value measurement. For example, management may have controls in place to:
    - Review and approve the use of the third-party pricing source, including consideration of the reputation, experience and objectivity of the third-party pricing source.
    - Determine the completeness, relevance and accuracy of the prices and pricing-related data.
- *The third-party pricing source's controls* – The controls and processes over valuations for the asset classes of interest to the auditor. For example, a third-party pricing source may have strong controls around how prices are developed, including the use of a formalised process for customers, both buy and sell side, to challenge the prices received from the pricing service, when supported by appropriate evidence, which may enable the third-party pricing source to constantly correct prices to more fully reflect the information available to market participants.

118. Possible approaches to gathering evidence regarding information from third-party pricing sources may include the following:

- For level 1 inputs, comparing the information from third-party pricing sources with observable market prices.
- Reviewing disclosures provided by third-party pricing sources about their controls and processes, valuation techniques, inputs and assumptions.
- Testing the controls management has in place to assess the reliability of information from third-party pricing sources.
- Performing procedures at the third-party pricing source to understand and test the controls and processes, valuation techniques, inputs and assumptions used for asset classes or specific financial instruments of interest.
- Evaluating whether the prices obtained from third-party pricing sources are reasonable in relation to prices from other third-party pricing sources, the entity's estimate or the auditor's own estimate.
- Evaluating the reasonableness of valuation techniques, assumptions and inputs.
- Developing a point estimate or a range for some financial instruments priced by the third-party pricing source and evaluating whether the results are within a reasonable range of each other.
- Obtaining a service auditor's report that covers the controls over validation of the prices.[31]

31 Some pricing services may provide reports for users of its data to explain their controls over pricing data, that is, a report prepared in accordance with ASAE 3402 *Assurance Reports on Controls at a Service Organisation*. Management may request, and the auditor may consider obtaining, such a report to develop an understanding of how the pricing data is prepared and evaluate whether the controls at the pricing service can be relied upon.

GS

119. Obtaining prices from multiple third-party pricing sources may also provide useful information about measurement uncertainty. A wide range of prices may indicate higher measurement uncertainty and may suggest that the financial instrument is sensitive to small changes in data and assumptions. A narrow range may indicate lower measurement uncertainty and may suggest less sensitivity to changes in data and assumptions. Although obtaining prices from multiple sources may be useful, when considering financial instruments that have inputs categorised at levels 2 or 3 of the fair value hierarchy, in particular, obtaining prices from multiple sources is unlikely to provide sufficient appropriate audit evidence on its own. This is because:

(a) What appear to be multiple sources of pricing information may be utilising the same underlying pricing source; and

(b) Understanding the inputs used by the third-party pricing source in determining the price may be necessary in order to categorise the financial instrument in the fair value hierarchy.

120. In some situations, the auditor may be unable to gain an understanding of the process used to generate the price, including any controls over the process of how reliably the price is determined, or may not have access to the model, including the assumptions and other inputs used. In such cases, the auditor may decide to undertake to develop a point estimate or a range to evaluate management's point estimate in responding to the assessed risk.

Audit Considerations When Management Estimates Fair Values Using a Model

121. Paragraph 13(b) of ASA 540 requires the auditor, if testing management's process of making the accounting estimate, to evaluate whether the method of measurement used is appropriate in the circumstances and the assumptions used by management are reasonable in light of the measurement objectives of the applicable financial reporting framework.

122. Whether management has used a third-party pricing source, or is undertaking its own valuation, models are often used to value financial instruments, particularly when using inputs at levels 2 and 3 of the fair value hierarchy. In determining the nature, timing and extent of audit procedures on models, the auditor may consider the methodology, assumptions and data used in the model. When considering more complex financial instruments such as those using level 3 inputs, testing all three may be a useful source of audit evidence. However, when the model is both simple and generally accepted, such as some bond price calculations, audit evidence obtained from focusing on the assumptions and data used in the model may be a more useful source of evidence.

123. Testing a model can be accomplished by two main approaches:

(a) The auditor can test management's model, by considering the appropriateness of the model used by management, the reasonableness of the assumptions and data used, and the mathematical accuracy; or

(b) The auditor can develop their own estimate, and then compare the auditor's valuation with that of the entity.

124. Where valuation of financial instruments is based on unobservable inputs (that is, level 3 inputs), matters that the auditor may consider include, for example, how management supports the following:

- The identification and characteristics of marketplace participants relevant to the financial instrument.
- How unobservable inputs are determined on initial recognition.
- Modifications it has made to its own assumptions to reflect its view of assumptions marketplace participants would use.
- Whether it has incorporated the best input information available in the circumstances.
- Where applicable, how its assumptions take account of comparable transactions.
- Sensitivity analysis of models when unobservable inputs are used and whether adjustments have been made to address measurement uncertainty.

125. In addition, the auditor's industry knowledge, knowledge of market trends, understanding of other entities' valuations (having regard to confidentiality) and other relevant price indicators informs the auditor's testing of the valuations and the consideration of whether the valuations appear reasonable overall. If the valuations appear to be consistently overly aggressive or conservative, this may be an indicator of possible management bias.

126. Where there is a lack of observable external evidence, it is particularly important that those charged with governance have been appropriately engaged to understand the subjectivity of management's valuations and the evidence that has been obtained to support these valuations. In such cases, it may be necessary for the auditor to evaluate whether there has been a thorough review and consideration of the issues, including any documentation, at all appropriate management levels within the entity, including with those charged with governance.

127. When markets become inactive or dislocated, or inputs are unobservable, management's valuations may be more judgemental and less verifiable and, as result, may be less reliable. In such circumstances, the auditor may test the model by a combination of testing controls operated by the entity, evaluating the design and operation of the model, testing the assumptions and data used in the model, and comparing its output to a point estimate or range developed by the auditor or to other third-party valuation techniques.[32]

128. It is likely that in testing the inputs used in an entity's valuation methodology,[33] for example, where such inputs are categorised in the fair value hierarchy, the auditor will also be obtaining evidence to support the disclosures required by the applicable financial reporting framework. For example, the auditor's substantive procedures to evaluate whether the inputs used in an entity's valuation technique (that is, level 1, level 2 and level 3 inputs) are appropriate, and tests of an entity's sensitivity analysis, will be relevant to the auditor's evaluation of whether the disclosures achieve fair presentation.

Evaluating Whether the Assumptions Used by Management Are Reasonable

129. An assumption used in a model may be deemed to be significant if a reasonable variation in the assumption would materially affect the measurement of the financial instrument.[34] Management may have considered alternative assumptions or outcomes by performing a sensitivity analysis. The extent of subjectivity associated with assumptions influences the degree of measurement uncertainty and may lead the auditor to conclude there is a significant risk, for example in the case of level 3 inputs.

130. Audit procedures to test the assumptions used by management, including those used as inputs to models, may include evaluating:

- Whether, and if so, how, management has incorporated market inputs into the development of assumptions, as it is generally preferable to seek to maximise the use of relevant observable inputs and minimise unobservable inputs;
- Whether the assumptions are consistent with observable market conditions, and the characteristics of the financial asset or financial liability;
- Whether the sources of market-participant assumptions are relevant and reliable, and how management has selected the assumptions to use when a number of different marketplace assumptions exist; and
- Whether sensitivity analyses indicate that valuations would change significantly with only small or moderate changes in assumptions.

See paragraphs A77 to A83 of ASA 540 for further considerations relative to evaluating the assumptions used by management.

131. The auditor's consideration of judgements about the future is based on information available at the time at which the judgement is made. Subsequent events may result in

32 ASA 540, paragraph 13(d), describes requirements when the auditor develops a range to evaluate management's point estimate. Valuation techniques developed by third parties and used by the auditor may, in some circumstances be considered the work of an auditor's expert and subject to the requirements in ASA 620.

33 See, for example, paragraph 15 of ASA 540 for requirements relative to the auditor's evaluation of management's assumption regarding significant risks.

34 See ASA 540, paragraph A107.

outcomes that are inconsistent with judgements that were reasonable at the time they were made.

132. In some cases, the discount rate in a present value calculation may be adjusted to account for the uncertainties in the valuation, rather than adjusting each assumption. In such cases, an auditor's procedures may focus on the discount rate, by looking at an observable trade on a similar security to compare the discount rates used or developing an independent model to calculate the discount rate and compare with that used by management.

Audit Considerations When a Management's Expert Is Used by the Entity

133. As discussed in Section I, management may engage a valuation expert to value some or all of their securities. Such experts may be brokers, investment bankers, pricing services that also provide expert valuation services, or other specialised valuation firms.

134. Paragraph 8 of ASA 500 contains requirements for the auditor when evaluating evidence from an expert engaged by management. The extent of the auditor's procedures in relation to a management's expert and that expert's work depend on the significance of the expert's work for the auditor's purposes. Evaluating the appropriateness of a management's expert's work assists the auditor in assessing whether the prices or valuations supplied by the management's expert provide sufficient appropriate audit evidence to support the valuations. Examples of procedures the auditor may perform include:

- Evaluating the competence, capabilities and objectivity of the management's expert for example: their relationship with the entity; their reputation and standing in the market; their experience with the particular types of instruments; and their understanding of the relevant financial reporting framework applicable to the valuations;
- Obtaining an understanding of the work of the management's expert, for example by assessing the appropriateness of the valuation technique(s) used and the key market variables and assumptions used in the valuation technique(s);
- Evaluating the appropriateness of that expert's work as audit evidence. At this point, the focus is on the appropriateness of the expert's work at the level of the individual financial instrument. For a sample of the relevant instruments, it may be appropriate to develop an estimate independently (see paragraphs 136 to 137 of this Guidance Statement on developing a point estimate or range), using different data and assumptions, then compare that estimate to that of the management's expert; and
- Other procedures may include:
    - Modelling different assumptions to derive assumptions in another model, then considering the reasonableness of those derived assumptions.
    - Comparing management's point estimates with the auditor's point estimates to determine if management's estimates are consistently higher or lower.

135. Assumptions may be made or identified by a management's expert to assist management in valuing its financial instruments. Such assumptions, when used by management, become management's assumptions that the auditor needs to consider in the same manner as management's other assumptions.

Developing a Point Estimate or Range

136. An auditor may develop a valuation technique and adjust the inputs and assumptions used in the valuation technique to develop a range for use in evaluating the reasonableness of management's valuation. Paragraphs 106 to 135 of this Guidance Statement may assist the auditor in developing a point estimate or range. In accordance with ASA 540,[35] if the auditor uses assumptions, or methodologies that differ from management's, the auditor shall obtain an understanding of management's assumptions or methodologies sufficient to establish that the auditor's range takes into account relevant variables and to evaluate any significant differences from management's valuation. The auditor may find it useful

35 See ASA 540, paragraph 13(c).

to use the work of an auditor's expert to evaluate the reasonableness of management's valuation.

137. In some cases, the auditor may conclude that sufficient evidence cannot be obtained from the auditor's attempts to obtain an understanding of management's assumptions or methodology, for example when a third-party pricing source uses internally developed models and software and does not allow access to relevant information. In such cases, the auditor may not be able to obtain sufficient appropriate audit evidence about the valuation if the auditor is unable to perform other procedures to respond to the risks of material misstatement, such as developing a point estimate or a range to evaluate management's point estimate.[36] ASA 705[37] describes the implications of the auditor's inability to obtain sufficient appropriate audit evidence.

Presentation and Disclosure of Financial Instruments

138. Management's responsibilities include the preparation of the financial report in accordance with the applicable financial reporting framework.[38] Financial reporting frameworks, including Australian Accounting Standards, often require disclosures in the financial report to enable users of the financial report to make meaningful assessments of the effects of the entity's financial instrument activities, including the risks and uncertainties associated with these financial instruments. The importance of disclosures regarding the basis of measurement increases as the measurement uncertainty of the financial instruments increases and is also affected by the level of the fair value hierarchy.

139. In representing that the financial report is in accordance with the applicable financial reporting framework, management implicitly or explicitly makes assertions regarding the presentation and disclosure of the various elements of financial statements and related disclosures. Assertions about presentation and disclosure encompass:

(a) Occurrence and rights and obligations—disclosed events, transactions, and other matters have occurred and pertain to the entity.

(b) Completeness—all disclosures that should have been included in the financial report have been included.

(c) Classification and understandability—financial information is appropriately presented and described, and disclosures are clearly expressed.

(d) Accuracy and valuation—financial and other information are disclosed fairly and at appropriate amounts.

The auditor's procedures around auditing disclosures are designed in consideration of these assertions.

Procedures Relating to the Presentation and Disclosure of Financial Instruments

140. In relation to the presentation and disclosures of financial instruments, areas of particular importance include:

- Financial reporting frameworks generally require additional disclosures regarding estimates, and related risks and uncertainties, to supplement and explain assets, liabilities, income, and expenses. The auditor's focus may need to be on the disclosures relating to risks and sensitivity analysis. Information obtained during the auditor's risk assessment procedures and testing of control activities may provide evidence in order for the auditor to conclude about whether the disclosures in the financial report are in accordance with the requirements of the applicable financial reporting framework, for example about:
    - The entity's objectives and strategies for using financial instruments, including the entity's stated accounting policies;

GS

36 See ASA 540, paragraph 13(d).

37 See ASA 705 *Modifications to the Opinion in the Independent Auditor's Report*.

38 See paragraphs 4 and A2 of ASA 200.

  - The entity's control framework for managing its risks associated with financial instruments; and
  - The risks and uncertainties associated with the financial instruments.
- Information may come from systems outside traditional financial reporting systems, such as risk systems. Examples of procedures that the auditor may choose to perform in responding to assessed risks relative to disclosures include testing:
  - The process used to derive the disclosed information; and
  - The operating effectiveness of the controls over the data used in the preparation of disclosures.
- In relation to financial instruments having significant risk,[39] even where the disclosures are in accordance with the applicable financial reporting framework, the auditor may conclude that the disclosure of estimation uncertainty is inadequate in light of the circumstances and facts involved and, accordingly, the financial report may not achieve fair presentation. ASA 705 provides guidance on the implications for the auditor's opinion when the auditor believes that management's disclosures in the financial report are inadequate or misleading.
- Auditors may also consider whether the disclosures are complete and understandable, for example, all relevant information may be included in the financial report (or accompanying reports) but it may be insufficiently drawn together to enable users of the financial report to obtain an understanding of the position or there may not be enough qualitative disclosure to give context to the amounts recorded in the financial statements. For example, even when an entity has included sensitivity analysis disclosures, the disclosure may not fully describe the risks and uncertainties that may arise because of changes in valuation, possible effects on debt covenants, collateral requirements, and the entity's liquidity. ASA 260[40] contains requirements and guidance about communicating with those charged with governance, including the auditor's views about significant qualitative aspects of the entity's accounting practices, including accounting policies, accounting estimates and financial statement disclosures.

141. Consideration of the appropriateness of presentation, for example on short-term and long-term classification, in substantive testing of financial instruments is relevant to the auditor's evaluation of the presentation and disclosure.

Other Relevant Audit Considerations

Written Representations

142. ASA 540 requires the auditor to obtain written representations from management and, where appropriate, those charged with governance whether they believe significant assumptions used in making accounting estimates are reasonable.[41] ASA 580[42] requires that if, in addition to such required representations, the auditor determines that it is necessary to obtain one or more written representations to support other audit evidence relevant to the financial report or one or more specific assertions in the financial report, the auditor shall request such other written representations. Depending on the volume and

39 ASA 540, paragraph 20, requires the auditor to perform further procedures on disclosures relating to accounting estimates that give rise to significant risks to evaluate the adequacy of the disclosure of their estimation uncertainty in the financial report in the context of the applicable financial reporting framework.

40 See ASA 260 *Communication with Those Charged with Governance.*

41 See ASA 540, paragraph 22. Paragraph 4 of ASA 580 *Written Representations* states that written representations from management do not provide sufficient appropriate audit evidence on their own about any of the matters with which they deal. If the auditor is otherwise unable to obtain sufficient appropriate audit evidence, this may constitute a limitation on the scope of the audit that may have implications for the auditor's report (see ASA 705).

42 See ASA 580, paragraph 13.

degree of complexity of financial instrument activities, written representations to support other evidence obtained about financial instruments may also include:

- Management's objectives with respect to financial instruments, for example, whether they are used for hedging, asset/liability management or investment purposes;
- Representations about the appropriateness of presentation of the financial report, for example the recording of financial instrument transactions as sales or financing transactions;
- Representations about the financial statements and note disclosures concerning financial instruments, for example that:
  - The records reflect all financial instrument transactions; and
  - All embedded derivative instruments have been identified;
- Whether all transactions have been conducted at arm's length and at market value;
- The terms of transactions;
- The appropriateness of the valuations of financial instruments;
- Whether there are any side agreements associated with any financial instruments;
- Whether the entity has entered into any written options;
- Management's intent and ability to carry out certain actions;[43] and
- Whether subsequent events require adjustment to the valuations and disclosures included in the financial report.

Communication with Those Charged with Governance and Others

143. Because of the uncertainties associated with the valuation of financial instruments, the potential effects on the financial report of any significant risks are likely to be of governance interest. The auditor may communicate the nature and consequences of significant assumptions used in fair value measurements, the degree of subjectivity involved in the development of the assumptions, and the relative materiality of the items being measured at fair value to the financial report as a whole. In addition, the need for appropriate controls over commitments to enter into financial instrument contracts and over the subsequent measurement processes are matters that may give rise to the need for communication with those charged with governance.

144. ASA 260 deals with the auditor's responsibility to communicate with those charged with governance in an audit of a financial report. With respect to financial instruments, matters to be communicated to those charged with governance may include:

- A lack of management understanding of the nature or extent of the financial instrument activities or the risks associated with such activities;
- Significant deficiencies in the design or operation of the systems of internal control or risk management relating to the entity's financial instrument activities that the auditor has identified during the audit;[44]
- Significant difficulties encountered when obtaining sufficient appropriate audit evidence relating to valuations performed by management or a management's expert, for example, where management is unable to obtain an understanding of the valuation methodology, assumptions and data used by the management's experts, and such information is not made available to the auditor by management' s expert;
- Significant differences in judgements between the auditor and management or a management's expert regarding valuations;

GS

43 Paragraph A80 of ASA 540 provides examples of procedures that may be appropriate in the circumstances.

44 ASA 265 *Communicating Deficiencies in Internal Control to Those Charged with Governance and Management* establishes requirements and provides guidance on communicating deficiencies in internal control to management and communicating significant deficiencies in internal control to those charged with governance. It explains that deficiencies in internal control may be identified during the auditor's risk assessment procedures in accordance with ASA 315 or at any other stage of the audit.

- The potential effects on the entity's financial report of material risks and exposures required to be disclosed in the financial report, including the measurement uncertainty associated with financial instruments;
- The auditor's views about the appropriateness of the selection of accounting policies and presentation of financial instrument transactions in the financial report;
- The auditor's views about the qualitative aspects of the entity's accounting practices and financial reporting for financial instruments; or
- A lack of comprehensive and clearly stated policies for the purchase, sale and holding of financial instruments, including operational controls, procedures for designating financial instruments as hedges, and monitoring exposures.

The appropriate timing for communications will vary with the circumstances of the engagement; however, it may be appropriate to communicate significant difficulties encountered during the audit as soon as practicable if those charged with governance are able to assist the auditor to overcome the difficulty, or if it is likely to lead to a modified opinion.

Communications with Regulators and Others

145. In some cases, auditors may be required,[45] or may consider it appropriate, to communicate directly with regulators or prudential supervisors, in addition to those charged with governance, regarding matters relating to financial instruments. Such communication may be useful throughout the audit. For example, in some jurisdictions, banking regulators seek to cooperate with auditors to share information about the operation and application of controls over financial instrument activities, challenges in valuing financial instruments in inactive markets, and compliance with regulations. This coordination may be helpful to the auditor in identifying risks of material misstatement.

Aus 145.1 The prudential supervisor in Australia for financial institutions is the Australian Prudential Regulation Authority (APRA). Prudential standards issued by APRA cover communications between the auditor and APRA. See, for example, APS 310 *Audit and Related Matters*, GPS 310 *Audit and Actuarial Reporting and Valuation* and LPS 310 *Audit and Actuarial Requirements*.

Conformity with International Pronouncements

This Guidance Statement conforms with International Auditing Practice Note (IAPN) 1000 *Special Considerations in Auditing Financial Instruments* issued by the International Auditing and Assurance Standards Board (IAASB), an independent standard-setting board of the International Federation of Accountants (IFAC).

Paragraphs that have been added to this Guidance Statement (and do not appear in the text of the equivalent IAPN) are identified with the prefix "Aus".

45 For example, ASA 250 *Consideration of Laws and Regulations in an Audit of a Financial Report* requires auditors to determine whether there is a responsibility to report identified or suspected non-compliance with laws and regulations to parties outside the entity. In addition, requirements concerning the auditor's communication to banking supervisors and others may be established in many countries either by law, by supervisory requirement or by formal agreement or protocol.

Appendix

Examples of Controls Relating to Financial Instruments

The following provides background information and examples of controls that may exist in an entity that deals in a high volume of financial instrument transactions, whether for trading or investing purposes. The examples are not meant to be exhaustive and entities may establish different control environments and processes depending on their size, the industry in which they operate, and the extent of their financial instrument transactions. Further information on the use of trade confirmations and clearing houses is contained in paragraphs 25–26 of this Guidance Statement.

As in any control system, it is sometimes necessary to duplicate controls at different control levels (for example, preventative, detective and monitoring) to avoid the risk of material misstatement.

The Entity's Control Environment

Commitment to Competent Use of Financial Instruments

The degree of complexity of some financial instrument activities may mean that only a few individuals within the entity fully understand those activities or have the expertise necessary to value the instruments on an ongoing basis. Use of financial instruments without relevant expertise within the entity increases the risk of material misstatement.

Participation by Those Charged with Governance

Those charged with governance oversee and concur with management's establishment of the entity's overall risk appetite and provide oversight over the entity's financial instrument activities. An entity's policies for the purchase, sale and holding of financial instruments are aligned with its attitude toward risk and the expertise of those involved in financial instrument activities. In addition, an entity may establish governance structures and control processes aimed at:

(a) Communicating investment decisions and assessments of all material measurement uncertainty to those charged with governance; and

(b) Evaluating the entity's overall risk appetite when engaging in financial instrument transactions.

Organisational Structure

Financial instrument activities may be run on either a centralised or a decentralised basis. Such activities and related decision making depend heavily on the flow of accurate, reliable, and timely management information. The difficulty of collecting and aggregating such information increases with the number of locations and businesses in which an entity is involved. The risks of material misstatement associated with financial instrument activities may increase with greater decentralisation of control activities. This may especially be true where an entity is based in different locations, some perhaps in other countries.

Assignment of Authority and Responsibility

Investment and Valuation Policies

Providing direction, through clearly stated policies approved by those charged with governance for the purchase, sale, and holding of financial instruments enables management to establish an effective approach to taking and managing business risks. These policies are most clear when they state the entity's objectives with regard to its risk management activities, and the investment and hedging alternatives available to meet these objectives, and reflect the:

(a) Level of management's expertise;

(c) Sophistication of the entity's internal control and monitoring systems;

(d) Entity's asset/liability structure;

(e) Entity's capacity to maintain liquidity and absorb losses of capital;

(f) Types of financial instruments that management believes will meet its objectives; and

GS

(g) Uses of financial instruments that management believes will meet its objectives, for example, whether derivatives may be used for speculative purposes or only for hedging purposes.

Management may design policies aligned with its valuation capabilities and may establish controls to ensure that these policies are adhered to by those employees responsible for the entity's valuation. These may include:

(a) Processes for the design and validation of methodologies used to produce valuations, including how measurement uncertainty is addressed; and

(b) Policies regarding maximising the use of observable inputs and the types of information to be gathered to support valuations of financial instruments.

In smaller entities, dealing in financial instruments may be rare and management's knowledge and experience limited. Nevertheless, establishing policies over financial instruments helps an entity to determine its risk appetite and consider whether investing in particular financial instruments achieves a stated objective.

Human Resource Policies and Practices

Entities may establish policies requiring key employees, both front office and back office, to take mandatory time off from their duties. This type of control is used as a means of preventing and detecting fraud, in particular if those engaged in trading activities are creating false trades or inaccurately recording transactions.

Use of Service Organisations

Entities may also use service organisations (for example asset managers) to initiate the purchase or sale of financial instruments, to maintain records of transactions for the entity or to value financial instruments. Some entities may be dependent on these service organisations to provide the basis of reporting for the financial instruments held. However, if management does not have an understanding about the controls in place at a service organisation, the auditor may not be able to obtain sufficient appropriate audit evidence to rely on controls at that service organisation. See ASA 402, which establishes requirements for the auditor to obtain sufficient appropriate audit evidence when an entity uses the services of one or more service organisations.

The use of service organisations may strengthen or weaken the control environment for financial instruments. For example, a service organisation's personnel may have more experience with financial instruments than the entity's management or may have more robust internal control over financial reporting. The use of the service organisation also may allow for greater segregation of duties. On the other hand, the service organisation may have a poor control environment.

The Entity's Risk Assessment Process

An entity's risk assessment process exists to establish how management identifies business risks that derive from its use of financial instruments, including how management estimates the significance of the risks, assesses the likelihood of their occurrence and decides upon actions to manage them.

The entity's risk assessment process forms the basis for how management determines the risks to be managed. Risk assessment processes exist with the objective of ensuring that management:

(a) Understands the risks inherent in a financial instrument before they enter into it, including the objective of entering into the transaction and its structure (for example, the economics and business purpose of the entity's financial instrument activities);

(b) Performs adequate due diligence commensurate with the risks associated with particular financial instruments;

(c) Monitors their outstanding positions to understand how market conditions are affecting their exposures;

(d) Has procedures in place to reduce or change risk exposure if necessary and for managing reputational risk; and

(e) Subjects these processes to rigorous supervision and review.

The structure implemented to monitor and manage exposure to risks should:

(a) Be appropriate and consistent with the entity's attitude toward risk as determined by those charged with governance;

(b) Specify the approval levels for the authorisation of different types of financial instruments and transactions that may be entered into and for what purposes. The permitted instruments and approval levels should reflect the expertise of those involved in financial instrument activities, demonstrating management's commitment to competence;

(c) Set appropriate limits for the maximum allowable exposure to each type of risk (including approved counterparties). Levels of allowable exposure may vary depending on the type of risk, or counterparty;

(d) Provide for the objective and timely monitoring of the financial risks and control activities;

(e) Provide for the objective and timely reporting of exposures, risks and the results of financial instrument activities in managing risk; and

(f) Evaluate management's track record for assessing the risks of particular financial instruments.

The types and levels of risks an entity faces are directly related to the types of financial instruments with which it deals, including the complexity of these instruments and the volume of financial instruments transacted.

Risk Management Function

Some entities, for example large financial institutions with a high volume of financial instrument transactions, may be required by law or regulation, or may choose, to establish a formal risk management function. This function is separated from those responsible for undertaking and managing financial instrument transactions. The function is responsible for reporting on and monitoring financial instrument activities, and may include a formal risk committee established by those charged with governance. Examples of key responsibilities in this area may include:

(a) Implementing the risk management policy set by those charged with governance (including analyses of the risks to which an entity may be exposed);

(b) Designing risk limit structures and ensuring these risk limits are implemented in practice;

(c) Developing stress scenarios and subjecting open position portfolios to sensitivity analysis, including reviews of unusual movements in positions; and

(d) Reviewing and analysing new financial instrument products.

Financial instruments may have the associated risk that a loss might exceed the amount, if any, of the value of the financial instrument recognised on the balance sheet. For example, a sudden fall in the market price of a commodity may force an entity to realise losses to close a forward position in that commodity due to collateral, or margin, requirements. In some cases, the potential losses may be enough to cast significant doubt on the entity's ability to continue as a going concern. The entity may perform sensitivity analyses or value-at-risk analyses to assess the future hypothetical effects on financial instruments subject to market risks. However, value-at-risk analysis does not fully reflect the extent of the risks that may affect the entity; sensitivity and scenario analyses also may be subject to limitations.

The volume and sophistication of financial instrument activity and relevant regulatory requirements will influence the entity's consideration whether to establish a formal risk management function and how the function may be structured. In entities that have not established a separate risk management function, for example entities with relatively few financial instruments or financial instruments that are less complex, reporting on and monitoring financial instrument activities may be a component of the accounting or finance function's responsibility or management's overall responsibility, and may include a formal risk committee established by those charged with governance.

The Entity's Information Systems

The key objective of an entity's information system is that it is capable of capturing and recording all the transactions accurately, settling them, valuing them, and producing information to enable the financial instruments to be risk managed and for controls to be monitored. Difficulties can

GS

arise in entities that engage in a high volume of financial instruments, in particular if there is a multiplicity of systems that are poorly integrated and have manual interfaces without adequate controls.

Certain financial instruments may require a large number of accounting entries. As the sophistication or level of the financial instrument activities increases, it is necessary for the sophistication of the information system to also increase. Specific issues which can arise with respect to financial instruments include:

(a) Information systems, in particular for smaller entities, not having the capability or not being appropriately configured to process financial instrument transactions, especially when the entity does not have any prior experience in dealing with financial instruments. This may result in an increased number of manual transactions which may further increase the risk of error;

(b) The potential diversity of systems required to process more complex transactions, and the need for regular reconciliations between them, in particular when the systems are not interfaced or may be subject to manual intervention;

(c) The potential that more complex transactions, if they are only traded by a small number of individuals, may be valued or risk managed on spreadsheets rather than on main processing systems, and for the physical and logical password security around those spreadsheets to be more easily compromised;

(d) A lack of review of systems exception logs, external confirmations and broker quotes, where available, to validate the entries generated by the systems;

(e) Difficulties in controlling and evaluating the key inputs to systems for valuation of financial instruments, particularly where those systems are maintained by the group of traders known as the front office or a third-party service provider and/or the transactions in question are non-routine or thinly traded;

(f) Failure to evaluate the design and calibration of complex models used to process these transactions initially and on a periodic basis;

(g) The potential that management has not set up a library of models, with controls around access, change and maintenance of individual models, in order to maintain a strong audit trail of the accredited versions of models and in order to prevent unauthorised access or amendments to those models;

(h) The disproportionate investment that may be required in risk management and control systems, where an entity only undertakes a limited number of financial instrument transactions, and the potential for misunderstanding of the output by management if they are not used to these types of transactions;

(i) The potential requirement for third-party systems provision, for example from a service organisation, to record, process, account for or risk manage appropriately financial instrument transactions, and the need to reconcile appropriately and challenge the output from those providers; and

(j) Additional security and control considerations relevant to the use of an electronic network when an entity uses electronic commerce for financial instrument transactions.

Information systems relevant to financial reporting serve as an important source of information for the quantitative disclosures in the financial report. However, entities may also develop and maintain non-financial systems used for internal reporting and to generate information included in qualitative disclosures, for example regarding risks and uncertainties or sensitivity analyses.

The Entity's Control Activities

Control activities over financial instrument transactions are designed to prevent or detect problems that hinder an entity from achieving its objectives. These objectives may be either operational, financial reporting, or compliance in nature. Control activities over financial instruments are designed relative to the complexity and volume of transactions of financial instruments and will generally include an appropriate authorisation process, adequate segregation of duties, and other policies and procedures designed to ensure that the entity's control objectives are met. Process flow charts may assist in identifying an entity's controls and lack of controls. This Guidance

Statement focuses on control activities related to completeness, accuracy and existence, valuation, and presentation and disclosure.

Authorisation

Authorisation can affect the financial statement assertions both directly and indirectly. For example, even if a transaction is executed outside an entity's policies, it nonetheless may be recorded and accounted for accurately. However, unauthorised transactions could significantly increase risk to the entity, thereby significantly increasing the risk of material misstatement since they would be undertaken outside the system of internal control. To mitigate this risk, an entity will often establish a clear policy as to what transactions can be traded by whom and adherence to this policy will then be monitored by an entity's back office. Monitoring trading activities of individuals, for example by reviewing unusually high volumes or significant gains or losses incurred, will assist management in ensuring compliance with the entity's policies, including the authorisation of new types of transactions, and evaluating whether fraud has occurred.

The function of an entity's deal initiation records is to identify clearly the nature and purpose of individual transactions and the rights and obligations arising under each financial instrument contract, including the enforceability of the contracts. In addition to the basic financial information, such as a notional amount, complete and accurate records at a minimum typically include:

(a) The identity of the dealer;

(b) The identity of the person recording the transaction (if not the dealer), when the transaction was initiated (including the date and time of the transaction), and how it was recorded in the entity's information systems; and

(c) The nature and purpose of the transaction, including whether or not it is intended to hedge an underlying commercial exposure.

Segregation of Duties

Segregation of duties and the assignment of personnel is an important control activity, particularly when exposed to financial instruments. Financial instrument activities may be segregated into a number of functions, including:

(a) Executing the transaction (dealing). In entities with a high volume of financial instrument transactions, this may be done by the front office;

(b) Initiating cash payments and accepting cash receipts (settlements);

(c) Sending out trade confirmations and reconciling the differences between the entity's records and replies from counterparties, if any;

(d) Recording of all transactions correctly in the accounting records;

(e) Monitoring risk limits. In entities with a high volume of financial instrument transactions, this may be performed by the risk management function; and

(f) Monitoring positions and valuing financial instruments.

Many organisations choose to segregate the duties of those investing in financial instruments, those valuing financial instruments, those settling financial instruments and those accounting/recording financial instruments.

Where an entity is too small to achieve proper segregation of duties, the role of management and those charged with governance in monitoring financial instrument activities is of particular importance.

A feature of some entities' internal control is an independent price verification (IPV) function. This department is responsible for separately verifying the price of some financial instruments, and may use alternative data sources, methodologies and assumptions. The IPV provides an objective look at the pricing that has been developed in another part of the entity.

Ordinarily, the middle or back office is responsible for establishing policies on valuation and ensuring adherence to the policy. Entities with a greater use of financial instruments may perform daily valuations of their financial instrument portfolio and examine the contribution to profit or loss of individual financial instrument valuations as a test of the reasonableness of valuations.

Completeness, Accuracy, and Existence

Regular reconciliation of the entity's records to external banks' and custodians' records enables the entity to ensure transactions are properly recorded. Appropriate segregation of duties between those transacting the trades and those reconciling them is important, as is a rigorous process for reviewing reconciliations and clearing reconciling items.

Controls may also be established that require traders to identify whether a complex financial instrument may have unique features, for example embedded derivatives. In such circumstances, there may be a separate function that evaluates complex financial instrument transactions at their initiation (which may be known as a product control group), working in connection with an accounting policy group to ensure the transaction is accurately recorded. While smaller entities may not have product control groups, an entity may have a process in place relating to the review of complex financial instrument contracts at the point of origination in order to ensure they are accounted for appropriately in accordance with the applicable financial reporting framework.

Monitoring of Controls

The entity's ongoing monitoring activities are designed to detect and correct any deficiencies in the effectiveness of controls over transactions for financial instruments and their valuation. It is important that there is adequate supervision and review of financial instrument activity within the entity. This includes:

(a) All controls being subject to review, for example, the monitoring of operational statistics such as the number of reconciling items or the difference between internal pricing and external pricing sources;

(b) The need for robust information technology (IT) controls and monitoring and validating their application; and

(c) The need to ensure that information resulting from different processes and systems is adequately reconciled. For example, there is little benefit in a valuation process if the output from it is not reconciled properly into the general ledger.

In larger entities, sophisticated computer information systems generally keep track of financial instrument activities, and are designed to ensure that settlements occur when due. More complex computer systems may generate automatic postings to clearing accounts to monitor cash movements, and controls over processing are put in place with the objective of ensuring that financial instrument activities are correctly reflected in the entity's records. Computer systems may be designed to produce exception reports to alert management to situations where financial instruments have not been used within authorised limits or where transactions undertaken were not within the limits established for the chosen counterparties. However, even a sophisticated computer system may not ensure the completeness of the recording of financial instrument transactions. Accordingly, management frequently put additional procedures in place to increase the likelihood that all transactions will be recorded.

APES 110

Code of Ethics for Professional Accountants

(Reissued December 2010: amended and compiled December 2011)

Issued by the Accounting Professional and Ethical Standards Board.

Note from the Institute of Chartered Accountants Australia

This note, prepared by the technical editor, is not part of APES 110.

Historical development

June 2006: APES 110 issued by the newly constituted Accounting Professional and Ethical Standards Board (APESB) to replace the profession's Code of Professional Conduct (Code). It did not, however, replace Section F.2 of the Code, 'Prospectuses and Reports on Profit Forecasts'. The Code was operative from 1 July 2006, or as otherwise provided within the Code. It was based on the International Federation of Accountants Code of Ethics for Professional Accountants.

December 2007: APES 110 amended to reflect the change to the definition of network firm in the Code issued by the International Ethics Standards Board for Accountants (IESBA) on which APES 110 is based. The change was operative from 1 July 2008.

February 2008: APES 110 amended to include changes to the auditor independence requirements of the *Corporations Act 2001*.

December 2010: APES 110 reissued to bring it into line with the amended Code issued by the IESBA which introduces the concepts of Public Interest Entities and Key Audit Partners. There is now a cooling-off period before Key Audit or Managing Partners can join public interest audit clients in certain positions and the partner rotation requirements are extended to all Key Audit Partners. The APESB has also added specific Australian requirements relating to inadvertent violations and multiple threats to auditor independence. The new Code is operative from 1 July 2011.

December 2011: APESB released an amending Standard that alters the definition of Public Interest Entity (PIE) in APES 110 and adds an Australian paragraph to provide guidance on which entities in Australia are, or are likely to be, Public Interest Entities. The amendment is effective from 1 January 2013.

The APESB issued a compiled version of APES 110 incorporating these amendments in December 2011.

Contents

Compilation Details

APES 110 *Code of Ethics for Professional Accountants* as amended

This compilation is not a separate Standard issued by Accounting Professional & Ethical Standards Board Limited (APESB). Instead, it is a compilation of APES 110 (December 2010) as amended or added to by subsequent APESB Standards, which are listed in the tables below.

APES 110 (December 2010) is effective from 1 July 2011 and supersedes the previous APES 110 issued in June 2006 (amended February 2008). The amendments listed in the Tables below and reflected in this compiled Standard are effective from 1 January 2013, with early adoption permitted. The compiled Standard takes into account amendments up to and including December 2011 and was prepared by the Technical Staff of APESB.

Table of Standards

Standard	Month issued	Operative date
Amendment to the Definition of Public Interest Entity in APES 110 *Code of Ethics for Professional Accountants* (issued December 2011)	December 2011	1 January 2013

Table of Amendments

Paragraphs affected	How affected	Amending Standard
290.25 – 290.26	amended	Definition of Public Interest Entity
Transitional Provisions 1 – 6	amended	Definition of Public Interest Entity
Conformity with International Pronouncements	amended	Definition of Public Interest Entity

Table of Additions

Paragraphs added	Amending Standard
AUST 290.26.1	Definition of Public Interest Entity

APES 110 *Code of Ethics for Professional Accountants*

Accounting Professional & Ethical Standards Board Limited (APESB) issued APES 110 *Code of Ethics for Professional Accountants* in December 2010.

This compiled version of APES 110 incorporates amendments contained in subsequent APESB Standards issued by the APESB up to and including December 2011 (see Compilation Details).

1 Scope and application

1.1 Accounting Professional & Ethical Standards Board Limited (APESB) issues APES 110 *Code of Ethics for Professional Accountants* (this Code). This Code is operative from 1 July 2011 and supersedes APES 110 *Code of Ethics for Professional Accountants* (issued in June 2006 and subsequently amended in February 2008. Earlier adoption of this Code is permitted. Transitional provisions relating to Public Interest Entities, partner rotation, non-assurance services, Fees – relative size, compensation and evaluation policies apply from the date specified in the respective transitional provisions (refer page 1952).

1.2 All Members in Australia shall comply with APES 110 including when providing Professional Services in an honorary capacity.

APES

1.3 All Members practicing outside of Australia shall comply with APES 110 to the extent to which they are not prevented from so doing by specific requirements of local laws and/or regulations.

1.4 This Code is not intended to detract from any responsibilities which may be imposed by law or regulation. AUASB has issued auditing standards as legislative instruments under the *Corporations Act 2001* (the Act). For audits and reviews under the Act, those standards have legal enforceability. To the extent that those auditing standards make reference to relevant ethical requirements, the requirements of APES 110 have legal enforceability due to Auditing Standard ASA 102 *Compliance with Ethical Requirements when Performing Audits, Reviews and Other Assurance Engagements*.

1.5 All references to Professional Standards, guidance notes and legislation are references to those provisions as amended from time to time.

1.6 In applying the requirements outlined in this Code, Members shall be guided, not merely by the words, but also by the spirit of this Code.

2 Definitions

In this *Code of Ethics for Professional Accountants* the following expressions have the following meanings assigned to them:

[AUST] ***AASB*** means the Australian statutory body called the Australian Accounting Standards Board that was established under section 226 of the *Australian Securities and Investments Commission Act 1989* and is continued in existence by section 261 of the *Australian Securities and Investments Commission Act 2001*.

Acceptable Level means a level at which a reasonable and informed third party would be likely to conclude, weighing all the specific facts and circumstances available to the Member at that time, that compliance with the fundamental principles is not compromised.

[AUST] ***Administration*** means an insolvency arrangement arising from an appointment, other than a members' voluntary liquidation, under which an insolvent entity operates.

Advertising means the communication to the public of information as to the services or skills provided by Members in Public Practice with a view to procuring professional business.

Assurance Client means the responsible party that is the person (or persons) who:

(a) In a direct reporting engagement, is responsible for the subject matter; or

(b) In an assertion-based engagement, is responsible for the subject matter information and may be responsible for the subject matter.

Assurance Engagement means an engagement in which a Member in Public Practice expresses a conclusion designed to enhance the degree of confidence of the intended users other than the responsible party about the outcome of the evaluation or measurement of a subject matter against criteria.

This includes an engagement in accordance with the *Framework for Assurance Engagements* issued by the AUASB or in accordance with specific relevant standards, such as International Standards on Auditing, for Assurance Engagements.

Assurance Team means:

(a) All members of the Engagement Team for the Assurance Engagement;

(b) All others within a Firm who can directly influence the outcome of the Assurance Engagement, including:

  (i) those who recommend the compensation of, or who provide direct supervisory, management or other oversight of the Assurance Engagement partner in connection with the performance of the Assurance Engagement;

  (ii) those who provide consultation regarding technical or industry specific issues, transactions or events for the Assurance Engagement; and

  (iii) those who provide quality control for the Assurance Engagement, including those who perform the Engagement Quality Control Review for the Assurance Engagement.

[AUST] *AuASB* means the Auditing and Assurance Standards Board which issued Australian auditing and assurance standards up to 30 June 2004, under the auspices of the Australian Accounting Research Foundation, a joint venture of CPA Australia and the Institute of Chartered Accountants in Australia.

[AUST] *AUASB* means the Australian statutory body called the Auditing and Assurance Standards Board established under section 227A of the *Australian Securities and Investments Commission Act 2001.*

Audit Client means an entity in respect of which a Firm conducts an Audit Engagement. When the client is a Listed Entity, Audit Client will always include its Related Entities. When the Audit Client is not a Listed Entity, Audit Client includes those Related Entities over which the client has direct or indirect control.

Audit Engagement means a reasonable Assurance Engagement in which a Member in Public Practice expresses an opinion whether Financial Statements are prepared, in all material respects (or give a true and fair view or are presented fairly, in all material respects,), in accordance with an applicable financial reporting framework, such as an engagement conducted in accordance with Auditing and Assurance Standards. This includes a statutory audit, which is an audit required by legislation or other regulation.

Audit Team means:

(a) All members of the Engagement Team for the Audit Engagement;

(b) All others within a Firm who can directly influence the outcome of the Audit Engagement, including:

  (i) those who recommend the compensation of, or who provide direct supervisory, management or other oversight of the Engagement Partner in connection with the performance of the Audit Engagement including those at all successively senior levels above the Engagement Partner through to the individual who is the Firm's senior or managing partner (chief executive or equivalent);

  (ii) those who provide consultation regarding technical or industry-specific issues, transactions or events for the Audit Engagement; and

  (iii) those who provide quality control for the engagement, including those who perform the Engagement Quality Control Review for the Audit Engagement; and

(c) All those within a Network Firm who can directly influence the outcome of the Audit Engagement.

[AUST] ***Auditing and Assurance Standards*** means:

(a) the AUASB standards, as described in ASA 100 *Preamble to AUASB Standards,* ASA 101 *Preamble to Australian Auditing Standards* and the *Foreword to AUASB Pronouncements*, issued by the AUASB, and operative from the date specified in each standard; and

(b) those standards issued by the AuASB which have not been revised and reissued (whether as standards or as guidance) by the AUASB, to the extent that they are not inconsistent with the AUASB standards.

[AUST] ***Australian Accounting Standards*** means the Accounting Standards (including Australian Accounting Interpretations) promulgated by the AASB.

Close Family means a parent, child or sibling who is not an Immediate Family member.

Contingent Fee means a fee calculated on a predetermined basis relating to the outcome of a transaction or the result of the services performed by the Firm. A fee that is established by a court or other public authority is not a Contingent Fee.

Direct Financial Interest means a Financial Interest:

- Owned directly by and under the control of an individual or entity (including those managed on a discretionary basis by others); or
- Beneficially owned through a collective investment vehicle, estate, trust or other intermediary over which the individual or entity has control, or the ability to influence investment decisions.

APES

Director or Officer means those charged with the governance of an entity, or acting in an equivalent capacity, regardless of their title.

Engagement Partner means the partner or other person in the Firm who is responsible for the engagement and its performance, and for the report that is issued on behalf of the Firm, and who, where required, has the appropriate authority from a professional, legal or regulatory body.

Engagement Quality Control Review means a process designed to provide an objective evaluation, on or before the report is issued, of the significant judgments the Engagement Team made and the conclusions it reached in formulating the report.

Engagement Team means all partners and staff performing the engagement, and any individuals engaged by the Firm or a Network Firm who perform procedures on the engagement. This excludes External Experts engaged by the Firm or a Network Firm.

Existing Accountant means a Member in Public Practice currently holding an audit appointment or carrying out accounting, taxation, consulting or similar Professional Services for a client.

External Expert means an individual (who is not a partner or a member of the professional staff, including temporary staff, of the Firm or a Network Firm) or organisation possessing skills, knowledge and experience in a field other than accounting or auditing, whose work in that field is used to assist the Member in obtaining sufficient appropriate evidence.

Financial Interest means an interest in an equity or other security, debenture, loan or other debt instrument of an entity, including rights and obligations to acquire such an interest and derivatives directly related to such interest.

Financial Statements mean a structured representation of Historical Financial Information, including related notes, intended to communicate an entity's economic resources or obligations at a point in time or the changes therein for a period of time in accordance with a financial reporting framework. The related notes ordinarily comprise a summary of significant accounting policies and other explanatory information. The term can relate to a complete set of Financial Statements, but it can also refer to a single Financial Statement, for example, a balance sheet, or a statement of revenues and expenses, and related explanatory note. The requirements of the financial reporting framework determine the form and content of the Financial Statements and what constitutes a complete set of Financial Statement. For the purposes of this Standard financial report is considered to be an equivalent term to Financial Statements.

Financial Statements on which the Firm will express an Opinion means in the case of a single entity, the Financial Statements of that entity. In the case of consolidated Financial Statements, also referred to as group Financial Statements, the consolidated Financial Statements.

Firm means:

(a) A sole practitioner, partnership, corporation or other entity of professional accountants;

(b) An entity that controls such parties, through ownership, management or other means;

(c) An entity controlled by such parties, through ownership, management or other means; or

(d) An Auditor-General's office or department.

Historical Financial Information means information expressed in financial terms in relation to a particular entity, derived primarily from that entity's accounting system, about economic events occurring in past time periods or about economic conditions or circumstances at points in time in the past.

Immediate Family means a spouse (or equivalent) or dependent.

Independence is:

(a) Independence of mind – the state of mind that permits the expression of a conclusion without being affected by influences that compromise professional judgment, thereby allowing an individual to act with integrity, and exercise objectivity and professional scepticism.

(b) Independence in appearance – the avoidance of facts and circumstances that are so significant that a reasonable and informed third party would be likely to conclude, weighing all the specific facts and circumstances, that a Firm's, or a member of the Audit or Assurance Team's, integrity, objectivity or professional scepticism has been compromised.

Indirect Financial Interest means a Financial Interest beneficially owned through a collective investment vehicle, estate, trust or other intermediary over which the individual or entity has no control or ability to influence investment decisions.

Key Audit Partner means the Engagement Partner, the individual responsible for the Engagement Quality Control Review, and other audit partners, if any, on the Engagement Team who make key decisions or judgments on significant matters with respect to the audit of the Financial Statements on which the Firm will express an Opinion. Depending upon the circumstances and the role of the individuals on the audit, "other audit partners" may include, for example, audit partners responsible for significant subsidiaries or divisions.

Listed Entity means an entity whose shares, stock or debt are quoted or listed on a recognised stock exchange, or are marketed under the regulations of a recognised stock exchange or other equivalent body.

[AUST] ***Member*** means a member of a professional body that has adopted this Code as applicable to their membership, as defined by that professional body.

Member in Business means a Member employed or engaged in an executive or non-executive capacity in such areas as commerce, industry, service, the public sector, education, the not for profit sector, regulatory bodies or professional bodies, or a Member contracted by such entities.

Member in Public Practice means a Member, irrespective of functional classification (e.g., audit, tax or consulting) in a Firm that provides Professional Services. This term is also used to refer to a Firm of Members in Public Practice and means a practice entity and a participant in that practice entity as defined by the applicable professional body.

Network means a larger structure:

(a) That is aimed at co-operation; and

(b) That is clearly aimed at profit or cost sharing or shares common ownership, control or management, common quality control policies and procedures, common business strategy, the use of a common brand-name, or a significant part of professional resources.

Network Firm means a Firm or entity that belongs to a Network.

Office means a distinct sub-group, whether organised on geographical or practice lines.

Professional Services means services requiring accountancy or related skills performed by a Member including accounting, auditing, taxation, management consulting and financial management services.

Public Interest Entity means:

(a) A Listed Entity; and

(b) An entity (a) defined by regulation or legislation as a public interest entity or (b) for which the audit is required by regulation or legislation to be conducted in compliance with the same Independence requirements that apply to the audit of Listed Entities. Such regulation may be promulgated by any relevant regulator, including an audit regulator.

Related Entity means an entity that has any of the following relationships with the client:

(a) An entity that has direct or indirect control over the client if the client is material to such entity;

(b) An entity with a Direct Financial Interest in the client if that entity has significant influence over the client and the interest in the client is material to such entity;

(c) An entity over which the client has direct or indirect control;

(d) An entity in which the client, or an entity related to the client under (c) above, has a Direct Financial Interest that gives it significant influence over such entity and the interest is material to the client and its related entity in (c); and

(e) An entity which is under common control with the client (a "sister entity") if the sister entity and the client are both material to the entity that controls both the client and sister entity.

Review Client means an entity in respect of which a Firm conducts a Review Engagement.

Review Engagement means an Assurance Engagement in which a Member in Public Practice expresses a conclusion whether, on the basis of the procedures which do not provide all the evidence that would be required in an audit, anything has come to the attention of the Member that causes the Member to believe that the Historical Financial Information is not prepared in all material respects in accordance with an applicable financial reporting framework such as an engagement conducted in accordance with Auditing and Assurance Standards on Review Engagements.

Review Team means:

(a) All members of the Engagement Team for the Review Engagement; and

(b) All others within a Firm who can directly influence the outcome of the Review Engagement, including:

(i) those who recommend the compensation of, or who provide direct supervisory, management or other oversight of the Engagement Partner in connection with the performance of the Review Engagement including those at all successively senior levels above the Engagement Partner through to the individual who is the Firm's senior or managing partner (chief executive or equivalent);

(ii) those who provide consultation regarding technical or industry specific issues, transactions or events for the engagement; and

(iii) those who provide quality control for the engagement, including those who perform the Engagement Quality Control Review for the engagement; and

(c) All those within a Network Firm who can directly influence the outcome of the Review Engagement.

Special Purpose Financial Statements means Financial Statements prepared in accordance with a financial reporting framework designed to meet the financial information needs of specified users.

Those Charged with Governance means the persons with responsibility for overseeing the strategic direction of the entity and obligations related to the accountability of the entity. This includes overseeing the financial reporting process.

Part A—General Application of the Code

SECTION 100

Introduction and Fundamental Principles

100.1 A distinguishing mark of the accountancy profession is its acceptance of the responsibility to act in the public interest. Therefore, a Member's responsibility is not exclusively to satisfy the needs of an individual client or employer. In acting in the public interest, a Member shall observe and comply with this Code. If a Member is prohibited from complying with certain parts of this Code by law or regulation, the Member shall comply with all other parts of this Code.

100.2 This Code contains three parts. Part A establishes the fundamental principles of professional ethics for Members and provides a conceptual framework that Members shall apply to:

(a) Identify threats to compliance with the fundamental principles;

(b) Evaluate the significance of the threats identified; and

(c) Apply safeguards, when necessary, to eliminate the threats or reduce them to an Acceptable Level. Safeguards are necessary when the Member determines that the threats are not at a level at which a reasonable and informed third party would be likely to conclude, weighing all the specific facts and circumstances available to the Member at that time, that compliance with the fundamental principles is not compromised.

A Member shall use professional judgment in applying this conceptual framework.

100.3 Parts B and C describe how the conceptual framework applies in certain situations. They provide examples of safeguards that may be appropriate to address threats to compliance with the fundamental principles. They also describe situations where safeguards are not available to address the threats, and consequently, the circumstance or relationship creating the threats shall be avoided. Part B applies to Members in Public Practice. Part C applies to Members in Business. Members in Public Practice may also find Part C relevant to their particular circumstances.

100.4 The use of the word "shall" in this Code imposes a requirement on the Member or Firm to comply with the specific provision in which "shall" has been used. Compliance is required unless an exception is permitted by this Code.

Fundamental Principles

100.5 A Member shall comply with the following fundamental principles:

(a) *Integrity* – to be straightforward and honest in all professional and business relationships.

(b) *Objectivity* – to not allow bias, conflict of interest or undue influence of others to override professional or business judgments.

(c) *Professional competence and due care* – to maintain professional knowledge and skill at the level required to ensure that a client or employer receives competent Professional Services based on current developments in practice, legislation and techniques and act diligently and in accordance with applicable technical and professional standards.

APES

(d) *Confidentiality* – to respect the confidentiality of information acquired as a result of professional and business relationships and, therefore, not disclose any such information to third parties without proper and specific authority, unless there is a legal or professional right or duty to disclose, nor use the information for the personal advantage of the Member or third parties.

(e) *Professional behaviour* – to comply with relevant laws and regulations and avoid any action that discredits the profession.

Each of these fundamental principles is discussed in more detail in Sections 110–150.

Conceptual Framework Approach

100.6 The circumstances in which Members operate may create specific threats to compliance with the fundamental principles. It is impossible to define every situation that creates threats to compliance with the fundamental principles and specify the appropriate action. In addition, the nature of engagements and work assignments may differ and, consequently, different threats may be created, requiring the application of different safeguards. Therefore, this Code establishes a conceptual framework that requires a Member to identify, evaluate, and address threats to compliance with the fundamental principles. The conceptual framework approach assists a Member in complying with the ethical requirements of this Code and meeting their responsibility to act in the public interest. It accommodates many variations in circumstances that create threats to compliance with the fundamental principles and can deter a Member from concluding that a situation is permitted if it is not specifically prohibited.

100.7 When a Member identifies threats to compliance with the fundamental principles and, based on an evaluation of those threats, determines that they are not at an Acceptable Level, the Member shall determine whether appropriate safeguards are available and can be applied to eliminate the threats or reduce them to an Acceptable Level. In making that determination, the Member shall exercise professional judgment and take into account whether a reasonable and informed third party, weighing all the specific facts and circumstances available to the Member at the time, would be likely to conclude that the threats would be eliminated or reduced to an Acceptable Level by the application of the safeguards, such that compliance with the fundamental principles is not compromised.

100.8 A Member shall evaluate any threats to compliance with the fundamental principles when the Member knows, or could reasonably be expected to know, of circumstances or relationships that may compromise compliance with the fundamental principles.

100.9 A Member shall take qualitative as well as quantitative factors into account when evaluating the significance of a threat. When applying the conceptual framework, a Member may encounter situations in which threats cannot be eliminated or reduced to an Acceptable Level, either because the threat is too significant or because appropriate safeguards are not available or cannot be applied. In such situations, the Member shall decline or discontinue the specific Professional Service involved or, when necessary, resign from the engagement (in the case of a Member in Public Practice) or the employing organisation (in the case of a Member in Business).

100.10 A Member may inadvertently violate a provision of this Code. Depending on the nature and significance of the matter, such an inadvertent violation may be deemed not to compromise compliance with the fundamental principles provided, once the violation is discovered, the violation is corrected promptly and any necessary safeguards are applied.

100.11 When a Member encounters unusual circumstances in which the application of a specific requirement of the Code would result in a disproportionate outcome or an outcome that may not be in the public interest, it is recommended that the Member consult with a member body or the relevant regulator.

Threats and Safeguards

100.12 Threats may be created by a broad range of relationships and circumstances. When a relationship or circumstance creates a threat, such a threat could compromise, or could be perceived to compromise, a Member's compliance with the fundamental principles. A circumstance or relationship may create more than one threat, and a threat may affect compliance with more than one fundamental principle. Threats fall into one or more of the following categories:

(a) Self-interest threat – the threat that a financial or other interest will inappropriately influence the Member's judgment or behaviour;

(b) Self-review threat – the threat that a Member will not appropriately evaluate the results of a previous judgment made or service performed by the Member, or by another individual within the Member's Firm or employing organisation, on which the Member will rely when forming a judgment as part of providing a current service;

(c) Advocacy threat – the threat that a Member will promote a client's or employer's position to the point that the Member's objectivity is compromised;

(d) Familiarity threat – the threat that due to a long or close relationship with a client or employer, a Member will be too sympathetic to their interests or too accepting of their work; and

(e) Intimidation threat – the threat that a Member will be deterred from acting objectively because of actual or perceived pressures, including attempts to exercise undue influence over the Member.

Parts B and C of this Code explain how these categories of threats may be created for Members in Public Practice and Members in Business, respectively. Members in Public Practice may also find Part C relevant to their particular circumstances.

100.13 Safeguards are actions or other measures that may eliminate threats or reduce them to an Acceptable Level. They fall into two broad categories:

(a) Safeguards created by the profession, legislation or regulation; and

(b) Safeguards in the work environment.

100.14 Safeguards created by the profession, legislation or regulation include:

- Educational, training and experience requirements for entry into the profession.
- Continuing professional development requirements.
- Corporate governance regulations.
- Professional standards.
- Professional or regulatory monitoring and disciplinary procedures.
- External review by a legally empowered third party of the reports, returns, communications or information produced by a Member.

100.15 Parts B and C of this Code discuss safeguards in the work environment for Members in Public Practice and Members in Business, respectively.

100.16 Certain safeguards may increase the likelihood of identifying or deterring unethical behaviour. Such safeguards, which may be created by the accounting profession, legislation, regulation, or an employing organisation, include:

- Effective, well-publicised complaint systems operated by the employing organisation, the profession or a regulator, which enable colleagues, employers and members of the public to draw attention to unprofessional or unethical behaviour.
- An explicitly stated duty to report breaches of ethical requirements.

Ethical Conflict Resolution

100.17 A Member may be required to resolve a conflict in complying with the fundamental principles.

100.18 When initiating either a formal or informal conflict resolution process, the following factors, either individually or together with other factors, may be relevant to the resolution process:

(a) Relevant facts;

(b) Ethical issues involved;

(c) Fundamental principles related to the matter in question;

(d) Established internal procedures; and

(e) Alternative courses of action.

Having considered the relevant factors, a Member shall determine the appropriate course of action, weighing the consequences of each possible course of action. If the matter remains unresolved, the Member may wish to consult with other appropriate persons within the Firm or employing organisation for help in obtaining resolution.

100.19 Where a matter involves a conflict with, or within, an organisation, a Member shall determine whether to consult with Those Charged with Governance of the organisation, such as the board of Directors or the audit committee.

100.20 It may be in the best interests of the Member to document the substance of the issue, the details of any discussions held, and the decisions made concerning that issue.

100.21 If a significant conflict cannot be resolved, a Member may consider obtaining professional advice from the relevant professional body or from legal advisors. The Member generally can obtain guidance on ethical issues without breaching the fundamental principle of confidentiality if the matter is discussed with the relevant professional body on an anonymous basis or with a legal advisor under the protection of legal privilege. Instances in which the Member may consider obtaining legal advice vary. For example, a Member may have encountered a fraud, the reporting of which could breach the Member's responsibility to respect confidentiality. The Member may consider obtaining legal advice in that instance to determine whether there is a requirement to report.

100.22 If, after exhausting all relevant possibilities, the ethical conflict remains unresolved, a Member shall, where possible, refuse to remain associated with the matter creating the conflict. The Member shall determine whether, in the circumstances, it is appropriate to withdraw from the Engagement Team or specific assignment, or to resign altogether from the engagement, the Firm or the employing organisation.

SECTION 110

Integrity

110.1 The principle of integrity imposes an obligation on all Members to be straightforward and honest in all professional and business relationships. Integrity also implies fair dealing and truthfulness.

110.2 A Member shall not knowingly be associated with reports, returns, communications or other information where the Member believes that the information:

(a) Contains a materially false or misleading statement;

(b) Contains statements or information furnished recklessly; or

(c) Omits or obscures information required to be included where such omission or obscurity would be misleading.

When a Member becomes aware that the Member has been associated with such information, the Member shall take steps to be disassociated from that information.

110.3 A Member will be deemed not to be in breach of paragraph 110.2 if the Member provides a modified report in respect of a matter contained in paragraph 110.2.

SECTION 120
Objectivity

120.1 The principle of objectivity imposes an obligation on all Members not to compromise their professional or business judgment because of bias, conflict of interest or the undue influence of others.

120.2 A Member may be exposed to situations that may impair objectivity. It is impracticable to define and prescribe all such situations. A Member shall not perform a Professional Service if a circumstance or relationship biases or unduly influences the Member's professional judgment with respect to that service.

SECTION 130
Professional Competence and Due Care

130.1 The principle of professional competence and due care imposes the following obligations on all Members:

(a) To maintain professional knowledge and skill at the level required to ensure that clients or employers receive competent Professional Service; and

(b) To act diligently in accordance with applicable technical and professional standards when providing Professional Services.

130.2 Competent Professional Service requires the exercise of sound judgment in applying professional knowledge and skill in the performance of such service. Professional competence may be divided into two separate phases:

(a) Attainment of professional competence; and

(b) Maintenance of professional competence.

130.3 The maintenance of professional competence requires a continuing awareness and an understanding of relevant technical, professional and business developments. Continuing professional development enables a Member to develop and maintain the capabilities to perform competently within the professional environment.

130.4 Diligence encompasses the responsibility to act in accordance with the requirements of an assignment, carefully, thoroughly and on a timely basis.

130.5 A Member shall take reasonable steps to ensure that those working under the Member's authority in a professional capacity have appropriate training and supervision.

130.6 Where appropriate, a Member shall make clients, employers or other users of the Member's Professional Services aware of the limitations inherent in the services.

SECTION 140
Confidentiality

140.1 The principle of confidentiality imposes an obligation on all Members to refrain from:

(a) Disclosing outside the Firm or employing organisation confidential information acquired as a result of professional and business relationships without proper and specific authority or unless there is a legal or professional right or duty to disclose; and

(b) Using confidential information acquired as a result of professional and business relationships to their personal advantage or the advantage of third parties.

140.2 A Member shall maintain confidentiality, including in a social environment, being alert to the possibility of inadvertent disclosure, particularly to a close business associate or a Close or Immediate Family member.

140.3 A Member shall maintain confidentiality of information disclosed by a prospective client or employer.

140.4 A Member shall maintain confidentiality of information within the Firm or employing organisation.

140.5 A Member shall take reasonable steps to ensure that staff under the Member's control and persons from whom advice and assistance is obtained respect the Member's duty of confidentiality.

140.6 The need to comply with the principle of confidentiality continues even after the end of relationships between a Member and a client or employer. When a Member changes employment or acquires a new client, the Member is entitled to use prior experience. The Member shall not, however, use or disclose any confidential information either acquired or received as a result of a professional or business relationship.

140.7 The following are circumstances where Members are or may be required to disclose confidential information or when such disclosure may be appropriate:

(a) Disclosure is permitted by law and is authorised by the client or the employer;

(b) Disclosure is required by law, for example:

(i) Production of documents or other provision of evidence in the course of legal proceedings; or

(ii) Disclosure to the appropriate public authorities of infringements of the law that come to light; and

(c) There is a professional duty or right to disclose, when not prohibited by law:

(i) To comply with the quality review of a member body or professional body;

(ii) To respond to an inquiry or investigation by a member body or regulatory body;

(iii) To protect the professional interests of a Member in legal proceedings; or

(iv) To comply with technical standards and ethics requirements.

AUST140.7.1 The circumstances described in paragraph 140.7 do not take into account Australian legal and regulatory requirements. A Member considering disclosing confidential information about a client or employer without their consent is strongly advised to first obtain legal advice.

140.8 In deciding whether to disclose confidential information, relevant factors to consider include:

(a) Whether the interests of all parties, including third parties whose interests may be affected, could be harmed if the client or employer consents to the disclosure of information by the Member;

(b) Whether all the relevant information is known and substantiated, to the extent it is practicable; when the situation involves unsubstantiated facts, incomplete information or unsubstantiated conclusions, professional judgment shall be used in determining the type of disclosure to be made, if any;

(c) The type of communication that is expected and to whom it is addressed; and

(d) Whether the parties to whom the communication is addressed are appropriate recipients.

SECTION 150

Professional Behaviour

150.1 The principle of professional behaviour imposes an obligation on all Members to comply with relevant laws and regulations and avoid any action or omission that the Member knows or should know may discredit the profession. This includes actions or omissions that a reasonable and informed third party, weighing all the specific facts and circumstances available to the Member at that time, would be likely to conclude adversely affects the good reputation of the profession.

150.2 In marketing and promoting themselves and their work, Members shall not bring the profession into disrepute. Members shall be honest and truthful and not:

(a) Make exaggerated claims for the services they are able to offer, the qualifications they possess, or experience they have gained; or

(b) Make disparaging references or unsubstantiated comparisons to the work of others.

Part B – Members in Public Practice

SECTION 200

Introduction

200.1 This Part of the Code describes how the conceptual framework contained in Part A applies in certain situations to Members in Public Practice. This Part does not describe all of the circumstances and relationships that could be encountered by a Member in Public Practice that create or may create threats to compliance with the fundamental principles. Therefore, the Member in Public Practice is encouraged to be alert for such circumstances and relationships.

200.2 A Member in Public Practice shall not knowingly engage in any business, occupation, or activity that impairs or might impair integrity, objectivity or the good reputation of the profession and as a result would be incompatible with the fundamental principles.

Threats and Safeguards

200.3 Compliance with the fundamental principles may potentially be threatened by a broad range of circumstances and relationships. The nature and significance of the threats may differ depending on whether they arise in relation to the provision of services to an Audit Client and whether the Audit Client is a Public Interest Entity, to an Assurance Client that is not an Audit Client, or to a non-assurance client.

Threats fall into one or more of the following categories:

(a) Self-interest;

(b) Self-review;

(c) Advocacy;

(d) Familiarity; and

(e) Intimidation.

These threats are discussed further in Part A of this Code.

200.4 Examples of circumstances that create self-interest threats for a Member in Public Practice include:

- A member of the Assurance Team having a Direct Financial Interest in the Assurance Client.
- A Firm having undue dependence on total fees from a client.
- A member of the Assurance Team having a significant close business relationship with an Assurance Client.
- A Firm being concerned about the possibility of losing a significant client.

APES

- A member of the Audit Team entering into employment negotiations with the Audit Client.
- A Firm entering into a Contingent Fee arrangement relating to an Assurance Engagement.
- A Member discovering a significant error when evaluating the results of a previous Professional Service performed by a member of the Member's Firm.

200.5 Examples of circumstances that create self-review threats for a Member in Public Practice include:

- A Firm issuing an assurance report on the effectiveness of the operation of financial systems after designing or implementing the systems.
- A Firm having prepared the original data used to generate records that are the subject matter of the Assurance Engagement.
- A member of the Assurance Team being, or having recently been, a Director or Officer of the client.
- A member of the Assurance Team being, or having recently been, employed by the client in a position to exert significant influence over the subject matter of the engagement.
- The Firm performing a service for an Assurance Client that directly affects the subject matter information of the Assurance Engagement.

200.6 Examples of circumstances that create advocacy threats for a Member in Public Practice include:

- The Firm promoting shares in an Audit Client.
- A Member acting as an advocate on behalf of an Audit Client in litigation or disputes with third parties.

200.7 Examples of circumstances that create familiarity threats for a Member in Public Practice include:

- A member of the Engagement Team having a Close or Immediate Family member who is a Director or Officer of the client.
- A member of the Engagement Team having a Close or Immediate Family member who is an employee of the client who is in a position to exert significant influence over the subject matter of the engagement.
- A Director or Officer of the client or an employee in a position to exert significant influence over the subject matter of the engagement having recently served as the Engagement Partner.
- A Member accepting gifts or preferential treatment from a client, unless the value is trivial or inconsequential.
- Senior personnel having a long association with the Assurance Client.

200.8 Examples of circumstances that create intimidation threats for a Member in Public Practice include:

- A Firm being threatened with dismissal from a Client Engagement.
- An Audit Client indicating that it will not award a planned non-assurance contract to the Firm if the Firm continues to disagree with the client's accounting treatment for a particular transaction.
- A Firm being threatened with litigation by the client.
- A Firm being pressured to reduce inappropriately the extent of work performed in order to reduce fees.
- A Member feeling pressured to agree with the judgment of a client employee because the employee has more expertise on the matter in question.
- A Member being informed by a partner of the Firm that a planned promotion will not occur unless the Member agrees with an Audit Client's inappropriate accounting treatment.

200.9 Safeguards that may eliminate or reduce threats to an Acceptable Level fall into two broad categories:

(a) Safeguards created by the profession, legislation or regulation; and

(b) Safeguards in the work environment.

Examples of safeguards created by the profession, legislation or regulation are described in paragraph 100.14 of Part A of this Code.

200.10 A Member in Public Practice shall exercise judgment to determine how best to deal with threats that are not at an Acceptable Level, whether by applying safeguards to eliminate the threat or reduce it to an Acceptable Level or by terminating or declining the relevant engagement. In exercising this judgment, a Member in Public Practice shall consider whether a reasonable and informed third party, weighing all the specific facts and circumstances available to the Member at that time, would be likely to conclude that the threats would be eliminated or reduced to an Acceptable Level by the application of safeguards, such that compliance with the fundamental principles is not compromised. This consideration will be affected by matters such as the significance of the threat, the nature of the engagement and the structure of the Firm.

200.11 In the work environment, the relevant safeguards will vary depending on the circumstances. Work environment safeguards comprise Firm-wide safeguards and engagement-specific safeguards.

200.12 Examples of Firm-wide safeguards in the work environment include:

- Leadership of the Firm that stresses the importance of compliance with the fundamental principles.
- Leadership of the Firm that establishes the expectation that members of an Assurance Team will act in the public interest.
- Policies and procedures to implement and monitor quality control of engagements.
- Documented policies regarding the need to identify threats to compliance with the fundamental principles, evaluate the significance of those threats, and apply safeguards to eliminate or reduce the threats to an Acceptable Level or, when appropriate safeguards are not available or cannot be applied, terminate or decline the relevant engagement.
- Documented internal policies and procedures requiring compliance with the fundamental principles.
- Policies and procedures that will enable the identification of interests or relationships between the Firm or members of Engagement Teams and clients.
- Policies and procedures to monitor and, if necessary, manage the reliance on revenue received from a single client.
- Using different partners and Engagement Teams with separate reporting lines for the provision of non-assurance services to an Assurance Client.
- Policies and procedures to prohibit individuals who are not members of an Engagement Team from inappropriately influencing the outcome of the engagement.
- Timely communication of a Firm's policies and procedures, including any changes to them, to all partners and professional staff, and appropriate training and education on such policies and procedures.
- Designating a member of senior management to be responsible for overseeing the adequate functioning of the Firm's quality control system.
- Advising partners and professional staff of Assurance Clients and Related Entities from which Independence is required.
- A disciplinary mechanism to promote compliance with policies and procedures.
- Published policies and procedures to encourage and empower staff to communicate to senior levels within the Firm any issue relating to compliance with the fundamental principles that concerns them.

200.13 Examples of engagement-specific safeguards in the work environment include:

- Having a Member who was not involved with the non-assurance service review the non-assurance work performed or otherwise advise as necessary.
- Having a Member who was not a member of the Assurance Team review the assurance work performed or otherwise advise as necessary.
- Consulting an independent third party, such as a committee of independent Directors, a professional regulatory body or another Member.
- Discussing ethical issues with Those Charged with Governance of the client.
- Disclosing to Those Charged with Governance of the client the nature of services provided and extent of fees charged.
- Involving another Firm to perform or re-perform part of the engagement.
- Rotating senior Assurance Team personnel.

200.14 Depending on the nature of the engagement, a Member in Public Practice may also be able to rely on safeguards that the client has implemented. However it is not possible to rely solely on such safeguards to reduce threats to an Acceptable Level.

200.15 Examples of safeguards within the client's systems and procedures include:

- The client requires persons other than management to ratify or approve the appointment of a Firm to perform an engagement.
- The client has competent employees with experience and seniority to make managerial decisions.
- The client has implemented internal procedures that ensure objective choices in commissioning non-assurance engagements.
- The client has a corporate governance structure that provides appropriate oversight and communications regarding the Firm's services.

SECTION 210
Professional Appointment

Client Acceptance

210.1 Before accepting a new client relationship, a Member in Public Practice shall determine whether acceptance would create any threats to compliance with the fundamental principles. Potential threats to integrity or professional behaviour may be created from, for example, questionable issues associated with the client (its owners, management or activities).

210.2 Client issues that, if known, could threaten compliance with the fundamental principles include, for example, client involvement in illegal activities (such as money laundering), dishonesty or questionable financial reporting practices.

210.3 A Member in Public Practice shall evaluate the significance of any threats and apply safeguards when necessary to eliminate them or reduce them to an Acceptable Level.

Examples of such safeguards include:

- Obtaining knowledge and understanding of the client, its owners, managers and those responsible for its governance and business activities; or
- Securing the client's commitment to improve corporate governance practices or internal controls.

210.4 Where it is not possible to reduce the threats to an Acceptable Level, the Member in Public Practice shall decline to enter into the client relationship.

210.5 It is recommended that a Member in Public Practice periodically review acceptance decisions for recurring client engagements.

Engagement Acceptance

210.6 The fundamental principle of professional competence and due care imposes an obligation on a Member in Public Practice to provide only those services that the

Member in Public Practice is competent to perform. Before accepting a specific client engagement, a Member in Public Practice shall determine whether acceptance would create any threats to compliance with the fundamental principles. For example, a self-interest threat to professional competence and due care is created if the Engagement Team does not possess, or cannot acquire, the competencies necessary to properly carry out the engagement.

210.7 A Member in Public Practice shall evaluate the significance of threats and apply safeguards, when necessary, to eliminate them or reduce them to an Acceptable Level. Examples of such safeguards include:

- Acquiring an appropriate understanding of the nature of the client's business, the complexity of its operations, the specific requirements of the engagement and the purpose, nature and scope of the work to be performed.
- Acquiring knowledge of relevant industries or subject matters.
- Possessing or obtaining experience with relevant regulatory or reporting requirements.
- Assigning sufficient staff with the necessary competencies.
- Using experts where necessary.
- Agreeing on a realistic time frame for the performance of the engagement.
- Complying with quality control policies and procedures designed to provide reasonable assurance that specific engagements are accepted only when they can be performed competently.

210.8 When a Member in Public Practice intends to rely on the advice or work of an expert, the Member in Public Practice shall determine whether such reliance is warranted. Factors to consider include: reputation, expertise, resources available and applicable professional and ethical standards. Such information may be gained from prior association with the expert or from consulting others.

Changes in a Professional Appointment

210.9 A Member in Public Practice who is asked to replace another Member in Public Practice, or who is considering tendering for an engagement currently held by another Member in Public Practice, shall determine whether there are any reasons, professional or otherwise, for not accepting the engagement, such as circumstances that create threats to compliance with the fundamental principles that cannot be eliminated or reduced to an Acceptable Level by the application of safeguards. For example, there may be a threat to professional competence and due care if a Member in Public Practice accepts the engagement before knowing all the pertinent facts.

210.10 A Member in Public Practice shall evaluate the significance of any threats. Depending on the nature of the Engagement, this may require direct communication with the Existing Accountant to establish the facts and circumstances regarding the proposed change so that the Member in Public Practice can decide whether it would be appropriate to accept the engagement. For example, the apparent reasons for the change in appointment may not fully reflect the facts and may indicate disagreements with the Existing Accountant that may influence the decision to accept the appointment.

210.11 Safeguards shall be applied when necessary to eliminate any threats or reduce them to an Acceptable Level. Examples of such safeguards include:

- When replying to requests to submit tenders, stating in the tender that, before accepting the engagement, contact with the Existing Accountant will be requested so that inquiries may be made as to whether there are any professional or other reasons why the appointment should not be accepted;
- Asking the Existing Accountant to provide known information on any facts or circumstances that, in the Existing Accountant's opinion, the proposed accountant needs to be aware of before deciding whether to accept the engagement; or
- Obtaining necessary information from other sources.

When the threats cannot be eliminated or reduced to an Acceptable Level through the application of safeguards, a Member in Public Practice shall, unless there is satisfaction as to necessary facts by other means, decline the engagement.

AUST210.11.1 A Member in Public Practice who is asked to replace an existing auditor or to accept nomination as a replacement auditor shall:

(a) Request the prospective client's permission to communicate with the existing auditor. If such permission is refused the Member shall, in the absence of exceptional circumstances, decline the Audit Engagement or the nomination; and

(b) On receipt of permission, request in writing of the existing auditor all information which ought to be available to enable the Member to make a decision as to whether the Audit Engagement or the nomination should be accepted.

210.12 A Member in Public Practice may be asked to undertake work that is complementary or additional to the work of the Existing Accountant. Such circumstances may create threats to professional competence and due care resulting from, for example, a lack of or incomplete information. The significance of any threats shall be evaluated and safeguards applied when necessary to eliminate the threat or reduce it to an Acceptable Level. An example of such a safeguard is notifying the Existing Accountant of the proposed work, which would give the Existing Accountant the opportunity to provide any relevant information needed for the proper conduct of the work.

210.13 An Existing Accountant is bound by confidentiality. Whether that Member is permitted or required to discuss the affairs of a client with a proposed accountant will depend on the nature of the engagement and on:

(a) Whether the client's permission to do so has been obtained; or

(b) The legal or ethical requirements relating to such communications and disclosure, which may vary by jurisdiction.

Circumstances where the Member is or may be required to disclose confidential information or where such disclosure may otherwise be appropriate are set out in Section 140 of Part A of this Code.

210.14 A Member in Public Practice will generally need to obtain the Client's permission, preferably in writing, to initiate discussion with an Existing Accountant. Once that permission is obtained, the Existing Accountant shall comply with relevant legal and other regulations governing such requests. Where the Existing Accountant provides information, it shall be provided honestly and unambiguously. If the proposed accountant is unable to communicate with the Existing Accountant, the proposed accountant shall take reasonable steps to obtain information about any possible threats by other means, such as through inquiries of third parties or background investigations of senior management or Those Charged with Governance of the client.

AUST210.15.1 The requirements of section 210 also apply where a Member in Public Practice is replacing or being replaced by an accountant who is not a Member.

SECTION 220

Conflicts of Interest

220.1 A Member in Public Practice shall take reasonable steps to identify circumstances that could pose a conflict of interest. Such circumstances may create threats to compliance with the fundamental principles. For example, a threat to objectivity may be created when a Member in Public Practice competes directly with a client or has a joint venture or similar arrangement with a major competitor of a client. A threat to objectivity or confidentiality may also be created when a Member in Public Practice performs services for clients whose interests are in conflict or the clients are in dispute with each other in relation to the matter or transaction in question.

220.2 A Member in Public Practice shall evaluate the significance of any threats and apply safeguards when necessary to eliminate the threats or reduce them to an Acceptable Level. Before accepting or continuing a client relationship or specific engagement, the Member in Public Practice shall evaluate the significance of any threats created by business interests or relationships with the client or a third party.

220.3 Depending upon the circumstances giving rise to the conflict, application of one of the following safeguards is generally necessary:

(a) Notifying the client of the Firm's business interest or activities that may represent a conflict of interest and obtaining their consent to act in such circumstances; or

(b) Notifying all known relevant parties that the Member in Public Practice is acting for two or more parties in respect of a matter where their respective interests are in conflict and obtaining their consent to so act; or

(c) Notifying the client that the Member in Public Practice does not act exclusively for any one client in the provision of proposed services (for example, in a particular market sector or with respect to a specific service) and obtaining their consent to so act.

220.4 The Member in Public Practice shall also determine whether to apply one or more of the following additional safeguards:

(a) The use of separate Engagement Teams;

(b) Procedures to prevent access to information (e.g., strict physical separation of such teams, confidential and secure data filing);

(c) Clear guidelines for members of the Engagement Team on issues of security and confidentiality;

(d) The use of confidentiality agreements signed by employees and partners of the Firm; and

(e) Regular review of the application of safeguards by a senior individual not involved with relevant client engagements.

220.5 Where a conflict of interest creates a threat to one or more of the fundamental principles, including objectivity, confidentiality, or professional behaviour, that cannot be eliminated or reduced to an Acceptable Level through the application of safeguards, the Member in Public Practice shall not accept a specific engagement or shall resign from one or more conflicting engagements.

220.6 Where a Member in Public Practice has requested consent from a client to act for another party (which may or may not be an existing client) in respect of a matter where the respective interests are in conflict and that consent has been refused by the client, the Member in Public Practice shall not continue to act for one of the parties in the matter giving rise to the conflict of interest.

SECTION 230

Second Opinions

230.1 Situations where a Member in Public Practice is asked to provide a second opinion on the application of Australian Accounting Standards, Auditing or Assurance Standards, reporting or other standards or principles to specific circumstances or transactions by or on behalf of a company or an entity that is not an existing client may create threats to compliance with the fundamental principles. For example, there may be a threat to professional competence and due care in circumstances where the second opinion is not based on the same set of facts that were made available to the Existing Accountant or is based on inadequate evidence. The existence and significance of any threat will depend on the circumstances of the request and all the other available facts and assumptions relevant to the expression of a professional judgment.

230.2 When asked to provide such an opinion, a Member in Public Practice shall evaluate the significance of any threats and apply safeguards when necessary to eliminate them or reduce them to an Acceptable Level. Examples of such safeguards include seeking client permission to contact the Existing Accountant, describing the limitations surrounding any opinion in communications with the client and providing the Existing Accountant with a copy of the opinion.

230.3 If the company or entity seeking the opinion will not permit communication with the Existing Accountant, a Member in Public Practice shall determine whether, taking all the circumstances into account, it is appropriate to provide the opinion sought.

SECTION 240

Fees and Other Types of Remuneration

240.1 When entering into negotiations regarding services, a Member in Public Practice may quote whatever fee is deemed appropriate. The fact that one Member in Public Practice may quote a fee lower than another is not in itself unethical. Nevertheless, there may be threats to compliance with the fundamental principles arising from the level of fees quoted. For example, a self-interest threat to professional competence and due care is created if the fee quoted is so low that it may be difficult to perform the engagement in accordance with applicable technical and professional standards for that price.

240.2 The existence and significance of any threats created will depend on factors such as the level of fee quoted and the services to which it applies. The significance of any threat shall be evaluated and safeguards applied when necessary to eliminate the threat or reduce it to an Acceptable Level. Examples of such safeguards include:

- Making the client aware of the terms of the engagement and, in particular, the basis on which fees are charged and which services are covered by the quoted fee.
- Assigning appropriate time and qualified staff to the task.

Contingent Fees

240.3 Contingent Fees are widely used for certain types of non-assurance engagements.[1] They may, however, create threats to compliance with the fundamental principles in certain circumstances[2]. They may create a self-interest threat to objectivity. The existence and significance of such threats will depend on factors including:

- The nature of the engagement.
- The range of possible fee amounts.
- The basis for determining the fee.
- Whether the outcome or result of the transaction is to be reviewed by an independent third party.

240.4 The significance of any such threats shall be evaluated and safeguards applied when necessary to eliminate or reduce them to an Acceptable Level. Examples of such safeguards include:

- An advance written agreement with the client as to the basis of remuneration.
- Disclosure to intended users of the work performed by the Member in Public Practice and the basis of remuneration.
- Quality control policies and procedures.
- Review by an independent third party of the work performed by the Member in Public Practice.

---

1 Contingent Fees for non-assurance services provided to Audit Clients and other Assurance Clients are discussed in Sections 290 and 291 of this Code.

2 APESB has prohibited the use of Contingent Fees in certain circumstances. These circumstances are described in the following APESB Standards:

APES 215 *Forensic Accounting Services*;

APES 225 *Valuation Services*;

APES 330 *Insolvency Services*;

APES 345 *Reporting on Prospective Financial Information Prepared in Connection with a Disclosure Document*; and

APES 350 *Participation by Members in Public Practice in Due Diligence Committees in connection with a Public Document.*

Referral fees and commissions

240.5 In certain circumstances, a Member in Public Practice may receive a referral fee or commission relating to a client. For example, where the Member in Public Practice does not provide the specific service required, a fee may be received for referring a continuing client to another Member in Public Practice or other expert. A Member in Public Practice may receive a commission from a third party (e.g., a software vendor) in connection with the sale of goods or services to a client. Accepting such a referral fee or commission creates a self-interest threat to objectivity and professional competence and due care.

240.6 A Member in Public Practice may also pay a referral fee to obtain a client, for example, where the client continues as a client of another Member in Public Practice but requires specialist services not offered by the Existing Accountant. The payment of such a referral fee also creates a self-interest threat to objectivity and professional competence and due care.

240.7 The significance of the threat shall be evaluated and safeguards applied when necessary to eliminate the threat or reduce it to an Acceptable Level. Examples of such safeguards include:

- Disclosing to the client any arrangements to pay a referral fee to another Member in Public Practice for the work referred.
- Disclosing to the client any arrangements to receive a referral fee for referring the client to another Member in Public Practice.
- Obtaining advance agreement from the client for commission arrangements in connection with the sale by a third party of goods or services to the client.

AUST240.7.1 A Member in Public Practice who is undertaking an engagement in Australia and receives a referral fee or commission shall inform the client in writing of:

- the existence of such arrangement;
- the identity of the other party or parties; and
- the method of calculation of the referral fee, commission or other benefit accruing directly or indirectly to the Member.

AUST240.7.2 The receipt of commissions or other similar benefits in connection with an Assurance Engagement creates a threat to Independence that no safeguards could reduce to an Acceptable Level. Accordingly, a Member in Public Practice shall not accept such a fee arrangement in respect of an Assurance Engagement.

240.8 A Member in Public Practice may purchase all or part of another Firm on the basis that payments will be made to individuals formerly owning the Firm or to their heirs or estates. Such payments are not regarded as commissions or referral fees for the purpose of paragraphs 240.5–240.7 above.

SECTION 250

Marketing Professional Services

250.1 When a Member in Public Practice solicits new work through Advertising or other forms of marketing, there may be a threat to compliance with the fundamental principles. For example, a self-interest threat to compliance with the principle of professional behaviour is created if services, achievements, or products are marketed in a way that is inconsistent with that principle.

250.2 A Member in Public Practice shall not bring the profession into disrepute when marketing Professional Services. The Member in Public Practice shall be honest and truthful and not:

(a) Make exaggerated claims for services offered, qualifications possessed, or experience gained; or

(b) Make disparaging references or unsubstantiated comparisons to the work of another.

If the Member in Public Practice is in doubt about whether a proposed form of Advertising or marketing is appropriate, the Member in Public Practice shall consider consulting with the relevant professional body.

SECTION 260

Gifts and Hospitality

260.1 A Member in Public Practice, or an Immediate or Close Family member, may be offered gifts and hospitality from a client. Such an offer may create threats to compliance with the fundamental principles. For example, a self-interest or familiarity threat to objectivity may be created if a gift from a client is accepted; an intimidation threat to objectivity may result from the possibility of such offers being made public.

260.2 The existence and significance of any threat will depend on the nature, value, and intent of the offer. Where gifts or hospitality are offered that a reasonable and informed third party, weighing all the specific facts and circumstances, would consider trivial and inconsequential, a Member in Public Practice may conclude that the offer is made in the normal course of business without the specific intent to influence decision making or to obtain information. In such cases, the Member in Public Practice may generally conclude that any threat to compliance with the fundamental principles is at an Acceptable Level.

260.3 A Member in Public Practice shall evaluate the significance of any threats and apply safeguards when necessary to eliminate the threats or reduce them to an Acceptable Level. When the threats cannot be eliminated or reduced to an Acceptable Level through the application of safeguards, a Member in Public Practice shall not accept such an offer.

SECTION 270

Custody of Client Assets

270.1 A Member in Public Practice shall not assume custody of client monies or other assets unless permitted to do so by law and, if so, in compliance with any additional legal duties imposed on a Member in Public Practice holding such assets.

270.2 The holding of client assets creates threats to compliance with the fundamental principles; for example, there is a self-interest threat to professional behaviour and may be a self-interest threat to objectivity arising from holding client assets. A Member in Public Practice entrusted with money (or other assets) belonging to others shall therefore:

(a) Keep such assets separately from personal or Firm assets;

(b) Use such assets only for the purpose for which they are intended;

(c) At all times be ready to account for those assets and any income, dividends, or gains generated, to any persons entitled to such accounting; and

(d) Comply with all relevant laws and regulations relevant to the holding of and accounting for such assets.

270.3 As part of client and engagement acceptance procedures for services that may involve the holding of client assets, a Member in Public Practice shall make appropriate inquiries about the source of such assets and consider legal and regulatory obligations. For example, if the assets were derived from illegal activities, such as money laundering, a threat to compliance with the fundamental principles would be created. In such situations, the Member may consider seeking legal advice.

SECTION 280

Objectivity—All Services

280.1 A Member in Public Practice shall determine when providing any Professional Service whether there are threats to compliance with the fundamental principle of objectivity resulting from having interests in, or relationships with, a client or its Directors, Officers or employees. For example, a familiarity threat to objectivity may be created from a family or close personal or business relationship.

280.2 A Member in Public Practice who provides an assurance service shall be independent of the Assurance Client. Independence of mind and in appearance is necessary to enable the Member in Public Practice to express a conclusion, and be seen to express a conclusion, without bias, conflict of interest, or undue influence of others. Sections 290 and 291 provide specific guidance on Independence requirements for Members in Public Practice when performing Assurance Engagements.

280.3 The existence of threats to objectivity when providing any Professional Service will depend upon the particular circumstances of the engagement and the nature of the work that the Member in Public Practice is performing.

280.4 A Member in Public Practice shall evaluate the significance of any threats and apply safeguards when necessary to eliminate them or reduce them to an Acceptable Level. Examples of such safeguards include:

- Withdrawing from the Engagement Team.
- Supervisory procedures.
- Terminating the financial or business relationship giving rise to the threat.
- Discussing the issue with higher levels of management within the Firm.
- Discussing the issue with Those Charged with Governance of the client.

If safeguards cannot eliminate or reduce the threat to an Acceptable Level, the Member shall decline or terminate the relevant engagement.

APES

[AUST] Preface: SECTIONS 290 and 291

SECTION 290 Independence – Audit and Review Engagements and

SECTION 291 Independence – Other Assurance Engagements

Section 290 of this Code addresses Independence requirements for Audit and Review Engagements, which are Assurance Engagements where a Member in Public Practice expresses a conclusion on Historical Financial Information.

Section 291 of this Code addresses Independence requirements for Assurance Engagements that are not Audit or Review Engagements of Historical Financial Information, referred to in this Code as Other Assurance Engagements.

The concept of Independence is fundamental to compliance with the principles of integrity and objectivity. This Code adopts a conceptual framework that requires the identification and evaluation of threats to Independence so that any threats created are eliminated or reduced to an Acceptable Level by the application of safeguards.

This approach contrasts with the rules adopted in legislation, which are often prescriptive in nature. Accordingly, Members and other readers of this Code should be aware that adherence to this Code does not ensure adherence to legislation and they must refer to such legislation to determine their legal obligations.

While this difference in approach makes precise comparisons to specific legislation, such as the *Corporations Act 2001*, difficult, the underlying principles of integrity and objectivity are consistent with objective and impartial judgement, when both approaches are tested in the context of all relevant facts by a reasonable person. Where APESB is aware that there is a more stringent requirement in the *Corporations Act 2001* an appropriate footnote reference has been included for the Members and other readers information. However, please note that not all applicable *Corporations Act 2001* requirements have been addressed and thus Members are referred to the *Corporations Act 2001* to determine their independence obligations when performing Audit and Review Engagements in accordance with the Act.

The statutory Independence of Auditors–General is provided for in legislation by the Parliament of each Australian jurisdiction in a number of ways. This includes defining the scope of an Auditor–General's mandate, the appointment and removal of an Auditor-General and the performance of his or her responsibilities. The requirements within this Code apply to Auditors-General and their senior Officers who are delegated or authorised to sign assurance reports and are Members, to the extent that they do not conflict with applicable legislation.

With regard to the use of the words "material" and "materiality" in Sections 290 and 291, it is not possible to give a definition which covers all circumstances where either word is used. In assessing materiality, a Member in Public Practice or a Firm shall consider both the qualitative and quantitative aspects of the matter under consideration which might have, or be seen to have, an adverse effect on the objectivity of the Member or Firm.

SECTION 290

Independence – Audit and Review Engagements

Contents

APES

Structure of Section

290.1 This section addresses the Independence requirements for Audit Engagements and Review Engagements, which are Assurance Engagements in which a Member in Public Practice expresses a conclusion on Financial Statements. Such engagements comprise Audit and Review Engagements to report on a complete set of Financial Statements and a single Financial Statement. Independence requirements for Assurance Engagements that are not Audit or Review Engagements are addressed in Section 291.

290.2 In certain circumstances involving Audit Engagements where the audit report includes a restriction on use and distribution and provided certain conditions are met, the Independence requirements in this section may be modified as provided in paragraphs 290.500 to 290.514. The modifications are not permitted in the case of an audit of Financial Statements required by law or regulation.

290.3 In this section, the term(s):

- "audit," "Audit Team," "Audit Engagement," "Audit Client" and "audit report" includes review, Review Team, Review Engagement, Review Client and review report; and
- "Firm" includes Network Firm, except where otherwise stated.

A Conceptual Framework Approach to Independence

290.4 In the case of Audit Engagements, it is in the public interest and, therefore, required by this Code of Ethics, that members of Audit Teams, Firms and, Network Firms shall be independent of Audit Clients.

290.5 The objective of this section is to assist Firms and members of Audit Teams in applying the conceptual framework approach described below to achieving and maintaining Independence.

290.6 Independence comprises:

Independence of Mind

The state of mind that permits the expression of a conclusion without being affected by influences that compromise professional judgment, thereby allowing an individual to act with integrity and exercise objectivity and professional scepticism.

Independence in Appearance

The avoidance of facts and circumstances that are so significant that a reasonable and informed third party would be likely to conclude, weighing all the specific facts and circumstances, that a Firm's, or a member of the Audit Team's, integrity, objectivity or professional scepticism has been compromised.

290.7 The conceptual framework approach shall be applied by Members to:

(a) Identify threats to Independence;

(b) Evaluate the significance of the threats identified; and

(c) Apply safeguards, when necessary, to eliminate the threats or reduce them to an Acceptable Level.

When the Member determines that appropriate safeguards are not available or cannot be applied to eliminate the threats or reduce them to an Acceptable Level, the Member shall eliminate the circumstance or relationship creating the threats or decline or terminate the Audit Engagement.

A Member shall use professional judgment in applying this conceptual framework.

290.8 Many different circumstances, or combinations of circumstances, may be relevant in assessing threats to Independence. It is impossible to define every situation that creates threats to Independence and to specify the appropriate action. Therefore, this Code establishes a conceptual framework that requires Firms and members of Audit Teams to identify, evaluate, and address threats to Independence. The conceptual framework approach assists Members in Public Practice in complying with the ethical requirements in this Code. It accommodates many variations in circumstances that create threats to

Independence and can deter a Member from concluding that a situation is permitted if it is not specifically prohibited.

290.9 Paragraphs 290.100 and onwards describe how the conceptual framework approach to Independence is to be applied. These paragraphs do not address all the circumstances and relationships that create or may create threats to Independence.

290.10 In deciding whether to accept or continue an engagement, or whether a particular individual may be a member of the Audit Team, a Firm shall identify and evaluate threats to Independence. If the threats are not at an Acceptable Level, and the decision is whether to accept an engagement or include a particular individual on the Audit Team, the Firm shall determine whether safeguards are available to eliminate the threats or reduce them to an Acceptable Level. If the decision is whether to continue an engagement, the Firm shall determine whether any existing safeguards will continue to be effective to eliminate the threats or reduce them to an Acceptable Level or whether other safeguards will need to be applied or whether the engagement needs to be terminated. Whenever new information about a threat to Independence comes to the attention of the Firm during the engagement, the Firm shall evaluate the significance of the threat in accordance with the conceptual framework approach.

290.11 Throughout this section, reference is made to the significance of threats to Independence. In evaluating the significance of a threat, qualitative as well as quantitative factors shall be taken into account.

AUST290.11.1 Where a Member in Public Practice identifies multiple threats to Independence, which individually may not be significant, the Member shall evaluate the significance of those threats in aggregate and the safeguards applied or in place to eliminate some or all of the threats or reduce them to an Acceptable Level in aggregate.

290.12 This section does not, in most cases, prescribe the specific responsibility of individuals within the Firm for actions related to Independence because responsibility may differ depending on the size, structure and organisation of a Firm. The Firm is required by APES 320 *Quality Control for Firms* to establish policies and procedures designed to provide it with reasonable assurance that Independence is maintained when required by relevant ethical requirements. In addition, Auditing and Assurance Standards require the Engagement Partner to form a conclusion on compliance with the Independence requirements that apply to the engagement.

Networks and Network Firms

290.13 If a Firm is deemed to be a Network Firm, the Firm shall be Independent of the Audit Clients of the other Firms within the Network (unless otherwise stated in this Code). The Independence requirements in this section that apply to a Network Firm apply to any entity, such as a consulting practice or professional law practice, that meets the definition of a Network Firm irrespective of whether the entity itself meets the definition of a Firm.

290.14 To enhance their ability to provide Professional Services, Firms frequently form larger structures with other Firms and entities. Whether these larger structures create a Network depends on the particular facts and circumstances and does not depend on whether the Firms and entities are legally separate and distinct. For example, a larger structure may be aimed only at facilitating the referral of work, which in itself does not meet the criteria necessary to constitute a Network. Alternatively, a larger structure might be such that it is aimed at co-operation and the Firms share a common brand name, a common system of quality control, or significant professional resources and consequently is deemed to be a Network.

290.15 The judgment as to whether the larger structure is a Network shall be made in light of whether a reasonable and informed third party would be likely to conclude, weighing all the specific facts and circumstances, that the entities are associated in such a way that a Network exists. This judgment shall be applied consistently throughout the Network.

290.16 Where the larger structure is aimed at co-operation and it is clearly aimed at profit or cost sharing among the entities within the structure, it is deemed to be a Network. However, the sharing of immaterial costs does not in itself create a Network. In addition, if the sharing of costs is limited only to those costs related to the development of audit methodologies, manuals, or training courses, this would not in itself create a Network. Further, an association between a Firm and an otherwise unrelated entity to jointly provide a service or develop a product does not in itself create a Network.

290.17 Where the larger structure is aimed at cooperation and the entities within the structure share common ownership, control or management, it is deemed to be a Network. This could be achieved by contract or other means.

290.18 Where the larger structure is aimed at co-operation and the entities within the structure share common quality control policies and procedures, it is deemed to be a Network. For this purpose, common quality control policies and procedures are those designed, implemented and monitored across the larger structure.

290.19 Where the larger structure is aimed at co-operation and the entities within the structure share a common business strategy, it is deemed to be a Network. Sharing a common business strategy involves an agreement by the entities to achieve common strategic objectives. An entity is not deemed to be a Network Firm merely because it co-operates with another entity solely to respond jointly to a request for a proposal for the provision of a Professional Service.

290.20 Where the larger structure is aimed at co-operation and the entities within the structure share the use of a common brand name, it is deemed to be a Network. A common brand name includes common initials or a common name. A Firm is deemed to be using a common brand name if it includes, for example, the common brand name as part of, or along with, its Firm name, when a partner of the Firm signs an audit report.

290.21 Even though a Firm does not belong to a Network and does not use a common brand name as part of its Firm name, it may give the appearance that it belongs to a Network if it makes reference in its stationery or promotional materials to being a member of an association of Firms. Accordingly, if care is not taken in how a Firm describes such memberships, a perception may be created that the Firm belongs to a Network.

290.22 If a Firm sells a component of its practice, the sales agreement sometimes provides that, for a limited period of time, the component may continue to use the name of the Firm, or an element of the name, even though it is no longer connected to the Firm. In such circumstances, while the two entities may be practicing under a common name, the facts are such that they do not belong to a larger structure aimed at co-operation and are, therefore, not Network Firms. Those entities shall determine how to disclose that they are not Network Firms when presenting themselves to outside parties.

290.23 Where the larger structure is aimed at co-operation and the entities within the structure share a significant part of professional resources, it is deemed to be a Network. Professional resources include:

- Common systems that enable Firms to exchange information such as client data, billing and time records;
- Partners and staff;
- Technical departments that consult on technical or industry specific issues, transactions or events for Assurance Engagements;
- Audit methodology or audit manuals; and
- Training courses and facilities.

290.24 The determination of whether the professional resources shared are significant, and therefore the Firms are Network Firms, shall be made based on the relevant facts and circumstances. Where the shared resources are limited to common audit methodology or audit manuals, with no exchange of personnel or client or market information, it is unlikely that the shared resources would be significant. The same applies to a common training endeavour. Where, however, the shared resources involve the exchange of people or information, such as where staff are drawn from a shared pool, or a common technical department is created within the larger structure to provide participating Firms with technical advice that the Firms are required to follow, a reasonable and informed third party is more likely to conclude that the shared resources are significant.

Public Interest Entities

290.25 Section 290 contains additional provisions that reflect the extent of public interest in certain entities. For the purpose of this section, a Public Interest Entity is:

(a) A Listed Entity*; or

(b) Any entity (a) defined by regulation or legislation as a public interest entity; or (b) for which the audit is required by regulation or legislation to be conducted in compliance with the same Independence requirements that apply to the audit of Listed Entities. Such regulation may be promulgated by any relevant regulator, including an audit regulator.

290.26 Firms shall determine whether to treat additional entities, or certain categories of entities, as Public Interest Entities because they have a large number and wide range of stakeholders. Factors to be considered include:

- The nature of the business, such as the holding of assets in a fiduciary capacity for a large number of stakeholders. Examples may include financial institutions, such as banks and insurance companies and pension funds;
- Size; and
- Number of employees.

AUST 290.26.1 The following entities in Australia will generally satisfy the conditions in paragraph 290.26 as having a large number and wide range of stakeholders and thus are likely to be classified as Public Interest Entities. In each instance Firms shall consider the nature of the business, its size and the number of its employees:

- Authorised deposit-taking institutions (ADIs) and authorised non-operating holding companies (NOHCs) regulated by the Australian Prudential Regulatory Authority (APRA) under the *Banking Act 1959*;
- Authorised insurers and authorised NOHCs regulated by APRA under Section 122 of the *Insurance Act 1973*;
- Life insurance companies and registered NOHCs regulated by APRA under the *Life Insurance Act 1995*;
- Disclosing entities as defined in Section 111AC of the *Corporations Act 2001*;
- Registrable superannuation entity (RSE) licensees, and RSEs under their trusteeship that have five or more members, regulated by APRA under the *Superannuation Industry (Supervision) Act 1993*; and
- Other issuers of debt and equity instruments to the public.

Related Entities

290.27 In the case of an Audit Client that is a Listed Entity, references to an Audit Client in this section include Related Entities of the client (unless otherwise stated). For all other Audit Clients, references to an Audit Client in this section include Related Entities over which the client has direct or indirect control. When the Audit Team knows or has reason to believe that a relationship or circumstance involving another Related Entity of the client is relevant to the evaluation of the Firm's Independence from the client, the Audit Team shall include that Related Entity when identifying and evaluating threats to Independence and applying appropriate safeguards.

APES

* *Includes a listed entity as defined in Section 9 of the Corporations Act 2001.*

Those Charged with Governance

290.28 Even when not required by the Code, applicable Auditing and Assurance Standards, law or regulation, regular communication is encouraged between the Firm and Those Charged with Governance of the Audit Client regarding relationships and other matters that might, in the Firm's opinion, reasonably bear on Independence. Such communication enables Those Charged with Governance to (a) consider the Firm's judgments in identifying and evaluating threats to Independence, (b) consider the appropriateness of safeguards applied to eliminate them or reduce them to an Acceptable Level, and (c) take appropriate action. Such an approach can be particularly helpful with respect to intimidation and familiarity threats.

Documentation

290.29 Documentation provides evidence of the Member's judgments in forming conclusions regarding compliance with Independence requirements. The absence of documentation is not a determinant of whether a Firm considered a particular matter nor whether it is Independent.

The Member shall document conclusions regarding compliance with Independence requirements, and the substance of any relevant discussions that support those conclusions. Accordingly:

(a) When safeguards are required to reduce a threat to an Acceptable Level, the Member shall document the nature of the threat and the safeguards in place or applied that reduce the threat to an Acceptable Level; and

(b) When a threat required significant analysis to determine whether safeguards were necessary and the Member concluded that they were not because the threat was already at an Acceptable Level, the Member shall document the nature of the threat and the rationale for the conclusion.

Engagement Period

290.30 Independence from the Audit Client is required both during the engagement period and the period covered by the Financial Statements. The engagement period starts when the Audit Team begins to perform audit services. The engagement period ends when the audit report is issued. When the engagement is of a recurring nature, it ends at the later of the notification by either party that the professional relationship has terminated or the issuance of the final audit report.

290.31 When an entity becomes an Audit Client during or after the period covered by the Financial Statements on which the Firm will express an Opinion, the Firm shall determine whether any threats to Independence are created by:

- Financial or business relationships with the Audit Client during or after the period covered by the Financial Statements but before accepting the Audit Engagement; or
- Previous services provided to the Audit Client.

290.32 If a non-assurance service was provided to the Audit Client during or after the period covered by the Financial Statements but before the Audit Team begins to perform audit services and the service would not be permitted during the period of the Audit Engagement, the Firm shall evaluate any threat to Independence created by the service. If a threat is not at an Acceptable Level, the Audit Engagement shall only be accepted if safeguards are applied to eliminate any threats or reduce them to an Acceptable Level. Examples of such safeguards include:

- Not including personnel who provided the non-assurance service as members of the Audit Team;
- Having a Member review the audit and non-assurance work as appropriate; or
- Engaging another Firm to evaluate the results of the non-assurance service or having another Firm re-perform the non-assurance service to the extent necessary to enable it to take responsibility for the service.

Mergers and Acquisitions

290.33 When, as a result of a merger or acquisition, an entity becomes a Related Entity of an Audit Client, the Firm shall identify and evaluate previous and current interests and relationships with the Related Entity that, taking into account available safeguards, could affect its Independence and therefore its ability to continue the Audit Engagement after the effective date of the merger or acquisition.

290.34 The Firm shall take steps necessary to terminate, by the effective date of the merger or acquisition, any current interests or relationships that are not permitted under this Code. However, if such a current interest or relationship cannot reasonably be terminated by the effective date of the merger or acquisition, for example, because the Related Entity is unable by the effective date to effect an orderly transition to another service provider of a non-assurance service provided by the Firm, the Firm shall evaluate the threat that is created by such interest or relationship. The more significant the threat, the more likely the Firm's objectivity will be compromised and it will be unable to continue as auditor. The significance of the threat will depend upon factors such as:

- The nature and significance of the interest or relationship;
- The nature and significance of the Related Entity relationship (for example, whether the Related Entity is a subsidiary or parent); and
- The length of time until the interest or relationship can reasonably be terminated.

The Firm shall discuss with Those Charged with Governance the reasons why the interest or relationship cannot reasonably be terminated by the effective date of the merger or acquisition and the evaluation of the significance of the threat.

290.35 If Those Charged with Governance request the Firm to continue as auditor, the Firm shall do so only if:

(a) the interest or relationship will be terminated as soon as reasonably possible and in all cases within six months of the effective date of the merger or acquisition;

(b) any individual who has such an interest or relationship, including one that has arisen through performing a non-assurance service that would not be permitted under this section, will not be a member of the Engagement Team for the audit or the individual responsible for the Engagement Quality Control Review; and

(c) appropriate transitional measures will be applied, as necessary, and discussed with Those Charged with Governance. Examples of transitional measures include:

- Having a Member review the audit or non-assurance work as appropriate;
- Having a Member, who is not a member of the Firm expressing the opinion on the Financial Statements, perform a review that is equivalent to an Engagement Quality Control Review; or
- Engaging another Firm to evaluate the results of the non-assurance service or having another Firm re-perform the non-assurance service to the extent necessary to enable it to take responsibility for the service.

290.36 The Firm may have completed a significant amount of work on the audit prior to the effective date of the merger or acquisition and may be able to complete the remaining audit procedures within a short period of time. In such circumstances, if Those Charged with Governance request the Firm to complete the audit while continuing with an interest or relationship identified in 290.33, the Firm shall do so only if it:

(a) Has evaluated the significance of the threat created by such interest or relationship and discussed the evaluation with Those Charged with Governance;

(b) Complies with the requirements of paragraph 290.35(b) – (c); and

(c) Ceases to be the auditor no later than the issuance of the audit report.

290.37 When addressing previous and current interests and relationships covered by paragraphs 290.33 to 290.36, the Firm shall determine whether, even if all the requirements could be met, the interests and relationships create threats that would remain so significant that objectivity would be compromised and, if so, the Firm shall cease to be the auditor.

290.38 The Member shall document any interests or relationships covered by paragraphs 290.34 and 36 that will not be terminated by the effective date of the merger or acquisition and the reasons why they will not be terminated, the transitional measures applied, the results of the discussion with Those Charged with Governance, and the rationale as to why the previous and current interests and relationships do not create threats that would remain so significant that objectivity would be compromised.

Other Considerations

290.39 There may be occasions when there is an inadvertent violation of this section. If such an inadvertent violation occurs, it generally will be deemed not to compromise Independence provided the Firm has appropriate quality control policies and procedures in place, equivalent to those required by APES 320 *Quality Control for Firms*, to maintain Independence and, once discovered, the violation is corrected promptly and any necessary safeguards are applied to eliminate any threat or reduce it to an Acceptable Level.

AUST290.39.1 Unless an inadvertent violation of this section is trivial and inconsequential, a Firm shall document and discuss it with Those Charged with Governance.

Paragraphs 290.40 to 290.99 are intentionally left blank.

Application of the Conceptual Framework Approach to Independence

290.100 Paragraphs 290.102 to 290.231 describe specific circumstances and relationships that create or may create threats to Independence. The paragraphs describe the potential threats and the types of safeguards that may be appropriate to eliminate the threats or reduce them to an Acceptable Level and identify certain situations where no safeguards could reduce the threats to an Acceptable Level. The paragraphs do not describe all of the circumstances and relationships that create or may create a threat to Independence. The Firm and the members of the Audit Team shall evaluate the implications of similar, but different, circumstances and relationships and determine whether safeguards, including the safeguards in paragraphs 200.12 to 200.15, can be applied when necessary to eliminate the threats to Independence or reduce them to an Acceptable Level.

290.101 Paragraphs 290.102 to 290.126 contain references to the materiality of a Financial Interest, loan, or guarantee, or the significance of a business relationship. For the purpose of determining whether such an interest is material to an individual, the combined net worth of the individual and the individual's Immediate Family members may be taken into account.

Financial Interests

290.102 Holding a Financial Interest in an Audit Client may create a self-interest threat. The existence and significance of any threat created depends on: (a) the role of the person holding the Financial Interest, (b) whether the Financial Interest is direct or indirect, and (c) the materiality of the Financial Interest.

290.103 Financial Interests may be held through an intermediary (e.g. a collective investment vehicle, estate or trust). The determination of whether such Financial Interests are direct or indirect will depend upon whether the beneficial owner has control over the investment vehicle or the ability to influence its investment decisions. When control over the investment vehicle or the ability to influence investment decisions exists, this Code defines that Financial Interest to be a Direct Financial Interest. Conversely, when the beneficial owner of the Financial Interest has no control over the investment vehicle or ability to influence its investment decisions, this Code defines that Financial Interest to be an Indirect Financial Interest.

290.104 If a member of the Audit Team, a member of that individual's Immediate Family, or a Firm has a Direct Financial Interest or a material Indirect Financial Interest in the Audit Client, the self-interest threat created would be so significant that no safeguards could reduce the threat to an Acceptable Level. Therefore, none of the following shall have a Direct Financial Interest or a material Indirect Financial Interest in the client: a member of the Audit Team; a member of that individual's Immediate Family; or the Firm.

290.105 When a member of the Audit Team has a Close Family member who the Audit Team member knows has a Direct Financial Interest or a material Indirect Financial Interest in the Audit Client, a self-interest threat is created. The significance of the threat will depend on factors such as: The nature of the relationship between the member of the Audit Team and the Close Family member; and The materiality of the Financial Interest to the Close Family member.

The significance of the threat shall be evaluated and safeguards applied when necessary to eliminate the threat or reduce it to an Acceptable Level. Examples of such safeguards include: The Close Family member disposing, as soon as practicable, of all of the Financial Interest or disposing of a sufficient portion of an Indirect Financial Interest so that the remaining interest is no longer material; Having a Member review the work of the member of the Audit Team; or Removing the individual from the Audit Team.

290.106 If a member of the Audit Team, a member of that individual's Immediate Family, or a Firm has a direct or material Indirect Financial Interest in an entity that has a controlling interest in the Audit Client, and the client is material to the entity, the self-interest threat created would be so significant that no safeguards could reduce the threat to an Acceptable Level. Therefore, none of the following shall have such a Financial Interest: a member of the Audit Team; a member of that individual's Immediate Family; and the Firm.

290.107 The holding by a Firm's retirement benefit plan of a direct or material Indirect Financial Interest in an Audit Client creates a self-interest threat. The significance of the threat shall be evaluated and safeguards applied when necessary to eliminate the threat or reduce it to an Acceptable Level[3]3.

290.108 If other partners in the Office in which the Engagement Partner practices in connection with the Audit Engagement, or their Immediate Family members, hold a Direct Financial Interest or a material Indirect Financial Interest in that Audit Client, the self-interest threat created would be so significant that no safeguards could reduce the threat to an Acceptable Level. Therefore, neither such partners nor their Immediate Family members shall hold any such Financial Interests in such an Audit Client.

290.109 The Office in which the Engagement Partner practices in connection with the Audit Engagement is not necessarily the Office to which that partner is assigned. Accordingly, when the Engagement Partner is located in a different Office from that of the other members of the Audit Team, professional judgment shall be used to determine in which Office the partner practices in connection with that engagement.

290.110 If other partners and managerial employees who provide non-audit services to the Audit Client, except those whose involvement is minimal, or their Immediate Family members, hold a Direct Financial Interest or a material Indirect Financial Interest in the Audit Client, the self-interest threat created would be so significant that no safeguards could reduce the threat to an Acceptable Level. Accordingly, neither such personnel nor their Immediate Family members shall hold any such Financial Interests in such an Audit Client.

290.111 Despite paragraphs 290.108 and 290.110, the holding of a Financial Interest in an Audit Client by an Immediate Family member of (a) a partner located in the Office in which the Engagement Partner practices in connection with the Audit Engagement, or (b) a partner or managerial employee who provides non-audit services to the Audit Client, is deemed not to compromise Independence if the Financial Interest is received as a result of the Immediate Family member's employment rights (e.g., through pension or share option plans) and, when necessary, safeguards are applied to eliminate any threat to Independence or reduce it to an Acceptable Level. However, when the Immediate Family member has or obtains the right to dispose of the Financial Interest or, in the case of a stock option, the right to exercise the option, the Financial Interest shall be disposed of or forfeited as soon as practicable.

290.112 A self-interest threat may be created if the Firm or a member of the Audit Team, or a member of that individual's Immediate Family, has a Financial Interest in an entity and an Audit Client also has a Financial Interest in that entity. However, Independence is deemed not to be compromised if these interests are immaterial and the Audit Client cannot exercise significant influence over the entity. If such interest is material to any party, and the Audit Client can exercise significant influence over the other entity, no safeguards could reduce the threat to an Acceptable Level. Accordingly, the Firm shall not have such an interest and any individual with such an interest shall, before becoming a member of the Audit Team, either:

(a) Dispose of the interest; or

(b) Dispose of a sufficient amount of the interest so that the remaining interest is no longer material.

290.113 A self-interest, familiarity or intimidation threat may be created if a member of the Audit Team, or a member of that individual's Immediate Family, or the Firm, has a Financial Interest in an entity when a Director, Officer or controlling owner of the

---

3 Refer to s 324CH(1) Items 10-12 of the *Corporations Act 2001* which prohibits this arrangement in respect of Audits performed in accordance with the Act.

Audit Client is also known to have a Financial Interest in that entity. The existence and significance of any threat will depend upon factors such as:

- The role of the professional on the Audit Team;
- Whether ownership of the entity is closely or widely held;
- Whether the interest gives the investor the ability to control or significantly influence the entity; and
- The materiality of the Financial Interest.

The significance of any threat shall be evaluated and safeguards applied when necessary to eliminate the threat or reduce it to an Acceptable Level. Examples of such safeguards include:

- Removing the member of the Audit Team with the Financial Interest from the Audit Team; or
- Having a Member review the work of the member of the Audit Team.

290.114 The holding by a Firm, or a member of the Audit Team, or a member of that individual's Immediate Family, of a Direct Financial Interest or a material Indirect Financial Interest in the Audit Client as a trustee creates a self-interest threat. Similarly, a self-interest threat is created when (a) a partner in the Office in which the lead Engagement Partner practices in connection with the audit, (b) other partners and managerial employees who provide non-assurance services to the Audit Client, except those whose involvement is minimal, or (c) their Immediate Family members, hold a Direct Financial Interest or a material Indirect Financial Interest in the Audit Client as trustee. Such an interest shall not be held unless:

(a) Neither the trustee, nor an Immediate Family member of the trustee, nor the Firm are beneficiaries of the trust;

(b) The interest in the Audit Client held by the trust is not material to the trust;

(c) The trust is not able to exercise significant influence over the Audit Client; and

(d) The trustee, an Immediate Family member of the trustee, or the Firm cannot significantly influence any investment decision involving a Financial Interest in the Audit Client.

290.115 Members of the Audit Team shall determine whether a self-interest threat is created by any known Financial Interests in the Audit Client held by other individuals including:

- Partners and professional employees of the Firm, other than those referred to above, or their Immediate Family members; and
- Individuals with a close personal relationship with a member of the Audit Team.

Whether these interests create a self-interest threat will depend on factors such as:

- The Firm's organisational, operating and reporting structure; and
- The nature of the relationship between the individual and the member of the Audit Team.

The significance of any threat shall be evaluated and safeguards applied when necessary to eliminate the threat or reduce it to an Acceptable Level. Examples of such safeguards include:

- Removing the member of the Audit Team with the personal relationship from the Audit Team;
- Excluding the member of the Audit Team from any significant decision-making concerning the Audit Engagement; or
- Having a Member review the work of the member of the Audit Team.

APES

290.116 If a Firm or a partner or employee of the Firm, or a member of that individual's Immediate Family, receives a Direct Financial Interest or a material Indirect Financial Interest in an Audit Client, for example, by way of an inheritance, gift or as a result of a merger and such interest would not be permitted to be held under this section, then:

(a) If the interest is received by the Firm, the Financial Interest shall be disposed of immediately, or a sufficient amount of an Indirect Financial Interest shall be disposed of so that the remaining interest is no longer material;

(b) If the interest is received by a member of the Audit Team, or a member of that individual's Immediate Family, the individual who received the Financial Interest shall immediately dispose of the Financial Interest, or dispose of a sufficient amount of an Indirect Financial Interest so that the remaining interest is no longer material; or

(c) If the interest is received by an individual who is not a member of the Audit Team, or by an Immediate Family member of the individual, the Financial Interest shall be disposed of as soon as possible, or a sufficient amount of an Indirect Financial Interest shall be disposed of so that the remaining interest is no longer material. Pending the disposal of the Financial Interest, a determination shall be made as to whether any safeguards are necessary.

290.117 When an inadvertent violation of this section as it relates to a Financial Interest in an Audit Client occurs, it is deemed not to compromise Independence if:

(a) The Firm has established policies and procedures that require prompt notification to the Firm of any breaches resulting from the purchase, inheritance or other acquisition of a Financial Interest in the Audit Client;

(b) The actions in paragraph 290.116 (a)–(c) are taken as applicable; and

(c) The Firm applies other safeguards when necessary to reduce any remaining threat to an Acceptable Level. Examples of such safeguards include:

- Having a Member review the work of the member of the Audit Team; or
- Excluding the individual from any significant decision-making concerning the Audit Engagement.

The Firm shall determine whether to discuss the matter with Those Charged with Governance.

AUST290.117.1 Unless an inadvertent violation of this section as it relates to a Financial Interest in an Audit Client is trivial and inconsequential, the Firm shall document and discuss it with Those Charged with Governance.

Loans and Guarantees

290.118 A loan, or a guarantee of a loan, to a member of the Audit Team, or a member of that individual's Immediate Family, or the Firm from an Audit Client that is a bank or a similar institution may create a threat to Independence. If the loan or guarantee is not made under normal lending procedures, terms and conditions, a self-interest threat would be created that would be so significant that no safeguards could reduce the threat to an Acceptable Level. Accordingly, neither a member of the Audit Team, a member of that individual's Immediate Family, nor a Firm, or Network Firm, shall accept such a loan or guarantee.

290.119 If a loan to a Firm from an Audit Client that is a bank or similar institution is made under normal lending procedures, terms and conditions and it is material to the Audit Client or Firm receiving the loan, it may be possible to apply safeguards to reduce the self-interest threat to an Acceptable Level. An example of such a safeguard is having the work reviewed by a Member from a Network Firm that is neither involved with the audit nor received the loan.

290.120 A loan, or a guarantee of a loan, from an Audit Client that is a bank or a similar institution to a member of the Audit Team, or a member of that individual's Immediate Family, does not create a threat to Independence if the loan or guarantee is made under normal lending procedures, terms and conditions. Examples of such loans include home mortgages, bank overdrafts, car loans and credit card balances.

290.121 If the Firm or a member of the Audit Team, or a member of that individual's Immediate Family, accepts a loan from, or has a borrowing guaranteed by, an Audit Client that is not a bank or similar institution, the self-interest threat created would be so significant that no safeguards could reduce the threat to an Acceptable Level, unless the loan or guarantee is immaterial to both (a) the Firm or the member of the Audit Team and the Immediate Family member, and (b) the client.

290.122 Similarly, if the Firm or a member of the Audit Team, or a member of that individual's Immediate Family, makes or guarantees a loan to an Audit Client, the self-interest threat created would be so significant that no safeguards could reduce the threat to an Acceptable Level, unless the loan or guarantee is immaterial to both (a) the Firm or the member of the Audit Team and the Immediate Family member, and (b) the client[4].

290.123 If a Firm or a member of the Audit Team, or a member of that individual's Immediate Family, has deposits or a brokerage account with an Audit Client that is a bank, broker or similar institution, a threat to Independence is not created if the deposit or account is held under normal commercial terms.

Business Relationships

290.124 A close business relationship[5] between a Firm, or a member of the Audit Team, or a member of that individual's Immediate Family, and the Audit Client or its management, arises from a commercial relationship or common Financial Interest and may create self-interest or intimidation threats. Examples of such relationships include:

- Having a Financial Interest in a joint venture with either the client or a controlling owner, Director, Officer or other individual who performs senior managerial activities for that client.
- Arrangements to combine one or more services or products of the Firm with one or more services or products of the client and to market the package with reference to both parties.
- Distribution or marketing arrangements under which the Firm distributes or markets the client's products or services, or the client distributes or markets the Firm's products or services.

Unless any Financial Interest is immaterial and the business relationship is insignificant to the Firm and the client or its management, the threat created would be so significant that no safeguards could reduce the threat to an Acceptable Level. Therefore, unless the Financial Interest is immaterial and the business relationship is insignificant, the business relationship shall not be entered into, or it shall be reduced to an insignificant level or terminated.

In the case of a member of the Audit Team, unless any such Financial Interest is immaterial and the relationship is insignificant to that member, the individual shall be removed from the Audit Team.

If the business relationship is between an Immediate Family member of a member of the Audit Team and the Audit Client or its management, the significance of any threat shall be evaluated and safeguards applied when necessary to eliminate the threat or reduce it to an Acceptable Level.

290.125 A business relationship[6] involving the holding of an interest by the Firm, or a member of the Audit Team, or a member of that individual's Immediate Family, in a closely-

4 Refer to s 324CH(1) Items 15, 16, 17 & 19 of the *Corporations Act 2001* which prohibits making or guaranteeing loans irrespective of materiality for audits performed in accordance with the Act.

5 Refer to s 324CH(1) of the *Corporations Act 2001* which prohibits certain relationships between a person or the Firm and the corporate Audit Client irrespective of materiality or the significance of the relationship or Financial Interest.

6 Refer to s 324CH(1) of the *Corporations Act 2001* which prohibits certain relationships between a person or the Firm and the corporate Audit Client irrespective of materiality or the significance of the relationship or Financial Interest.

held entity when the Audit Client or a Director or Officer of the client, or any group thereof, also holds an interest in that entity does not create threats to Independence if:

(a) The business relationship is insignificant to the Firm, the member of the Audit Team and the Immediate Family member, and the client;

(b) The Financial Interest is immaterial to the investor or group of investors; and

(c) The Financial Interest does not give the investor, or group of investors, the ability to control the closely-held entity.

290.126 The purchase of goods and services from an Audit Client by the Firm, or a member of the Audit Team, or a member of that individual's Immediate Family, does not generally create a threat to Independence if the transaction is in the normal course of business and at arm's length. However, such transactions may be of such a nature or magnitude that they create a self-interest threat. The significance of any threat shall be evaluated and safeguards applied when necessary to eliminate the threat or reduce it to an Acceptable Level. Examples of such safeguards include:

- Eliminating or reducing the magnitude of the transaction; or
- Removing the individual from the Audit Team.

Family and Personal Relationships

290.127 Family and personal relationships between a member of the Audit Team and a Director or Officer or certain employees (depending on their role) of the Audit Client may create self-interest, familiarity or intimidation threats. The existence and significance of any threats will depend on a number of factors, including the individual's responsibilities on the Audit Team, the role of the family member or other individual within the client and the closeness of the relationship.

290.128 When an Immediate Family member of a member of the Audit Team is:

(a) A Director or Officer of the Audit Client; or

(b) An employee in a position to exert significant influence over the preparation of the client's accounting records or the Financial Statements on which the Firm will express an Opinion,

or was in such a position during any period covered by the engagement or the Financial Statements, the threats to Independence can only be reduced to an Acceptable Level by removing the individual from the Audit Team. The closeness of the relationship is such that no other safeguards could reduce the threat to an Acceptable Level. Accordingly, no individual who has such a relationship shall be a member of the Audit Team.

290.129 Threats to Independence are created when an Immediate Family member of a member of the Audit Team is an employee in a position to exert significant influence over the client's financial position, financial performance or cash flows. The significance of the threats will depend on factors such as:

- The position held by the Immediate Family member; and
- The role of the professional on the Audit Team.

The significance of the threat shall be evaluated and safeguards applied when necessary to eliminate the threat or reduce it to an Acceptable Level. Examples of such safeguards include:

- Removing the individual from the Audit Team; or
- Structuring the responsibilities of the Audit Team so that the professional does not deal with matters that are within the responsibility of the Immediate Family member.

290.130 Threats to Independence are created when a Close Family member of a member of the Audit Team is:

(a) A Director or Officer of the Audit Client; or

(b) An employee in a position to exert significant influence over the preparation of the client's accounting records or the Financial Statements on which the Firm will express an Opinion.

The significance of the threats will depend on factors such as:

- The nature of the relationship between the member of the Audit Team and the Close Family member;
- The position held by the Close Family member; and
- The role of the professional on the Audit Team.

The significance of the threat shall be evaluated and safeguards applied when necessary to eliminate the threat or reduce it to an Acceptable Level. Examples of such safeguards include:

- Removing the individual from the Audit Team; or
- Structuring the responsibilities of the Audit Team so that the professional does not deal with matters that are within the responsibility of the Close Family member.

290.131 Threats to Independence are created when a member of the Audit Team has a close relationship with a person who is not an Immediate or Close Family member, but who is a Director or Officer or an employee in a position to exert significant influence over the preparation of the client's accounting records or the Financial Statements on which the Firm will express an Opinion. A member of the Audit Team who has such a relationship shall consult in accordance with Firm policies and procedures. The significance of the threats will depend on factors such as:

- The nature of the relationship between the individual and the member of the Audit Team;
- The position the individual holds with the client; and
- The role of the professional on the Audit Team.

The significance of the threats shall be evaluated and safeguards applied when necessary to eliminate the threats or reduce them to an Acceptable Level. Examples of such safeguards include:

- Removing the professional from the Audit Team; or
- Structuring the responsibilities of the Audit Team so that the professional does not deal with matters that are within the responsibility of the individual with whom the professional has a close relationship.

290.132 Self-interest, familiarity or intimidation threats may be created by a personal or family relationship between (a) a partner or employee of the Firm who is not a member of the Audit Team and (b) a Director or Officer of the Audit Client or an employee in a position to exert significant influence over the preparation of the client's accounting records or the Financial Statements on which the Firm will express an Opinion. Partners and employees of the Firm who are aware of such relationships shall consult in accordance with Firm policies and procedures. The existence and significance of any threat will depend on factors such as:

- The nature of the relationship between the partner or employee of the Firm and the Director or Officer or employee of the client;
- The interaction of the partner or employee of the Firm with the Audit Team;
- The position of the partner or employee within the Firm; and
- The position the individual holds with the client.

The significance of any threat shall be evaluated and safeguards applied when necessary to eliminate the threat or reduce it to an Acceptable Level. Examples of such safeguards include:

- Structuring the partner's or employee's responsibilities to reduce any potential influence over the Audit Engagement; or
- Having a Member review the relevant audit work performed.

APES

290.133 When an inadvertent violation of this section as it relates to family and personal relationships occurs, it is deemed not to compromise Independence if:

(a) The Firm has established policies and procedures that require prompt notification to the Firm of any breaches resulting from changes in the employment status of their Immediate or Close Family members or other personal relationships that create threats to Independence;

(b) The inadvertent violation relates to an Immediate Family member of a member of the Audit Team becoming a Director or Officer of the Audit Client or being in a position to exert significant influence over the preparation of the client's accounting records or the Financial Statements on which the Firm will express an Opinion, and the relevant professional is removed from the Audit Team; and

(c) The Firm applies other safeguards when necessary to reduce any remaining threat to an Acceptable Level. Examples of such safeguards include:

(i) Having a Member review the work of the member of the Audit Team; or

(ii) Excluding the relevant professional from any significant decision-making concerning the engagement.

The Firm shall determine whether to discuss the matter with Those Charged with Governance.

AUST290.133.1 Unless an inadvertent violation of this section as it relates to family and personal relationships is trivial and inconsequential, the Firm shall document and discuss it with Those Charged with Governance.

Employment with an Audit Client

290.134 Familiarity or intimidation threats may be created if a Director or Officer of the Audit Client, or an employee in a position to exert significant influence over the preparation of the client's accounting records or the Financial Statements on which the Firm will express an Opinion, has been a member of the Audit Team or partner of the Firm.

290.135 If a former member of the Audit Team or partner of the Firm[7] has joined the Audit Client in such a position and a significant connection remains between the Firm and the individual, the threat would be so significant that no safeguards could reduce the threat to an Acceptable Level. Therefore, Independence would be deemed to be compromised if a former member of the Audit Team or partner joins the Audit Client as a Director or Officer, or as an employee in a position to exert significant influence over the preparation of the client's accounting records or the Financial Statements on which the Firm will express an Opinion, unless:

(a) The individual is not entitled to any benefits or payments from the Firm, unless made in accordance with fixed pre-determined arrangements, and any amount owed to the individual is not material to the Firm; and

(b) The individual does not continue to participate or appear to participate in the Firm's business or professional activities.

290.136 If a former member of the Audit Team or partner of the Firm has joined the Audit Client in such a position, and no significant connection remains between the Firm and the individual, the existence and significance of any familiarity or intimidation threats will depend on factors such as:

- The position the individual has taken at the client;
- Any involvement the individual will have with the Audit Team;
- The length of time since the individual was a member of the Audit Team or partner of the Firm; and

7 Refer to s 324CK of the *Corporations Act 2001* regarding the 5 year cooling off period before a former Audit partner can be appointed as an Officer or Director of a Corporate Audit Client in circumstances where another former Partner of the Firm is already an Officer or Director of the corporate Audit Client.

- The former position of the individual within the Audit Team or Firm, for example, whether the individual was responsible for maintaining regular contact with the client's management or Those Charged with Governance.

The significance of any threats created shall be evaluated and safeguards applied when necessary to eliminate the threats or reduce them to an Acceptable Level. Examples of such safeguards include:

- Modifying the audit plan;
- Assigning individuals to the Audit Team who have sufficient experience in relation to the individual who has joined the client; or
- Having a Member review the work of the former member of the Audit Team.

290.137 If a former partner of the Firm has previously joined an entity in such a position and the entity subsequently becomes an Audit Client of the Firm, the significance of any threat to Independence shall be evaluated and safeguards applied when necessary to eliminate the threat or reduce it to an Acceptable Level.

290.138 A self-interest threat is created when a member of the Audit Team participates in the Audit Engagement while knowing that the member of the Audit Team will, or may, join the client some time in the future. Firm policies and procedures shall require members of an Audit Team to notify the Firm when entering employment negotiations with the client. On receiving such notification, the significance of the threat shall be evaluated and safeguards applied when necessary to eliminate the threat or reduce it to an Acceptable Level. Examples of such safeguards include:

- Removing the individual from the Audit Team; or
- A review of any significant judgments made by that individual while on the team.

Audit Clients that are Public Interest Entities

290.139 Familiarity or intimidation threats are created when a Key Audit Partner joins the Audit Client that is a Public Interest Entity as:

(a) A Director or Officer of the entity; or

(b) An employee in a position to exert significant influence over the preparation of the client's accounting records or the Financial Statements on which the Firm will express an Opinion.

Independence would be deemed to be compromised unless, subsequent to the partner ceasing to be a Key Audit Partner, the Public Interest Entity had issued audited Financial Statements covering a period of not less than twelve months and the partner was not a member of the Audit Team with respect to the audit of those Financial Statements[8].

290.140 An intimidation threat is created when the individual who was the Firm's Senior or managing partner (chief executive or equivalent) joins an Audit Client that is a Public Interest Entity as (a) an employee in a position to exert significant influence over the preparation of the entity's accounting records or its Financial Statements or (b) a Director or Officer of the entity. Independence would be deemed to be compromised unless twelve months have passed since the individual was the Senior or managing partner (chief executive or equivalent) of the Firm[9].

290.141 Independence is deemed not to be compromised if, as a result of a business combination, a former Key Audit Partner or the individual who was the Firm's former Senior or managing partner is in a position as described in paragraphs 290.139 and 290.140, and:

(a) The position was not taken in contemplation of the business combination;

8 Refer to s 324CI of the *Corporation Act 2001* for additional prohibitions on former Audit Partners joining corporate Audit Clients.

9 Refer to s 324CI of the *Corporation Act 2001* for additional prohibitions on former Partners joining corporate Audit Clients.

(b) Any benefits or payments due to the former partner from the Firm have been settled in full, unless made in accordance with fixed pre-determined arrangements and any amount owed to the partner is not material to the Firm;

(c) The former partner does not continue to participate or appear to participate in the Firm's business or professional activities; and

(d) The position held by the former partner with the Audit Client is discussed with Those Charged with Governance.

Temporary Staff Assignments

290.142 The lending of staff by a Firm to an Audit Client may create a self-review threat. Such assistance may be given, but only for a short period of time and the Firm's personnel shall not be involved in:

- Providing non-assurance services that would not be permitted under this section; or
- Assuming management responsibilities.

In all circumstances, the Audit Client shall be responsible for directing and supervising the activities of the loaned staff.

The significance of any threat shall be evaluated and safeguards applied when necessary to eliminate the threat or reduce it to an Acceptable Level. Examples of such safeguards include:

- Conducting an additional review of the work performed by the loaned staff;
- Not giving the loaned staff audit responsibility for any function or activity that the staff performed during the temporary staff assignment; or
- Not including the loaned staff as a member of the Audit Team.

Recent Service with an Audit Client

290.143 Self-interest, self-review or familiarity threats may be created if a member of the Audit Team has recently served as a Director, Officer, or employee of the Audit Client. This would be the case when, for example, a member of the Audit Team has to evaluate elements of the Financial Statements for which the member of the Audit Team had prepared the accounting records while with the client.

290.144 If, during the period covered by the audit report, a member of the Audit Team had served as a Director or Officer of the Audit Client, or was an employee in a position to exert significant influence[10] over the preparation of the client's accounting records or the Financial Statements on which the Firm will express an Opinion, the threat created would be so significant that no safeguards could reduce the threat to an Acceptable Level. Consequently, such individuals shall not be assigned to the Audit Team.

290.145 Self-interest, self-review or familiarity threats may be created if, before the period covered by the audit report, a member of the Audit Team had served as a Director or Officer of the Audit Client, or was an employee in a position to exert significant influence over the preparation of the client's accounting records or Financial Statements on which the Firm will express an Opinion[11]. For example, such threats would be created if a decision made or work performed by the individual in the prior period, while employed by the client, is to be evaluated in the current period as part of the current Audit Engagement. The existence and significance of any threats will depend on factors such as:

- The position the individual held with the client;
- The length of time since the individual left the client; and
- The role of the professional on the Audit Team.

10 Refer to s 9 Definition for 'Audit-critical employee' of the *Corporations Act 2001*.

11 Refer to s 324CH(1) Items 8 & 9 and s 324CF(5) Items 3, 4, 5 & 9 of the *Corporations Act 2001* regarding cooling-off period of 12 months immediately preceding the beginning of the audited period for a corporate Audit Client.

The significance of any threat shall be evaluated and safeguards applied when necessary to reduce the threat to an Acceptable Level. An example of such a safeguard is conducting a review of the work performed by the individual as a member of the Audit Team.

Serving as a Director or Officer of an Audit Client

290.146 If a partner or employee of the Firm serves as a Director or Officer of an Audit Client, the self-review and self-interest threats created would be so significant that no safeguards could reduce the threats to an Acceptable Level. Accordingly, no partner or employee shall serve as a Director or Officer of an Audit Client[12].

AUST290.146.1 If a partner or employee of the Firm were to serve as an Officer (including management of an Administration) or as a Director of an Audit Client, or as an employee in a position to exert direct and significant influence over the subject matter of the Audit Engagement, the threats created would be so significant no safeguard could reduce the threats to an Acceptable Level. Consequently, if such an individual were to accept such a position the only course of action is for the Firm to refuse to perform, or to withdraw from, the Audit Engagement.

290.147 The position of company secretary has different implications in different jurisdictions. Duties may range from administrative duties, such as personnel management and the maintenance of company records and registers, to duties as diverse as ensuring that the company complies with regulations or providing advice on corporate governance matters. Generally, this position is seen to imply a close association with the entity.

290.148 If a partner or employee of the Firm serves as company secretary for an Audit Client, self-review and advocacy threats are created that would generally be so significant that no safeguards could reduce the threats to an Acceptable Level. Despite paragraph 290.146, when this practice is specifically permitted under local law, professional rules or practice, and provided management makes all relevant decisions, the duties and activities shall be limited to those of a routine and administrative nature, such as preparing minutes and maintaining statutory returns. In those circumstances, the significance of any threats shall be evaluated and safeguards applied when necessary to eliminate the threats or reduce them to an Acceptable Level.

AUST290.148.1 As the company secretary of a company incorporated in Australia is an Officer under the *Corporations Act 2001*, no Partner or employee of a Firm shall act in the position of the company secretary of an Audit Client. If such an individual were to accept such a position the only course of action is for the Firm to refuse to perform, or withdraw from, the Audit Engagement.

290.149 Performing routine administrative services to support a company secretarial function or providing advice in relation to company secretarial administration matters does not generally create threats to Independence, as long as client management makes all relevant decisions.

Long association of senior personnel (including partner rotation) with an Audit Client

General Provisions

290.150 Familiarity and self-interest threats are created by using the same senior personnel on an Audit Engagement over a long period of time. The significance of the threats will depend on factors such as:

- How long the individual has been a member of the Audit Team;
- The role of the individual on the Audit Team;
- The structure of the Firm;
- The nature of the Audit Engagement;

APES

12 Refer to s 324CI of the *Corporations Act 2001* regarding prohibitions on Partners or employees serving as a Director or Officer of a corporate Audit Client.

- Whether the client's management team has changed; and
- Whether the nature or complexity of the client's accounting and reporting issues has changed.

The significance of the threats shall be evaluated and safeguards applied when necessary to eliminate the threats or reduce them to an Acceptable Level. Examples of such safeguards include:

- Rotating the senior personnel off the Audit Team;
- Having a Member who was not a member of the Audit Team review the work of the senior personnel; or
- Regular independent internal or external quality reviews of the engagement.

Audit Clients that are Public Interest Entities

290.151 In respect of an audit of a Public Interest Entity, an individual shall not be a Key Audit Partner for more than seven years[13]. After such time, the individual shall not be a member of the Engagement Team or be a Key Audit Partner for the client for two years. During that period, the individual shall not participate in the audit of the entity, provide quality control for the engagement, consult with the Engagement Team or the client regarding technical or industry-specific issues, transactions or events or otherwise directly influence the outcome of the engagement.

290.152 Despite paragraph 290.151, Key Audit Partners whose continuity is especially important to audit quality may, in rare cases due to unforeseen circumstances outside the Firm's control, be permitted an additional year on the Audit Team as long as the threat to Independence can be eliminated or reduced to an Acceptable Level by applying safeguards. For example, a Key Audit Partner may remain on the Audit Team for up to one additional year in circumstances where, due to unforeseen events, a required rotation was not possible, as might be the case due to serious illness of the intended Engagement Partner.

290.153 The long association of other partners with an Audit Client that is a Public Interest Entity creates familiarity and self-interest threats. The significance of the threats will depend on factors such as:

- How long any such partner has been associated with the Audit Client;
- The role, if any, of the individual on the Audit Team; and
- The nature, frequency and extent of the individual's interactions with the client's management or Those Charged with Governance.

The significance of the threats shall be evaluated and safeguards applied when necessary to eliminate the threats or reduce them to an Acceptable Level. Examples of such safeguards include:

- Rotating the partner off the Audit Team or otherwise ending the partner's association with the Audit Client; or
- Regular independent internal or external quality reviews of the engagement.

290.154 When an Audit Client becomes a Public Interest Entity, the length of time the individual has served the Audit Client as a Key Audit Partner before the client becomes a Public Interest Entity shall be taken into account in determining the timing of the rotation[14]. If the individual has served the Audit Client as a Key Audit Partner for five years or less when the client becomes a Public Interest Entity, the number of years the individual may continue to serve the client in that capacity before rotating off the engagement is seven years less the number of years already served. If the individual has served the Audit Client as a Key Audit Partner for six or more years when the client becomes a Public Interest Entity, the partner may continue to serve in that capacity for a maximum of two additional years before rotating off the engagement.

13 Refer to s 324DA of the *Corporations Act 2001* which has more restrictive Audit Partner rotation requirements for Listed Entities in Australia.

14 Refer to s 324DA of the *Corporations Act 2001* which has more restrictive Audit Partner rotation requirements for Listed Entities in Australia.

290.155 When a Firm has only a few people with the necessary knowledge and experience to serve as a Key Audit Partner on the audit of a Public Interest Entity, rotation of Key Audit Partners may not be an available safeguard. If an independent regulator[15] in the relevant jurisdiction has provided an exemption from partner rotation in such circumstances, an individual may remain a Key Audit Partner for more than seven years, in accordance with such regulation, provided that the independent regulator has specified alternative safeguards which are applied, such as a regular independent external review.

Provision of Non-assurance Services to Audit Clients

290.156 Firms have traditionally provided to their Audit Clients a range of non-assurance services that are consistent with their skills and expertise. Providing non-assurance services may, however, create threats to the Independence of the Firm or members of the Audit Team. The threats created are most often self-review, self-interest and advocacy threats.

290.157 New developments in business, the evolution of financial markets and changes in information technology make it impossible to draw up an all-inclusive list of non-assurance services that might be provided to an Audit Client. When specific guidance on a particular non-assurance service is not included in this section, the conceptual framework shall be applied when evaluating the particular circumstances.

290.158 Before the Firm accepts an engagement to provide a non-assurance service to an Audit Client, a determination shall be made as to whether providing such a service would create a threat to Independence. In evaluating the significance of any threat created by a particular non-assurance service, consideration shall be given to any threat that the Audit Team has reason to believe is created by providing other related non-assurance services. If a threat is created that cannot be reduced to an Acceptable Level by the application of safeguards, the non-assurance service shall not be provided.

290.159 Providing certain non-assurance services to an Audit Client may create a threat to Independence so significant that no safeguards could reduce the threat to an Acceptable Level. However, the inadvertent provision of such a service to a Related Entity, division or in respect of a discrete Financial Statement item of such a client will be deemed not to compromise Independence if any threats have been reduced to an Acceptable Level by arrangements for that Related Entity, division or discrete Financial Statement item to be audited by another Firm or when another Firm re-performs the non-assurance service to the extent necessary to enable it to take responsibility for that service.

290.160 A Firm may provide non-assurance services that would otherwise be restricted under this section to the following related entities of the Audit Client:

(a) An entity, which is not an Audit Client, that has direct or indirect control over the Audit Client;

(b) An entity, which is not an Audit Client, with a Direct Financial Interest in the client if that entity has significant influence over the client and the interest in the client is material to such entity; or

(c) An entity, which is not an Audit Client, that is under common control with the Audit Client.

If it is reasonable to conclude that (a) the services do not create a self-review threat because the results of the services will not be subject to audit procedures and (b) any threats that are created by the provision of such services are eliminated or reduced to an Acceptable Level by the application of safeguards.

290.161 A non-assurance service provided to an Audit Client does not compromise the Firm's Independence when the client becomes a Public Interest Entity if:

(a) The previous non-assurance service complies with the provisions of this section that relate to Audit Clients that are not public interest entities;

15 Refer to s 342A of the *Corporations Act 2001* which specifies that the Australian Securities and Investments Commission may grant extensions.

APES

(b) Services that are not permitted under this section for Audit Clients that are public interest entities are terminated before or as soon as practicable after the client becomes a Public Interest Entity; and

(c) The Firm applies safeguards when necessary to eliminate or reduce to an Acceptable Level any threats to Independence arising from the service.

Management Responsibilities

290.162 Management of an entity performs many activities in managing the entity in the best interests of stakeholders of the entity. It is not possible to specify every activity that is a management responsibility. However, management responsibilities involve leading and directing an entity, including making significant decisions regarding the acquisition, deployment and control of human, financial, physical and intangible resources.

290.163 Whether an activity is a management responsibility depends on the circumstances and requires the exercise of judgment. Examples of activities that would generally be considered a management responsibility include:

- Setting policies and strategic direction;
- Directing and taking responsibility for the actions of the entity's employees;
- Authorising transactions;
- Deciding which recommendations of the Firm or other third parties to implement;
- Taking responsibility for the preparation and fair presentation of the Financial Statements in accordance with the applicable financial reporting framework; and
- Taking responsibility for designing, implementing and maintaining internal control.

290.164 Activities that are routine and administrative, or involve matters that are insignificant, generally are deemed not to be a management responsibility. For example, executing an insignificant transaction that has been authorised by management or monitoring the dates for filing statutory returns and advising an Audit Client of those dates is deemed not to be a management responsibility. Further, providing advice and recommendations to assist management in discharging its responsibilities is not assuming a management responsibility.

290.165 If a Firm were to assume a management responsibility for an Audit Client, the threats created would be so significant that no safeguards could reduce the threats to an Acceptable Level. For example, deciding which recommendations of the Firm to implement will create self-review and self-interest threats. Further, assuming a management responsibility creates a familiarity threat because the Firm becomes too closely aligned with the views and interests of management. Therefore, the Firm shall not assume a management responsibility for an Audit Client.

290.166 To avoid the risk of assuming a management responsibility when providing non-assurance services to an Audit Client, the Firm shall be satisfied that a member of management is responsible for making the significant judgments and decisions that are the proper responsibility of management, evaluating the results of the service and accepting responsibility for the actions to be taken arising from the results of the service. This reduces the risk of the Firm inadvertently making any significant judgments or decisions on behalf of management. The risk is further reduced when the Firm gives the client the opportunity to make judgments and decisions based on an objective and transparent analysis and presentation of the issues.

Preparing Accounting Records and Financial Statements

General Provisions

290.167 Management is responsible for the preparation and fair presentation of the Financial Statements in accordance with the applicable financial reporting framework. These responsibilities include:

- Originating or changing journal entries, or determining the account classifications of transactions; and

- Preparing or changing source documents or originating data, in electronic or other form, evidencing the occurrence of a transaction (for example, purchase orders, payroll time records, and customer orders).

290.168 Providing an Audit Client with accounting and bookkeeping services, such as preparing accounting records or Financial Statements, creates a self-review threat when the Firm subsequently audits the Financial Statements.

290.169 The audit process, however, necessitates dialogue between the Firm and management of the Audit Client, which may involve (a) the application of accounting standards or policies and Financial Statement disclosure requirements, (b) the appropriateness of financial and accounting control and the methods used in determining the stated amounts of assets and liabilities, or (c) proposing adjusting journal entries. These activities are considered to be a normal part of the audit process and do not, generally, create threats to Independence.

290.170 Similarly, the client may request technical assistance from the Firm on matters such as resolving account reconciliation problems or analysing and accumulating information for regulatory reporting. In addition, the client may request technical advice on accounting issues such as the conversion of existing Financial Statements from one financial reporting framework to another (for example, to comply with group accounting policies or to transition to a different financial reporting framework such as International Financial Reporting Standards). Such services do not, generally, create threats to Independence provided the Firm does not assume a management responsibility for the client.

Audit Clients that are Not Public Interest Entities

290.171 The Firm may provide services related to the preparation of accounting records and Financial Statements to an Audit Client that is not a Public Interest Entity where the services are of a routine or mechanical nature, so long as any self-review threat created is reduced to an Acceptable Level. Examples of such services include:

- Providing payroll services based on client-originated data;
- Recording transactions for which the client has determined or approved the appropriate account classification;
- Posting transactions coded by the client to the general ledger;
- Posting client-approved entries to the trial balance; and
- Preparing Financial Statements based on information in the trial balance.

In all cases, the significance of any threat created shall be evaluated and safeguards applied when necessary to eliminate the threat or reduce it to an Acceptable Level. Examples of such safeguards include:

- Arranging for such services to be performed by an individual who is not a member of the Audit Team; or
- If such services are performed by a member of the Audit Team, using a partner or senior staff member with appropriate expertise who is not a member of the Audit Team to review the work performed.

Audit Clients that are Public Interest Entities

290.172 A Firm shall not provide to an Audit Client that is a Public Interest Entity accounting and bookkeeping services, including payroll services, or prepare Financial Statements on which the Firm will express an Opinion or financial information which forms the basis of the Financial Statements.

290.173 Despite paragraph 290.172, a Firm may provide accounting and bookkeeping services, including payroll services and the preparation of Financial Statements or other financial information, of a routine or mechanical nature for divisions or Related Entities of an

Audit Client that is a Public Interest Entity if the personnel providing the services are not members of the Audit Team and:

(a) The divisions or Related Entities for which the service is provided are collectively immaterial to the Financial Statements on which the Firm will express an Opinion; or

(b) The services relate to matters that are collectively immaterial to the Financial Statements of the division or Related Entity.

Emergency Situations – Audit Clients that are not Public Interest Entities

290.174 Accounting and bookkeeping services, which would otherwise not be permitted under this section, may be provided to Audit Clients that are not Public Interest Entities in emergency or other unusual situations when it is impractical for the Audit Client to make other arrangements. This may be the case when (a) only the Firm has the resources and necessary knowledge of the client's systems and procedures to assist the client in the timely preparation of its accounting records and Financial Statements, and (b) a restriction on the Firm's ability to provide the services would result in significant difficulties for the client (for example, as might result from a failure to meet regulatory reporting requirements). In such situations, the following conditions shall be met:

(a) Those who provide the services are not members of the Audit Team;

(b) The services are provided for only a short period of time and are not expected to recur; and

(c) The situation is discussed with Those Charged with Governance.

Valuation Services

General Provisions

290.175 A valuation comprises the making of assumptions with regard to future developments, the application of appropriate methodologies and techniques, and the combination of both to compute a certain value, or range of values, for an asset, a liability or for a business as a whole.

290.176 Performing valuation services for an Audit Client may create a self-review threat. The existence and significance of any threat will depend on factors such as:

- Whether the valuation will have a material effect on the Financial Statements.
- The extent of the client's involvement in determining and approving the valuation methodology and other significant matters of judgment.
- The availability of established methodologies and professional guidelines.
- For valuations involving standard or established methodologies, the degree of subjectivity inherent in the item.
- The reliability and extent of the underlying data.
- The degree of dependence on future events of a nature that could create significant volatility inherent in the amounts involved.
- The extent and clarity of the disclosures in the Financial Statements.

The significance of any threat created shall be evaluated and safeguards applied when necessary to eliminate the threat or reduce it to an Acceptable Level. Examples of such safeguards include:

- Having a Member who was not involved in providing the valuation service review the audit or valuation work performed; or
- Making arrangements so that personnel providing such services do not participate in the Audit Engagement.

290.177 Certain valuations do not involve a significant degree of subjectivity. This is likely the case where the underlying assumptions are either established by law or regulation, or are widely accepted and when the techniques and methodologies to be used are based on generally accepted standards or prescribed by law or regulation. In such circumstances, the results of a valuation performed by two or more parties are not likely to be materially different.

290.178 If a Firm is requested to perform a valuation to assist an Audit Client with its tax reporting obligations or for tax planning purposes and the results of the valuation will not have a direct effect on the Financial Statements, the provisions included in paragraph 290.191 apply.

Audit Clients that are Not Public Interest Entities

290.179 In the case of an Audit Client that is not a Public Interest Entity, if the valuation service has a material effect on the Financial Statements on which the Firm will express an Opinion and the valuation involves a significant degree of subjectivity, no safeguards could reduce the self-review threat to an Acceptable Level. Accordingly a Firm shall not provide such a valuation service to an Audit Client.

Audit Clients that are Public Interest Entities

290.180 A Firm shall not provide valuation services to an Audit Client that is a Public Interest Entity if the valuations would have a material effect, separately or in the aggregate, on the Financial Statements on which the Firm will express an Opinion.

Taxation Services

290.181 Taxation services comprise a broad range of services, including:

- Tax return preparation;
- Tax calculations for the purpose of preparing the accounting entries;
- Tax planning and other tax advisory services; and
- Assistance in the resolution of tax disputes.

While taxation services provided by a Firm to an Audit Client are addressed separately under each of these broad headings; in practice, these activities are often interrelated.

290.182 Performing certain tax services creates self-review and advocacy threats. The existence and significance of any threats will depend on factors such as (a) the system by which the tax authorities assess and administer the tax in question and the role of the Firm in that process, (b) the complexity of the relevant tax regime and the degree of judgment necessary in applying it, (c) the particular characteristics of the engagement, and (d) the level of tax expertise of the client's employees.

Tax Return Preparation

290.183 Tax return preparation services involve assisting clients with their tax reporting obligations by drafting and completing information, including the amount of tax due (usually on standardised forms) required to be submitted to the applicable tax authorities. Such services also include advising on the tax return treatment of past transactions and responding on behalf of the Audit Client to the tax authorities' requests for additional information and analysis (including providing explanations of and technical support for the approach being taken). Tax return preparation services are generally based on historical information and principally involve analysis and presentation of such historical information under existing tax law, including precedents and established practice. Further, the tax returns are subject to whatever review or approval process the tax authority deems appropriate. Accordingly, providing such services does not generally create a threat to Independence if management takes responsibility for the returns including any significant judgments made.

Tax Calculations for the Purpose of Preparing Accounting Entries

Audit Clients that are Not Public Interest Entities

290.184 Preparing calculations of current and deferred tax liabilities (or assets) for an Audit Client for the purpose of preparing accounting entries that will be subsequently audited by the Firm creates a self-review threat. The significance of the threat will depend on (a) the complexity of the relevant tax law and regulation and the degree of judgment necessary in applying them, (b) the level of tax expertise of the client's personnel, and (c) the materiality of the amounts to the Financial Statements. Safeguards shall

APES

be applied when necessary to eliminate the threat or reduce it to an Acceptable Level. Examples of such safeguards include:

- Using professionals who are not members of the Audit Team to perform the service;
- If the service is performed by a member of the Audit Team, using a partner or senior staff member with appropriate expertise who is not a member of the Audit Team to review the tax calculations; or
- Obtaining advice on the service from an external tax professional.

Audit Clients that are Public Interest Entities

290.185 In the case of an Audit Client that is a Public Interest Entity, a Firm shall not prepare tax calculations of current and deferred tax liabilities (or assets) for the purpose of preparing accounting entries that are material to the Financial Statements on which the Firm will express an Opinion.

Emergency Situations – Audit Clients that are not Public Interest Entities

290.186 The preparation of calculations of current and deferred tax liabilities (or assets) for an Audit Client that is not a Public Interest Entity for the purpose of the preparation of accounting entries, which would otherwise not be permitted under this section, may be provided to Audit Clients in emergency or other unusual situations when it is impractical for the Audit Client to make other arrangements. This may be the case when (a) only the Firm has the resources and necessary knowledge of the client's business to assist the client in the timely preparation of its calculations of current and deferred tax liabilities (or assets), and (b) a restriction on the Firm's ability to provide the services would result in significant difficulties for the client (for example, as might result from a failure to meet regulatory reporting requirements). In such situations, the following conditions shall be met:

(a) Those who provide the services are not members of the Audit Team;

(b) The services are provided for only a short period of time and are not expected to recur; and

(c) The situation is discussed with Those Charged with Governance.

Tax Planning and Other Tax Advisory Services

290.187 Tax planning or other tax advisory services comprise a broad range of services, such as advising the client how to structure its affairs in a tax efficient manner or advising on the application of a new tax law or regulation.

290.188 A self-review threat may be created where the advice will affect matters to be reflected in the Financial Statements. The existence and significance of any threat will depend on factors such as:

- The degree of subjectivity involved in determining the appropriate treatment for the tax advice in the Financial Statements;
- The extent to which the outcome of the tax advice will have a material effect on the Financial Statements;
- Whether the effectiveness of the tax advice depends on the accounting treatment or presentation in the Financial Statements and there is doubt as to the appropriateness of the accounting treatment or presentation under the relevant financial reporting framework;
- The level of tax expertise of the client's employees;
- The extent to which the advice is supported by tax law or regulation, other precedent or established practice; and
- Whether the tax treatment is supported by a private ruling or has otherwise been cleared by the tax authority before the preparation of the Financial Statements.

For example, providing tax planning and other tax advisory services where the advice is clearly supported by tax authority or other precedent, by established practice or has a basis in tax law that is likely to prevail does not generally create a threat to Independence.

290.189 The significance of any threat shall be evaluated and safeguards applied when necessary to eliminate the threat or reduce it to an Acceptable Level. Examples of such safeguards include:

- Using professionals who are not members of the Audit Team to perform the service;
- Having a tax professional, who was not involved in providing the tax service, advise the Audit Team on the service and review the Financial Statement treatment;
- Obtaining advice on the service from an external tax professional; or
- Obtaining pre-clearance or advice from the tax authorities.

290.190 Where the effectiveness of the tax advice depends on a particular accounting treatment or presentation in the Financial Statements and:

(a) The Audit Team has reasonable doubt as to the appropriateness of the related accounting treatment or presentation under the relevant financial reporting framework; and

(b) The outcome or consequences of the tax advice will have a material effect on the Financial Statements on which the Firm will express an Opinion;

The self-review threat would be so significant that no safeguards could reduce the threat to an Acceptable Level. Accordingly, a Firm shall not provide such tax advice to an Audit Client.

290.191 In providing tax services to an Audit Client, a Firm may be requested to perform a valuation to assist the client with its tax reporting obligations or for tax planning purposes. Where the result of the valuation will have a direct effect on the Financial Statements, the provisions included in paragraphs 290.175 to 290.180 relating to valuation services are applicable. Where the valuation is performed for tax purposes only and the result of the valuation will not have a direct effect on the Financial Statements (i.e. the Financial Statements are only affected through accounting entries related to tax), this would not generally create threats to Independence if such effect on the Financial Statements is immaterial or if the valuation is subject to external review by a tax authority or similar regulatory authority. If the valuation is not subject to such an external review and the effect is material to the Financial Statements, the existence and significance of any threat created will depend upon factors such as:

- The extent to which the valuation methodology is supported by tax law or regulation, other precedent or established practice and the degree of subjectivity inherent in the valuation.
- The reliability and extent of the underlying data.

The significance of any threat created shall be evaluated and safeguards applied when necessary to eliminate the threat or reduce it to an Acceptable Level. Examples of such safeguards include:

- Using professionals who are not members of the Audit Team to perform the service;
- Having a professional review the audit work or the result of the tax service; or
- Obtaining pre-clearance or advice from the tax authorities.

Assistance in the Resolution of Tax Disputes

290.192 An advocacy or self-review threat may be created when the Firm represents an Audit Client in the resolution of a tax dispute once the tax authorities have notified the client that they have rejected the client's arguments on a particular issue and either the tax authority or the client is referring the matter for determination in a formal proceeding, for example before a tribunal or court. The existence and significance of any threat will depend on factors such as:

- Whether the Firm has provided the advice which is the subject of the tax dispute;
- The extent to which the outcome of the dispute will have a material effect on the Financial Statements on which the Firm will express an Opinion;

APES

- The extent to which the matter is supported by tax law or regulation, other precedent, or established practice;
- Whether the proceedings are conducted in public; and
- The role management plays in the resolution of the dispute.

The significance of any threat created shall be evaluated and safeguards applied when necessary to eliminate the threat or reduce it to an Acceptable Level.

Examples of such safeguards include:

- Using professionals who are not members of the Audit Team to perform the service;
- Having a tax professional, who was not involved in providing the tax service, advise the Audit Team on the services and review the Financial Statement treatment; or
- Obtaining advice on the service from an external tax professional.

290.193 Where the taxation services involve acting as an advocate for an Audit Client before a public tribunal or court in the resolution of a tax matter and the amounts involved are material to the Financial Statements on which the Firm will express an Opinion, the advocacy threat created would be so significant that no safeguards could eliminate or reduce the threat to an Acceptable Level. Therefore, the Firm shall not perform this type of service for an Audit Client. What constitutes a "public tribunal or court" shall be determined according to how tax proceedings are heard in the particular jurisdiction.

290.194 The Firm is not, however, precluded from having a continuing advisory role (for example, responding to specific requests for information, providing factual accounts or testimony about the work performed or assisting the client in analysing the tax issues) for the Audit Client in relation to the matter that is being heard before a public tribunal or court.

Internal Audit Services

General Provisions

290.195 The scope and objectives of internal audit activities vary widely and depend on the size and structure of the entity and the requirements of management and Those Charged with Governance. Internal audit activities may include:

(a) Monitoring of internal control – reviewing controls, monitoring their operation and recommending improvements thereto;

(b) Examination of financial and operating information – reviewing the means used to identify, measure, classify and report financial and operating information, and specific inquiry into individual items including detailed testing of transactions, balances and procedures;

(c) Review of the economy, efficiency and effectiveness of operating activities including non-financial activities of an entity; and

(d) Review of compliance with laws, regulations and other external requirements, and with management policies and directives and other internal requirements.

290.196 Internal audit services involve assisting the Audit Client in the performance of its internal audit activities. The provision of internal audit services to an Audit Client creates a self-review threat to Independence if the Firm uses the internal audit work in the course of a subsequent external audit. Performing a significant part of the client's internal audit activities increases the possibility that Firm personnel providing internal audit services will assume a management responsibility. If the Firm's personnel assume a management responsibility when providing internal audit services to an Audit Client, the threat created would be so significant that no safeguards could reduce the threat to an Acceptable Level. Accordingly, a Firm's personnel shall not assume a management responsibility when providing internal audit services to an Audit Client.

290.197 Examples of internal audit services that involve assuming management responsibilities include:

(a) Setting internal audit policies or the strategic direction of internal audit activities;

(b) Directing and taking responsibility for the actions of the entity's internal audit employees;

(c) Deciding which recommendations resulting from internal audit activities shall be implemented;

(d) Reporting the results of the internal audit activities to Those Charged with Governance on behalf of management;

(e) Performing procedures that form part of the internal control, such as reviewing and approving changes to employee data access privileges;

(f) Taking responsibility for designing, implementing and maintaining internal control; and

(g) Performing outsourced internal audit services, comprising all or a substantial portion of the internal audit function, where the Firm is responsible for determining the scope of the internal audit work and may have responsibility for one or more of the matters noted in (a)–(f).

290.198 To avoid assuming a management responsibility, the Firm shall only provide internal audit services to an Audit Client if it is satisfied that:

(a) The client designates an appropriate and competent resource, preferably within senior management, to be responsible at all times for internal audit activities and to acknowledge responsibility for designing, implementing, and maintaining internal control;

(b) The client's management or Those Charged with Governance reviews, assesses and approves the scope, risk and frequency of the internal audit services;

(c) The client's management evaluates the adequacy of the internal audit services and the findings resulting from their performance;

(d) The client's management evaluates and determines which recommendations resulting from internal audit services to implement and manages the implementation process; and

(e) The client's management reports to Those Charged with Governance the significant findings and recommendations resulting from the internal audit services.

290.199 When a Firm uses the work of an internal audit function, Auditing and Assurance Standards require the performance of procedures to evaluate the adequacy of that work. When a Firm accepts an engagement to provide internal audit services to an Audit Client, and the results of those services will be used in conducting the external audit, a self-review threat is created because of the possibility that the Audit Team will use the results of the internal audit service without appropriately evaluating those results or exercising the same level of professional scepticism as would be exercised when the internal audit work is performed by individuals who are not members of the Firm. The significance of the threat will depend on factors such as:

- The materiality of the related Financial Statement amounts;
- The risk of misstatement of the assertions related to those Financial Statement amounts; and
- The degree of reliance that will be placed on the internal audit service.

The significance of the threat shall be evaluated and safeguards applied when necessary to eliminate the threat or reduce it to an Acceptable Level. An example of such a safeguard is using professionals who are not members of the Audit Team to perform the internal audit service.

APES

Audit Clients that are Public Interest Entities

290.200 In the case of an Audit Client that is a Public Interest Entity, a Firm shall not provide internal audit services that relate to:

(a) A significant part of the internal controls over financial reporting;

(b) Financial accounting systems that generate information that is, separately or in the aggregate, significant to the client's accounting records or Financial Statements on which the Firm will express an Opinion; or

(c) Amounts or disclosures that are, separately or in the aggregate, material to the Financial Statements on which the Firm will express an Opinion.

IT Systems Services

General Provisions

290.201 Services related to information technology ("IT") systems include the design or implementation of hardware or software systems. The systems may aggregate source data, form part of the internal control over financial reporting or generate information that affects the accounting records or Financial Statements, or the systems may be unrelated to the Audit Client's accounting records, the internal control over financial reporting or Financial Statements. Providing systems services may create a self-review threat depending on the nature of the services and the IT systems.

290.202 The following IT systems services are deemed not to create a threat to Independence as long as the Firm's personnel do not assume a management responsibility:

(a) Design or implementation of IT systems that are unrelated to internal control over financial reporting;

(b) Design or implementation of IT systems that do not generate information forming a significant part of the accounting records or Financial Statements;

(c) Implementation of "off-the-shelf" accounting or financial information reporting software that was not developed by the Firm if the customisation required to meet the client's needs is not significant; and

(d) Evaluating and making recommendations with respect to a system designed, implemented or operated by another service provider or the client.

Audit Clients that are Not Public Interest Entities

290.203 Providing services to an Audit Client that is not a Public Interest Entity involving the design or implementation of IT systems that (a) form a significant part of the internal control over financial reporting or (b) generate information that is significant to the client's accounting records or Financial Statements on which the Firm will express an Opinion creates a self-review threat.

290.204 The self-review threat is too significant to permit such services unless appropriate safeguards are put in place ensuring that:

(a) The Audit Client acknowledges its responsibility for establishing and monitoring a system of internal controls;

(b) The Audit Client assigns the responsibility to make all management decisions with respect to the design and implementation of the hardware or software system to a competent employee, preferably within senior management;

(c) The Audit Client makes all management decisions with respect to the design and implementation process;

(d) The Audit Client evaluates the adequacy and results of the design and implementation of the system; and

(e) The Audit Client is responsible for operating the system (hardware or software) and for the data it uses or generates.

290.205 Depending on the degree of reliance that will be placed on the particular IT systems as part of the audit, a determination shall be made as to whether to provide such non-assurance services only with personnel who are not members of the Audit Team and who have different reporting lines within the Firm. The significance of any remaining threat shall be evaluated and safeguards applied when necessary to eliminate the threat or reduce it to an Acceptable Level. An example of such a safeguard is having a Member review the audit or non-assurance work.

Audit Clients that are Public Interest Entities

290.206 In the case of an Audit Client that is a Public Interest Entity, a Firm shall not provide services involving the design or implementation of IT systems that (a) form a significant part of the internal control over financial reporting or (b) generate information that is significant to the client's accounting records or Financial Statements on which the Firm will express an Opinion.

Litigation Support Services

290.207 Litigation support services may include activities such as acting as an expert witness, calculating estimated damages or other amounts that might become receivable or payable as the result of litigation or other legal dispute, and assistance with document management and retrieval. These services may create a self-review or advocacy threat.

290.208 If the Firm provides a litigation support service to an Audit Client and the service involves estimating damages or other amounts that affect the Financial Statements on which the Firm will express an Opinion, the valuation service provisions included in paragraphs 290.175 to 290.180 shall be followed. In the case of other litigation support services, the significance of any threat created shall be evaluated and safeguards applied when necessary to eliminate the threat or reduce it to an Acceptable Level.

Legal Services

290.209 For the purpose of this section, legal services are defined as any services for which the person providing the services must either be admitted to practice law before the courts of the jurisdiction in which such services are to be provided or have the required legal training to practice law. Such legal services may include, depending on the jurisdiction, a wide and diversified range of areas including both corporate and commercial services to clients, such as contract support, litigation, mergers and acquisition legal advice and support and assistance to clients' internal legal departments. Providing legal services to an entity that is an Audit Client may create both self-review and advocacy threats.

290.210 Legal services that support an Audit Client in executing a transaction (e.g., contract support, legal advice, legal due diligence and restructuring) may create self-review threats. The existence and significance of any threat will depend on factors such as:

- The nature of the service;
- Whether the service is provided by a member of the Audit Team; and
- The materiality of any matter in relation to the client's Financial Statements.

The significance of any threat created shall be evaluated and safeguards applied when necessary to eliminate the threat or reduce it to an Acceptable Level. Examples of such safeguards include:

- Using professionals who are not members of the Audit Team to perform the service; or
- Having a professional who was not involved in providing the legal services provide advice to the Audit Team on the service and review any Financial Statement treatment.

290.211 Acting in an advocacy role for an Audit Client in resolving a dispute or litigation when the amounts involved are material to the Financial Statements on which the Firm will express an Opinion would create advocacy and self-review threats so significant that no safeguards could reduce the threat to an Acceptable Level. Therefore, the Firm shall not perform this type of service for an Audit Client.

290.212 When a Firm is asked to act in an advocacy role for an Audit Client in resolving a dispute or litigation when the amounts involved are not material to the Financial Statements on which the Firm will express an Opinion, the Firm shall evaluate the significance of any advocacy and self-review threats created and apply safeguards when necessary to eliminate the threat or reduce it to an Acceptable Level. Examples of such safeguards include:

- Using professionals who are not members of the Audit Team to perform the service; or
- Having a professional who was not involved in providing the legal services advise the Audit Team on the service and review any Financial Statement treatment.

290.213 The appointment of a partner or an employee of the Firm as General Counsel for legal affairs of an Audit Client would create self-review and advocacy threats that are so significant that no safeguards could reduce the threats to an Acceptable Level. The position of General Counsel is generally a senior management position with broad responsibility for the legal affairs of a company, and consequently, no member of the Firm shall accept such an appointment for an Audit Client.

Recruiting Services

General Provisions

290.214 Providing recruiting services to an Audit Client may create self-interest, familiarity or intimidation threats. The existence and significance of any threat will depend on factors such as:

- The nature of the requested assistance; and
- The role of the person to be recruited.

The significance of any threat created shall be evaluated and safeguards applied when necessary to eliminate the threat or reduce it to an Acceptable Level. In all cases, the Firm shall not assume management responsibilities, including acting as a negotiator on the client's behalf, and the hiring decision shall be left to the client.

The Firm may generally provide such services as reviewing the professional qualifications of a number of applicants and providing advice on their suitability for the post. In addition, the Firm may interview candidates and advise on a candidate's competence for financial accounting, administrative or control positions.

Audit Clients that are Public Interest Entities

290.215 A Firm shall not provide the following recruiting services to an Audit Client that is a Public Interest Entity with respect to a Director or Officer of the entity or senior management in a position to exert significant influence over the preparation of the client's accounting records or the Financial Statements on which the Firm will express an Opinion:

- Searching for or seeking out candidates for such positions; and
- Undertaking reference checks of prospective candidates for such positions.

Corporate Finance Services

290.216 Providing corporate finance services such as (a) assisting an Audit Client in developing corporate strategies, (b) identifying possible targets for the Audit Client to acquire, (c) advising on disposal transactions, (d) assisting finance raising transactions, and (e) providing structuring advice may create advocacy and self-review threats. The significance of any threat shall be evaluated and safeguards applied when necessary to eliminate the threat or reduce it to an Acceptable Level. Examples of such safeguards include:

- Using professionals who are not members of the Audit Team to provide the services; or
- Having a professional who was not involved in providing the corporate finance service advise the Audit Team on the service and review the accounting treatment and any Financial Statement treatment.

290.217 Providing a corporate finance service, for example advice on the structuring of a corporate finance transaction or on financing arrangements that will directly affect amounts that will be reported in the Financial Statements on which the Firm will provide an opinion may create a self-review threat. The existence and significance of any threat will depend on factors such as:

- The degree of subjectivity involved in determining the appropriate treatment for the outcome or consequences of the corporate finance advice in the Financial Statements;
- The extent to which the outcome of the corporate finance advice will directly affect amounts recorded in the Financial Statements and the extent to which the amounts are material to the Financial Statements; and
- Whether the effectiveness of the corporate finance advice depends on a particular accounting treatment or presentation in the Financial Statements and there is doubt as to the appropriateness of the related accounting treatment or presentation under the relevant financial reporting framework.

The significance of any threat shall be evaluated and safeguards applied when necessary to eliminate the threat or reduce it to an Acceptable Level. Examples of such safeguards include:

- Using professionals who are not members of the Audit Team to perform the service; or
- Having a professional who was not involved in providing the corporate finance service to the client advise the Audit Team on the service and review the accounting treatment and any Financial Statement treatment.

290.218 Where the effectiveness of corporate finance advice depends on a particular accounting treatment or presentation in the Financial Statements and:

(a) The Audit Team has reasonable doubt as to the appropriateness of the related accounting treatment or presentation under the relevant financial reporting framework; and

(b) The outcome or consequences of the corporate finance advice will have a material effect on the Financial Statements on which the Firm will express an Opinion;

The self-review threat would be so significant that no safeguards could reduce the threat to an Acceptable Level, in which case the corporate finance advice shall not be provided.

290.219 Providing corporate finance services involving promoting, dealing in, or underwriting an Audit Client's shares would create an advocacy or self-review threat that is so significant that no safeguards could reduce the threat to an Acceptable Level. Accordingly, a Firm shall not provide such services to an Audit Client.

Fees

Fees – Relative Size

290.220 When the total fees from an Audit Client represent a large proportion of the total fees of the Firm expressing the audit opinion, the dependence on that client and concern about losing the client creates a self-interest or intimidation threat. The significance of the threat will depend on factors such as:

- The operating structure of the Firm;
- Whether the Firm is well established or new; and
- The significance of the client qualitatively and/or quantitatively to the Firm.

The significance of the threat shall be evaluated and safeguards applied when necessary to eliminate the threat or reduce it to an Acceptable Level. Examples of such safeguards include:

- Reducing the dependency on the client;
- External quality control reviews; or
- Consulting a third party, such as a professional regulatory body or a Member, on key audit judgments.

APES

290.221 A self-interest or intimidation threat is also created when the fees generated from an Audit Client represent a large proportion of the revenue from an individual partner's clients or a large proportion of the revenue of an individual Office of the Firm. The significance of the threat will depend upon factors such as:

- The significance of the client qualitatively and/or quantitatively to the partner or Office; and
- The extent to which the remuneration of the partner, or the partners in the Office, is dependent upon the fees generated from the client.

The significance of the threat shall be evaluated and safeguards applied when necessary to eliminate the threat or reduce it to an Acceptable Level. Examples of such safeguards include:

- Reducing the dependency on the Audit Client;
- Having a Member review the work or otherwise advise as necessary; or
- Regular independent internal or external quality reviews of the engagement.

Audit Clients that are Public Interest Entities

290.222 Where an Audit Client is a Public Interest Entity and, for two consecutive years, the total fees from the client and its related entities (subject to the considerations in paragraph 290.27) represent more than 15% of the total fees received by the Firm expressing the opinion on the Financial Statements of the client, the Firm shall disclose to Those Charged with Governance of the Audit Client the fact that the total of such fees represents more than 15% of the total fees received by the Firm, and discuss which of the safeguards below it will apply to reduce the threat to an Acceptable Level, and apply the selected safeguard:

- Prior to the issuance of the audit opinion on the second year's Financial Statements, a Member, who is not a member of the Firm expressing the opinion on the Financial Statements, performs an Engagement Quality Control Review of that engagement or a professional regulatory body performs a review of that engagement that is equivalent to an Engagement Quality Control Review ("a pre-issuance review"); or
- After the audit opinion on the second year's Financial Statements has been issued, and before the issuance of the audit opinion on the third year's Financial Statements, a Member, who is not a member of the Firm expressing the opinion on the Financial Statements, or a professional regulatory body performs a review of the second year's audit that is equivalent to an Engagement Quality Control Review ("a post-issuance review").

When the total fees significantly exceed 15%, the Firm shall determine whether the significance of the threat is such that a post-issuance review would not reduce the threat to an Acceptable Level and, therefore, a pre-issuance review is required. In such circumstances a pre-issuance review shall be performed.

Thereafter, when the fees continue to exceed 15% each year, the disclosure to and discussion with Those Charged with Governance shall occur and one of the above safeguards shall be applied. If the fees significantly exceed 15%, the Firm shall determine whether the significance of the threat is such that a post-issuance review would not reduce the threat to an Acceptable Level and, therefore, a pre-issuance review is required. In such circumstances a pre-issuance review shall be performed.

Fees – Overdue

290.223 A self-interest threat may be created if fees due from an Audit Client remain unpaid for a long time, especially if a significant part is not paid before the issue of the audit report for the following year. Generally the Firm is expected to require payment of such fees before such audit report is issued. If fees remain unpaid after the report has been issued, the existence and significance of any threat shall be evaluated and safeguards applied when necessary to eliminate the threat or reduce it to an Acceptable Level. An example of such a safeguard is having an additional Member who did not take part in the Audit Engagement provide advice or review the work performed. The Firm shall determine whether the overdue fees might be regarded as being equivalent to a loan to the client and whether, because of the significance of the overdue fees, it is appropriate for the Firm to be re-appointed or continue the Audit Engagement.

Contingent Fees

290.224 Contingent Fees are fees calculated on a predetermined basis relating to the outcome of a transaction or the result of the services performed by the Firm. For the purposes of this section, a fee is not regarded as being contingent if established by a court or other public authority.

290.225 A Contingent Fee charged directly or indirectly, for example through an intermediary, by a Firm in respect of an Audit Engagement creates a self-interest threat that is so significant that no safeguards could reduce the threat to an Acceptable Level. Accordingly, a Firm shall not enter into any such fee arrangement.

290.226 A Contingent Fee charged directly or indirectly, for example through an intermediary, by a Firm in respect of a non-assurance service provided to an Audit Client may also create a self-interest threat. The threat created would be so significant that no safeguards could reduce the threat to an Acceptable Level if:

(a) The fee is charged by the Firm expressing the opinion on the Financial Statements and the fee is material or expected to be material to that Firm;

(b) The fee is charged by a Network Firm that participates in a significant part of the audit and the fee is material or expected to be material to that Firm; or

(c) The outcome of the non-assurance service, and therefore the amount of the fee, is dependent on a future or contemporary judgment related to the audit of a material amount in the Financial Statements.

Accordingly, such arrangements shall not be accepted.

290.227 For other Contingent Fee arrangements charged by a Firm for a non-assurance service to an Audit Client, the existence and significance of any threats will depend on factors such as:

- The range of possible fee amounts;
- Whether an appropriate authority determines the outcome of the matter upon which the Contingent Fee will be determined;
- The nature of the service; and
- The effect of the event or transaction on the Financial Statements.

The significance of any threats shall be evaluated and safeguards applied when necessary to eliminate the threats or reduce them to an Acceptable Level. Examples of such safeguards include:

- Having a Member review the relevant audit work or otherwise advise as necessary; or
- Using professionals who are not members of the Audit Team to perform the non-assurance service.

Compensation and Evaluation Policies

290.228 A self-interest threat is created when a member of the Audit Team is evaluated on or compensated for selling non-assurance services to that Audit Client. The significance of the threat will depend on:

- The proportion of the individual's compensation or performance evaluation that is based on the sale of such services;
- The role of the individual on the Audit Team; and
- Whether promotion decisions are influenced by the sale of such services.

The significance of the threat shall be evaluated and, if the threat is not at an Acceptable Level, the Firm shall either revise the compensation plan or evaluation process for that individual or apply safeguards to eliminate the threat or reduce it to an Acceptable Level. Examples of such safeguards include:

- Removing such members from the Audit Team; or
- Having a Member review the work of the member of the Audit Team.

290.229 A Key Audit Partner shall not be evaluated on or compensated based on that partner's success in selling non-assurance services to the partner's Audit Client. This is not intended to prohibit normal profit-sharing arrangements between partners of a Firm.

Gifts and Hospitality

290.230 Accepting gifts or hospitality from an Audit Client may create self-interest and familiarity threats. If a Firm or a member of the Audit Team accepts gifts or hospitality, unless the value is trivial and inconsequential, the threats created would be so significant that no safeguards could reduce the threats to an Acceptable Level. Consequently, a Firm or a member of the Audit Team shall not accept such gifts or hospitality.

Actual or Threatened Litigation

290.231 When litigation takes place, or appears likely, between the Firm or a member of the Audit Team and the Audit Client, self-interest and intimidation threats are created. The relationship between client management and the members of the Audit Team must be characterised by complete candour and full disclosure regarding all aspects of a client's business operations. When the Firm and the client's management are placed in adversarial positions by actual or threatened litigation, affecting management's willingness to make complete disclosures, self-interest and intimidation threats are created. The significance of the threats created will depend on such factors as:

- The materiality of the litigation; and
- Whether the litigation relates to a prior Audit Engagement.

The significance of the threats shall be evaluated and safeguards applied when necessary to eliminate the threats or reduce them to an Acceptable Level. Examples of such safeguards include:

- If the litigation involves a member of the Audit Team, removing that individual from the Audit Team; or
- Having a professional review the work performed.

If such safeguards do not reduce the threats to an Acceptable Level, the only appropriate action is to withdraw from, or decline, the Audit Engagement.

Paragraphs 290.232 to 290.499 are intentionally left blank.

Reports that Include a Restriction on Use and Distribution

Introduction

290.500 The Independence requirements in Section 290 apply to all Audit Engagements. However, in certain circumstances involving Audit Engagements where the report includes a restriction on use and distribution, and provided the conditions described in 290.501 to 290.502 are met, the Independence requirements in this section may be modified as provided in paragraphs 290.505 to 290.514. These paragraphs are only applicable to an Audit Engagement on Special Purpose Financial Statements (a) that is intended to provide a conclusion in positive or negative form that the Financial Statements are prepared in all material respects, in accordance with the applicable financial reporting framework, including, in the case of a fair presentation framework, that the Financial Statements give a true and fair view or are presented fairly, in all material respects, in accordance with the applicable financial reporting framework, and (b) where the audit report includes a restriction on use and distribution. The modifications are not permitted in the case of an audit of Financial Statements required by law or regulation.

290.501 The modifications to the requirements of Section 290 are permitted if the intended users of the report (a) are knowledgeable as to the purpose and limitations of the report, and (b) explicitly agree to the application of the modified Independence requirements. Knowledge as to the purpose and limitations of the report may be obtained by the intended users through their participation, either directly or indirectly through their representative who has the authority to act for the intended users, in establishing the nature and scope of the engagement. Such participation enhances the ability of the Firm to communicate with intended users about Independence matters, including the circumstances that are relevant to the evaluation of the threats to Independence and the applicable safeguards necessary to eliminate the threats or reduce them to an Acceptable Level, and to obtain their agreement to the modified Independence requirements that are to be applied.

290.502 The Firm shall communicate (for example, in an engagement letter) with the intended users regarding the Independence requirements that are to be applied with respect to the provision of the Audit Engagement. Where the intended users are a class of users (for example, lenders in a syndicated loan arrangement) who are not specifically identifiable by name at the time the engagement terms are established, such users shall subsequently be made aware of the Independence requirements agreed to by the representative (for example, by the representative making the Firm's engagement letter available to all users).

290.503 If the Firm also issues an audit report that does not include a restriction on use and distribution for the same client, the provisions of paragraphs 290.500 to 290.514 do not change the requirement to apply the provisions of paragraphs 290.1 to 290.231 to that Audit Engagement.

290.504 The modifications to the requirements of Section 290 that are permitted in the circumstances set out above are described in paragraphs 290.505 to 290.514. Compliance in all other respects with the provisions of Section 290 is required.

Public Interest Entities

290.505 When the conditions set out in paragraphs 290.500 to 290.502 are met, it is not necessary to apply the additional requirements in paragraphs 290.100 to 290.231 that apply to Audit Engagements for Public Interest Entities.

Related Entities

290.506 When the conditions set out in paragraphs 290.500 to 290.502 are met, references to Audit Client do not include its Related Entities. However, when the Audit Team knows or has reason to believe that a relationship or circumstance involving a Related Entity of the client is relevant to the evaluation of the Firm's Independence of the client, the Audit Team shall include that Related Entity when identifying and evaluating threats to Independence and applying appropriate safeguards.

APES

Networks and Network Firms

290.507 When the conditions set out in paragraphs 290.500 to 290.502 are met, reference to the Firm does not include Network Firms. However, when the Firm knows or has reason to believe that threats are created by any interests and relationships of a Network Firm, they shall be included in the evaluation of threats to Independence.

Financial Interests, Loans and Guarantees, Close Business Relationships and Family and Personal Relationships

290.508 When the conditions set out in paragraphs 290.500 to 290.502 are met, the relevant provisions set out in paragraphs 290.102 to 290.145 apply only to the members of the Engagement Team, their Immediate Family members and Close Family members.

290.509 In addition, a determination shall be made as to whether threats to Independence are created by interests and relationships, as described in paragraphs 290.102 to 290.145, between the Audit Client and the following members of the Audit Team:

(a) Those who provide consultation regarding technical or industry specific issues, transactions or events; and

(b) Those who provide quality control for the engagement, including those who perform the Engagement Quality Control Review.

An evaluation shall be made of the significance of any threats that the Engagement Team has reason to believe are created by interests and relationships between the Audit Client and others within the Firm who can directly influence the outcome of the Audit Engagement, including those who recommend the compensation of, or who provide direct supervisory, management or other oversight of the Audit Engagement Partner in connection with the performance of the Audit Engagement (including those at all successively senior levels above the Engagement Partner through to the individual who is the Firm's senior or managing partner (chief executive or equivalent)).

290.510 An evaluation shall also be made of the significance of any threats that the Engagement Team has reason to believe are created by Financial Interests in the Audit Client held by individuals, as described in paragraphs 290.108 to 290.111 and paragraphs 290.113 to 290.115.

290.511 Where a threat to Independence is not at an Acceptable Level, safeguards shall be applied to eliminate the threat or reduce it to an Acceptable Level.

290.512 In applying the provisions set out in paragraphs 290.106 and 290.115 to interests of the Firm, if the Firm has a material Financial Interest, whether direct or indirect, in the Audit Client, the self-interest threat created would be so significant that no safeguards could reduce the threat to an Acceptable Level. Accordingly, the Firm shall not have such a Financial Interest.

Employment with an Audit Client

290.513 An evaluation shall be made of the significance of any threats from any employment relationships as described in paragraphs 290.134 to 290.138. Where a threat exists that is not at an Acceptable Level, safeguards shall be applied to eliminate the threat or reduce it to an Acceptable Level. Examples of safeguards that might be appropriate include those set out in paragraph 290.136.

Provision of Non-Assurance Services

290.514 If the Firm conducts an engagement to issue a restricted use and distribution report for an Audit Client and provides a non-assurance service to the Audit Client, the provisions of paragraphs 290.156 to 290.231 shall be complied with, subject to paragraphs 290.504 to 290.507.

SECTION 291

Independence – Other Assurance Engagements

Contents

Paragraph

APES

Structure of Section

291.1 This section addresses Independence requirements for Assurance Engagements that are not Audit Engagements or Review Engagements. Additional Independence requirements for Audit and Review Engagements are addressed in Section 290. If the Assurance Client is also an Audit Client or Review Client, the requirements in Section 290 also apply to the Firm, Network Firms and members of the Audit Team or Review Team. In certain circumstances involving Assurance Engagements where the assurance report includes a restriction on use and distribution and provided certain conditions are met, the Independence requirements in this section may be modified as provided in 291.21 to 291.27.

291.2 Assurance Engagements are designed to enhance intended users' degree of confidence about the outcome of the evaluation or measurement of a subject matter against criteria. *Framework for Assurance Engagements* issued by the AUASB describes the elements and objectives of an Assurance Engagement and identifies engagements to which Auditing and Assurance Standards apply. For a description of the elements and objectives of an Assurance Engagement, refer to the Assurance Framework.

291.3 Compliance with the fundamental principle of objectivity requires being independent of Assurance Clients. In the case of Assurance Engagements, it is in the public interest and, therefore, required by this Code of Ethics, that members of Assurance Teams and Firms be independent of Assurance Clients and that any threats that the Firm has reason to believe are created by a Network Firm's interests and relationships be evaluated. In addition, when the Assurance Team knows or has reason to believe that a relationship or circumstance involving a Related Entity of the Assurance Client is relevant to the evaluation of the Firm's Independence from the client, the Assurance Team shall include that Related Entity when identifying and evaluating threats to Independence and applying appropriate safeguards.

A Conceptual Framework Approach to Independence

291.4 The objective of this section is to assist Firms and members of Assurance Teams in applying the conceptual framework approach described below to achieving and maintaining Independence.

291.5 Independence comprises:

Independence of Mind

The state of mind that permits the expression of a conclusion without being affected by influences that compromise professional judgment, thereby allowing an individual to act with integrity and exercise objectivity and professional scepticism.

Independence in Appearance

The avoidance of facts and circumstances that are so significant that a reasonable and informed third party would be likely to conclude, weighing all the specific facts and circumstances, that a Firm's, or a member of the Assurance Team's, integrity, objectivity or professional scepticism has been compromised.

291.6 The conceptual framework approach shall be applied by Members to:

- Identify threats to Independence;
- Evaluate the significance of the threats identified; and
- Apply safeguards when necessary to eliminate the threats or reduce them to an Acceptable Level.

When the Member determines that appropriate safeguards are not available or cannot be applied to eliminate the threats or reduce them to an Acceptable Level, the Member shall eliminate the circumstance or relationship creating the threats or decline or terminate the Assurance Engagement.

A Member shall use professional judgment in applying this conceptual framework.

291.7 Many different circumstances, or combinations of circumstances, may be relevant in assessing threats to Independence. It is impossible to define every situation that creates threats to Independence and to specify the appropriate action. Therefore, this Code establishes a conceptual framework that requires Firms and members of Assurance Teams to identify, evaluate, and address threats to Independence. The conceptual framework approach assists Members in Public Practice in complying with the ethical requirements in this Code. It accommodates many variations in circumstances that create threats to Independence and can deter a Member from concluding that a situation is permitted if it is not specifically prohibited.

291.8 Paragraphs 291.100 and onwards describe how the conceptual framework approach to Independence is to be applied. These paragraphs do not address all the circumstances and relationships that create or may create threats to Independence.

291.9 In deciding whether to accept or continue an engagement, or whether a particular individual may be a member of the Assurance Team, a Firm shall identify and evaluate any threats to Independence. If the threats are not at an Acceptable Level, and the decision is whether to accept an engagement or include a particular individual on the Assurance Team, the Firm shall determine whether safeguards are available to eliminate the threats or reduce them to an Acceptable Level. If the decision is whether to continue an engagement, the Firm shall determine whether any existing safeguards will continue to be effective to eliminate the threats or reduce them to an Acceptable Level or whether other safeguards will need to be applied or whether the engagement needs to be terminated. Whenever new information about a threat comes to the attention of the Firm during the engagement, the Firm shall evaluate the significance of the threat in accordance with the conceptual framework approach.

291.10 Throughout this section, reference is made to the significance of threats to Independence. In evaluating the significance of a threat, qualitative as well as quantitative factors shall be taken into account.

AUST291.10.1 Where a Member in Public Practice identifies multiple threats to Independence, which individually may not be significant, the Member shall evaluate the significance of those threats in aggregate and the safeguards applied or in place to eliminate some or all of the threats or reduce them to an Acceptable Level in aggregate.

291.11 This section does not, in most cases, prescribe the specific responsibility of individuals within the Firm for actions related to Independence because responsibility may differ depending on the size, structure and organisation of a Firm. The Firm is required by APES 320 *Quality Control for Firms* to establish policies and procedures designed to provide it with reasonable assurance that Independence is maintained when required by relevant ethical standards.

Assurance Engagements

291.12 As further explained in the Assurance Framework, in an Assurance Engagement the Member in Public Practice expresses a conclusion designed to enhance the degree of confidence of the intended users (other than the responsible party) about the outcome of the evaluation or measurement of a subject matter against criteria.

291.13 The outcome of the evaluation or measurement of a subject matter is the information that results from applying the criteria to the subject matter. The term "subject matter information" is used to mean the outcome of the evaluation or measurement of a subject matter. For example, the Framework states that an assertion about the effectiveness of internal control (subject matter information) results from applying a framework for evaluating the effectiveness of internal control, such as COSO[16] or CoCo[17] (criteria), to internal control, a process (subject matter).

APES

16 "Internal Control – Integrated Framework" The Committee of Sponsoring Organizations of the Treadway Commission.

17 "Guidance on Assessing Control – The CoCo Principles" Criteria of Control Board, The Canadian Institute of Chartered Accountants.

291.14 Assurance Engagements may be assertion-based or direct reporting. In either case, they involve three separate parties: a Member in Public Practice, a responsible party and intended users.

291.15 In an assertion-based Assurance Engagement, the evaluation or measurement of the subject matter is performed by the responsible party, and the subject matter information is in the form of an assertion by the responsible party that is made available to the intended users.

291.16 In a direct reporting Assurance Engagement, the Member in Public Practice either directly performs the evaluation or measurement of the subject matter, or obtains a representation from the responsible party that has performed the evaluation or measurement that is not available to the intended users. The subject matter information is provided to the intended users in the assurance report.

AUST291.16.1 The AUASB has issued *Framework for Assurance Engagements* which describes the nature of an Assurance Engagement. To obtain a full understanding of the objectives and elements of an Assurance Engagement it is necessary to refer to the full text of that document.

Assertion-based Assurance Engagements

291.17 In an assertion-based Assurance Engagement, the members of the Assurance Team and the Firm shall be independent of the Assurance Client (the party responsible for the subject matter information, and which may be responsible for the subject matter). Such Independence requirements prohibit certain relationships between members of the Assurance Team and (a) Directors or, Officers, and (b) individuals at the client in a position to exert significant influence over the subject matter information. Also, a determination shall be made as to whether threats to Independence are created by relationships with individuals at the client in a position to exert significant influence over the subject matter of the engagement. An evaluation shall be made of the significance of any threats that the Firm has reason to believe are created by Network Firm[18] interests and relationships.

291.18 In the majority of assertion-based Assurance Engagements, the responsible party is responsible for both the subject matter information and the subject matter. However, in some engagements, the responsible party may not be responsible for the subject matter. For example, when a Member in Public Practice is engaged to perform an Assurance Engagement regarding a report that an environmental consultant has prepared about a company's sustainability practices for distribution to intended users, the environmental consultant is the responsible party for the subject matter information but the company is responsible for the subject matter (the sustainability practices).

291.19 In assertion-based Assurance Engagements where the responsible party is responsible for the subject matter information but not the subject matter, the members of the Assurance Team and the Firm shall be independent of the party responsible for the subject matter information (the Assurance Client). In addition, an evaluation shall be made of any threats the Firm has reason to believe are created by interests and relationships between a member of the Assurance Team, the Firm, a Network Firm and the party responsible for the subject matter.

18 See paragraphs 290.13 to 290.24 for guidance on what constitutes a Network Firm.

Direct reporting Assurance Engagements

291.20 In a direct reporting Assurance Engagement, the members of the Assurance Team and the Firm shall be independent of the Assurance Client (the party responsible for the subject matter). An evaluation shall also be made of any threats the Firm has reason to believe are created by Network Firm interests and relationships.

Reports that Include a Restriction on Use and Distribution

291.21 In certain circumstances where the assurance report includes a restriction on use and distribution, and provided the conditions in this paragraph and in 291.22 are met, the Independence requirements in this section may be modified. The modifications to the requirements of Section 291 are permitted if the intended users of the report (a) are knowledgeable as to the purpose, subject matter information and limitations of the report and (b) explicitly agree to the application of the modified Independence requirements. Knowledge as to the purpose, subject matter information, and limitations of the report may be obtained by the intended users through their participation, either directly or indirectly through their representative who has the authority to act for the intended users, in establishing the nature and scope of the engagement. Such participation enhances the ability of the Firm to communicate with intended users about Independence matters, including the circumstances that are relevant to the evaluation of the threats to Independence and the applicable safeguards necessary to eliminate the threats or reduce them to an Acceptable Level, and to obtain their agreement to the modified Independence requirements that are to be applied.

291.22 The Firm shall communicate (for example, in an engagement letter) with the intended users regarding the Independence requirements that are to be applied with respect to the provision of the Assurance Engagement. Where the intended users are a class of users (for example, lenders in a syndicated loan arrangement) who are not specifically identifiable by name at the time the engagement terms are established, such users shall subsequently be made aware of the Independence requirements agreed to by the representative (for example, by the representative making the Firm's engagement letter available to all users).

291.23 If the Firm also issues an assurance report that does not include a restriction on use and distribution for the same client, the provisions of paragraphs 291.25 to 291.27 do not change the requirement to apply the provisions of paragraphs 291.1 to 291.159 to that Assurance Engagement. If the Firm also issues an audit report, whether or not it includes a restriction on use and distribution, for the same client, the provisions of Section 290 shall apply to that Audit Engagement.

291.24 The modifications to the requirements of Section 291 that are permitted in the circumstances set out above are described in paragraphs 291.25 to 291.27. Compliance in all other respects with the provisions of Section 291 is required.

291.25 When the conditions set out in paragraphs 291.21 and 291.22 are met, the relevant provisions set out in paragraphs 291.104 to 291.134 apply to all members of the Engagement Team, and their Immediate and Close Family members. In addition, a determination shall be made as to whether threats to Independence are created by interests and relationships between the Assurance Client and the following other members of the Assurance Team:

- Those who provide consultation regarding technical or industry specific issues, transactions or events; and
- Those who provide quality control for the engagement, including those who perform the Engagement Quality Control Review.

An evaluation shall also be made, by reference to the provisions set out in paragraphs 291.104 to 291.134, of any threats that the Engagement Team has reason to believe are created by interests and relationships between the Assurance Client and others within the Firm who can directly influence the outcome of the Assurance Engagement, including those who recommend the compensation, or who provide direct supervisory, management or other oversight, of the Assurance Engagement Partner in connection with the performance of the Assurance Engagement.

291.26 Even though the conditions set out in paragraphs 291.21 to 291.22 are met, if the Firm had a material Financial Interest, whether direct or indirect, in the Assurance Client, the self-interest threat created would be so significant that no safeguards could reduce the threat to an Acceptable Level. Accordingly, the Firm shall not have such a Financial Interest. In addition, the Firm shall comply with the other applicable provisions of this section described in paragraphs 291.113 to 291.159.

291.27 An evaluation shall also be made of any threats that the Firm has reason to believe are created by Network Firm interests and relationships.

Multiple Responsible Parties

291.28 In some Assurance Engagements, whether assertion-based or direct reporting, there might be several responsible parties. In determining whether it is necessary to apply the provisions in this section to each responsible party in such engagements, the Firm may take into account whether an interest or relationship between the Firm, or a member of the Assurance Team, and a particular responsible party would create a threat to Independence that is not trivial and inconsequential in the context of the subject matter information. This will take into account factors such as:

- The materiality of the subject matter information (or of the subject matter) for which the particular responsible party is responsible; and
- The degree of public interest associated with the engagement.

If the Firm determines that the threat to Independence created by any such interest or relationship with a particular responsible party would be trivial and inconsequential, it may not be necessary to apply all of the provisions of this section to that responsible party.

Documentation

291.29 Documentation provides evidence of the Member's judgments in forming conclusions regarding compliance with Independence requirements. The absence of documentation is not a determinant of whether a Firm considered a particular matter nor whether it is independent.

The Member shall document conclusions regarding compliance with Independence requirements, and the substance of any relevant discussions that support those conclusions. Accordingly:

(a) When safeguards are required to reduce a threat to an Acceptable Level, the Member shall document the nature of the threat and the safeguards in place or applied that reduce the threat to an Acceptable Level; and

(b) When a threat required significant analysis to determine whether safeguards were necessary and the Member concluded that they were not because the threat was already at an Acceptable Level, the Member shall document the nature of the threat and the rationale for the conclusion.

Engagement Period

291.30 Independence from the Assurance Client is required both during the engagement period and the period covered by the subject matter information. The engagement period starts when the Assurance Team begins to perform assurance services with respect to the particular engagement. The engagement period ends when the assurance report is issued. When the engagement is of a recurring nature, it ends at the later of the notification by either party that the professional relationship has terminated or the issuance of the final assurance report.

291.31 When an entity becomes an Assurance Client during or after the period covered by the subject matter information on which the Firm will express a conclusion, the Firm shall determine whether any threats to Independence are created by:

- Financial or business relationships with the Assurance Client during or after the period covered by the subject matter information but before accepting the Assurance Engagement; or
- Previous services provided to the Assurance Client.

291.32 If a non-assurance service was provided to the Assurance Client during or after the period covered by the subject matter information but before the Assurance Team begins to perform assurance services and the service would not be permitted during the period of the Assurance Engagement, the Firm shall evaluate any threat to Independence created by the service. If any threat is not at an Acceptable Level, the Assurance Engagement shall only be accepted if safeguards are applied to eliminate any threats or reduce them to an Acceptable Level. Examples of such safeguards include:

- Not including personnel who provided the non-assurance service as members of the Assurance Team;
- Having a Member review the assurance and non-assurance work as appropriate; or
- Engaging another Firm to evaluate the results of the non-assurance service or having another Firm re-perform the non-assurance service to the extent necessary to enable it to take responsibility for the service.

However, if the non-assurance service has not been completed and it is not practical to complete or terminate the service before the commencement of Professional Services in connection with the Assurance Engagement, the Firm shall only accept the Assurance Engagement if it is satisfied:

- The non-assurance service will be completed within a short period of time; or
- The client has arrangements in place to transition the service to another provider within a short period of time.

During the service period, safeguards shall be applied when necessary. In addition, the matter shall be discussed with Those Charged with Governance.

Other Considerations

291.33 There may be occasions when there is an inadvertent violation of this section. If such an inadvertent violation occurs, it generally will be deemed not to compromise Independence provided the Firm has appropriate quality control policies and procedures in place equivalent to those required by APES 320 *Quality Control for Firms*, to maintain Independence and, once discovered, the violation is corrected promptly and any necessary safeguards are applied to eliminate any threat or reduce it to an Acceptable Level. The Firm shall determine whether to discuss the matter with Those Charged with Governance.

AUST291.33.1 Unless an inadvertent violation of this section is trivial and inconsequential, the Firm shall document and discuss it with Those Charged with Governance.

Paragraphs 291.34 to 291.99 are intentionally left blank.

APES

Application of the Conceptual Framework Approach to Independence

291.100 Paragraphs 291.104 to 291.159 describe specific circumstances and relationships that create or may create threats to Independence. The paragraphs describe the potential threats and the types of safeguards that may be appropriate to eliminate the threats or reduce them to an Acceptable Level and identify certain situations where no safeguards could reduce the threats to an Acceptable Level. The paragraphs do not describe all of the circumstances and relationships that create or may create a threat to Independence. The Firm and the members of the Assurance Team shall evaluate the implications of similar, but different, circumstances and relationships and determine whether safeguards, including the safeguards in paragraphs 200.11 to 200.15 can be applied when necessary to eliminate the threats to Independence or reduce them to an Acceptable Level.

291.101 The paragraphs demonstrate how the conceptual framework approach applies to Assurance Engagements and are to be read in conjunction with paragraph 291.28 which explains that, in the majority of Assurance Engagements, there is one responsible party and that responsible party is the Assurance Client. However, in some Assurance Engagements there are two or more responsible parties. In such circumstances, an evaluation shall be made of any threats the Firm has reason to believe are created by interests and relationships between a member of the Assurance Team, the Firm, a Network Firm and the party responsible for the subject matter. For assurance reports that include a restriction on use and distribution, the paragraphs are to be read in the context of paragraphs 291.21 to 291.27.

291.102 Interpretation 2005-01 provides further guidance on applying the Independence requirements contained in this section to Assurance Engagements.

291.103 Paragraphs 291.104 to 291.120 contain references to the materiality of a Financial Interest, loan, or guarantee, or the significance of a business relationship. For the purpose of determining whether such an interest is material to an individual, the combined net worth of the individual and the individual's Immediate Family members may be taken into account.

Financial Interests

291.104 Holding a Financial Interest in an Assurance Client may create a self-interest threat. The existence and significance of any threat created depends on: (a) the role of the person holding the Financial Interest, (b) whether the Financial Interest is direct or indirect, and (c) the materiality of the Financial Interest.

291.105 Financial Interests may be held through an intermediary (e.g. a collective investment vehicle, estate or trust). The determination of whether such Financial Interests are direct or indirect will depend upon whether the beneficial owner has control over the investment vehicle or the ability to influence its investment decisions. When control over the investment vehicle or the ability to influence investment decisions exists, this Code defines that Financial Interest to be a Direct Financial Interest. Conversely, when the beneficial owner of the Financial Interest has no control over the investment vehicle or ability to influence its investment decisions, this Code defines that Financial Interest to be an Indirect Financial Interest.

291.106 If a member of the Assurance Team, a member of that individual's Immediate Family, or a Firm has a Direct Financial Interest or a material Indirect Financial Interest in the Assurance Client, the self-interest threat created would be so significant that no safeguards could reduce the threat to an Acceptable Level. Therefore, none of the following shall have a Direct Financial Interest or a material Indirect Financial Interest in the client: a member of the Assurance Team; a member of that individual's Immediate Family member; or the Firm.

291.107 When a member of the Assurance Team has a Close Family member who the Assurance Team member knows has a Direct Financial Interest or a material Indirect Financial

Interest in the Assurance Client, a self-interest threat is created. The significance of the threat will depend on factors such as

- The nature of the relationship between the member of the Assurance Team and the Close Family member; and
- The materiality of the Financial Interest to the Close Family member.

The significance of the threat shall be evaluated and safeguards applied when necessary to eliminate the threat or reduce it to an Acceptable Level. Examples of such safeguards include:

- The Close Family member disposing, as soon as practicable, of all of the Financial Interest or disposing of a sufficient portion of an Indirect Financial Interest so that the remaining interest is no longer material;
- Having a Member review the work of the member of the Assurance Team; or
- Removing the individual from the Assurance Team.

291.108 If a member of the Assurance Team, a member of that individual's Immediate Family, or a Firm has a direct or material Indirect Financial Interest in an entity that has a controlling interest in the Assurance Client, and the client is material to the entity, the self-interest threat created would be so significant that no safeguards could reduce the threat to an Acceptable Level. Therefore, none of the following shall have such a Financial Interest: a member of the Assurance Team; a member of that individual's Immediate Family; and the Firm.

291.109 The holding by a Firm or a member of the Assurance Team, or a member of that individual's Immediate Family, of a Direct Financial Interest or a material Indirect Financial Interest in the Assurance Client as a trustee creates a self-interest threat. Such an interest shall not be held unless:

(a) Neither the trustee, nor an Immediate Family member of the trustee, nor the Firm are beneficiaries of the trust;

(b) The interest in the Assurance Client held by the trust is not material to the trust;

(c) The trust is not able to exercise significant influence over the Assurance Client; and

(d) The trustee, an Immediate Family member of the trustee, or the Firm cannot significantly influence any investment decision involving a Financial Interest in the Assurance Client.

291.110 Members of the Assurance Team shall determine whether a self-interest threat is created by any known Financial Interests in the Assurance Client held by other individuals including:

- Partners and professional employees of the Firm, other than those referred to above, or their Immediate Family members; and
- Individuals with a close personal relationship with a member of the Assurance Team.

Whether these interests create a self-interest threat will depend on factors such as:

- The Firm's organisational, operating and reporting structure; and
- The nature of the relationship between the individual and the member of the Assurance Team.

The significance of any threat shall be evaluated and safeguards applied when necessary to eliminate the threat or reduce it to an Acceptable Level. Examples of such safeguards include:

- Removing the member of the Assurance Team with the personal relationship from the Assurance Team;
- Excluding the member of the Assurance Team from any significant decision-making concerning the Assurance Engagement; or
- Having a Member review the work of the member of the Assurance Team.

291.111 If a Firm, a member of the Assurance Team, or an Immediate Family member of the individual, receives a Direct Financial Interest or a material Indirect Financial Interest in an Assurance Client, for example, by way of an inheritance, gift or as a result of a merger, and such interest would not be permitted to be held under this section, then:

(a) If the interest is received by the Firm, the Financial Interest shall be disposed of immediately, or a sufficient amount of an Indirect Financial Interest shall be disposed of so that the remaining interest is no longer material, or

(b) If the interest is received by a member of the Assurance Team, or a member of that individual's Immediate Family, the individual who received the Financial Interest shall immediately dispose of the Financial Interest, or dispose of a sufficient amount of an Indirect Financial Interest so that the remaining interest is no longer material.

291.112 When an inadvertent violation of this section as it relates to a Financial Interest in an Assurance Client occurs, it is deemed not to compromise Independence if:

(a) The Firm has established policies and procedures that require prompt notification to the Firm of any breaches resulting from the purchase, inheritance or other acquisition of a Financial Interest in the Assurance Client;

(b) The actions taken in paragraph 291.111(a) – (b) are taken as applicable; and

(c) The Firm applies other safeguards when necessary to reduce any remaining threat to an Acceptable Level. Examples of such safeguards include:

(i) Having a Member review the work of the member of the Assurance Team; or

(ii) Excluding the individual from any significant decision-making concerning the Assurance Engagement.

The Firm shall determine whether to discuss the matter with Those Charged with Governance.

AUST291.112.1 Unless an inadvertent violation of this section as it relates to a Financial Interest is trivial and inconsequential, the Firm shall document and discuss it with Those Charged with Governance.

Loans and Guarantees

291.113 A loan, or a guarantee of a loan, to a member of the Assurance Team, or a member of that individual's Immediate Family, or the Firm from an Assurance Client that is a bank or similar institution, may create a threat to Independence. If the loan or guarantee is not made under normal lending procedures, terms and conditions, a self-interest threat would be created that would be so significant that no safeguards could reduce the threat to an Acceptable Level. Accordingly, neither a member of the Assurance Team, a member of that individual's Immediate Family, nor a Firm shall accept such a loan or guarantee.

291.114 If a loan to a Firm from an Assurance Client that is a bank or similar institution is made under normal lending procedures, terms and conditions and it is material to the Assurance Client or Firm receiving the loan, it may be possible to apply safeguards to reduce the self-interest threat to an Acceptable Level. An example of such a safeguard is having the work reviewed by a Member from a Network Firm that is neither involved with the Assurance Engagement nor received the loan.

291.115 A loan, or a guarantee of a loan, from an Assurance Client that is a bank or a similar institution to a member of the Assurance Team, or a member of that individual's Immediate Family, does not create a threat to Independence if the loan or guarantee is made under normal lending procedures, terms and conditions. Examples of such loans include home mortgages, bank overdrafts, car loans and credit card balances.

291.116 If the Firm or a member of the Assurance Team, or a member of that individual's Immediate Family, accepts a loan from, or has a borrowing guaranteed by, an Assurance Client that is not a bank or similar institution, the self-interest threat created would be so significant that no safeguards could reduce the threat to an Acceptable Level, unless the loan or guarantee is immaterial to both the Firm, or the member of the Assurance Team and the Immediate Family member, and the client.

291.117 Similarly, if the Firm, or a member of the Assurance Team, or a member of that individual's Immediate Family, makes or guarantees a loan to an Assurance Client, the self-interest threat created would be so significant that no safeguards could reduce the threat to an Acceptable Level, unless the loan or guarantee is immaterial to both the Firm, or the member of the Assurance Team and the Immediate Family member, and the client.

291.118 If a Firm or a member of the Assurance Team, or a member of that individual's Immediate Family, has deposits or a brokerage account with an Assurance Client that is a bank, broker, or similar institution, a threat to Independence is not created if the deposit or account is held under normal commercial terms.

Business Relationships

291.119 A close business relationship between a Firm, or a member of the Assurance Team, or a member of that individual's Immediate Family, and the Assurance Client or its management arises from a commercial relationship or common Financial Interest and may create self-interest or intimidation threats. Examples of such relationships include:

- Having a Financial Interest in a joint venture with either the client or a controlling owner, Director or Officer or other individual who performs senior managerial activities for that client.
- Arrangements to combine one or more services or products of the Firm with one or more services or products of the client and to market the package with reference to both parties.
- Distribution or marketing arrangements under which the Firm distributes or markets the client's products or services, or the client distributes or markets the Firm's products or services.

Unless any Financial Interest is immaterial and the business relationship is insignificant to the Firm and the client or its management, the threat created would be so significant that no safeguards could reduce the threat to an Acceptable Level. Therefore, unless the Financial Interest is immaterial and the business relationship is insignificant, the business relationship shall not be entered into, or shall be reduced to an insignificant level or terminated.

In the case of a member of the Assurance Team, unless any such Financial Interest is immaterial and the relationship is insignificant to that member, the individual shall be removed from the Assurance Team.

If the business relationship is between an Immediate Family member of a member of the Assurance Team and the Assurance Client or its management, the significance of any threat shall be evaluated and safeguards applied when necessary to eliminate the threat or reduce it to an Acceptable Level.

291.120 The purchase of goods and services from an Assurance Client by the Firm, or a member of the Assurance Team, or a member of that individual's Immediate Family, does not generally create a threat to Independence if the transaction is in the normal course of business and at arm's length. However, such transactions may be of such a nature or magnitude that they create a self-interest threat. The significance of any threat shall be evaluated and safeguards applied when necessary to eliminate the threat or reduce it to an Acceptable Level. Examples of such safeguards include:

- Eliminating or reducing the magnitude of the transaction; or
- Removing the individual from the Assurance Team.

Family and Personal Relationships

291.121 Family and personal relationships between a member of the Assurance Team and a Director or Officer or certain employees (depending on their role) of the Assurance Client, may create self-interest, familiarity or intimidation threats. The existence and significance of any threats will depend on a number of factors, including the individual's responsibilities on the Assurance Team, the role of the family member or other individual within the client, and the closeness of the relationship.

291.122 When an Immediate Family member of a member of the Assurance Team is:

(a) A Director or Officer of the Assurance Client, or

(b) An employee in a position to exert significant influence over the subject matter information of the Assurance Engagement,

or was in such a position during any period covered by the engagement or the subject matter information, the threats to Independence can only be reduced to an Acceptable Level by removing the individual from the Assurance Team. The closeness of the relationship is such that no other safeguards could reduce the threat to an Acceptable Level. Accordingly, no individual who has such a relationship shall be a member of the Assurance Team.

291.123 Threats to Independence are created when an Immediate Family member of a member of the Assurance Team is an employee in a position to exert significant influence over the subject matter of the engagement. The significance of the threats will depend on factors such as:

- The position held by the Immediate Family member; and
- The role of the professional on the Assurance Team.

The significance of the threat shall be evaluated and safeguards applied when necessary to eliminate the threat or reduce it to an Acceptable Level. Examples of such safeguards include:

- Removing the individual from the Assurance Team; or
- Structuring the responsibilities of the Assurance Team so that the professional does not deal with matters that are within the responsibility of the Immediate Family member.

291.124 Threats to Independence are created when a Close Family member of a member of the Assurance Team is:

- A Director or Officer of the Assurance Client; or
- An employee in a position to exert significant influence over the subject matter information of the Assurance Engagement.

The significance of the threats will depend on factors such as:

- The nature of the relationship between the member of the Assurance Team and the Close Family member;
- The position held by the Close Family member; and
- The role of the professional on the Assurance Team.

The significance of the threat shall be evaluated and safeguards applied when necessary to eliminate the threat or reduce it to an Acceptable Level. Examples of such safeguards include:

- Removing the individual from the Assurance Team; or
- Structuring the responsibilities of the Assurance Team so that the professional does not deal with matters that are within the responsibility of the Close Family member.

291.125 Threats to Independence are created when a member of the Assurance Team has a close relationship with a person who is not an Immediate or Close Family member, but who is a Director or Officer or an employee in a position to exert significant influence over the subject matter information of the Assurance Engagement. A member of the Assurance Team who has such a relationship shall consult in accordance with Firm policies and procedures. The significance of the threats will depend on factors such as:

- The nature of the relationship between the individual and the member of the Assurance Team;
- The position the individual holds with the client; and
- The role of the professional on the Assurance Team.

The significance of the threats shall be evaluated and safeguards applied when necessary to eliminate the threats or reduce them to an Acceptable Level. Examples of such safeguards include:

- Removing the professional from the Assurance Team; or
- Structuring the responsibilities of the Assurance Team so that the professional does not deal with matters that are within the responsibility of the individual with whom the professional has a close relationship.

291.126 Self-interest, familiarity or intimidation threats may be created by a personal or family relationship between (a) a partner or employee of the Firm who is not a member of the Assurance Team and (b) a Director or Officer of the Assurance Client or an employee in a position to exert significant influence over the subject matter information of the Assurance Engagement. The existence and significance of any threat will depend on factors such as:

- The nature of the relationship between the partner or employee of the Firm and the Director or Officer or employee of the client;
- The interaction of the partner or employee of the Firm with the Assurance Team;
- The position of the partner or employee within the Firm; and
- The role of the individual within the client.

The significance of any threat shall be evaluated and safeguards applied when necessary to eliminate the threat or reduce it to an Acceptable Level. Examples of such safeguards include:

- Structuring the partner's or employee's responsibilities to reduce any potential influence over the Assurance Engagement; or
- Having a Member review the relevant assurance work performed.

291.127 When an inadvertent violation of this section as it relates to family and personal relationships occurs, it is deemed not to compromise Independence if:

(a) The Firm has established policies and procedures that require prompt notification to the Firm of any breaches resulting from changes in the employment status of their Immediate or Close Family members or other personal relationships that create threats to Independence;

(b) The inadvertent violation relates to an Immediate Family member of a member of the Assurance Team becoming a Director or Officer of the Assurance Client or being in a position to exert significant influence over the subject matter information of the Assurance Engagement, and the relevant professional is removed from the Assurance Team; and

(c) The Firm applies other safeguards when necessary to reduce any remaining threat to an Acceptable Level. Examples of such safeguards include:

- Having a Member review the work of the member of the Assurance Team; or
- Excluding the relevant professional from any significant decision-making concerning the engagement.

The Firm shall determine whether to discuss the matter with Those Charged with Governance.

Employment with Assurance Clients

291.128 Familiarity or intimidation threats may be created if a Director or Officer of the Assurance Client, or an employee who is in a position to exert significant influence over the subject matter information of the Assurance Engagement, has been a member of the Assurance Team or partner of the Firm.

291.129 If a former member of the Assurance Team or partner of the Firm has joined the Assurance Client in such a position, the existence and significance of any familiarity or intimidation threats will depend on factors such as:

(a) The position the individual has taken at the client;

(b) Any involvement the individual will have with the Assurance Team;

APES

(c) The length of time since the individual was a member of the Assurance Team or partner of the Firm; and

(d) The former position of the individual within the Assurance Team or Firm, for example, whether the individual was responsible for maintaining regular contact with the client's management or Those Charged with Governance.

In all cases the individual shall not continue to participate in the Firm's business or professional activities.

The significance of any threats created shall be evaluated and safeguards applied when necessary to eliminate the threats or reduce them to an Acceptable Level.

Examples of such safeguards include:

- Making arrangements such that the individual is not entitled to any benefits or payments from the Firm, unless made in accordance with fixed pre-determined arrangements.
- Making arrangements such that any amount owed to the individual is not material to the Firm;
- Modifying the plan for the Assurance Engagement;
- Assigning individuals to the Assurance Team who have sufficient experience in relation to the individual who has joined the client; or
- Having a Member review the work of the former member of the Assurance Team.

291.130 If a former partner of the Firm has previously joined an entity in such a position and the entity subsequently becomes an Assurance Client of the Firm, the significance of any threats to Independence shall be evaluated and safeguards applied when necessary, to eliminate the threat or reduce it to an Acceptable Level.

291.131 A self-interest threat is created when a member of the Assurance Team participates in the Assurance Engagement while knowing that the member of the Assurance Team will, or may, join the client some time in the future. Firm policies and procedures shall require members of an Assurance Team to notify the Firm when entering employment negotiations with the client. On receiving such notification, the significance of the threat shall be evaluated and safeguards applied when necessary to eliminate the threat or reduce it to an Acceptable Level. Examples of such safeguards include:

- Removing the individual from the Assurance Team; or
- A review of any significant judgments made by that individual while on the team.

Recent Service with an Assurance Client

291.132 Self-interest, self-review or familiarity threats may be created if a member of the Assurance Team has recently served as a Director, Officer, or employee of the Assurance Client. This would be the case when, for example, a member of the Assurance Team has to evaluate elements of the subject matter information the member of the Assurance Team had prepared while with the client.

291.133 If, during the period covered by the assurance report, a member of the Assurance Team had served as Director or Officer of the Assurance Client, or was an employee in a position to exert significant influence over the subject matter information of the Assurance Engagement, the threat created would be so significant that no safeguards could reduce the threat to an Acceptable Level. Consequently, such individuals shall not be assigned to the Assurance Team.

291.134 Self-interest, self-review or familiarity threats may be created if, before the period covered by the assurance report, a member of the Assurance Team had served as Director or Officer of the Assurance Client, or was an employee in a position to exert significant influence over the subject matter information of the Assurance Engagement. For example, such threats would be created if a decision made or work performed by the individual in the prior period, while employed by the client, is to be evaluated in the current period as part of the current Assurance Engagement. The existence and significance of any threats will depend on factors such as:

- The position the individual held with the client;
- The length of time since the individual left the client; and
- The role of the professional on the Assurance Team.

The significance of any threat shall be evaluated and safeguards applied when necessary to reduce the threat to an Acceptable Level. An example of such a safeguard is conducting a review of the work performed by the individual as part of the Assurance Team.

Serving as a Director or Officer of an Assurance Client

291.135 If a partner or employee of the Firm serves a Director or Officer of an Assurance Client, the self-review and self-interest threats would be so significant that no safeguards could reduce the threats to an Acceptable Level. Accordingly, no partner or employee shall serve as a Director or Officer of an Assurance Client.

291.136 The position of Company Secretary has different implications in different jurisdictions. Duties may range from administrative duties, such as personnel management and the maintenance of company records and registers, to duties as diverse as ensuring that the company complies with regulation or providing advice on corporate governance matters. Generally, this position is seen to imply a close association with the entity.

291.137 If a Partner or employee of the Firm serves as Company Secretary for an Assurance Client, self-review and advocacy threats are created that would generally be so significant that no safeguards could reduce the threats to an Acceptable Level. Despite paragraph 291.135, when this practice is specifically permitted under local law, professional rules or practice, and provided management makes all relevant decisions, the duties and activities shall be limited to those of a routine and administrative nature, such as preparing minutes and maintaining statutory returns. In those circumstances, the significance of any threats shall be evaluated and safeguards applied when necessary to eliminate the threats or reduce them to an Acceptable Level.

291.138 Performing routine administrative services to support a company secretarial function or providing advice in relation to company secretarial administration matters does not generally create threats to Independence, as long as client management makes all relevant decisions.

Long Association of Senior Personnel with Assurance Clients

291.139 Familiarity and self-interest threats are created by using the same senior personnel on an Assurance Engagement over a long period of time. The significance of the threats will depend on factors such as:

- How long the individual has been a member of the Assurance Team;
- The role of the individual on the Assurance Team;
- The structure of the Firm;
- The nature of the Assurance Engagement;
- Whether the client's management team has changed; and
- Whether the nature or complexity of the subject matter information has changed.

The significance of the threats shall be evaluated and safeguards applied when necessary to eliminate the threats or reduce them to an Acceptable Level. Examples of such safeguards include:

- Rotating the senior personnel off the Assurance Team;
- Having a Member who was not a member of the Assurance Team review the work of the senior personnel; or
- Regular independent internal or external quality reviews of the engagement.

Provision of Non-assurance Services to Assurance Clients

291.140 Firms have traditionally provided to their Assurance Clients a range of non-assurance services that are consistent with their skills and expertise. Providing non-assurance services may, however, create threats to the Independence of the Firm or members of the Assurance Team. The threats created are most often self-review, self-interest and advocacy threats.

291.141 When specific guidance on a particular non-assurance service is not included in this section, the conceptual framework shall be applied when evaluating the particular circumstances.

291.142 Before the Firm accepts an engagement to provide a non-assurance service to an Assurance Client, a determination shall be made as to whether providing such a service would create a threat to Independence. In evaluating the significance of any threat created by a particular non-assurance service, consideration shall be given to any threat that the Assurance Team has reason to believe is created by providing other related non-assurance services. If a threat is created that cannot be reduced to an Acceptable Level by the application of safeguards the non-assurance service shall not be provided.

Management Responsibilities

291.143 Management of an entity performs many activities in managing the entity in the best interests of stakeholders of the entity. It is not possible to specify every activity that is a management responsibility. However, management responsibilities involve leading and directing an entity, including making significant decisions regarding the acquisition, deployment and control of human, financial, physical and intangible resources.

291.144 Whether an activity is a management responsibility depends on the circumstances and requires the exercise of judgment. Examples of activities that would generally be considered a management responsibility include:

- Setting policies and strategic direction;
- Directing and taking responsibility for the actions of the entity's employees;
- Authorising transactions;
- Deciding which recommendations of the Firm or other third parties to implement; and
- Taking responsibility for designing, implementing and maintaining internal control.

291.145 Activities that are routine and administrative, or involve matters that are insignificant, generally are deemed not to be a management responsibility. For example, executing an insignificant transaction that has been authorised by management or monitoring the dates for filing statutory returns and advising an Assurance Client of those dates is deemed not to be a management responsibility. Further, providing advice and recommendations to assist management in discharging its responsibilities is not assuming a management responsibility.

291.146 Assuming a management responsibility for an Assurance Client may create threats to Independence. If a Firm were to assume a management responsibility as part of the assurance service, the threats created would be so significant that no safeguards could reduce the threats to an Acceptable Level. Accordingly, in providing assurance services to an Assurance Client, a Firm shall not assume a management responsibility as part of the assurance service. If the Firm assumes a management responsibility as part of any other services provided to the Assurance Client, it shall ensure that the responsibility is not related to the subject matter and subject matter information of an Assurance Engagement provided by the Firm.

291.147 To avoid the risk of assuming a management responsibility related to the subject matter or subject matter information of the Assurance Engagement, the Firm shall be satisfied that a member of management is responsible for making the significant judgments and decisions that are the proper responsibility of management, evaluating the results of the service and accepting responsibility for the actions to be taken arising from the results of the service. This reduces the risk of the Firm inadvertently making any significant judgments or decisions on behalf of management. This risk is further reduced when the Firm gives the client the opportunity to make judgments and decisions based on an objective and transparent analysis and presentation of the issues.

Other Considerations

291.148 Threats to Independence may be created when a Firm provides a non-assurance service related to the subject matter information of an Assurance Engagement. In such cases, an evaluation of the significance of the Firm's involvement with the subject matter information of the engagement shall be made, and a determination shall be made of whether any self-review threats that are not at an Acceptable Level can be reduced to an Acceptable Level by the application of safeguards.

291.149 A self-review threat may be created if the Firm is involved in the preparation of subject matter information which is subsequently the subject matter information of an Assurance Engagement. For example, a self-review threat would be created if the Firm developed and prepared prospective financial information and subsequently provided assurance on this information. Consequently, the Firm shall evaluate the significance of any self-review threat created by the provision of such services and apply safeguards when necessary to eliminate the threat or reduce it to an Acceptable Level.

291.150 When a Firm performs a valuation that forms part of the subject matter information of an Assurance Engagement, the Firm shall evaluate the significance of any self-review threat and apply safeguards when necessary to eliminate the threat or reduce it to an Acceptable Level.

Fees

Fees – Relative Size

291.151 When the total fees from an Assurance Client represent a large proportion of the total fees of the Firm expressing the conclusion, the dependence on that client and concern about losing the client creates a self-interest or intimidation threat. The significance of the threat will depend on factors such as:

- The operating structure of the Firm;
- Whether the Firm is well established or new; and
- The significance of the client qualitatively and/or quantitatively to the Firm.

The significance of the threat shall be evaluated and safeguards applied when necessary to eliminate the threat or reduce it to an Acceptable Level. Examples of such safeguards include:

- Reducing the dependency on the client;
- External quality control reviews; or
- Consulting a third party, such as a professional regulatory body or a Member, on key assurance judgments.

291.152 A self-interest or intimidation threat is also created when the fees generated from an Assurance Client represent a large proportion of the revenue from an individual partner's clients. The significance of the threat shall be evaluated and safeguards applied when necessary to eliminate the threat or reduce it to an Acceptable Level. An example of such a safeguard is having an additional Member who was not a member of the Assurance Team review the work or otherwise advise as necessary.

Fees – Overdue

291.153 A self-interest threat may be created if fees due from an Assurance Client remain unpaid for a long time, especially if a significant part is not paid before the issue of the assurance report, if any, for the following period. Generally the Firm is expected to require payment of such fees before any such report is issued. If fees remain unpaid after the report has been issued, the existence and significance of any threat shall be evaluated and safeguards applied when necessary to eliminate the threat or reduce it to an Acceptable Level. An example of such a safeguard is having another Member who did not take part in the Assurance Engagement provide advice or review the work performed. The Firm shall determine whether the overdue fees might be regarded as being equivalent to a loan

APES

to the client and whether, because of the significance of the overdue fees, it is appropriate for the Firm to be re-appointed or continue the Assurance Engagement.

Contingent Fees

291.154 Contingent Fees are fees calculated on a predetermined basis relating to the outcome of a transaction or the result of the services performed by the Firm. For the purposes of this section, fees are not regarded as being contingent if established by a court or other public authority.

291.155 A Contingent Fee charged directly or indirectly, for example through an intermediary, by a Firm in respect of an Assurance Engagement creates a self-interest threat that is so significant that no safeguards could reduce the threat to an Acceptable Level. Accordingly, a Firm shall not enter into any such fee arrangement.

291.156 A Contingent Fee charged directly or indirectly, for example through an intermediary, by a Firm in respect of a non-assurance service provided to an Assurance Client may also create a self-interest threat. If the outcome of the non-assurance service, and therefore, the amount of the fee, is dependent on a future or contemporary judgment related to a matter that is material to the subject matter information of the Assurance Engagement, no safeguards could reduce the threat to an Acceptable Level. Accordingly, such arrangements shall not be accepted.

291.157 For other Contingent Fee arrangements charged by a Firm for a non-assurance service to an Assurance Client, the existence and significance of any threats will depend on factors such as:

- The range of possible fee amounts;
- Whether an appropriate authority determines the outcome of the matter upon which the Contingent Fee will be determined;
- The nature of the service; and
- The effect of the event or transaction on the subject matter information.

The significance of any threats shall be evaluated and safeguards applied when necessary to eliminate the threats or reduce them to an Acceptable Level. Examples of such safeguards include:

- Having a Member review the relevant assurance work or otherwise advise as necessary; or
- Using professionals who are not members of the Assurance Team to perform the non-assurance service.

Gifts and Hospitality

291.158 Accepting gifts or hospitality from an Assurance Client may create self-interest and familiarity threats. If a Firm or a member of the Assurance Team accepts gifts or hospitality, unless the value is trivial and inconsequential, the threats created would be so significant that no safeguards could reduce the threats to an Acceptable Level. Consequently, a Firm or a member of the Assurance Team shall not accept such gifts or hospitality.

Actual or Threatened Litigation

291.159 When litigation takes place, or appears likely, between the Firm or a member of the Assurance Team and the Assurance Client, self-interest and intimidation threats are created. The relationship between client management and the members of the Assurance Team must be characterised by complete candour and full disclosure regarding all aspects of a client's business operations. When the Firm and the client's management are placed in adversarial positions by actual or threatened litigation, affecting management's willingness to make complete disclosures self-interest and intimidation threats are created. The significance of the threats created will depend on such factors as:

- The materiality of the litigation; and
- Whether the litigation relates to a prior Assurance Engagement.

The significance of the threats shall be evaluated and safeguards applied when necessary to eliminate the threats or reduce them to an Acceptable Level. Examples of such safeguards include:

- If the litigation involves a member of the Assurance Team, removing that individual from the Assurance Team; or
- Having a professional review the work performed.

If such safeguards do not reduce the threats to an Acceptable Level, the only appropriate action is to withdraw from, or decline, the Assurance Engagement.

❖❖❖

Interpretation 2005-01 (Revised July 2009 to conform to changes resulting from the IESBA's project to improve the clarity of the Code)

Application of Section 291 to Assurance Engagements that are not Financial Statement Audit Engagements

This interpretation provides guidance on the application of the Independence requirements contained in Section 291 to Assurance Engagements that are not Financial Statement Audit Engagements.

This interpretation focuses on the application issues that are particular to Assurance Engagements that are not Financial Statement Audit Engagements. There are other matters noted in Section 291 that are relevant in the consideration of Independence requirements for all Assurance Engagements. For example, paragraph 291.3 states that an evaluation shall be made of any threats the Firm has reason to believe are created by a Network Firm's interests and relationships. It also states that when the Assurance Team has reason to believe that a Related Entity of such an Assurance Client is relevant to the evaluation of the Firm's Independence of the client, the Assurance Team shall include the Related Entity when evaluating threats to Independence and when necessary applying safeguards. These matters are not specifically addressed in this interpretation.

As explained in the International Framework for Assurance Engagements issued by the International Auditing and Assurance Standards Board, in an Assurance Engagement, the Member in Public Practice expresses a conclusion designed to enhance the degree of confidence of the intended users other than the responsible party about the outcome of the evaluation or measurement of a subject matter against criteria.

Assertion-based Assurance Engagements

In an assertion-based Assurance Engagement, the evaluation or measurement of the subject matter is performed by the responsible party, and the subject matter information is in the form of an assertion by the responsible party that is made available to the intended users.

In an assertion-based Assurance Engagement Independence is required from the responsible party, which is responsible for the subject matter information and may be responsible for the subject matter.

In those assertion-based Assurance Engagements where the responsible party is responsible for the subject matter information but not the subject matter, Independence is required from the responsible party. In addition, an evaluation shall be made of any threats the Firm has reason to believe are created by interests and relationships between a member of the Assurance Team, the Firm, a Network Firm and the party responsible for the subject matter.

Direct reporting Assurance Engagements

In a direct reporting Assurance Engagement, the Member in Public Practice either directly performs the evaluation or measurement of the subject matter, or obtains a representation from the responsible party that has performed the evaluation or measurement that is not available to the intended users. The subject matter information is provided to the intended users in the assurance report.

In a direct reporting Assurance Engagement Independence is required from the responsible party, which is responsible for the subject matter.

Multiple Responsible Parties

In both assertion-based Assurance Engagements and direct reporting Assurance Engagements there may be several responsible parties. For example, a public accountant in Public Practice may be asked to provide assurance on the monthly circulation statistics of a number of independently owned newspapers. The assignment could be an assertion based Assurance Engagement where each newspaper measures its circulation and the statistics are presented in an assertion that is available to the intended users. Alternatively, the assignment could be a direct reporting Assurance Engagement, where there is no assertion and there may or may not be a written representation from the newspapers.

In such engagements, when determining whether it is necessary to apply the provisions in Section 291 to each responsible party, the Firm may take into account whether an interest or relationship between the Firm, or a member of the Assurance Team, and a particular responsible party would create a threat to Independence that is not trivial and inconsequential in the context of the subject matter information. This will take into account:

- The materiality of the subject matter information (or the subject matter) for which the particular responsible party is responsible; and
- The degree of public interest that is associated with the engagement.

If the Firm determines that the threat to Independence created by any such relationships with a particular responsible party would be trivial and inconsequential it may not be necessary to apply all of the provisions of this section to that responsible party.

Example

The following example has been developed to demonstrate the application of Section 291. It is assumed that the client is not also a Financial Statement Audit Client of the Firm, or a Network Firm.

A Firm is engaged to provide assurance on the total proven oil reserves of 10 independent companies. Each company has conducted geographical and engineering surveys to determine their reserves (subject matter). There are established criteria to determine when a reserve may be considered to be proven which the Member in Public Practice determines to be suitable criteria for the engagement.

The proven reserves for each company as at December 31, 20X0 were as follows:

	Proven oil reserves thousands of barrels
Company 1	5,200
Company 2	725
Company 3	3,260
Company 4	15,000
Company 5	6,700
Company 6	39,126
Company 7	345
Company 8	175
Company 9	24,135
Company 10	9,635
Total	**104,301**

The engagement could be structured in differing ways:

Assertion-based engagements

A1 Each company measures its reserves and provides an assertion to the Firm and to intended users.

A2 An entity other than the companies measures the reserves and provides an assertion to the Firm and to intended users.

Direct reporting engagements

D1 Each company measures the reserves and provides the Firm with a written representation that measures its reserves against the established criteria for measuring proven reserves. The representation is not available to the intended users.

D2 The Firm directly measures the reserves of some of the companies.

Application of Approach

A1 Each company measures its reserves and provides an assertion to the Firm and to intended users.

There are several responsible parties in this engagement (companies 1-10). When determining whether it is necessary to apply the Independence provisions to all of the companies, the Firm may take into account whether an interest or relationship with a particular company would create a threat to Independence that is not at an Acceptable Level. This will take into account factors such as:

- The materiality of the company's proven reserves in relation to the total reserves to be reported on; and
- The degree of public interest associated with the engagement. (Paragraph 291.28.)

For example Company 8 accounts for 0.17% of the total reserves, therefore a business relationship or interest with Company 8 would create less of a threat than a similar relationship with Company 6, which accounts for approximately 37.5% of the reserves.

Having determined those companies to which the Independence requirements apply, the Assurance Team and the Firm are required to be independent of those responsible parties that would be considered to be the Assurance Client (paragraph 291.28).

A2 An entity other than the companies measures the reserves and provides an assertion to the Firm and to intended users.

The Firm shall be independent of the entity that measures the reserves and provides an assertion to the Firm and to intended users (paragraph 291.19). That entity is not responsible for the subject matter and so an evaluation shall be made of any threats the Firm has reason to believe are created by interests/relationships with the party responsible for the subject matter (paragraph 291.19). There are several parties responsible for the subject matter in this engagement (Companies 1-10). As discussed in example A1 above, the Firm may take into account whether an interest or relationship with a particular company would create a threat to Independence that is not at an Acceptable Level.

D1 Each company provides the Firm with a representation that measures its reserves against the established criteria for measuring proven reserves. The representation is not available to the intended users.

There are several responsible parties in this engagement (Companies 1-10). When determining whether it is necessary to apply the Independence provisions to all of the companies, the Firm may take into account whether an interest or relationship with a particular company would create a threat to Independence that is not at an Acceptable Level. This will take into account factors such as:

- The materiality of the company's proven reserves in relation to the total reserves to be reported on; and
- The degree of public interest associated with the engagement. (Paragraph 291.28).

For example, Company 8 accounts for 0.17% of the reserves, therefore a business relationship or interest with Company 8 would create less of a threat than a similar relationship with Company 6 that accounts for approximately 37.5% of the reserves.

Having determined those companies to which the Independence requirements apply, the Assurance Team and the Firm shall be independent of those responsible parties that would be considered to be the Assurance Client (paragraph 291.28).

D2 The Firm directly measures the reserves of some of the companies.

The application is the same as in example D1.

Part C – Members in Business

SECTION 300

Introduction

300.1 This Part of the Code describes how the conceptual framework contained in Part A applies in certain situations to Members in Business. This Part does not describe all of the circumstances and relationships that could be encountered by a Member in Business that create or may create threats to compliance with the fundamental principles. Therefore, the Member in Business is encouraged to be alert for such circumstances and relationships.

300.2 Investors, creditors, employers and other sectors of the business community, as well as governments and the public at large, all may rely on the work of Members in Business. Members in Business may be solely or jointly responsible for the preparation and reporting of financial and other information, which both their employing organisations and third parties may rely on. They may also be responsible for providing effective financial management and competent advice on a variety of business-related matters.

300.3 A Member in Business may be a salaried employee, a partner, Director (whether executive or non-executive), an owner manager, a volunteer or another working for one or more employing organisation. The legal form of the relationship with the employing organisation, if any, has no bearing on the ethical responsibilities incumbent on the Member in Business.

300.4 A Member in Business has a responsibility to further the legitimate aims of the Member's employing organisation. This Code does not seek to hinder a Member in Business from properly fulfilling that responsibility, but addresses circumstances in which compliance with the fundamental principles may be compromised.

300.5 A Member in Business may hold a senior position within an organisation. The more senior the position, the greater will be the ability and opportunity to influence events, practices and attitudes. A Member in Business is expected, therefore, to encourage an ethics-based culture in an employing organisation that emphasises the importance that senior management places on ethical behaviour.

300.6 A Member in Business shall not knowingly engage in any business, occupation, or activity that impairs or might impair integrity, objectivity or the good reputation of the profession and as a result would be incompatible with the fundamental principles.

300.7 Compliance with the fundamental principles may potentially be threatened by a broad range of circumstances and relationships. Threats fall into one or more of the following categories:

(a) Self-interest;

(b) Self-review;

(c) Advocacy;

(d) Familiarity; and

(e) Intimidation.

These threats are discussed further in Part A of this Code.

300.8 Examples of circumstances that may create self-interest threats for a Member in Business include:

- Holding a Financial Interest in, or receiving a loan or guarantee from the employing organisation.
- Participating in incentive compensation arrangements offered by the employing organisation.
- Inappropriate personal use of corporate assets.
- Concern over employment security.
- Commercial pressure from outside the employing organisation.

300.9 An example of a circumstance that creates a self-review threat for a Member in Business is determining the appropriate accounting treatment for a business combination after performing the feasibility study that supported the acquisition decision.

300.10 When furthering the legitimate goals and objectives of their employing organisations, Members in Business may promote the organisation's position, provided any statements made are neither false nor misleading. Such actions generally would not create an advocacy threat.

300.11 Examples of circumstances that may create familiarity threats for a Member in Business include:

- Being responsible for the employing organisation's financial reporting when an Immediate or Close Family member employed by the entity makes decisions that affect the entity's financial reporting.
- Long association with business contacts influencing business decisions.
- Accepting a gift or preferential treatment, unless the value is trivial and inconsequential.

300.12 Examples of circumstances that may create intimidation threats for a Member in Business include:

- Threat of dismissal or replacement of the Member in Business or a Close or Immediate Family member over a disagreement about the application of an accounting principle or the way in which financial information is to be reported.
- A dominant personality attempting to influence the decision making process, for example with regard to the awarding of contracts or the application of an accounting principle.

300.13 Safeguards that may eliminate or reduce threats to an Acceptable Level fall into two broad categories:

(a) Safeguards created by the profession, legislation or regulation; and

(b) Safeguards in the work environment.

Examples of safeguards created by the profession, legislation or regulation are detailed in paragraph 100.14 of Part A of this Code.

300.14 Safeguards in the work environment include:

- The employing organisation's systems of corporate oversight or other oversight structures.
- The employing organisation's ethics and conduct programs.
- Recruitment procedures in the employing organisation emphasising the importance of employing high calibre competent staff.
- Strong internal controls.
- Appropriate disciplinary processes.
- Leadership that stresses the importance of ethical behaviour and the expectation that employees will act in an ethical manner.

APES

- Policies and procedures to implement and monitor the quality of employee performance.
- Timely communication of the employing organisation's policies and procedures, including any changes to them, to all employees and appropriate training and education on such policies and procedures.
- Policies and procedures to empower and encourage employees to communicate to senior levels within the employing organisation any ethical issues that concern them without fear of retribution.
- Consultation with another appropriate Member.

300.15 In circumstances where a Member in Business believes that unethical behaviour or actions by others will continue to occur within the employing organisation, the Member in Business may consider obtaining legal advice. In those extreme situations where all available safeguards have been exhausted and it is not possible to reduce the threat to an Acceptable Level, a Member in Business may conclude that it is appropriate to resign from the employing organisation.

SECTION 310

Potential Conflicts

310.1 A Member in Business shall comply with the fundamental principles. There may be times, however, when a Member's responsibilities to an employing organisation and professional obligations to comply with the fundamental principles are in conflict. A Member in Business is expected to support the legitimate and ethical objectives established by the employer and the rules and procedures drawn up in support of those objectives. Nevertheless, where a relationship or circumstance creates a threat to compliance with the fundamental principles, a Member in Business shall apply the conceptual framework approach described in Section 100 to determine a response to the threat.

310.2 As a consequence of responsibilities to an employing organisation, a Member in Business may be under pressure to act or behave in ways that could create threats to compliance with the fundamental principles. Such pressure may be explicit or implicit; it may come from a supervisor, manager, Director or another individual within the employing organisation. A Member in Business may face pressure to:

- Act contrary to law or regulation.
- Act contrary to technical or professional standards.
- Facilitate unethical or illegal earnings management strategies.
- Lie to others, or otherwise intentionally mislead (including misleading by remaining silent) others, in particular:
  - The auditors of the employing organisation; or
  - Regulators.
- Issue, or otherwise be associated with, a financial or non-financial report that materially misrepresents the facts, including statements in connection with, for example:
  - The Financial Statements;
  - Tax compliance;
  - Legal compliance; or
  - Reports required by securities regulators.

310.3 The significance of any threats arising from such pressures, such as intimidation threats, shall be evaluated and safeguards applied when necessary to eliminate them or reduce them to an Acceptable Level. Examples of such safeguards include:

- Obtaining advice, where appropriate, from within the employing organisation, an independent professional advisor or a relevant professional body.
- Using a formal dispute resolution process within the employing organisation.
- Seeking legal advice.

SECTION 320

Preparation and Reporting of Information

320.1 Members in Business are often involved in the preparation and reporting of information that may either be made public or used by others inside or outside the employing organisation. Such information may include financial or management information, for example, forecasts and budgets, Financial Statements, management's discussion and analysis, and the management letter of representation provided to the auditors during the audit of the entity's Financial Statements. A Member in Business shall prepare or present such information fairly, honestly and in accordance with relevant professional standards so that the information will be understood in its context.

320.2 A Member in Business who has responsibility for the preparation or approval of the general purpose Financial Statements of an employing organisation shall be satisfied that those Financial Statements are presented in accordance with the applicable financial reporting standards.

AUST320.2.1 Where a Member in Business referred to in paragraph 320.2 is not satisfied that the Financial Statements of an employing organisation are presented in accordance with applicable Australian Accounting Standards, the Member shall:

(a) in all cases, notify Those Charged with Governance and document the communication; and

(b) qualify any declarations given by the Member in compliance with legislative and regulatory requirements or the organisation's reporting requirements.

320.3 A Member in Business shall take reasonable steps to maintain information for which the Member in Business is responsible in a manner that:

(a) Describes clearly the true nature of business transactions, assets, or liabilities;

(b) Classifies and records information in a timely and proper manner; and

(c) Represents the facts accurately and completely in all material respects.

320.4 Threats to compliance with the fundamental principles, for example, self-interest or intimidation threats to objectivity or professional competence and due care, are created where a Member in Business is pressured (either externally or by the possibility of personal gain) to become associated with misleading information or to become associated with misleading information through the actions of others.

320.5 The significance of such threats will depend on factors such as the source of the pressure and the degree to which the information is, or may be, misleading. The significance of the threats shall be evaluated and safeguards applied when necessary to eliminate them or reduce them to an Acceptable Level. Such safeguards include consultation with superiors within the employing organisation, the audit committee or Those Charged with Governance of the organisation, or with a relevant professional body.

320.6 Where it is not possible to reduce the threat to an Acceptable Level, a Member in Business shall refuse to be or remain associated with information the Member determines is misleading. A Member in Business may have been unknowingly associated with misleading information. Upon becoming aware of this, the Member in Business shall take steps to be disassociated from that information. In determining whether there is a requirement to report, the Member in Business may consider obtaining legal advice. In addition, the Member may consider whether to resign.

SECTION 330

Acting with Sufficient Expertise

330.1 The fundamental principle of professional competence and due care requires that a Member in Business only undertake significant tasks for which the Member in Business has, or can obtain, sufficient specific training or experience. A Member in Business shall not intentionally mislead an employer as to the level of expertise or experience possessed, nor shall a Member in Business fail to seek appropriate expert advice and assistance when required.

330.2 Circumstances that create a threat to a Member in Business performing duties with the appropriate degree of professional competence and due care include having:

- Insufficient time for properly performing or completing the relevant duties.
- Incomplete, restricted or otherwise inadequate information for performing the duties properly.
- Insufficient experience, training and/or education.
- Inadequate resources for the proper performance of the duties.

330.3 The significance of the threat will depend on factors such as the extent to which the Member in Business is working with others, relative seniority in the business, and the level of supervision and review applied to the work. The significance of the threat shall be evaluated and safeguards applied when necessary to eliminate the threat or reduce it to an Acceptable Level. Examples of such safeguards include:

- Obtaining additional advice or training.
- Ensuring that there is adequate time available for performing the relevant duties.
- Obtaining assistance from someone with the necessary expertise.
- Consulting, where appropriate, with:
  - Superiors within the employing organisation;
  - Independent experts; or
  - A relevant professional body.

330.4 When threats cannot be eliminated or reduced to an Acceptable Level, Members in Business shall determine whether to refuse to perform the duties in question. If the Member in Business determines that refusal is appropriate, the reasons for doing so shall be clearly communicated.

SECTION 340

Financial Interests

340.1 Members in Business may have Financial Interests, or may know of Financial Interests of Immediate or Close Family members, that, in certain circumstances, may create threats to compliance with the fundamental principles. For example, self-interest threats to objectivity or confidentiality may be created through the existence of the motive and opportunity to manipulate price sensitive information in order to gain financially. Examples of circumstances that may create self-interest threats include situations where the Member in Business or an Immediate or Close Family member:

- Holds a Direct or Indirect Financial Interest in the employing organisation and the value of that Financial Interest could be directly affected by decisions made by the Member in Business;
- Is eligible for a profit related bonus and the value of that bonus could be directly affected by decisions made by the Member in Business;
- Holds, directly or indirectly, share options in the employing organisation, the value of which could be directly affected by decisions made by the Member in Business;

- Holds, directly or indirectly, share options in the employing organisation which are, or will soon be, eligible for conversion; or
- May qualify for share options in the employing organisation or performance related bonuses if certain targets are achieved.

340.2 The significance of any threat shall be evaluated and safeguards applied when necessary to eliminate the threat or reduce it to an Acceptable Level. In evaluating the significance of any threat, and, when necessary, determining the appropriate safeguards to be applied to eliminate the threat or reduce it to an Acceptable Level, a Member in Business shall evaluate the nature of the Financial Interest. This includes evaluating the significance of the Financial Interest and determining whether it is Direct or Indirect. What constitutes a significant or valuable stake in an organisation will vary from individual to individual, depending on personal circumstances. Examples of such safeguards include:

- Policies and procedures for a committee independent of management to determine the level or form of remuneration of senior management.
- Disclosure of all relevant interests, and of any plans to trade in relevant shares to Those Charged with Governance of the employing organisation, in accordance with any internal policies.
- Consultation, where appropriate, with superiors within the employing organisation.
- Consultation, where appropriate, with Those Charged with Governance of the employing organisation or relevant professional bodies.
- Internal and external audit procedures.
- Up-to-date education on ethical issues and on the legal restrictions and other regulations around potential insider trading.

340.3 A Member in Business shall neither manipulate information nor use confidential information for personal gain.

SECTION 350

Inducements

Receiving Offers

350.1 A Member in Business or an Immediate or Close Family member may be offered an inducement. Inducements may take various forms, including gifts, hospitality, preferential treatment, and inappropriate appeals to friendship or loyalty.

350.2 Offers of inducements may create threats to compliance with the fundamental principles. When a Member in Business or an Immediate or Close Family member is offered an inducement, the situation shall be evaluated. Self-interest threats to objectivity or confidentiality are created when an inducement is made in an attempt to unduly influence actions or decisions, encourage illegal or dishonest behaviour, or obtain confidential information. Intimidation threats to objectivity or confidentiality are created if such an inducement is accepted and it is followed by threats to make that offer public and damage the reputation of either the Member in Business or an Immediate or Close Family member.

350.3 The existence and significance of any threats will depend on the nature, value and intent behind the offer. If a reasonable and informed third party, weighing all the specific facts and circumstances, would consider the inducement insignificant and not intended to encourage unethical behaviour, then a Member in Business may conclude that the offer is made in the normal course of business and may generally conclude that there is no significant threat to compliance with the fundamental principles.

350.4 The significance of any threats shall be evaluated and safeguards applied when necessary to eliminate them or reduce them to an Acceptable Level. When the threats cannot be eliminated or reduced to an Acceptable Level through the application of safeguards, a Member in Business shall not accept the inducement.

As the real or apparent threats to compliance with the fundamental principles do not merely arise from acceptance of an inducement but, sometimes, merely from the fact of the offer having been made, additional safeguards shall be adopted. A Member in Business shall evaluate any threats created by such offers and determine whether to take one or more of the following actions:

(a) Informing higher levels of management or Those Charged with Governance of the employing organisation immediately when such offers have been made;
(b) Informing third parties of the offer – for example, a professional body or the employer of the individual who made the offer; a Member in Business may however, consider seeking legal advice before taking such a step; and
(c) Advising Immediate or Close Family members of relevant threats and safeguards where they are potentially in positions that might result in offers of inducements, for example, as a result of their employment situation; and
(d) Informing higher levels of management or Those Charged with Governance of the employing organisation where Immediate or Close Family members are employed by competitors or potential suppliers of that organisation.

Making Offers

350.5 A Member in Business may be in a situation where the Member in Business is expected, or is under other pressure, to offer inducements to influence the judgment or decision-making process of an individual or organisation, or obtain confidential information.

350.6 Such pressure may come from within the employing organisation, for example, from a colleague or superior. It may also come from an external individual or organisation suggesting actions or business decisions that would be advantageous to the employing organisation, possibly influencing the Member in Business improperly.

350.7 A Member in Business shall not offer an inducement to improperly influence professional judgment of a third party.

350.8 Where the pressure to offer an unethical inducement comes from within the employing organisation, the Member shall follow the principles and guidance regarding ethical conflict resolution set out in Part A of this Code.

❖ ❖ ❖

Transitional Provisions

The Code is subject to the following transitional provisions:

Public Interest Entities

1. Section 290 of the Code contains additional Independence provisions when the Audit or Review Client is a Public Interest Entity. The additional provisions that are applicable because of the new definition of a Public Interest Entity and the requirements in paragraph 290.26 are effective on January 1, 2013. For partner rotation requirements, the transitional provisions contained in paragraphs 2 and 3 below apply.

Partner Rotation

2. For a partner who is subject to the rotation provisions in paragraph 290.151 because the partner meets the definition of the new term "Key Audit Partner," and the partner is neither the Engagement Partner nor the individual responsible for the Engagement Quality Control Review, the rotation provisions are effective for the Audits or Reviews of Financial Statements for years beginning on or after January 1, 2013. For example, in the case of an Audit Client with a calendar year-end, a Key Audit Partner, who is neither the Engagement Partner nor the individual responsible for the Engagement Quality Control Review, who had served as a Key Audit Partner for seven or more years (i.e., the audits of 2005 – 2011), would be required to rotate after serving for one more year as a Key Audit Partner (i.e., after completing the 2012 audit).

3. For an Engagement Partner or an individual responsible for the Engagement Quality Control Review who immediately prior to assuming either of these roles served in another Key Audit Partner role for the client, and who, at the beginning of the

first fiscal year beginning on or after January 1, 2012, had served as the Engagement Partner or individual responsible for the Engagement Quality Control Review for six or fewer years, the rotation provisions are effective for the audits or reviews of Financial Statements for years beginning on or after January 1, 2013. For example, in the case of an Audit Client with a calendar year-end, a partner who had served the client in another Key Audit Partner role for four years (i.e., the audits of 2003-2006) and subsequently as the Engagement Partner for five years (i.e., the audits of 2007-2011) would be required to rotate after serving for one more year as the Engagement Partner (i.e., after completing the 2012 audit).

Non-assurance services

4. Paragraphs 290.156-290.219 address the provision of non-assurance services to an Audit or Review Client. If, at the effective date of the Code, services are being provided to an Audit or Review Client and the services were permissible under the June 2006 Code (revised February 2008) but are either prohibited or subject to restrictions under the revised Code, the Firm may continue providing such services only if they were contracted for and commenced prior to July 1, 2012, and are completed before January 1, 2013.

Fees – Relative Size

5. Paragraph 290.222 provides that, in respect of an Audit or Review Client that is a Public Interest Entity, when the total fees from that client and its related entities (subject to the considerations in paragraph 290.27) for two consecutive years represent more than 15% of the total fees of the Firm expressing the opinion on the Financial Statements, a pre- or post-issuance review (as described in paragraph 290.222) of the second year's audit shall be performed. This requirement is effective for Audits or Reviews of Financial Statements covering years that begin on or after January 1, 2012. For example, in the case of an Audit Client with a calendar year end, if the total fees from the client exceeded the 15% threshold for 2012 and 2013, the pre- or post-issuance review would be applied with respect to the audit of the 2013 Financial Statements.

Compensation and Evaluation Policies

6. Paragraph 290.229 provides that a Key Audit Partner shall not be evaluated or compensated based on that partner's success in selling non-assurance services to the partner's Audit Client. This requirement is effective on January 1, 2013. A Key Audit Partner may, however, receive compensation after January 1, 2013 based on an evaluation made prior to January 1, 2013 of that partner's success in selling non-assurance services to the Audit Client.

❖ ❖ ❖

Conformity With International Pronouncements

APES 110 and the IESBA Code

APES 110 incorporates the *Code of Ethics for Professional Accountants* (IESBA Code) issued by the International Ethics Standards Board for Accountants (IESBA) in July 2009.

Compliance with the IESBA Code

The principles and requirements of APES 110 and the IESBA Code are consistent except for the following:

- The addition of a Scope and Application section in APES 110;
- The addition of paragraphs and definitions prefixed as AUST in APES 110. The additional definitions are of AASB, Administration, AuASB, AUASB, Auditing and Assurance Standards, Australian Accounting Standards and Member;
- APES 110 generally refers to Members whereas the IESBA Code refers to professional accountants;
- Defined terms are in title case in APES 110;
- APES 110 tailors the following IESBA defined terms to the Australian environment: Audit Engagement, Engagement Team, Financial Statements, Firm, Member in Public Practice, and Review Engagement;
- Paragraph 290.25 of APES 110 expresses Public Interest Entity in the singular form consistent with its definition in section 2;
- Paragraph 290.26 in APES 110 mandates Firms to determine whether additional entities are Public Interest Entities and the reference to member bodies has been removed ; and
- Unless strict requirements are met, APES 110 prohibits Members in Public Practice from providing accounting and bookkeeping services and preparing tax calculations for Audit Clients which are Public Interest Entities, even in emergency situations (refer paragraphs 290.172 – 290.173 and 290.185).

❖ ❖ ❖

Amendment to the Definition of Public Interest Entity in APES 110 *Code of Ethics for Professional Accountants*

(December 2011)

Contents

Section 2 Definitions

Public Interest Entity means:

(a) A Listed Entity; or

(b) An entity (a) defined by regulation or legislation as a public interest entity or (b) for which the audit is required by regulation or legislation to be conducted in compliance with the same Independence requirements that apply to the audit of Listed Entities. Such regulation may be promulgated by any relevant regulator, including an audit regulator.

Section 290 Independence – Audit and Review Engagements

[Paragraphs 290.1 – 290.24 of extant Section 290 remain unchanged.]

Public Interest Entities

290.25 Section 290 contains additional provisions that reflect the extent of public interest in certain entities. For the purpose of this section, a Public Interest Entity is:

(a) A Listed Entity*; or

(b) An entity (a) defined by regulation or legislation as a public interest entity; or (b) for which the audit is required by regulation or legislation to be conducted in compliance with the same Independence requirements that apply to the audit of Listed Entities. Such regulation may be promulgated by any relevant regulator, including an audit regulator.

290.26 Firms shall determine whether to treat additional entities, or certain categories of entities, as Public Interest Entities because they have a large number and wide range of stakeholders. Factors to be considered include:

- The nature of the business, such as the holding of assets in a fiduciary capacity for a large number of stakeholders. Examples may include financial institutions, such as banks and insurance companies and pension funds;
- Size; and
- Number of employees.

* *Includes a listed entity as defined in Section 9 of the Corporations Act 2001.*

AUST 290.26.1 The following entities in Australia will generally satisfy the conditions in paragraph 290.26 as having a large number and wide range of stakeholders and thus are likely to be classified as Public Interest Entities. In each instance Firms shall consider the nature of the business, its size and the number of its employees:

- Authorised deposit-taking institutions (ADIs) and authorised non-operating holding companies (NOHCs) regulated by the Australian Prudential Regulatory Authority (APRA) under the *Banking Act 1959*;

APES

- Authorised insurers and authorised NOHCs regulated by APRA under Section 122 of the *Insurance Act 1973*;
- Life insurance companies and registered NOHCs regulated by APRA under the *Life Insurance Act 1995*;
- Disclosing Entities as defined in Section 111AC of the *Corporations Act 2001*;
- Registrable superannuation entity (RSE) licensees, and RSEs under their trusteeship that have five or more members, regulated by APRA under the *Superannuation Industry (Supervision) Act 1993*; and
- Other issuers of debt and equity instruments to the public.

[Paragraph 290.27 – 290.514 remain unchanged.]

Effective Date:

The revisions are effective from 1 January 2013 with early adoption permitted.

❖ ❖ ❖

Transitional Provisions

The Code is subject to the following transitional provisions:

Public Interest Entities

1. Section 290 of the Code contains additional Independence provisions when the Audit or Review Client is a Public Interest Entity. The additional provisions that are applicable because of the new definition of a Public Interest Entity and the requirements in paragraph 290.26 are effective on January 1, 2013. For partner rotation requirements, the transitional provisions contained in paragraphs 2 and 3 below apply.

Partner Rotation

2. For a partner who is subject to the rotation provisions in paragraph 290.151 because the partner meets the definition of the new term "Key Audit Partner," and the partner is neither the Engagement Partner nor the individual responsible for the Engagement Quality Control Review, the rotation provisions are effective for the Audits or Reviews of Financial Statements for years beginning on or after January 1, 2013. For example, in the case of an Audit Client with a calendar year-end, a Key Audit Partner, who is neither the Engagement Partner nor the individual responsible for the Engagement Quality Control Review, who had served as a Key Audit Partner for seven or more years (i.e., the audits of 2005 – 2011), would be required to rotate after serving for one more year as a Key Audit Partner (i.e., after completing the 2012 audit).
3. For an Engagement Partner or an individual responsible for the Engagement Quality Control Review who immediately prior to assuming either of these roles served in another Key Audit Partner role for the client, and who, at the beginning of the first fiscal year beginning on or after January 1, 2012, had served as the Engagement Partner or individual responsible for the Engagement Quality Control Review for six or fewer years, the rotation provisions are effective for the audits or reviews of Financial Statements for years beginning on or after January 1, 2013. For example, in the case of an Audit Client with a calendar year-end, a partner who had served the client in another Key Audit Partner role for four years (i.e., the audits of 2003-2006) and subsequently as the Engagement Partner for five years (i.e., the audits of 2007-2011) would be required to rotate after serving for one more year as the Engagement Partner (i.e., after completing the 2012 audit).

Non-assurance services

4. Paragraphs 290.156-290.219 address the provision of non-assurance services to an Audit or Review Client. If, at the effective date of the Code, services are being provided to an Audit or Review Client and the services were permissible under the June 2006 Code (revised February 2008) but are either prohibited or subject to restrictions under the

revised Code, the Firm may continue providing such services only if they were contracted for and commenced prior to July 1, 2012, and are completed before January 1, 2013.

Fees – Relative Size

5. Paragraph 290.222 provides that, in respect of an Audit or Review Client that is a Public Interest Entity, when the total fees from that client and its related entities (subject to the considerations in paragraph 290.27) for two consecutive years represent more than 15% of the total fees of the Firm expressing the opinion on the Financial Statements, a pre- or post-issuance review (as described in paragraph 290.222) of the second year's audit shall be performed. This requirement is effective for Audits or Reviews of Financial Statements covering years that begin on or after January 1, 2012. For example, in the case of an Audit Client with a calendar year end, if the total fees from the client exceeded the 15% threshold for 2012 and 2013, the pre- or post-issuance review would be applied with respect to the audit of the 2013 Financial Statements.

Compensation and Evaluation Policies

6. Paragraph 290.229 provides that a Key Audit Partner shall not be evaluated or compensated based on that partner's success in selling non-assurance services to the partner's Audit Client. This requirement is effective on January 1, 2013. A Key Audit Partner may, however, receive compensation after January 1, 2013 based on an evaluation made prior to January 1, 2013 of that partner's success in selling non-assurance services to the Audit Client.

❖ ❖ ❖

Conformity With International Pronouncements

APES 110 and the IESBA Code

APES 110 incorporates the *Code of Ethics for Professional Accountants* (IESBA Code) issued by the International Ethics Standards Board for Accountants (IESBA) in July 2009.

Compliance with the IESBA Code

The principles and requirements of APES 110 and the IESBA Code are consistent except for the following:

- The addition of a Scope and Application section in APES 110;
- The addition of paragraphs and definitions prefixed as AUST in APES 110. The additional definitions are of AASB, Administration, AuASB, AUASB, Auditing and Assurance Standards, Australian Accounting Standards and Member;
- APES 110 generally refers to Members whereas the IESBA Code refers to professional accountants;
- Defined terms are in title case in APES 110;
- APES 110 tailors the following IESBA defined terms to the Australian environment: Audit Engagement, Engagement Team, Financial Statements, Firm, Member in Public Practice, and Review Engagement;
- Paragraph 290.25 of APES 110 expresses Public Interest Entity in the singular form consistent with its definition in section 2;
- Paragraph 290.26 in APES 110 mandates Firms to determine whether additional entities are Public Interest Entities and the reference to Member Bodies has been removed; and
- Unless strict requirements are met, APES 110 prohibits Members in Public Practice from providing accounting and bookkeeping services and preparing tax calculations for Audit Clients which are Public Interest Entities, even in emergency situations (refer paragraphs 290.172 – 290.173 and 290.185).

APES 205
Conformity with Accounting Standards

(Issued December 2007)

Issued by the Accounting Professional and Ethical Standards Board.

Note from the Institute of Chartered Accountants Australia

This note, prepared by the technical editor, is not part of APES 205.

Historical development

December 2007: APES 205 issued. It replaces Miscellaneous Professional Statement APS 1 and has been updated to reflect professional accountant responsibilities with respect to the preparation of general and special purpose financial statements under the current Australian financial reporting framework. It is operative from 1 July 2008.

Contents

1. Scope and application

1.1 Accounting Professional & Ethical Standards Board Limited (APESB) issues professional standard APES 205 *Conformity with Accounting Standards* (**the Standard**), which is effective from 01 July 2008.

1.2 APES 205 sets the standards for Members involved with the preparation, presentation, audit, review or compilation of Financial Statements, which are either General Purpose Financial Statements or Special Purpose Financial Statements, of entities in the private and public sectors. The mandatory requirements of this Standard are in **bold** type, preceded or followed by discussion or explanations in grey type. APES 205 should be read in conjunction with other professional duties of Members, and any legal obligations that may apply.

1.3 Members in Australia shall follow the mandatory requirements of APES 205 when they prepare, present, audit, review or compile Financial Statements.

1.4 Members outside Australia shall comply with the financial reporting framework applicable to the relevant jurisdiction when they prepare, present, audit, review or compile Financial Statements. However, where the Financial Statements are prepared in accordance with the Australian Financial Reporting Framework, Members shall comply with the requirements of this Standard.

1.5 Members shall be familiar with relevant professional standards and guidance notes when performing professional work. All Members shall comply with the fundamental principles outlined in the Code.

1.6 The Standard does not detract from any responsibilities which may be imposed by law.

1.7 All references to accounting, auditing and professional standards are references to those provisions as amended from time to time.

1.8 In applying the requirements outlined in APES 205, Members should be guided not merely by the words but also by the spirit of the Standard and the Code.

2. Definitions

For the purpose of this Standard:

AASB means the Australian statutory body called the Australian Accounting Standards Board that was established under section 226 of the *Australian Securities and Investments Commission Act 1989* and is continued in existence by section 261 of the *Australian Securities and Investments Commission Act 2001.*

Applicable Financial Reporting Framework means the financial reporting framework adopted by those charged with governance in preparing the Financial Statements.

Assurance Engagement means an Engagement in which a conclusion is expressed by a Member in Public Practice designed to enhance the degree of confidence of the intended users other than

APES

the responsible party about the outcome of the evaluation or measurement of a subject matter against criteria.

This would include an Engagement in accordance with *Framework for Assurance Engagements* issued by the Auditing and Assurance Standards Board (AUASB) or in accordance with specific relevant standards for Assurance Engagements.

AUASB means the Australian statutory body called the Auditing and Assurance Standards Board established under section 227A of the *Australian Securities and Investments Commission Act 2001.*

Audit Engagement means an Assurance Engagement to provide a reasonable level of assurance that a financial report is free of material misstatement, such as an Engagement in accordance with Australian auditing standards. This includes a statutory audit which is an audit required by legislation or other regulation, and other audits conducted for the purposes of the Corporations Act.

Australian Accounting Standards means the Accounting Standards (including Australian Accounting Interpretations) promulgated by the AASB.

Australian Financial Reporting Framework means the framework that uses Australian Accounting Standards as the Applicable Financial Reporting Framework and is adopted by those charged with governance when preparing Financial Statements.

Client means an individual, firm, entity or organisation to whom or to which Professional Services are provided by a Member in Public Practice in respect of Engagements of either a recurring or demand nature.

Code means APES 110 *Code of Ethics for Professional Accountants.*

Engagement means an agreement, whether written or otherwise, between a Member in Public Practice and a Client relating to the provision of services by a Member in Public Practice. However, consultations with a prospective Client prior to such agreement are not part of an Engagement.

Financial Statements means a structured representation of historical financial information, which ordinarily includes explanatory notes, intended to communicate an entity's economic resources or obligations at a point in time or the changes therein for a period of time in accordance with a financial reporting framework. The term can refer to a complete set of Financial Statements, but it can also refer to a single financial statement, for example, a balance sheet, or a statement of revenues and expenses, and related explanatory notes. The requirements of the financial reporting framework determine the form and content of the Financial Statements and what constitutes a complete set of Financial Statements.

For the purposes of this Standard financial report is considered to be an equivalent term to financial statements.

Firm means

(a) A sole practitioner, partnership, corporation or other entity of professional accountants;

(b) An entity that controls such parties;

(c) An entity controlled by such parties; or

(d) An Auditor-General's office or department.

Framework means the *Framework for the preparation and presentation of financial statements* issued by the AASB.

General Purpose Financial Statements means those intended to meet the needs of users who are not in a position to require an entity to prepare reports tailored to their particular information needs.

Member means a member of a professional body that has adopted this Standard as applicable to their membership as defined by that professional body.

Member in Public Practice means a Member, irrespective of functional classification (e.g. audit, tax, or consulting) in a Firm that provides Professional Services. The term is also used to refer to a Firm of Members in Public Practice and means a practice entity as defined by the applicable professional body.

Professional Bodies means the Institute of Chartered Accountants in Australia, CPA Australia and the National Institute of Accountants.

Professional Services means services requiring accountancy or related skills performed by a professional accountant including accounting, auditing, taxation, management consulting and financial management services.

Professional Standards mean all standards issued by Accounting Professional & Ethical Standards Board Limited and all professional and ethical requirements of the applicable Professional Body.

Reporting Entity means an entity in respect of which it is reasonable to expect the existence of users who rely on the entity's General Purpose Financial Report for information that will be useful to them for making and evaluating decisions about the allocation of resources. A Reporting Entity can be a single entity or a group comprising a parent entity and all the entities it controls.

Review Engagement means an Assurance Engagement to express a conclusion on whether, on the basis of the procedures which do not provide all the evidence that would be required in an audit, anything has come to the attention of the Member in Public Practice that causes the Member to believe that the historical financial information is not prepared in all material respects in accordance with an Applicable Financial Reporting Framework, which is an Engagement conducted in accordance with applicable assurance standards on Review Engagements.

Special Purpose Financial Statements means financial statements other than General Purpose Financial Statements.

Statements of Accounting Concepts mean SAC 1 *Definition of Reporting Entity* and *SAC 2 Objective of General Purpose Financial Reporting* issued by the AASB.

3. Fundamental responsibilities of Members

Public interest

3.1 **In accordance with Section 100.1 of the Code, Members shall observe and comply with their public interest obligations when they prepare, present, audit, review or compile Financial Statements.**

Professional competence and due care

3.2 **In accordance with Section 130 *Professional Competence and Due Care* of the Code, a Member in Public Practice who is performing professional work based on an Applicable Financial Reporting Framework shall ensure that the Member or the Firm has the requisite professional knowledge and skill or shall engage a suitably qualified external person. If a Member in Public Practice is unable to engage a suitably qualified person when required, the Member shall decline the Engagement.**

4. Responsibilities of Members in respect of the Reporting Entity concept

4.1 Members should take all reasonable steps to apply the principles and guidance provided in the Statements of Accounting Concepts and the Framework when assessing whether an entity is a Reporting Entity .

4.2 Statement of Accounting Concepts SAC 1 "Definition of Reporting Entity" provides guidance on circumstances in which an entity or economic entity should be identified as a Reporting Entity.

4.3 **Members who are involved in, or are responsible for, the preparation and/or presentation of Financial Statements of a Reporting Entity shall take all reasonable steps to ensure that the Reporting Entity prepares General Purpose Financial Statements.**

APES

5. Responsibilities of Members in respect of General Purpose Financial Statements

5.1 **Members shall take all reasonable steps to apply Australian Accounting Standards when they prepare and/or present General Purpose Financial Statements that purport to comply with the Australian Financial Reporting Framework.**

5.2 **Where Members are unable to apply Australian Accounting Standards pursuant to paragraph 5.1, they shall take all reasonable steps to ensure that any departure from Australian Accounting Standards, the reasons for such departure, and its financial effects are properly disclosed and explained in the General Purpose Financial Statements.**

5.3 If legislation, ministerial directive or other government authority requires a departure from Australian Accounting Standards, a Member should disclose that fact in the General Purpose Financial Statements as a reason for the departure.

5.4 Where a Member is unable to ensure proper disclosure of a departure from Australian Accounting Standards pursuant to paragraph 5.2, the Member should discuss the matter with the appropriate level of management of the relevant entity and document the results of these discussions.

5.5 **Members in Public Practice shall take all reasonable steps to ensure that Clients have complied with Australian Accounting Standards when they perform an Audit or Review Engagement or a compilation Engagement of General Purpose Financial Statements which purport to comply with the Australian Financial Reporting Framework.**

5.6 **Where a Member in Public Practice is unable to ensure that a Client complies with Australian Accounting Standards pursuant to paragraph 5.5, the Member shall consider Australian auditing standards applicable to Audit or Review Engagements or Professional Standards applicable to compilation Engagements.**

6. Responsibilities of Members in respect of Special Purpose Financial Statements

6.1 **Members who are involved in, or are responsible for, the preparation, presentation, audit, review or compilation of an entity's Special Purpose Financial Statements (except where the Special Purpose Financial Statements will be used solely for internal purposes) shall take all reasonable steps to ensure that the Special Purpose Financial Statements, and any associated audit report, review report or compilation report clearly identifies:**

- **(a) that the Financial Statements are Special Purpose Financial Statements;**
- **(b) the purpose for which the Special Purpose Financial Statements have been prepared; and**
- **(c) the significant accounting policies adopted in the preparation and presentation of the Special Purpose Financial Statements.**

6.2 **Where a Member in Public Practice is unable to ensure that a Client complies with an Applicable Financial Reporting Framework pursuant to paragraph 6.1, the Member shall consider Australian auditing standards applicable to Audit or Review Engagements or Professional Standards applicable to compilation Engagements.**

6.3 For all other Members, where the Member is unable to ensure that an entity complies with an Applicable Financial Reporting Framework pursuant to paragraph 6.1, the Member should discuss the matter with the appropriate level of management of the relevant entity and document the results of these discussions.

Conformity with International Pronouncements

The International Ethics Standard Board for Accountants (IESBA) has not issued a pronouncement equivalent to APES 205.

APES 210

Conformity with Auditing and Assurance Standards

(Issued September 2008: revised November 2011)

Issued by the Accounting Professional and Ethical Standards Board.

Note from the Institute of Chartered Accountants Australia

This note, prepared by the technical editor, is not part of APES 210.

Historical development

June 2006: APES 410 issued by the newly constituted Accounting Professional and Ethical Standards Board to replace APS 1.1. Operative from 1 July 2006.

September 2008: APES 410 reissued as APES 210. It established the responsibilities of members of the Institute, CPA Australia and the NIA in relation to compliance with Auditing Standards and the conduct of all Australian audit, review and assurance engagements of both financial and non-financial information.

November 2011: APES 210 updated and reissued to reflect changes to other auditing and ethical Standards. It is operative from the date of issue and has no international equivalent.

APES

Contents

1. Scope and application

1.1 Accounting Professional & Ethical Standards Board Limited (APESB) issues professional standard APES 210 *Conformity with Auditing and Assurance Standards* (the Standard), which is effective from the date of issue.

1.2 APES 210 sets the standards for Members to comply with Auditing and Assurance Standards when they conduct Assurance Assignments or Assurance Engagements. The mandatory requirements of this Standard are in bold type, preceded or followed by discussion or explanations in grey type. APES 210 should be read in conjunction with other professional duties of Members, and any legal obligations that may apply.

1.3 In undertaking work, including honorary work that is within the scope of an Assurance Engagement, a Member in Business is a Member in Public Practice for the purpose of this Standard.

1.4 Members in Australia shall follow the mandatory requirements of APES 210.

1.5 Members outside of Australia shall follow the provisions of APES 210 to the extent to which they are not prevented from so doing by specific requirements of local laws and/or regulations in the country in which they are working.

1.6 Members shall be familiar with relevant Professional Standards and guidance notes. All Members shall comply with the fundamental principles outlined in the Code.

1.7 The Standard is not intended to detract from any responsibilities which may be imposed by law or regulation.

1.8 All references to Professional Standards are references to those provisions as amended from time to time.

1.9 In applying the requirements outlined in APES 210, Members should be guided not merely by the words but also by the spirit of the Standard and the Code.

2. Definitions

For the purpose of this Standard:

Assurance Assignment means an Assignment in which a conclusion is expressed by a Member in Business designed to enhance the degree of confidence of the intended users about the outcome of the evaluation or measurement of a subject matter against criteria.

Assurance Engagement means an Engagement in which a conclusion is expressed by a Member in Public Practice designed to enhance the degree of confidence of the intended users other than the responsible party about the outcome of the evaluation or measurement of a subject matter against criteria.

This includes an Engagement in accordance with *Framework for Assurance Engagements* issued by the Auditing and Assurance Standards Board (AUASB) or in accordance with specific relevant standards, such as International Standards on Auditing, for Assurance Engagements.

Assignment means an instruction, whether written or otherwise, by an employer to a Member in Business relating to the provision of services by a Member in Business. However, consultations with the employer prior to such instruction are not part of an Assignment.

Auditing and Assurance Guidance means:

(a) the guidance statements and other guidance publications, as defined in the Foreword to AUASB Pronouncements, issued by the AUASB; and

(b) the auditing and assurance guidance statements and other guidance publications issued by the AuASB on behalf of CPA Australia and the Institute of Chartered Accountants in Australia.

Auditing and Assurance Standards means:

(a) the AUASB standards, as described in ASA 100 *Preamble to AUASB Standards*, ASA 101 *Preamble to Australian Auditing Standards* and the *Foreword to AUASB Pronouncements*, issued by the AUASB and operative from the date specified in each standard; and

(b) those standards issued by the AuASB, which have not been revised and reissued (whether as standards or as guidance) by the AUASB, to the extent that they are not inconsistent with the AUASB standards.

AuASB means the Auditing and Assurance Standards Board which issued Australian auditing and assurance standards up to 30 June 2004, under the auspices of the Australian Accounting Research Foundation, a joint venture of CPA Australia and the Institute of Chartered Accountants in Australia.

AUASB means the Australian statutory body called the Auditing and Assurance Standards Board established under section 227A of the *Australian Securities and Investments Commission Act 2001*.

Client means an individual, firm, entity or organisation to whom or to which Professional Services are provided by a Member in Public Practice in respect of Engagements of either a recurring or demand nature.

Code means APES 110 *Code of Ethics for Professional Accountants*.

Engagement means an agreement, whether written or otherwise, between a Member in Public Practice and a Client relating to the provision of Professional Services by a Member in Public Practice. However, consultations with a prospective Client prior to such agreement are not part of an Engagement.

Firm means

(a) A sole practitioner, partnership, corporation or other entity of professional accountants;

(b) An entity that controls such parties, through ownership, management or other means;

(c) An entity controlled by such parties, through ownership, management or other means; or

(d) An Auditor-General's office or department.

Member means a member of a professional body that has adopted this Standard as applicable to their membership, as defined by that professional body.

Member in Business means a Member employed or engaged in an executive or non-executive capacity in such areas as commerce, industry, service, the public sector, education, the not for profit sector, regulatory bodies or professional bodies, or a Member contracted by such entities.

Member in Public Practice means a Member, irrespective of functional classification (e.g. audit, tax, or consulting) in a Firm that provides Professional Services. The term is also used to refer to a Firm of Members in Public Practice and means a practice entity as defined by the applicable professional body.

Professional Services means services requiring accountancy or related skills performed by a Member in Public Practice including accounting, auditing, taxation, management consulting and financial management services.

Professional Standards means all standards issued by Accounting Professional & Ethical Standards Board Limited and all professional and ethical requirements of the applicable professional body.

3. Fundamental responsibilities of Members

Public interest

3.1 **In accordance with Section 100 *Introduction and Fundamental Principles* of the Code, Members shall observe and comply with their public interest obligations when they perform an Assurance Assignment or an Assurance Engagement.**

Independence

3.2 **When engaged to perform an Assurance Engagement, a Member in Public Practice shall comply with Section 290 *Independence – Audit and Review Engagements* or Section 291 *Independence – Other Assurance Engagements* of the Code, as applicable.**

Professional competence and due care

3.3 **In accordance with Section 130 *Professional Competence and Due Care* of the Code, a Member in Public Practice who is performing an Assurance Engagement shall ensure that the Member or the Firm has the requisite professional knowledge and skill or shall engage a suitably qualified external person. If the Member is unable to engage a suitably qualified person when required, the Member shall decline the Engagement.**

4. Auditing and Assurance Standards

4.1 **Except for the circumstances described in paragraph 4.2, a Member shall comply with Auditing and Assurance Standards.**

4.2 **Where legislation or other government authority requires a departure from Auditing and Assurance Standards, a Member shall disclose that fact in the Member's report. In these circumstances, a Member shall not assert compliance with any of those standards in the Member's report.**

5. Auditing and Assurance Guidance

5.1 A Member should follow relevant Auditing and Assurance Guidance.

Conformity with International Pronouncements

The International Ethics Standard Board for Accountants (IESBA) has not issued a pronouncement equivalent to APES 210.

Appendix 1

Summary of revisions to the previous APES 210 (Issued 30 September 2008)

APES 210 *Conformity with Auditing and Assurance Standards* originally issued on 30 September 2008 has been revised by APESB on 30 November 2011. A summary of the revisions is given in the table below.

Table of revisions*

Paragraph affected	How affected
2 – Definition of Auditing and Assurance Standards	Amended
2 – Definition of Firm	Amended
3.2	Amended

* *Refer Technical Update 2011/4*

APES 215

Forensic Accounting Services

(December 2008)

Issued by the Accounting Professional and Ethical Standards Board.

Note from the Institute of Chartered Accountants Australia

This note, prepared by the technical editor, is not part of APES 215.

Historical development

December 2008: APES 215 issued. It applies to forensic accountants giving or preparing evidence in legal proceedings, who are members of the three professional accounting bodies, both those working in the corporate sector and in government, and those in accountancy firms.

APES 215 applies from 1 July 2009 and replaced APS 11 'Statement of Forensic Accounting Standards' and GN 2 'Forensic Accounting'.

APES

Contents

1. Scope and application

1.1 Accounting Professional & Ethical Standards Board Limited (APESB) issues professional standard APES 215 *Forensic Accounting Services* (**the Standard**), which is effective for Engagements or Assignments commencing on or after 01 July 2009. Earlier adoption of this Standard is permitted.

1.2 APES 215 sets the standards for Members in the provision of quality and ethical Forensic Accounting Services. The mandatory requirements of this Standard are in **bold-type (black lettering)**, preceded or followed by discussion or explanations in normal type (grey lettering). APES 215 should be read in conjunction with other professional duties of Members, and any legal obligations that may apply.

1.3 Members in Australia shall follow the mandatory requirements of APES 215 when they provide Forensic Accounting Services.

1.4 Members outside of Australia shall follow the mandatory requirements of APES 215 to the extent to which they are not prevented from so doing by specific requirements of local laws and/or regulations.

1.5 Where a Professional Service which, when it commenced was not a Forensic Accounting Service, later becomes such a service, then the Member shall comply with the requirements of this Standard from that time onwards.

1.6 Where a Member is undertaking a Forensic Accounting Service, other than an Expert Witness Service, which later becomes an Expert Witness Service, the Member shall comply with the requirements of section 5 of this Standard from that time onwards.

1.7 Members shall be familiar with relevant professional standards and guidance notes when providing Professional Services. All Members shall comply with the fundamental principles outlined in the Code.

1.8 The Standard is not intended to detract from any responsibilities which may be imposed by law or regulation.

1.9 All references to Professional Standards, guidance notes and legislation are references to those provisions as amended from time to time.

1.10 In applying the requirements outlined in APES 215, Members should be guided not merely by the words but also by the spirit of the Standard and the Code.

2. Definitions

For the purpose of this Standard:

Assignment means an instruction, whether written or otherwise, by an Employer to a Member in Business relating to the provision of services by a Member in Business. However, consultations with the Employer prior to such instruction are not part of an Assignment.

Client means an individual, firm, entity or organisation to whom Professional Services are provided by a Member in Public Practice in respect of Engagements of either a recurring or demand nature.

Code means APES 110 *Code of Ethics for Professional Accountants*.

Consulting Expert means a Member who has been engaged or assigned to provide a Consulting Expert Service.

Consulting Expert Service means a Professional Service provided in the context of Proceedings, other than an Expert Witness Service, a Lay Witness Service or an Investigation Service. It includes acting as an adviser, an arbitrator, mediator, member of a professional tribunal, expert in an expert determination, referee or in a similar role.

Contingent Fee means a fee calculated on a predetermined basis relating to the outcome or result of a transaction or the result of the work performed. A fee that is established by a Court or other public authority is not a contingent fee.

Court means any body described as such and all other tribunals exercising judicial or quasi-judicial functions and includes professional disciplinary tribunals, industrial and administrative, statutory or parliamentary investigation and inquiries, royal commissions, arbitrations and mediations.

Employer means an entity or person that employs, engages or contracts a Member in Business.

Engagement means an agreement, whether written or otherwise, between a Member in Public Practice and a Client relating to the provision of services by a Member in Public Practice. However, consultations with a prospective Client prior to such agreement are not part of an Engagement.

Engagement Document means the document (i.e. letter, agreement or any other appropriate means) in which the Terms of Engagement are specified in a written form.

Expert Witness means a Member who has been engaged or assigned to provide an Expert Witness Service. As an Expert Witness, the Member may express opinions to the Court based on the Member's specialised training, study or experience on matters such as whether technical or professional standards have been breached, the amount of damages, the amount of an account of profits, or the amount of a claim under an insurance policy.

Expert Witness Service means a Professional Service provided in the context of Proceedings to give expert evidence in a Report or, in certain circumstances, orally.

Firm means

(a) A sole practitioner, partnership, corporation or other entity of professional accountants;

(b) An entity that controls such parties;

(c) An entity controlled by such parties; or

(d) An Auditor-General's office or department.

Forensic Accounting Services means Expert Witness Services, Lay Witness Services, Consulting Expert Services and Investigation Services.

Independence means

(a) Independence of mind - the state of mind that permits the provision of an opinion without being affected by influences that compromise professional judgment, allowing an individual to act with integrity, and exercise objectivity and professional scepticism; and

(b) Independence in appearance - the avoidance of facts and circumstances that are so significant a reasonable and informed third party, having knowledge of all relevant information, including any safeguards applied, would reasonably conclude a Firm's, or a member's, integrity, objectivity or professional scepticism had been compromised.

APES

Investigation Service means a Professional Service to perform, advise on, or assist with an investigation, whether or not in the context of Proceedings, in connection with allegations of, or concerns regarding conduct that may be illegal, unethical or otherwise improper.

Lay Witness means a Member who has been engaged or assigned to provide a Lay Witness Service.

Lay Witness Service means a Professional Service provided in the context of Proceedings to provide evidence other than expert evidence, whether orally or in the form of a Report or both. This service involves the Member giving evidence on matters within the Member's professional knowledge that are directly observed or perceived by the Member.

Member means a member of a professional body that has adopted this Standard as applicable to their membership, as defined by that professional body.

Member in Business means a Member employed or engaged in an executive or non-executive capacity in such areas as commerce, industry, service, the public sector, education, the not for profit sector, regulatory bodies or professional bodies, or a Member contracted by such entities.

Member in Public Practice means a Member, irrespective of functional classification (e.g. audit, tax or consulting) in a Firm that provides Professional Services. The term is also used to refer to a Firm of Members in Public Practice and means a practice entity as defined by the applicable professional body.

Proceedings means a matter before a Court, a matter which the Member has a reasonable expectation will be brought before a Court or a matter in which the Member is undertaking Professional Services to help make an assessment as to whether a matter should be brought before a Court.

Professional Standards means all Standards issued by Accounting Professional & Ethical Standards Board Limited and all professional and ethical requirements of the applicable professional body.

Professional Services means services requiring accountancy or related skills performed by a Member including accounting, auditing, taxation, management consulting and financial management services.

Report means a written report, affidavit or written statement that is for the purpose of communicating expert evidence or lay evidence in Court.

Terms of Engagement means the terms and conditions that are agreed between the Client and the Member in Public Practice for the Engagement.

3. Fundamental responsibilities of Members

3.1 **A Member providing a Forensic Accounting Service shall comply with Section 100 *Introduction and Fundamental Principles* of the Code and with relevant law.**

Public interest

3.2 **In accordance with Section 100 *Introduction and Fundamental Principles* of the Code, a Member shall observe and comply with the Member's public interest obligations when the Member provides a Forensic Accounting Service.**

3.3 **When engaged to perform a Forensic Accounting Service a Member shall be and be seen to be free of any interest which may be regarded as being incompatible with the fundamental principles of Section 110 *Integrity* and Section 120 *Objectivity* of the Code.**

3.4 **Members in Public Practice shall comply with Section 220 *Conflict of Interest* and Section 280 *Objectivity – All Services* of the Code.**

Professional Independence

3.5 **When a Member in Public Practice is engaged to perform a Forensic Accounting Service which requires Independence or where a Member in Public Practice purports to be independent when performing a Forensic Accounting Service, the Member shall comply with Independence as defined in this Standard.**

3.6 A Member in Public Practice shall determine whether the circumstances of the Forensic Accounting Service make the Engagement an Assurance Engagement under the *Framework for Assurance Engagements* issued by the Auditing and Assurance Standards Board (AUASB).

3.7 Where a Forensic Accounting Service is an Assurance Engagement, the Member in Public Practice shall comply with Section 290 *Independence – Assurance Engagements* of the Code.

3.8 If a Member in Public Practice is asked to provide a Professional Service to a Client where:

(a) the Member or the Member's Firm is providing or has provided an Expert Witness Service to the Client; or

(b) the Member or the Member's Firm is providing or has provided an Expert Witness Service to a different Client,

and the proposed Professional Service is related to the Expert Witness Service, and the Member determines that a reasonable and informed third party having knowledge of all the relevant information, including safeguards applied, would regard the objectives of the proposed Professional Service to be undertaken as being inconsistent with the objectives of the Expert Witness Service, then the Member shall decline the Engagement or the relevant part thereof.

3.9 There is no requirement, at law, that an Expert Witness be free of any relationship with parties to Proceedings. For example, there is no legal prohibition on a Member in Public Practice acting as an Expert Witness for a Client for whom the Member provides other Professional Services.

3.10 A Member who is providing an Expert Witness Service shall disclose matters in the Member's Report that will assist the Court to assess the degree of the Member's Independence.

Professional competence and due care

3.11 A Member providing a Forensic Accounting Service shall maintain professional competence and take due care in the performance of the Member's work in accordance with Section 130 *Professional Competence and Due Care* of the Code.

3.12 Forensic Accounting Services generally require a Member to have specialised training, study or experience. Before accepting an Engagement or Assignment to provide a Forensic Accounting Service, a Member should exercise professional judgement to determine if the Member is competent to provide the requested Forensic Accounting Service having regard to the Member's training, study or experience.

3.13 Where a Forensic Accounting Service or part thereof requires the consideration of matters that are outside a Member in Public Practice's professional expertise, the Member shall seek expert assistance or advice from a suitably qualified third party on those matters outside the Member's professional expertise or decline all, or that part of, the Forensic Accounting Service. Where the Member relies upon the advice of a third party, the Member shall disclose in any Report issued by the Member the name and qualifications of the third party and the area in the Report where the third party advice has been obtained.

3.14 In accordance with Section 330 *Acting with Sufficient Expertise* of the Code, a Member in Business shall only undertake Assignments for which the Member has, or can obtain, sufficient training or expertise and shall not intentionally mislead an Employer as to the level of expertise or experience possessed, nor shall a Member fail to seek appropriate expert advice and assistance when required.

3.15 If a Member acting as an Expert Witness expresses an opinion that is based on the work of another expert then the Member shall state in the Member's Report that the Member's opinion is based in part, on the assumption that the other expert's opinion is valid.

3.16 Where a Member performs a Forensic Accounting Service that involves acting as an investigator or as a decision-maker (as might be the case for certain Consulting Expert Services, such as acting as an arbitrator, mediator or referee), the Member may be required to observe some or all of the rules of procedural fairness (which collectively are referred to as "natural justice"). If a Member is not certain of the Member's legal obligations then the Member should consider taking legal advice.

Confidentiality

3.17 **In accordance with Section 140 *Confidentiality* of the Code a Member, who acquires confidential information in the course of professional work for a Client or Employer, shall not use that information for any purpose other than the proper performance of that professional work.**

3.18 Where a Client has given a Member in Public Practice permission to disclose confidential information to a third party, it is preferable that this permission is in writing. Where oral permission is obtained, a contemporaneous note should be made and kept on file by the Member recording the relevant details of the Client's permission.

4. Professional Engagement matters

4.1 **A Member in Public Practice shall document and communicate the Terms of Engagement in accordance with APES 305 *Terms of Engagement*.**

4.2 **A Member in Public Practice who is approached by a potential Client to undertake a Forensic Accounting Service shall comply with Section 210 *Professional Appointment* of the Code.**

5. Expert Witness Services

5.1 **If a Member in Public Practice is asked to provide an Expert Witness Service to a Client where:**

(a) the Member or the Member's Firm is providing or has provided another Professional Service to the Client; or

(b) the Member or the Member's Firm is providing or has provided another Professional Service to a different Client,

and the proposed Expert Witness Service is related to the other Professional Service, and the Member determines that a reasonable and informed third party having knowledge of all the relevant information, including safeguards applied, would regard the objectives of the proposed Expert Witness Service to be undertaken as being inconsistent with the objectives of the other Professional Service, then the Member shall decline the Engagement or the relevant part thereof.

5.2 **Subject to paragraph 5.3, if a Member in Business is asked to provide an Expert Witness Service to the Member's Employer where:**

(a) the Member or another employee of the Member's Employer has provided, or is providing, another service to the Employer which is related to the proposed Expert Witness Service; or

(b) the Member's Employer has an interest in the outcome of the Proceedings (whether as a party or otherwise),

and the Member determines that a reasonable and informed third party having knowledge of all the relevant information, including safeguards applied, would regard the objectives of the proposed Expert Witness Service to be undertaken as being inconsistent with the objectives of the other service, or if the Member's objectivity is impaired as a result of the Employer's interest in the outcome of the Proceedings, then the Member shall decline the Assignment or the relevant part thereof.

5.3 Paragraph 5.2 does not apply to a Member in Business who is employed by a government agency, where that agency has a statutory function of regulation, investigation, or law enforcement.

5.4 **A Member who is acting as an Expert Witness shall comply with the following:**

(a) the paramount duty to the Court which overrides any duty to the Client or Employer;

(b) a duty to assist the Court on matters relevant to the Member's area of expertise in an objective and unbiased manner;

(c) a duty not to be an advocate for a party;

(d) a duty to make it clear to the Court when a particular question or issue falls outside the Member's expertise.

5.5 A Member who is acting as an Expert Witness should comply with evidentiary and procedural requirements relating to Expert Witnesses.

The Report of an Expert Witness

5.6 **Subject to any legal requirements or restrictions, a Member providing an Expert Witness Service shall clearly communicate in any Report:**

(a) the instructions received, whether oral or written;

(b) any limitations on the scope of work performed;

(c) details of the Member's training, study and experience that are relevant to the matters on which the Member is providing expert evidence;

(d) the relationships, if any, the Member or the Member's Firm or the Member's Employer has with any of the parties to the Proceedings (including any of the matters referred to in paragraphs 3.8, 5.1, or 5.2) that may create a threat or a perceived threat to the Member's obligation to comply with the fundamental principles of the Code or the Member's paramount duty to the Court, and any appropriate safeguards implemented;

(e) the extent, if any, of reliance by the Member on the work of others;

(f) the opinions formed by the Member;

(g) whether an opinion is provisional rather than concluded, and, if so, the reasons why a concluded opinion has not been formed;

(h) the significant facts upon which the opinions are based;

(i) the significant assumptions upon which the opinions are based and the following matters in respect of each significant assumption:

(i) whether the Member was instructed to make the assumption or whether the Member chose to make the assumption; and

(ii) if the Member chose to make the assumption, then the reason why the Member made that choice;

(j) if the Member considers that an opinion of the Member may be misleading because a significant assumption is likely to mislead, then a statement to that effect and an explanation of why the assumption is likely to mislead;

(k) where applicable, that the Member's opinion is subject to the veracity of another person's Report upon which the Member's Report is based;

(l) the reasoning by which the Member formed the opinions, including an explanation of any method employed and the reasons why that method was chosen;

(m) a list of all documents and sources of information relied upon in the preparation of the Report;

(n) any restrictions on the use of the Report; and

(o) a statement that the Expert Witness Service was conducted in accordance with this Standard.

5.7 In providing an Expert Witness Service, a Member should consider whether APES 225 *Valuation Services* is applicable to the Engagement or Assignment. APES 225 requires, amongst other things, that a Member make certain disclosures in a Report.

5.8 If a Member is not certain whether a matter is a significant assumption or an opinion, the Member should consult the legal representative of the Member's Client or Employer.

6. False or misleading information and changes in opinion

6.1 A Member shall not knowingly or recklessly make a statement or cause another to make a statement in or in connection with a Forensic Accounting Service that, by its content or by an omission, is false or misleading.

6.2 If a Member who was engaged or assigned to provide an Expert Witness Service becomes aware that an opinion expressed by the Member in a Report or in oral evidence was based on information that was false, misleading or contained material omissions and that situation has not been subsequently disclosed in a Report or in oral testimony, the Member shall promptly inform, as appropriate, the legal representative of the Client, the Employer or the Court of the situation. The Member shall also consider whether it is necessary to issue a supplementary Report.

7. Quality control

7.1 A Member in Public Practice shall comply with the requirements of APES 320 *Quality Control for Firms*.

7.2 A Member in Business who undertakes a Forensic Accounting Service should utilise a system of quality control that includes appropriate policies and procedures taking into consideration the following elements of quality control:

(a) Leadership responsibilities for quality within the Employer;

(b) Ethical requirements;

(c) Human resources;

(d) Assignment performance; and

(e) Monitoring.

7.3 A Member performing a Forensic Accounting Service shall prepare working papers that appropriately document the work performed, including the basis on which, and the method by which, any calculations, determinations or estimates used in the provision of the Forensic Accounting Service have been made.

7.4 A Member should be aware that working papers generated as part of undertaking a Forensic Accounting Service may be required to be furnished to other parties or the Court as evidence. Where appropriate, a Member should maintain the chain of custody, including origin, possession and disposition of documents and other material, particularly originals, relevant to the Engagement or Assignment.

8. Professional fees

8.1 A Member in Public Practice providing a Forensic Accounting Service shall be remunerated for such service by way of professional fees computed in accordance with Section 240 *Fees and other Types of Remuneration* of the Code.

8.2 A Member in Public Practice shall not enter into a Contingent Fee arrangement or receive a Contingent Fee for:

(a) an Expert Witness Service; or

(b) a Forensic Accounting Service, other than an Expert Witness Service, that requires Independence or where the Member purports to be independent.

8.3 A Member in Business shall not enter into a contingent remuneration arrangement or receive contingent remuneration for an Expert Witness Service.

Conformity with International Pronouncements

The International Ethics Standard Board for Accountants (IESBA) has not issued a pronouncement equivalent to APES 215.

Appendix 1

Use of the terms "facts", "assumptions" and "opinions"

This Appendix analyses some examples to assist a Member determine whether a matter is a fact, an assumption or an opinion for the purposes of APES 215. Members are cautioned that the determination of whether a matter is a fact, an assumption or an opinion under this Standard is a matter to be judged based on the particular facts and circumstances. In part this arises because the character of the matter (i.e. whether it is a fact, an assumption or an opinion) may be confused with other ways of describing it (e.g. as an input to a calculation, a variable in an equation, an estimate, or an approximation). The examples contained in this Appendix are provided for illustrative purposes only. In all of the examples presented below it is assumed that there are no unmentioned facts which would be relevant to the consideration as to whether a matter is a fact, an assumption or an opinion.

Generally a fact can arise where the Expert Witness has applied specialised knowledge but has not applied any significant degree of expert judgement. However, where the Expert Witness applies a significant degree of expert judgement and draws an inference then the result will be an opinion.

The following are examples of how the work done by a Member may be characterised:

(a) The Member has been asked to calculate the cost of goods sold expense for a period based on balances for opening stock, purchases and closing stock that have already been agreed by the parties. In calculating the expense the Member applies specialised knowledge using a well-accepted method which is not controversial (i.e. that cost of goods sold expense is equal to opening stock plus purchases less closing stock). However, the calculation does not require the Member to apply any significant degree of expert judgement. In this case the figure calculated by the Member is a fact rather than an opinion (i.e. because it is in the nature of a scientific fact). On the other hand, if the Member were instructed to assume a figure for the cost of goods sold expense then that would be an assumption.

(b) The Member has been asked to quantify the lost profits that would have been earned by a business but for a breach of duty. Among other things, this may require the Member to choose a figure for the sales revenue that the business would have earned but for the breach of duty. The question of what would have happened to sales revenue but for the breach requires the Member to consider a situation that is hypothetical rather than real and which, therefore, cannot be a question of fact. If in assessing the figure for sales revenue the Member applies specialised knowledge and a significant degree of expert judgement then the Member will be expressing an opinion. On the other hand, if the Member were instructed to assume a figure for the sales revenue then that would be an assumption.

(c) The Member uses the Capital Asset Pricing Model (CAPM) to determine a discount rate for the valuation of a business using the discounted cash flow method. The Member must choose a figure for the beta, which is an input to the CAPM. In the normal course, the Member will choose a beta after having gathered relevant information and having performed relevant analyses. In assessing the figure for beta the Member will apply specialised knowledge and a significant degree of expert judgement. Therefore, the Member will be expressing an opinion. On the other hand, if the Member were instructed to assume a figure for the beta then that would be an assumption.

APES 220

Taxation Services

(Issued October 2009: revised March 2011)

Issued by the Accounting Professional and Ethical Standards Board.

Note from the Institute of Chartered Accountants Australia

This note, prepared by the technical editor, is not part of APES 220.

Historical development

October 2007: APES 220 'Taxation Services' issued to replace Miscellaneous Professional Statement APS 6 'Statement of Taxation Standards'. It focuses on the fundamental responsibilities of accountants in providing taxation services to clients and employers and is aligned with APES 110 'Code of Ethics for Professional Accountants'. It is operative from 1 July 2008.

March 2011: APES 220 was reissued in March 2011 to clarify the prohibition against members in public practice appropriating tax refunds as a means of settling fees without prior written consent from the client. It is operative from 1 May 2011, and has no international equivalent.

Contents

1. Scope and application

1.1 Accounting Professional & Ethical Standards Board Limited (APESB) has revised professional standard APES 220 *Taxation Services* (**the Standard**), which is effective from 1 May 2011.

1.2 APES 220 sets the standards for Members in the provision of quality and ethical Taxation Services. The mandatory requirements of this Standard are in **bold** type, preceded or followed by discussion or explanations in grey type. APES 220 should be read in conjunction with other professional duties of Members, and any legal obligations that may apply.

1.3 Members in Australia shall follow the mandatory requirements of APES 220 when they provide Taxation Services.

1.4 Members practising outside of Australia shall follow the provisions of APES 220 to the extent to which they are not prevented from so doing by specific requirements of local regulations and/or laws.

1.5 Members shall be familiar with relevant professional standards and guidance notes when providing Professional Services. All Members shall comply with the fundamental principles outlined in the Code.

1.6 The Standard is not intended to detract from any responsibilities which may be imposed by law.

1.7 All references to professional standards are references to those provisions as amended from time to time.

1.8 In applying the requirements outlined in APES 220, Members should be guided not merely by the words but also by the spirit of the Standard and the Code.

2. Definitions

For the purpose of this Standard:

Client means an individual, Firm, entity or organisation to whom or to which Taxation Services are provided by a Member in Public Practice in respect of Engagements of either a recurring or demand nature.

Code means APES 110 *Code of Ethics for Professional Accountants.*

Employer within the context of this Standard means an entity or person that employs, engages or contracts a Member in Business.

Engagement means an agreement, whether written or otherwise, between a Member in Public Practice and a Client relating to the provision of Professional Services by a Member in Public Practice. However, consultations with a prospective Client prior to such agreement are not part of an Engagement.

Firm means:

(a) A sole practitioner, partnership, corporation or other entity of professional accountants;

(b) An entity that controls such parties, through ownership, management or other means;

(c) An entity controlled by such parties, through ownership, management or other means; or

(d) An Auditor-General's office or department.

Member means a member of a professional body that has adopted this Standard as applicable to their membership, as defined by that professional body.

Member in Business means a Member employed or engaged in an executive or non-executive capacity in such areas as commerce, industry, service, the public sector, education, the not for profit sector, regulatory bodies or professional bodies, or a Member contracted by such entities.

Member in Public Practice means a Member, irrespective of functional classification (e.g. audit, tax or consulting) in a Firm that provides Professional Services. The term is also used to refer to a Firm of Members in Public Practice and means a practice entity as defined by the applicable professional body.

Professional Services means services requiring accountancy or related skills performed by a professional accountant including accounting, auditing, taxation, management consulting and financial management services.

Revenue Authorities include various levels of government authorities or similar institutions which have legislative powers to impose and/or collect taxes.

Taxation Law means a law and/or regulation of any level of government imposing a tax or otherwise dealing with tax, and includes any such laws and regulations that describe direct and indirect taxes, levies, surcharges, penalties or similar charges imposed by various levels of governments or similar institutions on economic transactions.

Taxation Services mean any services relating to ascertaining a Client's or Employer's tax liabilities or entitlements or satisfying their obligations under a Taxation Law, provided under circumstances where they can reasonably expect to rely on the services. This includes:

- preparation of a return, notice, statement, application or other document for lodgment with a Revenue Authority, and responding on behalf of a Client or Employer to requests for further information from a Revenue Authority;
- preparation of tax calculations to be used as the basis for the accounting entries in the financial statements;
- provision of tax planning and other tax advisory services; and
- assisting a Client or Employer in the resolution of tax disputes.

Writing means a mode of representing or reproducing words in a visible form, and includes words in an electronic format capable of being converted to printed text.

3. Fundamental responsibilities of Members

3.1 **Members providing Taxation Services shall at all times safeguard the interests of their Client or Employer provided that such services are delivered in accordance with Section 100 *Introduction and Fundamental Principles* of the Code and relevant Taxation Law.**

Public interest

3.2 **In accordance with Section 100.1 of the Code, Members shall observe and comply with their public interest obligations when they provide Taxation Services.**

Integrity and professional behaviour

3.3 **In accordance with the fundamental principles of integrity and professional behaviour contained in the Code, Members providing Taxation Services shall ensure that their own personal tax obligations and those of any associated entities for which the Member is responsible are properly discharged.**

Objectivity

3.4 **When providing Taxation Services Members shall be objective in accordance with Section 120 *Objectivity* of the Code. They shall maintain an impartial attitude and recommend options that meet the Client's or Employer's interests consistent with the requirements of the law.**

3.5 A Member may act as an advocate for a Client or Employer when representing or assisting them before certain tribunals. However, a Member acting in such a capacity before any court or tribunal should ensure that the Client or Employer is aware that the Member has an obligation not to mislead the court or tribunal and to safeguard his or her professional objectivity.

Confidentiality

3.6 **In accordance with Section 140 *Confidentiality* of the Code, a Member who acquires confidential information in the course of professional work for a Client or Employer shall not use that information for any purpose other than the proper performance of professional work for that Client or Employer.**

3.7 **Unless the Member has a legal obligation of disclosure, a Member shall not convey any information relating to a Client's or Employer's affairs to a third party without the Client's or Employer's permission.**

3.8 Where a Client has given a Member in Public Practice permission to disclose confidential information to a third party, it is preferable that this permission is in Writing. Where verbal permission is obtained, a contemporaneous note should be made and kept on file by the Member recording the relevant details of the Client's approval.

3.9 **Unless the Member has a legal obligation of disclosure, a Member shall not furnish to the Revenue Authorities any opinions or written advices of a third party who is acting in a specialist capacity on specific aspects of the Engagement, without the prior knowledge and express consent of that third party.**

3.10 **Where a Member provides confidential information in accordance with a legal obligation of disclosure, the Member shall notify the Client, Employer or relevant third party as soon as practical, provided that there is no legal prohibition against such notification.**

Professional competence and due care

3.11 **Members engaged in providing Taxation Services shall maintain professional competence and take due care in the performance of their work in accordance with Section 130 *Professional Competence and Due Care* of the Code.**

3.12 Competent Professional Service requires the exercise of sound judgment in applying professional knowledge and skill in the performance of such service. Due care imposes the obligation of acting diligently in accordance with applicable technical and professional standards when providing a Professional Service.

3.13 Members should therefore refrain from performing any services which they are not competent to carry out, unless expert advice and assistance is obtained to ensure that the services are performed to a standard agreed with the Client or Employer or as required by law.

3.14 **A Member shall maintain open, frank and effective communications with a Client or Employer. In this regard:**

(a) where appropriate having regard to the Member's agreed scope of work, a Member shall advise a Client or Employer of both the Member's and the Client's or Employer's rights, obligations and options available under the

APES

Taxation Law. A Member shall also advise the Client or Employer of their rights or options available under Taxation Law with respect to the seeking of a private ruling and the lodging of objections and appeals against adverse positions adopted by the Revenue Authorities; and

(b) in the context of Taxation Services requested, a Member shall advise a Client or Employer on the application of the Taxation Law, including any possible penalties and other legal tax consequence, so as to allow the Client or Employer to make an informed decision of the course of action to be taken.

3.15 A Member in Public Practice shall provide a Client with a statement in Writing that:

(a) the responsibility for the accuracy and completeness of the particulars and information provided by the Client rests with the Client;

(b) any advice given to the Client is only an opinion based on the Member's knowledge of the Client's particular circumstances; and

(c) a taxpayer has obligations under self assessment to keep full and proper records in order to facilitate the preparation of accurate returns.

3.16 The communication of the matters in paragraph 3.15 to the Client in Writing need not be in the form of a letter. For example, a standard format handout, brochure, leaflet or electronic communication is also acceptable.

3.17 Where the application of the Taxation Law is not certain, a Member shall not represent to a Client or Employer that the results of a Taxation Service (such as the tax or other revenue returns which the Member prepares or assists in preparing, or the tax advice the Member offers), are beyond challenge.

4. Preparation and lodgment of returns to Revenue Authorities

4.1 A Member shall prepare and/or lodge returns and other relevant documents required to be lodged with a Revenue Authority in accordance with the information provided by a Client or Employer, their instructions and the relevant Taxation Law.

4.2 Where appropriate a Member may accept a Client's or Employer's information, and is not responsible for its veracity. However, within the agreed scope of work a Member should obtain information which is sufficient to allow the Member to form a view as to the application of the law to that information and to be able to recommend the options available to the Client or Employer on how the information provided by them may be reflected in the relevant return or other document to be lodged. Where a Member reasonably believes that the information provided by the Client or Employer may be incomplete, false or misleading, the Member should have regard to the provisions of paragraph 7.3 of this Standard and the law.

4.3 Where a Member in Public Practice provides a tax lodgment service to another party and a significant portion of the work associated with the revenue returns and other relevant documents is not performed under the supervision of the Member in Public Practice, the Member in Public Practice shall perform sufficient reviews of the revenue returns and other relevant documents in accordance with this Standard and the Code prior to lodgment of these revenue returns.

5. Tax schemes and arrangements

5.1 The decision to enter into any tax scheme or arrangement will always be that of the Client or Employer.

5.2 Where appropriate, having regard to the Member's agreed scope of work, a Member shall give the Client or Employer sufficient information to enable the Client or Employer to be fully informed of the details of the scheme or arrangement and its current and future ramifications including the risks and uncertainties, particularly in relation to possible changes in Taxation Law.

5.3 A Member shall not knowingly or recklessly be associated with any arrangement which involves documents or accounting entries that are intended to misrepresent a transaction or which depend upon lack of disclosure for its effectiveness.

5.4 Member shall not promote, or assist in the promotion of, or otherwise encourage any tax schemes or arrangements where the dominant purpose is to derive a tax benefit and it is not reasonably arguable that the tax benefit is available under Taxation Law. Accordingly, a Member shall not provide advice on such a scheme or arrangement to a Client or Employer other than to advise that in the Member's opinion it is not effective at law.

5.5 Paragraph 5.4 does not preclude a Member from advising a Client or Employer on the resolution of such matters and providing other Taxation Services.

5.6 Provided that the provisions of paragraphs 5.3 and 5.4 do not apply, a Member may otherwise provide Taxation Services to a Client or Employer who has entered into a tax scheme or arrangement.

5.7 In respect of an entity that predominantly promotes tax schemes or arrangements, a Member shall not:

- **have any financial interest in such an entity; or**
- **render any Professional Service to such an entity where the Member knows that the Member's immediate or close family has a financial interest.**

6. Estimates

6.1 A Member shall not prepare or be associated with the preparation of returns or submissions to Revenue Authorities involving the use of estimates unless their use is generally accepted or under the circumstances it is impracticable to obtain exact data.

6.2 When estimates are used, a Member shall present them in such a manner as to avoid the implication of greater accuracy than in fact exists.

6.3 The Member shall consider whether the use of an estimate is reasonable in the particular circumstance. Where a Member has reason to believe an estimate is not reasonable the Member shall advise the Client or Employer of the risks and consequences of using the relevant estimate in the return or submission to be lodged with the Revenue Authorities.

7. False or misleading information

7.1 A Member shall not provide a Taxation Service to a Client or Employer if the Member finds that information on which the Taxation Service is to be based contains false or misleading information or omits material information and the Client or Employer is not prepared to appropriately amend it.

7.2 A Member shall not knowingly or recklessly make a statement or cause another to make a statement in or in connection with a Taxation Service that, by its content or by an omission, is false or misleading in a material manner.

7.3 Where a Member forms the view that a Taxation Service is based on false or misleading information or the omission of material information, the Member shall discuss the matter with the Client or Employer and advise them of the consequences if no action is taken.

7.4 Where a Member finds that a Client or Employer has filed returns or submissions in previous years (with which the Member may or may not have been associated) that contain materially false or misleading information or omit material information, the Member should discuss the matter with the Client or Employer and advise them of their responsibilities.

7.5 In the event of a Member subsequently becoming aware that information previously provided to a Revenue Authority by the Member, which the Member had no reason to believe at the time to be incorrect, is false or misleading, the Member should recommend that the Client or Employer make an appropriate disclosure or, alternatively, the Member should obtain authority from them to make the disclosure on their behalf.

7.6 **A Member in Public Practice who**

(a) **knows that a Client or the Member on behalf of the Client has filed a return or submission materially understating a tax liability to a Revenue Authority, and**

(b) **finds the Client unwilling to correct such understatement,**

shall consider the Firm's policies and procedures established in accordance with *Acceptance and Continuance of Client Relationships and Specific Engagements* of APES 320 *Quality Control for Firms* in determining whether to continue acting for the Client in a professional capacity.

7.7 Where a Member in Business is faced with similar circumstances, the Member is referred to Part C: Members in Business of the Code.

7.8 All references to false and misleading information in this section exclude information that is of an immaterial or inconsequential nature.

8. Professional engagement matters

8.1 **A Member in Public Practice shall provide the Client with an appropriate statement in Writing outlining the relevant terms of the Engagement to provide the Taxation Service in accordance with APES 305 *Terms of Engagement*.**

8.2 The provision of this statement to the Client in Writing need not be in the form of a letter. For example, a standard format handout, brochure, leaflet or electronic communication is also acceptable.

8.3 **A Member in Public Practice who is approached by a potential Client to undertake a Taxation Service shall comply with the requirements of Section 210 *Professional Appointment* of the Code.**

8.4 **A Member in Public Practice who has utilised the services of a third party in connection with the performance of a Taxation Service, such as a legal opinion to support the provision of taxation advice, shall not disclose the relevant opinion or the name of that third party without the prior consent of that party.**

8.5 **A Member consulting with others in relation to a Client's or Employer's affairs shall observe the requirements of Section 140 *Confidentiality* of the Code.**

9. Client monies

9.1 **A Member in Public Practice shall ensure prompt transmission of monies received on behalf of a Client from Revenue Authorities to the Client.**

9.2 **A Member in Public Practice shall not use, withhold or otherwise appropriate tax refunds to settle the fees of the Member or for any other use in lieu of their transfer directly to the Client, unless agreed to by the Client in Writing.**

9.3 **Where funds are to be banked by a Member in Public Practice on behalf of a Client, a Member shall use a separate bank account designated as a trust account and maintained in accordance with the requirements of the professional body to which the Member belongs.**

10. Professional fees

10.1 **A Member in Public Practice providing Taxation Services shall be remunerated for such services by way of professional fees computed in accordance with Section 240 *Fees and other Types of Remuneration* of the Code.**

11. Documentation

11.1 **A Member shall prepare working papers in accordance with this Standard that appropriately document the work performed, including aspects of the Taxation Service that have been provided in Writing in accordance with this Standard, and the basis on which, and the method by which, any calculations, determinations or estimates used in the provision of the Taxation Service have been made.**

11.2 A Member should adopt appropriate procedures for maintaining the confidentiality and safe custody of working papers and for retaining them for a period sufficient to meet the needs of the Member and in accordance with legal requirements of record retention.

11.3 Nothing in this Standard precludes the storage of documentation in appropriate electronic formats. Members contemplating the use of electronic storage should consider the legal implications of such forms of storage, which may vary by jurisdiction, and seek appropriate advice in this context.

Conformity with International Pronouncements

The International Ethics Standards Board for Accountants (IESBA) has not issued a pronouncement equivalent to APES 220.

Appendix 1

Summary of revisions to the previous APES 220

(Issued December 2007)

APES 220 *Taxation Services* originally issued in December 2007 has been revised by APESB in March 2011. A summary of the revisions is given in the table below.

Table of revisions*

Paragraph affected	How affected
9.2	Amended
Conformity with International Pronouncements	Added

* *Refer Technical Update 2011/1*

APES

APES 225
Valuation Services

(Issued July 2008: revised May 2012)

Issued by the Accounting Professional and Ethical Standards Board.

Note from the Institute of Chartered Accountants Australia

This note, prepared by the technical editor, is not part of APES 225.

Historical development

July 2008: APES 225 'Valuation Services' applies to all members in public practice and in business who provide an estimate of value for a business, business ownership interest, security or intangible asset to either a client or an employer. It is effective from 1 January 2009.

May 2012: APES 225 reissued to provide further guidance to practioners in respect of the three types of valuation services engagements and new requirements relating to engagement letters. It is effective for engagements commencing after 1 September 2012 with early adoption permitted.

Contents

1. Scope and application

1.1 Accounting Professional & Ethical Standards Board Limited (APESB) issues professional standard APES 225 *Valuation Services* (**the Standard**), which is effective for Valuation Engagements or Assignments commencing on or after 1 September 2012. Earlier adoption of this Standard is permitted.

1.2 APES 225 sets the standards for Members in the provision of quality and ethical Valuation Services. The mandatory requirements of this Standard are in **bold** type, preceded or followed by discussion or explanations in grey type. APES 225 should be read in conjunction with other professional duties of Members, and any legal obligations that may apply.

1.3 Members in Australia shall follow the mandatory requirements of APES 225 when they provide Valuation Services.

1.4 Members outside of Australia shall follow the mandatory requirements of APES 225 when they provide Valuation Services, to the extent to which they are not prevented from so doing by specific requirements of local laws and/or regulations.

1.5 Members shall be familiar with relevant professional standards and guidance notes when providing Professional Services. All Members shall comply with the fundamental principles outlined in the Code.

1.6 The Standard is not intended to detract from any responsibilities which may be imposed by law or regulation.

1.7 All references to professional standards and guidance notes are references to those provisions as amended from time to time.

1.8 In applying APES 225 Members should be guided not merely by the words but also by the spirit of the Standard and the Code.

2. Definitions

For the purpose of this Standard:

Assignment means an instruction, whether written or otherwise, by an Employer to a Member in Business relating to the provision of services by a Member in Business. However, consultations with the Employer prior to such instruction are not part of an Assignment.

Calculated Value means an estimate of value of a business, business ownership interest, security or intangible asset that results from a Calculation Engagement. A Calculated Value may either be a single amount or a range.

Calculation Engagement means an Engagement or Assignment to perform a Valuation and provide a Valuation Report where the Member and the Client or Employer agree on the Valuation Approaches, Valuation Methods and Valuation Procedures the Member will employ. A Calculation Engagement generally does not include all of the Valuation Procedures required for a Valuation Engagement or a Limited Scope Valuation Engagement.

Client means an individual, Firm, entity or organisation to whom or to which Valuation Services are provided by a Member in Public Practice in respect of Engagements of either a recurring or demand nature.

Code means APES 110 *Code of Ethics for Professional Accountants*.

Conclusion of Value means an estimate of value of a business, business ownership interest, security or intangible asset that results from a Valuation Engagement or a Limited Scope Valuation Engagement. A Conclusion of Value may either be a single amount or a range.

Contingent Fee means a fee calculated on a predetermined basis relating to the outcome or result of a transaction or the result of the work performed. A fee that is established by a court or other public authority is not a Contingent Fee.

Employer means an entity or person that employs, engages or contracts a Member in Business.

Engagement means an agreement, whether written or otherwise, between a Member in Public Practice and a Client relating to the provision of Professional Services by a Member in Public Practice. However, consultations with a prospective Client prior to such agreement are not part of an Engagement.

Firm means

(a) a sole practitioner, partnership, corporation or other entity of professional accountants;

(b) an entity that controls such parties, through ownership, management or other means;

(c) an entity controlled by such parties, through ownership, management or other means; or

(d) an Auditor-General's office or department.

Independence *means*

(a) Independence of mind - the state of mind that permits the provision of an opinion without being affected by influences that compromise professional judgment, allowing an individual to act with integrity, and exercise objectivity and professional scepticism; and

(b) Independence in appearance - the avoidance of facts and circumstances that are so significant a reasonable and informed third party, having knowledge of all relevant information, including any safeguards applied, would reasonably conclude a Firm's, or a member of the Engagement team's, integrity, objectivity or professional scepticism had been compromised.

Limited Scope Valuation Engagement means an Engagement or Assignment to perform a Valuation and provide a Valuation Report where the scope of work is limited or restricted. The scope of work is limited or restricted where the Member is not free, as the Member would be but for the limitation or restriction, to employ the Valuation Approaches, Valuation Methods and Valuation Procedures that a reasonable and informed third party would perform taking into consideration all the specific facts and circumstances of the Engagement or Assignment available to the Member at that time, and it is reasonable to expect that the effect of the limitation or restriction on the estimate of value is material. A limitation or restriction may be imposed by the Client or Employer or it may arise from other sources or circumstances. A limitation or restriction may be present and known at the outset of the Engagement or Assignment or may arise or become known during the course of a Valuation Engagement. A Limited Scope Valuation Engagement may also be referred to as a "restricted-scope valuation engagement" or an "indicative valuation engagement".

Member means a member of a professional body that has adopted this Standard as applicable to their membership, as defined by that professional body.

Member in Business means a Member employed or engaged in an executive or non-executive capacity in such areas as commerce, industry, service, the public sector, education, the not for profit sector, regulatory bodies or professional bodies, or a Member contracted by such entities.

Member in Public Practice means a Member, irrespective of functional classification (e.g. audit, tax or consulting) in a Firm that provides Professional Services. The term is also used to refer to a Firm of Members in Public Practice and means a practice entity as defined by the applicable professional body.

Premise of Value means an assumption regarding the most likely set of transactional circumstances that may be applicable to the subject valuation; e.g. going concern or liquidation.

Professional Services means services requiring accountancy or related skills performed by a professional accountant including accounting, auditing, taxation, management consulting and financial management services.

Terms of Engagement means the terms and conditions that are agreed between the Client and the Member in Public Practice for the Engagement.

Valuation means the act or process of determining an estimate of value of a business, business ownership interest, security or intangible asset by applying Valuation Approaches, Valuation Methods and Valuation Procedures. A Valuation does not involve the verification of information in respect of the business, business ownership interest, security or intangible asset being valued.

Valuation Approach(es) means a general way(s) of determining an estimate of value of a business, business ownership interest, security, or intangible asset using one or more Valuation Methods.

Valuation Engagement means an Engagement or Assignment to perform a Valuation and provide a Valuation Report where the Member is free to employ the Valuation Approaches, Valuation Methods, and Valuation Procedures that a reasonable and informed third party would perform taking into consideration all the specific facts and circumstances of the Engagement or Assignment available to the Member at that time. Where a Member has entered into a Valuation Engagement but during the course of performing the Valuation Engagement the Member becomes aware of a limitation or restriction that, if it had been known at the time the Engagement or Assignment was entered into, would have made the Engagement or Assignment a Limited Scope Valuation Engagement then the Valuation Engagement will become a Limited Scope Valuation Engagement.

Valuation Method(s) means, within Valuation Approaches, a specific way(s) to determine an estimate of value of a business, business ownership interest, security or intangible asset.

Valuation Procedures means the act, manner and technique of performing the steps of a Valuation Method.

Valuation Report means any written or oral communication by the Member containing a Conclusion of Value or a Calculated Value.

Valuation Service means a service provided by a Member to a Client or Employer in performance of a Valuation Engagement, Limited Scope Valuation Engagement or a Calculation Engagement.

3. Fundamental responsibilities of Members

3.1 **A Member providing a Valuation Service shall comply with Section 100 *Introduction and Fundamental Principles* of the Code and relevant law.**

3.2 **Members in Public Practice shall comply with Section 220 *Conflict of Interest* and Section 280 *Objectivity – All Services* in the Code.**

Public interest

3.3 **In accordance with Section 100 *Introduction and Fundamental Principles* of the Code, a Member shall observe and comply with the Member's public interest obligations when providing a Valuation Service.**

Professional Independence

3.4 **When engaged to perform a Valuation Service which requires Independence or purports to be independent, the Member in Public Practice shall comply with Independence as defined in this Standard.**

3.5 **A Member in Public Practice shall not act as an advocate in respect of a Valuation Service which requires Independence or purports to be independent.**

APES

Professional competence and due care

3.6 **A Member providing a Valuation Service shall maintain professional competence and take due care in the performance of the Member's work in accordance with Section 130 *Professional Competence and Due Care* of the Code.**

3.7 **Where a Valuation Service requires the consideration of matters that are outside a Member's professional expertise, the Member shall seek expert assistance or advice from a suitably qualified third party on those matters outside of the Member's professional expertise or decline the Valuation Service. The Member shall disclose in any Valuation Report or other relevant communications the extent of the reliance upon the advice of such a third party.**

3.8 **When planning to use the work of a suitably qualified third party, a Member shall assess the professional competence and objectivity of the third party, the engagement terms of the third party and on completion the appropriateness and reasonableness of the work performed.**

3.9 In undertaking a Valuation Service, a Member should consider the contents of any guidance in respect of Valuation matters issued by the professional accounting bodies and appropriate regulatory authorities.

Confidentiality

3.10 **In accordance with Section 140 *Confidentiality* of the Code, a Member who acquires confidential information in the course of professional work for a Client or Employer shall not use that information for any purpose other than the proper performance of professional work for that Client or Employer.**

3.11 **Unless the Member has a legal obligation of disclosure, a Member shall not convey any information relating to a Client's or Employer's affairs to a third party without the Client's or Employer's permission.**

3.12 Where a Client has given a Member in Public Practice permission to disclose confidential information to a third party, it is preferable that this permission is in writing. Where oral permission is obtained, a contemporaneous note should be made and kept on file by the Member recording the relevant details of the Client's approval.

3.13 **Where a Member provides confidential information in accordance with a legal obligation of disclosure, the Member shall notify the Client, Employer or relevant third party as soon as practicable, provided that there is no legal prohibition against such notification.**

4. Professional Engagement and other matters

4.1 **A Member in Public Practice shall document and communicate the Terms of Engagement to provide the Valuation Service in accordance with APES 305 *Terms of Engagement*.**

4.2 **A Member in Public Practice shall include the following in the Terms of Engagement:**

(a) **a statement as to which type of Engagement the Member has been engaged to perform;**

(b) **the definitions of a Valuation Engagement, a Limited Scope Valuation Engagement and a Calculation Engagement;**

(c) **for a Valuation Engagement, a statement that if the Member becomes aware during the course of performing the Valuation of a limitation or restriction that could have a material impact on the estimate of value, then the Engagement will become a Limited Scope Valuation Engagement;**

(d) **for a Calculation Engagement, a statement as to which Valuation Approaches, Valuation Methods and Valuation Procedures the Member has been engaged to perform;**

(e) **for a Valuation Service which requires Independence or purports to be independent, a statement confirming the Member's Independence and the Member's compliance with the Independence requirements of this Standard; and**

(f) **a statement that the Valuation Service will be conducted in accordance with this Standard.**

4.3 **A Member in Public Practice who is approached by a potential Client to undertake a Valuation Service shall comply with the requirements of Section 210 *Professional Appointment* of the Code.**

4.4 **A Member in Public Practice who has utilised the services of a third party in connection with the performance of a Valuation Service, such as a valuer of property, plant and equipment, shall not disclose the opinion or the name of that third party without the prior consent of that party unless the Member has a legal obligation of disclosure.**

4.5 **A Member shall gather sufficient and appropriate evidence by such means as inspection, inquiry, computation and analysis to provide reasonable grounds that the Valuation Report and the conclusions therein are properly supported. When determining the extent and quality of evidence necessary the Member shall exercise professional judgement, considering the nature of the Valuation, the type of Valuation Service and the use to which the Valuation Report will be put.**

5. Reporting

5.1 Generally when a Member in Public Practice provides a Valuation Service, the Member should prepare a written Valuation Report. However, this Standard recognises that a Member may issue a Valuation Report orally where instructed to do so by the Member's Client or where there are circumstances that would justify issuing a Valuation Report orally rather than in writing.

5.2 **Where a Member in Public Practice prepares a written Valuation Report in respect of a Valuation Service, the Valuation Report shall clearly communicate:**

(a) **The name of the party engaging the Member;**

(b) **A description of the business, business ownership interest, security or intangible asset being valued;**

(c) **The date at which the value has been determined;**

(d) **The date on which the Valuation Report has been issued;**

(e) **The purpose for which the Valuation Report has been prepared;**

(f) **The name and qualifications of the Member(s) responsible for the Valuation;**

(g) **The scope of the Valuation, including any limitations or restrictions;**

(h) **The Premise of Value adopted in the Valuation (e.g. going concern premise or liquidation premise);**

(i) **Whether the Valuation was undertaken by the Member acting independently or not;**

(j) **The Valuation Approach(es), Valuation Method(s) and Valuation Procedures adopted in determining the estimate of value and a description of how they were applied;**

(k) **The specific information on which the Member has relied and the extent to which it has been reviewed (e.g. the documents reviewed, the individuals interviewed, the facilities visited, the reports of other experts relied upon, and management representations);**

(l) **A description of the material assumptions applied in the Valuation and the basis for those assumptions;**

(m) **A Conclusion of Value for a Valuation Engagement or a Limited Scope Valuation Engagement, or a Calculated Value for a Calculation Engagement;**

(n) **All qualifications that materially affect the Conclusion of Value or Calculated Value;**

(o) **For a Limited Scope Valuation Engagement, that if a Valuation Engagement had been performed the results may have been different;**

(p) **For a Calculation Engagement, that if a Valuation Engagement had been performed the results may have been different;**

(q) **Where a Member has prepared a Valuation Report requiring Independence or purporting to be independent, that the compensation to be paid to the Member is not contingent on the conclusion, content or future use of the Valuation Report; and**

(r) **That the Valuation Service was conducted in accordance with this Standard.**

5.3 **Where a Member in Public Practice communicates the Valuation Report orally, the Member shall communicate the elements noted in paragraph 5.2, as appropriate in the circumstances, and document the oral communication, the reasons for issuing an oral report and the work performed in accordance with this Standard and the Firm's policies and procedures established under *Documentation* of APES 320 *Quality Control for Firms*.**

5.4 **In addition to the minimum requirements of a Valuation Report set out in paragraph 5.2, the Member in Public Practice shall consider including the following information in a Valuation Report, as appropriate:**

(a) **A description of other Valuation Approaches or Valuation Methods considered and the reasons why they were not considered relevant for the Valuation;**

(b) **Sufficient details of the Valuation calculations to allow a reader to understand how the Member determined the Conclusion of Value or Calculated Value;**

(c) **A summary of relevant financial information; and**

(d) **A summary of the relevant industry.**

5.5 A Member in Business who undertakes a Valuation Service should prepare a Valuation Report taking into consideration the requirements and guidance of paragraphs 5.1 to 5.4 of this Standard, as appropriate, and to the extent practicable.

6. Documentation

6.1 **A Member performing a Valuation Service shall prepare working papers that appropriately document the work performed, including the basis on which, and the method by which, any calculations, determinations or estimates used in the provision of the Valuation Service have been made.**

7. Use of a glossary of business valuation terms

7.1 **When issuing a Valuation Report, a Member shall clearly define the Valuation terms used.**

7.2 Members are encouraged to use as far as practicable terms that are in general use for Valuation Services. Members are referred to the *International Glossary of Business Valuation Terms* which are included in the valuation standards of the American Institute of Certified Public Accountants and the Canadian Institute of Chartered Business Valuators.

8. Professional fees

8.1 **A Member in Public Practice providing Valuation Services shall be remunerated for such services by way of professional fees computed in accordance with Section 240 *Fees and other Types of Remuneration* of the Code.**

8.2 **A Member in Public Practice shall not enter into a Contingent Fee arrangement or receive a Contingent Fee for a Valuation Service which requires Independence or purports to be independent.**

Conformity with International Pronouncements

The International Ethics Standard Board for Accountants (IESBA) has not issued a pronouncement equivalent to APES 225.

Appendix 1

Schematic and Examples

This Appendix contains a schematic and some examples to assist or determine whether a particular service is a Valuation Service for the purposes of APES 225 and, if so, whether the Engagement or Assignment is a Valuation Engagement, Limited Scope Valuation Engagement, or Calculation Engagement.

Members are cautioned that the determination of whether a particular service is a Valuation Service under this Standard is a matter to be judged based on the particular facts and circumstances. The examples contained in this Appendix are provided for illustrative purposes only and are not intended to be, and cannot be, all inclusive. The examples are not a substitute for reading the full text of APES 225 and applying the Standard to the particular circumstances to determine whether the Member is providing a Valuation Service. In all of the examples presented below it is assumed that there are no unmentioned facts which would be relevant to the consideration as to whether the service provided is a Valuation Service.

Schematic

The following schematic provides an overview of what constitutes a Valuation Service and what differentiates the three types of Engagement or Assignment.

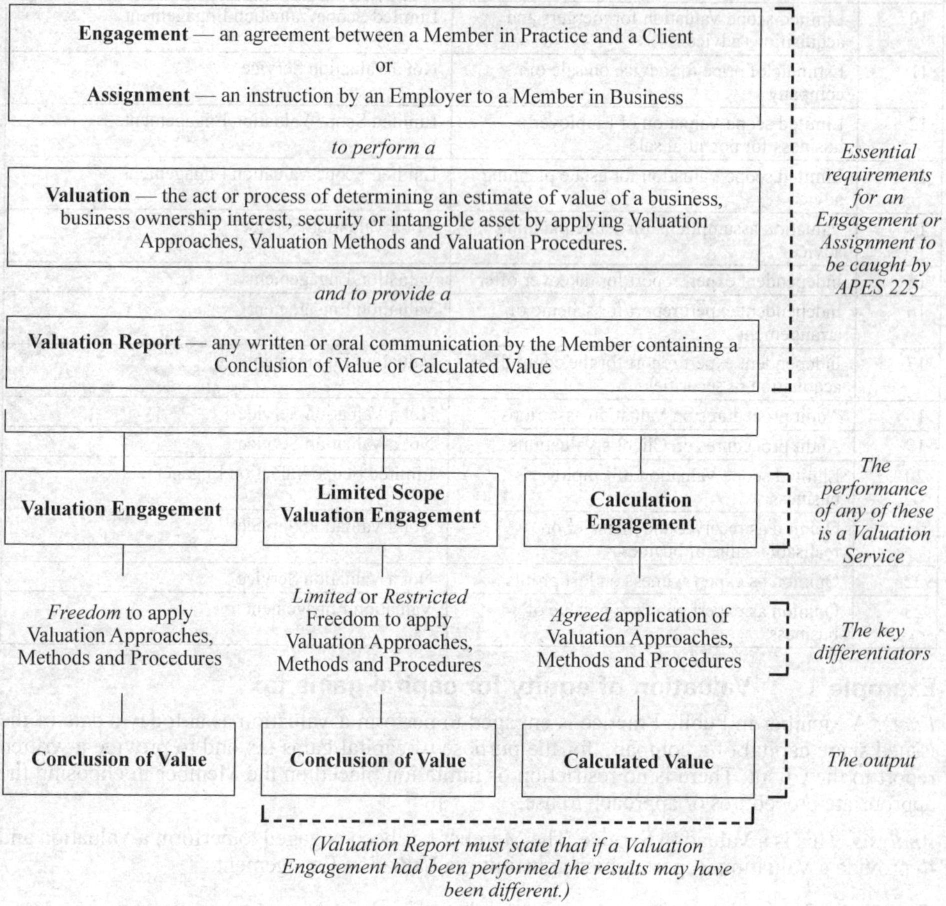

Examples

No	Title	Conclusion
1	Valuation of equity for capital gains tax	Valuation Engagement
2	Valuation of equity where industry not analysed	Limited Scope Valuation Engagement
3	Valuation Engagement becomes Limited Scope Valuation Engagement	Limited Scope Valuation Engagement
4	Valuation of equity for capital gains tax where Valuation date is eight years ago and information lost	Limited Scope Valuation Engagement
5	Valuation of equity for capital gains tax where records are sparse	Valuation Engagement
6	Valuation of equity for capital gains tax with limited time	Limited Scope Valuation Engagement
7	Valuation of shareholding for capital gains tax with assumption on the value of all equity	Limited Scope Valuation Engagement
8	Valuation of shareholding for capital gains tax with assumptions on the value of all equity and percentage discounts for the lack of control and marketability	Calculation Engagement
9	Valuation of Employer's intangible assets for tax consolidation	Valuation Engagement
10	Limited scope Valuation for mergers and acquisitions advice	Limited Scope Valuation Engagement
11	Estimate of price for advice on sale of a company	Not a Valuation Service
12	Limited scope Valuation of Employer's business for potential sale	Limited Scope Valuation Engagement
13	Limited scope Valuation for estate planning advice	Limited Scope Valuation Engagement
14	Valuation assumptions for estate planning advice	Not a Valuation Service
15	Independent expert report for takeover offer	Valuation Engagement
16	Independent expert report for scheme of arrangement	Valuation Engagement
17	Independent expert report for the compulsory acquisition of securities	Valuation Engagement
18	Audit procedures on Valuation assertions	Not a Valuation Service
19	Audit procedures on Client's Valuations	Not a Valuation Service
20	Limited scope Valuation of Employer's business	Limited Scope Valuation Engagement
21	Opinion as receiver and manager on realisable value of business	Not a Valuation Service
22	Opinion as expert witness on lost profits	Not a Valuation Service
23	Opinion as expert witness on value of business	Valuation Engagement

Example 1 Valuation of equity for capital gains tax

Facts: A Member in Public Practice is engaged to perform a Valuation as at today's date of the issued share capital of a company for the purpose of capital gains tax and to provide a written report to the Client. There is no restriction or limitation placed on the Member in choosing the appropriate procedures or approach to use.

Analysis: This is a Valuation Service. The Member has been engaged to perform a Valuation and to provide a Valuation Report, which constitutes a Valuation Engagement.

Example 2 Valuation of equity where industry not analysed

Facts: The facts are the same as for Example 1 except that the scope of work is limited in that the Member is instructed not to perform any analysis of the industry within which the business of the company operates. In the absence of this instruction the Member would have considered it appropriate to perform an analysis of the industry. The lack of analysis on the industry would reasonably be considered to have a material impact on the estimate of value.

Analysis: This is a Valuation Service. The Member has been engaged to perform a Valuation where the scope of work is limited or restricted, and to provide a Valuation Report, which constitutes a Limited Scope Valuation Engagement.

Example 3 Valuation Engagement becomes Limited Scope Valuation Engagement

Facts: The facts are the same as for Example 1 except that after agreeing the Terms of Engagement, which provides for a Valuation Engagement, during the course of performing the Valuation the Member becomes aware of a limitation. The Member intended to value the equity in the company using the income approach and for that purpose intended to estimate the company's expected future cash flows. The Member made relevant enquiries of the Client for the purpose of estimating the expected future cash flows. However, the Client decided not to respond to the Member's enquiries but instead instructed the Member to adopt the Client's existing forecast of cash flows so as to contain professional costs.

Analysis: This is a Valuation Service. The Member was initially engaged to perform a Valuation and to provide a Valuation Report, which constitutes a Valuation Engagement. The Client's subsequent instruction to adopt the Client's existing forecast of cash flows amounts to a limitation on the scope of work because it restricts the Member's freedom to employ the Valuation Procedures that are reasonable and appropriate taking into consideration all relevant facts and circumstances of the Engagement and the instruction could have a material impact on the estimate of value. Accordingly, from that moment the Engagement ceased to be a Valuation Engagement and became a Limited Scope Valuation Engagement.

Example 4 Valuation of equity for capital gains tax where Valuation date is eight years ago and information lost

Facts: The facts are the same as for Example 1 except that the valuation date is eight years ago and there is less information available now due to the subsequent destruction of many documents in accordance with the company's document retention policy and the departure of key staff. Despite this, there are some relevant documents, including financial statements for the three years up to the valuation date. The relative lack of information means that the Member is not able to choose the Valuation Approaches and Valuation Methods that the Member would otherwise consider appropriate, and is not able to apply Valuation Procedures to the extent to which the Member would otherwise consider appropriate.

Analysis: This is a Valuation Service. The Member has been engaged to perform a Valuation and provide a Valuation Report. A hypothetical seller and a hypothetical buyer standing at the valuation date eight years ago would have had more information available to them then than the Member has now for the purpose of performing a Valuation at a date eight years ago. The scope of work is limited or restricted because the relative lack of information restricts the Member's freedom to choose and apply Valuation Approaches, Valuation Methods and Valuation Procedures. Accordingly, the Engagement is a Limited Scope Valuation Engagement.

Example 5 Valuation of equity for capital gains tax where records are sparse

Facts: The facts are the same as for Example 1 except that the company maintains records that are very sparse (albeit compliant with legal requirements).

Analysis: This is a Valuation Service. The Member has been engaged to perform a Valuation and provide a Valuation Report. The sparse nature of the company's records does not amount to a limitation or restriction on scope because a hypothetical seller and a hypothetical buyer do not have any better information available to them. The fact of the sparse records is a characteristic of the company being valued and, therefore, is something that will be reflected in the estimate of value. The Engagement is a Valuation Engagement.

APES

Example 6 Valuation of equity for capital gains tax with limited time

Facts: The facts are the same as for Example 1 except that the Member is required to deliver a Valuation Report within a period of time that is too short to allow the Member to perform all of the Valuation Procedures that the Member otherwise considers appropriate.

Analysis: This is a Valuation Service. The Member has been engaged to perform a Valuation and provide a Valuation Report. The scope of work is limited or restricted because the short timeframe restricts the Member's freedom to choose and apply Valuation Procedures. Hence the Engagement is a Limited Scope Valuation Engagement.

Example 7 Valuation of shareholding for capital gains tax with assumption on the value of all equity

Facts: A Member in Public Practice is engaged to perform a Valuation of a shareholding in a company for the purpose of capital gains tax and to provide a written report to the Client. The Member is instructed to assume a particular figure for the value of all of the issued share capital of the company.

Analysis: This is a Valuation Service. The Member has been engaged to perform a Valuation and provide a Valuation Report where the scope of work is limited or restricted in that the Member is instructed to assume the value of all of the issued share capital. Otherwise the Member is free to apply the Valuation Approaches, Valuation Methods and Valuation Procedures the Member considers appropriate in determining an estimate of value of the shareholding. This freedom means the engagement is not a Calculation Engagement. The Engagement is a Limited Scope Valuation Engagement because the scope of work is limited or restricted.

Example 8 Valuation of shareholding for capital gains tax with assumptions on the value of all equity and percentage discounts for the lack of control and marketability

Facts: The facts are the same as for Example 7 except that in addition to being instructed to assume a particular figure for the value of all of the issued share capital of the company, the Member is instructed to assume particular percentage discounts for the lack of control and marketability associated with the shareholding.

Analysis: This is a Valuation Service. The Member has been engaged to perform a Valuation and provide a Valuation Report where the scope of work is limited or restricted in that the Member is instructed to assume the value of all of the issued share capital and to assume certain percentage discounts for the lack of control and marketability associated with the shareholding. The Engagement is a Calculation Engagement because the Member and the Client have agreed the Valuation Approaches, Valuation Methods and Valuation Procedures the Member will apply, thereby eliminating the Member's freedom to choose. The performance of the Calculation Engagement is a Valuation Service.

Example 9 Valuation of Employer's intangible assets for tax consolidation

Facts: A Member in Business is assigned by the Member's Employer to perform a Valuation of the intangible assets of a company acquired by the Employer for the purpose of tax consolidation and to provide a written report to the Employer.

Analysis: This is a Valuation Service. The Member has been engaged to perform a Valuation and to provide a Valuation Report, which constitutes a Valuation Engagement.

Example 10 Limited scope Valuation for mergers and acquisitions advice

Facts: A Member in Public Practice is engaged to provide mergers and acquisitions advice to a Client contemplating a potential acquisition of a business. Part of the instructions includes performing an indicative Valuation of the target business and providing an oral Valuation Report.

Analysis: This is a Valuation Service to the extent of the indicative Valuation. The Member has been engaged to perform an indicative Valuation and to provide a Valuation Report, which constitutes a Limited Scope Valuation Engagement.

Example 11 Estimate of price for advice on sale of a company

Facts: A Member in Public Practice is engaged to provide advice and assistance with respect to the sale of a company. As part of the sale process the Member is asked to provide generic valuation statistics and parameters relevant to the industry in which the company operates.

Analysis: This is not a Valuation Service. Even if some Valuation Procedures are conducted the Member has not been engaged to perform a Valuation or to provide a Valuation Report. The Member has been engaged to provide ancillary services related to the sale of a company.

Example 12 Limited scope Valuation of Employer's business for potential sale

Facts: A Member in Business is assigned by the Member's Employer to perform an indicative Valuation of a business owned by the Employer for the purpose of its potential sale and to provide an oral report to the Employer.

Analysis: This is a Valuation Service. The Member has been assigned to perform a Limited Scope Valuation and to provide a Valuation Report to the Member's Employer, which constitutes a Limited Scope Valuation Engagement.

Example 13 Limited scope Valuation for estate planning advice

Facts: A Member in Public Practice is engaged to provide estate planning advice. As a required input to providing that advice, the Member performs an indicative Valuation of a business and provides an oral Valuation Report to the Client.

Analysis: This is a Valuation Service to the extent of performing the indicative Valuation of the business and providing the Valuation Report, which constitutes a Limited Scope Valuation Engagement.

Example 14 Valuation assumptions for estate planning advice

Facts: A Member in Public Practice is engaged to provide tax advice in respect of an estate planning engagement. As part of the estate planning process, the Member provides assumptions of values of the assets to assess the potential tax consequences. The Member is not involved in determining the value of the estate.

Analysis: This is not a Valuation Service. Even if some Valuation Procedures are conducted the Member has not been engaged to perform a Valuation or to provide a Valuation Report. The Member has been engaged to provide tax advice in respect of estate planning.

Example 15 Independent expert report for takeover offer

Facts: A Member in Public Practice is engaged by a Client who is the target of a takeover offer to prepare an independent expert report on whether the takeover offer is "fair and reasonable". As noted in paragraph RG 111.10 of ASIC's Regulatory Guide 111 "Content of Expert Reports", an offer is "fair" if "the value of the offer price or consideration is equal to or greater than the value of the securities the subject of the offer". The Member will perform a Valuation of the securities for the purpose of assessing if the offer is "fair". In accordance with section 640 of the Corporations Act 2001, the independent expert's report will accompany the target's statement that will be sent to the shareholders of the Client.

Analysis: This is a Valuation Service to the extent of performing the Valuation of the securities and providing the Valuation Report. Although the Member has been engaged to express an opinion on whether the takeover offer is "fair and reasonable", the accepted meaning of "fair" (as stated in ASIC's Regulatory Guide 111) clearly implies that a Valuation is to be performed. Thus the Member has been engaged, in part, to perform a Valuation and to provide a Valuation Report, which constitutes a Valuation Engagement.

Example 16 Independent expert report for scheme of arrangement

Facts: A Member in Public Practice is engaged by a Client who is the target of a friendly takeover to be achieved by way of a scheme of arrangement, to prepare an expert's report on whether a scheme of arrangement is "in the best interests of the members of the company" in accordance with clause 8303 of Schedule 8 of the Corporations Regulations 2001. As noted in paragraph RG 111.16 of ASIC's Regulatory Guide 111 "Content of Expert Reports", in such a case the expert is expected to provide an opinion as to whether the proposal is "fair and reasonable" as that phrase is understood for the purpose of section 640 of the Corporations Act 2001. The Member will perform a Valuation of the securities for the purpose of assessing if the offer is "fair". The expert's report will, if the court directs, accompany the explanatory statement and notice of meeting sent to shareholders of the company.

Analysis: This is a Valuation Service to the extent of performing the Valuation of the securities and providing the Valuation Report. Although the Member has been engaged to express an opinion on whether the proposal is "in the best interests of the members of the company", accepted practice (as stated in ASIC's Regulatory Guide 111) implies that a Valuation is to be performed. Thus the Member has been engaged, in part, to perform a Valuation and to provide a Valuation Report, which constitutes a Valuation Engagement.

Example 17 Independent expert report for the compulsory acquisition of securities

Facts: A Member in Public Practice is engaged by a Client who has acquired 90% of the securities of a particular class of a company and wishes to issue a notice to acquire compulsorily the balance of the securities. The Member is engaged to provide an expert's report under section 667A of the Corporations Act 2001 on whether "the terms proposed in the notice give a fair value for the securities concerned". In accordance with section 664C, a copy of the expert's report will be sent to each holder of securities.

Analysis: This is a Valuation Service. The Member has been engaged to perform a Valuation and to provide a Valuation Report, which constitutes a Valuation Engagement.

Example 18 Audit procedures on Valuation assertions

Facts: A Member in Public Practice is engaged to perform an audit. The Member will perform procedures to test the valuation assertions (as defined in Australian Auditing Standard ASA 500 *Audit Evidence*) of the financial statement balances as part of the audit Engagement. The results of these procedures will be documented in the Member's working papers and will not be communicated to the Client.

Analysis: This is not a Valuation Service. The Member has not been engaged to perform a Valuation or to provide a Valuation Report. The Member has been engaged to perform an audit and the procedures to test the valuation assertions (as defined in the Auditing Standards) are only performed as part of the audit Engagement.

Example 19 Audit procedures on Client's Valuations

Facts: A Member in Public Practice is engaged to perform an audit. The Member will audit/review the valuation models or calculations prepared by the Client to test assets (including goodwill) for impairment as part of the Member's audit procedures in accordance with Auditing Standards. The procedures performed will be documented in the Member's working papers and will not be communicated to the Client.

Analysis: This is not a Valuation Service. The Member has not been engaged to perform a Valuation or to provide a Valuation Report. The Member has been engaged to perform an audit and the procedures to test impairment are only performed as part of the audit Engagement.

Example 20 Limited scope Valuation of Employer's business

Facts: A Member in Business is assigned to perform an indicative Valuation of the business of the Employer as part of the Employer's procedures in respect of testing assets (including goodwill) for impairment for financial reporting purposes.

Analysis: This is a Valuation Service. The Member has been assigned to perform an indicative Valuation and to provide a Valuation Report which constitutes a Limited Scope Valuation Engagement.

Example 21 Opinion as receiver and manager on realisable value of business

Facts: A Member in Public Practice is engaged by a secured creditor as a receiver and manager of the assets and undertaking of a company. In reporting to the Client the Member expresses an opinion on the amount that might be realised from the sale of the company's business.

Analysis: This is not a Valuation Service. Even if some Valuation Procedures are conducted the Member does not perform a Valuation and is not engaged to provide a Valuation Report. The Member has been engaged to perform an insolvency service and the opinion was expressed as part of performing that service.

Example 22 Opinion as expert witness on lost profits

Facts: A Member in Public Practice is engaged to act as an expert witness in litigation and to express an opinion on the quantum of damages suffered by the plaintiff as a result of an alleged wrong-doing by the defendant. The Member is instructed that the damages are to be determined by reference to lost profits and that the court must award damages as a once-off lump sum. In performing this task, the Member:

(a) will calculate the lost profits caused by the alleged wrong-doing by comparing the profits that the plaintiff would have earned but for the alleged wrong-doing with the profits that the plaintiff will earn given the alleged wrong-doing; and

(b) will calculate the present value of those lost profits.

The Member will provide a written report and may later give oral evidence at the court hearing.

Analysis: This is not a Valuation Service because the Member has not been engaged to perform a Valuation (i.e. the Member has not been engaged to determine an estimate of value of a business, business ownership interest, security or intangible asset).

Example 23 Opinion as expert witness on value of business

Facts: A Member in Public Practice is engaged to act as an expert witness in litigation and to express an opinion on the quantum of damages suffered by the plaintiff as a result of an alleged breach of contract by the defendant. The Member is instructed that the damages are to be determined by reference to the value of the plaintiff's business before the alleged breach of contract and the Member is instructed to express an opinion on that value. The Member will provide a written report and may later give oral evidence at the court hearing.

Analysis: This is a Valuation Service because the Member has been engaged to perform a Valuation and to provide a Valuation Report which constitutes a Valuation Engagement. It is a Valuation because the Member has been engaged to determine an estimate of value of a business by applying Valuation Approaches, Valuation Methods and Valuation Procedures.

Appendix 2

Summary of revisions to the previous APES 225 (Issued July 2008)

APES 225 *Valuation Services* originally issued in July 2008 has been revised by APESB in May 2012. A summary of the revisions is given in the table below.

Table of revisions*

Paragraph affected	How affected
1.1	Amended
2 – Definition of Calculation Engagement	Amended
2 – Definition of Firm	Amended
2 – Definition of Limited Scope Valuation Engagement	Amended
2 – Definition of Premise of Value	Added
2 – Definition of Valuation	Amended
2 – Definition of Valuation Engagement	Amended
3.8	Amended
4.2	Added
4.4	Amended
4.5	Amended
5.2(h)	Amended
5.2(i)	Amended
5.2(j)	Amended
5.2(k)	Amended
5.2(o)	Amended
5.2(p)	Amended
5.2(q)	Amended
5.2(r)	Amended
6.1	Amended
Appendix 1 (Schematic Diagram and 8 additional examples developed)	Amended
Appendix 2	Added

* *Refer Technical Update 2012/1*

APES 305
Terms of Engagement

(Issued December 2007: revised June 2009)

Issued by the Accounting Professional and Ethical Standards Board.

Note from the Institute of Chartered Accountants Australia

This note, prepared by the technical editor, is not part of APES 305.

Historical development

December 2007: APES 305 issued. From 1 July 2008 it was mandatory for all professional accountants working in public practice to document and communicate the terms of engagement when providing professional services to clients. APES 305 replaced APS 2 from that date.

June 2009: APES 305 reissued containing minor editorial amendments that did not alter the substance of the Standard.

APES

Contents

1. Scope and application

1.1 Accounting Professional & Ethical Standards Board Limited (APESB) issues the Standard APES 305 *Terms of Engagement* **(the Standard)**, which is effective for Engagements commencing on or after 01 July 2008.

1.2 APES 305 sets the standards in respect of Terms of Engagement for Members in Public Practice in the provision of quality and ethical Professional Services to Clients. The mandatory requirements of this Standard are in **bold** type, preceded or followed by discussion or explanations in grey type. In some instances there are specific standards applicable to Members in Public Practice issued by other standard setting bodies or specific requirements of statutes in respect of Terms of Engagement, for example ASA 210: *Terms of Audit Engagements* issued by the Auditing and Assurance Standards Board which governs audit Engagements. Compliance with these other standards or statutes should result in compliance with APES 305.

1.3 Members in Public Practice in Australia shall follow the mandatory requirements of APES 305 when they provide Professional Services to Clients.

1.4 Members in Public Practice outside of Australia shall follow the provisions of APES 305 to the extent to which they are not prevented from so doing by specific requirements of local laws and/or regulations.

1.5 Members in Public Practice shall be familiar with relevant professional standards and guidance notes when providing Professional Services. All Members shall comply with the fundamental principles outlined in the Code.

1.6 The Standard is not intended to detract from any responsibilities which may be imposed by law or regulation.

1.7 All references to professional standards, guidance notes and legislation are references to those provisions as amended from time to time.

1.8 In applying APES 305 Members in Public Practice should be guided not merely by the words but also by the spirit of the Standard and the Code.

2. Definitions

For the purpose of this Standard:

Client means an individual, firm, entity or organisation to whom or to which Professional Services are provided by a Member in Public Practice in respect of Engagements of either a recurring or demand nature.

Code means APES 110 *Code of Ethics for Professional Accountants*.

Engagement means an agreement, whether written or otherwise, between a Member in Public Practice and a Client relating to the provision of Professional Services by a Member in Public Practice. However, consultations with a prospective Client prior to such agreement are not part of an Engagement.

Engagement Document means the document (i.e. letter, agreement or any other appropriate means) in which the Terms of Engagement are specified in a written form.

Firm means (a) a sole practitioner, partnership, corporation or other entity of professional accountants;
(b) an entity that controls such parties through ownership, management or other means;
(c) an entity controlled by such parties through ownership, management or other means; or
(d) an Auditor-General's office or department.

Member means a member of a professional body that has adopted this Standard as applicable to their membership, as defined by that professional body.

Member in Public Practice means a Member, irrespective of functional classification (e.g. audit, tax, or consulting) in a Firm that provides Professional Services. The term is also used to refer to a Firm of Members in Public Practice and means a practice entity as defined by the applicable professional body.

Professional Services means services requiring accountancy or related skills performed by a professional accountant including accounting, auditing, taxation, management consulting and financial management services.

Terms of Engagement means the terms and conditions that are agreed between the Client and the Member in Public Practice for the Engagement.

3. Terms of Engagement for Professional Services

3.1 A Member in Public Practice shall document and communicate the Terms of Engagement when providing Professional Services to Clients.

3.2 The practice of documenting and communicating the Terms of Engagement should ensure that there is a clear understanding between the Client and the Member in Public Practice regarding the Terms of Engagement.

3.3 It is in the interests of both the Client and Member in Public Practice that the Member in Public Practice documents and communicates the Terms of Engagement, preferably before its commencement, to avoid misunderstandings with respect to the Engagement.

3.4 A Member in Public Practice shall document the Terms of Engagement in the Engagement Document.

3.5 The Terms of Engagement need not be in the form of a letter or agreement. For example, a standard format handout, brochure, leaflet or electronic communication is also acceptable.

3.6 The objectives and scope of some Engagements are established by law. Documentation of the Terms of Engagement cannot reduce obligations imposed by law. Where the Engagement is undertaken under Statute a Member in Public Practice should refer to the applicable provisions of the law in the Engagement Document.

4. General contents of an Engagement Document

4.1 The following is a guide to matters that should, for most Engagements, be considered for inclusion in an Engagement Document. Engagement Documents will vary according to the nature of the Engagement and the terms of appointment of the Member in Public Practice. The matters referred to below in paragraphs 4.2 to 4.10 should therefore be varied to meet the individual requirements and circumstances of each Engagement.

4.2 *Purpose*: The Engagement Document should explain that its purpose is to set out and confirm the understanding of the Member in Public Practice of the Terms of Engagement.

4.3 *Objectives of the Engagement*: A brief summary of the objectives of the Engagement including reference to the fact that:

(a) procedures to be performed will be limited exclusively to those related to the Engagement;

(b) neither an audit nor a review will be conducted and, accordingly, no assurance will be expressed (if applicable); and

(c) unless otherwise agreed, the Engagement cannot be relied upon to disclose irregularities, including fraud, other illegal acts and errors that may occur.

APES

4.4 *Scope of the Engagement*: Pertinent details of such matters as:

(a) time periods covered by the Engagement;

(b) period of appointment and time schedules;

(c) references to any legislation and professional standards that may be relevant to the Engagement;

(d) Client operations or procedures to be included in the Engagement;

(e) details of information to be provided by the Client;

(f) any limitations on the conduct of the Engagement; and

(g) other matters considered necessary or appropriate.

4.5 *Engagement output*: Details of reports or other anticipated outputs, including:

(a) expected timing;

(b) the intended use and distribution of reports;

(c) the nature of any anticipated disclaimer or arrangement that limits the liability of the Member in Public Practice (appropriate limitation of liability clauses for Members in Public Practice participating in Professional Standards Legislation schemes) with respect to the Client or any other user of the results of the Engagement.

4.6 *Relative responsibilities*: Responsibilities agreed upon, detailing those acknowledged to be the responsibility of:

(a) the Member in Public Practice, including reference to relevant confidentiality requirements and the impact of them on the quality review program of the relevant professional body to which the Member in Public Practice belongs;

(b) the Client, noting the fact that the Client is responsible for the completeness and accuracy of information supplied to the Member in Public Practice; and

(c) any third party.

4.7 *Involvement of other Members in Public Practice*: Where the work of another Member in Public Practice is to be used on some aspects of the Engagement, the details of this involvement should be documented in the Engagement Document.

4.8 *Fees and billing arrangements*: Reference to the basis of fees (e.g. time based billing, fixed price contracts, contingent fee arrangements or other similar agreement). Details of agreed upon billing schedules should also be included.

4.9 *Ownership of documents*: The Engagement Document should make clear who owns any documents produced as a result of the Engagement or provided by the Client for such a purpose including electronic data. If a Member in Public Practice has a policy of seeking to exercise a right of lien over such documents in the event of a dispute with the Client, this policy should be disclosed in the Engagement Document communicated to the Client including the process for dealing with disputes over the lien.

4.10 *Confirmation by the Client*: Request for a response from the Client confirming its understanding of the Terms of Engagement as outlined in the Engagement Document. It is preferable for this confirmation of Client acceptance of the Terms of Engagement to be obtained in a written form.

5. Recurring Engagements

5.1 For a recurring Engagement, the Member in Public Practice may decide not to send an Engagement Document on each occasion. The following factors may affect the decision of the Member in Public Practice to issue an Engagement Document:

(a) any indication that the Client misunderstands the objectives and scope of the Engagement;

(b) any significant changes in the Terms of Engagement;

(c) a recent change of Client management or ownership;

(d) a significant change in the nature or size of the Client's business; or

(e) legal requirements.

6. Limitation of liability

6.1 **A Member in Public Practice who is participating in a limitation of liability scheme shall be familiar with the relevant Professional Standards Legislation. A Member in Public Practice, who incorporates a limitation of liability provision in the Engagement Document, shall comply with the legislation and the relevant obligations (e.g. insurance, business assets, risk management, quality control etc.), imposed.**

6.2 **A Member in Public Practice who is a participant in a scheme under Professional Standards Legislation shall advise the Client that the Member's liability may be limited under the scheme.**

Conformity with International Pronouncements

The International Ethics Standard Board for Accountants (IESBA) has not issued a pronouncement equivalent to APES 305.

APES

APES 310
Dealing with Client Monies

(Issued December 2010)

Issued by the Accounting Professional and Ethical Standards Board.

Note from the Institute of Chartered Accountants Australia

This note, prepared by the technical editor, is not part of APES 310.

Historical development

December 2010: APES 310 was issued in December 2010 to replace Miscellaneous Professional Standard APS 10 'Trust Accounts'. It is effective from 1 July 2011 and has no international equivalent.

Contents

1. Scope and application

1.1 Accounting Professional & Ethical Standards Board Limited (APESB) issues professional standard APES 310 *Dealing with Client Monies* (**the Standard**), which is effective from 1 July 2011. This Standard supersedes APS 10 *Trust Accounts* and GN 3 *Operation of Trust Accounts*. Earlier adoption of this Standard is permitted.

1.2 APES 310 sets the standards for Members in Public Practice who Deal with Client Monies or who act as an Auditor of Client Monies. The mandatory requirements of this Standard are in **bold-type (black lettering)**, preceded or followed by discussion or explanations in normal type (grey lettering). APES 310 should be read in conjunction with other professional duties of Members and any legal obligations that may apply.

1.3 Members in Public Practice in Australia shall follow the mandatory requirements of APES 310 when they Deal with Client Monies or when they act as an Auditor of Client Monies.

1.4 Members in Public Practice practising outside of Australia shall follow the mandatory requirements of APES 310 to the extent to which they are not prevented from so doing by specific requirements of local laws and/or regulations.

1.5 Members in Public Practice shall be familiar with relevant Professional Standards and guidance notes when providing Professional Services. All Members shall comply with the fundamental principles outlined in the Code.

1.6 The Standard is not intended to detract from any responsibilities which may be imposed by law or regulation.

1.7 All references to Professional Standards, guidance notes and legislation are references to those provisions as amended from time to time.

1.8 In applying the requirements outlined in APES 310, Members in Public Practice should be guided not merely by the words but also by the spirit of the Standard and the Code.

APES

2. Definitions

For the purpose of this Standard:

Applicable Year-End Date means a date, which once determined cannot be changed without the approval of the applicable Professional Body. The Applicable Year-End Date must occur within 12 months of the month-end following the Member in Public Practice opening a Trust Account or the Member obtaining the authority to operate a Client Bank Account.

Auditing and Assurance Standards means:

- the AUASB standards, as described in ASA 100 *Preamble to AUASB Standards*, ASA 101 *Preamble to Australian Auditing Standards* and the *Foreword to AUASB Pronouncements*, issued by the AUASB, and operative from the date specified in each standard; and
- those standards issued by the AuASB which have not yet been revised and reissued (whether as standards or as guidance) by the AUASB, to the extent that they are not inconsistent with the AUASB standards.

AuASB means the Auditing and Assurance Standards Board which issued Australian Auditing and Assurance Standards up to 30 June 2004, under the auspices of the Australian Accounting Research Foundation, a joint venture of CPA Australia and the Institute of Chartered Accountants in Australia.

AUASB means the Australian statutory body called the Auditing and Assurance Standards Board established under section 227A of the *Australian Securities and Investments Commission Act 2001*.

Auditor of Client Monies means a Member in Public Practice who:

- has been engaged to perform an audit engagement of another Member in Public Practice's compliance with this Standard; and
- holds a certificate of public practice of one of the Professional Bodies.

Business Day means a day that is not a Saturday, Sunday, public holiday or bank holiday.

Client means an individual, firm, entity or organisation to whom or to which Professional Services are provided by a Member in Public Practice in respect of engagements of either a recurring or demand nature.

Client Bank Account means a Client's bank account held with a Financial Institution for which a Member in Public Practice, acting either solely or in conjunction with one or more people, holds a signing authority.

Client Monies means any Monies (in whatever form) coming into the control of a Member in Public Practice or any of the Member's Personnel which are the property of a Client and includes Monies to which the Member or the Member's Personnel have no present entitlement. "Control" means where a Member or any of the Member's Personnel, acting either solely or in conjunction with one or more people, can authorise the transacting of Client Monies.

Code means APES 110 *Code of Ethics for Professional Accountants*.

Deals (or Dealing) with Client Monies means to hold, receive or disburse Client Monies.

Deficiency means a deficit or shortfall of Client Monies, as disclosed by Records maintained by a Member in Public Practice, or in the records of a Financial Institution at which an account is held. However, it does not include any Deficiency which the Auditor of Client Monies is satisfied was caused solely by an error of a Financial Institution which has been subsequently rectified.

Financial Institution means a bank, building society, credit union or such other financial entity that is regulated by the Australian Prudential Regulation Authority (APRA) in accordance with the *Banking Act 1959*.

Firm means

(a) A sole practitioner, partnership, corporation or other entity of professional accountants;

(b) An entity that controls such parties through ownership, management or other means;

(c) An entity controlled by such parties through ownership, management or other means; or

(d) An Auditor-General's office or department.

Member means a member of a Professional Body that has adopted this Standard as applicable to their membership, as defined by that Professional Body.

Member in Public Practice means a Member, irrespective of functional classification (e.g., audit, tax or consulting) in a Firm that provides Professional Services. The term is also used to refer to a Firm of Members in Public Practice and means a practice entity as defined by the applicable Professional Body.

Monies means cash, foreign currency, any negotiable instrument and any security, the title to which is transferable by delivery (for example, bills of exchange and promissory notes), including delivery by electronic funds transfer.

Personnel for the purposes of this standard means employees, officers, directors, contractors or agents.

Professional Bodies means the Institute of Chartered Accountants in Australia, CPA Australia and the National Institute of Accountants.

Professional Standards means all standards issued by Accounting Professional & Ethical Standards Board Limited and all professional and ethical requirements of the applicable Professional Body.

Professional Services means services requiring accountancy or related skills performed by a Member in Public Practice including accounting, auditing, taxation, management consulting and financial management services.

Records means documentation evidencing the Dealing with Client Monies via a Trust Account or a Client Bank Account, or otherwise Dealing with Client Monies in accordance with a Client's instructions.

Trust Account means an account opened by a Member in Public Practice or by another party on behalf of the Member with a Financial Institution which is kept for the sole purpose of Dealing with Client Monies. A Trust Account can be in the form of:

- one or more accounts Dealing with Monies of one Client; or
- one or more accounts Dealing with Monies of multiple Clients.

3. Fundamental responsibilities of Members in Public Practice

3.1 **A Member in Public Practice who Deals with Client Monies or acts as an Auditor of Client Monies shall comply with Section 100 *Introduction and Fundamental Principles* of the Code and relevant law.**

3.2 **A Member in Public Practice who Deals with Client Monies or acts as an Auditor of Client Monies shall comply with Section 220 *Conflicts of Interest* and Section 280 *Objectivity – All Services* of the Code.**

Public interest

3.3 **In accordance with Section 100 *Introduction and Fundamental Principles* of the Code, a Member in Public Practice shall observe and comply with the Member's public interest obligations when the Member Deals with Client Monies or acts as an Auditor of Client Monies.**

Professional competence and due care

3.4 **A Member in Public Practice who Deals with Client Monies or acts as an Auditor of Client Monies shall maintain professional competence and exercise due care in the performance of the Member's work in accordance with Section 130 *Professional Competence and Due Care* of the Code.**

Confidentiality

3.5 **In accordance with Section 140 *Confidentiality* of the Code, a Member in Public Practice who acquires confidential information in the course of the Member's work for a Client shall not use that information for any purpose other than the proper performance of the professional work for that Client.**

Part A: Professional obligations of a Member in Public Practice who Deals with Client Monies

4. General principles

4.1 A Member in Public Practice who Deals with Client Monies shall comply with Section 270 *Custody of Client Assets* of the Code.

4.2 Subject to paragraphs 4.11, 4.12 and 6.7, a Member in Public Practice shall only Deal with Client Monies through a Client Bank Account or a Trust Account and only in accordance with the Client's instructions.

4.3 It is preferable that a Client's instructions are in writing. Where a Client gives an oral instruction, a contemporaneous note should be made and kept on file by the Member in Public Practice recording the relevant details.

4.4 A Member in Public Practice shall be accountable for all Client Monies and keep Client Monies separate from all other Monies of the Member.

4.5 A Member in Public Practice shall implement appropriate internal controls and procedures in respect of the operation of a Trust Account and a Client Bank Account. The Member shall take all reasonable steps to ensure that those internal controls achieve the following objectives:

(a) Client Monies are dealt with in accordance with the Client's instructions and this Standard;

(b) A Trust Account is properly safeguarded and accounted for; and

(c) A Client Bank Account is properly safeguarded against unauthorised access or use.

4.6 Subject to paragraph 4.7, a Member in Public Practice shall not obtain any benefit from Dealing with Client Monies, including benefits deriving from the deposit and/or investment of Client Monies, without prior written authority from the Client.

4.7 A Member in Public Practice shall only charge professional fees in respect of Dealing with Client Monies in accordance with Section 240 *Fees and Other Types of Remuneration* of the Code.

4.8 A Member in Public Practice shall bear any Financial Institution, statutory or other government charges in respect of a Trust Account.

4.9 A Member in Public Practice shall only deposit the Member's own funds to a Trust Account:

(a) to meet any charges made to the Trust Account where the Financial Institution has made such charges to the Trust Account in error, instead of to the Member's general bank account; or

(b) to meet a Financial Institution's prescribed minimum requirements for an ongoing account balance.

4.10 A Member in Public Practice who is acting as a trustee or under a power of attorney shall comply with the Member's legal and fiduciary duties as trustee or attorney when Dealing with Client Monies, and shall apply this Standard to the extent practicable.

4.11 A Member in Public Practice shall not:

(a) receive or pay into a Trust Account or a Client Bank Account; or

(b) disburse out of a Trust Account or a Client Bank Account

any Monies if the Member believes on reasonable grounds that they were obtained from, or are to be used for, illegal activities or that Dealing with the Monies is otherwise unlawful.

4.12 When Dealing with Client Monies, a Member in Public Practice shall not be involved in any money laundering transactions or in the utilisation of the proceeds of crime or terrorist financing.

5. Opening a Trust Account

5.1 **A Member in Public Practice who Deals in Client Monies shall open a Trust Account at a Financial Institution in the name of the Member or the Member's Firm and include the term "Trust Account" in its title, unless the Member has been authorised to operate a Client Bank Account.**

5.2 Paragraph 5.1 does not apply where a Member in Public Practice who does not wish to Deal in Client Monies receives Client Monies and dispatches them within 5 business days to the Client, drawer or sender as appropriate.

5.3 **A Member in Public Practice shall document the process followed to establish the identity of a Client and the source of Client Monies prior to Dealing with Client Monies.**

5.4 **A Member in Public Practice shall open and maintain a separate Trust Account where a Client requests one.**

5.5 **A Member in Public Practice shall not open a Trust Account with a Financial Institution unless its terms and conditions relating to Trust Accounts require that:**

(a) **all Monies standing to the credit of that account are held by the Member as Client Monies and that the Financial Institution is not entitled to combine the account with any other account, or to exercise any right to set-off or counterclaim against Monies in that account in respect of any sum owed to the Financial Institution on any other account; and**

(b) **any interest payable in respect of the account balance is credited to that account.**

5.6 **A Member in Public Practice shall retain a copy of the terms and conditions of the Financial Institution relating to a Trust Account as part of the Member's Records and, where requested, provide a copy to the Client within 10 Business Days of that request.**

5.7 **A Member in Public Practice shall inform the Client in writing:**

(a) **no later than at the time of initial deposit into a Trust Account, the details of the Financial Institution at which the Client Monies are to be held; and**

(b) **if there is a change to the existing Financial Institution arrangements, within 10 Business Days where the Client Monies are held.**

6. Dealing with Client Monies

Holding and receiving Client Monies

6.1 **Subject to paragraph 6.7, a Member in Public Practice shall deposit Client Monies into a Financial Institution within 3 Business Days of receipt.**

6.2 **A Member in Public Practice shall only hold Client Monies in a Trust Account for the period necessary to enable the purpose for which the Client Monies were received to be discharged.**

6.3 **A Member in Public Practice receiving Client Monies where the payee is no longer a Client, or the intended recipient is unknown to the Member, shall return the Monies within 10 Business Days to the drawer or sender as appropriate.**

6.4 **Where a Member in Public Practice is unable to disburse Client Monies to the Client, payee, drawer or sender, the Member shall comply with relevant legislation in respect of unclaimed Monies.**

6.5 **A Member in Public Practice shall record the following information for Client Monies received, or Monies received for deposit into a Client Bank Account:**

(a) **the name of the person from whom Monies were received;**

(b) **the amount of Monies;**

(c) **the Client for whose benefit Monies are held;**

(d) **the purpose for which Monies were received or other description of the Monies;**

APES

(e) the date on which Monies were received;

(f) the form in which Monies were received; and

(g) in relation to Client Monies of a kind referred to in paragraph 6.7, the location where the Monies are held.

6.6 **A Member in Public Practice shall issue an acknowledgement to the Client within 21 Business Days or as otherwise agreed with the Client containing the details specified in paragraph 6.5 and stating that the Member has deposited the Client Monies into a Trust Account or a Client Bank Account.**

6.7 **A Member in Public Practice who receives Client Monies that are not capable of being deposited into a Financial Institution shall safeguard the Monies against unauthorised use, record details in an appropriate register, and issue an acknowledgement to the Client within 21 Business Days containing the details specified in paragraph 6.5.**

6.8 Client Monies that are not capable of being deposited into a Trust Account or a Client Bank Account may include promissory notes or a coin collection. In such circumstances the requirements of paragraphs 4.1 and 6.7 apply.

Disbursement of Client Monies

6.9 **A Member in Public Practice shall disburse Client Monies within 3 Business Days of receipt of instructions in respect of the disbursement or in accordance with the terms of engagement.**

6.10 **Only a Member in Public Practice, or any persons authorised in accordance with paragraph 6.12, shall operate the Member's Trust Account.**

6.11 **A Member in Public Practice shall ensure that the Member has appropriate Records to support transacting electronic funds transfers from a Trust Account or a Client Bank Account.**

6.12 **In circumstances where a Member in Public Practice is not available to authorise Trust Account transactions in a timely manner, the Member shall delegate in writing the Member's authority to effect transactions to:**

(a) another Member in Public Practice;

(b) a solicitor holding a current practising certificate;

(c) a suitably competent person employed by the Member; or

(d) a manager of a branch of a Financial Institution.

6.13 **A Member in Public Practice who wishes to disburse Monies from a Trust Account or a Client Bank Account relating to professional fees and/or expenses due from a Client, shall obtain the Client's written approval prior to such disbursement.**

6.14 **A Member in Public Practice shall not make a disbursement to or on behalf of a Client from a Trust Account that exceeds the amount of funds standing to the credit of that Client.**

7. Documentation

7.1 **A Member in Public Practice shall maintain Records to appropriately document transactions in respect of Client Monies.**

7.2 **A Member in Public Practice shall ensure that all interest earned on Trust Accounts is credited to the relevant Client's account.**

7.3 **A Member in Public Practice shall retain Records that:**

(a) enable transactions involving Client Monies to be audited;

(b) disclose the financial position of Client Monies; and

(c) clearly identify the transactions made on behalf of each Client.

7.4 **Subject to legislative requirements, a Member in Public Practice shall retain and ensure that all documentation in respect of Client Monies is accessible for at least 7 years.**

7.5 Subject to legislative requirements, a Member in Public Practice shall take reasonable steps to ensure that the Client authorises the Member's Professional Body to have access to the Member's Records in respect of Client Monies for the purposes of an inspection, quality review or disciplinary proceedings of the applicable Professional Body.

7.6 A Member in Public Practice shall keep Records in such a manner as to disclose clearly:

(a) the details of all transactions involving Client Monies, including:

(i) details of all Client Monies paid direct to the Client, or to a third party nominated by the Client;

(ii) details of all cheques received and endorsed by the Member for disbursement to the Client, or to a third party nominated by the Client;

(iii) details of all electronic funds transfers of Monies received, and of Monies transferred direct to the Client, or to a third party nominated by the Client; and

(iv) details of any errors in transactions involving Client Monies;

(b) the details and basis of calculation of all interest earned on Client Monies held in a Trust Account and that the interest has been applied by the Member in accordance with paragraph 5.5(b);

(c) the financial position of a Member's Trust Account and Client's Bank Account and the Client Monies therein; and

(d) the signatories for each Client Bank Account authorised by the Client.

7.7 A Member in Public Practice shall reconcile the Trust Account Records to the Trust Account at least every 25 Business Days. The Member shall correct any differences or errors within 5 Business Days.

7.8 A Member in Public Practice shall provide a statement containing details of the Member's application of Client Monies and any interest earned on Client Monies, either to the Client or to such other person as directed by the Client:

(a) in respect of all transactions, at least annually;

(b) upon completion of the matter requiring the maintenance of the Trust Account or Client Bank Account;

(c) in respect of any transaction, upon written request from the Client; or

(d) when a Trust Account or Client Bank Account is closed or if the Member's authority to operate a Client Bank Account is revoked.

7.9 A Member in Public Practice shall issue the statements referred to in:

(a) paragraph 7.8(a) within 30 Business Days of the Applicable Year-End Date;

(b) paragraphs 7.8(b) and 7.8(d) within 25 Business Days;

(c) paragraph 7.8(c) within 5 Business Days.

7.10 Where a Client receives Client Bank Account statements directly from a Financial Institution, a Member in Public Practice shall provide to the Client details of transactions undertaken by the Member within 25 Business Days of the end of each month or as otherwise agreed with the Client.

7.11 A Member in Public Practice who operates a Client Bank Account shall ensure, except when the Client also transacts business through the Client Bank Account and receives statements directly from the Financial Institution, that the Member's Records for the Client Bank Account are reconciled to the Financial Institution statements at least every 25 Business Days. The Member shall take action to correct any difference or error identified during the reconciliation within 5 Business Days of such identification.

8. Audit of a Member in Public Practice's compliance with this Standard

8.1 **Subject to legislative requirements, a Member in Public Practice shall ensure that the Member's compliance with the requirements of this Standard is audited annually within 3 months of the Applicable Year–End Date.**

8.2 **A Member in Public Practice who Deals with Client Monies shall appoint another Member in Public Practice as Auditor of Client Monies to perform the audit pursuant to the requirements of this Standard.**

8.3 Paragraphs 8.1 and 8.2 do not apply to a Member in Public Practice in circumstances where a Trust Account is audited in accordance with *Trust Accounts Act 1973* (Qld) or similar legislative requirements.

8.4 **A Member in Public Practice whose compliance with this Standard is audited shall bear the cost of the audit.**

8.5 **A Member in Public Practice shall:**

(a) allow the Member's Professional Body or the Auditor of Client Monies access to the Member's Records; and

(b) assist the Member's Professional Body or the Auditor of Client Monies in the performance of their duties.

8.6 **A Member in Public Practice shall notify the applicable Professional Body and the Auditor of Client Monies within 5 Business Days of becoming aware of any Deficiency of Client Monies occurring in the Trust Account along with details of corrective action taken by the Member.**

8.7 **A Member in Public Practice who proposes to change the existing Auditor of Client Monies, shall first obtain the approval of the applicable Professional Body.**

8.8 **A Member in Public Practice shall appoint a replacement Auditor of Client Monies within 10 Business Days of the resignation or removal of the existing Auditor of Client Monies.**

8.9 **Where a Member in Public Practice ceases public practice and:**

(a) another Member in Public Practice is willing to accept the transfer of obligations to transact Client Monies in accordance with this Standard, the Member ceasing public practice shall obtain the written consent of the Client prior to the transfer; or

(b) no other Member in Public Practice is willing to accept the transfer of obligations to transact Client Monies or written consent in accordance with paragraph 8.9(a) has not been obtained, the Member or their legal representative shall return Client Monies to the Client.

8.10 **Where the circumstances described in paragraph 8.9 are applicable, a Member in Public Practice shall engage an Auditor of Client Monies to audit the Member's compliance with this Standard for the period where the Member was responsible for Client Monies which has not otherwise been subject to audit.**

8.11 **A Member in Public Practice shall ensure that the Member's compliance with this Standard is audited within 3 months of ceasing to Deal with Client Monies.**

Part B: Professional obligations of an auditor of a Member in Public Practice's compliance with this Standard

9. Professional obligations of an Auditor of Client Monies

9.1 **Subject to any legal requirements, a Member in Public Practice who acts as an Auditor of Client Monies shall perform the audit in accordance with Auditing and Assurance Standards.**

9.2 **An Auditor of Client Monies shall prepare the auditor's report in accordance with Auditing and Assurance Standards. If the report contains a modified opinion, the Auditor of Client Monies shall lodge the report with the applicable Professional Body within 15 Business Days of completion of the audit.**

9.3 Appendix 1 to this Standard contains an example of an audit report.

9.4 **An Auditor of Client Monies shall comply with Section 291 *Independence – Other Assurance Engagements* of the Code.**

9.5 **An Auditor of Client Monies shall not undertake an audit of another Member in Public Practice's compliance with this Standard in circumstances where a reasonable and informed third party having knowledge of all relevant information, including safeguards applied would determine that the independence of the Auditor of Client Monies is impaired as a result of a past, existing or proposed relationship.**

9.6 **An Auditor of Client Monies shall report any Deficiency of Client Monies to the Member's Professional Body within 5 Business Days upon becoming aware of the Deficiency.**

9.7 **An Auditor of Client Monies shall report to the Member's Professional Body within 10 Business Days of becoming aware of any material:**

(a) **failure by a Member to comply with paragraphs 6.1 or 6.9 of this Standard;**

(b) **uncorrected error reflected in a statement issued by a Financial Institution; or**

(c) **circumstances where Client Monies have not been transacted or maintained in accordance with this Standard.**

9.8 **Subject to legislative requirements, an Auditor of Client Monies shall retain relevant working papers for a period of at least 7 years.**

9.9 **A Member in Public Practice who wishes to resign from the position of Auditor of Client Monies shall first obtain the written approval of the applicable Professional Body.**

Conformity with International Pronouncements

The International Ethics Standard Board for Accountants (IESBA) has not issued a pronouncement equivalent to APES 310.

APES

Appendix 1
Example of an audit report

To [The applicable Professional Body]

Report on the compliance of [Member or Firm] with the requirements of APES 310

We have audited the compliance of [Member or Firm] with the requirements of APES 310 *Dealing with Client Monies* (APES 310) for the [year ended …. / …. / ….].

The Responsibility of [Member or Firm] for compliance with APES 310

[Member or Firm] is responsible for compliance with the requirements of APES 310. This responsibility includes establishing and maintaining internal controls relevant to compliance with the requirements of APES 310.

Auditor's Responsibility

Our responsibility is to express a conclusion on [Member or Firm]'s compliance with the requirements of APES 310. Our audit has been conducted in accordance with applicable Standards on Assurance Engagements including ASAE 3100 *Compliance Engagements* and with APES 310, in order to state whether, in all material respects, [Member or Firm] has complied with the requirements of APES 310 for the [year ended …. / …. / ….]. Our procedures included examination, on a test basis, of evidence supporting [Member or Firm]'s compliance with APES 310. We believe that the audit evidence we have obtained is sufficient and appropriate to provide a basis for our conclusion. ASAE 3100 also requires us to comply with the relevant ethical requirements, including independence requirements of APES 110 *Code of Ethics for Professional Accountants*.

Limitations on Use

This audit report has been prepared for [the applicable Professional Body] in accordance with APES 310. We disclaim any assumption of responsibility for any reliance on this report to any persons or users other than [the applicable Professional Body], or for any purpose other than that for which it is prepared.

Inherent Limitations

Because of the inherent limitations of any audit, it is possible that fraud, error or non compliance may occur and not be detected. An audit is not designed to detect all instances of non compliance with the requirements of APES 310, as an audit is not performed continuously throughout the [period] and the audit procedures performed are undertaken on a test basis. The conclusion expressed in this report has been formed on the above basis.

Independence

In conducting our audit, we have complied with the independence requirements of APES 110 *Code of Ethics for Professional Accountants.*

Conclusion

(A) Unqualified

In our opinion, [Member or Firm] has complied, in all material respects, with the requirements of APES 310 for the [year ended …. / …. / ….].

OR

(B) Qualified

In our opinion, except for [provide details of exceptions], [Member or Firm] has complied, in all material respects, with the requirements of APES 310 for the [year ended …. / …. / ….].

Address Member or Firm

Date

APES 315

Compilation of Financial Information

(Issued July 2008: revised November 2009)

Issued by the Accounting Professional and Ethical Standards Board.

Note from the Institute of Chartered Accountants Australia

This note, prepared by the technical editor, is not part of APES 315.

Historical development

July 2008: APES 315 'Compilation of Financial Information' replaced the Miscellaneous Professional Statement APS 9 'Statement on Compilation of Financial Reports' and was effective from 1 January 2009. It applies to members in public practice when they compile financial information including financial statements. It is consistent with the International ISRS 4410 'Engagements to Compile Financial Statements'.

APS 9 had been issued in May 1996, operative from 1 January 1997 to replace the old accountants' disclaimer.

November 2009: APES 315 revised and reissued. This revision includes a new paragraph 3.6 on confidentiality and paragraph 3.5 on independence has become a Standard.

APES

Contents

Paragraphs

1. Scope and application

1.1 Accounting Professional & Ethical Standards Board Limited (APESB) issues professional standard APES 315 Compilation of Financial Information (the Standard), which is effective for Engagements commencing on or after 01 January 2010. Earlier adoption of this Standard is permitted.

1.2 APES 315 sets the standards for Members in Public Practice who undertake Compilation Engagements in the provision of quality and ethical Professional Services. The mandatory requirements of this Standard are in **bold** type, preceded or followed by discussion or explanation in grey type. APES 315 should be read in conjunction with other professional duties of Members, and any legal obligations that may apply.

1.3 Members in Public Practice in Australia shall follow the mandatory requirements of APES 315 when they undertake Professional Services to Clients that are Compilation Engagements.

1.4 Members in Public Practice practising outside of Australia shall follow the provisions of APES 315 to the extent to which they are not prevented from so doing by specific requirements of local laws and/or regulations.

1.5 Members shall be familiar with relevant Professional Standards and guidance notes when providing Professional Services. All Members shall comply with the fundamental principles outlined in the Code.

1.6 The Standard is not intended to detract from any responsibilities which may be imposed by law or regulation.

1.7 All references to Professional Standards, guidance notes and legislation are references to those provisions as amended from time to time.

1.8 In applying the requirements outlined in APES 315, Members in Public Practice should be guided not merely by the words but also by the spirit of the Standard and the Code.

1.9 This Standard is directed towards Engagements to compile historical or prospective financial information.

1.10 The Standard should be applied to the extent practicable for Engagements to compile non-financial information.

1.11 This Standard is directed towards Members in Public Practice. However, Members in Business should apply this Standard to the extent practicable when they compile information for their employers especially in respect of regulatory reporting requirements and Compilation Reports prepared under ASIC Class Order CO 98/1417 *Audit relief for proprietary companies*.

2. Definitions

For the purpose of this Standard:

Applicable Financial Reporting Framework means in respect of an Engagement to prepare Financial Statements, the financial reporting framework adopted by Those Charged with Governance.

Australian Accounting Standards means the Accounting Standards (including Australian Accounting Interpretations) promulgated by the Australian Accounting Standards Board.

Client means an individual, firm, entity or organisation to whom or to which Professional Services are provided by a Member in Public Practice in respect of Engagements of either a recurring or demand nature.

Code means APES 110 *Code of Ethics for Professional Accountants*.

Compilation Engagement means an Engagement to compile financial information.

Compilation Report means a report prepared in accordance with this Standard.

Compiled Financial Information means a presentation of historical or prospective financial information in a specified form, without undertaking to express any assurance on the information. For the purposes of this Standard Compiled Financial Information includes Financial Statements.

Engagement means an agreement, whether written or otherwise, between a Member in Public Practice and a Client relating to the provision of Professional Services by a Member in Public Practice. However, consultations with a prospective Client prior to such agreement are not part of an Engagement.

Engagement Document means the document (i.e. letter, agreement or any other appropriate means) in which the Terms of Engagement are specified in a written form.

Financial Statements means a structured representation of historical or prospective financial information, which ordinarily includes explanatory notes, intended to communicate an entity's economic resources or obligations at a point in time or the changes therein for a period of time in accordance with a financial reporting framework. The term can refer to a complete set of Financial Statements, but it can also refer to a single financial statement, for example, a statement of financial position, or a statement of comprehensive income, and related explanatory notes. The requirements of the financial reporting framework determine the form and content of the Financial Statements and what constitutes a complete set of Financial Statements.

For the purposes of this Standard, the term financial report is considered to be equivalent to Financial Statements.

Firm means
(a) A sole practitioner, partnership, corporation or other entity of professional accountants;
(b) An entity that controls such parties;
(c) An entity controlled by such parties; or
(d) An Auditor-General's office or department.

General Purpose Financial Statements means those intended to meet the needs of users who are not in a position to require an entity to prepare reports tailored to their particular information needs.

APES

Independence means

(a) Independence of mind - the state of mind that permits the provision of an opinion without being affected by influences that compromise professional judgment, allowing an individual to act with integrity, and exercise objectivity and professional scepticism; and

(b) Independence in appearance - the avoidance of facts and circumstances that are so significant a reasonable and informed third party, having knowledge of all relevant information, including any safeguards applied, would reasonably conclude a Firm's, or a member of the Engagement team's, integrity, objectivity or professional scepticism had been compromised.

Member means a member of a professional body that has adopted this Standard as applicable to their membership as defined by that professional body.

Member in Business means a Member employed or engaged in an executive or non-executive capacity in such areas as commerce, industry, service, the public sector, education, the not for profit sector, regulatory bodies or professional bodies, or a Member contracted by such entities.

Member in Public Practice means a Member, irrespective of functional classification (e.g. audit, tax, or consulting) in a Firm that provides Professional Services. The term is also used to refer to a Firm of Members in Public Practice and means a practice entity as defined by the applicable professional body.

Professional Services means services requiring accountancy or related skills performed by a Member in Public Practice including accounting, auditing, taxation, management consulting and financial management services.

Professional Standards mean all Standards issued by Accounting Professional & Ethical Standards Board Limited and all professional and ethical requirements of the applicable professional body.

Special Purpose Financial Statements means Financial Statements other than General Purpose Financial Statements.

Terms of Engagement means the terms and conditions that are agreed between the Client and the Member in Public Practice for the Engagement.

Those Charged with Governance include those persons accountable for ensuring that the entity achieves its objectives with regard to reliability of financial reporting, effectiveness and efficiency of operations, compliance with applicable laws, and reporting to interested parties. Those Charged with Governance include management only when it performs such functions.

3. Fundamental responsibilities of Members in Public Practice

3.1 **Members in Public Practice undertaking Compilation Engagements shall comply with Section 100 *Introduction and Fundamental Principles* of the Code and relevant legislation.**

Public interest

3.2 **In accordance with Section 100 *Introduction and Fundamental Principles* of the Code, Members in Public Practice shall observe and comply with their public interest obligations when they undertake Compilation Engagements.**

Professional competence and due care

3.3 **Members in Public Practice undertaking Compilation Engagements shall maintain professional competence and take due care in the performance of their work in accordance with Section 130 *Professional Competence and Due Care* of the Code.**

Professional Independence

3.4 Independence is not a requirement for a Compilation Engagement.

3.5 **Where a Member in Public Practice is not independent, the Member shall make a statement to that effect in the Compilation Report.**

Confidentiality

3.6 **In accordance with Section 140 *Confidentiality* of the Code, a Member in Public Practice who acquires confidential information in the course of a Compilation Engagement for a Client shall not use that information for any purpose other than the proper performance of that Engagement.**

4. Objectives of a Compilation Engagement

4.1 The objective of a Compilation Engagement is for the Member in Public Practice to use accounting expertise, as opposed to auditing expertise, to collect, classify and summarise financial information. This will ordinarily entail reducing detailed data to a manageable and understandable form without a requirement to test the assertions underlying that information. The procedures employed are not designed and do not enable the Member to express any assurance on the financial information.

4.2 A Compilation Engagement may involve the preparation of Financial Statements (which may or may not be a complete set of Financial Statements). It may also involve compilation of other financial information without the compilation of Financial Statements.

4.3 Activities which fall outside the scope of APES 315 include:

(a) preparation of a taxation return and financial information prepared solely for inclusion in the taxation return;

(b) analysis of figures provided by a Client, in order to report to the Client. For example, providing advice on a Client's proposed purchase of another entity, using the other entity's Financial Statements;

(c) relaying information to a Client, without collection, classification or summarisation of the information.

5. Planning

5.1 **A Member in Public Practice shall plan the Compilation Engagement to ensure that the Engagement is conducted in accordance with this Standard and all applicable Professional Standards, laws and regulations.**

6. General Purpose or Special Purpose Financial Statements

6.1 **When undertaking a Compilation Engagement in respect of General Purpose Financial Statements or Special Purpose Financial Statements, a Member in Public Practice shall comply with the requirements of APES 205 *Conformity with Accounting Standards*.**

7. Defining the Terms of Engagement

7.1 **A Member in Public Practice shall document and communicate the Terms of Engagement in accordance with APES 305 *Terms of Engagement*.**

7.2 In addition to the *General contents of an Engagement Document of* APES 305 *Terms of Engagement*, a Member in Public Practice should consider the following matters for inclusion in the Engagement Document:

(a) nature of the Engagement including the fact that neither an audit nor a review will be carried out and that accordingly no assurance will be expressed;

(b) fact that the Engagement cannot be relied upon to disclose errors, illegal acts or other irregularities, for example, fraud or defalcations that may exist;

(c) nature of the information to be supplied by the Client;

(d) in respect of prospective financial information, the basis of forecasting;

(e) key assumptions relating to prospective financial information provided by the Client;

(f) in the event that the Member makes assumptions in forecasts these assumptions will be brought to the Client's attention;

APES

(g) fact that the Client is responsible for the accuracy and completeness of the information supplied to the Member and that an acknowledgement of such will be required in accordance with paragraph 11;

(h) basis of accounting on which the financial information is to be compiled and the fact that it, and any known departures there from, will be disclosed;

(i) requirement for General Purpose Financial Statements to be prepared in accordance with Australian Accounting Standards;

(j) intended use and distribution of the information, once compiled;

(k) form of any Compilation Report to be issued; and

(l) nature of any disclaimer or limitation of liability clause between the Member and the Client or the Member and any user of the Compiled Financial Information.

8. Procedures

8.1 A Member in Public Practice should obtain a general knowledge of the business and operations of the Client and should be familiar with the accounting principles and practices of the industry in which the Client operates and with the form and content of the financial information that are appropriate in the circumstances.

8.2 Other than as noted in this Standard, a Member in Public Practice is not ordinarily required to:

(a) make any inquiries of management to assess the reliability and completeness of the information provided;

(b) assess internal controls;

(c) verify any matters; or

(d) verify any explanations.

8.3 A Member in Public Practice who, on reasonable grounds, forms the view that the information supplied by the Client is materially false or misleading or the Client has omitted material information, shall consider performing the procedures noted in paragraph 8.2 and request the Client to provide any additional information required to complete the Engagement.

8.4 If the Client refuses to provide the additional information as requested under paragraph 8.3 or, having performed the procedures noted in paragraph 8.2, the Member in Public Practice concludes that the information supplied by the Client is materially false or misleading, the Member shall consider the Firm's policies and procedures established in accordance with *Acceptance and Continuance of Client Relationships and Specific Engagements* of APES 320 *Quality Control for Firms* in determining whether to continue acting for the Client in a professional capacity.

8.5 A Member in Public Practice shall perform sufficient reviews of the Compilation Engagement in accordance with Section 130 *Professional Competence and Due Care* of the Code and the Firm's policies and procedures established in accordance with *Engagement Performance* of APES 320 *Quality Control for Firms* prior to issuing the Compilation Report.

9. Misstatements

9.1 A Member in Public Practice shall consider whether the Compiled Financial Information is appropriate in form and content and free from obvious material misstatements.

9.2 In this Standard, material misstatements include the following:

(a) material mistakes in the application of the Applicable Financial Reporting Framework or an alternative financial reporting framework;

(b) non-disclosure of the financial reporting framework and any material departures there from; and

(c) non-disclosure of significant matters.

9.3 For the purpose of paragraph 9.2(a) examples of alternative financial reporting frameworks that may be applied to the presentation of Compiled Financial Information include, but are not limited to:

(a) a tax basis of accounting;

(b) the cash receipts and disbursements basis of accounting for cash flow information;

(c) the financial reporting provisions established by a regulator to meet the requirements of that regulator; and

(d) the financial reporting provisions of a contract, for example a loan agreement or trust deed.

9.4 If a Member in Public Practice forms the view, on reasonable grounds, that there are material misstatements in the Compiled Financial Information, the Member shall take all reasonable steps to agree appropriate amendments with the Client.

9.5 If such amendments are not made as requested under paragraph 9.4 and the Compiled Financial Information is considered to be misleading, the Member in Public Practice shall consider the Firm's policies and procedures established in accordance with *Acceptance and Continuance of Client Relationships and Specific Engagements* of APES 320 *Quality Control for Firms* in determining whether to continue acting for the Client in a professional capacity.

10. Documentation

10.1 A Member in Public Practice shall prepare working papers in accordance with this Standard that appropriately document the work performed, including aspects of the Compilation Engagement that have been provided in writing. The documentation prepared by the Member shall:

(a) provide a sufficient and appropriate record of the procedures performed for the Engagement;

(b) identify the sources of significant information the Member has used in the compilation of financial information; and

(c) demonstrate that the Engagement was carried out in accordance with this Standard and all other Professional Standards applicable to the Engagement, including policies and procedures established in accordance with APES 320 *Quality Control for Firms,* and any applicable ethical, legal and regulatory requirements.

11. Responsibility of the Client

11.1 A Member in Public Practice who undertakes a Compilation Engagement in respect of General Purpose or Special Purpose Financial Statements, shall obtain an acknowledgment from the Client of its responsibility for the reliability, accuracy and completeness of the accounting records and disclosure to the Member of all material and relevant information.

11.2 A Member in Public Practice who undertakes a Compilation Engagement other than those referred to in paragraph 11.1, should obtain an acknowledgement from the Client of its responsibility for the reliability, accuracy and completeness of the financial information and disclosure to the Member of all material and relevant information.

11.3 The acknowledgment referred to in paragraphs 11.1 and 11.2 may be provided by representations from the Client which cover the accuracy and completeness of the underlying accounting data and the complete disclosure of all material and relevant information to the Member in Public Practice.

12. Reporting on a Compilation Engagement

12.1 When a Member in Public Practice prepares Compiled Financial Information, the Member shall issue a Compilation Report, subject to the requirements of paragraph 12.3, in circumstances where:

(a) the Member's name is identified with the Compiled Financial Information;

(b) the Compiled Financial Information is for external use; or

(c) it is more likely than not that the intended user of the Compiled Financial Information may not understand the nature and scope of the Member's involvement with that information.

12.2 Generally when a Member in Public Practice compiles financial information for internal use by the Client, this Standard does not mandate the issue of a Compilation Report. In these circumstances the use of the Compiled Financial Information is restricted. The Member should include a reference that specifies that such Compiled Financial Information is "Restricted for internal use" or similar on each page of the Compiled Financial Information.

12.3 Where the Client has engaged another Member in Public Practice to audit or review the Compiled Financial Information in accordance with Australian auditing standards applicable to audit or review Engagements, the Member in Public Practice undertaking the Compilation Engagement shall consider the need to issue a Compilation Report. Where the Member decides not to issue a Compilation Report the Member shall document the rationale for that decision.

12.4 In the circumstances described in paragraph 12.3, if an audit or review report has been issued, this will override the need for the Member in Public Practice to issue a Compilation Report.

12.5 Where the circumstances described in paragraph 12.3 apply and the scope of the Compilation Engagement extends to significant subject matter not covered under the audit or review Engagement, the Member in Public Practice shall issue a Compilation Report for the subject matter not covered under the audit or review Engagement.

12.6 Where a Member in Public Practice issues a Compilation Report in accordance with paragraph 12.1 or 12.5, the Compilation Report shall contain the following:

(a) a title;

(b) an addressee;

(c) a statement that the Engagement was performed in accordance with this Standard;

(d) when relevant, a statement that the Member is not independent of the Client;

(e) identification of the Compiled Financial Information noting that it is based on the financial information provided by the Client (if applicable);

(f) the basis of any forecast information;

(g) key assumptions (applicable to prospective financial information only);

(h) a statement that the Client is responsible for the financial information compiled by the Member;

(i) a statement that neither an audit nor a review has been carried out and that accordingly no assurance is expressed on the Compiled Financial Information;

(j) if applicable, identification that the Member is reporting on a Special Purpose Financial Statement and the specific purpose for which it has been prepared;

(k) if applicable, a paragraph drawing attention to the disclosure of material departures from the applicable financial reporting framework;

(l) the date of the Compilation Report;

(m) the Member's or Firm's address;

(n) the Member's or Firm's name and signature;

(o) an appropriate disclaimer of liability.

12.7 Where a Member in Public Practice issues a Compilation Report in accordance with paragraph 12.1 or 12.5, the financial information compiled by the Member shall contain a reference such as "Unaudited", "Compiled without Audit or Review", or "Refer to Compilation Report" on each page of the Compiled Financial Information.

13. Communication of significant matters

13.1 A Member in Public Practice shall communicate to Those Charged with Governance of the Client any significant matters arising from the Compilation Engagement on a timely basis.

13.2 Communication should ordinarily be in writing. Where the communication occurs orally, a Member in Public Practice should record in the working papers a summary of the significant matters discussed.

13.3 If the Member in Public Practice obtains information that indicates that a material fraud, material misstatement or illegal act has occurred, the Member shall communicate these matters as soon as practicable to Those Charged with Governance of the Client.

13.4 Matters which should be communicated by the Member in Public Practice include:

(a) material misstatements identified during the Compilation Engagement and the appropriate amendments agreed with the Client in respect of the misstatements;

(b) additional information sought by the Member as a result of information supplied which contained material misstatements or was otherwise unsatisfactory;

(c) if additional information sought by the Member is not supplied:

(i) the effect that the lack of additional information may have on the Compiled Financial Information;

(ii) the effect of the lack of additional information on the Member's report; and

(iii) if appropriate, the fact that the Member proposes to withdraw from the Compilation Engagement as a result of the lack of additional information;

(d) any other matters that, in the Member's opinion, are significant in the context of the Compilation Engagement.

13.5 Where the Member in Public Practice obtains information that a material fraud, misstatement or illegal act has occurred and the Member has reason to believe that such an act is the result of actions of Those Charged with Governance of the Client, the Member shall consider the Firm's policies and procedures established in accordance with *Acceptance and Continuance of Client Relationships and Specific Engagements* of APES 320 *Quality Control for Firms* in determining whether to continue acting for the Client in a professional capacity.

14. Subsequent discovery of facts

14.1 Subsequent to the completion of the Compilation Engagement, the Member in Public Practice may become aware of facts that existed at the date of completion of the Compilation Engagement which may have caused the Member to believe that information supplied was materially false or misleading, had the Member been aware of such facts.

14.2 A Member in Public Practice shall consider the impact of subsequent discovery of facts on the Compiled Financial Information, discuss the matter with the Client, and take action appropriate in the circumstances. The Member shall document the reasons for the action taken by the Member.

14.3 If the Member in Public Practice believes that the Compiled Financial Information referred to in paragraph 14.2 needs to be revised, the Member shall take all reasonable steps to ensure that the Client takes the necessary steps to inform anyone who received the previously issued Compiled Financial Information of the situation.

14.4 When determining whether the Compiled Financial Information needs to be revised pursuant to paragraph 14.3, the Member in Public Practice should consider inter alia the duration of time between the issue of the Compiled Financial Information and the subsequent discovery of facts referred to in Paragraph 14.1, and the extent to which important decisions based on the Compiled Financial Information are still to be made.

14.5 If the Member in Public Practice becomes aware that the Client has not taken appropriate action in terms of paragraph 14.3, the Member shall notify Those Charged with Governance of the Client.

14.6 **If appropriate action is not taken by Those Charged with Governance of the Client, the Member in Public Practice shall consider the Firm's policies and procedures established in accordance with *Acceptance and Continuance of Client Relationships and Specific Engagements* of APES 320 *Quality Control for Firms* in determining whether to continue acting for the Client in a professional capacity.**

Examples of suggested Compilation Reports in respect of General Purpose and Special Purpose Financial Statements are contained in Appendix 1

Conformity with International Pronouncements

APES 315 and ISRS 4410

The basic principles and essential procedures of APES 315 and of ISRS 4410 *Engagements to Compile Financial Statements* issued by the International Auditing and Assurance Standards Board (IAASB) are consistent in all material respects, except that the scope and application and definitions are unique to APES 315 and except for the matters noted below:

- When undertaking a Compilation Engagement in respect of General Purpose or Special Purpose Financial Statements, APES 315 mandates that the Member in Public Practice needs to comply with APES 205 *Conformity with Accounting Standards*;
- The objectives of the Compilation Engagement (paragraph 4.1) and the requirement for Member to obtain a general knowledge of the business (paragraph 8.1) are included as guidance in APES 315;
- APES 315 requires that the Terms of Engagement be documented in accordance with APES 305 *Terms of Engagement*;
- APES 315 requires that the Compilation Report needs to include, where applicable, identification that the Member in Public Practice is reporting on Special Purpose Financial Statements and the specific purpose for which they have been prepared;
- APES 315 requires the inclusion of an appropriate disclaimer of liability in the Compilation Report;
- APES 315 addresses communication of significant matters to Those Charged with Governance of the Client and procedures to follow when facts are subsequently discovered which indicate that the Compiled Financial Information is materially misstated;
- APES 315 does not include a sample engagement letter; and
- APES 315 includes an example of a Compilation Report for each of General Purpose Financial Statements and Special Purpose Financial Statements. ISRS 4410 only includes an example of a Compilation Report for Financial Statements.

Appendix 1
Examples of Compilation Reports

Example 1

Example Compilation Report on an engagement to compile General Purpose Financial Statements.

COMPILATION REPORT TO [name of entity] ("the Client")

We have compiled the accompanying general purpose financial statements of [name of entity], which comprise the statement of financial position as at [30 June 20XX], the statement of comprehensive income, statement of changes in equity and statement of cash flows for the year then ended, a summary of significant accounting policies and other explanatory notes. These have been prepared in accordance with the *(the financial reporting framework/basis of accounting)* described in Note 1 to the financial statements.

The Responsibility of [Those Charged with Governance]

[Those charged with governance] of [name of entity] are solely responsible for the information contained in the general purpose financial statements and have determined that the *(financial reporting framework/basis of accounting)* used is appropriate to meet their needs and for the purpose that the financial statements were prepared.

Our Responsibility

On the basis of information provided by [Those charged with governance] we have compiled the accompanying general purpose financial statements in accordance with the *(financial reporting framework/basis of accounting)* and APES 315 *Compilation of Financial Information.*

Our procedures use accounting expertise to collect, classify and summarise the financial information, which [those charged with governance] provided, in compiling the financial statements. Our procedures do not include verification or validation procedures. No audit or review has been performed and accordingly no assurance is expressed.

The general purpose financial statements were compiled exclusively for the benefit of [those charged with governance]. We do not accept responsibility to any other person for the contents of the general purpose financial statements.

Independence (if required)

We are not independent of *[name of entity]* because *(reasons why not independent, for example, the member is a close relative of a director or proprietor of the entity).*

Address Member or Firm

Date

Example 2

Example Compilation Report on an engagement to compile Special Purpose Financial Statements.

COMPILATION REPORT TO [name of entity] ("the Client")

We have compiled the accompanying special purpose financial statements of [name of entity], which comprise the [statement of financial position] as at [30 June 20XX], the [statement of comprehensive income], [statement of changes in equity] and [statement of cash flows] for the year then ended, a [summary of significant accounting policies] and [other explanatory notes]. The specific purpose for which the special purpose financial statements have been prepared is set out in Note […].

The Responsibility of [Those Charged with Governance]

[Those charged with governance] of [name of entity] are solely responsible for the information contained in the special purpose financial statements and have determined that the *(financial reporting framework/basis of accounting)* used is appropriate to meet their needs and for the purpose that the financial statements were prepared.

APES

Our Responsibility

On the basis of information provided by [Those charged with governance] we have compiled the accompanying special purpose financial statements in accordance with the *(financial reporting framework/basis of accounting)* and APES 315 *Compilation of Financial Information.*

Our procedures use accounting expertise to collect, classify and summarise the financial information, which [those charged with governance] provided, in compiling the financial statements. Our procedures do not include verification or validation procedures. No audit or review has been performed and accordingly no assurance is expressed.

The special purpose financial statements were compiled exclusively for the benefit of [those charged with governance]. We do not accept responsibility to any other person for the contents of the special purpose financial statements.

Independence (if required)

We are not independent of *[name of entity]* because *(reasons why not independent, for example, the member is a close relative of a director or proprietor of the entity).*

Address Member or Firm

Date

Example 3

Example Compilation Report on an engagement to compile General Purpose Financial Statements with an additional paragraph that draws attention to a departure from the identified financial reporting framework.

COMPILATION REPORT TO [name of entity] ("the Client")

We have compiled the accompanying general purpose financial statements of [name of entity], which comprise the statement of financial position as at [30 June 20XX], the statement of comprehensive income, statement of changes in equity and statement of cash flows for the year then ended, a summary of significant accounting policies and other explanatory notes. These have been prepared in accordance with the *(the financial reporting framework/basis of accounting)* described in Note 1 to the financial statements.

The Responsibility of [Those Charged with Governance]

[Those charged with governance] of the [name of entity] are solely responsible for the information contained in the general purpose financial statements and have determined that the *(financial reporting framework/basis of accounting)* used is appropriate to meet their needs and for the purpose that the financial statements were prepared.

Our Responsibility

On the basis of information provided by [Those charged with governance] we have compiled the accompanying general purpose financial statements in accordance with the *(financial reporting framework/basis of accounting)* and APES 315 *Compilation of Financial Information.*

Our procedures use accounting expertise to collect, classify and summarise the financial information, which [those charged with governance] provided, in compiling the financial statements. Our procedures do not include verification or validation procedures. No audit or review has been performed and accordingly no assurance is expressed.

The general purpose financial statements were compiled exclusively for the benefit of [those charged with governance]. We do not accept responsibility to any other person for the contents of the general purpose financial statements.

Departure from the financial reporting framework

We draw attention to Note XX to the financial statements. [Those Charged with Governance] of [name of entity] have determined not to …… (E.g. capitalise leases in accordance with Australian Accounting Standard AASB 117 *Leases*) which is a departure from the applicable financial reporting framework.

Address Member or Firm

Date

APES 320

Quality Control for Firms

(Issued May 2006: reissued May 2009)

Issued by the Accounting Professional and Ethical Standards Board.

Note from the Institute of Chartered Accountants Australia

This note, prepared by the technical editor, is not part of APES 320.

Historical development

May 2006: APES 320 issued by the newly constituted Accounting Professional and Ethical Standards Board to replace APS 4 and 5. It was based on the International Standard for Quality Control ISQC 1 'Quality Control for Firms that Perform Audits and Reviews of Historical Financial Information, and Other Assurance and Related Services Engagements'. Systems of quality control in compliance with the Standard were required to be established by 1 July 2006.

May 2009: APES 320 reissued to reflect changing international Standards, in particular the International Standard or Quality Control ISQC 1, issued by the International Federation of Accountants (IFAC) in late 2008. It is operative from 1 January 2010.

September 2009: APESB issued a statement clarifying the meaning of the term 'Key Audit Partners'. The statement is included in this book behind APES 320.

Contents

Legal enforceability

The Auditing and Assurance Standards Board (AUASB) has issued auditing standards as legislative instruments under the Corporations Act 2001, effective for financial reporting periods, which commenced on or after 1 July 2006. For Corporations Act audits and reviews, those standards have legal enforceability. To the extent that those legally enforceable auditing standards make reference to the quality control requirements for Firms issued by a Professional Body, the requirements of APES 320 have the same level of legal enforceability in respect of Corporations Act audits and reviews. This is due to the linkages with Auditing Standards ASA 200 Overall Objectives of the Independent Auditor and the Conduct of an Audit in Accordance with Australian Auditing Standards and ASA 220 Quality Control for an Audit of a Financial Report and Other Historical Financial Information (or equivalent predecessor ASA's).

1. Scope and application

1.1 Accounting Professional & Ethical Standards Board Limited (APESB) issues professional standard APES 320 *Quality Control for Firms* (**the Standard**). Systems of quality control in compliance with this Standard are required to be established by 01 January 2010. Earlier adoption of this Standard is permitted.

1.2 APES 320 sets the standards for Members in Public Practice and Firms to establish and maintain a system of quality control at the Firm level in the provision of quality and ethical Professional Services. The mandatory requirements of this Standard are in **bold** type, preceded or followed by discussion or explanation in grey type. APES 320 should be read in conjunction with other professional duties of Members, and any legal obligations that may apply.

1.3 Members in Public Practice in Australia shall follow the mandatory requirements of APES 320.

1.4 Members in Public Practice practising outside of Australia shall follow the provisions of APES 320 to the extent to which they are not prevented from so doing by specific requirements of local laws and/or regulations.

1.5 Members shall be familiar with relevant Professional Standards and guidance notes when providing Professional Services. All Members shall comply with the fundamental principles outlined in the Code.

1.6 The Standard is not intended to detract from any responsibilities which may be imposed by law or regulation.

1.7 All references to Professional Standards, guidance notes and legislation are references to those provisions as amended from time to time.

1.8 In applying the requirements outlined in APES 320, Members in Public Practice should be guided not merely by the words but also by the spirit of the Standard and the Code.

1.9 In this Standard, Firms that have an Assurance Practice are required to apply the whole of APES 320 as applicable to their Assurance Practice and Assurance Engagements. Firms that do not have an Assurance Practice, or the non-assurance parts of Firms with an Assurance Practice, are required to apply all paragraphs of APES 320 where applicable other than those boxed and designated 'Assurance Practices only'. The application requirements are summarised in the flow chart in the Appendix to the Standard.

1.10 A Firm's Personnel may be required to comply with additional standards and guidance regarding quality control procedures at the Engagement level. For example in respect of Assurance Engagements, Auditing Standard ASA 220 *Quality Control for an Audit of a Financial Report and Other Historical Financial Information* (or equivalent predecessor ASA), issued by the Auditing and Assurance Standards Board establishes standards and provides guidance on quality control procedures for audits at the Engagement level.

2. Definitions

For the purpose of this Standard:

(a) ***Date of Report*** means the date selected by a Member in Public Practice to date a report.

(b) ***Engagement Documentation*** means the record of work performed, results obtained, and conclusions the Member in Public Practice reached (terms such as "working papers" or "workpapers" are sometimes used).

(c) ***Engagement Quality Control Review*** means a process designed to provide an objective evaluation, on or before the Date of Report, of the significant judgments the Engagement Team made and the conclusions it reached in formulating the report. The Engagement Quality Control Review process is for audits of financial statements of listed entities, and those other Engagements, if any, for which the Firm has determined an Engagement Quality Control Review is required.

(d) ***Engagement Quality Control Reviewer*** means a Partner, other person in the Assurance Practice, Suitably Qualified External Person, or a team made up of such individuals, none of whom is part of the Engagement Team, with sufficient and appropriate experience and authority to objectively evaluate the significant judgments the Engagement Team made and the conclusions it reached in formulating the report.

(e) ***Engagement Team*** means all Personnel performing the Engagement, and any individuals engaged by the Firm or a Network Firm who perform procedures on the Engagement. This excludes external experts engaged by the Firm or Network Firm.

(f) ***Firm*** means:

- A sole practitioner, partnership, corporation or other entity of professional accountants;
- An entity that controls such parties through ownership, management or other means;
- An entity controlled by such parties through ownership, management or other means; or
- An Auditor-General's office or department.

(g) ***Inspection*** means in relation to completed Engagements, procedures designed to provide evidence of compliance by Engagement Teams with the Firm's quality control policies and procedures.

(h) ***Listed Entity*** means an entity whose shares, stock or debt are quoted or listed on a recognised stock exchange, or are marketed under the regulations of a recognised stock exchange or other equivalent body.

(i) ***Monitoring*** means a process comprising an ongoing consideration and evaluation of the Firm's system of quality control, including a periodic Inspection of a selection of completed Engagements, designed to provide the Firm with Reasonable Assurance that its system of quality control is operating effectively.

(j) ***Network Firm*** or ***Network Assurance Practice*** means a Firm, practice or entity that belongs to a Network.

(k) ***Network*** means a larger structure:

(i) that is aimed at cooperation; and

(ii) that is clearly aimed at profit or cost-sharing or shares common ownership, control or management, common quality control policies and procedures, common business strategy, the use of a common brand name, or a significant part of professional resources.

(l) ***Partner*** means any individual with authority to bind the Firm with respect to the performance of a Professional Services Engagement.

(m) ***Personnel*** means Partners and Staff.

(n) ***Reasonable Assurance*** means in the context of this Standard, a high, but not absolute, level of assurance.

(o) ***Relevant Ethical Requirements*** means ethical requirements which the Engagement Team and Engagement Quality Control Reviewer are subject to, and which ordinarily comprise Parts A and B of the Code.

(p) ***Staff*** means professionals, other than Partners, including any experts the Firm employs.

(q) ***Suitably Qualified External Person*** means an individual outside the Firm with the competence and capabilities to act as an Engagement Partner, for example a Partner of another Firm, or an employee (with appropriate experience) of either a professional accountancy body whose members may perform audits and reviews of historical financial information, or other assurance or related services Engagements, or of an organisation that provides relevant quality control services.

AUST 2.1 For the purpose of this Standard:

(a) ***Assurance Engagement*** means an Engagement in which a conclusion is expressed by a Member in Public Practice designed to enhance the degree of confidence of the intended users other than the responsible party about the outcome of the evaluation or measurement of a subject matter against criteria.

This includes an Engagement in accordance with *Framework for Assurance Engagements* issued by Auditing and Assurance Standards Board (AUASB) or in accordance with specific relevant standards, such as International Standards on Auditing, for Assurance Engagements.

(b) ***Assurance Practice*** means the assurance division or section of a Firm, encompassing every Assurance Engagement conducted by the Firm, whether or not required to be conducted by a Registered Company Auditor and whether or not conducted by an individual auditor, an audit Firm or an audit company.

(c) ***Client*** means an individual, firm, entity or organisation to whom or to which professional services are provided by a Member in Public Practice in respect of Engagements of either a recurring or demand nature.

(d) ***Code*** means APES 110 *Code of Ethics for Professional Accountants*.

(e) ***Engagement*** means an agreement, whether written or otherwise, between a Member in Public Practice and a Client relating to the provision of Professional Services by a Member in Public Practice. However, consultations with a prospective Client prior to such an agreement are not part of an Engagement.

(f) ***Engagement Partner*** means the Partner or other person in the Firm who is responsible for the Engagement and its performance, and for the report that is issued on behalf of the Firm, and who, where required, has the appropriate authority from a professional, legal or regulatory body.

In public sector audit organisations, the term includes a suitably qualified person to whom the Auditor General has delegated Engagement Partner responsibilities.

(g) ***Independence*** means:

- Independence of mind – the state of mind that permits the provision of an opinion without being affected by influences that compromise professional judgment, allowing an individual to act with integrity, and exercise objectivity and professional scepticism; and
- Independence in appearance – the avoidance of facts and circumstances that are so significant a reasonable and informed third party, having knowledge of all relevant information, including any safeguards applied, would reasonably conclude a Firm's, or a member of the Engagement Team's, integrity, objectivity or professional scepticism had been compromised.

(h) ***Key Audit Partner*** means the Engagement Partner, the individual responsible for the Engagement Quality Control Review, and other audit Partners, if any, on the Engagement Team who make key decisions or judgments on significant matters with respect to the audit of the financial statements on which the Firm will express an opinion. Depending upon the circumstances and the role of the individuals on the audit, "other audit Partners" may include, for example, audit Partners responsible for significant subsidiaries or divisions.

(i) ***Professional Body(ies)*** means the Institute of Chartered Accountants in Australia, CPA Australia and the National Institute of Accountants.

(j) ***Professional Services*** means services requiring accountancy or related skills performed by a Member in Public Practice including accounting, auditing, taxation, management consulting and financial management services.

(k) ***Professional Standards*** means all standards issued by the Accounting Professional & Ethical Standards Board and all professional and ethical requirements of the applicable Professional Body.

(l) ***Member*** means a member of a Professional Body that has adopted this Standard as applicable to their membership as defined by that Professional Body.

(m) ***Member in Public Practice*** means a Member, irrespective of functional classification (e.g. audit, tax, or consulting) in a Firm that provides Professional Services. The term is also used to refer to a Firm of Members in Public Practice and means a practice entity as defined by the applicable Professional Body.

Objective

3. A Firm shall establish and maintain a system of quality control designed to provide it with Reasonable Assurance that the Firm and its Personnel comply with Professional Standards and applicable legal and regulatory requirements and that reports issued by the Firm or Engagement Partners are appropriate in the circumstances.

4. A system of quality control consists of policies designed to achieve the objectives set out in paragraph 3 and the procedures necessary to implement and monitor compliance with those policies.

5. The nature and extent of the policies and procedures developed by an individual Firm to comply with this Standard will depend on various factors such as the size and operating characteristics of the Firm, and whether it is part of a Network.

AUST 5.1 The policies and procedures developed by a Firm need not be complex or time-consuming to be effective. This Standard describes responsibilities for several different roles and functions within the Firm, including overall quality control and Monitoring. For a small Firm, it may be necessary for one person to perform more than one of these functions. In some circumstances, it may be appropriate to use the services of a Suitably Qualified External Person. When a Firm decides to use such a person, care should be taken to establish the legal responsibilities of the parties and to safeguard Client confidentiality.

Applying and complying with relevant requirements

6. Personnel within a Firm responsible for establishing and maintaining the Firm's system of quality control shall have an understanding of the entire text of this Standard, including its application and other explanatory material, to understand its objective and to apply its requirements properly.

7. A Firm shall comply with each requirement of this Standard unless, in the circumstances of the Firm, the requirement is not relevant to the services provided by the Firm.

Considerations specific to smaller Firms

8. This Standard does not call for compliance with requirements that are not relevant, for example, in the circumstances of a sole practitioner with no Staff. Requirements in this Standard such as those for policies and procedures for the assignment of appropriate Personnel to the Engagement Team (see paragraph 56), for review responsibilities (see paragraph 63), and for annual communication of the results of Monitoring to Engagement Partners within a Firm (see paragraph 117), are not relevant in the absence of Staff.

9. The requirements are designed to enable a Firm to achieve the objective stated in this Standard. The proper application of the requirements is therefore expected to provide a sufficient basis for the achievement of the objective. However, because circumstances vary widely and all such circumstances cannot be anticipated, the Firm shall consider whether there are particular matters or circumstances that require the Firm to establish policies and procedures in addition to those required by this Standard to meet the stated objective.

Elements of a system of quality control

10. A Firm shall establish and maintain a system of quality control that includes policies and procedures that address each of the following elements:

(a) Leadership responsibilities for quality within the Firm.

(b) Relevant Ethical Requirements.

(c) Acceptance and continuance of Client relationships and specific Engagements.

(d) Human resources.

(e) Engagement performance.

(f) Monitoring.

11. A Firm shall document its policies and procedures and communicate them to the Firm's Personnel.

12. In general, communication of quality control policies and procedures to Firm's Personnel includes a description of the quality control policies and procedures and the objectives they are designed to achieve, and the message that each individual has a personal responsibility for quality and is expected to comply with these policies and procedures. Encouraging Firm's Personnel to communicate their views or concerns on quality control matters recognises the importance of obtaining feedback on the Firm's system of quality control.

Considerations specific to smaller Firms

13. Documentation and communication of policies and procedures for smaller Firms may be less formal and extensive than for larger Firms.

Leadership responsibilities for quality within a Firm

14. A Firm shall establish policies and procedures designed to promote an internal culture recognising that quality is essential in performing Engagements. Such policies and procedures shall require the Firm's chief executive officer (or equivalent) or, if appropriate, the Firm's managing board of Partners (or equivalent), to assume ultimate responsibility for the Firm's system of quality control.

15. The Firm's leadership and the examples it sets significantly influence the internal culture of the Firm. The promotion of a quality-oriented internal culture depends on clear, consistent and frequent actions and messages from all levels of the Firm's management that emphasise the Firm's quality control policies and procedures, and the requirement to:

(a) Perform work that complies with Professional Standards and applicable legal and regulatory requirements; and

(b) Issue reports that are appropriate in the circumstances.

Such actions and messages encourage a culture that recognises and rewards high quality work. These actions and messages may be communicated by, but are not limited to, training seminars, meetings, formal or informal dialogue, mission statements, newsletters, or briefing memoranda. They may be incorporated in the Firm's internal documentation and training materials, and in Partner and Staff appraisal procedures such that they will support and reinforce the Firm's view on the importance of quality and how, practically, it is to be achieved.

16. Of particular importance in promoting an internal culture based on quality is the need for a Firm's leadership to recognise that the Firm's business strategy is subject to the overriding requirement for the Firm to achieve quality in all the Engagements that the Firm performs. Promoting such an internal culture includes:

(a) Establishment of policies and procedures that address performance evaluation, compensation, and promotion (including incentive systems) with regard to its Personnel, in order to demonstrate the Firm's overriding commitment to quality;

(b) Assignment of management responsibilities so that commercial considerations do not override the quality of work performed; and

(c) Provision of sufficient resources for the development, documentation and support of its quality control policies and procedures.

17. A Firm shall establish policies and procedures such that any person or persons assigned operational responsibility for the Firm's system of quality control by the Firm's chief executive officer or managing board of Partners has sufficient and appropriate experience and ability, and the necessary authority, to assume that responsibility.

18. Sufficient and appropriate experience and ability enables the person or persons responsible for the Firm's system of quality control to identify and understand quality control issues and to develop appropriate policies and procedures. Necessary authority enables the person or persons to implement those policies and procedures.

Relevant Ethical Requirements

19. A Firm shall establish policies and procedures designed to provide it with Reasonable Assurance that the Firm and its Personnel comply with Relevant Ethical Requirements.

20. Ethical requirements are contained in the Professional Standards. The Code establishes the fundamental principles of professional ethics, which include:

(a) Integrity;

(b) Objectivity;

(c) Professional competence and due care;

(d) Confidentiality; and

(e) Professional behaviour.

21. Part B of the Code illustrates how the conceptual framework is to be applied in specific situations. It provides examples of safeguards that may be appropriate to address threats to compliance with the fundamental principles and also provides examples of situations where safeguards are not available to address the threats.

22. The fundamental principles are reinforced in particular by:

- The leadership of the Firm;
- Education and training;
- Monitoring; and
- A process for dealing with non-compliance.

23. In complying with the requirements in paragraphs 19, 24–26, 29 and 31, the definitions of "Firm", "Network" and "Network Firms" used in the Relevant Ethical Requirements apply in so far as is necessary to interpret those ethical requirements.

Independence

24. A Firm shall establish policies and procedures designed to provide it with Reasonable Assurance that the Firm, its Personnel and, where applicable, others subject to Independence requirements (including Network Firm's Personnel) maintain Independence where required by Relevant Ethical Requirements. Such policies and procedures shall enable the Firm to:

(a) Communicate its Independence requirements to its Personnel and, where applicable, others subject to them; and

(b) Identify and evaluate circumstances and relationships that create threats to Independence, and to take appropriate action to eliminate those threats or reduce them to an acceptable level by applying safeguards, or, if considered appropriate, to withdraw from the Engagement, where withdrawal is possible under applicable law or regulation.

Assurance Practices only

25. A Firm shall establish policies and procedures that require:

(a) Engagement Partners to provide the Firm with relevant information about Client Engagements, including the scope of services, to enable the Firm to evaluate the overall impact, if any, on Independence requirements;

(b) Personnel to promptly notify the Firm of circumstances and relationships that create a threat to Independence so that appropriate action can be taken; and

(c) The accumulation and communication of relevant information to appropriate Personnel so that:

(i) the Firm and its Personnel can readily determine whether they satisfy Independence requirements;

(ii) the Firm can maintain and update its records relating to Independence; and

(iii) the Firm can take appropriate action regarding identified threats to Independence that are not at an acceptable level.

26. A Firm shall establish policies and procedures designed to provide it with Reasonable Assurance that it is notified of breaches of Independence requirements, and to enable it to take appropriate actions to resolve such situations. The policies and procedures shall include requirements for:

(a) Personnel to promptly notify the Firm of Independence breaches of which they become aware;

(b) The Firm to promptly communicate identified breaches of these policies and procedures to:

(i) The Engagement Partner who, with the Firm, needs to address the breach; and

(ii) Other relevant Personnel in the Firm and, where appropriate, the Network, and those subject to the Independence requirements who need to take appropriate action; and

(c) Prompt communication to the Firm, if necessary, by the Engagement Partner and the other individuals referred to in subparagraph (b)(ii) of the actions taken to resolve the matter, so that the Firm can determine whether it should take further action.

AUST 27. Guidance on threats to Independence and safeguards, including application to specific situations, is set out in the Code. The Code also requires threats to Independence that are not clearly insignificant to be documented and include a description of the threats identified and the safeguards applied to eliminate or reduce the threats to an acceptable level.

AUST 28. A Firm receiving notice of a breach of Independence policies and procedures should promptly communicate relevant information to Engagement Partners, others in the Firm as appropriate and, where applicable, experts contracted by the Firm and Network Firm Personnel, for appropriate action. Appropriate action by the Firm and the relevant Engagement Partner should include applying appropriate safeguards to eliminate the threats to Independence or to reduce them to an acceptable level, or withdrawing from the Engagement.

29. At least annually, a Firm shall obtain written confirmation of compliance with its policies and procedures on Independence from all Firm Personnel required to be independent by Relevant Ethical Requirements.

30. Written confirmation may be in paper or electronic form. By obtaining confirmation and taking appropriate action on information indicating non-compliance, the Firm demonstrates the importance that it attaches to Independence and makes the issue current for, and visible to, it's Personnel.

31. A Firm shall establish policies and procedures:

(a) Setting out criteria for determining the need for safeguards to reduce the familiarity threat to an acceptable level when using the same senior Personnel on an Assurance Engagement over a long period of time; and

(b) Requiring, for audits of financial statements of Listed Entities, the rotation of the Engagement Partner and the individuals responsible for Engagement Quality Control Review, and where applicable, others subject to rotation requirements, after a specified period in compliance with Relevant Ethical Requirements.

32. The Code discusses the familiarity threat that may be created by using the same senior Personnel on an Assurance Engagement over a long period of time and the safeguards that might be appropriate to address such threats.

APES

33. Determining appropriate criteria to address familiarity threats may include matters such as:
    (a) the nature of the Engagement, including the extent to which it involves a matter of public interest; and
    (b) the length of service of the senior Personnel on the Engagement.

    Examples of safeguards include rotating the senior Personnel or requiring an Engagement Quality Control Review.

34. The Code recognises that the familiarity threat is particularly relevant in the context of financial statement audits of Listed Entities. For these audits, the Code requires the rotation of Key Audit Partners after a pre-defined period, normally no more than five years, and provides related standards and guidance.

Considerations specific to public sector organisations

35. Statutory measures may provide safeguards for the Independence of public sector auditors. However, threats to Independence may still exist regardless of any statutory measures designed to protect their Independence. Therefore, in establishing the policies and procedures required by paragraphs 19, 24–26, 29 and 31, public sector auditors should have regard to the public sector mandate and address any threats to Independence in that context.

36. Listed entities as referred to in paragraphs 31 and 34 are not common in the public sector. However, there may be other public sector entities that are significant due to size, complexity or public interest aspects, and which consequently have a wide range of stakeholders. Therefore, there may be instances when a Firm determines, based on its quality control policies and procedures, that a public sector entity is significant for the purposes of expanded quality control procedures.

37. In the public sector, legislation may establish the appointments and terms of office of the auditor with Engagement Partner responsibility. As a result, it may not be possible to comply strictly with the Engagement Partner rotation requirements envisaged for listed entities. Nonetheless, for public sector entities considered significant, as noted in paragraph 36, it may be in the public interest for public sector audit organisations to establish policies and procedures to promote compliance with the spirit of rotation of Engagement Partner responsibility.

Acceptance and continuance of Client relationships and specific Engagements

38. A Firm shall establish policies and procedures for the acceptance and continuance of Client relationships and specific Engagements, designed to provide the Firm with Reasonable Assurance that it will only undertake or continue relationships and Engagements where the Firm:

(a) Is competent to perform the Engagement and has the capabilities, including time and resources, to do so;

(b) Can comply with Relevant Ethical Requirements; and

(c) Has considered the integrity of the Client and does not have information that would lead it to conclude that the Client lacks integrity.

39. Consideration of whether the Firm has the competence, capabilities and resources to undertake a new Engagement from a new or an existing Client involves reviewing the specific requirements of the Engagement and the existing Partner and Staff profiles at all relevant levels, and including whether:

- Firm's Personnel have knowledge of relevant industries or subject matters;
- Firm's Personnel have experience with relevant regulatory or reporting requirements, or the ability to gain the necessary skills and knowledge effectively;

- The Firm has sufficient Personnel with the necessary competence and capabilities;
- Experts are available, if needed;
- Individuals meeting the criteria and eligibility requirements to perform Engagement Quality Control Review are available, where applicable; and
- The Firm is able to complete the Engagement within the reporting deadline.

40. With regard to the integrity of a Client, matters to consider include, for example:
   - The identity and business reputation of the Client's principal owners, key management, related parties and those charged with its governance.
   - The nature of the Client's operations, including its business practices.
   - Information concerning the attitude of the Client's principal owners, key management and those charged with its governance towards such matters as aggressive interpretation of accounting standards and the internal control environment.
   - Whether the Client is aggressively concerned with maintaining the Firm's fees as low as possible.
   - Indications of an inappropriate limitation in the scope of work.
   - Indications that the Client might be involved in money laundering or other criminal activities.
   - The reasons for the proposed appointment of the Firm and non-reappointment of the previous Firm.
   - The identity and business reputation of related parties.

   The extent of knowledge a Firm will have regarding the integrity of a Client will generally grow within the context of an ongoing relationship with that Client.

41. Sources of information on such matters obtained by the Firm may include the following:
   - Communications with existing or previous providers of professional accountancy services to the Client in accordance with Relevant Ethical Requirements, and discussions with other third parties.
   - Inquiry of other Firm's Personnel or third parties such as bankers, legal counsel and industry peers.
   - Background searches of relevant databases.

42. A Firm shall establish policies and procedures that require:

(a) The Firm to obtain such information as it considers necessary in the circumstances before accepting an Engagement with a new Client, when deciding whether to continue an existing Engagement, and when considering acceptance of a new Engagement with an existing Client.

(b) If a potential conflict of interest is identified prior to accepting an Engagement from a new or an existing Client or during the conduct of an Engagement, the Firm to determine whether it is appropriate to accept or continue the Engagement.

(c) If issues have been identified, and the Firm decides to accept or continue the Client relationship or a specific Engagement, the Firm to document how the issues were resolved.

43. Deciding whether to continue a Client relationship includes consideration of significant matters that have arisen during the current or previous Engagements, and their implications for continuing the relationship. For example, a Client may have started to expand its business operations into an area where the Firm does not possess the necessary expertise.

44. A Firm shall establish policies and procedures on continuing an Engagement and the Client relationship, addressing the circumstances where the Firm obtains information that would have caused it to decline the Engagement had that information been available earlier. Such policies and procedures shall include consideration of:

(a) The professional and legal responsibilities that apply to the circumstances, including whether there is a requirement for the Firm to report to the person or

APES

persons who made the appointment or, in some cases, to regulatory authorities; and

(b) The possibility of withdrawing from the Engagement or from both the Engagement and the Client relationship.

45. Policies and procedures on withdrawal from an Engagement or from both the Engagement and the Client relationship should address issues that include the following:

- Discussing with the appropriate level of the Client's management and those charged with its governance the appropriate action that the Firm might take based on the relevant facts and circumstances.
- If the Firm determines that it is appropriate to withdraw, discussing with the appropriate level of the Client's management and those charged with its governance withdrawal from the Engagement or from both the Engagement and the Client relationship, and the reasons for the withdrawal.
- Considering whether there is a professional, legal or regulatory requirement for the Firm to remain in place, or for the Firm to report the withdrawal from the Engagement, or from both the Engagement and the Client relationship, together with the reasons for the withdrawal, to regulatory authorities.
- Documenting significant matters, consultations, conclusions and the basis for the conclusions.

Consideration specific to public sector audit organisations

46. In the public sector, auditors may be appointed in accordance with statutory procedures. Accordingly, certain of the requirements and considerations regarding the acceptance and continuance of Client relationships and specific Engagements as set out in paragraphs 38-45 may not be relevant. Nonetheless, establishing policies and procedures as described may provide valuable information to public sector auditors in performing risk assessments and in carrying out reporting responsibilities.

Human resources

47. A Firm shall establish policies and procedures designed to provide it with Reasonable Assurance that it has sufficient Personnel with the competence, capabilities and commitment to ethical principles necessary to:

(a) Perform Engagements in accordance with Professional Standards and applicable legal and regulatory requirements; and

(b) Enable the Firm or Engagement Partners to issue reports that are appropriate in the circumstances.

48. Personnel issues relevant to a Firm's policies and procedures related to human resources include, for example:

- Recruitment.
- Performance evaluation.
- Capabilities, including time to perform assignments.
- Competence.
- Career development.
- Promotion.
- Compensation.
- The estimation of Personnel needs.

Effective recruitment processes and procedures help the Firm select individuals of integrity who have the capacity to develop the competence and capabilities necessary to perform the Firm's work and possess the appropriate characteristics to enable them to perform competently.

49. Competence can be developed through a variety of methods, including the following:
- Professional education.
- Continuing professional development, including training.
- Work experience.
- Coaching by more experienced Staff, for example, other members of the Engagement Team.
- Independence education for Personnel who are required to be independent.

50. The continuing competence of a Firm's Personnel depends to a significant extent on an appropriate level of continuing professional development so that Personnel maintain their knowledge and capabilities. Effective policies and procedures should emphasise the need for continuing training for all levels of the Firm's Personnel, and should provide the necessary training resources and assistance to enable Personnel to develop and maintain the required competence and capabilities.

51. A Firm may use a Suitably Qualified External Person, for example, when internal technical and training resources are unavailable.

52. Performance evaluation, compensation and promotion procedures give due recognition and reward to the development and maintenance of competence and commitment to ethical principles. Steps a Firm may take in developing and maintaining competence and commitment to ethical principles include:

(a) Making Personnel aware of the Firm's expectations regarding performance and ethical principles;

(b) Providing Personnel with evaluation of, and counseling on, performance, progress and career development; and

(c) Helping Personnel understand that advancement to positions of greater responsibility depends, among other things, upon performance quality and adherence to ethical principles, and that failure to comply with the Firm's policies and procedures may result in disciplinary action.

Considerations specific to smaller Firms

53. The size and circumstances of a Firm will influence the structure of the Firm's performance evaluation process. Smaller Firms, in particular, may employ less formal methods of evaluating the performance of their Personnel.

Assignment of Engagement Teams

54. A Firm shall assign responsibility for each Engagement to an Engagement Partner and shall establish policies and procedures requiring that:

(a) The identity and role of the Engagement Partner are communicated to key members of Client management and those charged with governance;

(b) The Engagement Partner has the appropriate competence, capabilities and authority to perform the role; and

(c) The responsibilities of the Engagement Partner are clearly defined and communicated to that Partner.

55. Policies and procedures may include systems to monitor the workload and availability of Engagement Partners so as to enable these individuals to have sufficient time to adequately discharge their responsibilities.

56. A Firm shall establish policies and procedures to assign appropriate Personnel with the necessary competence and capabilities to:

(a) Perform Engagements in accordance with Professional Standards and applicable legal and regulatory requirements; and

(b) Enable the Firm or Engagement Partners to issue reports that are appropriate in the circumstances.

APES

57. A Firm's assignment of Engagement Teams and the determination of the level of supervision required, include for example, consideration of the Engagement Team's:

- Understanding of, and practical experience with, Engagements of a similar nature and complexity through appropriate training and participation;
- Understanding of Professional Standards and applicable legal and regulatory requirements;
- Technical knowledge and expertise, including knowledge of relevant information technology;
- Knowledge of relevant industries in which the Clients operate;
- Ability to apply professional judgment; and
- Understanding of the Firm's quality control policies and procedures.

Engagement performance

58. A Firm shall establish policies and procedures designed to provide it with Reasonable Assurance that Engagements are performed in accordance with Professional Standards and applicable legal and regulatory requirements, and that the Firm or the Engagement Partner issue reports that are appropriate in the circumstances. Such policies and procedures shall include:

(a) Matters relevant to promoting consistency in the quality of Engagement performance;

(b) Supervision responsibilities; and

(c) Review responsibilities.

59. A Firm promotes consistency in the quality of Engagement performance through its policies and procedures. This is often accomplished through written or electronic manuals, software tools or other forms of standardised documentation, and industry or subject matter-specific guidance materials. Matters addressed may include:

- How Engagement Teams are briefed on the Engagement to obtain an understanding of the objectives of their work.
- Processes for complying with applicable Engagement standards.
- Processes of Engagement supervision, Staff training and coaching.
- Methods of reviewing the work performed, the significant judgments made and the form of report being issued.
- Appropriate documentation of the work performed and of the timing and extent of the review.
- Processes to keep all policies and procedures current.

60. Appropriate teamwork and training assist less experienced members of an Engagement Team to clearly understand the objectives of the assigned work.

61. Engagement supervision includes the following:

- Tracking the progress of the Engagement;
- Considering the competence and capabilities of individual members of the Engagement Team, whether they have sufficient time to carry out their work, whether they understand their instructions and whether the work is being carried out in accordance with the planned approach to the Engagement;
- Addressing significant matters arising during the Engagement, considering their significance and modifying the planned approach appropriately; and
- Identifying matters for consultation or consideration by more experienced Engagement Team members during the Engagement.

62. A review consists of consideration of whether:

(a) The work has been performed in accordance with Professional Standards and applicable legal and regulatory requirements;

(b) Significant matters have been raised for further consideration;

(c) Appropriate consultations have taken place and the resulting conclusions have been documented and implemented;

(d) There is a need to revise the nature, timing and extent of work performed;

(e) The work performed supports the conclusions reached and is appropriately documented;

(f) The evidence obtained is sufficient and appropriate to support the report; and

(g) The objectives of the Engagement procedures have been achieved.

63. A Firm's review responsibility policies and procedures shall be determined on the basis that work of less experienced team members is reviewed by more experienced Engagement Team members.

Consultation

64. A Firm shall establish policies and procedures designed to provide it with Reasonable Assurance that:

(a) Appropriate consultation takes place on difficult or contentious matters;

(b) Sufficient resources are available to enable appropriate consultation to take place;

Assurance Practices only

(c) The nature and scope of, and conclusions arising from, such consultations are documented and agreed by both the individual seeking consultation and the individual consulted; and

(d) Conclusions resulting from consultations are implemented.

65. Consultation includes discussion at the appropriate professional level, with individuals within or outside the Firm who have specialised expertise.

66. Consultation uses appropriate research resources as well as the collective experience and technical expertise of the Firm. Consultation helps to promote quality and improves the application of professional judgment. Appropriate recognition of consultation in the Firm's policies and procedures helps to promote a culture in which consultation is recognised as a strength and encourages Personnel to consult on difficult or contentious matters.

67. Effective consultation on significant technical, ethical and other matters within the Firm, or where applicable, outside the Firm can only be achieved when those consulted:

- Are given all the relevant facts that will enable them to provide informed advice; and
- Have appropriate knowledge, seniority and experience,

and when conclusions resulting from consultations are appropriately documented and implemented.

Considerations specific to smaller Firms

68. A Firm needing to consult externally, for example, a Firm without appropriate internal resources may take advantage of advisory services provided by:

- Professional and regulatory bodies; or
- Commercial organisations that provide relevant quality control services.

Before contracting for such services, consideration of the competence and capabilities of the external provider helps the Firm to determine whether the external provider is suitably qualified for that purpose.

APES

Assurance Practices only

69. Documentation of consultations with other professionals that involve difficult or contentious matters that is sufficiently complete and detailed contributes to an understanding of:

    (a) The issue on which consultation was sought; and

    (b) The results of the consultation, including any decisions taken, the basis for those decisions and how they were implemented.

Engagement Quality Control Review

70. A Firm shall establish policies and procedures requiring, for appropriate Engagements, an Engagement Quality Control Review that provides an objective evaluation of the significant judgments made by the Engagement Team and the conclusions reached in formulating the report. Such policies and procedures shall:

(a) Require an Engagement Quality Control Review for all audits of financial statements of Listed Entities;

(b) Set out criteria against which all other audits and reviews of historical financial information, and other assurance and related services Engagements shall be evaluated to determine whether an Engagement Quality Control Review should be performed; and

(c) Require an Engagement Quality Control Review for all Engagements, if any, meeting the criteria established in compliance with subparagraph 70(b).

71. Criteria for determining which Engagements other than audits of financial statements of Listed Entities are to be subject to an Engagement Quality Control Review may include, for example:

- The nature of the Engagement, including the extent to which it involves a matter of public interest.
- The identification of unusual circumstances or risks in an Engagement or class of Engagements.
- Whether laws or regulations require an Engagement Quality Control Review.

Nature, timing and extent of the Engagement Quality Control Review

72. A Firm shall establish policies and procedures setting out the nature, timing and extent of an Engagement Quality Control Review. Such policies and procedures shall require that the Engagement report not be dated until the completion of the Engagement Quality Control Review.

73. A Firm shall establish policies and procedures to require the Engagement Quality Control Review to include:

(a) Discussion of significant matters with the Engagement Partner;

(b) Review of the financial statements or other subject matter information and the proposed report;

(c) Review of selected Engagement Documentation relating to significant judgements the Engagement Team made and the conclusions it reached; and

(d) Evaluation of the conclusions reached in formulating the report and consideration of whether the proposed report is appropriate.

74. An Engagement report is not dated until the completion of the Engagement Quality Control Review. However, documentation of the Engagement Quality Control Review may be completed after the Date of Report.

75. Conducting the Engagement Quality Control Review in a timely manner at appropriate stages during the Engagement allows significant matters to be promptly resolved to the Engagement Quality Control Reviewer's satisfaction on or before the Date of Report.

76. The extent of the Engagement Quality Control Review may depend, among other things, on the complexity of the Engagement, whether the entity is a Listed Entity, and the risk that the report might not be appropriate in the circumstances. The performance of an Engagement Quality Control Review does not reduce the responsibilities of the Engagement Partner.

77. For audits of financial statements of Listed Entities, a Firm shall establish policies and procedures to require the Engagement Quality Control Review to include consideration of the following:

(a) The Engagement Team's evaluation of the Firm's Independence in relation to the specific Engagement;

(b) Whether appropriate consultation has taken place on matters involving differences of opinion or other difficult or contentious matters, and the conclusions arising from those consultations; and

(c) Whether documentation selected for review reflects the work performed in relation to significant judgements and supports the conclusions reached.

78. Other matters relevant to evaluating the significant judgements made by the Engagement Team that may be considered in an Engagement Quality Control Review of an audit of financial statements of a Listed Entity include:

- Significant risks identified during the Engagement and the responses to those risks.
- Judgments made, particularly with respect to materiality and significant risks.
- The significance and disposition of corrected and uncorrected misstatements identified during the Engagement.
- The matters to be communicated to management and those charged with governance and, where applicable, other parties such as regulatory bodies.

These other matters, depending of the circumstances, may also be applicable for Engagement Quality Control Reviews for audits of financial statements of other entities as well as reviews of financial statements and other assurance and related services Engagements.

Considerations specific to public sector audit organisations

79. Although not referred to as Listed Entities, as described in paragraph 36, certain public sector entities may be of sufficient significance to warrant performance of an Engagement Quality Control Review.

Criteria for the eligibility of Engagement Quality Control Reviewers

80. A Firm shall establish policies and procedures to address the appointment of Engagement Quality Control Reviewers and establish their eligibility through:

(a) The technical qualifications required to perform the role, including the necessary experience and authority; and

(b) The degree to which an Engagement Quality Control Reviewer can be consulted on the Engagement without compromising the reviewer's objectivity.

81. What constitutes sufficient and appropriate technical expertise, experience and authority depends on the circumstances of the Assurance Engagement. For example, the Engagement Quality Control Reviewer for an audit of the financial statements of a Listed Entity is likely to be an individual with sufficient and appropriate experience and authority to act as an audit Engagement Partner on audits of financial statements of Listed Entities.

82. The Engagement Partner may consult the Engagement Quality Control Reviewer during the Engagement, for example, to establish that a judgment made by the Engagement Partner will be acceptable to the Engagement Quality Control Reviewer. Such consultation avoids identification of differences of opinion at a late stage of the Engagement and need not compromise the Engagement Quality Control Reviewer's eligibility to perform the role. Where the nature and extent of the consultations become significant the reviewer's objectivity may be compromised unless care is taken by both the Engagement Team and the reviewer to maintain the reviewer's objectivity. Where this is not possible, another individual within the Firm or a Suitably Qualified External Person should be appointed to take on the role of either the Engagement Quality Control Reviewer or the person to be consulted on the Engagement.

83. A Firm shall establish policies and procedures designed to maintain the objectivity of the Engagement Quality Control Reviewer.

84. Such policies and procedures should provide that the Engagement Quality Control Reviewer:

(a) Where practicable, is not selected by the Engagement Partner;

(b) Does not otherwise participate in the Engagement during the period of review;

(c) Does not make decisions for the Engagement Team; and

(d) Is not subject to other considerations that would threaten the reviewer's objectivity.

Considerations specific to smaller Firms

85. It may not be practicable, in the case of Firms with few Partners, for the Engagement Partner not to be involved in selecting the Engagement Quality Control Reviewer. Suitably Qualified External Persons may be contracted where sole practitioners or small Firms identify Engagements requiring Engagement Quality Control Reviews. Alternatively, some sole practitioners or small Firms may wish to use other Firms to facilitate Engagement Quality Control Reviews. Where a Firm contracts Suitably Qualified External Persons, the Firm should follow the requirements and guidance in paragraphs 80-83 and 87.

Considerations specific to public sector audit organisations

86. In the public sector, a statutorily appointed auditor (for example, an Auditor General, or other suitably qualified person appointed on behalf of the Auditor General) may act in a role equivalent to that of Engagement Partner with overall responsibility for public sector audits. In such circumstances, where applicable, the selection of the Engagement Quality Control Reviewer should include consideration of the need for Independence from the audited entity and the ability of the Engagement Quality Control Reviewer to provide an objective evaluation.

87. A Firm's policies and procedures shall provide for the replacement of the Engagement Quality Control Reviewer where the reviewer's ability to perform an objective review may be impaired.

Documentation of the Engagement Quality Control Review

88. A Firm shall establish policies and procedures on documentation of the Engagement Quality Control Review which require documentation that:

(a) The procedures required by the Firm's policies on Engagement Quality Control Review have been performed;

(b) The Engagement Quality Control Review has been completed on or before the Date of Report; and

(c) The reviewer is not aware of any unresolved matters that would cause the reviewer to believe that the significant judgments the Engagement Team made and the conclusions it reached were not appropriate.

Differences of opinion

89. A Firm shall establish policies and procedures for dealing with and resolving differences of opinion within the Engagement Team, with those consulted and, where applicable, between the Engagement Partner and the Engagement Quality Control Reviewer.

90. Such policies and procedures shall require that:

(a) Conclusions reached be documented and implemented; and

(b) The report not be dated until the matter is resolved.

91. Effective procedures encourage identification of differences of opinion at an early stage, provide clear guidelines as to the successive steps to be taken thereafter, and require documentation regarding the resolution of the differences and the implementation of the conclusions reached.

92. Procedures to resolve such differences may include consulting with another practitioner or Firm, or a professional or regulatory body.

Engagement Documentation

Completion of the assembly of final Engagement files

93. A Firm shall establish policies and procedures for Engagement Teams to complete the assembly of final Engagement files on a timely basis after the Engagement reports have been finalised.

94. Law or regulation may prescribe the time limits by which the assembly of final Engagement files for specific types of Engagement is to be completed. Where no such time limits are prescribed in law or regulation, paragraph 93 requires the Firm to establish time limits that reflect the need to complete the assembly of final Engagement files on a timely basis. In the case of an audit, for example, such a time limit would ordinarily not be more than 60 days after the date of the auditor's report.

95. Where two or more different reports are issued in respect of the same subject matter information of an entity, a Firm's policies and procedures relating to time limits for the assembly of final Engagement files address each report as if it were for a separate Engagement. This may, for example, be the case when the Firm issues an auditor's report on a component's financial information for group consolidation purposes and, at a subsequent date, an auditor's report on the same financial information for statutory purposes.

Confidentiality, safe custody, integrity, accessibility and retrievability of Engagement Documentation

96. A Firm shall establish policies and procedures designed to maintain the confidentiality, safe custody, integrity, accessibility and retrievability of Engagement Documentation.

97. Relevant Ethical Requirements establish an obligation for the Firm's Personnel to observe at all times the confidentiality of information contained in Engagement Documentation, unless specific Client authority has been given to disclose information, or there is a legal duty to do so. Specific laws or regulations may impose additional obligations on the Firm's Personnel to maintain Client confidentiality, particularly where data of a personal nature are concerned.

98. Whether Engagement Documentation is in paper, electronic or other media, the integrity, accessibility or retrievability of the underlying data may be compromised if the documentation could be altered, added to or deleted without the Firm's knowledge, or if it could be permanently lost or damaged. Accordingly, controls that the Firm designs and implements to avoid unauthorised alteration or loss of Engagement Documentation may include those that:

- Enable the determination of when and by whom Engagement Documentation was created, changed or reviewed;
- Protect the integrity of the information at all stages of the Engagement, especially when the information is shared within the Engagement Team or transmitted to other parties via the Internet;

- Prevent unauthorised changes to the Engagement Documentation; and
- Allow access to the Engagement Documentation by the Engagement Team and other authorised parties as necessary to properly discharge their responsibilities.

99. Controls that the Firm designs and implements to maintain the confidentiality, safe custody, integrity, accessibility and retrievability of Engagement Documentation may include the following:

- The use of a password among Engagement Team members to restrict access to electronic Engagement Documentation to authorised users.
- Appropriate back-up routines for electronic Engagement Documentation at appropriate stages during the Engagement.
- Procedures for properly distributing Engagement Documentation to the team members at the start of Engagement, processing it during Engagement, and collating it at the end of Engagement.
- Procedures for restricting access to, and enabling proper distribution and confidential storage of, hardcopy Engagement Documentation.

100. For practical reasons, original paper documentation may be electronically scanned for inclusion in Engagement files. In such cases, the Firm's procedures designed to maintain the integrity, accessibility, and retrievability of the documentation may include requiring the Engagement Teams to:

- Generate scanned copies that reflect the entire content of the original paper documentation, including manual signatures, cross-references and annotations;
- Integrate the scanned copies into the Engagement files, including indexing and signing off on the scanned copies as necessary; and
- Enable the scanned copies to be retrieved and printed as necessary.

There may be legal, regulatory or other reasons for a Firm to retain original paper documentation that has been scanned.

Retention of Engagement Documentation

101. A Firm shall establish policies and procedures for the retention of Engagement Documentation for a period sufficient to meet the needs of the Firm or as required by law or regulation.

102. The needs of a Firm for retention of Engagement Documentation, and the period of such retention, will vary with the nature of the Engagement and the Firm's circumstances, for example, whether the Engagement Documentation is needed to provide a record of matters of continuing significance to future Engagements. The retention period may also depend on other factors, such as whether local law or regulation prescribes specific retention periods for certain types of Engagements, or whether there are generally accepted retention periods in the jurisdiction in the absence of specific legal or regulatory requirements.

103. In the specific case of audit Engagements, the retention period would ordinarily be no shorter than seven years from the date of the auditor's report, or, if later, the date of the group auditor's report.

104. Procedures that a Firm adopts for retention of Engagement Documentation include those that enable the requirements of paragraph 101 to be met during the retention period, for example to:

- Enable the retrieval of, and access to, the Engagement Documentation during the retention period, particularly in the case of electronic documentation since the underlying technology may be upgraded or changed over time;
- Provide, where necessary, a record of changes made to Engagement Documentation after the Engagement files have been completed; and
- Enable authorised external parties to access and review specific Engagement Documentation for quality control or other purposes.

Ownership of Engagement Documentation

105. Unless otherwise specified by law or regulation, Engagement Documentation is the property of a Firm. The Firm may, at its discretion, make portions of, or extracts from, Engagement Documentation available to Clients, provided such disclosure does not undermine the validity of the work performed, or, in the case of Assurance Engagements, the Independence of the Firm or its Personnel.

Monitoring

Monitoring a Firm's quality control policies and procedures

106. A Firm shall establish a Monitoring process designed to provide it with Reasonable Assurance that the policies and procedures relating to the system of quality control are relevant, adequate, and operating effectively. This process shall:

(a) Include an ongoing consideration and evaluation of the Firm's system of quality control, including, on a cyclical basis, Inspection of at least one completed Engagement for each Engagement Partner;

(b) Require responsibility for the Monitoring process to be assigned to a Partner or Partners or other persons with sufficient and appropriate experience and authority in the Firm to assume that responsibility; and

(c) Require that those performing the Engagement or the Engagement Quality Control Review are not involved in inspecting the Engagements.

107. The purpose of Monitoring compliance with quality control policies and procedures is to provide an evaluation of:

- Adherence to Professional Standards and applicable legal and regulatory requirements;
- Whether the system of quality control has been appropriately designed and effectively implemented; and
- Whether the Firm's quality control policies and procedures have been appropriately applied, so that reports that are issued by the Firm or Engagement Partners are appropriate in the circumstances.

108. Ongoing consideration and evaluation of the system of quality control include matters such as the following:

- Analysis of:
  - New developments in Professional Standards and applicable legal and regulatory requirements, and how they are reflected in the Firm's policies and procedures where appropriate;

Assurance Practices only

  - Written confirmation of compliance with policies and procedures on Independence;

  - Continuing professional development, including training; and
  - Decisions related to acceptance and continuance of Client relationships and specific Engagements.
- Determination of corrective actions to be taken and improvements to be made in the system, including the provision of feedback into the Firm's policies and procedures relating to education and training.
- Communication to appropriate Firm's Personnel of weaknesses identified in the system, in the level of understanding of the system, or compliance with it.
- Follow-up by appropriate Firm's Personnel so that necessary modifications are promptly made to the quality control policies and procedures.

AUST109. In determining the scope of the Inspections, Firms may take into account quality reviews conducted by the Professional Bodies or regulator.

APES

Assurance Practices only

Inspection cycle policies and procedures may, for example, specify a cycle that spans three years. The manner in which the Inspection cycle is organised, including the timing of selection of individual Engagements, depends on many factors, such as the following:

- The size of the Firm.
- The number and geographical location of offices.
- The results of previous Monitoring procedures.
- The degree of authority both Personnel and offices have (for example, whether individual offices are authorised to conduct their own Inspections or whether only the head office may conduct them).
- The nature and complexity of the Firm's practice and organisation.
- The risks associated with the Firm's Clients and specific Engagements.

110. The Inspection process includes the selection of individual Assurance Engagements, some of which may be selected without prior notification to the Engagement Team. In determining the scope of the Inspections, the Firm may take into account the scope or conclusions of an independent external Inspection program such as conducted by the Professional Bodies or regulator. However, an independent external Inspection program does not act as a substitute for the Firm's own internal Monitoring program.

Considerations specific to smaller Firms

111. In the case of small Firms, Monitoring procedures may need to be performed by individuals who are responsible for design and implementation of the Firm's quality control policies and procedures, or who may be involved in performing the Engagement Quality Control Review. A Firm with a limited number of persons may choose to use a Suitably Qualified External Person or another Firm to carry out Engagement Inspections and other Monitoring procedures. Alternatively, the Firm may establish arrangements to share resources with other appropriate organisations to facilitate Monitoring activities.

Evaluating, communicating and remedying identified deficiencies

112. A Firm shall evaluate the effect of deficiencies noted as a result of the Monitoring process and determine whether they are either:

(a) Instances that do not necessarily indicate that the Firm's system of quality control is insufficient to provide it with Reasonable Assurance that it complies with Professional Standards and applicable legal and regulatory requirements, and that the reports issued by the Firm or Engagement Partners are appropriate in the circumstances; or

(b) Systemic, repetitive or other significant deficiencies that require prompt corrective action.

113. A Firm shall communicate to relevant Engagement Partners and other appropriate Personnel deficiencies noted as a result of the Monitoring process and recommendations for appropriate remedial action.

114. The reporting of identified deficiencies to individuals other than the relevant Engagement Partners need not include an identification of the specific Assurance Engagements concerned, although there may be cases where such identification may be necessary for the proper discharge of the responsibilities of the individuals other than the Engagement Partners.

115. Recommendations for appropriate remedial actions for deficiencies noted shall include one or more of the following:

(a) Taking appropriate remedial action in relation to an individual Assurance Engagement or member of Personnel;

(b) The communication of the findings to those responsible for training and professional development;

(c) Changes to the quality control policies and procedures; and

(d) Disciplinary action against those who fail to comply with the policies and procedures of the Firm, especially those who do so repeatedly.

116. A Firm shall establish policies and procedures to address cases where the results of the Monitoring procedures indicate that a report may be inappropriate or that procedures were omitted during the performance of the Assurance Engagement. Such policies and procedures shall require the Firm to determine what further action is appropriate to comply with relevant Professional Standards and applicable legal and regulatory requirements and to consider whether to obtain legal advice.

117. A Firm shall communicate at least annually the results of the Monitoring of its system of quality control to Engagement Partners and other appropriate individuals within the Firm, including the Firm's chief executive officer or, if appropriate, its managing board of Partners. This communication shall be sufficient to enable the Firm and these individuals to take prompt and appropriate action where necessary in accordance with their defined roles and responsibilities. Information communicated shall include the following:

(a) A description of the Monitoring procedures performed.

(b) The conclusions drawn from the Monitoring procedures.

(c) Where relevant, a description of systemic, repetitive or other significant deficiencies and of the actions taken to resolve or amend those deficiencies.

118. Some Firms operate as part of a Network and, for consistency, may implement some of their Monitoring procedures on a Network basis. Where Firms within a Network operate under common Monitoring policies and procedures designed to comply with this Standard, and these Firms place reliance on such a Monitoring system, the Firm's policies and procedures shall require that:

(a) At least annually, the Network communicate the overall scope, extent and results of the Monitoring process to appropriate individuals within the Network Firms; and

(b) The Network communicate promptly any identified deficiencies in the system of quality control to appropriate individuals within the relevant Network Firm or Firms so that the necessary action can be taken,

in order that Engagement Partners in the Network Firms can rely on the results of the Monitoring process implemented within the Network, unless the Firms or the Network advise otherwise.

Complaints and allegations

119. A Firm shall establish policies and procedures designed to provide it with Reasonable Assurance that it deals appropriately with:

(a) Complaints and allegations that the work performed by the Firm fails to comply with Professional Standards and applicable legal and regulatory requirements; and

(b) Allegations of non-compliance with the Firm's system of quality control.

As part of this process, the Firm shall establish clearly defined channels for Firm's Personnel to raise any concerns in a manner that enables them to come forward without fear of reprisals.

120. Complaints and allegations (which do not include those that are clearly frivolous) may originate from within or outside the Firm. They may be made by Firm's Personnel, Clients or other third parties. They may be received by Engagement Team members or other Firm's Personnel.

Assurance Practices only

121. Policies and procedures established for the investigation of complaints and allegations may include for example, that the Partner supervising the investigation:

- Has sufficient and appropriate experience;
- Has authority within the Firm; and
- Is otherwise not involved in the Engagement.

The Partner supervising the investigation may involve legal counsel as necessary.

122. If during the investigations into complaints and allegations, deficiencies in the design or operation of the Firm's quality control policies and procedures or non-compliance with the Firm's system of quality control by an individual or individuals are identified, the Firm shall take appropriate actions as set out in paragraph 115.

Considerations specific to smaller Firms

123. It may not be practicable, in the case of Firms with few Partners, for the Partner supervising the investigation not to be involved in the Engagement. These small Firms and sole practitioners may use the services of a Suitable Qualified External Person or another Firm to carry out the investigation into complaints and allegations.

Documentation of the system of quality control

124. A Firm shall establish policies and procedures requiring appropriate documentation to provide evidence of the operation of each element of its system of quality control.

125. The form and content of documentation evidencing the operation of each of the elements of the system of quality control is a matter of judgment and depends on a number of factors, including the following:

- The size of the Firm and the number of offices.
- The nature and complexity of the Firm's practice and organisation.

For example, large Firms may use electronic databases to document matters such as Independence confirmations, performance evaluations and the results of Monitoring Inspections.

126. Appropriate documentation relating to Monitoring should include, for example:

- Monitoring procedures, including the procedure for selecting completed Engagements to be inspected.
- A record of evaluation of:
  - Adherence to Professional Standards and applicable legal and regulatory requirements;
  - Whether the system of quality control has been appropriately designed and effectively implemented; and
  - Whether the Firm's quality control policies and procedures have been appropriately applied, so that reports that are issued by the Firm or Engagement Partners are appropriate in the circumstances.
- Identification of the deficiencies noted an evaluation of their effect, and the basis for determining whether and what further action is necessary.

Considerations specific to smaller Firms

127. Smaller Firms may use more informal methods in the documentation of their systems of quality control such as manual notes, checklists and forms.

128. **A Firm shall establish policies and procedures that require retention of documentation for a period of time sufficient to permit those performing Monitoring procedures to evaluate the Firm's compliance with its system of quality control, or for a longer period if required by law or regulation.**

129. **A Firm shall establish policies and procedures requiring documentation of complaints and allegations and the responses to them.**

Effective Date

130. Systems of quality control in compliance with this Standard are required to be established by 1 January 2010. Firms should consider the appropriate transitional arrangements for Engagements in process at that date.

❖ ❖ ❖

Conformity with International Pronouncements

APES 320 and ISQC 1

APES 320 incorporates ISQC 1 'Quality Control for Firms that Perform Audits and Reviews of Financial Statements, and Other Assurance and Related Services Engagements' issued by the IAASB. Words have only been changed where there is a need to accommodate Australian legislation and environment, and to fit within the structure of APES 320. These changes do not affect the substance of the requirements. Where paragraphs of APES 320 have no equivalent in the corresponding international standard, they are denoted with the letters "AUST" before the paragraph number.

Compliance with ISQC 1

The basic principles and essential procedures of APES 320 and ISQC 1 are consistent except for:

- The addition of paragraphs prefixed as AUST in APES 320; and
- The 'Scope and application section' included in APES 320 in accordance with APESB's drafting conventions.

APES

Appendix

Application requirements for Firms

The application requirements for Firms are summarised in the flow chart below.

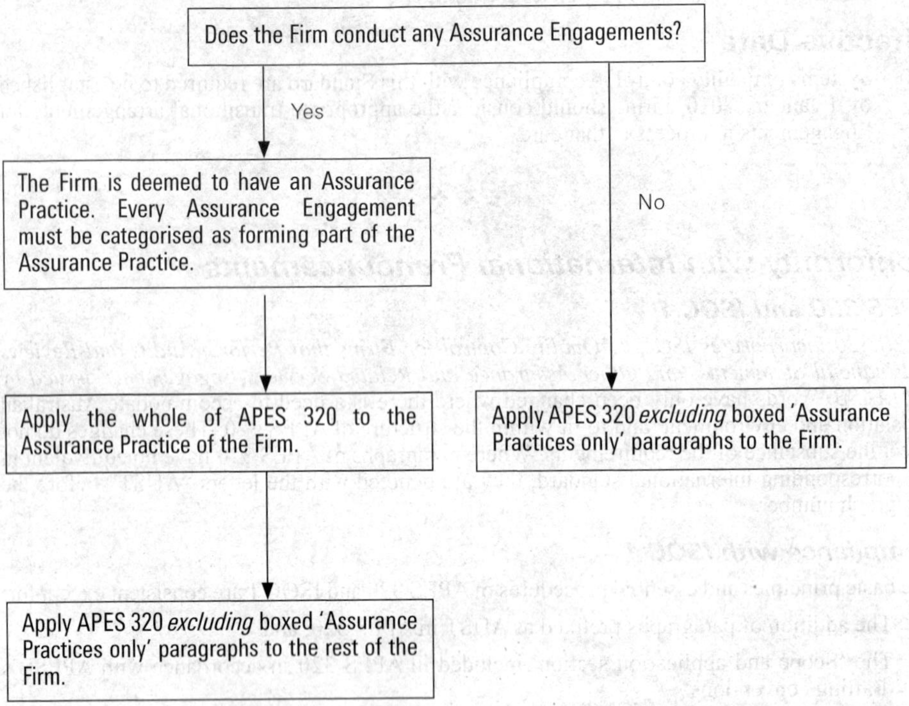

APES 320
APESB Technical Update
(Issued 17 September 2009)

Issued by the Accounting Professional and Ethical Standards Board.

APESB issues clarification in respect of Key Audit Partners

In May 2009, the Accounting Professional and Ethical Standards Board (APESB) issued a revised version of APES 320 *Quality Control for Firms* (APES 320) which will be effective from 1 January 2010. APES 320 has a mandatory requirement that in respect of listed entities, firms must establish rotation arrangements for the engagement partner, engagement quality control reviewer and others subject to rotation in accordance with relevant ethical requirements. APES 320 defines relevant ethical requirements as being Part A and B of APES 110 *Code of Ethics for Professional Accountants* (APES 110).

The revised APES 320 includes a definition of Key Audit Partner which is consistent with the recently issued IFAC Code of Ethics. The definition of Key Audit Partner in the new IFAC Code is broader than the requirements in the existing APES 110. For example, the broader definition will also capture partners responsible for key subsidiaries.

The existing APES 110 considers that in respect of listed entities the following personnel should be rotated after five financial years within a seven year period:

- Lead Engagement Partner;
- Audit Review Partner (if any); and
- Engagement Quality Control Reviewer

Stakeholders have raised concerns that the reference in APES 320 to Key Audit Partner can be read to mean that APES 320 is early adopting the broader definition of Key Audit Partner in the new IFAC Code. This is not the intention of the inclusion of the Key Audit Partner definition in APES 320. The purpose of the mandatory and guidance paragraphs is to refer to the rotation requirements established by the Code (APES 110) that are effective at the time.

Accordingly, until APESB issues the revised Code in line with the new IFAC Code and those provisions become effective, the Partners who are subject to rotation requirements will be the Lead Engagement Partner, Audit Review Partner and Engagement Quality Control Reviewer as defined in the existing APES 110.

APES 325
Risk Management for Firms

(Issued December 2011)

Issued by the Accounting Professional and Ethical Standards Board.

Note from the Institute of Chartered Accountants Australia

This note, prepared by the technical editor, is not part of APES 325.

Historical development

December 2011: APES 325 issued in December 2011. It contains a mandatory requirement to establish and maintain a risk management framework, together with supporting guidance. It is operative from 1 January 2013, when it will supersede the Institute's N3 'Risk Management Guidelines'. Early adoption is permitted.

Contents

1. Scope and application

1.1 Accounting Professional & Ethical Standards Board Limited (APESB) issues professional standard APES 325 *Risk Management for Firms* **(the Standard)**. A Risk Management Framework in compliance with this Standard is required to be established by Firms by 1 January 2013. Earlier adoption of this Standard is permitted.

1.2 APES 325 sets the standards for Members in Public Practice to establish and maintain a Risk Management Framework in their Firms in respect of the provision of quality and ethical Professional Services. Members have a responsibility, whether as owner, Partner or employee, to ensure that the Firm implements the requirements of the Standard. The level of responsibility will depend on the position held by each Member in the Firm, but as a minimum all Members should participate in the Firm achieving the objectives of the Standard. The Standard adopts the Firm as the overarching entity which must implement the requirements of the Standard, but it is the Firm's Members in Public Practice who have responsibility to ensure this occurs.

1.3 The mandatory requirements of this Standard are in **bold type (black lettering)**, preceded or followed by discussion or explanation in normal type (grey type). APES 325 should be read in conjunction with other professional duties of Members in Public Practice, and any legal obligations that may apply.

1.4 Members in Public Practice conducting the operations of a Firm in Australia shall follow the mandatory requirements of APES 325.

1.5 Members in Public Practice conducting the operations of a Firm outside Australia shall follow the provisions of APES 325 to the extent to which they are not prevented from so doing by specific requirements of local laws and/or regulations.

1.6 Members in Public Practice shall be familiar with relevant Professional Standards and guidance notes when providing Professional Services. All Members shall comply with the fundamental principles outlined in the Code.

1.7 The Standard is not intended to detract from any responsibilities which may be imposed by law or regulation.

1.8 All references to Professional Standards, guidance notes and legislation are references to those provisions as amended from time to time.

1.9 In applying the requirements outlined in APES 325, Members in Public Practice should be guided not merely by the words but also by the spirit of the Standard and the Code.

2. Definitions

For the purpose of this Standard:

Code means APES 110 *Code of Ethics for Professional Accountants.*

Engagement means an agreement, whether written or otherwise, between a Member in Public Practice and a Client relating to the provision of Professional Services by a Member in Public Practice. However, consultations with a prospective Client prior to such an agreement are not part of an Engagement.

Firm means:

(a) A sole practitioner, partnership, corporation or other entity of professional accountants;

(b) An entity that controls such parties through ownership, management or other means;

(c) An entity controlled by such parties through ownership, management or other means; or

(d) An Auditor-General's office or department.

Member in Public Practice means a Member, irrespective of functional classification (e.g. audit, tax, or consulting) in a Firm that provides Professional Services. The term is also used to refer to a Firm of Members in Public Practice and means a practice entity as defined by the applicable Professional Body.

Monitoring means a process comprising ongoing consideration and evaluation of the Firm's Risk Management Framework designed to provide reasonable confidence that the Firm's Risk Management Framework is operating effectively.

Network means a larger structure:

(i) that is aimed at co-operation; and

(ii) that is clearly aimed at profit or cost-sharing or shares common ownership, control or management, common quality control policies and procedures, common business strategy, the use of a common brand name, or a significant part of professional resources.

Partner means any individual with authority to bind the Firm with respect to the performance of a Professional Services Engagement.

Personnel means Partners and Staff.

Professional Services means services requiring accountancy or related skills performed by a Member in Public Practice including accounting, auditing, taxation, management consulting and financial management services.

Professional Standards means all standards issued by the Accounting Professional & Ethical Standards Board and all professional and ethical requirements of the applicable Professional Body.

Risk means the effect of uncertainty on objectives.

Risk Management means coordinated activities undertaken by a Firm, to direct and control the activities of the Firm with regard to Risk.

Risk Management Framework means the foundations[1] and organisational arrangements[2] for designing, implementing, Monitoring, reviewing and continually improving Risk Management throughout the Firm.

Staff means professionals, other than Partners, including any experts the Firm engages.

3. Objectives of a Risk Management Framework

3.1 An effective Risk Management Framework should assist a Firm to meet its overarching public interest obligations as well as its business objectives by:

(a) Facilitating business continuity;

(b) Enabling quality and ethical services to be rendered to clients; and

(c) Protecting the reputation and credibility of the Firm.

3.2 The Risk Management Framework should consist of policies designed to achieve the objectives set out in paragraph 3.1 and procedures necessary to implement and monitor compliance with those policies. The Risk Management Framework should be an integral part of the Firm's overall strategic and operational policies and practices and should take account of the Firm's Risk appetite.

3.3 A Firm's quality control policies and procedures, developed in accordance with APES 320 *Quality Control for Firms*, should be embedded within the Risk Management Framework.

---

1 The foundations include the policy, objectives, mandate and commitment to manage Risk.

2 The organisational arrangements include plans, relationships, accountabilities, resources, processes and activities.

This will facilitate a Firm complying with this standard and APES 320 and ensure consistency within the Firm's policies and procedures.

3.4 The requirements of the Standard are designed to enable a Firm to achieve the objectives stated in paragraph 3.1. The proper application of the requirements is therefore expected to provide a sufficient basis for the achievement of the objectives. However, because circumstances vary widely and all such circumstances cannot be anticipated, the Firm should consider whether there are particular matters or circumstances that require the Firm to establish policies and procedures in addition to those required by this Standard to meet the stated objectives.

4. Establishing and maintaining a Risk Management Framework for a Firm

4.1 **A Firm shall establish and maintain a Risk Management Framework taking into consideration its public interest obligations. The Firm shall periodically evaluate the design and effectiveness of the Risk Management Framework.**

4.2 **The Firm's Risk Management Framework shall include policies and procedures that identify, assess and manage key organisational Risks, which may include:**

- **(a) Governance Risks;**
- **(b) Business continuity Risks (including succession planning);**
- **(c) Business Risks;**
- **(d) Financial Risks;**
- **(e) Regulatory Risks;**
- **(f) Technology Risks**
- **(g) Human resources Risks; and**
- **(h) Stakeholder Risks.**

Additional Risks specific to the Firm can be identified through the use of other relevant standards or guidance.

4.3 The nature and extent of the policies and procedures developed by a Firm to comply with this Standard will depend on various factors such as the size and operating characteristics of the Firm and whether it is part of a Network.

4.4 **The Firm's chief executive officer (or equivalent) or, if appropriate, the Firm's managing board of Partners (or equivalent), shall take ultimate responsibility for the Firm's Risk Management Framework.**

4.5 The Firm's leadership and the examples it sets significantly influence the culture of the Firm. The adoption of an appropriate culture by a Firm is dependent on clear, consistent and frequent actions and messages from all levels within the Firm that emphasise the Firm's Risk Management policies and procedures.

4.6 **A Firm shall ensure that the Personnel assigned responsibility for establishing and maintaining its Risk Management Framework in accordance with this Standard have the necessary skills, experience, commitment and authority.**

4.7 Firms may refer to the following documents for guidance:

- *AS/NZS ISO 31000:2009 Risk Management – Principles and guidelines* which provides useful guidance to develop a framework for Risk Management: and
- For sole practitioners and small Firms, *Module 7: Risk Management of the Guide to Practice Management for Small and Medium-sized Practices* issued by the Small and Medium Practice Committee of the International Federation of Accountants.

APES

5. Monitoring a Firm's Risk Management policies and procedures

5.1 **A Firm shall establish a Monitoring process designed to provide reasonable confidence that the Risk Management policies and procedures relating to the Risk Management Framework are relevant, adequate and operating effectively and**

that instances of non-compliance with the Firm's Risk Management policies and procedures are detected.

5.2 A Firm shall establish a process whereby instances of non-compliance with the Firm's Risk Management policies and procedures are brought to the attention of the Firm's leadership who shall take appropriate corrective action.

5.3 A Firm's Monitoring process should include the requirements for the Firm:

(a) To undertake a review of the Firm's Risk Management Framework on a regular basis; and

(b) To designate from within the Firm's leadership a person or persons with sufficient and appropriate experience and authority the responsibility for ensuring that such regular reviews of the Firm's Risk Management Framework occurs.

6. Documentation

6.1 A Firm shall document its Risk Management Framework.

6.2 The form and content of documentation of the Risk Management Framework for a Firm is a matter of judgment and depends on a number of factors, including:

- The number of Personnel and offices of the Firm; and
- The nature and complexity of the Firm's practice and the services provided.

6.3 A Firm shall document its Risk Management policies and procedures and communicate them to the Firm's Personnel.

6.4 Communication of Risk Management policies and procedures to a Firm's Personnel should include a description of the policies and procedures, the objectives they are designed to achieve, and a message that each individual has a personal responsibility for Risk Management and is required to comply with the policies and procedures. In recognition of the importance of obtaining feedback on the Firm's Risk Management Framework and policies and procedures, the Firm's Personnel should be encouraged to communicate their views and concerns on Risk Management matters.

6.5 The documentation of a Firm's Risk Management Framework should include:

- Procedures for identifying potential Risks;
- The Firm's Risk appetite;
- Risks identified;
- Procedures for assessing and managing Risks;
- Treatment of identified Risks;
- Documentation processes;
- Procedures for dealing with non-compliance;
- Training of Staff in relation to Risk Management; and
- Procedures for regularly reviewing the Risk Management Framework.

6.6 A Firm shall retain all relevant documentation for a sufficient time to permit those performing the Firm's Monitoring process to evaluate its compliance with its Risk Management Framework and to comply with applicable legal or regulatory requirements for record retention.

6.7 A Firm shall document all instances of non-compliance with the Firm's Risk Management policies and procedures detected though its Monitoring process and the actions taken by the Firm's leadership in respect of those instances of non-compliance.

❖ ❖ ❖

Conformity with International Pronouncements

The International Ethics Standard Board for Accountants (IESBA) has not issued a pronouncement equivalent to APES 325.

APES 330
Insolvency Services

(Issued September 2009: revised November 2011)

Issued by the Accounting Professional and Ethical Standards Board.

Note from the Institute of Chartered Accountants Australia

This note, prepared by the technical editor, is not part of APES 330.

Historical development

September 2009: APES 330 issued. It has a greater focus on the independence of the practitioner and also contains guidance on providing expert witness services in the context of insolvency. It is operative for insolvency services commencing on or after 1 April 2010 and replaces APS 7 'Statement of Insolvency Standards' from that date. APS 7 was first issued in March 1984 by the Institute of Chartered Accountants in Australia and the Australian Society of Accountants (now CPA Australia). It was revised in 1989 and 1998.

November 2011: APES 330 revised to expand the relationships an insolvency practitioner must consider in assessing independence and to introduce the 'Network Firm' definition that is currently used in the APESB's 'Code of Ethics' in relation to auditor independence requirements. It is effective for insolvency services commencing on or after 1 April 2012, with early adoption permitted.

APES

Contents

1. Scope and application

1.1 Accounting Professional & Ethical Standards Board Limited (APESB) has revised professional standard APES 330 *Insolvency Services* (**the Standard**), which is effective for Insolvency Services commencing on or after 1 April 2012. Earlier adoption of this Standard is permitted.

1.2 APES 330 sets the standards for Members in Public Practice in the provision of quality and ethical Insolvency Services. The mandatory requirements of this Standard are in **bold-type (black lettering)**, preceded or followed by discussion or explanations in normal type (grey lettering). APES 330 should be read in conjunction with other professional duties of Members and any legal obligations that may apply.

1.3 Members in Public Practice in Australia shall follow the mandatory requirements of APES 330 when they provide Insolvency Services.

1.4 Members in Public Practice outside of Australia shall follow the mandatory requirements of APES 330 when they provide Insolvency Services, to the extent to which they are not prevented from so doing by specific requirements of local laws and/or regulations.

1.5 Members in Public Practice shall be familiar with relevant Professional Standards and guidance notes when providing Professional Services. All Members shall comply with the fundamental principles outlined in the Code.

1.6 The Standard is not intended to detract from any responsibilities which may be imposed by law or regulation.

1.7 All references to Professional Standards, guidance notes and legislation are references to those provisions as amended from time to time.

1.8 In applying the requirements outlined in APES 330, Members in Public Practice should be guided not merely by the words but also by the spirit of the Standard and the Code.

2. Definitions

For the purpose of this Standard:

Acceptable Level means a level at which a reasonable and informed third party would be likely to conclude, weighing all the specific facts and circumstances available to the Member in Public Practice at that time, that compliance with the fundamental principles of the Code is not compromised.

Administration means an insolvency arrangement arising from an Appointment, other than a members' voluntary liquidation, under which an insolvent Entity operates.

Appointee means a Member in Public Practice who is appointed to an Administration.

Appointment means the appointment of a Member in Public Practice as a Trustee in bankruptcy, a Trustee appointed under Section 50, a debt agreement administrator under Part IX, or a Trustee or controlling Trustee under Part X of the *Bankruptcy Act 1966*; or as a liquidator or provisional liquidator (other than a liquidator in a members' voluntary liquidation), a voluntary administrator, an administrator of a deed of company arrangement, a Controller, or a scheme manager under Chapter 5 of the *Corporations Act 2001*; or an appointment to provide Insolvency Services under any other legislation.

Approving Body means the body with authority to approve Professional Fees. Depending on the type of Appointment, this body will be the creditors, the secured creditor, the Committee or the court. In limited circumstances in an Appointment under the *Corporations Act 2001* or the *Bankruptcy Act 1966*, this approval is provided pursuant to those Acts.

Associate means an entity or person defined as an associate in the *Corporations Act 2001*.

Associated Entity means an Entity, including an unincorporated Entity such as a partnership, over which a Member in Public Practice has significant influence, that is neither a Controlled Entity nor an interest in a joint venture.

Close Family means a parent, child or sibling, who is not an Immediate Family member.

Code means APES 110 *Code of Ethics for Professional Accountants*.

Committee means a committee of inspection or committee of creditors.

Contingent Fee means a fee calculated on a predetermined basis relating to the outcome of a transaction or the result of the work performed. A fee that is established by a court or other public authority is not a Contingent Fee.

Controlled Entity means an Entity over which a Member in Public Practice has the power to govern the financial and operating policies of the Entity so as to obtain benefits from its activities.

Controller means a Member in Public Practice appointed as controller or managing controller under Part 5.2 of the *Corporations Act 2001*.

Engagement means an agreement, whether written or otherwise, between a Member in Public Practice and a client relating to the provision of Professional Services by a Member in Public Practice. However, consultations with a prospective client prior to such agreement are not part of an Engagement.

Entity means any legal, administrative or fiduciary arrangement, organisational structure or other party (including a person) having the capacity to deploy scarce resources in order to achieve objectives.

Expenses means the financial outlays incurred or paid by a Member in Public Practice to carry out an Administration. The term includes costs and disbursements.

Expert Witness means a Member in Public Practice who during the course of an Administration acts as an Expert Witness. As an Expert Witness, the Member may express opinions to the court based on the Member's specialised training, study or experience.

Financial Interest means an interest in an equity or other security, debenture, loan or other debt instrument of an Entity, including rights and obligations to acquire such an interest and derivatives directly related to such interest.

Firm means

(a) A sole practitioner, partnership, corporation or other entity of professional accountants;

(b) An entity that controls such parties through ownership, management or other means;

(c) An entity controlled by such parties through ownership, management or other means; or

(d) An Auditor-General's office or department.

Immediate Family means a spouse (or equivalent) or dependant.

Independence means

(a) Independence of mind - the state of mind that permits the provision of an opinion without being affected by influences that compromise professional judgment, allowing an individual to act with integrity, and exercise objectivity and professional scepticism; and

(b) Independence in appearance - the avoidance of facts and circumstances that are so significant a reasonable and informed third party, having knowledge of all relevant information, including any safeguards applied, would reasonably conclude a Firm's, or a member of the Engagement team's, integrity, objectivity or professional scepticism had been compromised.

Inducement means any benefit, whether monetary or not, given by a Member in Public Practice, the Member's Firm, Partners or an employee, or agent, consultant, or contractor of the Member, to an Entity which may in the view of a reasonable person influence that Entity's decision to refer, or to make, an Appointment.

An Inducement does not include:

- benefits of insignificant value in aggregate to the Entity which referred or made the Appointment;
- sponsorship of events or publications open to the public, or members of a professional body; or
- retainers or other similar payments to marketing consultants.

Insolvency Services means a Professional Service, excluding those in respect of members' voluntary liquidations, provided by a Member in Public Practice to an insolvent Entity under an Appointment.

Managerial Employee means an employee who acts in a managerial capacity within the structure of a Firm, including providing oversight, in the provision of services to clients.

Member means a member of a professional body that has adopted this Standard as applicable to their membership, as defined by that professional body.

Member in Public Practice means a Member, irrespective of functional classification (e.g. audit, tax or consulting) in a Firm that provides Professional Services. The term is also used to refer to a Firm of Members in Public Practice and means a practice entity as defined by the applicable professional body.

Network means a larger structure:

(a) That is aimed at co-operation; and

(b) That is clearly aimed at profit or cost sharing or shares common ownership, control or management, common quality control policies and procedures, common business strategy, the use of a common brand-name, or a significant part of professional resources.

Network Firm means a Firm or entity that belongs to a Network.

Office means a distinct sub-group, whether organised on geographical or practice lines.

Partner means any individual with authority to bind the Firm with respect to the performance of an Administration.

Pre-appointment Advice means any professional advice, whether giving an opinion or not, provided prior to an Appointment to an insolvent Entity or, if the insolvent Entity is a company, to its directors including advice given to advisors to the insolvent Entity or its directors.

Professional Fees means the amounts billed or to be billed by a Member in Public Practice on account of Professional Services performed or to be performed by the Member.

Professional Services means services requiring accountancy or related skills performed by a Member in Public Practice including accounting, auditing, taxation, management consulting and financial management services.

Professional Standards means all Standards issued by Accounting Professional & Ethical Standards Board Limited and all professional and ethical requirements of the applicable professional body.

Related Entity means an entity or person defined as a related entity in the *Bankruptcy Act 1966*.

Trustee means a person who administers a bankruptcy or Part X administration under the *Bankruptcy Act 1966*.

Witness Report means a written report, affidavit or written statement that is for the purpose of communicating expert evidence in a matter that is to be considered by a court.

3. Fundamental responsibilities of Members in Public Practice

3.1 **A Member in Public Practice providing an Insolvency Service shall comply with Section 100 Introduction and Fundamental Principles of the Code and relevant law.**

Public interest

3.2 **In accordance with Section 100 *Introduction and Fundamental Principles of the Code*, a Member in Public Practice shall observe and comply with the Member's public interest obligations when the Member provides an Insolvency Service.**

3.3 **A Member in Public Practice shall not advise an insolvent Entity (nor, if the Entity is a company, its directors) on how to cause assets to be unavailable in an Administration or to otherwise avoid the consequences of the insolvency.**

3.4 Paragraph 3.3 does not prevent a Member in Public Practice from providing Professional Services in respect of the structuring of the financial affairs of a solvent Entity.

Capacity and resources

3.5 **Prior to accepting an Appointment, a Member in Public Practice shall ensure that the Member has the capacity and has access to the necessary resources to conduct the proposed Administration in an effective and efficient manner.**

Professional competence and due care

3.6 **A Member in Public Practice providing an Insolvency Service shall maintain professional competence, take due care and act in a timely manner in the performance of the Member's work in accordance with Section 130 *Professional Competence and Due Care* of the Code.**

3.7 **When dealing with other practitioners in transitioning Appointments or where there are parallel Appointments, a Member in Public Practice shall be professional and co-operative, without compromising the Member's obligations in the Member's Appointment.**

3.8 **Where an Insolvency Service requires the consideration of matters that are outside the professional expertise of a Member in Public Practice, the Member shall seek expert assistance or advice from a suitably qualified third party, or decline the Insolvency Service. Where the Member relies on the advice of a third party, the Member shall disclose in relevant reports or communications the name and qualifications of the third party and the areas in which third party advice has been obtained. This obligation does not extend to legal advice where disclosure may result in a waiver of legal professional privilege.**

3.9 Relevant reports are those reports that include a reference to the subject matter for which expert assistance or advice has been obtained.

3.10 When planning to use the work of a suitably qualified third party, a Member in Public Practice shall assess the professional competence and objectivity of that third party, the appropriateness and reasonableness of the work performed, and the Professional Fees charged.

3.11 A Member in Public Practice shall take all reasonable steps to communicate with Entities affected by an Administration in a timely and clear manner as to the insolvency processes and the rights and obligations of the Entities.

3.12 In undertaking an Insolvency Service, a Member in Public Practice should consider any guidance issued by the professional accounting bodies and appropriate regulatory authorities.

Confidentiality

3.13 In accordance with Section 140 *Confidentiality* of the Code, a Member in Public Practice who acquires confidential information in the course of an Insolvency Service shall not use that information for any purpose other than the proper performance of that Insolvency Service.

Marketing

3.14 A Member in Public Practice providing an Insolvency Service shall comply with Section 250 *Marketing Professional Services* of the Code.

3.15 When placing an advertisement in respect of an Administration, a Member in Public Practice shall not use that advertisement to market the Member's Professional Services.

3.16 A Member in Public Practice shall not include slogans, logos, claims about the Member's Firm, or other promotional material in statutory advertisements.

3.17 A Member in Public Practice may include the Firm's logo in non statutory advertisements as long as that logo does not take prominence in the advertisement.

4. Professional Independence

4.1 Subject to paragraph 4.2, a Member in Public Practice accepting an Appointment or conducting an Administration shall maintain Independence.

4.2 A Member in Public Practice shall identify, evaluate and address threats to the Independence of the Member, prior to accepting an Appointment. Where the Member identifies a threat the Member shall not accept the Appointment, unless

- **the threat is trivial and inconsequential;**
- **the threat arises in circumstances or relationships that are permitted by this Standard; or**
- **the Member obtains court approval.**

4.3 A Member in Public Practice conducting an Administration shall:

- **act impartially in the discharge of the Member's duties and responsibilities; and**
- **ensure that the Member's personal interests do not conflict with the Member's duty to the creditors.**

4.4 For the purpose of this Standard, when seeking to identify relationships with an insolvent Entity, a Member in Public Practice shall take reasonable steps to identify and evaluate any threats the Member has reason to believe are created by the Firm's or Network Firms' interests and relationships with the insolvent Entity or its Related Entities. The Member shall consider the following matters when identifying relevant Network Firms:

(a) the geographical regions or countries in which the insolvent Entity or its Related Entities operate; and

(b) relationships with the directors or officers of the insolvent Entity or its Related Entities.

4.5 The following circumstances and relationships are not considered to create a threat to the Independence of a Member in Public Practice, who is considering accepting or continuing an Appointment:

(a) the Engagement of the Member, the Member's Firm or a Network Firm by a third party, who is not an Associate or Related Entity of an insolvent Entity, to investigate, monitor or advise on the affairs of the insolvent Entity on behalf of the third party; or

(b) the transition of an Appointment from one type of insolvency Administration to another under the relevant legislation, subject to the terms of that legislation, for example from an Appointment as administrator to voluntary liquidator under the *Corporations Act 2001*; or

(c) an Appointment as Controller of an insolvent Entity of which that Member or another Partner of the Member's Firm or Network Firm has been a Controller under a different debenture or where the Appointment has been made by the court; or

(d) advice provided by the Member, the Member's Firm or the Network Firm to the insolvent Entity prior to the Appointment which was limited to:

- the financial situation of the Entity;
- the solvency of the Entity;
- the consequences of insolvency for the Entity; or
- alternative courses of action available to the Entity.

4.6 Trivial or inconsequential relationships are not a bar to acceptance or retention of an Appointment by a Member in Public Practice. The Member is not required to list trivial or inconsequential relationships in the *Declaration of Independence, Relevant Relationships and Indemnities* referred to in paragraph 4.20. A relationship is trivial or inconsequential if it is remote, coincidental or insignificant.

4.7 Subject to paragraph 4.8, a Member in Public Practice shall not accept an Appointment, other than to act as a Controller, where the Member, the Member's Firm, a Network Firm or their Partners or those Managerial Employees in the Office in which the Member practises have, or have had, any of the following relationships:

(a) a Close or Immediate Family relationship with:

- **the insolvent Entity;**
- **a director or officer of the insolvent Entity; or**
- **an employee of or adviser to the insolvent Entity who is in a position to exert direct and significant influence over the insolvent Entity.**

(b) a close personal relationship with:

- **the insolvent Entity;**
- **a director or officer of the insolvent Entity; or**
- **an employee of or adviser to the insolvent Entity who is in a position to exert direct and significant influence over the insolvent Entity.**

(c) a material business relationship, including the holding of a material Financial Interest, whether directly or indirectly in or jointly with:

- **the insolvent Entity;**
- **a director or officer of the insolvent Entity; or**
- **an employee of or adviser to the insolvent Entity who is in a position to exert direct and significant influence over the insolvent Entity.**

(d) a material loan to or from or material guarantee to or from:

- **the insolvent Entity;**
- **a director or officer of the insolvent Entity; or**
- **an employee of or adviser to the insolvent Entity who is in a position to exert direct and significant influence over the insolvent Entity.**

APES

(e) **employment with the insolvent Entity in the preceding two years, in a position to exert direct and significant influence over the insolvent Entity.**

4.8 **In respect of prior relationships of the nature referred to in paragraphs 4.7(c) and (d), a Member in Public Practice shall evaluate any threats a prior relationship is likely to create to the Member's Independence. In performing this assessment, the Member shall determine whether a reasonable person considering all of the facts and circumstances would conclude that there are significant threats to the Member's Independence posed by a prior relationship. Factors to consider include the:**

- **nature of the prior relationship;**
- **time elapsed since the relationship ended; and**
- **reasons for the termination of the relationship.**

4.9 **Where a Member in Public Practice, in a capacity other than as an Appointee, has a controlling interest in, or the ability to influence, a business operating in the same, or principally the same market as the insolvent Entity, the Member shall evaluate the significance of any threats to Independence and, when necessary, apply safeguards to eliminate the threats or reduce them to an Acceptable Level. Where there are no safeguards that can eliminate the threats or reduce them to an Acceptable Level, the Member shall decline the Appointment.**

4.10 **A Member in Public Practice shall not accept an Appointment, other than to act as a Controller, where the Member, the Member's Firm or a Network Firm has during the prior two years provided a Professional Service to the insolvent Entity, unless the Professional Service is considered immaterial or is referred to in paragraph 4.5.**

4.11 A prior Professional Service is immaterial if it:

- was of limited scope, limited time and limited fees;
- will not be subject to review by the Member during the course of the Administration;
- will not affect the Member's ability to comply with the statutory and fiduciary obligations associated with the Administration; and
- does not create threats to the Member's ability to comply with the fundamental principles of the Code when performing the duties of the Administration.

4.12 **Where a Member in Public Practice is considering accepting an Appointment and two or more Firms or Network Firms have merged in the preceding two years, the Member shall evaluate any relationships that the Member is aware of or ought reasonably to be aware of which the insolvent Entity had with the Firm, previous Firm(s) or Network Firm(s) in the preceding two years in accordance with the requirements of this standard.**

4.13 **Where a Member in Public Practice is considering accepting an Appointment and has moved Firms in the preceding two years, the Member shall evaluate any relationships that the Member is aware of or ought reasonably to be aware of which the insolvent Entity had with the previous Firm or its Network Firms during the time that the Member was a Partner. Where there were prior relationships, the Member shall disclose the relationships in the *Declaration of Independence, Relevant Relationships and Indemnities*. Where the prior relationships pose significant threats to Independence and there are no safeguards that can eliminate the threats or reduce them to an Acceptable Level, the Member shall decline the Appointment.**

4.14 **If the insolvent Entity is a company, a Member in Public Practice shall not provide Pre-appointment Advice to both the Entity and its directors in their personal capacity, as the threat to Independence created would be so significant that no safeguard could reduce the threat to an acceptable level.**

4.15 The requirements of paragraph 4.14 do not prohibit a Member in Public Practice from providing general information on the insolvency process and the consequences of insolvency to both the Entity and its directors in their personal capacity.

4.16 A Member in Public Practice shall not accept an Appointment where the Member, the Member's Firm, a Network Firm or their Partners have provided Professional Services to the insolvent Entity or any other Entity which:

- **has reasonable potential to lead to litigation claims against the Member or the Member's Firm by a stakeholder of the Administration;**
- **is material to the Administration; or**
- **was related to the structuring of assets of the insolvent Entity in order to avoid the consequences of insolvency, even if that advice was provided at a time when the Entity was solvent.**

4.17 A Member in Public Practice shall not provide any Inducement to any Entity to secure an Appointment for the Member or to secure or prevent the Appointment or nomination of another person.

4.18 A Member in Public Practice shall not accept an Appointment or perform an Administration that involves:

(a) referral or other commissions, or monetary or non-monetary benefits;

(b) spotter's fees;

(c) understandings or requirements that work in the Administration will be given to a referrer; or

(d) any other such arrangements that restrict the proper exercise of the Member's judgement and duties.

4.19 A Member in Public Practice shall provide a *Declaration of Independence, Relevant Relationships and Indemnities* in respect of an Insolvency Service (excluding an Appointment as a Controller). The Member shall provide the Declaration in the first communication to the creditors and table it at the first meeting of the creditors.

4.20 A Member in Public Practice shall include the following in the *Declaration of Independence, Relevant Relationships and Indemnities*:

- **a declaration that the Member has undertaken an evaluation of the significance of any threats to Independence and that the Member determined that the Member is independent for the purpose of accepting the Appointment in accordance with the requirements of the relevant legislation and this Standard;**
- **a declaration setting out the circumstances of the Appointment including the number of meetings with the Insolvent Entity or its advisors and the period over which Pre-appointment Advice was provided, a summary of the nature of the issues discussed, the amount of any Professional Fees received for the Pre-appointment Advice and an explanation as to why such Pre-appointment Advice does not result in a conflict of interest or duty;**
- **a declaration setting out all relationships the Member, the Member's Firm, a Network Firm or their Partners or those Managerial Employees in the Office in which the Member practises, have had in the preceding two years with:**
  - **the insolvent Entity;**
  - **if the insolvent Entity is a company - an Associate of the company;**
  - **if the insolvent Entity is an individual:**
    - **an Immediate or Close Family member of the individual;**
    - **a spouse or dependant of an Immediate or Close Family member of the individual; or**
    - **any Entity with which the individual or any of the persons noted above are associated;**
  - **a former Appointee of the insolvent Entity; and**
  - **a person who has a charge over the whole or substantially the whole of the insolvent Entity's property and other assets;**

APES

and the reasons why these relationships, if any, do not result in a conflict of interest or duty;

- **a declaration of prior Professional Services provided in the preceding two years to the insolvent Entity by the Member, the Members' Firm, a Network Firm or their Partners, including the nature of the Professional Services, when the Professional Service was provided, the period over which the Professional Service was provided, the Professional Fees paid and the reasons why the Professional Service does not result in a conflict of interest or duty;**
- **a declaration that there are no other known prior Professional Services or other relationships that require disclosure; and**
- **a declaration of indemnities (other than statutory indemnities) and upfront payments, including the identity of each indemnifier or provider of an upfront payment (name and relationship with the insolvent Entity) and the extent and nature of each indemnity or upfront payment, a statement as to where the funds are being held, when and how the funds will be applied and that there are no other indemnities or upfront payments to be disclosed.**

4.21 **Where more than one Member in Public Practice is appointed to an insolvent Entity, all Appointees shall sign the *Declaration of Independence, Relevant Relationships and Indemnities* prior to its issue. Where this is not possible and a *Declaration of Independence, Relevant Relationships and Indemnities* is issued before all Appointees sign it, the Member shall:**

- **Provide an explanation in the *Declaration of Independence, Relevant Relationships and Indemnities* as to why all Appointees were not able to sign it; and**
- **Sign a replacement *Declaration of Independence, Relevant Relationships and Indemnities* as soon as possible and ensure that it is provided to creditors.**

4.22 **When circumstances or relationships giving rise to a threat to Independence are identified after the commencement of an Administration, a Member in Public Practice shall evaluate that threat and:**

(a) **continue performing the Administration if the Member determines that the threat would not have precluded the Member from accepting the Appointment had the threat been identified prior to the commencement of the Appointment. The Member shall amend the *Declaration of Independence, Relevant Relationships and Indemnities* and send it to all the creditors; or**

(b) **where the threat to the Independence of the Member would have precluded the Member from accepting the Appointment had the threat been identified prior to the commencement of the Appointment, the Member shall notify the court, all creditors and regulatory authorities as appropriate of the following:**

- **the nature of the threat;**
- **the key facts and circumstances;**
- **reasons why the circumstances or relationships giving rise to the threat were not identified prior to acceptance of the Appointment;**
- **the potential impact on the Independence of the Member;**
- **the status of the Administration;**
- **the costs of ceasing and transferring the Appointment; and**
- **Professional Fees and Expenses billed and any outstanding amounts; and**

(c) **in the circumstances described in paragraph 4.22 (b), apply to the court to either continue or resign from the Appointment.**

4.23 **Where a Member in Public Practice becomes aware that the *Declaration of Independence, Relevant Relationships and Indemnities* is out of date or inaccurate, the Member shall update the *Declaration* and provide it to the creditors or the**

Committee with the next communication and table it at the next meeting of the creditors or the Committee.

4.24 Where a Member in Public Practice is requested by an insolvent Entity, its directors or its creditors to consent to an Appointment to replace another person who has commenced the Administration, and the Member intends to agree to the request, the Member shall:

(a) give reasonable notice to the other person being not less than one business day prior to the meeting of creditors, except when the request is received within one business day before that meeting;

(b) not solicit proxies directly or indirectly and shall act, and be seen to act, in the creditors' interests;

(c) provide a *Declaration of Independence, Relevant Relationships and Indemnities* containing the information required by paragraph 4.20 at the meeting where the creditors decide whether to replace the other person; and

(d) disclose to the creditors the basis on which the Member proposes to charge Professional Fees and details of the Member's relationship with the Entity nominating the Member for the Appointment.

4.25 A Member in Public Practice should be aware that disclosure of matters in a *Declaration of Independence, Relevant Relationships and Indemnities*, and the tabling of such Declaration at a meeting of creditors, will not prevent a finding by a court, regulator or a professional body that a Member has breached the requirements of this Standard or the relevant law.

5. Professional Engagement matters

5.1 A Member in Public Practice who has accepted an Appointment is not required to provide an engagement document in accordance with APES 305 *Terms of Engagement*.

6. Dealings with property and other assets

6.1 A Firm which provides Insolvency Services shall establish policies and procedures which prohibit the Firm, a Network Firm, their Partners and employees, and the Close and Immediate Families, Controlled and Associated Entities of the Firm's and Network Firms' Partners and employees from acquiring or deriving a benefit from dealing with any assets including property which comes under the control of a Partner or employee due to an Appointment, without obtaining the prior approval of the court.

6.2 A Member in Public Practice shall not purchase property or other assets of an Administration without obtaining prior approval of the court.

6.3 A Member in Public Practice shall take all reasonable steps to ensure that the Member does not knowingly sell property or other assets of an Administration to the Member's Firm, a Network Firm, their Partners or employees, or to the Immediate and Close Families, Controlled or Associated Entities of the Member, the Firm's or Network Firms' Partners and employees without obtaining prior approval of the court.

6.4 Paragraphs 6.2 and 6.3 do not apply where the Member has accepted an Appointment in respect of a retail operation under Administration, and the assets are available for sale to the general public and no special treatment or preference over and above that granted to the general public is offered.

7. Expert Witness obligations

7.1 A Member in Public Practice who during the course of an Administration acts as an Expert Witness shall comply with the following:

(a) the paramount duty to the court which overrides any other duty;

(b) a duty to assist the court on matters relevant to the Member's area of expertise in an objective manner; and

(c) **a duty to make it clear to the court when a particular question or issue falls outside the Member's expertise.**

7.2 A Member in Public Practice who during the course of an Administration acts as an Expert Witness should comply with relevant evidentiary and procedural requirements relating to Expert Witnesses.

7.3 **Subject to any legal requirements or restrictions, a Member in Public Practice who during the course of an Administration acts as an Expert Witness shall clearly communicate in a Witness Report issued by the Member:**

(a) **the scope of work performed by the Member;**

(b) **any limitations on the scope of work performed;**

(c) **details of the Member's training, study and experience that are relevant to the matters on which the Member is providing expert evidence;**

(d) **the relationships, if any, the Member, the Member's Firm, or a Network Firm has with any of the parties to the proceedings that may create a threat or a perceived threat to the Member's obligation to comply with the fundamental principles of the Code or the Member's paramount duty to the court, and any appropriate safeguards implemented;**

(e) **the extent, if any, of reliance by the Member on the work of others;**

(f) **the opinions formed by the Member;**

(g) **whether an opinion is provisional rather than concluded, and, if so, the reasons why a concluded opinion has not been formed;**

(h) **the significant facts upon which the opinions are based;**

(i) **the significant assumptions upon which the opinions are based and the reasons why the Member made those assumptions;**

(j) **if the Member considers that an opinion of the Member may be misleading because a significant assumption is likely to mislead, then a statement to that effect and an explanation of why the assumption is likely to mislead;**

(k) **where applicable, that the Member's opinion is subject to the veracity of another person's report upon which the Member's Witness Report is based;**

(l) **the reasoning by which the Member formed the opinions, including an explanation of any method employed and the reasons why that method was chosen;**

(m) **a list of all documents and sources of information relied upon in the preparation of the Witness Report; and**

(n) **any restrictions on the use of the Witness Report.**

8. Professional Fees and Expenses

8.1 **A Member in Public Practice performing an Administration shall be remunerated for such service by way of Professional Fees in accordance with Section 240 *Fees and other Types of Remuneration* of the Code, subject to the limitations in paragraph 4.18.**

8.2 **A Member in Public Practice shall only claim Professional Fees and Expenses in respect of Professional Services performed or to be performed for an Administration which are necessary and proper.**

8.3 The term 'necessary' in paragraph 8.2 means professional work that is:

- directly connected with the Administration; and
- performed in accordance with the duties of the Appointment and Professional Standards.

8.4 The term 'proper' in paragraph 8.2 means professional work that is performed in an effective and efficient manner in an Administration.

8.5 **A Member in Public Practice shall claim as Professional Fees, and not as Expenses, any fees for Insolvency Services provided by the Member, the Member's Firm, a Network**

Firm or a third party to an Administration. Where the Member, the Member's Firm or a Network Firm provides Professional Services, other than Insolvency Services, the fees in respect of those services shall be claimed as Professional Fees.

8.6 A Member in Public Practice shall use the Member's commercial judgement, adopting the perspective of, and acting with the same care as, a reasonable person when incurring Expenses for the Administration.

8.7 A Member in Public Practice who has accepted an Appointment, other than as a Controller or a Trustee, shall obtain court approval when the Member makes a claim in respect of Professional Fees for any pre-appointment work performed in respect of an Appointment.

8.8 A Member in Public Practice shall not enter into an arrangement to receive a Contingent Fee for Insolvency Services if that arrangement:

- impairs the Member's Independence;
- results in the receipt of a Contingent Fee for performing professional work that the Member is required to complete under the relevant legislation governing an Appointment;
- is inconsistent with the fiduciary obligations of the Member; or
- results in the perception that the Member is acting in the Member's interests, rather than in the best interests of the creditors.

8.9 When considering whether a proposed Contingent Fee arrangement in a particular Administration meets the requirements of paragraph 8.8, a Member in Public Practice shall consider the following:

- funds available to the Administration;
- funding from alternative sources such as creditors or a litigation funder;
- the costs of the alternative sources of funds in comparison to the Contingent Fee arrangement;
- the risk associated with the tasks to be undertaken for the Contingent Fee; and
- the appropriateness of the amount of the proposed Contingent Fee in relation to the nature of the Administration and the risk associated with the task to be undertaken.

8.10 Where a Member in Public Practice enters into an arrangement to receive a Contingent Fee for Insolvency Services, the Member shall obtain approval from the Approving Body prior to commencement of Professional Services after having disclosed the following information:

- details of the arrangement including the nature of the contingency and how achievement of the contingency will be assessed;
- the Member's remuneration in the event the contingency is or is not achieved;
- when the Member's remuneration is expected to be drawn; and
- except in the case of an Appointment as a Controller, why the arrangement to receive a Contingent Fee is in the best interest of the creditors.

8.11 A Member in Public Practice who has accepted an Appointment, other than an Appointment as a Controller, shall provide the following information in the first communication to the creditors:

- the methods that may be used to calculate Professional Fees;
- the basis upon which Professional Fees will be charged for the Administration; and
- why the Member considers that the chosen method is suitable for the Administration.

8.12 Except in the case of an Appointment as a Controller, where the basis upon which Professional Fees for the Administration is time based a Member in Public Practice shall provide the creditors with the following additional information:

APES

- the scale of rates that will be used; and
- a best estimate of the costs of the Administration to completion, or to a specified milestone.

If subsequent to providing the best estimate of the costs of the Administration there is significant change to that estimate, the Member shall provide a new estimate to the creditors together with an explanation of the variance.

8.13 Where a Member in Public Practice has accepted an Appointment, other than as a Controller, and is seeking approval for Professional Fees from the Approving Body, the Member shall provide sufficient information so as to allow the Approving Body to make an informed assessment as to whether the remuneration is reasonable, and shall:

- provide details of how the Professional Fees are computed;
- provide a description of the Professional Services performed, or to be performed, broken down into broad categories, and the costs associated with each category;
- state the terms of the approval sought from the Approving Body;
- advise the total of Professional Fees previously determined and whether the Member will be seeking approval for additional Professional Fees in the future;
- advise when the Professional Fees will be drawn; and
- provide a summary of receipts and payments to and from the Administration bank account.

8.14 A Member in Public Practice shall only draw Professional Fees once the proper resolution, order, or authority has been obtained from the Approving Body and in accordance with the terms of approval.

8.15 Where a Member in Public Practice has entered into a fixed fee arrangement in respect of Professional Fees, the Member shall draw the fixed fee at the conclusion of the Administration or in amounts and at milestones specified by the Approving Body.

8.16 Where a Member in Public Practice seeks approval for the payment of prospective Professional Fees from the Approving Body, the Member shall specify the maximum amount of the Professional Fees that may be drawn before requiring further approval from the Approving Body. The Member shall draw on this prospective Professional Fee progressively as the work is completed.

8.17 Where a Member in Public Practice receives monies prior to acceptance of an Appointment to meet the costs of the proposed Administration, the Member shall ensure:

(a) the monies are held on trust;

(b) there are no conditions on the conduct or outcome of the Administration attached to the monies;

(c) full disclosure is made to creditors in the *Declaration of Independence, Relevant Relationships and Indemnities*; and

(d) approval of Professional Fees is obtained prior to them being withdrawn from the trust account.

9. Documentation and quality control

9.1 A Member in Public Practice shall comply with the requirements of APES 320 *Quality Control for Firms*.

9.2 A Member in Public Practice shall prepare working papers in accordance with this Standard that appropriately document the work performed, including aspects of the

Insolvency Service that have been provided in writing. The documentation prepared by the Member shall:

(a) provide a sufficient and appropriate record of the procedures performed for the Insolvency Service;

(b) identify threats to Independence, and how they have been evaluated and addressed including safeguards applied; and

(c) demonstrate that the Insolvency Service was carried out in accordance with this Standard and other applicable Professional Standards, including policies and procedures established in accordance with APES 320 *Quality Control for Firms*, and any applicable ethical, legal and regulatory requirements.

9.3 A Member in Public Practice may destroy the working papers referred to in paragraph 9.2 in accordance with the requirements of the *Corporations Act 2001* or *Bankruptcy Act 1966*.

Conformity with International Pronouncements

The International Ethics Standard Board for Accountants (IESBA) has not issued a pronouncement equivalent to APES 330.

Appendix 1

Summary of revisions to the previous APES 330 (Issued September 2009)

APES 330 *Insolvency Services* originally issued in September 2009 has been revised by APESB in November 2011. A summary of the revisions is given in the table below.

Table of revisions*

Paragraph affected	How affected
1.1	Amended
2 – Definition of Acceptable Level	Added
2 – Definition of Appointee	Added
2 – Definition of Appointment	Amended
2 – Definition of Network	Added
2 – Definition of Network Firm	Added
2 – Definition of Office	Added
2 – Definition of Pre-appointment advice	Added
2 – Definition of Trustee	Added
3.7	Added
3.8	Amended
3.9	Added
4.4	Added
4.5	Amended
4.6	Amended
4.7	Amended
4.8	Added
4.9	Added
4.10	Amended

* *Refer Technical Update 2011/3*

Paragraph affected	How affected
4.11	Amended
4.12	Added
4.13	Added
4.14	Amended
4.15	Added
4.16	Amended
4.19	Amended
4.20	Amended
4.21	Added
4.22	Amended
4.23	Amended
4.24	Amended
4.25	Amended
6.1	Amended
6.3	Amended
7.3(d)	Amended
8.1	Amended
8.5	Amended
8.7	Amended
8.9	Added
8.10	Amended
8.17	Amended

APES 345

Reporting on Prospective Financial Information Prepared in connection with a Disclosure Document

(Issued November 2008)

Issued by the Accounting Professional and Ethical Standards Board.

Note from the Institute of Chartered Accountants Australia

This note, prepared by the technical editor, is not part of APES 345.

Historical development

November 2008: APES 345 'Reporting on Prospective Financial Information prepared in connection with a Disclosure Document' applies to members in public practice when they are involved in engagements to prepare a report on or in connection with prospective financial information included in a disclosure document. It applies for engagements commencing on or after 1 July 2009, with early adoption permitted, and replaces F2 'Prospectuses and Reports on Profit Forecasts'.

APES

Contents

1. Scope and application

1.1 Accounting Professional & Ethical Standards Board Limited (APESB) issues professional standard APES 345 *Reporting on Prospective Financial Information prepared in connection with a Disclosure Document* (**the Standard**), which is effective for Engagements commencing on or after 01 July 2009. Earlier adoption of this Standard is permitted.

1.2 APES 345 sets the standards for Members in Public Practice in the provision of quality and ethical Professional Services in respect of Reporting Service Engagements. The mandatory requirements of this Standard are in **bold type (black lettering)**, preceded or followed by discussion or explanations in normal type (grey lettering). APES 345 should be read in conjunction with other professional duties of Members, and any legal obligations that may apply.

1.3 Members in Public Practice in Australia shall follow the mandatory requirements of APES 345 when they undertake Reporting Service Engagements for Clients.

1.4 Members in Public Practice practising outside of Australia shall follow the mandatory requirements of APES 345 to the extent to which they are not prevented from so doing by specific requirements of local regulations and/or laws in the country in which they are working.

1.5 Members in Public Practice shall be familiar with relevant Professional Standards and guidance notes when providing Professional Services. All Members shall comply with the fundamental principles outlined in the Code.

1.6 The Standard is not intended to detract from any responsibilities which may be imposed by law or regulation.

1.7 All references to Professional Standards are references to those provisions as amended from time to time.

1.8 In applying the requirements outlined in APES 345, Members in Public Practice should be guided not merely by the words but also by the spirit of the Standard and the Code.

1.9 The compilation of Prospective Financial Information does not, in itself, constitute a Reporting Service Engagement. APES 315 *Compilation of Financial Information* applies in these circumstances.

2. Definitions

For the purpose of this Standard:

Acceptable Level means a level at which a reasonable and informed third party would be likely to conclude, weighing all the specific facts and circumstances, that compliance with the fundamental principles is not compromised.

Assurance Engagement means an Engagement in which a conclusion is expressed by a Member in Public Practice designed to enhance the degree of confidence of the intended users other than the responsible party about the outcome of the evaluation or measurement of a subject matter against criteria.

This includes an Engagement in accordance with *Framework for Assurance Engagements* issued by the Auditing and Assurance Standards Board (AUASB) or in accordance with specific relevant standards, such as International Standards on Auditing for Assurance Engagements.

Client means an individual, firm, entity or organisation to whom or to which Professional Services are provided by a Member in Public Practice in respect of Engagements of either a recurring or demand nature.

Code means APES 110 *Code of Ethics for Professional Accountants*.

Disclosure Document means a disclosure document as defined in the *Corporations Act 2001*.

Engagement means an agreement, whether written or otherwise, between a Member in Public Practice and a Client relating to the provision of Professional Services by a Member in Public Practice. However, consultations with a prospective Client prior to such agreement are not part of an Engagement.

Engagement Document means the document (i.e. letter, agreement or any other appropriate means) in which the Terms of Engagement are specified in a written form.

Engagement Partner means the Partner or other person in the Firm who is responsible for the Engagement and its performance, and for the report that is issued on behalf of the Firm, and who, where required, has the appropriate authority from a professional, legal or regulatory body.

Engagement Period starts when the Firm accepts the Reporting Service Engagement and ends on the day the securities are allotted.

Engagement Team means all personnel performing an Engagement, including any experts contracted by the Firm in connection with that Engagement.

Financial Interest means an interest in equity or other security, debenture, loan or other debt instrument of an entity, including rights and obligations to acquire such an interest and derivatives directly related to such interest.

Firm means

(a) A sole practitioner, partnership, corporation or other entity of professional accountants;

(b) An entity that controls such parties;

(c) An entity controlled by such parties; or

(d) An Auditor-General's office or department.

Independence means

(a) Independence of mind – the state of mind that permits the provision of an opinion without being affected by influences that compromise professional judgement, allowing an individual to act with integrity, and exercise objectivity and professional scepticism; and

(b) Independence in appearance – the avoidance of facts and circumstances that are so significant a reasonable and informed third party, having knowledge of all relevant information, including any safeguards applied, would reasonably conclude a Firm's, or a member of the Engagement Team's integrity, objectivity or professional scepticism had been compromised.

Member in Public Practice means a Member, irrespective of functional classification (e.g. audit, tax, or consulting) in a Firm that provides Professional Services. The term is also used to refer to a Firm of Members in Public Practice and means a practice entity as defined by the applicable professional body.

APES

Partner means any individual with authority to bind the Firm with respect to the performance of an Engagement.

Product Disclosure Statement means a statement as defined in Part 7.9 of the *Corporations Act 2001*.

Professional Services means services requiring accountancy or related skills performed by a Member in Public Practice including accounting, auditing, taxation, management consulting and financial management services.

Professional Standards mean all standards issued by Accounting Professional & Ethical Standards Board Limited and all professional and ethical requirements of the applicable professional body.

Prospective Financial Information means financial information of a predictive character based on assumptions about events that may occur in the future and on possible actions by an entity.

Prospectus means a prospectus as defined in the *Corporations Act 2001*.

Reporting Service Engagement means an Engagement in which a Member in Public Practice prepares a report on or in connection with Prospective Financial Information where such Prospective Financial Information or part thereof and the related report are included in a Disclosure Document.

Those Charged with Governance includes those persons accountable for ensuring that the entity achieves its objectives, with regard to reliability of financial reporting, effectiveness and efficiency of operations, compliance with applicable laws, and reporting to interested parties. Those charged with governance include management only when it performs such functions.

3. Fundamental responsibilities of Members in Public Practice

3.1 **Members in Public Practice undertaking Reporting Service Engagements shall comply with Section 100 *Introduction and Fundamental Principles* of the Code and relevant legislation.**

3.2 **Members in Public Practice shall comply with Section 220 *Conflict of Interest* and Section 280 *Objectivity – All Services* in the Code.**

Public interest

3.3 **In accordance with Section 100 *Introduction and Fundamental Principles* of the Code, Members in Public Practice shall observe and comply with their public interest obligations when they provide Professional Services in respect of Reporting Service Engagements.**

Professional Independence

3.4 **When engaged to perform a Reporting Service Engagement which requires Independence or purports to be independent, a Member in Public Practice shall comply with Independence as defined in this Standard.**

3.5 **A Member in Public Practice shall consider whether the circumstances of the Reporting Service Engagement make the Engagement an Assurance Engagement under the *Framework for Assurance Engagements* issued by the Auditing and Assurance Standards Board.**

3.6 **Where a Reporting Service Engagement is an Assurance Engagement, the Member in Public Practice shall comply with Section 290 *Independence – Assurance Engagements* of the Code.**

3.7 **A Member in Public Practice shall not act as an advocate in respect of a Reporting Service Engagement which requires Independence or purports to be independent.**

Professional competence and due care

3.8 Members in Public Practice performing Reporting Service Engagements shall maintain professional competence and take due care in the performance of their work in accordance with Section 130 *Professional Competence and Due Care* of the Code.

3.9 Where a Reporting Service Engagement requires the consideration of matters that are outside the professional expertise of the Member in Public Practice, the Member shall seek expert assistance or advice from a suitably qualified third party or decline the Reporting Service Engagement. Where the Member relies upon the advice of a third party, the Member shall disclose in the Member's report the name and qualifications of the third party and the area in the report where the third party advice has been obtained.

3.10 When planning to use the work of a suitably qualified third party, a Member in Public Practice shall assess the professional competence and objectivity of that third party and the appropriateness and adequacy of the work performed.

3.11 In undertaking a Reporting Service Engagement, a Member in Public Practice should consider the contents of any guidance in respect of such services issued by the professional accounting bodies and appropriate regulatory authorities.

Confidentiality

3.12 In accordance with Section 140 *Confidentiality* of the Code, a Member in Public Practice who acquires confidential information in the course of a Reporting Service Engagement for a Client shall not use that information for any purpose other than the proper performance of the Reporting Service Engagement for that Client.

3.13 Unless a Member in Public Practice has a legal obligation of disclosure, the Member shall not convey any information relating to a Client's affairs to a third party without the Client's permission.

3.14 Where a Client has given a Member in Public Practice permission to disclose confidential information to a third party, it is preferable that this permission is in writing. Where oral permission is obtained, a contemporaneous note should be made and kept on file by the Member recording the relevant details of the Client's approval.

3.15 Where a Member in Public Practice provides confidential information in accordance with a legal obligation of disclosure, the Member shall notify the Client or the relevant third party as soon as practicable, provided that there is no legal prohibition against such notification.

4. Professional Engagement and other matters

4.1 A Member in Public Practice shall document and communicate the Terms of Engagement to provide the Reporting Service Engagement in accordance with APES 305 *Terms of Engagement*.

4.2 A Member in Public Practice who is approached by a potential Client to undertake a Reporting Service Engagement shall comply with the requirements of Section 210 *Professional Appointment* of the Code.

4.3 A Member in Public Practice who has utilised the services of a suitably qualified third party in connection with the performance of the Reporting Service Engagement shall not disclose the opinion or the name of that third party without the prior consent of that party unless the Member has a legal obligation of disclosure.

4.4 A Member in Public Practice shall gather sufficient and appropriate evidence by such means as inspection, inquiry, computation and analysis to ensure that the conclusions, for which the Member is responsible, are properly supported. When determining the extent and quality of evidence necessary, the Member shall exercise professional judgement, considering the nature of the Reporting Service Engagement, Terms of the Engagement and the use to which the Disclosure Document will be put.

5. Relationships that create threats to the fundamental principles

5.1 This section describes specific circumstances arising out of relationships with the Client, which may create threats to the fundamental principles in the Code. Consideration should always be given to what a reasonable and informed third party having knowledge of all relevant information, including safeguards applied, would reasonably conclude to be unacceptable. In situations when no safeguards are available to reduce the threat to an Acceptable Level, the only possible actions are to eliminate the activities or interest creating the threat, or refuse to accept or continue the Reporting Service Engagement.

5.2 Threats to the fundamental principles may be created by any of the following interests or relationships:

- Financial Interests;
- Loans and guarantees;
- Close business relationships with the Client;
- Employment relationships with the Client;
- Family and personal relationships.

6. The provision of other Professional Services

6.1 The provision of other Professional Services by a Member in Public Practice to the Client may create threats to compliance with the fundamental principles in the Code. Consequently, it is necessary to evaluate the significance of any threat created by the provision of such Professional Services. In some cases it may be possible to eliminate or reduce such threats by applying safeguards. In other cases no safeguards may be available to reduce the threats to an Acceptable Level. In such a situation, either the Reporting Service Engagement or the other Professional Services should not be carried out. In this Standard "other Professional Services" comprise any Engagement in which a Member provides Professional Services to a Client other than pursuant to a Reporting Service Engagement.

6.2 Prior to accepting an Engagement to provide other Professional Services, the Member in Public Practice shall consider and evaluate the significance of any threats identified. If the threats are other than insignificant, the Member shall consider and apply safeguards as necessary to reduce the threats to an Acceptable Level.

6.3 A Member in Public Practice shall refuse an Engagement to provide other Professional Services in circumstances where, the Engagement Partner responsible for the Reporting Service Engagement considers it probable that a reasonable and informed third party having knowledge of all relevant information including safeguards applied would regard the objectives of the Engagement to provide the other Professional Service, proposed to be undertaken during the Engagement Period, as being inconsistent with the objectives of the Reporting Service Engagement.

7. Documentation

7.1 A Member in Public Practice shall prepare working papers in accordance with this Standard that appropriately document the work performed, including aspects of the Engagement that have been provided in writing. The documentation prepared by the Member shall:

(a) provide a sufficient and appropriate record of the procedures performed for the Reporting Service Engagement;

(b) identify the source of significant information the Member has used in the conduct of the Reporting Service Engagement; and

(c) demonstrate that the Reporting Service Engagement was carried out in accordance with this Standard and all other Professional Standards applicable to the Reporting Service Engagement, including policies and procedures established in accordance with APES 320 *Quality Control for Firms*, and any applicable ethical, legal and regulatory requirements.

8. Reporting

8.1 A Member in Public Practice shall take all reasonable steps in accordance with the terms of Engagement to ensure that the Prospective Financial Information that is the subject of the Reporting Service Engagement does not contain false or misleading information, or omit material information.

8.2 A Member in Public Practice shall take all reasonable steps in accordance with the terms of Engagement, to ensure that the Disclosure Document clearly states the basis(es) and key assumptions used in forecasting the Prospective Financial Information.

8.3 If, subsequent to the issue of a Disclosure Document, the Member in Public Practice finds that information on which the Reporting Service Engagement is based contains false or misleading information or omits material information, the Member shall take all reasonable steps to ensure that the Client takes appropriate action to inform anyone who received the previously issued Disclosure Document of the situation.

8.4 If the Member in Public Practice becomes aware that the Client has not taken appropriate action in terms of paragraph 8.3, the Member shall notify Those Charged with Governance of the Client.

8.5 If the Member in Public Practice becomes aware that Those Charged with Governance have not taken action appropriate action in accordance with paragraph 8.4, the Member shall consider the Firm's policies and procedures established in accordance with *Acceptance and Continuance of Client Relationships and Specific Engagements* of APES 320 *Quality Control for Firms* in determining whether to continue acting for the Client in a professional capacity.

8.6 A Member in Public Practice shall not knowingly or recklessly make a statement or cause another to make a statement in or in connection with a Reporting Service Engagement that, by its content or by an omission, is false or misleading in a material manner.

9. Communication with Those Charged with Governance

9.1 The Member in Public Practice shall ensure that Those Charged with Governance of the Client, and any other persons or entities the Member is instructed to advise, are appropriately informed on a timely basis of all significant matters arising from the Reporting Service Engagement.

9.2 Matters communicated will generally include the key elements of the Member in Public Practice's consideration of significant matters such as:

- The principal threats, if any, to objectivity and Independence identified by the Member, including consideration of relationships between the Firm and the Client, its related entities and directors and any other entities directly involved in the transaction which is the subject of the Disclosure Document;
- Any safeguards adopted and the reasons why they are considered to be effective;
- The overall assessment of threats and safeguards; and
- Information about the general policies and processes within the Firm for maintaining objectivity and Independence.

10. Professional fees

10.1 A Member in Public Practice undertaking a Reporting Service Engagement shall be remunerated for such services by way of professional fees computed in accordance with Section 240 *Fees and other Types of Remuneration* of the Code.

10.2 A Member in Public Practice shall not enter into a Contingent Fee arrangement or receive a Contingent Fee for a Reporting Service Engagement requiring Independence or which purports to be independent.

11. Threatened and actual litigation

11.1 **Where litigation between the Client or its related entities and the Firm, which is other than insignificant, is already in progress, or where the Member in Public Practice considers such litigation to be probable, the Member shall consider the Firm's policies and procedures established in accordance with *Acceptance and Continuance of Client Relationships and Specific Engagements* of APES 320 *Quality Control for Firms* in determining whether to continue acting for the Client in a professional capacity.**

Conformity with International Pronouncements

The International Ethics Standard Board for Accountants (IESBA) has not issued a pronouncement equivalent to APES 345.

APES 350

Participation by Members in Public Practice in Due Diligence Committees in connection with a Public Document

(Issued December 2009: revised March 2011)

Issued by the Accounting Professional and Ethical Standards Board.

Note from the Institute of Chartered Accountants Australia

This note, prepared by the technical editor, is not part of APES 350.

Historical development

December 2009: APES 350 issued. It applies to members in public practice who serve on or report to a due diligence committee, as a member, observer or reporting person. The Standard deals with the initial appointment process, roles and obligations during the due diligence process, documentation and reporting and includes a standard due diligence sign-off letter. It applied from 1 February 2010. The International Ethics Standards Board for Accountants (IESBA) has not issued any international equivalent.

March 2011: APES 350 revised to include a new Materiality Letter as Appendix 2, explaining the nature of materiality. The revisions apply from 1 May 2011.

APES

Contents

1. Scope and application

1.1 Accounting Professional & Ethical Standards Board Limited (APESB) has revised professional standard APES 350 *Participation by Members in Public Practice in Due Diligence Committees in connection with a Public Document* (**the Standard**), which is effective for Engagements commencing on or after 1 May 2011. Earlier adoption of this Standard is permitted.

1.2 APES 350 sets the standards for Members in Public Practice in the provision of quality and ethical Professional Services to a Client which comprise participating in and/or reporting to a Due Diligence Committee, as a DDC Member, DDC Observer or Reporting Person in connection with a Public Document. The mandatory requirements of this Standard are in **bold type (black lettering)**, preceded or followed by discussion or explanations in normal type (grey lettering). APES 350 should be read in conjunction with other professional duties of Members, and any legal obligations that may apply.

1.3 Members in Public Practice in Australia shall follow the mandatory requirements of APES 350 when they provide Professional Services to a Client, which comprise participating in and/or reporting to a Due Diligence Committee as a DDC Member, DDC Observer or Reporting Person in connection with a Public Document issued in Australia. Where the transaction to which the Public Document relates is to be undertaken in whole or in part in a jurisdiction other than Australia or where the laws and/or regulations of a jurisdiction other than Australia apply to the Public Document, Members shall follow this Standard, except to the extent that this would cause a Member to breach the laws and/or regulations of such other jurisdiction.

1.4 Members in Public Practice practising outside of Australia shall follow the mandatory requirements of this Standard to the extent to which they are not prevented from so doing by specific requirements of local laws and/or regulations.

1.5 Members in Public Practice shall be familiar with relevant Professional Standards and guidance notes when providing Professional Services. All Members shall comply with the fundamental principles outlined in the Code.

1.6 The Standard is not intended to detract from any responsibilities which may be imposed by law or regulation.

1.7 All references to Professional Standards are references to those provisions as amended from time to time.

1.8 In applying the requirements outlined in APES 350, Members in Public Practice should be guided not merely by the words but also by the spirit of this Standard and the Code.

1.9 The Standard should be applied to the extent practicable where a Member in Public Practice provides Professional Services to a Client which comprise participating in and/or reporting to a Due Diligence Committee as a DDC Member, DDC Observer or Reporting Person in connection with an Engagement which is not in connection with a Public Document.

1.10 A Member in Public Practice may provide Professional Services to a Client in connection with a Due Diligence Committee in the role of a:

- DDC Member;
- DDC Member and Reporting Person;
- DDC Observer;
- DDC Observer and Reporting Person;
- Reporting Person.

These roles are defined in paragraph 2 and discussed in paragraph 5.1.

2. Definitions

For the purpose of this Standard:

Acceptable Level means a level at which a reasonable and informed third party would be likely to conclude, weighing all the specific facts and circumstances available to the Member in Public Practice at that time, that compliance with the fundamental principles of the Code is not compromised.

Assurance Client means the responsible party that is the person (or persons) who:

(a) In a direct reporting Engagement, is responsible for the subject matter; or

(b) In an assertion-based Engagement, is responsible for the subject matter information and may be responsible for the subject matter.

Assurance Engagement means an Engagement in which a Member in Public Practice expresses a conclusion designed to enhance the degree of confidence of the intended users other than the responsible party about the outcome of the evaluation or measurement of a subject matter against criteria.

This includes an Engagement in accordance with the *Framework for Assurance Engagements* issued by the Auditing and Assurance Standards Board (AUASB) or in accordance with specific relevant standards, such as International Standards on Auditing for Assurance Engagements.

Audit Client means an entity in respect of which a Firm conducts an Audit Engagement. When the Client is a Listed Entity, Audit Client will always include its related entities. When the Audit Client is not a Listed Entity, Audit Client includes those related entities over which the Client has direct or indirect control.

Audit Engagement means a reasonable assurance Engagement in which a Member in Public Practice expresses an opinion whether financial statements are prepared, in all material respects (or give a true and fair view or are presented fairly, in all material respects), in accordance with an applicable financial reporting framework, such as an Engagement conducted in accordance with Auditing and Assurance Standards. This includes a statutory audit, which is an audit required by legislation or other regulation such as the *Corporations Act 2001*.

Auditing and Assurance Standards means:

- In relation to reports for reporting periods commencing on or after 1 July 2006:
  - the AUASB Standards, as defined in the *Foreword to AUASB Pronouncements*, issued by the AUASB, and operative from the date specified in each standard; and

APES

    - those standards issued by the AuASB which have not yet been revised and reissued (whether as standards or as guidance) by the AUASB, to the extent that they are not inconsistent with the AUASB standards.
- In relation to reports for reporting periods commencing prior to 1 July 2006, the Auditing and Assurance Standards issued by the AuASB on behalf of CPA Australia and the Institute of Chartered Accountants in Australia.

AuASB means the Auditing and Assurance Standards Board which issued Australian Auditing and Assurance Standards up to 30 June 2004, under the auspices of the Australian Accounting Research Foundation, a joint venture of CPA Australia and the Institute of Chartered Accountants in Australia.

AUASB means the Australian statutory body called the Auditing and Assurance Standards Board established under section 227A of the *Australian Securities and Investments Commission Act 2001.*

Australian Financial Services Licence means a licence to provide financial services under Chapter 7 of the *Corporations Act 2001.*

Client means an individual, firm, entity or organisation to whom or to which Professional Services are provided by a Member in Public Practice in respect of Engagements of either a recurring or demand nature.

Code means APES 110 *Code of Ethics for Professional Accountants.*

Contingent Fee means a fee calculated on a predetermined basis relating to the outcome or result of a transaction or the result of the work performed. A fee that is established by a court or other public authority is not a Contingent Fee.

DDC Member means a Member in Public Practice who is engaged by a Client to provide Professional Services as a member of a Due Diligence Committee and who will participate in the Due Diligence Committee's decisions, sign all the collective reports and other documents issued by the Due Diligence Committee and in most instances will prepare a Due Diligence Sign-Off.

DDC Observer means a Member in Public Practice who is engaged by a Client to provide Professional Services as an observer to a Due Diligence Committee but who will not participate as a DDC Member and will not sign or be a party to any collective reports or documents issued by the Due Diligence Committee. As an observer a Member will:

- attend one or more meetings of the Due Diligence Committee but not undertake any due diligence enquiries or have reporting obligations to the Client or to the Due Diligence Committee; or
- attend one or more meetings of the Due Diligence Committee and undertake due diligence enquiries in relation to Financial Information and/or Other Specific Information and provide a report to the Client and/or the Due Diligence Committee. In certain circumstances, depending on factors such as timing and the scope of the Engagement, the Member may prepare a Due Diligence Sign-Off.

Disclosure Document means a disclosure document as defined in the *Corporations Act 2001.*

Due Diligence Committee means a committee established by Those Charged with Governance of a Client to co-ordinate and assist with the due diligence process to be undertaken by the Client in relation to a Public Document.

Due Diligence Planning Memorandum means the document prepared on behalf of a Client and signed by members of its Due Diligence Committee which sets out the due diligence process and reporting responsibilities. This document also specifies the respective individual and collective responsibilities of the participants in the due diligence process, including those of the members of the Due Diligence Committee.

Due Diligence Sign-Off means the letter or other appropriate written communication issued by a DDC Member or in certain cases a DDC Observer in connection with a Public Document when reporting to a Client and its Due Diligence Committee on the conclusions arising from the procedures conducted by a DDC Member or DDC Observer on Financial Information and/or Other Specific Information. (A form of Due Diligence Sign-Off which complies with the requirements of this Standard is set out in Appendix 1).

Engagement means an agreement, whether written or otherwise, between a Member in Public Practice and a Client relating to the provision of Professional Services by a Member in Public Practice. However, consultations with a prospective Client prior to such agreement are not part of an Engagement.

Engagement Document means the document (i.e. letter, agreement or any other appropriate means) in which the Terms of Engagement are specified in a written form.

Engagement Team means all personnel performing an Engagement, including any experts contracted by the Firm in connection with that Engagement.

Financial Information means historical, pro forma or prospective financial information or some combination of these as specified in the Engagement Document.

Firm means
(a) A sole practitioner, partnership, corporation or other entity of professional accountants;
(b) An entity that controls such parties through ownership, management or other means;
(c) An entity controlled by such parties through ownership, management or other means; or
(d) An Auditor-General's office or department.

Independence means:

(a) Independence of mind – the state of mind that permits the provision of an opinion without being affected by influences that compromise professional judgement, allowing an individual to act with integrity, and exercise objectivity and professional scepticism; and

(b) Independence in appearance – the avoidance of facts and circumstances that are so significant a reasonable and informed third party, having knowledge of all relevant information, including any safeguards applied, would reasonably conclude a Firm's, or a member of the Engagement Team's integrity, objectivity or professional scepticism had been compromised.

Listed Entity means an entity whose shares, stock or debt are quoted or listed on a recognised stock exchange, or are marketed under the regulations of a recognised stock exchange or other equivalent body.

Managerial Employee means an employee who acts in a managerial capacity within the structure of the Firm, including providing oversight, in the provision of services to Clients.

Materiality Letter means the letter or other appropriate written communication issued by a Member in Public Practice to a Client and its Due Diligence Committee that provides materiality guidance prepared with reference to applicable Auditing and Assurance Standards.

Member means a member of a professional body that has adopted this Standard as applicable to their membership as defined by that professional body.

Member in Public Practice means a Member, irrespective of functional classification (e.g. audit, tax, or consulting) in a Firm that provides Professional Services. The term is also used to refer to a Firm of Members in Public Practice and means a practice entity as defined by the applicable professional body.

Network means a larger structure:

(a) That is aimed at co-operation, and

(b) That is clearly aimed at profit or cost sharing or shares common ownership, control or management, common quality control policies and procedures, common business strategy, the use of a common branch-name, or a significant part of professional resources.

Network Firm means a Firm or entity that belongs to a Network.

Other Specific Information means specifically identified information, other than Financial Information, in a Public Document, which has been the subject of procedures performed by a Member in Public Practice as specified in the Engagement Document. Examples include specific tax-related information, environmental matters, and information technology matters.

Partner means any individual with authority to bind the Firm with respect to the performance of an Engagement.

Product Disclosure Statement means a statement as defined in Chapter 7 of the *Corporations Act 2001*.

Professional Services means services requiring accountancy or related skills performed by a Member in Public Practice including accounting, auditing, taxation, management consulting and financial management services.

Professional Standards means all standards issued by Accounting Professional & Ethical Standards Board Limited and all professional and ethical requirements of the applicable professional body.

Public Document means a Disclosure Document, Product Disclosure Statement or other documentation provided to shareholders, unit holders or holders of a relevant interest in an entity (or which is provided to management of an entity) in relation to a scheme of arrangement under Part 5.1 of the *Corporations Act 2001* or a takeover or compulsory acquisition under Chapter 6 of the *Corporations Act 2001*.

Reporting Person means a Member in Public Practice who is engaged by a Client to provide Professional Services and report to the Client and its Due Diligence Committee on a specific issue or area of enquiry, which has been identified by the Client or the Due Diligence Committee. A Reporting Person may also be a DDC Member or DDC Observer.

Terms of Engagement means the terms and conditions that are agreed between the Client and the Member in Public Practice for the Engagement.

Those Charged with Governance includes those persons accountable for ensuring that the entity achieves its objectives with regard to reliability of financial reporting, effectiveness and efficiency of operations, compliance with applicable laws and reporting to interested parties. Those Charged with Governance includes management only when it performs such functions.

3. Fundamental responsibilities of Members in Public Practice

3.1 **A Member in Public Practice providing Professional Services to a Client which comprise participating in and/or reporting to a Due Diligence Committee as a DDC Member, DDC Observer or Reporting Person in connection with a Public Document shall comply with Section 100 *Introduction and Fundamental Principles* of the Code and relevant law.**

3.2 **A Member in Public Practice providing Professional Services to a Client which comprise participating in and/or reporting to a Due Diligence Committee as a DDC Member, DDC Observer or Reporting Person in connection with a Public Document shall comply with Section 220 *Conflict of Interest* and Section 280 *Objectivity – All Services* of the Code.**

Public interest

3.3 **In accordance with Section 100 *Introduction and Fundamental Principles* of the Code, a Member in Public Practice shall observe and comply with the Member's public interest obligations when the Member provides Professional Services to a Client which comprise participating in and/or reporting to a Due Diligence Committee as a DDC Member, DDC Observer or Reporting Person in connection with a Public Document.**

Professional appointments

3.4 **A Member in Public Practice who is invited by a Client or potential Client to provide Professional Services which comprise participating in and/or reporting to a Due Diligence Committee as a DDC Member, DDC Observer or Reporting Person in connection with a Public Document shall comply with the requirements of Section 210 *Professional Appointment* of the Code.**

3.5 **A Member in Public Practice who is invited by a Client or potential Client to provide Professional Services which comprise participating in and/or reporting to a Due**

Diligence Committee as a DDC Member, DDC Observer or Reporting Person in connection with a Public Document shall determine whether there are threats to the Member's ability to comply with the fundamental principles of the Code prior to accepting the Engagement. Where the Member determines that there is a threat to the Member's ability to comply with the fundamental principles of the Code, the Member shall apply appropriate safeguards to eliminate the threat or reduce it to an Acceptable Level. Where appropriate safeguards are not available to reduce the threat to an Acceptable Level, the Member shall decline the Engagement or the relevant part thereof.

3.6 A Member in Public Practice who is invited by an Assurance Client to provide Professional Services which comprise participating in and/or reporting to a Due Diligence Committee as a DDC Member, DDC Observer or Reporting Person in connection with a Public Document shall consider Section 290 *Independence – Assurance Engagements* of the Code to determine whether the proposed Professional Services create threats to the Member's Independence. Where the Member determines that there is a threat to the Member's Independence, the Member shall apply appropriate safeguards to eliminate the threat or reduce it to an Acceptable Level. Where appropriate safeguards are not available to reduce the threat to an Acceptable Level, the Member shall decline the Engagement or the relevant part thereof.

3.7 A Member in Public Practice who is invited by an Audit Client to provide Professional Services which comprise participating in and/or reporting to a Due Diligence Committee as a DDC Member, DDC Observer or Reporting Person in connection with a Public Document shall comply with the applicable independence requirements of the *Corporations Act 2001*.

3.8 When considering the appropriateness of accepting a role as a DDC Member, DDC Observer or Reporting Person, a Member in Public Practice should consider matters such as:

(a) the responsibilities of the role;

(b) the circumstances and context of the role, including the proposed transaction to which the Public Document relates, the proposed timetable for the due diligence process, the availability of information and any limitations on the scope of the Professional Services to be provided. (This would usually be outlined in the Due Diligence Planning Memorandum);

(c) relevant experience and expertise of the other members of the Due Diligence Committee and other participants in the due diligence process, as membership of the Due Diligence Committee will generally create a relationship of cross reliance;

(d) whether providing the Professional Services would require the Member to hold an Australian Financial Services Licence; and

(e) where the Member's Firm or a Network Firm is the statutory auditor of a Listed Entity or disclosing entity in Australia or a foreign jurisdiction, whether independence obligations, in addition to the requirements of the Code, preclude the Member from accepting a role as a DDC Member, DDC Observer or Reporting Person, or limit the scope of the role the Member may perform.

3.9 If a Member in Public Practice is not certain about the legal implications of performing the role of a DDC Member, DDC Observer or Reporting Person, the Member should seek legal advice.

Professional Independence

3.10 When engaged to provide a Professional Service to a Client which requires Independence, a Member in Public Practice shall comply with Independence as defined in this Standard.

3.11 A Member in Public Practice shall consider whether an Engagement, or a specific element of an Engagement, is an Assurance Engagement under the *Framework for Assurance Engagements* issued by the AUASB.

APES

3.12 Where the Engagement is an Assurance Engagement, the Member in Public Practice shall comply with Section 290 *Independence – Assurance Engagements* of the Code.

Professional competence and due care

3.13 A Member in Public Practice performing Professional Services shall maintain professional competence and take due care in the performance of the Member's work in accordance with Section 130 *Professional Competence and Due Care* of the Code.

3.14 Where a Member in Public Practice has agreed to provide a Due Diligence Sign-Off in respect of Financial Information and/or Other Specific Information that requires the consideration of matters that are outside the professional expertise of the Member, the Member shall seek expert assistance or advice from a suitably qualified third party or decline the Engagement. Where the Member relies upon the advice of a third party in connection with a Due Diligence Sign-Off or other reports, the Member shall disclose in the Member's Due Diligence Sign-Off or other reports the name and qualifications of the third party and the subject matter on which the third party advice has been obtained.

3.15 When planning to use the work of a suitably qualified third party, a Member in Public Practice shall assess the professional competence and objectivity of that third party and the appropriateness and adequacy of the work performed.

3.16 A Due Diligence Committee will usually include or be assisted by advisers to the Client, including the Client's legal adviser. A Member in Public Practice who reports to a Due Diligence Committee is generally entitled to rely on the advice and opinions of those advisers. Accordingly, paragraphs 3.14 and 3.15 are not intended to require a Member to obtain separate advice on matters for which another adviser to or member of the Due Diligence Committee is responsible.

3.17 In performing a Professional Service, a Member in Public Practice should consider any guidance in respect of such services issued by the professional accounting bodies and appropriate regulatory authorities.

Confidentiality

3.18 In accordance with Section 140 *Confidentiality* of the Code, a Member in Public Practice who acquires confidential information in the course of professional work for a Client shall not use that information for any purpose other than the proper performance of the professional work for that Client.

3.19 Where a Member in Public Practice provides Professional Services to a Client which comprise participating in and/or reporting to a Due Diligence Committee, the proper performance of the work will generally require the Member to disclose confidential information of the Client to the Due Diligence Committee, subject to any overriding restrictions on disclosure of information (including those commonly referred to as ethical wall arrangements). Unless the Member has a legal obligation of disclosure, the Member should not disclose any information relating to the Client's affairs to a party, other than to a DDC Member, DDC Observer or Reporting Person, without the Client's prior written permission.

4. Professional Engagement and other matters

4.1 A Member in Public Practice shall document and communicate the Terms of Engagement to a Client in accordance with APES 305 *Terms of Engagement* and this Standard.

4.2 The Terms of Engagement prepared by a Member in Public Practice should specify:

(a) whether an investigating accountant's report or other report will be provided for inclusion in the Public Document and if so the Financial Information and/or Other Specific Information that will be the subject of the report and the nature and extent of assurance (if any) to be provided;

(b) where the Member will have a role in relation to the Due Diligence Committee, the nature of the role including whether the Member will be a DDC Member, a DDC Observer or a Reporting Person;

(c) the tasks to be undertaken by the Member in connection with the Public Document including the scope of work on the Financial Information and/or Other Specific Information upon which any Due Diligence Sign-Off is to be provided; and

(d) whether the Member will prepare a Due Diligence Sign-off and the proposed form of such sign off.

4.3 Where a Due Diligence Planning Memorandum assigns responsibilities to a Member in Public Practice that extend beyond those agreed in the Engagement Document, the Member shall:

(a) advise the Client, and if acceptable to both the Member and the Client, either amend and re-issue the Engagement Document or issue an addendum to the Engagement Document to reflect the additional responsibilities; or

(b) where those additional responsibilities conflict with, or are prohibited by, this Standard, or are not acceptable to the Member:

- **advise the Client and its Due Diligence Committee of the Member's responsibilities outlined in the Engagement Document and/or this Standard; and**
- **take all reasonable steps to have the Due Diligence Planning Memorandum amended so that it does not assign responsibilities to the Member that conflict with, or are prohibited by, this Standard or are beyond those agreed in the Engagement Document or addendum thereto.**

4.4 Where, after taking the steps outlined in paragraph 4.3, the Due Diligence Planning Memorandum still includes responsibilities that conflict with, or are prohibited by this Standard, the Member in Public Practice shall decline the Engagement to participate in, and/or report to, the Due Diligence Committee.

4.5 A Member in Public Practice should take all reasonable steps to ensure that the Public Document and other documents associated with the due diligence process (such as the Due Diligence Planning Memorandum) do not describe the role of the Member in a manner that may imply that the Member has undertaken procedures with respect to, accepted responsibility for, approved the disclosure of, or reported upon matters or information in the Public Document or other associated documents beyond what was agreed in the Engagement Document.

Materiality guidance

4.6 Where a Member in Public Practice agrees to provide materiality guidance, which a Client and its Due Diligence Committee will consider for application to the due diligence process in relation to a Public Document, the Member shall comply with applicable Auditing and Assurance Standards.

4.7 The materiality guidance provided by the Member in Public Practice should only set out the quantitative matters to be considered by the Client and the Due Diligence Committee and indicate that decisions as to quantitative and qualitative considerations concerning materiality in relation to a specific potential or proposed disclosure are the responsibility of the Client after consideration by its Due Diligence Committee.

4.8 A Member in Public Practice who is engaged to provide materiality guidance to a Client and its Due Diligence Committee shall issue a Materiality Letter to the Client and the Due Diligence Committee.

A form of the Materiality Letter is given in Appendix 2.

APES

5. Roles and obligations of a Member in Public Practice in a due diligence process in connection with a Public Document

5.1 A Member in Public Practice may be asked to undertake a variety of roles in relation to a due diligence process in connection with a Public Document as:

(a) a DDC Member which typically includes:

(i) attending meetings of the Due Diligence Committee;

(ii) considering information presented to the Due Diligence Committee;

(iii) participating in decisions of the Due Diligence Committee;

(iv) reading and commenting on drafts of the Public Document;

(v) performing procedures specified in an Engagement Document and preparing a Due Diligence Sign-Off; and

(vi) signing the Due Diligence Committee's report to Those Charged with Governance of the Client;

(b) a DDC Observer which typically includes attending some or all meetings of the Due Diligence Committee at the request of the Client and may include performing procedures specified in an Engagement Document and preparing a Due Diligence Sign-Off; or

(c) a Reporting Person reporting to the Client and its Due Diligence Committee on the results of procedures specified in an Engagement Document.

A Member in Public Practice may also be asked to undertake Professional Services for, and provide a report to, a Client on Financial Information and/or Other Specific Information relevant to a Public Document, without being a DDC Member, DDC Observer or Reporting Person.

Examples of such reports (which could alternatively be prepared as a Reporting Person) are:

- an assurance report applying relevant Auditing and Assurance Standards on specific Financial Information (usually known as an investigating accountant's report); and
- a tax report on the taxation implications for shareholders of a transaction contemplated in the Public Document;

either of which may or may not be prepared for inclusion in the Public Document.

5.2 A Member in Public Practice who accepts an Engagement to provide a Due Diligence Sign-Off or other reports to a Due Diligence Committee, whether as a DDC Member, DDC Observer, or Reporting Person shall specify in the Due Diligence Sign-Off or other reports the Financial Information and/or Other Specific Information in or relevant to the Public Document that the Member has performed procedures on, and the nature of those procedures.

5.3 Based on the work performed a Member in Public Practice may report in a Due Diligence Sign-Off that the Member is not aware of:

(a) the specified Financial Information and/or Other Specific Information being misleading or deceptive (including by omission) in the form and context in which they appear in the Public Document; and

(b) the due diligence enquiries set out in the Due Diligence Planning Memorandum adopted by the Due Diligence Committee as they relate to the Financial Information and/or Other Specific Information not constituting all enquiries which are reasonable in the circumstances so far as the Financial Information and/or Other Specific Information are concerned.

5.4 A Member in Public Practice who accepts an Engagement to report to a Due Diligence Committee, whether as a DDC Member, DDC Observer or a Reporting Person shall not report or advise on matters outside the Member's area of expertise.

5.5 Paragraph 5.4 precludes a Member in Public Practice from providing an opinion on:

(a) whether the Financial Information and/or Other Specific Information disclosed in a Public Document is sufficient and appropriate to satisfy the relevant disclosure requirements of the *Corporations Act 2001*, for example those set out in Division 4 of Part 6D.2. These are matters requiring the collective consideration of all of the members of the Due Diligence Committee, and are reported on in the Due Diligence Committee's report; or

(b) whether the Client has complied with other legal obligations such as continuous disclosure obligations.

5.6 Paragraph 5.4 does not preclude a Firm from providing legal advice and reporting in relation to a Public Document if the Firm has Partners and Managerial Employees who are suitably qualified lawyers.

5.7 A Member in Public Practice shall sign a report to Those Charged with Governance on:

(a) information in a Public Document of a general nature relating to financial, accounting, tax or any other matters; or

(b) the content of the Public Document as a whole; or

(c) the due diligence process in relation to (a) and (b),

only as a DDC Member and where that report is a report of the Due Diligence Committee which is approved and signed concurrently by the other members of the Due Diligence Committee.

5.8 The matters set out in paragraph 5.7 should be considered by the Due Diligence Committee using the collective knowledge and expertise of the committee as a whole. A Member in Public Practice will not have the requisite knowledge or expertise to make determinations in relation to, or report on, those matters independently of other Due Diligence Committee members. Paragraph 5.7 (a) does not preclude a Member acting as a Reporting Person from providing Professional Services in respect of the range of potential tax implications for shareholders/unit holders that may need to be described in the Public Document.

5.9 A Member in Public Practice providing Professional Services to a Client which comprise participation in and/or reporting to a Due Diligence Committee as a DDC Member, DDC Observer or Reporting Person shall bring to the attention of the Client and/or its Due Diligence Committee any significant concerns relating to the matters set out in paragraph 5.7 which come to the attention of the Member in performing the work set out in the Member's Terms of Engagement.

5.10 A Member in Public Practice who accepts an Engagement to provide a Due Diligence Sign-Off in relation to Financial Information shall not prepare the Financial Information which is the subject of the Due Diligence Sign-Off or any extracts, summaries or analysis thereof provided elsewhere in the Public Document.

5.11 Paragraph 5.10 does not preclude a Member in Public Practice from reviewing or commenting on drafts of the Public Document for the purpose of alerting the Client and the Due Diligence Committee to matters that may affect the Member's ability to provide the Due Diligence Sign-Off, and, if the Member is a DDC Member for the purposes of fulfilling the Member's duties as a DDC Member.

5.12 Where a Member in Public Practice accepts an Engagement to assist a Client or its Due Diligence Committee in any verification process in relation to information in the Public Document (other than disclosures and information relating to taxation law), the Member shall agree the specific procedures to be undertaken with the Client to provide such assistance.

5.13 A Member in Public Practice should only provide verification assistance in relation to information in the Public Document (other than disclosures and information relating to taxation law) by performing an agreed upon procedures Engagement. A Member should not accept responsibility for the verification of information in a Public Document (other than disclosures and information relating to taxation law). Those Charged with Governance of the Client are responsible for the inclusion of the Financial Information and Other Specific Information in the Public Document and are best placed to know whether there is new or additional information that might affect its proper verification.

5.14 **Where a Member in Public Practice accepts an Engagement to verify or assist a Client or its Due Diligence Committee with the verification of disclosures and information relating to taxation law, the Member shall exercise professional judgement in determining the nature, timing and scope of the procedures taking into consideration the Terms of Engagement.**

5.15 **Where a Member in Public Practice is a DDC Observer and has been requested to provide a Due Diligence Sign-Off, the Member shall consider the scope of any procedures the Member has agreed to perform in relation to the due diligence process in connection with the Public Document, and assess whether the scope of the procedures will enable the Member to provide a Due Diligence Sign-Off.**

5.16 The scope of the role and responsibilities of a Member in Public Practice as a DDC Observer should be specified in the Engagement Document. The role should also be described in the Due Diligence Planning Memorandum and should be consistent with that specified in the Engagement Document. As a DDC Observer, the Member is not a party to the Due Diligence Planning Memorandum or the Due Diligence Committee's report to the Client.

5.17 **A Member in Public Practice who performs an Assurance Engagement in connection with a Public Document shall comply with Auditing and Assurance Standards in accordance with APES 210 *Conformity with Auditing and Assurance Standards*.**

5.18 **A Member in Public Practice who performs a valuation service in connection with a Public Document shall comply with APES 225 *Valuation Services*.**

5.19 **A Member in Public Practice who performs a taxation service in connection with a Public Document shall comply with APES 220 *Taxation Services*.**

5.20 **A Member in Public Practice who performs Professional Services in connection with a Public Document that includes prospective financial information shall comply with APES 345 *Reporting on Prospective Financial Information Prepared in Connection with a Disclosure Document*.**

6. Documentation

6.1 **A Member in Public Practice shall prepare working papers in accordance with this Standard that appropriately document the work performed, including aspects of the Engagement that have been provided in writing. The documentation prepared by the Member shall:**

(a) provide a sufficient and appropriate record of the procedures performed for the Engagement;

(b) identify the source of significant information the Member has used in the conduct of the Engagement; and

(c) demonstrate that the Engagement was carried out in accordance with this Standard and all other Professional Standards applicable to the Engagement, including policies and procedures established in accordance with APES 320 *Quality Control for Firms*, and any applicable ethical, legal and regulatory requirements.

7. Reporting

7.1 **Before a Member in Public Practice provides a Due Diligence Sign Off to a Client and its Due Diligence Committee, the Member shall:**

(a) assess whether the scope of procedures undertaken in relation to the Financial Information and/or Other Specific Information is sufficient and appropriate for that purpose;

(b) consider the impact of any limitations on the scope of work; and

(c) ascertain that all material matters in relation to the Financial Information and/or Other Specific Information which arose during the course of the Member's work have been addressed by the Client or its Due Diligence Committee.

7.2 Where the procedures undertaken in relation to the Financial Information and/or Other Specific Information only comprise a limited level of enquiry and/or the procedures were undertaken pursuant to another Engagement completed in the past, a Member in Public Practice shall not issue a Due Diligence Sign Off containing the conclusions referred to in paragraph 7.3(k).

7.3 Where the requirements of paragraph 7.1 have been met and a Member in Public Practice provides a Due Diligence Sign-Off, it shall contain the following:

(a) the name of the party or parties engaging the Member;

(b) any other addressees of the Due Diligence Sign-Off (typically being the other members of the Due Diligence Committee);

(c) the date on which the Due Diligence Sign-Off has been issued;

(d) the purpose for which the Due Diligence Sign-Off has been prepared, including the Public Document and proposed transaction to which it relates;

(e) whether the Member has prepared the Due Diligence Sign-Off in the capacity of a DDC Member or DDC Observer;

(f) a statement that the Professional Services were conducted and the Due Diligence Sign-Off was prepared in accordance with this Standard;

(g) the Financial Information and/or Other Specific Information disclosed in the Public Document in relation to which the Member has undertaken procedures to which the Due Diligence Sign-Off relates;

(h) the scope of work performed in relation to the Financial Information and/or Other Specific information to which the Due Diligence Sign-Off relates;

(i) any limitations on the scope of work performed;

(j) the basis on which the statements in the Due Diligence Sign-Off are made, including specific reference to:

- **the scope of work performed;**
- **the materiality guidelines adopted by the Due Diligence Committee; and**
- **the extent, if any, of reliance by the Member on the work of others;**

(k) the conclusions of the Member in the form of negative statements as to whether having performed the scope of work, the Member has become aware of anything to cause the Member to believe that:

- **the Financial Information and/or Other Specific Information [as presented in identified sections of the Public Document] is misleading or deceptive (including by omission) in the form and context in which it appears; and**
- **the due diligence enquiries set out in the Due Diligence Planning Memorandum adopted by the Due Diligence Committee as they relate to the Financial Information and/or Other Specific Information do not constitute all inquiries which are reasonable in the circumstances so far as the Financial Information and/or Other Specific Information is concerned;**

(l) the significant assumptions upon which the conclusions of the Member are based;

(m) all qualifications to the conclusions of the Member; and

(n) any restrictions on the use and distribution of the Due Diligence Sign-Off.

A form of Due Diligence Sign-Off which complies with the requirements of this Standard is set out in Appendix 1. Members should note that this form of Due Diligence Sign-Off may require amendment if the Due Diligence Sign-Off is prepared by a Member as a DDC Observer.

7.4 Where a Member in Public Practice is asked to provide a Due Diligence Sign-Off in respect of a Public Document which has not been finalised, the Member shall consider:

(a) any amendments to the Due Diligence Sign-Off which may be required to reflect that the Public Document has not been finalised; and

(b) the information which has not been finalised in the draft Public Document,

to ensure that any sign off provided at that time is appropriate.

7.5 A substantially complete draft of a Public Document is often used as a confidential and restricted briefing document to seek the support of potential investors for the proposed transaction. In this situation, a Member in Public Practice may be requested to provide a Due Diligence Sign-Off in relation to the draft Public Document or to advise whether the Member would be able to provide a Due Diligence Sign-Off in relation to the draft Public Document if the Member was requested to do so at that time. In providing any such Due Diligence Sign-Off or providing any such advice, the Member should clearly state:

- any assumptions or qualifications relevant to the provision of the Due Diligence Sign-Off or the advice;
- the specific draft or version number of the Public Document to which the Due Diligence Sign-Off or the advice relates; and
- that the Due Diligence Sign-Off or the advice is subject to change as a result of events which occur or information which comes to the Member's attention between the date of the provision of the Due Diligence Sign-Off or the advice in relation to the draft Public Document and the date of the provision of any subsequent or final Due Diligence Sign-Offs in relation to the Public Document.

7.6 Where a Member in Public Practice is requested to provide to a Client and/or its Due Diligence Committee written status reports or interim reports in respect of specific work discussed in the Engagement Document (for example by way of a draft report, an oral presentation and/or by way of contributions to issues registers) or requested to provide on an interim basis detailed findings, the Member should include an appropriate disclaimer stating that such reports are provided for "information only" and are not suitable for reliance by the Client, the Due Diligence Committee or any other person.

7.7 Where a Client or its Due Diligence Committee requests a Member in Public Practice to make available to the Due Diligence Committee a previous report provided by the Member to the Client, or a report on work that is being undertaken by the Member for the Client for a purpose other than the transaction to which a Public Document relates (for example, a report on internal controls of the Client, or on acquisition due diligence procedures undertaken in relation to a business to be acquired by the Client), the Member should consider whether or not and on what basis such report(s) may be made available to the Due Diligence Committee, having regard to relevant factors, including:

(a) whether the information in the report (or on which it is based) remains current;

(b) whether the Member's approach to materiality in preparing the report was consistent with the materiality guidelines adopted by the Due Diligence Committee;

(c) the relevance of the report to the due diligence enquiries being undertaken by the Due Diligence Committee;

(d) the level of testing done on source information relied on by the Member in preparing the report; and

(e) whether Client consent has been obtained.

7.8 Where a Member in Public Practice is requested to provide consent to being named in a Public Document, or to the inclusion of the Member's report in the Public Document, the Member shall, prior to providing the consent, obtain the final draft of the Public Document to ensure that the form and context in which the Member's name and/or report appears is appropriate.

7.9 In accordance with the terms of a Due Diligence Planning Memorandum and/or relevant legislation, a Member in Public Practice shall bring to the attention of a Client and/or its Due Diligence Committee any material new circumstances relevant

to a Public Document of which the Member becomes aware subsequent to the issue of the Public Document.

7.10 The period to which any obligation referred to in paragraph 7.9 applies will usually be set out in the Due Diligence Planning Memorandum or relevant legislation.

8. Professional fees

8.1 A Member in Public Practice who performs Professional Services comprising participating in and/or reporting to a Due Diligence Committee as a DDC Member, DDC Observer or Reporting Person in connection with a Public Document, shall be remunerated for such services by way of professional fees computed in accordance with Section 240 *Fees and other Types of Remuneration* of the Code.

8.2 A Member in Public Practice shall not enter into a Contingent Fee arrangement or receive a Contingent Fee for a Professional Service which requires Independence or which purports to be independent.

Conformity with International Pronouncements

The International Ethics Standard Board for Accountants (IESBA) has not issued a pronouncement equivalent to APES 350.

Appendix 1

Due Diligence Sign-Off

[insert date]

The Due Diligence Committee,
each of its members and their representatives

Board of Directors
[insert name of the Client]
[insert address]

Dear Sirs,

[insert subject]

This Due Diligence Sign-Off is provided to you in relation to the [*describe Public Document*] to be issued by [*insert Client*] on [*insert date*] in connection with [*insert details of proposed transaction*] **(Offer/Transaction)**, and the work undertaken by us as a [DDC Member/ DDC Observer] pursuant to our Engagement Document with [Client] dated [insert date] (the **Engagement Document**).

Our services have been conducted and this Due Diligence Sign-Off has been prepared in accordance with APES 350 *Participation by Members in Public Practice in Due Diligence Committees in Connection with a Public Document.*

1. Introduction

We refer to the following financial information relating to the Client that is disclosed in the [*describe Public Document*]:

(a) [*specify relevant historical financial information on which the Member has performed a review*] for [*insert period*] as disclosed in Section [*insert*];

(b) [*specify relevant pro forma historical information on which the Member has performed a review*] for [*insert period*] as disclosed in Section [*insert*];

(c) [*specify relevant forecast financial information, if any on which the Member has performed a review*] for [*insert period*] as disclosed in Section [*insert*],

APES

(collectively **Financial Information**). [*Note –the definition of Financial Information should, where appropriate, be consistent with that used in any investigating accountant's report being provided by the Member in Public Practice*]

[The [other] information that is disclosed in the [*describe Public Document*], and to which this Due Diligence Sign-Off relates comprises the following:

(d) [*specify information which has been the subject of procedures specified in the Engagement Document*] disclosed in section [ ] of the [*describe Public Document*];

(e) [*insert as required*]

(collectively **Other Specific Information**).]

2. Scope of Work

As agreed with [*Client*] in the Engagement Document, in connection with the [*describe Public Document*] we have:

(a) [participated as a member of and been a Reporting Person to] [attended as an observer meetings of]the Due Diligence Committee (**DDC**) that has been established by the [Client] for the purposes of coordinating due diligence investigations as set out in the Due Diligence Planning Memorandum (**DDPM**) in connection with the [describe *Public Document*];

(b) prepared materiality guidance in a letter dated [*insert date*] for consideration by the [Client] and the DDC;

(c) conducted a review, in accordance with [ASRE 2405 or ASAE 3000 or other standards as appropriate], of the Financial Information furnished to us by the [Client];

(d) [assisted the Client in its verification of certain statements in the [*describe Public Document*] by performing the procedures set out in [*insert – eg "Appendix 2" or "the Engagement Document"*] as agreed by the Client (**Agreed Upon Procedures**);

(e) [prepared an investigating accountant's report (if applicable) on the Financial Information for inclusion in the [*describe Public Document*]];

(f) [prepared a letter on the tax implications of the proposed Offer/Transaction for Australian tax residents (if applicable) for inclusion in the [*describe Public Document*]]; and

(g) [*insert scope of work in relation to Other Specific Information being information which was not subject to the procedures in (d) above.*]

[Note: this is an example scope only, and should be tailored to reflect the agreed scope of the professional services]

Scope limitations

[insert scope limitations as relevant. For example, any limitations in access to financial records, key management personnel or information relating to a particular issue or particular accounting standard. See example limitation below for Agreed Upon Procedures work. Particular scope limitations may need to be inserted in relation to paragraph (c) in order to comply with Auditing Standards applying to review engagements]

The work referred to in paragraph (d) above was undertaken in accordance with Australian Auditing Standards applicable to Agreed Upon Procedures Engagements. The responsibility for determining the adequacy or otherwise of the Agreed Upon Procedures is that of the directors of the Client. That work did not constitute an audit or review in accordance with Australian Auditing Standards and consequently no assurance or audit opinion or review statement is expressed. Had we performed additional procedures or had we performed an audit in accordance with Australian Auditing Standards or a review in accordance with Australian Auditing Standards applicable to review engagements, other matters might have come to our attention that would have been reported to you.

3. Findings – Agreed Upon Procedures

[insert factual findings arising from Agreed Upon Procedures, including any exceptions noted]

4. Basis for Review Statement

The statement in section 5 (**Review Statement**) is made on the basis of:

(a) the procedures and other activities performed by us as described in section 2(c);

(b) the materiality criteria adopted by the Client and the DDC; and

(c) the assumptions and qualifications set out in this letter.

In making the Review Statement we only hold ourselves out as having expertise as [designation of applicable professional body] [in advising on Australian taxation matters (if applicable)]. We disclaim any skills or expertise in any other capacity.

5. Review Statement

Based on our review of the Financial Information, which is not an audit, and applying the materiality criteria adopted by the DDC, nothing has come to our attention that causes us to believe that:

(a) the Financial Information is misleading or deceptive (including by omission) in the form and context in which it appears; or

(b) the due diligence enquiries set out in the DDPM adopted by the DDC as they relate to the Financial Information do not constitute all enquiries which are reasonable in the circumstances so far as the Financial Information is concerned.

All matters in relation to the Financial Information which arose during the course of our work have been addressed by management of the [Client] or the DDC and, accordingly, there are no outstanding issues in relation to the Financial Information identified as part of our work which require the attention of the [Client] and the DDC.

6. Other Specific Information

[Insert appropriate statements and the basis for those statements, in relation to the Other Specific Information referred to in 2(g), if applicable.]

7. Assumptions

In making the Review Statement in this Due Diligence Sign-Off, we have assumed that:

(a) the representations made and the information (including responses to questions and questionnaires) provided by directors, officers, personnel and agents of the Client, other members of the DDC, and other persons reporting to the DDC, have been complete, true and accurate in all respects and were not misleading or deceptive;

(b) all persons who were interviewed, questioned or sent questionnaires were competent to answer all questions put to them, made complete and accurate disclosures in all matters and that there were no other persons who should have been interviewed, questioned or sent questionnaires in relation to the matters the subject of those questions;

(c) there were no relevant documents or information other than those which were disclosed, or provided by or on behalf of the Client to us which are relevant to the Financial Information;

(d) the report of [*insert name of third party expert*] dated [insert date] concerning [insert] [note: *qualifications of third party expert to be described*] is accurate and complete;

(e) all corporate records and other documents examined by us are genuine, complete, up-to-date and accurate and, without limitation, any minutes of the meetings of the Client examined by us correctly record the business of, and resolutions passed at, any such meeting and no relevant corporate records have been withheld from us (whether deliberately or inadvertently);

(f) all factual matters stated in any document provided to us are true and accurate; and

(g) the [describe Public Document] [insert date and final document version number] will be lodged with the Australian Securities and Investment Commission.

Nothing has come to our attention that causes us to believe that these assumptions are not reasonable. We have not taken any steps to validate these assumptions other than as may be specified in our scope of work in section 2.

8. Qualifications

Our Statements in this Due Diligence Sign-Off are subject to the following qualifications:

(a) we have no responsibility to update this Due Diligence Sign-Off for events and circumstances occurring after the date of this Due Diligence Sign-Off, other than as required under the terms of the Engagement Document;

(b) insofar as consideration of Australian accounting standards and other mandatory professional reporting requirements [and Australian tax laws] impact or formed part of our scope of work, in making the Statement in section 5 we have had regard to such Australian requirements as are in place as at 9am on the date of this letter;

(c) we make no statement, and express no opinion, on any matter such as legal matters requiring skills or expertise other than of an [accounting] [and/or] [Australian taxation] nature;

(d) the Statement in section 5 of this Due Diligence Sign-Off relates only to the Financial Information and does not relate to any additional statements in or concerning the [describe Public Document] that may be made by any person or any other conduct that any person may engage in concerning the [describe Public Document];

(e) the Statement in section 5 of this Due Diligence Sign-Off is limited to the knowledge of those partners, directors and employees of [insert Firm] who have provided the services [to Client] referred to in this letter, and we have made no enquiries of any [other] partner, director or employee of [*insert Firm*], or any of its related entities, who may have knowledge of matters relevant to the [*describe Public Document*] [through the provision of services to other Clients of [insert Firm], or whose knowledge may not be applied because of any ethical walls arrangements implemented in relation to our engagement by [Client] on this matter; and

(f) [We have relied on the accuracy and completeness of the report of [*insert name of third party expert*] dated [*insert date*] concerning [*insert*]. [*note: qualifications of third party expert to be described*].

9. Recipients of this Due Diligence Sign-Off

This Due Diligence Sign-Off is given solely for the benefit of:

(a) the Client and its representatives on the DDC;

(b) the directors of the Client; and

(c) each other member of the DDC and their representatives in their respective capacities as such,

(together referred to as the **Recipients**).

This Due Diligence Sign-Off is not intended for general circulation or publication and may not, without our prior written consent in each specific instance:

(a) be disclosed except to persons who, in the ordinary course of a Recipient's business have access to their papers and records and on the basis that such person will make no further disclosure of it and are not entitled to rely on it for any purpose;

(b) be filed with a government or other agency, or be quoted or referred to in any public document or domain; or

(c) be reproduced or used for any other purpose,

except as required by law, regulation or the rules of any Stock Exchange or government body or in connection with any enquiry conducted by a regulatory body or in the enforcement of the rights of, or in defence of any actual or potential claim against, a Recipient.

We do not accept any responsibility for any losses whatsoever occasioned by any Recipient or by any other party as a result of the circulation, reproduction or use of this Due Diligence Sign-Off contrary to the above paragraph.

Yours faithfully

Member or Firm

Appendix 2

Materiality Letter

The Due Diligence Committee, each of its members
and their representatives

Board of Directors

[Insert name of issuer]

[Insert address of issuer]

[Date]

Dear [ ]

Materiality guidance in relation to due diligence process of [Issuer]'s [Public Document]

We refer to our Engagement letter with [ ] dated [ ].

The purpose of this letter is to set out guidance with respect to the quantitative materiality thresholds for consideration by [Client and/or Issuer] and the Due Diligence Committee ("DDC") for the **[Prospectus /Product Disclosure Statement/Bidder Statement/Target Statement/ Explanatory Memorandum /Cleansing Notice or other Public Document**] proposed to be issued in connection with [describe proposed transaction] (the "Public Document") by [Issuer].

Decisions on materiality in relation to specific, potential or proposed disclosures are the responsibility of [Client] after consideration by the DDC. This letter contains specific guidance in relation to the quantitative factors of materiality. However, it does not contain any specific guidance in relation to the qualitative factors of materiality which by definition will be unique to the matter being considered.

Relevance of materiality guidelines

The guidance contained within this letter is based on requirements and guidance available in Australian Accounting Standards, AUASB Standards and AUASB Guidance Statements, and may not necessarily be directly applicable to all circumstances which may arise in relation to the Public Document.

Also, in the event of an alleged deficiency in the Public Document due to an alleged misleading or deceptive statement or omission or otherwise, the relevance or application of the concept of materiality may depend on the law that is alleged to have been breached, the available defences and the nature of the legal proceedings (i.e., criminal or civil). We recommend [Client and/or Issuer] seek legal advice on the extent to which materiality may or may not be relevant to the Public Document due diligence process in this instance.

Requirements and Application and Other Explanatory Material ("guidance") on applying the concept of materiality in the planning and performing of an audit of historical financial information is contained in Auditing Standard ASA 320 *Materiality in Planning and Performing an Audit* ("ASA 320") and Accounting Standard AASB 1031 *Materiality* ("AASB 1031"). The AUASB Glossary contains the following definition for 'Materiality':

"In relation to information, that if information is omitted, misstated or not disclosed, that information has the potential to affect the economic decisions of users of the financial report or the discharge of accountability by management or those charged with governance.".

Similarly AASB 1031 defines 'Materiality' as:

"Omissions or misstatements of items are material if they could, individually or collectively, influence the economic decisions of users taken on the basis of the financial statements. Materiality depends on the size and nature of the omission or misstatement judged in the surrounding circumstances. The size or nature of the item, or a combination of both, could be the determining factor."

In relation to applying materiality to pro forma adjustments to historical financial information, the following pronouncements have been considered:

- AGS 1062 *Reporting in Connection with Proposed Fundraisings*[1]; and
- Section 728 of the Corporations Act 2001 ("the Act") which determines that an offence has occurred if a misleading or deceptive statement, omission or new circumstance is materially adverse from the point of view of an investor[2],

with the provisions of the Act overriding the requirements of applicable AUASB Standards and AUASB Guidance Statements should they conflict or yield a different result[3].

The requirements and guidance contained in ASA 320 applies to historical financial information. A Due Diligence Committee dealing with prospective financial information may refer to ASA 320 for guidance when establishing materiality thresholds.

There is a relationship between materiality and risk. That is, the higher the risk of a statement being misleading or deceptive, or of an omission, the lower the materiality level. The DDC should take this relationship into account when determining the nature, timing and extent of due diligence procedures. The DDC should make a preliminary assessment of materiality to establish an appropriate quantitative materiality level to plan due diligence procedures.

Quantitative factors

Quantitative thresholds used as guidance for determining the materiality of the amount of an item or an aggregate of items are, of necessity, drawn at arbitrary levels. When establishing a preliminary quantitative materiality level, consideration needs to be given to:

- the reliability of management information;
- any factors which may indicate deviations from normal activities; and
- qualitative factors.

A percentage is ordinarily applied to a chosen benchmark as a starting point in determining materiality. When identifying an appropriate benchmark, regard is normally given to factors such as the elements of the financial information, items users are likely to focus on, the nature of the entity, its life cycle, industry and economic environment, the size of the entity, ownership and financing and the relative volatility of the benchmark. For uncorrected misstatements that are below the materiality level, an assessment is required of whether the cumulative result of these misstatements could have a material effect.

ASA 320 does not contain requirements that specify how to determine quantitative materiality thresholds, as their determination is a matter of professional judgement. Australian Accounting Standard AASB 1031 "Materiality" ("AASB 1031") adopts a similar approach to ASA 320 and explains the role of materiality in making judgements in the preparation and presentation of financial reports.

AASB 1031 states that in determining materiality both qualitative and quantitative factors need to be considered together and in particular circumstances, "either the nature or the amount of an item or aggregate of items could be the determining factor".

AASB 1031 provides a quantitative methodology as guidance for the determination of materiality in financial statements that states that:

1 As of March 2011 AUASB is revising this Standard.

2 There is no definition of "materiality" or "materially adverse" in the *Corporations Act 2001* (Cwlth). Given the absence of a legislative definition of materiality, it is widely accepted practice in Australia to consider the accounting definition of materiality in "Accounting Standard AASB 1031: *Materiality*".

3 *[If the Public Document is a Cleansing Notice, it may be desirable to include the following wording since S728 applies only to Disclosure Documents.]*

[Section [708AA/1012DAA] of the Act refers to the notion of "material" under subsection 11, which states that the Cleansing Notice to be lodged with the Australian Securities Exchange is defective if the Cleansing Notice is false or misleading in a material particular; or if the notice has omitted from it a matter or thing, the omission of which renders the notice misleading in a material respect. Given the similarities in references to the concept of materiality being applied to a misleading statement/particular or omission in both sections [708AA/1012DAA] and 728, AGS 1062 is still considered a useful source of guidance with regard to materiality where an offer is made under section [708AA/1012DAA].]

- an amount which is equal to or greater than 10% of the appropriate base amount may be presumed to be material unless there is evidence, or convincing argument, to the contrary; and
- an amount which is equal to or less than 5% of the appropriate base amount may be presumed not to be material unless there is evidence, or convincing argument, to the contrary.

As the above represents an aggregate materiality threshold the due diligence process should seek to identify individual matters or items that could have a material effect in aggregate. To facilitate this, the DDC should consider adopting an appropriate threshold for individual items to be identified and collected to assess whether in aggregate they may be material. General practice is to identify and collect individual items in a range of X% to Y% of the aggregate materiality threshold.

This quantitative methodology is in addition to, but not a substitute for, any qualitative assessment. The appropriate base amount will depend on the particular circumstances and AASB 1031 provides the following guidance in this respect:

(a) *the amount of an item or an aggregate of items relating to the statement of financial position is compared with the more appropriate of:*

(i) *the recorded amount of equity; and*

(ii) *the appropriate asset or liability class total; or*

(b) *the amount of an item or an aggregate of items relating to the statement of comprehensive income is compared with the more appropriate of the:*

(i) *profit or loss and the appropriate income or expense amount for the current reporting period; and*

(ii) *average profit or loss and the average of the appropriate income or expense amounts for a number of reporting periods (including the current reporting period); or*

(c) *the amount of an item or an aggregate of items relating to the statement of cash flows is compared with the more appropriate of the:*

(i) *net cash provided by or used in the operating, investing, financing or other activities as appropriate, for the current reporting period; and*

(ii) *average net cash provided by or used in the operating, investing, financing or other activities as appropriate, for a number of reporting periods (including the current reporting period).*

Clearly trends in key operating performance measures are as important as the absolute numbers.

AASB 1031 states that materiality "is a matter of professional judgement influenced by the characteristics of the entity and the perceptions as to who are, or are likely to be, the users of the financial report and their information needs. Materiality judgements can only be properly made by those who have the facts". It is within this context that the quantitative threshold guidelines noted above should be used.

Recommendations on quantitative materiality thresholds

Our recommendations on quantitative materiality thresholds to be adopted by the Due Diligence Committee are as follows:

Financial performance and cash flows

The process of due diligence should seek to identify, in respect of the financial performance and operating cash flows, misstatements in excess of $[ ] on the [net profit/profit before tax/ EBITDA] of [Issuer]. This level represents approximately [ ]% of the [average] [net profit/profit before tax/EBITDA] of [Issuer[for the year[s] [ended/ending] [ ] 20XX.

To ensure due consideration is given to individual items affecting the income statement and cash flow statement, which may aggregate to $[ ], all individual items greater than $[ ] should be identified for consideration.

APES

Balance Sheet

The process of due diligence in respect of the balance sheet should seek to identify a misstatement or reclassification of [Issuer]'s balance sheet or net assets of more than $[ ]. This level represents approximately X% of [the appropriate base] as at [ ] 20XX.

To ensure due consideration is given to individual items affecting the balance sheet, which may aggregate to $[ ], all individual items greater than $[ ] should be identified for consideration. These are items which are expected to affect the balance sheet only.

The quantitative materiality recommendations in this letter are provided as a guide only as recommendations covering every possible scenario, event or matter cannot be made. The overriding consideration in relation to each matter should be whether:

- the omission of the matter from the Public Document; or
- a misleading disclosure in relation to the matter,

would be likely to be considered to render the Public Document deficient in light of the legal disclosure requirements relevant to the Public Document.

Yours faithfully

Member

Appendix 3

Summary of revisions to the previous APES 350 (Issued December 2009)

APES 350 *Participation by Members in Public Practice in Due Diligence Committees in connection with a Public Document originally* issued in December 2009 has been revised by APESB in March 2011. A summary of the revisions is given in the table below.

Table of revisions*

Paragraph affected	How affected
1.1	Amended
2 – Definition of Other Specific Information	Amended
4 – Reference to Appendix 2	Added
5.7	Amended
5.9	Amended
5.12	Amended
5.13	Amended
5.14	Added
Appendix 1 – second paragraph	Amended
Appendix 1 – 2 (g)	Amended
Appendix 1 – 2 Scope limitations	Amended
Appendix 1 – 4	Amended
Appendix 1 – 5	Deleted
Appendix 1 – 6	Added
Appendix 1 – 7	Amended
Appendix 1 – 7 (c)	Amended
Appendix 1 – 8 (a)	Amended
Appendix 1 – 9 (a)	Amended
Appendix 1 – 9	Amended
Appendix 2	Added

* *Refer Technical Update 2011/2*

APES GN 40

Members in Business Guidance Note Ethical Conflicts in the Workplace – Considerations for Members in Business

(Issued March 2012)

Prepared and Issued by Accounting Professional and Ethical Standards Board.

Note from the Institute of Chartered Accountants Australia

This note, prepared by the technical editor, is not part of APES GN 40.

Historical development

March 2012: APES GN 40 issued. It provides assistance to members in business in addressing a range of ethical issues, including potential conflicts of interest arising from responsibilities to employers, their preparation and reporting of information, financial interests and whistle blowing.

APES GN 40 provides guidance on the application of fundamental principles contained in APES 110 'Code of Ethics for Professional Accountants' (the Code), and includes 21 case studies providing examples of ethical issues experienced in commercial, public and not-for-profit sectors. It includes a new section that provides guidance for members in business regarding their professional obligations in relation to whistleblowing. It supersedes GN1 'Members in Business Guidance Statement', which the APESB inherited from the accounting profession.

It has no international equivalent.

APES

Contents

1. Scope and application

1.1 Accounting Professional & Ethical Standards Board Limited (APESB) issues professional guidance note APES GN 40 *Ethical Conflicts in the Workplace – Considerations for Members in Business* (the Guidance Note). This Guidance Note supersedes GN 1 *Members in Business Guidance Statement*.

1.2 APES GN 40 provides guidance to Members in Business on the application of the fundamental principles contained within *Part A: General Application* and *Part C: Members in Business* of APES 110 *Code of Ethics for Professional Accountants* (the Code). The Guidance Note provides examples for Members in Business of situations that require professional judgment in the application of the principles of the Code.

1.3 Members in Business working in Australia should follow the guidance in APES GN 40 when they provide services to their Employer.

1.4 Members in Business working outside of Australia should follow the guidance in APES GN 40 to the extent to which they are not prevented from so doing by specific requirements of local laws and/or regulations.

1.5 The Guidance Note is not intended to detract from any responsibilities which may be imposed by law or regulation.

1.6 All references to Professional Standards and Guidance Notes are references to those provisions as amended from time to time.

1.7 Members in Business need to be familiar with relevant Professional Standards and Guidance Notes when providing Professional Services.

1.8 In applying the guidance outlined in APES GN 40, Members should be guided not merely by the words but also by the spirit of this Guidance Note and the Code.

2. Definitions

For the purpose of this Guidance Note:

Acceptable Level means a level at which a reasonable and informed third party would be likely to conclude, weighing all the specific facts and circumstances, that compliance with the fundamental principles is not compromised.

Code means APES 110 *Code of Ethics for Professional Accountants*.

Employer within the context of this Guidance Note means an entity or person that employs, engages or contracts a Member in Business.

Member means a Member of a Professional Body that has adopted this Guidance Note as applicable to their Membership as defined by that Professional Body.

Member in Business means a Member employed or engaged in an executive or non-executive capacity in such areas as commerce, industry, service, the public sector, education, the not for profit sector, regulatory bodies or Professional Bodies, or a Member contracted by such entities.

Professional Bodies means the Institute of Chartered Accountants in Australia, CPA Australia and the Institute of Public Accountants.

Professional Services means services requiring accountancy or related skills performed by a Member including accounting, auditing, taxation, management consulting and financial management services.

Professional Standards means all standards issued by Accounting Professional & Ethical Standards Board Limited and all professional and ethical requirements of the applicable Professional Body.

Those Charged with Governance means the persons with responsibility for overseeing the strategic direction of the entity and obligations related to the accountability of the entity. This includes overseeing the financial reporting process.

3. Fundamental responsibilities of Members in Business

3.1 The Code is the conceptual framework and foundation on which all APESB pronouncements are based. Compliance with and application of the Code is fundamental to the professional behaviour of Members in Business. Non-compliance with the Code can lead to disciplinary proceedings being initiated by the Professional Body to which the Member belongs.

3.2 Professional obligations and ethical requirements that Members in Business are required to comply with are based on the five fundamental principles of integrity, objectivity, professional competence and due care, confidentiality and professional behaviour in the Code.

3.3 The term Professional Services is defined in the Code as services requiring accountancy or related skills performed by a Member including accounting, auditing, taxation, management consulting and financial management services. Whilst a number of these services are typically performed by Members in Public Practice, services performed by Members in Business are also captured by the definition of Professional Services. Such services typically include those performed by financial accountants, tax accountants, financial analysts, financial planners, management accountants, internal auditors and financial controllers.

3.4 A Member in Business who provides Professional Services is required to comply with *Part A – General Application of the Code* and *Part C – Members in Business* including Section 100 *Introduction and Fundamental Principles* and any relevant law or regulation. Part C is specific to Members in Business and describes the application of the fundamental principles to some of the more commonly encountered situations that may create threats to compliance with the fundamental principles.

APES

4. Conceptual framework approach

4.1 Members in Business may encounter situations that give rise to threats to compliance with the fundamental principles. This Guidance Note uses the framework in the Code to assist Members to identify, evaluate and respond to threats to compliance with the fundamental principles. Members are required to implement safeguards to eliminate the threats or reduce them to an Acceptable Level so that compliance with the fundamental principles is not compromised. The Guidance Note provides a range of examples dealing with a variety of circumstances in which threats may arise and provides guidance on safeguards that may be adopted. Members should use the framework to address ethical issues arising from their work at an early stage to enable them to adopt appropriate safeguards which are suitable to the circumstance.

4.2 When considering situations that threaten compliance with the fundamental principles, Members in Business need to retain their objectivity and should use the following structured approach to ethical decision making:

i. Gather the facts and identify the problem or threat;

ii. Identify the fundamental principles involved;

iii. Identify the affected parties;

iv. Determine whether established organisational procedures and conflict resolution resources exist to address the threat to compliance with the fundamental principles;

v. Identify the relevant parties who should be involved in the conflict resolution process;

vi. Discuss the ethical issue and the conflict with the relevant parties, and in accordance with the prescribed procedures evaluate the significance of the threats identified and safeguards available;

vii. Consider courses of action and associated consequences;

viii. Consider whether to consult confidentially with external advisers such as an independent adviser, legal advisor and/or the Professional Body to which the Member belongs;

ix. Consider whether to consult Those Charged with Governance;

x. Decide on an appropriate course of action;

xi. Document all enquiries and conclusions reached; and

xii. implement the appropriate course of action. In the event that the Member believes that the threat to compliance with the fundamental principles has not been satisfactorily resolved, the Member should determine whether it is appropriate to resign.

The process to be followed as indicated above may vary with each particular circumstance and a flow diagram is set out below to provide guidance to a Member on how to arrive at an appropriate course of action:

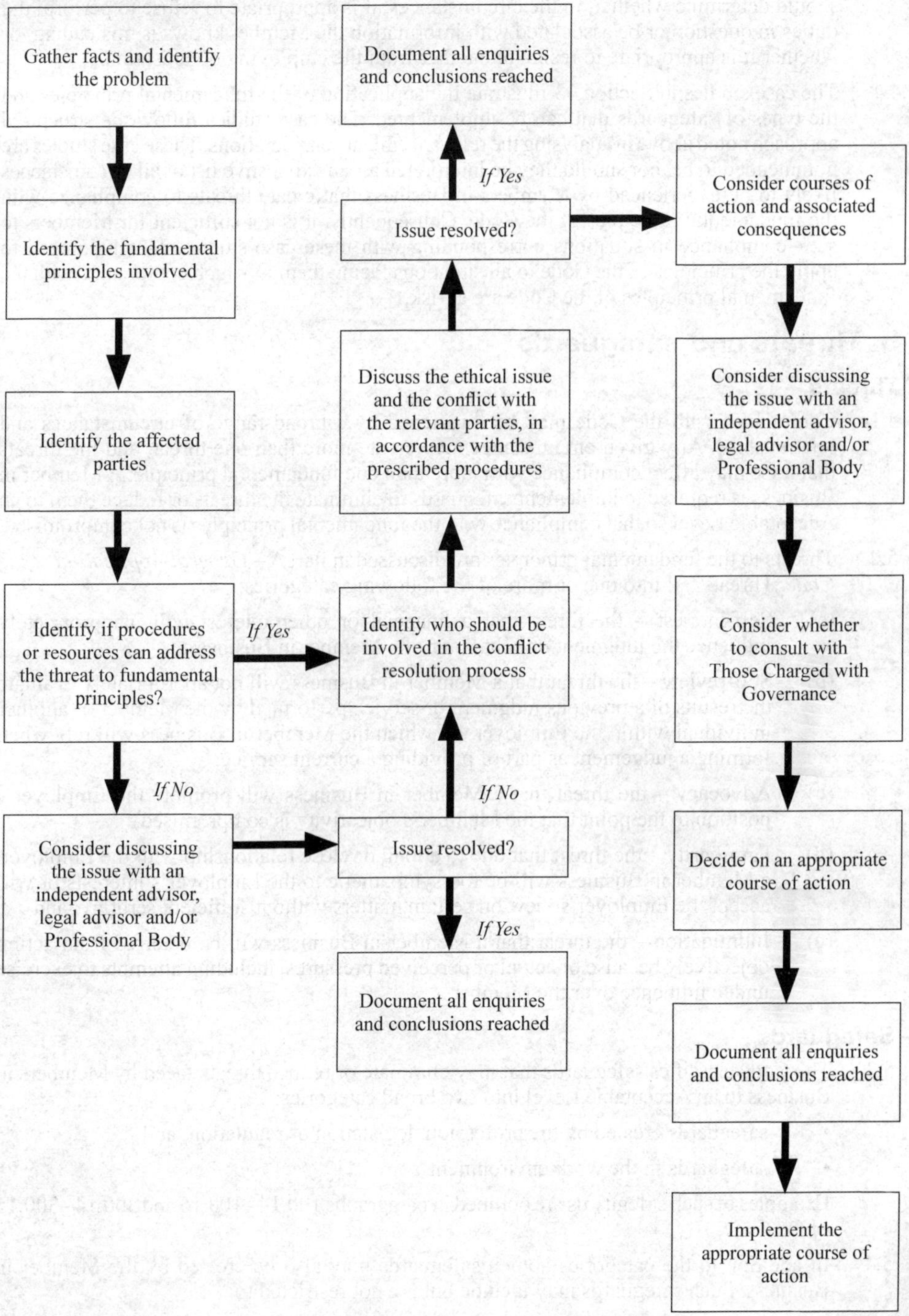

4.3 When resolving an ethical issue, a Member in Business should document the substance of the issue and details of any discussions held and conclusions reached concerning that issue. The Member should take qualitative as well as quantitative factors into account when evaluating the significance of an ethical issue, and be alert to the fact that reassessment of the issue may need to occur on an ongoing basis. If, after exhausting all relevant possibilities, the ethical issue remains unresolved, the Member should, where possible, refuse to remain associated with the matter creating the conflict. The Member should determine whether, in the circumstances, it is appropriate to refuse to perform the duties in question or be associated with information the Member knows is misleading, or whether it is appropriate to resign altogether from the employing organisation.

4.4 The case studies in Section 13 illustrate the application of the fundamental principles and the types of safeguards that can be implemented. The case studies follow the structured approach noted above in analysing the relevant ethical considerations. These case studies are not intended to be, nor should they be interpreted as, an exhaustive list of all circumstances likely to be experienced by Members in Business that create threats to compliance with the fundamental principles of the Code. Consequently, it is not sufficient for Members to seek compliance in situations corresponding with these case studies. Members need to apply the principles of the Code to all situations facing them in which compliance with the fundamental principles of the Code are at risk.

5. Threats and safeguards

Threats

5.1 Compliance with the Code may be threatened by a broad range of circumstances and relationships. Any given circumstance may create more than one threat, and the threats that arise may affect compliance with more than one fundamental principle. A Member in Business is required to implement safeguards to eliminate the threats or reduce them to an Acceptable Level so that compliance with the fundamental principles is not compromised.

5.2 Threats to the fundamental principles are discussed in Part A – *General Application of the Code*. Threats fall into one or more of the following categories:

(a) Self-interest – the threat that a financial or other interest will inappropriately influence the judgment or behaviour of a Member in Business;

(b) Self-review – the threat that a Member in Business will not appropriately evaluate the results of a previous judgment or service performed by the Member or another individual within the Employer, on which the Member in Business will rely when forming a judgement as part of providing a current service;

(c) Advocacy – the threat that a Member in Business will promote the Employer's position to the point that the Member's objectivity is compromised;

(d) Familiarity – the threat that due to a long or close relationship with the Employer, a Member in Business will be too sympathetic to the Employer's interests or will accept the Employer's view on certain matters without sufficient scrutiny; and

(e) Intimidation – the threat that a Member in Business will be deterred from acting objectively because of actual or perceived pressures, including attempts to exercise undue influence over the Member.

Safeguards

5.3 The Code classifies safeguards that may eliminate or reduce threats faced by Members in Business to an Acceptable Level into two broad categories:

- safeguards created by the profession, legislation or regulation; and
- safeguards in the work environment.

Examples of such safeguards are outlined in paragraphs 100.14 - 100.16 and 300.14 - 300.15 of the Code.

5.4 In addition to the categories above, safeguards may also be created by the Member in Business. Such safeguards may include but are not restricted to:

- keeping records of contentious issues and the action taken to resolve them;
- maintaining a broader perspective on how similar organisations function through establishing business relationships with other professionals; and
- using an independent advisor.

5.5 Discussion of ethical issues with the Professional Body to which the Member in Business belongs is strongly encouraged as the Professional Bodies are able to provide valuable advice in line with the behaviour expected of their Members and within the limits of acceptable practice and the law.

6. Overview of APES 110 PART C: Members in Business

6.1 APES 110 Part C illustrates how the conceptual framework contained in APES 110 Part A is to be applied by Members in Business.

6.2 APES 110 Part C Section 300 provides an overview of the various types of threats encountered by Members in Business in their work environment and appropriate safeguards that can be considered. In certain circumstances there may be no safeguards to reduce the threats to an Acceptable Level and the Member may need to consider refusing to perform the duties in question or resigning from the employing organisation (e.g. paragraphs 300.15, 320.6 and 330.4 of the Code).

6.3 APES 110 PART C Sections 310-350 specifies professional obligations of Members in Business in the following circumstances:

- Section 310 – Potential Conflicts;
- Section 320 – Preparation and Reporting of Information;
- Section 330 – Acting with Sufficient Expertise;
- Section 340 – Financial Interests; and
- Section 350 – Inducements.

7. Potential conflicts arising from responsibilities to the Employer

7.1 Potential conflicts may arise from the obligation of a Member in Business to comply with the fundamental principles of the Code whilst fulfilling responsibilities to the Employer. Ordinarily the Member is required to support the legitimate and ethical objectives established by the Employer and rules and procedures in support of those objectives. However, as a consequence of responsibilities to the Employer, the Member may be under pressure to act or behave in ways that could directly or indirectly threaten compliance with the fundamental principles of the Code.

7.2 Where potential conflicts arise, a Member in Business is required to comply with section 310 *Potential Conflicts* of the Code. Examples and the potential approaches to resolving such conflicts are shown in Case Studies 1 - 4.

8. Preparation and reporting of information to be used by internal and external parties

8.1 Members in Business are often involved in the preparation and reporting of information that may either be made public or used by others inside or outside the Employer. When preparing and reporting such information, Members are required to comply with section 320 *Preparation and Reporting of Information* of the Code.

8.2 A Member in Business is required to prepare or present information fairly, honestly and in accordance with relevant Professional Standards so that the information will be understood in its context. Threats to the Member's ability to do so may arise from pressure (intimidation or self-interest) to become associated with misleading information. Where the threats have been evaluated, safeguards such as those discussed in section 320 *Preparation and Reporting of Information* of the Code should be applied. Examples addressing the analysis of threats and application of safeguards are shown in Case Studies 5 - 9 and 20 - 21.

9. Member in Business's responsibility to Act with sufficient expertise

9.1 The fundamental principle of professional competence and due care requires that a Member in Business should only undertake tasks for which the Member has, or can obtain, sufficient specific training or experience. Members should not intentionally mislead Employers as to how much expertise or experience they have, nor should they fail to seek appropriate expert advice and assistance when required.

9.2 Where the ability of a Member in Business to perform duties with the appropriate degree of professional competence and due care is threatened by factors such as insufficient time, inadequate information, inadequate resources or insufficient knowledge, safeguards such as those in section 330 *Acting with Sufficient Expertise* of the Code should be applied. Examples addressing the need to act with sufficient expertise are provided in Case Study 10 and 19.

10. Financial interests of a Member in Business

10.1 Financial interests of a Member in Business or their immediate or close family members may give rise to threats to compliance with the fundamental principles of the Code. The Member is required to comply with section 340 *Financial Interests* of the Code in such circumstances. The Code requires the Member to evaluate the significance of such a threat, and the appropriate safeguards to be applied. The Member should examine the nature of the financial interest which includes considerations such as the significance of the interest and whether it is direct or indirect, as well as the value of the interest. An example showing considerations which may be applied by Members where financial interests threaten compliance with the fundamental principles of the Code is provided in Case Study 11. An additional example of personal financial gain for a Member is provided in Case Study 13.

11. Inducements offered to a Member in Business

11.1 Inducements refer to both the receiving of offers and making offers.

11.2 A Member in Business or an immediate or close family member may be offered an inducement such as gifts, hospitality, preferential treatment and inappropriate appeals to friendship or loyalty. Alternatively, a Member may experience pressure to offer inducements to subordinate the judgment of another individual or organisation, influence a decision making process or obtain confidential information.

11.3 Where threats to the fundamental principles arise from inducements, the Member in Business is required to follow the principles and guidance in Section 350 *Inducements* of the Code. Examples showing approaches that can be adopted by the Member where inducements threaten compliance with the fundamental principles of the Code are provided in Case Studies 12 - 14 and 18.

12. Disclosure of information and whistleblowing

Disclosure of information

12.1 In accordance with Section 140 *Confidentiality* of the Code, a Member in Business who acquires confidential information in the course of providing a Professional Service is prohibited from disclosing that information without proper and specific authority or unless there is a legal or professional right or duty to disclose it.

12.2 The *Privacy Act 1988* (Cth) (Privacy Act) prohibits the disclosure of personal information about an individual, other than in certain limited circumstances including circumstances where the individual has consented to the disclosure or the disclosure is required or authorised by or under law.

12.3 Whistleblower laws at Federal and State and Territory levels prohibit the disclosure of certain information obtained from and about a whistleblower unless such disclosure is required or authorised by such laws.

12.4 Examples of the disclosure of information that may in certain circumstances be required or authorised by the law include:

- reporting of suspected money laundering activities to AUSTRAC[1] in accordance with the *Anti-Money Laundering and Counter-Terrorism Financing Act 2006* (Cth); and
- where a Member in Business is authorised by the Member's Employer to receive whistleblower information, disclosure by the Member of such information to an authorised person under the *Corporations Act 2001* (Cth) (Corporations Act).

Protection of whistleblowers

12.5 Whistleblower laws in Australia provide whistleblowers with certain legal protection against liability for making certain disclosures and a specific process to follow when disclosing such information which may include, for example, information about a breach of the law by the business or persons in the business for or in which the whistleblower works. For example, under the Corporations Act whistleblowers will generally qualify for the protection if:

- the whistleblower is an officer, employee or contractor or employee of a contractor of the company ;
- the whistleblower first identifies themselves before making the disclosure (anonymous reports are not protected);
- the report is made by the whistleblower to a prescribed entity or person such as the Australian Securities and Investments Commission, a company auditor or member of an audit team conducting an audit of the company, a director, secretary or senior manager of the company or other person authorised by the company to receive such disclosure;
- the whistleblower had reasonable grounds to suspect that the information indicates that the company or an officer or employee of the company has or may have contravened a provision of the Corporations Act; and
- the report is made in good faith.

12.6 A Member in Business who is considering disclosing information about the Member's Employer or persons in the Employer's business in circumstances which would otherwise be a breach of the Member's professional obligation of confidentiality or statutory obligations is strongly advised to first obtain legal advice. Whistleblower laws establish the scope of the protection offered to the Member and the process which the Member is required to follow to obtain that protection. Where the Member needs further clarification or guidance concerning the Member's obligations under the Code, the Member should consult with the Member's Professional Body without disclosing confidential information.

Decision making process

12.7 Sometimes confidentiality, privacy and whistleblowing are the subject of internal business policies and procedures. In circumstances where a Member in Business is considering disclosing information, the Member should follow any relevant internal policies and procedures of the business which employs the Member. In addition to these requirements, where the Member is employed by a government entity or in the public sector, the Member is required to consider any public sector rules to which the Member is bound, prior to disclosing confidential information.

12.8 If the Employer does not have internal policies, procedures or rules that deal with the matter, a Member in Business should, amongst other things, consider the following when considering disclosing information about the Member's Employer or persons in the Employer's business in circumstances which would otherwise be a breach of their professional obligation of confidentiality:

(a) Statutory constraints and obligations on disclosure including those contained in Federal and State and Territory privacy and whistleblower laws;

(b) Statutory protection for whistleblowers contained in Federal and State and Territory whistleblower laws;

1 AUSTRAC is Australia's anti-money laundering and counter-terrorism financing regulator and specialist financial intelligence unit

APES

(c) Whether the information relates to conduct which constitutes a breach of or an offence under any laws ;

(d) Whether members of the public are likely to be adversely affected by the disclosure or non-disclosure of the information;

(e) The gravity of the matter, such as the size and extent of likely financial loss;

(f) The possibility or likelihood of repetition;

(g) The reliability and quality of the information available;

(h) The reasons for the Employer's unwillingness to disclose matters to the relevant authority;

(i) When the Employer gives authorisation to disclose information, whether or not the interests of all parties, including third parties whose interests might be affected, could be harmed;

(j) Whether or not all the relevant information is known and has been substantiated. Where the situation involves unsubstantiated or incomplete information and conclusions, professional judgment should be applied to determine the appropriate type of disclosure to be made, if any. The Member requires a reasonable belief that wrongdoing has occurred, before disclosure can be made;

(k) The type of communication that is expected and to whom it is addressed. In particular, the Member should be satisfied that the parties to whom the communication is addressed are authorised recipients; and

(l) The possible implications of disclosure for the Member and the Member's reputation.

12.9 Examples that address whistleblowing are included in Case Studies 15 - 17.

Prohibited dealing with information

12.10 A Member in Business should be aware that there are laws which make it an offence for a person to take certain actions in respect of documents or related material that are, or are reasonably likely to be, required in evidence in legal proceedings (whether in progress or to be commenced in the future). These actions include for example, destroying, concealing or rendering the documents or material illegible, undecipherable or unidentifiable or authorising or permitting another to do so.[2] The Member is strongly advised to take care to ensure that the Member does not take any prohibited action in respect of such information.

13. Case Studies

No	Title	Issues Discussed
1	Significant personal expenses claimed as company expenses	Potential conflicts
2	Council rates	Potential conflicts
3	Inappropriate small expense claim	Potential conflicts
4	Unlicensed software	Potential conflicts
5	Incorrect reporting of financial information	Preparation and reporting of information
6	Inappropriate capitalisation of research and development costs	Preparation and reporting of information
7	Inappropriate contractor claims	Preparation and reporting of information
8	Loss leaders or divisional failure?	Preparation and reporting of information
9	Satisfying the bank's lending criteria	Preparation and reporting of information/ Financial interests of a Member

2 See for example the *Crimes Act 1958 (Vic)*

No	Title	Issues Discussed
10	Valuing share options	Acting with sufficient expertise
11	Personal financial interest in a proposal	Financial interests of a Member
12	Inducements for non-disclosure of information	Inducements
13	Earnings management	Financial interests of a Member/ Inducement
14	Tender bids	Inducement
15	Non-disclosure to auditors and corrupt business practices	Whistleblowing
16	Inappropriate expense claims lodged by the Chief Executive	Whistleblowing
17	Inappropriate recording of patient attendance at a doctors' medical practice	Whistleblowing
18	Insider information	Public Sector - Inducement
19	Demonstrating due diligence in a voluntary position	Public Sector - Acting with sufficient expertise
20	Potential breach of not-for-profit status	Charitable organisation - Preparation and reporting of information
21	Ignorance is no excuse	Preparation and reporting of information/ Acting with sufficient expertise

Introduction

Case Studies have been presented to illustrate the application of a structured approach to the resolution of ethical issues. Members in Business should read the Case Studies whilst referring to the conceptual framework approach in Section 4, to gain an understanding of the process that should be adopted when faced with ethical issues in the workplace. The Case Studies are not intended to be conclusive but rather provide a framework that leads Members to a course of action that is consistent with the principles and requirements of the Code and this Guidance Note.

These Case Studies are fictitious and any similarities to actual events or circumstances are merely coincidental.

The presentation of each Case Study follows the following pattern:

- Case outline: basic facts are described;
- Fundamental principles of the Code: those identified as the key principles in the Case Study;
- Ethical decision making approach: selected steps from the conceptual framework approach in the Code; and
- Suggested possible courses of action are discussed.

Case Study 1 – Significant personal expenses claimed as company expenses

Potential Conflicts

Case outline

Alex (Member in Business) is the finance manager of an organisation. Alex is concerned that the Chief Executive has been making frequent interstate trips to Perth and charging expenses to the company. The trips and the activities undertaken appear to have only partial relevance to the company's activities. Alex is aware of the fact that the Chief Executive recently moved from Perth and still has a number of close family members residing there.

APES

Alex discusses the issue with the Chief Executive who explains that there is a verbal understanding with the Chairman of the company who is aware of the nature and purpose of the visits.

Fundamental principles of the Code

Integrity

Would processing the payments without an adequate explanation or supporting documentation be seen as being honest and fair?

Objectivity

How will the Member in Business demonstrate his objectivity, actual or perceived, in his dealings with the Chief Executive?

Professional competence and due care

How can allowing the expense payments to be processed without adequate explanation and supporting documentation be seen as acting with due skill, care and diligence?

Professional behaviour

How should the Member in Business proceed so as not to discredit himself? Would it be considered legal and acceptable to taxation authorities?

Ethical decision-making approach

Identify relevant facts

Has the Member in Business discussed the matter adequately to ensure the facts are correct? If so, is it possible to obtain support for the Chief Executive's understanding with the Chairman? Consider the company's policies and procedures, applicable accounting standards, best practice and applicable laws and regulations.

Identify affected parties

Key affected parties are the Member in Business, the Chief Executive, the Chairman and the Board. Other possible affected parties are the accounts payable department, human resources, internal audit, Australian Tax Office, audit committee, employees, shareholders and financial backers.

Determine whether a procedure of conflict resolution exists within the organisation

Consider the company's policies and procedures.

Consider who should be involved in the conflict resolution process

Who should be involved in the resolution of this matter and for what reason? What is the appropriate timing of their involvement? Are there trusted colleagues with whom the Member in Business can discuss his position? When do the Board and audit committee need to become involved?

Discuss the ethical dilemma with relevant parties

Does further discussion need to take place with the Chief Executive? Do the discussions need to extend to the Chairman?

Consider possible course of action

The Member in Business can discuss the issue further with his direct manager who may be in a position such as the Chief Financial Officer (CFO). Discussion could focus on the Member in Business obtaining clarity on the arrangement which may lead to documentary evidence supporting the understanding with the Chairman. If the issue is not resolved, the CFO and Member in Business may consider requesting evidence from the Chief Executive together and can explain that it is required to conform to the company's policies and procedures. If an appropriate response is not received, the Member in Business and CFO can request a meeting with the Chief Executive and the Chairman to clarify the issue. Where this is not successful, additional discussions with the Board, internal audit, audit committee or the external auditors may be required. All enquiries and conclusions reached should be documented by the Member in Business. Where such documentation is maintained, the Member in Business needs to consider the legal ramifications of doing so.

The Member in Business may also consider the ethical conflict resolution processes of his Professional Body.

Case Study 2 – Council rates

Potential Conflicts

Case outline

Jane (Member in Business) has just been appointed as the new financial controller of XYZ Ltd after 12 months of job hunting. Her first task is to prepare the annual financial report for the year ended 30 June 20X1.

Although XYZ Ltd appears solvent, when reviewing the figures, Jane notes that the company is in quite a weak cash position. She also notices that based on her limited understanding of the business, there appears to be an unusually high accruals figure. On discussion with the Managing Director (MD) Jane finds that the balance relates to 4 years of unpaid council rates. Further discussions reveal that the company has not received a rates notice since the breakup of the council and rezoning of the company premises, 4 years ago.

Jane is concerned about this matter and discusses it further with the Managing Director who becomes annoyed. He does not consider this to be a significant issue due to the fact that it is the council's mistake and not the company's. The company has been recording the amount in accordance with accounting standards and he believes that is the extent of the company's obligation. He then goes on to make it clear that the company's interests should be put first, particularly when the issue impacts the business's cash flow. Further if the company were to pay 4 years of back rates, its cash flow position would be severely weakened which may lead to potential job losses.

Fundamental principles of the Code

Integrity

How does the Member in Business maintain her integrity when she is being asked to undertake a course of action which she clearly has doubts about?

Objectivity

How would the Member in Business maintain her objectivity given that her Employer is operating under difficult economic conditions and has the added pressure of possibly disagreeing with her boss whom she hardly knows?

Confidentiality

Is there any basis on which the Member in Business could make disclosures given the Employer obviously believes that the company's non-payment of rates is confidential information.

Professional behaviour

How does the Member in Business proceed in order to not discredit herself?

Ethical decision-making approach

Identify relevant facts

Are there any other reasons why the company has not received a bill for rates? Can the Member in Business continue to merely accrue an estimate for the rates bill for the year? If not, does she go back to the Managing Director and advise that the company should contact the local council and inform them of the situation? Is there a supportive environment for open discussion of practical dilemmas without a recriminatory or 'blame' culture?

Identify affected parties

Key affected parties are the Member in Business, the Managing Director, the other directors, the company's employees, the shareholders (if different from the directors), the local council and the general public.

Determine whether a procedure of conflict resolution exists within the organisation

Consider the company's policies and procedures and applicable accounting standards.

Consider who should be involved in the conflict resolution process

Who should be involved in the resolution of this matter and for what reason? What is the appropriate timing of their involvement? Does the Member in Business have trusted colleagues with whom she can discuss her position? Is there anyone else within the company that the Member in Business should speak to regarding this matter? Are the other directors aware of this issue? Has the Member in Business discussed the matter with the Board?

Discuss the ethical dilemma with relevant parties

Do further discussions need to be held with the Managing Director or extend to other members of the Board?

Consider possible course of action

The Member in Business could try to use her interpersonal skills in a non-confrontational way to offer to find a solution to the underlying problem. She may consider explaining the potential consequences to the Managing Director if the error is discovered by the council. There may be interest or penalties imposed on the company which may impact on the company's good reputation. If at some future date there are plans to sell the company – any due diligence is likely to discover this non-payment of rates which could easily impact on a potential sale. Given all of this, the Member in Business could also highlight the need for the company to get legal advice on its obligations. The Member in Business could also ask the Managing Director to consider the company's moral obligation to the local community. All enquiries and conclusions reached should be documented by the Member in Business. Where such documentation is maintained, the Member in Business needs to consider the legal ramifications of doing so.

To resolve the problem, the Member in Business could suggest asking the local council to agree to a payment plan. It is unlikely that the council would want XYZ Ltd to go out of business potentially resulting in unemployment for a number of members of the community.

Case Study 3 – Inappropriate small expense claim

Potential Conflicts

Case outline

After several months of job searching, Jeremy (Member in Business) secured a position as a financial accountant with a sales company. The company is very small with only 12 employees, most of whom work in the sales area. Given the size of the company, there are very few formally documented policies and procedures in place. Two days before the completion of Jeremy's 3 month probationary period and formal performance review, Jeremy's supervisor, who is also a senior sales person, tells him that he incurred $175 expense entertaining a client the previous evening. He requests a cheque reimbursement and submits receipts from a restaurant and bar to support the amount. At the end of the day, the supervisor's wife comes to the office to meet her husband and drive him home. Jeremy overhears the wife talking to another employee about what a wonderful night she had last evening with her husband at dinner and at the bar.

Key fundamental principles and duties

Integrity

Can the Member in Business overlook the information he overheard and maintain his integrity?

Objectivity

How will the Member in Business manage the conflict between integrity and his desire to secure his job at the company at the completion of his probationary period?

Professional behaviour

Can the Member in Business ignore the information acquired and still satisfy the principle of professional behaviour?

Ethical decision-making approach

Identify relevant facts

Does the Member in Business have all of the facts? Can he discuss the nature of the expense further with the supervisor? What is the Member in Business's specific role in relation to expense claims and reimbursement? Is there an internal process for querying and reviewing expense claims?

Identify affected parties

The key affected parties are the Member in Business and the supervisor. Other possible affected parties are the supervisor's wife, the Australian Tax Office and other employees and stakeholders of the company.

Determine whether a procedure of conflict resolution exists within the organisation

Consider the company's policies and procedures, applicable accounting standards, best practice and applicable laws and regulations.

Consider who should be involved in the conflict resolution process

Who should be involved in the resolution of this matter and for what reason? What is the appropriate timing of their involvement? Does the Member in Business have trusted colleagues with whom he can discuss his position?

Discuss the ethical dilemma with relevant parties

Can further discussions be held with the supervisor to clarify the Member in Business's understanding? Does the Member in Business need to discuss the issue with anyone else in the company?

Consider possible course of action

The Member in Business may consider further discussions with the supervisor to clarify his understanding of the evening. He may approach such discussions in a non-confrontational manner and explain that he needs a complete understanding of the expense in order to appropriately classify it for financial reporting and taxation purposes. What client was entertained? Which account/product or service does this expense pertain to? If the Member in Business is unable to corroborate the expense claim he could highlight the implications of allowing inappropriate expense claims to continue such as Australian Tax Office investigations and potentially fines. Where this approach is unsuccessful the Member in Business may need to initiate discussions with another manager within the company to assist in resolution of the problem.

Case Study 4 – Unlicensed software

Potential Conflicts

Case outline

Jamie (Member in Business) is a young accountant with qualifications in accounting as well as in information technology. Jamie has recently been hired as an accounting assistant by a medium-sized retail company and is looking forward to the challenges the work force presents. On his first day at work, the financial controller hands Jamie a copy of Microsoft Office and asks him to install the software on 25 computers around the office. The financial controller states that the new software is required in order for Jamie to perform his accounting role. Jamie is about to commence the installation when he asks the financial controller if the company holds the licence for the software. The financial controller laughs and says Jamie has a lot to learn. He explains that the purchase of a licence would result in unnecessary expenditure with no added benefit to the company.

Key fundamental principles and duties

Integrity

Can the Member in Business overlook the fact that the company does not have the appropriate licences to use the software and maintain his integrity?

Objectivity

How will the Member in Business manage the conflict between integrity and his desire to secure his job at the company at the completion of his probationary period?

Professional behaviour

How should the Member in Business proceed in order to comply with relevant laws and avoid any action that discredits the profession?

Ethical decision-making approach

Identify relevant facts

Can the Member in Business discuss the matter further with the financial controller?

Identify affected parties

The key affected parties are the Member in Business, Microsoft Corporation, the financial controller and the company.

Determine whether a procedure of conflict resolution exists within the organisation

Consider the company's policies and procedures and applicable laws and regulations.

Consider who should be involved in resolution

Who should be involved in the resolution of this matter and for what reason? What is the appropriate timing of their involvement? Is there someone else within the organisation with which the Member in Business can discuss his position?

Discuss the ethical dilemma with relevant parties

Can further discussions be held with the financial controller to explain the risks of breaching copyright? Does the Member in Business need to discuss the issue with anyone else in the company?

Consider possible course of action

The Member in Business may consider further discussions with the financial controller to highlight the importance of obtaining a licence for use of the product. The Member in Business could highlight advantages such as support from the software provider and the tax deductible nature of the expense.

Case Study 5 – Incorrect reporting of financial information

Preparation and Reporting of Information

Case outline

Robyn (Member in Business) is the financial accountant in a company and is preparing the quarterly accounts. Robyn's immediate manager is a very forceful, domineering individual and Robyn has accepted his views over the last two years on the level of work in progress. The manager has instructed Robyn to report a 100% increase in work in progress during the current quarter. The year-end draft financial statements show that the company has only just met its business plan financial targets.

New evidence subsequently becomes available to suggest that something is clearly wrong and the work in progress had not increased at anywhere near the rate advised by Robyn's manager.

Fundamental principles of the Code

Integrity

Can the Member in Business show that the accounts are true and fair without amending them?

Objectivity

Given the manager is a forceful and intimidating individual, how would the Member in Business maintain her objectivity?

Professional competence and due care

Have the draft accounts been prepared in accordance with reporting requirements including applicable accounting standards, laws and regulations, and Professional Standards?

Professional behaviour

How should the Member in Business proceed so as not to discredit herself or the company?

Ethical decision-making approach

Identify relevant facts

Do other balances and analyses provide evidence that work in progress is incorrectly stated? For example, cost of sales analytical review, margin analysis and cash flows.

Identify affected parties

The Member in Business and her immediate manager are the key affected parties. Others that may be affected include other levels of management, recipient of the management accounts, users of the financial accounts, finance, purchasing, accounts payable, human resources, internal audit, audit committee, board, external auditors, shareholders, financial backers and the taxation office.

Determine whether a procedure of conflict resolution exists within the organisation

Consider the company's policies and procedures, applicable accounting standards, best practice and applicable laws and regulations.

Consider who should be involved in the conflict resolution process

Who should be involved in the resolution of this matter and for what reason? What is the appropriate timing of their involvement? The Member in Business may discuss the matter with her immediate line manager given the available evidence and possible consequences. Can the Member in Business discuss the matter with other affected parties such as the recipients of the management and financial accounts? What is the appropriate timing for such discussions?

Discuss the ethical dilemma with relevant parties

Does further discussion need to take place with the immediate manager? Do discussions need to extend to more senior levels of management?

Consider possible course of action

The Member in Business may corroborate the facts with other available documentation such as cost of sales calculations, previous stock counts and other financial information. The appropriate course of action such as undertaking a stock count can then be discussed with the Member in Business's immediate line manager. If the manager's response is not what the Member in Business considers appropriate, the matter may then be discussed with recipients of the management and financial accounts and the next level of management. Other steps could include, where appropriate, discussion with the senior management, internal audit, audit committee, the Board and external auditors.

In the case of a small business, the Member in Business may not have the ability to hold the detailed discussions suggested above. In this case, the main course of action would be to corroborate the facts and report in line with statutory requirements. The Member in Business may discuss the requirements with the line manager using facts as the basis for this discussion.

The Member in Business can also consider the ethical conflict resolution resources of her Professional Body. The Member in Business should also consider her employment options.

Case Study 6 – Inappropriate capitalisation of research and development costs

Preparation and Reporting of Information

Case outline

Nathan (Member in Business), the finance director of ABC Ltd, has become aware of a $1.5million investment in relation to a research and development (R&D) project. This project has not been properly assessed and therefore its chances of success are unknown. The company's policy on R&D clearly states that such costs are capitalised and deferred only where it is reasonable to expect a successful outcome and an associated revenue stream - a policy that is consistent with the *Income Tax Assessment Act 1997* research and development provisions.

Nathan approaches his long time good friend, Doug, the project leader, about the costs incurred and receives a response that there is no problem because he will provide some numbers that will keep the auditors happy.

It is only 1 week before the financial year-end and writing off the $1.5million at such a late stage would result in significant difficulties with the Board for Nathan. His relationship with Doug will also be impacted and he would be placed in a very precarious position with the Board.

APES

Fundamental principles of the Code

Integrity

How does the Member in Business maintain his integrity with the project leader, the Board and the auditors? Can the Member in Business retain his integrity without bringing the matter to the Board's attention?

Objectivity

How does the Member in Business remain objective as to the true nature of the research and development expenditure and their appropriate accounting treatment considering the long term friendship with the project leader?

Professional behaviour

How does the Member in Business proceed in order to not discredit himself?

Professional competence and due care

Have the accounts been prepared in accordance with applicable accounting standards, laws and regulations, and Professional Standards?

Ethical decision-making approach

Identify relevant facts

Should the Member in Business discuss the matter further with the project leader prior to taking the matter to the Board? What information will the Member in Business disclose to the auditors?

Other points to consider include whether there is a supportive environment for open discussion of practical dilemmas or is there a recriminatory or 'blame' culture in the company? Is there a problem with the company's internal controls in relation to the correct treatment of expenditure on R&D? Have similar incidences occurred in the past? Is there any commercial pressure on the project leader to defer expenditure items inappropriately?

Identify affected parties

The main affected parties are the Member in Business, the project leader, the directors, the company's employees and the shareholders (if different from the directors), and the Australian Taxation Office.

Determine whether a procedure of conflict resolution exists within the organisation

Consider the company's policies and procedures, applicable accounting standards, best practice and applicable laws and regulations.

Consider who should be involved in the conflict resolution process

Who should be involved in the resolution of this matter and for what reason? What is the appropriate timing of their involvement? Are there trusted colleagues with whom the Member in Business can discuss his position?

Discuss the ethical dilemma with relevant parties

Does further discussion need to take place with Doug? Do discussions need to be held with other levels of management and the Board?

Consider possible course of action

Commercial pressures on Doug may be forcing him to defer this expenditure. However, transparent reporting may require write-off of the $1.5 million. Initially the Member in Business may need to have further discussions with Doug to obtain a more comprehensive understanding of the project and its current status. The Member in Business should explain to Doug the potential implications of inappropriate treatment of the $1.5 million. Such implications would include a qualified audit report and its impact on the company. In addition, capitalisation of the costs is inconsistent with the requirements of the *Income Tax Assessment Act 1997* research and development provisions. This may lead to penalties and other negative consequences under the Act. If this approach fails then the Member in Business will have to approach senior management, the Chief Executive or the Board and explain the situation and work through how this issue can be resolved. The Member in Business could consider highlighting the expense as an exceptional item in order to provide a true and fair view.

Case Study 7 – Inappropriate contractor claims

Preparation and Reporting of Information

Case outline

William (Member in Business) is employed as the financial accountant in a medium-sized engineering firm. The firm specialises in the development and design of steel frames and pumps used to purify oil. Due to the fluctuation in demand the company maintains only a small permanent workforce with at times, up to 65% of the labour provided by external contractors.

William developed an innovative accounting system that analysed project costs against the work done and in doing so, found a significant fraud in contractor claims at the company. He incorporated the variances into his monthly report and approached the engineering manager with his findings. The engineering manager was clearly agitated by William's findings. He stated that William's job was to pay employees and creditors, meet statutory requirements, and that project reporting was the responsibility of project cost engineers.

Key fundamental principles and duties

Integrity

Can the Member in Business overlook his findings and maintain his integrity?

Objectivity

Knowing that something may be wrong, how can the Member in Business maintain his objectivity?

Confidentiality

Does the Member in Business have a legal or professional right or duty to disclose the information acquired? What whistleblowing obligations and protection does the Member in Business have?

Professional behaviour

How should the Member in Business proceed in order to comply with relevant laws and regulations and avoid any action that discredits the profession?

Professional competence and due care

Is the Member in Business able to check that his findings are correct?

Ethical decision-making approach

Identify relevant facts

Does the Member in Business have all of the facts? Is the new accounting system he developed performing a correct analysis? Can the results of the system be substantiated in an alternative way? Are there are other costs associated with employing contractors that may not have been taken into consideration (costs such as relocation costs)? Can the Member in Business discuss the matter further with the engineering manager or other recipients of his monthly report? What are the potential factors that would influence the engineering manager to conceal fraud in contractor claims?

Identify affected parties

The key affected parties are the Member in Business, the contractors, the engineering manager and the company itself. Other possible affected parties include the Australian Tax Office.

Determine whether a procedure of conflict resolution exists within the organisation

Consider the company's policies and procedures.

Consider who should be involved in resolution

Who should be involved in the resolution of this matter and for what reason? What is the appropriate timing of their involvement? Does the Member in Business have trusted colleagues with whom the Member can discuss his position?

Discuss the ethical dilemma with relevant parties

Can further discussions be held with the engineering manager? Do discussions need to be held directly with the contractors in question?

Consider possible course of action

The Member in Business should explain to the engineering manager the requirement to substantiate the alleged fraudulent claim and that the matter is to be investigated. The Member in Business may consider approaching the contractor in question with his findings and request supporting documentation for excess money paid. He would also then need to approach the relevant project cost engineer with the outcome so that the project can be appropriately costed. The Member in Business would also need to consider the fraudulent implications that arise from deceitful billing practices and determine whether any further sort of legal or other action is required. All enquiries and conclusions reached should be documented by the Member in Business. Where such documentation is maintained, the Member in Business needs to consider the legal ramifications of doing so. The Member in Business should consider reporting the outcomes to Those Charged with Governance.

Case Study 8 – Loss leaders or divisional failure?

Preparation and Reporting of Information

Case outline

Rebecca (Member in Business) is the accountant for the processed foods division of a manufacturing company. Rebecca's role involves the preparation of financial reports determined by corporate management to assist in the assessment of the team's performance. When preparing the regular financial reports Rebecca noticed some products appeared to have experienced lower sales in the last quarter. With further analysis she found that there were a significant number of products that had been sold at a net financial loss with some sold at below prime cost.

The company structure means that Rebecca reports to the divisional manager as opposed to the head office Chief Financial Officer (CFO). On reporting her results the divisional manager was agitated and advised Rebecca that her financial reports are not acceptable and inconsistent with general commercial practice. The manager then performed his own analysis of the division's products and concluded that all products were sold at positive margins. He did not provide Rebecca with any details of his study.

Key fundamental principles and duties

Integrity

Can the Member in Business overlook her findings and maintain her integrity?

Objectivity

Knowing that something may be wrong, how can the Member in Business maintain her objectivity?

Professional behaviour

How should the Member in Business proceed?

Professional competence and due care

Is the Member in Business able to check that her findings are correct?

Ethical decision –making approach

Identify relevant facts

Does the Member in Business have all of the facts? Does she need to consider other issues such as the overall profitability of the division and the necessity to produce complementary items to support profit leaders? Can the Member in Business discuss the matter further with the divisional manager?

Identify affected parties

The key affected parties are the Member in Business, the divisional manager and the company itself.

Determine whether a procedure of conflict resolution exists within the organisation

Consider the company's policies and procedures.

Consider who should be involved in resolution

Who should be involved in the resolution of this matter and for what reason? What is the appropriate timing of their involvement? Does the Member in Business have trusted colleagues with whom she can discuss her position?

Discuss the ethical dilemma with relevant parties

Can further discussions be held with the divisional manager? Do discussions need to be held with the head office CFO?

Consider possible course of action

The Member in Business may consider discussing the matter further with the divisional manager. She may approach the issue in a non-confrontational way by requesting that the manager provide her with feedback on what she did not consider as part of her analysis. Alternatively the Member in Business may approach the head office CFO directly to discuss the issue. All enquiries and conclusions reached should be documented by the Member in Business. The Member in Business should also ensure that she maintains a copy of her analysis.

Case Study 9 – Satisfying the bank's lending criteria

Preparation and Reporting of Information/Financial interests of a Member

Case outline

Sandra (Member in Business) is the Chief Financial Officer (CFO) of a large manufacturing company. It is November and the Chief Executive has just returned from a meeting with the company's bankers and calls Sandra into her office to discuss the results of negotiations. The Chief Executive explains that the company requires a significant capital injection in order to modernise its manufacturing equipment. This will enable the company to secure a large ongoing order from China which will result in all employees of the company receiving sizeable Christmas bonuses.

The Chief Executive explains to Sandra that the lending criteria of the bank require that the company demonstrate an adequate current and strong projected cash flow as well as a profitability level that will enable repayments of the loan to be made from an early date. The Chief Executive has told the bank that the company is in a strong position. However, Sandra knows that the company will not satisfy the bank's criteria. The Chief Executive has promised that Sandra (CFO) will deliver a financial report to the bank within 3 business days. The Chief Executive tells Sandra that it is up to her to decide the contents of the report.

Fundamental principles of the Code

Integrity

How does the Member in Business maintain her integrity with the Chief Executive and the bank?

Objectivity

How does the Member in Business remain objective as to the reporting on the company's financial status considering the pressure to misstate the accounts?

Professional behaviour

How does the Member in Business proceed in order to not discredit herself?

Ethical decision-making approach

Identify relevant facts

Can the Member in Business retain her integrity without reporting false information to the bank? Should the Member in Business discuss the matter further with the Chief Executive prior to presenting her report? What information will the Member in Business disclose to the bank?

Identify affected parties

The main affected parties are the Member in Business, the bank, the Chief Executive and the company's employees and the shareholders.

Determine whether a procedure of conflict resolution exists within the organisation

Consider the company's policies and procedures, applicable accounting standards, best practice and applicable laws and regulations.

Consider who should be involved in the conflict resolution process

Who should be involved in the resolution of this matter and for what reason? What is the appropriate timing of their involvement? Are there trusted colleagues with whom the Member in Business can discuss her position? The Member in Business should consider whether to consult confidentially with external advisers such as the Professional Body to which she belongs and whether to consult Those Charged with Governance.

Discuss the ethical dilemma with relevant parties

Does further discussion need to take place with the Chief Executive? Do discussions need to be held directly with the bank?

Consider possible course of action

Commercial pressures and the potential for personal financial gain by the Member in Business may encourage her to produce a report that satisfies the bank's criteria however this would be materially misrepresenting the company's position, which would mean that she would be in breach of the Code if they prepared or were associated with it. To produce such a report may actually jeopardise future borrowing activities of the company with this and other banks. The Member in Business may have additional discussions with the Chief Executive to explain the future implications of providing a report to the bank which misrepresents the company's position.

Case Study 10 – Valuing share options

Acting with Sufficient Expertise

Case outline

Olivia's Employer has requested that she (Member in Business) perform a valuation of share options. Olivia is not comfortable with the work as she does not have the required expertise to value options, and is uncertain about what to say to her Employer.

Fundamental principles of the Code

Professional competence and due care

Does the Member in Business have the necessary skills and experience to undertake the work?

Professional behaviour

How should the Member in Business proceed so as not to discredit herself or the company?

Ethical decision-making approach

Identify relevant facts

Can the Member in Business demonstrate her lack of expertise in this area and the potential impact on the company and offer alternatives? Consider the objective and time scale for the valuation in planning the next steps.

Identify affected parties

The Member in Business and the Employer are the key affected parties. Other parties that may be affected include the auditors, employees, human resources, shareholders and financial backers.

Determine whether a procedure of conflict resolution exists within the organisation

Consider the company's policies, procedures and guidelines, accounting standards, best practices, applicable laws and regulations.

Consider who should be involved in the conflict resolution process

Who should be involved in the resolution of this matter and for what reason? What is the appropriate timing of their involvement? Are there trusted colleagues with whom the Member in Business can discuss her position?

Discuss the ethical dilemma with relevant parties

Does further discussion need to take place with the Member in Business's manager? At what point will the Member in Business consider involving the next level of management?

Consider possible course of action

The Member in Business may consider discussing her concern about the lack of knowledge to value share options with her immediate manager. The Member in Business could suggest clearly defining the scope of the project and a course of action for addressing issues such as lack of knowledge or expertise. An appropriate course may be for example, employing a person with the necessary expertise. The focus during the discussion should be on the potential consequences to the business. The Member in Business could explain that employing a person with the necessary expertise does not affect her own obligation to ensure that the work is conducted in accordance with applicable accounting standards, laws and regulations. If the Member in Business does not consider her manager's reaction to be satisfactory, it may be appropriate to discuss the matter with the next level of management. If this response is not satisfactory, the Member in Business may need to involve internal audit, the audit committee and/or investment committee or the Board. Note that the substance of all discussions held, who was involved, what conclusions were reached and why, and her involvement should all be documented by the Member in Business. When doing so, the Member in Business may need to consider whether there are legal implications of maintaining such documentation in compliance with relevant laws and regulations.

The Member in Business could also consider the ethical conflict resolution resources of her Professional Body.

Case Study 11 – Personal financial interest in a proposal

Financial Interests

Case outline

Stella (Member in Business) has been appointed finance director of a public company which has difficulties attracting and retaining skilled staff. Stella's first task from the Board is to develop a benefits package to assist the company in overcoming this problem. Her own entitlement to benefits will also be in accordance with the new scheme. Based on extensive research and analysis, Stella concludes that in order to achieve the Board's objective, a significant increase in the whole range of benefits is required.

Fundamental principles of the Code

Integrity

In view of the Member in Business's personal interest, how will she ensure that her honesty remains unquestionable?

Objectivity

How will the Member in Business remain unbiased, and consider only the relevant facts, despite her personal interest in the benefits package?

Professional competence and due care

Does the Member in Business have all the necessary skills to draw up such a package?

Professional behaviour

How should the Member in Business proceed so as not to discredit her behaviour?

Ethical decision-making approach

Identify relevant facts

Consider the business's policies, procedures and guidelines, accounting standards, best practices, applicable laws and regulations. Is the information used for assessing the potential new benefits package independent? Who else has been involved in the proposal for the new benefits package?

Identify affected parties

The Member in Business and the Board are the key affected parties. Others that may be affected include employees, human resources, shareholders and financial backers.

APES

Determine whether a procedure of conflict resolution exists within the organisation

Consider the company's policies and procedures, applicable accounting standards, best practice and applicable laws and regulations.

Consider who should be involved in the conflict resolution process

Who should be involved in the resolution of this matter and for what reason? What is the appropriate timing of their involvement? Does the Member in Business have trusted colleagues with whom she can discuss her position? Has the Member in Business discussed the matter with the Board and/or human resources?

Discuss the ethical dilemma with relevant parties

Do further discussions need to take place with the Board or the directors individually prior to undertaking the task?

Consider possible course of action

Prior to explaining the findings to the Board, it may be advisable that the Member in Business informs the Board how she approached the project and who else was involved in the process (such as human resources). The Member in Business may find it helpful to document the substance of all discussions held, who was involved, what conclusions were reached and why, including her involvement. When maintaining such documentation, the Member in Business may need to consider the legal implications of doing so. When it is time to propose the new benefits package, the Member in Business may need to declare her conflict of interest. Findings may need to be presented to the Board by human resources or another independent party.

Case Study 12 – Inducements for non-disclosure of information

Inducement

Case outline

John (Member in Business) has been with his current employer for 8 months. However, things have not turned out well and he is moving on. John has significant concerns about the business conduct of the company, and believes there may be issues that require disclosure to the auditors or the regulator. A compromise agreement is currently being negotiated in which John will not receive a settlement if he reports any concerns, whereas if he agrees to a gagging clause then there will be a substantial payoff.

Fundamental principles of the Code

Integrity

What does the Member in Business need to do to demonstrate his integrity? How far does the Member in Business need to go?

Objectivity

How will the Member in Business manage the conflict between financial benefit and integrity?

Confidentiality

Is there any basis on which the Member in Business could make disclosures?

Ethical decision-making approach

Identify relevant facts

Are the Member in Business's concerns based on facts and does he have relevant facts to back his concerns? Are all the facts available or only a selection? Can the rest be established? Identifying the relevant facts could include understanding any requirements of legislation to make disclosures, and any protection that the Member in Business may seek from relevant legislation. Have any steps already been taken to try to resolve the Member in Business's concerns? Have these steps been documented?

Identify affected parties

The Member in Business and the Employer are the key affected parties. Other parties that may be affected are the regulator, auditor and the public, as well as Member in Business's family.

Determine whether a procedure of conflict resolution exists within the organisation

Given the nature of the dilemma, there may not be an internal conflict resolution process available. The Member in Business can also consider the ethical conflict resolution resources of his Professional Body.

Consider who should be involved in the conflict resolution process

Who should be involved in the resolution of this matter and for what reason? What is the appropriate timing of their involvement? Does the Member in Business have trusted colleagues with whom he can discuss his position? Can the Member in Business speak with his Employer about his concerns? Has the Member in Business made full disclosures to his solicitor, and received advice? Has the Member in Business discussed the matter with his family? Are there any external organisations that the Member in Business can contact such as public authorities?

Discuss the ethical dilemma with relevant parties

Do any additional discussions need to be held with the Member in Business's current Employer?

Consider possible course of action

There are two issues that need to be resolved:

1. How to address the matters of concern; and
2. How to achieve a satisfactory financial settlement.

Given the nature of the dilemma, the Member in Business may need to take advice early and often. The Member in Business may need to establish whether the facts support his concerns. If so, he may need to decide if there is a basis for disclosure and if so, what the value and consequences of that disclosure might be for the Member in Business and his family, the Employer, the industry and the profession. If the evidence available is considered sufficient, the Member in Business may resist the gagging clause, and argue for the concerns raised to be documented and considered by Those Charged with Governance of the company. The Member in Business should always ensure his family is aware of his concerns and actions, and their implications, without revealing confidential information.

The Member in Business may find it helpful to document the substance of all discussions held, who was involved, the conclusions reached and why, including his involvement. When doing so, legal implications of maintaining such documentation in compliance with relevant laws and regulations may need to be considered by the Member in Business.

Case Study 13 – Earnings management

Financial Interest of a Member/Inducement

Case outline

Phil (Member in Business) has been the accountant for a family business for a few years. The business has recently encountered some operating difficulties and associated financial difficulties. Subsequently a bank and a venture capitalist have invested and acquired over 35% of the company's shares. However, no board seats have been made available to the purchasers. The ongoing support of the bank and venture capitalist are dependent on the company's performance figures.

The Managing Director tells Phil that if he produces the 'right' figures he will receive a significant Christmas bonus and a 1% share option. The company is secretive, and as little information as possible is being given to the auditors and the investors.

Phil is preparing the quarterly management accounts and on review of the balances, believes that some figures are being 'massaged'. Phil has tentatively raised his concerns with the father and son Chairman and Chief Executive. Phil is then told that if he pursues the matter or fails to produce the 'right' figures, his bonus and share options will be forfeited.

Key fundamental principles and duties

Integrity

It is possible to support the business without being involved in reporting potentially misleading information?

Objectivity

How can the Member in Business avoid his professional judgment being influenced by the financial interest resulting from the bonus?

Professional behaviour

How will the Member in Business manage relationships with the affected parties?

Ethical decision-making approach

Identify relevant facts

Consider the business's policies, procedures and guidelines, accounting standards, applicable laws and regulations. The facts need to be double checked with a focus on significant figures in the accounts and their underlying assumptions. The Member in Business should consider whether the nature of the family business and its apparent secrecy means that he is not in possession of material facts.

Identify affected parties

The Member in Business, the family business, professional advisers, bankers and venture capitalists are the key affected parties. Others that may be affected are the Member in Business's own family and the profession.

Consider who should be involved in the conflict resolution process

Consider who should be involved in the resolution of this matter and for what reason? What is the appropriate timing of their involvement? Are there trusted colleagues or friends with whom the Member in Business can discuss his position? Can the Member in Business's Professional Body provide advice and provide assistance?

Discuss the ethical dilemma with relevant parties

Do further discussions need to take place with the Chairman and the Chief Executive?

Consider possible course of action

The Member in Business may approach the Chairman and Chief Executive and explain the long term implications of reporting inaccurate figures. He could focus discussions on the need to address the underlying business issues and the best way to address them to increase the long-term value of the company. Prior to having this discussion, the Member in Business may prepare realistic figures for presentation and explain the importance of presenting these for the company and his professional standing.

During the resolution process, Member in Business may find it helpful to document the substance of all discussions held, who was involved, what conclusions were reached and why, and his involvement. Note that the legal implications of maintaining such documentation in compliance with relevant laws and regulations may need to be considered. The Member in Business may also need to consider his employment options.

Case Study 14 – Tender bids

Inducement

Case outline

Paula (Member in Business) is a recently qualified professional accountant working in the accounting department of a property investment firm. The company is selling a piece of land and has stipulated that bids have to be submitted via email by 5pm of a specified date. All tender bids are to be considered as confidential and Paula is the initial point of contact for the tender bids. A few tender bids have been received prior to the deadline but not as many as initially anticipated.

At 4:30pm Paula receives a call from an anonymous prospective buyer who informs Paula that he is willing to pay a premium of 20% above the highest bid received by 4:55pm, provided he is informed beforehand of the highest bid received. The caller explains that in this way, all parties benefit. A higher fee is received for the land, the buyer does not have to make an unnecessarily high bid and Paula will be rewarded by the buyer for her hard work. He continues to explain that this type of activity is common in this industry and implies without naming names that other more senior personnel within the firm have taken advantage of these very generous financial terms in the past and would expect Paula to do the same.

Key fundamental principles and duties

Integrity

Can the Member in Business retain her integrity if she distorts the tender process? How does the Member in Business deal with the caller's allegations about more senior personnel within her company?

Objectivity

The Member in Business needs to consider the interest of all of the other parties involved in the tender process.

Confidentiality

How could one justify divulging confidential information to the callers in the interest of maximising the selling price of the land?

Professional behaviour

How does the Member in Business ensure that the she handles the client's allegations sensitively and professionally? Particularly given that the Member in Business has no knowledge of the accuracy of the allegations made by the caller?

Ethical decision-making approach

Identify relevant facts

Consider any further information the Member in Business may require to make a decision including consulting with relevant stakeholders of the company who may have a perspective on the tender process.

Identify affected parties

Key affected parties are the Member in Business, the caller, the directors and staff at the property investment firm, the bank, other creditors and other prospective buyers.

Determine whether a procedure of conflict resolution exists within the organisation

Consider the company's policies, procedures and guidelines, best practices, applicable laws and regulations.

Consider who should be involved in the conflict resolution process

Consider who should be involved in the resolution of this matter and for what reason? What is the appropriate timing of their involvement? The first issue is does the Member in Business immediately raise this with her manager before the caller phones back? Secondly, when the caller does phone back does the Member in Business transfer the call to her manager, does she get her manager to listen in to the conversation or does she merely deal with the caller?

Discuss the ethical dilemma with relevant parties

Does the Member in Business need to hold discussions with her manager or senior management of the company?

Consider possible course of action

From the given information, the company may benefit financially if the information is divulged. However, this is not certain as a late bid from another prospective buyer may yet be received prior to the deadline. The Member in Business needs to ensure that a fair tender process is held despite the short-term commercial pressure. The Member in Business also needs to ensure that any actions taken are within the confines of the law. The Member in Business may need to disclose the receiving of the call and the content of the discussion to Those Charged with Governance.

Case Study 15 – Non-Disclosure to auditors and corrupt business practices

Whistleblowing

Case outline

Sarah (Member in Business) is newly employed as an accounting systems manager and recently heard a rumour that the company recently paid a bribe to win overseas work. She has also noticed that the company culture appears to be that everyone has an attitude of getting away with as much as possible. Sarah goes to make her morning cup of coffee where she overhears a discussion with a divisional accountant about the fact that certain information had not been disclosed to the auditors. Sarah has not yet developed a strong working relationship with her line manager and as yet is not sure that her line manager will be supportive of her comments and desire to explore the accuracy of statements made.

Key fundamental principles and duties

Integrity

Can the Member in Business overlook the divisional accountant's comments, her impressions of organisational culture and the bribe allegedly paid to the overseas company and still demonstrate integrity?

Objectivity

Knowing that something may be wrong, how can the Member in Business maintain her objectivity?

Confidentiality

On what basis could or should the Member in Business make disclosures?

Professional behaviour

How should the Member in Business proceed so as not to discredit herself or the company?

Ethical decision-making approach

Identify relevant facts

Consider the business's policies, procedures and guidelines, accounting standards, best practices, applicable laws and regulations. Can the facts be corroborated with documentation or discussion with relevant parties? If proven would the conduct constitute a breach of any laws and if so, which ones? Is there an internal process for whistleblowing? Has the Member in Business taken the appropriate steps to understand her legal rights and responsibilities?

Identify affected parties

The Member in Business, the divisional accountant, the employee raising allegations about the bribe, the line manager and the auditor are the key affected parties. Other parties that may be affected are the company's other employees and where present, internal audit, the audit committee, the board, shareholders and financial backers.

Determine whether a procedure of conflict resolution exists within the organisation

Consider the company's policies and procedures and applicable laws and regulations.

Consider who should be involved in the conflict resolution process

Who should be involved in the resolution of this matter and for what reason? Do any confidentiality, privacy or whistleblower constraints prevent or restrict their involvement? What is the appropriate timing of their involvement? Has the Member in Business considered contacting her Professional Body for advice and guidance? Does the Member in Business have trusted colleagues with whom she can discuss her position? At what point will the Member in Business consider involving her line manager, the next level of management, the Board and the audit committee?

Discuss the ethical dilemma with relevant parties

Do further discussions with the divisional accountant need to take place? Similarly, do additional discussions need to be held with the employee raising bribery allegations?

Consider possible course of action

The Member in Business may consider checking the facts and discussing the matter with her immediate line manager. If the Member in Business feels that the response from the line manager is not satisfactory, the next step may be to discuss the matter further with the next level of management, internal audit, the audit committee or the Board.

The Member in Business's suspicions or rumours of criminal or corrupt activity are not sufficient for her to form a reasonable basis that wrongdoing has occurred. However, if there is evidence of wrongdoing, the Member in Business may contact her Professional Body (subject to confidentiality, privacy and whistleblower obligations) and consider obtaining legal advice. During the resolution process, it may be helpful to document the Member in Business's involvement in the resolution of the matter, the substance of all discussions held, the names of others involved, the decisions made by her and the basis for those decisions. When doing so, the Member in Business always needs to keep the legal considerations in mind.

Case Study 16 – Inappropriate expense claims lodged by the Chief Executive

Whistleblowing

Case outline

Crystal (Member in Business), the financial controller of the Australian division of an international company was reviewing the expense claims of senior management when she became aware of a claim from the Chief Executive Officer that was contrary to local tax laws. On further investigation, she found that this was not an isolated incident and claims of a similar nature added up to a significant amount. All claims were approved by the same international manager.

Key fundamental principles and duties

Integrity

Can the Member in Business overlook the Chief Executive Officer's expense claim and maintain her integrity?

Objectivity

Knowing that something may be wrong, how can the Member in Business maintain her objectivity?

Confidentiality

On what basis could or should the Member in Business make disclosures?

Professional behaviour

How should the Member in Business proceed so as not to discredit herself or the company?

Professional competence and due care

How can allowing the expense payments to be processed when they are contrary to local tax laws be seen as acting with due skill, care and diligence?

Ethical decision-making approach

Identify relevant facts

Does the Member in Business have all of the facts? Can the Member in Business discuss the matter further with the international manager that approved the expenses? If proven would the conduct constitute a breach of any laws and if so, which ones? Does the company have an internal process for whistle blowing? What steps has the Member in Business taken to understand her legal rights and responsibilities?

Identify affected parties

The key affected parties are the Member in Business and the Chief Executive Officer. Other possible affected parties are the Australian Tax Office, human resources, the Board and/or audit committee and other employees.

Determine whether a procedure of conflict resolution exists within the organisation

Consider the company's policies and procedures, applicable accounting standards, best practice and applicable laws and regulations.

Consider who should be involved in the conflict resolution process

Who should be involved in the resolution of this matter and for what reason? Do any confidentiality, privacy or whistleblower constraints prevent or restrict their involvement? What is the appropriate timing of their involvement? Does the Member in Business have trusted colleagues with whom she can discuss her position? Has the Member in Business discussed the matter with local management and/or human resources?

Discuss the ethical dilemma with relevant parties

Can further discussions be held with the international manager? Do discussions need to be held with the local senior management?

Consider possible course of action

The Member in Business may consider contacting the international manager who approved the expenses to clarify her understanding of the transactions. The Member in Business may consider quantifying the impact of the claims made by the Chief Executive from a taxation perspective and explain the problem to the international manager using this as a basis. The Member in Business could also then highlight the local implications of allowing such claims to continue. Implications may include fines from the Australian Taxation Office and unfavourable publicity to the company. Depending on the response received, the Member in Business may need to consider the likelihood of further assistance being provided by the international manager in relation to this wrongdoing and the impact that this may have on her actions. Enquiries of this nature, together with the details of the parties involved and reasons for any conclusions reached, should be documented by the Member in Business. The Member in Business may also consider raising the matter with the audit committee, once she has substantiated her belief that wrongdoing has occurred.

Case Study 17 – Inappropriate recording of patient attendance at a doctors' medical practice

Whistleblowing

Case outline

Rita (Member in Business) has recently returned to the workforce following maternity leave. She is employed as a part-time accountant for a local medical practice, reporting to a practice manager who is responsible for a number of doctors working together. In her second week on the job Rita noticed that one of the doctors appeared to treat more patients than were recorded in the electronic waiting room system used to manage patient attendance. It is the practice's policy that all doctors contribute to the practice half of their income earned from attending patients. Rita approached the doctor who suggested it was merely an oversight and that he would instruct the practice manager to update the records by the end of the week. At the end of the week Rita noticed that the patient attendance records had not been updated so she proceeded to update them herself. On Rita's return to work the following week, she noticed that the entries she made had been erased. When she approached the doctor about this, he snapped that her job was merely to record payments and expenses and any "business" matters were best left to those with the understanding of how to run a business. Rita has serious concerns about the doctor's actions in omitting to record patient attendances correctly.

Key fundamental principles and duties

Integrity

Can the Member in Business overlook the doctor's actions and maintain her integrity?

Objectivity

Knowing that something may be wrong, how can the Member in Business maintain her objectivity?

Confidentiality

On what basis could or should the Member in Business make disclosures?

Professional behaviour

How should the Member in Business proceed so as not to discredit herself?

Professional competence and due care

How can omission of patient attendance and therefore the costs and associated revenue be seen as acting with due skill, care and diligence?

Ethical decision-making approach

Identify relevant facts

Does the Member in Business have all of the facts? Is this merely a once-off or an ongoing practice by this doctor? Can she discuss the matter further with the doctor? If proven would the conduct constitute a breach of any laws and if so, which ones? Does the practice have an internal process for whistleblowing? What steps has the Member in Business taken to understand her legal rights and responsibilities? Has the Member in Business considered the application of Privacy laws to the handling of sensitive information within the personal health records of these patients and when and how these records can be amended?

Identify affected parties

The key affected parties are the Member in Business, the doctor concerned, other doctors of the practice and the patients whose records are not accurate. Other possible affected parties are the Australian Tax Office and Medicare.

Determine whether a procedure of conflict resolution exists within the organisation

Given the size of the practice, there may not be formal documented policies available. However, there may be a doctor who has the allocated responsibility for addressing staff issues.

Consider who should be involved in the conflict resolution process

Who should be involved in the resolution of this matter and for what reason? Do any confidentiality, privacy or whistleblower constraints prevent or restrict their involvement? What is the appropriate timing of their involvement? Does the Member in Business have trusted colleagues with whom she can discuss her position? Has the Member in Business discussed the matter with any of the other doctors?

Discuss the ethical dilemma with relevant parties

Can further discussions be held with the deceitful doctor? Do discussions need to be held with other doctors? Should she escalate matters given the doctor's previous brusque behaviour?

Consider possible course of action

The Member in Business may consider further discussions with the doctor concerned to clarify her understanding of the situation. Prior to discussions, the Member in Business may consider quantifying the impact of the doctor's behaviour and the likely impact over time. She may then decide to observe what happens over a longer period of time. All enquiries and conclusions reached may need to be documented by the Member in Business and when doing so, the Member in Business needs to be aware of the associated legal implications.

Case Study 18 – Insider information

Public Sector – Inducement

Case outline

Sally (Member in Business) is the head of internal audit in a public sector organisation which is about to tender for the contract for the internal audit service. She has been in her position for the duration of a five-year contract.

A new member of her team has been recruited in the normal course, from the department responsible for reviewing the tender contract. The new team member is employed in internal audit as a support administrator. Although he was not involved with the tender process, his former colleague and friend in the tendering department is responsible for the tender specification document and the evaluation process.

Sally's new employee had sight of some of the requirements and has offered to share with her information that may be of use when preparing the tender. However, this information is confidential and should not be seen by any of the tendering parties.

APES

It will be an open tender process for both external and internal providers. Bids from external providers are being encouraged. The evaluation process has been designed with this in mind.

If the contract is awarded externally, Sally, as the head of internal audit, will be unsure of her personal position in the organisation.

Sally understands the use of any insider knowledge of the tendering process would be inappropriate when preparing the tender proposal, but she feels she would have a better chance of success if she used this confidential information.

Key fundamental principles and duties

Integrity

How can the Member in Business demonstrate integrity despite the influence of the information available to her?

Objectivity

How can the Member in Business maintain her objectivity?

Confidentiality

How should the Member in Business act to maintain confidentiality?

Professional behaviour

How should the Member in Business proceed so as not to discredit herself?

Professional competence and due care

How can the Member in Business proceed in order to be seen as acting with due skill, care and diligence?

Ethical decision–making approach

Identify relevant facts

What are the risk factors here? What pressures is the Member in Business feeling to breach confidentiality principles? The Member in Business has a self-interest threat since her employment position with the company is uncertain if the internal audit contract is awarded to an external provider. The opportunity is present as a new member of her team has access to information that may better her chances. Having this information would compromise the probity of the tender process and increase the Member in Business's chances to the detriment of a fair and honest tender process.

Identify affected parties

The Member in Business, Employer and providers involved in the tender bid are the key affected parties.

Determine whether a procedure of conflict resolution exists within the organisation

Consider the company's policies, procedures and guidelines, best practices, applicable laws and regulations.

Consider who should be involved in the conflict resolution process

Who should be involved in the resolution of this matter and for what reason? What is the appropriate timing of their involvement? Are there trusted colleagues with whom the Member in Business can discuss her position?

Discuss the ethical dilemma with relevant parties

Should further discussion take place with the Member in Business's Professional Body?

Consider possible course of action

The Member in Business may consider disclosing this threat to the tendering department as well as any information she may already have received on the tender. The Member in Business could then discuss with her new team member from the tendering department the principles which would be compromised should she access this confidential information from the tender requirements and how it is her professional duty to follow these principles. She could also prevent the team member or his friend from providing her with any further confidential information on the tender. The Member in Business could consider discussing her concerns with Those Charged with Governance to determine why the contract tender has also gone to external providers and what that could potentially mean for her position with the company should an external party be appointed. The Member in Business could also examine her other employment options as a worst case scenario.

Case Study 19 – Demonstrating due diligence in an honorary position

Public Sector – Acting with Sufficient Expertise

Case outline

Tammy (Member in Business) has been appointed as a member of a School Board on a voluntary basis. She has also been appointed to the finance and buildings committee that awards building contracts. The membership of this committee includes a number of individuals with private sector experience and local businessmen. One is a local builder who has been a board member for a number of years and is well respected in the community and by the Board.

At Tammy's first meeting, the committee considers a report from the head teacher about the condition of the school hall and sets out a scheme of remedial building works with estimated costs. After discussion of the scheme, and recognising the need to move quickly if the work is to be carried out during the summer vacation, the board member who is the local builder offers to do the work at a competitive price and the other board members on the committee are minded to accept the offer.

However, although the offer has been made, the board members are not considering the use of a formal tender process or making any reference to governance arrangements that could exist for tenders. Tammy is concerned about the committee being unable to demonstrate reasonable decision making, stewardship of public money, and potential reputational risk.

Key fundamental principles and duties

Integrity

Can the Member in Business maintain her integrity without advising the committee of the need to demonstrate a proper decision-making process that would support any contracts awarded?

Objectivity

The information provided to her could result in the Member in Business saying nothing. How can she avoid the temptation to agree to the apparently easy solution and instead maintain objectivity?

Confidentiality

On what basis could or should the Member in Business make disclosures?

Professional behaviour

How should the Member in Business proceed so as not to discredit herself? Does this matter in cases where the employment is voluntary?

Professional competence and due care

How can the Member in Business demonstrate she is acting with due skill, care and diligence?

Ethical decision–making approach

Identify relevant facts

Does a voluntary position affect the level of professionalism that one must demonstrate? The Member in Business is new in her role and it can be assumed she is relatively unfamiliar with the policies, procedures and requirements of the School Board. On the surface it appears that the board member who is the builder seems to be the best person to perform the required works. Since the timeframe is short, using the builder board member's company could potentially facilitate the timely completion of the project, but only by bypassing tendering steps that maintain the probity of the process. Can the Member in Business act responsibly knowing that the tendering process would not stand up to outside scrutiny and considering that the project is dealing with public funds?

Identify affected parties

The key affected parties are the Member in Business, the School Board, parents, children, staff and other community stakeholders involved with the school.

Determine whether a procedure of conflict resolution exists within the organisation

Consider the company's policies, procedures and guidelines, best practices, applicable laws and regulations.

Consider who should be involved in resolution

Are there trusted colleagues or friends with whom the Member in Business can discuss her position? Can the Member in Business's Professional Body provide advice and provide assistance?

Discuss the ethical dilemma with relevant parties

Since the Member in Business sits on the School Board, would it be appropriate for her to discuss this with the finance and building committee members? Should she also discuss this with the Board? Should she consider consulting outside of the School Board?

Consider possible course of action

The Member in Business could bring the matter up before the finance and buildings committee and explain that, although it appears that the builder board member is the best candidate with a competitive bid, acceptance without following a proper tender process could be inappropriate. She could recommend that they follow a tendering process that is in accordance with good practice guidelines to explicitly demonstrate to the community a proper decision-making process that would support any contracts awarded. She may also need to explain to the board members that following a proper decision-making process would protect the committee members and the School Board from any potential reputational risk that the school did not properly award contracts, especially as it is funded by public money.

Case Study 20 – Potential breach of not-for-profit status

Charitable Organisations – Preparation and Reporting of Information

Case outline

Robert (Member in Business) is the Chief Financial Officer for a charitable organisation and has recently been informed by its auditor that preliminary analysis performed on the accounts indicates the organisation may have surpassed a legislative threshold for income from its commercial activities. It is uncertain how this came about, however it could potentially affect the organisation's tax exempt status with the Australian Taxation Office (ATO) as a registered charity. Robert has brought this matter to the attention of the Chief Executive who has expressed her fears of potential staff layoffs or a reduction in services occurring should there be penalties from the ATO or if the organisation loses its tax exempt status. Then the idea comes to him that the matter should be quietly managed in-house and that it should not be disclosed to the ATO since it was only an oversight in the current year.

Key fundamental principles and duties

Integrity

Can the Member in Business be involved in this decision and maintain his integrity? Is there a 'common sense' argument for not disclosing this unintentional slip to the authorities?

Objectivity

Can the Member in Business remain objective when deciding how to resolve this matter since his future position with the organisation may be at risk?

Confidentiality

On what basis could or should the Member in Business make disclosures?

Professional behaviour

How should the Member in Business proceed so as not to discredit himself?

Professional competence and due care

How can the Member in Business demonstrate he is acting with due skill, care and diligence?

Ethical decision-making approach

Identify relevant facts

The matter has yet to be analysed to ensure that preliminary findings are substantiated. The Member in Business should consider the alternatives. Is there any ethical discretion available in making a decision on this matter? Do the facts of the matter overrule any motives or intentions of the organisation when determining the tax implications? Would knowing the responsible party or their intentions affect the Member in Business's objectivity?

Identify affected parties

The key affected parties are the Member in Business, the auditor, the Employer, the management and staff, and the ATO.

Determine whether a procedure of conflict resolution exists within the organisation

Consider the company's policies, procedures and guidelines, best practices, applicable laws and regulations.

Consider who should be involved in resolution

Are there trusted colleagues or friends with whom the Member in Business can discuss his position? Can the Member in Business's Professional Body provide advice and provide assistance?

Discuss the ethical dilemma with relevant parties

Since the matter has already been discussed with the Chief Executive, should the Member in Business consider discussion with Those Charged with Governance?

Consider possible course of action

The Member in Business could investigate the auditor's findings in the first instance to determine whether there is any merit to the auditor's preliminary analysis. Should the auditor's findings be substantiated, the Member in Business may find it helpful to document the matter thoroughly and then consider whether to consult with internal or external taxation experts on how to approach the matter. The Member in Business may need to consider whether there is any legitimate means to deal with the matter and what long term repercussions would be on his professional reputation and on the organisation's reputation and future should they follow the Chief Executive's suggested solution and not disclose the matter to the ATO and its Australian Charities and Not-For-Profits Commission. Legitimate alternatives could be sought to limit the organisation's exposure to potential tax penalties or loss of charitable status. The Member in Business may find it useful to make inquiries on the ATO's powers to give relief in the event of loss of charitable status. Immediate contact with the ATO may be warranted in cases where timeliness of notification is a factor in the severity of the ruling by the authorities.

Case Study 21 – Ignorance is no excuse

Preparation and Reporting of Information/Acting with Sufficient Expertise

Case outline

Jill (Member in Business) is a long standing non-executive director for a large publicly listed property management group. The company has been taking advantage of readily available funds through short-term credit and rapidly increasing its portfolio of investment properties. Although this short-term debt has been easily converted into longer term less risky debt in the past, the tightening of the credit market due to a global financial crisis has left a large amount of debt which needs to be refinanced in the short term. Jill has reviewed the draft financial statements and notices that the split between current and non-current debt appears not to reflect this position. Jill makes inquiries of the Chief Financial Officer (CFO) whereupon she receives the response that the accounts have been reviewed by the CFO, the finance team, and preliminary sign-off has been obtained from the company auditor.

Key fundamental principles and duties

Integrity

Can the Member in Business overlook the available information and maintain her integrity?

Objectivity

Can the Member in Business rely on management and the auditor's judgment and remain objective when deciding how to resolve this matter since she is aware of differences?

Professional behaviour

How should the Member in Business proceed so as not to discredit herself?

Professional competence and due care

How can the Member in Business demonstrate she is acting with due skill, care and diligence? Should the Member in Business ask herself why her analysis is different to that of the others? How does the Member in Business ensure that a proper decision-making process is applied? How does she demonstrate the appropriate level of professional judgement?

Ethical decision–making approach

Identify relevant facts

Can the Member in Business rely on management and the company auditor without taking reasonable actions to understand the underlying information in the financial statements? The Member in Business is aware that significant events have taken place that are not disclosed in the accounts. What level of inquiry is required by non-executive directors of management in order to discharge their responsibilities?

Identify affected parties

The key affected parties are the Member in Business, the CFO, the company auditor, the Employer, the shareholders, and the securities regulator(s).

Determine whether a procedure of conflict resolution exists within the organisation

Consider the company's policies, procedures and guidelines, accounting standards, best practices, applicable laws and regulations.

Consider who should be involved in resolution

Are there trusted colleagues or friends with whom the Member in Business can discuss her position? Can the Member in Business's Professional Body provide advice and assistance? Is the Member in Business able to discuss the matter with a board member?

Discuss the ethical dilemma with relevant parties

Should the Member in Business raise this with the Board?

Consider possible course of action

The Member in Business may need to consider her professional and legal obligations in this matter and could perform further analysis to determine whether the split between current and non-current debt in the accounts is appropriate. If further review of the accounts indicates that the current/non-current split is not consistent with a true and fair view, then the Member in Business may need to make inquiries of the CFO and the auditor and then raise the matter as soon as possible with the Board. The Member in Business may find it helpful to document the matter thoroughly and may need to disclose her findings to the Board.

Conformity with International Pronouncements

The International Ethics Standard Board for Accountants (IESBA) has not issued a pronouncement equivalent to APES GN 40.

Acknowledgements

APESB gratefully acknowledges the publications listed below which provided insights into ethical issues faced by Members in Business and development of this Guidance Note. Further, some of the cases in this Guidance Note are based on scenarios described in these publications:

- *Molyneaux, David 2008, What do you do now? Ethical Issues Encountered by Chartered Accountants, The Institute of Chartered Accountants of Scotland*
- *The Institute of Chartered Accountants of Scotland Ethics Committee 2009, Shades of Grey. Ethical Dilemmas, retrieved 6th September 2010, http://www.icas.org.uk/site/cms/contentviewarticle.asp?article=6637*

- *ACCA (Association of Chartered Certified Accountants) 2008, Guidance on ethical matters for members in business, retrieved 25th March 2010, http://www.accaglobal.com/pubs/members/professional_standards/rules_standards/guidelines/ethical_matters.pdf*
- *CIPFA (The Chartered Institute of Public Finance & Accountancy) 2011 Ethics and You – A Guide to the CIPFA Standard of Professional Practice on Ethics, retrieved 5 January 2012, http://www.cipfa.org.uk/conduct/ethics.cfm*
- *CCAB (UK Consultative Committee of Accountancy Bodies) Ethical Dilemmas, Case Studies, retrieved January 25th, 2012, http://www.ccab.org.uk/reports.php#ethical*

Bibliography

High-profile examples of poor ethical behaviour in the corporate world

The following is a bibliography of actual examples of poor ethical behaviour in the corporate world:

ABC Learning

CPA Australia, January 2010, The ABC of a corporate collapse, retrieved March 2012, http://www.youtube.com/user/CPAaustralia#p/u/34/WIjQM18p2_k

http://www.youtube.com/watch?v=DIIrFV1p78Y&feature=related

http://www.youtube.com/watch?v=sMZExHXNlJQ&feature=related

http://www.youtube.com/watch?v=dvmnX4asuzs&feature=related

http://www.youtube.com/watch?v=a4rcGpRXD9I&feature=related

Bear Stearns

Norris, Floyd, April 2008 the Regulatory Failure behind the Bear Stearns Debacle, retrieved March 2012, http://www.nytimes.com/2008/04/04/business/04norris.html

Enron

BBC News World Edition, August 2002, Enron scandal at-a-glance, retrieved March 2012, http://news.bbc.co.uk/2/hi/business/1780075.stm

HIH Insurance

Marks, Kathy, April 2005, Director is jailed over scandal of 'Australian Enron, retrieved March 2012, http://www.independent.co.uk/news/world/australasia/director-is-jailed-over-scandal-of-australian-enron-6148162.html

Lehman Brothers

Investopedia Staff, Case Study: The Collapse of Lehman Brothers, retrieved March 2012, http://www.investopedia.com/articles/economics/09/lehman-brothers-collapse.asp

Opes Prime

Korporaal, Glenda, 2008, How Opes snared its rivals' clients, retrieved March 2012, http://www.news.com.au/business/how-opes-snared-its-rivals-clients/story-e6frfm1i-1111115971334

WorldCom

Scharff, M M, July 2005, WorldCom: A Failure of Moral and Ethical Values, retrieved March 2012, http://www.allbusiness.com/legal/trial-procedure-fines-penalties/13477699-1.html

Centro

Gettler, Leon, August 2011, Five management scandals: What you can learn, retrieved March 2012, http://www.smartcompany.com.au/managing-people/20110809-five-management-scandals-what-you-can-learn.html

APS 12
Statement of Financial Advisory Service Standards

(October 2005)

Note from the Institute of Chartered Accountants in Australia

This note, prepared by the technical editor, is not part of APS 12.

Historical development

October 2005: APS 12 was operative from 1 November 2005. It governs all aspects of financial advice provided by members of CPA Australia and the Institute of Chartered Accountants in Australia, including clear definitions in relation to fees and commissions, whether fees should be the preferred method of remuneration, and the banning of heavy initial-fee discounting. It provides an objective set of measures against which members, who are involved in the provision of financial advisory services, can be assessed.

The APS Miscellaneous Professional Standards 7, 9, 10, 11 and 12 are under review by the Accounting Professional and Ethical Standards Board. These Standards remain current until formally withdrawn.

Contents

Miscellaneous Professional Statement APS 12

Statement of Financial Advisory Service Standards

Part 1 – Introduction

1. Scope

1.1 CPA Australia and the Institute of Chartered Accountants in Australia ("the Institute") issue the following Statement of Financial Advisory Service Standards ("APS 12") which will become operative from 1 November 2005.

1.2 *Members* of CPA Australia and/or the Institute in public practice in Australia must follow the provisions of APS 12 when they provide *financial advice*.

***Members* in public practice outside Australia must follow the provisions of APS 12 to the extent that the provisions of APS 12 are not inconsistent with their local regulations and laws.**

All other *members* (including those outside of Australia) must follow the provisions of APS12 to the extent to which they are not prevented from so doing due to the specific requirements of an employer, AFS Licensee or local regulations and laws.

Where a *member* does not comply with a provision of APS 12, the *member must* document the departure from the Standard and note the reason/s for the non-compliance. In the case of a *member* not in public practice, the *member* should also bring the departure to the attention of their Employer or Licensee with a view to encouraging the Employer or Licensee to comply with the provisions of the Standard.

1.3 APS 12 covers the professional aspects of *financial advice* undertaken by a *member*, whether they are an AFS licensee or a *representative* in the provision of financial services under the Corporations Act (2001), or give *financial advice* which is not subject to licensing requirements.

1.4 *Members must be also familiar with all the other standards and By-laws applicable.*

1.5 *The Statement is not intended to detract from any responsibilities which may be imposed by law.*

1.6 *Members must also be familiar with and comply with any duties, obligations and responsibilities that apply under common law, the Corporations Act (2001) and other relevant legislation and the principles and practices of the AFS license holder, if any, whom the member represents.*

1.7 *Members providing* advice in the areas of mortgage broking, finance broking or the procurement of loans on behalf of clients, with the exception of gearing facilities arranged as a consequence of other *financial advisory services*, will not initially be required to meet the standards contained herein but are encouraged to use these standards as a guide to professional practice in these areas. Notwithstanding the above, APS 12 will still apply to all other areas of *financial advice* provided by the *member*. In addition, the Joint Code of Professional Conduct will continue to apply to all members.

1.8 All references to By laws, constitution, professional standards and legislation are references to those provisions as amended from time to time.

2. Purpose

2.1 *All members* are bound by the fundamental principles outlined in the Joint Code of Professional Conduct. This Statement has been developed to amplify the meaning of these principles as they apply to a *member's* role in the provision of financial advisory services.

2.2 The purpose of the Statement is to set a standard of professional best practice for *members* in the provision of quality and ethical financial advice to *clients*.

2.3 *Members* must follow the standards outlined in the Statement. *Members* should be guided in this regard not merely by the terms of the Statement, but also by its spirit.

3. Definitions

For the purpose of this Statement:

Australian Financial Services (AFS) License means the license granted by the Australian Securities and Investment Commission (ASIC) to a natural person or corporation to perform financial services, including the provision of financial product advice, within the scope of the specific license conditions attaching to that license.

Authorised Representative means a person or a corporation who is authorised by an AFS licensee to perform or deliver *financial advisory services* on its behalf.

Client means an individual, firm, entity or organisation to which *financial advisory services* are provided on a recurrent or an on demand basis.

Engagement means an agreement, whether written or otherwise, between a *member* and a *client* relating to the provision of professional services by the *member*. However, consultations with a prospective client prior to such agreement are not part of an *engagement*.

Fee for Service means a charge to clients based on the criteria as specified in Professional Statement F6 – Professional Fees, that being all of the following:

- the skill and knowledge required for the type of work;
- the level of training and experience of the person necessarily engaged in the work;
- the degree of responsibility applicable to the work, such as risk; and
- the time of all persons engaged in the work.

Financial Advice means any financial advisory service carried out by the *member*. These services include, but are not limited to:

i. Providing advice on financial products such as shares, managed funds, master funds, wrap accounts and life insurance carried out pursuant to an AFS License;

ii. The taxation aspects attaching to such advice;

iii. Dealing in financial products as defined in section 766C of the Corporations Act (2001); and

iv. The provision of *financial advice* not subject to AFS licensing, such as non product related advice on financial strategies or structures.

Financial Adviser means a natural person who provides *financial advice* to a *client*. The *financial adviser* will usually hold or represent an AFS Licensee in the provision of such advice (see *Representative*).

Financial Advisory Service means the provision of professional services by a *member* in the course of assisting *clients* to manage their financial affairs specifically related to wealth and retirement planning, personal risk management and allied advice. It includes the provision of financial services as defined in Section 766 of the Corporations Act (2001), and other *financial advisory services* for which a license may not be required (see *Financial Advice*).

Member means a *member* of CPA Australia and/or the Institute and where applicable includes his or her firm.

Representative means an *authorised representative* of an AFS Licensee, an employee or director of an AFS Licensee, an employee or director of a related body corporate of the Licensee or any other person acting on behalf of the AFS Licensee.

Statement of Advice (SoA) means any written advice to the *client* within the specific meaning of section 946A of the Corporations Act (2001).

Tax Advice means that where a *member* provides advice to a *client* on tax matters related only to the *financial* advice being provided to that *client*, then the *member* is deemed to be providing advice in their capacity as a *financial adviser*. Where the *member* is asked merely to provide tax advice to a *client* and is not undertaking any other *financial advisory services* then that *member* is not deemed to be providing advice as a *financial adviser*.

Part 2 – Ethical Code

The fundamental principles outlined in the Joint Code of Professional Conduct ("the Code") must be upheld by all *members*. APS 12 has been developed to amplify the meaning of these principles as they apply to a *member's* role in the provision of financial advisory services.

4. The Joint Code of Professional Conduct

4.1 The Code, which is mandatory for all *members*, recognises that the objectives of *members* involved in providing *financial advisory services* are to work to the highest standards of professionalism, to attain the highest levels of performance and generally to meet the public interest requirement.

4.2 These objectives require four basic needs to be met:

(i) Credibility

In the whole of society there is a need for credibility in information and information systems.

(ii) Professionalism

There is a need for individuals who can be clearly identified by *clients*, employers and other interested parties as professional persons in the provision of *financial advice*.

(iii) Quality of Services

There is a need for assurance that all services obtained from a *financial adviser* are carried out to the highest standards of performance and place the client's interests first.

(iv) Confidence

Users of the services of *financial advisers* should feel confident that there exists a framework of professional ethics which governs the provision of those services.

5. Fundamental Principles

The following fundamental principles of the Code form the basis of professional conduct by a *member* in the provision of *financial advisory services* and underpin the Standards that are set out in Part 3 of this Statement.

B1 The Public Interest;

B2 Integrity;

B3 Objectivity;

B4 Professional Independence;

B5 Confidentiality

B6 Technical and professional standards

B7 Competence and due care; and

B8 Ethical Behaviour.

Part 3 – The Standards

The Standards amplify the meaning of the fundamental principles of the Code and govern the professional responsibilities which a *member* must exercise in the course of providing financial advisory services.

The Standards are in **bold** type, followed by discussion or amplification in all other clauses. The Standards must be followed in conjunction with other professional duties of the *member*, any legal obligations that may apply including the Corporations Act (2001) and the principles and practices of the AFS Licensee whom the *financial adviser* may represent.

The appendices to this Statement are provided for assistance and further guidance on its practical application.

6. The Public Interest

6.1 ***Members* must at all times safeguard the interests of their *clients* and employers provided that they do not conflict with the duties and loyalties owed to the community and its laws.**

6.2 A distinguishing mark of the profession is the acceptance of its responsibility to the public. The accountancy profession's public consists of *clients*, credit grantors, governments, employers, employees, investors, the business and financial community and others who rely on the objectivity and integrity of *members* to maintain the orderly functioning of commerce and provide competent advice. This reliance imposes a public interest responsibility on *members*. The public interest is defined as the collective well-being of the community of people and institutions that the *members* serve.

6.3 The *member's* responsibility is not therefore exclusively to satisfy the needs of an individual *client* or employer. The standards of the accountancy profession are heavily determined by the public interest. For example, in relation to financial advisory services:

(i) *Members* help the public to identify and achieve their financial objectives through the provision of expert objective advice, so as to assist in the accumulation and protection of financial assets, and to ensure provision for retirement; and

(ii) *Members* have a responsibility to increase community confidence in *financial advice*. Advice must be of a high quality, objective, ethical and in the best interests of the *client*. The aim is to ensure confident and informed decision making by *clients*.

6.4 *Members* have an important role in society. Investors, creditors, employers and other sections of the business community, as well as government and the public at large, rely on *members* for sound financial accounting and reporting, effective financial management and competent advice on a variety of business, financial and taxation matters. The attitude and behaviour of *members* in providing such services have an impact on the economic well-being of the community.

6.5 *Members* can remain in this advantageous position only by continuing to provide the public with those unique services at a level which demonstrates that the public confidence is firmly founded. It is incumbent on *members* to ensure those services are executed at the highest level of performance and in accordance with ethical requirements that strive to ensure such performance. It is important that all stakeholders are satisfied that *members* are acting honestly and in good faith.

7. Integrity

7.1 ***Members* must be straightforward, honest and sincere in their approach to professional work.**

7.2 This includes a duty to be responsive and accountable, committed to acting responsibly, reliably and with respect in all professional relationships.

7.3 **Employed *members* must observe the terms of their employment, although these cannot require them to be implicated in any dishonest transaction.**

8. Objectivity

8.1 ***Members* must act fairly and must not allow prejudice, conflict of interest or bias to override their objectivity. When providing *financial advice*, they must maintain an impartial attitude and recommend solutions that meet the *client's* situation.**

8.2 *Members* serve in many different capacities and should demonstrate their objectivity in varying circumstances. *Members* in public practice may undertake reporting assignments and render tax and other management advisory services in addition to the provision of *financial advice* in industry, commerce, the public sector and education. They may also educate and train those who aspire to be admitted as *members*. Regardless of service or capacity, *members* should protect the integrity of their professional services, and maintain objectivity in their judgement.

8.3 ***Members* must identify and manage real and potential conflicts of interest.**

8.4 **A *member* must ensure that the conflict is disclosed to the *client* together with a detailed explanation of the circumstances and details of any safeguards that will be adopted to control the conflict. This allows, the *client* to make an informed decision as to whether to continue with the service. If the conflict cannot be adequately managed through controls and disclosure, the *member* must avoid the conflict by declining to provide the financial service or referring the client to another financial adviser.**

9. Professional Independence

9.1 **In providing *financial advice*, a *member* must uphold the principles of professional independence.**

9.2 ***Members* are reminded that there is a difference between meeting the standards of professional independence under APS 12 and the legal limitations to the use of the words independent, impartial or unbiased under section 923A of the Corporations Act. A *member* must not claim to be independent, impartial or unbiased or use the term/s independent, impartial or unbiased in their business or in any promotional literature unless their business operations strictly meet the provisions of section 923A Corporations Act (2001).**

9.3 Professional Statement F.1 of the Code applies to *financial advisory services* in the same manner as it applies to other forms of professional practice. Accordingly, APS 12 reiterates the professional aspects of independence as distinct from any requirements imposed by law.

9.4 Professional Independence requires:

Independence of mind: the state of mind that permits the provision of an opinion without being significantly affected by influences that compromise professional judgement, allowing an individual to act with integrity and exercise objectivity and professional scepticism.

Independence in appearance: The avoidance of facts and circumstances that are so significant that a reasonable and informed third party, having knowledge of all relevant information, including safeguards applied, would reasonably conclude a *member's* integrity, objectivity or professional scepticism had been compromised.

9.5 **A *member* providing financial advisory services must recognise the potential threats created by personal and business relationships; the acceptance of commission or other benefits; and financial involvements, which by reason of their nature or degree, might threaten his or her objectivity. In particular, the *member* must not be adversely influenced by third party remuneration in the preparation of advice to their *clients*.**

9.6 **The *member* must ensure that threats to independence are disclosed to *clients* so that the *member* can be seen to be free of any interest which might be regarded, whatever its actual effect, as being incompatible with integrity and objectivity. (*Members* are referred to Professional Statement F1 of the Code and Part 3 of APS 12 for its practical application.)**

9.7 **In accordance with Clauses 20 and 21 of this Statement the *member* must fully disclose all interests, both financial and non-financial earned from the sale of any financial product.**

9.8 **In recommending one financial product in preference to another, the *member* must make a recommendation which is appropriate to achieve the *client's* identified needs and objectives and explain the appropriateness of the recommendation in writing and in clear terms.**

9.9 **Further, the *member* must only recommend one financial product be replaced with another where it is appropriate to achieve the *client's* identified needs and objectives and it benefits the *client*. The reasons for the recommendation, a concise summary of the costs and benefits of the switch and the appropriateness of the transfer must be fully explained to the *client* in writing and in clear terms.**

10. Confidentiality

10.1 ***Members*** **must respect the confidentiality of information acquired in the course of their work which must not be used for any purposes other than the proper performance of professional duties for the** ***client.***

10.2 **Unless there is a legal or professional duty to disclose, a** ***member*** **must not convey or disclose any information relating to a** ***client's*** **affairs to a third party without the** ***client's*** **permission (*****Members*** **are referred to Professional Statement C5 of the Code for further information). When providing financial advisory services, an AFS Licensee whom the** ***member*** **represents is not deemed to be a third party.**

10.3 **Tax File Numbers ("TFN's") must only be collected, stored, used and secured in accordance with the Privacy Act 1988 and relevant taxation laws.**

10.4 ***Clients*** **may only be asked for a TFN where it is permitted by the law. A** ***member*** **must advise a** ***client,*** **that declining to quote a TFN is not an offence, but explain the consequences of not doing so.**

10.5 **Where a** ***member*** **receives a TFN in his/her capacity as a** ***financial adviser,*** **they must:**

(i) **Only use the TFN for a tax related purpose;**

(ii) **Ensure that the TFN information is protected and secure;**

(iii) **Ensure the TFN is only disclosed in accordance with the law;**

(iv) **Ensure that only authorised staff have access to TFN's and that access is restricted to the proper performance of duties;**

(v) **Make all staff aware of the need to protect the privacy of individuals in relation to TFN information; and**

(vi) **Dispose of TFN information, once it is no longer required by law or for the purposes of administration, by appropriate and secure means.**

11. Technical and Professional Standards

11.1 **A** ***member*** **engaged in** ***financial advisory services*** **must apply the same degree of skill, competence and diligence that is required to be exercised in performing any other professional work.**

11.2 ***Members*** **must also carry out their professional work in accordance with the technical and professional standards relevant to that work (*****Members*** **are referred to Section E of the Code for further information).**

11.3 **In agreeing to provide** ***financial advisory services*** **it is implied that there is a level of competence necessary to perform those services and that the knowledge, skill and experience of the** ***member*** **will be applied with reasonable care and diligence and in the best interests of the client.** ***Members*** **must therefore refrain from performing any services which they are not competent to carry out unless expert advice and assistance is obtained to ensure that the services are performed to a high standard.**

11.4 Further, a *member* has a continuing duty to maintain professional knowledge and skill at a level required to ensure that a *client* or employer receives the advantage of competent professional service based on up-to-date developments in practice, legislation and techniques.

11.5 ***Members*** **of CPA Australia must adhere to the minimum Continuing Professional Development (CPD) standards as outlined in the CPA Australia By-Laws paragraph 102.1(f). In addition, any** ***member*** **of CPA Australia who holds the CPA(FPS) specialist designation must meet the CPD standards outlined in By-Laws 802, 803 and 804.**

11.6 ***Members*** **of the Institute must adhere to the minimum Continuing Professional Education (CPE) requirements as set out in the Institute's Regulation 7 paragraph 1002. In addition, any** ***member*** **of the Institute holding a statutory registration in terms of Regulation 4 Para 702.1(i) is obliged to undertake at least 40% of this minimum CPE requirement in each of the appropriate speciality areas.**

12. Competence and Due Care

12.1 **A *member* engaged in financial advisory services must take reasonable professional care in the performance of their work.**

12.2 **A *member* must convey advice and recommendations to a *client* in writing and in a clear concise and effective manner.**

12.3 A *member* should communicate with the client in a way that builds a candid and trusting relationship, that assists the client in identifying and understanding his or her needs and objectives and that ensures clear, concise and effective explanations of the reasoning which led to the advice and the appropriateness of recommendations, to that client.

12.4 **A *member* must advise their *client* in writing that:**

(i) The *member* must make all reasonable enquiries in relation to the client's personal circumstances as required by law prior to the provision of advice, however the ultimate responsibility for the accuracy and completeness of the particulars and information supplied by the *client* to the *member*, rests with the client;

(ii) Any advice given to the *client* is an opinion only and is based on the *member's* knowledge of the particular circumstances; and

(iii) There are limitations attaching to financial advisory services and the *client* should not misinterpret an expression of opinion by the *member* as an assertion of fact.

13. Ethical Behaviour and other matters

13.1 ***Members* must conduct themselves in a manner consistent with the good reputation of their profession and refrain from any conduct which might bring discredit to their profession. It is important that stakeholders are satisfied that *members* are acting honestly and in good faith.**

13.2 It is important that *members* ensure *financial advisory services* are executed in accordance with ethical requirements. Should *members* encounter problems in identifying unethical behaviour and/or in resolving an ethical conflict they should refer to the guidelines for the resolution of ethical conflicts outlined in Joint Guidance Notes (GN1 – *Members in Business Guidance Statement*) and the assistance available from the accounting bodies to support *members* facing ethical dilemmas.

13.3 A *client* has an indisputable right to choose their *financial adviser* and to change to others should they so desire. If a *member* in public practice is approached by a potential *client* to take over their financial advisory work from another *member* in public practice the *members* must comply with the requirements of Sections D.6 and F.3 (*Changes in Professional Appointments*) of the Code.

13.4 *Members* consulting with each other in relation to their *clients'* affairs must observe the requirements of Sections D.7 and F.4 (*Referrals*) of the Code.

14. Incorrect or Misleading Information

14.1 **If a *member* knows or ought to know that *financial advice* is, or is likely to be, based on incomplete or inaccurate information, a *member* must immediately discuss the matter with their *client* and endeavour to persuade the *client* to correct any inaccuracy or omission involved and make reasonable other enquires with a view to ascertaining whether the information is correct in order to have the *financial advice* prepared on a factual basis, or where the financial advice has already been provided, to have it amended.**

14.2 **If the inaccuracy or omission is not rectified to the *member's* satisfaction, the *member* must provide a warning to the *client* in writing about the limitations of that advice and that the *client* should consider the appropriateness of the advice before acting on it.**

14.3 In those circumstances, the written advice should also contain a general summary of those aspects of the *client's* relevant circumstances that the *member* believes are inaccurate or incomplete. For financial advice given pursuant to an AFS License, the summary should be contained in the Statement of Advice.

14.4 If a *member* believes that a *client* has provided misleading information or that the advice will be based on misleading information, the *member* should consider not performing the service.

14.5 *Members* who are AFS Licensees must comply with their obligations under the Financial Transaction Reports Act (1988) in relation to due diligence, record keeping and reporting requirements including;

(i) The reporting of suspicious and other relevant cash transactions;

(ii) Verifying the identity of persons who are signatories to accounts; and

(iii) Preventing accounts from being opened or operated in a false name.

15. Terms of Engagement (Applicable to Members in Public Practice only)

15.1 The *member* must ensure that there is a clear and written understanding between the *client* and the *member* regarding the terms of engagement. Satisfaction of this requirement can be via:

- **a Terms of Engagement letter;**
- **an Authority to Proceed;**
- **a Client Agreement letter;**
- **a combination of the above; or**
- **another form of agreement which meets the criteria outlined in 15.2.**

15.2 *Members* must observe the requirement of APS2 Terms of Engagement in this regard when discussing new or recurring work with a *client*. At the very least the written contract for services should include:

(i) Fee and billing arrangements;

(ii) Service deliverables and timeframes;

(iii) Duration of the agreement/period of appointment (if known);

(iv) Expected frequency of contact; and

(v) Confidentiality provisions.

15.3 Where an AFS Licensee whom the *member* represents provides Engagement Letters which do not meet the standards of APS2, they will need to be amended to meet these standards. Where the AFS Licensee's requirements are stricter than the requirements of APS2 then the stricter requirements will prevail.

15.4 Appendix 2 contains a sample Letter of Engagement for use as a guide. It should be used in conjunction with the considerations outlined in APS2 and varied according to individual requirements and circumstances.

16. Estimates and Projections

16.1 A *member* must not prepare or be associated with the preparation of financial or investment projections involving the use of estimates unless their use is generally acceptable, or under the circumstances it is impracticable to obtain exact data.

16.2 When estimates are used, they must be presented in such a manner as to avoid the implication of greater accuracy than in fact exists. The *member* must be satisfied that the estimates are not unreasonable in the particular circumstances. Where estimates and/or projections are used there is to be a clear explanation to the *client*, in writing, as to why the specific estimate or projection rates used are appropriate and on what basis they are calculated.

17. Remuneration

17.1 *Members* providing *financial advice* must ensure that the *client* is clearly advised of the total cost of advice and that the total amount paid by the *client* by whatever means, fairly reflects the value of the work performed.

17.2 *Members* should adopt a *fee for service* approach as this is considered to be more consistent with the principles of professional independence. This applies to both initial and *ongoing* remuneration. Where the *member* accepts commissions or other incentives, the *member* is to adhere to Clauses 20 and 21 of this Statement. At a minimum, these benefits are to be fully and clearly disclosed to the *client* and the *client* is to receive appropriate advice for the total remuneration received. The *member* is referred to F6 (Professional Fees) of the Code for further information.

17.3 Where, due to unforeseen circumstances, the fee is, or is likely to be, greater than anticipated or expected by the *client*, the matter must be discussed with the *client* as soon as practicable, but always prior to billing.

18. Determining Fees (Applicable to Members in Public Practice only)

18.1 *Fees* must not be discounted for initial *engagements* where there is the intention of recovering these discounts through higher charges or the provision of additional services in the future.

18.2 Clause 18.1 does not apply to the following situations:

- Discounted or pro-bono work where there are not further subsequent charges or the subsequent charging level is consistent with the *members* usual fee schedule.
- Discounts on initial advice where it is expressly agreed with the *client* and the full cost of all initial and *ongoing* advice is disclosed at the time of the initial engagement.

18.3 The following would be considered a contravention of Clause 18.1:

- If a *member* were to advertise "free financial advice" or similar where the clear intention is to charge the client only be way of product placement fees or commissions.
- If a *member* provides free or heavily discounted financial planning advice where the intention is to recoup the fees through other services such as accounting or taxation services.

18.4 A mere standardised percentage basis applied to all funds under management or advice is not a *fee for service*.

18.5 In addition to the criteria specified in Professional Statement F6 of the Code - Professional Fees in setting or charging *fees for service*, *members* should consider:

(i) *Client* requirements;

(ii) Statutory duties;

(iii) Levels of expertise and responsibility required and the degree of complexity entailed;

(iv) Amount of time taken and effectively applied by the *member* and staff;

(v) The professional and financial risk associated with providing the advice; and

(vi) Any agreed fee basis.

19. Receipt of Fees (Applicable to Members in Public Practice only)

19.1 *Members* should not be restricted in how fees for service are received as Professional Independence comes from how *fees for service* are determined not how the fee is received. This means that *fees for service* can be collected via direct billing of the client or via the product or platform the client invests in.

19.2 Methods of receipt can include:

- Direct billing of client;
- Automatic debit from financial product, platform or administration service;
- Commission payments where they are offset against *fees for service* payable by the client;
- Converting an agreed fee for service into a percentage amount for the purpose of debiting against a financial product, platform or administration service.

20. Disclosure and Reporting Fees (Applicable to Members in Public Practice only)

20.1 A *member* must fully and accurately disclose in writing all interests, financial and nonfinancial, received or receivable by themselves, their AFS Licensee or a third party relating to the provision of advice given by the *member*. It includes payments and benefits to or from related parties that influence or might reasonably be capable of influencing advice and referral payments. Disclosure must be at a level of detail that a *client* would reasonably require for the purposes of deciding whether to act on the advice and must be clear, concise and transparent.

20.2 *Members* must disclose these interests as an amount in dollars, unless the item to be disclosed is the subject of an ASIC Class order.[1]

20.3 *Members* should report at least annually to all clients, all fees, commissions and other remuneration received on behalf of each client to demonstrate how *fees for service* are received and applied.

20.4 Where the *client* accepts the *engagement*, the *member* must ensure that the client receives a *Client* Fee Schedule containing a:

(i) Detailed description of all ongoing services offered;

(ii) Detailed description of all ongoing fees (including annual estimate);

(iii) Basis for the calculation of ongoing fees.

20.5 For *members* who hold an AFS License or represent an AFS Licensee, the obligation in Clause 20.4 will be deemed to have been met by the provision of a compliant Statement of Financial Advice, containing the relevant information.

20.6 If at any time after the initial advice there is a material change to the basis upon which a *member's* remuneration will be calculated, then a new *Client* Fee Schedule must be prepared and sent to the *client*.

20.7 All fees must be disclosed whether they are directly or indirectly paid by the *client*. Where a percentage calculation of a portfolio value is used for fee payment, an estimate should be used based on the annual opening balance of the *client's* account.

20.8 If a *member* is subject to a stricter requirement by the *AFS Licensee* they represent, or by having a stricter standard with the AFS License they hold, the *member* should apply that stricter standard.

20.9 Appendix 1 contains an example of best practice upfront fee disclosure for use as a guide. This should be varied according to individual requirements and circumstances.

21. Non cash and Alternative Remuneration (Applicable to Members in Public Practice only)

21.1 Alternative remuneration benefits, including soft dollar benefits received from third parties that place the interests of the *member* in significant conflict with those of the *client* must be avoided due to their potential to undermine the independence and professionalism of the advice.

1 The current ASIC Class Orders are C/O 04/1430 on Unknown facts and circumstances, C/O 04/1431 on Costs of derivatives, foreign exchange contracts, general insurance products and life risk insurance products, C/O 04/1432 on interest payable on deposit products, C/O 04/1433 on monetary benefits and interests and C/O 04/1435 on Amounts denominated in a foreign currency.

APS

21.2 ASIC[2] defines soft dollar benefits as all monetary and non-monetary benefits except direct client advice fees and basic monetary commissions that financial advisers and their licensees may receive if they recommend certain products. ASIC has identified certain types of soft dollar benefits that are often related to the sale of financial product to *clients* and are usually paid by third parties such as Fund Managers and Platform Providers as follows:

(i) Additional commission or benefits based on sales volumes;

(ii) Free or subsidised benefits such as:

- Rent for office or equipment,
- Computer hardware which would otherwise be purchased;
- Computer software which would otherwise be purchased;
- Meals or entertainment;
- Attendance at Adviser Conferences;
- Travel and accommodation to conferences or for personal use;
- Subscriptions to magazines, journals etc; and
- Other gifts or payments which may influence, or have the perception of influencing advice.

(iii) Sponsorship by a third party of an AFS Licensee or *representatives* function, seminar, conference or meeting;

(iv) "Buyer of Last Resort" agreements;

(v) Cash payments and/or goods not directly attributable to a direct *client* transaction;

(vi) Marketing Support payments;

(vii) Shares or options in the product provider;

(viii) Fee rebates or profit sharing arrangements;

(ix) Differential Splits.

21.3 The receipt of the following benefits, gifts or other incentives by a *member* from a third party related either directly or indirectly to the sale of product are banned:

- **Additional commission or benefits based on sales volumes unless they are rebated in full to the client;**
- **Preferential commission or benefits received for the sale of in house financial products;**
- **Free or subsidised office rental or equipment;**
- **Free or subsidised computer hardware;**
- **Free or subsidised computer software which is commercially available;**
- **Free or subsidised attendance (including travel and accommodation), or sponsorship of, conferences or functions of one or more days duration, conducted by a third party, where the principal eligibility is based on or related to business volumes written or held;**
- **Cash payments not directly attributable to a direct client action or sales volumes;**
- **Gifts over $300 in retail value.**

21.4 Alternative remuneration benefits received by a *member* from a third party relating to entertainment, conference attendance or sponsorship which are not volume based, that exceed $300 on the actual cash value or best estimated retail value, must be recorded by the *member* within 14 days of receipt, in an Alternative Remuneration Schedule, kept by them. Members must keep a record for five years after the receipt of a recordable benefit, or for five years after the last date of receiving a continuous or recurrent benefit.

2 Australian Securities and Investment Commission report on Soft Dollar Benefits – July 2004.

21.5 **The Alternative Remuneration Schedule must be made available for immediate inspection by *clients* or upon the request of CPA Australia or the Institute with 2 business days notice. Specific reference to the availability of the Alternative Remuneration Schedule is to be included in the *member's* Financial Services Guide and *Statement of Advice*, if a relevant recommendation is made.**

2.16 Appendix 3 contains a sample Alternative Remuneration Schedule for use as a guide. The Schedule should be varied according to individual requirements and circumstances, but should record any alternative remuneration benefits that have been received by the *member*. The Schedule should detail the company or provider of the benefit, the type of benefit, its estimated retail value and the date the benefit was received.

21.7 *Members* will be deemed to have satisfied the requirements of Clause 21.4 if they use or rely on an equivalent document provided by the AFS Licensee they represent.

21.8. Benefits, gifts or other incentives which are not banned under clause 21.3 and which are received by a *member* from one third party source but do not exceed $300 in total over any rolling 12 month period, will be deemed to be incidental and will not be subject to mandatory disclosure in the Alternative Remuneration Schedule. However, all benefits that influence or are capable of influencing advice, regardless of size, should be disclosed in the Financial Services Guide and *Statement Of Advice* if a relevant recommendation is made. For example, a Buyer of Last Resort agreement with a bias for certain brands must be disclosed in both the Financial Services guide and in the *Statement of Advice* if a relevant recommendation is made, whether or not the agreement is offered by a Product Provider of an AFS Licensee.

21.9 Where a *member* attends an educational event which is not subsidised and the event has a genuine educational or training purpose, disclosure is not required. Where the *member* attends an educational event in the capacity of a professional presenter, disclosure is not required.

21.10 *Members* should only use the term "Rebate" to describe an amount credited to the account of their *client*. Use of the term Rebate may otherwise be misleading and deceptive. An amount or payment retained by a product provider or an AFS Licensee should be more appropriately named a "Commission Payment."

21.11 For the purposes of Clause 21 the standard revenue splits applied by AFS Licensees to their representative will not be banned unless there is a product bias within the Licensees remuneration schedule, wherein the sale of certain products qualify for a higher split or additional benefits in comparison to other products.

Part Four – Administration

22. Notification

22.1 ***Members* must notify CPA Australia and/or the Institute when they:**

(i) Commence the holding of an *AFS License*;

(ii) Cease to hold an *AFS License*;

(iii) Become a Representative/Authorised Representative of an AFS Licensee ; or

(iv) Cease as a Representative/Authorised Representative of an AFS Licensee.

This must be done as soon as possible, but no later than the return of their annual membership renewal.

22.2 ***Members* must provide the full name of the AFS Licensee and the *AFS License* number and the effective date of the change as part of the notification required under Clause 22.1.**

APS

23. Monitoring Compliance (Applicable to Members in Public Practice only)

23.1 CPA Australia *members* compliance with this Statement will be assessed as part of CPA Australia's Quality Assessment Program.

23.2 Institute *members* may be subject to review in relation to their obligations under the Institute's Quality Review Program.

24. Enforcement

24.1 The Standards set out in this Statement are mandatory. Non-compliance can lead to disciplinary proceedings as provided in Clause 27 of CPA Australia's Constitution and By-Law 40 of the Institute.

24.2 Complaints regarding alleged breaches of the Statement by *members* shall be accepted from any individual or organisation by CPA Australia or the Institute, as relevant, for investigation and prosecution.

24.3 External complaint resolution schemes may have regard to the Statement when dealing with complaints against a *member*.

25. Transitional Arrangements

25.1 Where the items banned in Clause 21.3 are being received by a *member* as at the commencement date of APS 12, the *member* must by 31 December 2005 cease receipt of these items. In the meantime the *member* must comply with the disclosure and recording standards for these benefits.

Appendix One

Sample Fee Disclosure

- This table shows professional fees and other costs that you may be charged, together with commissions, benefits or interests we may receive from third parties in relation to the provision of services to you.
- We will advise you also of any incentives, bonuses or gifts provided to [the *member/firm*/AFS licensee] by any third party supplier. [the *member/firm*/AFS licensee] maintains an Alternative Remuneration Schedule and is available for you to view.
- Unless otherwise advised, all amounts disclosed are in dollar terms.
- The fees and costs shown may be collected in a number of ways including direct billing of you or received via the product or platform in which you invest.
- We will inform you promptly of any necessary changes to the fee structure or the billing arrangements.
- We will reconcile and report to you at least once yearly on all fees, commissions, remuneration and other benefits received.

Upfront Fees

	How and when paid/collected	Retained by our practice	Remitted to AFS Licensee	Amount/Total
Advice Preparation Fee				
Implementation Fee				
Transaction/ Investment costs.				
E.g.: stockbroker Portfolio service				
Commissions, other benefits or interests				
TOTAL upfront cost of advice				

Annual/Ongoing Service fees

	How and when paid/ collected	Retained by our practice	Remitted to Licensee	Total Annual Cost
Annual Service/ Advice fees				
Annual Wrap account fees				
Annual Portfolio management/ Investment Fees				
Annual Transaction costs ($50 per month)				
Commissions, other benefits or interests				
TOTAL in $				
TOTAL in % of funds invested				

Additional Fees

	How and when paid/collected	Retained by our practice	Remitted to AFS Licensee	Amount/Total
Switching Fee				
Implementation Fee				

APS

Appendix Two

Sample Terms of Engagement Letter

The following letter is for use as a guide in conjunction with the considerations outlined in this Statement and APS 2 Terms of Engagement. It should be varied according to the individual requirements and circumstances of both the *client* and the AFS licensee. Where appropriate, additional paragraphs may be included to address Limitation of Liability (*members* are referred to APS 2 Appendix 2).

To the *Client*,

Introduction

This letter is to confirm our understanding of the terms of our engagement and the nature and limitations of the services we will provide.

Purpose of the Engagement

NOTE: A brief summary of the purposes of the engagement should be included.

Examples of sentences which could be included follow:

1. *(Advisor's Licensee) holds an Australian Financial Services Licence to provide financial services and financial product advice and (Advisor) is our representative/authorised representative.*
2. *We have agreed to perform the following services on your behalf:*

   Here insert a clear description of the services to be provided which need to be tailored to the client's instructions. For example:

   A. *Advice in relation to…….*

   B. *Advice in relation to…….*
3. *The purpose of these services is to ………*
4. *The procedures we will perform will be limited to those related to this purpose.*
5. *A. To assist you in understanding our organisation more and the services we provide, we enclose the following information:*
   - *Our company brochure; and/or*
   - *A Financial Services Guide.*

   OR

   B. *We confirm that we have already provided you with information about our firm/ our Financial Services Guide.*

Scope of the engagement

NOTE: Here include pertinent details of such matters as:

1. Time periods covered by the *engagement*;
2. Period of appointment and time schedules;
3. Applicability of any legislation and of professional standards relevant to the *engagement*;

An example of a sentence which could be included here follows:

This engagement will be conducted in accordance with the relevant standards and ethical requirements of CPA Australia and/or the Institute of Chartered Accountants in Australia.

4. *Client* operations or procedures to be included in the *engagement*;
5. Details of information to be provided by the *client*;

An example of a sentence which could be included here follows:

Our advice to you must be based on your personal circumstances and financial objectives. To assist us in providing services to you we need you to provide details of:

- *Your relevant personal circumstances*
- *Your financial objectives and life goals*
- *Your financial situation and financial needs.*

If we believe that you have provided incorrect or incomplete information upon which the advice is to be based, we will immediately discuss the matter with you in order to correct any misstatement or omission involved. Should we continue to believe that our advice is based on information which is incomplete or inaccurate, you shall be warned in writing that the advice might have its limitations and you should consider the appropriateness of the advice before acting on it.

6. Other matters considered necessary or appropriate.

Service Deliverables/Timeframes

NOTE: Here you should insert details of statements of advice or other anticipated outputs, including:

1. Timeframes for the provision of advice;
2. The expected frequency of contact;
3. The intended use and distribution of written advice; and
4. The nature and effect of any anticipated disclaimer or arrangement that limits the liability of the *member* with respect to the *client* or any other user of the results of the *engagement*.

Example wording to be used under this heading follows:

Our services will be provided for the purposes noted above. We disclaim responsibility for any reliance on our advice for a purpose other than for which it was prepared. Our advice will contain a disclaimer to this effect.

We must also advise you that:

- Whilst we will make reasonable enquiries as to your personal circumstances, the responsibility for the accuracy and completeness of the particulars and information gathered in order to analyse your financial position and/or to prepare a financial plan or advice rests with you, the client.
- Any advice given to you is an opinion only and is based on our knowledge of the particular circumstances.
- There are limitations attaching to financial advice so you should not misinterpret an expression of opinion by us as an assertion of fact.

Relative Responsibilities

NOTE: Example wording to be used in this section follows:

The conduct of this engagement in accordance with the standards and ethical requirements of CPA Australia and the Institute of Chartered Accountants in Australia means that information acquired by us in the course of the engagement is subject to strict confidentiality requirements, in addition to our obligations under the Privacy Act 1988 (Cth) ("the Privacy Act"). That information will not be disclosed by us to other parties, without your express consent, except as required by law or professional obligation.

Our files may, however, be subject to review as part of the quality control review program of (insert CPA Australia and/or The Institute of Chartered Accountants in Australia as appropriate) which monitors compliance with professional standards by its members. We advise you that by signing this letter you acknowledge that, if requested, our files relating to this engagement will be made available under this program. Should this occur, we will advise you.

(The client) has agreed to arrange for reasonable access by us to the following people and documents, and is responsible for both the completeness and accuracy of the information supplied to us.

Fees and Billing Arrangements

NOTE: Here insert information for the client about fee arrangements.

Example wording to be used in this section follows:

The Financial Services Guide provides general information about our professional fees and how they will be disclosed to you.

Our written advice will provide information to you concerning the remuneration and benefits payable specifically for the services received by you.

In addition, our payment terms are as follows:

a)

b)

Where, due to unforseen circumstances, the fee is or is likely to be, greater than anticipated or expected, we will discuss the matter with you as soon as possible, but always prior to billing.

Other Matters

Here, information should be included about the following if appropriate:

Governing Law

Jurisdiction

Limitation of Liability

Indemnity

Severability

(Refer optional paragraphs in Appendix 2 of APS 2)

Confirmation of Terms

Please sign and return the attached copy of this letter to indicate that it is in accordance with your understanding of the arrangements. This letter will be effective for xxx (future years) unless we advise you of any change.

Yours sincerely.

Signature of Member
(name and title) Date

Acknowledged on behalf of (the client) by:

Signature of client
(name and title) Date

Appendix Three

Alternative Remuneration Schedule

Template Schedule for all non-cash and alternative remuneration or benefits received or receivable by a member.

AFS Licence holder	*Money Financial Planning*					
AFS Licence No	*11113333*					
Representative name	*A.N. Adviser*					
Date benefit received (Note 1)	**Source (Note 2)**	**Type (Note 3)**	**Description Note 4)**	**Provider of Benefit**	**Estimated RETAIL Value (Note 5)**	**Financial Category (Note 6)**
23 July 20XX	4	2	Complimentary subscription to XYZ publication	XYZ publishing	$100	E
2 October 20XX	2	2	Fund manager invitation to golf day and dinner	Australian Financial Management	$350	D
10 Jul 20XX	2	6	Compulsory orientation workshop for new product	Acme Wrap Account	$400	D
8 February 20XX	3	4	Buyer of Last Resort Agreement	Money Financial Planning	$500,000	A

EXAMPLES

Notes:

1. **Date benefit Received**

   Complete date benefit received – if received in full,

   Complete date benefit started – if benefit is on-going

   Complete date contract entered into – if benefit is deferred or at some future date

2. **Source**

   Type 1: For Product Manufacturer/Fund manager to AFS licensee.

   Type 2: For Product Manufacturer/Fund manager to Adviser.

   Type 3: For AFS Licensee to Adviser

   Type 4: For other Non Manufacturer or AFS licensee to Adviser

3. **Type**

1. Preferential commission or benefits based on sales volumes (Banned from 1 November 2005);
2. Free or subsidised office rental or equipment (Banned from 1 November 2005);
3. Free or subsidised computer hardware (Banned from 1 November 2005);
4. Free or subsidised computer software which is commercially available (Banned from 1 November 2005);
5. Free or subsidised attendance (including travel and accommodation), or sponsorship of, conferences or functions of one or more days duration, conducted by a third party, where the principal eligibility is based on or related to business volumes written or held (Banned from 1 November 2005);
6. Cash payments not directly attributable to a direct client action or sales volumes (Banned from 1 November 2005);
7. Gifts over $100 in retail value (Banned from 1 November 2005);
8. Entertainment/Meals;
9. Subscriptions to magazines, journals, industry associations;
10. Sponsorship by a third party of licensees, representatives or authorised representatives' function, seminar or meeting;
11. Other incentives or benefits which may have the ability to influence the advice of a member.

4. **Description**

Include a brief description of the purpose of the payment and/or benefit.

Provider of the Benefit

Include details related to the Provider of the Benefit.

5. **Estimated RETAIL value**

Include the actual value if known – or estimate the retail value of the benefit received or receivable. For future potential benefits, such as Buyer of Last Resort, a capital value based on the value as at the previous financial year end is to be used.

6. **Category of benefit**

Include the category of benefit based on the following schedule

A. Benefits in excess of $10,000, either in single payment or value of total benefits over a 12 month period.

B. Benefits between $2,500 and $9,999, either in a single payment or value of total benefits over a 12 month period.

C. Benefits between $500 and $2,499 either in a single payment or value of total benefits over a 12 month period.

D. Benefits between $300 and $499 either in a single payment or value of total benefits over a 12 month period.

E. Benefits less than $300 (disclosure not mandatory).

7. **Transitional Arrangements**

Where members are currently receiving benefits banned from 1 November 2005 they will have until 31 December 2005 to cease receiving those benefits. Following 1 November 2005 no new benefits that are banned will be allowed to commence.

A1
Supplemental Royal Charter

(22 August 2007)

ELIZABETH THE SECOND, by the Grace of God Queen of Australia and Her Other Realms and Territories, Head of the Commonwealth, GREETING:

WHEREAS His Majesty King George the Fifth on 19 June 1928 by Royal Charter (here called "the Original Charter") constituted a Body Politic and Corporate by the name of "The Institute of Chartered Accountants in Australia" (here called "the Institute") with perpetual succession and a Common Seal:

AND WHEREAS His Majesty in 1935 by Supplemental Royal Charter (here called "the First Supplemental Charter") authorised certain amendments to be made to the Original Charter:

AND WHEREAS WE in 1959 by Supplemental Royal Charter (here called "the Second Supplemental Charter") revoked Clauses 1 to 28 of the Original Charter and Clauses 1 and 2 of the First Supplemental Charter, and made new provisions for the governance of the Institute:

AND WHEREAS by Orders in Council dated 25 September 1964 and 9 June 1966 (here called "the Orders in Council") WE were pleased to allow certain amendments to the Second Supplemental Charter:

AND WHEREAS WE in 1973 by Supplemental Royal Charter (here called "the Third Supplemental Charter") revoked the Second Supplemental Charter and made new provisions for the governance of the Institute:

AND WHEREAS on 8 December 1987 WE have assigned to Our Governor-General of the Commonwealth of Australia all our powers and functions in respect of the issuing of Letters Patent:

(a) granting a Supplemental Charter to anyone in the Commonwealth of Australia to whom a Charter of incorporation has been granted by US or Our predecessors; or

(b) revoking, amending, or adding to, any Charter of incorporation or Supplemental Charter granted to anyone in the Commonwealth of Australia by US or Our predecessors,

and have authorised the Governor-General to exercise any of those powers and functions in Our name and on Our behalf:

AND WHEREAS in 1988 by Supplemental Royal Charter (here called "the Fourth Supplemental Charter") Our Governor-General granted, ordained and declared that the Institute continue to be a Body Politic and Corporate by the name of the Institute of Chartered Accountants in Australia with perpetual succession and a Common Seal but that save as aforesaid the Third Supplemental Charter be revoked but that nothing in such revocation would affect the validity or legality of any act, deed or thing done or executed under or pursuant to the provisions of the Original Charter or the Third Supplemental Charter and made new provisions for the governance of the Institute:

AND WHEREAS on 28 November 1997 by Supplemental Royal Charter (here called "the Fifth Supplemental Charter") Our Governor-General revoked the Fourth Supplemental Charter and made new provisions for the governance of the Institute:

AND WHEREAS on 23 August 2000 by Supplemental Royal Charter (here called "the Sixth Supplemental Charter") Our Governor-General revoked the Fifth Supplemental Charter and made new provisions for the governance of the Institute:

AND WHEREAS on 19 August 2005 by Supplemental Royal Charter (here called "the Seventh Supplemental Charter") Our Governor-General revoked the Sixth Supplemental Charter and made new provisions for the governance of the Institute:

AND WHEREAS the Institute has made representation to US as follows:

That since the grant of the Original Charter the Institute has pursued the aims and objects of the Charter and has sought to promote this standing, efficiency and usefulness of the profession of public accountancy;

That it has done so by fostering a high standard of professional education and competence and by requiring the observance of proper rules of conduct as a condition of membership; and that this has enabled the Institute to provide the Australian community with persons appropriately qualified to discharge the responsible roles demanded of public accountants as these have developed.

That since WE were last pleased to allow amendments to the Original Charter the membership of the Institute has continued to increase.

That it is the belief of the Institute that public recognition of members of the Institute and the governance of the Institute would be better achieved if certain amendments were made to the Original Charter as from time to time so amended or supplemented (here called "the Royal Charter").

AND WHEREAS the Institute has by that representation requested US to grant a Supplemental Charter for the above-mentioned purposes.

NOW THEREFORE WE do, by these Our Letters Patent issued in Our name by Our Governor-General of the Commonwealth of Australia, grant and declare as follows:

1 The Institute shall continue to be a Body Politic and Corporate by the name of The Institute of Chartered Accountants in Australia with perpetual succession and a Common Seal. Save as aforesaid, the Seventh Supplemental Charter shall be and is hereby revoked, but nothing in this revocation shall affect the validity or legality of any act, deed or thing done or executed under or pursuant to the provisions of the Original Charter or the Seventh Supplemental Charter.

Definitions

2 In this Our Supplemental Charter unless inconsistent with the subject or context:

(aa) "affiliate" means a natural person who is not entitled to be admitted to membership as a Fellow or Chartered Accountant but who has been admitted to membership of the Institute as an affiliate of a practice entity in accordance with the By-laws and the regulations made under Article 25.

(a) "Board" means the board of Directors of the Institute constituted under this Supplemental Charter and the By-laws;

(b) "the By-laws" means the By-laws contained in the Schedule hereto as amended or added to from time to time;

(c) "Director" means a person appointed to perform the duties of a director of the Institute;

(d) "Commonwealth of Australia" means Our Commonwealth of Australia and any territory or dependency in respect of which the Parliament of the Commonwealth or the Parliament of any State of the Commonwealth may make laws;

(da) "individual member" means a natural person who has been admitted to membership of the Institute as a Fellow or Chartered Accountant, and "individual membership" has a corresponding meaning;

(e) "practice entity" means any partnership, trust or body corporate or unincorporate in or through which persons who are members, or include a member or members, practise as public accountants;

(ea) "practice entity member" means a practice entity which is entitled under Articles 17 or 18 to describe itself as "Chartered Accountants" and which has been admitted to membership of the Institute;

(eb) "non-member practice entity" means a practice entity which has agreed to be bound by the standards of practice and professional conduct and by the discipline of the Institute;

(f) "public accountancy services" means such services as the Board may from time to time determine to be "public accountancy services";

(g) "public accountant" means a natural person:

(i) who maintains as a principal, whether on his or her own behalf or as a trustee and whether alone or with others, an office for the provision of one or more public accountancy services and who places that service or those services at the disposal of the community for remuneration, and not solely at the disposal of any individual, firm, trust or body of persons, corporate or unincorporate; or

(ii) who is a shareholder in, or a director of, a body corporate which, whether on its own behalf or as a trustee and whether alone or with others, maintains an office for the provision of one or more public accountancy services and which places that service or those services at the disposal of the community for remuneration, and not solely at the disposal of any individual, firm, trust or body of persons, corporate or unincorporate, and who, as an officer or employee of such body corporate or otherwise, provides or participates in the provision of such service or services on behalf of such body corporate; or

(iii) who is a beneficiary under a trust the trustee of which, whether alone or with others, maintains an office for the provision of one or more public accountancy services and places that service or those services at the disposal of the community for remuneration, and not solely at the disposal of any individual, firm, trust or body of persons, corporate or unincorporate, and who, as an officer or employee of such trustee or otherwise, participates in the provision of such service or services on behalf of such trustee.

(h) "registered graduate" means a person whose name is entered on the register of examination candidates maintained by the Institute and who has agreed to be bound by the provisions of this Our Supplemental Charter, the By-laws and the regulations made under Article 25;

(i) "Regional member" means a member enrolled on a Regional register constituted as prescribed in the By-laws;

(j) words importing the singular only include the plural and vice-versa, words importing the masculine gender only include the feminine and neuter genders and words importing persons include partnerships, trusts and corporations.

Principal Objects

3 The principal objects of the Institute shall be:

(a) to advance the theory and practice of accountancy in all its aspects;

(b) to recruit, educate and train a body of members skilled in such theory and practice;

(c) to preserve at all times the professional independence of accountants in whatever capacities they may be serving;

(d) to prescribe high standards of practice and professional conduct for, and to maintain the observance of such standards by:

(i) its members;

(ii) (Deleted August 2005)

(iii) non-member practice entities;

(iv) registered graduates;

(e) to prescribe disciplinary procedures and sanctions, to exercise disciplinary powers and to impose sanctions for the better observance of the standards of practice and professional conduct of the Institute by members, non-member practice entities and registered graduates;

(f) to do all such things as may advance the profession of accountancy, whether in relation to the practices of public accountants (including the provision by such practices, in addition to public accountancy services, of other services by persons from other professions) or in relation to industry, commerce, education, the public service or otherwise.

Ancillary Objects and Powers

4 In furtherance of the principal objects set out above, the Institute shall have the following ancillary objects and powers, namely:

(a) to implement and carry into effect, upon such terms and in such manner as the Institute may consider appropriate, steps to enable the accountancy profession so far as practicable to speak with an united voice on matters of professional, national and international importance and in this connection, inter alia, to co-operate and associate with any other institute, society or body of accountants, provided, however, that merger with another such institute, society or body of accountants shall require the approval of the Institute by resolution passed by a majority of not less than two thirds of the votes cast by the members entitled to vote who vote in a ballot conducted in accordance with the By-laws;

(b) to prescribe, in circumstances otherwise consistent with law, rules of professional conduct governing the formation and continuance of practice entity members and non-member practice entities, including practice entities which may offer other professional services in addition to public accountancy services, and to prescribe terms and conditions upon which such practice entities may describe themselves as "Chartered Accountants";

(c) (Deleted August 2005)

(d) to prescribe, in circumstances otherwise consistent with law, rules of professional conduct governing the participation or service by members in any partnership, trust or body corporate or unincorporate (other than a practice entity member) which, in the opinion of the Board, provides or purports to provide in Australia (except as ancillary to some other business) any services ordinarily provided by a member in practice as a public accountant;

(e) to prescribe, in circumstances otherwise consistent with law, rules of professional conduct governing the use of designations and descriptions by members and non-member practice entities;

(f) to prescribe, in circumstances otherwise consistent with law, rules of professional conduct governing the names under which members and non-member practice entities may provide one or more public accountancy services and the use which members may allow any person to make of their names in the provision of any such public accountancy service;

(g) to appoint examiners, to prescribe examinations for natural persons seeking to become members of the Institute, and to cause such examinations to be held, in each case, whenever in the opinion of the Board it is appropriate to do so, all as may be prescribed from time to time by the By-laws;

(h) to include amongst the sanctions to be prescribed for members pursuant to Article 3(e), and without limitation of the generality of that Article, the sanction of exclusion from membership and the sanction of the suspension of the right to any one or more or all of the benefits and privileges of membership;

(i) to purchase, take on lease or hire or in any other way acquire any real or personal property considered necessary for the use of members and others or for any purposes of the Institute and to sell, lease, mortgage or otherwise deal in any way with any such real or personal property;

(j) to construct, alter and maintain any buildings considered necessary for the use of members and others or for any purposes of the Institute and to provide the same and any buildings and rooms in the occupation of the Institute with all proper and necessary fixtures, fittings, furniture and other equipment;

(k) to maintain a library or libraries for the use of members and others;

(l) to publish or distribute books, pamphlets and journals relating to the affairs of the Institute or promoting and furthering the interests, usefulness and efficiency of members and others or of the accountancy profession generally;

(m) to make gifts or contributions for national, public, educational or charitable purposes;

(n) to make grants to universities or other educational establishments, to provide, finance and make grants for courses, lectures, classes or other tuition or for research and to establish scholarships or exhibitions and give prizes with a view to promoting or furthering the education, training or other interests of prospective members of the Institute;

(o) to organise, finance and maintain schemes for the granting of diplomas, certificates and other awards (with or without prior examination) to members of the Institute and of other professional bodies in any activities with which the accountancy profession is concerned and to provide for the use of designatory letters by persons granted such diplomas, certificates and awards; provided always that no such scheme shall become operative unless and until it shall have been approved by the Institute in general meeting;

(p) to make grants or other contributions to local or other societies having as an object the furtherance of any of the objects of the Institute;

(q) to pay remuneration to, and the expenses of, officials and employees of the Institute and to pay pensions and gratuities to, or to make other provision for, former officials and employees of the Institute and their dependants;

(r) to pay such sums for the remuneration of, allowances and for the expenses of officers of the Institute or Directors as may be permitted by the By-laws and to pay remuneration to and the expenses of any other persons (whether members of the Institute or not) who render services to the Institute;

(s) to make grants or otherwise render assistance to members of the Institute or their dependants in case of necessity;

(t) to assist any member of the Institute against whom a claim is made or who is involved in litigation in respect of any alleged act or omission by the member in the exercise of the member's profession as a Chartered Accountant in any case which, in the opinion of the Board, is of importance to the Institute or its members or the accountancy profession generally;

(u) to do, alone or in conjunction with others, the foregoing and all such other lawful things as may be incidental or conducive to promoting, furthering or protecting the interests, usefulness or efficiency of the Institute or its members or the accountancy profession generally.

Classes of Membership

5 (a) The members of the Institute shall be divided into 4 classes to be styled Fellows, Chartered Accountants, practice entity members, and affiliates, and such other classes as may be prescribed by the By-laws. Membership of each class shall carry such precedence, rights and obligations as provided hereinafter or by the By-laws from time to time.

(b) The persons who, at the date on which this Our Supplemental Charter becomes effectual in accordance with Article 26, are members of the Institute as Fellows, Chartered Accountants, practice entity members, or affiliates shall continue to be members of the Institute as Fellows, Chartered Accountants, practice entity members or affiliates as the case may be subject to the provisions of this Our Supplemental Charter and of the By-laws.

Fellows

6 Natural persons may be admitted to membership as Fellows of the Institute or may be advanced to that status on terms and conditions prescribed from time to time by the By-laws including, without limitation of the foregoing, terms and conditions in respect of training, examinations, nature and period of service or experience and fitness for membership.

Chartered Accountants

7 Natural persons may be admitted to membership as Chartered Accountants on terms and conditions prescribed from time to time by the By-laws including, without limitation of the foregoing, terms and conditions in respect of training, examinations, nature and period of service or experience and fitness for membership.

Practice entity members

7A Practice entities which are entitled under Articles 17 or 18 to describe themselves as "Chartered Accountants" may be admitted to membership on terms and conditions prescribed from time to time by the By-laws and the regulations made under Article 25.

Affiliates

7B Natural persons who are not entitled to be admitted to membership as Fellows or Chartered Accountants may be admitted to membership as affiliates of a practice entity on terms and conditions prescribed from time to time by the By-laws and the regulations made under Article 25.

Power to Refuse Admission

8 The Institute may by By-law provide that any person may be refused admission as a Chartered Accountant or as a Fellow or advancement to the status of a Fellow or may be delayed in such admission or advancement notwithstanding that such person may be otherwise entitled to be so admitted or advanced.

Registered Graduates

9 (a) Registered graduates may be granted such rights and privileges and shall be subject to such obligations as the Board may from time to time determine.

(b) The Board may from time to time prescribe the terms and conditions for registration as a registered graduate, including, without limiting the generality of the foregoing, terms and conditions in respect of educational qualification, fitness for registration and otherwise.

Board

10 There shall be a Board of the Institute consisting of natural persons, not more in number than shall be prescribed by the By-laws and elected or appointed in manner prescribed by the By-laws and one of the Directors shall be the President, and one shall be the Deputy President.

11 The members of the Institute and any other persons who, immediately prior to the time this Our Supplemental Charter becomes effective, are members of the Board of the Institute and the President and Deputy President shall, subject to the provisions of the By-laws, continue to hold office as members of the Board, President and Deputy President respectively.

12 (a) The Board shall be responsible for managing or directing the management of the affairs of the Institute and shall appoint and may remove, and shall determine the duties, salaries and remunerations of, the chief executive officer, solicitors, bankers, agents and other officers and employees of the Institute, and may make such arrangements and enter into such agreements with them or any of them as the Board shall think fit. The Board may also, in accordance with the provisions of this Our Supplemental Charter and of the By-laws, lawfully exercise all the powers of the Institute except as to such matters as are by this Our Supplemental Charter or by the By-laws directed to be transacted by or at a general meeting of the members of the Institute.

(b) All or any of the powers of the Board may be delegated to standing or other committees. Any such committee shall, in the exercise of the powers so delegated, comply with any regulations which may from time to time be imposed upon it by the Board but, subject thereto and to the By-laws, may sub-delegate all or any of its powers to sub-committees.

(c) The Board may also delegate any of its powers and responsibilities to any director or to an employee of the Institute or to any other person.

13 All powers which under the provisions of this Our Supplemental Charter may be exercised by the Board shall be exercised by it in accordance with, and subject to, the provisions of this Our Supplemental Charter and of the By-laws, and the exercise of all those powers shall be subject also to the control and regulation of any general meeting of the Institute, but not so as to make invalid any act done by the Board previously to any resolution being passed at a general meeting, and any act or proceeding of the Board shall not be invalidated or be illegal in consequence of there being any vacancy in the Board at the time of such act or proceeding being done or taken.

Payment of Subscriptions

14 (a) Every natural person or practice entity on his, her or its admission to and during his, her or its membership of the Institute shall pay such subscriptions, fees and other amounts as may be prescribed from time to time by the By-laws.

(b) Every registered graduate shall pay such subscription, fee and other amount as may be prescribed from time to time by the By-laws.

(c) Every non-member practice entity shall pay such subscription, fee and other amount as may be prescribed from time to time by the By-laws.

Regional Councils

15 The Institute may by By-law provide for the establishment of Regional Council of the Institute in any region of the Commonwealth of Australia to be elected or appointed in the manner provided in the By-laws. Such Regional Council shall exercise such functions and powers as are provided in the By-laws and shall do so subject to the provisions of this Our Supplemental Charter and the By-laws and subject to the control and regulation of the Board. The Institute may by By-law provide for the calling of meetings of Regional members with such powers and functions and subject to such conditions as may be prescribed by the By-laws.

Designations

16 An individual member of the Institute may designate himself or herself as a Chartered Accountant and may use after his or her name, in the case of a Fellow, the initials "F.C.A." (representing the words "Fellow Chartered Accountant"), and, in the case of a Chartered Accountant, the initials "C.A." (representing the words "Chartered Accountant"), provided that, when any such designation is used outside the Commonwealth of Australia, such designation shall be followed by the word "(Australia)" or its abbreviation "(Aust.)".

Descriptions as Chartered Accountants

17 A practice entity which is a partnership in which all the partners are individual or affiliate members may describe itself as "Chartered Accountants".

18 A practice entity, other than a partnership in which all the principals are individual or affiliate members, may describe itself as "Chartered Accountants" provided that it complies with the terms and conditions prescribed by the By-laws and the regulations made under Article 25.

Voting Rights

19 At every general or special meeting of the Institute or meeting of Regional members or on any ballot or poll, every individual member shall have such voting rights or such limited right of voting and there shall be such restrictions upon his or her right to vote as may be prescribed by the By-laws. Affiliates and practice entity members will not be entitled to vote at such meetings.

Cessation of Membership

20 If any person ceases for any cause whatever to be a member of the Institute, he, she or it shall not, nor shall his, her or its legal personal representatives, successors or assigns, have any interest in, or claim against, the funds or property of the Institute.

By-laws

21 Subject to the provisions of Article 22 hereof, the Institute may from time to time, by resolution approved by a ballot conducted in accordance with the By-laws, make such By-laws for the better execution of this Our Supplemental Charter, the furtherance of the objects of the Institute and generally for regulating the affairs of the Institute as to the Institute seem fit, and may from time to time rescind, vary or add to any By-laws and make others in their stead, but so that the By-laws for the time being be not in any respect repugnant to the laws of the Commonwealth of Australia or of any of the States or Territories comprised in the said Commonwealth or inconsistent with the express provisions of this Our Supplemental Charter.

22 No By-law or any rescission or variation thereof or addition thereto shall come into operation until the same shall have been submitted to and approved by Our Governor-General in and over Our Commonwealth of Australia or the person for the time being administering the Government of Our Commonwealth of Australia.

23 The Board of the Institute shall cause all such By-laws, when approved, to be printed and published together with the formal approval in the Official Gazette published by Our Government of Our Commonwealth of Australia.

24 Unless and until rescinded, varied or added to in accordance with the preceding Articles, the By-laws appended to this Our Supplemental Charter shall constitute the By-laws of the Institute.

Regulations

25 The Board may from time to time make such regulations as it thinks fit for the better execution of this Our Supplemental Charter or of the By-laws, the furtherance of the objects of the Institute and generally for regulating the affairs of the Institute and may rescind, vary or add to any such regulations, provided always that no such regulations shall be in any way inconsistent with the express provisions of this Our Supplemental Charter or of the By-laws. The regulations capable of being made under this Article include, without limitation of the foregoing, regulations prescribing rulings or providing guidance on the standards of practice and professional conduct, including the technical standards, which the Institute requires to be observed.

Application of income and assets of Institute

25A The assets and income of the Institute shall be applied solely in furtherance of the objects of the Institute as set out in Articles 3 and 4, and no portion of its assets or income shall be paid or transferred or distributed directly or indirectly, by way of dividend or otherwise, to the members of the Institute, provided that nothing in this Article shall prevent the payment in good faith of compensation to any member of the Institute in return for services actually rendered to the Institute, or in reimbursement of expenses incurred on behalf of the Institute, or as reasonable and proper rent for premises leased by any member to the Institute.

Winding up

25B In the event of the Institute being wound-up or dissolved, the amount that remains after such dissolution and the satisfaction of all debts and liabilities shall be transferred to another entity which has similar objects and which has rules prohibiting the distribution of assets and income to its members.

Alteration to Charter

26 The Institute may, by resolution passed by a majority of not less than two-thirds of such members as are entitled to vote and who vote in a ballot conducted in accordance with the By-laws, amend or add to this Our Supplemental Charter and such amendment or addition shall when allowed by US, Our Heirs or Successors become effectual so that this Our Supplemental Charter shall henceforth continue to operate as if it had originally been granted and made accordingly. This Article shall apply to this Our Supplemental Charter as amended or added to in manner aforesaid.

Application of Charter

27 This Our Supplemental Charter, the By-laws and the regulations made under Article 25 apply to all members and, where applicable, to all non-member practice entities and all registered graduates, wherever they may be within or without the Commonwealth of Australia, but subject to the provisions of any law of any country which is binding upon them. The funds of the Institute may be used outside the Commonwealth of Australia in any manner consistent with the objects and provisions of this Our Supplemental Charter and the By-laws.

28 As far as is consistent with the terms hereof, this Our Supplemental Charter shall be read as one with the Original Charter and henceforth shall operate as though it had been granted with the Original Charter.

AND LASTLY WE do grant and declare for US, Our Heirs and Our Successors that this Our Supplemental Charter shall be in all things valid and effectual in law according to its true intent and meaning and shall be taken, construed and adjudged in the most favourable and beneficial sense for the best advantage of the Institute as well in Our Courts of Record as elsewhere by all judges, justices, officers, ministers and other subjects of US, Our Heirs, and Our Successors, any non-recital, mis-recital or other omission, defect or thing to the contrary notwithstanding.

WITNESS under my hand and the }

Great Seal of Australia on }

22 August 2007 }

P M Jeffery

Governor-General

A2
By-Laws
(September 2010)

Section 1 – Preliminary

Commencement

1. These By-laws shall come into operation as from the date of their approval by the Governor-General of the Commonwealth of Australia pursuant to Article 22 of the Supplemental Charter.

Definitions

2. In the interpretation of the By-laws, unless the context or subject matter otherwise indicates or requires:

(a) Subject as hereinafter mentioned, words and expressions have the same meaning as in the Supplemental Charter and references herein to Fellows, Chartered Accountants, members and meetings shall be construed as having references to Fellows, Chartered Accountants, members and meetings of the Institute.

(b) "admission" in relation to membership of the Institute includes advancement in status and "admit" has a corresponding meaning.

(c) "Admission Regulations" means the regulations (if any) for the time being determined by the Board for the admission and readmission of persons to membership of the Institute, being regulations not inconsistent with the By-laws.

(d) "advancement in status" means the change in the class of a member from that of "Chartered Accountant" to "Fellow".

(e) "affiliate" and "affiliate member" means a natural person who participates with individual members in a practice entity, who is not a Fellow or Chartered Accountant or entitled to be admitted to membership as a Fellow or Chartered Accountant, who has been admitted to membership in accordance with the By-laws and the Regulations.

(f) "Audit Committee" means the committee established by the Board pursuant to By-law 129A.

(g) "Board" means the board of Directors of the Institute constituted under the Supplemental Charter and these By-laws.

(ga) "candidate member" means a registered graduate as referred to in the Supplemental Charter, who has been admitted to membership of the Institute as a candidate member;

(gb) "chartered firm" means a practice entity which is entitled under Articles 17 or 18 of the Supplemental Charter to describe itself as "Chartered Accountants".

(h) "Chief Executive Officer" means the chief executive officer of the Institute for the time being appointed by the Board under By-law 119B and includes any person for the time being discharging the duties of such officer or acting with his or her authority and on his or her behalf.

(i) "Director" means a person appointed to perform the duties of a director of the Institute.

(ia) "general purpose financial report" means a general purpose financial report comprising financial statements, notes to the financial statements and a directors' declaration.

(j) "individual member" means a natural person who has been admitted to membership as a Fellow or Chartered Accountant, and "individual membership" has a corresponding meaning.

(k) "month" means calendar month.

(l) "non-accountant" means a person who is not an accountant.

(m) "Overseas Member" means a member whose name appears on the Overseas Register.

(n) "Overseas Register" means the register of members whose registered address is outside the Commonwealth of Australia, to be maintained by the Chief Executive Officer under By-law 142.

(o) "post" means sending by post, facsimile transmission, email or document exchange, and "posted", "posting", "postal" and "postal ballot" have corresponding meanings.

(p) "practice entity" means any partnership, trust or body corporate or unincorporate in or through which persons who are members, or include a member or members, practise as public accountants.

(q) "practice entity member" means a chartered firm which has been admitted to membership of the Institute.

(r) "non-member practice entity" means a practice entity which has agreed to be bound by the standards of practice and professional conduct and by the discipline of the Institute.

(s) "prescribed" means prescribed by the Supplemental Charter or by the By-laws or by the Regulations.

(t) "Region" means each of the following regions of the Commonwealth of Australia:
   (i) New South Wales;
   (ii) Australian Capital Territory;
   (iii) Victoria;
   (iv) Tasmania;
   (v) Queensland;
   (vi) South Australia and Northern Territory;
   (vii) Western Australia.

(u) "Regional Council " means a Council for a Region constituted as prescribed in these By-laws and "Regional Councillor" means a member of a Regional Council.

(v) "Regional General Manager" means the general manager of the Institute in a Region appointed by the Chief Executive Officer and includes any person for the time being discharging the duties of such officer.

(w) "Regional meeting" means a meeting of the individual members and affiliate members enrolled on a Regional Register kept under the By-laws.

(x) "Regional Register" means the register of members in a Region to be maintained by the Chief Executive Officer under By-law 142.

(y) "registered address" of a member means his or her address on the National Register kept under the By-laws.

(z) "Regulations" means the regulations made by the Board from time to time under Article 25 of the Supplemental Charter.

(za) "special resolution of the Board " means a resolution passed by a majority of not less than three-fourths of the votes cast at a meeting of the Board at which a quorum is present.

(zb) "Supplemental Charter" means the Supplemental Charter as amended or added to from time to time.

(zc) "writing" includes printing, typing, lithography, microfilm, photocopying, facsimile transmission, electronic mail and other modes of representing or reproducing words in a visible form and "written" has a corresponding meaning.

(zd) words importing the singular only include the plural and vice-versa, words importing the masculine gender only include the feminine and neuter genders and "person" and words importing persons include partnerships, trusts and corporations.

(ze) a reference to a statute or other law includes regulations and other instruments under it and consolidations, amendments, re-enactments or replacements of any of them.

Interpretation of By-laws and regulations

3. If, in the opinion of the Board, any doubt arises as to the construction or interpretation of any of the By-laws, or of any of the regulations, the decision of the Board reduced to writing and recorded in the minute book shall be conclusive and binding on all members of the Institute. Due notice of such record shall be given by the Board to members by publication in the Institute's journal or otherwise as the Board may determine.

Use of Forms

4. Such forms as the Board may from time to time authorise shall be used in cases to which they are applicable, with such alterations or additions thereto, if any, as the Board may from time to time determine; and all notes and directions thereon shall be deemed part of the forms, and must be observed accordingly.

Section 2 – Membership

Classes

5. Membership of the Institute shall consist of:
   (a) the persons who, immediately before the date on which the Eighth Supplemental Royal Charter became effectual in accordance with Article 26, were Fellows, Chartered Accountants, affiliates or practice entity members;
   (b) the natural persons who, after such date, were or are admitted as Fellows or Chartered Accountants in conformity with the Institute's Royal Charter and By-laws as in force from time to time;
   (c) the natural persons who, after such date, were or are admitted to membership as affiliates of a practice entity in accordance with the By-laws and the Regulations;
   (d) the practice entities which, after such date, were or are admitted to membership in accordance with the By-laws and the Regulations; and
   (e) the natural persons who, after such date, were or are admitted to membership as candidate members.

Mode of Admission

6. All admissions of members shall be made by the Board.

Applicant to Satisfy

7. Subject to By-laws 12 and 18, every applicant for admission shall satisfy the Board, in such manner as the Board requires, that the applicant has fulfilled the prescribed conditions of such admission and shall also produce such evidence as the Board deems necessary of the applicant's fitness for such admission.

Discretion to Refuse

8. The Board may, in its absolute discretion and without giving any reason therefor, refuse to admit as a Fellow or Chartered Accountant a person whom it shall consider not to be a fit and proper person to be so admitted even if he or she has fulfilled the prescribed conditions of such admission.

Application for Admission

9. Every application for membership admission shall be made to the Board and shall be lodged with the Chief Executive Officer.

Conditions of Normal Admission and Advancement in Status

10. (a) A natural person shall be eligible for admission to membership of the Institute as a Chartered Accountant if, at the date of his or her application for such admission he or she:
   (i) has attained the age of 21 years;
   (ii) has passed the prescribed examinations;

(iii) has completed the prescribed period of service or experience in accountancy; and

(iv) otherwise complies, or upon admission will be able to and undertakes to comply, with the requirements of the Supplemental Charter, the By-laws and the Regulations.

(b) A Chartered Accountant may be advanced to the status of Fellow if, in the opinion of the Board, he or she is a fit and proper person to become a Fellow. In forming its opinion the Board shall have regard, inter alia, to the duration and quality of experience of the Chartered Accountant.

(c) A natural person shall be eligible for admission to membership of the Institute as an affiliate of a practice entity if, at the date of his or her application for such admission, he or she:

(i) is not a Fellow or Chartered Accountant or entitled to be admitted to membership as a Fellow or Chartered Accountant; and

(ii) complies, or upon admission will be able to and undertakes to comply, with the requirements of the Supplemental Charter, the By-laws and the Regulations insofar as they relate to affiliates.

(d) A chartered firm shall be eligible for admission to membership of the Institute as a practice entity member if, at the date of its application for such admission it complies, or upon admission will be able to and undertakes to comply, with the requirements of the Supplemental Charter, the By-laws and the Regulations insofar as they relate either to chartered firms or to practice entities generally.

(e) A natural person shall be eligible for admission to membership of the Institute as a candidate member if, at the date of his or her application for such admission:

(i) his or her name is entered on the register of examination candidates maintained by the Institute; and

(ii) he or she complies, or upon admission will be able to and undertakes to comply, with the requirements of the Supplemental Charter, the By-laws and the Regulations insofar as they relate to candidate members.

Normal Admission

11. The Board, on receiving an application, shall consider the same and the evidence in support thereof and shall make such investigation as it thinks fit. If the Board resolves that an applicant has satisfied the prescribed conditions of admission under By-law 10 and is a fit and proper person to be so admitted, it shall approve the application for admission and so admit the applicant.

Special Admissions

12. (a) If the Board resolves that, although an applicant has not satisfied the prescribed conditions of admission under By-law 10, he or she has satisfied the prescribed conditions of admission under the Admission Regulations and is a fit and proper person to be so admitted, it may approve the application for admission and so admit the applicant.

(b) The Board may at any time invite a person to become, and admit such a person as, a Fellow or Chartered Accountant on the grounds of his or her educational qualifications, expertise, experience in accountancy, or standing, although he or she has not satisfied either the prescribed conditions of admission under By-law 10 or the Admission Regulations.

(c) A person admitted under this By-law shall not be granted a certificate of public practice unless and until he or she shall have completed such period of service or experience in the practice of accountancy as the Board may prescribe.

13. (Deleted July 2000).

Notice of Admission

14. When a person has been admitted as a Fellow or Chartered Accountant or candidate member, the admission shall be recorded in the National and relevant Regional or Overseas Registers and a notice of his or her admission shall be sent by the Chief Executive Officer to the applicant.

When an affiliate or practice entity has been admitted as a member under By-law 10, a notice of their admission shall be sent by the Chief Executive Officer to the applicant. The admission of such a member shall be recorded in the National and in the relevant Regional or Overseas Registers.

Alternative Status on Admission

15. If an applicant for admission to membership as a Fellow is held by the Board not to be eligible for admission to membership as a Fellow but to be eligible for admission to membership as a Chartered Accountant, the Board may admit the applicant to membership as a Chartered Accountant if the applicant is willing to accept membership as a Chartered Accountant.

Notice of refusal and refund of fees

16. If an applicant is refused admission, a notice of his or her refusal shall be sent by the Chief Executive Officer to the applicant and any money lodged by the applicant with his or her application shall be refunded.

Commencing or Resuming Practice

17. (a) A member commencing or resuming practice as a public accountant or entering or re-entering employment with a member practicing as a public accountant or with a practice entity, in each case within the Commonwealth of Australia, shall forthwith notify the Chief Executive Officer.

(b) A member commencing or resuming practice as a public accountant or entering or re-entering employment with a member practising as a public accountant or with a practice entity, in each case outside the Commonwealth of Australia, shall forthwith notify the Chief Executive Officer.

Life and Honorary members

18. (a) (i) The Board may, on the motion of any Director other than the member proposed for election, elect any individual member as a Life member, and each Life member shall be entitled to all the privileges of membership without the payment of further annual subscription, fee or other amount: Provided that the number of Life members shall not at any time exceed 20.

(ii) The Board may likewise elect any natural person of prominence and standing as an Honorary member with the status of Fellow and each Honorary member shall be entitled to all the privileges of membership without the payment of any annual subscription, fee or other amount: Provided that the number of Honorary members shall not at any time exceed 10.

(b) Any Director intending to move for the election of a Life or Honorary member shall notify the Chief Executive Officer of his or her intention at least 30 days before the date of the meeting of the Board at which he or she intends to move the same. The Chief Executive Officer shall, not less than 14 days before the date of such meeting, dispatch notice of the motion by post to all other Directors.

Resignation

19. Any member may resign his or her membership by sending his or her resignation in writing together with all moneys owing by him or her to the Institute, whether for subscription, fee or other amount, to the Chief Executive Officer:

Provided that no resignation shall take effect unless and until it has been accepted by the Board. The Board may decline to accept the resignation of a member to whom a Notice of Disciplinary Action has been issued in accordance with By-law 45(a), or whose conduct, in the opinion of the Board, by virtue of matters brought to the attention of the Institute, may become the subject of professional conduct proceedings under Section 5.

Provided further that any member whose notice of resignation was not received by the Chief Executive Officer prior to 30 June in any year shall remain liable for any subscription, fee or other amount payable by him or her to the Institute in respect of the year ending the following 30 June, save that, in any case, the Board may in its absolute discretion remit the whole or any part of such subscription, fee or other amount.

Where the Board accepts the resignation of a member to whom a Notice of Disciplinary Action has been issued in accordance with By-law 45(a), or whose conduct, in the opinion of the Board, by virtue of matters brought to the attention of the Institute, may or (if the member had not resigned) may have become the subject of professional conduct proceedings under Section 5, the Institute may report the fact of the member's resignation and the issue of the Notice of Disciplinary Action (and the details of the allegations set out in the Notice of Disciplinary Action), or the details of such conduct and/or matters, as soon as practicable thereafter in the official publication of the Institute and on the Institute's website.

Readmission

20. The Board may, subject to such terms and conditions as it may think fit to impose:

(a) readmit to membership any person who has resigned or ceased for any reason to be a member;

(b) terminate the suspension of any member whose membership has been voluntarily suspended under By-law 21A.

Exclusion from membership

21. The Board may exclude a member if:

(a) under any legislation relating to mental health, he or she is certified, declared or found to be mentally ill or in need of treatment or care and control or incapable of managing his or her own affairs or is admitted to and remains in a hospital or other institution for the treatment of mental illness or a guardian is appointed to him or her or a trustee or administrator is appointed to his or her estate; or

(b) the member fails to pay any subscription, fee or other amount payable by the member to the Institute, including fees, fines and costs, within 3 months after the same has become due; or

(c) he or she fails to fulfil continuing professional education requirements as prescribed in the Regulations or (whether or not those requirements have been fulfilled) fails to notify the Institute of his or her compliance or otherwise for 2 consecutive years.

Such a member may be readmitted to membership under By-law 20.

Voluntary suspension of membership

21A. Any member may suspend his or her membership by sending written notice to that effect to the Chief Executive Officer specifying the period for which he or she wishes his or her membership to be suspended and the date from which the suspension is to take effect, and accompanying that notice with payment of all moneys owing by him or her to the Institute, whether for subscription, fee or other amount:

Provided that no suspension shall take effect unless and until it has been accepted by the Board. The Board may decline to accept the suspension of a member to whom a Notice of Disciplinary Action has been issued in accordance with By-law 45(a), or whose conduct, in the opinion of the Board, by virtue of matters brought to the attention of the Institute, may become the subject of professional conduct proceedings under Section 5.

Provided further that any member whose notice of suspension was not received by the Chief Executive Officer prior to 30 June in any year shall remain liable for any subscription, fee or other amount payable by him or her to the Institute in respect of the year ending the following 30 June, save that, in any case, the Board may in its absolute discretion remit the whole or any part of such subscription, fee or other amount.

During the period of a member's suspension, the member shall have none of the privileges or rights of a member.

A member's suspension may be terminated under By-law 20.

Where the Board accepts the voluntary suspension of a member whose conduct, in the opinion of the Board, by virtue of matters brought to the attention of the Institute, may or (if the member had not suspended his membership) may have become the subject of professional conduct proceedings under Section 5, the Institute may report the fact of the member's suspension and the details of such conduct and/or matters, as soon as practicable thereafter in the official publication of the Institute and on the Institute's website.

Section 3 – Examinations

Board to Prescribe Examinations

22. (a) Pursuant to Article 4(g) of the Supplemental Charter, the Board may prescribe examinations as a prerequisite for persons seeking admission to membership of the Institute (except practice entities and persons exempted under By-law 23) together with the educational qualifications for, and other conditions and matters to be satisfied by, persons seeking admission to any examinations conducted by the Institute.

(b) The Board may prescribe as any of the examinations or educational qualifications referred to in By-law 22(a), examinations conducted by any university, public education authority or other institution, whether in the Commonwealth of Australia or elsewhere.

(c) When the Board prescribes examinations conducted by the Institute, it shall also prescribe the subjects for such examinations.

(d) Subject to the By-laws, the Board may from time to time make Regulations for the holding and conduct of the examinations referred to in By-law 22(c) and may, by such Regulations prescribe the periods of service or experience (if any) required of candidates or any class of candidates and the fees payable by them for such examinations.

(e) (Deleted September 2002)

Exemptions from Examination

23. The Board may from time to time prescribe conditions under which exemption may be granted from any examinations or from any part thereof and may prescribe the fee or other amount payable therefor.

24 to 29 (Deleted September 2002)

Section 4 – Rights and Obligations of Members

Place of Business

30. On application for admission to membership, every applicant (being a natural person) shall, in writing under his or her hand inform the Chief Executive Officer of his or her place or principal place of business (whether as a principal or an employee) and the nature of such business and of his or her place of residence and shall thereafter advise the Chief Executive Officer of any change in these particulars.

On application for admission to membership, every applicant (being a practice entity) shall, in writing inform the Chief Executive Officer of its place or principal place of business and the nature of such business and shall thereafter advise the Chief Executive Officer of any change in these particulars.

Enquiries

31. The Board may from time to time require any member to satisfy the Board, in such manner as it requires, whether (in the case of a member being a natural person) he or she is, or is not, in practice as a public accountant or employed by a public accountant or a practice entity or (in the case of a member of any class of membership) whether any particulars regarding the member appearing on the National, Regional or Overseas Registers, as the case may be, are correct.

Certificate

32. (a) On the admission of any member, a certificate in the prescribed form shall, on payment of such fee, if any, as the Board may from time to time prescribe, be issued to such member certifying the member's class of membership.

(b) The certificate shall be under the Seal of the Institute and shall bear the signatures of the President or the Deputy President and of the Chief Executive Officer, which signatures may be printed reproductions, and its issue shall be recorded in a register to be kept for that purpose.

(c) Every such certificate shall remain the property of the Institute and the Board shall be at liberty at any time to call for, and compel, its production and delivery and the Board may alter or amend any such certificate or issue a new certificate in place thereof.

(d) The Board may charge such fee as it may from time to time prescribe for any such new certificate.

(e) Any person ceasing to be a member of the Institute shall, upon demand in writing by the Chief Executive Officer, return the former member's certificate of membership to the Chief Executive Officer for cancellation.

(f) If any member or former member neglects or refuses to deliver up the member's or former member's certificate on demand as aforesaid, the Institute may institute legal or other proceedings for its recovery.

Notification

33. (a) Unless exempted pursuant to the Regulations, every individual member shall before commencing to practise as a public accountant, lodge with the Chief Executive Officer an application for a certificate of public practice.

(b) Unless exempted pursuant to the Regulations, every individual member shall, upon ceasing to practise as a public accountant, forthwith send to the Chief Executive Officer, a notification to this effect.

Certificates of Public Practice

34. (a) A member shall not, without the consent of the Board, practise as a public accountant unless he or she has been issued with a current certificate of public practice or his or her application therefor has been approved or he or she is exempt from the obligation to hold such a certificate.

(b) The Board may prescribe Regulations for the issue and renewal of certificates of public practice and for any exemption from the obligation to hold such a certificate. Without limitation of the foregoing, the Board may prescribe the form of any application for such issue, renewal or exemption, any fee payable in respect thereof, the form and duration of any certificate of public practice and any conditions attaching thereto or to the issue or renewal thereof.

(c) Where a certificate of public practice has been issued or renewed (as the case may be) with attaching conditions and those conditions have not been satisfied within a period (not being less than 30 days) of the member being called upon to satisfy them by notice in writing from the Chief Executive Officer, the certificate of public practice shall, at the expiration of that period, be cancelled and accordingly cease to be a current certificate of public practice in terms of By-law 34(a).

(d) The certificate of public practice of a member upon whom any of the sanctions referred to in By-law 45(g)(i)(1), (2) or (3) has been imposed, shall, subject to any appeal under By-law 46, ipso facto, be cancelled and, accordingly, cease to be a current certificate of public practice in terms of By-law 34(a).

(e) A member whose certificate of public practice has been cancelled or who has otherwise ceased to be entitled to a certificate of public practice, shall, upon payment of the appropriate fee and subject to any conditions imposed by the Board be issued with a further certificate at such time as the Board may in its absolute discretion determine.

Rights at Meetings

35. Members shall be entitled to receive such notice of meetings and to exercise such voting power as is hereinafter prescribed both in relation to Regional meetings and in relation to meetings of members of the Institute. Members who are practice entities or affiliates or candidate members are not entitled to vote at Regional meetings or meetings of members of the Institute.

36. (a) A member of the Institute whose name, address and class of membership are not entered in the National Register shall not be entitled to be served with notice of, or to vote at, any meeting of the members of the Institute; and

(b) A member whose name, address and class of membership are not entered in a Regional Register shall not be entitled to be served with notice of, or to vote at, any meeting of the Regional members of that Region.

Employee members

37. A member in the employment of a public accountant or a practice entity shall not, without the written consent of his or her employer, undertake for remuneration any public accountancy services (as defined in Article 2(f) of the Supplemental Charter).

Liability

38. Any person who, for any reason, ceases to be a member shall nevertheless remain liable for, and shall pay to the Institute, all moneys which at the time of the person's ceasing to be a member were due from the person to the Institute.

Section 5 – Professional Conduct

39. (Deleted May 2004)

40. A member, non-member practice entity or candidate member shall be liable to disciplinary action in any of the following events, whether occurring before or after the coming into operation of these By-laws:

(a) if he, she or it has, in the opinion of either of the Tribunals referred to in By-law 41, failed to observe a proper standard of professional care, skill or competence in the course of carrying out his, her or its professional duties;

(b) if he, she or it has, before any court of law in any jurisdiction in Australia or elsewhere pleaded guilty to, or been found guilty of, any criminal offence which has not been set aside on appeal;

(c) if he, she or it has, in any civil proceedings before any court of law in any jurisdiction in Australia or elsewhere been found to have acted dishonestly and such finding has not been set aside on appeal;

(d) if he, she or it has pleaded guilty to, or been found guilty of, any statutory or other offence by a court of law, professional body, statutory or other regulatory authority in any jurisdiction in Australia or elsewhere which is not a crime but which, in the opinion of either of the Tribunals referred to in By-law 41, brings, or is likely to bring, discredit upon him, her or it, the Institute or the profession of accountancy and any such finding has not been set aside on appeal;

(e) if he, she or it has been the subject of an adverse finding in relation to his, her or its professional or business conduct or competence by any court of law, professional body, royal commission, statutory authority, regulatory authority, statutory body, commission or inquiry in any jurisdiction in Australia or elsewhere;

(f) if he, she or it has committed any breach of the Supplemental Charter, the By-laws or the Regulations (including the Regulations prescribing any ruling on the standards of practice and professional conduct, including the technical standards, required by the Institute to be observed);

(g) if he, she or it has failed to comply with any reasonable and lawful direction of any officer or organ of the Institute acting within the powers conferred by the Institute's Supplemental Charter, the By-laws or the Regulations and which relates to a matter concerning the good order and management of the Institute;

(h) if, in the case of a member (other than a practice entity member) or candidate member, he or she has become a bankrupt or has signed an authority authorising a registered trustee, a solicitor, the Official Trustee, or any other person able to be so authorized, to call a meeting of his or her creditors and/or to take over control of his or her property, or has given a written proposal for a debt agreement to the Official Receiver or any person authorised to receive such a proposal or has executed a personal insolvency agreement or has executed or otherwise entered into any agreement or arrangement, by whatever term called, with his or her creditors.

(i) if, in the case of a practice entity member or non-member practice entity, a resolution for the voluntary winding-up of such practice has been passed by its creditors or a winding-up order has been made in respect of it by a court of law or a compromise or scheme of arrangement between such practice entity and its creditors or a class of creditors has been agreed to or has been approved by a court of law or a receiver has been appointed of it or any of its assets or undertakings, or the practice entity enters into any other form of insolvency administration;

(j) if he, she or it has committed any act, omission or default which, in the opinion of either of the Tribunals referred to in By-law 41 brings, or is likely to bring, discredit upon himself, herself or itself, the Institute or the profession of accountancy.

41. (a) For the implementation of the procedures referred to in this Section, there shall be the following Tribunals:

(i) a Professional Conduct Tribunal appointed by the Board as hereinafter provided; and

(ii) an Appeal Tribunal appointed by the Board as hereinafter provided.

(b) The Professional Conduct Tribunal shall consist of not less than 20 natural persons comprised of:

(i) individual members of at least 10 years' standing; and

(ii) at least one non-accountant.

Such Tribunal shall not include any member of the Appeal Tribunal.

Not less than 4 members of the Professional Conduct Tribunal, a majority of whom shall be members of the Institute, and of whom at least one shall be a non-accountant, shall hear and determine any matter brought before it in accordance with the By-laws and shall exercise the powers and functions of such Tribunal.

(c) The Appeal Tribunal shall consist of not less than 6 natural persons comprised of:

(i) individual members of at least 10 years' standing who have served on the Professional Conduct Tribunal or are otherwise well acquainted with the Institute's professional conduct procedures; and

(ii) at least one non-accountant.

Such Tribunal shall not include any member of the Professional Conduct Tribunal.

Not less than 5 members of the Appeal Tribunal, a majority of whom shall be members of the Institute, and of whom at least one shall be a non-accountant, shall hear and determine any matter brought before it in accordance with the By-laws and shall exercise the powers and functions of such Tribunal.

42. Subject to the provisions of the Supplemental Charter and the By-laws the Professional Conduct Tribunal and the Appeal Tribunal may regulate their own procedures as they think fit including whether or not to hear any witness or admit any material and without giving any reason therefor. Without limiting the generality of the foregoing, each such Tribunal may, if it thinks fit:

(a) require the production for inspection by the Tribunal or any person appointed by it for such purpose, of any books, documents or papers in the possession or under the control of the member, non-member practice entity or candidate member whose conduct is the subject of a Notice of Disciplinary Action or in the possession or under the control of any other member, non-member practice entity or candidate member;

(b) require the member, non-member practice entity or candidate member whose conduct is the subject of a Notice of Disciplinary Action or any other member, non-member practice entity or candidate member, to provide all such information in relation to any such books, documents or papers or on any related matter as may reasonably be required by the Tribunal or by the person appointed for such purpose;

(c) require any member, non-member practice entity or candidate member other than any member, non-member practice entity or candidate member whose conduct is the subject of a Notice of Disciplinary Action to attend before the Tribunal and give evidence of any facts within his, her or its knowledge which relate to any Notice of Disciplinary Action against any member, non-member practice entity or candidate member;

(d) proceed with a hearing in the absence of a member, non-member practice entity or candidate member, where such member, non-member practice entity or candidate member, after being given notice to attend the hearing, fails without good cause to attend the hearing or, in the case of a practice entity, to be represented at the hearing.

43. (a) Any complaint made by a member of the Institute or by a member of the public concerning the conduct of a member, a non-member practice entity or a candidate member, shall be made to the Chief Executive Officer.

(b) On receipt of a complaint the Chief Executive Officer shall investigate the complaint and determine whether the matter should be referred to the Professional Conduct Tribunal.

(c) Where information comes to the attention of the Chief Executive Officer, which he or she considers may require consideration by the Professional Conduct Tribunal, he or she shall investigate the matter and determine whether the matter should be referred to the Professional Conduct Tribunal.

(d) Where the Chief Executive Officer commences an investigation under By-law 43(b) or (c) he or she shall be entitled in his or her absolute discretion to publicise the fact that an investigation is taking place, and to publicise the outcome of such investigation.

(e) Each complaint shall be in writing and shall, if the Chief Executive Officer so requires, be supported by such evidence, particulars or material as he or she considers necessary.

(f) (Deleted May 2004)

44. (a) The Chief Executive Officer, in investigating whether or not a matter should be referred to the Professional Conduct Tribunal, shall have the power to:

(i) undertake, or appoint any person or persons to undertake, whatever inquiries are deemed necessary provided that such person shall not thereafter be a member of the Tribunals referred to in By-law 41 formed to hear the particular matter being inquired into;

(ii) require the production of any books, documents or papers in the possession or under the control of the member, non-member practice entity or candidate member whose conduct is the subject of investigation or in the possession or under the control of any other member, non-member practice entity or candidate member;

(iii) require the member, non-member practice entity or candidate member whose conduct is being investigated or any other member, non-member practice entity or candidate member, to give all such information in relation to any such books, documents or papers or on any related matter as may reasonably be required by the Chief Executive Officer or by the person or persons he or she appoints for such purpose.

(b) If a complaint made by a member of the Institute or by a member of the public is subsequently withdrawn by the person who made it, the Chief Executive Officer may, in his or her sole discretion at any time prior to the commencement of the hearing by the Professional Conduct Tribunal determine that no further action be taken.

(c) If the Chief Executive Officer decides to refer a matter to the Professional Conduct Tribunal, he or she shall refer the matter to the Professional Conduct Tribunal together with all supporting material.

45. Where a complaint or matter is referred to the Professional Conduct Tribunal:

(a) The Chief Executive Officer shall give to the member, non-member practice entity or candidate member concerned:

(i) a Notice of Disciplinary Action setting out the alleged breaches or circumstances as referred to in By-law 40 and any particulars or materials in support; and

(ii) not less than 21 days notice of the date, time and place of the hearing before the Professional Conduct Tribunal.

(aa) The Chief Executive Officer may withdraw a Notice of Disciplinary Action at any time.

(ab) The Chief Executive Officer may amend a Notice of Disciplinary Action at any time, provided that he or she may not do so less than 21 days before the hearing, without the consent of the member, non-member practice entity or candidate member concerned.

(b) The member, non-member practice entity or candidate member receiving a Notice of Disciplinary Action or an amended Notice of Disciplinary Action shall not later than 7 days before the date of the hearing, provide in writing to the Chief Executive Officer:

(i) notice as to whether he, she or it will attend the hearing and, if represented, by whom;

(ii) a Statement of Defence to the Notice of Disciplinary Action;

(iii) the names of any witnesses he, she or it intends to call on his, her or its own behalf or whom he, she or it requires to attend the hearing; and

(iv) notice of any relevant fact or circumstance he, she or it wishes to bring to the attention of the Professional Conduct Tribunal.

Failure to comply with any or all of the above requirements shall not preclude the Professional Conduct Tribunal from proceeding to hear a Notice of Disciplinary Action at the appointed time.

(c) The Chief Executive Officer shall appoint a person or persons to present the case on behalf of the Institute.

(d) The Chief Executive Officer shall have the power to require any member, candidate member or representative of a practice entity (whether a practice entity member or a non-member practice entity) to attend and give evidence at the Professional Conduct Tribunal hearing.

(e) The Professional Conduct Tribunal shall give the member, affiliate, practice entity or candidate member concerned or his, her or its representative a reasonable opportunity of being heard and shall give due consideration to any material he, she or it may submit.

(f) The Professional Conduct Tribunal shall determine whether or not the allegations contained in the Notice of Disciplinary Action, or any part thereof, are established.

(g) If the Professional Conduct Tribunal makes a determination that the allegations contained in the Notice of Disciplinary Action, or any part thereof, are established, it may, having given the member, practice entity or candidate member a reasonable opportunity of being heard on the question of sanctions, impose any one or more of the following sanctions, namely:

(i) In the case of an individual member:

(1) exclusion from membership;

(2) cancellation of membership of the Institute for any period not exceeding 5 years with eligibility for re-instatement to membership on such terms and conditions as the Professional Conduct Tribunal may prescribe and on producing satisfactory evidence that during the period of suspension he or she has maintained his or her professional competence as required from time to time by the Regulations;

(3) cancellation of certificate of public practice;

(4) a declaration that the member is ineligible for a certificate of public practice for a period not exceeding 5 years and on such terms and conditions as to the

earlier termination of such period of ineligibility as the Professional Conduct Tribunal may prescribe;

(5) a fine of an amount not exceeding $100,000;

(6) a severe reprimand;

(7) a reprimand;

(8) a direction that the member obtains such advice relating to the conduct of his or her practice as the Professional Conduct Tribunal may prescribe;

(9) a direction that the member attend such continuing professional education course or courses as the Professional Conduct Tribunal may specify;

(10) a direction for payment of all or any portion of the costs and expenses incurred by the Institute in dealing with the Notice of Disciplinary Action.

(ii) In the case of an affiliate:

(1) exclusion from membership

(2) a fine not exceeding $100,000;

(3) a severe reprimand;

(4) a reprimand;

(5) a direction that the affiliate obtain such advice relating to the conduct of his or her practice as the Professional Conduct Tribunal may from time to time prescribe;

(6) a direction for payment of all or any portion of the costs and expenses incurred by the Institute in dealing with the Notice of Disciplinary Action.

(iii) In the case of a practice entity member, any one or more of the sanctions provided for an affiliate in By-laws 45(g)(ii)(1), (2), (3), (4), (5) and (6).

(iv) In the case of a non-member practice entity, any one or more of the sanctions provided for an affiliate in By-laws 45(g)(ii)(2), (3), (4), (5) and (6).

(v) In the case of a candidate member:

(1) a declaration that the candidate member is unfit to remain a candidate member;

(2) a declaration that the candidate member is ineligible for any period not exceeding 2 years to sit for any examination or examinations conducted by the Institute specified in such declaration;

(3) a declaration that the candidate member is disqualified from any examination or examinations of the Institute specified in such declaration;

(4) a declaration that the candidate member is ineligible to apply for membership for a period to be specified by the Professional Conduct Tribunal on such terms and conditions as to the earlier termination of such period of ineligibility as the Professional Conduct Tribunal may prescribe;

(5) a severe reprimand;

(6) a reprimand;

(7) a direction for payment of all or any portion of the costs and expenses incurred by the Institute in dealing with the Notice of Disciplinary Action.

(h) Notwithstanding that the Professional Conduct Tribunal determines that the allegations contained in a Notice of Disciplinary Action, or any part thereof, against the member, non-member practice entity or candidate member, are established, it may, at its discretion, not impose any sanctions.

(ha) If the Professional Conduct Tribunal determines that the allegations contained in the Notice of Disciplinary Action, or any part thereof, have or have not been established, it may give reasons for its determination, for any sanction which it imposes under By-law 45(g), and for any election under By-law 45(h) not to impose any sanctions.

(i) Notice in writing of the Professional Conduct Tribunal's determination and any sanction imposed (or of its election under By-law 45(h) not to impose any sanction), and of any reasons which the Tribunal has given for the determination and sanction (or exercise if its discretion under By-law 45(h) not to impose any sanction), shall be given by the Chief Executive Officer to the member, non-member practice entity or candidate member. Such notice shall also be given to the President.

(j) Unless notice of appeal is given in accordance with By-law 46(a) or (b), the determination and any sanction imposed by the Professional Conduct Tribunal (or the fact that it has elected under By-law 45(h) not to impose any sanction), and any reasons which the Tribunal has given for the determination and sanction (or exercise if its discretion under By-law 45(h) not to impose any sanction) shall be notified as follows:

  (i) in the case of a complaint made by a member of the Institute or a member of the public, to such member or member of the public;

  (ii) (Deleted May 2004)

  (iii) to the Board;

  (iv) to such other professional bodies and regulatory authorities as determined by the Professional Conduct Tribunal.

46. (a) Any member, non-member practice entity or candidate member against whom any determination has been made or upon whom any sanction has been imposed by the Professional Conduct Tribunal may, within 21 days after notice of such determination and sanction (or exercise of its discretion under By-law 45(h) not to impose any sanction) and of any reasons which the Tribunal has given for the determination and sanction (or exercise of its discretion under By-law 45(h) not to impose any sanction) being received, or in the ordinary course of post, would have been received by him, her or it, give notice of appeal to the Chief Executive Officer against any such determination or sanction or both. At the discretion of the Institute's President or failing him or her the Deputy President, later notice may be accepted. Each notice of appeal shall state the grounds of appeal and the grounds so stated shall not thereafter be amended except with the approval of the Appeal Tribunal.

(b) The President, or failing him or her the Deputy President, may, within 21 days after a determination has been made or a sanction imposed by the Professional Conduct Tribunal against a member, non-member practice entity or candidate member give notice of appeal to the Chief Executive Officer against any such determination or sanction, or both.

(c) As soon as practicable after receipt of a notice of appeal the Chief Executive Officer shall give to the member, non-member practice entity or candidate member not less than 21 days' notice of the date, time and place fixed for the hearing of the appeal. The Appeal Tribunal shall give the member, non-member practice entity or candidate member or his, her or its representative a reasonable opportunity of being heard.

(d) The member, non-member practice entity or candidate member appearing shall not later than 7 days before the date of the hearing provide in writing to the Chief Executive Officer:

  (i) notice as to whether he, she or it will attend the hearing and, if represented, by whom;

  (ii) the names of any witnesses he, she or it intends to call on his, her or its own behalf or whom he, she or it requires to attend the hearing; and

  (iii) notice of any relevant fact or circumstance he, she or it wishes to bring to the attention of the Professional Conduct Tribunal.

(e) The Chief Executive Officer shall appoint a person or persons to represent the Institute on the appeal.

(f) The Chief Executive Officer shall have the power to require any member (not being a practice entity member), candidate member or representative of a practice entity (whether a practice entity member or a non-member practice entity) to attend and give evidence at the Appeal Tribunal hearing.

(g) On each appeal the Appeal Tribunal shall have regard only to the material presented to the Professional Conduct Tribunal. At its discretion the Appeal Tribunal may hear any witness who appeared before the Professional Conduct Tribunal and receive additional material relevant to the complaint.

(h) On each appeal the Appeal Tribunal may affirm, vary or set aside any determination of the Professional Conduct Tribunal and may affirm, increase, reduce or set aside any sanction imposed and may impose any additional sanction or sanctions. The Appeal Tribunal may give reasons for its determination, for any increased or reduced sanctions, and for any additional sanctions imposed. A determination of the Appeal Tribunal shall take effect as from the date thereof unless some other date (not being earlier than the date of the determination or sanction appealed against) shall be specified in the determination. Notice in writing of any determination of the Appeal Tribunal, and of any reasons which the Appeal Tribunal has given for its determination and for any increased, reduced or additional sanction, shall, as soon as practicable, be given by the Chief Executive Officer to the member, non-member practice entity or candidate member and be notified as follows:

(i) in the case of a complaint made by a member of the Institute or a member of the public, such member or member of the public;

(ii) (Deleted May 2004)

(iii) the Board;

(iv) the Professional Conduct Tribunal;

(v) such other professional bodies and regulatory authorities as determined by the Appeal Tribunal.

47. (a) When any determination has been made against a member, non-member practice entity or candidate member by the Professional Conduct Tribunal, unless notice of appeal is duly given as provided in these By-laws and not subsequently withdrawn, the determination and any sanction imposed (or the fact of the Tribunal's election under By-law 45(h) not to impose any sanction), and any reasons which the Tribunal has given for the determination and sanction (or exercise of its discretion under By-law 45(h) not to impose any sanction), shall be reported in the official publication of the Institute and on the Institute's website.

(b) In the event of the Appeal Tribunal affirming or varying or setting aside any determination of the Professional Conduct Tribunal, or affirming, increasing, reducing or setting aside any sanction imposed by the Professional Conduct Tribunal, or imposing any additional sanction or sanctions, the determination of the Appeal Tribunal, any sanction imposed, and any reasons which the Appeal Tribunal has given for the determination and/or for any sanction imposed or which the Professional Conduct Tribunal has given for any determination and/or sanction (which has been affirmed by the Appeal Tribunal) or for the exercise of its discretion under By-law 45(h) not to impose any sanction, shall be reported as soon as practicable thereafter in the official publication of the Institute and on the Institute's website.

(c) Each report published as aforesaid shall include the name of the member, non-member practice entity or candidate member.

48. Where the Professional Conduct Tribunal or the Appeal Tribunal determines in favour of a member, non-member practice entity or candidate member, the determination may be published in such manner and form as may be authorised by the relevant Tribunal.

49. In the event of the name of a member being removed from the register, the member's certificate of membership and any certificate of public practice then held by the member shall be delivered up by the member to the Chief Executive Officer to be cancelled.

50. Where the matter to be heard relates to a member of either of the Tribunals referred to in By-law 41 or against a practice entity which employs that member or a practice entity in which that member has any interest or against any partner, officer, shareholder or employee of that same practice entity, that member shall not serve on the Tribunal which hears the matter.

51. Each of Tribunals referred to in By-law 41 may, on such terms as it thinks fit, authorise payment of the travelling and other out of pocket expenses, or any part thereof, of the member, non-member practice entity or candidate member whose conduct is the subject of a Notice of Disciplinary Action or of any witness or other person who has attended a meeting of such Tribunal convened for the hearing of a complaint against such member, affiliate, practice entity or candidate member.

Section 6 – Fees and Subscriptions

Prescription of Fees

52. (a) Every natural person and practice entity applying for admission (including advancement in status), and every member (other than a Life Member or an Honorary Member), shall pay such subscriptions, fees and other amounts as may be prescribed from time to time under the Regulations.

(b) Every non-member practice entity and candidate member shall pay such subscriptions, fees and other amounts as may be prescribed from time to time under the Regulations.

(c) (Deleted March 2009)

53. (Deleted March 2009)

Annual Subscriptions

54. (a) Annual subscriptions shall cover the period 1 July to 30 June and shall be payable in advance on 1 July in each year.

(b) (Deleted September 2002)

Disability

55. Should any individual member be disabled through ill-health or other sufficient cause from continuing to practice his profession, the Board may reduce or remit his or her annual subscription and other fee or amount payable by him or her from time to time and may also remit any arrears of subscription and other fee or amount due from that member.

Section 7 - Meetings of Members

Meetings of Regional members

56. Each Regional Council shall convene an annual general meeting of members enrolled on the Regional Register of that Region under By-laws 142 and 143 in the month of October in each year or in such other month as the Board may determine. Such meetings shall be called ordinary general Regional meetings.

57. Any Regional Council may, whenever it thinks fit and shall upon a requisition made in writing by 20 of such members, convene a special meeting of such members. Such meetings shall be called special general Regional meetings.

58. At every ordinary or special general Regional meeting the Regional Chair shall take the chair. If the office of Regional Chair is vacant or if the Regional Chair is not present at the time appointed for the meeting, the Vice-Chair of the Regional Council shall take the chair. If neither the Regional Chair nor the Vice-Chair is present, the members present shall choose one of their number to act as chair.

Meetings of members of Institute

59. The Board shall convene an annual general meeting of members of the Institute in the month of October in each year or in such other month as the Board may determine, provided that not more than 15 months shall elapse between 2 successive annual general meetings. Such meetings shall be called ordinary general Institute meetings.

60. The Board may, whenever it thinks fit and shall upon a requisition made in writing by 200 members entitled to vote, convene a special meeting of members of the Institute. Such meetings shall be called special general Institute meetings.

61. At every ordinary or special general Institute meeting the President shall take the chair.

If the office of President is vacant or if the President is not present at the time appointed for the meeting, the Deputy President shall take the chair. If neither the President nor the Deputy President is present, the individual members present shall choose one of their number to act as chair.

Meetings Generally

62. The succeeding By-laws in this Section shall apply to ordinary and special general Regional meetings and to ordinary and special general Institute meetings (except where otherwise provided therein). References therein to ordinary general meetings shall apply to ordinary general Regional meetings and ordinary general Institute meetings. References therein to special general meetings shall apply to special general Regional meetings and special general Institute meetings. References therein to meetings shall apply to any of such meetings and references therein to members, office bearers, officers and offices shall be taken to refer to those of a Region or of the Institute as the case may require.

63. Any requisition for a special general meeting shall specify the object of the meeting required and shall be signed by the members making the same and shall be deposited at the office. It may consist of several documents in like form each signed by one or more of the requisitionists. The meeting shall be convened for the purposes specified in the requisition and, if convened otherwise than by the Board or Regional Council as the case may be, for those purposes only.

64. (a) If the Board or Regional Council as the case may be within 30 days after the deposit of a requisition fails to convene a special general meeting to be held within 60 days after such deposit, the requisitionists may themselves convene a meeting to be held at the office or at some other convenient place in the city in which the office is situated within 90 days after such deposit.

(b) Any meeting convened under this By-law by the requisitionists shall be convened as nearly as possible in the same manner as that in which meetings are convened by the Board or Regional Council as the case may be.

65. (a) Subject to By-law 65(b), 21 days' notice specifying the place, day and hour of meeting and, in case of special business, the general nature of such business, shall be given of every meeting by notice served in accordance with By-law 149(a) on each member entitled to receive notices of meetings. Provided that where notice of any motion or business is accepted by the Chief Executive Officer or Regional General Manager pursuant to By-law 68 less than 30 days before the date of an ordinary general meeting, such notice shall be given to members entitled to receive notices of meetings of the proposed motion as the Board or Regional Council as the case may be shall deem fit and, in its discretion, the Board or Regional Council as the case may be may dispense with any such notice.

(b) With the consent in writing of two-thirds of the Directors or members of the Regional Council, as the case may be, a meeting (other than a meeting convened to consider the rescission or variation of or addition to the By-laws, or amendments or additions to the Supplemental Charter) may be convened by shorter notice and in any manner they think fit.

66. The accidental omission to give any notice or to send any voting paper to any member, or the non-receipt of any notice or voting paper by any member, shall not invalidate any resolution passed, any election held or other proceeding taken at any meeting.

67. The ordinary business of an ordinary general Institute meeting shall be to receive and consider the annual report of the Board, the general purpose financial report, and the report of the auditor, and to appoint an auditor. The ordinary business of an ordinary general Regional meeting shall be to receive and consider the reports of the Regional Council. All other business at an ordinary general meeting and all business at a special general meeting shall be deemed special.

68. A member or members entitled to vote wishing to bring before a meeting any motion or business not relating to the ordinary business of the meeting may only do so if 10 or more members give notice thereof in writing to the Board or Regional Council as the case may be, such notice to be in the hands of the Chief Executive Officer or Regional General Manager

as the case may be, not later than 60 days before the date fixed for such meeting, provided that the Chief Executive Officer or Regional General Manager as the case may be may, in his or her discretion, accept such notices up to 21 days before the date fixed for such meeting.

69. No motion or business shall be entertained or transacted at any meeting unless notice thereof has been properly given or dispensed with or unless the same shall, in the opinion of a majority of members personally present and entitled to vote, directly arise out of the motion or business properly before the meeting.

70. (a) 10 members personally present and entitled to vote shall constitute a quorum at an ordinary or special general meeting for the choice of a chair, the adjournment of a meeting, the reception and consideration of the annual report of the Board, the general purpose financial report, and the report of the auditor, and for the reception of the chair's declaration of the appointment of the auditor if one nomination only has been received for this office.

(b) In all other cases, 15 members personally present and entitled to vote shall constitute a quorum.

71. Subject to By-law 72, no business shall be transacted at any meeting unless the quorum requisite for such business shall be present at the commencement of the business.

72. If, within half an hour from the time appointed for a meeting a quorum is not present, the meeting, if convened upon such requisition as aforesaid, shall lapse. In any other case it shall stand adjourned to the next day at the same time and place and if, at such adjourned meeting, a quorum is not present, those members who are present shall be competent to transact the business for which the meeting was called.

Voting

73. Subject to By-law 74(a), at any meeting questions or resolutions which are submitted to the meeting for determination shall be decided in the first instance, by a show of hands.

74. (a) Except on a motion for adjournment or for the election of a chair, either the chair of the meeting or 10 members personally present and entitled to vote at such meeting may demand a poll.

(b) A poll shall be taken at the meeting in such manner as the chair of the meeting directs and the result of the poll shall be deemed to be the resolution of the meeting at which the poll was demanded.

(c) On a voting by show of hands or on a poll a chair shall be entitled to vote as a member, but shall have no additional or casting vote, and in all cases where there is an equality of votes, the question or resolution submitted to the meeting shall be deemed to have lapsed.

75. At any meeting, unless a poll is demanded, a declaration by the chair that a resolution has been carried or lost and an entry to that effect in the minute book shall be conclusive evidence of the fact without proof of the number or proportion of the votes recorded in favour of or against the resolution.

76. The chair of a meeting may, with the consent of the meeting, adjourn the same from time to time and place to place but no business shall be transacted at any adjourned meeting other than the business left unfinished at the meeting from which the adjournment took place unless, in the opinion of a majority of the members personally present and entitled to vote, the same shall directly arise thereat.

77. The demand for a poll shall not prevent the continuance of a meeting for the transaction of any business other than the question on which a poll has been demanded.

78. (a) The Board may at any time resolve that, in lieu of submitting a proposal to a meeting, it shall submit a resolution or resolutions to individual members by means of a postal or postal and electronic ballot which ballot shall be conducted as nearly as practicable in the manner set forth in this By-law.

(b) The Board shall appoint 5 members to be scrutineers, at least 3 of whom shall act as such.

(c) The Board shall set out the resolution or resolutions proposed by it in a notice to individual members and shall cause the notice and voting papers setting out the resolution or resolutions and containing full directions as to the method of voting to be posted or emailed (in the case of members who have advised the Institute of their email address) to all members who would have been entitled, if present, to vote at a meeting held on the day of the posting or emailing of the said notice and voting papers. Such notice and voting papers shall be sent to each such member in accordance with By-law 149(a).

(d) All members entitled to vote and wishing to vote on the resolution or (if there be more than one resolution) on any resolution, must do so by voting in the manner indicated in the directions and by posting the voting papers to the Institute or by voting online (in the case of members who have received the notice by email) in either case in accordance with the directions in the voting papers, so as to be received by the scrutineers not later than 21 days after the date of the notice from the Institute.

(e) Within 7 days after the last day upon which votes can be received under By-law 78(d), the scrutineers or at least 3 of them shall meet and examine the voting papers or voting papers and online votes.

(f) The voting papers and online votes may be examined either before or at such meeting of the scrutineers but may only be examined in the presence of at least one of the scrutineers. The scrutineers shall reject the vote of any member who at the date of such meeting was in arrears for more than 3 months in payment of any subscription, fee or other amount payable by him or her to the Institute or who has failed to observe the directions mentioned in By-law 78(c) (unless in their opinion he or she has clearly indicated the way in which he or she wishes to vote) and they may reject any other vote which, in their view, ought properly to be rejected. The scrutineers shall, as soon as practicable, report the result of the voting to the Chief Executive Officer and shall include in such report a statement of the number of votes rejected by them and the reasons for such rejection. The Chief Executive Officer shall arrange for the result of the postal or postal and electronic ballot to be given to members within a reasonable time after the receipt of such report, whether by publication in the Institute's journal or otherwise. The report of the scrutineers as to the result of the voting shall be conclusive. A resolution passed by such ballot shall have the same force and effect as if it were a resolution passed at a meeting of members held on the date of the report of the scrutineers.

(g) (Deleted August 2007)

79. (a) On a show of hands, every member personally present and entitled to vote shall have one vote.

(b) Upon a poll every member who is entitled to vote shall have one vote.

(c) Upon a postal ballot every member who is entitled to vote shall have one vote.

(d) Honorary members shall not be entitled to a vote.

(e) Affiliate members shall not be entitled to a vote.

(f) Practice entity members shall not be entitled to a vote.

(g) Candidate members shall not be entitled to a vote.

80. Votes on a poll may be given either personally or by attorney or proxy.

81. No person shall vote as attorney under power or as proxy who is not a member of the Institute and entitled to vote.

82. The instrument appointing a proxy or the power of attorney (if any) under which any proxy paper is signed or under which an attorney proposes to vote shall be deposited for verification with the Chief Executive Officer at the office not less than 48 hours before the time for holding the meeting or adjourned meeting (as the case may be) at which the proxy or attorney proposes to vote but no instrument appointing a proxy shall be valid after the expiration of 12 months from the date of its execution.

83. A vote given in accordance with the terms of a power of attorney or instrument of proxy shall be valid notwithstanding the previous death of the principal or revocation of the power of attorney or proxy, provided no intimation in writing of the death or revocation shall have been received at the office before the meeting.

84. Every instrument of proxy, whether for a specified meeting or otherwise, shall be in writing and as nearly as circumstances admit shall be in the form authorised by the Board under By-law 4. Instruments of proxy may be deposited with, or faxed or emailed to, or lodged electronically with, the Chief Executive Officer, in accordance with any directions in the applicable notice or voting paper issued by the Board or Regional Council.

85. A member shall not be entitled to be present or to vote on any question personally or by attorney or by proxy or as attorney or proxy for another member at any meeting or on any postal vote or to be reckoned in a quorum whilst he is in arrears for more than 3 months in payment of any subscription, fee or other amount payable by him or her to the Institute.

86. Unless he or she indicates to the contrary, a member voting shall be deemed to have voted for himself or herself and for all other members whose attorney or proxy he or she is but a member may cast separate votes for himself or herself and any such other member.

Section 8 - Regional Councils

87. (a) In addition to the Board there shall be, in each Region, Regional Council.

(b) Each Regional Council shall have such powers and duties as are prescribed by the By-laws or as may be prescribed from time to time by the Board.

Composition and term

88. (a) Each Regional Council shall comprise 6 members elected directly by the members of the Region provided that the Board may if so requested by a Regional Council from time to time, approve a Regional Council of 9 members, for such period as may be prescribed by the Board, provided that such approval will not be unreasonably withheld.

(b) Subject to By-laws 92, 93 and 95, the Regional Councillors will hold office for a term of 3 years from the 1 January immediately following their election, but will be eligible for re-election for further terms of 3 years in accordance with these By-laws.

89. (Deleted July 2000)

Eligibility for membership

90. (a) No member shall be eligible to be elected a Regional Councillor whilst he or she is in arrears in payment of any subscription, fee or other amount payable by him or her to the Institute and unless he or she is resident in and enrolled on the Regional Register of that Region under By-laws 142 and 143.

(b) No affiliate or practice entity member or candidate member shall be eligible to be elected a Regional Councillor.

91. (Deleted August 2007)

Rotation

92. One-third of the Regional Councillors for each Region shall retire from office each year, with effect as of 31 December in that year, but the retiring Councillors shall be eligible for re-election.

93. The Regional Councillors so retiring shall be those longest in office. As between 2 or more who have been in office an equal length of time, the Regional Councillors who retire shall, in default of agreement, be determined by lot.

94. (Deleted July 2000)

95. At each ordinary general Regional meeting eligible members shall be elected to fill all vacancies on the Regional Council occurring in terms of the By-laws.

Election

96. Subject to By-law 96A, the election of Regional Councillors shall be at an ordinary general Regional meeting and shall be conducted in accordance with the Regulations and procedures prescribed by the Board from time to time. Without limiting the generality of the foregoing:

(a) If the requisite number of candidates is nominated, the chair shall, at the meeting, declare them duly elected.

(b) If fewer than the requisite number of candidates are nominated, it shall be competent for the meeting, by resolution, to receive nominations for the number of places in excess of those for which nominations have been received and proceed to election in such manner as the chair directs.

96A. If more than the requisite number of candidates are nominated, a postal ballot or (at the election of the Board) postal and electronic ballot shall be conducted in accordance with the Regulations and the procedures prescribed by the Board from time to time.

Vacancies

97. In the event of any casual vacancy occurring in any Regional Council, the vacancy may be filled by the remaining Regional Councillors appointing an eligible member of the Institute to fill the vacancy but the member so appointed shall hold office only during the period for which the vacating Regional Councillor would have held office if no vacancy had occurred.

98. The continuing Regional Councillors may act notwithstanding any vacancy in a Regional Council, provided that, if the number of continuing Regional Councillors at any time is less than the quorum fixed for that Regional Council, such continuing Regional Councillors may act, but only for the purpose of filling the vacancies.

99. (Deleted July 2000)

Disqualification

100. The office of a Regional Councillor shall be vacated if he or she:

(a) dies or resigns that office by resignation in writing to that Regional Council;

(b) ceases to be a member of the Institute or any one of the sanctions referred to in By-laws 45(g)(i)(1) to (4) is imposed upon him or her;

(c) ceases to be enrolled on the Regional Register of that Region under By-laws 142 and 143;

(d) is absent from 2 or more consecutive ordinary meetings of the Regional Council without the leave of that Council and that Council resolves that his or her office be vacated;

(e) becomes liable to be excluded from membership under By-law 21(a);

(f) voluntarily suspends his or her membership under By-law 21A.

Meetings

101. The Regional Councils shall meet at such places and at such times as they may respectively determine.

101A. A Regional Council meeting may be held by conference telephone or videoconference technology or by using any other technology consented to by all the Regional Councillors for that Region which enables all participants to hear and participate in the proceedings. If a Regional Councillor is unable to attend a Regional Council meeting in person, he or she may, if a majority of the other Regional Councillors present at that or a previous meeting consent, participate in the meeting by telephone or any other technology approved by the other Regional Councillors. A Regional Councillor participating in such a Regional Council meeting, or so participating in a Regional Council meeting, will be deemed to have been present at the meeting and to have formed part of a quorum until the close of the meeting or until his or her link to the meeting is earlier disconnected. If any Regional Councillor so participating in a meeting intends to leave the meeting, or disconnect his or her link to it, prior to the close of the meeting, he or she must announce his or her intention to do so to the chair.

Notice

102. Notice of every meeting of a Regional Council shall be served in accordance with By-law 149 on each Regional Councillor, with the period of such notice being that approved by the Board from time to time.

Office Bearers

103. Within 60 days after each ordinary general Regional meeting, but not later than 31 December, the members who will be the Regional Councillors for that Region in the ensuing calendar year will meet and nominate from among their number, the proposed Chair and Vice-Chair for the ensuing calendar year.

103A. Each Regional Council shall as soon as practicable after 1 January in each year, appoint from among its Regional Councillors, a Chair and a Vice-Chair for that calendar year.

104. (Deleted July 2000)

Role and Powers of Regional Councils

104A. The role of Regional Council is to:

(a) provide advice to the Board on strategic policy and member issues;

(b) act as a link between the Board and the members in its Region;

(c) assist the Board in raising and maintaining the public profile of the Institute in its Region, including its profile with the relevant State and/or Territory governments; and

(d) implement in its Region, processes designed to attract and retain suitable Regional Council members.

105. Subject to the provisions of the Supplemental Charter and the By-laws, the Regional Councils shall have such powers and duties as may from time to time be specified or approved by the Board.

Committees

106. (a) Subject to the provisions of the Supplemental Charter and the By-laws, Regional Council may appoint committees (including branch committees) which may include persons other than Regional Councillors or members of the Institute and may:

(i) fix the quorum for such committees;

(ii) delegate any of its powers to any such committee; and

(iii) lay down rules for regulating the proceedings of such committees.

(b) By virtue of their offices, the Chair and Vice-Chair of Regional Council shall be members of all committees appointed by that Regional Council.

Section 9 – Board

Composition and term

107. (Deleted July 2000)

108. The Board shall comprise:

(a) 7 Directors directly elected by the members enrolled on the Regional Registers in accordance with By-law 108A; and

(b) any directors appointed by the Board under By-law 108C.

108A. In September, October or November each year, the members enrolled on each Regional Register kept under the By-laws shall, by postal ballot or (at the election of the Board) postal and electronic ballot, and in accordance with the Regulations and the procedures prescribed by the Board from time to time, elect a Director (unless and to the extent that the term of the existing Director elected by the members from that Region will continue for the following calendar year). To be so elected as a Director, a person must be an individual member of the Institute entitled to vote, enrolled on the relevant Regional Register, but need not be a member of the relevant Regional Council. The Directors so elected will hold office for a term of 3 years from the immediately following 1 January but will thereafter be eligible for re-election for further terms of 3 years pursuant to this By-law unless, at the time nominations close, the Director is in arrears in payment of any subscription, fee or other amount payable by the Director to the Institute.

108B. (Deleted August 2005)

108C. The Board may, in its discretion at any time, appoint no more than 4 additional Directors and in so doing shall have regard to the following matters:

(a) technical or administrative skills important to the Board;

(b) special or topical experience which may be required by the Board;

(c) under-representation on the Board of significant segments of the members of the Institute;

(d) the availability of potential future office bearers; and

(e) other factors necessary to achieve a balanced and effective Board.

A Director appointed under this by-law:

(f) need not be a member, unless there are at any time 2 non-member Directors who have been appointed under this by-law, in which case any additional Directors appointed under this by-law must be members;

(g) shall, subject to the By-laws, continue in office as a Director for a period of 3 years from the date of his or her appointment;

(h) shall be eligible for reappointment by the Board under this by-law for one further period of 3 years;

(i) may be removed from office by a resolution of the Board passed at a meeting convened with notice of its purpose;

(j) shall be ineligible for appointment as an office bearer of the Institute, if he or she is not a member.

108D. (Deleted August 2007)

Retirement and Removal

108E. A Director may retire from office by giving notice in writing to the Institute of that Director's intention to retire. A notice of resignation takes effect at the time which is the later of:

(a) the time of giving the notice to the Institute; or

(b) the expiration of the period, if any, specified in the notice.

108F. The office of a Director shall become vacant if the Director:

(a) dies, or resigns his or her office by sending his or her resignation in writing to the Board;

(b) becomes disqualified pursuant to the Corporations Act from managing corporations;

(c) is absent from 2 or more consecutive ordinary meetings of the Board without leave of the Board and the Board resolves that his or her office be vacated;

(d) is removed from office by the members at an ordinary or special general Institute meeting convened with notice of its purpose; or

(e) being a member of the Institute:

(i) ceases to be a member; or

(ii) has any one of the sanctions referred to in By-law 45(g)(i)(1) to (4) imposed upon him or her;

(iii) becomes liable to be excluded from membership under By-law 21(a); or

(iv) voluntarily suspends his or her membership under By-law 21A.

109 to 111 (Deleted July 2000)

Casual Vacancies

112. (a) Any casual vacancy occurring in the office of a Director elected pursuant to By-law 108A shall be filled by an individual member nominated by the Regional Council of the Region whose members elected the vacating Director, provided

that if the Regional Council does not fill the vacancy within 28 days after the vacancy occurs, the Board may appoint any member enrolled on the Regional Register of that Region to fill the vacancy.

(b) (Deleted August 2005)

113. The Director appointed to fill any casual vacancy shall hold the office only during the period for which the vacating Director would have held it if no vacancy had occurred.

114. The continuing Directors may act, notwithstanding any vacancy in the Board, provided that, if the number of continuing Directors at any time is less than the quorum fixed by the By-laws, such continuing Directors may act, but only for the purpose of filling the vacancy.

115. (Deleted July 2000)

116. (Deleted July 2000)

117. (Deleted July 2000)

Meetings

118. The Board shall meet at such time or times and at such place or places as it may determine and may regulate its own proceedings.

118A. A Directors' meeting may be held by conference telephone or videoconference technology or by using any other technology consented to by all the Directors which enables all participants to hear and participate in the proceedings. If a Director is unable to attend a Board meeting in person, he or she may, if a majority of the other Directors present at that or a previous meeting consent, participate in the meeting by telephone or any other technology approved by the other Directors. A Director participating in such a Board meeting, or so participating in a Board meeting, will be deemed to have been present at the meeting and to have formed part of a quorum until the close of the meeting or until his or her link to the meeting is earlier disconnected. If any Director so participating in a meeting intends to leave the meeting, or disconnect his or her link to it, prior to the close of the meeting, he or she must announce his or her intention to do so to the chair.

Office Bearers

119. Within 60 days after the declaration of the result of the last to be completed in each year of the postal ballots required by By-law 108A, but no later than 31 December, the members who will be the Directors in the ensuing calendar year shall meet and nominate from among their number, the proposed President and Deputy President for the ensuing calendar year.

119A. The Board shall as soon as practicable after 1 January in each year, appoint from among the Directors, a President and a Deputy President for that calendar year.

119B. The Chief Executive Officer of the Institute shall be appointed from time to time by the Directors.

Duration of Office

120. (a) The offices of President and Deputy President shall be vacated on 31 December in the year in which they are appointed or if the holder of either such office:

(i) dies, or resigns that office by resignation in writing to the Board;

(ii) becomes disqualified pursuant to the Corporations Act from managing corporations;

(iii) is removed from that office by special resolution passed at a special meeting of the Board convened with notice of the purpose;

(iv) ceases to be a Director.

(b) Any casual vacancy in any such offices shall be filled at a meeting of the Board to be held as soon as practicable after the occurrence of the vacancy and notice of the intention to fill such vacancy shall be given to all the Directors.

Convening of Meetings

121. A meeting of the Board may at any time be called by the order of the President or the Deputy President and shall be called by the Chief Executive Officer on receipt of a request in writing addressed to him or her by any 3 Directors.

Notice

122. Notice of every meeting of the Board shall be served in accordance with By-law 149 on each Director, with the period of such notice being that approved by the Board from time to time.

123. The notice shall specify the place, day and hour of meeting and shall contain, as far as practicable, a statement of the general nature of the business to be transacted at the meeting.

124. The accidental omission to give any notice or the non-receipt of any notice so served or the non-existence of any emergency shall not affect the validity of the proceedings at the meeting.

Chair of Meetings

125. At all meetings of the Board the President or, in his or her absence, the Deputy President shall preside. If at any meeting none of these office bearers shall be present at the time appointed for holding the same, the Directors present shall choose one of their number to be chair of that meeting.

Quorum and Voting

126. Subject to the requirements of the Supplemental Charter or the By-laws as to a special quorum in certain circumstances or as to a special majority:

(a) one half of the total number of the Directors plus one (or if that number is a fraction, the next highest whole number) shall constitute a quorum; and

(b) any question or resolution submitted to any meeting of the Board for determination shall be decided by a majority of votes of the Directors then present either in person or by proxy provided by the absent Director to another Director who is present in person at the meeting.

126A. The Chief Executive Officer is entitled to receive all papers which a Director is entitled to receive, and, unless and to the extent otherwise determined by the Board, to attend all meetings of the Board and fully participate in the discussions of the Board, but is not entitled to vote on any question or resolution before the Board.

127. The chair shall have a deliberative but not a casting vote and, in case of an equality of votes, the question or resolution submitted to the meeting shall be deemed to have lapsed.

Written Resolutions

128. (a) A resolution in writing a copy of which is served on every Director and signed by, or approved by an electronic mail message to the Chief Executive Officer to that effect from, at least three-fifths of those Directors shall (subject as hereinafter mentioned) be as valid and effectual as if it had been duly passed by those Directors at a duly convened Board meeting.

(b) No such resolution shall be valid or effectual if, within 21 days of the date of giving notice of the resolution to every Director in accordance with By-law 149, at least one-fifth of such Directors signify in writing under their hands their objection to the same. All such resolutions and objections shall be recorded in the minute book.

(c) This By-law does not apply to any resolution which, under the Supplemental Charter or the By-laws, is required to be passed by a specified number of Directors present at a meeting or by a specified majority of the Directors voting.

Establishment and Proceedings of Committees

128A. The Board may from time to time appoint such committees as it thinks fit for such purposes and with such powers, authorities and discretions as the Board may from time to time prescribe. Such committees may include persons other than Directors or members of the Institute.

129. Subject to the provisions of the Supplemental Charter and the By-laws, the Board may:

(a) fix the quorum of such committees;

(b) delegate any of its powers to any such committee; and

(c) lay down rules for regulating the proceedings of such committees.

129A. Without limiting the generality of By-law 128A, the Board shall appoint an audit committee to:

(a) ensure an appropriate level of diligence is applied to the review of financial performance, and in particular the annual accounts;

(b) review:

(i) end of financial year statements including general purpose financial report and related disclosures;

(ii) financial and other performance indicators and trends;

(iii) the findings and reports of the auditors;

(iv) risk management procedures; and

(v) extraordinary expenditures or financial issues;

(c) recommend auditors;

(d) address other matters referred by the Board from time to time; and

(e) report findings of the Committee to the Board.

130. (Deleted July 2000)

Sub-committees

131. Any committee formed by the Directors shall, in the exercise of the powers so delegated, comply with any regulations which, from time to time, may be imposed upon it by the Board but, and if and to the extent approved by the Board, and subject to any regulations imposed by the Board and to the provisions of the Supplemental Charter and the By-laws, may sub-delegate its powers to sub-committees.

132. (Deleted July 2000)

Powers of Board

133. In accordance with Article 12 of the Supplemental Charter, the affairs of the Institute shall be managed by or under the direction of the Board and for such purposes the Board shall, inter alia, exercise absolute and exclusive powers (but without prejudice to its right to delegate the same in accordance with the By-laws) in respect of the following:

(a) the receipt, control and disposition of the moneys and other property of the Institute, including all prescribed subscriptions, fees and other amounts payable to the Institute;

(b) the investment of any moneys received by or on behalf of the Institute in such investments as are authorised investments for trustees under the law of any of the States or Territories of the Commonwealth of Australia and also in any shares, stock, units, debentures or other securities of any nature whatsoever listed on any of the Australian or overseas recognised stock exchanges and in deposits through the official or short-term money markets with selected companies from time to time approved for that purpose by the Board, with power from time to time to realise or vary such investments;

(c) the appointment, removal or retirement of the Chief Executive Officer, agents and other officers and employees of the Institute and the remuneration of such persons;

(d) the appointment of solicitors to act for the Institute;

(e) the appointment of trustees to hold in trust for the Institute any property of the Institute;

(f) the institution of legal proceedings in respect of any matter concerning the affairs of the Institute, and the prosecution, defence, compounding or abandoning of any legal proceedings instituted by or against the Institute or against any of its office bearers, officers or employees;

(g) the appointment of bankers to the Institute;

(h) the promotion of improvements in the laws of the Commonwealth of Australia or any State or Territory thereof directly or indirectly affecting the profession of accountancy and the participation in public movements with a view to securing improvements in such laws;

(i) the promulgation of Regulations including, without limitation, Regulations prescribing rulings and providing guidance on the standards of practice and professional conduct, including the technical standards, which the Institute requires to be observed;

(j) the assistance of necessitous cases of members and their families, out of the funds of the Institute under its control.

133A. The Board may from time to time delegate any of its powers and responsibilities to a director or an employee of the Institute or any other person.

134. The Board may, from time to time, provide for the management of the affairs of the Institute at any place out of the Commonwealth of Australia or in any territory of the Commonwealth of Australia or in any special locality in the Commonwealth of Australia in such manner as it thinks fit.

Attorney

135. (a) The Board may, at any time and from time to time, appoint any person under the common seal of the Institute to be the attorney of the Board for such purposes and with such powers, authorities and discretion (not exceeding those vested in or exercisable by the Board under the Supplemental Charter or the By-laws) and for such period and subject to such conditions as the Board may from time to time think fit and the power of attorney may contain such provisions for the protection or convenience of persons dealing with the attorney as the Board thinks fit.

(b) Any such attorney may be authorised by the Board to sub-delegate all or any of the powers, authorities and discretions for the time being vested in him or her.

Power to Borrow

136. The Board may, from time to time, raise or borrow any moneys required for the purposes of the Institute and secure the repayment of the same by any means it thinks fit.

Remuneration of Directors, Reimbursement and Allowances

136A. The remuneration of the Directors shall be determined from time to time by the members of the Institute in general meeting.

137. The Board may pay the expenses incurred by Directors or other persons (whether or not members of the Institute) in attending meetings of the Board or of any committee or sub-committee thereof. The Board may also pay out of the funds of the Institute the expenses reasonably and properly incurred by the President or Deputy President or any other Director when acting in his or her official capacity for and on behalf of the Institute and may determine and pay the amount of any Presidential or other allowance.

Section 10 – Management

Chief Executive Officer and Regional General Managers

138. (a) The Chief Executive Officer shall have the powers and duties prescribed by the By-laws and the Regulations and, with the approval of the Board, may from time to time or at any time delegate all or any of such powers and duties to such person or persons and in such manner as may be so approved.

(b) A Regional General Manager shall have the powers and duties prescribed by the By-laws and the Regulations and, with the approval of the Chief Executive Officer, may from time to time or at any time likewise delegate all or any of such powers and duties.

Office

139. The office of the Institute shall be at such place in the Commonwealth of Australia as the Board may from time to time determine.

Regional Offices

140. Each Regional office shall be at such place in that Region as the Board may from time to time determine.

Minutes

141. (a) The Board and each Regional Council respectively shall cause minutes to be taken for the purpose of recording the proceedings at their meetings and at the meetings of the committees and sub-committees thereof respectively and at all meetings of members of the Institute and Regional meetings.

(b) The minutes of any meeting signed by the chair thereof or by the chair of the succeeding meeting shall be prima facie evidence of the transactions recorded in such minutes.

(c) The Regional General Manager of each Region shall, after every meeting of the Regional Council or of any committee or sub-committee thereof, send to the Chief Executive Officer copies of the minutes of such meetings when they have been approved by the chair thereof.

Registers

142. (a) The National, Regional and Overseas Registers shall be maintained under the control of the Chief Executive Officer and the information contained within the Regional Registers shall be provided to the respective Regional General Managers as and when required so as to enable Regional General Managers to comply with the requirements of these By-laws and otherwise.

(b) There shall be entered in the National Register the names, addresses and classes of membership of all individual members of the Institute; there shall be entered in each Regional Register the names, addresses and classes of membership of all individual members of the Institute whose registered address is in that Region, and there shall be entered in the Overseas Register the names, addresses and classes of membership of all individual members of the Institute whose registered address is outside the Commonwealth of Australia.

(c) Such other particulars shall be entered in the said Registers as the Board may from time to time prescribe.

Registered Address

143. The registered address of a member to be entered in the National Register and the relative Regional or Overseas Register shall be the member's place or principal place of business for the time being or, if a member has no place of business, his or her place of residence for the time being or such other place as the member may advise.

Change of Address

144. Every individual member of the Institute shall forthwith notify the Chief Executive Officer of any change required to be made in his or her registered address for the purpose of the preceding By-law.

Rectification

145. The Board may, if satisfied that any particulars appearing on any Register are incorrect, order their removal and may order that the Register be rectified by making such further or other entries as it deems necessary.

146. The Regional General Manager shall send to the Chief Executive Officer particulars of all information furnished to him or her by Regional members which is relevant for inclusion in the National and Regional Registers.

Evidence

147. Subject to the powers of the Board under By-law 145, the National Register shall be conclusive evidence of the particulars entered therein.

Closing of Registers

148. The National and each Regional Register may be closed for a period not exceeding 7 days immediately preceding the commencement of the period prescribed for service of notice of meetings of members of the Institute or of Regional members or the dispatch of voting papers pursuant to By-law 96(d) (as the case may be) and only those members whose names are entered in the relative Register at the time of such closing shall be entitled to be served with notice of meetings.

Service of Notices

149. (a) Any notice required to be given and any document required or permitted to be served or sent by any of the By-laws or Regulations and any voting paper may be served upon any member or person either personally or by sending it by post or facsimile transmission or electronic mail to him, her or it at his, her or its address as shown in the National Register or which has been notified in writing by the member or person to the Institute. Where a notice, document or voting paper is sent by post, service shall be deemed to be effected by properly addressing and posting an envelope or other package containing the notice, document or voting paper, and to have been made on the day after the date of its posting. Where a notice, document or voting paper is sent by facsimile transmission, service shall be deemed to be effected by properly addressing and transmitting the facsimile transmission and to have been made on the day following its dispatch (provided the sender shall have received a facsimile transmission report which indicates that the facsimile was sent in its entirety to the facsimile number of the addressee). Where a notice, document or voting paper is sent by electronic mail, service shall be deemed to be effected by properly addressing and transmitting the email and to have been made on the day of its transmission (provided the sender has not received an email transmission report which indicates that the email was not transmitted to the email address of the addressee).

(b) The non-receipt of such notice or voting paper shall not invalidate the proceedings of any meeting held in pursuance of such notice or in respect of which such voting paper was to be used.

(c) Where a given number of days' notice or notice extending over any other period is required to be given, the day of service shall, unless it is otherwise provided, be counted in such number of days or other period.

List of members

150. (a) The Board may in each year publish or cause to be published at the expense of the Institute or otherwise a list of the members of the Institute together with such other particulars in respect of the Institute or its objects as it deems advisable.

(b) In such list members may be distinguished in such way as the Board sees fit.

(c) Such list shall be supplied to members and others at such prices or gratuitously as the Board shall from time to time determine.

Bank Accounts

151. All moneys received on account of the Institute by the Board shall be paid forthwith into the bank appointed by the Board to the credit of the account of the Institute.

Records

152. The Board shall cause proper books and records to be kept of the moneys received and expended and accounts showing details of income and expenditure and of the Institute's assets and liabilities.

Accounts

153. The accounts of the Institute shall, unless and until otherwise determined by the Board, be closed annually as at 30 June.

154. The Board shall cause to be prepared for each financial year a general purpose financial report in accordance with Australian accounting standards which gives a true and fair view of the financial performance and position of the Institute. The Board shall cause the general purpose financial report to be audited by the auditor of the Institute not less than 28 days before each ordinary general Institute meeting.

155. Not less than 21 days before the ordinary general Institute meeting, the Board shall cause copies of the annual report of the Board, the general purpose financial report, and of the auditor's report to be:

(a) placed on the Institute's website with a communication to members that copies are available on the website, specifying the direct address on the website where the reports may be accessed; and

(b) posted to each member of the Institute who has so requested.

155A. (Deleted August 2007)

Auditor

156. If there is a vacancy in the office of auditor of the Institute, an auditor shall be elected as the auditor of the Institute by the members entitled to vote at the ordinary general meeting of the Institute.

157. (Deleted September 2002)

158. The auditor shall be an individual member of the Institute but no Director or Regional Councillor shall be eligible for election to the office of auditor.

159. In the event of the auditor being incapable of, or disqualified from, acting or, in the case of an extraordinary vacancy by death, resignation or otherwise, the Board shall appoint another auditor to fill the office until the next ordinary general meeting.

Indemnity

160. (a) Every Director and every Regional Councillor, Chief Executive Officer, and Regional General Manager and other officer of the Institute shall (notwithstanding any irregularity in their appointment) be indemnified by the Institute against, and it shall be the duty of the Board to pay out of the funds of the Institute vested in or under its control, all costs, losses and expenses which any such Director, Regional Councillor, Chief Executive Officer, Regional General Manager or other officer incurs or becomes liable to by reason of any contract entered into or act or deed done by him or her in discharge of his or her duties except in so far as the same shall happen from their own respective willful default.

(b) No such Director, Regional Councillor, Chief Executive Officer, Regional General Manager or other officer shall be liable for the acts of any other such person or for joining in any receipt or document or for any other act of conformity or for any loss or expense happening to the Institute unless the same happen from his or her own willful default.

(c) For the purposes of By-law 160 (a) and (b) "officer" means each:

(i) current or former employee of the Institute;

(ii) member of any committee, sub-committee, panel or taskforce established by or with the approval of the Board;

(iii) natural person appointed to a role to which the Board has resolved that the provisions By-law 160 should apply.

Irregularities

161. (a) All acts done by any meeting of the Board or by a committee thereof shall, notwithstanding that it be afterwards discovered that there was some irregularity in the appointment of any Director or of the committee or that such person was ineligible for appointment, be as valid as if that person had been duly appointed to be a Director or member of the committee and was eligible for appointment.

(b) The provisions of this By-law extend to sub-committees, panels and taskforces established by or with the approval of the Board, and to Regional Councils and to committees of Regional Councils.

Seal

162. The Common Seal of the Institute shall be in the custody of the Board and shall not be affixed to any document except by order of the Board and, subject to the By-laws, every document to which the Seal is affixed shall be signed by a Director and shall be countersigned by a second Director or the Chief Executive Officer or some other person appointed by the Board for the purpose.

G1
Fees

(March 1996)

Contents

Paragraphs

Guide to Members

Introduction

1 This statement is issued for the guidance of members in public practice in setting fees for professional services provided. The statement should be read in conjunction with the APES 110 – *Code of Ethics for Professional Accountants*, particularly Sections 290 and 291 in relation to Independence in relation to audit and assurance engagements and Section 240 *Fees and Other Types of Remuneration.*

Basic Principles

2 In setting fees, members must consider:

- client instructions;
- statutory duties;
- independence;
- levels of expertise and responsibility required and the degree of complexity entailed;
- amount of time taken and effectively applied by the member and staff; and
- any agreed fee basis.

3 Fees may be related to time, to the value of the service to the client or to commercial practice.

4 Where fees are not related to time:

- the member should send an engagement letter containing:
  - detailed description of engagement; and
  - details of the negotiated basis of the fee;
- the member should ensure that:
  - proper documentation of the agreed fee basis is retained; and
  - the fee basis is consistent with industry practice.

5 Fees for all engagements requiring independence must reflect fairly the work performed for the client and all the factors referred to in paragraph 2. (Refer also to APES 110 *Code of Ethics for Professional Accountants*, Sections 290 and 291 Independence). Subject to the consideration of threats to the fundamental principles discussed in Section 240, Sections 290 and 291, professional services may be provided on a contingency fee basis.

6 Before an assignment is undertaken, the client must be advised of the basis on which fees will be calculated, the billing arrangements and, where practical, the total of fees likely to be charged. Prompt advice must also be given of any necessary changes to the fee structure or billing arrangements.

7 Where it is likely that the fee may substantially increase in future periods, the client must be so advised.

8 The client must also be advised fully where the service provided by the member will result in commission being earned from a third party. Advice which may result in the earning of commission must be objective and in the best interest of the client.

9 Fees should not be discounted for initial engagements, with the intention of recovering those discounts through higher charges or the provision of additional services in future periods. Members must be able to demonstrate that the service has been of professional quality and adequately meets the client's requirements.

10 A member whose fees have not been paid may be entitled to retain certain books and papers of a client upon which he has been working, by exercising a lien, and may refuse to pass on information to the client or the member's successor until those fees are paid. Members should, however, consult their solicitors before seeking to exercise a lien in any but the most straightforward of cases and are referred to N1 *Books and Papers – Ownership, Possession and Disclosure*.

Determining Charge Rates

11 Fees calculated on a time basis should be set at a level which provides fair remuneration to the member and staff, having regard to their qualifications and experience.

12 Rates should be set having regard to:

- salaries to attract and retain skilled and competent staff;
- salary on-costs;
- overhead costs, including provision for adequate staff training and research;
- prospective charge-out time for professional and support staff; and
- appropriate notional principal salary and profit margin.

13 Hourly rates, based on the above information, would be calculated for each employee (or group of employees) and principal.

14 Hourly rates may vary according to the location of the practice. That is, they may include adjustment for isolation, remoteness and relative costs of living. In some areas there may be comparative advantages in these respects resulting in corresponding cost reduction.

Time Records

15 Adequate time records need to be maintained in order to calculate accurately effective and realistic fees, recognising circumstances where a high incidence of research time is encountered, where little prior notice is given or where, in providing special services such as for liquidations and investigations, staff having particular skills are required.

Narration on Accounts

16 Accounts must contain sufficient detail as to certainty about the services charged. All disbursements to be recovered should be detailed. Where appropriate, reference may be made to the engagement letter.

17 Where, due to unforeseen circumstances, the fee is, or is likely to be, greater than anticipated or expected by the client, the matter should be discussed with the client as soon as practicable, but always prior to billing.

Interim Billing

18 Good practice requires that, where a service is provided over an extended period, appropriate arrangements be made at the engagement stage to render interim accounts for work completed. Repetitive work should be billed regularly. In any event, accounts should be rendered as soon as possible after completion of the work. Interim billing results in the amounts of time expended to be reviewed regularly and any special work identified.

Retainers

19 Generally, a retainer fee basis is not encouraged because it is likely to be unfair to either the client or the member. However, there may be exceptional instances where such a basis is justified.

Fee Disputes

20 The Institute does not consider that its role is to arbitrate or mediate on a member's fee disputes. Members must ensure proper communications with their clients so as to avoid misunderstandings about fees charged. Good communication means keeping clients informed and involves keeping adequate records of work performed. The use of engagement letters setting out, in reasonable detail, the prospective fee basis is encouraged and, in this respect, members are referred to APES 305 *Terms of Engagement*.

N1 – Books and Papers:
Ownership, Possession and Disclosure

(April 1990)

Contents

Paragraph(s)

Ownership, Possession and Disclosure

This statement is issued to give guidance to members in practice on three matters:

A. *Ownership of Documents and Records* – which documents are owned by members and which are owned by their clients.

B. *Possession* – having established the ownership of documents, the question of possession arises. A member's exercise of a lien is discussed under this heading.

C. *Disclosure* – the obligations of a member to allow inspection of documents by taxation and other authorities.

A. Ownership

1 Introduction

The question of ownership of documents and records is largely a common sense matter. Ownership may be determined by reference to:

(a) the contract between the member and his client;

(b) the capacity in which the member acts in relation to his clients; and

(c) the purpose for which the documents and records exist or are brought into being.

A member's engagement will almost always result in a contract with his or her client. The contract may be written or oral and its terms may be express or implied. In any such contract the parties are free to agree on the ownership of documents and records already in existence or to be produced. Where the contract makes such provision, the question of ownership is settled by reference to the contract and it is not necessary to look further.

Where, as in most cases, the contract does not expressly deal with ownership of books and papers, the general rule is that documents brought into being by the member on the instructions of the client belong to the client. On the other hand, documents prepared, acquired or brought into being by the member solely for his own purposes as principal belong to the member. Most questions of ownership can be settled by reference to these principles, as set out below:

N1

2 Member's Working Papers

Documents which a member produces in the course of his work as principal which are not documents required by the Corporations Law or are not the end product of the engagement, belong to the member. If however, any of those working papers become an attachment to or form part of advice given to a client or are referred to or tabled at meetings, then they become part of the end product for which the client is being charged and therefore become the client's property.
(Amended 8.99)

3 Auditing

The end product of the members' work is to give an auditor's report. Documents prepared by the member solely for the purpose of carrying out his duties as auditor belong to the member. The ownership of documents or records is decided without reference to whether the audit is carried out under statutory provisions or not. If the work involved includes both auditing and accountancy, it may be necessary to consider the purpose for which the particular documents in question were prepared in order to determine their ownership.

4 Accountancy

By reference to the above principles, the question of ownership will depend on the nature of the accountancy work undertaken. For example, if the work is to prepare or write up a set of books for the client, the completed books belong to the client. If the work is to prepare for the client a profit and loss account and balance sheet from the client's books, the final accounts belong to the client, while the member's draft and office copy of those final accounts belong to the member. If, however, the client has specifically asked for drafts to be prepared for him, they will belong to the client as the drafts are the products which are required by the client. Analysis of banking accounts and correspondence with bankers and stock brokers for the purpose of producing accounts would normally belong to the member.

If the member's work is to produce final accounts from incomplete records, and he is not instructed by the client to work on the records themselves, schedules which he prepares for the purposes of producing the accounts would normally belong to the member. However, where financial records are required pursuant to statutory provisions (for example, records required by section 286 of the *Corporations Law*) those records belong to the client.

For the purpose of this Guidance Note, 'financial records' has the meaning ascribed to that phrase under s. 9 of the *Corporations Law* and would include any journals and ledgers prepared by a member for a client.
(Amended 8.99)

5 Taxation

Unlike many other areas of practice, a member will frequently be acting as the client's agent in taxation matters. For example, if the work is of a tax compliance nature such as the preparation and submission of accounts and tax returns, the accounts, schedules and computations belong to the client. This follows from the general rule that documents produced by an agent in the course of his engagement belong to the principal. If the work to be done is to give tax advice, the member is acting as principal and letters or documents giving that advice belong to the client. However, drafts, memoranda, notes and correspondence with solicitors in connection with that work belong to the member.

6 Communications Between a Member and His Client

Letters received by a member from his client belong to the member. A member's copy of any letter written to his client is made solely for his own purposes and also belongs to the member. Members' notes of instructions or interviews with the client belong to the member.

7 Communications with Third Parties

Where the member is acting as agent, such as liaising with the Taxation Office, all such documents belong to the client. Where the member obtains a document as principal, for example documents confirming the balance of an account between a third party and the client or the custody of securities, such documents would normally belong to the member. However, documents prepared by a third party as part of the engagement and sent to the member (other than at the member's expense) belong to the client. Where documents prepared by a third party are sent to a member, there may be particular documents which are solely for the member's benefit, in which event they would belong to the member.

(Amended 6.97)

B. Possession

8 Introduction

Having established the ownership of books and records, the owner is ordinarily entitled to possession of those documents if required. However, where work is performed for a client a lien over documents owned by the client may arise. A lien is the right of a person to retain possession of the owner's property until the owner pays what he owes to the person in possession. Except in rare circumstances, a lien does not give the person in possession the right to sell or otherwise dispose of the property, but only the right to retain it. The law recognizes two types of liens.

9 General Lien

A general lien is a lien over all property which can be retained until payment of the whole indebtedness by the owner to the person in possession on any account whatsoever. It applies whether or not the retained documents relate to the unpaid account or not. A general lien may be exercised by solicitors, bankers, mercantile agents and stockbrokers but it is unclear whether accountants enjoy a general lien. Members are advised against exercising such a lien until the matter is clarified in the Australian Courts.

10 Particular Lien

A particular lien is the right of one person to retain in his possession a particular piece of property until the debt incurred in respect of that property has been paid by the owner. Before a particular lien arises, the following circumstances must apply:

(a) The documents retained must be the property of the client who owes the money and not of a third party, no matter how closely connected with the client. This distinction is particularly important where members are retained by companies and also by the directors in relation to their personal affairs.

(b) The documents must have come into the possession of the member by proper means.

(c) Work must have been done by the member upon the documents or in producing them, not merely examined by the member for the purpose of the member's work; and

(d) The fees for which the lien is exercised must be outstanding in respect of such work and not in respect of other unrelated work.

The lien attaches to documents worked upon by the member during the period for which work fees are outstanding and applies notwithstanding that the documents may also contain work carried out in earlier periods, for example, company ledgers. It does not however extend to any separate documents containing earlier work for which payment has been made. Before discussing some of the special circumstances which apply to liens, it is worth noting that a lien exercised by a member will often have little more than nuisance value, particularly where the outstanding bill is disputed. Members are encouraged to resort to arbitration or other avenues where possible.

11 Statutory Books of Companies

Members cannot exercise a lien over books or documents of a registered company to the extent that they are required by statute or the company's articles to be available for public inspection, or to be kept at the registered office. Examples of such documents are the register of members and directors minute books.

12 Accounting Records of Companies

A lien cannot be exercised over any financial records required by section 286 of the *Corporations Law*. Under section 288, a company is required to make a hard copy of its financial records available within a reasonable time for inspection by certain persons *(Amended 8.99)*.

13 Receiver

The appointment of a receiver to any or all of a company's assets is believed not to affect the existence of a lien. The position is the same whether the receiver is appointed by the court (unless the court orders otherwise) or pursuant to deed.

14 Liquidator

An existing lien will not be lost on the appointment of a liquidator to a company, whether the liquidation is voluntary or not. However, no lien can arise over documents which come into a member's possession after the commencement of the liquidation.

Where the liquidation is involuntary, the court has the power to require an accountant to produce any books and papers in his custody. Production does not prejudice an existing lien, but thereafter the lien becomes valueless as the accountant becomes simply another creditor.

15 Bankruptcy

No person can claim a lien on the papers and documents of a bankrupt. Any documents retained by the member must be surrendered to the trustee in bankruptcy on request.

16 Defeat of a Lien

Where a member returns documents the subject of a lien to his client, or disposes of them to a third party, his lien is generally lost. However, in some instances the lien may be preserved, for example where the documents are produced pursuant to an order from the ASIC. This is discussed more fully in Part C – Disclosure.

Members should also be aware that where legal proceedings are commenced for the recovery of unpaid fees, the retained documents will frequently have to be disclosed prior to the hearing as part of normal Court procedures. To the extent that a client requires only the information contained in documents, rather that the document themselves, the benefit of any lien will be lost with such disclosure.

C. Disclosure

17 Introduction

A member owes a contractual duty of confidentiality to his client. Accordingly, if he discloses confidential information regarding his client's affairs to a third party without the approval of the client he will have breached his duty and be liable in damages to his client. The above statement is subject always to any overriding statutory provision permitting or requiring disclosure. However, the member should bear in mind the precise limits of any such statutory provision because if he oversteps those limits in making disclosure to a third party he will have breached his duty of confidentiality to his client.

18 Taxation

Section 263 of the *Income Tax Assessment Act 1936* basically confers on the Commissioner, and his authorised officers, the right to full and free access to all buildings, places, books, documents and other papers for the purposes of the Act and obliges the occupier of a building or place to provide reasonable facilities and assistance in this regard. Recent cases have clearly established that the Commissioner's power under Section 263 overrides a relevant duty of confidentiality but is still subject to the doctrine of legal professional privilege. Accordingly, it is essential that any documents which may be the subject of such privilege be identified prior to any access being given to the Commissioner or his officers.

The law in relation to Section 263 is uncertain in relation to a number of issues, some of which are the subject of current litigation. In order to assist members in their dealings with the Commissioner and his officers the Institute and others made lengthy submissions to the Commissioner which led to him issuing Additional Guideline A34 dealing with his powers of access under Section 263. While that Guideline is obviously of great benefit to members, it does not have the force of law and clients may have different views in respect of particular aspects of it which, if upheld, could render the member liable to damages for breach of his duty of confidentiality even if he has strictly complied with the Guideline. For this reason, it may be advantageous to a member if he could obtain the prior approval of each client (preferably in writing) to act in accordance with that Guideline and future Guidelines and/or to obtain the client's express approval to specific disclosures prior to them being made.

Members should carefully consider the terms of the Guideline and be familiar with it. However, some of the main points which may be noted are as follows:

(i) Documents are basically divided into three specific categories:

(a) 'Source Documents' Source documents are, in general terms, those which explain the basis and form part of the fabric of the transaction or arrangement including those prepared in connection with the conception, implementation and formal recording of the transaction or arrangement and which explain its setting, context and purpose. Examples are:

- traditional accounting records such as ledgers, journals, profit and loss accounts and balance sheets;
- the 'permanent' audit file; and
- tax working papers.

(b) 'Restricted Source Documents' These are a sub-category of source documents and, in general terms, include advice papers (including taxation advice) prepared or created prior to or contemporaneously with the relevant transaction or arrangement.

(c) 'Non Source Documents' These may generally be described as the balance of documents held by the member and examples of them would include:

- advice papers prepared subsequent to a transaction being completed which do not relate to the recording of the transaction in the accounts or the tax return;

- 'current' audit files (as contrasted to the 'permanent' audit file) relating to statutory audits, tax audits or due diligence investigations; and
- advice in respect of transactions that did not proceed.

(ii) The Commissioner has stated that:

(a) he should have full and free access to source documents (subject only to general restrictions such as legal professional privilege); and

(b) he should only have access to restricted source document or non source documents if:

- insufficient information on the relevant transaction or arrangement can be obtained from the taxpayer client;
- other records have been lost or destroyed or are otherwise unavailable or are not made available; or
- there is a suspicion of fraud, evasion or an offence under the Taxation Administration Act or any other illegal activity.

(iii) However, the Commissioner has further stated that if access is sought to restricted source or non source documents the following procedures are relevant:

(a) Tax Office access to such documents will only be sought with the written approval of the Deputy Commissioner of the relevant Office;

(b) the documents to which access is sought should be (to the extent practicable) clearly specified; and

(c) a reasonable time will be allowed to enable the member to consult with his client in relation to the proposed access.

(iv) The Commissioner also acknowledges that access to papers prepared by a member for a client in relation to legal proceedings (including an objection, appeal or review) under a taxation law are subject to the usual procedure for discovery and access to them will not be sought under Section 263.

It is important for members to bear in mind that Section 263 only relates to access to documents and does not authorise the Commissioner or his Officers to ask questions of the member. The power to ask questions and obtain information is conferred by Section 264 and it is important for members to note that the relevant request for information from the member must be in writing.

Power similar to those conferred on the Commissioner and his Officers under Section 263 of the *Income Tax Assessment Act 1936* are also conferred by:

(a) Section 127 of the *Fringe Benefits Tax Assessment Act 1986*;

(b) Section 109 *Sales Tax Assessment Act 1992*;

(c) Section 4 of the *Taxation (Unpaid Company Tax) Assessment Act 1982* (read in conjunction with Section 263 of the *Income Tax Assessment Act 1936*);

(d) Section 4 of the *Trust Recoupment Tax Assessment Act 1985* (read in conjunction with Section 263 of the *Income Tax Assessment Act 1936*);

(e) Section 38 *Superannuation Contributions Tax (Assessment and Collections) Act 1997*;

(f) Section 32 *Superannuation Contributions Tax (Members of Constitutionally Protected Superannuation Funds) Assessment and Collection Act 1997;*

(g) Section 76 *Superannuation Guarantee Administration Act 1992*;

(h) Section 26 *Termination Payments Tax (Assessment and Collection) Act 1997.*

(Amended 8.99)

19 Police Department

Police conducting an enquiry are generally entitled to information from a client's books and records and from the member's own documents. However, a search warrant is generally required before the Police can obtain possession of the books and records.

20 *Proceeds of Crime Act 1987* (Commonwealth)

This Act enables Police to require the production of documents and/or to search for and seize documents. In most cases the Police are required to obtain a warrant or an order of a Court prior to exercising the relevant powers. However, some provisions of the Act permit action to be taken with the consent of a relevant person. In this regard, Section 70 confers on a Police Officer power to enter premises, search and seize particular documents if he does so pursuant to a warrant or with the consent of the occupier of the premises. It would obviously be inadvisable for a member to give any such consent without the express approval of the relevant client having regard to the member's duty of confidentiality. It would be preferable for him to request the Officer to obtain the relevant warrant. Members should also bear in mind that every State (except Tasmania) has a statute entitled Crimes (Confiscation of Profits) Act. None of the State Acts have, at present, an equivalent to Section 70 although the Western Australian and Queensland Acts empower the police to obtain a court order to produce documents in a similar manner to the Federal Act. New South Wales members should be aware of the *Confiscation of Proceeds of Crime Act 1989* which empowers the police to confiscate documents discovered during the course of exercising a search warrant issued pursuant to the Act although such documents are not of the kind specified in the warrant. Where the police exercise this power, no consent will be required.

21 Australian Securities and Investments Commission

The ASIC can require an accountant in his capacity as agent, or auditor, to produce a company's books. Default in production empowers the Commission to apply for a search warrant authorising seizure of the documents.

22 Documents in Legal Proceedings

A valid subpoena issued against a member for the production of books and records or other documents in legal proceedings must generally be complied with. Court rules normally require subpoenas to be served in sufficient time to enable questions of legal professional privilege and confidentiality to be considered. It is therefore imperative that the client's attitude to production of the documents be ascertained and, if appropriate, legal advice sought on these matters.

23 Disclosure of Documents the Subject of a Lien

Normally, where possession of documents is given to a third party, any lien over the documents is lost. However where documents are produced to the ASIC pursuant to the Commission's order or a search warrant, the lien is reserved by statutory provisions. Documents produced pursuant to a special investigation by the Commission do not enjoy the same immunity. It is always open to a member to advise that documents are produced, subject to his right of lien. Whether this conditional production is effective to preserve the lien will vary from case to case.

N2
Money Laundering Guidelines

(February 1995)

Contents

Paragraph(s)

Money Laundering Guidelines

1 Issues Covered

- Money laundering is a serious crime.
- Helping a client to launder money may give rise to penalties of up to 20 years imprisonment.
- Duties of confidentiality and reporting.
- Clients may have obligations to report as "cash dealers".
- Corporations and other employers may incur criminal liabilities through the acts of their servants or agents.
- Accountants should not be involved in large cash transactions.
- Accountants should not allow themselves or their trust accounts to be used to achieve anonymity for their clients.
- Taking care to ensure that you know that your client is who he says he is.
- Where to report your concerns.
- Internal rules to assist your staff.

2 Introduction

These guidelines are designed to assist members to avoid, recognise and report, and thereby reduce the incidence of money laundering through the accountancy profession.

The guidelines have been developed by the Institute with the assistance of Commonwealth and State law enforcement agencies. They are regarded as the minimum required to assist in the reduction of money laundering. At the same time they take account of the duty of members to act in the interests of their clients.

N2

Compliance with these guidelines will not only assist in the reduction of money laundering, but also provide members with some protection from criminal prosecution, where they have been caught up in money laundering inadvertently or under duress.

The reduction in money laundering is an important element in the fight against organised crime, drug trafficking and tax evasion. As a part of the community, members have an obligation to do all they can to reduce the incidence of such activities.

These guidelines will not only assist members to avoid breaching current laws relating to money laundering, they also establish a scheme for the voluntary reporting of money laundering when this activity is detected.

Existing legislative schemes requiring the mandatory reporting of significant or suspicious transactions generally would not apply to accountants as such. However, the mandatory operating requirements do apply to members who are "cash dealers" within the meaning of the *Financial Transactions Reports Act 1988* (Commonwealth) discussed below. Compliance with these voluntary guidelines is a real and significant measure that the profession can put forward to counter calls for the application of mandatory requirements to its members. Similarly, failure to comply can be expected to result in the strengthening of calls for the application of mandatory requirements and government regulation.

Members should take all possible steps to comply with these guidelines. Depending upon the circumstances, a failure to do so could result in the member or the practice being liable to disciplinary action under one or more of the sub-paragraphs of By-Law 40.

3 Commonwealth Money Laundering Offences

The following is a brief description of the offences under Commonwealth law relating to money laundering. A more detailed description, including a full text of the legislative provisions, is contained within a paper prepared by Mr Andrew Throssell of the National Crime Authority, published in *Charter* of April 1995 and available from the Institute's Information and Research Service (1800 809 828).

The current Commonwealth money laundering offences are contained in sections 81 and 82 of the *Proceeds of Crime Act 1987 (Cth).*

Section 81 makes it an offence to engage in a transaction, or receive, possess, conceal, dispose of, or bring into Australia, money or property that is the proceeds of crime (i.e. proceeds of an indictable Commonwealth offence or an overseas offence that is equivalent to an Australian indictable offence). The offence carries a punishment of up to 20 years imprisonment and a fine of up to $200,000 or of up to $600,000 in the case of a body corporate. Section 82 makes it an offence to receive, possess, conceal, dispose of or bring into Australia, money or property that may be reasonably suspected of being the proceeds of crime. The offence carries a punishment of up to 2 years imprisonment and a fine of up to $5,000 or of up to $15,000 in the case of a body corporate.

In addition, section 6 of the *Crimes Act 1992* provides that any person who receives or assists another person, who is, to his knowledge, guilty of any offence against a law of the Commonwealth, in order to enable him to escape punishment or to dispose of the proceeds of the offence shall be guilty of an offence and subject to imprisonment for up to 2 years.

Section 85 of the *Proceeds of Crime Act 1987 (Cth)* deals with the liability of corporations for the acts of its directors, servants and agents, and of persons other than corporations for the acts of their servants and agents.

In relation to accountants, it is important to note that conduct engaged in by a servant or agent, within the scope of the actual or apparent authority of the servant or agent, will be deemed to have been engaged in by the employer and the state of mind of the servant or agent will be deemed to be that of the employer. Thus, if an employee of a firm commits a money laundering offence within the scope of his or her employment, the principals of the firm will also have committed the offence.

4 State and Territory Money Laundering Offences

Similar legislation relating to the proceeds of the State offences has been enacted in most State jurisdictions. Details of State legislation are contained in the abovementioned paper by the National Crime Authority.

5 Reporting Requirements

The *Financial Transaction Report Act 1988 (Commonwealth)* is administered by the Australian Transaction Reports and Analysis Centre (AUSTRAC) and imposes a reporting regime upon Cash Dealers (as defined in the Act), requiring them to report suspect transactions, significant cash transactions and international telegraphic transfers. Whilst accountants do not obviously fall within the definition of "cash dealer" in Section 3(1) of the *Financial Transactions Reports Act*, there is a view that they may fall within two limbs of the definition. Firstly, incorporated members' practices that are "financial corporations" within the meaning of the Constitution, and secondly, where the member is a trustee or manager of a unit trust. The terms "unit trust" and "unit trust scheme" are widely defined in the Act and where members offering investment services linked to their trust accounts allow moneys from the trust accounts to be deposited in interest-bearing accounts of various kinds, they may be held to be trustees of a unit trust scheme and therefore cash dealers under the Act. Members are referred to the discussion at pages 157 to 159 in *The Money Trail – Confiscation of Proceeds of Crime, Money Laundering and Cash Transaction Reporting*, Fisse, Fraser and Cross, 1992, The Law Book Company Ltd. Furthermore, a number of accountants are employed by companies that are cash dealers. In such cases, the knowledge of the accountant in relation to a transaction being conducted with his or her employer may give rise to an obligation for the employer to report that transaction.

The scheme of the *Financial Transaction Reports Act 1988* requires:

- **cash dealers to report on significant cash transactions (over $10,000) to AUSTRAC (the Act provides some specific exemptions) (Section 7).**
- **reports to be made of transfers of currency ($5,000 or more in value) into or out of Australia (Section 15).**
- **cash dealers to report on suspect transactions:**

  where the cash dealer has reasonable grounds to suspect that information the cash dealer has concerning the transaction may: be relevant to an investigation of an evasion or attempted evasion of a taxation law;

  be relevant to an investigation of, or prosecution of a person for, an offence against a law of the Commonwealth or a Territory: be of assistance in the enforcement of the *Proceeds of Crime Act 1987* (Section 16).

  Where a suspect transaction report is made under Section 16, the cash dealers (and the officer reporting) is taken, for the purposes of Sections 81 and 82 of the *Proceeds of Crime Act 1987* (the money laundering offences), not to have been in possession of that information at any time (Section 17).
- **cash dealers to report on international funds transfer instructions into and out of Australia (Section 17B). Protection against legal action being taken against a cash dealer or person reporting under Section 17B is provided by Sections 17D, 17E and 17F.**
- **that when a person opens an account or becomes a signatory to an account he or she must provide identification evidence (Section 18) and the cash dealer must retain that information (Sections 20 and 23). Sections 20A and 21 set out the identification evidence required.**
- **the Act also creates offences of opening or operating an account with a cash dealer in a false name (Section 24), failing to provide information (Section 28), providing false or misleading information (Section 29), providing incomplete information (Section 30) and conducting transactions so as to avoid transaction requirements (Section 31).**

N2

Each State and Territory has legislative provisions directly complementing the FTR Act under which cash dealers, who are carrying on business in each State and the NT, are required to report suspect transactions not reported under the FTR Act.

For details of other State and Territory legislation permitting the reporting of information by financial institutions, requiring the reporting of crimes and prohibiting the concealment of crimes, members are referred to the abovementioned National Crime Authority paper.

In New South Wales especially, failure to report a serious crime is itself a crime under Section 316 of the *Crimes Act 1900 (NSW).*

6 Accountant's Duty of Confidence

Accountants are usually in a fiduciary relationship with their clients. This means that they are under a duty to act in the interests of the client and in good faith. This duty implies that the accountant will not disclose confidential information acquired from or about the client, and especially not to disclose that information contrary to the client's orders or interest.

Even where the accountant and client are not in a fiduciary relationship, there will usually be an express or implied contractual duty of confidence.

However, it is clear law that "there is no confidence as to the disclosure of iniquity. You cannot make me the confidant of a crime or a fraud, and be entitled to close up my lips upon any secret which you have the audacity to disclose to me relating to any fraudulent intention on your part: such a confidence cannot exist." (*Garside v Outram* (1856) 26 LJ Ch 113).

For a detailed discussion of the law relating to this area, members are referred to the abovementioned National Crime Authority Paper.

In summary, an accountant's duty of confidence is overriden by the public interest in disclosure to the proper authorities of the commission of serious crimes or other iniquities. Money laundering certainly will fall within the category of "serious crime". Therefore, an accountant should disclose activity which he or she suspects on reasonable grounds to be money laundering to the proper authorities (Police, NCA, NSWCC, CJC etc).

However, where the member falls within the definition of "cash dealer" of the *Financial Transactions Reports Act* and suspects on reasonable grounds that he or she holds information about a transaction to which he/she is a party which contravenes the money laundering offences created by Sections 81 and 82 of the *Proceeds of Crimes Act*, disclosure should only be made to the Director of AUSTRAC. The Director of AUSTRAC has a discretion as to whether or not to distribute the information contained in the report to the law enforcement agencies referred to above as well as to other law enforcement agencies. Where the reporting requirements of the *Financial Transaction Reports Act* apply and are complied with, Section 16(5) protects members from actions for defamation and breach of confidence.

In normal circumstances, this disclosure will not give rise to any civil liability of the member. However, where doubt exists, legal advice should be sought.

7 Defamation

Apart from the situations referred to above where the legislation specifically protects members who comply with the reporting requirements from all civil proceedings, members will also be able to rely on the defence of qualified privilege to defamation proceedings brought against them provided:

- they had reasonable ground for believing that the money laundering information they reported was true; and
- the information is reported only to the appropriate law enforcement agencies.

  Qualified privilege is a defence only and does not prevent clients or others from commencing defamation proceedings against members. In this context, members are referred to the discussion in these guidelines on the notification requirements of their professional indemnity insurance policy.

Guidelines

Client Identification

8 Formal identification evidence for all clients should be obtained and recorded (this record would usually be in a central register).

It is recommended that the evidence be one or more of the following, preferably containing either a photograph or signature:

- Passport
- Driver's licence
- Identification Card issued by a Government Department or Educational Institution
- Land Title Document
- Credit Card or other bank identification
- Identification by employer from business records
- Group Certificate
- Identification by an acceptable referee

9 Where companies are being set up or transferred, identification evidence should be obtained and recorded in relation to all directors and shareholders.

10 Where trusts are being set up, a record should be kept of the settler and beneficiaries, and of any donors to the trust. (If your client is legitimate, there should not be concern about providing these details to you).

Trust Accounts

11 Formal identification evidence should be obtained for all clients depositing substantial sums through an accountant's trust account.

12 Records enabling the identification of the client for each transaction should be kept.

13 Transactions should not pass through an accountant's trust account without a legitimate commercial justification. The accountant's trust account should not be used to obtain anonymity for the client, especially where there are reporting requirements (e.g. for deposits of cash into bank accounts as contained in the *Financial Transactions Reports Act 1988*). A request by a client based upon a desire for anonymity should be regarded as suspicious.

14 If a client wishes an accountant to accept large sums of cash, either for deposit into a trust account or in payment of fees, the accountant should decline to receive the cash, requesting that the client obtain a bank cheque.

Involvement in Transactions

15 A member shall not associate himself or herself with any arrangement which involves documents or accounting entries that are intended to misrepresent the true nature of a transaction, the true source of funds, or the true ownership of an asset, or which depends upon lack of disclosure for its effectiveness.

16 A member shall not involve himself or herself with any arrangements to launder the proceeds of crime or any arrangement intended to be used to launder the proceeds of crime.

Reporting Transactions

17 While an accountant normally has a duty of confidence to his or her client, it is clear law that the duty does not extend to non-disclosure to the proper authorities of crimes. Thus, the duty of confidence is not breached by such disclosure.

18 A member, upon becoming aware of reasonable grounds to suspect that money laundering is occurring, should take steps to confirm those suspicions, and if the suspicions are not allayed, should then seek advice from the Institute's General Manager Professional Standards (02-92905627) as to the appropriate law enforcement agency to which the suspected money laundering should be reported.

AUSTRAC is committed to regular liaison with the Institute's General Manager Professional Standards with a view to assisting in the identification of suspected money laundering activity and in advising the Institute as to the proper agency or agencies to which such matters should be reported.

19 Where suspicious are formed that money laundering is taking place, regardless of the work being undertaken, the following factors should be taken into account in deciding whether to report.

- **There is no duty of confidence that binds a member not to report a crime that is being committed (the money laundering).**
- **When money laundering suspicions are formed, the source of the funds is not always apparent. If the funds could come from offences against Commonwealth laws, or from overseas, the member may be committing an offence (just on the basis of the suspicion) to transact those funds.**
- **There is a public interest (and, in some States, a legal duty) in favour of reporting money laundering (and other offences) to the proper authorities.**

It is not acceptable for an accountant, when confronted with a potential money laundering situation to simply decline to act and not report the matter.

20 If a member finds himself or herself to have been used in money laundering inadvertently or under duress, the situation should be remedied by reporting the matter as soon as possible.

21 Clients or employees of clients should not be informed of any money laundering suspicions, except after careful consideration and reference under the firm's usual procedures. Communication of money laundering suspicions may be made to a client's senior management, internal auditors, or other person responsible for reporting or monitoring money laundering, where the accountant has no reason to suspect that the person is implicated in the money laundering or may pass the information to the launderers.

However, where members make a report under the mandatory reporting requirements in legislation, such as the FTR Act, members should ensure that the legislation does not prohibit communication to clients. See for example, Section 16(5A) of the FTR Act.

22 Internal reporting procedures should be established, so that an employee with suspicions can identify the person to whom he or she should report those suspicions. This person must have access to information by which he or she can judge the reasonableness of the suspicion and should ensure that the information is passed to the proper authorities if appropriate.

23 Any report made should contain all information likely to be relevant to an investigation, including:

- suspect's full name, address, telephone number, date of birth, nationality, occupation, employer and any aliases known
- and identification reference seen or recorded
- details of transactions arousing suspicions, including amount, currency, source, destination, parties and bank accounts involved
- other relevant information, including the reason for suspicion.

24 Reports should be made in writing (in urgent cases by fax or by telephone), and a record should be kept of the communication, including the name of the agency and the person (name and position) the report was made to.

25 Before a report is made to an agency, the Institute's General Manager Professional Standards should be advised that a report is to be made, but not the details thereof. The Institute's General Manager Professional Standards will advise the name of the person in the agency to whom the report should be made and record the fact of the report and details of the agency to which it is to be made.

26 During an audit, an auditor should treat indications of possible money laundering similarly to indications of other offences (see AUS 210), taking into account the fact that the company could be liable to substantial fines and be liable to forfeiture of the laundered funds (usually resulting in the possible money laundering having a substantial impact on the

financial statements of the company). Money laundering through a company also distorts the financial statements through false entries to cover the laundering.

27 When a client is involved in a suspected incident of money laundering, the member should reconsider the reliability of all representations made in relation to the client. If the client is a corporation, the member should reconsider the reliability of all representations made by those involved in the laundering.

28 When a client is involved in a suspected incident of money laundering, all previous transactions should be reconsidered - are they now suspect, in light of the current knowledge of the member?

29 When a member has been involved, even inadvertently, in a money laundering transaction (for example, the member has received into his or her trust account "proceeds of crime") and/or has reported the client to the proper law enforcement authorities for suspected money laundering, the member should consider whether a circumstance has arisen which may possibly give rise to a claim against the member has arisen. If so, the member should notify his or her professional indemnity insurers of the circumstance.

30 Further advice and information can be provided upon request to the Institute's General Manager Professional Standards (02-92905627).

N3

Risk Management Guidelines

(April 1996)

Contents

Paragraph(s)

Risk Management Guidelines

A. Managing the Professional Liability of Accountants

The Institute's National Council directs members' attention to the most common situations where they may be sued for professional error. These notes explain how members can reduce the likelihood of claims being made against them and address the legal aspects of professional liability.

The Guidelines are based upon similar material provided by the Institute of Chartered Accountants in England and Wales to its members and National Council acknowledges the consent willingly provided by that Institute to use the material.

Introduction

1 The number and size of liability claims against accountants continue to increase. It is therefore important for members to manage the *extent* of their liability as accountants. Remember that claims can arise from errors committed in all areas of practice, with both small and large professional appointments being subject to significant claims. The basis of accountants' liabilities can arise from actions in tort, allegations of professional negligence, breaches of contract and breaches of statutory provisions, such as those under the Trade Practices Act.

A common feature of liability claims is the practitioner's apparent misunderstanding of the scope of, or responsibility for, the work to be done.

These notes are designed to help members avoid these misunderstandings, to identify the nature of any liability they may face professionally and to assist them to manage their exposure to it.

2 These notes only cover situations where members (or their employees or associates) risk liability as a result of providing professional services.

3 Remember that there is a contract between a member and a client, even if no written contract exists. The standard of work required by that contract is explained in paragraphs 2 and 3 of the Appendix.

Summary

4 Whilst it is impossible for members to avoid every situation where there is a possibility of a professional liability claim, there are ways to manage their potential liability. Consider the following methods:

(a) **define the scope and responsibilities of the engagement:**

(i) *to the client*, by agreeing to an engagement letter which:

- identifies the terms of the engagement (para. 6);
- defines only those specific tasks to be undertaken (paras 7 and 8);
- defines the responsibilities of the client, in particular specifying how and to what extent reliance is to be placed on the client or others (paras 9 and 10);
- specifies any limitations on the work to be undertaken (paras 11 to 14);

(ii) *to third parties*, by specifying in any report the precise nature of the work carried out and, as far as possible, the work not carried out, as well as any limitations on the work undertaken (para. 15);

(b) **define the purpose of reports:**

(i) by stating in the engagement letter the purpose for which the report has been prepared and that the client may not use the report for any other purpose (para. 17);

(ii) by stating in any report which may be seen by a third party the purpose for which it has been prepared and that it may not be relied on for any other purpose (paras 18 and 19);

(c) **restrict the use of the member's name:**

(i) by advising clients in the engagement letter of the need to obtain permission to use the member's name (para. 20);

(ii) by disallowing use of the member's name, where appropriate (para. 21);

(d) **identify those authorised to receive the report:**

(i) by a term in the engagement letter; and

(ii) by a warning in the report (paras 22 to 24);

(e) **limit or exclude liability:**

(i) to the client, by a term in the engagement letter (paras 25 to 27);

(ii) to third parties, by a disclaimer in any report (paras 28 to 33);

(f) **obtain an indemnity:**

(i) from the client and any third party (paras 34 to 36);

(ii) in connection with receiverships, trusts and secretarial work (paras 37 and 38);

(g) **define the scope of professional competence** to include only tasks within the member's competence (paras 39 and 40).

(h) **arrange for adequate insurance cover** (paras 42 to 50).

Each of these measures is discussed in more detail in the paragraphs referred to above.

Accepting New Clients

5 A senior and responsible person in the firm should be designated to evaluate such acceptance, or a committee formed for that purpose.

When the prospective client is a significantly large one, or where doubt exists as to acceptability, the matter should be discussed by all partners.

The responsible person in the firm should concentrate on the following:

- details about the integrity and reputation of the client, its directors and officers;
- whether the new relationship will be mutually beneficial;
- whether a formal pre-engagement review by a senior partner should be undertaken on a formalised basis;
- consideration of any major conflict that the firm might have through the engagement;
- whether the services required by the prospective client can be provided by the firm and are not illegal, in breach of regulation or professional ethics; and
- an assessment of the resources required for the new appointment.

The sources of information could include individuals within the firm, ASC records, stock exchange authority enquiries, press releases (through press agencies), enquiries, where permissible, of the prospective client's professional service providers and bankers and investigations of credit agencies such as Dun & Bradstreet.

Clearly, such enquiry would need to be discreet, with the potential client's consent being obtained where appropriate, and certainly not designed to alienate the prospective client. Such enquiry is a due diligence exercise but it should not prejudice the firm's commercial prospects.

The evaluation process should take into account the requirements of the Institute and, in particular, paragraph 6 of Professional Statement F.3, which requires the firm to communicate with the existing accountant before responding to an invitation to accept nomination or appointment involving recurring professional work hitherto carried out by another accountant.

It is recommended that, on completion of the evaluation, a file should be opened and full recommendations with supporting data should be maintained in such file.

Once the client has been accepted, a "post acceptance" evaluation process should be put in place. It is subsequent to the acceptance of the client that more information will become available and new clients may need to be monitored closely. This process may include:

- An analysis of developments in the client's industry;
- Consideration of the client's record of providing information and the accuracy of that information;
- Performance appraisals of the executives;
- Review of standards of record keeping;
- Review of the nature of management (whether it is consensual or dictated by one strong executive);
- Review of turnover of personnel;
- Investigation as to who the other professional advisers are;
- An understanding of the nature of the client's activities in the light of regulation and changing law, e.g. Trade Practices Act, laws relating to import/export etc.
- An understanding of the relationship between shareholders and management and constitution of the shareholding in the company;
- An understanding of the financial capitalisation and structure of the client; and
- Cashflow considerations.

Defining The Scope And Responsibilities Of The Engagement

(i) *To the Client:*

Identifying the terms of the engagement

6 Having agreed on the work to be performed, the terms of the engagement should be defined in an engagement letter. The engagement letter should identify in sufficient detail:

- the terms of the engagement, including the actual services to be performed;
- the sources and nature of any information to be provided; and
- to whom any report should be supplied.

The client should then sign and return a copy of the engagement letter (see APS 2 "Engagement Letters to Clients" and AUS204 "Terms of Audit Engagements").

Where the appointment results from a successful proposal, the proposal document itself will normally form the contract. However, if a separate engagement letter is prepared, it should specify the particular services or other terms that were agreed at the proposal stage. If the client later requests additional services or seeks to vary the terms of the agreement in any other way, then the resulting changes should similarly be agreed in writing and signed off by both the member and the client. Defining the specific tasks to be undertaken

7 As part of their professional work, members are often asked to give opinions and advice, including financial advice. When providing an opinion or advice, members should specify clearly in the engagement letter:

- the extent of the work to be undertaken, making particular reference to any information supplied by the client and relied on by the member in giving the advice or opinion, and
- the specific tasks to be undertaken and, where appropriate, the tasks which will not be undertaken.

8 If a member finds during the course of the engagement that it is unnecessary or impossible to perform all of the tasks anticipated, he or she should prepare and send a letter to the client specifying the changes to the scope of the work. This should be done before any report is submitted to the client. The changes should be accepted by the client and

N3

evidenced by a signed copy of the letter. If variations or amendments to the engagement contract are not mutually agreed the member could be in breach of contract.

The member should then make clear in the report precisely which tasks have and have not been undertaken. In any bills, the description of the work done should be consistent with the terms of the engagement letter (and any variation of it) and with the report.

Defining the responsibility to be undertaken by the client

9 If the client is to assume responsibility for doing any particular matter, then the member should make that fact clear in the engagement letter. For example, a report or statement may be prepared by a member for issue by the client in circumstances where the member could reasonably expect the client to check the document for completeness or accuracy before the client makes any use of it involving third parties. If a member considers that a particular document needs to be checked by the client, then the member should make this clear.

Ensuring that clients are aware of their responsibilities should help to avoid any later disputes.

10 Where the client has directly or indirectly determined the nature and scope of the procedures to be performed by a member as part of an engagement, the member should ensure that the engagement letter includes a statement that the client is assuming responsibility for the sufficiency of those procedures for the client's purposes.

However, if the member considers that the procedures may be insufficient for the client's purposes, then the member should not accept the engagement and should bring the shortfall in procedures to the attention of the client, as appropriate.

Specifying any limitations on the work to be done

11 If there are risks which attach to a particular engagement, it may be appropriate to alert the client to any limitations to the scope of the work to be done by the member. The most common example of this is where the client needs an immediate answer to a complicated problem.

In these circumstances, the member should consider whether it is appropriate to accept the engagement at the outset. If the member accepts the engagement, then the engagement letter (or at least the report) should make it clear that:

- the problem is a complex one;
- very little time has been given to study the problem;
- further time is required to consider matters in depth; and
- the opinion or advice given may need to be revised if further time were available.

The engagement letter should also make it clear that the client is responsible for the accuracy and completeness of the information supplied to the member. In all cases, the client should be warned about the risk of acting on the advice before further investigation can be carried out.

12 Rather than reporting on past performance, members are sometimes asked by clients to report on information relating to future performance.

There are many forms of forecast and projection on which a member may be asked to report. Because of the significant risk involved in reporting on any prospective financial information, members need to exercise particular care when deciding whether, and on what terms, to accept such engagements. Attention is directed to the contents of AUS804 "The Audit of Prospective Financial Information". Here are some examples of warnings which might be included in engagement letters and reports in such situations:

- *"The directors of [the company] are solely responsible for the projections and any assumptions based on those projections. The projections have been prepared to illustrate the consequences of [the project]. Since the projections relate to an extended period, actual results could be different because events and circumstances frequently do not occur as expected and do not therefore match the assumptions. The financial projections are, by their nature, not susceptible to audit, and we are unable to express an opinion as to the possibility that they will be achieved."*

- *"The directors of [the company] are solely responsible for the projections and any assumptions based on those projections. The financial projections cover an extended period for a company with no previous history and are based upon the directors' assumptions and estimates. The financial projections do not constitute a forecast, and they could be materially affected by changes in economic and/or other circumstances. For this reason, the actual [profits and cash flows] may vary considerably from those shown. The financial projections are, by their nature, not susceptible to audit, and we are unable to express an opinion as to the possibility that they will be achieved."*

13 Here are some other examples of situations where it may be appropriate to alert the client to limitations or restrictions on the scope of the member's work:

- an engagement undertaken in connection with a financing transaction where additional procedures may be necessary to enable the report user to reach a conclusion;
- a report based on the completion of certain agreed procedures which are not governed by professional standards (especially when the client or third party accepting responsibility for the sufficiency of the procedures may not fully understand the limitations of the work that they have requested);
- a report on financial information which contains significant uncertainties likely to be resolved in the near future. In this situation, it is appropriate to point out that the member has no responsibility to update the member's report in the light of subsequent events;
- a report on a presentation required to be prepared by the terms of a contract or a regulatory provision, particularly when there are indications that third parties may have differing views. In this situation, it is appropriate to note that any financial comments made do not touch on legal interpretation.

14 It is important to understand that properly worded statements and warnings of the kind considered in paragraphs 11 to 13 above may not be exclusions or restrictions of liability but rather definitions of the work undertaken and statements about the extent to which the client can rely on that work.

Such warnings and statements assist in protecting a member from professional liability claims based on the argument that the member's enquiries should have been different or more extensive. However, this is subject to the member clearly setting out the nature and extent of such enquiries in the report and preferably including this information in the client's engagement letter.

(ii) To Third Parties

15 Even though the engagement letter precisely sets out the definitions of the scope of the work and/or the limitations on that work, this is not enough to bind any third party who is not informed of the arrangement. As a result, members should ensure that they set out in their report, ideally by including in it a copy of the engagement letter, precise details of the work carried out and its purpose, any limitations on the work undertaken and, as far as possible, details of the work not carried out.

If this information is clearly set out in any report to which a third party may gain access, members may well gain some protection if a third party claims to have relied on the member's report.

Where members are aware that specific third parties will have access to their report, they should also consider asking those third parties to sign a copy of the engagement letter to indicate their acceptance of its terms. If this is not possible, members should make it clear to any third party that they make no representations about the adequacy of their procedures for the purposes of third parties.

The Resolution of Disputes

16 Members should consider including within the terms of their engagement the following: "Any disputes or disagreements arising out of or in connection with this engagement shall, upon the request of one or more of the parties to the dispute or disagreement, be referred to the sole arbitration of a person whom the parties have appointed. That person's decision shall be final and binding upon all of the parties, provided that the agreement to refer the dispute or disagreement to arbitration is made after the dispute or disagreement has arisen."

Defining the Purpose of Reports

17 Members may be able to limit their liability to the client by clearly restricting the use to which a report may be put. The restriction should be included in the engagement letter while also identifying the purpose for which the work has been requested. Whilst the wording of any such restriction will depend on the circumstances, an example is:

"This report/statement is intended solely for the information and use of the board and management of X Limited and Y Limited in connection with the proposed sale of Y Limited to A Limited and should not be used for any other purpose."

18 Where a document is drafted for initial discussions with the client, or with others, and is liable to be altered before it reaches its final form, the fact that it is a draft should be made clear. This serves to prevent any reliance on the draft document alone.

Ideally, the engagement letter should include a clause to the effect that where any document is marked "draft", or described in that way, then the client should not rely on any such document except with the member's written consent. In a similar way, where a member provides a client with a verbal report prior to a final report in writing, the member should make it clear in the engagement letter (and when giving the verbal report), that the verbal report is not definitive. The engagement letter should then go on to make the point that only the final written report will contain the member's definitive opinions and conclusions.

19 Where financial information is prepared, or reported on, by a member for a particular purpose, the member will not normally be liable to an unknown third party who relies on that information or report for any other purpose. However, members are advised to make the position clear by including in the financial information or report prepared by them, a statement of the purpose for which it was prepared along the lines of the example in para. 17.

Restricting the use of the member's name

20 Unless agreed, members should not allow their names to appear on any document issued by their client to any third party. Naturally, this does not include documents such as audited financial statements. It is recommended that a clause to this effect be included in the engagement letter.

21 Third parties often interpret the use of a member's name on a document as implying that an entity is financially sound. If a member becomes aware that a client plans to use his or her name in this way, the member should advise the client that the member's permission must first be obtained. In appropriate cases, it may be advisable to withhold permission.

Identifying the authorised recipients of reports

22 Restricting the use of reports, whether financial statements or otherwise, can reduce a member's exposure to third party claims. In some cases, however, it may be impossible to restrict the recipients of some documents such as auditor's reports under the Corporations Law and accountant's reports for listing purposes. Nevertheless, the implications of the duty of care owed to third parties are important for all members who produce or report upon financial statements or who provide reports of various other kinds (whether for a fee or not) which may be relied on by those third parties.

23 The contract between the member and the client (e.g. the letter of engagement) can specify that it is a term of the contract that the member's report or statement may not be circulated to third parties without the member's prior written consent. If the client does then circulate the document, the client may well be in breach of contract.

24 In addition, the reports or statements themselves may contain an instruction specifically restricting circulation. For example:

"Confidential. This report [statement] has been prepared for the private use of X [the client] only."

If a third party claims to have relied, without the member's consent, on a document marked in this way, the member may be able to avoid liability. This is on the basis that the third party was not someone the member had in mind as likely to suffer loss by any alleged error or shortcoming by the member.

A court faced with such a claim would likely look at the surrounding facts and what bearing those facts had on the parties' intentions. As a result, a document should only be marked in this way when the situation warrants it. Otherwise, the warning itself may possibly be devalued by indiscriminate use, especially when a document has a potentially wide audience, due to its nature.

Limiting or excluding liability

To the client

25 Even if a member limits or excludes liability in an agreement with a client, this may not always be legally effective. The relevant considerations here are set out in para. 10 of the Appendix.

The member should ensure that any letter of engagement accurately reflects at all times the scope of the agreement with the client, and this includes any provisions in the agreement to restrict or exclude the member's liability. Otherwise, if the terms of the member's retainer are later changed, questions may arise about the effectiveness of any new provisions in the agreement.

26 It may be appropriate in the agreement to exclude liability for any claim by the client involving fraud, misrepresentation or wilful default by the client or the client's employees. However, such clauses cannot form part of engagement letters for certain statutory audits (because of the general prohibition on any limitation of liability in s. 241 of the Corporations Law and other similar statutory provisions).

They may, however, be appropriate in non-statutory audit work and in non-audit engagements. Members who undertake statutory audits which are not governed by the Corporations Law should familiarise themselves with the relevant statutory provisions about liability so that they can determine whether or not they can limit liability.

27 Members should consider limiting the amount of their liability to the client (by negotiation) for all engagements. This is particularly so where the risks associated with a non-audit engagement are unacceptably high. However, this advice does not, of course, extend to the statutory audits mentioned earlier.

For example, a clause in the engagement letter can limit the amount of a claim by a client for breach of contract or negligence. The effect of such a clause will depend on:

- the adequacy of any consideration;
- the ongoing effect of the clause if the contract is terminated; and
- its justness in terms of the Contracts Review Act (see para. 10 in Appendix).

For NSW members the "liability capping" schemes envisaged in the *Professional Standards Act 1994* (NSW) may serve to limit their liability according to the terms of the scheme covering the member's professional association. In particular, members need to be aware of both the preconditions to this Act's operation and its limitations. For example, it does not apply to claims under federal legislation such as the Corporations Law and the Trade Practices Act.

Members' attention is also directed to Auditing Guidance Statement AGS 1014 "Privity Letter Requests".

N3

To third parties

28 Any attempt by a member to exclude or restrict liability to a third party will generally not be effective unless the third party is aware of the exclusion or restriction.

However, in some circumstances sec 9 of the Contracts Review Act may provide relief to third parties. Essentially, sec 9 permits the court to look at the fairness of the contract at the time it was made in the context of wide-ranging criteria. Some of those criteria focus on the parties' respective bargaining positions. There may be some situations where the absence of any bargaining power could place in doubt the effectiveness of any attempt to restrict or exclude liability.

29 Where a member prepares a report for a client and that report may be seen and relied upon by third parties, the member should include in the report a definition of the responsibilities of the engagement, the purpose of the report and its use (see para. 17).

In addition to this, the member may wish to exclude liability to third parties. If the member knows the identity of the third party, the member may be in a better position if he or she can sign a separate agreement with the third party, incorporating a fully negotiated exclusion or limitation of liability clause. Depending on whether or not the contract is enforceable, it may at least prevent third parties from arguing that they were unaware of the exclusions [see para. 28].

In addition, the member may include a disclaimer in the report to the effect that no responsibility to any third party who may rely on the report is accepted. If there are legal proceedings later, the presence in the report of such a disclaimer puts the onus on third parties of proving that their reliance on the report, despite the disclaimer, was reasonable.

However, members should avoid relying too heavily on disclaimers since Law, such as the Trade Practices and Fair Trading Acts, limit the effect of such disclaimers.

30 Where a member, having the client's authority, provides information directly to a third party, the effectiveness of any disclaimer of liability by the member will depend on the nature of the information itself.

For example, when providing information about creditworthiness, normal commercial practice is to state that while the information is provided in good faith, the member accepts no financial responsibility for the opinion expressed. As long as the information can be seen as clearly not the result of extensive knowledge or research by the member, such disclaimers will generally be effective.

31 Sometimes, however, a member may provide directly to a third party information which the third party (unless told otherwise) could reasonably expect to be the result of fairly extensive research. If a third party, directly or indirectly, requests such information, then the member owes that third party a duty of care when preparing and providing that information. For a disclaimer to be effective in these circumstances, it should outline the context in which the information is provided and the scope of the investigations and research performed.

32 Where third parties (e.g. potential purchasers, investors or lenders) request access to the working papers of the auditors of a target company or group, the auditors should only allow access if they are able to obtain from those third parties a signed disclaimer of any duty or liability as a result of the auditors providing access or information.

Further, client confidentiality must be preserved, with the client providing written permission and indemnity before access to working papers is provided to third parties. The disclaimer should be obtained both from those to whom access is granted (usually another firm of auditors) and from the potential purchasers, investors or lenders who make the request.

33 Where a document is prepared as a result of a member's own initiative (e.g. a newsletter or a textbook) and not as a result of a client's instructions or of any statutory requirement, it may be appropriate to include a disclaimer in the document. However, it would not be appropriate to place any substantial reliance on the disclaimer for any particular purpose.

The form that it should take will depend on the nature of the document itself, but a disclaimer along the following lines would generally be appropriate:

"No responsibility for loss to any person acting or refraining from acting as a result of any material in this publication can be accepted by [name of member, author or publisher]. Professional advice should be taken before applying the contents of this publication to your particular circumstances."

Obtaining an indemnity

From the client or a third party

34 To avoid a situation where a third party makes a claim against a member based on the contents of a document prepared by the member at the client's request, it may be appropriate to obtain an indemnity from the client for this purpose. Although such an indemnity will not necessarily prevent a third party from making a claim, it may, if properly worded, assist the member to transfer liability to the client for any loss suffered.

35 Indemnities may not be practical in situations where a report is likely to get wide circulation (e.g. accountants' reports in listing particulars or in an acquisition circular). However, where use of the report is restricted or where there is no requirement for a public statement about the auditor's involvement (e.g. in the case of preliminary announcements of results by listed companies), it may be reasonable to include an indemnity against loss suffered as a result of claims by third parties, including the costs of defending such claims.

36 Remember, however, that an indemnity does not prevent a claim from being made against the indemnified party. It merely gives that person a right to pass the liability on to another party. Obviously, if the indemnity is in some way ineffective or the party giving the indemnity has inadequate resources to meet the liability, then the indemnified party will be left unprotected.

Receiverships, trusts and secretarial work

37 As a result of sec 419 of the Corporations Law, where a member, acting as a receiver, enters into possession or assumes control of any property of a corporation for the purpose of enforcing any charge, the member is liable for the debts he or she incurs during the period of possession or control in connection with services rendered, goods purchased or property hired, leased, occupied or used.

Consequently, if a member appointed by a debenture holder to act in this capacity, has to manage a business, the member should ensure as far as possible that the person who appoints the member also provides full indemnity to cover the member against any loss arising out of the appointment. If no such indemnity can be obtained, then the member should attempt to ensure that any contract entered into on behalf of the business includes a clause absolving the member from any personal liability.

38 It is often prudent for a member who is appointed to act as a trustee or who is asked to carry out certain secretarial work (e.g. signing cheques), to obtain an appropriate indemnity.

If appointed as a trustee, the member can obtain a wide form of indemnity under the instrument creating the trust if the settler is willing to agree to include the indemnity in the trust deed. If the member is appointed to carry out certain secretarial work, then he or she should arrange for an indemnity to be obtained from the client.

Defining the scope of professional competence

39 When giving an opinion or advice on difficult or complicated issues (e.g. taxation rulings), members need to be aware of the consequences, financial or otherwise, if the opinion or advice proves to be wrong.

Although the law expects a member in general practice simply to bring a fair and reasonable degree of skill and competence to the problem on which he or she has been asked to advise, in certain situations this may extend to recognising the need to consult (with the client's approval) a specialist in the area in question.

There may also be situations when a member may choose to decline a particular assignment because, for example, he or she believes the matter on which advice is sought is outside the scope of the member's accountancy practice.

Members are reminded that one of the fundamental principles established in the Code of Professional Conduct at B.7 (Competence and Due Care) is that a member should not accept or perform work which the member is not competent to undertake unless he or she obtains the necessary advice and assistance to enable the work to be performed competently.

40 Where an engagement arises because of a separate commercial agreement between other parties, the member will not be able to vary the terms of the engagement without a variation of the separate agreement. Consequently, in such a situation the member should first ensure that the terms of his or her engagement, as defined in the agreement, are acceptable to all parties.

The member should decline to accept any engagement where the member is unable to fulfil the terms of any separate agreement or where the member considers that the risks of the engagement itself are too high. Problems which a member may wish to avoid include: owing a duty of care to a party known to be litigious, owing a duty of care to both sides of a transaction, and being required to perform limited procedures or merely a preparation-only engagement without any limitation clauses.

Conclusion

41 Members are reminded that even if they use their best endeavours to ensure that they adopt all the relevant measures outlined above, they may still run the risk of claims from clients or third parties.

Irrespective of whether or not these claims have merit, members should ensure that they have established proper procedures to identify and deal promptly with all claims, with notifications to their insurers and to seek appropriate legal advice as necessary.

It is critical that a clear, accurate and concise record of the member's work be retained. That record should include appropriate working papers, correspondence and filenotes.

A proper record provides useful evidence of what was said or done even if it was a long time ago. It can also be decisive in the determination or resolution of a dispute.

❖ ❖ ❖

Appendix: Legal Considerations

Defences to an Action for Negligence

1 It is a defence to an action for negligence to show:

(a) that no duty of care is owed to the plaintiff, or

(b) that there has been no breach of that duty, or

(c) that the negligence had not been an effective cause of the plaintiff's loss, or

(d) in the case of actions in tort, that no financial loss was suffered by the plaintiff, or

(e) that the action was statute-barred. The fourth defence does not apply to a claim in contract. Only nominal damages would be recoverable in such an action, and it is therefore unlikely to be brought in the first place.

Standard of work

2 When undertaking professional services, the member is expected under common law principles to exercise the appropriate level of skill and care when measured objectively. This obligation is underlined by s 71 of the Trade Practices Act and s 19 of the Sale of Goods Act to the extent that those Acts are relevant.

Any arrangement limiting or attempting to limit the standard of care expected can also impact on the scope of the retainer and the nature of any exclusions or disclaimers.

3 The skill and care required in any particular situation will be judged principally on the nature of the work agreed to be undertaken.

A member who undertakes work of an unusually specialised nature, or work of a kind where negligent performance is particularly likely to cause substantial loss, will usually be taken to have assumed a duty to exercise the higher degree of skill and care reasonably expected of any accountant undertaking such demanding work. This will especially be the case if members hold themselves out to be experienced in the kind of work in question.

In no case, however, is the duty likely to be absolute. Opinions expressed or advice given will not generate a liability merely because in the light of later events they prove to have been wrong. This is so even if they amounted to an error of judgement, provided that they were arrived at using the skill and care which was reasonable for an accountant undertaking such work.

Liability to third parties

4 Liability to third parties may arise where there is a duty of care in tort owed by the member. While an accountant will also generally owe a duty of care to the client, that duty is likely to be co-extensive with the member's contractual duty to the client.

5 Following *Caparo Industries plc v Dickman* [1990] 2 AC 605 HL, (see in particular pp 620H to 621A, and pp 638C to 638E), a duty of care to a particular third party may be owed by accountants where there are all of the following ingredients:

- foreseeability of damage to the third party
- a relationship of proximity or neighbourhood with that third party, and
- a situation where it would be fair, just and reasonable to impose a duty of a particular scope on the accountant

Although the courts have attempted to limit the circumstances in which a duty will be held to exist, it is wise to assume that it will exist in a situation where the member knows of the existence of a third party whom the member reasonably expects to receive and rely on the member's work for a particular transaction or purpose and to whom damage will be caused if the work has been done negligently.

The likelihood of a duty being imposed in this situation will increase where that third party has no other source of advice and where the purpose of the member's work is to induce the third party to take the particular action that the third party has later taken.

6 While each case will depend on its particular circumstances, the courts have recognised a number of circumstances in which a liability to third parties in tort will not generally arise. At the same time, the courts have indicated some of the material factors in deciding the issue:

Liability to shareholders/investors

(a) The House of Lords decided in *Caparo Industries plc v Dickman* (see above) that the auditors did not owe a duty of care to individual shareholders (whether or not they were existing shareholders) who bought shares in the company relying on the audited accounts.

(b) In *Al-Nakib Investments v Longcroft* (The Times, 4 May 1990) it was decided that a duty of care was owed to subscribers who relied on a prospectus but not to anyone else who bought shares in the market in reliance on the prospectus. Section 1009 of the Corporations Law extends liability for false or misleading statements in prospectuses to include experts, auditors and those generally involved in preparing prospectuses.

(c) The Court of Appeal decided in *James McNaughton Group v Hicks Anderson & Co* [1991] All ER 135 that the auditors of a target company did not owe a duty of care to an identified takeover bidder who relied on draft accounts. The accounts were produced for the target and not for the bidder, they were in draft rather than final form and it was not foreseeable that the bidder would not take independent advice.

N3

On the other hand, the same court held in *Morgan Crucible v Hill Samuel* [1991] Ch 295 that it was plainly arguable that a duty of care was owed to an identified bidder by auditors where extracts from financial statements were included in the defence document with a view to increasing the bid.

(d) In *Columbia Coffee & Tea Pty Ltd v Churchill (t/a Nelson Parkhill)* (1992) 29 NSWLR 179, Rolfe J of the Supreme Court of New South Wales examined a situation involving a company's decision to acquire shares in a second company on the basis of that second company's audited accounts and a subsequent special interim audit.

His Honour was satisfied that in light of the authorities (including *San Sebastian Pty Ltd v Minister Administering Environmental Planning and Assessment Act 1979 (NSW)* (1986) 162 CLR 340 and *R Lowe, Lippman Figdor & Franck v AGC (Advances) Ltd* [1992] 2 VR 671 that no duty of care was owed unless those authorities could be distinguished. Rolfe J distinguished these cases and found that a duty of care was owed based upon the firm's audit manual's recognition of "interested parties who read and rely upon our reports" in addition to the audit client.

(e) The decision of the Full Court of the Western Australian Supreme Court in *Edwards Karwacki v Jacka Nominees Pty Ltd* (1994) 15 ACSR 502 concerned the alleged failure of the auditors of Jacka Nominees Pty Ltd to detect the defalcations of the company's managing director. The discovery of those defalcations resulted in proceedings being brought against the auditors by:

- the company, and
- those who had invested in it.

The auditors applied to the Supreme Court of Western Australia for orders for summary judgement against the plaintiffs or orders striking out the statements of claim. Underpinning the auditors' position were the following arguments:

- in view of the size of the company, the managing director's fraud was the company's fraud and that gave the auditors a complete defence to the company's allegations, and
- the auditors were not responsible to the company's investors

At first instance and on appeal, the court dismissed the auditors' applications because:

- although it was strongly arguable that a managing director's fraud was the company's fraud in civil proceedings, it did not necessarily follow that fraud represented a complete defence. These issues were matters appropriately determined at a full hearing and not in the course of an application such as this; and
- although the notion that the auditors could be responsible to investors such as these was novel, reliance was not an essential factor in determining whether or not the auditors and investors were sufficiently linked to give rise to a duty of care. Factors which the investors pointed to included the auditors' statutory responsibility and obligations, the number of investors and the fact that they were a class whom the legislation was intended to protect. It was therefore arguable that they were owed a duty.

Liability to lenders

(f) In *Al Saudi Banque v Clark Pixley* [1989] 3 All ER 361 it was decided that auditors owed no duty of care to a bank lending money to a company in reliance on accounts, whether the bank was an existing creditor or not, where the auditors were not aware of the bank's existence nor of the fact that lenders were relying on the accounts.

(g) In *R Lowe, Lippman Figdor & Franck v AGC (Advances) Ltd* [1992] 2 VR 671 the Full Court of the Supreme Court of Victoria considered a claim by a financier for damages in circumstances where it had lent money to a company on the basis of the contents of that company's audited financial statements. The main judgement of the court was given by Brooking J who, having reviewed the authorities, including

San Sebastian Pty Ltd v Minister Administering Environmental Planning and Assessment Act 1979 (NSW) (see above), said:

"Where the plaintiff's claim for damages is based on a fraudulent misrepresentation, one thing he must prove is that the defendant made the representation with the intention that it be acted upon by the plaintiff or by a class of persons which will include the plaintiff: *Peek v Gurney* (1873) LR 6 HL 377; *Bradford Third Equitable Benefit Building Society v Borders* [1941] 2 All ER 205 (at p 211); *Commercial Banking Company of Sydney Ltd v R H Brown & Co* (1972) 126 CLR 337

"It cannot be said that in cases of negligent misstatement, a duty of care will exist only where the defendant made the statement with this intention. But in some cases the duty of care will not arise unless the statement was made with the intention mentioned.

"One of the things which the plaintiff had to prove in order to succeed in this case was that the defendant made the statement complained of with the intention that it be acted upon by the plaintiff or by a class which would include the plaintiff. This is not because, as regards negligent misstatements, the tort of negligence has the intention mentioned as an essential ingredient in common with the tort of deceit.

"It is because in a case like the present, there being no other combination of circumstances present sufficient to impose a duty of care, that duty will not arise unless the defendant made the statement with the intention mentioned." (at p 79)

In holding that the auditors owed no duty of care, His Honour concluded:

"In the present case, no finding was or could have been made that the purpose, or one of the purposes, of the auditors in making their report was to induce the plaintiff, or a class of persons to which it belonged, to act in reliance on the report.

"The only intention on the auditors' part in making their report [and] established in this case – and that only by inference – is an intention to discharge their statutory and contractual duties as Lyvetta's auditors by making the report required by the Companies Act. I am prepared to accept that they knew or believed that AGC would probably rely on the report in deciding what to do as regards Lyvetta's facility, but this knowledge or belief cannot be equated with an intention to induce AGC to act in reliance on the report.

"The learned primary judge thought it sufficient, for the existence of a duty of care, that the defendant knew that there was (as His Honour put it) a reasonable possibility that the plaintiff might rely on statements made by the defendant in its report for the purposes of its business relationship with Lyvetta. His Honour did not deal with the question whether it had to be or had been shown that the misstatement was made by the auditors with the intention of inducing the plaintiff, or a class to which it belonged, to act in reliance on it." (at p 682)

(h) In *Esanda Finance Corporation Ltd v Peat Marwick Hungerfords* (unreported, dated 14 February, 1994), Esanda Finance alleged that in the course of its financial dealings with Excel, it relied to its detriment upon audit reports prepared by the auditors, Peat Marwick Hungerfords. It alleged that those audits had been negligently prepared and that it had suffered damage as a result. Peat Marwick Hungerfords sought to strike out paragraphs of the statement of claim on the basis that those paragraphs did not disclose any basis upon which a duty of care was owed.

At first instance, Bollen J declined to strike out the paragraphs. Accordingly, Peat Marwick Hungerfords appealed.

On appeal, King CJ analysed the High Court decision in *San Sebastian Pty Ltd v Minister Administering Environmental Planning and Assessment Act 1979 (NSW)* (see above) and accepted that a number of factors, not necessarily involving an intention to induce, could give rise to a duty of care.

The only factors before him were statements in the accounting standards as to the group of people who might rely upon the audited accounts. They, in His Honour's opinion, did not reflect an assumption of responsibility sufficient on their own to give rise to a duty of care. His Honour also looked at the judgement of Rolfe J in *Columbia Coffee & Tea Pty Ltd v Churchill* (t/a Nelson Parkhill) (see above) and concluded that the passages in the auditors' audit manual to which Rolfe J had attached such significance, also failed to disclose that any responsibility had been assumed.

Consequently, His Honour (with whom Millhouse J agreed) directed that the relevant paragraphs of the statement of claim be struck out.

Olssen J took a narrower view of the circumstances in which a duty of care would arise and held that an assumption of responsibility by itself would not be enough, whether it took the form of the accounting standards or, as in *Columbia Coffee & Tea Pty Ltd v Churchill*, the audit manual or any other form.

He too was unable to find any factor or combination of factors upon which to base the existence of a duty of care and therefore directed that the relevant paragraphs be struck out.

Esanda Finance has appealed to the High Court of Australia. The Court's judgement is awaited.

(i) *Executor Trustee Australia Ltd & Ors v Peat Marwick Hungerfords* (1994) 15 ACSR 556 involved allegations that the defendant auditors had been negligent in their preparation of a number of reports and statements concerning the financial position of Excel Limited. The question that arose in this case was the extent to which the auditors were responsible to those who relied on the financial statements.

The auditors alleged that they were not responsible to those who invested on the basis of the financial statements, and accordingly they applied to the Supreme Court of South Australia to strike the claims out. In particular, the auditors argued that in making the statements they had made, there had been no intention to induce.

Bollen J refused to strike out any aspect of the statement of claim. In cases such as this, an intention to induce may create a sufficient degree of proximity but it was not an essential feature. An alternative feature could be the assumption of responsibility.

7 The implications of tortuous liability are important for all accountants who produce reports or statements of various kinds (whether for a fee or not) which are liable to be relied upon by persons other than those for whom they were originally prepared.

8 A member may sometimes be informed, before certain work is carried out, that a third party will rely upon the results. An example likely to be encountered in practice is a report on the business of a client which the member has been instructed to prepare for the purpose of it being shown to a potential purchaser or potential creditor of that business. In such a case it would be prudent for the member to assume that the same duty will be held to be owed to the third party as to the client unless the member has taken steps to disclaim liability (see paras 25-30 of these notes), in which case the liability may be reduced.

9 It is, however, important that members should appreciate that the precise ambit of the test in *Caparo Industries plc v Dickman* (see above) remains uncertain. For example, a duty of care to a third party may also arise when the member does not know that the work performed will in fact be relied upon by a particular third party but only knows that it is work of a kind which is liable in the ordinary course of events to be relied upon by a third party.

However, it will be more difficult for an unidentified third party to show a sufficient degree of proximity to meet the test.

In Australia, many of the questions about whether or not a duty is owed, are avoided by resort to the Trade Practices and Fair Trading Acts (particularly ss 52 and 42 respectively). For example, s. 52 of the Trade Practices Act says that: "A corporation shall not in trade and commerce, engage in conduct that is misleading or deceptive or is likely to mislead or deceive."

For example, an incorporated accounting practice may furnish a misleading report to a third party. In those circumstances, the third party could avoid intricate arguments about "duties of care" by simply pleading breaches of the Trade Practices Act.

The Federal Court has rejected the argument that the provision of professional services does not fall within the ambit of trade and commerce (see *Bond Corporation v Thiess Contractors Limited* (1987) 71 ALR 615).

Section 42 of the Fair Trading Act is an almost identical section but is not restricted to corporations or individuals in interstate trade or commerce.

Notwithstanding the scope of these sections, a plaintiff must still establish sufficient and reasonable reliance upon the alleged misrepresentation.

Excluding or limiting liability to a client

10 The following are the main relevant considerations.

Auditors Under the Corporations Law and Certain Other Statutes

Section 241 of the Corporations Law prohibits companies or their related bodies corporate from indemnifying, amongst others, their auditors in situations involving:

- claims by the company;
- claims by the related body corporate;
- claims involving lack of good faith;
- claims involving legal costs of an unsuccessful defence;
- claims involving a misuse of either information or position.

Any documents designed to indemnify the auditor against such matters will be void.

The precise operation and ambit of this section has yet to be examined by the courts. One of the difficulties facing auditors is reaching an agreement with their client company to include within its articles any indemnity, let alone one of the type envisaged by the section.

Section 1318 of the Corporations Law empowers a court to relieve, amongst others, an auditor from any liability in circumstances where the court is satisfied that the auditor has acted reasonably and should, in the circumstances, be excused. Courts which have looked at this section and its predecessor have tended to conclude that a finding of negligence prevents them from exercising those powers.

The *Contracts Review Act 1980* establishes a mechanism for judicial review of certain contracts and the granting of relief in respect of harsh, oppressive and unconscionable or unjust contracts. Where the court is satisfied that a contract, some of a contract's terms or one of those terms is unjust, s 7 of the Act empowers the court to, amongst other things, refuse to enforce the contract or vary its terms.

In determining whether to take any action along those lines, there are a number of factors which the court is allowed to take into account, including:

- any material inequity in the parties' bargaining power;
- the extent to which the contract's terms were the subject of negotiation;
- the extent to which the contract's terms can be complied with and are necessary for the protection of the parties' interests;
- the parties' ability to protect their respective interests;
- the parties' backgrounds;
- the contract's form and content;
- the availability of independent legal advice and the extent to which the contract's terms were explained;
- the existence of any undue influence, unfair pressure or unfair tactics;
- the parties' conduct in relation to similar contracts; and
- the commercial setting of the contract in question.

Although many of these considerations focus upon the parties to the contract, it is nevertheless feasible that where a contract's terms affect a third party, then that third party may be able to seek relief under the Act. Therefore, it is conceivable that a third party could successfully persuade the court that the terms of a retainer between a member and his or her client should not be enforced as against that third party.

B. Managing Risk – Professional Indemnity Cover Guide

42 Introduction

This guide will help members to gauge the adequacy of their practice's level of professional indemnity insurance. For convenience, this guide refers to 'firms', but it applies equally to other forms of practice. The nature and size of the firm will influence the degree of attention paid to the various aspects of this guide, but it is intended to be of use and relevance to all firms in terms of their practice work.

Regulation 4 of the Regulation in the Institute's section of the Member's Handbook deals with Certificates of Public Practice. The Regulation requires, amongst other things, that members who hold current Certificates of Public Practice or who are applying for such a Certificate, carry valid and binding professional indemnity insurance which meets the minimum requirements prescribed in Regulations 7PI.3.

The minimum requirements cover:

- which parties are to be the Insured;
- the Insurer's qualifications;
- coverage of the Insured's Profession and Business;
- the Period of Insurance;
- the Limit of the Indemnity;
- what is covered by the insurance;
- the extent to which an Insured must remain covered after ceasing to hold a Certificate of Public Practice (run-off cover).

These are the minimum requirements. Each member should review his or her practice to determine whether its features justify the member taking any further steps to ensure the practice's professional indemnity insurance is adequate.

43 Assessment of Risk

Before looking at the type of protection necessary to cover potential liabilities, a logical approach to risk assessment needs to be adopted. A firm should assess its risks at least annually, taking appropriate action as a result of that assessment. In particular, it should examine:

(a) its existing and intended areas of practice;

(b) its composition, experience and expertise;

(c) its management and internal control procedures;

(d) the possibility of being sued should anything go wrong and the possible size of any claim:
  - client by client, having regard to whether the work is ongoing or a one-off engagement;
  - client by client, having regard to the maximum potential exposure to the client's stakeholders;
  - generally talk through any concerns or problems with your partners or colleagues or with the PII broker.

(e) new and existing clients in terms of:
  - instructions received, the nature of the work to be carried out and the cooperation necessary to complete the task in a timely and accurate way;
  - credibility of management;

– quality of accounting, financial and management controls;
– type of business conducted by the client;

(f) economic factors, such as:
– rates of company insolvencies:
– types of business experiencing difficulty;
– the effect of current commercial circumstances on client's business.

(g) in the case of partnerships, delegation of risk assessment to responsible partner.

44 Reduction of Risk

If the firm identifies an area of the practice that poses high risk, the firm should:

(i) evaluate its ability to reduce the risk in terms of existing procedures;
(ii) adjust or reconsider that area of practice and its development;
(iii) retrain or employ staff to meet any staffing weaknesses;
(iv) review the engagement with clients in that area of practices; and
(v) apply risk management procedures, such as second partner review.

Generally, the firm should consider its quality control and assurance procedures, the problems these throw up and how they have been dealt with in the past.

45 Other Factors

(a) The firm must arrange professional indemnity insurance to cover:
 (i) all current staff and consultants and review insurance for subcontractors;
 (ii) all professional activities, including, for example, joint audit appointments;
 (iii) past and incoming partners and predecessors in business.

(b) The firm's claims history should be considered and a regular analysis of the causes of claims completed.

46 Amount and Extent of Liability Insurance

Having carried out the above assessment, the firm will need to decide how much insurance it needs. In making this decision the firm should:

(a) consider and attempt to quantify the firm's exposure, taking into account the worst case scenario;

(b) assess limits of insurance arranged by firms of a similar size and profile. Available sources such as inter-firm comparisons, information held by the firm's broker, and information held jointly with other firms by mutual arrangement should be considered;

(c) take expert advice on how much cover is available and what it costs;

(d) determine the sufficiency of the firm's own resources to meet claims, the availability of both personal and firm's assets and reserves set aside to meet known claims;

(e) take into consideration the long-tail nature of liability claims;

(f) recognise that the extent of losses can be substantially increased by interest, legal costs and inflation.

47 Forms of Insurance

Having decided how much insurance is needed, the firm should then consider the forms of insurance available. These include:

(a) Professional indemnity insurance. This insurance indemnifies the firm for claims made alleging breach of professional duty. Since professional indemnity insurance is a specialised form of insurance, the firm should use a broker with experience in this field.

(b) Directors & Officers insurance. This insurance indemnifies the assured for liabilities arising from errors in the management of corporate entities. It also provides reimbursement to the company where the company has obligations to indemnify its corporate officers. Whilst limited directors and officers' cover may be included under certain professional indemnity policies, it may be appropriate to ensure that separate adequate cover is secured for the whole board. This aspect should be carefully assessed with the firm's brokers.

(c) Trustees liability insurance. Trustees of, for example, superannuation funds, can now arrange separate cover to sit alongside the firm's professional indemnity insurance. There are pertinent reasons to investigate such cover with the firm's brokers. Since the firm's involvement may mean that partners wear more than one 'hat', the firm must make sure the insurance is put in place to cover all forms of exposure.

48 Other Insurance Considerations

(a) Self-Insured Excess

Careful selection of the appropriate level of excess, based on the partners' resources, including their borrowing capacity and the firm's assets must be made. The firm should consider its claims experience and the ability to meet excesses, if there are a number of claims. The minimum excesses specified under Regulation 7PI.3 must be taken into account.

(b) Captive/Mutual Arrangements

It is sometimes possible for a firm to cover liability through its own financial arrangements rather than through commercial insurers. The firm might effectively create its own insurance arrangements in this way, possibly with a group of other firms.

Expert legal, tax and insurance advice needs to be taken by the firm and sound management procedures would need to be in place to ensure that such arrangements met claims effectively.

49 Procedures for Identifying and Monitoring Claims

As well as taking steps to cover potential liabilities, the firm should look for ways to limit the possible damage caused by any existing claims, ensuring that the likelihood of such claims arising again is reduced as far as possible. The following steps would assist:

(a) regular and open discussion between partners and senior employees in order to identify any matters which may have led or may lead to a claim;

(b) the establishment of procedures to identify claims or potential claims and ensure that they are notified;

(c) monitoring of insurance arrangements to ensure that they remain effective; (e.g. notifications to insurers, review of limits, etc);

(d) regular claims review; and

(e) regular use of independent advisers such as insurance brokers, legal advisors and risk manager.

50 "Run-off" Cover

Paragraph 7PI.3(g) of Regulation 4A requires those members who cease public practice to ensure that they remain covered for at least the ensuing seven years from the date of cessation of practice. The firm and its retired partners must carefully assess the period of run-off cover in the light of limitation periods on those actions that could be brought against them and the firm.

Please Note

These Guidance Notes have been prepared for the information of members of the Institute of Chartered Accountants in Australia only. You should not act or omit to act on the basis of these Guidance Notes without first making such enquiries as the particular circumstances of your case may warrant.

N6

Reporting of Fraud and Other Illegal Acts

(July 2003)

Contents

N6

1. The Professional Accountant's Fiduciary Duty of Confidentiality

1.1 A member may act in a number of capacities, either as part of a practice or for an employer. In all such capacities a member owes a duty of confidentiality to the client or employer. Information that is disclosed to the member during an engagement or contract of service will be subject to the duty to keep the information confidential. When providing services to a client or employer, a member must be aware of such obligation. A member must ensure that the relationship with the client or employer is founded on trust, which implicitly requires the member to observe the obligations of confidentiality.

1.2 The duty of confidentiality, however, is not absolute. In certain circumstances a member may choose, or be compelled, to disclose information that is subject to the duty of confidentiality. The obligation to keep the information confidential may be overridden by statute. For example, there may be a statutory obligation to report fraud and other illegal acts. In carrying out an engagement, a member should be alert to the existence of any wrongdoing. In exceptional circumstances there may be occasions when disclosure of irregularity or wrongdoing may be required in the public interest, or in the member's own interest. These matters are discussed later in this guidance note.

2. Criminal Offences

2.1 In recent years there has been a steady growth in the number of criminal offences in connection with commercial operations. It is not practicable to set out all the offences that members may encounter in the course of their work, but they generally relate to the following areas:

(a) offences under criminal legislation – e.g. theft, obtaining an advantage by deception, false accounting and suppression of evidence, fraud and forgery;

(b) offences under the Corporations Law in relation to companies;

(c) offences in relation to participation in a criminal act – e.g. perjury, conspiracy, soliciting or inciting to commit crime and attempting to commit crime;

(d) offences in relation to direct and indirect taxation;

(e) offences relating to inside information under the Corporations Law;

(f) offences under the Trade Practices Act – e.g. in relation to exclusive dealing and misleading and deceptive conduct;

(g) offences under other legislation, including bankruptcy or insolvency offences, fraud on creditors, environmental protection and offences arising out of relations between employers and employees.

3. Members in Practice

3.1 Disclosure of Information by a Client to a Member

3.1.1 Where a member is engaged by a client to provide services and, in particular, to prepare or audit accounts or provide taxation services, the client should be notified that the member can do so only on the basis of full disclosure of all information relevant to the work in question. If the client will not agree, the member should not act for that client.

3.1.2 If, in issuing an opinion or report, a member forms a view that material information has not been disclosed, the member should consider whether there is a need to make reference to its absence in, or to qualify, the opinion or report. The member should, in these circumstances, also consider the option of discontinuing the engagement.

3.1.3 In the case of an auditor, there are specific obligations under the Corporations Law, e.g. an auditor must consider whether all information and explanations needed to form an opinion have been obtained.

3.1.4 It is an offence under the Corporations Law for an officer of a company, without lawful excuse, to obstruct an auditor of the company. Obstruction includes refusing or failing to give the auditor such information and explanations as the auditor desires for the purposes of audit.

3.2 Obligation to Disclose at law

3.2.1 A member must disclose information if compelled at law. For example, a member may be required to disclose confidential information under a court order in the form of a subpoena, under a search warrant or by reason of an overriding obligation under specific legislation such as the Corporations Law or Income Tax Assessment Act.

3.2.2 An auditor has a duty under section 332 (10) of the Corporations Law to inform the Australian Securities and Investment Commission, on becoming satisfied that there has been a contravention of the Corporations Law and the circumstances are such that, in the auditor's opinion, the matter has not been or will not be adequately dealt with by comment in the auditor's report on the financial statements or by bringing the matter to the notice of the directors.

3.2.3 The right to resist disclosure of information on the grounds of legal professional privilege will not normally be available to a member. Documents in the member's possession may, however, attract the privilege. Where a member is requested to disclose information at law, the member should consider whether privilege applies and seek legal advice.

3.2.4 In the event that a member is requested to disclose information that may tend to incriminate the member personally, the member usually has a right to a privilege against self-incrimination.

3.3 Disclosure in the Public Interest

3.3.1 There may be exceptional circumstances where a member forms the view that confidential information should be disclosed to an authority in spite of the absence of any court order or requirement under statute, because the member has formed the view that disclosure is in the public interest. No clear guidance has been given by the courts on the question of when it will be proper for a member to disclose confidential information to a third party on the grounds of public interest. In such a case, the member needs to assess the obligation to uphold public accountability and balance this against the duty to the client. Members should carefully consider whether breach of the duty of confidentiality to the client should be overridden. In most cases it would be appropriate for the member to seek legal advice or to consult the Institute's CA Advisory Groups (CAAGs) before making a decision.

3.4 Disclosure in the Member's Own Interest

3.4.1 There are circumstances where it will be necessary for a member to disclose confidential information in order to protect the member's own interests. It may be proper for a member to disclose the information in the absence of the client's authority in the following circumstances:

(a) to enable the member to defend a criminal charge or to be cleared of suspicion; or

(b) to resist proceedings for a penalty in respect of a taxation offence, for example in a case where it is suggested that the member assisted or induced a client to prepare or lodge incorrect returns or accounts; or

(c) to resist a legal action brought against the member by a client or some third party; or

(d) to enable the member to defend disciplinary proceedings or enquiry by the professional accounting bodies or other similar bodies.

3.4.2 A member should always consider whether it is appropriate to seek the client's prior consent to disclosure of the information and should seek legal advice before making any disclosure or approaching the client.

3.5 Prosecution of a Client or Former Client

3.5.1 A member should adopt a cautious approach if approached by the police, the Australian Taxation Office, the Australian Securities and Investment Commission or other public authority in connection with the potential prosecution of a client or former client. A member needs to assess the obligation to provide proper assistance to prosecuting authorities against the obligation of confidentiality to the client or former client. The member should first consider whether the information is confidential and whether the relevant authority is entitled to the information. A member should also consider whether the client or former client should be informed of the request for information.

3.5.2 In most cases the member will need to decide whether the authority has a right to the information and, if necessary, to seek legal advice to reach that decision.

3.5.3 If a member is required to attend court as a witness to disclose information that relates to a client, or is compelled to produce client documents under a subpoena, the member must generally comply. If the member is in any doubt about the obligation to disclose information, or to comply with a subpoena or other court process, the member should seek independent legal advice.

3.6 Suspicion of Unlawful Activity

3.6.1 A member who acquires knowledge during an engagement and who believes or suspects that a client, or an officer or employee of a client, may have been guilty of some default or unlawful act should, in the ordinary course of events, raise the matter with the management of the client at an appropriate level. If the concerns are not satisfactorily resolved, the member should consider reporting the matter to non-executive directors or to the client's audit committee, if there is one. Where this is not possible or this step fails to resolve the matter, a member should consider their professional duty and any other statutory obligation which may require the matter to be reported to a third party or statutory authority.

3.6.2 A member's response will depend on the capacity in which the member is acting. For instance, a member who has been appointed as an auditor will have different considerations from a member providing services on a non-audit engagement. Guidance is provided below on reporting suspected irregularity, fraud or unlawful acts to third parties.

3.7 Reporting an Irregularity, Fraud and Other Unlawful Act

3.7.1 Confidentiality is an implied term of a member's engagement contract with the client. For this reason, a member should not, as a general rule, disclose to unauthorised persons information about the client's affairs acquired during and as a result of a professional relationship.

3.7.2 In the absence of any statutory requirement, a member who becomes aware that a client has committed an unlawful act, or has failed to carry out some required legal duty, will generally not be obliged to disclose that state of affairs to any persons other than the directors of the client or some person having their authority. There will be circumstances where the failure to report the unlawful conduct may implicate the member who should then seriously consider whether that knowledge needs to be conveyed to the relevant authorities.

3.7.3 The obligation to disclose should be seriously considered and a member should have regard to the nature of the engagement, the engagement contract, the duty of confidentiality, obligations at law and under statute and general ethical obligations.

3.7.4 There will be exceptional circumstances where a member may conclude that it is proper to disclose information to a third party for the reason that it is in the public interest or for the member's own protection. This step should not be taken without full and proper consideration of the circumstances and the member should seek independent legal advice on whether the duty of confidentiality should be breached.

3.8 Failure to Report Criminal Offences

3.8.1 In dealing with a client's affairs, a member may become aware of conduct, which may be unlawful or criminal in nature.

3.8.2 A member should be aware that, in failing to report the matter to the relevant authorities or failing to act in a proper manner, the member may be liable to prosecution. For example, as a consequence, the member may be accused of:

(a) inciting a client to commit a criminal offence; or

(b) helping or encouraging a client in the planning or execution of a criminal offence which is committed; or

(c) concealing, destroying or fabricating evidence; or

(d) misleading the police by statements that are known to be untrue.

3.8.3 Where a member knows, suspects or believes that the client has committed, or intends to commit, a criminal offence, or the member is approached to give a statement to the police in respect of a client's affairs, legal advice should be sought about the issues involved.

3.9 Defamation

3.9.1 Where a member discovers any improper conduct, there is a need to consider the matter carefully before making statements or publicising any suspicion or belief. When reporting irregularities or unlawful activity, the nature of the information may damage the reputation of the client or another party and may render the member liable to an action for defamation. A member should be alert to the sensitivities of the information concerned and the need to ensure that, if information is disclosed without the authority of the client, it is correct and disclosure is justified in the circumstances. A member should seek independent legal advice if in any doubt.

3.9.2 In certain circumstances a person will have qualified privilege in proceedings for defamation, for statements where the maker of a statement has an interest or duty to make the statement to the recipient and the recipient has a corresponding interest or duty to receive it. Auditors have special protection for qualified privilege under the Corporations Law.

4 Members in Business

4.1 The Guidance set out above applies equally to a member in business. A member in this position may be presented with a situation where the duty to an employer conflicts with the ethical duty to disclose information to a third party. A member should first consider raising the suspected irregularity or improper conduct with management on a confidential basis. If the member forms the view that it would not be appropriate, independent legal advice should be sought on the position or, alternatively, the Institute's CA Advisory Groups (CAAGs) consulted.

5 General

5.1 Other legal systems

The discussion in this guidance note is in the context of the Australian legal system. Members should be alert to the fact that there are different requirements and obligations in other countries. Care is needed when members are working in other countries or dealing with people or organisations located there.

5.2 Professional advice for members – CA Advisory Group

5.2.1 To assist members to make the best possible decision in unfamiliar or challenging professional situations, including ethical dilemmas, the Institute has established CA Advisory Groups (CAAGs) in each region. Each CAAG is a collection of senior Institute members from the local region (NSW/ACT, QLD, VIC/TAS, SA/NT, WA) with a broad cross-section of professional and life experience and unblemished professional records. These members have been specially trained to provide confidential counseling and support on an informal basis.

5.2.2 Members may consult with a CAAG counsellor in confidence if they wish to discuss the circumstances connected with this guidance note.

5.2.3 Members in NSW and the ACT wishing to avail themselves of the service or wanting further information should, in the first instance, contact the Manager, Member Services NSW & ACT; whilst members in Queensland, Victoria/Tasmania, South Australia/ Northern Territory and Western Australia should contact their Regional Manager, during business hours.

5.3 Notification of Insurers

Circumstances, which give rise to issues involving criminality and unlawful conduct, are usually complex. In many cases the ramifications of the conduct and liabilities relating to it are uncertain. It is therefore important that members seek legal advice wherever appropriate. Given the nature of this type of conduct, a member should also consider notifying their insurer upon discovering or becoming aware of circumstances which suggest that illegal or unlawful activity has occurred, particularly if the member is concerned that it could be an activity which the member might have detected earlier.

N7
Arrangements to Cover the Incapacity or Death of a Sole Practitioner

(Revised May 2007)

Contents

Paragraph(s)

Arrangements to Cover the Incapacity or Death of a Sole Practitioner

Problems have arisen where a sole practitioner has become physically or mentally incapacitated and consequently unable to continue to manage the practice, or has died without making adequate arrangements for the conduct of the practice by others. The following guidance is intended to assist sole practitioners in identifying the solutions to the problems which will inevitably arise in the event of their incapacity or death. These problems may affect the member's family, clients, other members and firms who may be involved in the continuation of the practice, and the member's personal representatives.

General Considerations

1. All members in public practice have a duty to ensure that their practices are at all times properly supervised and conducted, including implementing arrangements to cover holidays and sickness of the practitioner. The problems which will inevitably arise where a sole practitioner ceases to be able to conduct the practice, because of continuing incapacity or death, are much more serious. The interruption of services resulting, in particular, from mental incapacity or death, will cause considerable difficulty and inconvenience to the member's clients, additional anxiety for his or her family, and reduction in the value of the practice or even its disintegration.

2. It is therefore vital for a sole practitioner to confront these problems and difficulties, preferably when first commencing practice, and to make arrangements appropriate to each of the following circumstances to enable the practice to be carried on with a minimum of dislocation:

   (a) short-term absence due to holiday or sickness;

   (b) continuing physical incapacity;

   (c) mental incapacity;

   (d) death.

   The arrangements in respect of (b), (c) and (d) should provide, as far as possible, for the practice to continue as a going concern by an appointed 'alternate' (see below) until such time as the sole practitioner recovers or a decision is made to dispose of the practice. Where the member is supervising the practice requirements of a Chartered Accountants Program candidate, or a student awaiting admission, these arrangements should include provision for notification of death or anticipated prolonged absence of the sole practitioner to the Institute so that provision can be made to ensure that the intending applicant's admission status is not placed in jeopardy.

3. The arrangements may be made with another sole practitioner or with a firm. According to legal advice obtained by the Institute, any effective arrangements will require specific legal measures, such as those described below. It is, however, first necessary to consider the specific legal problems associated with the provision of services in the following reserved areas of practice, if incapacity or death of a sole practitioner should occur.

Legal considerations arising in reserved areas

4. **Audit**

The Corporations Law allows a firm or an individual to act as an auditor of a company. In the case of a sole practitioner the individual practitioner will be appointed as auditor of a company. The individual appointee must oversee and sign off the audit. It is not permissible for another person who has not been appointed to sign an audit report.

There may be a situation where the sole practitioner has become physically (but not mentally) ill, and has completed the audit work save for the final review and signing of the audit report. In this instance an alternate who had been properly appointed by a power of attorney could, if satisfied with the audit work, carry out the review in consultation with the practitioner and sign the report on the authority of the practitioner. Temporary incapacity, mental or physical, would not necessarily terminate the appointment. In this situation the alternate (or sole practitioner where appropriate) should seek legal advice on the specific circumstances.

Where a sole practitioner who is an auditor dies or is mentally incapable, the audit appointment will be terminated and it will not be possible for an alternate to sign off an audit on their behalf.

5. **Trustee in Bankruptcy/Liquidator**

A sole practitioner who acts as trustee in bankruptcy, or liquidator, will be appointed in a personal capacity. In the event of incapacity or death of the appointee, a new appointee will need to be appointed. If an appointee dies, the appointment is automatically vacated. Specific procedures apply when appointing a new appointee. The procedures vary depending on the nature of the administration. An alternate or other 'substitute' is not automatically entitled to act in place of the sole practitioner. The appointment may need to be sanctioned by the Court, creditors or relevant committee. In certain circumstances it may be possible for an alternate to deal with a sole practitioner's resignation or vacation of office particularly as the representative of the sole practitioner's estate. If presented with these circumstances the alternate should seek legal advice.

6. **Tax Agent**

Where a sole practitioner acts as a tax agent there may be other employees in the firm who can continue to act as tax agent for clients during the period of incapacity. Where a partnership or company is registered as a tax agent, the person specified in the application for registration, as the nominee of the partnership, is registered as the nominee of the tax agent. Tax agents can register partners and employees as their nominees. Once registered, nominees may sign tax returns. It is not possible for the alternate to sign a tax return on behalf of the practitioner unless they are a registered nominee. Registered tax agents will need to notify the Tax Agents Board of any changes to nominees. If the alternate is a registered tax agent they can sign off in their own capacity.

7. **Investment Business Considerations**

The clients of sole practitioners who are authorised to carry on investment business may have investment commitments which the practitioner's incapacity or death could affect. Although there is no statutory requirement for these practitioners to make alternative arrangements in the event of their incapacity or death, it is advisable for them to do so.

In choosing an alternate for a practice which carries on investment business, the sole practitioner should choose an alternate who is licensed by the Australian Securities and Investments Commission ("ASIC") to carry on the investment business.

8. **Arrangements Needed**

The Institute has prepared a package outlining some of the issues a sole practitioner should consider in making arrangements for the continuity of their practice in the event of their future incapacity or death. It allows sole practitioners to determine for themselves, while competent, who will manage their practice and affairs in the event they are unable to do so.

The package recommends legal measures for the following arrangements:

(i) the appointment of an alternate as an attorney under a protected power of attorney (known as an enduring power of attorney) to enable that person to act during the sole practitioner's lifetime in the event of the practitioner's physical or mental incapacity; and

(ii) the appointment of an alternate as a special executor under the sole practitioner's will to attend to the affairs of the practice until it is sold, transferred or otherwise disposed of.

The package, Guidance on Incapacity or Death of a Sole Practitioner, is available on the Institute's website, charteredaccountants.com.au.

Glossary of Terms

Unless otherwise specified words and expressions have the same meaning in the Supplemental Charter, By Laws and Regulations.

Members should also have regard to the definitions contained in APES 110 *Code of Ethics for Professional Accountants*.

References herein to Fellows, Chartered Accountants, members and meetings shall be construed as having references to Fellows, Chartered Accountants, members and meetings of the Institute.

Admission in relation to membership of the Institute includes advancement in status and "admit" has a corresponding meaning.

Admission Regulations means the regulations (if any) for the time being determined by the Board for the admission and readmission of persons to membership of the Institute, being regulations not inconsistent with the By-laws.

Advancement in status means the change in the class of a member from that of "Chartered Accountant" to "Fellow".

Affiliate and **affiliate member** means a natural person who participates with individual members in a practice entity, who is not a Fellow or Chartered Accountant or entitled to be admitted to membership as a Fellow or Chartered Accountant, who has been admitted to membership in accordance with the By-laws and the Regulations.

Audit Committee means the committee established by the Board pursuant to By-law 129A.

Authorised representative means an individual member holding a Certificate of Public Practice with the Institute who is authorised by a non-member owner to act in a governance role of a practice entity.

Board means the board of Directors of the Institute constituted under this Supplemental Charter and the By-laws.

The By-laws means the By-laws contained in the Schedule to the Supplemental charter as amended or added to from time to time.

Candidate should be read as a reference to registered graduate.

Chartered firm means any partnership, trust or body corporate or unincorporate in or through which persons who are Members in public practice, or include a Member or Members in public practice, provide professional services to clients which is entitled to describe itself as "Chartered Accountants" in accordance with R9/1205.

Chief Executive Officer means the chief executive officer of the Institute for the time being appointed by the Board under By-law 119B and includes any person for the time being discharging the duties of such officer or acting with his or her authority and on his or her behalf.

Director means a person appointed to perform the duties of a director of the Institute.

Commonwealth of Australia means Our Commonwealth of Australia and any territory or dependency in respect of which the Parliament of the Commonwealth or the Parliament of any State of the Commonwealth may make laws.

Individual member means a natural person who has been admitted to membership as a Fellow or Chartered Accountant, and "individual membership" has a corresponding meaning.

Institute means The Institute of Chartered Accountants in Australia.

Member[1] means any applicant for or holder of:

- a Certificate of Public Practice; or
- affiliate membership; or
- practice entity membership.

Glossary

1 Regulation 4 Appendix 7PI.

Membership of the Institute shall consist of:

(a) the persons who, immediately before the date on which the Eighth Supplemental Royal Charter became effectual in accordance with Article 25, were Fellows, Chartered Accountants, affiliates or practice entity members;

(b) the natural persons who, after such date, are admitted as Fellows or Chartered Accountants in conformity with the Institute's Royal Charter and By-laws as in force from time to time;

(c) the natural persons who, after such date, are admitted to membership as affiliates of a practice entity in accordance with the By-laws and the Regulations; and

(d) the practice entities which, after such date, are admitted to membership in accordance with the By-laws and the Regulations.

Member in public practice means any member of the Institute who holds, or ought to hold, a Certificate of Public Practice and a practice entity member and an affiliate member.

Month means calendar month.

Non-accountant means a person who is not an accountant.

Non-member practice entity means a practice entity which is not admitted to membership of the Institute and is bound by the standards of practice and professional conduct and by the discipline of the Institute.

Overseas Member means a member whose name appears on the Overseas Register.

Overseas Register means the register of members whose registered address is outside the Commonwealth of Australia, to be maintained by the Chief Executive Officer under By-law 142.

Post means sending by post, facsimile transmission, email or document exchange, and "posted", "posting", "postal" and "postal ballot" have corresponding meanings.

Practice means a business providing professional services including services which require the holding of a current Certificate of Public Practice by the individual Member who is a Principal.

Practice entity means a partnership, an incorporated company, trust or any combination or partnership of these by or through which the member performs any of the functions of a member in public practice.

Practice entity member means a practice entity which is entitled under Articles 17 or 18 to describe itself as "Chartered Accountants" and which has been admitted to membership of the Institute.

Practice entity participant or **Participant** means a person who is a principal of a practice entity.

Practice entity representative means an individual member holding a Certificate of Public Practice with the Institute who is authorised by an applicant for Practice entity membership of the Institute to provide the undertakings required by Regulation 2.

Prescribed means prescribed by the Supplemental Charter or by the By-laws or by the Regulations.

Principal of a practice entity includes:

(a) in the case of a Practice Entity which is a partnership a partner of that partnership;

(b) in the case of a Practice Entity which is a body corporate, a director of that body corporate;

(c) in the case of a Practice Entity which is conducted as a trust, an individual who, as an officer or employee of the trustee of that trust or otherwise, provides or participates as a principal in the provision of the services provided by the practice entity; and

(d) an individual who, as an officer or employee of the practice entity, or otherwise, provides or participates as a principal in the provision of the services provided by the practice entity.

Principal in relation to a Practice means any person, who is a principal of the Practice or a principal, partner, director, officer or trustee of a related Entity of the Practice[1].

---

1 Regulation 4 Appendix 7PI.

Factors to consider in determining whether a person is a principal of a practice entity include whether:

- They have responsibility for the standard of professional work undertaken by the practice entity and management of the practice's activities, including: client selection and retention, determining the terms of the professional engagement, the type and quality of professional services provided, risk management, and the exercising of professional judgement in ethical and technical matters;
- Their individual acts are binding on the practice or other principals of the practice;
- They have the potential for personal liability for the practice's liabilities;
- They have a role in the governance of the practice;
- They have responsibility for signing off on professional engagements;
- They are acknowledged in the PI policy of the practice as a person responsible for professional engagements;
- They are promoted to clients and potential clients as the person responsible for professional engagements;
- The perception of clients and suppliers of the member is of a person who is able to bind the practice.
- A principal, partner, director, officer or trustee of a related entity of the practice may also be considered to be a principal of a practice entity.

Note: The absence of an equity holding in the practice by the member is **not** a conclusive factor in determining whether a member is a principal. Similarly an ownership interest in a practice is **not** necessarily the sole factor in determining whether a member is a principal of a practice entity. For example, an employee is not considered to be a principal merely where a share in ownership is incorporated into their employee remuneration package.

Public accountancy services

The Supplemental Royal Charter defines "public accountancy services" to mean such services as the Board may from time to time determine to be "public accountancy services".

The Board has determined such services to be accounting, auditing, management consulting, taxation, financial management and insolvency. With effect from 1 July 2005, the Board has determined that forensic accounting, risk management and corporate advisory services are **public accountancy services**.

Public accountant means a natural person:

(a) who maintains as a principal, whether on his own behalf or as a trustee and whether alone or with others, an office for the provision of one or more public accountancy services and who places that service or those services at the disposal of the community for remuneration, and not solely at the disposal of any individual, firm, trust or body of persons, corporate or unincorporate; or

(b) who is a shareholder in, or a director of, a body corporate which, whether on its own behalf or as a trustee and whether alone or with others, maintains an office for the provision of one or more public accountancy services and which places that service or those services at the disposal of the community for remuneration, and not solely at the disposal of any individual, firm, trust or body of persons, corporate or unincorporate, and who, as an officer or employee of such body corporate or otherwise, provides or participates in the provision of such service or services on behalf of such body corporate; or

(c) who is a beneficiary under a trust the trustee of which, whether alone or with others, maintains an office for the provision of one or more public accountancy services and places that service or those services at the disposal of the community for remuneration, and not solely at the disposal of any individual, firm, trust or body of persons, corporate or unincorporate, and who, as an officer or employee of such trustee or otherwise, participates in the provision of such service or services on behalf of such trustee.

Region means each of the following regions of the Commonwealth of Australia:

(i) New South Wales;

(ii) Australian Capital Territory;

(iii) Victoria;

(iv) Tasmania;

(v) Queensland;

(vi) South Australia and Northern Territory;

(vii) Western Australia.

Regional Council means a Council for a Region constituted as prescribed in these By-laws and "Regional Councillor" means a member of a Regional Council.

Regional General Manager means the manager of the Institute in a Region appointed by the Chief Executive Officer and includes any person for the time being discharging the duties of such officer.

Regional meeting means a meeting of the members enrolled on a Regional Register kept under the By-laws.

Regional member means a member enrolled on a Regional register constituted as prescribed in the By-laws.

Regional Register means the register of members in a Region to be maintained by the Chief Executive Officer under By-law 142.

Registered address of a member means his address on the National Register kept under the By-laws.

Registered graduate means a person whose name is entered on the register of examination candidates maintained by the Institute and who has agreed to be bound by the provisions of this Our Supplemental Charter, the By-laws and the regulations made under Article 25.

Regulations means the regulations made by the Board from time to time under Article 25 of the Supplemental Charter.

Related Entity means any partnership, company, corporation or trust carrying on the whole or any part of a practice[1].

Solicitation means an approach to a client or prospective client for the purpose of offering services and is considered a form of advertising.

Special resolution means a resolution passed by a majority of not less than three fourths of the votes cast at a meeting of the Board at which a quorum is present.

Supplemental Charter means the Supplemental Charter as amended or added to from time to time.

Writing includes printing, typing, lithography, microfilm, photocopying, facsimile transmission, electronic mail and other modes of representing or reproducing words in a visible form and "written" has a corresponding meaning.

Note:

(i) a reference to a statute or other law includes regulations and other instruments under it and consolidations, amendments, re-enactments or replacements of any of them.

(ii) words importing the singular only include the plural and vice-versa, words importing the masculine gender only include the feminine and neuter genders and words importing persons include corporations.

1 Regulation 4 Appendix 7PI.

R1

Regulations for the Chartered Accountants Program

(August 2012)

Contents

R1

Section I – General

1. About the Chartered Accountants Program

1.1.1 Structure

The Chartered Accountants Program consists of five modules.

The four technical modules are:

- Financial Accounting and Reporting (FIN)
- Management Accounting and Applied Finance (MAAF)
- Audit and Assurance (AAA)
- Taxation (TAX). There are currently separate modules for New Zealand and Australian tax.

The final module is Capstone.

1.2 Timetable

The timetable is based on three trimesters per year for the technical modules and two semesters per year for the Capstone. All of the modules are offered twice in a 12-month period.

The technical modules run over 12 weeks with a final examination in week 13.

The Capstone module runs over 14 weeks with a final examination in week 17.

1.3 Progression through the modules

The four technical modules can be completed in any order. A candidate must have successfully completed the four technical modules before he/she can enrol in the Capstone module.

The Capstone module can be completed upon successful completion of the four technical modules. It is strongly recommended that candidates have completed at least two years (full-time equivalent) of approved employment prior to undertaking the Capstone.

Candidates can enrol in only one module at a time.

1.4 Fees

The fee for each Chartered Accountants Program module is decided annually by the Institute's Board and must be paid at the time of enrolment in a module. Refer to the current fee schedule.

1.5 Exemptions

A candidate may apply for exemptions in accordance with the Institute's exemption policy.

1.6 Currency of the modules

A candidate who does not complete the Chartered Accountants Program within eight years of registration will be required to re-sit and successfully complete all required modules which fall outside this time limit.

1.7 Locations for module workshops, presentations and examinations

Candidates should elect their preferred workshop, presentation, and examination locations on enrolment for each module. The Institute will allocate candidates to locations and advise prior to the event. Due to the logistics of arranging workshops, presentations, and examinations the Institute can make no assurances that all candidates will be allocated to locations of greatest personal convenience.

2. Eligibility to register as a Chartered Accountants Program candidate

To register a candidate for the Chartered Accountants Program must have met the academic requirements, and be in approved employment.

2.1 Academic requirements

An applicant wishing to register as a Candidate for the Chartered Accountants Program must have satisfied the Academic requirements. These requirements are:

(a) An Institute accredited degree;

or

(b) An overseas qualification that has been accepted by the Institute as at least equivalent to an Australian or New Zealand Bachelor's degree;

or

(c) An accepted non-accounting degree.

and

(d) Passes in approved subjects covering the required topics. These subjects may be completed as part of an accredited degree or separately by way of approved subjects offered by tertiary education providers through a course or as single subjects.

2.1.1 Required topics

The Academic requirements prescribe the following required topics to be covered in the applicant's academic qualifications:

- Financial accounting
- Management accounting
- Finance
- Commercial and corporate law
- Taxation
- Audit and assurance
- Accounting Information systems
- Economics
- Quantitative methods
- Organisational management (NZICA only)

2.2 Practical experience Requirements

Applicants wishing to register as a candidate for the Chartered Accountants Program must be in approved employment in an Approved Training Employer (ATE) under the guidance of a mentor.

2.2.1 Requirements for approved employment

The requirements for approved employment are defined in the Practical Experience Requirements. In summary, these are:

(a) To be employed in an ATE for at least 17.5 hours per week. An ATE is an organisation that has met the standards for offering the type of work experience that fulfils the practical experience requirements for Chartered Accountants.

and

(b) To be employed in a relevant accounting role

and

R1

(c) To be mentored by a Chartered Accountant who is a member of the Institute or another recognised GAA body.

and

(d) To be undertaking development of required technical and non-technical competence to the levels outlined in the Institute logbook

2.2.2 **Practical experience prior to module study**

Whilst not mandatory, it is recommended that candidates undertake a period of employment in a relevant accounting role prior to commencing their first Chartered Accountants Program module.

2.2.3 **Module study out of approved employment**

In exceptional circumstances, candidates may apply to undertake up to two technical modules whilst out of approved employment.

Candidates must submit an application to complete a technical module out of approved employment as soon as they become aware of such circumstances.

Candidates must be in approved employment whilst studying the Capstone module.

3. Candidate registration for the Chartered Accountants Program

Candidates who meet the eligibility requirements outlined in Section 2 may apply to register for the Chartered Accountants Program.

3.1 **Jurisdiction of registration**

Candidates who live in New Zealand or Australia must register for the Chartered Accountants Program with the Institute in the country in which they live (as indicated by where they are resident for tax purposes). .

Candidates who do not live in New Zealand or Australia but completed the academic requirements in New Zealand or Australia must register for the Chartered Accountants Program in the country where they completed their study.

3.2 **Application for registration**

Applications for registration for the Chartered Accountants Program must be submitted on the Application Form and accompanied by:

(a) A certified copy of the candidate's academic transcript showing evidence of completion of the requirements outlined in section 2.1 of these Regulations.

and

(b) Notification that the candidate is in approved employment, in the form of an Agreement signed by the candidate, employer and mentor.

and

(c) (NZICA only) The Provisional Membership Application (if the candidate is not already a member).

3.3 **Confirmation of registration**

Once registration is approved a candidate will be provided with access to the Chartered Accountants Program orientation material and module enrolment information.

If an applicant is not eligible to register, they will be advised of the reason why.

4. Module enrolment

4.1 Requirements for module enrolment

Only registered candidates can enrol in a Chartered Accountants Program module.

Candidates are required to submit an enrolment application for each module no later than the enrolment closing date.

Refer to Section I: paragraph 1.3.

At the time of enrolment candidates are required to confirm that they are still in approved employment.

4.2 Jurisdiction of enrolment

A candidate may only enrol in a module where he/she is registered as a Chartered Accountants Program Candidate (refer to Section 3: paragraph 3.1)

Candidates who move their residence after they commence the Chartered Accountants Program may apply to transfer to study the program in their new country of residence. The modules they have already completed will be recognised.

Candidates cannot transfer their study part way through a module.

4.3 Enrolment fee

Payment of the required module fee must be made at the time of enrolment.

5. Module withdrawals

5.1 Notification of withdrawal from a module

A candidate may withdraw from a Chartered Accountants Program module at any time.

5.2 Impact of withdrawal from a module

A candidate who has formally withdrawn from a Chartered Accountants Program module will receive a result of 'Discontinued' for that module.

5.3 Refund of module fee

Module fee refunds will be paid according to the rates set out in the current fee schedule.

6. Assistance for candidates

The Institute may provide assistance for a candidate who has a disability or is experiencing circumstances that will impair his/her module assessment performance.

6.1 Request for assistance

A candidate who seeks assistance is required to make his/her request to the Institute. The Institute must receive the request at least one calendar month prior to the module commencement date.

Where the disability or circumstance arises after this time, candidates should contact the Institute as soon as possible.

6.2 Consideration of requests

The Institute will consider requests for assistance where:

(a) the request is specific as to the nature and extent of any assistance being sought;

and

(b) the request includes independent medical or other appropriate professional evidence of the candidate's disability or circumstance. This evidence must be dated within one month of the request made by the candidate. Any costs involved in obtaining such evidence will be met by the candidate;

and

(c) the request includes independent medical or other appropriate professional opinion as to the nature and extent of assistance required to satisfactorily compensate for the disability or circumstance.

R1

In such cases the Institute will determine the arrangements that shall be made for the candidate.

The Institute reserves the right to recover from the candidate all or part of the cost of any assistance provided.

7. Module Results

Candidates will receive a result for each module they enrol in. The result will be one of the following.

Result	**Candidate:**
Pass with Merit	Achieved within top 5% of module marks
Pass	Achieved required minimum module marks
Fail	Did not achieve required minimum module marks
Discontinued	Formally withdrew from the module after enrolments closed and prior to the exam date
Incomplete	Did not complete all module requirements and did not apply to withdraw from the module prior to the exam date

8. Special Consideration for Assessments

8.1 Special Consideration for examinations

8.1.1 Impaired examination performance

A candidate who sits an examination for any of the Chartered Accountant Program modules, but considers that his/her examination performance has been materially impaired by factors outside of his/her control, may make written application to the Institute for special consideration. This application must be accompanied by a medical and/or other appropriate independent statement that verifies the impairment experienced by the candidate. Such an independent statement must be dated no later than three days after the date of the final examination and the application must be received by the Institute within seven days of the final examination.

The application for Special Consideration will only be considered by the Institute if the candidate does not achieve a pass result for the module.

8.1.2 Missed examination

A candidate eligible to sit the final examination for any Chartered Accountants Program module, but who does not do so due to factors outside of his/her control, may make written application to the Institute to complete the technical module supplementary or capstone re-sit examination as their first attempt at no extra cost. This application must be accompanied by a medical and/or other appropriate independent statement that verifies the impairment experienced by the candidate. Such an independent statement must be dated no later than three days after the final examination and be received by the Institute within seven days of the final examination.

If a candidate misses a technical module supplementary examination or Capstone re-sit examination he/she is ineligible to apply for any further special consideration.

8.2 Special consideration for the Capstone workshop assessments

A candidate who, through factors outside of his or her control, either misses a workshop assessment, or whose workshop assessment performance is impaired, may make written application to the Institute for Special Consideration of the workshop assessment.

8.2.1 Missed Capstone workshop assessment

An application for special consideration in respect of a missed Capstone workshop assessment must be accompanied by a medical and/or other independent statement that verifies the reason why the candidate missed the assessment. Such independent statement must be dated no later than 3 working days after the date of the assessment for which special consideration is sought, and must be received by the Institute with 7 working days of the assessment.

The Institute will consider the application and decide whether the potential marks from the missed assessment can be reallocated to the final examination.

8.2.2 Impaired Capstone workshop performance

An application for special consideration in respect of an impaired Capstone workshop assessment must be accompanied by a medical and/or other independent statement that verifies the reason why the candidate's performance was impaired. Such independent statement must be dated no later than three days after the date of the assessment for which special consideration is sought, and must be received by the Institute with seven days of the assessment.

The application will be held until completion of the final examination and if applicable the Re-sit Examination. The candidate's final result will indicate the Institute decision (i.e. pass with Special Consideration or fail with Special Consideration).

9. Appeals

The Institute has a formal appeal process.

Should a candidate believe he/she has been treated unfairly or unjustly in terms of the Institute's processes and procedures in relation to these Regulations and has exhausted all possible remedies then the candidate is entitled to submit an appeal to the Institute.

Any appeal must be submitted in writing within 14 days of the related incident (28 days where the person is resident overseas).

Further details of the appeal process are available on request.

10. Chartered Accountants Program completion requirements and progression to membership

10.1 Completion requirements

A candidate will be deemed to have completed the Chartered Accountants Program when he/she has successfully completed all required modules.

10.2 Progression to full membership

To be eligible to apply for membership, candidates who have completed the Chartered Accountants Program must also have:

- completed at least three years full time (or part time equivalent) approved employment

and

- developed required technical and non-technical competence to the levels outlined in the Institute logbook

Refer to the Membership Regulations for detailed requirements.

11. Candidate Conduct

11.1 Professional conduct

Candidates are expected to conduct themselves with absolute integrity in every aspect of the Chartered Accountants Program.

Candidates are bound by the Institute's Rules/By Laws now in force or hereafter voted into existence and by the Code of Ethics now in force or amended from time to time.

11.2 Academic conduct

The Academic Conduct section outlines the expectations regarding academic conduct of candidates in the Chartered Accountants Program. It sets out what constitutes appropriate academic conduct, the process for investigating suspected breaches and the penalties for violations.

At enrolment, candidates must confirm they have read, understand and will abide by the Academic Conduct Regulations.

11.3 Online learning conduct

The Online Learning Conduct section outlines the expectations regarding the conduct of candidates in the Chartered Accountants Program. It sets out what constitutes appropriate conduct within the online learning environment, and the penalties for violations.

At enrolment, candidates must confirm they have read, understand and will abide by the Online Learning Conduct Regulations.

11.4 Assessment/examination conduct

The Assessment/Examination Conduct section outlines the expectations regarding the conduct of candidates undertaking Chartered Accountants Program assessments or examinations. It sets out what constitutes appropriate conduct in these situations, the process for investigating suspected breaches and the penalties for violations.

At enrolment, candidates must confirm they have read, understand and will abide by the Assessment/Examination Conduct Regulations.

12. Access to assessment material

Candidates may apply, within 2 weeks of the results release date, to access their written examination and workshop assessment material. A fee will be payable.

13. Reconsideration of final examination results

All final examination, supplementary examination (for technical modules), and re-sit examination (for Capstone) papers are subject to a rigorous review marking process prior to result release. No further reconsideration or remark is available post release of final module results

Section II: Regulations specific to the Technical Modules

14. Technical module structure

14.1 Technical modules run over 12 weeks with a final examination in Week 13.

14.2 During each technical module enrolled candidates have the option of attending a face to face lecture forum (ICAA only) or a virtual classroom on topics determined by the Institute. Candidates who wish to attend a face-to-face lecture forum or virtual classroom must register for these events.

15. Technical module assessment

15.1 The assessment structure for the technical modules is:

a.	Three (3) × Online Assessments	(up to 1hr each)	20%
b.	Final examination (3hrs 15mins)		80%

15.2 The online assessments in the technical modules are scheduled in Weeks 3, 6 and 9

15.3 The final examination is scheduled in Week 13 and is open-book

15.4 A supplementary examination will be offered for each technical module (refer to Section 17)

16. Technical module results

16.1 To pass a technical module, candidates are required to:

a. Achieve at least 50% of the total module marks

and

b. Achieve at least 50% (that is, at least 40 of the available 80 marks) of the total final examination (or supplementary examination) marks

17. Technical module supplementary examinations

17.1 Supplementary examinations are offered for the technical modules of the Chartered Accountants Program.

17.2 Candidates who meet one of the following eligibility criteria can apply to sit a technical module supplementary examination:

a. failed their final technical module

or

b. failed a technical module and achieved a minimum of 40% of the total examination marks (i.e. 32 marks out of 80 marks)

or

c. have applied for and been granted special consideration to sit the supplementary examination.

17.3 Eligible candidates must enrol online and pay the supplementary examination fee by the timetabled enrolment close date.

17.4 No late enrolment period applies to supplementary examinations.

17.5 No refunds apply to supplementary examinations

17.6 Supplementary examinations are offered in locations where there are sufficient candidate numbers. The Institute will advise of these locations 5 working days prior to the supplementary examination date.

Section III – Regulations specific to Capstone

18. About Capstone

18.1 Capstone is the fifth and final module of the Chartered Accountants Program. It is an integrated competency based module that may only be undertaken once the four technical modules have been successfully completed.

18.2 Whilst not mandatory, it is strongly recommended that candidates undertake a period of at least two years of approved employment prior to undertaking Capstone.

19. Capstone Structure

19.1 Capstone runs over 14 weeks with a final examination in Week 17.

19.2 Candidates are required to attend three face-to-face one day workshops held in weeks 5, 9 and 14. Attendance at these workshops is compulsory.

19.3 All candidates are required to attend the same workshop group over the three workshops.

19.4 Workshops will be offered in locations where there are 20 or more Capstone candidates able to meet together face-to-face. Candidates should elect their preferred location on enrolment. The Institute will allocate candidates to workshop locations and advise prior to the first workshop. Due to the logistics of arranging workshop groups the Institute can make no assurances that all candidates will be allocated to locations of greatest personal convenience.

19.5 Within their Workshop Group each candidate is placed in a Table Team of four or five candidates. All candidates will stay in the same Table Team for their three workshops.

20. Capstone Assessment

20.1 The assessment structure for Capstone is:

Assessments in workshops	40%
Workshop 1 - 10% (1 hour) – individual Workshop 2 - 15% (1½ hours) – individual Workshop 3 - 15% (1½ hours) – table team	
Final examination (3½ hours)	60%

20.2 The Capstone final examination will be an open book examination

20.3 There is a re-sit examination option for the Capstone (see Paragraphs 22 below)

21. Capstone Results

21.1 Capstone workshop results will be released to candidates prior to the final examination.

21.2 An overall pass mark of 60% or greater is required to pass the module.

22. Capstone Re-sit Examination Option

22.1 The Capstone Re-sit Examination option allows candidates who did not pass the module one opportunity to re-sit the final examination of the next immediate offering of Capstone.

22.2 All eligible candidates must enrol and if applicable pay the Re-sit Examination fee by the timetabled enrolment close dates.

22.3 No refunds apply to the Re-sit Examination

22.4 Candidates attempting the resit examination, carry forward their assessment results from the workshops. To pass Capstone using the Capstone Re-sit Examination, eligible candidates must achieve an examination mark, that when added to the workshop marks from their prior attempt at Capstone, equates to at least 60% of available marks.

Section IV – Candidate Code of Conduct

For further information visit charteredaccountants.com.au/Candidates/The-Chartered-Accountants-Program/Policies-and-Regulations.aspx.

Fees and Subscriptions

204 An applicant shall pay:

204.1 at the time of lodging the application, the prescribed fee; and

204.2 at the direction of the Institute, the subscription for the current year.

205 Where the application is by invitation of the Board (By-law 12(b)) no application fee will be payable.

Status on Admission

206 An applicant will be admitted as a Chartered Accountant or a Fellow as determined by the Board.

Applicant to be a Fit and Proper Person

207 In determining whether a person seeking to be admitted under By-law 12 is a fit and proper person to be admitted, the Institute may have regard to the matters identified in R2/105.

Interview

208 An applicant may be required to attend a personal interview.

Member of Approved Overseas Bodies

209 Special admission may apply to persons who are current financial members in good standing of one of the following overseas accounting bodies:

209.1 **Global Accounting Alliance Bodies**

A legally constituted State Authority in the United States of America (the person having CPA status) subject to appropriate service[1]

Canadian Institute of Chartered Accountants

Hong Kong Institute of Certified Public Accountants (members who have completed the HKICPA Qualifications Programme and trained under an Authorised Employer/Supervisor)

The Institute of Chartered Accountants in England and Wales

The Institute of Chartered Accountants in Ireland

New Zealand Institute of Chartered Accountants (members of the College of Chartered Accountants)

The Institute of Chartered Accountants of Scotland

The South African Institute of Chartered Accountants

Note: Members of these approved bodies must retain membership in good standing of the overseas accounting body. This may be subject to further verification.

209.2 **Other Approved Overseas Bodies**

Special admission may apply to persons who are current financial members in good standing of one of the following overseas accounting bodies who have met all requirements outlined in the current memorandum of understanding signed with each body[2]:

(i) The Malaysian Institute of Certified Public Accountants

(ii) The Institute of Chartered Accountants in India

209.3 An applicant shall have fulfilled the conditions of Special Admission as defined under Regulations R2/201-208.

1 Members of this body must demonstrate a satisfactory understanding of Australian Company and Taxation laws. The Institute will approve courses, which can be undertaken for this purpose.

2 and outlined in the membership section of the Institute's website.

209.4 An applicant shall have been admitted to the overseas accounting body by the usual education and professional examination requirements, not by special recognition or any other mutual recognition agreement.

209.5 An applicant shall have professional experience of not less than three (3) years in the case of an applicant who has graduated from a tertiary institution, or five (5) years in any other case, except where specific service requirements are defined under Regulation R2/209.2. Periods as an affiliate member of the Institute will be recognised in this context.

209.6 An application shall be supported by a recommendation for admission by at least two (2) individual members of this Institute who are not related to the applicant, and who either:

209.6.1 have been individual members for at least three (3) years, or

209.6.2 have been a member of the applicant's overseas professional body for at least five (5) years.

209.7 An applicant shall provide a reference from at least one (1) person from the country in which the membership was obtained to testify as to the applicant's overseas professional experience.

Member of Non-Approved Overseas Bodies

210 Persons who are members of non-approved overseas bodies will be required to complete the Chartered Accountants Program unless approved under Regulation R2/212.

Teacher of Accountancy

211 For the purpose of special admission of persons who are teachers of accountancy.

211.1 An applicant shall have fulfilled the conditions of special admission as defined under Regulations R2/201-208.

211.2 An applicant shall:

211.2.1 hold a Doctorate or Masters degree, with a major in Accounting or allied subject, acceptable to the Board, from a tertiary institution accredited by the Education Board; and

211.2.2 hold, both at the time of application and also when the application is considered by the Board, a position as a full-time teacher in a faculty offering a course accredited by the Institute for graduates and diplomates seeking admission to the Chartered Accountants Program, provided that:

(a) the position is that of lecturer, or a position of higher standing; and

(b) the position has been held at one or more accredited tertiary institutions for not less than five (5) years.

211.3 **References**

An applicant shall provide references from:

211.3.1 two (2) chartered accountants, who are not related to the applicant and who have known the applicant for at least two (2) years and who shall testify as to the applicant's character and integrity; and

211.3.2 two (2) academics, one of whom must be Head of the School or Dean of the Faculty in which the applicant is engaged and the second of at least equal status to the applicant but from another institution, who shall testify as to the applicant's professional ability.

Other forms of special admission

212 The Board may from time to time specify additional requirements to allow admission of an applicant under By-law 12.

Readmission (By-Law 20) Regulations

Lodgement of Application

301 Application for readmission under By-law 20 ("Readmission"), from any person who has resigned or otherwise ceased to be a member, including a person who has been excluded for non-payment of fees, shall be made to the Board.

Application Form

302 An applicant shall complete and personally sign the application form as issued by the Institute.

Fees and Subscriptions

303 An applicant shall pay:

303.1 at the time of lodging the application, the prescribed fee; and

303.2 at the direction of the Institute, the full subscription for the current year.

304 An applicant shall pay, at the direction of the Institute, a readmission fee of the sum total of subscriptions that would have been paid during the whole of the period since cessation of membership.

304.1 The readmission fee will be capped at an amount decided by the Institute and reviewed annually.

304.2 The readmission fee can be reduced, in extenuating circumstances, at the discretion of the Institute.

Status on Admission

305 An applicant who meets the conditions for readmission will be admitted as a Chartered Accountant or Fellow as determined by the Board, and:

(i) recommence their membership from the readmission approval date, such that periods of prior membership before readmission will not be aggregated with the recommenced period of membership for the satisfaction of any Institute requirement dependent on length of membership; or

(ii) if their exclusion was the result of non payment of fees and did not exceed 12 months, their membership will be considered to have continued from their original admission date.

Interview

306 An applicant may be required to attend a personal interview.

Applicant to be a Fit and Proper Person

307 Successful completion of all or any part of the Chartered Accountants Program will be required for an applicant who has not been engaged or employed in work considered by the Board to be accounting work for five (5) years or more prior to date of application. In determining whether a person seeking readmission is a fit and proper person, the Institute may consider:

307.1 the matters identified in R2/105;

307.2 whether the applicant is complying or will be able to comply with the Supplemental Charter, By-laws, Regulations prescribing rulings on the standards of practice and professional conduct, including the technical standards and other pronouncements of the Institute and, in particular, whether the applicant has been involved in any circumstance which would have constituted a breach of the Institute's ethical requirements since previously holding membership;

307.3 whether the applicant has undertaken Training & Development, as required of a member under Regulation R7, or will undertake such courses as may be required by the Board;

307.4 whether the applicant has such knowledge of or experience in accountancy in Australia as could reasonably be expected of a member of the Institute; and

307.5 whether the applicant meets any other requirements from time to time prescribed by the Board.

References

308 An applicant shall provide references from three (3) individual members of the Institute who shall testify as to the applicant's professional capacity, provided that:

308.1 at least one (1) of these individual members shall have known and had contact with the applicant for the whole of the period since cessation of membership; and

308.2 the other individual members shall have known the applicant for at least three (3) years.

Recommendation to the Board

309 Where an applicant for readmission does not fully comply with these Regulations recommendation may be made to the Board by Management that the application be approved. In such cases reasons shall be given as to why the recommendation is being made.

Reinstatement (By-Law 45) Regulations

Lodgement of Application

401 Application for reinstatement under By-law 45 from any person who has been suspended from membership for any period pursuant to By-law 45(g)(i)(2) shall be made to the Board.

Application Form

402 An applicant shall complete and personally sign the application form as issued by the Institute.

Fees and Subcriptions

403 An applicant for reinstatement will be required to pay a reinstatement fee.

Status on Reinstatement

404 An applicant who meets the conditions for reinstatement will:

(i) be reinstated to the status of "Chartered Accountant" unless the National Disciplinary Committee or the Appeal Committee has ordered to the contrary; and

(ii) recommence their membership from the reinstatement approval date.

Interview

405 An applicant may be required to attend a personal interview.

Satisfaction of Sanctions

406 An applicant seeking reinstatement as a member following suspension pursuant to By-law 45(g)(i)(2) will be required to satisfy the Board that all the conditions as laid down by the National Disciplinary Committee or the Appeal Committee, when suspended from membership, have been satisfied.

Bankruptcy

407 In the case of an applicant suspended from membership on the grounds of being an insolvent under administration, the Board will need to be satisfied that the applicant is no longer an insolvent under administration as defined in the Bankruptcy Act.

Affiliate Membership is not Transferable

516 Affiliate Membership is not transferable between practice entities.

517 Should an Affiliate member cease to be a practice entity participant of a practice entity their affiliate membership automatically ceases. On joining another practice entity as a practice entity participant a new application for affiliate membership will be required.

Recommendation to the Board

518 Where an applicant for approval as an Affiliate member does not fully comply with these Regulations, recommendation may be made to the Board by Management that the application be approved. In such cases reasons shall be given as to why the recommendation is being made.

Fees and Subscriptions

Application Fees

519 An applicant shall pay:

519.1 at the time of lodging the application, the prescribed fee; and

519.2 at the direction of the Institute, the subscription for Affiliate members for the current year.

Annual Fees

520 The annual fees payable by an Affiliate member shall be equivalent to fees for the individual members who are Practice entity participants in the practice entity.

PSC Levies

521 An Affiliate member shall pay, at the direction of the Institute, the PSC levy as prescribed by the Institute.

Regulations Relating to Approval for Practice Entity Membership

Lodgement of Application

601 Application shall be made to the Board or its delegated representative.

Application Form

602 A Practice entity representative shall:

602.1 complete and personally sign the application form as issued by the Institute; and

602.2 submit the application together with such accompanying documentation as required by the Institute.

Eligibility for Approval

603 Only a practice entity which may describe itself as "Chartered Accountant(s)" as defined under R9/1205 will be eligible for Practice Entity Membership, unless otherwise approved by the Board.

Practice Entity Representative's Undertakings

604 Practice Entity Membership shall only be approved where the following written undertakings are provided:

604.1 that the Institute will be notified immediately of:

604.1.1 any change of Practice entity representative; or

604.1.2 any change in directors, shareholders or principals of the practice entity which cause the practice entity member to cease to comply with the requirements of R9/1205; or

604.1.3 any change in practice entity name; and

604.2 that the practice entity representative will provide:

604.2.1 such information relating to claims data and/or professional indemnity insurance arrangements as may be requested from time to time to comply with the ongoing reporting requirements under Professional Standards legislation.

Obligations

605 Practice entities granted membership of the Institute must ensure that the conditions applying to that membership continue to be met. Failure to comply with the undertakings and obligations of Practice entity membership will lead to cessation of membership at the expiration of 30 days from the date of the breach.

The Institute's Limitation of Liability Scheme

606 The Institute's Limitation of Liability Scheme (the Scheme) applies to all practice entity members. A practice entity member is required to comply with the requirements of the Professional Standards Council (PSC) and Scheme then in force.

Professional Indemnity Insurance

607 On application and at the request of the Institute a Practice entity representative will confirm the existence of a contract of professional indemnity insurance which:

607.1 is valid and binding; and

607.2 meets at least the minimum requirements set out in the Appendix to R4.

Public Practice Regulations

608 A practice entity member is required to comply with the requirements of R9 – Regulations relating to public practice.

Quality Control

609 On application and at the request of the Institute a Practice entity representative will agree to comply with R4/715 and confirm that systems and procedures of quality control in accord with APES 320, and appropriate to the practice have been established and are maintained.

Change of Practice Entity Representative

610 It is the responsibility of the Practice entity member to ensure that at all times a Practice entity representative has been appointed and is authorised to provide the undertakings required in R2/604. Should the Practice entity representative no longer hold this position, a new Practice entity representative must be appointed within a commercially realistic timeframe. The Practice entity representative must provide the written undertakings required in R2/604 to the Institute within 30 days of their appointment.

Recommendation to the Board

611 Where an application for Practice entity membership does not fully comply with these Regulations, recommendation may be made to the Board by Management that the application be approved. In such cases reasons shall be given as to why the recommendation is being made.

Fees and Subscriptions

Application Fees

612 A Practice entity representative shall pay the prescribed fee at the time of lodging the application.

PSC Levies

613 A Practice entity representative shall pay, at the direction of the Institute, the PSC levy as prescribed by the Institute.

R3
Regulations Relating to Advancement to Fellowship

(Revised May 2010)

Contents

Paragraph(s)

Advancement To Fellowship

Recommendations

650 Recommendations for advancement to the status of Fellow are to be considered and approved by the General Manager, Chartered Accountants Program and Admissions.

Application Form

651 Nominations will be made by completion of the nomination form as issued by the Institute.

Eligibility for Advancement

652 Advancement to Fellowship is based on it being shown that a member has made a strong contribution to the profession and/or the community and is deserving of recognition.

652.1 A member may be nominated for advancement if the following criteria have been met. The member has:

652.1.1 demonstrated leadership in the profession as evidenced by the applicant's responsibilities in employment or public practice and by contribution/s made to the Institute and/or the community;

652.1.2 been a member of the Institute for a minimum continuous period of ten (10) years; and

652.1.3 held, while a member, a senior position in employment or in public practice; or a combination thereof, for at least seven (7) years.

652.2 Service as a member of an approved overseas body can be included when calculating the period required under Regulation 652.1.2 and 652.1.3.

Nominations

653 Nominations shall be made by two (2) Chartered Accountants who will testify as to the applicant's suitability for advancement in status based on the member having met the prescribed criteria indicated in Regulation 652.

Invitation by Regional Council

654 A Regional Council may make a recommendation to the General Manager, Chartered Accountants Program and Admissions that an invitation to advance to the status of Fellow be made to a member who has met the prescribed criteria indicated in Regulation 652.

Special Invitation/Nomination

655 If a member being nominated or invited has not fulfilled the prescribed criteria in Regulation 652.1.2 and 652.1.3, consideration can be given for advancement to Fellowship if it can be shown that the member has made a significant contribution to the accounting profession.

R4
Regulations Relating to Certificate of Public Practice

(Revised May 2012)

Contents

Introduction

701 By-law 34(a) provides that "A member shall not, without the consent of the Board, practise as a public accountant unless he or she has been issued with a current certificate of public practice or his or her application therefore has been approved or he or she is exempt from the obligation to hold such a certificate."

By-law 34(b) authorises the Board to prescribe Regulations for the issue and renewal of Certificates of Public Practice (CPPs) and for any exemption from the obligation to hold such a certificate.

Members Required to Hold a CPP

702.1 An individual member must apply for and be granted a CPP who:

(a) (i) undertakes any services which require the holding of any one of the following registrations/licences:

- Registered company auditor;
- Registered company liquidator;
- Registered trustee in bankruptcy;
- Australian Financial Services (AFS) license;

(ii) undertakes any services as an approved auditor of a self-managed superannuation fund;

(iii) undertakes any reviews of Second Tier Companies Limited by Guarantee in accordance with the *Corporations Act 2001.*

Or

(b) Undertakes services which require the holding of any one of the following registrations to the public for reward:

- Registered tax agent
- Registered BAS agent

(c) provides public accountancy services required under legislation or other statutory authority to the public for reward;

Or

(d) provides services as a Chartered Accountant to the public for reward;

Or

(e) is otherwise a principal of a practice entity which includes an individual who meets the criteria in (a), (b), (c) or (d) above;

Or

(f) conducts activities through an entity of which he or she is presently a principal, where that entity is covered by a professional indemnity policy also providing cover to an individual who meets any of the criteria in (a), (b), (c), (d) or (e) above.

In this Regulation the criteria comprised in (a) – (f) above are referred to as "relevant activities".

Overseas Members

702.2 An individual member must apply for and be granted a CPP who:

(a) seeks to provide relevant activities under R4/702.1 in an overseas country in which they are resident; and

(b) such services will be subject to Australian standards and legislation.

702.3 All such applicants under R4/702.2 are required to demonstrate to the satisfaction of the Institute the manner in which adherence will be achieved with the requirements of APES 320 and R4/715.

Commentary

The Supplemental Royal Charter defines "public accountancy services" to mean such services as the Board may from time to time determine to be "public accounting services". The Board has determined such services to be accounting, auditing, management consulting, taxation, financial management and insolvency. With effect from 1 July 2005, the Board has determined that forensic accounting, risk management and corporate advisory services are "public accountancy services".

R4/702.1(b) includes any conduct from which it may reasonably be inferred that the individual member is offering public accountancy services required under legislation or other statutory authority to the public as a principal for reward. For example, this includes but is not limited to, the role of:

- *an appropriately qualified accountant under the Estate Agents (General Accounts and Audit) Regulations 1997;*
- *a person approved to undertake an audit in accordance with the Residential Care Subsidy Principles 1997 of the Aged Care Act 1997.*

Providing services to the public for reward as a Chartered Accountant under R4/702.1(c) does not include a member:

- *using the post nominals CA, CA Financial Planning Specialist, FCA or FCA Financial Planning Specialist on their business card; or*
- *referring to membership of the Institute on their curriculum vitae or professional profile.*

Providing services to the public for reward as a Chartered Accountant under R4/702.1(c) applies where a member or practice entity of which they are a principal:

- *displays the description Chartered Accountant/s and/or the Chartered Accountants logo on letterhead, promotional material, electronic communications or websites; or*
- *is included in a listing or directory as a chartered firm or with the Chartered Accountants logo; or*
- *is conducted in a manner from which it may be reasonably inferred that the individual member or firm is obtaining a commercial benefit from membership of the Institute.*

Providing services on a pro bono or honorary basis is ***not*** *considered to be for reward.*

Factors to consider in determining whether a person is a principal of a practice entity (or its related entities) as referred to in R4/702.1(d) and (e) include whether:

- *They have responsibility for the standard of professional work undertaken by the practice entity and management of the practice's activities, including: client selection and retention, determining the terms of the professional engagement, the type and quality of professional services provided, risk management, the exercising of professional judgement in ethical and technical matters and signing on engagements;*
- *Their individual acts are binding on the practice or other principals of the practice;*
- *They have the potential for personal liability for the practice's liabilities;*
- *They have a role in the governance of the practice;*
- *They have responsibility for signing off on professional engagements;*
- *They are acknowledged in the professional indemnity policy of the practice as a person responsible for professional engagements;*
- *The perception of clients and suppliers of the member is of a person who is able to bind the practice.*

The absence of an equity holding in the practice by the member is ***not*** *a conclusive factor in determining whether a member is a principal. Similarly an ownership interest in a practice is not necessarily the sole factor in determining whether a member is a principal of a practice entity. For example, an employee is not considered to be a principal merely where a share in ownership is incorporated into their employee remuneration package.*

Lodgement of Application Form

703 Application shall be made to the Board and must be lodged prior to the date of intention to commence any relevant activities or a late lodgement fee will be incurred.

703.1 An applicant shall complete and personally sign the application form as issued by the Institute.

Monitored members

Commentary

Certain members who will not be required to hold a CPP have an obligation to be a monitored member. There are essentially two bases for holding the status of a monitored member – holding a statutory registration or licence that is not currently being utilised, or having previously held a CPP. Former CPP holders are obliged to be monitored members for a period of seven (7) years, corresponding to the period in which they are obliged to have run-off cover as specified in R4A/7PI.6. Where members are holding an unused statutory registration or licence identified in R4/704(a), their monitored member status continues while ever that registration or licence is held but not used. Some members may be monitored on both these bases concurrently.

704 An individual member who does not currently meet any of the criteria in R4/702.1 and

(a) holds any one of the following registrations/licences:

- Registered company auditor;
- Registered company liquidator;
- Registered tax agent;
- Registered trustee in bankruptcy;
- Registered BAS agent;
- AFS License;

Or

(b) is an authorised representative of an AFS Licensee;

Or

(c) met any of the criteria in R4/702.1 within the previous seven (7) years.

must apply to the Institute to be recognised as a monitored member.

Commentary

Members impacted by R4/704(a) should also consider their obligations under these registrations and licenses, in particular where such qualifications are not currently being used.

Members impacted by R4/704(c) should also consider the R4A/7PI.6 requirement that professional indemnity insurance be maintained through a period of not less than seven (7) years after ceasing practice.

Notification required

705 A member shall advise the Board in writing and such advice must be lodged within three (3) months of being granted status as any of the following:

- Registered company auditor;
- Registered company liquidator;
- Registered tax agent;
- Registered trustee in bankruptcy;
- Registered BAS agent;
- AFS Licensee;
- Authorised representative of an AFS Licensee.

Annual confirmation of this status is also required.

Commentary

Notification under R4/705 can be achieved by:

- *in the case of members meeting any of the criteria of R4/702.1, lodging an application for a CPP;*
- *in the case of members meeting any of the criteria of R4/704, applying to be recognised as a monitored member;*
- *in the case of annual confirmation, through the facility provided for membership subscription renewal.*

Pre-requisites to Holding a CPP

Service and Educational Requirements

706 An applicant shall have completed periods of service as defined hereunder.

(a) *Normal Admission under By-law 10(a)*

An individual member admitted under By-law 10(a) will have:

(i) demonstrated a satisfactory understanding of Australian Company and Taxation laws[1]; and

(ii) a minimum of two (2) years experience as an employee of a member in public practice; or

(iii) two (2) years post admission experience in public practice.

(b) *Special Admission under By-law 12*

An individual member admitted under By-law 12 will have:

(i) demonstrated a satisfactory understanding of Australian Company and Taxation laws[1]; and

(ii) a minimum of two (2) years Australian experience in public practice; or

(iii) a minimum of two (2) years experience in public practice post admission as a member of any one of the approved overseas bodies in R2/209.

Any service completed as an approved affiliate or affiliate member of this Institute will be deemed as service for the purposes of R4/706(b).

Public Practice Program

707 An applicant must have undertaken the Institute's Public Practice Program (PPP), or have completed an alternative course approved by the Institute, before commencing practice.

707.1 Where no course is available prior to commencement of practice an applicant must agree to undertake the PPP within six (6) months of the date on which approval to commence practice was granted by the Board, or at the earliest available date.

707.2 Should a member not complete the PPP within six (6) months of the date on which approval to practice was granted by the board, the Chief Executive Officer may suspend their CPP until the PPP is successfully completed.

707.3 An applicant applying for a CPP at a nil rate is not required to attend the PPP until the gross annual income from relevant activities referred to in R4/702 exceeds the amount prescribed in R4/723. When such income exceeds the amount prescribed, the applicant must agree to undertake the PPP, or an equivalent course approved by the Institute, within six (6) months of that date, or at the earliest available date.

707.4 An applicant who was previously the holder of a CPP and who ceased practice within a five (5) year period prior to the date of application is not required to undertake the PPP unless so sanctioned by the Professional Conduct Tribunal or the Appeal Tribunal.

707.5 The PPP will remain valid for five years from the time it is successfully completed by an applicant. If an application for a CPP is not received or finalised within the five years, the program must be undertaken again.

---

1 The Institute will approve courses, which can be undertaken for this purpose.

Commentary

A member who continues to practise whilst their CPP is suspended under R4/707.2 will be referred to Professional Conduct.

Training and Development

708 An applicant must demonstrate completion of Training and Development appropriate to the relevant activities referred to in R4/702 within the preceding two (2) years, otherwise the Board may require the applicant to undertake specific courses before a CPP may be granted.

Professional Indemnity Insurance

709 An applicant will confirm the existence of a contract of professional indemnity insurance which:

(a) is valid and binding; and

(b) meets at least the minimum requirements set out in the Appendix (R4A – Professional Indemnity Insurance) to these regulations.

Interview

710 An applicant may be required to attend a personal interview.

Consent of Employer

711 An applicant who is an employee of a member in public practice shall be required to include with the application the consent in writing of their employer.

Recommendation to the Board

712 Where an applicant for a CPP does not fully comply with these Regulations, the application may be approved on the basis of guidelines approved by the Board, from time to time.

Obligations of Holding a CPP

Professional Indemnity Insurance

713.1 A CPP holder must at all times have, or ensure that their practice has, a contract of professional indemnity insurance which:

(a) is valid and binding; and

(b) meets at least the minimum requirements set out in the Appendix (R4A – Professional Indemnity Insurance) to these regulations.

The Institute's Limitation of Liability Scheme

713.2 The Institute's Limitation of Liability Scheme (the Scheme) applies to all individual members who hold a CPP. An applicant is required to comply with the requirements of the Professional Standards Council and Scheme then in force.

Commentary

Participating members of the Scheme are members who are:

- *the holders of a CPP;*
- *affiliate members; and*
- *practice entity members.*

Training and Development

713.3 A CPP holder is required to undertake regular ongoing Training and Development as set out in R7/1002 of Regulation 7 *Regulations Relating to Training and Development*.

Public Practice Regulations

714 An applicant is required to comply with the requirements of Regulations relating to Public Practice R9.

714.1 An applicant shall provide:

(a) an example of the letterhead for the practice; and,

(b) where the intention is to practice from a residential address, a floor plan.

Commentary

Members should refer to the requirements of R9 Regulations relating to Public Practice for their ongoing public practice obligations. Matters dealt with include business stationery, electronic communications and business premises.

Quality Control

715 An applicant will confirm that systems and procedures of quality control in accord with APES 320 (and ASQC 1 where applicable), and appropriate to the practice, will be established and/or maintained and agrees to comply with the following conditions of holding a CPP:

715.1 Members who hold a CPP are required to undergo the quality review program from time to time in accordance with the policies and procedures laid down for the operation of the program.

715.2 In addition to any review conducted in accordance with R4/715.1, the Chief Executive Officer may at any time in their absolute discretion direct that a quality review be undertaken of all or part of a member's practice.

715.3 To enable the program to be conducted in an effective and timely manner members are required to co-operate with all reasonable requests by the Board, any committee or officer of the Institute or any person employed by the Institute to conduct a quality review, and to produce such documents or other materials in the member's possession as may be required to enable a review to be conducted.

715.4 If members do not produce such documents or other materials in their possession required in accordance with R4/715.3 and as reasonably requested by the Board, any committee or officer of the Institute or any person employed by the Institute to conduct a quality review, within 60 days of a request in writing, the Board may suspend their CPP until they provide the documents or other materials in their possession.

715.5 Members are required to meet the costs imposed by the Institute for a review undertaken in accordance with R4/715.1 and/or R4/715.2 of their practice.

Commentary

A member who continues to practise whilst their CPP is suspended under R4/715.4 will be referred to Professional Conduct.

Trust Accounts

716 An applicant will confirm that should a trust account be established:

(a) systems and procedures will be maintained in accord with the requirements of APS 10 – *Trust Accounts*/APES 310 *Dealing with Client Monies*; and

(b) all reasonable requests by the Board, any committee or officer of the Institute to produce documents or other materials as may be required to enable the member's adherence to the requirements of APS 10/APES 310 to be monitored will be responded to in a timely manner.

716.1 Should a member not produce such documents or other materials requested in accordance with Regulation R4/716(b) within 60 days of such written request, the Chief Executive Officer may suspend their CPP until they provide such documents, other materials or an explanation satisfactory to the Institute.

Commentary

A member who continues to practise whilst their CPP is suspended will be referred to Professional Conduct.

[Regulations R4/717 and R4/718 were removed with effect from 7 February 2011. It was resolved to retain the numbering of subsequent paragraphs to preserve the integrity of the cross-referencing of these provisions elsewhere in the Regulations.]

Renewal of CPPs

719 An individual member already granted a CPP must continue to ensure that the conditions applying to the certificate continue to be met and to confirm same through their annual membership subscription renewal.

CPP Fees and Levies Payable

Application and Subscription Fees and Levies

720 An applicant shall pay, at the time of approval of the application, such subscription fees and levies as prescribed by the Institute.

Late Lodgement Fee

721 Where the CPP application is lodged after the commencement of relevant activities an applicant shall pay, at the direction of the Institute, a late lodgment fee of 25% of the sum total of subscriptions that would have been paid during the period since the applicant commenced public practice. This fee will be capped at an amount decided by the Institute.

Annual Subscription Fees and Levies

722 The subscription fee is payable annually and shall cover the period 1 July to 30 June and shall be payable on 1 July each year, at the beginning of the relevant year. The Scheme levy is payable annually and shall initially be payable on application and thereafter on 1 July each year.

Amount Prescribed

723 The amount prescribed will be calculated on 1 July each year by rounding up to the nearest one thousand ($1,000) dollars the result of the following:

$$\frac{\text{Base amount} \times \text{CPI for the previous March quarter}}{\text{CPI for December 1999 quarter (124.1)}}$$

where "Base amount" is $20,000.

For permanently retired members the prescribed amount is doubled.

723.1 For the purposes of this Regulation "gross annual income" of participants in practice entities which provide relevant activities, includes both profit share and/or salary, however described.

Concessions for CPP holders

724.1 Where a CPP is held and:

i. the gross annual income of the applicant is $7,500 or less, a full concession applies and no fee is payable.

ii. the gross annual income of the applicant is less than the amount prescribed in R4/723 but is greater than $7,500 a partial concession applies and a fee of one-third (1/3) of the current fee is payable.

iii. Where relevant activities are provided by a member who is a full-time teacher of accountancy, a partial concession applies and a fee of one-third (1/3) of the current fee is payable.

724.2 Where an individual member is granted a CPP later than 1 July, the annual fee for the remainder of the fiscal year shall be calculated on a monthly pro rata of the annual fee.

724.3 No concession applies to the levy under the Scheme on all individual members who hold a CPP, affiliate and practice entity members.

Varying a CPP

725 Where a change in circumstances requires the individual member to vary the concession applicable to the CPP currently held the member will be required to meet all relevant obligations pertaining to the CPP.

726 Any CPP certificate previously held shall be returned to the Institute for cancellation.

727 If the individual member whose CPP is cancelled is required to again hold a CPP in the same financial year it shall be reissued without the application of R4/720.

Commentary

Members considering cancelling their CPP should also consider R4/713.2 The Institute's Limitation of Liability Scheme and R4/713.1 Professional Indemnity Insurance, particularly in regard to their status as a participating member of the Scheme and their obligation to hold run off cover. In addition, consideration should be given to the R4/704(c) obligation to be recognised as a monitored member.

Exemption

728 A member will not be required to hold a CPP if the member holds a current Public Practice Certificate issued by CPA Australia.

729 A member exempted from holding a CPP under R4/728 shall advise the Board annually of their continued entitlement to this exemption, or shall advise the Board immediately where they cease to hold a current Public Practice Certificate issued by CPA Australia.

Commentary

Where a member is granted an exemption under R4/728, the member's firm will then not be able to be compliant with R9/1205, and consequently will not be entitled to use the description 'Chartered Accountants' and the Chartered Accountants logo.

R4A
Professional Indemnity Insurance

(Revised August 2010)

Introduction

7PI This Regulation requires compulsory professional indemnity insurance for applicants for and holders of CPPs, affiliate memberships and practice entity memberships. Members holding CPPs, affiliate members and practising entity members are participating members in the limitation of liability schemes which do and will provide a limitation on the amount of damages depending on the nature of the engagement.

These requirements are consistent with the minimum standards of professional indemnity insurance set by the Professional Standards Council (PSC) for participants in professional standards schemes limiting liability and are a requirement of participation in these schemes. When a national liability-capping framework is in place, members may choose to obtain PI cover to the extent of the relevant limitation amount set out in the Scheme, depending on their circumstances. Until the approval of professional standards schemes in every state and territory, forming a national scheme, the compulsory insurance may not be adequate for many applicants, members and their firms. In the states or territories where a scheme has not yet been approved or where services are offered outside the occupational activities of accountants, each applicant, member and firm should take professional advice from insurance brokers or other advisers so that each can consider what is an adequate type and level of cover.

The Institute shall not be under any liability to any member or any other person arising out of any steps it takes or omits to take to ensure that members have complied with this Regulation, and in particular shall not be under any such liability in relation to verifying the existence of the insurance required by the Regulation.

7PI.1 In this Regulation:

(a) 'Member' means any applicant for or holder of:

a CPP; or

affiliate membership; or

practice entity membership.

(b) 'Practice' means a business providing professional services including services which require the holding of a CPP by the individual Member who is a Principal;

(c) 'Principal' in relation to a Practice means any person, who is a principal of the Practice or a principal, partner, director, officer or trustee of a Related Entity of the Practice;

(d) 'Related Entity' means any partnership, company, corporation or trust carrying on the whole or any part of a practice.

7PI.2 Each Member must have, or must ensure that each Practice has, a valid and binding contract of professional indemnity insurance which complies with the minimum requirements set out in Regulation 7PI.3. The insurance may have cover greater than those requirements.

7PI.3 The requirements for the professional indemnity insurance in Regulation 7PI.2 are as follows.

7PI.3.1 **Parties – Insured**

The insured must include:

(i) each Principal;

(ii) each Related Entity;

(iii) any person who is, or becomes, or ceases to be during the period of insurance a Principal or employee of the Practice or Related Entity;

(iv) any person who has ever been a Principal or employee of the Practice or Related Entity;

(v) in the event of the death or incapacity of any person in the above paragraphs, the legal personal representatives of that person.

7PI.3.2 **Parties – Insurer**

The insurer must be;

(i) authorised to carry on the insurance business under the *Insurance Act 1973* (Cth); or

(ii) an unauthorised foreign insurer (UFI) where:

(a) the insurance policy is to be arranged through an insurance broker or agent licensed in Australia.

(b) the UFI is to be domiciled in a member country of the International Association of Insurance Supervisors (IAIS) or other international organisation similarly reputed by the Australian Prudential Regulation Authority (APRA) or similar relevant Australian Authority.

(c) The UFI must have a minimum rating of "A" from AM Best, Moody's, Fitch Worldwide or Standard and Poor's or equivalent rating agencies.

(d) The proper law of the contract is Australian law.

(e) The legal system of the domicile country is subject to the treaty arrangements with Australia.

(f) The UFI has capacity for providing claims data of the type and standard generally available from the APRA in respect of domestic insurers.

(g) The insured also has an agreement with the insurer or broker, requiring the insurer or broker to provide claims data of the type and standard collected by APRA in respect of domestic insurers. The agreement must enable the data to be passed to the PSC; or

(iii) a captive or mutual which is duly authorized to carry on business in a foreign country.

7PI.3.3 **The Insured's Profession and Business**

The insurance must cover all services offered by an insured referred to in paragraph 7PI.3.1.

7PI.3.4 **The Period of Insurance**

The insurance must be either:

(i) for a period of not less than one year; or

(ii) for a period expiring on the next common expiry date for insurance placed under a scheme which requires all insurances under it to expire on a common expiry date.

7PI.3.5 **The Limit of Indemnity**

(i) The sum insured for the Practice must be:

(a) For jurisdictions where there is a limitation of liability scheme in place not less than either:

- $1 million where there is no individual engagement fee greater than $100,000, or

- the limitation amount for the category of service set out in the Institute scheme up to the monetary ceiling for the category of service set out in the Institute scheme;

or, in a state where there is no limitation of liability scheme in place:

(b) not less than $500,000

(ii) There may be an excess for each and every claim, but any such excess must not be more than:

(a) the amount calculated by multiplying the number of Principals of the Practice as at the beginning of the period of insurance, by $10,000, for each and every claim, or

(b) 3% of the total of the gross fee income of the Member and every Related Entity for the financial year immediately preceding the beginning of the period of insurance, whichever is the greater; and

(c) 5% of the indemnity cover required in 7PI.3.5

(iii) There must be cover for the costs and expenses, including legal costs and expenses, of investigating, defending and settling claims against the insured. Cost in addition cover is preferred. Where cost-in-addition cover is in place, the limit of indemnity will be the sum insured for the practice as set out in 7PI.3.5(i)

Where cost-in-addition cover is not in place, cost-inclusive cover must be for an indemnity limit not less than 25% greater than the amount of the required level of cover set out in 7PI.3.5(i) e.g. $1,250,000 where no fee for a single engagement exceeds $100,000.

7PI.3.6 **Cover**

(i) The insurance must cover either any civil legal liability or any act, error or omission of an insured who is providing the services for which a CPP is required, but the insurance may be subject to exceptions that are reasonably common for insurance of that type;

(ii) The insurance must not be cancellable by the insurer for innocent non-disclosure or misrepresentation, or by the insured at all;

(iii) The insurance must cover the insured against claims arising out of a dishonest act or omission of an insured (notwithstanding any misrepresentation or non-disclosure of such acts or omissions when effecting the insurance) but the insurer need not promise to indemnify any person committing, making or condoning any such dishonest act or omission or misrepresentation or non-disclosure in relation to it;

(iv) If the insurance has a retroactive date, it must be no later than seven (7) years before the beginning of the period of insurance;

7PI.4 (a) The Member must obtain a written statement of an insurance broker registered under the *Financial Services Reform Act 2001* (Cth) or the insurer under the insurance, certifying that on the basis of written information supplied to the broker in a proposal or otherwise by or on behalf of the Member insurance of the practice complies with the requirements of this Regulation.

(b) the member must ensure that any practice entity/ies relying on such professional indemnity insurance maintain the financial capacity and ability to meet the excess obligations under the contract of professional indemnity insurance, both at the time of renewal and throughout the course of the renewal period.

(c) The Member must provide to the Board, or its appointed delegate, such information and documents about or in evidence of the Practice's professional indemnity insurance as it requests.

(d) The Member must inform the General Manager, Standards & Public Affairs in writing within seven (7) days of becoming aware that his professional indemnity insurance, including the insurance referred to in this Regulation, has expired, been cancelled, avoided or otherwise become ineffective, such as potential exhaustion through notification of claims, unless within that period

(i) it has been renewed, or

(ii) he has concluded a valid and binding contract of professional indemnity insurance complying with this Regulation.

If, for a period of thirty (30) days, the individual member does not have insurance as required by this Regulation such member's CPP shall automatically be suspended until he arranges new insurance complying with this Regulation. Where an application has been made to the Board in accordance with 7PI.5 this period may be extended up to ninety (90) days.

7PI.5 The Board shall have discretion to issue a CPP or affiliate or practice entity membership to an applicant or member even if the applicant's or member's insurance does not comply with the requirements in Regulation 7PI.2. Without limiting the generality of this discretion, the Board may:

(a) issue CPPs or affiliate or practice entity memberships to applicants or members who have the required insurance in the form of a cover note or interim contract of insurance; or

(b) set criteria on the individual, affiliate or practice entity member and every Related Entity during the relevant period of insurance on which such exercise of discretion is conditional.

7PI.6 After ceasing to be a participating member of the Institute's Limitation of Liability Scheme, because the scheme expires, the member ceases to practice or retires or the practice entity merges with another practice, members must ensure that a valid and binding contract of professional indemnity insurance is maintained, through a period of not less than seven (7) years, where the member will not be covered by future policies.

R5
Regulations Relating to Rates of Subscription
(Revised September 2009)

Contents

Paragraph(s)

Regulations Relating to Rates of Subscription (By-Laws 53 and 54)

A member who retires or temporarily withdraws from practice as a public accountant, or from another business occupation, may apply for a reduction to the annual subscription fee.

A member granted a reduction in the annual subscription fee may, during the period of retirement or temporary withdrawal, retain the current class of membership and thereby be entitled to all the privileges of membership.

Late Fees

801 A member who fails to pay his annual subscription and/or fee for Certificate of Public Practice within two (2) months after the same has become due, shall be required to pay a late fee as determined by the Board.

Lodgement of Application for Concessional Subscription Rate

802 Application for a concessional rate of subscription (with the exception of an application for hardship) shall be made to the Customer Transactions Team. An application for hardship under 805.6 will be made to the Board.

Application Form

803 An applicant shall complete and personally sign the application form as issued by the Institute and shall pay at the time of such application the appropriate fee prescribed in these Regulations.

Annual Confirmation

804 A member who has been granted a concession may be required to confirm in writing annually to the Institute that circumstances relating to the concession remain unchanged.

Concessional Rate of Subscription

805 The following members, whether resident in Australia or overseas, may be considered as suitable applicants for a concessional rate of subscription.

805.1 **Low income**

Any member who is working with a gross annual income from personal exertion of not more than the amount prescribed in Regulation 723 will be required to make an annual payment of one-half of the current subscription.

805.2 **Career break**

Any member who has temporarily withdrawn from the workforce and who receives no income from personal exertion will be required to make an annual payment of one-tenth of the current subscription.

805.3 **Retired**

Any member who

(a) has retired permanently and derives no income from personal exertion; or

(b) is permanently unable to practise his profession

will be required to make an annual payment of one-tenth of the current subscription.

805.4 Any member of seventy-five (75) years of age may make application and will not be required to make payment of any further subscription fee or Certificate of Public Practice fee.

805.5 Any member who has been a member continuously for fifty (50) years may make application and will not be required to make payment of any further subscription fee.

805.6 **Hardship**

A member who demonstrates to the satisfaction of the Board that, because of personal hardship, special circumstances exist to warrant consideration by the Board of the granting of a concessional rate of subscription, may make application for such concession as a special case. When the concession is granted the member will not be required to make payment of any further subscription fee for the period of the concession.

805.7 **By-law 12(b)**

Where the member is admitted by invitation of the Board (By-law 12(b)) the subscription fee will be determined by the Board on an annual basis from the 1 July following admission.

Certificate of Public Practice

806 A member who has been granted a concessional rate of subscription under the terms of Regulation 805 must continue to meet their obligations, if any, to hold a Certificate of Public Practice in terms of the regulations relating to Certificates of Public Practice.

Training and Development

807 Any member who has been granted a concessional rate of subscription and holds a Certificate of Public Practice has an obligation to undertake Training and Development activities each year, as required under Regulation R7.

R6
Regulations Relating to Membership of the Information Technology (IT) Chapter

(Revised June 2004)

Introduction

From September 1996 until June 2004 it was open to members of the Institute to become members of the IT Chapter either as:

> **IT Chapter Subscribers**, being members and non-members interested in receiving information and a defined range of services from the IT Chapter, who paid a nominal subscription fee and were not subject to any rules or conditions of membership, or
>
> **IT Chapter Specialists**, being members who specialised in Information Technology, who successfully applied for specialist membership of the IT Chapter (based on criteria covering education, experience and peer review), and were thereby subject to various continuing conditions of membership and were recognised by the Institute as specialists in Information Technology.

In May 2004 the Board approved the disbanding of the specialist tier of the IT Chapter, making it the IT Special Interest Group, and the followings conditions now apply:

901 The IT Special Interest Group will consist of subscriber members being Institute members and non-members of the Institute interested in receiving information and a defined range of services from the IT Special Interest Group, who pay a nominal subscription fee and are not subject to any rules or conditions of membership.

902 The Institute no longer accredits members as IT Chapter Specialists.

903 Existing IT Chapter Specialists (that is, those members accredited as specialists as at 30 June 2004) shall be entitled to use the designation CA-IT Specialist on letterhead and stationery until 30 June 2006.

904 No specialist fees shall be levied from 1 July 2004.

905 All of the usual conditions of membership of the Institute shall apply to existing IT Chapter Specialists however the previous conditions of IT Chapter specialist membership shall not apply from 1 July 2004.

R7

Regulations Relating to Training and Development

(Revised May 2012)

Contents

Introduction

Training and Development is a vital element to all levels of membership in the Institute. It is recommended that individual and affiliate members plan ahead and design for themselves an integrated approach to their self development activities.

However, it is recognised that a number of "ad hoc" learning situations will present themselves and these will often provide valuable learning opportunities, both for new knowledge and skills and for revision. Individual and affiliate members should personally record their participation in all such activities in order that they may be able to comply with the reporting requirements of Regulation 1004.

The Principle of Training and Development

Training and Development is not just a response to immediate work or other needs. The benefits of work experience and other demands are recognised as being professionally very important. But these benefits are enjoyed by non-professionals as well. There are unique demands upon every professional to identify, develop, promote, maintain and improve upon knowledge and skills which constitute the dynamic expertise of the professions in a rapidly changing society. Often professional development comes not from reacting to change but by initiating it.

Individual and affiliate members who accept professional engagements or occupations imply that they have the necessary competencies to perform the work effectively. They must, therefore, refrain from undertaking or continuing any engagements which they are not competent to carry out unless they obtain adequate advice and assistance.

Becoming an individual or affiliate member of the Institute is but the first step in a lifelong process of education, training and development expected of chartered accountants.

The pace and volume of changing technology and knowledge means that every individual and affiliate member must allow sufficient time to absorb the range and depth of new material. By engaging in Training and Development, individual and affiliate members are making a positive investment in their future.

Individual and affiliate members have a continuing duty to maintain their professional knowledge and skill at a level required to ensure that their clients, or their employers, receive the advantages of competent professional services based on the latest developments in practice, law and business. When individual and affiliate members accept appointments to undertake professional services, or employment, the client or employer is entitled to rely on those persons as being professionally competent to perform the particular engagements or occupations.

Many means of meeting Training and Development requirements are available. Individual and affiliate members may use the resources of the Institute, their own resources, those of other organisations, or may prefer some combination. Training and Development activities are described in the commentary at (iii). They include attending an Institute course or workshop, completing a self-study program or some form of distance learning, participating in a local discussion group, enrolling in a short, or even long, tertiary education course, studying a specialist publication or audio or visual presentation or reading technical publications. Preparing and delivering a paper or address on a topic relevant to a member's profession or occupation are acceptable Training and Development activities. Training and Development can be pursued at home, in the city or the country, alone or with others in or outside working hours. In short, there is a great deal of flexibility in how to achieve Training and Development requirements. It is the result that counts. It is for the individual or affiliate member to decide the form and frequency of Training and Development to meet that member's particular requirements while meeting the minimum standards prescribed herein.

It is also for the individual or affiliate member to decide whether some particular activity was Training and Development or not. An article in a specialist journal may be professionally worthwhile to some and be recognised as a Training and Development activity. It may, however, be of no benefit to others who are already conversant with the material or where it is not relevant to the member's profession or occupation.

The hours outlined in Regulation 1002 are the minimum that individual and affiliate members are required to achieve to maintain their individual competencies. It is recommended that the time investment be in excess of these minimum levels.

The examples of Training and Development activities in the commentary at (iii) are provided to assist all individual and affiliate members. However, all professional education depends upon one thing: integrity. The professional is a member of a self-regulating profession which has standards, guidelines, provisions and resources for compliance and public recognition. But it is the final responsibility of the professional to interpret an activity and to judge within the guidelines whether the activity was personally and professionally developing. No professional can delegate fully all personal responsibility to a set of rules or pronouncements and still remain a professional. This personal responsibility is the life blood of a healthy professional body.

Persons Obliged to Undertake Training and Development

1001 It is the obligation of the following persons to undertake Training and Development in matters appropriate to their fields of practice or occupations (referred to in these Regulations as "individual and affiliate members obliged to undertake Training and Development"):

(a) All individual members who are obliged to pay annual subscriptions to the Institute in full (including overseas members), whether or not holding a certificate of public practice, but excluding those individual and affiliate members of at least 60 years of age as referred to below;

(b) All individual members who are required to hold either a full or concessional rate Certificate of Public Practice, whether or not paying an annual subscription in full;

(c) All affiliate members.

An individual member who is at least 60 years of age but does not hold a certificate of public practice is not obliged to complete any Training and Development. However, such member is still expected to maintain a level of competence appropriate to the position held, which may require completion of Qualifying hours.

Where an individual or affiliate member has been granted exemption for one or two years of the triennium, such member would be required to complete at least 30 hours of formal Training and Development per annum on a pro rata basis for the remaining period of the triennium.

Training and Development Requirements

1002 **Individual and affiliate members obliged to undertake Training and Development are required to achieve a minimum of 120 Qualifying hours (at least 90 hours of formal plus up to 30 hours of technical reading) over a three year period.**

At least 20 hours (including no more than 10 hours of technical reading) must be completed annually.

Over the three year period (the triennium) a maximum of 30 hours technical reading, referred to in the commentary at (iii)(n), may be claimed as Training and Development.

1002.1 **Any individual or affiliate member holding any registration/licence outlined in R4/702.1(a)(i) and R4/702.1(b) is obliged to undertake at least 40% of the minimum Training and Development requirement in each of the appropriate specialty areas (e.g. tax agents are required to undertake at least 40% of their hours in tax-related Training and Development etc.). This requirement is effective from 1 July 2004 other than for Registered BAS agents.**

(Sept 03)

1002.2 **From 1 July 2008, any individual or affiliate member signing a Self Managed Superannuation Fund (SMSF) audit report, is required to:**

(i) undertake at least 30 hours of their minimum Training and Development requirement over a three year period, comprising:

(a) at least eight (8) hours of formal superannuation training

(b) at least eight (8) hours of formal financial statement or compliance audit training

(c) at least four (4) hours of formal financial accounting training

(d) a maximum of ten (10) hours of technical reading related to this area.

This Training and Development is not limited to a focus on the audits of SMSFs; a combination of relevant courses is acceptable.

(ii) have completed, a course in the audit of SMSFs prior to undertaking or accepting a SMSF audit engagement.

1002.3 **From 1 July 2010, any individual or affiliate member who is not a registered company auditor and who is undertaking a review of a Second Tier Company Limited by Guarantee (STCLG), is required to:**

(i) undertake at least 30 formal hours of the minimum Training and Development requirement over a three year period, comprising any combination of courses on reviewing or auditing financial statements and financial accounting training.

(ii) have completed a course which includes reviews of financial statements prior to commencing STCLG reviews.

1002.4 **Where an individual or affiliate member is:**

- **a current member of one of the following Global Accounting Alliance (GAA) bodies:**
  - **American Institute of Certified Public Accountants;**
  - **Canadian Institute of Chartered Accountants;**
  - **Hong Kong Institute of Certified Public Accountants (members who have completed the HKICPA Qualifications Programme and trained under an Authorised Employer/Supervisor);**
  - **New Zealand Institute of Chartered Accountants (members of the College of Chartered Accountants);**
  - **The Institute of Chartered Accountants in England and Wales;**
  - **The Institute of Chartered Accountants in Ireland;**

- **The Institute of Chartered Accountants of Scotland;**
- **The South African Institute of Chartered Accountants; and**

- **resident in that GAA body's country,**

written evidence from that GAA body of compliance with their Continuing Professional Development obligations, is deemed as compliance with the requirements of 1002.

Where applicable, such members must meet the additional obligations of 1002.1 and 1002.2.

Commentary

Training and Development Activities

(i) Qualifying activities for Training and Development purposes should maintain and/or expand individual and affiliate members' capacity to enable them to discharge their professional obligations and should have the following characteristics:

- an organised, orderly framework developed from a clear set of objectives;
- a structure for imparting knowledge of an educational or technical nature; and
- require involvement by the participant.

Commonly accepted types of activity which meet these characteristics are lectures, courses, seminars, workshops, conventions, discussion groups, congresses, Professional Development Forums, symposiums, etc conducted by the Institute, other reputable bodies, educational institutions and in-house.

(ii) Where individual and affiliate members hold one or more statutory registrations (such as registered company auditor, registered company liquidator or registered tax agent) or hold themselves out to be a "specialist", (such as members of the IT and Financial Planning Chapter) they should plan their Training and Development with the objective of maintaining their levels of expertise appropriate to those areas of interest subject to Para 1002. Individual and affiliate members holding more than two statutory registrations or specialties must recognise that they are operating across a broad range of practice. To maintain competence in all areas, individual and affiliate members may be required to do more than the minimum hours required to adequately discharge their responsibilities to the public.

It is to be noted that the assessment of which subject area a particular activity falls into is a matter of self assessment. A single session on taxation may be a relevant tax course for a tax agent and yet be a relevant course on audit for a registered company auditor depending on the individual member's perspective. Each session can only be counted once.

(iii) Activities which will be recognised as qualifying for Training and Development purposes include the following:

(a) Congresses, Business Forums and conventions presented by the Institute or other professional accounting body;

National and State Congresses presented by a professional accounting body alone or in conjunction with other professional bodies, and designed to cater for a broad spectrum of member interests including those in particular occupational groupings, such as public accountants or government accountants;

(b) Courses, seminars, workshops, lectures and other professional educational activities presented by the Institute or other professional accounting body (one (1) hour or more);

Any of the range of technical activities organised by either body, alone or in conjunction with other organisations, regardless of whether arranged at National, State or other level;

(c) Meetings of Institute or other professional accounting body technical discussion groups (one (1) hour or more);

Formal meetings of Institute or other professional accounting body discussion groups which provide a structured forum for exchange of technical information relevant to individual and affiliate members with a common interest;

(d) Appropriate educational activities provided by the individual or affiliate member's employer or practice entity;

"In-house" courses, schools or similar activity arranged by the member's employer and presented either by that employer's staff, by individuals or organisations engaged by the employer, or a combination of these;

Training activities provided by employers are acceptable Training and Development providing they relate to the development, maintenance or expansion of professional competence. However, training involving purely administrative tasks of essentially a non-professional nature such as completing employer time sheets would not count towards Training and Development;

(e) Tertiary courses presented by educational institutions;

Courses conducted by tertiary institutions leading to a Degree, Diploma, or Post Graduate qualification, other than those undertaken as a pre-requisite for admission as a member of the Institute;

Contact time (lectures, exams and tutorials) may be claimed, as well as time spent in the research and writing of essays;

(f) Appropriate educational and developmental activities presented under the auspices of academic institutions, commercial establishments or other professional bodies (one (1) hour or more);

Extramural courses presented by tertiary institutions, seminars, courses, lectures, residential schools, conventions or other technical activities presented independently or jointly by tertiary institutions, commercial educational establishments or professional bodies;

(g) Researching and writing technical publications, preparation and delivery of technical papers;

Actual time engaged in researching material and writing technical publications may be claimed, whether the final product be in the form of a text book, an article in a professional journal or the presentation of an address. This should not include time devoted to layout, artwork, design or similar issues;

Time spent in preparation and presentation of lectures, courses and seminars and at workshops and discussion groups, may be claimed except for repeats of presentations which are substantially similar in form and content. The preparation and presentation of an address on a topic relevant to a member's profession or occupation may also be claimed. As a guide, three hours preparation may be claimed for each presentation hour, although this will obviously vary according to the complexity of the subject matter and the presenter's familiarity with the topic;

(h) Service on technical or research committees under the auspices of the Institute or other professional bodies or organisations;

Membership of technical or research committees or study groups where objectives are defined and specific contributions required of individual and affiliate members, usually involving both independent and collective study, review and analysis of designed material. For instance, Boards and Committees of the Australian or international standard-setting bodies; government sponsored advisory panels required to submit recommendations on issues concerning accountancy or finance; or course advisory committees established by educational institutions;

(i) Programmed self-study through a third party provider, including self-study video or audio packages;

Structured study programs designed for the individual which may or may not involve interaction with tutors or other individuals and may or may not include assignments, exercises or tests, whether or not these are submitted for assessment. Structured self-study courses may include several learning media and/or distance learning aids, e.g. notes combined with audio or video tapes; computerised or other electronic links;

(j) Participation in a Chartered Accountants Program module;

Qualifying hours may be claimed by satisfactorily completing a module, with the number of hours being directly related to the extent of the member's participation, up to a total of 60 hours per triennium but not exceeding 20 hours in any one year;

(k) Preparation of Chartered Accountants Program course material and participation as Chartered Accountants Program Focus Session Facilitators and assessment markers;

A maximum of 16 Qualifying hours may be claimed by Focus Session Facilitators per module, and a maximum of 7 Qualifying hours may be claimed by assessment markers;

(l) Participation as a Mentor for CA Candidates in the Chartered Accountants Program;

A maximum of 10 Qualifying hours per year may be claimed;

(m) Participation in a Quality Review conducted by the Institute or CPA Australia;

A maximum of 4 Qualifying hours may be claimed by individual and affiliate members who participate in their firm's Quality Review. This credit may be claimed by the member under review once every review cycle;

(n) Reading of Technical Literature.

Reading of professional journals, technical bulletins and releases and research projects to the extent of 30 hours per triennium may be claimed as Training and Development but not exceeding 10 hours in any one year;

Reading of new accounting and audit standards;

All of the aforesaid activities, except the reading of technical literature, would be regarded as formal Training and Development.

(iv) The trienniums will commence on 1 July in the year following the date of admission of a member (or date of approval of an affiliate) after 1 July 1994.

(v) In respect of those persons who are individual and affiliate members or affiliates as at 1 July 1994, the commencement date of their triennium shall be 1 July 1994 and the declaration referred to in Regulation 1004 will be due on 1 July each successive three years from the commencement dates.

Assessing Training and Development Hours

(vi) In assessing the time spent on Training and Development, individual and affiliate members obliged to undertake Training and Development should record only those hours spent directly on the Training and Development activity and only where the activity from which the member gains educational benefit is in excess of one (1) hour (in the case of discussion groups, etc).

(vii) Participation in courses provided by institutions and bodies other than the Institute and other professional accounting bodies is encouraged, where it is seen as a means of broadening the members' knowledge, skill, and expertise to the ultimate benefit of the individual and the profession, and may be claimed. As members of a professional body, those participating in the activity are in the best position to judge its relevance in terms of the foregoing. Accordingly, the Institute does not intend to impose a costly administrative infrastructure in an attempt to accredit all the many and varied avenues of Training and Development available to members, nor does it propose to enquire (other than on a selective basis - random or otherwise) of its members as to the activities attended during a year or triennium. Individual and affiliate members obliged to undertake Training and Development must be in a position to respond adequately to such enquiries.

(viii) Only the actual time during which a member participates in a recognised Training and Development activity may be claimed. For the purposes of an annual confirmation or triennial declaration, the aggregate time spent should be shown to the nearest hour.

(ix) Time spent in social, ceremonial or sporting events or in luncheons, dinners or informal functions associated with Training and Development activities but not forming part of the professional development segment, will not be recognised.

Recording of Training and Development Activities

1003 Individual and affiliate members obliged to undertake Training and Development are required to keep a personal record of the time spent on Training and Development activities to satisfy enquiries by the Board if called upon to do so.

Reporting of Training and Development Activities

1004 Individual and affiliate members obliged to undertake Training and Development will be required to provide details of the Training and Development activities undertaken -

(a) during the course of any year ended on 30 June; and

(b) during the course of their particular triennium ended on 30 June (as determined in the commentary at (iv) and (v).

in response to a written request from an officer of the Institute.

1004.1 Where an individual or affiliate member is:

- **a current member of another GAA body, and**
- **resident in that GAA body's country, and**
- **in compliance with that GAA body's CPD requirements**

written evidence of compliance from that GAA body will be accepted in response to such a written request from an officer of the Institute under R1004.

Commentary

(x) Letters will issue to individual and affiliate members obliged to undertake Training and Development, selected on a random basis, requesting details of all specialty registrations held together with details of Training and Development activities undertaken, including the date, organisation presenting the activity, description of the activity (refer Commentary paragraph (iii)) the specialty strand to which the activity belongs and, for each activity, the number of hours. Unless otherwise requested, supporting documentation is not required.

(xi) By-law 40(g) provides that a member (or affiliate) shall be liable to disciplinary action if he has failed to comply with any reasonable and lawful direction of any officer or organ of the Institute.

Exemptions

(xii) Individual and affiliate members obliged to undertake Training and Development who seek exemption from the requirement in Regulation 1002 must make written application for Exemption to the Chief Executive Officer, stating the grounds of their application and any special circumstances upon which they rely.

Exemption will apply to formal Qualifying hours only; technical reading must be maintained (to a maximum of 10 hours per year).

(xiii) The Chief Executive Officer, or nominee, may grant exemption if considered reasonable to do so in the light of any special circumstances contained in the application and shall notify the member of the decision.

(xiv) Notwithstanding anything contained herein to the contrary, the Chief Executive Officer, or nominee, may grant, on such terms and conditions as thought fit, a total or partial exemption from the provisions of this Regulation to any member who, in an application for an exemption sets out special circumstances that, in the opinion of the Chief Executive Officer or nominee, warrant such an exemption.

(xv) Exemption, once granted, will remain in force unless and until the special circumstances on which it was granted cease to exist and the onus is on the member to advise the Institute when the circumstances cease to exist.

(xvi) The following are examples of factors that would be relevant to the question as to whether special circumstances existed justifying the granting of an Exemption referred to at (xii) above:

(a) being on leave from professional duties for an extended period of time (e.g. parental or sabbatical leave); or

(b) a physical disability being such that the person would be unable to engage in Training and Development activities, or that it would be unreasonable to require the person to do so.

Advice and Guidance

(xvii) Individual and affiliate members seeking further advice on the types of activity recognised by the Institute are urged to discuss their concerns with the General Manager or their staff, who may nominate particular activities as being applicable and otherwise offer guidance.

R9
Regulations Relating to Public Practice

(Issued April 2008)

(Integrated R8 and R9)

Contents

Paragraph(s)

Introduction

For the purposes of this Regulation, a member in public practice includes individual members who hold or ought to hold a Certificate of Public Practice, affiliate and practice entity members.

This Regulation applies to all members in public practice regardless of whether the entity is entitled to use the description 'Chartered Accountant/s'.

General Principle

Members in public practice are responsible and accountable for their professional conduct and work. This principle applies notwithstanding the manner in which a member in public practice chooses to organise the professional work undertaken or the entity by or through which the work is carried out.

Practice Entities

1101 A member in public practice may perform by or through a partnership, an incorporated company, trust or any combination or partnership of these (each of which is below referred to as "practice entity") any of the functions of a member in public practice which the practice entity concerned is permitted by law to perform.

1102 A member in public practice shall not do, permit or cause to be done by or through a separate entity anything which the member would not be permitted to do as an individual or as a member in public practice.

1103 A member or members in public practice who conduct all or any part of a practice by or through a practice entity, or who use a practice entity for any of the purposes set out herein, shall be responsible for and accountable to the Institute for the conduct of that practice entity and shall cause it to comply with the Supplemental Charter, By-Laws and Regulations from time to time of the Institute. Accordingly, the Supplemental Charter, By-Laws and Regulations shall apply to a practice entity by or through which any member or members in public practice conduct all or any part of their practice.

1104 These Regulations shall have the same force, effect and application to a member in public practice whether the practice entity by or through which the member carries on business carries on that business or any function of that business on its own account, as a trustee or as an agent.

Requirement to Hold a Certificate of Public Practice

1105 Each individual member who is a practice entity participant must hold and continue to hold a current Certificate of Public Practice. Refer to Regulation 4 *Regulations Relating to Certificates of Public Practice*.

Professional Indemnity Insurance

1106 Each member in public practice must be insured under a contract of professional indemnity insurance providing cover and containing conditions as recorded under "Professional Indemnity Insurance" in R4/ 7PI.3.5.

Practice Management

Use of a Member's Name

1201 Members must preserve the integrity of the way in which their or their practice entity's name is used.

Use of Practice Names and Descriptions

1202 Members are prohibited from using a practice name which is false, misleading or deceptive. Practice names and descriptions must not reflect adversely on the profession.

1203 The words "Chartered" or "Chartered Accountants" must not form part of the practice name of a practice entity but may be used as a description where the conditions of Regulation 1205 are met.

Commentary

Further it is not appropriate to incorporate the words "Chartered" or "Chartered Accountants" in a registered symbol (such as a trade mark) as there is a risk that the description may be used where the conditions of R9/1205 are not met.

Sole practitioners – use of words denoting the plural

1204 The name and/or description of a practice entity which implies a greater number of practice entity participants than is, in fact, the case, is permissible only when the name of the participant is displayed with the name of the practice entity on all stationery, promotional materials, electronic communications and website of that practice entity.

Commentary

For example:

- Names such as "& Associates", "& Company (Co)" or "& Partners";
- Descriptions such as "Chartered Accountants".

Use of Description "Chartered Accountant(s)" and/or Chartered Accountants Logo

1205 The description "Chartered Accountant/s" and the Chartered Accountants logo may be used by a practice entity where:

(a) the following conditions are met:

- only individual or affiliate members or practice entities entitled to use the description "Chartered Accountant(s)" and the Chartered Accountants logo are the practice entity participants; and
- only individual or affiliate members have responsibility for the governance of the practice entity; and
- only individual or affiliate members have responsibility for the standard of professional work undertaken by the entity; and
- all such individual members hold and continue to hold a current Certificate of Public Practice with the Institute; and
- the number of affiliate members in a practice entity does not exceed the number of individual members who are practice entity participants; and

- the total share of affiliate members and their associated persons and entities in the capital, financial results and voting rights of the practice entity does not exceed one half (1/2) (loans by affiliate members and their associated persons and entities being treated as capital for such purpose); and
- any authorised representative/s of non-member owner/s who have responsibility for the governance of the practice entity are all individual member/s holding Certificates of Public Practice who have provided an undertaking acceptable to the Institute.

Or

(b) as approved by the Board.

1206 Where the Board forms the view that non-member owners are influencing the standard of professional work undertaken by the practice this is deemed to be a breach of R9/1205.

Unless approved by the Board, a breach of R9/1205 is deemed to be unprofessional conduct on the part of any members associated with the breach.

Where the breach of R9/1205 is a result of a change of member participants and the practice entity undertakes to remedy the defect within a commercially realistic timeframe there will be no deeming of unprofessional conduct.

Commentary

While recognising the evolving nature of the marketplace and the likelihood that innovative practice structures will arise in the future the Institute's focus has been on the principle of the individual responsibility of members for control over the standard of professional work. Rather than formulating a set of prescriptive rules the Institute relies on this principle to support and underpin the Chartered Accountants brand while guiding members in how they choose to structure their practice. If there is any doubt about whether an entity is entitled to use the description "Chartered Accountants" and the Chartered Accountants logo, guidance and advice should be sought from the Institute's Professional Standards Team. If necessary, specific approval can be given by the Board under R9/1205(b) to a particular structure.

Definitions and assumptions

Members should have regard to the Glossary of Terms when reading this Commentary, particularly Authorised representative, Chartered firm, Practice entity, Practice entity member, Practice entity participant, Practice entity representative, Principal of a practice entity and the factors to consider in determining whether a person is a Principal in relation to a practice entity (or its related entities).

Directors, including non-executive directors, trustees, authorised representatives of non-member owners, and practice entity representatives of a practice entity are assumed to be involved in the governance of the practice entity and in a position to influence the standard of professional work undertaken by that practice. Therefore in Chartered firms:

- all directors, including non-executive directors, and trustees must be individual members holding Certificates of Public Practice with the Institute, or affiliate members; and
- all practice entity representatives must be individual members holding Certificates of Public Practice with the Institute;
- all authorised representatives of non-member owners must be individual members holding Certificates of Public Practice with the Institute.

In such Chartered firms individual and affiliate members must exercise control in the following areas of practice management:

- client selection and retention;
- determining the terms of the professional engagement;
- the type and quality of professional services provided;
- risk management;
- the exercising of professional judgement in ethical and technical matters; and
- signing off engagements.

R9

Examples

Practice entities that are recognised as compliant with R9/1205 and described as Chartered firms include:

- an individual member, being a sole practitioner, practising in the member's own name, a firm name, through a company or through a trust;
- a partnership in which all the partners are individual or affiliate members, or practice entities entitled to use the description "Chartered Accountants" and the Chartered Accountants logo;
- a company in which all the directors are individual or affiliate members, and all the shareholders are individual or affiliate members, or practice entities entitled to use the description "Chartered Accountants" and the Chartered Accountants logo;
- a trust in which all the participants and the trustees are individual or affiliate members, or practice entities entitled to use the description "Chartered Accountants" and the Chartered Accountants logo;
- any combination or partnership of the above practice structures.

Chartered firms are entitled to use the description "Chartered Accountant(s)" and the Chartered Accountants logo and include those where all the Principals/practice entity participants are:

Principals/practice entity participants	**Practice structures – Chartered Firms**				
Individual member/s	Sole practitioner	Partnership	Company	Trust	Combination
Individual + affiliate members		Partnership	Company	Trust	Combination
Affiliate member/s*		Partnership *	Company *	Trust *	Combination*
Individual member/s + practice entity member/s		Partnership	Company	Trust	Combination
Affiliate member/s*+ practice entity member/s		Partnership *	Company *	Trust *	Combination*
Individual member/s + affiliate member/s + practice entity member/s		Partnership	Company	Trust	Combination
Individual member/s + practice entity/ies entitled to use the description "Chartered Accountants" and the Chartered Accountants logo		Partnership	Company	Trust	Combination
Affiliate member/s* + practice entity/ies entitled to use the description "Chartered Accountants" and the Chartered Accountants logo		Partnership *	Company *	Trust *	Combination*
Individual member/s + affiliate member/s + entity/ies entitled to use the description "Chartered Accountants" and the Chartered Accountants logo		Partnership	Company	Trust	Combination

* **only** where the practice entity associated with the affiliate member is recognised by the Institute as practising in conjunction with the practice entity that supported the affiliate member/s application for membership of the Institute.

R9/1205 does not permit the use of the description "Chartered Accountants" nor the Chartered Accountants logo by a practice entity in which individual, affiliate or practice entity members practise with non-member owners who are actively involved in the provision of professional services, unless the professional services provided by them are clearly distinguished from those provided by the member/s; for example, Chartered Accountants and Solicitors.

Generally in Chartered firms the role of non-member owners is limited to being a non-participating shareholder of a company or beneficiary of a trust; as such non-member owners could not be involved in the provision of professional services in a practice entity entitled to use the description "Chartered Accountants" nor the Chartered Accountants logo.

Practice entities that are unable to rely on the description Chartered Accountants under R9/1205 include:

Principals/practice entity participants	Practice structures				
Only Affiliate member/s	Sole practitioner	Partnership*	Company *	Trust *	Combination*
Individual member/s + Non-member/s		Partnership	Company	Trust	Combination
Affiliate member/s + Non-member/s		Partnership	Company	Trust	Combination

* **except** where the practice entity associated with the affiliate member is recognised by the Institute as practising in conjunction with the practice entity that supported the affiliate member/s application for membership of the Institute.

Board recognition

The Board has recognised Chartered firms as compliant with the principles of R9/1205 in the following circumstances:

(a) A share in ownership of the practice is incorporated into the employee remuneration package, where the shares or units issued to these employees are limited to a non-voting category of shareholding or interest. In such circumstances it is accepted that such employees do not exercise any control or influence, either directly or indirectly, over the standard of professional work undertaken by the practice and the responsibility to ensure that all aspects of the practice are conducted in accordance with the technical, professional and ethical standards laid down by the Institute remains that of the individual and affiliate member principals of the practice entity.

(b) Shares or units issued to employees do not represent a material interest in an entity whose ownership is widely held, such as a listed entity.

(c) Individual members are appointed to a governance role in a practice entity as authorised representative/s of non-member/s holding an equity interest where acceptable written undertakings are provided to the Institute acknowledging their responsibility for the reputation of the profession, the Institute and its members. Where it is accepted that such non-member owners are not otherwise involved in the provision of professional services, the practice entity is recognised as a Chartered firm. It is the responsibility of the individual and affiliate members of such a Chartered firm to ensure that the authorised representative/s of non-member owner/s are individual members holding Certificates of Public Practice with the Institute.

Common brand names

A common brand name includes common initials or a common name. A practice entity is considered to be using a common brand name if it includes, for example, the common brand name as part of, or along with, the business name of the practice entity, on the entity's business stationery or web site.

It is not acceptable to have different "offices" of Chartered firms practising under a common name using different descriptions (for example, Chartered Accountants, Certified Practising Accountants or Public Accountants) **unless** it can be demonstrated that they are quite separate entities. This distinction must be clearly evident to members of the public.

Monitoring

Chartered firms may be requested to provide appropriate evidence of compliance with R9/1205. Compliance with this requirement is monitored by the Institute to protect and safeguard the brand:

- in the approval process for practice entity membership under Regulation 2; and
- in the approval process for Certificates of Public Practice under Regulation 4; and
- as part of the Quality Review Program; and
- as part of the Institute's operational procedures to ensure the integrity and accuracy of the member database is maintained in accord with members' obligations under By-law A2/30.

Use of Designations and Descriptions

1207 The descriptions "Chartered", "Chartered Accountant(s)" and/or the Chartered Accountants Logo may not be used on any stationery or promotional material of the practice entity unless Regulations 1204 or 1205 are satisfied.

Business stationery and electronic communication

1208 The letterhead or website of:

– a member in public practice being a sole practitioner describing him/herself as a "Chartered Accountant" or using the Chartered Accountants logo;
– a practice entity describing itself as "Chartered Accountant(s)" or using the Chartered Accountants logo; or
– a member or an entity entitled to be described as "Chartered Accountant(s)" and use the Chartered Accountants logo

must not without the written consent of the Board, contain the name of any person who is not a practice entity participant, i.e. an individual member holding a Certificate of Public Practice or an affiliate member unless that person is clearly distinguished from the practice entity participant/s by the description used.

1209 The letterhead and websites of a practice entity having affiliate members must indicate for all practice entity participants, next to their respective names (if included on these items):

– for all members, their membership of the Institute, viz CA or FCA; and
– for all affiliate members, their membership of the Institute, viz Affiliate ICAA, and membership of other professional body (if any).

1210 Members are encouraged to use the description "Chartered Accountant(s)" and the Chartered Accountants logo. When entitled to do so and the member has the technical ability and experience, the member may use other designations and/or professional descriptions.

1211 A member in public practice must comply with the disclosure and style guide requirements of the Institute and Professional Standards Council then in force in the relevant state in which the member ordinarily resides.

Commentary

A member in public practice, being the holder of a solicitor's current practising certificate, may use the designation "Chartered Accountant and Solicitor".

Logotypes – logotypes in the form of designs or emblems (including combinations of the initial letters of a firm name) may be used on the letterheads, other stationery, electronic communications and website of members in public practice.

Chartered Accountants logo – members in public practice are prohibited from using the Chartered Accountants logo unless the practice entity is entitled to do so under R9/1205.

Affiliations – a member in public practice may indicate on his/her letterhead, other stationery, electronic communications and website any affiliations or representations with the other firms either in Australia or overseas.

Estimate of Profit Returns or Forecasts

1212 If an estimate of profit returns or forecasts is included in a document for external scrutiny, advertisement or publication seeking investment finance, the member's name shall not appear. Where the document for external scrutiny, advertisement or publication seeking investment finance does not contain such estimates, the member's name and address can be used in the advertisement only as an address for the receipt of enquiries.

Commentary

It is the responsibility of the member, practice entity or practice entity participant to ensure that any mention of their or its name in any document for external scrutiny, advertisement, or publication not prepared or distributed by the member, practice entity or practice entity participant contains only those references as are necessary from a professional viewpoint and do not include any laudatory or soliciting references except as may be required by law.

Where a member in public practice is engaged professionally by a client seeking investment moneys for a development project, every care should be exercised to ensure that an advertisement by the client seeking finance in no way indicates that the project is underwritten, recommended or promoted by the member in public practice unless the member has statutory authorisation to do so.

Advertising

1213 Advertising must not be false, misleading or deceptive or otherwise reflect adversely on the profession.

1214 Members in public practice must ensure that follow up communications are terminated when the recipient has so requested either directly to the member or through the Institute. Any continued contact is regarded as harassment which is considered to be unacceptable conduct.

Commentary

Forms of unacceptable advertising contemplated under this Regulation include those that:

(a) create false or unjustified expectations of favourable results;

(b) belittle others;

(c) imply the ability to influence any court, tribunal, regulatory agency or similar body or official thereof;

(d) consist of self-laudatory statements that are not based on verifiable facts;

(e) contain unidentified testimonials or endorsements;

(f) contain any representations that would be likely to cause a reasonable person to misunderstand or be deceived.

Members in public practice may approach potential clients personally or through direct mailing to make known the range of service that they offer.

Experience has shown that, before a member, being an employee (or partner), terminates employment (or partnership) to commence practice on his/her own account, the member should reach an understanding with the past employer (or ex-partners) concerning requests from the latter's clients. While it is a basic principle that an individual has an indisputable right to choose a professional advisor, there is a moral obligation on the new practising member not to do anything to disadvantage his/her previous employer or partner.

A member, who has had responsibility for particular clients within a firm and who resigns to conduct a separate practice, may be approached by a client of the previous practice to accept a future appointment. Before making any form of commitment, the departing member should contact the existing accountant to advise of the approach. The client should be advised to confer with their present accountant and only after being satisfied that this has been done should the departing member commence to follow the normal procedure for superseding another public accountant.

Problems often arise when employees of members leave to set up their own practice. Members are reminded of the possibility of utilising restrictive covenants in employment contracts, for which legal advice should be obtained.

Departing employees should recognise that client information obtained in the course of their employment, including client contact information, is subject to confidentiality, and is not available for use in soliciting prospective clients. By contrast, contact information obtained from publicly available resources is not so restricted.

Members in public practice will be held responsible for the form and content of any marketing, advertisement and promotion, whether placed or undertaken personally or by another person or organisation on behalf of a member's practice entity and for any marketing, advertising or promotion which the member either expressly or impliedly authorises.

For further marketing support refer to the Institute's web site at charteredaccountants.com.au

Office Premises

1215 The Institute requires that a member in public practice must provide an acceptable professional standard of facilities to ensure that communication with, and records of, clients are kept confidential. Where the member maintains an office open to the public within residential premises, that office must be in a location readily and separately accessible to the public.

Attention to Correspondence and Enquiries

1216 Members must reply to professional correspondence and enquiries expeditiously.

Books and Records

1217 Subject to any legal right of lien, a member in public practice must after a change in appointment has been effected, promptly make available for collection all books, papers, documents and other records belonging to the client.

Commentary

Members are referred to Guidance Note N1 – Books and Papers for guidance on the ownership, possession and disclosure of documents and records.

Following the appointment of another auditor, the outgoing auditor does not have any obligation to provide such information and advice to the incoming auditor as will enable the incoming auditor to substantiate the existence and value of assets and liabilities as at the end of the previous financial year. However, the outgoing auditor is encouraged to do so as a professional courtesy and with the knowledge and consent of the client. The audit working papers of the outgoing auditor are the property of that auditor and there is no obligation to make available any information contained therein.

Professional Fees

1218 Before undertaking an engagement, a member in public practice must:

(a) advise the client of the basis on which fees will be compiled; and

(b) clearly define the billing arrangement.

The member must advise the client without delay of any changes to the fee structure or billing arrangements which may become necessary during the course of an engagement or between engagements.

Commentary

It is not improper for a member in public practice to quote a fee known to be lower than that already charged by another practice, providing the engagement letter details the precise range of services and the likely level of future fees for those services.

The fact that there may be fees owing to an existing accountant is not a professional reason why a member in public practice should not accept an appointment.

Preparation of Legal Documents

1219 Members must not carry out work which is required by law to be performed by legal practitioners.

Commentary

Legislation in various States prohibits unqualified persons from preparing legal documents and members should ensure that they do not contravene these laws. If in doubt, refer the client to their solicitor or, if appropriate, obtain the client's approval to instruct a solicitor.

Client Complaints and Member Responsibility

1220 The Institute requires that a member in public practice must establish policies and procedures to deal appropriately with complaints and allegations that the work performed by the practice entity fails to comply with professional standards and regulatory and legal requirements.

Commentary

Complaints and allegations (which do not include those that are clearly frivolous) may be made by clients or other third parties. They may be received by engagement team members or other practice entity personnel.

It is the responsibility of members in public practice to ensure that clearly defined channels are established, documented and communicated to clients and other third parties to enable them to raise any concerns.

The practice entity must promptly investigate such complaints and allegations. Where appropriate the process set out in paragraphs 89 to 93 inclusive of APES 320 *Quality Control for Firms* is to be followed.

Where the results of the investigation indicate that the complaint is wholly or partly justified the practice entity shall take appropriate measures, as may be available, to resolve and settle the complaint. Such measures may include: remedial work, an apology, the reduction or refund of fees, the provision of information or otherwise.

1221 The Chief Executive Officer may, in his discretion, refer a complaint received by the Institute to a member in public practice for investigation and/or resolution by the practice entity.

1222 Failure by a member in public practice to promptly resolve a complaint, either direct by a client or other party, or referred under R9/1220 may of itself be grounds for disciplinary action under By-law 40(f).

R10
Regulations Relating to Membership of the Financial Planning Chapter

(Amended August 2009)

Contents

Introduction

1301 Joining the Financial Planning Chapter ("FP Chapter") is voluntary. The FP Chapter consists of two categories of participation, practicing and non-practicing. The FP Chapter is open to members of the Institute who specialise and those who are interested in financial planning. The Financial Planning Chapter has two categories of participation, described as:

(i) Financial Planning Chapter Members, being members who are interested in receiving information and a defined range of services from the Chapter, who pay a nominal subscription fee and are not subject to any rules or conditions of membership.

(ii) Financial Planning Chapter Specialists, being members who specialise in Financial Planning who successfully apply for specialist membership of the Chapter, are thereby subject to various continuing conditions of membership as defined in this regulation and are recognised by the Institute as specialists in Financial Planning.

These regulations have been developed by the National FP Chapter Committee and apply only to FP Chapter specialists (as defined in 1301 (ii) above).

In developing these regulations, the FP Chapter Committee has acknowledged the particular education, skills and knowledge base of a Chartered Accountant.

Lodgement of Application

1302 Applications for specialist membership of the FP Chapter should be forwarded to the Institute for consideration by the National FP Chapter Membership Panel.

Application Form

1303 An applicant shall complete and personally sign the application form as issued by the Institute.

Application Fees

1304 An applicant shall pay, upon approval of the application, such application and membership fees as are prescribed.

Entry Requirements for Specialist Membership

1305 An applicant must be a financial member of the Institute and must satisfy the following requirements:

Education

1305.1 Have met the Australian Securities and Investment Commission (ASIC) RG146 competency requirements for the following specialist knowledge and skills through the completion of ASIC approved training courses.

Generic knowledge and specialist knowledge areas:

- Generic
- Financial Planning
- Superannuation
- Managed investments
- Insurance
- Securities
- Derivatives

Provide evidence/documentation of meeting the continuing education requirements of ASIC RG146 and the Australian Financial services Licence (AFSL) holder.

Experience

1305.2 Provide evidence of being licensed to offer financial services advice.

Where an applicant holds a restricted licence, the National FP Chapter Membership Panel may consider the nature and extent of those restrictions in determining the application.

References

1305.3 Where an applicant is an authorised representative, the applicant must provide references from three (3) referees who can attest to the applicant's involvement in financial planning. Of those three (3) references:

(a) at least one (1) must be from a member of the Institute; and

(b) one (1) must be from the licence holder with whom the applicant is licensed.

Where the applicant is a licence holder, the applicant must provide references from two (2) referees who can attest to the applicant's involvement in financial planning. Of those two (2) references at least one (1) must be from a member of the Institute.

Interview

1305.4 An applicant may be required to attend an interview with the National FP Chapter Membership Panel.

Affiliates

1306 An affiliate of the Institute may apply and be accredited as a specialist member of the Chapter but in accordance with R2 an affiliate may not use the designation CA-Financial Planning Specialist.

Continuing Conditions of FP Chapter Membership

1307 All FP Chapter specialists will be obliged to meet the following conditions:

1307.1 Members of the Institute in public practice in Australia must follow the provisions of APS 12 when they provide financial advice.

Members in public practice outside Australia must follow the provisions of APS 12 to the extent that the provisions of APS 12 are not inconsistent with their local regulations and laws.

All other members (including those outside Australia) must follow the provision of APS 12 to the extent to which they are not prevented from doing so due to the specific requirements of an employer, AFSL holder or local regulations or law.

1307.2 Continue to be licensed to provide financial services advice. Where the FP specialist is no longer licensed he or she must contact the FP Membership Panel in writing and the FP Membership Panel shall have the discretion to waive this requirement for a period of up to twelve (12) months.

Ongoing Training and Development

1307.3 FP specialists are obliged to undertake FP-related Training and Development as part of their Training and Development requirements for the Institute as defined in Regulation R7 including at least 40% of the minimum Training and Development requirements in FP related areas. (Sept 03)

FP specialists will be required to complete, and may be required to submit a detailed analysis of their annual Training and Development to the Institute to demonstrate compliance. The analysis will outline:

(a) The type of Training and Development

(b) The date of undertaking

(c) Course provider

(d) Number of hours

Should an FP Chapter specialist fail to notify their Qualifying hours, up to two (2) reminder letters will be sent and if no response is received, three (3) months after the second letter, the specialist will be automatically removed from the FP Chapter specialist list and advised by letter.

Should an FP Chapter specialist appear not to have met the FP Chapter's requirement, a letter will be sent asking the specialist to prove that sufficient Training and Development has been attained. Should the specialist be unable to provide this proof or not respond within three (3) months to one further letter the specialist will be automatically removed from the FP Chapter specialist list and be advised by letter.

Professional Indemnity

1307.4 FP Specialists will be required to provide evidence of PI insurance held by the authorised representative and/or Australian Financial Services Licence Holder (AFSL).

AFSL Criteria

1307.5 AFSLs must continue to satisfy the licensing conditions as stipulated under the *Corporations Act 2001* and Regulations.

Annual Fees

1308 The prescribed annual fees payable by an FP Chapter specialist will be invoiced on an annual basis in conjunction with the Institute Membership Renewal process.

1309 Concessional rates of subscription as referred to in Regulation 805, also apply to FP Chapter specialist membership fees at the discretion of the National FP Chapter Committee.

1310 If an FP Chapter specialist is non-financial for more than three (3) months after receiving two (2) follow-up letters then the specialist is automatically removed from the Chapter specialist list regardless of the status of Institute membership.

Disciplinary Action

1311 Any matter concerning the professional conduct of a FP Chapter specialist will be dealt with in accordance with Section 5 of the By-laws.

1312 Any members excluded from the Institute's membership will be automatically excluded as a FP Chapter specialist.

Appeals and Reinstatements

1313 A member may appeal a decision regarding non-approval for FP Chapter specialist membership or their removal from the FP Chapter specialist list within three (3) months of the date of notification.

That appeal shall be heard by a committee constituted separately from the membership committee.

A member removed from the FP Chapter specialist list may seek readmission by submitting a new application for specialist membership to the membership committee.

Special Cases

1314 Members who do not fully comply with the regulations may apply to the National FP Chapter Committee for consideration as a special case admission.

❖❖❖

Appendix A – Financial Planning Training and Development Activities

Activities that will be recognised as qualifying for specialist FP Training and Development purposes must relate to financial planning and can include:

- Courses, seminars, workshops, lectures and other professional educational activities presented by the Institute or CPA Australia
- Meetings of Institute or CPA Australia technical discussion groups
- Attendance or involvement with technical discussion groups related to Financial Planning
- Appropriate educational activities provided by the member's employer or practice entity AFSL
- Study of courses conducted by tertiary institutions leading to a Degree, Diploma or Postgraduate qualification in a Financial Planning field
- Appropriate educational and developmental activities presented under the auspices of academic institutions, commercial establishments or other professional bodies
- Contributions to the Charter, Technical Bulletins or other FP Chapter publications on topics related to FP
- Preparation and presentation of professional development courses or conferences on FP related topics
- Service on technical or research committees of the Institute, CPA Australia, other professional bodies, government or industry in relation to policy or guidance in FP issues.

R11

Regulations Relating to Specialisation

(Issued August 2011)

Introduction

The Institute recognises that individual members may have undertaken specific study and gained experience within a recognised field of study and occupation, to such level that they would like to be recognised for their skills and experience in a particular field. Regulation 11 specifies the framework for recognising specialisation in a particular field, supported by appendices that detail the specific criteria to be met for each particular specialisation recognised by the Institute.

Definitions

1400.1 Specialisation is the term given to the recognition of individual members with skills and experience in a particular field, to such a level that they are recognised as specialists in that field. Ongoing education is required to maintain their recognition as a specialist.

1400.2 Certification is the process by which individual members undertake specific study and experience within a recognised field of study and occupation, to such level that they are recognised as qualified in the field, at a particular point in time. Unlike specialisation, there are no ongoing education requirements.

Eligibility

1401 Specialisation is only available to Individual Members of the Institute.

Pre-requisites for Specialisation

Application

1402 An Individual Member must apply for a specialisation in a form prescribed by the Institute.

Educational Requirements

1403 An Individual Member applying for specialisation must meet the specific educational pre-requisites required for the specialisation for which they are applying.

Verification of Educational Qualifications

1403.1 An Individual Member will be required to provide documentary evidence of their educational qualifications, as they relate to the application for specialisation.

Currency of Qualifications

1403.2 For the purposes of applying for specialisation, educational qualifications are deemed to be current for a period of 5 years, from date of completion.

Experience Requirements

1404 An Individual Member applying for specialisation must meet the specific service pre-requisites required for the specialisation for which they are applying.

References

1405 An Individual Member must provide written references, as per the specific requirements for the specialisation for which they are applying.

Application Form

1406 An applicant shall complete and personally sign the application form as issued by the Institute.

Lodgement of Application

1407 Application shall be made to the Board or their delegated representative.

Fees

Application Fee

1408 An Individual Member shall pay, at the time of application, the application fee as prescribed by the Institute.

Annual Fee

1409 An Individual Member shall pay, at the time of application and on an annual basis whilst they continue to hold the specialisation, the annual fee as prescribed by the Institute.

Amount Prescribed

1410 The amount prescribed will be calculated annually and individual members holding a specialisation will be notified of the annual fee via the annual membership subscription process.

Peer Review Fee

1411 An Individual Member shall pay, at the time of a peer review, such peer review fee as prescribed by the Institute.

Interview

1412 An Individual Member applying for specialisation may be required to participate in an interview as part of the application process.

Recommendation to the Board

1413 Where an applicant for a specialisation does not fully comply with these Regulations, recommendation may be made to the Board by Management that the application be approved. The Board may issue guidelines in relation to such recommendations.

Ongoing obligations

Training and Development

1414 An Individual Member holding a specialisation is obliged to undertake training and development specific to each of their fields of specialisation. Refer to Regulation R7.

Peer Review

1415 An Individual Member holding a specialisation must participate in a peer review, when requested by the Institute and pay any associated fee, as prescribed by the Institute.

1416 An Individual Member holding a specialisation must participate in a peer review, as a reviewer, when requested by the Institute.

Renewal of Specialisation

1417 An Individual Member granted a specialisation must continue to ensure that they meet the ongoing obligations of the specialisation and confirm the same through their annual membership subscription renewal.

Entitlements

1418 Individual members approved as a specialist are entitled to use the specified description, as detailed in the relevant specialisation appendix.

1419 Individual members will receive a certificate confirming their specialisation.

1420 Every such certificate shall remain the property of the Institute and the Board shall be at liberty at any time to call for, and compel, its production and delivery and the Board may alter or amend any such certificate or issue a new certificate in its place.

Consequences of Non-Compliance

1421 In the event that an Individual Member fails to meet one or more of the ongoing obligations of specialisation, their recognition as a specialist may be cancelled and this would remove their entitlements as specified in R11/1417 – R11/1419.

1422 Any matter concerning the professional conduct of a specialist will be dealt with in accordance with Section 5 of the By-laws. Where the Institute's Professional Conduct Tribunal delivers an adverse finding against an Individual Member holding a specialisation, the individual's specialisation will automatically be cancelled.

1423 Any Individual Member excluded from the Institute's membership will have their specialisation automatically cancelled.

Certificates of Public Practice

By-law 34(a) provides that "A member shall not, without the consent of the Board, practise as a public accountant unless he or she has been issued with a current certificate of public practice or his or her application therefore has been approved or he or she is exempt from the obligation to hold such a certificate."

By-law 34(b) authorises the Board to prescribe Regulations for the issue and renewal of Certificates of Public Practice (CPPs) and for any exemption from the obligation to hold such a certificate.

1424 Recognition as a specialist does not trigger the requirement to hold a Certificate of Public Practice. If an Individual Member otherwise meets the criteria in R4/702.1, they are required to hold a Certificate of Public Practice.

Appeals and Reinstatements

1425 An Individual Member may appeal a decision regarding non-approval for specialisation or the cancellation of their specialisation within three (3) months of the date of notification.

1426 An appeal shall be heard by a committee, as prescribed by the Board or their delegated representative.

1427 An Individual Member who cancels their specialisation or for whom the Institute cancels their specialisation, may reapply for the specialisation by submitting a new application for specialisation.

R11A
Regulations Relating to Specialisation in Self Managed Superannuation Funds

(Issued August 2011)

Introduction

The Self Managed Superannuation Funds Specialisation (SMSF Specialisation) recognises those Individual Members who have undertaken specific relevant study and gained experience in Self Managed Superannuation Funds, to such a level that they are recognised as having specialist skills in the field.

In addition to the requirements stated in R11 Regulations Relating to Specialisation:

Pre-requisites for SMSF Specialisation

There are two alternate pathways to meeting the education and experience pre-requisites for SMSF Specialisation.

1. Specialisation via Education and Practical Experience

Educational requirements

1500 An Individual Member applying for recognition as a Self Managed Superannuation Funds (SMSF) Specialist will be required to undertake study through an award program approved by the Institute for the purposes of specialisation.

Verification of Educational Qualifications

1500.1 An Individual Member applying for recognition as a Self Managed Superannuation Funds (SMSF) Specialist will be required to provide an academic transcript detailing the subjects undertaken and their successful completion.

Currency of qualifications

1500.2 For the purposes of applying for specialisation, successful completion of one of the specified subjects is deemed to be current for a period of five (5) years, from date of completion.

Experience requirements

1501 An Individual Member applying for recognition as a Self Managed Superannuation Funds (SMSF) Specialist is required to have a minimum of two (2) years practical experience within the previous five (5) years, where at least 40% of their employment was related to Self Managed Superannuation Funds.

2. Specialisation via Workshop Assessment and Practical Experience

Educational requirements

1502 An Individual Member applying for recognition as a Self Managed Superannuation Funds (SMSF) Specialist must complete a workshop as specified by the Institute and successfully complete the assessment component.

Verification of Educational Qualifications

1502.1 An Individual Member applying for recognition as a Self Managed Superannuation Funds (SMSF) Specialist will be required to provide documentary evidence of their successful completion of the workshop and assessment.

Currency of qualifications

1502.2 For the purposes of applying for specialisation, successful completion of the workshop and assessment component is deemed to be current for a period of five (5) years, from date of completion.

Experience requirements

1503 An Individual Member applying for recognition as a Self Managed Superannuation Funds (SMSF) Specialist is required to have a minimum of four (4) years practical experience within the previous ten (10) years, where at least 40% of their employment was related to Self Managed Superannuation Funds.

References

1504 An Individual Member applying for recognition as a Self Managed Superannuation Funds (SMSF) Specialist must provide two written references in support of their application for specialisation.

1504.1 At least one of these references must be from a Chartered Accountant with three (3) years membership or more who has known the applicant for 12 months or more.

1504.2 At least one of the references must attest to the individual member's skills and knowledge in superannuation and/or self managed superannuation funds.

Ongoing obligations

Training and Development

1505 An Individual Member holding a SMSF specialisation is obliged to undertake at least 40% of the minimum Training and Development requirement in Superannuation, with at least 20 hours specific to Self Managed Superannuation Funds.

1506 An Individual Member holding a SMSF specialisation is obliged to undertake Training and Development in accordance with Regulation R7.

Peer Review

1507 An Individual Member holding a SMSF Specialisation must participate in a peer review, when requested by the Institute and pay any associated fee, as prescribed by the Institute.

1508 An Individual Member holding a SMSF Specialisation must participate in a peer review, as a reviewer, when requested by the Institute.

Entitlements

1509 Individual members approved as a SMSF Specialist are entitled to use the description 'CA SMSF Specialist'. This is a description which can be used underneath their name, but does not constitute a designation or post-nominal.

1510 Individual members approved as a SMSF Specialist will receive a certificate confirming their specialisation.